DIRECTORY
OF
AMERICAN
SCHOLARS

DIRECTORY OF AMERICAN SCHOLARS

TENTH EDITION

VOLUME V

PSYCHOLOGY, SOCIOLOGY, & EDUCATION

Caryn E. Klebba, Editor

GALE GROUP

★

THOMSON LEARNING™

Detroit • New York • San Diego • San Francisco
Boston • New Haven, Conn. • Waterville, Maine
London • Munich

Caryn E. Klebba, *Editor*

Jason B. Baldwin, *Assistant Editor*

Contributing Editors: Alex Alviar, Claire M. Campana, Eric Hoss, Chris Lopez,
Christine Maurer, Jenai Mynatt, Jaime E. Noce, Kathleen E. Maki Potts, Amanda C. Quick

Lynne Maday, *Contributor*

Erin E. Braun, *Managing Editor*

Ralph Wiazowski, *Programmer/Analyst*
Venus Little, *Manager, Database Applications, Technical Support Services*

Dorothy Maki, *Manufacturing Manager*
Evi Seoud, *Production Manager*
NeKita McKee, *Buyer*

Data Capture Specialists: Nikkita Bankston, Cynthia A. Jones,
Frances L. Monroe

Mike Logusz, *Graphic Artist*

ISBN: 0-7876-5008-0 (Volume 1)
ISBN: 0-7876-5009-9 (Volume 2)
ISBN: 0-7876-5010-2 (Volume 3)
ISBN: 0-7876-5011-0 (Volume 4)
ISBN: 0-7876-5012-9 (Volume 5)
ISBN: 0-7876-5013-7 (Volume 6)
ISBN: 0-7876-5007-2 (set)
ISSN: 0070-5101

Printed in the United States of America
Published in the United States by Gale Group

CONTENTS

PREFACE

First published in 1942 under the auspices of the American Council of Learned Societies, the *Directory of American Scholars* remains the foremost biographical reference to American humanities scholars. With the tenth edition, the Gale Group has added social science scholars, recognizing the close relationship of the social sciences to the humanities.

The directory is arranged for convenient use in five subject volumes: Volume I: History, Archaeology, and Area Studies; Volume II: English, Speech, and Drama; Volume III: Foreign Languages, Linguistics, and Philology; Volume IV: Philosophy, Religion, and Law; Volume V: Psychology, Sociology, and Education. Each volume of biographical listings contains a geographic index. Volume VI contains an alphabetical index, a discipline index, an institutional index and a cumulative geographic index of scholars listed in the first five volumes.

The tenth edition of the *Directory of American Scholars* profiles more than 30,000 United States and Canadian scholars currently active in teaching, research, and/or publishing. The names of entrants were obtained from a variety of sources, including former entrants, academic deans, or citations in professional journals. In most cases, nominees received a questionnaire to complete, and selection for inclusion was made based on the following criteria:

1. Achievement, by reason of experience and training, of a stature in scholarly work equivalent to that associated with the doctoral degree, coupled with current activity in such work;

or

2. Achievement as evidenced by publication of scholarly works;

or

3. Attainment of a position of substantial responsibility by reason of achievement as outlined in (1) and (2).

Enhancements to the tenth edition include the addition of the fifth subject volume, Volume V: Psychology, Sociology, and Education,

and the renaming of Volume I to better reflect the disciplines covered within. An outline of the major disciplines within the social sciences and humanities has been added to each volume to assist in locating scholars associated with disciplines related to, but not named outright in the titles of the individual volumes. Please see page ix for this information. Those individuals involved in multiple fields are listed in all appropriate volumes.

The tenth edition of the *Directory of American Scholars* is produced by fully automated methods. Limitations in the printing method have made it necessary to omit most diacritics.

Individual entries can include: place and year of birth, *primary discipline(s), vital statistics, education, honorary degrees, past and present professional experience, concurrent positions, *membership in international, national and regional societies, honors and awards, *research interest, *publications, postal mailing and electronic mailing addresses. Elements preceded by an asterisk are limited as to the number of items included. If an entrant exceeded these limitations, the editors selected the most recent information. Biographies received in the offices of the Gale Group after the editorial deadline were included in an abbreviated manner whenever possible.

The editors have made every effort to include material as accurately and completely as possible within the confines of format and scope. However, the publishers do not assume and hereby disclaim any liability to any party for any loss or damage caused by errors or omissions in the *Directory of American Scholars*, whether such errors or omissions result from negligence, accident, or any other cause.

Thanks are expressed to those who contributed information and submitted nominations for the new edition. Many societies provided membership lists for the research process and published announcements in their journals or newsletters, and their help is appreciated.

Comments and suggestions regarding any aspect of the tenth edition are invited and should be addressed to The Editors, *Directory of American Scholars*, Gale Group, 27500 Drake Road, Farmington Hills, MI 48333-3535.

MAJOR HUMANITIES &
SOCIAL SCIENCE DISCIPLINES

*Volume I: History, Archaeology,
& Area Studies*

Aesthetics
Architecture
Archaeology
Area Studies
Art
Art History
Assyriology
Community Studies
Community Planning
Demography
Geography
History
International Studies
Urban Studies
Western Civilization

Volume II: English, Speech, & Drama

Advertising
Audiology
Bibliography
Cinema
Classical Literature
Communications
Composition (Language Arts)
Creative Writing
Drama
English Literature
Film Studies

Journalism
Library Science
Literary Theory
Literature
Marketing
Mass Communication
Media Studies
Music
Music History
Musicology
Performing Arts
Poetry
Rhetoric
Speech Communication
Speech-Language Pathology
Theater Studies

*Volume III: Foreign Languages,
Linguistics, & Philology*

Classical Languages
Comparative Literature
Foreign Languages
Foreign Literature Studies
Linguistics
Modern Languages
Philology
Romance Languages
Translation

Volume IV: Philosophy, Religion, & Law

Accounting
Business Administration
Corrections
Criminal Justice
Criminology
Economics
Epistemology
Ethics
Evangelism
Forensic Sciences
Government
Homiletics
International Relations
Missiology
Philosophy
Political Science
Public Affairs
Religious Studies
Statistics

Volume V: Psychology, Sociology, & Education

Adult Education
Anthropology
Behavioral Sciences
Child Development
Clinical Psychology
Counseling
Culture Studies
Education
Ethnology
Folklore
Gender Studies
Gerontology
Health Studies
Human Development
Language Education
Psychology
Social Work
Sociology
Women's Studies

ABBREVIATIONS

AAAS American Association for the Advancement of Science
AAUP American Association of University Professors
abnorm abnormal
acad academia, academic, academica, academie, academique, academy
accad accademia
acct account, accountant, accounting
acoust acoustical, accounstic(s)
adj adjunct, adjutant
actg acting
activ activities, activity
addn addition(s), additional
AID Agency for International Development
adjust adjust
admin administration, administrative
adminr administrator(s)
admis admissions
adv advisor(s), advisory
advan advance(d), advancement
advert advertisement, advertising
aerodyn aerodynamic(s)
aeronaut aeronautic(s), aeronautical
aesthet aesthetics
affil affiliate(s), affiliation
agr agricultural, agriculture
agt agent
AFB Air Force Base
AHA American Historical Association
akad akademi, akademia
Ala Alabama
Algem algemeen, algemen
allergol allergological, allergology
allgem allgemein, allgemeine, allgemeinen
Alta Alberta
Am America, Americain, American, Americana, Americano, Amerika, Amerikaansch, Amerikaner, Amerikanisch, Amerikansk
anal analysis, analytic, analytical
analog analogue
anat anatomic, anatomical, anatomy
ann annal(s)
anthrop anthropological, anthropology
anthropom anthropometric, anthropometrical, anthropometry
antiq antiquaire(s), antiquarian, antiquary(ies), antiquities
app appoint, appointed, appointment
appl applied
appln application

approx approximate, approximately
Apr April
apt apartment(s)
arbit arbitration
arch archiv, archiva, archive(s), archivio, archivo
archaeol archaeological, archaeology
archaol archaologie, archaologisch
archeol archeological, archeologie, archeologique, archeology
archit architectural, architecture
Arg Argentina, Argentine
Ariz Arizona
Ark Arkansas
asn association
asoc asociacion
assoc(s) associate(s), associated
asst assistant
Assyriol Assyriology
astrodyn astrodynamics
astron astronomical, astronomy
astronaut astronautical, astronautics
astronr astronomer
attend attendant, attending
atty attorney
audiol audiology
Aug August
auth author(s)
AV audiovisual
ave avenue

b born
BC British Columbia
bd board
behav behavior, behavioral, behaviour, behavioural
Bibl Biblical, Biblique
bibliog bibliografia, bibliographic, bibligraphical, bibliography(ies)
bibliogr bibliographer
bibliot biblioteca, bibliotec, bibliotek, bibliotheca, bibliothek, bibliothequeca
biog biographical, biography
biol biological, biology
bk(s) books
bldg building
blvd boulevard
bol boletim, boletin
boll bollettino
bor borough

bot botanical, botany
br branch
Brit Britain, British
Bro(s) Brother(s)
bull bulletin
bur bureau
bus business
BWI British West Indies

c children
Calif California
Can Canada, Canadian, Canadien, Canadienne
cand candidate
cartog cartografic, cartographical, cartography
cartogra cartographer
Cath Catholic, Catholique
CBS Columbia Broadcasting System
cent central
Cent Am Central America
cert certificat, certificate, certified
chap chapter
chem chermical, chemistry
chg charge
chemn chairman
Cie Compagnie
cient cientifica, cientifico
class classical
clin(s) clinic(s)
Co Companies, Company, County
coauth coauth
co-dir co-director
co-ed co-editor
co-educ co-educational
col(s) colegio, college(s), collegiate
collab collaboration, collaborative, collaborating, collaborator
Colo Colorado
Comdr Commander
com commerce, commercial
commun communication(s)
comn(s) commission(s)
comnr commissioner
comp comparative, comparee
compos composition(s)
comput computer, computing
comt committee
conf conference
cong congress
Conn Connecticut

conserv conservacion,conservation,
conservatoire, conservatory
consol consolidated, consolidation
const constitution, constitutional
construct construction
consult consultant, consulting
contemp contemporary
contrib contribute, contribution
contribur contributor
conv convention
coop cooperation, cooperative
coord coordinating, coordination
coordr coordinator
corresp corresponding
Corp Corporation
coun council, counsel, counseling
counr councillor, counselor
criminol criminology
Ct Court
ctr center
cult cultra, cultural, culturale, culture
cur curator
curric curriculum
cybernet cybernetics
CZ Canal Zone
Czeck Czechoslovakia

DC District of Columbia
Dec December
Del Delaware
deleg delegate, delegations
demog demographic, demography
demonstr demonstrator
dent dental, dentistry
dep deputy
dept department
Deut Deutsch, Deutschland
develop development
diag diagnosis, diagnostic
dialectol dialectology
dig digest
dipl diploma, diploma, diplomate, diplome
dir director(s), directory
  directory
Diss Abstr Dissertation Abstracts
dist district
distrib distributive
distribr distributors
div division, divorced
doc document, documentation
Dom Dominion
Dr Doctor, Drive
Drs Doctroandus

e east
ecol ecological, ecology
econ economic(s), economical, economy
ed edicion, edition, editor, editorial,
edizione
educ education, educational
educr educator(s)
Egyptol Egyptology
elec electric, electrical, electricity
  electrical
elem elementary
emer emeriti, emeritus
encour encouragement
encycl encyclopedia
employ employment
Eng England
environ environment, environmental
EPDA Education Professions Development
Act
equip equipment
ERIC Educational Resources Information
Center
ESEA Elementary & Secondary Education
Act

espec especially
estab established, establishment
estud estudante, estudas, estudianet,
estudio(s), estudo(s)
ethnog ethnographical, ethnography
ethnol ethnological, ethnology
Europ European
eval evaluation
evangel evangelical
eve evening
exam examination
examr examiner
except exceptional
exec executive(s)
exeg exegesis(es), exegetic, exegetical,
exegetics
exhib exhibition(s)
exp experiment, experimental, experimentation
exped expedition(s)
explor exploration(s)
expos exposition
exten extension

fac faculties, faculty
facil facilities, facility
Feb February
fed federal
fedn federation
fel(s) fellow(s), fellowship(s)
filol filologia, filologico
filos filosofia, filosofico
Fla Florida
FLES Foreign Languages in the Elementary
Schools
for foreign
forsch forschung, forschungen
found foundation
Fr Francais(s), French
Ft Fort

Ga Georgia
gen general, generale
geneal genealogical, genealogy
genoot genootschap
geod geodesy, geodetic
geog geografia, geografico, geographer(s),
geographic,
geographie, geographical, geography
geogr geographer
geol geologic, geological, geology
geophys geophysical
Ger German, Germanic, Germanisch,
Germany
Ges gesellschaft
gov governing, governors
govt government
grad graduate
Gr Brit Great Britain
guid guidance
gym gymnasium

handbk(s) handbooks
Hawaii
Hisp Hispanic, Hispanico, Hispano
hist historie, historia, historial, historic,
historica,
historical, historique, historische, history
histol histology, histological
Hoshsch Hoshschule
hon honorable, honorary
hosp(s) hospital(s)
hq headquarters
HumRRO Human Resources Research
Office
hwy highway

Ill Illinois

illum illuminating, illumination
illus illustrate, illustration
illusr illustrator
imp imperial
improv improvement
Inc Incorporated
incl include, included, includes, including
Ind Indiana
indust(s) industrial, industry(ies)
infor information
inst institut, instritute(s), institution(s),
instituto
instnl institutional, institutionalized
instr instruction, instructor(s)
instruct instructional
int internacional, international,
internazionale
intel intelligence
introd introduction
invest investigacion, investiganda,
investigation,
investigative
investr investigator
ist istituto
Ital Italia, Italian, Italiana, Italiano, Italica,
Italien,
Italienisch, Italienne, Italy

J Journal
Jan January
jour journal, journalism
jr junior
jurisp jurisprudence
juv juvenile(s)

Kans Kansas
Koninki koninklijk
Ky Kentucky

La Louisiana
lab laboratorie, laboratorio, laboratorium,
laboratory(ies)
lang language(s)
lect lecture(s)
lectr lecturer
legis legislacion, legislatief, legislation,
legislative,
legislativo, legislature, legislazione
lett letter(s), lettera, letteraria, letterature,
lettere
lib liberal
libr libary(ies), librerio
librn librarian(s)
lic license, lecencia
ling linguistic(s), linguistica, linguistique
lit liteary, literatur, literatura, literature,
littera,
literature
Ltd Limited

m married
mach machine(s), machinery
mag magazine
Man Manitoba
Mar March
Mariol Mariological, Mariology
Mass Massachusetts
mat matematica, matematiche, matematico,
matematik
math mathematics, mathematical, mathematics, mathematik,
mathematique(s), mathematisch
Md Maryland
mech mechanical
med medical, medicine
Mediter Mediterranean
mem member, memoirs, memorial
ment mental, mentally

metrop metropolitan
Mex Mexican, Mexicano, Mexico
mfg manufacturing
mfr manufacture, manufacturer
mgr manager(s)
mgt management
Mich Michigan
mid middle
mil military
Minn Minnesota
Miss Mississippi
mitt mitteilung
mkt market, marketing
MLA Modern Language Association of America
Mo Missouri
mod modern,moderna, moderne, moderno
monatsh monatsheft(e)
monatsschr monatsschrift
monogr monograph
Mont Montana
morphol morphologica, morphologie, morphology
mt mount, mountain(s)
munic municipal
mus museum(s)
musicol musicological, musicology

n north
nac nacional
NASA National Aeronautics & Space Administration
nat nationaal, national, nationale, nationalis, naturalized
NATO North Atlantic Treaty Organization
naz nazionale
NB New Brunswick
NC North Carolina
MCTE National Council of Teachers of English
NDak North Dakota
NDEA National Defense Education Act
NEA National Education Association
Nebr Nebraska
Ned Nederland, Nederlandsch
Nev Nevada
Neth Netherlands
Nfld Newfoundland
NH New Hampshire
NJ New Jersey
NMex New Mexico
no number
nonres nonresident
norm normal, normale
Norweg Norwegian
Nov November
NS Nova Scotia
NSW New South Wales
NT Northwest Territories
numis numismatic, numismatico, numismatique
NY New York
NZ New Zealand

occas occasional
occup occupation, occupational
Oct October
Ohio
OEEC Organization for European Economic Cooperation
off office, officer(s), official(s)
Okla Oklahoma
Ont Ontario
oper operation(s), operational, operative
ord ordnance
Ore Oregon
orgn organization, organizational

orient oriental, orientale, orientalist, orientalia
ornithol ornithological, ornithology

Pa Pennsylvania
Pac Pacific
paleontol paleontological, paleontology
PanAm Pan American
pedag pedagogia, pedagogic, pedagogical, pedagogico,
pedagogoie, pedagogik, pedagogique, pedagogy
Pei Prince Edward Island
penol penological, penology
phenomenol phenomenological, phenomenologie, phenomenology
philol philologica, philological, philologie, philologisch, philology
philos philosophia, philosophic, philosophical, philosophie, philosophique, philosophisch, philosophical, philosohpy, philosozophia
photog photographic, photography
photogr photographer(s)
phys physical
pkwy parkway
pl place
polit politica, political, politicas, politico, politics,
politek, politike, politique, politsch, politisk
polytech polytechnic
pop population
Pontif Pontifical
Port Portugal, Portuguese
postgrad postgraduate
PR Puerto Rico
pract practice
prehist prehistoric
prep preparation, preparatory
pres president
Presby Presbyterian
preserv preservation
prev prevention, preventive
prin principal(s)
prob problem(s)
probtn probation
proc proceding
prod production
prof professional, professor, professorial
prog program(s), programmed, programming
proj project, projective
prom promotion
prov province, provincial
psychiat psychiatria, psychiatric, psychiatrica, psychiatrie, psychiatrique, psychiatrisch, psychiatry
psychol psychological
pt point
pub pub, publique
publ publication(s), published, publisher(s), publishing
pvt private

qm quartermaster
quad quaderni
qual qualitative, quality
quart quarterly
Que Quebec

rd road
RD Rural Delivery, Rural Free Delivery Rural Free Delivery
rec record(s), recording
rech recherche
redevelop redevelopment
ref reference

regist register, registered, registration
registr registrar
rehabil rehabilitation
rel(s) relacion, relation(s), relative, relazione
relig religion, religious
rep representative
repub republic
req requirement(s)
res research, reserve
rev review, revised, revista, revue
rhet rhetoric, rhetorical
RI Rhode Island
Rt Right
Rte Route
Russ Russian
rwy railway

s south
SAfrica South Africa
SAm South America, South American
Sask Saskatchewan
SC South Carolina
Scand Scandinavian
sch(s) school(s)
scholar scholarship
sci science(s), scientia, scientific, scientifico, scientifique, scienza
SDak South Dakota
SEATO Southeast Asia Treaty Organization
sec secondary
sect section
secy secretary
sem seminaire, seminar, seminario, seminary
sen senator, sneatorial
Sept September
ser serial, series
serv service(s)
soc social, sociedad, sociedade, societa, societas, societate, societe, societet, society(ies)
soc sci social science(s)
sociol sociological, sociology
Span Spanish
spec special
sq square
sr senior
sr sister
St Saint, Street
sta station
statist statistical, statistics
Ste Sainte, Suite
struct structural, structure(s)
subcomt subcommittee
subj subject
substa substa
super superieur, superior, superiore
suppl supplement, supplementary
supt superintendent
supv supervising, supervision
supvr supervisor
supvry supervisory
surg surgical, surgery
surv survey
Swed Swedish
Switz Switzerland
symp symposium
syst system, systematic

tech technic(s), technica, technical, technicky, techniczny,
techniek, technik, technika, technikum, technique, technisch
technol technologic, technological, technologicke, technologico, technologiczny, technologie, technologika,

technologique, technologisch, technology
tecnol   technologia, technologica, technologico
tel telegraph(s), telephone
temp temporary
Tenn Tennessee
Terr Terrace
teol teologia, teologico
Tex Texas
textbk   textbook(s)
theol   theological, theologie, theologique, theologisch,
theology
theoret theoretic(al)
ther therapy
trans   transactions
transp   transportation
transl   translation, translator(s)
treas   treasurer, treasury
trop tropical
TV television
twp township

u und
UAR United Arab Republic
UK United Kingdom
UN United Nations

unemploy unemployment
UNESCO   United Nations Educational, Scientific & Cultural Organization
UNICEF   United Nations Children's Fund
univ(s) universidad, universite, university(ies)
UNRRA   United Nations Relief & Rehabilitation Administration
UNRWA   United Nations Relief & Works Agency
USA United States of America
US   United States
USPHS   United States Public Health Service
USSR Union of Soviet Socialist Republics
Utah

Va Virginia
var various
veg vegetable(s), vegetation
ver vereeniging, verein, vereingt, vereinigung
vet veteran, veterinarian, veterinary
VI Virgin Islands
vis visiting

voc vocational
vocab vocabulary
vol(s)   volume(s), voluntary, volunteer(s)
vchmn   vice chairman
vpres   vice president
Vt Vermont

w west
Wash Washington
wetensch wetenschappelijk, wetenschappen
WHO World Health Organization
WI   West Indies
wid widow, widowed, widower
Wis Wisconsin
wiss wissenschaft(en), wissenschaftliche(e)
WVa West Virginia
Wyo Wyoming

yearbk   yearbook(s)
YMCA Young Men's Christian Association
YMHA Young Men's Hebrew Association
YWCA Young Women's Christian Association
YWHA Young Women's Hebrew Association

z zeitschrift

xiv

Biographies

A

AANERUD, REBECCA J.
PERSONAL Born 10/16/1961, Buffalo, NY, m, 1982, 1 child **DISCIPLINE** WOMEN STUDIES, ENGLISH **EDUCATION** Univ Wash, BA, 90; MA, 93; PhD, 98. **CAREER** Instr to lectr, Univ Wash, 98-. **HONORS AND AWARDS** Phi Beta Kappa, 90; Doman Award for Excellence in Teaching, 97; Robert R and Mary Roberts Waltz Grad Fel, 97. **MEMBERSHIPS** MLA, Am Studies Asn, Nat Women Studies Asn. **RESEARCH** Critical Race Theory, Feminist Theory, US American Literature and Culture, Globalization, Film/television theory, Cultural Studies. **SELECTED PUBLICATIONS** Auth, "Fictions of Whiteness: Speaking the Names of Whiteness in US Literature," Essays in Soc and Cult Criticism, ed Ruth Frankenberg, (Duke Univ Pr, 97); auth, "Now More than Ever: James Baldwin and the Critique of White Liberalism," James Baldwin Now, ed Dwight McBride, (NY Univ Pr, 99); auth, "Thinking Again: This bridge called My back and the Challenge to Whiteness," This Bridge We Call Home, ed AnaLouise Keating and Gloria Anzaludua, Routledge, (forthcoming). **CONTACT ADDRESS** Dept Women Studies, Univ of Washington, PO Box 354345, Seattle, WA 98195. **EMAIL** raan@u.washington.edu

AANSTOOS, CHRISTOPHER
PERSONAL Born 04/04/1952, Saipan, d, 2 children **DISCIPLINE** PSYCHOLOGY **EDUCATION** Mich State Univ, BA, 74; Duquesne Univ, MA, 76; PhD, 82. **CAREER** Prof, State Univ W Ga. **HONORS AND AWARDS** Fel, Am Psychol Asn. **MEMBERSHIPS** APA. **CONTACT ADDRESS** Dept Psychol, State Univ of West Georgia, 1601 Maple St, Carrollton, GA 30117. **EMAIL** aanstoos@westga.edu

ABRAHAM, M. FRANCIS
PERSONAL Born 04/27/1939, Kerala, India, m, 1966, 2 children **DISCIPLINE** SOCIOLOGY, PSYCHOLOGY **EDUCATION** Gandhigram Rural Institute, MA, 64; Mich State Univ, PhD, 70. **CAREER** Grambling State Univ, 76-; Univ of Texas at Pan American, 72-73; Southhampton Col of Long Island Univ, 69-70. **HONORS AND AWARDS** Ford Foundation Fel, Bobbs-Merrill Awd for best PhD candidate MSU, 69. **RESEARCH** Third World Development, Peace Studies. **SELECTED PUBLICATIONS** Auth, Perspectives on Modernization, Univ Press of America, 80; auth, Modern Sociological Theory, Oxford Univ Press, 82; Sociological Thought: from Comte to Sorokin (co-author), Macmillan, 85; auth, Women, Development and Change,(co-editor) with S. Abraham, Wyndham Hall Press, 88; auth, Studies in Third World Development, (co-editor), Deep and Deep Publishers, 92; auth, The Agony of India, East West Books, Madras, 98. **CONTACT ADDRESS** Dept Sociology & Psychology, Grambling State Univ, 99 S Main St, Grambling, LA 71245. **EMAIL** fabraham@bayou.com

ABRAHAMS, CARYL
DISCIPLINE SOCIOLOGY **EDUCATION** Univ Fla, BA, 62; Univ Tex Austin, MSc SW, 70; PhD, 78. **CAREER** Lectr, Paisley Col of Tech, 74-75; asst prof, Laurentian Univ, 75-77; assoc prof, Univ of Toronto, 77-93; prof, Delta State Univ, 97-. **HONORS AND AWARDS** Fulbright Res Grant, 72-73; Hon Fel, Am Inst of Indian Studies, 73-73; World Who's Who of Women in Education, 78; Foremost Women of the Twentieth Century, 88; Donner Found Grant, 88; Delegate, World Summit for Soc Develop, 95; Kent and Janice Wyatt Fac Develop Fund Fel, 99. **MEMBERSHIPS** IUCISD; ACOSA; CDS; M/ASA. **RESEARCH** International, CD, RRA, PAR, SIA, Cross-Cultural, Social Dev. **SELECTED PUBLICATIONS** Auth, "Empowering Educators through Consultation: developing a new admissions process", Soc Develop Issues 11.1 (Spring 87); auth, "Social Impact Assessment: A Tool for Social Development", Soc Develop Issues 12.4 (Winter 89): auth, "Education for Social Welfare and Social Work", Annual J of the Siyane Col of Educ, vol 3, (Dec 89): coauth, "Transferring Technology through a Social Development Model of Consultation", Int Soc Work, 33.3 (90); coauth, "Self-Perceived Successful Adjustment of Sri Lankan Immigrants in Metropolitan Toronto (Ontario)", Polyphony, Vol 12 (90); coauth, Manual for Social Development Practice, Can Scholars Pr, (Toronto), 90; coauth, "Changchun City Civil Administration, People's Republic of China", Int Soc Work Vol 3-4, (91): 207-222; auth, "A Social Development Model for Community Practice", J of the Community Develop Soc 23.2 (92): coauth, "Social Work With Poor Women and their Children in Peru: Relevance of a Social Development Perspective", J of Applied Soc Sci 21.1 (Fall/Winter 96); coauth, "Sri Lankan Immigrants: Sinhalese and Burgher Communities", Encyclop of Can Peoples (forthcoming). **CONTACT ADDRESS** Dept Soc Sci, Delta State Univ, 1003 W Sunflower Rd, Cleveland, MS 38733. **EMAIL** carylmae@hotmail.com

ABRAMOVITZ, MIMI
PERSONAL Born 07/13/1941, New York, NY, m, 1962 **DISCIPLINE** SOCIAL WELFARE POLICY, WOMEN, POVERTY, WELFARE REFORM **EDUCATION** Univ Mich, BA, 63; Columbia Univ, MSW, 67; DSW, 81. **CAREER** Case wkr, Conn Wel Dept, 63-65; res asst, Comm Men Hlth, 67-68; ed, Yale Bk, 69-70; un org, NCDW, 70-71; res assoc, Yale Univ, 72-73; res dir, Corn Sch, 76-77; adj lectr, Hunter Col, 76-77; lectr, New York Univ, 78-79; adj asst prof, Ford Grad Sch, 79-81; asst prof, 81-85; assoc prof, 86-88, Hunt Coll; doc prog, CUNY, 89-; prof, Hunt Sch SW, 89-. **HONORS AND AWARDS** William J Branstrom Prize; Phi Kappa Phi; Phi Beta Kappa; MSW w Dist; NASW, PACE Awd; Outstand Bk Awd. **MEMBERSHIPS** NASW; CSWE; WC100; AWSW; SWHG; SWAA. **RESEARCH** Social welfare policy; welfare reform; poverty; women; work; poverty; social activism. **SELECTED PUBLICATIONS** Rev, "Wages for Housework," in Welfare's End, by Gwendolyn Mink, Progressive 62 (98): 41-43; rev, "Mothers of Invention," in The Myth of the Welfare Queen, by David Zuccino, Women's Rev Bks (97); auth, "Social Work and Social Reform: An Arena of Struggle, Soc Wor 43 (98): 512-527; auth, "Women: Get Ready for the Long Haul, Affilia 12 (96); auth, "Challenging the Myths of Welfare Reform From a Woman's Perspective, Soc Just 21 (94); auth, "Toward a Framework for Understanding Activism Among Poor and the Working Class Women in Twentieth Century America," in Whose Welfare? ed. Gwendolyn Mink (Ithaca: Cornell Univ Press, 99); coauth, "Playing by the Rules: Welfare Reform and the New Authoritarian State," in Without Justice for All, ed. Adolph Reed Jr (Boulder, CO: Westview Press, 99). **CONTACT ADDRESS** Sch of Soc Work, Hunter Col, CUNY, 129 East 79th St, New York, NY 10021. **EMAIL** iabramov@shiva.hunter.cuny.edu

ABRAMS, JANICE K.
DISCIPLINE EDUCATION **EDUCATION** Geneva Col, BSEd, 68; Univ PGH, MEd, 71; Indiana Univ PA, EdD, 90. **CAREER** Asst prof, Indiana Univ Pa, 89-91; assoc prof, Carlow Col, 92-. **HONORS AND AWARDS** Who's Who in Am Educ, 94. **MEMBERSHIPS** Kappa Delta Pi, Pi Delta Kappa, Pi Lambda Theta, Intl Reading Asn. **RESEARCH** Literacy, Perceptual conceptualization, Learning disabilities. **SELECTED PUBLICATIONS** Auth, An Analysis of Learning Disabilities and Childhood Depression in Pre-adolescent Students, 90. **CONTACT ADDRESS** Div Educ, Carlow Col, 3333 5th Ave, Pittsburgh, PA 15213.

ABRAMSON, DAVID M.
PERSONAL Born 07/25/1965, Chicago, IL **DISCIPLINE** ANTHROPOLOGY **EDUCATION** Wesleyan Univ, BA, 87; Ind Univ, MA, 94; PhD, 98. **CAREER** Assoc Instructor, Ind Univ, 95; Adj Fac, Butler Univ, 96; Adj Asst Prof and Post-Doc Fel, Brown Univ, 97-. **HONORS AND AWARDS** David C. Skomp Fel, IN Univ, 91-92; Travel Grant, IN Univ, 93; Fel, IN MacArthur Ctr, 93-94; Grant, Wenner-Gren Foundation, 94-95; Jacob K. Javits Fel, U.S. Dept Educ, 92-96; Fel, IN Univ, 96-97; Fel, ACTR/ACCELS, 98; Fel, NCEEER, 99-00. **MEMBERSHIPS** Am Anthropol Asn; Am Ethnol Asn; Asn for Polit and Legal Anthropol; Soyuz Res Network for Post-communist Cultural Studies. **RESEARCH** Political anthropology; Development and the politics of foreign aid; Postcolonial theory; collective identity; Transnationalism and globalization; Islam and politics; community and intimacy; Uzbekistan, Central Asia, former Soviet Union. **SELECTED PUBLICATIONS** Auth, "Renaming in Central Asia: A Process of History and Memory," The Turkish Studies Asn Bulletin, (93): 43-46; auth, "Remembering the Present: The Meaning of 1989's violence in Kokand today," Central Asia Monitor, (97): 18-21; auth, "A Critical Look at NGOs and Civil Society as Means to an End in Uzbekistan," Human Organization, (990: 240-250; auth, "Civil Society and the Politics of Foreign Aid in Uzbekistan," Central Asia Monitor, (99): 1-12. **CONTACT ADDRESS** Dept Anthropol, Brown Univ, 1 Prospect St, Providence, RI 02912-9127. **EMAIL** David_abramson@brown.edu

ABRAMSON, LYN
PERSONAL Born 02/07/1950, Benson, MN, s **DISCIPLINE** PSYCHOLOGY **EDUCATION** Univ Wisc, BA, 72; Univ Penn, PhD, 78. **CAREER** Asst Prof, SUNY, 78-80; Asst to Full Prof, Univ Wisc, 81-. **HONORS AND AWARDS** Early Career Awd, AAA; Kellett Mid-Career Awd. **MEMBERSHIPS** APA, SRP, AABT. **RESEARCH** Depression. **CONTACT ADDRESS** Dept Psychol, Univ of Wisconsin, Madison, 1202 W Johnson St, Madison, WI 53706.

ACHENBAUM, W. ANDREW
PERSONAL Born 03/02/1947, Philadelphia, PA, m, 1971, 2 children **DISCIPLINE** HISTORY; GERONTOLOGY **EDUCATION** Amherst Col, BA, 68; Univ Pa, MA, 70; Univ Mich, PhD, 76. **CAREER** Asst prof hist, Canisius Col, 76-80; asst res scientist, Inst Geront, Univ Mich, Ann Arbor, 78-80; Asst Prof Hist, Carnegie-Mellon Univ, 80-, Consult hist & humanities, Inst Gerontology, 77-78. **MEMBERSHIPS** Orgn Am Historians; Geront Soc; Soc Sci Hist Asn. **RESEARCH** United States social and cultural history; history of aging; social welfare. **SELECTED PUBLICATIONS** Auth, Old Age in The New Land: The American Experience Since 1790, Johns Hopkins Univ, 78; coauth, Old age and modernization, Gerontologist, 6/78; auth, From womb through bloom to tomb, Rev Am Hist, 6/78; coauth, Images of Old Age in America, 1790-Present, Inst of Gerontology, 78; auth, Modern Values and Aging America, Little Brown, 82. **CONTACT ADDRESS** Dept of Hist, Carnegie Mellon Univ, Pittsburgh, PA 15213.

ACHESON, JULIANNA
PERSONAL Born 04/20/1965, Rochester, NY, m, 1993, 2 children **DISCIPLINE** ANTHROPOLOGY **EDUCATION** Univ Maine, BA, 87; Univ Ariz, MA, 91; PhD, 97. **CAREER** Instr, Western Wash Univ, 95-; adj prof, Castleton State Col, 00-. **HONORS AND AWARDS** Tinker Grant, 89; IREX Scholar, 91, 99; Fulbright Fel, 92; Kukuchma Mem Lectr, 95; Western Wash Res Grant, 98. **MEMBERSHIPS** Soc for Applied Anthrop; Am Assoc for the Advan of Slavic Studies; Am Anthrop Assoc; Soc for the Anthrop of Europe; Rrural Sociol Assoc; AAUW; Czechoslovak Hist Conf. **RESEARCH** Slovakia, Central and Eastern Europe. **SELECTED PUBLICA-**

TIONS Auth, "Reflections on the Diachronism of Marshall Sahlins", Ariz Anthrop 2, 91; auth, "Nouvelle perspectives sur l'emigration et les retours selon le point de vue de la communaute de depart: analyse d'une cohorte du nord-ouest du Portugal", L'emigration: Une Response Universelle a une Situation de Crise?, Le Chable (Switzerland, 91); auth, We Haven't Eaten Fried Cheese Since the Revolution: Life After the Fall of Communism in Kojsov, Slovakia, Univ of Calif Pr, (forthcoming); auth, "Coping with an Uncertainty; Household Ecology in Rural Eastern Slovakia", Anthropology: Personal Encounters, ed Linda S Walbridge and April K Sievert, (forthcoming). **CONTACT ADDRESS** Dept Soc Sci, Castleton State Col, Leavenworth Hall, Castleton, VT 05735. **EMAIL** jacheson@cc.wwu.edu

ACHMITT, NEAL W.
PERSONAL Born 06/13/1944, Decorah, IA, m, 1968, 1 child **DISCIPLINE** PSYCHOLOGY **EDUCATION** Loras Cool, BA, 66; Purdue Univ, MS, 69; PhD, 72. **CAREER** Asst Prof, N Ky Univ, 72-74; From Asst Prof to Prof, Mich State Univ, 74-. **HONORS AND AWARDS** Fulbright Scholar, Univ Manchester; Distinguished SCI Contributions, SIOP; Distinguished Serv Contributions, SIOP. **MEMBERSHIPS** Am Psychol Asn, Acad of Management, Soc for Indust and Organizational Psychol. **RESEARCH** Personnel selection **SELECTED PUBLICATIONS** Coauth, "Likability and Similarity as Potential Sources of Predictor-Related Criterion Bias in Validation Research," Organizational Behav and Human Decision Processes, 68 (96): 272-286; coauth, "Relationship Between Culture and Responses to Biodata Employment Items," J of Applied Psychol, 82 (97): 113-129; coauth, "Video-based Versus Paper-And-Pencil Method of Assessment in Situational Judgement Tests: Subgroup Differences in Test Performance and Face Validity Perceptions," J of Applied Psychol, 82 (97): 143-159; coauth, "Applicant Reactions of Test Fairness: Integrating Justice and Self-Serving Bias Perspectives," Int J of Selection and Assessment, 6 (98): 232-239; coauth, "Parallel Test Development: A Procedure for Alternate Predictors and an Example," Personnel Psychol, 51 (98): 193-208; coauth, "Relationships Between Appropriateness Fit, Test Reactions, Test-Taking Motivation, Conscientiousness and Test Validity," Applied Psychol Measurement, 22 (99): 41-54; coauth, "Motivational and Contextual Influences on Training Effectiveness: A Field Study," Training Roes J, 4 (99): 11-26; coauth, "Developing Measures of Basic Job-Relevant English Proficiency for the Prediction of Job Performance and Promotability," J of Bus and Psychol (forthcoming). **CONTACT ADDRESS** Dept Psychol, Michigan State Univ, 135 Snyder, East Lansing, MI 48824. **EMAIL** schmitt@msu.edu

ACKERSON, BARRY J.
PERSONAL Born 06/24/1953, Ogdensburg, NY, m, 1976, 1 child **DISCIPLINE** SOCIAL WORK **EDUCATION** Univ Ala, Tuscaloosa, BA, 75; MSW, 78; PhD, 98. **CAREER** Center for the Study of Aging, Univ of Ala, 78, Col of Community Health Scis, 78; acting community placement dir, Bureau of M.I. Community Programs, 90-91; Ala Dept of Mental Health & Mental Retardation, Tuscaloosa and Montgomery, 90-97; adjunct fac, Univ of Ala, 94-98; asst prof, Univ of Ill at Urbana-Champaign, Sch of Soc Work, 98-. **HONORS AND AWARDS** Phi Beta Kappa; Phi Kappa Phi; graduated cum laude, Univ of Ala, 75; Doctoral Student Orgn Awd for Service and Leadership, 95; Nat Alumni Asn Fel, 97-98. **MEMBERSHIPS** NASW, ESWE, IAPSRS, Coun on Social Work Educ, Nat Alliance for the Mentally Ill (Champaign Co), Univ of Ala Social Work Soc. **RESEARCH** Adults with serious mental illness; social support; social competence. **SELECTED PUBLICATIONS** Coauth with S. A. Watkins, "Right-sizing: hospital-community collaboration to reduce inpatient beds," Discharge Planning Update, 14, 6 (94): 6-13; coauth with L. W. Badger, F. Buttell, and E. H. Rand, "The case for integration of social work psychosocial services into rural primary care practice," Health and Social Work, 22 (97): 20-29; auth, "Factors influencing life satisfaction in psychiatric rehabilitation," Psychiatric Rehabilitation J (winter 2000); coauth with W. D. Harrison, "Practitioners' perceptions of empowerment,." Families in Society (May/June 2000). **CONTACT ADDRESS** Dept Soc Work, Univ of Illinois, Urbana-Champaign, 1207 W Oregon, Urbana, IL 61801.

ADAMS, AFESA M.
PERSONAL Born 02/20/1936, Greenwood, MS, m, 1975 **DISCIPLINE** PSYCHOLOGY **EDUCATION** Weber State Col, BS, 1969; University of Utah, MS, 1973, PhD, 1975. **CAREER** University of Florida, asst professor, behavioral studies, 74-79, acting chair, behavioral studies, 76-78, assoc professor, psychology, 76-80; University of Utah, dept of family & consumer studies, chair, 80-83, assoc vice president, academic affairs, 84-89, assoc professor, family & consumer studies, adjunct assoc professor, dept of psychology; University of North Florida, College of Arts & Sciences, dean, 89-93; Professor of Psychology, 93- currently. **HONORS AND AWARDS** Beehive Lodge, Elks, community service award, 1986; Phi Kappa Phi; United Way, Great Salt Lake Area, recognition for community service award, 1986; Hall of Fame, Granite High School, 1987-88; Civil Rights Worker of the Year, NAACP SL Branch, 1988; Featured in State Office of Educational Equity Unit film, Building on a Legacy: Contemporary Pioneering Women, 1988. **MEMBERSHIPS** American Psychological Assn; Utah Council on Family Relations; Natl Council of Negro Women Inc; Southeastern Psychological Assn; American Psychological Assn; Gainesville Women's Health Center, board of directors; State of Utah, Divison of Children, Youth & Families Day Care, advisory board, 1980-83; Governor's Committee for Exec Reorganization, 1983-85; Governor's Task Force, study financial barriers to health care, 1983-84, employer sponsored child care, 1984; several publications and papers; Daniel Memorial Institute, Inc, board of directors, 1989; Jacksonville Community Council, Inc; Hubbard House Programs for Spouse Abuse, board of directors, 1992-94; Advocates for a Better Jacksonville, 1989-, Jacksonville Art Museum, bd of dirs, 1990-93; Jacksonville Women's Network, 1989-; Raines High School, advisory council, 1989-; Andrew Jackson High School, accreditation team, 1989-; JCCI Study, Young Black Males, management team, 1989-; Chair, Implementation Community: JCCI Young Black Males Study, 1989-; National Council on Family Relations, 1989-; Popular Culture Association, 1989-; American Association for High Education, 1989-93; JCCI, bd of dirs, 1993-, sec, 1994-95, president elect 1996-97; Leadership Jacksonville Class, 1994; LJ, bd of dirs, 1994-95; Florida Theatre, board of directors, 1994-, vice pres, 1996-; UNF/NW Link: A Service Learning Monitoring Program, 1995-. **CONTACT ADDRESS** Psychology Department, Univ of No Florida, St Johns Bluff Rd, S, Jacksonville, FL 32224-2645.

ADAMS, BEVERLY C.
PERSONAL Born 05/28/1952, Youngstown, OH, s, 1 child **DISCIPLINE** PSYCHOLOGY **EDUCATION** Univ Pittsburgh, PhD, 90. **CAREER** Asst Prof, Randolph-Macon Woman's Col, 97-. **MEMBERSHIPS** AERA; Psychonomics (Psychonomic Society), SRCD. **RESEARCH** Psycholinguistics; Sentence Processing; Technology & Gender. **SELECTED PUBLICATIONS** Auth, "A Trading relationship between reading skill and domain knowledge in children's text comprehension, by Adams, B.C., Bell, L.C., & Perfetti, C.A., Discomse Processes, 20, 95: 307-323; auth, "Lexical guidance in sentence processing?, by Adams, B.C., Clifton, Jr., C., & Mitchell, D.C., Disconmse Processes, 20, 98: 307-323. **CONTACT ADDRESS** Dept Psychology, Randolph-Macon Woman's Col, 2500 Rivermont Ave, Lynchburg, VA 24503. **EMAIL** badams@rmwc.edu

ADAMS, JEFFREY
DISCIPLINE PSYCHOLOGY **EDUCATION** Univ Calif, BA, 89; Calif State Univ, MA, 92; Univ Tenn, PhD, 96. **CAREER** Teaching Asst to Res Supervisor, Calif State Univ, 91-92; Teaching Assoc to Res Asst, Univ Tenn, 92-96; Asst Prof, High Point Univ, 96-. **HONORS AND AWARDS** Chancellor's Citation for Extraordinary Professional Promise, Univ TN, 96. **MEMBERSHIPS** Am Psychol Asn; Intl Network on Personal Relationships; Intl Soc for the Study of Personal Relationships; Nat Coun on Family Relations; SE Psychol Asn; Soc of SE Soc Psychol; Psi Chi. **RESEARCH** Commitment in close relationships, primarily on issues of conceptualization and measurement; Origins and dynamics of commitment in close relationships. **SELECTED PUBLICATIONS** Co-auth, "A psychometric exploration of marital satisfaction and commitment," Journal of Social Behavior and Personality, (95): 923-932; co-auth, "The assessment of trust orientation," Journal of Personality Assessment, (96): 305-322; co-auth, "The conceptualization of marital commitment: An integrative analysis," Journal of Personality and Social Psychology, (97): 1177-1196; co-auth, "The dynamics of interpersonal commitment and the issue of salience," in The handbook of interpersonal commitment and relationship stability, (Kluwer Acad Press, 99), 165-179; co-auth, "Interpersonal commitment in historical perspective," in The handbook of interpersonal commitment and relationship stability, (Kluwer Acad Press, 99), 3-33; co-ed, The handbook of interpersonal commitment and relationship stability, Kluwer Acad Press, 99; auth, "Future directions for commitment research," in The handbook of interpersonal commitment and relationship stability, (Kluwer Acad Press, 99), 503-520; auth, "Interpersonal commitment," in Encyclopedia of human emotions, Macmillan, 99; auth, "The Dimensions of Commitment Inventory," in A handbook of psychological tests, Edwin Mellen Press, in press. **CONTACT ADDRESS** Dept Beh Sci, High Point Univ, 933 Montlieu Ave, High Point, NC 27262. **EMAIL** jeadams@acme.highpoint.edu

ADAMS, KIMBERLY V.
DISCIPLINE 19TH-CENTURY BRITISH LITERATURE, BRITISH AND AMERICAN NOVEL, WOMEN'S STUDIES **EDUCATION** Harvard Univ, PhD. **CAREER** Instr, Rutgers, State Univ NJ, Camden Col of Arts and Sci. **HONORS AND AWARDS** Provost's Tchg Excellence Awd, 93. **RESEARCH** Feminist symbol. **SELECTED PUBLICATIONS** Auth, Feminine Godhead, Feminist Symbol: The Madonna in the Work of Ludwig Feuerbach, Anna Jameson, Margaret Fuller, and George Eliot, J of Feminist Stud in Relig; The Madonna and Margaret Fuller, Women's Stud. **CONTACT ADDRESS** Rutgers, The State Univ of New Jersey, New Brunswick, Camden Col of Arts and Sci, New Brunswick, NJ 08903-2101.

ADAMS, RICHARD E. W.
PERSONAL Born 07/17/1931, Kansas City, MO, m, 1955, 4 children **DISCIPLINE** ANTHROPOLOGY AND ARCHAEOLOGY **EDUCATION** BA, anthrop, Univ NMex, 53; MA, anthrop, Harvard Univ, 60; PhD, anthrop, 63. **CAREER** Asst prof to prof, anthrop, Univ Minn, 63-72; dean, humanities and social sci, Univ Tex San Antonio, 72-79; prof, anthrop, Univ Tex San Antonio, 80-. **HONORS AND AWARDS** Fulbright scholar, resident fel, Rochefeller Ctr, Bellagio, Italy, overseas fel, Churchill Col, Cambridge Univ, England; Nat Geographic Soc grant, 83-94; Nat Endowment for the Humanities grant, 85-94. **MEMBERSHIPS** Soc for Amer Archaeol; Registry of Prof Archaeol; Tex Archaeol Soc. **RESEARCH** New world archaeology; Primary ancient civilizations; Maya archaeology. **SELECTED PUBLICATIONS** Auth, Prehistoric Mesoamerica, Univ Ok Press, 92; coauth, "The Tombs of Rio Azul," National Geographic Res and Exploration (92); auth, The Ancient Civilizations of the New World, Westview Press, 97; auth, Rio Azul: An Ancient Maya City, Univ of Ok Press, 99; ed, The Origins of Maya Civilization; auth, Ancient Civilizations of the New World, Rio Azul. **CONTACT ADDRESS** Univ of Texas, San Antonio, 14070 Mint Tr., San Antonio, TX 78232-3509. **EMAIL** radams@utsa.edu

ADAMS, WILLIAM
PERSONAL Born 02/21/1923, Bloomington, IN, m, 1968, 6 children **DISCIPLINE** ANTHROPOLOGY **EDUCATION** Indiana Univ, AB, 44; MA, 49. **CAREER** Field Archaeologist, State of Indiana, Indian Historical Bureau, 45-47; Laboratory instr and Embalmer, Indiana Univ, 47-51; Student Archaeologist, Univ of Illinois, 49-; Zooarchaeologist, Univ of Michigan, 50; Teller and Dir, Bloomington National Bank, Executive Vice Pres and Director, Bloomington National Bank, 62-73; Pres and Chairman of Board, Bloomington National Bank, 73-80; Cnsultant, Bloominton National Bank, 80-82; Field Director, Royal Ontario Museum, 55-57; Lecturer in Zooarchaeology, Indiana Univ, 55-; Archaeologist and Zooarchaeologist, Indiana Gear Works Arctic Expedition, 57; Consultant and Supplier of Educational Specimens to Indianapolis Zoo, 80-92; Consultant and Supplier of Educational Specimens to Mesker Park Zoo. **HONORS AND AWARDS** Departmental Fac Improvement Grant for Catalog Revision for Zooarchaeology, 92; COAS grant for salvage of specimens from Valdez Oil Spill. **MEMBERSHIPS** Society of Professional Archaeologists; Society for Amer Archaeology; Southeastern Archaeological Conference; Indiana Academy of Science; Indiana Historical Society; Monroe County Historical Society; Trowel and Brush Society; National Audubon Society; smithsonian Associates; Old Library, Inc; Indiana Police League; Indiana Sheriffs Assoc; Indiana Chiefs of Police; Monroe County Auxiliary Police; Decade of Deputies. **RESEARCH** Amer Academy of Forensic Scientists; Indian Academy of Sciences; Aboriginal Medicine; Serology and Hitology of North American; Pleistocene Vertebrates. **SELECTED PUBLICATIONS** Auth, "Excavations at the Serpent Mound Group," Royal Ontario Museum, 56; auth, "Faunal remains from tenant farmer sites, Waverly Plantation, Mississippi," In Waverly Plantation: Ethnoarcheology of a tenant farming community," William Hampton Adams, ed. App.5, 437-451, National Technical Information Service, Washington, D.C., 80; auth, "In Bay Springs Mill: Historical; archeology of a rural Mississippi cotton milling community," William Hampton Adams, Steven D. Smith, David F. Barton, Timothy B. Riordan, and Stephen Poyper, App. 5, 477, National Technical Information Service, Washington, D.C.; auth, "The Kings Bay Plantation House and Kitchen," In Historical arcahaeology of Plantations of Kings Bay, Camden County, Georgia, Reports of Investigations 5, Dept of Anthropology, Univ of Florida Gainesville, 131-163, 87; auth, Foodways on the Plantations at Kings Bay: Hunting, Fishing, and Raising Food, 87, In Historical archaeology of Plantations of Kings Bay, Camden County, Georgia, Reports of Investigations 5, Dept of anthropology, Univ of Florida, Gainesville, 225-275, 87; auth, Faunal remains from the Palos Site Ck26, Cook County, Illinois, 88; auth, "Zooarchaeology in Indiana, the Past, the Present, and the Future," by Janis K. Kearney, Proceedings of the indiana Academy of Science, Indianapolis, 89; auth, "Holocene Bison Remains," from Greene County, Indiana, Proceedings of the Indiana Academy of science, in publication; **CONTACT ADDRESS** Dept Anthropology, Indiana Univ, Bloomington, 701 E Kirkwood Ave, Bloomington, IN 47405. **EMAIL** adamsw@indiana.edu

ADEKSON, MARY OLUFUNMILAYO
PERSONAL Born, Nigeria **DISCIPLINE** EDUCATION **EDUCATION** Brandeis Univ, BA, 75; Obafemi Univ, ME D, 87; Ohio Univ, PhD, 97. **CAREER** Teach, Nigeria, 68-88; act princ, Abe Tech Col, 78; coord guide serv, Min Edu, 84-88; pt lectr, Obafemi Univ, 86-88; vice prin, Olubuse HS, 87-88; grad asst, Ohio Univ, 88-91; contr wkr, 88-92; pt lectr, Univ Maryland, 93; adj prof, Bowie State Univ, 97-98; asst prof, St Bonaventure, 98-. **HONORS AND AWARDS** Gold Med, West African Athle Asn; Intl Peace Schl; Who's Who Med Hlth Care. **MEMBERSHIPS** ACA; AMHCA; AACD; CAN; ARCA; AMCD; OSNA; AGC. **SELECTED PUBLICATIONS** Auth, "Reclaiming the Lost Generation: Strategies for Working with African American Males," Advocate, AMHCA 17 (94); auth, "Positive Strategies for Working With Adolescents at Risk," Advocate, AMHCA 17 (94); auth, "The Interpersonal Techniques Used by Yoruba Traditional Healers of Nigeria: A Case

Study," Univ Microfilms (97); auth, "Family Theory Used by Yoruba Traditional Healers of Nigeria," in The Development of Family Therapy: A Global Perspective, forthcoming. **CONTACT ADDRESS** School Education, St. Bonaventure Univ, Saint Bonaventure, NY 14778.

ADETUNJI, JACOB
PERSONAL m, 1992, 3 children **DISCIPLINE** SOCIOLOGY **EDUCATION** Univ Calabar, Nigeria, BS, 85; Univ Ibadan, Nigeria, MS, 87; Australian Nat Univ, MA, 90; PhD, 95. **CAREER** Bell Res Fel, Harvard Ctr for Population and Development Studies, 93-95; DHS Fel, Macro Intl, 95-97; Res Fel, Univ Pa, 97-98; Asst prof, Bowling Green State Univ, 98-. **HONORS AND AWARDS** MacArthur Leadership Prog Fel Awd, 93-95; Population Council Fel, 93-94; Commonwealth Scholarship and Fel Awd, 88-93. **MEMBERSHIPS** Population Asn of Am, Am Sociol Asn, Intl Union for the Sci Study of Population, Union for African population Studies, African Studies Asn. **RESEARCH** Determinants of health and mortality differentials, HIV/AIDS, Population and socioeconomic development, African marriage systems and Determinants of unwanted fertility. **SELECTED PUBLICATIONS** Auth, "The impact of HIV/AIDS relative to other causes of adult deaths in sub-Saharan Africa," African Population Studies, (98): 17-35; auth, "Preserving the Pot and Water: Traditional Concept of Reproductive Health in a Nigerian Community," Social Science and Medicine, (96): 1561-1567; auth, "Infant Mortality and Mother's Education in Ondo State, Nigeria," Social Science and Medicine, (95): 253-263; auth, "Infant Mortality in Nigeria: Effects of Child's Place of Delivery, Mother's Education and Region of Residence," Journal of Biosocial Science, (94): 469-477; auth, "Church-based Obstetric Care in a Yoruba Community, Nigeria," Social Science and Medicine, (92): 1171-1178; auth, "Response of Parents to five Killer Diseases Among children in a Yoruba community, Nigeria," Social Science and Medicine, (91):1379-1387. **CONTACT ADDRESS** Dept Sociol, Bowling Green State Univ, 1001 E Wooster St, Bowling Green, OH 43403-0001. **EMAIL** adetunj@bgnet.bgsu.edu

ADLER, MARINA
PERSONAL Born Hanau, Germany **DISCIPLINE** SOCIOLOGY **EDUCATION** Univ Tenn, BA, 81; MA, 84; PhD, 90. **CAREER** Instructor, Univ Md, 84-89; Res Asst, Battelle Mem Inst, 88-90; Visiting Asst Prof to Assoc prof, Univ Md, 90-. **HONORS AND AWARDS** Irene Taeuber Awd, D.C. Sociol Soc, 87, 88; Pres Commission for Women's Awd for Excellence, Univ MD, 97. **MEMBERSHIPS** Am Sociol Asn; Sociol for Women in Soc; S Sociol Soc; Sektion Frauenforschung in den Sozialwissenschaften in der Deutschen Gesellschaft fur Soziologie; Intl Sociol Asn; E Sociol Soc. **RESEARCH** Cross-national work and family issues; Gender, the state, and social policy; Gender and race inequality; Quantitative and qualitative research methods. **SELECTED PUBLICATIONS** Co-auth, "Gender, Race, and Cultural Literacy: consequences for Academic performance," Teaching Sociology, (90: 850-854; co-auth, "Perceptions of Women's Opportunities in the Federal Republic of Germany and the United Kingdom," Mid-American Review of Sociology, (92): 45-60; auth, "Male-Female Power Differences at Work: a Comparison of Supervisors and policy Makers," Sociological Inquiry, (94): 37-55; co-auth, "East-West differences in Attitudes about Employment and Family in Germany," The Sociological Quarterly, (96): 401-416; co-auth, "Using and Interpreting Logistic Regression: A Guide for Teachers and Students," Teaching sociology, (96): 284-298; auth, "Xenophobia and Ethnoviolence in Contemporary Germany," Critical Sociology, (96): 29-52; auth, "Impact of German Unification on women in the rural East and West," Sociological Focus, (96): 291-310; co-auth, "Women's Work Values in Unified Germany: Regional Differences as Remnants of the Past," Work and Occupations, (97): 245-266; auth, "Social Change and Declines in Marriage and Fertility in the New German States," Journal of Marriage and the Family, (97): 37-49; auth, "Feminist Cross-national Research: Observations from a Research Project in Germany," Social Thought and Research, (97): 73-84. **CONTACT ADDRESS** Dept Sociol, Univ of Maryland, Baltimore, 1000 Hilltop Circle, Baltimore, MD 21250-0002. **EMAIL** Adler@umbc.edu

ADLER, PETER
PERSONAL Born 02/03/1952, Queens, NY, m, 1972, 2 children **DISCIPLINE** SOCIOLOGY **EDUCATION** Wash Univ, AM, 73; Univ Chicago, MA, 74; Univ Calif at San Diego, PhD, 80. **CAREER** Asst Prof, Univ of Tulsa, 80-86; Assoc Prof, Wash Univ at St. Louis, 86-87; Assoc Prof/Prof, Univ of Denver, 87-. **HONORS AND AWARDS** Distinguished Univ Lectr, Univ of Denver, 97-98. **MEMBERSHIPS** Am Sociol Asn, Soc for the Study of Soc Problems, Soc for the Study of Symbolic Interaction, Midwest Sociol Soc. **RESEARCH** Qualitative Methodology, Deviant Behavior, Social Psychology, Sociology of Sport. **SELECTED PUBLICATIONS** Coauth, "The Demography of Ethnography," J of Contemp Ethnog 24-1 (95); coauth, "Dynamics of Inclusion and Exclusion in Preadolescent Cliques," Soc Psychology Quart 35-2 (95); coauth, "Parent-as-Researcher: The Politics of Researching in the Personal Life," Qualitative Psychology 19-1 (96); coauth, "Preadolescent Clique Stratification and the Hierarchy of Identity," Sociol Inquiry 66-2 (96); coauth, Peer Power: Preadolescent Culture and Identity, Rutgers Univ Press (New Brunswick, NJ), 98; coauth, "Transience and the Postmodern Self: The Geographic Mobility of Resort Workers," The Sociol Quart 40-1 (99); coauth, "The Ethnographers' Ball Revisited," J of Contemp Ethnog 28-5 (99): coauth, "Resort Workers: Adaptations in the Leisure-Work Nexus," Sociol Perspectives 42-3 (99); coauth, Construction of Deviance: Social Power, Context, and Interaction, 3rd ed, Wasdworth (Belmont, CA), 00. **CONTACT ADDRESS** Dept Sociol, Univ of Denver, 2040 S Race St, Denver, CO 80210. **EMAIL** adler@spot.colorado.edu

ADOVASIO, J. M.
PERSONAL Born 02/17/1944, Youngstown, OH, w **DISCIPLINE** ANTHROPOLOGY **EDUCATION** Univ Ariz, BA, 65; Univ Utah, PhD, 70. **CAREER** Asst Prof, Youngstown State Univ, 70-71; Asst Prof to Assoc Prof, Univ Pittsburgh, 72-79; Adj Assoc Prof, Youngstown State Univ, 76-78; Assoc Prof to Prof, Univ Pittsburgh, 76-90; Prof to Inst Dir, Mercyhurst Col, 90-. **HONORS AND AWARDS** Honors Prog participant, Univ Ariz, 63-65; Phi Eta sigma; 62; Phi Beta Kappa, 66; Rhodes Scholarship, State of Ariz, 66; NDEA Fel, Univ Utah, 68-70; Sigma Xi, 76; Outstanding Young Men of Am, 78; Knight of the sovereign Military Order of Malta, 95; Grant, Nat Geog Soc, 93; Ires Grant, 94; Res Grant, Wenner Gren Foundation, 95. **MEMBERSHIPS** Am Anthropol Asn, Soc for Am Archaeol, Am Quaternary Asn, Am Asn for the Advancement of Sci, Soc for Penn Archaeol, NY Acad of Sci, Am Schools for Oriental Res. **RESEARCH** Primitive technology especially lithics, basketry and textiles; Early man in North America; The archaid (Mesolithic) stage in the Old and New World including subsistence, demography, technology, settlement patterns, etc.; Quaternary Paleoecology; Research methodology in the excavation of caves and rockshelters. **SELECTED PUBLICATIONS** Co-auth, "Basketry and Miscellaneous Perishable artifacts from Walpi Pueblo, Arizona," Ethnology Monographs Number 7, 85; co-auth, "Perishable Industries from Dirty shame rockshelter, Malheur county, Oregon," Ethnology Monographs 9, 86; co-auth, "Archaeological Investigations at 36BK549, Berks county Pennsylvania," University of Pittsburgh Anthropological Papers, 89; co-auth, "Environment and Excavations," Mercyhurst Archaeological Inst Reports of Investigations No. 1, 97; co-auth, "Archaeological Investigation of the Elk Creek site, Girard Township, Erie county, Pennsylvania," Mercyhurst Archaeological Inst Reports of Investigations No 2, 98; auth, "Paleoindians in Pennsylvania," in The Paleoindian Period in Pennsylvania, Penn Hist & Museum Commission, in press; auth, "Pennsylvania," in The early and Middle Woodland Periods in Pennsylvania, Penn Hist & Museum Commission, in press; auth, "The Appearance of Cultigens and the Early Woodland Period in southwestern Pennsylvania," Publications of the Ohio Archaeological Council, in press; auth, "Late Woodland adaptations on the Lake Erie Plain," in The Late Woodland Period in Pennsylvania, Penn Hist & Museum Commission, in press. **CONTACT ADDRESS** Dept Anthropol & Archaeol, Mercyhurst Col, 501 E 38th St, Erie, PA 16546. **EMAIL** adovasio@mercyhurst.edu

AFFINITO, MONA GUSTAFSON
PERSONAL Born 10/28/1929, Bristol, CT, d, 2 children **DISCIPLINE** PSYCHOLOGY **EDUCATION** Conn Col, BA, 51; Boston Univ, MA, 52; PhD, 64. **CAREER** Prof to dept chair, Southern Conn State Univ, 58-87; private practice, 78-. **MEMBERSHIPS** Am Psychol Asn, Conn Psychol Asn, Minn Psych Asn, Minn Women Psychol, Women in Psychol. **RESEARCH** Forgiveness, Women. **SELECTED PUBLICATIONS** Auth, Helping with Forgiveness Decisions, Manisses Commun Group, 98; auth, When to Forgive, New Harbinger Pub, 99. **CONTACT ADDRESS** Dept Psychol, Alfred Adler Inst of Minnesota, 1001 W Highway 7, Ste 311, Hopkins, MN 55305. **EMAIL** mona.affinito@mciworld.com

AGER, RICHARD D.
PERSONAL Born 10/01/1953, Ann Arbor, MI **DISCIPLINE** SOCIAL WORK **EDUCATION** Univ Mich, BA, 75; MSW, 80; PhD, 91. **CAREER** Teaching Fel, Univ MI, 90; Project Dir and Assoc Prof, Tulane Univ, 93-. **HONORS AND AWARDS** Grant, Tulane Univ, 94; Grant, LA Educ Quality Support Fund; Grant, CAP Alcohol and Other Drug Program; Grant, Fed Dept of Health, 98-00. **SELECTED PUBLICATIONS** Co-auth, "Unilateral relationship enhancement in the treatment of spouses of uncooperative alcohol abusers," American Journal of family Therapy, (90): 334-344; co-auth, "Treatment mediation and the spouse as treatment mediator," American Journal of Family Therapy, (91): 315-326; co-auth, "Nagging and other drinking control efforts of spouses of uncooperative alcohol abusers: Assessment and modification," Journal of Substance Abuse, (92): 309-318; co-auth, "The Spouse Enabling Inventory (SEI)," in Measures for clinical practice 2nd ed, Free Press, 94; co-auth, "The Spouse Sobriety Influence Inventory (SSII)," n Measures for clinical practice 2nd ed, Free Press, 94; co-auth, "The Life Distress Inventory (LDI)," in Measures for clinical practice 2nd ed, Free Press, 94; co-auth, "The Spouse Treatment Mediation Inventory (STMI)," in Measures for clinical practice 2nd ed, Free Press, 94; co-auth, "Measuring Spouse Sobriety Influence," Issues of Substance, (96): 6-7; co-auth, "Spouse enabling of alcohol abuse: Conception, assessment and modification," Journal of Substance Abuse, (96): 61-80; co-auth, "The Campus Affiliates Program: A case study in response to 'The university's responsibilities in troubled times'," American Behavior Scientist, (99): 827-839. **CONTACT ADDRESS** Dept Soc Work, Tulane Univ, 6823 St. Charles Ave, New Orleans, LA 70118. **EMAIL** ager@mailhost.tcs.tulane.edu

AGNE, KAREN J.
DISCIPLINE EDUCATION **EDUCATION** Southern Ill Univ, BS, 72; MS, 72; Univ Fla, PhD, 91. **CAREER** Instr, Southern Ill Univ, 82; Grad Teaching Assoc, Univ Fla, 87-91; Asst Prof, SUNY, 91-. **HONORS AND AWARDS** Distinguished Achievement Awd, Asn of Educ Pub, 99; Pi Lambda Theta Res Awd, 91; Nominated Outstanding Teaching Assoc, Univ Fla, 89; Phi delta Kappa Intl Prof Educ Soc, 89; Kappa Delta Pi Intl Honor Soc, 89; Pi Lambda Theta Nat Honor and professional Asn in Educ. **MEMBERSHIPS** Am Educ Res Asn, Phi Delta Kappa, Pi Lambda Theta, Kappa Delta Pi, Nat Asn for Gifted children, Creative Educ Foundation. **SELECTED PUBLICATIONS** Auth, Caring in the Classroom: The master teacher's way, forthcoming; co-auth, Creating a Caring classroom: A guide to teaching mastery, forthcoming; auth, "Caring: The Way of the Master Teacher," in Studying the Self Series, Vol 4: The role of Self in Teacher Development, SUNY Press, 98; auth, "Kill the Baby: Making All Things Equal," Educational Horizons, (99): 140-147; auth, "The dismantling of the Great American Public School," Educational Horizons, (98): 127-131; rev, of "Classroom Discipline and Management," by C.H. Edwards, Macmillan, 98; re, of "Management for Diverse classrooms: Understanding the Social Curriculum," Prentice-Hall Pub Co, 98; rev, of 'The RCM Plan: Responsible Classroom Management for Teachers and Students," Prentice-Hall Pub Co, 95; rev, of "Professional Core Case Studies for Teacher Decision-Making," by H Filler & G Greenwood, Macmillan Pub co, 94 **CONTACT ADDRESS** Dept Educ, SUNY, Col at Plattsburgh, 101 Broad St, Plattsburgh, NY 12901.

AHMED, ANSARUDDIN
PERSONAL m, 1 child **DISCIPLINE** SOCIOLOGY **EDUCATION** Univ Dhaka, BSS, 80; Univ Akron, MA, 85, PhD, 88. **CAREER** Asst prof, SUNY-MCC, 88-95; asst prof, Baldwin-Wallace Col, 95-98, assoc prof, 98-. **HONORS AND AWARDS** Numerous presentations at scholarly confs, res grants, prog evaluation projs, diversity workshops. **MEMBERSHIPS** Am Sociol Asn, Soc for the Advan of Socio-Econ, Asn for Social Econ. **RESEARCH** Socio-economic and community development. **SELECTED PUBLICATIONS** Coauth with David J. O'Brien and McKee McClendon, "Neighborhood Community and Quality of Life," J of the Community Develop Soc, vol 20, no 2 (fall 89); auth, "Testing Casual Interrelationships Between Population Dynamics, Factors of Technology, and Economic Growth," Nagarlok (Urban Affairs Quart), Vol XXIV, no 1, Center for Urban Studies, IIPA, New Delhi, India (Jan-March 92); auth, "Macrolevel Models of Comparative Economic Growth in Peripheral and Core Nations," The Asian Economic Rev, Indian Inst of Economics, Hyderabad, India (Dec 94). **CONTACT ADDRESS** Dept Sociol, Baldwin-Wallace Col, 275 Eastland Rd, Berea, OH 44017. **EMAIL** aahmed@bw.edu

AHN, TIMOTHY MYUNGHOON
PERSONAL Born 05/21/1953, Korea, m, 1978, 2 children **DISCIPLINE** CHRISTIAN EDUCATION **EDUCATION** Boston Univ, ThD, 94. **CAREER** Sr Pastor, Arcola Korean United Methodist Church. **CONTACT ADDRESS** S-62 Paramus Rd, Paramus, NJ 07652. **EMAIL** Wonseop@aol.com

AIELLO, T.
PERSONAL Born 01/07/1947, New York, NY, d **DISCIPLINE** SOCIAL WORK **EDUCATION** Juilliard School, BMus, 68; MSci, 69; Hunter Col, MSW, 79, NYU Elem Sch Soc Work, PhD, 93. **CAREER** Lectr to assoc prof, NY Univ, 91-. **HONORS AND AWARDS** Goddard Fel, NYU Sch of SW; Distinguished Teacher Awd, NY Univ, 98. **MEMBERSHIPS** NASW; NY State Clinical Soc, Soc Adolescent Psychiat. **RESEARCH** History of Psychoanalysis and social work. **SELECTED PUBLICATIONS** Rev, of "Adolescent Development: Psychopathology and Treatment", by H. Spencer Bloch, in J of Analytic Soc Work, 95; auth, "the history and influence of the psychoanalytic emigre community on clinical social work with children", Child and Adolescent Soc Work J, 98; auth, "Rationalization: A current theoretical conceptualization", A Dictionary of psychotherapy, Springer Pub, (NY), 98; auth, "Identity, Social Class and Intellect. Narrative of a Life History: The Treatment of a Young Asian Woman", Aspekte einer neven psychoanalyse: Ein selfstpsychologisher Austausch New York-Wien, Verlag Neue Psychoanalyse, (Wien), 99; coed, Love and Attachment, Jason Aronson, (Northvale, NJ), 99; auth, Child and adolescent treatment for social work practice: A relational perspective, Free Pr, (NY), 99; auth, "Identity: Dislocation and re-location in an Asian -American woman", Psychoanalysis and Psychotherapy, (00). **CONTACT ADDRESS** Sch of Soc Work, New York Univ, 2 Washington Sq N, New York, NY 10003.

AIKEN, LINDA H.
DISCIPLINE SOCIOLOGY, NURSING **EDUCATION** Univ Fla, BSN, 64; MN, 66; Univ Tex, PhD; Univ Wis, Postdoctoral Res Fel. **CAREER** Program Officer to Vice Pres, Robert Wood Johnson Foundation, 74-87; Prof, Univ Pa, 88-. **MEMBER-**

SHIPS Nat Acad of Sci, Nat Acad of Soc Insurance, Am Acad of Nursing, Am Sociol Asn. **RESEARCH** Health outcomes and policy. **SELECTED PUBLICATIONS** Auth, "Racial Differences in Access to Health Care: AIDS Care as a Case Illustration," in Problem of the Century: Racial Stratification in the US at the Millennium, Russell Sage, forthcoming; auth, "Hospital Organization and Culture: Impact on Outcomes," in The Future of the Hospital, London, forthcoming; auth, "Measuring Organizational Traits of Hospitals: The Revised Nursing Work Index," Nursing Research, forthcoming; auth, "The Magnet Nursing Services Recognition Program: A Comparison of Successful Applicants with Reputational Magnet Hospitals," American Journal of Nursing, 00; auth, "Organization and Outcomes of Inpatient AIDS Care," Medical Care, (99): 760-772; auth, "Accounting for Variation in Hospital Outcomes: A Cross-National Study," Health Affairs, (99): 256-259; auth, "Hospital Organization and Outcomes," Quality in Health Care, (98): 222-226; auth, "How the Organization and Staffing of Hospitals Affect Patient Outcomes," International Medical Forum, (98): 79-85; auth, "Review of Magnet Hospital Research: Established Findings and Implications for Professional Nursing Practice," Journal of Nursing Administration, (99): 9-19; auth, "Shaping systems to Promote Desired Outcomes: The Magnet Hospital Model," Journal of Nursing Administration, (99): 14-20. **CONTACT ADDRESS** Center for Health Outcomes & Policy Res, Univ of Pennsylvania, 420 Guardian Dr, Philadelphia, PA 19104-6096. **EMAIL** laiken@pop.upenn.edu

AINLEY, MARIANNE G.
PERSONAL Born Budapest, Hungary **DISCIPLINE** HISTORY OF SCIENCE, WOMEN'S STUDIES **EDUCATION** Sir George Williams Univ, BA, 64; Univ Montreal, MS, 80; McGill Univ, PhD, 85. **CAREER** Independent scholar, SSHRCC Can Strategic Grants Div, 86-87, 89-91; prin, Simone de Beauvoir Inst & Dir Women's Studs, Concordia Univ, 91-95; prof & ch, Women's Studies, Univ Northern BC, 95-. **MEMBERSHIPS** McGill Ctr Tchr Women; Soc Can Ornithol; Can Hist Educ Soc; Can Women's Stud Asn; Can Sci Tech Hist Asn; Can Res Inst Advan Women; Hist Sci Soc Am. **RESEARCH** Hist of Canaadian women and scientific work, feminist scientific biography, First Nations women and environmental knowledge, the hist of ornithology, and Candian environmental hist. **SELECTED PUBLICATIONS** Auth, Restless Energy: A Biography of Wiliam Rowan, 1891-1957, 93; auth, Louise de Kiriline Lawrence & the World of Nature: A Tribute in the Can Field Naturalist, 94; auth, Canadian Women's Contributions to Chemistry, 1900-1970, in Can Chem News, 94; auth, Despite the Odds, Essays on Canadian Women and Science, The Emergence of Canadian Ornithoogy - AN Historical Overview to 1950, in Contributions to the History of North American Ornithology, 95. **CONTACT ADDRESS** Women's Stud Prog, Univ of British Columbia, 3333 University Way, Prince George, BC, Canada V2N 4ZN. **EMAIL** ainley@unbc.ca

AKCA, ZEYNEP
PERSONAL Born 08/21/1950, Istanbul, Turkey, s, 1 child **DISCIPLINE** EDUCATION **EDUCATION** Hacettepe Univ, BA, 72; MA, 79; Univ Mo, PhD, 86. **CAREER** Adj Prof, Columbia Col, 89-91; Adj Prof, Lincoln Univ, 91-92; Asst Prof, Harris-Stowe State Col, 93-. **HONORS AND AWARDS** Ful Scholarship, UMC; An Apple for the Teacher Awd, Iota Phi Lambda Sorority. **MEMBERSHIPS** Am Psychol Asn, Coun of Exceptional Children, Alliance of the Mentally-ill, Mo Asn of Soc Welfare, Turkish Am Asn. **RESEARCH** At-risk children. **SELECTED PUBLICATIONS** Auth, Personality Characteristics of Sex Offenders. **CONTACT ADDRESS** Dept Teacher Educ, Harris-Stowe State Col, 3026 Laclede St, Saint Louis, MO 63103. **EMAIL** akcaz@hssc.edu

AKUBUKWE, DAVID
PERSONAL Born 10/25/1938, Omuma, Imo, Nigeria, m, 1969, 4 children **DISCIPLINE** SOCIOLOGY, SOCIAL WORK **EDUCATION** Texas Southern Univ, BA, 84; MA, 85; MA, 99; Texas A & M Univ, PhD, 93. **CAREER** Primary School Teacher, Oru LGA, 56-79; Headmaster, Umuhu Primary School, 79-80; Adjunct Prof, Texas Southern Univ, 94-95; Vis Asst Prof, Texas Southern Univ, 96-. **HONORS AND AWARDS** Who's Who Among Students in Am Universities and Colleges, 86. **MEMBERSHIPS** Society for the Study of Social Problems, Southwest Social Science Assoc, Nigerian Union of Teachers. **RESEARCH** Leadership & Social Power, News Coverage, Social Problems. **SELECTED PUBLICATIONS** Auth, Sociology: Concepts and Explanations, Opinion Research Ltd, 97; auth, Solution to Nigeria's Socio-Political and Economic Disaster: The Role of Leadership, Journal of Nigerian Affairs, 97. **CONTACT ADDRESS** Dept Sociology & Social Work, Texas So Univ, 3100 Cleburne St, Houston, TX 77004. **EMAIL** akubudave@aol.com

AL-MARAYATI, ABID AMIN
PERSONAL Born 10/14/1931, Baghdad, Iraq, 1 child **DISCIPLINE** POLITICAL SCIENCE, SOCIOLOGY, INTERNATIONAL LAW **EDUCATION** Bradley Univ, BA, 49-52, MA, 52-54; New York Univ, PhD, 54-59. **CAREER** Secy, Delegation Iraq, UN Gen Assembly, 55; secy, Delegation Yemen, UN Gen Assembly, 56-60; Instr, Govt, Univ Mass, 60; tech asst off, Int Atomic Energy Agency, Vienna, 60-62; assoc prof, SUNY, 62-64; res fel, Harvard Univ, 64-65; assoc prof, Ariz State Univ, 65-68; lectr & int educ consult, Am Inst For Trade, 65-68; PROF EMER, POLIT SCI, UNIV TOLEDO, 68-; vis prof, Univ Kuwait, 82-83; vis prof, Inst Public Admin, Riyadh, Saudi Arabia, 85-86; guest lectr, 90; vis prof, Beijing Stud Univ, 91. **MEMBERSHIPS** Assoc Student Educ; Middle East Studies Assoc N Amer; Phi Kappa Phi **RESEARCH** Psychological and Cultural Factors in the Iraq/Iran War; Shiism: A Study in Religion and Politics **CONTACT ADDRESS** Dept Polit Sci, Univ of Toledo, 2109 Terr View West, Toledo, OH 43607. **EMAIL** a_almarayati@yahoo.com

ALBA, RICHARD
PERSONAL Born 12/22/1941, 1942, m, 1976, 2 children **DISCIPLINE** SOCIOLOGY **EDUCATION** Columbia Col, AB, 63; PhD, 74. **CAREER** Asst prof, City Univ of NY, 74-77; asst prof, Cornell Univ, 77-80; assoc prof to prof, SUNY Albany, 80-. **HONORS AND AWARDS** Phi Beta Kappa; Fulbright Awd, 87-87, 93-94. **MEMBERSHIPS** Am Sociol Assoc; Eastern Sociol Soc; Population Assoc of Am. **RESEARCH** Race/ethnicity, immigration. **SELECTED PUBLICATIONS** Coauth, "Ethnicity in the American elite", Am Sociol Rev 47 (82): 373-83; auth, "The twilight of ethnicity among Americans of European ancestry: the case of Italians", Ethnic and Racial Studies 8 (85): 134-58; auth, Italian Americans: Into the Twilight of Ethnicity, Prentice-Hall, (Englewood Cliffs), 85; auth, Ethnic Identity: The Transformation of White America, Yale Univ Pr, (New Haven), 90; coauth, "Minority proximity to whites in suburbs: An individual-level analysis of segregation", Am J of Sociol 98 (93): 1388-1427; coauth, "Ethnische Ungleichheit im Deutschen Bildungssystem", Kolner Zeitschrift fur Soziologie und Sozialpsychologie 46 (94): 209-37; auth, "Assimilation's quiet tide", The Pub Interest 199 (95): 1-18; coauth, "Rethinking assimilation theory for a new era of immigration", Int Migration Rev 31 (97): 826-74; coauth, "Immigrant groups in the suburbs: A reexamination of suburbanization and spatial assimilation", Am Sociol Rev 64, (99): 446-60. **CONTACT ADDRESS** Dept Sociol, SUNY Albany, 1400 Washington Ave, Albany, NY 12222-1000. **EMAIL** r.alba@albany.edu

ALBERTS, DARLENE J.
PERSONAL Born 12/01/1941, Steubenville, OH, m, 1 child **DISCIPLINE** SOCIAL, BEHAVIORAL SCIENCE **EDUCATION** Franciscan Univ, BA, 60; Ohio State Univ, MA, 63; PhD, 73. **CAREER** Asst Prof, Ball State Univ, 63-65; Asst Prof, Murray State Univ, 65-69; Asst Prof, Iona Col, 73-78; Asst Prof, Bowling Green Univ, 80-88; Asst Prof, Ohio Dominican Col, 89-. **HONORS AND AWARDS** Phi Beta Kappa; Baconian Soc; Nat Defense Grant; Phi Alpha Theta. **MEMBERSHIPS** AHA, MESA, Islamic Soc; Ohio Humanities Assoc. **SELECTED PUBLICATIONS** Auth, "Faisal, France and Fantasy," Murray State Rev (69); auth, "Crisis in the Arab World," US Dept of State Bull (70); auth, "Arab Nationalism," US Dept of State For Affairs Doc (74); auth, King Hussein: The Consummate Politician, forthcoming. **CONTACT ADDRESS** Dept Soc and Behav Sci, Ohio Dominican Col, 1216 Sunbury Rd, Columbus, OH 43219.

ALBRECHT, GARY LOUIS
PERSONAL Born 09/29/1937, Port Townsend, WA, m, 3 children **DISCIPLINE** SOCIOLOGY **EDUCATION** Gonzaga Univ, MA, 61; Fordham Univ, MA, 65; Emory Univ, PhD, 70. **CAREER** Vis scholar, Ctr for Health Svc & Policy, N Western Univ, assoc prof, Univ Illinois, Schl of Pub Health, 79-80; prof, schl of pub health, prof, disability & human devel, 81-, Univ ILL. **HONORS AND AWARDS** Mary E. Switzer Dist res fel, Natl Inst on Disability & Rehabilitation Res; Scholar Res, Maison des Sciences de L'Homme, Paris; vis fel, Nuffield Col, Univ of Oxford, 92, 93, 96; Award for the Promotion of Human Welfare, 94; Freidson Award, 94. **MEMBERSHIPS** Soc for Res in Rehab (UK); Amer Sociol Assn; Amer Anthrop Assn; Grant Review Panel; NIDDR; US Dept Ed. **RESEARCH** Sociology of disability & rehabilitation; social context of AIDS epidemic; social interaction between the ill, the public, & professional staff. **SELECTED PUBLICATIONS** Auth, A Social Experience of Disability, Social Problems, McGraw Hill, 93; auth, A Sociological Evaluation of Our Experience With Aids: Research and Policy, ASA, Cong Briefing, 93; ed, Advances in Medical Sociology, Volume IV: A Reconsideration of Models of Health Behavior Change, JAI Press, 94; coauth, A Sociological Perspective of Health-Related Quality of Life Research, Advances in Med Sociol 5, 94; ed, Advances In Medical Sociology, Volume VI: Case and Case Management, JAI Press, 95; auth, Sociology, Encycl of Disability & Rehab, NY Macmillan, 96; coauth, Patient Satisfaction with an Emergency Department Chest Pain Observation Unit, Annals of Emerg Med 29, 97; coauth, Peer Intervention in Case Management Practice, J Case Manage 6:43, 97; auth, The Marketing of Rehabilitation Goods and Services, Health Illness & Healing: Soc, Soc Context & Self, Roxbury Press, 99. **CONTACT ADDRESS** School of Public Health, Univ of Illinois, Chicago, 1601 W Taylor St, Chicago, IL 60612. **EMAIL** Garya@uic.edu

ALDOUS, JOAN
PERSONAL Born Washington, DC, s **DISCIPLINE** SOCIOLOGY **EDUCATION** Kans State Univ, BS, 48; Univ Tex, MA, 49; Univ Minn, PhD, 63. **CAREER** From Asst Prof to Prof, Univ Minn, 63-74; Prof, Univ Ga, 74-75; Prof, Univ Notre Dame, 76-. **HONORS AND AWARDS** Ernest W. Burgess Awd, 88; Lilly Endowment for Curric Develop in Gender Studies, 89-92; NIMH Grad Fel, 90-93; AFS Found Grant, 00-01Phi Kappa Phi. **MEMBERSHIPS** ASA, Soc for Res in Child Develop, Nat Coun on Family Relations. **RESEARCH** Fathering, parent-child relationships. **SELECTED PUBLICATIONS** Auth, "New Views of Grandparents in Intergenerational Context," J of Family Issues, vol 16, no 1 (95): 104-122; auth, "Commentary: Development, Diversity and Converting Paths," J of Soc and Personal Relationships, vol 13, no 3 (96): 473-479; auth, "The Political Process and the Failure of the Child Labor Amendment," J of Family Issues, vol 18, no 1 (97): 71-91; auth, "Making Family Policy in Difficult Times," J of Family Issues, vol 18, no 1 (98): 4-6; auth, "Public Policy and Grandparents: Contrasting Perspectives," in Handbk on Grandparenting (Westport, CT: Greenwood Pr, 98), 230-246; coauth, "Fathering Over Time: What Makes the Difference?" J of Marriage and the Family, vol 60 (98): 809-820; auth, "The Changing Concept of Fatherhood," in The Family: Contemporary Perspectives and Challenges (Leuven, Belgium: Leuven Univ Pr, 98), 3-18; coauth, "Family Life and the Pursuit of Happiness: The Influence of Gender and Race," J of Family Issues, vol 20, no 2 (99): 155-180. **CONTACT ADDRESS** Dept Sociol, Univ of Notre Dame, 738 Flanner Hall, Notre Dame, IN 46556. **EMAIL** joan.aldous.1@nd.edu

ALDWIN, CAROLYN M.
PERSONAL Born 09/06/1953, Montgomery, AL, m, 1983 **DISCIPLINE** PSYCHOLOGY **EDUCATION** Clark Univ, BA; MA, 74; Univ Calif, PhD, 82. **CAREER** Lecturer, Univ Calif, 84-85; Res Psychologist, Va Clinic Boston, 85-90; Asst Prof to Prof, Univ Calif, 90-. **HONORS AND AWARDS** Jonas T Clark Scholarship, Clark Univ, 72-74; Regents Fel, Univ CA, 77; Fel, Nat Inst on Aging, 77-80; Chancellor's Awd, Univ CA, 81-82; Careeer Dev Awd, Univ CA, 84; FIRST Awd, Nat Inst on Aging, 89-95; Fel, Am Psychol Asn, 97. **MEMBERSHIPS** Am Psychol Asn; Gerontol Soc of Am; Soc of Beh Medicine. **RESEARCH** Adult Development and Aging; Health Psychology. **SELECTED PUBLICATIONS** Co-auth, "Age differences in stress, coping, and appraisal: Findings from the Normative Aging Study," Journals of Gerontology: Psychological Sciences, (96): 179-188; co-auth, "The development of coping resources in adulthood," Journal of Personality, (96): 91-113; co-auth, "A life-span perspective on the effects of military services," Journal of Geriatric Psychiatry, (97): 91-124; co-auth, "Age, cohort and period effects on alcohol consumption and problem drinking: Findings from the Normative Aging Study," Journal of Studies on Alcohol, (98): 712-722; co-auth, "Symptom trajectories following trauma exposure: Longitudinal findings from the Normative Aging Study," Journal of Nervous and Mental Disorders, (98): 522-528; auth, Stress, coping, and development: An integrative approach, Guilford Press, 99; coauth, "Hostility and the metabolic syndrome in older males: The Normative Aging Study," Sychosomatic Medicine, (00): 7-16. **CONTACT ADDRESS** Dept Human Dev, Univ of California, Davis, 1 Shields Ave, Davis, CA 95616. **EMAIL** cmaldwin@ucdavis.edu

ALEXANDER, ALEY E.
DISCIPLINE FOLKLORE **EDUCATION** Columbia Univ, PhD, 69. **CAREER** Prof, Plumber Col. **HONORS AND AWARDS** PBK **RESEARCH** Folklore **CONTACT ADDRESS** Hunter Col, CUNY, 695 Park Ave, New York, NY 10021. **EMAIL** aalexand@hejira.hunter.cuny.edu

ALEXANDER, BOBBY C.
PERSONAL Born 12/03/1950, Shreveport, LA **DISCIPLINE** ANTHROPOLOGY, RELIGIOUS STUDIES **EDUCATION** Baylor Univ, BA, 73; Union Theol Sem, M.Div, 76; Columbia Univ, MPhil, 81, & Union Theol Sem, PhD, 85. **CAREER** Tchng asst, 79-81, Barnard Col; adj lectr, 81-85, adj asst prof, 85-86, Hunter Col, CUNY; asst prof, 86-93, Southern Methodist Univ; lectr, 93-97, sr lectr, 97-, Univ Texas, Dallas; col master and asst dean for undergraduate studies,Sch of Social Sciences, 99-. **HONORS AND AWARDS** Student Choice Tchng Awd, schl of soc sci, Univ Texas Dallas, 96; Jr Scholar Awd SW Comm on Relig Stud, SW region of Amer Acad of Relig, 89-90; Res Asst Grant, AAR, 88-89; grant, US Department of Educ Fund for the Improvement of Post-secondary Educ, 99-002. **MEMBERSHIPS** Amer Anthrop Assn; AAR, Soc for Sci Stud of Relig. **RESEARCH** Relig & polit culture; religion in contemp Amer soc; religious community & its role as social network and adaptation in Mexican migrant workers in the US global economy. **SELECTED PUBLICATIONS** Ed asst, The Encycl of Relig, 84-86; auth, "Ceremony", Encycl of Relig, Macmillan, 87; art, Pentecostal Ritual Reconsidered: 'Antistructural' Dimension of Possession, J of Ritual Stud, 351:109, 89; art, Turner's Definition of Ritual Reconsidered: Grotowski's Experimental Theater as Secular Rituals of Spiritual Healing, Method & Theory in Stud of Relig, 3,1,31:62, 91; art, Correcting Misinterpretations of Turner's Theory: An African-American Pentecostal Illustration, J for Sci Stud of Relig, 30,1:26, 91; auth, Victor Turner Revisited: Ritual As Social Change, Scholars Press, AAR, 91; auth, Televangelism Reconsidered: Ritual in the Search for Human Community, Scholars Press, AAR, 91; auth, An Afterward on Ritual in Biblical Studies,

Semeia, 67:209, 95; ed, Listening: J of Religion and Culture, vol 33; ed, sect on ritual, Anthrop of Relig: A Handbk; auth, Ritual and Current Studies of Ritual: Overview, Anthrop of Relig: A Handbk, Greenwood Press, 97; auth, Televangelism Reconsidered: Ritual Within a Larger Social Drama, Rethinking Media, Relig, & Culture, Sage Pub, 97; auth, "A Pentecostal styled Mexican Mission in Dallas: An Illustration of Religious Diversity among New Latino Immigrants," Listeing, vol. 33, no. 3, pp 175-187. **CONTACT ADDRESS** School of Social Sciences, Univ of Texas, Dallas, PO Box 830688, Richardson, TX 75083. **EMAIL** bcalex@utdallas.edu

ALEXANDER, GEORGE P.
PERSONAL Born 12/10/1953, India, m, 1980, 1 child **DISCIPLINE** SOCIAL SERVICES, COMPARATIVE EDUCATION, CULTURAL STUDIES **EDUCATION** Fuller Theological Seminary, PhD, 90; Univ Calif at Los Angeles, Phd, 96. **CAREER** Assoc Prof of Intercultural Educators, Biola Univ, 94-; Prog Dir of PhD degrees, Biola Univ, 00-. **HONORS AND AWARDS** Who's Who Among America's Teachers, 99-00. **MEMBERSHIPS** Nat Asn of Ethnic Studies, Comparative and Int Educator Soc. **RESEARCH** Assimilation, acculturation and educational outcomes among Asian immigrants in the United States. **SELECTED PUBLICATIONS** Auth, New Americans: Asian Indians in the US, P & P Publ (Calif), 96; auth, Higher Education in India: Critical Issues and Trends, P & P Publ (Calif), 98. **CONTACT ADDRESS** Dept Cultural Studies, Biola Univ, 13800 Biola Ave, La Mirada, CA 90639-0002. **EMAIL** george_alexander@peter.biola.edu

ALEXANDER, JAMES
PERSONAL Born 09/04/1956, Chicago, IL, m, 1977, 2 children **DISCIPLINE** RELIGION, EDUCATION **EDUCATION** Central Mo Univ, BSE, 77, MSE, 82; St Thomas Theol Sem, MA, 85; Univ Ark, PhD, 95. **CAREER** Elementary teacher, 77-81; minister, 83-87; Chapter 1 Reading Teacher, 87-90; instr, ABE/GED, Dept of Corrections, 90-92; parochiol sch teacher, 92-95; asst prof, Lincoln Univ, 96-98; asst prof, Ky Wesleyan Col, 98-. **HONORS AND AWARDS** Theology Merit Scholar. **MEMBERSHIPS** IRA; Ky Reading Asn. **RESEARCH** Brain based teaching strategies, religion and public education. **SELECTED PUBLICATIONS** Auth, "A Strategy for Meaningful Phonics Instruction," The Mo Reader (spring 97); auth,"Multiple Intelligences Theory Applied to Reading Instruction," ERIC Document Reproduction Services ED402563; auth,"Religion Epistemology and the Public School," Relig and Ed (fall 97) and Relig and Politics, Am Political Sci Asn (summer 97); auth, "Reading Skill and Context Facilitation: A Classic Study Revisited," J of Ed Res (May/Jume 97); auth,"Reading and Postmodernism," Balanced Reading Instruction and ERIC/REC (in press). **CONTACT ADDRESS** Dept Ed, Kentucky Wesleyan Col, PO Box 1039, Owensboro, KY 42302. **EMAIL** jamesal@kwc.edu

ALEXANDER, JONATHAN F.
PERSONAL Born 10/02/1967, New Orleans, LA **DISCIPLINE** ENGLISH, WOMEN'S STUDIES **EDUCATION** La State Univ, BA, 89; MA, 91, PhD, 93. **CAREER** Lectr, Univ of S Colo, 94-98; asst prof, Univ of Cincinnati, 98-. **HONORS AND AWARDS** Harvey Milk Awd; Who's Who Among Am Teachers, 98, 00; Kairos Hypertext of the Year Awd, 98; Jonas B. Hebberhoffer Awd. **MEMBERSHIPS** MLA, NCTE, Popular Cult Assoc of Am. **RESEARCH** Writing Pedagogy, Computers and Composition, Sexuality Studies, Media Studies. **SELECTED PUBLICATIONS** Auth, "Out of the Closet and Into the Network: Sexual Orientation and the Computerized Classroom," Computers and Composition, (97); coauth, "The Pedagogy of Marking: Sexual Orientation in the Classroom," Feminist Teacher, (97); coauth, "Teacher Involvement and Transformative Power on a Gender Issues Discussion List," Meeting the Challenge: Innovative Feminist Pedagogues in Action, (99); auth, "Hypertext and Queer Theory," Kairos, (98); auth, "Beyond Identity: The Search for Queer Values and Community," Jour of Gay, Lesbian and Bisexual Identity, (01); auth, "Homo-pages and Queer Sites: Studying the Construction and Representation of Queer Identities on the World Wide Web," Int Jour of Sexuality and Gender Studies, forthcoming. **CONTACT ADDRESS** Univ of Cincinnati, PO Box 210205, Cincinnati, OH 45221. **EMAIL** jamma@fuse.net

ALEXANDER, THEODORE THOMAS, JR.
PERSONAL Born 11/24/1937, Los Angeles, CA, d **DISCIPLINE** EDUCATION **EDUCATION** Los Angeles Community Col, Los Angeles, CA, AA, electronics, 58; California State University, Los Angeles, CA, BA, education, 60, MA, education, 64; University of Southern California, Los Angeles, CA, EdD, education, 75. **CAREER** Los Angeles Board of Education, principal, 71-75, administrative; University of Southern California, adjunct associate professor, 71-; coord, 75-76, administrative consultant, 76-77, deputy area administrator, 77-78, asst dir, 78-82, asst superintendent, 82-00; Assoc Superintendent, 01. **HONORS AND AWARDS** USC Ebonics Support Group Outstanding Black Alumni Awd, 84; USC General Alumni Assn Tommy Statue Volunteer Service Awd, 84; National Achievement Awd, Lamba Kappa Mu Sorority, 85; Hilburn Awd, Human Relations Awd, City of Los Angeles Human Relations Committee, 69; Awd for Contribution to the field of education, The Assn of Black Law Enforcement Executives, 91; Community Service Awd, Kappa Alpha Psi National Awd, 88. **MEMBERSHIPS** President, Council of Black Administrators, 83-85; president, Education Alumni Assn, USC, 80-81; member, board of governors, General Alumni Assn, USC, 86-89; president, polemarch, Los Angeles Alumni Chapter Kappa Alpha Psi Fraternity, 86-89; president, Educare Support Group, USC, 85-86. **CONTACT ADDRESS** Los Angeles Board of Education, 450 N Grand, Rm G-353, Los Angeles, CA 90012.

ALFONSO, VINCENT C.
PERSONAL Born 08/26/1964, Brooklyn, NY, s **DISCIPLINE** PSYCHOLOGY **EDUCATION** Hofstra Univ, PhD, 90. **CAREER** Asst Prof, Fordham Univ. **HONORS AND AWARDS** Intl Who's Who, 98; Phi Beta Kappa, Brooklyn Col, 86. **MEMBERSHIPS** Am Psychol Asn, Am Psychol Soc, Nat Asn of School Psychol. **RESEARCH** Psychoeducational assessment, Early childhood psychology, subjective well-being. **SELECTED PUBLICATIONS** Auth, "Essentially, essential for WAIS-III users," Contemporary Psychology, in press; auth, "The course on individual cognitive assessment," School Psychology Review, in press; auth, "Assessment of cognitive functioning in preschoolers," in Assessing and screening preschoolers, New York, (99): 186-217; auth, "The impact of white counselor trainees' racial identity upon working alliance perceptions in same and cross racial dyads," Journal of counseling and development, (99): 324-329; auth, "Obesity and developmental disabilities: Pathogenesis and treatment," Journal of Developmental and Physical Disabilities, (98): 215-255; auth, "Common WISC-III examiner errors: Evidence from graduate students in training," Psychology in the Schools, (98): 119-125; auth, "The education of specialist level school psychologists: An unanswered challenge," Journal of Psychological practice, (97): 89-104; auth, "Issues and suggestions for training professionals in assessing intelligence," in Contemporary intellectual assessment: Theories, tests, and issues, (97): 326-344; auth, "Measurement of dependent variables," in Design and analysis of single case research, (96): 41-92. **CONTACT ADDRESS** Div of Psychol & Educ Services, Fordham Univ, 113 W 60th St, New York, NY 10023. **EMAIL** alfonso@fordham.edu

ALI, KAMAL HASSAN
PERSONAL Born 09/03/1944, Springfield, MA, m, 1966, 3 children **DISCIPLINE** EDUCATION **EDUCATION** Hunter Col, 1963-64; New York Univ, 1964-65; Univ of Massachusetts, Amherst, MEd, 1977, EdD, 1981. **CAREER** Human Resources Admin, sr human resource specialist, 67-71; Harlem East-Harlem Model Cities, project liason, 71-74; Univ of Massachusetts, Amherst, graduate research and teaching asst, 74-78; Vantage Consultants, Hartford, CT, training program developer, 78-79; Westfield State College, dir, minority/bilingual vocational teacher educ programs, 80-81, dir minority affairs, beginning 1981-, associate dean of academic affairs, currently. **HONORS AND AWARDS** Producer, host, cable television program "Coll Journal," Springfield, MA, 1983-; public speaking on educ, foreign policy, apartheid, 1984-86. **MEMBERSHIPS** Vice pres, Islamic Soc of Western Massachusetts, 1983-; Dunbar Community Center, chmn, bd of dir, 1984-86, chmn, New Bldg Comm, 1986-. **RESEARCH** Multicultural Education; curriculum dev; Islamic school dev. **SELECTED PUBLICATIONS** Author, "Islamic Education in the United States: An Overview of Issues, Problems and Possible Approaches," 1984, "The Shariah and Its Implications to Muslim School Planning," 1986, Amer Journal of Islamic Social Studies. **CONTACT ADDRESS** Office of Multicultural Devt, Westfield State Col, 577 Western Ave, Westfield, MA 01086. **EMAIL** kali@wisdom.wsc.ma.edu

ALLARD, M. JUNE
DISCIPLINE PSYCHOLOGY **EDUCATION** Mich State Univ, AB; MA; PhD. **CAREER** Teach, res, CISSR, Mich State Univ, 58-66; proj dir, res sci, American Univ, 66-67; sr staff, Operations Res, 67-69; prin sci, Leasco Sys, 69-70; res consul, priv, 66-; prof, 73-; ch, SBSD, 95-98; Worcester State Col, ch, 98-. **HONORS AND AWARDS** Sigma Xi; Psi Chi sec; Alpha Kappa Delta; Pi Gamma Mu, pres; Phi Kappa Phi; Alpha Lambda Delta; Alpha Sigma Lambda; Tau Gamma; Tau Sigma; Dir Intl Who's Who in Edu, Women of Sci, Woman of Year; Who's Who in Am, Men and Women, East, Women in Edu; Dist Ser Awd, 81, 84, 86; AAC Nat Fel; NSF Fel, 59-64. **MEMBERSHIPS** APA; Psi Chi Nat Hon Soc; WCHS; Girls' Inc. **SELECTED PUBLICATIONS** Coauth, Understanding Diversity: Readings, Cases and Exercises, Harper Collins (95); auth, Instructors Manuel to accompany Understanding Diversity: Readings, Cases and Exercises, Harper Collins (95); coauth, "Problems facing chronically mentally Ill elders receiving community-based psychiatric services: need for residential services," Adult Resid Care J 7 (93); coauth, "Community-based residential care for the chronically mentally ill elderly," Adult Resid Care J B (94); coauth, "Sleep deprivation and state college students," Soc Neurosci Abstracts 22 (96): 686; coauth, "Weekday vs weekend sleep patterns and daytime Sleepiness of college students," Soc Neurosci Abstracts 23 (97): 1848. **CONTACT ADDRESS** Dept Psychology, Worcester State Col, 486 Chandler St, Worcester, MA 01602. **EMAIL** jallard@worcester.edu

ALLEN, HENRY L.
PERSONAL Born 07/07/1955, Joiner, AR, m, 1979, 8 children **DISCIPLINE** SOCIOLOGY **EDUCATION** Wheaton Col, BA, 77; Univ Chicago, MA, 79; PhD, 88. **CAREER** Instr, Bethel Col, 82-87; assoc prof, Calvin Col, 87-91; asst prof, Univ Rochester, (1-98); assoc prof, Roch Inst Tech, 97-98; assoc prof, Wheaton Col, 98-. **HONORS AND AWARDS** Danforth Fel; Who's Who East, Edu, Am. **MEMBERSHIPS** NCSA. **RESEARCH** Mathematical sociology; sociology of higher education. **SELECTED PUBLICATIONS** Auth, "Workload and Productivity: Case Studies," in The NEA 1995 Almanac of Higher Education (Washington, DC: NEA Pub, 95); auth, "Faculty Workload and Productivity in the 1990s: Preliminary Findings," in NEA 1996 Almanac of Higher Education (Washington, D.C.: NEA Pub, 96); auth, "Risk and Failure as Preludes to Achievement," in Men to Men: Voices of African-American Males, ed. Lee June (Grand Rapids: Zondervan, 96); auth, "Faculty Workload and Productivity: Ethnic and Gender Disparities," in The NEA 1997 of Higher Education (Washington, DC: NEA Pub, 97); auth, "Tenure: Why Faculty, and the Nation, Need It," Thought and Action 2 (97): 75-88; auth, "Faculty Workload and Productivity: Gender Comparisons," in The NEA 1998 Almanac of Higher Education (Washington, DC: NEA Pub, 98); auth, "Evangelizing Professionals: Workers in the Field," in Evangelism and Discipleship in African-American Churches, ed. Lee June (Grand Rapids: Zondervan, 99); auth, "The Ideology of 'Equal Opportunity' in Modern School Systems," Quart J Ideology (99): 5-13; auth, "Workload and Productivity in an Era of Performance Measures," in The NEA 1999 Almanac Higher Education (Washington, DC: NEA Pub, 99), 27-44; auth, "Evangelism and Social Concerns in the 21st Century," Wheaton Mag (00): 20-21; auth, "Faculty Workload and Productivity in an Era of Organizational Restructuring," in The NEA 2000 Almanac of Higher Education (Washington, DC: NEA Pub, forthcoming). **CONTACT ADDRESS** Dept Sociology, Wheaton Col, Illinois, 501 College Ave, Wheaton, IL 60187. **EMAIL** henry.l.allen@wheaton.edu

ALLEN, IRVING L.
DISCIPLINE SOCIOLOGY **EDUCATION** Univ Iowa, PhD 65. **CAREER** Univ Connecticut, prof emer, 63-. **RESEARCH** Social History of Culture and Language **SELECTED PUBLICATIONS** The City in Slang: New York Life and Popular Speech, NY, Oxford Univ Press, 93. **CONTACT ADDRESS** Box 138, Storrs, CT 06268-0138.

ALLEN, LINDA
PERSONAL Born 04/04/1951, Cincinnati, OH, m, 1972, 1 child **DISCIPLINE** ANTHROPOLOGY **EDUCATION** Mount Mercy Col, BA, 87; Univ Iowa, MA, 89, PhD, 97. **CAREER** Asst prof of Anthropol, Kirkwood Community Col, 97-. **HONORS AND AWARDS** Nat Inst for Staff and Orgn Develop Excellence Awd, 2000. **MEMBERSHIPS** Am Anthropol Asn, Soc for Medical Anthropol, Soc for Soc Anthropol in Oceania. **RESEARCH** Migration, domestic violence, gender issues, area specialization- Micronesia. **SELECTED PUBLICATIONS** Auth, "Distance Learning, Web Sites, and Accreditation," The Col Student J, Vol 33, No 2; auth, "Subjective Gender Role Assessment Index for Use in the College Classroom," The Col Student J, Vol 33, No 4. **CONTACT ADDRESS** Dept Soc Sci, Kirkwood Comm Col, 209 Cedar Hall, PO Box 2068, Cedar Rapids, IA 52406.

ALLEN, PETER S.
PERSONAL Born 07/26/1944, Newton, MA, m, 1983, 4 children **DISCIPLINE** ANTHROPOLOGY **EDUCATION** Middlebury Col, AB, 66; Brown Univ, AM, 68; PhD, 74. **CAREER** Instructor to Prof, RI Col, 72-. **HONORS AND AWARDS** Fulbright-Hays Fac Res Grant, 79-80, 82-83; NEH Grant, 81-82; Grant, RI Committee for the Humanities, 87. **MEMBERSHIPS** Am Anthropol Asn; Archaeol Inst of Am; Modern Greek Studies Asn; Fulbright Alumni Asn; Soc for the Anthropol of Europe. **RESEARCH** Greece; Cyprus; Eurpoe; Modernization; Middle East; Urbanization; National Identity. **SELECTED PUBLICATIONS** Auth, Female Costume of the Sarakatsani, Haffenreffer Museum, 85; auth, "Dhali: A Traditional Community in Transition," in American Expedition to Idalion Cyprus 1973-1980, (Chicago, 89), 425-446; auth, "La Gestion des Conflits dans le Magne: de la Feodalite a l'adjudications," Droit et Cultures, (90): 83-99; co-auth, Archaeology on Film: A Comprehensive Guide to Audio-Visual Materials 2nd ed, Boston, 94; auth, "Finding Meaning in Modifications of the Environment: The Fields and Orchards of Mani," in Aegean Strategies: Studies of Culture and Environment on the European Fringe, (Rowman and Littlefield, 97), 259-270; auth, "Europe on Film," in Europe in the Anthropological Imagination, (Prentice-Hall, 97), 60-69. **CONTACT ADDRESS** Dept Anthropol & Geog, Rhode Island Col, 600 Mt Pleasant, Providence, RI 02908.

ALLEN, RHIANON
PERSONAL Born, United Kingdom, m, 1979, 3 children **DISCIPLINE** PSYCHOLOGY **EDUCATION** CUNY, PhD. 83. **CAREER** Res Sci, NYS Psychiat Inst, 81-86; asst Prof, Long Island Univ, 85-. **MEMBERSHIPS** APA, APS. **RESEARCH** Belief systems. **SELECTED PUBLICATIONS** Auth, "'Don't Go On My Property!': A Case Study in Transactions of User

Rights," Lang in Soc 24,3 (95): 349-372; coauth, "The Relationship between Anxiety and Problem-Solving Skills in Children With and Without Learning Disabilities," J of Learning Disabilities 29 (96): 439-446; coauth, "Unconscious Intelligence," in Companion to Cognitive Science, (Oxford, UK: Blackwell, 98), 314-330; coauth, "Rorschach Assessment of Annihilation Anxiety and Ego Functioning," Psychoanalytic Psychol 15 (98): 536-566; coauth, "Problem-Solving and External Representation of a Task," Brit J of Develop Psychol 16 (98): 505-517; coauth, "Achievement Motivation Orientation and Fear of Success in Asian American College Students," J of Clin Psychol 54 (98): 97-108; coauth, "Implicit and Explicit Learning," in The Nature of Cognition, (Cambridge: MIT Pr, 99), 475-513. **CONTACT ADDRESS** Dept Psychol, Long Island Univ, Brooklyn, 1 University Plaza, Brooklyn, NY 11201. **EMAIL** rhianon. allen@liv.edu

ALLEY, THOMAS R.
PERSONAL Born 10/20/1953, Bryn Mawr, PA, m, 2 children **DISCIPLINE** PSYCHOLOGY **EDUCATION** Penn State Univ, BA, 75; BS, 75; Univ Conn, MA, 79; PhD, 81. **CAREER** Lecturer, Univ Conn, 78-83; Vis Scholar to Vis Prof, 98-99; Asst Prof, to Prof, Clemson Univ, 84-. **MEMBERSHIPS** Am Psychol Soc, Beh and Brain Sci Assoc, Eastern Psychol Asn, Intl Soc for Ecol Psychol, Intl Soc for Human Ethology, NY Acad of Sci, Psychonomic Soc. **RESEARCH** Cognition, Ecological and evolutionary psychology, eyewitness testimonyk food preferences and aversions, Human ethology, Learning and memory, perceiving and recognizing faces, Perception and psychophysics, Psychosocial aspects of physical appearance. **SELECTED PUBLICATIONS** Auth, Social and Applied Aspects of Perceiving Faces, Hillsdale, NJ, 88; auth, "Variation in optimal human mating strategies: Effects of individual differences in competence and self-regulatory mechanisms," Behavioral & Brain Sciences, in press; auth, "A laser-based technique for measuring accuracy and distortion in judgments of linear dimensions," Behavior Research Methods, Instruments and Computers, in press; auth, "Reliability and accuracy in size judgments of objects and oneself," in Studies in Perception and Action, Mahwah, NJ, 99; auth, "The influence of physical state and color on perceived sweetness," Journal of Psychology, (98): 561-568; auth, "Attractiveness and the memorability of faces: Only a matter of distinctiveness?," American Journal of Psychology, (97): 81-92; auth, "'Body-image' distortion and accuracy of size perception for inanimate objects," in Studies in Perception and Action IV, Mahwah, NJ, 97; auth, "Can temporal direction affect memory for pictures of events?," in Studies in Perception and Action IV, Mahwah, NJ, 97. **CONTACT ADDRESS** Dept Psychol, Clemson Univ, 1 Clemson Univ, Clemson, SC 29634-0001. **EMAIL** alley@clemson.edu

ALLINGTON, RICHARD LLOYD
PERSONAL Born 05/13/1947, Grand Rapids, MI, m, 1980, 5 children **DISCIPLINE** EDUCATION **EDUCATION** Western Mich Univ, BA, 68; Mich St Univ, PhD, 73. **CAREER** Prof, 73-99, SUNY Albany; Fien Distinguished Prof of Educ, Univ of Florida, 00-. **HONORS AND AWARDS** Harris Awd, Intl Reading Asn; Johnston Awd, Center for Literacy and Disability; Pres Awd for re Excel, Who's Who in Amer Ed; Pres Natl Reading Conf; Bd of Dir, Intl Reading Asn; Res Grants from: Office of Ed Res and Improvement, Office of Special Ed and Rehabilitation, Natl Inst on Aging; Res Scientist at NRC, TLL & NRCELA. **RESEARCH** Literacy development; learning disabilities; education policy. **SELECTED PUBLICATIONS** Coauth, No Quick Fix: Rethinking Literacy Instruction In America's Elementary Schools, Tchrs Col Pres, 95; coauth, Schools That Work: All Children Readers And Writers, Longmans, 96; coauth, The Handbook of Special and Remedial Education, Elsevier Science, 96; auth, Help for Struggling Readers, Intl Reading Asn, 98; coauth, The Politics of literacy teaching: How Research Shaped Educational Policy-Making, Ed Resr, 99; auth, What really matters for struggling readers, Longmans, 00. **CONTACT ADDRESS** Univ of Florida, 2414 Norman Hall, Gainesville, FL 32611. **EMAIL** dickaufl@aol.com

ALONSO, ANA MARIA
PERSONAL Born 12/04/1955, Havana, Cuba, m, 1995, 1 child **DISCIPLINE** ANTHROPOLOGY **EDUCATION** Wellesley Col, BA, 78; Univ Chicago, MA, 82; PhD, 88. **CAREER** Asst prof, Univ of Tex, 88-91; asst prof to assoc prof, Univ Arizm 91-. **HONORS AND AWARDS** Grant, Soc Sci Res Coun, 83-85; Grant, Inter-Am Found, 83-85; Dissertation Writing Awd, Soc Sci Res Coun, 86; Fel, Pembroke Ctr for Teaching and Res on Women, Brown Univ, 87-88; Fel, Southwest Inst for Res on Women, Univ of Ariz, 90-91; Clara Lee Tanner Pub Fund, 93. **MEMBERSHIPS** Am Anthropol Asn; Asn of Latino/a Anthropol; Am Ethnol Soc; Asn for Latin Am Anthropol. **RESEARCH** State-formation; Nationalism; Gender; Ethnicity and Race; Social memory; History of Anthropology; Museums; The Social Organization and Representation of Space; Mexico; U.S.-Mexico Border; Social Movements; Resistance and Revolution. **SELECTED PUBLICATIONS** Auth, "Men in Rags and the Devil on the Throne: A Study of Protest and Inversion in the Post-Emancipation Trinidad Carnival," Plantation Society in the Americas, 90; auth, "Work and Gusto: Gender and Re-creation in a North Mexican Pueblo," in Workers' Expressions: Beyond Accommodation and Resistance, SUNY Press, 92; auth, "Gender, Power and Historical Memory: Discourses of

Serrano Resistance," in Feminists Theorize the Political, Routledge, 92; co-auth, "Silences: 'Hispanics,' AIDS and Sexual Practices," in The Lesbian and Gay Studies Reader, Routledge, 93; co-auth, "Multiple Selective Traditions in the Definition of agrarian Reform and Agrarian Struggle: the Ejido of Namiquipa, Chihuahua," in Everyday Forms of State Formation: Revolution and the Negotiation of Rule in Modern Mexico, Duke Univ Press, 94; auth, "Rationalizing Patriarchy: Gender, Domestic Violence and Law in Mexico," Identities, 95; auth, Thread of Blood: Gender, Colonialism and Revolution on Mexico's Northern Frontier, Univ Ariz Press, 95; auth, "u>S. Military Intervention, Revolutionary Mobilization and Popular Ideology in the Chihuahuan Sierra," in Rural Revolt: U.S. Intervention and the Domain of Subaltern Politics, Duke Univ Press, 98. **CONTACT ADDRESS** Dept of Anthropol, Univ of Arizona, 1009 E S Campus Dr, Bldg 30, Tucson, AZ 85721-0030. **EMAIL** alonso@u.arizona.edu

ALTALIB, OMAR
PERSONAL Born 05/16/1967, Arafa, Iraq, m, 1991 **DISCIPLINE** SOCIOLOGY **EDUCATION** George Mason Univ, BA, 89; Univ Chicago, MA, 93; PhD, 00. **CAREER** Res Asst, Nat Opinion Res Center, 92-95; Instructor, Daley Col, 98-99. **HONORS AND AWARDS** Nat Sci Foundation Grad Student Fel; Presidential Merit Scholarship. **MEMBERSHIPS** Am Sociol Asn. **RESEARCH** Sociology of the Family; Sociology of Education. **CONTACT ADDRESS** 12645 Alpine Dr, No 9, Alsip, IL 60803. **EMAIL** o-altalib@uchicago.edu

ALTEKRUSE, MICHAEL
PERSONAL Born 12/23/1939, Fort Wayne, IN, m, 1961, 3 children **DISCIPLINE** EDUCATION **EDUCATION** Ind Univ, BS, 62; MS, 65; EdD, 67. **CAREER** Prof, Southern Ill Univ, 67-92; Prof and Chair, Univ Nev, 92-95; Prof and Chair, Univ N Tex, 95-. **HONORS AND AWARDS** ACES Grad Student Mentor Awd, 89, 82; C.A. Micleman Awd, 90; Carbondale citizen of the Year, 79; Carbondale school District Hall of Fame, 81. **MEMBERSHIPS** Asn for Counselor Educ & Supervision, Am Coun Asn, Am Psychol Asn, Chi Sigma Iota. **SELECTED PUBLICATIONS** Auth, "Effectiveness of group supervision versus combined group and individual supervision with master-level counselor trainees," Counselor Education and Supervision, 00;' auth, "Community college counseling," Community College Journal, 00; auth, "Proposed guidance information technician: Is help on the way?," Texas Counselor's Network, (99): 4-5; auth, "ERIC announces new service," The ASCA Counselor, (99): 9; auth, "Counseling older adults," Educational Gerontology, (98): 303-307; auth, "Human development training centers of excellence for education and research," Guidance and Counseling, (96): 23-26; auth, "Supervisee's bill of rights," Counselor Supervision, 99. **CONTACT ADDRESS** Dept Counselor Educ, Univ of No Texas, PO Box 311337, Denton, TX 76203. **EMAIL** altkrs@unt.edu

ALTMAN, IRA
PERSONAL Born 03/17/1944, Kzyl-kya, Russia, m, 1969, 1 child **DISCIPLINE** SOCIOLOGY, PHILOSOPHY **EDUCATION** City Col of NY, BA, 66; Graduate School the City University of NY, MA, 74; PhD, 78. **CAREER** Instr-adjunct assoc prof, Queens's Col, 68; Hunter Col, 68; Lehman Col, 69-71; Brooklyn Col, 69-78; Long Island Univ, 70-71; Stevens Inst of Tech, 74-78; NY Inst Tech, 78-84; Pace Univ, 85-91; Yeshiva Univ, 90-92; Touro Col, 90-; Queensborough Community Col, 93-; Suffolk Community Col, 90-; ed, The City College Philosophy Journal, Logos, 65-67. **HONORS AND AWARDS** Special honors in theSocial Sciences (Social Sciences Honors Degree); the Marc Showitz Memorial Scholarship for Graduate Studies; univ fellowship; teaching assistantship; pres, The City Col Philos Soc (65); presented paper at the 18th annual spring meeting of the Long Island Philos Asn (82); invited to join a select delegation of philosophers to visit the Russian Republic and Hungary (95), China (96), India (96); invited paper based on his book "The Concept of Intelligence" at the Twentieth World Congress of Philosophy (98). **MEMBERSHIPS** Am Philos Asn, Long Island Philos Soc. **RESEARCH** Epistemology, critical thinking, ordinary language analysis, the philosophy of science, the philosophy of mind, **SELECTED PUBLICATIONS** Auth, The Concept of Intelligence: A Philosophical Analysis, Univ Press Am (97); Lectures in Philosophy, Am Heritage (96); Readings in Philosophy, McGraw-Hill (97); Lectures in Critical Thinking: A Beginner's Guide to Informal and Formal Logic, Copley (98); Exercise Manual for Lectures in Critical Thinking, McGraw-Hill (99). **CONTACT ADDRESS** Dept Social Sciences, Queensborough Comm Col, CUNY, 22205 56th Ave., Oakland Gardens, NY 11364-1432. **EMAIL** ialman@freewweb.com

ALTMAN, JOANNE
DISCIPLINE PSYCHOLOGY **EDUCATION** Franklin and Marshall Col, BA, 84; Temple Univ. MA, 87; PhD, 90. **CAREER** Instr, Psychology Temple Univ, 88-90; Adjunct Instr, Franklin and Marshall Col, 90; Asst Prof Washburn Univ, 91-99; Assoc Prof, Washburn Univ, 99-. **HONORS AND AWARDS** Psi Chi, Phi Kappa Phi, Who's Who Among Am Teachers, 96, 98, 00. **MEMBERSHIPS** Am Psychological Society (APS), Animal Behavior Society (ABS), American Zoological Assn (AZA) Consortium of Aquariums, Univ & Zoos,

Delta Society Human and Behavior and Evoluation Society, Int. Society for Comparative Psychology. **RESEARCH** Psychological well-being in captive wildlife; Animal-human interaction. **SELECTED PUBLICATIONS** Auth, The effect of resident cats on social and emotional behavior of elderly nursing home patients, Proceedings and Abstracts of the Annual Meeting of the Eastern Psychological Assoc, 87; auth, The human-avian bond, A.A.V. Today 2 (88): 143-145; auth, Cooper, iron, manganese and zinc content of hair from two populations of rhesus monkeys, Biological Trace Element Research, 53 (96): 167-183; auth, Calcium, magnesium and phosphorus content of hair from two populations of rhesus monkeys. Biological Trace Element Research, 53 (96): 147-165; auth, The Effects of Outlining as a Pedagogical Tool, Psychology, 33 (96): 52-55; auth, Animal Activity and visitor learning at the zoo, Anthrozoos, 11 (98): 12-21; auth, The effect of manipulatable on pacing and inactivity in captive bears, Journal of Applied Animal Welfare Science, 2 (99): 123-132; auth, Factors contributing to Sex Differences on the Mental Rotation Task, PSI CHI: Journal if Undergraduate Research, 5 (00): 29-35. **CONTACT ADDRESS** Dept Psychology, Washburn Univ of Topeka, 1700 SW College Ave, Topeka, KS 66621. **EMAIL** zzaltm@washburn.edu

ALVEY, RICHARD GERALD
PERSONAL Born 11/08/1935, Evansville, IN, m, 1967 **DISCIPLINE** FOLKLORISTICS, ENGLISH **EDUCATION** Univ Ky, BA, 69, MSLA, 70; Univ Pa, AM, 71, PhD(folkloristics), 74. **CAREER** Asst prof, 74-80, assoc prof folklore, Univ KY, 80-. **HONORS AND AWARDS** Mem, Coun on Exp Educ, 74-; Nat Endowment Humanities res grant, 76. **MEMBERSHIPS** Am Folklore Soc; Folklore Soc (British); Appalachian Studies Conf, 78; Asn Folklorists in South; Int Soc for Folk Narrative Res; bd mem, Appalachian Studies Conf, 78-. **RESEARCH** Folkloristics; Appalachian studies, regional studies; English. **SELECTED PUBLICATIONS** Auth, Phillips Barry and Anglo-American Folksong Scholarship, J Folklore Inst, 73; Folk beliefs about food & eating in Kentucky, Ky Hospitality, 76; A second look at the secondary ballad, Southern Folklore Quart, 78; Coyote tales, Enzyklopadie des Marchen **CONTACT ADDRESS** Dept of English, Univ of Kentucky, 500 S Limestone St, Lexington, KY 40506-0003.

AMAN, MICHAEL G.
PERSONAL Born 05/06/1945, Rochester, NY, m, 1974, 2 children **DISCIPLINE** PSYCHOLOGY **EDUCATION** Univ Windsor, BA, 68; Univ Ill, MA, 72; Univ Auckland, PhD, 79. **CAREER** Sen Res Fel, Medical Res Coun of New Zealand, 82-87; Assoc Prof to Prof, Oh State Univ, 87-. **RESEARCH** Pediatric psychopharmacology; Psychopharmacology of the Developmental disabilities. **SELECTED PUBLICATIONS** Co-auth, "The aberrant Behavior Checklist--Community: Factor validity and effect of subject variables for adults in group homes," American Journal on Mental Retardation, (95): 283-292; co-auth, "Psychotropic and anticonvulsant drugs in subjects with autism: Prevalence and patterns of use," Journal of the American Acad of Child and Adolescent Psychiatry, (95): 1672-1681; co-auth, "Consumer satisfaction with involvement in drug research: A social validity study," Journal of the American Academy of Child and Adolescent Psychiatry, (95): 940-945; co-auth, "Issues in the taxonomy of psychopathology in children and adolescents with mental retardation," Journal of Autism and Developmental Disorders, (95): 143-167; auth, "Stimulant drugs in the developmental disabilities revisited," Journal of Developmental and Physical Disabilities, (96): 347-365; co-auth, "Four-year follow-up of children with mental retardation and ADHD," Research in Developmental Disabilities, (96): 417-432; co-auth, "Psychometric evaluation of a measure of cognitive decline in elderly people with mental retardation," Research in Developmental Disabilities, (98): 63-71; co-auth, Psychotropic medications and developmental disabilities: The international consensus handbook, UAP, 98; co-auth, "Atypical antipsychotics in persons with developmental disabilities," Mental Retardation and Developmental Disabilities Research Reviews, 999): 253-263; co-auth, Practioner's guide to psychoactive drugs for children and adolescents, Plenum Press, 99. **CONTACT ADDRESS** Dept Psychol, Ohio State Univ, Columbus, 1581 Dodd Dr, The Nisonger Centre, Columbus, OH 3210-1296. **EMAIL** baman.1@osu.edu

AMARO, HORTENSIA
PERSONAL Born, Cuba **DISCIPLINE** PUBLIC HEALTH **EDUCATION** Univ Calif, BA, 75; MA, 77; PhD, 82. **CAREER** Asst Prof to Prof, Boston Univ, 83-. **HONORS AND AWARDS** Research Awd, Am Psychol Asn; Distinguished Contributors Awd, 93; Contributions to Women's Health Res Awd, Am Psychol Asn, 94; Contributions to Maternal and Child Health Awd, Boston, 95; Sci Pub Awd, Nat Asn of Women in Psychol, 96; Sci Contributions Awd, Am Public Health Asn, 96; MOM's Project Awd, MA Dept Public Health; Rafael Tavares Memorial Awd, New York, 98. **MEMBERSHIPS** Am Public Health Asn; Am Psychol Asn **SELECTED PUBLICATIONS** Co-auth, Impact of Ryan White care Act Title I on Capacity Building in Latino Community-based Organizations: findings from a Study from Two Cities, Boston Univ Press, 95; co-auth, "Panel I: Epidemiology of Ethnic Minority Health," Health Psychology, (95): 592-600; co-auth, "The health of Latino Youth: challenges for disease prevention," in Health Issues for Minority Adolescents, (Univ NE Press, 96),

80-115; co-auth, "Task Group I: Epidemiology of Minority Health," Journal of culture and Health, 96; co-auth, "Alcohol abuse and dependence in Latinos living in the USA: Validation of the CAGE (4M) Questions," Arch Intern Med, (99): 718-724; auth, "An Expensive Policy: The Impact of Inadequate Funding for Substance Abuse Treatment," American Journal of Public Health, (99): 657-659; co-auth, "Residential Substance Abuse Treatment with Latinas: Critical Issues and Challenges," Hispanic Journal of Behavioral Sciences, (99): 266-282; co-auth, "Frameworks for HIV prevention among Latina and African American women," Health Psychology: A Cultural Approach, in press; co-auth, "On the Margin: The Realities of Power and Women's HIV Risk Reduction Strategies," Journal of Sex Roles, in press; co-auth, "Participation of Latino Community-Based Organizations in the RWCA Process: A study of Two Metropolitan Areas, in press. **CONTACT ADDRESS** Sch Public Health, Boston Univ, 715 Albany St, Boston, MA 02118. **EMAIL** hamaro@bu.edu

AMIR, NADER
PERSONAL Born 09/21/1962, Iran, s **DISCIPLINE** PSYCHOLOGY **EDUCATION** Univ Ill, BS, 85; Stephen F. Austin State Univ, MA, 87; Chicago Med Sch, MS, 92; PhD, 95. **CAREER** Instructor, Stephen F. Austin State Univ, 85-87; Instructor, Univ Tex, 87-89; Instructor, Chicago Med Sch, 91-93; Asst Prof, Allegheny Univ, 95-98; Asst Prof, Univ Ga, 98-. **MEMBERSHIPS** APA; APS; AABT. **RESEARCH** Anxiety disorder. **SELECTED PUBLICATIONS** Co-auth, "Anxiety," in Encyclopedia of Mental Health, Academic Press, 98; co-auth, "Automatic activation and strategic avoidance of threat-relevant information in Social Phobia," Journal of Abnormal Psychology, (98): 285-290; co-auth, "Assessment of Psychology: Etiology and Nosology," in Comprehensive Clinical psychology, Pergamon, 98; co-auth, "Social Phobics evaluation of ambiguous situations," Behavior Research and Therapy, (98): 945-957; co-auth, "The Obsessive Compulsive Inventory: A Multi-Purpose Diagnostic Questionnaire Psychological Assessment, (98): 26-214; co-auth, "Cognitive Biases," in Social Phobia and Social Anxiety: An Integration, Allyn & Bacon, in press; co-auth, "Attentional biases for facial expression in social phobia: The use of the face-in-the-crowd paradigm," Cognition and Emotion, in press; co-auth, "Memory bias in generalized social phobia: Remembering negative emotional expressions," Journal of Anxiety Disorders, in press; co-auth, "Inflated perception of responsibility for harm in obsessive-compulsive disorder," Journal of Anxiety Disorders, in press; co-auth, "Family accommodation and rejection in relatives of OCD patients," Journal of Anxiety Disorders, in press **CONTACT ADDRESS** Dept Psychol, Univ of Georgia, Athens, GA 30602-3013. **EMAIL** amir@egon.psy.uga.edu

AMOS, ORIS ELIZABETH CARTER
PERSONAL Born Martinsville, VA, m **DISCIPLINE** EDUCATION **EDUCATION** VA State Col, BA 1951; OH State Univ, MA 1963, PhD 1971. **CAREER** VA Pub Schools, teacher, 51-55; Columbus OH Pub Sch, teacher, 63-66; OH State Univ, instr, 66-69; Otterbein Coll, asst prof, 71-75; Council for Exceptional Children, pres, 75; Coll of Educ, chmn Human Rel Comm, 75; Wright State Univ, prof of educ, 75-88; educ development consultant, 88-. **HONORS AND AWARDS** Named Outstanding Educator of Yr 1972; Awd for Distinguished Comm Serv Delta Sigma Theta Sorority 1972; Special Awd Serv to Black Students at Otterbein Coll 1973; Teacher Excellence Awd Wright State Univ 1979; Educator of Yr OH Fed Council of Exceptional Children 1982; Coord of Special Educ 1978-87; WSU Trustees Awd, 1987; Greene County Hall of Fame for Women, Greene County OH, 1988. **MEMBERSHIPS** Teachers Adv Comm State of OH 1975; adv Black Students Otterbein Coll 1975; adv bd Miami Valley Reg Res Ctr; adv bd Dayton Area United Cerebral Palsy Professional Serv; adv bd Sinclair Comm Coll Special Educ; Panel of Experts to review proposals St Bd of Educ Columbus, OH 1975; mem Delta Sigma Theta Sorority; Pi Lambda Theta Women's Honorary in Educ; Central Chapel Church Yellow Springs. **CONTACT ADDRESS** Education, Wright State Univ, Dayton, PO Box 416, Yellow Springs, OH 45387.

ANASTASI, JEFFREY S.
PERSONAL Born 02/22/1968, Austin, TX, m, 1994, 1 child **DISCIPLINE** PSYCHOLOGY **EDUCATION** State Univ NYork, Binghamton, BA, 90; MA, 93; PhD, 95. **CAREER** Asst prof, Francis Marion Univ, Florence, SC, 95-99, assoc prof, 99-. **MEMBERSHIPS** Assoc Member of the Psychonomic Soc, Pee Dee Natural Hist Soc, Southeastern Psychol Asn, Am Psychol Asn, Am Psychol Soc. **SELECTED PUBLICATIONS** Coauth with D. G. Payne and M. P. Toglia, "Recognition performance level and the magnitude of the misinformation effect in eyewitness memory," Psychonomic Bull & Rev, 1, 3 (95): 376-382; coauth with M. G. Rhodes, "The effects of a levels of activation manipulation on false recall," Psychonomic Bull & Rev, 6 (2000); coauth with M. G. Rhodes and M. C. Burns, "Distinguishing between memory illusions and actual memories utilizing phenomenological measurements and explicit warnings," Am J of Psychol, 100 (2000): 1-26; auth, "Source monitoring confusions: The effect of retention interval placement on the misleading post-event suggestibility effect," (in progress). **CONTACT ADDRESS** Dept Sociol & Psychol, Francis Marion Univ, PO Box 100547, Florence, SC 29501. **EMAIL** janastasi@fmarion.edu

ANDERMAN, ERIC M.
PERSONAL Born 06/22/1963, New York, NY, m, 1997, 1 child **DISCIPLINE** PSYCHOLOGY **EDUCATION** Harvard Univ, EdM, 86; Univ Mich, MA, 92; PhD, 94. **CAREER** Assoc Prof, Univ Ky, 94-. **HONORS AND AWARDS** Early Career Achievement Awd, APA. **MEMBERSHIPS** APA, AERA, SRA. **RESEARCH** Motivation during adolescence. **SELECTED PUBLICATIONS** Auth, "Motivation and School Reform," in Advances in Motivation and Achievement, vol 10 (Greenwich, CT: JAI Pr, 97), 303-337; auth, "The Middle School Experience: Effects on the Math and Science Achievement of Learning Disabled Adolescents," J of Learning Disabilities, 31 (98): 128-138; coauth, "Present and Possible Academic Selves During Early Adolescence," Elem Sch J, 100 (99): 2-17; auth, "Why Do Students Cheat?" Boys' Life (99): 2-17; coauth, "Social Influences on Sports Participation During Adolescence," J of Res and Develop in Educ, 33 (00): 85-94; coauth, "The Role of Motivation in Educational Psychology," Educ and Child Psychol (forthcoming). **CONTACT ADDRESS** Dept Psychol, Univ of Kentucky, 249 Dickey Hall, Lexington, KY 40506-0017. **EMAIL** eande1@pop.uky.edu

ANDERSON, DAVID ATLAS
PERSONAL Born 04/28/1930, Cincinnati, OH, m **DISCIPLINE** EDUCATION **EDUCATION** Rochester Inst of Tech, BFA 1960; Syracuse Univ, MA 1962; Union Grad School, PhD 1975. **CAREER** Urban League of Rochester, deputy exec dir 1967-70; State Univ of NY Brockport, lecturer Afro-Amer studies; Rochester Inst of Tech, visiting asst prof 1981-, dir parent educ, Rochester City School District. **HONORS AND AWARDS** Community Leadership Awd Urban League of Rochester 1982; Outstanding Community Serv, Health Assn of Rochester 1984; Distinguished Volunteer, Mental Health Assn Rochester 1986. **MEMBERSHIPS** Assoc Comm Health Univ of Rochester Medical Sch 1970-82; bd mem vice pres Mental Health Assoc 1980-86; lecturer Correctional Institutions at Sonyea and Oatka NY 1983-85; bd of dirs Rochester Museum & Sci Ctr 1986-90; Natl Assn of Black Storytellers, 1988-89. **CONTACT ADDRESS** Dir Parent Education, Rochester City Sch District, 131 W Broad St, Rochester, NY 14614.

ANDERSON, KEVIN
PERSONAL Born 10/28/1948, Jersey City, NJ, m, 1992, 1 child **DISCIPLINE** SOCIOLOGY **EDUCATION** Trinity Col, BA, 70; Queens Col (CUNY), MA, 80; City Univ NY (CUNY), PhD, 83. **CAREER** From Asst Prof to Assoc Prof, Northern Ill Univ, 85-. **HONORS AND AWARDS** DAAD Study Vis Grant, 94; Am Coun of Learned Soc Fel, 96-97. **MEMBERSHIPS** ASA, Am Soc of Criminology, Hegel Soc of Am. **RESEARCH** Sociological theory, history of social thought, criminological theory. **SELECTED PUBLICATIONS** Auth, Lenin, Hegel and Western Marxism: A Critical Study, Univ Ill Pr (Urbana, IL), 95; ed, Marx on Suicide, Northwestern Univ Pr (Evanston, IL), 99; ed, Erich Fromm and Critical Criminology: Beyond the Punitive Society, Univ Ill Pr (Urbana, IL), 00. **CONTACT ADDRESS** Dept Sociol, No Illinois Univ, Dekalb, IL 60115. **EMAIL** kanderson@niu.edu

ANDERSON, ROBERT T.
PERSONAL Born 12/27/1926, CA, m, 1973, 6 children **DISCIPLINE** ANTHROPOLOGY **EDUCATION** Univ Cal Berkeley, BA, 45, 49; MA, 53; PhD, 56; Univ Paris, D Soc, 59; Life Chiropractic Col, DC, 82; Univ Juarez, Mex, MD, 86. **RESEARCH** Medical anthropology; anthropology of religion. **SELECTED PUBLICATIONS** Coauth, "Culture and Pain," in The Puzzle of Pain, eds. G Levy, M de Vachon (Basel, Switzerland: Gordon and Breach Arts Intl, 94), 120-138; coauth, "Bonesetters and Curers in a Mexican Community: Conceptual Models, Status, and Gender," Med Anthro 17 (96): 23-38, auth, "African and Western Medicine: A Case Study," Harcourt Brace Pub (96): HVS video documentary, 8 min; auth, Magic, Science, and Health: The Aims and Achievements of Medical Anthropology, Harcourt Brace Pub (Fort Worth TX), 96; auth, "Creating Clinical Efficacy by the Delphi Process," Clin Acup Oriental Med 1 (99): 61-64; auth, "Human Evolution, Low Back Pain, and Dual-Level Control," in Evolutionary Medicine, eds. W Trevathan, E Smith, J McKenna (Oxford: Oxford Univ Press, 99): 333-349; auth, "A Case Study in Integrative Medicine: Alternative Theories and the Language of Biomedicine," J Altern Comple Med 5 (99): 165-173; auth, "Alternative and Conventional Medicine in Iceland: The Diagnosis and Treatment of Low Back Pain," Dir Health (Reykjavik: Iceland) in press; auth, "An Urban Medicine Woman and Integrated Medicine," J Alt Comple Med 6 (in press):1-4. **CONTACT ADDRESS** Dept Anthropology, Mills Col, 500 MacArthur Blvd, Oakland, CA 94613. **EMAIL** boba@mills.edu

ANDES, NANCY
DISCIPLINE SOCIOLOGY **EDUCATION** Kent State Univ, BA, 76; Cornell Univ, MA, 83; PhD, 84. **CAREER** Asst prof, Univ Conn, 84-90; vis prof, Univ Peruana Cayetano Heredia, 90; chair, asst prof Univ Alaska, 97-. **HONORS AND AWARDS** Who's Who of Am Women, 92; World's Who's Who of Women, 93-94; Intl Who's Who of Professional and Bus Women, 94; Ful Scholar to Peru, 90. **MEMBERSHIPS** Am Sociol Asn, Intl Sociol Asn, Pacific Sociol Asn. **RESEARCH** Social organization and Change: community contexts and health, Gender and class stratification; Research methods: statistical computing, Multivariate and graphical methods, Survey research; Medical sociology: Institutional determinants of mortality, Evaluation of community health prevention programs. **SELECTED PUBLICATIONS** Auth, "Parental Values towards Children: Social Status, Gender and Family Structural Differences," Journal of Human Values, (99): 157-167; auth, "Robust Strategies for Cluster Analyses," Bulletin de Methodologie Sociologique, (98): 31-47; auth, "Linking Publick Health Data using Geographic Information System Techniques: Alaskan Community Characteristics and Infant Mortality," Statistics in Medicine (95): 481-490; auth, "Society and indigenous Health Care: The Cases of Nepal and Alaska," Global Perspective on Health Care, (95): 268-276; auth, "Institutional Contexts and Mortality: The Case of Peru," Sociological Focus, (92): 295-309; auth, "Mortalidad Infantil y Contextos Comunitarios comunidades en Peru," Revista Peruana de Poblacion, (92): 81-106; auth, "Child Survival in Community Contexts," Cetral Issues in Anthropology X, (92): 16-22; auth, "Social Class and Gender: An Empirical Evaluation of Occupational Stratification and Gender," Gender & Society, (92): 231-251; auth, "Jackknife and Bootstrap Estimates for Cluster Validation: Examples using US Occupations," Bulletin de Methodologie Sociologique, (89): 29-43; auth, "Socio-economic, Bedical Care, and Public Health Contexts affecting Infant Mortality: A Study of Community-level Differentials in Peru," Journal of Health and Social Behaviour, (89): 386-397. **CONTACT ADDRESS** Dept Sociol, Univ of Alaska, Anchorage, 3211 Providence Dr, Anchorage, AK 99508. **EMAIL** afna@uaa.alaska.edu

ANDRE, MARIA CLAUDIA
PERSONAL Born 08/12/1959, Buenos Aires, Argentina, m, 1998, 1 child **DISCIPLINE** LATIN AMERICAN LITERATURE, 20TH CENTURY, GENDER STUDIES **EDUCATION** Univ del Salv, trans, interp, 84; SUNY, PhD, 95. **CAREER** Vis prof, Marist Col, 90-91; vis prof, Bard Col, 91-93; teach asst, SUNY, 92-95; assoc prof, Hope Col, 94-. **HONORS AND AWARDS** Sigma Delta Phi. **MEMBERSHIPS** LASA; MLA. **RESEARCH** Latin American women writer; Latin American politics; gender studies. **SELECTED PUBLICATIONS** Rev of "Intimas suculencias: tratado filoscfico de cocina by Laura Esquivel (Letras Femeninas, Univ Neb-Lin, forthcoming); auth, "Griselda Gambaro: feminismo e influencia en su narrativa," Confluencia J 14 (99); auth, "Entrevista a Luisa Valenzuela," Revista Atenea 476 (98); auth, "Entorno a canones, memorias y recuerdos : conversacion con Tununa Mercado" Alba de Am Inst Lit Cult Hisp16 (98); auth, "Entre el sicoanalisis y Ta literatura: conversación con Liliana Heker," Alba de Am 19 (OO); auth, "Entre los bordes de lo real y el desarrollo de la imaginacion: Entrevista con Liliana Heker," Alba de Am 19 (00); auth, "Entrevista a Luisa Valenzuela," Revista Hisp (00); auth, "Empowering the Feminine/Feminist/Lesbian Subject through the Lens: Representation of Women in Yo, Ta peor de todas," by Maria Luisa Bemberg's, in Tortilleras: Hispanic and Latina Lesbian Expression (Temple Univ Press, forthcoming). **CONTACT ADDRESS** Dept Modern, Classical Language, Hope Col, 137 East 12th St, Holland, MI 49423-3607. **EMAIL** andre@hope.edu

ANDREASEN, NANCY C.
PERSONAL 2 children **DISCIPLINE** PSYCHIATRY **EDUCATION** Univ Nebr, BA (summa cum laude), 58; Radcliffe Col, MA, 59; Univ Nebr, PhD, 63; Univ Iowa, MD, 70. **CAREER** Instr, English, Nebr Wesleyan, 60-61; instr, English, Univ Nebr, 62-63; asst prof English, 63-66, from asst prof to assoc prof psychiat, 73-81, prof psychiat, 81-, dir, Mental Health Clinical Res Ctr, 87-, Andrew H. Woods Prof Psychiat, 92-97, Andrew H. Woods Chair Psychiat, 97-, Univ Iowa; sr consult, Northwick Park Hospital, London, 83; Acad Vis, Maudsley Hospital, London, 86; Ed, Am J Psychiat; Assoc Ed, Schizophrenia Bull. **HONORS AND AWARDS** Sarnat Prize; Adolphmeyer Awd; C. Charles Burligame Awd; Dean Awd, Am Col Psychiat; Distinguished Service Awd, Am Col Psychiat; Fac Schol Awd, Univ Iowa; Fel, Royal Col Physicians and Surgeons of Canada; Fogarty Sr. Int Fel; Foundations' Fund Prize, Am Psychiat Asn; Fulbright Fel; Hall-Mercer Awd, Pa Hospital; Hibbs Awd, Am Psychiat Asn; Nelson Urban Res Awd, Iowa Mental Health Asn; Kempf Awd, Am Psychiat Asn; Kolb Awd, Columbia Univ; Marion Faye Spencer Awd; Menninger Awd for Psychiat Res; Merit Awd, Nat Inst Mental Health; Phi Kappa Phi; recipient of numerous other awards and grants. **MEMBERSHIPS** Am Med Asn; Acad Psychiat Consortium, Ctr Advanced Study Behavioral Sci; Am Psychopathol Asn (secy 81-87, vpres 87-88, pres 89-90); Am Psychiat Asn; Am Asn Advancement Sci; Am Col Neuropsychopharmacology; Am Col Psychiat; Inst Med; Int Soc Neuroimaging in Psychiat; Int Col Neuropsychopharmacol; Johnson County Med Soc; Nat Advisory Comt Med; Org Human Brain Mapping; Psychiat Res Soc (pres 85-86); Soc Biological Psychiat; Soc Neuroscience; World Psychiat Asn (Chair, Neuroimaging Section). **RESEARCH** Neuroimaging; cognitive and behavioral neuroscience; diagnosis, instrument development, and clinical assessment; schizophrenia. **SELECTED PUBLICATIONS** Coauth, Introductory Textbook of Psychiatry, Am Psychiat Press, 90, 2nd ed, 94; co-ed, Positive versus Negative Schizophrenia, Springer-Verlag, 90; ed, Schizophrenia: From Mind to Molecule, Am Psychiatric Press, 94; co-ed, Psychotic Continuum, Springer-Verlag, 94; author and editor of numerous articles

and other publications. **CONTACT ADDRESS** Dept Psychiat, Univ of Iowa, 200 Hawkins Dr., MHCRC, 2911 JPP, Lincoln, NE 52242.

ANDREASSI, JOHN L.
PERSONAL Born 10/23/1934, New York, NY, m, 1969, 3 children **DISCIPLINE** PSYCHOLOGY **EDUCATION** CUNY, BA, 56; Fordham Univ, MA, 59; Case Western Reserve Univ, PhD, 64. **CAREER** Res Psychologist US Navy, 64-65; dir of Cire Seraces Lab, Naval Training Devices Center, 65-67; prof, New York Univ, 67-73; prof, Baruch Col, CUNY, 73-. **HONORS AND AWARDS** Psi Chi; Presidential Awd for Scholarship, Baruch Col, 78; Government funded res on brain and behav, 70-85; ed-in-chief, Int J on Psychol, 88-. **MEMBERSHIPS** Am Psychol Asn, Int Org on Psychophysiology, Sigma Xi. **RESEARCH** Brain and behavior, stress and cardiovascular activity, perception. **SELECTED PUBLICATIONS** Auth, Psychophysiology: Human Behavior and Psychological Response, 4th ed, Manutah, NJ: Lawrence Fordham Asn (2000) **CONTACT ADDRESS** Dept Psychol, Baruch Col, CUNY, 17 Lexington Ave, PO Box G-4126, New York, NY 10010.

ANDREWS, ANTHONY P.
PERSONAL Born 08/23/1949, Washington, DC, m, 1989, 2 children **DISCIPLINE** ANTHROPOLOGY, ARCHAEOLOGY **EDUCATION** Harvard Univ, BA, 72; Univ Arizona, MA, 76; Univ Arizona, PhD, 80. **CAREER** Asst prof Anthro, Hamilton Col, 80-81; asst prof Anthro, New Col of USF, 81-85; assoc prof Anthro, New Col of USF, 85-89; prof Anthro, New Col of USF, 89-; Chair, Div of Soc Sci, New Col of USF, 89-95. **HONORS AND AWARDS** Magna Cum Laude, 72; multiple res grants; State of Florida Teaching Awd. **MEMBERSHIPS** Soc Am Archeol; Am Anthro Asn; Sociedad Mexicana de Antropologia; Sociedad Espanola de Estudios Mayas. **RESEARCH** Prehispanic and historical archaeology and ethnohistory of eastern Mesoamerica; historical cartography and history of Yucatan. **SELECTED PUBLICATIONS** Auth, A Preliminary Study of the Ruins of Xcaret, Quintano Roo, Mexico, Tulane Univ, 75; auth, Ecab: Poblado y Provincia del Siglo XVI en Yucatan, Instituto Nacional de Antropologia e Historia, Mexico, 79; auth, Arqueologia Historica en el Area Maya, Sociedad Mexicana de Antropologia, Mexico, 85; auth, Instituto Nacional de Antropologia e Historia, Mexico, 86; First Cities, St Remy/Smithsonian, 95; "A Brief History of Underwater Archaelogy in the Maya Area." Ancient Mesoamerica; "Late Postclassic Lowland Maya Archaeology." Jrnl World Prehistory. **CONTACT ADDRESS** Division of Soc Sci, New Col of the Univ of So Florida, Sarasota, FL 34243. **EMAIL** andrews@sar.usf.edu

ANDREWS, DONNA G.
PERSONAL Born 06/26/1959, La Grange, GA, m, 1999 **DISCIPLINE** EDUCATION **EDUCATION** N Ga Col, BS, 81; Ga State Univ, MEd, 86; PhD, 92. **CAREER** Teacher, Ga Public Schools, 81-87; Tech Asst, Ga State Univ, 87-92; Consultant, Ga Dept Educ, 92-96; Asst Prof, Piedmont Col, 96-. **MEMBERSHIPS** CEC; TASH. **RESEARCH** Autism; Transition; School Violence; Functional Communication. **CONTACT ADDRESS** Dept Educ, Piedmont Col, PO Box 10, Demorest, GA 30535. **EMAIL** dandres@piedmont.edu

ANDREWS, GREGG L.
PERSONAL Born 08/15/1950, Canton, OH, m, 1997, 3 children **DISCIPLINE** SOCIOLOGY **EDUCATION** Kent State Univ, AA, 76; BA, 81; Univ Akron, MA, 85; Kent State Univ, PhD, 95. **CAREER** Asst Exec Dir, The Twelve, Inc, 81-84; Exec Dir, United Way, 84-85; Dir of Spec Prog to Dean, Kent State Univ, 85-. **HONORS AND AWARDS** Zeisberger-Heckewelder Medal for Community Service, 98; Tuscarawas County Citizen of the Year, 99; Outstanding Young Men of Am. **SELECTED PUBLICATIONS** Auth, "Volunteer Satisfaction," Voluntary Action News, 85; co-auth, "Situational Facilities and Volunteer Work," Journal of Volunteer Administration, 88; co-auth, "Knowledge Based Economic Development," Economic Development Review, (99): 97. **CONTACT ADDRESS** Dept Arts & Sci, Kent State Univ, 330 Univ Dr NE, New Philadelphia, OH 44663. **EMAIL** gandrews@tusc.kent.edu

ANDREWS-MCCALL, MAXINE RAMSEUR
PERSONAL Born Fayetteville, NC **DISCIPLINE** EDUCATION **EDUCATION** Fayetteville State Univ, BS 1956; North Carolina Central Univ, MEd 1963; East Carolina Univ EdS 1975; Univ of NC at Greensboro, EdD 1985. **CAREER** Cumberland County Schools, teacher 1956-66, school social worker 1966-69; Elizabeth City State Univ, title III coord 1969-71; Fayetteville State Univ, adj prof 1985-; Sincerely Yours Writing & Specialty Svcs, proprietor 1986-; Cumberland County Schools, elem supervisor 1971-84, supervisor secondary educ 1984-90; Fayetteville State University, assistant professor/coordinator of secondary education, coordinator of educational administration/curriculum/instruction, director, teaching fellows program; coordinator, master of school admin degree program, currently. **HONORS AND AWARDS** Distinguished Alumnae Fayetteville State Univ Natl Assoc for Equal Oppor in Higher Educ 1986. **MEMBERSHIPS** Member, Natl Educ Assoc; member, Assoc for Supervision and Curriculum Div; member, NC Assoc for Educators; member, Phi Delta Kappa; member, NC Assoc of Administrators; member, Delta Sigma Theta Sor; member, NC Historical Preservation Soc; member, Fayetteville State Alumni Assoc; president, 1987-90, secretary, 1988-91, North Carolina Association of Supervision and Curriculum Development; Master of School Administration, Fay State University, coordinator, 1997-. **CONTACT ADDRESS** Coordinator, Master of School Administration Degree Program, Fayetteville State Univ, Fayetteville, NC 28301.

ANDRZEJEWSKI, JULIE
PERSONAL Born 09/17/1945, Tacoma, WA **DISCIPLINE** HUMAN RELATIONS **EDUCATION** Univ Wash, BA, 69; MA, 71; Univ N Col, EdD, 78. **CAREER** Prof, St. Cloud State Univ, 71-. **HONORS AND AWARDS** Phi Beta Kappa, Univ of Wash, 69; Lambda Lit Awd, 89; Distinguished Teacher Awd, St. Cloud State Univ, 89-90; Minn Women in Higher Educ Awd, 92; Grant; Minn State Univ, 94-96; Otto Bremer Found Grant, 97-00. **RESEARCH** Global human rights, social justice and environment issues; Prevention of harassment and hate crimes; Class, race, gender, disability, sexual orientation, religion, physical appearance and animal rights issues. **SELECTED PUBLICATIONS** Auth, "Teaching Controversial Issues in Higher Education: Pedagogical Techniques and Analytical Framework", in Practicing What We Teach: Confronting Issues of Diversity in Teacher Education, Ed, R. Martin, SUNY pr, 95; Auth, "Teaching and Learning Skills for Social Action", Infusion: Tools for Action and Education, Center for Campus Organizing (Cambridge, MA), 96; Auth, "The Myth of Reverse Discrimination", in Oppression and Social Justice: Critical Frameworks, Simon and Schuster, 96; Auth, "Knowledge and Skills for Social and Environmental Justice", in Oppression and Social Justice: Critical Frameworks, Simon and Schuster, 96; Auth, "Oppression and Social Justice: Critical Frameworks", in Oppression and Social Justice: Critical Frameworks, Simon and Schuster, 96; Auth, "Teaching for a Safe and Equitable Campus Environment", The Conversation, SCSU Face Center for Teaching Excellence, (Winter 98); Auth, "Collaborative Education Project Shows Promise for Preventing Harassment and Hate Crimes on Campus", The Conversation, SCSU Face Center for Teaching Excellence, (Fall 98); Auth, "Reflections on Political Bias in Traditional Education", A World of Difference Anti-Bias Study Guide, Anti-Defamation League of B'nai B'rith, 98; auth, "The Citizenship for Diversity Project: An Educational Model for Prevention of Harassment and Hate Crimes on Campus", Excellence in Teaching, (Spring 99); coauth, Education for Global Citizenship and Social Responsible, Monograph, John Dewey Project for Progressive Educ, Univ of Vermont (Spring 99); coauth, "Unveiling the Hidden Glass Ceiling: An Analysis of the Cohort Effect Claim," Am Sociol Rev, April 00. **CONTACT ADDRESS** Dept Human Relations, St. Cloud State Univ, 720 4th Ave S, Saint Cloud, MN 56301. **EMAIL** andrzejewski@stcloudstate.edu

ANTIA, KERSEY H.
PERSONAL Born 01/07/1936, Surat, India, m, 1966, 3 children **DISCIPLINE** PSYCHOLOGY **EDUCATION** Tata Inst of Social Svcs, MA; N.C. State Univ, MS, 69; Indiana Northern Univ, PhD, 74. **CAREER** Univ of N. C., res asst, 67-69; Behavior Systems Inc., Proj Dir, 69-70; State of IL, Clin Psychologist, 70-86; private practice as Psychologist, 86-. **MEMBERSHIPS** CPS, APS, SPM, AAP, AOS, AAR/WPR. **RESEARCH** Mind-body relations; interface between psychology and religion; interrelations and similarities between Zoroastrianism and Judeo-Christian traditions. **SELECTED PUBLICATIONS** Auth, Contributions of the Interview to the Selection of Higher-Level Personnel, Experimental Publication System, Wash. D.C. Am Psych Assoc, 69; auth, Job Satisfaction: Facts versus Fiction, Experimental Pub Sys, Wash D.C. Am Psych Assoc, 69; auth, A Dimensional Analysis of Instructor Ratings and Peer Nominations, Experimental Pub Sys, Wash D.C. Amer Psych Assoc, 70; auth, Consequences of Early Rejection and Social Deprivation on Later Speech Development, IL Jour of Speech & Hearing, 75; auth, Cognitive Climate of an Organization & Cognitive Style of Its Leader, Behavior, 93. **CONTACT ADDRESS** 8318 W. 138th Pl, Orland Park, IL 60462. **EMAIL** antia@juno.com

ANTON, HARLEY F.
PERSONAL Born 06/26/1951, McComb, MS, m, 1985 **DISCIPLINE** HISTORY, EDUCATION **EDUCATION** Samford, Univ, BA, 73; Louisiana State Univ, MA, 76. **CAREER** Instr, Louisiana State Univ, 80-87; asst prof, Middle Tenn State Univ, 88-. **HONORS AND AWARDS** Tenn Dev Educator of the Year, 97. **MEMBERSHIPS** NADE. **RESEARCH** Standardized testing, cognitive processing. **SELECTED PUBLICATIONS** Coauth, Key to Better College Reading, Townsend Pr, 96; coauth, Improving Reading Comprehension Skills, Townsend Pr, 94. **CONTACT ADDRESS** Dept Dev Studies, Middle Tennessee State Univ, 1301 E Main St, Murfreesboro, TN 37132-0001. **EMAIL** hanton@mtsu.edu

ANTONI, MICHAEL H.
PERSONAL Born 11/20/1955, Providence, RI, m, 1987, 1 child **DISCIPLINE** PSYCHOLOGY **EDUCATION** Univ RI, Kingston, BA, 79; Conn Col, New London, MA, 81; Univ Miami, Coral Gables, PhD, 86. **CAREER** Internship, Miami Veterans Admin Medical Center, 85-86; Clinical Psychology Licensure in State of Fla, 87; asst and assoc prof of Psychology, Univ Miami, Coral Gables, 87-95; investigator-Center for the Biopsychosocial Study of AIDS, 87-92; investigator-Sylvester Comprehensive Cancer Center, Miami, Fla, 90-; Sr investigator-Helen Dowling Cancer Inst, Rotterdam, Netherlands, 91-; prof, Psychol and Psychiatry, Univ Miami, Coral Gables, 96. **HONORS AND AWARDS** Young Investigator Awd, Soc of Behav Med, 93; Young Investigator Awd, Am Psychol Asn, Div 38, 93. **MEMBERSHIPS** Am Psychol Asn, Soc of Behav Med, Am Psychosomatic Soc, Int Soc of Behav Med. **SELECTED PUBLICATIONS** Coauth with G. van der Pompe and C. Heijnen, "Elevated basal cortisol levels and attenuated ACTH and cortisol responses to acute stress in women with metastatic breast cancer," Psychoneuroendocrinology, 21 (96): 361-374; coauth with S. Lutgendorf, G. Ironson, et al, "Cognitive behavioral stress management decreases dysphoric mood and Herpes Simplex Virus-Type 2 antibody titers in symptomatic HIV-seropositive gay men," J of Consulting and Clinical Psychol, 65 (97): 31-43; coauth with S. Lutgendorf, G. Ironson, et al, "Cognitive processing style, mood and immune function following HIV seropositivity notification," Cognitive Therapy and Res, 21 (97): 157-184; coauth with G. van der Pompe and C. Heijnen, "The relations of plasma ACTH and cortisol levels with the distribution and function of peripheral blood cells in response to a behavioral challenge in breast cancer: An empirical exploration by means of statistical modeling," Int J of Behav Med, 4 (97): 145-169; coauth with G. Ironson, C. Wynings, N. Schneiderman, A. Baum, M. Rodriquez, D. Greenwood, C. Benight, et al, "Post traumatic stress symptoms, intrusive thoughts, loss and immune function after Hurricane Andrew," Psychosomatic Med, 59 (97): 128-141; coauth with G. van der Pompe and C. Heijnen, "The effect of mild acute stress on immune cell distribution and natural killer cell activity in breast cancer patients," Biological Psychol, 48 (98): 21-35; coauth with G. van der Pompe and C. Heijnen, "The effects of surgical stress and psychological stress on the immune function of operative cancer patients," Psychology and Health (in press); coauth with T. Woods, G. Ironson, and D. Kling, "Religiosity is associated with affective and immune status in symptomatic HIV-infected gay men," J of Psychosomatic Res (in press); auth, "Psychoneuroimmunology," in A. Kazdin, ed, The Encyclopedia of Psychology, Am Psychol Asn and Oxford Univ Press (in press); coauth with N. Schneiderman, A. Baum, and G. Ironson, "Stress Management for HIV. Clinical Validation and Intervention Manual," Society of Behavioral Medicine Guidebook Series, NJ: Erlbaum (in press). **CONTACT ADDRESS** Dept Psychol, Univ of Miami, PO Box 248185, Miami, FL 33124.

ANTONIO, ROBERT
PERSONAL Born 06/20/1945, New Haven, CT, s **DISCIPLINE** SOCIOLOGY **EDUCATION** Miami of Oh, BA, 67; Notre Dame, MA, 70, PhD, 72. **CAREER** Asst prof, 71, assoc prof, 75, prof, 86-, Univ of KS. **HONORS AND AWARDS** Younger Humanist Fel-Natl Endowment of the Humanities, 74-75; Chancellors Club Awd for Teaching Excellence, 79; Chancellors Club Career Teaching Awd, 88; Chancellors Club Teaching Professorship, 89; Motor Board Honors Society-Outstanding Educator 75, 88, 91, 96. **MEMBERSHIPS** Amer Sociological Assn; Midwest Sociological Assn. **RESEARCH** Social Theory **SELECTED PUBLICATIONS** Auth, Max Weber, The Encyclopedia of Democracy, 95; Nietzsche's Antisociology: Subjectified Culture and the End of History, American Journal of Sociology, 95; Post-Fordism in the United States: The Poverty of Market Centered Democracy, Current Perspectives in Social Theory, 96; Mapping Postmodern Social Theory, in What is Social Theory? The Philosophical Debates, 98; Karl Marx, Blackwell Companion to the Major Social Theorists, 00. **CONTACT ADDRESS** Dept of Sociology, Univ of Kansas, Lawrence, 732 Fraser, Lawrence, KS 66045. **EMAIL** anto@falcon.cc.ukans.edu

ANTONUCCI, TONY C.
PERSONAL Born 09/09/1948, m, 1979, 2 children **DISCIPLINE** PSYCHOLOGY **EDUCATION** Hunter Col, BA, 69; Wayne State Col, MA, 72; PhD, 73. **CAREER** Teach asst, Wayne State Univ, 69-73; asst prof, Syracuse Univ, 73-79; asst prof, 79-88; asst res sci, 79-82; adj assoc prof, 82-90; assoc res sci, 82-90; fac assoc, 88-; assoc prof, 88-97; asst to dean, 96-98; prog dir, res sci, 90-; prof, 91-, Univ Michigan. **HONORS AND AWARDS** APA Fel; GSA Fel; Fogarty Sr Intl Fel; NIMH; Res Agen Uni Nat Intl Yr Old Pers, Mem; LASAC, Mem. **MEMBERSHIPS** SPSSI' APS; ISSBD; SRCD; GSA; APA; AAA. **RESEARCH** Social relations and well being across the life span. **SELECTED PUBLICATIONS** Coauth, "Extended Family Relationships," in Encyclopedia of Mental Health, ed. H Friedman (San Diego, CA: Acad Press, 98); coauth, "The negative effects of close social relations among older adults," Fam Rela 47 (98): 379-384; coauth, "The Family as a Context for Health and Well-being," Fam Rela 47 (98): 313-314; coauth, "The influences of gender and parental support in depressive symptomatology among African American & European American youth," Fam Rela 47 (98): 95-402; coauth, "Satisfaction with social networks: An examination of socioemotional selectivity theory of cohorts," Psych Aging 13 (98): 544-552; auth, "Psychological disorder and mortality in French older adults: Do social relations modify the relationship?" Am J Epidem 149 (99):116-126; coauth, "Attitudes toward Genetic

Testing and Fetal Diagnosis 1990-1996," J Health Soc Beh 40 (99): 429-445; coauth, "Marital status and risk of Alzheimer's Disease," Am Acad Neurol 53 (99):1953-1958; coauth, "Social support," in Encyclopedia of stress, ed. G Fink (San Diego, CA: Acad Press, in press); coauth, "The Impact of Positive and Negative Aspects of Marital Relationships and Friendships on Well-Being of Older Adults," App Devel Sci (in press); coauth, "Social Relations, Perceived Health and Life Satisfaction in Black America," in Health in Black America, eds. RC Gibson, JS Jackson (Newbury Park, CA: Sage Pub, in press); coauth, "Social networks, support, and integration," in Encyclopedia of Gerontology (San Diego, CA: Acad Press, in press.) **CONTACT ADDRESS** Dept Psychology, Univ of Michigan, Ann Arbor, 525 E Univ Ave, Ann Arbor, MI 48109.

APPEL, JAMES B.
PERSONAL Born 02/18/1934, New York, NY, w, 1965 **DISCIPLINE** PSYCHOLOGY **EDUCATION** Columbia Univ, AB, 55; Indiana Univ, PhD, 60. **CAREER** Post-Doctoral Res Fel, Inst for Psychiatric Res, Indiana Univ Sch of Med, 59-60; res asst, Yale Univ Sch of Med, 60-61, asst prof, 61-66; assoc prof, Univ of Chicago Sch of Med, 66-70; prof, Univ SC, 72-85; vis prof, Univ Col, London, July-Dec 78; Dir, Grad Progs in General-Experimental Psychology, Univ SC, 82-; vis res scientist, Nat Inst on Drug Abuse/Addiction Res Center, Baltimore, Md: March-May 86; Carolina Res Prof, Dept of Psychol, Univ SC, 86-. **HONORS AND AWARDS** NIH Fel, 59; Yale Univ, James Hudson Brown Memorial Fund, 60-61; NIH Res Grant, 63-65; NIH Biomedical Support Grant, 76-77, 79-80, 80-81; Licensed Beverage Industries, Inc, Res Support Grant, 64; Nat Sci Found Res Grants, 65-66, 67-68, 69-70; Nat Inst of Mental Health, Res Sci Develop Awd, 69-72; State of Ill Dept of Mental Health Res Grant, 70-72; Nat Inst of Mental Health Res Grants, 73-76, 73-79; Nat Inst of Drug Abuse Res Grants, 76-79, 80-89, 89-99; Univ SC Educ Found Res Awd, Col of Humanities and Soc Scis, 89; Nat Inst of Drug Abuse, Nat MERIT Awd89-99; Carolina distinguished Professorship, 86-. **MEMBERSHIPS** Am Asn for the Advancement of Sci, Am Col of Neuropharmacology, Am Psychol Asn, Behavioral Pharmacology Soc, Collegium Int Neuro-Psychopharmacologicum, Eastern Psychol Asn, Int Brain res Org, Sigma Xi, Soc for Neurosci, Soc for the Stimulus Properties of Drugs, SC Chapter of the Soc for Neurosci. **RESEARCH** Behavioral neuropharmacology: the relationship between in vitro drug effects and brain mechanisms; stimulus properties of CNS stimulant and hallucinogenic drugs; the effects of drugs on sensory and perceptual processes. **SELECTED PUBLICATIONS** Coauth with W. B. West, S. Livreri, B. B. Simon, M. Gooding, J. Buggy, "Stimulus effects of cocaine given centrally and systemically," Soc for Neurosci Abstract, 22 (96): 1583; coauth with B. B. Simon, "Effects of duloxetine, a dual serotonin and norepinephrine reuptake inhibitor, on the stimulus properties of cocaine and LSD," Soc for Neurosci Abstracts, 22 (96): 1584; coauth with B. B. Simon, "Dopaminergic and serotonergic properties of fluoxetine," Progress in Neuro-psychopharmacology and Biological Psychiatry, 21 (97): 169-181; coauth with B. B. Simon, "The role of DA in the Stimulus effects of Cocaine and nomifensine," Soc for Neurosci Abstracts, 23 (97): 987; coauth with W. B. West and J. Buggy, "Differences in the stimulus properties of LSD in the Nac, ventricles, dorsal raphe and fimbria striatum," Soc for Neurosci Abstracts, 23 (97): 1499; coauth with W. B. West, W. G. Rolandi, T. Alici and K. Pechersky, "Increasing the selectivity of drug discrimination procedures," Behavioral Pharmacology, 9 (98): 102; coauth with W. B. West, W. G. Rolandi, T. Alici and K. Pechersky, "Increasing the selectivity of drug discrimination procedures," Pharmacology, Biochemistry, and Behavior, 64 (99): 353-358; coauth with M. E. Chachich, W. B. West, and J. McLaughlin, "Differential substitution of dopaminergic drugs in a cocaine-Other Drug discrimination procedure," Soc for Nerurosci Abstracts, 25 (99): 1873; coauth with W. B. West, A. Lou, K. Perchersky, and M. E. Chachich. "Antagonism of a PCP drug discrimination by hallucinogens and related drugs," Neuropsychopharmacology (in press); coauth with W. B. West, K. C. Ross, M. E. Chachich, F. Howard, and J. R. Coleman, "Possible neuroprotective effects of LSD on PCP-enhanced audiogenic seizures," Soc for Neurosci Abstracts, 25 (99): 61. **CONTACT ADDRESS** Dept Psychol, Univ of So Carolina, Columbia, 512 Pendleton St, Columbia, SC 29208. **EMAIL** appel@sc.edu

APPELBAUM, PAUL S.
PERSONAL Born 11/30/1951, Brooklyn, NY, m, 1974, 3 children **DISCIPLINE** BIOLOGY, MEDICINE AND PSYCHIATRY **EDUCATION** Columbia Col, AB, 72; Harvard Med Sch, MD, 76. **CAREER** Asst to assoc prof, psychiat and law, Univ Pittsburgh, 80-84; assoc prof, psychiat, Harvard Med Sch, 84-85; A.F. Zeleznik distinguished prof, psychiat, Univ Mass Med Sch, 85-; chair, dept of psychiat, Univ Mass Med Sch, 92-; fel, Ctr for Advan Study in the Behavioral Sci, 96-97. **HONORS AND AWARDS** Pfizer vis prof, Md Psychiat Res Ctr, Univ Md, 98; Edward J. Strecker, MD award, Inst of Pa Hospital and Jefferson Med Col, 97; Fritz Redlich fel, Ctr for Advan Study in the Behavioral Sci, 96-97; Manfred S. Guttmacher award, Amer Psychiat Asn and Amer Acad of Psychiat, 83, 96 2000; Will Solimene award, Amer Med Writers Asn, 95; Pfizer vis prof, dept of psychiat, Univ Calif Davis, 95; Saleem Shah Mem award, State Mental Health Forensic Dir Asn, 93. **MEMBERSHIPS** Amer Med Asn; Intl Acad of Law and Mental Health; Mass Psychiat Soc; Amer Soc of Law, Med and Ethics; Amer Acad of Psychiat and the Law; Pa Psychiat Soc; Mass Psychiat Soc; Amer Psychiat Asn. **RESEARCH** Violence, its prediction and control; Ethical issues in general medical and psychiatric practice; Legal regulation of medical practice; Phenomenology of delusions. **SELECTED PUBLICATIONS** Co-auth, Assessing Competence To Consent To Treatment: A Guide for Physicians and Other Health Professionals, Oxford Univ Press, 98; co-ed, Trauma & Memory: Clinical & Legal Controversies, Oxford Univ Press, 97; auth, Almost a Revolution: Mental Health Law and the Limits of Change, Oxford Univ Press, 94; co-auth, Violence by people discharged from acute psychiatric inpatient facilities and by others in the same neighborhoods, Arch Gen Psychiat, 98; co-auth, C: The MacCAT-T: A clinical tool to assess patients' capacities to make treatment decisions, Psychiat Svc, 97; auth, A theory of ethics for forensic psychiatry, Jour Amer Acad Psychiat Law, 97; auth, Almost a revolution: an international perspective on the law of involuntary commitment, Jour Amer Acad Psychiat Law, 97; co-auth, Capacities of hospitalized, medically ill patients to consent to treatment, Psychosomatics, 97; co-auth, Twenty years after Tarasoff: reviewing the duty to protect, Harvard Rev Psychiat, 96; co-auth, Constructing competence: formulating standards of legal competence to make medical decisions, Rutgers Law Rev, 96; co-auth, Psychotherapists' duties to third parties: Ramona and beyond, Amer Jour Psychiat, 95; co-auth, Moral stage of reasoning & the misperceived duty to report past crimes (misprision), Intl Jour Law Psychiat, 95; co-auth, Boundaries in psychotherapy: model guidelines, Psychiat: Interpersonal and Bio Processes, 95; coauth, Clinical Handbook of Psychiatry and the Law, 3rd Ed, 00. **CONTACT ADDRESS** 55 Lake Ave. N, Worcester, MA 01655. **EMAIL** appelbap@ummhc.org

ARAFAT, IBTIHAJ
PERSONAL Born Nablus, Palestine, s **DISCIPLINE** SOCIOLOGY **EDUCATION** OSU, BS, 67; MS; 68; PhD, 70. **CAREER** Edu expert, UNESCO, 57-64; prof, CUNY City Col, 70-; UNFPA sr demog expert, 78-80, 87-90; consul, UN, 91, 92, 96. **HONORS AND AWARDS** UNESCO Fel, 57; Vis Schl, Middle States; Alturas Awd; IIE Awd. **MEMBERSHIPS** PAA; SAA. **RESEARCH** Population; social problems; women's studies; Middle Eastern studies. **SELECTED PUBLICATIONS** Auth, Sex Roles; auth, Methods of Research; auth, Population; auth, Thinking About Population: An Introduction to Modern Demography, 95; auth, Palestinian Culture, forthcoming; auth, House Husbands, forthcoming. **CONTACT ADDRESS** Dept Sociology, City Col, CUNY, Convent Ave at 138th St, New York, NY 10031.

ARAOZ, DANIEL L.
PERSONAL Born 04/23/1930, Buenos Aires, Argentina, m, 1991, 2 children **DISCIPLINE** COUNSELING, PSYCHOLOGY **EDUCATION** Gonzaga Univ, BA, 52; MA, 54; Col Mt St Vincent, PhL, 54; Alm Col, STL, 64; Univ Santa Clara, MST, 61; Columbia Univ, MA, 64; EdD, 69. **HONORS AND AWARDS** AIPP, Fel. **MEMBERSHIPS** APA. **RESEARCH** Mind body influences. **SELECTED PUBLICATIONS** Auth, Hypnosis and Sex Therapy, Brunner/Mazel, 82; auth, Reengineering Yourself, Adams Pub, 94; auth, Solution-Oriented Brief Therapy, Brunner/Mazel, 95; auth, The New Hypnosis, Brunner/Mazel, 85. **CONTACT ADDRESS** Dept Counselor Education, Long Island Univ, C.W. Post, 720 Northern Blvd, Greenvale, NY 11548. **EMAIL** taoist23@argentinamail.com

ARCHER, CHALMERS, JR.
PERSONAL Born 04/21/1938, Tchula, MS, s **DISCIPLINE** EDUCATION **EDUCATION** Saints Junior Col, Associate, art; Tuskegee Inst, Alabama, BS 1972, MEd 1973; Auburn University, Alabama, PhD 1979; Univ of Alabama, Post Doctorate Certificate, 1979; MIT, Cambridge MA, Certificate 1982. **CAREER** Saints Jr College, asst to the pres, 68-70; Tuskegee Inst, asst vice pres & asst prof 1970-83; Northern Virginia Community College, admin/prof, 83-; Jackson Advocate, contributing editor. **HONORS AND AWARDS** Honorary Doctorate of Letters, Saints Jr Coll, Lexington MS, 1970; Phi Delta Kappa Awd for Leadership; Exemplary Research & Program Development, 1981; cited for community contribution; lectured at Cambridge Univ, England, and five major universities on teaching and learning interdisciplinary studies, 1988-89; architect of Comp Counseling Ctr & Weekend College at Tuskegee Inst; Architect of Reading & Language Arts Special Emphasis Curriculum for public schs; developed successful multi-level Educ Alliance to Adv Equal Access with public schs; author of 22 educational & other publications; participated in President-elect Clinton's "A Call for Reunion" Opening Ceremony; President Clinton's Task Force, Americans for Change, charter member; Democratic National Committee; Clinton/Gore Rapid Response Team. **MEMBERSHIPS** Natl Assn of Coll Deans, Registrars, and Admissions Officers; Phi Delta Kappa; Kappa Delta Pi; APGA; Life Member, NAACP; charter mem Kiwanis Intl of Macon Coll; AAUP; AACRAO; Southeastern Assoc of Community Coll; Cooperative Educ; vice pres, Saints Jr Coll Alumni; past bd mem, Natl Consortium for the Recruitment of Black Students from Northern Cities; past chmn, State of Alabama's Steering Comm for Advanced Placement of High School Students; consultant, Department of Education on Retention, 1990-92. **SELECTED PUBLICATIONS** Author: Growing Up Black in Rural Mississippi, 1992; On the Shoulders of Giants, 00; Growing Up With the Green Berets, 00. **CONTACT ADDRESS** Manassas Campus, No Virginia Comm Col, 6901 Sudley Rd, Manassas, VA 20109-7435. **EMAIL** drarcher97@aol.com

ARDELT, MONIKA
PERSONAL Born 04/29/1960, Wiesbaden, Germany, m, 1990, 2 children **DISCIPLINE** SOCIOLOGY **EDUCATION** Johann Wolfgang Goethe-Univ Frankfurt/Main (Germany), MA, 87; Univ NC, Chapel Hill, PhD, 94. **CAREER** Res assoc, J. W. Goethe-Univ Frankfurt/Main (Germany), 87-88; asst prof, Univ Fla, 94-. **HONORS AND AWARDS** Distinguished Grad Student Howard W. Odum Awd, Dept Sociol, UNC-CH, 94; Brookdale Nat Fel Awd, 99. **MEMBERSHIPS** Am Sociol Asn, Southern Sociol Soc, The Gerontological Soc of Am. **RESEARCH** Adult human development; aging and the life course; death and dying; family and society, stress and coping/mental health; social psychology, quantitative and qualitative data analysis. **SELECTED PUBLICATIONS** Coauth with Glen H. Elder, Rand D. Conger, and E. Michael Foster, "Families Under Economic Pressure," J of Family Issues, 13, 1 (92): 5-37; coauth with Glen H. Elder and E. Michael Foster, "Children in the Household Economy," in, R. Conger and G. H. Elder, eds, Families in Troubled Times: Adapting to Change in Rural America, New York: Aldine-DeGruyter (94); coauth with Glen H. Elder and Elizabeth B. Robertson, "Families Under Economic Pressure," in , R. Conger and G. H. Elder, eds, Families in Troubled Times: Adapting to Change in Rural America, New York: Aldine-DeGruyter (94); coauth with G. H. Elder, Jacquelynne Eccles, and Sarah Lord, "Inner City Parents Under Economic Pressure: Perspectives on the Strategies of Parenting," J of Marriage and the Family, 57 (95): 771-784; auth, "Wisdom and Life Satisfaction in Old Age," J of Gerontology: Psychol Scis, 52B, 1 (97): P15-P27; auth, "Social Crisis and Individual Growth: The Long-Term Effects of the Great Depression," J of Aging Studies, 12, 3 (98): 291-314; coauth with Glen H. Elder, Jr, "Family Influences and Adolescents' Lives," in F. F. Furstenberg, Jr, J. S. Eccles, G. H. Elder, Jr, T. Cook, and A. Sameroff, eds, Managing to Make It: Urban Families and Adolescent Success, Chicago, ILL: Univ Chicago Press (99); coauth with G. H. Elder, Jr, "Household, Kinship, and the Life Course: Research Question, Embeddedness, and Human Agency," in M. B. Spencer, G. K. Brookins, and W. Allen, eds, Beginnings: The Social and Affective Development of Black Children, 2nd ed, Hillsdale, NY: Erlbaum (in press); coauth with Jacquelynne S. Eccles, "Effects of Mothers' Parental Efficacy Beliefs and Promotive Parenting Strategies on Inner-City Youth," J of Family Issues (in press); auth, "Antecedents and Effects of Wisdom in Old Age: A Longitudinal Perspective on Aging Well," Res on Aging (in Press); auth, "Intellectual Versus Wisdom-Related Knowledge: The Case for a Different Kind of Learning in the Later Years of Life," Ed Gerontology: An Int J of Res and Practice (in press). **CONTACT ADDRESS** Dept Sociol, Univ of Florida, PO Box 117330, Gainesville, FL 32611-7330. **EMAIL** Ardelt@soc.ufl.edu

ARIES, ELIZABETH J.
PERSONAL Born 09/24/1947, Chicago, IL, m, 1974, 2 children **DISCIPLINE** PSYCHOLOGY **EDUCATION** Univ Mich, BA, 69; Harvard Univ, MA, PhD, 73. **CAREER** Asst Prof, Yale Univ, 73-75; Prof, Amherst Col, 75-. **HONORS AND AWARDS** Phi Beta Kappa. **MEMBERSHIPS** Am Psychol Asn; Am Psychol Soc. **RESEARCH** Gender and communication; Identity development at adolescence. **SELECTED PUBLICATIONS** Auth, Men and Women in Interaction: Reconsidering the differences, Oxford Univ Press, 96; auth, "Gender differences in interaction: A re-examination," in Sex and gender differences in communication, (Lawrence Earlbaum Pub, 98); auth, Adolescent Behavior: Readings and Interpretations, McGraw-Hill, 01. **CONTACT ADDRESS** Dept Psychol, Amherst Col, 555 Bay Rd, Amherst, MA 01002. **EMAIL** ejaries@amhers.edu

ARIKER, SHIRLEY
PERSONAL Born Norwich County, m, 1982, 1 child **DISCIPLINE** SOCIAL WORK **EDUCATION** Univ Conn, BA, 62; MA, 66; NY Univ, MSW, 87. **CAREER** Prof, State Univ of NYork & Empire State Col. **HONORS AND AWARDS** Excellence in Mentoring. **MEMBERSHIPS** Nat Asn of Soc Workers of NY State, Clinical Soc Workers--NY Sch for Psychoanalytic Psychotherapy. **SELECTED PUBLICATIONS** Auth, "Prisoners," New Catholic World; auth, "A Class Consciousness," Radical Teacher. **CONTACT ADDRESS** Dept Human Services, SUNY Metropolitan Ctr, 225 Varick St, New York, NY 10014. **EMAIL** shirley.ariker@esc.edu

ARMITAGE, SUSAN
PERSONAL Born 05/17/1937 **DISCIPLINE** US WOMEN'S HISTORY **EDUCATION** Univ London, PhD, 68. **CAREER** Prof, Washington State Univ. **HONORS AND AWARDS** Dist Fulbright Scholar, Moscow State Univ, 95. **RESEARCH** Women in the U.S. West. **SELECTED PUBLICATIONS** Coauth, Out of Many, Prentice Hall, 94; co-ed, The Women's West, 87; So Much To Be Done: Women Settlers on the Mining and Ranching Frontier, 90; Writing the Range: Race, Class, and Culture in the Women's West, 98. **CONTACT ADDRESS** Dept of History, Washington State Univ, 301 Wilson Hall, PO Box 644030, Pullman, WA 99164-4030. **EMAIL** armitage@wsu.edu

ARMSTRONG, CHRISTOPHER
PERSONAL Born 07/26/1945, Bethesda, MD, m, 1975, 1 child **DISCIPLINE** SOCIOLOGY **EDUCATION** Washington & Lee Univ, MA, 67; Univ Penn, PhD, 74. **CAREER** Asst to Full Prof, Bloomsburg Univ, 74-. **HONORS AND AWARDS** Who's Who Worldwide; Intl Who's Who of Professionals. **MEMBERSHIPS** E Sociol Soc, S Sociol Soc. **RESEARCH** New England Boarding Schools; Ethnic History. **CONTACT ADDRESS** Dept Sociol & Soc Work, Bloomsburg Univ of Pennsylvania, 400 E 2nd St, Bloomsburg, PA 17815.

ARNETT, CARLEE
PERSONAL Born 08/13/1964, Trenton, NJ, m, 1991, 2 children **DISCIPLINE** GERMAN STUDIES, SECOND LANGUAGE ACQUISITION **EDUCATION** Mt Holyoke Col, BA, 87; Univ Calif, Berkeley, MA, 91; Univ Mich, PhD, 95. **CAREER** Vis asst prof, coordr, Ohio State Univ, 97-98; asst prof, dir, Univ Ariz, 98-00; asst prof, Univ of Calif, Davis, 00-. **HONORS AND AWARDS** Rackham Dissertation Fel, Frank X. Braun Tchg Prize, Univ Mich, 94. **MEMBERSHIPS** Modern Lang Asn; Soc Germanic Philol; Am Asn Tchrs German. **RESEARCH** German syntax; second language acquisition; older Germanic languages. **SELECTED PUBLICATIONS** Auth, Perfect Auxiliary Selection in the Old Saxon Heliand, 97; auth, German Impersonal Passives, 97; auth, "Perfect Auxiliary Selection in the Old Saxon Heliand," Am J of Germanic Ling and Lit 9 (97); coauth, "The Professionalization of Teaching Assistants: Can it be accomplished?," Unterrichtspraxis/Teaching German 33 (00); auth, "Cognitive Approach to the Passive in Old Saxon," Am J of Germanic Ling and Lit 12 (00). **CONTACT ADDRESS** Dept of German, Univ of California, Davis, 1 Shields Ave, 622 Sproul Hall, Davis, CA 95616-8606. **EMAIL** clarnett@ucdavis.edu

ARNOLD, DEAN E.
PERSONAL Born 08/02/1942, Sioux Falls, SD, m, 1968, 2 children **DISCIPLINE** ANTHROPOLOGY **EDUCATION** Wheaton Col, BA, 64; Univ IL Urbana, MA, 67; PhD, 70. **CAREER** Asst prof, Pa State Univ, 69-72; asst prof to prof, Wheaton Col, 73-. **HONORS AND AWARDS** Aldeen Fund Grants; Ford Found Grant; Nat Defense For Lang Fel, 66-69; Fulbright Scholar, 72-73, 84; Wheaton Col Grants; Vis Fel, Clare Hall, Cambridge, 85; Awd for Excellence in Ceramic Studies, Soc for Am Anthrop, 96; Werner-Gren Found Grant, 97; NEH Grant, 95-97. **MEMBERSHIPS** Royal Anthrop Inst of Great Britain and Ireland; Am Anthrop Assoc; Soc for Am Anthrop; Am Assoc for the Advan of Sci; Inst of Andean Studies; Fulbright Alumni Assoc. **SELECTED PUBLICATIONS** Coed, Cognitive studies of Southern Mesoamerica, SIL Museum of Anthrop, (Dallas, TX), 77; auth, Ceramic theory and cultural process, Cambridge Univ Pr, 85; auth, Ecology of Ceramic Production in an Andean Community, Cambridge Univ Pr, 93; coauth, "Factors Affecting Standardization", Ceramic Production and Distribution: An Integrated Approach, ed Geoge J Bey III and Christopher A Pool, Westview Pr, (Boulder, 92): 93-113; auth, "Comments on Section II", Chemical Characteristics of Ceramic Pastes in Archaeology, ed Hector Neff, Prehistory Pr, (Madison, 92): 159-166; auth, "Carry identification when conducting field research", Mistakes that social scientists make: Error and redemption in the research process, ed Richard A Seltzer, St Martin Pr, (NY, 95): 79-81; auth, "Field Work in Mexico", La Tinaja: A Newsletter of Archaeol Ceramics 11.1 (97): 1-3; auth, "Ceramic Ethnoarchaeology at Ticul, Yucatan Mexico, Soc for Archaeol Sci Bulletin 21, (98): 1-2; auth, "Ancient Andean Ceramic Technology: An Ethnoarchaeological Perspective", Andean Ceramics: Technology, Organization, and Approaches, ed Izumi Shimada, Univ of Pa, (98): 353-367; auth, "Advantages and Disadvantages of Vertical-half Molding Technology: Implications for Production Organization", Pottery and People: A Dynamic Interaction, ed James M. Skibo and Gary M. Feinman, Univ of Utah Pr, (Salt Lake City, 99): 50-80; coauth, "Testing Interpretative Assumptions of Neutron Activation Analysis: Contemporary Pottery in Yucatan, 1964-1994", Material Meanings: Critical Approaches to the Interpretations of Material Culture, ed Elizabeth Chilton, Univ of Utah Pr, (Salt Lake City, 99): 61-84. **CONTACT ADDRESS** Dept Sociol and Anthrop, Wheaton Col, Illinois, 501 College Ave, Wheaton, IL 60187. **EMAIL** dean.e.arnold@wheaton.edu

ARNOLD, EDWIN P.
PERSONAL Born 07/09/1945, Beaver Falls, PA, m, 1968, 2 children **DISCIPLINE** EDUCATION **EDUCATION** Geneva Col, BS, 67; Duquesne Univ, MA, 72; Univ Houston, EdD, 81. **CAREER** Dir, Public Sch, 67; assoc dir, Slippery Rock State Univ, 69-73; asst dir, Univ Houston, 74; chemn, Grove City Col, 75-. **MEMBERSHIPS** Am Band Masters Asn; PMEA; CBDNA; MENC. **CONTACT ADDRESS** Grove City Col, Grove City, PA 16127. **EMAIL** eparnold@gcc.edu

ARNOLD, GORDON
DISCIPLINE EDUCATION **EDUCATION** Clark Univ, BA cum laude, 76; Univ Rhode Island, M.L.S., 82; Boston Col, PhD, 94. **CAREER** Assoc Prof of Liberal Arts, Montserrat Col of Art, 94-; Adjunct Research Assoc, Center for Polig Analysis, Univ of Massachusetts at Dartmouth, 96-; Research Assoc, New England Research Center for Higher Education, Univ Mass at Boston, 90-96; Librarian and Assoc Dean, Montserrat Col of Art, 89-96. **HONORS AND AWARDS** Beta Phi Mu, (International Library Science Honor Society). **MEMBERSHIPS** Assoc for the Study of Higher Education, Amer Political Science Assoc. **RESEARCH** Organization theory; higher education in American society; media and education. **SELECTED PUBLICATIONS** Coauth, "Implementing Change," Chapter in Handbook on the Undergraduate Curriculum, edited by Jerry G. Gaff and James L. Ratcliff, San Francisco: Jossey-Bass; auth, "The Politics of Curriculum Reform," Chapter in Revitalizing General Education in a Time of Scarcity, edited by S. Kanter, Z. Gamson & H. London, Needham, MA: Allyn & Bacon, 97; auth, "The Ecology of Curriculum Reform," Change 29 4, 97: 18-23; auth, "The Emergence of Faculty Unions at the Public Universities of Southern New England," Labor Studies Journal 22 4: 62-87; auth, "The Politics of Faculty Unionization: The Experience of Three Universities," Westport, CT: Bergin & Garvey. **CONTACT ADDRESS** Dept Liberal Arts, Montserrat Col of Art, PO Box 62, Beverly, MA 01915-0062. **EMAIL** garnold@montserrat.edu

ARONOFF, MYRON J.
PERSONAL Born 03/01/1940, Kansas City, MO, m, 1962, 2 children **DISCIPLINE** ANTHROPOLOGY, POLITICAL SCIENCE **EDUCATION** Miami Univ, BA, 62; UCLA, MA, 65, PhD, 76; Manchester Univ, PhD, 69. **CAREER** Res fel, Manchester Univ, 65-69; lectr, 70-73, sr lectr, 73-76, assoc prof, 76-77, Tel Aviv Univ; assoc prof, 77-81, prof, 81-90, prof II of political science & anthropology, 90-, Rutgers Univ. **HONORS AND AWARDS** SSRC-UK 1969-71; Ford Found, 72-73; ACLS & SSRC, 82-83; Neth Inst Advan Stud fel, 74-75 & 96-97. **MEMBERSHIPS** Int Union Anthrop & Ethnol (vpres 93-2003); Am Polit Sci Asn; Am Anthrop Asn; Asn Polit & Legal Anthrop (pres 85-87); Asn Israel Stud (pres 85-87). **RESEARCH** Political culture; collective identity-ethnicity & nationalism; literature & politics; politics of espionage; Israeli culture & politics; Israel-Palestinian relations. **SELECTED PUBLICATIONS** Auth, The Spy Novels of John le Carre: Balancing Ethics and Politics, St. Martins, 99; auth, Power and Ritual in the Israel Labor Party, M E Sharpe, 93; coauth, Explaining Domestic Influences on Current Israeli Foreign Policy: The Peace Negotiations, The Brown Jour World Affairs, 96; The Peace Process and Competing Challenges to the Dominant Zionist Discourse, The Middle East Peace Process, SUNY Press, 98; Domestic Determinants of Israeli Foreign Policy: The Peace Process from the Declaration of Principles to the Oslo II Interim Agreement, The Middle East and the Peace Process: The Impact of the Oslo Accords, Univ Press Fla, 98. **CONTACT ADDRESS** Political Studies Dept, Rutgers, The State Univ of New Jersey, New Brunswick, Hickman Hall-Douglas Campus, PO Box 270, New Brunswick, NJ 08903-0270. **EMAIL** maronoff@rci.rutgers.edu

ARONSON, ELLIOT
PERSONAL Born 01/09/1932, Revere, MA, m, 1954, 4 children **DISCIPLINE** SOCIAL PSYCHOLOGY **EDUCATION** Brandeis Univ, BA 54; Wesleyan Univ, MA 56; Stanford Univ, PhD 59. **CAREER** Asst prof, Harvard Univ, 59-62; prof, Univ Minn, 62-66; prof, Univ Texas Austin, 66-74; from prof to prof emeritus, Univ Cal Santa Cruz, 74-. **HONORS AND AWARDS** AAAS Dist Res Awd; APA Dist Res Awd; SESP Dist Res Awd; 3 Dist Teaching Awd, APA, UCSC most Fav Teacher, U of T; Donald Campbell Awd; Prof of the Year CASE; Guggenheim Fel; Gordon Allport Prize; Dist Sci-Lect APA; Dist Sci Career Awd; Bernhard Dist Vis Prof Williams Coll **MEMBERSHIPS** APA; APS; SPSSI; SESP; AAAS Fel. **RESEARCH** Social influence; prejudice reduction; cognitive dissonance. **SELECTED PUBLICATIONS** coauth, Age of Propaganda, W H Freeman & Co (NYork), 92; coauth, Social Psychology: Vol 1, 2, 3, Elgar Ltd (London), 93; coauth, Social Psychology: The Heart and the Mind, Harper Collins (Nyork), 94, 2nd ed, Longman, 3rd ed, 99; auth, On Baseball and Failure, Dialogue, 95; coauth, Cooperation the Classroom: The Jigsaw Method, Longman (NYork), 97; auth, The giving away of psychology - and condoms, APS Observer, 97; coauth, Whe Exemplification Fails: Hypocrisy and the motive for self-integrity, JPSP, 97; auth, "The theory of cognitive dissonance: The evolution and vicissitudes of an idea," in The Message of Social Psychology, eds, C. McCarty and S. A. Haslam (London: Blackwell, 97); auth, "Dissonance Hypocrisy and the Self-Concept," in Cognitive Dissonance Theory: Revival Revisions and Controversies, Amer Psych Asn (Wash DC), 98; coauth, "The experimental method in social psychology," in The Handbook of Social Psychology, eds, G. Lindzey D. Gilbert and S. Fiske (NYork: Random House, 98); auth, The Social Animal, Worth (NYork), 8th ed, 99; auth, Nobody Left to Hate, Freeman (NYork), 00. **CONTACT ADDRESS** Dept of Psychology, Univ of California, Santa Cruz, 136 Tree Frog Lane, Santa Cruz, CA 95060. **EMAIL** elliot@cats.ucsc.edu

ARRIZON, ALICIA
DISCIPLINE WOMAN'S STUDIES, ETHNIC STUDIES **EDUCATION** Ariz State Univ, BA, 84; MA, 86; Stanford Univ, PhD, 92. **CAREER** Teaching fel, Stanford Univ, 89-90; asst prof to assoc prof, Univ Calif Riverside, 92-. **HONORS AND AWARDS** Dorothy Danforth Compton Fel, 90-9; Choice Bk Award, 00. **MEMBERSHIPS** NACCS; ATHE; WTP; MLA; ASTR. **RESEARCH** US Latin literature and culture studies; contemporary Latin America; critical and feminist theory; art and visual culture; theater and performance; ethinticity, race, gender and sexualities. **SELECTED PUBLICATIONS** Auth, "Contemporizing Performance: Mexican, California and the Padua Hills Theater," Mester 22 (94); auth, "Josefina Niggli (1910-1983)," in The New Handbook of Texas (Austin: THA, 96); auth, "Chicanas en la Escena: Teatralidad y Performance," Ollantay Theater Mag 4 (96); auth, "Soldaderas and the Staging of the Mexican Revolution," J Performance Studies (98); auth, Latina Performance: Traversing the Stage, Ind Univ Pr (Bloomington), 99; auth, "Transculturation and Gender in U.S. Latina Performance," Theater Res Int 24 (99); co-ed, Latinas on Stage, Third Woman Pr (Berkeley), 00; auth, "Mythical Performativity," Theater J (00). **CONTACT ADDRESS** Dept Ethnic Studies, Univ of California, Riverside, Riverside, CA 92512. **EMAIL** alicia.arrizon@ucr.edu

ASBURY, JO ELLEN
PERSONAL Born 08/25/1956 **DISCIPLINE** PSYCHOLOGY **EDUCATION** Univ Pittsburgh, PhD, 85. **CAREER** Instructor, Cmty Col of Allegheny Cty, 81-84; Lecturer, Anne Arundel Cmty Col, 87-89; Asst Prof to Assoc Prof, Bethany Col, 90-. **MEMBERSHIPS** Am Psychol Asn. **RESEARCH** Domestic violence; Qualitative Methodologies; Self-Efficacy and Human Agency; Multicultural issues. **SELECTED PUBLICATIONS** Auth, "Overview of focus group research," Qualitative Health Research, (95): 414-420; auth, "What do we know now about spouse abuse and child sexual abuse in families of color in the United States," in Family Violence: Prevention and Treatment, 2nd ed, (Thousand Oaks, 99), 148-167. **CONTACT ADDRESS** Dept Psychol, Bethany Col, West Virginia, RR 1, Bethany, WV 26032. **EMAIL** j.asbury@mail.bethanywv.edu

ASCENCAO, ERLENE M.
PERSONAL Born 04/08/1954, Manaus, Brazil, d **DISCIPLINE** PSYCHOLOGY **EDUCATION** Reinhardt Col, AA, 78; Berry Col, BA, 80; Emory Univ, MA, 82; PhD, 86; Univ Tenn, PhD, 95. **CAREER** Asst Prof, Tenn St Univ, 98-; Clinical Asst Prof, Meharry Med Col, 00-. **HONORS AND AWARDS** Who's Who Among Am Jr Col; Outstanding Young Woman of Am, Emory Univ, 82; Chancellor's Awd for Excellence in Teaching, Univ Tenn, 92-93; Awd for Outstanding Clinical Work, Luton Ment Health Serv, 97. **MEMBERSHIPS** STP, SPSEMI, APA. **RESEARCH** Multiculturalism, diversity and mental health issues, diversity and behavioral medicine, HIV/AIDS patients. **SELECTED PUBLICATIONS** Coauth, "Depressions and Locus of Control in Minority College Women," Career Opportunities in Res Educ and Training, ongoing Proj (98-); coauth, Psychological, Psychosocial and Cultural Factors and HIV Disease for Latino Clients," APA Nat Conf (00); coauth, The Effects of Healing Touch on Salivary IgA and Health Enhancement of HIV Positive Clients, 00. **CONTACT ADDRESS** Dept Psychol, Tennessee State Univ, 3500 John A Merritt, Nashville, TN 37209. **EMAIL** eascencao@tnstate.edu

ASHLEY, DAVID
PERSONAL Born 12/12/1950, London, England, m, 2 children **DISCIPLINE** SOCIOLOGY **EDUCATION** Univ York, BA, 72; Univ Pittsburgh, PhD, 79. **CAREER** Prof, Univ Wyo **HONORS AND AWARDS** Vera and Walter Morris foundation Grant, 89; Am Coun of Learned Soc Travel Grant, 86; Owens Fel, 77; Mellon Fel, 73. **RESEARCH** Social Theory. **SELECTED PUBLICATIONS** Auth, Sociological Theory: Classical Statements 5th ed, Boston,, 00; auth, History Without a Subject: The Postmodern condition, Westview Press, 97; auth, Mao's children in the New China. Voices from the Red Guard Generation, Routledge, in press; auth, "Postmodern society," The Meaning of Sociology. A Reader, Prentice-Hall, (99): 360-363; auth, "Mathematics, Postmodernism and the Loss of Certainty," Current Perspectives in Social Theory, Jai Press, 96; auth, "Postmodernism and Anti-Foundationalism," Postmodernism and social Inquiry, New York, 94; auth, "Postmodernism and the social Science," The social Science Journal, (91): 279-287; auth, "Class Struggle in the People's Republic of china Before and After Tiananmen Square," Humanity and Society, (91): 156-182; auth, "Playing with the Pieces: The Fragmentation of Social Theory," Critical Theory Now, (91): 70-97; auth, "Marx and the Excess of the Signifier. Domination as Production and as simulation," sociological Perspectives, (90): 129-146. **CONTACT ADDRESS** Dept Sociol, Univ of Wyoming, PO Box 3293, Laramie, WY 82071. **EMAIL** ashleywy@uwyo.edu

ASHTON, NANCY
PERSONAL Born 04/20/1950, New Brunswick, NJ, s, 1 child **DISCIPLINE** PSYCHOLOGY **EDUCATION** Smith Col, BA, 72; Univ Fla, MA, 74; PhD, 76. **CAREER** Admin Asst, Smith Col, 72; Adj Prof, Univ Fla, 73-76; Asst Prof, Kearney State Col, 76-77; Assoc Prof, Richard Stockton Col, 77-. **HONORS AND AWARDS** Career Development Awd, Stockton State Col, 89; Merit Awd, Stockton State Col, 81, 88; Psi Chi, Stockton State Col, 80; Sigma XI; Sloan Fel, Smith Col, 71. **MEMBERSHIPS** Am Psychol Asn, Am Psychol Soc, Eastern Psychol Asn. Nat Women's Studies Asn, Soc for the Advancement of Soc Psychol, Soc for the Psychol Study of Soc issues. **RESEARCH** Gender; Prosocial behavior; Quantitative reasoning; Environmental psychology. **SELECTED PUBLICA-**

TIONS Auth, "Infusing Quantitative reasoning in Women's Studies courses," Drew Univ, 00; auth, "Integration of Mathematical concepts With Social Science concepts," in Proceedings of the Second Regional Conference on Quantitative Reasoning Across the Disciplines, Richard Stockton Col, 99; auth, "Bad Girls/Good Girls: Women, Sex and Power in the Nineties, Rutgers Univ Press, 96; auth, "Abortion Politics", "Abortion Wars", and "Reproduction, Ethics and the Law," NWSA Journal, (98): 224-228; rev, of "Knowledge, Difference & Power, Revising Herself and Between Voice and Silence" by Goldberger, Josselson, Taylor et al, Transformations, (97): 145-151; auth, "Eyewitness Accuracy and Gender," Psychological Reports, (96): 94; auth, "Gender, Self-esteem and perception of own attentiveness," Perceptual and Motor Skills, (96): 1105-1106. **CONTACT ADDRESS** Dept Soc & Beh Sci, Richard Stockton Col, PO Box 195, Pomona, NJ 08240. **EMAIL** ashtonn@stockton.edu

ASPELL, PATRICK JOSEPH
PERSONAL Born 06/21/1930, Boston, MA, m, 1979, 1 child **DISCIPLINE** PHILOSOPHY, PSYCHOLOGY **EDUCATION** Oblate Col, BA, 56; Cath Univ Am, STL & MA, 57, PhD(philos), 59; Univ Redlands, MA, 79; US Int Univ, PhD(psychol), 82. **CAREER** From instr to assoc prof philos, Oblate Col, 59-70, chmn dept, 68-81, prof, 70-81; Lectr philos, Cath Univ Am, 61-63; vis asst prof, Univ Tex, San Antonio, 80-81; publisher, Lfewings, Ltd.; vice pres, Aspell Empowerment Enter, Inc. **MEMBERSHIPS** Christian Asn Psychol Stud. **RESEARCH** History of philosophy; theories of knowledge; metapsychol; psychol. **SELECTED PUBLICATIONS** Auth, A critique of Santayana's epistemology, Mod Schoolman, 61; Objective knowledge according to Ralph Barton Perry, New Scholasticism, 62; Plato and Anaxagoras, In: The New Cath Encycl, McGraw, 67; History of Philosophy, coauth, Readings in Ancient Western Philosophy, 70, Ancient Western Philosophy, 71, auth, Medieval Western Philosophy, 78 & Readings in Medieval Western Philosophy, 78, Appleton; auth, The Enneagram Personality Portraits: Enhancing Professional Relationships; The Enneagram Inventory and Profile, Enhancing Team Performance, Improving Problem-Solving Skills, Leadership Styles and the Enneagram, Jossey Bass; auth, What Drives You Crazy?, Human Resource Dev Press. **CONTACT ADDRESS** 247 Barbara Dr, San Antonio, TX 78216. **EMAIL** pat@aspell.com

ASSAR, NANDINI NARAIN
PERSONAL Born Kanpur, India **DISCIPLINE** SOCIOLOGY **EDUCATION** Delhi Univ, India, BA; Binghamton Univ, MA, 92; Virginia Tech, PhD, 00. **CAREER** Lectr, Binghamton Univ, 92; instr, Virginia Tech, 98-00. **HONORS AND AWARDS** Joel Robinson Schlp, 91; NSEP Fel, 94; NSF Stp; Fac Dev Gnt, CEUT, 97, 99. **MEMBERSHIPS** ASA; SWS; AWD; ABS. **RESEARCH** Race; ethnicity; women in development; immigration. **SELECTED PUBLICATIONS** Auth, "Patels in Budget Motels: An Indian-American Success Story," in Current Research on Occupations and Professions, ed. Helena Z Lopata (JAI Press: Greenwich, CT, 98); auth, "Gender Hierarchy in Motel Work: A Macrosociological and Microeconomical Analysis," in Advances in Gender Research, eds. Vasilikie Demos, Marcia Texler Degal (JAI Press: Greenwich, CT, 98); auth, "Immigration Policy, Cultural Norms and Gender Relations Among Indian-American Motel Owners," in Gender and Immigration, eds. Gregory A Kelson, Debra L DeLaet (Macmillan Press: UK, 99). **CONTACT ADDRESS** Dept Interdisciplinary Studies, Virginia Polytech Inst and State Univ, 351 Lane Hall, Blacksburg, VA 24061. **EMAIL** nassar@vt.edu

ATANDA, ALFRED W.
PERSONAL Born 10/20/1940, Ghana, m, 1964, 7 children **DISCIPLINE** PSYCHOLOGY **EDUCATION** Jersey City State Col, BA; Rutgers Univ, EdM; EdD. **CAREER** Assoc Prof, Ocean County Col. **RESEARCH** Intelligence debate. **SELECTED PUBLICATIONS** Auth, Twisted Intelligence Theory, forthcoming. **CONTACT ADDRESS** Dept Soc Sci, Ocean County Col, PO Box 2001, Toms River, NJ 08754. **EMAIL** aatanda@ocean.cc.nj.us

ATANG, CHRISTOPHER
PERSONAL Born 10/30/1938, m, 1972, 5 children **DISCIPLINE** CURRICULUM **EDUCATION** Univ Wis, BS, 66; Ind Univ, MS, 73; Iowa State Univ, PhD, 84. **CAREER** From Asst Prof to Assoc Prof, 97-. **HONORS AND AWARDS** Medallion Awd, Phi Delta Kappa. **MEMBERSHIPS** Tex Assoc of Col Teachers, Tex Educ Assoc. **RESEARCH** Cognitive style and learner-centered learning. **SELECTED PUBLICATIONS** Auth, Vision for Development in Cameroon in 2050; auth, A Breach of Trust: The Annexation of the Southern Cameroons, 97. **CONTACT ADDRESS** Dept Curric, Texas So Univ, 3100 Cleburne St, Houston, TX 77004. **EMAIL** nchifor@hotmail.com

ATKINS, KATHLEEN
PERSONAL Born 01/29/1953, Columbus, MS, s, 1 child **DISCIPLINE** EDUCATION **EDUCATION** Miss Univ, BS, 75; MEd, 78; Univ S Miss, DEd, 87. **CAREER** Adj Instructor, Miss Univ for Women, 78-84; Adj Instructor to Doctoral Asst, Univ S Miss, 85-87; Asst Prof to Assoc Prof, Univ Cent Ark, 88-. **MEMBERSHIPS** Am Asn of Col for Teacher Educ; Asn of Teacher Educ; Coun for Exceptional Children; Asn for Persons with Severe Disabilities. **SELECTED PUBLICATIONS** Co-auth, "Counseling special populations for transition services," in Counseling special populations: Research and practice perspectives, (JAI Press, 95), 35-63; co-auth, "Counseling factors and strategies for working with parents and families of children with disabilities," in Counseling special populations: Research and practice perspectives, (JAI Press, 95), 65-98; co-auth, "Professional development through university and public school collaboration," in Modeling Professional Development: An Arkansas Perspective, 96; co-auth, "Portfolio assessment: An individualized approach for general and special education," in Advances, practices, and concerns in special education, (JAI Press, 98), 55-76. **CONTACT ADDRESS** Dept curriculum & Instruction, Univ of Central Arkansas, 201 Donaghey Ave, Conway, AR 72035-5003.

ATKINSON, HARLEY
PERSONAL Born 06/08/1951, Grand Prarie, Canada, m, 1995, 2 children **DISCIPLINE** RELIGIOUS EDUCATION **EDUCATION** Trinity Western Univ, AA, 75; Can Bible Col, BRE, 80; Biola Univ Talbot Sch Theol, MA, 85; EdD, 89. **CAREER** Minister of Youth, Red Deer Alliance Church, 80-83; assoc prof of Christian Educ, Toccoa Falls Col, 89-. **MEMBERSHIPS** North Am Professors of Christian Educ, Youth Ministry Educators. **SELECTED PUBLICATIONS** Auth, "Dewey's Process of Reflective Thinking and Christian Education," Christian Educ J vol IX, 3 (89); auth, "Identifying Reasons for Non participation in CE Classes in CMA Churches of the South Pacific District," Christian Educ J vol XIII, 3 (93); auth, "Reinforcement in Learning: Integrating Skinner and Scripture," Christian Educ J vol XIV, 1 (93); auth, "Factors Motivating Participation in Adult Christian Education Opportunities in C & MA Churches of the South Pacific District," Christian Educ J vol XIV, 2 (94); ed, Handbook of Young Adult Religious Education, Relig Education Press (Birmingham, AL), 95; auth, Ministry With Youth In Crisis, Relig Educ Press (Birmingham, AL), 97; auth, Teaching Youth With Confidence, Evangelical Training Asn (Wheaton, IL), 00. **CONTACT ADDRESS** Dept Christian Educ, Toccoa Falls Col, PO Box 800-157, Toccoa, GA 30577.

ATKINSON, MICHAEL
PERSONAL Born 07/02/1942, Midland, TX **DISCIPLINE** LITERARY THEORY, ARCHETYPAL PSYCHOLOGY & LITERATURE **EDUCATION** Rice Univ, BA, 64; PA State Univ, MA, 67, PhD(English), 70. **CAREER** Assoc Prof English, Univ Cincinnati, 70-. **MEMBERSHIPS** MLA; AAUP; Midwest Mod Lang Asn; Popular Culture Asn. **RESEARCH** American renaissance; contemporary poetics. **SELECTED PUBLICATIONS** Auth, Collective Preconscious & Found Footage Film as an Inexhaustable Source of the Underground, Film Comment, Vol 29, 1993; Genuine B-Noir & Films of Director James B. Harris, Sight and Sound, Vol 3, 1993; Ousmane Sembene & The Film Director and African Cinema-We-Are-No-Longer-In-The-Era-of-Prophets, Film Comment, Vol 29, 1993; Between Worlds & Surrealists, Film and Hathaway, Henry 'Peter Ibbetson', Film Comment, Vol 29, 1993; The 'Tattooed Woman in Heavens Flower Shop', MI Quart Rev, Vol 32, 1993; Head Case & Arnaud Desplechin La 'Sentinelle', Film Comment, Vol 29, 1993; 'Airfield', Literary Rev, Vol 36, 1993; The 'Mask', wirh C. Russell, Sight and Sound, Vol 4, 1994; The Night Countries of the Brothers Quay & Film Directors, Film Comment, Vol 30, 1994; 'Highway Patrolman', with A. Cox, Film Comment, Vol 30, 1994; 'Death and the Compass', Film Comment, Vol 30, 1994; Regulation of Science by Peer Review, Studies in Hist and Philos of Sciencs, Vol 25, 1994; Crossing ther Frontiers--with Everyone from Psychos to Scholars Hitting the Highway, Has the Road Movie Found New Wheels, Sight and Sound, Vol 4, 1994; The Faber Book of Movie Verse, with P. French and K. Wlaschin, Film Comment, Vol 30, 1994; The 'Paper', with R. Howard, Sight and Sound, Vol 4, 1994; A 'Perfect World', with C. Eastwood, Sight and Sound, Vol 4, 1994; Son of Apes & 'Planet of the Apes' Film Serials, Film Comment, Vol 31, 1995; Delirious Inventions--Why Have Comics and Cartoons from 'Popeye' Onwards So Often Been Translated into Live Action Movies, Sight and Sound, Vol 5, 1995; 'Jefferson in Paris', with J. Ivory, Sight and Sound, Vol 5, 1995; Earthly Creatures & Peter Jackson Horror Film "Heavenly Creatures', Film Comment, Vol 0031, 1995; The 'Specialist', with L. Llosa, Sight and Sound, Vol 5, 1995; 'Tommy Boy', with P. Segal, Sight and Sound, Vol 5, 1995; 'Beach Red' -, with C. Wilde, Film Comment, Vol 32, 1996; Naked Prey--The Cinema of Cornel Wilde, Introduction & Conclusions, Vol 32, 1996; 'Aeon Flux', Film Comment, Vol 32, 1996; Songs of Crushed Love--TheCinema of Stanley Kwan, Film Comment, Vol 32, 1996; 'No Blade of Grass', with C. Wilde, Film Comment, Vol 32, 1996; Best of 96 & Movies, Film Comment, Vol 33, 1997; 'Lumiere et Compagnie', with S. Moon, Film Comment, Vol 33, 1997. **CONTACT ADDRESS** Dept of English, Univ of Cincinnati, P O Box 210069, Cincinnati, OH 45221-0069.

ATLAS, JOHN WESLEY
PERSONAL Born 08/15/1941, Lake Providence, LA, m **DISCIPLINE** EDUCATION **EDUCATION** Grambling Coll, BS 1963; Wayne State Univ, MEd 1968, EdD 1972. **CAREER** LA Schools, music teacher, 63-65; Detroit Public Schools, music teacher, 65-67, guidance counselor, 67-70, asst prin, 70-72; Gov State Univ, prof, 72-73; Oakland Univ, assoc prof, 73-. **MEMBERSHIPS** Mem Amer Personnel & Guidance Assn; mem Assn for Non-White Concerns in Personnel & Guidance; mem Omega Psi Phi Frat; Topical Conf on Career Educ for Handicapped Indiv 1979. **SELECTED PUBLICATIONS** "Consulting, Affecting Change for Minority Students" Jour of Non-White Concerns in Pers & Guidance Wash, DC 1975; publ "Effects of Crystal & Bolles on Vocational Choice" Jour of Emp Counsel Wash, DC 1977; publ "Career Planning Need of Unemployed Minority Persons" Jour of Emp Counseling Wash, DC 1978; book chap "The Role of Counseling & Guidance in Facilitating Career Educ Needs of Handicapped". **CONTACT ADDRESS** Sch of Human & Educ Serv, Oakland Univ, Rochester, MI 48309.

ATTEBERY, LOUIE WAYNE
PERSONAL Born 08/14/1927, Weiser, ID, m, 1947, 2 children **DISCIPLINE** ENGLISH & AMERICAN LITERATURE, FOLKLORE **EDUCATION** Col ID, BA, 50; Univ Mont, MA, 51; Univ Denver, PhD, 61. **CAREER** Teacher English, Middleton High Sch, ID, 49-50, Payette High Sch, 51-52, Nyssa High Sch, Ore, 52-55 & East High Sch, Denver, 55-61, chmn dept, 61; from asst prof to assoc prof, 61-69, chmn dept, 68-73 & 76-78, Prof English, Col of ID, 69-98, prof emer, 98-; Prin lectr, Summer Inst Am Studies, 63-70, dir, 66-70; Bruern fel, Univ Leeds, 71-72; consult, EXPO 74, acting vice pres for acad affairs, 83-84. **MEMBERSHIPS** Western Lit Asn; Western Hist Asn; Am Folklore Soc. **RESEARCH** The epistemology of Western American literature; the cement truck urban belief tale; the Oregon cowboy: a continuing search for authenticity. **SELECTED PUBLICATIONS** Auth, Governor jokes, Southern Folklore Quart, 12/69; The American West and the Archetypal Orphan, Western Am Lit, fall 70; It was a DeSoto, J Am Folklore, 10-12/70; The Fiddle Tune: An American Artifact, Readings in Am Folklore, 79; auth, The College of Idaho: A Centennial History, The College of Idaho, 91; auth, Sheepmay safely Graze, Univ of Idaho, 93; auth, The Most of What we Spend: A Biography of Robert L. Hendren, Jr., West Shore Press, 97; auth, Albertson College of Idaho: The Second Hundred Years, Albertson College of Idaho, 99; auth, J.R. Simplot: A Billion the Hard Way, Caxton Press, 00. **CONTACT ADDRESS** Dept of English, Albertson Col of Idaho, Caldwell, ID 83605. **EMAIL** lattebery@albertson.edu

ATWOOD, JOAN DELORES
PERSONAL Born Long Island, NY, 5 children **DISCIPLINE** FAMILY STUDIES, HEALTH **EDUCATION** Stat Univ NY at Stony Brook, BA, 73; MA, 75; MA, 77; DPhil, 81; Adelphi Univ, Master Soc Work, 84; Post-Doctoral Training, Salvador Minuchin, 88-91; Post-Doctoral Training, Harville Hendrix Relationship Inst, 92-. **CAREER** Teaching asst & tutor, Stat Univ NY, 73-76; from adj asst prof to asst prof, State Univ NY, 74-84; prof & dir of grad prog in marriage and family therapy, Hofstra Univ, 84-; dir, Long Island Family Therapists, 82-; dir, Hofstra Univ Marital and Family Therapy Clinic, 90-. **HONORS AND AWARDS** Phi Alpha Sigma, Suffolk Community Col; Dean's List, State Univ NY at Stony Brook; Magna Cum Laude, State Univ NY at Stony Brook; Fac Development Grants, Hofstra Univ; Long Island Marriage and Family Therapist of the Year Awd, 92. **MEMBERSHIPS** Am Psychol Asn, Am Asn of Marriage and Family Therapists, Am Asn for Counseling and Development, Am Sociol Asn, Soc for the Sci Study of Sex, Nat Orgn of Soc Workers, Am Asn of Sex Educators, Counselors, and Therapists, Asn for Clinical Sociologists, Sociologists for Women in Soc, Fel of the ctr for Int Tech Coop. **RESEARCH** Differentiation of Self, Attitudes About Single Parents and Children of Divorce, Couples and Finance. **SELECTED PUBLICATIONS** Auth, Family Scripts, Taylor and Francis, Inc. (Chicago, IL), 96; auth, Challenging Family Therapy Situations: A Social Constructionist Perspective, Springer (New York), 97; coauth, "The Feminization of Poverty: Issues and Therapeutic Concerns," j of Feminist Family Therapy 9.2 (97): 195-208; coauth, "Multiple sclerosis and social constructionism," in Couples: A Medley of Models, ed. Barbar Jo Brothers (NY: The Haworth Press, 98); coauth, "Multiple Sclerosis: A Social Constructionist Approach," J of Couples Therapy 7.2, 3 (98): 117-136; auth, "Sex Therapy," in Joseph Wecksler, An Introduction to Marriage and Family Therapy (NY: The Haworth Press, 00). **CONTACT ADDRESS** Dept Counselor Educ, Hofstra Univ, 1000 Fulton Ave, Hempstead, NY 11550.

AULL, FELICE
PERSONAL Born 08/12/1938, Vienna, Austria, m, 1962, 1 child **DISCIPLINE** MEDICAL EDUCATION **EDUCATION** Barnard Col, AB, 60; Cornell Univ, PhD, 64; NY Univ, MA, 01. **CAREER** Instr, to assoc prof, NY Sch of Med, 66-. **HONORS AND AWARDS** NIH Fel, 60-64, 65-66; NIH Prin Investigator, 68-80; Lewis Thomas Sco Fel, 00-. **MEMBERSHIPS** MLA, Am Soc for Bioethics and Humanities, Am Pysiol Soc, Biophysical Soc, Soc of General Physiologies, NY Acad of Sci, AAAS, Assoc for Women in Sci. **RESEARCH** Cultural dislocation, illness/exile, borderlands, cosmopolitanism, illness narrative, physician memories and physician poetry. **SELECTED PUBLICATIONS** Ed, Literature, Arts, and Medicine Database, NY Univ, 93-; auth, "Commentary on 'The Ship Pounding' and 'The Sick Wife,'" Acad Med, 72/3 (97): 194; auth,

"Commentary on 'Ma, A Memoir,'" Acad Med 73/1 (98): 66; auth, "Resources for Teaching Literature and Medicine, Teaching Lit ad Medicine, MLA, 00; auth, "Commentary on 'Across the Border' and 'Emigration,'" Acad Med 75/11 (00): 1114. **CONTACT ADDRESS** Sch of Med, New York Univ, 550 First Ave, New York, NY 10016. **EMAIL** aullf01@popmail.med.nyu.edu

AUSTIN, JOHN
PERSONAL Born 12/03/1949, Appomattox, VA, m, 1973, 2 children **DISCIPLINE** SOCIAL WORK **EDUCATION** Virginia Commonwealth Univ, PhD, 84; Univ Pa, Advanced Certificate, 79; Virginia Commonwealth Univ, MSW, 74; Bowie State Col, BS, 73; Community Col Baltimore, AA, 70. **CAREER** Prof and Chair, Delaware State Univ, 97-; Prof (Admissions Director for Social Work), Norfolk State Univ, 76-97; Instr & Chair of Sociology (Director of Social Welfare Program), Hampton Univ, 74-76. **HONORS AND AWARDS** Post Doctorate Fellowship in HIV-AIDS, Univ of Michigan's Institute for Survey Research, 95; CSWE Minority Scholar, Virginia Commonwealth Univ; SRS Scholar, Virginia Commonwealth Univ. **MEMBERSHIPS** Council on Social Work Education; National Assoc of Social Workers. **RESEARCH** Prevention; HIV-AIDS; Substance Abuse; Health Promotion. **SELECTED PUBLICATIONS** Auth, "Building Health Coalitions in the Black Community, by R. Braithwarte, S. Taylor and John Austin, London: Sage, 00. **CONTACT ADDRESS** Dept Social Work, Delaware State Univ, 1200 N Dupont Hwy, Dover, DE 19901. **EMAIL** jaustin@dsc.edu

AUSTIN, PATRICIA
DISCIPLINE EDUCATION **EDUCATION** Agnes Scott Col, BA, 72; Univ NH, MAT, 73; Univ New Orleans, PhD, 87. **CAREER** Asst prof, Tulane Univ, 92-94; assoc prof, Univ of New Orleans, 94-. **MEMBERSHIPS** Int Reading Assoc; Nat Coun of Teachers of English; Am Libr Assoc; Soc of Book Writers and Illustrators. **RESEARCH** Children's literature, Writing. **SELECTED PUBLICATIONS** Auth, "Math Books as Literature: Which Ones Measure UP?", New Advocate 11.2 (98): 119-133; auth, "In the Shadow of Expectation: Teachers and Learners at Risk", Clearing House 71.4 (98): 214-216; auth, "Talking with Tomie", Teaching and Learning Lit 7.5 (98): 47-58; coauth, "Are We There Yet? A Vacation Listening Guide to Adult Audio Books That Kids Enjoy Too", Book Links 7.6 (98): 16-20; auth, "Author and Illustrator Studies in the Classroom", Book Links, 8.1 (98): 55-62; coauth, "Making Connections in the Life and Work of Walter Dean Myers", Teaching and Learning Lit 8.1 (98): 42-54; coauth, "Simons Says: Open Up the World of Science", J of Youth Serv in Libr, 12.3 (99): 29-33; coauth, "The Audio Argument or Sound Advice about Literature", New Advocate 12.3 (99): 241-247; auth, "The Story Behind the Artist and her Stories: An Interview with Peggy Rathmann", New Advocate 12.4 (99): 305-313; coauth, "Williams' Doll Revisited", Lang Arts 77.4 (99): 324-330. **CONTACT ADDRESS** Dept Curric and Instr, Univ of New Orleans, 2000 Lakeshore Dr, New Orleans, LA 70148-0001.

AVALOS, HECTOR
PERSONAL Born 10/08/1958, Nogales, Mexico, m, 1979 **DISCIPLINE** ANTHROPOLOGY **EDUCATION** Univ Ariz, BA, 82; Harvard Div School, MTS, 85; Harvard Univ, PhD, 91. **CAREER** Carolina Minor postdoc fel, 91-93, Univ of NC; Asst Prof, 93-98, Assoc Prof, Dir Latino Stud, Iowa State Univ. **HONORS AND AWARDS** Prof of the Year, Early Excell research Awd. **MEMBERSHIPS** SBL, AAR. **RESEARCH** History of medicine, science & religion **SELECTED PUBLICATIONS** Auth, Illness and Health Care in the Ancient Near East, The role of The Temple in Greece, Mesopotamia and Israel, in: Harvard Semitic Monographs, Atlanta Scholars Press, 95; Daniel 9: 24-25 and Mesopotamian Temple Rededications, in: J of Biblical Lit, 98; Can Science Prove that Prayer Works? in: Free Inquiry, 97; The Gospel of Lucas Gavilan as Postcolonial Biblical Exegesis, in: Semeia, 96; A Ladino Version of the Targum of Ruth, in: Estudios Biblicos, 96; Ancient Medicine, In Case of Emergency Contact Your Local Prophet, in: Bible Review, 95; The Biblical Sources of Columbus's Libro de las profecias, in: Traditio, 94; auth, Health Care and the Rise of Christianity, Hendrickson Press (Peabody, MA), 99. **CONTACT ADDRESS** Religious Studies Program, Iowa State Univ of Science and Tech, 402 Catt Hall, Ames, IA 50011. **EMAIL** havalos@iastate.edu

AYALA-ALCANTAR, CHRISTINA
PERSONAL Born 04/20/1968, Artesia, CA, m, 1999 **DISCIPLINE** PSYCHOLOGY **EDUCATION** Univ LaVerne, BA; BS, 90; Calif State Univ, MA, 92; Mich State Univ, PhD, 98. **CAREER** Asst Prof, Univ LaVerne, 98-. **HONORS AND AWARDS** Who's Who Among Students in Am Univ & Col, 90; Psi Chi Service Awd, Univ LaVerne, 90; Academic Awd, Univ LaVerne, 89. **MEMBERSHIPS** Soc for Cmty Res and Action. **RESEARCH** Latinas and HIV/AIDS; Latina sexuality; Public policy and people with developmental disabilities; Multiracial feminism. **CONTACT ADDRESS** Dept Psychol, Univ of La Verne, 1950 3rd St, LaVerne, CA 91750. **EMAIL** rodriguc@ulv.edu

AYRES, JOHN J. B.
PERSONAL Born 08/02/1939, Ocean City, MD, m, 1961, 2 children **DISCIPLINE** PSYCHOLOGY **EDUCATION** Col William and Mary, BA, 61; Univ Ky, MA, 63, PhD, 65. **CAREER** Captain U.S. Army Medical Service Corps, Army Natick Laboratories, Natick, Mass, 65-67; vis prof, Western Washington State Col, Bellingham, Washington, 73-74; vis prof, Univ Haw, Honolulu, 82; asst to full prof, Univ Mass, Amherst, 67-. **HONORS AND AWARDS** Grad with honors in psychol, 61; NSF Predoctoral Fel, summer 63; named honorary Adelphian, 68; Grants from the Nat Inst of Mental Health and from the Nat Sci Found; nominated by Dept of Psychol, Univ Mass, Amherst, for Am Psychol Asn's Distinguished Teaching Awd, 84; nominated Editor-Elect of the J of Experimental Psychol: Animal Behavior Processes, 89, 95; nominated Editor-Elect of Animal Learning & Behavior, 93, 96; nominated for Univ Distinguished Teaching Awd, 97, 98. **MEMBERSHIPS** Eastern Psychol Asn, The Psychonomic Soc, Am Psychol Soc, Asn for Behavior Analysis. **RESEARCH** Pavlonian conditioning; animal learning and behavior. **SELECTED PUBLICATIONS** Coauth, "One-trial context fear conditioning as a function of the interstimulus interval," Animal Learning & Behavior, 23 (94): 400-410; coauth, "Conditioned stimulus determinants of conditioned response form in Pavlonian fear conditioning," J of Experimental Psychol: Animal Behavior Processes, 22 (96): 87-104; coauth, "One-trial simultaneous and backward excitatory fear conditioning in rats: Lick suppression, freezing, and rearing to CS compounds and their elements," Animal Learning & Behavior, 25 (97): 210-220; coauth, "Converging evidence for one-trial context fear conditioning with an immediate shock: Importance of shock potency," J of Experimental Psychol: Animal Behav Processes, 23 (97): 312-324; auth, "Fear conditioning and avoidance," in Learning and Behavior Therapy, ed. W. O'Donohue (MA: Allyn & Bacon, 98), 122-145; coauth, "Blocked and overshadowed stimuli are weakened in their ability to serve as blockers and second-order reinforcers in Pavlonian fear conditioning," J of Experimental Psychol: Animal Behav Processes, 25 (99): 45-67. **CONTACT ADDRESS** Dept Psychol, Univ of Massachusetts, Amherst, PO Box 37710, Amherst, MA 01003. **EMAIL** joeayres@psych.umass.edu

AZZOLINA, DAVIS S.
PERSONAL Born 05/22/1957, East Orange, NJ, s **DISCIPLINE** FOLKLORE **EDUCATION** Univ Penn, BA, 78, MA, 91, PhD, 96; Columbia Univ, MS, 79; **CAREER** Ref asst, 78-79, Butler Libr, Columbia Univ; ref-col devel libr, Fondren Lib, Rice Univ; ref libr, 82-86, Eisenhower Library, John Hopkins Univ; adj asst prof, 97-, Univ Penn; ref libr, 86-, Van Pelt Libr, Univ Penn. **RESEARCH** Folklore, gay studies, Mormonism **CONTACT ADDRESS** Reference Libr, Univ of Pennsylvania, 3420 Walnut St, Philadelphia, PA 19104.

B

BA-YUNUS, ILYAS
PERSONAL Born 12/17/1932, Karachi, Pakistan, m, 1966, 1 child **DISCIPLINE** SOCIOLOGY **CAREER** Prof, Dept of Sociol, SUNY Cortland. **MEMBERSHIPS** Am Sociol Asn, Asn of Muslim Soc Scis. **RESEARCH** Demography, law and Islamic sociology. **SELECTED PUBLICATIONS** Auth, major contributions to 100 Years of American Sociology; auth, Islamic Sociology; auth, Ideological Dimensions of Islam: Making Sense Out of History; several journal articles. **CONTACT ADDRESS** Dept Sociol, SUNY, Col at Cortland, PO Box 2000, Cortland, NY 13045. **EMAIL** Bayunus@cortland.edu

BABBITT, BEATRICE C.
DISCIPLINE LEARNING DISABILITIES; MATHEMATICS DISABILITIES; ASSISTIVE TECHNOLOGY **EDUCATION** UCLA, PhD, 86. **CAREER** Assoc prof, dir, technol related grant, coordr, grad prog, dir, tchr educ, Univ Nev, Las Vegas. **SELECTED PUBLICATIONS** Auth, Hypermedia: Making the mathematics connection, Intervention in Schl and Clinic, 93; Cross-disciplinary training in assistive technology, Proc of the 10th Annual Int Technol and Persons with Disabilities Conf, Calif State Univ, Northridge, 95; coauth, Using hypermedia to improve the mathematics problem-solving skills of students with learning disabilities, J of Learning Disabilities, 29, 96. **CONTACT ADDRESS** Dept of Spec Educ, Univ of Nevada, Las Vegas, 4505 Maryland Pky, Las Vegas, NV 89154-3014. **EMAIL** babbitt@nevada.edu

BABER, CEOLA ROSS
PERSONAL Born 11/30/1950, Selma, AL, m, 3 children **DISCIPLINE** EDUCATION **EDUCATION** CA State Univ Sacramento, BA 1972; Stanford Univ, MA 1975; Purdue Univ, PhD 1984. **CAREER** Sequoia Union HS Dist, teacher 1974-78; Tuskegee Univ, project coord/instructor 1979-80; Purdue Univ, rsch assoc 1980-81, dir/asst prof 1984-89; Univ of North Carolina-Greensboro, School of Education, asst assoc prof 1989-; assoc prof 95-; assoc dean, 99-. **HONORS AND AWARDS** Consortium of Doctors Distinguished Women of Color Awd, 91; UNCG Alumni Teaching Excellence Awd, 93; Who's Who Among America's Teachers, 98. **MEMBERSHIPS** American Educational Research Association; National Association of Multicultural Education; National Council for Social Studies; Kappa Delta Pi; Delta Kappa Gamma International Education Society; INTASC Social Studies Standards Committee, 98-01; Theory and Research in Social Education, 99-; Guilford County Schs Restructuring Committee, 99-00; NCATE Bd of Examiners, 99-04; . **RESEARCH** Equity education, secondary education. **SELECTED PUBLICATIONS** Auth, Black Studies for White Students, Momentu 17 (1) (87): 26-28; auth, The artistry and artifice of Black communication, eds. G. Gay & W. Baber, Expressively Black: The cultural basis of ethnic identity, Praeger (87): 75-108; auth, Ethnic identity development and literacy education, Reading Psychology, 13 (1), 92; auth, Wholistic literacy instruction for at risk students, Reading Psychology, 92; auth, A holistic basic skills curriculum for at-risk students, Current Issues in Middle Level Education, 94; auth, Teaching about diversity, Graham, NC: North Carolina Coun for the Social Studies, 94; auth, Leaders of color as catalysts for community building in a multicultural society, Theory and Research in Social Education, 95; auth, Teaching and learning English, social studies, and science together: An experiment in secondary teacher education at UNCG, North Carolina Journal of Teacher Education, 96; auth, Oral history: Engaging students in community-based learning, in B. Hatcher & S.S. Beck (eds.), Learning opportunities beyond the school 2nd ed, Onley, MD: Asn for Childhood Educ Int, 97; auth, Multicultural education, in Kazdin, A.E. (ed.) Encyclopedia of Psychology, American Psychological Asn and Oxford Univ Pr, 00. **CONTACT ADDRESS** Univ of No Carolina, Greensboro, PO Box 26171, Greensboro, NC 27402-6171. **EMAIL** crbaber@uncy.edu

BABROW, AUSTIN S.
PERSONAL Born 08/31/1954, NY, m, 2 children **DISCIPLINE** HEALTH COMMUNICATION, PERSUASION **EDUCATION** Univ Ill, PhD, 86. **CAREER** Assoc prof, Purdue Univ. **SELECTED PUBLICATIONS** Auth, The many meanings of "uncertainty" in illness: Toward a systematic accounting, Babrow, A. S., Kasch, C. R., & Ford, L A., Health Communication 10 (98): 1-24; auth, Colloquy: Developing multiple-process theories of communication, Babrow, A. S., Human Communication Research 25 (98): 152-155; auth, Dialysis patients' preferences for family-based advance care planning. Annals of Internal Medicine, Hines, S. C., Glover, J. J., Holley, J. L., Babrow, A. S., Badzek, L. A., & Moss, A. H., 130 (99): 825-828; auth, From "reducing" to "coping with" uncertainty: Reconceptualizing the central challenge in breast self-exams. Social Science & Medicine, Babrow, A. S., & Kline, K. N., 00. **CONTACT ADDRESS** Dept of Commun, Purdue Univ, West Lafayette, 1366 Lib Arts & Educ Bldg 2114, West Lafayette, IN 47907-1080. **EMAIL** ababrow@sla.purdue.edu

BACIGALUPE, GONZALO
PERSONAL Born 11/23/1958, Chile, m, 1984, 2 children **DISCIPLINE** EDUCATION **EDUCATION** Licentiate, Pontifical Catholic Univ, 84; MA, 86; Univ Mass, EdD, 94. **CAREER** Asst Prof, Nova Southeastern Univ, 94-96; Consultant, Roxbury Comprehensive Community Health Center, 97-00; Clinical Staff, Harvard Med School, 97-99; Res Affil to Asst Prof, Univ Mass, 96-. **HONORS AND AWARDS** Career Development Awd, Dept Health & Human Service, 99-00; Training Awd, Family Therapy Network, 97; Res Fel, Mauricio Gaston Inst, 97; Ford Foundation, Univ Mass, 97. **MEMBERSHIPS** Am Asn for Marriage and Family Therapy, Am Psychol As, Am Orthopsychiat Asn, Coun on Contemporary Families, Am Coun Asn, Am Prof Soc of the Abuse of Children, Am Public Health Asn, Asn for Family Therapy and Systemic Practice in the UK; Asn for Women in Psychol, Chilean Psychol Asn, Chilean Soc of Clinical Psychol, Intl Family Therapy Asn, Latin Am Studies Asn, Mass Teachers Asn, Nat Educ Asn. **RESEARCH** Latino families; Health care quality and access; Family therapy training and supervision; Team consultation, Trauma and violence. **SELECTED PUBLICATIONS** Auth, "Family violence in Chile: political and legal dimensions in a period of democratic transition," Violence Against Women, (00): 429-450; auth, "El Latino: Transgressing the macho," in Family therapy with Hispanics: toward appreciating diversity, Allyn & Bacon, 00; auth, "family therapy supervision with Latino(a) therapists," Family therapy with Hispanics: toward appreciating diversity, Allyn & Bacon, 00; auth, "Treinamento e consultoria em terapia sistemica transcultural: Uma visao poscolonialista," Nova Perspectiva Sistemica, (99): 5-23; auth, "Personality in interpersonal and systemic theories," in Advanced Personality, Plenum Press, 98; auth, "Excrevendo na terapia: Uma abordagem participativa," Nova Perspectia Sistemica, (98): 45-55; auth, "Introduction to Special Issue: consulting and training in the land of others," Journal of Systemic Therapies, (98): 1-2; auth, "Cross-cultural systemic therapy consultation and training: a postcolonial view," Journal of Systemic Therapies, (98): 31-43; auth, "Writing in therapy: a participatory approach," Journal of Family Therapy, (96): 361-373. **CONTACT ADDRESS** Dept Educ Admin, Univ of Massachusetts, Boston, 100 Morrissey Blvd, Boston, MA 02125.

BADER, CAROL H.
PERSONAL Born 09/14/1949, Navasota, TX, m, 1973, 1 child **DISCIPLINE** EDUCATION **EDUCATION** La Tech Univ, BA, 71; Purdue Univ, MA, 73; La State Univ, EdS, 75; PhD, 78. **CAREER** Teaching Asst, Purdue Univ, 71-73; Teacher,

Donaldsonville High School, 73-74; Reading Chairman, St Amant elementary School, 74-76; consultant, Exxon Co, 76-78; Reading Coordinator, LSU Developmental Reading Laboratory, 78-87; Director of Developmental Studies, Middle Tenn State Univ, 87-. **HONORS AND AWARDS** Intl Who's Who of Pub Service, 00; Who's Who 2000-2001 Millennium Ed, 00; commitment to NADE Awd, 99; dictionary of Intl Biography 27th Ed, 99; Who's Who in the South and Southwest, 99-00; Outstanding People of the 20th Century, 99-00; Who's Who of Am Women, 21st Ed, 99-00; dictionary of Intl Biography, 26th Ed, 98; Who's Who in the world, 16th Ed, 98-99; Intl Women of the Year, 98-99; Who's Who in the south and Southwest, 97-98; Who's Who, Exec Ed, 95-96; John Champaigne Awd, MTSU Developmental Studies Dept, 93; Outstanding Advising Awd, MTSU's Developmental Studies Advisors, 96; Educator of the Year, Tenn Asn for Developmental Educ, 92; Grateful Recognition of Services Performed, LSU, 87; Phi Delta Kappa Outstanding Initiate Paper, 78; Phi Kappa Phi Nat Honor Fraternity. **MEMBERSHIPS** Phi Delta Kappa Nat Honorary Educ Fraternity, Phi Kappa Phi Nat Honor Fraternity, Intl Reading Asn, Tenn Asn for Developmental Educ, Nat Asn for Developmental Educ, Am Asn of Univ Prof. **RESEARCH** Developmental Studies, Attention Deficit disorders, Evaluation, Retention. **SELECTED PUBLICATIONS** auth, "Study Abroad during the summer of 2000," NADE Newsletter, (99): 3; auth, "Learning disabilities/ADHD and Accommodations in the Math Classroom," Proceedings of the TNADE Annual Conference, 95; auth, "Public Relations: Making videos to Promote Your Program," Proceedings of the 18th Annual Conference of the National Association for Developmental Education, 95; auth, Keys for reading Improvement, Townsend press, 94; auth, "Writing Assignments: The Right Tool for Improving Math skills?," Selected NADE Conference proceedings, 94; auth, Improving Reading comprehension skills, Townsend Press, 92; auth, "A Cumulative Study of Retention of former Developmental Students in college Level Algebra and composition at MTSU: 1985-1991," TNADE Bulletin, (92): 2-3; auth, "The Development, Implementation, and Evaluation of a Reading Program at an Open-Admissions, Four-Year State University," Innovative Learning Strategies: 1985-1986, 86; auth, "Visual Screening of Developmental Students: Mildred, Are You Blind Yet?," National Association of Developmental Educators Newsletter, 83. **CONTACT ADDRESS** Dept Developmental Studies, Middle Tennessee State Univ, 1301 E Main St, Murfreesboro, TN 37132-0001. **EMAIL** cbader@mtsu.edu

BAEZA, J.
PERSONAL Born 12/25/1942, Shafter, TX, s, 2 children **DISCIPLINE** PSYCHOLOGY **EDUCATION** Ariz State Univ, BS, 79; Univ IA, MA, 83; PhD, 89. **CAREER** Res Asst, Iowa City, 85-89; Instructor, Gateway Col, 90-91; Asst Prof, S Ill Univ, 91-96; Assoc Prof, Kansas City Cmty Col, 98-. **MEMBERSHIPS** Asn of Hispanics Higher Educ. **RESEARCH** Domestic Violence; Child Abuse; Educations Methodology. **CONTACT ADDRESS** Dept Soc Sci, Kansas City Kansas Comm Col, 7250 State Ave, Kansas City, KS 66112. **EMAIL** baeza@toto.net

BAGWELL, GEORGE
PERSONAL Born 12/02/1949, Littlefield, TX, m, 1979 **DISCIPLINE** ANTHROPOLOGY, PSYCHOLOGY **EDUCATION** San Diego State Univ, BA, 71; MA, 73. **CAREER** Division Dir, 78-82, Dean of the Campus, 82-88, Prof, Colo Mountain Col, 88-. **HONORS AND AWARDS** Fac Mem of the Year, Colo Mt Col; Colo Distance Educator of the Year, Telecommunication Cooperative of Colo, 99; Proclamation of Outstanding Accomplishments, City of Steamboat Springs, 84,88. **MEMBERSHIPS** American Anthropological Assoc, American Psychological Assoc. **RESEARCH** Pedagogy in distance education. **SELECTED PUBLICATIONS** Auth, "Our Cool College,", Steamboat Magazine, 88; auth, Reports of Visits, North Central Assoc Accreditation Agency. **CONTACT ADDRESS** Dept Arts & Sciences, Colorado Mountain Col, Alpine, 1330 Bob Adams Dr, Steamboat Springs, CO 80487. **EMAIL** lbagwell@coloradomtn.edu

BAILEY, ADRIENNE YVONNE
PERSONAL Born 11/24/1944, Chicago, IL **DISCIPLINE** EDUCATION **EDUCATION** Mundelein Coll, BA 1966; Wayne State Univ, MEd 1968; Northwestern Univ, PhD 1973. **CAREER** Chicago Bd of Educ, Deneen Elementary School, teacher Social Studies, English, French, Math, 66-67; So Shore YMCA, Chicago, neighborhood youth corps supvr, 67; Circle Maxwell YMCA, Chicago, program coordinator, 67-68; Detroit Bd of Educ, substitute teacher, 68-69; Gov Office of Human Resources, Chicago, educ coord, 69-71; Northwestern Comm Educ Proj, Northwestern Univ, univ coord, 72-73; Chicago Comm Trust, Chicago, sr staff assoc, 73-81; College Bd NY, vice pres acad affairs, 81-. **HONORS AND AWARDS** Merit Awd, NW Alumni Assn 1981; Diamond Jubilee Recognition, Phi Delta Kappa 1981; Certificate of Recognition, Phi Delta Kappa NW Univ Chapter 1980; Salute IL Serv, Federal Savings & Loan Bank 1980; Meritorious Serv Awd, Educ Commission of the State NAEP 1980; Human Relations Awd, IL Educ Assn 1980; attendance at White House Celebration for the Signing of S210 Creating a Dept of Educ, 1979; Kizzy Awd for Outstanding Contributions in Educ 1979; Outstanding Achievement Awd in Educ, YWCA of Metro Chicago 1978; Distinguished Serv Awd, Ed Commission of the State 1977; 1 of 10 Outstanding Young Citizens Awd, Chicago Jaycees 1976; Community Motivation Awd HU MA BE Karate Assoc 1975; 1 of 10 Outstanding Young Persons Awd, IL Jaycees 1975; 1of 100 Outstanding Black Women in AmAwd, Operation PUSH 1975; Commencement Speaker Mundelein Coll 1975; Image Awd for Outstanding Contributions in Field of Educ, League of Black Women 1974; Recognition Awd, Black Achiever of Indust YMCA of Metro Chicago 1974; TTT Fellowship, Northwestern Univ 1971-73; MDEA Inst in French, Univ of ME 1966; Special Service Awd, Natl Alliance of Black School Educators, 1987. **MEMBERSHIPS** Gov Educ Adv Comm 1983-87, Natl Comm on Secondary Schooling for Hispanics 1983-85, Educ & Career Devel Advisory Comm Natl Urban League 1982-, visiting comm Grad School of Educ Harvard Univ 1977-83; advisory panel Phi Delta Kappa Gallup Poll of the Publics Attitudes Toward Public Educ 1984; policy comm School of Educ Northwestern Univ 1983-; bd of trustees Hazen Found, New Haven CT, 1977-87; bd of trustees So Educ Found, Atlanta GA, 1983-; Natl Task Force on State Efforts to Achieve Sex Equity 1980-83, chmn advisory comm Council on Found Internship & Fellowship Program for Minorities & Women 1980-82; adv comm Inst for Educ Finance & Govt Stanford Univ 1980-85; bd of dir Assn of Black Found Exec 1975-87; IL State Bd of Educ 1974-81, pres1978-79; Natl Assn of State Bds of Educ; commiss 1981, steering comm 1974-79, exec comm 1977-75, 1978-79 Educ Commiss of the States; Natl Assessment of Educ Program Policy Comm 1976-80; task force Desegregation Strategies Project 1976-81; bd of dir Council on Foundations 86; META 86; editorial bd, The Kappan (Phi Delta Kappan); Governor's Advisory Comm on Black Affairs, NY, co-chair, Educ sub-Committee 1986-; bd of dir The Negro Ensemble, NY, 1987-; bd of trustees Marymount Coll 1988-89; bd of trustees The Foundation Center 1989-. **SELECTED PUBLICATIONS** Auth, "Comm Coll Capability Project," IL Bd of Higher Educ 1972; "Citizens in Public Ed in Chicago" Citizen Action in Educ 1976; "Agenda for Action" Educ Leadership 1984; "Top 100 Black Business & Professional Women," Dollars & Sense Magazine, 1985. **CONTACT ADDRESS** Acad Affairs, Col Board Publ, 45 Columbus Ave, New York, NY 10023.

BAILEY, CHARLES RANDALL
PERSONAL Born 02/07/1938, Plain City, OH, m, 1970, 2 children **DISCIPLINE** MODERN EUROPEAN HISTORY & HISTORY OF EDUCATION **EDUCATION** Oh Univ, BA, 60; Univ Chicago, MA, 62, PhD(hist), 68. **CAREER** Instr hist, Juniata Col, 62-63; asst prof, 67-78, Assoc Prof Hist, State Univ NY Col Geneseo, 78-, Nat Endowment for Humanities fel, Univ NC, Chapel Hill, 78-79. **MEMBERSHIPS** AHA; Soc Fr Hist Studies. **RESEARCH** Eighteenth-century French education. **SELECTED PUBLICATIONS** Auth, French Secondary Education, 1763-1790: The Secularization of Ex-Jesuit Colleges, Am Philos Soc, 78; Municipal colleges: Small-town secondary schools in France prior to the revolution, Fr Hist Studies, 82. **CONTACT ADDRESS** Dept of Hist, SUNY, Col at Geneseo, 1 College Cir, Geneseo, NY 14454-1401.

BAILEY, FREDERICK GEORGE
PERSONAL Born 02/24/1924, United Kingdom, m, 1949, 2 children **DISCIPLINE** SOCIAL ANTHROPOLOGY **EDUCATION** Manchester, PhD. **CAREER** Emer, Univ Cal San Diego; Guggenheim fel, 77. **HONORS AND AWARDS** S C Roy Memorial Gold Medal distinguished services to anthrop in India. **MEMBERSHIPS** Am Acad Arts Sci. **RESEARCH** Micro-politics; India; Peasants. **SELECTED PUBLICATIONS** Auth The Kingdom of Individuals, Cornell Univ Press, 94; The Witch-Hunt, Cornell Univ Press, 94; The Civility of Indifference, Cornell Univ Press, 96; The Need for Enemies, Cornell Univ Press, 98. **CONTACT ADDRESS** Dept of Anthropology, Univ of California, San Diego, La Jolla, CA 92093. **EMAIL** fbailey@UCSD.edu

BAILEY, VELDA
PERSONAL Born 04/29/1940, Goodland, KS, m, 1962, 2 children **DISCIPLINE** EDUCATION **EDUCATION** Mesa Col, AA, 60; Univ N Colo, BA, 62; MA, 65. **CAREER** Teacher, Mancos Pub School, 62-65; Lead Teacher, Mesa Valley Schools, 65-82; Coordinator, Grad Site Mesa State Col, 82-. **CONTACT ADDRESS** Grad Site Coordinator, Mesa State Col, PO Box 2647, Grand Junction, CO 81502-2647. **EMAIL** vbailey@mesastate.edu

BAILYN, LOTTE
PERSONAL Born 07/17/1930, Vienna, Austria, m, 1952, 2 children **DISCIPLINE** SOCIAL PSYCHOLOGY **EDUCATION** Swarthmore Col, BA, 51; Harvard Univ, MA, 53, PhD, 56; Univ of Piraeus, Honorary Doctorate, 00. **CAREER** Res assoc, Grad Sch of Educ, Harvard, 56-57; instr, Dept Econ and Soc Sci, MIT, 57-58; res assoc, 58-64, lectr, 63-67, Dept Soc Rel, Harvard Univ; from res assoc to sr lectr, prof, Sloan Sch of Mgt, MIT, 69-91, T. Wilson Prof, 91- ; vis scholar, Dept Social and Econ Stud, Imperial Col of Sci and Technol, London, 82, scholar in res, Rockefeller Found Study and Conf Ctr, Bellagio, Italy, 83; vis univ fel, Dept of Mgt Studies, Univ Auckland, NZ, 84; vis scholar, Univ Cambridge, 86-87; acad vis, Mgt School, Imperial Col of Sci Technol and Med, London, 91, 95; Matina S Horner distinguished vis prof, 00; Radliffe Col, 95-97; Chair, MIT Faculty, 97-99. **HONORS AND AWARDS** Phi Beta Kappa Sigma Xi; listed, Who's Who in America. **MEMBERSHIPS** Acad Mgt; Am Psych Asn (Fellow); Am Social Asn. **RESEARCH** Impact of orgn practices on employee lives, gender in orgns. **SELECTED PUBLICATIONS** Auth, Living with Technology: Issues at Mid-Career, MIT Press, 80; coauth, Working with Careers, Columbia Univ, 84; auth, Breaking the Mold: Women, Men, and Time in The New Corporate World, Free Press, 93. **CONTACT ADDRESS** Sloan School of Management, Massachusetts Inst of Tech, E52-585, Cambridge, MA 02142. **EMAIL** lbailyn@mit.edu

BAIRD-OLSON, KARREN P.
PERSONAL Born 07/25/1936, Lewiston, UT, d, 3 children **DISCIPLINE** SOCIOLOGY **EDUCATION** Mont State Univ, BS, 62; Univ Mont, MA, 84; Univ N Mex, PhD, 94. **CAREER** Instr, Fort Peck Assiniboine and Sioux Cmty Col, 77-79; Teaching Asst, Univ Mont, 82-84; Teaching Asst, Univ N Mex, 86-89; Instr to Asst Prof, Kans State Univ, 89-98; Asst Prof, Univ Central Fla, 98-. **HONORS AND AWARDS** Outstanding Fac of the Year Awd, Kans State Univ, 93; Participant, Conf on US Security and the Soviet Challenge, 79; Grant, Native Am Cultural Awareness Prog, 73-74; Fel, Nat Inst of Mental Health, 84-86. **MEMBERSHIPS** Am Asn of Univ Prof, Am Indian Prof Asn, Am Sociol Asn, Honors Program Student Asn of the ASA, Pacific Sociol Asn, Mid-South Sociol Asn, Nat Asn of Ethnic Studies, SW Soc Sci Asn, Victim Offender Mediation Asn **SELECTED PUBLICATIONS** Auth, "Reflections of an AIM Activist: Has IT all Been Worth It?," American Indian Culture and Research Journal, (94): 233-252; auth, "Survival Roles of Plains Indian Reservation Women," Family Perspectives, (93): 445-470; auth, "Reflections of an AIM Activist," in No Middle Ground, New York Univ Press, 97; auth, "ASA Candidate Profiles," The Network Newsletter, 92; auth, "A Quantification of Bigotry, Betrayal, and a Blend of Both," MAP Newsletter, 92; auth, "Hmong Bicultural Program Evaluation: Corvalis, Montana, Univ Mont 92; auth, The Survival Strategies of Plains Indian Women Coping with Structural and Interpersonal Victimization on a Northwest Reservation, Harper and Row Pub, forthcoming. **CONTACT ADDRESS** Dept Sociol, Univ of Central Florida, PO Box 1613600, Orlando, FL 32816-1360.

BAKEMAN, ROGER
PERSONAL Born 05/28/1939, Auburn, KY, s **DISCIPLINE** PSYCHOLOGY **EDUCATION** Univ Tex, PhD, 73. **CAREER** Asst Prof, Ga State Univ, 73; Assoc Prof, Ga State Univ, 78; Prof, Ga State Univ, 84. **HONORS AND AWARDS** Fel, Div of Am Psychol Asn; Fel, Am Psychol Soc. **MEMBERSHIPS** Am Asn for the Advan of Sci, Am Asn of Univ Prof, APA, APS, Int Soc on Infant Studies, Soc for Res in Child Develop. **RESEARCH** Social development of infants and toddlers, observational methodology and data analysis. **SELECTED PUBLICATIONS** Coauth, "When Ns do not Justify the Means: Small Samples and Scientific Conclusions," in Communication and Language Acquisition: Discoveries from Atypical Development (97): 35-48; coauth, "Detecting Sequential Patterns and Determining their Reliability with Fallible Observers," Psychological Methods, 2 (97): 357-370; coauth, "Observing Interaction: An Introduction to Sequential Analysis, 2nd ed, (Cambridge Univ Pr, 97); coauth, "Maternal Drug Use During Pregnancy: Are Preterm and Fullterms Affected Differently?" Developmental Psychology, 34 (98): 540-554; coauth, "Determining the Power of Multiple Regression Analyses both with and without Repeated Measures,' Behavior Research Methods, Instruments and Computers, 31 (99): 150-154. **CONTACT ADDRESS** Dept Psychol, Georgia State Univ, 33 Gilmer St, SE, Atlanta, GA 30303. **EMAIL** bakeman@gsu.edu

BAKER, CHRISTINA L.
PERSONAL Born 08/18/1939, Gastonia, NC, m, 1961, 4 children **DISCIPLINE** WOMEN'S STUDIES **EDUCATION** Furman Univ, BA, 61; Duke Univ, MA, 52; Union Inst, PhD, 91. **CAREER** From Instr to Prof, Univ of Maine, 78-; Maine State Rep, Dist 117, 97-. **HONORS AND AWARDS** Presidential Outstanding Teacher Awd, 92; Champion for C Awd, Maine C Alliance, 99; Flamming Fel, 99; Trustee Professorship, Univ of Maine at Augusta, 00. **RESEARCH** Women's History. **SELECTED PUBLICATIONS** Auth, In a Generous Spirit: A First-Person Biography of Myra Page, Univ of Ill, 96; coauth, The Conversation Begins: Mothers and Daughters Talk about Living Feminism, Bantam, 96. **CONTACT ADDRESS** Dept Lib Arts, Univ Col of Bangor, 214 Texas Ave, Bangor, ME 04401-4367. **EMAIL** cbaker@maine.edu

BAKER, DAVID V.
PERSONAL Born 02/12/1951, San Francisco, CA, m, 1991, 3 children **DISCIPLINE** SOCIOLOGY **EDUCATION** Calif State Univ, Northridge, BA, 79; Univ Calif, Riverside, MA, 85, PhD, 87; Calif Southern Law Sch, JD, 2001. **CAREER** Assoc prof and chair, Riverside Community Col, 87-; adjunct assoc prof, Chapman Univ, 91-; vis lectr, Univ Calif, Riverside, 94-95. **HONORS AND AWARDS** Nat Endowment for the Humanities, summer sem for col teachers, 91, 95. **MEMBERSHIPS** Acad of Criminal Justice Scis, Calif Sociol Asn, Am Soc of Criminology, Western Soc of Criminal Justice Eds, Pacific Sociol Asn. **RESEARCH** Capital punishment, racism in

the U.S. criminal justice system, social inequality. **SELECTED PUBLICATIONS** Auth, Race, Racism and the Death Penalty in the United States, Vande Vere Pubs (91); auth, Perspectives on Race and Ethnicity in American Criminal Justice, West Pub (94); auth, Sources: Notable Selections in Race and Ethnic Relations, Dushkin Pub (95); auth, "Racism, Capital Punishment, and the United States Supreme Court," in D. Dunn and D. Waller, eds, Analyzing Social Problems: Essays and Exercises, Wadsworth (96): 107-116; auth, Sources: Notable Selections in Race and Ethnic Relations, 2nd ed, Dushkin Pub (98); auth, "A Descriptive Profile and Socio-Historical Analysis of Female Executions in the United States: 1632-1997," Women and Criminal Justice, 10, 3 (99): 57-93; auth, "Slave Executions in the United States: A Descriptive Analysis of Social and Historical Factors," The Soc Sci J, 36, 1 (99): 1-31; auth, Sources: Notable Selections in Crime, Criminology, and Criminal Justice, Dushkin Pub Group (2000); auth, Structured Inequality in American Society: Critical Discussions on the Continuing Significance of Race, Ethnicity, Gender, and Class, Prentice-Hall (2000); auth, "Latinos and the United States Criminal Justice System," The Justice Professional, 11, 4 (2000). **CONTACT ADDRESS** Dept Behav Scis, Riverside Comm Col, 4800 Magnolia Ave, Riverside, CA 92506-1299. **EMAIL** dvbaker@rccd.cc.ca.us

BAKER, LEE D.
PERSONAL Born 04/24/1966, San Diego, CA, m, 1997, 1 child **DISCIPLINE** ANTHROPOLOGY **EDUCATION** Portland State Univ, BS, 89; Temple Univ, MA, PhD, 94; Univ Ghana, Cert, 95. **CAREER** Asst Prof, Duke Univ, 95-99; Asst Prof to Assoc Prof, Columbia Univ, 97-99; Assoc Prof, Duke Univ, 99-. **HONORS AND AWARDS** Temple Univ Nominee, Coun of Grad Sch Dissertation Awd, 94; Gallery of Success, Temple Univ, 98; MacDonald Summer Fel, Columbia Univ, 99. **MEMBERSHIPS** NY Acad of Sci; Am Anthropol Asn; Nat Coun of Black Studies. **RESEARCH** The coterminous disourse of law and science and how it shapes notions of race and structures racial inequality; History of anthropology in the United States; Aboriginal experiences in Australia and the African American experience in the United States. **SELECTED PUBLICATIONS** Auth, "Cultural Creolization and the Constitution of Ethnicity Amongst Aboriginal Professionals in Dampierland, Western Australia," in Foragers in Context: Long Term, Regional and Historical Perspectives in Hunter-Gatherer Studies, MI, 91; auth, "The Location of Franz Boas Within the African American Struggle," Critique of Anthropology, (94): 199-217; auth, "Savage Inequality: Anthropology in the Erosion of the Fifteenth Amendment," Transforming Anthropology, (94): 28-33; co-auth, "Race, Racism, and the History of U.S. Anthropology," Transforming Anthropology, (94): 1-7; auth, "Racism in Professional Settings: Forms of Address as Clues to Power Relations," Journal of Applied Behavioral Sciences, (95): 186-201; auth, "Unraveling the Boasian Discourse: The Racial Politics of 'Culture' in School Desegregation, 1944-1954," Transforming Anthropology, (98): 15-32; auth, From Savage to Negro: Anthropology and the Construction of Race, 1896-1954, Univ CA Press, 98; auth, "Racism in Professional Settings: Forms of Address as Clues to Power Relations," in Race & Ideology: Language, Symbolism, and Popular Culture, (Wayne State Univ Press, 99), 115-132; auth, "Research, Reform, and Racial Uplift: The Mission of the Hampton Folklore Society," History of Anthropology, 00; auth, "Afrocentricity and the American Dream," in Theorizing Black Studies, (Columbia Univ Press, 00). **CONTACT ADDRESS** Dept Cultural Anthropol, Duke Univ, 114B Social Science, PO Box 90091, Durham, NC 27708-0091. **EMAIL** ldbaker@acpub.duke.edu

BAKER, LINDA D.
PERSONAL Born 08/10/1942, NC, m, 1960, 3 children **DISCIPLINE** CHILD DEVELOPMENT **EDUCATION** Lenoir Rhyne Col, BA, 84; Lenoir Rhyne Col, MA, 89. **CAREER** Asst/Staff Psychol, psychiat hosp, 84-93; Prof, Catawba Valley Community Col, 93-. **HONORS AND AWARDS** Psychol Awd, undergraduate sch; St Proj Commt for Curric Improvement for Psychol/Sociol. **MEMBERSHIPS** NBCC, ACA, APA Div 2, APS, NAMP. **RESEARCH** Child development. **CONTACT ADDRESS** Dept Arts & Sci, Catawba Valley Comm Col, 2550 US Hwy 70 SE, Hickory, NC 28602. **EMAIL** lbaker@cvcc.cc.nc.us

BAKER, PARRIS
PERSONAL Born 11/24/1957, Erie, PA, m, 1997, 1 child **DISCIPLINE** SOCIOLOGY **EDUCATION** Gannon Univ, BA-BSW, 92; Case Western Reserve Univ, MSSA-MSW, 95. **CAREER** Asst prof, Gannon Univ. **HONORS AND AWARDS** Gannon Univ Awd for Acad Achievement. **MEMBERSHIPS** NASW; CAC; CCS. **RESEARCH** Fathers and families, group efficacy. **CONTACT ADDRESS** Dept Sociol, Gannon Univ, 109 University Sq, Erie, PA 16541. **EMAIL** bakerp@gannon.edu

BAKER, RONALD LEE
PERSONAL Born 06/30/1937, Indianapolis, IN, m, 1960, 2 children **DISCIPLINE** FOLKLORE **EDUCATION** IN State Univ, Terre Haute, BS, 60, MA, 61; IN Univ, Bloomington, PhD(folklore), 69. **CAREER** Instr English, Univ IL, Urbana, 63-65; teaching assoc, English & Folklore, IN Univ, Ft Wayne, 65-66; from instr to assoc prof, 66-76, prof English, IN State Univ, Terre Haute, 76-, chnmn dept, 80-; Vis lectr English, Univ IL, Urbana, 72-73; vis assoc prof folklore, IN Univ, Bloomington, 75, vis prof, 78; ed, Midwestern Folklore, 75-98; ed, The Folklore Historian, 90-. **HONORS AND AWARDS** Res/Creativity Awd, IN State Univ, 90; fel, Am Folklore Soc, 96. **MEMBERSHIPS** Am Folklore Soc; Am Name Soc; MLA; Hoosier Folklore Soc. **RESEARCH** American folklore; narrative folklore; folklore and literary relations; namelore; Indiana folklore. **SELECTED PUBLICATIONS** Auth, Folklore in the Writings of Rowland E Robinson, Bowling Green Univ, 73; coauth, Indiana Place Names, IN Univ, 75; auth, Hoosier Folk Legends, IN Univ, 82; Jokelore: Humorous Folktales from Indiana, IN Univ, 86; French Folklife in Old Vincennes, ICTE/HFS, 89; ed, The Study of Place Names, ICTE/HFS, 91; auth, From Needmore to Prosperity: Hoosier Place Names in Folklore and History, IN Univ, 95; auth, "Homeless, Friendless, and Penniless: The WPA Interviews with Former Slaves Living in Indiana," in Univ, 00. **CONTACT ADDRESS** Dept of English, Indiana State Univ, 210 N 7th St, Terre Haute, IN 47809. **EMAIL** ejrlb@root.indstate.edu

BAKER, THOMAS E.
PERSONAL Born 06/15/1941, New York, NY, m, 1969, 1 child **DISCIPLINE** SOCIOLOGY, CRIMINAL JUSTICE **EDUCATION** Va Commonwealth Univ, AA, MS; East Stroudsburg Univ, Med, MS; Marywood Univ, CAGS Psychology and Counseling; PA State Univ, Advanced Study Adult Ed; Temple Univ, Educational Leadership. **CAREER** Assoc prof, Univ Scranton, 75-; Lt. Col. (Ret.) US Army Reserve Military Police Corps; Special Agent and Commander , US Army Criminal Investigation Command; police consultant to local law enforcement agencies, police administration, police testing, and COPPS grants. **HONORS AND AWARDS** Phi Epsilon Kappa; Kappa Delta Pi; Pi Gamma Mu; Scholarship Awd, Mich State Univ, Police Community Relations; Outstanding Honor Academic Graduate, Montgomery County Police Acad, Md; Dean's list student, Va Commonwealth Univ; Who's Who in Am Law Enforcement; Directory of Distinguished Americans; Who's Who in America; Who's Who in the East; Outstanding Young Men of America; Who's Who in the Northeast. **MEMBERSHIPS** Police and Criminal Psychology; Nat Asn of Chiefs of Police; Southern Criminal Justice Asn; The American Legion; Disabled American Veterans. **RESEARCH** Psychological personality profiling; police administration; criminal investigation; crime prevention; organized crime; community-oriented and problem-solving policing; police grantsmanship; crime analysis. **SELECTED PUBLICATIONS** Author of more than 40 articles in professional journals. **CONTACT ADDRESS** Dept Sociol, Univ of Scranton, 800 Linden St, Scranton, PA 18510.

BALCH, WILLIAM
PERSONAL Born 04/03/1946, New York, NY, d, 1 child **DISCIPLINE** PSYCHOLOGY **EDUCATION** Haverford Col, BA, 68; Univ Minn, PhD, 76. **CAREER** Instructor, Davidson Col, 76-77; Fel, Univ Conn, 77-78; Asst Prof to Prof, Penn State Univ, 78-. **MEMBERSHIPS** Am Psychol Soc; E Psychol Soc. **RESEARCH** Mood and memory; Music and memory. **SELECTED PUBLICATIONS** Co-auth, "Music-dependent memory in immediate and delayed recall," Memory & Cognition, (92): 21-28; auth, "Effect of class standing on students' predictions of their final exam scores," Teaching of Psychology, (92): 136-141; co-auth, "Music-dependent memory: The roles of tempo change and mood mediation," Journal of Experimental Psychology: Learning, Memory, and Cognition, (96): 1354-1363; auth, "Practice versus review exams and final exam performance," Teaching of Psychology, (98): 181-185; co-auth, "Dimensions of mood in mood-dependent memory," Journal of Experimental Psychology: Learning, Memory, and Cognition, (99): 70-83. **CONTACT ADDRESS** Dept Psychol, Pennsylvania State Univ, Altoona, 3000 Ivyside Pk, Altoona, PA 16601. **EMAIL** wrb3@psu.edu

BALDO, TRACY D. BOSTWICK
PERSONAL Born 10/21/1964, Marion, IN, m, 1995 **DISCIPLINE** PSYCHOLOGY **EDUCATION** Purdue Univ, BS, 86, MS, 89, PhD, 90. **CAREER** Asst prof, Auburn Univ, 90-91; assoc prof, Univ Northern Colo, 91-99, prof, 99-, Div Dir, 98-. **HONORS AND AWARDS** Nat Certified Counselor; Licensed Prof Counselor; Outstanding Service Awd, Colo Col Coun Asn, 95; Prof of the Year, Grad Student Asn, 96; nominated for the M. Lucile Harrison Prof of Excellence Awd, 98, 99; Recipient of Outstanding University Women Awd, 99. **MEMBERSHIPS** Am Coun Asn, Asn for Coun Educ and Supervision, Colo Coun Asn, Colo Asn for Coun Educ and Supervision, Am Mental Health Coun Asn. **RESEARCH** Sexual assaults, counselor training. **SELECTED PUBLICATIONS** Coauth, "Concurrent validity of the Relationship with Father Inventory," Psychol Reports, 83 (98): 403-409; coauth, "Interpersonal process recall and solution focused process recall in the supervision of counselors," J for the Ala Coun Asn, 23, 2 (98): 26-31; coauth, "Facilitating the transition from individual sessions to systemic family sessions: Issues of supervision and training," The Family J: Coun and Therapy for Couples and Families, 5 (98): 257-262; coauth, "Narcissistic measures of Lutheran clergy who self-reported committing sexual misconduct," Pastoral Psychol, 47, 2 (98): 81-96; coauth, "Family sculpting in supervision of family therapy," The Family J: Coun and Therapy for Couples and Families, 6 (98): 231-234; coauth, "The rural school counselor: Professional issues, roles, and training," Ala Coun Asn J, 24, 1 (98): 20-27; coauth, "A gender based solution-focused genogram case: He and she across the generations," The Family J: Coun and Therapy for Couples and Families, 7 (99): 177-180; coauth, "The efficacy of eye movement desensitization and reprocessing in the treatment of test anxiety among college students," J of Col Coun (in press). **CONTACT ADDRESS** Dept Prof Psychol, Univ of No Colorado, McKee 248, Greeley, CO 80639. **EMAIL** baldo@unco.edu

BALL, RICHARD E.
PERSONAL Born 10/31/1937, Pasadena, CA, m, 1962, 2 children **DISCIPLINE** SOCIOLOGY **EDUCATION** Calif State Univ, Long Baech, BA, 61; Univ Fla, MA, 75, PhD, 80. **CAREER** Vis asst prof, Erskine Col, 77-78; asst prof, Univ West Ala, 78-79; prof, Ferris State Univ, 80-. **HONORS AND AWARDS** Fulbright Scholar, Japan, 93-94, 98-99; Marvin Olsen Awd, Mich Sociol Asn, 96; Marqui's Who's Who in the Midwest, 96-97, 98-99. **MEMBERSHIPS** Mich Sociol Asn. **RESEARCH** African American family, Asian-Americans. **SELECTED PUBLICATIONS** Auth, Marital Status, Household Structure, and Life Satisfaction of Black Women," Soc Problems, 30, 4, 400-409 (April 83); auth, "Family and Friends: A Supportive Network for Low-Income American Black Families," J of Comp Family Studies, 30, 4, 51-65 (April 83); auth, "Parental Role Satisfaction of Black Mothers in the United States," Int J Sociol of the Family, 14, 1, 33-46 (spring 84); auth, "Marital Status and Life Satisfaction of Black Men," J of Soc and Personal Relationships, 1, 4, 459-70 (Dec 84); auth, "Marital Status and Life Satisfaction Among Black Americans," J of Marriage and the Family, 48, 2, 389-94 (May 86); auth, "Black Husbands' Satisfaction with Their Family Life," J of Marriage and the Family, 48, 4, 849-55 (Nov 86); auth, "Satisfaction With Family Life of Married Black Americans," Mich Sociol Rev, 3, 45-53 (fall 89); auth, "Marriage: Conducive to Greater Life Satisfaction for American Black Women?," in Robert Stapler, ed, The Black Family: Essays and Studies, 4th ed, Wadsworth (91); auth, "Children and Marital Happiness of Black Americans," J of Comp Family Studies, 24, 2, 203-18 (summer 93); auth, "The American Family at the Millenium," J of Am Studies, 30, 2, 447-55 (winter 98). **CONTACT ADDRESS** Dept Soc Sci, Ferris State Univ, 820 Campus Dr, Big Rapids, MI 49307-2225. **EMAIL** ballr@ferris.edu

BANDY, JOE
PERSONAL Born 08/30/1967, Nashville, TN, m, 1997 **DISCIPLINE** SOCIOLOGY **EDUCATION** Rhodes Col, Memphis, BA, 89; Univ Calif, Santa Barbara, MA, 93; PhD, 98. **CAREER** Teaching assoc/lectr, Univ Calif, Santa Barbara, 93-97; asst prof, Bowdoin Col, Brunswick, Maine, 98-. **HONORS AND AWARDS** Psi Chi; Mortar Board; Academic Senate Res Grant, Univ Calif, Santa Barbara, 97; Dept of Sociol Res and Travel Grants, Univ Calif, Santa Barbara, 96-97. **MEMBERSHIPS** Am Sociol Asn, Soc for the Study of Soc Problems, Latin Am Studies Asn, Southern Sociol Asn, Pacific Sociol Asn, Inst for Policy Studies, Center for Political Ecology. **SELECTED PUBLICATIONS** Auth, "Managing the Other of Nature; Sustainability, Spectacle, and Global Regimes of Capital in Ecotourism," Public Culture, 8, 3 (96): 539-66; auth, "Reterritorializing Borders: Transnational Environmental Justice Movements on the US-Mexico Border," Race, Gender, and Class, 5, 1 (97): 80-103; auth, Border Crossings: Transnational Movements for Alternative Development and Radical Democracy in the U.S./Mexico Border Region-A Summary Report, issued to field contracts and colleagues (April 99); auth, "Bordering the Future: Resisting Neoliberalism in the Borderlands," Critical Sociol (forthcoming); auth, "Reterritorializing Borders: Transnational Environmental Justice Movements on the US-Mexico Border," reprint forthcoming as a chapter in Environmental Injustice and Race, Gender and Class Issues, eds Robert Bullard, Dorceta Taylor, and Glenn Johnson (2000). **CONTACT ADDRESS** Dept of Sociol/Anthropol, Bowdoin Col, 7000 Col Station, Brunswick, ME 04011-8470. **EMAIL** jbandy@bowdoin.edu

BANERJEE, LEENA
DISCIPLINE PSYCHOLOGY **EDUCATION** Va Polytech & State Univ, PhD, 85. **CAREER** Assoc Prof, Calif School of Professional Psychol. **HONORS AND AWARDS** Member, Human Resources Honors Committee. **MEMBERSHIPS** Am Asn of Marriage and Family Therapy. **RESEARCH** Multiculturalism & American national cultural identity; Program development; Evaluation & Direct service consultation issues for foster children and families. **CONTACT ADDRESS** Dept Psychol, California Sch of Professional Psychology, Los Angeles, 1000 S Fremont Ave, Alhambra, CA 91803. **EMAIL** lbanerjee@mail.cspp.edu

BANICH, MARIE T.
PERSONAL Born 08/06/1957, New York, NY **DISCIPLINE** PSYCHOLOGY **EDUCATION** Tufts Univ, BA, 78; Univ Chicago, PhD, 85. **CAREER** Asst Prof to Full Prof, Univ Ill at Urbana, 85-00; Full Prof, Univ Colo, 00-. **HONORS AND AWARDS** Arnold O. Beckman Res Awd, 86; Beckman Fel, Univ Ill, 89; Psi Chi Undergrad Teaching Awd, Univ Ill, 91; Ar-

nold O. Beckman Res Awd, 94. **MEMBERSHIPS** Cognitive Neurosci Soc; Am Psychol Soc; Intl Soc for Beh Neurosci; Intl Neuropsychol Soc. **RESEARCH** Cognitive neuroscience of attention utilizing brain mapping techniques such as functional magnetic resonance imaging and event-related potentials. **SELECTED PUBLICATIONS** Auth, Neuropsychology, Houghton-Mifflin, 97; auth, "fMRI studies of Stroop tasks reveal unique roles of anterior and posterior brain systems in attentional selection," J of Cognitive Neurosci, 00; auth, "Prefrontal regions play a predominant role in imposing an attentional "set": Evidence from fMRI," Cognitive Brain Research, 00; auth, "The Cerebral hemispheres cooperate to perform complex but not simple tasks," Neuropsychology, 00; auth, "One of twenty question for the twenty-first century: How do brain regions interact and integrate information?" Brain and Cognition, 00. **CONTACT ADDRESS** Dept Psychol, Univ of Colorado, Boulder, UCB 345, Boulder, CO 80309. **EMAIL** mbanich@psych.colorado.edu

BANK, BARBARA J.
PERSONAL Born 12/13/1939, Chicago, IL, m, 1976 **DISCIPLINE** SOCIOLOGY **EDUCATION** Ill State Univ, BS, 61; Univ IA, MA, 68; PhD, 74. **CAREER** Instructor to Assoc Prof and Dept Chair, Univ Mo, 69-84; Visiting Fel, Australian Nat Univ, 84-85, 88; Assoc Prof, Mo London Prog, London, 92; Visiting Fel, Australian Nat Univ, 93; Prof, Univ Mo, 99-. **HONORS AND AWARDS** Alumnae Anniv Awd, Univ MO, 84; Fulbright Sen Scholar Awd, 85; Purple Chalk Teaching Awd, Univ MO, 98; Grant, Univ MO Graduate Res Coun, 98-99. **MEMBERSHIPS** Am Educ Res Asn; Am Sociol Asn; Asn for the Study of Higher Educ; Intl Network on Personal Relationships; Intl Soc for the Study of Personal Relationships; Midwest Sociol Soc; Nat Women's Stud Asn; Sociol for Women in Soc. **RESEARCH** Social Psychology; Sociology of Gender; Sociology of Youth and Education. **SELECTED PUBLICATIONS** Co-auth, "First-Semester Grades, Thought Modes, and Undergraduate Persistence," Contemporary Educational Psychology, (94): 416-429; auth, "Student Friendships and conflict in School," in International Encyclopedia of Education, Pergamon Press, 94; auth, "Friendships in Australia and the United States: From Feminization to a More Heroic Image," Gender & Society, (95): 79-98; auth, "Gendered Accounts: Undergraduates Explain Why They Seek Their Bachelor's Degrees," Sex Roles, (95): 527-544; auth, "Introduction: Some Paradoxes of Gender Equity in Schooling," in Gender, Equity, and Schooling: Policy and Practice, Garland Pub, 97; co-ed, Gender, Equity, and Schooling: Policy and Practice, Garland Pub, 97; auth, "Peer Cultures and Their Challenge for Teaching," in The International Handbook of Teachers & Teaching, (Kluwer Acad Pub, 97), 879-937; co-auth, "Social Psychological Theories in Education," in The International Encyclopedia of the Sociology of Education, (Pergamon Press, 97), 32-42; auth, "Some Dangers of Binary Thinking: Comment on 'Why Smart People Believe that Schools Shortchange Girls'," Gender Issues, (99): 83-86; co-auth, "Gender and Friendship: Why Are Men's Same-Sex Friendships Less Intimate and Supportive?", Personal Relationships, in press. **CONTACT ADDRESS** Dept Sociol, Univ of Missouri, Columbia, 109 Sociol Bldg, Columbia, MO 65211-1100. **EMAIL** BankB@missouri.edu

BANKS, JAMES ALBERT
PERSONAL Born 09/24/1941, Marianna, AR, m **DISCIPLINE** EDUCATION **EDUCATION** Chicago City Col, AA, 1963; Chicago State University, BE, 1964; Michigan State University, MA, 1967, PhD, 1969. **CAREER** Joilet Illinois Public Schools, teacher, 65; Francis W Parker School, teacher, 65-66; University of Michigan, visiting prof of education, summer 75; The British Academy, UK, visiting lecturer, 83; Monash University, Australia, visiting prof of education, 85; University of Washington-Seattle, assoc prof, 71-73, prof of education, 73-, chairman, dept of curriculum & instruction, 82-87, College of Education, prof, currently. **HONORS AND AWARDS** Golden Key Natl Honor Society, honorary member, 1985; Distinguished Scholar/Researcher on Minority Education, American Education Research Assn, 1986. **MEMBERSHIPS** Natl Defense Education Act; Spencer fellow, Natl Academy of Education, 1973-76; Natl fellow, W K Kellogg Foundation, 1980-83; Rockefeller Foundation Fellowship, 1980; bd of dirs, Social Science Education Consortium, 1976-79; bd dir, Assn for Supervision & Curriculum Development, 1976-80; Natl Council for the Social Studies, vice president, 1980, president elect, 1981, president, 1982, bd of dirs, 1980-84. **SELECTED PUBLICATIONS** We Americans, Our History and People, two vol, 82; Teaching Strategies for the Social Studies, 4th ed, 90; co-auth, Multicultural Education in Western Societies, 86; Teaching Strategies for Ethnic Studies, 4th ed, 87; Multiethnic Education Theory and Practice, 2nd ed, 88; March Toward Freedom: A History of Black Americans, 78; co-auth, Multicultural Education: Issues and Prespectives, 89. **CONTACT ADDRESS** Col of Education, DQ-12, Univ of Washington, Seattle, WA 98195-0001.

BANKS, WILLIAM MARON, III
PERSONAL Born 09/22/1943, Thomasville, GA **DISCIPLINE** EDUCATION **EDUCATION** Dillard Univ, B 1963; Univ of KY, Doctorate 1967. **CAREER** Attebury Job Corps Center, supr counselor & psychol, 67; Howard Univ, counselor psychol, 67-70, dept chairperson, 72-75; Univ of CA at Berkeley, prof, 70-, provost, 88-89. **HONORS AND AWARDS** Summer Scholars Awd US Civil Serv Commn; Univ of CA Regents Fellowship; Instructional Improve Grant; American Book Awd, 1996. **MEMBERSHIPS** Mem Soc for Psychol Study of Soc Issues; Soc for Study of Soc Problems; Amer Personnel & Guid Assn; chairperson Univ of CA Afro-Amer Studies Consortium 1979-81; Assn of Black Psychologists. **SELECTED PUBLICATIONS** articles monographs on effects of racial differences in psychotherapy & counseling; auth, "Black Intellectuals." **CONTACT ADDRESS** Univ of California, Berkeley, 682 Barrows, Berkeley, CA 94720. **EMAIL** bilbankssociety@rates.berkeley.edu

BANKSTON, CARL L.
PERSONAL Born 08/08/1952, New Orleans, LA, m, 1986, 3 children **DISCIPLINE** SOCIOLOGY **EDUCATION** Southern Methodist Univ, BS, 75; Univ California, Berkeley, MA, 80; Louisiana State Univ, Phd, 95. **CAREER** Supervisor, Philippine Refugee Processing Center, 85-90; Morong, Bataar, The Philippines, 85-90; Asst Prof, Univ of Southwestern Louisiana, 95-99; Asst Prof, Tulane Univ, 99-. **HONORS AND AWARDS** Phi Kappa Phi Emergent Researcher Awd, 97; Outstanding Paper Awd, Louisiana Education Research Assoc, 99; Thomas and Znaniecki Awd for Outstanding Book, Am Sociological Assoc, 99. **MEMBERSHIPS** Amer Sociological Assoc; Southern Sociol Assoc; Mid-South Sociol Assoc. **RESEARCH** International Migration; Race and ethnicity; Sociology of Education; Sociology of Religion. **SELECTED PUBLICATIONS** Auth, "Science, Technology and the Third World: An Annotated Bibliography," by Shrum, Wesley, Carl L. Bankston III, and Stephen Voss, Metuchen, NJ: Scarecrow Press, 95; auth, "The Effects of Minority Language Literacy on the Academic Achievement of Vietnamese Youth in New Orleans," by Bankston, Carl L. III and Min Zhou, Sociology of Education 68, 95: 1-17; auth, "Majority African American Schools and the Perpetuation of Social Injustice: The Influence of De Facto Segregation on Academic Achievement," by Bankston, Carl L. III and Stephen J. Caldas, Social Forces, 75, 96: 535-556; auth, "Propositions for a Structural Analysis of Creolism," by Henry, Jacques and Carl L. Bankston III, Current Anthropology, 39, 98: 558-566; auth, "Family Structure, Schoolmates, and the Racial Inequalities of Schools," by Bankston, Carl L. III and Stephen J. Caldas, Journal of Marriage and the Family, 60, 98: 715-723; auth, "Growing Up American: How Vietnamese Children Adapt to Life in the United States," by Zhou, Min and Carl L. Bankston III, New York: Russell Sage Foundation, 98; auth, "Endogamy among Louisiana Cajuns: A Social Class Explanation," by Bankston, Carl L. III, and Jacques Henry, Social Forces, 77, 99; auth, "Radical and Ethnic Relations in America," by Bankston, Carl L. III, 3 vols, Pasadena, Ca: Salem Press; auth, "Sociology Basics," by Bankston, Carl L. III, Ed, 2 vols, Pasadena, Ca.: Salem Press, 00; auth, "Straddling Two Social Worlds: The Experience of Vietname Refugee Children in the United States," by Zhou, Min and Carl L. Bankston III, New York: ERIC Clearinghouse on Urban Education, 00; **CONTACT ADDRESS** Dept Sociology, Tulane Univ, New Orleans, LA 70118. **EMAIL** cbankst@mailhost.tcs.tulane.edu

BAR, ROSANN
PERSONAL Born 04/09/1960, Jersey City, NJ, m, 1989, 3 children **DISCIPLINE** SOCIOLOGY **EDUCATION** Caldwell Col, BA, 82; Columbia Univ, MA, 84; MPhil, 85; PhD, 93. **CAREER** Vis Lecturer, Rutgers Univ, 88-92; Instr, Hunter Col, 92-93; Lecturer to Asst Prof, 89-. **HONORS AND AWARDS** Outstanding Young women of Am, 97; Product of the Year Awd, Globe Fearon educational Pub, 96; Robert J Levin Prize, Columbia Univ, 85; President's Fel, Columbia Univ,84-85. **MEMBERSHIPS** Am Sociol Asn, Eastern Sociol Asn, Nat Coun on Family Relations. **SELECTED PUBLICATIONS** Auth, "Israeli-Americans," Racial and Ethnic Relations in America, Salem Press, 99; auth, "Sabotage," Racial and Ethnic Relations in America, Salem Press, 99; auth, "Epithet Transfer," Racial and Ethnic relations in America, Salem Press, 99. **CONTACT ADDRESS** Dept Sociol, Caldwell Col, 9 Ryerson Ave, Caldwell, NJ 07006. **EMAIL** rbar@caldwell.edu

BAR-YOSEF, OFER
PERSONAL Born 08/29/1937, Jerusalem, Israel **DISCIPLINE** ANTHROPOLOGY **EDUCATION** Hebrew Univ, Israel, BA, MA, 65; PhD, 70. **CAREER** From assoc prof to prof, Hebrew Univ, 73-88; prof, 88-, Harvard Univ. **MEMBERSHIPS** AAA; GSA; SAA; SAS. **RESEARCH** Paleolithic; Neolithic; Origin of Agriculture. **SELECTED PUBLICATIONS** Coed, Late Quaternary Chronology and Paleoclimates in the Eastern Mediterranean, Radiocarbon and the American School of Prehistoric Research, Peabody Museum (Harvard Univ), 94; co-ed, The Definition and Interpretation of Levallois Technology, Prehistory Press (Madison), 95; co-ed, An Early Neolithic Village in the Jordan Valley, Part I: The Archaeology of Netiv Hagdud, Am Sch Prehist Res 43, Peabody Museum (Harvard Univ: Cambridge, 97); co-ed, Seasonality and Sedentism: Archaeological Perspectives from Old and New World Sites, Peabody Museum (Harvard Univ), 98; co-ed, Neanderthals and Modern Humans in Western Asia, Plenum: NY (98); co-ed, "The chronology of the Middle Paleolithic of the Levant," in Neanderthals and Modern Humans in Western Asia, Plenum: NY (98): 39-56; auth, "Early colonization's and Cultural continuities in the Lower Paleolithic of Western Asia," in Early Human Behavior in Global Context: The Rise and Diversity of the Lower Paleolithic Record, eds. MD Petraglia, R Korisettar (Routledge: London, 98): 221-279; auth, "On the nature of transitions: the Middle to Upper Paleolithic and the Neolithic Revolution," Cambridge Arch J 8 (98): 141-177; auth, "Symbolic expressions in Later Prehistory in the Levant - why are so few?," in Beyond Art, eds. M Conkey, O Soffer, D Stratmann, N Jablonski (Memoirs of the California Academy of Sciences: San Francisco, 98); coauth, "The big deal about blades: laminar technologies and human evolution," Am Anthro 101 (99): 322-338; auth, "The Natufian culture in the Levant, threshold to the origins of agriculture," Evolu Anthro 6 (98): 159-177. **CONTACT ADDRESS** Dept Anthropology, Harvard Univ, Peabody Museum, Cambridge, MA 02138. **EMAIL** obaryos@fas.harvard.edu

BARAKAT, LAMIA
DISCIPLINE SOCIOLOGY, PSYCHOLOGY **EDUCATION** Villanova Univ, BA, 85;Univ SC, PhD, 91. **CAREER** Mental Health Consult, Columbia Area Mental Health Center, 86-87; Psychol, Dept of Youth Serv, 89; staff therapist, Univ of SC, 87-90; psychol intern, Univ of Med and Dent of NJ, 90-91; asst psychol, Children's Hosp of NJ, 91-93; staff psychol, Children's Choice, Inc., 93; fac, Villanova Univ, 92-95; psychol, Children's Hosp of Philadelphia, 93-96; asst prof, Drexel Univ, 96-. **HONORS AND AWARDS** Am Psychol Asn Diss Awd; **MEMBERSHIPS** Am Psychol Assoc; Pa Psychol Assoc; Philadelphia Neuropsychology Soc; Soc of Pediatric Psychol. **RESEARCH** Pediatric psychology, psychosocial aspects of chronic illness in children. **SELECTED PUBLICATIONS** Coauth; "Optimism, appraisals and coping in the adjustment of mothers and their children with spina bifida", Jour of Child and Fam Studies (95):303-320; coauth, "Management of death in children", Ped in Rev (95):419-424; coauth," Self-reported and observed distress and coping by mothers of children with leukemia during painful procedures", The Am Jour of Family Therapy (96):236-250;coauth, "Families surviving childhood cancer; A comparison of post traumatic stress symptoms with families of healthy children", Jour of Ped Psychol (97):843-859; coauth, "Family issues related to cognitive aspects of chronic illness in children", Cognitive Aspects of Chronic Illness in Children, (99); coauth, "The impact of childhood hypothalamic/chiasmatic brain tumors on child adjustment and family functioning", Children's Health Care, (00); coauth, "Interest Box: Family and child adjustment to cognitive aspects of cancer in children", Prin of Neuropsychol, (00); coauth, Promoting positive health attitudes and behaviors: Preliminary evaluation of a peer health education program (forthcoming); coauth, "Child Health Psychology", Health Psychol, (forthcoming). **CONTACT ADDRESS** Dept Sociol Psychology, Drexel Univ, 3141 Chestnut St, Philadelphia, PA 19104. **EMAIL** lamia.p.barakat@drexel.edu

BARFIELD, THOMAS J.
PERSONAL Born 04/21/1950, Atlanta, GA **DISCIPLINE** ANTHROPOLOGY **EDUCATION** Univ Pa, BA, 72; Harvard Univ, MA, 74, PhD, 78. **CAREER** Vis asst prof, Wellesley Col, 81-82; asst prof, Harvard Univ, 82-85, assoc prof, 86-89, vis prof, spring 92; prof and chairman, Boston Univ, 89-. **RESEARCH** Pastoral nomadism in the Near East and Central Eurasia, political economy, cultural ecology, ethno-archaeology, anthropological approaches to historical method, indigenous domestic architecture, ethnicity. **SELECTED PUBLICATIONS** Coauth with Russell Barber, The Amphitheater Site: A Late Archaic Settlement in Watertown, MA, Cambridge, MA: Harvard Inst for Conservation Archaeol (82); auth, The Perilous Frontier: Nomadic Empires and China, Cambridge, MA and Oxford: Blackwell (89, first paperback, 92, reprinted 94, 96); auth, "Tribe and State Relations: The Inner Asian Perspective," in Tribes and State Formation in the Middle East, ed by Philip Khoury and Joseph Kostiner, Berkeley: Univ Calif Press (91): 153-185; coauth with Albert Szabo, Afghanistan: An Atlas of Indigenous Domestic Architecture, Austin: Univ of Tex Press (91); auth, " 'The Centrality of Central Asia': A Dialogue with Frank," Studies in History, 8/1 (n.s.) (92): 101-106, reprinted in Bull of Concerned Asian Scholars, 24/2 (92): 76-79; auth, The Nomadic Alternative, Englewood Cliffs, NJ: Prentice-Hall (93); auth, "The Devil's Horsemen: Steppe Nomadic Warfare in Historical Perspective," in Studying War: Anthropological Perspectives, ed by S. P. Reyna and R. E. Downs, Amsterdam: Gordon and Breach (94): 157-182; auth, "Prospects for Plural Societies in Central Asia," Cultural Survival Quart, 18/2 (94): 48-51; auth, "The Afghan Morass," Current Hist, 95, 597, (96): 38-43; exec ed, The Dictionary of Anthropology, Oxford: Blackwell (97). **CONTACT ADDRESS** Dept Anthropol, Boston Univ, 232 Bay State Rd, Boston, MA 02215. **EMAIL** barfield@bu.edu

BARKAN, ELLIOTT ROBERT
PERSONAL Born 12/15/1940, Brooklyn, NY, m, 1994, 3 children **DISCIPLINE** AMERICAN HISTORY, ETHNIC STUDIES **EDUCATION** Queens Col, NYork, BA, 62; Harvard Univ, MA, 64, PhD(hist), 69. **CAREER** Instr hist, Pace Col, 64-68; from asst prof to prof, 68-74, Full Prof Hist, CA State Col, San Bernardino, 74-, Consult, Los Angeles City Sch Syst, 73-74; Calif State Univ Soc Sci Res Council's Field Inst fel, 82-83; vis prof, Summer Inst, Amerika House, Falkenstein, West Germany, 78; VP/Pres. Elect of the I&EHS, Fulbrights &

India, 83, England, 87-8; & Norway 93. **MEMBERSHIPS** AHA; Orgn Am Historians; Immigration & Ethnic Hist Soc. **RESEARCH** Comparative American ethnic history & contemporary immigration. **SELECTED PUBLICATIONS** ed, Edmund Burke on the American Revolution, Harper, 66; auth, The Emergence of a Whig Persuasion: Conservatism, Democratism, and the New York State Whigs, NY Hist, 10-71; James Barbour (1775-1842), In: Encyclopedia of Southern History, 76; Proximity and Commuting Immigration, In: American Ethnic Revival, 77; French Canadian Americans, In: Harvard Encyclopedia of American Ethnic Groups, 80; The Price of Equality: Comparative American Ethnic History, Prentice-Hall; coauth (with Nikolas Khokhlov), Socio Economic Data Indices of Naturalization Patterns in the United States, A Theory Revisited, Ethnicity, 6/80; auth, Asian & Pacific Migration, Greenwood, 92; Race, Religion, and Nationality in American Society-A Model of Ethnicity-From Contact to Assimilation-Response, J of Am Ethnic Hist, Vol 14, 95; The White Peril-Foreign Relations and Asian Immigration to Australia and North-America, 1919-1978, with S. Brawley, J of Am Hist, Vol 82, 95; And Still They Come, Harland Davidson, 96; Peopling Indiana-The Ethnic Experience, with R. M. Taylor and C. A. McBirney, J of Am Hist, Vol 84, 97; ed., A Nation of Peoples, Greenwood, 99; co-ed, U.S. Immigration & Naturalization Laws and Issues, Greenwood, 99; ed., Making It in America, forthcoming 00, ABC-Clio. **CONTACT ADDRESS** Dept of Hist, California State Univ, San Bernardino, 5500 University Pky, San Bernardino, CA 92407-7500. **EMAIL** ebarkan@csusb.edu

BARKER, LEWIS M.
PERSONAL Born 05/01/1942, York, NE, m, 1981, 4 children **DISCIPLINE** PSYCHOLOGY, NEUROSCIENCE **EDUCATION** Occidental Col, AB, 64; Fla State Univ, MA, 71, PhD, 72. **CAREER** Asst to full prof, Baylor Univ, 72-; past dir, PhD progs in Experimental Psychol, Neuroscience. **HONORS AND AWARDS** Psi Chi Teaching Awds, 5 years; Outstanding Prof, Baylor Univ, 98; Doctoral Graduate Awd of Distinction, Fla State Univ, 98 (1st recipient of 650 grads); Doctoral prog direction, original research, editing books, writing college textbooks. **MEMBERSHIPS** Am Psychol Soc, Psychonomic Soc, Comparative Cognition Soc. **RESEARCH** Appetite, learning, evolutionary psychology. **SELECTED PUBLICATIONS** Coed with M. R. Best and M. Domjan, Learning Mechanisms in Food Selection, Baylor Univ Press, Waco, Tx (77); ed, The Psychobiology of Human Food Selection, AVI Pub, Westport, Ct (82), also pub by Ellis Horwood, Ltd, Chichester (82); auth with C. A. Weaver, "Conditioning flavor preferences in rats: Dissecting the 'medicine effect'," Learning and Motivation, 22 (91): 311-328; auth, Learning and Behavior: Biological, Psychological, and Sociocultural Perspectives, 3rd ed, Upper Saddle River, NJ: Prentice Hall (2001); auth, Psychology, Upper Saddle River, NJ: Prentice Hall (2001). **CONTACT ADDRESS** Dept Psychol & Neurosci, Baylor Univ, Waco, PO Box 97334, Waco, TX 76798. **EMAIL** Lewis_Barker@Baylor.edu

BARLOW, DAVID H.
DISCIPLINE PSYCHOLOGY **EDUCATION** Univ Notre Dame, AB, 64; Boston Col, MA, 66; Univ Vt, PhD, 69. **CAREER** Adj prof, Albany Med Col, 80-96; Dir of Clinical Training, SUNY, 82-96; prof, SUNY, 96-; res prof, Boston Univ, 98-. **HONORS AND AWARDS** Fritz Redlich Fel, 97-98; Awd, Am Psychol Assoc, 00; Awd, Mass Psychol Assoc, 00; Gen Hosp of the Chinese People's Liberation Army, 00; Awd, Calif Psychol Assoc. **MEMBERSHIPS** Assoc for Behav Analysis, Am Psychol Assoc, AAAS, Behav Therapy and Res Soc, Soc for Psychotherapy Res, NY State Psychol Assoc. **RESEARCH** The nature and treatment of anxiety and its disorders. **SELECTED PUBLICATIONS** Coauth, Single case experimental designs: Strategies for studying behavior change, Pergamon Pr, (NY), 84; auth, Anxiety and its disorders: the nature and treatment of anxiety and panic, Guildford Pr, (NY), 88; coauth, Chronic anxiety, generalized anxiety disorder, and mixed anxiety depression, Guilford Publ, (NY) 91; coauth, Mastering stress: A Lifestyle Approach, Am Health Publ Co, (TX), 91; coauth, Mastery of your anxiety and worry: Client workbook, Graywind Publ, (San Antonio, TX), 92; coauth, Casebook in Abnormal Psychology, Brooks/Cole, (CA), 96; coauth, The scientist practitioner: Research and accountability in the age of managed care, Allyn & Bacon, (Needham Heights, MA), 00; ed, Clinical handbook of psychological disorders: A step-by-step treatment manual, Guilford Pr, (NY), in press. **CONTACT ADDRESS** Centre for Anxiety and Related Disorders, Boston Univ, 648 Beacon St, 6th Flr, Boston, MA 02215-2013. **EMAIL** dhbarlow@bu.edu

BARLOW, K. RENEE
DISCIPLINE ANTHROPOLOGY, ARCHAEOLOGY, BEHAVIORAL ECOLOGY **EDUCATION** Brigham Young Univ, BS, 84; Univ Utak, MA, 93, PhD, 97, **CAREER** Mus asst, Brigham Young Univ Mus Peoples and Cultures, 81- 83; Archaeologist, Salt Lake City, 85-90; archaeologist, Northwest Archaeol Consult, Seattle, 96; adj instr, Univ Utah/princ investigator, Univ Archeol Ctr, 93-98; cur collect, Edge of the Cedars Mus, Utah State Div Pks & Rec, 98-. **CONTACT ADDRESS** Edge of the Cedars State Park, 4159 S 570 E, Apt I, Salt Lake City, UT 84107-2043. **EMAIL** NRDPR.rbarlow@state.ut.us

BARLOW, WILLIAM B.
PERSONAL Born 02/25/1943, Fort Rucker, AL, d **DISCIPLINE** EDUCATION **EDUCATION** San Francisco State University, BA, 1968; University of California at Santa Cruz, MA, 1974, PhD, 1983. **CAREER** Mount Vernon College, assistant professor, 76-80; Howard Univ, Prof, 80-. **HONORS AND AWARDS** Schomburg, NEH Fellowship, 1991-92; University of Mississippi, NEH Fellowship, 1986. **MEMBERSHIPS** Union of Democratic Communication, steering committee, 1977-; International Association for Study of Popular Music, steering committee, 1989-; International Association for Mass Communication Research, 1986-. **SELECTED PUBLICATIONS** From Cakewalks to Concert Halls, 1992; co-author with Jan Dates, Split Image: African-Americans in the Mass Media, 1990; Looking Up at Down: The Emergence of Blues Culture, 1989. **CONTACT ADDRESS** Department of Radio/TV/Film, Howard Univ, Washington, DC 20059.

BARMAN, JEAN
PERSONAL Born 08/01/1939 **DISCIPLINE** HISTORY, EDUCATION **EDUCATION** Macalester Col, BA, 61; Harvard Univ, MA, 63; Univ Calif Berkeley, MLS, 70; Univ BC, EdD, 82. **CAREER** Prof, Educational Studies, Univ BC **HONORS AND AWARDS** Can Hist Educ Asn Founders' Prize, 89, 92-93; Can Hist Asn Reg Hist Prize, 92; UBC Alumni Prize Soc Sci, 92; Killam res fel, 92-93; UBC Killam Tchg Prize, 96. **MEMBERSHIPS** Can Hist Asn. **RESEARCH** Canadian Educational and Social History; British Columbia History; Private Education and Canada; Aboriginal Schooling; Qualitative Research Methodology. **SELECTED PUBLICATIONS** Auth, "British Columbia Local Histories: A Bibliography," Victoria: British Columbia Heritage Trust, (91), 196; auth, "The West beyond the West: A History of British Columbia," University of Toronto Press, (91), 429; auth, "History of Canadian Childhood and Youth: A Bibliography," Westport, CT: Greenwood Press, (92), 492; auth, "Contemporary Canadian Childhood and Youth: A Bibliography," Westport, CT: Greenwood Press, (92), 486; auth, "First Nations Eduation in Canada: The Circle Unfolds," Vancouver; UBC Pres, (95), 355; auth, "Children, Teachers and Schools in the History of British Columbia," ed. Barman, J., Sutherland, N. and Wilson, J.D. Calgary: Detselig, (95), 426; auth, "Writing the History of Northern British Columbia," (Lakehead University, 96), 298-335; auth, "I walk my own track in life & no mere male can bump me off it': Constance Lindsay Skinner and the Work of History," in Creating Historical Memory: English-Canadian Women and the Work of History," ed. Beverly Boutilier and Alison, (Prentice Vancouver: UBC Press, 97); auth, "British Columbia: Historical Interpretations," ed. Barman J., McDonald, R.A.J., and Wade J., Burnaby: Open Learning Agency, 97; auth, "Families vs. Schools: Children of Aboriginal Descent in British Columbia Classrooms of the Late Nineteenth Century," ed. Edgar-Andre Montigny and Lori Chambers, Family Matters: Papers in Post-Confederation Canadian Family History, (Toronto: Canadian Scholars' Press, 98), 73-89. **CONTACT ADDRESS** Educ Studies Dept, Univ of British Columbia, Vancouver, BC, Canada V6T 1Z4. **EMAIL** jean.barman@ubc.ca

BARNES, DANIEL RAMON
PERSONAL Born 05/16/1940, Fillmore, NY, m, 1989, 4 children **DISCIPLINE** AMERICAN LITERATURE, FOLKLORE **EDUCATION** St Bonaventure Univ, BA, 62; Univ KS, MA, 66; Univ KY, PhD(English), 70. **CAREER** From instr to asst prof, 68-73, Assoc Prof English, OH State Univ, Columbus, 73-, Consult, Smithsonian Inst Festival of Am Folklore, 71; Asst Prof, 73-95; ed, Motif: Int Newslett Res in Folklore & Lit, 81-; Emeritus Prof, 95-, Visiting Prof, Oberlin College, 97, Ohio U, 98-99. **HONORS AND AWARDS** Invited as 1985 Nordic Institute Lecturer In Folklore; elected Folklore Fel, Finnish Acad Sci and Letters, 90. **MEMBERSHIPS** MLA; Am Folklore Soc; Asn Anthrop Study of Play; Int Soc Folk Narrative Res; Folklore Soc Britain. **RESEARCH** Nineteenth century American literature; folklore and literature; folklore and folklife. **SELECTED PUBLICATIONS** Auth, Ford and the Slaughtered Saints: A New Reading of The Good Soldier, Mod Fiction Studies, summer 68; Folktale Morphology and the Structure of Beowulf, Speculum, 70; Physical Fact and Folklore: Hawthorne's Egotism, or the Bosom Serpent, Am Lit, 71; The Bosom Serpent: A Legend in American Literature and Culture, J Am Folklore, 72; Toward the Establishment of Principles for the Study of Folklore and Lliterature, Southern Folklore Quart, 79; Telling it Slant: Emily Dickinson and the Proverb, Genre, summer 79; auth, "Interpreting Urban Legends," ARV: Sccandinavian Yearbook of Folklore, 84. **CONTACT ADDRESS** Dept of English, Ohio State Univ, Columbus, 164 W 17th Ave, Columbus, OH 43210-1326.

BARON, STEVEN H.
PERSONAL Born 07/29/1961, Norristown, PA, m, 1984, 2 children **DISCIPLINE** PSYCHOLOGY **EDUCATION** Montgomery Co Community Col, AS, 80; **HONORS AND AWARDS** Who's Who of Am Teachers, 00. **RESEARCH** Imagery, sport psychology, pharmacology. **SELECTED PUBLICATIONS** Auth, "Coaching the Athlete, Teaching the Parent," Calif Assoc of Independent Schs Newsletter (86): 11-13; auth, "Anxiety in Youth Sports," Anxiety (97): 3-5; coauth, "Is Depression Associated with IL-2 Treatment?" A Clin Report of Completed Suicide, JAOA (93); coauth, "Algorithm for the Diagnosis and Treatment of Depression," JAOA (93); coauth, "Behavioral Effects of Smoking Cessation of an Adolescent, In-Patient, Psychiatric Unit," JACN (95); coauth, "Recognition and Diagnosis of Depression and Anxiety in the Primary Care Setting," JAOA (95); coauth, "Is Doping Out of Control? Echoes From the Underground," Doping Control Newsletter-USOC (96); coauth, "Pharmacoeconomic Issues in Treating Depression," JAOA (97); auth, "Getting Psyched About Soccer," Touchline (99); auth, "The Coach as a Teacher," Touchline (99). **CONTACT ADDRESS** Dept Soc Sci, Montgomery County Comm Col, PO Box 400, Blue Bell, PA 19422.

BARR, MARLEEN SANDRA
PERSONAL Born 03/01/1953, New York, NY **DISCIPLINE** WOMEN & LITERATURE **EDUCATION** State Univ NYork Albany, BA, 74; Univ MI, MA, 75; State Univ NYork Buffalo, PhD(English), 79. **CAREER** Asst Prof English, VA Polytech Inst & State Univ, 79-, Consult, Educ Testing Serv, 82 & Coun Wis Writers Annual Awards Competition, 82. **MEMBERSHIPS** MLA; Northeast Mod Lang Asn; Popular Cult Asn. **RESEARCH** Science fiction studies; contemporary American literature. **SELECTED PUBLICATIONS** Ed, Future Females: A Critical Anthology, Bowling Green Univ, Popular Press, 81; contribr, The Feminine Eye, 82, Frederick Ungar Co; auth, Science Fiction and the Fact of Women's Repressed Creativity, Extrapolation, spring 82; A Nerw Species-Gender and Science in Science-Fiction, with R. Roberts, Science-Fiction Studies, Vol 20, 93. **CONTACT ADDRESS** Dept English, Virginia Polytech Inst and State Univ, Blacksburg, VA 24061. **EMAIL** mbarr@vt.edu

BARRETT, BARNABY B.
DISCIPLINE CLINICAL PSYCHOLOGY **EDUCATION** Harvard Univ, PhD, 76; Inst Advanced Study of Human Sexology, DHS, 94. **CAREER** Dir, Midwest Inst of Sexology; prof, Wayne State Univ. **RESEARCH** Sexuality; Psychoanalytic Psychology; Anthropology; Cultural Studies. **SELECTED PUBLICATIONS** Auth, Psychoanalysis and The Postmodern Impulse, 93. **CONTACT ADDRESS** Dept of Family Medicine, Wayne State Univ, Detroit, MI 48202. **EMAIL** aa0888@wayne.edu

BARRETT, TRACY
PERSONAL Born 03/01/1955, Cleveland, OH, m, 1983, 2 children **DISCIPLINE** ITALIAN; WOMEN'S STUDIES **EDUCATION** Brown Univ, ABM 76; Univ Calif-Berkeley, MA, 79; PhD, 88. **CAREER** Teaching asst to assoc, Univ Calif-Berkeley, 78-83; Lectr to sr lectr ital, Vanderbilt Univ, 84- . **HONORS AND AWARDS** Ital-Am Fel, 78; Distinguished Teaching Asst, 82; NEH, 94; Harriett S. Billiam Awd Exc Teaching, 96. **MEMBERSHIPS** Am Assn Teachers Ital; Am Coun Teaching For Lang; Auth Guild Soc Children's Book Writers & Illusr. **RESEARCH** Medieval Women Authors, Children's Literature. **SELECTED PUBLICATIONS** Auth, Growing Up in Colonial America, Millbrook Press, 95; auth, "Album Quilts" Quilt World, (96); auth, "Virginia," Celebrate the States, Benchmark Books, (97); auth "Tennessee," Celebrate the States, Benchmark Books, (98); auth, Kidding Around Nashville, John Muir Publ, 98; auth, "Kentucky," Celebrate the States, Benchmark Books, (99); auth, Anna of Byzantium, Bantam Doubleday Dell, 99. **CONTACT ADDRESS** Dept Fr & Ital, Vanderbilt Univ, 2201 W End Ave, Nashville, TN 37235-0001. **EMAIL** tracy.barrett@vanderbilt.edu

BARRETT-LARIMORE, RITA L.
PERSONAL Born 11/30/1961, Richmond, VA, m, 1995, 2 children **DISCIPLINE** PSCYHOLOGY **EDUCATION** Winston-Salem Stave Univ, BA, 84; Univ S Carolina, MA, 87; PhD, 95. **CAREER** Res Assoc, Yale Univ, 98; Lecturer to Asst Prof, Morgan State Univ, 98-. **MEMBERSHIPS** Am Psychol Asn. **RESEARCH** The study of the behavioral pharmacology of CNS stimulants, their interaction with neural processing and the development on animal models of human disease states. **SELECTED PUBLICATIONS** Auth, "Analysis of the discriminative stimulus effects of cocaine and the cocaine analogue WIN 35,428 in rats using cumulative dosing," Dissertation abstracts international, 95; co-auth, "Potentiation of cocaine-like effects of dopamine receptor agonists," Soc for neuroscience abstract, 89; co-auth, "Impact of self-administered cocaine and cocaine cues on extracellular striatal dopamine in rhesus monkeys," Journal of neurochemistry, in press; co-auth, "Pharmacological evaluation of dimethylheptyl analogs of delta-9-THC: reassessment of the putative three-point cannabinoid-receptor interaction," Drug and alcohol dependence, (94): 231-240; co-auth, "Pharmacological and environmental determinants of relapse to cocaine-seeking behavior," Pharmacology, biochemistry and behavior, in press; co-auth, "Discriminative stimulus effects of CP 55,940 and structurally dissimilar cannabinoids in rats," Neuropharmacology, (95): 669-676. **CONTACT ADDRESS** Dept Psychol, Morgan State Univ, 1700 E Cold Springs Lane, Baltimore, MD 21251.

BARRIGA, ALVARO
PERSONAL Born 11/21/1965, Santiago, Chile, m, 1992 **DISCIPLINE** PSYCHOLOGY **EDUCATION** Ohio State Univ, BA, 89; MA, 94; PhD, 96. **CAREER** Psychology Intern, Richalnd Hospital, 93-95; Psychologist, Auberle, 97-; Assoc Prof

of Psychology, Seton Hill Col, 96-. **HONORS AND AWARDS** Univ Minority Fel, 90-91, Graduate Alumni Research Awd, 94-95, Licenced Psychologist, 99-. **MEMBERSHIPS** Am Psychological Assoc, Society for Research in Child Development. **RESEARCH** Social Cognition in Adolescent Psychopathology. **SELECTED PUBLICATIONS** Auth, Measuring cognitive distortion in antisocial youth: Development and preliminary validation of the"How I Think" questionaire, Aggressive Behavior, 22 (96): 333-343; auth, Developing the helping skills and prosocial motivation of aggressive adolescents in peer group programs, Aggression and Violent Behavior, 1 (96): 283-305; auth, Relations between self-serving cognitive distortions and overt vs. covert antisocial behavior in adolescents, Aggressive Behavior, 24 (98): 335-346; auth, Cognitive distortion and problem behaviors in adolescents, Criminal Justice and Behavior, 27 (00): 36-56. **CONTACT ADDRESS** Dept Psychology, Seton Hill Col, 1 Seton Hill Dr, Greensburg, PA 15601. **EMAIL** barriga@setonhill.edu

BARRON, SHEREE S.
PERSONAL Born 06/25/1947, Aragon, GA, d, 3 children **DISCIPLINE** PSYCHOLOGY **EDUCATION** Kennesaw State Univ, BS, 87; Auburn Univ, MS, 91; PhD, 93. **CAREER** Teaching Asst, Auburn Univ, 88-93; Asst Prof to Assoc Prof and Chair, Ga Col & State Univ, 93-. **HONORS AND AWARDS** Phi Kappa Phi Honor Soc, 99; Excellence in Teaching Awd, Ga, 97-98; WhoÛs Who among Am Teachers, 98. **MEMBERSHIPS** Am Psychol Asn, Am Psychol Soc, Asn, for Behavior Analysis, Asn for Women in Psychol, Ga Asn for Women in Educ, SE Psychol Asn, Southern Regional Chapt of Asn for Women in Psychol, SE Asn for Behavior Analysis. **RESEARCH** Teaching of Psychology, Women's Studies Issues, Developmental Disabilities. **SELECTED PUBLICATIONS** Auth, "The effects of peanut butter on ruminating," American Journal of Mental Retardation, (91): 631-645; auth, "Examination of a Mock Jury Trial: Assessing the Deliberation Process", 97; auth, "Variables that Influence Homesickness," 97; auth, "An empirical Evaluation of the Effects of Extra Credit," 97; auth, "Developing an Educational Program for victims of domestic violence," 98; auth, "How Teachers Influence Students," 98; auth, "Alternatives to the Lecture: Peer Teaching in Small Groups," 98; auth, "A Critical Examination of the Use of Independent Studies in USG Schools," 98. **CONTACT ADDRESS** Dept Psychol, Ga Col & State Univ, Campus Box 090, Milledgeville, GA 31061. **EMAIL** sbarron@mail.gcsu.edu

BARRY, BERT
PERSONAL Born 03/11/1954, St Louis, MO, m, 1989, 3 children **DISCIPLINE** ENGLISH AS A SECOND LANGUAGE **EDUCATION** Washington Univ, BA, 76; MA, 80; Saint Louis Univ, PhD, 95. **CAREER** Teacher, Annunciation School, 77-81; instr, Meramac Community Col, 82-97; Dir of Int Svc, Webster Univ, 96-. **MEMBERSHIPS** MLA, NAFSA, Inst of Int Educ, Teachers of Eng to Speakers of Other Lang, Int Educ Counc of St Louis. **RESEARCH** Folktales, Intercultural Communications, Modern and Post-Modern Poetry. **CONTACT ADDRESS** Dept ESL, Webster Univ, 270 E Lockwood Ave, Saint Louis, MO 63119-3194. **EMAIL** barrybe@webster.edu

BARSTOW, ANNE LLEWELLYN
PERSONAL Born 06/22/1929, Jacksonville, FL, m, 1952, 3 children **DISCIPLINE** MEDIEVAL & WOMEN'S HISTORY **EDUCATION** Univ Fla, BA, 49; Columbia Univ, MA, 64, PhD(medieval hist), 78. **CAREER** Asst prof, 70-79, Assoc Prof Medieval Hist, State Univ NY, Col Old Westbury, 79-, Lectr, Relig Dept, NY Univ, 70-73 & Episcopal Divinity Sch, 78. **MEMBERSHIPS** Am Acad Relig; AHA; Inst Res Hist; Feminist Theol Inst. **RESEARCH** Late medieval radical female mysticism: Joan of Arc; history of compulsory celebacy laws for priesthood; the churches' attitudes towards clergy wives. **SELECTED PUBLICATIONS** Auth, Early Goddess Religions, In: An Introductin to the Religion of the Goddess, Seabury Press, 82; Anglican Clergy Wives after the Reformation, In: Women in New Worlds, Vol II, Abingdon Press, 82; Married Priests and the Reforming Papacy: The Eleventh-Century Debates, 82 & Joan of Arc and Radical Mysticism, Edwin Mellen Press; Womens Lives in Medieval Europe-A Sourcebook, E. Amt, ed, Church Hist, Vol 63, 94; The Albigensian Crusades, with J. R. Strayer and C. Lansing, Church Hist, Vol 63, 94; Ways of Lying-Dissimulation, Persecution, and Conformity in Early Modern Europe, with P. Zagorin, Am Hist Rev, Vol 99, 94; Backlash & Excerpts From the Speeches to 1992 Republican National Convention on the Nature, Manifestations and Effects of the Feminist Movement in the Last 30 Years, J of Feminist Studies in Religion, Vol 10, 94; Confession and Community in 17th-Century France-Catholic and Protestant Coexistence in Aquitaine, with G. Hanlon, Church Hist, Vol 64, 95; Women Religious-The Founding of English Nunneries After the Norman Conquest, with S. Thompson, Church Hist, Vol 64, 95; The Oldest Vocation-Christian Motherhood in the Middle Ages, with C. W. Atkinson, Church Hist, Vol 64, 95; Growing Up in Medieval London-The Experience of Childhood in History, with B. A. Hanawalt, Church Hist, Vol 64, 95; From Virile Woman to Womanchrist-Studies in Medieval Religion and Literature, with B. Newman, Church Hist, Vol 65, 96; The Law of the Father-Patriarchy in the Transition From Feudalism to Capitalism, with M. Murray, Am Hist Rev, Vol 102, 97. **CONTACT ADDRESS** 606 W 122 St, New York, NY 10027.

BART, BENJAMIN FRANKLIN
PERSONAL Born 12/21/1917, Chicago, IL, m, 1942, 3 children **DISCIPLINE** FRENCH LITERATURE, LANGUAGE EDUCATION **EDUCATION** Harvard Univ, AB, 38, AM, 46, PhD, 47. **CAREER** Instr Romance lang, Harvard, 47; asst prof, Pomona Col, 47-50; asst prof, Univ MI, 50-56; from assoc prof to prof, Syracuse Univ, 56-67; Prof French, Univ Pittsburgh, 67-, Dir Comp Lit Prog, 74-, Ford Found fel, 52-53; Am Coun Learned Socs grants-in-aid, 60, 61, & 63; Am Philol Soc grant, 74; Camargo Found fel, 81; Nat Endowment for Humanities fel, 81. **MEMBERSHIPS** Am Asn Teachers Fr; MLA. **RESEARCH** French 19th century literature; the teaching of French. **SELECTED PUBLICATIONS** **CONTACT ADDRESS** Dept of French, Univ of Pittsburgh, Pittsburgh, PA 15260.

BARTEL, LEE R.
PERSONAL Born 04/04/1948, Steinbach, MB, Canada **DISCIPLINE** MUSIC EDUCATION **EDUCATION** Univ Man, BA, 73, MEd, 84; Brandon Univ, BMus, 75; Univ Ill, PhD, 88. **CAREER** High sch & univ mus tchr, 69-76; prof & mus dept ch, Steinbach Bible Col, 75-85; dir develop, 86-87, assoc prof & ch music education, Univ Toronto, 87-, founder & dir, Can Mus Educ Res Ctr, 89-. **MEMBERSHIPS** Am Educ Res Asn; Can Univ Mus Soc; Int Soc Mus Educ; Mus Educ Nat Conf; Ont Mus Educ Asn. **RESEARCH** Research methods, evaluation, social psychology, choral music, and alternative methods in secondary music. **SELECTED PUBLICATIONS** Coauth, A Guide to Provincial Music Curriculum Documents since 1980, 93; coauth, Get Into Guitar, 73; ed, A College Looks Forward, 87; ed, Research Perspectives on Music Education (monograph ser); ed, Can J Res Mus Educ, 93-. **CONTACT ADDRESS** Music Educ Div, Univ of Toronto, Toronto, ON, Canada M5S 1A1. **EMAIL** lbartel@eps.utoronto.ca

BARTKOWSKI, JOHN
PERSONAL Born 04/06/1966, Milwaukee, WI **DISCIPLINE** SOCIOLOGY **EDUCATION** St Mary's Univ, BA, 87; Univ Tex, MA, 93; PhD, 97. **CAREER** Teaching Asst to Instr, Univ Tex; Instr to Prof, Miss State Univ. **HONORS AND AWARDS** Nominated for Best Article Awd; Gallagher Awd, Asn for the Sociol of Religion, 95; Who's Who Among Students in am Univ and Col, 88; Marianist Young Scholar Awd, St Mary's Univ, 84-87. **MEMBERSHIPS** Am Sociol Asn, Southwestern Soc Sci Asn **RESEARCH** Sociology of the family; sociology of gender; sociology of religion; social theory; qualitative methodology; cultural sociology. **SELECTED PUBLICATIONS** Auth, Remaking the Godly Marriage: Gender Negotiation in Evangelical Families, Cambridge Univ Press, 00; co-auth, "Distant patriarchs or Expressive dads? The discourse and Practice of Fathering in conservative Protestant families," the sociological quarterly, in press; co-auth, "To Veil or not to Veil? A Case Study of Identity Negotiation among Muslim Women in Austin, Texas," Gender & Society , in press; co-auth, "Breaking Walls, Raising Fences: Masculinity, Intimacy, and accountability among the Promise Keepers," sociology of religion, (00): 121-130; auth, "One step forward, One Step Back: Progressive Traditionalism and the Negotiation of domestic Labor within Evangelical Families," Gender Issues, (990: 40-64; auth, "The Evangelical Family Paradox: conservative Rhetoric, Progressive Practice," the Responsive community, (990: 34-39; co-auth, "Religious Organizations, anti-Poverty relief, and Charitable Choice: A feasibility study of faith-Based Welfare Reform in Mississippi," PricewaterhouseCoopers Endowment, 99; co-auth, "Conservative versus Mainstream Models of Childrearing in Popular Manual," in feuds about the family: conservative, Centrist, Liberal, and feminist perspectives, Prentice Hall, 99; co-auth, "The Conservative Protestant Family paradox: conservative Rhetoric, Progressive practice," The Brookings Review, 99. **CONTACT ADDRESS** Dept Sociol, Mississippi State Univ, PO Box C, Mississippi State, MS 39762. **EMAIL** bartkowski@soc.msstate.edu

BARTLE, ELIZABETH E.
PERSONAL Born 05/27/1953, NE **DISCIPLINE** SOCIOLOGY **EDUCATION** Nebr Wesleyan Univ, 71-73; Univ Nebr at Lincoln, BSW, 76; Univ Nebr at Omaha, MSW, 93; Univ Kans, PhD, 97. **CAREER** Case worker/group home supervisor, Nebr Center for Children & Youth, 75-82; home healthcare worker, Home Services for Independent Living, 83-84; youth counselor, Youth Service System, 87; grad teaching asst, Univ of Nebr at Omaha, 92-93; grad teaching asst & instr, Univ of Kans, 93-94; grad teaching asst, Univ of Kans, 95; adj fac, Ariz State Univ, 97; instr & res specialist, Univ of Ill at Urbana-Champaign, 97-98; asst prof, Calif State Univ at Northridge, 98-. **RESEARCH** Women, welfare and work; lesbians and hate crimes. **SELECTED PUBLICATIONS** Auth, "Exposing and Reframing Welfare Dependency," J of Sociol & Soc Welfare (98); auth, "Lesbians and Hate Crimes," J of Poverty (forthcoming); coauth, "Supporting the Move From Welfare to Work: What Women Say," Affilia (forthcoming); coauth, "An Ethnographic Study of an Empowerment-oriented Family Service Agency (forthcoming). **CONTACT ADDRESS** Dept Sociol, California State Univ, Northridge, 18111 Nordhoff St, Northridge, CA 91330-8318. **EMAIL** elizabeth.bartle@csun.ed

BARTLE-HARING, SUZANNE
PERSONAL Born 03/21/1962, PA, m, 1996, 1 child **DISCIPLINE** HUMAN DEVELOPMENT, FAMILY **EDUCATION** Pa State Univ, BS, 84; Univ Conn, MA, 87; Univ Conn, PhD, 90. **CAREER** Res Assoc, Mayatech Corp, 90; Vis Prof, Va Tech, 91-92; Assoc Prof, Ohio State Univ, 92-. **MEMBERSHIPS** Am Assoc of Marriage and Family Therapists, Nat Coun on Family Rel. **RESEARCH** Distance regulation within the family system as it relates to development. **SELECTED PUBLICATIONS** Coauth, "Family System Dynamics, Identity Development and Adolescent Alcohol Use: Implications for Family Treatment," Family Rel, 38 (89): 258-265; coauth, "A Model of Parenting Style, Adolescent Individuation and Adolescent Self-Esteem," J of Adolescent Res, 4 (89): 283-298; coauth, "Similarity Between Parents' and Adolescents' Levels of Individuation," Adolescence, 26 (91): 913-924; auth, "The Degree of Similarity of Differentiation of Self Between Partners in Dating and Married Couples: Preliminary Evidence," Contemp Family Ther, 15 (93): 467-484. Coauth, "Individuation and Relationship Violence," The Am J of Family Ther, 22 (94): 222-236; coauth, The Behavioral and Emotional Reactivity Index: Preliminary Evidence for Construct Validity from Three Studies," Family Rel, 44 (96): 267-277; coauth, "The Process of Divorce," in Research and Theory in Family Science (Brooks/Cole, 95): 271-283; auth, "Family of Origin and Interpersonal Contributions to the Interdependence of Dating Partners' Trust," Personal Rel, 3 (96): 197-209; auth, "The Relationships Among Parent-Adolescent Differentiation, Sex Role Orientation and Personal Adjustment in Late Adolescence and Early Adulthood," J of Adolescence, 20 (97): 553-565; coauth, "Family Systems in Flux: clinical Implications of Life Span Transitions," in Families Across Time: A Life Course Perspective, (Roxbury, 00). **CONTACT ADDRESS** Dept Human Develop & Family, Ohio State Univ, Columbus, 190 N Oval Mall, Columbus, OH 43210. **EMAIL** bartle.2@osu.edu

BARTLETT, MARIA
PERSONAL Born 11/03/1946, San Francisco, CA, s **DISCIPLINE** SOCIAL WORK **EDUCATION** Univ Ill at Chicago, PhD, 90. **CAREER** Assoc prof, Humboldt Univ, 99-. **HONORS AND AWARDS** Governor's Awd for Teaching Excellence, 97. **MEMBERSHIPS** Soc for Soc Welfare Activism. **RESEARCH** Women, Curricula, Values and Ethics, Aging, Health, International Social Work, Environmentalism. **SELECTED PUBLICATIONS** Auth, Married Widows: The Wives of Men in Long Term Care, Garland Publ, 93; coauth, "Moral Reasoning and Alzheimer's Care: Exploring Complex Weavings Through the Narrative," J of Aging Studies 7.4 (93): 409-421; coauth, "Hispanic Men and Long Term Care: The Wives' Perspective," J of Multicultural/Social Work 3.4 (94): 77-88; auth, "Married Widows: The Wives of Men in Long Term Care," J of Women and Aging 6.1 (94): 91-106; coauth, Teaching Feminist Practice: Support, Transition, Change," Affilia 3.4 (95): 442-457; coauth, "What Happens to Patients After Nursing Home Placement?," Soc Work and Health Care 22.1 (95): 69-79; auth, "A Life Story: Told Through the Voice of Dementia," Reflections: J of the Helping Professions 2.1 (96): 3-5. **CONTACT ADDRESS** Dept Soc Work, Humboldt State Univ, 1 Harpst St, Arcata, CA 95521. **EMAIL** mb20@axe.humboldt.edu

BARTON, BETH
PERSONAL Born 06/25/1966, Washington, DC, m, 1995, 2 children **DISCIPLINE** PSYCHOLOGY **EDUCATION** Ripon Col, BA, 88; Univ Wisconsin, MS 92; PhD, 93. **CAREER** Res prog mgr, Univ Wisconsin, 92-93; res spec, Virginia Med Cen, 94; instr, Coastal Carolina Comm Col, 94-. **HONORS AND AWARDS** Psi Chi, Nat Hon Soc; Phi Sigma Iota, Nat Hon Soc. **MEMBERSHIPS** AERA; APA; STP. **RESEARCH** Educational motivation; smoking cessation. **SELECTED PUBLICATIONS** Coauth, "Psychometric properties and validity of the Obsessive-Compulsive Drinking Scale," Alcoholism: Clin Exper Res (94); coauth, "Development and initial validation of a measure of drinking urges in abstinent alcoholics," Alcoholism: Clin Exper Res 19 (95): 600-606; coauth, "Naltrexone and brief counseling to reduce heavy drinking," Am J Add 3 (94): 91-99; coauth, "Development and initial validation of a measure of alcohol urges in abstinent alcoholics," Bio Psych 35 (94): 693; coauth, "Attitudes of family practice residency program directors toward mandatory preemployment drug testing," Fam Med 29 (97): 625-628. **CONTACT ADDRESS** Dept Humanities, Coastal Carolina Comm Col, 444 Western Blvd, Jacksonville, NC 28546. **EMAIL** bartonb@coastal.cc.nc.us

BARTON, SALLY H.
PERSONAL Born Memphis, TN, 1 child **DISCIPLINE** PSYCHOLOGY **EDUCATION** Univ Ut, BA, 71; MSW, 73; PhD, 78; Brigham Young Univ, PhD, 85. **CAREER** Medical Staff, Utah Valley Reg Medical Center, 85-; Assoc Prof to Prof and Assoc Dean, Brigham Young Univ, 83-. **HONORS AND AWARDS** Diplomat. Am Board of Group Psychol, 99; Fel, Acad of Clinical Psychol, ABPP, 94; Chair, Psychol Licensing Board, State of Utah, 94; Delegate, Asn of State and Provincial Psychology Boards,; Diplomat, Am Board of Professional Psychology, 91. **MEMBERSHIPS** Am Psychol Asn, Am Group Psychotherapy Asn, Utah Psychol Licensing Board **RESEARCH** Group psychotherapy process and outcome research; Women's issues. **SELECTED PUBLICATIONS** Auth, "A

Qualitative examination of Borderline personality (BPD) disordered patient: Interpersonal dynamics and underlying paradoxes," Journal of Personality Disorder, in press; auth, "Therapeutic focusing in time-limited group psychotherapy," Journal of Group dynamics, (97): 254-266; auth, "Origins of BPD: cronus eating his children," Journal of the American Academy of Psychoanalysis, (96): 499-513; auth, "Mormons and psychotherapy," in Handbook on religion and mental health, Academic Press, 98; auth, "Infanticide: When mothers murder," in Lethal Violence: A sourcebook on fatal domestic, acquaintance and stranger aggression, CRC Press, 96; auth, "Women and divorce," in Finding happiness and wholeness after divorce,; Deseret Books, 97; auth, "Psychology as foil to religion: A reformulation of dualism," Dialogue: A Journal of Mormon Thought, (97): 65-72. **CONTACT ADDRESS** Dept Psychol, Brigham Young Univ, PO Box 25543, Provo, UT 84602. **EMAIL** shb@email.byu.edu

BARUCH, ELAINE HOFFMAN
PERSONAL Born New York, NY, 1 child **DISCIPLINE** ENGLISH, WOMEN'S STUDIES **EDUCATION** Queens Col, NYork, BA, 54; Radcliffe Col, MAT, 55; Columbia Univ, PhD(English, comp lit), 66. **CAREER** Lectr English, Queens Col, NY, 60-62 from instr to asst prof, 67-77, Assoc Prof English to prof emer, York Col, NY, 78-, Gen ed, Women's Studies Ser, Everett/Edwards Cassette Curric, 74-. **MEMBERSHIPS** MLA. **RESEARCH** Seventeenth century. **SELECTED PUBLICATIONS** **CONTACT ADDRESS** Dept of English, York Col, CUNY, 150-14 Jamaica Ave, Jamaica, NY 11451.

BARUSCH, AMANDA S.
PERSONAL Born 09/08/1955, Long Beach, CA, m, 1983, 2 children **DISCIPLINE** SOCIAL WORK **EDUCATION** Reed Col, BA, 77; Univ Calif Berkeley, MSW, 81; PhD, 85. **CAREER** Instructor, Univ Guam, 84-85; Asst Prof to Full Prof, Univ Ut, 85-. **HONORS AND AWARDS** Fel, Gerontol Soc of Am; McPhee Awd, 99. **MEMBERSHIPS** Coun on Soc Work Educ. **RESEARCH** Aging; Poverty; Women. **SELECTED PUBLICATIONS** Co-auth, "Characteristics of long-term welfare recipients: Just like you and me?," Social Work, forthcoming; co-auth, "Mental Health Service Utilization Among Frail, Low-Income Elders: Perceptions of Home Service Providers and Elders in the Community," forthcoming; co-auth, "Factors predicting life satisfaction of frail, low income elders," Journal of Gerontology and Social Work; auth, "Serving Older Men: dilemmas and Opportunities," Geriatric Care Management Journal, (00): 31-36; co-auth, "Depressive Symptoms Among the Frail Elderly: Physical and Psycho-social Correlates," International Journal of Aging and Human Development, (99): 107-125; co-auth, "Managed Care: A Critical Overview," Journal of Health and Social Policy, (990: 21-36; auth, "Religion, age and adversity: Religious experiences of low-income, elderly women," Journal of Sociology and Social Welfare, (99): 125-141; auth, "Self-concepts of low-income older women: Not old or poor, but fortunate and blessed," International Journal of Aging and Human Development, (97): 269-282; co-auth, "Spouse caregivers and the caregiving experience: Does cognitive impairment make a difference?," Journal of Gerontological Social Work, (96): 93-106; auth, "Programming for family care: Mandates, incentives and rationing," Social Work, (95): 315-322. **CONTACT ADDRESS** Grad Sch of Soc Work, Univ of Utah, 201 S 1460 E 250S, Salt Lake City, UT 84112. **EMAIL** abarusch@socwk.utah.edu

BASDEN, B. H.
PERSONAL Born 02/10/1940, Coeur d'Alene, ID, m, 1962, 2 children **DISCIPLINE** EXPERIMENTAL PSYCHOLOGY **EDUCATION** UCSB, PhD, 69. **CAREER** Prof, 73-, Cal State Univ. **MEMBERSHIPS** APA; APS; PS. **RESEARCH** Human Memory. **SELECTED PUBLICATIONS** Coauth, Directed Forgetting: A contrast of methods and interpretations, in: JM Goldberg, CM MacLeod, eds, Intl Forgetting: Interdisciplinary Approaches, Lawrence Erlbaum Pub, 98; coauth, Laboratory Experiences in Introductory Psychology, Dubuque IA, Kendall-Hunt Pub, 97; coauth, Study Guide to accompany, Psychology, Forth Edition, by Roedier, Capaaldi, Paris, Polivy, LA, West Pub, 96; Directed Forgetting: A further comparison of the list and item methods, Memory, 96; coauth, Retrievalinhibition in directed forgetting and posthypnotic amnesia, Intl J Clinical and Exper Hypnosis, 94; coauth, Cross language priming in word fragment completion, J Memory and Lang, 94; coauth, A comparison of group and individual remembering: Does group participation disrupt retrieval?, J Exper Psychol, Learning Mem Cognition, 97. **CONTACT ADDRESS** Dept Psychology, California State Univ, Fresno, NYS PH 11, Fresno, CA 93740-8019. **EMAIL** barbb@csafresno.edu

BASKIND, DAVID
PERSONAL Born 01/01/1967, Cleveland, OH, m, 1997 **DISCIPLINE** PSYCHOLOGY **EDUCATION** Miami Univ, BA, 89; Bowling Green State Univ, MA, 92; PhD, 95. **CAREER** Asst prof, Delta Col, 95-. **MEMBERSHIPS** APA, AAUP; APA; CAPA. **SELECTED PUBLICATIONS** Coauth, "Relations among basic processes, beliefs, and performance: A lifespan perspective", Basic and applied memory: Research on practical aspects of memory, eds D. Hermann, M. Johnson, C. McEvoy, C. Hertzog and P. Hertel, Erlbaum (Hillsdale, NJ), 96; coauth, Test bank to accompany 'the Developing Person Through Childhood and Adolescence (Fifth Edition)', Worth Pub, (NY), 00. **CONTACT ADDRESS** Dept Soc Sci, Delta Col, 6263 Mackinaw Rd, University Center, MI 48710-0001. **EMAIL** debaskin@alpha.delta.edu

BASSETT, RODNEY
PERSONAL Born 06/22/1951, Oregon City, OR, m, 1978, 2 children **DISCIPLINE** PSYCHOLOGY **EDUCATION** Seattle Pacific Univ, BA, 73; Ohio State Univ, MA, 75, PhD, 77. **CAREER** Prof, Roberts Wesleyen Col, 77-; contrib ed, J of Psychol and Theology, 89-; bk rev ed, J of Psychol and Christianity, 91-; contrib ed, Res on Christian Higher Ed, 93-. **HONORS AND AWARDS** Univ Fel, Ohio State Univ, 73-77; nominee for a Grad Assoc Teaching Awd, Ohio State Univ, 76; Barbara S. Muller Awd for Teaching Excellence, Roberts Wesleyen Col, 78; Fac Awd for Prof Accomplishments, Roberts Wesleyan Col, 92. **MEMBERSHIPS** Am Psychol Asn, Christian Asn for Psychol Studies, Soc for Personality and Social Psychol, Soc for the Sci Study of Relig. **RESEARCH** Intergration of psychology and Christianity, psychology of religion. **SELECTED PUBLICATIONS** Coauth, with K. Perry, R. Repass, E. Silver, and T. Welch, "Perceptions of God among persons with mental retardation: A research note," J of Psychol and Theol, 22, 45-49 (94); coauth with P. C. Hill, "The ACE model of emotions: Living Jesus Christ while experiencing emotions," J of Psychol and Theol, 26, 232-246 (98); coauth, with H. L. Smith, R. J. Newell, and A. H. Richards, "Thou shalt not like sex: Taking another look at religiousness and sexual attitudes," J of Psychol and Christianity, 18, 205-216 (99); coauth with E. Hodak, J. Allen, D. Bartos, J. Grastorf, L. Sittig, and J. Strong, "Homonegative Christians: Loving the sinner but hating the sin?" J of Psychol and Christianity (in press). **CONTACT ADDRESS** Dept Soc Sci, Roberts Wesleyan Col, 2301 Westside Dr, Rochester, NY 14624. **EMAIL** bassettr@roberts.edu

BATE, BRIAN R.
PERSONAL Born 07/04/1940, Cleveland, OH, d, 2 children **DISCIPLINE** PSYCHOLOGY **EDUCATION** Princeton Univ, 58-61; Western Reserve Univ, Cleveland, OH, AB, 63, MS, 65; Case Western Reserve Univ, PhD, 72. **CAREER** Psychologist/marriage and family counr, 72-96; instr, Cuyahoga Community Col, Western Campus, 69-70, asst prof, 70-73, assoc prof, 73-77, prof, 77-. **HONORS AND AWARDS** Nat Merit Scholar, 58-61 and 62-63; developed and taught the first underclass-level behavior modification course in the USA, 70-77; credited in 18 authors' general psychology texts; listed in: Dictionary of Int Biography, Who's Who Among Human Service Professionals, Marquis' Who's Who in Scci and Engineering, Who's Who in the Midwest, Who's Who in Medicine and Healthcare, Who's Who in America (96-99). **MEMBERSHIPS** Am Psychol Asn, Gestalt Inst of Cleveland, Cuyahoga Community Col Speakers Bureau, Am Fed of Musicians, Edelweiss Ski Club, Cleveland Buddhist Temple. **CONTACT ADDRESS** Cuyahoga Comm Col, Western, 11000 W Pleasant Val, Cleveland, OH 44130-5199.

BATESON, MARY CATHERINE
PERSONAL Born 12/08/1939, New York, NY, m, 1960, 1 child **DISCIPLINE** ANTHROPOLOGY, ENGLISH **EDUCATION** Radcliffe Col, BA, 60; Harvard Univ, PhD, 63. **CAREER** Instr, Harvard Univ, 63-66; asst to assoc prof, Ateneo de Manila Univ, 66-68; sr res fel, Brandeis Univ, 68-69; assoc prof, Northeastern Univ, 69-71; vis lectr, Univ Tehran, 72-74; vis prof, Northeastern Univ, 74-75; prof, Damavand Col, 75-77; dean of social sci and humanities, Univ Northern Iran, 77-79; vis scholar, Harvard Univ, 79-80; prof, Amherst Col, 80-86; dean of fac, Amherst Col, 80-83; vis prof, Spelman Col, 96; Guggenheim fel, 87-88, fieldwork in Israel, 89, Clarence J. Robinson prof, George Mason Univ, 87- ; schlr-in-res, Radcliffe Inst for Adv Studies, Harvard Univ, 00-01. **MEMBERSHIPS** Amer Anthrop Asn; Lindisfarne Asn; Authors Guild, PEN. **SELECTED PUBLICATIONS** Co-ed, Approaches to Semiotics: Indiana University Conference on Paralinguistics and Kinesics, Moulton, 64; auth, Structural Continuity in Poetry: A Linguistic Study of Five Pre-Islamic Odes, Moulton, 70; auth, Our Own Metaphor: A Personal Account of a Conference on the Effects of Conscious Purpose on Human Adaptation, Knopf, 72, 2nd ed, Smithsonian Pr Paperback, 91; auth, With a Daughter's Eye: A Memoir of Margaret Mead and Gregory Bateson, Morrow, 84; co-auth, Angels Fear: Towards an Epistemology of the Sacred, Macmillan, 87; co-auth, Thinking AIDS, Addison-Wesley, 88; auth, Composing a Life, Atlantic Monthly Pr, 89; auth, Peripheral Visions: Learning Along the Way, HarperCollins, 94; auth, Full Circles, Overlaping Lives: Culture and Generation in Transition, Random House, 00. **CONTACT ADDRESS** Dept of Anthrop & English, George Mason Univ, Fairfax, 201 East Bldg, Fairfax, VA 22030-4444. **EMAIL** mcatb@attglobal.net

BATTLE-WALTERS, KIMBERLY
PERSONAL Born 09/04/1967, Los Angeles, CA, s **DISCIPLINE** SOCIOLOGY; SOCIAL WORK **EDUCATION** Southern Calif Col, BA, 89; Temple Univ, MSW, 91; Univ Fla, PhD, 97. **CAREER** Asst prof, Azusa Pac Univ, 97-00. **HONORS AND AWARDS** Black Fac Teaching Fel Awd, Univ Fla, 94-97; Provost Awd Schol & Serv, Azusa Pac Univ, 00. **MEMBERSHIPS** Baccalaureate Soc Work Prog Dir; Am Sociol Asn; Nat Coun Family Rel. **RESEARCH** Race & ethnicities, Ethics & religious issues, Marriage & family/singles, Urban issues, Social work. **SELECTED PUBLICATIONS** Auth, "National coalition of 100 black women/men", The African Encycl Supplement, (NY: Marshall Cavendish), 97; auth, "Transracial adoption", The African Encycl Supplement, (NY: Marshall Cavendish), 97; auth, "Head Start", The African Encycl Supplement, (NY: Marshall Cavendish), 97; auth, "Welfare reform", The African Encycl Supplement, (NY: Marshall Cavendish), 97; auth, "Aid to families with dependent children", The African Encycl Supplement, (NY: Marshall Cavendish), 97; coauth, "They think you ain't much of nothing: The social construction of the welfare mother", Jour of Marriage and the Family 60, (98):849-865; coauth, "Welfare mothers welcome reform, urge compassion", Family Relations 48, (99):197-206; auth, Dispelling the Myth, (00). **CONTACT ADDRESS** Dept Soc Work, Azusa Pacific Univ, 901 E Alosta Ave, Azusa, CA 91702. **EMAIL** KWALTERS@APU.EDU

BAUM, WILLIAM M.
PERSONAL Born 12/08/1939, New York, NY, m, 1980, 5 children **DISCIPLINE** PSYCHOLOGY **EDUCATION** Harvard Col, AB, 61; PhD, 66. **CAREER** Res Fel, Harvard Univ, 67-70; Asst Prof, Harvard Univ, 70-74; From Asst to Full Prof, Univ of NH, 77-99. **HONORS AND AWARDS** Phi Beta Kappa; Sigma Xi; Harvard Col Scholar, 57-61; Nat Sci Found Grad Fel, 62-65; NATO Post-doctoral Fel, 65-66; Nat Sci Found Post-doctoral Fel, 66-67; Res Fel, Harvard Univ, 67-70; NSF Grant, 74, 81, 87; Univ of NH Instructional Develop Grant, 88; Univ NH Fac Scholar Awd, 90; Univ of NH Summer Fel, 87, 90. **MEMBERSHIPS** Animal Behav Soc, Human Behav and Evolution. **RESEARCH** Choice, Foraging, Evolution, Culture. **SELECTED PUBLICATIONS** Auth, Understanding Behaviorism: Science, Behavior, and Culture, Addison-Wesley-Longman (NY), 94; coauth, "Comparing locomotion with lever-press travel in an operant simulation of foraging," J of Exp Analysis of Behav 68 (97): 177-192; auth, "The trouble with time," in Investigations in behavioral epistemology, ed. L.J. Hayes and P.M. Ghezii (Context Press, 97); coauth, "Competition, travel and ideal free distribution," J of Exp Analysis of Behav 69 (98): 227-245; coauth, "Optimality and concurrent variable-interval variable-ratio schedules," J of Exp Analysis of Behav 71 (99): 75-89; coauth, "Choice, contingency discrimination, and foraging theory," J of Exp Analysis of Behav 71 (99): 355-373; coauth, "Choice in variable environment: Every reinforcer counts," J of Exp Analysis of Behav (in press); auth, "Choice of Mating Tactics and Constrained Optimality," Behav and Brain Sci (in press); rev, of Handbook of Behaviorism, ed by William O'Donohue and Richard Kitchener, J of Appl Behav Analysis (in press); coauth, "Behavior analysis, evolutionary theory, and the corporal discipline of children," in Corporal punishment of children in theoretical perspective, ed. M. Donnelly and M. Straus (Yale Univ Press, in press). **CONTACT ADDRESS** Dept Psychology, Univ of New Hampshire, Durham, 125 Technology Dr, Conant Hall, Durham, NH 03824. **EMAIL** wbaum@pacbell.net

BAXTER, LAURIE RAE
DISCIPLINE EDUCATIONAL PHILOSOPHY **EDUCATION** Holland Col Sch Art & Design, AA; Fairhaven Col, BA; W Wash Univ, Med; Ohio State Univ, PhD. **CAREER** Instr, Univ Brit Columbia; Univ Ariz; Ohio State Univ; prof. **RESEARCH** Cross-cultural aesthetics media and film studies. **SELECTED PUBLICATIONS** Past sr ed, contrib, Can Rev of Art Edu: Research and Issues; pub(s), Jour Aesthetic Edu; Stud in Edu; Jour Multi-Cult and Cross-Cult Res in Art Edu. **CONTACT ADDRESS** Dept of Commun and Soc Found(s), Univ of Victoria, PO Box 3045, Victoria, BC, Canada V8W 3P4. **EMAIL** lbaxter@uvic.ca

BEAMAN, MARIAN L.
PERSONAL Born 07/24/1941, PA, m, 1967, 2 children **DISCIPLINE** EDUCATION **EDUCATION** E Mennonite Univ, BA, 63; Univ N Fla, Med, 86. **CAREER** Adj prof to prof, Fla Community Col at Jacksonville, 87-. **HONORS AND AWARDS** Fac Develop Awd, Consortium for Community College Devlop, Ann Arbor, MI, 96; Outstanding Fac Awd Nominee, Fla Community Col, 97, 98. **MEMBERSHIPS** Nat Coun of Teachers of English; Int alliance of Teacher Scholars; Kappa Delta Pi Honor Soc. **RESEARCH** Learning communities, Cooperative Learning in Higher education. **SELECTED PUBLICATIONS** Auth, "Illusion: Parts I and II", Cases on College Teaching and Learning, Fla Community Col, 94; auth, "A Sense-able Approach to Classical Argument, Teaching English in the Two-Year Col, 95. **CONTACT ADDRESS** Dept Humanities and Fine Arts, Florida Comm Col, Jacksonville, 11901 Beach Blvd, Jacksonville, FL 32246-6624. **EMAIL** mbeaman@fccj.org

BEAN, JUDITH M.
PERSONAL Born 01/01/1945 **DISCIPLINE** ENGLISH, WOMEN'S STUDIES **EDUCATION** Sam Houston State Univ, BA, 62; MA, 88; Texas A and M Univ, PhD, 92. **CAREER** Lectr, Texas A and M Univ, 92-93; vis prof, Prairie View A and M Univ, 93-94; assoc prof, Tex Woman's Univ, 94-. **HONORS AND AWARDS** Who's Who Among Ameri-

ca's Teachers, 96, 98. **MEMBERSHIPS** MLA, Margaret Fuller Soc, Ling Asn of the SW, Soc for the Study of Am Women Writers, CCC. **RESEARCH** American Women's Literature, Women's Discourse and Rhetoric, Sociolinguistics. **SELECTED PUBLICATIONS** Auth, "The Evolution of the Inchoatives 'Go to' and 'Get to,'" SECOL Rev, 91; auth, "Gender, Politeness and Discourse Management in Same-sex and Cross-sex Opinion-Poll Interviews," Jour of Pragmatics (92); auth, "True Grit and All the Rest: The Expression of Regional and Individual Identity in Molly Ivin's Discourse," Southwestern Am Lit, (93); coauth, "Workplace Reasons for Saying You're Sorry: Discourse Management and Apology," Discourse Processes, (94); auth, "Texts From Conversation: Margaret Fuller's Influence on Emerson," Studies in the Am Renaissance, (94); auth, "Conversations as Rhetoric in Margaret Fuller's Woman in the Nineteenth Century," In Her Own Voice: Nineteenth-Century American Women Essayists, (97); coauth, "Self-Expression and Linguistic Variation," Language in Society, (97); auth, "A Presence Among Us: Margaret Fuller's Place in nineteenth-Century Oratorical Culture," Fuller's Cultural Critique: Her Age and Legacy, (98); auth, "Margaret Fuller and Julia Ward Howe: A Woman-to-Woman Influence," (99); coed, Margaret Fuller, Critic: Writings from the New York Tribune, 1844-1846, 00. **CONTACT ADDRESS** Dept English, Speech and For Lang, Texas Woman's Univ, Denton, TX 76204-5829. **EMAIL** jbean@twu.edu

BEAN, SUZANNE M.
PERSONAL Born 12/02/1957, Greenwood, MS, m, 1989, 2 children **DISCIPLINE** EDUCATION **EDUCATION** Delta State Univ, BS, 79; Univ Southern Miss, MEd, 86; PhD, 89. **CAREER** Teacher, Miss, 79-84; Admin Asst, Univ Southern Miss, 85-89; asst prof to prof, Miss Univ for Women 90-. **HONORS AND AWARDS** Fac Member of the Year, Miss Univ for Women, 97-98. **SELECTED PUBLICATIONS** Coauth, Girls and Young Women Leading the Way; coauth, Girls and Young Women Inventing; coauth, Girls and Young Women Entrepreneurs, coauth, Leadership for Students: A Practical Guide; coauth, Adventures and Challenges: Real Life Stories by Girls and Young Women. **CONTACT ADDRESS** Educ and Human Sci, Mississippi Univ for Women, 1100 College St, W-Box 1637, Columbus, MS 39701.

BEATIE, BRUCE A.
PERSONAL Born 03/04/1935, Oakland, CA, m, 1990, 2 children **DISCIPLINE** MEDIEVAL, FOLK, AND POPULAR LITERATURE **EDUCATION** Univ Calif, Berkeley, AB, 59; Univ Colo, MA, 60; Harvard Univ, PhD(comp lit), 67. **CAREER** Asst prof Ger, Univ Colo, 64-67, asst prof Ger & comp lit, 67-68; assoc prof, Univ Rochester, 68-70; chmn, Dept Mod Lang, 70-77, Prof Ger,Cleveland State Univ, 70-88, Prof Comp & Medieval Studies, 89-. **HONORS AND AWARDS** Germanistic Society of Am, fel, 63-64; Nat Endowment for Humanities younger scholar fel, 70. **MEMBERSHIPS** Midwest MLA; AAUP, Sci Fiction Res Assoc, Int Arthurian Soc. **RESEARCH** Medieval comparative literature; popular and traditional narrative; folklore. **SELECTED PUBLICATIONS** Auth, Arthurian films and Arthurian texts: problems of reception and comprehension, Arthurian Interpretations, Spring 88; Arthur C. Clarke and the alien encounter: The background of Childhood's End, Extrapolation, Spring 89; E.E. Smith, In: Twentieth Century Science Fiction Writers, 3rd ed, St. James, 91; The broken quest: the Perceval romances of Chretien de Troyes and Eric Rohmer, In: The Arthurian Revival: Essays on Form, Tradition, and Transformation, Garland, 92; coauth, Reflected images in two Mexican poems of 1957: Piedra de sol by Octavio Paz and Misterios gozosos by Rosario Castellanos, Revista / Review Interamericana 26, 96; author of several other articles. **CONTACT ADDRESS** Dept of Mod Lang, Cleveland State Univ, 1983 E 24th St, Cleveland, OH 44115-2440. **EMAIL** b.beatie@popmail.csuohio.edu

BEAUCHAMP, HEATHER
PERSONAL Born 04/03/1970, Hudson, NY, m, 1994, 1 child **DISCIPLINE** PSYCHOLOGY **EDUCATION** SUNY, PhD. **CAREER** Asst Prof, State Univ NYork (SUNY). **HONORS AND AWARDS** Fac-Student Summer Grant. **MEMBERSHIPS** APA. **RESEARCH** False memories. **SELECTED PUBLICATIONS** Coauth, "Teachers' Attitudes and Policies Regarding Children's Play," Psychol in the Schs, 33 (96): 61-69. **CONTACT ADDRESS** Dept Psychol, SUNY, Col at Potsdam, 44 Pierrepont Ave, Potsdam, NY 13676.

BEAUDRY, MARY CAROLYN
PERSONAL Born 11/25/1950, Great Lakes, IL **DISCIPLINE** HISTORICAL ARCHAEOLOGY, ANTHROPOLOGY, MATERIAL CULTURE STUDIES **EDUCATION** Col William & Mary, BA, 73; Brown Univ, MA, 75; PhD, 80. **CAREER** Assoc Prof Archaeol, Boston Univ, 90-; Dir, Spencer-Peirce Little Archaeol Proj, Newbury, MA, 86. **HONORS AND AWARDS** Recipient of three grants for the Nat Endowment for the Humanities; NEH fel for Advanced Study at Winterthur Mus and Libr, 94-95. **MEMBERSHIPS** Council for Northeast Hist Archaeol; Soc Hist Archaeol (pres, 89); Soc Indus Archaeol; Soc Post-Medieval Archaeol; Registry of Prof Archaeol; World Archaeol Congress. **RESEARCH** Historical archaeol of landscapes and households; comparative colonialism; culture contact; minorities and women; ceramic analysis and typologies; foodways; method and theory; public outreach. **SELECTED PUBLICATIONS** Coauth, Living on the Boott: Historical Archaeology at the Boott Mills Boardinghouses, Lowell, Massachusetts, Univ MA Press, 86; ed, Documentary Archaeology in the New World, Cambridge Univ Press, 88; coed, The Art and Mystery of Historical Archaeology, CRC Press, 92. **CONTACT ADDRESS** Dept of Archaeol, Boston Univ, Boston, MA 02215. **EMAIL** beaudry@bu.edu

BECHTEL, ROBERT
PERSONAL Born 10/19/1932, Pottstown, PA, m, 1972, 2 children **DISCIPLINE** PSYCHOLOGY **EDUCATION** Susquehanna Univ, BA, 62; Univ Kansas, MA, 65; PhD, 67. **CAREER** Inst Comm Stud, 65-69; GKS Men Health Found, 69-74; Environ Res Devel Found, 74-80; Univ Ariz, 76-. **HONORS AND AWARDS** Fel APA; Environ Des Res Asn Awd. **MEMBERSHIPS** APA; AAA; EDRA. **RESEARCH** Ecological and environmental psychology. **SELECTED PUBLICATIONS** Auth, Environment and Behavior: An Introduction, Sage Pub (97); coauth, Methods in Environmental and Behavioral Research, Van Nostrand (89); auth, Enclosing Behavior, Dowd Hutchinson and Ross (79). **CONTACT ADDRESS** Dept Psychology, Univ of Arizona, PO Box 210068, Tucson, AZ 85721-0068.

BECHTOLD, BRIGITTE
PERSONAL Born 04/27/1946, Braunschweig, Germany, m, 1989, 2 children **DISCIPLINE** SOCIOLOGY, ANTHROPOLOGY **EDUCATION** Univ Brussels, Belgium, LIC, 67; Mich State Univ, MA, 70; Univ Pa, PhD, 82. **CAREER** Senior Economist, Minimum Wage Study Commission, 79-81; prof, Central Mich Univ, 82-. **HONORS AND AWARDS** Ontario Grad Fel, 70-72; Fel, Univ of Pa, 72-75; Alan Warehime Distinguished Prof, Susquehamma Univ, 87-88; Phi Beta Delta, Pi Del Tau Phi, Kappa Hu Epsilon, Omicron Delta Epsilon. **MEMBERSHIPS** Union for Radical Polit Econ; Int Assoc for Feminist Econ, Int Virginia Wolf Soc. **RESEARCH** Game theory, gender and labor markets, infanticide, methodology in economics. **SELECTED PUBLICATIONS** Auth, "A Methodologist's Econometric Model Selection" Int Advances in Econ Res I.2 (95):119-128; auth, "Gunnar Myrdal" in An Encycl of Keynesian Econ, ed Thomas Cate, Geoff Harcourt and David C. Colander, Edward Elgar Pub, (96):495-462; auth, Economy and Society: the Long View of Economic Ideas and Institutions, Stipes Pub (Champaign, IL), 96; rev, of "Bringing It All Back Home: Class, Gender and Power in the Modern Household" by Fraad, Resnick and Wolff, Rev of Radical Polit Econom 28.4 (96): 148-151; coauth, "Endogenous Generation of Parenting Preferences by Interaction of an Internal and an External Game", Rev of Radical Polit Econ, 30.3 (98); coauth, "Social Services for Immigrant Women in European Nations: Lessons from the Council of Europe's Project on Human Dignity and Social Exclusion" in Gender, Migration and Public Policy, eds Gregory Kelson and Debra DeLaet, New York Univ Pr and Macmillan Pub, (99), 198-212; rev, of "Fondements et Limites du Capitalisme" by Louis Gill, Rev of Radical Polit Econ, 31.2 (99):8-11; auth, "The practice of Econometrics: A Feminist Critique, Rev of Radical polit Econ, 31.3 (99):40-52; auth, "The European Economy at Century's End", Rev of Radical Polit Economics, (forthcoming); auth, "Infanticide in 19th Century France: A Quantitative Interpretation", Rev of Radical Polit Econom (forthcoming). **CONTACT ADDRESS** Dept Sociol and Anthrop, Central Michigan Univ, 137 Anspach Hall, Mount Pleasant, MI 48859-0001. **EMAIL** brigitte.h.bechtold@cmich.edu

BECK, LOIS
PERSONAL 1 child **DISCIPLINE** ANTHROPOLOGY **EDUCATION** Portland State Univ, BA, 67; Univ Chicago, MA, 69; PhD, 77. **CAREER** Asst prof, Amherst Col, 73-76; asst prof, Univ Utah, 76-80; assoc prof to prof, Washington Univ, 80-. **HONORS AND AWARDS** Sigma Xi; Fulbright-Hays Fac res Gnt; NEH; SSRC. **MEMBERSHIPS** MESA; SIS. **RESEARCH** Anthropological research in Iran; nomadic pastoralism; tribe-state relationships; Islam and politics; gender. **SELECTED PUBLICATIONS** Co-ed, Women in the World, Harvard Univ Press (78); auth, The Qashqa'I of Iran, Yale Univ Press (86); auth, Nomad: A Year in the Life of a Qashqa'I Tribesman in Iran, Univ Cal Press (91). **CONTACT ADDRESS** Dept Anthropology, Washington Univ, 1 Brookings Dr, Box 1114, Saint Louis, MO 63130-4862. **EMAIL** lbeck@artsci.wustl.edu

BECK, SYLVEN S.
PERSONAL Born 12/04/1949, New York, NY, d, 1 child **DISCIPLINE** EDUCATION **EDUCATION** Marymount Manhattan Col, BA, 72; City Col, SUNY, MS, 74; George Washington Univ, EdE, 81. **CAREER** Instr, George Washington Univ, 80-81, asst prof/dir, 81-92, assoc prof/dir, 92-. **HONORS AND AWARDS** Grad Res Awd, 81; Philanthropy Awd, 91; Sylven Seid Beck Endowment Fund for Elem Ed, 96. **MEMBERSHIPS** Nat Asn Asian & Pacific Am Eds, AERA, ATE, Nat Science Teachers Asn. **RESEARCH** Diversity issues, clinical supervision, elementary science education. **SELECTED PUBLICATIONS** Coauth with D. Wizer, "Using online discussions to study diversity," J of Computing in Teacher Ed, 13, 1 (96): 6-11. **CONTACT ADDRESS** Dir, Elem Ed, The George Washington Univ, 2134 G St NW, Room 406, Washington, DC 20052. **EMAIL** sbeck@gwu.edu

BECKER, GARY J.
PERSONAL Born 04/20/1931, Atlantic City, NJ, m, 1976, 3 children **DISCIPLINE** EDUCATION **EDUCATION** Trinity Christian Col, AB, 73; Calvin Theol Sem, MDiv, 81; Mich State Univ, PhD, 91. **CAREER** Missionary, Christina Reformed World Missions, 77-84; Assoc prof, Gordon-Conwell Theol Sem, 86-95; Prof and Acad Dean, Calvin Theol Sem, 95-. **HONORS AND AWARDS** Am Bible soc Awd, Calvin Theol Sem; Hinman Grad Fel, Mich State Univ; Phi Kappa Phi, 86; Two Thousand Notable Am Men 2nd ed, 94. **MEMBERSHIPS** Am Soc of Missiol, Evangelical Missiol Soc, N Am Prof of Christian Educ. **RESEARCH** Intercultural relations; Philosophy of Education; Missions, history and theology. **SELECTED PUBLICATIONS** Rev, of "Bill Wallace of China," by Jesse Fletcher, Church History, in press; auth, "Disciple, Follower," in Baker dictionary of Christian Education, in press; auth, "The Christian Reformed Church and World Cultures," Calvin Seminary forum, (99): 6-7; auth, "Trusting Enough to Rest," The New Bethesda Bulletin, (98): 2-3; rev, of "Models of the Kingdom," by Howard Snyder, Missiology, (96): 129; co-auth, "Engaging the Other in a Global Village," Theological Education: Supplement 1 Fundamental Issues in Globalization, (90): 52-85. **CONTACT ADDRESS** Dept Pastoral Ministry, Calvin Theol Sem, 3233 Burton St SE, Grand Rapids, MI 49546-4301.

BECKER-SLATON, NELLIE FRANCES
PERSONAL Born 08/31/1921, Providence, RI, m, 1950 **DISCIPLINE** EDUCATION **EDUCATION** NYork Univ, BS Occup Therapy 1946; CA State Clge at Los Angeles, Tchrs Credential 1952; Pepperdine Univ, MA 1975; Claremont Grad Schl, PhD 1988. **CAREER** Hines VA Hosp in Chicago IL, Sawtelle VA Hosp in Los Angeles CA, occup therapist 1947-50; CA Eagle, family edit 1948-51; Pittsburgh Courier, contrib writer 1951-52; LA Unified Sch Dist Reg D, multicultural adult educ tchr 1972-77; Frances Blend School for Visually Handicapped, sci coord 1973-75; Westminster Elem Sch, multicultural coord 1978-79; Walgrove Elem Sch and Charnock Elem Sch, intgrtn coord 1979-80; LA Unified Sch Dist, educ prof writer; Westminster Elementary, 80-. **HONORS AND AWARDS** Resolution comm work LA City Cncl 1985; Women of the Year LA Sentinel Newspaper 1962; author writers award Our Authors Study Club 1966; comm work Natl Assc for coll Women; Sci Authors Radio Station KDAY 1965; comm work Westminster Presb 1973; Senate Resolution State of California 199. **MEMBERSHIPS** Dir Comm Sci Workshops 1960-69; former pres Intl Scribbles West 1960-65; Chap 587 Council for Excep Children; former bd mem LA Reading Assn; Amer Folklore Soc; LA CA Genealogical Soc; EDUCARE; Linguistics Soc of Amer; Alpha Kappa Alpha Sor; co-founder Doctoral Support Group 1982; mem Western Folklore Soc, NAPPS and SCC-LYP; Afro-Amer Genealogical Soc of Southern California; Los Angeles Urban League; co-founder, pres Association of Pan African Doctoral Scholars 1981-92; Daughters of American Revolution; Hollywood Chapter of California, 1996 . **SELECTED PUBLICATIONS** author Bacteria and Viruses Prentice Hall; author On My Own Harcourt Brace-Jovanovich. **CONTACT ADDRESS** Los Angeles Unified Schl Dist, 1010 Abbot Kinney Blvd, Venice, CA 90291.

BEEVI, MARIAM
PERSONAL s **DISCIPLINE** LITERATURE, WOMEN'S STUDIES **EDUCATION** Univ Calif Irvine, BA, 94; MA, 96; PhD, 00. **MEMBERSHIPS** MLA, AAAS, AAS. **RESEARCH** Diaspora, Visual Studies, Psychoanalysis, Sexuality. **SELECTED PUBLICATIONS** Auth, "The Passing of Literary Traditions: The Figure of the Woman from Vietnamese Nationalism to Vietnamese American Transnationalism," Amerasia Jour 23.2 (97): 27-53. **CONTACT ADDRESS** Dept English, Univ of California, Irvine, 435 Hum Instructional Bldg, Irvine, CA 92697-0001. **EMAIL** mbeeri@uci.edu

BELKNAP, JOANNE
PERSONAL Born 05/08/1958, Denver, CO, p, 1991, 1 child **DISCIPLINE** SOCIOLOGY **EDUCATION** Univ Colo, BA, 81; Mich State Univ, MS, 83; PhD, 86. **CAREER** Asst prof to assoc prof, Univ Cincinnati, 86-98; assoc prof, Univ Colo, 98-. **HONORS AND AWARDS** Teaching Awd, Univ Cincinnati, 96; Col of Educ Service Awd, Univ Cincinnati, 91; Univ Cincinnati's Racial Awareness Pilot Project Fac Awd, 90; Distinguished Scholar Awd, Am Soc of Criminol, 97; Elizabeth Moen "Walk the Talk" Awd, Univ Colo, 00. **MEMBERSHIPS** Am Soc of Criminol. **RESEARCH** Feminist Criminology (women and girls as victims and offenders). **SELECTED PUBLICATIONS** Auth, "Women in Conflict: An Analysis of Women Correctional Officers," in The Criminal Justice System and Women, 2nd ed, (McGraw-Hill, 95), 404-420; co-auth, "Understanding incarcerated Girls: The Results of a Focus Group Study," Prison J, (97): 381-404; co-auth, "High School Students' Adherence to Rape Myths and the Effectiveness of High School Rape Awareness Programs," Violence Against Women, Vol 4, (98): 308-328; co-auth, "In Their Own Words: Battered Women's Assessment of Systemic Responses," Violence and Victims, (98): 3-20; co-auth, "Police Responses to Battering in a Pro-Arrest Jurisdiction," Justice Quart, (99): 249-273; auth, The Invisible Woman: Gender, Crime, and Justice, 2nd ed, Wadsworth Pub Co, 01. **CONTACT ADDRESS** Dept Sociol, Univ of Colorado, Boulder, 219 Ketchum Hall, Campus Box 327, Boulder, CO 80309. **EMAIL** joanne.belknap@colorado.edu

BELL, BARBARA MOSALLAI
PERSONAL Born 11/19/1937, Indianapolis, IN, m, 1975, 3 children **DISCIPLINE** PSYCHOLOGY **EDUCATION** PhD 63, MA 59, Univ of Tehran. **CAREER** Prof Psychol Univ of Iran, Therapist, Private Practice, Houston, Writer. **MEMBERSHIPS** Writer's Guild of Las Vegas, Intl Wonens Writers Guild. **RESEARCH** Psychol-in most all fields. **SELECTED PUBLICATIONS** Auth of,The Peacock Princess, 95; True Story of my Life in Iran. **CONTACT ADDRESS** 3001 Lake East Dr Apt 1137, Las Vegas, NV 89117. **EMAIL** B. Bell26846@AOL.com

BELL, DIANE
PERSONAL Born 06/11/1943, Melbourne, Australia, d, 2 children **DISCIPLINE** ANTHROPOLOGY **EDUCATION** Frankstons Tchr Col, Victoria, TPTC, 61; Monash Univ, Victoria, BA, 76; Australian Nat Univ, PhD, 81. **CAREER** Henry R Luce Prof Relig, Econ Develop & Soc Justice, Holy Cross Col, 89-98; dir Womens Stud Prog & Prof Anthrop, George Wash Univ, 99-; **HONORS AND AWARDS** Finalist Staley Awd **MEMBERSHIPS** Am Anthrop Asn; Am Acad Relig; Australian Anthrop Soc; Australian Inst Aboriginal & Torres Straits Is Stud. **RESEARCH** Indigenous peoples; Land rights; Law reform; Radical Feminist theory and practice; Human rights; Comparative religion. **SELECTED PUBLICATIONS** Auth, Daughters of the Dreaming, Univ Minn Press, 83; coed Gendered Fields: Women, Men & ethnography, Routledge, 93; coed Radically Speaking: Feminism Reclaimed, Spinifex Press, 96; Ngarrindjeri Wurruwarrin: A World that is, was, and will be, Spinifex Press, 98. **CONTACT ADDRESS** Women's Studies Prog, The George Washington Univ, Funger Hall, Rm 506-J, Washington, DC 20052. **EMAIL** dbell@gwu.edu

BELL, KATIE ROBERSON
PERSONAL Born 06/14/1936, Birmingham, AL, m **DISCIPLINE** EDUCATION **EDUCATION** AL State Coll, BS 1956, EdS 1977; Wayne State Univ, MSLA 1973; Univ of AL, PhD 1982. **CAREER** Tuskegee Inst HS, librarian 56-59; Parker HS, asst librarian 59-70, librarian 70-73; AL State Univ, asst ref lib 73-74, coord of user serv 74-75, coord lib educ 75-; So AL Reg Inserv Educ Ctr, dir, 85; AL State Univ, Prof of Lib Educ, 85-. **HONORS AND AWARDS** Cert of Honor Birmingham Classroom Teachers Assoc 1970; Educator of the Year Area of Instructional Leadership/ Univ of AL 1981; Identification of Activities in Staff Capstone Journal 1982; Development Progs for Secondary Educ Teachers. **MEMBERSHIPS** Consultant ESAA Task Force ASU & Mobile Sch System 1979-82; Comm Tutorial Prog/Links Inc 1982-84; evaluator Natl Council for the Accreditation of Teacher Educ 1983-; bd mem pres elect AL Instructional Media Assoc 1984-; counselor Nu Epsilon Chap Kappa Delta Pi 1984-; evaluator S Assn of Schs & Colls 1985-; bd mem Montgomery Comm Council of the United Way 1985-; area director, The Links, Inc., southern area director, 1991-94. **CONTACT ADDRESS** Library Educ, Alabama State Univ, 915 S Jackson St, Montgomery, AL 36195.

BELL, LINDA
PERSONAL Born 07/12/1944, Austin, TX, m, 1965, 3 children **DISCIPLINE** PSYCHOLOGY **EDUCATION** Oberlin Col, BA, 67; Univ Tex Austin, MA, 68; Duke Univ, PhD, 73. **CAREER** Peace Corps, 68-70; prof, Univ of Houston Clear Lake, 76-; vis res, Nat Inst of Mental Health in Japan, 85-87. **HONORS AND AWARDS** Grant, NIMH, 76-77, 77-83; Res Grant, Hogg Found for Mental Health, 78-82; Awd for Contr to Family Therapy in Tex; Res Awd Res Fund, Japanese Min of Health and Welfare, 87-89; Res Grant, Univ of Houston Clear Lake, 88-98. **MEMBERSHIPS** Am Psychol Assoc; Nat Counc on Family Rel; Am Family Therapy Acad; Am Assoc for Marriage and Family Therapy. **RESEARCH** Family process and individual development - U.S. and Japan. **SELECTED PUBLICATIONS** Coauth, "Family climate and the role of the female adolescent: Determinants of adolescent functioning" in Family Studies Yearbook Vol II, ed D.H. Olson and B.C. Miller (Beverly Hills: Sage, 84), 295-303; coauth, "Peer relationships of adolescent daughters: A reflection of family relationship patterns: Family Relations 37 88): 171-174; coauth, "Micro and Macro measurement of family systems concepts", Family Psychol 3, (89): 137-157; coauth, "Experienced closeness and distance among family members", Contemporary Family Therapy 13, (91): 231-245; coauth, "Family functioning of adolescents' families: Studies of assessment of family health", Japanese Jof Family Therapy 8, (91): 40-53; auth, "Comparison: Western and Japanese Therapists", Japanese Jof Psychotherapy 17, (91): 328-332; auth, "Song without words", in The Evolving Therapist, eds R. Simon, C. Barrilleaus, M.S. Wylie and L.M. Markowitz, (NY: Guildford, 92): 48-53; coauth, Connection and individuality in Japan and the United States, Gender, culture and conception of family health", Jof Gender, Culture and Health 1 (96): 277-294; auth, "Start with Meditation", in 101 More Interventions in Family Therapy, ed t. Nelson and T. Tepper, (NY: Haworth, 98): 52-56; coauth, "Japanese and U.S. marriage experiences", Jof Comp Family Studies 32, 00. **CONTACT ADDRESS** Dept Human Sci, Univ of Houston, 2700 Bay Area Blvd, Houston, TX 77058-1098. **EMAIL** belllinda@cl.uh.edu

BELL, LINDA A.
PERSONAL Born 08/06/1940, Daytona Beach, FL **DISCIPLINE** FEMINIST THEORY, EXISTENTIALISM, ETHICS, CONTINENTAL PHILOSOPHY **EDUCATION** Emory Univ, PhD, 73. **CAREER** Prof, Ga State Univ. **SELECTED PUBLICATIONS** Auth, Visions of Women; Sartre's Ethics of Authenticity; Rethinking Ethics in the Midst of Violence: A Feminist Approach to Freedom. **CONTACT ADDRESS** Georgia State Univ, Atlanta, GA 30303. **EMAIL** wsilab@langate.gsu.edu

BELL, REVA PEARL
PERSONAL Born 08/17/1925, Marshall, TX, m **DISCIPLINE** EDUCATION **EDUCATION** Bishop Coll, BS 1947; TX Christian Univ, MEd 1965; TX Woman's Univ, PhD 1980. **CAREER** Ft Worth Public Schools, teacher, curriculum writer, curriculum content analyst, head teacher early childhood learning center; SW Educ Devel Lab, curriculum coord; TX Christian Univ, instructor. **HONORS AND AWARDS** Concepts & lang prog co-author SW Educ Devel Lab 1974; Getting Started co-author Natl Educ Lab Publishers 1975; Natl Sic Found Grant N TX State Univ. **MEMBERSHIPS** Consult SW Educ Devel Lab; consult Indian & Migrants Div OCD; consult Early Childhood Parent Prog; treas/bd of dirs Winnie-the-Pooh Day Care Ctr 1978-79; day care ctr educ chairperson task force Amer Heart Assn 1979-; Curriculum Guide for Early Childhood Ft Worth Pub Schs 1972. **CONTACT ADDRESS** Texas Christian Univ, 2900 S University Dr, Fort Worth, TX 76129.

BELL, SUSAN GROAG
PERSONAL Born, Czechoslovakia **DISCIPLINE** HISTORY OF WOMEN **EDUCATION** Stanford Univ, AB, 64; Univ Santa Clara, MA, 70. **CAREER** Adj lectr, Univ Santa Clara, 71-81; Lectr Hist, Stanford Univ, 82-, Senior scholar, Instr, Res on Women & Gender, Stanford Univ, 78-. **MEMBERSHIPS** AHA; Conf British Studies; Coord Comt Women in the Hist Profession; Western Asn Women Historians; Garden Hist Soc. **RESEARCH** European and British women's intellectual history; history of women as gardeners; history of women and literacy. **SELECTED PUBLICATIONS** Auth, Christine de Pizan, 1364-1430: Humanism and the Problem of a Studious Woman, Feminist Studies, 76; Lady Warwick: Aristocrat, Socialist Gardener, San Jose Studies, 82; Medieval Women Bookowners: Arbiters of Lay Piety and Ambassadors of Culture, Signs: J of Women in Culture and Soc, 82; coauth, Women, the Family and Freedom: 1750-1950; The Debate in Documents, 2 Vols, Stanford Univ Press; coauth, Revealing Lives: Autobiography, Biography and Gender, Albany, NY, State Univ of New York press, 90;' auth, Between Worlds, In Cxechoslovakia, England and Americ: A Memoir, New York, E P Dutton/William Abrahams 91; auth, " A Lost Tapestry: Margaret of Savoy's "Cite Des Dames," Une Femme de Lettres au Moven Age: Etudes autour de Christine De Pizan, Orleans , France, Editions paradigme, 95; auth, "A New Approach to the Influence of Christine de Pizan: The Lost Tapestries of "The City of Ladies," Actes du colloque d' Orleans, Juillet 1995, Etudes christiniennes, vol 3, Paris, Honore Champion, (98): 7-11; auth, "Vanessa's Garden," Singular Continuities, Stanford Univ Press, 00. **CONTACT ADDRESS** Inst for Research on Women and Gender, Stanford Univ, Stanford, CA 94305-8640. **EMAIL** groagbel@stanford.edu

BELLAMY, EVERETT
PERSONAL Born 12/29/1949, Chicago, IL, d **DISCIPLINE** EDUCATION **EDUCATION** University of Wisconsin, BS, 1972, MS, 1974; Cleveland State University, JD, 1980; Cleveland-Marshall Col of Law. **CAREER** University of Wisconsin, graduate assistant; Cleveland State University, coordinator of student activities; Charles Hamilton Houston Pre-Law Institute, instructor and assistant executive director; Georgetown University Law Center, assistant dean, adjunct professor. **HONORS AND AWARDS** Honors Cert, Montgomery County, MD, 1996. **MEMBERSHIPS** National Bar Association, 1986-; American Bar Association, 1984-; National Conference of Black Lawyers, DC Chapter, chairperson, 1981-83; Phi Alpha Delta Law Fraternity International, 1980-. **SELECTED PUBLICATIONS** "The Status of the African American Law Professors," 1990; "Academic Enhancement and Counseling Programs," 1991; Where We Stand: African American Law Professors Demographies, 1992. **CONTACT ADDRESS** Law Ctr, Georgetown Univ, 600 New Jersey Ave, Ste 308, Washington, DC 20001. **EMAIL** bellamy@law.georgetown.edu

BELPEDIO, JAMES R.
PERSONAL Born 01/07/1942, Virginia, MN, m, 4 children **DISCIPLINE** EDUCATION **EDUCATION** Va Jr Col, AS, 62; Bemidji State Col, BS, 64; E Mich Univ, MA, 71; Univ NDak, PhD, 95. **CAREER** Teacher, Kearsley High School, 64-70; Grad Teaching Asst and Intern to Res Asst, Univ NDak, 70-73; Prof, Becker Col, 73-. **MEMBERSHIPS** Popular Culture Asn; N Eng Popular Culture Asn; N Eng Hist Asn; The Hist Soc; Wilson Assoc. **RESEARCH** U.S. History; Civil War; World War I Era; American Cinema, all aspects; History of Commercial Radio, 1920-1955. **SELECTED PUBLICATIONS** Auth, "Orville Babcock, Soldier, Engineer," in The Encyclopedia of the American Civil War, 99; auth, "Ding Dong School," in Encyclopedia of Chicago History, 99; auth, "Audrey Meadows," in The Encyclopedia of Popular Culture, 99; auth, "Bell Telephone Hour," in The Encyclopedia of Popular Culture, 99; auth, "Edward Asner," in The Encyclopedia of Popular Culture, 99; auth, "Judy Holliday," in The Encyclopedia of Popular Culture, 99; auth, "The Lone Ranger," in The Encyclopedia of Popular Culture, 99; auth, "The Maltese Falcon," in The Encyclopedia of Popular Culture, 99; auth, "Michael Landon," in The Encyclopedia of Popular Culture, 99; auth, "Mildred Pierce," in The Encyclopedia of Popular Culture, 99; auth, "Rex Beach," in The Encyclopedia of Popular Culture, 99; auth, "Rose Marie," in The Encyclopedia of Popular Culture, 99; auth, "Shane," in The Encyclopedia of Popular Culture, 99; auth, "Tyne Daly," in The Encyclopedia of Popular Culture, 99. **CONTACT ADDRESS** Dept Gen Educ, Becker Col, Worcester, 61 Sever St, Worcester, MA 01609-2165. **EMAIL** jbelpedio@beckercollege.edu

BENDA, BRENT B.
PERSONAL Born 03/02/1945, Winslow, AZ, m, 1999 **DISCIPLINE** SOCIAL WORK **EDUCATION** Southwest Mo State Univ, BS, 68; Univ Wis Madison, MSSW, 72; PhD, 79. **CAREER** Asst prof, Univ Pittsburgh Sch of Soc Work, 79-82; asst prof, Va Commonwealth Univ Sch of Soc Work, 82-89; from asst prof to prof, Univ Ark at Little Rock Sch of Soc Work, 89-. **HONORS AND AWARDS** Col Fac Excellent Awd in Res & Scholar, 92, 96, & 98. **SELECTED PUBLICATIONS** Coauth, "Testing the Deviance Syndrome Perspective among Boot Camp Participants," J of Criminal Justice 25 (97): 409-424; coauth, "Race and Gender Differences in Theories of Sexual Behavior among Rural Adolescents Residing in AFDC Families," Youth & Soc 30 (98): 59-88; coauth, "A Study of Recidivism of Serious and Persistent Offenders among Adolescents," J of Criminal Justice 27 (99): 111-126; coauth, "Examination of an Integrated Theoretical Model of Exercise Behavior," Am J of Health Behav 23 (99): 381-392; coauth, "Religiosity and Violence: Are They Related After Considering Demographic and Theoretical Factors?," J of Criminal Justice (in press); auth, "Rejoinder to Jonathan Caulkins: The statistical prediction conundrum," Int J of Forecasting (in press); coauth, "Alcohol and Crime among Religious Youth," Alcoholism Treatment Quart (in press). **CONTACT ADDRESS** Dept Soc Work, Univ of Arkansas, Little Rock, 2801 S University Ave, Little Rock, AR 72204.

BENDER, EILEEN TEPER
PERSONAL Born 12/01/1935, Madison, WI, m, 1956, 3 children **DISCIPLINE** AMERICAN LITERATURE, MODERN FICTION, WOMEN'S STUDIES **EDUCATION** Northwestern Univ, BSJ, 56; Notre Dame Univ, PhD(English), 77. **CAREER** Assoc lectr English, Ind Univ, South Bend, 66-68, dir grant & spec proj, 76-78, asst chair Arts & Sci, 78-80, actg chair, 80; asst instr English, Yale Univ, 72-73; Asst Prof English, Notre Dame UNIV, 80-85; Prof English, IN Univ South Bend, 85; Mem adv bd, Danforth Found Grad Fel Prog, 78-81; mem, Ind Comt for Humanities, 78-82; selection comt, Rhodes Scholar Prog, 79-82; consult, Young Fel Sem, Carnegie Corp, 80; selection comt, Charlotte Newcombe Fel Prog, 81-84; Academic Advisor to the Pres, IN, 89-95. **HONORS AND AWARDS** Faculty Colloquium on Excellence in Teaching, (FACET), 89; IU Sylvia Bowman Awd, 95; Lundquist Facutly Fellow, IUSB, 95; Carnegie Prof of the Year, 99. **MEMBERSHIPS** Soc Values Higher Educ; MLA; Danforth Asn; AAHE. **RESEARCH** Contemporary Amer novelists; modern English and Amer women writers; post contemporary narrative strategies; Nature American Literature. **SELECTED PUBLICATIONS** Auth, Hist As Womans Game, 'Bellefleur' As Texte De Jouissance, Soundings, Vol 0076, 93. **CONTACT ADDRESS** Indiana Univ, South Bend, South Bend, IN 46634-7111. **EMAIL** ebender@iusb.edu

BENDER, NATHAN E.
PERSONAL Born 09/29/1957, Amherst, OH, s **DISCIPLINE** ANTHROPOLOGY, LIBRARY SCIENCE **EDUCATION** Ohio State Univ, BA, 80; Univ Wash, MA, 83; Kent State Univ, MLS, 86. **CAREER** Libr Western Hist Collections, Univ Okla, 86-89; Head, spec collections, Mont State Univ Librs, 89-94; curator, head spec collections, WV Univ Librs, 94-97; curator, McCracken Res Libr, Buffalo Bill Hist Ctr, 97-. **MEMBERSHIPS** Am Library Asn, Soc of Am Archivists, Am Indian Library Asn, Am Folklore Soc. **RESEARCH** The American Native Press, Native American syllabaries, Wester American folklore and literature, history of technology, archaeology, western frontier photographers. **SELECTED PUBLICATIONS** Auth, "A Bibliographic Note on the Siwinowe Kesibwe," Native Pr Res Journal 4 (87): 25-27; auth, "The Moccasin, Songs of the Navajo Sea and the Cult Archaeology of Harry E. Miller," Native Pr Res Journal 9 (89): 1-10; auth, "The Library Division of the Western History Collections," in American Indian Resource Materials in the Western History Collections, Univ of Oklahoma, ed. Donald L. DeWitt, Univ of Oklahoma Pr, 90; auth, "Libraries Celebrate the Western States Centennials, 1989-90," coauth with Gregg Sapp, Public Libraries Quarterly, 91; auth, "Cherokee Shorthand: As Derived from Pitman Shorthand and in Relation to the Dot-Notation Variant of the Sac and Fox Syllabary," American Indian Culture and Res Journal, 91. **CONTACT ADDRESS** McCracken Research Library, Buffalo Bill Histol Ctr, 720 Sheridan Ave, Cody, WY 82414. **EMAIL** nbender@bbhc.org

BENESON, WAYNE A.
PERSONAL Born 12/10/1948, Minneapolis, MN, m, 1999, 4 children **DISCIPLINE** VIOLENCE PREVENTION IN SCHOOLS **EDUCATION** Univ Calif, BA, 70; Univ Ky, MA, 74; Univ Idaho, PhD, 88. **CAREER** Instr, Univ Idaho, 86-88; assoc prof, Ill State Univ, 88-. **HONORS AND AWARDS** Grant, The Township of Bloomington and Victim Offender Reconciliation Program, 96; Local Area Network grant, 97; VORP grant, 97; prog grant, Ill Violence Prevention Authority, 99; internal univ grant, 99. **MEMBERSHIPS** PDK, ASCD, AERA, Holmes Partnership. **RESEARCH** Professional development schools, violence prevention in schools and community, staff development. **SELECTED PUBLICATIONS** Coauth with M. Carlson, "Faith Development of Children at a Glance," in M. Snyder, M. Grundy, S. Farneth, M. Clark, and M. Carlson, eds, Opening Doors to Quaker Worship, Philadelphia: Friends General Conf (94); coauth with E. Steinbeck, "An opportunity for ownership: Developing a sense of community in a rural middle school," Middle Sch J, 26(1), 21-23 (94); coauth with B. Kollus and T. Wheeler, "A public policy program for NAME: Taking Action for our future," The Fourth R., 58,1,8-11 (95); auth, "Recognizing the spiritual space in a conflict," The Fourth R., 74, 14-15 (96); auth, "Preface to 'Training peer mediators in the college and university setting: A trainer's guide' by Richard T. Olshak, Campus Judicial Consulting, Inc., San Francisco, CA (97); auth, "Can empathy be taught? A chapter in the Conflict Management Resource Guide for Elementary School, The Ohio Commission on Dispute Resolution and Conflict Management (97); auth, "Training scenarios for ethics and cross-cultural conflict," in R. T. Polshak, ed, Training peer mediators in the college and university setting: A trainer's guide, 2nd ed, by Richard T. Olshak, Campus Judicial Consul;ting, Inc., San Francisco, CA (98); auth, "Ethical Standerds in Mediation: Perception to Theory to Practice," in R. T. Olshak, ed, Training peer mediators in the college and university setting, College Station, Tex: Asn for Student Judicial Affairs (99). **CONTACT ADDRESS** Dept Curric Instr, Illinois State Univ, 1 Campus Box 5330, Normal, IL 61790-5330. **EMAIL** wabenens@ilstu.edu

BENIGER, JAMES R.
PERSONAL m, 1984, 2 children **DISCIPLINE** COMMUNICATIONS AND SOCIOLOGY **EDUCATION** Harvard Univ, BA; Univ CA at Berkeley, MS, MA, PhD. **CAREER** Assoc prof, Univ Southern CA, 85-; res asst, Bureau Soc Sci Res, WA; lectr, UC-Berkeley; asst prof, Princeton Univ & vis assnt prof, Yale Univ. past consult, Off Technol Assessment, US Cong. **HONORS AND AWARDS** Asn Am Publ award; Phi Kappa Phi Fac Recognition Awd; NY Times Bk Rev, Notable Paperback Yr, 89; Nat Newspaper Fund fel. **MEMBERSHIPS** Past mem ed bd, Publ Opinion Quart, J Commun, Critical Stud in Mass Commun, Commun Theory & Knowledge; past assoce ed, Commun Res & auth, Far Afield; past bd, Overseers Gen Soc Survey, NORC, Univ Chicago & 2 yr elected terms, publ ch & sec-treas, Am Asn Publ Opinion Res. **SELECTED PUBLICATIONS** Auth, The Control Revolution: Technological and Economic Origins of the Information Society, Harvard UP, 86 & Trafficking in Drug Users: Professional Exchange Networks in the Control of Deviance, Cambridge UP, hardcover, 83 & paperback, 84; publ on, technol & soc change, mass media and publ opinion, popular cult & the arts. **CONTACT ADDRESS** Annenberg School for Commun, Univ of So California, University Park Campus, Los Angeles, CA 90089.

BENINGER, RICHARD J.
PERSONAL Born 02/11/1950, Walkerton, ON, Canada, s, 2 children **DISCIPLINE** PSYCHOLOGY **EDUCATION** Univ W Ont, BA, 73; McGill Univ, MA, 74; PhD, 77. **CAREER** Asst prof to prof, Queens Univ, 80-. **HONORS AND AWARDS** Fel, Univ BC; Career Scientist, ON Ministry of Health, 82-87, 87-92; Fel, AAAS, 92; Fel, IBNS, 95; Fel, APS, 97. **MEMBERSHIPS** Am Asn for the Adv of Sci; Am Psychol Soc; Can Asn for Neurosci; Can Col of Neuropsychopharmacol; Can Soc for Brain, Beh and Cognitive Sci; Can Soc for Neurosci; Europ Beh Pharmacol Soc; Intl Beh Neurosci Soc; Soc for Neurosci; S Ont Neurosci Asn. **RESEARCH** Neurotransmitters and behavior; Signaling pathways and learning and memory; Cognitive effects of antipsychotic medications. **SELECTED PUBLICATIONS** Co-auth, "Microinjections of flupenthixol into the caudate-putamen but not the nucleus accumbens, amygdala or frontal cortex of rats produce intra-session declines in food-rewarded operant responding," Beh Brain Res, (93): 203-212; co-auth, "Picolinic acid blocks the neurotoxic but not the neuroexcitant properties of quinolinic acid in the rat brain: Evidence from turning behavior and tyrosine hydroxylase immunohistochemistry," Neuroscience, (94): 603-612; co-auth, "Dopamine D1-like agonists impair responding for conditioned reward in rats," Beh Pharmacol, (95): 785-793; co-auth, "The endogenous cannabinoid receptor agonist anandamide impairs memory in rats," Beh Pharmacol, (96): 276-284; co-auth, "Behavioral effects of clozapine and dopamine receptor subtypes," Neurosci and Biobehav Rev, (97): 531-558; co-auth, "Psychopharmacology of conditioned reward: Evidence for a rewarding signal at D1-like dopamine receptors," Psychopharmacology, (99): 95-110; co-auth, "Inhibition of unconditioned activity, locomotor sensitization, and conditioned activity produced by intra-accumbens amphetamine," Beh Pharmacol, (00): 365-376. **CONTACT ADDRESS** Dept Psychol, Queen's Univ at Kingston, 50 Arch St, Kingston, ON, Canada K7L 3L6.

BENJAMIN, LOIS
PERSONAL Born Eatonton, GA, s **DISCIPLINE** SOCIOLOGY **EDUCATION** Clark Col, BA, 66; Univ Calif, MA, 69; PhD, 75. **CAREER** Asst Prof, Univ Fla, 76-81; Assoc Prof and Res Dir, Central State Univ, 81-90; Prof, Hampton Univ, 90-. **HONORS AND AWARDS** 2000 Outstanding Intellectuals of the 20th Century, O'Neill D Swanson Awd, Central State Univ, 87; Nominated as outstanding teacher, Univ Tampa, 78. **MEMBERSHIPS** Asn of Black Sociol, Am Sociol Asn, Southern Sociol Soc. **RESEARCH** Racial, Ethnic, class and Gender Stratification; The black Middle class; black Male/Female Relations; Qualitative Research Methods; Race, Racism, and Ethnic Relations. **SELECTED PUBLICATIONS** Auth, Three Black Generations at the Crossroads: Community, Culture, and Consciousness, Burnham Pub, in press; ed, Black Women in the Academy: Promises and Perils, Univ Press of Fla, 97; co-auth, "African American children in Predominantly White Educational Settings: The Identity Dilemma," SIG Monograph, 94; auth, "Strength Through Diversity," The Hampton Roads, 92; auth, "The Civil Rights Movement and Today's Blacks," Black Opinion, 92; auth, The black elite: Facing the color Line in the Twilight of the Twentieth Century, Nelson-Hall Pub, 91. **CONTACT ADDRESS** Dept Sociol, Hampton Univ, Hampton, VA 23668. **EMAIL** xeniao@erols.com

BENNION, J.
PERSONAL Born 10/02/1964, Salt Lake City, UT, d, 2 children **DISCIPLINE** ANTHROPOLOGY **EDUCATION** Portland State Univ, MA, 90; Univ Ut, PhD, 96. **CAREER** Asst Prof, Ut Valley State Col, 97-. **HONORS AND AWARDS** Dean's Scholarship Awd. **MEMBERSHIPS** Am Anthropol Asn. **RESEARCH** Polygyny; Alternative sex, marriage and family. **CONTACT ADDRESS** Dept Beh Sci, Utah Valley State Col, 800 W Univ Pkwy, Orem, UT 84097. **EMAIL** bennioja@uvsc.edu

BENSON, JOHN S.
PERSONAL Born 08/19/1958, Moline, IL, m, 1982, 2 children **DISCIPLINE** EDUCATION **EDUCATION** Gustavus Adolphus Col, BA, 80; Mankato State Univ, BSc, 82; Univ Minn, MA, 90; PhD, 96. **CAREER** Teacher, Laredo ISD, 82-84; teacher, Wilson Center, 84-85; teacher, Columbus School, 85-88; asst prof, Moorhead State Univ, 94-. **MEMBERSHIPS** Asn of Am Geogr, Nat Coun for Geog Educ, Nat Asn for Soc Studies. **RESEARCH** Medical geography, Africa, Migration, Sense of Place issues. **SELECTED PUBLICATIONS** Auth, "Using an Inquiry Approach to Teach Pre-Service Teachers about Facts, Concepts, and Generalizations," The Social Studies, (89): 227-231; auth, "Centerville/Centreville: An Exercise in Mental Mapping," Journal of Geography, 00. **CONTACT ADDRESS** Dept Elem Educ, Moorhead State Univ, 1104 7th Ave S, Moorhead, MN 56563-0002. **EMAIL** bensonj@mhd1.moorhead.msus.edu

BENSON, LEGRACE
PERSONAL Born 02/23/1930, Richmond, VA, w, 1952, 3 children **DISCIPLINE** ART; PHILOSOPHY; PERCEPTUAL PSYCHOLOGY **EDUCATION** Meredith Coll, AB, 51; Univ Georgia Athens, MFA, 56; Cornell Univ, PhD, 74. **CAREER** Asst prof, Cornell Univ, 68-71; assoc prof/assoc dean for special programs, Wells Coll, 71-77; assoc dean, SUNY-Empire State Coll, 77-80; coordinator of arts, humanities and communications study, center for distance learning, SUNY-Empire State Coll, 81-92. **HONORS AND AWARDS** Empire State Coll Excellence in Scholarship, 92. **MEMBERSHIPS** Natl Coalition of Independent Scholars; Haitian Studies Assn; Coll Art Assn; Latin Amer Studies Assn; Arts Council African Studies Assn; African Studies Assn; Canadian Assn Latin Amer and Caribbean Studies. **RESEARCH** Arts and Culture of Haiti; adult distance learning **SELECTED PUBLICATIONS** Auth, The Utopian Vision in Haitian Painting, Callaloo, Spring 92; Journal of Caribbean Studies, Observations on Islamic Motifs in Haitian Visual Arts, Winter 92/Spring 93; The Arts of Haiti Considered Ecologically, Paper for Culture Change and Technology in the Americas conference, Nov 95; Three Presentations of the Arts of Haiti, Journal of Haitian Studies, Autumn 96; Habits of Attention: Persistence of Lan Ginee in Haiti, in The African Diaspora African Origins and New-world Self-fashioning, 98; How Houngans Use the Light from Distant Stars; Muslim and Breton Survivals in Haitian Voudou Arts, 99; The Artists and the Arts of Haiti in Their Geographical and Conversational Domains, 99. **CONTACT ADDRESS** 314 E. Buffalo St., Ithaca, NY 14850-4227. **EMAIL** legracebenson@clarityconnect.com

BENSON, WARREN S.
PERSONAL Born 08/23/1929, Chicago, IL, m, 1953, 2 children **DISCIPLINE** HISTORY OF EDUCATION **EDUCATION** NW Col, BA, 52; Dallas Theol Sem, ThM, 56; SW Baptist Theol Sem, MRE, 57; Loyola Univ Chicago, PhD, 75. **CAREER** Min of Education, Winnetka Bible Church, 57-62; Min of Youth & Education, First Covenant Church, Minn, 62-65; Min of Education, Lake Ave Congregational Church, Pasedena, 65-69; Assoc prof, Christian Education, Dallas Theol Sem, 74-78; asst prof, Christian Education, Trinity Evangelical Divinity School, Deerfield, 70-74 & 78-. **HONORS AND AWARDS** Distinguished Prof of Christian Education (NAPCE) **MEMBERSHIPS** N Amer Prof Christian Education; Asn Prof & Res Relig Educ **SELECTED PUBLICATIONS** Coauth, A History and Philosophy of Christian Education, Moody Press; coed, Youth Education in the Church, Moody Press; The Complete Book of Youth Ministry, Moody Press; auth, Leading the Church in Education, Word Publishing. **CONTACT ADDRESS** Trinity Evangelical Divinity Sch, 2065 Half Day Rd., Deerfield, IL 60015.

BENTON, STEPHEN L.
PERSONAL Born 04/20/1955, Lincoln, NE, m, 1979, 2 children **DISCIPLINE** PSYCHOLOGY **EDUCATION** Univ Neb, BA, 77; MA, 80; PhD, 83. **CAREER** Asst Prof to Prof, Kans State Univ, 83-; Chair, Counseling & Educ Psychology, Kans State Univ, 88-90; Ed, Educ Psychol Rev, 90-. **HONORS AND AWARDS** Grad Fac Teaching Awd, Col of Educ, 98; Notable Grad, Univ Neb Lincoln Teachers Col, 98; Awd of Excellence, Univ Neb, 97. **MEMBERSHIPS** Am Psychol Asn, Am Educ Res Asn, Phi Kappa Phi . **RESEARCH** Cognitive and motivational processes involved in academic writing and studying, alcohol/drug abuse prevalence and prevention. **SELECTED PUBLICATIONS** Auth, "The Levin and O'Donnell proposal is a good first step," Issues in Education: Contributions from Educational Psychology, in press; auth, "What are the buildings saying? A study of first year undergraduate students' attributions about college campus architecture," NASPA Journal, in press; auth, "Psychological foundations of elementary writing instruction," in Handbook of academic learning: construction of knowledge, Academic Press, 97; auth, "Individual differences in interest and narrative writing," Contemporary Educational Psychology, (96): 305-324; auth, "Implementing a drug prevention program: A comparative case study of two rural Kansas schools," Journal of Alcohol and Drug Education, (95): 26-48; auth, "Students' perceptions of parents' and teachers' qualities of interpersonal relations," Journal of Youth and Adolescence, (96): 787-802. **CONTACT ADDRESS** Dept Psychol, Kansas State Univ, 369 Bluemont Hall, Manhattan, KS 66506. **EMAIL** leroy@ksu.edu

BERARDO, FELIX MARIO
PERSONAL Born 02/07/1934, Waterbury, CT, m, 1979, 2 children **DISCIPLINE** SOCIOLOGY **EDUCATION** Univ CT, BA (Sociology), 61; FL State Univ, PhD (Sociology & Anthropology, High Honors and Distinction), 65. **CAREER** Asst prof Sociology and Rural Sociology, Washington State Univ, 65-69; assoc prof Sociology, 69-73, assoc chair, 72-77, prof Sociology, Univ FL, 73-, dept chair, 85-91; ed, J of Marriage and the Family, 75-81, assoc ed, 72-75, 82-85; assoc ed, Int J of Sociology of the Family, 70-92; assoc ed, The Family Coordinator, 71-75; assoc ed, Social Forces, 76-79; assoc ed, Death education, 79-86; assoc ed, J of Aging Studies, 86-; consult ed, Death studies, 86-92; ed adv bd, Population Res and Policy Rev, 80-90, Sage Family Studies Abstracts, 81-, Sociological Inquiry, 91-. **HONORS AND AWARDS** Phi Beta Kappa, Phi Kappa Phi, Univ CT; Alpha Kappa Delta, FL State Univ; Arthur Peterson Awd in Death Education, 86; One of Ten Family Sociologist in America, recognition by NCFR, 87; One of Top Publishers of Family Studies in refereed professional journals from 80-87, Univ NE, 88; nominated for Pres, Southern Sociol Soc, 88; Certificate of Recognition, Nat Coun on Family Relations, 88; nominated for Pres, Nat Coun on Family Relations, 89; nominated for Assoc Dean, CLAS, 95; recognized as "Very Important Professor," Career Resource Center, 90; nominated, Publications Vice-Pres, Nat Coun on Family Relations, 95; awarded fel status, Gerontological Soc of Am, 92; selected to be included in Profiles in Gerontology: Biographical Dictionary of Sociology; invited by Pres, Japanese Sociol Soc, to visit Japan to consult with faculty in Tokyo Metropolitan Inst; listing found in many bibliographical directories. **MEMBERSHIPS** Am Sociol Asn (sec, Family Section); Nat Coun on Family Relations (Section chmn; chair, Pub Bd Chair, Strategic Planning Comm); Southern Sociological Soc (Section chair; Chmn, Fl Membership Comm, Chair, Program Comm); Gerontological Soc of Am, fel; Southeastern Coun on Family Relations (Chair, Nomination's Comm); FL Coun on Family Relations (Pres). **RESEARCH** Family soc; family gerontology; soc gerontology; soc of death & survivorship; life transitions; soc of risk. **SELECTED PUBLICATIONS** Coed, "Emerging Conceptual Frameworks in Family Analysis," New York: Macmillan, 66; ed, "Violence and the Family, Special Issue of Journal of Marriage and the Family," (November 71): pp. 621-731; ed, "The Family and Aging, Special Issue of The Family Coordinator: Journal of Education, Counseling and Service," (January, 72): pp. 3-122; coauth, "The Family: Its Structure and Interaction, New York: Macmillan, 73; ed., "Decade Review: Family Research, 1970-1979, Minneapolis, MN: National Council on Family Relations, (80): pp. 1-283; coed, "Emerging Conceptual Frameworks in Family Analysis," New Edition, New York: Preager, 81; ed, "Late Life Transitions, The Annals of the American Academy of Political and Social Sciences, (November 82); 187 pgs; ed, "Survivorship: the Other Side of Death and Dying," Special Issue of Death Education, (1985): 1-110; coed, "Death: Facing the Facts," 2nd Edition, New York: Hemisphere, A subsidiary of Harper & Row, 88; ed, "Privacy and the Family," Special Issue of Journal of Family Issues, (January 98): 118 pgs. **CONTACT ADDRESS** Dept of Sociology, Univ of Florida, 3113 Turlington Hall, P O Box 117330, Gainesville, FL 32611-7330. **EMAIL** fberardo@soc.ufl.edu

BERG, JAMES J.
PERSONAL Born 07/01/1964, Superior, WI **DISCIPLINE** EDUCATION **EDUCATION** Univ Minn, BA, 86; MA, 92; PhD, 96. **CAREER** Vis lectr, Univ Minn, 96-97; dir, asst prof, Univ Maine, 99-00; prog dir, Minn State Col and Univ, 00-. **HONORS AND AWARDS** Finalist, Lambda Lit Awd for Gay Studies, 01. **MEMBERSHIPS** MLA, Am Assoc for Higher Educ, Prof and Org Dev Network. **RESEARCH** Christopher Isherwood and 20th Century Gay Literature, Literature and Film. **SELECTED PUBLICATIONS** Coed, The Isherwood Century: Essays on the Life and Work of Christopher Isherwood, Univ of Wis Pr, 00; coed, Conversations with Christopher Isherwood, Univ Pr of Miss, 01. **CONTACT ADDRESS** Minnesota State Univ, St. Paul, 1450 Energy Park Dr, Ste 300, Saint Paul, MN 55108. **EMAIL** bergjj@yahoo.com

BERG, WILLAIM J.
PERSONAL Born 10/26/1942, Dunkirk, NY, m, 1986, 4 children **DISCIPLINE** FRENCH STUDIES, LANGUAGE, EDUCATION **EDUCATION** Hamilton Col, BA, 64; Princeton Univ, MA, 66; PhD, 69. **CAREER** Asst prof to prof to dept chmn, Univ Wis Madison, 67-. **HONORS AND AWARDS** Vilas Assoc, 91-93; Hon Fel, 94; Malverson Baslom Profshp, 95-00; Excellence Teaching Chancellor's Awd, 95. **MEMBERSHIPS** MLA; ACTFL. **RESEARCH** French literature; literature and painting; technology in teaching. **SELECTED PUBLICATIONS** Co-ed, Poemes, Pieces, Prose, Schofer/Rice, 73; co-auth, Images, 89; co-auth, Emile Zola Revisited, 92; auth, The Visual Novel, 92; co-auth, Gustave Flaubert, 97; co-auth, Paroles, 99. **CONTACT ADDRESS** For Lang Dept, Univ of Wisconsin, Madison, 750 Van Hise Hall, Madison, WI 53706. **EMAIL** wjberg@facstaff.wisc.edu

BERG-WEGER, MARLA
PERSONAL Born 07/13/1956, Smith Center, KS, m, 1981, 2 children **DISCIPLINE** SOCIAL WORK **EDUCATION** Kans State Univ, BSc, 78; MD, 83; Washington Univ, PhD, 93 **CAREER** Training Outreach Coordr, Kans State Univ Center for Aging, 78; Soc Worker, Kans Dept of Soc Rehab Serv Junction City, 78-82; Mil Outreach Coordr, Crisis Center Inc, Manhattan Kans, 82-84; Med Soc Work Consult, Abilene Home Health Serv Kans, 83; Intake Therapist, Pawnee Mental Health Serv Manhattan Kans, 83-84; Med Soc Worker, Southeastern Gen Hosp Lumberton, NC, 85; Assoc Dirc of Behav Sci, Asst Dir of Geriatrics, Community Med Coordr, Duke-Fayyetteville Are Health Educ Center family Practice Residency NC, 85-90; Assoc Dir of Field Educ, Coordr of Continuing Educ and Lectr, George Warren Brown Sch of Soc Work at Wash Univ, St. Louis, Missouri, 93-95; Asst Prof, Dir of Practicum, St. Louis Univ, Sch of Soc Serv, St. Louis, Missouri, 95-. **HONORS AND AWARDS** Duke Fayetteville Family Med Residency Teacher of the Year,88, 90; Pembroke State Univ Field Instr of the Year, 90; Who's Who Among Human Serv Professionals, 90; Fac Achievement Awd-Asn for Gerontology Educ in Soc Work, 98; YMCA Saint Louis Univ Women's Commission Leadership Awd, 99; Who's Who in the World, 00. **MEMBERSHIPS** Coun on Soc Work Educ, Nat Asn of Soc Workers, Asn for Gerontology Educ - Soc Work, Alzheimers Asn, Family Support Coun, Baccalaureate SW Pgm Directors. **RESEARCH** Family caregiving of the elderly, Social work field education. **SELECTED PUBLICATIONS** Auth, Daughters Caring for Elderly Parents: Stress or Choice?, Garland Publi Co (NY), 96; auth, "Thoughts on the doctoral process," in Completing your thesis or dissertation, auth. F. Pyrczak (Los Angeles CA: Pyrczak Publ, 99), 29-31; coauth, The Practicum Companion for Social Work: Integrating Class and Field Work, Allyn & Bacon (Boston), 00; coauth, "Human service non-profit agencies: Studying the impact of policy changes, " J of Sociomonia (in press); coauth, "Social welfare policy changes and social work practice," Advances in Soc Work Practice (in press); coauth, "Using the Caregiver Well-Being Scale across the caregiving continuum, " J of Soc Serv Res (forthcoming); coauth, "Living with and caring for older family members: Issues related to caregiver well-being," J of Gerontological Soc Work 32-3 (in press); coauth, "Community Participation: Identifying Influences and a Plan," in Favorite Counseling and Therapy Homeworks, 51 Therapists Share Their Most Creative Strategies, ed. H.G. Rosenthal (Washington DC: Accelerated Develop, in press); coauth, "Achieving wellness: Developing a self-care plan," in Active Learning Exercises for Social Work and the Human Services, ed. C. Solomon (Boston: Allyn & Bacon, forthcoming); coauth, "Caregiver Well-Being Scale," in Program Evaluation, auth. D. Royse (Pac Grove, CA: Brooks/Cole Publ Co, in press). **CONTACT ADDRESS** Sch of Soc Serv, Saint Louis Univ, 3550 Lindell Blvd, Saint Louis, MO 63103.

BERGER, BENNET MAURICE
PERSONAL Born 05/01/1926, New York, NY, d, 4 children **DISCIPLINE** SOCIOLOGY **EDUCATION** Hunter Col, BA, 50; Univ Cal Berk, PhD, 58. **CAREER** Univ IL, Urbana, Asst Prof, Assoc Prof, 59-63; Univ Cal Davis, Assoc Prof, Prof, 63-73; Univ Cal San Diego, Prof, 73-91, Prof Emer, 91-. **HONORS AND AWARDS** NIMH Grant, 70-73; NEH fel, 81-82. **MEMBERSHIPS** Am Sociol Asn. **RESEARCH** Youth, culture, theory. **SELECTED PUBLICATIONS** An Essay On Culture, 95; Authors of Their own Lives, ed, 90; The Survival of a Counterculture, 81; Looking For America, 71; Working Class Suburb, 68. **CONTACT ADDRESS** Univ of California, San Diego, Dept Sociology, San Diego, CA 92037. **EMAIL** bberger@weber.ucsd.edu

BERGER, RONALD J.
PERSONAL Born 01/03/1951, Los Angeles, CA, m, 1989, 3 children **DISCIPLINE** SOCIOLOGY **EDUCATION** Univ Calif at Los Angeles, BA, 73; MA, 75; PhD, 80. **CAREER** Inst, Calif State Univ at Long Beach, 76-77; vis lectr, Univ of Calif at Riverside, 79-81; from asst prof to prof, Univ of Wis at Whitewater, 81-. **HONORS AND AWARDS** Outstanding Res Awd, Univ of Wis at Whitewater, 94. **MEMBERSHIPS** Acad of Criminal Justice Sci, Am Soc of Criminology, Am Sociol Asn, Midwest Sociol Soc, Nat Coun on Crime & Delinquency, Soc for the Study of Soc Problems. **RESEARCH** Holocaust and Genocide Studies, Sociological Criminology. **SELECTED PUBLICATIONS** Auth, "Agency, Structure, and Jewish Survival of the Holocaust: A Life History Study," Sociol Quart 36 (95): 15-36; co-ed, Rape and Society: Readings on the Problem of Sexual Assault, Westview Press, 95; auth, Constructing a Collective Memory of the Holocaust: A Life History of Two Brothers' Survival, Univ Press of Colo, 95; ed, The Sociology of Juvenile Delinquency 2nd ed, Nelson-Hall, 96; auth, "The Politics of Collective memory: The Holocaust in Israel and West Germany," Perspectives on Social Problems Vol 8, JAI Press, 96; coauth, "Competing Perspectives on Cross-National Crime: An Evaluation of Theory and Evidence," Issues in Comparative Criminology, Ashgate, 97; coauth, "Altruism Amidst the Holocaust: An Integrated Social Theory, perspectives on Social Problems Vol 10, JAI Press, 98; coauth, Crime, Justice, and Society: Criminology and the Sociological Imagination, McGraw-Hill, forthcoming. **CONTACT ADDRESS** Dept Sociol, Univ of Wisconsin, Whitewater, 800 W Main St, Whitewater, WI 53190-1705. **EMAIL** bergerr@mail.uww.edu

BERGSTROM, ANNA
PERSONAL Born 03/25/1961, Sweden **DISCIPLINE** FRENCH, FRENCH EDUCATION, SPANISH **EDUCATION** Univ Wis-Madison, BA, 83, MA, 86; Penn State Univ, PhD, 95. **CAREER** Vis lectr, Dept Fr & Ital, Ind Univ, 93-95; ASST PROF, DEPT FOR LANG, LIT, UNIV DEL, 95-. **HONORS AND AWARDS** Mortar Board Outstanding Prof Awd Distinction, 98 **MEMBERSHIPS** Am Asn Appl Ling, Europ Second Lang Acquisition, Am Asn Teachers of Fr, Del Coun on the Teaching of For Lang. **RESEARCH** Appl ling, second lang acquisition, acquisition of temporality. **SELECTED PUBLICATIONS** Auth, L'influence des distinctions aspectuelles sur l'acquisition des temps en francais langue etrangere," Acquisition et Interaction en Langue Etrangere, No. 9; coauth, "Tense and Aspect in SLA and FLL: Learner Narratives in English (SL) and French (FL)," Can Modern Lang Rev, No. 52; review, "Semantique de la temporalite en fracais," The French Reivew, Apr 98. **CONTACT ADDRESS** Dept For Lang & Lit, Univ of Delaware, 326 Smith Hall, Newark, DE 19716. **EMAIL** bergstro@udel.edu

BERK, BERNARD B.
PERSONAL Born 02/09/1934 **DISCIPLINE** SOCIOLOGY **EDUCATION** Univ Calif at Los Angeles, BA, 56; Univ Mulugair, MA, 57; PhD, 61. **CAREER** Vis Prof, Univ Calif, Los Angeles, 61-93; Research Social Scientist, State of CA, 63-69; Vis Prof Univ of New Hampshire, Lecturer, Univ of CA, 64-73; Assoc Prof, CA State Univ, 74; Vis Prof, Univ of New Hampshire, 91-92. **HONORS AND AWARDS** Phi Kappa Phi Honor Society, Horace H. Rackham Scholarship, National Institute of Mental Health Pre-Doctoral Research Fellow, 59-91; "Outstanding Prof" Awd for Distinguished Service from the Asn Student Body, Univ of CA at Los Angeles, 61. **MEMBERSHIPS** ASA American Sociology Assoc, Section member on Theory ASA, Section member on Criminology, Pacific Sociological Assoc, Sociologists for Women in Society. **RESEARCH** Social Factors and Mental Illness, 67, Dept Mental Hygiene, Data Repository of Studies on Deviance, 67, UCSB Cohort Study of Patient Admissions, 68, Dept Mental, Hygiene, Evaluation of Training Psychiatric Supervisors, 68, Dept of Mental Hygiene, Turnover of Psychiatric Adies, 68, Dept of Mental Hygiene, Informal Organization of Adolescent Patients on Psychiatric Wards, 68, Dept of Mental Hygiene, Changes in Self Conceptions Among Hospitalized Patients, 69, Dept of Mental Hygiene, Sociology of Depression (with A. Linsky), 71, UNH, Deviant Behavior. **SELECTED PUBLICATIONS** Auth, "A Comparative Study of Corrections Campt Goals and Client Attiltudes," 60; auth, "Informal Organizatin and Leadership Among Inmates in Treatment and Custodial Prison Camps: A Comparative Study," Thesis. 61; auth, "Organizational Goals and Inmate Organization," American Journal of Sociology, 5 (66); auth, "Evaluation of Training Program for Psychiatric Aides," CA Mental Health Research Digest 6 (68): 79; auth, "Sociology of Mental Health and Mental Illness," The Clinical Psychologist, XXII, (69); auth, "Mental Illness Among Chinese: Myth or Realtiy," with Luch Cheng Hirata, Journal of Social Issues 29 (75); auth, "Selection Versus Role Occupancy as Determinants of Role Related Attitudes Among Psychiatric Aides," with Victor Goertzel, Journal of Health and Social Behavior, 16 (75); auth, "Staff Stability and Organizational Effectiveness," Pacific Sociology Review, 20 (77). **CONTACT ADDRESS** Dept Sociology, California State Univ, Los Angeles, 5151 State Univ Dr, Los Angeles, CA 90032.

BERKELEY, ISTVAN S. N.
DISCIPLINE COGNITIVE SCIENCE **EDUCATION** Univ Leeds, England, BA, 87; Univ Alberta, Can, MA, 90, PhD, 97. **CAREER** Inst, Athabasca Univ, 95; res asst, Univ Alberta, 94-96; lectr, 96-97; ASST PROF, UNIV SOUTHWESTERN LA, 97-. **CONTACT ADDRESS** Univ of Southwestern Louisiana, PO Box 43770, Lafayette, LA 70504. **EMAIL** istvan@usl.edu

BERKMAN, JOYCE A.
PERSONAL Born 11/20/1937, San Jose, CA, m, 1962, 2 children **DISCIPLINE** HISTORY, WOMEN'S STUDIES **EDUCATION** Univ Calif, Los Angeles, BA, 58; Yale Univ, MA, 59, PhD, 67. **CAREER** Instr, Conn Col, 62-63; instr, 66-68, asst prof, 68-80,Danforth Found assoc, 75-; Assoc Prof Hist, Univ Mass, 80-; Prof of Hist., 00-; Adjunct Prof of Women's Studies, 00-. **HONORS AND AWARDS** Distinguished Teacher Awd, Univ Mass, 80. **MEMBERSHIPS** Am Hist Assoc; Berkshire Orgn Women Historians; Conf Brit Historians; Northeast Victorian Studies Asn; New Eng Hist Asn; Nat Women's Studies Asn. **RESEARCH** 19th and 20th century British and American women's history; African-American women's history; Victorian social and intellectual history; historical methodology; European Women's History. **SELECTED PUBLICATIONS** Auth, The Healing Imagination of Olive Schreiner: Beyond South African Colonialism, Univ Mass Press, 89; co-ed, African American Women and the Vote, Univ mass Press, 97; co-ed, Contenplating Edith Stein, Univ of Notre Dame Press, forthcoming. **CONTACT ADDRESS** Univ of Massachusetts, Amherst, Amherst, MA 01003-0002. **EMAIL** jberkman@history.umass.edu

BERKOWITZ, STEPHEN DAVID
PERSONAL Born 11/26/1942, New York, NY, m, 1973, 2 children **DISCIPLINE** SOCIOLOGY **EDUCATION** Univ Mich, AB, 65; Brandeis Univ, PhD, 75. **CAREER** Asst prof, Univ Sask, 71-73; vis asst prof, Memorial Univ, 78; asst prof, Univ Toronto, 73-81; lectr to prof, Univ Ver, 80--; vis scholar, Harvard Univ, 88-89; prof, Univ Ft Hare, SA, 97-99. **HONORS AND AWARDS** NIHM; Alpha Kappa Delta. **MEMBERSHIPS** ASA; CSAA; INSNA. **RESEARCH** Structural analysis; political economy; comparative organization; family/ethnic structure; epidemiology; sociology of religion. **SELECTED PUBLICATIONS** Coauth, Multicultural Education in Colleges and Universities: A Transdisciplinary Approach, LEA (Hillsdale, NJ), 98; coauth, Social Structures: A Network Approach, JAI Press (Greenwich, CT), 97 2nd ; coauth, An Introduction to Structural Analysis, Westview Press (Boulder, C0), forthcoming; coauth, "Corporate Control and Enterprise Structure in the Canadian Economy:1972-1987," Social Networks 17 (95): 111-127; coauth, "Scholars, Sects, and Sanghas: Recruitment to Asian Based Meditation Groups in North America," SA: J Sociology of Religion 49 (88): 136-170; coauth, "A Goodness of Fit Index for Blockmodels," Social Networks 2 (80): 219-34; coauth, "Structural and Non-Structural Models of Elites," Canadian J Sociology 5 (80): 13-30; coauth, "Multicultural, Transdisciplinary Education: An Introduction," Multicultural Education in Colleges and Universities: A Transdisciplinary Approach (Hillsdale, NJ: LEA, 98); coauth, "Towards A Transdisciplinary Conceptualization of Multicultural Studies," Multicultural Education in Colleges and Universities: A Transdisciplinary Approach (Hillsdale, NJ: LEA, 98). **CONTACT ADDRESS** Dept Sociology, Univ of Vermont, 31 S Prospect St, Burlington, VT 05405-1704. **EMAIL** sberkowi@zoo.uvm.edu

BERLEANT, RIVA
PERSONAL m, 1958, 3 children **DISCIPLINE** ANTHROPOLOGY **EDUCATION** State Univ NY, BA, 56; Long Island Univ, MS, 67; State Univ NY, PhD, 74. **CAREER** Instr, CUNY, 73-78; asst prof to prof emeritus, Univ Conn, 80-. **HONORS AND AWARDS** Woodrow Wilson Dissertation Fel, 72-73; Soc Sci Res Coun Fel, 79-80; Fulbright, Brazil,92. **MEMBERSHIPS** Am Anthropol Asn, soc for Caribbean Studies, Soc of Folkdance Hist, Asn of Caribbean Hist. **RESEARCH** Caribbean society and history, slavery and plantations, Mahican Indians in colonial period, Seneca Indians and Genesee Valley landscape history. **SELECTED PUBLICATIONS** Auth, Antigua and Barbuda: a Critical Bibliography, Oxford, 95; auth, Montserrat: A Critical Bibliography, Oxford, 91; ed, the keeping of Animals: adaptation and social Relations in Livestock-Producing communities, 83; auth, "Amhican-Moravian Mission Town and their built Environments," in Essays in architectural anthropology, (forthcoming); auth, "Women, Work, and Gender in the Caribbean: Recent Research," Latin American Research Review, (99): 201-211; auth, "The White Minority and the emancipation Process in Montserrat, 1811-1827," New West Indian Guide, (96): 1-29; auth, "From Labor to peasantry in Montserrat after the End of slavery," in Small Islands, Large Questions: society and Individual in the Caribbean after Emancipation, London, 95; auth, "Merging domains and Women's roles in Barbuda and dominica," in Women and Change in the Caribbean, Bloomington, 92; auth, "Free labor and the Economy in Seventeenth-Century Montserrat," The William and Mary Quarterly, (89): 539-564. **CONTACT ADDRESS** Dept Anthropol, Univ of Connecticut, Storrs, Storrs, CT 06268. **EMAIL** rberleant@uconn.cted.net

BERNSTEIN, IRA H.
PERSONAL Born 08/10/1938, New York, NY, m, 1961, 2 children **DISCIPLINE** PSYCHOLOGY **EDUCATION** Univ Mich, BA, 59; Vanderbilt Univ, MA, 61; PhD, 63. **CAREER** USPHS, NIMH Teaching Fel, Vanderbilt Univ, 59-63; Res Assoc and Instr, Univ of Ill, 63-64; From Asst Prof to Prof, Univ tex Arlington, 64-; Vis Prof, Univ of N Tex, 71; Adj prof, Univ Tex Southwestern Med Sch at Dallas, 76-79; Clinical Prof, Univ Tex Southwestern Med Sch at Dallas, 81-89; Asst Provost/Dir of Inst Res, Univ Tex Arlington, 94-95. **HONORS AND AWARDS** Cert of Merit, Am Med Asn, 69; Awd, Am Acad of Ophthalmology and Otalaryngology, 69. **MEMBERSHIPS** APA, Int Soc for Psychophysics, Psychonomic Soc, Soc for Appl Multivariate Res, Soc for Personality Assesment. **RESEARCH** Psychometric Theory, Multivariate Analysis, Perception, Psychophysics, Computers and Data Processing. **SELECTED PUBLICATIONS** coauth, "On the utility of the West Haven-Yale Multidimesional Pain Inventory (MPI)," Spine 20 (95): 956-963; coauth, "Proactive and retroactive priming in serial target detection," J of Exp Psychology: Human Perception and Performance 22 (96): 1482-1495; coauth, "The effect of grouping on metacontrast masking," in Proceedings of the Twelfth Annual Meeting of the International Society for Psychophysics, ed. S. Masin (Padua, Italy: Univ of Padua, 96), 281-286; coauth, "On the dimensionality of the Buss/Perry Aggression Questionnaire," Behavior Res and Ther 35 (97): 563-568; coauth, Computer Literacy: Getting the most from your PC," Sage Publ (Thousand Oaks, CA), 98; coauth, "Predictors of potential drug interactions," Hosp Pharmacy 33 (98): 835-840; coauth, "Pharmacist recognition of potential drug interactions," Am J of Health-System Pharmacy 56 (99): 1524-1599; coauth, "Some determinants of diagnosis and neuroleptic administration among schizophrenic and mood disordered VA patients," Multivariate Exp Clinical Res (in press); auth, "Projects in Experimental Psychology: Software for several classical perception experiments,"in Behavior Research Methods, Instruments, and Computers, in press; coauth, Statistical data analysis for the personal computer, Sage Publ (Thousand Oaks, CA), forthcoming. **CONTACT ADDRESS** Dept Psychology, Univ of Texas, Arlington, PO Box 19528, Arlington, TX 76019-0528. **EMAIL** Bernstein@uta.edu

BERUBE, MAURICE R.
PERSONAL Born 05/24/1933, Portland, ME, m, 1999, 3 children **DISCIPLINE** EDUCATION **EDUCATION** Fordham Col, BA, 54; New York Univ, MA, 65; Union Grad School, 75, PhD. **CAREER** Teacher, 60-64, ed & teacher, Union Grad School, 68-76; Queens Col, 68-76; Old Dominion Univ, 79-. **HONORS AND AWARDS** Va Cultural Laureate; Univ & Col Outstanding Teacher, Old Dominion Univ; Eminent Scholar; listed in Who's Who in Am Ed. **MEMBERSHIPS** Am Ed Res Asn. **RESEARCH** Educational history; policy. **SELECTED PUBLICATIONS** Auth, American School Reform, 94; American Presidents and Education, 91; Teacher Politics, 88; Education and Poverty, 84; The Urban University in America, 78. **CONTACT ADDRESS** 2107 Claremont Ave, Norfolk, VA 23507. **EMAIL** mberube@odu.edu

BERUBE, MICHAEL
PERSONAL Born 09/26/1961, New York, NY, m, 2 children **DISCIPLINE** EDUCATION **EDUCATION** Univ Va, PhD, 89; **CAREER** Instr, 89-94, assoc prof, 94-95, prof, 96- , Dir, Ill Program for Res in Hum, 97- , Univ Ill, Urbana-Champaign. **SELECTED PUBLICATIONS** Auth, Marginal Forces/ Cultural Centers: Tolson, Pynchon, and the Politics of the Canon, Cornell, 92; auth, Public Access; Literary Theory and American Cultural Politics, Verson, 94; co-ed, Higher Education Under Fire: Politics, Economics, and the Crisis of the Humanities, Routledge, 95; auth, Life As We Know It: A Father, A Family, and an Exceptional Child, Pantheon, 96; auth, The Employment of English: Theory, Jobs, and the Future of Literary Study, NYU, 98. **CONTACT ADDRESS** Univ of Illinois, Urbana-Champaign, 805 West Pennslyvania Ave, Urbana, IL 61801. **EMAIL** m-berube@uiuc.edu

BESTHORN, FRED H.
PERSONAL Born 12/23/1951, KS, m, 2 children **DISCIPLINE** SOCIAL WORK **EDUCATION** Sterling Col, BS, 73; Grace Theol Sem, MDiv, 78; Univ Kans, MSW, 91; PhD, 97. **CAREER** Adj Prof, Allen County Community Col, 94-96; Adj Prof to Asst Prof, Washburn Univ, 95-. **HONORS AND AWARDS** Nominated Dorothy Hoagland Outstanding Dissertation and Res Awd, Univ Kans, 97; Argersinger Awd, Univ Kans, 98; Phi Kappa Phi Honor Soc, 91.; Outstanding Law-Enforcement Officer of the Year, 85; Commendation for Outstanding Life Saving Response, 82. **MEMBERSHIPS** Nat Asn of Soc Workers, Coun on Social Work Educ, Inst of Noetic Sci, Phi Kappa Phi Honor Soc, Am Psychotherapy Asn, Am Asn of Univ Prof. **RESEARCH** Applying Radical Ecological Theory to Social Work practice settings; The association between Spirituality and Human Well-being; Social Policy Analysis of Antipoverty and Public Assistance Programs; The viability and effectiveness of Macro-Level interventions to a broad assortment of individual and familial issues. **SELECTED PUBLICATIONS** Auth, "Reconceptualizing social work's person-inenviroment perspective: Explorations in radical environmental thought,: Dissertation Abstracts International, (97): 4067; auth, "Seeking connections with land and nature: Rural migration and the simple life," in Proceedings of the Sixth Annual Nonpoint Source Pollution Confernce,98; auth, "Lessons from nature: The suburban dilemma," The Great Plains Review, (98): 51-54; co-auth, "Opinions/perspectives/beliefs: Nature as professional resource - A new ecological approach to helping, " Kansas Chapter NASW, (99): 15; auth, "Adoption the gracious miracle, The Great Plains Review, (99): 74-77; auth, "Transpersonal psychology and deep ecological philosophy: Exploring linkages and applications for social work," Social Thought: Journal of Religion and Social Work, in press; co-auth, "Rethinking environment: Deep ecology and social work practice," Journal of Teaching in Social Work,00; auth, "The oppression of women and nature: Ecofeminism as a framework for a social justice oriented social work, Social Work, forthcoming; auth, "Rethinking the concept of self: Radical environmental philosophy and social work practice," Journal of Progressive Human Services, forthcoming. **CONTACT ADDRESS** Dept Soc Work, Washburn Univ of Topeka, 1700 SW Col Ave, Topeka, KS 66621. **EMAIL** zzbest@washburn.edu

BETHEL, ELIZABETH RAUH
PERSONAL Born 08/27/1942, Grosse Pointe, MI **DISCIPLINE** SOCIOLOGY; COMMUNICATION **EDUCATION** Univ Oklahoma, PhD, 74. **CAREER** Lander Univ, prof, sociol, 74-; Univ Madras, Fulbright lectr, 90. **MEMBERSHIPS** ASA; SSS; NWU. **RESEARCH** African Am Culture; Southern US Culture; Global Ethnic Culture. **SELECTED PUBLICATIONS** Black Communities, in Neil Larry Schumsky, ed, American Cities and Suburbs: An Encyclopedia, Clio, pub 98; Journals and Voices: Mosaics of Community, in Documenting Cultural Diversity in the Resurgent American South, in: Margaret R Dittemore and Fred J Hay, eds, Am Lib Asn, 97; AIDS: Readings on a Global Crisis, Allyn and Bacon, 95; numerous other pub. **CONTACT ADDRESS** Dept Sociology, Lander Univ, Greenwood, SC 29646. **EMAIL** ebethel@lander.edu

BETTINGER, ROBERT L.
PERSONAL Born 05/08/1948, Berkeley, CA, m, 1969, 1 child **DISCIPLINE** ANTHROPOLOGY **EDUCATION** Univ Calif, BA, PhD, 75. **CAREER** Asst prof, 75-79, assoc prof, 79-80, NYU; asst prof, 80-82, assoc prof, 82-88, prof, 88-, Univ Calif, Davis. **HONORS AND AWARDS** Dist fac award, 92; dist alumni award, 94, Univ Calif Riverside. **MEMBERSHIPS** Soc Amer Anthropology **RESEARCH** Prehistory; hunter-gatherers; evolutionary theory. **SELECTED PUBLICATIONS** Art, Doing Great Basin Archaeology Recently: Coping with Variability, J of Archaeol Res, NY Plenum, 93; coauth, Prehistoric Settlement Categories and Settlement Systems in the Alashan Desert of Inner Mongolia, PRC J Anthrop Archaeol, 94; auth, How, When, and Why Numic Spread, Across the West: Human Population Movement and the Expansion of the Numa, Univ Utah Press, 94; auth, Prehistory of the Crooked Creek area, Crooked Creek Guidebook, Univ Calif White Mountain Res Station Pub, 94; coauth, The Numic Spread: a Computer Simulation, Amer Antiquity, 95; coauth, Simulating the global human expansion in the late Pleistocene, J Archaeol Science, 95; coauth, Settlement Patterns Refected in Assemblages from the Pleistocene/Holocene Transition in North Central China, J Archaeol Science, 95; coauth, Serum albumin phenotypes at Stillwater: Implications for Population History in the Great Basin, Antropol Papers Amer Museum of Nat Hist, 95; coauth, Style, Function and Cultural Evolutionary Processes, Darwinian Archaeol, Plenum, 96; coauth, The State of Evolutionary Archaeology: Evolutionary Correctness or the Search for the Common Ground, Darwinian Archaeol, Plenum, 96; coauth, Central Place Models of Acorn and Mussell Processing, J Archaeol Science, 97; coauth, Evolutionary Implications of Metrical Variation in Great Basin Projectile Points, Rediscovering Darwin: Evolutionary Theory & Archaeol Explanation, Archaeol Papers Amer Anthropol Assn, 97; coauth, New Dates for the North China Mesolithic, Antiquity, 97; auth, Cultural, Human, and Historical Ecology in the Great Basin: Fifty Years of Ideas about Ten Thousand Years of Prehistory, Advances in Hist Ecology, Columbia Univ Press, 98; auth, A Hunter-Gatherer Landscape: Southwest Germany in the Late Paleolithic and Mesolithic, Plenum, 98. **CONTACT ADDRESS** Dept of Anthropology, Univ of California, Davis, Davis, CA 95616. **EMAIL** rlbettinger@ucdavis.edu

BEVIN, TERESA
PERSONAL Born 12/19/1949, Cuba, d **DISCIPLINE** PSYCHOLOGY, SOCIOLOGY **EDUCATION** Montgomery Col, MHA, 79; George Wash Univ, BA, 81; Univ Md, MA, 83; Med, 85. **CAREER** Coordr, Nat Med Center, 87-90; Psychotherapist, Montgomery Co, 90-95; Prof, Montgomery Col, 85- **HONORS AND AWARDS** Sigma Delta Pi. **MEMBERSHIPS** Mental Health Adv Comt, Montgomery Col Fac Coun. **RESEARCH** Learning styles through different cultures. **SELECTED PUBLICATIONS** Auth, "Multiple Traumas of Refugees: Near Drowning and Witnessing of Maternal Rape," Children in Crisis, Guilford Publ (91); auth, "Violent Deaths of Parents: Case of Marty," in Helping Bereaved Children (NY: Guilford Publ, 93); auth, Havana Split, Arte Publico Pr (Houston, TX), 98. **CONTACT ADDRESS** Dept Lang, Montgomery Col, Takoma Park, 7600 Takoma Ave, Takoma Park, MD 20912-4141. **EMAIL** tbevin@mc.cc.md.us

BEYELER, JULIA M.
PERSONAL Born 11/13/1938, Orrville, OH, m, 1961, 3 children **DISCIPLINE** EDUCATION **EDUCATION** Goshen Col, BS, 60; Kent State Univ, MEd, 65; Univ Akron, PhD, 95. **CAREER** Teacher, Wooster City Schools, 65-74; adj prof, Univ of Akron, 77-. **HONORS AND AWARDS** Award, Ohio Board of Regents, 98. **MEMBERSHIPS** AERA; IRA; NTA. **RESEARCH** Student learning, applications of learning theory to practice. **SELECTED PUBLICATIONS** Auth, "Reluctant Readers: Case Studies of Reading and Study Strategies in Introduction of Psychology", Learning Assistance Rev 3 (98): 5-19; auth, "Services for Academic Success: Tutoring, Testing, Teaching, Tracking", Official Proceedings of the Nat Tutoring Assoc, (99): 83-91. **CONTACT ADDRESS** Dept Soc Sci, Univ of Akron, Wayne Col, 1901 Smucker Rd, Orrville, OH 44667. **EMAIL** juliabeyeler@uakron.edu

BEYER, DAVID W.
PERSONAL Born 10/03/1949, Sioux Falls, SD, s **DISCIPLINE** MUSIC EDUCATION **EDUCATION** North Tex State Univ, MME, 72. **CAREER** Independent scholar, bibl chronol, unaffiliated, San Diego/Newport Beach, Calif. **MEMBERSHIPS** Soc of Bibl Lit. **RESEARCH** Biblical chronology; Josephus studies. **SELECTED PUBLICATIONS** Auth, Josephus Reexamined: Unraveling the Twenty-second Year of Tiberius, Chronos Kairos Christos II, Vardaman, Mercer Univ Press, 98; auth, Finegan's Reliance on Early Manuscript Discoveries of Beyer, 284, 292, 301, Handbook of Biblical Chronology, Hendrickson Publ, 98. **CONTACT ADDRESS** 204 N. El Camino Real E-401, Encinitas, CA 92024.

BHATIA, KUNDAN LAI
PERSONAL Born 02/01/1930, India, m, 1959, 2 children **DISCIPLINE** SOCIOLOGY **EDUCATION** Ind Univ, PhD, 71. **CAREER** Prof, Slippery Rock Univ. **MEMBERSHIPS** Am Sociol Asn, PA Sociol Ans, Intl Sociol Asn. **RESEARCH** Emergence of Middle Class in India and South Asia; Sociological Organizations; Racial Change. **CONTACT ADDRESS** Dept Sociol & Anthropol, Slippery Rock Univ of Pennsylvania, 14 Maltby Dr, Slippery Rock, PA 16057.

BIAFORA, FRANK
PERSONAL Born 03/23/1965, Morgantown, WV, s **DISCIPLINE** SOCIOLOGY, ANTHROPOLOGY **EDUCATION** Univ Fla, BA, 86; MA, 88; Univ Miami, PhD, 91. **CAREER** Assoc Prof, St Johns Univ, 93-. **HONORS AND AWARDS** Fac Develop Grant, St Johns Univ, 96; Outstanding Young Am Awd, 98; Drug Abuse Grant, CSAT, 98-; 4-Year Grant, St Johns Univ/Dept Educ, 99; Serv Learning Grant, St Johns Univ, 99; Ronald McNair Scholars Grant, 99-. **MEMBERSHIPS** ASA, ASC, APHA, SSSB, ACJS. **RESEARCH** Crime and delinquency, substance use/abuse and treatment, sociological research methods and statistics. **SELECTED PUBLICATIONS** Auth, "Differences in Depressive Symptoms Between Blacks and Whites: A Test of Differential Exposure and Vulnerability to Stressful Life Events," in Normal and Pathological Develop in a Diverse Soc: In Search of a Paradigm (New York: Jason Aronson Pr, 99); auth, "'Just the Facts, Ma'am,': The Supreme Court Says 'No' to Media Ride-Alongs," J of Criminal Justice and Pop Cult 7:1 (99): 15-25; auth, "Censoring the Press: The Supreme Court Rules on Media Ride-Alongs," Picturing Justice (99); coauth, "A Longitudinal Study of Drug Treatment in a Long-Term Care Facility," J of Substance Abuse Treatment (forthcoming). **CONTACT ADDRESS** Dept Sociol & Anthrop, St. John's Univ, 8000 Utopia Pkwy, Jamaica, NY 11439.

BIASCO, FRANK
PERSONAL Born 01/15/1928, Chicago, IL, m, 1953, 5 children **DISCIPLINE** PSYCHOLOGY **EDUCATION** Wheaton Col, AB, 53; Loyola Univ, MSW, 56; Ind Univ, EdD, 65. **CAREER** Asst prof, State Univ of NY and Oswego, 66-68; assoc prof, Fla State Univ, 68-70; Dir Student Services, Duval Co Public Schs, Jacksonville, Fla, 70-71; assoc prof, Univ West Fla, 71-, coordr, Coun Psychol Prog, 71-75, coordr, Sch Psychol Program, 86-89. **HONORS AND AWARDS** President of Nat Org on Testing; President of State Org (Fl) on Counselor Trainees; Fel, Am Orthopsychiatric Asn; Phi Delta Kappa; Pi Gamma Mu; listed in: Am Men of Sci, Community Leaders of Am, Leaders in Educ, Dictionary of Int Biogaphy, Contemporary Authors, Library of Human Resources; Outstanding Service to the Community Awd, Neighborhood Youth Corps; Distinguished Service Awd, Action 76; Pacesetter Awd, Escambia Co, Fla, 78; Meritorious Service to Education, Phi Delta Kappa, NW Fla Chapter, 80; nominated for Professional of the Year, Chamber of Commerce Awd, 86. **MEMBERSHIPS** APA, FPA, NWFLPA; NEA; Am Legion; Veterans of Foreign Wars. **RESEARCH** Attitudinal research. **SELECTED PUBLICATIONS** Auth, "Teacher, where are you?," Guidance Clinic, 12 (80): 16; coauth, "Effects of group counseling with military prisoners or selected personality traits," The J for Specialists in Group Work, 5, 1 (80): 15-19; coauth, "Increasing appreciation of authority figures among naval confinees through group counseling," Corrective and Social Psychiatry, 27, 2 (81): 96-98; coauth, "Community service as applied psychology college credit," Col Student J, 16, 2 (82): 121-123; coauth, "Personality differences between successfully and unsuccessfully treated drug abusers," Social Behavior and Personality, 11 (83): 105-

111; coauth, "College students' attitudes toward abortion," Col Student J, 23, 3 (89): 1-4; coauth, "College students' attitudes toward AIDS," Col Student J, 25, 3 (91): 394-400; coauth, "College students' attitudes toward drinking and driving," 26, 2 (92): 1-3; auth, "College students' attitudes toward UFOs," Col Student J, (2000); coauth, "College students' attitudes toward Binge Drinking," Col Student J (in press). **CONTACT ADDRESS** Dept Psychol, Univ of West Florida, 11000 Univ Pkwy, Pensacola, FL 32514. **EMAIL** Fbiasco@ATT.net

BIBACE, ROGER
PERSONAL Born 03/04/1926, Alexandria, Egypt, m, 1960, 3 children **DISCIPLINE** PSYCHOLOGY **EDUCATION** Univ Brit Colum, BA, 49; Clark Univ, PhD, 56. **CAREER** Lecturer to Prof, Clark Univ, 57-. **HONORS AND AWARDS** Distinguished Teacher Awd, Soc of Teachers in Family Medicine, 76; Who's Who in the East; Who's Who in Science and Technol; Who's Who in Am Educ; Intl Who's Who in Medicine; Intl Who's Who in Educ; Who's Who Among Human Service Prof. **MEMBERSHIPS** Am Psychol Asn; E Psychol Asn; MA Psychol Asn; N Eng Psycho Asn; Am Assn for the Adv of Sci; Am Asn of Univ Prof; Soc of Teachers of Family Medicine. **SELECTED PUBLICATIONS** Co-auth, "A Developmental Analysis of Prisoners' Conceptions of AIDS," Criminal Justice and Behavior: An International Journal of Correctional Psychology, (92): 174-188; co-auth, "A Developmental Analysis of Female Prisoners' Conceptions of AIDS," Criminal Justice and Behavior: An International Journal of Correctional Psychology, (93): 240-253; auth, "The Family Therapist as consultant: Alliances, Agency, Autonomy," Family Systems Medicine, 94; co-auth, "Dating couples and Their Relationships: Intimacy and Contraceptive Use," Adolescence, (99): 1-7; co-auth, "Children and Medicines: What They Want to Know and How They Want to Learn," Journal of Social and Administrative Pharmacy, (99): 38-52; co-auth, "Educational research traids: Accomplishment with efficiency," in Partnerships in Research, clinical and Educational Settings, (Ablex Pub Co, 99), 73-76; co-auth, "contrasting transmission and partnership models of teaching and learning," in Partnerships in Research, Clinical and Educational Settings, (Ablex Pub Co, 99), 91-104; auth, "Pediatric asthma: Assessing and changing behavior," in Partnerships in Research, Clinical and Educational Settings, (Ablex Pub Co, 99), 199-208; auth, "Faculty physician groups," in Partnerships in Research, Clinical and Educational Settings, (Ablex Pub co, 99), 235-240; auth, "A partnership ideal," in Partnerships in Research, Clinical and Educational Settings, (Ablex Pub co, 99), 275-306. **CONTACT ADDRESS** Dept Psychol, Clark Univ, 950 Main St, Worcester, MA 01610. **EMAIL** rbibace@ziplink.net

BICKEL, JULIA M.
DISCIPLINE EDUCATION **EDUCATION** Ball State Univ, BSEd, 69; MAEd, 74; Ind State Univ, PhD, 00. **CAREER** Dir Assessment, Ind Univ E, 91-93; Dir Learning Cent, Ivy Tech State Col, 94-. **RESEARCH** Student retention; Higher education administration. **SELECTED PUBLICATIONS** Auth, The Perceptions of Senior Administrators as they relate to student retention issues. **CONTACT ADDRESS** Dept Gen Educ, Ivy Tech State Col, Northeast, 3800 N Anthony Blvd, Fort Wayne, IN 46805-1430. **EMAIL** jbickel@ivy.tech.in.us

BIDWELL, CHARLES E.
PERSONAL Born 01/24/1932, Chicago, IL, m, 1932, 1 child **DISCIPLINE** SOCIOLOGY **EDUCATION** Univ Chicago, AB, 50; AM, 53; PhD, 56. **CAREER** Lecturer, Harvard Univ, 59-61; Asst Prof to Prof, Univ Chicago, 61-. **HONORS AND AWARDS** Guggenheim Fel; Fel, Am Asn for the Advancement of Sci. **MEMBERSHIPS** Nat Acad of Educ, Sociol Res Asn, Ma Sociol Asn, Am Educ Res Asn, AAAS. **RESEARCH** Sociology/Education. **SELECTED PUBLICATIONS** Auth, "The School as a Formal Organization," in Handbook of Organizations, Rand McNally, 65; auth, "School District Organization and Student Achievement," American Sociological Review, (75): 55-70; auth, "Conceptualizing and Measuring the Effects of School and Schooling," American Journal of Education, (80): 401-430; auth, The Organization and its Ecosystem: A Theory of Structuring in Organizations, JAI Press, 85; auth, Structuring in Organizations: Ecosystem Theory Evaluated, JAI Press, 87; auth, "An Ecological Theory of Organizational Structuring," in Continuities in Sociological Human Ecology, Plenum Press, 98; auth, "Working: Perceptions and Experiences of American Teenagers," in Youth Experience and Development: Social Influences and Educational Challenges, 98; auth, "School as Context and Construction: A Social Psychological Approach to the Study of Schooling," in Handbook of the Sociology of Education, Plenum Press, 99; auth, "Sociology and the Study of Education," in Issues in Education Research: Problems and Possibilities, 99; auth, "The Collegial Focus: Teaching Fields, Colleague Relationship, and Instructional Practice in American High Schools," Sociology of Education, (99): 234-256. **CONTACT ADDRESS** Dept Sociol, Univ of Chicago, 1126 E 59th St, Chicago, IL 60637. **EMAIL** c_bidwell@uchicago.edu

BIEGEL, DAVID E.
PERSONAL Born 07/03/1946, New York, NY, d, 1 child **DISCIPLINE** SOCIOLOGY **EDUCATION** City Col NY, BA, 67; Univ Md, MSW, 70; PhD, 82. **CAREER** From Asst Prof to Assoc Prof, Univ Pittsburgh, 80-86; Vis Sen Res Assoc, Univ Pittsburgh, 87-88; Prof, Case Western Res Univ, 88-. **HONORS AND AWARDS** VISTA Fels Prog, Univ Md, 68-70; Fac Fel, Univ Pittsburgh, 83; Who's Who Among Human Serv Professionals, 88; Fel, Gerontological Soc of Am, 92-; Res Fel, Ohio Dept of Ment Health, 90-91; Who's Who in the Midwest, 26th Ed, 98-99; Who's Who in Am, 54th Ed, 00; Who's Who in Med and Health Care, 3rd Ed, 00. **SELECTED PUBLICATIONS** Auth, "Facilitators and Barriers to Small Group Participation," J of the Calif Alliance for the Ment Ill, 4:4 (95): 18-20; coauth, "Overcoming Barriers faced by African-American families with a Family Member with Mental Illness," Family Rels 46:2 (97): 163-178; coauth, "Barriers to the Use of Mental Health Services by African-American and Hispanic Elderly Persons," J of Applied Gerontological Soc Work 29:1 (97): 23-44; coauth, "Predictors of Psychiatric Re-Hospitalization for Persons with Serious and Persistent Mental Illness," Psychiat Rehab J 22:2 (98): 155-166; coauth, "The Impact of Family Caregiver Attitudes on the Use of Community Services for dementia Care," J of Applied Gerontology 18:2 (99): 201-221; coauth, "Concept Mapping in Mental Health: Uses and Adaptations," Evaluation and Prog Planning, 24:4 (99); coauth, Innovations in Practice and Service Delivery with Vulnerable Populations Across the Lifespan, Oxford UP (New York), 00. **CONTACT ADDRESS** Dept Sociol, Case Western Reserve Univ, 10900 Euclid Ave, Cleveland, OH 44106.

BIGGS, SHIRLEY ANN
PERSONAL Born 03/09/1938, Richmond, VA, m **DISCIPLINE** EDUCATION **EDUCATION** Duquesne U, BEd 1960; Univ of SC, MEd 1972; Univ of Pittsburgh, EdD 1977. **CAREER** Pittsburgh Public School, teacher, 61-68; Benedict Coll, instructor, 68-72, reading specialist consultant, 72-; Univ of Pittsburgh, faculty in school of educ, 74-, asso prof, asst dean for student affairs 86-, director of affirmative action, minority affairs, 89-. **HONORS AND AWARDS** honored for literacy research activities by the Pittsburgh City Council 1986; editor Innovative Learning Strategies, 1989-90; Intl Reading Assn, 1989-90. **MEMBERSHIPS** Pres Gerald A Yoakam Reading Cncl 1978-79; chmn research div Pittsburgh Literacy Coalition 1984-; mem Intl Reading Assoc 1973-; mem Nat Reading Conference; director of research Coalition for the Advancement of Literacy Pittsburgh, 1985-; chair College Reading Improvement Group, International Reading Association, 1990-; chair, Pittsburgh Peace Institute, 1997-; Natl Conference on Research in Language and Literacy. **SELECTED PUBLICATIONS** Auth, "The Plight of Black Males in American Schools: Separation May not be the Answer;" auth, "Building on Strengths: Closing the Literacy Gap;" auth, "African American Adult Reading Performance: Progress in the Face of Problem;" ed, Journal of College Literacy and Learning (formerly Forum for Reading); co-auth, Administrators Reference Manual: Bridging Assessment and Instruction, 1998; "Minority Student Retention: A Framework for Discussion and Decision-making," 98; co-auth, Students Self Questioning and Summarizing, 84; Co-auth, Reading to Achieve, Strategies for Adult Coll; 83. **CONTACT ADDRESS** Sch of Education, Univ of Pittsburgh, 5TO1 Forbes Quandrangle, Pittsburgh, PA 15260.

BILMES, JACK
PERSONAL Born 08/09/1940, Astoria, NY, m, 1963, 1 child **DISCIPLINE** ANTHROPOLOGY **EDUCATION** Brandeis Univ, BA, 61; Yale Univ, MA, 68; Stanford Univ, MA, 70; PhD, 74. **CAREER** Vis asst prof to prof, Univ of Haw, 73-. **HONORS AND AWARDS** NY State Regents Scholar, 57; Yale Univ Fel, 63; Nat Defense For Lang Fel, 64; Nat Inst General Med Sci Res Grant, 68-73; Fujio Matsuda Scholar, 88-89; UH Research Grants, 88-89, 90, 92; Guggenheim Found Grant, 88-89; Wenner-Gren Found Grant, 88-89; Danish Res Acad Grant, 92; Aalborg Univ Grant, 94, 98. **MEMBERSHIPS** Am Anthrop Assoc; Int Pragmatics Assoc. **RESEARCH** Discourse and Interaction, Ethnomethodology and Social Action Theory, Thailand, Bali. **SELECTED PUBLICATIONS** Coauth, "Following Instructions", Quarterly Newsletter of the Lab or Comparative Human Cognition 6, 84: 81-87; auth, "Freedom and Regulation: An Anthropological Critique of Free Market Ideology", Res in Law and Econ 7, (85): 123-147; auth, Discourse and Behavior, Plenum Pr, 86; auth, "Category and Rule in Conversation Analysis", Papers in Pragmatics 2, (88): 25-59; auth, "Referring to Internal Occurrences: A Reply to Coulter", J for the Theory of Soc Behav (92): 253-262; auth, "Dividing the Rice: A Microanalysis of the Mediator's Role in a Northern Thai Negotiation", Lang in Soc 21, (92): 569-602; auth, "Ethnomethodology, Culture, and Implicature: Toward an Empirical Pragmatics", Pragmatics 3, (93): 387-409; auth, "Constituting Silence: Life in the World of Total Meaning", Semiotica 98, (94): 73-87; auth, "Being Interrupted", Lang in Soc 26, (97): 1-25; auth, "Questions, Answers, and the Organization of Talk in the 1992 Vice-Presidential Debate: Fundamental Considerations", Res in Lang and Soc Interaction 32 (99). **CONTACT ADDRESS** Dept Anthrop, Univ of Hawaii, Honolulu Comm Col, 2424 Maile Way, Honolulu, HI 96822. **EMAIL** bilmes@hawaii.edu

BILODEAU, LORRAINE
PERSONAL Born 12/09/1935, Holyoke, MA **DISCIPLINE** ELEMENTARY EDUCATION; RELIGIOUS EDUCATION; LIBRARY SCIENCE AND INFORMATION **EDUCATION** Catholic Teachers Col; BS, 69; Fairfield Univ, MA, 75; Dominican Univ, MLS, 88. **CAREER** Tchr, Rhode Island Catholic Sch; DRE dir, St. Leo the Great; librn, dir, Anna Maria Col. **MEMBERSHIPS** ALA; NEACRL; CLA; NECLA. **RESEARCH** Geneology and icons. **CONTACT ADDRESS** Mondor-Eagen Library, Anna Maria Col, Paxton, MA 01612-1198. **EMAIL** lbilodeau@annamaria.edu

BINDER, AMY J.
PERSONAL Born 10/01/1964, Minneapolis, MN, m, 1999 **DISCIPLINE** SOCIOLOGY **EDUCATION** Stanford Univ, BA, 86; Northwestern Univ, MA, 92; PhD, 98. **CAREER** Adjunct instr, Northwestern Univ, 96-97; asst prof, Univ of Southern Calif, Los Angeles, 98-. **HONORS AND AWARDS** Robert F. Winch Memorial Awd, Northwestern Univ, 93, 97; Recipient, Diss Year Grant, Northwestern Univ, 96; Recipient, Spenser Found Small Grants Prog, 2000-01; Panel presenter on USC Fac Inst for Service Learning, 2000; mem, selection comt for the Grace Ford Salvatori Scholarship, USC; reviewer for: Am J of Sociol, Contemporary Sociol, Law and Soci Inquiry, Sociol Forum, Social Problems. **MEMBERSHIPS** Am Sociol Asn, Pacific Sociol Asn **RESEARCH** Education, culture, social movements, organizational sociology, media, race. **SELECTED PUBLICATIONS** Auth, "Constructing Racial Rhetoric: Media Depictions of Harm in Heavy Metal and Rap Music," Am Sociol Rev, vol 58 (Dec 93); coauth with James Rosenbaum, "Do Employers Really Need More Educated Youth?," Sociol of Educ (Jan 97); auth, "Friend and Foe: Boundary Work and Collective Identity in the Afrocentric and Multicultural Curriculum Movements in American Public Education," in The Cultural Territory of Race: Black and White Boundaries, Michele Lamont, ed, Univ of Chicago Press/ Russell Sage Found (99); auth, "Why Do Some Curricular Challenges 'Work' While Others Do Not? The Case of Three Afrocentric Challenges: Atlanta, Washington, DC, and New York State," Sociol of Educ (forthcoming); rev of Image Politics: The New Rhetoric of Environmental Activism for the Am J of Sociol (forthcoming). **CONTACT ADDRESS** Dept Sociol, Univ of So California, 3620 S Vermont Ave, Los Angeles, CA 90089-0259. **EMAIL** abinder@usc.edu

BINDON, JAMES R.
PERSONAL Born 11/23/1947, San Francisco, CA, m, 1969, 1 child **DISCIPLINE** ANTHROPOLOGY **EDUCATION** Univ Calif Berkeley, AB, 73; Pa State Univ, MA, 75; PhD, 81. **CAREER** Asst Prof to Prof and Chair, Univ Ala, 78-. **MEMBERSHIPS** Am anthropol Asn; Am Asn of Phys Anthropol; Human Biol Asn. **RESEARCH** Biological Anthropology; Human Population Biology; Lifestyle Measurement; Cultural Consensus; Nutrition; Growth and Development; Infant Feeding; Obesity; Diabetes; Hypertension. **SELECTED PUBLICATIONS** Co-auth, "Life style, modernization, and adaptation among Samoans," Collegium Anthropologicum, (91): 101-110; co-auth, "Social Status and growth: Theoretical and Methodological considerations," MASCA Res Papers, Vol 9, (92): 67-76; auth, "Polynesian responses to modernization: Overweight and obesity in the South Pacific," in Social Aspects of Obesity, (Gordon and Breach, 95), 227-251; auth, "Coming of age of human adaptation studies in Samoa," in Human Adaptability: Past, Present, and Future, (Oxford Univ Press, 97), 126-156; co-auth, "Social Context and Psychosocial Influences on Blood Pressure among American Samoans," Am J of Phys Anthropol, (97): 7-18; co-auth, "Bergmann's rule and the thrifty genotype," Am J of Phys Anthropol, (97): 201-210. **CONTACT ADDRESS** Dept Anthropol, Univ of Alabama, Tuscaloosa, 16 ten Hoor Bldg, Tuscaloosa, AL 35487. **EMAIL** jbindon@tenhoor.as.ua.edu

BIRAN, MIA W.
PERSONAL Born 06/24/1948, Haifa, Israel, d **DISCIPLINE** PSYCHOLOGY **EDUCATION** Univ Haifa, Israel, BA, 73; MA, 77; Rutgers Univ, PhD, 80. **CAREER** TA, Univ of Haifa, 71-77; clinical psychologist, Rutgers Univ, 80-82; asst prof to assoc prof, Miami Univ, 83-. **HONORS AND AWARDS** Am Asn of Univ Women Int Fel, 78; Grants, Miami Univ, 94, 95, 97, 98. **MEMBERSHIPS** Am Psychol Assoc; Ohio Psychol Assoc. **RESEARCH** Anxiety disorders, eating disorders, stress, acculturation. **SELECTED PUBLICATIONS** Rev, of "Handbook of Cognitive Therapy Techniques" by R.E. McMullin, Contemp Psychol 34 (89): 287; auth, "Successful treatment of agoraphobia and resourcefulness", Learned Resourcefulness, ed M. Rosenbaum, Springer (NY), 90; rev of "Psychological Treatment of Panic", by D.H. Barlow and J.A. Cerny, Contemp Psychol 35, (90: 898-899; auth, "Personality patterns and tendency for somatization", Psychol Psychoanalyst, XV.2 (95): 39; rev, of "Disorders of the self: New Therapeutic Horizons", by J.F. Masterson and R. Klein, Contemp Psychol 42, (97): 628-629. **CONTACT ADDRESS** Dept Psychol, Miami Univ, 122 Benton Hall, Oxford, OH 45056. **EMAIL** biranmw@muohio.edu

BIRCHETTE, WILLIAM ASHBY, III
PERSONAL Born 05/09/1942, Newport News, VA, s **DISCIPLINE** EDUCATION **EDUCATION** St Augustine's Col, BA 1964; VA State Univ, MEd 1973; Univ of VA, EdD 1982. **CAREER** Wilson City Public Schools; Delaware Tech & Community College; Banneker Jr HS, principal, DC Public Schools;

Hampton Univ, instructor; asst to reg supt, DC Public Schools; Magruder Middle School, principal 1983-87; Reservoir Middle School, principal 1988-90; Vasguard Middle School, VA Dept of Education, principal, 89; Southern Vance High School, Vance County Schools, principal, 90-92; Isle of Wight County Schools, assistant superintendent for instruction, 92-97; Spotsylvania County Schools, supervisor English, language arts, 98-. **HONORS AND AWARDS** Outstanding Leadership Awd 1978; Citizen Involvement in Education 1980; Charles Stewart Mott Fellow 1980; Education Fellow Univ of VA; Principal, Vanguard Middle School, VA Dept of Education 1987; Author, "Guidelines for Middle Schools in Virginia," (VASSP Journal) 1988; Contributions (Executive Educator) 1988; Twenty-Five Outstanding High Schools, NC Dept of Ed, principal, 1991. **MEMBERSHIPS** Phi Delta Kappa; ASCD; Natl Comm Educ Assn; VA Comm Educ Assn; advisory bd Hampton Roads Boys Club; bd of directors Youth Programs-Mall Tennis Club; Omega Psi Phi; member NAACP; pres Peninsula Council of Urban League; pres, PTPA; An Achievable Dream, bd of dirs. **CONTACT ADDRESS** Spotsylvania County Schools, 6717 Smith Station Rd, Spotsylvania, VA 22553.

BIRNBAUM, NORMAN
PERSONAL Born 07/21/1926, New York, NY, 2 children **DISCIPLINE** SOCIOLOGY **EDUCATION** Williams Col, BA, 47; Harvard Univ, PhD, 58. **CAREER** Lectr, London School of Econ and Polit Sci, 53-59; fel, Nuffield Col, Oxford Univ, 59-64; vis prof, Univ Strasbourg, 64-66; prof, Grad Fac of Political and Soc Sci, New School for Social Res, 66-68; prof, Amherst Col, 68-79; mellon Prof Hum, 79-81, Univ Prof, 81- , Georgetown Univ Law Center. **HONORS AND AWARDS** Guggenheim Found fel; mem, Inst for Advanced Study; vis scholar, Giovanni Agnelli Found; vis fel, Wissenschaftskolleg; dir d-Etudes Associe, Ecole des Hautes Etudes en Sciences Sociales; Fulbright Distinguished Chair, Univ Bologna; founding ed board, New Left Review, London, 59; ed board, Partisan Rev, 71-83; ed board, The Nation, 76- . **RESEARCH** Modern industrial society; modern social movements; religion and society. **SELECTED PUBLICATIONS** Auth, Crisis of Industrial Society, 69; auth, Toward A Critical Sociology, 71; auth, The Radical Renewal, 88; auth, Searching for the Light, 93; auth, After Progress, 00. **CONTACT ADDRESS** Law Ctr, Georgetown Univ, 600 New Jersey Ave NW, Washington, DC 20001. **EMAIL** birnbaum@law.georgetown.edu

BLACK, BEVERLY M.
DISCIPLINE SOCIAL WORK **EDUCATION** Univ Wisc, BA, 75; MS, 77; Univ Tex, PhD, 89. **CAREER** Asst Prof, St Edward's Univ, 86-87; Visiting Asst Prof, Fla Intl Univ, 88-89; Asst Prof, Tex Christian Univ, 89-91; Visiting Asst Prof to Asst Prof, Fla Intl Univ, 91-95; Assoc Prof, Wayne State Univ, 95-. **HONORS AND AWARDS** Grant, MI Dept of Community Health, 98-99, 99-02; Feminist Scholar Awd, Coun of Soc Work Educ, 98; Grant, MI Dept Community Health, 97-98; Grant, Wayne State Univ, 97; Fin Awd, Wayne State Univ, 96; Fin Awd, TX Christian Univ, 89-90. **MEMBERSHIPS** SEMARN; Coun on Soc Work Educ; Nat Asn of Woc Workers; Nat Hospice Org; Soc for Soc Work and Res. **RESEARCH** Sexual Assault and Dating Violence Prevention; Volunteerism; Attitude Change; Homophobia; Sexism. **SELECTED PUBLICATIONS** Auth, "Attitudes toward international issues: The influence of social work education," Social Work and Social Services Review: An International Journal of Applied Research, (97): 39-52; co-auth, "Treating tuberculosis: The essential role of social work," Social Work in Health Care, (98): 51-68; co-auth, "The relationship between attitudes: Homophobia and sexism among social work students," Affilia: Journal of Women and Social Work, (98): 166-189; co-auth, "From attitude change to effective practice: Exploring the relationship," Journal of Social Work Education, (99): 87-100; co-auth, "Age differences in volunteer participation," The Journal of Volunteer Administration, (99): 38-47; co-auth, "Attitudes and behaviors of social work students toward lesbians and gay male clients: Can panel presentations make a difference?," Journal of Gay and Lesbian Social Services, (99): 47-68; co-auth, "Age-related variation in roles performed by hospice volunteers," Journal of Applied Geronotology, (99): 519-537; co-auth, "Volunteerism and older adults: Implications for social work practice," Journal of Gerontological Social Work, in press; co-auth, "Evaluating a psychoeducational sexual assault prevention program," Research on Social Work Practice, in press; co-auth, "Gender and moral reasoning: African American youth respond to dating dilemmas," Journal of Human Behavior in the Social Environment, in press. **CONTACT ADDRESS** Sch of Soc Work, Wayne State Univ, 112 Cohn Bldg, Detroit, MI 48202.

BLACK, WESLEY O.
PERSONAL m, 2 children **DISCIPLINE** YOUTH EDUCATION **EDUCATION** Hardin - Simmins Univ, BM, 68; Southwestern Baptist Theol Sem, MA, 75, PhD, 85. **CAREER** Prof, Southwestern Baptist Theol Sem, 83-. **HONORS AND AWARDS** Min Youth, Ctr Baptist Church, 70-71; First Baptist Church, Duncan, 73-81; North Side Baptist Church, 75-81; youth consult, Baptist Sunday Sch Bd, 81-83. **MEMBERSHIPS** N Amer Prof Christian Edu; Youth Ministry Educator's Forum; Baptist Rel Edu Assn Southwest; S Baptist Rel Edu Assn. **SELECTED PUBLICATIONS** Auth, Introduction to Youth Ministry, Holman, 91. **CONTACT ADDRESS** Sch Theol, Southwestern Baptist Theol Sem, PO Box 22000, Fort Worth, TX 76122-0418. **EMAIL** wob@swbts.swbts.edu

BLAIN, ROBERT R.
PERSONAL Born 10/29/1938, Holyoke, MA, m, 1984, 3 children **DISCIPLINE** SOCIOLOGY **EDUCATION** Univ Mass, BA, 60; Harvard Univ, MA, 64; Univ Mass, PhD, 67. **CAREER** Instr to Asst Prof, The Ohio State Univ, 66-68; Assoc to Full Prof, Southern Ill Univ at Edwardsville, 68-. **HONORS AND AWARDS** Cert of Excellence, State of Ill Historical Soc. **RESEARCH** Wealth and Poverty. **SELECTED PUBLICATIONS** Auth, "On Humans' psychological reductionism," Sociol Inquiry 4 1 (Winter 71): 3-25; auth, "An Alternative to Parsons' four-function paradigm as a basis for developing general sociological theory," Am Sociol Rev 36 (Aug 71): 678-692; auth, "Parsons' hierarchy of control and the codification variable of the ICL theory," Indian J of Soc Res 15 (Aug and Dec 74): 179-189; auth, "The information chain theory of cooperation," Int J of Comp Sociol 26 (Mar-June 85): 75-89; auth, "United States Public and Private Dept: 1791-2000," Int Soc Sci J 114 (Nov 870: 577-591; auth, The Historic Cooperative Village of Declare: A Centennial Collection, 90; auth, "Defining exchange rate parity in terms of GDP per hour work," Appl Behav Sci Rev 4-1 (96): 55-79; auth, A History of Cooperative Village of Declare: Expansion of Centennial Collection, 97; auth, National wealth and poverty, 98; auth, "An instrument panel for spaceship earth," The Int J of Humanities and Peace 15-1 (99): 52-54. **CONTACT ADDRESS** Dept Sociol, So Illinois Univ, Edwardsville, PO Box 1455, Edwardsville, IL 62026-1455. **EMAIL** rblain@siue.edu

BLAIR, ROBERT G.
PERSONAL Born 11/07/1958, Bloomington, IN, m, 1990, 3 children **DISCIPLINE** SOCIAL WORK **EDUCATION** Wash State Univ, BA, 85; Univ Utah, MSW, 87, PhD, 96. **CAREER** Asst prof, Moorehead State Univ, 97-. **HONORS AND AWARDS** Golden Key Nat Honor Soc. **MEMBERSHIPS** Nat Asn Soc Workers. **RESEARCH** Cambodian refugees, resiliency, prevention. **SELECTED PUBLICATIONS** Auth, "Integrating Disability: My Journey," Reflections: Narratives of Professional Helping, 5, 4 (99): 7-15; auth, "Risk Factors Associated with PTSD and Major Depression among Cambodian Refugees in Utah," Health and Social Work: J of NASW, 25, 1 (2000): 23-30; auth, "Mental Health Needs among Cambodian Refugees in Utah," J of Int Soc Work (April 99). **CONTACT ADDRESS** Dept Sociol, Morehead State Univ, 150 Univ Blvd, Morehead, KY 40351. **EMAIL** r.blair@morehead-st.edu

BLAKE, J. HERMAN
PERSONAL Born 03/15/1934, Mt. Vernon, NY, m **DISCIPLINE** SOCIOLOGY **EDUCATION** NYork Univ, BA 1960; Univ CA, MA 1965, PhD 1973. **CAREER** Univ CA, asst prof, 66-70, assoc prof, 70-74; UCSC, prof, 74-84; Oakes Coll UCSC, founding provost, 72-84; Tougaloo Coll, pres, 84-87. **HONORS AND AWARDS** Named among Top 100 Emerging Young Leaders in Higher Educ Amer Council of Educ 1978. **MEMBERSHIPS** Mem Amer Sociol Assn, Population Assn of Amer, Pacific Sociol Assn; bd trustee Save the Children Fedn; bd trustee Penn Comm Serv Fellowships Woodrow Wilson 1960, John Hay Whitney 1963; mem Population Council 1964; Danforth Found 1964; Rockefeller Found 1965; Ford Found 1970. **SELECTED PUBLICATIONS** Co-author "Revolutionary Suicide" 73. **CONTACT ADDRESS** Dept Sociology, Swarthmore Col, Swarthmore, PA 19081.

BLAKE, MICHELLE
PERSONAL Born 10/20/1953, Memphis, TN, m, 1987 **DISCIPLINE** SOCIOLOGY **EDUCATION** Christian Brothers Univ, BA, 75; Univ Louisville, MSSW, 91; Fla State Univ, PhD, 98. **CAREER** Adj Prof, Fla A&M Univ, 93-94, 96; Teaching Asst, Fla State Univ, 93-97; Asst Prof, Instr, Univ S Ind, 97-. **MEMBERSHIPS** NASW, CSWE, NAPT. **CONTACT ADDRESS** Dept Sociol, Univ of So Indiana, 8600 Univ Blvd, Evansville, IN 47712.

BLAKELY, EVERETT
PERSONAL Born 02/24/1941, AR **DISCIPLINE** SOCIAL WORK **EDUCATION** Univ Mich, BA, 72; Univ Mich, MSW, 75; Hawthorne Univ, DSW, 95. **CAREER** Clinical Social Work, twenty-seven years, Community Mental Health Systems. **MEMBERSHIPS** Soc of Clinical and Soc Work, Am Psychotherapists Asn. **RESEARCH** Mental health policy and service delivery. **SELECTED PUBLICATIONS** Auth, Characteristics of Homeless Victims; auth, Values, Attitudes and Tracking; auth, The Decline of Common Sense and Rise of Mental Illness; auth, Capital Punishment and Social Work Values; auth, Thoughtless Youth Killers; auth, Religious Ethics and Professional Practice. **CONTACT ADDRESS** Dept Social Work, Univ of Michigan, Flint, 303 E Kearsley St, Flint, MI 48502.

BLAKESLEE, SPENCER
PERSONAL Born 01/23/1935, Minneapolis, MN, m, 1989, 1 child **DISCIPLINE** SOCIOLOGY **EDUCATION** Univ Minn, AS, 70; BA, 72; MA, 75; Northeastern Univ, PhD, 97. **CAREER** Lectr, Northeastern Univ, 90-97; asst prof, Framingham State Col, 98-. **HONORS AND AWARDS** Stotsky Holocaust Mem Awd, 93. **MEMBERSHIPS** ASA; Eastern Sociol Soc; Assoc Jewish Studies. **RESEARCH** Social Identity and Sociol Processes, Social Perspectives on Holocaust, Antisemitism, Racism and Violence. **SELECTED PUBLICATIONS** Auth, "The Holocaust in a Sociological Perspective", in Handbook of Genocide: Theories, Cases, and Implications, An International Perspective, ed Jack Nusan Porter, Am Sociol Assoc, (Wash, DC), 99; auth, The Death of American Antisemitism, Praeger, (Westport, CT), 00; auth, "Sociological Properties of the Shoah", in Mini-Encyclopedia of the Holocaust: Sociological and Sexual Themes, Brill, (Holland) (forthcoming). **CONTACT ADDRESS** Dept Sociol, Framingham State Col, 100 State St, Framingham, MA 01702. **EMAIL** sblake@mail2.gis.net

BLALOCK, CARMEN FOUNTAIN
PERSONAL Born 12/16/1947, Birmingham, AL, 1 child **DISCIPLINE** SOCIOLOGY, EDUCATION **EDUCATION** Univ Ala, BS, 70; MA, 72; EdD, 83. **CAREER** Women and Girls Dir, YMCA, Tuscaloosa, Ala, 71-72; Proj Dir, 74-77, Div Chairperson for Soc Sci, 90-93, instr, 72-, and Distance Educ Coordr, Calhoun Community Col, 97-. **MEMBERSHIPS** Am Asn of Univ Women, Ala Community Col Asn, Southern Sociol Asn, Mid-South Sociol Asn, CHA: The Asn for Horsemanship Safety and Education, Sierra Club, Ala Water Watch. **SELECTED PUBLICATIONS** Auth, "Building Community: The Tale of a Trail," Endurance News, Vol 27, No 6 (96): 30-31; auth, "Local Equestrian Team Fares Well," Endurance News, Vol 27, No 11 (96): 8; auth, "On the Ground in the Nineties," Ala-Miss Sociol Asn, UNA, Florence, Ala (97); auth, "Angels Cry White Tears," Trail Blazer (March/April 97): 45; auth, "Institutional Effectiveness and Distance Learning," TeleLearning, Austin Tex, (99). **CONTACT ADDRESS** Dept Soc Sci, Calhoun Community Col, PO Box 2216, Decatur, AL 35609.

BLAND, SIDNEY RODERICK
PERSONAL Born 10/31/1936, Caroleen, NC, m, 1962, 2 children **DISCIPLINE** WOMEN'S HISTORY, AMERICAN HISTORY **EDUCATION** Furman Univ, BA, 59; Univ Md, College Park, MA, 61; George Washington Univ, PhD(Am civilization), 72. **CAREER** Asst prof, 65-72, assoc prof, 72-81, Prof Hist, James Madison Univ, 81-, Co-chmn, Am Studies Comt, 73-; grant, Am Philos Soc, 81. **RESEARCH** Militancy in the woman suffrage movement in the early twentieth century; women in Southern history; late 19th-early 20th century American history. **SELECTED PUBLICATIONS** Auth, Aspects of Woman Suffrage Militancy in England, 1905-1914, Studies & Res, 3/70; New life in an Old Movement: The Great Suffrage Parade of 1913, Records, Columbia Hist Soc, 71-72; Mad Women of the Cause: The National Women's Party and the South, Furman Univ Studies, 12/80; Lucy Burns, In: Notable American Women: The Modern Period, Harvard Univ Press, 80; Fighting the Odds: Militant Suffragists in South Carolina, SC Hist Mag, 1/81; Never Quite as Committed as We'd Like: The Suffrage Militancy of Lucy Burns, J Long Island Hist, XXII, No 2, spring 81. **CONTACT ADDRESS** Dept of Hist, James Madison Univ, Harrisonburg, VA 22801.

BLASI, ANTHONY J.
PERSONAL Born 04/03/1946, Dayton, OH, s **DISCIPLINE** SOCIOLOGY **EDUCATION** St Edmond's Univ, BA, 68; Univ Notre Dame, MA, 71; Univ Notre Dame, Phd, 74; Univ St Michael's Col, MA, 84; Collegium Christi Regis, STL, 85; Univ Toronto, ThD, 86. **CAREER** Asst prof, Univ Louisville, 76-78; assoc prof, Daemen Col, 78-80; asst prof, Univ Hawaii, 86-90; assoc prof, Muskingum Col, 90-94; assoc prof, Tenn State Univ, 94-99, prof, Tenn State Univ, 99-. **MEMBERSHIPS** ASA, Asn for the Sociol of Relig, Religious Res Asn, Soc for the Sci Study of Relig, Southern Sociol Soc. **RESEARCH** Sociology of relig. **SELECTED PUBLICATIONS** Coauth, Toward an Interpretive Sociology, 78; auth, Segregationist Violence and Civil Rights Movements in Tuscaloosa, 80; auth, A Phenomenological Transformation of the Social Scientific Study of Religion, 85; auth, Early Christianity as a Social Movement, 89; auth, Making Charisma: The Social Construction of Paul's Public Image, 91; auth, A Sociology of Johannine Christianity, Edwin Mellen Press, 96; auth, "George Herbert Mead's Transformation of his intellectual Context," in The Tradition of the Chicago Sch of Sociol (98): 149-178; auth, "American Ritual and American Gods," in The Am Ritual Tapestry (98): 109-116; auth, "L'ideologic de 'Eglise chretienne primitiv dans l'Epitre de Saint Paul aux Romains et la lettre de recommandation de Phebee," Soc Compass 464 (99): 507-520; auth, Organized Religion and Seniors' Mental Health, 99. **CONTACT ADDRESS** Dept Sociol, Tennessee State Univ, 3500 John A Merritt, Nashville, TN 37209-1561. **EMAIL** blasi3610@cs.com

BLATT, SIDNEY JULES
PERSONAL Born 10/15/1928, Philadelphia, PA, m, 1951, 3 children **DISCIPLINE** PSYCHOLOGY **EDUCATION** Univ of Chicago, PhD, 57. **CAREER** PROF, YALE UNIV, 60-. **HONORS AND AWARDS** Sigmund Freud Prof, Zachs Prof of Art Hist, Hebrew Univ, 88-89; Fulbright Sr Res Fel, 88-89;

Bruno Klopfer Awd for Distinquished Res Contributions; Distinguished Scientific Contributions Awd, Division 39, Am Psychol Assoc.; **MEMBERSHIPS** Asn of Medical School Profs of Psychol; Am Psychol Asn; Distinguished Res Contriburs. **RESEARCH** Mental representations and their role in personality development; psychopathology and the therapeutic process. **SELECTED PUBLICATIONS** Co-ed, The Self in Emotional Distress: Cognitive and Psychodynamic Perspectives, Guilford Press, 93; coed, Depression and the Self, In Session: Pyschotherapy in Practice, John Wiley & Sons, 97; coauth, Therapeutic Change: An Object Relations Perspective, Plenum, 94; coauth, The Prediction of Therapeutic Response to the Long-term Extensive Treatment of Seriously Disturbed Young Adults, Psychotherapy Res, 95; coauth, Developmental Lines, Schemas, and Archtypes, Am Psychol, 95; coauth, Differential Vulnerability of Dependency and Self-criticism Among Disadvantaged Teenages, J of Res on Adolescence, 95; coauth, Relatedness and Self Definition: A Dialectic Model of Personality Development, Development and Vulnerabilities in Close Relationships, Lawrence Erlbaum Assocs, 96; coauth, Precursors of Relatedness and Self-definition in Mother-Infant Interaction, Pschoanalytic Perspectives on Developmental Psychol, APA, 96; coauth, A Psychodynamic Approach to the Diagnosis of Psychopathology, Making Diagnosis Meaningful, APA Press, 98; coauth, Attachment Styles and Parental Representations, J of Personality & Soc Psychol, 98. **CONTACT ADDRESS** Depts of Psychol and Psychiat, Yale Univ, 25 Park St, New Haven, CT 06519. **EMAIL** sidney.blatt@yale.edu

BLAU, JUDITH R.
PERSONAL Born 09/27/1942, Elansius, MI, m, 1968, 2 children **DISCIPLINE** SOCIOLOGY **EDUCATION** Univ Chicago, BA, 64, MA, 67; Northwestern Univ, PhD, 72; **CAREER** Asst Prof to Assoc Prof, State Univ NY - Albany, 78-88; Prof, 88-97, Gillian T. Cell Prof, Univ NC - Chapel Hill, 97-. **MEMBERSHIPS** Am Sociol Asn; Int Sociol Asn; Southern Sociol Soc. **RESEARCH** Education; art; organization. **SELECTED PUBLICATIONS** Auth, Left-Brain v. Right-Brain Mistakes, Mistakes Social Scientists Make, St. Martin's Press, 95; The Toggle Switch of Institutions: Religion and Art in the U.S. in the Nineteenth and Early Twentieth Century, Soc Forces, 96; coauth, Black and White Students in Two-Year Colleges, Thought & Action. Spring 96; Second-Order Cultural Effects of Civil Rights on Southern Nonprofit Organizations, Nonprofit & Voluntary Sector Quart 25, 96; auth, Organizations as Overlapping Jurisdictions Restoring Reason in Organizational Accounts, Admin Sci Quart, 96; coauth, Historically Black Organizations in the Nonprofit Sector, Nonprofit and Voluntary Sector Quart, 96; The Duality of Church and Faith, Sociol Perspectives 4, 97; ed, Blackwell Companion to Sociology, Blackwell, 01. **CONTACT ADDRESS** Univ of No Carolina, Chapel Hill, Hamilton Hall, CB# 3210, Chapel Hill, NC 27599-3210. **EMAIL** judith_blau@unc.edu

BLEE, K. M.
DISCIPLINE SOCIOLOGY **EDUCATION** Univ Wisc, PhD, 82. **CAREER** Prof of sociol, dir of women's studies, assoc dean of col of art and sci, Univ Ky, 81-96; prof of sociol and hist and dir of women's studies, Univ Pittsburgh, 96-. **RESEARCH** Gender; Racism; Politics. **SELECTED PUBLICATIONS** Auth, No Middle Ground, NY Univ Press, 98; auth, Women of the Klan, Univ Calif Press, 91. **CONTACT ADDRESS** Univ of Pittsburgh, 2603 FQ, Pittsburgh, PA 15260. **EMAIL** kblee@pitt.edu

BLEVINS, GREGORY A.
PERSONAL Born 01/27/1947, South Bend, IL, m, 1979, 1 child **DISCIPLINE** SOCIOLOGY **EDUCATION** Lake Mich Col, AS, 68; Western Mich Univ, BS, 70; MA, 74; PhD, 79. **CAREER** Instr, Western Mich Univ, 79-81; Asst Prof, Univ S Dak, 81-82; Prof, Governors State Univ, 82-. **MEMBERSHIPS** Intl Coalition for Addiction studies Educ **RESEARCH** Alcohol and drug Abuse. **SELECTED PUBLICATIONS** Coauth, "A Scenario for the Future: Implications of Academic Education on the Next Generation of Counselors," The Counselor, 97; auth, Substance Abuse: Current Concepts Study Guide 3rd ed, Governors State Univ, 95; auth, "Pharmacology of Abused Drugs," in Handbook on Substance Abuse, Aspen Press, 94; coauth, Substance Abuse Counseling: an Individualized Approach 2nd ed, Cole Pub Co, 94. **CONTACT ADDRESS** Dept Health Occupations, Governors State Univ, 1 Univ Pkwy, Park Forest, IL 60466.

BLOCK, JOYCE
PERSONAL Born 12/29/1951, New York, NY, m, 1984, 2 children **DISCIPLINE** PSYCHOLOGY **EDUCATION** Grad Cen, CUNY, PhD, 82. **CAREER** Clinical Psychol, 82; Post Doct Fellow, Psychol, Down State Med Cen, 85; Adj Prof, Notre Dame Univ, St Mary's Col. **MEMBERSHIPS** Am Psychol Asn **SELECTED PUBLICATIONS** Motherhood as Metamorph, Dutton, 90; Family Myths, Simon & Schuster, 94. **CONTACT ADDRESS** 300 North Michigan St, South Bend, IN 46601.

BLOCKLEY, MARY EVA
PERSONAL Born 01/10/1956, Mt Vernon, IL **DISCIPLINE** EDUCATION **EDUCATION** Bryn Mawr Col, BA, 77; Yale Univ MA, 78, MPhil, 79, PhD, 84; **CAREER** Asst, Universite de Geneve, 81-82; instr English, Smith Col, 82-84; lectr, English, Yale Col, 84-85; asst prof, 85-92, assoc prof, 92- , English, Univ Texas Austin. **HONORS AND AWARDS** Fel, Yale Univ, 77-81; NEH Summer Stipend 87; NEH Fel, 89-90; Univ Texas Faculty Res Asst, 90, 96; URI Grant, 86. **MEMBERSHIPS** Ger Ling Asn; Int Soc Anglo-Saxonists; LSA; Mediaeval Acad Am; MLA. **RESEARCH** Old English syntax; history of the English language; English philology. **SELECTED PUBLICATIONS** Auth, Klaeber's Relineations of Beowulf and Verses Ending in Words Without Categorical Stress, Rev English Stud, 95; auth, Apposition and the Subjects of Clause-Initial Verbs, in Baker, ed, Words and Works, Univ Toronto, 98; auth, Caedmon's Conjunction: Caedmon's Hymn 76 Revisited, Speculum, 98; auth, Aspects of Old English Poetic Syntax: Where Clauses Begin, 00; coauth, A Biography of the English Language, 3d ed, Harcourt, 2001. **CONTACT ADDRESS** Dept of English, Univ of Texas, Austin, Austin, TX 78712-1164. **EMAIL** blockley@utxvms.cc.utexas.edu

BLOUNT, MARCELLUS
DISCIPLINE AMERICAN AND AFRICAN-AMERICAN LITERARY AND CULTURAL STUDIES **EDUCATION** Williams Col, BA, 80; Yale Univ, PhD, 87. **CAREER** English and Lit, Columbia Univ **HONORS AND AWARDS** Stephen H. Tyng Grant; res fel carter g. woodson inst; vis fel wesleyan's ctr afro-am studies; rockefeller fel ctr study black lit & cult. **SELECTED PUBLICATIONS** Coauth, In a Broken Tongue: Rediscovering African-American Poetry. **CONTACT ADDRESS** Columbia Univ, 2960 Broadway, New York, NY 10027-6902.

BLUM, LAWRENCE A.
PERSONAL Born 04/16/1943, Baltimore, MD, m, 1975, 3 children **DISCIPLINE** PHILOSOPHY; EDUCATION **EDUCATION** Princeton Univ, BA, 64; Harvard Univ, PhD, 74. **CAREER** Prof, Univ of Mass at Boston, 73- ; vis assoc prof, Univ of Calif, 84; vis prof, Stanford School of Educ, 90; vis prof, Columbia Univ, 90. **HONORS AND AWARDS** Chancellor's Distinguished Scho Awd, Univ of Mass, 81, 94; NEH fel for Col Tchrs, 86-87; Fel in Harvard Prog in Ethics and the Professions, 92-93. **MEMBERSHIPS** Am Philos Asn; Asn for Moral Educ; Philos of Educ Soc; Am Soc for Polit & Legal Philos. **RESEARCH** Moral philosophy; Multicultural education; Race studies; Moral education. **SELECTED PUBLICATIONS** Auth, Friendship, Altruism, and Morality, 80; Moral Perception and Particularity, 94; Community and Virtue, How Should One Live?, ed R. Crisp, 96; Altruism and Egoism, Dictionnaire de philosophie morale, 96; Community, Philos of Educ: An Encyclopedia, ed J.J. Chambliss, 96; Race, Racism, and Pan-African Identity: Thoughts on K. Anthony Appiah's In My Father's House, New Polit Sci, double issue 38/39, 97; Multicultural Education as Values Education, Harvard Proj on Schooling and Children Working Paper, 97; Altruism and Benevolence, Encyclopedic Dictionary of Bus Ethics, eds P. Werhane and R.E. Freeman, 97; Schindler's Motives, Psychoculture: Rev of Psychology and Cult Studies, vol 1, no 2, 97; Recognition, Value, and Equality: A Critique of Charles Taylor's and Nancy Fraser's Accounts of Multiculturalism, Theorizing Multiculturalism: A Guide to the Current Debate, ed C. Willett, 98; Racial Integration Revisited, Norms and Values: Essays In Honor of Virginia Held, eds J. Graf Habera and M. Halfon, 98; coauth, A Truer Liberty: Simone Weil and Marxism, 89. **CONTACT ADDRESS** Dept of Philosophy, Univ of Massachusetts, Boston, 100 Morrissey Blvd., Boston, MA 02125. **EMAIL** lawrence.blum@umb.edu

BLUM, TONI L.
PERSONAL Born 10/27/1962, Alamogordo, NM, m, 1991, 2 children **DISCIPLINE** PSYCHOLOGY **EDUCATION** Bethany Col, BA, 85; Ohio St Univ, MA, 88; PhD, 94. **CAREER** From Asst Prof to Assoc Prof, Stetson Univ, 91-. **HONORS AND AWARDS** Who's Who in Am Cols and Univs, 85; Psi Chi; Sigma Xi. **MEMBERSHIPS** APS, CUR, SEPA. **RESEARCH** Metacognition, cognitive skills measurement, decision strategy selection. **SELECTED PUBLICATIONS** Coauth, "Enhancing an Object-Oriented Curriculum: Metacognitive Assessment and Training," Frontiers in Educ (99); coauth, "The Assessment of Cognitive Skills for Computer Science Educ," Frontiers in Educ (99); coauth, "Unique Invulnerability Measurement in Skydivers: Scale Validation," Psi Chi J of Undergrad Res (95). **CONTACT ADDRESS** Dept Psychol, Stetson Univ, De Land, 421 N Woodland Blvd, Deland, FL 32720. **EMAIL** tblum@stetson.edu

BOCHNOWSKI, MICHAEL
PERSONAL Born 08/04/1938, Brooklyn, NY **DISCIPLINE** RELIGIOUS EDUCATION **EDUCATION** New York Univ, PhD, 93. **CAREER** Dir relig educ, Ft Belvoir, Va, 86- . **HONORS AND AWARDS** Res fel, Yale Divinity Sch; U.S. Army Chief of Chaplains Writing Awd Competition, 96. **MEMBERSHIPS** Am Asn Christian Counr; Relig Educ Asn. **RESEARCH** Religion and worship. **CONTACT ADDRESS** 8637 Beerman Pl, Alexandria, VA 22309-1616. **EMAIL** smbphd@aol.com

BOCK, PHILIP K.
PERSONAL Born 08/26/1934, New York, NY, m, 1976, 3 children **DISCIPLINE** SOCIAL ANTHROPOLOGY **EDUCATION** Harvard Univ, PhD, 62. **CAREER** Asst prof to prof emer, Univ New Mexico, 62-92. **HONORS AND AWARDS** Woodrow Wilson Fel; Harvard Univ Fel; Danforth Fel; NSF and NEA awds; Univ New Mexico Pres Prof, 85-90. **MEMBERSHIPS** Am Anthrop Asn; Soc for Psychol Anthrop. **RESEARCH** Social anthropology; musicology; cognitive psychology; Shakespeare and Elizabethan culture. **SELECTED PUBLICATIONS** Auth, Shakespeare and Elizabethan Culture, Schocken, 84; auth,The Formal Content of Ethnography, International Museum of Cultures, 86; auth, Rethinking Psychological Anthropology, Freeman, 88; ed, and auth two chap, Handbook of Psychological Anthropology, Greenwood, 94. **CONTACT ADDRESS** Dept of Anthropology, Univ of New Mexico, Albuquerque, Albuquerque, NM 87131. **EMAIL** pbock@unm.edu

BODKIN, THOMAS E.
PERSONAL Born 10/20/1968, Chattanooga, TN, s **DISCIPLINE** ANTHROPOLOGY **EDUCATION** Univ Tenn, Chattanooga, BA, 92; Univ Tenn, Knoxville, MA, 95. **CAREER** Adjunct fac, Univ Tenn, Chattanooga; Forensic anthropologist, Hamilton Co Medical Examiner Office, 97-. **HONORS AND AWARDS** Phi Kappa Phi; Lambda Alpha; Alpha Soc; Beta Beta Beta: Sigma Chapter; Mortar Board: Quadrangle Chapter; Outstanding Sr Awd, Univ Tenn, Chattanooga; Golden Key: Chattanooga Chapter; Outstanding Student Awd, Univ Tenn Chattanooga. **MEMBERSHIPS** Am Asn of Forensic Sci, Am Asn of Physical Anthropology, Tenn Anthropol Asn. **RESEARCH** Forensic anthropology. **SELECTED PUBLICATIONS** Auth of over 40 anthropology reports prepared for court. **CONTACT ADDRESS** Dept Sociol & Anthropol, Univ of Tennessee, Chattanooga, 615 McCallie Ave, Chattanooga, TN 37403. **EMAIL** TomB@mail.hamiltontn.gov

BOIVIN, MICHAEL
PERSONAL Born 07/28/1955, Detroit, MI, m, 1978, 4 children **DISCIPLINE** PSYCHOLOGY **EDUCATION** Spring Arbor Col, BA, 76; W Mich Univ, MA, 78; PhD, 80; Univ Mich, MA, 94. **CAREER** Faculty, Spring Arbor Col, 79-96; Prof, Ind Wesleyan Univ, 96-. **HONORS AND AWARDS** Sen Res Awd, Fulbright Scholar, Zaire, 96; Visiting Researcher, St. Andrews Univ; John Templeton Oxford Seminar, 99. **MEMBERSHIPS** Christian Asn for Psychol Studies. **RESEARCH** Developmental neuropsychology. **SELECTED PUBLICATIONS** Auth, "Modality specificity of memory span tasks among Congolese children: A developmental perspective," Journal of Clinical and Experimental Neuropsychology, (99): 375-384; auth, "An ecological paradigm for a health behaior analysis of 'Konzo', a paralytic disease of Zaire from toxic cassava," Social Science & Medicine, (97): 1853-1862; co-ed, "Theme Issue: Christianity and Homosexuality," Christian Scholar's Review, (97); auth, "WARA Research Fellow report: Effects of cerebral malaria and other illnesses on the neuropsychological development of Senegalese children," West African Research Association Newsletter, (97): 16-17; auth, "Final report on the advanced research training seminar on mediational intervention for sensitizing caregivers programme in Sherbrooke, Quebec," International Journal of Psychology, (96): 270-272; auth, "Validating a cognitive ability testing protocol with Lao children for community development applications," Neuropsychology, (96): 588-599; auth, "Ue of the K-ABC in cognitive ability testing with African children," International Journal of Disability, Development, and Education, (96): 5-24; auth, "Economic advantage and the cognitive ability of rural children in Zaire, Africa," Journal of Psychology, (96): 95-107; auth, "Use of the Tactual Performance Test for cognitive ability testing with African children," Neuropsychology, (95): 409-417; auth, The accidental anthropologist: A Fulbright scholar unloads his cultural baggage in Zaire, Spring Arbor College Press, 95. **CONTACT ADDRESS** Dept Beh Sci, Indiana Wesleyan Univ, 4201 S Wash St, Marion, IN 46953. **EMAIL** mboivin@indwes.edu

BOLAND, JAMES M.
PERSONAL Born 08/18/1942, Hammond, IN, m, 1962, 3 children **DISCIPLINE** EDUCATION **EDUCATION** Ind Univ, BS, 68; Ball State Univ, MAE, 70, EdD, 72. **CAREER** Teacher, Hammond Public Sch, 68-69; asst prof of educ, Ball State Univ; asst dean of Student Services, 76, assoc prof of Educ, Indiana Univ Northwest, Dir, Educ Field Experiences and Placement, 78-90, 96-98, Dir, Indiana Univ NW Testing Bureau, 88-99. **HONORS AND AWARDS** Division of Educ Teaching Awd, Indiana Univ NW, 81, 83, 83, 84; Alumni Asn Distinguished Educator Awd, Indiana Univ NW, 90; Teaching Excellence Recognition Awd (TERA), Indiana Univ NW, 98-99. **MEMBERSHIPS** Ind Sch Psychols Asn, Ind Asn of Teacher Educ, Am Personnel & Guidance Asn, Kappa Delta Pi, Phi Delta Kappa. **RESEARCH** Inclusion. **SELECTED PUBLICATIONS** Coauth, Foundations of Education in A Field-Based Setting, Univ Press of Am, Washington, DC (76); coauth, "The Predictability of College Graded Point Averages," J of Educ Opportunity Progs (Nov 8, 76); coauth, "Ethnicity as a Background Factor in College Education," Urban Educ, XIII, Vol 1 (April 78): 65-70; auth, "So you want to get a Student Testes: Tips for the Building Administrator," Catalyst: The J of the

Nebr Coun of Sch Adminr, Vol 4, No 2 (winter 81): 43-45; auth, "Retrenchment: Panacea or Placebo?," Action in Teacher Educ: The J of the Asn of Teacher Educs, Vol 3, Nos 2 and 43 (summer/fall 81): 85-89; auth, "Tips on How to Relax," Sch and Community, The Mag of the Missouri State Teachers Asn (Oct 81): 34-35, 51. **CONTACT ADDRESS** Div of Educ, Indiana Univ, Northwest, 3400 Broadway, Gary, IN 46408. **EMAIL** jboland@iun.haw1.iun.indiana.edu

BOLES, DAVID B.
PERSONAL Born 08/31/1952, Columbus, OH, m, 1987, 2 children **DISCIPLINE** PSYCHOLOGY **EDUCATION** Mich State Univ, BS, 74; Univ Oregon, MS, 77, Doctor Philos, 79. **CAREER** Vis asst prof, New Col of the Univ of South Fla, 79-80; vis asst prof, Univ Tex, Arlington, 80-81; vis asst prof, Univ Calgary, 81-82; vis ast prof, Ill State Univ, 82-83; res assoc, Univ Ill, Urbana-Champaign, 83-84; vis res assoc, Instituto di Psicologia, CNR (Nat Res Coun), Rome, Italy, summer 84; asst to assoc prof, Rensselaer Polytech Inst, 84-2000; assoc prof, Univ Ala, 2000-. **HONORS AND AWARDS** Acting chair, Dept Psychol, Rensselaer Polytech Inst, 91-93 (acting co-chair, 96); Human Factors Grad Prog Dir, Dept Psychol, Rensselaer Polytech Inst, 89-99; mem, Int Sci Adv Bd, International Encyclopedia of Ergonomics and Human Factors (under compilation). **MEMBERSHIPS** Am Psychol Soc, Human Factors Soc, Psychonomic Soc. **RESEARCH** Cognitive neuroscience, cognitive resources, individual differences, hemispheric asymmetry, human factors. **SELECTED PUBLICATIONS** Auth, "Parameters of the Bilateral effect," in F. L. Kitterle, ed, Hemispheric Communication: Mechanisms and Models, Hillsdale, NJ: Lawrence Erlbaum Assocs (95); coauth with S. J. Pasquarette, "Correlated auditory asymmetries in lexical and nonlexical tasks," Cortex, 32 (96): 537-545; coauth with T. A. Karner, "Hemispheric differences in global versus local processing: Still unclear," Brain and Cognition, 30 (96): 232-243; auth, "Factor analysis and the cerebral hemispheres: 'Unlocalized' functions, " Neuropsychologia, 34 (96): 723-736; auth, "Multiple resource contributions to training," Proceedings of the Human Factors and Ergonomics Soc, 41st Annual Meeting (97): 1176-1179; coauth with M. B. Law, "A simultaneous task comparison of differentiated and undifferentiated hemispheric resource theories," J of Experimental Psychol: Human Perception and Performance,24 (98): 204-215; auth, "Relationships among multiple task asymmetries: I, A critical review," Brain and Cognition, 36 (98): 253-267; auth, "Relationships among multiple task asymmetries: II. A large-sample factor analysis, Brain and Cognition, 36 (98): 268-289; auth, "The role of target task pre-exposure in resource training," Proceedings of the Human Factors and Ergonomics Soc, 43rd Annual Meeting 999): 1166-1170; auth, "The 'lumping' and 'splitting' of function and brain," Brain and Cognition (in press). **CONTACT ADDRESS** Dept Psychol, Univ of Alabama, Tuscaloosa, PO Box 870348, Tuscaloosa, AL 35487. **EMAIL** dboles@bama.edu

BOLICH, GREG
PERSONAL Born 07/07/1953, Spokane, WA **DISCIPLINE** PSYCHOLOGY **EDUCATION** Seattle Pac Univ, BA, 74; Seattle Pac Univ, MCM, 75; Western Evangelical Sem, MA, 77; Gonzaga Univ, PhD, 83; Union Inst, PhD, 93. **CAREER** instr, Inland Empire Sch of the Bible, 74-76; Lectr-at-Large, Fuller Theol Sem, 80; Adminr, Gonzaga Univ, 81-83; Fac, Eastern Wash Univ, 83-93; Fac, Cleveland Community Col, 93-. **HONORS AND AWARDS** Outstanding Young Man of Am, 77; Who's Who in Am Ed. **MEMBERSHIPS** APA, North Carolina Psychol/Sociol Fac Asn. **RESEARCH** Psychological research and humanities research, developing educational web site resources. **SELECTED PUBLICATIONS** Auth, Karl Barth and Evangelicalism, InterVarsity Pr, 80; Auth, Authority and the Church, Univ Pr of Am, 82; "On Dating James: New Perspectives on an Ancient Problem," doctoral diss, Gonzaga Univ Pr, 83; Auth, The Christian Scholar: An Introduction to Theological Research, Univ Pr of Am, 86; coauth, Introduction to Religion, Kendall/Hunt Pr, 88; coauth, God in the Docket: The Problem of Good and Evil, Kendall/Hunt Pr, 92; Biological Foundations for a Psychobiology of Abuse Trauma, Monograph, Union Inst, 93; Auth, Brick by Brick on the Road to Oz: Metaphors for Recovery from Sexual Abuse Trauma, Monograph, Union Inst, 92; Auth, Psyche's Child: The Story of Psychology, Kendall/Hunt Pr, 00. **CONTACT ADDRESS** Dept of Lib Arts, Cleveland Comm Col, 137 S Post Rd, Shelby, NC 28152. **EMAIL** bolich@cleveland.cc.nc.us

BOLING, BECKY
DISCIPLINE WOMEN WRITERS **EDUCATION** Northwestern State Univ, PhD. **CAREER** Literature, Carleton Col. **SELECTED PUBLICATIONS** Areas: Griselda Gambaro, Carlos Fuentes, Gabriel Garcia Marquez, Ana Lydia Vega, and Luisa Valenzuela. **CONTACT ADDRESS** Carleton Col, 100 S College St., Northfield, MN 55057-4016.

BOLLAND, O. NIGEL
PERSONAL Born 09/18/1943, Great Britain, m, 1966, 2 children **DISCIPLINE** SOCIOLOGY **EDUCATION** Hull, BA, 66; McMaster, MA, 67; Hull, PhD, 76. **CAREER** Res fel, Inst of Soc and Econ Res, Univ West Indies, Jamaica, 68-72; Prof, Colgate Univ, 72- . **HONORS AND AWARDS** NEH Fellowship, 94. **MEMBERSHIPS** Soc for Caribbean Studies; Caribbean Studies Asoc; Asoc of Caribbean Hist. **RESEARCH** Colonialism and labor in the Caribbean and Central America. **SELECTED PUBLICATIONS** auth, Belize: A New Nation in Central America, 86; Colonialism and Resistance in Belize: Essays in Historical Sociology, 88; Colonialismo y resistencia en Belice: Ensayos de sociologia historia, 92; On the March: Labour Rebellions in the British Caribbean, 1934-39, 95; Struggles for Freedom: Essays on Slavery, Colonialism, and Culture in the Caribbean and Central America, 97. **CONTACT ADDRESS** Dept of Sociology and Anthropology, Colgate Univ, Hamilton, NY 13346. **EMAIL** nbolland@mail.colgate.edu

BOLLENDORF, ROBERT F.
PERSONAL Born 09/11/1946, Kenosha, WI, m, 1998, 4 children **DISCIPLINE** OCCUPATIONAL EDUCATION **EDUCATION** St Joseph's Col, Collegeville, Ind, BA; Southern Ill Univ, Carbondale, MS; Northern Ill Univ, De Kalb, EdD. **CAREER** Ill Dept of Corrections, 70-71; Col of Du Page, 71-. **HONORS AND AWARDS** Graduated cum laude, honor soc, Ill Community Col Trustees Asn Teacher of the Year. **MEMBERSHIPS** Am Coun Asn, IAODAPCA, IAEDP. **RESEARCH** Addiction. **SELECTED PUBLICATIONS** Auth, Sober Spring, Acta Pubs; auth, Flight of the Loon, Acta Pubs. **CONTACT ADDRESS** Dept Occup Ed, Col of DuPage, 425 22nd St, Glen Ellyn, IL 60137. **EMAIL** bollen@cdnet.cod.edu

BOLLONG, CHARLES A.
PERSONAL Born 01/22/1955, Burnaby, BC, Canada **DISCIPLINE** ANTHROPOLOGY **EDUCATION** Simon Fraser Univ, BA, 79; Univ Otago, New Zealand, MA, 83; Southern Methodist Univ, MA, 89; PhD, 96. **CAREER** Curator, Queen Victoria Museum, Zimbabwe, 84-87; fac, Pima Community Col, 93-99; asst prof, Univ Ariz, 99-. **MEMBERSHIPS** Soc of Africanist Archaeol, Soc for Am Archaeol, Zimbabwe Prehisbory Soc. **RESEARCH** Hunter-gatherer and pastoralist interactions in southern Africa as reflected in ceramic technologies. **SELECTED PUBLICATIONS** Coauth, "Context and dating of pre-European livestock in the upper Seacow river Valley," Annals of the S Africa Museum, (93); coauth, "Direct dating and identity of fibre temper in pre-contact Bushman (Basarwa) pottery," Jour of Archaeol Sci, (94); auth, "Analysis of Site Stratigarphy and Formation processes using Patterns of Pottery Sherd Dispersion," Jour of Field Archaeol, (94); coauth, "Later Stone Age ceramic stratigraphy and direct dates on pottery: a comparison," Southern African Field Archaeol, (96); coauth, "Lustering of ceramic elemental data from PIXE analysis: A case study using herder-hunter pottery," Jour of Archaeol Sci, (97); coauth, Khoikhoi and Bushman pottery in the Cape Colony: Ethnohistory and Later Stone Age Ceramics of the South African Interior," Jour of Anthrop Archaeol, (97); coauth, "Later Stone Age hunter-herder interactions reflected in ceramic distributions in the upper Seacow River valley," S African Jour of Sci, (99). **CONTACT ADDRESS** Dept Anthrop, Univ of Arizona, Tucson, AZ 85721. **EMAIL** cbollong@email.arizona.edu

BOLOGNA, M.
PERSONAL Born 05/25/1963, Port Chester, NY, s **DISCIPLINE** SOCIAL WORK **EDUCATION** SUNY, BA, 85; MSW, 89; PhD, 00. **CAREER** Instructor, Col of St Rose, 94-; Consultant, Clearview Center, 96-; Consultant, Equinox Domestic Violence Services, 97-. **HONORS AND AWARDS** Service Awd, Col of St Rose. **RESEARCH** Family Violence. **CONTACT ADDRESS** Dept Soc Work, Col of Saint Rose, Albany, NY 12203. **EMAIL** mbol563@aol.com

BOLSTERLI, MARGARET JONES
PERSONAL Born 05/10/1931, Watson, AR, 2 children **DISCIPLINE** ENGLISH, CULTURAL HISTORY **EDUCATION** Univ Ark, BA, 53; Wash Univ, MA, 53; Univ Minn, PhD(English), 67. **CAREER** Asst prof English, Augsburg Col, 67-68; Prof English, Univ Ark, 68-, Nat Endowment Humanities Younger Humanist Award, 70-71; Ark Endowment Humanities grant, 80-81. **MEMBERSHIPS** MLA; SCent Mod Land Asn; Am Asn State & Local Hist. **RESEARCH** Nineteenth century Britain; the American south; women's studies. **SELECTED PUBLICATIONS** Auth, Porter,Katherine,Anne and Texas, Mod Fiction Stud, Vol 0038, 92; An Interview with Bolsterli,Margaret,Jones, Ark Hist Quart, Vol 0055, 96; Warren,Robert,Penn And The American Imagination--Mod Fiction Stud, Vol 0038, 92. **CONTACT ADDRESS** Dept of English, Univ of Arkansas, Fayetteville, Fayetteville, AR 72701.

BOND, MEG
PERSONAL Born 05/08/1952, La Jolla, CA, 2 children **DISCIPLINE** PSYCHOLOGY **EDUCATION** Stanford Univ, BA, 74; Univ Ore, MA, 76; PhD, 83. **CAREER** Instructor, Univ Ore, 79-81; Res Assoc and Assoc Dir to Adj Asst Prof, Univ Ill, 82-88; Asst Prof, Lesley Col, 88-89; Asst Prof to Prof, Univ Mass, 89-. **HONORS AND AWARDS** Contributions to Diversity and Excellence Awd, Univ MA, 96; University in the city Scholar, Univ MA, 97-98. **MEMBERSHIPS** Am Psychol Asn. **SELECTED PUBLICATIONS** Auth, "Prevention and the ecology of sexual harassment: Creating empowering climates," Prevention in Human Services, (95): 147-173; co-auth, "Workforce diversity: Emerging interdisciplinary challenges," New Solutions, (97): 41-57; auth, "The multi-textured lives of women of color," American Journal of Community Psychology, (97): 733-744; co-auth, "The ecology of diversity in organizational settings: Lessons from a case study," Human Relations, (98): 589-623; co-auth, "Dilemmas at work," Journal of Management Inquiry, (98): 252-269; auth, "Gender, race, and class in organizational settings," American Journal of Community Psychology, (99): 327-355; co-auth, "Stories of relative privilege: Power and social change in feminist community psychology," American Journal of community Psychology, in press; co-auth, "Methodological issues and challenges for a feminist community psychology," American Journal of Community Psychology, in press **CONTACT ADDRESS** Dept Psychol, Univ of Massachusetts, Lowell, 1 University Ave, Lowell, MA 01854. **EMAIL** Meg_Bond@uml.edu

BONDER, BETTE R.
PERSONAL m, 2 children **DISCIPLINE** HEALTH SCIENCES **EDUCATION** Northwestern Univ, PhD, 74. **CAREER** Asst prof, Towson State Univ, 79-83; prof, Cleveland State Univ, 89-. **HONORS AND AWARDS** Fel, Am Occupational Therapy Asn. **MEMBERSHIPS** AOTA, APA, GSA. **RESEARCH** Meaning of occupation, culture and occupation. **SELECTED PUBLICATIONS** Auth, Psychopathology and Function, 2nd ed, Thorofare, NJ: Slack (95); auth, "Psychosocial components of function," C. Christiansen, C. Baum, eds, Occupational Therapy, 2nd ed, Thorofare, NJ: Slack (97); coauth with C. Zadorozny and R. Martin, "Dressing in Alzheimer's Disease: Procedural memory and Executive function," Clinical Gerontologist, 19 (98): 88-92; auth, "Run (or walk briskly) for your life: Exercise in later life," The Gerontologist, 38 (98): 757; coauth with L. Martin, "Personal meanings of occupation for women in later life," Women and Aging (in press); co-ed with L. Wagner, Functional Performance in Older Adults, 2nd ed (in press). **CONTACT ADDRESS** Dept Health Scis, Cleveland State Univ, 1983 E 24th St, Cleveland, OH 44115. **EMAIL** b.bonder@popmail.csuohio.edu

BONEVA, BONKA
PERSONAL Born 11/20/1950, Plovdiv, Bulgaria, m, 1984, 1 child **DISCIPLINE** SOCIOLOGY, ETHNOLOGY **EDUCATION** Univ Sofia, Dipl Sociol, 73; Bulgarian Acad Sci, PhD, 89; Univ Pittsburgh, MS, 98. **CAREER** Vis Schol, Northwestern Univ, 88-89; Vis Schol, Univ Pittsburgh, 94-95; Senior Researcher, Inst Sociol, Bulgarian Acad of Sci, 76-98; Post Doctoral Fel, Carnegie Mellon Univ, 98-. **HONORS AND AWARDS** Fel, Am Coun of Learned Soc, 88-89; Res Fel, NATO, 93-94; Fel, Woodrow Wilson Int Ctr for Schol, 95. **MEMBERSHIPS** AAASS, APA, AWP, EAESP, SPSSI. **RESEARCH** Social and ethnic identities, human motivation, personality in culture, motives to migrate. **SELECTED PUBLICATIONS** Coauth, "Ethnicity in Pirin Macedonia: Blurred Categories, Emergent Minority," Balkanistica 9 (96): 156-165; coauth, "East-West European Migration and the Role of Motivation in Emigration Desires," Migracijske teme 13 (97): 335-362; auth, "Ethnicity and the Nation: The Bulgarian Dilemma," in Linguistic Minorities in Central and East Europe, Miltilingual Matters Publ, LTD (98): 80-97; coauth, "Achievement, Power and Affiliation Motives as Clues to (E)migration Desires: A Four-Countries Comparison," European Psychologist 3 (98): 2-8. **CONTACT ADDRESS** Dept Comput Sci, Carnegie Mellon Univ, 5000 Forbes Ave, Pittsburgh, PA 15213-3890. **EMAIL** bboneva@andrew.cmu.edu

BONNER, MARY WINSTEAD
PERSONAL Born 04/20/1924, Nash Co, NC, m, 1956 **DISCIPLINE** EDUCATION **EDUCATION** St Pauls University, BS (cum laude) 1946, LhD, 1979; VA State University, MS 1952; New York Univ 1953-67; Southern Univ 1953, 1954; OK State Univ, EdD 1968; Univ of KS, Post Doct 1974; Univ of California Berkeley 1974; Instde Fililogia Satillo Mexico, further study 1984. **CAREER** Greensville Cty VA, instr, 46-52; So Univ, instr, 52-57; St Louis Publ Schools, instr, 57-64; OK State Univ, grad asst, 65-66; USC, vstg prof, 68; Norfolk State Coll, vstg prof, 71-73; Emporia State Univ, prof, prof emeritus, 86. **HONORS AND AWARDS** European Tour England, Belgium, Holland, Germany, France, Switzerland 1983; tour of Soviet Union & Warsaw Poland 1974, Spain 1976, Mexico 1979, Venezuela 1981, Caribbean 1986; Hall of Fame Sigma Gamma Rho; Cert of Achievement in Spanish Emporia State Univ 1978; languages Spanish, French, Russian; Outstanding Aluma St Pauls Coll 1979, 1984; creation of Bonner-Bonner Lecture Series, Emporia State Univ; Emporia State Univ, Ruth Schillinger Awd, 1998. **MEMBERSHIPS** Mem Sigma Gamma Rho, Amer Assn of Univ Women, Natl Council of Negro Women, natl Spanish Hon Soc, Sigma Delta Pi 1979, International Platform Assn, Panel of American Women, KS Children's Service League, Retired Teachers Assn; asst dir, ast district coordinator 1989-90, editor state newsletter 1991-92, Hospital Auxiliaries of Kansas; secretary, Emporia Retired Teachers Assn 1988-89; bd of dirs, Societas Docta; mem, Lyon County Board of Corrections 1990-91; mem, Lyon County Planning Committee 1991-92. **CONTACT ADDRESS** Emporia State Univ, 1200 Commercial St, Emporia, KS 66801.

BONTATIBUS, DONNA
PERSONAL Born 02/14/1968 **DISCIPLINE** DEVELOPMENTAL STUDIES **EDUCATION** Albertus Magnus Col, BA, 90; Univ RI, MA, 92; PhD, 95. **CAREER** Adj Fac, Univ, RI, 94; Adj Fac, Univ New Haven, 93-96; Instr, Branford Hall Career Institute, 94-98; Adj Fac, Middlesex Community Technical Col, 93-98; Adj Fac, Southern Conn State Univ, 97-98; Instr, Norwalk community Col, 98-. **HONORS AND AWARDS** Who's Who Among Grad Students, 96; Phi Kappa Phi Honor Soc, Univ RI, 95; Dorothy E Schoelzel Memorial Scholarship, 94; Teaching Assistantship, Univ RI, 94; Summa cum Laude, Albertus Magnus Col, 90; Who's Who among Col Students, 90. **MEMBERSHIPS** NE Mod Lang Asn, Mod Lang Asn, Soc of Early Americanists. **RESEARCH** Women's Literature before 1900 **SELECTED PUBLICATIONS** Auth, "Poet Elizabeth Whitman and Hannah Webster Foster's: A Late 18th Century New England Web of Connections," curious Room, 00; auth, "American Women Writers: Writing History, Rewriting Their future," Eighteenth Century: A Current Bibliography, 99; auth, The Seduction Novel of the Early Nation, Mich State Univ Press, 99; auth, "Reconnecting with the Past: Personal Hauntings in Margaret Atwood's The Robber Bride," Papers on Language and Literature, (98): 358-371; auth, "Susanna Rowson," Literary Sketches, 95; auth, "Mercy Warren," Literary Sketches, 95; auth, "Louisa May Alcott," Literary Sketches, 95. **CONTACT ADDRESS** Dept Develop Studies, Norwalk Comm-Tech Col, 188 Richards Ave, Norwalk, CT 06854-1634.

BONVILLAIN, NANCY
PERSONAL Born 08/03/1945, Pittsburgh, PA **DISCIPLINE** ANTHROPOLOGY, LINGUSTICS **EDUCATION** Hunter Col, City Univ NY, BA, 66; Columbia Univ, NY, PhD, 72. **CAREER** Asst Prof, Mich State Univ, E Lansing, 71-73; Asst Prof, Livingston Col, Rutgers Univ, 73-74; Asst Prof, Sarah Lawrence Col, Bronxville, NY, 75-76; Adj Asst Prof, York Col, Queens NY, 75-76; Adj Asst Prof, Kingsborough Community Col, Brooklyn NY, 75-76; Asst/Assoc Prof, SUNY Stony Brook, 76-92; Acting Chairperson, Anthrop Dept, SUNY, Stony Brook, 81; Vis Assoc Prof, Columbia Univ NY, 81-82; Adj Prof, New Sch for Soc Res, NYork City, 79-93; Adj Prof, SUNY Purchase, 93, 94; Fac, Simon's Rock Col of Bard, Mass, 96-; Adj, Berkshire Community Col, Mass, 96-; Anthrop, Summer Session, Columbia Univ, 82-. **HONORS AND AWARDS** Phi Beta Kappa, 67; Res Fel, Nat Endowment for the Humanities, 74-75. **MEMBERSHIPS** Am Anthrop Asn, Ling Soc of Am. **RESEARCH** Native American Cultures, Histories and Languages, Mohawk Linguistics. **SELECTED PUBLICATIONS** Auth, Women and Men: cultural constructs of gender, Prentice Hall (Englewood Cliffs, NJ), 93, 97, 01; auth, The Hopi, Chelsea House Publ (NY), 94; auth, Black Hawk, Sac Rebel, Chelsea House Publ (NY), 94; auth, The teton Sioux, Chelsea House Publ (NY), 94; auth, The Haidas, Millbrook Press (Brookfield, CT), 94; auth, The Sac and Fox, Chelsea House Publ (NY), 95; auth, The Navajos, Millbrook Press (Brookfield, CT), 95; auth, The Zuni, Chelsea House Publ (NY), 95; auth, Native American Religion, Chelsea House Publ (NY), 96; auth, The Cheyenne, Millbrook Press (Brookfield, CT), 96; auth, The Santee Sioux, Chelsea House Publ (NY), 97; auth, Native American Medicine, Chelsea House Publ (NY), 98; auth, Native Nations: cultures and histories of Native North America, Prentice Hall (Upper Saddle River, NJ), in press. **CONTACT ADDRESS** Dept Soc Sci, Simon's Rock Col of Bard, 84 Aford Rd, Great Barrington, MA 01230.

BOOS, FLORENCE SAUNDERS
PERSONAL Born 11/11/1943, Santa Barbara, CA, m, 1965, 1 child **DISCIPLINE** ENGLISH LITERATURE, WOMEN'S STUDIES **EDUCATION** Univ Mich, BA, 64; Harvard Univ, AM, 65; Univ Wis, PhD, 72. **CAREER** Instr English, Univ Sask, 70-71; asst prof, 73-77, assoc prof, 77-81, Prof English, Univ Iowa, 82-, Old Gold fel, Univ Iowa, 74 & 79, fac res grant, 75-76; bibliog, Women & Lit, 74-77, assoc ed, 75-80; Bunting fel, 80-81; Univ Iowa fac scholar, 81-84; Fulbright sr lectr, Univ Iceland, fall 85; NEH fel, Univ Iowa, summer 92. **HONORS AND AWARDS** Woodrow Wilson Nat fel, 64-65; Douglas Stuart fel, Queen's Univ, 66-67; Fac scholar award, Univ Iowa, 75, 90; Fac development assignment, Univ Iowa, 97. **MEMBERSHIPS** Midwest Victorian Studies Asn; MLA; Women's Caucus Mod Lang; Res Soc Victorian Periodicals; Hopkins Soc. **RESEARCH** Social and cultural history of Britain from the eighteenth century to the present; Victorian poetry. **SELECTED PUBLICATIONS** Auth, Catharine Macaulay's Letters on Education 1790: An Early Feminist Polemic, Univ Mich Papers Woman's Studies, No 2; The Poetry of Dante Gabriel Rossetti: A Critical and Source Study, Mouton, The Hague, 75, reprinted, in Nineteenth-Centruy Literature Criticism, Gale Res Co, 83; ed, Socialist Diary, Windhover Press, 81; The Juvenillia of William Morris, William Morris Soc, 82; ed, Bibliography of Women and Literature, 1975-80, 2 vol, Holmes and Meier, 88; ed & contrib, Socialism and the Literary Artistry of William Morris, Univ Mo Press, 90; The Design of William Morris's The Earthly Paradise, Edwin Mellen Press, 91; ed, & contrib, History and Community: Essays in Victorian Medievalism, Garland Publ, 92; guest ed, William Morris: 1896-1996, Victorian Poetry, winter 96; The Earthly Paradise by William Morris, vol I and II, Garland Publ, 00. **CONTACT ADDRESS** Dept of English, The Univ of Iowa, 308 English Phil Bld, Iowa City, IA 52242-1492. **EMAIL** florence-boos@uiowa.edu

BOOXBAUM, RONNIE
PERSONAL Born 02/14/1947, New York, NY, d, 2 children **DISCIPLINE** ANTHROPOLOGY **EDUCATION** Univ Conn, BA, 69; Northeastern Univ, MA, 92; Univ Mass, PhD, 95. **CAREER** Prof, Holyoke Community Col, 94-. **HONORS AND AWARDS** Outstanding Community Service Awd, Amherst, 94; Leslie White Awd, 91. **MEMBERSHIPS** Am Anthropol Asn. **RESEARCH** Refugee resettlement, transnationalism, adaptation, Southeast Asia, American Ethnic Communities. **SELECTED PUBLICATIONS** Auth, "The Meaning of Ethnicity in American Society: A Perspecitve from Two Case Studies of the Jewish Community," in Ethnicity and its Identity in the USA, (Ibaraki, Japan) 81; auth, "Jewish Communities inWestern Massachusetts, A Preliminary Study:, in Ethnicity and Cultural Pluralism in the USA, (Ibaraki, Japan) 78. **CONTACT ADDRESS** Dept Soc Sci, Holyoke Comm Col, 303 Homestead Ave, Holyoke, MA 01040. **EMAIL** booxbaum@external.umass.edu

BORCHARD, KURT
PERSONAL Born Fairbanks, AK **DISCIPLINE** SOCIOLOGY **EDUCATION** Univ Alaska, BA, 90; Univ Colorado, MA, 93; Univ Nevada, PhD, 98. **CAREER** Asst prof, Univ Nebr, Kearney, 98-. **HONORS AND AWARDS** Res Ser Coun Fac Grant, Univ NE, 99. **MEMBERSHIPS** MSS; PSA; SSSI. **RESEARCH** Homelessness; criminology/deviance; qualitative methods; social psychology; cultural studies. **SELECTED PUBLICATIONS** Ref, "Between a Hard Rock and Postmodernism: Opening the Hard Rock Hotel and Casino," J Cont Ethnography 2 (98): 242-269; ref, "Lost in the Funhouse: U.S. Youth Culture and its Commodification." Social Alternatives (Australia)2 (99): 8-10; ref, "Fear of and Sympathy toward Homeless Men in Las Vegas," Humanity and Society 1 (00): 3-18; auth, "Simpsons as Subculture: Multiple Technologies, Group Identity and Authorship," in Selected Papers From the Annual Meetings of the Society for the Interdisciplinary Study of Social Imagery, eds. Steven Kaplan, Will Wright (Pueblo: Univ Southern Colorado Press, 94); rev, "Creating Born Criminals," Sociol Res Online (98); rev, "Commodity Your Dissent," Soci Inquiry (99); rev, "Highway Patrolman," J Crim Just Pop Culture (99): 38-40; rev, "Shelter Blues," Sociol Inquiry (99). **CONTACT ADDRESS** Dept Sociology, Univ of Nebraska, Kearney, Copeland Hall 120, Kearney, NE 68849-1295. **EMAIL** borchardk@unk.edu

BORCHERT, SUSAN D.
PERSONAL Born 03/02/1947, Columbus, OH, m, 1982 **DISCIPLINE** SOCIOLOGY **EDUCATION** Oh State Univ, PhD, 79. **CAREER** Assoc Prof, Lake Erie Col, 84-. **HONORS AND AWARDS** Grant, Am Asn for State & Local Hist, 81, 83; NEH Summer Fel, 81. **MEMBERSHIPS** Sociol for Women in Soc; Inst for Women's Policy Res. **RESEARCH** Intersection of race, social class and gender. **SELECTED PUBLICATIONS** Auth, "Parental Leave: a sensible, pro-family initiative," Forum, The Plain Dealer, (90): 9; auth, "Elizabeth Ross Haynes," African American Women: a bibliographical dictionary, 93; auth, "Catherine Deaver Lealtad," African American Women: a bibliographical dictionary, 93; auth, "Josephine Pinyon," African American Women: a bibliographical dictionary, 93; auth, "Adelle Ruffin," African American Women: a bibliographical dictionary, 93; co-auth, Lakewood the first Hundred Years, 1889-1989, 2nd ed, Donning Pub Co, 94. **CONTACT ADDRESS** Dept Soc Sci, Lake Erie Col, 391 W Washington St, Painesville, OH 44077. **EMAIL** sbrochert@lec.edu

BORER, HAGIT
DISCIPLINE SYNTAX, MORPHOLOGY, LANGUAGE ACQUISITION **EDUCATION** MIT, PhD. **CAREER** Prof, Univ Southern Calif. **RESEARCH** Comparative syntax; interaction between syntax & morphology; language acquisition. **SELECTED PUBLICATIONS** Auth, Parametric Syntax: Case Studies in Semitic &Romance Languages, Foris Publ, Dordrecht, 84; Restrictive Relatives in Modern Hebrew, Natural Lang & Ling Theory 2, 84; I-Subjects, Ling Inquiry 17 3, 86; Anaphoric AGR, in The PRO Drop Parameter, Reidel, Dordrecht, 89; The Causative- Alternative: A Case Study in Parallel Morphology, J Ling Rev, 92; The Ups & Downs of Hebrew Verb Movement, Natural Lang and Ling Theory 13, 95; coauth, The Maturation of Syntax, in Parameter Setting, Reidel, Dordrecht, 87. **CONTACT ADDRESS** Dept of Linguistics, Univ of So California, University Park Campus, Los Angeles, CA 90089. **EMAIL** borer@almaak.usc.edu

BORG, MARIAN J.
PERSONAL Born 02/25/1965, New York, NY, m, 1998 **DISCIPLINE** SOCIOLOGY **EDUCATION** Univ VA, PhD, 94. **CAREER** Asst prof, Univ Fla, 94-. **HONORS AND AWARDS** Fac Teaching Awd, 99. **MEMBERSHIPS** Am Soc of Criminol, Am Sociol Asn. **RESEARCH** Social Control, Deviance, Criminology, Conflict Management. **SELECTED PUBLICATIONS** Auth, "Expressing Conflict, Neutralizing Blame and Making Concessions in Small Claims Mediation," Law and Policy, (forthcoming); auth, "Recent Research on Capital Punishment: Changing the Nature of Contemporary Death Penalty Debates," Annual Review of Sociology, (forthcoming); auth, "Drug Testing in Organizations: Applying Horwitz's Theory of the Effectiveness of Social Control," Deviant Behavior, (00): 123-154; auth, "Using Violence as Social Control: Applying a Theory of Conflict Management to Juvenile Disputes," Univ Fla Journal of Law and Public Policy, (99): 313-339; auth, "The Effect of Vicarious Homicide Victimization on Support for Capital Punishment: A Test of Black's Theory of Law," Criminology, (98): 537-568. **CONTACT ADDRESS** Dept Sociol, Univ of Florida, PO Box 117330, Gainesville, FL 32611. **EMAIL** mborg@soc.ufl.edu

BORNET, BRUNO
PERSONAL Born 09/25/1965, Paris, France, m, 1994, 2 children **DISCIPLINE** PSYCHOLOGY **EDUCATION** Loyola Univ, BA, 87; MA, 90; Univ N Mex, PhD, 98. **CAREER** Prof, Univ N Mex; Director, Santa Fe Cmty Col. **HONORS AND AWARDS** Nominated, Teaching Excellence Awd, Santa Fe Cmty Col, 98, 99. **MEMBERSHIPS** Am Psychol Asn, Am Anthropol Asn. **RESEARCH** Philosophy of psychology; Cross-cultural psychology, sociology; Race and ethnicity; Prejudice and discrimination; Child development; Human sexuality. **CONTACT ADDRESS** Dept Arts & Sci, Santa Fe Comm Col, New Mexico, 6401 Richards Ave, Santa Fe, NM 87505. **EMAIL** brunocom@aol.com

BOROCZ, JOZSEF
DISCIPLINE SOCIOLOGY **EDUCATION** Kossuth Lajos Univ, MA, 82; Eotvos Lorand Univ, Trans Dip, 90; John Hopkins Univ, PhD, 92. **CAREER** Asst prof, Univ Cal, Irvine, 92-95; asst prof, Rutgers Univ, 95-. **MEMBERSHIPS** ASA; ECSA; AASS; HAS; SSHA. **RESEARCH** Comparative-historical sociology; social change; socio-economic and political transformations after state socialism; sociology of economic knowledge; 'eastern enlargement' of the European Union. **SELECTED PUBLICATIONS** Auth, Leisure Migration: A Sociological Study on Tourism, Pergamon Press (Oxford, UK), 96; co-ed, A New World Order? Global Transformation in the Late 20th Century, Greenwood Press, 95; co-ed, Gender and Nation, East Euro Politics Soc 8 (94): 223-3 16; coauth, "Who You Know. . .: Earnings Effects of Formal and Informal Social Network Resources under Late State Socialism, Hungary, 1986-87." J Socio-Econ 27 (98): 403-27; coauth, "Housing Advantages for the Better-Connected? Institutional Segmentation, Settlement Type and Network Effects in Late State-Socialist Housing Equalities," Soc Forces 76 (98): 1275-1304; coauth, "Business Elites in Central and Eastern Europe: Continuity and Change, Pre-Socialist and Socialist Legacies," in Elites after State Socialism: Theory and Analysis, eds. John Higley, Gyorgy Lengyel (Rowman and Littlefield, 99); auth, "From Comprador State to Auctioneer State: Property Change, Realignment and Peripherialization in Post-State-Socialist Central Europe," in States and Sovereignty in the Global Economy, eds. David A Smith, Dorothy Solinger, Steven Topik (London: Routledge, 99); auth, "Reaction as Progress: Economists as Intellectuals," in Intellectuals and Politics in Central Europe, ed. Andras Bozoki (Budapest: Cen Euro Univ Press, 99); auth, "Informality and Nonprofits in Central European Capitalism," Voluntas (00); auth, "Informality Rules." East Euro Politics Soc (00). **CONTACT ADDRESS** Dept Sociology, Rutgers Univ, 54 Joyce Kilmer Dr, Piscataway, NJ 08854-8045. **EMAIL** jborocz@rci.rutgers.edu

BORSKY, SUSAN
PERSONAL Born 01/23/1948, Miami, FL, m, 1966, 2 children **DISCIPLINE** PSYCHOLOGY **EDUCATION** FL Atlantic Univ, BA, 93; MA, 95; PhD, 98. **CAREER** Vis asst prof, Northern Ariz Univ, 98-99; asst prov, Univ of N Florida, 99-. **HONORS AND AWARDS** Susan Dewar Awd for Acad Excellence, 93; Newell Doct Fel, 97; Gertrude Makowsky Mem Scholarship, 96. **MEMBERSHIPS** Am Psychol Soc. **RESEARCH** Perception and Language processing. **SELECTED PUBLICATIONS** Auth, "Context Independent Sentence Processing" in Sentence Processing: A Cross-Linguistic Perspective, San Diego, 98; auth, "The Temporal Unfolding of Local Acoustic Information and Sentence Context," Journal of Psycholinguistic Research, (00): 155-168; auth, "How to milk a coat: The effect of acoustic and semantic informatin on phoneme categorization," Journal of the Acoustical Society of America, (98): 2670-2676; auth, "On-line examination of language performance in normal and neurologically impaired adults," American Journal of Speech and Language Pathology, (98): 49-60. **CONTACT ADDRESS** Dept Psych, Univ of No Florida, 4567 St. Johns Blf S, Jacksonville, FL 32224. **EMAIL** sborsky@unf.edu

BORSTEL, FREDERICO VON
PERSONAL Born 02/22/1950, Mexico, m, 1979, 1 child **DISCIPLINE** EDUCATION DEVELOPMENT **EDUCATION** Univ Minn, BA, 72; Allende Inst, MA, 74; Univ Am, MA, 77; Univ Toronto, PhD, 82. **CAREER** Adj Assoc Prof, U S Int Univ, 86-97; From Assoc Prof to Prof, Newsch of Arts & Archit, 89-. **HONORS AND AWARDS** Fulbright Sr Scholar, 00-01. **RESEARCH** Planning and design for schools, colleges and universities, instructional program design, teacher training, organizational analysis. **SELECTED PUBLICATIONS** Auth, Planning, Research and Design for a Masters Degree Program in Business Administration for Baja, California, Univ Phoenix Pr, 92; auth, A Theoretical Framework for Productive Education, UNESCO (Paris), 93; auth, Thesis Integration Project: A

Thesis and Research Development System for Arts and Science, Newsch of Archit, 95-99. **CONTACT ADDRESS** Dept Lib Arts, Newsch of Architecture, 1249 F St, San Diego, CA 92101-6634.

BOTTOMS, BETTE L.
PERSONAL Born 05/25/1964, Richmond, VA, m **DISCIPLINE** PSYCHOLOGY **EDUCATION** Randolph-Macon Woman's Col, Lynchburg, VA, BA, 86; Univ Denver, MA, 89; SUNY at Buffalo, PhD, 92. **CAREER** Asst prof, 92-96, assoc prof, Dept of Psychology, Univ IL, Chicago, 97-. **HONORS AND AWARDS** Am Psychol/Law Soc First Place Dissertation Awd, 93; UIC-Amoco Silver Circle Teaching Excellence Awd, 97; UIC Teaching Recognition Prog Awd, 97; UIC Teaching Excellence Awd, 98; Saleem Shah Early Career Awd for Psychology and Law Research, 98. **MEMBERSHIPS** Phi Beta Kappa; Sigma Xi; Psi Chi; APA; Midwestern Psychol Asn; Soc for Applied Res in Memory and Cognition; Soc for the Psychological Study of Social Issues; Am Psychol/Law Soc; Am Professional Soc on the Abuse of Children; Int Soc for the Prevention of Child Abuse and Neglect; Children's Healthcare is a Legal Duty, Inc. **RESEARCH** Psychology and law; children's eyewitness testimony. **SELECTED PUBLICATIONS** Auth, with P R Shaver, G S Goodman, and J J Qin, In the Name of God: A Profile of Religion-Related Child Abuse, J of Social Issues, 51, 95; with B M Schwartz-Kenney, and G S Goodman, Techniques for Improving Children's Person Identification Accuracy, Child Maltreatment, 1, 96; with C A Carter and M Levine, Linguistic and Socio-Emotional Influences on the Accuracy of Children's Reports, Law and Human Behavior, 20, 96; with P R Shaver and G S Goodman, An Analysis of Ritualistic Child Abuse Allegations, Law and Human Behavior, 20, 96; with G S Goodman, International Perspectives on Child Witnesses: An Introduction to the Issues, Criminal Justice and Behavior, 23, 96; with K R Diviak and S L Davis, Juror's Reactions to Satanic Ritual Abuse Allegations, Child Abuse and Neglect, 21, 97; with S L Davis, The Creation of Satanic Ritual Abuse, J of Social and Clinical Psychology, 16, 97; with J J Qin, G S Goodman, and P R Shaver, Repressed Memories of Ritualistic and Religion-Related Child Abuse, in S J Lynn & K McConkey, eds, Truth in Memory, Guilford, 98; ed, with G S Goodman, International Perspectives on Child Abuse and Children's Testimony: Psychological Research and Law, Sage, 96; numerous other publications, several forthcoming. **CONTACT ADDRESS** Dept of Psychology, Univ of Illinois, Chicago, 1007 West Harrison St, MC 285, Chicago, IL 60607-7131. **EMAIL** bbottoms@uic.edu

BOUCHER, JERRY
PERSONAL Born 09/11/1939, KN, m **DISCIPLINE** PSYCHOLOGY **EDUCATION** San Francisco State Col, BA, 65; Univ Calif, PhD, 71. **CAREER** Asst res psychologist, Univ Calif, 71-73; res assoc, East-West Center, 73-89; adj prof, Univ San Francisco, 94-. **HONORS AND AWARDS** Fel. **MEMBERSHIPS** Am Psychol Asn, Intl Asn for Cross-Culture, Acad for Intercultural Res. **RESEARCH** Emotion, Ethnic conflict **SELECTED PUBLICATIONS** Auth, "Foreign Language learning, ethnic identity, and cross-cultural communication," in Psychology in International Perspective, 92; auth, "Themes and models of conflict," in Ethnic Conflict: International Perspectives, 87; auth, Ethnic Conflict: International Perspectives, Beverly Hills, 87; auth, "Concepts of depression across culture and language groups," International Journal of Intercultural Relations, (86): 321-346; auth, "Judgments of emotions from antecedent situations in four cultures," in From a Different Perspective: Studies of Behavior Across Cultures, 86. **CONTACT ADDRESS** Dept Psych, Univ of San Francisco, 2130 Fulton St, San Francisco, CA 94117. **EMAIL** boucherj@usfca.edu

BOURGUIGNON, ERIKA EICHHORN
PERSONAL Born 02/18/1924, Vienna, Austria, w, 1950 **DISCIPLINE** ANTHROPOLOGY **EDUCATION** Queens Coll, BA, 45; Univ Conn, grad study, 45; Northwestern Univ, PhD, 51. **CAREER** Instr, Ohio State Univ, 49-56; asst prof, Ohio state Univ, 56-60; assoc prof, Ohio State Univ, 60-66; prof, Ohio State Univ, 66-90; act ch, Anthrop, 71-72; Dept Chair, 72-76; PROF EMER, OHIO STATE UNIV, 90-. **HONORS AND AWARDS** Doctor of Humane Letters, Honorary degree, Queens College CUNY, 00. **MEMBERSHIPS** Am Anthrop Asn; Ctrl State Anthrop Soc; Ohio Acad Sci; World Psychiat Asn; Am Ethnol Soc; Antrop Soc for Psychol; Phi Beta Kappa; Sigma Xi **RESEARCH** Psychological Anthrpology. **SELECTED PUBLICATIONS** Edr, Margaret Mead: The Anthropologist in America-Occasional Papers in Anthropology, Ohio State Univ, 86; auth, A Memoir of 1939 by Bronka Schneider, Ohio St Univ Press, 98. **CONTACT ADDRESS** Dept Anthrop, Ohio State Univ, Columbus, 199 E N Broadway st., Columbus, OH 43214-4111. **EMAIL** bourguignon.1@osu.edu

BOURNE, LYLE E.
PERSONAL Born 04/12/1932, Boston, MA **DISCIPLINE** PSYCHOLOGY **EDUCATION** Brown Univ, BA, 53; Univ Wis, MS, 55; PhD, 56. **CAREER** Asst Prof to Assoc Prof, Univ Utah, 56-63; Assoc Prof to Prof, Univ Colo, 63-. **HONORS AND AWARDS** Listed in Who's Who in America; Listed in Am Men and Women of Sci; Listed in Who's Who in Am Educ; Francis Whelan Scholar, Brown Univ, 76; USPHS Res Scientist

Awd, 71-76; Soc Sci Writing Awd, Univ Colo, 88; Dept Outstanding Service Awd, 93-94. **MEMBERSHIPS** Am Psychol Asn, Sigma Xi, Psychonomic Soc, Cognitive Sci Soc, Rocky Mountain Psychol Asn, Am Psychol Soc, The Soc for Applied Res in Memory and Cognition. **SELECTED PUBLICATIONS** Auth, "The strategic basis of performance to binary classification tasks: Strategy choices and strategy transitions," Journal of Memory and Language, (99): 223-252; auth, "Cross modality priming between odors and odor-congruent words," Am Journal of Psychology, (99): 175-186; auth, "Obituary: Bruce Rowland Ekstrand (1940-1996)," American Psychologist, (99): 66-67; auth, "Cycle of Blame or Just World: Effects of Legal Verdicts on Gender Patterns in Rape Myth Acceptance and Victim-empathy," Psychology of Women Quarterly, (98): 575-588; auth, "Effects of cortical polarization on mental arithmetic," Cognitive Brain Research, (98): 49-56; auth, "Extensive practice in mental arithmetic and practice transfer over a ten month retention interval," Mathematical Cognition, (98): 21-46; auth, Psychology: Behavior in context, New York, 98; auth, Einfuhrung in die Psychologie, Frankfurt, 92; auth, Psychology: A Concise Introduction, New York, 88; auth, Cognitive Processes, 2nd ed, Englewood clifs, 86; auth, Psychology: Its principles and meanings, 5th ed, New York, 85. **CONTACT ADDRESS** Dept Psychol, Univ of Colorado, Boulder, Boulder, CO 80309-0345. **EMAIL** lbourne@psych.colorado.edu

BOWE, FRANK
PERSONAL Born 03/29/1947, Danville, PA, m, 1974, 2 children **DISCIPLINE** EDUCATION **EDUCATION** Western Md Col, BA, 69; Gallaudet Grad School, MA, 71; NY Univ, PhD, 76. **CAREER** Teacher, Central Susquehanna Intermediate Univ, 71-72; Res Sci, NYork Univ, 72-76; Exec Dir, Am Coalition of Citizens with Disabilities, 76-81; pres, FBA Inc, 81-84; Dir Res, US Archit and Transp Barriers compliance Board, 84-87; Reg Comnr, US Dept of Educ, 87-89; prof, Hofstra Univ, 89-. **HONORS AND AWARDS** Distinguished Alumnus Awd, NY Univ, 79; Hon LLD, Gallaudet Col, 81; Am with Disabilities Act Awd, 91; Distinguished Serv Awd, Pres of the US, 92; Nat Hall of Fame for People with Disabilities, 84; Distinguished Teacher of the Year Awd, Hofstra Univ, 96. **MEMBERSHIPS** Alliance for Public Technol; Am Assoc of People with Disabilities; AAUP; Counc for Exceptional Children; Nat Assoc for Deaf; Telecommunication for the Deaf Inc. **SELECTED PUBLICATIONS** Auth, Changing the Rules, T.J. Pub, 86; auth, Equal Rights for Americans with Disabilities, Franklin Watts, 92; auth, Birth to Five: Early Childhood Special Education, Thomson Learning, 95, 00; auth, Physical, Sensory, and Health Disabilities: An Introduction, Prentice Hall, Merrill Educ, 00; auth, Universal Design in Education: Teaching Nontraditional Students, Greenwood Pub Group, (forthcoming). **CONTACT ADDRESS** Dept Counr Educ, Hofstra Univ, 110 Mason Hall, 124 Hofstra Univ, Hempstead, NY 11549. **EMAIL** frank.bowe@hofstra.edu

BOWER, BEVERLY LYNNE
PERSONAL Born 09/10/1951, Washington, DC, m **DISCIPLINE** EDUCATION **EDUCATION** Univ of KS, BS Ed 1973; Emporia State Univ, MLS 1980; Florida State University, Tallahassee, FL, PhD, 1992. **CAREER** Lansing Jr High School, reading teacher 73-74; Chillicothe HS, French/English teacher 74-75; Dept of Defense Dependent Schools, French/English teacher 75-80; Pensacola Jr Coll, librarian 80-84; Pensacola Jr Coll, dir lrc serv 85-92; University of SC, College of Education, asst professor, 93-96; Florida State Univ, Coll of Educ, Asst Prof, 97-. **HONORS AND AWARDS** Natl Achievement Scholar; Leaders Program, Amer Assn of Women in Community & Junior Colleges, 1989; Florida State University Fellowship, 1990-91; USC Mortar Board Outstanding Teacher Awd, 1994. **MEMBERSHIPS** Sec West FL Library Assn 1981-83; mem ALA-JMRT Minorities Recruitment Comm 1982-83, FL Library Assn, community college caucus chair/chair-elect 1986-88; FL Assn of Comm Coll, regional dir 1987; chapter president, Florida Assn of Community Colleges, 1988; bd of directors, YWCA Pensacola, 1989-91; AAWCC, founding chapter president; AAWCC, 1990-96; ASHE, 1991-; CSCC, bod, 1998; FSU Hardee Ctr, bd of governors, 1997-. **CONTACT ADDRESS** Col of Educ, Florida State Univ, Tallahassee, FL 32306.

BOWER, GORDON
PERSONAL Born 12/30/1932, Scio, OH, m, 1957, 3 children **DISCIPLINE** PSYCHOLOGY **EDUCATION** Western Reserve Univ, BA, 54; Yale Univ, MS, 56; PhD, 59. **CAREER** Asst prof to prof, Stanford Univ, 59-. **HONORS AND AWARDS** Nat Acad of Sci; Am Acad of Arts and Sci. **MEMBERSHIPS** APA; APS; WPA; Cog Sci Soc; Psychernomics Soc. **RESEARCH** Learning, memory, behavior modification, emotion. **SELECTED PUBLICATIONS** Auth, Theories of Learning, 3rd, 4th, 5th eds; coauth, Human Associative Memory; coauth, Attention in Learning; coauth, Asserting Yourself. **CONTACT ADDRESS** Dept Psychol, Stanford Univ, Stanford, CA 94305. **EMAIL** gordon@psych.stanford.edu

BOWSER, BENJAMIN PAUL
DISCIPLINE SOCIOLOGY **EDUCATION** Franklin and Marshall Col, BA, 69; Cornell Univ, PhD, 76. **CAREER** Asst prof, SUNY, Binghamton, 72-75; asst dean, Cornell Univ, 75-

82; dir, MEO, Boulder, 82-83; dir Santa Clara Univ, 83-85; asst to dir, Stanford Univ, 85-86; res dir, BHPF, San Francisco, 90-91; prof, Cal State Univ, Hayward, 86-. **HONORS AND AWARDS** Rockefeller Fel; SSA Hon; Field Poll Fac Fel; James A Nakano Citation, Outstand Sci Paper; Outstand Prof of Year; Pres Dist Fel. **MEMBERSHIPS** ASHA; AWAC. **SELECTED PUBLICATIONS** Co-ed, Impacts of Racism on White Americans, Sage Pub (Thousand Oaks), 96; ed, Racism and Anti-Racism in World Perspective, Sage Pub (Thousand Oaks), 95; co-ed, Toward the Multicultural University, Praeger Press (Westport, CN), 95; co-ed, Confronting Diversity Issues on Campus, Sage Pub (Thousand Oaks), 93; ed, Black Male Adolescents: Parenting and Education in Community Context, UP of America (Lanham, Md), 91; co-ed, Census Data with Maps for Small Areas of New York City, 1910-1960. [Microfilm and Guide] Research Pub (Woodbury, CT), 81; coauth, "Background to Crack Cocaine Addiction and HIV High Risk Behaviors: Another AIDS Epidemic," Am J Drug Alcohol Abuse 23 (97): 67-78; auth, "African American Men as Injection Drug Users: An Application of Alienation Theory to Addiction and Treatment," J Res on Minority Affairs 6 (96): 85-101; coauth, "Crack Cocaine Smokers who Turn to Drug Injection: Characteristics, Factors Associated with Injection, and Implications for HIV Transmission," Drug and Alcohol Dependence 42 (96): 85-92; coauth, "Intersecting Epidemics: Crack Cocaine Use and HIV Infection Among Inner-City Young Adults, New England J Medicine 331 (94): 1422-1427. **CONTACT ADDRESS** Dept Sociology, California State Univ, Hayward, 3103 Meiklejohn Hall, Hayward, CA 94542.

BOYCHUK, TERRY
PERSONAL Born 07/28/1964, Saskatoon, Canada, s **DISCIPLINE** SOCIOLOGY **EDUCATION** Carleton Col, Northfield, MN, BA, 86; Princeton Univ, MA, 90, PhD, 94. **CAREER** Asst prof, Center for Health Policy Res and Ed, Duke Univ, 93-96; asst prof, Dept Sociol, Macalester Col, 96-. **HONORS AND AWARDS** Phi Beta Kappa, Carleton Col, 86; John D. Rockefeller III Fel, Yale Univ, 90. **MEMBERSHIPS** Am Sociol Asn, Asn Can Studies in the United States. **RESEARCH** Historical and comparative sociology, political sociology, social policy, non-profit organizations. **SELECTED PUBLICATIONS** Auth, The Making and Meaning of Hospital Policy in the United States and Canada, Ann Arbor, MI: Univ Mich Press (99); coauth with Frank Dobbin, "National Employment Systems and Job Autonomy," Organization Studies , 20, 2 (99): 257-291. **CONTACT ADDRESS** Dept Sociol, Macalester Col, 1600 Grand Ave, Saint Paul, MN 55105. **EMAIL** boychuk@macalester.edu

BOYD, CANDY DAWSON
PERSONAL Born 08/08/1946, Chicago, IL, d **DISCIPLINE** LANGUAGE ARTS **EDUCATION** Northeastern Illinois State University, BA, 1967; University of California, Berkeley, CA, MA, 1978, PhD, 1982. **CAREER** Overton Elementary School, Chicago, IL, teacher, 68-71; Longfellow School, Berkeley, CA, teacher, 71-73; University of California, Berkeley, CA, extension instructor in language arts, 72-79; St Mary's College of California, Moraga, CA, extension instructor in language arts, 72-79; Berkeley Unified School District, Berkeley, CA, district teacher trainer in reading and communication skills, 73-76; St Mary's College of California, Moraga, CA, lecturer to assistant professor, 76-83, chair of reading leadership elementary education, and teacher effectiveness programs, 76-87, tenured assoc prof, 83-91, prof, 91-94; Masters Programs in Reading & Special Educ, Chair, 94-. **HONORS AND AWARDS** First Distinguished Professor of the Year, St Mary's College, 1992; author, Circle of Gold, Scholastic, 1984; Coretta Scott King Awd Honor Book for Circle of Gold, American Library Association, 1985; Outstanding Bay Area Woman, Delta Sigma Theta, 1986; **MEMBERSHIPS** Member, St Mary's College Rank and Tenure Committee, 1984-87; member, multiple subjects waiver programs committee, review committee, State of California Commission on Teacher Credentialing, 1985-, advisory committee for multiple subject credential with an early childhood emphasis, State of California Commission on Teacher Credentialing, 1986-87. **SELECTED PUBLICATIONS** Author, Breadsticks and Blessing Places, Macmillan, 85, published in paperback as Forever Friends, Viking, 86; author, Charlie Pippin, Macmillan, 1987; author, Chevrolet Saturdays, Macmillan, 1993; author, Fall Secrets, Puffin, 1994; A Different Beat, 1994; author, Daddy, Daddy, Be There, Philomel, 1995; Spotlight on Literature Program, McGraw-Hill, 1995. **CONTACT ADDRESS** Sch of Education, Saint Mary's Col, California, Box 4350, Moraga, CA 94575.

BOYD, ROBERT
PERSONAL Born Ft Lauderdale, FL **DISCIPLINE** SOCIOLOGY **EDUCATION** Univ North Carolina, PhD, 89. **CAREER** Assoc prof, Miss State Univ. **MEMBERSHIPS** ASA. **RESEARCH** Sociology; demography; race relations. **CONTACT ADDRESS** Dept Sociology, Mississippi State Univ, PO Box C, Mississippi State, MS 39762. **EMAIL** boyd@soc.msstate.edu

BOYLAND, JOYCE TANG
DISCIPLINE PSYCHOLOGY **EDUCATION** Harvard Col, AB, 86; Univ Calif Berkeley, MA, 92; Phd, 96. **CAREER** Fel, Carnegie Mellon Univ, 96-98; Asst Prof, Alverno Col, 98-. **CONTACT ADDRESS** Dept Beh Sc, Alverno Col, PO Box 343922, Milwaukee, WI 53234.

BRABECK, MARY M.
PERSONAL Born 07/26/1945, Oakridge, TN, m, 1967, 2 children **DISCIPLINE** EDUCATION **EDUCATION** Univ Minn, BA, 67; St. Cloud State Univ, MS, 70; Univ Minn, PhD, 80. **CAREER** Instructor, Univ Minn, 71-75; Instructor, Salve Regina Col, 76-80; Asst Prof to Prof and Dean, Boston Col, 80-. **RESEARCH** Intellectual and ethical development; Gender and culture; Values and conceptions of the moral self; Human rights education; Service learning; Inter-professional collaboration; Professional ethics. **SELECTED PUBLICATIONS** Co-auth, "What we do not know about Women's Ways of Knowing," in Psychology of Women: Ongoing Debates, (Yale Univ Press, 96), 261-269; co-auth, "Interprofessional collaboration for children and families: Opportunities for counseling psychology in the 21st century," The Counseling Psychologist, (97): 615-636; auth, "The moral self, values and circles of belonging," in Women's Ethnicities: Journeys through Psychology, (Westview Press, 96), 145-165; co-auth, "Feminist theory and psychological practice," in Shaping the future of feminist psychology: Education, research, and practice, (Am Psychol Asn Press, 97), 15-35; co-auth, Racial Ethical Sensitivity Test: Scoring manual and videotape, Boston Col, 98; co-auth, "Changing the Culture of the University to Engage in Outreach Scholarship," in University-Community Collaborations for the Twenty-First Century: Outreach Scholarship for Youth and Families, (Garland Pub, 98), 335-364; co-auth, "Ethics and collaborative practice in public schools," in Collaborative Practice: School and Human Service Partnerships, (Praeger Pub, 99), 285-297; co-auth, "Introduction," in Practicing Feminist Ethics in Psychology, (Washington, 00), 3-15; co-auth, "Feminist Ethics: Lenses for Examining Ethical Psychological Practice," in Practicing Feminist Ethics in Psychology, (Am Psychol Asn, 00), 17-35; ed, Practicing Feminist Ethics in Psychology, Am Psychol Asn, 00. **CONTACT ADDRESS** Peter & Caroly Lynch Sch of Educ, Boston Col, Chestnut Hill, 140 Commonwealth Ave, Chestnut Hill, MA 02467. **EMAIL** Brabeck@bc.edu

BRACKETT, KIMBERLY P.
PERSONAL Born 06/01/1968, Jacksonville, FL, m, 1992 **DISCIPLINE** SOCIOLOGY **EDUCATION** Jacksonville Univ, BS, 90; Univ Fla, MA, 93; Univ Fla, PhD, 96. **CAREER** Asst Prof, Auburn Univ, 96-. **MEMBERSHIPS** ASA, Southern Sociol Soc, Nat Coun on Family Rel, AL-MS Sociol Assoc. **RESEARCH** Social Psychology, gender, family. **SELECTED PUBLICATIONS** Rev, "Handbook of Marriage and Family," for Family Rel 45 (96): 4; auth, "Small Group and Collaborative Exercises," Marriages and Families, 6th ed, Wadsworth Publ Co(CA: 96); auth, "Small Group and Collaborative Exercises," Marriages and Families, 7th ed, Wadsworth Publ Co(CA: 99); auth, CNN Marriage and Collaborative Video Guide and Questions, Wadsworth Publ Co, 00; auth, "Facework Strategies Among Romance Fiction Readers," The Soc Sci J (forthcoming). **CONTACT ADDRESS** Dept Sociol, Auburn Univ, PO Box 244023, Montgomery, AL 35124. **EMAIL** kbrackett@mickey.aum.edu

BRADLEY, JOSEPHINE
PERSONAL Born 03/07/1940, Greensboro, NC, w, 1963, 3 children **DISCIPLINE** WOMENS STUDIES **EDUCATION** NC Col, BA, 63; Mich State Univ, MSN, 66; Emory Univ, MA, 94; PhD, 95. **CAREER** Assoc prof, Tusculum Col, 83-88; asst prof, Agnes Scott Col, 93-97; asst prof, Clark Atlanta Univ, 97-. **HONORS AND AWARDS** Teacher of the Year, Tusculum Col; Who's Who Among College and University Students. **MEMBERSHIPS** Assoc of Social and Behav Scientist; Assoc of Black Sociol. **RESEARCH** Africana Women's autobiography, school desegregation, Black Women's Spirituality. **SELECTED PUBLICATIONS** Coauth, "White Pain Pollen: An Elite Biracial Daughter's Quandry" in Sex, Love, Race: Crossing boundaries in N Am Hist, ed Martha Hodes, (NY: NY Univ Pr, 99). **CONTACT ADDRESS** Africana Women's Studies, Clark Atlanta Univ, 223 James Brawley SW, Atlanta, GA 30314. **EMAIL** jobradley@mindspring.com

BRANDT-WILLIAMS, ANN
PERSONAL Born 11/12/1946, Indianola, IA, m, 1993, 4 children **DISCIPLINE** PSYCHOLOGY **EDUCATION** Parkview Methodist Hospital, Nursing Diploma, 67; Purdue Univ, BSN, 77; Northern Ariz Univ, MA, 84; Ariz State Univ, PhD, 95. **CAREER** Glendale Community Col, 84-. **MEMBERSHIPS** Am Psychol Assoc; Western Psychol Assoc; AAUP; Psi Beta. **SELECTED PUBLICATIONS** Coauth, "Staying in College: Moderators of the Relation between Intention and Institutional Departure", J of Higher Educ, 96; coauth, "Learning Through Community", The Forum: Maricopa Center for Learning and Instruction, 99. **CONTACT ADDRESS** Dept Psychol, Glendale Comm Col, Arizona, 6000 W Olive Ave, Glendale, AZ 85302. **EMAIL** ann.brandt-williams@gcmail.maricopa.edu

BRAUD, WILLIAM
PERSONAL Born 11/26/1942, New Orleans, LA, m, 1981 **DISCIPLINE** PSYCHOLOGY **EDUCATION** La State Univ, BA, 64; Univ Iowa, MA, 66; PhD, 67. **CAREER** Assoc prof, Univ Houston, 67-75; sen res assoc, Mind Sci Foundation, 75-92; prof, Inst of Transpersonal Psych, 92-. **HONORS AND AWARDS** NSF and NDEA Fel; Teaching Excellence Awd, Univ Houston; Awd for Outstanding Contribution, Parapsychological Asn. **MEMBERSHIPS** Asn for Transpersonal Psychol, Parapsychol Asn, Am Soc for Psych Res, Acad of Relig and Psychical Res. **RESEARCH** Transpersonal psychology; Spirituality; Alternative ways of knowing; Novel research methods; Epistemology; Attention; Intention; Imagination; Consciousness studies; Mystical experience. **SELECTED PUBLICATIONS** Auth, "Wellness implications of retroactive intentional influence: Exploring an outragious hypothesis," Alternative Therapies in Health and Medicine, (00): 37-48; auth, Transpersonal research methods for the social sciences: Homoring human experience, Thousand Oaks, 98; auth, "Can research be transpersonal?" Transpersonal Psychology Review, (98): 9-17; auth, "Parapsychology and spirituality: Implication and application," in Body, Mind, and spirit: Exploring the parapsychology of spirituality, Charlottesville, (97): 135-152; auth, "Distant intentionality and healing: Assessing the evidence," Alternative Therapies, (97): 62-73; auth, "An experience of timelessness," Exceptional Human Experience, (95): 64-66; auth, "Attention focusing facilitated through remote mental interaction," Journal of the American Society for Psychical Research, (95): 103-115; auth, "Can our intentions interact directly with the physical world?" European Journal of Parapsychology, (94): 78-90; auth, "Honoring our natural experiences," Journal of the American Society for Psychical Research, (94): 293-308; auth, "Reaching for consciousness: Expansions and complements," Journal of the American Society for Psychical Research, (94): 185-206. **CONTACT ADDRESS** Dept Psychol, Inst of Transpersonal Psychology, 744 San Antonio Ave, Palo Alto, CA 94303. **EMAIL** wbraud@itp.edu

BREINES, WINIFRED
DISCIPLINE SOCIOLOGY **EDUCATION** Univ Wisc, BA, 63; Cornell Univ, MCP, 65; Brandeis Univ, PhD, 79. **CAREER** Prof, Northeastern Univ, Boston, Dept Sociol and Anthropol. **RESEARCH** Social movements, gender, race, women's studies, America Post WWII. **SELECTED PUBLICATIONS** Auth, The Great Refusal: Community and Organization in the New Left, Rutgers Univ Press; auth, Young, White, and Miserable: Growing Up Female in the Fifties, Beacon Press; coed with Alexander Bloom, Takin' it To the Streets: A Sixties Reader, Oxford Univ Press; auth, The Trouble Between Us: White Women, Black Women, the Movement Years (forthcoming). **CONTACT ADDRESS** Sociology/Anthropology 500 Ho, Northeastern Univ, 360 Huntington Ave, Boston, MA 02115.

BRENNAN, LINDA
PERSONAL Born 02/22/1961, Los Angeles, CA, s **DISCIPLINE** ACTING, VOICE, SPEECH, PSYCHOLOGY **EDUCATION** Calif State Univ, BA, 85; Brandeis Univ, MFA, 88; Antioch Univ, MA, 94. **CAREER** Chair, AM Acad of Dramatic Arts W Voice & Speech Dept; staff therapist, Verougo Mental Health; voice & dialect coach. **MEMBERSHIPS** Calif Asn of Marriage and Family Therapists, Screen Actors Guild, Voice and Speech Teachers Asn, Am Fedn of Television & Radio Artists. **CONTACT ADDRESS** Dept Drama, American Acad of Dramatic Arts, West, 600 Playhouse Alley, Pasadena, CA 91101-5218.

BRETTELL, CAROLINE B.
PERSONAL Born 06/11/1950, Montreal, PQ, Canada, m, 1973 **DISCIPLINE** ANTHROPOLOGY **EDUCATION** Yale Univ, BA 71; Brown Univ, MA 72, PhD 78. **CAREER** Brown Univ, tech asst 71-74; Univ TX, instr 77-78, Res assoc 79-80; Univ IL vis asst prof 81; De Paul Univ, instr 82; Loyola Univ, lectr vis asst 83-87; The Newberry Library, Res assoc proj dir 84-88; S Meth Univ, vis assoc prof 88-91, assoc prof 91-93, dir womens stud 89-94, prof anthropo 93-, chair dept anthropo 94. **HONORS AND AWARDS** Alice Palmer Fellowship, declined; Lichtstern Fell; NEH; Newberry Lib Fell; Nat Res Ser Awd; Gulbenkian Foun Fell; Soc Sci Res Fell; Woodrow Wilson Foun doc Fell; CA Coun Doc Fell; Univ Fell Brown; John Chester Adams Cup Yale; numerous research grants. **MEMBERSHIPS** Coun Euro Stud; SSHA; Soc Span Portug Hist Stud; Amer Ethnological Soc; AAA. **RESEARCH** Relig, migration, immigration, gender issues. **SELECTED PUBLICATIONS** Auth, "Migration Theory: Talking Across Disciplines," ed. With James Hollifield, New York Routledge, 00; auth, Writing Against the Wind: A Mother's Life History," Wilmington, Scholarly Resources, 99; Gender and Health: An International Perspective, ed with Carolyn Sargent, Prentice Hall, 96; When They Read What We Write: The Politics of Ethnography, ed vol, Westport CT, Bergin and Garvey, Greenwood 93; Fieldwork in the Archives: Methods and Sources in Historical Anthropology, in: H Russell Bernard, ed, Handbook of Mthods In Anthropology, Altamira Press, 98; Historical Perspectives on Infant Mortality in Northwestern Portugal, in: Small Wars: The Cultural Politics of Childhood, Nancy Scheper-Hughs and Carolyn Sargent, eds, Berkeley, Univ Of CA Press, 98; numerous bks, chapters and articles. **CONTACT ADDRESS** Dept of Anthrop, So Methodist Univ, Dallas, TX 75275. **EMAIL** cbrettel@mail.smu.edu

BRIGGS, CHARLES L.
PERSONAL Born 04/08/1953, Albuquerque, NM, m, 1996, 2 children **DISCIPLINE** ANTHROPOLOGY **EDUCATION** Colo Col, BA, 74; Univ Chicago, MA, 78, PhD, 81. **CAREER** Asst prof to prof, anthrop, chemn dept 90-94, Vassar Col, 80-95; Andrew W. Mellon Fac Fel in Hum, Comm on Degrees in Folklore and Mythology, 83-84; vis asst prof, SUNY Albany, anthrop, 86; lectr, Dept Folklore, Univ Penn, 89; vis assoc prof and acting chemn, Dept Perf Stud, NY Univ, 91-92; prof ethnic stud, Univ Calif, San Diego, 95- . **HONORS AND AWARDS** Phi Beta Kappa; tuition fel, 75-76; training fel, NIMH, 76-79; James Mooney Awd, So Anthrop Soc, 78; Mellon Fac Fel, 83-84; fel, NEH, 89-90; Chicago Folklore Prize, 89; fel, Am Folklore Soc Fellows, 90; fel, John Simon Guggenheim Mem Found, 94-95; fel Woodrow Wilson Int Ctr for Scholars, 97-98. **MEMBERSHIPS** Am Anthrop Asn; Am Ethnolog Soc; Am Folklore Soc; Am Stud Asn; Int Pragmatics Asn; Latin Am Indian Lit Asn; Latin Am Stud Asn; Ling Soc of Am; NY Folklore Soc; Soc for Cult Anthrop; Soc for Ling Anthrop; Soc for Stud of the Indigenous Lang of the Am. **SELECTED PUBLICATIONS** Coauth, Hispano Folklore of New Mexico: The Lorin W. Brown Federal Writers' Project Manuscripts, Univ New Mexico, 78; auth, The Wood Carvers of Cordova, New Mexico: Social Dimensions of an Artistic Revival, Univ Tenn, 80; auth, Learning How to Ask: A Sociolinguistic Appraisal of the Role of the Interview in Social Science Research, Cambridge, 86; co-ed, Land, Water, and Culture: New Perspectives on Hispanic Land Grants, Univ New Mexico, 87; auth, Competence in Performance: The Creativity of Tradition in Mexicano Verbal Art, Univ Penn, 88; co-ed, The Lost Gold Mine of Juan Mondragon: A Legend of New Mexico Performed by Melaquias Romero, Univ Az, 90; ed, Disorderly Discourse: Narrative, Conflict, and Social Inequality, Oxford, 96. **CONTACT ADDRESS** Dept of Ethnic Studies, Univ of California, San Diego, 9500 Gilman Dr, La Jolla, CA 92093-0522. **EMAIL** clbriggs@weber.ucsd.edu

BRINER, WAYNE
PERSONAL Born 07/07/1959, Peoria, IL, s, 2 children **DISCIPLINE** PSYCHOLOGY **EDUCATION** Sangamon Univ, BA, 82; MA, 83; Northern Ill, PhD, 87. **CAREER** Adj instr, Golden Gate Univ, 89; adj instr, Tulane Univ, 89-90; Res Scientist, House Ear Inst, 89-92; adj instr, Antioch Univ, 91-92; adj instr, West Coast Univ, 91; asst prof, Univ Neb, Kearney, 92-94; assoc prof, 95-. **HONORS AND AWARDS** Postdoc Fel, Tulane Sch Of Med; Pratt-Hines Schlp Awd; Univ Neb Teach Awd; UNK Creat Teach Awd. **MEMBERSHIPS** CTUP; NCUR; CUS; NSAS; Psi Chi; Sigma Xi; SEBM. **RESEARCH** Birth defects. **SELECTED PUBLICATIONS** Auth, "The Treatment of Tinnitus or 'Can they do anything to all those crickets in my head?' " SHHH J 12 (91): 10-13; rev of "The Metronomic Society," by M Young, Sci Books Films 25: 21-22; rev of, 'The Modular Brain," by R Restak, Sci Bokks Film 31: 5; rev of "Enchanted Looms," by R Cotterill, Sci Books Films 35: 105; auth, "A behavioral nosology for phantom auditory sensation (tinnitus)," Psychol Reports 77 (95): 27-34; auth, "Animal demonstrations of human conditions for the physiological psychology laboratory," J Instruc Psychol 23 (96): 183-188; coauth, "The arnold-chiari malformation in curly tail mice," Med Sci res 25 (97): 729-730; coauth, "Fighting and exploratory behavior in isolation-reared rats," Aggression Behavior 25 (99): 211-223. **CONTACT ADDRESS** Dept Psychology, Univ of Nebraska, Kearney, 905 W 25th St, Kearney, NE 68847.

BRISCOE, DAVID L.
PERSONAL Born 10/14/1950, Mars Hill, NC, m, 1994 **DISCIPLINE** SOCIOLOGY **EDUCATION** Univ Ark, BA, 80; MA, 85; Southern Ill Univ, PhD, 93. **CAREER** Instr, Southern Ill Univ, 90-92; Asst prof to Assoc Prof, Univ Ark 92-. **HONORS AND AWARDS** James E.West Fel, Boy Scouts of Am, Who's Who among Am's Teachers, 6th ed; Men of Achievement, 17th ed; Dictionary of Leading am, 00; UALR Golden Apple Awd; Sigma Xi; Kappa Delta Pi; Phi Theta Kappa; Psi Chi; Alpha Epsilon Lambda; Alpha Phi Sigma; Alpha Kappa Delta; Phi Alpha Theta; Sigma Tau Delta; Pi Sigma Alpha; alpha Sigma Lambda. **SELECTED PUBLICATIONS** Co-auth, Plain Talk: The Future of Little Rock's Public Schools, 97; auth, Tenant Farming as a Modified Version of American Slavery, forthcoming; auth, The social Interpretation of Social Experience Through Verse, forthcoming. **CONTACT ADDRESS** Dept Sociol, Univ of Arkansas, Little Rock, 2801 S University Ave, Little Rock, AR 72204.

BROAD, DAVID B.
PERSONAL Born 10/30/1946, Brooklyn, NY, m, 1989, 2 children **DISCIPLINE** SOCIOLOGY **EDUCATION** Univ Houston, BS, 71, MA, 73; Regents Col, BA, 78; Canisius Col, MS, 88; State Univ NYork at Buffalo, PhD, 86. **CAREER** Instr, Buffalo State Col, 77-84; asst prof, Canisius Col, 84-87; assoc prof, Adams State Col, 87-89; prof, William Penn Col, 89-91; prof, Tenn State Univ, 91-98; dean, Elgin Commun Col, 98-. **HONORS AND AWARDS** Tchr Year, 97, Tenn State Univ; Gold Medal, 87, Empire State Games. **MEMBERSHIPS** Am Sociol Asn; Popular Culture Asn. **RESEARCH** American class structure; popular culture. **SELECTED PUBLICATIONS** Auth, art, The Parent Trap: A Myth of the Reunited Self, 95; auth, art, The Social Register: Directory of America's Upperclass, 96; coed, Student, Self and Society: Stories From the Lives of Learners, 96; auth, art, Sheena, Queen of the Jungle: White Goddess of the Dumont Era, 97; auth, art, Annie Oakley: Women, Legend and Myth, 98. **CONTACT ADDRESS** Elgin Comm Col, Elgin, IL 60123. **EMAIL** dbroad@elgin.cc.il.us

BRODWIN, PAUL E.
PERSONAL Born 01/30/1958, Baltimore, MD, s **DISCIPLINE** ANTHROPOLOGY **EDUCATION** Swarthmore Col, BA, 81; Harvard Univ, PhD, 91. **CAREER** Asst Prof, Univ Wis, 91-; Adj Prof, Med Sch Wis, 97-. **MEMBERSHIPS** Am Anthrop Asn. **RESEARCH** Medical anthropology, social theory, comparative bioethics. **SELECTED PUBLICATIONS** ed, Biotechnology and Culture: Bodies, Anxieties, Ethics, Ind Univ Pr, 00; Auth, Medicine and Morality in Haiti: The Contest for Healing Power, Cambridge Univ Pr, 00. **CONTACT ADDRESS** Dept Anthrop, Univ of Wisconsin, Milwaukee, PO Box 413, Milwaukee, WI 53201. **EMAIL** brodwin@uum.edu

BROOKE, ROGER
PERSONAL Born 05/07/1953, South Africa, m, 1979, 3 children **DISCIPLINE** PSYCHOLOGY **EDUCATION** Univ Capetown, BA, 76; Rhodes Univ, BA, 77; Univ Witwatessrand, MA, 83; Rhodes Univ, PhD, 89. **CAREER** Clinic Psychol, Duquesne Univ, 83-. **MEMBERSHIPS** APA. **RESEARCH** Psychotherapy, phenomenology. **SELECTED PUBLICATIONS** Auth, Jung and Phenomenology, Routledge (New York, NY), 91; auth, Pathways into the Jungian World, Routledge (New York, NY), 00. **CONTACT ADDRESS** Dept Psychol, Duquesne Univ, 600 Forbes Ave, Pittsburgh, PA 15282-0001. **EMAIL** brooke@duq.edu

BROOKS-GUNN BROOKS-GUNN, JEANNE
PERSONAL Born 12/09/1946, Bethesda, MD, m, 1 child **DISCIPLINE** PSYCHOLOGY **EDUCATION** Conn Col, BA, 69; Harvard Univ, EdM, 70; Univ Penn, PhD, 75. **CAREER** Adj Prof to Asst prof, Columbia Univ, 75-85; Adj Prof, Univ Pa, 85-90; Prof, to Founding Dir Inst on Child and family Policy, Columbia Univ, 91-. **HONORS AND AWARDS** Gallagher Lectureship, Soc for Adolescent Medicine, 99; Hammer Awd, Fed Interagency Forum on Child and Family Statistics, 98; Nicholas Hobbs Awd, Am Psychol Asn, 97; John P Hill Awd, Soc for Res on Adolescence, 96; William Goode Book Awd, Am Sociol Asn, 88; Phi Delta Kappa Dissertation Awd; Phi Lambda Theta; Phi Delta Kappa; Honors Awd in Undergraduate Major. **MEMBERSHIPS** Am Asn for the Adv of Sci, Am Educ Res Asn, Am Psychol Asn, Am Psychol Soc, NY Acad of Sci, soc for Res in child Development, Soc for Res in Adolescence, Soc for Beh Pediatrics. **SELECTED PUBLICATIONS** Co-ed, Escape from poverty: What makes a difference for children?, Cambridge Univ Press, 95; co-ed, Consequences of growing up poor, Russell Sage press, 97; co-ed, Transitions through adolescence: Interpersonal domains and context, Erlbaum Pub, 96; auth, Girls' experience of adolescence, Harvard Univ Press, forthcoming; co-ed, Conflict and cohesion in families: Causes and consequences, Erlbaum Pub, 99; co-ed, Neighborhood Poverty: context and consequences for children Vol I, Russell Sage, 97; co-ed, Policy implications in studying neighborhoods Vol II, Russell Sage Press, 97; co-co-auth, "Marriage and the baby carriage: Historical change and intergenerational continuity in early parenthood," in Negotiating adolescence in times of social change, Cross-national perspectives on developmental process and social intervention, Cambridge Univ Press, in press; co-auth, "Profiles of grandmothers who help care for their grandchildren in the United States," Family Relations, in press; co-auth, "Early childhood intervention programs: what about the family?," in Handbook on early childhood intervention 2nd ed, Cambridge Univ Press, in press; co-auth, "Famlywork: Welfare changes, parenting and young children," in Exits from poverty, Cambridge Univ Press, in press; co-auth, "antecedents and consequences: Racial socialization in Black girls' families," in Telling the untold story: Racial socialization among ethnic families of color, in press. **CONTACT ADDRESS** Dept Human Development, Columbia Univ, 525 W 120th St, New York, NY 10027. **EMAIL** brooks-gunn@columbia.edu

BROSNAHAN, LEGER
PERSONAL Born 12/11/1929, Kansas City, MO, m, 1967, 2 children **DISCIPLINE** ENGLISH, LITERATURE, COMPOSITION, ESL **EDUCATION** Georgetown Univ, AB, 51; Harvard Univ, MA, 52; PhD, 58. **CAREER** Instr, Northwestern Univ, 57-61; asst prof, Univ of Hawaii-Manoa, 61-63; asst prof, Univ of Md at Col Park, 65-68; from assoc prof to prof, Ill State Univ, 68-. **MEMBERSHIPS** ALSC, NAS, MSA, AAUP, MLA. **RESEARCH** English Language, Literature, Composition, ESL, Comparative Medieval Literature. **SELECTED PUBLICATIONS** Auth, Around the World in English, Kenkyusha, 74; auth, Japanese and English Gesture, Taishukan, 88; auth, Chinese and English Gesture, BLCUP, 91; auth, Standard American English Behavior, Dongyang Munhuasa, 98. **CONTACT ADDRESS** Dept English, Illinois State Univ, 1 Campus PO Box 4240, Normal, IL 61790. **EMAIL** lnbrosna@ilstu.edu

BROUDY, HARRY S.
PERSONAL Born 07/27/1905, Filipowa, Poland, m, 1947, 1 child **DISCIPLINE** PHILOSOPHY OF EDUCATION **EDUCATION** Boston Univ, AB, 29; Harvard Univ, MA, 33, PhD, 35. **CAREER** Supvr adult educ, Mass Dept Educ, 36-37; prof philos educ, Mass State Col North Adams, 37-49, Framingham, 39-57; Prof Philos, Univ Ill, Urbana, 57-, Lectr, Cornell Univ, 62; Boyd H Bode lectr, Ohio State Univ, 63; ed, Educ Forum, 64-73; fel Ctr Advan Study Behav Sci, 67-68; consult, Educ Res Coun Am, Cleveland, 66-80; distinguished vis prof, Mem Univ St John's Nfld, 74, Calif State Univ, Los Angeles, 78; Emens distinguished prof, Ball State Univ, 82. **HONORS AND AWARDS** DH, Oakland Univ, 69, Mass State Col, 81; DHL, Eastern Ky State Univ, 79. **MEMBERSHIPS** Philos Educ Soc (pres, 54); Asn Realistic Philos (pres, 55-56); Am Philos Asn; Metaphys Soc; Am Soc Aesthet. **RESEARCH** Aesthetic education; uses of schooling in nonschool situations; Polanyi's tacit knowing. **SELECTED PUBLICATIONS** Auth, Thoughts on Art Education, J Aesthetic Educ, Vol 0027, 93. **CONTACT ADDRESS** Col of Educ, Univ of Illinois, Chicago, Chicago, IL 60680.

BROWMAN, DAVID L.
PERSONAL Born Missoula, MT, m, 1965, 3 children **DISCIPLINE** ANTHROPOLOGY **EDUCATION** Univ Mont, BA, 63; Univ Washington, MA, 66; Harvard Univ, PhD, 70. **CAREER** Teaching tutor, Harvard Univ, 69-70; Asst to Full Prof, Washington Univ, 70-. **HONORS AND AWARDS** Fel, AAAS; Fel, AAA. **RESEARCH** Andean prehistory; Origins of agriculture; Pastoralism; History of science. **CONTACT ADDRESS** Dept Anthropol, Washington Univ, 1 Brookings Dr, Saint Louis, MO 63130. **EMAIL** dlbrowma@artsci.wustl.edu

BROWN, BEATRICE S.
PERSONAL Born 07/14/1950, Louisville, KY, s **DISCIPLINE** PSYCHOLOGY **EDUCATION** Addis Ababa Univ, psychology, Ethiopia, 1990-; Cornell Univ, Cooperative Nutrition Program, PhD Doctoral/Elected Research Visiting Faculty Member, certificate, 1991; Postgraduate Ctr for Mental Health, New York, certificate, 1995; certificate, Albert Einstein College of Medicine" Advances in the Treatment of Schizophrenia, 98; Albert Einstein College of Medicine & Montefiore Medical Center Post Doctoral Course in Geriatric Psychopathology and Treatment, 98. **CAREER** City Coll, City Univ, NY, adjunct prof, 89-; Upper Manhattan Mental Health Ctr, children day treatment unit dir, 89-91; Jewish Board of Family & Children Svcs, residential treatment facility girls unit dir, 94-; Central Brooklyn Coordinating Council Inc, mental health unit psychologist, 97-. **HONORS AND AWARDS** American Psychological Assn, Full Membership Status, 1995; Black Psychologists Assn, 1998. **MEMBERSHIPS** BSB Wholistic Psychological Center, Inc, founder, dir, CEO, 1997; The Childrens Annex Multi-Media Communications Project, 99. **RESEARCH** Emotion of Anger/Conflict, Resolution & Degrees of Anger & Love **SELECTED PUBLICATIONS** Auth, The Seven Law Curriculum for Positive Thinking in Children & Adolescents, Brown Educational Institute, 89; auth, Essence Total Makeover, Chapt 5, " Mental Wellness, Random House/ Crown, 99. **CONTACT ADDRESS** PO Box 172, Mount Vernon, NY 10552. **EMAIL** dochsb10552@yahoo.com

BROWN, FRANK
PERSONAL Born 05/01/1935, Gallian, AL, m **DISCIPLINE** EDUCATION **EDUCATION** AL State Univ, BS 1957; OR State Univ, MS 1962; Univ of CA at Berkeley, MA 1969, PhD 1970; Harvard University, Institute for Educational Management, fellow, 1988. **CAREER** NY State Commiss on Ed, assoc dir, 70-72; Urban Inst CCNY, dir 1971-72; Cora P Maloney Coll SUNY Buffalo, dir 1974-77; SUNY Buffalo, prof 1972-83; Univ of NC Chapel Hill, School of Ed, dean 1983-90; Institute for Research in Social Science, Chapel Hill, NC, dir, educational research policy studies project, 90-; Cary C Boshamer, professor of education, 90-; University of California, Berkeley, CA, visiting scholar, 90-91. **HONORS AND AWARDS** Grad Fellowship OR State Univ 1961-62; Grad Fellowship Univ of CA Berkeley 1968-70; Rockefeller Found Scholars Awd 1979-80; Langston Hughes Inst Awd, Outstanding Service & Leadership; SUNY Buffalo Special Awd, Achievement in Research, Teaching & Service; Tar Heel of the Week, Raleigh News & Observer; Amer Educ Research Assn Awd, Dedicated Service & Leadership; numerous other awards; Publ 5 books, monographs & 110 articles; Fellow, Harvard Univ Institute for Educational Management 1988; Book Series Editor, Educational Excellence, Diversity, and Equity, Corwin Press, 1991-. **MEMBERSHIPS** Rho Lambda Chapter of Alpha Phi Alpha Fraternity, Buffalo, New York, president, 1977-78; Western New York Black Educators Association and the National Urban Education Conference, co-founder, 1975-83; State University of New York at Buffalo; Black Faculty Association, co-founder, 1972; Buffalo Urban League, board of directors, 1978-81; Langston Hughes Institute-Black Cultural Center for Western New York and Buffalo, board of directors, 1978-83; Buffalo School Desegregation Case, Federal District of Western New York, consultant and researcher, 1976-83; vice pres Div A of American Ed Research Assn 1986-88; bd of dirs, American Assn of Colleges of Teacher Education 1988-92; board of directors, National Organization for Legal Problems in Education, 1990-93. **CONTACT ADDRESS** Dir, Educ Research, Univ of No Carolina, Chapel Hill, Manning Hall, CB #3355, Chapel Hill, NC 27599-3355. **EMAIL** fbrown@email.unc.edu

BROWN, JOHN A.
PERSONAL Born 01/10/1934, Evanston, IL, m, 1987, 2 children **DISCIPLINE** ANTHROPOLOGY **EDUCATION** Univ Chicago, BA, 54; Univ Chicago, MA, 58; Univ Chicago, PhD, 65. **CAREER** From Asst Prof to Assoc. Prof, Mich State Univ, 69-71; From Assoc. Prof to Prof, Northwestern Univ, 71-. **HONORS AND AWARDS** Feel, Nat Endowment Humanities, 87-88; Vis Feel, Cambridge Univ, 87-88; Feel, Am Assoc. for the Advancement of SCI, 90; Distinguished Serv Awd, Soc for Am Archaeology, 99. **MEMBERSHIPS** Am Anthrop Assoc., Am Assoc. for the Advancement of SCI, Soc for Am Archaeology. **RESEARCH** Cross-cultural study of mortuary practices for social analysis, evolutionary processes leading to social and cultural complexity in the Eastern Woodlands of North America, iconographic analysis of the Southeastern Ceremonial Complex religion. **SELECTED PUBLICATIONS** Ed, "Approaches to the Social Dimensions of Mortuary Practices," Memoirs of the Soc for Am Archaeol, no 25 (71); co-ed, Prehistoric Hunters and Gatherers: The Emergence of Cultural Complexity, Acad Pr (New York, NY), 85; coauth, Ancient Art of the American Woodland Indians, Henry N. Abrams, Inc (New York, NY), 85; auth, "The Spiro Ceremonial Center: The Archaeology of Arkansas Valley Caddoan Culture in Eastern Oklahoma," Memoirs of the Museum of Anthrop, no 29, Univ Mich (96); auth, "The Archaeology of Ancient Religion in the Eastern Woodlands," Annual Rev of Anthrop, 26 (97): 465-485. **CONTACT ADDRESS** Dept Anthrop, Northwestern Univ, 1810 Hinman Ave, Evanston, IL 60208-0809. **EMAIL** jabrown@nwu.edu

BROWN, JOHN ANDREW
PERSONAL Born 07/17/1945, Birmingham, AL, m, 1993 **DISCIPLINE** EDUCATION **EDUCATION** Daniel Payne College, AA, 1965; Columbia University, 1966; Dartmouth College, 1966; Miles College, BA, 1967; Yale University Divinity School, MDiv, 1970, STM, 1972. **CAREER** Yale Univ Divinity Sch, assoc prof 1970-73; Trinity Coll Hartford, asst prof rel/dir ICS prog 1973-76; CT Coll New London, vstg prof rel 1974-75;The Coll of New Rochelle at NY, theol sem adj prof rel 1980-; Audrey Cohen College, prof/adm, 79-93, adjunct prof of business ethics, 88-93, special asst to the vice pres/dir of staff development, 91-93; Miles Coll, adjunct prof of history, 94-; Lawson State Community Coll, adjunct prof of history, philosophy and religion, 94-; Univ of Alabama at Birmingham, consultant, 94. **HONORS AND AWARDS** Carnegie Fellowship Columbia Univ 1966; Richard Allen Awd; Rockefeller Protestant Fellowship Theological Education 1967-70; Oliver E Daggett Prize Yale Corp 1969; Research Fellowship Yale Univ 1971-72; mem Pi Gamma Mu; Fellowship UTS Black Econ Develop Fund 1976; Biog sketch in Yale Univ 1985 Alumni Directory; The College of New Rochelle, en Years of Outstanding Teaching and Contributions to the College, 1989, Awd for Fourteen Years of Outstanding Teaching and Service to the College, 1993; Audrey Cohen College, Crystal Awd, 1991; Phi Theta Kappa Inc, Alpha Epsilon Gama Chapter, Awd for Outstanding Service, 1996. **MEMBERSHIPS** Consultant Trinity Coll 1973, Manchester Comm Coll1976; educ admin Bronx Extension Site-Coll for Human Serv 1986-; mem NY Urban League, Alpha Phi Alpha,NAACP, ASALH, Yale Alumni Associates of Afro-Americans, AAUP. **CONTACT ADDRESS** Professor, Social Science Dept, Lawson State Comm Col, 3060 Wilson Rd, Birmingham, AL 35221.

BROWN, JUDITH K.
PERSONAL Born 10/31/1930, Frankfurt, Germany, w, 1957, 2 children **DISCIPLINE** ANTHROPOLOGY **EDUCATION** Cornell Univ, BS, 52; Harvard Univ, MEd, 54; Inst Educ, Univ London, Certificate in Child Develop, 55; Harvard Univ, EdD, 62; Bunting Inst, Radcliffe Col, Post-doctoral Fel, 67-69. **CAREER** Lectr, Oakland Univ, 64-66, asst prof, 69-75, assoc prof, 75-83, prof, 83-; vis scholar, Inst for Res on Women and Gender, Stanford Univ, winter 89; vis res assoc, Dept of Anthropol, Bryn Mawr Col, winter 93; vis scholar, Prog in Human Develop, Grad Sch of Educ, Harvard Univ, winter 97. **HONORS AND AWARDS** Nat Inst of Health, Div of Human Develop and Aging, 90-93; Who's Who in Am Educ, 92-93; Int Authors and Writers Who's Who, 93; Dict of Am Biog, 94; The World's Who's Who of Women, 95; Who's Who in the World, 97. **MEMBERSHIPS** Am Anthropl Asn, Am Asn for Univ Profs, Soc for Psychol Anthropol, Asn for Anthropol & Gerontology. **RESEARCH** Cross-cultural studies of middle aged women, women's economic activities and wife abuse. **SELECTED PUBLICATIONS** Co-ed with Jeanette Dickerson-Putman, Women among Women: Anthropological Perspectives on Female Age Hierarchies, Champaign, Ill: Univ Ill Press (98); auth, "Lives of Middle-Aged Women," in Women in the Third World: An Encyclopedia of Contemporary Issues, Nelly Stromquist, ed, New York: Garland (98): 246-251; coauth, "Women's Age Hierarchies: An Introductory Overview," in Women among Women: Anthropological Perspectives on Female Age Hierarchies, Jeanette Dickerson-Putman and Judith K. Brown, eds, Urbana, Ill: Univ Ill Press (98); coauth, "Being in Charge: Older Women and Their Younger Female Kin," in Women among Women: Anthropological Perspectives on Female Hierarchies, Jeanette Dickerson-Putman and Judith K. Brown, eds, Urbana, Ill: Univ Ill Press (98): 100-123; coauth, "A Bibliography for the Cross-Cultural Study of Women's Lives," in Women among Women: Anthropological Perspectives on Female Hierarchies, Jeanette Dickerson-Piutman and Judith K. Brown, eds, Urbana, Ill: Univ Ill Press (98): 124-140; co-ed with Dorothy Counts and Jacquelyn Campbell, To Have and to Hit: Anthropological Perspectives on Wife-Beating, Champaign, Ill: Univ of Ill Press (99); auth, "Introduction: Defini-

tions, Assumptions, Themes and Issues," in To Have and to Hit: Anthropological Perspectives on Wife-Beating, co-ed with Dorothy Counts and Jacquelyn Campbell, Champaign, Ill: Univ of Ill Press (99): 3-26. **CONTACT ADDRESS** Dept Anthropol & Sociol, Oakland Univ, Rochester, MI 48309-4495. **EMAIL** brown@oakland.edu

BROWN, MARY ELLEN
PERSONAL Born 01/06/1939, d, 2 children **DISCIPLINE** FOLKLORE **EDUCATION** Mary Baldwin Col, BA, 60; Univ of Pa, MA, 63; PhD, 68. **CAREER** Asst prof, Ind State Univ, 70-72; asst prof to prof, Ind Univ, 72-. **HONORS AND AWARDS** Res Fel, Edinburgh Univ, 78, 79; ACLS Grant, 79, 84; Res Funds, IND Univ, 80-82, 87-89, 93, 97; Title VI Summer Lang Fel, 91, 93; Sr Fac Fel, 91-92; Fulbright Res, 98. **MEMBERSHIPS** Am Folklore Soc; Assoc for Scottish Lit Study. **RESEARCH** Auth, "Some Continuities Between Oral and Written Literature", Proceedings of the Folklore Soc Centenary Celebration, ed Venetia Newall, (80): 272-277; auth, Burns and Tradition, Macmillan Pr, (London), 84; auth, "Tannahill as Local Poet", Paisley Poets, ed Stuart James and Gordon McCrae, Univ of Paisley Libr; (93): 25-36; auth, "The Mechaism of the Ancient Ballad: William Motherwell's Explanation", Oral Tradition II (96): 175-198; auth, "All is Not Narrative or Whole: The Real Scottish Repertoire", Ljudske alade med zrocilom in sodobnostjo/Ballads between tradition and modern times, ed Marjetka Golezco, Zolozba ZRC SAZU, (Lolozba), 98; auth, "Introduction", "Achebe, Chinua", "Aesop's Fable", Encyclopedia of Folklore and Literature, ABC-CLIO, (Santa Barbara, CA), 98; ed, Encyclopedia of Folklore and Literature, ABC-CLIO, (Santa Barbara, CA), 98; auth, The Bedesman and the Hodbearer: The Epistolary Friendship of Francis James Child and William Walker, Elphinstone Inst, (Aberdeen), (forthcoming); auth, Cultural Nationalism, Conservatism, Antiquarianism: William Motherwell's Querel with change, Univ Pr of Ky, (forthcoming); auth, "The Harvard Professor and the Pawnbroker: FJ Child and Will Walker: Collaboration in the Ballad", Bridging the Cultural Divide: Our Common Heritage, Georg Olms Verlag A G (Hildesheim), (forthcoming). **CONTACT ADDRESS** Folklore Inst, Indiana Univ, Bloomington, 504 N Fess Ave, Bloomington, IN 47408-3822. **EMAIL** brown2@indiana.edu

BROWN, MICHAEL FOBES
PERSONAL Born 07/06/1950, Syracuse, NY **DISCIPLINE** CULTURAL ANTHROPOLOGY **EDUCATION** Princeton Univ, BA, 72; Univ of Mich, PhD, 81. **CAREER** LAMBERT PROF OF ANTHROPOLOGY & LATIN AM STUDIES, WILLIAMS COL, 80-. **HONORS AND AWARDS** Smithsonian fel, 83; NEH fel, 88; Weatherhood Scholar, School of Am Res, 93. **MEMBERSHIPS** Am Anthropological Asn; Am Ethnological Soc. **RESEARCH** Religion; human ecology; social movements; cultural/intellectual property. **SELECTED PUBLICATIONS** Auth, Tsewa's Gift: Magic and Meaning in an Amazonian Society, Smithsonian Inst Press, 86; auth, Facing the State, Facing the World: Amazonia's Native Leaders and the New Politics of Identity, L'Homme, 93; auth, On Resisting Resistance, Am Anthropologist, 96; auth, The Channeling Zone: American Spirituality in an Anxious Age, Harvard Univ Press, 97; auth, Can Culture Be Copyrighted?, Current Anthropology, 98; auth, The New Alienists: Healing Shattered Selves at Century's End, Paranoia Within Reason, Univ of Chicago Press, 98; coauth, War of Shadows: The Struggle for Utopia in the Peruvian Amazon, Unis of Calif Press, 91. **CONTACT ADDRESS** Dept of Anthropology & Sociology, Williams Col, Williamstown, MA 01267-2606. **EMAIL** mbrown@williams.edu

BROWN, OLA M.
PERSONAL Born 04/07/1941, Albany, GA, s **DISCIPLINE** EDUCATION **EDUCATION** Albany State Coll, BS 1961; Univ of GA, MEd 1972, EdS 1973, EdD 1974. **CAREER** Thomas County Schools, Thomasville GA, teacher, 61-67; Dougherty County Schools, Albany GA, teacher, 67-71; Univ of GA Athens, grad asst, 72-74; Valdosta State Coll GA, prof of educ, 74-91; Dept Head, Early Childhood and Reading Education, 80-90; dept head, professor emerita, currently. **HONORS AND AWARDS** Educ Instr of Yr Student GA Assn of Educ (VSC) 1975; WH Dennis Meml Awd Albany State Coll 1976; Ira E Aaron Reading Awd S Central GA Council of IRA 1977. **MEMBERSHIPS** Mem Phi Delta Kappa Educ Frat 1975-; recording sec GA Council of Intl Reading Assn 1977-79; treas GA Assn of Higher Educ (GAE Affl) 1977-80; mem Amer Assn of Univ Prof 1977-80; vice pres 1979-80, pres 1980-81 GA Council of Intl Reading Assn; state coordinator Intl Reading Assn 1988-91. **CONTACT ADDRESS** Dept Head, Valdosta State Univ, 1500 N Patterson St, Valdosta, GA 31698.

BROWN, RICHARD H.
PERSONAL Born 05/12/1940, New York, NY, m, 1968, 1 child **DISCIPLINE** SOCIOLOGY **EDUCATION** Univ of Calif Berkeley, BA, 61; Columbia Univ, MA, 65; Univ of Calif San Diego, PhD, 73. **CAREER** Instr, Calif State Univ, 71-72; p'rof, Univ of Md, 75-. **HONORS AND AWARDS** Fulbright Lectr, Colombia, 93. **RESEARCH** Power/knowledge, culture, identity and globalization, comparative history study of modernity and postmodernity. **SELECTED PUBLICATIONS** Auth, A Poetic for Sociology: Toward a Logic of Discovery for the Human Sciences, Cambridge Univ Pr, 77; auth, Society as Text: Essays on Rhetoric, Reason and Reality, Univ of Chicago Pr, 87; auth, Social Science as Civil Discourse: Essays on the Invention, Uses and Legitimization of Social Theory, Univ of Chicago Pr, 89; auth, Toward a Democratic Science: Scientific Narration and Civil Communication for a Democratic Society, Yale Univ Pr, 98; coauth, Is the United States a Postmodern Society? Culture, Capitalism and the Prospects for Democracy in America, Yale Univ Pr, 99; auth, Culture, Capitalism and Democracy in America, (forthcoming). **CONTACT ADDRESS** Dept Sociol, Univ of Maryland, Col Park, 2112 Art-Sociology, College Park, MD 20742-0001. **EMAIL** rbrown@bss1.umd.edu

BROWN, ROBERT
DISCIPLINE DISTANCE LEARNING **EDUCATION** Univ Md, PhD, 77. **CAREER** Okla St Univ. **HONORS AND AWARDS** Best Collection Essays Technical Scientific Comm; Frank R. Smith Awd Outstanding Jour Article; dean, arts & sciences **SELECTED PUBLICATIONS** Coauth, Technical Writing for Non-Native Speakers of English; Auth, Harcourt-Brace, 95; Team Conferences: Full Collaboration in the Report Writing Process," in A Publications Management: Essays for Professional Communicators; Rethinking the Approach to Communication Training, Technical Communication, 94. **CONTACT ADDRESS** Oklahoma State Univ, Stillwater, 101 Whitehurst Hall, Stillwater, OK 74078.

BROWN, STEVEN M.
PERSONAL Born Philadelphia, PA, m, 1975, 2 children **DISCIPLINE** JEWISH EDUCATION AND STUDIES **EDUCATION** Jewish Theol Sem Am, BA, BHL; Columbia Univ, MA, EdD. **CAREER** Prin, Cent Hebrew HS Long Island, NY; head tchr to headmaster, N Brch Solomon Schechter Day School, 73-75; educ dir, Adath Jeshurun, Elkins Park, Pa; dir, Melton Res Ctr Jewish Educ, 96; dean William Davidson Grad Schl Jewish Educ, Jewish Theol Sem Am. **HONORS AND AWARDS** Jewish educ workshops, Israel and Argentina; exec bd, Jewish Educ Assembly; pres, Solomon Schechter Day Schl Principals Coun; bd dir, Jewish Comm Rel Coun Philadelphia; bd dir, Adath Jeshurun. **MEMBERSHIPS** Asn Supervision and Curr Devel; Jewish Fed Greater Philadelphia. **SELECTED PUBLICATIONS** Auth, L'Ela--L'Ela: Higher and Higher--Making Jewish Prayer Part of Us; Reclaiming Our Legacy.* Marbeh Torah, Marbeh Chaim-The More Torah, The More Life; Willing, Learning, and Striving, A Course for Teaching Jewish Youth Based on Emet Ve-Emunah; Approaches to the Numinous, Learn Torah With.Dr Brown. **CONTACT ADDRESS** Jewish Theol Sem of America, 3080 Broadway, New York, NY 10027. **EMAIL** stbrown@jtsa.edu

BROWN, SUSAN G.
PERSONAL Born 02/10/1951, Wichita, KS, m, 1999, 1 child **DISCIPLINE** SOCIOLOGY **EDUCATION** Tulane Univ, PhD, 83. **CAREER** From Asst Prof to Prof, Univ Hawaii, 85-. **MEMBERSHIPS** AAAS, ABS. **RESEARCH** Animal behavior, evolution of gender, women's health. **SELECTED PUBLICATIONS** Coauth, "The Behaviour of a Rare Male Phenotype of the Unisexual Gecko, 'Lepidodactylus Lugubris'," The Herpetological J 6 (96): 69-73; coauth, "The Relationship Between Calcium Gland Size, Fecundity and Social Behavior in the Unisexual Geckos, 'Lepidodactylus Lugubris' and 'Hemidactylus Garnotii'," Int J of Comparative Psychol (97); coauth, "Faeces Avoidance Behavior in Unisexual and Bisexual Geckos," The Herpetological J (forthcoming); coauth, Relations Between Menstrual Cycle Phase, Coitus and Women's Health Problems, forthcoming; auth, Women and Health: A Sociological, Epidemiological and Cross-Cultural Approach to Women's Health, forthcoming. **CONTACT ADDRESS** Dept Sociol, Univ of Hawaii, Hilo, 200 W Kawili St, Hilo, HI 96720. **EMAIL** susanb@hawaii.edu

BROWNE, DALLAS L.
PERSONAL Born 10/09/1944, Chicago, IL, m, 4 children **DISCIPLINE** ANTHROPOLOGY **EDUCATION** Univ Illinois-Urbana, Phd, 83; Univ Illinois-Urbana, MA, 71; Northeastern Illinois Univ, BA, 67. **CAREER** Pres, Council on Foreign Relations, St. Louis Committee, 99-; Board of Directors, Katherine Dunham Museum; Board of Directors, Eugen Redmond Writers Society. **HONORS AND AWARDS** NDF Fellowships; Ford Foundation; Foreign Area Fellowship; Rockefeller Grant; Teacher of the Year Awd, Student Government, York College CUNY, 89; International Student Advisor of the Year, Southern Illinois Univ, 95; Outstanding Student Advisor Awd, SIUE, 97; Delta Sigma Theta, Outstanding Teacher of the Year Awd SIUE, 98. **MEMBERSHIPS** AAUP (Amer Assoc of Univer Prof); NEA-IEA; World Affairs Council; Amer Anthropolical Assoc; African Studies Assoc; Urban Anthropology Society; Mid-West Assoc of Latin Amer Studies. **RESEARCH** Biography of Allison Davis; Urban Cultural Change in East Africa; African Cultural Retention Latin America. **SELECTED PUBLICATIONS** Auth, "Allison Davis: Across Class and Culture," in I. Harrison, ed. Afr-Am Pioneers in Anthropology, 99; auth, "Culture, Power, and Genocide in Rwanda," in Meghan O'Meara, ed., History Behind the Headlines Chapter 7, 00. **CONTACT ADDRESS** Dept Anthropology, So Illinois Univ, Edwardsville, PO Box 1451, Edwardsville, IL 62026-1451. **EMAIL** dbrowne@siue.edu

BROWNELL, SUSAN E.
PERSONAL Born 10/08/1960, Bethesda, MD, s **DISCIPLINE** ANTHROPOLOGY **EDUCATION** Univ Va, BA, 82; Univ Calif, PhD, 90. **CAREER** Asst Prof to Assoc Prof, Univ of Mo, 94-. **MEMBERSHIPS** Res Coun of the Intl Olympic Comt. **RESEARCH** China, Sports, Gender, Nationalism, the Body. **SELECTED PUBLICATIONS** Auth, Chinese Femininities/Chinese Masculinities: A Reader, Univ of Calif Press, (forthcoming); Auth, Training the Body for China: Sports in the Moral Order of the People's Republic, Univ of Chicago Press, 95; Auth, "Mainstreaming Gender, Washing Away Feminism", Bulletin of Concerned Asian Scholars 31 (99): 29-40; Auth, "The Body and the Beautiful in Chinese Nationalism: Sportswomen and Fashion Models in the Reform Era", China Information (99): 36-58; Auth, "'China Bashing' at the Olympic Games: Why the Cold War Continues in Sports Journalism", Shorenstein Papers in East Asian Studies 9 (96): 1-4. **CONTACT ADDRESS** Dept Anthrop, Univ of Missouri, St. Louis, 8001 Natural Bridge, Saint Louis, MO 62121. **EMAIL** sbrownell@umsl.edu

BROWNLEY, MARTINE WATSON
PERSONAL Born 07/27/1947, Spartanburg, SC **DISCIPLINE** ENGLISH LITERATURE; WOMEN'S STUDIES **EDUCATION** Agnes Scott Col, BA, 69; Harvard Univ, AM, 71, PhD(English), 75. **CAREER** Goodrich C. White Prof of English and Winship Distinguished Res Prof, Emory Univ, 96-. **HONORS AND AWARDS** Recognition Awd, Am Asn Univ Women, 78; Fel for Univ Teachers, NEH, 88-89. **MEMBERSHIPS** MLA; Am Soc 18th Century Studies; Southeastern Am Soc 18th Century Studies. **RESEARCH** 17th & 18th century British literary historiographers; Women's studies. **SELECTED PUBLICATIONS** Ed., Mothering the Mind, Holmes & Meier, 84; Auth, Clarendon and the Rhetoric of Historical Form, U of Penn P, 85; ed., Women and Autobiography, Scholarly Resources, 99; auth, Deferrals of Domain: Contemporary Women Novelists and the State, St. Martin's P, 00. **CONTACT ADDRESS** Dept of English, Emory Univ, 537 Kilgo Cir N-317, Atlanta, GA 30322. **EMAIL** mbrown1@emory.edu

BRUHN, JOHN GLYNDON
PERSONAL Born 04/27/1934, Norfolk, NE, s **DISCIPLINE** MEDICAL SOCIOLOGY **EDUCATION** Univ Nebr, BA, 52-56, MA, 56-58; Yale Univ, PhD, 58-61; Harvard Grad Sch Edu, MLE, 97. **CAREER** Resr, Nebr Sch Med, 58; resr, Yale Univ, Conn Dept Mental Health, 58-59; instr, Sociol, South Conn Coll, 60-61; res couns, Yale Univ, 61; resr sociol, Dept Psychol Med, Univ Edinburgh, Scotland, 61-62; instr, Med Sociol, Univ Okla, 62-63; asst prof, Dept Psych & Behav Sci, Univ Okla, 63-64;asst prof, Prevent Med & Public Health, Univ Okla Med Ctr, 64-67; clin investr, Okla Med Res Found, 65-67; assoc prof, Sociol Med, Univ Okla Med Ctr, 67-72; assoc prof, Human Ecol, Sch Health, Univ Okla Med Ctr, 67-69; prof & ch, Dept Human Ecol, Sch Health, Univ Okla Med Ctr, 69-72; assoc dean, Univ Tx Med Br-Galveston, 72-81; prof, Prevent Med & Commun Health, Univ Tx Med Ctr, 71-91; dean, Sch Allied Health Sci, Univ Tx Med Br, 81-91; vpres, Acad Affs & Res, Univ Tx -El Paso, 91-95; prof, Coll Nurs & Health Sci, Univ Tx-El Paso, 91-95; adj prof, Mgt & Policy Sci, Univ Tx Health Sci Ctr, 91-95; Provost, Dean, Prof, Sociol, Sch Behav Sci & Educ, Penn State Harrisburg, 95-99; adj prof, health sciences, NM State Univ, Las Cruces, 99-. **RESEARCH** Organizational behavior; organizational ethics. **SELECTED PUBLICATIONS** Coauth, Handbook of Clinical Sociology, Plenum Pub Co, 91; coauth, Managing Boundaries in the Health Professions, Charles C Thomas, 93; coauth, Perspectives on Life-Threatening Illness for Allied Health Professionals, Haworth Press, 93; coauth, Clinical Sociology: An Agenda for Action, Plenum Publ, 96; co-edr, Border health: Challenges for the United States and Mexico, Garland Publ, 97. **CONTACT ADDRESS** 8864 East Surrey Ave, Scottsdale, AZ 85260-7613. **EMAIL** jjgbruhn@azlink.com

BRUMFIEL, ELIZABETH M.
PERSONAL Born 03/10/1945, Chicago, IL, m, 1967, 1 child **DISCIPLINE** ANTHROPOLOGY **EDUCATION** Univ Mich, BA, 65; UCLA, MA, 69; Univ Mich, PhD, 76. **CAREER** Volunteer, Peace Corps, 66-67; res asst to teaching fel, Univ Mich, 67-72; lectr, E Mich Univ, 70-77; asst prof to prof, Albion Col, 77-. **HONORS AND AWARDS** Mellon Found Grant, Albion Col, 81; Scholar of the Year, Albion Col, 91; Citation, Brown Univ 92; Fel, Am Asn for the Adv of Sci, 93; NEH Fel, 94; Fel, Ctr for Adv Study in the Beh Sci, 94-95. **MEMBERSHIPS** Am Anthropol Asn; Soc for Am Archaeol; Am Asn for the Adv of Sci; Asn for Feminist Anthropol; Soc for Econ Anthropol; Sigma XI. **RESEARCH** Gender, class and factional dynamics in prehistoric cultures; Mesoamerican prehistory and ethnohistory; Aztec women. **SELECTED PUBLICATIONS** Auth, "Weaving and cooking: Women's production in Aztec Mexico" in Engendering Archaeology: Women and prehistory, (London, 91), 224-251; auth, "Breaking and Entering the Ecosystem--Gender, Class, and Faction Steal the Show," Am Anthropol, (92): 5451*-567; co-ed, Factional Competition and Political Development in the New World, Cambridge Univ Press, 94; ed, Economic Anthropology of the State, Univ Press of Am, 94; auth, "Figurines and the Aztec state: Testing the effectiveness of ideological domination," in Gender in Archaeology: Essays in Research and Practice, (Univ Pa Press, 96), 143-166; auth,

"The quality of tribute cloth: The place of evidence in archaeological argument," Am Antiquity, (96): 453-462; auth, "Huitzilopochtli's thirst: Aztec ideology in the archaeological record," Cambridge Archaeol J, (98): 3-13; auth, "Aztec hearts and minds: Religion and the state in the Aztec empire," in Imperial Designs: Comparative Dynamics of Early Empires, (Cambridge Univ Press, in press), 283-309; ed, Production and Power at Postclassic Xaltocan, Univ Pittsburgh Press, in press. **CONTACT ADDRESS** Dept Anthropol & Sociol, Albion Col, 611 E Porter St, Albion, MI 49224. **EMAIL** ebrumfiel@albion.edu

BRUNER, EDWARD M.
PERSONAL Born 09/28/1924, New York, NY, m, 1948, 2 children **DISCIPLINE** ANTHROPOLOGY **EDUCATION** Univ Chicago, PhD 54; OH State Univ, MA 50, BA 48. **CAREER** Asst prof, Yale Univ, 54-60; from assoc prof to prof emeritus, Univ Ill, 61-94. **HONORS AND AWARDS** Campus Awd for Tchg; Pres, AES; pres, SHA; fel, Center for Advanced Study, 60-61. **MEMBERSHIPS** AAA; SHA; AES; SCA. **RESEARCH** Tourism, culture change, interpretive anthropology, Indonesia. **SELECTED PUBLICATIONS** Tourism in Ghana: The Representation of Slavery and the Return of the Black Diaspora, Amer Anthro; 96; Tourism in the Balinese Borderzone, In Displacement, Diaspora and Geographies of Identity, ed, Smadar Lavie and Ted Sewdenburg, Durham, Duke Univ Press, 96; Maasai on the Lawn: Tourist Realism in East Africa, with Barbara Kirshenblatt-Gimblett, Cultural Anthropology, 94; numerous publications. **CONTACT ADDRESS** Dept of Anthrop, Univ of Illinois, Urbana-Champaign, 607 South Mathews, Urbana, IL 61801. **EMAIL** ebruner@uiuc.edu

BRUNO, JAMES EDWARD
PERSONAL Born 12/12/1940, Brooklyn, NY, m, 1980, 2 children **DISCIPLINE** EDUCATION, ECONOMICS, ENGINEERING **EDUCATION** UCLA, PhD, 68. **CAREER** Prof Education, UCLA. **HONORS AND AWARDS** EUCLAN Res Awd. **MEMBERSHIPS** AERA; ORSA. **RESEARCH** Temporal orientation and human behavior; Decision analysis-operations research; Information referenced testing and assessment. **SELECTED PUBLICATIONS** Coauth, Item Banking: Interactive Testing and Self Assessment, Springer-Verlag, Berling, 93; auth, Time in the Lifetime of a Teacher: Educational Leadership in an Era of Time Scarcity, Corwin Press, 97. **CONTACT ADDRESS** Dept of Education, Univ of California, Los Angeles, 1032A Moore Hall, Los Angeles, CA 90095. **EMAIL** jbruno@ucla.edu

BRUNVAND, JAN HAROLD
PERSONAL Born 03/23/1933, Cadillac, MI, m, 1956, 4 children **DISCIPLINE** FOLKLORE **EDUCATION** Mich State Univ, BA, 55, MA, 57; Ind Univ, PhD, 61. **CAREER** Asst prof English, Univ Idaho, 61-65; assoc prof, Southern Ill Univ, 65-66; assoc prof, 66-71, Prof English, Univ Utah, 71-, Fulbright grant & Guggenheim Found fel, Romania, 70-71, Int Res & Exchanges Bd grant, Romania, 73-74 & 81; ed, J Am Folklore, 76-80. **MEMBERSHIPS** Am Folklore Soc. **RESEARCH** The folktale; Romanian folklore; American folklore. **SELECTED PUBLICATIONS** Auth, A Dictionary of Proverbs and Proverbial Phrases From Books Published by Indiana Authors Before 1890, Ind Univ, 61; The folktale origin of The Taming of the Shrew, Shakespeare Quart, autumn 66; The Study of American Folklore, Norton, 68, 2nd ed, 78; A Guide For Collectors of Folklore in Utah, Univ Utah, 71; The study of Romanian folklore, J Folklore Inst, 72; Folklore: A Study and Research Guide, St Martins, 79; Readings in Am Folklore, 79 & The Vanishing Hitchhiker: American Urban Legends and Their Meanings, 81, Norton. **CONTACT ADDRESS** Dept of English, Univ of Utah, Salt Lake City, UT 84112.

BRUSTEIN, WILLIAM
PERSONAL Born 07/13/1947, Fairfield, CT, m, 1981, 2 children **DISCIPLINE** SOCIOLOGY **EDUCATION** Univ Conn, BA, 69; John Hopkins SAIS, MA, 71; Univ Washington, MA, 77; PhD, 81. **CAREER** Asst prof, Univ Utah, 81-87; assoc prof, 87-88; assoc prof Univ Minn, 89-94; dept ch, 95-98; cen dir, 92-95; prof, 94-. **HONORS AND AWARDS** Who's Who in world; Fulbright Fel; Phi Beta Kappa; Acad Dist Teach; Superior Teach Awd; Morse Amoco Awd; Dist Teach Awd; ASA, James S Coleman Dist Cont to Rational-Choice Schlp. **MEMBERSHIPS** ASA; APSA; ISA. **RESEARCH** Political extremism; Interwar fascism and Nazism; Anti-Semitism; Xenophobia; Sociological theory; social change. **SELECTED PUBLICATIONS** Auth The Logic of Evil: The Social Origins of the Nazi Party, 1925-1933, Yale Univ Press (New Haven, CT), 96; auth, The Social Origins of Political Regionalism: France, 1849-1981, Univ Cal Press (Berkeley), 88; auth, Roots of Hate: Popular Anti-Semitism in Europe Before the Holocaust, Cambridge Univ Press (Cambridge and NY), in press; ed, "Nazism as a Social Phenomenon," Am Behavioral Sci 41(98); auth, "Who Joined the Nazis and Why?" Am J Sociol 103 (97): 216-221; auth, "The Nazi Party and the German New Middle Class, 1925 to 1933." Am Behavioral Sci 41 (98): 1238-1262; coauth, "Joining the Nazi Party: Explaining the Political Geography of NSDAP Membership, 1925-1933." Am Behavioral Sci 41 (98): 1305-1324; auth, "The Costs and Benefits of Joining an Extremist Party: Membership in the pre-1933 Nazi Party." Res Polit Sociol 8 (98): 35-56; coauth, "Interwar Fascist Popularity in Europe and the Default of the Left," Euro Sociol Rev 15 (99): 25-44; auth, "Introduction: Nazism as a Social Phenomenon." Am Behavioral Sci 41 (99): 1189-1192; auth, "Anti-Semitism in Europe: Before the Holocaust." In Fremdenfeindlichkeit, Rechtsextremismus, Jugendgewalt: Intl Soziol Psychol Perspektiven, ed. Klaus Boelinke, Daniel Fuss, John Hagan (forthcoming). **CONTACT ADDRESS** Dept Sociology, Univ of Minnesota, Twin Cities, 267 19th Ave, Minneapolis, MN 55455. **EMAIL** brustein@atlas.socsci.umn.edu

BRYAN, JESSE A.
PERSONAL Born 06/15/1939, Red Springs, NC, m, 1950 **DISCIPLINE** EDUCATION **EDUCATION** Johnson C Smith Univ, Undergrad Degree 1964; Univ of GA, Grad Studies 1964; Temple Univ, MEd 1968; Univ of Toledo, PhD 1977. **CAREER** Admissions Glassboro State Coll, numerous positions & assoc dir 1969-70; Student Field Experience Office Univ of Toledo, admin asst 1970-71; Univ of Toledo, dir upward bound 1971-73; Bloomsburg Univ, dir center for acad devel 1973-87, dir, Dept of Dev Instr, beginning 1987, retired. **HONORS AND AWARDS** Special Recognition Ed Opportunity Ctr, Ctr for Acad Devel; Two Advisory Awds Third World Cultural Soc; Advisory Awd Kappa Alpha Psi Lambda Alpha; Vol Leader Awd Young Men's Christian Assoc; special award from former students. **MEMBERSHIPS** Mem Kappa Alpha Psi Fraternity 1961-; mem Phi Delta Kappa 1972-; dir Act 101 Program 1973-; mem Act 101 Exec Comm 1973-83; Black Conf on Higher Educ 1973-; mem Western Reg of Act 101 1978-; mem Kiwanis Intl 1979-; pres Equal Educ Oppor Program 1980-. **CONTACT ADDRESS** Professor Emeritus, Bloomsburg Univ of Pennsylvania, Waller Administration Bldg Room #14, Bloomsburg, PA 17815.

BRYANT, BUNYAN I.
PERSONAL Born 03/06/1935, Little Rock, AR, m, 1993 **DISCIPLINE** EDUCATION **EDUCATION** Eastern MI Univ, BS, 1958; Univ of MI, Social Work, MSW, 1965; Univ of MI, Education, PhD, 1970. **CAREER** Univ of MI, School of Natural Resources & Environment, prof. **HONORS AND AWARDS** MLK Dreamkeeper Awd; Distinguished Leadership to the Environmental Justice Movement Awd; Environmental Justice Advisory Council; Recognition Awd; Sch of Natural Resources Outstanding Teacher Awd. **MEMBERSHIPS** League of Conservation, bd mem; USEPA Clean Air Act, advisory comm. **SELECTED PUBLICATIONS** Auth, Race & the Indicence of Environmental Hazards, Westview Press, Baulder, 1992; Author/editor, Environmental Justice: Issues, Policies & Solutions, 1995. **CONTACT ADDRESS** Professor, Univ of Michigan, Ann Arbor, 430 E University, Dana Bldg, Rm 1536, Ann Arbor, MI 48109. **EMAIL** bbryant@umich.edu

BUCKLEY, THOMAS
PERSONAL Born 05/28/1942, Louisville, KY, m, 1979, 1 child **DISCIPLINE** ANTHROPOLOGY **EDUCATION** Harvard, BA, 75; Univ Chicago, MA, 77; PhD, 82. **CAREER** Asst prof to assoc prof, Univ Mass at Boston, 82--. **HONORS AND AWARDS** NIH; APS; Com of Mass; Fel,; Soc for Values in Higher Ed; Ford Foundation Teaching Fel. **MEMBERSHIPS** Am Anthropol Asn. **RESEARCH** N american Indians; Gender; Advocacy; History of anthropology. **SELECTED PUBLICATIONS** Auth, "The Shaker Church in Native northwestern California," Native american Culture and Research Journal, (97); auth, "The pitiful history of little events: The epistemological and moral contexts of Kroeber's Californian ethnology, 1900-1915," History of anthropology Vo.8, (96): 257-297; auth, "Yurok doctors and the concept of shamanism," California Indian Shamanism, (92); auth, Blood Magic: The Anthropology of Menstruation, Univ of Calif Press: Los Angeles, 88; auth, "Kroeber's theory of culture areas and the ethnology of northwest California," Anthropological Quarterly, (88): 15-26; auth, "Suffering in the cultural construction of others: Robert Spott and A.L. Kroeber," American Indian Quarterly, (88): 437-445; auth, "Dialogue and shared authority: Informants as critics," Central Issues in Anthropology, (87): 13-23; auth, "Yurok speech registers and ontology," Language in Society, (84): 467-488; auth, "Menstruation and the power of Yurok women: Methods in cultural reconstruction," American Ethnologist,(82): 47-60. **CONTACT ADDRESS** Dept Anthropol, Univ of Massachusetts, Boston, 100 Morrissey Blvd, Boston, MA 02125. **EMAIL** thomas.buckley@umb.edu

BUFFORD, RODGER K.
PERSONAL Born 12/23/1944, Santa Rosa, CA, m, 1968, 2 children **DISCIPLINE** PSYCHOLOGY **EDUCATION** Kings Col, BA, 66; Univ Illinois, MA, 70; PhD, 71. **CAREER** Asst prof, 71-76, Amer Univ; chmn, dept of psychology, 76-77 Huntington Col; part-time inst,77-81, dept of counseling and psychological stud, Georgia St Univ; assoc prof, Psychological Studies Inst, 77-81, dir of clinical training, 80-81, psychological stud inst; psychologist, 80-82, Atlanta Counseling Center; psychologist, 82-, Western Psychological and Counseling Svc; assoc prof, 82-86, prof & chmn, 86-90, div of clinical psychology, Western Conservative Baptist Sem; prof & chmn, grad school of clinical psychology, 90-95, prof, & dir of research and integration, 95-97; Prof and dir of training; George Fox Univ; **HONORS AND AWARDS** Exemplary Paper in Humility Theology for 1997 Awd in Religion and the Human Behavioral Sciences, John Templeton Found; Templeton Found Awd - 1993 Call for Papers in Humility Theology Program. **MEMBERSHIPS** Who's Who in the World, 84-98; Who's Who in Med and Healthcare, 97-98; Who's Who in Science and Eng, 96-97; Who's Who in the West, 84-99; Who's Who among Human Svc Prof, 85; Who's Who in Frontier Science and Tech, 84-85; Who's Who in the South an Southwest, 77-78; Who's Who among Students, 65-66; Amer Men and Women of Science, 95-96; Personalities of the South, 75-76; Who's Who Among Students in Amer Col and Univ. **RESEARCH** Theoretical and empirical integration of psychology and Christian faith, including empirical psychology of religion, and esp empricial investigation of spiritual wellbeing and maturity, spiritual interventions in psychotherapy, and spiritual outcomes of psychotherapy. **SELECTED PUBLICATIONS** Auth, The Human Reflex: Behavioral Psychology in Biblical perspective, Harper and Row, 81; auth, Counseling and the Demonic, Word Books, 88; coauth, Norms for the Spiritual Well-being Scale, Jour of Psych and Theol, 91; art, Reflections on Christian counseling, CAPS W Newsletter 19, 92; art, Looking Over the Horizon: Presidential reflections, CAPS W Newsletter 20, 93; art, Faith that Hurts, CAPS W Newsletter 19, 93; coauth, Effects of Cognitive-Behavioral Marriage Enrichment On Marital Adjustment Of Church Couples, Jour of Psych and Theol 24, 96; art, Managed Care; What good is it? OPA Newsgram, 96; art, The Scientist as Christian or Atheist, Persp on Science & Christian faith 48, 96; art, Consecrated Counseling: Reflections on the Distinctives of Christian Counseling, Jour of Psych and Theol 25, 97; art, Personal Knowledge and Truth: A Response to Sorenson's Leper Metaphor, Internet Pub, Christian Asn for Psychol Stud, 97; coauth, Evolutionary Psychology: A Paradigm Whose Time May Come, Persp on Science and Christian Faith 50, 98; auth, Bufford, R.K., Aversion therapy. In D.G. Benner and P.C. Hill, eds, Baker encylopedia of psychology and counseling (Grand Rapids, MI: Baker), 99; auth, Bufford, R.K., Behavior modification. In D.G Benenr and P.C. Hill eds., Baker Encyclopedia of psychology and counseling (Grand Rapids, MI: Baker), 99; auth, Bufford, R.K., Behavioral psychology. In D.G. Benner and P.C. Hill, eds., Baker encyclopedia of psychology and counseling, 2nd ed. (Grand Rapids, MI: Baker), 99; auth, Bufford, R.K., Exorcism. In D.G. Benner and P.C. Hill, eds., Baker encyclopedia of psychology and counseling, 2nd ed. (Grand Rapids, MI: Baker), 99; auth, Bufford, R.K., Flooding. In D.g. Benner and P.C. Hill, eds., Baker encyclopedia of psychology and counseling, 2nd ed. (Grand Rapids, MI: Baker), 99; auth, Bufford, R.K., Models of mental illness. In D.G.Benner and P.C. Hill, eds. (Grands, Rapids, MI: Baker), 99; auth, Combs, C.W., Campbell, C.D., Bufford, R.K., & Halter, L.L. Effects of cognitive-behavioral marriage enrichment: A controlled study. Marriage and Family: A Christian Journal, 3 (00): 99-111; auth, Houston, B.M., Bufford, R.K., & Johnson, W.B. Distinctive components and perceived sources of gain in Christian counseling. Journal of Psychology and Christianity, 18 (00): 238-253. **CONTACT ADDRESS** Grad School of Clinical Psychology, George Fox Univ, 414 N. Meridian, Newberg, OR 97132-2697. **EMAIL** rbufford@georgefox.edu

BULGER, PEGGY A.
PERSONAL Born 12/13/1949, Albany, NY, m, 1979, 2 children **DISCIPLINE** FOLKLORE, FOLKLIFE **EDUCATION** Western KY, MA 75; Univ Penn, PhD 92. **CAREER** Bureau of Florida Folklife progs, admin, 75-89; Southern Arts Feder, Dir prog, sr prog off, 89-. **HONORS AND AWARDS** Wayland D Hand Prize; fel, Brit Coun For Exch; Emply of Prom Awd FL. **MEMBERSHIPS** Am Folklore Soc; North Am Folk Music Dance Allian. **RESEARCH** Southern culture and folk arts; celtic folklore. **SELECTED PUBLICATIONS** South Florida Folklife, with Tina Bucuvalas and Stetson Kennedy, Jackson, Univ Miss Press, 94; Musical roots of the South, ed, Atlanta GA, Southern Arts Fed, 92, several pub. **CONTACT ADDRESS** 607 Philadelphia Ave., Takoma Park, MD 20912-4111. **EMAIL** pbulger@southarts.org

BULL, BARRY L.
PERSONAL Born 08/29/1947, Billings, Mont, m, 1971, 2 children **DISCIPLINE** PHILOSOPHY, EDUCATION **EDUCATION** Yale Univ, BA, 69; Univ Va, MA, 70; Univ Idaho, MAT, 72; Cornell Univ, PhD, 79. **CAREER** Asst Prof, Wellesley Col, 79-84; Asst Prof to Assoc Prof, Univ Haw, 86-89; Assoc Prof, Univ Minn, 89-90; Assoc Prof to Full Prof, Ind Univ, 90-. **HONORS AND AWARDS** Francis I. Dupont Fel, Univ Va, 69-70; Fel, Univ Idaho, 71-72; Fel, Am Coun of Learned Soc, 82-83; Mellon Fel, 83-84; Phi Kappa Phi; Phi Delta Kappa; Dean's Medallion, Ind Univ, 00. **MEMBERSHIPS** Philos of Educ Soc; Intl Network of Philos of Educ; Am Educ Res Asn. **RESEARCH** The ethics of education policy generally, currently focusing on the adoption and implementation of national curriculum and achievement standards. **SELECTED PUBLICATIONS** Auth, "The limits of teacher professionalization," in The moral dimensions of teaching, Jossey-Bass, 90; co-auth, "The pedagogic nature of subject matter knowledge," Am Educ Res J, 91; co-auth, The Ethics of multicultural and bilingual education, Teachers Col Press, 92; coauth, Education in Indiana: An overview, Ind Educ Policy Center, 94; co-auth, Professional development and teacher time: Principles, guidelines, and policy options for Indiana, Ind Educ Policy Center, 94; co-auth, Learning together: Professional development for better schools, Ind Educ Policy Center,, 96; co-

auth, Planning together: Professional development for teachers of all students, Ind Educ Policy Center,, 97; auth, "School reform in Indiana since 1980," In Hoosier schools: Past and Present, Ind Univ Press, 98; auth, "Political philosophy and the balance between central and local control of schools," in Balancing local control and state responsibility for K-12 Education, 00. **CONTACT ADDRESS** Dept Educ, Indiana Univ, Bloomington, Education 4240, Bloomington, IN 47405. **EMAIL** bbull@indiana.edu

BULLOUGH, ROBERT V., JR.
PERSONAL Born 02/12/1949, Salt Lake City, UT, m, 1976, 4 children **DISCIPLINE** EDUCATIONAL STUDIES; HISTORY **EDUCATION** Univ of Utah, BS, 71, MEd, 73; Ohio State Univ, PhD, 76. **CAREER** Prof, Educ Stud, Univ of Utah, 76-99; prof emeritus, Educational Studies, Univ Utah, 99-; prof, teacher educ, Brigham Young Univ. **HONORS AND AWARDS** Phi Beta Kappa; Phi Kappa Phi, 71; AACTE Outstanding Writing Awd, 97. **MEMBERSHIPS** Am Educ Res Asn; Prof of Curriculum; Phi Delta Kappa. **RESEARCH** Teacher development; curriculum studies; lives of children. **SELECTED PUBLICATIONS** Auth, Trends in teacher education reform in America: A personal perspective, Teacher Educators' Annual Handbook, Queensland Univ of Tech, 87-97, 93; co-auth, Becoming a Student of Teaching: Methodologies for Exploring Self and School Context, Garland Publishing Inc, 95; auth, Professorial dreams and mentoring: A personal view, Teachers and mentors: Profiles of distinguished 20th century professors of education, Garland Publishing Inc, 257-267, 96; auth, Becoming a Teacher: Self and the social location of teacher education, Int Handbook of Tchrs and Tchng, Kluwer Acad Publishers, 87-148; auth, Practicing theory and theorizing practice in teacher education, Purposes, passion, & pedagogy in teacher education, The Falmer Press, 13-21, 97; co-auth, First year teacher--after eight years: An inquiry into teacher development, Tchrs Col Press, 97; auth, Musing on life writing: Biography and case studies in teacher education, Writing educational biography: Adventures in qualitative research, Garland Publishing, 19-32, 98; auth, Children's Lives - On the Other Side of Teacher's Desk, Teachers Col Pr, 00. **CONTACT ADDRESS** 413 4th Ave, Salt Lake City, UT 84103. **EMAIL** bob_bullough@byu.edu

BURCH, HOBART
PERSONAL Born 07/29/1932, Appleton, WI, m, 1991, 3 children **DISCIPLINE** SOCIOLOGY **EDUCATION** Princeton Univ AB, 53; Un Theol Sem, M Div, 56; Columbia Univ, MS, 58; Brandeis Univ, PhD, 65. **CAREER** Yth wkr, pub asst wkr, chap, comm org, consul, 50-58; dir, Coun Churches, 58-62; consul, EGFA, 62-64; fed govt, 64-69; sec, minist, 69-74; exec dir, NSWA, 74-76; dir, Univ Nebraska, 76-81; prof, 76-. **MEMBERSHIPS** NASW. **RESEARCH** Social policy and planning; social ethics. **SELECTED PUBLICATIONS** Auth, The Why's of Social Policy, Praeger (NY), 91; auth, Basic Social Policy and Planning, Haworth (NY), 96; auth, Social Welfare Policy Analysis and Choices, Haworth (NY), 99, coauth, Bubba Justice in Key West, Dageford Press (Lincoln), 99. **CONTACT ADDRESS** School Social Work, Univ of Nebraska, Omaha, 6001 Dodge St, Omaha, NE 68182-0293.

BURGER, MARY WILLIAMS
PERSONAL Born North Little Rock, AR **DISCIPLINE** EDUCATION **EDUCATION** University of Arkansas, BA (magna cum laude), 1959; Colorado State University, MA, English lit, 1961; Washington University, PhD, modern literature, 1973; Harvard University, certified in education management, 1978. **CAREER** Lincoln University, instructor, English, 61-66; University of Missouri, instructor, asst professor, English, 66-69, 73-75; University of Maryland, asst provost/asst vice pres, 75-84; Tennessee State University, vice pres for academic affairs, professor, English, starting 1984; California State Univ Sacramento, Vice Pres for Academic Affairs, currently. **MEMBERSHIPS** Consultant, Natl Education Assn, 1973; reviewer, Middle States Assn of Colleges & Schools, 1974-75; consultant, Urban Behavioral Research Assn, 1974-79; consultant, Midwest Center for EEO, 1974-75; Alpha Kappa Mu; Alpha Kappa Alpha; Phi Kappa Phi; Sister Cities of Baltimore-Garnga Liberia; College Language Assn; State Planning Committee ACE/NIP. **SELECTED PUBLICATIONS** Black Viewpoint, New American Library, 1971; Ford Foundation Fellow, Washington University, 1972-73; Images of Black Women Sturdy, Black Bridges, Doubleday, 1979; Improving Opportunity for Black Students, NAFEO Proceedings, 1983; Sister Cities, Intl TAP Grant, Gbarnga Liberia, 1983. **CONTACT ADDRESS** California State Univ, Sacramento, 6000 J St, Sacramento, CA 95819-2605.

BURGHARDT, GORDON M.
PERSONAL Born 10/11/1941, Milwaukie, WS, m, 1983, 3 children **DISCIPLINE** PSYCHOLOGY **EDUCATION** Univ Chicago, SB, 63; PhD, 66. **CAREER** Vis Sci, J F Kennedy Ctr for Res, 72; Res Assoc, Smithsonian Tropical Res Inst, 78-94; Instr, Univ Chicago, 66-67; From Asst Prof to Prof, Univ Tenn, 68-. **HONORS AND AWARDS** Col Arts and Sci Fac Public Serv Awd, 99; UTK Travel Awd, 99; UTK Sci Alliance Res Funding Awd, 97-00. **SELECTED PUBLICATIONS** Coauth, The Well-Being of Animals in Zoo and Aquarium Sponsored Research, Scientists Ctr for Animal Welfare (Greenbelt, MD), 96; coauth, "The Genetics of Dietary Experience in a Restricted Natural Population," Psychol Sci 11 (00): 69-72; coauth, "Chemical Stimuli from Potential Prey and Predators: Behavioral Responses by Hatchling Racers (Coluber Constrictor) from Two Geographically Distinct Populations," Amphibia-Reptilia (forthcoming); coauth, "Does Prey Matter: Geographic Variation in Antipredator Responses of Hatchlings o f a Japanese Natricine Snake, Rhabdophis Tigrinus," J of Comparative Psychol (forthcoming); auth, "Play: Attributes and Neural Substrates." in Handbk of Behavioral Neurobiology, vol 15 (forthcoming); auth, The Genesis of Animal Play, MIT Pr (Cambridge, MA), forthcoming; coauth, The Cognitive Animal: Empirical and Theoretical Perspectives on Animal Cognition, MIT Pr (Cambridge, MA), forthcoming. **CONTACT ADDRESS** Dept Psychol, Univ of Tennessee, Knoxville, 312 Austin Peay Bldg, Knoxville, TN 37996-0001. **EMAIL** gburghar@utk.edu

BURKE, KEVIN
DISCIPLINE SPORT PSYCHOLOGY **EDUCATION** Belmont Abbey Col, BA, 82; E Carolina Univ, MA, 84; Fla State Univ, PhD, 88. **CAREER** Instructor, Tallahassee Col, 86-88; Instructor, Appalachian State Univ, 88-89; Asst Prof, Ill State ;Univ, 89-91; Asst Prof, N Ill Univ, 91-94; Instructor, Southeastern Col, 94-96; Assoc Prof, Ga Southern Univ, 96-. **HONORS AND AWARDS** Teaching Awd, GA Southern Univ, 98-99; Scholarship Awd, GA Southern Univ, 97-98; Outstanding Teaching Fel, E Carolina Univ, 82-83. **MEMBERSHIPS** Asn for the Adv of Applied Sport Psychol; GA Asn for Health, Phys Educ, Recreation and Dance. **SELECTED PUBLICATIONS** Auth, "Evaluation of the tennis serve in physical education classes," Strategies, (90): 8-18; auth, "Dealing with Sports Officials," Sport Psychology Training Bulletin, (91): 1-6; auth, "Computerized consulting in sport psychology: some experiences with youth baseball, softball, and teeball," Perceptual and Motor Skills, (94): 538; co-auth, "Structural charting and perceptions of momentum in intercollegiate volleyball," Journal of Sport Behavior, ((5): 167-182; co-auth, "Psychological factors associated with alcohol use by high school athletes," Journal of Sport Behavior, (95): 195-208; co-auth, "Encouragement during maximal exercise testing of Type A and Type B scorers," Perceptual & Motor Skills, (97): 507-512; co-auth, "Momentum in sport: A real or illusionary phenomenon for spectators," International Journal of Sport Psychology, (97): 79-96; co-auth, "Perceptions of momentum in college and high school basketball: An exploratory, case study investigation," Journal of Sport Behavior, (99): 303-309; co-auth, "An exploratory investigation of the perceptions of anxiety among basketball officials before, during, and after the contest," Journal of Sport Behavior, in press. **CONTACT ADDRESS** Dept Kinesiol, Georgia So Univ, Statesboro, GA 30460-8076. **EMAIL** kevburke@gsaix2.cc.GaSoU.edu

BURLING, ROBBINS
PERSONAL Born 04/18/1926, Minneapolis, MN, d, 1951, 3 children **DISCIPLINE** ANTHROPOLOGY & LINGUISTICS **EDUCATION** Yale Univ, BA, 50; Harvard Univ, PhD, 58. **CAREER** From instr to asst prof anthrop, Univ Pa, 57-63; assoc prof, 63-67, Prof Anthrop & Ling, Univ Mich, Ann Arbor, 67-; Fulbright Found lectr, Rangoon, Burma, 59-60; fel, Ctr Advan Studies Behav Sci, 63-64; Guggenheim Found fel, 71-72; vis prof, Univ Gothenburg, Sweden, 79-80; Fulbright Found Lectr, Shillong, India, 96-97. **MEMBERSHIPS** Am Anthrop Asn; Ling Soc Am; Asn Asian Studies. **RESEARCH** Anthropology; linguistics. **SELECTED PUBLICATIONS** Auth, Rengsanggri, Family and Kinship in a Garo Village, Univ Pa, 63; Hill Farms and Padi Fields, Prentice-Hall, 65; Man's Many Voices, 70 & English in Black and White, 73, Holt; The Passage of Power, Acad Press, 74; Sounding Right, Newbury House, 82; Learning a Field Language, Univ Mich Press, 84; Patterns of Language, Acad Press, 92; The Strong Women of Modhupur, Dhaka: Univ Press Ltd, 97. **CONTACT ADDRESS** Dept of Anthrop, Univ of Michigan, Ann Arbor, 500 S State St, Ann Arbor, MI 48109-1382. **EMAIL** rburling@umich.edu

BURLINGAME, GARY M.
DISCIPLINE PSYCHOLOGY **EDUCATION** Andrews Univ, BS, 78; Univ Ut, MS, 81; PhD, 83. **CAREER** Core Fac, Assoc Dir, Asst Prof to prof, Brigham Young Univ, 83-. **HONORS AND AWARDS** Fel, Am Psychol Asn; Who's Who in Am Col and Univ; Who's Who in Human Service Professionals. **MEMBERSHIPS** Am Psychol Asn, Intl Soc for Psychotherapy Res, Soc for the Study of Chaos Theory in Psychol and Life Sci, Am Group Psychotherapy Asn, Utah Psychol Asn. **RESEARCH** Group Psychotherapy, measurement and methodology. **SELECTED PUBLICATIONS** Auth, "Group Psychotherapy," in Encyclopedia of Psychology, Oxford Univ Press, in press; auth, "The Hill Interaction Matrix: Therapy through dialogue," in Process in Therapeutic Groups: A handbook of system analysis, in press; auth, "Does Group Psychotherapy Work?," in A Guide for starting psychotherapy groups, Academic Press, 99; auth, "Youth Outcome Questionnaire," in The use of psychological testing for treatment planning and outcome assessment, Lawrence Erlbaum Assoc, 99; auth, "How to evaluate a mental health outcome measure," in The 1997 Behavioral Outcomes and Guidelines Sourcebook, New York, 97; auth, "The Thera-peutic application of groups: From Pratt's 'thought control classes' to modern group psychotherapy," Journal of Group Dynamics, in press; auth, "Book review: The measurement and management of clinical outcomes in mental health," Psychotherapy Practice and Research, (99): 83-84; auth, "Reading disability subtypes: The test of memory and learning," Archives of Clinical Neuropsychology, 99; auth, "The measurement and management of clinical outcomes in mental health," Psychotherapy Practice and Research, 98; auth, "Comparative efficacy of individual and group psychotherapy: A meta-analytic perspective," Group Dynamics: Theory, Research, & Practice, (98): 101-117. **CONTACT ADDRESS** Dept Psychol, Brigham Young Univ, PO Box 25543, Provo, UT 84602.

BURNS, MARY T.
PERSONAL Born 07/11/1929, Louisville, KY, s **DISCIPLINE** EDUCATION **EDUCATION** St Louis Univ, MA, 68; Univ Cincinnati, EdS, 71; EdD, 74. **CAREER** Teach, St Patrick, 50-60; teach, St Mary's, 61-63; teach, St Vincent's, 63-67; principal, LaSalette Acad, 69-72; prof, Spalding Univ, 74-82; dept ch, 82-84; dean, 84-. **HONORS AND AWARDS** Who's Who in Am Edu, Edu Admin, Contemp Achiev, Am Women, Prof Bus Women; Dist Ser Awd; Hall of Fame, Outstand Achiev Edu Leadershp; AACTE Spec Consultant and Pres, 91-. **MEMBERSHIPS** Pi Mu Epsilon; Delta Epsilon Sigma; Pi Lambda Theta; ATEDC; AACTE; KACTE; Phi Delta Kappa; WSA; KCPEA; AASA; NASSP; KASSP; NEA. **SELECTED PUBLICATIONS** Auth, "In the Winners Circle," KATE NL (88); auth, "Spalding's Great Idea for Principals," Spalding Univ News (89); auth, "A Challenge to Vision and Leadership," Comm Kacte NL (92); auth, "Experiences and Cultural Differences in India," 99; auth, **CONTACT ADDRESS** School of Education, Spalding Univ, 851 S 4th St, Louisville, KY 40203.

BURR, CAROL E.
PERSONAL Born 01/16/1943, Hasbrook Heights, NJ, m, 1987, 2 children **DISCIPLINE** WOMENS STUDIES **EDUCATION** Middlebury Col, BA, 65; Columbia Univ, MA, 68; Case Western Reserve Univ, PhD, 75. **CAREER** Instructor, Cleveland State Univ, 65-67; Teaching Fel, Case Western Reserve Univ, 68-70; Asst to Assoc Prof, Calif State Univ, 70-. **HONORS AND AWARDS** Oustanding Service Awd, Carnegie Foundation, 89. **MEMBERSHIPS** MLA. **RESEARCH** Women Writers. **CONTACT ADDRESS** Dept Multicultural & Gender Studies, California State Univ, Chico, 400 W 1st St., Chico, CA 95929-0001.

BURRIGHT, RICHARD B.
PERSONAL Born 08/10/1934, Freeport, IL, m, 1957, 2 children **DISCIPLINE** PSYCHOLOGY **EDUCATION** Univ Ill, BA, 59; MS, 62; PhD, 66. **CAREER** Act asst prof, Harpur Col, SUNY, 63-66; asst prof, 66-69; assoc prof, 69-85; prof, 85-. **HONORS AND AWARDS** NIMH; NSF; NIH, 85-88, 87-90; EPA; DARPA. **MEMBERSHIPS** APA; AAAS; BGA; EPA; NYAS; Sigma Xi. **RESEARCH** Neural, environmental, genetic, nutritive, and life-span correlates of behavior related to the integration and utilization of sensory information in both brain-damaged and 'normal' organisms. **SELECTED PUBLICATIONS** Coauth, "Psychotherapy with the brain injured adult," Psycho Priv Prac 16 (97); 33-44; coauth," The malingering of Multiple Sclerosis and mild traumatic brain injury," Brain Injury (97): 343-352; coauth, "The relationship of daily stress and health-related behaviors to adolescents cholesterol levels," Adolescence 33 (98): 447-460; coauth, "Chapman-Cook speed reading test: Performance of college student," Perceptual Motor Skills 86 (98): 687-690; coauth, "Performance of psychiatric patients on the Gordon Diagnostic System," ADHD/Hyperactivity NL (98): 2-3; coauth, "Prevalence of traumatic brain injury in psychiatric and nonpsychiatric subjects," Brain Injury 12 (98): 207-214; coauth, "Sub acute Pb exposure during development and unbaited tunnel maze performance in mace," Pharm Biochem Behav 59 (98): 183-189; coauth, "K-FAST and WRAT-3: Are they really different?" Clin Neuropsycho (99): x-y; coauth, "Psychiatric treatment outcome following traumatic brain injury," Brain Injury, in press; coauth, "Behavioral differences between psychiatric patients with confirmed versus non-confirmed traumatic brain injuries," forthcoming. **CONTACT ADDRESS** Dept Psychology, SUNY, Binghamton, PO Box 600, Binghamton, NY 13902. **EMAIL** burright@binghamton.edu

BURRIS-KITCHEN, DEBORAH J.
PERSONAL Born 08/07/1960, Lafayette, IN, m, 1988, 1 child **DISCIPLINE** BEHAVIORAL SCIENCE **EDUCATION** Purdue Univ, BA, 88; Ball State Univ, MA, 90; Western Mich Univ, PhD, 95. **CAREER** Prof, Univ La Verne, 95-. **HONORS AND AWARDS** Alpha Kappa Delta. Grad Student of the Year, Western Mich Univ, 95. **MEMBERSHIPS** ASC, ASA, PSA. **RESEARCH** Political economy, race, drugs, crime. **SELECTED PUBLICATIONS** Auth, Female Gang Participation: The Role of African-American Women in the Informal Economy, Mellen Pr, 97; auth, "Assessing Campus Climate of Cultural Diversity," Col Student J (forthcoming). **CONTACT ADDRESS** Dept Behavior Sci, Univ of La Verne, 1950 3rd St, La Verne, CA 91750. **EMAIL** kitchend@ulv.edu

BURRISON, JOHN A.
PERSONAL Born 10/11/1942, Philadelphia, PA, s **DISCIPLINE** FOLKLORE **EDUCATION** Penn St Univ, BA, 64; Univ Penn, MA, 66, PhD, 73. **CAREER** Prof, dir, folklore cur, Georgia St Univ. **HONORS AND AWARDS** Governor's Award in the Humanities, 87. **MEMBERSHIPS** Am Folklore Soc **RESEARCH** Folklore, US Southern British Isles, specialization in folk pottery **SELECTED PUBLICATIONS** Auth, Brothers in Clay: The Story of Georgia Folk Pottery, Univ of Ga Press, 83; auth, Storytellers: Folktales and Legends From the South, Univ of Ga Press, 89; auth, Shaping Traditions: Folk Arts in a Changing South, Univ of Ga Press, 00. **CONTACT ADDRESS** Dept of English, Georgia State Univ, Univ Plaza, Atlanta, GA 30308-3083.

BURSON, HERBERT I.
PERSONAL Born 07/22/1957, Montgomery, AL **DISCIPLINE** SOCIAL WORK **EDUCATION** Huntingdon Col, BA, 79; Univ Ala, MSW, 87; PhD, 01. **CAREER** Soc Work Sup, Montgomery County Dept of Human Resources, 87-93; Public Health Soc Worker, Ala Dept of Public Health, 95-96; Instr, Auburn Univ, 96-. **HONORS AND AWARDS** Fel, Univ Ala, 98-99; Phi Kappa Phi; Alpha Beta. **MEMBERSHIPS** CSWE. **RESEARCH** Child Welfare: History, Policy and Practice; Social Welfare History and Policy; Feminist theory. **CONTACT ADDRESS** Dept Sociol, Anthropol and Soc Work, Auburn Univ, 9030 Haley Center, Auburn, AL 36849. **EMAIL** bursohi@mail.auburn.edu

BURSTON, DANIEL
PERSONAL Born 12/12/1954, Naharia, Israel, m, 1990, 2 children **DISCIPLINE** PSYCHOLOGY **EDUCATION** York Univ, PhD, 85; PhD, 89. **CAREER** Assoc prof, Duquesne Univ, 98-. **RESEARCH** History of the mental health professions, philosophy and psychology. **SELECTED PUBLICATIONS** Auth, The Legacy of Erich Fromm, Harvard Univ Pr, (Cambridge), 91; auth, The Wing of Madness: The Life and Work of R.D. Laing, Harvard Univ Pr, (Cambridge), 96; AUTH, "Laing and Heidegger On Alienation", J of Humanistic Psychol 38.4 (98): 80-93; auth, "Erich Fromm: Humanism and Psychoanalysis" and "R.D. Laing: Existentialism and Psychoanalysis", , Humanistic and Transpersonal Psychology, ed D. Moss, Greenwood Pr, (Westport, CT), 99; auth, "Archetype and Interpretation", Psychoanalytic Rev 86.1 (99): 35-62; auth, "Erich Fromm", The Freud Encyclopedia, ed, Edwin Erwin, Garland, (forthcoming); auth, "Otto Rank", Encyclopedia of Psychology, ed Raymond Fancher, Oxford Univ Pr, (forthcoming); auth, The Crucible of Experience: R.D. Laing and The Crisis of Psychotherapy, Harvard Univ Pr, (Cambridge), 00. **CONTACT ADDRESS** Dept Psychol, Duquesne Univ, 600 Forbes St, Pittsburgh, PA 15282-0001. **EMAIL** burston@duq.edu

BURTON, CHARLES E.
PERSONAL Born 07/22/1933, Birmingham, AL, m, 1955, 3 children **DISCIPLINE** SOCIOLOGY **EDUCATION** Univ Tenn, PhD, 76. **CAREER** ch, Univ of Al Dept of Sociol, 76-82; Assoc Prof, McMurry Univ, 83-87; part-time Prof, Univ of Tex, 90-. **MEMBERSHIPS** Soc for the Study of Soc Prob. **RESEARCH** Poverty, homelessness. **SELECTED PUBLICATIONS** Auth, The Poverty debate, Greenwood-Praeger Publ, 92. **CONTACT ADDRESS** Dept Soc Sci, Univ of Texas, Dallas, PO Box 830688, Richardson, TX 75083. **EMAIL** emory.burton@gte.net

BURTON, J. D.
PERSONAL Born 05/28/1959, Mankato, MN **DISCIPLINE** HISTORY OF EDUCATION **EDUCATION** St Olaf Coll, BA, 81; Univ Chicago, MA, 85; Coll of William & Mary, MA, 89; PhD, 96. **CAREER** Res Assoc, De Paul Univ, 85-88; Sr Res Asoc, Asoc Dir Inst Plan Res, De Paul Univ91-92; Dir Inst Plan Res, De Paul Univ, 92-94; Dir, Mgt Support De Paul Univ, 94-96; dir acad support De Paul Univ, 96-. **MEMBERSHIPS** Orgn of Am Historians; Hist of Educ Soc; Soc Sci Hist Asn; Asn for the Stduy of Hist Educ. **RESEARCH** History of Education; History of Higher Education; Colonial New England. **SELECTED PUBLICATIONS** Auth, Crimson Missionaries: Harvard College and the Robert Boyle trust, The New England Quart, 94; Harvard Tutors: The Beginning of an Academic Profession, Hist of Higher Educ Annual, 96; Philanthropy and the Origins of Educational Cooperation: Harvard College, the Hopkins Trust and the Cambridge Grammar School, The Hist of Educ Quart, 97; coauth, Data Linking: A Model of Student Outcomes Assessment, A Collection of Papers on Self-Study and Institutional Improvement, 94; Faculty Vitality in the Comprehensive University: Changing Context and Concerns, Res and Higher Educ, 96; From Retention to Satisfaction: New Outcomes for Assessing the Freshmen Experience, Res in Higher Educ, 96. **CONTACT ADDRESS** DePaul Univ, 2320 N Kenmore Ave, Chicago, IL 60614. **EMAIL** jburton@wppost.depaul.edu

BURTON, MICHAEL L.
PERSONAL Born 06/06/1942, Long Beach, CA, m, 1979, 4 children **DISCIPLINE** ANTHROPOLOGY **EDUCATION** MIT, BS, 64; Stanford, PhD, 68. **CAREER** Prof, Univ Calif, Irvine, 69-. **HONORS AND AWARDS** Stirling Awd, AAA, 76. **MEMBERSHIPS** AAA; SAA; ASAO; SEA; SCCR. **RESEARCH** Economic anthropology; ecological anthropology; gender; households; food systems. **SELECTED PUBLICATIONS** Coauth, "Balanced Designs for Triads Tests," Social Science Research 5 (76): 247-267; coauth; "Sex Differences in Maasai Cognition of Personality and Social Identity," Am Anthr 81 (79): 841-873; coauth, "Sexual Division of Labor in Agriculture," Am Anthro 86 (84): 568-583; coauth, "Navajo Attitudes Toward Development and Change," Am Anthro 86 (84): 885-904; coauth, "Regions Based on Social Structure," Current Anthropology 37 (96): 87-123; coauth, "The Meanings of Work: Pacific Policy Implications of Globalization," in press, The Contem Pacific. **CONTACT ADDRESS** Dept Anthropology, Univ of California, Irvine, Irvine, CA 92697-0001. **EMAIL** mlburton@uci.edu

BUSCH, LAWRENCE M.
PERSONAL Born 03/27/1945, New York, NY, m, 1966, 2 children **DISCIPLINE** SOCIOLOGY **EDUCATION** Hofstra Univ, BA, 65; Cornell Univ, MS, 72; PhD, 74. **CAREER** Asst Prof to Full Prof, Univ of Kentucky, 74-90; Prof - Univ Distinguished Prof, Mich State Univ, 90-. **HONORS AND AWARDS** Award for Outstanding Res, Rural Sociol Soc. **MEMBERSHIPS** Rural Sociol Soc, Soc for Soc Studies of Sci, Agriculture, Food and Human Values Soc. **RESEARCH** Food and agricultural standards, agricultural policy. **SELECTED PUBLICATIONS** Coauth, Making Nature, Shaping Culture: Plant Biodiversity in Global Context, Univ of Nebr Press (Lincoln), 95; coauth, "The Blackleg Epidemic in Canadian Rapeseed as a "Normal Agricultural Accident'," Ecol Appln 7-4 (97): 1350-1356; coauth, "Beyond Political Economy: Actor Networks and the Globalization of Agriculture," Rev of Int Polit Econ 4-4 (97): 688-708; coauth, "Technology Policy in a Rapidly Changing World," in Visions of American Agriculture, ed. W. Lockeretz (Ames: Iowa State Univ Press, 97), 205-219; coauth, "Can Cooperatives Survive the Privatization of Biotechnology in U.S. Agriculture?," in Privatization of Information and Agricultural Industrialization, ed. Steven A. Wolf (Boca Raton, FL: CRC Press, 98); auth, "Networks and Agricultural Development: The Case of Soybean Production and Consumption in Brazil," Rural Sociol 63-3 (98): 349-371; auth, "Beyond Politics: Rethinking the Future of Democracy," Rural Sociol 64-1 (99): 2-17; auth, The Eclipse of Morality: Science, State and Market, Aldine DeGruyter (Hawthrone, NY), 99; coauth, "Who Cares if the Rat Dies? Rodents, Risks and Humans in the Science of Food Safety," in Illness and the Environment: A Reader in Contested Medicine, ed. S. Kroll- Smith, P. Brown, and V. Gunter (NY: NY Univ Press, forthcoming); auth, "The Moral Economy of Grades and Standards," J of Rural Studies (forthcoming). **CONTACT ADDRESS** Dept Sociol, Michigan State Univ, 316 Berkey Hall, East Lansing, MI 48824. **EMAIL** lawrence.busch@ssc.msu.edu

BUSH, HARRY H.
PERSONAL Born 01/25/1926, Berlin, Germany, m, 1958 **DISCIPLINE** SOCIOLOGY **EDUCATION** Univ Chicago, BA, 51; Ind Univ, MA, 58; Univ Pa, PhD, 69. **CAREER** Univ Miss Saint Louis, 66-. **MEMBERSHIPS** Midwest Sociol Soc. **RESEARCH** Sociological Theory, Sociology of Ideology. **SELECTED PUBLICATIONS** Auth, Sociology, Race and Ethnicity: A Critique of American Ideological Intrusions Upon Sociological Theory, Gordon & Breach, (NY), 79; auth, "Social Constructions of Relevance: Ideological Bents of Client-Friendly Sociology", Quarterly J of Ideology, 9.2, (85): 1-16; auth, "On Vertical Drift and the Quest for theoretical Integration in Sociology", Soc Epistemology 3.3 (89): 229-246; auth, "Social Movements and Social Problems: Toward a Conceptual Rapprochement", Research in Social Movements, Conflicts and Change, Vol 17, eds, L. Kriesberg, M. Dobkowski and I. Walliman, JAI Pr, (Greenwich, CT), (94): 247-284; auth, Social Problems and Social Movements: An Exploration into the Sociological Construction of Alternative Realities, Humanities Pr, (Atlantic Highlands, NJ), 95; auth, "Book Revieew: Social Movements and Social Classes", Soc Forces 75.1 (96): 356-357; auth, "A Scatter of Sociologies: Vertical Drift and the Quest for Theoretical Integration in Sociology", The Living Legacy of Marx, Durkheim and Weber: Applications and Analyses of Classical Sociological Theory by Modern Social Scientists, ed Richard Altschuler, Gordian Knot Books, (NY, 98): 537-565; auth, "Dominant Group" and "Racial vs Ethnic", Racial and Ethnic Relations in America, ed Carl L. Blankston III, Salem Pr, (Pasadena, 00): 326-327, 843-844. **CONTACT ADDRESS** Dept Sociol, Univ of Missouri, St. Louis, 8001 Natural Bridge, Saint Louis, MO 63121.

BUTLER, J. COREY
PERSONAL Born 07/26/1966, Chicago, IL, m, 1989 **DISCIPLINE** PSYCHOLOGY **EDUCATION** Knox Col, BA, 89; Univ Maine, PhD, 94. **CAREER** Asst prof, Mary Crest Int Univ, 95-97; asst prof, Southwest State Univ, 97-2000. **HONORS AND AWARDS** Edith Powers Van Dyke Awd. **MEMBERSHIPS** Am Psychol Asn, Am Psychol Soc. **RESEARCH** Personality and social psycholohy. **SELECTED PUBLICATIONS** Coauth with R. M. Ryckman, B. Thornton, and R. L. Bouchard, "Assessment of the full content of physique stereotypes via a free-response format," J of Soc Psych, 133, 147-162 (93); coauth with R. M. Ryckman, "Perceived and ideal physiques in male and female university students," J of Soc Psychol, 133, 751-752 (93); coauth with R. M. Ryckman and J. C. Butler, "Personality correlates of the hypercompetitive attitude scale: Validity tests of Horney's theory of neurosis," J of Personality Assessment, 62, 84-94 (94); coauth with R. M. Ryckman, R. L. Bouchard, and G. W. Crompton, "Stereotypes of extremely muscular individuals' romantic relationships with partners of varying physiques," J of Psychol, 128, 353-356 (94); coauth with R. M. Ryckman, B. Thornton, and M. A. Lindner, "Assesment of physique subtype stereotypes," Genetic, Social, and General Monographs, 123, 101-128 (97); auth, "Factor analysis of physique-stereotyped traits," J of Soc Psychol, 137, 392-394 (97); auth, "Personality and emotional correlates of right-wing authoritarianism," Personality and Individual Differences,28, 1-14 (2000). **CONTACT ADDRESS** Dept Soc Sci, Southwest State Univ, 1501 State St, Marshall, MN 56258. **EMAIL** butler@ssu.southwest.msus.edu

BUTLER, REBECCA BATTS
PERSONAL Born Norfolk, VA **DISCIPLINE** EDUCATION **EDUCATION** Temple U, DEd 1965; Temple U, MEd 1958; Glassboro State Coll, BS 1942. **CAREER** Camden Public Schools, elementary teacher, 37-51, supvr of guidance, 66-68, dir adult comm prog, 69-74; Camden Secondary School, teacher, 51-59; NJ State Dept of Educ, 68-69; Glassboro State Coll, adj prof; Organized Special Service School for Unwed Mothers Camden City, Public Schools, director. **SELECTED PUBLICATIONS** Auth, "Portraits of Black Role Models In The History of Southern New Jersey"; "My Thoughts I Write," 1990; auth, "Bronze Stars of the Delaware Valley," 00. **CONTACT ADDRESS** 15 Eddy Lane, Cherry Hill, NJ 08002.

BUZZELL, TIMOTHY
DISCIPLINE SOCIOLOGY **EDUCATION** Drake Univ, BA, 83; MPA, 85; Iowa State Univ, PhD, 91. **CAREER** Iowa Justice Planning Agency, 83-87; Governor's Alliance on Substance Abuse, 87-88; Iowa Center for Comm and civi Educ, 88-96. **MEMBERSHIPS** Am Sociol Assoc; Midwest Sociol Soc. **RESEARCH** Crime and Delinquency, Sociology of Law, Political Sociology. **CONTACT ADDRESS** Dept Hist, Poli Sci, Sociol, Baker Univ, PO Box 65, Baldwin City, KS 66006.

BYARS, JACKIE L.
PERSONAL Born 01/05/1951, Harlingen, TX, m, 1983 **DISCIPLINE** FILM & TELEVISION STUDIES, AMERICAN CULTURE, WOMEN'S STUDIES **EDUCATION** Univ Tx at Austin, BA, 74, MA, 76, PhD, 83; Univ Calif School of Criticism & Theory, summer, 77; Inter-Univ Center for Film & Critical Studies, 80-81. **CAREER** Vis asst prof, 83-84, asst prof, Dept of Commun Arts, Univ Wis-Madison, 85-90; Andrew W. Mellon postdoctoral fel & lectr, Dept of the Hist of Art, Bryn Mawr Col, 84-85; asst prof, Dept of Radio-Television-Film, Tx Christian Univ, 90-91; vis asst prof, Dept of Commun, St. Mary's Col of Calif, 91-92; dir, women's studies prog, 94-97, Co-Dir, Film Studies Prog, 95-, Assoc Prof, Dept of Commun, Wayne State Univ, 92-. **MEMBERSHIPS** Soc for Cinema Studies; Union for Democratic Commun; Nat Commun Asn; Int Asn for Mass Commun Res. **RESEARCH** The representation of difference in mediated texts; the relation between corporate practices and screen representations; landcapes and communication. **SELECTED PUBLICATIONS** Auth, All That Hollywood Allows: Re-reading Gender in 1950s Melodrama, Univ of NC Press & Routledge, 91; The Prime of Ms. Kim Novak: Struggling Over the Feminine in the Star Image, The Other 50s: Interrogating Midcentury Am Icons, Univ of Ill Press, 97; Feminism, Psychoanalysis, and Female-Oriented Melodramas of the 1950s, Multiple Voices in Feminist Film Theory and Criticism, Univ of Minn Press, 93; Gazes/Voices/Power: Expanding Psychoanalysis for Feminist Film and Television Theory, Female Spectators: Looking at Film and Television, Verso, 88; Reading Feminine Discourse: Prime-Time Television in the U.S., Commun, 87; coauth, Telefeminism: The Lifetime Cable Channel, Critical Studies in Mass Commun, forthcoming; Once in a Lifetime: Narrowcasting to Women, Camera Obscura, May-Sept-Jan, 94-95; Reading Difference: The Characters at Frank's Place, Women Making Meaning: The New Feminist Scholar in Commun, Routledge, 92. **CONTACT ADDRESS** Dept of Commun, Wayne State Univ, 585 Manoogian Hall, Detroit, MI 48202. **EMAIL** jbyars@aol.com

BYNUM, DAVID ELIAB
PERSONAL Born 01/26/1936, Louisville, KY, m, 1966, 2 children **DISCIPLINE** EASTERN EUROPEAN ORAL LITERATURE **EDUCATION** Harvard Univ, AB, 58, Am, 62, PhD(Slavic lang & lit), 64. **CAREER** From instr to asst prof Slavic & gen educ & asst cur, Harvard Univ, 64-72, cur, Milman Parry Collection oral lit, 72-78, lectr oral lit, 73-78; prof mod lang & chmn dept, The Citadel, 80-82; Prof Mod Lang & Dean Col Arts & Sci, Cleveland State Univ, 82-, Consult, subcomt E Cent & Southeast Europ studies & mem adv comt libr needs, Am Coun Learned Soc, 67-72; assoc bibliogr, MLA, 67-, exec comt, div anthrop approaches to lit, 78-82, deleg assembly, 80-82; chmn bd tutors in folklore & mythology, Harvard Univ, 68-77, managing ed, Publ Milman Parry Collection, 73-, exec officer, Ctr Study Oral Traditions, 74-78, mem, Standing Comt African Studies, 74-78, tutor folklore & myth, John Winthrop House, 77-80; prin investr, Nat Endowment for Humanities Prog Dev Grant, 72-74; Guggenheim fel, 79-80; chmn, Comt to Rev Daniel Lib, 81-. **MEMBERSHIPS** MLA; Am Folklore

Soc; Am Asn Advan Slavic Studies; Am Asn Southern European Studies; Comp Lit Asn. **RESEARCH** Oral traditions; narrative; East European literatures. **SELECTED PUBLICATIONS** **CONTACT ADDRESS** Dept Religious Studies, Cleveland State Univ, 1983 E 24th St, Cleveland, OH 44115.

BYRNE, WILLIAM
PERSONAL Born 08/07/1932, Poughkeepsie, NY, m, 1968, 2 children **DISCIPLINE** BEHAVIORAL SCIENCES **EDUCATION** Hobart Col, BA, 55; Univ Denver, MA, 66; Univ Denver, PhD, 71. **CAREER** Teacher, Arlington Central Schs, 57-60; Dir Athletics, Oakwood Friends Sch, 60-65; Dir Counr, Marycrest High Sch, 66-67; Prof, Orange Co Community Col, 71-. **HONORS AND AWARDS** SUNY Chancellor's Awd for Excellence in Teaching, 93. **MEMBERSHIPS** Am Sociol Asn, Eastern Sociol Asn. **RESEARCH** Swedish social democracy. **CONTACT ADDRESS** Dept Soc and Behav Sci, Orange County Comm Col, 115 South St, Middletown, NY 10940. **EMAIL** altext@banet.net

C

CADES, STEVEN
PERSONAL Born 01/10/1942, Philadelphia, PA, m, 1968, 2 children **DISCIPLINE** SOCIOLOGY **EDUCATION** Rutgers Univ, BA, 68; MA, 72; PhD, 75. **CAREER** Instructor to Asst Prof, Catholic Univ of Am, 72-77; Assoc Prof to Prof, WA Col, 77-. **MEMBERSHIPS** Am Sociol Asn. **RESEARCH** Urban Family. **CONTACT ADDRESS** Dept Sociol & Anthropol, Washington Col, 300 Washington Ave, Chestertown, MD 21620. **EMAIL** scades@washcoll.edu

CAHN, EDGAR S.
DISCIPLINE EDUCATION LAW AND PROPERTY **EDUCATION** Swarthmore Col, BA, 56; Yale Univ, MA, 57, PhD, 60, JD, 63. **CAREER** Prof; tchs in, Publ Entitlements Clin; codean, Antioch Sch Law, 71-80; a vis scholar, Columbia Univ(s) Ctr, Study of Human Rights; sr res fel, Southeast FL Ctr on Aging, FL Int Univ; distinguished vis scholar, London Sch Econ, 86. **HONORS AND AWARDS** Co-founder, Nat Legal Serv prog; innovative concept of, ser credits or time dollars, as an economic strategy for addressing soc prob(s) is being implemented in 36 states and in Sweden, Japan & Can. **SELECTED PUBLICATIONS** Auth, Hunger; USA; Time Dollars; Our Brothers' Keeper: The Indian in White America; articles on, zoning, int law, public interest law, legal educ. **CONTACT ADDRESS** School of Law, Univ of District of Columbia, 4200 Connecticut Ave Northwest, Washington, DC 20008.

CALCAGNETTI, DANIEL J.
DISCIPLINE PSYCHOLOGY **EDUCATION** Moravian Col, BS, 79; Rensselaer Polytech Inst, MS, 82; Temple Univ, MA, 85; PhD, 86. **CAREER** Res Instr, 91-92; Asst Prof, Northeastern Univ, 92-93; From Asst Prof to Assoc Prof, Fairleigh Dickinson Univ, 93-. **HONORS AND AWARDS** Teacher of the Year, 99; Who's Who Among Am Teachers, 00. **MEMBERSHIPS** Soc for Neurosci. **RESEARCH** The role of neurochemical systems in control of behavior, brain mechanisms regulating analgesia, reward, feeding/drinking, stress, Pavlovian conditioning and stimulus discrimination. **SELECTED PUBLICATIONS** Coauth, "Blockade of Cocaine-Induced Conditioned Place Preference: Relevance to Cocaine Abuse Therapeutics," Life Sci 56:7 (95): 475-483; coauth, "Olfactory Bulbectomy Disrupts the Expression of Cocaine-Induced Conditioned Place Preference," Physiol and Behav 53:3 (96): 597-604; coauth, "Natural Plant Hallucinogen Profiles: A Functional Bibliography," J of Psychol and the Behav Sci 11 (97): 55-68. **CONTACT ADDRESS** Dept Psychol, Fairleigh Dickinson Univ, Florham-Madison, 285 Madison Ave, Madison, NJ 07940. **EMAIL** robinc@enter.net

CALDWELL, M. MILFORD
PERSONAL Born 02/20/1928, SC, m **DISCIPLINE** EDUCATION **EDUCATION** SC State Coll, BS 1949; SC State Coll, MS 1950; OH State U, PhD 1959; OH State U, Post Doctoral Fellow. **CAREER** DE State Coll, prof of educ; Elizabeth City State Univ, prof of educ, 61-62; OH State Univ, asst prof of educ, 59-61. **MEMBERSHIPS** Pres Assn of Coll & Sch of Educ in State Univ & Land-Grant Colls; past pres DE Acad of Sci; mem Am Assn of Higher Edn; gov comm of Vocational Edn; mem Century Club YMCA; NAACP; Phi Alpha Theta; Gamma Sigma Delta; Phi Delta Kappa. **CONTACT ADDRESS** 1200 N Dupont Hwy, Dover, DE 19901. **EMAIL** mcald@erols.com

CALDWELL, SARAH
PERSONAL Born 09/18/1957, Berkeley, CA, m, 1 child **DISCIPLINE** ANTHROPOLOGY **EDUCATION** Univ Calif, Berkeley, BA, 87, MA, 88, PhD, 95. **CAREER** Asst prof, anthrop and relig, Univ Mich, Ann Arbor, 95-98; asst prof, relig, Calif State Univ, Chico, 98- . **HONORS AND AWARDS** NEH Younger Scholars Prog, 86; Univ medal for most distinguished grad sr, Univ Calif, Berkeley, 87; Javits grad fel, 87-91; Fulbright-Hays fel, 92; Ruth C. Boyer Prize, 93; diss writing fel, 93-94; Robert Stoller Found prize, 95; Mich Soc of Fel, postdoc fel, 95-98. **MEMBERSHIPS** Am Acad Relig; Am Anthrop Asn; Am Asn of Univ Women; Am Ethnol Soc; Asn for Asian Stud; Asn for the Psychoanalysis of Culture and Soc; Soc for Psychol Anthrop; Soc for Tantric Stud. **RESEARCH** South Asia; Hinduism; performance; folklore; anthropology of religion; ritual; gender and sexuality; feminist psychoanalysis; cognition; abuse and trauma. **SELECTED PUBLICATIONS** Auth, Geza Roheim's Theory of the Dream Origin of Myth, Psychoanalytic Stud of Soc, 88; auth, Bhagavati: Ball of Fire, in Hawley, ed, Devi: Goddesses of India, Univ Calif, 96; contribur, Claus, ed, South Asian Folklore: An Encyclopedia, Garland, in press; auth, The Bloodthirsty Tongue and the Self-Feeding Breast: Homosexual Fellatio Fantasy in a South Indian Ritual Tradition, in Vaidyanathan, ed, Vishnu on Freud's Desk: A Hunduism and Psychoanalysis Reader, Oxford, 99; auth, Transcendence and Culture: Anthropologists Theorize Religion, Relig Stud Rev, 99; auth, Waves of Beauty, Rivers of Blood: Constructing the Goddess' Body in Kerala, in Pintchmann, ed, In Search of Mahadevi: Constructing the Identity of the Hindu Great Goddess, SUNY, 00; auth, On Terrifying Mother: Sexuality, Violence, and Worship of the Goddess Kali in Kerala, Delhi: Oxford Univ, 99. **CONTACT ADDRESS** Dept of Religious Studies, California State Univ, Chico, Chico, CA 95929-0740. **EMAIL** scaldwell@csuchico.edu

CALGARO, W.
PERSONAL Born 08/29/1950, Chicago, IL, m, 1982, 2 children **DISCIPLINE** SOCIOLOGY **EDUCATION** Univ Md, AA, 72; Governors State Univ, BA, 73, MA, 74, MA, 75. **CAREER** 25 years as educator overseas and at community cols; fac sociol, Ill Prairie State Col, 93-, special projects: workplace literacy and inted. **HONORS AND AWARDS** Univ of Padsa, Italy, 72; Univ of Buenos Aires, Argentina, 95; Univ of Tel Aviv, Israel, 97; Fel Awded UNESCO/Earthwatch, Paraguay, 95, Chimacoco Tribe; fel, Awded UNESCO/Earthwatch, Israel, 97, archeol dig of Yasseh Yam; Minority Student Awd 99 and Fac of the ., Jan 99. **MEMBERSHIPS** Altrusa, COTA, Earthwatch, et al. **RESEARCH** Hunting and gathering indigenous tribes, South America. **SELECTED PUBLICATIONS** Auth, "Never Too Late Too... " J for Teaching for Success, Calif (Jan 99). **CONTACT ADDRESS** Dept Soc Sci, Prairie State Col, 202 S Halsted, Chicago Heights, IL 60411. **EMAIL** wcalgaro@prairie.ccil.us

CALHOUN, LEE A.
PERSONAL Born 08/16/1947, Mobile, AL **DISCIPLINE** SOCIOLOGY **EDUCATION** Univ Toledo, BA 1969; Notre Dame, MA 1971; Univ MI, MA 1972; Univ of MI, PhD Candidate. **CAREER** Herring-Guerden Assoc, S Bend IN, consultant, 71; Dept of Sociology Notre Dame, teacher asst, 71; Dept of Sociology Univ MI, teaching fellow, 72; Afram Assoc, Ann Arbor MI, owner, 72; Howard Univ, lectr, 73-. **MEMBERSHIPS** Mem Am Acad Polit & Social Sci; inst Soc Ethics Life Sci; Am Soc Pub Adminstrn; Nat conf Black Polit Scintists; Univ Toledo Alumni Assn; Notre Dame Alumni Assn Alpha Kappa Delta; Sociology Honor Soc; NASSPAA Fellowship 1971-73; fellowship Univ MI 1972. **CONTACT ADDRESS** Dept Polit Sci, Howard Univ, Washington, DC 20059.

CALLAGHAN, GLENN MCKEE
PERSONAL Born 10/31/1968, Fullerton, CA, s **DISCIPLINE** PSYCHOLOGY **EDUCATION** Univ Calif at Irvine, BA; Univ Nev, PhD. **CAREER** Asst prof, San Jose State Univ, 98-. **MEMBERSHIPS** Am Psychol Asn, Asn for Advancement of Behav Therapy. **RESEARCH** Psychotherapy process and Outcome, Depression. **SELECTED PUBLICATIONS** Coauth, "Language in dreaming and regional EEG alpha power," Sleep 19 (96): 232-235; coauth, "A radical behavioral understanding of the therapeutic relationship in effecting change," Behav Therapy 27 (96): 623-641; coauth, "The importance of the principle of clinical significance--Defining significant to whom and for what purpose," Psychotherapy Res 6 (96): 133-143; coauth, "Useful constructions of the client-therapist relationship, Psychotherapy 33 (96): 381-390; auth, "The clinical utility of client dream reports from a radical behavioral perspective, The Behav Therapist 19 (96): 49-52; coauth, "REM sleep eye movement counts correlate with visual imagery in dreaming: A pilot study," Psychophysiology 34 (97): 377-381; coauth, "Multiple concurrent supervision and the potential confusion," The Behav Therapist 21 (98): 20-22; auth, "Generic and specific considerations for internship applicants of behavioral orientation," The Behav Therapist 21 (98): 29-31; coauth, "Epistemological barriers to radical behaviorism," The Behav Analyst 21 (98): 307-320. **CONTACT ADDRESS** Dept Psychology, San Jose State Univ, 1 Washington Square, San Jose, CA 95192-0001.

CALLICUTT, JAMES W.
PERSONAL Born 08/21/1928, Memphis, TN, m, 1950, 4 children **DISCIPLINE** SOCIAL WORK **EDUCATION** Memphis State Col, BS, 51; Univ Tenn, MSSW, 58; Brandeis Univ PhD, 69. **CAREER** Assoc to prof, Univ Tex Arlington, 68-; vis prof, Lancashire Polytechnic, 85-86. **HONORS AND AWARDS** Social Worker of the Year, Tarrant County Unit, NASW/Tex, 93; Lifetime Achievement Awd, Tarrant County Unit, NASW/Tex, 98. **MEMBERSHIPS** Nat Assoc of Soc Workers; Counc on soc Work Educ. **RESEARCH** Mental Health Policy and Services, Social Work Education, Professions. **SELECTED PUBLICATIONS** Coauth, "Milieu Concept in Out-Patient Treatment", Mental Hygiene 51.3 (67): 449-451; ed, Health Care Issues in the 80's: Social Work's Contributions in Physical and Mental Health, Univ of Tex Arlington, 80; coauth, "Fees for Counseling Services: Why Charge Them?", Admin in Mental Health, 9.2 (81): 100-122; auth, "Contemporary Settings and the Rise of the Profession in Mental Health", Social Work and Mental Health, eds J.W. Callicutt and P.J. Lecca, Free Pr, (NY, 83): 30-41; coed, Social Work and Mental Health, Free Pr, NY, 83; auth, "Mental Health Services", Encycl of Soc Work, 18th Ed, Nat Assoc of Soc Workers, (NY, 87): 125-135; coauth, "Patient Advocacy Groups in Mental Health: A Systems Perspective", Nat Soc Sci Perspective J 8.2 (95): 159-168; auth, "Overview of the Field of Mental Health", Mental Health Policy and Practice Today, eds T.R. Watkins and J.W. Callicutt, Sage, (Thousand Oaks, CA) (97): 3-16; coauth, "Personnel: The Professionals and Their Preparation, Mental Health Policy and Practice Today, eds T.R. Watkins and J.W. Callicutt, Sage (Thousand Oaks, CA), (97): 69-85; coed, Mental Health Policy and Practice Today, Sage, (Thousand Oaks, CA), 97; auth, "Social Policies and Mental Health", The Handbook of Social Policy, eds J. Midgley, M.B. Tracy and M. Livermore, Sage, (Thousand Oaks, CA), 00. **CONTACT ADDRESS** Dept Soc Work, Univ of Texas, Arlington, Box 19129, Arlington, TX 76019-0001. **EMAIL** callicutt@uta.edu

CAMERON, CATHERINE M.
DISCIPLINE ANTHROPOLOGY **EDUCATION** York Univ, BA, 70; MA, 73; Univ Ill, PhD, 82. **CAREER** Asst prof, 83-90, assoc prof, Cedar Crest Col, 90- **HONORS AND AWARDS** Numerous articles on tourism, economic change, music, and the arts. **MEMBERSHIPS** Am Anthropol Asn. **RESEARCH** Industrial communities, tourism, museum studies, music, the Caribbean. **SELECTED PUBLICATIONS** Auth, "My (New) Hidden Agenda in Teaching Introductory Anthropology," FOSAP Newsletter, 5, 1 (96): 14-17; auth, Dialectics in the Arts: The Rise of Experimentalism in American Music, Westport, Ct: Praeger (96); auth, "Dilemmas of the Cross-Over Experience: Tourism Work in Bethlehem, Pennsylvania," in Erve Chambers, ed, Tourism and Culture: An Applied Perspective, Albany, NY: State Univ of NY Press (97): 163-181; auth, "Thanksgiving Feast Is America's Most Unifying Cultural Tradition," The Morning-Call (Nov 26, 98): A47; auth, "The Not-so-New Social History; Review of 'The New History in an Old Museum', by Richard Handler and Eric Gable, Anthropology and Humanism, 23, 2 (98): 4-5; coauth with John B. Gatewood, "Excursions into the Un-Remembered Past: What People Want from Visits to Historical Sites," submitted for a special issue of Public Historian, Steven Lubar and Stephen Cutcliffe, eds (forthcoming); coauth with John B. Gatewood, "Seeking Numinous Experiences in the Un-Remembered Past," submitted to Human Organization (forthcoming); auth, "Emergent Industrial Heritage: The Politics of Selection," submitted to J of Museum Anthropol, 23, 3 (2000). **CONTACT ADDRESS** Dept Sociol & Anthropol, Cedar Crest Col, 100 Col Dr, Allentown, PA 18104. **EMAIL** ccameron@cedarcrest.edu

CAMERON, MARY M.
PERSONAL Born 01/09/1956, Utica, NY, m, 2000 **DISCIPLINE** ANTHROPOLOGY, WOMEN'S STUDIES **EDUCATION** Russell Sage Col, BS, 78; Mich State Univ, MA, 88; PhD, 93. **CAREER** Volunteer, Am Peace Corps, 78-81; teacher, Bishop Maginn High Sch, 81-83; libr asst, res asst, TA, asst ombudsman, Mich State Univ, 83-92; asst to assoc prof, Auburn Univ, 92-. **HONORS AND AWARDS** Scholarship, Russell Sage Col, 74-78; Fel, Mich State Univ, 83-84, 87, 87-88; 84-85; Sigma Xi Grant, 85, 88; World Bank Grant, 89; Fulbright-Hays Grant, 88-89; Grant, Auburn Univ, 93; Ill NWSA Book Award, 94; Phi Beta Delta, 95; Breeden Teaching Award, Auburn Univ, 97; Fac Achievement Award, Auburn Univ, 98; Grant, Auburn Univ, 98, 00; Fulbright Sr Fel, 99-00. **MEMBERSHIPS** Asian Studies Asn, Nepal Studies Asn, Inst for Biodiversity Conserv in Nepal, WHID, Am Anthrop Asn, Soc for Feminist Anthrop, Soc for Applied Anthrop, Soc for Cult Anthrop, Nat Women's Studies Asn, NOW, Am Botanical Coun, Auburn Group in Ecol. **RESEARCH** Cultural Anthropology, Nepal and Sough Asia, rural southern America, urban northern America, Gender and culture, medical anthropology, cast and gender politics, Ayurvedic medicine, international alternative movements, farmers and artisans, women and international development, agrarian change, the human body and culture. **SELECTED PUBLICATIONS** Auth, "Biodiversity Conservation and Economic Development in Nepal's Khaptad National Park Region: Untouchables as Entrepreneurs and Conservation Stewards," Himalayan Res Bull 15.2 (95): 56-63; auth, "Transformations of Gender and Caste Divisions of Labor in Rural Nepal: Land, Hierarchy, and The Case of Untouchable Women," Jour of Anthrop Res 51.3, (95): 215-46; auth, "Biodiversity and Medicinal Plants in Nepal: Involving Untouchables in Conservation and Development," Human Org 55.1, (96): 84-92; auth, "The Riti-Bhagya System in Western Nepal: Farmers and Artisans, Caste and Gender," Peoples of the Himalayas: Ecology, Culture, Development and Change, ed KD Mahanta, (NY: Kamla-Raj Enterprise, 97): 189-94; auth, "applied Research in Anthropology: Biodiversity and Untouchables in Nepal," Society, Culture and the Environment, 2nd ed, ed Paul Starr (NY: Am Heritage Customs Publ, (97): 93-98; auth, On the Edge of the Auspicious:

Gender and Caste in Nepal, Univ Ill Pr, (Champaign, IL), 98; auth, "Negotiating Marriage in Nepal: Bride price and Untouchable Women's Work," Til Death Do Us Part: A Multicultural Approach to Marriage, ed Robin Miller and Sandra Browning, (Stamford, CT: JAI Pr, 99). **CONTACT ADDRESS** Dept Sociol, Anthrop and Soc Work, Auburn Univ, 7018 Haley Center, Auburn, AL 36849. **EMAIL** camermm@auburn.edu

CAMP, DAVID A.
PERSONAL Born 01/25/1956, Enio, OK, m, 1984, 2 children **DISCIPLINE** SOCIOLOGY **EDUCATION** Northeastern State Univ, BA, 79; OK State Univ, MA, 91; PhD, 95. **CAREER** Teaching asst, OK State Univ, 90-95; asst prof, Northeastern State Univ, 95-97; asst prof, Culver-Stockton Col, 97-. **HONORS AND AWARDS** Larry Perkins Teaching Awd, OK State Univ, 94; Phoenix Awd, OK State Univ, 93; Outstanding Scholarship, OK State Univ, 91-92. **SELECTED PUBLICATIONS** Auth, "Chaos and the Withering Family. Explaining American Criminality," Journal of Humanity and Society 21, (97): 190-198; auth, "Evaluation of FORT," Journal of the Oklahoma Criminal Justice Research Consortium, 96; auth, "Incarceration and Correctional Alternatives, 95; auth, "Oklahoma Incarceration Rates by Race," Journal of the Oklahoma Criminal Justice Research Consortium, 94; auth, "Socialization of Energy Beliefs and Attitudes," Free Inquiry Journal of Sociology, 94; auth, "Chapter Introductions for Social Ecology and Socialization," Sociology Readings and Activities, 92; auth, "Problems of Global Overpopulation," Sociology Readings and Activities Manual, 92; auth, "Youth Education in Social Skills: Operation Manual," Social Skills Training for Youth, 87. **CONTACT ADDRESS** Dept Soc & Beh Sci, Culver-Stockton Col, 1 Col Hill, Canton, OH 63435.

CAMPBELL, GREGORY R.
DISCIPLINE ANTHROPOLOGY **EDUCATION** Univ Calif, Los Angeles, BA, 79 (History and Anthropol); Univ Okla, Norman, MA, 82, PhD, 87; Univ Calif, Los Angeles, Inst Am Cultures, Postdoctoral Diploma, 88. **CAREER** Asst prof, Univ Mont, Missoula, 88-91, assoc prof, 92-98, prof, 99-. **HONORS AND AWARDS** Publication Awd, The Mansfield Library, Univ Mont, 90, 99; Teaching Service Awd, Davidson Honors Col, Univ Mont, 91; Merit Awd, Teaching and Res, Dept of Anthropol, Univ Mont, 91, 95, 97; Awded continuous tenure, Dept of Anthropol, Univ Mont, 94; Ethnologist/Ethnohistorian, Fort Lemhi Shoshone Indian Community Federal Recognition Project, 96-98; Univ Res Grant, Univ Mont, 97-98; Fac Res Fel in Western Studies, Ctr for the Rocky Mountain West, Univ Mont, 99-2000. **MEMBERSHIPS** Nat Asn for Ethnic Studies, Am Anthropol Asn, Am Soc for Ethnohistory, Soc for North Am Anthropol. **RESEARCH** Native North America, race and ethnicity, political economy, demographic anthropology, social epidemiology, social organization, ethnohistory. **SELECTED PUBLICATIONS** Auth, "Little Wolf" and "Morning Star," in Encyclopedia of the American West, Vols 2 and 3, New York: Macmillan Reference, USA (96): 891, 1040; auth, "Race," in Encyclopedia of Social Issues, John K. Roth, ed, Vol 5, Pasadena: Marshall Cavendish Corp (97): 1300-1303; auth, "Critical Race Theory," in Encyclopedia of Multiculturalism, Vol 7, Pasadena: Salem Press (98): 1955-1957; auth, "Living in a State of Race: Race and Racism in the Post-Civil Rights Era," in Many Americas: Critical Perspectives on Racism, Ethnicity, and Cultural Identity, Gregory R. Campbell, ed, Ames: Kendall/Hunt Pub Co (98): 291-312; ed, Many Americas: Critical Perspectives on Racism, Ethnicity, and Cultural Identity, Ames: Kendall/Hunt Pub Co (98); auth, "Many Americas: The Intersection of Class, Race, and Ethnic Identity," in Many Americas: Critical Perspectives on Racism, Ethnicity, and Cultural Identity, Gregory R. Campbell, ed, Ames: Kendall/Hunt Pub Co (98): 3-38; auth, "Plains Indians," in Encyclopedia of North American History, 11 vols, John S. Super, ed, Tarrytown: Marshall Cavendish Corp (99): 491-496; auth, Native Peoples of the Northwestern Plains: An Ethnohistory of Cultural Persistence and Change, Moscow: Univ Idaho Press (submission, Winter 99); auth, "The Big Horn Medicine Wheel: A Sacred Landscape and the Struggle for Religious Freedom," European Rev of Native Am Studies, 13, 2 (2000): 21-35. **CONTACT ADDRESS** Dept Anthropol, Univ of Montana, Missoula, MT 59812.

CAMPBELL, HOWARD B.
PERSONAL Born 05/04/1957, Lansing, MI, m **DISCIPLINE** ANTHROPOLOGY **EDUCATION** Univ Wisc, PhD, 90. **CAREER** Assoc prof, Univ TX El Paso, 91-2000. **MEMBERSHIPS** Am Anthrop Asn. **RESEARCH** Mexico. **SELECTED PUBLICATIONS** Auth, Zapotec Struggles, Smithsonian Inst Press (93); auth, Zapotec Renaissance, Univ NM Press (94). **CONTACT ADDRESS** Dept Sociol and Anthrop, Univ of Texas, El Paso, 500 W University Ave, El Paso, TX 79968-0001. **EMAIL** hcampbel@utep.edu

CAMPBELL, JOHN W.
PERSONAL Born 12/07/1941, Jersey City, NJ, m, 1961, 4 children **DISCIPLINE** EDUCATION **EDUCATION** Mt St Mary's Col, BS, 64; Univ Del, MEd, 68; Pa State Univ, EdD, 71. **CAREER** From Asst to Assoc Prof, Univ Nev, 71-78; Vis Prof, Mt St Mary's Col, 78-95; Prof, Mt St Mary's Col, 95-. **MEMBERSHIPS** CEC, AERA, EERA, PDK, PLT. **RESEARCH** Student learning, teacher behavior, student discipline. **SELECTED PUBLICATIONS** Coauth, "The Effects of Video Tape Recordings on the Learning Characteristics of Mentally Retarded Children," The Pointer, 22 (77): 42-47; coauth, "The Effects of Language Training on Math Skills of the Mentally Retarded," Ment Retardation, 16 (78): 167-168; auth, "Evaluation of Physical Fitness Training Programs for Retarded Boys," J for Spec Educators of the Mentally Retarded, 14 (78): 78-82; auth, "Faculty Involvement in the Revision of the Core Curriculum: A Renewed Commitment to the Liberal Arts," Educ Record (83): 57-60; auth, "Developing Meaningful Procedures for Evaluation College Teaching," Md Assoc for Higher Educ J (84); coauth, "Can Colleges Go Back to a Core Curriculum?" Planning for Higher Educ, 19 (90): 9-16; auth, "A Comparison of Teacher Efficacy Among Pre-Service and In-Service Teachers in Scotland and America," Educ, 117 (96): 3-11; auth, "Elementary Teacher Attitudes About Full Inclusion: A Pilot Study," J of Res in Educ, 7 (97): 62-67; auth, Individualizing Instruction for the Educationally Handicapped: Teaching Strategies in Remedial and Special Education, Charles C. Thomas (Springfield, IL), 98; auth, Student Discipline and Classroom Management, Charles C. Thomas (Springfield, IL), 99. **CONTACT ADDRESS** Dept Educ, Mount Saint Mary's Col and Sem, 16300 Old Emmitsburg, Emmitsburg, MD 21727.

CANTOR, NORMAN FRANK
PERSONAL Born 11/19/1929, Winnipeg, MB, Canada, m, 1957, 2 children **DISCIPLINE** MEDIEVAL & ENGLISH LEGAL HISTORY, HISTORICAL SOCIOLOGY **EDUCATION** Univ Man, BA, 51; Princeton Univ, MA, 53, PhD, 57. **CAREER** From instr to asst prof hist, Princeton Univ, 55-60; vis prof, Johns Hopkins Univ, 60; from assoc prof to prof, Columbia Univ, 60-66; prof, Brandeis Univ, 66-68, Leff prof, 68-70; chmn dept, State Univ NY, Binghamton, 70-74, distinguished prof hist, 70-76, provost for grad studies, 75-76, vpres acad affairs, 75-76; vchancellor acad affairs & prof hist, Ill-Chicago Circle, 76-78; dean fac arts & sci, 78-81, prof hist, 78-81, Prof Hist & Sociol, New York Univ, 81-; Can Coun fel, 60; Am Coun Learned Soc fel, 60; consult, Bar Asn NYC, 63-67; consult, Encycl Britannica, 64-65; consult, Life mag, 66-68; vis prof, Brooklyn Col, 72-73, Adelphi Univ, 87; Fulbright prof, Tel Aviv, 87-88; consult, NEH 73, 89-91. **HONORS AND AWARDS** Nat Book Critics Circle Nomination, 91; NY Public Libr Awd, 97; Fel Royal Hist Soc, 74; lld, univ winnipeg, 73. **MEMBERSHIPS** AHA; AAUP. **RESEARCH** Medieval cultural history; legal history; comparative European history. **SELECTED PUBLICATIONS** Inventing the Middle Ages, Morrow, 91; Civilization of the Middle Ages, HarperCollins, 93; The Sacred Chain, HarperCollins, 94; Medieval Lives, HarperCollins, 94; The Medieval Reader, 95; The Jewish Experience, HarperCollins, 95; The American Century, HarperCollins, 97; Imagining the Law, HarperCollins, 97. **CONTACT ADDRESS** Dept Hist, New York Univ, 53 Washington Sq S, New York, NY 10012-4556.

CAO, LIQUN
PERSONAL Born 07/31/1958, Nanjing, China, m, 1 child **DISCIPLINE** SOCIOLOGY **EDUCATION** Univ Cincinnati, PhD, 93. **CAREER** Visiting Prof, Miami Univ, 92-93; Asst Prof, Salem State Col, 93-94; Asst Prof to Assoc Prof, E MI Univ, 94-. **HONORS AND AWARDS** Jr Scholar Paper Competition Awd, South Korea, 98; Outstanding Student Paper Awd, Kansas City, 93; Lois Elliot Grad Stud Res Awd, Univ Cincinnati, 92. **MEMBERSHIPS** Acad of Crim Justice Sci; Am Soc of Criminol; Am Sociol Asn; Asn of Chinese Prof of Soc Sci in the U.S.; Midwestern Crim Justice Asn. **RESEARCH** Comparative criminology; Social control; Police and theory. **SELECTED PUBLICATIONS** Co-auth, "Prison disciplinary tickets: A test of the deprivation and importation models," Journal of Criminal Justice, (97): 103-113; co-auth, "The social Determinants of Gun Ownership: Self-Protection in an Urban Environment," criminology, (97): 629-657; co-auth, "Public confidence in the police: A comparative study between Japan and America," Journal of Criminal Justice, (98): 279-289; co-auth, "Shoplifting: A test of an integrated model of strain, differential association, and seduction theories," Sociology of Crime, Law, and Deviance, (98): 65-83; co-auth, "Political conservatism and confidence in the police: A comparative analysis," Journal of Crime and Justice, (98): 71-76; co-auth, "Confidence in the police among industrialized nations," in International Criminal Justice: Issues in a Global Perspective, (Allyn and Bacon, 00), 71-81; auth, "Security in Taiwan," in Taiwan in the 21st Century: Mainland Chinese Scholars Looking Ahead, World Scientific Pub, 00; auth, "Determinants of citizen complaints against police abuse of power," Journal of Criminal Justice, forthcoming; co-auth, "A test of Lundman's organizational product thesis with data on citizen complaints," Policing: An International Journal of Police Strategy and Management, forthcoming; co-auth, "Inequality and crime in China," in Social Change and Crime in China, Greenwood Press, forthcoming. **CONTACT ADDRESS** Dept Sociol & Anthropol, Eastern Michigan Univ, 712 Pray Harrold, Ypsilanti, MI 48197. **EMAIL** soc_cao@online.emich.edu

CAPRA, CARL J.
PERSONAL Born 08/18/1948, Kansas City, MO, s, 1 child **DISCIPLINE** BEHAVIORAL SCIENCE **EDUCATION** Rockhurst Col, BA, 70; Cent Mo State Univ, MSE, 80; Univ Kans, MA, 89. **CAREER** Asst Prof, Rockhurst Univ, 88-. **HONORS AND AWARDS** Midwest Coach of the Year, NAIA, 97-98. **MEMBERSHIPS** NIRSA; USGA; PGA Partner's Club. **RESEARCH** Basketball. **SELECTED PUBLICATIONS** Auth, Scholastic Coach, 85; auth, The Basketball Clinic, 85. **CONTACT ADDRESS** Dept Beh Sci, Rockhurst Col, 1100 Rockhurst Rd, Kansas City, MO 64110. **EMAIL** carl.capra@rockhurst.edu

CAPUTI, JANE
PERSONAL Born 10/27/1953, Brooklyn, NY **DISCIPLINE** AMERICAN STUDIES, WOMENS STUDIES **EDUCATION** Boston Col, BA, 74; Simmons Col, MA, 77; Bowling Green State Univ, PhD, 82. **CAREER** Prof, Amer Studies, Univ Nmex, 95-97; prof, women's studies, Fla Atlantic Univ, 97-. **HONORS AND AWARDS** Emily Toth Awd, for The Age of Sex Crime, 88; Honorable Mention, Carl Bode Awd, Amer Culture Asn, for The New Founding Fathers: The Lore and Lure of the Serial Killer, 91; Kathleen Gregory Klein Awd, Popular Culture Asn, for American Psychos: The Serial Killer in Contemporary Fiction, 92. **RESEARCH** New spiritualities; Violence against women; Popular culture. **SELECTED PUBLICATIONS** Auth, Unthinkable Fathering: Connecting Incest and Nuclearism, Hypatia: A Journal of Feminist Philosophy, vol 9, no 2, 102-122, 94; auth, American Psychos: The Serial Killer in Contemporary Fiction, Jour of Amer Culture, 16, no 4, 101-112, 93; auth, The Heart of Knowledge: Nuclear Themes in Native American Thought and Literature, Amer Indian Culture and Res Jour, 14, no 4, 1-27, 92; auth, Gossips, Gorgons & Crones: The Fates of the Earth, Bear and Co, 93; co-auth, Websters' First New Intergalactic Wickedary of the English Language, Beacon Press, Boston, 87; auth, The Age of Sex Crime, Bowling Green State Univ Popular Press, Bowling Green, Oh, 87; auth, The Seocnd Coming of Diana," National Womens Studies Asn Journal 11:2, (99): 103-123. **CONTACT ADDRESS** Women's Studies, Florida Atlantic Univ, Boca Raton, FL 33431. **EMAIL** jcaputi@fau.edu

CARDENAS, MARIA DE LA LUZ RODRIGUEZ
PERSONAL Born 09/03/1945, Laredo, TX, m, 1971, 3 children **DISCIPLINE** HISTORY, WOMEN'S STUDIES **EDUCATION** Tex Woman's Univ, BA, 69; MA, 74; Colegio de Mex, Cert Women's Study, 94. **CAREER** Instr, Laredo Community Col, 70-; Staff Develop Office, Laredo Community Col, 74-76; Asst to Acad Dean, Laredo Community Col, 76-81; St. Augustine High Sch Life Vocations/Hist/Rel, 81-88; Laredo Community Col Dir of Familias Pueden, Ford Found, 96-. **HONORS AND AWARDS** Fel for Master' Degree, Summer Inst in Mex City, Grant; Ford Found Rural Community Col Initiative, 96-99; Pathfinder Awd, Tex A&M Int Univ 99-00; S Tex Writing Proj, 00-02. **MEMBERSHIPS** Tex Community Col Teachers, AAUW, Delta Kappa Gamma, Tex State Hist Asn, Int Good Neighbor Coun, Las Mujeras, Laredo Comn for Women, Domestic Violence Coalition, Tex State Cath Hist Conf. **RESEARCH** Women's history, Hispanic educational models, Women vowed religions, Church history, Women in politics. **SELECTED PUBLICATIONS** Auth, "Anglo-American Relations, 1844-46,"; auth, "Laredo Vietnam Causalities & their Families," 93, 97; auth, "Jovita Perez, First Woman Licensed Custom House Broker in U.S.;" auth, "Fearless Voices in a Common Struggle, Laredo Women in Politics;" auth, "The Role of the Laity-Diocese of Corpus Christi Synod Doc;" auth, "Familias Pueden," LCC's Rural Community Col Initiative; auth, "Hispanic Women in Communication, Texas Tamaulipas Border." **CONTACT ADDRESS** Dept Soc and Behav Sci, Laredo Comm Col, 1 W End Wash, Laredo, TX 78040. **EMAIL** lrcardenas@laredo.cc.tx.us

CARDINAL, BRADLEY J.
PERSONAL Born 05/31/1963, Everett, WA, m, 1988 **DISCIPLINE** SPORTS PSYCHOLOGY **EDUCATION** Temple Univ, PhD, 93; Eastern Washington Univ, MS, 87; Eastern Washington Univ, BA/Ed., 85. **CAREER** Asst Prof, Dept of Exercise and Sport Science, 97-; Co-Director, Sport and Exercise Psychology Laboratory, 97-; Faculty Affiliate Gerontology Program, Oregon State Univ, 97-; Asst Prof, Coord, Health Education Program, Division of Health, 93-; Faculty Affiliate, Institute of Gerontology, Wayne State Univ, 97; Asst Prof, Director of The Body Shop Fitness-Wellness Center, Department Education, Health and Recreation, Eastern Washington Univ, 90. **HONORS AND AWARDS** Mabel Lee Awd, Am Alliance for Health, Physical Education, Recreation, and Dance, 98; Fellow, Am College of Sports Medicine; 98; Young Alumni Achievement Awd, College of Health, Physical Education, Recreation, and Dance Alumni Association, Temple Univ, 96; Certificate of Recognition, Detroit Health Department, Worksite and Community Health Promotion Program, 96; Fellow, Research Consortium, Am Alliance for Health, Physical Education, Recreation, and Dance, 95; Public Relations Awd, Pennsylvania State Association for Health, Physical Education, Recreation and Dance, 93; Dr. Art Broten Young Scholar's Awd, Western College Physical Education Society, 90. **MEMBERSHIPS** Amer Alliance for Health, Physical Education, Recreation and Dance (Life Member); Amer College of Sports Medicine; Assoc for the Advancement of Applied Sport Psychology; Eta Sigma Gamma, National Professional Health Science Honorary (Life Member); National Assoc for Physical Education, in Higher Education; Oregon Alliance for Health, Physical Edu-

cation, Recreation and Dance; Washington Alliance for Health, Physical Education, Recreation and Dance. **SELECTED PUBLICATIONS** Auth, "Readability analysis of written informed consent forms used in exercise and sport psychology research," by Cardinal, B.J., Martin, J.J., & Sachs, M.L., Research Quarterly for Exercise and Sport, 67, (96): 360-362; auth, "Evaluation of the revised physical activity readiness questionnaire in older adults," by Cardinal, B.J., Esters, J., & Cardinal, M.K., Medicine and Science in Sports and Exercise, 28, (96): 468-472; auth, "Dietary profiles of elite female marathon runners," Journal of Physical Education and Sport Sciences, 10, (97): 1-13; auth, "Evaluation of the KASPER pilot program for at risk 3rd 7 4th grade students," by Bertolini, S.L., & Cardinal, B.J., Michigan Association for Health, Physical Education, Recreation, and Dance Journal, (97): 32-34; auth, "Assessing the physical activity readiness of inactive older adults," by Cardinal, B.J., Adapted Physical Activity Quarterly, 14, (97): 65-73; auth, "Construct validity of stages of change for exercise behavior," by Cardinal, B.J., American Journal of Health Promotion, 12, (97): 68-74; auth, "Are overweight physical educators at a disadvatage in the labor market?" by Melville, D.S., & Cardinal, B.J., A random survey of hiring personnel, The Physical Educator, 54 (97): 216-221; auth, "Application of the transtheoretical model of behavior change to preadolescents physical activity and exercise behavior," by Cardinal, B.J., Engels, H.-J., & Zhu, W, Pediatric Exercise Science, 10, (98): 69-80; auth, "Interaction between stage of exercise and relapse," by Cardinal, B.J., Journal of Human Movement Studies, 34, (98): 175--185; auth, "Increasing children's physical activity," by Cardinal, B.J. Journal of Physical Education, Recreation and Dance, 71, (00): 26-29. **CONTACT ADDRESS** Dept Exercise & Sport Science, Oregon State Univ, 220 Langton Hall, Corvallis, OR 97331. **EMAIL** brad.cardinal@orst.edu

CARLISLE, HARRY J.
PERSONAL Born 10/05/1932, Santa Barbara, CA, m, 1957, 3 children **DISCIPLINE** PSYCHOLOGY **EDUCATION** Univ Calif, Santa Barbara, BA, 59; Univ Calif, Santa Barbara, MA, 60; Univ Washington, Seattle, 64; Univ Pa Medical School, Postdoctoral Research Fellow, 64-65. **CAREER** Prof of Psychology, Univ of Calif, 77-; Research Physiologist, St. George's Hospital Medical School, Univ of London, 85-89; Assoc Prof of Psychology, Univ of Calif, 70-77; Research Fellow, Institute of Animal Physiology, 71-72; Asst Prof of Psychology, Univ of Calif, 65-70. **MEMBERSHIPS** Am Phsysio Soc; Soc for Newrosci; AAAS. **RESEARCH** Regulation of Food intake and body temperature. **SELECTED PUBLICATIONS** Auth, "Effect of ambient temperature on paradoxical metabolic responses to norepinephrine," by Zylan, K.D. & Carlisle, H.J., Pharmacology, Biochemistry & Behavior, 93, 43: 577-582; auth, "Thermoregulatory responses to B-agonists at low ambient temperature in the rat," by Carlisle, H.J. & Stock, M.J. Experimental Physiology, 93, 78: 775-786; auth, Thermoregulatory effects of beta-adrenoceptors: Effects of selective agonist and the interaction of antagonists with isoproterenol and BRL 35135 in the cold," by Carlisle, H.J. & Stock, M.J., Journal of Pharmacology and Experimental Therapeutics, 93, 266, 775-786; auth, "Effects of B-adrenoceptor agonists and antagonists on thermoregulaion in the cold in lean and obese Zucker rats," by Carlisle, H.J., Dubuc, P.U. & Stock, M.J., Pharmacology, Biochemistry & Behavior, 93, 46, 953-958; auth, "Thermal preference behaviour following B-agonist stimulation," in A.S. Milton, by Carlisle, H.J., Rothberg, S. & Stock, M.J., Temperature Regulation: Advances in Pharmacological Sciences, Birkhauser, Basel, 247-251, 1994; auth, "Effects of epinephrine on thermoregulatory behavior in lean and obese Zucker rats in the cold," by Carlisle, H.J., Dubuc, P.U. & Stock, M.J., Pharmacology, Biochemistry & Behavior, 95, 51, 255-261; auth, "Temperature-dependent effects of a-adrenergic agonists and antagonist in the cold," by Carlisle, H.J. & Stock, M.J., Pharmacology, Biochemistry & Behavior, 95, 51, 263-270; auth, "Temperature-dependent effect of ephedrine in the cold," by Carlisle, H.J. & Stock, M.J., Physiology & Behavior, 96, 0, 1147-1150; auth, "Effects of a1-adrenoceptor and Ca channel inhibition of norepinephrine-induced thermoregulatory behavior in the cold," by Carlisle, H.J. & Stock, M.J., Pharmacology, Biochemistry & Behavior, 97, 57, 185-189; auth, "Thermal preference behavior following clonidine, norepinephrine, isoproternol and ephedrine, by Carlisle, H.J. & Stock, M.J., Frost, T.S., Physiology & Behavior, 99, 66, 585-589. **CONTACT ADDRESS** Dept Psychology, Univ of California, Santa Barbara, 552 University Rd, Santa Barbara, CA 93106. **EMAIL** carlisle@psych.ucsb.edu

CARLSMITH, LYN
PERSONAL Born 10/07/1932, Portland, OR, w, 1963, 3 children **DISCIPLINE** PSYCHOLOGY **EDUCATION** Stanford Univ, BA, 54; MA, 59; Harvard Univ, PhD, 63. **CAREER** Res assoc, Yale Univ, 63-65; Yth Div Prog, 70-78; sr lect, Stanford Univ, 78-00. **HONORS AND AWARDS** NIH Fel, 58-63. **MEMBERSHIPS** APS. **RESEARCH** Social development of children, adolescents, adults. **SELECTED PUBLICATIONS** Auth, "Effect of Early Father Absence on Scholastic Aptitude," Harvard Edu Rev (64); auth, Instructor's Manual for Hilgard and Atkinson, Introduction to Psychology (67 and 71). **CONTACT ADDRESS** Dept Psychology, Stanford Univ, Stanford, CA 94305. **EMAIL** lyn@psych.stanford.edu

CARMACK, ROBERT M.
PERSONAL Born 02/24/1934, AZ, m, 1981, 5 children **DISCIPLINE** ANTHROPOLOGY **EDUCATION** Univ Calif, LA, BA, 60, MA, 62, PhD, 65. **CAREER** Asst Prof, Ariz State Univ, 64-66; Asst Prof, Univ Calif, San Diego, 67-70; Prof, SUNY, 70-. **HONORS AND AWARDS** SUNY Pres Excellence. **MEMBERSHIPS** AA; CIHMA; Inst Meso-American Stud. **RESEARCH** Political Anthropology; Central America, Mayan Studies, Ethnohistory. **SELECTED PUBLICATIONS** Co-ed, Historia Antigua de America Central: Del Poblamiento a la Conquista, FLASCO, 93; ed, Soplos del viento en Buenos Aires: La antropoliogia de un canton brunca de Costa Rica, Univ de Costa Rica, 94; auth, Rebels of Highland Gautemala, Univ Okla Press, 95; co-ed, The Legacy of Mesoamerica: History and Culture of a Native American Civilization, Prentice Hall, 95; auth, Introduction to Cultural Anthropology: A World Systems Approach, McGraw-Hill, 95; Historia social de los K'ichee, Cholsamaj, 98. **CONTACT ADDRESS** Dept Anthrop, SUNY, Albany, 1400 Washington Ave, Albany, NY 12222. **EMAIL** rcarmack@csc.albany.edu

CARMAZZA, ALFONSO
PERSONAL Born 06/22/1946, Aragona, Italy, m, 3 children **DISCIPLINE** PSYCHOLOGY **EDUCATION** McGill Univ, BA, 70; Johns Hopkins Univ, PhD, 74. **CAREER** Asst to prof, Johns Hopkins Univ, 74-87; prof, Univ de Geneve, 86-87; adj prof, Univ of Md, 89-93; prof, chair, Johns Hopkins Univ, 87-93; McLaughlin Dist prof, Dartmouth Med Sch, 93-95; prof, Harvard Univ, 95-. **HONORS AND AWARDS** Javits Neuroscience Investigator Awd, 89; Doctor Honoris Causa, Belgium 93; J.L. Signoret Prize, Ipsen Found, 96; NEH Grants. **RESEARCH** Neglect dyslexia, dysgraphia, psychology of language, lexical access, aphasia. **SELECTED PUBLICATIONS** Coauth, "Is lexical selection in bilinguals language specific? Further evidence from Spanish-English bilinguals", Bilingualism: Lang and Cognition 2 (99): 231-244; coauth, "Lexical selection in bilinguals: Do words in the bilingual's two lexicons compete for selection?", J of Memory and Lang 41 (99): 365-397; coauth, "The gender congruity effect: Evidence from Spanish and Catalan", Lang and Cognitive Processes 14, (99): 381-391; coauth, "Mechanisms of spatial attention revealed by hemispatial neglect", Cortex 35, (99): 433-442; auth, "Lexicon, neural basis", MIT Encyclop of the Cognitive Sciences, eds R.A. Wilson and F.C. Keil, MIT Pr, 99; coauth, "Sublexical conversion procedures and the interaction of phonological and orthographic lexical forms", Cognitive Neuropsychology 16, (99): 557-572; coauth, "The selection of determiners in noun phrase production", J of Experimental Psychol: Learning, Memory and Cognition 25, (99): 907-922; coauth, "Deficits in lexical access and semantic processing: Implications for models of normal language", Psychonomic Bull and Rev 6, (99): 5-27; auth, "Aspects of lexical access: Evidence from aphasia", Language and the Brain: Representation and Processing, eds Y. Grodzinsky, L. Shapiro and D. Swinney, Acad Pr, (San Diego), 00; auth, "The organization of conceptual knowledge in the brain", The New Cognitive Neurosciences, ed M.S. Gazzaniga, MIT Pr, (00). **CONTACT ADDRESS** Dept Psychol, Harvard Univ, 33 Kirkland St, William James Hall 930, Cambridge, MA 02138. **EMAIL** caram@wjh.harvard.edu

CARMEL, SIMON J.
PERSONAL Born 04/30/1938, Baltimore, MD, s **DISCIPLINE** SOCIOLOGY **EDUCATION** Gallaudet Univ, BA, 61; Am Univ, MA, 80; PhD, 87. **CAREER** Physicist, Nat Bureau Standards, 61-81; Adj Asst Prof, Gallaudet Univ, 82-87; Assoc Prof, Nat Tech Inst for Dear, 88-. **HONORS AND AWARDS** Fulbright Scholar Awd, Russia, 93; Edward Miner Gallaudet Awd, Gallaudet Univ, 97; Strathmore's Who's Who, 98. **MEMBERSHIPS** Am Anthropol Asn; Am Folklore Soc; Phi Delta Kappa; Soc for the Anthropol in Cmty Col; Nat Asn of the Deaf. **RESEARCH** Deaf culture; Deaf folklore; Different sign languages; Deaf communities. **SELECTED PUBLICATIONS** Auth, International CISS Ski Technical Signs for Racers and Officials, Copenhagen, 90; auth, "A Checklist of Dictionaries of National Sign Languages of Deaf People," Sign Language Studies, (92): 232-252; auth, "Deaf Folklore," in American Folklore: An Encyclopedia, (Garland Pub, 96), 197-200; auth, Deaf-lore: Deaf People, Culture and Identity, 01. **CONTACT ADDRESS** Dept Cultural Studies, Nat Tech Inst for Deaf, 52 Lomb Memorial Dr, Rochester, NY 14623. **EMAIL** sjcnah@rit.edu

CARNEY, VIRGINIA I.
PERSONAL Born 05/27/1941, Maryville, TN, m, 1963, 7 children **DISCIPLINE** ENGLISH, NATIVE STUDIES, WOMEN'S STUDIES **EDUCATION** Tenn Temple Univ, BA, 69; Cleveland State Community Col, AND, 78; Univ Alaska, MA, 90; Univ Ky, PhD, 00. **CAREER** Teacher, Nassau Christian Acad, 73-74; nurse, Bradley Mem Hosp, 78-80; nurse, Humana Hosp, 80-83; office nurse, 83-86; adj prof, Univ of Alaska, 90-93; TA, Univ of Ky, 93-97; asst prof, E Ky Univ, 98-. **HONORS AND AWARDS** S Reg Educ Board Diss Fel, 97-98; Scholars for the Dream Awd, 97; Ellershaw Awd, 98; Frances C. Allen Fel, 98; Fac Grant, E Ky Univ, 99-00; Chi Omega Outstanding Prof Awd, 00. **MEMBERSHIPS** Assoc for the Study of Am Indian Lit, Conf on Col Comp and Commun, MLA, NCTE, Wordcraft Circle of Native Writers and Storytellers. **RESEARCH** Letters and speeches of Eastern Band Cherokee Women, Black Indians. **SELECTED PUBLICATIONS** Auth, "These Are Our Mountains, Too!" Appalachian Heritage, (95); auth, "Cherokee/Appalachian Communities: Remembering the Pattern, Re-Spinning the Web," Jour of Appalachian Studies, (97); auth, "I Used to be a Hillbilly; Now I'm Appalachian," One Hundred Years of Appalachian Visions, Appalachian Imprints, (KY: Berea, 97); auth, "Native American Loanwords in American English," Wicazo SA Rev, (97); auth, Dancing on New Ground: The Life of Morningstar Conner, Unole Pr, (Wallingford, KY), 97; auth, "The Speeches of Nanye'hi (Nancy Ward) and Kitteuha," Speakers of the Eastern Woodlands, Greenwood Publ, (NY, 00); auth, "Irrepressible Voices: The As-Told-To Stories of Pretty Shield and Lee Maracle," Native Am Lit Strategies for the New Millennium, (01); auth, "A Time for Healing," The People Who Stayed Behind, (01). **CONTACT ADDRESS** Dept English, Eastern Kentucky Univ, 467 Case Annex, Richmond, KY 40475-3021. **EMAIL** engcarne@acs.eku.edu

CARPENTER, CAROLE
DISCIPLINE FOLKLORE **EDUCATION** Dalhousie Univ, BA, 66; Univ Pa, MA, 68, PhD, 75. **CAREER** Dean's asst, Univ Pa, 66-69; lectr, 71-74, asst prof, 74-78, Assoc Prof, Univ York, 78-. **HONORS AND AWARDS** Awd Excellence Tchr, Fac Arts, York Univ, 87; Writing award, Asn Can Studs, 93. **MEMBERSHIPS** Folklore Studs Asn Can; Am Folklore Soc; Hum Soc Sci Fedn Can. **SELECTED PUBLICATIONS** Auth, "Folklore as a Tool of Multiculturalism," in Stella Hryniuk, Twenty Years of Multiculturalism: Successes and Failure, (Winnipeg: St John's Press, 92): 149-160; auth, "The Intangible Heritage of Muskoka," in D.A. Robertson and R.F. Willimson, Final Phase 1 Report of the Master Plan of Archaeological Rresoureces of the District Municipality of Muskoka, (Toronto: Archaeological Ser, 92): 155-164; auth, "Developing an Appreciation for the Cultural Signigicance of Childlore," Children's Folklore Rev 17:1, (94), 19-29; auth, "The Ethnicity Factor in Anglo-Canadian Folkloristics," in Canadian Music: Identity & Hegemony, Toronto: Candian Scholars Press, (94); auth, "Evaluating and Conserbing the Intangible Heritage of Muskoka," in Conservation and Management Guidline, Report of the Master Plan of the Archaeological Res of the Dist Municipality of Muskoka and the Wahta Mohawks vol 3, (Toronto: Archaeological Serv Inc, 94): 77-125; rev, on "Publishing Folklore," Can Children's Lit 21:1, (95): 55-62; auth, "Enlisting Children's Literature in the Goals of Multiculturalism," Mosaic 29:3, Speical Issue, Idols of Otherness: The Rhetoric and Reality of Multicultualism, (96): 53-73; auth, In Our Own Image:The Child, Canadian Culture and Our Furture, Toronto: Robarts Centre for Canadian Studies, Youk Univ, 96; auth, "Use It of Lose It: Conserving Traditions Through Heritage Planning for Tourism," in Gwenda Beed Davey and Susan Faine, Traditions and Tourism: The Good, The Bad and the Ugly, (VI: National Centre for Autralian Studies, 96): 17-24; auth, "Arthur Huff Fauset: Campaigner for Social Justice," in Ira E. Harrison and Faye V Harrison, African-Am Pioneers in Anthropology, Urbana-Champaign and Chicago: Illionois Univ Press, 98. **CONTACT ADDRESS** Dept of Humanities, York Univ, 4700 Keele St, North York, ON, Canada M3J 1P3. **EMAIL** carolec@yorku.ca

CARRINGER, ROBERT L.
PERSONAL Born 05/12/1941, Knoxville, TN, m, 1968 **DISCIPLINE** FILM STUDIES, CULTURAL STUDIES, AMERICAN STUDIES **EDUCATION** Univ Tenn, AB, 62; Johns Hopkins Univ, MA, 64; Ind Univ, PhD, 70. **CAREER** Prof English & Film Studies, Univ Ill, Urbana, 70-, fel, Fac Study Second Discipline (Cognitive psychol), 90-91; assoc, Center for Advan Studies, 83-84; NEH res ed grant, 86-87; Getty Scholar, 96-97. **HONORS AND AWARDS** Undergrad Instr Awd, 79; Amoco Curric Develop Awd, 80; Distinguished Prof Awd, 85; Apple Computer Curric Innovation Awd, 88. **MEMBERSHIPS** Soc Cinema Studies; Univ Film Asn; Film Div, Mod Lang Asn; Film Studies Sect, Midwest Mod Lang Asn. **RESEARCH** American film; American Literature. **SELECTED PUBLICATIONS** Auth, Circumscription of space and the form of Poe's Arthur Gordon Pym, PMLA, 5/74; Citizen Kane, The Great Gatsby, and some conventions of American narrative, Critical Inquiry, winter 75; Rosebud, dead or alive, PMLA, 3/76; coauth, Ernst Lubitsch, G K Hall, 78; auth, The Scripts of Citizen Kane, Critical Inquiry, fall 78, ed, The Jazz Singer, Univ Wis, 79; auth, Orson Wells and Gregg Toland, Critical Inquiry, summer 82; ed, Citizen Kane, Criterion Laserdisc 84, rev ed, 92; auth, The Making of Citizen Kane, Univ Calif, 85, rev ed, 96; ed, The Magnificent Ambersons, Criterion Laserdisc, 84, rev ed, 92; auth, The Magnificent Ambersons: A Reconstruction, Univ Calif, 93; Designing Los Angeles: Richard Sylbert, Wide Angle, 98; Hollywood's LA, in Looking at Los Angeles, Getty, 00. **CONTACT ADDRESS** Dept of English, Univ of Illinois, Urbana-Champaign, 608 S Wright St, Urbana, IL 61801-3613. **EMAIL** fergus@uiuc.edu

CARTER, BARBARA LILLIAN
PERSONAL Born 06/20/1942, Mexia, TX, s **DISCIPLINE** EDUCATION **EDUCATION** Fisk Univ, AB 1963; Brandeis Univ, MA 1967, PhD 1972; Harvard Univ Inst of Educ Mgmt, attended 1984. **CAREER** Federal City College, asst prof 1969-72, assoc provost and assoc prof 1972-77; Univ of District of Columbia, assoc vice pres and prof 1977-80, vice pres for academic affairs 1980-81; Spelman Coll, vice pres for academic af-

fairs and dean 1981-, acting dean 1986-87. **HONORS AND AWARDS** Woodrow Wilson Fellow 1963; Phi Beta Kappa 1963; Fellow Natl Inst of Mental Health 1964-67; Aspen Institute for Humanistic Studies Fellowship 1981. **MEMBERSHIPS** Mem Amer Sociological Assoc 1969-; bd dirs YWCA of Atlanta 1982-; bd dirs United Way of Atlanta 1985-, Public Broadcast Assoc 1985-; bd trustees Atlanta Coll of Art 1986-; bd of trustees Chatham Coll. **SELECTED PUBLICATIONS** Coauth, "Protest, Politics and Prosperity" 1978. **CONTACT ADDRESS** Vice Pres for Academic Afrs, Spelman Col, 350 Spelman Ln SW, Atlanta, GA 30314.

CARTER, DAVID G., SR.
PERSONAL Born 10/25/1942, Dayton, OH, m, 1999, 3 children **DISCIPLINE** EDUCATION **EDUCATION** Central State Univ, BS 1962-65; Miami Univ, MEd 1967-68; The OH State Univ, PhD 1969-71. **CAREER** Dayton City Schools, 6th grade tchr, 65-68, asst prin, 68-69, elem prin, 69-70, unit facilitator, 70-71; Dayton Publ Schools, serv unit dir (dist supt), 71-73; Wright State Univ, adj prof, 72; Penn State Univ, asst prof dept of educ admn, 73-75, assoc prof dept educ admn, 75-77; Univ of CT, Storrs, CT, assoc prof dept educ admin, 77-79, prof dept educ admn, 80-, assoc dean/sch educ, 77-82, assoc vice pres acad affairs, 82-88; Eastern CT State Univ, Willimantic, CT, pres, 88-; Corporator, Liberty Bank, 99-; Dir, Liberty Bank, 00-. **HONORS AND AWARDS** NAACP, Roy Wilkins Civil Rights Awd, 1994; Connecticut American Legion 39th Americanism Awd, 1994; Inducted into the Donald K Anthony Achievement Hall of Fame, 1993; Distinguished Alumnus, Central State University, Wilberforce, OH, 1988; Selected Young Man of the Year Dayton Jr C of C 1973; Selected Man of the Year by the African American Affairs Commission, 00. **MEMBERSHIPS** Commission's Division III NCAA, chair, 1994-97; Urban League of Greater Hartford, bd of dirs, 1994-97; Consult Professional Devel Assoc 1979-80; consult Milwaukee Pub Schools 1980; consult Syracuse Univ Research Corp 1976; consult PA Dept of Educ 1973-77; consult So Ea Delco Sch Dist 1973-83; consult Booz-Allen and Hamilton Inc 1972-73; bd trustees Dayton Museum of Natl Hist 1973; mem Centre Cnty Mental Hlth and Mental Retardation Adv Bd 1974-76; mem Adv Cncl to the Bd of Mental Health for Program Dev 1977-80; mem Governor's Task Force on Jail and Prison Overcrowding 1980; bd dir New Engl Reg Exch 1981-86; corporator Windham Meml Comm Hosp 1982; trustee Windham Meml Comm Hosp 1984; dir Windham Healthcare Sys Inc 1984; mem Phi Delta Kappa; mem Amer Educ Rsch Assn; mem NAACP; mem Pi Lambda Theta; mem Phi Kappa Phi; bd dir Natl Organiz on LegalProbl in Education 1980-83; ed bd Journal of Equity and Leadership 1980; mem Good Samaritan Mental Health Adv 1968-73. **SELECTED PUBLICATIONS** Auth, "Students Rights and Responsibilities, Challenge or Revolt" Penn School Master Journal for Secondary Principals 1974; auth, "Implications of Teacher Performance Appraisal" The Penn School Master 1975; co-auth, "Minority Students, Ability Grouping and Career Development" Journal of Black Studies with Frank Brown and J John Harris, 1978; auth, "Race, Language and Sex Discrimination" in A Digest of Supreme Court Decisions Affecting Education, 1978. **CONTACT ADDRESS** Eastern Connecticut State Univ, 83 Windham St, Willimantic, CT 06226-2295. **EMAIL** carter@ecsu.ctstateu.edu

CARTER, DONALD
PERSONAL Born 08/22/1955, Oakland, CA, m, 1987, 2 children **DISCIPLINE** ANTHROPOLOGY **EDUCATION** Univ Calif, BA, 83; Univ Chicago, MA, 88; Univ Chicago, PhD, 92. **CAREER** Vis Asst Prof, Johns Hopkins Univ, 95-99; Vis Asst Prof, Stanford Univ, 98-99; Asst Prof, Johns Hopkins Univ, 98-. **HONORS AND AWARDS** CIC Fel, Univ Chicago, 84-87; CIC Int Study Fel, Turin, Italy, 86; Fulbright Fel, 89-90; Stanford Humanities Ctr Fel, Stanford Univ, 98-99. **MEMBERSHIPS** AAA, Asn of Africanist Anthrop, ABA, SAE, SHA, WARA. **RESEARCH** Critical race theory, disapproval, West Africa, modern Italy. **SELECTED PUBLICATIONS** Rev, Strangers and Traders: Yoruba Migrants, Markets and the State in Northern Ghana by J S Eades, Edinburgh UP (N Ghana), 93; rev, Cultural Change and the New Europe: Perspectives on the European Community, Westview Pr (Boulder CO), 93; auth, "Blue Routes: African, Diaspora Mourid and Elsewhere," in Global Transformations (Routledge, forthcoming); coauth, "Speaking for the Subject," in Families in the Field (forthcoming). **CONTACT ADDRESS** Dept Anthrop, Johns Hopkins Univ, Baltimore, 3400 N Charles St, Baltimore, MD 21218.

CARTER, JUDY L.
PERSONAL Born 06/07/1942, McCormick, SC, m, 1968 **DISCIPLINE** EDUCATION **EDUCATION** Paine College, Augusta, GA, BA, 1967; Augusta College, Augusta, GA, MEd, 1976; University of South Carolina, Columbia, SC, EdD, 1981. **CAREER** Richmond County Bd of Ed, Augusta, GA, teacher, 67-76; Paine College, Augusta, GA, instructor, 76-80; University of South Carolina, Aiken, SC, dir of student teaching, 80-84; Paine College, Augusta, GA, chair, div of education, 84-. **HONORS AND AWARDS** Teacher of the Year, Paine College, 1979-80; Graduate Advisor of the Year, Alpha Kappa Alpha Sorority Inc, 1988; Minority Teacher Recruitment Project, Consortium for the Advancement of Private Higher Education, 1988-90; Outstanding Community Leader, Wrights Enterprise, 1990. **MEMBERSHIPS** Vice-president, Alpha Kappa Alpha Sorority Inc, 1985-87; president, The Augusta Chapter of Links Inc, 1986-89; chairperson, Georgia Advisory Council, 1988-89; director, Bush Faculty Development Program, 1988-; site coordinator, Ford Teacher-Scholar Program, 1990-; member, Georgia Assn of Colleges for Teacher Education, 1985-. **CONTACT ADDRESS** Paine Col, 1235 15th St, Augusta, GA 30910-2799.

CARTER, NANCY CORSON
PERSONAL Born 03/28/1943, Williamsport, PA, m, 1967, 1 child **DISCIPLINE** AMERICAN & WOMEN'S STUDIES **EDUCATION** Susquehanna Univ, BA, 65; Univ Iowa, MA, 68, PhD(Am Civics), 72. **CAREER** Dir, Learning Resources Ctr, 74-76, asst prof Am Studies, 76-78, asst prof Lit & Humanities, 78-79, asst prof Lit & Creative Writing, Eckerd Col, 79-; prof Humanities, 91; fel, Cross-Disciplinary Inst, Summer, 75 & Inst Ecumenical & Cult Res, St John's Univ, Fall, 77; Fla Corresp, Art Voices/South, 78-82; poet-in-schs, Pinellas County Arts Coun, 81. **HONORS AND AWARDS** Dana Fellow, Southeastern Consortium Humanities Program, Emory Univ, 89-90; Visiting Prof, Duke Univ School of the Environment, 95-96. **MEMBERSHIPS** Soc Values Higher Educ; Am Studies Asn; Southeast Women's Studies Asn; MLA. **RESEARCH** Writings of Doris Lessing, especially mythical and evolutionary aspects; interdisciplinary approaches to theme and process of the spiritual journey; psycho-historical, mythical and spiritual ramifications of Jean Houston's work. **SELECTED PUBLICATIONS** Contribr poems, Survivor's Box, Possum Press, 77; 1970's images of the machine and the garden: Kosinski, Crews & Pirsig, Soundings: An Interdisciplinary J, 78; Artist profiles for Florida artists issue: Beckett, Crane, Hodgell, Rigg, Art Voices/South, 79; Demeter & Persephone in Margaret Atwood's novels: Mother-daughter transformations, J Anal Psychol, 10/79; coauth, Spirit of Eve: The Art of Marion Beckeet (videotape), produced on WEDU, 81; Journey toward wholeness: A meditation on Doris Lessing's The Memoirs of a Survivor, J Evolutionary Psychol, 8/81; Dragon Poems, Lewiston/Queenston/Lampeter: Mellen Poetry Press, 93. **CONTACT ADDRESS** Lett Collegium Eckerd Col, 4200 54th Ave S, Saint Petersburg, FL 33711-4744. **EMAIL** carternc@eckerd.edu

CARTWRIGHT, LISA
DISCIPLINE FILM AND MEDIA STUDIES, GENDER STUDIES **EDUCATION** Yale Univ, PhD. **CAREER** Assoc prof; taught at, Yale Univ. **HONORS AND AWARDS** Chicago Hum Inst Rockefeller fel; Univ Chicago Pembroke Ctr for Tchg and Res on Women fel & Brown Univ Alumna, Whitney Mus Am Art Independent Study Prog. **RESEARCH** Modernist modes of visual representation in US med sci. **SELECTED PUBLICATIONS** Auth, Screening the Body: Tracing Medicine's Visual Culture; co-ed, The Visible Woman: Imaging Technologies, Inscribing Science; articles on, film modernism and sci, med imag ing and gender, media and commun technol-(s) in health care & soc transformation through technol art and activism. **CONTACT ADDRESS** Dept of Eng, Univ of Rochester, 601 Elmwood Ave, Ste. 656, Rochester, NY 14642. **EMAIL** lisac@troi.cc.rochester.edu

CASH, ROBERT W.
PERSONAL Born 09/04/1932, Newark, NJ, m, 1960, 3 children **DISCIPLINE** PSYCHOLOGY **EDUCATION** Denison Univ, BA, 54; Univ Iowa, MA, 57; Mich State Univ, MA, 65; Univ Arizona, EdD, 70. **CAREER** Prof, Cal State Univ Long Beach, 70-00; prof emer, 00-. **HONORS AND AWARDS** Dist Univ Teach Awd; Fulbright Schol, 92-93. **MEMBERSHIPS** APA; ACA; ACES. **RESEARCH** Communication skills in human resources development. **SELECTED PUBLICATIONS** Auth, School Counseling: Past, Present, Future; auth, Career Education in the United States. **CONTACT ADDRESS** Dept Edu Psychology, California State Univ, Long Beach, 1250 N Bellflower, Long Beach, CA 90840-0001. **EMAIL** rcash@csulb.edu

CASHWELL, SUSAN T.
PERSONAL Born 06/28/1963, Wurthsmith AFB, MI, m, 1996, 3 children **DISCIPLINE** SOCIAL WORK **EDUCATION** N Mich Univ, BSW, 94; Fla State Univ, MSW, 95; PhD, 99. **CAREER** Grants Coordinator, Valdosta State Univ, 98-00; Asst Prof, Auburn Univ, 00-. **HONORS AND AWARDS** Outstanding Grad Student, Fla State Univ, 98; Gorman Scholar Awd, Fla State Univ, 95; Outstanding Grad Sen, N Mich Univ, 94. **MEMBERSHIPS** Nat Asn of Soc Workers; Coun on Soc Work Educ; Soc for Soc Work Res; Baccurleate Prog Dir Asn. **RESEARCH** Welfare reform; Child welfare; Caregiving. **SELECTED PUBLICATIONS** Auth, "To Grandmas house we go: Providing services to grandparents raising grandchildren in rural America," in Conference Proceedings: The Changing Face of Rural America, The 24th Annual National Institute on Social Work and Human Services in Rural America, 99; auth, "Getting the short end of the stick: Family caregivers, professional caregivers, and care receivers in rural America," n Conference Proceedings: The Changing Face of Rural America, The 24th Annual National Institute on Social Work and Human Services in Rural America, 99; auth, "Smoke and Mirrors: The shifting dependency of former rural welfare mothers," Rural Soc Work, in press. **CONTACT ADDRESS** Dept Soc Work, Auburn Univ, 7030 Haley Center, Auburn, AL 36830. **EMAIL** cashwswa@auburn.edu

CASILE, WILLIAM
PERSONAL Born 03/19/1948, Pittsburgh, PA, d, 2 children **DISCIPLINE** COUNSELING **EDUCATION** Duquesne Univ, BS, 70; Univ Pittsburgh, MEd, 72; PhD, 80. **CAREER** Asst Prof to Assoc Prof, Duquesne Univ, 80-. **HONORS AND AWARDS** Allegheny Sch Sci Educ and Tech Making Sci Work Awd, 98; Education Awd, West Oxfordshire, 97; Professional Adv Awd, 95; Quality Excellence Awd, ASSET Leadership Team, 94; Hunkle Foundation Fac Dev Awd, 93, 89, 87; President's Awd, Duquesne Univ, 91; Presidential Merit Increment Awd, Duquesne Univ, 91-92; Grant, Duquesne Univ, 88; Top Five Teacher Awd, Duquesne Univ, 87; Nat Distinguished Service Registry, 87. **MEMBERSHIPS** Allegheny Cty Coun Asn; PA Coun Asn; PA Asn for Spec in Group Work; PA Asn for Coun Educ & Supervisors; PA Asn for Multicultural Coun & Dev; Am Coun Asn; Asn for Coun Educ & Supervision; Asn for Spec in Group Work; Asn of Multicultural Coun & Dev; Am Sch Coun Asn; Chi Sigma Iota; Asn for Supervision and Curriculum Dev; PA Sci Teachers Asn; Nat Sci Teachers Asn. **RESEARCH** Continuing professional development for counselors; Supervision training; Relationships between organizational leadership and outcomes. **SELECTED PUBLICATIONS** Auth, "I traveled to Oxford--a kindred journey," Norham Centre for Leadership Studies Monograph, 94; co-auth, "Evaluation of 1995 implementation of continuous progress instruction in the Fox Chapel School District, Duquesne Univ, 96; auth, "A decade of expanding the network and nature of leadership," in Leadership in Schools: developments in the national curriculum, student achievement and community schools, Oxford, 98; co-auth, "Collaborative leadership and partnership management," in New directions for School Leadership, Jossey-Bass, 98. **CONTACT ADDRESS** Dept Coun, Duquesne Univ, 600 Forbes Ave, Pittsburgh, PA 15282-0001. **EMAIL** Casile@duq.edu

CASSARA, SHIRLEY
PERSONAL Born 12/04/1949, Brockton, MA, m, 1984, 2 children **DISCIPLINE** BEHAVIORAL SCIENCE **EDUCATION** Bard Col, BA, 71; NY Univ, MA, 73; Univ Mass at Amherst, EdD, 83. **CAREER** Prof, Bunker Hill Community Col, 74-; Certified Parent Effectiveness Training Instr, 90-; adj prof, Wheelock Col Grad Sch, 90-. **HONORS AND AWARDS** Master Teacher Awd, Nat Inst for Staff and Organizational Development, 85; Master Presenter Awd, Nat Inst for Staff and Organizational Development, 98; Dedicated Service Awd, Bunker Hill Community Col, 99. **MEMBERSHIPS** Am Psychotherapy Asn, Int Soc of Infant Studies, Am Counseling Asn. **RESEARCH** Classroom Assessment, Teaching Improvement Strategies, Stress Management, Temperament Styles. **SELECTED PUBLICATIONS** Auth, Power of Relaxation (audio), 92; co-ed, Teaching for Our Times: A Journal of Good Teaching Practice, 99. **CONTACT ADDRESS** Dept Behav Sci, Bunker Hill Comm Col, 250 Rutherford Ave, Boston, MA 02129. **EMAIL** profcassara@hotmail.com

CASTENELL, LOUIS ANTHONY, JR.
PERSONAL Born 10/20/1947, New York, NY, m **DISCIPLINE** EDUCATION **EDUCATION** Xavier Univ of LA, BA Educ, 68; Univ of Wis Milwaukee, MS Educ Psych, 73; Univ of IL, PhD Educ Psych, 80. **CAREER** Univ of WI-Milwaukee, academic adv 1971-74; Xavier Univ, dir alumni affairs 1974-77, asst prof 1980-81, dean, Cincinnati Educ Col, 90; dean grad sch; Univ of Cincinnati, dean, Col of Educ; dean, Univ of Georgia Col of Educ, 99. **HONORS AND AWARDS** Craig Rice Scholarship Xavier Univ, 68; Fellowship Univ of IL, 77-78; Fel Natl Inst of Mental Health, 78-80; over 15 published works on aspects of educ; Am Educational Studies Asn, Critic's Choice Awds, 93; Presidential Awd, Networking Together Inc, 96; Critic's Choice Awd from the Am Educ Stud Asn. **MEMBERSHIPS** Human Rights and Academic Freedom AERA; Ronald McDonald House of La; NAACP; Children Museum of Cincinnati; Nat Asn of State Universities and Land Grant Col; Am Asn for Higher Educ. **RESEARCH** Race and diversity in testing, learning, social growth and other aspects of educ. **CONTACT ADDRESS** Univ of Cincinnati, Athens, GA 30602.

CASTILLO, ED
PERSONAL Born 08/25/1947, San Jacinto, CA, d, 2 children **DISCIPLINE** AMERICAN ANTHROPOLOGY, U.S. HISTORY **EDUCATION** Univ Calif, Riverside, BA, 69; Univ Calif, Berkeley, MA, 74, PhD, 77. **CAREER** Prof & dept chmn, Native Am Stud, 72- , Univ Calif, Berkeley, Univ Calif, Santa Cruz, Sonoma State Univ. **HONORS AND AWARDS** Outstanding Fac of the Year, 74; Fac Meritorious Performance Awd, 89-90; Awd for Academic Excellence, 98; listed in Who's Who, 99. **MEMBERSHIPS** Am Indian Hist Soc; Am Hist Soc, Pacific Branch; Am Indian and Alaskan Native Prof Asn. **RESEARCH** California Indian history; North American Indian history. **SELECTED PUBLICATIONS** Auth, History of the Impact of Euro-American Exploration and Settlement on the Indians of California, and, Recent Secular Movements Among California Indians, 1900-1973, in Handbook of North American Indians, v.8, California, Smithsonian Inst, 78; coauth, A Bibliography of California Indian History, Ballena, 78; contribur, The Missions of California: A Legacy of Genocide, American Indian Historical Society, 87; auth, The Ethnography and History of the California Indians, in Champagne, ed, The Native North American Indian Almanac, Gale, 94; auth, The Language

of Race Hatred, in Bean, ed, The Ohlone Past and Present: Native Americans of the San Francisco Bay Region, Ballen, 94; coauth, Indians, Franciscans and Spanish Colonization: The Impact of Franciscan Missionaries on the Indians of California, Univ New Mexico, 95; auth, Mission Indian Federation: Protecting Tribal Soverignty, 1919-1967, in Davis, ed, The Encyclopedia of Native Americans in the 20th Century, Garland, 95; auth, California Overview, in Encyclopedia of Native American Tribes, Gale, 98; auth, The Indians of Southern California, Bellerophon, 98. **CONTACT ADDRESS** Sonoma State Univ, 1501 E Colati Blvd, Rohnert Park, CA 94928.

CASTONGUAY, LOUIS G.
PERSONAL Born 10/14/1959, Vaudreuil, QC, Canada, m, 1992 **DISCIPLINE** PSYCHOLOGY **EDUCATION** Univ Sherbrooke, BA, 81; Univ Montreal, MPs, 84; SUNY PhD, 92. **CAREER** Assoc prof, Pa State Univ. **HONORS AND AWARDS** Sigma Xi, 90; Winner, Grad Student Paper Competition, Am Psychol Assoc, 93; Early Career Contribution Awd, 98; Jack D Krasner Mem Awd, 98. **MEMBERSHIPS** Am Psychol Assoc; Soc for Psychotherapy Res; Soc for the Explor of Psychotherepy Integration. **RESEARCH** Psychotherapy process and outcome. **SELECTED PUBLICATIONS** Coauth, "Integrating interpersonal assessment and adult attachment using SASB", Europ J of Psychol Assessment 15, (99): 206-220; coauth, "Reflecting on current challenges and new directions in psychotherapy: What can be learn from dialogues between clinicians, researchers, and policy makers?", J of Clinical Psychol/In Session 55, (99): 1407-1413; coauth, "Contemporary challenges and new directions in psychotherapy: An introduction", J of Clinical Psychol/In Session 55 (99): 1321-1323; coauth, "Assessing the role of treatment manuals: Have they become necessary but non-sufficient ingredients of change?", Clinical Psychol: Sci and Practice 6, (99): 449-455; coauth, "Psychotherapy for depression: Current and future directions in research, theory, practice, and public policy", J of Clinical Psychol/In Session 55 (99): 1347-1370); coauth, "Compulsive checking behaviors in generalized anxiety disorder", J of Clinical Psychol (forthcoming); coauth, "Psychotherapy Research", Encyclopedia of Psychology and Neuroscience, eds, W.E. Craighead and C.B. Nemeroff, Wiley, (NY), (forthcoming), coauth, "Les mecanismes de base en psychotherapie", Psychiatrie clinique: Approche bio-psycho-sociale, eds P. Lalonde and F. Grunberg, Gaetan Morin, (forthcoming); auth, "Training in Psychotherapy Integration: Introduction to current efforts and future visions" and "A common factors approach to psychotherapy training", J of Psychotherapy Integration, (forthcoming); auth, **CONTACT ADDRESS** Dept Psychol, Pennsylvania State Univ, Univ Park, 308 Moore, University Park, PA 16802.

CASTRICANO, JODEY
DISCIPLINE CULTURAL STUDIES **EDUCATION** Simon Fraser, BA, MA; British Columbia, PhD. **CAREER** Asst Prof **RESEARCH** Cultural studies, feminist theory, queer theory, psychoanalysis, poststructuralism, contemporary Am lit, the gothic, popular culture. **SELECTED PUBLICATIONS** Auth, If a Building Is a Senctence, So Is A Body: Kathy Acker's Empire of the Senseless and Postcolonial Gothic; Rude Awakenings--or, What happens When a Lesbian Reads the Hieroglyphics of Sleep in Djuna Barnes Nightwood; West Coast Line, 94. **CONTACT ADDRESS** Dept of English, Wilfrid Laurier Univ, 75 University Ave W, Waterloo, ON, Canada N2L 3C5. **EMAIL** jcastric@wlu.ca

CASTRO, RUSSELL A.
PERSONAL Born 09/25/1957, Galveston, TX, m, 1998, 1 child **DISCIPLINE** SOCIOLOGY **EDUCATION** Univ Colo at Boulder, BA, 87; MA, 91. **CAREER** Lectr, Univ Colo, 91; ed asst, Royal Dutch Acad of Sci, 91-92; lectr, Delgado Community Col, 93-94; res assoc, Xavier Univ, 94-95; adj prof, Southeastern La Univ, 96-. **HONORS AND AWARDS** Listed in Who's Who Among America's Teachers 00: America's Best Students Select America's Best Teachers, 00. **MEMBERSHIPS** Nat Mortar Board Soc, Soc for the Study of Soc Problems, Am Sociol Asn, New Orleans Lit Renaissance Project. **RESEARCH** Occupational Displacement, Retirement's Impact on Identity, Comparative Policy Analysis, Emergent Dynamics of Cyber Communication. **SELECTED PUBLICATIONS** Auth, "The Rise and Fall of NORML as a Professional Social Movement Organization: A Case Study Exploration Through Collective Action Mapping," The Int J on Drug Policy 2.3 (90); auth, "Substance Control policy Recommendations," in State of Am Soc, ed. Suzanne K. Steinmetz (IN: Family Res Inst, 91); auth, "Behind Closed Doors at the Mouse Cafe: A Subcultural Enclave of Coffee Shop Suppliers in Amsterdam," Contemporary Drug Problems 22.3 (95); auth, "Drug Use, Cultures and Subcultures," in Encyclopedia of Criminology and Deviant Behavior, ed. Clifton D. Bryant (London & NY: Taylor & Francis Pub Co., 00). **CONTACT ADDRESS** Dept Sociol, Soc Work & Criminal Justice, Southeastern Louisiana Univ, 500 Western Ave, Campus Box 686, Hammond, LA 70402-0686. **EMAIL** rcastro@selu.edu

CATALANO, RICHARD F.
DISCIPLINE SOCIOLOGY **EDUCATION** Univ Wisconsin, BA, 73; Univ Washington, MA, 76; PhD, 82. **CAREER** Assoc dir, 87-; prof, Univ Washington, 95-. **HONORS AND AWARDS** Outstand Contr Excell Awd, 96. **MEMBERSHIPS** ASC; SSC; CSWE; SPR. **RESEARCH** Positive and problem development among youth; Etiology and prevention; cultural similarities and differences in etiology and program effects. **SELECTED PUBLICATIONS** Coauth, The nature of school bullying: A cross-national perspective, Routledge (NY), 99; coauth, Parents who care: A step-by-step guide for families with teens, Developmental Res and Prog (Seattle), 97; coauth, "Delinquent behavior," in Ambulatory Pediatrics, eds. M Green, RJ Weitzman (Philadelphia: WB Saunders, 99); coauth, "The contribution of gang membership to delinquency beyond delinquent friends," in Data Analysis for Criminal Justice and Criminology, eds. J McKean, B Byers (Allyn & Bacon, 98); coauth, "Effectiveness of primary prevention interventions with high-risk youth," in Cost benefit/cost effectiveness research of drug abuse prevention: Implications for programming and policy, eds. WJ Bukoski, RI Evans (Rockville, MD: National Institute on Drug Abuse, 98); coauth, "Benefits and costs of a family-focused methadone treatment and drug abuse prevention program: Preliminary findings," in Cost benefit/cost effectiveness research of drug abuse prevention: Implications for Programming and policy, eds. WJ Bukoski, RI Evans (Rockville, MD: Nat Inst Drug Abuse, 98); coauth, "Comparative study on bullying: US country report," in The nature of school bullying: A cross-national perspective, eds. Y Morita, PK Smith, RF Catalano, J Junger-Tax, D Olweus, P Slee (NY: Routledge, 99); coauth, "Comparative study on bullying: Canada. country report, in The nature of school bullying: A cross-national perspective, eds. Y Morita, PK Smith, RF Catalano, J Junger-Tax, D Olweus, P Slee (NY: Routledge, 99). **CONTACT ADDRESS** School of Social Work, Univ of Washington, PO Box 354900, Seattle, WA 98195-4900. **EMAIL** catalano@u.washington.edu

CATANIA, A. CHARLES
PERSONAL Born 06/22/1936, New York, NY, m, 1962, 2 children **DISCIPLINE** PSYCHOLOGY **EDUCATION** Columbia Col, AB (NYork State Regents Scholarship, Phi Beta Kappa, Highest Honors with Distinction in Psychology), 57; Columbia Univ, MA, 58; Harvard Univ, PhD (Psychology), 61. **CAREER** Teaching asst, Columbia Col, 56-58; res tech, Bell Telephone Labs, summer 58; res fel in Psychol, Harvard Univ, 60-62; Sr Pharmacologist, Smith Kline and French Labs, 62-64; asst prof, 64-66, assoc prof, 66-69, prof and dept chair, Univ Col of Arts and Science, New York Univ, 69-73; prof, Univ of MD, Baltimore County, 73-; prof fel, Univ Wales, 86-87, vis res fel, 89-; vis prof, Keio Univ, Tokyo, Japan, July 92. **HONORS AND AWARDS** Nat Science Found fel, 58-60; British Coun fel, 86; James McKeen Cattell Sabbatical Awd, 86-87; Fulbright Sr Res fel (US-UK), 86-87; Outstanding contrib to Behavior Analysis, Northern CA Asn for Behavior Analysis, 90; Outstanding Scientific Contributions to Psychology Awd, MD Psychol Asn, 93; The Don F Hake Basic/Applied Res Awd, div 25 of the Am Pyschol Asn, 98; Master lect, Animal Learning and Behavior, Am Psychol Asn, 98. **MEMBERSHIPS** Soc for the Experimental Analysis of Behavior (Pres, 66-67, 81-83; bd of dirs, 66-74, 78-86, 87-95, 97-2005); Am Psychol Soc (Fellow, div 3, 25, 28; Distinguished vis prog, Div 25, Experimental Analysis of Behavior, prog co-chair, 76, pres, 76-79, exec comm, 81-84, Pres elect, 96-98); Eastern Psychol Soc; Asn for Behavioral Analysis (pres, 81-84, chair pub bd, 91-95; Language Origins Soc (prog chair, 96 Annual Meeting, bd of dird, 97); Am Psychol Asn (charter member and fel); Phi Beta Kappa; Psychonomic Soc; Sigma Xi. **RESEARCH** Analysis of behavior; experimental psychology; psychology of learning; language and verbal behavior. **SELECTED PUBLICATIONS** Ed, Contemporary Research in Operant Behavior, Scott Foresman, 68, Spanish ed, Editorial Trillas, 80; ed with T A Brigham, Handbook of Applied Behavior Analysis: Social and Instructional Processes, Irvington, 78; ed with S Harnad, The Selection of Behavior: the Operant Behaviorism of B F Skinner, Cambridge Univ Press, 88; ed with P N Hineline, Variations and Selections: An Anthology of Reviews from the Journal of the Experimental Analysis of Behavior, Bloomington, IN: Soc for the Experimental Analysis of Behavior, 96; auth, Learning, 4th ed, Prentice-Hall, 98; numerous other publications (about 175 in all). **CONTACT ADDRESS** Dept of Psychology, Univ of Maryland, Baltimore County, 10545 Rivulet Row, Columbia, MD 21044-2420. **EMAIL** catania@umbc.edu

CAUGHEY, JOHN L.
DISCIPLINE ETHNOGRAPHY AND AMERICAN STUDIES **EDUCATION** Harvard Col, BA, 63; Univ PA, MA, 67, PhD, 70. **CAREER** Am Stud Dept, Univ Md **RESEARCH** Ethnographic, comp investigation of contemp cult as syst of meaning. **SELECTED PUBLICATIONS** Auth, Imaginary Social Worlds: A Cultural Approach, Univ Nebr Press, 84; On the Anthropology of America, Epilogue to Symbolizing America, Univ Nebr Press, 86; Gina as Steven: The Social and Cultural Dimensions of a Media Relationship, Visual Anthrop Rev, Special issue on Culture/Media, 94; Imaginary Social Relationships, Media Jour: Reading and Writing About Popular Culture, Allyn and Bacon, 95; Personal Identity on Faanakkar, Pieces of The Personality Puzzle: Readings in Theory and Research, W W Norton and Co, 97. **CONTACT ADDRESS** Am Stud Dept, Univ of Maryland, Col Park, Taliferro Hall, College Park, MD 20742-8821. **EMAIL** jc29@umail.umd.edu

CHAMBLISS, WILLIAM J.
PERSONAL Born 12/09/1933, Buffalo, NY, m, 1988, 3 children **DISCIPLINE** SOCIOLOGY **EDUCATION** UCLA, BA, 55; Ind Univ, PhD, 62. **CAREER** Visiting Prof, Univ Wisc, 66-67; Visiting Prof, Univ Ibadan, 69-70; Visiting Prof, Univ Uppsala, 71; Visiting Prof, London School of Economics & Polit Sci, 70-71; Visiting Prof, Univ Oslo, 74-75; Visiting Prof, Univ Stockholm, 75-76; Visiting Prof, Univ Mo, 78; Prof, George Washington Univ. **HONORS AND AWARDS** Major achievement Awd, Am Soc of Criminol, 95; Bruce Smith Sr. Awd, Acad of Criminal Justice Sci, 86; Distinguished Scholarship, Am Sociol Asn, 85; Fulbright Res Fel, 89-90; Augustus Scholar, Nat Ctr on Inst and alternatives. **MEMBERSHIPS** Am Soc Criminol, Soc for the Study of Racial Problems. **RESEARCH** Crime; Law and Politics. **SELECTED PUBLICATIONS** Auth, Power, Politics and Crime, Westview Press, 99; auth, sociology: second Ed, Longman, 97; co-auth, Sociology, Harper/Collins, 95; co-ed, Making Law: The State, Law and Structural contradictions, Ind Univ Press, 94; co-auth, Criminal Law, Criminology and Criminal Justice: a Case Book, Menlo Park, 90; auth, On the Take: From Petty Crooks to Presidents, Ind Univ Press, 89; auth, Exploring Criminology, Macmillan, 88. **CONTACT ADDRESS** Dept Sociol, The George Washington Univ, 2035 H St NW, Washington, DC 20052-0001.

CHANDLER, THEODORE A.
PERSONAL Born 05/21/1932, Indianapolis, IN, m, 1962, 3 children **DISCIPLINE** PSYCHOLOGY **EDUCATION** Northwestern Univ, BS, 54; Univ Chicago, MA, 57; Univ Mich, PhD, 71. **CAREER** Prof, Kent State Univ, 71-. **HONORS AND AWARDS** Phi Delta Kappa Awd, Who's Who in Am Educ, Who's Who in Ohio, Who's Who in the Midwest, Men of Achievement, Leaders in Educ, Who's Who Among Human Service Professionals, Dictionary of Intl Biography. **MEMBERSHIPS** Am Psychol Asn, Am Educ Res Asn, Am Soc of Clinical Hypnosis **RESEARCH** Motivation and learning, Attributional processes. **SELECTED PUBLICATIONS** Auth, "The human services training effectiveness postcard: A tool for research and evaluation of human services training," Professional Development, (99): 43-56; auth, "Empowering Teachers, Empowering Principals," NASSP Bulletin, (99): 117-118; auth, "Use of reframing as a classroom strategy," Education, (98): 365-367; auth, "The mind-body connection: Beyond tradition," Administrative Radiology Journal, (98): 8-9; auth, "Self esteem and causal attributions," Genetic, Social, and General Psychology Monographs, (97): 479-491; auth, "Managing motivation," Small Business News, (97): 42; auth, "Semantic differential comparisons of attributions and dimensions among respondents from seven nations," Psychological Reports, (96): 747-758; auth, "Techniques for optimizing MRI relaxation and visualization," Administrative Radiology Journal, (96): 16-18; auth, "Undermining the Academy," College Student Journal, (96): 54-56; auth, "The relationship among attributions, divergent thinking and retention of nonsense syllables and non-related words," Psychology in the Schools, (93): 91-96. **CONTACT ADDRESS** School Psychol, Kent State Univ, PO Box 5190, Kent, OH 44242-0001.

CHANDLER, THEODORE ALAN
PERSONAL Born 09/19/1949, St. Louis, MO **DISCIPLINE** EDUCATION **EDUCATION** Northwest MO State Univ, BS 1973; Southern IL Univ Edwardsville, MA 1980; Univ of FL, PhD 1986. **CAREER** Cleveland HS, secondary teacher 76-79; New Student Life-SIU Edwardsville, consul 80; SIU Edwardsville, grad teaching asst 79-80; Univ of FL, grad teaching asst 80-83; Sex Equity in Voc Ed, project asst, 83; FL Keys Comm Coll, prof & ea/co coord 83-90, Arts & Sciences Division, Chmn, 90-. **HONORS AND AWARDS** Top Ranked Paper Competitive FL Speech Comm Assn 1982; Outstanding Young Men of Amer Jaycees 1984; Teaching Excellence Awds SIU-E, 1980, Univ of FL, 1983; Outstanding Faculty Member Phi Theta Kappa 1989-90. **MEMBERSHIPS** Mem FL Speech Comm Assn 1981-; mem Speech Comm Assn 1980-; mem Southern Speech Comm Assn 1981-; mem FL Assn of Equal Oppor Profs 1983-; mem Tennessee Williams Fine Arts Ctr Founders Soc, Key West, 1985-; board of directors Helpline Inc, secretary 1992-93, president 1993-94; AIDS Help Inc, volunteer, 1988-93. **CONTACT ADDRESS** Arts & Sci Div, Florida Keys Comm Col, 5901 W College Rd, Key West, FL 33040.

CHANG, EDWARD T.
PERSONAL Born 05/06/1956, Inchon, Korea, m, 1985, 1 child **DISCIPLINE** ETHNIC STUDIES **EDUCATION** UC Berkeley, PhD, 90; Asian American Studies, MA, Univ Calif at Los Angeles; Sociology, BA, UC Berkeley, 82. **CAREER** Asst Prof, Calif State Univ, Pomona, Ethnic and Women's Studies, 90-92; Asst Prof, UC Riverside, Ethnic Studies, 92-98; Assoc Prof, UC Riverside, Ehnic Studies, 98-. **HONORS AND AWARDS** President's Awd, Republic of Korea, 95; John Anson Ford Awd, LA County Human Relations Commision, 95; Education Awd, UCLAC higher education, 95; Distinguished Korean Am Awd, SUNY at Stony Brook, 93. **MEMBERSHIPS** Association for Asian American Studies; National Association for Ethnic Studies. **RESEARCH** Korean-Black Relations; LA Civil Unrest; Multiracial Coalition Building; Korean American Studies. **SELECTED PUBLICATIONS** Auth, Edward T. Chang and Jeanette Diaz-Veizades, "Ethnic Peace in the American City: Building Community in Los Angeles and Beyond, New York: NYU Press, 99; auth, Edward T. Chang and Janet C. Chang, "Following the Footsteps of Korean Americans, Los Angeles: The Pacific Institute for Peacemaking, 95;

auth, Edward T. Chang and Russell Leong, Los Angeles-Struggles Toward Multiethnic Community, Seattle: Univ of Washington Press, 95; auth, Angie Chung and Edward, "Third World Liberation to Multiple Oppression Politics: A Contemporary Approach to Interethnic Coalitions," Social Justice, 99; auth, "New Urban Crisis: Korean-African American Relations" in Koreans in the Hood: Conflict with African Americans, Baltimore: Johns Hopkins Univ Press, 99. **CONTACT ADDRESS** Dept Ethnic Studies, Univ of California, Riverside, Riverside, CA 92521-0001. **EMAIL** edch@pop.ucr.edu

CHANG, MEI-I
PERSONAL Born 03/05/1963, Taipei, Taiwan, s **DISCIPLINE** PSYCHOLOHY **EDUCATION** Indiana State Univ, Psy D, 96. **CAREER** Asst prof, Calif Sch of Prof Psychol, 94-. **HONORS AND AWARDS** Ind State Univ Scholarship, 89-93; Washington Univ Scholarship, 81-82, 83-87; Washington Univ Dean's List, 86-87. **MEMBERSHIPS** Am Psychol Asn, Wellesley Center for Women, Asn Women in Psychol, Calif Psychol Asn, San Diego Psychol Asn. **RESEARCH** Multicultural identity development, resilience trauma, women's issues. **SELECTED PUBLICATIONS** Coauth with A. S. Kaufamn, "An empirical study of resilience in battered women," manuscript submitted (98); coauth with M. Thatcher, "Women's resilience program: From concept ro reality," San Diego Psychol Asn Newsl, 8(9), 1-4 (Oct 99); coauth, with A. S. Kaufman, "A conceptual and empirical approach toward understanding of resilience in battered women," Violence Against Women (in Press); coauth with Y. Kawahara, "Asian American Psychology in the 21st Century: Southern Calif AAPA Conf, " Asian Am Psychol (Feb 2000). **CONTACT ADDRESS** Dept Psychol, California Sch of Professional Psychology, San Diego, 6160 Cornerstone E, San Diego, CA 92121-3725. **EMAIL** mchang@mail.cspp.edu

CHANG, PATRICIA
PERSONAL Born 03/18/1962, San Francisco, CA, m, 1991, 3 children **DISCIPLINE** SOCIOLOGY **EDUCATION** Univ Calif, BA, 82; Stanford Univ, MA, 87; PhD, 93. **CAREER** Post Doct, Center for Social and Religious Research, 93-95; Researcher, Inst for Church Life Notre Dame, 95-96; Asst Prof, Univ Notre Dame, 97-. **MEMBERSHIPS** Am Sociol Asn, Asn for the Sociol of Relig, Soc for the Sci Study of Relig, Relig Res Asn. **RESEARCH** Book Manuscript: The Politics of moral order; Institutional and environmental effects on decision making in Protestant denominations. **SELECTED PUBLICATIONS** Auth, "Credentialism Across Creeds: clergy Education and Stratification Across Protestant Denominations," Journal for the Scientific Study of Religion, forthcoming; auth, "Crowded Pulpits: observations and Explanations of the Clergy Over Supply in the Protestant Churches, 1950-1993," Journal for the Scientific Study of Religion, (99): 398-410; auth, "Effects of Marital Status on Clergy Earnings," Sociology of Religion, 99; auth, Clergywomen: An Uphill Calling, Westminster Press, 98; auth, "Female Clergy in the Contemporary Protestant Church: A Current Assessment," Journal for the Scientific Study of Religion, (97): 565-573; auth, "In Search of A Pulpit: The Effects of Sex Differences and Temporal Contexts on the Transition to First Clergy Job," Journal for the Scientific Study of Religion, (97): 614-627; auth, "Church-Agency Relationships in the Black Community," Nonprofit and Voluntary Sector Quarterly, (94): 91-105; auth, "The International Labor Organization and the Welfare State: Institutional Effects on national Welfare Spending, 1960-1980," International Organizations, (93): 235-263. **CONTACT ADDRESS** Dept Sociol, Univ of Notre Dame, 25 O Shaugnssy Hall, Notre Dame, IN 46556. **EMAIL** chang.23@nd.edu

CHAO, PAUL K.
PERSONAL Born 12/26/1919, Cheng-ting, China, m, 1972 **DISCIPLINE** ANTHROPOLOGY **EDUCATION** Cambridge Univ, Eng, M Lit, 67; New York Univ, PhD, 36. **CAREER** Maryland State Col, Univ Maryland, 67-69; William Patterson Univ, 69-90; Prof Emer. **HONORS AND AWARDS** Pacific Cultural Found Gnt. **MEMBERSHIPS** RAI; Mem Fitzwilliam Coll; Mem Needham Res Inst. **RESEARCH** Chinese culture; family; geography; myth and folklore. **SELECTED PUBLICATIONS** Auth, Women Under Communism: Family in Russia and China, General Hall Inc (NY), 77; auth, Chinese Kinship, Routledge (London) 84; auth, The Changing Geography of China, Commercial Press (Hong Kong), 90; auth, Totemism and Taboo in China, Hsing-Hua Pub (NY), 98; transl, "La Sorcellerie," forthcoming. **CONTACT ADDRESS** Dept Anthropology, William Paterson Univ of New Jersey, 300 Pompton Rd, Wayne, NJ 07470.

CHAPMAN, JUDITH G.
PERSONAL Born 10/22/1949, Kane, PA, m, 1971, 2 children **DISCIPLINE** PSYCHOLOGY **EDUCATION** St Bonaventure Univ, BA, 71; MA, 75; Syracuse Univ, PhD, 87. **CAREER** Asst Prof to Full Prof and Dean of Col of Arts and Sci, Saint Joseph's Univ, 88-. **HONORS AND AWARDS** Merit Awd, Saint Joseph's Univ, 94; Sigma Xi, Sci Res Soc, 89; Delta Epsilon sigma, Nat Scholastic Honor Soc, 70; Psi Chi, Nat Honor Soc, 69. **MEMBERSHIPS** Am Psychol Asn, Am Psychol Soc, Eastern Psychol Asn, Sigma Xi, Soc for Personality and Soc Psychol, Soc for the Advancement of Soc Psychol. **RESEARCH** Group processes: social behavior in interdependent situations; small group behavior, with a special interest in the application of self-attention theory to describe the effects of the group on the individual; Blushing: the relationship of self-consciousness and social anxiety to blushing propensity and awareness of blushing and the impact that awareness has on psychological and physiological responses; Volunteerism: the motivational bases of volunteerism and relationships between motives and satisfaction with volunteer service; Media Influenc4e: the impact of the media on perceptions of the relative importance of social issues, with special interest in how the media defines 'reality' with regard to social biases and prejudices. **SELECTED PUBLICATIONS** Auth, Educating students to make a difference: community based service learning, Haworth Press, 99; auth, "Collegiate service-learning: Motives underlying volunteerism and satisfaction with volunteer service," Journal of Prevention and Intervention in the Community, (99): 19-33; auth, "An Introduction to community-based service-learning," Journal of Prevention and Intervention in the Community, (99): 1-3; auth, "Faculty and student participation and perceptions of service-learning outcomes," Journal of Prevention and Intervention in the Community, (90: 183-196; auth, "Can the media create public opinion? A social identity approach," Current directions in Psychological Science, (99): 152-155; auth, "Social value orientations and decisions to take proenvironmental action," Journal of Applied Social Psychology, (98): 675-697; auth, "Service learning and the carative treatment model," Journal of Continuing Higher Education, (97): 34-38; auth, "Motivational Bases of volunteerism and Satisfaction with Volunteer Service: A Collegiate Sample," in Service-Learning: Linking Academics and the Community, 96; auth, "Motivational loss in small task groups: Free-riding on a cognitive task," Genetic, Social, and General Psychology Monographs, (93): 55-73. **CONTACT ADDRESS** Col of Arts & Sci, Saint Joseph's Univ, 5600 City Ave, Philadelphia, PA 19131.

CHASE HANKINS, JUNE
PERSONAL Born 08/13/1944, Wichita Falls, TX, m, 1969, 1 child **DISCIPLINE** AFRICAN AMERICAN WOMEN NOVELISTS **EDUCATION** Southwestern Univ, BA, Univ AR, MA; TX A&M Univ, PhD. **CAREER** Southwest Tex State Univ **HONORS AND AWARDS** NEH Grant; Two NEH Summer Inst Grants. **MEMBERSHIPS** Soc for Tech Commun; Toni Morrison Soc. **RESEARCH** T. Morrison. **SELECTED PUBLICATIONS** Auth, Making Use of the Literacy Debate. **CONTACT ADDRESS** Southwest Texas State Univ, 601 University Dr, San Marcos, TX 78666-4604. **EMAIL** jh20@swt.edu

CHATTOPADHYAY, ARPITA
PERSONAL Born 09/12/1958, Bombay, India, m, 1986 **DISCIPLINE** SOCIOLOGY **EDUCATION** Calcutta Univ, BSc, 79; Delhi Univ, MSc, 82; Brown Univ, PhD, 97. **CAREER** Asst prof, Kansas State Univ, 98-. **HONORS AND AWARDS** Population Coun Fel; UN Develop Prog Fel. **MEMBERSHIPS** Am Sociol Assoc; Population Assoc of Am; Int Union for the Sci Study of Population. **RESEARCH** Demography, Inequality, gender role/differentials, migration. **SELECTED PUBLICATIONS** Auth, "Work or Family: Incorporating Rural Women in the Urban Labor Markets of Malaysia", PRB Fel Prog Res Paper Series, (Washington, DC), 96; auth, "Family Migration and the Economic Status of Women in Malaysia", Int Migration Rev 31.2 (97): 338-352; auth, "Gender, Migration and Career Trajectories in Malaysia", Demography, 35.3, (98): 335-344; coauth, "Changes in Familial Support for the Elderly in Taiwan: 1963-1992", J of Comp Fam Studies 30.3 (99): 523-537; auth, "Gender Differences in the Socioeconomic Outcome of Family Migration: the Role of Family Decision Making Versus Labor Market Stratification", Gender Issues, (forthcoming). **CONTACT ADDRESS** Dept Sociol and Anthrop, Kansas State Univ, 207 Waters Hall, Manhattan, KS 66506.

CHEN, JOHN C.
PERSONAL Born 04/30/1949, Augusta, GA **DISCIPLINE** PSYCHIATRY **EDUCATION** Loma Linda Univ, MA 74; Claremont Grat Univ, PhD, 84; Univ Calif Los Angeles, JD, 87. **CAREER** Adj instr, philos, Fullerton Col, 89-90; adj asst prof, psychiat, Charles Drew Univ, 98- ; clinical asst prof, psychiat, Univ Calif, Los Angeles, 98- . **MEMBERSHIPS** APA; ABA; Soc for the Exploration of Psychothepy Integration; Chinese Hist Soc of Am; Calif Hist Soc. **RESEARCH** Philosophy of psychotherapy; Chinese American history; pediatric psychopharmacology. **SELECTED PUBLICATIONS** Auth, Reversal of Fortune: Images of America's Chinese, 1937-1944: The Dominance of California in DeWitt, ed, Readings in California Civilization, 4th ed. **CONTACT ADDRESS** 745 E Valley Blvd, PMB 120, San Gabriel, CA 91776. **EMAIL** jcchendrew@aol.com

CHEN, SHEYING
PERSONAL Born 11/20/1955, People's Republic of China, m, 1984, 2 children **DISCIPLINE** SOCIOLOGY, SOCIAL WORK **EDUCATION** Changsha Metallurgical Col, Undergrad Diploma, 80; Zhongshan Univ, Guangzhou, Postgrad Diploma, 86, MA, 88; Univ Calif at Los Angeles Sch Public Policy & Soc Res, MSW, 93, PhD, 96. **CAREER** Asst lectr, Hunan TV Univ, China, 80-84; instr, Univ Hong Kong, 90-91; lectr, City Univ of Hong Kong, 90-91; asst prof, Zhongshan Univ, Guangzhou, 86-92; asst prof, Calif State Univ, Los Angeles, 9/94 to 12/94; asst prof, Col of Staten Island, 96-. **HONORS AND AWARDS** Guangdong Soc Sci Res Excellence Awd, 89; Univ Hong Kong Scholarship, 89-90; Univ Hong Kong Res grants, 90, 91; Univ Calif at Los Angeles Fel, 91-96; Dr. Lo Kwee Seong Educ Found Awd, 92; The Gold Fel, 92-93; CSI Prog Develop Awds, 97, 98, 99, 2000; Public Policy and Development Strategy: An International Comparative Study, 98-2007; CCK Found Conf Travel grant, 99; Outstanding Prof Permanent Residency Awded by U. S. INS, 97; First Feliks Gross Endowment Awd for Outstanding Scholarly Achievement Awded by CUNY Acad, 98; honoree at Chancellor's Reception, CUNY, 98; honoree at President's Reception, CSI, 97, 98. **MEMBERSHIPS** Coun on Soc Work, Int Sociol Asn, Am Sociol Asn, Am Asn for Chinese Studies, Chinese Am Educ Res and Develop Asn, Am Fedn of Teachers, Nat Asn of Soc Workers, NY State Soc Work Educ Asn, UCLA Soc Welfare Alumni Asn, CUNY Acad for the Humanities and Scis, CUNY Prof Staff Congress, Chinese Asn of Sci and Technol, Guangdong Asn of Sociol, Guangdon Asn of Civil Affairs Admin. **RESEARCH** Comparative social policy and developmental strategy, urban issues and special economic zones, China; behavioral, social, and cross-cultural study of health/mental health practice, community care, family, and aging; and research methodology and technology; research in higher and professional education (interdisciplinary). **SELECTED PUBLICATIONS** Coauth with Y. Sui, et al, Social Work: A Teachers' Resource Book, Beijing: Civil Affairs Admin Col (in Chinese) (90); transl, Introducing Social Work and Social Work Education in China, Jinan: Shandong Sch of Civil Affairs Admin (91); coauth with Z. Wu and A. Li, Social Work, Beijing: Chinese Soc Press (in Chinese) (92); auth, Social Policy of the Economic State and Community Care in Chinese Culture: Aging, Family, Urban Change, and the Socialist Welfare Pluralism, Brookfield, VT: Ashgate (96); auth, Measurement and Analysis in Psychosocial Research: The Failing and Saving of Theory, Brookfield, Vt: Ashgate (97); auth, Mastering Research: A Guide to the Methods of Social and Behavioral Sciences, Chicago: Nelson-Hall Pubs (98); auth, "Community Care for the Elderly," Int Perspectives in Sociol (99); coauth with J. E. Lubben, "Social Networks and Health: Measurement and Analysis Issues," Advances in Medical Sociol (in press); coauth with Y. E. Lu and J. Mishne, Culturally Competent Clinical Practice: Theories, Models, and Intervention Guidelines, Northvale, NJ" Jason Aronson Pubs (forthcoming 2000); auth, Understanding Chinese Policy: A Rugged Path for a Nation (under review); coauth with Y. E. Lu and D. Lum, "Cultural Competency and Achieving Styles in Social Work: A Conceptual and Empirical Exploroation," J of Multicultural Soc Work (in press). **CONTACT ADDRESS** Dept Sociol & Psychol, Col of Staten Island, CUNY, 2800 Victory Blvd, Staten Island, NY 10314. **EMAIL** sheyingchen@yahoo.com

CHEN, YIWEI
PERSONAL Born 05/06/1968, China, m, 1995, 1 child **DISCIPLINE** PSYCHOLOGY **EDUCATION** Nanjung Univ, BA, 89; MA, 92; Ga Inst Technol, MS, 95; PhD, 98. **CAREER** Asst Prof, Bowling Green State Univ, 98-. **HONORS AND AWARDS** Grad Res Awd, Am Psychol Asn, 95; Grad Student Honoree, Ga Inst of Technol, 97. **MEMBERSHIPS** Am Psychol Asn, Gerontol Soc of Am. **RESEARCH** Social cognition and aging; Memory and aging; Mental control and health promotion. **SELECTED PUBLICATIONS** Co-auth, "Unwanted thought: age differences in the correction of social Judgments," Psychology and aging, in press; co-auth, "Evidence for content-specificity of causal attributions across the adult life span," Aging, Neuropsychology, and cognition, (98)L 241-263; auth, "Unwanted memory: Age differences in susceptibility to the influence of false information on social judgments," Ga Inst of Technol, 98; co-auth, 'Age differences in stages of attributional processing," Psychology and aging, (970: 694-703; co-auth, "Everyday problem solving across the adult life span: The influence of domain-specificity and cognitive appraisal," Psychology and Aging, (970: 684-693; co-auth, "Interrole conflict as a function of life stage, gender, and gender-related personality attributes," Sex Roles, (97): 155-174; co-auth, "Adaptive cognition and aging," Am Behavioral Scientist, (96): 231-248. **CONTACT ADDRESS** Dept Psychol, Bowling Green State Univ, 1001 E Wooster St, Bowling Green, OH 43403-0001.

CHESTNUT, DENNIS EARL
PERSONAL Born 05/17/1947, Green Sea, SC **DISCIPLINE** EDUCATION, PSYCHOLOGY **EDUCATION** East Carolina Univ, BA Psych & Soc 1965-69, MA Clinical Psych 1971; Univ of utah, Doc Prog Clin Psy 1971-74; NYork Univ, PhD Comm Psych 1982. **CAREER** Camden Co MH Ctr, psychological consul 1974-75; Neuse Mental Health Ctr, qual assurance consult 1975-77; Medgar Evers Coll CUNY, instr psychology 1979-81; East Carolina Univ, asst prof psychol 1974-, prof of psychol. **HONORS AND AWARDS** Outstanding Sr Dept of Sociology E Carolina Univ 1969; NIMH Fellow Univ Utah 1971-74; NIMH Fellow NY Univ 1978; NEH Summer Stipend for study of Southern Black Culture 1982. **MEMBERSHIPS** Pres Young People's Holiness Assoc United Pentecostal Holiness Churches of Amer Inc; Alpha Phi Alpha Frat; natl treas Assoc of Black Psychologists 1983-84; organizational liaison Assoc for Humanistic Psychology 1983-84; s regional rep

Assoc of Black Psychologists 1984-85; mem at large bd of dirs Assn for Humanistic Psychology 1984-85; reg rep NC Group Behavior Soc 1981-; vice bishop United Pentecostal Holiness Churches of Amer 1981-; pastor Mt Olive Holiness Church Tabor City NC 1984-; treas NC Assoc Black Psychologists; mem Pitt Cty Mental Health Assoc; pres NC Chap Assoc Black Psychologists 1986-87; dir Minority Affairs Assoc for Humanistic Psychology 1986-; co-chmn Natl Black Family Task Force of the Assoc of Black Psychologists. **CONTACT ADDRESS** Prof of Psychology, East Carolina Univ, Greenville, NC 27834.

CHIA, ROSINA
PERSONAL Born 02/24/1939, Hong Kong, China, d, 2 children **DISCIPLINE** PSYCHOLOGY **EDUCATION** Nat Taiwan Univ, BS, 62; Univ Mich, MA, 63; Univ Mich, PhD, 69. **CAREER** From Lectr to Prof, E Carolina Univ, 68-. **HONORS AND AWARDS** Phi Kappa Phi; Sigma Xi; Psi Chi; Omicron delta Kappa, Phi Beta Delta; Who's Who of Am Women; World's Who's Who of Women Educr; Who's Who of Sino-Am; World's Who's Who of Am Women; Outstanding Scientist of 20th-Century. **MEMBERSHIPS** IACCP, ICP, APA, AAAP. **RESEARCH** Cross-cultural research between Chinese and Americans. **SELECTED PUBLICATIONS** Coauth, "Differences in Source and Modes in Locus of Control for Chinese and Americans," in Psychol and Educ in the 21st-Century (Edmonton, Canada: ICP Pr, 97); coauth, "Differentiation in the Source of Internal Control for Chinese," J of Soc Behav and Personality 13 (98): 565-578; coauth, "Gender and Racial Differences in Mathematical Performance," J of Soc Psychol 139 (99): 677-689; coauth, "Social Interaction Differences Between Chinese and Americans," Psychol Beitrage 41 (99): 84-90. **CONTACT ADDRESS** Dept Psychol, East Carolina Univ, 1000 E 5th St, Greenville, NC 27858. **EMAIL** chiar@mail.ecu.edu

CHIANG, LINDA H.
PERSONAL Born Taipei, Taiwan, m, 1974, 2 children **DISCIPLINE** EDUCATION **EDUCATION** National Taiwan Normal Univ, BA, 72; Ball State Univ, MA, 87; EdD, 90. **CAREER** Instr, Ball State Univ, 90; Asst Prof of Education, Anderson Univ, 91-95; Assoc Prof of Education, Anderson Univ, 95-00; Prof of Education, Anderson Univ, 00. **HONORS AND AWARDS** Phi Tau Phi Scholastic Society, Secretary/Treasurer, Indiana Chinese Professional Assoc, Board member/Treasurer, Grants, both for internal and external for research. **MEMBERSHIPS** Midwest Educational Research Assoc, Indiana Chinese Professional Assoc. **RESEARCH** Multicultural education, Teaching styles/learning styles. **SELECTED PUBLICATIONS** Auth, Multicultural Education, 97; auth, Ethnic Thoughts and Behavior, 97; auth, Globalization and Confucianism in Chinese Society. **CONTACT ADDRESS** Dept Education, Anderson Univ, 1100 E 5th St, Anderson, IN 46012. **EMAIL** lhchiang@anderson.edu

CHILDS, FRANCINE C.
PERSONAL Born Wellington, TX, s **DISCIPLINE** EDUCATION **EDUCATION** Paul Quinn Col, BS 62; East Tex State Univ, MEd 70, EdD 75. **CAREER** Wiley Coll, dean of students 1970-72; East TX State Univ, part-time project dir special svcs/full time doctorial student 1972-74; Ohio Univ, prof afro-amer studies 1974-85, chair/prof afro-amer studies 1985-. **HONORS AND AWARDS** Paul Quin Coll Outstanding Alumni 1982; Individual Witness for Peace & Justice Awd 1985; OU Higher Educ Mgmt Develop Prog 1985-86; Outstanding Black Alumni Awd 1986; Fulbright Hays Scholarship 1986; Peace Corp Black Educator of Year, 1988-89; Anna Cooper Presidential Awd, 1992; Phenomenal Woman Awd, 1996; Marcus Foster Distinguished Educators Awd, 1996; Ohio University Honorary Alumni Awd, 1997. **MEMBERSHIPS** Local pres & advisor OH Univ Chap NAACP 1971-; mem League of Women Voters 1977-; educ chair OH Conf of Branches NAACP 1978-; natl coord Booker T Washington Alumni Assoc 1982-; prayer coord Athens Christian Women Club 1984-86; workshop leader Ohio Bapt Women Aux Convention 1985-; local conf host and prog-comm Natl Cncl on Black Studies 1987; National Alliance of Blk School Education; Mt Zion Baptist Ch, assoc pastor, currently. **CONTACT ADDRESS** Prof African Amer Studies, Ohio Univ, 302 Lindley, Athens, OH 45701.

CHIN, JEFFREY C.
DISCIPLINE ANTHROPOLOGY, SOCIOLOGY **EDUCATION** Univ Mich, PhD, 83. **CAREER** Prof, Ly Moyne Col, 83-. **HONORS AND AWARDS** Carnegie Nat Schol, 99-00. **MEMBERSHIPS** Am Soc Asn. **RESEARCH** Scholarship of teaching and learning, social psychology. **CONTACT ADDRESS** Dept Anthrop & Sociol, Le Moyne Col, 1419 Salt Springs Rd, Syracuse, NY 13214. **EMAIL** chin@mail.lemoyne.edu

CHIRAYATH, VERGHESE J.
PERSONAL Born 12/10/1941, Kerala, India, m, 1970, 2 children **DISCIPLINE** SOCIOLOGY **EDUCATION** Univ Scranton, BS, 66; Univ Ill, AM, 69; Cornell Univ, PhD, 74. **CAREER** From Instr to Assoc Prof, John Caroll Univ, 70-; Dir Hon Prog, John Caroll Univ, 83-85; Dir Int Studies Center, John Caroll Univ, 90-; Univ Ombudsperson, Racial Harassment, John Caroll Univ, 93-. **HONORS AND AWARDS** George Graulel Fac Fel, 77-78, 89-90; Cleveland Fac Fel, 89; Grant to establish Segundo Montes Mem Lect, Detroit Province Soc of Jesus, 89; Cert of Awd for Educ, Com on Cath Community Action, 92. **MEMBERSHIPS** Cleveland Coun on World Affairs, UN Asn, Greater Cleveland Chap, Nat Asn of For Student Affairs, N Central Sociol Asn, Soc for Appl Sociol. **RESEARCH** Corporate wrongdoing, the global economy, changing nature of immigration (both legal and illegal) and its impact on American society. **SELECTED PUBLICATIONS** Coauth, "Recent Immigrants to the U.S.: Their Assimilation," in American Ethnic Revival, ed. J. Klinton (Aurora, Ill: Soc Sci and Sociol Resources, 77); auth, "The Stranger in Our Midst," Caroll Bus Bul (Summer/Fall 77); auth, Domestic Implications of the New Immigration for the U.S. and Other Host Societies: Occupations and Services,: Book II, Res Inst on Immigration and Ethnic Studies, Smithsonian Inst (Wash DC), 79; auth, "Illegal Immigration: Economic and Legal Issues," Caroll Bus Bul (Spring 79); auth, "The Role of Budgetary Allocations in the United Way Agencies," in Politics, Public Policy, and the Voluntary Sector (Kansas City, MO: Asn of Voluntary Action Scholars, 87); auth, "Sociological Explanations of Unites States Assimilation: Some Insights from the Chinese Community in Cleveland," in The Western Reserve: Edited Readings, ed. Ruth P. Miller (Cleveland, OH: John Caroll Univ Dept of Sociol, 88); coauth, "Middle East Realpolitik, Nation-building, and the Palestine Question," Mich Sociol Rev (Fall 90). **CONTACT ADDRESS** Dept Sociol, John Carroll Univ, 20700 N Park Blvd, Cleveland, OH 44118. **EMAIL** vchirayath@jcu.edu

CHIRBAN, JOHN T.
PERSONAL Born 06/24/1951, Chicago, IL, m, 1992, 3 children **DISCIPLINE** PSYCHOLOGY **EDUCATION** Hellenic Col, BA, 73; Holy Cross Sch Theol, MDiv, 75; Harvard Univ, ThM, 76; ThD, 80; Boston Univ, PhD, 90. **CAREER** Prof of Psychol, Hellenic Col/Holy Cross Sch of Theol, 83-, chemn, Dept of Human Develop, 79-; adj instr, Mass Sch of Prof Psychol, 96-; clinical instr in Psychol, Harvard Medical Sch, 96-; instr, The Couples and Family Training Prog, The Cambridge Hospital, 97-98. **RESEARCH** Integration of medicine, psychology, and religion. **SELECTED PUBLICATIONS** Contribur, "Developmental stages in eastern orthodox christianity," Ken Wilbur, ed, Transformations of Consciousness, Boston: Shambala, New Sci Libr, Random House (86); auth, The Interactive-Relational Approach to Interviewing: Applications with Lucille Ball and B. F. Skinner, Ann Arbor, Mich: Univ Microfilms Int (91); ed and contribur, Health and Faith: Medical, Psychological and Religious Dimensions, Lanham, Md: Univ Press of Am (91); ed and contribur, Healing: When Medicine, Psychology and Religion Come Together, Brookline, Mass: Holy Cross Press (91); ed and contribur, Ethical Dilemmas: Crises in Faith and Modern Medicine, Lanham, Md: Univ Press of Am (94); ed and contribur, Clergy Sexual Misconduct: Orthodox Christian Perspectives, Brookline, Mass: Hellenic Col Press (94); ed and contribur, Personhood: Deepening the connections Between Body, Mind, and Soul, Westport, Ct: Greenwood Pub Group-Bergin & Garvey (96); auth, Interviewing in Depth: The Interactive-Relational Approach, Thousand Oaks, Calif: Sage Pubs (96); ed and contribur, Sickness or Sin: Spiritual Discernment and Differential Diagnosis (2000). **CONTACT ADDRESS** Dept Human Development, Hellenic Col, 50 Goddard Ave, Brookline, MA 02445. **EMAIL** jchirban@hms.harvard.edu

CHOPE, ROBERT C.
PERSONAL Born 04/06/1945, Detroit, MI, s **DISCIPLINE** PSYCHOLOGY **EDUCATION** Harvard Univ, BA, 67; San Francisco State Univ, MA, 68; Univ Minn, PhD, 74. **CAREER** Prof, San Francisco State Univ, 75-. **MEMBERSHIPS** APA, ACA, W Asn for Coun. **RESEARCH** Career psychology. **SELECTED PUBLICATIONS** Auth, Dancing Naked: Breaking through the emotional limits that keep you from the job you want, New Harbinger Pub, 00. **CONTACT ADDRESS** Dept Counseling, San Francisco State Univ, 1600 Holloway Ave, San Francisco, CA 94132. **EMAIL** rcchope@sfsu.edu

CHORAJIAN, LEVON
PERSONAL Born 08/09/1942, East Orange, NJ, m, 1979, 4 children **DISCIPLINE** SOCIOLOGY **EDUCATION** Temple Univ, BA, 64; Univ Mich, MA, 65; Brandeis Univ, PhD, 74. **CAREER** Prof, Univ of Mass Lowell, 70-; chairman, Zoryan Inst for Contemp Armenian Res and Documentation, 93-. **HONORS AND AWARDS** Fulbright Lectr, Armenian SSR, 86-87; Fulbright Lectr, Armenia, 96. **MEMBERSHIPS** Am Sociol Assoc; Soc for Armenian Studies; Soc for the Study of Social Problems. **RESEARCH** Political Sociology, Mass Media, Racial and Ethic Studies. **SELECTED PUBLICATIONS** Ed, Readings in Critical Sociology, 89; ed, The Hand in Your Pocket May Not Be Your Own, 91; coauth, The Caucasian Knot, 94; trans, of Armenia in Crisis, 95; coed, Studies in Comparative Genocide, 99; coauth, "Selling Supreme Court Nominees: The Case of Ruth Bader Ginsburg," Critical Sociol 23.3 (97):3-32. **CONTACT ADDRESS** Dept Sociol, Univ of Massachusetts, Lowell, 1 University Ave, Lowell, MS 01854.

CHRISLER, JOAN C.
PERSONAL Born 01/01/1953, Teaneck, NJ, m, 1976 **DISCIPLINE** PSYCHOLOGY **EDUCATION** Fordham Univ, BS, 75; Yeshiva Univ, MA; PhD, 86. **CAREER** Prof, Conn Col, 87-. **HONORS AND AWARDS** Florence L Denmark Nat Fac Advisor Awd, 00; Psi Chi; Fel, Am Psychol Soc, 99; Distinguished Publication Awd, Asn for Women in Psychol, 97; Christine Ladd Franklin Awd, AWP, 96; Fel, Am Psychol Asn, 94. **MEMBERSHIPS** Am Psychol Soc, Asn for Women in Psychol, Am Asn of Univ Prof, Soc for Menstrual Cycle Res, Soc for Beh Medicine, Intl Council of Psychol. **RESEARCH** Health psychology; Psychology of women and gender. **SELECTED PUBLICATIONS** Auth, "A comparison of eating attitudes and behaviors among adolescent and young women with type 1 diabetes and phenylketonuria," Journal of Developmental and Behavioral Pediatrics, in press; auth, "Does feminism serve a protective function against eating disorders?," Journal of Lesbian Studies, (99): 141-148; auth, "Innovative methods: Resources for research, teaching, and publishing," Psychology of Women quarterly, (99): 431-456; auth, "Women and weight: Gendered messages on magazine covers," Sex Roles, (99): 647-655; auth, "Psychometric evaluation of the Menstrual Joy Questionnaire," Psychological Reports, (99): 135-136; auth, "Menarche stories: Reminiscences of college students from Lithuania, Malaysia, Sudan, and the United States," Health Care for Women International, (98): 101-110; auth, "Is a little (psychiatric) knowledge a dangerous thing? The impact of premenstrual dysphoric disorder on perceptions of premenstrual women," Psychology of Women Quarterly, (97): 315-322; auth, "Body esteem, eating attitudes, and gender-role orientation in children," Current Psychology, (96): 235-248; auth, "Politics and women's weight," Feminism & Psychology, (96): 181-184; auth, "Body stereotyping and stigmatization of obese persons by first graders," Perceptual and Motor skills, (95): 909-910. **CONTACT ADDRESS** Dept Psychol, Connecticut Col, 270 Mohegan Ave, New London, CT 06320. **EMAIL** jcchr@conncoll.edu

CHRISTENSEN, JOHN E.
PERSONAL m, 3 children **DISCIPLINE** SPECIAL EDUCATION AND COMMUNICATION DISORDERS **EDUCATION** Dana Col, BS; Univ Nebr, Omaha, MS; Univ Kans, PhD. **CAREER** Asst prof, 80-86, dir, Speech-Lang-Hearing prog, 83-88, assoc prof, 86-, chair, dept Spec Educ & Commun Disorders, Univ Nebr, Omaha, 88-98; Acting Dean, College of Education, 98-99; Dean, College of Education, 99-00. **MEMBERSHIPS** Am Speech-Language-Hearing Assoc; Nebraska Assoc of Colleges for Teacher Education; Phi Delta Kappa; Nebraska Speech-Language-Hearing Assoc; Nebraska Council of School Administrators; Am Assoc of Colleges for Teacher Education. **RESEARCH** Pre-referral practices. **SELECTED PUBLICATIONS** Coauth, Policy Issues Concerning Public School Choice and Special Education Programs, Case In Point: J of Coun of Adminr, 6(1), 91 auth, The Reality of Outcomes-Oriented Accredition, The International Electronic Journal for Leadership in Learning, vol. 3, n 13, 99; auth, "Principals' Perceptions of Pre-Referral Student Assistance Teams," Educational Research Service Spectrum, (00) 14-19. **CONTACT ADDRESS** Univ of Nebraska, Omaha, 60th & Dodge Sts, Kayser Hall 334, Omaha, NE 68182-0161. **EMAIL** John_Christensen@unomaha.edu

CHRISTIE, ALICE
PERSONAL Born 06/19/1945, New York, NY, d, 1 child **DISCIPLINE** EDUCATION **EDUCATION** Denison Univ, BA, 67; Boston Univ, MEd, 70; Ariz State Univ, PhD, 95. **CAREER** Exec Dir, CED, 87-88; Teaching Asst to Asst Prof, Ariz State Univ W, 84-. **HONORS AND AWARDS** Prof of the Year, ASU, 99; Teacher of the Year, 99. **MEMBERSHIPS** NCTE, ISTE, AACE, SITE. **RESEARCH** Technology and Gender; Technology and Literacy; Educational Uses of the Internet and Techology. **SELECTED PUBLICATIONS** Auth, "Can technology help teachers and students break down gender stereotypes?", in Technology and Teacher Educational Annual Proceedings of SITE 96 (96): 31-35; auth, "Using telecommunications to break down gender stereotypes," Ninth Annual Proceedings of the International Qualitative Research, 96; auth, "Using email within a classroom based on feminist pedagogy," Journal of Research on Computing in Education 28 (97); auth, "Using telecommunications to increase gender equity in technology use," Sixth Annual Proceedings of the International Society of Technology in Education Conference on Telecommunications and Multimedia in Education, 97; auth, "Using Technology to Enhance Literacy in Elementary School Children," Nineteenth Annual Proceedings of the National Educational Computing Conference, (98): 81-91; auth, "Girls, Boys and Computing: Gender Considerations, CLICK!: Computers and Learning in Classrooms K-6, 98. **CONTACT ADDRESS** Sch of Educ, Arizona State Univ, West, PO Box 37100, Glendale, AZ 85306. **EMAIL** alice.christie@asu.edu

CHU, MAYLING M.
DISCIPLINE SOCIAL WORK **EDUCATION** Ariz State Univ, PhD, 95. **CAREER** Asst Prof, Auburn Univ, 95-96; Asst Prof, Calif State Univ, 96-. **MEMBERSHIPS** NASW, CSWE, ASC. **RESEARCH** Juvenile Justice; Social Work with Minority; International Social Work Policy. **CONTACT ADDRESS** Dept Soc Work, California State Univ, Stanislaus, 801 W Monte Vista Ave, Turlock, CA 95382. **EMAIL** mchu@stan.csustan.edu

CHURCH, DAN M.

PERSONAL Born 04/20/1939, NC, m, 1963, 2 children **DISCIPLINE** TWENTIETH-CENTURY THEATER AND FILM, TECHNOLOGY AND LANGUAGE ACQUISITION **EDUCATION** Wake Forest Col, BA, 61; Middlebury Col, MA, 62; Univ Wis, PhD, 68. **CAREER** Asst prof Fr, Antioch Col, 65-67; asst prof, 67-70; assoc prof, 70-01; dir, Vanderbilt-in-Fr, 74-76; dir, Workshop on the Quest Authoring Syst, 86; dir, Mellon Regional fac develop sem, 86; dir, lang lab, Vanderbilt Univ, 88-96; emeritus, 01. **MEMBERSHIPS** Comput Assisted Lang Instr Consortium; chemn, Courseware Develop Spec Interest Gp. **SELECTED PUBLICATIONS** Auth, Interactive Audio for Foreign-Language Learning, Lit & Ling Comp, V, 2; AndrQ Barsacq, Gaston Baty, and Roger Planchon, Theatrical Directors: A Biographical Dictionary, Greenwood Press, 94; rev, GramDef French, CALICO J, 98. **CONTACT ADDRESS** Vanderbilt Univ, 636 Timber Lane, Nashville, TN 37215. **EMAIL** dan.m.church@vanderbilt.edu

CIENA, MEL

PERSONAL Born New York, NY, s **DISCIPLINE** PSYCHOLOGY **EDUCATION** San Jose State Univ, BA, 71; MA, 74; Stanford Univ, MA, 76; PhD, 98. **CAREER** Instr, West Valley Col, 74-91; prof, Univ San Francisco, 91-. **HONORS AND AWARDS** Phi Delta Kappa; Stanford Fel; Distinguished Lecture Awd, San Francisco, 98; Outstanding instructor, San Jose, 86; Hall of Fame, San Jose Col, 87; Nat Sci Foundation Res Fel, Stanford Univ. **MEMBERSHIPS** Am Asn of Univ Prof, Child Dev Consortium, Stanford Alumni Asn. **RESEARCH** Motivation and orientation for 2nd language acquisition (neurological, biological and psychological). **SELECTED PUBLICATIONS** Auth, Parental Attitude/Behavior: Student Workbook for Discussion Groups, San Jose City Col Press, 84; auth, A glossary of Development and Overview of Developmental Stages and Theories, Calif Pub, 80; ed, The Developing Child 3rd ed, Harper and Row Pub, 80; auth, Lifespan Development, Conception through Old Age, (forthcoming). **CONTACT ADDRESS** Dept Psych, Univ of San Francisco, 2130 Fulton St, San Francisco, CA 94117. **EMAIL** ciena@usfca.edu

CIOCHON, RUSSELL L.

PERSONAL Born 03/11/1948, Altadena, CA, m, 1986 **DISCIPLINE** ANTHROPOLOGY **EDUCATION** Univ Calif Berkeley, MA, 74, PhD 86. **CAREER** Lectr, Univ North Carolina, Charlotte, 78-81; res paleontol, Univ Calif, Berkeley, 82-83; res assoc, Inst Human Origins, Berkeley, 83-85; res assoc, SUNY Stony Brook, 85-86; asst prof, Univ Iowa, 87-90, assoc prof, 90-96, prof, 96-, ch, Dept of Anthrop, Univ Iowa. **HONORS AND AWARDS** Res grant Smithsonian Foreign Currency Prog, 78; Leakey Found, 87. **MEMBERSHIPS** AAAS, Am Anthrop Asn; Am Asn Phys Anthrop; Soc Syst Biol; Phi Beta Kappa. **RESEARCH** Paleoanthropology, human evolution, primate evolution, archaeology of Asia. **SELECTED PUBLICATIONS** Ed, Human Evolution Source Book, 93; auth/ed, Integrative Paths to the Past, 94; auth, Evolution of the Cercopithecoid Forelimb, 93; co-ed, Oxford Series in Human Evolution, 95-. **CONTACT ADDRESS** Dept of Anthropology, Univ of Iowa, 114 Macbride Hall, Iowa City, IA 52242-1322. **EMAIL** russell-ciochon@uiowa.edu

CISSELL, WILLIAM B.

PERSONAL Born 04/21/1941, KY, m, 1967, 1 child **DISCIPLINE** HEALTH STUDIES **EDUCATION** Southern ill Univ Carbondale; Univ Calif Los Angeles, MSPH, 70; Southern ill Univ Carbondale, PhD, 77. **CAREER** Asst Prof, Univ of Tex Austin, 77-79; Asst to Assoc Prof, E Tenn State Univ, 79-89; Chair Dept of Health Studies, Tex Woman's Univ, 89-98; Prof, Tex Woman's Univ, 98-. **HONORS AND AWARDS** Distinguished Fel Awd SOPHE, 86; Distinguished Serv Awd Eta Sigma Gamma, 87; Past-President's Awd, Texas Chap SOPHE, 95; Outstanding fac member, Red Bud Awds, Tex Woman's Univ; Distinguished Career Serv Awd, Tex Chap SOPHE, 97; Commendation on Admin Serv, Tex Woman's Univ, 99; Phi Kappa Phi. **MEMBERSHIPS** Soc for Public Health Educ, Am Asn for Health Educ, am Sch Health Asn, Eta Sigma Gamma Hon Soc, N Am Regional Orgn/ Int Union for Health Promotion and Educ, Phi Kappa Phi Hon Soc, Golden Key Hon Soc. **RESEARCH** Professional Preparation and Quality Assurance within the Health Education Profession, History of the Health Education Profession. **SELECTED PUBLICATIONS** Coauth, "Professionalism and academic job announcements in health education," Wellness Perspectives: Research, Theory, Practice 10-4 (94): 40-48; coauth, "Attachment and bonding in adoptive families," in American family: Life and health, ed. Robert D. Patton (Palo Alto, CA: Third Party, 95); coauth, "Texas guidelines: A case study in state attention to standards for professional preparation," The Eta Sigma Gamma Monograph Ser 13-2 (95): 36-44; auth, Texas guidelines: A case study in state attention to standards for professional preparation," Overview of the development of graduate health education standards, The Eta Sigma Gamma Monograph Ser 13-2 (95): 44-52; coauth, "A critical analysis of the CHES credentialing issue: Bridging the gap between vision and outcomes," J of Health Educ 29-4 (98): 213-220; coauth, "Role modeling: A dilemma for the health education specialist," Health Educ and Behav 26-5 (99): 621-622; coauth, "Evaluating the Texas Woman's University distance education program: A case study," Educ Technology and Soc, URL: http://grouper.ieee.

org/groups/ltsc/ifets/periodicalvol_3_99/v_399.html (July 99). **CONTACT ADDRESS** Dept Health Studies, Texas Woman's Univ, PO Box 425499, Denton, TX 76204-5499.

CLAASSEN, CHERYL

PERSONAL Born 07/24/1953, Syracuse, NY, 1 child **DISCIPLINE** ANTHROPOLOGY **EDUCATION** Univ Ark, BA, BSW, 75; Harvard Univ, PhD, 82. **CAREER** Archaeol, State of NC, 79-80; dir, Seasonality Lab, Center for Archaeol Res and Development, Peabody Museum, Harvard Univ, 81-82; Charles Phelps Taft postdoctoral res fel, Univ Cincinnati, 82-83; vis prof, Anthropology, Universidad de las Americas, 90-91; asst to assoc prof, anthropology, 83-94, Prof of Anthropology, Appalachian State Univ, 94-; Res Assoc, Center Fro Am Archael, 95-. **HONORS AND AWARDS** Certificate of Commendation, Am Asn for State & Local Hist; NSF grant, 85, 87, & 93; Am Philos Soc Grant, 87. **MEMBERSHIPS** Soc for Am Archaeol; Southeastern Archaeol Conf. **RESEARCH** Gender; sociology of archaeology; shells; symbolic landscapes, Eastern U.S. **SELECTED PUBLICATIONS** Auth, Shells for the Archaeologist, Cambridge Univ Press, 98; Black and White Women at Irene: A Revised View, Where We've Been: Early Women Archaeologists in the Southeast, Univ of Fl Press, 98; Washboards, Pigtoes, and Muckets: Historic Musseling in the Mississippi Watershed, Hist Archaeol, 94; Looking for Gender in Appalachian Prehistory, Archaeol of Appalachia, NY State Museum Monographs in Archaeol, 98; Challenges in Gendering Southeastern Prehisotry, Gender and Southeastern Prehistory, 98; Changing Venue: Proposals About Women's Lives in Prehistoric North America, Women in Prehistory: North Am and Mesoamerica, Univ of Pa Press, 97; Social Organization of the Shell Mound Archaic, The Middle and Late Archaic in the Southeastern U.S., Univ of Fl Press, 96; Research Problems with Shell from Shell Mound Archaic Sites, Of Caves in Shell Mounds, Univ of Ala Press, 96; coauth, Women in the Ancient Americas: Archaeologists, Gender, and the Making of Prehistory, Women in Prehistory: North Am and Mesoamerica, Univ of Pa Press, 97; co-ed, Women in Prehistory: North America and Mesoamerica, Univ of Pa Press, 97; ed, Dogan Point: An Archaic Shell-Matrix Site on the Hudson, Archaeol Services, 95; Women in Archaeology, Univ of Pa Press, 94; Exploring Gender Through Archaeology, Prehist Press, 92. **CONTACT ADDRESS** Dept of Anthropology, Appalachian State Univ, Boone, NC 28608.

CLARK, ANNA

DISCIPLINE MODERN BRITAIN HISTORY, EUROPEAN WOMEN'S HISTORY, HISTORY OF SEXUALITY **EDUCATION** Rutgers Univ, PhD, 87; Harvard, BA; Univ of Essex, MA. **CAREER** Assoc prof, Univ NC, Charlotte; assoc prof, Univ of Minn. **HONORS AND AWARDS** N Am Conf on Brit Stud Prize in the Hum. **RESEARCH** Gender and Politics in late 18th and Early 19th Century Britain; domesticity and the Poor Laws in the 19th Century. **SELECTED PUBLICATIONS** Auth, Women's Silence, Men's Violence: Sexual Assault in England, 1770-1845, Pandora, 87; auth, The Struggle for the Breeches: Gender and the Making of the British Working Class, Univ Calif Press 95; auth, "Anne Lister's Construction of Lesbian Identity," Journal of the History of Sexuality, 96; auth, "Wilkes and d'Eon: the Politics of Masculinity, 1763-1778," Eighteenth-Century Studies, 98. **CONTACT ADDRESS** Dept of Hist, Univ of Minnesota, Twin Cities, 774 Social Science Bldg, 267 19th Ave S, Minneapolis, MN 55455. **EMAIL** clark106@umn.edu

CLARK, GRACIA

PERSONAL Born 06/11/1952, Seattle, WA **DISCIPLINE** ANTHROPOLOGY **EDUCATION** Stanford Univ, BA, 84; Cambridge, PhD, 94. **CAREER** Asst prof, Univ Wisc, Parkside, 85-87; asst prof, Univ Mich, Ann Arbor, 87-94; asst prof, Indiana Univ, Bloomington, 94-. **HONORS AND AWARDS** President, Soc for Economic Anthropol. **MEMBERSHIPS** Soc for Economic Anthropol. **SELECTED PUBLICATIONS** Auth, Onions Are My Husband, Univ Chicago Press (94). **CONTACT ADDRESS** Dept Anthropol, Indiana Univ, Bloomington, 701 E Kirkwood Ave, Bloomington, IN 47405. **EMAIL** gclark@indiana.edu

CLARK, JAMES J.

PERSONAL Born 10/12/1958, Binghamton, NY, m, 1991, 3 children **DISCIPLINE** SOCIOLOGY **EDUCATION** Sienna Col, BA, 80; Univ Ky, MSW, 83; Univ Chicago, PhD, 95. **CAREER** Dir, Cath Soc Serv Bur, 84-89; Assoc Prof, Univ Ky, 91-. **HONORS AND AWARDS** Lyndhurst Found Prize, 87; Fel, Nat Inst of Ment Health, 89; Res Comt Awd, Univ Ky, 94. **RESEARCH** Forensic mental health and substance use research. **SELECTED PUBLICATIONS** Coauth, "The Mental Health Expert: Eight Steps to Integrating a Specialist into the Case," Criminal Justice 11 (96): 2-13; coauth, " A View from the Trenches: Training the New Law Graduates to Practice Law," Univ of Cincinnati Law J 65 (97): 381-422; auth, "Dilemmas at the Nexus: Criminal Law and the Mental Health Professions," J of Law and Soc Work 6 (98): 43-56; coauth, "Developing a Rural Therapy: A Qualitative Investigation," Substance Use and Misuse (99); coauth, "Practicum Instruction: Warning Signs of Boundary Problems and What to Do About Them," J of teaching in Soc Work (99); coauth, "Heading Off

Boundary Problems: Clinical Supervision as Risk Management," Psychiat Serv 50 (99): 1435-1439; coauth, Structured Behavioral Outpatient Rural Therapy: A Treatment Manual for Rural Substance Abuse, Univ Ky Pr (Lexington, KY), forthcoming. **CONTACT ADDRESS** Dept Sociol, Univ of Kentucky, 500 S Limestone St, Lexington, KY 40506-0027.

CLARK, MARY MORRIS

PERSONAL Born 12/28/1941, Tuscaloosa, AL, 3 children **DISCIPLINE** LINGUISTICS, AFRICAN LANGUAGES **EDUCATION** Univ NH, BA, 62; Univ Mass, PhD(ling), 78. **CAREER** Teacher English, math & sci, US Peace Corps, Nigeria, 64-65; instr, Sch for Int Training, 75-78; Asst Prof Ling, English Dept, Univ NH, 78- **MEMBERSHIPS** Ling Soc Am; African Ling Soc; North Eastern Ling Soc; Teachers of English to Speakers of Other Lang; NCTE. **RESEARCH** The use of tone and intonation in languages; the interaction of phonology with other parts of the grammar; applications of linguistics in language teaching. **SELECTED PUBLICATIONS** Auth, Classification of Adults for Family Studies of Developmental Language Disorders, Jour Speech and Hearing Res, Vol 0039, 96; Guilty if Charged--A Response to the Bernstein, Richard Account of the Silva, Donald Case at the University-of-New-Hampshire--An Exchange, NY Rev Bk(s), Vol 0041, 94. **CONTACT ADDRESS** English Dept, Univ of New Hampshire, Durham, 125 Technology Dr, Durham, NH 03824-4724. **EMAIL** mmc@christa.unh.edu

CLARK, SANZA BARBARA

PERSONAL Born 07/03/1940, Cleveland, OH, d **DISCIPLINE** EDUCATION **EDUCATION** Kent State Univ, BA 1967; Duquesne Univ, MA 1970; Howard Univ, CAS 1980; Univ of IL, PhD 1985. **CAREER** Univ of Pittsburgh, Swahili instructor 1969-72; Tanzanian Min of Natl Educ, educ officer IIA 1972-78; University of Illinois, statistical consultant, 80-83; OH State Univ, Swahili instructor 1983-84; Cleveland State Univ, assoc prof educ/rsch 1985-. **HONORS AND AWARDS** Mem Phi Delta Kappa Professional Soc; mem Phi Kappa Phi Honor Soc; Guide-Formulas-Hypothesis Testing Univ of IL 1982; Effects-Parental Educ & Sch on Ach Univ of IL 1985; Ed Refugees in Tanzania Comp & Intl Educ Soc 1986; Honoree, Outstanding African-American Women, 1996; Queen Mother Awd, Excellence in Service & Community, 1996. **MEMBERSHIPS** Pres Orchard Family Housing Council 1981-83; pres Parents for Quality Educ 1986-87; chmn, Mali Yetu Alternative Educ School 1988-; trustee, Center for Human Services, 1989-91. **SELECTED PUBLICATIONS** "African-American Research," The State of Black Cleveland, 1989; "Persistence Patterns of African-American College Students," Readings on the State of Education in Urban America, 1991; "An Analysis of African-American First Year College Student Attitudes & Attrition Rates," Journal of Urban Education, 1992; "The Great Migration," Mali Yetu, 1993; "The Schooling of Cultural and Ethnic Subordinate Groups," Comparative Education Review, 1993; "Rediscovering Our Roots in Ghana, Africa," Mali Yetu, 1995. **CONTACT ADDRESS** Cleveland State Univ, Cleveland, OH 44115.

CLARK, TERRY NICHOLS

PERSONAL Born 11/26/1940, Chicago, IL **DISCIPLINE** SOCIOLOGY **EDUCATION** Bowdoin Col, BA, 62; Columbia Univ, MA, 65, PhD, 67. **CAREER** Asst prof, 66-71, assoc prof, 71-85, prof, 85-, chmn, Sociology Program, 89-, Univ of Chicago; Sr Study Dir, Nat Opinion Res Ctr, 74-; vis assoc prof, Yale Univ, 72; vis scholar, Centre Universitaire Internat Paris, 65, 69; Brookings Instr, 75; Coord Fiscal Austerity and Urban Innovation Project US and World; Dir Comparative Study Community Decision-making, Univ of Chicago, 67-; chmn, Comm on Community Res and Devel Soc for Study Social Problems, 70-71; vis res, Urban Inst Pub Fin Group WA Summer 70; consul to Office Policy Devel and Res HUD, WA, summer 75. **MEMBERSHIPS** Amer Sociology Asn; Intl Sociology Asn; The Tocqueville Soc. **SELECTED PUBLICATIONS** Auth, A Mayors Financial Management Handbook, 82; coauth, City Money Political Processes Fiscal Strain and Retrenchment, 83; coauth, Policy Responsiveness and Fiscal Strain in 51 American Communities A Manual for Studying City Politics Using the MORC Permanent Community Sample, 83; auth, Coping with Urban Austerity Research in Urban Policy, 84. **CONTACT ADDRESS** Univ of Chicago, 1126 East 59th St, 326 Soc Sci Bldg, Chicago, IL 60637. **EMAIL** tnclark@uchicago.edu

CLARK, VEVE A.

PERSONAL Born 12/14/1944, Jamaica, NY **DISCIPLINE** EDUCATION **EDUCATION** Univ of CA Berkeley, PhD; Queens Coll NYork, MA; Univ de Nancy France, Cert d'Etudes Superieures; Queens Coll NYork, BA. **CAREER** Univ of CA Berkeley, lecturer 1974-79; Tufts Univ, assoc prof 1980-90; Univ of California, Berkeley, associate professor, 91-. **HONORS AND AWARDS** Natl Endowment for the Arts Grants for Maya Deren Proj & Katherine Dunham Proj 1980-81; Merrill Ingram Found Writing Grant for Deren Proj 1982; Mellon Faculty Rsch Awd Tufts Univ 1983-84; co-editor The Legend of Maya Deren, Film Culture NY 1985; Gussenheim Fellow, 1987; Brown University Fellow, Rites and Reason and Univ Massachusetts, Boston, MA, 1988. **MEMBERSHIPS** Archivist The Katherine Dunham Fund 1977-; coord Africa & The

New World Program at Tufts Univ 1981-; bd mem Fenway Comm Devel Corp 1981-83. **CONTACT ADDRESS** Univ of California, Berkeley, 660 Barrows Hall, Berkeley, CA 94720-2572.

CLAYTON, OBIE
PERSONAL Born 02/26/1954, Meridian, MS, m, 1984, 2 children **DISCIPLINE** SOCIOLOGY **EDUCATION** Millsaps Col, BA, 76; Emory Univ, MA, 78; PhD, 81. **CAREER** Instr, Millsaps Col, 78; asst prof, Morehouse Col, 79-81; asst prof, Univ of Mass at Boston, 82-86; assoc prof, The Atlanta Univ, 86-88; assoc prof and grad fac fel, Univ of Nebr at Omaha, 88-92; dir, Morehouse Res Inst, 92-; ed, Challenge: A J of Res on African Am Men, Morehouse Res Inst, 92-; assoc prof, Morehouse Res Inst, 92-; vice provost for res, Morehouse Res Inst, 96-98. **HONORS AND AWARDS** Listed in Who's Who in Am Colleges and Universities; Spivak Awd, Am Sociol Asn; Am Sociol Asn Fel, ETA Sigma Phi, Omicron Delta Kappa, C. Wright Mills Awd, Millsaps Col; Lilly Found Awd, Millsaps Col; Emory Univ Fel. **MEMBERSHIPS** Asn of Behav and Soc Scientists, Am Sociol Asn, Ga Sociol Soc, Southern Sociol Soc, Acad of Criminal Justice Sci, Am Soc of Criminology, Mid-south Sociol Asn, Nat Coun of Univ Res Administrators. **RESEARCH** Criminology, Statistics, Urban Poverty, Demography. **SELECTED PUBLICATIONS** Coauth, "The Administration of Justice," African-Americans: Essential Perspectives, Auburn House Press (Westport, CT), 93; auth, "The Black Family in Atlanta," The Status of Blacks in Atlanta, Clark Atlanta Univ Press (Atlanta, GA), 94; auth, "The Church and Social Change: Accomodation, Moderation or Protest?" Daedalus 1 (95); auth, "Immigrants, Economic Opportunity and Political Influence: Perception of Native Born Americans," Challenge 1 (96); ed, An American Dilemma Revisited: Race Relations in A Changing World, Russell Sage, 96; auth, African American Fathers and their Families in Contemporary American Society, Russell Sage Found, 99. **CONTACT ADDRESS** Dept Sociol, Morehouse Col, 830 Westview Dr SW, Atlanta, GA 30314. **EMAIL** oclayton@morehouse.edu

CLEMMER, LINDA
PERSONAL Born 05/04/1954, Duckhill, MS, m, 1970, 2 children **DISCIPLINE** EDUCATION **EDUCATION** Blue Mountain Col, BS, 81; Univ Miss, Med, 91; Univ Miss, EdD, 98. **CAREER** Teacher, North Tippah Sch Dist, 81-89; Teacher, Benton Co Sch Dist, 89-94; Libr, Instr, Blue Mountain Col, 94-98; Asst Prof, Col of the Ozarks, 98-. **HONORS AND AWARDS** Who's Who Among Am Teachers; STAR Teacher, 86, 92. **MEMBERSHIPS** ACEI, IRA, Delta Kappa Gamma. **RESEARCH** ADHD, gender equity. **CONTACT ADDRESS** Dept Educ, Col of the Ozarks, PO Box 472, Point Lookout, MO 65726. **EMAIL** clemmer@cofo.edu

CLIFFORD, GERALDINE JONCICH
PERSONAL Born 04/17/1931, San Pedro, CA, w, 1969 **DISCIPLINE** HISTORY OF AMERICAN EDUCATION **EDUCATION** Univ Calif, Los Angeles, AB, 54, MEd, 57; Columbia Univ, EdD(hist educ), 61. **CAREER** Lectr hist & soc found educ, Univ Calif, Santa Barbara, 61-62; from asst prof to assoc prof educ, 62-72, res & travel grant, 63, assoc dean, Sch Educ, 76-80, chmn, Dept Educ, 78-81, Prof Hist Educ, Univ Calif, Berkeley, 72-, Guggenheim fel, 65-66; humanities res fel, 73-74 & 81-82; Rockefeller Humanities fel, Rockefeller Found, 77-78. **HONORS AND AWARDS** Phi Beta Kappa, Willystine Goodsell Awd (for service to women in education). **MEMBERSHIPS** AHA; Am Studies Asn; Hist Educ Soc (pres, 76-77); Am Educ Studies Asn; Am Educ Res Asn (vpres, 73-75). **RESEARCH** Autobiographical sources in the history of American education; women in educational history; nineteenth century American schools and colleges; history of the American Women teacher. **SELECTED PUBLICATIONS** Ed, Psychology and the Science of Education, Columbia Univ, 62; auth, The Sane Positivist: A Biography of E L Thorndike, Wesleyan Univ, 68; Edward Lee Thorndike: A biography, In: New International Encyclopedia of the Social Sciences, Crowell Collier & Macmillan, 68; A history of the effects of research on teaching, In: Second Handbook, Rand McNally, 73; The Shape of American Education, Prentice-Hall, 76; Home and school in nineteenth century America, Hist Educ Quart, 78; ed, School: A Brief for Professional Education, Chicago 99; auth, Lone Voyagers, Feminist Press, 89. **CONTACT ADDRESS** Sch of Educ, Univ of California, Berkeley, 1501 Tolman Hall, Berkeley, CA 94720-1671.

CLOUGH, WULFSTAN
PERSONAL Born 04/19/1952, Wilmington, DE **DISCIPLINE** MEDIEVAL LITERATURE, FOLKLORE **EDUCATION** Univ Del, BA, 74; MA, 77; Univ Notre Dame, PhD, 84; St Vincent Sem, MDiv. **CAREER** Teaching asst, Univ Del, 75-77; teaching asst, Univ Notre Dame, 78-82; instr, Univ Del, 85-90; asst prof, St Vincent Col, 96-. **HONORS AND AWARDS** Ernest P. Dobson Awd, 99; Univ Notre Dame Res Fel, Teaching Fel, 78-82, 82-84; Univ Del, Teaching Fel, 75-77. **MEMBERSHIPS** MLA; CCL; NCTE; Mythopoeic Soc. **RESEARCH** Medieval and renaissance literature; myth and folklore; film; fantasy and science fiction. **SELECTED PUBLICATIONS** Co-ed, The Vercelli Homilies: Translations from the Anglo-Saxon, Univ Pr Am, 90; auth, "Oliier, Branagh, and the BBC: Three Henry V's on Film," Lit Conf (00); auth, "Einstein and Religion: What Do We Know?" ACTC Conf (forthcoming). **CONTACT ADDRESS** English Dept, Saint Vincent Col, Latrobe, PA 15650-2667. **EMAIL** wclough@stvincent.edu

COAN, RICHARD W.
PERSONAL Born 01/24/1928, Martinez, CA, d, 4 children **DISCIPLINE** CLINICAL PSYCHOLOGY **EDUCATION** Univ of Southern Calif, PhD, 55. **CAREER** Res Assoc in Psychol, Univ Ill, 55-57; Asst Prof to Prof of Psychol, Univ of Ariz, 57-89; Prof Emeritus, Univ Ariz, 89-. **MEMBERSHIPS** Am Psychol Asn. **RESEARCH** Psychology of myths & tales; human personality; symbolism. **SELECTED PUBLICATIONS** Auth, The optimal personality, an empirical and theoretical analysis, Routledge & Kegan Paul, 74; auth, Hero, artist, sage, or saint? A survey of views on what is variously called mental health, normality, maturity, self-actualization and human fulfillment, Univ Colombia Press, 77; auth, Psychologists: Personal and theoretical pathways, Irvington, 79; auth, Psychology of adjustment: Personal experience development, Wiley, 83; auth, Human consciousness and its evolution: A multidimensional view, Greenwood, 87. **CONTACT ADDRESS** 4158 E Waverly St, Tucson, AZ 85712.

COBB, JEANNE B.
PERSONAL Born 04/05/1948, Thomasville, NC, m, 1974, 2 children **DISCIPLINE** EDUCATION **EDUCATION** Western Carolina Univ, BS, 70; Univ Tenn, MS, 71; EdD, 92. **CAREER** Asst Prof, Univ N Tex, 97-. **HONORS AND AWARDS** Fel, Emory Univ, 76; Chancellor's Citation, Univ Tenn, 92; Outstanding Student, Univ Tenn, 92-93; Who's Who in Am Women, 00; Who's Who in Am, 00. **MEMBERSHIPS** IRA, NCTE, NRC, NAEYC, OTER, NAECTE, ATE, TSRA, ACEI, ILA. **RESEARCH** Strategies for improving literacy achievement of at risk readers. **SELECTED PUBLICATIONS** Coauth, "Community: No Magic Formula," The Writing Teacher 9:3 (96): 19-20; auth, "The Social Contexts of Tutoring: Mentoring the Older At-Risk Student," Reading Horizons 39:1 (98): 49-75; auth, "Impact of Major Field of Study on Tutors' Performance: A Literacy Intervention Program for At-Risk Fourth Graders," J of Reading Educ 24:2 (99); coauth, "Preservice teachers' Assessment of the Use of Centers as an Aspect of Developmentally Appropriate Practice in First Grade Classrooms," J of Early Childhood Teacher Educ (00); auth, "Listening Within the Social Contexts of Tutoring: An Essential Component of the Mentoring Relationship with Older At-Risk Readers," Int J of Listening (00); auth, "Graduates of Professional Development School Programs: Perceptions of the Teacher as Change Agent," The Teacher Educr (00); auth, "The Impact of a Professional Development School on Preservice Teacher Preparation, Inservice Teacher Professionalism and Elementary Aged Children," Action in Teacher Educ (00). **CONTACT ADDRESS** Dept Educ, Univ of No Texas, PO Box 311337, Denton, TX 76203. **EMAIL** jcobb@coefs.coe.unt.edu

COBBLE, DOROTHY SUE
PERSONAL Born 06/28/1949, Atlanta, GA, m, 1997, 3 children **DISCIPLINE** WOMEN'S STUDIES, LABOR STUDIES **EDUCATION** Univ Calif, Berkeley, BA, 72; Stanford Univ, PhD, 86. **CAREER** Dept chair and Dir, Labor Studies Dept, City Col of San Francisco, 80-86; assoc prof, Rutgers Univ, 86-. **HONORS AND AWARDS** H. Gutman Book Awd, 92; Rutgers Univ Bd of Trustees Res Awd, 92; ALCS and NEH Res Awds; Funding Dir, Centre for Women and Work, 930-96; Woodrow Wilson Fel, 99-2000. **MEMBERSHIPS** Org of Am Hists, Industrial Relations Res Asn. **RESEARCH** American labor and women's history; women and work; service work. **SELECTED PUBLICATIONS** Auth, Dishing It Out: Waitresses and Their Unions in the Twentieth Century, Urbana: Univ Ill Press (91); ed, Women and Unions: Forging A Partnership, Ithaca: Cornell Univ ILR Press (93); auth, "Lost Ways of Organizing: Reviving the AFL's Direct Affiliate Strategy," Industrial Relations, 36, no 3 (July 97): 278-301; auth, "The Next Unionism: Structural Innovations for a Revitalized Labor Movement," Labor Law J, 48, no 8 (Aug 97): 439-443; auth, "Knowledge Workers and the New Unionism," Thought and Action: The National Education Association Higher Education Journal, 15, no 2 (fall 99): 19-24; auth, "A Spontaneous Loss of Enthusiasm': Workplace Feminism and the Transformation of Women's Service Jobs in the 1970's," Int Labor and Working-Class Hist, 56 (fall 99): 23-44; coauth, "Historical Perspectives on Representing NonStandard Workers," in Non-Traditional Work Arrangements and the Changing Labor Market, ed by Francoise Carre, et al, Wisc: Industrial Relations Res Asn (2000). **CONTACT ADDRESS** Dept Labor and Industrial Relations, Rutgers, The State Univ of New Jersey, New Brunswick, PO Box 5062, New Brunswick, NJ 08903-5062.

COCHRAN, ROBERT
PERSONAL Born 05/24/1943, Lake Forest, IL, m, 5 children **DISCIPLINE** FOLKLORE **EDUCATION** Univ Toronto, PhD. **CAREER** English and Lit, Univ Ark. **HONORS AND AWARDS** Dir, Ctr Ark & Regional Studies. **SELECTED PUBLICATIONS** Auth, Vance Randolph: An Ozark Life, Ill, 85; Samuel Beckett: A Study of the Short Fiction, G K Hall, 91; A Mountain Life: Walter Williams of Newton County, Ark, 92; "Unable to Sleep, The Father Fills Page After Page," Quart, 91; "Deliberate Valediction: Williams' 'Pictures from Brueghel'," Tenn Quart, 94; Our Own Sweet Sounds: A Popular History of Arkansas Music, Ark, 96; auth, Music's Esiee: Western Swing Fiddler Frrankie Kelly, 97; auth, Singing in Zion: Music and Song In the Life of An Arkansas Family, Arkansas U Press, 99. **CONTACT ADDRESS** Univ of Arkansas, Fayetteville, CARS: Old Main 506, Fayetteville, AR 72701. **EMAIL** rcochran@comp.uark.edu

CODLING, JIM
PERSONAL Born 11/28/1949, Lloydminster, SK, Canada, m, 1982, 2 children **DISCIPLINE** HISTORY, PHILOSOPHY, EDUCATION **EDUCATION** Univ Saskatchewan, B Ed, 72; Knox Col, M Div, 76; Convent Sem, Th M, 81; Mississippi State Univ, M Ed, 89; Concordia, St Louis, Th D, 90. **CAREER** Prof, Mary Holmes Col, 91-. **HONORS AND AWARDS** Concordia Res Fel; Fisher Prize, Knox Coll; Fac Mem of the Year, 94; Res, 94; Teach, 95. **MEMBERSHIPS** Convent Presbytery. **RESEARCH** Ethics; Reformation History; Local Histories. **SELECTED PUBLICATIONS** Auth, 'The New Deal in Public Policy," 97; auth, Cross Cultural Missions, Coast to Coast (92); auth, Why So Many Churches, Coast to Coast (94). **CONTACT ADDRESS** Dept Soc Science, Education, Mary Holmes Col, PO Box 1257, West Point, MS 39773 1257.

COFFIN, TRISTRAM POTTER
PERSONAL Born 02/13/1922, San Marino, CA, m, 1944, 4 children **DISCIPLINE** ENGLISH AND FORKLORE **EDUCATION** Haverford Col, BS, 43; Univ Pa, AM, 47, PhD, 49. **CAREER** From instr to assoc prof English, Denison Univ, 49-58; assoc prof English & folklore, 58-64, vdean, Grad Sch Arts & Sci, 65-68, prof English, 64-84, Prof Emer English and Folklore, Univ PA, 84- . **HONORS AND AWARDS** Guggenheim fel, 53. **MEMBERSHIPS** MLA; Am Folklore Soc (secy-treas, 60-65, 2nd vpres, 67-); Folklore Soc England. **RESEARCH** Anglo-American ballad; folk literature; American Indian and Negro. **SELECTED PUBLICATIONS** Auth, Index to the Journal of American Folklore, Univ Tex Press, 58; co-ed Folklore in America, 67; auth, Uncertain Glory, 71; auth, The Old Ball Game, 71; The Book of Christmas Folklore, Seabury, 73; co-ed, Folklore from the Working Folk of America, Doubleday Anchor, 73; auth, The Female Hero, Seabury, 75; The British Traditional Ballad in North America, Am Folklore Soc, 77; The Proper Book of Sexual Folklore, Seabury, 78; coauth, The Parade of Heroes, Doubleday Ancho, 78; Great Game for a Girl, Exposition, 80; co-ed, Folklore of the American Holidays, Editions I & II & III. **CONTACT ADDRESS** PO Box 509, Wakefield, RI 02880.

COFIELD, ELIZABETH BIAS
PERSONAL Born 01/21/1920, Raleigh, NC, m **DISCIPLINE** EDUCATION **EDUCATION** Hampton Inst, BS; Columbia U, MA; diploma in adminstrn & supervision. **CAREER** Wade County Bd of Commrs, Juan Medford co commr, 72; Shaw Univ, prof of educ. **MEMBERSHIPS** Elected to Raleigh Sch Bd 1969-72. **CONTACT ADDRESS** Education, Shaw Univ, 118 E South St, Raleigh, NC 27602.

COGAN, KAREN D.
PERSONAL Born 09/20/1963, Redondo Beach, CA, m, 1989, 2 children **DISCIPLINE** PSYCHOLOGY **EDUCATION** Univ Calif at Los Angeles, BA, 85; MS, 87; Ohio State Univ, PhD, 91. **CAREER** Psychologist/Adj Prof, Southern Methodist Univ, 91-92; Psychologist, Pvt Practice, 92-; Psychologist/Asst Prof, Univ of N Tex, 92-. **HONORS AND AWARDS** Univ Calif, Los Angeles, Outstanding Sr Awd. **MEMBERSHIPS** Am Psychol Asn, Asoc for Advancement of Appl Sport Psychology. **RESEARCH** Sport Psychology, Women's Issue, Sexual Abuse, Eating Disorders. **SELECTED PUBLICATIONS** Coauth, "Psychological and physiological effects of controlled intensive training and diet on collegiate rowers," Int J of Sport Psychology 22 (91): 165-180; coauth, "Sport Consultation: An evaluation of a season long intervention with a collegiate women's gymnastics team," The Sport Psychologist 9 (95): 282-296; coauth, "Consultation with college student-athletes," Col Student J 30 (95): 9-16; coauth, "Gender differences in perceived effectiveness of sport psychology consultants," The Sport Psychologist 10 (96): 132-139; coauth, "Counseling Women Athletes," in Counseling College Student Athletes: Issues and Interventions, ed. E.F. Etzel, A.P. Ferrante, and J.W. Pinkey (Morgantown, WV: Fitness Infor Technology, 96); coauth, "Diversity in athletics," in Exploring Sport and Exercise Psychology, ed. J. Van Raalte and B. Brewer (Washington, DC: Am Psychol Asn, 96); auth, "Putting the 'clinical' into sport psychology consulting," The Psychotherapy Patient 10 (98): 131-144; coauth, Sport psychology library: Gymnastics, Fitness Infor Technology (Morgantown, WV), 00. **CONTACT ADDRESS** Dept Psychology, Univ of No Texas, PO Box 311280, Denton, TX 76203. **EMAIL** Cogan@dsa.admin.unt.edu

COHEN, ANDREW D.
PERSONAL Born 03/14/1944, Washington, DC, m, 1968, 2 children **DISCIPLINE** EDUCATION **EDUCATION** Harvard Univ, BA, 65; Stanford Univ, MA, 71; Stanford Univ, PhD, 73. **CAREER** Peace Corps volunteer, Bolivia, 65-67; Teaching Fel, Stanford Univ, 70-72; Coordr, English Placement Exam,

UCLA, 72-75; Asst Prof, UCLA,72-75; Sr Lectr, Hebrew Univ Jerusalem, 75-79; Dir, Ctr Applied Ling, Hebrew Univ, 76-80; Academic Head, Dept English as a Foreign Lang, Hebrew Univ, 77-78; Assoc Prof Applied Ling, Hebrew Univ, 79-91; Vis Prof, UCLA, 80-81; Dir, Ctr Applied Ling Res, Hebrew Univ, 81-91; Fulbright Lectr and Researcher, Brazil, 86-87; Vis Scholar, Univ Hawaii, 96-97; Vis Scholar, Tel Aviv Univ, 97; Prof, Univ Minn. **HONORS AND AWARDS** Distinguished Scholar in Residence, Ga State Univ; Melton Fel, Johns Hopkins Univ; Bush Faculty Develop Program on Excellence in Teaching, Univ Minn; Distinguished Lectr Program, Temple Univ, Japan; Fulbright Researcher and Lectr, Brazil. **MEMBERSHIPS** TESOL; AAAL; MinneTESOL; ILTA; ACTFL; AILA **RESEARCH** Bilingual and immersion education; language assessment; language learning and use strategies; speech acts; applied linguistic research methods. **SELECTED PUBLICATIONS** Auth, The Role of Instructors in Testing Summarizing Ability, A New Decade of Language Testing: Collaboration and Cooperation, TESOL, 93; coauth, The Production of Speech Acts by EFL Learners, TESOL Qrt, 27 (1), 93; auth, Assessing language ability in the classroom, 2nd ed, Newbury House/Heinle & Heinle, 94; ed, Focusing on Language and Language Processing: Beyond Test Scores, Language Testing, 11 (2), 94; auth, The Language Used to Perform Cognitive Operations During Full Immersion Math Tasks, Language Testing, 11 (2), 94; auth, Research Methodology in Second Language Acquisition, Erlbaum, 94; auth, SLA Theory and Pedagogy: Some Research Issues, Second Language Acquisition Theory and Pedagogy, Lawrence Erlbaum, 95; auth, In Which Language Do/Should Multilinguals Think?, Language, Culture and Curriculum, 8 (2), 95; auth, The Role of Language of Thought in Foreign Language Learning, Working Papers in Educational Linguistics, 11 (2); auth, Investigating the Production of Speech Act Sets, Speech Acts Across Cultures: Challenges to Communicate in a Second Language, Mouton de Gruyter, 96; auth, Developing the Ability to Perform Speech Acts, Second Language Acquisition, 18 (2), 96; Cohen, A. D., Strategies in learning and using a second language, Harlow, Essex: Longman, 98; ed, Bachman, L. F. & Cohen, A. D., Interfaces between second language acquisition and language testing research, Cambridge, UK: Cambridge Univ Press, 98; auth, Cohen, A. D. & Brooks-Carson, A., Research on direct vs. translated writing: Students' strategies and their results, Modern Language Journal, 85, 169-188, 01. **CONTACT ADDRESS** Dept of English as a Second Language, Univ of Minnesota, Twin Cities, 331E Nolte Center, Minneapolis, MN 55455. **EMAIL** adcohen@tc.umn.edu

COHEN, BURTON I.
PERSONAL Born 05/02/1931, Chicago, IL, m, 1954, 3 children **DISCIPLINE** RELIGIOUS EDUCATION **EDUCATION** Univ Chicago, MA, PhD; Roosevelt Univ, BA. **CAREER** Dir, Camp Ramah, 59-89; assoc prof, 57-. **HONORS AND AWARDS** JTSA Nat Comn Service Awd; JEA Behrman House Lifetime Achievement Awd. **MEMBERSHIPS** United Synagogue Comn Jewish Educ; Nat Exec Comt Jewish Educr Assembly. **SELECTED PUBLICATIONS** Auth, Case Studies in Jewish School Management, Behrman House, 92; ed, Women and Ritual: An Anthology, Nat Ramah, 86; co-ed, Studies in Jewish Education and Judaica in Honor of Louis Newman, Ktav, 84. **CONTACT ADDRESS** Dept of Jewish Educ, Jewish Theol Sem of America, 3080 Broadway, New York, NY 10027. **EMAIL** bucohen@jtsa.edu

COHEN, JONATHAN ALLAN
PERSONAL Born 12/04/1939, Troy, NY, m, 1995, 3 children **DISCIPLINE** PSYCHIATRY **EDUCATION** Univ Cal LA, BS 63, Sch Med, MD 67. **CAREER** Private Practice, psychiatry and psychoanalysis, 74-. **MEMBERSHIPS** APA; FAS; PNHP. **RESEARCH** Psychoanalytic theory and practice. **SELECTED PUBLICATIONS** Auth, Apart for Freud: Notes for a Rational Psychoanalysis, SF, City Lights Press, in press, 00; Freudianism and the human moral system. In: Against Normalization, eds, C. Ware A. Molino, SF, City Lights Press, 98; A View of the Moral Landscape of Psychoanalysis, Jour of Amer Acad Psychoanalysis, 94. **CONTACT ADDRESS** 2005 Franklin St., Suite 500, Denver, CO 80205-5401. **EMAIL** jon.cohen@interfold.com

COHEN, LINDSEY
PERSONAL Born 06/24/1968, Atlanta, GA, m, 1997, 1 child **DISCIPLINE** PSYCHOLOGY **EDUCATION** Univ Ga, PhD, 98. **CAREER** Asst Prof, Wash State Univ, 98-. **HONORS AND AWARDS** Florene M Young Clinical Awd, Univ Ga, 95-96, 98; Univ Wide Scholar and Merit Suppl Awd, Univ Ga, 97-98; Boardman Awd, Univ Ga, 98; Zimmer Res Awd, Univ Ga, 98; A S Edwards Awd, Univ Ga, 98. **MEMBERSHIPS** APA, SPP, AABT. **RESEARCH** Pediatric psychology, children's stress and coping during medical procedures. **SELECTED PUBLICATIONS** Coauth, "Current Status and Future Directions in Acute Pediatric Pain Assessment and Treatment," J of Pediatric Psychol 24 (99): 150-152; coauth, "The Encyclopedia of Parenting Theory and Research," Greenwood Publ Group (99): 157-159; coauth, "Comparative Study of Distraction Versus Topical Anesthesia for Pediatric Pain Management During Immunizations," Health Psychol 18 (99): 591-598; coauth, "Easier Said Than Done: What Parents Say They Do and What They Do During Children's Immunizations," Children's Health Care 29 (00): 79-86; coauth, "The Influence of Parental Reassurance and Distraction on Children's Reactions to an Aversive Medical Procedure," Children's health Care (forthcoming). **CONTACT ADDRESS** Dept Psychol, Washington State Univ, PO Box 644820, Pullman, WA 99164-4820. **EMAIL** cohenl@wsu.edu

COHEN, MARJORIE G.
PERSONAL Born 02/17/1944, Franklin, NJ **DISCIPLINE** POLITICAL SCIENCE, WOMEN'S STUDIES **EDUCATION** Iowa Wesleyan Col, BA, 65; NY Univ, MA, 69; York Univ, PhD 85. **CAREER** Lectr, 71-82, prof, York Univ, 84-86; prof, Ont Inst Stud Educ, 86-91; Ruth Wynn Woodward Endowed Prof, 89-90; Chair, Women's Stud & Prof Political Science & Women's Stud, Simon Fraser Univ, 91-. **HONORS AND AWARDS** Marion Porter Prize Feminist Res, 85; York Univ Fac Grad Stud Dissertation Prize, 85; Laura Jamieson Bk Prize, 89. **MEMBERSHIPS** Ed bd, Can Forum, 77-85; ed bd, Labour/Le Travail, 91-94; Nat Action Comt Status Women. **SELECTED PUBLICATIONS** Auth, Free Trade and the Future of Women's Work: Manufacturing and Service Industries, 87; auth, Women's Work, Markets and Economic Development in Nineteenth Century Ontario, 88; coauth, Canadian Women's Issues, Vol I, Strong Voices 93, Vol II, Bold Visions, 95. **CONTACT ADDRESS** Dept of Women's Stud, Simon Fraser Univ, Burnaby, BC, Canada V5A 1S6. **EMAIL** marjorie_cohen@sfu.ca

COHEN, MYRON L.
PERSONAL Born 06/24/1937, Jersey City, NY, m, 1996 **DISCIPLINE** ANTHROPOLOGY **EDUCATION** Columbia Col NYork, BA 58; Columbia Univ, MA 63, PhD 67. **CAREER** Columbia Univ, lectr, asst prof, assoc prof, prof 66 to 97-. **HONORS AND AWARDS** Sr Sch Res Fell 2; Chiang Chinakuo Foun Fell; Henry Luce Foun. **MEMBERSHIPS** FAAA; RAI; AAS **RESEARCH** Family organization; social organ; political organ; econ culture; religion; China; East Asia. **SELECTED PUBLICATIONS** Auth, Asia Case Studies in the Social Sciences: A Guide for Teaching, Armonk NY, M E Sharpe 92; House United, House Divided: The Chinese Family in Taiwan, NY, CUP 76; Commodities and Contracts In Late Imperial China: Economic Culture in a Qing-Period South Taiwan Community, in: Locating Capitalism in Time and Space: Global restructuring Power and Identity, ed, David L. Nugent, Stanford CA, SU Press, forthcoming; North China Rural Families: Changes During the Communist Era, Etudes Chinoises, Bull Assoc Fran, Vol 17, No 1-2, p 59-154, 99; State and Society Under Qing 1644-1911, in: Asia in Western and World History: A Guide for Teaching, eds, Ainslie T. Embree Carol T. Gluck, Armonk NY, M E Sharpe 97; The Hakka or Guest People: Dialect as a Sociological Variable in Southeastern China, in: Guest People Hakka Identity in China and Abroad, ed, Nicole Constable, Seattle, UWP 96. **CONTACT ADDRESS** Dept of Anthropology, Columbia Univ, New York, NY 10027. **EMAIL** mlc5@columbia.edu

COHN, BERNARD SAMUEL
PERSONAL Born 05/13/1928, Brooklyn, NY, m, 1950, 4 children **DISCIPLINE** ANTHROPOLOGY, HISTORY **EDUCATION** Univ Wis, BA, 49; Cornell Univ, PhD(anthrop), 54. **CAREER** Res assoc anthrop, Univ Chicago, 56-57; fel hist, Rockefeller Found, 57-59; asst prof, Univ Chicago, 59-60; assoc prof anthrop, Univ Rochester, 60-64; assoc prof, 64-67, chmn dept anthrop, 69-71, Prof Anthrop & Hist, Univ Chicago, 67-, Guggenheim fel, 64-65; vis prof, Univ Mich, 66-67; fel, Ctr Advan Study Behav Sci, 67-68; Richards lectr, Univ Va, 65; Am Coun Learned Soc-Soc Sci Res Coun fel, Comt Southern Asia, 73-74; Am Inst Indian Studies fel, 74-75; NSF grant, 75-77. **MEMBERSHIPS** Am Anthrop Asn; Asn Asian Studies; Royal Anthrop Inst; Am Soc Ethnohist; AHA. **RESEARCH** History of South Asia; comparative colonial systems; representations of authority in colonial India. **SELECTED PUBLICATIONS** Auth, The Sepoy and the Raj--The Indian Army, 1860-1940, Intl Hist Rev, Vol 0017, 95. **CONTACT ADDRESS** Dept of Anthrop, Univ of Chicago, Chicago, IL 60637.

COLARELLI, STEPHEN MICHAEL
DISCIPLINE PSYCHOLOGY **EDUCATION** Northwestern Univ, BA, 73; Univ Chicago, MA, 79; NYork Univ, PhD, 82. **CAREER** Dir of Grad Progs in Industrial/Organizational Psychology, Dept Psychology, Central Mich Univ, Mt. Pleasant, 90-96; Prof (Fulbright Fel), Dept of Psychology, Univ Zambia, Lusaka, 95; Prof, Central Mich Univ, 94-. **HONORS AND AWARDS** Phi Beta Delta; Who's Who in Sci and Engineering, 94-95 ed; Fulbright Fel, 95; Central Mich Univ Fac Res and Creative Endeavors Res Grant, 97. **MEMBERSHIPS** Acad of Management, Am Psychol Soc, Asn for Politics and Life Scis, Behavioral and Brain Scis Soc, Human Behavior and Evolution Soc, Int Soc for Human Ethology, Soc for Industrial/Organizational Psychol, Soc for the Evolutionary Analysis of Law. **SELECTED PUBLICATIONS** Couth with K. O'Hara and T. A. Beehr, "Organizational centrality: A third dimension of intraorganizational career movement," J of Applied Behav Sci, 30 (94): 198-216; coauth with G. A. Adams and T. C. Elacqua, "The employment interview as a sociometric selection technique," J of Psychotherapy, Psychodrama and Sociometry, 47 (94): 99-113; auth, "Establishment and job context influences on the use of hiring practices," Applied Psychology: An Int Rev, 45 (96): 153-176; coauth with M. S. Montei, "Some contextual influences on training utilization," J of Applied Behav Sci, 32 (96): 306-322; auth, "Psychological interventions in organizations: An evolutionary perspective," Am Psychol, 53 (98): 1044-1056; auth, "Evolution, the criterion problem, and complexity," Behv and Brain Scis (in press). **CONTACT ADDRESS** Dept Psychol, Central Michigan Univ, 100 W Preston Rd, Mount Pleasant, MI 48859-0001. **EMAIL** s.colarelli@cmich.edu

COLATRELLA, CAROL
DISCIPLINE CULTURAL STUDY OF AMERICAN AND EUROPEAN LITERATURE **EDUCATION** Rutgers Univ, PhD, 87. **CAREER** Assoc prof, exec dir, Soc for Lit & Sci, Ga Inst of Technol. **RESEARCH** Herman Melville's fictions. **SELECTED PUBLICATIONS** Auth, Evolution, Sacrifice, and Narrative: Balzac, Zola, and Faulkner; coed, Cohesion and Dissent in America. **CONTACT ADDRESS** Sch of Lit, Commun & Cult, Georgia Inst of Tech, Skiles Cla, Atlanta, GA 30332. **EMAIL** carol.colatrella@lcc.gatech.edu

COLBURN, KENNETH
PERSONAL Born 08/26/1950, Plainfield, NJ, m, 1980, 2 children **DISCIPLINE** SOCIOLOGY **EDUCATION** Rutgers Univ, AB, 72; York Univ, MA, 74; PhD, 80. **CAREER** Asst prof to full prof, 88-. **HONORS AND AWARDS** Phi Kappa Phi; Alpha Kappa Delta. **MEMBERSHIPS** Am Sociol Asn, North Central Sociol Asn, Midwest Sociol Asn, Acad of Criminal Justice. **RESEARCH** Urban and community sociology, Deviance, Theory. **CONTACT ADDRESS** Dept Sociol & Criminal Justice Dept Sociol & Criminal Justice, Butler Univ, 4600 Sunset Ave, Indianapolis, IN 46208. **EMAIL** kcolburn@butler.edu

COLE, PHILLIS B.
PERSONAL Born 11/22/1944, St. Charles, IL, m, 1972, 2 children **DISCIPLINE** WOMEN'S STUDIES, AMERICAN STUDIES **EDUCATION** Oberlin Col, BA, 66; Harvard Univ, MA, 67; PhD, 73. **CAREER** Asst prof to vis res scholar, Wellesley Col, 73-89; res assoc to lectr, Harvard Univ, 84-88; assoc prof to prof, Pa State Del County, 89-. **HONORS AND AWARDS** NEH, 80-81, 93; Woodrow Wilson Found, 66-67; Ford Found, 67-73; Charles Warren Ctr, 80-81; Mellon Found, 82-83; Ellis Found, 85; Pa State Inst, 91, 98; James Russell Lowell Prize, 99; Choice Outstanding Bk, 98; Acad Excellence Award, 01; Phi Beta Kappa. **MEMBERSHIPS** MLA; ALA; ASA; RWES; SSAWW; Margaret Fuller Soc; Thoreau Soc. **RESEARCH** American Transcendentalism; American women writers; 19th-century reform rhetoric; autobiography and diary. **SELECTED PUBLICATIONS** Auth, "Emerson, England, and Fate," English Inst Essays (75); auth, "The Purity of Puritanism: Transcendentalist Readings of Milton," Studies Romanticism (78); auth, "The Advantage of Loneliness: Mary Moody Emerson's Almanacs," Harvard English Studies (82); auth, "From the Edwardses to the Emersons," CEA Crit (87); auth, The American Writer and the Condition of England, Garland Pr, 87; auth, "Men and Women Conversing: The Emersons in 1837," Univ Rochester Pr (97); auth, Mary Moody Emerson and the Origins of Transcendentalism: A Family History, Oxford Univ Pr, 98; auth, "The Nineteenth-Century Women's Rights Movement and the Canonization of Margaret Fuller," ESQ (98); auth, "Woman Questions: Emerson, Fuller, and New England Reform," MHS (99); auth, "Stanton, Fuller, and the Grammar of Romanticism," New Eng Quart (00). **CONTACT ADDRESS** Humanities Dept, Pennsylvania State Univ, Delaware County, 25 Yearsley Mill Rd, Media, PA 19063. **EMAIL** pbc2@psu.edu

COLE, STEPHEN
PERSONAL Born 06/01/1941, New York, NY, m, 1987, 2 children **DISCIPLINE** SOCIOLOGY **EDUCATION** Columbia Univ, BA, 62; PhD, 67. **CAREER** Asst prof, Columbia Univ, 67-68; asst prof, SUNY at Stony Brook, 68-70, assoc prof, 70-73, prof, 73-95, leading prof, 95-; res assoc, Center for the Soc Scis, Columbia Univ, 77-88; vis prof, Center for Am Studies, Univ of Warsaw, Poland, 87; chair of Sociol, Dept of Anthropol and Sociol, Univ of Queensland, Australia, 95-97. **HONORS AND AWARDS** Ford Found Fac Res Fel, 71-72; Guggenheim Found Fel, 78-79; Fel, Ctr for Advanced Study in the Behavioral Scis, Stanford, Calif, 78-79; mem, Sch of Soc Sci, Inst for Advanced study, Princeton, NJ, 92-93; Vis Scholar, Russell Sage Found, 97-98; Grants from: the Coun of Ivy League Presidents, the Andrew W. Mellon Found, and the Ford Found. **SELECTED PUBLICATIONS** Coauth with Jonathan R. Cole, "The Ortega Hypothesis," Science 1978 (October 72): 368-375; coauth with Jonathan R. Cole, Social Stratification in Science, Chicago: The Univ of Chicago Press (73, paperback ed, 81); coauth with Leonard Rubin and Jonathan R. Cole, Peer Review in the National Science Foundation: Phase I, Washington, DC: Nat Acad of Scis (78); coauth with Jonathan R. Cole, Peer Review in the National Science Foundation: Phase II, Washington, DC: Nat Acad of Scis (81); coauth with J. R. Cole and G. Simon, "Chance and Consensus in Peer Review," Science 215 (Jan 22, 82): 344-348; auth, "The Hierarchy of the Sciences?," Am J of Sociol 89 (83): 111-139; auth, "Sex Discrimination and Admission to Medical School: 1929-1984," Am J of

Sociol, 92 (86): 549-567; auth, Making Science: Between Nature and Society, Cambridge: Harvard Univ Press (92, paperback ed 95). **CONTACT ADDRESS** Dept Sociol, SUNY, Stony Brook, Stony Brook, NY 11794. **EMAIL** scole@notes.cc.sunysb.edu

COLEMAN, JOHN ALOYSIUS
PERSONAL Born 03/27/1937, San Francisco, CA **DISCIPLINE** SOCIOLOGY OF RELIGION **EDUCATION** St Louis Univ, BA, 60, MA, 61; Univ Santa Clara, STM, 68; Univ Calif, Berkeley, PhD(sociol), 74. **CAREER** Asst prof relig & soc, Jesuit Sch Theol & Grad Theol Union, Berkeley, 74-77; res fel, Woodstock Ctr, Georgetown Univ, 77-78; Asst Prof Relig & Soc, Jesuit Sch Theol & Grad Theol Union, Berkeley, 78-, Fel social ethics, Univ Chicago Divinity Sch, 73-74. **MEMBERSHIPS** Cath Theol Soc Am; Am Acad Relig; Am Soc Christian Ethics. **RESEARCH** Sociology of comparative Catholicism; history of social Catholicism; human rights. **SELECTED PUBLICATIONS** Auth, On Being the Church in the United-States--Contemporary Theological Critiques of Liberalism, Theol Stud, Vol 0057, 96; Religion and Politics in Latin-America--Liberation-Theology and Christian Democracy, Jour Rel, Vol 0073, 93; Pious Passion--The Emergence of Modern Fundamentalism in the United-States And Iran--Comparative-Studies in Religion and Society, Theol Stud, Vol 0055, 94; Sociology and Social-Justice--The Case-Study of Fichter, Joseph Sj Research, Sociol Rel, Vol 0057, 96. **CONTACT ADDRESS** Graduate Theol Union, 2465 Le Compte Ave, Berkeley, CA 94709.

COLEMAN, KAREN J.
PERSONAL Born 04/10/1967, Madrid, Spain, m **DISCIPLINE** PSYCHOLOGY **EDUCATION** Wash State Univ, BS, 90; Univ Ga, MS, 92; PhD, 94. **CAREER** Asst res prof, Univ at Buffalo, 96-97; asst prof, Univ of Tex at El Paso. 97-. **HONORS AND AWARDS** Principal investigator, "Measuring Physical Activity ion Hispanic Women," El Paso Border Res Ctr, 2000; principal investigator, "El Paso Child and Adolescent Trail for Cardiovascular Health Program Evaluation," Am Heart Asn, 2001. **MEMBERSHIPS** Soc of Behav Med, Am Col of Sports Med, Soc for Cross-Cultural Res, Am Asn for the Advancement of Sci. **RESEARCH** Physical activity as a behavior; success in promoting the adoption of an active lifestyle for optimal health benefits; behavioral and physiologic change; behavior modification techniques to ensure exercise adherence; the study of the reinforcing value of exercise relative to other alternatives. **SELECTED PUBLICATIONS** Coauth with D. A. Raynor and L. H. Epstein, "Effects of proximity on the choice to be physically active or sedentary," Res Quart for Exercise and Sport, 69 (98): 99-103; coauth with L. H. Epstein, "Application of Generalizability Theory to measurement of activity in males who are not regularly active: a preliminary report," Res Quart for Exercise and Sport, 69 (98): 58-63; coauth with H. R. Raynor, D. M. Mueller, F. J. Cerny, J. M. Dorn, and L. H. Epstein, "Providing sedentary adults with choices for meeting their exercise goals," Preventative Med, 28 (99): 510-519; couth with E. C. Gonzalez and T. Cooley, "An objective measure of reinforcement and its implications for physical promotion in sedentary Hispanic and Anglo women," Annals of Behavioral Med (in press). **CONTACT ADDRESS** Dept Psychol, Univ of Texas, El Paso, 500 W Univ Ave, El Paso, TX 79968-0001. **EMAIL** kcoleman@miners.utep.edu

COLEMAN, PRISCILLA K.
PERSONAL Born 03/31/1961, Scranton, PA, m, 1983, 3 children **DISCIPLINE** PSYCHOLOGY **EDUCATION** Southern Conn State Univ, BA, 86; James Madison Univ, MA, 92; WV Univ, PhD, 98. **CAREER** Instr, James Madison Univ, 93-95; res specialist, James Madison Univ, 97-98; asst prof, Univ of the South, 98-. **HONORS AND AWARDS** Phi Kappa Phi, 97; Eberly Doctoral Res Awd, 97; Soc for Res in Child Dev Stud Travel Awd, 97. **MEMBERSHIPS** Am Psychol Asn, Soc for Res in Child Dev, Am Psychol Soc. **RESEARCH** Parenting, Socio-emotional development in infancy, psychological effects of abortion. **SELECTED PUBLICATIONS** Auth, "The relationship between deception and power in college students' dating relationships: An exploratory study," Journal of Sex and Marital Therapy, (in press); auth, "College students' attitudes toward abortion and commitment to the issue," Social Science Journal, (in press); auth, "Parenting self-efficacy among mothers of school-age children: Conceptualization, measurement, and predictors," Family Relations, (forthcoming); auth, "Self-efficacy and parenting quality: Findings and future application," Developmental Review, (98): 47-85; auth, "Infant attachment as a dynamic system," Human Development, (in press); auth, "Attitudes toward abortion and interest in the issue as determinants of perceptions of the appropriate level of male involvement in abortion decisions," Journal of American College Health, (99): 164-172; auth, "The quality of abortion decisions and college students' reports of post-abortion emotional sequel and abortion attitudes," Journal of Social and Clinical Psychology, (98): 425-442; auth, "The relationship between prenatal expectations and postnatal attitudes among first-time mothers," Journal of Reproductive and Infant Psychology, (99): 27-39; auth, "The influence of intercultural experiences and second language proficiency on college students' cross-cultural adaptability," International Education, (98): 217-224. **CONTACT ADDRESS** Dept Psychol, Univ The South, 735 Univ Ave, Sewanee, TN 3783-1000. **EMAIL** pcoleman@sewanee.edu

COLLINS, DEREK B.
PERSONAL Born 08/24/1965, Washington, DC, m, 1990, 2 children **DISCIPLINE** COMPARATIVE LIT; CLASSICS; FOLKLORE & MYTHOLOGY **EDUCATION** Univ CA, Los Angeles, MA, 91; Harvard Univ, PhD, 97. **CAREER** Asst Prof Classics, Univ Texas at Austin, 97-. **HONORS AND AWARDS** Nat Academy of Sciences, Ford Found, Doctoral Dissertation fel, 9/96--6/97. **MEMBERSHIPS** Am Philos Asn; Classical Asn of the Middle West and South; Am Folklore Soc. **RESEARCH** Greek lit; comparative lit (German); witchcraft. **SELECTED PUBLICATIONS** Trans, Greek selections in the Appendix to Claude Calame, The Craft of Poetic Speech in Ancient Greece, Cornell Univ Press, 95; auth, The Myth and Ritual of Ezili Freda in Hurston's Their Eyes Were Watching God, Western Folklore 55, 96; trans with J. Orion, Claude Calame, Young Women's Choruses in Ancient Greece: Their Morphology, Religious Role, and Social Functions, Lanham, MD, Rowman & Littlefield Pubs, 97; auth, Fatum, in the Dictionaire International des Termes Litteraitres, gen ed, Jean-Marie Grassin, A. Francke-Berne, Saur-Vg Pub, Berne, Munich, Paris, New York, 97; On the Aesthetics of the Deceiving Self in Nietzsche, Pindar, and Theognis, Nietzsche-Studien 26, 97; Review of Jacob Rabinowitz, The Rotting Goddess: The Origin of the Witch in Classical Antiquity, Scholia 7 (ns), 16, 98; Immortal Armor: The Concept of Alke in Archaic Greek Poetry, Lanham, MD, Rowman & Littlefield Pubs, 98; Hesiod and the Divine Voice of the Muses, Arethusa, forthcoming, 99. **CONTACT ADDRESS** Dept of Classical Studies, Univ of Michigan, Ann Arbor, 2160 Angell Hall, 435 S State St, Ann Arbor, MI 48109-1003. **EMAIL** dbcollin@umich.edu

COLLINS, ELSIE
PERSONAL Born Durham, NC, d **DISCIPLINE** EDUCATION **EDUCATION** DE St Coll, BA 1945; Columbia U, MA 1952; Union Grad Sch, PhD 1977. **CAREER** Trenton State Coll, asst prof, 71-; Trenton, NJ, asst dir of COP, 71; Natl Teachers Corp, Trenton NJ, team leader, 68-71; Core Curr Jr High School, Trenton NJ, teacher, 61-62, 64-68, demonstration teacher, 65-68; Trenton State Coll, supvr summer semester for teachers, 65-75; Dover DE Jr & Sr High Schools, teacher, 45-59; Beth Jacob Jewish High School New York City, teacher, 60-61; Consult Serv & In-serv Workshops Trenton; Teahcer Educ NJ State Dept Higher Educ, 67-72; Afro-Amer Studies, 69-76; Urban Educ Curriculum Spec, 72-. **HONORS AND AWARDS** Valedictorian high sch schlrship high honor DE St Coll; scholarship student of music Tchrs Coll Columbia Univ 1950-57; soloist St Paul United Meth Ch Trenton 1967-; publ "Poverty & the Poor" 1968; contributed to Devl of Urban Educ Series Prob of Amer Soc 1966-68; special award World Who's Who of Women in Educ 1977-78; Internatl Artists & Fellows of Distinction 1980. **MEMBERSHIPS** Mem Community Leaders & Noteworthy Am 1979; mem Doctorate Assn of NY Educators 1980; mem Amer Assn Univ Women 1954-60; current membrshp New Jersey HistSoc Am Assn Negro Mus; NAACP; Urban Leag Couns of Soc Studies NEA NJEA Poverty Law Ctr AKA Assn for Superv & Curriculum Devel. **CONTACT ADDRESS** Trenton State Col, 371 Education Bldg, Trenton, NJ 08625.

COLSTON, HERBERT L.
PERSONAL Born 09/21/1966 **DISCIPLINE** PSYCHOLOGY **EDUCATION** Purdue Univ, BS, 89; Univ Calif, MS, 93; PhD, 95. **CAREER** Part-Time Fac, Calif State Univ, 97; Instr, Univ Calif, 97; Asst Prof, Univ Wis, 97-. **HONORS AND AWARDS** Jason Albrecht Outstanding Young Sci Awd, Soc for Text and Discourse, 98. **SELECTED PUBLICATIONS** Auth, "Salting a Wound or Sugaring a Pill: The Pragmatic Functions of Ironic Criticism," Discourse Processes, 23 (97): 25-45; auth, "I've Never Seen Anything Life It: Overstatement, Understatement and Irony," Metaphor and Symbol, 12 (97): 43-58; coauth, "Analogy and Irony: Rebuttal to 'Rebuttal Analogy'," Metaphor and Symbol, 13 (98): 69-75; rev, "Metaphor: Implications and Applications," Metaphor and Symbol, 14 (99): 77-80; auth, "'Not Good' is 'Bad,' But 'Not Bad' is 'Not Good': An Analysis of Three Accounts of Negation Asymmetry," Discourse Processes, 28 (99): 237-256; auth, "'Dewey Defeats Truman': Interpreting Ironic Restatement," J of Lang and Soc Psychol, 19 (00): 44-63. **CONTACT ADDRESS** Dept Psychol, Univ of Wisconsin, Parkside, Kenosha, WI 53141-2000. **EMAIL** herbert.colston@uwp.edu

COLVIN, MARK
PERSONAL Born 10/01/1947, San Marcos, TX, m, 1984, 2 children **DISCIPLINE** SOCIOLOGY, ANTHROPOLOGY **EDUCATION** Univ Colorado, PhD, 85. **CAREER** Asst Prof of Sociology, George Mason Univ, 86-92; Assoc Prof of Sociology, 92-00. **HONORS AND AWARDS** Special Mention for ASA Book Awd, 93; Am Sociological Assoc. **MEMBERSHIPS** American Sociology Assoc, American Society of Criminology. **RESEARCH** Crime, Delinquency and Corrections. **SELECTED PUBLICATIONS** Auth, The Penitentiary in Crisis, SUNY Press, 92; auth, Penitentiaries, Reformatories, and Chain Gangs, St. Martin's Press, 97; auth, Crime and Coercion, St, Martin's Press, 00. **CONTACT ADDRESS** Dept Sociology & Anthropology, George Mason Univ, Fairfax, 4400 Univ Dr, Fairfax, VA 22030. **EMAIL** mcolvin@gmu.edu

COMAROFF, JEAN
PERSONAL Born Edinburgh, m, 1967, 2 children **DISCIPLINE** ANTHROPOLOGY **EDUCATION** Cape Town, BA; London Sch of Econ, PhD. **CAREER** Asst Prof, Univ Chicago, 79-87; Prof, 87-96; Bernard E & Ellen C Sunny Distinguished Science Prof & Ch, 96. **HONORS AND AWARDS** Gordon Laing Prize, Best Book; teaching awards; MLA award, best Special Issue J, 00. **MEMBERSHIPS** African Stud Asn; Am Anthrop Asn. **RESEARCH** Ritual, body; medicine; colonialism & history in Southern Africa (Tswana peoples). **SELECTED PUBLICATIONS** Auth, Body of Power, Spirit of Resistance: The Culture and History of a South African People, Univ Chicago Press, 85; co-auth, Of Revelation and Revolution: Christianity, Colonialism, and Consciousness in South Africa, Univ Chicago Press, 91, vol II, 97; co-auth, Ethnography and the Historical Imagination, Westview Press, 92; co-ed, Modernity and its Malcontents: Ritual and Power in Africa, Univ Chicago Press, 93; co-ed, Civil Society, Moral Community and Public Sphere in Africa, in press; auth, Millennial Capitalism and the Culture of Neo-Liberalism, Duke Univ Press, 01. **CONTACT ADDRESS** Dept of Anthrop, Univ of Chicago, 1126 E 59th St, Chicago, IL 60637.

COMER, JOHN
PERSONAL Born 12/07/1946, Memphis, TN, m, 1969, 4 children **DISCIPLINE** SOCIOLOGY, THEOLOGY, PHILOSOPHY **EDUCATION** Auburn Univ, BS, 68, MBA, 69; Univ of the South, MDiv, 75. **CAREER** Pastoral theology, 75-00; university chaplain, 79-85; chaplain, Marion Military Inst, 98-00. **HONORS AND AWARDS** Algeron Sidney Sullivan Awd, Auburn Univ, 68; Paul Harris Fel, Rotary Int, 92; Who's Who in South and Southwest; Who's Who in Religion in Am; Who's Who in Teaching in Am. **MEMBERSHIPS** Omicron Delta Kappa, Omicron Delta Epsilon, Delta Sigma Rho, Tau Kappa Alpha, Scabbord and Blade. **RESEARCH** Psychology, sociology, statistics. **CONTACT ADDRESS** Dept Hist & Soc Sci, Marion Military Inst, 1101 Washington St, Marion, AL 36756-3213.

COMOR, EDWARD
PERSONAL Born Toronto, ON, Canada **DISCIPLINE** POLITICAL ECONOMY OF COMMUNICATION AND CULTURE **EDUCATION** Univ Toronto; BA; Univ Leeds, MA; York Univ, PhD. **CAREER** Prof, Am Univ. **HONORS AND AWARDS** Chair, Int Communication Section of the Int Studies Asn, 00-01. **MEMBERSHIPS** Int Studies Asn; Int Asn for Media and Communication Res; Int Communication Asn; Asn for Evolutionary Economics. **RESEARCH** United States foreign communication policy; The mediating role of free trade treaties and other international institutions; The political economic implications of the internet; auth, The Writings and methodology of Harold A. Innis. **SELECTED PUBLICATIONS** Ed/contribur, The Global Political Economy of Communications, St. Martin's Press, 94, 96; auth, Communication, Commerce and Power, St. Martin's Press, 98. **CONTACT ADDRESS** American Univ, 4400 Massachusetts Ave, Washington, DC 20016. **EMAIL** ecomor@american.edu

COMSTOCK, GEORGE ADOLPHE
PERSONAL Born 05/17/1932, Seattle, WA, d **DISCIPLINE** COMMUNICATIONS, SOCIAL PSYCHOLOGY **EDUCATION** Univ Wash, BA, 54; Stanford Univ, MA, 58, PhD(commun), 67. **CAREER** Asst prof jour, NY Univ, 67-68; social psychologist, Rand Corp, 68-70 & NIMH., 70-72; sr social psychologist, Rand Corp, 72-77; prof commun, S I Newhouse Sch Pub Commun, 77-79, S I Newhouse Chair Pub Commun, Syracuse Univ, 79- . **HONORS AND AWARDS** Sr sci adv, US Surgeon Gen Sci Adv Comt TV & Social Behavior, 70-72. **MEMBERSHIPS** Asn Educ Jour and Mass Commun; Am Asn Pub Opinion Res; Soc Psychol Study Social Issues. **RESEARCH** Behavioral effects of televised portrayals; influence of mass media on society. **SELECTED PUBLICATIONS** Co-ed, Media Content and Control, Vol I, Television and Social Learning, Vol II, Television and Adolescent Agressiveness, Vol III, Television in Day-to-day Life, Vol IV, Television's Effects: Further Explorations, Vol V, In: Television and Social Behavior, US Govt Printing Off, 72; coauth, Television and Human Behavior: The Research Horizon, Future and Present, & auth, Television and Human Behavior: The Key Studies, Rand Corp, 75; coauth, Television and Human Behavior, Columbia Univ, 78; auth, Television in America, 2nd ed, Sage, 91; auth, Evolution of American Television, Sage, 89; auth, Television and the American Child, Academic, 91; co-auth, Television: What's on, Who's Watching, and What It Means. **CONTACT ADDRESS** Pub Commun, Syracuse Univ, Syracuse, NY 13210.

CONGDON, KRISTIN G.
PERSONAL Born 10/09/1948, Boston, MA, m, 1970 **DISCIPLINE** ART-ART EDUCATION, FOLKLORE, ART HISTORY **EDUCATION** PhD Univ of Oregon, 83; MS IN Univ, 72; BA Valparaiso Univ, 70. **CAREER** Prof of Art, Univ of Central FL, Orlando, Coordinator AA Hist Prog 88-present; Asst Prof, AA Edu Bowling Green State Univ,OH, 84-87. **HONORS AND AWARDS** Natl Art Edu Assoc, Zeigfeld Awd, Res of the Year Awd, Southeastern Region's Natl Art Edu Assoc Higher Edu Div Natl Art Educator of the Year Awd, NAEA Barkan Awd. **MEMBERSHIPS** Am Folklore Assoc, Col Art

Assoc, Intl Soc for Edu through AA, Natl Art Edu Assoc, Woman's Caucus for AA. **RESEARCH** Commun AAS Soc Eco, Feminist& AA Criticism, Folklore At/Traditional AA, Art and Eco multi-cultural Edu. **SELECTED PUBLICATIONS** Review ed,: Indigenous Teaching(Webb-based Pub) 98-present; Member, Review Bd, The Journal of Gender Issues in Art and Education, 96-present; Outside Review Ed, Aouthern Folklore, 93-95; Member Ed Advisory Bd, Studies in Art Education, 91-95; Journal of Multi-cultural and Cross-cultural Research in Art Education, 87-present; Asst Ed: Journal of Social Theory and Art Education, 90-91; Browne, R Browne P, Congdon, KG et al, The Encyclopedia of Popular Culture in the United States, NY ABC-CLIO Publishing Co, in press. **CONTACT ADDRESS** Col of Arts and Sci, Univ of Central Florida, Orlando, FL 32816. **EMAIL** kcongdon@pegasus.cc.ucf.edu

CONIGLIARO, VINCENT
PERSONAL Born 07/20/1928, Palermo, Italy, m, 1983, 4 children **DISCIPLINE** PSYCHIATRY **EDUCATION** Gonzaga Col, BA, 46; Palermo Med School, MD, 51; Milan Neuropsychiatric Ins, MS, 53; Postgrad Center New York, Cert in Psychoanalysis, 63. **CAREER** Lecturer, School of Theology for Laymen, New York, 61-63; Asst prof, Fordham Univ, 63-66; Co-founder of Grad School of Pastoral Counseling, Iona Col, 63-68; Assoc Prof to Prof, Fordham Univ, 66-, Dean, Training Inst for Mental Health, 78-. **MEMBERSHIPS** Am Asn of Univ Prof, Am Psychiat Asn, NY County Psychia Asn, Nat Med Asn, Manhattan Cent Med Asn, Acad of Relig and Mental Health, Guild of Catholic Psychiat, Am Geriatrics Asn, Royal Soc for the Promotion of Health, Soc of Grad of Ital Med Schools. **SELECTED PUBLICATIONS** Auth, "In Days of Time-limited Psychotherapeutic Modalities, is Freudian Thinking Obsolete?," Crisis Intervention, 97; auth, The Dream as a tool in Psychodynamic Psychotherapy: The royal Road to the Unconscious, Intl Univ Press, 97; auth, "September Reflections: Allegretto ma non Troppo," Newsletter of the Assoc of the Training Institute for Mental health Practitioners, 76; auth, "The Tyranny of Looks. Psychologic and socio-Cultural Considerations on Physical Attractiveness and Sex Appeal," Cosmopolitan, April 75; auth, Pastoral Counseling: Psychologist or Confessor?, Il Giornala Di Sicilia, 70. **CONTACT ADDRESS** Dept soc Service, Fordham Univ, 113 W 60th St, New York, NY 10023.

CONKLIN, JOHN E.
PERSONAL Born 10/02/1943, Oswego, NY, m, 1982, 4 children **DISCIPLINE** SOCIOLOGY, CRIMINOLOGY **EDUCATION** Cornell Univ, AB, 65; Harvard Univ, PhD, 69. **CAREER** Res assoc, Center for Criminal Justice, Harvard Law Sch, 69-70; asst prof to prof, Tufts Univ, 70-, chair, Dept Sociol and Anthropol, 81-86, 90-91. **HONORS AND AWARDS** Phi Beta Kappa, 65; Bobbs-Merrill Awd for outstanding grad student, 67; AB, cum laude, 65; Nat Defense Ed Act Title IV Fel, 65-68. **MEMBERSHIPS** Am Sociol Asn, Am Soc Criminol. **RESEARCH** Criminal behavior, art theft. **SELECTED PUBLICATIONS** Sr auth with Dermot Meagher, "The Percentage Deposit Bail System: An Alternative to the Professional Bondsman," J of Criminal Justice, 1, 299-317 (winter 73); auth, The Impact of Crime, NY: Macmillan Pub Co (75); auth, "Robbery, Elderly, and Fear: An Urban Problem in Search of a Solution," in Jack and Sharon S. Goldsmith, eds, Crime and the Elderly, Lexington, MA: D. C. Heath and Co, 99-110 (76); auth, Illegal but Not Criminal: Business Crime in America, Englewood Cliffs, NJ: Prentice-Hall, Inc (77); auth, Sociology: An Introduction, 2nd ed, NY: Macmillan (87, also, 1st ed, 84); auth, "Crime and Punishment," in The United States of America: A Handbook , Oxford, England: Facts on File, Inc (92); auth, Art Crime, Westport, CT: Praeger (94); ed, New Perspectives in Criminology, Boston: Allyn & Bacon (96); auth, "Art Theft," in Encyclopedia of Crime and Deviant Behavior, Volume 2: Crime and Juvenile Delinquency, Philadelphia: Taylor and Francis (2000); auth, Criminology, 7th ed, Boston: Allyn & Bacon (2001). **CONTACT ADDRESS** Dept Sociol & Anthropol, Tufts Univ, Medford, 520 Boston Ave, Medford, MA 02155. **EMAIL** jconklin@emerald.tufts.edu

CONNOLLY, THOMAS J.
PERSONAL Born 03/01/1954, Fargo, ND, m, 1982, 1 child **DISCIPLINE** ANTHROPOLOGY, ARCHAEOLOGY **EDUCATION** Univ Oregon, PhD, 86 **CAREER** Research div dir, State Mus Anthrop, Univ Oregon, 86- **MEMBERSHIPS** Soc Amer Archaeol; Soc Calif Archaeol; Assoc Ore Archaeologist; Plains Archaeol Soc **RESEARCH** Archaelogy of Western North America **SELECTED PUBLICATIONS** "Radiocarbon Evidence Relating to Northern Great Basin Basketry Chronology." Jour Calif & Great Basin Anthrop, 98; "Newberry Crater: A Ten-Thousand-Year Record of Human Occupation and Environmental Change in the Basin-Plateau Borderlands." Univ Utah Anthro Papers; "Oregon Wet Site Basketry: A Review of Structural Type." Contribution to the Archaeology of Oregon, 95-97; coauth, "Population Dynamics on the Northwestern Great Basin Periphery: Clues from Obsidian Geochemistry," Jrnl of Calif and Great Basin Antrho 19 (2) (97): 241-250; coauth, "Mapping the Mosier Mounds: The Significance of Rock Feature Complexes on the Southern Columbia Plateau," Jrnl of Archaeological Sce, 24 (97): 289-300; coauth, "Comments on 'America's Oldest Basketry,'" Radiocarbon 41 (3) (99): 309-313. **CONTACT ADDRESS** Dept Anthro, Univ of Oregon, Eugene, OR 97403. **EMAIL** connolly@darkwing.uoregon.edu

CONRAD, CHERYL D.
DISCIPLINE BEHAVIORAL NEUROSCIENCE **EDUCATION** Univ Calif Irvine, BS, 86; BS, 86; Univ Ill Urbana, PhD, 94. **CAREER** Postdoc Fel, Rockefeller Univ, 94-97; Asst Prof, Ariz State Univ, 97-. **HONORS AND AWARDS** Fel, Nat Inst of Health, 88, 94, 96; Grant, Ariz State Univ, 00; Incentive Awd, Ariz State Univ, 00; Doolen Scholar, Univ Ill; Outstanding Teacher, Univ Ill; Who's Who in Am Women. **MEMBERSHIPS** Soc for Neurosci; Soc for Behav Neurosci; Am Psychol Soc; NY Acad of Sci. **RESEARCH** Stress; Learning and Memory; Hippocampl function; Emotion. **SELECTED PUBLICATIONS** Co-auth, "Selective hippocampal granule cell loss after adrenalectomy: Implications for spatial memory," J of Neurosci, 93; co-auth, "Dentate gyrus destruction and spatial learning impairment after corticosteroid removal in young and middle-aged rats," Hippocampus, 95; co-auth, "Chronic restraint stress impairs rat spatial memory on the Y-Maze and this effect is blocked by tianeptine pre-treatment," Behav Neurosci; 96; co-auth, "Prevention of stress-induced morphological and cognitive consequences," Europ Neuropsychopharmacol, 97; co-auth, "Effects of Type I and Type II corticosteroid receptor agonists on exploratory behavior and spatial memory on the Y-Maze," Brain Research, 97; co-auth, "Support for a bimodal role for Type II adrenal steroid receptors in hippocampus-dependent spatial recognition memory," Neurobiol of Learning and Memory, 99; co-auth, "Repeated restraint stress enhances fear conditioning, independently of causing hippocampal CA3 dendritic atrophy," Behav Neurosci, 00; co-auth, "Acute stress increases neuropeptide Y (NPY) mRNA within the arcuate nucleus and hilus of the dentate gyrus,' Molecular Brain Res, 00. **CONTACT ADDRESS** Dept Psychol, Arizona State Univ, Box 1104, Tempe, AZ 85287-1104. **EMAIL** conradc@asu.edu

CONRAD, MARGARET R.
PERSONAL Born 12/14/1946, Bridgewater, NS, Canada **DISCIPLINE** HISTORY, WOMEN'S STUDIES **EDUCATION** Acadia Univ, BA, 67; Univ Toronto, MA, 68, PhD, 79. **CAREER** Ed, Clark, Irwin Publ, 68-69; lectr to assoc prof, 69-87, Prof History, Acadia Univ, 87-; adj prof, Dalhousie Univ, 91-; Nancy Rowell Jackman Chair Women's Stud, Mt St Vincent Univ, 96-98. **HONORS AND AWARDS** Fel, Royal Soc Canada, 95. **MEMBERSHIPS** Asn Can Stud; Can Hist Asn; Can Res Inst Advan Women; Can Women's Stud Asn; Planter Stud Ctr. **RESEARCH** History of Atlantic Canada. **SELECTED PUBLICATIONS** Auth, Recording Angels, 83; auth, George Nowlan: Maritime Conservative in National Politics, 86; coauth, Twentieth Century Canada, 74; coauth, Women at Acadia University: The First Fifty Years 1884-1934, 83; coauth, No Place Like Home: The Diaries and Letters of Nova Scotia Women 1771-1938, 88; coauth, History of the Canadian Peoples, 2 vols, 93, 2nd ed 97; supv ed, New England Planters in Maritime Canada, 93; ed, They Planted Well, 88; ed, Making Adjustments: Change and Continuity in Planter Nova Scotia, 91; ed, Intimate Relations, 95; co-ed, Atlantis: A Women's Stud J, 75-85; co-ed, Can Hist Rev, 97-. **CONTACT ADDRESS** History Dept, Acadia Univ, Wolfville, NS, Canada B0P 1X0. **EMAIL** margaret.conrad@acadiau.ca

CONYNE, ROBERT
PERSONAL Born 05/21/1944, Amsterdam, NY, m, 1960, 2 children **DISCIPLINE** PSYCHOLOGY **EDUCATION** Syracuse Univ, AB, 66; Purdue Univ, MS, 68; PhD, 70. **CAREER** Asst to Full Prof, Univ Cincinnati, 74-. **HONORS AND AWARDS** Fel, ASGW; Prof Adv Awd,ASGW; Who's Who in the Midwest; Who's Who of Emerging Leaders in Am. **MEMBERSHIPS** Am Psychol Asn; Am Psychol Soc; Am Psychol Soc. **RESEARCH** Group Work; Prevention; Ecology and Counseling. **SELECTED PUBLICATIONS** Auth, Failures in Group Work, Gage, 99. **CONTACT ADDRESS** Dept Sch Psychol & Coun, Univ of Cincinnati, PO Box 210002, Cincinnati, OH 45221-0001. **EMAIL** conynerk@mail.uc.edu

COOK, ANNE E.
PERSONAL Born 08/23/1973, Keokuk, IA, s **DISCIPLINE** PSYCHOLOGY **EDUCATION** La State univ, BA, 95; Univ NH, MA, 97; Univ NH, MST, 00; Univ NH, PhD, 00. **HONORS AND AWARDS** Phi Beta Kappa; 3 UNH Summer Fels. **MEMBERSHIPS** APA, Soc for Text & Discourse, **RESEARCH** Cognitive psychology, discourse comprehension, memory. **SELECTED PUBLICATIONS** Coauth, "What is Readily Available During Reading? A Memory-Based Text Processing View," Discourse Processes, 26 (98): 109-129; coauth, "Semantic and Episodic Effects on Bridging Inferences," Discourse Processes (forthcoming); coauth, "The Psychology of Knowledge Activation in Text Comprehension and Problem Solving," The Int Encycl of the Soc and Behav Sci (forthcoming). **CONTACT ADDRESS** Dept Psychol, Univ of New Hampshire, Durham, 125 Technology Dr, Conant Hall, Durham, NH 03824. **EMAIL** aecook@alberti.unh.edu

COOK, SHARON
PERSONAL Born 04/30/1965, Rocky Mount, NC, m, 1991, 1 child **DISCIPLINE** PSYCHOLOGY, SOCIOLOGY **EDUCATION** NC Central Univ, BA, 86; Univ NC Chapel Hill, MSW, 95; Univ NC Greensboro, PhD, currently enrolled. **CAREER** Prog Dir at Forsyth-Stakes Mental Health, 90-95; Instr to Asst Prof, Winston Salem State Univ, 95-. **HONORS AND AWARDS** Annie Kizer Bost Awd, Univ NC Chapel Hill, 95; Kappa Delta Pi Honor Soc, 99; Who's Who Among America's Teachers, 99; Wachovia Teaching Excellence Awd, 99. **MEMBERSHIPS** Nat Asn of Soc Workers, NC Asn for Res in Educ. **RESEARCH** Social Welfare Policy, College Retention among African Americans, Social Welfare History. **SELECTED PUBLICATIONS** Auth, "Giving Decades of Quiet Service: Mary Eliza Church Terrell," in African American Leadership in Social Welfare: An Empowerment Tradition (NASW Press, 00). **CONTACT ADDRESS** Dept Soc Sci, Winston-Salem State Univ, 601 S M L King Dr, Winston-Salem, NC 27110-0001. **EMAIL** nccooks@aol.com

COOKSEY, ELIZABETH C.
PERSONAL Born, United Kingdom, m, 1988, 2 children **DISCIPLINE** SOCIOLOGY **EDUCATION** Oxford Univ, BA, 82; Brown Univ, MA, 84; PhD, 88. **CAREER** Asst Prof, Ohio State Univ, 91-98; Assoc Prof, Ohio State Univ, 98-. **HONORS AND AWARDS** Fel, Univ NC, 88-91. **MEMBERSHIPS** PAA, ASA, SSS. **RESEARCH** Fertility, adolescent sexual behavior. **SELECTED PUBLICATIONS** Auth, "The Epidemiology of Fetal Loss," Int Planned Parenthood Federation Med Bull, 21 (87): 2-4; auth, "We've Come A Long Way . . . Maybe," in A Celebration of the Education of Women, (Oxford Univ Pr, 93); Rev, "Not Yet Pregnant: Infertile Couples in Contemporary America," Contemp Sociol, 22 (93): 409-410; auth, "Fatherhood and Apple Pie," Family Policy Bull (96): 15; coauth, "Family Disruption and the Cognitive and Behavioral Development of Children in Longitudinal Data from Britain and the USA," Working Paper #50, Soc Statistics Res Unit, City Univ Pr (London, UK), 98: coauth, "A Socio-Demographic Profile of Fathers in Britain and the United States," Demography 35 (98): 217-228; coauth, "Parenting From a Distance: The Effects of Paternal Characteristics on Contact Between Nonresidential Fathers and Their Children," Demography 35 (98): 187-200; coauth, "Young Adult Occupational Achievement: Early Expectations Versus Behavioral Reality," Work and Occups 26 (99): 220-263; coauth, "Diverse Family Living Situations and Child Development: A Multilevel Analysis Comparing Longitudinal Evidence from Britain and the United States," Int J of Law, Policy and the Family, 13 (99): 292-314; Rev, "Making Ends Meet: How Single Mothers Survive Welfare and Low-Wage Work," Pop Studies 54 (NY: Russell Sage Found, 00). **CONTACT ADDRESS** Dept Sociol, Ohio State Univ, Columbus, 190 N Oval Mall, 300 Bricker Hall, Columbus, OH 43210. **EMAIL** cooksey.1@osu.edu

COOLEY, TIMOTHY
PERSONAL Born 10/15/1962, Norfolk, VA **DISCIPLINE** ETHNOMUSICOLOGY **EDUCATION** Wheaton Conserv Music, Wheaton Col (Ill), B Mus, 85; Northwestern Univ, M Music, 87; Brown Univ, PhD, 99. **CAREER** Adjunct Instr, Rhode Island Col, 95-98; Lectr, Univ Cal, 98-. **HONORS AND AWARDS** Wilk Prize for Res in Polish Music, 97, for Authentic Troupes and Inauthentic Tropes; Polish Music Reference Center, Univ S Cal-Los Angeles; Graduate Fel, 97, Brown Univ, 97; James T Koetting Prize, 96, for Authenticity on Trial in Polish Contest Festivals; Northeast Chapter, Soc for Ethnomusicol Int Res and Exchanges Board: Individual Advanced Res Fel in Eastern Europ Studies, Poland, 94-95; Am Council of Learned Societies: Predissertation Travel Grant Program in Eastern European Studies, Poland, 1992, East European Language Training Grant, Poland, 1993; Polish Am Teachers Asn: Summer Sessions Scholarship, Jagiellonian Univ, Poland, 1993; Kosciuszko Found: Summer Sessions Scholarship, Jagiellonian Univ, Krakow, Poland, 1992, 2) Study Abroad Scholarship, Inst of Art, Polish Acad of Sciences, Warsaw, Poland, 1994, 3) Dissertation writing grant, 95-96; Pi Kappa Lambda, 87; Presser Scholar; Wheaton Col Conservatory, 84-85; Nat Asn of Teachers of Singing, First Place, performance competition, 84. **MEMBERSHIPS** Soc for Ethnomusicol; Am Musicol Soc; Int Coun for Traditional Music; Am Folklore Soc. **RESEARCH** Music cult Eastern Europe, Middle East, Oceania, Multicult Am, Ethnicity. **SELECTED PUBLICATIONS** Music of the Polish Tatra Mountain Gorale in Chicago, forthcoming; Am Musical Atlas, ed Jeff Todd Titon, Schirmer Books; United States of America, European-Am music, Polish, forthcoming, Janice Kleeman; In The New Grove Dictionary of Music and Musicians, rev ed; Macmillan; Authentic Troupes and Inauthentic Tropes, 98; Polish Music J, Online, 1(1), Univ S Cal; Shadows in the Field: An Introduction, 97; co-ed, In Shadows in the Field: New Perspectives for Fieldwork in Ethnomusicology, Oxford Univ Press; co-ed, Shadows in the Field: New Perspectives for Fieldwork in Ethnomusicology, 97, Oxford Univ Press; Dance, Ritual, and Music, 95; asst ed, Warsaw: Inst of Art, Polish Acad of Sciences; Fire in the Mountains: Polish Mountain Fiddle Music, v1, The Karol Stoch Band. CD with extensive notes, Shanachie Entertainment Corp, 97; Fire in the Mountains: Polish Mountain Fiddle Music, v2; The Great Highland Bands, CD with extensive notes, Shanachie Entertainment Corp, 97; Polish Village Music: Historic Polish-American Recordings 1927-1933, CD song transcriptions and translations, Arhoolie Productions, Inc, 95; auth, "Folk Festival as Modern Ritual in the Polish Tatra Mountains," The World of Music, 41, 3, (99): 31-55; auth, "Creating an 'Authentic' Folk Music of the

Polish Tatras," in After Chopin: Essays in Polish Music, ed Maria Anna Harley, Polish Music History Series, Vol 6, forthcoming. **CONTACT ADDRESS** Dept of Music, Univ of California, Santa Barbara, Santa Barbara, CA 93106-6070. **EMAIL** cooley@humanitas.ucsb.edu

COOMBS, ROBERT H.
PERSONAL Born 09/16/1934, Salt Lake City, UT, m, 1958, 7 children **DISCIPLINE** SOCIOLOGY **EDUCATION** Univ Utah, MS, 58, MS, 59; Washington State Univ, PhD, 64. **CAREER** Instr, 63-64 and asst prof, 64-66, sociol, Iowa State Univ; asst prof, 66-68, assoc prof, 68-70, sociol, Wake Forest Univ; res specialist, Calif Dept Mental Hygiene, 70-73; from assoc res sociol to prof is residence at highest level, UCLA Neuropsychiatric Inst/Dept of Psychiat and Biobehavioral Sci, 70- . **HONORS AND AWARDS** Phi Kappa Phi; Alpha Kappa Delta; NSF fel, 62, 63; US Congress Citation for Exemplary Project, 75, 76; delegat, White House Conf on Children and Youth, 78; Kappa Delta Pi; Sigma Xi; fel, AAAS, 91; fel, Am Psychol Soc, 91; award for Excellence in Educ, 92; distinguished Faculty Educ Awd, 92; fel, Am Asn of Applied and Preventive Psychol, 94. **MEMBERSHIPS** Am Sociol Asn; Int Sociol Asn; World Federation for Mental health; AAAS; World Federation for Medical Educ; Am Pshchol Soc; Am Asn of Applied and Preventive Psychol; Am Psychotherapy Asn. **RESEARCH** Professional socialization in medicine; substance abuse. **SELECTED PUBLICATIONS** Coauth, Handbook of Drug Abuse Prevention: A Comprehensive Strategy to Prevent the Abuse of Alcohol and Other Drugs, Allyn & Bacon, 95; auth, Drug-Impaired Professionals, Harvard Univ, 97; auth, Surviving Medical School, Sage, 98; auth, Cool Parents/Drug-Free Kids, Center Press, forthcoming; auth, Addiction Recovery Tools: A Practitioner's Handbook, forthcoming; auth, Drugs, Addiction, and Society, Allyn & Bacon, forthcoming; auth, Women Surgeons: Breaking the Sex Barriers, forthcoming; coauth, Seasons of Marriage: A Thirty-Year Developmental Study of Physicians' Wives, forthcoming. **CONTACT ADDRESS** School of Medicine, Univ of California, Los Angeles, 760 Westwood Plz, Los Angeles, CA 90024-1759. **EMAIL** rcoombs@mednet.ucla.edu

COOMBS, ROBERT STEPHEN
PERSONAL Born 02/10/1952, Hampton, VA, m, 1979, 2 children **DISCIPLINE** PSYCHOLOGY, MINISTRIES **EDUCATION** Carson-Newman Col, BA, 74; Southern Baptists Theol Sem, MD, 77; PhD Ministry, 88; PhD Philos, Univ Tenn, 94. **CAREER** Assoc Pastor, W Hills Baptist Church Knoxville, 79-90; Dir of Clinical Prog, Knox Area Rescue Ministries Knoxville, 90-92; Adj Prof, Univ of Tenn Knoxville, 93-97; Adj Prof, Carson-Newman Col Jefferson City Tenn, 95-97; Minister, Norris Religious Fel, 94-97; Adj Prof, Univ of Tenn Chattanooga Tenn, 97-98; Adj Prof, Southern Adventist Univ Coldale Tenn, 97-; Therapist, Hiwassee Mental health Cleveland Tenn, 99-. **HONORS AND AWARDS** Phi Sigma Tau, Kappa Omicron Nu, Alpha Phi Omega, Distinguished Teacher Awd, Univ of Tenn Knoxville, 96. **MEMBERSHIPS** Boys' Work Committee, Knox Co Asn of Baptists, 81-83; UNICEF Knox Co, 81-83; Detoxification Rehabil Inst, 81-84; Homeless Coalition Knoxville, 91-92; Inter-Agency Coun on the Homeless, 91-92; Norris Ministerial Asn, 95-97; Int Counc OF Community Churches Editorial 95-97; YMCA, 96-97; Nat Coun on Family Relations, 94-00. **SELECTED PUBLICATIONS** Auth, "The Breakfast Club, "in Group Mag (Group Publ, Loveland, CO), 85; auth, Of Such is the Kingdom, Baker Book House (Grand Rapids, MI), 87; auth, Concise Object Sermons for Children, Baker Book House (Grand Rapids, MI), 89; auth, Enlightening Object Sermons for Children, Baker Book House (Grand Rapids, MI), 92; auth, Building an Effective Youth Program, Community Church Press (Chicago, IL), 95; auth, "I Can See Clearly Now, in Group Mag (Group Publ, Loveland, CO), 96; co-ed, The Inclusive Pulpit Vol I and Vol II, Community Church Press (Chicago, IL), 96,96; auth, "Family Works Column," Cleveland Daily Banner (99). **CONTACT ADDRESS** Dept Educ and Psychology, Southern Adventist Univ, PO Box 370, Collegedale, TN 37315. **EMAIL** DrRCoombs@aol.com

COONEY, MARK
PERSONAL Born 03/16/1955, Dublin, Ireland, m, 1982, 2 children **DISCIPLINE** SOCIOLOGY **EDUCATION** Nat Univ Ireland, BCL, 76; Harvard Law Sch, SJD, 88; Univ Va, PhD, 91. **CAREER** Lect, Univ Col Dublin, 78-80; lect, Univ Zimbabwe, 84-86; Assoc Prof, Univ Ga, 91-. **MEMBERSHIPS** ASA, Am Soc of Criminol, Law and Soc Assoc. **RESEARCH** Sociology of law, conflict management. **SELECTED PUBLICATIONS** Auth, "Behavioral Sociology of Law: A Defense," Mod Law Rev 49: 262-271; auth, "Racial Discrimination in Arrest," chap 5, in Virginia Rev of Socio, vol 1: Law and Soc Control (Greenwich: JAI Pr, 92); auth, "The Informal Social Control of Homicide," J of Legal Pluralism 34 (94): 31-59; auth, "Evidence as Partisanship," Law and Soc Rev 27 (94): 833-859; auth, "Legal Sociology and the New Institutionalism," Studies in Law, Polit and Soc 15 (95): 85-101; auth, "Hunting Among Police and Predators: The Enforcement of Traffic Law," Studios in Law, Polit and Soc 16 (97): 165-188; auth, "The Decline of Elite Homicide," Criminol 35 (97): 381-407; auth, From War to Tyranny: Lethal Conflict and the State," Am Sociol Rev 62 (97): 316-338; auth, "The Dark Side of Community: Moralistic Homicide and Strong Social Ties," Sociol Focus 31 (98): 135-153; auth, Warriors and Peacemakers: How Third Parties Shape Violence, NY Univ Pr, 98. **CONTACT ADDRESS** Dept Sociol, Univ of Georgia, Athens, GA 30602. **EMAIL** mcooney@arches.uga.edu

COOPER, CHRIS
PERSONAL Born 06/23/1963, New York, NY, s **DISCIPLINE** SOCIOLOGY **EDUCATION** Amer Univ, PhD, 94; New Eng School Law, JD, 95. **CAREER** Police off; atty; prof. **HONORS AND AWARDS** Fulbright Scholar, 96. **MEMBERSHIPS** Soc Prof in Dispute Resolution; Acad Criminol Justice Sci. **RESEARCH** Policing, Mediation. **SELECTED PUBLICATIONS** Auth, Mediation and Arbitration by Patrol Police Officers, Rowman & Littlefield, (99). **CONTACT ADDRESS** Dept Sociol & Anthrop, Saint Xavier Univ, 3700 W 103 St, Chicago, IL 60655-3105. **EMAIL** cooper@sxu.edu

COOPER, HARRIS M.
PERSONAL Born 04/13/1951, New York, NY, m, 1975, 2 children **DISCIPLINE** PSYCHOLOGY **EDUCATION** State Univ NYork at Sony Brook, BA, 72; Univ Conn, MA, 74; PhD, 75. **CAREER** Instr, Colgate Univ, 76-77; asst prof and res assoc, Center for Res in Soc Behavior, Univ of Mo-Columbia, 77-80, assoc prof, 80-85, prof, 85-, Frederick A. Middlebush Prof of Psychology, 91-94. **HONORS AND AWARDS** Raymond B. Cattell Early Career Awd for Programmatic Res, Am Educ Res Asn, 84; Gold Chalk Awd, Excellence in Grad Educ, Univ Mo-Columbia, 92; Interpretive Scholarship Awd, Am Educ Res Asn, 97. **MEMBERSHIPS** Am Asn for the Advancement of Sci, Am Psychol Asn, Am Psychol Soc, Am Educ Res Asn, Midwestern Psychol Asn, Soc for the Advancement of Soc Psychol, Soc for Experimental Soc Psychol, Soc for Philos and Psychol, Soc for the Soc Studies of Sci. **SELECTED PUBLICATIONS** Coauth with T. L. Good, Pygmalion grows up: Studies in the expectation communication process, NY: Longman (83); auth, Homework, NY: Longman (89); coauth with T. Cook, D. Cordray, H. Hartmann, L. Hedges, R. Light, T. Louis, and F. Mosteller, Meta-analysis for explanation: A casebook, NY: Russell Sage Found (92); auth, The battle over homework: An administrators guide to sound and effective policies, Newbury Park, CA: Corwin Press (94); coauth with L. V. Hedges, The Handbook of research synthesis, NY: Russell Sage Found (94); auth, Synthesizing research: A guide for literature reviews, 3rd ed, Thousand Oaks, CA: Sage (98); coauth with K. Charlton, J. Valentine, and L. Muhlenbruck, Making the Most of Summer School, Monograph Series of the Soc for Res in Child Develop, Malden, MA: Blackwell (in press). **CONTACT ADDRESS** Dept of Psychol, Univ of Missouri, Columbia, McAlester Hall, Columbia, MO 65211. **EMAIL** cooperh@missouri.edu

COOPER, JOEL
PERSONAL Born 12/03/1943, New York, NY, m, 1966, 3 children **DISCIPLINE** PSYCHOLOGY **EDUCATION** City Col NY, BA, 65; Duke Univ, PhD, 69. **CAREER** Asst prof to prof, 69-. **MEMBERSHIPS** APA; APS; SESP; SPPI; SPSP; EPA. **RESEARCH** Attitudes, attitude change, cognitive dissonance theory, social psychological processes in psychotherapy, social impact of computer technology, computer use and gender, psychology and law. **SELECTED PUBLICATIONS** Coauth, Understanding Social Psychology, Dorsey Pr, (Homewood, IL), 91; coauth, "Gender differences in children's reactions to success and failure with computers", Computers in Human Behav 13.2 (97): 267; auth, "Unlearning Cognitive Dissonance: Toward an understanding of the development of cognitive dissonance", J of Exp Soc Psychol 34 (98): 562-575; coed, Attribution Processes, Person Perception, and Social Interaction: The Legacy of Edward E. Jones, Am Psychol Assoc (Washington, DC), 98; auth, "Unwanted Consequences and the Self: In Search of the Motivation for Dissonance Reduction", in Cognitive dissonance: Progress on a pivotal theory in social psychology, ed E. Harmon-Jones and J. Mills, APA, (Washington, DC), 99; coauth, Social Psychology, Nelson-Hall Pub, (Chicago, IL), 00; coauth, "The role of group identity in dissonance processes", Attitudes, Behavior and Social Context, Erlbaum Assoc (Mahwah, NJ), 00; coauth, "Cognitive Dissonance", Int Encycl of Soc and Behav Sci, (forthcoming); coauth, "Reactions to Mock Jurors to Testimony of a Court Appointed Expert", Behav Sci and the Law, (forthcoming); coauth, "A self-standards model of dissonance", J of Exp Soc Psychol, (forthcoming). **CONTACT ADDRESS** Dept Psychol, Princeton Univ, 1-S-5 Green Hall, Princeton, NJ 08544-0001. **EMAIL** jcoops@princeton.edu

COPELAND, ANNE P.
PERSONAL Born 09/03/1951, Pittsburgh, PA, m, 1984, 2 children **DISCIPLINE** PSYCHOLOGY **EDUCATION** Eckerd Col, BA, 73; Am Univ, MA, 75; PhD, 77. **CAREER** Asst prof, Kent State Univ, 77-79; assoc prof to adj assoc prof, Boston Univ, 79-; exec dir, Interchange Inst, 97-. **MEMBERSHIPS** Am Psychol Asn; Soc for Intercultural Educ, Training, and Res. **RESEARCH** Families in intercultural transition. **SELECTED PUBLICATIONS** Co-auth, Studying families, Sage Pub, 91; co-auth, Separating Together: Families and Parental Divorce, Guilford Pub, 97. **CONTACT ADDRESS** Dept Psychol, Boston Univ, 64 Cummington St, Boston, MA 02215. **EMAIL** annec@bu.edu

COPELAND, ROBERT M.
PERSONAL Born 05/12/1943, Hendersonville, NC **DISCIPLINE** EDUCATION **EDUCATION** Livingstone Coll, BS, 1964; Oregon State Univ, MS, 1971; Oregon State Univ, PhD, 1974. **CAREER** Coll of Liberal Arts & Sciences, Univ of IL, assoc dean, 86-96, asst dean, 74-86; exc and senior assoc dean, 96-; Oregon State Univ, teacher, counselor, 71-74; Ebenezer Ave School Rock Hill SC, teacher, 68-70; Sunset Park School, Rock Hill, SC, teacher, coach, 64-68. **HONORS AND AWARDS** fellow, Natl Science Found, 1970-71, Ford Found, 1971-72, Natl Fellowships Fund, 1972-74; Pres, Natl Assn of Acad Affairs Administrators 1987. **MEMBERSHIPS** Mem, Natl Science Teacher's Assn, Natl Educ Assn, Assn for Educ of Teachers of Sci, Urbana Council Comm for Training of Teachers of Science, Alpha Phi Alpha, Phi Delta Kappa Hon Soc, Amer Coll Personnel Assn, Assn for Council & Devel; member, National Academic Advisory Association, 1988-. **CONTACT ADDRESS** Col Liberal Arts and Scis, Univ of Illinois, Urbana-Champaign, 702 S Wright Street, Urbana, IL 61801.

CORLEY, CONSTANCE SALTZ
PERSONAL Born 07/09/1954, St Louis, MO **DISCIPLINE** PSYCHOLOGY **EDUCATION** Webster Col, BA, 75; Univ Mich, MSW, 78; MA, 81; PhD, 82. **CAREER** Adj Instr, Univ NC, 81-86; Asst Prof, Duke Univ, 83-86; Asst Prof, Yale Univ, 87-89; Asst Prof, Southern Ct State Univ, 86-89; Assoc Prof, Va Commonwealth Univ, 89-92; From Assoc Prof to Prof, Univ Md, 92-. **HONORS AND AWARDS** Rackham Block Grant, Univ Mich, 76-77; Health Serv Res Fel, Vet Admin, 80-81; Fel, Gerontological Soc of Am, 94-; Phi Alpha Hon Soc, 89-:AGE-SW Leadership Awd, 98. **MEMBERSHIPS** Am Soc on Aging, AGE-SW, Asn for Gerontology in Higher Educ, Coun on Soc Work Educ, Gerontological Soc of Am, Md Gerontological Asn, Nat Asn of Soc Workers, Soc for Soc Work Res, Southern Gerontological Soc. **RESEARCH** Aging, teamwork, mind-body-spirit wellness, rehabilitation. **SELECTED PUBLICATIONS** Auth, "Rehabilitation," in Encycl of Aging, 2nd ed (95); coauth, "Interdisciplinary Teams in Health Care: Integration of Family Caregivers," Soc Work in Health Care, 22 (96): 59-70; auth, "Promoting Clinical and Research Skills in Evaluating Interdisciplinary Teams," Gerontological and Geriatrics Educ, 16 (96): 79-90; auth, "From Issues to Actions," J of Gerontological Soc Work, 27 (97): 89-95; auth, "The Aging Family," J of Gerontological Soc Work, 27 (97): 55-64; coauth, "Streamlining Outpatient Geriatric Assessment: Essential Social, Environmental and Economic Variables," Soc Work in Health Care, 27 (97): 1-14; ed, Social Work Response to the 1995 White House Conference on Aging: From Issues to Action, Haworth Pr (New York, NY), 97; coauth, "Substance Use Disorders," in Med Aspects of Disability: A Handbk for the Rehab Professionals, 2nd ed (New York: Springer, 99); auth, Social Work Leadership: Interdisciplinary Education in a Changing Practice Environment, Springer Pr (New York, NY), forthcoming. **CONTACT ADDRESS** Dept Psychol, Univ of Maryland, Columbia, 6402 Cardinal Ln, Columbia, MD 21044. **EMAIL** csaltz@ssw.umaryland.edu

CORRUCCINI, ROBERT
PERSONAL Born 05/21/1949, Takoma Park, MD, m, 1982, 2 children **DISCIPLINE** ANTHROPOLOGY **EDUCATION** Colo Univ, BA, 71; Univ Calif Berkeley, PhD, 75. **CAREER** Prof, S Ill Univ, 78-. **HONORS AND AWARDS** Outstanding Scholar, SIU, 94. **MEMBERSHIPS** AAPA; HBC; AAA. **RESEARCH** Dental Anthropology; Statistics. **CONTACT ADDRESS** Dept Anthropol, So Illinois Univ, Carbondale, S IL Union, Carbondale, IL 62901.

COSTANZA, STEPHEN E.
PERSONAL Born 12/03/1969, Chalmette, LA, s **DISCIPLINE** CRIMINAL JUSTICE, SOCIOLOGY **EDUCATION** Louisiana State Univ, PhD, 98. **CAREER** Asst prof, Southeastern La Univ, 98-. **HONORS AND AWARDS** ICPSR Stipend, 96; LA Dept Forest Grant, 99; SLU Grant, 99. **MEMBERSHIPS** MSSA; SSI; ACJA. **RESEARCH** Quantitive sociology; crime history. **SELECTED PUBLICATIONS** Auth, "History of Organized Crime In America," Encycl Crime Dev Behavior (00). **CONTACT ADDRESS** Dept Sociology, Southeastern Louisiana Univ, 500 Western Ave, Hammond, LA 70402.

COSTLEY, KEVIN
PERSONAL Born 07/27/1954, Joplin, MO, m, 1986, 2 children **DISCIPLINE** EDUCATION **EDUCATION** Mo S State Col, BS, 75; Pittsburgh State Univ, MS, 78; Kans State Univ, PhD, 82. **CAREER** Adj Fac, Mo S State Col, 96-; Prof, Messenger Col, 96-. **HONORS AND AWARDS** Outstanding Young Men of Am; Little Theatre Critic's Choice Awd, Joplin; Who's Who Among Students in Am Col and Univ; MSSC Outstanding Sen Awd Nominee. **MEMBERSHIPS** MSSC Coun for Exceptional Children. **SELECTED PUBLICATIONS** Auth, "Attitudes of Southeast Kansas Public School Superintendents Toward the Academically Gifted and Programs for the Gifted," 82; auth, "A Glance at Early Childhood Creativity," Early Childhood Monographs, 98; auth, "Adjudication: That Vital Part of Piano Performance," Piano Guild Notes, 99; auth, "Motivation and Motivational Techniques in Piano Lessons,"

Music Educator's Journal, 99; auth, "Musical and Academic Achievement of Young Children: Is There a Relationship Between Parent and Teacher Involvement?," Child Development, 99; auth, "There's Nothing More Exciting That a Piano Recital," Clavier, 00. **CONTACT ADDRESS** Dept Liberal Arts, Messenger Col, PO Box 4050, Joplin, MO 64803-4050.

COTE, NATHALIE
PERSONAL Born, IL, s **DISCIPLINE** PSYCHOLOGY **EDUCATION** Furman Univ, BA, 88; Vanderbilt Univ, MS, 92; PhD, 98. **CAREER** Res assoc, Learning Technol Center, Vanderbilt Univ, TN, 97-98; asst prof of Psychol, Belmont Abbey Col, 98-. **HONORS AND AWARDS** Phi Beta Kappa; Psi Chi; Harold Stirling Vanderbilt Grad Scholar; Susan W. Gray Awd for Excellence in Scholarly Writing. **MEMBERSHIPS** Am Psychol Asn, Am Psychol Soc, Soc for the Teaching of Psychol, Am Educ Res Asn, European Asn for Res on Learning and Instr, Mid-South Educ Res Asn, Am Asn of Univ Women. **SELECTED PUBLICATIONS** Coauth, "Paragraphing, reader, and task effects on discourse comprehension," Discourse Processes, 20 (95): 273-305; coauth with C. E. Hmelo, "The development of self-directed learning strategies in problem-based learning," in D. C. Edelson and E. A. Domeshek, eds, Proceedings of the Second Int Conf for the Learning Scis, Evanston, Il (July 96); coauth, "Extending capacity-constrained construction integration: Toward 'smarter' and flexible models of text comprehension," in B. K. Britton and A. C. Graesser, eds, Models of text comprehension, Hillsdale, NJ: LEA (96); auth, with the Cognition and Technol Group at Vanderbilt, "Looking at technology in context: A framework for understanding technology and education research," in D. C. Berliner and R. C. Calfee, eds, Handbook of Educational Psychology, NY: MacMillan Pub (96); coauth, "Students making sense of informational text: Relations between processing and representation," Discourse Processes, 25 (98): 1-53; coauth with S. R. Goldman, "Building representations of informational text: Evidence from children's think-aloud protocols," in H. van Oostendorp and S. R, Goldman, eds, The construction of mental representations during reading, Mahewah, NJ: Erlbaum (99). **CONTACT ADDRESS** Dept Psychol, Belmont Abbey Col, 100 Belmont Mt Holly, Belmont, NC 28012. **EMAIL** cote@crusader.bac.edu

COTERA, MARIA E.
PERSONAL Born 07/17/1964, Austin, TX, m, 1999 **DISCIPLINE** AMERICAN STUDIES, WOMEN'S STUDIES, LATINO STUDIES **EDUCATION** Univ Tex, BA, 86; MA, 94; Stanford Univ, PhD, 00. **CAREER** Asst prof, Univ Mich, 00-. **HONORS AND AWARDS** Postdoc Fel Univ Mich, 00-01; Dis Fel Ford Found, 99-00; Am Dis Fel, AAUW Edu Found, 00; Grad Res Opp Awd, 99; Dis Res Fel, Sch Hum Sci, Stan Univ, 99; Escobedo Sum Res Fel, Cen Chicana Res, Stan Univ, 97; Prog Dev Fel, Grad Opp Prog, Univ Tex, 93-94; Tex Achiev Awd, 82-86; Frederick Cervantes Stud Premio, Nat Asn Chicano/Chicana Stud, 99; James W. Lyons Awd Ser to the Stan Comm, 98-99; Dean of Stud, Stan Univ, 99; Galarza Prize for Excel, Stan Cen Chicana/o Res, 96. **MEMBERSHIPS** MLA; ASA; NACCS. **RESEARCH** Writing by women of color; ethnic and racial consciousness in the inter-war years, 1920-1940; Latina/o studies; American Indian studies; women's studies; comparative approaches to ethnic studies. **SELECTED PUBLICATIONS** Co-ed, Caballero, Tex AM Press, 95; auth, contrb, "Refiguring the 'American Congo:' Jovita Gonzdlez, John Gregory Bourke and the Battle Over Ethnohistorical Representations of the Borderlands," in Recovering a Mexican American, West Lit Ser (00); auth, contrb, "Engendering a 'Dialectics of Our America:' Jovita Gonzalez' Pluralist Dialogue as Feminist Testimonio," Las Obreras: The Politics of Work and Family, UCLA Chi Stud Res Cent (00); auth, contrb, "Jovita Gonzalez Mireles" in Latinas in the United States, Hist Encycl (forthcoming); auth, "Deconstructing the Corrido Hero, Caballero and its Gendered Critique of Nationalist Discourse," Mex Am Persp (95). **CONTACT ADDRESS** Am Cultures Prog, Univ of Michigan, Ann Arbor, 419 S State St, 2402 Mason Hall, Ann Arbor, MI 48109. **EMAIL** mcotera@umich.edu

COTTER, JOHN LAMBERT
PERSONAL Born 12/06/1911, Denver, CO, m, 1941, 2 children **DISCIPLINE** HISTORICAL ARCHEOLOGY, ANTHROPOLOGY **EDUCATION** Univ Denver, BA, 34, MA, 35; Univ Pa, PhD(anthrop), 59. **CAREER** Supvr, Archaeol Surv Ky, 38-40; archaeologist, US Nat Park Serv, 40-77; res & writing, 77-, Adj assoc prof Am Civilization, Univ Pa, 60-79, Assoc Cur, Am Hist Archaeol, Univ Mus, 70-79, Emer Assoc Cur, 79-; ed, Bibliog Hist Archaeol. **HONORS AND AWARDS** J A Mason Awd, Archaeol Soc Pa, 74; D E Finley Awd, Nat Trust for Hist Preserv, 78. **MEMBERSHIPS** Fel Am Anthrop Asn; fel AAAS; Soc Prof Archaeologists; Archaeol Inst Am; Soc Hist Archaeol (pres, 66-67). **RESEARCH** Archaeology of historical American sites and their conservation; archaeology of prehistoric American sites, and conservation. **SELECTED PUBLICATIONS** Coauth, Archaeology of Bynum Mounds, 52 & auth, Archaeological Excavations at Jamestown, Virginia, 58, Govt Printing Off; ed, Bibliography of Historical Sites Archaeology, Univ Microfilms, 66; Handbook for Historical Archaeology, J L Cotter, 68; auth, Above Ground Archaeology, Govt Printing Off, 74; contribr, chap 5, In: The Study of American Culture, Everett-Edwards, 78; contribr, chap 5, In: Historical Archaeology: A Guide, Baywood, 78; auth, Premier etablissement Francais en Acadie: St Croix, Dossiers de l'Archeologie, 78. **CONTACT ADDRESS** Univ Museum, 34th & Spruce Sts, Philadelphia, PA 19174.

COTTLE, THOMAS J.
PERSONAL Born 01/22/1937, Chicago, IL, m, 1964, 3 children **DISCIPLINE** PSYCHOLOGY; SOCIOLOGY **EDUCATION** Harvard Univ, BA; Univ Chicago, MA, PhD. **CAREER** Boston Univ, prof 90-; Harvard Med Sch, lectr 75-90; Harvard Univ, asst prof, asst chemn; Amherst Col, vis prof; Wesleyan Univ, vis prof; Boston Univ, lectr; Columbia Col, vis prof; Radcliffe Inst, instr; Duquesne Univ, dist vis prof. **HONORS AND AWARDS** Young Psychologist Awd; Guggenheim Fel; Pioneer Fel; Nat Bdcst Tele Awd; Amer Can Soc Awd; PA Awd; Emmy Awds; Gabriel Awd; Tom Phillips Awd; Cit Par Choice Awd; Derose/Hinkhouser Awd; Amer Women Rad/TV Awd; MA Alli Mentally Ill; presently a regular contributor to midday news, wcvb-tv, abc, boston; actively appearing on: the tom cottle show; tom cottle up close; tom cottle soap box; good morning america; today show; 20/20; john davidson show; hour magazine; david suskind show; nov **SELECTED PUBLICATIONS** Auth, Private Lives and Public Accounts; A Family Album; Busing; Children in Jail; Children's Secrets; Hidden Survivors; The Voices of School; Time's Children; Like Fathers Like Sons; Barred From School; Perceiving Time; The Abandoners; The Present of things Future, coath; Getting Married, coauth; Black Children White Dreams; Black Testimony; et al. **CONTACT ADDRESS** School of Education, Boston Univ, 605 Commonwealth Ave, Boston, MA 02215. **EMAIL** tcottle@bu.edu

COUCH, JAMES
PERSONAL Born 03/16/1946, St Louis, MO, m, 1968, 3 children **DISCIPLINE** PSYCHOLOGY **EDUCATION** Trinity Univ, BA, 68; Univ Mass, MS, 71; PhD, 72 **CAREER** Prof to Dept Head, James Madison Univ, 79-. **MEMBERSHIPS** Am Psychol Asn, Am Psychol Soc, Va Psychol Asn. **RESEARCH** Eyewitness testimony; Jury behavior. **SELECTED PUBLICATIONS** Auth, Computer use in psychology: A directory of software, American Psychological Asn, 92; auth, Hardware, software, and the Mental Health Professional, American Psychological Asn, 91; auth, Computer use in psychology: A directory of software, American Psychological Asn, 88; auth, A laboratory manual for Psychological Statistics, Kinko's Pub, 88; auth, Fundamentals of statistics for the Behavioral Sciences, West Pub, 87; auth, Instructors Manual for Fundamentals of statistics for the Behavioral Sciences, West pub, 87; auth, Computer use in psychology: A directory of software, American Psychological Asn, 87; auth, Knowledge of eyewitness identification issues: An update, forthcoming; auth, "Another psychometric evaluation of the Just world Scale," Psychological Reports, (98): 1283-1286; auth, "Using the Internet in instruction: A homepage for statistic," Psychological Reports, (97): 999-1003 **CONTACT ADDRESS** Dept Psychol, James Madison Univ, 800 S Main St, Harrisonburg, VA 22807-0002. **EMAIL** couchjv@jmu.edu

COUGHLAN, REED
PERSONAL Born 08/07/1948, Port Jervis, NY, m, 1983, 1 child **DISCIPLINE** SOCIOLOGY **EDUCATION** Middlebury Col, BA; SUNY Binghamton, MA; PhD. **CAREER** Fac, Empire State Col, SUNY, 74-; prof, 91-. **HONORS AND AWARDS** Chancel Awd, Excel in Teach, SUNY; Empire State Coll Found Awd, Excel Schol. **RESEARCH** Ethnic conflict, N Ireland, Cyprus, Balkans. **SELECTED PUBLICATIONS** Auth, "Cyprus: From Corporate Autonomy to the Search for Territorial Federalism," Autonomy and Ethnicity: Negotiating Competing Claims in Multi-Ethnic States, ed. Yash Guy (London, Cambridge Univ Press, forthcoming); coauth, "The Poverty of Primordialism: The demystification of Ethnic Attachments," Ethnic and Racial Stud 16 (93): 183-203; co-ed, Economic Dimensions of Ethnic Conflict, Intl Perspectives, NY, Martins Press, 91). **CONTACT ADDRESS** Dept Social Science, SUNY, Empire State Col, 207 Genesee St, Utica, NY 13501. **EMAIL** reed.coughlan@esc.edu

COUNTS, M. REID
PERSONAL Born 09/12/1970, Columbia, SC **DISCIPLINE** SOCIOLOGY, CRIMINOLOGY **EDUCATION** Univ SC, BS, 92; MCJ, 94; PhD, 99. **CAREER** Lect, Univ Nebr, 97-99; Asst Prof, Univ Nebr, 99-00; Asst Prof, Univ SC, 00-. **MEMBERSHIPS** Acad of Criminal Justice Sci. **RESEARCH** School violence, ritualistic crime, juvenile justice. **SELECTED PUBLICATIONS** Coauth, The Evolution of School Disturbance in America, Praeger, 98. **CONTACT ADDRESS** Dept Sociol, Univ of Nebraska, Kearney, 905 W 25th St, Kearney, NE 68847. **EMAIL** countsm@uncwil.edu

COURAGE, RICHARD A.
PERSONAL Born 01/15/1946, Brooklyn, NY, m, 1969, 2 children **DISCIPLINE** ENGLISH EDUCATION **EDUCATION** Columbia Univ, PhD, 90 **CAREER** Assoc Prof English, Asst Chair English Dept, Westchester Community Coll, 90-. **HONORS AND AWARDS** State Univ NY Chancellor's Awd for Exc; Nat Inst forStaff & Org Dev. **MEMBERSHIPS** Nat Coun Teachers Eng; Hudson Valley Writing Proj; Mod Lang Asn. **RESEARCH** Literacy, African-Am lit. **SELECTED PUBLICATIONS** Auth, Dangerous Narrative, in College Composition and Commun, Feb 96; auth, Interaction of Public and Private Liteacies, in College Composition and Commun, Dec 93; auth, Basic Writing: End of a Frontier, in J Teaching Writing, Fall/Winter 90; auth, James Baldwin's Go Tell It on the Mountain: Voices of a People, in CLA J, june 89. **CONTACT ADDRESS** Westchester Comm Col, Valhalla, NY 10595. **EMAIL** rac46@aol.com

COURTNEY, RICHARD
PERSONAL Born 06/04/1927, Newmarket, England, m, 1952, 2 children **DISCIPLINE** DRAMA, EDUCATION **EDUCATION** Univ Leeds, BA, 51, dipl educ, 52. **CAREER** Sr lectr drama, Trent Park Col, Inst Educ, Univ London, 58-67; assoc prof, Univ Victoria, BC, 68-71; prof, Univ Calgary, 71-74; Prof Educ, Ont Inst Studies in Educ, 74-, Ed, Discussions in Develop Drama, Univ Calgary, 71-74; chmn, Nat Inquiry into Arts & Educ in Can, 75-80; vis fel, Melbourne State Col, 79. **HONORS AND AWARDS** Queen's Silver Jubilee Medal, 77. **MEMBERSHIPS** Fel Royal Soc Arts; Can Conf Arts (pres, 73-76); Can Child & Youth Drama Asn (pres, 70-72); Am Soc Aesthetics; Am Theatre Asn. **RESEARCH** Developmental drama, the relationship of enactment to philosophy, ethnology, education, psychology and sociology. **SELECTED PUBLICATIONS** Auth, Tree,Beerbohm and Knight,G.Wilson--Reply to Pearce,Brian, New Theatre Quart, Vol 0013, 97. **CONTACT ADDRESS** Dept of Curric, Ontario Inst for Studies in Education, Toronto, ON, Canada M5S 2L6.

COURTNEY, SEAN
PERSONAL Born 03/04/1948, Cork, Ireland, m, 2 children **DISCIPLINE** EDUCATION **EDUCATION** Univ Col Cork Ireland, BA; MA; Northern Ill Univ, EdD. **MEMBERSHIPS** AERA, AAACE, POD Network. **RESEARCH** New forms of pedagogical design; Teaching, learning in higher education. **SELECTED PUBLICATIONS** Co-auth, Characteristics of adults as learners and implications for computer-based systems for information and instruction, Minn Dept of Economic Sec, 99; co-auth, Transforming Your Teaching: A Guide to Helping Adults Learn, forthcoming; auth, "The Sixth Floor: Museum Experiences as Learning Environments," Resources in Education, 98; auth, "Transforming the classroom: Technology and the culture of learning," in Creating alternative Learning cultures: Culture, Cognition, and Learning, Ellenville, 98. **CONTACT ADDRESS** Dept Educ Psychol, Univ of Nebraska, Lincoln, PO Box 880345, Lincoln, NE 68588. **EMAIL** scourtney@unl.edu

COWEN, JOHN EDWIN
PERSONAL Born 09/03/1940, Jersey City, NJ, m, 1964, 2 children **DISCIPLINE** EDUCATION **EDUCATION** St Peter's Col, BS, 62; Jersey City Col, MA, 65; Teachers Col, EdD, 73. **CAREER** Asst Prof, Fairleigh Dickinson Univ, 95-. **HONORS AND AWARDS** Phi Delta Kappa; President's Awd, Int Reading Asn; Bergen Co Superintendent's Awd, Distinguished Educr. **MEMBERSHIPS** NJRA, Int Reading Asn, ALA, WJASCD, ATE, ASCD. **RESEARCH** Standards, early childhood literacy, disparity of racial and ethnic achievement, teaching reading through the arts. **SELECTED PUBLICATIONS** Auth, English Teacher's Portfolio of Multicultural Activities, CARE, 96; auth, E E Cummings' Lyricism, Today," J of the E E Cummings Soc, no 5 (96); auth, "The Poet as Visual Artist," Life, the Sunday Chronicle, 5:7-8 (97); coauth, Reading in the Content Areas: Strategies for Success, Globe Fearon Educ Publ (Upper Saddle River, NY), 99; auth, "Essential Elements of a Balanced Reading Program," The Reading Instruction J, NJRA (00); auth, "Using Louise M Rosenblatt's 'Aesthetic Stance' to Teach Children How to Read a Poem," The Reading Instruction J 45:4-7 (00). **CONTACT ADDRESS** Dept of Educ, Fairleigh Dickinson Univ, Florham-Madison, 285 Madison Ave, Madison, NJ 07940-1006. **EMAIL** cowtra@aol.com

COWLES, LOIS ANNE FORT
DISCIPLINE SOCIAL WELFARE, SOCIAL WORK **EDUCATION** Ind Univ, Bloomington, AB, 55; MA, 64; Ind Univ, Indianapolis, MSW, 66; Univ Wis, Madison, PhD, 90. **CAREER** Asst prof, Indiana State Univ, Terre Haute, 89-93; assoc prof, Idaho State Univ, 93-. **HONORS AND AWARDS** Kappa Kappa Gamma Rehabilitation Educ Grant, 65; Methodist Hospital Soc Work Educ Grant, 64; U. S. Public Health Service Res Training Grant, 79; Univ of Wisc Teaching Assistantship, 83; I.S.U. Phi Kappa Phi Honor Soc, bd mem, mem 96. **MEMBERSHIPS** Acad of Certified Soc Workers, Clinical Soc Worker (Indiana Health Profs Bureau), Nat Asn of Soc Workers, Coun on Social Work Educ, Soc for Soc Work Leadership in Health Care, Asn for Gerontology in Higher Educ, SAGE: The Section on Aging of the C.S.W.E., Idaho Womens Network. **SELECTED PUBLICATIONS** Auth, "The concept of caring," Networking, 4, 2 (summer 91): 1-3; coauth with M. J. Lefcowitz, "Interdisciplinary expectations of the medical social worker role in the hospital setting," Health and Soc Work, 17, 1 (92): 57-65; coauth with M. J. Lefcowitz, "Interdisciplinary expectations of the medical social worker in the hospital setting: Part II," Health and Social Work, 20, 4 (95): 279-286; auth, Social Work in the Health Field: A Care Perspective, Haworth Press (99); **CONTACT ADDRESS** Dept Sociol, Idaho State Univ, 921 S 8th Ave, Box 8114, Pocatello, ID 83209-0001.

COX, JOSEPH W.
PERSONAL Born 05/26/1937, Hagerstown, MD, m, 1963, 3 children **DISCIPLINE** EARLY AMERICAN HISTORY, HIGHER EDUCATION **EDUCATION** Univ Md, BA, 59, PhD(hist), 67. **CAREER** Asst hist, Univ Md, 60-64; assoc dean English, hist & soc sci, Towson State Univ, 69-72, dean eve col & summer session, 72-75, dir fac develop, 75-77, prof hist, 64-81, vpres acad affairs & dean univ, 77-81; VPres Acad Affairs, Northern Ariz Univ, 81-, Consult on col governance, Bd Trustees, Md State Cols, 68; consult on fac teaching awards, Pa State Dept Educ, 76-78. **MEMBERSHIPS** Am Asn Higher Educ; AAUP. **RESEARCH** Early American history; Maryland history; history of higher education; cultural philanthropy in 19th century America; the Historical Society movement. **SELECTED PUBLICATIONS** Contribr, Racial sensitivity: A model program, Am Personnel & Guide Asn, 70; auth, Champion of Southern Federalism: Robert Goodloe Harper, Kennikat, 72; coauth, Programs that don't lock you in: The flexible degree structure, Col Mgt, 73; auth, The second bachelor's program, Md Higher Educ, 73; The Army Corps of Engineers in the Early National Era 1781-1812, Govt Printing Off, 78; The Origins of the Md Historical Society, Md Hist Mag, 79; Surviving the 1980's, Nacubo, 81. **CONTACT ADDRESS** Dept of History, No Arizona Univ, Flagstaff, AZ 86001.

COXWELL, MARGARET
PERSONAL Born 03/28/1943, Seattle, WA, d, 2 children **DISCIPLINE** EDUCATION **EDUCATION** Mont State Univ, BS, 65; Med, 89; PhD 95. **CAREER** Assoc pfor, Northern State Univ, 95-. **HONORS AND AWARDS** Prof of the Month, Mont State Univ, 94; prof of the year, Northern State Univ, 95. **MEMBERSHIPS** ASCD, NAEYC, NCTM, Phi Delta Kappa, Delta Kappa Gamma, IRA. **RESEARCH** Teaching and learning styles, brain-based learning. **SELECTED PUBLICATIONS** Auth, The Nitty Gritty Language Arts Methods Book, 99. **CONTACT ADDRESS** Dept Elem & Secon Educ, No State Univ, 1200 S Jay St, Aberdeen, SD 57401. **EMAIL** coxwellm@northern.edu

CRABTREE, CLARIE
PERSONAL 2 children **DISCIPLINE** AMERICAN LITERATURE AND FOLKLORE **EDUCATION** Trinity Col, BA; Fordham Univ, MA; Wayne State Univ, PhD. **CAREER** Fulbright sr lectr, Romania, 94-95; Prof, 97-. **HONORS AND AWARDS** Dir, women's stud prog. **MEMBERSHIPS** MLA, Detroit Writers' Guild. **RESEARCH** William Faulkner. **SELECTED PUBLICATIONS** Pub(s), on Faulkner, and women writers sich as Erdrich, Hurston, and Toni Morrison. **CONTACT ADDRESS** Dept of Eng, Univ of Detroit Mercy, 4001 W McNichols Rd, PO BOX 19900, Detroit, MI 48219-0900. **EMAIL** crabtrec@udmercy.edu

CRAFTS, AMY
PERSONAL Born 12/01/1959, Waltham, MA, m, 1990 **DISCIPLINE** SPORT PSYCHOLOGY **EDUCATION** Brown Univ, BA, 82; Smith Col, MA, 84; Union Inst, PhD, 98. **CAREER** Assoc Prof, New Eng Col, 88-. **MEMBERSHIPS** Am Polarity Therapy Asn. **RESEARCH** Body-centered therapies; Holistic health; Spiritual well-being. **CONTACT ADDRESS** Dept Kinesiol, New England Col, Henniker, 26 Bridge St, Henniker, NH 03242.

CRAIG, JOHN ELDON
PERSONAL Born 07/23/1941, Sherbrooke, PQ, Canada, m, 1975 **DISCIPLINE** MODERN EUROPEAN HISTORY, COMPARATIVE EDUCATION **EDUCATION** Bowdoin Col, AB, 62; Stanford Univ, AM, 63, PhD, 73. **CAREER** Actg instr hist, Stanford Univ, 67; actg asst prof, Univ Va, 67-73; asst prof, 75-81, assoc prof, Educ, Univ Chicago, 81-. **MEMBERSHIPS** AHA; Conf Group Cent Europ Hist; Soc Fr Hist Studies; Soc Sci Hist Asn; Int Sociol Asn. **RESEARCH** Modern European social history; educational expansion in developed and developing countries. **SELECTED PUBLICATIONS** Auth, Maurice Halbwachs a Strasbourg, Rev Fr Sociol, Vol 20, 273-292; "On the Development of Educational Systems," American Journal of Education, 89; The Expansion of Education, Rev Res in Educ, 9: 151-213; Die Durkheim-Schule und die Annales, Gerschichte der Soziologie, Suhrkamp (4 vols), 3: 298-322; Higher Education and Social Mobility in Germany, 1850-1930, The Transformation of Higher Learning, 1850-1930, Klett-Cotta, 82; coauth (with N. Spear), Explaining Educational Expansion: An Agenda for Historical and Comparative Research, & Rational Actors, Group Processes, and the Development of Educational Systems, The Sociology of Educational Expansion, Sage, 82; auth, Scholarship and Nation Building: The Universities of Strasbourg and Alsatian Society, 1870-1939, Univ Chicago Press, 84. **CONTACT ADDRESS** Dept of Educ, Univ of Chicago, 5835 Kimbark Ave, Chicago, IL 60637-1684. **EMAIL** j-craig@uchicago.edu

CRAIG, WENDY M.
PERSONAL Born 04/28/1962, Toronto, ON, Canada, s **DISCIPLINE** PSYCHOLOGY **EDUCATION** Univ BC, BA, 85; York Univ, MA, 89; PhD, 93. **CAREER** Asst prof to assoc prof, Queen's Univ, 93-. **HONORS AND AWARDS** Can Inst for Health Res Investigator Award. **MEMBERSHIPS** Am Psychol Asn; Can Psychol Asn; Soc for Res in Child Develop; Soc for Res in Adolescence. **RESEARCH** Aggression; Victimization; Bullying; Adolescence; Peer relationships; Childhood; Children's mental health; Sexual harassment; Girls' aggression; Juvenile delinquency. **SELECTED PUBLICATIONS** Co-auth, "Peer processes in bullying and victimization: An observational study," Exceptionality Educ in Can, (95): 81-05; co-auth, "Kindergarten predictors of boys' stable behavior problems at the end of elementary school," J Abnormal Child Psychol, (95): 751-766; co-auth, "Developmental Juvenile Delinquency Prevention," Europ J on Criminal Res Policy, (97): 34-49; co-auth, "Observations of bullying and victimization in the schoolyard," Can J of School Psychol, (97): 41-60; co-auth, "Observations of aggressive and nonaggressive children on the school playground," Merrill Palmer Quart, (98): 55-76; auth, "The relationship among bullying, victimization depression, anxiety, and aggression in elementary school children," Personality and Individual Differences, (98): 123-130; co-auth, "Emotional regulation and display in classroom bullying: Characteristic expressions of affect, coping styles and relevant contextual factors," Soc Develop, (00): 226-244; co-auth, "Observations of bullying on the playground and in the classroom," Intl J Sch Psychol, (00): 22-36. **CONTACT ADDRESS** Dept Psychol, Queen's Univ at Kingston, 62 Arch St, Kingston, ON, Canada K7L 3N8. **EMAIL** craigw@psyc.queensu.ca

CRAMER, ELIZABETH P.
PERSONAL Born 01/16/1961, Englewood, NJ, m, 1 child **DISCIPLINE** SOCIAL WORK **EDUCATION** Binghamton Univ, BA, 83; Univ Mich, MSW, 84; Univ SC, PhD, 95. **CAREER** Asst Director, Domestic Violence Project, Inc, 87-92; Instr, Eastern Mich Univ, 91-92; Teaching Asst and Adj Instr, Univ SC, 92-95; Asst Prof, Va commonwealth Univ, 95-. **HONORS AND AWARDS** Feminist Scholarship Awd, Coun on Soc Work Educ, 00; community Services Asn Awd, Va Commonwealth Univ; Outstanding Grad Student, Univ SC; Naiad Press Nat Women's studies Asn Scholarship, 94. **MEMBERSHIPS** Acad of Certified Soc Workers; Asn for the Advancement of Soc Work with Groups, Inc; Coun of Soc Work Educ; Nat Asn of soc Workers; Nat Clearinghouse for the Defense of Battered Women; Nat Coalition Against Domestic Violence; Nat Gay and Lesbian Task Force; Nat Women's Studies Asn; Virginians for Justice. **RESEARCH** Domestic violence; Lesbian/gay issues; Group methods. **SELECTED PUBLICATIONS** Auth, "Variables that predict verdicts in domestic violence case," Journal of Interpersonal Violence, (99): 1137-1150; auth, "Hate crime laws and sexual orientation," Journal of Sociology and Social Welfare, (99): 5-24; auth, "Attitudes and behaviors of social work students toward lesbian and gay male clients: Can panel presentations make a difference?," Journal of Gay and Lesbian Social Services, (99): 47-68; auth, "From attitude change to effective practice with gay male and lesbian clients: Exploring the relationship," Journal of Social Work Education, (99): 87-100; auth, "Parallel identity Development processes for persons with nonvisible disabilities and lesbian, gay, and bisexual persons," Journal of Gay, Lesbian, and Bisexual Identity, (99): 23-37; auth, "Effects of an educational unit about lesbian identity development and disclosure in a social work methods course," Journal of Social Work Education, (97): 49-72; auth, "Strategies for reducing social work students' homophobia," in Overcoming heterosexism and homophobia: Strategies that work, Columbia Univ Press, 97; auth, "Lesbian and bisexual women," in Teaching racial, ethnic, an cultural diversity in social work: A collection of model course outlines, 00; auth, "Small Groups," in Dimensions of human behavior. Person and environment, Pine Forge Press, 99; auth, "Learning from Les Ms.," in Letters to our children: Lesbian and gay adults speak to the new generation, 97; rev, of "Social Work with Lesbians, Gays, and Bisexuals: A Strengths perspective," The Lesbian Review of Books, 00. **CONTACT ADDRESS** Dept Soc Work, Virginia Commonwealth Univ, Box 842027, Richmond, VA 23284. **EMAIL** ecramer@titan.vcu.edu

CRANE, DIANA
PERSONAL Born 04/05/1933, Toronto, ON, CAN, m, 1965, 1 child **DISCIPLINE** SOCIOLOGY **EDUCATION** Radcliff Coll, AB, 53; Columbia Univ, MA, 61; PhD, 64. **CAREER** Asst prof, Yale Univ, 64-68; asst prof, John Hopkins Univ, 68-72; assoc prof, Univ Penn, 73-. **HONORS AND AWARDS** Pres Fel, Columbia Univ, 62-63, 63-64; Guggenheim Fel, 74-75; Mem, Adv studt, Princeton NJ, 76-77; Phi Beta Kappa, 77; Fulbright Res Awd, 87-88; Bellagio Study Con Cen, 99. **MEMBERSHIPS** ASA; ESA. **RESEARCH** Sociology of arts, culture, and cultural policy. **SELECTED PUBLICATIONS** Auth, Invisible Colleges: Diffusion of Knowledge in Scientific Communities, University of Chicago Press (Chicago) 72; auth, The Sanctity of Social Life: Physicians' Treatment of Critically ill Patients, Russell Sage Foundation (New York), 75, Paperback edition, Transaction Books (New Brunswick, NJ), 77; auth, The Transformation of the Avant-Garde: The New York Art World, 1940-1985, Univ of Chicago Press (Chicago), 87, Paperback edition, 1988, Chinese edition: Yuan-Liou Pub Com (Taipei, Taiwan), 95; auth, The Production Culture: Media and the Urban Arts, Sage (Newbury Park, CA), 92; ed, The Sociology of Culture: Emerging Theoretical Perspectives, Basil Blackwell (Oxford, UK), 94, Korean edition: Ilushin Publishing Co (Seoul, Korea), 98; auth, Fashion and its Social Agendas: Class, Gender, and Identity in Clothing, Univ of Chicago Press (Chicago, IL), 00. **CONTACT ADDRESS** Dept Sociology, Univ of Pennsylvania, 3718 Locust Walk, Philadelphia, PA 19104. **EMAIL** craneher@sas.upenn.edu

CRANK, JOE N.
DISCIPLINE SPECIAL EDUCATION; SCHOOL PSYCHOLOGY **EDUCATION** Southern Ill Univ, BA; Ill State Univ, MS; Univ Kans, PhD. **CAREER** Coordr, schl psychol prog, Univ Nev, Las Vegas. **SELECTED PUBLICATIONS** Auth, Decisions, decisions, decisions: Solving personal problems, Intervention in Schl and Clinic, 23, 88; Surface Counseling Instructors Manuel, Ctr for Res and Learning, KU, 95; coauth, A self-instructional surface-counseling program: Development and validation, Learning Disabilities, 1 (3), 90; Visual depictions as information organizers for enhancing achievement of students with learning disabilities, Learning Disabilities Res and Pract, 8 (3), 93; Surface Counseling, Edge Enterprises, 95. **CONTACT ADDRESS** Dept of Spec Educ, Univ of Nevada, Las Vegas, 4505 Maryland Pky, PO Box 453014, Las Vegas, NV 89154-3014. **EMAIL** crank@nevada.edu

CREED, GERALD
DISCIPLINE ANTHROPOLOGY **EDUCATION** Duke Univ, BA, 76-80; Ohio State Univ, vis stud, 84-85; Yale Univ, vis stud, 85; CUNY, PhD, 92. **CAREER** Asst prof, Hunter Col, 92-97; assoc prof, 98-. **HONORS AND AWARDS** Bulgarian Stud Asn Bk Prize; Outstand Schl Achie, Feliks Gross End Awd; NSF Gnt; Fulbright-Hays Doc Diss Res; Wenner-Gren Found Anthrop Res. **SELECTED PUBLICATIONS** Auth, Domesticating Revolution: From Socialist Reform to Ambivalent Transition in a Bulgarian Village, Penn State Univ Press (University Park, PA), 98; co-ed, Knowing Your Place: Rural Identity and Cultural Hierarchy, Routledge (NY) 97; auth, "Agriculture and the Domestication of Industry in Rural Bulgaria, Am Ethnol 22 (95): 528-548; auth, "The Politics of Agriculture: Identity and Socialist Sentiment in Bulgaria," Slavic Rev 54 (95): 843-868; auth, "An Old Song in a New Voice: Decollectivization in Bulgaria," in East European Communities: The Struggle for Balance in Turbulent Times, ed. David Kideckel (Boulder, CO: Westview Press, 95), 25-46; auth, "Uncommon Research on the Common European Home: Understanding the New Europe," Rev Anthro 27 (98): 251-267; auth, "Deconstructing Socialism in Bulgaria" in Uncertain Transition: Ethnographies of Change in the Postsocialist World, eds. Michael Burawoy, Katherine Verdery (Lanham, MD: Rowan and Littlefield, 99): 223-243. **CONTACT ADDRESS** Dept Anthropology, Hunter Col, CUNY, 695 Park Ave, New York, NY 10021. **EMAIL** gereed@shiva.hunter.cuny.edu

CREW, B. KEITH
PERSONAL Born 08/02/1955, Biloxi, MS, m, 1992, 2 children **DISCIPLINE** SOCIOLOGY, ANTHROPOLOGY **EDUCATION** Univ Ky, PhD, 87. **CAREER** Assoc Prof, Univ N Iowa, 92-. **MEMBERSHIPS** ASA, Am Soc of Criminologists, Acad of Criminal Justice Sci, Midwest Sociol Soc. **RESEARCH** Law and social control, crime. **SELECTED PUBLICATIONS** auth, "Responding to Student Writing in the Undergraduate Sociology Course," Crossover: The Writing Across the Curriculum Newsletter (90): auth, "Acting like cops: The Social Reality of Crime and Law on Television Police Dramas," in Marginal Conventions: Popular Culture, Mass Media and Social Deviance, (Bowling Green, OH: Popular Pr, 90); auth, Sex Differences in Criminal sentencing: Chivalry or Patriarchy?" Justice Quart 8,1 (91): 59-83; auth, "Race Differences in Felony Charging and Sentencing: Toward an Integration of Decision-Making and Negotiation Models," J of Crime and Justice 14,1 (91): 99-122; coauth, "Dating Violence and Social Learning Theory: A Multivariate Analysis," Violence and Victims 7,1 (92): 3-14; coauth, "A Comparison of Transfer and Non-Transfer Students Majoring in Criminology and Criminal Justice," J of Criminal Justice Ed 4,1 (93): 133-151; auth, "Warning: Contents of this Course May Be Offensive," in Teaching the Sociol of Deviance, (Am Soc Assoc, 99), 16-19; auth, "Nuts, Sluts and 'perverts' Revisited: The Role of the Deviance Course in the Contemporary Sociology Curriculum," in Teaching the Sociol of Deviance (Am Soc Assoc, 99), 5-8; coauth, "Kidnapping," Encycl of Criminol and Deviant Behav, Taylor and Francis (forthcoming); auth, "Mass Media and Crime," Encycl of Criminol and Deviant Behav, Taylor and Francis (forthcoming). **CONTACT ADDRESS** Dept Sociol & Anthrop, Univ of No Iowa, Cedar Falls, IA 50614-0513.

CRIM, ALONZO A.
PERSONAL Born 10/01/1928, Chicago, IL, m **DISCIPLINE** EDUCATION **EDUCATION** Roosevelt Coll, BA 50; Univ of Chicago, MA 58; Harvard Univ, EdD 69. **CAREER** Chicago Pub Schs, teacher, 54-63, supr, 68-69; Whittier Elem Sch, principal, 63-65; Adult Educ Ctr, 65; Wendell Phillips HS, 65-68; Compton Union HS, 69-70; Compton Unified Sch Dist, 70-73; Atlanta Pub Sch, 73-88; GA State Univ, prof, beginning 88; prof emer, Spelman College. **HONORS AND AWARDS** Eleanor Roosevelt Key Awd Roosevelt Univ 74; Vincent Conroy Awd Harvard Grad Sch 70; Distingushed Educators Awd Teacher's Coll Columbia Univ 80; Father of the Year Awd in Educ SE Region of the US 81; Honor of the Yr Awd in Patriotism Military Order of World Wars 81; Hon life mem IL Congress of Parents and Teachers 82; One of North Amer 100 Top Execs The Executive Educator magazine 84; Big Heart Awd

GA Special Olympics 85; The Golden Staff Awd GA State Univ; Volunteer of the Year YMCA of Metro Atlanta; Horace Mann Bond Cup Fort Valley Coll 85; Abe Goldstein Human Relations Awd Anti-Defamation League 85; Distinguished Public Relations Awd GA Chap of the Public Relations Soc of Amer 86; hon DL degree Newberry Coll, hon doctor of public serv degree Gettysburg Coll, Honorary Degree Georgetown Univ; Honorary Degree Princeton Univ; Honorary Degree Harvard Univ; Honorary Degree Tuskege Univ; Honorary Degree Columbia Univ. **MEMBERSHIPS** Mem various offices and committees, Amer Assn Sch Admin; Natl Alliance Black Sch Superintendents; Natl Alliance Black Sch Educ; Harvard Grad Sch Educ; Jr Achievement Gr Atlanta; So Council Intl & Pub Affairs; Educ Prog Assn Amer; GA Council Economic Educ; Amer Cancer Soc; GA Assn Sch Superintendents; Atlanta YMCA; Natl EdD Prog Educ Leaders; Rotary Club; Atlanta Council for Intl Visitors; Atlanta Area Scout Council's Expo; Phi Beta Kappa; life mem NAACP; mem Amer Assn of Sch Administrators; mem Kappa Alpha Psi, Kappa Boule, Phi Delta Kappa. **CONTACT ADDRESS** Education Dept, Spelman Col, 350 Spelman Ln, SW, Box 63, Atlanta, GA 30314-4399.

CRISMORE, AVAN G.
PERSONAL Born 10/07/1929, Chicago, IL, m, 1949, 6 children **DISCIPLINE** ENGLISH, EDUCATION **EDUCATION** St. Francis Univ, BS, 64; MEd, 66; Univ IL, PhD, 85. **CAREER** Teacher, Norwell High School, 64-80; Dir, Univ of IL, 83; assoc to asst prof, Ind Univ Bloomington, 84; prof, Ind Univ Purdue Ft Wayne, 85-. **HONORS AND AWARDS** WhoÛs Who Among Am Teachers; Int Student Org Awd for Teaching ESL. **MEMBERSHIPS** NCTE; Am Educ Res Assoc; Int Reading Assoc; Rhetoric Soc of Am; AILA. **RESEARCH** Visuals - 2 dimensional, Metadiscourse, Critical Thinking, English for Second Language-Controshire Rhetoric. **SELECTED PUBLICATIONS** Coauth, "On the reefs: The verbal and visual rhetoric of Darwin's other big theory", Rhetoric Soc Quarterly 21.2 (91): 11-25; rev, of "Writing: Invitation and Response" by Vincent Ruggeriero and Patrica Morgan, Focuses: Writing Theory and Practices 6.2 (93): 145-147; coauth, "Metadiscourse in persuasive writing: A study of texts written by American and Finnish university students", Written Commun 10.1 (93): 39-71; coauth, "A quantitative contrastive study of metadiscourse: Problems in design and analysis of data", Papers and Studies in Contrastive Linguistics, Vol 28, ed J. Fisiak, Adam Mickiewicz Univ, (Poznam, Poland), (93): 137-151; auth, "Learning about metadiscourse", Encycl of English studies and language arts, Vol I, Nat Counc of Teachers of English, (93): 801-803; coauth, "Attitudes toward English in Malaysia", World Englishes 15.3 (96): 319-335; coauth, "Effects of hedges and gender on attitudes of readers in the United States toward material in a scientific textbook", Culture and Styles of Academic Discourse, ed A. Duszak, de Gruyeter, (Berlin/NY, 97): 222-247; coauth, "Hedges and readers: Effects on attitudes and learning", Hedging and Discourse: Approaches to the analysis of a pragmatic phenomenon in academic texts, eds R. Markkanen and H. Schroder, de Gruyter, (Berlin/NY), 97; coauth, "Collaborative learning in Malaysian postsecondary classrooms", TESOL J, 97; auth, "Visual Rhetoric in an Indiana University Foundation Annual Report", IU Center for Philanthropy working paper series, 98. **CONTACT ADDRESS** Dept English, Indiana Univ-Purdue Univ, Fort Wayne, 2010 E Coliseum Blvd, Fort Wayne, IN 46805-1445. **EMAIL** crismore@ipfw.edu

CROISSANT, JENNIFER L.
PERSONAL Born 08/07/1965, Bellefonte, PA, m, 1999 **DISCIPLINE** SCIENCE AND TECHNOLOGY STUDIES, SOCIOLOGY **EDUCATION** Penn State, BS, 87; MIT, SM, 89; RPI, PhD, 94. **CAREER** Asst Prof, Univ Ariz, 95-. **MEMBERSHIPS** Soc for Soc Studies of Sci; Am Sociol Asn. **CONTACT ADDRESS** Dept Sci, Univ of Arizona, CSTS/MSE, Bldg 12, Tucson, AZ 85721. **EMAIL** jlc@u.arizona.edu

CRONIN, CHRISTOPHER
PERSONAL Born 02/27/1958, NJ, s **DISCIPLINE** PSYCHOLOGY **EDUCATION** Univ Wis Madison, BS, 80; Univ Del, MA, 84; PhD, 85. **CAREER** Asst prof, Transylvania Univ, 91-94; lectr, Flinders Univ, S Australia, 95-96; prof, chair, Saint Leo Univ, 96-. **MEMBERSHIPS** Am Psychol Assoc; Fla Acad of Sci; Am Assoc of Coun and Develop; Who's Who Among Human Serv Prof. **SELECTED PUBLICATIONS** Auth, "Adolescent reports of parental spouse abuse in military and civilian families", J of Interpersonal Violence 10.1 (95): 117-122; auth, "Religiosity, religious affiliation and alcohol and drug use among American college students living in Germany, Int J of the Addictions 30.2 (95): 231-238; coauth, "Effects of modeling on the use of nonsexist language among high school freshpersons and seniors", Sex Roles 33.11-12, (95): 819-830; auth, "Harm reduction for alcohol-use-related problems among college students", Substance Use and Misuse 31, (96): 2029-2037; auth, "Reasons for drinking versus outcome expectancies in the prediction of college student drinking", Substance Use and Misuse 32.10, (97): 1287-1311; coauth, "Two measures of sensation seeking as predictors of alcohol use among high school males", Personality and Individual Differences 22.3 (97): 393-401; ed, Military Psychology; An Introduction, Simon & Schuster (Needham Heights, MA), 98; auth, "Introduction to military psychology" and "The future of military psychology", Military Psychology: An Introduction, ed C. Cronin, Simon & Schuster, (Needham Heights, MA), 98; coauth, "Division 19 needs assessment results", Milit Psychol 15.1 (98): 5-11. **CONTACT ADDRESS** Div of Soc Sci, Saint Leo Univ, PO Box 6665, Saint Leo, FL 33574. **EMAIL** christopher.cronin@saintleo.edu

CROSBY, MARGAREE SEAWRIGHT
PERSONAL Born 11/21/1941, Greenville, SC, m, 1963 **DISCIPLINE** EDUCATION **EDUCATION** South Carolina State University, BS, 1963; Clemson University, MEd, 1973; University of Massachusetts/Amerst, EdD, 1976. **CAREER** School District of Greenville County, headstart tchr, summers, 65, 66, elementary tchr, 64-68, reading resource tchr, 68-74; University of Massachusetts, teaching asst, CUETEP coordinator, 74-76; University of South Carolina, Spartanburg, asst professor, 76-77; Clemson University, associate professor, 77-. **HONORS AND AWARDS** SC Pageant, 1992 SC Women Achievement Awd, The First Awd, 1992; Fifty Most Influential Black Women of South Carolina, 1992; Greenville News/Hayward Mall, Order of the Jessamine Awd, 1991; American Association of University Women, Women in History Who Make a Difference, 1982; Greenville Middle School, Outstanding Educator and Service Awd, 1992; Regional Positive Image Awd, 1993; International Citizen of the Year, Omega Psi Phi Fraternity Inc, 1994, Cleveland, OH; Appointed Woman of Achievement, South Carolina Governor's Office, 1994. **MEMBERSHIPS** National Association of Black Educators, 1991-; National Association of Black Reading and Language Arts Educators; Greenville Hospital System Board of Trustees, chairperson, nominating committee, 1991-97; Governor's Blue Ribbon Committee on Job Training, 1985; SC Council of International Reading Association, board of directors, chairperson, conf pro comm, 1992; Sunbelt Human Advancement Resources, Project RISE advisory board, 1988-; Clemson University, university self study committee, 1986; Affirmative Action Committee; Elementary Curriculum Committee, chairperson, 1992, department head search committee, 1985, faculty search committee, chairman, 1988. **SELECTED PUBLICATIONS** Groomed and trained over 1500 young men and ladies for presentation to society in Debutante Cotillion, AKA, Beautillion (Jack & Jill), 1968-; trained and developed over 500 AFDC mothers for gainful employment in the hospitality sector, 1984-88; principal investigator, A Survey of Principal Attitudes Toward Ability Grouping/Tracking in the Public School of So St, 1991; coordinator, Multi-Cultural Enhancement Project, 1992; "Cooperative Learning," "Alternatives to Tracking and Ability Grouping," Natl Council for Teachers of English and the Natl Dropout Prevention Center. **CONTACT ADDRESS** College of Education, Tillman Hall, Clemson Univ, PO Box 340709, Clemson, SC 29634-0001.

CROSS, DOLORES E.
PERSONAL Born 08/29/1938, Newark, NJ, d **DISCIPLINE** EDUCATION **EDUCATION** Seton Hall University, South Orange Newark, NJ, BS, 1963; Hofstra University, Hempstead, NYork, MS 1968; The University of Michigan, Ann Arbor, MI, PhD, 1971. **CAREER** Northwestern University, Evanston, IL, assistant professor in education & director of master of arts in teaching, 70-74; Claremont Graduate School, Claremont CA, assoc prof in education & dir of teacher education, 74-78; City Univ of New York, New York, NY, vice chancellor for student aff & spec programs, 78-81; New York State Higher Education Service Corp, Albany, NY, president, 81-88; University of Minnesota, Minneapolis, MN, associate provost & assoc vice pres for acad affairs, 88-90; Chicago State University, Chicago, IL, president, 90-97; Morris Brown College, President, 98-. **HONORS AND AWARDS** Honorary Doctorate of Law, Skidmore College, 1988; Honorary Doctorate of Law, Marymount Manhattan, 1984; John Jay Awd, New York State Commission of Independent Colleges and Universities, 1989; NAACP, Muriel Silverberg Awd, New York, 1987; Honorary Doctorate, Hofstra University, Elmhurst College. **MEMBERSHIPS** Member, Women Executives in State Government; advisory board member, Assn of Black Women in Higher Education; member, NAACP; member, American Educational Research Assn, 1990-; vice chr, American Association for Higher Education; vice chr, Campus Compact, Senior Consultant South Africa Project. **CONTACT ADDRESS** GE Fund, 3135 Easton Turnpike, Fairfield, CT 06431.

CROW, BEN
PERSONAL Born 06/18/1947, United Kingdom, m, 1987, 2 children **DISCIPLINE** SOCIOLOGY **EDUCATION** Central London Polytechnic, BSc, 70; Univ Edinburgh, PhD, 80. **CAREER** Lectr, Open Univ, 84-92; vis assoc prof, Univ Calif Berkeley, 94-95; asst prof, Univ Calif Santa Cruz, 96-. **RESEARCH** Water, Food, Development. **SELECTED PUBLICATIONS** Coed, Rural Livelihoods: Crises and Responses, Oxford Univ Pr, 92; auth, Sharing the Ganges: the Politics and Technology of River Development in South Asia, Sage, (Delhi and CA), 95; auth, "New actors and new space for environmental agreement", Water Nepal 6.1 (98): 25-41; auth, "Development and Underdevelopment", Encyclopedia of Political Economy, ed P. O'Hara, Routledge, (London, 98); auth, "Researching the Market System in Bangladesh", Agricultural Markets from Theory to Practice: Field Experience in Developing Countries, ed B. Harris-White, Macmillan (London, 99); auth, "Why is agricultural growth uneven? Class and the agrarian surplus in Bangladesh", Sonar Bangla? Agricultural Growth and Agrarian Change in West Bengal and Bangladesh, Eds B. Rogaly, B. Harriss-White and S. Bose, Sage, 99; auth, "Understanding famine and hunger", Poverty and Development into the 21st Century, eds T. Allen and A. Thomas, Oxford Univ Pr, (forthcoming), auth, "Class and Market in Rural Bangladesh", Festschrift for A R Desai, eds J. Banaji and M. Desai, Oxford Univ Pr, (forthcoming); auth, Market and Class in Rural South Asia, Macmillan Pr, (forthcoming). **CONTACT ADDRESS** Dept Sociol, Univ of California, Santa Cruz, 1156 High St, Santa Cruz, CA 95064.

CROWDER, DIANE GRIFFIN
PERSONAL Born Denison, TX **DISCIPLINE** FRENCH, WOMEN'S STUDIES **EDUCATION** TX Christian Univ, BSEd, 70; Univ Wis, MA, 72; PhD, 77. **CAREER** Asst Prof to Full Prof, Cornell Col, 77-. **HONORS AND AWARDS** Richard & Norma Small Chair for Distinguished Senior Fac, Cornell Col, 00; McConnell Grant, 99; Mellon Grant, 98; Awd for Outstanding Achievement in the Advancement of Women in Higher Education, IA, 97. **MEMBERSHIPS** Mod Lang Asn, Nat Women's Studies Asn. **RESEARCH** Feminist theory, Queer theory, Contemprary French novel. **SELECTED PUBLICATIONS** Auth, "Lesbians and the (Re/De)Construction of the Female Body", in Queer Looks (NY: Haworth); auth, "Amazons", The Gay and Lesbian Literary Heritage (95); transl Colette Guillaumin, "The Constructed Body", Reading the Social Body, (Univ of IA Press, 1993); auth, "Separatism and Feminist Utopian Fiction", Sexual Practice/Textual Theory: Lesbian Cultural Criticism (93): 237-250. **CONTACT ADDRESS** Dept Modern & Classical Lang, Cornell Col, 600 1st St W, Mount Vernon, IA 52314. **EMAIL** dcrowder@cornell-iowa.edu

CROWLEY-LONG, KATHLEEN
PERSONAL Born 09/18/1958, Troy, NY, m, 1980, 2 children **DISCIPLINE** PSYCHOLOGY **EDUCATION** Syracuse Univ, BA, 80; State Univ NY (SUNY), MS, 83; State Univ NY (SUNY), PhD, 87. **CAREER** Asst Prof, Col of St Rose, 86-93; Asst Prof, Univ Hartford, 93-97; Assoc Prof, Col of St Rose, 97-. **HONORS AND AWARDS** Psi Chi, 92-; Teacher of the Year Awd, Col of St Rose Student Assoc, 93. **MEMBERSHIPS** Am Psychol Assoc, Soc for Psychol of Women. **RESEARCH** Gender development, teaching of psychology, parenting. **SELECTED PUBLICATIONS** Auth, "Making Room for Many Feminisms," Psychol of Women Quart (98). **CONTACT ADDRESS** Dept Psychol, Col of Saint Rose, 432 Western Ave, Albany, NY 12203. **EMAIL** crowleyk@mail,strose.edu

CRUMBLEY, DEIDRE H.
PERSONAL Born 12/12/1947, Philadelphia, PA, s **DISCIPLINE** ANTHROPOLOGY, RELIGION & CULTURE **EDUCATION** Temple Univ, BA, 70; North Western, MA, 84, PhD, 89; Harvard, MTS. **CAREER** Jr res fel, 82-84, African Studies Dept; Univ of Ibadan Nigeria West Africa, 82-86; jr lectr, 84-86, Arecheology & Anthropology; Rollins Col, 88-91, Anthropology; Univ FL, Anthropology, 91-98; asst prof, 98, NC State Univ, Africana Studies, Multidisciplinary Studies Div. **HONORS AND AWARDS** Lilly Fel, 79; Fubright Hays, 85; Ford Post doc fel, 91. **MEMBERSHIPS** Amer Anthropological Assn; Amer Acad Religion; **RESEARCH** Religion and change in Africa and the African disapora **SELECTED PUBLICATIONS** Auth, West African Journal of Archeology & Anthropology, vol 16, Ibadan, Nigeria, 88; Impurity and Power: Women in Aladura churches, Africa, 92; Even a Woman: Sex Roles and Mobility in an Aldura Hierarchy, Sept 14, 1988; "Also Chosen: Jews in the Imagination of a Black Storefront Church" IN: Anthropology and Humanism (apublication of the American Anthropological Association) vol 25, issue #1, April 00, pp 6-23; "On Being First: Dogma, Disease and Domination in the Rise of an African Church" In: Religion (an international journal on religion, culture, and society based in London and Berkeley) Volume 30 issue #2-April pp 169-184. **CONTACT ADDRESS** Africana Studies/Div of Multidisciplinary Studies, No Carolina State Univ, Raleigh, NC 27695-7107. **EMAIL** deidre_crumbley@ncsu.edu

CRYSTAL, STEPHEN
PERSONAL Born 10/00/1946, Washington, DC **DISCIPLINE** HEALTH **EDUCATION** Univ Chicago, BS, 68; Harvard Univ, MA, 75; PhD, 81. **CAREER** Dir, NYork City Human Resources Admin Ctr for Human Services Res and Development, 78-95; asst prof & chief Division of Health Car Science, Univ Calif San Diego, 85-87; vis prof, Harvard Medical Sch, 95-96; clinical/adjunct appointments, Univ Ccalif San Diego & Rober Wood Johnson Sch of Medicine, 87-; from assoc res prof to res prof, Rutgers Univ Inst for Health, 87-; chair div on aging, Rutgers Univ, 87; dir of AIDS res group, Rutgers Univ, 87-. **HONORS AND AWARDS** Nat Merit Scholar; John Kendrick Prize, Int Asn for Res in Income and Wealth; Women's Health Res Leadership Awd, 99; ABT Asn Public Policy Res Prize; Nat Sci Found Grad Fel Univ Scholar, Harvard Univ. **MEMBERSHIPS** Am Sociol Asn, Am Public Helath Asn, Gerontological Soc of Am, Am Econcomic Asn. **RESEARCH** HIV/AIDS Research, Aging and Long Term Care and Research. **SELECTED PUBLICATIONS** Auth, "Managed Care and HIV Disease," Am J of Managed Care 2.1 (96): 90-91; coauth, "Health Insurance Coverage at Midlife:

Characteristics, Costs, and Dynamics," Health Care Financing Rev 18.3 (97): 123-148; coauth "Health Care Needs and Services Delivery for Older Persons with HIV/AIDS: Issues and Research Challenges," Res on Aging 20 (98): 739-759; coauth, "Home care Use and Expenditures Among Medicaid Beneficiaries with AIDS," Health Care Financing Rev 20 (99): 1-17; coauth, "Incidence and Duration of Hospitalizations Among Persons with AIDS: An Event Approach," Health Services Res 33 (99): 1611-1638; coauth, "Out of Pocket Health Care Costs Among Older Americans," J of Gerontology: Soc Sci (00); coauth, "Social Support, Conflict, Coping and Distress Among Persons with HIV/AIDS," J of Applied Soc Psychology (in press). **CONTACT ADDRESS** Inst for Health, Health Care Policy and Aging Res, 30 College Ave, New Brunswick, NJ 08901. **EMAIL** scrystal@rci.rutgers.edu

CSIKSZENTMIHALYI, MIHALY
PERSONAL Born 09/29/1934, Fivme, Italy, m, 1961, 2 children **DISCIPLINE** PSYCHOLOGY **EDUCATION** Univ Chicago, PhD, 64. **CAREER** Chr Dept Sociology & Anthropology, Lake Forest, IL, 64-69; Prof & Chr, Dept Psychology, Univ Chicago, 70-; fel, Am Acad Art Sci, Am Acad Educ, Hungarian Acad Sci. **HONORS AND AWARDS** Doctor of Sciences, H.C., Fulbright Senior Scholar **RESEARCH** Psychology of creativity; Enjoyment; Cultural evolution. **SELECTED PUBLICATIONS** Flow=The Psychology of Optimal Experience, 90; The Evolving Self, 93; Creativity, 96; Finding Flow, 97. **CONTACT ADDRESS** Drucker Graduate School of Management, 1021 Dartmouth Avenue, Claremont, CA 91711. **EMAIL** miska@cgu.edu

CUBIE, MICHAEL
PERSONAL Born 11/02/1948, San Francisco, CA, d, 1 child **DISCIPLINE** PHILOSOPHY, PSYCHOLOGY **EDUCATION** San Jose State Univ, BA, 79; MS, 84; Wright Inst, PhD, 88. **CAREER** Counselor, Seven Step Found, 76-78; Counselor, Meadows Boys Home, 80-83; therapist, Bill Wilson Crisis Center, 84-89; counselor, County Health Dept, 87-89; Dir, STEPS Alcohol Prog, 89-90, clinical psychologist, Agnews Develop Center, 90-93, instr, Masters Inst, 93-00, instr, W Valley Col, 93-00. **MEMBERSHIPS** Nat Assoc of Black Psychol; Bay Area Assoc of Black Psychol; Nat Caucus and Center on Black Aged; Nat Black Child Develop Inst. **RESEARCH** Racism and societal institutions, cross cultural psychology, cultural-historical approaches in definitions of psychological functioning, impact of brain lesion on psychological and behavioral functioning. **SELECTED PUBLICATIONS** Auth, The Relationship of Employment and Education to the Role of the Black Father; auth, The Missing Link In the Afro-Centric Perspective. **CONTACT ADDRESS** Dept Counseling, West Valley Col, 14000 Fruitvale Ave, Saratoga, CA 95070-5640. **EMAIL** michael_cubie@wymccd.cc.ca.us

CUELLAR, JOSE
DISCIPLINE ETHNIC STUDIES **EDUCATION** Calif St Univ, Long Beach, BA, 69; Univ Calif, Los Angeles, MA, 71; PhD, 77. **CAREER** Vis Asst Prof, Univ Calif, 78-79; Assoc Prof, San Diego St Col, 80-85; Assoc Prof, Stanford Univ, 85-88; Vis Prof, Univ Calif, 89-. **HONORS AND AWARDS** Outstanding Chicano Fac Awd, Stanford Univ, 86; WAMMIE Awd Winner, 91; Rockefeller Humanities Gateways Fel, Guadeloupe Cult Arts Ctr, 97-98; **SELECTED PUBLICATIONS** 24 j articles, book chapters, essays and 11 book rev published in professional j and texts like Minority Aging; Essential Curricula Content for Selected Health and Allied Health Professions; Hispanic Elderly in Transition. **CONTACT ADDRESS** Dept Ethnic Studies, San Francisco State Univ, 1600 Holloway Ave, San Francisco, CA 94132-1722.

CULLINAN, BERNICE ELLINGER
PERSONAL Born 10/12/1926, Hamilton, OH, d, 2 children **DISCIPLINE** EDUCATION, SOCIOLOGY, PSYCHOLOGY **EDUCATION** Ohio State Univ, BSc, 48, MA, 51, PhD, 64. **CAREER** Elementary teacher, Ohio Public Schools, 46-59; instr, 59-64, asst prof, Ohio State Univ, 64-67; study dir, The Critical Reading Project, USOE, 64-67; prof, NYU, 67-97; Editor-in-Chief, Wordsong Books, Boyds Mills Press, 90-. **HONORS AND AWARDS** Reading Hall of Fame, Int Reading Asn, 89; Arbuthnot Awd, 89; Who's Who in Am Ed, 91; Jeremiah Ludington Awd, 92; Citation for Outstanding Contribution to Literacy, Ind Univ, 95; Col of Education Hall of Fame, 95, Charlotte Huck Prof of Children's Lit, Ohio State Univ, 97; pres, Reading Hall of Fame, Int Reading Asn, 98. **MEMBERSHIPS** Chair, Selection Comm Ezra Jack Keats New Writer Award; editorial board, The New Advocate; advisor, IRA Teachers' Choices Project; Advisory Board, Ranger Rick Magazine; Board of Trustees, Highlights Found; Advisory Board, the Arthur Series, WGBH Boston Children's Programming. **RESEARCH** Childrens poems; literacy initiatives in the United States; development of children's responses to literature; young black children's language & reading competence. **SELECTED PUBLICATIONS** Auth, Let's Read About..Finding Books They'll Love to Read, Scholastic, 93; 75 Authors & Illustrators Everyone Should Know, Children's Book Coun, 94; coauth, Helping Your Child Learn to Read, U.S. Dept of Ed, 93; Three Voices: Invitation to Poetry Across the Curriculum, Stenhouse, 95; Language, Literacy, & the Child, Second Edition, Harcourt Brace, 97; Literature and the Child, Fourth Edition, Harcourt Brace, 98; ed, Fact and Fiction: Literature Across the Curriculum, Int Reading Asn, 93; Pen in Hand: Children Become Writers, Int Reading Asn, 93; Children's Voices: Talk in the Classroom, Int Reading Asn, 93; A Jar of Tiny Stars: Poems by NCTE Award-Winning Poets, Wordsong/NCTE, 96. **CONTACT ADDRESS** 10 E 40th St., New York, NY 10016. **EMAIL** BerniceCullinan@Worldnet.att.net

CULYER, RICHARD
PERSONAL Born, MD, m, 1969, 1 child **DISCIPLINE** EDUCATION **EDUCATION** Fla State Univ, PhD, 73. **CAREER** Fac, Appalachian state Univ, 66-72; asst dir , Right to Read, Fla, Dept of Ed, 73-74; prof ed, Coker Col, 96-. **HONORS AND AWARDS** Golden Apple Awd-TV Channel 13; First 10-year Citation for Contributions to Reading (NC Reading Asn); Young Man of the Year, Kings Mountain, NC; listed in 10 biographical references; pres, NCRA; state coord, NCRA; Ed conf proceedings, 10 years; speaker on over 200 occasions; established schoolwide reading programs in three states. **MEMBERSHIPS** IRA, Phi Delta Kappa, NCTE, Col Reading Asn, Nat Ed Asn. **RESEARCH** Establishing schoolwide reading programs, strategies for at-risk children, comprehension. **SELECTED PUBLICATIONS** Coauth with Dr. Gail B. Culyer, Preventing Reading Failure: A Practical Approach; auth, Ideas for Developing Comprehension; auth, Grouping: How, Why, When?; coauth with Dr. Edwin H. Smith; Teaching Reading to Adults; over 700 publications including: weekly columnist for newspaper (parent suggestions); many sets of materials for children; many monographs (over 80) for educators. **CONTACT ADDRESS** Dept Ed, Coker Col, 300 E Col Ave, Hartsvill, SC 29550. **EMAIL** Rculyer@pascal.coker.edu

CUMMINGS, WILLIAM K.
PERSONAL Born 10/18/1943, Raleigh, NC, m, 1997 **DISCIPLINE** COMPARATIVE EDUCATION, GLOBAL STUDIES **EDUCATION** Univ Mich, BA, 65; Harvard Univ, MA, 68; PhD, 72. **CAREER** Lectr, Harvard Univ, 86-92; prof of Comparative Educ and Dir, Center for Comparative and Global Studies in Educ, SUNY Buffalo, 92-. **HONORS AND AWARDS** Woodrow Wilson Fel, 65; Nat Inst of Mental Health Fel, 70-72; Fulbright Scholar to Japan, 75, 96; Outstanding Performance Awd from Nat Sci Found, 86; Pres of Comparative and Int Educ Soc, 98-99. **MEMBERSHIPS** AERA, CIES. **SELECTED PUBLICATIONS** Coauth with Gail Chambers, Profiting from Education, NY: Inst of Int Educ (90); auth, The Changing Academic Marketplace and University Reform in Japan, NY: Garland Pub (90); co-ed with Philip G. Altbach, The Challenge of Eastern Asian Education: Implications for America, Albany: SUNY Press (97); co-ed with H. Dean Nielsen, Quality of Education for All: Community-Oriented Approaches, NY: Garland Pub, Inc (97); ed, Service University in Comparative Perspective, Higher Education, vol 35, 1 (98); co-ed, Quality Education in Ethiopia: Vision for the Twenty-First Century, Addis Ababa: Addis Ababa Univ Press (99). **CONTACT ADDRESS** Center for Comparative and Global Studies in Educ, SUNY, Buffalo, 428 C Baldy Hall, Buffalo, NY 14260. **EMAIL** wkcum@usa.net

CUNNIGEN, DONALD
PERSONAL Born 02/16/1952, m, 1985 **DISCIPLINE** SOCIOLOGY **EDUCATION** Tougaloo Col, BA, 74; Univ NH, MA, 76; Harvard Univ, AM, 79, PhD, 88. **CAREER** Asst prof, Univ Pa, 88-92; asst prof, Univ Mo-Columbia, 92-93; asst prof, Univ RI, 93-99, assoc prof, 99-. **HONORS AND AWARDS** Sociol Spectrum Awd, 99; Asn of Soc & Behav Scis, Pres, 99. **MEMBERSHIPS** Asn Black Sociols, Asn of Soc & Behav Scis, Am Sociol Asn, Southern Sociol Soc. **RESEARCH** Race relations, social movements & social change, sociology of education. **SELECTED PUBLICATIONS** Auth, "Working for Racial Integration: The Civil Rights Activism of Bishop Duncan Montgomery Gray of Mississippi, " Anglican & Episcopal Hist (98); auth, "Bringing the Revolution Down Home: Republic of New Africa in Mississippi," Sociol Spectrum (99). **CONTACT ADDRESS** Dept Sociol & Anthropol, Univ of Rhode Island, 10 Chaffee Rd, Kingston, RI 02881. **EMAIL** dcunn@uriacc.uri.edu

CUNNINGHAM, JACK R.
DISCIPLINE CHRISTIAN EDUCATION **EDUCATION** Cent Baptist Col BA; Mid-Am Sem, MA; SW Baptist Theol Sem, PhD. **CAREER** Adj instr, Cent Baptist Col; instr, Inst Christian Stud Southwestern Sem; admin distance edu, Sem Extension of the S Baptist Convention; J.M. Frost assoc prof, S Baptist Theol Sem; vis prof on sabbatical summer 00. **RESEARCH** Areas of experiential learning assessment, distance education and adult education. **SELECTED PUBLICATIONS** Auth, ed, ten teachers' and study guides on the subjects of Old Testament, New Testament and teaching; pub(s), on non-traditional education methodology. **CONTACT ADDRESS** Sch Christian Edu and Leadership, So Baptist Theol Sem, 2825 Lexington Rd, Louisville, KY 40280. **EMAIL** jcunningham@sbts.edu

CUNNINGHAM, JAMES J.
PERSONAL Born 04/19/1938, Pittsburgh, PA, m **DISCIPLINE** EDUCATION **EDUCATION** BS, 1964; MA, 1967; EdS, 1969; DEd, 1971. **CAREER** Elementary school teacher, 64-66; Washington DC, counselor, prin 66-68; Fed City Coll, Washington DC, 68-71; Assoc Cont Res & Analysis Inc, Washington DC, consultant 69; Fed City Coll, dir of admissions 71; HEW/DE, Washington DC, consultant 71; Moton Consortium on Adm & Financial Aid, co-dir 71-72; TX Southern Univ, dean of students, prof of educ 72-74; Mankato State Coll, Mankato MN, vice pres student servs, prof of educ 74; TX Southern Univ Houston, special asst to the pres 86, prof of graduate educ, vice pres institutional advancement. **MEMBERSHIPS** Mem Natl Assn for Higher Edn; Personnel Guidance Assn; Assn of Coll Adm Counselors; DC Couns Assn; Elem Classroom Tchrs Assn; Natl Tchrs Assn; TX Personnel Serv Adminstrs; MN State Coll Student Assn; MN Student Serv Adminstrn; NAACP. **CONTACT ADDRESS** Graduate Education, Texas So Univ, Houston, TX 77004.

CUNNINGHAM, KEITH K.
PERSONAL Born 04/28/1939, Beardstown, IL, m, 1959, 2 children **DISCIPLINE** FOLKLORE **EDUCATION** Western IL Univ, BS, 59; Miss Sch Relig, BD, 63; Univ Mo, MA, 66; Ind Univ, PhD, 76. **CAREER** Teacher, Harrisburg High Sch, 65-66; prof, Moberly Jr Col, 66-69; instr to prof, Northern Ariz Univ, 69-. **HONORS AND AWARDS** Outstanding Fac Member Awd, Northern Ariz Univ, 73; Printer's Devil Awd, Am Folklore Soc, 87. **MEMBERSHIPS** Am Folklore Soc; Int Soc for Contemp Legend Res. **RESEARCH** Ethnography, Narrative Research. **SELECTED PUBLICATIONS** Auth, The Oral Tradition of the American West: Adventure, Courtship, Family, and Place in Traditional Recitation, August House Pr, (Little Rock, Ark), 90; auth, "It was the (Untranslatable): A Native American Legend Interpreted from a Cross-Cultural Perspective", Folklore 102.1 (91): 89-96; coauth, "He Just Fell Over Dead: Navajo Humor, Navajo Hozho", Spoken in Jest: Studies in Culture and Humour, Sheffield Acad Pr, (Sheffield, Eng, 91): 15-29; auth, "Navajo, Mormon, Zuni Graves: Navajo, Mormon, Zuni Ways", Cemeteries and Gravemarkers: Voices of American Culture, Utah State Univ Pr, (Logan, UT, 92): 197-215; auth, American Indians' Kitchen-Table Stories: Contemporary Conversations with Cherokee, Sioux, Hopi, Osage, Navajo, Zuni, and Members of Other Nations, August House Pr, (Little Rock, Ark), 92; auth, "The People of Rimrock Bury Alfred Lorenzo: Tri-Cultural Funerary Practice", Ethnicity and the American Cemetery, Popular Culture Pr, (Bowling Green, OH, 93): 173-192; auth, "The Effects of a Folklorist Residency Upon Student Self-Esteem: A Descriptive Study", Schools, Communities and the Arts: A Research Compendium, Morrison Inst for Pub Policy, (Tempe, AZ, 95): 57-59; auth, "Concho: The People of the Santo Nino", J of the Southwest 38.4 (97): 37-62; auth, Two Zuni Artists: A Tale of Art and Mystery, Univ Pr of Miss, (Jackson, Miss), 98. **CONTACT ADDRESS** Dept English, No Arizona Univ, PO Box 6032, Flagstaff, AZ 86011.

CUNNINGHAM, WILLIAM DEAN
PERSONAL Born 08/09/1937, Kansas City, MO, d **DISCIPLINE** EDUCATION **EDUCATION** Univ of KS, BA 1959; Univ of TX, MLS 1962, PhD 1972. **CAREER** Federal Aviation Agency, chief library serv 65-67; Topeka Public Library, head adult serv 67-68; US Dept of Educ, prog officer 68-71; Howard Univ, dir univ libraries 70-73; Univ of MD Coll of Library & Information Services, asst prof 73-. **HONORS AND AWARDS** Citations from Dept of Education, FAA, ASALA. **MEMBERSHIPS** Mem Amer Library Assn 1970-, Assn for the Study of Afro-Amer Life and History 1974-; bd dirs Soul Journey Enterprises 1974-; mem Natl Black Heritage Council 1984-. **SELECTED PUBLICATIONS** Auth, Blacks in Performing Arts; co-auth, Black Guide to Washington. **CONTACT ADDRESS** Libr & Info Servs, Univ of Maryland, Col Park, 4105 Hornbake Library, College Park, MD 20742.

CURET, LUIS ANTONIO
PERSONAL Born 10/20/1960, San Juan, PR, m, 1990, 2 children **DISCIPLINE** ANTHROPOLOGY, ARCHAEOLOGY **EDUCATION** Arizona State Univ, PhD, 92. **CAREER** Asst prof, Gettysburg Col, 93-96; asst prof, Univ of Colorado, Denver, 96- . **HONORS AND AWARDS** Res awd, Univ Colorado, 98. **MEMBERSHIPS** Soc for Am Archaeol; Sigma Xi Sci Soc; Int Asoc Caribbean Archaeol; Asociacion Puertorriquencia de Antropologos y Arqueologos. **RESEARCH** Caribbean and Mesoamerica; complex societies. **SELECTED PUBLICATIONS** Auth, Ceramic Production Areas and Regional Studies: An Example From La Mixtequilla, Veracruz, Mexico, in J of Field Archaeol, 93; auth, Prehistoric Demographic Changes in the Valley of Maunabo, Puerto Rico: A Preliminary Report, in Proc of the 14th Int Cong for Caribbean Archaeol, 93; coauth, Post classic Changes in Veracruz, Mexico, Ancient Mesoamerica, 94; auth, Ideology, Chiefly Power, and Material Culture: An Example from the Greater Antilles, Latin Am Antiq, 96; auth, Technological Changes in Prehistoric Ceramics from Eastern Puerto Rico: An Exploratory Study, in J of Archaeol Sci, 97; auth, New Formulae for Estimating prehistoric Populations for Lowland South America and the Caribbean, in Antiquity, 98; coauth, Poder e ideologia: el control del simbolismo en los cacicazgos tempranos de Puerto Rico, Historia y Sociedad, 98; coauth, Mortuary Practices, Social Development and Ideology in Precolumbian Puerto Rico, Latin Am Antiq, in press; coauth, Informe Preliminar del Proyecto Arqueologico del Centro Indigena de Tibes, Ponce, Puerto Rico, in Proc of the 16th Int Cong

for Caribbean Archaeol, in press. **CONTACT ADDRESS** Dept of Anthropology, Univ of Colorado, Denver, Campus Box 103, PO Box 173364, Denver, CO 80217-3364. **EMAIL** lcuret@carbon.cudenver.edu

CURRAN, SARA R.
PERSONAL Born 03/24/1961, Beirut, Lebanon, m, 1987, 1 child **DISCIPLINE** SOCIOLOGY **EDUCATION** Univ Mich, BS, 83; NCar State Univ, MS, 90; PhD, 94 **CAREER** Asst Prof, Princeton Univ, 96-. **HONORS AND AWARDS** Awd, President's Standing Committee, Princeton Univ, 99; Mellon Foundation Fel, Univ WA, 94-; Rockefeller Foundation Dissertaion Fel, 92-94; Howard W. Odum Grad Stud Awd, Univ NC, 92; Andrew W. Mellon Foundation, 92; NRSA Predoctoral Awd, Univ NC, 89-; Gamma sigma Delta, NC State Univ, 89. **MEMBERSHIPS** Am Sociol Asn; Population Asn of Am; Intl Union for the Sci Study of Population; Asn for Asian Studies. **RESEARCH** Migration and Development; Intrahousehold and Intergenerational Relations; Aging; Economic Sociology; Population, Social Organization and the Environment. **SELECTED PUBLICATIONS** Auth, "Uneven Development in North Carolina? Job Quality Differences Between Local and NonLocal Firms," Rural Sociology, (91): 4; auth, "Review of Political Economy of Health Care in Southeast Asia," Journal of Developing Societies, 93; auth, "Review of The Family, The Market, and The State in Aging Societies," Professional Geographer, 95; auth, "Community and contraceptive Choice in Rural Thailand: A Case Study of Nang Rong," Demography, 96; auth, "Review of Population and Development: A Critical Introduction," contemporary Sociology, (99): 201-202. **CONTACT ADDRESS** Dept Sociol, Princeton Univ, 2-N-1 Green Hall, Princeton, NJ 08544-0001. **EMAIL** Curran@princeton.edu

CURRY, ALLEN
PERSONAL Born Pennsylvania, PA, m, 1965, 2 children **DISCIPLINE** CHRISTIAN EDUCATION **EDUCATION** Temple Univ, Ed.D. **CAREER** VP/AA; Hugh and Sally Reaves prof. **HONORS AND AWARDS** Dir, Edu Svc(s), cord, Production, Great Commn Publ. **SELECTED PUBLICATIONS** Auth, The God We Love and Serve. **CONTACT ADDRESS** Dept of Christian Education, Reformed Theol Sem, Mississippi, 5422 Clinton Blvd, Jackson, MS 39209-3099. **EMAIL** acurr@rts.edu

CURTIS, WILLIAM H.
PERSONAL Born 06/25/1930, Philadelphia, PA, s **DISCIPLINE** PSYCHOLOGY **EDUCATION** Mt St Mary's Col, BA, 61; St Mary's Sem, STB, 63; Loyola Col, MEd, 64; Walden Univ, PhD, 75. **CAREER** Adj Instructor, Georgetown Univ, 65-66; Instructor, Cmty Col Philadelphia, 66-67; Prof to Dept Chair, Camden County Col, 67-. **HONORS AND AWARDS** Charter Fac Plaque, Camden County Col. **MEMBERSHIPS** Am Psychol Asn, Am Soc of Clinical Hypnosis. **RESEARCH** Projective techniques in clinical assessment. **CONTACT ADDRESS** Dept Psychol, Camden County Col, PO Box 200, Blackwood, NJ 08012. **EMAIL** wcurtis@camdencc.edu

CUTTER, WILLIAM
PERSONAL Born 02/09/1937, St. Louis, MO, m, 1970, 1 child **DISCIPLINE** MODERN HEBREW LITERATURE, EDUCATION **EDUCATION** Yale Univ, AB, 59; Hebrew Union Col, Ohio, MA, 65; Univ Calif, Los Angeles, PhD(Near Eastern lit), 71. **CAREER** From instr to asst prof Hebrew lit, 65-71, asst dean col, 65-69, dir sch educ, sch Judaic studies, 69-76, assoc prof, 71-76, Prof Hebrew Lit Educ, Hebrew Union Col, Calif, 76-. **MEMBERSHIPS** Cent Conf Am Rabbis; AAUP; Asn Jewish Studies; Nat Asn Temple Educr; Nat Comn Jewish Educ. **RESEARCH** Hebrew literature between 1880 and 1940; contemporary Jewish religious education; American Jewish fiction. **SELECTED PUBLICATIONS** Auth, numerous articles and essays. **CONTACT ADDRESS** Sch of Educ, Hebrew Union Col-Jewish Inst of Religion, California, Los Angeles, CA 90007. **EMAIL** cutter@usc.edu

D

D'ANGELO, RAYMOND
PERSONAL Born 08/01/1947, Vineland, NJ, m, 1981, 2 children **DISCIPLINE** SOCIOLOGY **EDUCATION** Duquesne Univ, BA, 69; New School for Social Res, MA, 73; Bryn Mawr Col, PhD, 83. **CAREER** Prof to Dept Chair, St Joseph's Col, 73-. **HONORS AND AWARDS** NSF Grant; NEH Grant; NIC Awd; Delta Epsilon Sigma Honor Soc. **MEMBERSHIPS** Org of Am Hist, Am Sociol Asn. **RESEARCH** The Civil Rights movement, Popular culture, Historic preservation. **SELECTED PUBLICATIONS** Auth, The American Civil Rights Movement: Readings and Interpretations, McGraw-Hill, 00; auth, "Public Opinion and the Civil Rights Movement," in Civil Rights in the United States, Macmillan, 99; auth, Student Workbook for Data analysis, 96; auth, "Sports Gambling and the Media: Who Supports Whom?," ARENA Review, Journal for the Study of Sport and Sociology, 87; auth, "The Social Organization of Sports Gambling," Proceedings of the Sixth National Conference on Gambling and Risk-Taking, The Gambling Studies, 85; auth, The Social Organization of Sports Gambling: A Study in Deviance and Convention, 83. **CONTACT ADDRESS** Dept Soc Sci, St. Joseph's Col, New York, 245 Clinton Ave, Brooklyn, NY 11205-3602.

D'ANTONIO, WILLIAM
PERSONAL Born 02/07/1926, New Heaven, CT, m, 1950, 6 children **DISCIPLINE** SOCIOLOGY **EDUCATION** Yale Univ, BA, 48; Univ Wis, MA, 53; Mich State Univ, PhD, 58. **CAREER** Instr, Mich State Univ, 57-59; Asst to Full Prof, Univ of Notre Dame, 59-71; Dept Head, Univ of Notre Dame, 66-71; Prof, Univ of Conn, 71-86; Dept Head, Univ of Conn, 71-76; Adj Res Prof, Life Cycle Inst, Cath Univ, 93-. **HONORS AND AWARDS** Res Grant, Soc Sci Res Coun; Res Grant, Dept of Health and Human Serv; Res Grant, Lilly Endowment; Res Grant, Louisville Inst; Phi Kappa Phi Nat Honor Soc; Aida Tomeh Distinguished Serv Awd, N Central Sociol Asn, 91; Stuart A. Rice Merit Awd, DC Sociol Soc, 95. **MEMBERSHIPS** Am Sociol Asn, A Asn of Univ Professors, Int Inst of Sociol. **RESEARCH** Family and Religion, Authority and Decision Making, Small groups within large organizations. **SELECTED PUBLICATIONS** Auth, "Personal Autonomy and Concern for the commons: The Communitarian Challenge," Va Soc Sci J 31 (96): 11-21; coauth, "The Catholic Vote in Election'96,", Public Perspective (June/July 97): 45-48; coauth, Laity: American and Catholic, Transforming the Church, Sheed and Ward (Kansas City), 96; co-ed, Ecology, Society and the Quality of Social Life, Transaction Publ Co (New Brunswick), 96; coauth, The Catholic Experience of Small Christian Communities, Paulist Press (NY), 00. **CONTACT ADDRESS** Dept Sociol, Catholic Univ of America, 620 Michigan Ave NE, Washington, DC 200064-0002. **EMAIL** Dantonio@cua.edu

D'AOUST, JEAN-JACQUES
PERSONAL Born 01/03/1924, Alfred, ON, Canada, m, 1987, 5 children **DISCIPLINE** PSYCHOLOGY OF DEVELOPMENT, WORLD RELIGIONS **EDUCATION** Univ Ottawa, BA, B Ph, 46; St Vincent Sem, MA, 60; Yale Univ, MA, 65; M Ph, 66; PhD, 68; Slippery Rock Univ, MA, 87. **CAREER** Coord, Unied Rel Init; adj prof, Marshall Univ, Ashland Com Coll; assoc prof, Ashland Com Col, ret. **HONORS AND AWARDS** Can Coun Arts Fel; Kent Fel; Yale Univ Fel. **MEMBERSHIPS** ACR; APS; SVHE. **RESEARCH** Psychology of development; world religions; Biblical research; Jesus seminars. **CONTACT ADDRESS** Dept Social Science, Ashland Comm Col, 1400 College Rd, Ashland, KY 41101.

D'HEURLE, ADMA J.
PERSONAL Born 06/21/1924, Lebanon, m, 1950, 3 children **DISCIPLINE** PSYCHOLOGY **EDUCATION** Am Univ Beirut, AB, 47; Smith Col, MA, 48; Univ Chicago, PhD, 53. **CAREER** Asst Prof, St. Xavier Col, 54-58; Lecturer, Stanford Univ, 72-73; Adj Prof, Long Island Univ, 75-80; Vis Prof, Univ of Uppsala, 80-81; Vis Prof, Univ of Turku, 87, 89, 90; Asst Prof to Prof, Mercy Col, 61-. **HONORS AND AWARDS** Alumni Gold Medal, Mercy Col, 98; Res Grant, Finnish Peace Inst, 90; Teaching Excellence and Campus Leadership Awd, Mercy Col, 95; Nominee for Prof of the Year, Council for Adv and Sup of Educ, 87; Fulbright Grant, 87; Am Men and Women of Sci, 78; Sr Gratia Maher Awd, Mercy Col, 68, 74. **MEMBERSHIPS** Am Psychol Asn, Am Psychol Soc, Am Asn of Univ Prof, Ibsen Asn of Am, Psychol for Soc Responsibility, Soc for Cross-Cultural Res, Soc for the Adv of Scand Studies, World Fed for Mental Health. **RESEARCH** Comparative socialization, Peace education. **SELECTED PUBLICATIONS** Rev, of "La Derniere Migration" by Janine Matillon, World Literature Today, 99; auth, "Language and the Culture of Peace," The Acorn: Journal of the Gandhi-King Society, (98): 33-42; auth, "Primers as socializing agents: A Comparison of American and Finnish reading Materials for Grades Three to Six," Comparative Education Review, (95): 280-298; auth, "Birgitta Trotzig: Portrait", Scandanavian Studies, (95): 247-251; auth, Peace-Mindidness of the Super Powers as Perceived in Four Countries, Tampere, 94; auth, "A Daughter's Memoir Review of Alva Myrdal by Sissela Bok," Scandinavian Studies, 92; auth, "Vampire and Child Savior Motifs in the Tales of Isak Dinesen," in Of Mice and Women: Aspects of Female Aggression, Academic Press, 92; auth, "Time's Disinherited Children: Childhood, Regression and Sacrifice," Ibsen News and Comment, 91; auth, "Birgitta Trotzig: Poet, Novelist and Essayist," Dictionary of Scandinavian Literature, Greenwood Press, 90. **CONTACT ADDRESS** Dept Beh Sci, Mercy Col, 555 Broadway, Dobbs Ferry, NY 10522.

DAANE, MARY
PERSONAL Born 12/14/1946, Sheboygan, WI, m, 1990, 2 children **DISCIPLINE** EDUCATION **EDUCATION** Upsala Col, BA, 69; Seton Hall Univ, EdMA, 79; NY Univ, PhD, 90. **CAREER** Instr, Columbia Univ, 89; asst prof, Union County Col, 90-91; assoc prof, Waycross Col, 91-97; dept dir, Hudson County Cmty Col, 97-. **HONORS AND AWARDS** WhoÛs Who in Am, 00. **MEMBERSHIPS** NCTE Am Coun of Higher Educ, Intl Reading Asn. **RESEARCH** Reading, Metacognition, Metalinguistics, Rhetoric and composition, Adult learners. **SELECTED PUBLICATIONS** Auth, "Writing Reality: Composition, Metaphor, and Cosmology," Journal of the Assembly for Expanded Perspectives on Learning, 96; auth, "Using Story Summaries to Enhance Comprehension and Writing Skills," Focus 18, 94; auth, "Good Readers Make Good Writers: a description of four college students," Journal of Reading, 91. **CONTACT ADDRESS** Dept Gen Educ, Hudson County Comm Col, 901 Bergen Ave, Jersey City, NJ 07306-4301. **EMAIL** mdaane@mail.hudson.cc.nj.us

DABBS, JENNIFER B.
PERSONAL Born 10/24/1964, McComb, MS, m, 1990 **DISCIPLINE** SOCIOLOGY **EDUCATION** Centenary Col, BA, 86; Univ Pittsburgh, MA, 88; Univ N Tex, PhD, 94. **CAREER** Asst Prof to Prof and Dept Co-Ord, La Col, 95-. **HONORS AND AWARDS** Who's Who Among Am Teachers, 00, 96. **MEMBERSHIPS** Am Sociol Asn; Nat Coun on Family Relationships; Alpha Kappa Delta. **RESEARCH** Teaching Sociology. **CONTACT ADDRESS** Dept Soc & Beh Sci, Louisiana Col, 1140 Col Dr, Pineville, LA 71360. **EMAIL** dabbs@lacollege.edu

DALE, HELEN
PERSONAL Born 02/06/1945, Chicago, IL, 2 children **DISCIPLINE** ENGLISH EDUCATION **EDUCATION** NYork Univ, MA; Univ Wis Madison, PhD. **CAREER** Fac. **HONORS AND AWARDS** Phi Beta Kappa; Promising Res Nat Awd, finalist; NCTE; Steve Cahir Awd for Outstanding Res in Writing--Am Ed Res Assoc. **RESEARCH** Composition theory; collaborative writing; ethics of qualitative research; the links between theory and practice for student teachers; collaborative self-study as reform in teacher education; high school/university literacy partnerships. **SELECTED PUBLICATIONS** Auth, Co-authoring in the Classroom: Creating an Environment for Effective Collaboration; auth, "Collaborative Wrinting Interactions in One Ninth-Grade Classroom," J of Educational Res 87.6, (94), 334-344; auth, "Dilemmas of Fidelity: Qualitative research in the Classroom," Ethics and representation in Qualitative Studies of Literacy, Urbana, IL: NCTE, (96), 77-94; auth, The Influence of Co-authoring on the Writing Process," J of teaching Writing 15.1, (96), 65-79; auth, "Letters of Intent: Collaborative Self-Study as Reform in Teacher Education," The Heart of the Matter: Teacher Ed Reform Perspectives and Possibilities, (98), 81-99; auth, "Creating Literacy Communities: high school/ University Partnerships," English J, (98), 53-58. **CONTACT ADDRESS** Dept of English, Univ of Wisconsin, Eau Claire, Hibbard Hall 412, PO Box 4004, Eau Claire, WI 54702-4004. **EMAIL** dalehn@uwec.edu

DALEY, JAMES
PERSONAL Born 09/09/1940, Pittsburgh, PA, s **DISCIPLINE** PSYCHOLOGY **EDUCATION** Calif State Univ, BA, 68; Wright Inst, MA, 70; PhD, 73. **CAREER** Psychologist, Diablo Valley Col, 70-. **HONORS AND AWARDS** Danforth Scholar, Stanford Univ, 78. **RESEARCH** Infectious disease and W.H.O. **SELECTED PUBLICATIONS** Auth, AIDS: What is Now Known; auth, Education and Support for People with AIDS; auth, AIDS and Mental Health; auth, Psychology and Human Services. **CONTACT ADDRESS** Div Soc Sci, Diablo Valley Col, 321 Golf Club Rd, Pleasant Hill, CA 94523.

DALEY, JAMES G.
DISCIPLINE SOCIAL WORK **EDUCATION** Wofford Col, BS, 74; Univ SC, MSW, 77; Fla State Univ, PhD, 86. **CAREER** Chief, USAF, 86-96; asst prof, Southwest Miss State Univ, 96-. **MEMBERSHIPS** Coun on Soc Work; Nat Assoc of Soc Workers; Acad of Certified Soc Workers. **SELECTED PUBLICATIONS** Auth, "Clinical instruments for assessing family health", Family Health: A Holistic Approach to Social Work Practice, eds F.K. Yuen and J.T. Pardeck, Auburn House, (99): 81-100; ed, Social Work Practice in the Military, Haworth Pr, (Bingingham, NY), 99; auth, "Military Social Work Practice: Putting it all Together", "Understanding the Military as an Ethnic Identity", "Understanding Life in the Air Force", "Career Progression and Grooming", and "Military Social Work Practice in Mental Health Programs", Social Work Practice in the Military, ed J.G. Daley, Haworth Pr, (Bingingham, NY), 99; auth, "Applications of family measurement scales to gay and lesbian families", A Professional's Guide to Understanding Gay and Lesbian Domestic Violence, Edwin Mellen Pr, (Lewiston, 99): 277-286; coauth, "A factor analysis of the family assessment device", Family Process (forthcoming); coauth, "The Lesbian Partner Abuse Scale", Res in Soc Work Practice (forthcoming). **CONTACT ADDRESS** Dept Soc Work, Southwest Missouri State Univ, Springfield, 901 S National Ave, Springfield, MO 65804-0095. **EMAIL** jgd768f@mail.smsu.edu

DANE, BARBARA
PERSONAL Born 09/13/1939, New York, NY, m, 1979 **DISCIPLINE** SOCIAL WORK **EDUCATION** Fordham Univ, PhD, 85. **CAREER** Assoc prof, NYork Univ, Sch Sco Work, 90-. **HONORS AND AWARDS** Fac Schl Awd. **MEMBERSHIPS** NASN. **RESEARCH** Bereavement; AIDS; secondary trauma. **SELECTED PUBLICATIONS** Coauth, "Resident Guests: Social Workers in Host Settings," Soc Work (91); auth," Counseling Bereaved Middle Aged Children: Parental Suicide Survivors," J Clinical Social Work (91); auth, "Adult Children with AIDS: Anticipatory Mourning of Middle Aged Parents," J Families in Society (91); coauth, "AIDS and Dying:

The Teaching Challenge," J Teach Social Work (90); coauth, "AIDS: A Curriculum and Teaching Model," J Social Work Edu (90); coauth, "Minority Survivors of Persons With AIDS: The Teaching Imperative." J Multicultural Social Work Practice (93); coauth, Health Care Professionals Coping with Grief." In AIDS in the 21st Century (94); auth, KeeshaÜs secret: My mommy died of AIDS, Centering Corp (Omaha, NE), forthcoming; auth, "Child welfare workers: An innovative approach for interacting with secondary trauma," J Social Work Edu (00); auth, "Thai Women: Mediation to cope with the stressors of living with HIV/AIDS," J Religion & Health (forthcoming). **CONTACT ADDRESS** School of Social Work, New York Univ, New York, NY 10003.

DANESHPOUR, MANIJEH
PERSONAL Born 04/11/1969, Iran, m, 1984, 2 children **DISCIPLINE** PSYCHOLOGY **EDUCATION** Univ Utah, BS, 90; MS, 92; Univ Minnesota, PhD, 96. **CAREER** Asst prof, dir, St Cloud State Univ. **MEMBERSHIPS** Am Asn Mar Fam Coun. **RESEARCH** Stress and coping for individuals, couples and families. **SELECTED PUBLICATIONS** Auth, Muslim Family and Family Therapy, J Mar Fam Ther. **CONTACT ADDRESS** Dept Psychology, St. Cloud State Univ, 720 4th St, Edu Bldg B249, Saint Cloud, MN 56301. **EMAIL** mdanespour@stcloudstate.edu

DANIEL, E. VALENTINE
DISCIPLINE ANTHROPOLOGY **EDUCATION** Amherst Col, BA, 71; Univ Chicago, MA, 73; PhD, 79. **CAREER** Prof, Univ of Mich, 90-97; Prof, Dir Southern Asian Inst, Columbia Univ, 97-. **MEMBERSHIPS** Asn of Am Anthropologists, Asn of Asian Studies. **RESEARCH** Semiotic Anthropology, Philosophical Anthropology, South Asia. **SELECTED PUBLICATIONS** Auth, "Tea Talk: Violent Measures in the Discursive Practices of Sri Lanka's Estate Tamils," Comp Studies in Soc and Hist 15-3 (93); coauth, Annual Review or Anthropology, Vol 22 to Vol 27, Annual Rev Inc (Palo Alto), 92-97; auth, "The Individual in Terror," in Embodiment and Experience: The Existential ground of culture and self, ed. Tom Csordas (Cambridge: Cambridge Univ Press, 94); coauth, "Introduction," in Culture/Contexture: Essays in Anthropology and Literary Study, ed. E. Valentine Daniel and Jeffrey Peck (Barkeley: Univ of Calif Press, 96); auth, "Crushed Glass," in Culture/Contexture: Essays in Anthropology and Literary Study, ed. E. Valentine Daniel and Jeffrey Peck (Barkeley: Univ of Calif Press, 96); coauth, "Introduction," in Mistrusting Refugee, ed. E. Valentine Daniel and John Chr. Knudsen (Barkeley: Univ of Calif Press, 96); coauth, "Formations, Forms and Transformations," in Mistrusting Refugee, ed. E. Valentine Daniel and John Chr. Knudsen (Barkeley: Univ of Calif Press, 96); auth, Charred Lullabies: Chapters in an Anthropology of Violence, Princeton Univ Press (Princeton), 97; auth, "The Limits of Culture," in Near Ruins, ed. Nicholas B. Dirks, (Minn: Univ of Minn Press. 98); auth, "Nation and Alienation," in Violence and Subjectivity, ed. Veena Das (Berkeley: Univ of Calif Press, 99); auth, "The Refugee: a discourse on displacement," in Anthropology and the World, ed. Jeremy Mc Clancy (Chicago: Univ of Chicago Press, 00). **CONTACT ADDRESS** Dept Anthrop, Columbia Univ, 2960 Broadway, New York, NY 10027. **EMAIL** evd7@columbia.edu

DANZER, GERALD
PERSONAL Born 11/09/1938, Chicago, IL, m, 1960, 3 children **DISCIPLINE** HISTORY, EDUCATION **EDUCATION** Concord Col, BS, 59; Nwest Univ, MA, 61; PhD, 67. **CAREER** Prof, Univ Ill, 67-. **HONORS AND AWARDS** James Harvey Robinson Prize; 87, 90. **MEMBERSHIPS** AHA; OAH; AAG; NCSS. **RESEARCH** History of Cartography; historical geography; cities and the built environment; state and local history. **SELECTED PUBLICATIONS** Auth, People Space and Time, 86; auth, World History: An Atlas, 98; auth, Public Places: Exploring Their History, 87; auth, Discovering World History Through Maps and Views, 96. **CONTACT ADDRESS** Dept History, Univ of Illinois, Chicago, 851 South Morgan St, Box 723, Chicago, IL 60607-7042. **EMAIL** gdanzer@uic.edu

DANZGER, M. HERBERT
PERSONAL Born 12/11/1934, m, 1959, 4 children **DISCIPLINE** SOCIOLOGY **EDUCATION** Yeshiva Univ, BA 56; Columbia Univ, MA, 62; PhD, 68. **CAREER** Res Asst and Teaching Asst, Columbia Univ, 58-59; Lecturer, CUNY, 60-65; Instructor, SUNY, 65-67; Lecturer to Asst Prof, Herbert Lehman Col, 67-68; Sen Lecturer, Bar Ilan Univ, 71-72; Assoc Prof, CUNY, 72-75; Prof, Hebrew Univ, 75-76; Prof and Chair, Herbert Lehman Col, 74-. **HONORS AND AWARDS** Fulbright Fel, 75-76; Lucius Littaur Foundation, 96, 93; Memorial Foundation of Jewish Culture, 91; Nat Sci Foundation, 71; Grant, Nat Sci Foundation, 73; Nat Inst of Mental Health, 67-68 **MEMBERSHIPS** Am Sociol Asn; Asn for Sociol Relig; Asn for Jewish Studies; E Sociol Soc. **RESEARCH** Sociology of Religion; Sociology of Jews and Judaism; Social movements; Sociology of convension and identity. **SELECTED PUBLICATIONS** Auth, "Martin Buber," in The Encyclopedia of Religion and the Social Sciences, (Altimira Press, 98), 64-65; auth, "Jewish-Christian Relations and Anti-Semitism," in The Encyclopedia of Religion and the Social Sciences, (Altimira Press, 98), 247-250; auth, "Jews," in The Encyclopedia of Religion and the Social Sciences, (Altimira Press, 98), 250-251; auth, "Judaism," in The Encyclopedia of Religion and the Social Sciences, (Altimira Press, 98), 253-260; auth, "The Impact of Dominant Versus Minority Status on Religious Conversion Processes," in Prophetic Religions, Mobilization, and Social Action in the Twenty-First Century, (Breenwood Pub, 98), 174-182; auth, "The Return to Traditional Judaism of Russian Emigres in Israel and the United States," in Religion in a Changing World, (Greenwood Pub, 98), 11-21; auth, "The Rebirth of Judaism in Kiev After Babi Yaar and Communism: The Interplay of Family and Religion," in Family, Religion and Social change in Diverse Societies, (Oxford Univ Press, 99); auth, "Community Conflict and Residential Desegregation: The Outcomes of Civil Rights Events, 1955-1965," in Dispute Resolution: Emerging Research Agendas From the city University of New York, John Jay Press, 00; auth, "Returning to Traditional Judaism," in The Companion to Judaism Selected Readings," Oxford Pub, 00; auth, "The Revival of Traditional Forms of Judaism: A Global Perspective," in The Blackwell Reader in Judaism, Oxford, forthcoming. **CONTACT ADDRESS** Dept Sociol & Soc Work, Lehman Col, CUNY, 250 Bedford Park W, Bronx, NY 10468. **EMAIL** mhdlc@cunyvm.cuny.edu

DARLING, CAROL
PERSONAL Born 04/13/1946, Virginia, MN, m, 1989 **DISCIPLINE** FAMILY LIFE EDUCATION **EDUCATION** Univ Minn, BS, 68; Utah State Univ, MS, 72; Mich State Univ, PhD, 79. **CAREER** Teach, dept ch, Pub Sch Sys, 68-71; teach asst, Utah State Univ, 71-72; instr, 72-73; instr, Univ Minn, 73-76; res asst, Mich State Univ, 76-78; teach asst, 78-79; admin asst, 78-79; asst prof to prof, Fla State Univ, 79-. **HONORS AND AWARDS** Phi Kappa Phi; Kappa Omicron Nu; Phi Upsilon Omicron; Omicron Delta Kappa; Pi Lambda Theta; Sigma Epsilon Sigma; Mortar Bd Chimes; Seminole Awd; NCFR Ser Awd; Fulbright Schl; Univ Excell Teach Awd; Dist Teach Awd; TIP Awd; PEP Awd; NCFR Excell Teach Awd; Ernest G Osborne Awd; Excell Coll Univ Teach Awd. **MEMBERSHIPS** NCFR; SSSS; AAFCS; NAEYC; Fulbright Asn; Groves Conf Marr Fam. **RESEARCH** Human sexuality; family life education; cultural diversity/multicultural education; stress in clergy families. **SELECTED PUBLICATIONS** Coauth, "A call to the profession: Serving culturally diverse individuals and families," J Family Consumer Sci 89 (97): 36-45; auth, :From Structured Beginnings to creative Ends: Preparing Graduate Students as Educators," Fam Sci Rev 10 (97): 322-342; coauth, "Sexual contacts: Experiences, thoughts, and fantasies of adult male survivors of child sexual abuse," J Sex and Marital Thera 23 (97): 305-316; coauth, "Using "family groups" in family life education: The role of cooperative learning," J Family and Consumer Sci Edu 16 (98): 16-26; coauth, "Professional development of students: Understanding the process of becoming a Certified Family Life Educator," Family Sci Rev 2 (98): 2-13; coauth, "Multicultural education in collegiate family and consumer sciences programs: Developing cultural competence," J Family and Consumer Sci 90 (98): 42-48; coauth, Self perceptions of female sexuality. In Handbook of sexuality-related measures, eds. C Davis, W Yarber, R Bauserman, 0 Scheer, S Davis (244-248) (Newbury Park, CA: Sage Pub, 98); coauth, Female sexual response patterns: Grafenberg spot/area and ejaculation. In Handbook of sexuality-related measures, eds. C Davis, W Yarber, R Bauserman, 0 Scheer, S Davis "(213-218) (Newbury Park, CA: Sage Pub, 98); coauth, "Family focus on cultural diversity: The role of home economics," in A Five-Year Retrospective of the Massachusetts Avenue Building Assets Fund Grants Program: 92-96 (39-42) (Alexandria, VA: Am Asn Family Consumer Sci, 98); coauth, "Quality of life: Perceptions of African Americans," J Black Studies 30 (00): 422-427. **CONTACT ADDRESS** Dept Child & Family Sciences, Florida State Univ, Tallahassee, FL 32306-1491. **EMAIL** cdarling@mailer.fsu.edu

DARLING, ROSALYN
PERSONAL Born 05/28/1946, New York, NY, m, 1969, 2 children **DISCIPLINE** SOCIOLOGY **EDUCATION** Univ Conn, PhD, 78. **CAREER** Exec Dir, Beginnings Inc, 79-94; Assoc Prof, Ind Univ of Pa, 94-. **MEMBERSHIPS** Am Sociol Asn, Soc for disability Studies, Soc for the Study of Soc Problems, Soc for Applied Sociol. **RESEARCH** Children with disabilities; Human services. **SELECTED PUBLICATIONS** Auth, The Partnership Model in Human Services: Sociological Foundations and Practices, Plenum Pub, 00; auth, Ordinary Families, Special Children: A Systems Approach to Childhood Disability, Guilford Press, 97; auth, Families in Focus: Sociological Methods in Early Intervention, Pro-Ed, 96; auth, Families, Physicians, and Children with Special Health Needs: Collaborative Medical Education Models, Greenwood Pub, 94; auth, "The Value of a Pre-Internship Observation Experience," Teaching Sociology, (98): 341-346 **CONTACT ADDRESS** Dept Sociol, Indiana Univ of Pennsylvania, 102 McElhaney Hall, Indiana, PA 15705-0001. **EMAIL** rdarling@grove.iup.edu

DARLINGTON, RICHARD B.
PERSONAL Born 11/16/1937, Woodbury, NJ, m, 1989, 2 children **DISCIPLINE** PSYCHOLOGY **EDUCATION** Swarthmore Col, BA, 59; Univ Minn, PhD, 63. **CAREER** Asst Prof to Prof, Cornell Univ, 63-. **HONORS AND AWARDS** Fel, Am Asn for the Advancement of Sci; Who's Who in Am. **MEMBERSHIPS** Soc for Neuroscience. **RESEARCH** Behavioral statistics and measurement; Allometry. **SELECTED PUBLICATIONS** Co-auth, "Pre-school programs and later school competence low-income families," Science, (80): 202-220; auth, Regression and Linear Models, McGraw-Hill, 90; co-auth, "Linked regulari development and evolution of mammalian brains," Science, 95. **CONTACT ADDRESS** Dept Psychol, Cornell Univ, 211 Uris Hall, Ithaca, NY 14853. **EMAIL** rbd1@cornell.edu

DASGUPTA, NILANJANA
PERSONAL Born 10/10/1969, Calcutta, India **DISCIPLINE** PSYCHOLOGY **EDUCATION** Smith Col, AB, 92; Yale Univ, MS, 94, MPhil, 96, PhD, 98. **CAREER** Postdoctoral fel, Univ Washington, 97-99; asst prof, New Sch for Soc Res, 99-. **HONORS AND AWARDS** Yale Grad Fel, Yale Diss Fel, summa cum laude, Psi Chi, Phi Beta Kappa, Sigma Xi, 92; grant-in-aid, Soc for the Psychol Study of Soc Issues, 96. **MEMBERSHIPS** Am Psychol Asn, Am Psychol Soc. **RESEARCH** Social psychology, stereotyping, prejudice and discrimination. **SELECTED PUBLICATIONS** Coauth with M. R. Babaji, "The consciousness of social beliefs: A program of research on stereotyping and prejudice," in V. Y. Yzerbyt, G. Lories and B. Dardenne, eds Metacognition: Cognitive and social dimensions, Great Britain: Sage Pubs (98); coauth with R. P. Abelson, J. Park, and M. R. Banaji, "Perceptions of the collective other," Personality and Social Psychology Rev, 2 (98): 243-250; coauth with M. R. Banaji and R. P. Abelson, "Group entitativity and group perception: Associations between physical features and psychological judgement," J of Personality and Soc Psychol, 77 (99): 991-1003; coauth with D. E. McGhee, A. G. Greenwald, and M. R. Babaji, "Automatic preference for White Americans: Eliminating the familiarity explanation," J of Experimental Psychol (in press). **CONTACT ADDRESS** Dept Psychol, New Sch for Social Research, 65 5th Ave, New York, NY 10003.

DASH, IRENE GOLDEN
PERSONAL Born New York, NY, 2 children **DISCIPLINE** ENGLISH DRAMATIC LITERATURE, WOMEN'S STUDIES, AMERICAN THEATRE **EDUCATION** Beaver Col, BA; Columbia Univ, MA, PhD(English), 72. **CAREER** Lectr English, Queensborough Community Col, City Univ NY, 70-71; lectr, 72-74, Asst Prof English, Hunter Col, City Univ NY, 74-, Int corresp, World Shakepeare Bibliog, 81. **HONORS AND AWARDS** NEH Research Fellowship, 83-84; NEH Travel Grant 86; Folger Library Fellowship, 89-90; ACLS Travel Grant, 96; Lucius Littauer Grant, 96; Invited to Intl Shakespeare Conf, 94, 96, 98,00. **MEMBERSHIPS** Shakespeare Asn Am; Am Soc 18th Century Studies; Am Name Soc; NCTE; Am Soc Theatre Res. **RESEARCH** Shakespeare's women. **SELECTED PUBLICATIONS** Wooing, Wedding, & Power: Women in Shakespeare's Plays, Columbia VP, 81, paper 84; auth, Single-Sex Retreats in 2 Early-Modern Dramas--Shakespeare,William and Cavendish, Margaret--Loves Labors Lost and the Convent of Pleasure, Shakespeare Quart, Vol 0047, 96; Women's Worlds in Shakespear's Plays, Univ of Delaware Pr, 97; "Holiday, Judy." Jewish Women in America: An Historical Encyclopedia, Vol 1, Routledge, 97. **CONTACT ADDRESS** 161 W 16th St, New York, NY 10011. **EMAIL** idash1@aol.com

DASHEFSKY, ARNOLD
PERSONAL Born 09/09/1941, Philadelphia, PA, m, 1968, 2 children **DISCIPLINE** SOCIOLOGY **EDUCATION** Temple Univ, BA, 64; MA, 66; Univ Minn, PhD, 69. **CAREER** Prof, Univ Conn, 69-. **HONORS AND AWARDS** Wilstein Inst, Boston; Conn Acad of Arts & Sci. **MEMBERSHIPS** Am Asn Univ Prof, Am Sociol Asn, Asn for Jewish Studies, Soc for the Scientiic Study of Religion. **RESEARCH** Sociol Studies in race and ethnic relations, social psychology, Jewish studies. **SELECTED PUBLICATIONS** Auth, Jewish Choices: American Jewish Denominationalism, SUNY Press: Albany, 98; auth, Ethnic Identification Among American Jews, Lexington, 93; auth, Americans Abroad: A Comparative Study of Emigrants From the United States, New York, 92; auth, "The Quest for Continuity in the North American Jewish Community," Freedom and Responsibility, (98): 379-391; auth, "A Study of Jewish Denominational Preferences: Summary Findings," American Jewish Yearbook, Vol 97, (97): 115-137. **CONTACT ADDRESS** Dept Sociol, Univ of Connecticut, Storrs, 344 Mansfield Road U68, Storrs, CT 06269-2068.

DASILVA, FABIO B.
PERSONAL Born 09/01/1934, Brazil, s **DISCIPLINE** SOCIOLOGY **EDUCATION** Foundation School Sociol, Sao Paulo, MA, 59; Univ Sao Paulo, MA, 60; Univ Fla, PhD, 63. **CAREER** Asst Prof to Assoc Prof, Univ Tex, 64-67; Vis Prof to Prof, Univ Notre Dame, 67-. **MEMBERSHIPS** ASA, ISA, SPEP **RESEARCH** Continental thought, Culture (Music). **SELECTED PUBLICATIONS** Co-auth, All Music: Essays in the Hermeneutics of Music, Ashbury, 98; auth, Her Voices: Hermeneutics of the Feminine, Univ Press of Am, 98; co-auth, Sociology and Interpretation, SUNY, 98. **CONTACT ADDRESS** Dept Sociol, Univ of Notre Dame, 810 Flanner Hall, Notre Dame, IN 46556. **EMAIL** fabio.b.dasilva.1@nd.edu

DAVENPORT, GENE LOONEY
PERSONAL Born 10/09/1935, Sylacauga, AL, d, 2 children **DISCIPLINE** PSYCHOLOGY, RELIGION, OLD TESTAMENT, BIBLICAL THEORY **EDUCATION** Birmingham-Southern Col, BA(psychol), 57; Vanderbilt Divinity School, BD, 60; Vanderbilt Univ, PhD(religion:Old Testament, Biblical theol), 68. **CAREER** Prof of Relig, Lambuth Univ, 63-. **MEMBERSHIPS** Soc of Biblical Lit. **RESEARCH** Apocrypha and pseudepigrapha; theol of culture; Sermon on the Mount; the Book of Revelation. **SELECTED PUBLICATIONS** Auth, The Eschatology of the Book of Jubilees, E J Brill, 71; The Anointed of the Lord in Psalms of Solomon 17, Ideal Figures in Ancient Israel, Scholars Press; Into the Darkness: Discipleship in the Sermon on the Mount, Abingdon Press, 88. **CONTACT ADDRESS** Dept of Relig and Philos, Lambuth Univ, Jackson, TN 38301. **EMAIL** davenpor@lambuth.edu

DAVID, GERALD
PERSONAL Born 08/05/1941, Brooklyn, NY, m, 1967, 6 children **DISCIPLINE** PHD-CLINICAL PSYCHOLOGY, DHL-MODERN PHILOSOPHY **EDUCATION** Dr. of Hebrew Literature, 75, Bernard Reval Graduated School, Yeshiva Univ, Professional License, 72, New York State Department of Educ Specialization, PhD, 71, Ferkauf Graduate School, Yeshiva Univ, Professional Diploma, 68, New York State Dept of Educ, Ordination(Semicha), 66, Rabbi Isaac Elechanan Theol Seminary, Yeshiva Univ, Master of Sci in Educ, 66, City Univ of New York, Naster of Sci in Educ, 65, Ferkauf Graduate School, Yeshiva Univ, BA, 63, Yeshiva College. **CAREER** Admin Supvr and Clin Psychol positions, 66-present, New York City Bd of Educ, Supv, Diry and Psychol positions at Ohel Family Serv, 79-present. **HONORS AND AWARDS** Hon Pres-Jewish Community Council at Rockaways, Hon Chm-JASH Senior Center, Hon Chm-Jewish Services Co-ulitius. **MEMBERSHIPS** Amer Psychological Associates. **RESEARCH** Pshchol, Philos, Rel. **SELECTED PUBLICATIONS** Man's Search for Immortality: A Positivist Approach, Yeshiva Univ Press, 78, "Preschool Intellectual Assessment with the Ammons Quick Test",in Psychology in the Schools, 75, 12, 430-431, "The Effects of Special Class Placement on Multiple Disabled Children", in Reading Improvement, 75, 14, 138-143, " The Russians: A New Community in Our Midst", in Proceedings of the Association of Orthodox Jewish Scientists, 82, " A Study of the Needs of Russian Immmigrant Youth", 80, Research Study Monograph sponsored by Ahudath Israel of Amer, funded by the New York City Youth Bd. **CONTACT ADDRESS** 861 East 27th St., Brooklyn, NY 11216.

DAVID, KEITH R.
PERSONAL Born 08/20/1929, Arkansas City, KS, m, 1949, 4 children **DISCIPLINE** SOCIOLOGY AND PHILOSOPHY **EDUCATION** Okla Baptist Univ, BA; Wichita State Univ, MA; Southern Ill Univ, PhD. **CAREER** Detail engr, Boeing Airplane Co, 48-51; Baptist minister, 51-69; lectr, philos, 60-61, dept of eng res, eng grade 3, 54-60, Wichita State Univ; doctoral asst, 62-64, lectr, philos, 64-69, Southern Ill Univ; asst prof to assoc prof to full prof, philos, William Jewell Col, 69-98. **HONORS AND AWARDS** Outstanding Facul Mem, William Jewell Col, 84; Profile in Excellence, Okla Baptist Univ, alumni office, 91; Prof emer, William Jewell Col, 94. **MEMBERSHIPS** Amer Philos Asn; Baptist Philos Teachers Asn. **RESEARCH** American philosophy; Philosophy of religion; Medical ethics. **SELECTED PUBLICATIONS** Auth, Historical Note: The Paul Carus Collection, The Monist, 75; auth, Percept and Concept in William James, The Philos of William James, Felix Meiner Verlag, 76; eng res publ, Aerodynamics, dept of defense, 55-58, Wichita State Univ, dept of eng res. **CONTACT ADDRESS** 1029 Broadmore Ln., Liberty, MO 64068.

DAVIES, IVOR KEVIN
PERSONAL Born 12/19/1930, Birmingham, England, m, 1966, 2 children **DISCIPLINE** PSYCHOLOGY **EDUCATION** Univ Birmingham, UK, BA, 52, MA, 54; Univ Illinois, MSc, 53; Univ Nottingham, UK, PhD, 67. **CAREER** Prof, educ, adj prof, Bus Admin, Indiana Univ. **HONORS AND AWARDS** Cadbury Prize; fel, Br Psychol Soc; fel, Col of Preceptors. **MEMBERSHIPS** Br Psychol Soc; Am Psychol Asn; Inst of Dir, UK. **RESEARCH** Strategic thinking; needs analysis and assessment; human error. **SELECTED PUBLICATIONS** Auth, Management of Learning, McGraw-Hill, 73, auth, Organization of Training, McGraw-Hill; auth, Objectives in Curriculum Design, McGraw-Hill, 76; auth, Instructional Technique, McGraw-Hill, 81. **CONTACT ADDRESS** 2447 Rock Creek Dr, Bloomington, IN 47401. **EMAIL** davies@indiana.edu

DAVIES, JAMES
PERSONAL Born 02/22/1948, Freetown, Sierra Leone, m, 1975, 2 children **DISCIPLINE** SOCIOLOGY **EDUCATION** MM Teachers Col, HTC, 69; St. Augustine Col, BA, 77; NC Central Univ, MA, 79; Univ Okla, PhD, 88. **CAREER** Lect, NC Central Univ, 80-82; Lect, MM Teachers Col, 82-85; Res Asst, Univ Okla, 85-88; From Asst Prof to Prof, NC Central Univ, 88-. **HONORS AND AWARDS** Who's Who in Am Teachers, 5th & 6th eds. **MEMBERSHIPS** RSS, SSS, NCFR **SELECTED PUBLICATIONS** Auth, "The Effects of Kinship Ties on Parental Attitudes Toward Early Childhood Dependency," Family Perspective 22 (88): 61-72; auth, "General Assistance Among U.S. Cities: A Test of Alternative Hypotheses," Sociol Spectrum 10 (90): 283-299; auth, "The Influence of Racial Inequality, Economy Deprivation and Sex Ratio on the Incidence of Female-Headed Families Among U.S. Cities," Family Perspective 27 (93): 109-125; auth, "Impact of a Shrinking Job Market on the Incidence of Female-Headed Families," Nat J of Sociol 10 (96): 15-34. **CONTACT ADDRESS** Dept Sociol, No Carolina Central Univ, 1801 Fayetteville St, Durham, NC 27707. **EMAIL** jdavies928@aol.com

DAVIES, KIMBERLY A.
PERSONAL Born 06/14/1965, Columbus, OH, s **DISCIPLINE** SOCIOLOGY **EDUCATION** Oh State Univ, BA, 88, BA, 88, MA, 90, PhD, 96. **CAREER** Asst prof, Dept Sociol, Augusta State Univ, 96-. **HONORS AND AWARDS** Ohio State Univ: Sociol Grad Res Support Awd Grant, 95, Intense Summer Res Fel, 95, Most Supportive Colleague Awd, 95-96; Fac Res and Develop Grants, Augusta State Univ, 96, 97, 98, 99 (total of eight); Outstanding Paper Awd, Acad of Criminal Justice Scis, March 97. **MEMBERSHIPS** Acad of Criminal Justice Scis, Am Soc of Criminology, Am Sociol Asn, Ga Sociol Soc, Mid-South Sociol Asn, Nat Women's Studies Asn, Southern Criminal Justice Asn. **RESEARCH** Gender, race and crime; homicide; measurement of crime; structural determinants of crime; teaching sociology; violence toward women. **SELECTED PUBLICATIONS** Auth, "An Exercise on Police Ticketing Decisions and Chivalry," " Sociology 510: Suggested Books," and "Oral Book Report Assignment Guidelines," in Teaching About Women in Criminal Justice and Criminology Courses: A Resource Guide Vol II, eds. Christine Rasche and Lynne Goodstein (OH: The Div of Women and Crime, Am Soc of Criminology, 95); auth, "Voluntary Exposure to Pornography and Men's Attitudes Toward Feminism and Rape," The J of Sex Res, 34 (97): 131-137; coauth,1999 Majors in Criminal Justice and Sociology Survey Report, Technical Report (99); coauth, Hyde Park Neighborhood Survey Report, Technical Report (99); auth, "Suicide as Deviant Behavior," in The Encyclopedia of Criminology and Deviant Behavior, Vol IV, ed by Charles Faupel (2000); coauth, "No Sissy Boys ere: A Content Analysis of the Representation of Masculinity in Elementary School Reading Textbooks," Sex Roles (forthcoming). **CONTACT ADDRESS** Dept Sociol, Augusta State Univ, 2500 Walton Way, Augusta, GA 30904. **EMAIL** kdavies@aug.edu

DAVIS, EDWARD L.
PERSONAL Born 12/06/1943, Union Bridge, MD, m **DISCIPLINE** EDUCATION **EDUCATION** Morgan State Univ, BS 1965; OH Univ, MS 1967; Johns Hopkins Univ, MS 1973; NC State Univ, PhD 1977. **CAREER** Morgan State Univ Math Dept, instr, 70-73; Univ of Cincinnati Coll of Business, asst prof, 76-80; Atlanta Univ Graduate School of Business, assoc prof, 80-88; Clark Atlanta University, chmn decision science dept, 88-95, Business School, acting dean, 95-. **HONORS AND AWARDS** MD Senatorial Fellowship 1961-65; Balt Colt Found Scholarship 1961-65; So Fellowship Found 1973-76; Volunteer of the Year City of Raleigh 1974. **MEMBERSHIPS** Mem Operations Rsch Soc of Amer 1974-; mem Transport Rsch Bd 1980-; mem Alpha Phi Alpha Frat 1961-; task force mem Atlanta C of C 1982-; Operations Rsch Soc of Amer 1973-; Amer Inst for Decision Sci 1980-; Transp Rsch Bd 1980-. **CONTACT ADDRESS** Clark Atlanta Univ, James P Brawley at Fair St, Atlanta, GA 30314.

DAVIS, GARY A.
PERSONAL Born 07/28/1938, Salt Lake City, UT, m, 1961, 3 children **DISCIPLINE** PSYCHOLOGY **EDUCATION** Univ Wisc-Madison, PhD, 65. **CAREER** Prof of Educ Psychol, Univ Wisc-Madison, 65-94. **HONORS AND AWARDS** Wilhelm Wundt Awd from XXII Int Congress of Psychol, 80; E. Paul Torrance Creativity Awd, 99. **MEMBERSHIPS** APA; AERA; NAGC; CEP. **RESEARCH** Creativity; gifted education; character education. **SELECTED PUBLICATIONS** Auth, Handbook of Gifted Education, 2nd ed, 97; auth, Education of the Gifted and Talented, 4th ed, 98; auth, Creativity is Forever, 4th ed, 98. **CONTACT ADDRESS** PO Box 222, Cross Plains, WI 53528. **EMAIL** gadavis1@facstaff.wisc.edu

DAVIS, GLORIA-JEANNE
PERSONAL Born 02/06/1945, Gary, IN, m **DISCIPLINE** EDUCATION **EDUCATION** Eastern KY Univ, BBA 1970, MBA 1971; IL State Univ, PhD 1986. **CAREER** Caterpillar Tractor Co, analyst/machine shop training, 74-78; Bloomington City Hall, financial advisor, 78-84; IL Central Coll, Inst/Business Dept, 86-; IL State Univ, Univ Affirmative Action Officer, 84-, Asst to Pres for Affirmative Action and Equal Opportunity, 88-96; Mitsubishi Motors, Dir Opportunity Programs, 96-. **HONORS AND AWARDS** Administrator of the Year Awd, Black Student Union, 1987; Educ Administration & Foundations Advisory Council, Recognition Awd, 1990; Administrative Professional Distinguished Service Awd, Administrative Professional Staff, 1991; MacMurray Coll, NAACP, Civil Rights Awd, 1994. **MEMBERSHIPS** ISU Toastmasters, pres, 1990, 1992, mem, 1989-; IL Affirmative Action Officers Assn, pres, 1986-88, mem, 1988-; Assn of Black Academic Employees, pres, 1987-89, 1990-91, mem, 1986-; ISU Recruitment & Retention Committees, chair, 1988-89, mem, 1987-96; Admini Professional Grievance Panel, elected mem, 1985-96; IL Committee on Black Concerns in Higher Educ, steering comm secretary, 1984-93, co chair annual conference, 1993, steering comm mem, 1984-96; IL State Univ Black Colleagues Assn, campus liaison, 1986-96; North Central Assn of Coll & School Self Study, mem, 1993-96; Natl Collegiate Athletic Assn Self Study, mem, 1993-96; McLean Cty AIDS Task Force, bd of dirs, 1993-. 1993-; Institute for Collaborative Solutions, bd of dirs, 1997-; Bloomington Liquor Commission, commissioner, 1997-. **CONTACT ADDRESS** Opportunity Programs, Mitsubishi, 100 N Mitsubishi Motorway, Normal, IL 61761.

DAVIS, JAMES O.
PERSONAL Born 04/06/1943, MO, m, 1969, 3 children **DISCIPLINE** PSYCHOLOGY **EDUCATION** Okla State Univ, PhD, 72. **CAREER** Prof, SW Missouri State Univ, 72-. **HONORS AND AWARDS** Univ Res Awd, 97. **MEMBERSHIPS** APS. **RESEARCH** Prenatal influences in psychopathology. **SELECTED PUBLICATIONS** Coauth, "Nature, nurture and twin research strategies," Current Directions in Psych 6 (97): 117-121; coauth, "Prenatal growth markers in schizophrenia: A monozygotic co-twin control study," Am J Psychiatry 151 (96): 1166-1172; coauth, "Famine and schizophrenia: First trimester malnutrition or second trimester beriberi," Biological Psychiatry 40 (96): 1-3; auth, "Genetic anticipation," Am J Psychiatry 153 (96): 450-451; coauth, "Prenatal development of monozygotic twins and concordance for schizophrenia," Schizophrenia Bulletin 21 (96): 357-366; coauth, "Monozygotic twin chorion type and concordance for schizophrenia: Genes or germs?" Schizophrenia Bulletin 21 (95): 13-18. **CONTACT ADDRESS** Dept Psychology, Southwest Missouri State Univ, Springfield, 901 S National, Springfield, MO 65804. **EMAIL** jod103f@mail.smsu.edu

DAVIS, MOLLY F.
PERSONAL Born Shreveport, LA, m, 1982, 3 children **DISCIPLINE** SOCIAL WORK **EDUCATION** La State Univ, BA, 71; Tulane Univ, MSW, 73; Fla State Univ, EdD, 84. **CAREER** Assoc prof, Univ of W Fla, 76-84; assoc prof, George Mason Univ, 87-. **HONORS AND AWARDS** NIHM Fel, Phi Alpa; Serv Learning Fel/ Va Addictions Tech Transfer Ctr Grant, 99. **MEMBERSHIPS** AAUP; Youth Outreach Task Force; Coun on Soc Work Educ; Nat Assoc of Prevention Prof; Human Serv Alliance; Quantico Civilian Mil Coun; Va Higher Educ Consortium; Nat Assoc of Soc Workers. **SELECTED PUBLICATIONS** Auth, "Understanding normal aging: The foundation for design of living environments for aged persons", J of Independent Living 2.2 (88); auth, "Prevention programs: Building strengths in communities", Prevention and Promotion Bull, 87; auth, "A triumph of community spirit", Current Municipal Problems 15.4 (89); coauth, "Assessing BSW programs: An outcome driven approach", J of Soc Work Educ 31.1 (95); auth, Guide to Personal Safety Risk Management Manual, George Mason Univ Pr, 95; coauth, "Worker Safety; Practical Applications for Human Services", Am Humane Assoc 12.4 (97); coauth, "The Perspectives of Substance Abuse Professionals on Licensure", VATTC Newsletter, 97; auth, "Managing Personal Safety Risk for Social Work Students in the Practicum", IHC Pub, (New Orleans), 98; auth, "Managing Personal Safety Risk for Service Learning Students", IHC Pub, (New Orleans), 98; auth, Social Work and The Web, Brooks/Cole, (forthcoming); auth, Human Behavior: Macros Social Environment, Brooks/Cole, (forthcoming). **CONTACT ADDRESS** Dept Soc Work, George Mason Univ, Fairfax, 4400 University Dr, Fairfax, VA 22030.

DAVIS, NATHAN T.
PERSONAL Born 02/15/1937, Kansas City, KS, m **DISCIPLINE** ETHNOMUSICOLOGY **EDUCATION** Univ KS, BME 1960; Wesleyan U, CT, PhD Ethnomusicology. **CAREER** Club St Germain, Paris, prof debut with Kenny Clark 63; Donald Byrd, Blue Note Club Paris, 63; Chat Que Peche, Eric Dolphy, Paris, 64; toured Europe with Art Blakly & New Jazz Messengers, 65; Europe & Amer, recorded several albums as leader; total 10 LP's as leader; Belgium Radio-TV, staff composer. **HONORS AND AWARDS** Honorary Doctorate of Humane Letters, Florida Memorial College. **MEMBERSHIPS** Mem SACEM, Soc of Composers, Paris, France; co-chmn ed com Inst of Black Am Music; mem Afro-Am Bi-Cen Hall of Fame; est & created PhD degree prog in Ethnomusicology, Univ Pittsburgh; created Jazz Program at Univ Pittsburgh; created Jazz Program Paris-Am Acad Paris. **CONTACT ADDRESS** Music Dept, Univ of Pittsburgh, 4337 Fifth Ave, Pittsburgh, PA 15260. **EMAIL** ndavis+@pitt.edu

DAVIS, ROBERT LEIGH
DISCIPLINE ENGLISH AND EDUCATION **EDUCATION** Stanford Univ, BA, 78; MA, 81; Univ Calif Berkeley, PhD, 92. **CAREER** Eng tchr, Serra High Sch, San Mateo, Calif, 80-85; instr, Golden Gate Univ, San Francisco, Calif, 85-92; grad student instr, Univ Calif Berkeley, 85-92; asst prof eng, Wittenburg Univ, 92-. **HONORS AND AWARDS** BA with distinction, Stanford Univ, 78; fel, NEH Summer Sem for Secondary Sch Tchrs, Co Col, 84; Tchr of the Year, Serra High Sch, San Mateo, Calif, 85; Benjamin Putnam Kurtz Graduate Essay

Prize, Univ Calif Berkeley, 89; highest distinction, comprehensive oral exam, Univ Calif Berkeley, 89; Omicron Delta Kappa Excellence in Tchr, Wittenburg Univ, 96; Southwest Oh Coun of Higher Educ Facult Excellence, 97. **SELECTED PUBLICATIONS** Auth, Whitman and the Romance of Medicine, Berkeley and Los Angeles, Univ Calif Press, 97; Articles, The Lunar Light of Student Writing: Portfolios and Literary Theory, Situating Portfolios: Four Perspectives, ed Kathleen Blake Yancy and Irwin Weiser, Provo, Ut State Univ Press, 97; Review Essay: Richard Selzer's Raising the Dead, Lit and Med, 13:2, fall, 94; America, Brought to Hospital: The Romance of Medicine and Democracy in Whitman's Civil War, The Wordsworth Cir, 24:2, winter, 94; Deconstruction and the Prophets of Literary Decline, The Chicago Tribune, Op-Ed, 29 March 94; The Art of the Suture: Richard Selzer and Medical Narrative, Lit and Med, 12:2, fall, 93; Whitman's Tympanum: A Reading of Drum-Taps, The Amer Transcendental Quart, 6:3, fall, 92; Medical Representation in Walt Whitman and William Carlos Williams, The Walt Whitman Quart Rev, 6:3, winter, 89; That Two-Handed Engine and the Consolation of Lycidas, Milton Quart, 20:2, May, 86. **CONTACT ADDRESS** Wittenberg Univ, 3388 Petre Rd., Springfield, OH 45502.

DAVIS, ROBERT PAUL
PERSONAL Born 07/03/1926, Malden, MA, m, 1953, 3 children **DISCIPLINE** EDUCATION **EDUCATION** Harvard Univ, AB, 47, MD , 51, AM, 55; Brown Univ, AM, 67. **CAREER** Intern, 51-52, asst med, 52-55, sr asst res phys, 55-56, ch res phys, 56-57, Peter Brent Brigham Hosp; jr fel, 52-55, Soc of Fellows Harvard; asst med, 56-57, Harvard Med School; asst prof med, 57-59, Univ NC; asst prof med, 59-66, assoc prof, 67, Albert Einstein Col Med; career sci, 62-67, Health Res Coun, NY; asst vis phys, 59-65, assoc vis phys, 66-67, Bronx Munic Hosp Center; phys in ch, 67-74, dir renal and metabolic diseases, 74-79, Miriam Hosp, Providence; prof med sci, 67-84, prof emeritus, 84-, chmn sect in med div biol & med scis, 71-74, Brown Univ; vis sci, 65-66 Ins Biol Chem of Univ Copenhagen; ensign, USNR, 44-46, Lt (jg) MC, 51; past mem, Corp Butler Hosp, Jewish Family & Childrens Serv; mem sci adv coun NE Reg Kidney Prog; v chmn RI Advisory Comm Med Care & Ed Found, chmn med adv bd, RI Kidney Found; past bd dirs Assoc Alumni Brown Univ; member med adv bd N Eng sect Am Liver Found, 86-; trustee, N Eng Organ Bank, Boston, 69-, treas, 70-; pres End-Stage Renal Disease Coord Coun Network 28, N Eng, 78-79; assoc ed, RI Med J, 71-80. **HONORS AND AWARDS** Traveling fel, Commonwealth fund, 65-66; Willard O. Thompson Memorial traveling scholar, ACP, 65; fel AAAS, ACP. **MEMBERSHIPS** Am Fed Clin Res; Am Soc Transplant Physicians; Harvey Soc; Biophys Soc; NY Academy Medicine; Am Heart Asn; NY Academy Science; Am Soc Cell Biology; Soc Gen Physiologists; Am Physiol Soc; Am Soc Artificial Internal Organs; Int Soc Nephrology Clin; Diabetes Soc RI (pres 70-71); Providence, RI Med Socs; Am Soc Nephrology; Am Soc Pediatric Nephrology; Soc for Health and Human Values; Am Philos Asn; Phi Beta Kappa; Sigma XI. **CONTACT ADDRESS** Brown Univ, 245 Waterman St, Ste 400B, Providence, RI 02906-5215. **EMAIL** robert_paul_davis@brown.edu

DAVIS, RONALD LEROY
PERSONAL Born 09/22/1933, Cambridge, OH **DISCIPLINE** AMERICAN CULTURAL HISTORY **EDUCATION** Univ Tex, BA, 55, MA, 57, PhD(hist), 61. **CAREER** Asst prof hist, Kans State Teachers Col (Emporia State Univ), 61-62; asst prof humanities, Mich State Univ, 62-65; from asst prof to assoc prof, 65-72, PROF HIST, SOUTHERN METHODIST UNIV, 72-; Mich State Univ All-Univ res grant, 63-64, Univ Grad Coun grant, 67-68; dir oral hist prog on performing arts, Southern Methodist Univ, 72-; dir, DeGolyer Inst Am Studies, 74- **HONORS AND AWARDS** Phi Beta Kappa. **MEMBERSHIPS** Orgn Am Historians; Western Hist Asn. **RESEARCH** American cultural history, particularly history of American music, theater, and film. **SELECTED PUBLICATIONS** Auth, A History of Opera in the American West, Prentice-Hall, 64; Opera in Chicago, Appleton, 66; Culture on the Frontier, SW Rev, fall 68; Sopranos and Six-Guns: The Frontier Opera House as a Cultural Symbol, Am West, 11/70; ed, The Social and Cultural Life of the 1920's, Holt, 72; auth, A History of Music in American Life, Krieger Publ Co, 80-82; Hollywood Beauty: Linda Darnell and the American Dream, Univ OK Press, 91; The Glamour Factory, SMU Press, 93; John Ford: Hollywood's Old Master, Univ Ok Press, 95; Celluloid Mirrors: Hollywood and American Society Since 1945, Harcourt Brace, 97; Duke: The Life and Image of John Wayne, Unvi OK Press, 98; auth, La Scala West: The Dallas Opera Under Kelly and Rescigno, SMU Press, 00. **CONTACT ADDRESS** Dept of Hist, So Methodist Univ, P O Box 750001, Dallas, TX 75275-0001. **EMAIL** rldavis@mail.smu.edu

DAVISON, NANCY R.
DISCIPLINE AMERICAN CULTURE **EDUCATION** Smith, BA, 66; Univ Mich, MA, 73, PhD, 80. **CAREER** ARTIST, PRINTMAKER & GALLERY OWNER **MEMBERSHIPS** Am Antiquarian Soc **SELECTED PUBLICATIONS** Author, American Sheet Music Illustration: Reflections of the Nineteenth-Century, Clements Library Exhibition, 73; auth, "Andrew Jackson in Cartoon and Caricature," American Printmaking Before 1876: Fact, Fiction, and Fantasy, Lib Congress, 75; auth, "Bickham's Musical Entertainer and Other Curiosities," in Eighteenth-Century Prints in Colonial America: To Educate and Decorate, Colonial Williamsburg Found, 79; auth, E. W. Clay and the American Caricature Business, in Prints and Printmakers of New York State, 1825-1940, Syracuse Univ Press, 86; York Beach Activity Book, Blue Stocking, 96. **CONTACT ADDRESS** PO Box 1257, York Beach, ME 03910.

DAWES, ROBYN M.
PERSONAL Born 07/23/1936, Pittsburgh, PA, m, 1999, 2 children **DISCIPLINE** PHILOSOPHY, PSYCHOLOGY **EDUCATION** Harvard Univ, BA, 58; Univ Mich, MA, 60; PhD, 63. **CAREER** Prof, Carnegie Mellon Univ, 90-; Acting Head, Dept of Soc and Decision Sci, Carnegie Mellon Univ, 95-96; The Olof Palme Vis Prof, Univ of Stockholm and Goteborg, 99; The Charles J. Queenan Jr Univ Prof, Carnegie Mellon Univ, 97-. **HONORS AND AWARDS** James McKean Sabbatical fel, 78-79; Fel, Ctr for Advanced Study in Behav Sci, 80-81; Outstanding Empirical Paper Awd, Second Int Conf on Socio-Economics, Wash DC, 90; William James Book Awd, APA, 90; Fel, Ctr for rationality and Interactive Decision Making, Univ of Jerusalem, 94; Honorary Degree of Doctor of Philos, Goteborg Univ, Fac of Soc Sci, 99. **RESEARCH** Behavioral decision making, social choice and irrationality. **SELECTED PUBLICATIONS** Auth, "Qualitative consistency masquerading as quantitative fit," in Structures and Norms in Science, ed. M.L. Dalla Chiara et all (The Netherlands: Kluwer Acad Publ, 97), 387-390; auth, "Standards for psychotherapy, in Encyclopedia of Mental Health Vol 3 (98): 589-597; coauth, "Anticipated versus actual reactions to HIV test results," Am J of Psychology 112 (99): 297-311; auth, "A message from psychologists to economists. Mere predictability doesn't matter like it should (without a good story appended to it), " J of Econ Behav and Orgn 39-1 (99): 29-40; auth, "Two methods for studying the incremental validity of Rorschach variable, " Psychol Assessment 11-3 (Sep 99): 297-302; auth, "A theory of irrationality as a 'reasonable' response to an incomplete specification," Synthese (in press); auth, "Clinical versus actuarial prediction," in International Encyclopedia of Social and Behavioral Science (in press); auth, "Problems of probabilistic thinking, " in International Encyclopedia of Social and Behavioral Science (in press); coauth, Rational Choice in an Uncertain World: 2nd ed, forthcoming; auth, Irrationality in Everyday Life, Professional Arrogance, and Outright Lunacy, forthcoming. **CONTACT ADDRESS** Dept Decision Sciences, Carnegie Mellon Univ, 500 Forbes Ave, Pittsburgh, PA 15213. **EMAIL** rd1b@andrew.cmu.edu

DE BOER, GEORGE E.
PERSONAL Born 11/03/1944, Paterson, NJ, w, 2 children **DISCIPLINE** EDUCATION **EDUCATION** Hope Col, BA, 66; Univ Iowa, MAT, 68; Northwestern Univ, PhD, 72. **CAREER** Instr, Northwestern Univ, 68-71; teach, HS, 71-74; asst prof, 74-82; assoc prof, 82-90; prof, 91-, Colgate Univ. **HONORS AND AWARDS** Who's Who in Am Edu, the East; **MEMBERSHIPS** AERA; NSRST; NSTA. **SELECTED PUBLICATIONS** Auth, A History of ideas in science education: Implications for practice, Teach Coll Press (NY), 91; rev of "Children's Mathematical Frameworks 8-13: A Study of Classroom Teaching," by David C Johnson, Colgate Scene (93); coauth, Research on goals for the science curriculum. In Handbook of research on science teaching, Macmillan (NY), 94; coauth, The goals of the science curriculum. In Redesigning the Science Curriculum, Colorado: BSCS (Colorado Springs), 95; auth, "Historical perspectives on scientific literacy," in Scientific Literacy, eds. W Graeber, C Bolte (Kiel, Germany: Inst Sci Edu, 97); rev "Conjuring Science: Scientific Symbols and Cultural Meanings," in American Life, by Christopher P Toumey , Colgate Scene (97); auth, "What we have learned and where we are headed: Lessons from the Sputnik era," Am Phy Soc (98); auth, Student-centered teaching in a standards-based world: Finding a sensible balance, J Sci Edu (99). **CONTACT ADDRESS** Dept Education, Colgate Univ, 13 Oak Dr, Hamilton, NY 13346. **EMAIL** gdeboer@mail.colgate.edu

DE CARO, FRANK
PERSONAL Born 04/22/1943, New York, NY, m, 1970 **DISCIPLINE** FOLKLORE **EDUCATION** St Francis Col, BA, 63; Johns Hopkins Univ, MA, 64; Ind Univ, PhD, 72. **CAREER** From asst prof to prof, La State Univ at Baton Rouge, 70-; vis asst prof, Univ Tex, 73-74. **HONORS AND AWARDS** Fulbright Awd, India, 66; Am Asn for State & Local Hist Awd of Excellence, 90; Found for Hist La Preservation Awd, 98; La Endowment for the Humanities La Humanities Book Awd, 99. **MEMBERSHIPS** Am Folklore Soc, La Folklore Soc. **RESEARCH** Folklore. **SELECTED PUBLICATIONS** Auth, "From Sea to Shining Sea: Popular Presentation of American Folklore and Its Problems," Southern Folklore 52 (95): 69-77; ed, The Folktale Cat, Barnes and Noble, 95; coauth, "'In This Folk-Lore Land': Race, Class, Identity, and Folklore Studies in Louisiana," J of Am Folklore 109 (96): 31-59; coauth, British Voices from South Asia, La State Univ Libraries (Baton Rouge, LA), 96; coauth, "Strategies of Presentation and Control at Disney's EPCOT: 'Field Notes' on Tourism, Folk Ideas, and Manipulating Culture," Southern Folklore 54 (97): 26-39; ed, Louisiana Sojourns: Travelers' Tales and Literary Journeys, La State Univ Press (Baton Rouge, LA and London), 98. **CONTACT ADDRESS** Dept English, La State Univ at Baton Rouge, Baton Rouge, LA 70803-5001. **EMAIL** fdecaro@lsu.edu

DE OLLOS, IONE Y.
PERSONAL Born 03/27/1951, McCook, NE, m, 1981 **DISCIPLINE** SOCIOLOGY **EDUCATION** Neb Wesleyan Univ, BS, 73; E Ky Univ, MS, 78; Univ SDak, MSS, 84; Ariz State Univ, PhD, 93. **CAREER** Instr, Ariz State Univ, 90-91; instr, Ga State Univ, 92-94; instr, Clayton State Col, 93-94; instr, Oglethorpe Univ, 94; asst prof to assoc prof, Ball State Univ, 94-. **HONORS AND AWARDS** Phi Kappa Phi; Alpha Kappa Delta; Grant, Ball State Univ, 95, 97, 99, 00; Fel Ball State Univ, 00; Who's Who in Am, 95, 00; Int Book of Honor, 99; World Who's Who of Women, 93-01. **MEMBERSHIPS** ASA, Soc for the Study of Social Problems, Nat Counc on Family Relations, Pacific Sociol Assoc, Gerontological Soc of Am. **RESEARCH** The impact of crises on the family, the role of the physical structure of the house as a repository for memorabilia and place of ritual activity for families. **SELECTED PUBLICATIONS** Coauth, "The aged in the United States: Kinship and household" and "Types of household composition among the elderly in the United States and Hungary: A comparison," Kinship and Aging, ed Peter Somlai, Hungarian Acad of Sci, (Budapest: 97): 216-264, 7-54; coauth, "Increasing knowledge on family issues: A research agenda for 2000," Mental retardation in the year 2000, ed. L. Rowitz, Springer-Verlag, (92): 69-84; auth, On becoming homeless: The shelterization process for homeless families, Univ of Am Pr, (Lanham, MD), (97); coauth, "Do elderly Americans want a national healthcare system? An investigation into the debate," Sociol Abstracts, (99); coauth, "How far is too far? The effect of geographic distance on the expectation of receiving assistance from children," Sociol Abstracts, 99; coauth, "Older adults' attitudes on right-to-die in Middletown, USA," Gerontologist 39, (99); coauth, "The Internet as an information resource for older adults," Jour of Educ Tech Systems 28.2 (99-00): 107-120; coauth, "Aging Childless Individuals and Couples: Suggestions for New Directions in Research," Sociol Inquiry, forthcoming; coauth, "A survey analysis of age, attitudes and usage of computers ten years later," Gerontologist, forthcoming. **CONTACT ADDRESS** Dept Sociol, Ball State Univ, Muncie, IN 47306. **EMAIL** ideollos@gw.bsu.edu

DE RIOS, MARLENE DOBKIN
PERSONAL Born 04/12/1939, New York, NY, m, 1969, 2 children **DISCIPLINE** ANTHROPOLOGY **EDUCATION** Univ Cal Riverside, PhD 72. **CAREER** Cal State Univ Fullerton, prof 69 to 98-; Univ Cal Irvine, assoc prof 87-. **HONORS AND AWARDS** Fulbright Fel; NIMH post doc Fel. **MEMBERSHIPS** AAA; APA **RESEARCH** Comparative Healing Systems; Shamanism; Latino Mental Health Issues; Hallucinogens. **SELECTED PUBLICATIONS** Auth, Amazon Healer, The Life and Times of an Urban Shaman, Bridport, England, Prism Press, 92; Hallucinogens: Cross-cultural Perspective, Albuquerque NM, U of NM press, 84, reprinted, Bridport, Eng, Prism Press, 90; Adolescent Drug Use in Cross-cultural Perspective, coauth, Jour of Drug Issues, 92. **CONTACT ADDRESS** 2555 E Chapman Ave, No 407, Fullerton, CA 92831. **EMAIL** septrion@aol.com

DE VRIES, BRIAN
DISCIPLINE GERONTOLOGY **EDUCATION** Univ BC, BA, 80; MA, 84; PhD, 88. **CAREER** Asst Prof, Univ BC, 889-96; Vesting Asst Prof, Pacific Grad School, 95, 96; Vesting Scholar, Univ Calif, 95-96; Adj Prof, Univ Tex, 89-; Assoc Prof, San Francisco State Univ, 97-. **HONORS AND AWARDS** Just Desserts Awd for Outstanding Student Service, 95; Soc Sci and Humanities Res Coun, 88-89; BC Gerontol Asn Awd, 86; Morris Belkin Awd, 85. **MEMBERSHIPS** Gerontol Soc of Am, Can Asn on Gerontol, Calif Coun on Gerontol and Geriatrics. **RESEARCH** Narratives of the self; Life review and Guided Autobiography; Grief and bereavement (accounts of loss); Integrative complexity (content/structural analysis); Friend and family relationships over the life-span. **SELECTED PUBLICATIONS** Ed, End of life issues: interdisciplinary and multidimensional perspectives, Springer Pub, 99; co-ed, Narrative gerontology: Theory, research, and practice, in press; auth, "Friendship in childhood and adulthood: Lessons across the life span," International Journal of Aging and Human Development, in press; co-auth, "Definitions of friendship in the third age: age, gender, and study location effects," Journal of Aging studies, in press; co-auth, "Integrating personal reflection and group-based enactments," Journal of Aging Studies, (99): 109-199; co-auth, "Recovery from the perspective of the bereaved: Personal assessments and sources of distress and support," End of life issues: Interdisciplinary and multidimensional perspectives, 99; co-auth, "Friendship at the end of life," in annual Review of Gerontology and Geriatrics, Springer Pub, in press; auth, "A review of 'Person, Self and Moral Demands: Individualism contested by collectivism'," Political Psychology, in press. **CONTACT ADDRESS** Dept Gerontol, San Francisco State Univ, 1600 Holloway Ave, San Francisco, CA 94132. **EMAIL** bdevries@sfsu.edu

DEAK, GEDEON O.
PERSONAL Born 09/20/1967, Buffalo, NY, m, 2 children **DISCIPLINE** LANGUAGE DEVELOPMENT **EDUCATION** Vassar Col, BA, 90; Univ Minnesota, Phd, 95. **CAREER** Asst Prof, Vanderbilt Univ, 95-99; Asst Prof, UCSD, 99-. **HONORS AND AWARDS** APS Student Research Competition Awd; U of MN Doctoral Dissertation Fellowship; Eva

O. Miller Doctoral Fellowship; U of MN Graduate School Fellowship; APA Dissertation Research Awd; NAE/Spencer Foundation Postdoctoral Fellowship; Nicholas Hobbs Society Grant. **MEMBERSHIPS** APS, Cognitive Development Society; IASCL; Jean Piaget Society; Psychonomics Society; SRCD. **RESEARCH** Cognitive Development; Language Development. **SELECTED PUBLICATIONS** Auth, "Hedgehogs, foxes, and the acquisition of verb meaning," by Maratsos, M. & Deak G., In M. Tomasello & W. Merriman, eds., Beyond names for things: Children's acquisition of verbs, Hillsdale, NJ: Lawrence Erlbaum Associates, 95; auth, "The effects of task comprehenion on preschoolers' and adults' categorization choices," Journal of Experimental Child Psychology, 60, 95: 393-427; auth, "The dynamics of preschooles' categorization choices," by Deak, G. & Bauer, P.J., Child Development, 67, 740-767; auth, "On having complex representations of things: Preschoolers use multiple words for objects and people," by Deak, G.O. & Maratsos, M., Development Psychology, 34, 224-240; auth, "The growth of flexible problem solving: Preschool children use changing verbal cues to infer multiple word meanings," by Deak, G.O., Journal of Cognition and Development, 1, 157-192; auth, "Chasing the fox of word learning: Why "constraints" fail to capture it," Developmental Review, Deak, G.O., 20, 29-80. **CONTACT ADDRESS** Dept of Cognitive Science, Univ of California, San Diego, 9500 Gilman Dr, La-Jolla, CA 92093-0515. **EMAIL** deak@atscogsci.ucsd.edu

DEAL, TERRANCE E.
PERSONAL Born 08/31/1939, m, 1975, 1 child **DISCIPLINE** EDUCATION ADMINISTRATION, SOCIOLOGY **EDUCATION** Univ LaVerne, BA, Hist, Phys Educ, 57-61; Calif State Col-LA, MA, Educ Admin, Soc Sci, 61-66; Stanford Univ, PhD, 68-70. **CAREER** Tchr, Fremont Jun High Sch, 61-66; tchr, Pacific Grove High Sch, 66-68; admin asst to Supt Schs, Pacific Grove Unified Sch Dist, 70; prin, Community-Centered High Sch, Pacific Grove, CA, 70-71; dir, Athenian Urban Center, San Francisco, CA, 71-72; asst prof, Univ British Columbia, 73; lectr, Sch Educ, Stanford Univ, 72-76; asst prof, Admin & Policy Analysis, Stanford Univ, 76-77; assoc prof, Admin, Plan & Soc Policy, Harvard Univ, 77-83; PROF, EDUC & HUMAN DEVELOP, PEABODY COLL VANDERBILT UNIV, 83-; co-dir, Nat Center Educ Leadership, Vanderbilt/Harvard, 88-94. **MEMBERSHIPS** Mich Found Educ Leadership-Kellog Found; Center for Support of Prof Practice in Educ; Nat Bd Advisors; Round Table; Corp Family Solution; Phi Delta Kappa; Am Educ Res Asn **SELECTED PUBLICATIONS** Coauth, Becoming a Teacher-Leader: From Isolation to Collaboration, Corwin Press, 94; coauth, Becoming a School Board Member, Corwin Press, 95; coauth, Leading With Soul: An Uncommon Journey of Spirit, Jossey-Bass, 95; coauth, Reframing Organizations: Artistry, Choice, and Leadership, Jossey-Bass, 97; coauth, Corporate Celebration: Play, Purpose, and Profit at Work, Berrett-Koehler Pub, 98. **CONTACT ADDRESS** Peabody Col, Vanderbilt Univ, Box 514 Peabody, Nashville, TN 37203.

DEANGELO, LEANNA M.
PERSONAL Born 08/18/1962, Independence, MO, m, 1999 **DISCIPLINE** PSYCHOLOGY **EDUCATION** Sierra Nev Col, BA; Pepperdine Univ, MA; Saybrook Inst, PhD. **CAREER** Fac mentor, Capella Univ. **MEMBERSHIPS** APA. **RESEARCH** Magical contagion; psychoneuroimmunology; health psychology. **SELECTED PUBLICATIONS** Auth, "Stereotypes and Stigma: Biased Attributions in Matching Persons With drawings of Viruses?," Intl J Aging (00); auth, "Medical Meditation: Some Theoretical and Practical Concepts," J Clin Psychol in Med Settings (00); auth, The Psychology of Germs, MIT (Cambridge) in press. **CONTACT ADDRESS** Dept Psychology, Capella Univ, 2441 E Bagnell St, Springfield, MO 65804. **EMAIL** lmdeangelo@hotmail.com

DEATON, ROBERT L.
PERSONAL Born 07/21/1936, Beaumont, TX, m, 1966, 2 children **DISCIPLINE** SOCIAL WORK **EDUCATION** Univ Ut, MSW, 64; Univ Nev, EdD, 80. **CAREER** Training Spec, Dept Fam Services, Ut, 67-69; Asst Prof to Prof Emeritus, Univ Mont, 69-. **HONORS AND AWARDS** Soc Worker of the Year, MT, 92; Fac Service Awd, Univ MT, 99. **MEMBERSHIPS** Nat Asn of Soc Workers. **RESEARCH** The family; Child welfare; Stress management; Trauma and PTSD. **SELECTED PUBLICATIONS** Auth, Planning and Managing Death Issues in the Schools, Greenwood Pub, 94. **CONTACT ADDRESS** Dept Soc Work, Univ of Montana, Missoula, MT 59812-0001.

DECI, EDWARD
PERSONAL Born 10/14/1942, New York, NY, s **DISCIPLINE** PSYCHOLOGY **EDUCATION** Hamilton Col, AB, 64; Univ of London, 65; Univ of Pennsylvania, MBA, 67; Carnegie-Mellon Univ, MS, 68; PhD, 70. **CAREER** Faculty Member, Univ of Rochester, 70-; Prof, Univ of Rochester, 78-. **HONORS AND AWARDS** Grants from National Institute of Mental Health; National Science Foundation; National Institute of Child Health; Human Development. **MEMBERSHIPS** Amer Psychological Assoc. **RESEARCH** Human Motivation; Human Freedom. **SELECTED PUBLICATIONS** Auth, "Human autonomy: The basis for true self-esteem," by Deci, E.L. & Ryan, R.M., In M. Kernis ed., Efficacy, agency, and self-esteem, 95: 31-49, New York: Plenum; auth, "Elements within the competitive situation that affect intrinsic motivation," by Reeve, J., & Deci, E.L., Personality and Social Psychology Bulletin, 96: 24-33; auth, "Motivational predictors of weight loss and weight-loss maintenance, by Williams, G.C., Grow, V.M., Freedman, Z.R., Ryan, R.M., & Deci, E.L., Journal of Personality and Social Psychology, 96:115-126; auth, "Internalization of biopsychosocial values by medical students: A test of self-determination theory, by Williams, G.C., & Deci, E.L., Journal of Personality and Social Psychology, 70, 96: 767-779; auth, "All goals are not created equal: An organismic persopective on the nature of goals and their regulation," by Ryan, R.M., Sheldon, K.M., Kasser, T., & Deci, E.L., In P.M. Gollwitzer & J.A. Bargh, eds, The Psychology of Action: Linking Cognition and Motivation to Behavior, pp 96: pp 7-26, New York: Guilford; auth, "Internali-zation within the family: The self-determination theory perspective, by Grolnick, W.S., Deci, E.L., & Ryan, R.M., In J.E. Grusec & L. Kuczynski, eds, Parenting and children's internalization of values: A handbook of contemporary theory, 97, pp 135-161, New York: Wiley; auth, "Autonomous Regulation and Adherence to Long-term Medical Regimens in Adult Outpatients," by Williams, G.C., Rodin, G.C. Ryan, R.M. Grolnick, W.S., & Deci, E.L., Health Psychology, 17, 98: 269-276; auth, "A meta-analytic review of experiements examining the effects of extrinsic rewards on intrinsic motivation," by Deci, E.L., Koestner, R., & Ryan, R.M., Psychological Bulletin, 125, 99, 627-668; auth, "The American Dream in Russia: Extrinsic aspirations and well-being in two cultures," by Ryan, R.M., Chirkov, V.I., Little, T.D., Sheldon, K.M., Timoshina, E., & Deci, E.L., Personality and Social Psychology Bulletin, 25, 99: 1509-1524; auth, "Self-determination theory and the facilitationof intrinsic motivation, social development, and well-being," by Ryan, R.M., & Deci, E.L., American Psychologist, 55, 68-78. **CONTACT ADDRESS** Dept Psychology, Univ of Rochester, Rochester, NY 14627. **EMAIL** deci@atspsych.rochester.edu

DEEGAN, MARY JO
PERSONAL Born 11/22/1946, Chicago, IL, s **DISCIPLINE** SOCIOLOGY **EDUCATION** Univ Chicago, PhD, 75. **CAREER** Prof, Univ of Nebr, 75-. **HONORS AND AWARDS** Who's Who in Am; Choice Awd for book "Jane Addams and the Men and the Chicago School." **MEMBERSHIPS** Am Sociol Asn, Charlotte Perkins Gilman Soc, Harriet Martineary Soc. **RESEARCH** Classical and Contemporary Theory, Women, Physical Disability. **SELECTED PUBLICATIONS** Co-ed, Women and Disability: The Double Handicap, Transaction Books (New Brunswick, NJ), 85; co-ed, Women and Symbolic Interaction, Allen and Unwin (Winchester, MA), 87; co-ed, A Feminist Ethic for Social Science Research, Edwin Mellen Press (Lewiston, NY), 88; auth, Jane Addams and the Men and the Chicago School, 1892-1918, Transaction Press (New Brunswick, NJ), 88; auth, American Ritual Dramas: Social Rules and Cultural Meanings, Greenwood Press (Wesport, CA), 89; ed, Women in Sociology: A Bio-Bibliographical Sourcebook, Greenwood Press (NY), 91; co-ed and intro, With Her in Ourland, by Charlotte Perkins Gilman, Greenwood Press (Wesport, CA), 97; ed, The American Ritual Tapestry, Greenwood Press (Wesport, CA), 98; ed and intro, Play, School, and Society, by George Herbert Mead, Peter Lang (NY), 99. **CONTACT ADDRESS** Dept Sociol, Univ of Nebraska, Lincoln, 71 Oldfather, PO Box 880324, Lincoln, NE 68588-0324.

DEFILIPIS, NICK A.
PERSONAL Born 10/04/1949, Chicago, IL, m, 1990 **DISCIPLINE** PSYCHOLOGY **EDUCATION** Northwestern Univ, BA, 71; Univ IA, MA, 74; PhD, 76. **CAREER** Teaching Asst, Univ IA, 72-74; Asst in Educ, Univ S Fla Med Sch, 75-76; Asst Prof, Augusta State Univ, 76-80; Adj Fac, DeKalb Cmty Col, 89-91; Prof, Ga Sch of Prof Psychol, 90-. **MEMBERSHIPS** Nat Register of Health Service Providers in Psychol; Am Psychol Asn; GA Psychol Asn; Nat Acad of Neuropsychol; Am Board of Prof Neuropsychol; Am Acad of Neuropsychol; Intl Neuropsychol Soc; Am Board of Prof Psychol; Acad of Clinical Psychol. **SELECTED PUBLICATIONS** Auth, "A History of childhood hyperactivity," Insight, (86): 20-22; co-auth, "Mature concerns for clinical psychology: The exorbitant cost of success," The Psychotherapy Bulletin, 89; co-auth, "Personality correlates of functional cerebral asymmetry in preschool children," Clinical Neuropsychology, (83): 14-15; co-auth, "The effects of time of exposure on Tactual Performance Test Memory and Location scores," Applied Neuropsychology, (97): 247-248; co-auth, "Proposed schedule of usual and customary test administration times," The Clinical Neuropsychologist, (99); 13. **CONTACT ADDRESS** Dept Psych, Georgia Sch of Professional Psychology, 990 Hammond Dr NE, Atlanta, GA 30328. **EMAIL** nickdefi@aol.com

DEFIORE, JOANN
PERSONAL Born 02/05/1968, NJ, m, 1999, 1 child **DISCIPLINE** SOCIOLOGY **EDUCATION** Catholic Univ Am, BA, 90; Univ MD, MA, 92; PhD, 95. **CAREER** Prof, Whitman Col, 95-96; prof, Univ Wash-Bothell, 96-. **MEMBERSHIPS** Am Sociol Asn. **RESEARCH** Race, Class and Gender, Friendship - community, Ecological thought. **SELECTED PUBLICATIONS** Auth, "Given an opportunity to reach out: heterogeneous participation in optional service-learning projects," Teaching Sociology, (forthcoming); auth, "Macro-Level Consequences of the Demand for Female Labor," American Journal of Sociology (98); auth, "All Women Benefit in an Integrated Labor Market: The Effect of Occupational Gender Integration on the Gender Earnings Ratio," American Sociological Review, (97): 714-734; auth, "Same Data, Different Conclusions: Comment on Annette Bernhardt, Martina Morris, and Mark S. Handcock," American Journal of Sociology, (96): 1143-1162; auth, "What is a Profession?", Professions: Key Issues, (97); auth, "Gender Inequality in Nonmetropolitan and Metropolitan Areas," Rural Sociology, (96): 272-288; auth, "Occupational Gender Segregation and the Earnings Gap: changes in the 1980s," Social Science Research, (95): 439-454; auth, "Occupations Gender Desegregation in the 1980s," Work and Occupations, (95): 1-25. **CONTACT ADDRESS** Dept Liberal Arts, Univ of Washington, 22011 26th Ave SE, Bothell, WA 98021. **EMAIL** jdefiore@u.washington.edu

DEFLEM, MATHIEU
PERSONAL Born 05/20/1962, Maaseik, Belguim **DISCIPLINE** SOCIOLOGY, ANTHROPOLOGY **EDUCATION** Katholieke Universiteit Leuven Belgium, MA, 86; Univ Hull England, MA, 90; Univ Colo, PhD, 96. **CAREER** Vis asst prof, Kenyon Coll, 96-97; asst prof, Purdue Univ, 97-. **MEMBERSHIPS** Am Sociol Asn; Soc for the Study of Social Problems; Am Soc for Criminology; Law and Soc Asn; Acad of Criminal Justice Sci; Europ Community Studies Asn. **RESEARCH** Law and Social Control; Comparative and Historical Sociology; Sociological Theory. **SELECTED PUBLICATIONS** Auth, Law Enforcement in British Colonial Africa: A Comparative Analysis of Imperial Policing in Nyasaland, the Gold Coast, and Kenya, Police Stduies, 94; Social Control and the Theory of Communicative Action, Int J of the Sociol and Law, 94; Corruption, Law and Justice: A Conceptual Clarification, J of Criminal justice, 95; International Policing in 19th Century Europe: The Police Union of German States, 1851-1866, Int Criminal Justice Rev, 96; Surveillance and Criminal Statistics: Historical Foundations of Governmentally, Studies in Law, Politics and Society, 97; The Boundaries of Abortion Law: Systems Theory from parsons to Luhmann and Habermas, Social Forces, 98; coauth, Profit and Penalty: An Analysis of the Corrections-Commercial Complex, Crime and Delinquency, 96; The Myth of Post-National Identity: Popular Support for European Unification, Social Forces es, 96; ed, Habermas, Modernity and Law, 96. **CONTACT ADDRESS** Dept of Sociology, Purdue Univ, West Lafayette, Stone Hall, West Lafayette, IN 47907-1365. **EMAIL** DeflemM@soc.purdue.edu

DEITRICK, LYNN
PERSONAL Born Harrisburg, PA, 1 child **DISCIPLINE** ANTHROPOLOGY **EDUCATION** Univ S Fla Tampa, PhD, 01. **CAREER** Grad Asst, Prog Evaluation, Cheles Center for Healthy Mothers and babies, Central Hillsborough Healthy Start Project, Tampa, Fla; Adj Teaching Fac, Univ S Fla Sarasota. **HONORS AND AWARDS** Sihma Theta Tau-Nat Nursing Hon Soc. **MEMBERSHIPS** Am Anthrop Soc, Soc for Appl Anthrop. **RESEARCH** Women's and Childrens Health Issues, Program Evaluation. **CONTACT ADDRESS** Dept Soc Sci, Univ of So Florida, 5700 N Tamiami Trail, Sarasota, FL 34243. **EMAIL** Ldeitrick@aol.com

DEL CAMPO, ROBERT L.
PERSONAL Born 10/24/1949, Yonkers, NY, m, 1972, 1 child **DISCIPLINE** FAMILY AND CONSUMER SCIENCE **EDUCATION** State Univ NYork, BS, 71; Va Tech, MS, 73; Fla State Univ, PhD, 75. **CAREER** Prof, Eastern Mich Univ, 75-88; prof of Family and Child Sci, N Mex State Univ, 88-, head, Dept of Human, Environmental and Consumer Scis, 88-93. **HONORS AND AWARDS** Tenure, 79; Who's Who Among Teachers, 98. **MEMBERSHIPS** Am Asn for Marriage and Family Therapy, Nat Coun on Family Relations, Int Family Therapy Asn. **RESEARCH** The interface of work and family in minority populations. **SELECTED PUBLICATIONS** Coauth with D. Del Campo, "Adult Caregivers and Aging Family Members," Conf Proceedings: Annual Meeting of the Tex Asn for Marriage and Family Therapy (Jan 2000); coauth with D. Del Campo, Taking Sides: Clashing Views on Controversial Issues in Childhood and Society, 3rd ed, Guilford, Ct: Dushkin/McGraw Hill Pub Co (2000); coauth with D. Del Campo, Instructor's Manual for Taking Sides: Clashing Views on Controversial Issues in Childhood and Society, 3rd ed, Guilford, Ct: Dushkin/McGraw Hill Pub Co (2000); coauth with A. E. Crnkovic and R. Steiner, "Mental Health Professionals' Perceptions of Women's Experiences of Family Violence," Contemporary Family Therapy (June 2000); coauth with D. Del Campo and M. DeLeon, "Recent Literature of Adult Caregivers & Aging Family Members," The Forum for Family & Consumer Issues (in press). **CONTACT ADDRESS** Dept Family & Consumer Sci, New Mexico State Univ, PO Box 3470, Las Cruces, NM 88003. **EMAIL** rdelcamp@nmsu.edu

DELANEY, CAROL L.
PERSONAL Born 12/12/1940, New York, NY, d, 1 child **DISCIPLINE** ANTHROPOLOGY **EDUCATION** Harvard Div School, MTS, 73; Univ Chicago, MA, 78; PhD, 84. **CAREER** Asst dir, Harvard Univ, 85-87; asst prof, assoc prof, 95-, Stanford Univ. **HONORS AND AWARDS** Nat Jewish Bk Awd;

Fulbright Schl. **MEMBERSHIPS** AAA; AEA; AAR; MES; TSA. **RESEARCH** Gender; religion; culture theory; Turkey. **SELECTED PUBLICATIONS** Auth, Abraham on Trial: The Social Legacy of Biblical Myth, Princeton Univ Press, 98; coed, Naturalizing Power: Essays, Feminist Cultural Analysis, Routledge, 95; auth, The Seed and The Soil: Gender and Cosmology, Turkish Vill Soc(Univ Cal, Berkeley), 91. **CONTACT ADDRESS** Dept Cultural, Social Anthropology, Stanford Univ, Stanford, CA 94305.

DEMARR, MARY JEAN
PERSONAL Born 09/20/1932, Champaign, IL **DISCIPLINE** ENGLISH, WOMEN'S STUDIES **EDUCATION** Lawrence Col, BA, 54; Univ Ill, Urbana, AM, 57, PhD(English), 63. **CAREER** Asst prof English, Willamette Univ, 64-65; from asst prof to assoc prof, 65-75, prof english and Women's studies, Ind State Univ, Terre Haute, 75-95, prof emeritus, 95-. **HONORS AND AWARDS** Phi Beta Kappa; Phi Kappa Phi; George N. Dove Award for "Outstanding Contribution to the Serious Study of Mystery and Crime Fiction," 95; MidAmerica Award for "Distinguished Contributions to the Study of Midwestern Literature," 00. **MEMBERSHIPS** MLA; Mod Humanities Res Asn; NCTE; AAUP; Popular Cult Asn. **RESEARCH** American literature; women's studies. **SELECTED PUBLICATIONS** Contributor and ed, Annual Bibliography of English Language and Literature, Modern Humanities Research Asn (Leeds, England), 66-69, 70-73; 74-92; coauth, The Adolescent in the American Novel Since 1960, Frederick Ungar Publishing Co (NYork), 86; auth, "Chopin,Kate Reconsidered--Beyond the Bayou," Jour Pop Cult (94); auth, "The Darkness of the Women': Two Short Stories by Ruth Suckow," MidAmerica XXI (94): 112-121; ed, In the Beginning: First Novels in Mystery Series, Popular Press (Bowling Green, OH), 95; auth, "Clifford D. Simak's Use of the Midwest in Science Fiction," MidAmerica XXII (95): 108-121; auth, Colleen McCullough: A Critical Companion, Greenwood Press (Westport, CT), 96; auth, "True-Crime Books: Socio/Psycho-Babble or Socially Redeeming Voyeurism?" Clues (96): 1-18; auth, Barbara Kingsolver: A Critical Companion, Greenwood Press (Westport, CT), 99; auth, "Dana Stabenow's Alaska Mysteries," Diversity and Detective Fiction, ed. Kathleen Gregory Klein (Bowling Green, OH, Popular Press, 99), 115-129. **CONTACT ADDRESS** Dept of English, Indiana State Univ, Terre Haute, IN 47809. **EMAIL** mjd594@msn.com

DEMBO, RICHARD
PERSONAL Born 01/04/1940, New York, NY, m, 1967, 2 children **DISCIPLINE** SOCIOLOGY, CRIMINOLOGY **EDUCATION** NY Univ, BA, 61; Columbia Univ, MA, 65; NY Univ, PhD, 70. **CAREER** Assoc Prof, Clarkson Col, 76-78; Sen Res Assoc, Univ Denver, 79-81; Assoc Prof, Univ Denver, 80-81; Prof, Univ S Fla, 81-00. **HONORS AND AWARDS** Who's Who in Sci and Engineering, 96-97; Int Dir of Distinguished Leadership, 97; Who's Who in the World, 98. **MEMBERSHIPS** Am Soc of Criminology, ASA, Acad of Criminal Justice Sci. **RESEARCH** Develop and test juvenile interventions, alcohol and drug use, research methodology and statistics. **SELECTED PUBLICATIONS** Coauth, "Gender Differences in Service Needs Among Youths Entering a Juvenile Assessment Center: A Replication Study," J of Correctional Health Care, 2 (95): 191-216; coauth, "Juvenile Health Service Centers: An Exciting Opportunity to Intervene with Drug Involved and Other High Risk Youth," in Intervening with Drug Involved Youth, (Newbury Park, CA: Sage, 96); coauth, "A Family Empowerment Intervention for Families of Juvenile Offenders," Aggression and Violent Behavior: A Rev J, 1 (96): 205-216; coauth, "Drug Use and the Delinquent Behavior Among High Risk Youths," J of Child and Adolescent Substance Abuse, 6 (97): 1-25; coauth, "The Relationships Between Youths' Identified Substance Use, Mental Health or Other Problems at a Juvenile Assessment Center and Their Referrals to Needed Services," J of Child and Adolescent Substance Abuse, 6 (97): 23-54; coauth, "The Hillsborough County, Florida Juvenile Assessment Center: A Prototype," The Prison J, 78 (98): 439-450; coauth, "A Longitudinal Study of the Impact of a Family Empowerment Intervention on Juvenile Offender Psychosocial Functioning: A First Assessment," J of Child and Adolescent Substance Abuse, 8 (98): 15-54; coauth, "Predictors of Recidivism to a Juvenile Assessment Center: A Three Year Study," J of Child and Adolescent Substance Abuse, 7 (98): 57-77; coauth, "Engaging High Risk families in Community Based Intervention Services," Aggression and Violence: A Rev J, 4 (99): 41-58; coauth, "Criminal Justice Responses to Adolescent Substance Abuse," in Prevention and Societal Impact of Drug and Alcohol Abuse, (Mahwah, NJ: Lawrence Erlbaum Assoc, 99); **CONTACT ADDRESS** Dept Sociol, Univ of So Florida, 4202 E Fowler Ave, Tampa, FL 33620. **EMAIL** jac@gate.net

DEMKO, DAVID
PERSONAL m, 2 children **DISCIPLINE** PSYCHOLOGY, SOCIOLOGY, EDUCATION **EDUCATION** W Va Univ, BA, 70; MA, 76; Univ Mich, PhD, 82. **CAREER** Prof, Miami Dade Community Col, 91-; Prof, Nova S Eastern Univ, 92-; ed-in-chief, Age Ventura News Serv, www.demko.com, 97-; Prof, Fla Atlanic Univ, 99-. **HONORS AND AWARDS** Outstanding Fac Awd, Phi Theta Kappa Student Hon Soc, 94, 97, 99; Student Govt Teaching Excellence Awd, 97, 98, 99. **MEMBERSHIPS** World Future Soc, Nat Dir of Syndicated Columnists.

RESEARCH Gerontology, School Reform. **SELECTED PUBLICATIONS** Ed, Aging America Newsletter, ISSN 1088-5889; ed and publ, Nationally Syndicated Columnist, Syndication Dir, 91-00; auth, articles in J of Hearing Care and Technology, 95. **CONTACT ADDRESS** Dept Behav Sci, Miami-Dade Comm Col, 11380 NW 27th Ave, Miami, FL 33167. **EMAIL** david@demko.com

DEMONE, HAROLD WELLINGTON
DISCIPLINE SOCIOLOGY **EDUCATION** Tufts Col, BA, 48; Tufts Univ, MA, 49; Brandeis Univ, PhD, 66. **CAREER** Instr, dept of sociology, Tufts Univ, 49-54; exec dir, NH Div on Alcoholism, State Dept of Health, 54-56; Comnr on Alcoholism, 56-59, Special Asst to the Comnr of Public Health, 59-60, Commonwealth of Mass; Exec Dir, The Medical Found Inc, 60-67; Exec Vice Pres, United Community Planning Corp, 67-77; Dean, School of Soc Work, Rutgers Univ, 77-87; Prof II, School of Social Work and Graduate Sociology Dept, Rutgers Univ, 77-92; PROF II EMERITUS, 92-; VISITING SCHOLAR, HELLER GRAD SCHOOL, BRANDEIS UNIV, 97-; LECTR, BOSTON COL GRAD SCHOOL OF SOCIAL WORK, 98-. **HONORS AND AWARDS** Alpha Kappa Delta, 51; Pi Gamma Mu, 49; Mass Asn for Mental Health Awd, 66; Mass Psychological Asn Awd, 66; Mass Asn for Retarded Children Awd for Special Recognition, 67; Mass Public Health Asn Lemuel Shattuck Awd, 75; The Joshua A. Guberman Lectr in Law and Social Policy, 86; NASW Social Work Pioneer, Nat Asn of Soc Workers, 97; Tufts Univ Alumni Asn Distinguished Service Awd, 98. **MEMBERSHIPS** Nat Asn for Soc Workers, 66-; Int Coun on Soc Welfare, 78-; Coun on Soc Work Ed, 77-; Am Public Health Asn, 57-; Soc for the Study of Soc Problems, 52-; Nonprofit and Voluntary Sector Quarterly, occasional reviewer, 98-. **SELECTED PUBLICATIONS** Coauth, Alcoholism and Society, Oxford Univ Press, 62; coauth, Administrative and Planning Techniques in Human Service Organizations, Behavioral Pubs, 73; coauth, A Handbook of Human Service Organizations, Behavioral Pubs, 74; auth, Stimulating Human Services Reform, Aspen Systems Corp, 78; coauth, Social Work Past, A Twenty-five-Year History of the Graduate School of Social Work, Rutgers, 83; coauth, Services for Sale: Purchasing Health and Human Services, Rutgers Univ Press, 89; co-ed & contribur, The Privatization of Human Services Vol 1: Policy and Practice Issues, Springer Pub Company, 98; co-ed, The Privatization of Human Services Vol 1: Case Studies in the Purchase of Human Services, 98. **CONTACT ADDRESS** Graduate School of Social Work, Rutgers, The State Univ of New Jersey, New Brunswick, 536 George St, New Brunswick, NJ 08903.

DENBOW, JAMES R.
PERSONAL Born 12/14/1946, IA, m, 1969, 2 children **DISCIPLINE** ANTHROPOLOGY **EDUCATION** Univ Ill, BA, 69; Univ Ind, 76; PhD, 83. **CAREER** Cur, Nat Mus of Botswana, 79-82; Sen Cur, Nat Mus Botswana, 82-86; Assoc Prof, Univ Tex, 86-. **RESEARCH** African prehistory and anthropology. **SELECTED PUBLICATIONS** Coauth, "The Early Stages of Food Production in Southern Africa and Some Potential Linguistic Correlations," in Sprache und Geschichte Afrika, vol 1 (86), 83-103; coauth, "The Advent and Course of Pastoralism in the Kalahari," Science 234 (86): 1509-15; auth, "A New Look at the Later Prehistory of the Kalamari," J of African Hist 27 (86): 3-29; auth, "After the Flood: A Preliminary Account of Geological, Linguistic and Archaeological Investigations in the Okavango Region of Northern Botswana," in Contemporary Studies on Khoisan (Hamburg: Helmut Buske, 87), 181-214; coauth, "Uncovering Botswana's Past," Nat Museum Gaborone (90); auth, "Congo to Kalahari: Data and Hypotheses about the Political Economy of the Western Stream of the Early Iron Age," African Archaeological Rev (90): 139-175; coauth, "Paradigmatic History of San-Speaking Peoples and Current Attempts at Reconstruction," Current Anthrop (90): 489-524; coauth, "Paintings Like Engravings: Rock Art at Tsodilo," in Contested Images: Diversity in Southern African Rock Art Res (Johannesburg: Witwatersrand Univ Pr, 94), 131-158; auth, "Material Culture and the Dialectics of Identity in the Kalahari: AD 700-1700," in Beyond Chiefdoms: Pathways to Complexity in Africa, (Cambridge Univ Pr, 99), 110-123; auth, "Heart and Soul: Glimpses of Ideology and Cosmology in the Iconography of Tombstones from the Loango Coast of Central Africa," J of Am Folklore 112 (99): 404-423. **CONTACT ADDRESS** Dept Anthrop, Univ of Texas, Austin, University of Tex, Austin, TX 78712. **EMAIL** jdenbow@mail.utexas.edu

DENDINGER, DONALD
PERSONAL Born 10/04/1937, Coleridge, NE, w, 1975, 2 children **DISCIPLINE** SOCIOLOGY **EDUCATION** Creighton Univ, BA, 59; St Thomas Sem, MS, 62; Univ Md, MSW, 71; Univ Denver, PhD, 77. **CAREER** Priest, Archdiocese of Omaha, NE, 63-75; Prof, Univ Neb, 77-. **HONORS AND AWARDS** Soc Worker of the Year, Nat Asn of Soc Workers, 96. **MEMBERSHIPS** Nat Assoc of Soc Workers, Nat Assoc for Develop Educ. **RESEARCH** Recruiting, retaining and graduating under-represented students. **SELECTED PUBLICATIONS** Coauth, "The Goodrich Scholarship Program, A Retention Model for Low Income Students," Non Traditional and Interdisciplinary Progs Conf, George Mason Univ Pr (88); coauth, "Recruiting and Teaching Low Income Students: Toward the Development of a Model," Int Third World Studies J

and Rev, 7 (89); coauth, "Assessing Supervisory Skills," The Clinical Supvr, vol 7 (89); coauth, "Minority Faculty Development: Making the Commitment," The Non Traditional and Interdisciplinary Progs Conf, George Mason Univ Pr, 90; auth, "The Weekend Format for Graduate Students: Student Perceptions," The Non Traditional and Interdisciplinary Progs Conf, George Mason Univ Pr, 92. **CONTACT ADDRESS** Dept Sociol, Univ of Nebraska, Omaha, 6001 Dodge St, Omaha, NE 68182-0002. **EMAIL** dendinger@unomaha.edu

DENMARK, FLORENCE L.
PERSONAL Born 01/28/1931, Philadelphia, PA, m, 1973, 6 children **DISCIPLINE** PSYCHOLOGY **EDUCATION** Univ Penn, AB, 52; AM, 54; PhD, 58. **CAREER** Lectr, Queens Col, 59-66; prof, Hunter Col, CUNY, 64-90; dist prof, Pace Univ, 88-; adj prof, Grad Cen, CUNY, 90-. **HONORS AND AWARDS** Recog Cert, Psi Chi, 72, 75, 78, 81, 83, 85; Geo N Shuster Fac Awd; SESP Mem; Mellon Schl; Kurt Lewin Awd; FOPW Awd; First Nat Dist Ser Awd, Psi Chi; Outstand Wom Sci Awd; Nat Intl Achiev Awd Dist Career Awd; Wilhelm Wundt Awd; APA Cent Awd; Carolyn Wood Sherif Awd; Allen V Williams Awd; Margaret Flot Washburn Awd; Interam Awd; Dist Intl Psychol Awd; Psi Chi Dist Mem; Phi Alpha Theta; Sigma Xi; Phi Beta Kappa; Who's Who in Am, East, Women in Edu; Am Men and Women of Sci. **MEMBERSHIPS** APA; NYSPA; NYAS; EPA; CSSP; ICP; Psi Chi; AWP; COGDOP; SASP; AWS; ISP; IOSG; ACLS. **RESEARCH** Social psychology including the psychology of women and gender; minority group achievement; leadership and status; cross-cultural and international research. **SELECTED PUBLICATIONS** Co-ed, Psychology of Women: A handbook of issues and theories, Greenwood Press, (Westport, CT), 93; co-ed, Violence and the Prevention of Violence, Praeger (Westport, CT), 95; co-ed, Females and autonomy: A life-span perspective, Allyn and Bacon (Boston, MA), 99; coauth, Engendering Psychology, Allyn and Bacon (Boston, MA), forthcoming; auth, "Women and Psychology: An international perspective," Am Psychol 53 (98): 465-473; coauth, "Bereavement and stress of a miscarriage: As it affects the couple," Omega 37 (98): 315-325; auth, "Enhancing the development of adolescent girls," in Beyond Appearance: A new Look at Adolescent Girls, eds. NG Johnson, MC Roberts, J Worell (Washington, DC: APA, 99); auth, "Older Women's Lives: Myths and Realities," La Psicologia (99). **CONTACT ADDRESS** Dept Psychology, Pace Univ, New York, 1 Pace Plaza, New York, NY 10038. **EMAIL** fdenmark@pace.edu

DENNIS, RUTLEDGE M.
PERSONAL Born 08/16/1939, Charleston, SC, d, 4 children **DISCIPLINE** SOCIOLOGY **EDUCATION** SC State Univ, BA, 66; Wash State Univ, MA, 69; PhD, 75. **CAREER** Dir, African Studies Prog/Asst Prof/Assoc Prof, Va Commonwealth Univ, 71-89; Prof, George Mason Univ, 89-. **HONORS AND AWARDS** Who's Who in Am; Who's Who Among African Am; Alpha Kappa Mu Hon Soc; Sigma Xi; Outstanding Educator of Am; Ford Found Fel; Reise-Melton Awd; Jewish Educators Awd; Distinguished Leadership Awd, African Am Studies Prog, Va Commonwealth Univ; Alpha Phi Alpha Acad Achievement Awd. **MEMBERSHIPS** Asn of Black Sociologists, Soc for Study of Soc Probl, Southern Sociologists, Eastern Sociologists. **RESEARCH** Theory, Social Stratification, Race and Ethnicity, Urban Political Sociology. **SELECTED PUBLICATIONS** Coauth, Afro-Americans: A Social Science Perspective, Univ Press of Am (Wash, DC), 76; coauth, The Politics of Annexation: Oligarchic Power in a Southern City, Schenkman Publ Co (Cambridge), 82; ed, Research in Race and Ethnic Relations Vol 6, JAI Press Inc (Greenwich, CT), 91; co-ed, Race and Ethnicity in Research Methods, Sage Publ (Newbury Park), 93; ed, Racial and Ethnic Politics, Research in Race and Ethnic Relations Vol 7, JAI Press Inc (Greenwich, CT), 94; ed, The Black Middle Class, Research in Race and Ethnic Relations Vol 8, JAI Press Inc (Greenwich, CT), 95; ed, W.E.B. Du Bois: The Scholar as Activist, Research in Race and Ethnic Relations Vol 9, JAI Press Inc (Greenwich, CT), 96; ed, Black Intellectuals, Research in Race and Ethnic Relations Vol 10, JAI Press Inc (Greenwich, CT), 97. **CONTACT ADDRESS** Dept Sociol & Anthrop, George Mason Univ, Fairfax, 4400 Univ Dr, Fairfax, VA 22030. **EMAIL** rdenni1@gmu.edu

DENTAN, ROBERT K.
PERSONAL Born 08/28/1936, New Haven, CT, m, 1972, 3 children **DISCIPLINE** ANTHROPOLOGY **EDUCATION** Yale Univ, BA, 58; PhD, 65. **CAREER** Prof, Ohio State Univ, 64-68; prof, SUNY/Buffalo, 68-. **HONORS AND AWARDS** Anthropol Fund for Urgent Res. **MEMBERSHIPS** Am Anthropol Asn, Asian Studies Asn, Am Asn Advancement of Sci. **RESEARCH** (Non)violence, Oppression. **SELECTED PUBLICATIONS** Auth, "Spotted Doves at War: The Praak Sangkiil," Asian Folklore Studies, 00; auth, Semai: In Endangered Peoples of East and Southeast Asia, Greenwood Pub Group, 00; auth, "Untransfiguring Death," Review of Indonesian and Malaysian Affairs 33, (99): 16-65; auth, Malaysia and the 'Original People': A Case Study of the Impact of Development on Indigenous Peoples, Boston, 97; auth, "The Persistence of Received Truth: How the Malaysian Ruling Class Constructs Orange Asli. In Indigenous Peoples and the State: Politics, Land, and Ethnicity in the Malaysan Peninsula and Borneo," Monograph 46/Yale Univ, (97): 98-134; auth, "Bad Day at Bukit Pekan,:

American Anthropologist 97, (95): 225-231; auth, "Stewards of the Green and Beautiful World," in Dimensions of traditions and development in Malaysia, 95. **CONTACT ADDRESS** Dept Anthropol, SUNY, Buffalo, PO Box 610005, Buffalo, NY 14261-0005. **EMAIL** rkdentan@acsu.buffalo.edu

DEPILLARS, MURRY NORMAN
PERSONAL Born 12/21/1938, Chicago, IL, m **DISCIPLINE** EDUCATION **EDUCATION** JC Wilson Coll, AA Fine Arts 1966; Roosevelt Univ, BA Art Educ 1968, MA Urban Studies 1970; PA State Univ, PhD Art Educ 1976. **CAREER** Mast Inst, Chicago comm on urban opportunity div of training, 68; Univ of IL Chicago, educ asst program asst dir, 68-71; numerous art exhibits throughout the US; VA Commonwealth Univ Richmond, dean school of art; Chicago State Univ, exec vp for planning and mgmt, currently. **HONORS AND AWARDS** Elizabeth Catlett Mora Awd of Excellence Natl Conf of Artists 1977; Special Arts Awd & Art Educ Awd Branches for the Arts 1980; Man of Excellence Plaque Ministry of Educ Republic of China 1980; Excellence in the Educ Preservation & Promotion of Jazz Richmond Jazz Soc 1981; Outstanding Admin Awd Black Student Alliance 1982; Outstanding Achievement in the Arts Branches for the Arts 1982; Alumni Fellow Penn State Univ 1989. **MEMBERSHIPS** Bd of dir & illustrator 3rd World Press Chicago 1960-; bd of dir & art dir Kuumba Workshop Chicago 1969-; bd of dir & contributing ed Inst of Positive Educ Chicago 1970-; adv bd Journal of Negro Educ Washington 1973-; bd of dir N Amer Zone & co-chmn Upper So Region 2nd World Black & African Festival of Arts & Culture 1973-74; pres Natl Conf of Artists Richmond 1973-77; mem Intl Council of Fine Arts Deans 1976-; hmn of bd Natl Conf of Artists NY 1977; First Sino/Amer Conf on the Arts Taipei Taiwan 1980; arts commission Natl Assoc of State Univ & Land Grant Colls 1981-88; consultant Natl Endowment for the Humanities 1982-84; cons Corp of the Public Broadcasting & the Annenberg School of Communications 1983; OH Eminent Scholars Program Panel OH Bd of Regents1983-84; consult The O Paul Get-Trust 1984; Natl Endowment for the Arts Expansion Arts Program 1985-; Natl Jazz Serv Org 1985-; US Info Agency Acad Specialist to Malaysia 1985; Africobra 1985-; arts adv bd Coll Bd 1984-85; chmn, coordinator comm The Richmond Jazz Festival 1984-; art & architectural review bd Commonwealth of VA 1986-. **CONTACT ADDRESS** Exec VP, Planning and Mgmt, Chicago State Univ, 9501 S King Dr, Chicago, IL 60628.

DEREZOTES, DAVID S.
PERSONAL Born 11/15/1951, Chicago, IL, s, 2 children **DISCIPLINE** SOCIAL WORK **EDUCATION** Iowa State Univ, BS, 74; San Diego State Univ, MSW, 80; Intl Col, PhD, 84; Univ Calif, PhD, 89. **CAREER** Prof, Univ Utah. **RESEARCH** Advanced generalist practice. **SELECTED PUBLICATIONS** Auth, Advanced generalist social work practice: An inclusive approach, Sage Pub, 99; co-auth, Preventing adolescent abuse, Lexington Books, 90; co-auth, "The association between child maltreatment and self-esteem," in The social importance of self-esteem, Univ Calif Press, 89; auth, "Transpersonal social work with couples: A compatibility-intimacy model," Social Thought, forthcoming; auth, "The taboo against being a psychotherapist, "Reflections: Narratives of Professional Helping, forthcoming; co-auth, "Evaluation of yoga and meditation trainings with adolescent sex offenders," Child and Adolescent Social Work Journal, forthcoming; auth, "Social work practice with parenting: Issues, paradigms, and recommendations," Journal of Applied Social Sciences, (96): 25-35; auth, "Evaluation of ht e Late Nite Basketball Program," Child and Adolescent Social Work Journal, (96): 33-50; co-auth, "Spirituality and religiosity in practice: In-depth interviews of social work practitioners," Social Thought: Journal of Religion in the Social Services, (95): 39-56; auth, "Spiritual and religious factors in practice: Empirically-based recommendations for social work education," Arete, (95): 1-15 **CONTACT ADDRESS** Grad School of Soc Work, Univ of Utah, 201 S 1460 E 250S, Salt Lake City, UT 84112.

DEROSE, LAURIE
PERSONAL Born 04/07/1968, Elmhurst, IL, m, 1990, 2 children **DISCIPLINE** SOCIOLOGY **EDUCATION** Brown Univ, AB, 90; MA, 92; PhD, 95. **CAREER** Res assoc, World Hunger Prog, Brown Univ, 95-98; vis asst prof, Brown Univ, 94-97; asst prof, Univ MD, 98-. **HONORS AND AWARDS** Peter K. New Student Res Prize, honorable mention, The Soc for Applied Anthropology, 95. **MEMBERSHIPS** Population Asn of Am; Am Sociol Asn; Population Reference Bureau; District of Columbia Sociol Soc. **RESEARCH** Fertility transition in Sub-Sahara Africa, demographic effects of education decline and female labor force participation, reproductive decision-making. **SELECTED PUBLICATIONS** Coauth with Ann E. Biddlecom, "A Cross-National Study of Virgin Births," J of Irreproducible Results 38, no. 3: 9-14 (May/June 93); coauth with Martin Brockerhoff, "Parental Education and Child Survival: Can the DHS Tell Us Anything New?," Health Transition Rev 4, no. 2: 192-196 (Oct. 94); coauth with Martin Brockerhoff, "Child Survival in East Africa: The Impact of Preventative Health Care," World Development 24, no. 12: 1841-1857 (Dec. 96); coauth with Ellen Messer and Sara Millman, "Who's Hungry? And How Do We Know?," Tokyo: United Nations Press (98). **CONTACT ADDRESS** Dept Sociol, Univ of Maryland, Col Park, 2112 Art-Sociology Bldg, College Park, MD 20742. **EMAIL** lderose@socy.umd.edu

DESCARTES, RENE
PERSONAL Born 02/02/1944, Brooklyn, NY, m, 1967, 3 children **DISCIPLINE** ANTHROPOLOGY **EDUCATION** SUNY Buffalo, BA, 70; SUNY Albany, MA, 72; MLS, 91; MA, 98; New Sch for Soc Res, PhD, 81. **CAREER** Assoc Prof, SUNY, 93-. **RESEARCH** Early Civilizations; Agricultural Systems; Latin America. **CONTACT ADDRESS** Dept Soc Sci, SUNY, Col of Agr and Tech at Cobl, Cobleskill, NY 12043.

DESMANGLES, LESLIE GERALD
PERSONAL Born 09/28/1941, Port-au-Prince, Haiti, m, 1968, 3 children **DISCIPLINE** ANTHROPOLOGY OF RELIGION **EDUCATION** Eastern Col, BA, 64; Eastern Baptist Theol Sem, MDiv, 67; Temple Univ, PhD(anthop relig), 75. **CAREER** Instr, Eastern Col, 69-70; instr, Ohio Wesleyan Univ, 70-75 & asst prof, 75-76; asst prof, DePaul Univ, 76-78; assoc prof Relig, Trinity Col, 78-, instr, Ohio Univ, 75-76; consult, Miami Univ of Ohio, 73-74 & Hispanic Health Coun of Hartford, 81-; Nat Endowment for Humanities & Trinity Col res grant, 80; dir, Prog Intercult Studies, Trinity Col, 81-. **HONORS AND AWARDS** United States Embassy Awd in Port-au-Prince for valuable contribution in promoting mutual understanding between Haiti and the United States; Haitian-Am Alliance Awd; 2000 Teacher of the Year. **MEMBERSHIPS** Asn Sociol Relig; Am Acad Relig; Caribbean Studies Asn; Pres, Haitian Studies Asn. **RESEARCH** African traditional religions; Caribbean religions. **SELECTED PUBLICATIONS** Auth, African interpretations of the Christian cross in Haitian Vodun, Sociol Analysis, 76; Rites baptismaux: Symbiose du Vodou et du Catholicisme a Haiti, Concilium, 77; The way of Vodun death, J Relig Thought, 80; Vodun baptismal rites, J Inter-Denominational Theol Ctr, 81; The Faces of the Gods: Vodou and Roman Catholicism in Haiti, Univ of NC Press, 93. **CONTACT ADDRESS** Dept Relig & Intercult, Trinity Col, Connecticut, 300 Summit St, Hartford, CT 06106-3186. **EMAIL** leslie.desmangles@mail.trincoll.edu

DEUTSCHER, IRWIN
PERSONAL Born 12/24/1923, New York, NY, m, 1950, 2 children **DISCIPLINE** SOCIOLOGY **EDUCATION** Univ Missouri, PhD, 58. **CAREER** Prof, Dir of Youth Dev Ctr, Syracuse Univ, 59-68; prof, Case Western Reserve Univ, 68-75; prof,Univ Akron, 75-84, prof emer, 84- . **HONORS AND AWARDS** Annondale Mem Medal for Distinguished Service to Indian Anthropology, 97; Am Sociol Asn Distinguished Career Awd, 97; Lee Founders Awd, Soc for the Study of Social Problems, 97; Distinguished Alumnae Awd, Univ of Missouri, 98; Lifetime Achievement Awd, Sociol Practice Asn, 98. **MEMBERSHIPS** Am Sociol Asn; Soc for Appl Sociol; Soc for the Study of Social Problems; Int Sociol Asn; District of Columbia Sociol Soc. **RESEARCH** Program evolution; reduction of ethnic violence worldwide, applied sociology. **SELECTED PUBLICATIONS** Coauth, Sentiments and Acts, Aldine/deGruyter, 93; auth, Making a Difference: The Practice of Sociology, Transaction Books, 99 . **CONTACT ADDRESS** 4740 Conn Ave NW #1007, Washington, DC 20008. **EMAIL** ideutscher@cs.com

DEVINE, MARY E.
DISCIPLINE POPULAR CULTURE **EDUCATION** AB, 60, PhD, 64, Loyola Univ. **CAREER** Asst Prof, Michigan State Univ, 64-69; Assoc Prof, 69-75, Prof, 75-, Salem State Col. **CONTACT ADDRESS** 28 Village St, Marblehead, MA 01945. **EMAIL** mary.devine@salem.mass.edu

DEVITIS, JOSEPH
PERSONAL Born 04/24/1945, Baltimore, MD, m, 1988, 1 child **DISCIPLINE** HUMAN DEVELOPMENT **EDUCATION** Johns Hopkins Univ, BA, 67; MEd, 69; Bowie State Univ, MA, 85; Univ Ill, PhD, 92. **CAREER** Instr, Univ Tenn, 72-88; Prof, State Univ NY, 88-. **HONORS AND AWARDS** Choice Awd, Am Libr Assoc, 85, 92. **MEMBERSHIPS** Am Educ Studies Assoc, Soc of Profs of Educ, Philos of Educ Soc. **RESEARCH** Educational policy and reform, moral development, helping professions. **SELECTED PUBLICATIONS** Coauth, Theories of Moral Development, Charles C. Thomas, 85; ed, Women, Culture and Morality: Selected Essays, Peter Lang Publ, 87; co-ed, Building Bridges for Educational Reform: New Approaches to Teacher Education, Iowa State Univ Pr, 89; coauth, Helping and Intervention, Irvington, 91; coauth, Competition in Education, Charles C. Thomas, 92; co-ed, School Reform in the Deep South: A Critical Appraisal, Univ Ala Pr, 92; coauth, Theories of Moral Development, 2nd Ed, Charles C. Thomas, 94; coauth, The Success Ethic, Education and the American Dream, State Univ NY, 96; co-ed, To Serve and Learn: The Spirit of Community in Liberal Education, Peter Lang Publ, 98. **CONTACT ADDRESS** Dept Human Develop, SUNY, Binghamton, PO Box 6000, Binghamton, NY 13902. **EMAIL** jdevitis@binghamton.edu

DEWSBURY, DONALD A.
PERSONAL Born 08/11/1939, Brooklyn, NY, d, 2 children **DISCIPLINE** PSYCHOLOGY **EDUCATION** Bucknell Univ, AB, 61; Univ Mich, PhD, 65. **CAREER** From Asst Prof to Prof, Univ Fla, 66-. **HONORS AND AWARDS** Phi Beta Kappa; Phi Sigma; C T Morgan Serv Awd; Sigma Xi Sr Fac Awd; Awd, Animal Behav Soc. **MEMBERSHIPS** APA, APS, HSS, ABS. **RESEARCH** History of psychology. **SELECTED PUBLICATIONS** Ed, Unification Through Division: Histories of Divisions of the American Psychological Association, Vol 1, APA (Wash, DC), 96; auth, Unification Through Division: Histories of Divisions of the American Psychological Association, Vol 2, APA (Wash, DC), 97; auth, Unification Through Division: Histories of Divisions of the American Psychological Association, Vol 3, APA (Wash, DC), 98; auth, Unification Through Division: Histories of Divisions of the American Psychological Association, Vol 4, APA (Wash, DC), 99; auth, "Curt Paul Richter," in Am Nat Biog, vol 18 (Oxford UP, 99), 469; auth, "The Proximate and the Ultimate: Past, Present and Future," Behav Processes 46 (99): 189-199; auth, Unification Through Division: Histories of Divisions of the American Psychological Association, Vol 5, APA (Wash, DC), forthcoming. **CONTACT ADDRESS** Dept Psychol, Univ of Florida, PO Box 112250, Gainesville, FL 32611. **EMAIL** dewsbury@psych.ufl.edu

DHARWADKER, APARNA
PERSONAL Born 06/14/1955, Jaipur, India, m, 1976, 2 children **DISCIPLINE** LITERARY AND CULTURAL STUDIES **EDUCATION** Univ Rajasthan, BA, 75; Delhi Univ, MA, 77; Pa State Univ, PhD, 90. **CAREER** Instr, Univ of Il Chicago, 87-89; instr, Univ of Ga Athens, 89-91; asst to assoc prof, Univ of Okla, 91-. **HONORS AND AWARDS** Folger Fel, 84; Newberry Libr Fel, 87; Okla Found for Humanities Grant, 93; AIIS Res Fel, 98; NEH Res Fel, 98. **MEMBERSHIPS** MLA; Am Soc for Theatre Res; Am Soc for Eighteen-Century Studies. **RESEARCH** Postcolonial studies, comparative modern drama and theatre, restoration and 18th century British literature. **CONTACT ADDRESS** Dept English, Univ of Oklahoma, 900 Asp Ave, Norman, OK 73019-4050. **EMAIL** adhar@ou.edu

DI PARDO, ANNE
PERSONAL Born 06/14/1953, Eugene, OR, m, 1974, 1 child **DISCIPLINE** ENGLISH, EDUCATION **EDUCATION** Calif State Univ, BA, 75; Univ Calif at Los Angeles, MA, 76; Univ Calif at Berkeley, EdD, 91. **CAREER** Assoc prof, Univ of Iowa, 91-. **HONORS AND AWARDS** Post0doctoral fel, Nat Acad of Educ; NCTE Promising Researcher Awd; NWCA Outstanding Scholar Awd. **MEMBERSHIPS** NCTE, AERA, NCRLL. **RESEARCH** Literacy Practices, Issues in Teachers' Professional Lives. **SELECTED PUBLICATIONS** Auth, A Kind of Passport: A Basic Writing Adjunct Program and the Challenge of Student Diversity, NCTE, 93; auth, Teaching n Common: Challenges to Joint Work in Classrooms and Schools, Teachers Col Press, 99. **CONTACT ADDRESS** Dept English, Univ Iowa, N246 Lindquist Ctr, Iowa City, IA 52242. **EMAIL** anne-dipardo@uiowa.edu

DIAMOND, ELIN
DISCIPLINE FEMINIST THEORY AND FEMINIST THEATER, AMERICAN DRAMA, EARLY MODERN DRAMA **EDUCATION** Brandeis, BA; Univ Calif, Davis, MA, PhD. **CAREER** Prof Eng, Rutgers, The State Univ NJ, Univ Col-Camden. **RESEARCH** Drama and performance; dramatic theory; critical theory. **SELECTED PUBLICATIONS** Auth, Unmaking Mimesis: Essays on Feminism and Theater; Performance and Cultural Politics; ed, Printer's Comic Play. **CONTACT ADDRESS** Dept of Lit in Eng, Rutgers, The State Univ of New Jersey, New Brunswick, Murray Hall 205B, New Brunswick, NJ 08903. **EMAIL** ediamond@rci.rutgers.edu

DIAMOND, SIGMUND
PERSONAL Born 06/14/1920, Baltimore, MD, m, 1945, 2 children **DISCIPLINE** HISTORY, SOCIOLOGY **EDUCATION** Johns Hopkins Univ, AB, 40; Harvard Univ, PhD (US hist), 53. **CAREER** Reader-coder, Off Facts and Figures, Washington, DC, 42; head radio intel unit, Bd Econ Warfare, 42-43; int rep, United Auto Workers-Cong Indust Orgn, Mich, 43-49; from asst prof to assoc prof, 55-63, Prof Sociol and Hist, Columbia Univ, 63-, Fel, Ctr Advan Studies Behav Sci, 59-60; ed, Polit Sci Quart, 63-73; sr res fel, Newberry libr, Ill, 67; vis prof, Hebrew Univ, Jerusalem, 69-70; mem panel III, comt brain sci, Nat Res Coun, 72-; Fulbright prof, Tel-Aviv Univ, 75-76; deleg, Am Coun Learned Soc, 78-80. **MEMBERSHIPS** Conf Jewish Social Studies; Inst Early Am Hist and Cult; AHA; Econ Hist Asn; Am Sociol Asn. **RESEARCH** Sixteenth and 17th century theories of human nature and social organization; comparative studies of colonization in the New World; sociology of the arts. **SELECTED PUBLICATIONS** Auth, Whos Afraid of George and Marthas Parlor, Lit Film Quart, Vol 24, 96; Mothers in the Margins--Hardy, Thomas, Lawrence,D. H., And Suffragisms Discontents, Colby Quart, Vol 32, 96; Menand Review of Hershberg Book on Conand, James,B.--A Comment, NY Rev Books, Vol 41, 94; Diamond, Sara, Womens Stud Interdisciplinary J, Vol 25, 96. **CONTACT ADDRESS** Dept of Sociol, Columbia Univ, New York, NY 10027.

DIAO, WEI
PERSONAL m, 1 child **DISCIPLINE** SOCIOLOGY **EDUCATION** Univ Toronto, PhD, 76. **HONORS AND AWARDS** Fulbright Int Studies Grant, 98. **RESEARCH** Chinese Diaspora, History of Chinese Civilization, Social Policy. **SELECTED PUBLICATIONS** Auth, Inquality v Social Policy: The Sociology of Welfare, 83; coauth, Choices and Chances: Sociology for Everyday Life, 90. **CONTACT ADDRESS** Humanities Div, No Seattle Comm Col, 9600 College Way N, Seattle, WA 98103-3514. **EMAIL** wdjao@sccd.ctc.edu

DIAZ, HECTOR L.
PERSONAL Born 02/23/1957, Juncos, Puerto Rico, m, 1993, 4 children **DISCIPLINE** SOCIOLOGY **EDUCATION** Antillean Col, BA, 78; Case Western Reserve Univ, MS, 81; Univ Ill, PhD, 95. **CAREER** Asst Prof, Atlantic Union Col, 92-94; Assoc Prof, Loma Linda Univ, 94-96; Assoc Prof, Andrews Univ, 97-. **HONORS AND AWARDS** Scholar, Nat Inst of Ment Health, 85-86; Scholar, Ill Consortium for Educ Opportunities, 90-92; Martin Luther King/Rosa Parks/Cesar Chavez Fel, 98-99. **MEMBERSHIPS** Coun on Soc Work Educ **RESEARCH** Social capital, economic development, policy studies, international social welfare. **SELECTED PUBLICATIONS** Auth, "Acculturation, Stress and Alcohol Drinking Among Puerto Ricans in the United States," in Ponencias de la III Convencion Nacional de Trabajo Social 1995 (95); auth, "Interventions Against Distress: Remedial vs. Developmental Approaches," Adventist Develop Dialog, 1 (97): 25-32. **CONTACT ADDRESS** Dept Sociol, Andrews Univ, 100 US Highway 31, Berrien Springs, MI 49104-0001. **EMAIL** hdiaz@andrews.edu

DIAZ-DUQUE, OZZIE FRANCIS
PERSONAL Born 09/17/1951, Guanajay, Cuba **DISCIPLINE** LANGUAGE EDUCATION **EDUCATION** Queens Col, City Univ New York, BA, 73; Univ Iowa, MA, 75, PhD, 80. **CAREER** Instr Span, 73-82, Asst Prof Span & Port, Univ Iowa, 82-, Med interpreter Am sign lang, Hosps & Clinics, Univ Iowa, 80-; consult & lectr, Col Nursing, Univ Iowa, 77, lectr, Col Med, 74- **HONORS AND AWARDS** Haney Medal, NY City Student Art League, 71; Sigma Delta Pi, Nat Hisp Honor Soc, 72; Magna Cum Laude, Queens Col, CUNY, 73; Outstanding Schol, Univ Iowa, 80; Certificate of Merit, Lyons Club, Iowa City, 83; Volunteer of the Year, State of Iowa Gubernatorial Awd, JCAC, 87; Certificate of Merit, Bureau of Business Practice, 89; U.S. Surgeon General's Certificate of Merit, 93; Staff Excellence Awd, Univ Iowa, 93. **MEMBERSHIPS** MLA; Am Med Writers Asn; Am Transl Asn. **RESEARCH** Foreign language teaching techniques; communication in medical settings; vocal music and literature. **SELECTED PUBLICATIONS** Auth, Manual de Transplante de Hidago, Transplant Unit, Dept Surgery, Univ Iowa Hospitals and Clinics, 96; Why don't I?, Iowa Rev, 9/96; Selections of poetry, Lambda Publ, 12/96; ed and consult, Spanish for Medical Personnel, Jarvis and Lebredo, Houghton Mifflin, 96; auth, Trauma Cerebral: Manual de informacion, Dept Neurology, Univ Iowa Hospitals and Clinics, 97; coauth, Interpreting in Health Care Settings, New Physician Mag, 2/97; Poetry and essay in Looking Queer: An Anthology, Hawthorne Press, 98; author of numerous other articles. **CONTACT ADDRESS** Dept Span & Port, Univ of Iowa, 111 Phillips Hall, Iowa City, IA 52242. **EMAIL** odduque@blue.weeg.uiowa.edu

DIAZ-LEFEBVRE, RENE
PERSONAL Born 08/19/1950, Tucson, AZ, m, 2000 **DISCIPLINE** PSYCHOLOGY **EDUCATION** Pima Col, AA, 72; Univ Redland, BA, 74; Calif State Univ, MA, 76; Union Grad School, PhD, 82. **CAREER** Counselor, Pima Col, 74-75; Asst to Dean, Johnston Col, 75-76; Director, Mt San Jacinto Col, 76-77; Counselor, Gavilan Col, 77-83; Coordinator, S Mountain Cmty Col, 84-85; Prof, Rio Salao Cmty Col, 85-91; Prof, Glendale Cmty Col, 91-. **HONORS AND AWARDS** Who's Who in the World, 95-96; Who's Who Among Am Teachers, 90, 98, 00; Who's Who in the West, 96-97; Who's Who in Am Educ, 92-93, 96-97. **RESEARCH** Intelligence; Creativity. **SELECTED PUBLICATIONS** Auth, Coloring Outside the Lines: Applying Multiple Intelligences and Creativity in Learning, John Wiley & sons, 99; auth, "I Can Never Go Back.," the forum: sharing Information On teaching and Learning, 98; co-auth, "What if They Learn differently: Applying Multiple Intelligence Theory in the Community College," Leadership Abstracts, 98; co-auth, "coloring Outside the Lines: applying the Theory of Multiple Intelligences to the community College Setting," community College Journal, 97; auth, "Unlocking the Motivation, the Desire, and the Joy to Learn," Innovation abstracts, 97; auth, "Give Them an Inch.Honors Students as Teachers," The National Honors Report, 95; auth, "Students as Psychological Consumers," Innovation Abstracts, 92; auth, "Reach Out and Touch someone: Effective Retention Strategies With the Adult Distance Learner," conference Proceeding, 92; auth, "I Just Didn't Have Enough time.Assisting the Busy Adult student Develop Critical Reading and Thinking skills," Adult Learning, 90. **CONTACT ADDRESS** Dept Psychol, Glendale Comm Col, Arizona, 6000 W Olive Ave, Glendale, AZ 85302.

DIBABA, MAMO
DISCIPLINE EDUCATION **EDUCATION** BS, MA, PhD. **CAREER** Spring Arbor Col **SELECTED PUBLICATIONS** Auth, Teaching Philosophy and Style: Theory and practice from concept to application. **CONTACT ADDRESS** Spring Arbor Col, 106 E Main St, Spring Arbor, MI 49283.

DICKEL, CHARLES TIMOTHY
PERSONAL Born 11/04/1946, Portland, OR, m, 1973, 3 children **DISCIPLINE** EDUCATION **EDUCATION** Whitman Col, BA, 68; Ind Univ, MS, 71; DEd, 73. **CAREER** Asst Prof to Prof and Dean, Creighton Univ, 76-. **HONORS AND AWARDS** Eugene Marx Awd, Whitman Col, 68; Fel, IN Univ, 69-70; Creative and Innovative Awd, N Am Asn for Summer session, Creighton Univ, 80; First Annual Dean's Awd for Excellence in Teaching, Creighton Univ, 85; Who's Who in am Educ, 89-90, 96-97; Teacher of the Year Awd, Burlington Northern Foundation, Omaha NE, 92; Outstanding Advisor Awd, Creighton Univ, 93; Alpha Phi Teacher Recognition Awd, Creighton Univ, 96; Achievement Awd for Outstanding Mission contribution, Creighton Univ, 96; Fel, U.S. West Acad Dev and Technol Ctr, Creighton Univ, 97-98; William f. Kelley Achievement Awd for Outstanding Contribution, Creighton Univ, 98, 99. **MEMBERSHIPS** Am Coun Asn; Asn for Adult Dev and Aging; Asn for Coun Educ and Supervision; Asn for Supervision and Curriculum Dev; NE Asn for Coun Educ and Supervision; NE Coun Asn; Nat Catholic Educ Asn. **RESEARCH** Adult development; Teaching effectiveness; Impact of poverty on human development; Prevention in creating mental health; **SELECTED PUBLICATIONS** Auth, Primary prevention for counselors and teachers 2nd ed, Omaha, 95; auth, "A Tribute to 'Mrs. Keyser'," Nebraska Library Asn Quarterly, 95): 18-21; co-auth, "Unity: Developing relationships between school and community counselors," The Professional School Counselor, (98): 95-102; auth, "Why Creighton?," Update: University College, (98): 1-2; co-auth, "School counseling and referrals: A negotiated beginning," The Texas Asn for Counseling and development Journal, (99): 44-51; auth, "A word from the Dean," Update: University College, (99): 1-2; auth, "Who am I? What am I about? And Where am I going?," Update: University College, (99): 1-2; auth, "A meaning-filled work life," Update: University College, (00): 1-2. **CONTACT ADDRESS** Dept Educ, Creighton Univ, 2500 California Plaza, Omaha, NE 68178-0001. **EMAIL** ctdickel@creighton.edu

DICKERSON, JOYCE
PERSONAL Born 02/04/1951, AL, m, 1992, 3 children **DISCIPLINE** SOCIOLOGY **EDUCATION** Tuskegee Univ, BS, 72; Univ Ala, MS, 74; PhD, 85. **CAREER** Asst Prof, Grambling St Univ, 92-93; Vis Prof, Fla A&M Univ, 93-95; Asst Prof, NC A&T St Univ, 95-. **HONORS AND AWARDS** Kappa Delta Pi, 81; Who's Who Among Human Serv Professionals, 92; Outstanding Serv Awd, Fla A&M Univ, 95; Grants, U S Dept Health and Human Serv, 98; Outstanding Leadership Awd, NC A&T St Univ, 98. **MEMBERSHIPS** CSWE, ACSW, ASBSWE, YFG. **RESEARCH** Family violence, community and school violence and cross-cultural social work practice. **SELECTED PUBLICATIONS** Auth, Crime Rates at Selected HBCUs: A Male Incentive Curriculum Model, NCRTL (Lansing, MI), 97; auth, Domestic Violence Database: A Resource Manual, NC A&T St Univ Pr (Greensboro, NC), 98; auth, Domestic Violence Training Curriculum Manual, NC A&T St Univ Pr (Greensboro, NC), 98; auth, "Margaret Murray Washington: Rural Woman Organizer," in African-Am Leadership in Soc Welfare Hist: An Empowerment Tradition, NASW Pr (forthcoming). **CONTACT ADDRESS** Dept Sociol, No Carolina Agr and Tech State Univ, 201 Gibbs, Greensboro, NC 27411. **EMAIL** dickersj@ncat.edu

DIEM, RICHARD A.
PERSONAL Born Kansas City, MO, m, 2 children **DISCIPLINE** EDUCATION **EDUCATION** Bradley Univ, BS; S Ill Univ, MS; Colo State Univ, MA; Northwestern Univ, PhD. **CAREER** Clinical Prof, N Ill Univ, 74-75; Asst Prof, Univ Tex, 75-81; Distinguished Visiting Lecturer, Tex Women's Univ, 82-83; Sen Fulbright Res, Escola Superior de Educaco de Viseu Portugal, 83-84; Assoc Prof to Prof, Univ Tex, 81-. **HONORS AND AWARDS** Kezai Koho Japan Foundation Fel; Korea Foundation Fel; Fulbright Sen Lecturer Res Awd, Portugal; Fulbright Sen Lecturer Res Awd, Korea; Nat Sci Foundation Fel; Nat Coun for the Soc Studies Outstanding Trade Book Awd. **MEMBERSHIPS** Nat Coun for the Soc Studies; Am Educ Res Asn; SW Educ Res Asn; Am Asn for Urban Educ. **RESEARCH** Educational applications of technology; Ethnographic research methodology; Educational policy; social studies education; Secondary education. **SELECTED PUBLICATIONS** Auth, Using Computers as a Resource, Franklin and Watts, 83; auth, Computers in Schools: A Guide to Research, Garland Pub, 88; auth, Technology and Teacher Education, Austin, 98; auth, "Information Technology and Civic Education," in Technology and Social Studies - Issues and Applications, SUNY Press, 97; auth, "Microcomputer Technology in Educational Environments: Three Case Studies," Journal of Educational Research, 86; auth, "Student/Teacher Reactions to a Technology Based Learning Intervention Within School Environments," The High School Journal, 95; auth, "Technology and Measures of Self-Esteem in Secondary Students Identified as a At-Risk," Journal of At-Risk Issues, 98; auth, "Technology and Elementary Social Studies: Possibilities, Prospects, Realities," Social Studies and the Young Learner, 99. **CONTACT ADDRESS** Dept Educ, Univ of Texas, San Antonio, 6900 N Loop 1604 W, San Antonio, TX 78249. **EMAIL** rdiem@utsa.edu

DIETLER, MICHAEL
PERSONAL Born 03/19/1952, Washington, DC, m, 1985 **DISCIPLINE** ANTHROPOLOGY **EDUCATION** Stanford Univ, AB, 74; Univ Calif Berkeley, MA, 76, PhD, 90. **CAREER** Asst to assoc prof, Yale Univ, 90-95; assoc prof, Univ Chicago, 95-. **MEMBERSHIPS** Amer Athrop Asn; Soc for Amer Archaeol; Europ Asn of Archaeol; Soc Prehist Fr. **RESEARCH** Archaeology of Europe (Celtic iron age); Colonialism; Material culture; Ethnoarchaeology. **SELECTED PUBLICATIONS** Auth, A tale of three sites: the monumentalization of Celtic oppida and the politics of collective memory and identity, World Archaeol, 30, 72-89, 98; Consumption, agency and cultural entanglement: theoretical implications of a Meditteranean colonial encounter, Studies in Culture Contact: Interaction, Culture Change, and Archaeology, pp 288-315, Carbondale, Univ Southern Ill Press, 98; co-auth, Habitus, techniques, style: an integrated approach to the social understanding of material culture and boundaries, The Archaeology of Social Boundaries, pp 232-263, Wash, DC, Smithsonian, 98; auth, The Iron Age in Meditterranean France: colonial encounters, entanglements, and transformations, Jour of World Prehist, 11, 269-357, 97; L'art du vin chez les Gaulois, Pour la Sci, 237, 68-74, 97; Archaeology, Encycl of Soc and Cult Anthrop, pp 45-51, London, Routledge, 96; auth, Feasts and commensal politics in the political economy: food, power, and status in prehistoric Europe, Food and the Status Quest: An Interdisciplinary Perspective, pp 87-125, Oxford, Berghahn Publ, 96; auth, Early Celtic socio-political relations: ideological representation and social competition in dynamic comparative perspective, Celtic Chiefdom, Celtic State: The Evolution of Complex Social Systems in Prehistoric Europe, pp 64-71, Cambridge, Cambridge Univ Press, 95; auth, The cup of Gyptis: rethinking the colonial encounter in Early Iron Age Western Europe and the relevance of world-systems models, Jour of Europ Archaeol, 3, 2, 89-111, 95; co-auth, Habitus et reproduction sociale des techniques: l'intelligence due style en archeologie et en ethnoarcheologie, De la prehistoire aux missiles balistiques: l'Intelligence sociale des techniques, pp 202-227, Paris, La Decouverte, 94; co-auth, Ceramics and ethnic identity: ethnoarchaeological observations on the distribution of pottery styles and the relationship between the social contexts of production and consumption, Terre cuite et societe: la ceramique, document technique, economique, culturel, XIVe Rencontre Internationale d'Archaeologie et d'Historoire d'Antibes, pp 459-472, Juan-les-Pins, Editions APDCA, 94; auth, Our ancestors the Gauls: archaeology, ethnic nationalism, and the manipulation of Celtic identity in modern Europe, Amer Anthrop, 96, 584-605, 94; auth, Quenching Celtic thirst, Archaeol, 47, 3, 44-48, 94. **CONTACT ADDRESS** Dept. of Anthropology, Univ of Chicago, 1126 E. 59th St., Chicago, IL 60637. **EMAIL** mdietler@anthro.spc.uchicago.edu

DIETZ, THOMAS
PERSONAL Born 08/17/1949, Kent, OH, m, 1991, 2 children **DISCIPLINE** SOCIOLOGY **EDUCATION** Kent State Univ, BGA, 72; Univ Calif, PhD, 79. **CAREER** Prof, George Mason Univ. **HONORS AND AWARDS** Fel, Am Asn for the Adv of Sci; Distinguished Contribution Awd, Am Sociol Asn. **MEMBERSHIPS** Soc for Human Ecology. **RESEARCH** Human Ecology; Human Dimensions of Global Change; Environmental values and valuation; Cultural evolution. **SELECTED PUBLICATIONS** Co-ed, Environmentally significant Consumption: Research directions, Nat Acad Press, 97; co-ed, Human Ecology: Crossing Boundaries, Soc for Human Ecology, 93; co-auth, The Risk Professionals, Russell Sage foundation, 87; co-ed, Handbook for Environmental Planning: The Social Consequences of Environmental Change, Wiley-Interscience, 77; co-auth, "Climate Change and Society: Speculation, Construction and Scientific Investigation," International Sociology, (98): 421-455; co-auth, "Science, Values and Biodiversity," BioScience, (98): 441-444; co-auth, "Effects of Population and affluence on CO2 Emissions," Proceedings of the National Academy of Science, (97): 175-179; co-auth, "Toward a Theory of Choice: Socially embedded Preference Construction," Journal of Socio-Economics, (95): 261-279. **CONTACT ADDRESS** Dept Sociol & Anthrop, George Mason Univ, Fairfax, 4400 Univ Dr, Fairfax, VA 22030. **EMAIL** tdietz@gmu.edu

DIGGS, WILLIAM P.
PERSONAL Born 10/19/1926, Columbia, SC, m **DISCIPLINE** SOCIOLOGY **EDUCATION** Friendship Jr Coll Rock Hill SC, 1943; Morehouse College, AB 1949; Atlanta U, MA 1951; Colgate-Rochester Div Sch, BD 1955; MDiv 1972. **CAREER** Friendship Jr Coll, Rock Hill SC, instructor 50-52; Friendship Jr Coll, instructor Sociology 55-61; Galilee Baptist Church, York SC, pastor 55-62; Second Baptist Church, Leroy NY, student pastor 54-55; Benedict Coll, Columbia SC, asst prof Sociology 64-74; Trinity Baptist Church, Florence SC & Morris Coll, Sumter SC, minister, asst prof Sociology. **HONORS AND AWARDS** Valedictorian HS class; honorary DD Friendship Jr Coll 1973; Honorary LHD Morris Coll 1973; hon-

ored by Trinity Bapt Ch Florence; recognition of dedicated service ch & community 1969; honored Zeta Phi Beta Sorority Inc; Florence outstanding leadership civic econ comm involvement 1971; citz of the yr Chi Iota Chap Omega Psi Phi Frat 1976; outst achvmt & serv Omega Psi Phi Frat 1976. **MEMBERSHIPS** Am Assn of Univ Prof; Alpha Kappa Delta Honorary Sociological Soc; pres Florence Br NAACP 1970-74; life mem NAACP; mem Community Relations Com Relations Florence, SC; chmn Community Action Agency Florence Co; mem Area Manpower Bd; mem Florence Co Bd of Health; mem trustee bd Friendship Jr Coll; mem trustee bd Morrisl Coll. **CONTACT ADDRESS** 124 W Darlington St, Florence, SC 29501.

DIGIACOMO, SUSAN
PERSONAL Born 05/24/1951, MA, m, 1985 **DISCIPLINE** ANTHROPOLOGY **EDUCATION** Univ Mass, BA, 73; MA, 76; PhD, 85 **CAREER** Adj Prof, Univ Mass; Vis Asst Prof, Middlebury Co. **HONORS AND AWARDS** Res Fel, Spanish Ministry of Educ & Sci, 93; Res Fel, Harvard Med School, 88-90; Fulbright Res Grant, 87; Travel Grant, Nat Sci Foundation, 81; Stipend, European Studies Prog, Univ Mass, 77. **RESEARCH** Spain; Nationalism in Catalonia; Cultural studies of medicine **SELECTED PUBLICATIONS** Auth," Language Ideological Debates in an Olympic City: Barcelona, 1992-1996," in Language Ideological Debates: Studies in Linguistic Historiography, 99; aut, "Catalan is Everyone's Thing: Normalizing a Nation," in Language, Ethnicity and the State: Regional and Minority Languages in Europe, St Martins Press, forthcoming; auth, "Catalonia: A Nation Without a State," in Endangered Peoples: Europe, Greenwood Pub, forthcoming; auth, "Becoming Real: Illness and/as the Making of an Anthropologist," in The Wounded Ethnographer: Illness and Disability as Sources of Professional Creativity, Gordon and Breach Pub, forthcoming; auth, "Spaniard," in American Immigrant Cultures: Builders of a Nation, Simon & Schuster, 97; auth, "Metaphor als Krankheit, Postmoderne Dilemmata in der Reprasentation von Korper, Geist und Krankheit," in Anatomien medizinischen Wissens, Fisher Taschenbuch, 96; auth, "Can There be a Cultural Epidmiology?," Medical Anthropology Quarterly, (99): 436-457; auth, "The New Internal Colonialism" International Journal of Qualitative Studies in Education, (99): 263-268; auth, "Homage from Catalonia," The Volunteer: Journal of the Veterans of the Abraham Lincoln Brigade, (98): 6-8; **CONTACT ADDRESS** Dept Sociol & Anthropol, Middlebury Col, Middlebury, VT 05753. **EMAIL** sdigiaco@middlebury.edu

DIL, NASIM
DISCIPLINE SPECIAL EDUCATION; EARLY CHILDHOOD SPECIAL EDUCATION **EDUCATION** Univ Peshawar, BA, 54; Univ Punjab, Pakistan, MA, 57; Ind Univ, Bloomington, MS, 69, PhD, 71. **CAREER** Prof, Univ Nev, Las Vegas, 77. **HONORS AND AWARDS** Distinguished Service Awd, Teacher Education Division of the Council for Exceptional Children, 99. **MEMBERSHIPS** CEC, AERA, ATE, AACP-DM, PLT, CPREA. **SELECTED PUBLICATIONS** Auth, Nonverbal communication in young children, Topics in Early Childhood Spec Educ, 4, 84; coauth, Improvement in arithmetic self-concept through combined positive reinforcement, peer interaction, and sequential curriculum, J of Sch Psychol, 9, 71; Available special education faculty positions in higher education, J of Tchr Educ and Spec Educ, 16, 93; Co-auth, Effective Personal Preparation Strategies for Specialized Education, SSEPC Monograph, Vol II, (97). **CONTACT ADDRESS** Dept of Spec Educ, Univ of Nevada, Las Vegas, 4505 Maryland Pky, Las Vegas, NV 89154-3014. **EMAIL** dil@ccmail.nevada.edu

DILLON, MICHELE
PERSONAL Born 09/13/1960, Ireland, m, 1989, 2 children **DISCIPLINE** SOCIOLOGY **EDUCATION** Univ Col, Dublin, B, 80, M, 83; Univ Calif, Berkeley, PhD, 89. **CAREER** Assoc prof, Yale Univ, 93-. **HONORS AND AWARDS** Book rev ed, J for the Sci Study of Rel; ed bd, Sociol Theory. **MEMBERSHIPS** Am Sociol Asn, Soc for the Sci Study of Rel. **RESEARCH** Culture, religion, Catholicism. **SELECTED PUBLICATIONS** Auth, Debating Divorce: Moral Conflict in Ireland, Lexington: Univ Press of Ky (93); auth, "Cultural Differences in the Abortion Discourse of the Catholic Church: Evidence from Four Countries," Sociol of Rel, 57: 25-36 (96); auth, "Divorce and Cultural Rationality," in M. Peillon and E. Slater, eds, Encounters with Modern Ireland, Dublin: Inst of Public Admin (97); auth, "Rome and American Catholics," The ANNALS of the Am Acad of Political and Soc Sci, vol 558 (July 98); auth, "The Catholic Church and Possible 'Organizational-Selves': The Implications for Institutional Change," J for the Sci Study of Relig, 38: 386-397 (99); auth, "The Authority of the Holy Revisited: Habermas, Religion, and Emancipatory Possibilities," Sociol Theory, 17: 290-306 (99); auth, "Catholic Identity: Balancing Reason, Faith, and Power, NY: Cambridge Univ Press (99); auth, entries on "The Vatican," "Encyclical," "Sacraments," "Annulment," "Relic," "Afterlife," in Wade Clark Roof, ed, The Encyclopedia of Contemporary American Religion, NY: Macmillan Ref (2000); auth, "Pierre Bourdieu, Religion, and Misrecognition," Cultural Studies: An Annual Rev (under review); coauth with Paul Wink, "Religious involvement and health outcomes in late adulthood: Findings from a longitudinal study," in T. Plante & A. Sherman, eds, Faith and Health, NY: Guilford (in press). **CONTACT ADDRESS** Dept Sociol, Yale Univ, PO Box 208265, New Haven, CT 06520. **EMAIL** michele.dillon@yale.edu

DILLON, WILTON STERLING
PERSONAL Born 07/13/1923, Yale, OK, m, 1956, 1 child **DISCIPLINE** ANTHROPOLOGY **EDUCATION** BA, Univ of Calif, Berkeley, 51; PhD, Columbia Univ NYork, 61; Post Graduate Studies, Univ of Paris and Univ of Leyden, 51-52. **CAREER** Info Spec, Civil Info and Edu Sec Supreme Comdr Allied Powers, Tokyo, 46-48; Lectr on Hum Sci, Hobart and William Smith Col Geneva, NY, 53-54; Letcr in Japanese Studies, Fordham Univ, MY, 54; Dir of Clearinghouse for Res in Hum Org, Soc for Applied Anthro, 63; Staff Dir Sci Org Devel Bd Natl Acad of Sci, Washington, DC, 63069; Dir of Symposia and Seminars and Intersisciplinary Studies, Smithsonian Inst, 69-. **HONORS AND AWARDS** Grant Found Res award for field work in Fance, 56; Ford Found award for field work in West Africa, 58; Excellence Awd OK Baptist Univ, 89; Acheivement Awd Am for Indian Opportunity, 90; Presidential Scholar Univ Alabama, Tuscaloosa. **MEMBERSHIPS** Soc for Applied Anthro; Am Anthro Assoc; Am Assoc for the Advan Of Sci; Inst for Psychiatry and Foreign Affairs; Inst for Intercultural Studies; Lit Soc of Wash; Inst for Current World Affairs. **RESEARCH** Sci diplomacy; cross-cultural commun; gift exchange; Anthro of Knowledge; Kinship and Soc; Hist of Anthro. **SELECTED PUBLICATIONS** Gifts and Nations: The Obligation to Give, Receive and Repay, The Hague and Paris: Mouton 68; The Cultural Drama: Modern Identities and Social Ferment, Dillon, Wilton S ed, Wash; Smithsonian Institution Press, 74; The Statue of Liberty Revisited: Making A Universal Symbol, Dillon, Wilton S and Kotler, Neil G, eds, Wash: Smithsonian Institution Press, 93; Margaret Mead and Government: American Anthropologist vol 82 No 2, 80; The Flow of Ideas Between Africa and America: Bulletin of the Atomic Scientists, 66; Margaret Mead: President-Elect, 74. Science. **CONTACT ADDRESS** Smithsonian Inst, Washington, DC 20560. **EMAIL** mcelroym@op.si.edu

DILLY, BARBARA J.
PERSONAL Born 07/30/1949, Charles City, IA, s **DISCIPLINE** ANTHROPOLOGY **EDUCATION** Univ Calif at Los Angeles, BA, 88; Univ Calif at Irvine, PhD, 94. **CAREER** Adj prof, Univ Northern Iowa, 98-00. **HONORS AND AWARDS** Environmental Educator of the Year Awd, Iowa Sierra Club, 97. **MEMBERSHIPS** Am Anthrop Asn, Asn for Applied Anthrop, Am Folklore Soc. **RESEARCH** Food Production, Rural Communities, Agriculture & Religion, Rural Gender Roles, Applied Anthropology, Rural Folklore. **SELECTED PUBLICATIONS** Auth, "The Globalization of Environmentalism: Eco-Tourism, Economic Development and Cultural Preservation in the Guyanese Rainforest," in Globalization and the Rural Poor in America, ed. William M. Loker (CO: Lynne Rienner Pub, 99). **CONTACT ADDRESS** Dept Sociol & Anthrop, Univ of No Iowa, Cedar Falls, IA 50614-0001. **EMAIL** dilly@uni.edu

DIMOND, ROBERTA R.
PERSONAL Born 03/25/1940, Bakersfield, CA, m, 1970, 3 children **DISCIPLINE** SPORT PSYCHOLOGY **EDUCATION** Stanford Univ, AB, 62; MA; Univ of Pa, MS; EdD. **CAREER** Lectr, Temple Univ; prof, Del Valley Col. **HONORS AND AWARDS** Newhouse Found Scholar; Nat Teachers Awd. **MEMBERSHIPS** AAUP; Am Psychol Assoc; USTA; MADD; WWF; Alpha Sigma Chi; Phi Kappa Sigma. **RESEARCH** Sport psychology. **SELECTED PUBLICATIONS** Auth, Racial and Gender Bias in Vocational Counseling; auth, Sports Motivational Cues; auth, Dream Interpretations. **CONTACT ADDRESS** Dept Lib Arts, Delaware Valley Col, 700 E Butler Ave, Doylestown, PA 18901.

DINNERSTEIN, MYRA
PERSONAL Born 04/19/1934, Philadelphia, PA, m, 1961, 2 children **DISCIPLINE** WOMEN'S STUDIES **EDUCATION** Univ Pa, AB, 56; Columbia Univ, MA, 63, PhD (hist), 71. **CAREER** Lectr hist, Univ Ariz, 71-74, Chariperson Women's Studies, Univ Ariz, 75-, Consult, Nat Endowment for Humanities and Fund for Improvement of Postsecondary Educ, 79-, Nat Rev Bd, Project on Women in the Curric, Mont State Univ, 81-, Pres, Nat Adv Bd, New Dir Young Women, 81-. **MEMBERSHIPS** AHA; Nat Women's Studies Asn. **RESEARCH** American women's history. **SELECTED PUBLICATIONS** Auth, The Overworked American--The Unexpected Decline of Leisure, J Am Hist, Vol 79, 93. **CONTACT ADDRESS** Univ of Arizona, 1 University of AZ, Tucson, AZ 85721-0001. **EMAIL** myrad@u.arizona.edu

DIRENZO, GORDON JAMES
PERSONAL Born 07/19/1934, North Attleboro, MA, m, 1968, 3 children **DISCIPLINE** SOCIOLOGY **EDUCATION** Univ Notre Dame, BA, 56, AM, 57, PhD, 63. **CAREER** Instr, Univ Portland, 61-62; asst prof of sociology, Fairfield Univ, 62-66; assoc prof of sociology, 66-70; Univ Del, Prof of Sociology, 70-. **HONORS AND AWARDS** Fulbright-Hays Prof of Sociology, Univ Rome, 68-69, Univ Bologna, 80-81. **MEMBERSHIPS** Am Sociol Asn; Am Psychol Asn. **RESEARCH** Interaction of personality systems and social systems. **SELECTED PUBLICATIONS** Auth, Personality and Society, Simon & Shuster, 98; The Social Individual, Ginn Press, 96; Human Social Behavior, Hold, Rinehart & Winston, 90; We, the People: American Character and Social Change, Greenwood Press, 77; Personality and Politics, Doubleday and Company, 74; Personality, Power and Politics, Univ of Notre Dame Press, 67; Concepts, Theory and Explanation in the Behavioral Sciences, Random House, 66. **CONTACT ADDRESS** Dept of Sociology, Univ of Delaware, Newark, DE 19716. **EMAIL** gdirenzo@udel.edu

DITTES, JAMES EDWARD
PERSONAL Born 12/26/1926, Cleveland, OH, m, 1948, 4 children **DISCIPLINE** PSYCHOLOGY OF RELIGION **EDUCATION** Oberlin Col, BA, 49; Yale Univ, BD, 54, MS, 55, PhD(psychol), 58. **CAREER** Instr sci, Am Sch, Turkey, 50-52; from instr to assoc prof relig, 55-67, prof psychol relig, Yale Univ, 67-, chm dept relig studies, 75-82; ed, J Sci Studies Relig, 66-71. **HONORS AND AWARDS** Guggenheim fel, 65-66; Fulbright res fel, Rome, 65-66; Nat Endowment for Humanities sr fel, 72-73. **MEMBERSHIPS** Soc Sci Studies Relig (pres, 72-73); Am Acad Relig. **RESEARCH** Motivation and vocational dilemmas of clergymen; development and decay of self-transcending commitments; continuity between biography and theology of major religious figures. **SELECTED PUBLICATIONS** Coauth, Psychological Studies of Clergymen, Nelson, 65; auth, The Church in the Way, Scribners, 67; Psychology of Religion, In: Handbook of Social Psychology, Addison-Wesley, 69; Minister on the Spot, United Church, 70; Bias and the Pious, Augsburg, 73; Beyond William James, In: Beyond the Classics, Harper, 73; The Investigator as an Instrument of Investigation, In: Encounter With Erikson, Scholars, 77; When People Say No, Harper, 79; The Male Predicament, Harper, 85; Driven by Hope, Westminster John Knox, 96; Men At Work, Westminster John Knox, 96; Pastoral Counseling, Westminster John Knox, 99; auth, Re-Calling Ministry, Choice, 99. **CONTACT ADDRESS** Dept of Religious Studies, Yale Univ, PO Box 208287, New Haven, CT 06520-8287. **EMAIL** james.dittes@yale.edu

DIZARD, JAN
PERSONAL Born 09/04/1940, Duluth, MN, m, 1963, 2 children **DISCIPLINE** SOCIOLOGY **EDUCATION** Univ Minn, BA, 62; Univ Chicago, MA, 63; PhD, 67. **CAREER** Instr, Univ Chicago; asst prof, Univ Calif Berkeley, 65-69; asst prof to prof, Amherst Col, 69-. **MEMBERSHIPS** Am Sociol Asn. **RESEARCH** The family; Environmental sociology; Sociology of conflict and conflict resolution. **SELECTED PUBLICATIONS** Co-auth, The Minimal Family, Univ Mass Press, 90; co-ed, Guns in America: A Reader, NY Univ Press, 99; auth, Going Wild: Hunting, Animal Rights and the Contested Meaning of Nature, Univ Mass Press, 99; auth Mortal Stakes: The Fate of Hunting in Modern Society, Univ Mass Press, (forthcoming). **CONTACT ADDRESS** Dept Anthropol and Sociol, Amherst Col, 205 Morgan Hall, PO Box 2226, Amherst, MA 01002-5000. **EMAIL** jedizard@amherst.edu

DOAN, JAMES E.
PERSONAL Born 04/11/1953, Palo Alto, CA **DISCIPLINE** FOLKLORE, CELTIC STUDIES, MEDIEVAL LITERATURE **EDUCATION** Univ Calif, BA, 75; MA, 77; Harvard Univ, MA, 78; PhD, 81. **CAREER** Assoc prof, dean, Chamberlayne Jr. Col, 81-88; prof, Nova Southeastern Univ, 88-. **HONORS AND AWARDS** NEH, 84; British Coun, 93, 96; Nova Southeastern Univ Fac Awd, 01. **MEMBERSHIPS** MLA, Am Conf for Irish Studies, Int Assoc for the Study of Irish Lit. **RESEARCH** Folklore, Celtic Studies, Medieval Literature, Irish-American Studies. **SELECTED PUBLICATIONS** Auth, The Romance of Cearbhall and Fearbhlaidh, Dolmen Pr, 85; auth, Women and Goddesses in Early Celtic History, Myth and Legend, Northeastern Univ, 87; auth, Cearbhall O Dalaigh: An Irish Poet in Romance and Oral Tradition, Garland Pr, 90; auth, Early Celtic, Irish and Mediterranean Connections, Tema, Cagliari, Italy, 96; auth, The Otherworld Journey: A Celtic and Universal Theme, Princess Grace Libr, Monaco, 98; auth, "How the Irish and Scots Became Indians: Colonial Traders and Agents and the Southeastern Tribes," New Hibernia Rev, (99); auth, "The Voyage of St Brendan: Otherworld Tale, Christian Apologia or Medieval Travelog?" ABEI Jour, (00); auth, "Revisiting the Blasket Island Memoirs," Irish Studies Rev, (00); coauth, "Reverine Crossings: Gender, Identity and the Reconstruction of National Mythic Narrative in the Crying Game," Cult Studies, (01). **CONTACT ADDRESS** Dept Lib Arts, Nova Southeastern Univ, Fort Lauderdale, 3301 College Ave, Ft Lauderdale, FL 33314. **EMAIL** doan@nova.edu

DOAN, LAURA L.
PERSONAL Born 07/16/1951, San Diego, CA **DISCIPLINE** ENGLISH, WOMEN'S STUDIES **EDUCATION** Univ San Diego, BA, 73; San Francisco State Univ, MA, 75; Univ Chicago, PhD, 83. **CAREER** Asst prof, Stetson Univ, 83-89; prof, SUNY Geneseo, 89-. **HONORS AND AWARDS** NEH Fel, 97-98; Robert W MacVittie Supported Prof, 99-02. **MEMBERSHIPS** MLA, N Am Conf on Brit Studies. **RESEARCH** Lesbian and Gay Studies, History of Sexuality, Modern/Contemporary British Literature and Culture. **SELECTED PUBLICATIONS** Ed, Old Maids to Radical Spinsters: Unmarried Women in the Twentieth-Century Novel, Univ of Ill Pr, 91; ed, The Lesbian Postmodern, Columbia Univ Pr, 94; coed, Sexology in Culture: Labelling Bodies and Desires, Univ Chicago Pr, 98; coed, Sexology Uncensored: The Documents of Sexual

Science, Univ Chicago Pr, 98; coed, Palatable Poison: Critical Perspectives on the Well of Loneliness, Columbia Univ Pr, 01; auth, Fashioning Sapphism: The Origins of a Modern English Lesbian Culture, Columbia Univ Pr, 01. **CONTACT ADDRESS** Dept English, SUNY, Col at Geneseo, Geneseo, NY 14454. **EMAIL** doan@geneseo.edu

DOBRIN, ARTHUR
PERSONAL Born 08/22/1943, Brooklyn, NY, m, 1964, 3 children **DISCIPLINE** SOCIOLOGY **EDUCATION** City Col NY, BA, 65; NY Univ, MA, 71; Adelphi Univ, (DSW)PhD, 88. **CAREER** Prof, Hofstra Univ, 98-. **RESEARCH** Moral development, Kenyan women writers. **SELECTED PUBLICATIONS** Auth, "The Role of Agrarian Cooperatives in the Development of Kenya," Studies in Comparative Int Develop, (Rutgers Univ: Sage Publ, 70); auth, Salted with Fire, Oxford Univ Pr (Nairobi, Kenya, Africa), 90; auth, Malaika, the Jomo Kenyatta Foundation (Nairobi, Kenya, Africa), 98; auth, Ethical People and How They Get To Be That Way, Ethica Pr, 98; auth, After Uhuru: Kenya Stories, Cross-Cult Commun, 98; auth, Tea in a Blue Cup, Cross-Cult Commun, 99; auth, 40 Things You Can Do To Raise a Moral Child, Penguin/Putnam (forthcoming). **CONTACT ADDRESS** Sch Univ Studies and New Col, Hofstra Univ, 1000 Fulton Ave, Hempstead, NY 11550-1030.

DOLAN, RONALD
PERSONAL Born 10/19/1939, Hammond, IN, m, 1969, 2 children **DISCIPLINE** SOCIAL WORK **EDUCATION** West Kentucky State Univ, BA, 66; Univ Denver, MSW, 69; Ball State Univ, Ed D, 78. **CAREER** Prof, Ball State Univ, 71-. **HONORS AND AWARDS** Lilly Open Fel; Sagamore Wabash Awd, 96; Kirkpatrick Achiev Awd; Appt Alt Del, White House Conf Aging, 95. **MEMBERSHIPS** NASW; NCPEA; AATH; ASA. **RESEARCH** Domestic violence; elderly. **SELECTED PUBLICATIONS** Coauth, "Area agencies on aging and the prevention of elder abuse: The results of a national study," J Elder Abuse and Neglect 3 (91): 21-40; coauth, "The relative contributions of occupational groups in the discovery and treatment of elder abuse and neglect," J Gerontol Soc Work 17 (91): 183-199; coauth, "Improving the physicians to elder abuse and neglect: Contributions of a model program," Gerontol Soc Work 19 (93): 35-47; coauth, "A test of public reactions to alleged abuse," J Elder Abuse and Neglect, 9 (98): 42-65; rev, "The dimensions of elder abuse: perspectives for practitioners," J Elder Abuse and Neglect 1O (99): 172-174; auth, "Adult protective service investigators: Indiana's response to endangered adults," Victimization Elderly and Disabled 2 (99): 38-44. **CONTACT ADDRESS** Dept Social Work, Ball State Univ, 2000W University, Muncie, IN 473306-0002. **EMAIL** rdolon@bsu.edu

DOLON, RONALD
PERSONAL Born 10/19/1939, Hammond, IN, m, 2 children **DISCIPLINE** SOCIAL WORK **EDUCATION** W Ky State Univ, BA, 66; Univ Denver, MSW, 69; Ball State Univ, EdD, 78. **CAREER** Soc worker, Ind, 65-71; asst prof to prof, Ball State Univ, 71-. **HONORS AND AWARDS** Social Worker of the Year Award, Nat Asn of Social Workers, 00; Sagamore of the Wabash, 96; Kirkpatrick Achievement Award, Kirkpatrick Memorial Conf on Aging Muncie Ind, 96; Lilly Endowment Fac Open Fel, 87-88; We-ness Award, Ball State Univ, 86; Nominee, Outstanding Teacher Award, 86-87. **MEMBERSHIPS** Nat Asn of Soc Workers; Nat Committee for the Prevention of Elder Abuse. **RESEARCH** Older Battered Women; Elder Abuse and Neglect; Caregiver Stress; Humor as Stress Management. **SELECTED PUBLICATIONS** Co-auth, "Breaking the cycle of family violence: Services for children in shelters for battered women," Free Inquiry in Creative Sociology, (91): 31-36; co-auth, "Area agencies on aging and the prevention of elder abuse: The results of a national study," J of Elder Abuse and Neglect, (91): 21-40; co-auth, "The relative contributions of occupational groups in the discovery and treatment of elder abuse and neglect," J Geronotol Soc Work, (91): 183-199; co-auth, "Elder mistreatment," in Crisis Intervention in Criminal Justice and Social Services, (Springfield, 91), 113-146; co-auth, "Improving the responses of physicians to elder abuse and neglect: Contributions of a model program," J Gerontol Soc Work, (93): 35-47; co-auth, "A test of public reactions to alleged abuse," J Elder Abuse and Neglect, (98): 42-65; auth, "Adult protective service investigators: Indiana's response to endangered adults," Victimization of the Elderly and Disabled, (99): 38-44; co-auth, "Perceptions of adult protective service workers of the support provided by criminal justice professions in cases of elder abuse," J Elder Abuse and Neglect, (00): 71-94. **CONTACT ADDRESS** Dept Soc Work, Ball State Univ, North Quad 112, Muncie, IN 47306. **EMAIL** rdolon@gw.bsu.edu

DOMINOWSKI, ROGER L.
PERSONAL Born 02/21/1939, Chicago, IL, m, 1984, 4 children **DISCIPLINE** PSYCHOLOGY **EDUCATION** DePaul Univ, BA, 60, MA, 63; Northwestern Univ, PhD, 65. **CAREER** Instr, Asst Prof, DePaul Univ, 62-66; Asst Prof, Prof, Univ Ill at Chicago, 66-. **HONORS AND AWARDS** Postdoctoral Res Fellow, Univ Aberdeen, Scotland, 72-73; Excellence in Tchng Awd, Univ Ill at Chicago, 98. **MEMBERSHIPS** Am Psychol Soc; Brit Psychol Soc; Sigma Xi; Psychonomic Soc. **RE-**

SEARCH Psychology of problem solving, reasoning, & creativity; teaching processes. **SELECTED PUBLICATIONS** Co-auth, History of research on thinking and problem solving, Thinking and Problem Solving: Handbook of Cognition and Perception, 2nd ed, Acad Press, 1-35, 94; co-auth, Insight and problem solving, The nature of Insight, MIT Press, 31-62, 95; auth, Productive problem solving, The creative cognition approach, MIT Press, 73-96, 95; co-auth, Metacognition and problem solving: A process oriented approach, J of Experimental Psychol: Learning, Memory, & Cognition, 21, 205-223, 95; auth, Verbalization and problem solving, Metacognition in educational theory and practice, 98. **CONTACT ADDRESS** Dept of Psychol, m/c 285, Univ of Illinois, Chicago, 1007 W Harrison St, Chicago, IL 60617. **EMAIL** rdomin@uic.edu

DONADEY, ANNE
DISCIPLINE FRENCH, WOMEN'S STUDIES **EDUCATION** Universite de Nice, France, BA, 84; MA, 85; Northwestern Univ, PhD, 93. **CAREER** Lectr, Univ Tex Austin, 85-87; TA, Northwestern Univ, 88-93; asst to assoc prof, Univ Iowa, 93-01; assoc prof, San Diego State Univ, 01-. **HONORS AND AWARDS** Diss Recognition Awd, Northwestern Univ, 91; Awd, Iowa Cult Affairs Coun, 95-96; Awd, Obermann Ctr for Adv Studies Humanities Symposium Awd, 95-96; Who's Who in the Midwest, 96, 98-99. **MEMBERSHIPS** African Lit Assoc, AAUW, AATF, AAUP, Midwest Mod Lang Assoc, MLA, Women in Fr. **RESEARCH** Postcolonial literature (especially North African and Caribbean women writers), postcolonial theory, feminist theory and criticism, colonialism, race and gender in France and the US. **SELECTED PUBLICATIONS** Auth, "Assia Djebar's Poetics of Subversion," L'Esprit createur 33.2 (93): 107-17; auth, "'Une certaine idee de la France': The Algeria Syndrome and Struggles over 'French' Identity," Identity Papers: Contested Nationhood in Twentieth-Century France, ed Steven Unger and Tom Conley, Univ of Minn Pr, (Minneapolis, 96): 215-32; auth, "Rekindling the Vividness of the Past Assia Djebar's Films and Fiction," World Lit Today 70.4 (96): 885-92; coed, Empire and Occupation and the Francophone World, Studies in Twentieth-Century Literature 23.1 (99); auth, "Cultural Multilingual Strategies of Postcolonial Literature: Assia Djebar's Algerian Palimpsest," World Lit Today 74.1 (00): 27-36; auth, "'Y' a bon Banania': Ethics and Cultural Criticism in the Colonial Context," Fr Cult Studies 11.1.31, (00): 9-29; auth, "Portrait of a Maghrebian Feminist as a Young Girl: Fatima Mernissi's 'Dreams of Trespass,'" Edebiyat: Jour of Middle Eastern Lit 11.1 (00): 85-103; auth, "Anamnesis and National Reconciliation: Re-Membering October 17, 1961," Immigrant Narratives in Contemporary France, ed Susan Ireland and Patrice J Proulx, Greenwood Pr, (01): 47-56; auth, Recasting Postcolonialism: Women Writing between Worlds, Heinemann, 01. **CONTACT ADDRESS** European Studies, San Diego State Univ, 5500 Campanile Dr, San Diego, CA 92182.

DONAT, PATRICIA
DISCIPLINE EDUCATION **EDUCATION** Univ Northern Iowa, BA, 86; Univ NC, MA, 90; Univ NC, PhD, 95. **CAREER** Dir, Univ NC, 93-95; Asst Prof, Miss Univ for Women, 95-. **HONORS AND AWARDS** Who's Who Among Am Teachers, 98, 99; IMAGE Outstanding Teacher of the Year Awd, 99; MUW Student Appreciation Awd, 99; Psi Chi. **MEMBERSHIPS** APA, Southeastern Psychol Assoc., Miss Professional Educr Assoc. **RESEARCH** Gender, violence against women. **SELECTED PUBLICATIONS** Coauth, "Diversity in the Rural Poor: Differences Between Households With and Without Telephones," Public Health Nursing, 12 (95): 386-392; coauth, "An Examination of the Attitudes Underlying Sexual Coercion Among Acquaintances," in Sexual Coercion in Dating Relationships (Binghamton, NY: Haworth Pr, 96), 27-47; coauth, "A Feminist Redefinition of Rape and Sexual Assault: Historical Foundations and Change," in Gender Violence: Interdisciplinary Perspectives (NY: New York Univ Pr, 97), 184-193; coauth, "Perceptions of Women's Sexual Interest and Acquaintance Rape: The Role of Sexual Overperception and Affective Attitudes," Psychol of Women Quart, 23 (99): 691-705; coauth, "RE-examining the Issue of Nonconsent in Acquaintance Rape," in Sexuality, Society and Feminism (Wash, DC: Am Psychol Assoc., 00), 355-376. **CONTACT ADDRESS** Dept Educ, Mississippi Univ for Women, PO Box W-1637, Columbus, MS 39701. **EMAIL** pdonat@muw.edu

DONOHUE, BRADLEY C.
PERSONAL Born 09/17/1965, New York, NY, m, 1988, 2 children **DISCIPLINE** PSYCHOLOGY **EDUCATION** Univ Kans, BA, 89; Nova Southeastern Univ, PhD, 95. **CAREER** Instr to Adj Prof, Broward Community Col, 94-96; Adj Prof, Nova Southeastern Univ, 96-98; Asst Prof, Univ Nev, 98-. **HONORS AND AWARDS** Who's Who among Am Teachers, 00; alumni Asn Awd, UNLV, 99; New Investigator Awd, UNLV, 99; Col of Liberal Arts Res Awd, UNLV, 99; Univ Fac Travel Committee Awd, UNLV, 99; Prof of the Year, Broward Community Col, 96-97; Good Citizen Awd, Winn Dixie, Inc, 95; Psi Chi Nat Honor Soc, 87-88; Nat PAL Light Heavyweight Boxing Champion, 86; Ranked #5 in the US, boxing light-heavy weight division, 86. **MEMBERSHIPS** Asn for the Advancement of Beh Therapy. **RESEARCH** Substance abuse, Domestic violence, Sports psychology. **SELECTED PUBLICATIONS** Auth, "Identification of Neuropsychological sub-

types in a sample of delinquent adolescents," Journal of Psychiatric Research, in press; auth, "Satisfaction of parents with their substance abusing and conduct-disordered youth," Behavior Modification, in press; auth, "The relationship of anxiety and child maltreatment," Journal of Family Violence, in press; auth, "Adolescents and their parents: A critical review of measures to assess their satisfaction with one another," Journal of Clinical Psychology review, in press; auth, "Prevalence and treatment of substance abuse in the mentally retarded population: an empirical review," Journal of Psychoactive Drugs, in press; auth, "Satisfaction of conduct-disordered and substance abusing youth with their parents," Behavior Modification, in press; auth, "Substance refusal skills in a population of adolescents diagnosed with conduct disorder and substance abuse," Addictive Behaviors, (99): 37-46; auth, "Role-play Assessment of Social Skills in conduct-disordered and Substance Abusing Adolescents: An empirical Review," Journal of Child and Adolescent Substance Abuse, (99): 1-29; auth, "Development of an ecobehavioral treatment program for child maltreatment," Behavioral Interventions, (99): 55-82; auth, "Improving initial session attendance in conduct disordered and substance abusing adolescents: A controlled study," Journal of child and Adolescent Drug Abuse, (98): 1-13; auth, "Behavioral treatment of conversion disorder in adolescence: A case example of globus hystericus," Behavior Modification, (97): 231-251; auth, "Relationship of depressions with measures of social functioning in adult drug abusers," Addictive Behaviors, (96): 211-216. **CONTACT ADDRESS** Dept Psychol, Univ of Nevada, Las Vegas, PO Box 455030, Las Vegas, NV 89154. **EMAIL** donohueb@nevada.edu

DONOHUE, JOHN WALDRON
PERSONAL Born 09/17/1917, New York, NY **DISCIPLINE** HISTORY & PHILOSOPHY OF EDUCATION **EDUCATION** Fordham Univ, AB, 39; St Louis Univ, MA, 44; Woodstock Col, STL, 51; Yale Univ, PhD, 55. **CAREER** Teacher high sch, NY, 44-47; from assoc prof to prof hist & philos of educ, Sch Educ, Fordham Univ, 55-70, adj prof, 77-80; Assoc Ed, America, 72- . **HONORS AND AWARDS** Mem, Society of Jesus, 39- ; ordained Roman Catholic priest, 50; Trustee, Fordham Univ, 69-77, 78-87, St Peter's Col, 80- ; St Louis Univ, 67-81. **MEMBERSHIPS** Philos Educ Soc; Nat Cath Ed Asn. **RESEARCH** Theory of Christian education; contemporary problems concerning religion and education. **SELECTED PUBLICATIONS** Auth, Work and Education, Loyola Univ, 59; Jesuit Education: An Essay on the Foundations of Its Idea, Fordham Univ, 63; St Thomas Aquinas and Education, Random, 68; Catholicism and Education, Harper, 73. **CONTACT ADDRESS** America 106 W 56th St, New York, NY 10019.

DONOVAN, AINE
PERSONAL Born 04/25/1956, Boston, MA, m, 1997, 1 child **DISCIPLINE** EDUCATION **EDUCATION** Univ San Francisco, Ed D, 95. **CAREER** Asst prof, US Nav Acad. **MEMBERSHIPS** PES; AME; APA. **RESEARCH** Moral education. **SELECTED PUBLICATIONS** Auth, Ethics for the Military Leader, Pearson Pub, 99; auth, "Celestial Navigation with a Moral Compass," J Just Car Edu (99); auth "The Case for Ethics Education," Shipmate (94); auth, "Leading by Example," Char Quart 2 : 5. **CONTACT ADDRESS** Dept Leadership Ethics, Law, United States Naval Acad, 112 Cooper Rd, Annapolis, MD 21402. **EMAIL** adonovan@nadn.navy.mil

DORGAN, HOWARD
PERSONAL Born 07/05/1932, Ruston, LA, m, 1961, 2 children **DISCIPLINE** COMMUNICATION AND APPLACHIAN ETHNOGRAPHY **EDUCATION** Univ Tex, El Paso, BA, 53; Univ Tex, Austin, MFA, 57; La State Univ, PhD, 71. **CAREER** Asst prof speech, lamar Univ, 66-69; assoc prof commun, 71-77, prof commun, 77-98, prof emeritus commun, 98-, Appalachian State Univ; ed, Southern Commun Jour, 81-84; exec sec, Southern Commun Asn, 85-90; pres, Southern Commun Asn, 91-92; pres, Appalachian Studies Asn, 95-96. **HONORS AND AWARDS** Trustees Award for Excellence in Teaching, 75; Outstanding Fac Award, 93; Thomas Wolfe Literary Award, 93; Southern Commun Outstanding Service Award, 95; Appalachian Consortium Distinguished Service Award, 98; Appalachian Studies Distinguished Service Award, 00. **MEMBERSHIPS** Southern Commun Asn; Appalachian Consortium; Appalachian Studies Asn. **RESEARCH** Southern rhetoric and public address; Appalachian religious traditions. **SELECTED PUBLICATIONS** Coed, The Oratory of Southern Demagogues, LSU Press, 82; coed, A New Diversity in Contemporary Southern Rhetoric, LSU Press, 87; auth, Giving Glory to God in Appalachia, Univ of Tenn Press, 87; auth, The Old Regular Baptists of Central Appalachia, Univ of Tenn Press, 89; auth, Airwarves of Zion, Univ Tenn Press, 93; Auth, In the Hands of a Happy God, Univ of Tenn Press, 97. **CONTACT ADDRESS** Dept of Commun, Appalachian State Univ, Boone, NC 28608. **EMAIL** dorganch@appstate.edu

DORNAN, READE W.
PERSONAL Born 12/07/1940, Denver, CO, m, 1964, 2 children **DISCIPLINE** ENGLISH EDUCATION **EDUCATION** Univ Colo, BA, 63; Mich State Univ, MA, 80; PhD, 88. **CAREER** Teacher, Hinckley High School, 63-65, Fleur du Lac School, 65-66, Garden School, Malaysia, 72-74; adj asst prof,

Univ Mich, 85-95; vis prof, Purdue Univ, 95-96; lectr, 96-98, tchg asst, 78-85, Mich State Univ; asst prof, Cent Mich Univ, 98- . **HONORS AND AWARDS** Phi Beta Kappa; SLATE Rep Nat Coun Teachers English. **MEMBERSHIPS** Ctr Exten Lang & Thinking; Ger Soc Contemp Theatre & Drama English; Int Reading Asn; Mod Lang Asn & Midwest Mod Lang Asn; Nat Coun Teachers English and Mich Coun TE; Soc Values Higher Educ. **RESEARCH** Literacy, Drama in education, Whole language for secondary students, young adult literature. **SELECTED PUBLICATIONS** Auth, "Women Playwrights Since 1975", Oxford Companion to Women's Writing in the US, Oxford Univ Press, 95; auth Arnold Wesker Revisited. NY: Twayne, Simon & Schuster, 95; auth, "Omaha Magic Theatre: Not Corn, But Babes Unchained." Contemp Drama in English, Spring, 97; auth "Looking for Commonalties: The Pragmatist's Approach to Our Differences." J of Midwest Mod Lang Asn, Spring, 97; co-auth, Multiple Voices, Multiple Texts: Reading in the Secondary Content Areas, Heinemann Boynton/Cook, 97; ed, Arnold Wesker: A Casebook, NY: Garland, 98. **CONTACT ADDRESS** Dept English, Central Michigan Univ, 206 Anspach Hall, Mount Pleasant, MI 48859-0001. **EMAIL** reade.dornan@cmich.edu

DORSEL, THOMAS N.
PERSONAL Born 05/11/1946, Cincinnati, OH, m, 1970, 5 children **DISCIPLINE** PSYCHOLOGY **EDUCATION** Univ Notre Dame, BA, 68; Univ Ky, MS, 70; Univ NMex, PhD, 74. **CAREER** Prof, Western Carolina Univ, 74-86; Prof, Francis Marion Univ, 86-. **MEMBERSHIPS** SCPA **RESEARCH** Clinical health and sport psychology. **SELECTED PUBLICATIONS** 1 Book and 25 Publ. **CONTACT ADDRESS** Dept Psychol, Francis Marion Univ, PO Box 100547, Florence, SC 29501. **EMAIL** tdorsel@fmarion.edu

DOTY, DALE V.
PERSONAL Born 04/11/1954, Rochester, NY, m, 1989, 3 children **DISCIPLINE** PSYCHOLOGY **EDUCATION** Univ Rochester, BS, 74; MA, 76; Univ Calif, PhD, 90. **CAREER** Assoc Prof, Monroe Community Col, 87-; Adj Prof, St. John Fisher Col, 93-. **RESEARCH** Developmental Psychology. **CONTACT ADDRESS** Dept Psychology, St. John Fisher Univ, 3690 E Ave, Rochester, NY 14618. **EMAIL** ddoty@monroecc.edu

DOUDNA, MARTIN KIRK
PERSONAL Born 06/04/1930, Louisville, KY, m, 1962, 3 children **DISCIPLINE** ENGLISH LITERATURE, AMERICAN CULTURE **EDUCATION** Oberlin Col, AB, 52; Univ Louisville, MA, 59; Univ Mich, PhD (Am cult), 71. **CAREER** Asst prof English, Mackinac Col, 66-69; assoc prof, 71-78, Prof English, Univ Hawaii, Hilo, 78-. **MEMBERSHIPS** MLA; Thoreau Soc; Thoreau Lyceum. **RESEARCH** Nineteenth century American literature; American liberalism and radicalism; American magazine journalism. **SELECTED PUBLICATIONS** Auth, Nay Lady Sit, The Dramatic and Human Dimensions of Comus, Anq A Quart J Short Articles Notes Revs, Vol 8, 95. **CONTACT ADDRESS** Humanities Div, Univ of Hawaii, Hilo, Hilo, HI 96720.

DOUGLASS, MELVIN ISADORE
PERSONAL Born 07/21/1948, Manhattan, NY, s **DISCIPLINE** EDUCATION **EDUCATION** Vincinnes University, AS, 1970; Tuskegee Institute, BS, 1973; Morgan State University, MS, 1975; New York University, MA, 1977; Columbia University, EdM, 1978, EdD, 1981. **CAREER** Queensboro Society for the Prevention of Cruelty to Children Inc, child care worker, 73-75; Public School 401-X, dean of students/teacher, 73-75; Amistad Child Day Care Center, school age program director, 76-77; Beck Memorial Day Care Center, administrative director, 83-84; Department of Juvenile Justice, primary school department chair, 84-85, ombudsman, 85-88; John Jay College of Criminal Justice, adjunct instructor, 88-89; Stimson Middle School, Chairperson, Boys Track Head Coach, 88-; College of New Rochelle, Instructor, 93-. **HONORS AND AWARDS** Grad Scholarship Columbia Univ 1978; Kappa Delta Pi Honor Soc in Educ inducted 1978; Service Awd NY City Transit Branch NAACP 1986; Citation for Comm Serv NYS Governor Mario Cuomo 1986; Citation Awd New York City Mayor Edward Koch 1986; Citation of Honor Queens Borough Pres Claire Shulman 1986; City Council Citation Awd, New York City Councilman Archie Spigner 1988; Civil Rights Awd, New York City Transit Branch NAACP 1988; Black Winners: A History of Spingarn Medalists 1984; Famous Black Men of Harvard 1988; Jefferson Awd, American Institute for Public Service, 1987; Omega Man of the Year Awd, Nu Omicron Chapter, 1987; Cert of Ordination, Cross Roads Baptist Church, NYC, 1990; State of New York Legislative Resolution, Senator Alton R Waldon Jr, 1991; Alumni Faculty Citation Awd, Vincennes University, 1991. **MEMBERSHIPS** Pres, founder Jamaica Track Club 1973-; bd of dirs Nu Omicron Chap of Omega Psi Phi Day Care Ctr 1984-; mem Prince Hall Masonry; pres bd of dirs New York City Transit Branch NAACP 1984-90; co-chairperson Educ Comm NY State Conf of NAACP 1986-89; chairperson Anti-Drug Comm Metro Council of NAACP Branches 1986-89; Jamaica East/West Adolescent Pregnancy Prevention Consortium 1986-89; basileus Nu Omicron Chap Omega Psi Phi Frat 1987-88; board of directors, Queens Council on the Arts 1983-86; bd of dirs Black Experimental Theatre 1982-; bf of dirs The United Black Men of Queens County Inc 1986-89; S Huntington Chmns' Assn, 1988-; Queens adv bd, New York Urban League, 1988-93; Amer Federation of Sch Administrators, 1988-; Council of Administrators and Supervisors, 1988-; Natl Black Child Devel Institute, 1982-; National Education Association, 1973-; community adv bd, The City of New York Dept of Correction, The Queens House of Detention for Men, 1991-94; community adv bd, Public School 40, Queens, NY, 1992-; bd of dirs Long Island Tuskegee Alumni Assn, 1986-, vp, 1987-89; bd of dirs, Dance Explosion, 1987-; area policy bd no 12, Subunit 2, 1987-; Ancient Arabic Order of Nobles of the Mystic Shrine. Licensed to preach, Calvary Bapt Ch, Jamaica NY, 1987. **SELECTED PUBLICATIONS** Written numerous publications, including: "Developing Successful Black Students," Feb 5, 1994, "Dr. Gerald W. Deas: More Than Pills," Feb 24, 1995, New York Amsterdam News; Social Studies Sixth Grade Teacher's Curriculum Guide, co-written with A. Sheppard, South Huntington School Dist, 1992. **CONTACT ADDRESS** English and Social Studies, Stimson Junior High Sch, Oakwood Rd, Huntington Station, NY 11746.

DOW, JAMES RAYMOND
PERSONAL Born 01/02/1936, D'Lo, MS **DISCIPLINE** GERMAN FOLKLORE **EDUCATION** MS Col, BA, 57; Univ IA, MA, 61, PhD(Ger), 66. **CAREER** Instr Ger, Univ IA, 64-66; asst prof, Univ WY, 66-70; asst prof, 71-74, assoc prof, 74-80, prof Ger, IA State Univ, 80-. **RESEARCH** Hermann Hesse's Marchen; Romantic Kunstmarchen; American-German folkloristic studies. **SELECTED PUBLICATIONS** Co-ed, Internationale Volkskundliche Bibliographie, 82; German Volkskunde; Nazification of an Academic Discipline; Volkische Wissenschaft. **CONTACT ADDRESS** Dept of Foreign Lang and Lit, Iowa State Univ of Science and Tech, Ames, IA 50011-0002. **EMAIL** jrdow@iastate.edu

DOWNS, LOUIS
PERSONAL Born 01/16/1948, Grand Junction, CO, m, 1983, 3 children **DISCIPLINE** EDUCATIONAL PSYCHOLOGY **EDUCATION** S Ore State col, MS, 87; Ore State Univ, PhD, 97. **CAREER** Cons, Pres, Psychotherapist/Counseling Northwest, 87-97; asst prof, Calif State Univ San Bernardino, 97-. **HONORS AND AWARDS** Phi Kappa Phi, 87; Phi Theta Kappa, 90; Ore Laurels Scholar, 96; Beta Delta, 00. **MEMBERSHIPS** Am Counseling Assoc; Assoc for Counselor Educ and Supervision. **RESEARCH** Ethical preparation of counselors and counselor educators. Educational intervention with fetal alcohol syndrome and children. **SELECTED PUBLICATIONS** Auth, "For the common good", W Wind Rev 2, (87):78-87; auth, "A holistic approach to chemical dependence counseling", Ore Counseling Assoc Newsletter 2, 93; coauth, "gender issues in Human Services counseling supervision", Human Serv Educ 18.1 (98):39-48; auth, The Educational counselor's Role in alternative Education", The Clearinghouse 73.2 (99):118-120; auth, "Ethics training in counselor education programs and its relationship to professional practice: A National Survey", Counselor Educ and Supervision, (forthcoming). **CONTACT ADDRESS** Dept Educ Psychol, California State Univ, San Bernardino, 5500 University Pky, San Bernardino, CA 92407. **EMAIL** ldowns@csusb.edu

DOYEL, D.
PERSONAL Born 08/24/1946, Lindsay, CA, m, 1983 **DISCIPLINE** ANTHROPOLOGY, PSYCHOLOGY AND EDUCATION **EDUCATION** BA, 69, Std Sec Credential, 70, MA, 72, Calif State Univ Chico; Univ Ariz, PhD, 77. **CAREER** Dir, Navajo Nation Archaeol Mus Div, 79-82, cons archael, 82-83, dir, Cty Phoenix Archaeol and Pueblo Grande Mus, 84-89; cons archaeol, Estrella Cult Res, 90-93; prin investr, Archaeol Consult Serv Ltd, 93-. **HONORS AND AWARDS** Outstanding Supv, Navajo Nation, 81; Who's Who in the West, 92-; Who's Who Intl, 95-. **MEMBERSHIPS** Soc Amer Archaeol, Ariz Archaeol Hist Soc, charter mem, Mus Assoc Ariz, 83; charter mem, Planetary Soc, 80; Sigma Xi, 78-. **RESEARCH** Archaeological Research (Southwest U.S.); Cultural Ecology; Southwest Ethnography; Museum Interpretation and Administration. **SELECTED PUBLICATIONS** Auth, Hohokam Exchange and Interaction, Chaco and Hohkam: Prehistoric Regional Systems in the American Southwest, ed P.L. Crown and W.J. Judge, Sch Amer Res, Santa Fe, Nmex, pp 225-252, 91; Hohokam Cultural Evolution in the Phoenix Basin, Exploring the Hohokam: Prehistoric Desert Peoples of the American Southwest, ed G.J. Gumerman, Univ Nmex Press, Albuquerque, Nmex, pp 231-278, 91; Interpreting Prehistoric Cultural Diversity in the Arizona Desert, Culture and Contact: Charles C. Di Peso's Gran Chichimeca, ed A. Woosley and J. Ravesloot, Univ Nmex Press, Albuquerque, Nmex, pp 39-64, 94; coauth, Processes of Aggregation in the Prehistoric Southwest, Themes in Southwestern Prehistory: Grand Patterns and Local Variations in Culture Change, ed G. Gumerman, Sch Amer Res, Santa Fe, Nmex, pp 109-134, 94; On Rivers and Boundaries in the Phoenix Basin, Arizona, Kiva, 8, 455-474, 93; Auth, Charles C. Di Peso: Expanding the Frontiers of American Archaeology, Amer Antiq, 59, 9-20, 94; coauth, Archaeomagnetic Dating and the Bonito Phase Chronology, Jour Archaeol Science, 21, 651-658, Acad Press Ltd, London, 94; auth, Resource Mobilization and Hohokam Society: Analysis of Obsidian Artifacts from the Gatlin Site, Kiva, 62, 45-60, 96; Ed, Anasazi Regional Organization and the Chaco System, Anthrop Papers of the Maxwell Mus, no 5, Albuquerque, Nmex, 92; The Hohokam Village: Site Structure and Organization, Amer Asn for the Advan of Science, SWARM Div, Glenwood Springs, Colo, 87. **CONTACT ADDRESS** PO Box 60474, Phoenix, AZ 85082-0474. **EMAIL** ddoyel@doitnow.com

DOYLE, CHARLES CLAY
PERSONAL Born 07/20/1943, Marlin, TX **DISCIPLINE** ENGLISH, FOLKLORE **EDUCATION** Univ Tex, Austin, BA, 64, PhD (English), 69. **CAREER** Asst prof, Univ Southern Calif, 69-74; asst prof, 74-79, Assoc Prof English, Univ GA, 79-. **MEMBERSHIPS** MLA; Am Folklore Soc; Am Dialect Soc; Amici Thomae More; Male-dicta: Int Res Ctr Verbal Aggression. **RESEARCH** Renaissance literature; European and American folklore; the English language. **SELECTED PUBLICATIONS** Auth, More Epigrams in the 16th Century and 17th Century 94p; Bourbon Nugae and More Epigrammata, Moreana, Vol 32, 95; The Long Story of the Short End of the Stick , Am Speech, Vol 69, 94; Another Elliptic with aand an Elliptic to, Am Speech, Vol 72, 97; Duck Butter Redux , Am Speech, Vol 72, 97; The Proverbial Hole in the Ground, Anq A Quart J Short Articles Notes Revs, Vol 8, 95; He That Will Swear Will Lie, Chaucer Rev, Vol 32, 97. **CONTACT ADDRESS** Dept of English, Univ of Georgia, 0 Georgia University, Athens, GA 30602-0001. **EMAIL** cdoyle@arches.uga.edu

DOYLE, CHARLOTTE
DISCIPLINE PSYCHOLOGY **EDUCATION** Temple Univ, AB, 59; Univ Mich, AM, 61; PhD, 65. **CAREER** Instr, Univ Mich, 63-64; Asst Prof, Cornell Univ, 64-66; From Asst Prof to Prof, Sara Lawrence Col, 66-. **MEMBERSHIPS** APA, APS, CLA, ACBW. **RESEARCH** The creative process in writing and other arts, the creative process and the young child, the narrative study of women's public lives. **SELECTED PUBLICATIONS** Auth, "Truth in Children's Books and Other Adult Fictions," The Westchester Writer 11:3 (96); auth, "Mother's Day, 1992," Psychol and the Arts Newsletter, summer issue, page 3 (97); auth, YOU CAN'T CATCH ME, The Growing Tree Ser, HarperCollins (New York), 98; auth, "The Writer Tells: The Creative Process in the Writing of Literary Fiction," Creativity Res J 11:1 (98): 29-36; auth, "Creative Minds at Play," Scholastic Parent & Child 5:1 (98): 36-41; auth, "Psychology, Definition of," Encycl of Psychol, APA (99). **CONTACT ADDRESS** Dept Psychol, Sarah Lawrence Col, 1 Mead Way, Bronxville, NY 10708. **EMAIL** cdoyle@mail.slc.edu

DOYLE, KENNETH
PERSONAL Born 03/02/1943, Menominee, MI, d, 1 child **DISCIPLINE** PSYCHOLOGY **EDUCATION** Univ Minn, PhD, 72. **CAREER** Assoc prof **RESEARCH** Psychology of money. **SELECTED PUBLICATIONS** Auth, Wealth Accumulation and Management, 91-00; coauth, Communication in the Language of Flowers, Horticulture Tech, 94; ed, The Meanings of Money, 92; auth, The Social Meanings of Money and Property, 99; ed, Ethnicity and Money, (in press). **CONTACT ADDRESS** Sch of Jour and Mass Commun, Univ of Minnesota, Twin Cities, 206 Church St SE, 111 Murphy Hall, Minneapolis, MN 55455. **EMAIL** kendoyle@umn.edu

DOYLE, MARY BETH
PERSONAL Born 05/31/1962, NJ **DISCIPLINE** EDUCATIONAL PSYCHOLOGY **EDUCATION** SUNY, Buffalo, BS, 86, MS, 90; Univ Minn, PhD, 95. **CAREER** Proj coordr, Severe Handicaps Tech Assistance Prog, SUNY, Buffalo, 88091; Proj coodr, Inst on Community Integration, Univ Minn, 91-94; Proj coodr, Inst on Commmunity Integration, Univ Minn, 94-95; asst prof ed, Trinity Col, 95-. **HONORS AND AWARDS** Who's Who Among America's Teachers, 99. **MEMBERSHIPS** Asn for Supervision and Leadership, Asn for Persons with Severe Handicaps, Coun for Exceptional Children, J of the Asn for Persons with Severe Handicaps (guest reviewer). **RESEARCH** Inclusive education, paraprofessionals. **SELECTED PUBLICATIONS** Auth, The Paraprofessional's Guide to the Inclusive Classroom: Working as a Team, Baltimore: Brookes Pub (97); coauth with D. Guerney, in M. S. Fishbaugh, ed, Collaboration guide for early career educators, Baltimore: Brookes Pub (in press); coauth with B. Sirvis and D. Alcouloumre, in D. L. Ryndak, ed, Assessment for students with physical disabilities and health impairments who are in regular class, Allyn & Bacon (in press). **CONTACT ADDRESS** Dept Ed, Trinity Col, Vermont, 208 Colchester Ave, Burlington, VT 05401. **EMAIL** mbdoyle@charity.trinityvt.edu

DRACHMAN, VIRGINIA GOLDSMITH
PERSONAL Born 01/12/1948, New York, NY, 2 children **DISCIPLINE** AMERICAN MEDICAL & WOMEN'S HISTORY **EDUCATION** Univ Rochester, BA, 70; State Univ NYork, Buffalo, MA, 74, PhD, 76. **CAREER** Assoc prof hist med & hist women, Tufts Univ, 77, Rockefeller Found fel hist & women med movement, 77-78. **HONORS AND AWARDS** ACLS Ford, 88; NSF Law & Soc Sci, 88; NEH Summer Fel, 94. **MEMBERSHIPS** AHA; Orgn Am Historians; Am Studies Asn. **RESEARCH** Women in med. **SELECTED PUBLICATIONS** Auth, Women Lawyers & the Origins of Professional Identity in America: The Letters of the Equity Club, 1887-1890,

Univ Mich Press, 94; Sisters in Law: Women Lawyers in Modern American History, Harvard Univ Press, 98; Hospital with a Heart: Women Doctors and the Paradox of Separation at the New England Hospital, 1862-1969, Cornell Univ Press, 98. **CONTACT ADDRESS** Dept of Hist, Tufts Univ, Medford, 520 Boston Ave, Medford, MA 02155-5555. **EMAIL** drachman@tiac.net

DRAKE, ROGER A.
PERSONAL Born Bremerton, WA, m, 1979 **DISCIPLINE** PSYCHOLOGY **EDUCATION** W Wash Univ, BA, 66; Univ Iowa, MA, 69; Univ Tenn, PhD, 81. **CAREER** Ful prof, Sheffield Hellam Univ Yorkshire, 81-82; vis prof, John Hopkins Univ, 88-89; prof, S State Col, 69-. **HONORS AND AWARDS** Intl Res Grant, NATO, 86-91; Biomedic Sabbatical grant, 88-89; Sci Review Panel, NTDCR, 99; Adv Methods Training grant, Nat Inst on Aging, 99-00. **MEMBERSHIPS** Soc for Neuroscience, Soc for Personality and Soc Psychol. **RESEARCH** Neurobiology of emotion, Persuasion, Optimism, Risk. **SELECTED PUBLICATIONS** Auth, "Processing persuasive arguments: Discounting of truth and relevance as a function of agreement and manipulated activation asymmetry," Journal of research in Personality, (93): 184-196; auth, "Complex experimental designs: Interactions," Survey of social science: Psychology, (93): 625-630; auth, "Cognitive spatial-motor processes: Specification of the direction of visually guided isometric forces in two-dimensional space: Time course of information transmitted and effect of constant force bias," Experimental Brain research, (91): 446-452; auth, "Some dynamic properties of attitude structures: Context-induced response facilitation and polarization," Journal of Personality and social Psychology, (91): 193-202; auth, "Self-serving biases in causal attributions as a function of altered activation asymmetry," International Journal of Neuroscience, (89): 199-204; auth, "Effects of gaze manipulation on aesthetic judgments: Hemisphere priming of affect," Acta psychologica, (87): 91-99; auth, "Induced lateral orientation and persuasibility," Brain and cognition, (85): 156-164; auth, "Lateral asymmetry of personal optimism," Journal of Research in Personality, (84): 497-507. **CONTACT ADDRESS** Dept Beh and Soc Sci, Western State Col of Colorado, 600 N Adams St, Gunnison, CO 81231-0001. **EMAIL** rdrake@western.edu

DRENNAN, ROBERT D.
PERSONAL Born 10/15/1947, m, 1974, 1 child **DISCIPLINE** ANTHROPOLOGY **EDUCATION** Princeton Univ, AB, 69; Univ Mich, MA, 70; PhD, 75. **CAREER** Asst Prof to Prof and Dept Chair, Univ Pittsburgh, 77-. **MEMBERSHIPS** Am Anthropol Asn; Am Asn for the Adv of Sci; Sociedad Colombiana de Arqueologia; Soc for Am Archaeol; Soc for East Asian Archaeol. **RESEARCH** Origins and development of complex societies, especially at the chiefdom level; Archeological data management and analysis; Computer applications to archeology, especially graphics; Regional settlement analysis; Mesoamerica; Northern South America; China **SELECTED PUBLICATIONS** Auth, "Imports and Exports in Classic Mesoamerican Political Economy: The Tehuacan Valley and the Teotihuacan Obsidian Industry," in Research in Economic Anthropology, (90): 177-199; auth, "Prehispanic Trajectories of Social Change in Mesoamerica, Central America, and Northern South America," in chiefdoms: Power, Economy, and Ideology, (Cambridge Univ Press, 91), 263-287; co-auth, "Regional Dynamics of chiefdoms in the Valle de la Plata, Colombia," Journal of Field Archaeology, (91): 297-317; co-ed, Prehispanic Chiefdoms in the Valle de la Plata, Vol II: Ceramics--Chronology and Craft Production, Univ Pittsburgh, 93; auth, "Mortuary Practices in the alto Magdalena: The social context of the 'San Agustin culture," in Tombs for the Living: Andean Mortuary Practices, (Dumbarton Oaks, 95), 79-110; auth, "Social Inequality and agricultural resources in the Valle de la Plata, Colombia," in Foundations of Social Inequality, Plenum Press, 95; auth, "Chiefdoms in Northern South America," Journal of World Prehistory, (95): 301-340; auth, "Betwixt and Between in the Intermediate Area," Journal of Archaeological Research, (96): 95-132; auth, Statistics for Archaeologists: A Commonsense Approach, Plenum Press, 96. **CONTACT ADDRESS** Dept Anthropol, Univ of Pittsburgh, 3H01 Forbes Quad, Pittsburgh, PA 15260. **EMAIL** drennan+@pitt.edu

DRESSER, N.
PERSONAL Born 10/28/1931, Los Angeles, CA, m, 1951, 3 children **DISCIPLINE** FOLKLORE **EDUCATION** UCLA, MA 72; BA 70. **CAREER** Cal State Univ LA, 25 year Faculty Member, Eng Amer Studies 72-92; LA Times columnist of Multicultural Manners, and full time write of books, 92-. **HONORS AND AWARDS** John Anson Ford Awd; Smithsonian Inst Awds; NEH. **MEMBERSHIPS** AFS; CFS; ISAZ; CHSSC; WGAw. **RESEARCH** Multicultural communication, customs and beliefs; human animal relations; vampires. **SELECTED PUBLICATIONS** Auth, Multicultural Celebrations: Today's Rules of Etiquette for Life's Special Occasions, Three Rivers Press, 99; The Horse Bar Mitzvah, Companion Animals and Us: Exploring the Relationships Between People and Pets, Cambridge Univ Press, 00; We Don't Ask They Don't Tell, The Intl Soc for Anthrozoology NewsL, 98; The M Word, Western Folklore, 98; Multicultural Manners: New Rules of Etiquette for a Changing Society, NY, John Wiley & Sons, 96; Korean ed 97; Vampires, American Folklore: An Encycl, Hamden CT, Garland Pub, 96; Our Own Stories: Readings for Cross-cultural Communication, 2nd ed, White Plains NY, Longman Pub, 95; The Case of the Missing Gerbil, Western Folklore, 94; Into the Light: Romania Stakes Its Claim to Dracula, The World and I, 95; First World Dracula Congress, Sky, 95; Multicultural Manners, twice mthly Los Angeles Times. **CONTACT ADDRESS** Dept of English, California State Univ, Los Angeles, 5151 State Univ Dr, Los Angeles, CA 90032. **EMAIL** norined@earthlink.net

DRUGAN, ROBERT C.
PERSONAL Born 01/26/1957, Morristown, NJ, m, 1983, 2 children **DISCIPLINE** PSYCHOLOGY **EDUCATION** Susquehanna Univ, BA, 79; Univ Colo, Boulder, MA, 81, PhD, 84. **CAREER** Teaching asst, Univ Colo, Boulder, 79-81, NIMH Res Trainee, 81-82, Res asst, 83-84; Mead-Johnson Postdoctoral Res Fel, NIMH, Bethesda, Md, 85-86; NIMH Postdoctoral Res Fel (Nat Res Service Award), 86-88; asst prof, Brown Univ, Providence, RI, 88-95; asst prof, Univ New Hampshire, Durham, 95-98, assoc prof, 98-. **HONORS AND AWARDS** Pi Gamma Mu, 77; Psi Chi, 77; Charles E. Lyle Senior Psi Chi Awd, Susquehanna Univ, 79; Grad Student Found Fund Awd, Univ Colo, 82; NIMH Nat Res Service Awd, 85-87; Sigma Xi, 88; Alfred P. Sloan Res Fel, 89-91; NIH-sponsored Psychoneuroimmunology Workshop Competition Winner (with D. Townson), 98; NIMH Special Emphasis Panel Member: Hypothalamic-Pituitary-Adrenal (HPA) Axis Regulation, 99. **MEMBERSHIPS** Am Asn for the Advancement of Sci, Soc for Neurosci, Eastern Psychol Asn, Sigma Xi, Int Soc for Psychoneuroendocrinology. **RESEARCH** Psychopharmacology, neuropharmacology and behavior: neurobiology/neurochemistry of inescapable stress-induced deficits, endogenous systems responsible for the protective effects of coping with stress (benzodiazepine/GABA receptor complex), neurobiology of stress resilience, peripheral benzodiazepine receptors, psychoneuroimmunology. **SELECTED PUBLICATIONS** Auth, "Peripheral benzodiazepine receptors: Molecular pharmacology to possible physiological significance in stress-induced hypertension," Clinical Neuropharmacology, 19 (96): 475-496; coauth, "Analysis of the importance of controllable versus uncontrollable stress on subsequent behavioral and physiological functioning," Brain Res Protocols, 2 (97): 69-74; auth, "Coping with traumatic stress interferes with memory of the event: A new conceptual mechanism for the protective effect of stress control," in Trauma and Event Memory, L. Williams and V. Banyard, eds, Sage Pubs, Thousand Oaks, CA (99): 245-256; coauth, "FG 7142- and restraint-induced alterations in the ataxic effects of alcohol and midazolam in rats are time dependent," Pharmacology, Biochemistry and Behavior, 62 (99): 45-51; coauth, "Effects of chlordiazepoxide and FG 7142 on a rat model of diencephalic amnesia as measured by delayed-matching-to-sample performance," Psychopharmacology, 142 (99): 413-420; auth, "The neurochemistry of stress resilience and coping: A quest for nature's own antidote to illness," in The Science of Optimism and Hope, Templeton Press, Radnor, Pa (in press); auth, "The use of the triadic design to produce behavioral learned helplessness in rats," Current Protocols in Neuroscience, John Wiley and Sons, Inc (in press). **CONTACT ADDRESS** Dept Psychol-Conant Hall, Univ of New Hampshire, Durham, 125 Technology Dr, Durham, NH 03824.

DRULINER, MARCIA M.
PERSONAL Born 12/18/1946, Auburn, NE, s **DISCIPLINE** LINGUISTICS, EDUCATION **EDUCATION** Nebr Wesleyan, BA, 69; Univ Nebr, MSE, 74; Marquette Univ, Doctor Philos, 92. **CAREER** Lect, Univ Nebr, Lincoln, 91-93; assoc prof, Concordia Col, Bronxville, NY, 93-95; asst prof, Northwestern Col, Orange City, Iowa, 98-. **HONORS AND AWARDS** PiLambda Theta; Who's Who Among America's Teachers; Who's Who in America; Universidad de Madrid, summer study prog in Spain; Instituto Antonio Machado, summer study prog in Spain; Universidad de Guadalajara, summer study prog in Mexico; CEUCA, summer study prog in Bogota, Columbia. **MEMBERSHIPS** Nat Asn Multicultural Ed, Delta Kappa Gamma, Philos of Ed Soc, AmAsn Teachers of Spanish & Portuguese, Lutheran Ed Asn. **RESEARCH** Paulo Freire and education for critical consciousness. **CONTACT ADDRESS** Dept Teacher Ed, Northwestern Col, Iowa, 101 7th St S W, Orange City, IA 51041. **EMAIL** druliner@nwciowa.edu

DU TOIT, BRIAN M.
PERSONAL Born 03/02/1935, Bloemfoutein, South Africa, m, 1958, 3 children **DISCIPLINE** ANTHROPOLOGY **EDUCATION** Univ Pretoria, BA, 56; MA, 61; Univ Ore, PhD, 63. **CAREER** Lectr, Univ of Stellenbosch, 64-65; Lectr, Univ of Cape Town, 66; Asst Prof to Prof, Univ of Fla, 66-. **HONORS AND AWARDS** Sigma Xi, 63; Asn of Current Anthropol, 64; Fel Of African Studies Asn, 69; President's Scholar, Univ of Fla, 76-77; Fel of Soc for Appl Anthrop, 79; Phi Kappa Phi, 95. **MEMBERSHIPS** Soc for Appl Anthrop, African Studies Asn. **RESEARCH** Medical Anthropology, Aging, HIV/AIDS, Africa, Melanesia. **SELECTED PUBLICATIONS** Auth, "Compassion, Truth and Clarity: An Appreciation of South African Anthropologist Monica Hunter Wilson," Occasional Papers 2, Inst of Nyakyusa-Ngonde Studies (96); auth, "Ethnomedical (Folk) Healing in the Caribbean," J of Caribbean Studies 12-1 (97): 95-109; auth, "Immigrant Communities: European Communities," in Encyclopedia of Sub-Saharan Africa (NY: Simon and Schuster, 97); auth, "Afrikaners," in Encyclopedia of Cultures and Daily Life (Pepper Pike, OH: Eastwood Publ, 97); auth, Human Sexuality: Cross-Cultural Readings, McGraw-Hill Col Custom Ser (NY), 98; auth, The Boers in East Africa: Ethnicity and Identity, Bergan & Garvey (Westport), 98; auth, "Modern Folk Medicine in South Africa," S African J of Ethnol 21-4 (98): 145-152; auth, "Ethnicity and Human Rights: Appealing to different Loyalties," Human Peace and Human Rights 12 - 1(99): 10-15; auth, Ethnicity and Nationalism: Spanners in the wheel of Human Rights, forthcoming; auth, Religion and the Adjustment of Displaces Peoples, forthcoming; coauth, Ethnicity, Drug Use, and HIV/AIDS in South Africa, forthcoming. **CONTACT ADDRESS** Dept Anthrop, Univ of Florida, PO Box 117305, Gainesville, FL 32611. **EMAIL** bdutoit@anthro.ufl.edu

DUBE, THOMAS M. T.
PERSONAL Born 12/25/1938, Essexvale, Zimbabwe, m **DISCIPLINE** EDUCATION **EDUCATION** Univ of Lesotho, BA 1958; Univ of So Africa, UED 1960; CW Post Coll of Long Island U, MS 1963; Univ of Chgo, MA 1972; MI State U, MA 1974; Uof Rochester, EdD 1969; Cooley Law Sch, JD. **CAREER** Western MI Univ, asst prof Social Science; Geneva Coll PA, asst prof; Rochester NY, pre-school teacher; Ministry of African Educ, Rodesia Africa, high school teacher, elementary school teacher. **MEMBERSHIPS** Mem Rhodesian African Tchrs Assn; vol activities in Black Comm Rochester, Pittsburg, Kalamazoo; mem Assn of African Studies in Am; founder mem JairosJiri Inst for Physically-Handicapped; founder, mem, asst prin Mpopoma African Comm HS. **CONTACT ADDRESS** 337 Moore Hall, Kalamazoo, MI 49001.

DUBIN, S. C.
PERSONAL Born 11/05/1949, Kansas City, MO **DISCIPLINE** SOCIOLOGY **EDUCATION** Univ Chicago, PhD 82, MA 76; Univ Missouri, BA 71. **CAREER** SUNY Purchase Col, lectr, asst prof, assoc prof, prof, 86 to 98-; Yale Univ, post doc fel, 83-84; Univ Chicago, post doc fel, 83. **HONORS AND AWARDS** Phi Beta Kappa; Phi Eta Sigma; NY Times Notable Book of the Year; Gustavas Myers Soc Outstanding Book. **MEMBERSHIPS** ASA **RESEARCH** Sociology of art; culture; mass media; censorship; deviant and social control; freedom of expression issues. **SELECTED PUBLICATIONS** Auth, Displays of Power: Memory and Amnesia in the American Museum, NYU Press, 99; Arresting Images, Impolitic Art, Uncivil Actions, Routledge, 92; Bureaucratizing the Muse: Public Funds and the Cultural Worker, U of Chicago Press, 87. **CONTACT ADDRESS** Social Science Division, SUNY, Col at Purchase, Purchase, NY 10577.

DUCK, STEVE
PERSONAL Born Keynsham, England, m, 1987, 4 children **DISCIPLINE** PSYCHOLOGY **EDUCATION** Oxford Univ, BA, 68, MA, 72; Sheffield Univ, PhD, 71. **CAREER** Lectr, Glasgow Univ, 71-73; lectr, 73-78, sr lectr, 78-86, Univ of Lancaster; DANIEL & AMY STARCH PROF, UNIV OF IOWA, 86-. **HONORS AND AWARDS** GR Miller Book Awd, SCA, 96; Fel, APA, APS, ICA, AAAPP; Berscheid-Hatfield Distinguished Mid-Career Achievement Awd, INPR, 98. **MEMBERSHIPS** Int Network on Personal Relationships; Int Soc Indy Personal Relationships; Nat Commun Asn; Int Soc Study Personal Relationships. **RESEARCH** Personal relationships; personal construct theory. **SELECTED PUBLICATIONS** Auth, Meaningful Relationships, 94; auth, Handbook of Personal Relationships, 2nd ed, Wiley, 97; auth, Human Relationships, 3rd ed, 98; auth, Relations to Others, 2nd ed, Open Univ, 99. **CONTACT ADDRESS** Commun Studies Dept, Univ of Iowa, 105-BCSB, Iowa City, IA 52242. **EMAIL** steve-duck@uiowa.edu

DUCKWORTH, ELEANOR R.
PERSONAL Born 10/29/1935, Montreal, QC, Canada, s **DISCIPLINE** EDUCATION **EDUCATION** Colby Col, BA, 57; Univ de Paris, Certificat Propendeutique, 58; Univ de Geneve, Diplome, 59, 60; Licence, 60; Doctorate, 77. **CAREER** Lectr, MIT, 78-81; Assoc prof to prof, 81-; chair, 93-96. **HONORS AND AWARDS** AERA Awd, 88; Dr of the Univ, Univ of Ottawa, 93. **MEMBERSHIPS** Study Comm on Undergrad Educ and Educ of Teachers; Center for Collaborative Educ. **RESEARCH** Subject Matter Learning, Curriculum, Teacher Education. **SELECTED PUBLICATIONS** Auth, The African Primary Science Program: An Evaluation and Extended Thoughts, NDak Study Group on Evaluation, 78; auth, Inventing Density, NDak Study Group on Evaluation, 86; auth, The Having of Wonderful Ideas and Other Essays on Teaching and Learning, Teachers Col Pr, (NY), 87; coauth, Science Education: A Minds-On Approach for the Elementary Years, Lawrence Erlbaum Assoc, (Hillsdale, NJ), 90; auth, "Twenty-four, Forty-two and I Love You: Keeping it Complex", Harvard Educ Rev 61, (91): 1-24; auth, "A Constructivist Perspective on Teaching and Learning Science", Constructivism: Foundations, Perspectives and Practice, ed Fosnot, Teachers Col Pr, 96; coauth, Teacher to Teacher: Learning From Each Other, Teachers Col Pr, (NY), 97; ed, People Learning, Teachers Col Pr, (forthcoming). **CONTACT ADDRESS** Dept Learning and Teaching, Harvard Univ, 13 Applian Way, 226 Longfellow Hall, Cambridge, MA 02138. **EMAIL** eleanor_duckworth@gse.harvard.edu

DUGAW, DIANNE M.
PERSONAL Born 08/24/1948, Seattle, WA **DISCIPLINE** ENGLISH, FOLKLORE **EDUCATION** Univ Portland, BA, 72; Univ Colo, MMus, 74; Univ Calif at Los Angeles, PhD, 82. **CAREER** Vis lectr, Univ Calif, 82-85; asst prof, Univ Colo, 85-90; from assoc prof to prof, Univ Ore, 91-. **MEMBERSHIPS** Am Soc for Eighteenth-Century Studies, MLA, Am Folklore soc, Calif Folklore Soc, Northwest Soc for Eighteenth-Century Studies. **RESEARCH** British and American Folklore and Popular Culture (especially folk songs), Seventeenth- and Eighteenth-Century British Literature and Culture. **SELECTED PUBLICATIONS** Auth, Warrior Women and Popular Balladry, 1650-1850, Cambridge Univ Press, 89 & 96; ed, The Anglo-American Ballad, Garland Press, 95; auth, "Deep Play": John Gay and the Invention of Modernity, Univ Del Press, 00. **CONTACT ADDRESS** Dept English, Univ of Oregon, 1286 Univ Ore, Eugene, OR 97403.

DUKES, RICHARD L.
PERSONAL Born 11/15/1946, Toledo, OH, m, 1969, 3 children **DISCIPLINE** SOCIOLOGY **EDUCATION** Calif State Univ, Northridge, BA; Univ S Calif, PhD, 73. **CAREER** Assoc Prof to Prof, Univ Colo Colorado Springs, 77-. **HONORS AND AWARDS** Univ Teaching Awd, 83. **MEMBERSHIPS** N Am Simulation and Gaming Asn, Am Sociol Asn. **RESEARCH** Youth, Evaluation Research, Simulation and Gaming. **SELECTED PUBLICATIONS** Auth, Worlds Apart, Klumer (Dordrecht, Netherlands), 90. **CONTACT ADDRESS** Dept Sociol, Univ of Colorado, Colorado Springs, 1420 Austin Bluffs, Colorado Springs, CO 80918. **EMAIL** rdukes@mail.uccs.edu

DULANY, DON E.
PERSONAL Born 12/09/1928, Shreveport, LA, m, 1955, 1 child **DISCIPLINE** PSYCHOLOGY **EDUCATION** AB, Univ TN, 48; PhD, Univ MI, 55. **CAREER** Inst, Univ MI, 52; Active Duty U S Army, 54-56; Lecturer Psychol, FL State Univ; Extension for Overseas Military Personel, 55-56; Assit Prof, Univ IL, 56-59; Faculty Res Fellow Graduate Coll, 57; Res Fellow, Harvard Univ, 58; Assoc Prof, 59-64; Prof, Univ IL, 64; Affiliate, Beckman Inst, 90-. **HONORS AND AWARDS** Graduate Student Org Awd for Excellence in Graduate Teaching, 74; Psi Chi Awd for Excellence in Undergraduate Teaching, 84, 88; Mabel Kirkpatrick Hohenboken Awd for Excellence In Teaching in Psychol, 92; William F. Prodasy Awd for Distinguished Teaching in the Coll of Liberal Arts and Sci, 94. **MEMBERSHIPS** Amer Psycholo Soc Fellow; Amer Psychol Assoc Fellow Div 3 Experimental Psychol; Psychonomic Soc; Assoc for the Sci Study of Consciouseness; Soc Philos and Psycholo; Sigma Xi. **RESEARCH** Cognitive Phsychol; consciousness and non-conscious processes; intentions formation; casusal reasoning. **SELECTED PUBLICATIONS** Dulany, D E; 97; Scientific approaches to conciousness, Mahwah NJ, Lawrence Erlbaum Assoc, Dulany D E, (in press 98); Encylopedia of Psychology, Washington and NY, Amer Psychol Assoc and Oxford Univ Press, Dulany,D.E. (in press 98); Behavioral and Brain Sciences, Consciousness in theories of explicit and implicit Psychonomic Soc Chicago, 96; Ed, American Journal of Psychology, 88-; Graduate Study Committee, 94-98; Chair Livrary Committee, 95-97. **CONTACT ADDRESS** Depy of Psycholo, Univ of Illinois, Urbana-Champaign, Champaign, IL 61820. **EMAIL** d-dulanye@uiuc.edu

DUMOND, D. E.
PERSONAL Born 03/23/1929, Childress, TX, m, 1950 **DISCIPLINE** ANTHROPOLOGY, ARCHAEOLOGY **EDUCATION** Univ New Mexico, BA, 49; Mexico City College, MA, 57; Univ Oregon, PhD, 62. **CAREER** Asst Prof, Assoc Prof, Prof, 62-94, Univ Oregon; Dir 77-96, OR State Museum of Anthropology; Dir 82-96, U of OR Museum Nat Hist; Prof Emeritus of Anthropology. **HONORS AND AWARDS** SSRC Fel; NEH Fel; Japan Soc Promo Sci Fel; SI Fel; Arctic Inst NA Elec Fel; AAAS Elec Fel; AAA Career Achv Awd. **MEMBERSHIPS** AAA; SAA; AAA. **RESEARCH** Archaeology and Ethnohistory of the American Arctic; Archaeology and Ethnohistory of Mexico. **SELECTED PUBLICATIONS** Auth, The Machete and the Cross: Campesino Rebellion in Yucatan, Lincoln, Univ of NE Press, 97; Poison in the Cup: The South Alaskan Smallpox Epidemic of 1835, in: Chin Hills to Chiloquin: Papers Honoring the Versatile Career of Theodore Stern, edited, Univ of Oregon Anthro Papers, 96; Holocene Prehistory of the Northernmost North Pacific, J World Prehistory, 95; co auth, Paugvik: A Nineteenth Century Native Village on Bristol Bay Southwestern Alaska, Fieldiana Anthro, Field Museum of Natural History, Chicago, 95; auth, Western Arctic Culture, a section in the article, The Arctic, Encyc Britannica, Macropaedia, 93; co auth, Holocene Prehistory of the Northernmost North Pacific. **CONTACT ADDRESS** Dept of Anthropology, Univ of Oregon, Eugene, OR 97403-1218. **EMAIL** ddumond@oregon.uoregon.edu

DUMONT, LLOYD F.
PERSONAL Born 04/29/1951, Philadelphia, PA, m, 1984, 4 children **DISCIPLINE** SOCIOLOGY, CRIMINAL JUSTICE **EDUCATION** Gloucester County Col, AA, 73; Glassboro State Col, BA, 92; St Joseph's Univ, MS, 95. **CAREER** Police Off, Wash Twp Police, 74-76; County Detective, Gloucester County, 76-89; Spec Agent, Pa State Bureau, 89-90; Lieutenant, Wash Twp Police, 90-99; Adj Prof, Gloucester County Col, 92-; Adj Prof, Rowan Univ, 95-98; Adj Prof, Fairleigh Dickinson Univ, 00-; Adj Prof, Gloucester County Police Acad, 00-. **MEMBERSHIPS** Intl Asn of Chiefs of Police; NJ Narcotics Officers Asn; Intl Narcotics Officers Asn; VIDOCQ Soc; Am Soc of Law Enforcement Trainers. **SELECTED PUBLICATIONS** Auth, "Recognizing Post Shooting Trauma," Law and Order Magazine, 99; auth, "Minimizing Undercover Violence," Law and Order Magazine, 00. **CONTACT ADDRESS** Dept Sociol/Criminal Justice, Fairleigh Dickinson Univ, 1400 Tanyard Rd, Sewell, NJ 08080. **EMAIL** ldumont@gccnj.edu

DUNDES, ALAN
PERSONAL Born 09/08/1934, New York, NY, m, 1958, 3 children **DISCIPLINE** FOLKLORE **EDUCATION** Yale Univ, BA, 55, MAT, 58; Ind Univ, Bloomington, PhD(folklore), 62. **CAREER** Instr English, Univ Kans, 62-63; from asst prof to assoc prof anthrop, 63-68, prof anthrop & folklore, Univ Calif, Berkeley, 68-, Guggenheim fel, 66-67; Nat Endowment for Humanities, sr fel, 72-73. **HONORS AND AWARDS** Sigillo d'Oro (Seal of Gold), the Pitre Prize for Lifetime Achievement in Folklore, 93; Distinguished Teaching Awd, 94. **MEMBERSHIPS** Am Folklore Soc; Am Anthrop Asn. **RESEARCH** Symbolism; structuralism. **SELECTED PUBLICATIONS** Auth, The Morphology of North American Indian Folktales, Acad Sci Fennica, Helsinki, 64; ed, The Study of Folklore, 65 & Mother Wit from the Laughing Barrel: Readings in the Interpretation of Afro-American Folklore, 73, Prentice-Hall; coauth, La Terra in Piazza: An Interpretation of the Palio Siena, Univ Calif Press, 75; Urban Folklore from the Paperwork Empire, Am Folklore Soc, 75; compiler, Folklore Theses and Dissertations in the United States, Univ Tex Press, 76; auth, Interpreting Folklore, Ind Univ Press, 80; coauth, The Art of Mixing Metaphors, Acad Sci Fennica, Helsinki, 81. Auth, Life is Like a Chicken Coop Ladder, Columbia Univ Press, 84; Parsing Through Customs, Univ Wisc Press, 87; Cracking Jokes, Ten Speed Press, 87; coauth, When You're Up to Your Ass in Alligators, Wayne State Univ Press, 87, auth, Folklore Matters, Univ Tenn Press, 89; coauth, Never Try to Teach a Pig to Sing, Wayne State Univ Press, 91; coauth, Sometimes the Dragon Wins, Syracuse Univ Press, 96; auth, From Game to War, Univ Press KY, 97; Two Tales of Crow and Sparrow, Rowman & Littlefield, 97; Holy Writ as Oral Lit: The Bible as Folklore, Rowman & Littlefield, 99; Coauth, Why Don't Sheep Shrink When It Rains, Syracuse Univ Press, 00. **CONTACT ADDRESS** Dept of Anthropology, Univ of California, Berkeley, 232 Kroeber Hall, Berkeley, CA 94720-3711.

DUNHAM, ROGER
PERSONAL Born 09/29/1947, Seattle, WA, m, 1969, 6 children **DISCIPLINE** SOCIOLOGY **EDUCATION** Univ Wash, BA, 69; Wash State Univ, MA, 75; PhD, 77. **CAREER** Asst prof, Univ Miami, 77; assoc prof, 83; prof, 89-; assoc ch, 00-. **MEMBERSHIPS** ASA; ASC; CSLS; ERD; ISA. **SELECTED PUBLICATIONS** Coed, Crime and Justice in America: Present Realities and Future Prospects, Prentice-Hall (Englewood Cliffs, NJ), 97; coauth, The Force Factor: Measuring Police Use-of-Force Relative to Suspect Resistance, Police Research Evalu Ser: Police Exec Res Forum (Washington DC), 97; coauth, Understanding Police Use-of-Force: The Force Factor and Implications for Policy and Training, Police Res Eval Ser: Police Exec Res Forum (Washington DC), in press; coauth, Police Pursuits: What We Know, Police Res Eval Ser: Police Exec Res Forum (Washington DC), 00; coauth, "High-Speed Pursuit: The Offender's Perspective," Crim Justice Behavior 25 (98): 30-45; coauth, "On the Study of Neighborhoods and the Police," in Community Policing: Contemporary Readings, eds. Geoffrey Alpert, Alex Piquero (Prospect Heights, IL: Waveland Press, 98); coauth, "Policing in the Wake of Hurricane Andrew: Comparing Citizen's and Police Priorities," Policing: Intl J 21 (98): 330-338; coauth, "Force Factor: Measuring and Assessing Police Use of Force and Suspect Resistance," Use of Force by Police: Overview of National and Local Data: US Dept Justice, Nat Inst Justice/Bureau Justice Stats (Wash, DC, 99), 45-60; coauth, "Integrated Theories of Crime and Delinquency," in Historical, Conceptual and Theoretical Issues, eds. Peter Adler, Patti Adler, Jay Corzine, Encyclopedia of Criminology and Deviant Behavior (London: Taylor and Francis Pub, 00); coauth, "Family and Crime/Delinquency," in Crime and Juvenile Delinquency, eds. David Luckenbill and Dennis Peck, Encyclopedia of Criminology and Deviant Behavior (London: Taylor and Francis Pub, 00). **CONTACT ADDRESS** Dept Sociology, Univ of Miami, PO Box 24862, Miami, FL 33124. **EMAIL** rdunham@umiami.ir.miami.edu

DUNN, ANNIE M.
PERSONAL Born 10/20/1929, SC, m, 1962, 1 child **DISCIPLINE** PSYCHOLOGY **EDUCATION** Montgomery Col, AA, 71; Univ Md, BS, 78; MEd, 81; PhD, 93 **CAREER** Coordinator, Res Project Georgetown Univ Hosp, 87-88; Prof, Montgomery Col, 89-. **MEMBERSHIPS** Phi Kappa Phi, Am Soc on Aging. **RESEARCH** Mental health counseling and crisis intervention; Individual and group sessions and marital counseling; PTSD counseling and education; Death education and suicide prevention; Drug and alcohol counseling. **SELECTED PUBLICATIONS** Auth, "Extraversion-Introversion and Spatial Intelligence," Perceptual and Motor Skills, (93): 19-24; co-auth, "Spatial Intelligence and the Six-Factor Personality Questionnaire," Perceptual and Motor Skills, (96): 1235-1240; auth, "An Exploratory Study of Undergraduates' Attributions of Success or Failure on Spatial Tests," Perceptual and Motor Skills, (99): 695-702. **CONTACT ADDRESS** Dept Soc Sci, Montgomery Col, Takoma Park, 7600 Takoma Ave, Tacoma Park, MD 20912.

DUNN, IVY D.
PERSONAL Born 05/01/1950, Chicago, IL, m, 1986 **DISCIPLINE** PSYCHOLOGY **EDUCATION** Chicago State Univ, BA, 71; Univ S Calif, MS, 80; Univ Tex Dallas, PhD, 91. **CAREER** Software training consult, Phillips Data Syst, 80-82; proj manager, Tex Instruments, 83-86; adj instr, Paul Quinn col, 90-92; res assoc, Univ of IL, 93-95; adv committee, Am Psychol Assoc Minority Fel Prog, 93-97; fac adv, Marine Biol Lab, 95; res assoc, Auditory Neuroscience Lab, 95-98; adj instr to asst prof, Chicago State Univ, 95-; proj couns, NASA/Fla A&M Univ, 98. **HONORS AND AWARDS** Fel, SW Medi School, 90-92; Am Psychol Asn Serv Awd, 98. **MEMBERSHIPS** Soc for Neuroscience; Women in Neuroscience. **SELECTED PUBLICATIONS** Auth, "Classification of complex-partial seizure patients using the P300 auditory evoked response and working memory ability", Diss Abstracts Int 53, (92), 1216; coauth, "P300 activation time: a noninvasive tool for presurgical evaluation in temporal lobe epilepsy", Soc for Neuroscience Abstracts 18.1, (92), 905; coauth, "Scalp-recorded P300 reflects seizure spread in epileptic patients", Am Epilepsy Soc Abstracts 128, (92); coauth, "The effects of difficulty level and sensory modality on P300 scalp distribution", Int Soc for Brain Electro-Magnetic Topography Proceedings 222, 94; auth, "P300 latency at cortical sites in visual and auditory oddball paradigms", Soc for Neuroscience Abstracts 18.2, (95):905; auth, "People of color in the neurosciences: a directory", the Assoc of Neuroscience Depts and Progs, Wash DC, 96; coauth, "Achievement in the midst of adversity: People of color in the Neurosciences", Soc for Neuroscience Abstracts, 97. **CONTACT ADDRESS** Chicago State Univ, 9501 S King Dr, Chicago, IL 60628.

DURHAM, JOSEPH THOMAS
PERSONAL Born 11/26/1923, Raleigh, NC, m **DISCIPLINE** EDUCATION **EDUCATION** Morgan State Coll, AB (honors) 1948; Temple Univ, EdM 1949; Columbia Univ, EdD 1963. **CAREER** New Lincoln School, teacher 1956-58; Southern Univ, prof 1958-60; Coppin State Coll, chmn educ 1960-63; Albany State Coll, dean & prof 1963-65; Coppin State Coll, dean of college 1965-68; IL State Univ, assoc dean educ 1968-72; Howard Univ, dean of school of educ 1972-75; Coppin State Coll Baltimore, dean of educ 1975-76; MD State Bd for Higher Educ, dir inst approval; Comm Coll of Baltimore, pres, 85-90; Morgan State Univ, prof; Coppin State Coll, Lecturer, currently. **HONORS AND AWARDS** Fellow General Educ Bd 1953-54; Fellow Danforth Found 1975; Commissioner Montgomery Co Human Relations 1983-86; Presidential Leadership Medallion, Univ of Texas, 1989. **MEMBERSHIPS** Mem Phi Delta Kappa; mem Alpha Phi Alpha; visiting prof Univ of New Hampshire 1966. **SELECTED PUBLICATIONS** "The Story of Civil Rights as Seen by the Black Church" DC Cook Publishing Co 1971. **CONTACT ADDRESS** Lecturer in Education, Coppin State Col, Baltimore, MD 21216.

DURNIN, JOHN H.
PERSONAL Born 07/09/1937, Salem, OR, m, 3 children **DISCIPLINE** EDUCATION **EDUCATION** West Ore State Univ, BA, 63; Univ Utah, MS, 66; Univ Penn, PhD, 71. **CAREER** Teacher, Sinslaw School, Ore, 63-64; teacher, Washoe Cnty Sch Dist, Nev, 65-66; lecturer, Univ Pa, 69-72; educ spec, Navy Personnel Res Dev Center, 76-77; Full prof, Gazi Univ, Turkey, 83-85; vis prof, Australian Cath Univ, 91; assoc prof, Villanova Univ, 72-00. **HONORS AND AWARDS** Phi Delta Kappa; Phi Kappa Phi; Ful Scholar; Outstanding Leadership in Educ, Penn; Energy Educ Awd, Penn; four Chaplin Legion of Honor. **MEMBERSHIPS** Am Educ Res Asn, Nat coun of Teachers of Mathematics, Asn for Adv of computing in Educ, Penn Asn for Supervision and Curric Dev. **RESEARCH** Problem Solving and Technology in Education. **SELECTED PUBLICATIONS** Auth, Perspectives on Turkish education: An inside view, Indiana Univ Turkish Studies Series, Bloomington, 98; auth, "Developing ethical praxis: Hermeneutics, reflective practice and educational ethics," Journal of Structural Learning, (95): 215-230; auth, "Teaching problem solving processes in elementary school mathematics," Journal of Structural Learning, (97): 53-69; auth, "In-service teachers pre-service teachers technology," Ed-Media, (99): 1781-1783. **CONTACT ADDRESS** Dept of Educ, Villanova Univ, 800 E Lancaster Ave, Villanova, PA 19085. **EMAIL** john.durnin@villanova.edu

DUST, MARGARET C.
PERSONAL Born 08/01/1947, East Chicago, IL, s **DISCIPLINE** PSYCHOLOGY **EDUCATION** Loyola Univ, BA, 69; Purdue Univ, BA, 77; Ill Inst Tech, MS, 85; Andrews Univ, PhD, 95. **CAREER** Visiting Asst Prof, Purdue Univ, 78-90; Instructor to Assoc Prof, Chicago State Univ, 90-. **HONORS AND AWARDS** Teacher of the Year, Purdue Univ, 80, 89, 90; Phi Kappa Phi Honor Soc; Pi Lambda Theta Honor Soc; Who's Who Among Am Teachers, 96, 98, 01; Fac Excellence Awd,

98-99; Nat Sci Foundation Grant. **MEMBERSHIPS** APA; ASA; Soc for Computers in Psychol. **RESEARCH** Minorieties and diversity. **SELECTED PUBLICATIONS** Auth, "A Veteran's Album, 1969-1970," in A Veteran's Album: A Photographic Book on the vietnam War, Turner Pub Co, 94; co-auth, Personality Profiles of Policemen and Civilians, 95; co-auth, African American Women and Self-Esteem, 95. **CONTACT ADDRESS** Dept Psychol, Chicago State Univ, 9501 S King Dr, Chicago, IL 60628. **EMAIL** bij6med@csu.edu

DWORKIN, ANTHONY G.
PERSONAL Born 11/22/1942, Los Angeles, CA, m, 1966, 1 child **DISCIPLINE** SOCIOLOGY **EDUCATION** Occidental Col, AB, 64; Northwestern Univ, MA, 66; PhD, 70. **CAREER** Instr/Asst Prof, Univ of Mo, 68-73; Assoc Prof to Prof, Univ of Houston, 73-; Dept Chair, Univ of Houston, 88-94; Res Dir, Tex Center for Univ Sch Partnership, 91-97; Dir, Sociol of Educ Res Group, 97-. **HONORS AND AWARDS** Phi Beta Kappa, 64; Woodrow Wilson Fel, Dissertation Fel, 64-68; NSF and US Dept of Educ Grants; Tex Educ Agency Grants. **MEMBERSHIPS** Am Sociol Asn, Southwestern Soc Sci Asn, Southwestern Sociol Asn, Soc for the Study of Social Problems, Midwest Sociol Soc. **RESEARCH** Sociology of education, race, ethnic, and gender relations. **SELECTED PUBLICATIONS** Auth, Giving Up on Schools: Student Dropouts and Teacher Burnouts, Corwin/Sage (Newbury Park, CA), 91; coauth, "Teacher Burnout in the Face of Reform: Some Caveats in 'Breaking the Mold'," in Investing in U.S. Schools: Directions for Educational Policy, ed. Bruce Anthony Jones and Kathryn M. Borman (Norwood, NJ: Ablex, 94), 68-86; auth, "Teacher Burnout," in International Encyclopedia of Education, 2nd ed, ed. T. Husen and T. N. Postlethwaite (Oxford: Pergamon Press, 94); auth, "Teacher burnout with an epilogue," in International Encyclopedia of Education, 2nd ed, CR-ROM, ed. T. Husen and T. N. Postlethwaite (Oxford: Pergamon Press, 96), International Encyclopedia of the Sociology of Education, ed. L. Saha (Oxford: Elsevier, 98); auth, ""Teacher burnout," in International Handbook of Teachers and Teaching, ed. B.J. Biddle, T.L. Good, and I.V. Goodson (Dordrecht, The Netherlands: Kluwer, 97), and in La ensenanza y los profesores, vol 3 (La ensenanza en un muno en transformacion), (Madrid: Paidos, 00); coauth, The Minority Report: An Introduction to Race, Ethnic, Gender Relations, 3rd Edition, Harcourt Brace (Fort Worth), 99; auth, "A Scale to Assess Teacher Burnout," in Handbook on Tests and Measurement in Education and the Social Sciences, 2nd Ed, ed. L.K. Bishop and P.E. Lester (Lancester, PA: Technomic Publc Co, forthcoming); coauth, "Case studies in race and ethnic relations," in Case Studies and Social Problems, ed. N. Dolch and L. Deutschman (General Hall, forthcoming); auth, "Teacher Burnout: A Structural Approach," in Education and Sociology: An Encyclopedia, ed. D.L. Levinson, P.W. Cookson Jr, and A.R. Sadovnik (NY: Garland Publ, forthcoming); coauth, "Modeling the Effects of Changing Demography on Student Learning: Application Designed to Change School District Practices," in Challenges of Urban Education, ed. K. McClafferty, C.A. Torres, and T. Mitchell (Albany, NY: SUNY Press, 00). **CONTACT ADDRESS** Dept Sociol, Univ of Houston, 4800 Calhoun Rd, Houston, TX 77204-0001. **EMAIL** gdworkin@jetson.uh.edu

DWYER, JOHANNA
PERSONAL Born 10/20/1938, Syracuse, NY, s **DISCIPLINE** NUTRITION SCIENCES, GERONTOLOGY **EDUCATION** Cornell Univ, BS, 60; Univ Wisc, MS, 62; Harvard Sch Public Health, MSc 68, DSc, 69. **CAREER** Dir, Frances Stern Nutrition Center, 74-; prof, Tufts Sch of Med and Nutrition, 83-; Sr Scientist, Jean Mayer Human Nutrition Research Center on Aging, Tufts, 88-. **HONORS AND AWARDS** BS with honors, Cornell Univ, 60; Inst of Medicine; Nat Acad of Scis; Bd of Trustees, ILSI N Am; published 1 book, 150 original research articles, and 200 review articles. **MEMBERSHIPS** Am Dietetic Asn, Am Soc for Nutrition Scis. **RESEARCH** Nutrition. **SELECTED PUBLICATIONS** Coauth with Van de Bree MBM, and L. J. Eaves, "Genetic and environmental influences on the food patterns of twins aged 50+ y," AJCN, 70 (99): 456-465; coauth with J. Eliasi, "Dietary assessment, dietary guidelines and diets," in D. Heber, ed, Human Nutrition and Obesity, Vol 5, Atlas of Clinical Endocrinology (99): 180-198; auth, "Chapter 22: Early diet and later growth outcomes: from cradle to ripe old age," in F. E. Johnston, B. Zerni, and P. B. Eveleth, eds, Human Growth in Context, Smith Gordon: London, UK (99): 259-271; auth, "Nutrition 101: the concept of nutritional status and guides for nutrition intakes, eating patterns, and nutrition," in J. E. Rippe, Lifestyle Medicine, Butterworth (99): 135-148; auth, "Nutrition for Women in the Childbearing Years: Year 2000 and Beyond," Nutrition in Clinical Care, 2, 1 (99): 2-5; coauth with E. H. J. Kim, K. M. Schroeder, and R. F. Houser, "Two small surveys, 25 years apart, investigation motivations of dietary choice in 2 groups of vegetarians in the Boston area," J of the Am Dietetic Asn, 5 (May 99): 598-601; auth, "Nutrition in the community: the art and science of delivering services," Am J of Clinical Nutrition, 70 (99): 1; coauth with J. Eveland, "Hyperhomocysteinemia and other risk factors for cardiovascular disease in kidney transplant recipients, dialysis, and chronic renal failure patients," Nephrology Incite (winter 2000): 22-26; auth, "Nutrition," in A. E. Kazdin, ed, Encyclopedia of Psychology, Oxford Univ Press, England (2000): 1002-1013; auth, "Moderated discussion in Symposium on functional foods," in J. Milner, ed, Am J of Clinical Nutrition (in press). **CONTACT ADDRESS** Frances Stern Nutrition Center, New England Medical Center, 750 Washington St, Box 783, Boston, MA 02111. **EMAIL** jdwyer@lifespan.org

DYBOWSKI, BRIAN
PERSONAL Born 09/20/1938, Austin, TX, s **DISCIPLINE** PHILOSOPHY, PSYCHOLOGY **EDUCATION** Col Santa Fe (then St Michael's Col), BS, 61; Aquinas Inst, MA, 68; PhD, 70; Ohio State Univ, PhD, 73; St Mary's Univ, MA, 92; Univ St Thomas, Spirituality diploma, 92. **HONORS AND AWARDS** Manuel Lujan Awd for Excellence in Teaching; Fairfax Awd for Outstanding Teaching. **MEMBERSHIPS** Catholic Philos Asn, Fel of Catholic Scholars. **RESEARCH** Learning, Epistemology, Cognitive Psychology. **CONTACT ADDRESS** Dept Soc Sci, Col of Santa Fe, 1600 Saint Michaels Dr, Santa Fe, NM 87505-7615. **EMAIL** bdybowski@csf.edu

DYKE, DORIS J.
PERSONAL Born, ON, Canada **DISCIPLINE** EDUCATION **EDUCATION** Queen's Univ, BA, 59; Univ Toronto, BEd, 61, MEd, 63; Columbia Univ & Union Theol Sem, MA, 62, EdD, 67. **CAREER** Sch tchr, Ont, 12 yrs; assoc prof, Col Ed, Univ Sask, 64-72; assoc prof, Univ Louisville, 72-73; prof & dean of educ, Dalhousie Univ, 73-77; Prof & Dir M.R.E. Studs, Emmanuel Col, 77-95. **HONORS AND AWARDS** Sr Res Awd, ATS, 89. **MEMBERSHIPS** Can Theol Soc; Asn Prof Res Relig Educ; Royal Soc Arts; Phil Educ Soc. **SELECTED PUBLICATIONS** Auth, God's Grace on Fools, God's Pity on God in Can Women's Studs, 87; auth, Crucified Women, 91; co-ed, Education and Social Policy: Local Control of Education, 69. **CONTACT ADDRESS** Univ of Toronto, 82 Admiral Rd, Toronto, ON, Canada M5R 2L6.

DYSON, ROBERT HARRIS, JR.
PERSONAL Born 08/02/1927, York, PA **DISCIPLINE** ANTHROPOLOGY, ARCHAEOLOGY **EDUCATION** Harvard College, BA magna cum laude 50; Harvard Univ, PhD 66; Univ Penn, MA hon 71. **CAREER** Univ Penn, asst prof, assoc prof, 54-94; prof emer, Univ Penn Museum, asst, assoc, curator, curator emer, 54-95, dir, dir emer, 82-94; Univ Penn Arts Sci, dean, 79-82. **HONORS AND AWARDS** R H Dyson Ch Endow, NEA; Elect Cors Mem; Elect APA; Elect Cors Mem Deutchees Arch. **MEMBERSHIPS** AIAP; AIIS; AIA; Brit Sch Arch Iraq; Brit Sch Arch Iran; Brit Sch Arch Turkey; SAA. **RESEARCH** Archaeol and prehistory; Near East and Iran; paleoecoogy; technology; archit; cultural change; hist of Near Eastern archaeol; chronology; and urbanization. **SELECTED PUBLICATIONS** Auth, Triangle-Festoon Ware Reconsidered, Iranica Ant, in press 99; The Achaemenid Triangle Ware of Hasanlu IIIA, Anatolian Iron Ages, BIAT, 98; Hasanlu, ditto vol 2, 97; History of the Field: Archaeology in Persia, The Oxford Encycl of the Near East, OUP, 97. **CONTACT ADDRESS** Near East Laboratory, Univ of Pennsylvania, Philadelphia, PA 19104. **EMAIL** robertd@sas.upenn.edu

DYTELL, RITA
PERSONAL Born 05/09/1943, New York, NY, m, 1965, 1 child **DISCIPLINE** HEALTH STUDIES **EDUCATION** City Col NY, BA, 64; CUNY, PhD, 70. **CAREER** Sen Res Sci, NYork Univ, 70-71; Asst Prof, NYork Inst Tech, 74-81; From Asst Prof, to Prof, Col of Mt St Vincent, 85-. **HONORS AND AWARDS** Fac Develop Summer Grant, Col of Mt St Vincent, 94-95; Sigma Xi. **MEMBERSHIPS** Soc of Behav Med, APA, Soc for the Psychol Study of Soc Issues, EPA. **SELECTED PUBLICATIONS** Coauth, "A Casual Analysis of the Interrelationship Among Exercise, Physical Fitness and Well-Being," Tech Report (92); coauth, "Multidimensional Health Locus of Control, Health Values and Health Behaviors Among Males and Females," Navy Tech Report (92); coauth, "Stability of Health Behaviors and Physical Fitness Over Three years," Navy Tech Report (92): coauth, "Dual Earner Families. The Importance of Work Stress and Family Stress for Psychological Well-Being," J of Occupational Health Psychol, vol 1, no 2 (96): 211-223; coauth, "Mother's and Father's Stress and Well-Being: Same or Different?" Ann of Behav Med 20 (98); coauth, "Parental Work Stress and Family Well-Being," Ann of Behav Med 21 (99); coauth, "Parents Do Matter: Adolescent Stress and Well-Being," Ann of Behav Med (00). **CONTACT ADDRESS** Dept Health Studies, Col of Mount Saint Vincent, 6301 Riverdale Ave, Bronx, NY 10471. **EMAIL** rdytell@cmsv.edu

DZAMBA, ANNE
PERSONAL m, 1987 **DISCIPLINE** HISTORY, WOMEN'S STUDIES **EDUCATION** Swarthmore Col, BA, 60; Univ Del, PhD, 73. **CAREER** Prof of hist and women's studies, chairperson, hist dept, West Chester Univ, Pa, 95-99. **SELECTED PUBLICATIONS** Auth (as Anne Dzamba Sessa), Richard Wagner and the English, and various articles. **CONTACT ADDRESS** Dept Hist, West Chester Univ of Pennsylvania, 700 S High St, West Chester, PA 19383-0003.

DZIEGIELEWSKI, SOPHIA
PERSONAL Born 10/27/1955, Brooklyn, NY, m, 1988, 3 children **DISCIPLINE** SOCIAL WORK **EDUCATION** Univ Cen Flor, BA, 81; Flor State Univ, MSW, 86; PhD, 90. **CAREER** Nurse, US Air Force, 74-76; dir, Gold Age Hlth Care, 78-81; asst dir, Dom Abuse Coun, 82-84; sr eval, GCLSH, 85-86; soc wkr, HPC, 86-87; instr, Flor State Univ, 87-89; asst prof, Martin Army Hosp, 89-92; adj prof, Univ Tenn, 92-95; assoc prof, Meharry Med Col, 92-95; assoc prof, Univ Alabama, 95-97; creator, ed train, Siri Prod, 90-; ten prof, Univ Cen Flor, present. **HONORS AND AWARDS** Jean Rayfield Awd; NASW Soc Wkr of the Year; US PHS Prog Dir Awd; US Army Achiev Medal; Alzheim Asn Outstand Profess Cont Awd; NASW, Stud MSW Soc Wkr of the Year. **MEMBERSHIPS** NASW; CSWE; **SELECTED PUBLICATIONS** Coauth, "Smoking Cessation: Increasing Practice Understanding and Time-Limited Intervention Strategy," J Contemp Human Ser (99); coauth, "EMDR as a Time-Limited Intervention for Body Image Disturbance and self-esteem: A Single Subject Case Study Design," J Psycho Indep Pract (99); coauth, "Self-Directed Treatment for Panic Disorder: A Holistic Approach," J Res Soc Work Eval (00); coauth, "The Measurement of Patient Satisfaction in a Public Hospital in Ankara," Health Serv Manage Res (in press); coauth, "Involuntary Sterilization and Mentally Retarded: Revisited," Human Rights Rev 3 (00); coauth, "Short-Term Treatment: Models and Methods," in Advances in Mental Health Research: Implications for Practice, by J Williams, K Ell (Wash, DC: NASW Press, 98); coauth, "Gender Issues in Family Therapy, in Family Practice: Brief Systems Methods for Social Workers," by C Franklin, C Jordan (Pacific Grove, CA: Brooks/Cole Pub, 98); coauth, "Sexual Desire and Arousal Disorders, in Handbook of Empirical Social Work Practice, Volume 1, Mental Disorders," by B Thyer, J Wodarski (NY: John Wiley & Sons, 98); auth, Clinical, Advanced, Intermediate: Preparation for Social Work Licensure Exam, Sin Prod (Orlando, FL), rev ed, 99; coauth, "Procedures for Evaluating Time-Limited Crisis Intervention," in Crisis Intervention Handbook, ed. A Roberts (New York: Oxford Univ Press, in press); auth, The Changing Face of Health Care Social Work: Professional Practice in the Era of Managed Care, Springer Pub (98); coauth, Introduction to Social Work: The Peoples' Profession, forthcoming; coauth, Clinical Assessment and Psychopharmacology: A Social Work Perspective, Springer Pub, forthcoming; coauth, Human Growth and Development: An Empirical Approach, Springer Pub, forthcoming. **CONTACT ADDRESS** Dept Social Work, Univ of Central Florida, PO Box 163358, Orlando, FL 32816-3358. **EMAIL** sdziegie@mail.ucf.edu

DZUBACK, MARY ANN
PERSONAL Born 03/17/1950, Chattanooga, TN, m, 1983 **DISCIPLINE** HISTORY; EDUCATION **EDUCATION** Franconia Col, BA, 74; Columbia Univ, PhD, 87. **CAREER** From asst prof to assoc prof, Wash Univ, 87-. **HONORS AND AWARDS** Rockefeller Arch Ctr grant; Spencer Found grant, Wash Univ fac res grant, Oberlin Col Arch grant. **MEMBERSHIPS** Hist of Educ Soc; Am Educ Res Asn, Am Hist Asn; Org of Am Hists; Hist of the Behavioral Scis Asn. **RESEARCH** Soc and intellectual hist of educ and higher educ; Women's hist, gender and cult. **SELECTED PUBLICATIONS** Auth, Robert M. Hutchins: Portrait of an Educator, 91; various articles. **CONTACT ADDRESS** Dept of Education, Washington Univ, 1 Brookings Dr, Campus Box 1183, Saint Louis, MO 63130. **EMAIL** madzubac@artsci.wash.edu

E

EACHRON, ANN MAC
PERSONAL Born 10/10/1944, Ithaca, NY, d, 2 children **DISCIPLINE** SOCIAL WORK **EDUCATION** Cornell Univ, BA, 67, PhD, 75; Univ Pittsburgh, MSW, 69. **CAREER** Assoc Sam & Rose Ginfold prof hum develop, Brandeis Univ, 75-84; prof school soc work, Ariz State Univ, 84- . **HONORS AND AWARDS** Phi Kappa Phi **MEMBERSHIPS** Nat Asn Soc Workers. **RESEARCH** Program design and effectiveness in the human services, Indian Child Welfare. **CONTACT ADDRESS** School Soc Work, Arizona State Univ, PO Box 871802, Tempe, AZ 85287. **EMAIL** ann.maceachron@asu.edu

EAGLY, ALICE H.
PERSONAL Born 12/25/1938, Los Angeles, CA, m, 1962, 2 children **DISCIPLINE** PSYCHOLOGY **EDUCATION** Harvard Univ, AB, 60; Univ Mich, MA, 63; PhD, 65. **CAREER** Prof, Northwestern Univ, 95-. **HONORS AND AWARDS** Phi Beta Kappa, 59; Nat Merit Scholar, 56-60; Phi Beta Kappa Sen Prize, Harvard Univ, 60; Fulbright Fel, 60-61; Sigma Xi, 65; Citation as Distinguished Leader Awd, APA, 94; Sabbatical Awd, James McKeen Cattell Fund, 98-99; Distinguished Sci Awd, 99. **MEMBERSHIPS** APA, SESP, MPA, ISP, AWP. **RESEARCH** Attitudes, gender and sex differences. **SELECTED PUBLICATIONS** Coauth, The Psychology of Attitudes, Harcourt Brace Jovanovich (Ft Worth, TX), 93; coauth, Psicologia in las Americas, Sociedad Interamericana de Psicologia (Caracas, Venezuela), 99; coauth, "The Impact of Attitudes on Memory: An Affair to Remember," Psychol Bull 125 (99): 64-89; coauth, "Gender-Stereotypic Images of Occupations Correspond to the Sex Segregation of Employment," Personality and Soc Psychol Bull 25 (99): 413-423; coauth, "The Origins of Sex Differences in Human Behavior: Evolved Dispositions Versus Social Roles," Am Psychol 54 (99): 408-423; coauth, "Quantitative Synthesis of Social Psychological Research," in Handbk

of Res Methods in Soc Psychol (00): 496-528; coauth, "Why Counterattitudinal Messages are as Memorable as Proattituddinal Messages: The Importance of Active Defense Against Attack," Personality and Soc Psychol Bull (forthcoming); coauth, "Do Attitudes Affect Memory? Tests of the Congeniality Hypothesis," Current Directions in Psychol Sci (forthcoming). **CONTACT ADDRESS** Dept Psychol, Northwestern Univ, 102 Swift Hall, Evanston, IL 60208-0001. **EMAIL** eagly@nwu.edu

EARLE, KATHLEEN ALISON
PERSONAL Born 08/17/1944, Syracuse, NY, m, 1979, 3 children **DISCIPLINE** SOCIAL WORK, SOCIAL WELFARE **EDUCATION** SUNY, Albany, BA, 67; MSW, 76; Rockefeller Col, PhD, 96. **CAREER** Res assoc, SUNY, 76-77; NYS Off Men Health, 77-79; pol anal, NYS Comm, 79-80; admin, Camray Corp, 81-83; anal, NYS Men Health, 83-87; soc wkr, Eddy Long THHC, 87-88; anal, res, NYS Men Health, 87-95; asst prof, Univ So Maine, 96-. **HONORS AND AWARDS** NICWA Grant; Fac Sen Res Grant, USM; USM Seed Money; FSR Grant; Found Mem, Soc Social Work Res. **MEMBERSHIPS** AOA; NASW; NICWA; SSW. **RESEARCH** Mental health; American Indians; child welfare. **SELECTED PUBLICATIONS** Auth, "The Greater Bangor Communities for Children Project: A Community that Cares," Bangor Daily News (98); auth, "The Harvest Festival," Families in Soc 80 (99): 213-215; auth, "Cultural Diversity and Mental Health: the Haudenosaunee of New York State," in Multicultural Issues in Social Work, Practice and Research, eds. PL Ewalt, EM Freeman, AE Fortune, DL Poole, SL Witkin (Washington DC: NASW Press, 99); auth, "Cultural Diversity and Mental Health: the Haudenosaunee of New York State," in Social Welfare and Social Work, ed. V E Faherty (Guilford, CT: Dushkin/McGraw Hill, 00); coauth, "Outpatient Suicide: an Emerging Profile," Hospital Comm Psych 45 (96): 123-126; coauth, "Seclusion Use With Children and Adolescents in Public Psychiatric Hospitals," Am J Orthopsych 65 (95): 238-244; coauth, "Mental Health Services Recipients: Their Role in Shaping Organizational Policy," Administration and Policy in Mental Health 23 (96): 547-553; coauth, "Predictors of the Use of Restraint and Seclusion in Public Psychiatric Hospitals," Admin Policy in Mental Health 23 (96): 527-532; coauth, "Child Abuse and Neglect in Indian Country: Policy Issues," Fam Soc 81 (00): 49-58; coauth, Promising Practices: Cultural Strengths and Challenges in Implementing a System of Care Model in American Indian Communities, Child, Adolescent and Family Branch/Center for Mental Health Services, Substance Abuse and Mental Health Services Admin (Washington DC), in press. **CONTACT ADDRESS** Dept Social Work, Univ of So Maine, PO Box 9300, Portland, ME 04104. **EMAIL** kearle@usm.maine.edu

EASTER, MARILYN
PERSONAL Born 01/06/1957, Oklahoma City, OK, m **DISCIPLINE** EDUCATION **EDUCATION** University of Colorado, BA; Denver University, MA, MSW; University of San Francisco, EdD. **CAREER** Marketing By Marilyn, consultant, 79-82; General Dentistry, mktg mgr, 82-; Amador Adult School, instr, 83-85; Chabot Col, instr, 85-87; Calif State Univ, instructor, 87-91; St Mary's Col, assoc prof , 94-99, prof/chair of health services, student advisor mktg mgr, human sevices, Col of Notre Dame, 95-99; adjunct prof of Marketing, Calif State Univ, Hayward, 87-99; prof, Marketing, MIS & Decision science programs, San Jose State Univ, San Jose, CA, 00-. **HONORS AND AWARDS** Outstanding Dissertation Awd, 93; Outstanding Student Council Leadership Awd, 92; Emmy Nominee, Affirmative Action Pro 209, 97; NAFEO, Conference Speaker, 98; Teacher Excellence, Key Note Speaker, 98; Outstanding Prof Recognition, Spring Gala, Col of Notre Dame, 98; Who's Who Among African Americans, 98; United States team member to participate in the Educational Res Ambassadors Prog in China, 99 & 00. **MEMBERSHIPS** Col of Notre Dame, SAFE, chair, 97-; Am Soc of Training & Dev, 99-; Phi Delta Kappa Fraternity, 91-; Calif State Teachers Asn, 93-; NAACP, 97-; Col of Notre Dame, steering comm, co-chair, 97-; Nat School Safety Center, 98-; Nat Asn for Equality in Higher Education, 98-; Calif Professors Asn, 94-; Phi Delta Kappa Fraternity, 92-; Am Res Asn, 90-. **SELECTED PUBLICATIONS** Auth, The ABCs of Mktg a Successful Business, 86; auth, Stress and Coping Mechanism Among Female Dentists, 91; auth, Evaluation of Higher Education, A Case Study, 92; auth, Picking the Perfect School, 93; auth, A Triangulated Research Design for Studying Stress, 93; auth, "Effectiveness of Diversity Training," Center for the Study of Diversity Training and Learning (99); auth, "Technology in Education: Curriculum Implications," University of San Francisco (99); auth, "Racism and Elitism in Higher Education," National Association of African American Studies and the National Association of Hispanic & Latino Studies (99); auth, "Recruitment and Retention in Higher Education: Using Technology," National Association for Equality in Higher Education (99). **CONTACT ADDRESS** Col of Business, San Jose State Univ, One Washington Sq., San Jose, CA 95192-0065. **EMAIL** measter@msn.com

EASTMAN, CAROL M.
PERSONAL Born 09/27/1941, Boston, MA **DISCIPLINE** LINGUISTICS, ANTHROPOLOGY **EDUCATION** Univ Mass, BA, 63; Univ Wis, PhD (ling), 67 **CAREER** Asst prof anthrop and ling, 67-73, assoc prof, 73-79, Prof Anthrop, Univ Wash, 79-, Vis prof, Univ Nairobi, 79-80; Adj Prof Ling and Women Studies, Univ Wash, 79-. **MEMBERSHIPS** Ling Soc Am; fel African Studies Asn; Am Anthrop Asn; Current Anthrop. **RESEARCH** Bantu linguistics and literature; Northwest Indian languages; language and culture. **SELECTED PUBLICATIONS** **CONTACT ADDRESS** Dept of Anthrop, Univ of Washington, Seattle, WA 98195.

EBERLY, MARY B.
PERSONAL Born 11/23/1965, Oshkosh, WI, s **DISCIPLINE** PSYCHOLOGY **EDUCATION** Mich State Univ, BS, 88; Oh State Univ, MA, 91; PhD, 95. **CAREER** Asst prof, Rockhurst Col, 94-96; asst Prof, Oakland Univ, 96-, **MEMBERSHIPS** Ohio State Univ Grad Student Alumni Res Award, 93; Ohio State Univ Seed Grant awarded to Raymond Montemayor, PhD, in support of Mary Eberly's research, 96; Presidential Grant for Fac Develop, Rockhurst Col, 96; Oakland Univ Fac Res Fel, 97; Univ Recognition for Teaching Excellence at the President's Annual Fac Recognition Luncheon, 99. **SELECTED PUBLICATIONS** Coauth with D. J. Flannery, R. Montemayor, and J. Torquati, "Unraveling the ties that bind: Affective expression and perceived conflict in parent-adolescent interactions," J of Social and Personal Relationships, 10 (93): 495-509; coauth with R. Montemayor and D. J. Flannery, "Variations in adolescent helpfulness toward parents in a family context," J of Early Adolescence, 13 (93): 228-244; coauth with R. Montemayor and D. J. Flannery, "effects of pubertal status and conversation topic on parent and adolescent affective expression," J of Early Adolescence, 13 993): 431-447; coauth with D. J. Flannery and R. Montemayor, "The influence of parent negative emotional expression on adolescents' perceived perceptions of their relationships with their parents," Personal Relationships, 1 (94): 259-274; coauth with R. Montemayor, "Doing good deeds: An examination of adolescent prosocial behavior in the context of parent-adolescent relationships," J of Adolescent Res, 13 (98): 403-432; coauth with R. Montemayor, "Chores," in C. Smith, ed, Encyclopedia of Parenting, Westport, Ct: Greenwood Press/Plenum (99); coauth with R. Montemayor, "Adolescent affection and helpfulness toward parents: A 2-year follow-up," J of Early Adolescence, 19 (99): 226-248. **CONTACT ADDRESS** Dept Psychol, Oakland Univ, 208 Pryale, Rochester, MI 48309.

ECKART, MICHELLE
PERSONAL Born 08/13/1947, Chicago, IL, m, 1971, 3 children **DISCIPLINE** EDUCATIONAL PSYCHOLOGY **EDUCATION** Roosevelt Univ, BA, 71; St Cloud State Univ, BS, 87, MS, 88; Univ North Dakota, PhD, 93. **CAREER** Ed specialist, 2 yr learning disabilities prog, Univ Minn, Twin Cities; lect, 1 yr, emotional/behav disabilities prog, Univ Minn, Twin Cities; academic adv, 1 yr, special educator licensure progs, Univ Minn, Twin Cities; supervisor, learning disabilities practicum and lect LD prog, 5 yrs, Univ Minn; supervisor, special educator practicum, 5 yr ed progs, Univ ND; LD teacher 3 yr, Onamia Elementary Sch; coord, 1 yr, academic learning center, St Cloud Univ. **HONORS AND AWARDS** 3 Teaching licenses; 1 administrative license; Grad teaching assistantships: Univ ND, 94, St Cloud State, 94; Bd of Higher Ed Scholarship, State of North Dakota, 92; Excellence in Teaching Awd, presented by Minn Asn of Elementary Sch Principals. **MEMBERSHIPS** CEC. **RESEARCH** Teacher education, special education and the arts, overidentification of Native Americans in special education. **CONTACT ADDRESS** Ed Psychol, Univ of Minnesota, Twin Cities, 178 Pillsbury Dr S E, 204 Burton Hall, Minneapolis, MN 55455. **EMAIL** eckar001@umn.edu

ECKSTEIN, SUSAN
PERSONAL Born New York, NY, m, 1977, 2 children **DISCIPLINE** SOCIOLOGY **EDUCATION** Beloit Col, BA, 63; Columbia Univ, PhD, 71. **CAREER** Lectr to prof, Boston Univ, 77-; adj prof, Boston Col, 95; adj prof, Columbia Univ, 89; vis asst prof, Univ Calif Santa Barbara, 74. **HONORS AND AWARDS** Outstanding Book Awd, Am Sociol Asn, 95; Choice's Outstanding Acad Books Awd, 95; Lourdes Casal Awd, 83; NECLAS Awd, 82; Metcalf Teaching Awd, Boston Univ, 93. **MEMBERSHIPS** Am Sociol Asn; N Eng Coun on Latin Am; Latin Am Studies Asn. **RESEARCH** Latin America: political economy. **SELECTED PUBLICATIONS** Auth, Back from the future: Cuba under Castro, Princeton Univ Press, 94; ed, Power & Popular Protest: Latin American Social Movements, Univ Calif Press, 02; co-ed, Politics of Injustice in Latin America, Univ Calif Press, 02. **CONTACT ADDRESS** Dept Sociol, Boston Univ, 96 Cunningham St, Boston, MA 02215. **EMAIL** seckstei@bu.edu

EDGETTE, J. JOSEPH
PERSONAL Born 06/08/1942, Philadelphia, PA, s **DISCIPLINE** EDUCATION **EDUCATION** West Chester State Col, BS, 66; Univ Penn, MS, 71; MA, 77; PhD, 82. **CAREER** Teacher, Ridley School District, 66-79; Adj Lecturer, Villanova Univ, 79-84; Assoc prof, Widener Univ, 79-. **HONORS AND AWARDS** Phi Beta Delta, 99; Sigma Tau Delta, 98; Knights of St James Fraternity, 96; 2000 Outstanding Scholars of the 20th Century, 99; Kappa Delta Pi Chi Service Awd, 98; Awd of Appreciation, Chester-Upland School district, 98; Outstanding Teacher Awd, School of Human Services, 96; Who's Who Among Am Teachers, 96. **MEMBERSHIPS** Nat Coun of Teachers of English, Penn Coun of Teachers of English, Am Folklore Soc, Penn Folklore Soc, Western Folklore Soc, Children's Folklore Section of the Am Folklore Soc, Educ Section of the Am Folklore Soc, Mid-Atlantic Folklore Soc, PACTE , Am Asn for Col for Teacher Educ, Asn of Grad Liberal Studies Prog, Asn for Supervision and Curriculum Development, Penn Asn, of Col and Teacher Educ, Asn for Gravestone Studies, Am Culture Asn, Phi Kappa Phi, Kappa Delta Pi. **SELECTED PUBLICATIONS** Auth, "Now I lay me down to sleep.: and Their Meaning on Children's Gravemarkers," Children's Folklore Review, 99; auth, "Fields of Folklore: Essays in Honor of Kenneth S Goldstein,": Canadian Folklore Canadien, 98; auth, "A Review of John Barry Brown's Soul in Stone: Cemetery Art from America's Heartland in the Annals of Iowa, 95; auth, "Cemetery Association," in Invisible Philadelphia: Community Through Voluntary Organization, John Hopkins Univ Press, 95; auth, "The Epitaph and Personality Relevation," Cemeteries and Gravemarkers Voices of American Culture, UMI Research, 89; auth, "The Wood Family: Generations of Stone Carvers in Delaware County," Craft and Community: Traditional Arts in Contemporary Society, Penn Heritage Affairs Commission, 88; auth, "Rebirth of the Renaissance Man, and Woman: Master's Program Addresses Renewed Interest in the Liberal Studies," Impact, (86): 13-14; auth, "The Gravemarker and Oral Tradition," New Jersey Folklore, (85): 7-12; auth, "From Generation to Generation: Philadelphia's Wood Family Stone Carvers," Impact, (85): 12-14, 24; auth, "The Wood Family of Philadelphia: Four Generations of Stonecarving," By Land and by Sea: Studies in the Folklore of Work and Leisure Honoring Horace P. Beck on his Sixty-Fifth Birthday, Legacy Books, 85. **CONTACT ADDRESS** Dept Educ, Widener Univ, Pennsylvania, 1 University Pl, Chester, PA 19013.

EDULJEE, NINA
PERSONAL Born 12/20/1963, India, m, 1991 **DISCIPLINE** PSYCHOLOGY **EDUCATION** Univ Ga, MA, 88; Univ Bombay, Psychol, 94; Temple Univ, PhD, 95. **CAREER** Grad asst to instr, Temple Univ, 88-94; Instr, West Chester Univ, 94; asst prof, St. Joseph's Col, 94-. **HONORS AND AWARDS** Psi Chi Honor Society; Nat Scholar, India, 84-85. **MEMBERSHIPS** New England Psych Assoc; Soc for Cross-Cultural Res; Am Educ Res Assoc; Cheiron, ASCD. **RESEARCH** Cross-cultural research on students attitudes towards computers. **SELECTED PUBLICATIONS** Coauth, "Elementary vs Secondary School Teachers Retraining to Teach Computer Science", J of Res on Computing in Educ 27.3 (95): 336-347. **CONTACT ADDRESS** Dept Psychol, Saint Joseph's Col, Maine, 278 Whites Bridge Road, Standish, ME 04084. **EMAIL** neduljee@sjcme.edu

EDWARDS, CARLA
PERSONAL Born 11/14/1955, Manhatten, KS **DISCIPLINE** PSYCHOLOGY **EDUCATION** Univ Mo, PhD. **CAREER** Psychologist, Adolescent Corrections at CSC Tarkio Acad; asst prof, Northwest Mo State Univ. **RESEARCH** Addictions, Trauma Survivors **SELECTED PUBLICATIONS** Coauth, "Rosalie Raynor Watson: The mother of a behaviorist's sons," Psychol Reports 65 (89): 163-169; coauth, "The development of a graduate student handbook intended to facilitate socialization processes," Am Psychol Asn Student Affiliate Newsletter (93); coauth, "Characteristics of counselor self-disclosure in the therapy process," J of Counseling and Development Vol 7 (94): 384-389; auth, "I was born in 1955: An essay on gender roles," Lynx 1.1 (98): 8; auth, "Single-session counseling," The Counseling Interviewer (99):; 8-11; coauth, "Traumagenic dynamics in adult women survivors of childhood sexual abuse vs. Adolescent male sex offenders with similar histories," J of Offender Rehabilitation (in press). **CONTACT ADDRESS** Dept Sociol & Psychol, Northwest Missouri State Univ, 800 University Dr, Maryville, MO 64468. **EMAIL** edwards@mail.nwmissouri.edu

EDWARDS, GRACE TONEY
DISCIPLINE APPALACHIAN LITERATURE & FOLKLORE, AMERICAN LITERATURE, COMPOSITION **EDUCATION** Appalachian State Univ, BS, MA; Univ VA, PhD. **CAREER** Prof, dir, Appalachian Reg Stud Ctr, ch, Appalachian Stud prog, Radford Univ. **SELECTED PUBLICATIONS** Auth, Emma Belle Miles: Feminist Crusader in Appalachia, in the anthology Appalachia Inside Out; Our Mother's Voices: Narratives of Generational Transformation, in the J of Appalachian Stud. **CONTACT ADDRESS** Radford Univ, Radford, VA 24142. **EMAIL** gedwards@runet.edu

EDWARDS, HARRY
PERSONAL Born 11/22/1942, St. Louis, MO, m **DISCIPLINE** SOCIOLOGY **EDUCATION** San Jose State, BA 1964; Cornell U, MA 1966, PhD 1972. **CAREER** San Jose State, instructor Sociology 66-68; Univ of Santa Clara, instructor Sociology 67-68; Univ of CA Berkeley, asst prof Sociology 70-77, assoc prof Sociology, prof Sociology. Served as consultant with producers of sports relatedprograms on NBC, CBS, ABC and PBS TV networks; sports commentary for Natl Public Radio via satellite to Washington DC; interview/commentary prog on KPFA-Radio Berkeley CA; consulted/appeared on camera for BBC TV (British), CBC TV (Candaian) West German TV for CBS' "60 Minutes", CNN's "Sports Focus", NBC's "Nightly News", ABC's "Sportsbeat" and "Nightline", PBS's

"James Michner's World", Turner Sports Nework ESPN "SportsForum" and numerous local & relgional TV productions foing on issues relating to sports & society; participated in lecture & consulting fair at Natl Sports Inst Oslo Norway, Natl Sports Inst Moscow USSR; consultant San Francisco 49ers and Golden State Warriors. **HONORS AND AWARDS** NAACP Educ Incentive Scholarship CA State Univ 1960; Athletic Scholarship CA State Univ 1960; Woodrow Wilson Fellowship 1964; Man of Yr Awd San Francisco Sun Reporter 1968; Russwurm Awd Natl Newspaper Publishers Assoc 1968; fellowship Cornell Univ 1968; Dist Scholar in Res fall 1980 OR State Univ; Miller Scholar in Res fall 1982 Univ of IL Champaign/ Urbana Charleston Gazette; Dist Scholar in Res spring 1983 Norwegian Coll of Physical Educ & Sports Oslow Norway; Dist Schlr Spring 1984 Univ of Charleston; Dist Visiting Scholar fall 1984 IN St Univ. **SELECTED PUBLICATIONS** Contributed editorials to Los Angeles Times, NY Times, San Francisco Examiner, Oakland Tribune, Chicago Sun-Times, Black Scholar, East St Louis Monitor, Milwaukee Courier, Newsday, Los Angeles Hearld Examiner, Sports Illustrated, Sports & Athletes & Inside Sports. **CONTACT ADDRESS** Sociology Dept, Univ of California, Berkeley, 410 Barrows Hall, Berkeley, CA 94720.

EDWARDS, JAY D.
PERSONAL Born 09/05/1937, Chicago, IL, m, 1963, 1 child **DISCIPLINE** ANTHROPOLOGY **EDUCATION** Lycoming Col, BA, 63; Tulane Univ, MA; 65, PhD, 70. **CAREER** Assoc grad faculty, School of Arch, full prof athrop, dir, Fred B. Kniffen Cultural Resources Lab, La State Univ. **HONORS AND AWARDS** Study of historic preservation of Whitney Plantation and planning of La's Creole Plantation Cultures, 91-93; grant, Program for Cultural Cooperation between Spain's Ministry of Culture and the U.S.'s universities, 93; subventions, Ella West Freeman Found and Kemper and Leila Williams Found, 96. **RESEARCH** Cultural anthropology; folklore; vernacular architecture; the Caribbean; Louisiana. **SELECTED PUBLICATIONS** Coauth, Cajun Country, Jackson, 91; auth, The Origins of Creole Architecture, Winterthur Portfolio, 94; coauth, A Creole Lexicon: Architecture, Landscape, People, LSU Press, 98; auth, What Louisiana's Architecture Owes to Hispaniola (and What it does not), Louisiana Cultural Vistas, 99. **CONTACT ADDRESS** Dept of Geography & Anthropology, Louisiana State Univ and A&M Col, Baton Rouge, LA 70803. **EMAIL** gaedwa@lsu.edu

EDWARDS, JOY
PERSONAL Born 02/10/1942, Big Spring, TX, m, 1966, 1 child **DISCIPLINE** EDUCATION **EDUCATION** Baylor Univ, BA, 63; TX Christian Univ, M.Ed, 67; TX Woman's Univ, PhD, 73. **CAREER** Prof, TX Wesleyan Univ, 73-. **MEMBERSHIPS** Asn for Supv & Curric Dev, Phi Delta Kappa, Learning Disability Asn. **CONTACT ADDRESS** Dept Educ & Psych, Texas Wesleyan Univ, 7113 Deer Hollow, Fort Worth, TX 76132. **EMAIL** edwardsj@txwes.edu

EDWARDS, VIVIANE
PERSONAL Born Charlo, NB, Canada **DISCIPLINE** SECOND LANGUAGE EDUCATION **EDUCATION** Univ NB, BA, 63, BEd, 66, MEd, 85. **CAREER** Coord, Second Lang Svcs, Prov NB, 72-85; Prof Educ, Univ New Brunswick 85-, dir Second-Lang Educ Ctr 85-. **HONORS AND AWARDS** Merit Awd, Univ New Brunswick, 90. **MEMBERSHIPS** Can Asn Immersion Tchrs; Can Asn Second-Lang Tchrs. **SELECTED PUBLICATIONS** Auth, French Immersion Process, Product and Perspective in Can Mod Lang Rev, 92; auth, Touch of .. Class! in Can Mod Lang Rev, 94. **CONTACT ADDRESS** Second-Language Educ Centre, Univ of New Brunswick, Fredericton, Fredericton, NB, Canada E3B 6E3. **EMAIL** vedwards@unb.ca

EELLS, GREGORY T.
PERSONAL Born 01/31/1967, Fairfield, IL, m, 1992, 2 children **DISCIPLINE** PSYCHOLOGY **EDUCATION** Greenville Col, BA, 89; Eastern Ill Univ, MA, 91; Okla State Univ, PhD, 96. **CAREER** 4 Years at the Univ of Southern Miss, counseling Center as a licensed psychologist, 2 years as Center Director, also, adjunct prof in psychol. **HONORS AND AWARDS** APA Sci directorate travel Awd; licensed psychologist; BA, Greenville Col, cum laude, 89. **MEMBERSHIPS** Am Psychol Asn, Miss. **RESEARCH** Counseling utilization, public perception of counseling, spirituality and counseling. **SELECTED PUBLICATIONS** Coauth with D. L. Boswell, "The validity of Rorschach inanimate movement and diffuse shading responses as measures of anxiety and frustration," Perceptual and Motor Skills, 78 (94): 1299-1302; coauth with A. F. Carlozzi, K. S. Bull, and J. D. Hurlburt, "Empathy as related to creativity, dogmatism, and expressiveness," J of Psychol, 129 (95): 365-377; coauth with R. N. Williams, D. E. McIntosh, R. S. Dean, and H. Hendrie, "Neuropsychological Subgroups of Dementia of the Alzheimer's Type," Int J of Neuroscience, 87 (96): 79-90; coauth with B. Blackenship, A. F. Carlozzi, L. Barnes, and K. Perry,"Adolescent client perceptions of and reactions to reframe and symptom prescription techniques," J of Mental Health Coun, 20 (98): 172-182; coauth with J. P. Miller, "The effects of degree of religiosity on attitudes toward professional counseling," J of Psychol and Christianity, 17 (98): 248-256; coauth with D. R. Fuqua and D. L. Boswell, "Factors in client's selection of mental health providers," Psychol Reports, 85 (99): 249-254. **CONTACT ADDRESS** Dept Psychol, Univ of So Mississippi, PO Box 5025, Hattiesburg, MS 39406. **EMAIL** Gregory.Eells@usm.edu

EICHENBAUM, HOWARD
PERSONAL Born 10/16/1947, Chicago, IL, m, 1985, 2 children **DISCIPLINE** PSYCHOLOGY **EDUCATION** Univ Mich, BS, 69; PhD, 75. **CAREER** Dept assoc, Univ Mich, 74-75; fel, MIT, 75-77; asst prof, Wellesley Col, 77-91; res affiliate, MIT, 78-91; prof, Univ NC, 91-93; prof, SUNY Stony Brook, 93-96; prof and dir, Boston Univ, 96-. **HONORS AND AWARDS** Res Serv Award, MIT, 75-77. **MEMBERSHIPS** Soc for Neurosci; AAAS. **RESEARCH** Neurobiology of learning and memory. **SELECTED PUBLICATIONS** Co-auth, "Conservation of hippocampal memory function in rats and humans," Nature, (96): 255-257; co-auth, "Functional organization of the hippocampal memory system," Proc Nat Acad Sci, (96): 13500-13507; co-auth, "The hippocampus and memory for orderly stimulus relations," Proc Nat Acad Sci, (97): 7109-7114; auth, "Declarative memory: Insights from cognitive neurobiology," Ann Rev of Psychol, (97): 547-572; co-auth, "Abnormal hippocampal representations in alpha-CaMKII (T286A) and CREB (alpha/delta-) mice," Science, (98): 867-869; co-auth, "The global record of memory in hippocampal neuronal activity," Nature, (99): 613-616; co-auth, "Cross model associative representations in the rodent orbitofrontal cortex," Neuron, (99): 349-359; auth, "A cortical-hippocampal system for declarative memory," Nature Rev Neurosci, (00): 41-50; co-auth, From Conditioning to Conscious Recollection: Memory Systems of the Brain, Oxford Univ Press, 01. **CONTACT ADDRESS** Dept Psychol, Boston Univ, 64 Cummington St, Boston, MA 02215. **EMAIL** hbe@bu.edu

EIGEN, MICHAEL
DISCIPLINE PSYCHOLOGY **EDUCATION** New Sch Soc Res, PhD, 74. **CAREER** Psychologist 30 years. **MEMBERSHIPS** NPA for Psychoanalysis and post doctoral program, NYU. **SELECTED PUBLICATIONS** Auth, The Psychotic Core; The Electrified Tightrope; Psychic Deadness; Toxic Nourishment; The Psychoanalytic Mystic; Reshaping the Self; Coming Through the Whirlwind; several hundred articles. **CONTACT ADDRESS** Apt 101A, New York, NY 10024. **EMAIL** mikeigen@aol.com

EISENSTEIN, HESTER
PERSONAL Born 10/14/1940, New York, NY **DISCIPLINE** SOCIOLOGY **EDUCATION** Radcliffe Col, BA, 61; Yale Univ, PhD (hist), 67. **CAREER** From instr to asst prof hist, Yale Univ, 66-70; asst prof hist, 70-72, Coord Exp Col, Barnard Col, Columbia Univ, 70-96; prof, Queen's Col, 96-; dir, Women's Studies Prog, Queen's Univ, 96-00; Spivack grant, Barnard Col, Columbia Univ, 75. **MEMBERSHIPS** AHA; Nat Women's Studies Asn. **RESEARCH** Gender and globalization in relation to the international women's movement. **SELECTED PUBLICATIONS** Auth, Inside Agitators: Australian Femocrats and the State (Temple Univ Press, 96); auth, Gender Shock: Practicing Feminism on Two Continents (Beacon, 91); auth, Contemporary Feminist Thought (G.K. Hall, 83). **CONTACT ADDRESS** Dept of Sociology, Queens Col, 65-30 Kissena Bvld, Flushing, NY 11367. **EMAIL** hester_eisenstein@qc.edu

EISNER, WENDY
PERSONAL Born 04/05/1953, New York, NY, s, 1 child **DISCIPLINE** PSYCHOLOGY **EDUCATION** Wellesley Col, BA, 75; Columbia Univ, MA, 79; Hunter Col CUNY, PhD, 87. **CAREER** Adj fac, Neurophysiology, The Rockefeller Univ, 88-96; instr to assoc prof, Nassau Community Col, 88-. **HONORS AND AWARDS** Nat Merit Scholar, 71; Phi Beta Kappa, 75; Sigma Xi, 84; Biopsychology Prog of CUNY Distinguished Student Awd, 84; Helena Rubenstein Found Tuition Grant, 85; NCC of SUNY Distinguished Fac Achievement Awd, 97; NCC Student Org of Latinos (SOL) Sponsor-an-Educator Awd, 99; Am Biographical Inst Prof Women's Advisory Bd, 99; Int Who's Who of Prof & Business Women, 6th ed, 99. **MEMBERSHIPS** Int Asn of Empirical Aesthetics, Am Psychol Asn . **RESEARCH** Vision, psychology of art. **SELECTED PUBLICATIONS** Coauth, "Contrast-dependent responses in the human visual system: Childhood through adulthood," Int J of Neuroscience, 80 (95): 181-201; coauth, "Lateral interactions within on and off pathways: A VEP analysis," Supplement to Investigative Opthamology & Visions Science, 37, 3 (96); auth, "Achieving gender equity in science education," Women's Studies Quart. Curriculum Transformation in Community Colleges: Focus on Introductory Courses, Vol XXIV, 3 & 4 (fall/ winter 96): 84-87; co-ed, Gender equity in the classroom: A science education model, NCC Printing & Pubs (97); auth, Feelings & Visions: The psychology of visual art, American Heritage (97). **CONTACT ADDRESS** Dept Psychology, Nassau Comm Col, 1 Education Dr, Garden City, NY 11530.

EKBANTANI, GLAYOL
PERSONAL Born Tehran, Iran, s, 1 child **DISCIPLINE** ESL **EDUCATION** Univ Ill, MA, 74; Univ Ill, PhD, 81. **CAREER** Dir and Prof, St Johns Univ, 92-. **MEMBERSHIPS** TESOL **RESEARCH** Assessment and program evaluation. **SELECTED PUBLICATIONS** Auth, Portfolio Assessment in Teacher Training, 97; auth, Assessment of Business Terminology Through Picture Ads, 98; auth, Engaging ESL Faculty in Self-Assessment, 98; auth, Turning the Table with Faculty Evaluating the Director, 99. **CONTACT ADDRESS** Dept ESL, St. John's Univ, 8000 Utopia Pkwy, Jamaica, NY 11439-0001. **EMAIL** ekbatang@stjohns.edu

ELDRIDGE, DARYL
PERSONAL m, 2 children **DISCIPLINE** FOUNDATIONS OF EDUCATION **EDUCATION** Drury Col, BA, 73; Southwestern Baptist Theol Sem, MARE, 77, PhD, 85. **CAREER** Dean; prof, Southwestern Baptist Theol Sem, 84-. **HONORS AND AWARDS** J.P. Price Awds, 77; Albert G. Marsh Awd, 82; Outstanding Young Men Am, 79; min youth and music, fbc, 72-73; min edu and youth, parkview baptist church, 73-75; min edu and youth, parkview baptist church, 77-80; min edu, tate springs, baptist church, 80-84; min edu, hurst baptist church, 91-96. **SELECTED PUBLICATIONS** Ed, Teaching Ministry of the Church, Broadman & Holman, 95; auth, Why Youth Should Study Doctrine, Equipping Youth, 90; Creative Ways to Study Doctrine, Article. Equipping Youth, 90; How Teenagers Learn at Church, Church Admin, 86. **CONTACT ADDRESS** School Edu Ministries, Southwestern Baptist Theol Sem, PO Box 22000, Fort Worth, TX 76122-0418. **EMAIL** dre@swbts.swbts.edu

ELFIMOV, ALEXEI
PERSONAL Born 04/11/1966, Tselinograd, Union Soviet Socialist Republic, m, 1995 **DISCIPLINE** ANTHROPOLOGY **EDUCATION** Moscow State Univ, BA, 92; Rice Univ, PhD, 98. **CAREER** Lect anthropol, Rice Univ, 98-2000. **HONORS AND AWARDS** Award of the Res Inst for the Study of Man grant, 95; Awd of the Soros Found grant, 92. **MEMBERSHIPS** Am Asn for the Advancement of Slavic Studies. **RESEARCH** Social theory, anthropology, Russia, Europe, USA. **SELECTED PUBLICATIONS** Auth, "Clifford Geertz's Theory of Cultural Interpretation," Etnograficheskoe Obozrenie, no 3 (92); auth, "The State of the Discipline in Russia," Am Anthropol, vol 99 (97); auth, Academics and the Production of Intellectual Discourse of Modernity in Russia, Late Editions, vol 7, Univ of Chicago Press (2000) **CONTACT ADDRESS** Dept Anthropol, Rice Univ, 6100 Main St, Houston, TX 77005. **EMAIL** elfimov@rice.edu

ELIOT, JOHN
PERSONAL Born 10/28/1933, Washington, DC, m, 1959, 3 children **DISCIPLINE** EDUCATION, PSYCHOLOGY **EDUCATION** Harvard Col, AB, 56; Harvard Univ, AMT, 58; Stanford Univ, EdD, 66; Wash Theol Union, Masters, 99. **CAREER** Teacher, Lincoln Public Schs, 58-61; Asst Prof, Northwestern Univ, 66-69; Assoc Prof, Univ Md, 69-78; Prof, Univ Md, 78-. **HONORS AND AWARDS** Distinguished Vis Schol, Univ Leeds, 75; Fel, Am Psychol Asn. **MEMBERSHIPS** APA, APS. **RESEARCH** Human development, educational psychology, nature of explanation in the study of cognition, the nature and measurement of spatial intelligence. **SELECTED PUBLICATIONS** Auth, Human Development and Cognitive Processes, Holt, Rinehart and Winston (New York, NY), 71; auth, Int Dir of Spatial Tests, NFER, 83; auth, Eliot-Price Test, 76; auth, SEK Test, 8; auth, Models of Psychol Space, Springer-Verlag (New York, NY), 87; auth, Gestalt Completion, 99. **CONTACT ADDRESS** Dept Ed & Psychol, Univ of Maryland, Silver Spring, 2705 Silverdale Dr, Silver Spring, MD 20906-5322. **EMAIL** je10@umail.umd.edu

ELKIND, PAMELA D.
PERSONAL Born 07/27/1943, Worcester, MA, m, 1989, 2 children **DISCIPLINE** SOCIOLOGY **EDUCATION** Boston Univ, BA, 65; MA, 72; Northeastern Univ, PhD, 83. **CAREER** Vis prof, Worcester Polytech Inst, 75-76; adj prof, Northeastern Univ, 79; vis prof, Clark Univ, 80-81; vis prof, Dartmouth Col, 81; prof, Eastern Wash Univ, 81-. **RESEARCH** Environment and energy, social impact assessment, medical sociology, rural communities, urban sociology, research methods, evaluation research, applied sociology, sociological practice and family. **CONTACT ADDRESS** Dept Sociol, Eastern Washington Univ, M/S 38, 314 Patterson Hall, Cheney, WA 99004.

ELLENS, JAY HAROLD
PERSONAL Born 07/16/1932, McBain, MI, m, 1954, 7 children **DISCIPLINE** PSYCHOLOGY; RELIGION **EDUCATION** Calvin Coll, BA, 53; Calvin Theol Sem, MDiv, 56; Princeton Theol Sem, ThM. 65; Wayne State Univ, PhD, 70; Univ Mich, PhD. **CAREER** Univ tchg, 65-85; clin psychol, 70-; Presby Theol, Pastor, Pastoral Counr, 56- ; US Army Chaplain (COL), 55-92; Princeton tchg fel; Finch lectr, Fuller; Wheaton Distinguished lectr; Stob lectr ethics and religion; distinguished lectr, Austin Theol Sem. **HONORS AND AWARDS** Meritorious Serv Medals (4), Legion Merit, numerous for serv, unit, merit citations, medals, ribbons (16), US Army. **MEMBERSHIPS** CAPS; SBL; AAR; AIA; ROA; MOWW; AL. **RESEARCH** Psychology of human development; Christians origins and their roots in ancient Judaism. **SELECTED PUBLICATIONS** auth Models of Religious Broadcasting, 74; God's Grace and Human Health, 82; Turning Points

in Pastoral Care, 89; Christian Perspectives on Human Development, 90; coauth, Interpretation of Bible, 97. **CONTACT ADDRESS** 26707 Farmington Road, Farmington Hills, MI 48334-4329. **EMAIL** jharoldellens@Juno.com

ELLIOTT, MARTA
PERSONAL Born 03/23/1964, OH, s, 2 children **DISCIPLINE** SOCIOLOGY **EDUCATION** Ohio State Univ, BA, 88, BA, 90; Johns Hopkins Univ, PhD, 94. **CAREER** Asst prof of Sociol, Univ Nevada, Reno, 96-. **MEMBERSHIPS** Am Sociol Asn, Am Public Health Asn, Pacific Sociol Asn. **RESEARCH** Survey deign and analysis, sociology of mental health and illness, sociology of education. **SELECTED PUBLICATIONS** Coauth with Toby Parcel, "The Determinants for Young Women's Wages: Comparing the Effects of Individual and Occupational Labor Market Characteristics," Soc Sci Res, 25 (96): 240-259; auth, "Impact of Work, Family and Welfare Receipt on Women's Self-Esteem and Young Adulthood," Soc Psychol Quart, 59, 1 (96): 80-95; coauth with John F. Packham, "When Do Single Mothers Work?: An Analysis of the 1990 U. S. Census Data," J of Sociol and Soc Welfare 25, 1 (98): 39-60; auth, "School Finance and Opportunities to Learn: Does Money Well Spent Enhance Student's Achievement?," Sociol of Ed, 71, 3 (98): 223-245; auth, "The Stress Process in Neighborhood Context," Health and Place (forthcoming). **CONTACT ADDRESS** Dept Sociol, Univ of Nevada, Reno, N Virginia Ave, Reno, NV 89557-0001. **EMAIL** melliott@unr.edu

ELLIS, CAROLYN SUE
PERSONAL Born 10/13/1950, Luray, VA, m, 1995 **DISCIPLINE** SOCIOLOGY, COMMUNICATION **EDUCATION** The Col Wiilliam & Mary, BA, 73; State Univ NYork, Stony Brook, MA, 77; PhD, 81. **CAREER** Asst prof, Univ South Fla, 81-85, assoc prof, 85-94, Co-Dir for Inst for Interpretive Human Studies, Col of Arts and Scis, 90-, joint appt, Special Educ, assoc mem, Inst on Aging, Courtesy appt, Gerontology, 96-, prof, Dept of Sociol, 94-, prof, Dept of Commun, 96-. **HONORS AND AWARDS** Nominated for Cooley Awd, Soc for the Study of Symbolic Interaction, 95; Provost's Salary Awd for Outstanding Career Performance, 95; the USF Grad Student Commun Asn Outstanding Fac Recognition Awd, 97-98; Dow Vis Scholar, Saginaw Valley State Univ, spring 99; Teaching Incentive Prog Awd, USF, 98; Univ Teaching Awd, USF, 99; Merit Pay Awd, USF, 99; HUB Awd, Outstanding fac Awd, selected by USF Commun graduating MA students, 98-99; Feminist Mentor Awd, given by Soc for the Study of Symbolic Interaction, 2000. **MEMBERSHIPS** Am Sociol Asn, Int Soc for Res on Emotions, Soc for the Study of Symbolic Interaction, Midwest Sociol Soc, Nat Commun Asn, Int Soc for the Study of Interpersonal Relationships. **RESEARCH** Qualitative methods, ethnography, emotions, health and illness, interpersonal relationships, race and emotions, narrative inquiry, interpretive social science, death and dying, writing lives. **SELECTED PUBLICATIONS** Auth, Fisher Folk: Two Communities on Chesapeake Bay, Lexington, Ky: The Univ Press of Ky (86); auth, Final Negotiations: A Story of Love, Loss, and Chronic Illness, Philadelphia: Temple Univ Press (95); co-ed with A. Bochner, Composing Ethnography: Alternative Forms of Qualitative Writing, AltaMira Press (96); co-ed with A. Bochner, Taking Ethnography into the Twenty-First Century, special issue of J of Contemporary Ethnography, Vol 25, No 1 (April 96): 1-168; auth, "What Counts as Scholarship in Communication? An Autoethnographic Response," Am Commun J (on-line), Vol 1, Issue 2 (Feb 14, 98); coauth with A. Bochner, "Bringing Emotional and Personal Narrative into Medical Social Science," Health, Vol 3, No 3 (99): 229-237; coauth with A. Bochner, "Which Way to Turn?," J of Contemporary Ethnography, Vol 28, No 5 (99): 485-499; auth, "He(art)ful Autoethnography," Qualitative Health Res, Vol 9, No 5 (99): 653-667; auth, "Creating Criteria: An Ethnographic Short Story," Qualitative Inquiry, Vol 6, No 2 (in press); auth, Doing Autoethnography: A Methodological Novel, Walnut Creek, Calif: AltaMira Press (forthcoming). **CONTACT ADDRESS** Dept of Commun, Univ of So Florida, 4202 E Fowler Ave, CIS 1040, Tampa, FL 33620-7800. **EMAIL** cellis@chumal.cas.usf.edu

ELLIS, SUSAN
PERSONAL Born Pocatello, ID, 3 children **DISCIPLINE** ANTHROPOLOGY **EDUCATION** Univ Utah, PhD, 97. **CAREER** Heritage Col 87-; outstanding fac award; Newberry Libr fel; Templeton Found award. **MEMBERSHIPS** Am Schools Oriental Res; Near E Archaeol Soc. **RESEARCH** Pottery technology; Ethmoarchaeology; Georgraphic information systems; Palynology; Museology. **SELECTED PUBLICATIONS** Auth January 1994: Preliminary Pollen Report for 1992 Excavation Abila of the Decapolis, Jordan, Near E Archaeol Soc Bull; Household Styles and Pottery Use in Modern Egypt: Patterns for Archaeology, Am Schools Oriental Res, 94; Replication of Rammeside Pottery Styles by a Modern Egyptian Potter, Am Schools Oriental Res, 95. **CONTACT ADDRESS** 4911 Cherokee, Pocatello, ID 83686. **EMAIL** ellis_s@heritage.edu

ELLSWORTH, PHOEBE C.
PERSONAL Born 01/22/1944, Hartford, CT, m, 1979, 2 children **DISCIPLINE** PSYCHOLOGY **EDUCATION** Bryn Mawr Col, AB, 63; Radcliffe Col, AB, 66; Stanford Univ, PhD, 70. **CAREER** Asst Prof, Stanford Univ, 70-71; Asst Prof, Yale Univ, 71-75; Vis Asst Prof, Stanford Univ, 73-74; From Assoc Prof to Prof, Yale Univ, 75-81; Prof, Stanford Univ, 81-87; Prof, Univ Mich, 87-. **HONORS AND AWARDS** Phi Beta Kappa; Outstanding Res Awd, Univ Mich, 96; Sen Fel, Mich Soc Fels, 92-96; Distinguished Lectr, Am Psychol Asn, 99. **MEMBERSHIPS** APA, APS, SESP, APLA, LSA, Am Asn of Applied and Preventive Psychol, AALS, AAAS. **RESEARCH** Motivation and emotion, law and human behavior, law and society, personality and social psychology, child development, experimental social psychology. **SELECTED PUBLICATIONS** Auth, "Some Reasons to Expect Universal Antecedents of Emotion," in The Nature of Emotion: Fundamental Questions (New York: Oxford UP, 95), 150-154; auth, "Levels of Thought and Levels of Emotion," in The Nature of Emotion: Fundamental Questions (New York: Oxford UP, 95), 192-196; coauth, "Who Should Stand Next to the Suspect?" J of Applied Psychol 80 (95): 525-531; coauth, "Psychology and Law," in The Handbk of Soc Psychol, 4th ed (McGraw-Hill, 98), 684-731; coauth, "Through the Looking Glass Darkly? When Self Doubts Turn Into Relationship Insecurities," J of Personality and Soc Psychol 75 (98): 1459-1480; coauth, "Sentimental Stereotypes: Emotional Expectations for High and Low Status Group Members," Personality and Soc Psychol Bull (forthcoming); auth, "Jury Reform at the End of the Century: Real Agreement, Real Changes," J of Law Reform (forthcoming); coauth, " Juror Comprehension and Public Policy: Perceived Problems and Proposed Changes," Psychol, Public Policy and Law (forthcoming). **CONTACT ADDRESS** Dept Psychol, Univ of Michigan, Ann Arbor, 525 E University Ave, Hutchins Hall, Ann Arbor, MI 48109-1109. **EMAIL** pce@umich.edu

ELNAJJAR, HASSAN
PERSONAL Born 03/13/1950, Gaza, m, 1973, 5 children **DISCIPLINE** SOCIOLOGY **EDUCATION** Univ Ga, PhD, 93. **CAREER** Asst Prof, Dalton State Col, 91-. **MEMBERSHIPS** ASA; GSA. **RESEARCH** Immigration; Gulf War. **CONTACT ADDRESS** Dept Soc Sci, Dalton Col, 213 N Col Dr, Dalton, GA 30720.

ELSBERND, MARY
PERSONAL Born 07/09/1946, Decoral, IA **DISCIPLINE** CATHOLIC SOCIAL TEACHINGS, SOCIAL ETHICS; WOMEN'S STUDIES; GOSPEL OF JOHN **EDUCATION** Briar Cliff Col, BA, 68; St. John's Univ, MA, 77; Katholieke Univ Leuven, Belgium, Sacrae Theologiae Baccalauraum, 82, Sacrae Theologiae Licentiatam, 83, BA, 81, MA, 82, PhD, 85, Sacrae Theologiae Doctor, 86. **CAREER** Asst prof, 92-96, assoc prof Pastoral Stud in Social Ehtics, 96- , Grad Dir Master Div prof, 95, Loyola Univ; asst prof Theology, 85-89, assoc prof, 89-92, Briar Cliff Col; Instr Theol, Briar Cliff Col, 79-80; Rel tchr in Wahlert and Aquin Catholic High Schools, 68-79; French Tchr Aquin Cath High Sch, 68-73; vis guest prof, Katholieke Univ Leuven, fac Moral Theol and Women's Stud, 97; Vrij asst for the Moral Theol Dept, Katholieke Univ, 84; res asst with Ctr of Concern, Wash DC, summer 90; fac mem in the Sioux City Diocesan Church Ministries Prog, 88-92; dir, Briar Cliff Peace Stud Prog, 87-92; **HONORS AND AWARDS** Study leave, Loyola Univ, Chicago, Fall 97; Loyola Univ Scholar Recipient to Faith and the Intellectual Collegium, Summer 95; Res Support Grant, Summer 94, Loyola Univ, for Young Adult Volunteer Proj; Briar Cliff Col nominee to NEH, summer grant, 92; Briar Cliff nominee for Kellogg Natl Fel Prog for the development fo "effective and broad leadership skills and abilities: 89; Briar Cliff Col finalist for Burlington Northern Outstand Tchr, 87; Vrij Asst for the Moral Theol Dept, Katholieke Univ Leuven, 84; Acad Scholar Katholieke Univ Leuven, 81-85. **MEMBERSHIPS** Cath Theol Soc Am; AAR; Soc Christian Ethics; Cath Comm on Intell Cultural Affairs. **RESEARCH** Justice and John; Women's Leadership. **SELECTED PUBLICATIONS** Auth, Papal Statements on Rights, A Historical Contextual study of Encyclical Teaching from Pius VI to oPius XI (1791-1939), Ann Arbor, MI: Univ Microfilms, Inc., 85; auth, "Rights Statements, A Hermeneutical Key to Continuing Development in Magisterial Teaching, in Ephemerides Theologicae Lovanienses LXII, (86): 308-332; co-auth, "What's at Stake? American Women Religious Naming Ourselves Women," in Claiming Our Truth, Reflections on Identity by Am Women Religious, (Washington, DC: LCWR, 88); auth, A Theology of Peacemaking, A Vision, A Road, A Task, Lanham, MD: Univ Press of Am, 88; coauth, When Love is not Enough, The Practice of Justice, Collegeville: The Liturgical Press, (forthcoming); coauth, Integrating Catholic Heritage, Catholic Teacher Supplement to The World Around Us, New York: Macmillan/McGraw-Hill, 91; auth, "Work and Workers," in Louvain Studies 19, (94): 212-234; auth, "And Whatever Happened to Octogesima adveniens, 4?" in Theological Studies 56, (95): 39-60; auth, "The Reinterpretation of Gaudium et spes in Vertatis Splendor," in Bibiotheca Ephemeridum Theooogicarum Lovaniensium, (forthcoming); auth, "Theorectical Foundations of Interactive leadership in Catholic Social Teachings". **CONTACT ADDRESS** Institute of Pastoral Studies, Loyola Univ, Chicago, 6525 N Sheridan Rd, Chicago, IL 60626. **EMAIL** melsber@luc.edu

EMERY, KITTY
PERSONAL Born 09/05/1963, Barbados, s **DISCIPLINE** ANTHROPOLOGY **EDUCATION** Trent Univ, BSc, 86; Univ Toronto, MA, 90; Cornell Univ, MA, 93; PhD, 97. **CAREER** Teaching Asst, Univ Toronto, 87-88; Teaching Asst, York Univ, 89-90; Teaching Asst to Instructor, Cornell Univ, 93-96; Asst Prof, SUNY, 97-. **HONORS AND AWARDS** Soc Sci and Humanities Res Coun Fel, 98-99; Soc Sci Humanities Res Coun of Can Fel, 92-99; Cornell Univ Sage Doctoral Fel, 92-96. **RESEARCH** Mesoamerican archaeology; Environmental archaeology; Zooarchaeology; Latin American cultural heritage management (environmental emphasis). **SELECTED PUBLICATIONS** Co-auth, "Ancient and modern Maya exploitation of the jute snail," Latin American Antiquity, (90): 170-183; co-auth, "Arqueologia, epigrafia y el descubrimiento de una tumba real en el centro ceremonial de Dos Pilas, Peten," Utz'ib, (91): 14-28; co-auth, "Between Mountains and Sea: Investigations at Piedras Negras," Mexicon, 98; auth, "Temporal trends in ancient Maya animal use: Zooarchaeological studies of Postclassic and Colonial period faunal assemblages from Lamanai and Tipu, Belize," in Reconstructing Ancient Maya Diet, Univ UT Press, 99; auth, "Fauna of Ancient Mexico and Central America," in The Archaeology of Ancient Mexico and Central America: An Encyclopedia, Garland Pub, in press; co-auth, "Isotopic Analysis of Ancient Deer Bone: Biotic Stability in Collapse Period Maya Land-Use," Journal of Archaeological Science, in press; co-auth, "Freshwater Snail Use in the Maya Lowlands: Application of Foraging Strategy Models," Journal of Archaeological Science, in press; co-ed, Maya Zooarchaeology: New Directions in Method and Theory, UCLA Press, in press; auth, "Dietary, Environmental, and Societal Implications of Ancient Maya Animal Use in the Petexbatun: A Zooarchaeological Perspective on the Collapse," Vanderbilt Univ Press, in press. **CONTACT ADDRESS** Dept Anthropol, SUNY, Col at Potsdam, 44 Pierrepoint Ave, Potsdam, NY 13676. **EMAIL** emerykf@potsdam.edu

EMIGH, REBECCA JEAN
DISCIPLINE SOCIOLOGY **EDUCATION** Columbia Univ, BA, 84; MA, 85; Univ Chicago, MA, 90; PhD, 93. **CAREER** Dir, Center for Comparative Social Analysis, Univ Calif, Los Angeles, 99; Fac affiliate, Developmental Studies Prog, Univ Calif, Los Angeles, 93-; Fac affiliate, Center of Medieval and Renaissance Studies, Univ Calif, Los Angeles, 93-; asst prof, of Sociol with a joint appointment in the Dept of Statistics, Univ of Calif, Los Angeles, 93-. **HONORS AND AWARDS** Ford Found Grant, 98-2000; World Bank Grant, 99-2000; Ctr for German and European Studies Grant, Univ of Calif, Berkeley, 99; Nat Sci Found Grant, 99-2000; Univ Calif, Los Angeles, Academic Senate Grant, 99-2000; ISOP Fac Small Grant Awd, Univ Calif, Los Angeles, 99-2000; Career Development Awd, Univ Calif, Los Angeles, 99-2000. **MEMBERSHIPS** Am Sociol Asn, Soc for Comparative Res, Population Asn of Am, Soc Sci Hist Asn, Am Sociol Asn, Am Statistical Asn. **SELECTED PUBLICATIONS** Auth, "Traces of Certainty: Recording Death and Taxes in Fifteenth-Century Tuscany," The J of Interdisciplinary Hist, XXX (II, Autumn 99): 181-198; auth, "The Length of Leases: Short-Term Contracts and Long-Term Relationships," Viator, 30 (99): 345-382; auth, "Means and Measures: Productive Comparisons of Agricultural Output of Sharecropping and Smallholding in Fifteenth-Century Tuscany," Social Forces, 78, 2 (99): 461-491; auth, "The Gender Division of Labor: The Case of Tuscan Smallholders," Continuity and Change (forthcoming); coauth with Rosemary L. Hopcroft, "Divergent Paths of Agrarian Change: Eastern England and Tuscany Compared," The J of European Economic Hist (in press); auth, "Economic Outcomes: Forms of Property Rights or Class Capacities? The Example of Tuscan Sharecropping," The European J of Sociol (forthcoming); coauth and ed with Ivan Szelenyi, Poverty, Ethnicity, and Gender in Eastern Europe During the Market Transition, Greenwood Press (forthcoming); coauth with Eva Fodor and Ivan Szelenyi, "The Racialization and Feminization of Poverty?" in Poverty, Ethnicity, and Gender in Eastern Europe During Market Transition, Greenwood Press (forthcoming). **CONTACT ADDRESS** Dept Sociol, Univ of California, Los Angeles, PO Box 951551, Los Angeles, CA 90095-1551. **EMAIL** emigh@bigstar.sscnet.ucla.edu

EMIHOVICH, CATHERINE A.
PERSONAL Born 06/04/1948, Tonawanda, NY, m, 1974, 2 children **DISCIPLINE** EDUCATION **EDUCATION** Syracuse Univ, BS, 70; SUNY, MA, 80; PhD, 83. **CAREER** Adj Asst Prof, SUNY, 80-82; Asst Prof, Univ SC, 82-87; Assoc Prof, Fla State Univ, 87-94; Assoc Prof to Prof, SUNY, 94-. **HONORS AND AWARDS** Distinguished Alumni Awd, SUNY. **MEMBERSHIPS** AERA, AAA, Coun on Anthropol and Educ. **RESEARCH** Race, class and gender equity in education; Professional development in teacher education; School-liked integrated services. **SELECTED PUBLICATIONS** Co-auth, "Introduction to critical thinking," Educational Foundations, (99): 3-9; auth, "Compromised positions: The ethics and politics of designing research in the postmodern age," in Accuracy or advocacy: The politics of research in education, Educational Policy, 99; auth, "Framing teen parenting: Cultural and social contexts," Education and Urban Society, (98): 139-156; auth, "Boys will be boys: Young Males' perceptions of women, sexuality, and prevention," Education and Urban Society, (98): 172-188; auth, "Distancing passion: Narratives in social science," qualitative Studies in Education ,(95): 37-48; co-auth, Transforming schools and schools of education: A new vision for preparing educators, Corwin Press, 98; co-auth, Sex, kids and politics: Health services in schools, Teachers Col Press, 97;

auth, "Bodytalk: Discourses of sexuality among adolescent African-American girls," in Kids talk: strategies language practices in later childhood, Oxford Univ Press. **CONTACT ADDRESS** Dept Educ Psychol, SUNY, Buffalo, PO Box 601000, Buffalo, NY 14260-0001.

ENDERS, VICTORIA L.
PERSONAL Born 05/08/1944, Stamford, TX, m, 1995, 3 children **DISCIPLINE** WOMENS STUDIES **EDUCATION** Hills Col, BA, 66; Columbia Univ, MA, 67; Univ Calif, PhD, 84. **CAREER** Asst to assoc prof, Northern Ariz Univ, 85-. **MEMBERSHIPS** SSPHS, NACS, WSPH, SFHS, SWWH, WAWH. **RESEARCH** European cultural history, Women, France and Spain, Modernism **SELECTED PUBLICATIONS** Auth, Constructing Spanish Womanhood: Female Identity in Modern Spain, New York, 99. **CONTACT ADDRESS** Dept Womens Studies, No Arizona Univ, PO Box Nau, Flagstaff, AZ 86011-0001. **EMAIL** victoria.enders@nau.edu

ENGEL, MARTIN
PERSONAL Born 12/27/1929, Mannheim, Germany, m, 1958, 3 children **DISCIPLINE** EDUCATION **EDUCATION** Syracuse Univ, BA, 51, PhD, 61; Harvard Univ, MA, 53. **CAREER** Asst art hist, Syracuse Univ, 56-59, instr, 60-61; asst prof humanities, Monteith Col, Wayne State Univ, 61-62; from asst prof to assoc prof hist and fine arts, Carnegie-Mellon Univ, 62-69; sr prog officer, Arts and Humanities Prog, US Off Educ, 69-72; Sr Prog Officer Educ Res and Develop, Nat Inst Educ, 72-; Arts and Humanities Adv, Nat Inst Educ, Dept Health, Educ, Welfare, 76-, Consult, Nat Endowment Humanities, 69-71 and Harcourt Brace Jovanovich, 73; adv bd, Rockefeller Brothers Fund, 80-. **MEMBERSHIPS** Nat Art Educ Asn. **RESEARCH** Cognitive processes in the arts; education policy in arts and humanities; research management. **SELECTED PUBLICATIONS** Auth, The European Novel--History of its Poetics, Archiv Studium Neueren Sprachen Literaturen, Vol 230, 93; Aesthetics of Modernism, Archiv Studium Neueren Sprachen Literaturen, Vol 233, 96; Aesthetics of Modernism, Archiv Studium Neueren Sprachen Literaturen, Vol 233, 96; Early Realism and the Legacy of Romanticism--Myth, Dream and Fairy Tales in Immermann, Karl Works, Zeitschrift Deutsche Philologie, Vol 114, 95; The European Novel--History of its Poetics, Archiv Studium Neueren Sprachen Literaturen, Vol 230, 93; Translated Life--Rimbaud Biography in its German Translations by Klammer, Karl, Zech, Paul, and Wolfenstein, Alfred, Germanisch Romanische Monatsschrift, Vol 43, 93. **CONTACT ADDRESS** National Inst of Educ, Washington, DC 20208.

ENGEL, SCOTT
PERSONAL Born 03/22/1968, Los Angeles, CA, m, 1992, 1 child **DISCIPLINE** PSYCHOLOGY **EDUCATION** Sonoma State Univ, BA, 90; MA, 91. **CAREER** Instructor, Miles Cmty Col, 91-. **HONORS AND AWARDS** Who's Who Among Col Teachers. **MEMBERSHIPS** Phi Theta Kappa. **RESEARCH** Psycholinguistics; Plautdietsch (Low German) Language. **CONTACT ADDRESS** Dept Philos & Psychol, Miles Comm Col, 2715 Dickinson St, Miles City, CT 59301. **EMAIL** engels@po.mec.cc.mt.us

ENGLAND, MICHEAL
PERSONAL Born 09/14/1954, Beloit, WI, m, 1976 **DISCIPLINE** EDUCATION **EDUCATION** Andrews Univ, BS, 77; Western Carolina Univ, MA, 80; Walla Walla Col, MEd, 86; Andrews Univ, EDD, 96. **CAREER** Teacher, Captain Gilmer Elem Sch, 77-81. **HONORS AND AWARDS** Who's Who Am Teachers, 98, 00; Phi Delta Kappa; Pi Lambda Theta. **MEMBERSHIPS** Asn Supv Curric Develop (ASCD). **RESEARCH** School Reform, Staff development, Brain- compatible teaching. **SELECTED PUBLICATIONS** Auth, Fantastic Field Day Flings, 93; auth, Positively Phenomenal Physicality, 94; auth, Multiple Intelligence Resource Manual, 98. **CONTACT ADDRESS** Dept Educ and Psychology, Southwestern Adventist Univ, PO Box 567, Keene, TX 76059-0567. **EMAIL** englandm@swau.edu

ENGLER, RUSSELL
PERSONAL Born 01/29/1957, Ridgewood, NJ, m, 1987, 2 children **DISCIPLINE** LAW, LEGAL EDUCATION **EDUCATION** Yale Col, BA, 79; Harvard Law Sch, JD, 83. **CAREER** Clerk, U.S. Circuit Court of Appeals, 83-84; staff atty, Brooklyn Legal Serv, 84-93; asst prof to prof and dir, New Eng Sch of Law, 93-; lectr, Harvard Law Sch, 99-00. **MEMBERSHIPS** Bar Member in Mass, NY and Md; Boston Bar Asn; Mass Bar Asn; Asn of Am Law Sch; Clinical Legal Educ Asn. **RESEARCH** Poverty Law; Public Interest Law; Legal Ethics. **SELECTED PUBLICATIONS** Auth, "Out of sight and Out of Line: The Need for Regulation of Lawyers' Negotiations with Unrepresented Poor Persons," Calif L Rev, 97; auth, "And Justice For All--Including the Unrepresented Poor: Revisiting the Roles of the Judges, Mediators, and Clerks," Ford L Rev, 99. **CONTACT ADDRESS** New England Sch of Law, 154 Stuart St, Boston, MA 02116.

ENGLISH, LEONA
PERSONAL Born 11/10/1963, NF, Canada **DISCIPLINE** EDUCATION **EDUCATION** Memorial Univ Newfoundland, BA, 84, BEd, 84; Univ Toronto, MRE, 89; Columbia Univ, EdD, 94. **CAREER** Asst Prof, St. Francis Xavier Univ, 96-. **MEMBERSHIPS** (CASAE), Asn of Prof and Res in Relig Educ, Am Asn of Adult and Continuing Educ, Can Asn for the Study of Adult Educ, Relig Educ Asn of Canada and the US. **RESEARCH** Adult education, informal learning, mentoring, postmodernity. **SELECTED PUBLICATIONS** Auth, Mentoring in Religious Education, 98; auth, "Mentoring for Adult Religious Educators," in Caravan, 98; "The Tradition of Teresa of Avila and its Implications for Mentoring of Religious Educators," 96. **CONTACT ADDRESS** St. Francis Xavier Univ, PO Box 5000, Antigonish, NS, Canada B2G 2W5. **EMAIL** lenglish@stfx.ca

ENTERLINE, LYNN
DISCIPLINE GENDER STUDIES, CLASSICAL, MEDIEVAL, AND EARLY MODERN LITERATURE **EDUCATION** Cornell, PhD. **CAREER** Instr, Vanderbilt Univ. **RESEARCH** Theories of rhetoric, language, and poetics from the classical period through the 17th century; contemporary intersections between feminist, queer, materialist and psychoanalytic critiques of literature and culture. **SELECTED PUBLICATIONS** Auth, The Tears of Narcissus: Melancholia and Masculinity in Early Modern Writing; The Rhetoric of the Body in Renaissance Ovidian Poetry. **CONTACT ADDRESS** Vanderbilt Univ, Nashville, TN 37203-1727.

EPPERSON, DOUGLAS
DISCIPLINE PYSCHOLOGY **CAREER** Asst Prof to Assoc Prof and Assoc Chair, Iowa State Univ, 79-. **HONORS AND AWARDS** Res Grant, Sci and Humanities; Grant, Dept of Public Instruction, 94-96; Grant, ISU Office of the President, 99-01. **MEMBERSHIPS** Am Psychol Asn, Am Psychol Soc, Midwestern Psychol Asn, Iowa Psychol Asn, Asn for the Treatment of Sexual Abusers. **SELECTED PUBLICATIONS** Co-auth, "The experience and expression of anger: Relationships with gender, gender-role socialization, and mental health functioning," Journal of counseling Psychology, (96): 158-165; auth, "Women's career development: Can theoretically derived variables predict persistence in engineering majors?," Journal of Counseling Psychology, (97): 173-183; auth, "A multiple groups analysis of predictors of higher-level career aspirations among women in mathematics, science, and engineering majors," Journal of Counseling Psychology, (98): 483-496; auth, "Perceived causes of success and failure: Are women's attributions related to satisfaction and persistence in engineering majors," Journal of Research in Science Teaching, (99): 663-676; co-auth, "Minnesota Sex Offender Screening Tool (MnSOST)," Minnesota Dept of Corrections, 95; co-auth, "Minnesota Sex Offender Screening Tool - Revised (MnSOST-R)," Minnesota Dept of Corrections, 98. **CONTACT ADDRESS** Dept Psychol, Iowa State Univ, 1 Iowa State Univ, Ames, IA 50011-3180.

ERDENER, YILDIRAY
DISCIPLINE FOLKLORE, ETHNOMUSICOLOGY **EDUCATION** Indiana Univ, MA, PhD, 87. **CAREER** Instr, Defense Lang Inst Monterey Calif, 85-86; Instr, Univ of Calif Berkeley, 86-87; Res, Scholar in Residence, "Shifting Gears, the meaning of work,", 88-91; Asst Prof, Univ of tex at Austin, 93-. **HONORS AND AWARDS** Fulbright-Hays Doctoral Dissertation Abroad; Inst of Turkish Studies; Nat Endowment for the Humanities. **MEMBERSHIPS** Am Folklore Soc, Soc of Asian Music. **RESEARCH** Minstrel tradition of Turkey and Central Asia, Shamanism in Siberia and Central Asia, Middle Eastern Music. **SELECTED PUBLICATIONS** Auth, Muzik Formlari (The Forms of Music), 76; auth, "Turkish Minstrels in Song Duel ," Int Folklore Rev (93): auth, The Song Contests of Turkish Minstrels, Garland Publ, 95. **CONTACT ADDRESS** Dept of Middle Eastern Lang and Cultures, Univ of Texas, Austin, Austin, TX 78712-1013. **EMAIL** y.erdener@mail.utexas.edu

ERDMANS, MARY PATRICE
PERSONAL Born 06/14/1959, MI, s **DISCIPLINE** SOCIOLOGY **EDUCATION** Saint Mary's Col, BA, 81; Northwestern Univ, MA, 87, PhD, 92. **CAREER** Res Asst, Center for Urban Affairs and Policy Res, Northwestern Univ, 88-90; instr, Krakow Industrial Soc, Poland, 90; instr, Northwestern Univ, 90-92; asst prof, Univ NC, Greensboro, 92-98, assoc prof, 98-; vis assoc prof, Col of the Holy Cross, Worcester, MAS, 99-2000. **HONORS AND AWARDS** Diss Year grant, Northwestern Univ, 90-91; res grant, Buehler Ctr on Aging, Northwestern Univ, 92; Polish Am Who's Who, 92-; UNCG Res Coun New Fac grant, 92-93; UNCG Excellence Found Summer Res grant, 93, 95; Undergrad Res Asst, UNCG, 93-94, 96-97; Kohler Fund travel grant, UNCG, 94; Linda Carlisle Fac Res Grant in Women's Studies, 99; Oskar Halecki Prize, Polish Am Hist Asn, 99. **MEMBERSHIPS** Am Sociol Asn, Southern Sociol Asn, Midwest Sociol Soc, Asn for Humanist Sociol, Immigration Hist Soc, polish Am Hist Asn, Polish Inst of Arts and Scis, Polskie Towarzystwo Socjologiczne. **SELECTED PUBLICATIONS** Rev of The Power of Symbols Against the Symbols of Power by Jan Kubik, Contemporary Sociol, 24, 4 (95): 354-55; auth, "Illegal Home Care Workers: Polish Immigrants Caring for American Elderly," Current Res on Occupations and Profs, 9 (96): 267-292; auth, "How to Read Sociological texts," Ch 32 in The Student's Companion to Sociol, ed by Jon Gubbay, Chris Middleton, and Chet Ballard, Oxford: Blackwell Pubs (97); auth, "Immigrants, Wakacjusze, and Refugees: The New Polish Cohort," Fiedorczyk Lecture Series, Central Conn State Univ, New Britain, CT (97); auth, "The Transformation of the Polish National Alliance: From Immigrant to Ethnic Organization," in Ethnicity. Culture, City: Polish-Americans in the USA: Cultural Aspects of Urban Life 1870-1950 in Comparative Perspective, ed by Thomas Gladsky, Adam Walaszek and Malgorzata M. Wawryliewicz, Warsaw: Oficyna Akademicka (98); auth, Opposite Poles: Immigrants and Ethnics in Polish Chicago, 1976-1990, University Park, PA: Penn State Press (98); rev of Immigration, Stress, and Readjustment by Zeev Ben-Sira, Contemporary Sociol (99); auth, "Portraits of Emigration: Sour Milk and Honey in the Promised Land," Sociol Inquiry, 69, 3 (99): 337-363; auth, "Stanislaus Can't Polka: Polish Newcomers in Established Polish American Communities," in Race and Ethnic Relations, ed by Peter Kivisto and Georgeanne Rundblad, Thousand Oaks, CA: Pine Forge Press (forthcoming); auth, "Polonia and the New Century: We Will Not Fade Away," in Polish Americans, ed by M. B. Biskupski, James Pula, Thomas Napierkowski and Stanislaus Blejwas, NY: Hippocrene Books (forthcoming). **CONTACT ADDRESS** Dept Sociol and Anthropol, Col of the Holy Cross, One College St, Worcester, MA 01610.

ERICKSON, MARTHA F.
PERSONAL Born 04/18/1946, Chairton, IA, m, 1970, 2 children **DISCIPLINE** PSYCHOLOGY **EDUCATION** Iowa State Univ, BS, 67; Univ Minn, MA, 75; PhD, 84. **CAREER** Dir, Univ of Minn, 91-; advisor to VP Gore for annual family policy conf, 94-. **HONORS AND AWARDS** Friend of the Col Awd, Univ of Minn, 94; Comnr Awd, DHHS; Alumni Merit Awd, Iowa State Univ, 98; Carolyn Helman Lichtenberg Crest Awd, Pi Beta Phi Int, 00. **MEMBERSHIPS** Am Prof Soc on Abuse of Children; Am Psychol Assoc; Family Resource Coalition; Minn Psychol Assoc; Nat Assoc of School Psychol; Soc for Res in Child Develop. **RESEARCH** Parent-child attachment, child abuse prevention, community-based approaches to strengthening families. **SELECTED PUBLICATIONS** Coauth, "Considering Attachment Issues in Permanency Decisions", CASCW News 12; (98): 1-12; coauth, "The Children, Youth and Family Consortium: A University of Minnesota/ Community Partnership", University-Community Collaborations for the Twenty-first Century: Outreach Scholarship for Youth and Families, eds R. Lerner and L. Simon, Garland, (NY, 98): 186-201; coauth, "A broad and dynamic partnership: Minnesota's Children, Youth and Family Consortium", Serving Children and Families through Community-University Partnerships: Success Stories, eds T.R. Chibucos and R. Lerner, Kluwer Acad Pub, (Boston, 99): 231-236; coauth, "An international conference and an open file", Prospects, XXIX.2 (99): 167-179; auth, "Seeing is Believing (video)", Irving B. Harris Center for Infant and Toddler Develop, Univ of Minn, 99; coauth, "Steps toward effective, enjoyable parenting: Facilitators' Guide", Irving B. Harris Center for Infant and Toddler Develop, Univ of Minn, 99; coauth, Infants, toddlers and families: A framework for support and intervention, Guilford Pub, (NY), 99; auth, "The Children, Youth and Family Consortium: A University of Minnesota/Community Partnership", Social Change, Public Policy, and Community Collaborations: Training Human Development Professionals for the Twenty-First Century, eds PA. Ralston et al, Kluwer Acad Pub, (Boston, 00): 71-83; coauth, "Child neglect", APSAC Handbook on Child Maltreatment, eds J. Briere et al, Sage, (forthcoming); auth, "Abandonment", Parenthood in America: An Encyclopedia, eds M. Bornstein et al, ABC-CLIO (forthcoming). **CONTACT ADDRESS** Children, Youth & Family Consortium, Univ of Minnesota, Twin Cities, 200 Oak St SE, Minneapolis, MN 55455. **EMAIL** mferick@tc.umn.edu

ERICKSON, REBECCA J.
PERSONAL Born 04/03/1962, Berkeley, CA **DISCIPLINE** SOCIOLOGY **EDUCATION** Indiana Univ, BA, 84; Wash State Univ, MA, 86; PhD, 91. **CAREER** Asst prof, 91-96; assoc prof, 96-, Univ Akron. **HONORS AND AWARDS** Phi Beta Kappa; James F Short Jr, Res Awd; Fav Fac Mem; Teach Awd, Buchtel Coll. **MEMBERSHIPS** ASA; NCFR. **RESEARCH** Work and family; sociology of emotions; social psychology of the self. **SELECTED PUBLICATIONS** Co-ed, Social Perspectives on Emotion, JAI Press (Greenwich, CT) 97; co-ed, "Putting Emotions to Work (or, Coming to Terms with a Contradiction in Terms)," Soc Persp on Emotion (97): 3-18; co-ed, "Real Life Applications," Soc Persp on Emotion 4 (97): 19-33; co-ed, "For Love or Money?: Work and Emotional Labor in a Social Movement Organization," Socl Persp on Emotion 4 (97): 317-346; coauth, "Inauthenticity and Depression: Assessing the Consequences of Interactive Service Work," Work and Occ 24 (97): 188-213; coauth, "Doing for Others on the Job: The Affective Requirements of Service Work, Gender, and Emotional Well-being," Soc Prob 44 (97): 235-256; auth, "The Importance of Authenticity for Self and Society," Symbolic Interaction 18 (95): 117-136; coauth, "The Consequences of Caring: Exploring the Links Between Women's Job and Family 'Emotion Work'," Sociol Quart 36 (95): 301-324; auth, "Our Society, Our Selves: Becoming Authentic in an inauthentic

World," Adv Devel J 6 (94): 27-39; auth, "Reconceptualizing Family Work: The Effect of Emotion Work on Perceptions of Marital Quality." J Mar Fam 55 (93): 888-900. **CONTACT ADDRESS** Dept Sociology, Univ of Akron, 302 Buchtel Mall, Akron, OH 44325-0002. **EMAIL** rericks@uakron.edu

ERICSSON, K. ANDERS
PERSONAL Born 10/23/1947, Bromma, Sweden, m, 1986, 2 children **DISCIPLINE** PSYCHOLOGY **EDUCATION** Univ Stockholm, Sweden, BA, 70, PhD, 76. **CAREER** Asst prof, Univ Stockholm, 74-75; Head of human factors group, Inst of Aviation Med, Linkoping, Sweden, 75-79 (on leave 77-79); Post doctoral fel/res assoc, Carnegie-Mellon Univ, Pittsburgh, 77-80; asst prof, Univ Colo, Boulder, 80-86; vis sci, Max Planck Inst for Human Develop and Educ, Berlin (4 months), 86; assoc prof, Univ Colo, Boulder (on leave 87-89), 86-92; assoc res prof, Max Planck Inst for Human Develop and Educ, Berlin, 87-89; prof, Univ Colo (approved leave without pay during 93), 92-93; prof, Conradi Eminent Scholar, The Fla State Univ, 92-. **MEMBERSHIPS** Psychonomic Soc, Cognitive Sci Soc, Am Psychol Soc, Am Psychol Asn. **RESEARCH** The analysis of verbal reports on thinking, protocol analysis, exceptional memory performance, the structure and acquisition of expert performance, the role of deliberate practice in attaining expert levels of performance. **SELECTED PUBLICATIONS** Co-ed, Toward a general theory of expertise: Prospects and limits, Cambridge: Cambridge Univ Press (91); coauth, Protocol analysis; Verbal reports as data (revised ed), Cambridge, Mass: Bradford books/MIT Press (93); coauth, "The role of deliberate practice in the acquisition of expert performance," Psychol Rev, 100, 3 (93): 363-406; coauth, "Long-term working memory," Psychol Rev, 102, 2 (95): 211-245; coauth, "Expert and exceptional performance: Evidence on maximal adaptations on task constraints," Annual Rev of Psychol, 47 (96): 273-305; ed, The road to excellence: The acquisition of expert performance in the arts and sciences, sports, and games, Mahweh, NJ: Erlbaum (96); coauth, "Maintaining excellence: Deliberate practice and elite performance in young and older pianists," J of Experimental Psychol: General, 125 (96): 331-359; auth, "The Scientific Study of Expert Levels of Performance: General Implications for Optimal Learning and Creativity," High Ability Studies, 9, 1 (98): 75-100. **CONTACT ADDRESS** Dept Psychol, Florida State Univ, PO Box 3061270, Tallahassee, FL 32306-1270. **EMAIL** ericsson@psy.fsu.edu

ERIKSON, FRITZ JOHN
PERSONAL Born 03/04/1957, Mt Pleasant, MI, m, 1980, 2 children **DISCIPLINE** EDUCATION, PSYCHOLOGY **EDUCATION** Western Mich Univ, BS, 80; Univ Northern Colo, MA, 84; EdD, 87. **CAREER** Chair and Prof of Education and Psychology, Dept of Educ, Mich Technol Univ, 97-. **MEMBERSHIPS** Am Psychol Asn, Asn for Supervision and Curriculum Develop, Am Educ Res Asn. **RESEARCH** Assessing foreign trained Math and Science teachers for teaching in U.S. Schools; forecasting athletic and academic performance. **SELECTED PUBLICATIONS** Coauth, Creating Effective Schools: An Inservice Program for Enhancing School Learning Climate and Achievement, 2nd ed, Holmes Beach,, Fl: Learning Pubs (97); coauth, Sub Survival: A Handbook for the Substitute Elementary Teacher, 2nd ed, Holmes Beach, Fl: Learning Pubs (97); coauth, The Internet Primer: Getting Started on the Internet, Version 3 , Chicago, Il: McGraw-Hill Higher Educ (98); coauth, Netscape Communicator and the World Wide Web, Chicago,Il: McGraw-Hill Higher Educ (98); coauth with John A. Vonk, Microsoft Internet Explorer and the World Wide Web, Chicago, Il: McGraw-Hill Higher Educ (99); coauth with Danna O. Downing, School Volunteers Handbook, Holmes Beach, Fl: Learning Pubs (2000). **CONTACT ADDRESS** Dept Educ and Psychol, Michigan Tech Univ, 1400 Townsend Dr, Houghton, MI 49931. **EMAIL** ferickso@mtu.edu

ESPELAGE, DOROTHY
PERSONAL Born 09/14/1968, Alliance, OH **DISCIPLINE** PSYCHOLOGY **EDUCATION** Va Commonwealth Univ, BS, 91; Radford Univ, MA, 93; Ind Univ, PhD, 97. **CAREER** Asst prof, Univ of IL, 97-. **HONORS AND AWARDS** Phi Eta Sigma; Psi Chi; Phi Kappa Phi; Paul Munger Awd, 96; Grants, Univ of IL, 97-98; 99-00; R. Stewart Jones Awd, 98; Arnold O Beckman Awd, 98; Bureau of Educ Res Fac Fel, 99-00. **MEMBERSHIPS** Am Psychol Assoc; Am Educ Res Assoc; Soc for Res on Adolescence; Acad for Eating Disorders. **SELECTED PUBLICATIONS** Coauth, "Using multimedia to teach conflict resolution skills to young adolescents", Am J of Preventative Med 12.2 (96): 65-74; coauth, "Course Development in Multicultural Counseling", Multicultural Counseling Competencies: Assessment, Education and Training, and Supervision, eds D.B. Pope-Davis and H.F. Coleman, Sage Pub, (Thousand Oaks, CA); coauth, "Role strain in couples with and without a child with a chronic illness: Associations with marital satisfaction, intimacy, and daily mood", Health Psychol 17, (98): 112-124; coauth, "A computer-based violence prevention intervention for young adolescents: A pilot Study", Adolescence 33 (98): 785-95; coauth, "Factors associated with bullying behavior in middle school students", J of Early Adolescence 19, (99): 341-361; coauth, "Examining the social environment of middle school students who bully", J of Couns and Develop, (forthcoming); coauth, "The effectiveness of a multimedia violence prevention program for early adolescents", Am J of Health Behav (forthcoming); coauth, "Measuring Adherence to Medial Treatment in childhood Chronic Illness: Considering Multiple Methods and Sources of Information", Clinical Psychol in Med Settings, (forthcoming); coauth, Assessment of problematic situations and coping strategies in women with eating disorders: Reliability and validity of a role-play inventory", J of Psychopathology and Behav Assessment (forthcoming). **CONTACT ADDRESS** Dept Educ Psychol, Univ of Illinois, Urbana-Champaign, 1310 S 6th St, Champaign, IL 61820. **EMAIL** espelage@uiuc.edu

ESTES, RICHARD J.
PERSONAL Born 06/20/1942, Philadelphia, PA, d, 3 children **DISCIPLINE** CULTURAL STUDIES, SOCIAL WORK **EDUCATION** LaSalle Col, BA, 65; Univ Pa, MSW, 67; postgraduate, Menniger Found, 67-68; Univ Calif at Berkeley, DSW/PhD, 73. **CAREER** Consulting fac member, Ctr for Training in Community Psychiatry and Mental Health Admin, 71-73; from instr to prof, Univ Pa Sch of Soc Work, 73-; consult & advisor, Univ Pa Sch of Allied Health Professions, 74-75; assoc member of ctr, Univ Pa Ctr for E Asian Studies, 96-; member of fac comt, Univ Pa Ctr for African Studies, 96-. **HONORS AND AWARDS** Social Worker of the Year Awd, Pa Chapter of the Nat Asn of Soc Workers, 92; Distinguished Fulbright Scholar, Yonsei Univ, 94; Alumni Recognition Awd, Univ Pa, 96; Distinguished Recent Contribution to Soc Work Educ Awd, Coun on Soc Work Educ, 97; Int Rhoda G. Sarnat Awd of the Nat Asn of Soc Workers for Distinguished Contribution to the Public Image of Soc Work, 97; Best Article in 1996 Soc Indicators Res Awd, Int Soc of Quality of Life Studies, 97. **MEMBERSHIPS** Acad of Certified Soc Workers, Am Public Health Asn, Coun on Soc Work Educ, Fulbright Asn, Int Asn of Schs of Soc Work, Int Coun on Soc Welfare, In Soc for Quality-of-Life Studies, Inter-University Consortium for Int Soc Development, Nat Asn of Soc Workers. **RESEARCH** International and Comparative Social Development, Comparative Social Welfare, Social Indicators, Strategic and Long Range Planning, Private Philanthropy, The Shifting "Welfare Mix": The Public/Private Partnership in human Services, Dynamics of Inter-Cultural Education, Evaluative Research, Application of Information and Computer Technology to Human Service Organizations. **SELECTED PUBLICATIONS** Coauth, Towards a Social Development Strategy for the ESCAP Region, United Nations Economic and Soc Comn for Asia and the Pacific, 92; auth, Internationalizing Social Work Education: A Guide To Resources For A New Century, Univ Pa Sch of Soc Work, 92; auth, "Trends in European Social Development, 1970-1994," Soc Indicators Res 38.6 (97): 1-19; auth, "Social Work, Social Development and Community Welfare Centers in International Perspective," Int Soc Work 40.1 (97): 43-55; coauth, "The Structure of American Philanthropy," Charity News (96); auth, "Trends in World Development, 1970-95: Development Prospects For a New Century," J of Developing Societies 14.1 (98): 11-39; auth, Resources for Social and Economic Development: A Guide to the Scholarly Literature, Univ Pa Sch of Soc Work, 98; auth, "Social development trends in the successor states to the former Soviet Union: The Search for a new paradigm," in Challenges of Transformation and Transition From Centrally Planned to Market Economies, ed. Kempe R. Hope, Jr. (United Nations Ctr for Regional Development, 98), 13-30; auth, "Informational tools for social workers: Research in the global age," in Innovations in Global Social Work: All Our Futures, ed. Chathapuran S. Ramanathan & Rosemary J. Link (Brooks/Cole Publ Co., in press). **CONTACT ADDRESS** Sch of Soc Work, Univ of Pennsylvania, 3701 Locust Walk, Philadelphia, PA 19104-6214. **EMAIL** restes@ssw.upenn.edu

ETHRIDGE, ROBERT WYLIE
PERSONAL Born 11/12/1940, Monroe, MI, 3 children **DISCIPLINE** EDUCATION **EDUCATION** Western MI Univ, AB 1962, AM 1970; Univ of MI Ann Arbor, PhD 1979. **CAREER** Detroit Public Schools, teacher 62-69; Western MI Univ, area coordinator housing 69-72, admin asst to pres 72-79, sec bd of trustees 79-81; Emory Univ, coordinator of equal opportunity programs, 81, asst vice pres 82-92, Assoc VP, 92-, Adj Asst Prof, 82-. **HONORS AND AWARDS** Achievement Awd Northern Province KAY 1961-62; Community Bldg Awd Black Monitor 1985; Citation for Public Service-Kalamazoo 1979; GA Public Relations Assn 1985; 2nd annual Civil and Human Rights Awd-Intl, 1988; Proclamation State of Michigan House of Representatives, 1988; Assn of Official Human Rights Agencies. **MEMBERSHIPS** Mem CUPA, NACUBO 1981-, NAACP 1981-; 2nd vice pres 1981-82, 1st vice pres 1982-84 Amer Assoc for Affirmative Action; bd mem Natl Assault on Illiteracy Program 1983-; financial subcomm United Way 1984-; pres Amer Assoc for Affirmative Action 1984-88; bd mem American Contract Compliance Assn; mem Leadership Conference on Civil rights; United Way-Health Services Council 1984-; United Way-Admissions Panel 1984-; AAAA Natl Conf Planner 1982-84; mem Natl Inst for Employment Equity 1986-; chairman of the bd, Amer Contract Compliance Assoc, 1987-89; pres, Onyx Society of Western Michigan Univ, 1989-91; president, American Assn for Affirmative Action, 1990-92; bd of dirs, Western MI Univ Alumni Assn, 1989-, vp, 1993-94, pres, 1994-96; Community Friendship Inc, bd of dirs, 1994-96, treas, 1996-97; Georgia Nursing Foundation, bd of dirs, 1994-95; WMU Onyx Society, pres, 1994-96, 1997-; 100 Black Men of Dekalb, bd of dirs, 1997-98; Leadership Atlanta, membership comm, 1997-98; Race Relations Comm, 1997-98. **CONTACT ADDRESS** Emory Univ, 110 Administration Bldg, Atlanta, GA 30322. **EMAIL** eeorwe@emory.edu

EUBANKS, EUGENE E.
PERSONAL Born 06/06/1939, Meadville, PA, m **DISCIPLINE** EDUCATION **EDUCATION** Edinboro St U, BA 1963; MI St U, PhD 1972. **CAREER** University of Missouri-KC, School of Education, prof, currently, dean 79-89; Univ of DE, prof of educ admin 72-74; Cleveland Pub Schs, tchr & admnstr 63-70. **HONORS AND AWARDS** Articles published: A Study of Teacher Perception of Essential Teacher Attributes, 1974; Big-City Desegregation since Detroit, 1975; Rev Jesee L Jackson & PUSH Program for Excellence in Big-City Schools, 1977. **MEMBERSHIPS** Consult Cleveland Found; consult KC Pub Schs; consult MO St Dept Edn; consult NAACP Sch Desegregation Suit in Cleveland OH; Nat Allinc Blk Sch Edctrs; Natl Conf Profs Educ Admin; Phi Delta Kappa; Am Assn of Univ Profs; NAACP; PUSH; Urban League; pres, AACTE, 1988; mem, Natl Policy Bd of Educ Admin, 1988. **CONTACT ADDRESS** Sch Educ, Univ of Missouri, Kansas City, 5100 Rockhill Rd, Kansas City, MO 64110.

EVANS, DAVID
PERSONAL Born 11/20/1962, Springfield, MA, m, 2000 **DISCIPLINE** PSYCHOLOGY **EDUCATION** Westfield State Col, BA, 85; Tufts Univ, MA, 91; Boston Univ, PhD, 94. **CAREER** Res Fel, Yale Univ, 93-95; Asst Prof, Univ of New Orleans, 95-98; Asst Prof, Bucknell Univ, 98-. **MEMBERSHIPS** SRCD; APA; ACPP. **RESEARCH** Developmental Psychopathology; Obsessive-Compulsive Behavior in Childhood; Adolescent Self-Concept. **SELECTED PUBLICATIONS** Coauth, "Ritual, habit and perfectionism: The prevalence and development of compulsive-like behavior in normal young children," Child Development, (97): 58-68; auth, "Development of the self in mental retardation," in Handbook of development and mental retardation, Cambridge Univ Press, 98; co-auth, "Intellectual development in children with Down syndrome," in Down syndrome: A review of current knowledge, (Whurr Pub, 99), 124-132; co-auth, "Neuropsychological models of childhood obsessive-compulsive disorder," The Child and Adolescent Psychiatric Clinics of North America, (99): 513-531; coauth, "Rituals, fears and phobias in young children: Insights from development, psychopathology and neurobiology," Child Psychiatry and Human Development, (99): 261-276; auth, "Rituals and other syncretic tools: Insights from Werner's comparative psychology," in Heinz Werner and his relevance for research and theory in the 21st century," Journal of Adult Development, 00; co-auth, "Developmental aspects of psychological defenses: Their relation to self-complexity, self-perception and symptomatology in adolescents," child Psychiatry and Human Development, 00; co-auth, "Compulsive-like behavior in individuals with Down syndrome: Its relation to MA level, adaptive and maladaptive behavior," Child Development, (00): 288-300; co-auth, "The mysterious myth of attention deficits in mental retardation and other defect stories: Developmental lessons not yet learned," International Review of Mental Retardation Research, in press. **CONTACT ADDRESS** Dept Psychol, Bucknell Univ, Lewisburg, PA 17837. **EMAIL** dwevans@bucknell.edu

EVANS, DONNA BROWDER
PERSONAL Born Columbus, OH, d **DISCIPLINE** EDUCATION **EDUCATION** Oh State Univ, BS, 58; MS, 64; PhD, 70. **CAREER** Univ of Cincinnati, asst prof 1969-73; Univ of Maine, prof/grad dean, 73-83; Skidmore Coll, prof/chair dept of educ 1983-87, Wayne State Univ, prof/dean of educ 1987-91; Univ of North Florida, Prof/Dean, 91-95; Dean, Col of Educ, Oh State Univ, 00-. **MEMBERSHIPS** Mem Alpha Kappa Alpha Sor Detroit Chapt; mem Coalition of 100 Black Women Albany 1984-87; mem Amer Assoc of Univ Women Saratoga Springs 1984-87; mem Links Inc Jacksonville Chap 1987-; bd of dirs Assoc Black Educators/Profs 1985-87; bd of dirs Soroptomist Intl 1985-87; bd dir Lake George Opera Festival; bd dir Task Force Against Domestic Violence Saratoga Spngs; Sophisticates Savannah Chap 1988-, Carrousels, Detroit Chap 1988-; Junior Achievement, Jacksonville, board of directors, 1991-. **SELECTED PUBLICATIONS** Reviewer Brooks Cole Publishing Co 1980-; editorial bd Journal of Reality Therapy 1984-; publications "Success Oriented Schools in Action" 1981, "A Conversation with William Glasser" 1982, "Opening Doors to the Future Through Education" 1984, "Reality Therapy, A Model for Physicians Managing Alcoholic Patients" 1984, "Curriculum Not Either-Or", 1991. **CONTACT ADDRESS** Educ Dean's Office, Ohio State Univ, Columbus, 1945 N High St, 127 Arps Hall, Columbus, OH 43210. **EMAIL** Evans.650@osu.edu

EVANS, GARY W.
PERSONAL Born 11/22/1948, Summit, NJ, m, 1984, 3 children **DISCIPLINE** HUMAN ECOLOGY **EDUCATION** Colgate Univ, AB, 71; Univ Mass, Amherst, MS, 73, PhD, 75. **CAREER** Fac, Univ Calif, Irvine, 75-92; fac, Cornell, 92-. **HONORS AND AWARDS** Fulbright Fels, 82, 99; Nat Res Service Awd, NICHD, 98-99. **MEMBERSHIPS** APA, APS, EDRA. **RESEARCH** Environmental stress, poverty and chil-

dren. **SELECTED PUBLICATIONS** Auth, "Environmental cognition," Psychol Bull, 88 (80): 259-287; ed, Environmental Stress, NY: Cambridge Univ Press (82); coauth with S. Cohen, D. Stokols, and D. S. Krantz, Behavior, health and environmental stress, NY: Plenum (86); coauth with S. Carrere, "Traffic congestion, perceived control, and psychophysiological stress among urban bus drivers," J of Applied Psychol, 76 (91): 658-663; coauth with S. J. Lepore, "Household crowding and social support: A quasi-experimental analysis," J of Personality and Soc Psychol, 65 (93): 308-316; coauth with S. Hygge and M. Bullinger, "Chronic noise and psychological stress," Psychol Sci, 6 (95): 333-338; coauth with S. J. Lepore, "Moderating and mediating processes in environment-behavior research," in G. T. Moore and R. W.Marans, eds, Advances in environment, behavior, and design, Vol 4 , NY: Plenum (97): 255-285; co-ed with G. Johansson, "Studies of urban mass transit operators," J of Occupational Health Psychol, 3 (98): 99-187; coauth with S. J. Lepore, B. R. Shejwal and M. N. Palsane, "Chronic residential crowding and children's well being: An ecological perspective," Child Develop, 69 (98): 1514-1523; auth, "Environmental stress and health," in A. Baum, T. Revenson, and J. E. Singer, eds, Handbook of health psychology, Hillsdale, BNJ: Erlbaum (in press). **CONTACT ADDRESS** Dept Human Ecology, Cornell Univ, Van Rensselaer Hall, Ithaca, NY 14853. **EMAIL** GWE1@cornell.edu

EVANS, JAMES L.
PERSONAL Born 08/231/1927, Paris, MO, w, 1973 **DISCIPLINE** ENGLISH, SOCIOLOGY **EDUCATION** Cen Mo State Col, BA, BS, 50; Univ Colo, MA, 55; Univ Tex Austin, MA, 64; PhD, 67. **CAREER** U.S. Army Med Corp, 51-53; teacher, pub sch, 55-60; teacher, Laredo Jr Col, 61-64; teacher asst to asst prof to assoc prof to prof to emer, Univ Tex, 65-. **HONORS AND AWARDS** Alum Asn Master Prof, 98; Who's Who Am Teachers, 96; Emeritus, 97. **MEMBERSHIPS** MLA; TKS; WCPM; Ellen Glasgow Soc; HCHS. **RESEARCH** Beadle Dime novels of 1800s; literature and history of American West; sources of place names; Willa Cather; travel and travel literature of Europe. **SELECTED PUBLICATIONS** Auth of 12 articles on Beadle Dime Novels, Round-Univ Pr (87-98); auth, "Ethnic Tensions in the Lower Rio Grande Valley to 1860," in American Folklore (Utah Pr, 76); auth, "Teaching My Antonia to Non-English Majors from Spanish to-Speaking Homes," in Approaches to Teaching My Antonia (MLA, 89). **CONTACT ADDRESS** PO Box 672, McAllen, TX 78505-0672.

EVANS, JOHN
PERSONAL Born 11/27/1950, Seneca, SC, s **DISCIPLINE** SOCIAL WORK **EDUCATION** Univ Tex, Arlington, PhD, 94. **CAREER** Adj Prof, Eastfield Col, Mesquite Tex, 98-. **MEMBERSHIPS** LMSW. **RESEARCH** Families, Appalachian life/poverty. **SELECTED PUBLICATIONS** Auth, Album of Appalachian folklore and Music, Case Study. **CONTACT ADDRESS** Dept Soc Sci, Eastfield Col, 3737 Motley Dr, Mesquite, TX 75150.

EVANS, WAYNE
PERSONAL Born 04/19/1938, Rosebud, SD, m, 2000, 4 children **DISCIPLINE** EDUCATION **EDUCATION** Univ SDak, EdD, 76. **CAREER** Assoc Prof, Univ SDak, 69-. **HONORS AND AWARDS** Outstanding Indian Student Counselor; Outstanding Indian Educ; Outstanding Young Man of Am. **MEMBERSHIPS** Coun on Higher Educ, SDak Educ Assoc. **RESEARCH** Culture, teaching across cultures. **SELECTED PUBLICATIONS** Auth, Native American in Science and Math Curriculum, 98; auth, Virtual Rural Communities Development: Human Links That Sustain Web Links, 00. **CONTACT ADDRESS** Dept Educ, Univ of So Dakota, Vermillion, 414 E Clark St, Vermillion, SD 57069. **EMAIL** wevans@usd.edu

EVERSON, GEORGE D.
PERSONAL Born 09/18/1953, Salt Lake City, UT, m, 1991, 1 child **DISCIPLINE** ANTHROPOLOGY **EDUCATION** Humbolt State Univ, BA, 82; Univ Cal, MA, 91; Univ Cal, PhD, 95. **CAREER** Prof, Univ Cal, 95-. **MEMBERSHIPS** SOPA, ROPA, Regist of Prof Archeol. **RESEARCH** Archeoastronomy, North American prehistory, Mesoamerican and Andean civilizations, cultural geography, military history. **SELECTED PUBLICATIONS** coauth, "The Desert Tortoise in the Prehistory of the Southwestern Great Basin and Adjacent Areas," in J of California and Great Basin Anthropology 11(2) (89): 175-202; coauth, "Archaeological Investigations at the Oak Creek Canyon Site (Caker-1998), Tehachapi Mountains," in Pacific Coast Archaeological Society Quarterly 28(1) (92): 43-66; coauth, "Investigations at Four Small Archaeological Sites in Rosamond, Kern County, California," in Archaeological Studies in Rosamond, Western Mojave Desert, California (93): 34-47; **CONTACT ADDRESS** Dept Antrop, California State Univ, San Bernardino, 5500 Univ Pkwy, San Bernardino, CA 92407. **EMAIL** deverson@mail.csusb.edu

EWELL, BARBARA CLAIRE
PERSONAL Born 03/10/1947, Baton Rouge, LA **DISCIPLINE** ENGLISH RENAISSANCE AND WOMEN'S LITERATURE **EDUCATION** Univ Dallas, BA, 69; Univ Notre Dame, PhD (English), 74. **CAREER** Asst prof English, Loyola Univ South, 74-75; instr, Newcomb Col, 75-76; asst prof, Univ Col, Tulane Univ, 76-79; Asst Prof English, Univ Miss, 79-, Lectr and instr, writing workshops, Mobil, Erns and Erns and Save the Children Conf, 77-79; consult, Allen Johnson and Assoc, 77-79; Prof of English, City College, Loyola Univ, 84-; Visiting prof, Fordham Univ, 94. **HONORS AND AWARDS** National Endowment for the Humanities, dir, summer seminar, 88; Louisana Endowment for the Humanities, 92; Fulbright Comission/CIES, Sr. Lecture Awd, Universidad Catolica, Santiago Chile, fall 92; NEH Faculty Focus Group, picturing America, Loyola Univ, 99; Monticello Col Found fel, Newberry libr, 82-83. **MEMBERSHIPS** MLA, Women's Caucus; SCent Mod Lang Asn; Nat Women's Studies Asn; NCTE; SCent Renaissance Asn. **RESEARCH** Michael Drayton and related poets; Kate Chopin in the context of 19th century popular fiction; women writers of the English Renaissance. **SELECTED PUBLICATIONS** Auth, Kate Chopin, Ungar (New York), 86; co-ed, New Orleans Review: Special Issue on Louisiana Women Writers, 15:1 (Spring 88); auth, "Kate Chopin and the Dream of Female Selfhood," in Beyond the Bayou: Essays on Kate Chopin (Louisiana State UP, Baton Rouge, 92), 157-65; ed, Louisiana Women Writers: New Critical Essay and a Comprehensive Bibliography, LSU Press (Baton Rouge), 92; auth, "Telling Stories, Teaching Narrative: A Progressive Writing Assignment," Teaching Faulkner 5 (Spring 94):1-2; auth, "Making Places: Kate Chopin and the Art of Fiction," Louisiana Literature 11 (Spring 94):157-71; co-auth, "Creating Conversations: A Model for Interdisciplinary Team-Teaching," College Teaching 48.4 (Fall 95):127-131; ed, Performance for a Lifetime: A Festschrift Honoring Dorothy Brown: Essays on Women, Religion, and the Renaissance, Loyola (New Orleans), 97; co-auth, "Taking on the World: Women and the Fulbright Program," National Women's Studies Journal (Spring 98); Guest ed, Ocentennial of The Awakening Special Issue, The Southern Quarterly (spring 99). **CONTACT ADDRESS** Dept of English, Loyola Univ, New Orleans, 6363 St. Charles Ave., New Orleans, LA 70118. **EMAIL** bewell@loyno.edu

EYAL, GIL
PERSONAL Born 01/20/1965, Israel, m, 1998 **DISCIPLINE** SOCIOLOGY **EDUCATION** Tel-Aviv Univ, BA, 89; MA, 91; Univ Calif at Los Angeles, MA, 92; PhD, 97. **CAREER** Instr, teach fel, Univ Calif, Los Angeles, 94; grad res, 95, 96; asst prof, 97-. **HONORS AND AWARDS** Pauley Fel; Peace Scholarshp; Grad Res Fel; Dist Fel; Trv, Res Grant; Fieldwork Fel; Mellon Fel; Chancellor's Fel; Fac Res Grant, 97, 99. **MEMBERSHIPS** ASA; AIS. **RESEARCH** Sociology of Knowledge; sociology of intellectuals; Eastern Europe. **SELECTED PUBLICATIONS** Auth, "Anti-Politics and the Spirit of Capitalism: Dissidents, Monetarists and the Czech Transition to Capitalism," Theory and Soc (forthcoming); coauth, Making Capitalism without Capitalists: Class Formation and Elite Struggles in Post-Communist Central Europe, Verso (London), 98; coauth, "Das Zweite Bildungsburgertum: Die Intellektuellen im Ubergang vom Sozialismus zum Kapitalismus in Mitteleuropa," in Eliten im Wandel. Politische Fuhrung, wirtschatfliche Macht and Meinungsbildung im neuen 0steuropa, eds. Magarditsch A Hatschikjan, Franz Lothar Altmann (Verlag Ferdinand Schoningh, 98): 62-101; coauth, "The Theory of Post-Communist Managerialism: Elites and Classes in the Post-Communist Transformation," New Left Rev 222 (97): 60-92; auth, "The Discursive Origins of Israeli Separatism: The Case of the Arab Village," Theory and Society 25 (96): 389-429; coauth, "The Social Composition of the Communist Nomenklatura: A Comparison of Russia, Poland and Hungary," Theory and Society 24 (95): 723-750; auth, Pastors and Prognosticators: The New Class and the Break-up of Czechoslovakia, forthcoming; auth, "Intellectuals in Public: The Social Origins of Commentary on Middle Eastern Affairs in Israel," [Hebrew] Teoria ve-Bikoret (Theory and Criticism), forthcoming. **CONTACT ADDRESS** Dept Sociology, Univ of California, Berkeley, 410 Barrows Hall, Berkeley, CA 94720-1980.

EYER, DIANE E.
PERSONAL Born 03/21/1944, Buffalo, NY, m, 1991 **DISCIPLINE** HUMAN DEVELOPMENT **EDUCATION** Univ Pa, PhD, 88. **CAREER** Lecturer, Univ of Pa; Asst Prof, Temple Univ. **HONORS AND AWARDS** Schol & Res assistanceships. **MEMBERSHIPS** Cheiron Soc; Hist of Childhood and Youth Soc. **RESEARCH** History & sociology of psychology, especially child development; history of american childhood. **SELECTED PUBLICATIONS** Auth, Mother-Infant Bonding: A Scientific Fiction, Yale, 92; auth, Maternal Infant Bonding: A Scientific Fiction, Human Nature, 5:1, 69-94, 94; auth, The Attachment Myth, Women, Men, and Gender: Ongoing Debates, Yale Univ Press, 96; auth, Motherguilt: How Our Culture Blames Mothers for What's Wrong With Society, Random House, 96. **CONTACT ADDRESS** 320 Centre Ave, Newtown, PA 18940. **EMAIL** eyerbyer@voicenet.com

F

FABER, DANIEL R.
PERSONAL Born 05/20/1961, Chicago, IL, m, 1989, 2 children **DISCIPLINE** SOCIOLOGY **EDUCATION** Univ Ky, BA, 83; Univ Calif, MA; 87; PhD, 89. **CAREER** Asst Prof, Northeastern Univ, 90-. **HONORS AND AWARDS** Travel Fel, Marion and Jasper Whiting Foundation Boston, 00; Res Fund Awd, Aspen Inst, 99; RSDF Awd, Northeastern Univ, 99; Outstanding Academic Book, Choice Magazine, 93; Grant, Res and Scholarship Development Fund, 94. **RESEARCH** US and International Environmental Politics; Political Economy. **SELECTED PUBLICATIONS** Auth, Environment Under fire: Imperialism and the Ecological Crisis in Central America, Monthly Review Press, 93; ed, The struggle for Ecological Democracy: Environmental Justice Movements in the United states, Guilford Press, 98; auth, "The Struggle for Ecological Democracy and Environmental Justice," in The Struggle for Ecological Democracy: Environmental Justice Movements in the United States, Guilford Press, 98; auth, "The Political Ecology of American Capitalism: New Challenges for the Environmental Justice Movement," in The Struggle for Ecological Democracy: Environmental Justice Movements in the United States, Guilford Press, 98; auth, "Capitalism and the Crisis of Environmentalism," in Toxic Struggles: The Theory and Practice of Environmental Justice, New Society Pub, 93; auth, "La Liberacion del Medio Ambiental: The rise and Fall of Revolutionary Ecology in Nicaragua, 1979-1999," Capitalism, Nature, Socialism, (99): 45-80; auth, "The New Scientific Paradigms: A Socialist Critique of Marcello Cini," Capitalism, Nature, Socialism,, (92): 105-110; auth, "The Ecological Crisis of Latin America: A Theoretical Introduction," Latin American Perspectives, (92): 3-16; auth, "Imperialism, revolution, and the Ecological Crisis of Central America," Latin American Perspectives, (92): 17-44; auth, "Central America: A Disaster that Was Waiting to Happen," Z Magazine, (99): 5-6 **CONTACT ADDRESS** Dept Sociol/Anthropol, Northeastern Univ, 360 Huntington Ave, Boston, MA 02115. **EMAIL** dfaber@gis.net

FALGOUT, SUZANNE
PERSONAL Born 10/22/1949, New Orleans, LA, m, 1995 **DISCIPLINE** ANTHROPOLOGY **EDUCATION** Univ Oregon, PhD, 84; MA, 78; Univ New Orleans, BA, 76. **CAREER** Prof of Anthropology, Univ of Hawaii-West Oahu, 92-; Social Sciences Division Chair, 99-00. **MEMBERSHIPS** Amer Anthropological Assoc; Assoc for Social Anthropology in Oceania. **RESEARCH** Micronesia; World War II in the Pacific. **SELECTED PUBLICATIONS** Auth, "The Typhoon of War," with Lin Poyer and Laurence Carucci, UH Press; auth, "American Anthropology and Micronesia, "with Robert Kiste, UH Press. **CONTACT ADDRESS** Dept Social Science, Univ of Hawaii, West Oahu, 96-129 Ala Ike, Pearl City, HI 96782. **EMAIL** falgout@hawaii.edu

FALK, JOHN L.
PERSONAL Born 12/27/1927, Toronto, ON, Canada, m, 1965, 1 child **DISCIPLINE** PSYCHOLOGY **EDUCATION** McGill Univ, BA, 50; MA, 52; Univ Ill, PhD, 56. **CAREER** Prof of Psychol, Rutgers Univ, 69-. **HONORS AND AWARDS** Res Sci Awd, 90-99; Nat Inst on Drug Abuse Solvay Awd for Psychopharmacology, 97. **MEMBERSHIPS** Am Col of Neuropsychopharmocology, Col on Problems of Drug Dependence. **RESEARCH** Behavior analysis; drug dependence. **SELECTED PUBLICATIONS** Coauth, "Pharmacokinetic-pharmacodynamic modeling of the psychomotor stimulant effect of cocaine after intravenous administration: Timing performance deficits," J Pharmacol Exp Ther, 288 (99): 535-543; coauth, "Within-subject variability in cocaine pharmacokinetics and pharmacodynamics after intraperitoneal in comparison with intravenous cocaine administration," Exp Clin Psychopharmocol, 7 (99): 3-12; coauth, "Sensitization of operant behavior to oral cocaine with increasing- and repetitive-dose regimens," Behav Pharmocol, 10 (99): 15-26; coauth, "Establishing oral preference for quinine, phencyclidine and caffeine solutions in rats," Behav Pharmacol, 10 (99): 27-38; coauth, "Cocaine pharmacodymanics after intravenous and oral administration: Relation to pharmacokinetics," Psychopharmacology, 144 (99): 323-332; coauth, "Pharmacokinetic determinants of cocaine's differential effects on locomotor and operant behavior," Europ J Pharmacol, 381 (99): 85-92; coauth, "Dose-dependent effects but not sensitization of DRL 45-s performance by oral d-amphetamine with cumulative- and repeated-dosing regimens," Behav Pharmacol, 10 (99): 739-746; coauth, "Establishing preference for lidocaine solution to water: comparison between a fading and an abrupt-removal procedure for withdrawing a compound vehicle," Behav Pharmacol, 10 (99): 803-808; auth, "Addictive behavior with and without pharmacologic action: Critical role of stimulus control," NIDA Monogr (in press). **CONTACT ADDRESS** Dept Psychol, Rutgers Univ, Piscataway, NJ 08854-8020. **EMAIL** jfalk@rci.rutgers.edu

FALLDING, HAROLD J.
PERSONAL Born 05/03/1923, Cessnock, Australia **DISCIPLINE** SOCIOLOGY, RELIGION **EDUCATION** Univ Sydney, BS, 50, BA, 51, Dip Ed, 52, MA, 55; Australian Nat Univ, PhD, 57. **CAREER** High sch tchr, Australia, 52-53; sr res fel, Univ Sydney, 56-58; sr lectr, Univ NSW, 59-62; vis assoc prof, grad sch Rutgers, State Univ NJ, 63-65; prof sociol, 65-88, DISTINGUISHED PROF EMER, UNIV WATERLOO, 89-. **MEMBERSHIPS** Clare Hall, Cambridge Univ; Stratford Shakespearean Found Can; Am Sociol Asn; Can Soc Sociol Anthrop; Asn Sociol Relig; Int Sociol Asn; Int Conf Sociol Relig; Can Inst Int Affairs. **SELECTED PUBLICATIONS**

Auth, The Sociological Task, 68; auth, The Sociology of Religion: An Explanation of the Unity and Diversity in Religion, 74; auth, Drinking, Community and Civilization: The Account of a New Jersey Interview Study, 74; auth, The Social Process Revisited: Achieving Human Interests through Alliance and Opposition, 90; auth, Collected Poetry, 97. **CONTACT ADDRESS** 40 Arbordale Walk, Guelph, ON, Canada N1G 4X7.

FALVO, DONNA R.

PERSONAL Born 03/17/1945, Tuscola, IL, m, 1 child **DISCIPLINE** PSYCHOLOGY **EDUCATION** Ill Univ, PhD, 78. **CAREER** Dir, Behav Sci, Southern Ill Univ Carbondale Sch of Med; Prof, Coordr rehabil Coun Training Prog, Southern Ill Univ Carbondale. **HONORS AND AWARDS** Mary Switzer Scholar - Wash DC, 86; Fac Woman of Distinction Awd, 94; Sigma Xi. **MEMBERSHIPS** Am Rehabil Coun Asn, Am Psychol Asn. **RESEARCH** Patient Compliance. **SELECTED PUBLICATIONS** Auth, "Risk: Sexually Transmitted Disease," J of Appl Rehabil Coun 25-1 (94): 43-49; auth, Effective Patient Education: A Guide to Increased Compliance, Aspen (Gaitehrsburgh, MD), 94; auth, "Psychological Adjustment," in Encyclopedia of Rehabilitation, ed. A. Dell Orto and M. Marinelli (MacMillan, 95); auth, "Educational Evaluation: What are the Outcomes?," Advances in Renal Replacement Ther 2-3 (95): 227-233; coauth, "The informed patient poses a different challenge," Patient Care 30-16 (96); 128-138; coauth, "Medical aspects of disability: Functional limitations and employment," The Rehabil Prof 6-6 (98): 26-30; auth, "Medical Aspects of Aging and Disability," in Directions in Gerontological Nursing (New York, NY: Hatherleigh Co, 98); auth, "Assistive Technology," in Professional Counseling: Transition into the next Millennium, ed. Charlotte Dixon and William G. Emener (Springfield, IL: Charles C. Thomas, 99); auth, Medical and Psychological Aspects of Disability, 2nd ed, Aspen (Gaithersburg, MD), 99; coauth, "Patient Education," in Textbook of Family Medicine, 6th ed, ed. Robert Rakel (Philadephia, PA: W.B. Saunders, 00). **CONTACT ADDRESS** Rehabil Coun, So Illinois Univ, Carbondale, Southern Ill Union, Carbondale, IL 62901. **EMAIL** dfalvo@siu.edu

FANT, GENE C., JR.

PERSONAL Born 06/30/1963, Laurel, MS, m, 1989, 2 children **DISCIPLINE** ENGLISH, EDUCATION **EDUCATION** James Madison Univ, BS, 84-; Old Dominion Univ, MA, 87; New Orleans Baptist Theolog Sem, Mdiv, 91; Univ Southern Miss, MED, 95, PhD, 95. **CAREER** Asst dir, Univ Southern Miss, 94-95; asst prof, dir, Miss Col, 95-; assoc prof, ch, Dept of Eng, Miss Col, 99-. **HONORS AND AWARDS** Dave-Maher Prize, 94; Linwood Orange Award & Fel, 94; Who's Who in the World, 99; doctoral fel, usm. **MEMBERSHIPS** MLA; SCMLA; Conf on Christianity and Lit; Miss Philol Asn; Int Arthurian Society. **RESEARCH** Medieval/Renaissance English literature; Bible as literature; popular culture. **SELECTED PUBLICATIONS** Auth, Petrarchan Hagiography, Gender, and Subjectivity in Mary Wroth's Pamphilia to Amphilanthus, 95; auth, art, Pun's on the Name of the Beloved in Wroth's Pamphilia to Amphilanthus, 96; auth, art, Peachwood Remembered: The Photography of Marian Stark Gaines, 97; auth, art, John Stewart Bryan, Eugene S. Pulliam, Theodore Lothrop Stoddard, 98; coauth, Expectant Moments, 99. **CONTACT ADDRESS** Mississippi Col, Clinton, PO Box 4022, Clinton, MS 39058. **EMAIL** fant@mc.edu

FARARO, THOMAS J.

PERSONAL Born 02/11/1933, New York, NY, m, 1955, 2 children **DISCIPLINE** SOCIOLOGY **EDUCATION** Syracuse Univ, PhD, 63. **CAREER** From Assoc Prof to Distinguished Prof, Univ of Pittsburgh, 67-. **MEMBERSHIPS** Sociol Res Asn, Am Sociol Asn. **RESEARCH** Theoretical and Mathematical Sociology. **SELECTED PUBLICATIONS** Coauth, "The Emergence of Computational Sociology," The J of Math Sociol (special issue on Sociol Algorithms, ed. D. Heise) Vol 20 2-3 (95): 79-87; auth, "Foundational Problems in Theoretical Sociology," in James S. Coleman, ed. J. Clark (Falmer Press, 96); coauth, "Status and Participation in Task Groups: A Dynamic Network Model," The Am J of Sociol 101-5 (96): 1366-1414; coauth, "Social Structure, Networks, and E-State Structuralist Models," The J of Math Sociol 21-1/2 (96): 57-76; coauth, "Generating Symbolic Interaction: Production System Models," Sociol Methods and Res 25-1 (96): 60-102; auth, "Reflections on Mathematical Sociology," Sociol Forum 12-1 (97): 73-101; coauth, "Synthesizing Theories of Deviance and Control: With Steps Toward a Dynamic Network Model," in Status, Network and Structure: Theory Development in Group Processes, ed. J. Szmatka, J. Skvoretz and J. Berger (Stanford Univ Press, 97), 362-386; coauth, "The Theory of Solidarity: An Agenda of Problems," in The Problem of Solidarity, ed. P. Doreian and T. Farao (Gordon and Breach, 98); co-ed, The Problem of Solidarity, Gordon and Breach, 98; coauth, "Advances in Generative Structuralism: Structured Agency and Multilevel Dynamics," J of Math Sociol 24 (99): 1-65. **CONTACT ADDRESS** Dept Sociol, Univ of Pittsburgh, 2G24 Forbes Quad, Pittsburgh, PA 15260.

FARGANIS, JAMES

PERSONAL Born 12/15/1933, New York, NY, m, 1970, 2 children **DISCIPLINE** SOCIOLOGY **EDUCATION** Brooklyn Col, BA, 56; Penn State Univ, MA, 58; Cornell Univ, PhD, 65. **CAREER** Prof, Vassar Col, 70-98; vis prof, New School Univ, 98-. **HONORS AND AWARDS** Fulbright Scholar; NEH Fel. **MEMBERSHIPS** Am Sociol Assoc. **RESEARCH** American society, Social theory, Postmodernism. **SELECTED PUBLICATIONS** Auth, The Classic Tradition to Post-Modernism, McGraw Hill, 99. **CONTACT ADDRESS** Dept Sociol, New Sch for Social Research, 65 - 5th Ave, New York, NY 10003.

FARLEY, ROY C.

PERSONAL Born 02/21/1942, Dierks, AR, m, 1969, 2 children **DISCIPLINE** GRADUATE EDUCATION **EDUCATION** Henderson State Univ, BA, 64; Univ Cent Ark, MS, 72; Univ Ark, EdD, 78. **CAREER** Res Sci, Ark Rehab Res & Training Center, 74-99; Asst Prof, Univ Ark, 74-99; Prof, Univ Ark, 99-. **HONORS AND AWARDS** Res Awd, Am Rehab Asn; **MEMBERSHIPS** Am Coun Asn, Assoc of Counr Ed and Supv. **RESEARCH** Career development, counseling strategies. **SELECTED PUBLICATIONS** Coauth, "Service Delivery Strategies for Promoting Employment Outcomes in Menz, F.," Lessons for Improving Employment of People with Disabilities from Vocational Rehabilitation Research, Nat Asn of Rehab Res and Training Centers (97): 119-134; coauth, Native Americans with Disabilities: Power Strategies for Cross Cultural Service Delivery, NAMRC, Auburn Univ, 98; coauth, Go for the Gold: Empowerment Training to Enhance Client Participation in the Rehabilitation Process, 95; coauth, "The Intake Interview," Case Management and Rehabilitation Counseling - Procedures and Techniques, (98): 33-50; coauth, "Effects of a Career Assessment and Planning Intervention on the Vocational Development of Secondary Students with Disabilities," Vocation Evaluation and Work Adjustment J, Spring 1999, vol 32, no 1 (99): 15-21; coauth, "Enhancing the Career Exploration and Job-Seeking Skills of Secondary Students with Disabilities," Career Development for Exceptional Individuals, Spring 1999, vol 22, no 1 (99). **CONTACT ADDRESS** Grad Ed, Univ of Arkansas, Fayetteville, 134 Grad Ed Bldg, Fayetteville, AR 72701. **EMAIL** rfarley@comp.uark.edu

FARMER, P.

PERSONAL Born 10/26/1959, North Adams, MA, m, 1997, 1 child **DISCIPLINE** ANTHROPOLOGY **EDUCATION** Harvard Univ, MD, 90, PhD, 90. **CAREER** Assoc prof, Harvard Med Schl. **HONORS AND AWARDS** MacArthur Fel, 93-98; Wellcome Medal, 92; Eileen Bashes Prize, 96. **MEMBERSHIPS** Amer Anthrop Assn; Amer Col of Internal Med; Intl Union Against Tuberculosis. **RESEARCH** AIDS, TB, Social inequalities. **SELECTED PUBLICATIONS** Auth, AIDS and Accusation, Univ Calif Press, 92; auth, Uses of Haiti, Comm Courage, 94; auth, Women, Poverty and AIDS, Common Courage, 96; auth, Infections and Inequalities, Univ Calif Press, 98; auth, Pathologies of Power, Univ Calif Press, 99. **CONTACT ADDRESS** 113 Rivers St, Cambridge, MA 02139. **EMAIL** partnersma@aol.com

FARRER, CLAIRE RAFFERTY

PERSONAL Born 12/26/1936, New York, NY, d, 1 child **DISCIPLINE** ANTHROPOLOGY & FOLKLORE **EDUCATION** Univ CA, Berkeley, BA, 70; Univ TX, Austin, MA, 74, PhD, 77. **CAREER** Am Folklore Soc, Smithsonian Inst, Austin, TX, 73-74; res assoc, Joint Senate-House Committee on Prison reform, TX, summer 74; academic fel, Whitney M Young Memorial Found, Inc, NY, 74-75; NEA Folk Arts Prog, Washington, DC, 76-77; Weatherhead Resident fel, School of Am Res, 77-78; asst prof, anthropol, Univ IL, Urbana-Champaign, 78-85; coord of Certificate prog in Applied Anthropol and asoc prof, 85-89, prof, Anthropology, CA State Univ, Chico, 89-; vis prof, Rijksuniversiteit-Gent, Belgium, spring 90; dir, Center for Multicultural and Gender Studies, CSU-Chico, 94; exec dir/ business manager, Western Folklore, CA Folklore Soc, 94-98; Hulbert Endowed chair and vis prof of Southwest Studies, Hulbert Center for Southwest Studies, the Colorado Col, Colorado Springs, CO, spring 97. **HONORS AND AWARDS** Phi Kappa Phi; Sigma Xi; Advanced Sem, School of Am Res, Santa Fe, NM, 78; Univ IL-Urbana: res bd, 79, 83, Center for Advanced Study, 82, Excellent Teacher, 80, Outstanding Teacher, 84, 85; Am Philos Soc, Phillips Fund, 82; Am Coun of Learned Socs grant, 84; CA State Univ, Chico, res, 86-88, Professional Promise Awd, 87, Professional Achievement Awd, 87, 93, Outstanding Prof Awd, 93-94, Student Internship Service grant, 89; NEH travel grant, 88; Phi Eta Sigma, Oustanding Teacher Awd, 91, hon member, 91; Golden Key Nat Honor Soc, 93, summer res fel, 95; Recipient, First Annual MAGGIE Awd for Outstanding Women Leaders, 93; CHOICE Outstanding Academic Book, 93; Book, Thunder Rides a Black Horse: Mescalero Apaches and the Mythic Present, nominated for a Spur Awd and a PEN literary writing award, 94; several other various res grants; listed in several honorary publications including numerous editions of Who's Who. **MEMBERSHIPS** Am Anthropological Asn; Am Ethnological Soc; Am Folklore Soc; Am Soc for Ethnohistory; Authors Guild; CA Folklore Soc; Int Soc for Archaeostonomy & Astronomy in Culture; Royal Anthropol Inst; Soc for the Anthropology of Consciousness; Soc for Cultural Anthropol; Soc for Humanistic Anthropol; Southwestern Anthropol Asn; Traditional Cosmology Soc. **RESEARCH** Ritual; ethnoastronomy; Mescalero Apaches; Whiteriver Apaches. **SELECTED PUBLICATIONS** Auth, Thunder Rides a Black Horse: Mescalero Apaches and the Mythic Present,Waveland Press, 94, 2nd ed, Waveland Press, 96; Who Owns the Words?: An Anthropological Prespective on Public Law 101-601, J of Arts, Management, Law, and Society, 94; Turning the Storm, in Bridges to Humanity: Narratives on Anthropology and Friendship, Bruce Grindal and Frank Salamone, eds, Waveland Press, 95; On Singers and Lineages: Response to Rushforth, Am Ethnologist, 95; review essay of When They Read What We Write, Caroline B Brettell, ed, On the Production of Knowledge, Hein Streefkers, and The Politics of Ethnolgraphic Reading and Writing, Henk Driessen, ed, Am Anthropol, 96; Bloed en Paarden: Culturele Evenementen in Belgie-Een Antropologische Analyse van een Vreemde Cultuur, Cultuur en Migratie, 96; numerous books, book chapters, journal and encyclopedia articles, monographs, reviews, and other publications. **CONTACT ADDRESS** Dept of Anthropol, California State Univ, Chico, Chico, CA 95929-0400. **EMAIL** cfarrer@csuchico.edu

FAWCETT, BILL

DISCIPLINE ANTHROPOLOGY **EDUCATION** Univ NM, BA, 75; Univ Wyo, MA, 80; Univ MA, Amherst, PhD, 87. **CAREER** Assoc Prof, Ut State Univ, 90-. **HONORS AND AWARDS** Fel, Am Anthropol Asn. **RESEARCH** Archaeology and Ethnohistory; East Africa; Western North America. **CONTACT ADDRESS** Dept Sociol, Soc Work & Anthropol, Utah State Univ, 0730 Univ Blvd, Logan, UT 84322-0730. **EMAIL** bfawcett@wpo.hass.usu.edu

FEAGIN, JOE R.

PERSONAL Born 05/06/1938, San Angelo, TX, m, 1960, 2 children **DISCIPLINE** SOCIOLOGY **EDUCATION** Baylor Univ, BA, 60; Harvard Univ, PhD, 66. **CAREER** Prof, Univ Tex, 70-90; Grad Res Prof, Univ Fla, 90-. **MEMBERSHIPS** Am Sociol Asn. **RESEARCH** Racial and Gender Discrimination. **SELECTED PUBLICATIONS** Co-auth, A Case for the Case Study, 91; co-auth, White Racism: The Basics, 94; co-auth, Racial and Ethnic Relations, 98; auth, The New Urban Paradigm: Critical Perspectives on the City, 00; co-auth, The First R: How Children Learn Race and Racism, 00; auth, Racist America: Roots, Current Realities and Future Reparations, 00. **CONTACT ADDRESS** Dept Sociol, Univ of Florida, PO Box 117330, Gainesville, FL 32611.

FEAR, MARCIA B.

PERSONAL Born 06/02/1952, Youngstown, OH, s, 2 children **DISCIPLINE** PSYCHOLOGY **EDUCATION** Youngstown State Univ, BA, 75; MS, 80; Ohio State Univ, PhD, 88. **CAREER** Prog Director, Ohio State Univ, 85-94; adj asst prof, Ohio State Univ, 90-94; asst prof, Northwestern Okla State Univ, 96-. **HONORS AND AWARDS** Who's Who Among Human Serv Prof, 85-86; Who's Who in the Midwest, 94; Who's Who of Am Women, 95; Who's Who in Am, 95; World Who's Who of Women, 95. **MEMBERSHIPS** Am Coun Assoc; AAUW; Phi Kappa Phi; Int Platform Assoc; Nat Assoc for Women in Educ; Nat Board for Certified Counselors; Nat Coun for Res on Women; Okla Coun Assoc. **RESEARCH** Counselor Preparation, Equity. **SELECTED PUBLICATIONS** Coauth, "Math + Science + Girls = Vocational preparation for girls: A difficult equation to balnce", Ohio State univ, (columbus, 92); auth, "Sexual Harassment: Understand it, talk about it, post a policy against it", Ohio State Univ, (Columbus, 92); auth, "Bringing multiculturism to education", Ohio State Univ, 93; coauth, "Male issues in vocational education, Ohio State Univ (Columbus, 93). **CONTACT ADDRESS** Dept Psychol, Northwestern Oklahoma State Univ, 709 Oklahoma Blvd, Alva, OK 73717. **EMAIL** mbfear@nwosu.edu

FEDER, KENNETH L.

PERSONAL Born 08/01/1952, New York, NY, m, 1981, 2 children **DISCIPLINE** ANTHROPOLOGY **EDUCATION** SUNY Stonybrook, BA, 73; Univ Conn, MA, 75; PhD, 82. **CAREER** Central CT State Univ, 77-; Full Prof, Anthropology Dept, 90-. **HONORS AND AWARDS** Excellence in Teaching Awd, 93. **RESEARCH** American Prehistory, Archaeological Methods. **SELECTED PUBLICATIONS** Auth, A Village of Outcast: Historical Archaeology and Documentary Research at the Lighthouse Village, Mayfield Publishing, 94 (Mountain View, CAï; auth, Ten years after: Surveying misconceptions about the human past, CRM (Cultrual Resource Management) 18 (95): 10-14; auth, Archaeology and the Paranormal, In the Encyclopedia of the Paranormal, ed. By G. Stein, Prometheus Books (Buffalo) 96; auth, Indians and archaeologists: Conflicting views of myth and science, Skeptic 5 (97): 74-80; auth, Perceptions of the past: Survey results-how students perceive the past, General Anthropology 4 (98): 8-12; auth, Archaeology and Afrocentrism: An attempt to set the record straight, A Current Bibliography on African Affairs 29 (98-99): 199-210; auth, Native American archaeology in Connecticut after conduct. In The Archaeology of Connecticut, edited by W.F. Keegan and K.N. Keegan, Bibliopola Press; Storrs, (Connecticut, 99), 60-64; auth, Frauds, Myth,s and Mysteries: Science and Pseudoscience in Archaeology, Mayfield Publishing, Mountain View, CA, 99; auth, The Past in Perspective: An Introduction to Human Prehistory, Mayfield Publishing, Mountain View, CA, 99; auth, Lessons From the Past: A Reader in Introductory Archaeology, Mayfield Publishing, Mountain View, CA, 99.

CONTACT ADDRESS Dept Anthropology, Central Connecticut State Univ, 1615 Stanley St, New Britain, CT 06053. EMAIL feder@mail.ccsu.edu

FEIFER, IRWIN
PERSONAL Born 11/07/1934, Brooklyn, NY, m, 1963, 2 children **DISCIPLINE** PSYCHOLOGY, SOCIOLOGY **EDUCATION** Brooklyn Col, BA, 55; MA, 57; NY Univ, PhD, 70. **CAREER** Dir Office of Evaluation and Research, Brooklyn Col, 55-57; Teaching and Res Fel, Univ Pa, 57-58; Clinical Assoc, Brooklyn Col, 58-60; Dir to Prof and Assoc Dean, LaGuardia Community Col, 71-. **HONORS AND AWARDS** Founders Day Awd, NY Univ, US Army citation; US Dept of Labor Awd; Phi Beta Kappa; Psi Chi; Pi Mu Epsilon. **MEMBERSHIPS** Am Psychol Soc, Am Psychol Asn, Eastern Psychol Asn, Cooperative Educ Asn, NY State Cooperative Educ Assoc, US Dept of Labor's Nat Manpower Advisory Committee, NY Psychol Asn, Am Soc for Training and Development, Metropolitan Asn of applied Psychol, Am Management Asn, Advisory Board of the NY Sate Educ Dept. **RESEARCH** Cultural diversity in the classroom and on-the-job. **SELECTED PUBLICATIONS** Coauth, The Integration of cooperative Education and The Liberal Arts, Canadian Asn of Cooperative Educ, 86; auth, "Measurement; supplement or substitute for Judgment," Journal of Cooperative Education, 80; auth, "Maximizing Cooperative Education through Internship Seminars," Journal of cooperative Education, 75; co-auth, "Maximizing Your Training Efficiency: The Application of Behavioral Principles to Job Training (Training Manual and Workbook Exercises), New York, 72; **CONTACT ADDRESS** Dept Soc Sci, LaGuardia Comm Col, 3110 Thomson Ave, Long Island City, NY 11101.

FELDMAN, HEIDI M.
PERSONAL Born 02/24/1949, Philadelphia, PA, 2 children **DISCIPLINE** DEVELOPMENTAL PSYCHOLOGY; MEDICINE **EDUCATION** Univ Penn, BA, 70; PhD, 75; Univ Calif, MD, 79. **CAREER** Asst prof, Univ Pittsburgh, 84-90; dir, Child Develop Unit, Children's Hospital of Pittsburgh, 84-93; interim dir, Dept Communication Disorders, Children's Hospital of Pittsburgh, 86-87; dir, Down Syndrome Center, Children's Hospital of Pittsburgh, 89-91; assoc prof Pediatrics, Univ of Pittsburgh School of Medicine, 90-; division chief, General Acad Pediatrics, Children's Hospital of Pittsburgh, 93-; secondary appt, Dept Communication Science & Disorders, School of Health & Rehabilitation Sciences, Univ Pittsburgh, 96-; vchair, fac & prog develop, dept of pediatrics, Univ Pittsburgh, Sch of Med, 00- ; prof pediatrics, Univ Pittsburgh, Sch of Med, 00- . **HONORS AND AWARDS** Phi Beta Kappa, 70; Miles S Murphy Awd for Distinction in Psychology, 70; Mortar Board Senior Women's Honor Soc, Univ Pa, 69-70; Ntl Sci Found Fel, 72-75; Frank-Arendsee-Feldman Found for Medical Res and Scholar, 78; Soc for Pediatric Res Member, 92-96; Soc Pediatric Res Senior Member, 96-. **MEMBERSHIPS** Amer Women's Med Assoc, 82-85; Mass Med Soc, 82-83; Boston Inst for Parents, Infants, and Children, 83-84; Fac Assoc School of Med, Univ Pittsburgh, 84-; Soc Developmental-Behavioral Pediatrics, 85-; Soc Res in Child Dev, 85-; Amer Acad Pediatrics, 86-. **SELECTED PUBLICATIONS** A playroom observation procedure to assess children with mental retardation and ADHD, Jour Abnormal Child Psychol, 98; Caring for children with special needs, Contemporary Pediatrics, 98; Teaching pediatric residents about early intervention and special education, Jour Developmental & Behavioral Pediatrics, 97. **CONTACT ADDRESS** Gen Acad Pediatrics, Children's Hospital of Pittsburgh, One Children's Pl, 3705 Fifth Ave, Pittsburgh, PA 15213. **EMAIL** feldmanh@pitt.edu

FELDMAN, MAURICE A.
PERSONAL Born 10/06/1949, New York, NY, 2 children **DISCIPLINE** PSYCHOLOGY **EDUCATION** City Col CUNY, BA; McMaster Univ, PhD. **CAREER** Asst prof, Univ W Ont, 75-80; lectr, St Clair Col, 77; acting dir, Southwestern Regional Centre, 79-80; project dir to prog dir, Surrey Place Centre, 80-91; lectr to asst prof, Univ Toronto, 90-94; assoc prof to prof, Queen's Univ, 94-. **HONORS AND AWARDS** Brit Psychol Soc Travel Fel, 01; Vis Scholar, Univ Sydney, 01. **MEMBERSHIPS** Ont Col of Psychol; Can Registry of Health Serv Providers in Psychol; am Asn of Mental Retardation; Can Psychol Asn; Asn for Beh Analysis Intl; Ont Asn on Develop Disabilities; Ont Asn for Beh Analysis. **RESEARCH** Developmental Disorders; Psychopathology and Disabilities; Child Maltreatment; Early Intervention. **SELECTED PUBLICATIONS** Auth, "Balancing freedom from harm and the right to treatment in persons with developmental disabilities," in Current perspectives in the use of nonaversive and aversive interventions with developmentally disabled persons, (Sycamore Press, 90), 261-271; co-auth, "Comparison of staff training strategies to promote generalized teaching skills," J of Applied Beh Analysis, (92): 165-179; co-auth, "Effectiveness of home-based early intervention on the language development of children of parents with mental retardation," Res in Develop Disabilities, (93): 387-408; auth, "Parenting education for parents with intellectual disabilities: A review of outcome studies," Res in Develop Disabilities, (94): 299-332; co-auth, "Comprehensive assessment of severe behavior disorders," in Treatment of severe behavior problems: Models and methods in developmental disabilities, (Pacific Grove, 97), 23-48; co-auth, "Effects of maternal mental retardation and poverty on intellectual, academic, and behavioral status of school-age children," Am J on Mental Retardation, (97): 352-364; auth, "Preventing child neglect: Child-care training for parents with intellectual disabilities," Infants and Young Children, (98): 1-11; co-auth, "Using self-instructional pictorial manuals to teach child-care skills to mothers with intellectual disabilities," Beh Modification, (99): 480-497; co-auth, "Behavior problems in young children with or at risk for developmental delay," J of Child and Family Studies, (00): 247-261; ed, Essential reader in early intervention, Blackwell, in press. **CONTACT ADDRESS** Dept Psychol, Queen's Univ at Kingston, 50 Arch St, Kingston, ON, Canada K7L 3L6. **EMAIL** feldman@psyc.queensu.ca

FELLMAN, ANITA C.
PERSONAL Born 05/13/1942, Chicago, IL **DISCIPLINE** WOMEN'S STUDIES **EDUCATION** Oberlin Col, BA, 64; Univ Mich, MA, 65; Northwestern Univ, PhD, 69. **CAREER** Lecturer, Dept of History, Univ of British Columbia, 69-71; Adjunct Prof, Women's Studies, Simon Fraser Univ, 74-88; Dir of Women's Studies and Assoc Prof of History, Old Dominion Univ, 88-. **HONORS AND AWARDS** Laura Jamieson Prize, Canadian Research Institute for the Advancement of Women, 87. **MEMBERSHIPS** Amer Historical Assoc; Organization of American Historians; Canadian Historical Assoc. **RESEARCH** US and Canadian Women's History; Amer Cultural and intellectual history. **SELECTED PUBLICATIONS** Co-auth, "Making Sense of Self: Medical Advice Literature in Late Nineteenth-Century America," Philadelphia: Univ of Pennsylvania Press, 81; auth, "Rethinking Canada: The Promise of Women's History," Toronto: Copp Clark, 86, 91, Toronto: Oxford University Press, 97; auth, "Ourselves as Students: Multicultural Voices in the Classroom," Carbondale: Southern Illinois University Press, 96. **CONTACT ADDRESS** Dept Women's Studies, Old Dominion Univ, Norfolk, VA 23529. **EMAIL** afellman@odu.edu

FELLMAN, GORDON
PERSONAL Born 05/10/1934, Omaha, NE, m, 1999 **DISCIPLINE** SOCIOLOGY **EDUCATION** Antioch Col, BA, 57; Harvard Univ, PhD, 64. **CAREER** Instr/lectr, Harvard Univ, 63-64; asst prof to prof, Brandeis Univ, 64-. **HONORS AND AWARDS** Chair, Peace and Conflict Studies Program, Brandeis Univ, 90-. **MEMBERSHIPS** AAUP; Am Sociol Assoc. **RESEARCH** War and peace, psychoanalytic sociology, empowerment, politics. **SELECTED PUBLICATIONS** Coauth, The Deceived Majority: Politics and Protest in Middle America, Trans-Action Pr, (New Brunswick), 73; auth, "Leaf in the Wind, Jayaprakash Narayan as Politician and as Saint", Psychohistory Rev 9.3 (81): 183-213; auth, "Freedom from Work, Freedom to Work: Contribution and Fulfillment in Post-Industrial Society, Part I", Changing Work, (Spring 86); auth, "Brandeis in the Balance", Tikkun, Nov/Dec 90; coauth, The Nuclear Seduction: Why The Arms Race Doesn't Matter, and What Does, Univ of Calif Pr, (Berkeley), 90; auth, "The Truths of Frankenstein: Technologism and Images of Destruction", Psychohistory Rev 19.2, (Winter 91): auth, "On the Fetishism of Publications and the Secrets Thereof", Academe, (Jan/Feb 95); auth, "Tibet: A Culture in Exile", Peacework, (Sept 95); auth, "The Prize of Authenticity", Writing Sociol 3.2, (Fall 95); auth, Rambo and the Dalai Lama: The Compulsion to Win and Its Threat to Human Survival, SUNY Pr, (Albany), 98. **CONTACT ADDRESS** Dept Sociol, Brandeis Univ, 415 South St, Waltham, MA 02453. **EMAIL** fellman@brandeis.edu

FELTEY, KATHRYN M.
PERSONAL Born 08/01/1954, Long Island, NY, s, 1 child **DISCIPLINE** SOCIOLOGY **EDUCATION** Wright State Univ, Dayton, Oh, BA, 78, MA, 82; Oh State Univ, Columbus, PhD, 88. **CAREER** Asst prof, Univ Akron, Ohio, 88-92, assoc prof, 92-, Dir, Undergrad Studies, Dept Sociol, 95-97, Dir, Women's Studies Prog, Interdisciplinary Progs, 97-99. **HONORS AND AWARDS** Pioneer Awd, Univ Akron, 93; listed in: Who's Who in the Midwest, Who's Who of Am Women, Who's Who in the World, World Who's Who of Women, 91-99; Acad of Management, Best Article Awd, 99. **MEMBERSHIPS** North Central Sociol Asn, Sociols for Women in Soc, Soc for Applied Sociol, Inst for Women's Policy Res, Am Sociol Asn, Nat Coun on Family Relations. **RESEARCH** Homeless women and children, violence in interpersonal relationships, citizen participation. **SELECTED PUBLICATIONS** Auth, "Single-Parents," in Encyclopedia of Marriage and the Family, ed by David Levinson, NY: MacMillan (95); coauth, "Role Exit from Home to Homeless," Free Inquiry in Creative Sociol, 24 (96): 1-10; rev of Violence Between Intimate Partners: Patterns, Causes and Effects, ed By Albert P. Cardelli, Boston: Allyn & Bacon (97), J of Marriage and the Family (98); coauth, "The Questions of Participation: Toward Authentic Public Participation in Public Administration," Public Administration Rev, 48 (98): 317-326; coauth, "Women, Power, and Change in Sociology and Beyond: Sociologists for Women in Society," Sociol Spectrum, 18 (98): 211-228; coauth, "From Victim to Survivor: Recovered Memories and Identity Transformation," in Trauma and Memory, ed by Linda Williams and Victoria Banyard, Sage Pubs (99): 161-174; coauth, " 'The Only Thing You Really Got . Is This Minute': Homeless Women Re-visioning the Future," in Reclaiming the Future: Women's Strategies for the 21st Century, ed by Somer Brodribb, Canada: Gynergy Books (99). **CONTACT ADDRESS** Dept Sociol, Univ of Akron, 248 Olin Hall, Akron, OH 44325-1905. **EMAIL** FELTEYK@UAKRON.EDU

FENG-CHECKETT, GAYLE
PERSONAL Born 12/08/1952, Los Angeles, CA, m, 1994, 3 children **DISCIPLINE** ENGLISH, ESL **EDUCATION** Univ Redlands, BA, 74; Univ N Dak, MA, 76. **CAREER** Instr, Concordia Col, 78-80; instr, St Louis Community Col, 86-93; prof, St Charles County Community Col, 93-. **HONORS AND AWARDS** Golden Apple Awd, St Peters Chamber of Commerce. **MEMBERSHIPS** TESOL; MCCA; NCTE; TYCA; CWA; M/MLA. **RESEARCH** Teaching English as a second language, teaching/learning for developmental writers, critical thinking. **SELECTED PUBLICATIONS** Coauth, "The Write Start: Sentence to Paragraph", The Write Start: Paragraph to Essay" in Develop Writing Textb Series, Addison Wesley Longman. **CONTACT ADDRESS** Dept English, Saint Charles County Comm Col, PO Box 76975, Saint Peters, MO 63376-0092. **EMAIL** gfeng@chuck.stchas.edu

FENNESSEE, W. T.
PERSONAL Born 04/09/1951, Mt Pleasant, TN, s **DISCIPLINE** PSYCHOLOGY **EDUCATION** Austin Peay State Univ, BS, 74; Univ Tenn, MS, 76; Southern Ill Univ, RhD, 87. **CAREER** Asst Prof and Coordinator, Rhode Island Col, 87-88; Asst Prof and Coordinator, Murray State Univ, 89-93; Asst Prof and Director, Ala A & M Univ, 95-. **MEMBERSHIPS** Am Couns Asn, Nat Rehabilitation Asn, Asn of Higher Educ and Disability, Intl Asn of Marriage and Family Coun, Am Rehabilitation Asn. **CONTACT ADDRESS** Dept Beh Sci, Alabama A&M Univ, PO Box 580, Normal, AL 35762. **EMAIL** wfennessee@aamu.edu

FENTON, WILLIAM NELSON
PERSONAL Born 12/15/1908, New Rochelle, NY, m, 1936, 3 children **DISCIPLINE** ANTHROPOLOGY, ETHNOHISTORY **EDUCATION** Dartmouth Col, AB, 31; Yale Univ, PhD (anthrop), 37 Hon Degree: LLD, Hartwick Col, 68. **CAREER** Community worker among Senecas, US Indian Serv, 35-37; from instr to asst prof anthrop, St Lawrence Univ, 37-39; assoc anthropologist, Bur Am Ethnol, Smithsonian Inst, 39-43, sr ethnologist, 43-51; exec secy anthrop and psychol, Nat Acad Sci-Nat Res Coun, 52-54; asst comnr, NY State Mus and Sci Serv, NY State Educ Dept, 54-68; res prof, 68-74, distinguished prof, 74-79, Emer Prof Anthrop, State Univ NY Albany, 79-, Secy war comt, Smithsonian Inst, 42-44, res assoc ethnogeog bd, 43-45; mem comn lang and areal implications, Comn Armed Forces Educ Prog, Am Coun Educ, 46; trustee, Mus Am Indian, Heye Found, New York City, 76-80 and 82-; dean Iroquois Studies, 80. **HONORS AND AWARDS** Cornplanter Medal for Iroquois Research, 65; LL.D. Hartwick College, 68; Citizen Laureate award, Univ at Albany Foundation, 78; Wilbur Cross Medal, Yale Univ Graduate School, 99. **MEMBERSHIPS** Am Anthrop Asn; Am Folklore Soc (pres, 59-60); Am Ethnol Soc (pres, 59); Am Soc Ethnohist (pres, 62). **RESEARCH** Iroquois studies. **SELECTED PUBLICATIONS** Auth, The Iroquois Eagle Dance: an Offshoot of the Calumet Dance. Bureau of American Ethnology Bulletib 156, Washington, DC, 53; auth, American Indian and White Relations to 1830: Needs and Opportunities for Study, Chapel Hill: Univ of NC Press 57; auth, The False faces of the Iroquois, Norman Oklahoma: The Univ of OK Press, 87; auth, The Great Law and the Longhouse: A Political History of the Iroquois Confederacy, Norman, OK: The Univ of OK Press, 98. **CONTACT ADDRESS** 7 N Helderberg Pkwy, Slingerlands, NY 12159. **EMAIL** wnfenton@yahoo.com

FERBER, ABBY L.
DISCIPLINE SOCIOLOGY **EDUCATION** Am Univ, BA, 87; Univ Ore, MS, 91; PhD, 94. **MEMBERSHIPS** Am Sociol Asn, Social for Women in Soc, Soc for the Study of Soc Problems, Northwest Coalition Against Malicious Harassment, Mountain States Network against Bigotry, Coalition for Human Dignity; Pacific Sociol Asn, Pi Gamma Mu. **RESEARCH** Gender; Race and ethnicity; contemporary social theory; White supremacist and right-wing social movements. **SELECTED PUBLICATIONS** Auth, Common Ground: University Students of Color Speak Out, Rowman and Littlefield, forthcoming; auth, White Man Falling: Race, Gender, and White Supremacy, Rowman and Littlefield, 98; auth, "Reading Right: The Western Tradition in White Supremacist Discourse," Sociological Focus, forthcoming; auth, "White Men are this Nation': Right Wing Militias and the Restoration of Rural American Masculinity,": Rural Sociology, forthcoming; auth, "Teaching About the Organized White Supremacist Movement," ASA Teaching Resources: Guide to Teaching Hate Crimes, American Sociological Association, 00; auth, "White supremacy and the Threat of Multiracial Identity," Colorlines in the 21st Century, forthcoming; auth, "Intersectionality and White Masculinity," Gender Stratification: Social Construction and Structural Accounts, Roxbury Press, forthcoming; auth, "Racial Warriors and Weekend Warriors: The Construction of Masculinity in Mythopoetic and White Supremacist Discourse,": Men and Masculinities, forthcoming; auth, "The Construction of Race, Gender, and Class in White Supremacist Discourse," Race, Gender and Class, (99): 67-89. **CONTACT ADDRESS** Dept Sociol, Univ of Colorado, Colorado Springs, 1420 Austin Bluffs, Colorado Springs, CO 80918.

FERERE, GERARD ALPHONSE
PERSONAL Born 07/21/1930, Cap Haitian, Haiti, m **DISCIPLINE** EDUCATION **EDUCATION** Naval Acad of Venezuela, Ensign, 53; Villanova Univ, MA, 67; Univ of PA, PhD, 74. **CAREER** Haitian Navy, naval officer 53-58; Haiti, language teacher 58-63; St Joseph's Univ, prof 64-. **MEMBERSHIPS** Coalition for Haitian Concerns, Haitian American commissioner, Pennsylvania Heritage Affairs Commission. **CONTACT ADDRESS** Dept of Foreign of Lang and Lit, Saint Joseph's Univ, City Ave at 54th St, Philadelphia, PA 19131. **EMAIL** ferere@sju.edu

FERNQUIST, ROBERT M.
PERSONAL Born San Francisco, CA, m, 1987, 4 children **DISCIPLINE** SOCIOLOGY **EDUCATION** Brigham Young, BA, 89, MS, 90; Indiana Univ, PhD, 96. **CAREER** Adjunct prof, Mont State Univ, 93-96; asst prof, Ferrum Col, 96-97; ast prof, Central Mo State Univ, 97-. **HONORS AND AWARDS** Fee scholarship for doctoral studies at Indiana Univ/ **MEMBERSHIPS** Am Sociol Asn, Midwest Sociol Soc, Mo Sociol Asn. **RESEARCH** Suicide. **SELECTED PUBLICATIONS** Coauth with Phillips Cutright, "Societal Integration and Age-Standardized Suicide Rates in 21 Developed Countries, 1955-1989," Soc Sci Res, 27 (98): 109-127; auth, "Gender Equality and the Sex Differential in Suicide Rates Using Gender-Age Standardized Data," Archives of Suicide Res, 5 (99): 255-260; auth, An Aggregate Analysis of Professional Sports, Suicide, and Homicide Rates: 30 U. S. Metropolitan Areas, 1971-1990," Aggression and Violent Behav, 5 (2000); coauth with Phillips Cutright, "The Effects of Societal Integration, Period, Region, and the Culture of Suicide on Male Age-Specific Suicide Rates: 20 Developed Countries, 1955-1989," Soc Sci Res, 29 (2000): 148-172; coauth with Phillips Cutright, "Societal Integration, Culture, and Period: Their Impact on Female Age-Specific Rates in 20 Developed Countries, 1955-1989," Sociol Focus (2000); auth, "An Examination on Cross-National Lethal Violence Rates and Suicide-Homicide Ratios: Are LVR and SHR Worthwhile," Archives of Suicide Res (forthcoming); auth, "The Impact of the 1994-1995 Professional Baseball and Hockey Strikes on National Suicide and Homicide Rates," Archives of Suicide Res (forthcoming); auth, "Problem Drinking in the Family and Youth Suicide," Adolescence (forthcoming); coauth with Phillips Cutright,"Egalitarianism, the Economy and the Percent Male of Total Suicide: An Exploratory Analysis of Nine European Countries, 1975-1987," Omega, the J of Death and Dying (forthcoming); coauth with Phillips Cutright,"Firearms and suicide: The American experience, 1926-1996," Death Studies (forthcoming). **CONTACT ADDRESS** Dept Sociol & Soc Work, Central Missouri State Univ, Wood 203, Warrensburg, MO 64093. **EMAIL** Fernquist@cmsu1.cmsu.edu

FERRARO, KENNETH K.
PERSONAL Born 10/13/1954, Pittsburgh, PA, m, 1978, 3 children **DISCIPLINE** SOCIOLOGY **EDUCATION** St Vincent Col,Latrobe, PA, BA, 76; Duquesne Univ, MA, 78; Univ Akron, OH, PhD, 81. **CAREER** Asst prof, Univ NC, Wilmington, 81-84; asst prof, Northern Ill Univ, DeKalb, 84-87, Dir Gerontology Prog, 86-90, assoc prof, 87-90; assoc prof, Purdue Univ, 90-94, prof, 94-, Dir Gerontology Prog, 95-. **HONORS AND AWARDS** Grad with honors, St Vincent Col, 76; Who's Who Among Students in Am Cols and Univs, 76. **RESEARCH** Health, gerontology, health inequality, religion and health, minority health. **SELECTED PUBLICATIONS** Auth, "Women's Fear of Victimization: Shadow of Sexual Assault?," Soc Forces, 75 (96): 667-690; ed, Gerontology: Perspectives and Issues, 2nd ed, New York: Springer Pub (97); coauth with Ya-ping Su, "Social Relations and Health Assessments Among Older People: Do the Effects of Integration and Social Contributions Vary Cross-Culturally?," J of Gerontology: Soc Scis, 52B (97): S27-S36; coauth with Melissa M. Farmer and John A. Wybraniec, "Health Trajectories: Long-Term Dynamics Among Black and White Adults," J of Health and Soc Behav, 38 (97): 38-54; coauth with Melissa M. Farmer, "Distress and Perceived Health: Mechanisms of Health Decline," J of Health and Soc Behav, 38 (97): 298-311; auth, "Firm Believers? Religion, Body Weight, and Well-Being," Rev of Relig Res, 39 (98): 224-244; coauth with Ya-ping Su, "Financial Strain, Social Relations, and Psychological Distress Among Older People: A Cross-Cultural Analysis," J of Gerontology: Soc Scis 54B (99): S3-S15; coauth with Melissa M. Farmer, "Utility of Health Data from Social Surveys: Is There a Gold Standard for Measuring Morbidity?," Am Sociol Rev, 64(99): 303-315; coauth with Tara L. Booth, "Age, Body Mass Index, and Functional Illness," J of Gerontology: Soc Scis, 54B (99): S339-S348; coauth with Ya-ping Su, "Physician-Evaluated and Self-Reported Morbidity for Predicted Disability," Am J of Public Health, 90 (2000): 103-108. **CONTACT ADDRESS** Dept Sociol & Anthropol, Purdue Univ, West Lafayette, 1365 Stone Hall, West Lafayette, IN 47907-1365. **EMAIL** ferraro@purdue.edu

FERRIS, ALAN
PERSONAL Born 12/11/1964, Columbus, NE, m, 1989, 2 children **DISCIPLINE** PSYCHOLOGY **EDUCATION** Kans State Univ, MS, 90; PhD, 92; Univ Neb, BS, 98. **CAREER** Asst Prof, Mt Marty Col, 92-99; Assoc Prof, Mt Marty Col, 99-. **MEMBERSHIPS** Midwest Psychol Asn, APA, Soc for the Teaching of Psychol. **RESEARCH** Teaching and learning, health psychology, religion. **SELECTED PUBLICATIONS** Auth, "Student Attitudes Towards Portfolios to Encourage Journal Reading," Res in Educ (98). **CONTACT ADDRESS** Dept Community Serv, Mount Marty Col, Yankton, 1105 W 8th St, Yankton, SD 57078. **EMAIL** aferris@mtmc.edu

FERRO, TRENTON R.
PERSONAL Born 02/08/1939, Yuma, AZ, m, 1964, 4 children **DISCIPLINE** ADULT EDUCATION **EDUCATION** Concordia Sr Col, BA, 61; Concordia Theol Sem, MDiv, 65, STM, 66; Univ Calif-Berkeley, MA, 75; Northern Ill Univ, EdD, 89. **CAREER** Inst, Northern Ill Univ, 85-87; adj prof, Nat Col Educ, 88-89; asst prof, Ball State Univ, 89-90; asst prof, 90-95, Assoc prof, 95-, dept chmn, 99-; Ind Univ Penn. **HONORS AND AWARDS** Fel, Project for the Study of Adult Learning, 92. **MEMBERSHIPS** Am Asn Adult & Continuing Educ; Comn Prof Adult Educ; Relig Educ Asn; Penn Asn Adult Continuing Educ. **RESEARCH** Adult learning and development; program planning and evaluation; volunteerism; adult religious education; educational gerontology. **SELECTED PUBLICATIONS** Auth, AKC Judges Institute Instructional Design and Teaching Manual, Am Kennel Club, 91; co-ed, Proceedings of the Pennsylvania Adult and Continuing Education Research Conference, 94,95,98,01; co-ed, Proceedings of the Eastern Regional Adult and Continuing Education Research Conference, 99; auth, 6 reviews in mental measurements yearbooks; auth, of numerous articles, book chapters, and other publications. **CONTACT ADDRESS** Indiana Univ of Pennsylvania, 234 Stouffer Hall, Indiana, PA 15705-1087. **EMAIL** trferro@grove.iup.edu

FETTERLEY, JUDITH
PERSONAL Born 11/28/1938, New York, NY **DISCIPLINE** AMERICAN LITERATURE, WOMEN'S STUDIES **EDUCATION** Swarthmore Col, BA, 60; Ind Univ, MA, 66, PhD (English), 69. **CAREER** Asst prof English, Univ Pa, 67-73; asst prof, 73-78, ASSOC PROF ENGLISH, STATE UNIV NY, ALBANY, 78-. **MEMBERSHIPS** Nat Women's Studies Asn; MLA. **RESEARCH** Nineteenth century Am Lit; American women writers; Mark Twain. **SELECTED PUBLICATIONS** Auth, The sanctioned rebel, Studies Novel, fall 71; Disenchantment: Tom Sawyer in Huckleberry Finn, PMLA, 72; Yankee Showman and reformer: The character of Mark Twain's Hank Morgan, Tex Studies Lang & Lit, 73; Beauty as the beast: Fantasy and fear in I, The Jury, J Popular Cult, 75; Growing up female in The Old Order, Kate Chopin Newslett, 76; The temptation to be a beautiful object: Double standard and double bind in The House of Mirth, Studies Am Fiction, 77; The Resisting Reader: A Feminist Analysis of American Fiction, Ind Univ, 78. **CONTACT ADDRESS** Dept of English, SUNY, Albany, Albany, NY 12222.

FIEBERT, MARTIN S.
PERSONAL Born 06/06/1939, New York, NY, m, 2000, 2 children **DISCIPLINE** PSYCHOLOGY **EDUCATION** Queens Col, BS, 60; Univ Rochester, PhD, 65. **CAREER** Prof, Cal State Univ at Long Beach. **MEMBERSHIPS** APS, AMSA. **RESEARCH** Interracial dating, men as victims of partner abuse, Transpersonal psychology. **SELECTED PUBLICATIONS** Coauth, " College women who initiate assaults on their male partners and the reasons offered for such behavior," Psych Report 80 (97): 583-590; coauth, "Gender Stereotypes: A Bias Against Men," J Psych 131 (97): 407-410; coauth, " In and Out of Freud's Shadow: A Chronology of Adler's Relationship with Freud," Individual Psych 53 (97): 241-269; auth, "References Examine Assaults by Women on their Spouses/ Partners," Sexuality and Culture 1 (97): 273-286; coauth, "Sexual Coercion: Men Victimized by Women," J Men's Stud 6 (98): 127-133; coauth, "Assessing African-American and Jewish Intergroup Perceptions and Attitudes," Perc Motor Skills, 88 (99): 253-258. **CONTACT ADDRESS** Dept of Psychology, California State Univ, Long Beach, 1250 N Bellflower, Long Beach, CA 90840-0001. **EMAIL** mfiebert@usclb.edu

FIELD, MARK G.
PERSONAL Born 06/17/1923, Switzerland, m, 1948, 4 children **DISCIPLINE** SOCIOLOGY **EDUCATION** Harvard Col, BA, 48; Harvard Univ, MA, 50, PhD, 55. **CAREER** Assoc prof, Univ Ill, 61-62; from prof to prof ermer, Boston Univ, 62-; res fel & assoc, Davis Ctr for Russ Stud, Harvard Univ, 62-; adj prof, Sch of Public Health, Univ Harvard, 88-. **MEMBERSHIPS** Am Sociol Asn; Am Asn Advan Slavic Stud; Soc Europeenne de Culture. **RESEARCH** Sociology of health care; health crisis in the former Soviet Union; comparative health care systems; cultural aspects of health. **SELECTED PUBLICATIONS** Ed, Success and Crisis in National Health Care Systems: A Comparative Approach, Routledge, 89; co-ed, The Political Dynamics of Physician Manpower Policy, Amsterdam, 90; coauth, Cultural Images of Health: A Neglected Dimension, Nova Science, 95; auth, The Health Crisis in the Former Soviet Union: A Report from the Post-War Zone, Soc Sci and Med, 95; coatuh, The Current State of Health Care in the Former Soviet Union: Implications for Health Care Policy and Reform, Am J of Public Health, 96; auth, Health in Russia: The Regional and National Dimensions, in Stavrakis, ed, Beyond the Monolity: The Emergence of Regionalism in Post-Soviet Russia, Woodrow Wilson Ctr, 97; coauth, From Assurance to Insurance in Russian Health Care: The Problematic Transition, Am J Pub Health, 98; co-ed, Russia's Torn Safety Nets: Health and Social Welfar During the Transition, St. Martin's Pr, 00. **CONTACT ADDRESS** Davis Center for Russian Studies, Harvard Univ, 1737 Cambridge St, Cambridge, MA 02138. **EMAIL** mfield@hsph.harvard.edu

FIELDS, MILTON
PERSONAL Born 04/26/1941, Millport, AL, m, 1965, 1 child **DISCIPLINE** ELEMENTARY EDUCATION, SUPERVISION, SCHOOL ADMINISTRATION, READING **EDUCATION** Free Will Baptist Bible Coll, BA, 67; Univ Ala-Birmingham, BS, 76; Univ S Ala, MED, 80; Univ S Miss, PhD, 83. **CAREER** Asst Prin, EscatAwarpa Elem School, Moss Point, Miss, 76-83; Chairman of Bd Post Sec Prog for Ment Retared Adults, Columbus, Miss, 83-86; Prin, Carrollton Elem School, Carrollton, Ala, 86-88; Prin, Caledonia and W Lowndes Middle School, Columbus, Miss, 88-92; Prin, Fairview Elem School, Columbus, Miss, 92-94; Chm, Dept of Teacher Education, Free Will Baptist Bibl Coll, Nashville, Tenn, 94-98; Acad dean, Free Will Baptist Bibl Coll, Nashville, Tenn, 98; Accreditation Auditor, Miss State Dept of ed, 89-94; SACS evaluator, K-12, 89-94, College, 99-; Educ. Study Commission, National Assoc of Free Will Baptists, 99-. **HONORS AND AWARDS** Who's Who Among Outstanding Americans, 95-96; Outstanding District Pub School Administrator, 91. **MEMBERSHIPS** Coll Rep Metrop Coun of Teacher Educrs; Tenn Asn of Independent Lib Arts Colls 95-99; Pres 99-00; Tenn Asn of Techer Educrs; Exec Bd of TATE Secy. **RESEARCH** Christian Education; Communication Anxiety; Motivations. **SELECTED PUBLICATIONS** Auth, Decision-making, Mgt. Educ articles, Contact, 72; Decision-making, Mgt, Educ articles, Contact, 82; auth, Anxiety Among Elementary Teachers According to Various Formats and Levels of Written Memoranda, 83; Educ artciles, Free Will Baptist Bibl Coll Bull, 94. **CONTACT ADDRESS** Free Will Baptist Bible Col, 3606 West End Ave, Nashville, TN 37025. **EMAIL** sara@fwbbc.edu

FIEMA, ZBIGNIEW
PERSONAL Born 03/07/1957, Poland, s **DISCIPLINE** ARCHAEOLOGY; ANTHROPOLOGY **EDUCATION** Univ Utah, PhD, 91 **CAREER** Assoc Instr, 86-92, Univ Utah; Visiting Prof, Univ Helsinki, Finland, 96-97; Chief Archaelogist, American Center of Oriental Research, Jordan, 92-97. **HONORS AND AWARDS** Phi Kappa Phi Honors Soc, Univ Utah **MEMBERSHIPS** Amer Schools of Oriental Research; Archaelogical Inst of Amer. **RESEARCH** Culture History of the Roman & Byzantine East; complex societies; archaelogical methodology **SELECTED PUBLICATIONS** Coauth, Report on the Petra Scrolls Project, Journal of Archaelogy, 95; Auth, Military Architecture and Defense System in Roman-Byzantine Southern Jordan. A Critical Appraisal of Recent Interpretations, Studies in the Archaeology and History of Jordan V, 95; Sr Coauth, The Petra Church Project 92-94, The Roman and Byzantine Near East: Some Recent Archaeological Research, 95; Auth, Nabataean and Palmyrene Commerce - The Mechanisms of Intensification, The Proceedings of the International Conference on Palmyra and the Silk Road, 96; Les papyri de Petra, Le Monde de la Bible, 97; Report on the Petra Church Project, American Journal of Archaeology, 97; Petra Romana et Byzantina, Petra - Antike Felsstadt zwischen Arabischer Tradition und Griechischer Norm, 97; At-Tuwan - The Development and Decline of a Classical Town in Southern Jordan, Studies in the History and Archaeology of Jordan VI, 97; Report on the Roman Street in Petra Project, American Journal of Archaeology, 98. **CONTACT ADDRESS** Dept. of Philosophy Stewart Building, Univ of Utah, University of Utah, Salt Lake City, UT 84112.

FIGONE, ALBERT J.
PERSONAL Born 03/04/1938, s **DISCIPLINE** SPORTS PSYCHOLOGY **EDUCATION** Humboldt State Univ, 91; Arizona State Univ, 95; Univ Utah, PhD, 73-76; San Francisco State Univ, MA, 66-68; Univ Wyoming, BS, 58-60; Col San Mateo, AA, 57-58. **CAREER** Asst Prof, Humboldt State Univ, 80; Assoc Prof, 84; Graduate Coord, 85-90; Promotion to Prof 90; Social Science Teacher/Head Baseball Coach, Livermore High School 78-80; Asst Prof of Physical Education/Head Baseball Coach/Asst Football Coach, 70-78; Mathematics Teacher/Social Science Teacher/Physical Education Teacher/Head Baseball Coach/Asst Football Coach/Assistant Track Coach/Junior Varsity Basketball Coach/, Terra Nova High School, 96-70. **MEMBERSHIPS** National Assoc for Physical Education in Higher Education (NAHPE); North Amer Society for Psychology of Sport and Physical Activity (NASPA); North American Society for the Sociology of Sport (NASS); Humboldt County Historical Society (HCHS); Amer Italian Historical Assoc (AIHA); International Society of Sport Psychology (ISSP); Amer Alliance for Health, Physical Education, Recreation, and Dance (AAHPERD); Amer Baseball Coaches Assoc (ABCA); Pacific Coast League Historical Society (PCLHS); California Historical Society (CHS); North Amer Society for Sport History (NASSH); California Assoc for Health, Physical Education, Recreation, & Dance (CAHPERD); Society for American Baseball Research (SABR); Assoc for the Advancement of Applied Sport Psychology (AAASP). **SELECTED PUBLICATIONS** Auth, "The art of pitching with control," Figone, A.J., California Association for Health, Physical Education, Recreation and Dance (CAHPERD) Journal, (99 May,

June); auth, "When the physical breaks down, try a little A.S.P. (Applied Sport Psychology)," Figone, A.J., Scholastic Coach and Athletic Director, (99, May); Auth, "Using a systematic offensive rating system for baseball and softball," Figone, A.J., Strategies: A journal for Sport and Physical Educators, (99, May, June); auth, "Baseball's piotal era, 1945-1951," Figone, A.J., for the Sociology of Sport Journal (SSJ)," (99, Summer); rev, "Onward to victory: The crisis that shaped college" Figone, A.J., for the Sociology of Sport Journal (SSJ), (99, Summer); auth, "Research, writing, and publishing for the right reasons," Figone, A.J., Journal of Health, Physical Education, Recreation and Dance (JOPERD), (99, fall); rev, "Relocating teams and expanding leagues in profesiona sports: How the major leagues respond to market conditions," Figone, A.J., for the Journal of Sport History (JSH), (00, January); auth, "Why don't practitioners use research? Selected explanations," Figone, A.J., California Association for Health, Physical Education, Recreation and Dance (CAHPERD) Journal, (00, Feb); auth, "Reasons coaches do not use applied sport psychology," Figone, A.J., California Association for Health, Physical Education, Recreation, and Dance (CAHPERD) Journal Times, (00, March); auth, "Beward of the post-mortem," Figone, A.J., California Association for Health, Physical Education, Recreation, and Dance (CAHPERD) Journal Times, (00, May). **CONTACT ADDRESS** Dept Health Physical Educ, Humboldt State Univ, 1 Harpst St, Arcata, CA 95521. **EMAIL** ajf2@humboldt.edu

FILINSON, RACHEL
PERSONAL Born 08/25/1956, Chicago, IL, m, 1984, 2 children **DISCIPLINE** SOCIOLOGY **EDUCATION** Univ Ill, BA, 77; Univ Stirling, MSc, 79; Univ Aberdeen, PhD, 82. **CAREER** Asst Prof, Purdue Univ, 84-87; Prof, RI Col, 87-. **HONORS AND AWARDS** Res Fel, Med Res Coun Inst of Med Soc, 79-82; NIMH Postdoctoral Fel, Univ Mo, 82-84. **MEMBERSHIPS** Assoc of Gerontology in Higher Educ. **RESEARCH** Cross-cultural aging, aging policy. **SELECTED PUBLICATIONS** Auth, "Religious Programming for Nursing Home Residents," J of Jewish Communal Serv, 71 (95): 333-339; auth, "A Survey of Grass Roots Advocacy Organizations for Nursing Home Residents," J of Elder Abuse & Neglect, 7 (95): 75-91; auth, "Legislating community Care: The British Experience with U S Comparisons," The Gerontologist, 37 (97): 333-341; auth, "The Impact of the Community Care Act--Views from the Independent Sector," Health & Soc Care in the Community, 6 (98): 241-250; coauth, "A Cross-National Test of Propositions from the Neo-Pluralist Perspective on Social Security Expenditures," J of Aging and Soc Policy, 10 (98): 49-66; auth, "Consumer Empowerment Through Education," Educ Gerontology, 25 (99): 155-165. **CONTACT ADDRESS** Dept Sociol, Rhode Island Col, 600 Mt Pleasant, Providence, RI 02908.

FILLER, JOHN W.
DISCIPLINE EARLY CHILDHOOD SPECIAL EDUCATION **EDUCATION** Peabody Col, PhD. **CAREER** Coordr, doctoral stud, Univ Nev, Las Vegas. **SELECTED PUBLICATIONS** Auth, A coment on inclusion: Research and Social Policy, Soc for Res in Child Develop Policy Rpt, 10, 96; coauth, Perceived importance of social skills: A survey of teachers, parents and other professionals, J of Spec Educ, 25, 91. **CONTACT ADDRESS** Dept of Spec Educ, Univ of Nevada, Las Vegas, 4505 Maryland Pky, Las Vegas, NV 89154-3014. **EMAIL** jfiller@nevada.edu

FINE, ELIZABETH C.
PERSONAL Born 12/20/1948, Cincinnati, OH, m, 1977, 1 child **DISCIPLINE** PERFORMANCE STUDIES, FOLKLORE **EDUCATION** Univ Tex, Austin, BS, 71, PhD (commun), 78; Univ Calif, Berkeley, MA, 73. **CAREER** Lect and asst prof, Univ Il, Urbana 77-79; asst and assoc prof Virginia Tech , 79-; dir, Humanities Progms, Center for Interdisciplinary Studies, Virginia Tech, 99-, asst and assoc prof, Virginia Interdiciplinary Studies, Virginia Tech, 99-. **HONORS AND AWARDS** Woodrow Wilson Fel, 71; Oustanding Dissertation Awd, Univ of Texas at Austin, 78-79; The Lilla A Heston Awd for Outstanding Scholarship in Interpretation and Performance Studies, presented by the Speech Communn Asn, 93; Third Place, Chicago Folklore Prize 85; Choice's Outstanding Academic Book of 85. **MEMBERSHIPS** Nat Commun Assoc, Am Folklore Soc **RESEARCH** Performance Studies, Appalachian Studies, African American Folklore. **SELECTED PUBLICATIONS** Auth, The Folklore Text: From Performance to Print, Bloomington: Indiana Univ Press, 84,94; auth, Fine Elizabeth and Speer, Jean Haskell, eds Performance, Culture and Identity, NY: Prager, 92; auth, " Lazy Jack": Coding and Contexualizing Resistance in Appalachia and the South: Place, Gender, Pedagogy, Vol 11, (3), 99: 112-137; auth, Leading Proteus Captive." Teaching Oral Traditions, MLA, 98, 59-71. **CONTACT ADDRESS** Dept of Commun Studies, Virginia Polytech Inst and State Univ, Blacksburg, VA 24060. **EMAIL** bfine@vt.edu

FINK, DEBORAH R.
PERSONAL Born 10/13/1944, Lincoln, NE, m, 1966, 2 children **DISCIPLINE** ANTHROPOLOGY **EDUCATION** Doane Col, Crete, NE, BA, 65; Univ NE, Lincoln, MA, 67; IA State Univ, Ames, MS, 74; Univ MN, Minneapolis, PhD, 79. **CAREER** Lect, Grinnell Col, 80; asst prof, anthropol, IA State, 80-81, adjunct prof, 83; adjunct asst prof, Women's Studies, Univ IA, 84-85; Rockefeller fel, Rural Women and Feminist Issues, 88-89; independent scholar, 89-. **HONORS AND AWARDS** Cum laude graduation, Doane Col, 65; graduate res grant, IA State, 73; MacMillan fel, Univ MN, 77; Doctoral dissertation fel, Univ MN, 78-79. **MEMBERSHIPS** Am Anthropological Asn; Central States Anthropol Asn; Soc for Applied Anthropol; Nat Coalition of Independent Scholars. **RESEARCH** Rural studies; cross-cultural study of women; labor studies. **SELECTED PUBLICATIONS** Auth, Open Country, Iowa: Rural Women, Tradition and Change, SUNY Press, 86; Agrarian Women: Wives and Mothers in Rural Nebraska 1880-1940, Univ NC Press, 92; review, All Will Yet Be Well: The Diary of Sarah Gillespie Huftalen, 1873-1952, by Suzanne L Bunkers, ND Hist, 95; review, Chasing Rainbows: A Recollection of the Great Plains, 1921-1975, by Gladys Leffler Gist, ed by James Marten, Great Plains Quart, 95; What Kind of Woman Would Work in Meatpacking, Anyway? World War II and the Road to Fair Employment, Great Plains Res, 95; World War II and Rural; Women, in IA Hist Reader, ed by Marvin Bergman, Ames: State Hist Soc of IA in assoc with IA State Univ Press, 96; Reoganizing Production: Gender and Control in Iowa Meatpacking, in Unionizing The Jungles: Labor and Community in the Twentieth-Century Meatpacking Industry, ed by Shelton Stromquist and Marvin Bergman, Univ IA Press, 97; review, The Prairie Winnows Out Its Own, by Paula M Nelson, WI Mag of Hist, 97; review, Troublesome Creek: A Midwestern, by Jeanne Jordan and Steven Asher, H-Rural, 8, Sept 97; review, Farm Boys: Lives of Gay Men from the Rural Midwest, collected and edited by Will Fellows, Annals of IA, 97; review, A Most Comfortable Dinner-18th Century Foods to Subsist a Great Number of Persons at a Small Expense, collected by Clarissa F Dillon, The Independent Scholar, 98; review, The Danish Revolution, 1500-1800: An Ecohistorical Interpretation, by Thorkild Kjaergaard, trans by David Hohnen, H-Rural, 98; Cutting Into the Meatpacking Line: Workers and Change in the Rural Midwest, Univ NC Press, 98; several publications forthcoming. **CONTACT ADDRESS** 222 S Russell, Ames, IA 50010. **EMAIL** afink@iastate.edu

FINK, VIRGINIA
PERSONAL Born 12/02/1947, Springfield, OH, m, 1968, 2 children **DISCIPLINE** SOCIOLOGY **EDUCATION** Oh Univ, BSN, 84; MA, 86; Univ Va, PhD, 93. **CAREER** Instructor, Univ Colo, 96-. **MEMBERSHIPS** SSSR; Pacific Sociol Asn. **RESEARCH** Gender and Religion. **SELECTED PUBLICATIONS** Auth, "Patriliny: A Major Religious Bar in the Cage of Patriarchy," Journal of Feminist Studies in Religion, forthcoming. **CONTACT ADDRESS** Dept Sociol, Univ of Colorado, Colorado Springs, 1420 Austin Bluffs, Colorado Springs, CO 80918. **EMAIL** vfink@brain.uccs.edu

FINKELSTEIN, BARBARA
PERSONAL Born 03/22/1937, Brooklyn, NY, m, 1959, 2 children **DISCIPLINE** AMERICAN HISTORY, HISTORY OF EDUCATION **EDUCATION** Columbia Univ, BA, 59; MA, 60; EdD, 70. **CAREER** Lectr hist educ, Brooklyn Col, 61-62; asst prof, 70-74, assoc prof, 74-83, prof, 83- , hist educ, dir, Ctr Stud Educ Policy & Human Values, 79- , Univ Md, College Park; Nat Endowment for Humanities fel, 75-76; contrib ed, J Psychohist, 77- ; Japan Soc for Promotion of Sci fel, 91-92; ser ed, Reflective Hist, Teachers Col Press, Columbia Univ, 94- ; adv bd, US Ed, Pedagogica Hist, 89- ; Int Adv Bd, Hist of Educ, 96- . **HONORS AND AWARDS** Critic's Choice Awd, Am Educ Studies Asn, 81; recipient Key to the City of Osaka, 87; Am Educ Press Asn Awd, 89; Distinguished Int Service Awd, Univ Md, 94-95; Outstanding Woman of the Year, Univ Md, 97-98. **MEMBERSHIPS** Am Educ Studies Asn (pres, 81-82); Hist Educ Soc (pres, 98-99); Am Educ Res Asn (vpres, 89-91); Soc Res Child Develop. **RESEARCH** Family and education in historical perspective; childhood history in nineteenth century United States; learners and learning in American History; comparative cultural studies. **SELECTED PUBLICATIONS** Auth, Governing the Young: Teacher Behavior in Popular Primary Schools in Nineteenth Century United States, Taylor & Francis, 89; auth, Dollars and Dreams: Classrooms as Fictitious Message Systems, 1790-1930, Hist of Educ Q, 91; auth, Perfecting Childhood: Horace Mann and the Origins of Public Education in the United States, Biography, 91; auth, Education Historians as Mythmakers, Rev of Res in Educ, 92; auth, The Evolving Terrain of Teaching: Classroom Management in the United States, 1790-1990, in, Classroom Practices and Politics in Cross Cultural Perspective, Garland, 97; coauth, Discovering Culture in Education: An Approach to Cultural Education Program Evaluation and Design, 98; ed and contribur, Hidden Messages: Instructional Materials for Cultural Teaching and Learning, Intercultural, 98. **CONTACT ADDRESS** Dept of Educ Policy, Univ of Maryland, Col Park, College Park, MD 20742-0001. **EMAIL** bf6@umail.umd.edu

FINNEY, BEN RUDOLPH
PERSONAL Born 10/01/1933, San Diego, CA, m, 1996, 2 children **DISCIPLINE** ANTHROPOLOGY **EDUCATION** Univ Calif Berkeley, BA, history, economics, anthropology, 55; Univ Hawaii, MA, anthropology, 59; Harvard Univ, PhD, anthropology, 64. **CAREER** Sr statistician, Kaiser Steel Corp, Industrial Engineering Dept, 56; Aviation ground officer, US Naval Reserve, active duty, 57; manufacturing analyst, General Dynamics Corp, Industrial Engineering Dept, Convair Div, mfg analyst, 56, 58; resident tutor, Harvard Coll, Lowell House, 60-61, 62-64; teaching fellow, 60-61, 62-64, visiting scholar, 79-80, Harvard Univ, Dept of Anthropology; asst prof, Univ Calif, Santa Barbara, Dept of Anthropology, 64-67; visiting fellow, New Guinea Res Unit, 67, sr res fellow, Dept Pacific History, Res School of Pacific Studies, 68-70, Australian Natl Univ; visiting scholar, Harvard Univ, Dept Anthropology, 79-80; res assoc, Bishop Museum, Dept Anthropology, 89-; bd dirs, Bernice Pauahi Bishop Museum, 93-99; visiting lecturer, French Univ Pacific, 96-; chair, 94-, Dept Space & Society, Summer Session Program, visiting lecturer, 96-, Master Space Studies Program, Intl Space Univ; sr fellow, 71-72, res assoc, 72-76, Technology and Development Inst, East-West Center, (half-time appt with Univ Hawaii), Univ Hawaii; assoc prof, 70-73, prof, 73-00, chair, 86-95, prof emeritus, 01-, Dept of Anthropology, Univ of Hawaii. **HONORS AND AWARDS** Regent's Medal, Univ Hawaii, 97; Tsiolkovsky Medal, Tsiolkovsky State Museum of the History of Commun, 95; French Univ of the Pacific Medal, 95; Royal Inst of Navigation Bronze Medal, 94. **MEMBERSHIPS** Founding pres, Polynesian Voyaging Soc; Amer Assn for the Advancement of Sci; Intl Acad of Astronautics; Amer Anthropological Assn; Societe des Etudes Oceaniennes; Polynesian Soc; Space Studies Inst; Hawaiian Acad of Sci. **RESEARCH** Human Exploration; experimental Polynesiavoyaging; humanity and space; globalization and social change. **SELECTED PUBLICATIONS** Auth, From Sea to Space, 92; auth, "The Other One-Third of the Globe," Journal of World History, v 5, n 2, 94; auth, Voyage of Rediscovery: A Cultural Odyssey through Polynesia, 94; coauth, Tsiolkovsky, Russian Cosmism and Extraterrestrial Intelligence," Quarterly Journal of the Royal Astronomical Society, v 36, 95; auth, "Colonizing an Island World," in Prehistoric Settlement of the Pacific, Transactions of the American Philosophical Society, v. 86, n 86, 97; auth, "Putting Voyaging Back into Polynesian Prehistory," in Oceanic Culture History: Essays in Honour of Roger Green, New Zealand Journal of Archaeol Special Publication, 97; auth, "Will Space Change Humanity?" in Fundamentals of Space Life Sciences, v 2, 97; auth, "Experimental Voyaging, Oral Tradition and Long Distance Interaction in Polynesia," in Prehistoric Interaction in Oceania: an Interdisciplinary Approach, New Zealand Archaeol Assn Monograph 21, 98; auth, "Nautical Cartography and Traditional Navigation," in The History of Cartography, Vol2, part 3, Cartography in Traditional African, American, Artics, Australian, and Pacific Societies (Univ of Chicago Press, 98); auth, "The Sin at Awarua," The Contemporary Pacific 11 (99); auth, "SETI, Consilience, and the Unity of Knowledge," in When SETI Succeeds: The Impact of High-Information Contact, (A Humanity 3000 Knowledge Workshop, The Foundation for the Future, 00). **CONTACT ADDRESS** Dept of Anthropology, Univ of Hawaii, Manoa, 2424 Maile Way, SSB 346, Honolulu, HI 96822. **EMAIL** bfinney@hawaii.edu

FIREBAUGH, GLENN
PERSONAL Born Charleston, VA, m, 1970, 3 children **DISCIPLINE** SOCIOLOGY **EDUCATION** Ind Univ, BA, 74; PhD, 76. **CAREER** Asst Prof to Assoc Prof, Vanderbilt Univ, 76-88; Prof, Penn State Univ, 88-. **HONORS AND AWARDS** NIMH Fel, IN Univ, 72-76; Distinction in the soc Sci Awd, Penn State Univ, 00. **MEMBERSHIPS** Am Sociol Asn; Population Asn of Am. **RESEARCH** Trends in world inequality. **SELECTED PUBLICATIONS** Co-auth, "The artifact Issue in Deterrence research," Criminology, (90): 347-367; co-auth, "Confidence in Science: The Gender Gap," soc Sci Quarterly, (92): 101-113; co-auth, "Vote Turnout of Nineteenth amendment women: the enduring effect of disenfranchisement," am Journal of Sociol, (95): 972-996; auth, "Development sociology as we approach the Twenty-first Century," Intl Journal of Sociol and Soc Policy, (97): 90-96; co-auth, "Who Supports Marketization and Democratization in Post-communist Romania," Sociological Forum, (98): 521-541; auth, "Empirics of World Income Inequality,' Am Journal of Sociol, (99): 1597-1630; auth, Analyzing Repeated Surveys, Sage Pub, 97. **CONTACT ADDRESS** Dept Sociol, Pennsylvania State Univ, Univ Park, 201 Oswald Tower, University Park, PA 16802. **EMAIL** firebaug@pop.psu.edu

FIRESTONE, JUANITA M.
PERSONAL Born 01/30/1947, Wurzburg, Germany, m, 1995, 2 children **DISCIPLINE** PSYCHOLOGY, SOCIOLOGY **EDUCATION** Black Hills State Univ, BS, 79; Univ Tex, MA, 82; PhD, 84. **CAREER** Assoc Prof, Univ Tex, 94; Prof, Univ Tex, 00-. **HONORS AND AWARDS** UT Syst Chancellor's Res Awd, 91; Outstanding Fac Mem, Univ Tex, 92; Univ Fac Res Awd, 93-94; Joint Fac-Grad Student Summer Grant, 97; UTSA Fac Res Grant, 98; Who's Who Among Am Teachers, 97-98; President's Distinguished Res Awd, 98-99. **MEMBERSHIPS** ASA, Am Inst of Biol Sci, Southwestern Soc Sci Assoc, Sociol for Women in Soc, Golden Key Nat Hon Soc. **RESEARCH** Gender issues, military sociology, survey research, quantitative analysis. **SELECTED PUBLICATIONS** Auth, "Changes in Predictors of Gender Role Ideologies Among Women: A Multivariate Analysis," Sex Roles, 38 (98): 239-252; auth, "Trends in Gender Equity in Retention and Promotion of Officers," Free Inquiry in Creative Sociol, 26 (98): 1-4; auth, "Exploring Violence and Abuse in Gay Male Relationships," Violence and Victims, 13 (98): 1-15; auth, Predicting Unsafe Sexual behavior Among Individuals with HIV/AIDS," Sociol Pract, 1 (99): 175-

191; auth, "Gender Role Ideology and the Gender Based Differences in Earnings," J of Family and Econ Issues, 20 (99): 191-216; auth, "Changes in Patterns of Sexual harassment in the US Military: A Comparison of the 1988 and 1995 DoD Surveys," Armed Forces & Soc, 25 (99): 613-634; auth, "Women, Men and Job Satisfaction in Academia: Perceptions of a Glass Ceiling," in The Women-Centered Univ: Interdisciplinary Perspectives (Univ Pr of Am, 99), forthcoming; auth, "Warfare and Military Studies, Overview," in Encycl of Violence, Peace and Conflict (San Diego, CA: Acad Pr, 99), forthcoming; auth, "Intimate Violence Among Mexican Origin Women: Correlates of Abuse," J of Gender, Cult and Health, 4 (99): 119-134; auth, "Economic Context and Multiple Abuse Techniques," Violence Against Women, 6 (00): 49-67. **CONTACT ADDRESS** Dept Soc Sci, Univ of Texas, San Antonio, 6900 N Loop 1604 W, San Antonio, TX 78249. **EMAIL** jfirestone@utsa.edu

FISCHER, JEROME M.
PERSONAL Born 10/03/1954, Anaconda, MT, m, 1985 **DISCIPLINE** EDUCATION, ADULT COUNSELING **EDUCATION** Mont Tech, BA, 79; Eastern Mont Col, MS, 90; Southern Ill Univ, RhD, 92. **CAREER** From Asst Prof to Assoc Prof, Univ Idaho, 93-. **HONORS AND AWARDS** Fac Awd, 96-97; Fac Awd, 98-99. **MEMBERSHIPS** NCRE, ACA, NRA, IRA, ARCA, NRCA. **RESEARCH** Ethics in rehabilitation counseling, multicultural counseling, civil rights for people with disabilities, families of children with disabilities. **SELECTED PUBLICATIONS** Coauth, "The Re-Employment of the Sexual Addict/Offender Counseling Program: An Evaluation," Human Serv Educ 14 (96): 33-36; coauth, "University Students' Knowledge of Civil Rights Laws Pertaining to People with Disabilities," J of Applied Rehabil Coun 27:4 (96): 25-29; coauth, "Evaluating the Effectiveness of a Multicultural Counseling Ethics and Assessment Training," J of Applied Rehibil Coun 28 (97): 15-19; coauth, "Perceptions of Cooperative Education: A Comparison of Students with and without Disabilities," J of Coop Educ 32:1 (98): 25-35; coauth, "Perspectives in Counseling Skills and Techniques for Cultural Competence: An Evaluation," MPAEA J of Adult Educ 26:2 (98): 13-24. **CONTACT ADDRESS** Dept Educ, Univ of Idaho, 375 S Line St, Moscow, ID 82844-0001. **EMAIL** jfischer@uidaho.edu

FISHER, GENE A.
PERSONAL Born 02/25/1937, New Haven, CT, d, 1 child **DISCIPLINE** SOCIOLOGY **EDUCATION** Ind Univ, MA, 84; Univ Ariz, PhD, 78. **CAREER** Post-doc Fel, Ind Univ, 82-84; Asst Prof to Assoc Prof, Univ Mass, 84-. **MEMBERSHIPS** Am Sociol Asn, Editorial Board of Soc Psychol Quarterly, Editorial Board of Journal of Health and Soc Behavior, Reviewer of: Sociol Methodology, Sociol Methods and Res, Soc Sci, Res, Psychol Bulletin, Journal of Math Sociol, Soc Problems, Sociol Forum, Am Sociol Review, Sociol Theory, Journal of Health and Soc Behavior, and Social Forces. **SELECTED PUBLICATIONS** Auth, "The dissolution of Joint Living Arrangements among Single parents and children: Does Welfare make a difference," Social Science Quarterly, forthcoming; auth, "Caribbean Blacks in Comparative perspective," Journal of Ethnic and Migration Studies, (99): 187-212; auth, "Hazards of the Market: The Continuity and Dissolution of Interorganizational Market Relationships," American Sociological Review, (98): 147-177; auth, "Theoretical and Methodological Elaborations of the Circumplex Model of Personality Traits and Emotions," in Circumplex Models of Personality and Emotions, Washington, 97; auth, "A State Network of Family Support Services: The Massachusetts Family Support Demonstration Project," Evaluation and Program Planning, (96): 27-39; auth, "Measuring Worker Cognitions about Parents of Children with Mental and Emotional Disabilities," Journal of Emotional and Behavioral Disorders, (94); 99-108; auth, "Evaluation of Rhode Island's supported Housing projects," in Proceedings, Third Annual Conference on State Mental Health Agency Services Research, 93; auth, "Informal Systems of Care for the Chronically Mentally Ill," Community Mental Health Journal, (92): 413-425; rev of "Careers and Creativity: social Forces in the Arts," by Harrison C White, Contemporary Sociology, (94): 880-882. **CONTACT ADDRESS** Dept Sociol, Univ of Massachusetts, Amherst, Amherst, MA 01003. **EMAIL** fisher@soc.umass.edu

FISHER, JAMES F.
PERSONAL Born 06/05/1950, KS, d, 2 children **DISCIPLINE** ANTHROPOLOGY **EDUCATION** Princeton Univ, BA, 62; Univ Chicago, MA, 67; PhD, 72. **CAREER** Prof, Carleton Col, 71-. **MEMBERSHIPS** AA, Explorers Club, Nepal Studies Asn. **RESEARCH** Himalayas, Nepal, Tibet. **SELECTED PUBLICATIONS** Auth, Introductory Nepali, Univ Mo 65; ed, Himalayan anthropology: the Indo-Tibetan Interface, Mouton Pub, 78; auth, Trans-Himalayan Traders: Economy, Society, and Culture in Northwest Nepal, Univ Calif press, 86; ed, Occasional papers in Sociology and Anthropology, Tribhuvan Univ Press, 87; auth, Sherpas: Reflections on Change in Himalayan Nepal, Univ Calif Press, 90; auth, Living Martyrs: Individuals and Revolution in Nepal, Oxford Univ Press, 97; auth, "Tourism and Education in Highland Nepal," in Development and Rural south Asia, Univ of Chicago, 97; auth, "Remarks at launch of Living Martyrs," in Tanka Prasad Acharva Smriti-Grantha, Katmandu, 97; rev of "Himalayan Herders," a film by John and Naomi Bishop, American Anthropologist, 98. **CONTACT ADDRESS** Dept Sociol & Anthropol, Carleton

Col, 1 N Col St, Northfield, MN 55057. **EMAIL** jfisher@carleton.edu

FISHER, LEONA W.
PERSONAL Born 08/22/1944, CA **DISCIPLINE** ENGLISH LITERATURE, WOMEN'S STUDIES **EDUCATION** Stanford Univ, BA; Univ Santa Barbara Ca, MA, PhD. **CAREER** Prof. **HONORS AND AWARDS** CHLA 1st runner-up, Best Critical Article, 90; Res grant, 94; CASE, Silver Medal, 85; Bronze Medal, 86; Bibliog Soc of Am, 00. **MEMBERSHIPS** MLA, Children's Lit Assoc, Nineteenth-Century Studies Assoc. **RESEARCH** Children's Literature, Victorian literature, women writers, nonfiction prose, 19th century drama, feminist theory. **SELECTED PUBLICATIONS** Auth, "Mystical Fantasy for Children: Silence and Community," 90; Lemn, Dickens, and 'Mr. Nightingale's Diary': A Victorian Farce, 88; "Mark Lemon's Three Farces on the 'Woman Question'," 88; "The Challenge of Women's Studies: Questions for a Transformed Future at Georgetown," 90. **CONTACT ADDRESS** English Dept, Georgetown Univ, PO Box 571131, Washington, DC 20057-1131. **EMAIL** fisherl@georgetown.edu

FISHERKELLER, JOELLEN
DISCIPLINE EDUCATION & COMMUNICATION **EDUCATION** Univ CA, Berkeley, PhD, 95. **CAREER** Asst prof, New York Univ, 95-. **RESEARCH** Young people; media cultures; media education. **SELECTED PUBLICATIONS** Auth, The Hidden Persistence of Immigrant Drop Outs: Distortions, Blank Spots and Blind Spots in Research on Schooling Careers, with Donald A Hansen and Vicky Johnson, Int J of Educational; Research, Pergamon Press, vol 23, no 1, 95; Representing Student's Thinking About Nutrient Cycles in Ecosystems, Bidimensional Coding of a Complex Topic, with Kathleen Hogan, J of Research in Science Teaching, vol 33, no 9, 96; Review of Children and the Movies: Media Influence and the Payne Fund Controversy, by Garth S Jowett, Ian C Jarvie, and Kathryn H Fuller, Cambridge Univ Press, 96, J of Commun, autumn 97; Review of Writing Superheroes: Contemporary Childhood, Popular Culture, and Classroom Literacy, by Anne Haas Dyson, Teachers Col Press, 97, Anthropology and Education Quart, 97; Learning from Young Adolescent TV Viewers, NJ J of Commun, fall 97; Everyday Learning About Identities Among Young Adolescents in TV Culture, Anthropology and Ed Quart, vol 28, no 4, winter 97; Learning About Power and Success: Young Adolescents Interpret TV Culture, The Commun Rev, March 98. **CONTACT ADDRESS** Dept of Culture and Commun, New York Univ, 239 Greene St, Rm 735, New York, NY 10003-6674. **EMAIL** jf4@is2.nyu.edu

FITE, KATHLEEN E.
PERSONAL Born 06/26/1948, Houston, TX, s **DISCIPLINE** EDUCATION **EDUCATION** SW Tex State Univ, BS, 69; MEd, 70; Univ N Tex, EdD, 72. **CAREER** Director, Center for the Study of Basic Skills, 80; Director, Race Desegregation Training Inst, 82-83; Director, Elementary Educ, 83-84; Prof, SW Tex State Univ, 73-. **HONORS AND AWARDS** Who's Who in Am, Who's Who in Am Educ, Who's Who of Am Women, Who's Who of the World, San Marcos Women's Hall of Fame, Key of Excellence Awd. **MEMBERSHIPS** Asn for Childhood Educ Intl, Asn for Supervision and Curriculum Development. **RESEARCH** Emerging literacy, Technology, Teacher training, Learning/Brain. **CONTACT ADDRESS** Dept Curriculum & Instruction, Southwest Texas State Univ, 601 Univ Dr, San Marcos, TX 78666.

FITTIPALDI, SILVIO EDWARD
PERSONAL Born 11/09/1937, Philadelphia, PA **DISCIPLINE** RELIGION, PSYCHOLOGY **EDUCATION** Villanova Univ, AB, 60; Augustinian Col, MA, 64; Temple Univ, PhD (relig), 76. **CAREER** Instr relig, Villanova Univ, 72-76, asst prof, 76-82, chmn dept, 77-80. **MEMBERSHIPS** Col Theol Soc; Cath Theol Soc Am; Friends Conf Relig and Psychol; Asn Humanistic Psychol. **RESEARCH** The encounter of world religions; religion and psychology; mysticism. **SELECTED PUBLICATIONS** Auth, Freedom in Roman Catholicism and Zen Buddhism, In: Liberation, Revolution and Freedom, Seabury, 75; co-ed, From Alienation to At-One-Ness, Villanova Univ, 78; auth, How to Pray Always Without Always Praying, Fides/Claretian, 78; Buddhist Sutras and Enlightenment in Contemporary Zen, Horizons, fall 78; The Zen of Ethics, In: Essays in Morality and Ethics, Paulist Press, 80; Human Consciousness and the Christian Mystic: Teresa of Avila, In: The Metaphors of Consciousness, Plenum, 81; Teaching religion as a spiritual process, In: The Journey of Western Spirituality, Scholars Press, 81; Zen Mind, Christian Mind, Empty Mind, J Ecumenical Studies, 82. **CONTACT ADDRESS** 1325 S Broad St, Philadelphia, PA 19147.

FITZPATRICK, ELLEN
DISCIPLINE MODERN AMERICA, WOMEN'S HISTORY, INTELLECTUAL HISTORY **EDUCATION** Brandeis Univ, PhD. **CAREER** Assoc prof, Univ NH, 97-. **HONORS AND AWARDS** Charles Warren Ctr fel, Harvard Univ; Andrew Mellon fac fel in the Hum, Harvard Univ; Spencer Found grant; NEH grant. **RESEARCH** Reinventing history: American historians and the memory of modern history. **SELECTED PUBLICATIONS** Auth, Endless Crusade: Women Social Scientists

and Progressive Reform; auth, Muckraking: Three Landmark Articles; ed, Century of Struggle by Eleanor Flexner; coauth, America in Modern Times. **CONTACT ADDRESS** Univ of New Hampshire, Durham, Durham, NH 03824. **EMAIL** effitz@mediaone.net

FITZPTRICK, KEVIN MICHAEL
PERSONAL Born 03/10/1956, Lebanon, PA, m, 1985, 3 children **DISCIPLINE** SOCIOLOGY **EDUCATION** Susquehanna Univ, BA, 78; Univ SC, Columbia, MA, 80; SUNY, Albany, PhD, 85. **CAREER** Asst prof, 85-91, assoc prof, Univ of Ala at Birmingham, 91-. **HONORS AND AWARDS** Univ of Ala Birmingham Excellence in Teaching Awd, 94. **MEMBERSHIPS** ASA, APSA, SSS. **RESEARCH** Mental health, youth-adolescence, urban sociology. **SELECTED PUBLICATIONS** Coauth with Mark La Gory and Ferris Ritchey, "Criminal Victimization Among the Homeless," Justice Quart, 10 (93): 353-368; coauth with Jeffrey Clair and Mark LaGory, "Psychosocial Support and Caregiver Depression: Sociological Variations on a Gerontological Theme," Sociol Perspectives, 38 (95): 195-216; coauth with Marylyn Wright, "Gender Differences in Medical School Attrition Rates, 1973-1992," J of the Am Med Women's Asn, 50 (95): 204-206; auth, "Fighting Among America's Youth: A Risk and Protective Factors Approach," J of Health and Soc Behavior, 38 (97): 131-148; auth, "Aggression and Environmental Risk Among Low-Income, African-American Youth," J of Adolescent Health, 21 (97): 172-178; coauth with Sean-Shong Hwang, "Class Differences in Racial Attitudes: A Divided Black America?," Sociol Perspectives, 41 (98): 367-380; coauth with Michele Wilson, "Exposure to Violence and Post-Traumatic Stress Symptomatology Among Abortion Clinic Workers," J of Traumatic Stress, 12 (99): 227-242; auth, "Violent Victimization Among America's School Children," J of Interpersonal Violence, 14 (99): 1055-1069; coauth with Mark La Gory and Ferris Ritchey, "Dangerous Places: Exposure to Violence and Its Mental Health Consequences for the Homeless," Am J of Orthopsychiatry, 69 (99): 438-447. **CONTACT ADDRESS** Dept Sociol, Univ of Alabama, Birmingham, 1530 3rd Ave S, Birmingham, AL 35294-3350.

FLACKS, RICHARD
PERSONAL Born 04/26/1938, Brooklyn, NY, m, 1959, 2 children **DISCIPLINE** SOCIAL PSYCHOLOGY **EDUCATION** Brooklyn Col, BA 58; Univ Michigan, PhD 64. **CAREER** Univ Chicago, asst prof 64-69; Univ Cal SB, prof, 69-, ch, 75-80. **HONORS AND AWARDS** Dist Tchg Awd; Richard Flacks Internship in Students Affairs. **MEMBERSHIPS** ASA; SSSI; SSPP; SPSSI. **RESEARCH** Social movements; Political Consciousness, college students cultures. **SELECTED PUBLICATIONS** Auth, Cultural Politics and Social Movements, co-ed, Temple Univ Press, 95; auth, Beyond the Barricades: The Sixties Generation Grows up, coauth, Temple Univ Press, 89; Reviving Democratic Activism: Thoughts about strategy in a dark time, in: David Trend, ed, Radical Democracy: Identity Citizenship and the State, Routledge, 96; auth, Who Supports the Troops? Vietnam and the Gulf War and the Making of Collective Memory, coauth, Social Problems, 95; auth, The Party's Over-so what's to be done? Social Res, 93; auth, Students Behaving Badly, NY Times, 00. **CONTACT ADDRESS** Dept of Sociology, Univ of California, Santa Barbara, Santa Barbara, CA 93106. **EMAIL** flacks@alishaw.ucsb.edu

FLINT, MARCHA
PERSONAL Born 09/18/1932, New London, CT, d, 2 children **DISCIPLINE** PSYCHOLOGY **EDUCATION** Hunter Col, BA, 60; NY Univ, MA, 64; CUNY, Grad Center, PhD, 74; Rutgers Univ Grad Sch Applied & Prof Psychology, Psy M, 98. **CAREER** Instr, Hunter Col, Lehman Col, 64-68; asst prof, Montclair State Univ, 68-74, assoc prof, 74-88, full prof, 88-. **HONORS AND AWARDS** Sr Researcher, South East Asia, Fulbright Fel, 85-86; Alpha Lambda, Beta chapter, 87-; Ed bd, Menopause, 93-; Sigma Delta Epsilon, Kappa chapter, 94-; Psy D candidate, Rutgers Univ, Grad Sch of Applied Psychol; Who's Who Among Am Teachers, 98; ed bd, Climacteric, 99-. **MEMBERSHIPS** Human Biology Coun-Fel, Am Anthropol Asn Fel, NY Acad of Scis, N Am Menopause Soc, Int Menopause Soc. **RESEARCH** Menopause cross-culturally, women's physical and mental health. **SELECTED PUBLICATIONS** Coauth with R. Samil, "Cultural and subcultural meanings of the menopause," in M. Flint, F. Kronenberg and W. Utian, eds, Multidisciplinary Perspectives on the Menopause, NY: New York Acad of Scis (90); auth, "Global aspects of the menopause," in G. Berg and J. Hammer, Modern Management of the Menopause, NY: Pantheon Press (94); coauth with L. Lieberman, " A Tribute to Edward E. Hunt," Am J of Human Biology, 7, 4 (95): 423; auth, "Secular Trends in Menopause Age," J of Psychosomatic Obstetrics & Gynocology, 18 (97): 65-72. **CONTACT ADDRESS** Dept Anthropology DI-408, Montclair State Univ, 1 Normal Ave, Montclair, NJ 07043. **EMAIL** flintm@mail.montclair.edu

FLINT-FERGUSON, JANIS
PERSONAL Born 06/06/1953, Chicago, IL, m, 1978 **DISCIPLINE** EDUCATION **EDUCATION** N Cent Col, BA, 75; Ill State Univ, MS, 85; PhD, 93. **CAREER** Res Asst to Grad Asst, Ill State Univ, 87-90; Instructor, Gibson City Jr/Sr High School,

79-90; Consultant, N Eng League of Middle Sch, 98-; Assoc Prof and Dept Chair, Gordon Col, 90-. **HONORS AND AWARDS** Col Educator of the Year, MA Asn of Teacher Educ, 97; Who's Who in the East, 99-00; Who's Who in Am, 98-99; Who's Who in Am Educ, 89-90, 92-93, 94-95, 96-97, 98-99. **MEMBERSHIPS** NE MA Reg Middle Grades Alliance; N Eng League of Middle Sch; Nat Coun of Teachers of Eng. **RESEARCH** Adolescent literature; Middle School philosophy and organization; Writing and rhetoric. **SELECTED PUBLICATIONS** Co-auth, "Making Evaluation a Part of the Learning Process," Journal of Reading, (87): 140-145; co-auth, "Grammar in Context: Why and How," English Journal, (90): 66-70; co-auth, "Articulation--An Idea that Works," Language Arts Journal of Michigan, 94; co-auth, Instructor's Manual (Readings are Writing), Prentice-Hall, 95; co-auth, Readings Are Writings, Prentice-Hall, 95; auth, "Foreword," Special Education Careers, 95; auth, "And Now a Word from our Sponsors . . .," English Journal, 95; auth, "Exemplary Practices: Gordon College," Meeting the Standards: Improving Middle Level Teacher Education, NMSA, 96; co-auth, Yonder Mountain: Teacher's Guide, Gordon Col Press, 99; auth, "Being and Becoming a Real Writer Through Reading the Manuscripts of Robert Cormier," OH Journal of the English Language Arts, 99. **CONTACT ADDRESS** Dept Educ, Gordon Col, Massachusetts, 255 Grapevine Rd, Wenham, MA 01984. **EMAIL** flint@gordon.edu

FLIPPEN, J. BROOKS
PERSONAL Born 12/13/1959, Norfolk, VA, m, 1989, 2 children **DISCIPLINE** SOCIOLOGY **EDUCATION** Wash & Lee Univ, BA, 82; Univ Richmond, MA, 88; Univ Md, PhD, 94. **CAREER** Res Asst, Univ Richmond, 86-87; Teaching Asst, Univ Md, 87-90; Adj Instr, Trinity Col, 90-95; From Asst Prof to Assoc Prof, Southeastern Okla St Univ, 95-. **HONORS AND AWARDS** Phi Alpha Theta; Outstanding Scholar Awd, Sch of Arts and Letters, 95. **MEMBERSHIPS** OAH, AHA, ASEH, FHS, SHGAPE, OAPH. **RESEARCH** 20th Century American environmental politics. **SELECTED PUBLICATIONS** Auth, "The Nixon Administration, Politics and the Call of the Wild," Environ Hist Rev, vol 19, no 2 (95): 37-54; auth, "Containing the Urban Sprawl: The Nixon Administration's Land Use Policy," Presidential Studies Quart, vol 26, no 1 (96): 197-207; auth, "A Truly Historic Time: Wildlife Management, Politics and the Nixon Administration," Human Dimensions of Wildlife, vol 2, no 2 (97): 50-59; auth, "Pests, Pollution and Politics," Agricultural Hist, vol 71, no 4 (97): 101-112; auth, "Mr Hickel Goes to Washington," Alaska Hist, vol 12, no 2 (98): 1-22; auth, Nixon and the Environment, Univ NMex Pr (Albuquerque, NM), 00. **CONTACT ADDRESS** Dept Sociol, Southeastern Oklahoma State Univ, Durant, OK 74701. **EMAIL** bflippen@sosu.edu

FLOYD, SAMUEL A., JR.
PERSONAL Born 02/01/1937, Tallahassee, FL, m, 1956, 3 children **DISCIPLINE** MUSIC EDUCATION **EDUCATION** Florida A&M Univ, BS, 57; Southern Ill Univ, MME, 65, PhD, 69. **CAREER** Instr, Fla A&M Univ, 62-64; Instructor, Dept of Music, Florida A&M University, Asst Dir of Bands, Florida A&M University, 62-64; Instructor, Assoc Prof, Southern Ill Univ Carbondale, 64-78; instr/assoc prof, Music, South Ill Univ, Carbondale, 65-78; dir, Inst Res Black Am Music, Fisk Univ, 78-83; Dir, Center Black Music Res, Columbia Coll, 83-. **MEMBERSHIPS** Coll Music Soc; A, Musicol Soc; Sonneck Soc Am Music; Am Musicological Society; Coll Music Society; Council Member, 78-80; College Music Society; Pi Kappa Lambda; Soc for Am Music. **RESEARCH** Music in Black Diaspora. **SELECTED PUBLICATIONS** "Eileen Jackson-Southern: Quiet Revolutionary," New Perspectives on Music: Essays in Honor of Eileen Southern, Harmonie Park Press, 92; "Troping the Blues: From Spirituals to the Concert Hall," Black Music Res Jour, 93; The Power of Black Music, Oxford Univ Press, 95; auth, "The Power of Black Music," New York: Oxford University Press, 95; ed. International Dictionary of Black Composers, 2 vols, Chicago: Fitzroy Dearborn Publishers, 99; auth, "Troping the Blues: From Spirituals to the Concert Hall," Black Music Research Journal 13, no. 1, Spring 93: 31-50; auth, "Black Music in the Circum-Caribbean," American Music 17, no. 1, Spring 99, pp. 1-37. **CONTACT ADDRESS** Center Black Music Res, Columbia Col, Illinois, 600 S Mich Ave, Chicago, IL 60605. **EMAIL** sfloyd@popmail.colum.edu

FOLLICK, EDWIN D.
PERSONAL Born 02/04/1935, Glendale, CA, m, 1986 **DISCIPLINE** SOCIOLOGY, RELIGION **EDUCATION** Calif State Univ Los Angeles, BA, 56, MA, 61; Pepperdine Univ, MA, 57, MPA, 77; St Andrews Theol Col, PhD, 58, DTheol, 58; Univ S Calif, MS, 63, MEd, 64, AdvMEd, 69; Blackstone Law, LLB, 66, JD, 67; Cleveland Chiropractic Col, Los Angeles, DC, 72; Academia Theatina, PhD, 78; Antioch Univ, Los Angeles, MA, 90. **CAREER** Instr, Libr Admin, Los Angeles City Sch, 57-68; law libr, Glendale Univ Col of Law, 68-69; col librn, 69-74, dir of educ & admis, 74-84, prof of jurisprudence, 75-, dean student aff, 76-92, dean of educ, 89-, Cleveland Chiropractic Col Los Angeles Campus; assoc prof, Newport Univ, 82; extern prof theology, St Andrews Theol Col, London, 61; Chapalin, Cleveland Los Angeles Campus, 85-; Chaplain of Cleveland Col Multicampus System, 00-. **HONORS AND AWARDS** Undergraduate honors in educ & svc & leadership; three sabbatical leaves which included grants to visit the Soviet Union & China twice; Who's Who in America, 99. **MEMBERSHIPS** ALA; NEA; Amer Assoc Law Librns; Amer Chiropractic Assoc; Int Chiropractors Assoc; Int Platform Assoc; Phi Delta Kappa, Sigma Chi Psi; Delta Tau Alpha. **RESEARCH** Sociological & religious implications of health. **SELECTED PUBLICATIONS** Auth, The Law and Chiropractic: Administrative Discretion-A Concluding Summary, Part 7, Chiropractic Education: A Management Analysis of Professional Study for the 1990s, Part 1-4, Digest of Chiropractic Economics, 80-92. **CONTACT ADDRESS** 6435 Jumilla Ave, Woodland Hills, CA 91367. **EMAIL** follicke@cleveland.edu

FOLLMAN, JOHN C.
PERSONAL Born 12/15/1927, Omaha, NE, d, 5 children **DISCIPLINE** EDUCATION **EDUCATION** Univ Nebr, BA; Univ Omaha, MA; Ind Univ, PhD. **CAREER** Asst Prof, Wis State Univ, 64-66; Asst Prof, Univ S Fla, 66-69; Assoc Prof, Univ S Fla, 69-73; Prof, Univ S Fla, 73-. **MEMBERSHIPS** Am Educ Res Asn, Fla Educ Res Asn, Nat Coun on Measurement in Educ. **RESEARCH** Correlations, critical thinking, evaluation of faculty teaching, research and service, evaluation of teaching, scholastic aptitude and achievement, scoring of English compositions. **SELECTED PUBLICATIONS** Coauth, "Graphics Variables and Reliability of Level of Essay Grades," Am Educ Res J, 8 (71): 365-373; auth, Cornucopia of Correlations," Am Psychologist, 39, 701-702; auth, "Pedagogue--Paragon and Pariah--20% of the Time--Implications on Merit Pay," Am Psychologist, 39 (84): 1069-1070; auth, "The Enhancement of Children's Vocabularies," The Clearing House, 63 (90): 329-332; auth, "The Conundrum of Class Size at the College Level," The Col Quart, 2 (94): 13-17. **CONTACT ADDRESS** Dept Educ, Univ of So Florida, 4202 Fowler Ave, EDU 380 E, Tampa, FL 33620.

FONER, NANCY
PERSONAL Born New York, NY, m, 1 child **DISCIPLINE** ANTHROPOLOGY **EDUCATION** Branders Univ, BA, 66; Univ Chicago, PhD, 71. **CAREER** Prof, State Univ of NY, 85-. **RESEARCH** Immigration to US, Caribbean Diaspora, Aging. **SELECTED PUBLICATIONS** Auth, The Caregiving Dilemma: Work in and American Nursing Home, Univ of Calif Press, 94; auth, From Elles Island to JFK: New York's Two Great Waves of Immigration, Yale Univ Press, 2000. **CONTACT ADDRESS** Dept Soc Sci, SUNY, Col at Purchase, 735 Anderson Hill Rd, Purchase, NY 10577.

FORMAN, MICHAEL LAWRENCE
PERSONAL Born 06/30/1940, Kansas City, MO, m, 1963, 4 children **DISCIPLINE** LIMGUISTICS, ANTHROPOLOGY **EDUCATION** John Carroll Univ, AB, 61; Cornell Univ, PhD, 72. **CAREER** Asst researcher, Pac & Asian Ling Inst, 68-69, acting asst prof, 69-72, asst prof, 72-73, chmn Southeast Asian studies, 77-80, Assoc Prof Ling, Univ Hawaii, Manoa, 73-, Second Language Acquisition faculty; assoc ed, Oceanic Ling; co-ed, The Carrier Pidgeon, 93-96; contribr, Biography: An Interdisciplinary Quart. **HONORS AND AWARDS** Nat Endowment for Humanities study fel, 74-75; Soc Sci Res Inst, 80-82, 93-95; Excellence in Teaching Awd, Univ Hawaii Board of Regents, 84, Univ Hawaii Col Lang, Ling, & Lit, 84; Robert W. Clapton Awd for Distinguished Community Service, 86. **MEMBERSHIPS** Am Anthrop Asn; Ling Soc Am; Ling Soc Philippines. **RESEARCH** Child language acquisition; pidginization and creolization; Philippine descriptive linguistics. **SELECTED PUBLICATIONS** Auth Kapampangan Grammar Notes, 71 & Kapampangan Dictionary, 71, Univ Hawaii; coauth, Riddles: Expressive models of interrogation, Ethnology, Vol X , Nov 4 & In: Directions in Sociolinguistic Holt, 72; ed, World Englishes 2000, Univ Hawaii Press, 97. **CONTACT ADDRESS** Dept of Ling, Univ of Hawaii, Manoa, 1890 E West Rd, Honolulu, HI 96822-2318. **EMAIL** forman@hawaii.edu

FORSYTH, DAN W.
PERSONAL Born 02/23/1947, Winnipeg, MA, Canada **DISCIPLINE** ANTHROPOLOGY **EDUCATION** UCLA, BA, 70; Univ Chicago, MS, 76; Univ Calif, PhD, 83. **CAREER** Visiting Prof, Univ Oslo; 93-94; Prof, Univ S Colo, 95-. **HONORS AND AWARDS** Boyer Prize. **MEMBERSHIPS** Am Anthropol Asn; Soc for Psychol Anthropol. **CONTACT ADDRESS** Dept Sociol & Anthropol, Univ of So Colorado, 2200 Bonforte Blvd, Pueblo, CO 81001.

FORTE, ALLEN
PERSONAL Born 12/23/1926, Portland, OR, m, 1998 **DISCIPLINE** THEORY OF MUSIC EDUCATION **EDUCATION** Columbia Univ, BA, 50, MA, 52. **CAREER** Instr music, Columbia Teachers Col, 54-59; instr music theory, Mannes Col Music, 57-59; from instr to assoc prof, Yale Univ, 59-64; prof music, Mass Inst Technol, 67-68; Prof Music, Yale Univ, 68-, Battell Prof Teory of Music, 91-; Dir Grad Studies Music, 70-77; Ed, J Music Theory, 60-67; Gen Ed Composers of the 20th c Yale Univ Press, 80-. **HONORS AND AWARDS** MA, Yale Univ, 68 MUS DOC, Eastman School of Music 78; Pres, Society for Music Theory, 77-82; Fellow, American Academy of Arts and Sciences 95; Lifetime Member, Society for Music Theory, 95; Festschrift: Music Theory in Concept and Practice, 97; Wallace Berry Book Publ Awd, 97; ma, yale univ, 68. **MEMBERSHIPS** Soc for mus Theory, Am Musicol Soc. **RESEARCH** Theory of tonal music; Scenkerian analysis; 18th and 19th century music theory; early 20th cavant-garde music; formal music theory; American popular song 1920-50. **SELECTED PUBLICATIONS** Auth, "Tonal Harmony in Concept and Practice," 62; auth, "The Structure of Atonal Music," 73; auth, "The American Popular Ballard of the Golden Era, 95; auth, "The Atonal Music of Anton Webern," 98; auth, "The Structural Origin of Exact Tempi in the Brahms-Haydn Variations," Music Review May 57; auth, "Aspects of Rhythm in Webern's Atonal Music, Music Theory Spectrum, vol 2," 80; auth, "Middleground Motives in the Adagietto of Mahler's Fifth Symphony," 19th Century Music, vol. viii, 84; auth, "New Approaches to the Linear Analysis of Music," Jnl of Mus Teory vol 36, 92; auth, "The Golden Thread: Octatonic, Jnl of Mus Theory," Music Analysis vol 10 91; auth, "Concepts of Linearity in Schoenberg's Atonal Music, Jnl of Mus Theory vol 36, 92; auth, "The Golden Thread: Octatonic Music in Webern's Early Songs," Bailey ed, Webern Studies, 96; auth, "Reflections upon the Gershwin-Berg Connection," The Musical Quarterly, vol 83, 99. **CONTACT ADDRESS** Dept of Music, Yale Univ, P O Box 208310, New Haven, CT 06520. **EMAIL** allen.forte@yale.edu

FORTIER, TED
PERSONAL Born 08/01/1953, Spokane, WA, s **DISCIPLINE** ANTHROPOLOGY **EDUCATION** Washington State Univ, PhD, 95. **CAREER** Res, Dept Natural Resources, 95-97; asst prof, Seattle Univ, 97- . **HONORS AND AWARDS** Mellon fel, 98. **MEMBERSHIPS** Am Acad Relig; Am Anthrop Asn; Soc for Cultural Anthrop. **RESEARCH** Indians of North America; epistemology; culture change; religion. **SELECTED PUBLICATIONS** Auth, Blue Print for Parish Social Ministry, Spokane Diocese, 96; auth, Searching for the Past, Companions, 96; auth, James Schneiders, Coeur d'Alene Council Fires, 97; coauth, Cultural Memory: The Presence of a People, Orbis, 99. **CONTACT ADDRESS** Dept of Sociol, Seattle Univ, Casey 305, Seattle, WA 98122. **EMAIL** tedf@seattleu.edu

FORTNER-WOOD, CHERYL
PERSONAL Born 10/16/1969, Washington, DC, m, 1 child **DISCIPLINE** PSYCHOLOGY **EDUCATION** Col Charleston, BS, 91; W Carolina Univ, MA, 94; Purdue Univ, PhD, 97. **CAREER** Lecturer, Univ Wisc, 96-98; Asst Prof, Winthrop Univ, 98-. **MEMBERSHIPS** SRCD; APA; ISIS; NAEYC **RESEARCH** Attachment; Childcare. **SELECTED PUBLICATIONS** Co-auth, "Research in Review: Adult-child relationships in early childhood programs," Young children, (95): 69-78; co-auth, "Child Care: The Debate," in Continuing Issues in Early childhood Education, (Prentice, 97), 87-102; co-auth, "Adult-child relationships in early childhood programmes," in Research Information for Teachers, (New Zealand Coun for Educ Res, 97), 1-4; co-auth, "The parent-caregiver relationship scale: Rounding out the relationship system in infant child care," Early Education & Development, (97): 83-100; co-auth, "Measuring exploratory behavior in toddlers: Tests and the natural environment," Journal of Genetic Psychology, (97): 495-497; co-auth, "The context of infant attachment in family child care," Journal of Applied developmental Psychology, (99): 319-336. **CONTACT ADDRESS** Dept Psychol, Winthrop Univ, 128 Kinard, Rock Hill, SC 29733. **EMAIL** fortnerc@winthrop.edu

FORTUNATO, VINCENT J.
PERSONAL Born 05/17/1956, Freeport, NY, d **DISCIPLINE** PSYCHOLOGY **EDUCATION** Univ Albany, SUNY, PhD, 96. **CAREER** Asst prof, Univ of Southern Miss, 97-. **MEMBERSHIPS** SIOP; APA; Acad of Management. **RESEARCH** Attitudes in the work place, mood at work, work-related stress, work motivation. **SELECTED PUBLICATIONS** Coauth, "Nursing informatics needs assessment: Are distance programs needed?", Nursing Res 23, (98): 1-5; coauth, "Taking the strain out of negative affectivity: Development and initial validation of scores on a strain-free measure of negative affectivity", Educ and Psychol Measurement 59, (99): 77-97; coauth, "An examination of the discriminant validity of the Strain-free Negative Affectivity scale", J of Occupational and Org Psychol 72, (99): 1-17; coauth, "Positive affectivity as a moderator of the task characteristics-perceived task characteristics relationship", J of Applied Soc Psychol (forthcoming). **CONTACT ADDRESS** Dept Psychol, Univ of So Mississippi, PO Box 5025, Hattiesburg, MS 39406.

FORTUNE, ANNE E.
PERSONAL Born 06/27/1945, New Haven, CT, m **DISCIPLINE** SOCIAL WORK **EDUCATION** Univ Chicago, AB, 70; AM, 75; PhD, 78. **CAREER** Asst Prof, George Warren Brown School of Social Work, Washington Univ, 77-82; Assoc prof, Va commonwealth Univ, 82-89; Assoc Prof to Prof, 88-. **MEMBERSHIPS** Council on Soc Work Educ, Nat Asn of Soc Workers, Acad of Cert Soc Workers, Soc for Soc Work and Research. **RESEARCH** Outcomes of social work practice; Social work education. **SELECTED PUBLICATIONS** Auth, Research in Social Work, 3rd ed, Columbia Univ press, 99; auth, Teaching Research: an Instructor's Manual for Research in social Work 3rd ed, Columbia Univ Press, 99; co-ed, Multicultural Issues in Social Work Vol II, NASW Press, 98; auth, "Termi-

nation in Direct Practice," in Encyclopedia of Social Work 19th ed, NAWS Press, 95; auth, "Further Explorations of the Liaison Role: a View from the Field," in Social Work Field Education: Views and Visions, Kendall/Hunt Publishing Co., (95): 273-293; auth, "Field Education," in The Foundations of Social Work Knowledge, Columbia Univ Press, (94): 151-194; auth, "Commentary: Ethnography in Social Work," in Qualitative Research in Social Work, Columbia Univ Press, (94): 63-67. **CONTACT ADDRESS** School of Soc Welfare, SUNY, 1400 Washington Ave, Albany, NY 12222-1000. **EMAIL** rfortune@csc.albany.edu

FOSSHAGE, JAMES L.
PERSONAL Born 09/09/1940, Durango, CO, m, 1963, 1 child **DISCIPLINE** PSYCHOLOGY **EDUCATION** Univ Colo., BA, 62; Columbia Univ, PhD, 68. **CAREER** Fac, Nat Inst for the Psychotherapies, 72-; Prof, New York Univ. **HONORS AND AWARDS** Phi Beta Kappa; NIP Contribution to Psychoanalysis. **MEMBERSHIPS** Am Psychol Asn, Asn for Autonomous Psychoanalytic Inst. **RESEARCH** Dreams. **CONTACT ADDRESS** Nat Inst for the Psychotherapies, 330 W 58th St, New York, NY 10019. **EMAIL** fosshage@psychoanalysis.net

FOSTER, DAVID W.
PERSONAL Born 09/11/1940, Seattle, WA, m, 1966, 1 child **DISCIPLINE** SPANISH, WOMEN'S STUDIES **EDUCATION** Univ of Wash, BA, 61; MA, 63; PhD, 64. **CAREER** Teaching Asst to instr, Univ of Wash, 61-64; vis instr, Fresno State Col, 62; vis asst prof, Vanderbilt Univ, 64; asst prof, Univ of Mo, 64-66; fulbright prof, Inst del Profesorado Superior en Lenguas Vivas, Universidad Nacional de La Plata, 67; asst prof to prof, Ariz State Univ, 70-; fulbright prof, Univ de Buenos Aires, 73; Inter-American Development Bank Prof of Ling, Univ Catolica de Chile, 75; fulbright prof, univ Federal do parana, 85; fulbright prof, Univ Catolica del Uruguay, 88; vis prof, Univ of Calif at Los Angeles, 89; vis prof, Univ of Ariz, 89. **HONORS AND AWARDS** Outstanding Graduate Mentor, Graduate Col, 89; res of the year, Alumni Asn, 94. **RESEARCH** Urban culture in Latin America, with emphasis on issues of gender construction and sexual identity, Jewish culture. **SELECTED PUBLICATIONS** Auth, Violence in Argentine Literature: Cultural Responses to Tyranny, Univ of Mo Press, 95; auth, Sexual Textualities: Essays on Queer/ing Latin American Writing, Univ of Tex (Austin, TX), 97; auth, Espacio escenico y lenguaje, Galerna (Buenos Aires, Mexico), 98; auth, A Funny Dirty Little War/No habra mas penas ni olvido, Flicks Books (Trowbrdige, Eng), 98; coauth, Culture and Customs of Argentina, Greenwood Press (Westport, CT), 98; coauth, The Writer's Reference Guide to Spanish, Univ of Tex Press (Austin, TX), 99; auth, Gender and Society in contemporary Brazilian Cinema, Univ of Tex Press (Austin, TX), 99. **CONTACT ADDRESS** Dept Lang and Lit, Arizona State Univ, PO Box 870202, Tempe, AZ 85287-0202. **EMAIL** david.foster@asu.edu

FOSTER, MARK A.
PERSONAL Born 02/27/1956, New York, NY, s **DISCIPLINE** SOCIOLOGY **EDUCATION** Nassan Community Col, AA, 76; Univ Ga, AB, 78; Long Island Univ, MA, 81; Miss State Univ, PhD, 84. **CAREER** Asst Prof, Clinch Valley Col, 85-89; Asst Prof, Macon Col, 89-93; Assoc Prof, Johnson Cmty Col, 93-. **HONORS AND AWARDS** Alpha Kappa Delta; Phi Alpha Theta. **MEMBERSHIPS** Asn for Bahaii Studies. **RESEARCH** Religion. **CONTACT ADDRESS** Dept Humanities & Soc Sci, Johnson County Comm Col, 12345 College Blvd, Overland Park, KS 66210. **EMAIL** owner@fosterservices.com

FOX, LINDA CHODOSH
PERSONAL Born 05/20/1943, Charlottesville, VA, m, 1967, 2 children **DISCIPLINE** SPANISH, WOMEN'S STUDIES **EDUCATION** Douglass Col, BA, 65; Ind Univ, Bloomington, MA 67; Univ Wis-Madison, PhD(Span), 74. **CAREER** Lectr, 71-74, asst prof Span, Ind Univ-Purdue Univ, Fort Wayne, 74-95; assoc prof Span, 96-; dir of Women's Studies, 82-88; 95, newsletter ed, Feministas Unidas: A coalition of feminist scholars in Span, Span-Am, Luso-Brazilian, Afro-Port & Chicano-Riqueno Studies; 81-96. **HONORS AND AWARDS** Phi Beta Kappa, 65; Sigma Delta Pi Honorary, 65; Outstanding Teacher Awd Indiana U-Purdue U, Fort Wayne, 96; Best Teachers in America; 98; Zonta Summit Awd, 00. **MEMBERSHIPS** MLA; Am Asn Teachers Span & Port; Assoc Lit Hisp Femenina; Feministas Unidas. **RESEARCH** Power in the family and beyond: Dona Perfecta and Bernarda Alba as manipulators of their destinies; characterization of women in Hispanic literature. **SELECTED PUBLICATIONS** Auth, Vision of Cain and Abel in Spain's generation of 1898, CLA J, 6/78; Las lagrimas y la tristeza en el Lazarillo de Tormes, Revista Estudios Hisp, 10/79; Making Bonds, Breaking Bonds: The Mother-Daughter Relationship in Chicana Poetry 1975-1985, in En homenaje a Victoria Urbano, ed, Adelaida Lopez de Martinez, Madrid: Editorial Fundamentos, 93; From Chants to Borders to Communion: Pat Mora's Journey to Nepantla, Bilingual Review, Revista Bilingue, Sept-Dec, 96; auth, "Four imaginarios femeninos in Pat Mora's 'Cuarteto Mexicano,'" in The Americas Review, valedictorian issue, 99. **CONTACT ADDRESS** Dept of Mod Foreign Lang, Indiana Univ-Purdue Univ, Fort Wayne, 2101 Coliseum Blvd E, Fort Wayne, IN 46805-1499. **EMAIL** fox@ipfw.edu

FRAGER, ROBERT
PERSONAL Born 06/20/1940, New York, NY, m, 1983, 4 children **DISCIPLINE** PSYCHOLOGY **EDUCATION** Reed Col, BA, 61; Harvard Univ, Phd, 67. **CAREER** Vis Lecturer in Psychol, UC Berkeley, 68-69; Asst Prof Psych, UCSC, 69-74; Founding Pres, Institute for Transpersonal Psych 75; Prof of Psychol, 75-. **HONORS AND AWARDS** Pres, Association for Transpersonal Psych, 83-85. **RESEARCH** Sufism; Psychology of Religion. **SELECTED PUBLICATIONS** Auth, "Essential Sufism," San Francisco: Harper SanFrancisco, with James Fadiman; auth, "Personally and Personal Growth," 4th ed, NY: Longman, with James Fadiman; auth, "Love is the Wine: Teachings of a Sufimaster in America," Los Angeles: Philosophical Research Soc.; auth, "Heart Self and Soul: A Sufi Psychology of Growth, Balance and Harmony," Wheaton, IL: Quest. **CONTACT ADDRESS** Dept Psychology, Inst of Transpersonal Psychology, 744 San Antonio Ave, Palo Alto, CA 94303.

FRANK, JOHN DAVID
PERSONAL Born 10/17/1963, Elmhurst, IL **DISCIPLINE** SOCIOLOGY **EDUCATION** Univ Chicago, AB, 85; Stanford Univ, PhD, 95. **CAREER** Asst prof to assoc prof, Harvard Univ, 95-. **SELECTED PUBLICATIONS** Coauth with Evan Schofer and John Charles Torres, "Rethinking History: Change in the University Curriculum, 1910-90," Sociol of Ed, 67: 231-242 (Oct 94); coauth with John W. Meyer and David Miyahara," The Individualist Polity and the Centrality of Professionalized Psychology: A Cross-National Study," Am Sociol Rev, 60:360-377 (June 95); coauth with John W. Meyer, Ann Hironaka, Evan Schofer, and Nancy Brandon Tuma,"The Structuring of a World Environmental Regime, 1870-1990," Int Org, 51: 623-651 (autumn 97); auth, "Science, Nature, and the Globalization of the Environment, 1870-1990," Soc Forces, 76: 409-435 (Dec 97), reprinted in R. Scott Frey, ed, The Environment and Society Reader, Needham Heights, MA: Allyn & Bacon (97); coauth with Deborah Barrett, "Population Control for National Development: From World Discourse to National Policies," in Constructing World Culture: International Nongovernmental Organizations Since 1875, ed John Boli and George M. Thomas, Stanford, CA: Stanford Univ Press (99); coauth with Elizabeth H. McEneaney, "The Individualization of Society and the Liberalization of State Policies on Same-Sex Sexual Relations, 1984-1995," Social Forces, 77:911-944 (March 99); auth, "The Social Bases of Environmental Treaty Ratification, 1900-1990," Sociol Inquiry, 69: 523-550 (fall 99); coauth with Suk-Ying Wong, John W. Meyer, and Francisco O. Ramirez, "Embedding National Society: Worldwide Changes in University History Curricula, 1895-1994," Comparative Ed Rev, 44: 29-53 (Feb 2000); coauth with Ann Hironaka and Evan Schofer, "The Nation-State and the Natural Environment Over the Twentieth Century," Am Sociol Rev, 65: 96-116 (Feb 2000); coauth with Ann Hironaka and Evan Schofer, "Environmentalism as a Global Institution," Am Sociol Rev, 65:122-127 (Feb 2000). **CONTACT ADDRESS** Dept Sociol, Harvard Univ, William James, Cambridge, MA 02138. **EMAIL** frankdj@wjh.harvard.edu

FRANTZ, BARBARA
PERSONAL Born, Germany, m, 2 children **DISCIPLINE** GERMAN, FEMINIST STUDIES **EDUCATION** Univ Calif Santa Barbara, BA, 89; MA, 91; PhD, 95. **CAREER** Lectr, Calif Poly San Luis Obispo, 95-. **HONORS AND AWARDS** Teaching Asst of the Year Awd, UCSB, 94; General Affiliates Dissertation Fel, 94; Grad Student Fee Fel, 94, 95; Hayman Fel Awd, 95. **MEMBERSHIPS** AATG, Calif For Lang Teachers Asn, MLA, Women in Ger, Prof Women's Asn. **RESEARCH** Issues related to women, age, gender, Social issues related to women. **SELECTED PUBLICATIONS** Auth, "Jewish Working Women in Weimar Fiction: being a Flapper was not for Everyone," in Weimas Culfare: Issues of Modernity and the Metropolis, ed. C. Gannon and S. Melto, 94; contrib, Feminist Encyclopedia of German Literature, Greenwood Publ Press, 97; auth, Gertrud Kolmar's Prose, Peter Lang Publ (NY), 97. **CONTACT ADDRESS** Dept Mod Lang, California Polytech State Univ, San Luis Obispo, 1 Grand Ave, San Luis Obispo, CA 93407-9000. **EMAIL** bfrantz@calpoly.edu

FRASIER, MARY MACK
PERSONAL Born 05/17/1938, Orangeburg, SC, m **DISCIPLINE** EDUCATION **EDUCATION** SC State Coll, BS 1958; SC State Coll, MEd 1971; Univ of CT, PhD 1974. **CAREER** Univ of GA, Department of Education, professor, psychology, National Research Center on the Gifted and Talented, assoc dir, 74-; SC State Coll, dir special serv for disadvantaged students in insts of higher educ 71-72; Wilkinson High School, Orangeburg SC, instructor Choral Music 58-71. **MEMBERSHIPS** President, GA Federation-Council for Exceptional Children, 1977-78; exec bd, Nat Assn for Gifted Children 1977-81; National Association for Gifted Children, president, 1983-91; bd of govs, The Assn for the Gifted 1978-80; Pi Lambda Theta, 1973; Delta Sigma Theta Sorority Athens Alumnae Chap, 1974-; Phi Delta Kappa, 1979-; Kappa Delta Pi, 1990. **SELECTED PUBLICATIONS** Articles pub in "The Gifted Child Quarterly, Journal for the Education of the Gifted Exceptional Children"; chap in book "New Voices in Counseling the Gifted" Kendall-Hunt 1979. **CONTACT ADDRESS** 325 Aberhold, Athens, GA 30602.

FREED, BARBARA
DISCIPLINE FRENCH AND SECOND LANGUAGE ACQUISITION **EDUCATION** Univ Pa, PhD. **CAREER** Languages, Carnegie Mellon Univ. **SELECTED PUBLICATIONS** Auth, The Linguistic Consequences of Study Abroad Experiences. In preparation for the "Studies in Bilingualism Series.". John Benjamins Publ Co; Foreign Language Acquisition Research and The Classroom, Lexington, MA: D. C. Heath & Co, 91; The Foreign Language Requirement in Teaching Languages at College: Curriculum and Content, NTC Publ Gp, 92; Language Learning in a Study Abroad Context: The Effects of Interactive and Non-Interactive Out-of Class Contact on Grammatical Achievement and Oral Proficiency, 90. **CONTACT ADDRESS** Carnegie Mellon Univ, 5000 Forbes Ave, Pittsburgh, PA 15213.

FREEDHEIM, DONALD K.
PERSONAL Born 07/31/1932, Cleveland, OH, m, 1958, 3 children **DISCIPLINE** PSYCHOLOGY **EDUCATION** Miami Univ, AB, 54; Duke Univ, PhD, 60. **CAREER** Asst prof to prof, Case Western Reserve Univ, 60-. **HONORS AND AWARDS** Sigma Xi; Psi Chi; Omicron Delta Kappa; Distinguished Psychologist Awd, APA, 91; Psychol of the Year Awd, Cleveland Psychol Assoc, 91; Distinguished Practitioner, Nat Acad of Practice, 96. **MEMBERSHIPS** Am Psychol Assoc; Cleveland Psychol Assoc; Ohio Psychol Assoc; Soc for the Exploration of Psychotherpay Integration; Int Coun of Psychol; Am Assoc on Mental Retardation; Am Orthopsychiatric Assoc; Nat Register of Health Service Providers in Psychol. **SELECTED PUBLICATIONS** Auth, "Historical perspectives on Psychotherapy", Annals of the NY Acad of Sci, 727 (94): 123-132; coauth, The Anatomy of Psychotherapy, Am Psychol Assoc, (Washington, DC), 95; coauth, "Training issues in clinical psychology", Beginning Skills and Professional Issues in Clinical Psychology, eds E. Walker and J. Matthews, Allyn and Bacon, (97): coauth, "Responding therapeutically to patient anger", Independent Practitioner, 17, (97): 99-101; coauth, "Training in psychotherapy during graduate school", Psychotherapy in Private Practice, 17, (98): 3-18; coauth, Clinical Child Documentation Sourcebook, Wiley & Sons, (NY), 99; auth, "Theories, Clinical Psychology" and "Psychiatry", Encyclopedia of Psychology, Oxford Univ Pr, (NY), 00; ed, History of Psychology, Wiley & Sons, (NY), (forthcoming). **CONTACT ADDRESS** Dept Psychol, Case Western Reserve Univ, 10900 Euclid Ave, Cleveland, OH 44106-7123. **EMAIL** dkf@cwru.edu

FREEHLING, WILLIAM W.
PERSONAL Born 12/26/1935, Chicago, IL, m, 1971, 4 children **DISCIPLINE** AMERICAN CULTURAL HISTORY **EDUCATION** Harvard Univ, AB, 58; Univ Calif-Berkeley, MA, 59; Berkeley, PhD, 63. **CAREER** Tchg fel, Berkeley, 59-60 & 62-63; instr Univ S Carolina, 61-62; instr, Harvard Univ, 63-64; asst prof to prof, Univ Mich, 64-72; prof, Johns Hopkins Univ, 72-91; Thomas B. Lockwood Prof Am Hist, SUNY, Buffalo, 91-94; Otis A. Singletary Chr in Hum, Univ Kentucky, 94- . **HONORS AND AWARDS** Woodrow Wilson fel, Guggenheim fel, 69-70, nHF fel, 68; Horace Rockham fel, 70-71; Owsley Prize; Bancroft Prize, Nevins Prize; Univ Mich Russel Prize. **MEMBERSHIPS** Am Hist Soc; S Hist Asn; Orgn Am Hist; Am Antiq Soc; Soc Am Hist; Soc Hist of Early Repub; The Hist Soc. **RESEARCH** History of American furniture; History of the Civil War era. **SELECTED PUBLICATIONS** Auth, The Reintegration of American History: Slavery and the Civil War, NY, 94; The Road to Disunion, Disunionists at Bay, 1776-1854, NY, 90; ed, Secession Debated: Georgia's Showdown in 1860, NY, 93; rev, David Gollaher, Ddorothea Dix, Lexington Herald-Leader, 96; auth, "The South versus Te South: How AntiConfederate Southerners Shaped the Course of the Civil War," NY 01. **CONTACT ADDRESS** Singletary Chair in the Humanities, Univ of Kentucky, 1715 Patterson Office Tower, Lexington, KY 40506-0027. **EMAIL** wwfree0@pop.uky.edu

FREEMAN, BERNICE
PERSONAL Born 08/08/1909, La Grange, GA **DISCIPLINE** ENGLISH EDUCATION **EDUCATION** Tift Col, AB, 30; Univ NC, Chapel Hill, MA, 32; Columbia Univ, EdD(English educ), 52. **CAREER** Teacher high schs, Ga, 30-42; instr and critic, Demonstration High Sch, Ga Col, Milledgeville, 42-48, asst prof and prin, 48-51; co-dir, Ga Educ Ctr, 50-51; instructional supvr, Troup County Schs, Ga, 51-67; from assoc prof to prof educ, West Ga Col, 67-74, coordr, 69-73, chmn, Dept Sec Educ, 73-74; RETIRED., Mem high sch sect comt, NCTE, 52-54, mem bd dir elem sect, 66-69; mem, Publ and Constructive Studies Comt, Dept Rural Educ, NEA, 58-65, mem exec bd, 64-69, mem exec comt, 65-69. **MEMBERSHIPS** NCTE; NEA; MLA; SAtlantic Mod Lang Asn. **RESEARCH** The short story as a means of identifying a place; the Georgia short story. **SELECTED PUBLICATIONS** Auth, Precise Moments, Georg Rev, Vol 47, 93. **CONTACT ADDRESS** 305 Park Ave, La Grange, GA 30240.

FREEMAN, STEPHANNY FUMI
PERSONAL Born 11/27/1969, Chicago, IL, m, 1998 **DISCIPLINE** EDUCATION **EDUCATION** Univ Calif at Los Angeles, BA, 90; MEd, 91; PhD, 97. **CAREER** Res Educationist; Univ Calif, Los Angeles, 98-. **HONORS AND AWARDS** Fel,

UCA. 97-00. **RESEARCH** Social-emotional development in children with disabilities 9specifically Down syndrome and Autism), Classroom placement/practice of children with disabilities, reading in children with Down syndrome. **SELECTED PUBLICATIONS** Coauth, "Attention regulation by children with Down syndrome: Coordinated joint attention and social referencing looks", Am J on Mental retardation 100.2 (95): 128-136; coauth, "Friendships in children with developmental disabilities" Early Educ and Develop 9.4 (98): 341-355; coauth, "Parental perspectives on inclusion: Effects of autism and Down syndrome", J of Autism and Develop Disorders 29.4 (99): 297-305; coauth, "Satisfaction and desire for change in educational placement for children with Down syndrome: Perceptions of parents", Remedial and Special Educ 20.3 (00): 143-151. **CONTACT ADDRESS** Grad School of Educ, Univ of California, Los Angeles, PO Box 951521, Los Angeles, CA 90095-1521. **EMAIL** sfreeman@mednet.ucla.edu

FREEMAN, YVONNE
DISCIPLINE BILINGUAL EDUCATION **EDUCATION** Taft Col, AA; Univ CA-Santa Barbara, BA; Stanford Univ, MA; Univ AZ, MA, PhD. **CAREER** Prof; div hd, Fresno Pacific Col. **HONORS AND AWARDS** Bd dir(s), Whole Lang Umbrella. **MEMBERSHIPS** Mem, Nat Conf Res Lang and Lit; Ctr Expansion of Lang and Thinking; Mod Lang Assn; Intl Reading Assn; CA Reading Assn; Tchr(s) Eng to Speakers of Other Lang; CA TESOL; Nat Coun Tchr(s) Eng; Nat Assn Bilingual Edu; CA Assn Bilingual Edu. **RESEARCH** Effective practices for tchg Eng to lang minority students. **SELECTED PUBLICATIONS** Co-auth, Report Card on Basal Readers, Richard C Owen, 88; Whole Language for Second Language Learners, N.H.: Heinemann, 92; Between Worlds: Access to Second Language Acquisition, Heinemann, 94; Teaching Reading and Writing in the Spanish/English Bilingual Classroom, Heinemann, 97. **CONTACT ADDRESS** Div Lang, Lit and Cult, Fresno Pacific Col, 1717 S Chestnut, Fresno, CA 93702. **EMAIL** yfreeman@fresno.edu

FREIMUTH, VICKI S.
DISCIPLINE HEALTH COMMUNICATION **EDUCATION** FL State Univ, PhD. **CAREER** Prof, Univ MD. **RESEARCH** Public's search for and use of health information. **SELECTED PUBLICATIONS** Co-auth, College Students' Awareness and Interpretation of the AIDS Risk, Sci, Tech, and Human Values 12, 87; Searching for Health Information: The Cancer Information Service Experience, Univ Pa Press, 89. **CONTACT ADDRESS** Dept of Commun, Univ of Maryland, Col Park, 4229 Art-Sociology Building, College Park, MD 20742-1335.

FREISCHLAG, JERRY A.
PERSONAL Born 02/08/1942, Nashua, NH, m, 1961, 4 children **DISCIPLINE** SPORT PSYCHOLOGY **EDUCATION** Ithaca Col, BA, 64; Stanford Univ, MA, 67; Florida State Univ, PhD, 71. **CAREER** Prof of Kinesiology, CA State Univ, 69-. **HONORS AND AWARDS** Danforth Foundation Assoc, Life Fellow of AAHPERD Research Consortium. **MEMBERSHIPS** AAHPERD **RESEARCH** Psychology of exercise and sport. **SELECTED PUBLICATIONS** Auth, "International Journal of Sport Psychology," Selected psycho-social characteristics of marathoners, 12 (81): 282-288; auth, "The Physician and Sportsmedicine, " Weight loss, body composition and health of high school wrestlers, 12 (84): 121-126; auth, "The Chronicle of Physical Education in Higher Education, (90): 10-14; auth, "Violence in Sports," ed. Keith Henschen and William Straub, Sport: Psychology: An Analysis of Athlete Behavior (Mouvement Pub: Ithaca, NY), 95. **CONTACT ADDRESS** Dept Kinesiology, California State Univ, San Bernardino, 5500 Univ Parkway, San Bernardino, CA 92407. **EMAIL** jfreisch@csusb.edu

FRENCH, LAURENCE
PERSONAL Born 03/24/1941, Manchester, NH, m, 1971 **DISCIPLINE** PSYCHOLOGY **EDUCATION** Univ NH, BA, 68; MA, 70; PhD, 75; Univ Neb, PhD, 81. **CAREER** Asst Prof, Western Carolina Univ, 72-77; Asst Prof, Univ Neb, 77-80; Staff Psychologist, NH Neuropsychiat Hosp, 80-89; From Assoc Prof to Prof, Western NMex Univ, 89-. **HONORS AND AWARDS** Bassett Memorial Awd; Grad Fac Fel; Ford Cross-Cult Res Awd; Educr of the Year Awd, NIDA Res Awd. **MEMBERSHIPS** APA, Am Soc of Criminology. **RESEARCH** Violence, international social and criminal justice, assessment, American Indians. **SELECTED PUBLICATIONS** Auth, Counseling American Indians, Univ Pr of Am, 97; auth, The Qualla Cherokee: Surviving in Two Worlds, Edwin Mellen Pr, 98; auth, Addictions and Native Americans, Praeger, 00. **CONTACT ADDRESS** Dept Soc Sci, Western New Mexico Univ, PO Box 680, Silver City, NM 88062. **EMAIL** frenchl@silver.wnmu.edu

FRENCH, RICHARD FREDERIC
PERSONAL Born 06/23/1915, Randolph, MA **DISCIPLINE** MUSIC, RELIGION **EDUCATION** Harvard Univ, BS, 37, MA, 39. **CAREER** Mem Soc Fellows, Harvard Univ, 41-42, 46-47, asst prof music, 47-51; vpres, Assoc Music Publ, NY, 51-59; pres, NY Pro Musica, 58-70; prof sacred music, Union theol Sem, 66-73; Prof Music, Inst Music and Worship, Yale Univ, 73-, Trustee, Brooklyn Music Sch, 60-70 and Schola Mu-

sicae Liturgicae, NY, 73-; adj prof sacred music, Union theol Sem, 73-77. **MEMBERSHIPS** Am Musicol Soc. **RESEARCH** Music and liturgy; Russian; graduate educational curricula. **SELECTED PUBLICATIONS** Auth, Libraries, History, Diplomacy, and the Performing Arts--Essays in Honor of Smith, Carleton, Sprague, Notes, Vol 49, 93. **CONTACT ADDRESS** Sch of Music, Yale Univ, New Haven, CT 06520. **EMAIL** rfrench@pantheon.yale.com

FRENCH, SANDRA
PERSONAL Born 03/26/1943, Ames, IA, d **DISCIPLINE** SOCIOLOGY **EDUCATION** Iowa State Univ, BS, 65; Tulane Univ, MA, 78; PhD, 80. **CAREER** CAAO, Indiana Univ, 88-90; asst prof, 80-90; dir, 97-98; assoc prof, 91-. **HONORS AND AWARDS** Fst Fac Fel; Teach Excell Recog Awd. **MEMBERSHIPS** NCSA; ASA; SWS; NCCSW. **RESEARCH** Women in professions; relationship violence; welfare reform; post polio syndrome. **SELECTED PUBLICATIONS** Coauth, "Implications for Changes in Affirmative Action: The Case of Public Accounting," J Accou Ethics Pub Pol 2 (99): 286-309; coauth, Women in Public Accounting," in Women and Work: A Reader, eds. Paul J Dubeck, Kathryn Borman (New Brunswick, N.J: Rutgers Univ Press, 97): 202-205; coauth, "Academic Mentors as Gatekeepers," in Women and Work: A Reader, eds. Paul J Dubeck, Kathryn Borman (New Brunswick, N.J: Rutgers Univ Press, 97): 347-350; coauth, "Social Policy and Women in Public Accounting: A Cross-Cultural Comparison," Intl Adv Econ Res (96); coauth, "Violent Environment: Implications for Relationships," Ind Acad Soc Sci (95). **CONTACT ADDRESS** Dept Social Services, Indiana Univ, Southeast, 4201 Grant Line Rd, New Albany, IN 47150. **EMAIL** sfrench@iuo.edu

FREYMEYER, ROBERT H.
PERSONAL Born 12/09/1951, Wadsworth, OH, m, 1987, 2 children **DISCIPLINE** SOCIOLOGY **EDUCATION** Vanderbilt Univ, BA, 73; Col William and Mary, MA, 76; Univ Cincinnati, PhD, 79. **CAREER** Vis asst prof, Lander Col, 79-81; asst prof, Gettysburg Col, 81-84; asst prof to prof and chair, Presbyterian Col, 84-. **HONORS AND AWARDS** Fulbright-Hayes Group Awd Participant, summer 85; Fulbright-Hayes Awd, summer 87. **MEMBERSHIPS** Am Sociol Asn; Population Asn Am; Southern Sociol Soc; Southern Demographic Asn; SC Sociol Asn; NC Sociol Asn. **RESEARCH** Southern culture, demographic change, family issues. **SELECTED PUBLICATIONS** Auth, "In-migration and Changing Southern Political Orientations," The Rev of Regional Studies (83); coauth with P. Neal Ritchey, "Spatial Distribution of Opportunities and Magnitude of Migration," Sociol Perspectives (85); auth, "The Consequences of Migration for a Southern Community," Perspectives on the Am South, vol. 3 (85); auth, "Population Policy and the State of Israel," in Curriculum Projects for the Jerusalem Seminar on Ancient and Modern Israel, Jrerusalem: Ministry of Ed (summer 87); auth, "The Social and Demographic Characteristics of Southern Politicians," Sociol Spectrum (87); coauth with Barbara E. Johnson, "Replicating Family Size: Does Growing Up in a Single Parent Family Matter," Sociol Focus (89); auth, "Migration and Regional Distinctiveness: Attitudinal Differences Among Northerners," Mich Sociol Rev (92); auth, "Geographic Mobility," in Encyclopedia of American Social History, Charles Schribner's Sons (93), revised and reissued as Schribner's American History and Culture on CD-ROM (98); auth, "Rape Myths and Religiosity,: Sociol Spectrum (97); auth, "Mobility," The Oxford Companion to United States History, Oxford Univ Press (forthcoming). **CONTACT ADDRESS** Dept Sociol, Presbyterian Col, 503 S Broad St, Clinton, SC 29325. **EMAIL** rhfreym@presby.edu

FRIEDENBERG, JAY
PERSONAL Born 10/28/1966, New York, NY, s **DISCIPLINE** PSYCHOLOGY **EDUCATION** Boston Univ, BA, 88; Univ Va, MA, 91; PhD, 95. **CAREER** Asst Prof, Manhattan Col, 95-. **MEMBERSHIPS** Asn for Res in Vision and Ophthalmol; Psychonomic Soc; E Psychol Asn. **RESEARCH** Visual perception; facial attractiveness; symmetry detection; Perception of two-body center of mass. **SELECTED PUBLICATIONS** Auth, "Intricate Consciousness," Objectivity, (93): 29-67; co-auth, "Detection of Symmetry and Perceptual Organization: The Way a Lock-and-Key Process Works," Acta Psychologica, (97): 119-140; co-auth, "Double-blind Study of Possible Proximity Effect of Sucrose on skeletal Muscle Strength," Perceptual and Motor Skills, (99): 966-968; auth, "Coactivation, Pop-out, and Symmetry affect Line Discrimination," Perceptual and Motor Skills, (00): 111-120. **CONTACT ADDRESS** Dept Psychol, Manhattan Col, 4513 Manhattan College, Bronx, NY 10471. **EMAIL** jfrieden@manhattan.edu

FRIEDLANDER, JUDITH
PERSONAL Born 04/10/1944, New York, NY, m, 1997 **DISCIPLINE** ANTHROPOLOGY **EDUCATION** Univ Chicago, BA, 66; MA, 69; PhD, 73; Harvard Univ, MA, 67. **CAREER** Asst prof, SUNY, 72-90; prof, Hunter Col, CUNY, 90-93; prof, New School for Soc Res, 93-. **HONORS AND AWARDS** Woodrow Wilson Fel, 66; Elsie Clewes Parsons Student Competition Awd, 69; Grants, NDEA, Rockefeller Found, NEH, Wenner Gren Found; Eberstad Prof, New School for Soc Res, 93-. **MEMBERSHIPS** Am Anthrop Assoc. **RESEARCH** Eth-

nicity, Nationalism, Education in Mexico, France and the US. **SELECTED PUBLICATIONS** Auth, Being Indian in Hueyapan: A Study of Forced Identity in Contemporary Mexico, St Martin's Pr, (NY), 75; coed, Women in Culture and Politics: A Century of Change, Ind Univ Pr, (Bloomington), 86; auth, Vilna on the Seine, Yale Univ Pr, (New Haven), 90; transl, of "The Defeat of the Mind", by Alain Finkielkraut, Columbia Univ, Pr, (NY), 95; auth, "Yiddish Literature in French Translation: The Pioneering Role of Rachel Ertel", Nat Counc of Jewish Women, 96; auth, "Reflections of a Jewish Feminist", Festschrift in Honor of Rabbi Mordecai Waxman, Jewish Theo Sem, (NY), 99; transl, of "In the Name of Humanity", by Alain Finkielkraut, Columbia Univ Pr, (NY), 99; auth, "The Six-Day War and the Jewish Question in France", Avraham Harman Inst of Contemporary Jewry, (Jerusalem), (forthcoming); auth, "Alain Finkielkraut", Columbia History of Twentieth Century French Thought, ed Lawrence Kritzman, Columbia Univ Pr, (NY), (forthcoming). **CONTACT ADDRESS** Dept Anthrop, New Sch for Social Research, 65 5th Ave, New York, NY 10003.

FRIEDMAN, MONROE P.
PERSONAL Born 10/06/1934, New York, NY, m, 1956, 3 children **DISCIPLINE** PSYCHOLOGY **EDUCATION** Brooklyn Col, BS, 56; Univ Tenn, PhD, 59. **CAREER** Asst prof to prof, Eastern Mich Univ, 64-. **HONORS AND AWARDS** Phi Kappa Phi; Sigma Xi; Bronze Prize, Int Consumer Film Competition, 75; Awds, NEH, 81, 87; Distinguished Fac Awd, Eastern Mich Univ, 80; US Rep, Int Asn of Applied Psychol, 88-; Applied Consumer Econ Res Awd, 91, 97; Chair, Distinguished Fel Awds Committee, Am Coun on Consumer Interests. **SELECTED PUBLICATIONS** Auth, "Experiential Consumption: A Little Information May Not Be a Good Thing", Consumer Interests Annual 43, (97): 82-83; auth, "Cigarette Smoking by Children in Developing Countries: A Problem Whose Time Has Come?", Consumer Interests Annual, 44, (98): 234; auth, "No One is Always Right, Including the Customer", J of Bus Ethics 17, (98): 883-884; auth, "Coping with Consumer Fraud: The Need for a Paradigm Shift", J of Consumer Affairs 32, (98): 1-12; auth, Consumer Boycotts: Effecting Change through the Marketplace and the Media, Routledge (NY), 99; rev, of "Greenspeak: A Study of Environmental Discourse", by Rome Harre, Jens Brockmeier and Peter Muhlhausler, Population and Environ Psychol Bulletin, 25 (99): 8-9; auth, "Ethical Dilemmas Associated with Consumer Boycotts", J of Soc Philos, (forthcoming); auth, "A Hundred Years of Consumer Boycotts", Consumer Interests Annual, (forthcoming); rev of "The Overspent American" by Juliet B Schor, J of Socio-Economics (forthcoming). **CONTACT ADDRESS** Dept Psychol, Eastern Michigan Univ, 537 Mark Jeffersen, Ypsilanti, MI 48197. **EMAIL** psy_friedman@online.emich.edu

FRIEDMAN, NORMAN
PERSONAL Born 04/10/1925, Boston, MA, m, 1945, 2 children **DISCIPLINE** ENGLISH, PSYCHOLGOY **EDUCATION** Harvard Univ, AB, 48, AM, 49, PhD (English), 52; Adelphi Univ, MSW, 78. **CAREER** From instr to assoc prof English, Univ Conn, 52-63; assoc prof to full prof english, Queens Col and Grad Center, CUNY, 63-88; Am Coun Learned Soc grants, 59 and 60; Fulbright lectr, Univs Nantes and Nice, 66-67; consult, PMLA. **HONORS AND AWARDS** Bowdoin Prize, 48; Northwest Rev Annual Poetry Prize, 63; Borestone Mountain Poetry Awds, 64, 67. **MEMBERSHIPS** MLA, NCTE, ALA, NASW. **RESEARCH** Literary criticism and critical theory; Victorian and modern literature; psychology and literature. **SELECTED PUBLICATIONS** Auth, E.E. Cummings: The Art of His Poetry, Baltimore: Johns Hopkins Press, London: Oxford University Press, 60; auth, Poetry: An Introduction to Its Form and Art, with Charles A. McLaughlin, New York: Harper, 61; auth, Logic, Rhetoric, and Style, with Charles A. McLaughlin, Boston: Little, Brown, 63; auth, E.E. Cummings: The Growth of a Writer, Carbondale: Southern Illinois University Press, 64; auth, E.E. Cummings: A Collection of Critical Essays, Englewood Cliffs, New Jersey: Prentice-Hall Spectrum Books, Twentieth Century Views, 72; auth, Form and Meaning in Fiction, Athens: University of Georgia Press, 75; auth, The Magic Badge: Poems 1953-1984, Austin, Texas: Slough Press, 84; auth, The Intrusions of Love, Poems, Lewiston, NY: Mellen Poetry Press, 92; auth, (Re)Valuing Cummings: Further Essays on the Poet, 1962-1993, Gainsville: University Press of Florida, 96. **CONTACT ADDRESS** 33-54 164 St, Flushing, NY 11358-1442. **EMAIL** nfriedman18@aol.com

FRIEDMAN, SAUL S.
PERSONAL Born 03/08/1937, Uniontown, PA, m, 1964, 3 children **DISCIPLINE** HOLOCAUST & MIDDLE EAST EDUCATION **EDUCATION** Kent State Univ, BA, 59; Ohio State Univ, MA, 62, PhD (hist), 69. **CAREER** Asst prof, 69-74, assoc prof, 74-80, Prof Hist, Youngstown State Univ, 80-; Univ Res Prof, Youngstown State, 76; dir, Holocaust and Judaic Studies prog, 98-. **HONORS AND AWARDS** Ohio Humanties Council Lifetime Achievement Awd, 98; Cleveland Regional Emmy Awds, 86, 88, 89, 91, 97; Brandeis Awd, Youngstown Zionist Dist, 89; Triumphant Spirit Awd for Edu, 99; Distinguished Univ Prof, YSU, 76, 82, 86, 90, 92. **MEMBERSHIPS** NEA. **RESEARCH** Holocaust; Zionism and Arab nationalism; Jews in Arab lands. **SELECTED PUBLICATIONS** auth, No Haven for the Oppressed: Official U.S. Policy toward European Jewish Refugees, 1933-1945, Wayne State, 72; auth, Pogrom-

chik: The Assassination of Simon Petlura, Hart, 76; auth, The Incident at Massena: The Blood Livel in American, Stein & Day, 78; auth, Amcha: An Oral Testament of the Holocaust, Univ Press of Am, 79; auth, Land of Dust: Palestine at the turn of the Century, Univ Press, 82; auth, The Oberammergau Passion Play: A Lance against Civilization, Southern IL, 84; auth, Without Future: The Plight of Syrian Jewry, Praeger, 89; auth, The Terezin Diary of Gonda Redlich, Kentucky, 92; auth, Holocaust Literature, Greenwood, 94; auth, Jews and the American Slave Trade, Transaction, 97. **CONTACT ADDRESS** Dept of Hist, Youngstown State Univ, One University Plz, Youngstown, OH 44555-0002.

FRIEDRICH, PAUL
PERSONAL Born 10/22/1927, Cambridge, MA, m, 1996, 6 children **DISCIPLINE** LINGUISTICS, ANTHROPOLOGY, POETRY **EDUCATION** Harvard Univ, BA, 50, MA, 51; Yale Univ, PhD, 57. **CAREER** Res assoc, Russ Res Ctr, 49-50; asst prof anthrop, Harvard Univ, 57-58; asst prof jr ling, Deccan Col, India, 58-59; asst prof anthrop, Univ Pa, 59-62; assoc prof, 62-67, prof anthrop & ling, Univ Chicago, 67-; prof anthrop, ling & soc thought, 92. **MEMBERSHIPS** Ling See Am; Amer Anthro Assoc; Amer Acad Arts & Sci . **RESEARCH** Homeric Greek; Russian, Comp. Poetics. **SELECTED PUBLICATIONS** Auth, Russia and Eurasia, Encyclopedic 1 World, Cultures, 94; auth, Music in Russian Poetry, Lang, 98. **CONTACT ADDRESS** Dept of Anthrop, Univ of Chicago, 1126 E 59th St, Chicago, IL 60637-1539.

FRINK, HELEN
DISCIPLINE WOMEN'S STUDIES **EDUCATION** Univ NH, 68; Univ Chicago, MA, 71, PhD, 75. **CAREER** Asst prof, Keene State Col, 74-79; assoc prof, SUNY, Albany, 79-81; prof, Keene State Col, 81-. **HONORS AND AWARDS** Phi Beta Kappa, 68; cum laude, PhD, 75. **MEMBERSHIPS** MLA, AATG, Women in German, Nat Women's Studies Asn. **SELECTED PUBLICATIONS** Auth, Animal Symbolism in Hofmannsthal's Works, NY and Berne: Peter Lang (85); auth, These Acworth Hills, Acworth, NH (89); auth, Alstead Through the Years, Portsmouth, NH: Peter Randall (92); auth, Women After Communism: the East German Experience (forthcoming). **CONTACT ADDRESS** Dept Modern Langs, Keene State Col, 229 Main St, Keene, NH 03435-0001. **EMAIL** hfrink@keene.edu

FROMAN, LARRY
PERSONAL Born 01/01/1948, Bronx, NY, m, 1974, 2 children **DISCIPLINE** PSYCHOLOGY **EDUCATION** City Col NY, BA, 68; Wayne State Univ, MA, 72; PhD, 77. **CAREER** Coor, Michigan dept Edu, 69-71; consul, psych, Detr, 74-75; APAC Fel, 75-76; res assoc, US Conf May, 76-77; res assoc, MDRC, 78-80; vis psychol, NIDA, 89; assoc prof, Towson Univ, 80-. **HONORS AND AWARDS** NSF Schlp; NIMH Schlp; APA Fel; Psi Chi Outstand Fac Awd; Alpha Sigma Lambda Teach Awd; Outstand Teach, TU; Grad Fac Teach Awd. **MEMBERSHIPS** ASTD; SHRM; AAER. **RESEARCH** Educational leadership. **SELECTED PUBLICATIONS** Coauth, "The Untapped Resource: Perspectives on Attitude and Policy Change," Worklife 4 (88): 18-19; coauth, "Research on Drugs in the Workplace," NIH Guide 25 (90); auth; "Industrial Organizational Psychology," in Psychology, ed. C Morris (Englewood Cliffs, NJ: Prentice-Hall, 93); auth, "Adult Learning in the Workplace," in Handbook of Adult Lifespan Learning, ed. J. Sinnott (NY: Greenwood Press, 94). **CONTACT ADDRESS** Dept Psychology, Towson State Univ, 8000 York Rd, Baltimore, MD 21252. **EMAIL** lfroman@towson.edu

FROSE, VICTOR
PERSONAL Born 06/09/1940, Neuendorf, Ukraine **DISCIPLINE** LANGUAGE EDUCATION **EDUCATION** Univ BC, BEd, 67; Western Wash State Col, MEd, 67; Univ Minn, PhD, 77. **CAREER** Asst prof to prof, Univ Man, 70-79; PROF LANGUAGE EDUCATION, UNIV BRITISH COLUMBIA, 86-, dept head, 86-96. **SELECTED PUBLICATIONS** Auth/co-ed, An Experience-Based Approach to Language and Reading, 77; auth/co-ed, Research in the Language Arts, 81; auth/co-ed, Whole-Language, 90, 94; auth/co-ed, A Language Approach to Reading, 91; auth/co-ed, Language Across the Curriculum, 97; co-ed, Eng Quart, 85-91. **CONTACT ADDRESS** Dept of Lang Educ, Univ of British Columbia, Vancouver, BC, Canada V6T 1Z4. **EMAIL** csf@telus.net

FROST, CHRISTOPHER J.
PERSONAL Born 06/04/1953, TX, m, 1989, 3 children **DISCIPLINE** PSYCHOLOGY **EDUCATION** Baylor Univ, BA, 75; MA, 80; PhD, 84. **CAREER** Vis Prof, Midway Col, 90-91; Sen Res Schol and Lect, Univ Bucharest, 95-96; Asst Prof, Southwest Tex State Univ, 87-93; Assoc Prof, Southwest Tex State Univ, 94-99; Assoc Prof, Al Akhawayn Univ, 98-99; Prof, Southwest Tex State Univ, 00-. **HONORS AND AWARDS** Outstanding Teacher of the Year, Midway Col, 91; Presidential Endowment for Excellence in Teaching, Southwest Tex State Univ,92; Merrick Endowment Teaching Enhancement Awd, 93; FIPSE Competitive Grant, Inst for Integrative Studies, 94; Hon Mem, Golden Key Hon Soc; Fulbright Schol and Sen Lect, Fulbright Comn, 96; Distinguished Speaker and Favorite Prof, Alpha Chi, 97; Int App, Al Akhawayn Univ, 98. **MEMBERSHIPS** APA, AAAPP, Inst for the Humanities at Salado, AHS, Soc for the Sci Study of Relig, Assoc for Integrative Studies, Int Coun of Psychol, Fulbright Assoc. **RESEARCH** Psychology in interdisciplinary perspective, psychology in social context, cross-cultural studies, organizational psychology, psychology of religion, competing perspectives on mental health, clinical psychology, personality and identity, psychology applied to teaching and learning. **SELECTED PUBLICATIONS** Auth, Religious Melancholy or Psychological depression? Univ Pr of Am (Lanham, MD), 85; auth, "Melancholy as an Alternative to the Psychological Label of Depression," The Int J for the Psychol of Relig 2,2 (92): 71-85; auth, "Reality Construction and Presentational Language: A Social-Cognitive Perspective on Prejudice," Humanity and Soc 16,2 (92): 197-216; coauth, "Church Attendance, Meaningfulness of Religion and Depressive Symptomology Among Adolescents," J of Youth and Adolescence 22,5 (93): 559-568; coauth, "Psychoanalytic Psychotherapy and the Tragic Sense of Life and Death," Bull of the Menninger Clin 59,2 (95): 145-159; auth, The University in Your Life: Instructor's Manual, McGraw-Hill/Brown & Benchmark (Guilford, CT), 96; coauth, "Using Technology to Make Connections in the Core Curriculum," The J of Technol studies 24,2 (98): 38-43; coauth, "Simone Weil: On Politics, Religion and Society," Sage Publ Ltd (London, UK), 98; coauth, "Romanian and American Life Aspirations and Their Relation to psychological Well-Being." J of Cross-Cultural Psychol (forthcoming). **CONTACT ADDRESS** Dept Psychol, Southwest Texas State Univ, 601 University Dr, San Marcos, TX 78666. **EMAIL** frosty@swt.edu

FRUNDT, HENRY
PERSONAL Born 05/22/1940, Blue Earth, MN, m, 1970, 6 children **DISCIPLINE** SOCIOLOGY **EDUCATION** St Louis Univ, BA, 64; MA, 67; Rutgers Univ, PhD, 75. **CAREER** Program Developer, US Dept of Labor, 69; Instructor, Univ Wisc, 69-71; Consultant, UN Center on Transnational Co, 78-85; Consultant, Am Univ, 81-82; Consultant, Nat Coun of Churches, 75-78; Lecturer, Universidad Rafael Landivar, 87-88; Prof and Director, Ramapo Col, 73-. **HONORS AND AWARDS** Fulbright Fel, 87-88; Fel, OAS Scholarship, 82; Who's Who in Am. **MEMBERSHIPS** Latin Am Studies Asn; Mid-Atlantic Latin Am Studies Asn. **RESEARCH** Social movements in Central America; US Labor; Food and Agriculture. **SELECTED PUBLICATIONS** Auth, "Guatemala in Search of Democracy," Journal of Interamerican Studies and World Affairs, 90; auth, "Multiculturalism and the New World Order," NJ Journal on Multicultural Education, 93; auth, "The Rise and Fall of AIFLD in Guatemala," Social and Economic Studies, 95; auth, "Trade and Cross-Border Labor strategies in the Americas," Economic and Industrial Democracy, 96; auth, Trade Conditions and Labor Rights: US Initiatives, Dominican and Central American Responses, Univ Press of FL, 98; auth, "Cross-Border Organizing in the Apparel Industry: lessons from Central America and the Caribbean," Labor Studies Journal, 99. **CONTACT ADDRESS** Dept Soc Sci, Ramapo Col of New Jersey, 505 Ramapo Valley Rd, Mahwah, NJ 07430.

FRUZZETTI, ALAN
PERSONAL Born 12/23/1959, MA, m, 2000, 3 children **DISCIPLINE** PSYCHOLOGY **EDUCATION** Brown Univ, BA, 82; Univ WA, MS, 89; PhD, 93. **CAREER** Asst Prof to Assoc Prof and Assoc Chair, Univ Nev, 94-. **MEMBERSHIPS** Am Psychol Asn; Am Psychol Soc; Asn for the Advancement of Beh Therapy; Asn for Beh Analysis; Soc for Psychotherapy Res; Intl Soc for Dialectical Beh Therapy. **RESEARCH** Psychopathologs and family interactions; Treatment of Serious Disorders. **SELECTED PUBLICATIONS** Auth, "Observing intimacy," Couples Research and Therapy, (97): 3, 7-8; co-auth, "Supervision in Dialectical Behavior Therapy," in Handbook of psychotherapy supervision, (Wiley Pub, 97), 84-100; auth, "The case against prescription privileges for psychologists: Issues and implications," in Prescription privileges for psychologists, (Context Press, 98), 74-78; co-auth, "Dialectical Behavior Therapy - Family skills training," Family Process, (99): 399-414; co-auth, "Ethics in couples and family therapy," in Ethics in psychotherapy, in press; co-auth, "Domestic violence: Assessment, prediction and intervention," in Handbook of Forensic Psychology, in press; co-auth, "Dialectical behavior therapy with batterers: Rationale and procedures," Cognitive and Behavioral Practice, in press; auth, "Dialectical behavior therapy for borderline personality disorder," in comprehensive handbook of psychotherapy: cognitive, behavioral, functional approaches, in press; co-auth, "Dialectical Behavior Therapy with couples and families, Guilford Press, in press. **CONTACT ADDRESS** Dept Psychol, Univ of Nevada, Reno, N Virginia Ave, Reno, NV 89557-0001. **EMAIL** aef@unr.edu

FRY, CHRISTINE L.
PERSONAL Born 04/24/1943, m, 1967 **DISCIPLINE** ANTHROPOLOGY **EDUCATION** Wagner Col, NYork, BA, 65; Univ Ariz, MA, 69, PhD, 73. **CAREER** Prof, anthropology, 84-, Loyola Univ Chicago. **HONORS AND AWARDS** Kalish Awd for Innovative Publication, 94. **MEMBERSHIPS** Amer Anthropological Asn; Asn for Anthropology & Gerontology; Gerontological Soc of Amer. **RESEARCH** Aging; older people in communities **SELECTED PUBLICATIONS** Coauth, The Aging Experience: Diversity and Commonality Across Cultures, Sage Pub, 94; art, Kin and Kindred: the First and Last Source of Support, Adult Intergenerational Rel: Effects of Societal Change, Springer Pub, 94; art, Kinship and Individuation, Adult Intergenerational Relations: Effects of Societal Change, Springer Pub, 94; art, Age and the Life Course, Aging Experience: Diversity and commonality Across Cultures, Sage Pub, 94; art, Age, Aging and Culture, Handbook of Aging and the Social Sciences, 4th ed, Academic Press, 95; art, Cross-Cultural Perspectives on Aging, Gerontology: Perspectives & Issues 2nd ed, Springer, 97; art, Culture and the Meaning of a Good Old Age, Cultural Contexts of Aging, 2nd ed, Greenwood Press, 97; art, Anthropological theories of age, Handbook of Theories of Aging, Springer Pub, 98. **CONTACT ADDRESS** Dept of Sociology and Anthropology, Loyola Univ, Chicago, Chicago, IL 60626. **EMAIL** Cfry@luc.edu

FRYE, CHERYL A.
PERSONAL Born 05/05/1966, m, 1991 **DISCIPLINE** PSYCHOLOGY **EDUCATION** Tufts Univ, PhD, 92. **CAREER** Prof, Conn Col, 95-98; Prof, SUNY, 98-. **HONORS AND AWARDS** NSF Career Grant, 96-01. **MEMBERSHIPS** Soc Neuroscience. **RESEARCH** Steroids **CONTACT ADDRESS** Dept Psychol, SUNY Albany, 1400 Washington Ave, Albany, NY 12222-1000. **EMAIL** cafrye@cnsunix.albany.edu

FUKURAI, HIROSHI
PERSONAL Born 10/22/1954, Japan, m, 1992 **DISCIPLINE** SOCIOLOGY, LEGAL STUDIES **EDUCATION** Calif State Univ, BS, 79; Univ Calif at Riverside, MA, 82; PhD, 85. **CAREER** From asst prof to assoc prof, Univ Calif at Santa Cruz, 90-. **MEMBERSHIPS** Am Soc of Criminology, Am Sociol Asn, Am Statistical Asn. **RESEARCH** Law & Society, Statistics, Race Relations, the Pacific Rim. **SELECTED PUBLICATIONS** Coauth, Common Destiny: Japan and the United States in the Global Age, McFarland & Company, Inc. (Jefferson, NC), 90; coauth, Race and Jury: Racial Disenfranchisement and the Search for Justice, Plenum Publ Corp., 93; auth, "Is O. J. Simpson Verdict and Example of Jury Nullification? Jury Verdicts, Legal Concepts, and Jury Performance in a Racially Sensitive Criminal Case," Int J of Applied and Comparative Criminal Justice 22 (98): 185-210; auth, "Social Deconstruction of Race and Affirmative Action in Jury Selection," La Raza Law J (99); auth, "Further affirmative action strategies for racial and ethnic equality in the jury system: The case study of Eugene "Bear" Lincoln trail and the Native American jury," Chican/Latino Law Rev (99); auth, "Rethinking the representative jury requirement: Jury representatives and cross-sectional participation from the beginning to the end of the jury selection process," Int J of Applied and Comparative Criminal Justice (99); auth, "Where did Hispanic jurors go? Computer graphics and statistical analysis of Hispanic participation in grand juries in California," Western Criminology Rev, forthcoming; auth, Anatomy of the McMartin Child Molestation Case: Pretrial Publicity, Jury Selection, Prosecutorial Misconduct, and Future Reforms in Child Sexual Abuse Cases, Harvard Univ Pr, forthcoming; auth, The Racialized Jury Boxes: Affirmative Action in Jury Selection and Racially Mixed Juries, SUNY Univ Pr, forthcoming. **CONTACT ADDRESS** Dept Sociol, Univ of California, Santa Cruz, 1156 High St, Santa Cruz, CA 95064. **EMAIL** hiroshi@cats.ucsc.edu

FULLARD, WILLIAM
DISCIPLINE EDUCATIONAL PSYCHOLOGY **EDUCATION** Haverford Col, AB, 59; Univ PA, AM, 65; PhD, 68. **CAREER** Prof or Educational Psychology, Temple Univ, 82; Ctr Assoc, Ctr for Research in Human Development and Education, Temple Univ, 86. **HONORS AND AWARDS** Postdoctoral Research Fellow, Yale Univ, 68-96. **MEMBERSHIPS** Am Psychological Assoc, Society for Research in Child Development. **RESEARCH** Temperament: Development of assessment instruments for childern and adults, Sexuality: Developemnt of assessment instruments for knowledge, attitudes and behavior in adolescents and yound adults, Adolescent Pregnancy and Parenting: Program development and evaluation: Parenting practices and child outcomes, Child development: Knowledge and attitudes about child development: Effects of early experience, Day Care, Historical perspectives. **SELECTED PUBLICATIONS** Auth, Latent-variable confirmatory factor analysis of the Adolescent Temperament Questionnaire, Journal of Adolescent Research, 10 (95): 246-277; auth, The Sexual Knowledge and Attitude Test for Adolescents, in C.M. Davis, W.L. Yarber, R. Bauseman, G. Shreer, & S.L. Davis eds., Handbook of sexuality-related measures, Thousand Oaks (CA: Sage), 98. **CONTACT ADDRESS** Dept Educational Psychology, Temple Univ, 1301 Cecil B Moore, Philadelphia, PA 19122.

FULLMER, ELISE M.
PERSONAL Born 09/29/1953, Salt Lake City, UT **DISCIPLINE** SOCIAL WORK **EDUCATION** Univ Utah, BS, 85; MSW, 88; SUNY, Albany, PhD, 92. **CAREER** Assoc prof, Univ of NC Charlotte, 92-. **HONORS AND AWARDS** Phi Kappa Phi. **MEMBERSHIPS** NAWS. **RESEARCH** Aging. **SELECTED PUBLICATIONS** Coauth, "Living outside the system: An exploration of older families who do not use day programs", Lifespan development and mental retardation: Implications for individuals, their families, and the human service system, eds M.M. Seltzer, M.W. Krauss and M.;. Janicki, Am Assoc of Mental Retardation, (94), coauth, "Assisting older

families of adults with lifelong disabilities", Enabling Aging Families: Directions for Practice and Policy, eds, G.C. Smith, S. Tobin, E.A. Robertson-Tchabo and P.W. Power, Sage Pub, (Beverly Hills), 95; coauth, "Elderly mothers caring for offspring with mental retardation at home", Am J of Mental Retardation 99, (95): 487-499; auth, "Challenging biases against families of older gays and lesbians", Enabling Aging Families: Directions for Practice and Policy, eds G.C. Smith, S.S. Tobin, E.A. Robertson-Tchabo and P.W. Power, Sage Pub, (Beverly Hills), 95; coauth, "Significant relationships among older women: Cultural and personal constructions of lesbianism", J of Women and Aging 8 3/4, (96): 75-89; coauth, "Older mothers caring for their daughters and sons with mental retardation who do not use day services", J of Physical Develop Disabilities 9, (97): 153-172; coauth, "The effects of offspring gender on older mothers caring for their sons and daughters with mental retardation", The Gerontologist 37.6 (97): 1-9; coauth, "Sexual orientation and occupation as status", Advances in Group Process Vol 15, ed J. Skvoretz, 98; auth, "Working an extra step: Recover and aging of an ethnic minority lesbian", Commun in Recovery: Multiple Perspectives, eds, L.J. Eastland, S. Herndon and Jeanine Barr, Hampton Pr, 99; coauth, "Negating Identity: the Social Construction of Older Lesbians", J of Women and Aging, (forthcoming). **CONTACT ADDRESS** Dept of Soc Work, Univ of No Carolina, Charlotte, 9201 University City, Charlotte, NC 28223.

FUNK, JOEL D.
PERSONAL Born 05/25/1946, New Brunswick, NJ, m, 1972, 3 children **DISCIPLINE** PSYCHOLOGY **EDUCATION** Rutgers Univ, BA, 67; Clark Univ, MA, 74; PhD, 77. **CAREER** Instr to prof, Plymouth State Col, 75-. **HONORS AND AWARDS** Phi Beta Kappa; Phi Kappa Phi. **MEMBERSHIPS** Assoc for Transpersonal Psychol; Soc for Res in Adult Develop. **RESEARCH** Higher States of Development, Near-death experience. **SELECTED PUBLICATIONS** Rev, of "The Moebius Seed" by Steven Rosen, ReVision 8.2 (96): 91-92; auth, "Spiritual development and spiritual pathology II: Person to Person", J of Psychol and Judaism 11.1 (87): 15-29; auth, "The QCS method", Plymouth State Col J on Writing Across the Curric 1.1 (89): 56-63; auth, "Post-formal cognitive theory and developmental stages of musical composition", Adult development 1, Comparisons and applications of adolescent and adult developmental models eds C. Armon, M. Commons, J. Sinnott, F. Richards, Praeger, (NY, 89): 3-30; rev, of "Conscious Evolution" by Janet Lee Mitchell, Anthrop of Consciousness 1.3-4, (90): 35-36; rev, of "What Survives" Contemporary Explorations of Life After Death", J of Near-Death Studies 10.4 (92): 247-253; auth, "Unanimity and disagreement among transpersonal psychologists", Transcendence and mature thought in adulthood: The further reaches of human development", eds M. Miller and S. Cook-Greuter, Rowman and Littlefield, (Lanham, MD, 94): 3-36; auth, "Naturopathic and allopathic healing: a developmental comparison", Townsend Letter for Doctors and Patients, Issue 147, (Oct 95): 50-58; auth, "Inspired Creativity", Creativity, spirituality, and transcendence: Paths to integrity and wisdom in the mature self, eds M. Miller and S. Cook-Greuter, Ablex Pub, (Greenwich, CT, 00): 55-72. **CONTACT ADDRESS** Dept Psychol, Plymouth State Col of the Univ System of New Hampshire, 17 High St, Plymouth, NH 03264. **EMAIL** jfunk@mail.plymouth.edu

FURMAN, DAVID M.
PERSONAL Born 01/14/1960, Erie, PA, m, 1990, 3 children **DISCIPLINE** SOCIAL WORK **EDUCATION** Wheaton Col, BA, 82; Univ Denver, JD, 89; MSW, 89. **CAREER** Public defender, 90-94; attny, 95-, adj prof, lecturer, Denver Univ, 95-, magistrate, Denver Juvenile Court, 99-. **SELECTED PUBLICATIONS** Auth, Law in Social Work Practice 2nd ed, Nelson-Hall: Chicago, 99; auth, "The role of the guardian in juvenile delinquency cases," The Colorado Lawyer, (98): 53-56. **CONTACT ADDRESS** Grad School of Soc Work, Univ of Denver, 2148 S High St, Denver, CO 80210.

G

GABEL, CREIGHTON
PERSONAL Born 04/05/1931, Muskegon, MI, m, 1952, 3 children **DISCIPLINE** ARCHAEOLOGY, ANTHROPOLOGY **EDUCATION** Univ Mich, AB, 53, AM, 54; Univ Edinburgh, PhD(prehist archaeol), 57. **CAREER** From instr to asst prof anthrop, Northwestern Univ, 56-63; assoc prof, 63-69, Prof Anthrop, Boston Univ, 69-, NSF grants, Northern Rhodisia, 60-61 and Kenya, 66-67; res assoc, African Studies Ctr, 63-; chmn anthrop, Boston Univ, 70-72 and 76-; Sr Fulbright Hays award, Liberia, 73. **MEMBERSHIPS** Soc Am Archaeol; S African Archaeol Soc; Soc Africanist Archaeologists Am. **RESEARCH** Prehistoric archaeology Old World, expecially Africa; hunter-gatherers and early agricultural societies. **SELECTED PUBLICATIONS** Ed/contribr, Man Before History, Prentice-Hall Inc, 64; auth, Stone Age Hunters of the Kafue, Boston Univ, 65; analysis of Prehistoric Economic Patterns, Holt,. Rinehart & Winston, 67; co-ed/contribr, Reconstructing African Culture History, Boston Univ, 67. **CONTACT ADDRESS** African Studies Ctr, Boston Univ, 10 Lenox St, Brookline, MA 02146.

GADDY, STEPHANIE
PERSONAL Born 03/18/1959, Normal, IL, m, 1979, 3 children **DISCIPLINE** EDUCATION **EDUCATION** Ill State Univ, BS, 89; MS, 95; ABD- Educ D, 00. **CAREER** Fac, Lincoln Col, 93-. **HONORS AND AWARDS** Kappa Delta Pi Honor Soc, Who's Who of Am Col Teachers. **MEMBERSHIPS** Int Reading Asn, Ill reading Coun, Asn for Supervision and Curric Develop. **RESEARCH** Literacy, Intrinsic motivation, Lifelong learning. **SELECTED PUBLICATIONS** Auth, "Creating a desire to read," Innovations Abstracts (98); auth, "Pow.Wow-Motivating students in writing," Innovations Abstracts (00). **CONTACT ADDRESS** Dept Humanities and Soc Sci, Lincoln Col, 300 Keokuk St, Lincoln, IL 63656. **EMAIL** sagaddy@lincolncollege.edu

GADSDEN, GLORIA Y.
PERSONAL Born 12/30/1968, New York, NY **DISCIPLINE** PSYCHOLOGY, SOCIOLOGY **EDUCATION** Barnard Col, AB; Univ Penn, MA; PhD. **CAREER** Adj prof, Univ Pa, 96-98; lectr, Nassau Comm Col, 97-98; asst prof, Fairleigh Dick Univ, 00-. **HONORS AND AWARDS** Outstand Fac; Heritage Awd. **MEMBERSHIPS** ASA; SWS. **RESEARCH** Gender and sexuality; deviance; race and ethnic relations; family. **SELECTED PUBLICATIONS** Auth, "The Male Voice in Women's Magazines," Gender Issues, 00. **CONTACT ADDRESS** Dept Social Science, Fairleigh Dickinson Univ, Florham-Madison, 285 Madison Ave, Mio5B, Madison, NJ 07940. **EMAIL** gadsden@alpha.fdu.edu

GAFFNEY, PATRICK D.
PERSONAL Born 08/20/1947, Pasco, WA, s **DISCIPLINE** ANTHROPOLOGY **EDUCATION** Univ Notre Dame, BA, 69, MTh, 72; Univ Chicago, MA, 77, PhD, 82. **CAREER** Assoc prof and chair, Univ Notre Dame, 80-; guest prof, Philosophy Center Jinja, Uganda, 92-94. **MEMBERSHIPS** Phi Beta Kappa, Am Anthropol Asn; Middle east Studies Asn, African Studies Asn. **RESEARCH** Religion and politics, human rights, conflict and peace making, Middle East and Africa. **SELECTED PUBLICATIONS** Auth, The Prophet's Pulpit: Islamic Preaching in Contemporary Egypt, Univ Calif (94); coauth, Breaking Cycles of Violence: Conflict Prevention and Intrastate Crisis, Kumarian Press (99). **CONTACT ADDRESS** Dept Anthropol, Univ of Notre Dame, 314 O Shaugnssy Hall, Notre Dame, IN 46556. **EMAIL** Patrick.D.Gaffney.1@nd.edu

GAINEY, RANDY R.
PERSONAL Born 05/11/1963, Atlanta, GA, s **DISCIPLINE** SOCIOLOGY, CRIMINAL JUSTICE **EDUCATION** Univ Wash, PhD, 95. **CAREER** Asst Prof, Old Dom Univ, 95-. **MEMBERSHIPS** Am Soc of Criminology, ASA. **RESEARCH** Fear of crime, sentencing, alternative punishments. **SELECTED PUBLICATIONS** Coauth, "Participation in a Parent Training Program for Methadone Clients," Addictive Behav, 20 (95): 117-125; coauth, "Reducing Parental Risk Factors for Children's Substance Misuse: Preliminary Outcomes with Addicted Parents," Substance Use & Misuse, 32 (97): 699-721; coauth, ""A Meta-Analysis of Patient Factors Associated with Continued Drug Use During and After Treatment for Opiate Addiction," Addiction, 93 (98): 73-92; coauth, "How Monitoring Punishes," J of Offender Monitoring, 12 (99): 23-26; coauth, "Attitudes Towards Electronic Monitoring Among Monitored Offenders and Criminal Justice Students," J of Offender Monitoring, 29 (99): 195-208; coauth, "Electronic Monitoring Directors' Attitudes About Good Time," J of Criminal Justice (forthcoming). **CONTACT ADDRESS** Dept Sociol, Old Dominion Univ, Norfolk, VA 23529.

GALANTER, MARC
PERSONAL Born 02/18/1931, Philadelphia, PA, m, 1967, 3 children **DISCIPLINE** LAW, SOCIOLOGY OF LAW **EDUCATION** Univ Chicago BA, 50, MA, 54, JD, 56. **CAREER** Instr law, Univ Chicago, 56-57; asst prof, Stanford Univ, 58-59; from vis asst prof to assoc prof soc sci, Univ Chicago, 59-71; prof law, State Univ NY Buffalo, 71-76; vis prof, 76-77, Prof Law & S Asian Studies, Law Sch, Univ Wis, 77-; Centennial Prof Law, London Sch of Economics, 00; ed, Law & Soc Rev, 72-76; mem comt on law & soc sci, Soc Sci Res Coun, 75-84; mem adv panel for law & soc sci prog, NSF, 76-78; consult, Ford Found, New Delhi, 81-84; chmn, Int Union Anthrop Ethnol Sci Comn on Folk Law & Legal Pluralism, 81-83; pres, Law & Soc Asn, 83-85; Dir, disputes processing res prog, 84-; Dir, Inst Legal Studies, 90-98. **HONORS AND AWARDS** Kalven Prize, Law & Soc Asn; Hon prof, Nat Law Sch India; Sr fel, Law & Modernization Prog, Yale Univ, 70-71; Nat Endowment for Humanities, 79-80; fel, Van Leer Jerusalem Found, 80; Guggenheim Found fel, 85-86; fel, Center Advan Studies Behavioral Sci, 97-98. **MEMBERSHIPS** Law & Soc Asn; Am Law Inst; Am Acad Arts & Sci. **RESEARCH** Law and soc change; lawyers, litigation; law and relig. **SELECTED PUBLICATIONS** Auth, Religious freedoms in the United States: A turning point, Wis Law Rev, 66; The abolition of disabilities: Untouchability and the law, In: The Untouchables in Contemporary India, Univ Ariz, 72; auth, Why the haves come out ahead: Speculations on the limits of legal change, 74; Justice in many rooms: Courts, private ordering and indigenous law, J Legal Pluralism, 81; Reading the Landscape of Disputes, UCLA Law Rev, 83; Competing Equalities, Law, and the Backward Classes in India, Univ of Calif Press, 1984; Law and Society in Modern India, Oxford Univ Press, 89; Tournament of lawyers, Univ Chicago Press, 91; News from Nowhere, Denver Law Rev, 92; Real World Torts, Md Law Rev, 96. **CONTACT ADDRESS** Law Sch, Univ of Wisconsin, Madison, 975 Bascom Mall, Madison, WI 53706-1301. **EMAIL** msgalant@facstaff.wisc.edu

GALENZA, BRUCE D.
PERSONAL Born 07/08/1950, Camrose, AB, Canada, m, 1988, 3 children **DISCIPLINE** PSYCHOLOGY **EDUCATION** Univ Alberta, PhD, 93. **CAREER** Asst Prof, Univ Alberta, 86-93; Asst Prof, Westmar Univ, 93-97; Asst Prof, Glenville State Col, 97-. **MEMBERSHIPS** Am Psychol Asn. **RESEARCH** Critical thinking in Higher Education. **CONTACT ADDRESS** Dept Soc Sci, Glenville State Col, 200 High St, Glenville, WV 26351. **EMAIL** galenza@glenville.edu

GALVIN, KATHLEEN
PERSONAL Born 07/29/1949, m, 2 children **DISCIPLINE** ANTHROPOLOGY **EDUCATION** Colo State Univ Fort Collins, BA, 71; MA, 79; State Univ NY Binghamton, PhD, 85. **CAREER** Consult, Norweg Agency for Int Develop, Oslo, Norway, Nairobi, Kenya, 85-86; Vis Scientist, Int Lab for Res on Animal Disease, Nairobi, Kenya, 91; From Res Scientists to Sr Res Scientists, Colo State Univ, 85-; From Instr to Assoc Prof, Colo State Univ, 88-; **HONORS AND AWARDS** Distinguished Dissertation Awd in the Soc Sci, State Univ of NY at Binghamton, 85; Vis Res Fel, Univ of Witwatersrand, S Africa, 95-96; Nat Sci Found Fel in Environ Biol, 88; Crash course in Arc View GIS, 98. **MEMBERSHIPS** Am Asn of Phys Anthropologists, Human Biol Asn, Am Anthropol Asn, Soc for Appl Anthrop. **RESEARCH** Human ecology, Human adaptability, Human Dimensions of Global Environmental Change, Arid and semiarid tropical ecosystems, Pastoralism, Household economics, Diet and nutritional status of African pastoralists, International development, Africa, US, Mongolia. **SELECTED PUBLICATIONS** Auth, "Nutritional ecology of pastoralists in dry tropical Africa," Am J of Human Biol 4-2 (92): 209-221; coauth, "Climate patterns and land use practices in the dry zones of east and west Africa," BioScience 44-5 (94): 340-349; coauth, "Global Impact of land use change: Linkages between the social natural sciences," BioScience 44-5 (94): 300-304; co-ed, African pastoralist Systems: AN Integrated Approach, Lynne Rienner (Boulder), 94; auth, "Nomadism," in Encyclopedia of Cultural Anthropology, ed. D> Levinsosn and M. Ember (New York, NY: Henry Holt and Co, 96), 859-863; coauth, "Diet, nutrition and the pastoral strategy," in Nutritional Anthropology: Biocultural Perspectives on Food and Nutrition, ed. A.H. Goodman, D.L. Dufour and G.H. Pelto (Mountain View, CA: Mayfield Publ Co, 99): coauth, "Dietary intake and nutritional status," in Turkana Herders and Dry Savanna. Ecology and biobehavioral response of nomads to an uncertain environment, ed. M.A. Little and P.W. Leslie (Oxford: Oxford Univ Press, 99), 125-245; coauth/panelist, Making Climate Forecasts Matter. Panel on Human Dimensions of Seasonal-to-Interannual Climate Variability, Nat Acad Press (Wash DC), 99; coauth, "Generalizing El Nino effects upon Maasai livestock using hierarchical clusters of vegetation patterns. Photogrammmetric Engineering and Remote Sensing," (in press). **CONTACT ADDRESS** Dept Anthrop, Colorado State Univ, Fort Collins, CO 80523-0001. **EMAIL** kathy@nrel.colostate.edu

GAMACHE, GERALD L.
PERSONAL Born 12/30/1942, Des Moines, IA, s **DISCIPLINE** PSYCHOLOGY **EDUCATION** Pensacola Jr Col, AA, 74; Univ N Fla, BA, 75; MA, 76; Old Dominion Univ, PhD, 86. **CAREER** Adj Fac, Old Dominion Univ, 77-86; Psychologist, U>S. Army, 86-89; Adj Fac, Univ Denver, 89-91; Asst Prof, Flagler Col, 91-. **HONORS AND AWARDS** Phi Delta Kappa; Cert of Achievement, Nat Board for Cert Coun; Psi Chi Nat Honor Soc; Phi Delta Kappa Honor Soc; Fe, Am Col of Forsenic Examiners; Merit Achievement Awd, U.S. Army; Merit Awd, Phi Delta Kappa; Outstanding Young Am. **MEMBERSHIPS** Am Counseling Asn; Am Mental Health Coun Asn; Am Psychol Asn; Am Psychol Soc; Huyman Factors and Ergonomics Soc; Phi Delta Kappa; Psi Chi. **RESEARCH** Organizational performance; Personnel systems; Human performance; Physical abilities and demands analysis; safety systems; human engineering; ground accident analysis; system inadequacies and human error. **SELECTED PUBLICATIONS** Co-auth, Dictionary of Psychometric Terms and Psychometric Tests, Sharenko Press, 96; co-auth, State and Parameter Estimation in Human Engineering, forthcoming; co-auth, Human Factor and Ergonomics in the Workplace, forthcoming. **CONTACT ADDRESS** Dept Soc Sci, Flagler Col, PO Box 1027, Saint Augustine, FL 32085-1027. **EMAIL** gamachj@aug.com

GAMBURD, GERALDINE
PERSONAL Born 01/19/1927, Sodus, NY, w, 1 child **DISCIPLINE** ANTHROPOLOGY **EDUCATION** Univ Rochester, BA, 48; Univ Mich, MA, 58; Columbia Univ, PhD, 72. **CAREER** Anthropol, Goddard Col, 66-67; Instr, SUNY, 70-71; Asst Prof to Prof, Univ Mass, 71-. **HONORS AND AWARDS** Healy Awd, 93; Res Grant, Am Inst of Ceylon Studies, 68; For Lang scholarship, Nat Defense, 67; NY State Regents Scholar-

ship, 64-67, 44-48. **MEMBERSHIPS** Nm Anthropol Asn, Soc for South Asian Studies, Sri Lanka Soc Sci Asn, Urban Studies Asn. **RESEARCH** Peace studies, Sustainable development, Cooperativism. **SELECTED PUBLICATIONS** auth, Understanding Terrorism: Culture and sharing - An essential Relationship; Matters of violence: Reflections on social and Political Violence in Sri Lanka, 97; auth, "Values, Actions and Prerequisites of Peace," International Colloquium of The Alliance for a Responsible and Solidary World, 96; auth, "Violence in Sri Lanka: Its sources and discourses," Second World Congress on Violence and Human Coexistence, 92; auth, "Power and Women's Space in Sri Lanka," Nivedini: A Sri Lankan Feminist Journal, 94; auth, "Understanding Terrorism: Culture and Sharing - An essential Relationship?," PRAVADA, 94; auth, "Sri Lanka: The fallacy of the trickle-down theory or Health, Ecology and Participatory Democracy in Sri Lanka," Lank Guardian, 89. **CONTACT ADDRESS** Dept Anthropol & Sociol, Univ of Massachusetts, Dartmouth, 285 Old Westport Rd, North Dartmouth, MA 02747. **EMAIL** ggamburd@umassd.edu

GANESAN, INDIRA
DISCIPLINE WOMEN'S STUDIES, ENGLISH **EDUCATION** Vassar Col, 82; Univ Iowa, 84. **HONORS AND AWARDS** Phi Beta Kappa; Granta Finalist, 97; Fel, FAWC, Radcliffe Coll. **MEMBERSHIPS** MLA; AWD. **RESEARCH** Creative writing; women's studies; ethnic studies. **SELECTED PUBLICATIONS** Auth, The Journey, Alfred and Knopf, 90; auth, Inheritance, Alfred and Knopf, 98. **CONTACT ADDRESS** Dept Humanities, Long Island Univ, Southampton Col, 239 Montauk Hwy, Southampton, NY 11968-4100. **EMAIL** igaresan@southampton.livnet.edu

GANS, HERBERT J.
PERSONAL Born Cologne, Germany **DISCIPLINE** SOCIOLOGY **EDUCATION** Univ Chicago, 47, MA, Soc & Soc Sci, 50; Univ Pa, PhD, Plan & Soc. **CAREER** Plan, publ & priv agencies, 50-53; lectr, Dept City Plan, Univ Pa, 53-64; assoc/adj prof, Teachers Coll, 64-69; prof, Soc & Plan, Urban Stud & Plan, MIT, 69-71; prof, Sociol, Columbia Univ, 71-85; Robert S Lynd Prof, Columbia Univ, 85-. **HONORS AND AWARDS** Guggenheim fel, 77; German Marshall Fund Fel, 84; Sr Fel, Gannett Ctr for Media studies, 85-86; Visting Scholar, russell sage found, 89; Sr Fel, Media Studies Ctr, 96; Honorary Mem, german Soc, Assn,97. **MEMBERSHIPS** Coun of the Am Soc Assoc. **RESEARCH** Urban & community studies; Urban poverty & antipoverty plan; Social plan, Social politics; Ethnicity. **SELECTED PUBLICATIONS** Auth, The Urban Villagers, Free Press, 62; auth, People and Plans, Basic Books, 68; auth, More Equality, Pantheon Books, 73; auth, Popular Culture and High Culture , Basic Books, (74), rev, 99; auth, Deciding What's News, Pantheon Books, 79; auth, Middle American Individualism, Free Press, (88), rev. in paper back, Oxford Press, 91; auth, People, Plans and Policies: Essays on Poverty, Racism and Other National Urban Problems, Columbia Univ Press and Russell Sage Fndn, 91; auth, The War Against the Poor: The Underclass and Antipoverty Policy, Basic Books, 95; auth, Making Sense of America: Sociological Analyses and Essays, Rowman & Littlefield, 99. **CONTACT ADDRESS** Dept Sociol, Columbia Univ, 404 Fayerweather Hall, New York, NY 10027.

GARAVALIA, LINDA
PERSONAL Born 12/18/1961, Atlanta, GA, m, 1998 **DISCIPLINE** EDUCATIONAL PSYCHOLOGY **EDUCATION** Clemson Univ, BA, 83, MA, 86; Univ SC, PhD, 96. **CAREER** Res asst, Univ SC, 98-99; asst prof, Valdosta State Univ, 96-99; asst prof, Univ MO, Kansas City, 99-. **HONORS AND AWARDS** Outstanding Grad Student Awd, Dept of Ed Psych, Univ SC, 96; Distinguished Res Awd Recipient, SCEPUR, 2000. **MEMBERSHIPS** AERA, APA. **RESEARCH** Self-regulation, motivation, assessment, effective classroom practices. **SELECTED PUBLICATIONS** Coauth with L. S. Schwartz, Ten common classroom practices that undermine student success," Occup Ed Forum, 24 (2), 34-43 (97); coauth with M. Gredler, "Students' perceptions of self-regulatory and other-directed study strategies: A factor analysis," Psychol Reports, 86, 102-108 (2000); coauth with J. Hummel, L. Wiley, and W. Huitt, "The Course Syllabus: Faculty and student perceptions of important syllabus components," J on Excellence in College Teaching (in press). **CONTACT ADDRESS** Sch of Ed, Univ of Missouri, Kansas City, 5100 Rockhill Rd, Kansas City, MO 64110. **EMAIL** Garavalial@umkc.edu

GARCIA, WILLIAM BURRES
PERSONAL Born 07/16/1940, Dallas, TX **DISCIPLINE** MUSIC EDUCATION **EDUCATION** Prairie View A&M Univ, music courses 1958-61; N TX State Univ, BMus 1962, MMus Ed 1965; Univ of IA, PhD 1973; Howard Univ, NEH Fellow 1973-74; Carnegie-Mellon Univ, College Mgmt Prog 1984. **CAREER** Philander Smith Coll, instructor of music 1963-64; Langston Univ, asst prof of music 1965-69; Miles Coll, assoc prof of music 1974-77; Talladega Coll, acting academic vice pres 1982-83; prof of music 1977-, chmn of music dept 1977-, chmn of humanities div 1981-85; Selma Univ, acad dean 1986-. **HONORS AND AWARDS** Doctoral Fellowship Grants S Fellowships Fund Inc 1969-73; Ford Found Fellowship Grant for Dissertations in Ethnic Studies 1971-72; Out-

standing Educators of Amer 1975; lecture, "John Wesley Work, Choral Composer" Ethnic Music Workshop Coll of Fine Arts 1974; lecture "John Wesley Work, Black Amer Composer" Afro-Amer Music Workshop Ctr for African & Afro-Amer Studies Atlanta Univ 1975; paper, "African Elements in Afro-Amer Music" Anniston Museum of Natl History AL 1982. **MEMBERSHIPS** Mem Phi Mu Alpha Sinfonia 1965; bd Div of Higher Educ Disciples of Christ 1978-81; bd Talladega Arts Council 1981-; life mem Amer Choral Dirs Assn; mem Amer Choral Found; mem Amer Musicological Soc; mem Coll Music Soc; mem Intl Heinrich Schutz Soc; mem Natl Assn of Teachers of Singing; mem Thomas Music Study Club of Natl Assn of Negro Musicians. **SELECTED PUBLICATIONS** "Church Music by Black Composers, A Bibliography of Choral Works" Black Perspective in Music 1974. **CONTACT ADDRESS** Academic Dean, Selma Univ, 1501 Lapsley St, Selma, AL 36701.

GARDNER, HOWARD E.
PERSONAL Born 07/11/1943, Scranton, PA, m, 1982, 4 children **DISCIPLINE** PSYCHOLOGY **EDUCATION** Harvard Univ, AB, 65; PhD, 71. **CAREER** Adjunct res prof, Boston Univ Sch of Medicine, 87-; co-dir, Harvard Project Zero, 72-, chair, steering comt, 95-; Adjunct prof, Harvard Univ, 91-, prof of Educ, Harvard Grad Sch of Educ, 86-98, John H. and Elizabeth A. Hobbs Prof of Cognition and Educ, 98-. **HONORS AND AWARDS** Presidential Citation, Am Psychol Asn, 98; The Walker Prize, Museum of Sci, Boston, Mass, 99; Golden Plate Awd, Am Acad of Achievement, Washington, DC, 99; 14 Honorary Doctorates. **MEMBERSHIPS** Authors' Guild, Am Asn for the Advancement of Sci, Nat Acad of Educ, Am Acad of Arts and Scis, Soc for Res in Child Develop, Am Educ Res Asn, Acad of Asphasia, Int Neuropsychol Symposium. **SELECTED PUBLICATIONS** Auth, with the collaboration of E. Laskin, Leading Minds: An anatomy of leadership, NY: Basic Books (95); auth, Extraordinary Minds: Portraits of exceptional individuals and an examination of our extraordinariness, NY: Basic Books (97); auth, The Disciplined Mind: What All Students Should Understand, NY: Simon & Schuster (99); auth, Intelligence Reframed: Multiple Intelligences for the 21st Century, NY: Basic Books (99). **CONTACT ADDRESS** Dept Human Develop, Harvard Univ, 13 Appian Way, Cambridge, MA 02138. **EMAIL** Howard@pz.harvard.edu

GARDNER, RICK M.
PERSONAL Born 08/10/1943, Fresno, CA, m, 1967, 2 children **DISCIPLINE** PSYCHOLOGY **EDUCATION** Univ Nev, MA, 67; PhD, 69. **CAREER** Instr, Univ Nev, 68; Asst Prof, Univ Southern Colo, 69-74; Assoc Prof, Univ Southern Colo, 74-78; Vis Prof, Univ Mainz, 87; Prof, Univ Southern Colo, 78-91; Prof, Univ Colo, 91-. **MEMBERSHIPS** APS. **RESEARCH** Perception, psychophysics, body image. **SELECTED PUBLICATIONS** Coauth, "Influence of Somatotype on Perceived Personality Traits: A Computer-TV Video Approach," J of Soc Behav and Personality 9,3 (94): 555-563; coauth, "A Comparison of Three Psychophysical Techniques for Estimating Body Size Perception," Perceptual & Motor Skills 80 (95): 1379-1390; coauth, "The Role of Sensory and Nonsensory Factors in Body Size Estimations of Eating Disorder Subjects," J of Clin Psychol 52,1 (96): 3-15; auth, "Methodological Issues in Assessment of the Perceptual Component of Body Image Disturbance," Brit J of Psychol 87 (96): 1-11; auth, "Misconceptions About Classical Psychophysics and the Measurement of Response Bias," Perceptual & Motor Skills 84 (97): 587-594; coauth, "Developmental Changes in Children's Body Image," J of Soc Behav and Personality 12,4 (97): 1019-1036; coauth, "Methodological Concerns When Using Silhouettes to Measure Body Image," Perceptual & Motor Skills 86 (98): 387-395; coauth, "Body Size Estimations in Children Six Through Fourteen: A Longitudinal Study," Perceptual & Motor Skills 88 (99): 541-545; coauth, "Gender and Ethnic Differences in Children's Judgements of Perceived and Ideal Body Size in Self and Others," Psychol Record 49 (99): 555-564; coauth, "Body Size Estimations, Body Dissatisfaction and Ideal Size Preferences in Children Six Through Fourteen," J of Youth and Adolescence 28, 5 (99): 603-618. **CONTACT ADDRESS** Dept Psychol, Univ of Colorado, Denver, Campus Box 173, PO Box 173364, Denver, CO 80217.

GARFINKEL, ALAN
PERSONAL Born 09/06/1941, Chicago, IL, m, 1965, 2 children **DISCIPLINE** SPANISH EDUCATION **EDUCATION** Univ Ill, Urbana, BA, 63, MA, 64; Ohio State Univ, PhD(educ), 68. **CAREER** Teacher Span, Waukegan Twp High Sch, Ill, 64-66; asst prof foreign lang educ, Okla State Univ, 69-72; asst prof, 72-74, Assoc Prof Foreign Lang Educ, Purdue Univ, West Lafayette, 72-, Asst Dir, Div Sponsored Prog, 81-85, Ed Notes and News, Mod Lang J, 74--90; prof of Span and edu, Purdue Univ, 93-. **HONORS AND AWARDS** Fulbright, US Dept of State Academic Specialist. **MEMBERSHIPS** Am Coun Teaching Foreign Lang; MLA; Nat Soc Studies Educ; Am Asn Teachers Span & Port; Rotary Int. **RESEARCH** Language teaching methodology and curriculum; language teacher education; continuing education. **SELECTED PUBLICATIONS** Coauth, Explorando en la Cast de los Monstruos, Teacher's Discovery (Auburn Hills, MI), 97; auth, Capitan Cataplum y Sargento Sapo . .., Carlex (Rochester, MI), 00; articles and revs in Hispania, Foreign Lang Annals, and Modern Lang Jrnl. **CONTACT ADDRESS** FLL/SC, Purdue Univ, West Lafayette, West Lafayette, IN 47907-1359. **EMAIL** alangarf@purdue.edu

GARIBALDI, ANTOINE MICHAEL
PERSONAL Born 09/26/1950, New Orleans, LA, s **DISCIPLINE** EDUCATION **EDUCATION** Howard Univ, BA (magna cum laude) 1973; Univ of Minnesota, PhD 1976. **CAREER** Holy Comforter-St Cyprian DC, elem teacher 1972-73; Univ of Minnesota Coll of Educ, rsch asst 1973-75; St Paul Urban League St Acad, principal 1975-77; Natl Inst of Educ, rsch admin 1977-82; Xavier Univ of Louisiana, Dept of Educ, chmn, prof of educ, 82-89, dean, 89-91, College of Arts and Sciences, vice pres for academic affairs, 91-96; Howard Univ, Provost and Chief Academic Officer, 96-00. **HONORS AND AWARDS** Educational Testing Service, Sr Fellow. **MEMBERSHIPS** Amer Psychological Assn (Fellow); Amer Educ Rsch Assn; Assn of Black Psychologists; Phi Delta Kappa; Alpha Phi Alpha; Phi Kappa Phi; pres Univ of Minnesota Black Studies Psychological Assn 1974-75; US Army Sci Bd 1979-83; lecturer Howard Univ School of Educ 1981; assoc editor Amer Educ Rsch Journal 1982-84; consultant US Dept of Educ 1983-85; New Orleans Library Bd 1984-93, chairman, 1991-93; Journal of Negro Education, board of directors; co-chmn, Mayor's Foundation for Educ, 1987-90; co-chmn, educ comm, Urban League of Greater New Orleans, 1984-90; American Library Association; Alpha Kappa Mu, Psi Chi; Center for Education of African-American Males, board of directors, 1991-92; Metropolitan Area Committee, board of directors, 1992-96, education fund board, 1991-96. **SELECTED PUBLICATIONS** Author, works include: The Decline of Teacher Production in Louisiana 1976-83; Attitudes Toward the Profession, 1986; Southern Education Foundation monograph, 1986; Educating Black Male Youth: A Moral and Civic Imperative, 1988; editor: Black Colleges and Universities: Challenges for the Future, 1984; "Teacher Recruitment and Retention: With a Special Focus on Minority Teachers", National Education Association, 1989; co-editor: The Education of African-Americans; more than 70 chapters and articles in professional journals and books. **CONTACT ADDRESS** Educational Testing Service, Rosedale Rd, Princeton, NJ 08541. **EMAIL** agaribaldi@cts.org

GARNER, ROBERTA
PERSONAL m, 2 children **DISCIPLINE** SOCIOLOGY **EDUCATION** Univ of Chicago, AB, 62, AM, 63, PhD, 66. **CAREER** Asst prof, Queens Col, 66-67; asst prof, Barnard Col, 67-69; lectr, Univ of Chicago, 69-71; PROF, DEPAUL UNIV, 71-. **HONORS AND AWARDS** IREX fel, 88; Woodrow Wilson, 63; Phi Beta Kappa, 62. **MEMBERSHIPS** Am Soc Asn. **RESEARCH** Social theory, political sociology; social change; sociology of education; collective behavior. **SELECTED PUBLICATIONS** Auth, Contemporary Movements and Ideologies, McGraw-Hill, 96; coauth, Social Movement Theory and Research: An Annotated Bibliographical Guide, Magill Bibliog, The Scarecrow Press, & Salem Press, 97; ed, Social Theory: Continuity and Confrontation, Peterborough, ON: Broadview Press, 00. **CONTACT ADDRESS** Dept of Sociology, DePaul Univ, 2320 N Kenmore, Chicago, IL 60614. **EMAIL** rgarner@wppost.depaul.edu

GAROFALO, V. JAMES
PERSONAL Born 07/06/1939, Oneida, NY, m, 1966, 4 children **DISCIPLINE** EDUCATION **EDUCATION** Albright Col, BA, 61; Colgate Univ, MAT, 62; Syracuse Univ, PhD, 69. **CAREER** Instr, Columbia Sch of Soc Work, 65-66; Grad Asst, Syracuse Univ, 66-67; Dir, Univ Md, 68-71; Coordr Univ Wis, 74-77; Dir, SUNY, 77-79; Middle Sch Teacher, Who Public Schs, 87-96; Reading Consult, Wyo Public Schs, 96-; Prof, Aquinas Col, 79-. **MEMBERSHIPS** Int Reading Assoc, Mich Reading Assoc, Mich Educ Assoc, Wyo Educ Assoc, Nat Coun of Teachers of English, Friends of Nigeria, Am Indian Sci and Engineering Soc. **SELECTED PUBLICATIONS** Auth, History of the Oneida Carrying place from 1746-1783, Colgate Univ Pr (Hamilton, NY), 62; auth, Reading Instruction for the Agricultural Migrant's Children, SUNY Pr (Geneseo, NY), 66; auth, Standard Achievement Test Norm Tables for Migrant Children, Center for Migrant Studies (Geneseo, NY), 68; auth, Evaluation of Migrant Summer School Programs Supported by the New York Upstate Department of Education, Center for Migrant Studies (Geneseo, NY), 68; auth, A Migrant Teacher's Idea Book, SUNY Pr (Geneseo, NY), 68; auth, Perceptual Disability Screening Test Study, Clarksdale Pr (Clarksdale, MS), 72; auth, University Without Walls-Special Services Report, Univ Wis Pr (Greenbay, WI), 74; auth "Reading Attitudes and Perceptions of 7th-8th Grade Students: Part I of a Research Report," Mich Reading J 28,2 (94): 7-16; auth, "Reading Attitudes and Perceptions of 7th-8th Grade Students: Part II of a Research Report," Mich Reading J 28,2 (95): 29-40; auth, Conductive Education Seven Week Summer Program-1997 Grand Rapids, Michigan: A Description of Behaviors and Attitudes Before and After the Program, Aquinas Col Pr (Grand Rapids, MI), 97; **CONTACT ADDRESS** Dept Educ, Aquinas Col, Michigan, 1607 Robinson Rd, SE, Grand Rapids, MI 49506. **EMAIL** garogv@aquinas.edu

GARRETT, ALINE M.
PERSONAL Born 08/28/1944, Martinville, LA **DISCIPLINE** EDUCATION **EDUCATION** Univ SW LA, BA, 66; Oberlin OH, AM, 68; Univ MA, PhD, 71. **CAREER** Univ of Southwestern LA Lafayette, assoc prof Psychology 71; Univ of MA Amherst, grad res asst; Summer School Faculty USL, teacher 70 & 69; Psychometrist Lafayette Parish Schools, summer 67;

Project Head Start, Lafayette LA, teacher 66; prof and Dept Head, Univ of Louisiana. **HONORS AND AWARDS** Faculty advisor Nat Honor Soc; outstanding black citizen award So Consumers Educ Found Field of Educ, 75; res grant to do family res HEW Office Child Devel, 74-75; SEPA Vist Women Prog, 74-. **MEMBERSHIPS** Am Psychol Asn; Nat Asn Black Psychol; Soc for Res in Child Devel; Psi Chi; SE Psychol Asn; LA Psychol Asn; Nat Council Black Child Devel; Lafayette Chap Epilepsy Found; Alpha Lambda Delta. **CONTACT ADDRESS** Psychology Dept, Univ of Louisiana, Girard Hall Room 206E, PO Box 43131, Lafayette, LA 70504-3131. **EMAIL** psychology@louisiana.edu

GARRETT, GERALD R.
PERSONAL Born Mt. Vernon, WA **DISCIPLINE** SOCIOLOGY, CRIMINOLOGY, ADDICTIONS **EDUCATION** Whitman Col, AB, 62; Washington State Univ, MA, 66; Washington State Univ, PhD, 71. **CAREER** Vis prof, Univ of Alaska, 78; vis prof, Wash State Univ, 77-78, 94, 96, 99; Asst prof to prof , Univ Mass, Dir, grad prog in Applied Sociology, 81-84, Dir, Alcohol & Substance Abuse Studies, 86-, Dir, Center for Criminal Justice, Univ Mass, 92-98. **HONORS AND AWARDS** Distinguished Leadership, International Coalition of Addiction Studied Education; Outstanding Service, Northeastern Asn of Criminal Justice Sciences. **MEMBERSHIPS** Northeastern Asn of Criminal Justice Sci; Int Coalition of Addictions Studies Ed; Eastern Sociological Soc. **RESEARCH** Alcohol and other drugs; homelessness; alcohol/drug-related crime; deviance. **SELECTED PUBLICATIONS** Coauth, Substance Use and Abuse Among UMASS Boston Students, 98; Crime, Justice, and Society, General-Hall Inc, 96; Responding to the Homeless, Plenum Pub, 92; Manny: A Criminal-Addict's Story, Houghton-Mifflin, 77; Women Alone, Lexington Books, 76; auth, Working with the Homeless, Center for Commun Media, 90. **CONTACT ADDRESS** Dept. of Sociology, Univ of Massachusetts, Boston, 100 Morrissey Blvd., Boston, MA 02125-3393. **EMAIL** skymen@juno.com

GARRISON, MARY ELIZABETH
PERSONAL Born 03/30/1960, Vallejo, CA, m, 1986, 2 children **DISCIPLINE** SOCIAL WORK **EDUCATION** Benedictine Col, BA, 82; Iowa State Univ, MS, 84; PhD, 90. **CAREER** Asst Prof, Univ of Akron, 89-93; from Asst to Assoc Prof, La State Univ, 93-. **HONORS AND AWARDS** Fac Teaching Awd, La State Univ Baton Rouge, La State Univ Baton Rouge; Tiger Athletic Found Teaching Awd, Col of Agr. **MEMBERSHIPS** Nat Coun on Family Rel, Grove's Conf on Marriage and Family. **RESEARCH** Family stress and coping. **SELECTED PUBLICATIONS** Coauth, "Nutrition knowledge of health care providers in Lebowa, South Africa: Implications for nutrition services delivery," J of Human Nutrition and Dietetics 10 (97): 295-303; coauth, "Nephrologists' and internal medicine physician's expectations of rental dietitians and general clinical dietitians," J of AM Dietetic Asn 97 (97): 1389-1393; auth, "Family stress process, " La Agr 41 (98): 19-10; coauth, "Assessment of nutrition education needs related to increasing dietary calcium intake in low income Vietnamese mothers using focus group discussions," J of Nutrition and Educ 30 (98): 155-163; coauth, "Examining proximal processes in young children's home environments: A preliminary report," Family and Consumer Sci Res J 27 (98): 3-34; auth, "Determinants of the quality of life in rural families," The J of Rural Health 12 (98): 146-153; coauth, "The influence of daily hassles, managerial behavior, and role balance on health status," Family Econ and Resource Management Biennial 3 (99): 44-45; coauth, "Writing across the curriculum in family and consumer sciences: A curriculum showcase," Family Econ and Resource Management Biennial 3 (99): 65; coauth, "Focus groups discussions: Three examples from family and consumer science research," Family and Consumer Sci Res J 28 (99): 428-450; coauth, "Preserving the family: Marital conflict and domestic violence," in Handbook of Empirical Social Work Practice: Vol 2 (NY: Wiley and Sons), 225-240. **CONTACT ADDRESS** Sch of Human Ecol, La State Univ Baton Rouge, Baton Rouge, LA 70803-0001.

GARRISON, RONILUE B.
PERSONAL Born 03/18/1941, St Joseph, MO, m, 1965, 2 children **DISCIPLINE** EDUCATION **EDUCATION** William Jewell Col, AB, 63; Kans Univ, MS, 66; Univ Mo, EJS, 92; PhD, 97. **CAREER** Teacher, Reg Educ, 63-66; Teacher, Spec Educ, 66-80; Prof, William Jewell Col, 80-. **HONORS AND AWARDS** Christa McAullite Pioneer in Educ Awd, KC North Camber of Commerce. **MEMBERSHIPS** NCTM; ASCD; Phi Delta Kappa; NSTA. **RESEARCH** Curriculum Integration. **CONTACT ADDRESS** Dept Educ, William Jewell Col, 500 College Hill, Liberty, MO 64068.

GARROUTTE, EVA
PERSONAL Born 12/29/1962, Johnson City, NY, s **DISCIPLINE** SOCIOLOGY **EDUCATION** Princeton Univ, PhD, 93 **CAREER** Asst Prof, 92-98, Univ of Tulsa; Prof, 98-pres, Boston Col **HONORS AND AWARDS** Ford Found Fel **MEMBERSHIPS** Am Soc Assoc; Am Acad of relig **RESEARCH** Cultural Analysis; Sociology of Religion; Sociology of Science; Race & Ethnicity **SELECTED PUBLICATIONS** Auth, "When Scientists Saw Ghosts and Why They Stopped," Vocabularies of Public Life, 92; Auth, "American Indian Education and the Ideology of Western Science," Proceedings, 92 **CONTACT ADDRESS** Dept of Sociol, Boston Col, Chestnut Hill, Chestnut Hill, MA 02478. **EMAIL** eva.garroutte@bc.edu

GARTH, PHYLLIS HAM
PERSONAL Born 03/24/1952, Brooklyn, NY, m, 1983, 2 children **DISCIPLINE** SOCIAL WORK **EDUCATION** Olive-Harvey Col, Diploma Art, 72; Roosevelt Univ, BA, 73; Governors State Univ, MA, 75, Univ Chicago, MSW, 90; Northern Ill Univ, EdD, 96. **CAREER** Police officer, Chicago, 77-95; exec dir, PEAP Chicago, 80-88; project training specialist, Harold Wah Col, 89-94; lecturer, Univ Chicago, 94-; asst prof, George Williams Col, 97-. **MEMBERSHIPS** Sisters of Color Intl. **RESEARCH** Intersection of race, class, gender and sexual orientation, Race, Racism and oppression, Human/Cultural diversity. **SELECTED PUBLICATIONS** Auth, "Human Diversity in Law Enforcement, The Intersection of Race, Class and Gender: Implications for Education and Training," Critical Issues in Law Enforcement Education, McGraw-Hill: New York, (in press); auth, "Community Policing in Urban America: Implications for Training and Education," Critical Issues in Law Enforcement Education, McGraw-Hill: New York, (in press); auth, "Feminist Theory and The Social Construction of Knowledge; The Intersection of Race, Class and Gender. An Afrocentric Feminist Educational Perspective," Adult Education Research Conf, Univ Tenn, (94): 25-32; auth, "A New Knowledge: Feminism From An Afrocentric Perspective," Transforming Educational Practice, (94): 8-13; auth, "Community and Institutional Responses to the Youth Gang Problem: Case Studies Based on Field Visits and Other Materials, 90; auth, "The Future of Maxwell Street Market: Community Assistance Panel Report, Chicago, 89. **CONTACT ADDRESS** Dept Social Work, Aurora Univ, 347 S Gladstone, Aurora, IL 60506. **EMAIL** pgarth@admin.aurora.edu

GARY, LAWRENCE E.
PERSONAL Born 05/26/1939, Union Springs, AL, m, 1969, 3 children **DISCIPLINE** SOCIAL WORK **EDUCATION** Tuskegee Inst, BS, 63; Univ Mich, MPA, 64; MSW, 67; PhD, 70. **CAREER** Lecturer to asst prof, Univ Mich, 68-70; asst to VP, Howard Univ, 71-72; assoc prof to full prof, Howard Univ, 72-. **HONORS AND AWARDS** Outstanding Fac Awd, Howard Univ, 72; Publication Awd, NABSE, 83; Labor of Love Awd, Nat Head Start Asn, 84; Alumni Merit Awd, Tuskegee Univ, 91; Distinguished Fac Res Awd, Howard Univ, 95; Distinguished Recent Contrib to Soc Work Awd, CSWE, 96; Excellence Awd for Teaching, Howard Univ, 97. **MEMBERSHIPS** Am Public Health Asn, Coun on Soc Work Educ, Am Orthopsychiatric Asn, Groves Conf on Marriage, Nat Asn of Black Soc Workers, Nat Asn of Soc Workers, Nat Coun on Fam Relations; Soc Welfare Hist Group, Soc for Soc Work and Res. **RESEARCH** Human Behavior, Mental Health, Family and Marriage, Public Policy. **SELECTED PUBLICATIONS** Auth, "The Protective factor model: Strengths oriented prevention for African American families," Cultural Competence for Health Care Professionals Working with African American Communities: Theory and Practice, (98): 81-105; auth, "Correlates of health related behaviors in older African American adults: Implications for health promotion," Family and community Health Journal, (96):43-57; auth, "African American Males perceptions of racial discrimination: A sociocultural analysis," Social Work Research, (95): 207-217; auth, Major depression in a community sample of African Americans," American Journal of Psychiatry, (95): 373-378; auth, "Health Status," The Sociology of African Americans: A Reader, (94): 347-363; auth, "Religious involvement and Health status among African American Males," Journal of the National Medical Association, (94): 825-831; auth, "The history of social work education for Black people 1900-1930," Journal of Sociology and Social Welfare," (94): 67-81; auth, "African American males and success," The Sphinx, (93): 4-7. **CONTACT ADDRESS** Dept Soc Work, Howard Univ, 2400 6th St NW, Washington, DC 20059-0002. **EMAIL** lgary@fac.howard.edu

GATES, BARBARA TIMM
PERSONAL Born 08/04/1936, Sheboygan, WI, d, 2 children **DISCIPLINE** ENGLISH LITERATURE, WOMEN'S STUDIES **EDUCATION** Northwestern Univ, BA, 58; Univ Del, MA, 61; Bryn Mawr Col, PhD(English), 71. **CAREER** Lectr English, Widener Col, 65-67; from asst prof to Alumni Distinguished prof, Univ Del, 71-. **HONORS AND AWARDS** Univ Del res grants, 72, 76, 79 and 81; Danforth assoc, 73-; Lindback Awd for Excellence in Teaching, Univ Del, 74; consult Excellence in Teaching and Distinguished Acad Serv, Dept Educ, Commonwealth Pa, 75-76; Am Philos Soc grant, 76; DIMER res grant, 77; Am Coun Learned Soc grant, 79; Nat Endowment for Humanities grant, 81; fel, Center for Advanced Study, Univ Deleware; E. Arthur Trabant Awd for Promoting Equity at the Univ Deleware, 92; CASE Prof of the Year, Carnegie Found, 95. **MEMBERSHIPS** MLA; AAUP; Dickens Soc; Northeastern Mod Lang Asn; Bronte Soc. **RESEARCH** Victorian literature; early romanticism. **SELECTED PUBLICATIONS** Auth, Victorian Suicide: Mad Crimes and Sad Histories, Princeton Univ Pr (Princeton), 88; ed, Critical Essays on Charlotte Bronte, G. K. Hall (Boston), 89; ed, J of Emily Shore, Univ Va Pr (Charlottsville), 91; co-ed, Natural Eloquence: Women Resinscribe Science, Univ Wisconisn Pr (Madison), 97; auth, Kindred Nature: Victorian and Edwardian Women Tell Nature's Story, Univ Chicago Pr (Chicago), 98; numerous scholarly articles, reviews, and presentations. **CONTACT ADDRESS** Dept of English, Univ of Delaware, Newark, DE 19711.

GATEWOOD, ALGIE C.
PERSONAL Born 12/17/1951, Wadesboro, NC, m, 1973 **DISCIPLINE** EDUCATION **EDUCATION** Livingstone Coll, BA Social Science/History 1970-74; Appalachian State Univ, MA Higher Educ/Coll Admin 1976-77; UNC-Charlotte, Certificate in Guidance & Counseling 1982; North Carolina State University, EdD; 1988-94; Winthrop Univ, School Administration Licensing. **CAREER** Anson Comm Coll, dir of human resources devel, 74-81; dir of inst research, 80-81, acting dean of students, 81-82, dean of students, 82-97; Univ of NC, Gen Admin, 97-. **HONORS AND AWARDS** Bd mem emeritus, Anson Regional Medical Services, 1997; bd mem of the year, Anson Regional Medical Services, 1996; nominated John B. Grenzebach Awd, CASE, 1996; Martin Luther King Jr. Education Awd from Association of Univ. Women of Anson. Honored by establishment of the Dr. A.C. Gatewood Scholarship, Alpha Pi Chi Sorority & Women Action Club. **MEMBERSHIPS** Phi Beta Sigma Fraternity; trustee Ebenezer Baptist Church; 1980-; NC Foundation for Advanced Health Programs, vp; Anson Regional Medical Services, bd mem emeritus; past mem, Anson County Bd of Education; NC Contract Prgms for Denistry, Medicine, and Optometry, comm mem; NC Allied Health Council; NC Trustees Assn, past mem **SELECTED PUBLICATIONS** Auth, "A Model for Assessing the Fund-Raising Effectiveness of Comm Coll Non-profit Foundations in NC"; "A Comparative Analysis & Evaluation of Comm Coll non-profit Foundations in NC," "The Student Recruitment and Retention Manual. **CONTACT ADDRESS** General Administration, Univ of No Carolina, Chapel Hill, UNC Research Triangle Park Bldg, Research Triangle Park, NC 27709. **EMAIL** gatewood@ga.unc.edu

GATHERCOAL, KATHLEEN
PERSONAL Born 11/12/1958, Philadelphia, PA **DISCIPLINE** PSYCHOLOGY **EDUCATION** Franklin & Marshall Col, BA, 81; Case Western Reserve Univ, MA, 85; PhD, 85; Sch Optometry at Univ Calif at Berkeley, post-grad res, 87. **CAREER** Teaching asst, Franklin & Marshall Col, 80-81; res asst, Perceptual Development Lab at Case Western Reserve Univ, 81-85; post grad researcher, Infant Vision Lab at Univ Calif at Berkeley, 85-87; asst prof, Ind University/Purdue Univ at Indianapolis, 87-93; adj asst prof, Ind Univ, 91-93; assoc grad fac, Ind Univ, 92-93; from asst prof to assoc prof, George Fox Col, 93-; Dept of Psychol Co-chair, George Fox Col, 94-96; dir of res for Grad Sch of Clinical Psychol, George Fox Col, 99-. **HONORS AND AWARDS** Psi Chi, 80-; Predoctoral fel, NICHD, 81-85; listed in Who's Who of Am Women; listed in The World's Who of Women. **MEMBERSHIPS** Am Psychol Asn, Western Psychol Asn, Int Soc for Infant Studies, Soc for Res in Child Development, Friends Asn for Higher Educ. **RESEARCH** Infant Face Perception, Post-modern Theory. **SELECTED PUBLICATIONS** Coauth, "Simulus energy does not account for 2-month-olds' face preferences," J of Experimental Psychol: Human Perception and Performance 13 (87): 594-600; auth, "Specific vs. non-specific face recognition device," in Developmental neurocognition: Speech and face processing in the first year of life, eds. B. de Boysson-Bardies, S. de Schonoen, p. Jusczyk, P. Macneilage, & j. Morton (The Netherlands: Kluwer Academic Pub, 93); auth, "Postmodern change and psychology," in Implications of postmodernism for Christian psychological therapy, symposium at the meeting of the Christian Asn for Psychological Studies, 98; auth, "A postmodern theory of self," presented to the Templeton Regional Workshop on Sci and Relig, 98; auth, "A three-dimensional demonstration of embryogenesis," in Teaching demonstrations and activities from Teaching of Psychology, eds. D. Johnson and M.E. Ware (NJ: Lawrence Erlbaum Associates, Inc., in press). **CONTACT ADDRESS** Dept Soc Sci, George Fox Univ, 414 N Meridian St, Newberg, OR 97132. **EMAIL** kgatherc@georgefox.edu

GAVIN, ROSEMARIE JULIE
PERSONAL Born 01/26/1917, Tropico, CA **DISCIPLINE** EDUCATION, ENGLISH **EDUCATION** Univ Calif, Los Angeles, BEd, cum laude, 39; Cath Univ Am, MA, 52; Stanford Univ, PhD(educ), 55. **CAREER** Teacher, Notre Dame High Schs, Calif, 42-51; prof educ & English, Col Notre Dame, Calif, 51-, dir grad studies, 63-, Acad Dean, 68-83, dir teacher educ, 52-70 & evening div, 55-65; deleg, Int Chap of Sisters of Notre Dame de Namur, Rome, 68 & 69; mem bd trustees, Col Notre Dame, Calif & Asn Independent Calif Cols & Univs, 68-. **HONORS AND AWARDS** BEd cum laude. **MEMBERSHIPS** AAUP; Am Asn Higher Educ; Nat Soc Study Educ; Nat Cath Educ Asn. **RESEARCH** Individualized instruction; single campus plan. **SELECTED PUBLICATIONS** Auth, Training Teachers of Secondary School English in Catholic Colleges for Women, Cath Educ Rev, 2/56; Chief Influences Shaping the Poetic Imagery of Thomas Merton, Renascence, 57; Hopkins' The Candle Indoors, Explicator, 2/62. **CONTACT ADDRESS** Col of Notre Dame, 1500 Ralston Ave, Belmont, CA 94002-1997. **EMAIL** Sr.Gavin@cnd.edu

GAYLES-FELTON, ANNE RICHARDSON
PERSONAL Born 06/04/1923, Marshallville, GA, w, 1991 **DISCIPLINE** SECONDARY EDUCATION **EDUCATION** Fort Valley State Col, BS, 43; Columbia Univ, MA, 49; Ind Univ, EdD, 61. **CAREER** Teacher, Lamson Richardson High Sch, 43-44; teacher, Industrial High Sch, 45-46; nursery sch teacher, 46; teacher, Luther Sch, 46-48; teacher, Luther Sch, 48-49; head, dept of sociol at Ark Baptist Col, 49-50; instr, Fort Valley State Col, 50-51; prof & dir of student teaching, Stillman Col, 51-52; instr, Fort Valley State Col, 52-54; asst prof & supvr, 54-57; prof, Fla A & M Univ, 57-; exchange prof, Fla State Univ, 75-78. **HONORS AND AWARDS** Teacher of the Year, Fla A & M Univ, 90-91; Soc Sci Educator Awd, Fort Valley State Col, 92; Dean's Distinguished Academic And Service Awd, Fla A & M Univ, 99; Phi Delta Kappa; Pi Gamma Mu; Alpha Kappa Mu; Kappa Delta Pi; Delta Sigma Theta; Pi Lambda Theta. **MEMBERSHIPS** Asn of Teacher Educators, Int Coun on Educ for Teaching, Soc of Professors of Col Teaching, Am Asn of Cols for Teacher Educ, Nat Asn of Multicultural Educ. **RESEARCH** Multicultural Education, Instructional Improvement in Higher Education/Teacher Education, Professional Laboratory Experiences, Increasing Teaching Effectiveness and Upgrading Student Learning in Secondary Schs. **CONTACT ADDRESS** Dept Secondary Educ, Florida A&M Univ, 1500 Wahnish Way, Tallahassee, FL 32307. **EMAIL** afelton@famu.edu

GEAREY, AMELIA J.
DISCIPLINE CHRISTIAN EDUCATION **EDUCATION** State Univ NYork, BS; Fla State Univ, MS, PhD. **CAREER** Asst prof, 90; asst dir, Ctr Ministry of Tchg; assoc ed, Episcopal Children's Curriculum; assoc prof, 92; dir, Ctr Ministry of Tchg; ed, Episcopal Curriculum for Youth; prof, 00. **SELECTED PUBLICATIONS** Auth, Episcopal Children's Curriculum Director's Guide, Morehouse, 98; The Theological Challenge of Writing Curriculum, Engaging the Curriculum, 97; Young Children and the Expression of Faith, NAES, Worship in Episcopal Schools; Teaching Teenagers: The Joy and the Challenge, Youth and Young Adults. **CONTACT ADDRESS** Virginia Theol Sem, 3737 Seminary Rd, Alexandria, VA 22304. **EMAIL** AGearey@vts.edu

GEARY, DAVID
PERSONAL Born 06/07/1957, Providence, RI, m, 1982, 2 children **DISCIPLINE** PSYCHOLOGY **EDUCATION** Univ Santa Clara, BS, 79; Calif State Univ, MS, 81; Univ Calif, MA, 84; PhD, 86. **CAREER** Visiting Asst Prof, Univ Tex, 86-87; Asst Prof to Prof, Univ MO, 87-. **HONORS AND AWARDS** Excellence for Res Awd, MENSA Foundation, 92; Chancellor's Awd, 96. **MEMBERSHIPS** Am Asn for the Adv of Sci; Am Psychol Soc; Soc for Res in Child Development; Evolution and Human Beh Soc. **RESEARCH** Sexual selection and biological sex differences; Learning disabilities; Intelligence; Development of mathematical competencies. **SELECTED PUBLICATIONS** Auth, "Learning disabilities in elementary mathematics: An overview for educators," Perspectives, 00; co-auth, "Numerical and arithmetical cognition: A longitudinal study of process and concept deficits in children with learning disability," Journal of Experimental Child Psychology, 00; co-auth, "Evolutionary developmental psychology," Child Development, (00): 57-65; auth, "Evolution and proximate expression of human paternal investment," Psychological Bulletin, (00): 55-77; co-auth, "Numerical and arithmetical deficits in learning disabled children: Relation to dyscalculia and dyslexia," Aphasiology, in press; auth, "Sexual selection and sex differences in social cognition," in Biology, society and behavior: Gender differences in cognition, Ablex, in press; co-auth, "Sex differences in spatial cognition, computational fluency, and arithmetical reasoning," Journal of Experimental Child Psychology, in press; auth, "Arithmetical development: Commentary and future directions," in The development of arithmetic concepts and skills: Constructing adaptive expertise, Erlbaum, in press; co-auth, "Mathematics and science achievement: A psychological perspective," in A psychology of education reform: Psychological perspectives on improving America's schools, am Psychol Asn, in press; auth, "Darwinism, schooling, and mathematics: How an understanding of evolution can inform instructional practices," in Curriculum wars: Alternative approaches to reading and mathematics, Brookings Inst, in press. **CONTACT ADDRESS** Dept Psychol, Univ of Missouri, Columbia, McAlester Hall 100B, Columbia, MO 65211-0001.

GEDICKS, ALBERT J.
PERSONAL Born 09/04/1948, New York, NY, s **DISCIPLINE** SOCIOLOGY **EDUCATION** Univ Wis, BA, 72; MS, 74; PhD, 79. **CAREER** From acad staff to prof, Univ Wis La Crosse, 85-. **HONORS AND AWARDS** Phi Kappa Phi, Univ Wis, 70; George Floro Awd for Outstanding Service to the Discipline of Sociol, Wis Sociol Asn, 97; Soc Justice Awd, Wis Community Fund, 97; Friend of Indian Educ Awde, Wis Indian Educ Asn, 97. **MEMBERSHIPS** AM Sociol Asn, Midwest Sociol Soc, Wis Sociol Asn. **RESEARCH** Environmental Sociology, Race and Ethnic Relations, Political Sociology, Sociology of Film. **SELECTED PUBLICATIONS** Auth, The New Resource Wars: Native and Environmental Struggles Against Multinational Corporations, South End (Boston, MA), 93. **CONTACT ADDRESS** Dept Sociol & Anthrop, Univ of Wisconsin, La Crosse, 1725 State Street, La Crosse, WI 54601. **EMAIL** gedicks.albe@uwlax.edu

GEERTZ, CLIFFORD
PERSONAL Born 08/23/1926, San Francisco, CA, m, 1987, 2 children **DISCIPLINE** ANTHROPOLOGY **EDUCATION** Antioch Col, AB 50; Harvard Univ, PhD 56. **CAREER** Univ Chicago, asst prof to prof, anthrop 60-70; Oxford Univ, Eastman prof 78-79; Princeton Univ, prof of soc sci 70-; Harold F Linder, Prof Soc Sci, Inst for Adv Stud 82. **HONORS AND AWARDS** Hon Doctorates from Harvard, Northern, Chicago, Brandeis, Yale, Princeton, Cambridge, Georgetown Universities and from the following Colleges, Bates, Knox, Swarthmore, Williams, and New Sch for Soc Res; Soc Sci Prize, Amer Acad Arts Sci; NBCC Prize; Fukuoka Asian Cultural Prize. **MEMBERSHIPS** Fell, AAAS, APS, NAS; Corresponding Fell, Brit Acad; Hon Fell, Royal Anthro Inst GB and IRE; AAA; Assn for Asian Stud; MESA. **RESEARCH** Econ develop, soc hist, sociology of relig, organization of traditional marketplaces, peasant agriculture. **SELECTED PUBLICATIONS** Auth, Availale Light, 00; After the Fact, 95; Works and Lives, 88; Local Knowledge, 83; The Interpretation of Cultures, 73; Islam Observed, 68. **CONTACT ADDRESS** Sch of Soc Sci, Inst for Advanced Studies, Princeton, NJ 08540. **EMAIL** geertz@ias.edu

GEIER, CONNIE
PERSONAL Born 04/19/1952, SD, m, 1974, 2 children **DISCIPLINE** EDUCATION **EDUCATION** N State Univ, MS; EdD. **CAREER** Asst Prof, N State Univ, 97-. **HONORS AND AWARDS** Outstanding Fac Member of the Year, N State Univ, 99-00; Outstanding Grad Student of the Year, Univ SD, 96-97. **MEMBERSHIPS** Phi Delta Kappa; Asn for Supervision and Curriculum Development. **RESEARCH** Brain-based Learning; Reflective Writing; Assessment. **SELECTED PUBLICATIONS** Auth, "Students' Reflections on the Importance of Children's Literature in Elementary Classrooms," The Reader: Journal of the Arkansas Reading Council, 00; auth, "Student Teachers' Concerns," in Writing for Learning Journal: A Collaborative Writing-Across-the-Curriculum Project, N State Univ, 97. **CONTACT ADDRESS** Dept Elem & Sec Educ, No State Univ, 1200 S Jay St, Aberdeen, SD 57401. **EMAIL** geierc@wolf.northern.edu

GEISELMAN, PAULA
PERSONAL Born 06/30/1944, OH, s **DISCIPLINE** PSYCHOLOGY **EDUCATION** Ohio Univ, AB, 71; MS, 76; Univ Calif, PhD, 83. **CAREER** Adj and Assoc Prof, La State Univ, 91-. **HONORS AND AWARDS** Psi Chi Awd, 69; Sigma Xi, 83; St of La Govr's Awd, 94; Fel, IBNS, 95; Soc for Neuroscience Abstract Awd, SNA, 97. **MEMBERSHIPS** AAAS, WN, NYAS, APA, NAASO, APS. **SELECTED PUBLICATIONS** Coauth, "Perception of Sweetness Intensity Determines Women's Hedonic and Other Perceptual Responsiveness to Chocolate Food," Appetite 31 (98): 37-48; coauth, "Reliability and Validity of a Macronutrient Self-Selection Paradigm and a Food Preference Questionnaire," Psychol and Behav 63:5 (98): 919-928; auth, "Female Sex Hormones in the Control of Food Intake: Relationships to Preferences for Sweet Tastants and Fatty Foods, Especially Chocolate," Women's Health: Prevention is the Best Med (forthcoming); auth, "Interrelationships Among Nutritional, Behavioral and Physiological Aspects of Appetite and Hunger Motivation in the Control of Food Intake and Body Weight," in Meeting the Challenges of the Med and Psychosoc Aspects of Obesity and Weight Control (forthcoming). **CONTACT ADDRESS** Dept Psychol, La State Univ, Baton Rouge, LA 70803-0001.

GEIST, CHARLES R.
PERSONAL Born 10/29/1946, Pasadena, CA, s **DISCIPLINE** PSYCHOLOGY **EDUCATION** Univ San Diego, BS, 68; Univ Mont, MA, 73; PhD, 75. **CAREER** From Assoc Prof to Prof, Univ Alaska, 79-. **HONORS AND AWARDS** Who's Who Among Students in Am Univs, 68; Sigma Xi, 73; Outstanding Young Educ Awd, 78; Psi Chi, 79; Int Book of Hon, 82; Int Men of Achievement, 82; Who's Who in the West, 82. **MEMBERSHIPS** APA, ABS, WPA. **RESEARCH** Psychology, research methods and cross-cultural testing, developmental psychology. **SELECTED PUBLICATIONS** Coauth, "A Comparison of the Psychological characteristics of Smokers, Ex-Smokers and Nonsmokers," J of Clinical Psychol 46 (90): 102-105; coauth, "Latency of Auditory Event-Related Potential P3 Correlates with Forward Digit Span in an Alaskan Subarctic Sample," Perceptual and Motor Skills 72 (91): 820-822; coauth, "Geophysical Variables and Behavior: LXX Testing Electromagnetic Explanations for a Possible Psychokinetic Effect of Therapeutic Touch on Germinating Corn Seed," Psychol Reports 70 (92): 891-896; coauth, "Effect of Second Language Study of Phonemic Discrimination and Auditory Event-Related Potentials in Adults," Perceptual and Motor Skills 87 (98): 447-456; coauth, "Effect of Lavender Aromatherapy on Exercise Recovery," Psychol Reports 88 (98): 756-758; coauth, "Effect of Brief Exposure of Media Advertising on Self-Consciousness and Body Self-Consciousness," Psychol Reports (forthcoming). **CONTACT ADDRESS** Dept Psychol, Univ of Alaska, Fairbanks, PO Box 756480, Fairbanks, AK 99775.

GELBER, STEVEN MICHAEL
PERSONAL Born 02/21/1943, New York, NY, m, 1990, 2 children **DISCIPLINE** AMERICAN SOCIAL & CULTURAL HISTORY **EDUCATION** Cornell Univ, BS, 65; Univ Wis-Madison, MS, 67, PhD, 72. **CAREER** Prof hist, Univ Santa Clara, 69. **MEMBERSHIPS** Orgn Am Hist; AHA. **RESEARCH** Am business thought; cult hist. **SELECTED PUBLICATIONS** Auth, Business Ideology and Black Employment, Addison-Wesley, 73; Black Men and Businessmen, Kennikat, 74; co-auth, New Deal Art: California, de Saisset Mus, 76; auth, California's new deal murals, Calif Hist, 79; Culture of the work place and the rise of baseball, J Social Hist, 82; Their hands are all out playing: business and amateur baseball, 185-1917, Jour Sports Hist, spring 84; The eye of the beholder: Images of California by Dorothea Lange and Russell Lee, Calif Hist, fall 85; Sequoia seminar: Th origins of religious sectarianism, Calif Hist, spring 90; Co-auth (with Martin Cook), Saving the Earth: The history of a middle-class millenarian movement, Univ Calif Press, 90; A job you can't lose: Work and hobbies in the Great Depression, J Social Hist, summer 91; Free market metaphor: The historical dyanics of stamp collecting, Comparative Studies in Society and Hist, 10/92; Do-it-yourself: Constructing, repairing and maintaining domestic masculinity, Am Quart, 3/97; Hobbies: Productive learning and the culture of work in America, Columbia Univ Press, 99. **CONTACT ADDRESS** Dept of Hist, Santa Clara Univ, 500 El Camino Real, Santa Clara, CA 95053-0285. **EMAIL** sgelber@scu.edu

GELFAND, ELISSA DEBORAH
PERSONAL Born 01/26/1949, New York, NY, 1 child **DISCIPLINE** FRENCH STUDIES, WOMEN'S STUDIES **EDUCATION** Barnard Col, BA, 69; Brown Univ, MA, 72, PhD, 75. **CAREER** Prof Eng, Ecole Active Bilingue, Paris, 73-75; asst prof, 75-81, assoc prof, 81-88, Prof French, Mount Holyoke Col, 88-, Dir, Women's Studies Prog, 82-84, 98-, Instr French, Alliance Ft Providence, RI, 71-73; instr English, Int House, Paris, 73; Andrew W Mellon fel interdisciplinary res, 79. **HONORS AND AWARDS** Dorothy Rooke McCulloch Chair in Romance Languages 92-; Faculty Research Fellowship, 88-89. **MEMBERSHIPS** Ed bd, Women in French Studies; Am Asn Tchr(s) Ft; MLA; Northeast Mod Lang Asn; Nat Women's Studies Asn; Women's Caucus Mod Lang. **RESEARCH** Feminist theory, women's and gender studies; prison lit; Interwar French Jewish writers. **SELECTED PUBLICATIONS** Auth, Alberline Sarrazin: A control case for femininity in form, Fr Rev, 12/77; A response to the void: Madame Roland's memoires particuliers and her imprisonment, Romance Notes, 79; translr, texts by B Groult, F Parturier & D Pogg,: In: New French Feminisms, Univ MA Press, 80; auth, Women prison writers in France: Twice criminal, Mod Lang Studies, 80-81; Imprisoned women: Toward a socio-literary feminist analysis, Yale Fr Studie, 81; Imagination in Confinement: Women Writers from French Prisons, Cornell Univ Press, 83; coauth, French Feminist Criticism: An Annotated Bibliography, Garland Press, 85; Albertine Sarvazin, Dictionary of Literary Biography, 89; Gender and Me Rise of te Novel, The French Review, 88; Resetting the Margins: The Outsider in French Literature and Culture, Critical Issues in Foreign Language Instruction, 91; Feminist Criticism, French, Encyclopedia of Contemporary Literary Theory, 93; Clara Malraux, Dictionaire literaire des femmes de langue francaise, 97. **CONTACT ADDRESS** Dept of French, Mount Holyoke Col, 50 College St, South Hadley, MA 01075-1461. **EMAIL** egelfand@mtholyoke.edu

GELHART, ROBERT
PERSONAL Born 06/10/1944, Susanville, CA, m, 1999 **DISCIPLINE** PSYCHOLOGY **EDUCATION** Central Wash State Univ, BEd, 59; Med, 61; Univ Southern Calif, EdD, 68. **CAREER** Asst prof, Northern Colo Univ, 66-68; prof, Univ Nev, 68-75; prof, Pepperdine Univ, 75-. **HONORS AND AWARDS** Luckman Distinguished Teaching Fel, 96-00; Community Leaders of Am; Am Biographical Inst; Who's Who in the West; Marquis Who's Who. **MEMBERSHIPS** The Compendium: Persons of Eminence in the Field of Exceptional Children, Asn Adv Behav Therapy, Academic Therapy Pub. **RESEARCH** Cognitive behavior therapy, Anxiety, Depression. **SELECTED PUBLICATIONS** Auth, Comorbid Risk Factors Influence on Intervention Effectiveness of Cognitive-Behavioral Treatment of Depression (in press); auth, Group Cognitive-Behavioral Therapy of Depression and the Interaction of Demographic Variables, (in press); auth, Expert Witness Report: Saling v Irvine Unified School District Negligent grounds maintenance as the proximate cause of foot injury on school property, Orange County CA, 98; auth, Expert Witness Report: Negligent supervision as the proximate cause of a spine injury during a school supervised extra curricular activity, Ridgecrest CA, 97; auth, Expert Witness Report: Chen v Huntington Beach City School District. Negligent supervision as the proximate cause of a broken nose occurring during a fight in a physical education locker room, Orange County CA, 97; auth, Expert Witness Report: Mora v Capistrano Unified School District Middle-school aged girl sexually attacked by fellow student during teacher absence, Orange County CA, 97; auth, Expert Witness Report: Goldfarb v Orange Unified School District Negligent supervision as the proximate cause of a shoulder injury occurring during a physical education class flag football game, Orange County CA, 96; auth, Expert Witness Report: Wrongful death of an 11 year old boy due to negligent supervision, Los Angeles CA, 96; auth, Expert Witness Report: Negligent supervision as the proximate cause of a head injury to an 11 year old girl during a school supervised soft ball game, Bakersfield CA, 96; auth, Expert Wit-

ness Report: Negligent supervision as the proximate cause of a leg injury during a physical education class, Los Angeles CA, 96. **CONTACT ADDRESS** Dept Psychol, Pepperdine Univ, 400 Corporate Point, Culver City, CA 90230. **EMAIL** rgelhart@pepperdine.edu

GELO, DANIEL J.
PERSONAL Born 02/07/1957, Orange, NJ, m, 1982, 2 children **DISCIPLINE** BEHAVIORAL SCIENCE **EDUCATION** Rutgers Col, BA, 79; Rutgers Univ, MA, 82; Rutgers Univ, MPhil, 83; Rutgers Univ, PhD, 86. **CAREER** Assoc Prof, Univ Tex, 94-. **HONORS AND AWARDS** Distinguished Achievement Awd, Univ Tex, 94; Outstanding Teaching Awd, Univ Tex, 96; Res Grant, Univ Tex, 99; Who's Who in the World; Who's Who in the S and Southwest; Int Who's Who of Professionals; Who's Who Among Am Teachers, Who's Who Among Young Am Professionals; Who's Who Among Emerging Leaders in Am; Who's Who in Sci and Engineering. **MEMBERSHIPS** AAA, AFS, ASE, NAASA. **RESEARCH** American Indian cultures and societies, symbolism. **SELECTED PUBLICATIONS** Auth, "Powwow Patter: Indian Emcee Discourse on Power and Identity," J of Am Folklore 112 (99): 40-57; auth, Comanches in the New West 1896-1908, Tex UP (Austin, TX), 99; auth, "'Comanche Country and Ever Has Been': A Native Geography of the Nineteenth-Century Comancheria," Southwestern Hist Quart (forthcoming); auth, Kickapoo-Comanche Relations and the Texas Frontier, forthcoming; auth, Comanche Belief: Symbol and Knowledge on the Southern Plains, Tex UP (Austin, TX), forthcoming; auth, Indians of the Great Plains, forthcoming. **CONTACT ADDRESS** Dept Behav Sci, Univ of Texas, San Antonio, 6900 N Loop 1604 W, San Antonio, TX 78249. **EMAIL** dgelo@utsa.edu

GEMMILL, ROBERT H.
PERSONAL Born 01/20/1944, Provo, UT, m, 1970, 2 children **DISCIPLINE** SOCIOLOGY **EDUCATION** Univ Ut, BS, 67; BS, 69; MS, 69; Our Lady of the Lake Univ, MSW, 77; Univ Ut, DSW, 85. **CAREER** Asst Prof, Baylor Univ, 71-76; Instructor, Walter Reed Army Med Center, 85-92; Asst Prof, Nat Catholic Sch of Soc Services, 85-92; Asst Prof, Med Col of Ga, 92-; Asst Prof, Augusta State Univ, 98-. **HONORS AND AWARDS** Who's Who Worldwide; Order of Military Med Merit, 92; Prefix A, Army Med Dept, 92; Who's Who Among Human Service Prof, 93. **RESEARCH** Language structure of women and its influence in therapy and evaluation of child abuse cases. **SELECTED PUBLICATIONS** Auth, "Managing Psychosocial Programs," in AIDS: A Health Care Management Response, Aspen Pub, 88; co-auth, "Advocacy function in Social Work Case Management," in Social Work Case Management, Aldine de Gruyter Pub, 92; co-auth, "Social Work Service to Army Repatriated Prisoners of War," The Journal of the United States Army Medical Dept, 92; co-auth, "Social Work Service to Army Repatriated Prisoners of War," in Perspectives on the Gulf War, 93; co-auth, "Look-Back Investigation After Human Immunodeficiency Virus Seroconversion in a Pediatric Dentist," The Journal of Infectious Diseases, (94): 1-8; Auth, Spouse Abuse Manual: Assessment, Diagnosis and Treatment, Cornell Univ Press, 97; auth, Child Abuse Manual: Assessment, Diagnosis and Treatment, Cornell Univ Press, 98. **CONTACT ADDRESS** Dept Sociol, Augusta State Univ, 2500 Walton Way, Augusta, GA 30904. **EMAIL** bobgyap@aol.com

GEMS, GERALD R.
PERSONAL Born 03/21/1947, Chicago, IL, 2 children **DISCIPLINE** PHYSICAL EDUCATION **EDUCATION** Northeastern Ill Univ, BA, 77; Univ Ariz, MS, 80; Univ Md, PhD, 89. **CAREER** Dean of Students Summer Program, Webb Schools, 84-94; Athletic director, Webb Schools, 79-85; Teaching Asst, Univ Md, 85-88; Assoc Prof to Prof and Dept Chair, North Central Col, 88-. **HONORS AND AWARDS** Ill Humanities Coun, "Roads Scholar", 99-00; Dissinger Awd, North Centrl Col, 96; NEH Grant, DePaul Univ, 95; Lilly foundation grant, 92; Phi Alpha Epsilon, Nat Honor Soc, 86-87; Phi Theta Kappac, Nat Honor Soc, 74-75; Dean's Honor List, Mayfair Col, 73-75. **MEMBERSHIPS** Org of Am Hist, Am Alliance for Health, Phys Educ, Recreation and Dance, Nat Asn of Sport and Phys Educ, N Am Soc for Sport Hist, Sport Sociol Acad, Sport Art Acad, Sport Philos Acad, Nat Asn for Girls' and Women's Sport, Curriculum and Instruction Acad, Professional Football Res Asn, Nat Geog Soc, Nat Asn for Ethnic Studies, Chicago Hist Soc. **SELECTED PUBLICATIONS** Auth, For Pride, Profit and Patriarchy: Football and the Incorporation of American Cultural Values, Scarecrow Press, forthcoming; auth, Windy City Wars: Labor, Leisure, and Sport in the Making of Chicago, Scarecrow Press, 97; ed, Sports in North America: A Documentary History, Vol 5, 1880-1900, Academic International Press, 95; auth, "The Rise of Sport at a Jewish Settlement House: The Chicago Hebrew Institute, 1908-1921" in Sports and the American Jew, Syracuse Univ Press, 98; auth, "Selling Sport and Religion in American Society: Bishop Sheil and the Catholic Youth Organization," in The New American Sport History, Univ Ill Press, 96; auth, "Sport in a Multicultural World," in Models of Interdisciplinary, 96; auth, "Sports, War, and Ideological Imperialism," Peace Review, (99): 573-578; auth, "A Response to Playing Indian," American Indian Culture and Research Journal, (99): 133-135; auth, "Montana's Professional Football Team," Coffin Corner, (98): 22-23 **CONTACT ADDRESS** Dept Phys Educ, No Central Col, PO Box 3063, Naperville, IL 60566. **EMAIL** grg@noctrl.edu

GENTRY, ATRON A.
PERSONAL Born El Centro, CA **DISCIPLINE** EDUCATION **EDUCATION** Pasadena City Clge, AA 1958; CA State Polytechnic Clge, 1959; CA State Univ at Los Angeles, BA 1966; Univ of MA, EdD 1970. **CAREER** Apple Creek State Inst OH, asst supr 75-76; Cleveland State Hosp OH, supr 76-78; Hull Clge of Higher Educ Hull England, visiting prof 81; Univ of MA, prof of educ; Visiting Professor in Beijing Tchrs Coll 86. **HONORS AND AWARDS** Citizen of the Year Omega Psi Frat 1967; Urban Srv Awd Ofc of Econ Apport US Govt 1966; Urban Educ The Hope Factor Philadelphia Sounder 1972; The Politics of Urban Educ for the 80's Natl Assn of Sec Schl Principals 1980; Dedication & Service, Boston Secondary School Project l987; The Dr. Carter G. Woodson Memorial Uplift Awd Tau Iota Chapter, Omega Psi Fraternity 1988; Crispus Attucks Awd, National Committee for Commemoration of America's Revolutionary War Black Patriot, 1991. **MEMBERSHIPS** Assc dean Schl of Educ Univ of MA 1971-72, 1972-75, dir of the Center for Urban Educ 1968-71; staff mem 1984 Olympic Games L A Olympic Org Comm 1984; Kentucky Colonel 1974; mem Phi Delta Kappa 1971; Dir of Boston Scndry Schls Project, a collaborative prgm between Univ of Mass at Amherst & Boston Secondary Schls. **SELECTED PUBLICATIONS** Author, Learning to Survive: Black Youth Look for Education and Hope; Co-editor, Equity and Excellence in Education. **CONTACT ADDRESS** Educ Dept, Univ of Massachusetts, Amherst, Amherst, MA 01002.

GEORGE, LUVENIA A.
PERSONAL Born 02/26/1934, Chicago, IL, m, 1953, 2 children **DISCIPLINE** ETHNOMUSICOLOGY **EDUCATION** Howard University, BMEd, 1952; University of Maryland College Park, MEd, 1969; University of Maryland Baltimore County, PhD, 1995. **CAREER** District of Columbia Public Schools, music teacher, 54-92; Smithsonian Institution, research scholar, 93-94, coordinator DE youth proj, 94-. **HONORS AND AWARDS** African-American Museum, Hall of Fame Inductee, 1997. **MEMBERSHIPS** Sargent Presbyterian Church, organist, 1960-, elder, 1991-; District of Columbia Music Education Association, pres, 1970-72; District of Columbia Choral Directors Association, pres, 1978-80. **SELECTED PUBLICATIONS** Author: "Teaching the Music of Six Different Cultures," 2nd ed, 1987; Lucie Campbell in "We'll Understand It Better Bye & Bye," 1992; Duke Ellington: "Composer Beyond Category," 1993; "The Source of African-American Music," 1991. **CONTACT ADDRESS** CProgram in African-American Culture, Smithsonian Inst, 14th & Constitution Ave, NW, Washington, VT 20560. **EMAIL** lgeogal@hotmail.com

GEORGES, ROBERT A.
PERSONAL Born 05/01/1933, Sewickley, PA, m, 1956, 1 child **DISCIPLINE** FOLKLORE, LINGUISTICS **EDUCATION** Ind State Col, BS, 54; Univ Pa, MA, 61; Ind Univ, PhD, 64. **CAREER** Teacher English, Bound Brook High Sch, NJ, 54-56; Southern Regional High Sch, Manahawkin, 58-60; from instr to asst prof English, Univ Kans, 63-66; from asst prof to assoc prof English and folklore, 66-76, vchmn, Folklore and Mythology Group, 67-68, chmn 68-76, PROF ENGLISH and FOLKLORE, UNIV CALIF, LOS ANGELES, 76-, Guggenheim fel, 69-70. **MEMBERSHIPS** MLA; Ling Soc Am; Am Folklore Soc. **RESEARCH** Narrating process; narrative analysis; conceptual foundations of folklore and mythology studies. **SELECTED PUBLICATIONS CONTACT ADDRESS** Folklore and Mythology Studies Univ of Calif Los, Los Angeles, CA 90024.

GERRITZ, E. KEITH
PERSONAL Born 08/26/1937, St Cloud, MN, m, 1959, 4 children **DISCIPLINE** PSYCHOLOGY **EDUCATION** Univ Minnesota, BA, 59; Columbia Univ, PhD, 70. **CAREER** Instr, Grinnell Col, 68-70; asst prof, 70-71; assoc prof, 71-74; prof, Wilmington Col, 75-. **HONORS AND AWARDS** NIMH Fel. **MEMBERSHIPS** APA. **RESEARCH** Teaching of psychology; bystander intervention; social behavior of small rodents in a laboratory open field. **CONTACT ADDRESS** Dept Psychology, Wilmington Col, Ohio, 251 Ludovic St, Wilmington, OH 45177.

GERSON, KATHLEEN
PERSONAL Born 08/06/1947, Montgomery, AL, m, 1981, 1 child **DISCIPLINE** SOCIOLOGY **EDUCATION** Stanford Univ, BA, 69; Univ CA at Berkeley, MA, 74, PhD, 81. **CAREER** Asst prof, 80-87, New York Univ; visiting scholar, Russel Sage Found, 87-88, assoc prof, 88-94, dir of undergraduate studies in sociology, 90-96, prof, 95-present, New York Univ. **HONORS AND AWARDS** NYU Presidential Fel, 85; finalist C. Wright Mills and William J. Goode Book Awds, 86; SWS Feminist Lecturer on Women and Social Change (awarded annually by the Sociologists for Women in Society to a senior scholar who has made a major contribution, 98; research grant, The Alfred P. Sloan Found. **MEMBERSHIPS** Amer Sociol Assn; Easter Sociol Soc; Council on Contemporary Families; Council of Research Advisors, Ctr for Families; Ford Found Project on the Integration of Work, Family, and Community; Sloan Found Research Network on Work Redesign and Work/Family, 95-96; Soc for the Study of Social Problems; Sociologist for Women in Society. **RESEARCH** Gender; the family; families and work; gender and the moral order; Amer Families in transition; the life course and human development; social and individual change processes; qualitative research methods. **SELECTED PUBLICATIONS** Auth, No Man's Land: Men's Changing Commitments to Family and Work, 93; Hard Choices: How Women Decide About Work, Career, and Motherhood, 85; The Social Construction of Fatherhood, in Parenting: Contemporary Issues and Challenges, 97; An Institutional Perspective on Generative Fathering: Creating Social Supports for Parenting Equality, in Generative Fathering: Beyond Deficit Perspectives, 97; Do Americans Feel Overworked? Comparing Actual and Ideal Working Time, in Work and Family: Research Informing Policy, 98; Gender and the Future of the Family: Implications for the Post-Industrial Workplace, pp. 11-21, in Challenges for Work and Family in the 21st Century, 98; Who are the Overworked Americans? Review of Social Economics (Special Issue on The Overworked American Debate, 98; auth, "Resolving Family Dilemmas and Conflicts: Beyond Utopia," Contemporary Sociology, 29, 1: 180-188; auth, "Children of the Gender Revolution," In Restructuring Work and the Life Course," University of Toronto Press. **CONTACT ADDRESS** New York Univ, 269 Mercer St, 4th Fl, New York, NY 10003. **EMAIL** gerson@mail.soc.nyu.edu

GEVIRTZ, RICHARD N.
PERSONAL Born 01/25/1944, Chicago, IL, m, 1969, 2 children **DISCIPLINE** PSYCHOLOGY **EDUCATION** Univ Wisc, BS, 66; De Paul Univ, MA, 69; PhD, 71. **CAREER** Assoc prof, St. Mary's Col, 71-80; prof, Calif School for Professional Psychol, 80-. **HONORS AND AWARDS** BCIA Certificate of Recognition; Phallin Fellow. **MEMBERSHIPS** APA, AAPB, BSC, ISARP. **RESEARCH** Applied psychophysiology. **SELECTED PUBLICATIONS** Coauth with R. Gadler, abstract, "Evaluation of Needle Electromyographic Response to Emotional Stimuli," Applied Psychophysiology and Biofeedback, 22, 137 (97); coauth with S. Banks, D. Jacobs, and D. Hubbard, "Effects of autogenic relaxation training on EMG activity in myofascial trigger points," J of Musculoskeletal Pain, 6, #4 (98); coauth abstract, with P. Humphreys, " A comparison of self-regulation techniques versus dietary fiber alone in the treatment of recurrent abdominal pain (RAP) in children," Applied Psychophysiology and Biofeedback, 23, 118 (98); coauth abstract with B. Wiederhold and M. Wiederhold, "Enhancing treatment of specific phobias with virtual reality and physiological feedback," Applied Psychophysiology and Biofeedback, 24 (2), 140 (99); coauth abstract with M. Stevens, M. Wiederhold, and L. Verity, "Chronic fatique syndrome: A chronobiologically oriented, controlled treatment outcome study," Applied Psychophysiology and Biofeedback, 24 (2), 129 (99); coauth abstraxt with J. Armm, D. Hubbard, and E. Harpin, "The Relationship between personality characteristics and local muscle tenderness development in first year psychology graduate students: A prospective study," Applied Psychophysiology and Biofeedback, 24 (2), 125 (99); coauth abstract with J. Muse, "The effects of a psychological stressor on nEMG activity while performing a typing task in good and poor ergonomic positions," Applied Psychophysiology and Biofeedback, 24 (2), 120 (99); coauth abstract with L. Mertz, "Spectral analysis of heart rate in subtypes of asthmatics," Applied Psychophysiology and Biofeedback, 24 (2), 119 (99); auth, "Physiology of Stress," in D. Kenney, J. Carlson, J. Sheppard, and F. J. McGuigan, eds, Stress and Health: Research and Clinical Applications, Harwood Academic Pubs, Sydney, Australia (2000); auth, "Resonant frequency training to restore homeostasis for treatment of psychophysiological disorders," Biofeedback, 27 (4), 7-9 (2000). **CONTACT ADDRESS** Dept Psychol, California Sch of Professional Psychology, San Diego, 6160 Cornerstone E, San Diego, CA 92121. **EMAIL** rgevirtz@mail.cspp.edu

GHOSH, RATNA
DISCIPLINE EDUCATION **EDUCATION** Univ Calcutta, BA, 60; Univ Calgary, MA, 73, PhD, 76. **CAREER** Vis prof, Univ Calgary, 76-77; vis prof, OISE, 77; asst prof, 77-81, assoc prof, 81-88, Prof, McGill Univ 88-. **HONORS AND AWARDS** Killam predoctoral schol, Univ Calgary, 74; Dame Merit, Order Saint John Jersualem, Knights Malta, 93; Woman Distinction, YWCA, 96. **MEMBERSHIPS** Shastri Indo-Can Inst; Can Human Rights Found; Nat Adv Comt Develop Educ Soc; Comparative & Int Educ Soc. **SELECTED PUBLICATIONS** Auth, Multicultural Policy and Social Integration: South Asian Canadian Women in Indian J Gender Studs, 94; auth, Overview on Women & Development in Women's Studs Encyclopedia, 96; auth, Redefining Multicultural Education, 96. **CONTACT ADDRESS** Dept of Education, McGill Univ, 3700 McTavish St, Montreal, QC, Canada H3A 1Y2. **EMAIL** ghosh@education.mcgill.ca

GIACOBBE, GEORGE A.
PERSONAL Born 11/24/1943, St Louis, MO, m, 1977, 2 children **DISCIPLINE** TEACHER EDUCATION **EDUCATION** Univ Tulsa, BA, 66; Am Univ, MEd, 70; Univ Ga. PhD, 73. **CAREER** Music therapist aide, Hissom Memorial Center, 66-67; clinical psychol tech, Walter Reed Gen Hosp, 68-69; teacher, Tulsa Pub Schools, 72-75; asst prof to assoc prof, Va Commonwealth Univ 75-. **HONORS AND AWARDS** Kappa Delta Pi; Psi Chi; Awd, Charterhouse School, 97; Awd, Nat Asn of Peer Group Agencies. **MEMBERSHIPS** Phi Delta Kappa; Coun for Exceptional Children; Assoc of Teacher Educators.

RESEARCH Success of students with emotional disturbance, music and students with emotional disturbance. **CONTACT ADDRESS** Dept Teacher Educ, Virginia Commonwealth Univ, Oliver Hall, Room 2098, Richmond, VA 23284-2020.

GIBBS, TYSON
DISCIPLINE ANTHROPOLOGY **EDUCATION** Dartmouth Col, BA, 73; Univ Fla, Gainesville, MA, 77, PhD, 79, Certificate in Gerontology, Gerontology Center, 79. **CAREER** Instr, Univ SC, Columbia , 80-81, adjunct asst prof and asst prof, 81-83; asst prof, Dept of Preventative Med, Meharry Medical Col, Nashville, Tenn, and assoc dir, Center on Aging, Academic Affairs, Meharry Medical Col, 83-87; asst prof, Ga State Univ, 91-92; assoc prof, West Ga Col, Carrollton, 92-93; asst prof, Clinical Med, Geriatric Center, Emory Univ Sch of Med, Atlanta, 93-94; asst prof, Inst of Anthropol, Univ North Tex, Denton, 95-97, assoc prof, 98-. **HONORS AND AWARDS** Grad Coun Fel, Univ Fla, Gainesville, 75; Nat Fel Fund, Ford Found, 76-79; Whitney Young Scholar (declined), 79-80; SC Children's Scholar, 82; proj dir, "Gerontology at Meharry Med Col," 84-86; Proj Dir, Private Coun of Atlanta (declined by employer), 94-95; Proj Dir, Nat Cancer Inst, 93-95; Univ N Tex Fac Grant, 95-96; Assoc Dir, Housing & Urban Develop, 97-99. **SELECTED PUBLICATIONS** Auth, A Guide to Ethnic Health Collections in the United States, Greenwood Pubs, Westport, Conn (96); auth, " Issues of Ethnicity and Culture in the Workplace," High Plains Applied Anthropol, 16 (96): 196-202; auth, "Portrait of Minority," in Diversity and Culture, ed Larry Naylor, Bergin and Garvey, Westport, Conn (97); coauth, "Afrocentrism in the 21st Century," The Western J of Black Studies, 21 (97): 173-179; coauth, Division of Education and Research Handbook, Dept of Family Med, Tex Col of Osteopathic Med (99); coauth, Institute of Anthropology Handbook, Inst of Anthropol, Univ N Tex (99); coauth, TAPESTRY Handbook, Office of Equity and Diversity, Univ of N Tex (99). **CONTACT ADDRESS** Sch of Community Service, Univ of No Texas, PO Box 311340, Denton, TX 76203.

GIBSON, JENNIFER
PERSONAL Born 03/30/1972, Stephenville, TX, s, 1 child **DISCIPLINE** PSYCHOLOGY **EDUCATION** Tarleton State Univ, BS, 95; MEd, 97. **CAREER** Lecturer, Tarleton State Univ, 97-. **MEMBERSHIPS** SW Psychol Asn. **CONTACT ADDRESS** Dept Educ & Psychol, Tarleton State Univ, Box T-0820, Stephenville, TX 76402-0001. **EMAIL** jgibson@tarleton.edu

GIELE, JANET Z.
PERSONAL Born 08/23/1934, Mediva, OH, m, 1957, 2 children **DISCIPLINE** SOCIOLOGY **EDUCATION** Earlham Col, AB, 56; Harvard Univ, AM, 58; PhD, 61. **CAREER** Instr, Wellesley Col, 62-70; Fel, Radcliffe Col, 70-75; lecturer to assoc prof, Brandeis Univ, 76-89; prof, Brandeis Univ, founding director to acting dean, Heller School, 90-94; vis scholar, Wellesley Col, 99-00. **HONORS AND AWARDS** Woodrow Wilson Fel, 56-57; Phi Beta Kappa, 62; Bunting Fel, 70-72; Ford Foundation Fac Fel, 74-75; CEW Scholar Awd, 86-87; Gender Roles Grant, 87-88; Outstanding Alumni Awd, 90; German Marshall Fund Res Fel, 92-93; Rockefeller Foundation Resident Fel, 93; Radcliffe Fel, 99. **SELECTED PUBLICATIONS** Auth, Women's Work and Women's Lives: The Continuing Struggle Worldwide, Westview Press: Boulder, 92; auth, Women in the Middle Years: Current Knowledge and Directions for Research and Policy, Wiley: New York, 82; auth, Women and the Future: Changing Sex Roles in Modern America, Free Press: New York, 78; auth, Women:Roles and Status in Eight Countries, Wiley: New York, 77. **CONTACT ADDRESS** Dept Soc Welfare, Brandeis Univ, 415 South St, Waltham, MA 02453. **EMAIL** giele1@brandeis.edu

GIELEN, UWE P.
PERSONAL Born 08/15/1940, Berlin, Germany, s **DISCIPLINE** PSYCHOLOGY **EDUCATION** Wake Forest Univ, MA, 68; Harvard Univ, PhD, 76. **CAREER** From Instr to Asst Prof, CUNY, 73-80; Assoc Prof, St Francis Col, 80-87; Prof, St Francis Col, 87-; Dir, Inst for Int and Cross-Cultural Psychol, St Francis Col, 98-; Vis Prof, Univ Padua, 95-00. **HONORS AND AWARDS** Fel, Am Psychol Assoc; Fel, Am Psychol Soc; Kurt Lewin Awd; Wilhelm Wundt Awd, NY State Psychol Assoc. **MEMBERSHIPS** Int Coun of Psychol, Soc for Cross-Cultural Res, APA, APS. **RESEARCH** International and cross-cultural psychology, moral reasoning, Tibetan Buddhism. **SELECTED PUBLICATIONS** Co-ed, The Kohlberg Legacy for the Helping Professions; co-ed, Psychology in International Perspective: 50 Years of the International Council of Psychologists; co-ed, Cross-Cultural topics in Psychology, 2nd ed; coauth, Advancing Psychology and Its Applications: International Perspectives; coauth, The Family and Family Therapy in International Perspective; co-ed, Psychology in the Arab Countries; coauth, International Approaches to the Family and Family Therapy; co-ed, International Perspectives on Human Development. **CONTACT ADDRESS** Dept Psychol, St. Francis Col, 180 Remsen St, Brooklyn, NY 11201. **EMAIL** ugielen@hotmail.com

GIFFORD, BERNARD R.
PERSONAL Born 05/18/1943, Brooklyn, NY, m **DISCIPLINE** EDUCATION **EDUCATION** Long Island Univ, BS 1965; Univ of Rochester Med Sch, MS 1968; Univ of Rochester Med Sch, PhD 1972. **CAREER** Univ of California at Berkeley, prof, currently; Academic Systems Corp, chmn, currently; Russell Sage Found, resident scholar, beginning 77; New York City Public School System, deputy chancellor & chief of business affairs office 73-77; New York City Rand Inst, pres 72-73. **HONORS AND AWARDS** Phi Beta Kappa. **MEMBERSHIPS** Adv Com, John F Kennedy Inst of Politics, Harvard Univ; bd of visitors, City Coll of NY; bd of trustees, NY Univ; acad adv com, US Naval Academy; consultant, CA Supreme Court, 1978-79; consultant, Asst Sec for Com Planning & Devt, Dept of Housing & Urban Devt, 1979; consultant, Natl Acad of Public Admin, 1979-80; consultant, Natl Inst of Educ; bd of dirs, NY Urban Coalition; bd of trustees, German Marshall Fund of US; editorial bd, Urban Affairs Quarterly; bd of edit advs NY Affairs; editorial bd, NY Educ Quarterly; editorial bd, policy Analysis; appointed adj prof, public admin, Columbia Univ, 1975-77; appointed adj lecturer, Public Policy, John F Kennedy School of Govt, Harvard Univ, 1977-78; appointed adjunct & visiting prof, Dept of Urban Studies &Planning, Hunter Coll, City Univ oY, MA Inst of Tech; US Atomic Energy Comm, Fellow in Nuclear Science, 1965-71. **SELECTED PUBLICATIONS** Co-author, "Revenue Sharing & the Planning Process" 1974; author, "The Urbanization of Poverty: A Preliminary Investigation of Shifts in the Distribution of the Poverty Population by Race Residence & Family Structure," 1980; numerous other publications. **CONTACT ADDRESS** Dept Educ, Univ of California, Berkeley, Tolman Hall, Berkeley, CA 94720.

GILBERT, BENNIE RUTH
PERSONAL d **DISCIPLINE** PSYCHOLOGY **EDUCATION** Univ Kans, PhD, 73. **CAREER** Prof, Stephens Col, 69-. **MEMBERSHIPS** APA **RESEARCH** Social Psychology; Gerontology. **CONTACT ADDRESS** Dept Psychol, Stephens Col, 1200 E Broadway, Columbia, MO 65215-0001. **EMAIL** brgilbert@wc.stephens.edu

GILBERT, EDWARD R.
PERSONAL Born 03/17/1935, Sharon, PA, m, 1959, 4 children **DISCIPLINE** PSYCHOLOGY **EDUCATION** Dickinson Col, BA, 57; Penn State Univ, MS, 58; Temple Univ, EdD, 65. **CAREER** Prof, albright Col, 58-; adj prof, Temple Univ, 62-88; psychol, Personnel Sci Center, 68-; teacher, Wilson School Dist, 70-80; instr, Lancaster Gen Hosp School of Nursing, 81-87. **HONORS AND AWARDS** Phi Delta Kappa; Presidential Citation, 75; Christian R. and Mary F. Lindback Awd, 78; Alpha Sigma Lambda, 85; Bronze Key Awd, 88; Jacob Awd, 88; Alumni Asn Ser Awd, 95; Who's Who among Am Teachers, 98. **MEMBERSHIPS** Citizens Advisory Comm; Blue Spruce Found. **CONTACT ADDRESS** Dept Psychol, Albright Col, PO Box 15234, Reading, PA 19612.

GILBERT, JAMES L.
PERSONAL Born 02/02/1970, Marietta, GA, m, 1996 **DISCIPLINE** PSYCHOLOGY **EDUCATION** Univ W Al, BS, 76; MS, 96. **CAREER** Vis prof, Univ W Al; staff, Pain Treatment Ctr. **HONORS AND AWARDS** EMS Instr of the Year, 97; Prof of the Year, 98. **MEMBERSHIPS** Int Critical Incident Stress Found; Int Assoc of Police Counselors/Chaplains; Amer Psychol Assoc. **RESEARCH** Critical incident stress etiology & treatment. **CONTACT ADDRESS** Pain Treatment Center, 1314 19th Ave., Meridian, MS 39301. **EMAIL** james_805@lycos.com

GILBERT, SANDRA MORTOLA
PERSONAL Born 12/27/1936, New York, NY, m, 1957, 3 children **DISCIPLINE** ENGLISH LITERATURE, WOMEN'S STUDIES **EDUCATION** Cornell Univ, BA, 57; NYork Univ, MA, 61; Columbia Univ, PhD, 68. **CAREER** Assoc prof and prof, Univ of Calif, Davis, 75-85; prof, Princeton Univ, 85-89; prof, Univ of Calif, Davis, 89. **HONORS AND AWARDS** Morrison Poetry Prize, Cornell Univ, 55; Guilford Essay Prize, Cornell Univ, 57; Van Rensselaer Poetry Prize, Columbia Univ, 64; Res Asst grant, CA State Hayward Found, 69-70; IN Univ Summer Fac Fel, 74; Univ CA Hum Inst, summer 76, 78; Finalist, Assoc Writing Prog Contest, 76-77; Univ CA Prog Develop Award, summer 79; Nominee, Nat Bk Critics' Circle Award, 80; Runner-up, Pulitzer Prize in Non-Fiction, 80; Eunice Tietjens Mem Prize, Poetry, 80; NEH Summer Seminar, Univ Calif Davis, summer 81; Univ CA Tchg Develop Award, summer 81; Gildersleeve Professorship, Barnard Col, Columbia Univ, fall 82; Joseph Warren Beach Lectr, Univ MN, May 84; Fac, School of Criticism & Theory, Northwestern Univ, Summer 84; USA Today, People Who Made a Difference, 85; Ms., Woman of the Year Award, 86; D. Litt., Wesleyan Univ, June 88; Paley Lectr, The Hebrew Univ, Jerusalem, 90; Charity Randall Award, Int Poetry Found, 1/90; Danz lectr, Univ WA Seattle, 92; Paterson Prize, 95; Union League Prize, 96; Fel, Am Acad Arts and Sci, 97. **MEMBERSHIPS** MLA. **RESEARCH** Nineteenth & 20th century Brit lit; mod poetry; feminist critical theory. **SELECTED PUBLICATIONS** Auth, Acts of Attention: The Poems of D.H. Lawrence, Cornell, 73; revised ed, Southern Illinois, 90; coauth, The Madwoman in the Attic: The Woman Writer and the Nineteenth-Century Literary Imagination, Yale, 79; auth, In the Fourth World: Poems, Alabama/AWP Poetry Series, 79; co-ed, Shakespeare's Sisters: feminist Essays on Women Poets, IU, 79; auth, The Summer Kitchen: Poems, Heyeck, 83; auth, Emily's Bread: Poems, Norton, 84; auth, Kate Chopin's The Awakening and Selected Stories, Penguin, 84; co-ed, The Norton Anthology of Literature by Women: The Tradition in English, Norton, 85; co-edd, A Guide to the Norton Anthology of Literature by Women, 85; co-ed, No Man's Land: The Place of the Woman Writer in the Twentieth Century, Vol. I, The War of the Words, Yale, 87. **CONTACT ADDRESS** Dept of Eng, Univ of California, Davis, Davis, CA 95616-5200. **EMAIL** sgilbert@ucdavis.edu

GILES, JERRY
PERSONAL Born 01/02/1943, Manti, UT, m, 1967, 8 children **DISCIPLINE** LEARNING ENHANCEMENT **EDUCATION** BA, Univ Utah, 68; MA, 71; Trades and Industry Certificate, Salt Lake Community Col, 75. **CAREER** Teacher, Granite Sch District, 68-72; instr to prof, Salt Lake Community Col, 72-; instr, Management Systems Corp, 85-86; instr, Univ of Phoenix Utah Division, 86-. **HONORS AND AWARDS** Teaching Excellence Awd, Salt Lake Community Col, 86; NISOD Teaching Excellence Awd, 94; Local Service Awd, Ut Asn for Adult, Community, and Continuing Educ, 98. **MEMBERSHIPS** ASCD, NADE, SWADE, UAACCE. **RESEARCH** Brain Research Applied to Education, Multiple Intelligences. **SELECTED PUBLICATIONS** Auth, The Vicious Circle of Life: Who Made Up These Rules Anyway?, 88; auth, Personal Productivity Planner (software), 88; auth, "Creative Values and Self-Image," ERIC, 95. **CONTACT ADDRESS** Dept Developmental Educ, Salt Lake Comm Col, 4600 S Redwood Rd, Salt Lake City, UT 84123-3145. **EMAIL** gilesje@slcc.edu

GILES, LINDA
PERSONAL Born Bloomington, IL, s **DISCIPLINE** ANTHROPOLOGY **EDUCATION** Univ Pittsburgh, BA, 70; Univ Tex Austin, MA, 76; PhD, 89. **CAREER** Asst prof, Il State Univ, 90-. **HONORS AND AWARDS** Fel, Wenner-Gren Found for Anthrop Res; Fel, Am Asn of Univ Women; Fel, NSF; Fel, Soc Sci Res Coun; Fel, Fulbright-Hayes. **MEMBERSHIPS** Am Anthrop Assoc; African Studies Assoc. **RESEARCH** Spirit possession, Swahili coastal area in East Africa, religion and symbolic students, African art and artifacts. **SELECTED PUBLICATIONS** Auth, "Possession Cults on the Swahili Coast: A Re-examination of Theories of Marginality", Africa 57.2 (87): 234-58; auth, "The Dialectic of Spirit Production: A Cross-Cultural Dialogue", Mankind Quarterly XXIX.3 (89): 243-65; rev, "Politics and Spirit Possession", of The Possessed and Dispossessed: Spirits, Identity, And Power in a Madagascar Migrant Town by Lesley Sharp, Am Anthrop 93.3 (95): 577-78; auth, "Sociocultural Change and Spirit Possession on the Swahili Coast of East Africa", Anthrop Quarterly 68.2 (95): 89-106; coauth, The African Collection: Art and Artifacts at Illinois State University, CD-ROM, IL State Univ, 96; auth, "Spirit Possession and the Symbolic Construction of Swahili Society", in Spirit Possession, Modernity, and Power, eds Heike Behrend and Ute Luig, James Curry, (London), 99. **CONTACT ADDRESS** Dept Sociol and Anthrop, Illinois State Univ, 1 Campus, Box 4660, Normal, IL 61790-4660. **EMAIL** llgiles@mail.ilstu.edu

GILGEN, ALBERT R.
PERSONAL Born 09/19/1930, Akron, OH, m, 1954, 3 children **DISCIPLINE** PSYCHOLOGY **EDUCATION** Princeton Univ, BA, 52; Kent State, MA, 63; Mich State, PhD, 65. **CAREER** Beloit Col, asst, assoc prof, 65-73; Univ Northern Iowa, prof dept hd, Psych, 73-93, prof, 93-. **HONORS AND AWARDS** Fulbright Hays Exch Lectr, Galway Ireland; Distg Schol, Univ N Iowa. **MEMBERSHIPS** APA (Fellow), APS (Fellow), Who's Who in America. **RESEARCH** Hist of Psychol **SELECTED PUBLICATIONS** Auth, American Psychology since World War II: A Profile of the Discipline, 82, Westportauth, International Handbook of Psychology, 87, Gilgen, A.R. and Gilgen, C.K. (Eds.) Westport, CT. Greenwood Press; Soviet and American Psychology during World War II, with C K Carol, VA Koltsova, Y N Olenik, Westport CT Greenwood Press, 97; Post Soviet Perspectives on Russian Psychology, with V A Koltsova, Y N Olenik, C K Gilgen, Westport Ct Greenwood Press, 96; Chaos Theory in Psychology, with F D Abraham, eds, Westport CT Greenwood Press, 95. **CONTACT ADDRESS** Dept Psychology, Univ of No Iowa, Cedar Falls, IA 50613. **EMAIL** albert.gilgen@uni.edu

GILL, DAVID G.
PERSONAL Born 03/16/1924, Vienna, Austria, m, 1947, 2 children **DISCIPLINE** SOCIAL WELFARE **EDUCATION** Hebrew Univ, Israel, BA, 57; Univ Penn, MSW, 58; DSW, 63. **CAREER** Asst prof to prof, Brandeis Univ, 64-; vis prof, Washington Univ, 75-. **HONORS AND AWARDS** UN Schl; US Child Bureau res Gnt; Levinson Found Res Gnt; Human Ser Awd, 99; NASW Soc Wkr of the year Awd,00. **MEMBERSHIPS** NASW; AOA. **RESEARCH** Social economic justice; humanization of work; prevention of domination and exploitation; prevention of structural violence. **SELECTED PUBLICATIONS** Auth, Violence Against Children, Harvard Univ Press, 70, 73; auth, Unraveling Social Policy, Schenkman, 73, 76, 81, 90, 92; auth, The Challenge of Social Equity, Schenk-

man, 76; auth, Beyond the Jungle, Schenkman and G K Hall, 79; auth, Confronting Justice and Oppression, Columbia Univ Press, 79; ed, Child Abuse and Violence, AMS Press, 79; co-ed, Toward Social and Economic Justice, Schenkman, 85; co-ed, The Future of Work, Schenkman, 87. **CONTACT ADDRESS** Dept Social Welfare, Brandeis Univ, 415 South St, Waltham, MA 02453. **EMAIL** gil@binah.cc.brandeis.edu

GILL, DIANE L.
PERSONAL Born 11/07/1948, Watertown, NY, s **DISCIPLINE** PSYCHOLOGY, SPORT STUDIES **EDUCATION** SUNY Cortland, BS, 70; Univ Ill Urbana-Champaign, MS, 74; PhD, 76. **CAREER** Univ of Waterloo Dept of Kinesiology, 76-78; Univ of Iowa, 79-86; Univ of NC at Greensboro, Dept of Exercises and Sport Sci, 87-. **HONORS AND AWARDS** Distinguished Alumni, SUNY Cartland, 91; Southern District AAMPERD Scholar, 96-97; Nat Asn for Girls and Women's Sports NC Pathfinder Awd, 97-98. **MEMBERSHIPS** Am Psychol asn, Asn for the Advancement of Appl Sport Psychology, N Am Soc for Psychology and Sport and Phys Activ. **RESEARCH** Social Psychology of Sport and Exercise, Gender and Cultural Diversity. **SELECTED PUBLICATIONS** Auth, Psychological dynamic of sport and exercise, 2nd ed, 00; articles in J of Sport and Exercise Psychology, The Sport Psychol, Sex Roles, Res Quart for Exercise and Sport. **CONTACT ADDRESS** Dept of Exercises and Sport Sci, Univ of No Carolina, Greensboro, PO Box 26169, Greensboro, NC 27402-6169. **EMAIL** diane_gill@uncg.edu

GILLETT, MARGARET
PERSONAL Born Wingham, Australia **DISCIPLINE** EDUCATION **EDUCATION** Univ Sydney, BA, 50, Dip Educ, 51; New South Wales Tchr Cert, 52; Russell Sage, Troy, NY, MA, 58; Columbia Univ, EdD, 61. **CAREER** Tchr, Eng & Hist, 51-53, educ off, 54-57, Australia; asst prof, educ, Dalhousie Univ, 61-62; assoc prof, educ, 64-67, ch, dept hist & philos educ, 66-68, prof, 67-82, Macdonald Prof Educ, 82-94, Prof Emer, McGill Univ, 95-. **HONORS AND AWARDS** 75th Anniversary Medal, contrib feminism & higher educ Women, Russell Sage NY, 91; Women Distinction, YWCA, 94; LLD, Univ Sask, 88. **MEMBERSHIPS** Comp Int Educ Soc Can; Am Educ Studs Asn; Can Hist Educ Asn; Can Res Inst Advan Women; Can Women's Studs Asn. **SELECTED PUBLICATIONS** Auth, A History of Education: Thought and Practice, 66; auth, We Walked Very Warily: A History of Women at McGill, 81; auth, Dear Grace: A Romance of History, 86; coauth, A Fair Shake Revisited, 96. **CONTACT ADDRESS** 3700 McTavish St, Montreal, QC, Canada H3A 1Y2. **EMAIL** ingi@musich.mcgill.ca

GILMARTIN, BRIAN G.
PERSONAL Born 05/18/1940, Newark, NJ, s **DISCIPLINE** PSYCHOLOGY **EDUCATION** Univ CO, BA, 62; Univ Utah, MS, 65; Univ Iowa, PhD, 76. **CAREER** Asst prof, Humboldt State Univ, 69-73; vis prof, Va Tech Univ, 75-76; vis prof, Auburn Univ, 79-80; asst prof, Westfield State Univ, 80-87; vis prof, E Tenn State Univ, 87-88; prof, Montana State Univ, 88-. **RESEARCH** Shyness; parenting; effects of dog ownership on family life and on morale; neuropsychology of personality; book and several articles on sexual spouse sharing. **SELECTED PUBLICATIONS** Auth, Inside Swinging Families: The Gilmartin report (78); auth, Shyness and Love (87); auth, The Shy Man Syndrome (89). **CONTACT ADDRESS** Dept Humanities and Soc Sci, Montana State Univ, Northern, PO Box 7751, Havre, MT 59501.

GILSON, JOAN
PERSONAL Born 08/20/1945, Kansas City, MO, m, 1965, 2 children **DISCIPLINE** HIGHER EDUCATION ADMINISTRATION, ENGLISH LANGUAGE, LITERATURE **EDUCATION** Univ Ark, BA, 65; Univ Missou, MA, 85; PhD, 94. **CAREER** Instr, Univ Missou, 82-95; adj assoc prof, John CCC, 95-. **HONORS AND AWARDS** Sosland Awd; Helen Kemper Doc Fel; Outstand Edu Diss; Leiberman Awd. **RESEARCH** Teaching of writing; organizational cultures. **SELECTED PUBLICATIONS** Auth, "The Service Learning Journal: A Resource Guide for Teachers," Am Asn Comm Coll (99); auth, From Weet to RW Jones: Letters from Home, 1861-1863 (93); auth, "An Overview of Student Development Theories: Their Relevance for Today's Student, " ERIC (91); auth, "Reconstructive Reflective Teaching: A Review of the Literature," ERIC (90); auth, "Values Education: Collaborative Efforts Between Academic Affairs and Student Services," ERIC (90); auth, "The Written English Proficiency Test at The University of Missouri-Kansas City," ERIC (91); coauth, "Collaborative Revision Groups and the Basic Writer," ERIC (88). **CONTACT ADDRESS** Dept Communications, Johnson County Comm Col, 12345 College Blvd, Shawnee-Mission, KS 66210-1283. **EMAIL** jgilson@jccc.net

GINSBERG, ELAINE KANER
PERSONAL Born 02/29/1936, New York, NY, d, 3 children **DISCIPLINE** AMERICAN LITERATURE, WOMEN WRITERS **EDUCATION** Trinity Univ, BA, 57; Univ Okla, MA, 66, PhD(English), 71. **CAREER** Instr, Univ Okla, 67-68; asst prof, 68-75, assoc prof English, 75-84, chmn dept, 78-84; asst vp, W VA Univ, 84-89; fel, Am Antiquarian Soc, 76, 90; chair, Grad Studies Forum, SAtlantic Mod Lang Asn, 81-82; evaluator, Humanities Found of WVa, 81-; consultant Evaluator, North Cen Assn of Cols and Schools, 89. **MEMBERSHIPS** MLA; Am Studies Asn; pres Women's Caucus of Mod Lang Assn, 98. **RESEARCH** American fiction; British and American women writers; Colonial American literature. **SELECTED PUBLICATIONS** Auth, The female initiation theme in American literature, Studies in Am Fiction, 75; Style and identification in Common Sense, WVa Philol Papers, 77; contribr, American Literature, 1764-1789, Univ Wis Press, 77; American Women Writers: A Critical Reference Guide, Vols I, II & IV, Frederick Ungar Publ Co, 79-82; Toward the Second Decade, Greenwood Press, 81; co-ed, Virginia Woolf: Centennial Essays, Whitston Publ Co, Inc, 83; contrib Anti-Feminism in the Acedemy, Fuoutlege, 96; ed, Passing and the Fictions of Identity, Duke Univ Pr, 96. **CONTACT ADDRESS** Dept of English, West Virginia Univ, Morgantown, PO Box 6296, Morgantown, WV 26506-6296. **EMAIL** eginsber@wvu.edu

GINSBERG, LEON
PERSONAL Born 01/14/1936, San Antonio, TX, m, 1983, 5 children **DISCIPLINE** SOCIAL WORK **EDUCATION** Trinity Univ, BA, 57; Tulane Univ, MSW, 59; Univ Okla, PhD, 66. **CAREER** Asst Prof to Assoc Prof, Univ Okla, 63-68; Prof and Dean, WV Univ, 68-84; Distinguished Prof and Chancellor, Univ SC, 84-. **HONORS AND AWARDS** Distinguished West Virginian, 84; Outstanding Alumni, Tulane Univ, 89; Rhoda G Sarnal Awd, Nat Asn of Soc Workers, 98. **MEMBERSHIPS** Nat Asn of Soc Workers, Coun Soc Work Educ. **RESEARCH** Social policy; Social research **SELECTED PUBLICATIONS** Co-ed, New Management in Human Services, 2nd ed, NASW Press; auth, Social Work Almanac 2nd ed, NASW Press, 95; auth, Social Work in Rural Communities 3rd ed, VA Coun on Soc Work Educ, 98; auth, Careers in Social Work, Allyn and Bacon, 98; auth, Conservative Social Welfare Policy, Nelson-Hall, 98; auth, Understanding Social Problems, Policies, and Programs 3rd ed, Univ SC Press, 99. **CONTACT ADDRESS** Dept Soc Work, Univ of So Carolina, Columbia, Columbia, SC 29225-0001. **EMAIL** leon.ginsberg@sc.edu

GISH, NANCY K.
PERSONAL Born 09/28/1942, Circleville, OH **DISCIPLINE** ENGLISH AND WOMAN'S STUDIES **EDUCATION** PhD, Eng, Univ Michigan, 73. **CAREER** Univ Southern Maine, Dir woman's Studies Prog, 95-, Prof, 85, Assoc Prof, 82-85, Asst Prof, 80-82; Dir Womans Studies, 87-89, Acting Dir Women's Studies Prog, Univ So ME, 85-86; Asst Prof, Univ Penn, 73-79; Coordin Rhetoric Inst, Univ Penn, 78-79; Lect, Univ Michigan, 72-73; Instr, Wayne State Univ, 66-72. **HONORS AND AWARDS** Russell Chair in Edu and Philos, 92-94; Schol to Sch of Criticism and Theory, 87; Univ southern ME Summer Faculty Fellowship, 84; Convocation Schol, 82-83; NEH Fellow, 79-80. **MEMBERSHIPS** MLA; ME Women's Studies Consortium. **RESEARCH** Mod and Contemp Poetry; Ident and Subjectivity; Scot Lit and Cult; Women's Poetry; Cross-cultural poetic Experimentation. **SELECTED PUBLICATIONS** Hugh MacDiarmid: Man and Poet, Nat Poet Found, Orono, Univ Edinburgh P, Edinburgh, 92; The Waste Land: A Poem of Memory and Desire, Twyane, Boston, 88; Hugh MacDiarmid: The Man and His Work, Macmillan, London, 84; Time in the Poetry of T S Elliot, Macmillan, London, 81. **CONTACT ADDRESS** 53 Lawn Ave, Portland, ME 04103. **EMAIL** ngish@usm.maine.edu

GITTINS, ANTHONY
PERSONAL Born 02/16/1943, Manchester, United Kingdom, s **DISCIPLINE** THEOLOGY, ANTHROPOLOGY **EDUCATION** Edinburgh, Scotland, MA, Soc Anthropol, 72, MA, Linguistics, PhD, Anthropol, 77. **CAREER** Head of Mission Dept, Missionary Inst London, 80-84; assoc prof, Cath Theol Union, Chicago, 84-90, prof, 90-98, Bishop Fx Ford Prof (Chair), 98-. **HONORS AND AWARDS** Frai Fel, Royal Anthropol Inst; Bishop Fx, Ford Prof of Missiology. **MEMBERSHIPS** RAI, ASA, CTSA, AAA, AMS, APS, MWPM. **RESEARCH** Inculturation; theological method; contemporary theology in Africa; theological anthropology. **SELECTED PUBLICATIONS** Auth, Bread for the Journey, Orbis (93); auth, Gifts and Strangers, Paulist (98); auth, Reading the Clouds, Liguori (99); auth, Life and Death Matters, Steyler (2000). **CONTACT ADDRESS** Dept Theol, Catholic Theol Union at Chicago, 5401 S Cornell Ave, Chicago, IL 60615-5664. **EMAIL** tgittins@ctu.edu

GLADDEN, JOHN W.
PERSONAL Born 01/17/1937, McAlester, OK, m, 1988, 1 child **DISCIPLINE** PSYCHOLOGY **EDUCATION** Univ Okla, BA, 58; Okla State Univ, MS, 60; PhD, 65. **CAREER** Assoc Prof, Tex Tech Univ, 66-67; Superintendent, Lubbock State Sch, 66-85; Chief Psychol, Pauls Valley State Sch, 85-88; Adj Fac, Tarleton Univ, 91-. **HONORS AND AWARDS** Fel, AAMR. **MEMBERSHIPS** AAMR. **RESEARCH** Mental Retardation; Psychopathology. **CONTACT ADDRESS** Dept Soc & Beh Sci, Tarleton State Univ, Box 1416, Killeen, TX 76540. **EMAIL** j-kgladden@htcomp.net

GLASCO, ANITA L.
PERSONAL Born 10/24/1942, Kansas City, KS **DISCIPLINE** EDUCATION **EDUCATION** U Univ So CA, AB 1964; Harvard Univ Law Sch, JD 1967. **CAREER** Univ of Chicago Law Sch, master of comparative law 70; Southwestern Univ Sch of Law, prof of law 75-; SW, Asso prof of law 72-75; Smith & Glascod partner 71-72; Lewis & Clark Coll, visting prof of law 75; Univ of Wash, visting prof of law 74; Univ of TN knoxville, vis prof of law 80. **HONORS AND AWARDS** Outst Young Woman of Am honoree 1971. **MEMBERSHIPS** Mem CA State Bar Assn 1968-; mem Black Women Lawyers Assn; mem CA Assn of Black Lawyers; chpn Elect of Minority Groups Sect of Assn of Am Law Schs1977; chmn Minority Groups Sect of Assn of Law Schs 1978; fellow Inst French Lang & Civil Univ of Geneva 1968; fellow Inst of French Lang & Civil Univ ofPau 1969; fellow Inst French Lang & Civil Univ of Paris 1969; comparative law fellow Univ of Aix-Marseilles 1969-74. **CONTACT ADDRESS** Southwestern Univ Sch of Law, 675 S Westmoreland, Los Angeles, CA 90005.

GLASER, DANIEL
PERSONAL Born 12/23/1918, New York, NY, m, 1946, 1 child **DISCIPLINE** SOCIOLOGY **EDUCATION** Univ Chicago, AB, 39, AM, 47, PhD, 54. **CAREER** US Army, 42-46; US Mil Govt Ger Prison Branch, 46-49; Sociol-actuary, Ill Parole & Pardon Bd, 49-54; asst prof to prof & ch, Sociol Dept, Univ Ill-Urbana, 54-68; Rutgers Univ on 3/4 leave to NY State Narcotic Addiction Control Comn, Res Comnr, 68-69; prof sociol, 70-89, prof emer, 89- , Univ Southern Calif; sr res assoc, Soc Sci Res Inst, 78-; vis assoc prof, UCLA, 61; vis prof Ariz State Univ, 63-64; distinguished Emer award, U S Cal, 95. **HONORS AND AWARDS** Annual Awd John Howard Asn, 65; E H Sutherland Awd, 76; August Vollmer Awd, 90; Richard A McGee Awd, 87; distinguished sociol pract award, 95. **MEMBERSHIPS** Ill Acad Criminol; Am Sociol Asn; Am Soc Criminol; Am Justice Inst; Pac Sociol Asn. **RESEARCH** To expand practical knowledge that canalleviate mankind's problems, seek not just precision, but the grounding of facts in abstract explanatory principles. **SELECTED PUBLICATIONS** Ed, Handbook of Criminology, 74; auth Crime in Our Changing Society, 78; Encyclo Crime and Justice, 83; Evaluation Research and Decision Guidance, 88; Preparing Convicts for Law-Abiding Lifes: The Pioneering Penology of Richard A McGee, 95. **CONTACT ADDRESS** 901 S Ogden Dr., Los Angeles, CA 90036-4411.

GLASER, ROBERT
PERSONAL Born 01/18/1921, Providence, RI, m, 1945, 2 children **DISCIPLINE** PSYCHOLOGY **EDUCATION** City Col NY, BS, 42; Indiana Univ, MA, 47, PhD, 49. **CAREER** Univ Prof, Dept Psychology, Univ of Pittsburgh, 72-, Dir, Learning Research Development Center, 63-97, Dir Emeritus, 97-. **HONORS AND AWARDS** Doctor of Science, Honoris Causa: Univ of Leuven, Belgium, Indiana Univ; John Simon Guggenheim Fel, 75; E. L. Thorndike Awd for Distinguished Psychological Contributions to education, 81; CUNY Awd for Outstanding Contributions to the Advancement of Psychology, 89; James McKeen Cattell Fel Awd for Distinguished Scientific Contributions and their Applications, Am Psychol Soc, 93; Distinguished Prof Achievement Awd, Nat Soc for Performance and Instruction, 95; Chancellor's Distinguished Res Awd, Univ Pittsburgh, 95; ROUNDTABLE Honoree, Vanderbilt Univ, 96; Distinguished Achievement Awd, Univ of Calif, Los Angeles, Ctr for the Study of Evaluation, 97; Distinguished Lifetime Contribution to Evaluation, Measurement, and Statistics, Am Psychol Asn, 97; E. F. Lindquist Awd, Am Educ Res Asn, 98; Franklin V. Taylor Awd, Div 21, Am Psychol Asn, 98; Educ Testing Service 1998 Awd for Distinguished Service to Measurement. **MEMBERSHIPS** AERA, APA, APS, NAE. **RESEARCH** Cognitive psychology. **SELECTED PUBLICATIONS** Ed, Advances in instructional psychology, Vol 4, Hillsdale, NJ: Lawrence Erlbaum Assocs (93); auth, "Changing the agency for learning: acquiring expert performance," in A. Ericsson, ed, The road to excellence: The Acquisition of expert performance in the arts and sciences, sports and games, Mahwah, NJ: Erlbaum (96): 303-311; co-ed with L. Schauble, Innovations in Learning: New environments for education, Mahwah, NJ: Lawrence Erlbaum Assocs (96); co-ed with S. Vosniadou, E. De Corte, and H. Mandel, International perspectives on the design of technology-supported learning environments, Mahwah, NJ: Lawrence Erlbaum Assocs (96); auth, "Instructional technology and the measurement of learning outcomes: Some questions," in J. M. Notterman, ed, The evolution of psychology, Washington, DC: Am Psychol Asn (97): 337-342; auth, " 'The Vision thing': Educational Research and AERA in the 21st Century, Part 3: Perspectives on the research-practice relationship," Educational Researcher, 26 (7), 24 (97); auth, "Education for all: Access to learning and achieving usable knowledge," Prospects, XXVIII, 1 (98): 7-20; coauth with G. P. Baxter, "Cognition and construct validity: Evidence for the nature of cognitive performance in assessment situations," in H. Braun & D. Wiley, eds, Under construction: The role of construct in psychological and educational measure. A Feschrift in honor of Sam Messick, Mahwah, NJ: Erlbaum (in press); ed, Advances in instructional psychology, Educational design and cognitive science, Vol 5, Mahwah, NJ: Lawrence Erlbaum Assocs (in press). **CONTACT ADDRESS** Learning Research and Development Center, Univ of Pittsburgh, 3939 O'Hara St, Rm 835, Pittsburgh, PS 15260. **EMAIL** Glaser@pitt.edu

GLASS-COFIN, BONNIE
PERSONAL Born 02/16/1957, St Louis, MO, m, 1980, 1 child **DISCIPLINE** SOCIOLOGY **EDUCATION** Whitman Col, BA, 80; Univ Calif, Los Angeles, MA, 85; PhD, 92. **CAREER** Assoc Prof, Ut St Univ, 93-. **HONORS AND AWARDS** Emerging Scholar Awd, 97; Fulbright Scholar, 97-98. **MEMBERSHIPS** AAA. **RESEARCH** Gender, Shamanism, medical anthropology, ethnohistory, Latin America, feminist anthropology. **SELECTED PUBLICATIONS** Coauth, "La Brujeria en la Costa Norte del Peru del Siglo XVIII -- El Casa de Maria de la O," J of Latin Am Lore, 17 (91): 103-130; auth, "Male and Female Healing in Northern Peru: Metaphors, Models and Manifestations of Difference," J of Ritual Studies, 10.1 (96): 63-91; auth, "Engendering Peruvian Shamanism Through Time: Insights from Ethnohistory and Ethnography," Ethnohist, 46.2 (99): 205-238; auth, "Reflections on the Experience of Healing: Whose Logic? Whose Experience," in Healing Logics (Logan: Ut St UP, forthcoming). **CONTACT ADDRESS** Dept Sociol, Utah State Univ, 730 University Blvd, Logan, UT 0730. **EMAIL** glasscob@cc.usu.edu

GLASSMAN, RONALD
PERSONAL Born 06/01/1937, New York, NY, m, 1972, 2 children **DISCIPLINE** SOCIOLOGY **EDUCATION** Queens Col, BA, 59, Ohio State Univ, MA, 60; New Sch for Soc Res, PhD, 68. **CAREER** Asst prof, Queens Col, 65-67; asst prof, Conn Col for Women, 68-72; asst prof, Herbert Lehman Col, 73-78; prof, William Paterson Univ, 80-; adj prof, NYU, Great Books 95-, vis prof, Wesleyan Univ, 98-. **HONORS AND AWARDS** UNESCO Travel Grant, 85; NEH Scholar, 85, 88, 92; Fel, Princeton Univ, 90-91. **MEMBERSHIPS** Am Sociol Assoc; Am for Democratic Action; Nat Max Weber Colloquium. **SELECTED PUBLICATIONS** Auth, Democracy and Equality, Praeger, (NY), 88; auth, "Weberian Sociology, Modernity, and Social Theory," The Renascence of Sociological theory, eds Etzkowitz and Glassman, Peacock (Woodson, IL), 89; coauth, A Democracy Agenda for the Year 2000, Democracy Project, (NY), 89; coed, The Renascence of Sociological Theory, Peacock (Woodson, IL), 89; auth, China in Transition: Communism, Capitalism, Democracy, Praeger, (NY), 90; auth, "A Weberian Analysis of China in Transition", Theory, Culture and Society, Vol 7, Sage, (London), 90; coauth, For Democracy; The Noble Character and Tragic Flaws of the Middle Class, Greenwood Pr, (Westport, CT), 93; auth, The Middle Class and Democracy in Socio-Historical Perspective, E.J. Brill (Netherlands), 95; auth, The Middle Class and Democracy and Global Perspective, Macmillan, (London, England), 96; auth, Caring Capitalism: The Welfare State on a Middle Class Base, Macmillan, (London, England), 99. **CONTACT ADDRESS** Dept Sociol, William Paterson Col of New Jersey, 300 Pompton Rd, Wayne, NJ 07470.

GLAZER, ILSA M.
PERSONAL Born 07/28/1940, New York, NY, d, 2 children **DISCIPLINE** BEHAVIORAL SCIENCE **EDUCATION** Brooklyn Col, CUNY, BA; Brandeis Univ, MA, 68; Univ Sussex, D Phil, 77. **CAREER** Asst prof, SUNY, Stony Brook; Univ Haifa, Israel; Univ Zambia; Assoc prof, CUNY, Kingsborough, 93-. **HONORS AND AWARDS** NIMH; Ford Fel; Fulbright Fel; Res Grants; Phi Beta Kappa. **MEMBERSHIPS** AAA. **RESEARCH** Human rights of Israeli women; Zambian women in social change. **SELECTED PUBLICATIONS** Coauth, "On Aggression, Human Rights, and Hegemonic Discourse: The Case of a Murder for Family Honor in Israel," Sex Roles: A Journal of Research (94), vol.30, no 3; auth, "Into the 21st Century: An Urban Studies Handbook for the Global Village," (95); auth, "A Cloak of Many Colors: Jewish Feminism and Feminist Jews in America," in Women: A Feminist Perspective (95); auth, "Beyond the Competition of Tears: Black-Jewish Conflict Containment in a New York Neighborhood," in Cultural Variation in Conflict Resolution: Alternatives for Reducing Violence (97); auth, "Alcohol and Politics in Urban Zambia: The Intersection of Gender and Class," in African Feminism: The Politics of Survival in Sub Saharan Africa [97]; auth, "Family: Religious and Legal Systems: Judaic traditions," Women's Studies Intl Encyc (in press). **CONTACT ADDRESS** Dept Behavioral Sciences, Kingsborough Comm Col, CUNY, 2001 Oriental Blvd, Brooklyn, NY 11235. **EMAIL** iglazer@kbcc.cuny.edu

GLAZIER, STEPHEN D.
PERSONAL Born 06/10/1949, New London, CT, m, 1975, 1 child **DISCIPLINE** ANTHROPOLOGY, SOCIOLOGY, THEOLOGY **EDUCATION** Eastern Col, AB, 71; Princeton Theol Sem, MDiv, 74; Univ of Ct, PhD, 81. **CAREER** Prof, Grad Studies, Univ of Nebr, Kearney, 94-; vis prof, Univ of Nebr at Lincoln, 2000-. **HONORS AND AWARDS** Teaching Fel, Am Acad of Relig/Lilly Found Workshops, 97-98; Delegate, Consciousness Studies Summer Inst, Univ of Ariz and the Fetzer Inst, 97; Prog ed, Anthropol of Relig Section, 97th Annual Meeting, Am Anthropol Asn, 98; Vice-Pres, Anthropol of Relig Section, Am Anthropol Asn, 98-2000; Secretary, Soc for the Sci Study of Relig, 98-2001. **MEMBERSHIPS** Am Anthropol Asn, Royal Anthropol Inst, Soc for the Anthropol of Relig, Soc for the Sci Study of Relig, Soc des Americanistes de Paris, Caribbean Studies Asn. **RESEARCH** Anthropology (four subfields), religion, race and ethnicity, ethnohistory, Caribbean and Latin America, ethnomusicology, folklore. **SELECTED PUBLICATIONS** Ed, Anthropology of Religion: A Handbook, Westport, CT: Greenwood (97); auth, "Foreword," special issue: Turkic and Siberian Shamanism in the Former USSR, E. J. N. Fridman, guest ed, Anthropol of Consciousness, vol 10, no 4 (99); auth, "William Wallace Fenn," "John Mifflin Brown," and "Benjamin W. Arnett," in American National Biography, J. A. Garraty, gen ed, New York: Oxford Univ Press (99); auth, "Anthropology and Theology: The Legacies of a Link," Explorations in Anthropology and Theology, 2nd ed, F. A. Salome and W. R. Adams, ed, Lanham, Md: Univ Press of Am (99); auth, "Anti Anti-Reductionism: Biological and Cognitive Approaches to the Anthropology of Religion," Guest ed's intro, special issue, Zygon (2000); auth, "After the Falls: Pilgrimage and Healing in Post Colonial Trinidad," Yearbook of Cross-Cultural Medicine and Psychotherapy, vol 10, M. Winkelman and J. Dubisch, guest eds (200); coauth, "Understanding Caribbean Religions," Ch 10 in Understanding Caribbean Culture, T. d'Agostino and R. Hillman, eds, Kingston, Jamaica: Ian Randle, Boulder, Co: Kynn Riener (2000); ed, Anthropology and Contemporary Religions, Westport, Ct: Greenwood (2000); gen ed, Encyclopedia of Religion and Society (Volume V): African and African American Religions, New York and London: Routledge (2001). **CONTACT ADDRESS** Dept Sociol and Anthropol, Univ of Nebraska, Kearney, 905 W 25th St, Kearney, NE 68847. **EMAIL** glaziers@unk.edu

GLENN, CECIL E.
PERSONAL Born 12/18/1938, Nashville, TN, m **DISCIPLINE** EDUCATION **EDUCATION** BA; MA; PhD 1975. **CAREER** Univ of CO, prof Social Science, head Ethnic Studies; Chicago Dept of Educ, Public Health Serv Civil Rights Envolvement, 10 yrs; teahcer 15 yrs; Higher Educ, area urban sociologist 5 yrs; Mental Health Inc, serv in mental health field chmn 5 yrs. **HONORS AND AWARDS** Recip awds Nat Alliance of Business 1975; Mt Plains Comm Coll Ldshp 1974; Partners corrective progs 1974. **MEMBERSHIPS** Chmn Malcolm X Mental Inc; mem NAACP. **CONTACT ADDRESS** Dept of Ethnic Studies, Univ of Colorado, Denver, Campus Box 134, PO Box 173364, Denver, CO 80217-3364. **EMAIL** cglenn@carbon.cudenver.edu

GLISKY, ELIZABETH LOUISE
PERSONAL Born 10/28/1941, Toronto, ON, Canada, m, 1962, 4 children **DISCIPLINE** PSYCHOLOGY **EDUCATION** Univ Toronto, BA, 62; PhD, 83. **CAREER** Asst prof, Univ of Ariz, 89-95, assoc prof, 95-99, prof, 99-; Ed rev bd, J of Clinical and Experimental Neuropsychol, 95-; ed rev bd, J of the Int Neuropsychol Soc, 99-; Exec ed, Neuropsychol Rehabilitation, 99-; Pres, Rocky Mountain Psychol Asn, 99-2000. **HONORS AND AWARDS** Univ of Toronto Postdoctoral Awd to Research Fel, 83-86; Provost's Teaching Awd, Univ of Ariz, 89-90; Office of the Vice Provost for Academic Affairs grant, 94; Nat Inst on Aging grant, 97-2002; The James S. McDonnell Found grant, 97-99. **MEMBERSHIPS** APA, APS, INS, Psychonomic Soc, Cognitive Neurosci Soc, Int Neuropsychol Soc. **RESEARCH** Remediation of organic memory disorders, memory and aging, cognitive and neural correlates of memory, rehabilitation of brain-injured individuals, frontal lobe function and memory, learning and memory in normal and pathological populations. **SELECTED PUBLICATIONS** Coauth with M. A. McDaniel, S. R. Rubin, M. J. Guynn, and B. C. Routhieaux, "Prospective memory: A neuropsychological study," Neuropsychol, 13 (99): 103-110; coauth with S. Z. Rapcsak, S. L. Reminger, A. W. Kaszniak, and J. F. Comer, "Neuropsychological mechanisms of false facial recognition following frontal lobe damage," Cognitive Neuropsychol, 16 (99): 267-292; coauth with S. R. Rubin, C. Van Petten, and W. M. Newberg, "Memory conjunction errors in younger and older adults: Event-related potential and neuropsychological data," Cognitive Neuropsychol, 16 (99): 459-488; coauth with M. L. Glisky, "Memory rehabilitation in the elderly," in D. T. Stuss, G. W. Wincour, and I. H. Robertson, eds, Cognitive neurorehabilitation, London, UK: Cambridge Univ Press (00); coauth with A. W. Kaszniak, S. L. Reminger, and S. Z. Rapcsak, "Conscious experience and autonomic response to emotional stimuli following frontal lobe damage," in S. R. Hameroff, A. W. Kaszniak, and D. J. Chalmers, eds, "Toward a science of consciousness III: The third Tuscon discussions and debates, Cambridge, MA: MIT Press (99); auth, "Neuropsychology: Interventions," in A. E. Kazdin, ed, Encyclopedia of Psychology, Washington, DC and New York: Am Psychol Asn and Oxford Univ Press (2000). **CONTACT ADDRESS** Dept Psychol, Univ of Arizona, PO Box 210068, Tuscon, AZ 85721-0068. **EMAIL** glisky@u.arizona.edu

GLOBERMAN, ERMA
PERSONAL Born Brooklyn, NY, 2 children **DISCIPLINE** SOCIAL WORK **EDUCATION** CUNY, BA, 78; NY Univ, MSW, 81. **CAREER** Therapist, Peninsula Counseling Center, 83-92; Admin Supervisor, Jewish Board of Family & Children's Services, 92-96; Adj Assoc Prof, N Y Univ, 90-. **HONORS AND AWARDS** Fel, New York Univ, 80. **MEMBERSHIPS** NASW, Board Cert Diplomate, Psi Chi, Alpha Sigma Lambda. **RESEARCH** Family Systems. **CONTACT ADDRESS** School of Soc Work, New York Univ, 2 Washington Sq N, New York, NY 10003. **EMAIL** egloberman@aol.com

GLOWIENKA, EMERINE FRANCES
PERSONAL Born 03/09/1920, Milwaukee, WI **DISCIPLINE** PHILOSOPHY, SOCIOLOGY **EDUCATION** Marquette Univ, BA, 42, MA, 51, PhD(Philos), 73; St Louis Univ, PhD-(Sociol), 56. **CAREER** Elem & sec teacher, Acad Sacred Heart, Ill, 45-53; instr Philos & Sociol, Barat Col, 55-58; assoc prof Sociol & chmn dept, Duchesne Col, 61-62; prof Sociol & Social Welfare, San Francisco Col Women, 62-70, chmn dept, 61-70; asst prof Philos, Univ San Diego, 71-74; prof Philos & Sociol & chairperson Dept, Gallup Br Col, Univ NMEX, 74-, prof Philos, Gallup Diocesan Sem, 74-. **MEMBERSHIPS** Am Philos Asn; Am Cath Philos Asn; Soc Women Philos. **RESEARCH** Ethics; metaphysics; personalization. **SELECTED PUBLICATIONS** Auth, Social philosophy as a synthesis of the social sciences, Am Cath Sociol Rev, Fall 63; Notes on consciousness in matter, New Scholasticism, Fall 69; Why do we teach?, Mod Soc, 1/70; A brighter side of the new genetics, Bioscience, 2/75; The counsel of poverty: Gospels versus acts, Rev Relig, 3/75; On demythologizing philosophy, Southwest Philos Studies, 4/81; Aquinas With the Realists and the Conceptualists, Southwest Philosophical Studies, 18, 96; auth, "Person as 'That Which Is Most Perfect in Nature'," Southwest Philosophical Studes, vol 20 (98): 56-65; auth, Personization: The Moral Norm for Today, Gallup, New Mexico, The Indian Trader Inc Publisher, 99; auth, "On Knowing the Act of Knowing," Southwest Philosophical Studies, vol 22, 00 (forthcoming). **CONTACT ADDRESS** Dept of Philos Gallup Br Col, Univ of New Mexico, Gallup, 200 College Rd, Gallup, NM 87301-5603.

GMELCH, GEORGE
PERSONAL Born 12/28/1945, New York, NY, m, 1969, 1 child **DISCIPLINE** ANTHROPOLOGY **EDUCATION** Stanford, BA, 68; UCSB, PhD, 75. **CAREER** McGill Univ, Asst Prof, 73-75; SUNY, Albany, Asst Prof, 75-80; Union Coll, Prof, 80-present. **MEMBERSHIPS** Amer Anthro Assoc **RESEARCH** Cultural Anthro; Caribbean; Ireland, tourism; Sport, Urban Anthro, Oral Hist; work. **SELECTED PUBLICATIONS** The Ball Players, 00; In The Ballpark, 98; The Parish Behind God's Back, 97; The Irish Tinker's, 87; Urban Life 93. **CONTACT ADDRESS** Dept of Anthro, Union Col, New York, Schenectady, NY 12308. **EMAIL** gmelchg@union.edu

GMELCH, SHARON BOHN
PERSONAL Born 06/02/1947, Balboa, Panama, m, 1968, 1 child **DISCIPLINE** CULTURAL ANTHROPOLOGY **EDUCATION** Univ Calif, Santa Barbara, BA, 69, MA, 71, PhD, 75. **CAREER** PROF, ANTHROP, UNION COLL. **HONORS AND AWARDS** Book of the Year, Irish Book Publisher's Asn, 76; Silver Apple, Nat Educational Film and Video Festival, 92; Honoree, Soc for Visual Anthrop, 92; Honoree, Margaret Mead Film Festival, 93. **MEMBERSHIPS** Am Anthrop Asn **RESEARCH** Ethnicity; Cultural change; Gender; Visual anthropology; Biography **SELECTED PUBLICATIONS** Tinkers and Travellers: Ireland's Nomads, Mc-Gill Univ Press, 76; edr, Irish Life and Traditions, Syracuse univ Press, 86; Nan: The Life of an Irish Travelling Woman, Waveland Press, 91; coauth, A Matter of Respect, co-produced with Ellen Frankenstein, 92; The Parish Behind God's Back: The Changing Culture of Rural Barbados, Univ Mich Press, 97; Gender on Campus: Issues for College Women, Rutgers Univ Press, 98. **CONTACT ADDRESS** Dept Anthrop, Union Col, New York, Schenectady, NY 12308. **EMAIL** gmelchs@union.edu

GODDU, TERESA
DISCIPLINE AMERICAN LITERATURE AND CULTURE **EDUCATION** Univ Pa, PhD. **CAREER** Instr, Vanderbilt Univ. **RESEARCH** American literature; American cultural study; African American literature. **SELECTED PUBLICATIONS** Auth, Gothic America, Columbia UP, 97. **CONTACT ADDRESS** Vanderbilt Univ, Nashville, TN 37203-1727.

GOFORTH, CAROL R.
PERSONAL Born 10/12/1960, Fayetteville, AR, m, 1992, 4 children **DISCIPLINE** PSYCHOLOGY, LAW **EDUCATION** Univ AR, BA, 81; JD, 84. **CAREER** Assoc attorney, Doerner, Stuart, Saunders, Daniel & Anderson, OK, 84-89; adjunct prof, Col Law, Univ Tulsa, 87-88; instr, Seton Hall Parma prog, Parma, Italy, summer 90; asst prof law, 89-92, assoc prof law, School of Law, Seton Hall Univ, Newark, NJ, 92-93; from vis assoc prof law to Clayton N. Little prof law, Univ Ark School of Law, Fayettsville, 93-. **HONORS AND AWARDS** Selected AR Bar Found Prof, June 98; Clayton N. Little Prof Law, June 00. **MEMBERSHIPS** Am Bar Asn; AR Bar Asn; Am Law Inst. **RESEARCH** Corporate law; securities law; limited liability companied; limited liability partnerships. **SELECTED PUBLICATIONS** Co-auth, with L Beard, The Arkansas Limited Liability Company, M & M Press, 94; auth, Limited Liability Partnerships: Does Arkansas Need Another Form of Business Enterprize?, 1995 AR L Notes 57; The Rise of the Limited Liability Company: Evidence of a Race Between the States, but Heading Where?, 45 Syracuse L Rev, 1193, 95; What is She? How Race Matters, and Why It Shouldn't, 46 DePaul Univ L Rev 1, 96; Limiting the Liability of General Partners in LLPs: An Analysis of Statutory Alternatives, 75 OR L Rev 1139, 97; Continuing Obstacles to Freedom of Choice for Management Structure in LLC's, 1 Lewis & Clark J of Small and Emerging Bus L, 165, 97; Limited Liability Partnerships: The Newest

Game in Town, AR L Notes 25, 97; An Update on Arkansas Limited Liability Companies: New Tax Regulations and New State Laws, 1997 AR L Notes 11; Reflections on What Lawyers Should Reflect On, 30 So TX L Rev, 585, 98; co-auth, with Michael L Closen and Gary S Rosin, Agency & Partnership, Problems and Statutes, supp 96 & supp 97; with Michael L Closen and Gary S Rosin, Agency and Partnership, Cases and Materials, supp 96 & supp 97; auth, The Revised Uniform Partnership Act: Ready or Not, Here It Comes, Ark Law Notes 47 (99); with L Beard, Arkansas LLCs. LLPs, LLLPs, M & M Press, forthcoming; auth, Treatment of LLC Membership Interests Under the Arkansas Securities Act, 1998 AR L Notes, 33; Not In My Back Yard! Restrictive Covenants as a Basis for Opposing the Construction of Cellular Towers, 46 Buffalo L Rev, 705; auth, A Bad Call: Preemtion of State and Local Governmental Authority to Regulate Wireless Communication Facilities on the Basis of Radio Frequency Emissions, NYork Law School Law Review (forthcoming); auth, Use of Simulations and Client Based Exercises in the Basic Course, 34 Ga Law Review (forthcoming). **CONTACT ADDRESS** School of Law, Univ of Arkansas, Fayetteville, Fayetteville, AR 72701. **EMAIL** goforth@comp.uark.edu

GOGGIN, WILLIAM
PERSONAL Born 07/24/1947, Denver, CO, m, 1968, 2 children **DISCIPLINE** PSYCHOLOGY **EDUCATION** Rice Univ, BA, 70; Ind Univ, PhD, 79. **CAREER** Instr, Hartwick Col, 75-78; Asst Prof, Kent State Univ, 79-80; Prof, Univ S Miss, 80-. **HONORS AND AWARDS** Nat Inst of Ment Health Fel, 70-73; Summer Res Grant, 85; Summer Teaching Grant, 93. **MEMBERSHIPS** APA, Soc for Personality and Soc Psychol. **RESEARCH** Personality, social psychology. **SELECTED PUBLICATIONS** Coauth, "Design and Development of a Modified Paired-Associate Learning Test," Archs of Clinical Neuropsychol, 9 (94): 183; coauth, "Assessing Spatial Learning and Memory Using Corsis Block-Tapping Test," Archs of Clinical Neuropsychol, 9 (94): 117; coauth, "Knowledges Work Groups as Social Groups: A Critical Analysis of the Symposium Contributions Based on the Cooperative Theory of Groups," in Advances in Interdisciplinary Studies of Work Teams, vol 2 (Greenwich, CT: JAI Pr, 95); coauth, "The Escape Theory of Suicide in College Students: Testing a Model that Includes Perfectionism," Suicide and Life-Threatening Behav, 26 (96): 181-186; coauth, "A Multifaceted Concept of Group Maturity, Its Measurement and Relationship to Group Performance," Small Group Behav (forthcoming). **CONTACT ADDRESS** Dept Psychol, Univ of So Mississippi, PO Box 5025, Hattiesburg, MS 39406. **EMAIL** william.goggin@usm.edu

GOLD, ANN G.
PERSONAL Born 12/08/1946, Chicago, IL, m, 1981, 3 children **DISCIPLINE** ANTHROPOLOGY **EDUCATION** Univ Chicago, BA, 75, MA, 78, PhD, 84. **CAREER** Vis asst, adj asst, acting asst, Mellon fel, South Asian Studies, Cornell Univ, 85-93; asst prof, 93-96, prof, Syracuse Univ, relig, 96-. **HONORS AND AWARDS** Fulbright Res scholar, 92-93; Spencer Found major grant, 96-97; NEH fel for univ teachers, 97-98. **MEMBERSHIPS** AAA; AAR; AAS. **RESEARCH** South Asia; Religion; Environment; Oral traditions; Gender. **SELECTED PUBLICATIONS** Co-auth, Listen to the Heron's Words: Reimagining Gender and Kinship in North India, Univ Calif Press, 94; auth, A Carnival of Parting: The Tales of King Bharthari and King Gopi Chand As Sung and Told by Madhu Natisar Nath of Ghatiyali, Rajasthan, India, Univ Calif Press, 92; auth, Fruitful Journeys: The Ways of Rajasthani Pilgrims, Univ Calif Pres, 88; article, Outspoken women: Representations of Female Voices in a Rajasthani Folklore Community, Oral Traditions, 98; auth, Wild Pigs and Kings: Remembered Landscapes in Rajasthan, Amer Anthrop, 97; auth, Khyal: Changed Yearnings in Rajasthani Women's Songs, Manushi, 96; auth, The Jungli Rani and Other Troubled Wives in Rajasthani Oral Traditions, From the Margins of Hindu Marriage, Oxford Univ Press, 95; auth, Mother Ten's Stories, Relig of India in Practice, Princeton Univ Press, 95; auth, Magical Landscapes and Moral Orders: New Readings in Religion and Ecology, Relig Studies Rev, 95; auth, Of Gods, Trees and Boundaries: Divine Conservation in Rajasthan, Folk, Faith and Feudalism, Rawat Publ, 95; auth, Gender, Violence and Power: Rajasthani Stories of Shakti, Women as Subjects: South Asian Histories, Univ Press of Va, 94; auth, Yatra, Jatra, and Pressing Down Pebbles: Pilgrimage within and beyond Rajasthan, The Idea of Rajasth, Manohar Publ, 94; auth, Drawing Pictures in the Dust: Rajasthani Children's Landscapes, Childhood, 94. **CONTACT ADDRESS** Dept of Religion, Syracuse Univ, 501 Hall of Languages, Syracuse, NY 13244-1170. **EMAIL** aggold@syr.edu

GOLD-NEIL, VALERIE L.
PERSONAL Born 03/16/1950, Casa Grande, AZ, m, 1999, 2 children **DISCIPLINE** PSYCHOLOGY **EDUCATION** Tex Tech, BA, 79; EdD, 89. **CAREER** Prof, Irvine Valley Col, 93-. **HONORS AND AWARDS** Humanitarian of the Year Awd, Orange Cty CA, 93; Woman of the Year, Lubbock TX, 87; Diplomate, Am Psycholtherapy Asn. **MEMBERSHIPS** CPA; APA. **SELECTED PUBLICATIONS** Co-auth, "Identification of AIDS and Other Related Attitudes," Journal of Social Psychology, (92): 129-130; co-auth, "The Effects of a Gay/Lesbian Panel Discussion on Student Attitudes Toward Gay Men, Lesbians and Persons with AIDS," Journal of Sex Education & Therapy, (93): 47-63; auth, "Why HIV Women Should Speak Out," Lifetimes, 94; dir, "An Invitation to Listen," 95. **CONTACT ADDRESS** Dept App Psychol, Irvine Valley Col, 5500 Irvine Cent Dr, Irvine, CA 92618. **EMAIL** valgn@home.com

GOLDBERG, HERBERT
PERSONAL Born 07/14/1937, Berlin, Germany, d, 1 child **DISCIPLINE** PSYCHOLOGY **EDUCATION** Adelphi Univ, PhD, 63. **CAREER** Prof, Calif State Univ, 65-. **HONORS AND AWARDS** Phi Beta Kappa, CCNY, 58. **MEMBERSHIPS** APA. **RESEARCH** Gender. **SELECTED PUBLICATIONS** Co-auth, Creative Aggresion; auth, The Hazards of Being Male; auth, The New Male; auth, The New Male-Female Relationship; auth, The Inner Male; auth, What Men Really Want; co-auth, Money Madness. **CONTACT ADDRESS** Dept Psychol, California State Univ, Los Angeles, 5151 State Univ Dr, Los Angeles, CA 90032.

GOLDBERG, STEVEN
PERSONAL Born 10/14/1941, New York, NY, m, 1999 **DISCIPLINE** SOCIOLOGY **EDUCATION** CUNY Grad Center, PhD. **CAREER** CUNY City Col. **MEMBERSHIPS** Am Sociol Assoc. **RESEARCH** Logic of Scientific Questions. **SELECTED PUBLICATIONS** Auth, The Inevitability of Patriarchy, William Morris, 73; auth, When Wish Replaces Thought, Prometheus Books, 91; auth, Why Men Rule, Open Court, 93; auth, "The Erosion of the Social Sciences in Dumbing Down: Essays on the Strip-Mining of American Culture, eds Katherine Washburn and John Thorton, Norton, (NY, 96), 97-114; auth, "Truth and Consequences (On Scientific Method)", Chronicles 20.7 (96): auth, "Is Patriarchy Inevitable", Nat Rev 11 (96): 32-36; auth, "Defending Choice", Society, (97); auth, "The Logic of Patriarchy", Gender Issues 17.3 (99): 53-69. **CONTACT ADDRESS** Dept Sociol, City Col, CUNY, 160 Convent Ave, New York, NY 10031.

GOLDBERGER, LEO
PERSONAL Born 06/28/1930, Vukovar, Yugoslavia, m, 1970, 1 child **DISCIPLINE** PSYCHOLOGY **EDUCATION** McGill Univ, BA, 51; NYork Univ, PhD, 58. **CAREER** Res Psychologist, NY Hospital-Cornell Medical Center, 53-54; ASST PROF TO PROF, DIR OF RES CENTER OF MENTAL HEALTH, DEPT OF PSYCHOL, NYU, 56-. **HONORS AND AWARDS** NIMH Res Career Development Awd, 63-68; Knight's Cross, Queen of Denmark, 93. **RESEARCH** Psychoanalysis; stress & coping; Holocaust rescuers. **SELECTED PUBLICATIONS** Auth, Handbook of Stress, Free Press, 93; auth, The Rescue of the Danish Jews, NYU Press, 87; auth, Psychoanalysis & Contemporary Thought, Quart, 77-. **CONTACT ADDRESS** Dept of Psychology, New York Univ, 6 Washington Pl., New York, NY 10003. **EMAIL** leo.goldberger@nyu.edu

GOLDFARB, JEFFREY C.
DISCIPLINE LIBERAL STUDIES, COMPARATIVE POLITICS **EDUCATION** Univ Chicago, PhD, 77. **CAREER** Prof, Eugene Lang Col. **RESEARCH** Soc of cult; comp polit; phenomenological soc; relationship between cult, polit, and democratic institutions. **SELECTED PUBLICATIONS** Auth, After the Fall: The Pursuit of Democracy in Central Europe, 92; The Cynical Society: The Culture of Politics and the Politics of Culture in American Life, 91; Beyond Glasnost: The Post-Totalitarian Mind, 89; On Cultural Freedom: An Exploration of Public Life in Poland and America, 82; The Persistence of Freedom: The Sociological Implications of Polish Student Theater, 80. **CONTACT ADDRESS** Eugene Lang Col, New Sch for Social Research, 66 West 12th St, New York, NY 10011.

GOLDIN, MILTON
PERSONAL Born 01/08/1927, Cleveland, OH, m, 1950, 2 children **DISCIPLINE** MUSICOLOGY; PSYCHOLOGY **EDUCATION** New York Univ, BA, 53, MA, 55. **CAREER** Admin dir, Amer Choral Found, 55-61; assoc dir devel, Brookdale Hosp Ctr 63-66; fund raising campaign dir, Wash Sq. Col and Grad Sch, Arts and Sci, NYU, 66-67; VP Oram Assoc, Inc, 67-72, Exec VP, 72-75; fund raising counc, 75-78; pres, The Milton Goldin Co, 78-; mgr, Amor Artis Chorale and Orch, 61-78; contributing ed, periodicals, 96-. **HONORS AND AWARDS** ASCAP Deems Taylor award, 70; Phi Beta Kappa; Psi Chi; Mu Sigma **MEMBERSHIPS** National Coalition of Independent Scholars (NCIS) **RESEARCH** German economy 1917-1952; american philanthropy; environmental history. **SELECTED PUBLICATIONS** Auth, The Music Merchants, 69; auth, Why They Give, 76; PS, Goldhagen and the Holocaust, Jan 97; The Earth Times, The New York-New Jersey Follies, Mar 97; The Genocide Forum, Allianz's First Trial, Sept 97; History Today, Financing the SS, June 98; Gannett Newspapers, Tourism Isn't Going to Make Up for GM Loss, June 98. **CONTACT ADDRESS** 266 Crest Dr, Tarrytown, NY 10591-4328. **EMAIL** MiltonG525@aol.com

GONZALES, GAIL
PERSONAL Born 12/26/1957, Bryan, TX, m, 1989, 2 children **DISCIPLINE** PSYCHOLOGY **EDUCATION** Southwest Tex State Univ, BA, 79; Univ Tex, MA, 82; PhD, 83. **CAREER** Prof, Dir of Prof Develop and Employee Rel Pima Col, 92-. **HONORS AND AWARDS** Who's Who Among Am Teachers, 00. **MEMBERSHIPS** Am Psychol Asn. **RESEARCH** Faculty Development, Health Psychology. **SELECTED PUBLICATIONS** Coauth, "The Faculty Learning Academy," Innovation Abstracts vol XX, 25 (98). **CONTACT ADDRESS** Dept Psychology, Pima Comm Col, 5901 S Calif Santa Cruz, Tucson, AZ 85709-6030. **EMAIL** ggonzales@pimacc.pima.edu

GONZALEZ, NORMA E.
PERSONAL Born Tucson, AZ, m, 6 children **DISCIPLINE** ANTHROPOLOGY **EDUCATION** Univ Ariz, BA; MA; PhD. **CAREER** Asst res anthropol to assoc res prof, Univ Ariz, 92-. **MEMBERSHIPS** Coun of Anthropol and Educ; Am Anthropol Asn; am Educ Res Asn; Asn of Latina and Latino anthropol; Soc for Ling Anthropol. **RESEARCH** Educational anthropology; applied anthropology; linguistic anthropology; child language socialization; household ethnography; community/school linkages; Mexican-origin populations; critical theory; women's narratives. **SELECTED PUBLICATIONS** Auth, "Contestation and Accommodation in Parental Narratives," Educ and Urban Soc, (96): 54-70; co-auth, "Teaching Anthropological Methods to Teachers: The Transformation of Knowledge," in The Teaching of Anthropology: Problems, Issues and Decisions, Mayfield Pub, (97): 353-359; auth, "Blurred Voices: Who speaks for the subaltern?" in Becoming a Language Educator, (Lawrence Erlbaum and Assoc, 97), 75-83; co-auth, "Teachers as social scientists: Learning about culture from household research," in Race, Ethnicity and Multiculturalism, (Garland Pub, 97), 89-114; co-auth, "Bridging Funds of Distributed Knowledge: Creating Zones of Practices in Mathematics," J of Educ for Students Placed at Risk, (01): 115-132; co-auth, "Between Home and School Mathematics Practices," in Classroom Diversity: Connecting Curriculum to Students' Lives, 01; co-ed, Classroom Diversity: Connecting Curriculum to Students' Lives, Heinemann Press, 01; auth, I am my language: Discourses of women and children in the borderlands, Univ Ariz Press, (forthcoming). **CONTACT ADDRESS** Dept Anthropol, Univ of Arizona, PO Box 210030, Tucson, AZ 85721-0030.

GOODING, DIANE
PERSONAL Born 07/27/1963, New York, NY, s **DISCIPLINE** PSYCHOLOGY **EDUCATION** Harvard Univ, AB, 85; Hennepin County Med Center, Psychol Predoctoral Internship, 93; Univ Minn, PhD, 96. **CAREER** Asst prof, Univ Wisc, 96-. **HONORS AND AWARDS** Young Investigator Awd, 99; NAMI Res Awd, Wisc, 99; A.J. Cooper Fel, Univ Wisc, 95-96; NIMH Neurobehavioral Res Training Fel, 93-95; Ford Foundation Dissertation Fel, 91-92; NIMH Minority Res Training Fel, 90-91; CIC Minorities Fel, 87-90; Elizabeth Cary Agassiz Certificate of Merit, Radcliffe Col, 84; Sigma Xi, 98; NY Acad of Sci, 92; Phi Kappa Phi, 89. **MEMBERSHIPS** Intl Soc for Psychiat Genetics, Soc for Res in Psychopathol, Am Psychol Soc, Am Psychol Asn, Intl Soc for Women in Cognitive Neuroscience, Soc for Psychophysiol Res. **RESEARCH** Schizophrenia and spectrum disorders, Biological bases of psychotic disorders, At-risk populations, Oculomotor behavior, Neuropsychology, Behavioral genetics. **SELECTED PUBLICATIONS** Auth, "Smooth pursuit and visual fixation in psychosis-prone individuals," Psychiatry Research: Neuroimaging, in press; auth, "Working Memory and Wisconsin Card sorting Test performance in schizotypic individuals: a Replication and Extension," Psychiatry Research, (00): 161-170; auth, "Wisconsin Card Sorting Test deficits in schizotypic individuals," Schizophrenia Research, (99): 201-209; auth, "Smooth pursuit and saccadic eye movement performance in a prefrontal leukotomy patient," Journal of Psychiatry & Neuroscience, (99): 462-467; auth, "The role of executive funcioning in saccade generation. Commentary on Findlay & Walker's model of saccade generation," Behavioral and Brain Sciences, (99): 686-687; auth, "Perceptual biases in psychosis-prone individuals," Journal of Abnormal Psychology, (99): 283-289; auth, "Antisaccade task performance in questionnaire-identified schizotypes," Schizophrenia Research, (99): 157-166; auth, "Nailfold capillary plexus visibility in relation to schizotype," Schizophrenia Research, (98): 207-212; auth, "Schizophrenia through the lens of a developmental psychopathology perspective," in Manual of Developmental Psychopathology, New York, (95): 535-580. **CONTACT ADDRESS** Dept Psychol, Univ of Wisconsin, Madison, 1202 W Johnson St, Madison, WI 53706. **EMAIL** dgooding@facstaff.wisc.edu

GOODMAN, LOUIS
PERSONAL Born 12/06/1942, New York, NY, m, 1965, 2 children **DISCIPLINE** SOCIOLOGY, ECONOMICS **EDUCATION** Dartmouth Col, BA; Northwestern Univ, MA, PhD. **CAREER** Asst Prof, Yale Univ, 69-75; dir, Latin Am & Caribbean Prog, Soc Sci Res Coun, 72-78; lect, Yale Univ, 78-81; dir, Latin Am Prog, Woodrow Wilson Int Ctr Scholars, 81-86; prof, Am Univ, dean Sch Int Service, 86-. **HONORS AND AWARDS** Dir, Latin Am Prog, Woodrow Wilson Int Ctr Scholars; Dir, Latin Am & Caribbean Prog,Soc Sci Res Coun. **RESEARCH** Impact of transnational corporations on National development, Civil-Military Relations, Democracy Building. **SELECTED PUBLICATIONS** Auth, Small Nations, Giant Firms: Capital Allocation Decisions in Transnational Corporations, Holmes and Mier, 87; The Military and Democracy in Latin America, D.C. Heath-Lexington, 90; Lessons from the Venezuelan Experienc, Johns Hopkins, 95. **CONTACT AD-**

DRESS American Univ, 4400 Massachusetts Ave, Washington, DC 20016.

GOODMAN, WILLIAM
PERSONAL Born 09/08/1961, New Hyde Park, NY, m, 1989, 1 child **DISCIPLINE** PSYCHOLOGY **EDUCATION** Am Univ, BA, 83; Univ Pa, MSW, 85; Hofstra Univ, MA, 90; PhD, 93. **CAREER** Instr, Norwalk Community Col; licensed psychologist, Old Greenwich & Fairfield, CT. **MEMBERSHIPS** Am Psychol Asn. **RESEARCH** Client Attitudes Toward Mutual Health Professionals, Efficacy of Psychotherapy. **SELECTED PUBLICATIONS** Auth, Kennedy and Clinton: A Psychohistorical Analysis, in press. **CONTACT ADDRESS** Dept Soc & Behav Sci, Norwalk Comm-Tech Col, 188 Richards Ave, Norwalk, CT 06854.

GOODMAN-DELAHUNTY, JANE
PERSONAL Born 02/17/1952, Johannesburg, South Africa, 1 child **DISCIPLINE** PSYCHOLOGY, LAW **EDUCATION** Univ Witwatersrand, Johannesburg, S Africa, BA, 72, MA, 73; Univ Seattle Sch of Law, JD, 83; Univ Wa Seattle, PhD, 86. **CAREER** Assoc, 83-84, Bricklin & Gendler, Seattle; trial atty, 84-88, US Equal Employ Opportunity Comm, Seattle; litigation atty, 89-92, Frank & Rosen, Seattle; mediator, arbitrator, 94-, Judicial Arbitration & Mediation Svc, Endispute, Calif; admin judge, 92-, US Equal Employ Opportunity Comm; Assoc Prof, Univ of New South Wales, 00. **HONORS AND AWARDS** Conrad Linder Mem Awd, 73; Amer Jurisprudence Awd, 82, 83; PhD Scholar, 83; Grad Res Fel, 85; Dissertation Prize, 87; Special Commendation, 88; Pres, Amer Psychol-Law Soc, 94; Chairman's Innov Awd, 95; Amer Psychol-Law Soc Fel, 96. **MEMBERSHIPS** Amer Bar Assoc; Amer Judicature Soc; Amer Psychol Assoc; Amer Psychol-Law Soc; Amer Psychol Soc; Int Assoc Applied Psychol; Int Cong Law & Mental Health; Law & Soc Assoc; San Diego Psych-Law Soc; Seattle-King Co Bar Assoc; Soc for Psychol Study of Soc Issue; Wa St Bar Assoc. **RESEARCH** Psychol & law; scientific & expert evidence; employ discrimination; sexual harassment; cultural diversity; collective & political violence; dispute resolution; procedural & distributive justice; causal reasoning; decision-making; stereotyping; eyewitness reliability; jury behavior. **SELECTED PUBLICATIONS** Art, Employment Discrimination and Stereotyping, Encyclopedia of psychology, Oxford Univ Press, Amer Psychol Assoc, 99; art, Civil law: Employment and Discrimination, Perspectives on Psychology and Law: The State of the Discipline, Plenum Press, 99; art, Pragmatic Considerations Supporting the Reasonable Victim Standard in Hostile Workplace Sexual Harassment Cases, Psychology, Public Policy & Law, 99, coauth, Juror Decisions About Damages in Employment Discrimination Cases, Behavioral Sci & the Law, 99; art, Same-Sex Harassment: Implications of The Oncale Decision for Forensic Evaluations of Plaintiffs, Behavioral Sci & the Law, 99. **CONTACT ADDRESS** 2407 Calle Madiera, San Clemente, CA 92672. **EMAIL** jg-d@pacbell.net

GOODYEAR, RUSSELL
PERSONAL Born 07/26/1941, Pine Bluff, AR, m, 1993, 3 children **DISCIPLINE** SPANISH, FOLKLORE **EDUCATION** Marion Inst, ASc, 61; Henderson State Col, BA, 63; Univ Ark, MA, 70; Univ Ark, PhD, 77. **CAREER** Prof, Sul Ross State Univ, 77-93; Prof, Midland Col, 93-. **HONORS AND AWARDS** Teacher of the Year, Midland Col, 94-95; Teacher of the Year, Midland Col, 97-98. **MEMBERSHIPS** Tex Folklore Soc, W Tex Hist Asn, Tex St Hist Asn. **RESEARCH** Folklore and Hispanic literature. **SELECTED PUBLICATIONS** Auth, A Critical Anthology of Cuban Short Stories in Translation, 77; auth, Republic of Mexico: Decimal Coinage, 92. **CONTACT ADDRESS** Dept Lang & Fine Arts, Midland Col, 3600 N Garfield St, Midland, TX 79705-6329. **EMAIL** rhgoodyear@midland.cc.tx.us

GOOSMAN, STUART
DISCIPLINE ETHNOMUSICOLOGY **EDUCATION** Univ WA, PhD. **CAREER** Asst prof; affil fac, Univ Ctr for African & African-Am Stud. **RESEARCH** African Diapora; jazz and popular music; politics and music. **SELECTED PUBLICATIONS** Publ on topics that range from, black group vocal harmony to George Clinton, rap & hip-hop, Juan Luis Guerra & Louis Moreua Gottschalk. **CONTACT ADDRESS** School of Music, Univ of Texas, Austin, 2613 Wichita St, Austin, TX 78705.

GORDON, AARON Z.
PERSONAL Born 10/11/1929, Port Gibson, MS, d **DISCIPLINE** EDUCATION **EDUCATION** Univ Mi, BS 1952; Wayne State U, MA 1956; Univ Mi, PhD 1974. **CAREER** Ft Monmouth, Assoc Officers Signal Course 52; Communications Center Qualification Course, 52; Teletype Operators School, asst officer in charge; Message Center Clk School, officer in charge; SW Signal School Training Center, Camp San Luis Obispo CA; 3rd Infantry Div AFFE Korea, communication center officer, asst cryptographic officer 53-54; Br Officers Advance Signal Officers Course, 63; Command & Gen Staff Coll Ft Levenworth; ICAF, 74; Air War Coll Maxwell Air Force Base; personnel Officer 65; S1 5064 USAR Garr, 67-69; 5032 USAR School, branch officer advanced course instructor 69-71, dir 71-73. **HONORS AND AWARDS** Bronze Star Decoration; co-holder worlds record Outdoor Distance Medley Relay; co-holder world's record Indoor Distance Medley Relay; co-holder am record Indoor Two Mile & Relay 1951. **MEMBERSHIPS** Mem Hlth & Curriculum Wrkshp Detroit Pub Schs 1963; co-author Guide to Implementation of Unit of Smiking & Hlth 1963; asst dist ldr E Dist & Dist Ldr 1961-63; com chmn Hlth & Phys Ed Tchrs Inst Day E Dist 1964; sch dist rep Last Two Millage Campaigns Educ TV Tchr Channel 56 Detroit Pub Schs 1964; mem Detroit Orgn Sch Admnstrs & Suprs; Phi Delta Kappa; pgm chmn Detroit Sch Mem's Clu Metro; Detroit Sco Black Educ Admn; Natl All Black Ed; MI Assc Elem Sch Admn Region 1; com mem Midwest Dist AAHPR Conv Detroit 1964; mem Pgmd Educ Soc Detroit 1965; speaker Blue Star Mothers Detroit1963; Carter CME Ch Detroit; bd dir mem Troop 775 BSA 1964; participating guest Focus Negro Life & History Six Wk Work Shop 1967; coordntr Annual Spelling Bee 1967; participant MaximizingBenefits from Testing Workp Test Admn 1968; participant Ed Admn Workshop 1970-73; dir Professional Skills Dev Workshop Metro Detroit Soc Black Ed Admn Ann Arbor 1973; spkr Hampton Sch Detroit 1973; spkr Joyce Sch Grad 1973. **CONTACT ADDRESS** 15000 Trojan, Detroit, MI 48235.

GORDON, LYNN
DISCIPLINE LINGUISTICS AND TESOL **EDUCATION** Univ Calif, Los Angeles, PhD. **CAREER** Assoc prof, Washington State Univ. **SELECTED PUBLICATIONS** Auth, Maricopa Morphology and Syntax, 86. **CONTACT ADDRESS** Dept of English, Washington State Univ, 1 SE Stadium Way, PO Box 645020, Pullman, WA 99164-5020. **EMAIL** gordonl@wsunix.wsu.edu

GORDON, LYNN DOROTHY
PERSONAL Born 11/25/1946, New York, NY, m, 1981, 2 children **DISCIPLINE** AMERICAN HISTORY, WOMEN'S STUDIES **EDUCATION** Columbia Univ, AB, 68; Univ Chicago, MA, 74, PhD, 80. **CAREER** Teacher social studies, Sweet Home Jr High Sch, 69-73; assoc master of arts prog, Univ Chicago, 74-77; instr educ, Bowdoin Col, 77-78; instr hist, Northern Ill Univ, 79-80; lectr, Princeton Univ, 80-82; from asst prof to assoc prof Educ & Hist, 82-98; Assoc Dean Warner Grad Sch Educ, Univ Rochester, 89-91. **HONORS AND AWARDS** Loewenstein-Wiener Fel Am Jewish Arch, 84; Spencer Found Fel, 91-92; Flora Stone Mather Vis Prof, Case W Reserve Univ, 96. **MEMBERSHIPS** Orgn Am Historians; Nat Women's Studies Asn; Hist Educ Soc (Pres 93); Women Historians Midwest; Berkshire Conf Women Hist. **RESEARCH** History of education and higher education; women's hist; ethnicity and immigration; 20th Century Am Hist. **SELECTED PUBLICATIONS** Auth, Coeducation on two campuses: Berkeley and Chicago 1890-1912, Woman's Being, Woman's Place, 79; Women and the anti-child labor movement in Illinois, Compassion and Responsibility, Univ Chicago, 80; Gender & Higher Education in the Progressive Era, Yale Univ, 90; Why Dorothy Thompson Lost Her Job, Hist Educ Quart, Fall, 94; Race, Class and the Bonds of Womanhood at Spelman Seminary, 1881-1923, Hist Higher Educ Annual, 89. **CONTACT ADDRESS** Dept History, Univ of Rochester, Rochester, NY 14627. **EMAIL** lngo@troi.cc.rochester.edu

GORDON, MILTON A.
PERSONAL Born 05/25/1935, Chicago, IL, m **DISCIPLINE** EDUCATION **EDUCATION** Xavier Univ New Orleans, BS 1957; Univ of Detroit, AM 1960; IL Inst of Tech, PhD 1968. **CAREER** Univ of Chicago Math Lab Applied Science, Education; Chicago Public School System, Education; Loyola Univ of Chicago, Education; IL Inst of Tech, Education; Univ of Detroit, Education; Chicago State Univ, prof of math 78-; Coll of Arts & Science, dean 78-. **HONORS AND AWARDS** Honorary registrar of West Point Mil Acad 1973; **MEMBERSHIPS** Dir Afro-Amer Studies Prog Loyola Math Assoc of Amer, Chicago Math Club, African Assoc of Black Studies, Sigma Xi, Assoc of Social & Behavioral Sci; mem City of Evanston Youth Commiss; chmn Archdiocese of Chicago School Bd 1977-79; bd dir Dem Party of Evanston; mem State of IL Data Comm, Phi Delta Kappa, Amer Conf of Acad Deans, Counc of Coll & Arts & Sci NSF 1964, IL Inst of Tech, Afro-Amer Studies KY State Coll 1971; Rice Univ 1972, Univ of WI 1972, Amer Men & Women of Sci 1972. **SELECTED PUBLICATIONS** Auth, "Enrollment Analysis of Black Students in Inst of Higher Ed from 1940-72"; "Correlation Between HS Performance & ACT & SAT Test Scores by Race & Sex". **CONTACT ADDRESS** Dean, Col Arts & Science, 6525 N Sheridan Rd, Chicago, IL 60626.

GOREHAM, GARY
PERSONAL Born Ft Leavensworth, KS, m, 2 children **DISCIPLINE** SOCIOLOGY, ANTHROPOLOGY **EDUCATION** SD State Univ, PhD, 85. **CAREER** Assoc prof, chair, Dept Sociol & Anthropol, ND State Univ, Fargo. **RESEARCH** Rural sociology. **SELECTED PUBLICATIONS** Ed, The Encyclopedia of Rural America: The Land and People, ABC-CLIO (97). **CONTACT ADDRESS** Dept Sociol & Anthropol, No Dakota State Univ, PO Box 5075, Fargo, ND 58105. **EMAIL** goreham@plains.nodak.edu

GORFAIN, PHYLLIS
PERSONAL Born 10/09/1943, Houston, TX, M, 1965 **DISCIPLINE** ENGLISH, FOLKLORE **EDUCATION** Butler Univ, BA, 65; Univ Calif, Berkeley, MA, 67, PhD(English), 73. **CAREER** ASSOC PROF ENGLISH, OBERLINE COL, 71-, Am Coun Learned Soc study fel, 75-76. **MEMBERSHIPS** MLA. **RESEARCH** Shakespeare; folklore and literature; African folklore. **SELECTED PUBLICATIONS** Coauth, Ambiguity and exchange the double dimension of Mbeere Riddles, J Am Folklore, 76; auth, Puzzle and artifice: The riddle as metapoetry in Pericles, Shakespeare Surv, 76; Riddles and reconciliation: The formal unity of All's Well That Ends Well, J Folklore Inst, 76; Riddles and the tragic structure of Macbeth, Miss Folklore Regist, 76; Toward a folkloristic approach to Shakespearean drama, Southern Folklore Quart, 77. **CONTACT ADDRESS** Dept of English, Oberlin Col, 135 W Lorain St, Oberlin, OH 44074-1076.

GORING, WILLIAM S.
PERSONAL Born 02/01/1943, NY, m **DISCIPLINE** EDUCATION **EDUCATION** Univ Columbia, BA 1959; Univ San Francisco, JD 1963. **CAREER** Mutual of NY Secur; Minority Educ Devel Univ of San Francisco, dir; Special Opportunity Scholarship Programs Univ of CA Berkeley, exec dir; E Bay Home Care Serv Inc, part owner 75; Trio Educ Disadvantage Health Educ & Welfare, task force chmn. **CONTACT ADDRESS** 1511 Linden, Oakland, CA 94607.

GORSKI, PHILIP
PERSONAL Born 07/19/1963, Livermore, LA, m, 1989, 2 children **DISCIPLINE** SOCIOLOGY **EDUCATION** Deep Springs College, AA, 83; Harvard College, BA, 86; Univ Cal Berkeley, PhD, 96. **CAREER** Asst Prof, 96-, Univ Wisconsin Madison. **HONORS AND AWARDS** IRH UW-M; Adv Stud Cen UM; SSRC Berlin Prog; SSRC West Europe. **MEMBERSHIPS** ASA; SSHA; AHA. **RESEARCH** Comparative Historical Sociology; Sociology of Religion; Early Modern European History. **SELECTED PUBLICATIONS** Auth, Historicizing the Secularization Debate: Church State and Society in Late Medieval and Early Modern Europe, 1300-1700, Amer Soc Rev, forthcoming; auth, The Protestant Ethic and the Spirit of Bureaucracy, Amer Soc Rev, 95; auth, Calvinism Confessionalism and State-Formation in Early Modern Europein: George Steinmetz ed, State/Culture, Ithaca NY, Cornell U Press, 98; Calvinism and Democracy: Populism Pacification and Resistance in the Dutch Republic 1555-1787, in: Carl Lankowski ed, Breakup Breakdown Breakthrough: Germany's Tortuous Path to Modernity, NY Berghahn, forthcoming; coauth, The German Left: Red Green and Beyond, NY, Oxford U Press, 93. **CONTACT ADDRESS** Dept of Sociology, Univ of Wisconsin, Madison, Madison, WI 55760. **EMAIL** pgorski@ssc.wisc.edu

GORSUCH, RICHARD L.
PERSONAL Born 05/14/1937, Wayne, MI, m, 1961, 2 children **DISCIPLINE** PSYCHOLOGY, RELIGION **EDUCATION** Tex Christian Univ, AB, 59; Univ Ill, MA, 62, PhD, 65; Vanderbilt Univ, MDiv, 68. **CAREER** Res asst, Univ Ill, 59-61; acting psychol trainee, State Hospital North, Orofino, summer 60; postdoctoral fel, Nat Inst of Mental Health, Public Health Service, 61-63; res assoc, Vanderbilt Univ, 63-65, instr, 65-66; Kennedy Asst prof of psychol, Kennedy Center for Res on Ed & Human Develop, George Peabody Col for Teachers, 68-70, assoc prof, 70-73; assoc prof, Inst of Behav Res, Tex Christian Univ, 73-75; assoc prof to prof, Univ Tex, 75-79; prof psychol, Fuller Theol Sem, 79-. **HONORS AND AWARDS** Diplomate in assessment (Charter mem, ABEP status in development); Fel, Am Psychol Asn, Pres, Div 36, 90-91; Mem, Coun of Representatives, 84-85, 89-90; William James Awd, Am Psychol Asn, 86; pubs in measurement/methodology, personality & soc psychol, psychol of rel and substance abuse. **MEMBERSHIPS** Am Psychol Asn, Soc of Multivariate Experimental Psychol, Soc for the Sci Study of Relig, Relig Res Asn. **RESEARCH** Multivariate statistics and psychology of religion. **SELECTED PUBLICATIONS** Auth, Factor Analysis, Hillsdale, NJ: Lawrence Erlbaum Assoc, Pub (83); coauth with S. McPherson, "Intrinsic/Extrinsic Measurement: I/E-Revised and Single-Item Scales," J for the Sci Study of Relig, 28, 3 (89): 348-354; auth, "Religious aspects of substance abuse and recovery," J of Soc Issues, 51, 2 (95): 65-83; auth, "Exploratory factor analysis: Its role in item analysis," J of Personality Assessment, 68, 3, (97): 532-560; auth, "Toward motivational theories of intrinsic religious commitment," in B. Spilka & D. N. McIntosh, eds, The psychology of religion: Theoretical approaches, Boulder, CO: Westview Press (97); auth, UniMult: for Univariate and Multivariate Data Analysis, (computer prof and guide) Pasadena, CA: Unimult (90-99). **CONTACT ADDRESS** Dept Psychol, Fuller Theol Sem, 180 N Oakland, Pasadena, CA 91001.

GOSS, THERESA CARTER
PERSONAL Born 08/22/1932, Latham, AL, m **DISCIPLINE** EDUCATION **EDUCATION** AL State Univ Montg, BS; NC Central Univ Durham, MLS; Nova Univ Ft Lauderdale, EdD. **CAREER** Jackson State Univ, librarian 54-55; FL A&M Univ, librarian 56; Pinellas HS, librarian 56-66; St Petersburg Jr Coll, librarian 66-81; MM Bennett Library SPSC, dir 81-. **HONORS AND AWARDS** Girl Scout Leadership Awd 1959; PCPTa

Awd for Outstanding Serv 1960; Religious Comm Serv Awd 1961; SOUL Awd for Outstanding Serv 1971; Library Bd Mem Awd City of Clearwater 1976; Alpha Kappa Alpha Awd Outstanding Accomplishments 1979; "Model Library Serv for the Hearing Handicapped" Major Applied Rsch Project Ft Lauderdale Nova Univ 1978, various other publications; Kappa Alpha Psi Awd; Links Awd for Outstanding Serv in Library Science; pres Clearwater Adult Adv Comm. **MEMBERSHIPS** Mem League of Women Voters 1957-; mem Amer Assn of Univ Women 1958-; mem NAACP 1964-; mem Amer Assn of Univ Prof 1979-; mem Women's Adv Com Eckerd Coll 1979-; mem FL Library Assn, Amer Library Assn, Southeast Library Assn, FL Assn of Comm Coll, Phi Delta Kappa, Amer Assn of Univ Women; mem Alpha Kappa Alpha Sor, Links Inc, Silhouettes of Kappa Alpha Psi; Clearwater Airport Authority; Pinellas Co Arts Council. **CONTACT ADDRESS** MM Bennett Library, 6605 5th Ave N, Saint Petersburg, FL 33710.

GOSSY, MARY S.
DISCIPLINE FEMINIST THEORY AND GOLDEN AGE LITERATURE, PROSE NARRATIVE, PSYCHOANALYTIC, THEORY AND LITERATURE **EDUCATION** Bryn Mawr, BA, Harvard Univ, MA, PhD. **CAREER** Assoc prof, Rutgers, The State Univ NJ, Univ Col-Camden. **RESEARCH** Feminist theories and practices of representation, especially in lit. **SELECTED PUBLICATIONS** Auth, The Untold Story: Women and Theory in Golden Age Texts, 89; Freudian Slips: Woman, Writing, the Foreign Tongue, 95. **CONTACT ADDRESS** Dept of Span and Port, Rutgers, The State Univ of New Jersey, New Brunswick, New Brunswick, NJ 08903. **EMAIL** mgossy@rci.rutgers.edu

GOTTDIENER, MARK
PERSONAL Born 05/19/1943, New York, NY, m, 1969, 2 children **DISCIPLINE** SOCIOLOGY **EDUCATION** SUNY, PhD, 73. **CAREER** Asst prof, Univ NY, 73-77; assoc to full prof, Univ Calif, 77-94; full prof, SUNY Buffalo, 94-. **MEMBERSHIPS** Am Sociol Asn. **RESEARCH** Urban Semiotics, Cultural Studies. **SELECTED PUBLICATIONS** Auth, Las Vegas: Social Production of an All American City, Blackwell; auth, The Theming of America, Perseus Press; auth, The New Urban Sociology, McGraw-Hill; auth, Postmodern Semiotics, Blackwell. **CONTACT ADDRESS** Dept Sociol, SUNY, Buffalo, PO Box 604140, Buffalo, NY 14260-0001.

GOUINLOCK, JAMES
DISCIPLINE PHILOSOPHICAL ANTHROPOLOGY **EDUCATION** Columbia Univ, PhD, 69. **CAREER** Prof emer, Philos, Emory Univ. **SELECTED PUBLICATIONS** Auth, John Dewey's Philosophy of Value; Excellence in Public Discourse; and Rediscovering the Moral Life: Philosophy and Human Practice; Ed, The Moral Writings of John Dewey; Coed, Ethics in the History of Western Philosophy. **CONTACT ADDRESS** Dept of Philos, Emory Univ, Atlanta, GA 30322.

GOULD, DANIEL
PERSONAL Born 01/04/1952, Oswego, NY, m, 1979, 2 children **DISCIPLINE** PHYSICAL EDUCATION **EDUCATION** SUNY, BS, 73; Univ WA, MS, 74; Univ Ill, PhD, 78. **CAREER** Asst Prof to Assoc Prof, Mich State Univ, 77-82; Assoc Prof, Kans State Univ, 82-84; Assoc Prof, Univ Ill, 84-88; Prof, Univ NCar, 88-. **HONORS AND AWARDS** Dept Undergrad Scholar, SUNY, 72-73; Nominee for Teacher-Scholar Awd, MI State Univ, 80-81, 81-82; Man of the Year, USA Wrestling, 85; Lillian M. Wellner Distinguished Scholar, Frostburg State Univ, 89; Fel, Am Acad of Kinesiol and Phys Educ; Hall of Fame, Nat Asn for Sport and Phys Educ, 99. **MEMBERSHIPS** Am Acad of Kinesiol and Phys Educ; Am Alliance of Health, Phys Educ, Recreation and Dance; Am Col of Sports Med; Am Psychol Asn; Asn for the Advancement of App Sport Psychol; Intl Soc for Sport Psychol; N Am Soc for the Psychol of Sport and Phy Act; Stress and Anxiety Res Soc. **RESEARCH** Stress-athletic performance relationship; Sources of athletic stress; Athlete motivation; Sport psychological skills training use and effectiveness. **SELECTED PUBLICATIONS** Co-auth, "Coping strategies utilized by National Champion figure skaters," Research Quarterly for Exercise and Sport, (93): 453-468; co-auth, "Sport Psychology: The Griffith era (1920-1940)," The Sport Psychologist, (95): 391-405; auth, "Personal motivation gone awry: Burnout in athletes," Quest, (96): 275-289; co-auth, "Burnout in competitive junior tennis players, III. Individual differences in the burnout experience," The Sport Psychologist, (97): 257-276; co-auth, "Coping with season-ending injuries," The Sport Psychologist, (97): 379-399; co-auth, "People helping people? Examining the social ties of athletes coping with burnout and injury stress," Journal of Sport and Exercise Psychology, (97): 368-395; co-auth, "An examination of mental skills training in junior tennis coaches," The Sport Psychologist, (99): 127-143; co-auth, "Factors affecting Olympic performance: Perceptions of athletes and coaches from more and less successful teams," The Sport Psychologist, (99): 371-395. **CONTACT ADDRESS** Dept Phys Educ, Univ of No Carolina, Greensboro, 1000 Spring Garden, Greenboro, NC 27412-0001. **EMAIL** drgould@uncg.edu

GOVER, YERAH
PERSONAL Born 06/05/1931, Athens, Greece, m, 3 children **DISCIPLINE** CULTURAL STUDIES **EDUCATION** SUNY, BA, 81; CUNY, MA, 89; PhD, 92. **CAREER** Adj asst prof, CUNY. **HONORS AND AWARDS** Honorary Award, John D and Catherine T MacArthur Found, 96; Adv Res Grant, Soc Sci Res Coun, 94. **MEMBERSHIPS** MLA; Am Middle E Studies Asn. **RESEARCH** Ideological impositions on culture as represented in literature and film specifically in relation colonialism and post-colonialism. **SELECTED PUBLICATIONS** Auth, Zionism: The Limits of Moral Discourse in Israel's Hebrew Fiction, Minn Univ Press, 94. **CONTACT ADDRESS** Dept Soc and Cultural Studies, Queens Col, CUNY, 11045 71st Rd, Forest Hills, NY 11375-4960. **EMAIL** garyerah@yahoo.com

GRABER, ROBERT
PERSONAL Born 04/30/1950, Lansing, MI, m, 1972, 2 children **DISCIPLINE** ANTHROPOLOGY **EDUCATION** Ind Univ, AB, 73; Univ Wisc, MS, 76; PhD, 79. **CAREER** Asst prof, Millsaps Col, 79-81; asst prof to full prof, Truman State Univ, 81-. **HONORS AND AWARDS** Phi Beta Kappa, Phi Kappa Phi. **MEMBERSHIPS** Am Anthropol Asn, Soc for Am Archeol. **RESEARCH** Cultural evolution. **SELECTED PUBLICATIONS** Auth, Valuing Useless Knowledge: An Anthropological Inquiry into the Meaning of Liberal Education, Thomas Jefferson Univ Press, 95; auth, A Scientific Model of Social and Cultural Evolution, Thomas Jefferson Univ Press, 95; auth, Meeting Anthropology Phase to Phase: Growing Up, Spreading Out, Crowding In, Switching On, Cardina Acad Press, 00. **CONTACT ADDRESS** Dept Soc Sci, Truman State Univ, 100 E Normal St, Kirksville, MO 63501. **EMAIL** rgrager@truman.edu

GRACE, CHRISTOPHER R.
PERSONAL m, 1987, 2 children **DISCIPLINE** PSYCHOLOGY **EDUCATION** Colo State Univ, MS, 88; Color State Univ, PhD, 88. **CAREER** Asst Prof, Biola Univ, 88-; Asst Provost, Biola Univ, 99-. **MEMBERSHIPS** APS. **RESEARCH** Helping behavior, moral beliefs and behavior. **SELECTED PUBLICATIONS** Coauth, "Effects of Compliance Techniques on Spontaneous and Asked-For Helping," J of Soc Psychol 128 (88): 525-532; coauth, "Psychotherapists' Management of Confidentiality, Burnout and Affiliation Needs: A National Survey," Psychotherapy in Private Pract 13(2) (94): 1-17; coauth, "Introduction to Special Issue," J of Psychol and Theol 23(4) (95): 1-2; coauth, "Excellence in Pedagogy: Some Obstacles to Integration for the Christian Psychology Professor," J of Psychol and Theol 23(4) (95): 3-9; coauth "The Perils and Promises of Teaching Integration in Introductory Psychology," J of Psychol and Theol 23(4) (95): 10-15; auth, "Clearing Away Centuries of Soot: Science, Religion and the 17th-Century Puritans," Fac Dialogue 26 (96); coauth, "Effects of Perceived Ethnicity on Ratings of Speaker/Teacher Effectiveness," Res on Christian Higher Ed 5 (98): 125-139; coauth, "Differential Self-Focused Attention and Helping Behaviors," Psychol Reports (forthcoming). **CONTACT ADDRESS** Dept Psychol, Biola Univ, 13800 Biola Ave, La Mirada, CA 90639-0001.

GRAFF, GERALD E.
PERSONAL Born 06/28/1937, Chicago, IL **DISCIPLINE** ENGLISH, EDUCATION **EDUCATION** Univ of Chicago, AB, 59; Stanford Univ, PhD, 63. **CAREER** Asst prof, Univ of NMex, Albuquerque, 63-66; from asst prof to prof, 66-90, chmn, English Dept, 77-83, Northwestern Univ; George M. Pullman Distinguished Service Prof of English and Educ, 90-99, dir, Master of Arts Prog in the Humanities, 96-99, Univ of Chicago; dean, Curric and Instr, Col of Lib Arts and Sci, prof, Dept of English, Univ of Ill at Chicago, 00-. **HONORS AND AWARDS** Am Bk Award, Before Columbus Found, 93. **RESEARCH** Problem of academic discourse for students, literary & cultural theory, history of education, pedagogy and curriculum. **SELECTED PUBLICATIONS** Auth, Poetic Statement and Critical Dogma, Northwestern Univ Press, 70; coed, W.B. Scott, Chicago Letter and Other Parodies, Ardis, 78; auth, Literature Against Itself: Literary Ideas in Modern Society, Univ of Chicago Press, 79; coed, Criticism in the University, Northwestern Univ Press, 85; coed, Scott, Parodies, Etc. and So Forth, Northwestern Univ Press, 85; auth, Professing Literature: An Institutional History, Univ of Chicago Press, 87; coed, The Origins of Literary Studies in America: A Documentary Anthology, Routledge, Chapman & Hall, 88; auth, Beyond the Culture Wars: How Teaching the Conflicts can Revitalize American Education, Norton, 92; auth, "Hiding It from the Kids," Col English 62 (99): 242-254; auth, "Scholars and Soundbites: The Myth of Academic Difficulty," PMLA 115 (00): 1041-1052. **CONTACT ADDRESS** Col of Liberal Arts and Sci, Univ of Ill at Chicago, 601 S Morgan St, 410 Univ Hall, Chicago, IL 60607-7104.

GRAHAM, CYNTHIA A.
PERSONAL Born 10/16/1957, Montreal, QC, Canada, m, 1992, 2 children **DISCIPLINE** PSYCHOLOGY **EDUCATION** Univ Scotland, BA, 79; Univ Glasgow, Scotland, M.A.S., 82; McGill Univ, PhD, 90. **CAREER** Lectr, Univ Edinburgh, 93-95; adjunct asst prof, Dept Psychol, and asst prof, Dept of Psychiatry, Ind Univ, 96-. **MEMBERSHIPS** Soc for the Sci Study of Sexuality, Am Psychol Asn, Int Acad of Sex Research, British Menstrual Cycle Res Group, World Res Network on the Sexuality of Women and Girls, Portuguese Soc of Clinical Sexology, Soc for Menstrual Cycle Res, Can Psychol Asn. **RESEARCH** Fragrance as a modulator of sexual arousal in women; sexual behavior and knowledge about HIV/AIDS; the effects of steroidal contraceptives on the well-being and sexuality of women. **SELECTED PUBLICATIONS** Coauth, "The effects of steroidal contraceptives on the well-being and sexuality of women: A double-blind, placebo-controlled, two centre study of combined and progestogen-only methods," Contraception, 52 (95): 363-369; coauth, "Crisis intervention," in An Introduction to the Psychotherapies, ed S. Bloch, 3rd ed, Oxford: Oxford Univ Press (96); coauth, "A comparison of retrospective interview assessment vs. daily ratings of sexual interest and activity in women," in J. Bancroft, ed, Researching Sexual Behavior: Methodological issues, Bloomington: Indiana Univ Press (97); auth, "Birth control," in G. Brannigan, R. Allgeier, & E. Rice Allgeier, eds, The Sex Scientists, New York: Harper & Collins (97); auth, "What is emotion?," in M. Porter, B. Alder, & C. Abraham, eds, Psychology and Sociology Applied to Medicine, Edinburgh: Churchill Livingstone (98); coauth, "Effects of fragrance on female sexual arousal and mood across the menstrual cycle," Psychophysiology, 37 (2000): 76-84. **CONTACT ADDRESS** Dept Psychol, Indiana Univ, Bloomington, 1101 E 10th St, Bloomington, IN 47405. **EMAIL** cygraham@indiana.edu

GRAHE, JON E.
PERSONAL Born 11/21/1970, Portsmouth, VA, m, 1995, 1 child **DISCIPLINE** PSYCHOLOGY **EDUCATION** Shippensburg Univ, BA, 92; Univ Toledo, MA, 94; PhD, 97. **CAREER** Vis asst prof, Monmouth Col, 97-99; asst prof and chair, Monmouth Col, 00-. **MEMBERSHIPS** MPA, APS, APA. **RESEARCH** Interpersonal perception, accuracy. **SELECTED PUBLICATIONS** Coauth, "Nominal and Interactive Groups: Effects of Preinstruction and Deliberations on Decisions and Evidence Recall in Complex Trials," J of Applied Psychol 80 (95): 1-10; coauth, "Dyad Rapport and the Accuracy of its Judgment Across Situations: A Lens Model Analysis," J of Personality and Soc Psychol 71 (96): 110-129; coauth, "The Silent Treatment: Perceptions of its Behaviors and Associated Feelings," Group Processes & Intergroup Relations 1 (98): 117-142; coauth, "The Importance of Non-verbal Cues for Judging Rapport," J of Nonverbal Behavior 23 (99); coauth, "The Scarlet Letter: An Examination of Social Ostracism," J of Personal and Interpersonal Loss (in press); coauth, "Teaching Experimental Methods: A reliable experiment that will bring smiles to your students' faces," Teaching of Psychol (in press). **CONTACT ADDRESS** Dept Psychol, Monmouth Col, 700 E Broadway, Monmouth, IL 61462. **EMAIL** jgrahe@monm.edu

GRANROSE, CHERLYN SKROMME
PERSONAL Born 11/23/1942, MI, d, 3 children **DISCIPLINE** BEHAVIORAL SCIENCES, PSYCHOLOGY **EDUCATION** Univ Mich, BS, 64; MS, 66; Kans State Univ, MS, 77; Rutgers Univ, PhD, 81. **CAREER** Admin Asst, Div of Biol, Univ of Ga, 67-71; Instr, Lab Resources Admin, Div of Biol, Kans State Univ, 74-78; Instr, Dept of Psychol, Rutgers Univ, 79-80; Assoc Prof, Dir of Leadership Skill Assessment, Sch of Management, Clarkson Univ, 87-88; Asst and Assoc Prof, Sch of Bus and Management, Temple Univ, 81-93; Vis Fulbright Lectr, Sch of Management, Wuhan Univ, 97; Vis Fulbright Lectr, Sch of Management, Jilin Univ, 97; Vis Fulbright Lectr, Sch of Bus Admin, Renmin Univ of China, 98; Prof, Sch of Behav and Orgn Sci, Claremont Grad Univ, 93-. **HONORS AND AWARDS** Rackham Grad Scholar, Univ of Mich, 65-66; Danforth Assoc, Univ of Ga, 68-72; Phi Kappa Phi, Kans State Univ, 77; Sigma Xi, Rutgers Univ, 80; Univ Fel, Honor Scholar, Rutgers Univ, 78-81; Fulbright-Hays Summer Sem Abroad Prog Korea/Taiwan, 88; Radcliffe Res Fel, Temple/Murray Lib, 90-91; Fulbright Res Fel, Singapore, 91; Fulbright Lect Fel, PRC, 97-98. **RESEARCH** International Career Management, Employee Participation in Organizational Decision Making, Women's Work/Family Decision Making. **SELECTED PUBLICATIONS** Coauth, Science, Sex and Society, WEEAP, US DHEW, Educ Develop Center, (Newton, MA), 79; coauth, Job Saving Strategies: Worker Buyouts and QWL, Upjonh Inst (Kalamazoo, MI), 89; coauth, Work-Family Role Choices for Women in Their 20s and 30s, Praeger (Westport, CT), 96; auth, "Planning to combine work and childrearing," in Women at Work: A Handbook, ed. P.J. Dubeck and K. Borman (NY: Garland Publ, 96), 401-404; coauth, "Global boundaryless careers: Models from Chinese family businesses," in Boundaryless Careers: Work, mobility and learning in the new organizational era (London: Oxford Univ Press, 96), 201-217; ed, Careers of East Asian Managers, Quorum (Westport, CT), 97; co-ed, Cross Cultural Work Groups, Sage (Newbury Park, CA), 97; coauth, "Changing organizational cultures in Chinese firms, " in the Handbook of Organizational Culture and Climate, ed. N.M. Ashkanasy, C. Wilderom and M.F. Peterson (Thousand Oaks, CA: Sage, 00); auth, "Alternative ways of describing time in cross cultural careers research, " in Trends in Organizational Behavior Vol 7, ed. D. Rousseau and C. Cooper (Chichester, NY: Wiley, forthcoming); **CONTACT ADDRESS** Sch of Behav and Orgn Sci, Claremont Graduate Sch, 123 8th St, Claremont, CA 91711. **EMAIL** cherlyn.granrose@cgu.edu

GRANT, BARRY KEITH
PERSONAL Born New York, NY, m, 1947 **DISCIPLINE** FILM, POPULAR CULTURE **EDUCATION** State Univ NY

Buffalo, BA, 69, PhD(English, Am lit & film), 75. **CAREER** Lectr, 75-76, asst prof, 76-81, ASSOC PROF FILM AND POPULAR CULT, BROCK UNIV, 81-, CHMN, DEPT FINE ARTS, 82-, Asst dir, Media Study, Buffalo, 74-75; film critic, CJQR-FM, St Catharines, Ont, 80-; reader, Post-Script: Essays in Film and the Humanities, 82-. **HONORS AND AWARDS** Recipient of the Brock Univ Distinguished Scholar Awd, 99. **MEMBERSHIPS** MLA; Popular Cult Asn; Film Studies Asn Can; Soc Educ Film and TV. **RESEARCH** American film; science fiction; popular music; film theroy; history; criticism; film and literature; genre studies; popular culture; cultural studies; Canadian cinema; documentary film; screen education. **SELECTED PUBLICATIONS** Auth, Film Study in the Undergraduate Curriculum ed. New York: Modern Language Association (Options for Teaching Series), 83; auth, "Purple Passages or Fiestas in Blue?: Notes Toward an Aesthetics of Jazz Vocalese." Popular Music and Society 18, no. 1 (94): 125-143; auth, The Dread of Difference: Gender and the Horror Film ed. Austin: University of Texas Press, 96; auth, Frederick Wiseman's "Near Death" London: Flicks Books, forthcoming 99; auth, The Films of Peter Jackson (Studies in New Zealand Culture Series), London: Nottingham Trent Univ, UK: Kakapo Books, forthcoming 99; auth, "'Sensuous Elaboration': Speculation and Spectacle in the Science Fiction Film." Alien Zone II: Cultural Theory and Contemporary Science Fiction Cinema, ed. Annette Kuhn (London: Verso, forthcoming 1999); auth, "Two Rode Together: John Ford, Fenimore Cooper, and Generic Cycling." John Ford: A Reappraisal ed. Gaylyn Studlar and Matthew Bernstein (Washington: Smithsonian Institute, forthcoming 1999). **CONTACT ADDRESS** Communications, Popular Culture & Film, Brock Univ, 500 Glenridge Ave., Thistle Complex, room 146K, Saint Catharines, ON, Canada L2S 3A1. **EMAIL** bgrant@spartan.ac.BrockU.CA

GRANTHAM, D. WESLEY
PERSONAL Born 01/13/1944, Atlanta, GA, m, 1988, 3 children **DISCIPLINE** HEARING SCIENCE, PSYCHOACOUSTICS **EDUCATION** Oberlin Col, AB, 67; Ind Univ, PhD, 75. **CAREER** Postdoc fel, Northwestern Univ, 75-78; asst prof, Loyola Univ, 78-80; adj asst prof, Vanderbilt Univ Med Cen, 80-87; adj assoc prof, 87-97; dir res, 87-; prof, 98-. **HONORS AND AWARDS** Regional Scholar; Phi Beta Kappa; Dept Fel of the Year; TAASLP Res Awd; ASA Fel; Nominated for Mentoring Awd, 97. **MEMBERSHIPS** ASA; ARO. **RESEARCH** Auditory perception; Binaural hearing. **SELECTED PUBLICATIONS** Coauth, "Fringe effects in modulation making," J Acoustical Soc Am 91 (92): 3451-3455; auth, "Adaptation to auditory motion in the horizontal plane: Effect of prior exposure to motion on motion detectability," Perception & Psychophysics 52 (92): 144-150; auth, "Spatial hearing and related phenomena," in Handbook of Perception and Cognition: Hearing, ed. BCJ Moore (Academic, San Diego, 95); auth, "Left-right asymmetry in the buildup of echo suppression in normal hearing adults," J Acoustical Soc Am 99 (96): 118-1123; auth, "Auditory motion perception: Snapshots revisited," in Binaural and Spatial Hearing in Real and Virtual Environments, eds. TR Anderson, RH Gilkey (Lawrence Erlbaum: Mahwah, NJ, 97): 295-313; coauth; "Echo suppression and discrimination suppression aspects of the precedence effect," Perception & Psychophysics 57 (97): 1108-1117; auth, "Auditory motion aftereffects in the horizontal plane: The effects of spectral region, spatial sector, and spatial richness," Acustica/Acta Acustica 84 (98): 337-347; coauth, "The effect of a free field auditory target's motion on its detectability in the horizontal plane," J Acoustical Soc Am 102 (97): 1907-1910; coauth, "Cross-spectral and temporal factors in the precedence effect: Discrimination suppression of the lag sound in free-field," J Acoustical Soc Am 102 (97): 2973-2983; coauth; "Effects of earplugs and protective headgear on auditory localization ability in the horizontal plane," H. Factors 41 (99): 282-294. **CONTACT ADDRESS** Dept Speech, Hearing Sciences, Vanderbilt Univ, VUMC Medical Center, Station 17-8700, Nashville, TN 37232-8700. **EMAIL** d.wesley. grantham@vanderbilt.edu

GRASSBY, RICHARD
PERSONAL Born 11/29/1935, Darjeeling, m, 1999 **DISCIPLINE** SOCIOLOGY **EDUCATION** Oxford Univ, BA, 57; MA, 61. **HONORS AND AWARDS** PS Allen Res Fel; Vis Prof, Bryn Mawr; NEH, 96; Woodrow Wilson Fel, 97; IAS, Fel, Princeton; Marques Lothian Hist Prize. **RESEARCH** The economic, demographic, social and cultural history of pre-industrial societies, primarily those of England and it dependencies with special reference to business, the family, and material culture. **SELECTED PUBLICATIONS** Auth, "Marine painting as fine art," Am Neptune 54 (94): 245-51; auth, "The decline of falconry in early modern England," Past and Present 157 (97): 37-62; auth, "Love, property and kinship," Eng Hist Rev 113 (98): 335-50; auth, The English Gentleman in Trade: The life and works of Sir Dudley North 1641-1691, Oxford Univ Press, 94; auth, Ship, Sea and Sky: The Marine Art of James Edward Buttersworth 1817-1894, Rizzoli Intl Press, 94; auth, The Business Community of Seventeenth Century England, Cambridge Univ Press, 95; auth, The Idea of Capitalism Before the Industrial Revolution, Rowan and Littlefield, 99; auth, Kinship and Capitalism: Marriage, Family and Business in the English-speaking World, 1580-1740, Woodrow Wilson Cen Press and Cambridge Univ Press, 00. **CONTACT ADDRESS** 10007 Brookmoor Dr, Silver Spring, MD 20901-2711. **EMAIL** rgrassby@compusnet.com

GRAVES, MICHAEL W.
PERSONAL Born 10/27/1952, Belleville, IL **DISCIPLINE** ANTHROPOLOGY **EDUCATION** Univ Wash, BA, 71; Univ Ariz, PhD, 81. **CAREER** Asst prof of anthropology, 81-85, dir, Micronesian Res Center, 85-86, Univ Guam; asst prof of anthropology, 86-89, assoc prof of anthropology, 89-95, full prof, 95-, special asst to sr vp and exec vice chancellor, 96- Univ Hawaii at Manoa . **HONORS AND AWARDS** Men of Achievement, biographee, 93-98. **MEMBERSHIPS** Soc for Amer Archaeol; Indo Pacific Assn; Archaeol Inst of Am; Amer Anthropological Assn. **RESEARCH** Archael of Oceania and Asia; archaeol method and theory. **SELECTED PUBLICATIONS** Coauth, "Seriation as a Method of Chronologically Ordering Architectural Design Traits: An Example from Oceania," Archaeology in Oceania, v 31, 96; coauth, "Dryland Agricultural Expansion and Intensification in Kohala, Hawai'i Island," Antiquity, v 70, 96; coauth, "Integration of Global Positioning Systems in Archaeological Field Research: A Case Study from North Kohala, Hawai'i Island," SAA Bulletin, v 16, 98; auth, "The Study of Prehistoric Puebloan Pottery Designs: The Intellectual Tradition of Southwestern Archaeol," The Journal of Archaeol Method and Theory, v 4, 1998; coauth, "The Tongan Maritime Expansion: A Case Study in the Evolutionary Ecology of Social Complexity," Asian Perspectives, v 37, 98. **CONTACT ADDRESS** Office of Senior Vice Pres and Exec Vice Chancellor, Univ of Hawaii, Manoa, 2444 Doc St, Honolulu, HI 96822. **EMAIL** mgraves@hawaii.edu

GREEK, MORGAN S. J.
PERSONAL Born 02/11/1925, Jacksonville, FL, m, 1954, 2 children **DISCIPLINE** EDUCATION **EDUCATION** Jones Business Col, BS; Univ Miami, B ed; Fla State Univ, MS. **CAREER** Instr, Jones Bus Col, 50-51; teach, Landon HS, 51-58; vis instr, Stetson Univ, 59, 61; res dir, Appalachian Sch camp, 62, 63; eng curr, Duval Cnty Pub Sch, 64; teach, Lees-Mcrae Col Camp, 65; dept ch, Englewood HS, 58-65; pt instr, Jacksonville Univ, 63-81; res prof, res teach, Fla State Univ, 65-70; pt instr, Fla AM Univ, 75-76; pt instr, Univ N Fla, 76-81; asst prof, Stetson Univ, 79-85; prof, City Col Chicago, 85-88; prof, Cen Tex Col, 87; vis prof Jacksonville Univ, 87-. **MEMBERSHIPS** ATEA; FTEA; AASD; FASCD; Phi Delta Kappa; Kappa Delta Pi; Fulbright Alum Asn; FATSS. **SELECTED PUBLICATIONS** Coauth, "Job Descriptions for Officers of the Florida Asn of Teacher Education," 83; coauth, Guidelines for Student Teachers in Florida, 84. **CONTACT ADDRESS** Dept Education, Jacksonville Univ, 2800 Univ Blvd N, Jacksonville, FL 32211.

GREELEY, ANDREW M.
PERSONAL Born 02/05/1928, Chicago, IL **DISCIPLINE** SOCIOLOGY, ENGLISH LITERATURE, RELIGION **EDUCATION** St Mary Lake Sem, STL, 54; Univ Chicago, MA, Soc, 61, PhD, 62. **CAREER** Sr stud dir, Nat Opinion Res Center, Univ Chicago, 62-68; prog dir, High Educ, univ Chicago, 68-70; lectr, Soc dept, Univ Chicago, 63-72; Prof, Soc, Univ Ariz, 78-; Prof, Soc Sci, Univ Chicago, 91-. **SELECTED PUBLICATIONS** Religion as Poetry, Trans Publ, 95; Sociology and Religion: A Collection of Readings, Harper Collins Coll Publ, 95; coauth, Common Ground, Pilgrim Press, 96; coauth, Forging a Common Future, Pilgrim Press, 1997; I Hope You're listening God, Crossroads Publ, 97. **CONTACT ADDRESS** Nat Opinion Res Center (NORC), Univ of Chicago, 1155 E 60th St, Chicago, IL 60637. **EMAIL** agreel@aol.com

GREEN, GEORGE
PERSONAL Born 01/26/1937, Urbana, IL, m, 1977, 4 children **DISCIPLINE** HISPANIC LITERATURE, LINGUISTICS, TRANSLATION, FOLKLORE **EDUCATION** Columbia Univ, BA, 68; MA, 71; MPhil, 74; PhD, 76. **CAREER** Prof, Univ Tex at Brownsville, 76-. **HONORS AND AWARDS** NDF, 71. **MEMBERSHIPS** Ed Bd, Novosantanderino; Ed Bd, Mesquite Rev. **RESEARCH** Latin American poetry and novel, esp Mexico and Central America; 19th and 20th Centuries. **SELECTED PUBLICATIONS** Auth, El Lenguaje Poetico De Ruben Dario, Univ America (Managua, Nicaragua), 99. **CONTACT ADDRESS** Dept Arts, Sci, Univ of Texas, Brownsville, 1614 Ridgely Rd, Brownsville, TX 78520-4964.

GREEN, JESSE DAWES
PERSONAL Born 02/09/1928, Chippewa Falls, WI, m, 1950, 3 children **DISCIPLINE** AMERICAN STUDIES, HISTORY OF ANTHROPOLOGY **EDUCATION** Reed Col, BA, 51; Univ Calif, Berkeley, MA, 57; Northwestern Univ, PhD(English), 72. **CAREER** Asst prof compos and lit, Univ Cincinnati, 64-68; prof to prof emer, Chicago State Univ, 68-. **HONORS AND AWARDS** Summer grant, National Endowment for Humanities, 76 and 81; fel, National Endowment for Humanities, 82-83. **RESEARCH** History of consciousness; literature and anthropology. **CONTACT ADDRESS** Dept of English, Chicago State Univ, Chicago, IL 60628. **EMAIL** j-green1@csu.edu

GREEN, MALINDA HENDRICKS
PERSONAL Born 10/25/1950, Alva, OK, m, 1986, 3 children **DISCIPLINE** EDUCATIONAL PSYCHOLOGY **EDUCATION** Northwestern Okla State Univ, BA, 71, MA, 76; Univ Okla, PhD, 89. **CAREER** Classroom teacher, Medicine Lodge High Sch, Kans, 71-75; classroom teacher, Luling High Sch,

Tex, 80-81; classroom teacher, Breckenridge High Sch, Tex, 81-84; guidance counr, North Barber Count, Medicine Lodge, Kans, 84-86; career counr, Inst for Employment & Career Planning, Univ of Okla, Norman, 86-87; grad teaching asst, Univ Okla, Norman, 87-89; adjunct instr, 89; asst prof, Univ Central Okla, 89-94; assoc prof, 94-98, prof, 98-. **HONORS AND AWARDS** Teacher of the Year for Col of Ed, Univ of Central Okla; Pres, Okla Asn of Teacher Eds, 94-95; mem of Exec Bd, 94-96; State Delegate, Asn of Teacher Eds, 95; Pres, Rocky Mountain Ed Res Asn, 98-99, Pres-Elect, 99-2000; licensed Psychologist through the State Bd of Examiners of Psychologists. **MEMBERSHIPS** Am Ed Res Asn, Am Psychol Soc. **RESEARCH** Sex differences, cultural impact on learning. **SELECTED PUBLICATIONS** Coauth with Jennifer J. Endicott, "Profile of Mature Women Electing Professional Education," The J of Ed Philos & Hist, 44 (94); auth, "Influences of Job Type, Job Status, and Gender on Achievement Motivation," Current Psychol, 14, 2 (95): 159-164; coauth with Jennifer J. Endicott and Sheldon N. Russell, "Conceptual Framework as Basis for the University of Central Oklahoma Initial Teacher Preparation Program," The Tower Rev, 14, 1 (95): 6-14; coauth with Sheldon Russell, "A Comparison of Students Based upon Teacher Preparation Programs," The Okla Teacher Ed, 3, 1 (96): 32-49; coauth with Will Anderson, "UCO and the Issue of Diversity," The Tower Rev, 14, 1 (96-97): 40-50; coauth with Sheldon Russell, "Using Adolescent Gender Role as a Motivational Tool in the Classroom," J: Okla Asn of Supervision and Curriculum Devel, 9, 1 (98): 44-46; auth, "Listening to the Voices of the Teachers Following the Murray Building Incident," OATE J: The J of the Okla Asn of Teacher Eds, 2 (98): 24-34; ed, RMERA 1998: Abstracted Proceedings, Rocky Mountain Ed Res Asn Annual Meeting, Edmond, Okla (98); coauth with Bryan Duke, "Getting Students 'Hooked': Using Theatrics to Encourage Student Investment in Learning," OATE J: The J of the Okla Asn of Teacher Eds, 3 (99): 14-22; coauth with Robin Harris and Dennis Frisby, "The Oklahoma TeleScience Project," OATE J: The J of the Okla Asn of Teacher Eds (spring 2000). **CONTACT ADDRESS** Dept Teacher Ed, Univ of Central Oklahoma, 100 N Univ Dr, PO Box 176, Edmond, OK 73034-5209. **EMAIL** mgreen@ucok.edu

GREEN, RONALD K.
PERSONAL Born 03/16/1936, Oakland, CA, m, 1959, 1 child **DISCIPLINE** SOCIAL WORK **EDUCATION** Linfield Col, BA, 59; Columbia Univ, MS, 63; Calif State Univ, MPA, 70; Univ Tenn, JD, 77. **CAREER** Asst prof and Dir, Office of Res and Public Service, Univ of Tenn Col of Soc Work, 74-80, assoc prof, 80-85; instr and Dir, Prof Develop and Res, Mandel Sch of Applied Soc Scis, Case Western Reserve Univ, Cleveland, 89-94, 89-94, asst dean and instr, 95-96; prof and chair, Dept Soc Work, Winthrop Univ, Rock Hill, SC, 96-. **HONORS AND AWARDS** Nat Inst of Mental Health Grad Fel, 62; Outstanding Young Man in America, 68; Soc Worker of the Year, Knox Area Branch, Tenn Chapter, NASW, 77; Dir, Soc Agency of the Year, Knox Area Branch, Tenn Chapter, NASW, 81; Who's Who Among Human Service Profs, 92. **MEMBERSHIPS** Coun on Soc Work Educ; Nat Asn of Soc Workers, SC Chapter. **SELECTED PUBLICATIONS** Coauth with Alice K. Johnson, Michael D. Bremseth, and Elizabeth Tracy, "No Home, No Family: Homeless Children in Rural Ohio," Human Services in the Rural Environment, Vol 19, Nos 2/3 (fall/winter 95-96); coauth with Kimberly Strom, "If You Offer it They Will Come; Continuing Education Programs on Poverty," J of Continuing Soc Work Educ, Vol 6, No 4 (Sept 96); auth, Handbook of Federal Policy Materials Related to Public Human Services Training Funding, Nat Staff Develop and Training Asn, APWA, Washington, DC (March 96, rev Oct 96); coauth with Richard L. Edwards, "Welfare Reform: Implications for Professional Development in Social Work," Prof Develop in Soc Work, Vol 1, No 1 (spring/summer 98); coauth with Paul K. Dezendorf, "The Impact of Electronic Social Work (ESW) on Rural Practice," in Goutham M. Menon and Nancy K. Brown, eds, 3rd Annual Technology Conference for Social Work Education and Practice, Conference Proceedings, Col of Soc Work, Univ SC (99); coauth with Paul K. Dezendorf, "Using Technology-Enhanced Community Support Networks," in Iris Carlton-LaNey, Richard L. Edwards and P. Nelson Reid, eds, Preserving and Strengthening Small Towns and Rural Communities, NASW Press (99); coauth with Paul K. Dezendorf, "Strengthening Community Coalitions with Internet-based Communications," in J. Finn and G. Holden, eds, Human Services Online: A New Area for Service Delivery, Hayworth Press, Inc (in press); coauth with Paul K. Dezendorf, "Strengthening Community Coalitions with Internet-based Communications," Computers in Human Services (in press). **CONTACT ADDRESS** Dept Soc Work, Winthrop Univ, 701 W Oakland Ave, Rock Hill, SC 29733-0001. **EMAIL** greenr@winthrop.edu

GREENBAUM, MICHAEL B.
PERSONAL Born, NJ, m, 4 children **DISCIPLINE** JEWISH EDUCATION AND STUDIES **EDUCATION** Univ Miami, BS; Jewish Theol Sem, MA; Columbia Univ, PhD, 94. **CAREER** Asst prof, vice chancellor, and CEO, Jewish Theol Sem. **HONORS AND AWARDS** Secy, Nat Ramah Comm; secy, Joint Ret Bd Conser Mvmt; secy, Morningside Area Alliance; evaluator, Nat Comm Accrediting; evaluator, Mid States Asn Cols and Schls. **MEMBERSHIPS** E Asn Col and Univ Bus Officers. **RESEARCH** Louis Finkelstein. **SELECTED PUBLI-**

CATIONS Auth, The Finkelstein Years, Tradition Renewed: A History of The Jewish Theological Seminary, 97. **CONTACT ADDRESS** Jewish Theol Sem of America, 3080 Broadway, New York, NY 10027. **EMAIL** migreenbaum@jtsa.edu

GREENBERG, STEVEN
PERSONAL Born 08/21/1952, Boston, MS, m, 1977, 4 children **DISCIPLINE** EDUCATION **EDUCATION** NE Univ, BS, 75, Med, 79; Bridgewater State Col, CAGS, 90; Univ Mass, EdD, 90. **CAREER** Teacher, Randolph Pub School, 76-77; educ super, Baird Center, 78-81; principal, Unifed School Dist 482, 81-82; teacher, Sharon Pub School, 82-87; admin, Maynard Pub School, 87-88; prof, Bridgewater State Col, 88-. **MEMBERSHIPS** Nat Assoc of Lab Scholars. **RESEARCH** Use of technology in the elementary classroom, student self-esteem. **SELECTED PUBLICATIONS** Auth, Creating a multicultural, nón-graded integrated curriculum writing model, Mass, 92; auth, "Written expression skills taught through student success, Nat Assoc of Lab Schools Jour, 92. **CONTACT ADDRESS** Dept Elem and Early Childhood Educ, Bridgewater State Col, 135 Hart Hall, Bridgewater, MA 02325-0002. **EMAIL** sgreenberg@bridgew.edu

GREENFIELD, LIAH
PERSONAL Born 08/22/1954, Vladivostock, USSR, m, 1979, 1 child **DISCIPLINE** SOCIOLOGY, POLITICAL SCIENCE **EDUCATION** Hebrew Univ Jerusalem, BA, 76; MA, 78; PhD, 82. **CAREER** Asst to The John L. Loeb Assoc Prof of Sociol and Soc Studies, Harvard Univ, 85-94; vis assoc prof, Dept of Political Sci, MIT, fall 92; univ prof and prof of Sociol and Political Sciences, Boston Univ, 94-; vis prof, Ecole des Hautes Etudes en Sciences Sociales, Paris, spring 97 **HONORS AND AWARDS** Ford Found Grant for Grad Res, 80-81; Mellon Fel, 85-86; John M. Olin Fac Fel, 87-88; Inst for Advanced Study, Princeton, mem, 89-90; Grant from the Nat Coun for Soviet & East European Res, 91-94; United Nations, "expert on mission" to UNRISD and UNDP, invited speaker on ethnic conflict at a preparatory conference for the World Summit on Social Development, Aug 17-19, 94; Nat Intelligence Coun, consult, participant in the workshop "New fundamentals of Global Relations," Sept 21, 94; United Nations, Vienna Office, expert consult, invited speaker on ethnic conflict at the meeting organized by the UNPROFOR in Yugoslavia, Jan 16-17, 95; Woodrow Wilson Int Centre for Scholars, Fel, 97-98; Earhart Found Fel, 97-98. **MEMBERSHIPS** Nat Sci Found, Am Sociol, Israeli Sociol, Critical Rev, Encyclopedia of Nationalism (Academic Press), Am Sociol Asn. **RESEARCH** Nationalism; modern society, politics, and economy; philosophy and methodology of social sciences. **SELECTED PUBLICATIONS** Auth, Nationalism: Five Roads to Modernity, Harvard Univ Press (92); auth, "The Origins and Nature of American Nationalism in Comparative Perspective," Knud Krakau, ed, The American Nation--National Identity--Nationalism, Berlin: JFK Institut fuer Nordamerikastudien, Freie Univ (97): 19-53; auth, "Metodologies en l'esrudi del nacionalisma," transl by Esther Sala Miralles, in Nacionalismes I cienties socials, Editorial Meditterrania (97): 239-248. Auth, "Is Nationalism Legitimate? A Sociological Perspective on a Philosophical Question," Can J of Philos, Supplementary Vol 22 (98): 93-108; auth, Nacionalismo: Cinco Caminhos para a Modernidade (Portuguese), Publicacoes Europa-America, Bibliotec Universitaria (98); auth, "Is Nation Unavoidable? Is Nation Unavoidable Today?," in Hanspeter Kriese, et al, eds, Nation and National Identity: The European Experience in Perspective, Zurich: Verlag Ruegger (99); auth, Nacionalisme I Modernitat, Catarroja: Editorial Afers, Universitat de Valencia (99); auth, Then Spirit of Capitalism: Nationalism and Economic Growth (completed June 99); auth, National Consciousness, the Intelligentsia, and Political Change in Russia: An Interpretation of a Culture (in progress); auth, "Etymology, Definitions, Types," lead theoretical essay, Encyclopedia of Nationalism, vol 1 (in press). **CONTACT ADDRESS** The University Professors, Boston Univ, 745 Commonwealth Ave, Boston, MA 02215.

GREENHILL, PAULINE
PERSONAL Born 03/23/1955, Peterborough, ON, Canada **DISCIPLINE** ANTHROPOLOGY, WOMEN'S STUDIES **EDUCATION** Trent Univ, BA, 76; Memorial Univ Nfld, MA, 81; Univ Texas Austin, PhD, 85. **CAREER** Asst prof, 86-90, assoc prof, Can stud, Univ Waterloo, 90-91; women's stud, 91-96, Prof Anthropology & Women's Stud, Univ Winnipeg, 96-; assoc ed, Canadian Folklore canadien, 96-. **HONORS AND AWARDS** SSHRCC grants; Erica & Arnold Rogers Awd Excellence Res Schol; Chicago Folklore Prize, 89; Can Ethnic Stud res grant. **MEMBERSHIPS** Can Women's Stud Asn. **SELECTED PUBLICATIONS** Auth, So We Can Remember: Showing Family Photographs, 81; auth, Lots of Stories: Maritime Narratives from the Creighton Collection, 85; auth, True Poetry: Traditional and Popular Verse in Ontario, 89; auth, Ethnicity in the Mainstream, 94; co-ed, Undisciplined Women: Tradition and Culture in Canada, 97. **CONTACT ADDRESS** Women's Stud, Univ of Winnipeg, Winnipeg, MB, Canada R3B 2E9. **EMAIL** pauline.greenhill@uwinnipeg.ca

GREENWOOD, DAVYDD J.
PERSONAL Born 09/28/1942, Pueblo, CO, m, 1965, 1 child **DISCIPLINE** ANTHROPOLOGY **EDUCATION** Grinnell

Col, BA, 64; Univ Pittsburgh, PhD, 70. **CAREER** Asst Prof to Prof, 70-. **HONORS AND AWARDS** Phi Beta Kappa, Corresponding member, Spanish Royal Acad of Moral and Political Sci. **MEMBERSHIPS** Am Anthropol Asn, am Ethnol Soc, Nat Asn for the Practice of Anthropol. **RESEARCH** Action research, Ethnic conflict, Political economy, Spain. **SELECTED PUBLICATIONS** Auth, "Reconstructing the Relationships between Universities and Society through Action Research," in Handbook of Qualitative Research, 2nd ed, forthcoming; auth, "Action Research Versus Academic Taylorism: Recreating University-Society Relationships," in Proceedings of the Fred emery memorial Conference, forthcoming, auth, "Differences about difference: Learning from Europe about Identity Politics in the United States," Arts and Sciences Newsletter, Cornell University, (00): 1,5; co-auth, " Action Research, Science, and the Co-optation of Social Research," Studies in cultures, Organizations and Societies,99; auth, "The Inhumanities and Inaction Research in Anthropology, Society for Humanistic Anthropology," Anthropology Newsletter, (99): 56; auth, "Postmodernismo y positivismo en el estudio de la ethnicidad: antropologos teorizando versus antropologos practicando su profesion, en Beatriz Ruiz y Jose Maria Cardesin," Antropologia hoy: teoria, tecnicas y tacticas, (99): 193-209; auth, Hondarribia: Riqueza ingrata: comercializacion y colapso de la agricultura, Universidad del Pais Vasco, 98; co-ed, La democracia y la diferencia: culture, poder y preprentacion en los Estados Unidos y en Espana, Madrid, 98; ed, Action Research: From Research to Writing in the Scandinavian Action Research Program, amsterdam, 99. **CONTACT ADDRESS** Dept anthropol, Cornell Univ, 215 McGraw Hall, Ithaca, NY 14853.

GREENWOOD, THERESA M. WINFREY
PERSONAL Born 12/28/1936, Cairo, IL, m, 1960, 2 children **DISCIPLINE** EDUCATION **EDUCATION** Millikin Univ, BA music educ 1959; Ball State Univ, EdM 1963, EdD 1976. **CAREER** E Chicago Pub Schools, music teacher 59-61; Muncie Pub Schools, teacher 62-68; Ball State Univ, acad counselor 71-72; Ball State Univ Burris Lab School, asst prof educ 79-, teacher of gifted/talented program 86-; Middle School Teacher, 98-. **HONORS AND AWARDS** Soc Studies Grant 1982; Commendation IN Gov Orr 1982; NAACP Awd 1980; IN All-Amer Family Awd Family Weekly Mag, Eastern Airlines 1972; fellowship Natl Fellowship Funds Emory Univ 1973-76; BSU Minority Achievement Awd, minority Student Development, 1989, currently developing "Tap the Gap," a progam for at-risk students; developing innovative elementary parent partnership; Team program "Connections" for Christa McAuliffe Fellowship; Ford Fellowship 1975- 76 for doctorate; Eli Lilly Foundation, France, 1989; Teacher of the Year, runner-up, Indiana Dept of Educ, 1982-83; Disney Presents The American Teacher Telecast, 1994; Geraldine R Dodge Grant to design and host "A Celebration of Teaching Conf for Minorities," 1994; Indiana Teacher of the Year Finalist, 1994; Video Report Card,developed and innovated for Christa McAuliffe Fellowship; AAUW Round Table Panelist Natl Gender Study "Gender Bias in the Classroom," 1991; "Women of the Rainbow," Indianapolis Minority Chamber of Commerce, 1992; Served on the Search Committee for Superintendent of University Schools, 1994; Unsung Heros Awd, 1998; Fulbright Memorial Scholar to Japan, 1998; "Wood, Paint and a Good Idea: Young Entrepreneurs," The Technology Teacher, 1998; "Traveling Teddy Bears Teach More Than Geography," Teddy Bear Review, 1999, Ball Univ, Jewish Studies Fellowship, 1998; Presentation, "Young Entrepreneurs," 61st Int Technol Educ Asn Conf, 99; Panel Mem, Ball State Univ "Legacy 21" project, 95, 96; Presentation, Nat Asn of Laboratory Schools, 82, 84, 93, 94, 98; Guest Speaker, Anderson Univ, 96-98; Co-presenter, "Team Teaching Approach for Cardiovascular Training and Relevant Academic Activities," NALS, New Orleans, 98; Co-presenter, "Global Games and the Seven Intelligences," NALS, Phoenix, 97. **MEMBERSHIPS** Past pres Sigma Alpha Iota 1958; music adjudicator NISBOVA 1961-; bd of dir United Way, ARC, Huffer Day Care, WIPB-TV 1969-75; mem Kappa Delta Pi 1972-73; mem & state sec Natl League Amer Pen Women 1973-78; testified White House Conf on Families 1980; mem Eastern IN Community Choir; ed bd White River State Park 1983; judge Social Study History Days; adv bd Social Studies Council Natl Publ 1982; recipient Ind & MI Electric Co Mini-Grant 1987; Kodak (Newsletter Pub 1985 & Prie Time Newsletter Pub) 1986; editorial bd Natl Soc Studies Journal; speaker HS Young Writers Conf 1986; media volunteer Pan-American Games 1987. **SELECTED PUBLICATIONS** Feature Story, Ball State University Research Publication Bene Facta; published, Psalms of a Black Mother, Warner Press ,1970, Gospel Graffiti, M Evans, NY, 1978, weekly newspaper column, Muncie Eve Press; Poems, "Black Like It Is/Was," 1974, "Break Thru (Upper Room Anthology)," 1972, "Crazy to be Alive in Such a Strange World," 1977; bibliographic, Ladies Home Journal, 1976, Essence Mag, 1975, Church Herald, 1972; article, "Cross-Cultural Educ for Elementary School," The Social Studies Teacher, 1983; published poems in the Saturday Even ing Post, 1974; students gained extensive publicity for "Dear-World" letters to Pres Reagan & Gen Sec Mikhail Gorbachev during Washington Summit (exhibited 10 months at World's Largest Children Museum), 1988; writing, "Open Letter to Miss Crawford, Diary of a Black Girl Growing Up in America," Madison County Magazine, March 1991; Published: Technology Horizons Education Journal, "Let's Pop Some Corn and Watch Your Report Card;" Principal Magazine (NAESP), 1995;

Inerviewed for Indianapolis Star and Ball State Information Bureau for national wire services for views on "The Status of Minorities in Teaching" and "Black Creativity and Education;" Created and Produced Educational television show, "What's In The Attic?"; Presented at state and national Gifted Conferences, Indianapolis and Salt Lake City, Utah (Young Entrepreneurs Project); Panel for local PBS telecast, "Parents, The Early Years," 1992; Developed a theoretical, Multiple Intelligence Model based on African Proverbs. **CONTACT ADDRESS** Burris Lab School, Ball State Univ, 2000 Univ, Muncie, IN 47306. **EMAIL** tgreenwo@gw.bsu.edu

GREIL, ARTHUR L.
PERSONAL Born 04/24/1949, Baltimore, MD, m, 1974, 2 children **DISCIPLINE** SOCIOLOGY **EDUCATION** Syracuse Univ, BA, 71; Rutgers Univ, MA, 74; PhD, 79. **CAREER** Instr to full prof, Alfred Univ, 77-. **HONORS AND AWARDS** Who's Who in Am, Contemporary Authors. **MEMBERSHIPS** Am Sociol Asn, Soc for the Study of Soc problems, Sociol for Women in Soc, Soc for the Sci study of Religion. **RESEARCH** Infertility, New Religious Movements, Quasi-religion and para-religion. **SELECTED PUBLICATIONS** Auth, "Infertility and Psychological Distress: A Critical Review of the Literature," Social Science and Medicine, (97):1679-1704; auth, "Sacred claims: The 'Cult Controversy' as a Struggle over the right to the Religious label," Religion and the Social Order Vol 6, (96): 47-63; auth, "Explorations along the Sacred Frontier: Notes on Para-religions, Quasi-religions, and Other Boundary Phenomena," Religions and the Social Order Vol 2, (93): 153-172; auth, Not Yet Pregnant: Infertile couples in Contemporary America, Rutgers Univ Press, 91; auth, "Is Alcoholics anonymous a Religious Organization?: Meditations on Marginality," Sociological Analysis, (89): 41-51; auth, "Infertility: His and Hers," Gender & Society, (88): 172-199; auth, "Social Cocoons: Encapsulation and Identity Transformation," Sociological Inquiry, (84): 260-278; auth, Georges Sorel and Sociology of Virtue, Univ Press of America, 81. **CONTACT ADDRESS** Dept Soc Sci, Alfred Univ, 1 Saxon Dr, Alfred, NY 14802. **EMAIL** fgreil@alfred.edu

GRIFFIN, BETTY SUE
PERSONAL Born 03/05/1943, Danville, KY, d **DISCIPLINE** EDUCATION **EDUCATION** Fisk Univ, BS 1965; OR State Univ, MEd 1976, EdD 1985. **CAREER** Overbrook HS Philadelphia, teacher 1968-70; Model Cities Portland OR, placement dir 1970-72; OR State Univ, dir, field prog 1972-, prof educ psych, dir tchr training prog; KY Dept of Education, dir beginning teacher internship prog 1986-89; Exec Advisor, KY Dept of Education. **HONORS AND AWARDS** Bd mem OR Governors Commiss 1978; Danford Fellow OR State Univ; mem Faculty Networking Stanford Univ 1980; OR Governors Commn on Black Affairs 1985; Governors Scholars Selection Committee 1986; National Forum for Black Public Admin: Eli Fellow. **MEMBERSHIPS** Mem Outstanding Young Women of Ame 1977; ed consult Portland Public Schools 1978-; mem KY Col Assoc 1979, Delta Sigma Theta, Soroptomist; Scholarship committee YMCA Black Achievers; Phi Kappa Phi; Eastern Star. **CONTACT ADDRESS** Office of Instruction, Kentucky Dept of Education, 500 Merd Capital Plaza Tower #1728, Frankfort, KY 40601.

GRIFFIN, WENDY
PERSONAL Born 09/23/1941, Evanston, IL, s **DISCIPLINE** WOMEN'S STUDIES **EDUCATION** Univ Calif Irvine, BA, 78; MA, 82; PhD, 85. **CAREER** Assoc prof, Calif State Univ Long Beach. **HONORS AND AWARDS** BA, magna cum laude, 77. **MEMBERSHIPS** ASR, SSSR. **RESEARCH** Goddess spirituality, elofeminism. **SELECTED PUBLICATIONS** Coauth with Tanice G. Foltz, "Into the Darkness: An Ethnographic Study of Witchcraft and Death," Qualitative Sociol, Vol. 13, no. 3, 211-234 (fall 90), reprinted (95), in Deviance: A Symbolic Interactionist Approach, ed Nancy J. Herman, Dix Hills, NY: General Hall, Inc., reprinted 2000, in Extreme Methods: Innovative Approaches to Social Science Research, ed Richard Tewsbury and J. MitchellMiller, Allyn and Bacon (Plenum Pub); auth, "The Embodied Goddess: Feminist Witchcraft and Female Divinity," Sociol of Relig, vol. 56, no. 1, 35-49 (95); coauth with Tanice G. Foltz, "She Changes Everything She Touches: Ethnographic Journeys of Self Discovery," in Composing Ethnographies, eds Carolyn Ellis and Arthur Bochner, Los Angeles: Altamira Press, 301-330 (96); ed, Daughters of the Goddess: Studies of Healing, Identity and Empowerment, Walnut Creek: Altamira Press (99); auth, "An American Paean for Diana: An Unlikely Feminist Hero," in The Mourning for Princess Diana, ed Tony Walter, Oxford: Berg Pubs, 241-252 (99); auth, "Maiden, Mother AND Crone," in Witchcraft and Magic in Twentieth-Century United States, ed Helen A. Berger, Univ PA Press (2000); auth, "Spirituality" and "Wicca," entries in Contemporary American Religion, ed Wade Clark Roof, NY: Macmillan Reference (2000). **CONTACT ADDRESS** Dept Womens Studies-Fo2 226, California State Univ, Long Beach, 1250 N Bellflower, Long Beach, CA 90840-0001. **EMAIL** wgriffin@csulb.edu

GRIMES, TRESMAINE
PERSONAL Born 08/03/1959, New York, NY, m, 1984, 2 children **DISCIPLINE** PSYCHOLOGY **EDUCATION** Yale

Univ, BA, 80; New School for Social Research, MA, 82; Columbia Univ, MPhil and PhD, 90. **CAREER** Asst prof, 91-96; chair of dept, 98-. **HONORS AND AWARDS** Outstanding Young Women of Am; Outstanding Teacher of the Year; SC Psychol Asn, 98; Who's Who in America, Who's Who Among Am Teachers. **MEMBERSHIPS** Am Psychol Asn, SE Psychol Asn, SC Psychol Asn, Soc for the Teaching of Psychol. **RESEARCH** High risk children and youth, Drug abuse, Ethnic minorities. **SELECTED PUBLICATIONS** Auth, "Bias and Alternatives in Psychological Testing," Journal of Negro Education, (80): 350-360; auth, "In search of the truth about history, sexuality, and Black women: An interview with Gail E. Wyatt," Teaching of Psychology, (99): 66-69; auth, "Creating opportunities for service learning through the applied psychology course," ERIC Document Reproduction Service, (98): 424-504; auth, "HBCUs and Psychology Education: Toward the 21st Century," ERIC Document Reproduction Service, (96): 405-523; auth, "Personal Touch: Mentoring Minorities in Psychology," ERIC Document Reproduction Service, (96): 405-524. **CONTACT ADDRESS** Dept Sociol & Psychol, So Carolina State Univ, 300 Col St NE, Orangeburg, SC 29117-0001. **EMAIL** tgrimes@alphal.scsu.edu

GRIMSTED, DAVID ALLEN
PERSONAL Born 06/09/1935, Cumberland, WI, m, 1960, 3 children **DISCIPLINE** AMERICAN CULTURAL HISTORY **EDUCATION** Harvard Univ, AB, 57; Univ Calif, Berkeley, MA, 58, PhD, 63. **CAREER** Actg instr, Am hist, Univ Calif, Berkeley, 62-63; asst prof, Bucknell Univ, 63-67; fel, Charles Warren Ctr, Harvard Univ, 67-68; Assoc Prof Am Hist, Univ MD, College Park, 68-, Nat Endowment for Humanities fel, 67-68. **HONORS AND AWARDS** Recipient of a Citation for Excellent Teaching, Univ Commencement, 88; Research grants from NEH, the Charles Warren Ctr at Harvard, ACLS, and an IREX grant to the former USSR. **MEMBERSHIPS** Am Studies Asn; Orgn Am Historians; AHA. **RESEARCH** Nineteenth century American cultural history; Jacksonian America. **CONTACT ADDRESS** Dept of Hist, Univ of Maryland, Col Park, 3434 30th St, NW, Washington, DC 20008. **EMAIL** dg33@umail.umd.edu

GRINGERI, CHRISTINA E.
PERSONAL Born, PA, m, 2 children **DISCIPLINE** SOCIAL WORK **EDUCATION** Clark Univ, BA, 78; Univ Wisc, MSW, 86; PhD, 90. **CAREER** Lecturer, Univ Wisc, 89; Asst Prof to Asst Prof and Director of Women's Studies, Univ Utah, 90-. **HONORS AND AWARDS** Silberman Fund, 96; Teaching Excellence Awd, 96; Fac Fel, 96, Vilas Grad Fel, 87; Jonas Hall Scholarship, 78. **RESEARCH** Women and work, Poverty issues, Microenterprise development, Rural community development. **SELECTED PUBLICATIONS** Auth, "Cashing in on Social Capital: Subsidizing Low-wage Work in Rural Areas," Social Development, forthcoming; auth, "Waiting for my job to come back: Rural Underemployment in Seasonal Economies," Rural Sociology, in press; auth, "The Poverty of Hard Work: Multiple Jobs and Low Wages in Family Economies of Rural Utah Households," Social Work, 99; auth, "Making Cadillacs and Buicks for General Motors: Homework as Rural Development in the Midwest," in Invisible No More, routledge Press, 96; auth, "Understanding Changes in Rural Labor Markets," in The American Countryside: Rural People and Places, Univ Press of Kansas, 95; auth, Getting By: Women Homeworkers and Rural Economic Development, Univ Press of Kansas, 94; auth, "Assembling Genuine GM Parts: Rural Homeworkers and Economic Development," Economic Development Quarterly, (94): 147-157; auth, "Work Structures and Rural Poverty," in Persistent poverty in Rural America, Westview Press, 93. **CONTACT ADDRESS** School of Soc Work, Univ of Utah, 201 S 1460 E 250S, Salt Lake City, UT 84112. **EMAIL** cgringeri@socwk.utah.edu

GRISEL, JUDITH E.
PERSONAL Born 06/05/1963, Dover, DE, s **DISCIPLINE** PSYCHOLOGY **EDUCATION** Fla Atlantic Univ, BA, 88; Univ Colo, MA; PhD, 93. **CAREER** Fel, Ore Health Sci, 94-97; Asst Prof, Reed Col, 96-97; Asst Prof, Furman Univ, 97-. **HONORS AND AWARDS** NEH Grant. **MEMBERSHIPS** Soc for Neurosci, NY Acad of Sci, Am Asn for the Advancement of Sci. **RESEARCH** Neuroscience; Biological basis of drug addiction. **SELECTED PUBLICATIONS** Co-auth, "Quantitative trait loci affecting ethanol metabolism in the BXD recombinant inbred mouse strains," Pharmacogenetics, forthcoming; auth, "Mapping quantitative trait loci (QTL)," Alcohol Health and Research World, forthcoming; co-auth, "Effects of supraspinal orphanin FQ/nociceptin," Peptides, in press; co-auth, Increased Ethanol Administration in Beta-Endorphin Deficient Mice," NIAAA Monograph, in press; co-auth, "Toward a Functional Characterization of Orphanin FQ/Nociceptin: Parametric and Organismic considerations, " Eur.Journal Pain, (98): 278-280; co-auth, "Parallel activation of multiple spinal opiate systems appears to mediate 'non-opiate' street-induced analgesias," Brain Research, (92): 99-108; co-auth, "Opioid and nonopioid interactions in two forms of stress-induced analgesia," Pharmacology Biochemistry & Behavior, (93): 161-172; co-auth, "Route of morphine administration modulates conditioned analgesic tolerance and hyperalgesia," Pharmacology Biochemistry & Behavior, (94): 1029-1035; co-auth, "Molecular Biology of Alcoholism and Drug Abuse," in Encyclopedia of Molecular Biology, 95. **CONTACT ADDRESS** Dept Psychol, Furman Univ, 3300 Poinsett Hwy, Greenville, SC 29613-1000. **EMAIL** judy.grisel@furman.edu

GRISSETT, BARBARA
PERSONAL Born 10/21/1947, TN, m, 1985, 4 children **DISCIPLINE** SOCIOLOGY, SOCIAL WORK **EDUCATION** Southern Col, BS, 68; Univ Tex at Arlington, MSSW, 81; PhD, 92. **CAREER** Asst prof, E Tex State Univ, 88-96; assoc prof, E Tex State Univ & Tex A & M at Commerce, 96-00. **HONORS AND AWARDS** Soc Worker of the Year, 99; listed in Who's Who in Col & Univ Fac, 00. **MEMBERSHIPS** NASW, CSWE, BPD. **RESEARCH** Child Welfare. **SELECTED PUBLICATIONS** Auth, "Social Work Practica," in Managing Inter-Disciplinary Departments, eds. L. A. Furr and W. E. Thompson (DC: American Sociol Asn, 92), 68-79; coauth, "Effects of Parental Divorce on Children's Financial Support for College," in The Economics of Divorce: The Effects on Parents and Children, ed. Craig A Everett (NY: The Haworth Press, Inc., 94), 155-166; coauth, "The Effects of Parental Divorce on Children's Financial Support for College," J of Divorce and Remarriage 22.1/2 (94): 155-166; auth, "The Couvade," in Human Behavior and the Social Environment, ed. L. A. Furr (Allyn and Bacon, 96); auth, "Family Diversity," in Human Behavior and the Social Environment, ed. L. A. Furr (Allyn and Bacon, 96). **CONTACT ADDRESS** Dept Soc Work, Texas A&M Univ, Commerce, PO Box 3011, Commerce, TX 75429. **EMAIL** barbara_grissett@tamu-commerce.edu

GROFMAN, BERNARD N.
PERSONAL Born 12/02/1944, Houston, TX **DISCIPLINE** POLITICAL SCIENCE, SOCIAL PSYCHOLOGY **EDUCATION** Univ Chicago, BS, mathematics, 66, MA, political sci, 68, PhD, political sci, 72. **CAREER** Instructor, political sci, 70-71, adjunct asst prof, applied mathematics, 75, asst prof, 71-76, SUNY at Stony Brook; visiting lecturer, political sci, Univ Mannheim (Germany), 73; visiting asst prof, School of Social Scis, visiting asst prof, 75-76; Univ Calif, assoc prof of political sci, 76-80; guest scholar, Brookings Institution, Governmental Studies Program, 84; visiting prof, Univ Wash, Seattle, Dept of Political Sci, 85; fellow, Center for Advanced Study in the Behavioral Sciences, 85-86; visiting prof, Univ Mich, 89; scholar-in-residence, Inst for Legal Studies, Kansai Univ, Japan, 90; prof of political sci and social psychol, Univ Calif, Irvine, 80-. **HONORS AND AWARDS** Pi Sigma Alpha Awd, Best Paper, Annual Meeting of the Midwest Political Science Assn, 79; co-chair, American Political Science Assn, Conf Group on Representation and Electoral Systems, 82-85; Carl B. Allendoerfer Awd (corecipient), for mathematical writing for undergraduates, Mathematical Assn of Am, 85; chair, Amer Political Science Assn, Section on Representation and Electoral Systems, 91-93; designation by the Gustavus Myers Center for the Study of Human Rights in North Amer of Controversies in Minority Voting (book) as one of the outstanding books on intolerance published in North America in 1992; Richard Fenno Prize co-recipient, for the best book published in 1994 in the field of legislative studies (Quiet Revolution in the South) , Legislative Studies Section of the Amer Political Science Assn, 95; Lauds and Laurels Awd for Professional Achievement, UCI Alumni Assn, 95; Awd for Teaching Innovation in the School of Social Sciences, UCI Dean for Undergraduate Education, 96. **MEMBERSHIPS** Chair, American Political Science Assn, Section on Representation and Electoral Systems, 91-93; Inst for Math and Behavioral Sci, 90-. **RESEARCH** Mathematical models of group and individual decision making with a focus on electoral behavior and voter choice and issues connected with representation and redistricting; individual and group information processing and decision heuristics; political propaganda, particularly political cartooning and satire; law and social science, particularly in the domain of civil rights; use of computers as a teaching aid. **SELECTED PUBLICATIONS** Ed, Political Gerrymandering and the Courts, 90; co-editor, Controversies in Minority Voting: The Voting Rights Act in Perspective, 92; ed, Information, Participation and Choice: An Economic Theory of Democracy in Perspective, 93; co-editor, Quiet Revolution in the South: The Voting Rights Act, 1965-1990, 94; ed, Legislative Term Limits: Public Choice Perspectives, 96; ed, Race and Redistricting, 98. **CONTACT ADDRESS** Dept of Political Science, Univ of California, Irvine, 3151 Social Science Plaza, Irvine, CA 92697-5100. **EMAIL** bgrofman@uci.edu

GRONBJERG, KIRSTEN ANDERSON
PERSONAL Born 03/08/1936, Denmark, m, 1970 **DISCIPLINE** SOCIOLOGY **EDUCATION** Pitzer Col, Claremont, CA, BA (Sociol), 68; Univ Chicago, MA (Sociol), 70, PhD (Sociol), 74. **CAREER** Res asst, Pitzer Col, 68; lab asst, Univ Chicago, 68-69; lect in Sociol, Hofstra Univ, 71-73; lect in Sociol, 73-74, asst prof, SUNY at Stony Brook, 74-76; vis prof, School of Social Service Administration, Univ Chicago, 87-88; asst prof of Sociol, 76-78, assoc prof of Sociol, 78-86, prof of Sociol, 86-96, chair, Dept of Sociol and Anthropol, 96, Loyola Univ of Chicago; adjunct prof, in Univ Center on Philanthropy, 97-, School of Public and Environmental Affairs, IN Univ: assoc dean for Academic Affairs, 97-, prof, 97-. **HONORS AND AWARDS** Numerous grants and fellowships from the following sources: Woods Fund, Chicago, Field Found, Chicago, Chicago Community Found, Lyloa Univ, Aspen Inst, prog on non-profit orgs at Yale Univ, Joyce Found, Am Coun of Learned Soc, Ford Res grants, Univ Chicago, SUNY, Albion small fund, Chapin Hall Center for Children, and others, 65-97; Honorable mention, Staley-Robeson-Ryan-St Lawrence Prize, 94; Chmn's Awd, United Way of Chicago, 95; Distinguished Service Awd, past-pres, ARNOVA, 95; ARNOVA Awd for Distinguished Book in Nonprofit and Voluntary Action Res, 95; Architect, Advocate, Advisor Tribute, United Way/Crusade of Mercy, 96; honorable mention, Competition for Outstanding Article in "Nonprofit and Voluntary Sector Quarterly," for The United Way at the Crossroads: Community Planning and Allocation, 97; Academic Leadership Program fl, Committee on Institutional Cooperation, 98-99; honorary mention, Virginia A. Hodgkinson Res Prize, for Mapping Small Religious Nonprofit Organizations: An Illinois Profile, 99. **MEMBERSHIPS** Asn for Res on Nonprofit Orgs and Voluntary Action; Joint Task Force of the Nat Asn for Schools of Public Affairs and the Nonprofit Academic Centers Coun; Am Sociol Asn; ASA Section on Community and Urban Sociol; Midwest Sociol Soc; Soc for the Study of Social Problems; Int Sociol Asn; ISA Res Comm on Poverty, Social Welfare and Social Policy; IL Sociol Asn; Am Soc for Public Admin: Asn for Public Policy Analysis and Management; Asn for Public Policy Analysis and Management, 89-; Population Asn of Am; Am Political Science Asn; Int Soc for Third-Sector Res, 91-; Nat Asn of Schools of Public Affairs and Administration; institutional rep, School fo Public and Environmental Affairs, 99. **RESEARCH** Charity and nonprofit orgs; orgs and org change; public and private welfare systems; comparative social policies. **SELECTED PUBLICATIONS** Auth, Understanding Nonprofit Funding: Managing Revenues in Social Service and Community Development Organizations, Jossey-Bass Inc Pubs, 93; The NTEE: Human Service and Regional Applications, Nat Center for Charitable Statistics, Voluntas 5, 94; Structure and Adequacy of Human Service Facilities: Challenges for Nonprofit Managers, with Ami Nagle, Nonprofit Management and Leadership, 5, 94; Child Welfare Contracting: Market Forces and Leverage, with Ted Chen and Matthew Stagner, Soc Sci Rev, 69, 95; State and Local Funding for Nonprofit Organizations, in Dilemas of Fiscal Reform: Paying for State and Local Government, ed by Lawrence B Joseph, Center for Urban Res and Policy Studies at the Univ Chicago, 96; the United Way System at the Crossroads: Community Planning and Allocation, with Lori Harmon, Aida Olkkonen, and Asif Raza, Nonprofit and Voluntary Sector Quart 25, 96; Transaction Costs in Social Contracting: Lessons from the USA, The Contract Culture in Public Service: Studies from Britain, Europe, and the USA, ed by Perri and Jeremy Kandall, Arena/Ashgate Pub, 97; coauth, "Mapping Small Religious Nonprofit Organizations: An Illinois Profile," Nonprofit and Voluntary Sector Quart 27 (98): 13-31; auth, "Markets, Politics, and Charity: Nonprofits in the Political Economy," in Private Actiona and the Public Good, ed. Walter W. Powell and Elisabeth Clemens (New Haven, CT: Yale Univ Pr, 98), 137-150; coauth, "Small Religious Nonprofits in Illinois," in Financing Am Religion, ed. Mark Chaves and Sharon L. Miller (Walnut Creek, CA: AltaMira Pr, 99), 139-146; coauth, "Nonprofit Organizations and Public Policies in the Delivery of Human Services," in Philanthropy and the Nonprofit Sector in a Changing Am, ed. Charles Clotfeiter and Thomas Ehrlich (Bloomington, IN: Indiana Univ Pr, 99), 139-172; coauth, "Philanthropic Funding of Human Services: Solving Ambiguity Through the Two-Stage Competitive Process," Nonprofit and Voluntary Sector Quart 29 (00): 9-40; Varieties of Nonprofit Funding Sources: Trends and Dimensions, in Financing the Nonprofit Sector, ed by Alan Abramson, forthcoming; **CONTACT ADDRESS** Office of the Dean, Scho of Public and Env Affairs, Indiana Univ, Bloomington, 10th and Fee Ln, Bloomington, IN 47405. **EMAIL** kgronbj@indiana.edu

GROOME, THOMAS H.
PERSONAL Born 09/30/1945, Dublin, Ireland, m, 1985, 1 child **DISCIPLINE** RELIGIOUS EDUCATION **EDUCATION** St Patrick's Sem IR, Mdiv (equiv.), 68; Fordham Univ, MA, Rel/Edu, 71; Union Theol SEM, Doc Rel/Edu, 75. **CAREER** Prof Theol, presently, Boston College. **HONORS AND AWARDS** The Emmaus Awd for Catechetical Leadership from NPCD, 99; Leadership in Catechesis award from NCCL, 97. **MEMBERSHIPS** AAR; CTSA; APRRE. **RESEARCH** Interface of Ideology and Contemporary Culture. **SELECTED PUBLICATIONS** Auth, Educating for Life: A Spiritual Vision for Every Teacher and Parent, Allen TX, Thomas Moore Press, 98; auth, Christian Religious Education: Sharing Our Story and Vision, San Francisco: Jossey Bass, 98; Language for a Catholic Church, KA City, Sheed and Ward, 91; primary auth of new revised, Coming to Faith, series, WH Sadlier, 95. **CONTACT ADDRESS** Inst of Religious Education, Boston Col, Chestnut Hill, Chestnut Hill, MA 02167. **EMAIL** groomet@bc.edu

GROTH, MILES
PERSONAL Born 12/04/1946, Greensburg, PA **DISCIPLINE** PHILOSOPHY; PSYCHOLOGY **EDUCATION** Franklin and Marshall Col, AB; Fordham Univ, PhD. **CAREER** Asst prof, dept of psychology, Wagner Col; existential psychotherapy & psychoanalysis, private practice. **HONORS AND AWARDS** Outstanding Educators in Amer, 76. **MEMBERSHIPS** Amer Philos Asn; Soc Existential Anal; Amer Heidegger Conf; Asn Study Philos Unconscious; Int Soc Phenomenol & Human Sci. **RESEARCH** Heidegger; Existential analysis **SELECTED PUBLICATIONS** Auth, Preparatory Thinking in Heideggers

Teaching, Philos Libr, 87; Newsletter of the Society for Existential Analysis, 96; Existential Therapy on Heideggerian Principles, Jour Soc Existential Anal, 97; Some Precursors of Poppers Evolutionary Theory of Knowledge, Philos Sci, 97; Acknowledgement on the Conferment of the National Hebel Memorial Prize, Delos, 97; The Voice That Thinks: Heidegger Studies, Eadmer Press, 97; Listening with the Mind's Ear, Heidegger's Philosophy of Translation, Prometheus Books, 2000. **CONTACT ADDRESS** Dept of Psychology, Wagner Col, 111 Parker Hall, Staten Island, NY 10301. **EMAIL** mgroth@wagner.edu

GUARNACCIA, CHARLES A.
PERSONAL Born 03/15/1957, Hackensack, NJ, m, 1984, 3 children **DISCIPLINE** PSYCHOLOGY **EDUCATION** Steven Inst Tech, BS, 79; Ariz State Univ, BS, 83; MA, PhD, 90. **CAREER** Engineer, Motorola, 79-82; res asst, Ariz State Univ, 84-89; instr, Univ N Tex, 90-91; asst prof, 91-98; assoc prof, 98-. **HONORS AND AWARDS** UNT Fac Fel; Grad Res Grant; Baywood Pub Awd. **MEMBERSHIPS** APA; GSA. **RESEARCH** Life stress and coping; life stress and adaptation of older adults; life stress and adaptation of cancer and other medical patients and their family members; public health psychology; grief and bereavement; research methodology. **SELECTED PUBLICATIONS** Rev of, Alcoholism and Aging: An Annotated Bibliography and review, Clin Geron 16 (93); coauth, "The scientific study of Adlerian theory," in Interventions and Strategies in Counseling and Psychotherapy, eds. RE Watts, J Carlson (NY: Francis and Taylor, 99); coauth, "Age cohort differences in perceptions of funerals," in End of Life Issues: Interdisciplinary and multidimensional perspectives (NY: Springer, 99); coauth, "Hematological cancer patients' quality of life: Self versus intimate or non-intimate confidant reports," Psycho-Oncology 8 (99): 546-552; coauth, "Influence of perceived preventability of the death and emotional closeness to the deceased: A test of Bugen's Model," Omega: J Death and Dying (99): 261-276; coauth, "The relationship of cause of death to attitudes towards funerals and bereavement adjustment," Omega J Death and Dying 38 (99): 275-290; coauth, "A model of psychological distress for mothers of children with attention-deficit hyperactivity disorder (ADHD)," J Child Fam Stud 8 (99): 27-45; coauth, "Differences Between Mexican Women and US Born Older Women of Mexican Descent on Breast Cancer Screening Health Beliefs and Behaviors," Health Care Women Intl, forthcoming. **CONTACT ADDRESS** Dept Psychology, Univ of No Texas, PO Box 311280, Denton, TX 76203. **EMAIL** guarnacc@unt.edu

GUARNIERI, NANCY M.
PERSONAL Born 03/02/1935, Philadelphia, PA, m, 1957, 3 children **DISCIPLINE** EDUCATION **EDUCATION** Allegheny Col, BA, 53; Temple Univ, MEd, 59; Vanderbilt Univ, EdD, 88. **CAREER** Prof, Tidewater Comm Col. **MEMBERSHIPS** Nat Center for Montessori Educ; Community Col Consortium for Early Childhood; Southeastern Assoc for Early Childhood Educ; ACCESS; Southeastern Assoc for Children Under Six. **RESEARCH** Montessori education. **CONTACT ADDRESS** Dept Soc Sci, Tidewater Comm Col, 1700 College Cres, Virginia Beach, VA 23456. **EMAIL** tcguarn@tc.cc.va.us

GUGLER, JOSEF
PERSONAL Born 04/08/1933, The Hague, Netherlands **DISCIPLINE** SOCIOLOGY **EDUCATION** Munich Univ, Germany, MA, 55; Cologne Univ, Germany, PhD, 59. **CAREER** Lectr, Makerere Univ Col, Uganda, 64-70; vis prof, Lovanium Univ, Zaire, 68; vis lectr, Univ Col, Tanzania, 68; assoc prof, Univ Conn, 69-; vis prof, Regensburg Univ, Germany, vis prof, Mainz Univ, Germany, 83-84; prof, Bayreuth Univ, Germany, 86-91. **HONORS AND AWARDS** Grant, Cologne Univ, 57-58; Grant, Ger Res Asn, Fel, Am Inst of Indian Studies, 80-81; Grant, Ger Res Asn, 87, 89. **MEMBERSHIPS** Int Sociol Assoc Res Committees; Ass Int des Sociol de Langue Fr; Am Sociol Assoc; African Studies Assoc. **RESEARCH** Cities in poor countries, Literature and film in Africa. **SELECTED PUBLICATIONS** Ed, Urban Growth in Subsaharan Africa, Nkanga 6, (Kampapa: Makerere Inst of Soc Res, 70); coauth, "Urbanization and Social Change in West Africa" in Urbanization in Developing Countries, Cambridge Univ Pr, 78; coauth, Cities, Poverty, and Development: Urbanization in the Third World, Oxford Univ Pr, 82; ed, The Urbanization of the Third World, Oxford Univ Pr, 88; ed, Literary Theory and African Literature - Theorie litteraire et litterature africaine, (NJ: Transaction, 94); ed, The Urban Transformation of the Developing World, Oxford Univ Pr, 96; ed, Cities in the Developing World, Oxford Univ Pr, 97; auth, "Wole Soyinka's Konti's Harvest from Stage to Screen: Four Endings to Tyranny", Can Jour of African Studies 31 (97):32-49; coauth, "Ousmane Sembene's Xala: The Novel, the Film and Their Audiences", Res in African Lit 29 (98):147-158; auth, "African Writing Projected onto the Screen: Sambizanga, Xala and Kongi's Harvest", African Studies Rev 42 (99):79-104. **CONTACT ADDRESS** Dept Sociol, Univ of Connecticut, Storrs, 344 Mansfield Road, U2068, Storrs, CT 06269-2068. **EMAIL** josef.gugler@uconn.edu

GUIDO, JOSEPH
PERSONAL Born 04/21/1953, Providence, RI, s **DISCIPLINE** PSYCHOLOGY **EDUCATION** Brown Univ, AB, 75; Dominican House Studies, MDiv, 80; STL, 82; Harvard Univ, Edm, 88; EdD, 94. **CAREER** Roman Catholic Priest, Dominican Friars of St. Joseph Province, 81- **HONORS AND AWARDS** Who's Who Among America's Teachers, 00. **MEMBERSHIPS** American Psychological Association, Society for the Scientific Study of Religion. **RESEARCH** Psychotherapy, adult development, psychopathology, psychology of religion. **SELECTED PUBLICATIONS** Auth, "Beyond Broken Promises: Healing the Wound of Sexual Assault on Campus," America 181 (8), 99; auth, "Schooling the Soul: A Psychological Perspective on the Implicit Theology of Roman Catholic Candidates for Ministry (Toronto: Regis College, 97). **CONTACT ADDRESS** Dept Psychology, Providence Col, 549 River Ave, Providence, RI 02918-0001. **EMAIL** jguido@providence.edu

GUILMET, GEORGE
PERSONAL Born 02/08/1947, Seattle, WA, m, 1980 **DISCIPLINE** ANTHROPOLOGY **EDUCATION** Univ Wash, BS, 69; MA, 73; Univ Calif, Los Angeles, PhD, 76. **CAREER** Lectr, Calif State Col, 76-77; asst prof to prof, Univ of Puget Sound, 77-. **HONORS AND AWARDS** Grant, Carnegie Found, 74; Grant, Univ of Puget Sound, 77-79, 83-84; 86, 88; Martin Nelson Awd, 89, 93; John Lantz Sr Fel, 91; Oustanding People of the 20th Century, 00. **MEMBERSHIPS** Am Anthrop Assoc; Fed of Small Anthrop Prog; Soc for Psychol Anthrop; Soc for Philos and Tech; Pacific NW Hist guild. **RESEARCH** American Indian and Alaska Natives Mental Health, Cognitive and Affective Development among American Indians and Alaska Natives, Psychological Impact of Technocultural Change; Ethics and Technocultural Change. **SELECTED PUBLICATIONS** Auth, "Impact of the Computer Revolution on Human cognition", Cultural Futures Res 8.1 (83): 45-56; auth, "Health Care and Health Care Seeking Strategies among Puyallup Indians", Culture, Med and Psych 8.4 (84): 349-369; coauth, "Cultural Lessons for Clinical Mental Health Practice: The Puyallup Tribal Community", Am Indian and Alaska Native Mental Health Res 1.2 (87): 32-49; auth, "The Effects of Traditional Eskimo Patterns of Cognition on the Acceptance or Rejection of Technological Innovation", Research in Philosophy and Technology, ed Paul T Durbin, JAI Pr, (Greenwich, 85); 149-159; coauth, "Mental Health Care in a General Health Care System: The Experience of the Puyallup", Behavioral Health Issues among American Indians and Alaska Natives: Explorations on the Frontiers of the Biobehavioral Science, J of National Center of Am Indian and Alaska Native Mental Health Res, (88): 290-324; coauth, The People Who Give More: Health and Mental Health Among the Contemporary Puyallup Indian Tribal Community, Am Indian and Alaska Native Mental Health Res J, 89; coauth, "Puyallup", Native America in the Twentieth Century: An Encyclopedia, ed Mary B Davis, Garland (NY, 95): 520-522; auth, "The Safe Futures Initiative at Chief Leschi Schools: A School-Based Tribal Response to Alcohol-Drug Abuse, Violence-Gang Violence, and Crime on an Urban Reservation", Am Indian Cult and Res J 22.4 (98): 407-440. **CONTACT ADDRESS** Dept Sociol and Anthrop, Univ of Puget Sound, 1500 N Warner St, Tacoma, WA 98416-0130. **EMAIL** guilmet@ups.edu

GULLACE, NICOLETTA F.
DISCIPLINE MODERN BRITAIN, EUROPEAN SOCIAL HISTORY, WOMEN'S HISTORY **EDUCATION** Univ Calif, Berkeley, PhD. **CAREER** Asst prof, Univ NH, 95-. **HONORS AND AWARDS** Fulbright-Hays fel, UK; Mellon dissertation fel; Charlotte Newcombe fel; Olin postdoctoral fel in Mil and Strategic Hist; Hortense Cavis Shepherd Professorship, 99-02. **RESEARCH** Gender, popular culture, and political ideology; the cultural construction of warfare, particularly issues of propaganda, public opinion, and the rhetoric of international law. **SELECTED PUBLICATIONS** Auth, White Feathers and Wounded Men: Female Patriotism and the Memory of the Great War, J of Brit Stud; Women and the Ideology of War: Recruitment, Propaganda, and the Mobilization of Public Opinion in Britain, 1914-1918, Univ Calif, Berkeley; Sexual Violence and Family Honor: British Propaganda and International Law during the First World War, Am Hist Rev, 97. **CONTACT ADDRESS** Univ of New Hampshire, Durham, Durham, NH 03824. **EMAIL** nfg@hopper.unh.edu

GULLICKSON, GAY LINDA
PERSONAL Born 07/04/1943, Portland, OR **DISCIPLINE** WOMEN'S STUDIES, EUROPEAN HISTORY **EDUCATION** Pomona Col, BA, 65; Yale Univ, BD, 68, STM, 70; Univ NC, Chapel Hill, PhD(hist), 78. **CAREER** Teacher relig, Day Prospect Hill Sch, 69-72; asst prof hist, Skidmore Col, 78-81; Andrew Mellon fel, Univ Pittsburgh, 81-82; Asst Prof Hist, Univ MD, 82-, Teaching assoc, Danforth Found, 80-. **MEMBERSHIPS** AHA; Social Sci Hist Asn. **RESEARCH** The French textile industry; rural industrialization; sexual divisions of labor and women's work. **SELECTED PUBLICATIONS** Auth, Property, Production, and Family in Neckarhausen, 1700-1870, Soc Hist, Vol 0018, 93; The Land and the Loom--Peasants and Profit in Northern France, 1680-1800, J Econ Hist, Vol 0054, 94; Industry and Politics in Rural France--Peasants of the Isere, 1870-1914, Am Hist Rev, Vol 0100, 95; Art and the French Commune--Imagining Paris after War and Revolution, Am Hist Rev, Vol 0101, 96; The Flour War--Gender, Class, and Community in Late Ancien-Regime French Society, J Interdisciplinary Hist, Vol 0027, 96; European Women and Preindustrial Craft, J Interdisciplinary Hist, Vol 0028, 97. **CONTACT ADDRESS** Dept of Hist, Univ of Maryland, Col Park, 2115 Francis Scott Key Hall, College Park, MD 20742. **EMAIL** gg17@umail.umd.edu

GUMPERZ, JOHN J.
DISCIPLINE LINGUISTICS, ANTHROPOLOGY **EDUCATION** Univ Cincinnati, BA, 47; Univ Mich, PhD(Ger ling), 54. **CAREER** Instr ling, Cornell Univ, 52-54; from instr to assoc prof S Asian lang and ling, 56-67, Prof Anthrop, Univ Calif, Berkeley, 67-, Ford Found fel ling, India, 54-56; mem comt sociolinguistics, Soc Sci Res Coun, 66-73; Trainers of Teachers of Teachers comt, Berkeley sch bd, 69-71. **MEMBERSHIPS** Ling Soc Am; Am Anthrop Asn; Ling Soc India; AAAS. **RESEARCH** Sociolinguistics; linguistics and cognitive anthropology; applied linguistics. **SELECTED PUBLICATIONS** Auth, Treacherous Words--Gender and Power in Academic Assessment, Folia Linguistica, Vol 0030, 96. **CONTACT ADDRESS** Dept of Anthrop, Univ of California, Berkeley, 232 Kroeber Hall, Berkeley, CA 94720.

GUNDAKER, G.
DISCIPLINE ANTHROPOLOGY **EDUCATION** Bennington Col, BA, 72; E Tenn State Univ, MFA, 77; Columbia Univ, Ed D, 88; Yale Univ, PhD, 92. **CAREER** Asst prof, 93-00; assoc prof, William and Mary Col, 00-. **HONORS AND AWARDS** Land Arch Fel; CCSAC Fel; SAR Fel. **MEMBERSHIPS** ASA; AAA; AFS; CAA; AAR. **RESEARCH** Education; art; culture; religion. **SELECTED PUBLICATIONS** Auth, Signs of Diaspora/Diaspora Signs: Literacies, Creolization, and Vernacular Practice, Oxford Univ Press, 98; ed, Keep Your Head to the Sky: Interpreting African American Home Ground, Univ Princeton, 98. **CONTACT ADDRESS** Dept Anthropology, Col of William and Mary, PO Box 8795, Williamsburg, VA 23187.

GUSTERSON, HUGH
PERSONAL Born 01/28/1959, United Kingdom, s **DISCIPLINE** ANTHROPOLOGY **EDUCATION** Cambridge UK, BA, 80; Univ Pa, MSc, 82; Stanford Univ, PhD, 92. **CAREER** Weatherherd Fel, Sch of Am Res Santa Fl, 91-92; from Assoc to Asst Prof, Mass Inst of Technology, 92-. **HONORS AND AWARDS** Levitan Prize, Mass Inst of Technology. **MEMBERSHIPS** Am Anthrop Asn, Soc for Soc Study of Sci, Soc for Cult Anthrop, Am Ethnol Asn. **RESEARCH** Cultural Theory, Science Studies, Security Studies. **SELECTED PUBLICATIONS** Auth, Nuclear Rites: A Weapons Laboratory at the End of the Cold War, Univ of Calif Press, 96; auth, "Comment on 'Controlling Processes: Tracing the Dynamic Processes of Power' by Laura Nader," Current Anthrop 38-5 (97); coauth, "An Internet Experiment," Anthrop Newsletter 39-2 (98): 19; auth, "Reimagining Russian Nuclear Weapons Scientists," Anthrop of E Europe Rev 16-1 (98): 27-30; auth, "Nuclear Weapons and the Other in the Western Imagination," Cult Anthrop 14-1 (99): 111-143; auth, "Presenting The Creation: Dean Acheson and the Rhetorical Legitimization of NATO," Alternatives 24 (99): 39-57; auth, "(Anti)nuclear Pilgrims," Anthropologiska Studier 62-62 (99): 61-66; auth, "Feminist Militarism," Polit and Legal Anthrop Rev 22-2 (99): 17-26; auth, "Los Alamos: A Summer Under Siege," Bull of the Atomic Scientists 55-6 (99): 36-41; co-ed, Cultures of Insecurity: States, Communities, and the Production of Danger, Univ of Minn Press, 99. **CONTACT ADDRESS** Dept Anthrop, Massachusetts Inst of Tech, 77 Massachusetts Ave, Cambridge, MA 02139-4301.

GUTEK, GERALD LEE
PERSONAL Born 07/10/1935, Streator, IL, m, 1965, 2 children **DISCIPLINE** HISTORY OF EDUCATION **EDUCATION** Univ Ill, Urbana, BA, 57, MA, 59, PhD(educ), 64. **CAREER** From instr to asst prof educ, 63-68, assoc prof found of educ, 68-72, chmn dept found of educ, 69-72, Prof Hist and Found of Educ, Loyola Univ Chicago, 72-, Am Philos Soc res grant, 68; partic, Foreign Policy Asn Proj Modernization in India, 69. **MEMBERSHIPS** Hist Educ Soc; Philos Educ Soc; Nat Coun Social Studies; Orgn Am Historians. **RESEARCH** History of the Pestalozzian Movement in the United States; educational theory. **SELECTED PUBLICATIONS** Auth, Pestalozzi and Education, Random, 68; The Educational Theory of George S Counts, Ohio State Univ, 70; An Historical Introduction to American Education, Crowell, 70; A History of the Western Educational Experience, Random, 72; Philosophical Alternatives in Education, Merrill, 74; Joseph Neef: The Americanization of Pestalozzianism, Univ Ala, 78. **CONTACT ADDRESS** Found of Educ, Loyola Univ, Chicago, Chicago, IL 60611.

GUTHMAN, CHRISTINE A.
PERSONAL Born 02/17/1937, Grenada, West Indies, w, 1969, 8 children **DISCIPLINE** HEALTH SCIENCES **EDUCATION** Brooklyn Col, BS, 64; Columbia Univ, MPH, 68; NY Univ, DPhil, 87. **CAREER** Asst prof, Stony Brook Univ, 74-76; special asst to the county exec, Suffolk County Govt, 88-90; prof, Suffolk County Community Col, 90-; academic chair of Health Sci, Suffolk County Community Col, 95-98. **HONORS AND AWARDS** Health Educ Awd, Nat Asn of business and Professional Women, 85; Long Island Black Educator's Asn

Awd, 93; Sensitivity Training Awd, Suffolk County Police Dept, 97. **MEMBERSHIPS** Am Public Health Asn, Am Asn of Health, Physical Education, Recreation, and Dance. **RESEARCH** Socioeconomic Factors and Health Care, Sexual Assault, Healing Racism. **SELECTED PUBLICATIONS** Auth, "After the Rape: Guidelines in the AIDS Era," The Nursing Spectum 6.5 (94); auth, Rx for Healing Racism, Allette World Press (Huntington, NY), 00. **CONTACT ADDRESS** Dept Health Occupations, Suffolk County Comm Col, Western, 1001 Crooked Hill Rd, Brentwood, NY 11717. **EMAIL** guthmac@sunysuffolk.edu

GUTHRIE, SHARON R.
PERSONAL Born 01/07/1950, Ventura, CA, s **DISCIPLINE** PHYSICAL EDUCATION **EDUCATION** Univ Calif, BA, 72; Calif State Univ, BA, 75; MA, 75; MA, 82; Oh State Univ, PhD, 85. **CAREER** Asst Prof to Assoc Prof, Calif State Univ, 90-. **HONORS AND AWARDS** Women Studies Awd, 95; Phi Beta Delta Honor Soc, 91; Outstanding Teaching Awd, DePaul Univ,; Delta Psi Kappa Awd, 84-86; Phi Kappa Phi, Dean's Scholar. **RESEARCH** The interaction of physical activity and self-perception; sport sociology (e.g., gender, disability, sexual orientation), sport/exercise psychology (body image, self-concept) **SELECTED PUBLICATIONS** auth, "Disability and Sport: A Sociological Analysis," in Textbook of Sports Medicine, in press; auth, "The Effects of Three Types of Physical Activity on the Physical Self Worth and Global Self Esteem of College Women: A test of Fox and Corbin's hierarchical model of self," Journal of Sport and Exercise Psychology, forthcoming; auth, "Managing imperfection in a perfectionistic culture: Physical activity and disability management among women with disabilities," Quest, (99): 369-381; auth, "Interactive interview with Pat Griffin regarding her book,' Strong Women, Deep Closets: Lesbians and Homophobia in Women's Sport," Quest, (99): 289-301; auth, "Building feminism: A Review of three books: Leslie Heywood's Bodymakers, Maria Lowe's Women of Steel, and Pamela Moore's Building Bodies," International Review for Sport Sociology, (99): 427-430; auth, "Women and Self defense," in International Encyclopedia of Women and Sport, Macmillan, 99; auth, Feminism and the Female body: Liberating the Amazon within, Lynne Rienner Pub, 98; auth, "Defending the Self: Martial arts and women's self-esteem," Women in Sport and Physical Activity Journal, (97): 1-28; auth, "Women with disabilities: Transgressive challenges to the normative body," Perspectives: Journal of the Western Society of Physical Education for College Women, 97; auth, "Liberating the Amazon: Empowering women through feminist education with the martial arts," Perspectives: Journal of the Western Society of Physical Education of College Women, (97): 57-65. **CONTACT ADDRESS** Dept Kinesiol & Phys Ed, California State Univ, Long Beach, 1250 N Bellflower, Long Beach, CA 90840-0001. **EMAIL** guthrie@csulb.edu

GUTOWSKI, CAROLYN
PERSONAL Born Pittsburgh, PA **DISCIPLINE** RELIGION, GERONTOLOGY **EDUCATION** LaRoche Col, BA, 69; Duquesne Univ, MAT, 73; Walden Univ, PhD, 90. **CAREER** Adj prof, MaryMount Univ, 94-; teacher, Pittsburgh parochial schs, 61-; founder, dir, Bonaventure Soc Svcs Ctr, 76-80; prof coord, Ctr App Res and the Apostolate, 87-88; prog coord Nat Inst for the Family, 80-87; Exec Dir, Advisory Neighborhood Comm 3-C, 92-98; Dir of Prog, National Institute for the Family. **MEMBERSHIPS** Am Acad Rel; Am Soc Aging; Environ Alliance Senior Involvement; N Am Coalittion Rel & Ecology (NACRE). **RESEARCH** Grandparenting; spirituality and aging. **SELECTED PUBLICATIONS** Auth, Grandparents are Forever, Paulist Press, 94; auth, The Regenerative Role of Grandparents, AARP/Cornell Univ, 91; auth, Grandparents are Forever, Catholic Woman, Sept 94. **CONTACT ADDRESS** 8101 Connecticut Ave, N410, Chevy Chase, MD 20815. **EMAIL** gutgeist@ioip.com

GUTWIRTH, MADELYN
PERSONAL Born 01/04/1926, Brooklyn, NY, m, 1948, 3 children **DISCIPLINE** FRENCH LITERATURE, WOMEN'S STUDIES **EDUCATION** Brooklyn Col, BA, 47; Bryn Mawr Col, MA, 49, PhD(French), 58. **CAREER** Instr French, Haverford Col, 50-51; assoc prof, 66-69, Prof French, West Chester State Col, 69-, FAC Coordr, Arts and Sci, 79-, Vis lectr French, Univ Pa, 67-68; Am Count Learned Soc fel, 71-72. **MEMBERSHIPS** MLA; Northeast Mod Lang Asn (pres, 73-74); Am Soc 18th Century Studies; Soc d'Etudes Staeliennes; AAUP. **RESEARCH** Madame de Stael; Romanticism; the 18th century. **SELECTED PUBLICATIONS** Auth, Madame de Stael's debt to Phedre: Corinne, Studies Romanticism, spring 64; Madame de Stael, Rousseau and the woman question, PMLA, 1/71; co-ed, Sources et Reflets de l'Histoire de France, Oxford Univ, 71; auth, Corinne et l'esthetique du camee, Acta Collogue de Clermont sur le preromantisme, 72; Madame de Stael, Novelist, Univ Ill, 78; Laclos and le sexe: The rack of ambivalence, Studies Voltaire & 18th Century, 80; Femme, Revolution et mode epistolaire, Cahiers Staeliens, 81. **CONTACT ADDRESS** Dept of Foreign Lang, West Chester Univ of Pennsylvania, West Chester, PA 19380.

GUY-SHEFTALL, BEVERLY
PERSONAL Born 06/01/1946, Memphis, TN, d **DISCIPLINE** WOMEN'S STUDIES **EDUCATION** Spelman Col, BA, 66; Atlanta Univ, MA, 68; Emory Univ, PhD. **CAREER** Prof and Dir, Spelman Col. **MEMBERSHIPS** NWSA; ASA; Nat Coun for Res on Women. **RESEARCH** Black Women's History; Women's History; Black Feminism. **CONTACT ADDRESS** Dept Womens Studies, Spelman Col, 350 Spelman Lane, Atlanta, GA 30314. **EMAIL** bsheftall@aol.com

H

HABERMAS, RONALD T.
PERSONAL Born 09/20/1951, Detroit, MI, m, 1973, 3 children **DISCIPLINE** RELIGIOUS EDUCATION, HUMAN DEVELOPMENT **EDUCATION** William Tyndale Col, BA, 73; North Am Baptist Sem, MDiv, 76; Wheaton Grad Sch, MA, 82; Mich State Univ, PhD, 85. **CAREER** Assoc prof, Liberty Univ, 82-87; assoc prof, Columbia Biblical Sem, 87-93; Mc Gree Prof of Biblical Studies, John Brown Univ, 93-. **HONORS AND AWARDS** Richards Awd in Christian Ministry, Wheaton Grad Sch, 82; Fel, Mich State Univ, 83; Mc Gree Prof of Biblical Studies, John Brown Univ, 93-. **MEMBERSHIPS** North Am Profs of Christian Ed. **RESEARCH** Foundations of religious education; human development; education. **SELECTED PUBLICATIONS** Coauth with Klaus Issler, Teaching for Reconciliation: Foundations and Practice of Christian Educational Ministries, Baker Book House (92); coauth with Klaus Issler, How We Learn: A Teacher's Guide to Educational Psychology, Baker Book House (94); coauth with David Olshine, Tag-Team Youth Ministry: 50 Practical Ways to Involve Parents and Other Caring Adults, Standard Pub (95); coauth with David Olshine, Down But Not Out Parenting: 50 Ways to Win With Your Teen, Standard Pub (95); coauth with Joyce Armstrong Carroll, Jesus Didn't Use Worksheets: A 2000 Year Old Model for Good Teaching, Absey & Co (96); coauth with David Olshine, "How to Have a REAL Conversation With Your Teen, Standard Pub (98); auth, Raising Teens While They're Still in Preschool: What Experts Advise for Successful Parenting, Col Press (98). **CONTACT ADDRESS** Bibllical Studies, John Brown Univ, 2000 W Univ St, Siloam Springs, AR 72761-2112. **EMAIL** Rhabermas@acc.jbu.edu

HACKETT, DAVID H.
DISCIPLINE AMERICAN RELIGIOUS HISTORY, SOCIOLOGY OF RELIGION **EDUCATION** Emory Univ, PhD, 86. **CAREER** Assoc prof. **RESEARCH** Gender and American culture, American catholicism. **SELECTED PUBLICATIONS** Auth, Religion and American Culture: A Reader, Routledge, 95; Gender and Religion in American Culture, 1870-1930, Rel and Amer Cult, 95; The Silent Dialogue: Zen Letters to a Trappist Monk, Continuum, 96. **CONTACT ADDRESS** Dept of Relig, Univ of Florida, 226 Tigert Hall, Gainesville, FL 32611. **EMAIL** dhackett@religion.ufl.edu

HAGAN, WILLIE JAMES
PERSONAL Born 12/17/1950, Montgomery, AL, m, 1979 **DISCIPLINE** EDUCATION **EDUCATION** Mitchell College, New London, CT, AS, 1971; University of Connecticut, Storrs, CT, BA, 1973, MA, 1975, PhD, currently. **CAREER** Dept of Higher Education, Hartford, CT, asst dir of legislative services; Univ of Connecticut, Storrs, CT, dir of government relations, 86-90, acting vice president, 90, Associate Vice Pres, 90-. **MEMBERSHIPS** Member, Government Relations and Communications Officers, 1982-87. **CONTACT ADDRESS** External Affairs, Univ of Connecticut, Storrs, U-166, Storrs, CT 06268.

HAGAR, HOPE
PERSONAL Born 12/01/1941, Willmar, MN, m, 1964 **DISCIPLINE** SOCIAL WORK **EDUCATION** Hamline Univ, BA, 63; Univ IA, MSW, 70; Univ Wisc, PhD, 90. **CAREER** Asst Prof to Assoc Prof and Chair, Univ Wisc, 74-. **MEMBERSHIPS** Soc for Res in Child Dev; Jean Piaget Soc; WI Coun on Soc Work Educ. **RESEARCH** Moral development. **CONTACT ADDRESS** Dept Soc Work, Univ of Wisconsin, La Crosse, 1725 State St, La Crosse, WI 54601.

HAIL, JIM G.
PERSONAL Born 05/15/1936, Amarillo, TX, m, 1954, 3 children **DISCIPLINE** PSYCHOLOGY **EDUCATION** W Tex State, BS, 70; MA, 71; Baylor Univ, EdD, 82. **CAREER** Prof, Mc Lennan Community Col, 71-. **HONORS AND AWARDS** Psi Chi; Alpha Chi; Psi Beta; Phi Delta Kappa. **MEMBERSHIPS** Am Psychol Asn, Am Col of Forensic Examiners. **SELECTED PUBLICATIONS** Auth, "About Humanistic Behaviorism," The Baylor Educator VI (Winter 81-82): 5-8; auth, "The Effects of Immediate Feedback on Retention in the An Academic Setting," Community/Jr Col Res Quart VIII (84): 225-232; auth, Test Bank to Accompany Psychology, Spencer Rathus, Holt, Rinerhart, and Winston, 88, 90; Auth, Test Bank to Accompany Essentials of Psychology, 2 ed, Spencer Rathus, Holt, Rinerhart, and Winston, 88; auth, Test Bank form B to Accompany Psychology Science, Behavior and Life, Crooks and Stein, Holt, Rinerhart, and Winston, 89. **CONTACT ADDRESS** Dept Soc Sci, McLennan Comm Col, 1400 Col Dr, Waco, TX 76708. **EMAIL** jgh@mcc.cc.tx.us

HAJJAR, LISA
DISCIPLINE SOCIOLOGY **EDUCATION** Tufts Univ, BA, 83; Georgetown Univ, MA, 88; Am Univ, PhD, 95. **CAREER** Vis asst prof, Swarthmore Col, 95-99; asst prof, Morehouse Col, 99-. **HONORS AND AWARDS** Malcolm W. Kerr Diss Awd, 95. **MEMBERSHIPS** MESA, LSA, ASA. **RESEARCH** Law, Human Rights, Contemporary Middle East. **SELECTED PUBLICATIONS** Auth, "Sovereign Bodies, Sovereign States and the Problem of Torture," Studies in Law, Politics and Society, (forthcoming); auth, "Speaking the Conflict, or How the Druze Became Bi-lingual: A Study of Druze Translators in the Israeli Military Courts," Ethnic and Racial Studies 23 (00); auth, "Alternatives to an International Criminal Court," Middle East Report, (98); auth," Between a Rock and a Hard Place: Arab Women, Liberal Feminism and the Israeli State," Middle East Report, (98); auth, "(Re)Made in the USA: Middle East Studies in the Global Era," Middle East Report, (97); auth, "Cause Lawyering in Transnational Perspective: National Conflict and Human Rights in Israel/Palestine," Law and Society Review, (97); auth, " Making Identity Policy: Israel's Interventions among the Druze," Middle East Report, (96); auth, "Zionist Politics and the Law: The Meaning of the Green Line," Arab Studies Journal, (94); auth, "Gender, Ethnocentricity and Middle East Studies," News from Within, (93); auth, "Who is a Druze," News from Within, (93). **CONTACT ADDRESS** Dept Sociol, Morehouse Col, 830 Westview Ave SW, Atlanta, GA 30307. **EMAIL** lhajjar@morehouse.edu

HALE, JANICE ELLEN
PERSONAL Born 04/30/1948, Ft. Wayne, IN, d, 1984, 1 child **DISCIPLINE** EDUCATION **EDUCATION** Spelman Coll, BA 1970; Interdenominational Theol Center, MRE 1972; GA State Univ, PhD 1974. **CAREER** Early Childhood Educ Clark Coll, Asso Prof; Dept of Psychology Yale Univ, Res assoc; Afro-Am Studies Prog, Lecturer 80-81; Cleveland State Univ, Assoc Prof; Wayne State University, Prof, 00-. **HONORS AND AWARDS** Winner of Spencer Found Grant, 50 Future Leaders, Ebony Mag, 78, Nominated for Pulitzer Prize, 95 **MEMBERSHIPS** Visions for Children, African-American Early Childhood Educ Res Demonstration Prog; Natl Assn for the Educ of Young Children, 88-92, Nat Coun for Black Child Dev, N.C. Asn for the Educ of Young Children, **SELECTED PUBLICATIONS** Auth, Christian Education for Black Liberation: In For You Who Teach in the Black Church, 73; Auth, The Woman's Role: The Strength of Black Families in the 1st World, An International Journal of Black Thought, 77; Auth, Black Children, Their Roots, Culture and Learning Styles, John Hopkins Univ Press (revised), 86; Auth, Unbank the Fire: Visions for the Education of African-American Children, Johns Hopkins University, Press, 94. **CONTACT ADDRESS** Early Childhood Educ, Wayne State Univ, 213 Educ Bldg, Detroit, MI 48202. **EMAIL** janiceehale@cs.com

HALL, CATHY W.
PERSONAL Born 05/11/1951, Rome, CA, m, 1972, 1 child **DISCIPLINE** PSYCHOLOGY **EDUCATION** Emory Univ, BA, 72; MEd, 74; Univ Ga, EdS, 77; PhD, 82. **CAREER** Asst Prof, Fort Hays Univ, 83-87; Asst Prof to Full Prof, E Carolina Univ, 87-. **HONORS AND AWARDS** Who's Who of Am Women; Who's Who in Medicine and Health Care. **MEMBERSHIPS** Am Psychol Asn; Nat Asn of Sch Psychol; SE Psychol Asn; Intl Coun of Psychol; Nat Acad of Neuropsychol. **RESEARCH** Social Skills in Relation to Special Learners; Resiliency factors. **SELECTED PUBLICATIONS** Co-auth, "Response to Biggs' Comments," Psychological Reports, (97): 1040-1042; co-auth, "a comparison of visual and auditory processing tests on the Woodcock-Johnson Tests of Cognitive Ability, Revised and the Learning Efficiency Test-II," Psychology in the Schools, (97): 321-328; co-auth, "Social perception in students with learning disabilities and attention deficit/hyperactivity disorder," Journal of Nonverbal Behavior, (98): 125-134; co-auth, "Temporal stability of the Learning Efficiency Test-II," Perceptual and Motor Skills, (98): 219-224; auth, "Meningitis and Encephalitis," in Health-related disorders in children and adolescents, (am Psychol Asn, 98); co-auth, "Gender and racial differences in mathematical performance," The Journal of Social Psychology, (990: 677-689; co-auth, "Perception of nonverbal social cues by regular education, ADHD, and ADHD/LD students," Psychology in the Schools, (99): 505-514; co-auth, "College students' perception of facial expressions," Perceptual and Motor Skills, (99): 763-770; auth, "Computer-assisted instruction in reducing errors in scoring of the WISC-III," Psychological Reports, (99): 825-833. **CONTACT ADDRESS** Dept Psychol, East Carolina Univ, 1000 E 5th St, Greenville, NC 27858. **EMAIL** hallc@mail.ecu.edu

HALL, GENE E.
PERSONAL Born 06/19/1941, Rutland, VT, m, 1965, 2 children **DISCIPLINE** EDUCATION **EDUCATION** Catleton State Col, BS, 64; Syracuse Univ, MS, 65; PhD, 68. **CAREER** Prof, Proj and Ctr Dir, R&D Ctr for Teacher Educ, Univ Tex-Austin, 68-86; prof, Univ Fla, 86-88; dean, Univ Northern Col, 88-93; prof, 88-99; prof, Univ Nev-Las Vegas, 99- . **MEMBERSHIPS** Am Educ Res Asoc. **RESEARCH** Change proven in organizations; leadership during change; implementation evaluation; teacher education r&d and policy. **SELECTED PUBLICATIONS** Auth with S.M. Hord, Change in Schools: Facilitating the Process, 87; auth, The Local Education Change

Process and Policy Implementation, J Res Sci Teaching, 92; co-auth, Supervision and Organizational Development, Handbook of Research on Supervision, 98; co-auth, Introduction to the Foundations of American Education, 99. **CONTACT ADDRESS** Col of Education, Univ of Nevada, Las Vegas, 4505 Maryland Pkwy, Las Vegas, NV 89154. **EMAIL** ghall@ccmail.nevada.edu

HALL, JOHN R.
PERSONAL Born 04/23/1946, Louisville, KY, m, 1998 **DISCIPLINE** SOCIOLOGY **EDUCATION** Yale Univ, BA, 68; Univ Wash, PhD, 75. **CAREER** Asst to assoc prof, Univ of Miss, 76-89; prof, Univ Cal Davis, 89-. **MEMBERSHIPS** Am Sociol Assoc; Soc Sci Hist Assoc. **RESEARCH** Religion, culture, economic development, social movements. **SELECTED PUBLICATIONS** Auth, The Ways Out: Utopian Communal Groups in an Age of Babylon, Int Libr of Sociol, Routledge and Kegan Paul (London, 78); auth "World system holism and colonial Brazilian Agriculture: a critical case analysis", Latin Am Res Rev 19, (84): 43-69; auth, Gone From the Promised Land: Jonestown in American Cultural History, Transaction Books, (New Brunswick, NJ), 87; auth, "Social organization and pathways of commitment: types of communal groups, rational choice theory, and the Kanter thesis" Am Sociol Rev 53 (88): 679-92; auth, "The patrimonial dynamic in colonial Brazil", in Brazil and the World-System, ed Richard Graham, Univ of Tex Pr, (91): 57-88; auth, "The capital(s) of culture: a non-holistic theory of status situations, class, gender, and ethnicity", in Cultivating Differences: Symbolic Boundaries and the Making of Inequality, eds Michele Lamont and Marcel Fournier, Univ of Chicago Pr, 92; coauth, Culture" Sociological Perspectives, Prentice-Hall, (Englewood Cliffs, NY), 93; ed, Reworking Class, Cornell Univ Pr, (Ithaca, NY), 97; auth, Cultures of Inquiry: From Epistemology to Discourse in the Methodological Practices of Sociolhistorical Research, Cambridge Univ Pr, (Cambridge), 99; coauth, Apocalypse Observed: Religious Movements and Violence in North America, Europe and Japan, Routledge (London), 00. **CONTACT ADDRESS** Dept Sociol, Univ of California, Davis, 1 Shields Ave, Davis, CA 95616. **EMAIL** jrhall@ucdavis.edu

HALL, RONALD
DISCIPLINE SOCIAL WORK **EDUCATION** Shaw Col, BA, 76; Univ Detroit, MCS, 78; Univ Mich, MSW, 84; Atlanta Univ, PhD, 89. **CAREER** Asst Prof, Mich State Univ. **RESEARCH** Skin color discrimination, **SELECTED PUBLICATIONS** Auth, "Blacks who pass," in Brotherman: The Odyssey of Black Men in America--An Anthology, Ballantine Books, 95; auth, "The Bleaching Syndrome: African Americans' Response to Cultural Domination vis-a-vis Skin color," Journal of black Studies, (95): 172-184; auth, "Occupational aspirations among African Americans: A case for Affirmative Action," Journal of Sociology and Social Welfare, (96): 117-128; coauth, The Basketball Ethos as Exacerbation of Sudden Cardiac Disease Among Young African-American Males, David Walker Res Inst, 97; co-auth, Ownership, Responsibility and Accountability for Student Achievement, Alpine Guild, 98; auth, "Human behavior in the Biracial social environment: Towards a comprehensive identity model" Loyola Journal of Social Sciences, (98): 1-11; auth, "The myth of third world solidarity: Hypergamy by skin color as a vehicle of racism vis-a-vis African-Americans," Psychologia, (99): 1-23; auth, "Identity and the physiological evolution of Eurasians in North America: toward a lifespan human development model," Asian Profile, (99): 537-543; auth, "Western Assimilation of Asian Women: Manifestations of Male Domination," Loyola Journal of Social Sciences, (990: 19-30; auth, "The Bleaching Syndrome: As per racism in the new millennium," Psychologia, (99): 1-20. **CONTACT ADDRESS** Sch of Soc Work, Michigan State Univ, 254 Baker Hall, East Lansing, MI 48824. **EMAIL** hallr@pilot.msu.edu

HALL, WAYNE W.
DISCIPLINE EDUCATION **EDUCATION** Park Col, BA, 68; St Mary's Univ, MA, 76; Univ Houston, EdD, 86 **CAREER** Adj Fac, Rollins Col, 79-83; Adj Fac, Houston Cmty Col, 85-88; Fac, San Jacinto Col, 88-. **RESEARCH** Educational Technology. **CONTACT ADDRESS** Dept Beh Sci, San Jacinto Col, Central, 8060 Spencer Hwy, Pasadena, TX 77505. **EMAIL** whall@sjcd.cc.tx.us

HALLER, ARCHIBALD O.
PERSONAL Born 01/15/1926, San Diego, CA, m, 1989, 5 children **DISCIPLINE** SOCIOLOGY **EDUCATION** Hamline Univ, BA, 50; Univ Minn, MA, 51; Univ Wisc, PhD, 54. **CAREER** Prof Emeritus Sociology, Univ Wisc, 94-; Distinguished vis prof Rural Sociology, Ohio St Univ, 82-83; prof Sociology, Univ Wisc, 65-94; assoc prof to prof Sociology, Mich St Univ, 56-65; res assoc Sociology, Univ Wisc, 54-56. **HONORS AND AWARDS** Order of Merit, Grand Officer, Govt Brazil, 81; Fulbright Fel to Brazil, 62, 74, 79, 83, 87, 88, 89; Distinguished Rural Sociologist, Rural Sociological Soc, 90. **MEMBERSHIPS** Amer Sociological Assoc Fel 59-; Am Assoc for the Advancement of Sci Fel, 75;Industrial Relations Res Assoc, 76-; Intl Industrial Relations Assoc, 76-; Intl Rural Sociological Assoc; Intl Sociological Assoc for Rural Sociology; Latin Amer Res Assoc; Midwest Sociological Soc; NY Acad of Sci; Rural Sociological Soc; Sigma Xi; Sociological Res Assoc **RESEARCH** Societal Stratification Structures; Social Status Allocation Processes; Socioeconomic Development. **SELECTED PUBLICATIONS** Concepts and Indicators of Development: An Empirical Analysis, Jour of Developing Societies, 98; The Socioeconomic Development Levels of the People of Amazonian Brazil-1970 and 1980, Jour Developing Areas, 96; Social Structure and Behavior: Essays in Honor of William Hamilton Seward, Academic Pr, 82. **CONTACT ADDRESS** Dept of Rural Sociology, 350 Agriculture Hall, Madison, WI 53706. **EMAIL** haller@ssc.wisc.edu

HALONEN, JANE S.
PERSONAL Born 07/14/1950, South Bend, IN, m, 1976 **DISCIPLINE** PSYCHOLOGY **EDUCATION** Butler Univ, Indianapolis, BA, 72; Univ Wis, Milwaukee, MS, 76; PhD, 80. **CAREER** Owner and clinical affiliate, Phoenix Clinic, 88-95; prof, Alverno Col, 81-98; Dir, Sch of Psychol, James Madison Univ, 98- **HONORS AND AWARDS** Phi Kappa Phi; NSF Undergraduate Fel, 71; Butler Univ Distinguished Alumni Awd, 95; Texty Awd, Textbook Authors Asn, 96; Ruth Hubbard Cousins Lectr for Psi Beta, 97; Distinguished Teaching Awd, Am Psychol Foun, 2000. **MEMBERSHIPS** Am Psychol Asn, Soc for the Teaching of Psychol, Coun of Teachers of Undergrad Psychol, Am Psychol Soc, Am Asn of Higher Educ, Improving Univ Teaching, Midwestern Psychol Asn, Educational Testing Service. **RESEARCH** Critical thinking, college success, faculty development. **SELECTED PUBLICATIONS** Auth, "The critical thinking companion for introductory psychology," NY: Worth (96); coauth with M. J. Reedy and P. C. Smith, Psychology: The active learner (CD-ROM), Madison, WI: Brown and Benchmark (96); coauth with J. W. Santrock, "The psychology of adjustment," Madison, WI: Brown and Benchmark (97); auth, "Becoming an independent thinker," in P. I. Hettich, ed, Learning skills for college and career, Pacific Grove, CA: Brooks-Cole (92/97); coauth with J. W. Santrock, Your guide to college success, Belmont, CA: Wadsworth (98); coauth with J. W. Santrock, Psychology: Contexts and Applications, Boston, MA: McGraw Hill (98); coauth with C. Gray, The critical thinking companion for introductory psychology, 2nd ed, Worth: NY (in production); coauth with S. F. Davis, The many faces of psychology research in the 21st century, Washington, DC: Am Psychol Asn (in press). A **CONTACT ADDRESS** Dept Psych & Educ Msc 7401, James Madison Univ, 800 S Main St, Harrisonburg, VA 22807-0002. **EMAIL** halonejx@jmu.edu

HALPERIN, D.
PERSONAL Born 09/01/1934, New York, NY, m, 1968, 3 children **DISCIPLINE** PSYCHOLOGY **EDUCATION** Harvard Col, BA, 55; Univ Va Med Sch, MD, 60. **CAREER** Assoc clinical prof, Mt Sinai Sch of Med; adjunct assoc prof, John Jay Col of Criminal Justice. **HONORS AND AWARDS** Certified in psychoanalyses in group; Distinguished contributions to psychoanalysis, CCAPS; mem, adv bds, AFF. **MEMBERSHIPS** APA, AGPA, Am Acad Psychoanalysis, AAPL. **RESEARCH** False memory syndrome, cults. **SELECTED PUBLICATIONS** Auth, Psychodynamic..are, Sect & Colt (85); auth, Group Therapy: New .. (89); auth, Group Therapy with Children and Adolescents. **CONTACT ADDRESS** Dept Psychol, John Jay Col of Criminal Justice, CUNY, 445 W 59th St, New York, NY 10019.

HALVERSON, SUSAN E.
PERSONAL Born 11/23/1948, Echo, MN, d, 3 children **DISCIPLINE** EDUCATION **EDUCATION** Southwest St Univ, BS, 81; Regent Univ, MA, 83; Col William & Mary, EdS, 96; PhD, 99. **CAREER** Asst Prof, Portland St Univ, 99-. **HONORS AND AWARDS** Chi Sigma Iota. **MEMBERSHIPS** ACA, ASCA, AAMFT, ACES. **RESEARCH** Marriage and family counseling, school counseling, counselor education. **SELECTED PUBLICATIONS** Auth, "'And Now I'm Addicted!': A Counselor's Plan to Teach Kids About Addiction," Professional Sch Coun, 3:2 (99): 147-149; coauth, "The Helping Relationship," in Introd to Coun (Needhan Heights, MA: Allyn & Bacon, forthcoming). **CONTACT ADDRESS** Dept Educ, Portland State Univ, PO Box 751, Portland, OR 97207.

HAMILTON, EDWIN
PERSONAL Born 07/24/1936, Tuskegee, AL, m, 1960 **DISCIPLINE** EDUCATION **EDUCATION** Tuskegee Univ, BS 1960, MEd 1963; The Ohio State Univ, PhD 1973. **CAREER** Macon County Schools, dir 1965-70; Ohio State Univ, rsch asst 1971-73; FL International Univ, prof 1973-74; Howard Univ, prof 1974-. **HONORS AND AWARDS** Fulbright Scholar (Nigeria) CIES/USIA 1982-83; Writer's Recognition Univ of DC 1984; Certificate of Appreciation Phi Delta Gamma Johns Hopkins Univ 1986; Certificate of Awd Phi Delta Kappa Howard Univ 1987-89; Distinguished Alumni Citation NAFEO/Tuskegee Univ, 1988; President's Awd Howard Univ, PDK, 1989; designed study-travel to China Tour, 1989. **MEMBERSHIPS** Mem AAACE/ASTD 1975-87; presidential assoc Tuskegee Univ 1980-; mem Intl Assoc CAEO/ICA 1984-87; rsch rep Phi Delta Kappa Howard Univ 1986-87; adjunct prof Univ of DC 1986; educ leader Professional Seminar Consultants's (Russia) 1986; adjunct prof OH State Univ 1987; pres, Howard Univ PDK, 1989-89; elections judge, P G Bd of Elections, Upper marlboro, MD, 1986-87; chief elections judge, 1988-95. **CONTACT ADDRESS** Professor of Education, Howard Univ, Washington, VT 20059.

HAMILTON, RICHARD FREDERICK
PERSONAL Born 01/18/1930, Kenmore, NY, m, 1957, 2 children **DISCIPLINE** SOCIOLOGY **EDUCATION** Univ Mich, 47-48; Univ Chicago, AB, 50; Columbia Univ, MA, 53; PhD, 63. **CAREER** Res asst, Columbia Univ, 53-54; instr, U.S. Army, 54-56; free-lance writer, 56-57; instr, Skidmore Col, 57-59; instr, Harpur Col, 59-64; asst prof, Princeton Univ, 64-66; from assoc prof to prof, Univ Wis, 66-70; prof, McGill Univ, 70-86; from prof to prof emeritus, Ohio State Univ, 86-. **HONORS AND AWARDS** Scholar, NY State, 47; Scholar, Univ Chicago, 50; grant, Columbia Univ, 53; three grants, State Univ NY Res Found, 60-63; five grants, Princeton Univ Comt on Res, 64-65; fac res grant, Soc Sci Res Coun, 66; res comt grant, Univ Wis, 67-68; fac res grant, Soc Sci Res Coun, 68; Nat Sci Found grant, 69-71; Canada Coun Grant, 70-73 & 74-78; five grants, McGill Univ Res Comt, 70-74; grant, Soc Sci and Humanities Res Coun of Canada, 79-86; seed grant, Ohio State Univ, 88; Distinguished Scholar Awd, Ohio State Univ, 93. **RESEARCH** Political Sociology, Historical Sociology, Comparative Institutions. **SELECTED PUBLICATIONS** Auth, The Social Misconstruction of Reality: Validation and Verification in the Scholarly Community, Yale Univ Press, 96; auth, Marxism, Revisionism, and Leninism: Explication, Assessment and Commentary, Praeger, forthcoming; auth, Mass Society, Pluralism, and Bureaucracy: Explication, Assessment and Commentary, Praeger, forthcoming. **CONTACT ADDRESS** Dept Sociol, Ohio State Univ, Columbus, 1501 Neil Ave, Columbus, OH 43201-2602. **EMAIL** hamilton.1@osu.edu

HAMMOND, JAMES MATTHEW
PERSONAL Born 07/10/1930, Keanansville, NC, m **DISCIPLINE** PSYCHOLOGY **EDUCATION** Oakwood Coll, BA 1953; SC State Coll, MSc 1960; Catholic Univ of Amer, MA 1975; Friendship Coll, DDiv 1963; S IL Univ, PhD 1973. **CAREER** Atkins HS, guidance counselor 1960-61; Sci Dept Bekwai Teachers Coll, chair 1961-68; Seventh Day Adventist Church of Sierra Leone, pres 1968-70; SDA Church of North Ghana, exec dir 1972-74; Metro Family Life Council, mem 1979; Pan African Develop Coop, bd mem 1981; MD Psychological Assoc, mem 1982-; Columbia Union Coll, chair/prof of psychology. **HONORS AND AWARDS** UNESCO Fellow United Nations Organs 1972; Phi Delta Kappa mem SIU Chap 1972. **MEMBERSHIPS** Mem Metro Family Life Council 1979; bd mem Pan African Develop Coop 1981; mem MD Psychological Assoc 1982; chaplain (maj) Civil Air Patrol 1983. **CONTACT ADDRESS** Chair/Prof of Psychology, Columbia Union Col, 7600 Flower Ave, Takoma Park, MD 20912.

HAMPTON, BARBARA L.
DISCIPLINE ETHNOMUSICOLOGY **EDUCATION** Columbia Univ, PhD. **CAREER** Prof & dir, Grad Prog in Ethnomusicol. **MEMBERSHIPS** Served on, nat exec bd, Soc for Ethnomusicol. **SELECTED PUBLICATIONS** Contribur, Garland Encycl World Mus; JVC Anthology Mus and Dance in the Americas & Int Encycl of Dance; ed, Through African-Centered Prisms and Mus and Gender. **CONTACT ADDRESS** Dept of Music, Hunter Col, CUNY, 695 Park Ave, New York, NY 10021.

HAMPTON, GRACE
PERSONAL Born 10/23/1937, Courtland, AL **DISCIPLINE** EDUCATION **EDUCATION** Art Inst Chicago, BAE 1961; IL State U, MS 1968; AZ State U, PhD Dec 1976. **CAREER** IL State Univ, prof Art Educ; Northern IL Univ; School Art Inst Chicago; CA State Univ Sacramento; Univ of OR. **MEMBERSHIPS** Mem Nat Art Educ Assn; Nat Conf of Black Artist; Artist-in-residence Hayden House Phoenix; presented papes local & natl conferences; del Festac 1977. **CONTACT ADDRESS** Art Dept, California State Univ, Sacramento, Sacramento, CA 95819.

HAMPTON, ROBERT L.
PERSONAL Born 11/18/1947, Michigan City, IN, m **DISCIPLINE** SOCIOLOGY **EDUCATION** Princeton Univ, AB 1970; Univ of Michigan, MA 1971, PhD 1977. **CAREER** Connecticut Coll, asst prof 74-83; Harvard Med School, lectr of ped 81-93; Connecticut Coll, assc prof 83-89, prof 89-94, dean, 87-94; professor of Family Studies, professor of Sociology, 94-; Acad Affairs, assoc provost, dean for undergraduate studies, currently. **HONORS AND AWARDS** Danforth Assc Danforth Found 1979; NIMH Post Doc Flwshp 1980; NRC Flwshp Natl Rsrch Cncl 1981; Rockfeller Flwshp Rockefeller Found 1983. **MEMBERSHIPS** Consultant Urban Inst 1975; consultant Women in Crisis 1979-82; consultants Childrens Hospital Boston 1982; mem exec com Peguot Comm Found 1983-86; chr Oprtns Dev Corp 1977-78; pres of bd Child & Family Agency 1987-90; New London County Child Sexual Abuse Task Force; United Way of Southeastern Connecticut, 1992-95; Prince Georges County Superintendent of Schools, advisory comm; Inst for Women's Policy Research, advisory comm. **CONTACT ADDRESS** Univ of Maryland, Col Park, College Park, MD 20742-5031. **EMAIL** rhampton@deans.umd.edu

HANDEL, GERALD
PERSONAL Born 08/08/1924, Cleveland, OH, m, 1956, 2 children **DISCIPLINE** SOCIOLOGY **EDUCATION** Univ Chicago, AB, 47; IBID, AM, 51; PhD, 62. **CAREER** Res

assoc, asst dir, vic pres, Soc Res Inc, 56-66; sr staff assoc, Cen Urb Edu, 66-67; prof, CUNY, 67-. **HONORS AND AWARDS** ASA Mem; Assoc Ed, J Marr Family, 63-69; Assoc Ed, Soc Inq, 97-. **MEMBERSHIPS** ASA; SSSI; ESS. **RESEARCH** The life course; childhood socialization; family interaction. **SELECTED PUBLICATIONS** Ed, Childhood Socialization, Aldine de Gruyter (Hawthorne, NY), 88; auth, "Abandoned Ambitions: Transition to Adulthood in the Life Course of Working-Class Boys," in Sociological Studies of Child Development, ed. Spencer Cahill (JAT Press: Greenwich, CT), 91; co-ed, The Psychosocial Interior of the Family, Aldine de Gruyter (Hawthorne, NY), 94; coauth Family Worlds, Univ Press of Am (Lanham, MD), 95; auth, Making a, Life in Yorkville. Experience and Meaning in the Life-Course Narrative of an Urban Working-Class Man (Westport, CT: Greenwood Press, 00) **CONTACT ADDRESS** Dept Sociology, City Col, CUNY, 160 Convent Ave, New York, NY 10031. **EMAIL** geraldhandel@earthlink.net

HANSEN, BARBARA L.
PERSONAL Born 09/27/1935, Indianapolis, IN, s **DISCIPLINE** ENGLISH EDUCATION **EDUCATION** Ball State Univ, BS, 63; MA, 64; PhD, 71. **CAREER** Grad teaching asst to instr, Ball State Univ, 63-72; asst prof to prof, Univ of Cincinnati, 72-. **HONORS AND AWARDS** Venture Club National Awd for Outstanding Handicapped Student, 62; doctoral teaching fel, Ball State Univ, 67-68; Midwest Awd, President's Comt for the Handicapped, 72; Fac Achievement Awd, Univ of Cincinnati, 94; listed in The World Who's Who of Women, International Who's Who in Educ, and Who's Who Among America's Teachers. **SELECTED PUBLICATIONS** Coauth, Developing Sentence Skills, Prentice-Hall Inc., (Englewood Cliffs) 90; auth, "Commentary," Col Teaching (91); auth, "Is No an Outdated Word?," Children Today (91): 18-21; auth, "The Road Less Traveled," Careers & the Disabled (93); auth, Picking Up the Pieces: Healing Ourselves After Personal Loss, Taylor Pub Co. (Dallas, TX), 91 and Harper Collins Pub Co. (New York), 93; coauth, Simplified Sentence Skills, NTC/Contemporary Pub (Lincolnwood), 97; auth, The Strength Within: Cultivating Habist of Wholeness, Hope, and Joy, Hidden Spring/Paulist Press (Mahwah, NJ), 00. **CONTACT ADDRESS** Dept English, Univ of Cincinnati, 9555 Plainfield Rd, Cincinnati, OH 45236-1007.

HANSEN, KAREN V.
PERSONAL Born 04/23/1955, Chico, CA, m, 1985, 2 children **DISCIPLINE** SOCIOLOGY **EDUCATION** Univ Calif, Santa Barbara, BA, 77; MA, 79; Univ Calif, Berkeley, PhD, 89. **CAREER** Instr, Univ of Calif Berkeley, 88; asst prof to assoc prof, Brandeis Univ, 89-; Mellon Fac Fel, Harvard Univ, 92. **HONORS AND AWARDS** Gertrude Jaeger Prize, 88; Woodrow Wilson Res Grant, 88; Regent's Fel, Univ of Calif Berkeley, 88-89; NEH Grants, 91, 99; Am Philos Soc Grant, 92; Marver and Sheva Bernstein Fel, 83-94; vis scholar, Radcliffe Col, 95-96; Mazer Grant, 98; Norwegian Royal Ministry of Foreign Affairs Grant, 98. **SELECTED PUBLICATIONS** Coed, Women, Class and the Feminist Imagination; A Socialist-Feminist Reader, Temple Univ Pr, 90; auth, A Very Social Time: Crafting Community in Antebellum New England, Univ of Calif Pr, 94; coauth, "Surveying the Dead Informant: Quantitative Analysis and Historical Interpretation", Qualitative Sociol 18.2 (95): 227-236; auth, "No Kisses Is Like Youres': An Erotic Friendship Between African-American Women During the Mid-Nineteenth Century", Gender and Hist, 7.2 (95): 153-182; auth, "Rediscovering the Social: Visiting Practices in Antebellum New England and the Limits of the Public/Private Dichotomy", Public and Private in Thought and Practice: Perspectives on a Grand Dichotomy, eds Krishan Kumar and Jeff Weintraub, Univ of Chicago Pr, (97): 268-302; auth, "Masculinity, Caregiving, and Men's Friendship in Antebellum New England", Families in the U.S.: Kinship and Domestic Politics, eds Karen V. Hansen and Anita Ilta Garey, Temple Univ Pr, (98): 575-585; coed, Families in the U.S.: Kinship and Domestic Politics, Temple Univ Pr, 98; auth, "Historical Sociology and the Prism of Biography: Lillian Wineman and the Trade in Dakota Beadwork, 1893-1929", Qualitative Sociol 22.4 (99): 353-368; coauth, "Sociability and Gender: Visiting Patterns of Working People in Nineteenth-Century New England, "Soc Sci Hist, (forthcoming; **CONTACT ADDRESS** Dept Sociol, Brandeis Univ, 415 South St, Waltham, MA 02453. **EMAIL** khansen@brandeis.edu

HANSEN, WILLIAM F.
PERSONAL Born 06/22/1941, Fresno, CA, m, 1994, 1 child **DISCIPLINE** CLASSICAL STUDIES, FOLKLORE **EDUCATION** Univ Calif, Berkeley, BA, 65, PhD, 70. **CAREER** From asst prof to prof, Class Stud & Folklore, Inst, Indiana Univ Bloomington, 70-; assoc dean fac, Indiana Univ Bloomington, 86-92; chemn, Class Stud, Indiana Univ Bloomington, 97-; co-dir, Program in Mythology Stud, 98-. **HONORS AND AWARDS** Phi Beta Kappa, 65; NEH Younger Hum Fel, 72-73; Am Coun Learned Soc fel, 77-78, 92. **MEMBERSHIPS** Am Philol Asn; Class Asn of the Middle West and South; Am Folklore Soc; Calif Folklore Soc; Hoosier Folklore Soc; Int Soc for Folk-Narrative Res; Int Soc for Contemp Legend Res. **RESEARCH** Mythology; folklore; early Greek epic; early fiction. **SELECTED PUBLICATIONS** Auth, The Theft of the Thunderweapon: A Greek Myth in Its International Context,

Classica et Mediaevalia, 95; auth, Abraham and the Grateful Dead Man, in Bendix, ed, Folklore Interpreted: Essays in Honor of Alan Dundes, Garland, 95; auth, The Protagonist on the Pyre: Herodotean Legend and Modern Folktale, Fabula, 96; auth, Phlegon of Tralles' Book of Marvels, Univ Exeter, 96; auth, Homer and the Folktale, in Morris, ed, A New Companion to Homer, Brill, 97; auth, Idealization as a Process in Ancient Greek Story-Formation, Symbolae Osloenses, 97; auth, Mythology and Folktale Typology: Chronicle of a Failed Scholarly Revolution, J of Folklore Res, 97; ed, Anthology of Ancient Greek Popular Literature, Indiana, 98. **CONTACT ADDRESS** Classical Studies Dept, Indiana Univ, Bloomington, 1020 E Kirkwood Ave, Bloomington, IN 47405-7103. **EMAIL** hansen@indiana.edu

HANSON, ALLAN
PERSONAL Born 05/17/1939, Dixon, IL, m, 3 children **DISCIPLINE** ANTHROPOLOGY **EDUCATION** Princeton Univ, AB, 61; Univ Chicago, MA, 63; PhD, 66. **CAREER** Prof, Univ of Kans, 66-; chair, 83-88. **HONORS AND AWARDS** Nat Sci Found Fel, 61-66; Nat Inst of Mental Health Res Grant, 67; Kans City Asn of Trusts and Found Grant, 67; Andrew Mel Fel, 72-73; Am Coun of Learned Soc Fel, 76-77; Fulbright Awd, 80; NEH Grant, 82-83; Spencer Found Grant, 89; Intra-Univ Vis Prof, Unif of Kans, 83; Phi Beta Kappa. **MEMBERSHIPS** Am Anthrop Assoc; Assoc for Soc Anthrop in Oceania; Soc for Cult Anthrop; Polynesian Soc; Societe des Etudes Oceaniennes; Pacific Arts Assoc. **RESEARCH** Symbolic anthropology, postmodernism, cultural impact of technological developments, art, contemporary American society, New Zealand Maori, Polynesian and Oceanic ethnology. **SELECTED PUBLICATIONS** Auth, Rapan Lifeways: Society and History on a Polynesian Island, Little, Brown, (Boston), 70; auth, Meaning in Culture, Routledge & Kegan Paul, (London), 75; coauth, Counterpoint in Maori Culture, Routledge & Kegan Paul, (London), 83; coauth, The Art of Oceania: A Bibliography, G.K. Hall, (Boston), 84; coed, Art and Identity in Oceania, Univ of Haw Pr, (Honolulu), 90; auth, Testing Testing: Social Consequences of the Examined Life, Univ of Calif Pr, (Berkeley), 93; auth, "Developing Abilities - Biologically?", Talent in Context: Historical and Social Perspectives on Giftedness, eds R.C. Friedman and K.B. Rogers, Am Psychol Assoc, (98): 39-60; auth, "Zero Effect: the Year 2000 Computer Crisis", Society 32.2 (99): 68-74; auth, "Where Have All the Abnormal People Gone?", Humanist (00): 29-32; auth, "How tests Create What They Are Intended to Measure", Assessment: Social Practice and Social Product, ed Ann Filer, Falmer Pr, (London), (forthcoming). **CONTACT ADDRESS** Dept Anthrop, Univ of Kansas, Lawrence, 1 Univ of Kans, Lawrence, KS 66045-1500. **EMAIL** hanson@ukans.edu

HANSON, DAVID J.
PERSONAL Born 08/10/1941, Orlando, FL, m, 1964, 1 child **DISCIPLINE** SOCIOLOGY **EDUCATION** Fla State Univ, BA, 63; Syracuse Univ, MA, 67; PhD, 72. **CAREER** Asst prof, 68; dir, 89-95; prof, 95-, SUNY. **HONORS AND AWARDS** Mellon Awd, Excel Teach; NSSA Awd Excel; Who's Who in World, and Education. **MEMBERSHIPS** NYSA; ESS. **RESEARCH** Alcohol use and abuse. **SELECTED PUBLICATIONS** Auth, Alcohol Education: What we must do, Praeger Pub (Westport, CT), 96; auth, Preventing Alcohol Abuse: Alcohol Culture and Control, Praeger Pub (Westport, CT), 95; ed, Stand! Drugs and Society, Coursewise Pub (St Paul, MN), 99; auth, "Historical Overview of Alcohol Abuse, in Prevention and Societal Impact of Drug and Alcohol Abuse, eds R T Ammerman, Peggy J Ott, Ralph E Tarter (Mahwah, NJ and London, Eng: Lawrence Erlbaum Assoc Pub, 99); coauth, "Drinking Behavior: Taking Personal Responsibility," in Drug Use in America: Social, Cultural, and Political Perspectives, ed. Peter Venturelli (NY, Jones and Bartlett, 94); auth, Wayne Bidwell Wheeler, Am Nat Biography, Oxford Univ Press (NY), 99; coauth, "Reduction of consumption theory: a test using the drinking patterns and problems of collegians in the United States, Coll Stud J (99); auth, "The Role of Formal Education," in Learning to Drink, eds. Grant Marcus (NY: Intl Council on Alcohol Policies, in press). **CONTACT ADDRESS** Dept Sociology, SUNY, Col at Potsdam, 44 Pierrepont Ave, Potsdam, NY 13676. **EMAIL** hansondj@potsdam.edu

HANSON, MARCI J.
DISCIPLINE EDUCATION **EDUCATION** Univ Ore, BA, 70; Penn State Univ, MS, 74; Univ Ore, PhD, 78. **CAREER** Res Scientist, Princeton, 78-79; Program Dir, San Francisco Special Infant Services, 79-95; Prof, San Francisco State Univ, 82-. **HONORS AND AWARDS** Phi Beta Kappa. **MEMBERSHIPS** CEC, DEC, SRCD, NAEYC, SRCD. **RESEARCH** Early intervention with young children who are at risk or disabled; Family systems and services. **SELECTED PUBLICATIONS** Co-auth, "Entering Preschool: Family and Professional Experiences in this transition process," Journal of Early Intervention, in press; co-auth, "Key influences on the initiation and implementation of inclusive preschool programs," Exceptional Children, in press; auth, "Early Transitions for children and families: Transitions from infant/toddler services to preschool education," ERIC Digest, 99; co-auth, "Can I play with you? Peer culture in inclusive preschool classrooms," JASH, (99): 69-84; co-auth, "On the forms of inclusion: Context and individualized service delivery models," Journal of Early Interven-

tion, (990: 185-199; co-auth, "The culture of inclusion: Recognizing diversity at multiple levels," Early Childhood Research Quarterly, (98): 185-209; co-auth, "Communities, Families and Inclusion," Early Childhood Research Quarterly, (98): 125-150; co-auth, "Language, culture and disability: Interacting influences on preschool inclusion," Topics in Early Childhood Special Education, (97): 307-336; co-auth, "Finding friends at school and at home: Parents' strategies for helping preschoolers develop friendships," Exceptional Parent, (97): 24-26; co-auth, "The impact of changing roles on relationships between professionals in inclusive programs for young children," Early Education and Development, (97): 67-82. **CONTACT ADDRESS** Dept Spec Educ, San Francisco State Univ, 1600 Holloway Ave, San Francisco, CA 94132. **EMAIL** mjhanson@sfsu.edu

HANSON, SANDRA L.
PERSONAL Born 01/20/1963, Minneapolis, MN, m, 1980, 1 child **DISCIPLINE** SOCIOLOGY **EDUCATION** Mankato State Univ, BA, 75; Penn State Univ, MA, 78; PhD, 81. **CAREER** Asst Prof, Univ Mo, 81-82; Asst Prof, Case Western Reserve Univ, 82-84; Sen Res Analysts, Decision Resources Corp, 84-86; Asst Prof to Assoc Prof, Catholic Univ, 86-. **RESEARCH** GENDER: Gender, family and achievement; women in science; gender, sports and science; minority women in science; women in science across cultures; religion and gender in comparative context; ACHIEVEMENT: Role of family background, gender, schools, personal experiences, and values in determining chances of dropping out of high school, high school achievement, and labor market experiences; gender influences on educational aspirations and math/science school and work experiences; FAMILY: Work and the family; stratification of women in the labor force; consequences of women's labor force participation for the family; extended kin relations; family background and school achievement; adjustment to divorce; socialization and gender construction; family involvement in teen pregnancy programs; family and success for women scientists; AGING: Sources of variation in filial responsibility norms; extended kin networks; age as social structure; generations and change; DEMOGRAPHY: Patterns of female labor force participation and the family; antecedents and consequences of childless and one-child families; antecedents of adolescent pregnancy; cohorts, history and periods; QUANTITATIVE METHODS: Experience in survey design; training and experience in structural equation models, log linear analysis, probit and logistic models, and latent structure analysis, as well as other more traditional quantitative techniques; experience with secondary data sets including GSS, NELS, HSB, LSAY, SIMS, SISS, TIMS, and ISSP. **SELECTED PUBLICATIONS** Auth, "Gender, Families, and Science: Influences on Early Science Training and Career Choices," Journal of Women and Minorities in Science and Engineering, forthcoming; auth, "Catholicism, country, and the Construction of Gender: Catholic Women in Poland and the US," Polish Sociological Review, forthcoming; auth, "Women in Male domains: Sport and Science," Sociology of Sport Journal, (99): 92-110; auth, "Women, Sport, and Science: Do Female Athletes Have an Advantage?", Sociology of Education, (98): 93-110; auth, "Gender, Family resources and Success in Science," Journal of Family Issues, (96): 83-113; auth, Lost Talent: Women in the Sciences, Temple Univ Press, 96; auth, "Gender Stratification in The Science Pipeline: A Comparative Analysis of Seven Countries," Gender and Society, (96): 271-290; auth, "Lost Talent: Unrealized Educational Aspirations and Expectations Among US Youth," Sociology of Education, (94): 159-183. **CONTACT ADDRESS** Dept Sociol, Catholic Univ of America, 620 Mich Ave NE, Washington, DC 20064-0002.

HARDEMAN, CAROLE HALL
PERSONAL Born Muskogee, OK, 1 child **DISCIPLINE** EDUCATION **EDUCATION** Fisk Univ, BA Music; Univ of OK, MA 1975, PhD Ed Admin 1979; Harvard Univ, MLE Program, 1988. **CAREER** Univ of OK, Coll of Educ & Human Relations, adj prof 80-85; Southwest Center for Human Relations Studies, exec dir 82-85; Adroit Publ Inc, pres; LeMoyne-Owen College, vice president for academic affairs, 90-92, vp for research and development 92-97; Langston Univ, Assoc Dean of Graduate Studies, 97-. **HONORS AND AWARDS** Regents Doct Fel OK State Regents for Higher Ed 1975-79; Outstanding Fac/Staff Univ of OK 1984; Commiss by Nat Ctr for Ed Stat US Dept of Ed Rsch & Stat Div to write paper addressing policy issues & admin needs of Am ed syst through the year 2001; Spec Consult for Sci Projects Harvard Univ; Roscoe Dungee Awd for Excellence in Print Journalism OK Black Media Assoc 1984; editor, NABSE; Journal, NABSE Res Roundtable Monographs, editor; Tennessee Higher Education Commission Community Svc Awd, 1997; NABSE Higher Education Awd, 99. **MEMBERSHIPS** Exec bd Nat Alliance/Black School Ed 1996-; founder OK Alliance for Black School Educators 1984; mem Links Inc, Jack & Jill Inc, NABSE, Urban League, NAACP, NAMPW, AASA, ASCD, AERA, Alpha Kappa Alpha, YWCA, Assoc of Women in Math; keynote speaker, Univ of DE, Univ of Pittsburgh, Univ of OK, State Dept of Ed-PA, DC Public Schools, Chicago IL, New Orleans Chap One, Las Vegas; Natl Task Force on Multicultural Ed; member, Memphis Arts Council Committee of 100; bd of dir, Planned Parenthood; bd of dirs, Southern Region of Planned Parenthood, exec bd, 1994-; Memphis in May, Memphis Literacy

Council. **RESEARCH** Effective Pedogogy for Urban Learners; Classroom Management in Urban Schools; The Philosophies of W.E.B. Dubois Revistes. **SELECTED PUBLICATIONS** Auth, Sounds of Science, Textbooks, MATHCO Textbooks. **CONTACT ADDRESS** Graduate Studies, Langston Univ, 4205 Lincoln Blvd, Oklahoma City, OK 73105. **EMAIL** chhardeman@lunet.edu

HARDGRAVE, BILLY D.
PERSONAL Born 10/11/1941, Fayetteville, AR, m, 1960, 5 children **DISCIPLINE** BEHAVIORAL SCIENCE **EDUCATION** Pensacola Junior Col, Associate Arts, 70; Univ West Florida, Bachelor Arts, Psychology, 73; Univ Northern Colorado (CSAP), Master Arts, Psychology, Guidance and Counseling, 79; Univ Northern Colorado, Doctor Education, Counselor Education, 89. **CAREER** Counselor/Advisor, Aims Community Col, Greeley, CO, 85; Prof, Psychology, Aims Community Col, 87-99; Prof/Co-Chair, Psychology, Aims Community Col, 99-00. **HONORS AND AWARDS** Colo Career Development Assn Awd: Best Career Coun Prof in Colo, 91; Colo Counseling Assn Awd: Exemplary Counseling Program Awd, 92; Colo School Counselor Assn: Lance Huffman Awd for Outstanding Contributions and leadership, 93; Aims speakers Bureau distinguished service Awd, 87-88; PJC-Honors; WWF, Summa Cum Laude; UNC, Golden Key National Honor Society. **MEMBERSHIPS** Amer Counseling Assn (ACA); Assn for Coun Ed & Supervision (ACES); National Career Development Assn (NCDA). **RESEARCH** Freshman Retention through orientation and career planning. **SELECTED PUBLICATIONS** Coauth, "Career/Life Planning (A manual for Life's Choices)," articles in the Journal of Colorado Assn: for Comm and Development, 87 and 89, a college career planning system: A course model and career counselors must do SDB counseling. **CONTACT ADDRESS** Dept Social & Behavioral Sci, Aims Comm Col, 5401 20th St, Greeley, CO 80634. **EMAIL** b.hardgrave@aims.edu

HARDY, R. REED
PERSONAL Born 04/12/1944, McKeesport, PA, m, 1967, 2 children **DISCIPLINE** PSYCHOLOGY **EDUCATION** Clarion State Univ, BA; West Va Univ, MA; PhD. **CAREER** Assoc prof, St. Norbert Col, 74-. **HONORS AND AWARDS** Who's Who Among Students, 66; Who's Who in Am, 93; Fac-Student Collab Res Awd, 99. **MEMBERSHIPS** Am Pyschol Assoc; Assoc of Behav Analysis; Midwestern Psychol Assoc. **RESEARCH** Optimal Human Development, Multi-Cultural Personal Growth. **SELECTED PUBLICATIONS** Auth, "Chapter continuity and visibility on campus: An advisor's touch", Eye on Psi Chi, 1.2 (97): 13; auth, Zen Master: Practical Zen by an American for Americans, St. Norbert Col Pub, 99. **CONTACT ADDRESS** Dept Psychology, St. Norbert Col, 100 Grant St, De Pere, WI 54115. **EMAIL** hardrr@mail.snc.edu

HARING, LEE
PERSONAL Born 06/30/1930, New York, NY **DISCIPLINE** FOLKLORE **EDUCATION** Haverford Col, AB, 51; Columbia Univ, AM, 52, PhD, 61. **CAREER** Asst prof Eng, Guilford Col, 53-56; lectr, 57-61, from instr to asst prof, 61-72, assoc prof, 72-80, prof eng, Brooklyn Col, 80-, Lectr speech, Greensboro Col, 55-56; lectr Eng, City Col NY, 56; admin secy, African Prof, Friends World Inst, 67-69. **MEMBERSHIPS** Am Folklore Soc; Soc Ethnomusicol; Int Folk Music Coun. **RESEARCH** African folk narrative; Am folklore and folk narrative. **SELECTED PUBLICATIONS** Ed, Treasure chest of American folk song, 61 & Folk banjo styles, 62, Elektra Rec; auth, The Gypsy Laddie Hargail Music, 62; ed, Folk Songs for Guitar, Novello, 64; A college course in the ballad, NY Folklore Quart, 67; Performing for the interviewer, Southern Folklore Quart, 72; East African oral narrative, Res African Lit, fall 72. **CONTACT ADDRESS** Dept of Eng, Brooklyn Col, CUNY, 2901 Bedford Ave, Brooklyn, NY 11210-2813.

HARKIN, MICHAEL E.
PERSONAL Born 08/16/1958, Muncie, IN, m, 1984, 3 children **DISCIPLINE** ANTHROPOLOGY **EDUCATION** Unv NC, BA, 80; Univ Chicago, MA, 84; Univ Chicago, PhD, 88. **CAREER** Vis Asst Prof, Univ Wyo, 89-90; Vis Asst Prof, Mont State Univ, 90-91; Asst Prof, Emory Univ, 91-93; From Asst Prof to Assoc Prof, Univ Wyo, 93- **HONORS AND AWARDS** Louise Asher Fel, Univ Chicago; Extraordinary Merit Awd for Res, Univ Wyo, 97; NEIT Fel, 99; Can Studies Sen Fel, 00. **MEMBERSHIPS** Am Anthrop Assoc, Am Soc for Ethnohist, Am Soc for Psychol Anthrop. **RESEARCH** Ethnohistory, political symbols, religion, North American Indians. **SELECTED PUBLICATIONS** Auth, "Modernist Anthropology and Tourism of the Authentic," Ann of Tourism Res, 32 (95): 650-670; co-ed, "Native American Women's Responses to Christianity," Ethnohist, 43 (96); auth, "Past Presence: Conceptions of History in Northwest Coast Studies," Arctic Anthrop, 33 (96): 1-15; auth, "A Tradition of Invention: Modern Ceremonialism on the Northwest Coast," in Present is Past: Some Uses of Tradition Among Native Societies in North America and New Zealand (Univ Pr of Am, 97), 97-112; auth, The Heiltsuks: Dialogues of History and Culture on the Northwest Coast, Univ Neb Pr, 97; auth, "Ethnoscience," Encycl of Semiotics, Oxford Univ Pr (98): 221-222; auth, "Whales, Chiefs and Giants: An Exploration into Nuuchah-nulth Politcal Thought," Ethnol, 37 (98): 317-332; ed, "With My Own Eyes: A Lakota Woman Tells Her People's Story," by Susan Bordeaux Bettelyoun and Josephine Waggoner, J of the Royal Anthrop Inst, no 5 (99): 4-5; auth, "Sacred Place, Scarred Space," Wicazo Sa Rev, 15 (00): 71-105; auth, "Staged Encounters: Indians and Tourism," Ethnohist (forthcoming); **CONTACT ADDRESS** Dept Anthrop, Univ of Wyoming, PO Box 3431, Laramie, WY 82071. **EMAIL** harkin@uwyo.edu

HARMON-JONES, EDDIE A.
PERSONAL Born 01/14/1968, Florence, AL, m, 1993, 1 child **DISCIPLINE** PSYCHOLOGY **EDUCATION** Univ Ala, BS, 90; Univ Kans, MA, 92; Univ Ariz, PhD, 95. **CAREER** Res Fel, Univ Tex Galveston, 95-96; Visiting Asst prof, Univ Tex Arlington, 96-97; Asst Prof, Univ Wisc, 97-. **HONORS AND AWARDS** John Ost Awd, Univ AL, 90; Grant, Univ AZ, 94; Grant, Am Psychol Asn, 97; Grant, WI Alumni Res Foundation, 98, 99; Grant, Nat Inst of Ment Health, 99. **MEMBERSHIPS** Am Psychol asn; Am Psychol Soc; Soc for personality and Social Psychol; Soc for Res in Psycholphysiol. **RESEARCH** Socail Psychology; Motivation; Emotion; Pychophysiology. **SELECTED PUBLICATIONS** Co-auth, "By faith alone: Religious agitation and cognitive dissonance," Basic and Applied Social Psychology, (97): 17-31; co-auth, "Impulsiveness, aggression, reading, and the P300 of the event-related potential," Personality and Individual Difference, (97): 439-445; co-auth, "Terror management and cognitive experiential self theory: Evidence that terror management occurs in the experiential system," Journal of Personality and Social Psychology, (97): 1132-1146; co-auth, "Anger and prefrontal brain activity; EEG asymmetry consistent with approach motivation despite negative affective valence," Journal of Personality and Social Psychology, (98): 1310-1316; co-auth, "An introduction to the theory of cognitive dissonance, its revisions, and current controversies," in cognitive Dissonance: Perspectives on a pivotal theory in social psychology, (Washington, 99), 3-21; auth, "Toward un understanding of the motivation underlying dissonance processes: Is feeling personally responsible for the production of aversive consequences necessary to cause dissonance effects?," in cognitive Dissonance; Perspectives on a pivotal theory in social psychology, (Washington, 99(, 71-99; auth, "A cognitive dissonance theory perspective on the role of emotion in the maintenance and change of beliefs and attitudes," in The effects of emotions upon the formation and strength of beliefs, Cambridge Univ Press, in press; auth, "An update on dissonance theory, with a focus on the self," in Psychological perspectives on self and identity, Washington, in press; co-auth, Cognitive Dissonance: Progress on a pivotal theory in social psychology, Am Psychol Asn, 99; auth, "Cognitive dissonance and experienced negative affect: Evidence that dissonance increases experienced negative affect even in the absence of aversive consequences," Personality and Social Psychology Bulletin, in press. **CONTACT ADDRESS** Dept Psychol, Univ of Wisconsin, Madison, 1201 W Johnson St, Madison, WI 53706. **EMAIL** eharmonj@facstaff.wisc.edu

HARPER, GARY F.
PERSONAL Born 06/05/1948, Orange, NJ, m, 1970, 2 children **DISCIPLINE** EDUCATION **EDUCATION** Allegheny Col, BA, 70; Bowling Green State Univ, Ohio, MA, 73; Kent State Univ, 76. **CAREER** Asst to assoc prof, SUNY Col , Fredonia, 77-90, Dean, Div of Ed Studies, 94-96, Prof of Ed, 96-. **MEMBERSHIPS** Am Ed Res Asn, Asn for Behav Analysis, Coun for Exceptional Children. **RESEARCH** Peer-assisted and cooperative learning. **SELECTED PUBLICATIONS** Coauth with B. Mallette, L. Maheady, A. Bentley, & J. Moore, "Retention and Treatment Failure in Classwide Peer Tutoring: Implications for Further Research," J of Behav Ed, 5 (95): 399-414; coauth with L. Maheady & B. Mallette, "The Pair Tutoring Program: A Potentially Replicable Early Field-Based Experience to Prepare Preservice General Educators to Work with Students with Special Needs," Teacher Ed and Special Ed, 19, 4 (96): 277-97; coauth with M. Karnes, D. Collins, L. Maheady & B. Mallette, "Using Cooperative Learning Strategies to Improve Literacy Skills in Social Studies," Reading & Writing Quart: Overcoming Learning Difficulties, 13 (97): 37-51; coauth with L. Maheady, B. Mallette, and M. Karnes, "Peer Tutoring and the Minority Child with Disabilities," Preventing School Failure, 43 (99): 45-51; coauth with L. Maheady, "Classwide Student Tutoring Teams: Aligning Course Objectives, Student Practice Activities and Testing," Proven Practice in the Prevention and Remediation of School Problems,1,2 (99): 55-59, 84-85; coauth with L. Maheady & B. Mallette, "The effects of reciprocal peer coaching on preservice general educators' instruction of students with special learning needs," Teacher Ed and Special Ed, 22 (99): 201-216; coauth with L. Maheady , B. Mallette, and M. Karnes, "The Instructional Assistants Program: A Potential Entry Point for Behavior Analysis in Education?," Ed & Treatment of Children, 22 (99): 447-469. **CONTACT ADDRESS** Sch of Ed, SUNY, Col at Fredonia, 138 Central Ave, Fredonia, NY 14063. **EMAIL** harper@fredonia.edu

HARPER, WILLIAM
PERSONAL Born 11/11/1944, Glendale, CA, m, 4 children **DISCIPLINE** PHYSICAL EDUC **EDUCATION** Calif State Univ, BA, 65; Univ S Calif, PhD, 71. **CAREER** Asst Prof to Assoc Prof, Emporia State Univ, 69-79; Assoc Prof to Prof, Purdue Univ, 79-. **HONORS AND AWARDS** Outstanding Fac Awd, Emporia State Univ, 78-79; MCL Excellence in Teaching Awd, Purdue Univ, 81; AMOCO Outstanding Undegraduate Teaching, Nominee, Purude Univ, 82, 85; Book of Great Teachers, Purdue Univ, 99. **MEMBERSHIPS** Am alliance for Health, Phys Educ, Recreation and Dance; Nat Asn for Phys Educ in Higher Educ; Phi Epsilon Kappa. **RESEARCH** Sport and leisure studies; Modern technology on the direction of sport and leisure; Grantland Rice. **SELECTED PUBLICATIONS** Co-auth, "Thoreau on leisure: A wide halo of ease", Popular Culture Review, (97): 121-137; auth, "The future of leisure: Making leisure work," Leisure Studies, (97): 189-198; auth, "A lesson from Minerva," Quest, (99): 102-115; auth, How You Played the Game: The Life of Grantland Rice, Univ MO Press, 99. **CONTACT ADDRESS** Dept Health, Kinesiol and Leisure Studies, Purdue Univ, West Lafayette, West Lafayette, IN 47907. **EMAIL** wharper@purdue.edu

HARPOLD, TERRY
DISCIPLINE LITERATURE, COMMUNICATION, AND CULTURE **EDUCATION** Univ Pa, PhD, 94. **CAREER** Asst prof, mem, Ctr for New Media Educ and Res, & Graphics, Visualization, & Usability Ctr, Ga Inst of Technol. **RESEARCH** Postmodern culture and literature. **SELECTED PUBLICATIONS** Publications include discussions of hypertextual narrative form and its graphical representations, the "inverted landscapes" of author J.G. Ballard, and the obscured political economies of cartographic depictions of the Internet. **CONTACT ADDRESS** Sch of Lit, Commun & Cult, Georgia Inst of Tech, Skiles Cla, Atlanta, GA 30332. **EMAIL** terry.harpold@lcc.gatech.edu

HARRE, H. ROMANO
PERSONAL Born 12/18/1927, New Zealand, m, 1948, 1 child **DISCIPLINE** PSYCHOLOGY **EDUCATION** Auckland Univ, BSc, 48, MA, 53; Oxford Univ, BPh, 56, MA, 59. **CAREER** King's Col, Auckland, 48-53; Punjab Univ, Pakistan, 54; Leicester Univ, 58-60; Oxford Univ, 60-96; vis prof, Georgetown Univ, 88-. **HONORS AND AWARDS** Honorary doctorates from Brussels, Helsinki, and Lima. **MEMBERSHIPS** Am Psych Soc; Br Soc for Philos of Sci. **RESEARCH** Philosophy of science, language and thought, philosophy of psychology. **SELECTED PUBLICATIONS** Auth, Personal Being: a Theory for a Corporal Psychology, Blackwell, 83; Physical Being: a Theory for a Corporal Psychology, Blackwell, 91; auth, Social Being: a Theory for a Social Psychology II, Blackwell, 93; coauth, The Discursive Mind, Sage, 94; coed, The Emotions: Social, Cultural, and Physical Dimensions of the Emotions, Sage, 96. **CONTACT ADDRESS** Dept of Psychol, Georgetown Univ, 303A White Gravenor, Box 571001, Washington, DC 20057. **EMAIL** harreh@gunet.georgetown.edu

HARRINGTON, ROBERT
PERSONAL Born 07/26/1948, Meelford, MA, m, 1981, 4 children **DISCIPLINE** PSYCHOLOGY **EDUCATION** Boston Univ, AB, 70; Boston State Col, Med, 75; Univ Iowa, PhD, 80. **CAREER** Prof, Univ of Kans, 80- **HONORS AND AWARDS** Award for Best Res Paper, Asn for Psychol and Educ Res, Kans. **MEMBERSHIPS** Am Psychol Asn, Asn for Psychol and Educ Res Kans, Nat Asn for Sch Psychologists. **RESEARCH** Personality Assesment, Children's Behavioral Problems. **CONTACT ADDRESS** Dept Educ Psychology, Univ of Kansas, Lawrence, Lawrence, KS 66045-1500.

HARRIS, EDWARD E.
PERSONAL Born 02/27/1933, Topeka, KS **DISCIPLINE** EDUCATION **EDUCATION** Lincoln Univ, AB 1954; Univ IA, AM 1958, PhD 1963; Univ Wis, post grad 1972. **CAREER** IN Univ, Purdue Univ Indianapolis, assoc prof sociology 68-; CA State Coll, asst prof 65-68; Prairie View A&M Coll, TX, assoc prof 63-64. **MEMBERSHIPS** Mem Am & No Central Sociological Assns ed bd Coll Student Journal 1971-. **SELECTED PUBLICATIONS** Contrib articles to professional jrnls. **CONTACT ADDRESS** Indiana Univ-Purdue Univ, Indianapolis, Indianapolis, IN 46208.

HARRIS, J. GORDON
PERSONAL Born 11/01/1940, LA, m, 1967, 2 children **DISCIPLINE** GERONTOLOGY, BIBLICAL STUDIES **EDUCATION** Baylor Univ, BA, 62; SW BTS Sem, BD, 65; ThM, 67; S Sem, PhD, 70; Hebrew Col, MA, 81. **CAREER** Prof, BT Sem, Philippines, 70-75; prof, N Am Baptist Sem, 75-; Acad VP, 82-95; Dir, 95-. **HONORS AND AWARDS** Outstanding Young Men in Am; Who's Who in Relig, 77; Distinguished Am in 20th Century; Pres, Lions Club; Pres, NAPH; Pres, Upper Midwest SBL/AAR. **MEMBERSHIPS** NAPH; NABPR; Soc of Bibl Lit; Am Soc of Ageing. **RESEARCH** Hebrew Scriptures, Joshua, prophets, wisdom literature; Gerontology, spirituality and aging, Bible and aging. **SELECTED PUBLICATIONS** Auth, Biblical Perspectives on Aging, Fortress, 87; Auth, Joshua, NI Biblical Commentary, Hendrikson, 00. **CONTACT ADDRESS** Dept Relig, No American Baptist Sem, 1525 S Grange Ave, Sioux Falls, SD 57105-1526. **EMAIL** gharris@nabs.edu

HARRIS, JANICE HUBBARD
PERSONAL Born 03/30/1943, Los Angeles, CA, m, 1966, 2 children **DISCIPLINE** BRITISH FICTION; WOMEN'S STUDIES; POST COLONIAL STUDIES **EDUCATION** Stanford Univ, AB, 65; Brown Univ, PhD, 73. **CAREER** Instr English, Tougaloo Col, 69-73; from asst prof English to prof, 75-, assoc dean arts sci, 83-84, dir univ honors prog, 82-86, dir women's studies, 95-99, Univ Wyo. **HONORS AND AWARDS** Danforth Teaching fel, 81. **MEMBERSHIPS** MLA; Nat Women's Studies Asn; Women's Caucus Mod Lang. **RESEARCH** Modern British fiction; women's studies; Post-Colonial Literatures. **SELECTED PUBLICATIONS** Auth, D H Lawrence and Kate Millett, Mass Rev, summer 74; Our mute, inglorious mothers, Midwest Quart, 4/75; Insight and experiment in D H Lawrence's early short fiction, Philol Quart, summer 76; Sexual antagonism in D H Lawrence's early leadership fiction, Mod Lang Studies, spring 77; The moulting of the plumed serpent, Mod Lang Quart, 3/79; Bushes, bears and the beast in the jungle, Studies in Short Fiction, spring 81; Gayl Jones' Corregidora, Frontiers, Vol 3; Feminist Representations of Wives and Work: An Almost Irreconcilable' Edwardian Debate, Women's Stud, 93; Challenging the Script of the Heterosexual Couple: Three Marriage Novels by May Sinclair, Papers on Lang & Lit, 93; Wifely Speech and Silence: Three Marriage Novels by H G Wells, Stud in Novel, 94; Edwardian Stories of Divorce, Rutgers Univ, 96. **CONTACT ADDRESS** Dept English, Univ of Wyoming, PO Box 3353, Laramie, WY 82071-3353. **EMAIL** jharris@vwyo.edu

HARRIS, JOSEPH
DISCIPLINE FOLKLORE AND ENGLISH **EDUCATION** Univ Ga, BA; Univ Frankfurt; Cambridge Univ, England; Harvard Univ, AM, PhD. **CAREER** Prof. **RESEARCH** Tradition and language. **SELECTED PUBLICATIONS** Co-ed, Prosimetrum: Cross-Cultural Perspectives on Narrative in Prose and Verse, 97. **CONTACT ADDRESS** Dept of English, Harvard Univ, 8 Garden St, Cambridge, MA 02138. **EMAIL** harris@fas.harvard.edu

HARRIS, JOSEPH JOHN, III
PERSONAL Born 10/10/1946, Altoona, PA, m, 1988 **DISCIPLINE** EDUCATION **EDUCATION** Highland Park College, AS, 1967; Wayne State University, BS, 1969; University of Michigan at Ann Arbor, MS, 1971, PhD, 1972. **CAREER** Detroit Public Schools, teacher, assistant principal, 68-73; Highland Park Public School, consulting proj dir, 73; Pennsylvania State Univ, asst prof, 73-76; Indiana Univ, assoc profr, 76-83, prof, chair, center dirr, 83-87; Cleveland State Univ, prof, dean, 87-90; Univ of KY, Prof, Dean, 90-. **MEMBERSHIPS** Editorial board, CSU Magazine, 1989-; board of trustees, Greater Cleveland Literacy Coalition, 1988-; advisory board, National Sorority of Phi Delta Kappa, 1988-; board of trustees, National Public Radio Affiliate-WCPNW, 1988-; board of directors, Marotta Montessori School/Cleveland, 1987-90; National Organization on Legal Problems in Education, board of directors, 1988-91; Lexington Arts and Cultural Center, board of directors; Holmes Group Ed Schools, E Lansing, board of directors. **SELECTED PUBLICATIONS** Author: "Education, Society & the Brown Decision," Journal of Black Studies, 1982; "The Outlaw Generation," Educational Horizons, 1982; "Identifying Diamond in the Rough," The Gifted Child Today, 1990; "Public School-Univ Collaboration," Community Education Journal, 1989; "The Resurrection of Play in Gifted...," Journal for the Education of the Gifted, 1990; "The Elusive Definition of Creativity," The Journal of Creative Behavior, 1992; "Dissonance in the Education Ecology," Metropolitan Universities, 1991; "The American Achievement Ideology and Achievement Differentials Among Preadolescent Gifted and Nongifted African-American Males and Females," Journal of Negro Education, 1992. **CONTACT ADDRESS** Col of Education, Univ of Kentucky, 103 Dickey Hall, Lexington, KY 40506-0017.

HARRIS, SANDRA M.
PERSONAL Born 01/11/1959, Hollandale, MS, m, 1997, 3 children **DISCIPLINE** EDUCATIONAL PSYCHOLOGY **EDUCATION** San Bernadino Valley Col, Calif, AA, 83, AS, 87; Community Col of the Air Force, AAS, 87, AAS, 90; Calif State Univ, BA, 89, MA, 90; Auburn Univ, MS, 98, PhD, 99. **CAREER** Grad res asst, Calif state Univ, 89-91; statistical consult, Troy State Univ, 91-92; adjunct fac, Chapman Univ, Calif, 93; adjunct fac, Troy State Univ, 94-98; Interactive Courseware Lead Instructional Systems Designer, Cubic Applications, Inc, 97-; asst prof, Troy State Univ, Montgomery, 99-. **HONORS AND AWARDS** Tactical Airlift Command Extensive Educ Achievement Awd, 84; Calif State Univ Grad Equity Fel, 90; Noncommissioned Officer's Asn Military Excellence Awd, 91; Prof Military Educ Achievement Awd, 92; Troy State Univ African Am Fel Recipient, 94; U.S. Air Force Commendation Medal, 96; U.S. Air Force Meritorious Service Medal, 97; warren E. Willingham Grad Res Fels, 97, 98. **MEMBERSHIPS** Am Asn of Univ Women, Am Educ Res Asn, Am Psychol Asn, Mid-South Educ Res Asn, Nat Asn for Sch Psychologists, Nat Coun on Measurement in Educ, Psychometric Soc. **RESEARCH** Achievement motivation; retention in higher education; minority issues; mentoring. **SELECTED PUBLICATIONS** Auth, Factor influencing pursuit of higher education: Validating a questionnaire, Washington, DC: ERIC Clearinghouse on Higher Education, ERIC Document Reproduction Service No ED 425 689 (98). **CONTACT ADDRESS** Dept Educ & Psychol, Troy State Univ, Montgomery, PO Drawer 4419, Montgomery, AL 36103. **EMAIL** SFCLL997@msn.com

HARRIS, WALTER, JR.
PERSONAL Born 01/27/1947, Suttles, AL, m, 1976 **DISCIPLINE** EDUCATION **EDUCATION** Knoxville College, Knoxville, TN, BS, 1968; Michigan State University, East Lansing, MI, MM, 1969, PhD, 1979; Harvard University, Cambridge, MA, diploma, 1990. **CAREER** Knoxville College, Knoxville, TN, dir, choral activities, chair, music dept, dir, division arts and humanities; Arizona State Univ, Tempe, AZ, coord, undergraduate studies, music, asst dean, College of Fine Arts, acting dean, College of Fine Arts, associate dean, College of Fine Arts, interim asst vice pres academic affairs, Vice Provost, currently. **HONORS AND AWARDS** Luce Fellow, Luce Foundation, 1977; NEH Fellow, 1974; Pi Kappa Lamda Honorary Fraternity, Michigan State University, 1968. **MEMBERSHIPS** President, Arizona Alliance for Arts Education, 1991-93; member, board of trustees, Phoenix Boys Choir, 1990-; member, board of directors, Phoenix Symphony Orchestra, 1990-; member, International Council of Fine Arts Deans, 1985-; regional chairperson, American Choral Directors Assn, 1987-. **CONTACT ADDRESS** Academic Affairs, Arizona State Univ, Off of the Sr VP & Provost, Adm 211, Tempe, AZ 85287-2803.

HARRIS, WILLA BING
PERSONAL Born 03/12/1945, Allendale, SC, m, 1972 **DISCIPLINE** EDUCATION **EDUCATION** Bennett Coll, BA 1966; Bloomsburg State Coll, MEd 1968; Univ of IL, EdD 1975. **CAREER** White Haven State School & Hospital, classroom teacher, 67-69; Albany State Coll, instructor, 69; SC State Coll Orangeburg, asst prof & suprv of graduate practicum students, 69-70; Univ of Illinois at Urbana-Champaign, Upward Bound, head counselor, 71, asst to major advisor, 71-73; Barber-Scotia Coll, asst prof of educ & psychology 1975-76; Alabama State Univ, Montgomery, coord, Central AL Regional Educ In-Serv Center, coord 1985-88, dir, Rural & Minority Special Educ Personnel Preparation, 88, assoc prof & coord for special educ, 76-, dir of emotional conflict, teacher preparation program, 90-98. **HONORS AND AWARDS** USOE Fellow Univ of IL 1970-73; Ford Found Fellow Univ of IL 1972-73; Ed of Year AL Assoc Retarded Citizens 1982; Outstanding Educ, Montgomery County Assn for Retarded Citizens, 1982; Volunteer Services Awd, Montgomery County Assn for Retarded Citizens, 1985; Distinguished Alumni Awd, C V Bing High School, Allendale, SC, 1988. **MEMBERSHIPS** Consult Head Start 1977-80, 1984-85; lay delegate annual conf AL-West FL Conf United Meth Church 1980-90; bd of dir United Meth Children's Home Selma AL 1984-94, 1996; ASU Credit Union 1984-87, Nellie Burge Comm Ctr 1985-91; mem Amer Assoc on Mental Deficiency-Mental Retardation, AAUP, AL Consortium of Univ Dirs Spec Ed, Black Child Devel Inst, Council for Excep Children, Council for Children with Behavior Disorders, Div for Children with Commun Disorders, Div for Mental Retardation, Teacher Ed Div, IL Admin of Spec Ed, Kappa Delta Pi, Natl Assoc for Ed of Young Children, Natl Assoc for Retarded Citizens, Montgomery Cty Assoc for Retarded Citizens, Phi Delta Kappa, ASU Grad Faculty, AL State Univ Woman's Club, Montgomery Newcomers Club, Tot'n'Teens, Peter Crump Elem SchoolPTA State & Natl Chapt,tropolitan United Methodist Church, Adult II Sunday School Class, Committee Chmn Fund Raising Choir Robes, Organizer of United Meth Youth Fellow, Admin Bd; jurisdictional coordinator, Black Methodists for Southeastern Jurisdiction Church Renewal, 1989-; board member/finance chair, National Black Methodists for Church Renewal, 1989-; president/board of directors, United Methodist Children's Home, 1990-94. **CONTACT ADDRESS** Prof of Spec Educ, Alabama State Univ, Box 288, Montgomery, AL 36101-0271.

HARRIS, WILLIAM MCKINLEY, SR.
PERSONAL Born 10/29/1941, Richmond, VA, m, 4 children **DISCIPLINE** EDUCATION **EDUCATION** Howard U, BS Physics 1964; Univ Washington, MUP Urban Plng 1972, PhD Urban Plng 1974. **CAREER** Cntr for Urban Studies Western Washington State Clg, dir 73-74; Black Studies Dept Portland St U, chrmn 74-76; Off Afro Am Afrs, dean 76-81; Univ of Virginia, prof of city planning, 87-; planning consultant, 87-. **HONORS AND AWARDS** Fellow, Am Inst of Certified Planners; Danforth Assc Danforth Found VA 1980; outstanding serv Comm Dev Soc VA 1984; Citizen Ambassador Program, delegation leader to China, 1992, 1994; Monticello Community Action Agency, Teacher of the Year, 1990; Portland, Oregon Citizen of the Year, 1975. **MEMBERSHIPS** Charlottesville Planning Commission, 1981-; Charlottesville Bd of Zoning Appeals, 1991-; TJ United Way, bd of dirs, 1990-; Am Inst of Certified Planners, 1978-; Am Planning Assn, 1976-; NAACP, 1964-; People to People's Citizen Ambassador Program, 1993-; Dev Training Inst, bd mem, 1988-. **SELECTED PUBLICATIONS** Author of: "Environmental Racism: A Challenge to Community Development," Journal of Black Studies, 1995; "African American Economic Development in Baltimore," The Urban Design and Planning Magazine, 1993; "Technology Education for Planners: A Century for African and People of African Descent," African Technology Forum, 1992; "Professional Education of African Americans: A Challenge to Ethical Teaching," Business and Professional Ethics Journal, 1990; Black Community Development, 1976; Charlottesville Little League Basketball, coach, championships, 1982, 1988, 1992. **CONTACT ADDRESS** Dept Urban & Regional Planning, Jackson State Univ, 3825 Ridgewood Rd, Box 23, Jackson, MS 39211. **EMAIL** umharris@mail1.jsums.edu

HARRISON, ALGEA OTHELLA
PERSONAL Born 02/14/1936, Winona, WV **DISCIPLINE** EDUCATION **EDUCATION** Bluefield State Coll, BS (Magna Cum Laude) Ed 1956; Univ of MI, MA Ed 1959, PhD Psych, Ed 1970. **CAREER** Detroit Public School System, teacher; Inkster School System, Rsch Design, Urban Action Needs Analysis, Wayne County Headstart Program, MI Dept of Educ, consultant 62-66; Highland Park School System, school diagnostician 68-69; Oakland Univ, prof currently. **HONORS AND AWARDS** Horace Rackham Predoctoral Fellow 1969-70; US Publ Health Grants, 1965-68; graduated second highest mem of class. **MEMBERSHIPS** Mem Amer Psych Assoc, MI Psych Assoc, Assoc of Black Psych, Soc for Rsch in Child Devel, Assoc of Soc & Behavioral Sci; bd trustees New Detroit Inc, Roeper City & Cty Schools; mem Founders Soc, Your Heritage House A Black Museum, Natl Org for Women, Child Care Coord Council. **CONTACT ADDRESS** Psychology Dept, Oakland Univ, Rochester, MI 48309.

HARRISON, DON K., SR.
PERSONAL Born 04/12/1933, Nashville, NC, m **DISCIPLINE** EDUCATION **EDUCATION** North Carolina Central Univ, BA 1953; Wayne State Univ, MA 1958; Univ of Michigan, PhD 1972; Licensed Psychologist. **CAREER** Univ of Michigan Rehabilitation Rsch Inst, assoc prof and dir 76; Univ of Michigan Rehabilitation Counseling Educ, assoc prof and dir 75; Guidance and Counseling Program, Univ of Michigan, chmn 74-77; Guidance and Counseling Program, Univ of Michigan, asst prof 72-76; Vocational Rehabilitation, Wayne State Univ, adjunct asst prof 72. **HONORS AND AWARDS** Outstanding Srv Awd MI Prsnl & Guid Assn 1976. **MEMBERSHIPS** Dir PRIME Inc Detroi MI 1970-80; mem Am Psychol Assn; mem Personnel & Guidance Assn Rehab Couns Traineeship Rehab Srv Admin 1975. **CONTACT ADDRESS** Rehabilitation Research, Univ of Michigan, Ann Arbor, 1360 School of Educ, Ann Arbor, MI 48109.

HARRISON, ROBERT M.
PERSONAL Born 01/21/1929, Jaffna, Sri Lanka, m, 1984, 3 children **DISCIPLINE** PSYCHOLOGY **EDUCATION** Oberlin Col, AB, 51; Pa State Univ, MS, 53; PhD, 57. **CAREER** Res assoc, Harvard Med Sch, 59-91; ass prof, Univ Mass Amherst, 62-66; assoc prof, Boston Univ, 66-. **HONORS AND AWARDS** Fel, Mass Mental Health Center, 57-59; Fel, McLean Hospital. **MEMBERSHIPS** Am Psychol Asn; Am Psychol Soc; E Psychol Asn; Mass Psychol Asn; Sigma Xi. **RESEARCH** Testing psychoanalytic hypotheses of the unconscious; Measuring affect recognition; Headache; Pregnancy outcome and early infancy. **SELECTED PUBLICATIONS** Co-auth, "The effect of sensory deprivation and ego-strength on a measure of autistic thinking," J of Personality Assessment, (90): 694-703; co-auth, "Affect in early memories of borderline patients," J of Personality Assessment, (91): 75-83; auth, "Atypical emotions in relationships as correlates of the MMPI," J of Psychol, (94): 165-175; co-auth, "Maternal depressive symptoms affect infant cognitive development in Barbados," J of Child Psychol and Psychiat, (00): 747-751. **CONTACT ADDRESS** Dept Psychol, Boston Univ, 64 Cummington St, Boston, MA 02215. **EMAIL** hunter@bu.edu

HARROD, HOWARD L.
PERSONAL Born 06/09/1932, Holdenville, OK, m, 1971, 2 children **DISCIPLINE** SOCIOLOGY OF RELIGION **EDUCATION** Oklahoma Univ, BA, 60; Duke Univ, BD, 60; Yale Univ, STM, 61, MA, 63, PhD, 65. **CAREER** Asst prof, Howard Univ, 64-66; assoc prof, Drake Univ, 66-68; prof, social ethics and sociol, relig, Vanderbilt Univ, 68- . **HONORS AND AWARDS** Rockefeller Doctoral Fel, 62-63; NEH, 67; Am Coun Learned Soc Fel, 81-82; Vanderbilt Univ Fel, 87-88; Rockefeller Fel, 88. **MEMBERSHIPS** Soc for the Sci Study of Relig; Soc for Values in Higher Ed; Am Acad of Relig; Soc for the Sci Study of Relig; Soc of Christian Ethics; Plains Anthrop Soc. **RESEARCH** Religion and culture; Northern Plains religions. **SELECTED PUBLICATIONS** Auth, Mission among the Blackfeet, Univ Okl, 71; auth, The Human Center: Moral Agony in the Social World, Fortress, 81; auth, Renewing the World: Plains Indians Religion and Morality, Univ Ariz Pr, 92; auth, Becoming and Remaining a People: Native American Religions on the North Plains, Univ Ariz Pr, 95; auth, numerous articles and book ch. **CONTACT ADDRESS** Divinity School, Vanderbilt Univ, Nashville, TN 37240. **EMAIL** howard.harrod@vanderbilt.edu

HARROLD, FRANCIS B.
PERSONAL Born 05/06/1948, Indianapolis, IN, m, 1981, 2 children **DISCIPLINE** ANTHROPOLOGY **EDUCATION** Loyola Univ Chicago, BA, 70; Univ Chicago, MA, 74; PhD, 78. **CAREER** Vis Asst Prof, Univ of Victoria, 78-80; From Asst Prof to Prof, Univ Tex at Arlington, 80-; Chair of Dept of Sociol and Anthrop, Univ Tex at Arlington, 95-. **MEMBERSHIPS**

Soc for Am Archaeol, Am Archaeol Asn. **RESEARCH** Paleolithic Arhaeol, modern human origins, popular beliefs about the past. **SELECTED PUBLICATIONS** Coauth, "Creationism, cult archaeology, and other pseudoscientific beliefs: a study of college students," Youth and Soc 17 (86): 396-421; auth, "Une reevaluation du Chatelperronien," Bul de la Societe Prehistorique Ariege-Pyrenees XLI (86):151-169; co-ed, Cult Archaeology and Creationism: Understanding Pseudoscientific Beliefs about the Past, Univ of Iowa Press (Iowa), 87, expanded ed, 95; auth, "Mousterian, Chatelperronian, and Early Aurignacian: Continuity or Discontinuity?," in The Human Revolution: Behavioral and Biological Perspectives on the Origins of Modern Humans, ed. P. Mellars and C. Stringer (Univ of Edinburgh Press, Princeton Univ Press, 89), 677-713, and in The Human Evolution Sourcebook, ed. J, Fleagle and R. Chiochon (Englewood Cliffs, NJ: Prentice Hall, 92); coauth, The Creationist Movement in Modern America, Twayne Publ (Boston), 90; auth, "The elephant and the blind men: paradigms, data gaps, and the Middle-Upper Paleolithic transition in southwestern France," in Perspectives on the Past: Theoretical Biases in Mediterranean Hunter-Gatherer Research, ed. G. Clark (Philadelphia, Univ of Pa Press, 91), 164-182; auth, "Variability and function among Gravette points from southwestern France," in Hunting and Animal Exploitation in the Later Paleolithic and Mesolithic of Europe, ed. G. Peterkin, H. Bricker and P. Mellars (Wash: Archaeol Papers of the Am Anthrop Asn, 4, 92), 69-81; coauth, "The influence of group processes on pseudoscientific belief: 'knowledge industries' and the legitimization of threatened worldviews," in Advances in Group Processes Vol 10, ed. E. Lawer, B. Markovsky, J. O'Brien, and K. Heimer (NY: JAI Press, 93), 133-162; coauth, "A paradigm's worth of difference? Understanding the impasse over modern human origins," The Yearbk of Phys Anthrop 40 (96): 113-138. **CONTACT ADDRESS** Sociol Dept, Univ of Texas, Arlington, Box 19599, Arlington, TX 76019-0001. **EMAIL** harrold@uta.edu

HARSH, CONSTANCE D.
DISCIPLINE 19TH CENTURY ENGLISH LITERATURE, WOMEN AND LITERATURE **EDUCATION** Univ PA, BA, MA, 82, PhD, 87. **CAREER** Instr, Bryn Mawr Col; assoc prof, Colgate Univ, 88-. **MEMBERSHIPS** MLA; RSVP. **RESEARCH** Victorian fiction, John Cowper Powys. **SELECTED PUBLICATIONS** Auth, Subversive Heroines: Feminist Resolutions of Social Crisis in the Condition-of-England Novel, Univ Mich Press, 94; Gissing's In the Year of Jubilee and the Epistemology of Resistance, SEL, 94; Thyrza: Romantic Love and Ideological Co-Conspiracy, Gissing Jour, 94); Gissing's The Unclassed and the Perils of Naturalism, ELH, 92; auth, "Reviewing New Women Fiction in the Daily Press," VPR 00; auth, "Eliza Lynn Linton as a New Women Novelist," Rebel of the Family, Broadview Press 01. **CONTACT ADDRESS** Dept of Eng, Colgate Univ, 13 Oak Drive, Hamilton, NY 13346. **EMAIL** charsh@mail.colgate.edu

HART, JULIE
PERSONAL Born 11/10/1953, Columbus, OH, m, 1973, 2 children **DISCIPLINE** SOCIOLOGY **EDUCATION** Ohio Univ, BS, 81; Univ Notre Dame, MA, 91, MA, 93, PhD, 95. **CAREER** Asst prof, Bethel Col, 94-. **HONORS AND AWARDS** Summa cum laude, Univ Notre Dame; Outstanding Nursing Student Awd, Ohio Univ, 81; Diss Year Fel, Univ Notre Dame, 93-94; Helping Hand Awd, Bethel Col, 99. **MEMBERSHIPS** Am Sociol Asn, Peace Studies Asn. **RESEARCH** Intergroup conflict, nonviolent direct action. **SELECTED PUBLICATIONS** Auth, "The Impact of a Peer Mediation Program on an Elementary School Environment," J of Peace and Change (97); auth, "Palestinian Authority in Washington Report on the Middle East," (Oct 99). **CONTACT ADDRESS** Bethel Col, Kansas, 300 E 27th St, North Newton, KS 67117. **EMAIL** jhart@bethelks.edu

HART, STEPHEN
PERSONAL Born 02/14/1946, Chicago, IL, m, 1977 **DISCIPLINE** SOCIOLOGY **EDUCATION** Univ Calif, PhD, 79; Univ Calif, MA, 68; Harvard Col, AB, 67 **CAREER** Frontier Science & Tech Res Found Analysis, 98-; Center Theolog Inquiry, 97; Center Study Amer Relig Princeton Univ, 97; Ntl Endowment Humanities Fel, 96; adjunct asst prof, State Univ New York-Buffalo, 93-; freelance contract res, 90- **RESEARCH** Religion; Culture; Politics; Social Movements **SELECTED PUBLICATIONS** Cultural Dilemmas of Progressive Politics: Styles of Engagement among Grassroots Activists, Univ Chicago Pr, 99; What Does the Lord Require? How American Christians Think about Economic Justice, Oxford Pr, 96; "The Cultural Dimension of Social Movements: A Theoretical Reassessment and Literature Rev," Sociology of Relig, 96 **CONTACT ADDRESS** 185 Admiral Rd, Buffalo, NY 14216. **EMAIL** sahart@buffalo.edu

HART, SUSAN J.
PERSONAL Born 10/26/1962, San Antonio, TX, m, 1987, 1 child **DISCIPLINE** PHYSICAL EDUCATION **EDUCATION** Southwestern Univ, BS, 84; Tarleton State Univ, MEd, 90; Tex A & M Univ, PhD, 96. **CAREER** Asst prof, Tex A & M Univ, 95-97; asst prof, NMex State Univ, 98-. **HONORS AND AWARDS** Lolas Halverson Awd for Outstanding Young Investigator in Motor Development, 97. **MEMBERSHIPS** Am Alliance for Health, Physical Education, Recreation, and Dance. **RESEARCH** Motor Development. **SELECTED PUBLICATIONS** Coauth, "Probing Previc's theory of postural control (foot dominance), Brain and Cognition 30.3 (96): 351-353; coauth, "A Question of Foot Dominance," The J of General Psychol 123.4 (96): 289-296; coauth, "Brief communication: Bilateral footedness and task complexity," Int J of Neuroscience 88 (96): 141-146; coauth, "Examining the mobilizing feature of footedness," Laterality 2.1 (97): 17-26; coauth, "Examining the mobilizing feature of footedness," Perceptual and Motor Skills 86 (98): 1339-1342; coauth, "Perceived job stress of teachers and teacher-coaches," Tex Asn HPERD J (99). **CONTACT ADDRESS** Dept Physical Educ, New Mexico State Univ, PO Box 30001, Las Cruces, NM 88003. **EMAIL** shart@nmsu.edu

HARTLEY, LOYDE HOBART
PERSONAL Born 07/21/1940, Parkersburg, WV, m, 1962, 3 children **DISCIPLINE** SOCIOLOGY OF RELIGION **EDUCATION** Otterbein Col, AB, 62; United Theol Sem, BD, 65; Emory Univ, PhD, 68. **CAREER** Lectr, Emory Univ, 67-68; Assoc Prof and Society, Union College, 68- 71; Prof of Religion and Society, Lancaster Theo Sem, 71-; Dir of Doctoral Studies, 71-74; dir, doctoral studies, 73-75, Dean of the Seminary, 75-82, Lancaster Theol Sem; Dean of the Seminary, LTS, 75-82. **MEMBERSHIPS** Am Sociol Assn; Soc Sci Studies Relig; Relig Res Assn. **RESEARCH** Religious beliefs and attitudes; organization of religious groups; professional characteristics of clergy. **SELECTED PUBLICATIONS** Auth, The Placement And Deployment Of Ministers in the United Church of Christ, Res Ctr Relig & Soc, Pa, 73; auth, Understanding Church Finances, Pilgrim Press, 84; auth, Cities and Churches, Scarecrow Press; 92. **CONTACT ADDRESS** Lancaster Theol Sem, 555 W James St, Lancaster, PA 17603-2830. **EMAIL** lhartley@lts.org

HARTMANN, DOUGLAS R.
PERSONAL Born 07/16/1967, Marshall, MO, m, 1993, 2 children **DISCIPLINE** SOCIOLOGY **EDUCATION** Univ Chicago, BA, 89, MA, 90; Univ Calif San Diego, PhD, 97. **CAREER** Asst prof, Sociology, Univ Minn, 97-. **MEMBERSHIPS** Am Sociol Asn. **RESEARCH** Race/ethnicity, sociology of culture, theory, American society. **SELECTED PUBLICATIONS** Auth, "The Chicago Public School Senior Survey: Student Perception and High School Reality," Metropolitan Opportunity Project directed by Gary Orfield, Working Paper Number 14 (summer 88); auth, "The Politics of Race and Sport: Resistance and Domination in the 1968 African American Olympic Protest Movement," Ethnic and Racial Studies, 19, 3 (July 96): 548-66, reprinted in Practicing Inequalities: Critical Inquiries, ed by Judith Howard and Jodi O'Brien, London: Basil Blackwell (98): 337-359; coauth with Stephen Cornell, Ethnicity and Race: Making Identities in a Changing World," Pine Forge Press: Thousand Oaks, CA (98); auth, "Toward a Race-Critical Sociology," Critica: A J of Critical Essays, Univ Calif, San Diego Critica Monograph Series (spring 99): 21-32; coed with Roderick A. Ferguson, "Rethinking Race, Troubling Empiricism," special volume of Critica: A J of Critical Essays, Univ Calif, San Diego: Critica Monograph Series (spring 99); auth, "Race, Sport and the Sociology of Culture," Culture, 14, 2 (winter 2000): 1-6; auth, "Rethinking the Relationships between Sport and Race in American Culture: Golden Ghettos and Contested Terrain," Sociol of Sport J (forthcoming). **CONTACT ADDRESS** Sociol, Univ of Minnesota, Twin Cities, 267 119th Ave S, 909 Soc Sci Bldg, Minneapolis, MN 55455. **EMAIL** hartmann@atlas.socsci.umn.edu

HARTSOUGH, CAROLYN
PERSONAL Born 05/09/1942, Orange, CA, m, 1965, 1 child **DISCIPLINE** PSYCHOLOGY **EDUCATION** UC Berkeley, BA, 64; MA, 66; PhD, 73. **CAREER** Asn res educr and co-dir, hyperactivity follow-up study: young adults, UC Berkeley, 73-; coordr, sch psychol training program, UC Berkely, 90-. **HONORS AND AWARDS** Phi Beta Kappa, Junior Year Inst; Pi Lamba Theta, Hon Educ Soc. **MEMBERSHIPS** AERA, APA, Bay Area Women Evaluators. **RESEARCH** ADHD through the life course, program evaluation. **SELECTED PUBLICATIONS** Coauth, "Students identified as seriously emotionally disturbed in school-based day treatment: Cognitive, psychiatric and special education characteristics," Behav Disorders 20(4), (95): 238-252; coauth, "Tracking procedures and attrition containment in a long term follow-up of a community-based ADHD sample," J of Child Psychol and Psychiat and Allied Disciplines 37(6), (96): 705-713; coauth, "An analysis of practices used to support new teachers: What helps?" Teacher Educ Quart 24(2), (97): 41-52; coauth, "Prospective study of tobacco smoking and substance abuse among samples of ADHD and non-ADHD samples," Learning Disabilities 31(6), (98): 533-544; coauth, "Development and scaling of a preservice teacher rating instrument," J of Teacher Educ 49(2), (98): 132-139; coauth, "Operation promise: Empowering inner city youth," in Advances in Youth Development Programming, ed. M. T. Braverman, R. M. Carlos and S. M. Stanley, in press; coauth, "A comparison of self-report of criminal involvement and official arrest records for individuals with Attention Deficit Hyperactivity Disorder," Aggressive Behav, in press; coauth, "Childhood ADHD subtypes as predictors of adult criminal activity," J of Child Psychol and Psychiat and Allied Disciplines, in press. **CONTACT ADDRESS** Dept Educ, Univ of California, Berkeley, 4327 Tolman Hall, Berkeley, CA 94720. **EMAIL** carolynh@socrates.berkeley.edu

HARTWELL, STEPHANIE
PERSONAL Born 03/02/1968, Newton, MA **DISCIPLINE** SOCIOLOGY **EDUCATION** Yale Univ, PhD. **CAREER** Asst Prof, Univ Mass. **MEMBERSHIPS** ASA. **SELECTED PUBLICATIONS** Coauth, "Assessing the Value of a Short-Term Residential Drug Treatment Program for Homeless Men," J of Addictive Diseases, vol 14 #4 (95): 21-39; coauth, "Alcohol and Drug Abuse Among Connecticut Youth: Implications for Adolescent Medicine and Public Health," Conn Med, no 9 (97): 577-586; auth, "Treatment Seeking Patterns of Chronic Recidivists," Qualitative Health Res, vol 8, no 4 (98): 497-510; coauth, "Reducing Alcohol Misuse in the Workplace," The Exchange, Employee Assistance Res Suppl (98): 6-8; auth, "The Working Life of Homeless Street Addicts," The J of Substance Use, vol 4 (99): 10-15; coauth, "Models of Care: Massachusetts' Forensic Transition Program," Psychiat Servs, vol 50 (99): 1220-1222; auth, "Not All Work is Created Equal: Homeless Substance Abusers and Marginal Employment," Res in the Sociol of Work (00). **CONTACT ADDRESS** Dept Sociol, Univ of Massachusetts, Boston, 100 Morrissey Blvd, Boston, MA 02125. **EMAIL** stephanie.hartwell@umb.edu

HARVEY, LEWIS O., JR.
PERSONAL Born 07/01/1942, Bellefonte, PA, m, 1994, 3 children **DISCIPLINE** PSYCHOLOGY **EDUCATION** Williams Col, BA, 64; Pa State Univ, MS, 66; PhD, 68. **CAREER** Instr, Univ Md Soesterberg, 70; asst prof, Mass Col of Optometry, 70-74; res assoc, MIT, 70-74; asst prof to prof, Univ Colo, 74-; guest prof, Ludwig-Maximilian Univ, 81-82, 83, 85; guest prof Klinikum der AlbertLudwigsUniversitat, 91-92; guest prof, Univ Nijmegen, 01. **HONORS AND AWARDS** Alexander von Humboldt Stipendium; Fac Assembly Teaching Award, Boulder; Fel, Am Psychol Asn; Fel, am Psychol Soc. **MEMBERSHIPS** Am Psychol Asn; Am Psychol Soc; Psychonomics Soc; Optical Soc of Am; Asn for Res in Vision and Ophthalmology. **RESEARCH** Vision; Visual perception; Psychophysics; Signal detection theory. **SELECTED PUBLICATIONS** Coauth, "Visual masking at different polar angles in the two dimensional Fourier plane,: J of the Optical Soc of Am, (90): 116-127; co-auth, "Contrast thresholds for identification of numeric characters in direct and eccentric view," Perception and Psychophysics, (91): 495-508; co-auth, "Spatial distortions in visual perception," Gestalt Theory, (91): 210-231; co-auth, "Application of signal detection theory to weather forecasting behavior," Monthly Weather Rev, (92): 863-883; co-auth, "Making better use of scientific knowledge: separating truth from justice," Psychol Sci, (92): 80-87; auth, "The critical operating characteristic and the evaluation of expert judgment," Org Beh and Human Decision Processes, (92): 229-251; co-auth, "Cortical magnification theory fails to predict visual recognition," Europ J of Neurosci, (94): 1583-1588; co-auth, "Senescent changes in acotopic contrast sensitivity," Vision Res, (99): 3728-3736. **CONTACT ADDRESS** Dept Psychol, Univ of Colorado, Boulder, 345 UCB, Boulder, CO 80309-0345. **EMAIL** lharvey@psych.colorado.edu

HARVEY, RICHARD D.
PERSONAL Born 09/17/1968, Culver City, CA, m, 1996, 3 children **DISCIPLINE** PSYCHOLOGY **EDUCATION** Central State Univ, BA, 90; Univ Kans, MA, 92; PhD, 95. **CAREER** Asst Prof, St. Louis Univ, 95-. **HONORS AND AWARDS** Who's Who in Am. **MEMBERSHIPS** Am Psychol Asn, Gateway Industrial/Orgn Psychology Soc. **RESEARCH** Oppression, Identity, Organizational Culture, Christianity. **SELECTED PUBLICATIONS** Coauth, "Friendship pair similarity as a measure of group value," Group Dynamics: Theory, Res, and practice 1 (97): 1-11; coauth, "Perceived discrimination among African-Americans: Attributions, group identifications, and consequences for well-being," J of Personality and Soc Psychology 77 (99): 135-149; coauth, "Group-identity based self-protective strategies: The sigma of race, gender, and garlic," Europ J of Soc Psychology (in press); auth, "Individual differences in the phenomenological impact of social stigma," J of Soc Psychology (in press); coauth, "Collective guilt and shame as motivation for White support of Black programs," J of Appl Soc Psychology (in press); coauth, "Hostile environments, stereotype threat, and math performance among undergraduate women," Current Psychology (in press). **CONTACT ADDRESS** Dept Psychology, Saint Louis Univ, 221 N Grand Blvd, Saint Louis, MO 63103. **EMAIL** harveyr@slu.edu

HASKELL, GUY H.
PERSONAL Born 03/08/1956, New York, NY, m, 1988, 2 children **DISCIPLINE** FOLKLORE ANTHROPOLOGY **EDUCATION** IN Univ, PhD, 85; MA, 79; State Univ of NYork, Stony Brook, BA, 76. **CAREER** Visiting Asst Prof, Dept Middle Eastern Studies, Emory Univ, 94-; Dir Judaic and Near Eastern Studies, Oberlin Coll, 88-94; Asst Prof, Judaic and Near Eastern Studies, Oberlin Coll, 88-94; Lecurer, Jidaic and Near Eastern Studies; Dir, Judaic and Near Easter Studies Program House, Oberlin Coll, 85-88; Assoc Inst, Dept of Near Eastern Langs and Cultures, IN Univ, 82-85; Interim Dir B'nai B'rith Hillel Found, IN Univ, 81-82; Assoc Inst, Folklore Dept, IN Univ, 79-80; Assoc Inst, Dept of Near Eastern Langs and Cul-

tures, IN Univ, 78-79. **HONORS AND AWARDS** Phi Beta Kappa, Emory Univ Recognition for Excellent Teaching, 98; H.H. Powers Travel Grant, Bugaria and Israel, 92; Lilly Endowment Curricc Devel Frant for Minority Concerns, 91; Mellon Freshman-Sophomore Colloquium Devel Grant, 90; Grant in Aid Oberlin Coll Acculturation and Ethnicity in Israel-The Second Generation of Jews form Bulgaria, Tel Aviv, 86; Grant in Aid, IN Univ, 84; Dissertation Writing Grant, IN Univ, 83; Title VI Foreign Lang Fellowshop Arabic, 77; Hon BA, State Univ of NY,Stony Brook. **MEMBERSHIPS** Chair Comm for the Anthro of Jews and Judaism; Amer Anthro Assoc; Exec Board Gen Anthro Div; Chair Jewish Folklore and Ethnology Section, Amer Folklore Soc Section, Cord Folklore and Anthro Assoc for Jewish Studies; Assoc for Israel Studies; Israel Anthro Assoc; Bulgarian Studies Assoc; Natl Assoc of Pfor of Hebrew; Midwest Jewish Studies Assoc; Assoc for the Social Sci Study of Jewry; World Congress of Jewish Studies. **RESEARCH** Immigration; Ethnicity; Israeli Soc Sci; Jews of Bulgaria. **SELECTED PUBLICATIONS** From Sofia to Jaffa: The Jews of Bulgaria and Israel; Jewish Floklore and Anthro Series; ed, with a preface by Raphael Patai, Detroit Wayne State Univ Press, 94; Steven Sowman Choice 32, pp5729, 95; Jean Carasso Letter Sepharad, 95; pp8-10, Carol Silverman Jewish Folklore and Ethnology Review 17, 95; Walter Weiker Contemporary Jewry 16, 95; Committee for the Anthropology of Jews and Judaism: Background, Anthro of Rel Section, ed, Andrew Buckser Anthropology Newsletter Vol 39 No 4, 98; The Dossolution of Sephardic Cultrue in Bulgaria in Yeddish and Norman Stillman eds, From Iberia to Diaspora: Studies in Sephardic History and Culture, Leiden: Brill Forthcoming ,98; The hws of Bulgaria and the Final Solution, Jewish Folklore and Ethnology Review Vol 20 No 1, 98; Committee for the Anthropology of Jews and Judaism, Anthropology Newsletter Vol 38 No 5, 97; Publication Board General Anthropology Beneral Anthro Div Amer Anthro Assoc, Ed Board Jewish Folklore and Anthro Series, Wayne State Univ Press, (Dan Ben-Amos,ed in Chief), Joelle Bahloul, The Arcjitecture of Memory in Religious Studies Review, forthcoming. **CONTACT ADDRESS** Dept of Middle Eastern Studies, Emory Univ, Callaway S317, Atlanta, GA 30022. **EMAIL** ghaskel@emory.edu

HASLETT, TAMMY
PERSONAL Born 04/18/1970, Johnstown, PA, m, 1991 **DISCIPLINE** PSYCHOLOGY **EDUCATION** Univ Akron, PhD, 91. **CAREER** Psychologist, Nulton Diagnostic and Treatment Center; Adj Asst Prof, Univ Pittsburgh. **MEMBERSHIPS** APA, Gerontol Soc of Am. **RESEARCH** Creativity; Outcome Measures; Intelligence. **CONTACT ADDRESS** Dept Nat Sci, Univ of Pittsburgh, Johnstown, 450 Schoolhouse Rd, Johnstown, PA 15904.

HASSENGER, ROBERT
PERSONAL Born 03/02/1937, Sioux City, IA, m, 1979, 6 children **DISCIPLINE** SOCIOLOGY **EDUCATION** Univ Notre Dame, BA, 59; Univ Chicago, PhD, 65. **CAREER** Asst prof, Univ Notre Dame, 65-71; assoc prof, Kalamazoo Col, 71-72; assoc prof to prof, SUNY Empire State Col, 72-, fac chair, 96-2000. **HONORS AND AWARDS** SUNY Empire State Col Fac Lect, 95; SUNY Empire State Col Found Awd for Excellence in Scholar, 94. **MEMBERSHIPS** Soc for Values in Higher Ed. **RESEARCH** Social policy, social change, higher education. **SELECTED PUBLICATIONS** Auth, The Shape of Catholic Higher Education, Univ Chicago Press (67); over 100 published articles, chapters and reviews. **CONTACT ADDRESS** Center for Distance Learning, SUNY, Empire State Col, 3 Union Ave, Saratoga Springs, NY 12866. **EMAIL** rlh61@hotmail.com

HATFIELD, ELAINE
PERSONAL Born 10/22/1937, Detroit, MI, m, 1982 **DISCIPLINE** PSYCHOLOGY **EDUCATION** Univ Mich, BA, 59; Stanford Univ, PhD, 63. **CAREER** Asst to Assoc Prof, Univ Minn, 63-66; Assoc Prof, Univ Rochester, 66-67; Assoc Prof to Prof, Univ Wisc, 67-81; Guest Res Prof, Mannheim West Germany, 72; Prof and Chair, Univ Haw, 81-. **MEMBERSHIPS** Soc for the Sci Study of Sex. **RESEARCH** Love, Emotion, Human sexuality. **SELECTED PUBLICATIONS** Auth, a New Look at Love, Univ Press of America, 78; auth, Psychology of Emotion, Harcourt Press, 92; auth, Love, Sex and Intimacy: Their Psychology, Biology, and History, HarperCollins, 93; auth, Emotional Contagion, Cambridge Univ Press, 94; auth, Love and Sex: Cross-Cultural Perspectives, Allyn & Bacon, 96. **CONTACT ADDRESS** Dept Psychol, Univ of Hawaii, Honolulu Comm Col, 2430 Campus Rd, Honolulu, HI 96822. **EMAIL** elaineh1@aol.com

HATTERY, ANGELA J.
PERSONAL Born 07/05/1966, San Antonio, TX, m, 1988, 2 children **DISCIPLINE** SOCIOLOGY **EDUCATION** Carleton Col, BA; Univ Wisc-Madison, MS, 91, PhD, 96. **CAREER** Asst prof, Ball State Univ, 96-98; asst prof, Wake Forest Univ, 98-. **HONORS AND AWARDS** Nat Coun of Family Relations/sage, student/new prof book Awd, 98. **MEMBERSHIPS** Am Sociol Asn, Southern Sociol Asn, Soc for the Study of Social Problems, Midwest Sociol Soc, Sociols for Women in Soc. **RESEARCH** Gender, work, family, volunteerism. **SELECTED PUBLICATIONS** Auth, Social Problems: Sociology 220: A Course Guide, Univ Wisc Press (95); coauth with Emily W. Kane, "Men's and Women's Perceptions of Non-Consensual Sexual Intercourse," Sex Roles, 33 (95): 785-802; coed with Ione Y. DeOllos, Principles of Sociology: A departmental reader, 3rd ed, Fort Worth, TX: HarCourt Brace Custom Pub (98); auth, Women, Work, and Family, Sage (spring 2000); auth, "Social Class Stratification Project," in Active Learning Exercises for Introductory Sociology,ed by Kathleen McKinney, Barbara Heyl, and Frank D. Beck, Pine Forge Press (forthcoming); several papers under review. **CONTACT ADDRESS** Dept Sociol, Wake forest Univ, PO Box 7808, Winston-Salem, NC 27109. **EMAIL** hattery@wfu.edu

HAUCK, PAUL A.
PERSONAL Born 09/15/1924, Germany, m, 1953, 3 children **DISCIPLINE** PSYCHOLOGY **EDUCATION** Drew univ, BA 48; Univ UT, MA 51, PhD 53. **CAREER** Rock Island IL, Clinical Psychologist, 68-; Peoria Mental Health Clinic, Chief Psychol. **HONORS AND AWARDS** Dist Psychol Awd; Fell of APA; Outstanding Educ of Am; frequent visitor on radio and television. **MEMBERSHIPS** UMVPA; APA **SELECTED PUBLICATIONS** The Rational Management of children, Libra Press; the following from Westminster Press, Reason in Pastoral Counseling, Over Coming Frustration and Anger, Overcoming Depression, Overcoming worry and Fear, Brief Counseling with RET, Overcoming Jealousy and Possessiveness, How to get the Most Out of Life, Overcoming the rating game, The Three Faces of Love, Marriage is a Loving Business, How to stand Up for Yourself, How to Cope with People Who Drive You Crazy. **CONTACT ADDRESS** Safety Building, suite 302, Rock Island, IL 61201.

HAUPT, EDWARD
PERSONAL Born 12/28/1936, Bronx, NY, d, 1960, 3 children **DISCIPLINE** PSYCHOLOGY **EDUCATION** Univ Minn, BEng, 59; New York Univ, PhD, 69. **CAREER** Lab Psychologist, NIMH, 64-67; Asst Prof, Hampton Inst, 67-69; Asst Prof to Prof, Montclair State Univ, 69-. **MEMBERSHIPS** Am Psychol Asn. **RESEARCH** History of early experimental psychology. **SELECTED PUBLICATIONS** Auth, "The first Memory Drum," American Journal of Psychology, in press; auth, "Origins of American psychology in the work of G.E. Muller: Classical psychophysics and serial learning," in Psychology: Theoretical-historical perspectives, 98; auth, "Building a cybermuseum of early instruments and procedures with the 1903 Eduard Zimmermann catalog as an example," Behavioral Research Methods, Instrumentation, and computers, (98): 320-326; auth, "From whence comes experimental psychology? An alternative family tree," Caudernos Argentinos de Historia de la Psychologia de Argentinia, (97): 53-78; co-auth, "Modeling of human visual system dynamics affecting the visual evoked potential," in Modeling and control in biomedical systems. Proceedings of the IFAC Symposium, (94): 513-516; co-auth, "Distinct pattern of spacial frequency response by normal, recovered optic neuritis, and normal fellow eyes to a new linearly-variable neutral density filter," Graefe's archive, (93): 79-83. **CONTACT ADDRESS** Dept Psychol, Montclair State Univ, 1 Normal Ave, Montclair, NJ 07043. **EMAIL** haupt@email.njin.net

HAUSBECK, KATE
PERSONAL Born 10/11/1967, Buffalo, NY **DISCIPLINE** SOCIOLOGY **EDUCATION** SUNY, Buffalo, BA, 89; MA, 91; PhD, 97. **CAREER** Grad Student Instr, SUNY, 91-94; Vis Fac, SUNY, 94-95; Asst Prof, Univ Nev, 95-. **HONORS AND AWARDS** Excellence in Teaching Awd, St Univ NY (SUNY), 91-92; Distinguished Teacher Awd, Univ Nev, 99. **RESEARCH** Theory: contemporary, Postmodern, feminist, Classical, gender studies. **SELECTED PUBLICATIONS** Coauth, "Special Topics: Sociology of the Sex Industry," in The Sociol of Sexuality and Sexual Orientation: Syllabi and Teaching Materials (Wash, DC: ASA Pr, 97); coauth, "McDonaldization of the Sex Industry? The Business of Sex," in Primis Social Prob (McGraw Hill Publ, 99); coauth, "Inside Nevada's Brothel System," in Sex for Sale (New York: Routledge, 99), 217-243; coauth, "Prostitution-Nevada," in Encycl of Criminology and Deviant Behav, vol 3, Sexual Deviance (Taylor and Francis, 00); coauth, "Just Beneath the Surface: Re-Reading Geoscience, Re-Scripting the Knowledge/Power Nexis," Women's Studies Quart, 28:1-2 (00); auth, "Girls of Grit and Glitter in the City of Women: Las Vegas as Playground of Paradox," in The Grit Behind the Glitter (CA: Univ Calif Pr, 00); rev, Making Sense of Pornography, by Joanna Phoenix, Contemp Sociol, St Martins Pr (forthcoming). **CONTACT ADDRESS** Dept Sociol, Univ of Nevada, Las Vegas, PO Box 455033, Las Vegas, NV 89154. **EMAIL** hausbeck@nevada.edu

HAUSENBLAS, HEATHER ANN
PERSONAL Born 04/07/1970, Sudbury, ON, Canada, m, 2000 **DISCIPLINE** PHYSICAL EDUCATION, PSYCHOLOGY **EDUCATION** McMaster Univ, BA, 92; BA, 93; Univ W Ont, PhD, 98. **CAREER** Asst Prof, Univ Fla, 98-. **HONORS AND AWARDS** Sport Sci Awd, Intl Olympic Committee, 98; Young Sci Awd, Can Psychomotor Learning & Sport Psychol Asn, 96; P.L. Newbriggings Prize, Hamilton, 92. **MEMBERSHIPS** AASP; NASPSPA; SCAPPS; AED; APA. **SELECTED PUBLICATIONS** Co-auth, "Social influence and exercise: A meta-analysis," Journal of Sport & Exercise Psychology, (96): 1-16; co-auth, "The relationship between group cohesion and self-handicapping in female and male athletes," Journal of Sport & Exercise Psychology, (96): 132-143; co-auth, "Application of the theories of reasoned actioned and planned behavior in exercise: A meta-analysis," Journal of Sport & Exercise Psychology, (97): 47-62; co-auth, "Imagery use by athletes: Development of the sport Imagery Questionnaire," International Journal of Sport Psychology, (98): 73-89; co-auth, "Psychological commitment to exercise and eating disorder symptomology among female aerobic instructors," The Sport Psychologist, (98): 180-190; co-auth, "Group influences on eating and dieting behaviors in male and female residence members," College Student Journal, (98): 585-589; co-auth, "Social physique anxiety and eating disorder correlates among female athletic and nonathletic populations," Journal of Sport Behavior, (99): 502-513; co-auth, "Eating disorder indices and athletes: An integration," Journal of Sport & Exercise Psychology, (99): 230-258; co-auth, "When a comment is much ado about little: A reply to the Spence," Journal of Sport & Exercise Psychology, (99): 382-388. **CONTACT ADDRESS** Dept Exercise Sci, Univ of Florida, PO Box 118205, Gainesville, FL 32611.

HAUSER, ROBERT M.
PERSONAL Born 09/03/1942, Chicago, IL, m, 2 children **DISCIPLINE** SOCIOLOGY **EDUCATION** Univ Chicago, BA, 63; Univ Mich, MA, 66; PhD, 68. **CAREER** Res Asst, Johns Hopkins Univ, 59-62; Res Asst, Jack Meltzer Assoc, 62-63; Res Asst, Univ Mich, 64-65; Asst Prof, Brown Univ, 67-69; Asst Prof to Full Prof, Univ Wisc, 69-81; Vis Prof, Inst for Adv Study, Vienna, 80; Prof, Univ Wisc, 81-; Vis Prof, Univ Bergen, 83-84. **HONORS AND AWARDS** Metropolitan community Res Fel, Univ Mich, 63-64; Nat Inst of Mental health Fel, Univ Mich, 65-67; Phi Kappa Phi, 65; Sociol Res Asn, 72; HI Romnes Fac Fel, Univ Wisc, 76; Nominee for the Alan T Waterman Awd, Univ Wisc, 76; Fel, Am Asn for the advancement of Sci, 77; Fel, Ctr for Advanced Study in the Behavioral Sci, 77-78; Fel, Am Statistical Asn, 78; Who's Who in Am, Who's Who in Am Sci, Who's Who in the World, Paul F. Lazarsfeld Awd, Am Sociol Asn, 86. **MEMBERSHIPS** Nat Acad of Sci, Am Sociol Asn, Midwest Sociol Asn, Wisc Sociol Asn, Population Asn of am, Am Statistical Asn, Am Educ Res Asn, Soc for the Study of Soc Biol, Am Asn for the Advancement of Sci, Am Asn of Univ Prof, Soc Sci Hist Asn, Alpha Kappa Delta. **RESEARCH** Ed, Indicators of Children's Well-Being, Russell Sage Foundation, 97; ed, High Stakes: Testing for Tracking, promotion, and Graduation, Nat Acad press, forthcoming; auth, "Social Stratification Across Three Generations: New Evidence from the Wisconsin Longitudinal Study," American Sociological Review, (97): 561-572; auth, "Verbal Ability and Socioeconomic Success: A Trend analysis," Social Science Research, (97): 331-376; auth, "Trends in Black-White Test Score Differences: I. Uses and Misuses of NAEP/SAT Data," in The Rising Curve: Long-term Gains in IQ and Related Measures,98; auth, "The WORDSUM Vocabulary Test," in The Rising curve: Long-term Gains in IQ and Related measures,98; auth, " Does the Gender composition of Sibships Affect Educational Attainment?," Journal of Human Resources, (98): 644-657; auth, "choosing a Measure of Occupational Standing: How Useful are composite Measures in Analyses of Gender Inequality in Occupational Attainment?," Sociological methods and Research, (98): 3-76; auth, "Socioeconomic Achievements of Siblings in the Life course: new Findings from the Wisconsin Longitudinal Study," Research on aging, forthcoming; auth, "Occupational Status, Education, and social Mobility in the Meritocracy," Meritocracy and Inequality, forthcoming. **CONTACT ADDRESS** Dept Sociol, Univ of Wisconsin, Madison, 1180 Observatory Dr, Madison, WI 53706. **EMAIL** hauser@ssc.wisc.edu

HAVIR, LINDA
PERSONAL Born, MN **DISCIPLINE** SOCIOLOGY **EDUCATION** Univ Minn, BA, 68; MA, 71; PhD, 88. **CAREER** Res analyst, Minn Dept of Corrections, 71-72; adj instr, Univ Minn, 71-75; from instr to prof, St Cloud State Univ, 72-; chair, St Cloud Univ Dept of Sociol & Anthrop, 93-. **HONORS AND AWARDS** Award for Outstanding Res in the Sr Ctr Field, Nat Coun on the Aging, Inc., 94; SCSU Assessment Mini-grant, 98; Service-learning grant, Minn Campus Compact and Minn Higher Educ Services Offices, 97-99. **MEMBERSHIPS** Am Sociol Asn, Midwest Sociol Soc, Am Soc on Aging. **RESEARCH** Aging Issues, Gambling and Older People, Rural Aging, Rural Health Issues. **SELECTED PUBLICATIONS** Auth, "Banking for the Mature Market," in Encyclopedia of Financial Gerontology, eds. Lois Vitt and Jurg Siegenthaler (Greenwood Publ, 95); auth, "An Assessment of the Needs of Older Adults Living in Central Minnesota," Central Minn Coun on Aging, 95; auth, But Will They Use It? Social Service Utilization by Rural Elderly, Garland Publ (New York), 95. **CONTACT ADDRESS** Dept Sociol & Anthrop, St. Cloud State Univ, 720 4th Ave S, Saint Cloud, MN 56301.

HAWDON, JAMES E.
PERSONAL Born 02/11/1963, Tarentown, PA, m, 1998 **DISCIPLINE** SOCIOLOGY **EDUCATION** Penn State, BA, 85; Univ Virginia, MA, 88; PhD, 92. **CAREER** Asst prof, Clemson Univ, 92-97; GS dir, 95-; assoc prof, 97-. **MEMBERSHIPS** ASS; SSS. **RESEARCH** Crime; deviance' historical comparative. **SELECTED PUBLICATIONS** Auth, Emerging Organizational Forms: The Proliferation of Intergovernmental Organi-

zations in the Modern World System, Greenwood Pub Grp (96); auth, ed, "Recent Developments in the World-System," J Sociol Soc Pol 17 (96); auth, "Daily Routines and Crime: Using Routine Activities as Measures of Hirschi's Involvement," Youth Soc 30 (99): 395 - 415; auth, "Cycles of Deviance: Structural Change, Moral Boundaries, and Drug Use, 1880-1990," Socio Spectrum 16 (96):183-207; coauth, "Marital Status and General-life Satisfaction: A Cross-National Comparison," Intl J Comp Sociol 39 (98): 224-236; coauth, "Community Programs and Violence: Assessing an Anti-violence Program," Nat Fund Collab Viol Preven Rep 14 (98): 3-5; auth, "Penetrating the Illegal Economy of Crack Dealing," Quali Socio 21 (98): 91-96. **CONTACT ADDRESS** Dept Sociology, Clemson Univ, Clemson, SC 29634-0001. **EMAIL** hawdonj@clemson.edu

HAWKINS, DORISULA WOOTEN
PERSONAL Born 11/15/1941, Mt. Pleasant, TX, m **DISCIPLINE** EDUCATION **EDUCATION** Jarvis Christian Coll, BS 1962; East TX State Univ, attended 1965; Prairie View A&M Univ, MS 1967; TX A&M Univ, attended 1970; Univ of Houston, EdD 1975. **CAREER** Jarvis Coll, sec & asst public relations dir 62-63; Roxton School Dist, instructor business 63-66; Prairie View A&M Univ, assoc prof, 66-96, head general business dept 76-88; Jarvis christian Coll, dev officer, 96-97, prof business administration, 97-. **HONORS AND AWARDS** Dist Business Tchr of the Yr TBEA 1981; Disting Alumnus Jarvis Coll 1982; nominee State Tchr of Yr TBEA 1982; Disting Alumni Citation (NAFEO) 1986. **MEMBERSHIPS** Adv bd Milady Publishing Co; exec bd mem TX Assn of Black Personnel in Higher Educ 1978-83; bd mem TX Bus Educ (TBEA) Assn 1978-83; pres Alpha Kappa Alpha 1982-85; chmn TX Business Tchr Educ Cncl 1985-87; mem Natl Bus Educ Assoc; mem Jarvis Christian Coll Bd of Trustees, 1986-88; pres Natl Alumni Assoc 1986-88. **SELECTED PUBLICATIONS** "Can Your Office Administration be Justified" TX Business Educator 1979. **CONTACT ADDRESS** Jarvis Christian Col, PO Box 1470, Hawkins, TX 75765-0893.

HAWKINS, JOHN P.
PERSONAL Born 06/13/1946, La Grande, OR, m, 1969, 4 children **DISCIPLINE** ANTHROPOLOGY **EDUCATION** Univ Chicago,PhD, 78 **CAREER** Prof, Brigham Young Univ, 74-. **HONORS AND AWARDS** NIMH Fel, NSF Fel, Woodrow Wilson Fel. **MEMBERSHIPS** Am Anthrop Asn. **RESEARCH** U.S. Army, Gautemalan society. **SELECTED PUBLICATIONS** Auth, Army of Hope, Army of Alienation: Culture and Contradiction in the U.S. Army Communities of Cold War Germany, Praeger Pr, 00. **CONTACT ADDRESS** Dept Anthrop, Brigham Young Univ, 945 Swkt, Provo, UT 84602.

HAWTHORNE, BERTON J.
PERSONAL Born Waterford, MI **DISCIPLINE** PSYCHOLOGY **EDUCATION** Univ Mich, BA, 93; Mich State Univ, MA, 95; Univ of Detroit, PhD, 99. **CAREER** Asst prof, Mich State Univ, 97-. **HONORS AND AWARDS** Phi Beta Kappa; Teaching Award, MSU, 98. **MEMBERSHIPS** HNA, APA, AAS, GGS. **RESEARCH** Stress and individual performance in sport, Motivation and behavior within and across teams. **SELECTED PUBLICATIONS** Coauth, Stress and the Body, Garland Publ, 97; coauth, Blood, Sweat, and Tears: Motivation and Behavior in Sports, Garland Publ, 98; coauth, "Collegiate Athletes and Competition," J of Psychol Studies 5 (98): 44-52. **CONTACT ADDRESS** Dept Psychol, Michigan State Univ, East Lansing, MI 48824.

HAY, FRED J.
PERSONAL Born 10/03/1953, Toccoa, GA, m, 1983, 1 child **DISCIPLINE** ANTHROPOLOGY; LIBRARY SCIENCE **EDUCATION** Rhodes Col, BA, 75; Univ Va, MA, 81; Fl St Univ, MLIS, 87; Univ Fl, PhD, 85. **CAREER** Asst prof, St Cloud St Univ, 85-86; librn, asst prof, Ks St Univ, 88-89; librn, Harvard Univ, 89-94; prof, librn, Appalachian St Univ, 94-. **HONORS AND AWARDS** Douglas W. Bryant Fel, 92-93; Brenda McCullum Mem Prize, Amer Folklore Soc, 97. **MEMBERSHIPS** Amer Anthrop Assoc; Appalachian Stud Assoc; Amer Libr Assoc; Assoc of Col & Res Libr; Assoc of Black Anthrop; Progressive Librn Guild. **RESEARCH** Appalachia, African-American cultures; Black music; soc sci bibliogr & documentation, southern US, Caribbean. **SELECTED PUBLICATIONS** Auth, Tozzer Library: How to Access the World's Largest Anthropology Bibliography, Cult Anthrop Methods Newsletter, 92; OCLC: An Essential Tool for Anthropological Documentation, Cult Anthrop Methods Newsletter, 93; The Significance of Caribbeanist Anthropology: A Bibliographic History, Ref Svc Rev, 95; coed, Documenting Cultural Diversity in the Resurgent American South: Collectors, Collecting and Collections; Assoc of Col & Res Libr; ed, auth, When Night Falls: Kric! Krac!, Libr Unlimited, 98; auth, "The Sacred/Profane Dialectic in Delta Blues as Exemplified in Excerpts from the Life and Lyrics of Sonny Bay Williamson," Phylon (87); auth, "Microethnography of a Haitian Boutique," Social and Economic Studies (90); auth, "The Subject Specialist in the Academic Library," Jrnl of Academic Librarianship (90); auth, African American Community Studies from North America, Garland, 91. **CONTACT ADDRESS** W. L. Evry Appalachian Col, Appalachian State Univ, Belk Library, Boone, NC 28608. **EMAIL** hayfj@appstate.edu

HAYES, CHARLES LEONARD
PERSONAL Born 12/16/1921, Baton Rouge, LA, m **DISCIPLINE** EDUCATION **EDUCATION** Leland Coll, AB 1947; Loyola U, EdM 1949; Univ No CO, EdD 1958. **CAREER** Chicago, teacher 48-49; NC A&T State Univ, instr 49-52, asst prof, 52-56, prof, 58-61, chmn 61-66; George Washington Univ, ace fellow, 66-67; US Office of Educ HEW, chief 67-69; Albany State Coll, pres 69-80; NC A&T State Univ, chmn beginning 80, adjunct faculty, currently. **MEMBERSHIPS** Am Assn of Univ Profs; Assn of Higher Edn; NEA; Phi Delta Kappa; Am Personnel & Guidance Assn; Am Coll Personnel Assn; Assn of Counselor Educators & Suprs; NC Psychol Assn; Kappa Delta Pi; bd dir Albany Urban League; Albany USO Council; exec bd Chehaw Council Boy Scouts of Am; Nat Conf of Christian& Jews; YMCA; Citizens Adb Com; mem Drug Action Council, Volunteers to the Courts. **CONTACT ADDRESS** No Carolina Agr and Tech State Univ, 1601 E Market St, Greensboro, NC 27411.

HAYES, EDWARD L.
PERSONAL m, 3 children **DISCIPLINE** CHRISTIAN EDUCATION **EDUCATION** Westmont Col, BA; Dallas Theol Sem, ThM; Univ Denver, PhD. **CAREER** Prof, pres Denver Sem, 93. **HONORS AND AWARDS** Baptist minister, First Baptist Church of Montebello, Calif; exec dir, Mount Hermon Assn, 79-92. **RESEARCH** Teaching, preaching, administering and fundraising. **SELECTED PUBLICATIONS** Auth, The Focused Life and Other Devotion; Words to Live By and The Focused Life. **CONTACT ADDRESS** Denver Conservative Baptist Sem, PO Box 10000, Denver, CO 80250.

HAYES, LEOLA G.
PERSONAL Born Rocky Mount, NC, m **DISCIPLINE** EDUCATION **EDUCATION** BS; MA; MS prof diploma; PhD 1973. **CAREER** William Paterson Coll of NJ, chmn Special Educ Dept, currently; Fair Lawn NJ, supervisor, spl educ, 57-64; Fair Lawn NJ, teacher of handicapped children; Blind Chicago, consultant, 54-57; Blind NY Inst for Blind, teacher, 53-54. **HONORS AND AWARDS** Recipient: Human Relations Awd, Natl Bus & Professional Women; Nat Comm Ldrs Awd; Hannah G Solomon Awd; Ernest Melly Awd. **MEMBERSHIPS** CEC; Vocational Rehab Soc; AAMD; NJEA; Drug Abuse Prog 1973-; Young People Counseling Session, Alpha Kappa Alpha Sorority. **CONTACT ADDRESS** Spec Educ, William Paterson Col of New Jersey, 300 Pompton Rd, Wayne, NJ 07470.

HAYES, STEVEN C.
PERSONAL Born 08/13/1948, Philadelphia, PA, m, 1987, 3 children **DISCIPLINE** PSYCHOLOGY **EDUCATION** Loyola Marymount Univ, BA, 70; W Va Univ, Morgantown, MA, 74, PhD, 77. **CAREER** Instr to assoc prof, Univ NC at Greensboro, 76-86; prof and Dir of Clinical Training, Univ of Nevada, Reno, 86-93, Univ of Nevada Found Prof, 92-, chair, 94-. **HONORS AND AWARDS** Fel, Am Psychol Soc, 89; Fel, Am Asn of Applied and Preventative Psychol, 91; Univ of Nevada Found Prof, 92; Univ of Nevada, Reno, Outstanding Researcher of the Year, 97; Univ and Community Col System of Nevada Regents' Researcher of the Year, 2000; W Va Univ Col of the Arts and Sci Alumnus of the Year, 2000; Don F. Hake Awd for Exemplary Contributions to Basic Behav Res and Its Applications, Div 25, Am Psychol Asn, 2000. **MEMBERSHIPS** Am Psychol Asn, Am Asn of Applied and Preventative Psychol, Asn for Advancement of Behavior Therapy, Asn for Behav Analysis, Western Psychol Asn, Soc for the Experimental Analysis of Behavior, Soc for Psychotherapy Res. **RESEARCH** The development of an experimentally-based analysis of the nature of the human language and cognition and its application to the understanding and alleviation of human suffering. **SELECTED PUBLICATIONS** Coauth, Acceptance and Commitment Therapy: An experiential approach to behavior change, NY: Guilford Press (99); coauth, The Scientist-Practitioner: Research and accountability in the age of managed care, 2nd ed, NY: Allyn & Bacon (99); coauth, Acceptance and Commitment Therapy: A manual for the treatment of emotional avoidance, 2nd ed, Reno, NV: Context Press (99); coauth, Organized behavioral healthcare: Issues and prospects, NY: Academic (in press); coauth, "Derived relational responding as learned behavior," in S. C. Hayes, D. Barnes-Holmes, & B. Roche, eds, Relational Frame Theory: A Post-Skinnerian Account of Human Language and Cognition, Reno, NV: Context Press (in press); auth, "Acceptance and change," in N. J. Smelser & P. B. Baltes, eds, International Encyclopedia of the Social and Behavioral Sciences, Oxford, England: Pergamon (in press); coauth, "Applied behavior analysis," in S. Turner, eds, Encyclopedia of psychology, NY: Elsevier Science (in press). **CONTACT ADDRESS** Dept Psychol/296, Univ of Nevada, Reno, N Virginia Ave, Reno, NV 89557-0062. **EMAIL** hayes@scs.unr.edu

HAYMAN, CAROL
PERSONAL Born 02/18/1953, Ft Walton Beach, FL, m, 1 child **DISCIPLINE** ANTHROPOLOGY **EDUCATION** Univ Tex, BAA, BFA, MA. **CAREER** Tex Lutheran Univ, 6 years; instr of Anthropology, Austin Community Col, 90-. **MEMBERSHIPS** Cultural Survival, Austin Visual Arts Asn, The Rock Art Found, Tex Archaeol Soc, Tex Photographic Soc. **RESEARCH** Indigenous rights, textiles, photography. **CONTACT ADDRESS** Dept Soc & Behav Sci, Austin Comm Col, 1212 Rio Grande St, Austin, TX 78701. **EMAIL** chayman@austin.cc.tx.us

HAYNES, JAMES H.
PERSONAL Born 11/27/1953, Pensacola, FL, s **DISCIPLINE** EDUCATOR **EDUCATION** Pensacola Jr Coll, AA 1973; Morehouse Coll, BA 1975; Georgia State Univ, MEd 1977; Univ of IA, PhD 1979. **CAREER** Atlanta Public Sch System, teacher, 75-77; Philadelphia Training Center, asst dir, 79-80; FL A&M Univ, dir of planning 1980-83; Morgan State Univ, dir of inst research, 83-84, vice pres of planning, 84, Title III Coord, 88-. **HONORS AND AWARDS** Honorary membership in Promethean Kappa Tau, Phi Delta Kappa, Phi Alpha Theta; Governor's Citation for services to youth in Baltimore community; Mayor's Citation for services to youth in Baltimore city. **MEMBERSHIPS** Woodrow Wilson Nat'l Fellowship Foundation, 1980; Title III Prog Bowie State Coll, counsultant 1984-; Assoliation of Minority Hlth Profession Sch, consultant 1982; supervisor of admin for NTE, GMAT 1984-; Alpha Phi Alpha, Baltimore Morehouse Alumni Club, sec; NAACP; Morehouse Coll Nat'l Alumni Assoc; board of directors, Baltimore Employment Network. **CONTACT ADDRESS** Morgan State Univ, Cold Spring Ln & Hillen Rd, Baltimore, MD 21239.

HAYWARD, DOUGLAS
PERSONAL Born 06/24/1940, Midland, ON, Canada, m, 1961, 3 children **DISCIPLINE** CULTURAL STUDIES, ANTHROPOLOGY, MISSIOLOGY **EDUCATION** Westmont Col, BA; Fuller Theol Sem, MA; Univ Calif, Santa Barbara, MA; PhD. **CAREER** Assoc Prof, Biola Univ, 89-. **HONORS AND AWARDS** Who's Who Among Am Teachers, 96, 98, 00; Marquis Who's Who in the World, 17th Ed, 00. **MEMBERSHIPS** ASM, WMS, ASAO. **RESEARCH** Anthropological study of religion, Christianity and culture, socio-religious change. **SELECTED PUBLICATIONS** Auth, Vernacular Christianity Among the Mulia Dani: An Ethnography of Religious Belief Among the Western Dani of Irian Jaya, Indonesia, UP of Am (Lanham, MD), 97; auth, "Selected Bibliography of Pre-Industrial Peoples for Church Workers," J of Frontier Missions, vol 14:4 (97): 199-203; auth, "Sociology of Religion," in Evangelical Dict of World Missions (Grand Rapids, MI: Baker Publ Co, 00); auth, "Satanism, Satanism," in Evangelical Dict of World Missions (Grand Rapids, MI: Baker Publ Co, 00); auth, "Wicca, Wiccan," in Evangelical Dict of World Missions (Grand Rapids, MI: Baker Publ Co, 00); auth, "Neopagan, Neopaganism," in Evangelical Dict of World Missions (Grand Rapids, MI: Baker Publ Co, 00); auth, "Totem and Totemism," in Evangelical Dict of World Missions (Grand Rapids, MI: Baker Publ Co, 00); auth, "Saturday Night in Pasadena: A Case Study of Harvest Rock Church," in The Relig of Generation X. (Routledge Pr, forthcoming). **CONTACT ADDRESS** Dept Cult Studies, Biola Univ, 13800 Biola Ave, La Mirada, CA 90639-0001. **EMAIL** doug_hayward@peter.biola.edu

HAZELRIGG, LAWRENCE E.
PERSONAL Born 10/16/1941, St Joseph, MO, m, 1975, 3 children **DISCIPLINE** SOCIOLOGY **EDUCATION** Univ Mo, BA, 63; Fla State Univ, MS, 64; Univ Tex, PhD, 70. **CAREER** From Asst Prof to Assoc Prof, Ind Univ, 70-80; Prof, Fla State Univ, 80-. **HONORS AND AWARDS** Res Sci Awd, Nat Sci Found, 75-79. **MEMBERSHIPS** Nat Sci Found. **RESEARCH** Processes of allocation, socialization, decision making, organizational rationalities. **SELECTED PUBLICATIONS** Auth, "Reading Goffman's Framing as Provocation of a Discipline." Human Studies 15 (92): 239-264; Auth, "Constructionism and Practices of Objectivity," in Reconsidering Social Constructionism (NY: Aldine de Guyter, 93), 485-500; auth, Social Science and the Challenge of Relativism, 3 vols, Univ Fla Pr (Gainesville, FL), 89, 95; auth, "Marx and the Meter of Nature," Rethinking Marxism 6 (93): 104-122; auth, "Gender, Race/Ethnicity and Poverty in Later Life," J of Aging Studies 9 (95): 43-63; coauth, Ending A career in the Auto Industry, Plenum Pr (New York, NY), 96; auth, "Perceived Income Inadequacy Among Older Adults," Res on Aging 19 (97): 69-107; auth, "A Multilevel Model of Early-Retirement Decisions Among Auto Workers in Plants with Different Futures," Res on Aging 21 (99): 275-303; auth, "Fueling the Politics of Age," Am Soc Rev 64 (99): 570-576; auth, "Scaling the Semantics of Satisfaction," Soc Indicators Res 49 (00): 147-180. **CONTACT ADDRESS** Dept Sociol, Florida State Univ, PO Box 3062270, Tallahassee, FL 32306. **EMAIL** lhazelri@garnet.acns.fsu.edu

HEALEY, WILLIAM C.
PERSONAL Born 05/07/1935, Jefferson City, MO, m, 1957, 2 children **DISCIPLINE** COMMUNICATIVE DISORDERS, SPECIAL EDUCATION **EDUCATION** Univ Mo, PhD, 63. **CAREER** Ch, dept Spec Educ, Univ Nev, Las Vegas; Prof, Univ of Nevada. **HONORS AND AWARDS** Board of Regents Outstanding Faculty Member Awd; Families for Effective Autism Treatment "Outstanding Leadership and Service" Awd; Beam of Light Awd for Outstanding Service, Clark County School District; Outstanding Collaborator Awd, Gallaudet Univ, Honor Board Awd for Outstanding Lifelong Leadership, Arizona Assoc for the Gifted and Talented: President Jimmy Carter Appointee to the Commission on Mental Health; and Appointee by US Commissioner of Education, Dr. Ernest Boyer

to Task Force on Basic Skills. **RESEARCH** Effective Treatments of Children with Disabilities; Basic Belief Systems of School Administrators. **SELECTED PUBLICATIONS** Auth, Monitoring and mainstreaming amplification units for the children: The need for standard practices, NSSHLA J, 18, 91; Inclusion in childhood services: Ethics and endocratic oughtness, in Hayes, L, Hayes, G, Moore, S, & Ghezzi, P, Ethics and Developmental Disabilities, Context Press, 94; What administrators want from special education teachers, CEC Today, 95; auth, Stages of Adjustment in Parents of Children with a Handicap, Journal of Defectology, Defectology Association of Yugoslavia, 98; auth, Early Intervention Programs for Children with Disabilities in Korea, International Journal of Disability, Development, and Education, 99. **CONTACT ADDRESS** Dept of Spec Educ, Univ of Nevada, Las Vegas, 4505 Maryland Pky, Las Vegas, NV 89154-3014. **EMAIL** healey@nevada.edu

HEATH, DWIGHT BRALEY
PERSONAL Born 11/19/1930, Hartford, CT, m, 1 child **DISCIPLINE** SOCIAL AND CULTURAL ANTHROPOLOGY **EDUCATION** Harvard Univ, AB, 52; Yale Univ, PhD (anthropology), 59. **CAREER** Prof of Anthropology, Brown Univ, 59-; various years, part-time vis prof of anthropology at Univ WI, Universidad de Costa Rica; frequent consultant to govt and international organizations around the world. **HONORS AND AWARDS** Frequent res grants: Nat Science Found; Nat Inst on Alchohol Abuse & Alchoholism; Wenner-Gren Found; Fulbright; Soc Sci res Coun; et al. **MEMBERSHIPS** Crosscultural and historical perspectives on alcohol & drugs; social hist; political socialization; ethnography. **SELECTED PUBLICATIONS** Author of several books on Pilgrims at Plymouth; Latin American cultures & societies; alcohol in sociocultural perspective; historical dictionary of Bolivia; International Handbook on Alcohol and Culture, Greenwood, 95; The World of Drink, Taylor & Francis, 99. **CONTACT ADDRESS** Dept of Anthropology, Brown Univ, Box 1921, Providence, RI 02912-1921. **EMAIL** Dwight_Heath@Brown.edu

HEATH, ROBIN L.
PERSONAL Born 10/07/1946, Prince Rupert, BC, Canada, s **DISCIPLINE** ANTHROPOLOGY **EDUCATION** Univ Ky, PhD, 98. **MEMBERSHIPS** Am Anthrop Asn; Am Public Health Asn; Asn Anthrop and Gerontology. **RESEARCH** Brain and behavior; humor. **SELECTED PUBLICATIONS** Coauth, Lay Concepts of Stroke in Kentucky, What Works? Synthesizing Effective Biomedical and Psychosocial Strategies for Healthy Families in the 21st Century, Ind Univ, 94; Prosodic Characteristics of Speech Pre and Post Right Hemisphere Stroke, Brain and Lang 51, 95; Cognitive Model of Stroke, Indian J Gerontology, 96; Farm Youth and Horse-Related Injuries: A Case for Safety Helmets, J Agromedicine 5, 98; The Interpersonal Management of Crying Among Survivors of Stroke, Sociological Spectrum 18, 98. **CONTACT ADDRESS** Anthrop Dept, Univ of Kentucky, Lafferty Hall, Lexington, KY 40536. **EMAIL** rlheat00@ukcc.uky.edu

HECHTER, MICHAEL
PERSONAL Born 11/15/1943, Los Angeles, CA, m, 1983, 2 children **DISCIPLINE** SOCIOLOGY **EDUCATION** Columbia Univ, AB, 66, PhD, 72; Univ Oxford, MA, 94. **CAREER** Asst to full prof, Univ Washington, 70-84; prof, Univ Ariz, 84-94; Univ Lectr and Fel, New Col, Oxford, 94-96; prof, Univ Ariz, 96-99; prof, Univ Washington, 99-. **HONORS AND AWARDS** Vis Fel, Russell Sage Found, 88-89; Elected, Sociol Res Asn, 92; Fel, Ctr for Advanced Studies in the Behav Scis, 98-99. **MEMBERSHIPS** Am Sociol Asn. **RESEARCH** Theory, political sociology, nationalism. **SELECTED PUBLICATIONS** Ed, The Microfoundations of Macrosociology, Philadelphia: Temple Univ Press (83); auth, Principles of Group Solidarity, Berkeley & London: Univ Calif Mesa (87); co-ed, Social Institutions, NY and Berlin: Aldine de Gruyter (98); co-ed, The Origin of Values, NY: Aldine de Gruyter (93); auth, Internal Colonialism, New Brunswick and London: Transaction Pubs (99); auth, Containing Nationalism, Oxford and NY: Oxford Univ Press (2000); co-ed, Social Works, NY: Russell Sage Found (in press); author of many articles in prof journals. **CONTACT ADDRESS** Dept Sociol, Univ of Washington, PO Box 353340, Seattle, WA 98195-3340. **EMAIL** Hechter@u.washington.edu

HEFLIN, JOHN F.
PERSONAL Born 04/07/1941, Sweetwater, TX, m **DISCIPLINE** EDUCATION **EDUCATION** NM Highlands Univ, BA 1963; Stanford Univ, MA 1972, PhD 1977. **CAREER** Portland State Univ, asst prof educ admin, 76-; OR Dept D, EEO program coord, 74-76; Stanford Univ, asst to dean, 71-74; Merced Union High School, Merced, CA, teacher/coach, 65-70; US Dept Interior Denver, CO, cartographer 64-65. **HONORS AND AWARDS** NW Association of Black Elected Officials; Foundation Leadrship Development Program fellow 1970-71. **MEMBERSHIPS** Portland Urban League; OR Assembly for Black Affairs; OR Alliance of Black School Educators; CA Teachers Assn; OR Educators Assn; NEA; Natl Cnl Social Studies; Policy Student Orgn; Phi Delta Kapp; bd dir Mid-Peninsula Task Force Integrated Ed; Am Ed Research Assn; ed dir NAACP; Natl Alliance of Black School Educators; ntl chmn Rsrch Focus on Black Ed (Am Ed Research Assn); commis-

sioner Portland Metro Human Realtions Committee; Assn for Supervision & Curriculm Dev. **CONTACT ADDRESS** Portland State Univ, PO Box 751, Portland, OR 97207.

HEFNER, CARL
PERSONAL Born 04/19/1942, Latrobe, PA, m **DISCIPLINE** ANTHROPOLOGY **EDUCATION** Univ Haw, PhD, 94. **CAREER** Instr, Univ of Haw, 86-. **HONORS AND AWARDS** Excellence in Teaching Awd, Univ of Haw, 96; listed in Who's Who Amongst America's Teachers, 98; Ctr for Asia Pacific exchange Awd. **MEMBERSHIPS** Asn for Asian Studies. **RESEARCH** Indonesia, Southeast Asia, Visual Anthropology, Web-based Instruction. **SELECTED PUBLICATIONS** Auth, Ludruk: Folk Theatre of Java; auth, Vietnam: History and Culture. **CONTACT ADDRESS** Dept Soc Sci, Univ of Hawaii, Kapiolani Comm Col, 4303 Diamond Head Rd, Honolulu, HI 96816. **EMAIL** hefner@hawaii.edu

HEGGINS, MARTHA JEAN ADAMS
PERSONAL Born 05/09/1942, Florence, SC, 1 child **DISCIPLINE** TEACHER EDUCATION **EDUCATION** SC State Univ, BS, 64; Bank Street Col Educ, MS, 69; Rutgers Univ, EdD, 75. **CAREER** Instr, SC State Univ, 69-70, asst dir and instr, 70-71; Dir, Demonstration Day Care Learning Center, New Brunswick Public Schs, NJ, 72-75; assoc prof, SC State Univ, 77-81, prof and coordr of Early Childhood Education, 85-; Dir, Proj PRIMER (Pre-Sch Readiness and Intervention Managing Educ Resources), 97-. **HONORS AND AWARDS** SC State Univ: Teacher of the Year, 77-78, 82-83, 91-92, Teacher of the Teacher Awd, 82-83, Distinguished Fac Chair, 82-83; organizer, founder and pres, Nat Black Child Development Inst, 90-92; 1999 SC State Univ: President's Circle, Excellence in Service Awd, Certificate of Service Awd for Thirty Years of Service, Quarter-Century Club Appreciation Awd (25)Years; listed in: Annual Cornell Empowerment and Family Support Network Dictionary, Who's Who Among America's Teachers, Who's Who in the South and Southwest, Who's Who of Am Women, The World Who's Who of Women, Directory of Distinguished Americans. **MEMBERSHIPS** Southern Asn of Children Under Six, Nat Black Children Develop Inst, Phi Delta Kappa, Kappa Omnicron Nu Honor Soc, Nat Asn for the Educ Int, SC Coun of the Int Reading Asn, SC Asn of Teacher Educators, SC Asn for Supervision and Curriculum Develop, SC Asn for the Educ of Young Children, SC Early Childhood Asn. **RESEARCH** A Study of Head Start Training and Social Skills Development in Rural Children in South Carolina, submitted to the 1890 Research and Extension program, South Carolina State Univ, January 2000. **SELECTED PUBLICATIONS** Auth, A Study of Minority Early Childhood Leadership in Rural South Carolina: Final Report, submitted to the Center for the Study of the Black Experiences Affecting Higher Education, Clemson Univ, Clemson, SC (93); auth, "Beyond the ABC's: A Point of View Number One Goal 2000," The South Carolina Program for the Recruitment and Retention of Minority Teachers, SCSU, Orangeburg, SC, Vol 1 (95); coauth with Gwen Niilampti, Conflict Resolution- A Manual for Teaching Conflict Resolution Skills, SC Stet Univ, Orangeburg, SC (96); coauth with Gwen Nall-Niilampti, Conflict Resolution, Violence Prevention, Peace Education- A Paradigm for Early Childhood Education in the 21st Century, 4th ed, Orangeburg, SC: New Millennium Pubs (2000). **CONTACT ADDRESS** Dept Teacher Educ, So Carolina State Univ, 300 Col St NE, Orangeburg, SC 29117-0001. **EMAIL** MEHEGGINS@scsu.edu

HEGMON, MICHELLE
DISCIPLINE ANTHROPOLOGY **EDUCATION** Univ Va, BA, 81; Univ Mich, MA, 84; PhD, 90. **CAREER** Postdoctoral Fel and Res Collaborator, Smithsonian Inst, Conserv Anal Lab, Wash DC, 90-91; Res Analyst, Crow Canyon Archaeol Center, Cortez, Colo, 91; Asst Prof, NMex State Univ, Las Cruces, 91-95; Asst/Assoc Prof, Ariz State Univ, Tempe, 95-. **MEMBERSHIPS** Am Anthrop Asn, Am Asn of Univ Prof, Ariz Archaeol and Hist Soc, Sigma Xi Found, Soc for Am Archaeol. **RESEARCH** Archeology, US Southwest, Material culture, Social Theory. **SELECTED PUBLICATIONS** Co-ed, The Architecture of Social Integration in Prehistoric Pueblos, Occasional Papers, Crow Canyon Archaeol Center (Cortex, Colo), 89; auth, "Archaeological Research on Style," Annual Rev of Anthrop 21 (92): 517-536; auth, "Pueblo I Ceramic Production in Southwestern Colorado: Analyses of Igneous Rock Temper," The Kiva 60 (95): 371-390; auth, The Social Dynamics of Pottery Style in the Early Puebloan Southwest, Occasional Papers 5, Crow Canyon Archaeol Center (Cortex, Colo), 95; coauth, "Production for Local Consumption and Exchange: Comparisons of Early Red and White Ware Ceramics in the San Juan Region," in The Organization of Ceramic Production in the American Southwest, ed. B.J. Mills and P.L. Crown (Tucson: Univ of Ariz Press, 95), 30-62; coauth, "Gender, Anatomical Knowledge, and Pottery Production: Implications of an Anatomically Unusual Birth Depicted on Mimbres Pottery from Southwestern New Mexico," Am Antiquity 61 (96): 747-754; coauth, "The Production of San Juan Red Ware in the Northern Southwest: Insights Into Regional Interaction in Early Puebloan Prehistory," Am Antiquity 62 (97): 449-463; auth, "Technology, Style, and Social Practices: Archaeological Approaches," in Archaeology of Social Boundaries, ed. M. Stark (Wash, DC: Smithsonian Inst Press, 98), 264-279; coauth, "Mimbres Aban-

donment and Regional Reorganization," Am Anthropologist 100 (98): 1-15; ed, The Archaeology of Regional Interaction: Religion, Warfare and Exchange in the American Southwest, Univ Press of Colo (Niwot), 99. **CONTACT ADDRESS** Dept Anthrop, Arizona State Univ, PO Box 872402, Tempe, AZ 85287. **EMAIL** michelle.hegmon@asu.edu

HEILMAN, SAMUEL C.
PERSONAL Born 05/26/1946, Karlsruhe, Germany, m, 1969, 4 children **DISCIPLINE** SOCIOLOGY, ANTHROPOLOGY **EDUCATION** Brandeis Univ, BA, 68; New Sch for Soc Res, MA, 70; Univ Pa, PhD(sociology), 73. **CAREER** Instr, St. Joseph's Univ, 72-73; instr, Univ Pa, 72-73; from asst prof to assoc prof, 73-82, prof, sociology, 82-, Harold Proshansky Chair in Jewish Studies, 93-, grad chair, Dept Sociology, 76-78, chair dept, 79-80, dir, Jewish Studies Prog, 80-86, dir, Ctr for Jewish Studies, 80-87, Queens Col, City Univ New York; vis prof, Max Weinreich Ctr for Advanced Jewish Studies, YIVO Inst Jewish Res, 76; vis prof, Hebrew Univ Jerusalem, 79, 88; vis prof, Tel Aviv Univ, 84; Vis Fulbright Prof, Universities of New South Wales, Sydney, and Melbourne, 86; Fel, Inst for Advanced Study, Jerusalem, 91-92. **HONORS AND AWARDS** Grad Fac Fel, New Sch for Social Res, 68-70; Teaching Fel in Soc Psychol, Univ Pa, 70-71; Dissertation Fel, Univ Pa Ctr for Urban Ethnography, 72-73; Distinguished Fac Awd, CUNY, 85, 87, 94; The Present Tense Mag Lit Awd for best book of the year in the religious thought category, for The Gate Behind the Wall, 84; Nat Jewish Book Awd, for A Walker in Jerusalem, 86; recipient of numerous grants. **SELECTED PUBLICATIONS** Auth, Synagogue Life: A Study in Symbolic Interaction, Univ Chicago Press, 76; auth, The People of the Book: Drama, Fellowship and Religion, Univ Chicago Press, 83; auth, The Gate Behind the Wall, Summit Books/Simon & Schuster, 85; coauth, A Walker in Jerusalem, Summit Books/Simon & Schuster, 86, 2nd ed, J.P.S. 95; coauth, Cosmopolitans and Parochials: Modern Orthodox Jews in America, Univ Chicago Press, 89; auth, Defenders of the Faith: Inside Ultra-Orthodox Jewry, California, 99; auth, Portrait of American Jews: The Last Half of the Twentieth Century, Univ Wash Press, 95; auth, When A Few Dies, California, 01. **CONTACT ADDRESS** Dept Sociology, Queens Col, CUNY, 6530 Kissena Blvd, Flushing, NY 11367. **EMAIL** Scheilman@yahoo.com

HEINZ, JOHN P.
PERSONAL Born 08/06/1936, Carlinville, IL, m, 1967, 2 children **DISCIPLINE** LAW, SOCIOLOGY **EDUCATION** Wash Univ, AB, 58; Yale Univ, LLB, 62. **CAREER** Teaching fel, Wash Univ, 58-59; atty, Off Secy Air Force, 62-65; from asst prof to prof, 65-88, Owen L. Coon Prof Law, Northwestern Univ, 88-, Prof Soc, 87-; dir Russell Sage prog law & soc sci, Northwestern Univ, 68-70, dir res, Sch Law, 73-74; consult, Ill Judicial Conf, 71-73; pres, John Howard Asn, 74-75; mem res adv comt, Am Judicature Soc, 75-77; affiliated scholar, Am Bar Found, 75-; mem, bd trustees, Law & Soc Asn, 78-81; exec dir, Am Bar Found 82-86. **HONORS AND AWARDS** Harry Kalven Prize of the Law and Soc Asn, for distinguished research on law and society, 87; Distinguished Alumni Achievement Awd, Washington Univ, 98; recipient of numerous research grants. **MEMBERSHIPS** Law & Soc Asn; Am Bar Asn. **RESEARCH** Law and the behavioral sciences; the legal profession; criminal law. **SELECTED PUBLICATIONS** Coauth, A theory of Policy Analysis and some Preliminary Applications, In: Policy Analysis of Political Science, Markham, 70; Public Access to Information, Transaction Bks, 79; Chicago Lawyers: The Social Structure of the Bar, Russell Sage Found & Am Bar Found, Basic Book, 82, rev ed, Northwestern Univ Press and Am Bar Found, 94; The Hollow Core: Private Interests in National Policy Making, Harvard Univ Press, 93; The Constituencies of Elite Urban Lawyers, Law & Soc Rev, vol 31, 97; auth or coauth of numerous other journal articles. **CONTACT ADDRESS** Sch of Law, Northwestern Univ, 357 E Chicago Ave, Chicago, IL 60611-3069. **EMAIL** j-heinz@nwu.edu

HEINZE, RUTH-INGE
PERSONAL Born 11/04/1919, Berlin, West Germany **DISCIPLINE** RELIGION, ASIAN FOLKLORE **EDUCATION** Univ Calif, Berkeley, BA, 69, MA, 71, PhD(Asian studies), 74. **CAREER** Ed text bks, Follett Publ Co, Chicago, 55-56; lectr anthrop, Exten Course, Berlin, 63-73; producer, Radio Broadcast Berlin, 63-68; lectr English, Univ Chiang Mai, Thailand, 72; Res Assoc, Ctr South & Southeast Asia Studies, Univ Calif, Berkeley, 73-, Am Inst Indian Studies travel grant, 75; lectr Southeast Asia, Univ San Francisco, 75-76; Fulbright res fel, Inst Southeast Asian Studies, Singapore, 78-79; dir & ed newslett, Asian Folklore Studies Group; nat dir, Independent Scholars Asia, 81- **MEMBERSHIPS** Asn for Asian Studies; Asian Folklore Studies Group; Independent Scholars Asia; Int Asn Study Asian Med. **RESEARCH** Historical and functional analysis of religious practices in South and Southeast Asia; psychological anthropology; translation of foreign texts. **SELECTED PUBLICATIONS** Auth, The Rock Art of Utah, Am Indian Culture Res J, Vol 0019, 95. **CONTACT ADDRESS** Ctr for South & Southeast Asia Studies, Univ of California, Berkeley, 260 Stephens Hall, Berkeley, CA 94720.

HELLAND, JANICE
PERSONAL Born 04/28/1943, Lethbridge, AB, Canada, 2 children **DISCIPLINE** WOMEN'S STUDIES, ART HISTORY **EDUCATION** Univ Lethbridge, BA, 73; Univ Vict, MA, 84; PhD, 91. **CAREER** Asst prof, Memorial Univ, 88-91; asst prof, Concordia Univ, 91-. **HONORS AND AWARDS** Queen's Univ Nat Schl, 99-04; Concordia Res Fel, 99; Univ Edin, Res Fel, 95; **MEMBERSHIPS** UAAC; AAH. **RESEARCH** 19th century women artists (British and Irish); textile arts; 19th-century home arts and industries (Britain and Ireland); Arts & Crafts Movement. **SELECTED PUBLICATIONS** Auth, Professional Women Painters in Nineteenth-Century Scotland: Commitment, Friendship, Pleasure (London: Ashgate/Scolar, 00): 212; auth, The Studios of Frances and Margaret Macdonald (Manchester Univ Press, 96): 207; auth, Collaborative Work among The Four," in Wendy Kaplan, ed. Charles Rennie Mackintosh (London: John Murray and New York: Abbeville, 96): 89-112; auth, "Culture, Politics, Identity in the Paintings of Frida Kahlo," in The Expanding Discourse: Feminism and Art History, eds. Norma Broude and Mary Garrard (NY: Harper Collins, 92): 397-407; auth, "Gender and Opposition in Frances Macdonald's Art," in Glasgow Girls: Women in Art and Design, 1880-1920, ed. Jude Burkhauser (Edinburgh: Canongate, 90): 128-131 and 250-251; auth, "A Sense of Extravagance: Margaret Macdonald's Gesso Panels, 1900-1903," Vis Cult Brit 2 (01): 1-15; auth, "'Quaint and curious': Scottish Textiles at Turin, 1902," J Scot Soc Art Hist 5 (00): 51-8; auth, "Artistic Advocate: Mary Rose Hill Burton and the Falls of Foyers" in Scottish Economic and Social History, vol 17, Part 2 (97): 127-147; auth, "Locality and Pleasure in Landscape: A Study of Three Nineteenth-Century Scottish Watercolourists," in Rural History: Economy, Society, Culture, vol 8 (97): 149-164; auth, "The Critics and the Arts and Crafts: The Instance of Margaret Macdonald and Charles Rennie Mackintosh," Art Hist 17 (94): 205-223. **CONTACT ADDRESS** Inst Women's Studies, Queen's Univ at Kingston, 99 University Ave, Kingston, ON, Canada K7L 3N6. **EMAIL** hellandj@post.queensu.ca

HELLE, ANITA
DISCIPLINE ENGLISH EDUCATION **EDUCATION** Univ Puget Sound, BA, 70, MA, 72; Univ Ore, PhD, 86. **CAREER** Engl, Oregon St Univ. **SELECTED PUBLICATIONS** Auth, Reading Women's Autobiographies and Reconstructing Knowledge, Narrative and Dialogue in Education, Tchrs Col Press, 91; Reading the Rhetoric of Curriculum Transformation, NWSA Jour, 94; William Stafford: On the Poet, His vocation, and Cultural Literacy, NCTE, 94. **CONTACT ADDRESS** Oregon State Univ, Corvallis, OR 97331-4501. **EMAIL** ahelle@orst.edu

HELLER, JANET
PERSONAL Born 07/08/1949, Milwaukee, WI, m, 1982 **DISCIPLINE** ENGLISH, LITERATURE, LINGUISTICS, CREATIVE WRITING, WOMEN'S STUDIES **EDUCATION** Oberlin Col, 67-70; Univ Wis at Madison, BA, 71; MA, 73; Univ Chicago, PhD, 87. **CAREER** Ed, Primavera, 73-92; coord of the Writing Prog, Univ of Chicago, 76-81; instr, Northern Ill Univ, 82-88; asst prof, Nazareth Col, 89-90; asst prof, Grand Valley State Univ, 90-97; asst prof, Albion Col, 98; asst prof, Western Mich Univ, 99-. **HONORS AND AWARDS** Winner, Friends of Poetry Contest, Kalamazoo, 89; listed in Directory of Am Poets & Fiction Writers, 79-. **MEMBERSHIPS** MLA, Mich Col English Asn, Soc for the Study of Midwestern Lit. **RESEARCH** Nineteenth-Century British Literature, Contemporary American Poetry, Prose Non-fiction, the Drama, Linguistics Applied to Literature, Women's Studies (Women Writers, Literature & Social Sciences, American Literature Since 1800). **SELECTED PUBLICATIONS** Auth, Coleridge, Lamb, Hazlitt, and the Reader of Drama, 90; articles have appeared in Poetics, Concerning Poetry, Lan and Style, Theatre J, Shakespeare Bulletin, The Eighteenth Century, PBSA, Libr Quart, Twentieth Century Lit, and others; poetry has appeared in Anima, Cottonwood, Organic Gardening, Ky Poetry Rev, Earth's Daughters, Lilith, Modern Maturity, and others. **CONTACT ADDRESS** Dept English, Western Michigan Univ, 1201 Oliver St, Kalamazoo, MI 49008-3804. **EMAIL** janet.heller@wmich.edu

HELMINIAK, DANIEL A.
PERSONAL Born Pittsburgh, PA **DISCIPLINE** EDUCATIONAL PSYCHOLOGY, SYSTEMIC THEOLOGY **EDUCATION** Boston Coll Andover Newton Theol Sch, PhD, 79; Univ Tex, Austin, PhD, 84. **CAREER** Asst prof, Oblate Sch Theol, 81-85; pastoral couns, 89-95; asst prof, State Univ W Ga, 95-97; psychotherapist, Pittsburgh Pastoral Inst, 97-98; coord educ, Consumer Credit & Counseling Svcs, 98-99; asst prof, State Univ West Georgia, 00-. **HONORS AND AWARDS** Catholic Journalist Book Awds hon mention, 87. **MEMBERSHIPS** Am Acad Rels; Am Asn Pastoral Counrs; Am Psychol Asn Cath Theol Soc Am; Soc Sci Stud Rel; Soc Sci Stud Sexuality. **RESEARCH** Midlife transition; relationship of psychol and theol; spirituality; sexual integration. **SELECTED PUBLICATIONS** Auth, Spiritual Development: An Interdisciplinary Study, Loyola Univ Press, 87; auth, What the Bible Really Says About Homosexuality, Alamo Square Press, 94; auth, The Same Jesus: A Contemporary Christology, Loyola Univ Press, 96; auth, The Human Cove of Spirituality: Mind as Psyche and Spirit, State Univ NY Press, 96; auth, Religion and the Human Sciences: An Approach via Spirituality, State Univ NY; auth, What the Bible Really Says About Homosexuality, revised edition, Alamo Square Pr, 00. **CONTACT ADDRESS** Psychology Dept, State Univ of West Georgia, Carrollton, GA 30118. **EMAIL** dhelmini@westga.edu

HELWEG, ARTHUR W.
PERSONAL Born 06/01/1940, Kalamazoo, MI, m, 1999, 2 children **DISCIPLINE** ANTHROPOLOGY **EDUCATION** Miami Univ (Ohio), BS, 62; Mich State Univ, MA, 70; PhD, 77. **HONORS AND AWARDS** Fulbright Res Grant, India, England, Australia, 79, 80; Fulbright Teaching Grant, Romania, 91-92; Smithsonian Institution Grant, India, 81-82, Theodore Saloutos Awd, Immigration Hist Soc, 90. **MEMBERSHIPS** Am Anthropol Asn, Asn for Asian Studies. **RESEARCH** Immigration, South Asia, East Europe; Economic development. **SELECTED PUBLICATIONS** Auth, Struggling with the Communist Legacy, Boulder, 98; ed, Punjab in Perspective: Proceedings of the Research Committee on Punjab Conference, 1987, Mich State Univ, 91; auth, An Immigrant Success Story: East Indians in America, Univ Penn Press, 90; auth, Facing East/Facing West: North America and the Asia/Pacific Region of the 1990s, Western Mich Press, 90; auth, Sikhs in England, 2nd ed, Oxford Univ Press, 86; auth, Social Soundness Assessment of the Lakhra Coal Mine and Power Generation Project, US Agency for Intl Development, 85; auth, Sikhs in England: The Development of a Migrant community, Oxford Univ Press, 79; auth, "Scholarship vs. Religion: The Sikh Case at Home and Abroad," Journal of Sikh Studies, (98): 1-15; auth, "Revitalization in a Sikh Community," The Guru Gobind Singh Journal of Religious studies, (94): 3-4, 10-25. **CONTACT ADDRESS** Dept Anthropol, Western Michigan Univ, 1201 Oliver St, Kalamazoo, MI 49008. **EMAIL** helweg@wmich.edu

HELWEG-LARSEN, MARIE
PERSONAL Born 04/01/1963, Copenhagen, Denmark, s, 1 child **DISCIPLINE** PSYCHOLOGY **EDUCATION** Calif State Univ, Northridge, BA, 89; Univ Calif, Los Angeles, MA, 90, PhD, 94. **CAREER** Vis asst prof, Univ of Fla, 96-98; vis scholar, Nat Inst of Public Health, Denmark, summers 97, 98, 99; asst prof, Dept of Psychol, Transylvania Univ, 98-. **HONORS AND AWARDS** Ad hoc reviewer for: Psi Chi J of Undergrad Res, Personality and Soc Psychol Bull, Health Psychol, J of Applied Psychol, J of Soc and Clinical Psychol, Environment and Behavior, Basic and Applied Soc Psychol, J of Personality and Soc Psychol, J of Applied Psychol, and Conf for the Soc of Southeastern Soc Psychols. **MEMBERSHIPS** Am Psychol Asn, Soc for Personality and Social Psychol, Soc of Southeastern Soc Psychols, Soc for the Psychol Study of Soc Issues. **SELECTED PUBLICATIONS** Coauth, "Prevalence estimates and adolescent risk behavior: Cross-cultural differences in social influence," J of Applied Psychol, 80 (95): 107-121; coauth with B. E. Collins, "A social-psychological perspective on the role of knowledge about AIDS in AIDS prevention," Current Direction in Psychol Sci, 6 (97): 23-26, reprinted in Annual Editions: Social Psychology 1999/2000, Dushkin/McGraw-Hill, Guilford, Ct; coauth, "To picture or not to picture: Levels of erotophobia and breast self-examination brochure techniques," J of Applied Soc Psychol, 27 (97): 2200-2212; auth, "Students do not overestimate their life expectancy: An alternative demonstration of unique invulnerability," Teaching of Psychol, 26 (99): 215-217; auth, "(The Lack of) optimistic biases in response to the Northridge earthquake: The role of personal experience," Basic and Applied Soc Psychol, 21 (99): 119-129; coauth with M. Kjoller, "Suicidal ideation and suicide attempts among adult Danes," Scandinavian J of Public Health (in Press); coauth with C. Howell, "Effects of erotophobia on the persuasiveness of condom advertisements containing strong or weak arguments," Basic and Applied Soc Psychol (in press); auth, J. A. Shepperd, "The optimistic bias: Moderators and measurement concerns," Personality and Soc Psychol Rev (in press). **CONTACT ADDRESS** Dept Psychol, Transylvania Univ, 300 N Broadway, Lexington, KY 40508-1797. **EMAIL** mhelweglarsen@transy.edu

HENDERSON, GEORGE
PERSONAL Born 06/18/1932, Hurtsboro, AL, m **DISCIPLINE** EDUCATION **EDUCATION** Wayne State U, BA 1957, MA 1959, PhD 1965. **CAREER** Church Youth Svc, soc caseworker, 57-59; Detroit Housing Commn, soc economist, 60-61; Detroit Urban League, com serv dir, 61-63; Detroit Mayors Youth Commn, pgm dir, 63-64; Detroit Pub Sch, asst supt, 65-67; Univ of OK, prof of human relations, currently. **HONORS AND AWARDS** Citation for Achievements in Human Relations, Oklahoma State Senate, 1978; Distinguished Community Serv Awd, Urban League of Oklahoma City, 1981; Citation for Affirmative Action Activities in Higher Educ, Oklahoma House of Representatives, 1984; David Ross Boyd Distinguished Prof, Univ of Oklahoma, 1985; Civilian Commendation, Tinker AFB, Oklahoma, 1986; Outstanding Faculty Awd, Univ of Oklahoma Black People's Union, 1987; Outstanding Contributions, Osan Air Base, Korea, 1987; Trail Blazer Awd, Oklahoma Alliance for Affirmative Action, 1988; Outstanding Teacher, Univ of Oklahoma Black Alumni Assn, 1988; Human Rights Awd, Oklahoma Human Rights Commission, 1989; Oklahoma Black Public Administrators Excellence Awd, 1990; Martin Luther King Jr Awd, Univ of Oklahoma College of Health Black Student Assn, 1990; Regent's Distinguished Professor, University of Oklahoma, 1989; Distinguished Service Awd, University of Oklahoma, 1992; American Association for Higher Education, Black Caucus Awd for Educational Service, 1992; Cultural Diversity in the Workplace, 1994; Social Work Interventions, 1994; Migrant, Immigrants & Slaves, 1995; Human Relations Issues in Management, 1996. **MEMBERSHIPS** Disting visiting prof USAF Acad 1980-81; consult US Dept of Def, US Dept of Justice, US Commn on Civil Rights, Social Sec Admin, Am Red Cross; mem Kappa Alpha Psi Frat; mem Am Sociological Assn; mem Assn of Black Sociologist; mem Assn for Supr & Curriculum Devel. **SELECTED PUBLICATIONS** "Understanding Indigenous and Foreign Cultures", 1989; "Values in Health Care,", 1991; "Police Human Rel" 1981; "Transcultural Hlth Care" 1981; "Physician-Patient Communication" 1981; "The State of Black OK" 1983; "The Human Rights of Profsnl Helpers" 1983; "Psychosocial Aspects of Disability" 1984; "Mending Broken Children" 1984; "College Survival for Student Athletes," 1985; "Intl Business & Cultures" 1987; "Our Souls to Keep," 1998; **CONTACT ADDRESS** Col of Liberal Studies, Univ of Oklahoma, 1700 Asp Ave, Ste 226, Norman, OK 73072.

HENDRICK, IRVING GUILFORD
PERSONAL Born 08/30/1936, Los Angeles, CA, m, 1996, 3 children **DISCIPLINE** HISTORY OF EDUCATION **EDUCATION** Whittier Col, AB, 58, MA, 60; Univ Calif, Los Angeles, EdD, 64. **CAREER** Teacher, jr high sch, Calif, 59-62; asst prof educ, Flint Col, Univ Mich, 64-65; from asst prof to assoc prof, 65-74, prof educ, 74-, assoc dean, sch educ, 75-, Univ Calif, Riverside; Ex officio mem, Calif Comn Teacher Prep & Licensing, 77-. **MEMBERSHIPS** Hist Educ Soc; Am Educ Res Assn; Nat Soc for Study Educ. **RESEARCH** History of education in the United States; history of minority group education in the United States; history of teacher education and certification requirements. **SELECTED PUBLICATIONS** Auth, The Development of a School Integration Plan in Riverside, California, Riverside Sch Study, 68; auth, The Education of Non-Whites in Clifornia, 1849-1970, R & E Res Assocs, 75; art, Federal Policy Affecting the Education of Indians in California, Hist Educ Quart, summer 76; auth, California Education, Boyd & Fraser, 80. **CONTACT ADDRESS** Sch of Educ, Univ of California, Riverside, 900 University Ave, Riverside, CA 92521-0001. **EMAIL** irving.hendrick@ucr.edu

HENLY, JULIA
PERSONAL Born 07/06/1965, St Paul, MN, m, 1993, 1 child **DISCIPLINE** SOCIAL SERVICE, SOCIAL PSYCHOLOGY, SOCIAL WELFARE **EDUCATION** Univ Wis, BA, 88; Univ Mich, MSW, 91; PhD, 94. **CAREER** Asst prof, Univ Calif, Los Angeles, 95-97; asst prof, Univ Chicago, 97-. **MEMBERSHIPS** SSWR; SPSSI; APPAM. **SELECTED PUBLICATIONS** Auth, "The significance of social context: The case of adolescent parenting in the African American community," J Black Psych 19 (93): 461-477; auth, "Comparative research on adolescent childbearing: Understanding race differences," African Am Res Persp 2 (95): 70-81; coauth, "Creating social reality: Informational social influence and the content of stereotypic beliefs," Personality Soc Psych Bul 22 (96): 598-610; coauth, Confronting welfare stereotypes: Characteristics of General Assistance Recipients and Post-Assistance Employment," Soc Work Res (96): 217-227; coauth, "The Future of child welfare, in Social Work in the 21st Century," eds. M Reisch, E Gambrill (Pine Forge Press, 97); auth, "The complexity of support: The impact of family structure and provisional support on African-American and white adolescent mothers," Am J Comm Psych 25 (97): 629-655; auth, "Barriers to Finding and Maintaining Jobs: The Perspectives of Workers and Employers in the Low-Wage Labor Market," in Hard Labor: Women and Work in the Post-welfare Era, eds. Joel F Handler, Lucie White (NY: ME Shappe, Inc, 99); auth, "Mismatch in the Low-Wage Labor Market: Job Search Perspective," in The Low-Wage Labor Market: Challenges and Opportunities for Economic Self-Sufficiency (U.S. Dept Health Human Ser, Wash, DC: U.S. Govt Printing Off, forthcoming). **CONTACT ADDRESS** School of Social Service, Univ of Chicago, 969 E 60th St, Chicago, IL 60637.

HENNING, NELSON
PERSONAL Born 04/21/1949, Evansville, IN, m, 1971, 3 children **DISCIPLINE** SOCIAL WORK **EDUCATION** Southern Ill Univ, BSW, 76; Univ Ill, MSW, 77; Univ Pittsburgh, PhD, 86. **CAREER** Mental health Adminr, Shapiro Developmental Center, Kankakee, Ill, 77-78; USAF military soc worker, 78-95; assoc prof, Cedarville Univ, 95-. **HONORS AND AWARDS** NIMH fel, 76-77; mem, Acad of Certified Soc Workers; licensed Independent Soc Worker; mem, Chi Gamma Iota; presented numerous workshops in the areas of family dynamics and alcoholism. **MEMBERSHIPS** Nat Asn Soc Workers, North Am Asn for Christians in Soc Work, Am Asn of Christian Couns, Ohio Chapter of Soc Work Eds. **RESEARCH** Alcoholism, aspects of spirituality. **SELECTED PUBLICATIONS** Auth, "The U.S. Air Force's Rehabilitation Program, in Proceedings of the One Hundred and Seventeenth Annual Congress of Correction of the American Correctional Association, College Park, MD: Am Correctional Asn; auth, "Ebenezar Rockwood Hoar," in Encyclopedia of the Supreme Court, Salem Press: Pasadena, CA (2000). **CONTACT ADDRESS** Dept Hist

& Soc Sci, Cedarville Col, PO Box 601, Cedarville, OH 45314. **EMAIL** henningn@cedarville.edu

HENRY, CAROLYN S.
PERSONAL Born 01/31/1955, Newton, KS **DISCIPLINE** COUNSELING **EDUCATION** Okla Christian Col, BSE, 76; Okla State Univ, 77; Univ Tenn, MS, 81; PhD, 84. **CAREER** Director of Career Planning, Pepperdine Univ, 77-80; Asst Prof, S Dak State Univ, 85-88; Asst Prof to Prof and Interim Head, 88-. **HONORS AND AWARDS** Outstanding Fac Mentor, Okla state Univ, 96; Lela O'Toole Res Awd, Okla Asn of family and consumer Sci, 95; Okla A & M Regents' distinguished Teaching Awd, Okla State Univ, 93; New Professional of the Year Awd, Okla Coun of Family Relations, 90. **MEMBERSHIPS** Nat Coun on Family Relations, Am Asn of Marriage and Family Therapy, Soc, for Res on Adolescence **RESEARCH** Adolescents and families; Family stress and coping. **SELECTED PUBLICATIONS** Auth, Adolescent perceptions of interparental conflict, stressors, and coping as predictors of adolescent family life satisfaction," Sociological Inquiry, (99): 599-620; auth, "Family stressor events, family coping strategies, and adolescent adaptation in farm and ranch families," Adolescence, (99): 147-168; auth, "Adolescent social competence and parental satisfaction," Journal of Adolescent Research, (97): 389-409; auth, "Predictors of life satisfaction among low-income rural youth," Journal of Adolescence, (97): 443-450; auth, "The double ADCX model and children's adaptation to parental divorce," Journal of Divorce and Remarriage, (97): 17-37; auth, "Adolescents' perceptions of family system characteristics, parent-adolescent dyadic behaviors, adolescent qualities, and adolescent empathy," Family Relations, (96): 283-292; auth, "Family characteristics as predictors of adolescent substance use," Adolescence, (96): 59-77; auth, "Family resources and adolescent family life satisfaction in remarried family households," Journal of Family Issues, (95): 765-786; auth, "Adolescent social competence, parental qualities, and parental satisfaction," American Journal of Orthopsychiatry, (95): 49-262. **CONTACT ADDRESS** Dept child & Family Studies, Oklahoma State Univ, Stillwater, Stillwater, OK 74078-0001.

HENRY, MILDRED M. DALTON
PERSONAL Born Tamo, AR **DISCIPLINE** EDUCATION **EDUCATION** AM&N College, 71; Southern IL Univ, 76; Southern IL Univ Carbondale, PhD, 83. **CAREER** AM&N Coll, sec bus office 1949-51; St Paul Public Library, library asst 1956-58; AM&N Coll, lib asst/secty 1968-71; Pine Bluff School Dist, music teacher 1971-75; Southern IL Univ Edwardsville, library asst 1975; Watson Chapel School Dist, counselor 1976-77; Univ of AR at Pine Bluff, counselor 1978-80; Southern IL Univ at Carbondale, grad asst 1981; Carbondale Elem Sch Dist, teacher 1981-83; CA State Univ San Bernardino, asst prof 1983-. **HONORS AND AWARDS** Leadership Awds Atlanta Univ & UCLA 1978 & 1979; Citizen of Day Radio Station KOTN Pine Bluff 1980; Dean's Fellowship Southern IL Univ Carbondale 1980-81; Outstanding Scholastic Achievement Black Affairs Council SIUC 1981. **MEMBERSHIPS** Adv bd Creative Educators Inc Riverside; city commissioner Fontanta CA; exec bd Rialto/Fontana NAACP; Provisional Educ Services Inc; Amer Assn of Univ Profs; Natl Educ Assn; CA Faculty Assn; CA Teachers Assn; CA Assn of Counseling Develop; Assn of Teacher Educators; CA Black Faculty and Staff Assn; CA State Employees Assn, Inland Empire Peace Officers Assn; NAACP; Natl Council of Negro Women; steering comm San Bernardino Area Black Chamber of Commerce; San Bernardino Private Industry Council. **SELECTED PUBLICATIONS** Auth, "Setting Up a Responsive Guidance Program in a Middle School" The Guidance Clinic 1979. **CONTACT ADDRESS** California State Univ, San Bernardino, College of Education, 5500 University Pkwy, San Bernardino, CA 92407. **EMAIL** henry@csusb.edu

HENRY, SAMUEL DUDLEY
PERSONAL Born 10/09/1947, Washington, DC, m, 1988 **DISCIPLINE** EDUCATION **EDUCATION** DC Teachers Coll, BS 1969; Columbia Univ, MA 1974, EdD 1978. **CAREER** Binghamton, eng/soc studies teacher 1971-73; HMLI Columbia Univ Teachers Coll, rsch assoc 1975-77; Sch of Ed Univ MA Amherst, asst prof 1977-78; Race Desegregation Ctr for NY, NJ, VI & PR, dir 1978-81; San Jose State Univ, dir of Equal Opportunity & Affirmative Action; CSU Northridge, Northridge CA, School of Education, assoc dean (acting) 1988-; San Jose State Univ, San Jose CA, School of Social Sciences, assoc dean 1987-88, assistant vice pres for Student Affairs, 89-92; Portland State University, executive director, Portland Educational Network, 92-94; Urban Fellow and Associate Professor of Education, beginning 1994-; Depaun Univ, chair of ed dept, 98-99; chair of curriculum and instruction, GSE, PSU. **HONORS AND AWARDS** Outstanding Serv Awd Disabled Students SJSU 1982-83; Commendation Curr Study Comm East Side Union HS Dist 1984; AA in Higher Educ/2nd Annual Conf on Desegregation in Postsecondary 1984. **MEMBERSHIPS** Exec bd Greenfield Secondary Sch Comm 1977-79; sponsor Harlem Ebonetts Girls Track Team 1980-81; exec bd Santa Clara Valley Urban League 1982-83; exec bd CAAAO,CA Assoc of Affirmative Action Off 1983-84; mem Prog Comm No CA Fair Employ Roundtable 1983-85; mem ASCD Assoc of Supr of Curr Ser 1984-85; mem bd of dirs Campus Christian Ministry 1984-85; San Jose Roundtable, chair-drug prevention task force. **RESEARCH** Culture contact in education. **CONTACT ADDRESS** Chair of Curriculum & Instruction, Associate Professor of Education, PO Box 751, Portland, OR 97207-0751. **EMAIL** henrys@pdx.edu

HENSLEY, ROBERT B.
PERSONAL Born 08/14/1965, Chicago Heights, IL, s **DISCIPLINE** PSYCHOLOGY **EDUCATION** Kirkwood Community Col, AA, 86; Univ Northern Iowa, BA, 90; MA, 92. **CAREER** Instr, Kirkwood Community Col, 92-; Instr, Mount Meroy Col, 95-; **HONORS AND AWARDS** Psi Chi, 87; Kappa Delta Pi, 87; Phi Alpha Theta, 89; Outstanding Young Men in Am, 98; Who's Who in Am, 00. **MEMBERSHIPS** Midwestern Psychol Asn, Am Psychol Asn. **RESEARCH** Relationship termination adjustment, childhood attachment, self-efficiency in marriage. **SELECTED PUBLICATIONS** Auth, "Relationship Termination and the FAOS: A Comparative Study," J of Divorce and Remarriage 25 (96): 139-150. **CONTACT ADDRESS** Dept Soc Sci, Kirkwood Comm Col, PO Box 2068, Cedar Rapids, IA 52406.

HERMAN, RANDOLPH W.
PERSONAL Born 10/15/1946, Washington, DC, m, 1969, 2 children **DISCIPLINE** SOCIOLOGY **EDUCATION** Vanderbilt Univ, BA, 68; Univ Md, MSW, 70; Massey Univ NZ, MPhil, 84; Univ St Thomas, EdD, 99. **CAREER** Assoc Prof, Massey Univ NZ, 79-90; Director, Personal Performance Inc, 90-92; Director, Minn Aids Project, 92-94; Asst Prof, Univ St Thomas, 94-. **MEMBERSHIPS** NASW; CSWE. **RESEARCH** Gerontology-Advanced Planning; HIV/AIDS; Case Managers; Men-Anger and Violence. **CONTACT ADDRESS** Dept Sociol, Univ of St. Thomas, Minnesota, 2115 Summit Ave, Saint Paul, MN 55105. **EMAIL** wrherman@stthomas.edu

HERNANDEZ, ARTHUR E.
PERSONAL Born 08/04/1954, San Antonio, TX **DISCIPLINE** PSYCHOLOGY, PHILOSPHY **EDUCATION** St. Mary's Univ, BA, 75; MA, 78; Univ Tex San Antonio, MA, 82; Tex A&M Univ Col Station Tex, PhD, 87. **CAREER** Instruct Specialist, Chemn of English Dept, Edgewood Independent Sch Dist San Antonio Tex, 76-79; Consult, Alamo Are Teacher's Center, San Antonio Tex, 79; Teacher, San Antonio Independent Sch Dist, 79-80; Educ Specialist, Acad of Health Sci, Ft. Sam Houston Tex, 80-82; Teaching Asst, Tex A&M Univ, Col Station Tex, 83; Assoc Sch Psychologist, San Antonio Independent Sch Dist, 84-85; Project Dir, Tex A&M Univ, Col Station Tex, 85-88; Dir of Enrichment Serv, Hisp Asn of Col and Univ, 88-89; Lectr, Our Lady of the Lake Univ, San Antonio Tex, 89; Instr, Incarnate Word Col, San Antonio Tex, 89; Assoc Prof, Univ of Tex San Antonio, 89-; Dir Interdisciplinary Studies Prog, Univ of Tex at San Antonio, 98-. **HONORS AND AWARDS** IWW, Kellags Found Fel, 99-01. **MEMBERSHIPS** Am Educ Res Asn, Nat Asn of Sch Psychologists. **RESEARCH** Measurement, evaluation, multiculturalism. **SELECTED PUBLICATIONS** Auth, "Do Role Models Influence Self Efficacy and Aspiration in Mexican American At-Risk Females," Hisp J of Behav Sci 17-2 (95); coauth, "The Role of Student, Instructor and Administrator Perceptions of Effective Teaching," J of Excellence in Col Teaching 6-3 (96); auth, "Attention Deficit Disorder/Hyperactivity Disorder: A Primer," Prof Med Asst (Nov/Dec 96); coauth, We the People, Houghton Mifflin Elem Soc Studies Ser, 97; auth, "Percentiles: Debunking The Myths," Prof Med Asst (Mar/Apr 97); coauth, "A Pilot Study of the Bienstar Health Program: A Diabetes Risk Factor Prevention," J of Sch Health 68-2 (98): 62-67; auth, "Observational Learning: Modeling and Patient Education," Prof Med Asst (Jan/Feb 98); coauth, "Bienstar: A Diabetes Risk Factor Modification Program," Diabetes 48, suppl 1 (99): A305; auth, Success in the Classroom: Maximizing the Opportunity of American Diversity, Houghton Mifflin Publ Co (Boston), in press; ed, Appleseeds, Cobblestone Publ Co (Peterborough, NH), in press. **CONTACT ADDRESS** Dept Educ, Univ of Texas, San Antonio, 6900 N Loop 1604 W, San Antonio, TX 78249. **EMAIL** aehernandez@utsa.edu

HERNANDEZ, JUAN E.
PERSONAL Born 03/08/1938, Mayaguez, PR, m, 3 children **DISCIPLINE** SOCIOLOGY **EDUCATION** Univ Puerto Rico, BA, 62, MA, 70; NY Univ, PhD, 82. **CAREER** Prof, Inter Am Univ Puerto Rico, 83-. **HONORS AND AWARDS** New Encycl of Puerto Rico, 93; Who's Who Among Am Teachers, 94. **MEMBERSHIPS** LASA; Int Sociol Assoc; Sociol of Migration Res Comm; Academia Puertorriquena de la Historia. **SELECTED PUBLICATIONS** Auth, "Migracion de retorno o circulacion de obreros boricuas?", Revista de Ciencias Sociales, Rio Piedras, Puerto Rico, 85; auth, "Reintegration of Circulating Familes in Southwestern Puerto Rico", Int Migration Rev XXIV.2 (86); auth, "Migratory Trends in Puerto Rico: 1950 to the Present", Cambridge Surv of World Migration, Cambridge Univ Pr, 95. **CONTACT ADDRESS** Dept Soc Sci, Inter American Univ of Puerto Rico, San German, PO Box 1544, San German, PR 00683.

HERRICK, SUSAN
PERSONAL Born 11/29/1947, New York, NY **DISCIPLINE** SOCIOLOGY **EDUCATION** Queens Col, BA; Hunter Col, MA; Univ NH, MA; PhD. **CAREER** Assoc prof, West Liberty State Col, 95-. **HONORS AND AWARDS** Nat Inst of Mental Health Fel, Univ NH. **MEMBERSHIPS** WV Sociol Asn. **RESEARCH** Family and Work Role Conflicts, Effects of Early Day Care of Children on Family roles and child development. **SELECTED PUBLICATIONS** Auth, Directory of Regional Educational Resource Organizations in the Mid-Atlantic Region, Philadelphia, 92; auth, Syllabus and Successful Introductory Sociology Assignments, Washington, 96; auth, "Initiatives for Families: Research, Policy, Practice, and Education," National Council on Family Relations, 95. **CONTACT ADDRESS** Dept Soc & Beh Sci, West Liberty State Col, PO Box 457, West Liberty, WV 26074. **EMAIL** herricks@wlsc.wvnet.edu

HERSEN, MICHEL
PERSONAL Born 01/14/1940, Brussels, Belgium **DISCIPLINE** PSYCHOLOGY **EDUCATION** Queen's Col, BA, 61; Hofstra Univ, MA, 63; State Univ NYork, PhD, 66; VA Hosp (Yale Univ Sch Med Prof) Post-Doctoral, 65-66. **CAREER** Prof and Dean, Sch of Prof Psychol, Pacific Univ; Interim Dean of Psychol, NOVA Southeastern Univ; Dir of NOVA Community Clinic for Older Adults; ed and co-ed of seven journals; ed and co-ed of 126 books; auth and coauth of 94 book chapters; over 224 articles published. **HONORS AND AWARDS** ABPP Lifetime Achievement Awd; elected president of the Asn for the Advancement of Behavior Therapy, 76; George M. Estabrook Distinguished Service Awd, Hofstra Univ, 87. **RESEARCH** Behavior modification and geropsychology. **SELECTED PUBLICATIONS** Coauth, "An overview of managed mental health care: Past, present & future," in A. J. Kent, M. Hersen, eds, A Psychologist's guide to managed mental health care, Mahwah, NJ, Lawrence Erlbaum Assocs, Pubs (2000); coauth, "Historical perspectives," in G. Goldstein, M. Hersen, eds, Handbook of psychological assessment, 3rd ed, Oxford, England: Elsevier Sci, Ltd (2000); coauth, "Introduction," in V. B. Van Hasselt, M. Hersen, eds, Aggression and violence: An introductory text, Needham Heights, Mass: Allyn & Bacon (2000); coauth, "Historical overview," in M. Hersen, R. T. Ammerman, eds, Advanced abnormal child psychology, 2nd ed, Mahwah, NJ: Erlbaum & Assocs, Inc (2000); co-ed, Handbook of gender, culture, and health, Mahwah, NJ: Lawrence Erlbaum & Assocs, Inc (in press); co-ed, Issues in the psychology of women, NY: Kluwer Academic/Plenum Press (in press); co-ed, Effective brief therapies, NY: Academic Press (in press). **CONTACT ADDRESS** Chief Academic Dean, Pacific Univ, 2004 Pacific Ave, Forest Grove, OR 97116. **EMAIL** hersenm@pacificu.edu

HERSHENSON, DAVID B.
PERSONAL Born 08/30/1933, Boston, MA, m, 1957, 2 children **DISCIPLINE** PSYCHOLOGY **EDUCATION** Harvard Univ, AB, 55; Boston Univ, AM, 60; PhD, 64. **CAREER** Asst prof, prof, Ill Inst Tech, 65-77; prof, dean, Boston Univ, 77-82; prof, Univ Maryland, 82-. **HONORS AND AWARDS** AMHCA Res of Year Awd; ARCA, Dist Prof Awd; APA Fel. **MEMBERSHIPS** ACA; APA. **RESEARCH** Work adjustment; rehabilitation counseling; theory development. **SELECTED PUBLICATIONS** Coauth, Community counseling: Contemporary Theory and Practice, Allyn and Bacon (Needham Hts, MA), 96; coauth, Mental health counseling: Theory and practice, Pergamon (Elmsford, NY), 87; coauth, "Trends affecting rehabilitation counselor education," Rehab Edu 12 (98): 277-238; auth, "Systemic, ecological model for rehabilitation counseling," Rehab Coun Bul 42 (98): 40-50; auth, "Human growth and development," in. Preparation Guide for the national counselor examination, ed LC Loesch (Greensboro, NC: Cen Creden Edu, 98); coauth, "Vocational and' career development in rehabilitation," Rehab Edu 13 (99): 105-112; coauth, "Vocational rehabilitation and community reintegration of the wounded combatant," in Textbook of military medicine: Part IV. Surgical combat casualty care: Rehabilitation of the injured combatant, eds. TR Dillingham, PV Belandres (Wash, DC: Off Surg Gen, US Army, 99); auth, "Toward a cultural anthropology of disability and rehabilitation." Rehab Coun Bul (in press); coauth, "Causal attributions of disabilities and the choice of rehabilitation approaches," Rehab Coun Bul 43 (00): 106-112. **CONTACT ADDRESS** Dept Counseling, Personnel Serv, Univ of Maryland, Col Park, 3214 C Benjamin Bldg, College Park, MD 20742-1100. **EMAIL** dh21@umail.umd.edu

HERSHENSON, MAURICE
PERSONAL Born 05/27/1933, Brooklyn, NY, m, 1955, 2 children **DISCIPLINE** PSYCHOLOGY **EDUCATION** Brooklyn Col, BA, 55; MA, 60; Yale Univ, PhD, 64. **CAREER** Asst prof to assoc prof, Univ Wis, 63-68; assoc prof to prof, Brandeis Univ, 68-. **RESEARCH** Visual space perception. **SELECTED PUBLICATIONS** Auth, Visual Space Perception: A Primer, MIT Press, 98; auth The Moon Illusion, Erlbaum, 89. **CONTACT ADDRESS** Dept Psychology, Brandeis Univ, 415 South St, Waltham, MA 02453. **EMAIL** hershenson@brandeis.edu

HERSHEY, DANIEL
PERSONAL Born 02/12/1931, New York, NY, m, 1965, 2 children **DISCIPLINE** GERONTOLOGY **EDUCATION** Cooper Union, BS, 53; Univ Tenn, PhD, 61. **CAREER** PROF, UNIV CINCINNATI, 62-. **HONORS AND AWARDS** Fulbright fel, 75 & 91; Tau Beta Pi teaching award, 70 & 72, 1st

place, Cincinnati Eds Assn fiction writing, 75; Clinical Research Awd, Amer Soc **MEMBERSHIPS** Int Soc for Systems Sciences; Amer Aging Assn; Amer Inst Chemical Engineers; Am Soc Bariatric Physicians. **RESEARCH** Aging, Evolving Systems, Living humans and Inanimate corporations and the universe. **SELECTED PUBLICATIONS** Ed, Chemical Engineering in Medicine and Biology, Plenum, 67; auth, In God We Trust, Vantage, 67; ed, Blood Oxygenation, Plenum, 70; auth, Everyday Science, Doubleday, 71; Transport Analysis, Plenum, 73; Lifespan and Factors Affecting It, CC Thomas, 74; A New Age-Scale for Humans, Lexington Books, 80; Must We Grow Old: From Pauling to Prigogine to Toynbee, Basal Books, 84; Diagnosing and Organizational Bureaucracy, Basal Books, 97; Entropy, Infinity, and God, Basal Books, 97. **CONTACT ADDRESS** 726 Lafayette Ave., Cincinnati, OH 45220-1053. **EMAIL** daniel@basaltech.com

HERSHEY, DOUGLAS
PERSONAL Born 06/25/1958, Berkeley, CA, m, 1990 **DISCIPLINE** PSYCHOLOGY **EDUCATION** Calif State Univ Northridge, BA, 85; Univ S Calif, MA, 87; OhD, 90. **CAREER** Lectr, Univ S Calif, 86-89; Asst Prof, George Mason Univ, 90-96; Asst Prof, Okla State Univ, 96-. **HONORS AND AWARDS** Nat Inst of Again Predoctoral Res Traineeship, Univ of S Calif, 86-90; Outstanding Fac Awd, Okla State Univ, 99. **RESEARCH** Cognitive aging psychology, Retirement planning and decision making. **SELECTED PUBLICATIONS** Coauth, "Analysis of structure and discriminative power of the Mattis Dementia Rating Scale," J of Clinical Psychology 52 (96): 395-409; coauth, "The Research Methods Script," Teaching of Psychology 23 (96): 97-99, and in Handbook for teaching statistics and research methods, 2nd ed, ed. M.E. Ware, and C.L. Brewer (Mahwah, NJ: Erlbaum Press), 193-196; coauth, "Conceptions of the psychological research process: Script variation as a function of training and experience," Current Psychology 14 (96): 293-312; auth, "Age differences in confidence ratings on a complex financial decision making task," Exp Aging Res 23(97): 257-273; coauth, "Perceptions of wisdom associated with selected occupations and personality characteristics," Current Psychology 16 (97): 115-130; coauth, "Challenges of training pre-retirees to make sound financial planning decision," Educ Gerontology 24 (98): 447-470; coauth, "The use of correspondence in the classroom," in Activities Handbook, Vol IV, ed. L.T. Benjamin et al (Wash, DC: Am Psychol Asn, 99); coauth, "Age Differences on a procedurally oriented test of practical problem solving," J of Adult Develop 6 (99): 87-104; coauth, "Cognitive aging psychology: Significant advances, challenges, and training issues," Educ Gerontology 25 (99): 349-364. **CONTACT ADDRESS** Dept Psychology, Oklahoma State Univ, Stillwater, Stilwater, OK 74078-0001. **EMAIL** hershey@okway.okstate.edu

HERZBRUN, MICHAEL B.
PERSONAL Born 01/15/1943, Cleveland, OH, m, 1973, 1 child **DISCIPLINE** PSYCHOLOGY **EDUCATION** Hiram Col, BA, 64; Oh State Univ, MA, 68; Hebrew Un Univ, MAHL, 73; Ord, 75; Univ Rochester, EdD, 91. **CAREER** Coun, St John Fisher Col, 90-; Rabbi, Temple Emanuel, 85-. **HONORS AND AWARDS** Who's Who Am Teach; Hon Doc. **MEMBERSHIPS** CCAR; RBA; ACA; ASERVIC. **RESEARCH** Religious development; professional ethics. **SELECTED PUBLICATIONS** Auth, "Circumcision: The Pain of the fathers," CCAR J 38 (91): 1-13; auth, "Pain and Circumcision," CCAR J 40 (93): 61-62; auth, "Religious consensus between adolescents and their fathers within the Jewish community," J Sci Stud Rel 43 (93): 163-168; auth, "The silent minority: Non believers in the reform Jewish community," CCAR J 45 (98): 48-56; auth, "Loss of faith: A qualitive analysis of Jewish non-believers," Coun Val 43 (99): 129-141. **CONTACT ADDRESS** Dept Psychology, St. John Fisher Col, 3690 East Ave, Rochester, NY 14618. **EMAIL** herzbrun@sjfc.edu

HESLEP, ROBERT DURHAM
PERSONAL Born 12/18/1930, Houston, TX, m, 1964, 2 children **DISCIPLINE** PHILOSOPHY OF EDUCATION **EDUCATION** Tex Christian Univ, AB, 55; Univ Chicago, AM, 57, PhD(philos educ), 63. **CAREER** Teacher, Harvard Sch Boys, Chicago, 58-63; instr philos educ, Pestalozzi-Froebel Teachers Col, Chicago, 59-61; assoc prof educ found & philos, Edinboro State Col, 63-65; assoc prof, 65-72, prof philos of educ, Univ GA, 72-, consult, Res for Better Sch, 76-77; adv, Nat Soc for Study Educ, 76-77; mem, Philos of Educ Soc Comn to Analy Am Educ, 74-75. **MEMBERSHIPS** Philos Educ Soc (pres, 76-77; Southeast Philos Educ Soc (pres, 71-72). **RESEARCH** The concept of action; philosophy of mind; political philosophy; moral education. **SELECTED PUBLICATIONS** Auth, Thomas Jefferson & Education, Random, 69; ed, Philosophy of Education, 1971, Philos Educ Soc, 71; co-ed, Social Justice and Preferential Treatment, Univ Ga, 77; auth, The Mental in Education: A Philosophical Study, Univ Ala Press, 81; auth, Education in Democracy, Iowa State Univ Press, 89; auth, Moral Education for Americans, Praeger, 95; auth, Philosophical Thinking in Educational Practice, Praeger, 97. **CONTACT ADDRESS** Col of Educ, Univ of Georgia, 308 River's Crossing, Athens, GA 30602-0001. **EMAIL** rheslep@uga.edu

HESSLER, RICHARD M.
PERSONAL Born 08/25/1941, Los Angeles, CA, m, 1963, 4 children **DISCIPLINE** SOCIOLOGY **EDUCATION** Loyola Univ Los Angeles, Calif, BA, 63; Univ Pittsburgh, PhD, 70. **CAREER** Instr to asst prof, Univ Pittsburgh, 67-69; asst prof, Tufts Univ, 69-71; assoc prof, Univ Mo, Columbia, 71-74, prof, 74-. **HONORS AND AWARDS** Pi Gamma Mu, Loyola Univ, 62; Nat Defense Educ Act Fel, Univ Pittsburgh, 64-67; Fulbright Scholar to Sweden, 77-78; Outstanding Dedication and Achievement Awd for Teaching, Student Body, Sch of Med, UMC, April 86; Res Leave, Univ of Mo, Columbia, 93, 99. **MEMBERSHIPS** Pi Gamma Mu. **RESEARCH** Gerontology, comparative health care systems. **SELECTED PUBLICATIONS** Coauth with Andrew C. Twaddle, A Sociology of Health, St Louis, Mo: C. V. Mosby Co (77, 2nd ed, 87, Macmillan & Co); coauth with James Guinn, Dan Huesgen, and Linda Wolter, "Research Entry: A 20-year Longitudinal Study of The Rural Elderly," Qualitative Sociol, 12, 3 (89): 261-77; coauth with S. H. Pazaki, Richard W. Madsen, and Robert L. Blake, "Predicting Morality Among Independently Living Rural Elderly: A 20-year Longitudinal Study," Sociol Quart, 31, 2 (90): 253-267; auth, Social Research Methods, St Paul, Mn, West Pub Co (92); coauth with Kristina Freerks, "Privacy Ethics in the Age of Disclosure: Sweden and America Compared," Am Sociol, 26, 2 (95): 1-19; coauth with Suli Jia, Richard Madsen and Hooshang Pazaki, "Gender, Social Networks and Survival Time: A 20-Year Study of the Rural Elderly," Archives of Gerontology and Geriatrics (forthcoming); auth, "The Rise and Fall of American Medicine," The Korean J of Am Hist (98): 217-235; auth, "Per Mediation: A Qualitative Study of Youthful Frames of Power and Influence," Mediation Quart (98): 187-198; auth, "Cross-cultural analysis of longevity among Swedish and American elders: the role of social networks in the Gothenburg and Missouri longitudinal studies compared," Archives of Gerontology and Geriatrics, 28 (99): 131-148. **CONTACT ADDRESS** Dept Sociol, Univ of Missouri, Columbia, 205 Sociol, Columbia, MO 65201.

HESTER, THOMAS R.
PERSONAL Born 04/28/1946, Crystal City, TX, m, 1966, 2 children **DISCIPLINE** ANTHROPOLOGY **EDUCATION** Univ Cal, PhD, 72; Univ Texas at Austin, BA, 69. **CAREER** Act Asst Prof, Univ Calif, Berkeley, 72-73; Asst Prof, Assoc, Prof, 73-87; Prof, Univ Tex, San Antonio, 78; Prof, Anthropology, Univ Tex, Austin, 87-. **HONORS AND AWARDS** Accademia Nazionale di Lincei, 98; Fel, Tex Archeol Soc. **MEMBERSHIPS** Texas Archeol Soc, Soc for American Archaeology, Plains Anthropological Conf. **RESEARCH** Archaeology: North America; Maya; ancient technologies. **SELECTED PUBLICATIONS** Auth, Ethnology of Texas Indians, 91; auth, Maya Stone Tools, 91; auth, Continuing Archaeol at Colha, Beliize, 94; auth, Field Methods in Archaeology, Mayfield, 97; auth, Stone Artifacts of Texas Indians, Gulf, 99. **CONTACT ADDRESS** Dept Anthropology, Univ of Texas, Austin, O Univ of Texas, Austin, TX 78712. **EMAIL** t.r.hester@mail.utexas.edu

HEUCHERT, J. W.
PERSONAL Born 10/12/1955, Belfast, South Africa, m, 1999, 1 child **DISCIPLINE** PSYCHOLOGY **EDUCATION** Univ Pretoria, BA, 81; BA hon, 83; Univ Witwatersand, H Ed, 82; Geo State Univ, MS, 85; Boston Univ, MA, 87; PhD, 90. **CAREER** Asst prof, Bost Univ,89-91; sr lectr, Potche Univ, 92-94; sr lectr, Univ Witwaters, 95-98; assoc prof, Alleg Col, 98-. **HONORS AND AWARDS** Fulbright Fel, 84, 90. **MEMBERSHIPS** PSSA; NWPPS. **RESEARCH** Personality; psychopathology; social identity. **SELECTED PUBLICATIONS** Rev of "Personality: Analysis and interpretation of lives," SA J Psychol 28 (98): 1; ed, "History and methods of psychology," in Psychology and the health sciences (Zoekop: Belfast, 98); auth, "The applicability of the five factor model of personality in a South African sample," in South Africa beyond transition: Psychological well-being, ed. L Schlebusch, Psycho Soc South Africa (Pretoria, 98); coauth, "Personality and self esteem of a group of students," in South Africa beyond transition: Psychological well-being, ed. L Schlebusch, Psycho Soc South Africa (Pretoria, 98); coauth, "Personality and psychological symptomatology of a group of students," in South Africa beyond transition: Psychological well-being, ed. L Schlebusch, Psycho Soc South Africa (Pretoria, 98); coauth, "Personality and conservatism," in South Africa beyond transition: Psychological well-being, ed. L Schlebusch, Psycho Soc South Africa (Pretoria, 98); coauth, "The five-factor model in South African college students," Am Behavioral Sci, in press; coauth, "The relationship between serotonin and performance on the TCI," Psychiatry Res, in press; coauth, "Community psychology as a paradigm for social change in South Africa," in Community psychology in the South: Theory, methods and practice, ed. M Seedat, forthcoming; coauth, "The relationship between personality and mood: comparison of the BDI and the TCI," Personality and Individual Differences, forthcoming. **CONTACT ADDRESS** Dept Psychology, Allegheny Col, 520 N Main St, Meadville, PA 16335. **EMAIL** jheucher@alleg.edu

HEWETT, STEPHENIE M.
PERSONAL Born 04/26/1958, Aiken, SC, m, 1979, 2 children **DISCIPLINE** EDUCATION **EDUCATION** Clemson Univ, BA, 79, Med, 85; NM State Univ, EdD, 88. **CAREER** Asst prof, Teacher Educ Div, The Citadel, 88- . **HONORS AND AWARDS** Outstanding Young Wom Am Awd; Young Centennial Res Awd; Who's Who Am Educ. **RESEARCH** Students with reading disabilities and/or brain injuries. **SELECTED PUBLICATIONS** Auth, Content area reading strategy, Sharing Edeas in MiddleSchool Reading, 2,3; 90; auth, A Literature Review of Basic Skills Programs, Educ Issues, 1, 51-58, 90; auth, The Impaoct of the Components of Writing Instruction on Student's Writing Achievement, Writing Teacher, 5, 18-20, 91; co-auth, Development of an individual study program based on learning styles, The Oklahoma Reader, 27, 10-12, 92; co-auth, School violence: Student remedies, Nat Forum Educ Admin & Supvr J, 12, 47-53, 94; co-auth, An Alternative college preparatory program for high risk students, Am Sec Educ, 23, 30-32, 94; auth Supplemental reading to enhance subject area understanding, Okla Reader, 33, 4-5, 97. **CONTACT ADDRESS** Dept Educ, The Citadel, The Military Col of So Carolina, 648 Oak Marsh Dr, Mount Pleasant, SC 29464. **EMAIL** HewettS@Citadel.edu

HEYNS, BARBARA
PERSONAL Born 07/17/1953, TX, s **DISCIPLINE** SOCIOLOGY **EDUCATION** Univ Calif Berkeley, BA, 74; Univ Chicago, MA, 75; PhD, 77. **CAREER** Prof, Harvard Univ, 77-79; prof, Univ of Calif Berkeley, 79-89; prof, NY Univ, 89-. **HONORS AND AWARDS** Fulbright Fel, 89-91; Fel, Jean Monneyy, Italy, 95-96. **RESEARCH** Eastern European Transition. ASA, SASE, SWS. **CONTACT ADDRESS** Dept Sociol, New York Univ, 269 Mercer St, New York, NY 10003. **EMAIL** barbara.heyns@nyu.edu

HICKS, RONALD E.
PERSONAL Born 08/26/1940, Kingman, IN, m, 1982, 4 children **DISCIPLINE** ANTHROPOLOGY **EDUCATION** Purdue Univ, BA, 63; Univ Penn, PhD, 75. **CAREER** Asst Prof to Prof and Dept Chair, Ball State Univ, 76-. **MEMBERSHIPS** Am Anthropol Asn, Soc for Am Archaeol, Archaeol Inst of Am, Royal soc of Antiquaries of Ireland. **RESEARCH** Cognitive and landscape archaeology; Pre-Christian Ireland. **SELECTED PUBLICATIONS** Auth, "Beyond alignments," Archaeoastronomy & Ethnoastronomy News, (93): 1, 4; ed, Native American Cultures in Indiana, Ball State Univ, 92; auth, "The Year at Drombeg," in World archaeoastronomy, Cambridge Univ Press, 89; co-auth, Site distribution and physiographic zones along the Big Blue river glacial sluiceway, Ind Acad of Sciences, (88): 75-81. **CONTACT ADDRESS** Dept Anthropol, Ball State Univ, 2000 W Univ, Muncie, IN 47306-0002. **EMAIL** rhicks@bsu.edu

HILDRETH, GLADYS JOHNSON
PERSONAL Born 10/15/1933, Columbia, MS, m **DISCIPLINE** EDUCATION **EDUCATION** So Univ Baton Rouge LA, BS 1953; Univ of Wis Madison, MS 1955; MI State Univ East Lansing, PhD 1973. **CAREER** So Univ, assoc prof, 60-68; LA State Univ School of Human Ecology, prof family studies, 74-90; Texas Woman's Univ, Denton, TX, prof, 90-. **HONORS AND AWARDS** Grad School Fellowship MI State Univ Human Ecology 1970; Thelma Porter Fellowship MI State Univ Human Ecology 1970; Recipient of the LA Home Econ Assn Disting District & State Serv Awd 1986; Nominated for Amer Council on Educ Fellow; Distinguished Faculty Fellowship Awd, Louisiana State University; Distinguished Service Awd, Southeast Council on Family Relations; Natl Council of Family Rel, Marie Peters Ethnic Minority Awd. **MEMBERSHIPS** Chmn jr div adv council LA State Univ 1979-80; state chmn aging serv LA Home Econ Assn 1978-80; consult Natl Assn for Ed of Young Children 1974-; Ctr for the Family Amer Home Econ Assn 1977-79; Delta Sigma Theta 1970-; mem Phi Upsilon Omicron So Univ Home Econ, Omicron Nu MI State Univ Human Ecology; National Council on Family Relations; Sect, TCFR; Texas Consortium On Geriatric Education. **CONTACT ADDRESS** Family Sciences, Texas Woman's Univ, Denton, TX 76205.

HILL, CLARA E.
PERSONAL Born 09/13/1948, Shivers, MS, m, 2 children **DISCIPLINE** PSYCHOLOGY **EDUCATION** Southern IL Univ, BA, 70; MA, 72; PhD, 74. **CAREER** Asst prof to prof, Univ of Md, 74-. **HONORS AND AWARDS** Res Awd, Univ of Md, 82, 86; Computer Incentive Awd, Univ of Md, 85; Fel, Am Psychol Assoc; Participant, NIHM Workshops, 83, 86, 90; Improvement of Instruction Awd, 89; Who's Who in Am; Who's Who in the World. **MEMBERSHIPS** Soc for Psychotherpay Res; Am Psychol Assoc; Soc for the Exploration of Psychotherapy Integration; Assoc for the Study of Dreams. **SELECTED PUBLICATIONS** Auth, Therapist techniques and client outcomes: Eight cases of brief psychotherapy, Sage, (Newbury Park, CA), 89; auth, Working with dreams in psychotherapy, Guilford Pr, (NY), 96; coauth, Helping skills: Facilitating exploration, insight, and action, Am Psychol Assoc, (Washington, DC), 99; coauth, "Describing the face of transference: Psychodynamic therapists' recollections of transference in successful long-term therapy," J of Coun Psychol 46, (99): 257-267; auth, "Bruce Fretz: A leader with quiet grace and tact", Coun Psychol, (forthcoming); coauth, "Structured brief therapy with a focus on dreams or loss for clients with troubling dreams and recent losses", J of Coun Psychol 47, (forthcoming); coauth,

"the effects of including the action state in dream interpretation", J of Coun Psychol (forthcoming); coauth, Rogerian therapy; Where has it been and where is it going?", J of Clinical Psychol, (forthcoming); auth, "Working with dreams in psychotherapy: what do we know empirically?", Psychotherapy Bulletin, (forthcoming); coauth, "Client concealment and self-presentation in therapy: A reaction to Kelly", Psychol Bulletin (forthcoming). **CONTACT ADDRESS** Dept Psychol, Univ of Maryland, Col Park, 1147 Zoology, College Park, MD 20742-001. **EMAIL** hill@psyc.umd.edu

HILL, JONATHAN D.
PERSONAL Born 02/21/1954, Charlotte, NC, m, 2000, 2 children **DISCIPLINE** ANTHROPOLOGY **EDUCATION** Univ Chicago, BA, 76; Indiana Univ, PhD, 83. **CAREER** Vis asst prof, Dept of Anthropology, 83-86, Univ of Georgia; asst prof, 86-90, assoc prof, 90-96, Dept of Anthropology, SIUC; vis assoc prof, 93-94, Dept of Anthropology, UCLA; prof, Dept of Anthropology, 96-, Chair, Dept of Anthropology, SIUC, 99-. **HONORS AND AWARDS** NDEA Title VI Fellowship in Portuguese and Latin Amer Studies, Indiana Univ, 77-78; Fulbright-Hays Training Grant, Doctoral Dissertation Abroad Program to Venezuela, 80-81; Fulbright-Hays Fac Res Abroad Grant to Venezuela, 84-85; Smithsonian Postdoctoral Fellowship, 87-88; Cultural Survival Grant for fieldwork in Columbia, 89; Office of Res and Development S IL Univ for fieldwork and archival res in Venezuela, 93; National Endowment for the Humanities Summer Research Stipend, Wenner-Gren Foundation for fieldwork in Venezuela, 98. **MEMBERSHIPS** Amer Anthrop Asn; Amer Ethnological Soc; Amer Soc for Ethnohistory; Cult Survival Scholars Network; Latin Amer Stud Asn; NY Acad of Sciences; Soc for Cultural Anthrop; Soc for Ethnomusicology; Soc for Linguistic Anthrop. **RESEARCH** Ethnology, ecology and history of Lowland South America; ethnomusicology; performance studies; symbolic and semiotic anthropology; nationalism and ethnicity; critical studies of culture; power and history. **SELECTED PUBLICATIONS** Ed, Anthropological Discourses and the Expression of Personhood in South American Inter-Ethnic Relations, S Amer Indian Stud, Bennington Col, 93; auth, Keepers of the Sacred Chants The Poetics of Ritual Power in an Amazonian Soc, Univ of Arizona Press, 93; ed, History Power and Identity Ethnogenesis in the Americas 1492-1992, Univ of Iowa Press, 96; art, Introduction Ethnogenesis in the Americas 1492-1992, History Power and Identity Ethnogenesis in the Americas After 1492, Univ of Iowa Press, 96; art, Northern Arawakan Ethnogenesis and Historical Transformations, History Power and Identity Ethnogenesis in the Americas After 1492, Univ of Iowa Press, 96; art, South America Tropical Forests, Encyclopedia of Cultural Anthropology, Henry Holt Co, 96; auth, Indigenous Peoples and the Rise of Independent Nation-States, Cambridge History of Native Peoples of the Americas, Vol. III, Pt. 2, 704-764. **CONTACT ADDRESS** Dept of Anthropology, So Illinois Univ, Carbondale, Mail Code 4502, Carbondale, IL 62901-4502. **EMAIL** jhill@siu.edu

HILL, KIM R.
PERSONAL Born 07/06/1953, San Diego, CA, m, 1982, 2 children **DISCIPLINE** ANTHROPOLOGY **EDUCATION** Univ Ut, PhD, 83. **CAREER** Prof, Univ Nmex, 00-. **RESEARCH** Human evolutionary ecology, hunter-gatherers, lowland South America. **SELECTED PUBLICATIONS** Coauth, Ache Life History: The Ecology and Demography of a Foraging People, Aldine Pr, 96; coauth, "The Evolutionary Ecology of Childhood Asthma," in Evolutionary Med (Oxford, UK: Oxford Univ Pr, 99); coauth, "The Ache of Paraguay," in The Cambridge Encycl of Hunters and Gatherers (Cambridge: Cambridge Univ Pr, 99), 92-96; coauth, "Life History Traits in Humans: Theory and Empirical Studies," Annual Rev Anthrop 28 (99): 397-430; coauth, "Sustainability of Ache Hunting in the Mbaracayu Reserve, Paraguay," in Sustainability of Hunting in Tropical Forests (NY: Columbia Univ Pr, 00); coauth, "A Test of the 'Showing Off' Hypothesis," Current Anthrop 41 (00): 124-125; coauth, "The Evolution of Intelligence and the Human Life History," Evolutionary Anthrop (forthcoming); coauth, "'It's a Wonderful Life': Signaling Generosity Among the Ache of Paraguay," Evolutionary Anthrop (forthcoming); coauth, "Food Transfers Among Hiwi Foragers of Venezuela," J of Human Ecol (forthcoming); coauth, "Cooperative Food Acquisition by Ache Foragers," in Coop in Animals and Humans (forthcoming). **CONTACT ADDRESS** Dept Anthrop, Univ of New Mexico, Albuquerque, 1 University Campus, Albuquerque, NM 87131-0001. **EMAIL** kimhill@unm.edu

HILL, MICHAEL R.
PERSONAL Born 11/06/1944, Louisville, KY, m, 1982 **DISCIPLINE** SOCIOLOGY **EDUCATION** Municipal Univ Omaha, BA, 67; Univ Nebraska-Lincoln, MA, 69; PhD, 82; PhD, 89. **CAREER** Asst res dean, Col Design, Iowa State Univ, 79-80; vis prof, Iowa State Univ, 78-81; vis prof, Univ Minn-Duluth, 85-86; vis prof, Albion Col, 86-87; adj prof, Univ Nebraska, 91-; adj prof, Iowa Western Comm Col, 95- ; ed, Sociological Origins, 99-. **HONORS AND AWARDS** Gamma Theta Upsilon, 65; Omicron Delta Kappa, 67; Sigma Xi, 85; 1st Place, Parson Conf, Harvard Univ, 88; Alpha Kappa Delta, 96. **MEMBERSHIPS** ISA; ASA; Harriet Martineau Socio Soc. **RESEARCH** History of Sociology; Sociological Theory; Qualitative Research Methods; Human Spatial Behavior. **SELECTED PUBLICATIONS** Auth, Walking, Crossing Streets and Choosing Pedestrian Routes, Univ Nebraska Studies (84); co-ed, Women and Symbolic Interaction, Allen and Unwin (87); ed, How to Observe Morals and Manners, by Harriet Martineau, Transaction Books (89); auth, Archival Strategies and Techniques, Sage Publications (93); ed, With Her in Ourland: Sequel to Herland, by Charlotte Perkins Gilman, Greenwood Press (97). **CONTACT ADDRESS** Dept Social Science, Iowa Western Comm Col, 2700 College Rd, PO Box 4-C, Council Bluffs, IA 51503.

HILL-MILLER, KATHERINE CECELIA
PERSONAL Born 01/24/1949, Granite City, IL, m, 1982, 1 child **DISCIPLINE** MODERN BRITISH & WOMEN'S LITERATURE **EDUCATION** Fordham Univ, BA, 71; Columbia Univ, MA, 72, MPhil, 74, PhD(English), 79. **CAREER** Teaching fel, Columbia Univ, 74; lect, Kingsborough Comm Col, 72-73; asst prof, Col William & Mary, 77-80; asst prof 80-84, assoc prof 84-89, PROF ENGLISH, CW POST CAMPUS LONG ISLAND UNIV, 89-; dir, poetry ctr, 82-85, DIR WRITING, CW POST CTR, 93-; guest lect, Rheinische Friedrich-Wilhelms-Universitat, Bonn, 86. **HONORS AND AWARDS** Dir, NEH Summr Sem; Virginia Woolf's Major Novels, 94,96,00. **MEMBERSHIPS** MLA; Virginia Woolf Soc. **RESEARCH** Virginia Woolf; experimental fiction; women writers. **SELECTED PUBLICATIONS** Auth, My Hideous Progeny: Mary SHelley, William Godwin, and the Father-Daughter Relaationship, Univ Del Press, 95; auth, The Bantam Book of Spelling, Bantam Books, 86; co-auth, Writing Effective Paragraphs, Harper and Row, 74; auth, Virginia Woolf's Places: A Guide to Some English Literary Landscapes, Duckworth Publishers, fothcoming; auth, Virginia Woolf and Leslie Stephen: History and Literary Revolution, Pubs of the Mod Lang Asn, 96, no 3, 81. **CONTACT ADDRESS** Dept of English, Long Island Univ, C.W. Post, Greenvale, NY 11548. **EMAIL** fkcmiller@aol.com

HILLEBRAND, JOHN D.
PERSONAL Born 05/22/1956, Springfield, VA, s **DISCIPLINE** SOCIOLOGY **EDUCATION** Univ Calif, Davis, BA, 78; Univ Calif, San Diego, MA, 80; Calif Community Col Teaching Credential, Sociol, 83; Univ Calif, San Diego, PhD, 91. **CAREER** Lectr, Southwest Mo State Univ, 91-93; asst prof, Northwestern State Univ of La, 94-. **HONORS AND AWARDS** Summer fel in economics, Inst for Humane Studies, Menlo Park, 81; res grant, Inst for Human Studies, Menlo Park, Calif, 81; co-principal investigator, Bd of Regents Support Fund Grant, 99; Who's Who Among America's Teachers, 2000. **MEMBERSHIPS** Alpha Kappa Delta, MidSouth Sociol Asn, Am Acad of Prof Sociol Practitioners. **RESEARCH** Deviance, research methodology, marriage and the family, social psychology, American society. **SELECTED PUBLICATIONS** Contribr, Creative Interviewing by Jack D. Douglas, Sage (85); coauth, Love, Intimacy, and Sex, by Jack D. Douglas and Freda Atwell with the assistance of John Hillebrand, Sage (88); contribr, The Myth of the Welfare State, by Jack D. Douglas, Transaction Books (89); rev of The Politics and Morality of Deviance, Nachman Ben-Yehunda (90), in Deviant Behavior, Vol 11, No 3 (90); rev of The Trials of Oscar Wilde, Michael Foldy (97), in Deviant Behavior, Vol 20, No 3 (99): 291-298; rev, Male on Male Rape, Michael Scarce (98), in Deviant Behavior, Vol 20, No 3 (99): 291-298; rev essay, "Closing in On Intimacy," Family Relations, Vol 48, No 2(April 99): 217-221; rev, Qualitative Research Methods for the Social Sciences, Bruce L. Berg (98), in Teaching Sociol, Vol 28, No 1 (Jan 2000). **CONTACT ADDRESS** Dept Soc Sci, Northwestern State Univ of Louisiana, 350 Sam Sibley Rd, Natchitoches, LA 71497-0003. **EMAIL** Hillebrand@alpha.nsula.edu

HILLIER, SUSAN
DISCIPLINE PSYCHOLOGY **EDUCATION** Univ Calif, PhD, 88. **CAREER** Prof, Sonoma State Univ, 88-. **MEMBERSHIPS** ASA, APA. **RESEARCH** Self-concept development in later life, Narrative as research method. **SELECTED PUBLICATIONS** Auth, Making connections: Internet Guide to Marriage and Relationships Studies, McGraw Hill, 00; auth, Aging, the Individual, and Society, Wadsworth Pub, 99; auth, Marriage and Family: The Quest for Intimacy, 4th ed, McGraw Hill, 99. **CONTACT ADDRESS** Dept Psychol, Sonoma State Univ, 1801 E Cotati Ave, Rohnert Park, CA 94928. **EMAIL** hillier@sonoma.edu

HILLIS, RICK
PERSONAL Born 03/02/1966, Nipawin, ON, Canada, m **DISCIPLINE** PHYSICAL EDUCATION, POETRY **EDUCATION** Univ Sask, BEd, 70; Univ Iowa, MFA, 84. **CAREER** Lectr, Stanford Univ, 90-93; writer in residence to asst prof, Reed Col, 94-00. **HONORS AND AWARDS** Stegner Fel; Drue Heinz Fiction Prize. **MEMBERSHIPS** PEN. **SELECTED PUBLICATIONS** Auth, The Blue Machines at Night, 88; auth, Limbo River, 90. **CONTACT ADDRESS** Dept English, Reed Col, 3203 SE Woodstock Blvd, Portland, OR 97202-8138. **EMAIL** rick.hillis@reed.edu

HILPERT, BRUCE
PERSONAL Born 08/18/1950, Ft Campbell, KY, d, 1 child **DISCIPLINE** ANTHROPOLOGY **EDUCATION** Univ Ariz, BA, 72; MA, 77. **CAREER** Curator to registrar, Ariz Hist Soc, 78-85; curator, Ariz State Museum, Univ Ariz, 85-. **HONORS AND AWARDS** Special Achievement Awd, Ariz State Museum, 94; Special Achievement Awd, Ariz Archaeol and Hist Soc, 92. **MEMBERSHIPS** Am Asn of Museums; Museum Asn of Ariz. **RESEARCH** Prehistory of the Southwest; Ethnography of the Southwest; Museum Evaluation. **SELECTED PUBLICATIONS** Auth, Paths of Life: American Indians of the Southwest, 96; auth, The Chaco Handbook: An Encyclopedic Guide, Univ Ut Press, in press. **CONTACT ADDRESS** Dept Anthropol, Univ of Arizona, 1009 E South Campus Dr, Bldg 30, Tucson, AZ 85721-0030. **EMAIL** hilpert@u.arizona.edu

HIMMELGREEN, DAVID
PERSONAL Born 12/26/1959, New York, NY, m, 1990, 2 children **DISCIPLINE** ANTHROPOLOGY **EDUCATION** State Univ NYork, BA, 83; MA, 87; PhD, 94. **CAREER** Vis Asst Prof, SUNY, 93-94; Assoc Dir of Res, Hispanic Health Coun, 94-98; Vis Asst prof, Univ S Fla, 98-. **HONORS AND AWARDS** Certificate of Recognition, Univ Conn, 97-98. **MEMBERSHIPS** Am Public Health Asn, Am Anthropol Asn, Human Biol Asn, Coun on Nutritional Anthropol. **RESEARCH** Maternal and child health, nutritional assessment, food insecurity and hunger, child growth and development, obesity and chronic disease (e.g., diabetes, cardiovascular disease), hypertension, nutrition education, nutrition and HIV/AIDS, HIV/AIDS prevention evaluation, and behaviorally based intervention research. **SELECTED PUBLICATIONS** Auth, "Food insecurity among low-income Hispanics in Hartford, Connecticut: implications for public health policy," Human organization, in press; auth, "Latinos, hunger, and nutrition," The Hispanic Outlook in Higher Education, 99; auth, "A comparison of the nutritional status and food security of inner-city drug-using and non-drug using Latino women," American Journal of Physical Anthropology, (98): 351-361; auth, "HIV, AIDS, and other health risks: Findings from a multi-sit national study. An introduction," American Journal of Drug and Alcohol Abuse, (98): 187-197; auth, "Poverty, Food insecurity and Obesity--What we don't know and need to find out," Anthropology Newsletter, (97): 12-13; auth, "Food insecurity at home: considerations for applied research in the USA," Communicator, The Official Publication of the Council on Nutritional Anthropology, (96): 8-13; auth, "Taking care of yourself when you are an addict: Food habits of addicted Hispanic women in Hartford, Connecticut," Medical Anthropology, (99): 281-298; auth, "Knowledge of folic acid and neural tube effects among inner-city residents: have they even heard of it?," Journal of the American Dietetic Association, (99): 80-83; auth, "Prenatal and prenatal factors associated with breast-feeding initiation among inner-city Puerto Rican women," Journal of the American Dietetic Association, 657-663; auth, "Variation in drug injection frequency among out-of-treatment drug users: A national study," American Journal of Drug and Alcohol Abuse, (98): 321-341; auth, "Changing the environment of AIDS risk: findings on syringe exchange and pharmacy sale of syringes in Hartford, CT," Medical Anthropology, (98): 107-130; auth, "Community-based AIDS prevention: preliminary outcomes of a program for African American and Latino injection drug users," Journal of Drug Issues, (96): 561-590. **CONTACT ADDRESS** Dept Anthropol, Univ of So Florida, 4202 Fowler Ave, Tampa, FL 33620.

HINES, VIRGINIA E.
PERSONAL Born 10/03/1954, Monroe, MI, d, 2 children **DISCIPLINE** TEACHER EDUCATION **EDUCATION** Grand Valley State Univ, B Ph, 76; Salem-Teiko Univ, MA, 91; West Virginia Univ, EdD, 94. **CAREER** Coord, DC PS, 78-91; asst prof, Plattsburgh State Univ, 94-98; asst prof, Lake Superior State Univ, 98-. **HONORS AND AWARDS** Dist Fac, 00; Kappa Delta Phi; Phi Delta Kappa. **MEMBERSHIPS** AERA; EERA; SIG, TERS; ASCD; Kappa Delta Phi. **RESEARCH** Curriculum theories and practice; use of telecommunicated journals in teacher education. **SELECTED PUBLICATIONS** Coauth, "Gaining Insight into K-12 educator's telecommunications learning experiences via qualitive inquiry," Intl J Edu Tech (96); auth, When the Wind was Singing Freedom: Reflections on Thomas Jefferson College, Mich St Press (forthcoming). **CONTACT ADDRESS** Dept Teacher Education, Lake Superior State Univ, 650 Easterday Ave, Sault Ste. Marie, MI 49783.

HINKES, MADELINE J.
PERSONAL Born 07/22/1955, Chicago, IL, 1 child **DISCIPLINE** ANTHROPOLOGY **EDUCATION** Northwestern Univ, BA, 75; Univ Kans, MA, 77; Univ Ariz, PhD, 83. **CAREER** Fac, Pima Community Col, Tuscon, Ariz, 78, 79; instr, teaching asst, and res assoc, Univ Ariz, 78-82; adjunct fac, San Diego Mesa Col, 94-98; adjunct fac, Nat Univ, San Diego, 94-; asst prof, San Diego Mesa Col, to present; Chief Forensic Anthropologist for San Diego Co Medical Examiner's Office, to present. **HONORS AND AWARDS** US Army Commander's Awd for Civilian Service, 86; US Navy Certificate of Recognition, 87; US Army Commendation for Meritorious Achievement, 87; US Army Special Achievement & Meritorious Service Awd, 87. **MEMBERSHIPS** Am Acad of Forensic Scis, Nat Found for Mortuary Care, Am Soc of Forensic Odontology, Am Bd of Forensic Anthropol. **RESEARCH** Human variation, forensic science, accident investigation, museum studies, natural history. **SELECTED PUBLICATIONS** Rev of Mortal Remains: A True Story of Ritual Murder, by Henry Scammell, Am

J of Physical Anthropol, 87 (92): 237; auth, Revised Anthropology Protocol for US Army Central Identification Laboratory, Hickam Air Force Base, Hawaii (92); auth, "Realities of Racial Determination in a Forensic Setting," in Race, Ethnicity, and Applied Bioanthropology, C. C. Gordon, ed, NAPA Bull, 13 (93): 48-53, Am Anthropol Asn, Washington, DC; auth, "Wind Mountain Osteological Analysis," in Mimbres Mogollon Archaeology, A. I. Woosley and A. J. McIntyre, eds, Univ N Mex Press, Albuquerque (96): 373-388; auth, "Dental Anthropology, Racial Odontology," in Forensic Odontology News, 17, 1 (98): 6; coauth, "Anthropological Analysis of the Human Remains Excavated from the Mesheikh Site during the Harvard-Boston Egyptian Expedition of 1912," (in press); auth, "Human Skeletal Remains from el-Kurru, Egypt," Boston Mus of Fine Arts (in press). **CONTACT ADDRESS** Dept Behav Sci, San Diego Mesa Col, 7250 Mesa Col Dr, San Diego, CA 92111. **EMAIL** Mhinkes@sdccd.cc.ca.us

HINRICHS, BRUCE
PERSONAL Born 10/26/1945, Minneapolis, MN, d, 2 children **DISCIPLINE** BEHAVIORAL SCIENCE **EDUCATION** Univ Minn, PhD, 73. **CAREER** Prof, Century Col, 88-. **HONORS AND AWARDS** Hon Fel, Univ Wis; Teacher in Residence, Univ Ill. **MEMBERSHIPS** Am Psychol Asn. **RESEARCH** Cognitive neuroscience and film studies, modern art. **SELECTED PUBLICATIONS** Auth, "Chaos and Cosmos: The Search for Meaning in Modern Art," The Humanist (March/April, 95): 22-28; Auth, "A Trip to the Movies: 100 Years of Film as Art," The Humanist (January/February, 96): 7-13; Auth, Film Art: Readings, St. Paul Century Coll, (96); Auth, "Brain Research and Folk Psychology," The Humanist (March/April, 97): 26-31; Auth, "Computing the Mind," The Humanist (March/April, 98): 26-30; Auth, "Spider Webs of Silken Thread: Memory and Brain," Communitas (April, 99); Auth, Film and Art, J Pr (99); Auth, Mind as Mosaic: The Robot in the Machine, J Pr (00); Auth, "The Art That Isn't: The Severed Head of Cinema," The Humanist (forthcoming). **CONTACT ADDRESS** Dept of Behav Sci, Century Comm and Tech Col, 3401 Century Ave N, White Bear Lake, MN 55110. **EMAIL** b.hinrichs@cctc.cc.mn.us

HISLOPE, KRISTI A.
PERSONAL Born 11/14/1969, Somerset, KY **DISCIPLINE** SPANISH, ESL **EDUCATION** Morehead State Univ, BS, 92; Univ Ky, MA, 94; Purdue Univ, PhD, 01. **CAREER** TA, Univ Ky, 92-95; Instr, Lexington Community Col, 95; TA, Purdue Univ, 95-01; ESL instr, Purdue Village Eng as a Second Lang School, 98-01; asst prof, N Ga Col and State Univ, 01-. **HONORS AND AWARDS** Purdue Res Grant, 97, 99-01. **MEMBERSHIPS** Am Assoc of Applied Ling, Am Assoc of Teachers of Span and Port, MLA, Am Coun on the Teaching of Foreign Lang. **RESEARCH** Teaching Spanish to Spanish-Speakers, Writing Processes, Written Focus-on-Form methods for grammar acquisition, second language acquisition, Spanish linguistics, ESL. **SELECTED PUBLICATIONS** Coauth, "(Re)experiencing hegemony: The linguistic imperialism of Robert Phillipson," Int Jour of Applied Ling 8.2 (98); coauth, "Hegemonic Discourse Revisited," Int Jour of Applied Ling 9.1, (99); coauth, "A Study of syllable final /r/ neutralization in Puerto Rican Spanish," Romance Lang Annuals 10, (99); auth, "Issues in Teaching Writing in Spanish to Hispanic Bilinguals at the University Level," Multiplicities: Mediating Cultural Productions, (Purdue Univ, 00). **CONTACT ADDRESS** FLL Dept, 134 Stanley Coulter Bldg, West Lafayette, IN 47906. **EMAIL** hislopek@omni.cc.purdue.edu

HO, TRUC-NHU
PERSONAL Born 06/25/1945, Hue, Vietnam, d, 1 child **DISCIPLINE** SOCIOLOGY **EDUCATION** Univ Mich, BA; Cal State Univ, Sacramento, MA; Rutgers Univ, PhD, 92. **CAREER** Asst prof, Univ NC, Pembroke, 98-. **HONORS AND AWARDS** Fel, Rutgers Univ. **MEMBERSHIPS** Am Soc Criminology; World Soc Victimology; Acad Crim Just Sci. **RESEARCH** Art theft; domestic violence; violence against women. **SELECTED PUBLICATIONS** Auth, "Prevention of Art Theft at Commercial Art Galleries," Studies On Crime and Crime Prevention (98); auth, "Art Theft in NYC," Empirical Stud of the Arts (98). **CONTACT ADDRESS** Dept Sociology, Univ of No Carolina, Pembroke, PO Box 1510, Pembroke, NC 28372. **EMAIL** hotruc@sassette.uncp.edu

HOARD, R. J.
PERSONAL Born 04/03/1956, Chicago Heights, IL, m, 1984, 3 children **DISCIPLINE** ANTHROPOLOGY **EDUCATION** Univ NE, Lincoln, BA (anthropol), 82; Univ OR, MA (Anthropol), 85; Univ MO, Columbia, PhD (Anthropol), 92. **CAREER** Grad teaching asst, field school inst, Dept of Anthropol, Univ OR, 84-85; grad instr, grad teaching asst, Dept of Anthropol, Univ MO, Columbia, 86-91; Instr, Dept of Social and Behavioral Sciences, 98; Archaeological Field Dir, Missouri Dept of Transportation, 92-00; State Archeologist, Kansas State Hist Soc, 00-. **HONORS AND AWARDS** Grant-in-aid, Soc of the Sigma Xi, 89. **MEMBERSHIPS** Soc for Am Archaeology; Plains Anthropol Soc; MO Archaeol Soc; Human Behavior and Evolution Soc. **RESEARCH** Archaeology, primarily early agricultural societies; geographic emphasis: North Am (midwest); res foci: ceramic technology, materials science, archaeometry, Late Woodland. **SELECTED PUBLICATIONS** Coauth, "Neutron Activation Analysis of Stone from the Chadron Formation and a Clovis Site on the Great Plains," J of Archaeol Sci 19 (92): 655-665; coauth, "Source Determination of White River Group Silicates From Two Archaeological Sites in the Great Plains," Am Antiquity 58 (93): 698-710; coauth, "Materials Science and Midwestern Pottery: Generating Data for a Selectionist Framework," J of Archaeol Method and Theory 1 (94): 259-304; coauth, "Additional Comments on Neutron Activation Analysis of Stone From the Great Plains: Reply to Church," J of Archaeol Sci 22 (95): 7-10; coauth, "A Materials Science Approach to Understanding Limestone-Tempered Pottery From the Midwest," J of Archaeol Sci 22 (95): 823-832; coauth, "Ceramic Vessels," in Burkemper: A Study of Middle and Late Woodland Subsistence and Ceramic Technology in the Central Mississippi River Valley (IL State Museum Reports of Investigations, no 52, 96), 91-144; coauth, "The Origins and Evolution of Rock Fences in Missouri," Material Culture 30.1 (98): 1-22; coauth, "Late Woodland Archaeology in Missouri," in Late Woodland Societies: Tradition and Transformation Across the Midcontinent, ed. T.E. Emerson, D. McElrath, and A. Fortier (Univ of Nebraska Press, Lincoln, 00); auth, "Late Woodland in Central Missouri: The Boone Phase," in Late Woodland Societies: Tradition and Transformation Across the Midcontinent, ed. T.E. Emerson, D. McElrath, and A. Fortier (Univ of Nebraska Press, Lincoln, 00); coauth, "Limestones as Tempering Agent in Prehistoric Midwestern Pottery," in Explanations of Change: Case Studies in Evolutionary Archaeology, ed. Robert C. Dunnell and Robert D. Leonard (Univ of Utah, Salt Lake, forthcoming). **CONTACT ADDRESS** Cultural Resources, Kansas State Hist Soc, 6425 S.W. 6th Avenue, Topeka, KS 66615-1099. **EMAIL** rhoard@ kshs.org

HOBFOLL, STEVEN E.
PERSONAL Born 09/25/1951, Chicago, IL, m, 1977, 3 children **DISCIPLINE** PSYCHOLOGY **EDUCATION** Uni Ill, BS, 73; Univ S Fla, MA, 75; PhD, 77. **CAREER** Adj Prof, US Intl Univ, 77-79; Psychologist, anchorage children's Center, 77-79; Lecturer to Assoc Prof, Ben Gurion Univ, 80-83; Assoc Prof to Prof, Tel Aviv Univ, 83-88; Vis Prof, DePaul Univ, 86-87; Prof, Kent state Univ, 87-. **HONORS AND AWARDS** Commendation Awd, SE Psychol Asn, 75; Peer Recognition Awd, Ohio Dept of Health, 90; Scholarly Contribution Awd, Kent State Univ, 93; Distinguished Scholar, Kent State Univ, 99; Berscheid-Hatfield Awd, 99. **RESEARCH** Stress, Women's Health promotion. **SELECTED PUBLICATIONS** Auth, "Conservation of resources: A stress theory based on the primacy of resource loss," in The encyclopedia of stress, San Diego, in press; auth, "Loss, resources, and resiliency in close interpersonal relationships," in Loss and Trauma: General and Close Relationship Perspectives, New York, in press; auth, "Comparing men's and women's loss of perceived social and work resources following psychological distress," Journal of Social and Personal Relationships, in press; auth, "Money doesn't talk it swears: How economic stress and resistance resources impact inner-city women's depressive mood,," American Journal of Community Psychology, in press; auth, "Ways of coping among low-income inner city somen: the multiaxial model of coping," African American research Perspectives, (00): 30-40; auth, "Reducing AIDS risk among inner-city women: A review of the collectivist empowerment AIDS Prevention (CE-AP) program," Journal of the European academy of Dermatology and Venereology, (99): 166-174; auth, "When it rains it pours: The greater impact of resource loss compared to gain on psychological distress," Personality and Social Psychology Bulletin. (99): 1172-1182; auth, Stress, culture, and community: The psychology and philosophy of stress, new York, 98; ed, Traumatic stress: From theory to practice, New York, 95; ed, Extreme stress and communities: Impact and Intervention, Dordrecht, 95; auth, Work won't love you back: A survival guide for dual career couples, New York, 94; ed, Family helath psychology, Washington, 92. **CONTACT ADDRESS** Dept Psychol, Kent State Univ, PO Box 5190, Kent, OH 44242-0001. **EMAIL** shobfoll@kent.edu

HOBLER, BRUCE
PERSONAL Born 03/19/1938, Balto, MD, m, 1960, 1 child **DISCIPLINE** SOCIAL WORK **EDUCATION** Kenyon Col, AB, 60; Univ Pa, MSW, 64; Univ Maryland, PhD, 71. **CAREER** Social Work Supervisor, Dept of Mental Retardation, 66-70; Clinical Dir. Dept of Mental Retardation, 70-73; Superintendent, Sunland Training Ctr, 73-74; Superintendent & Education Dir, DE Dept of Correction, 76-97; Assoc Professor, Delaware State Univ, 97-. **MEMBERSHIPS** Correctional Education Assoc, Council of Directors of Correctional Education, Council on Social Work Education. **RESEARCH** Correctional Education Programs. **SELECTED PUBLICATIONS** Auth, Future Perspectives in Correctional Education, auth, National Newsletter in Correctional Education, auth, Region II-Director's Symposium; Assessing Correctional Education; auth, Delaware Educates Incarcerated Fathers, 99; auth, Correctional Education, 99. **CONTACT ADDRESS** Dept Social Work, Delaware State Univ, 1200 N Dupont Hwy, Dover, DE 19901. **EMAIL** lhobler@atsplus.net

HOBSON, MATTHEW L.
PERSONAL Born 06/27/1954, Des Moines, IA, m, 1975, 2 children **DISCIPLINE** HEALTH **EDUCATION** Univ Northern Iowa, BA, 76; MA, 93. **CAREER** Adj prof, Univ of Northern Iowa, 95-99. **MEMBERSHIPS** Iowa Public Health Assoc. **RESEARCH** Human Diseases and Sexuality. **CONTACT ADDRESS** Design, Family and Consumer Sci, Univ of No Iowa, Latham 235, Cedar Falls, IA 50614-0001. **EMAIL** mhobson@health.state.ia.us

HOCK, ROGER R.
DISCIPLINE PSYCHOLOGY **EDUCATION** Univ Calif, PhD, 89. **SELECTED PUBLICATIONS** Co-auth, "Acquiring skill through job experience," in Frontiers of Industrial and Organizational Psychology, Vol I, Jossey Bass, 86; auth, "Professional burnout among public school teachers," Public Personnel Management, (88): 167-189; auth, LaserPsych: Introductory psychology on laser disk, Prentice Hall, 93; auth, Forty studies that changed psychology: Explorations into the history of psychological research (Third Edition), Prentice Hall, 99; auth, The human sexuality digest: A custom-publishing database, Pearson Custom Pub, 00; co-auth, It's my life now: Starting over after an abusive relationship or domestic violence, Routledge, 00. **CONTACT ADDRESS** Dept Psychol, Mendocino Col, Ukiah, CA 95482.

HOCKINGS, PAUL E.
PERSONAL Born 02/23/1935, Hertford, United Kingdom, m, 1998 **DISCIPLINE** ANTHROPOLOGY **EDUCATION** Univ Sydney, BA, 57; Univ Toronto, MA, 60; Univ Calif, Berkeley, PhD, 65. **CAREER** Asst Prof, Univ Calif, Los Angeles, 65-69; Res Dir, MGM Documentary London, 69; Prof, Univ Ill at Chicago, 70-; Ed in Chief, Visual Anthrop, 91-. **MEMBERSHIPS** Am Anthrop Asn, Royal Anthrop Inst, Soc for Visual Anthrop. **RESEARCH** South Asian ethnography and history, Dravidian languages, Visual anthropology. **SELECTED PUBLICATIONS** Co-ed, Cinematographic Theory and New Dimensions in Ethnographic Film, Nat Musem of Ethnol (Osaka), 88; auth, Counsel from the Ancients: A Study of Badaga Proverbs, Prayers, Omens and Curses, Mounton de Gruyter (Berlin), 88; ed, Blue Mountains: The Ethnography and Biogeography of a South Indian Region, Oxford Univ Press (New Delhi etc), 89; ed, Encyclopedia of World Cultures, Vol III South Asia and Vol V East and Southeast Asia, G.K. Hall (Boston), 92; coauth, A Badaga-English Dictionary, Mounton de Gruyter (Berlin and NY), 92; ed, Principles of Visual Anthropology, Mounton de Gruyter (Berlin and NY), 95; auth, Bibliographie generale sur les Monts Nilgiri de l'Inde du sud 1603-1996 – A Comprehensive Bibliography for the Nilgiri Hills of Southern India 1603-1996 – Eine umfassende Bibliographie der Nilgiri-Berge Sudindiens, Universite Michel de Montaigne (Bordeaux), 97; auth, Kindreds of the Earth: Badaga Household Structure and Demography, Sage Publ (New Delhi, London and Thousand Oaks), AltaMira Press (Walnut Creek, CA), 99; auth, "Mortuary Ritual of the Badagas of Southern India," Fieldiana (Anthrop Ser) 32 (Chicago: Field Museum, 00). **CONTACT ADDRESS** Dept Anthrop, Univ of Illinois, Chicago, 1007 W Harrison St, Chicago, IL 60607. **EMAIL** ooty@uic.edu

HOEFEL, ROSEANNE
DISCIPLINE AMERICAN LITERATURES, RHETORIC, POETRY AND WOMEN'S STUDIES **EDUCATION** Ohio State Univ, PhD. **CAREER** Assoc prof, Alma Col; assoc dean, Col of Letters and Science, Univ of Wisc, Osh Kosh. **HONORS AND AWARDS** Barlow Awd for Fac Excellence. **SELECTED PUBLICATIONS** Her articles have appeared in Stud in Short Fiction, Emily Dickinson J, Transformations, Phoebe, Feminisms and The Women's Stud Rev. **CONTACT ADDRESS** Letters & Sciences, Dean's Office, Univ of Wisconsin, Oshkosh, Alma, MI 48801. **EMAIL** hoefel@uwosh.edu

HOEFER, RICHARD
DISCIPLINE SOCIAL WORK, POLITICAL SCIENCE **EDUCATION** Univ Kans, BSW, 79, MSW, 81; Int Grad Sch, Univ Stockholm, Diploma, 82; Univ Mich, MA, 84, PhD, 89. **CAREER** Lectr, Univ Mich, Ann Arbor, 88-89; res assoc, Center for Governmental Studies, Northern Ill Univ, DeKalb, 89-92; asst prof, Northern Ill Univ, 89-92; assoc dir, Center for Res, Evaluation and Technol, Sch of Soc Work, Univ Tex at Arlington, 94-, asst prof, Univ Tex at Arlington, 92-95, assoc prof, 95-. **HONORS AND AWARDS** Dept of Labor Human Resources Management Training Grant, 80-81; Senator James B. Pearson Overseas Study Fel, 81-82; Swedish Inst Fel, 82; Nat Inst of Mental Health Fel, 82-83; Univ Mich Rackham Predoctoral Grant, 86-87; American-Scandinavian Found Fel, 86-87; Fulbright-Hays Fel, 86-87; Fernando G. Torgerson Awd, Sch of Soc Work, Univ Tex, Arlington, May 98; Soc Worker of the Year, Tarrant Co Unit of the Tex Chapter of the Nat Asn of Soc Workers, March 99. **MEMBERSHIPS** Nat Asn of Soc Workers, Coun for Soc Work Educ, Asn for Community Orgn and Soc Admin, The Soc Welfare Policy and Policy Practice Group, Asn for Res on Nonprofit Orgns and Voluntary Action, Int Soc for Third Sector Res. **RESEARCH** Nonprofit organization management, work and life issues, program evaluation, nonprofit advocacy, American social welfare policy, Swedish social policy. **SELECTED PUBLICATIONS** Auth, "A Conceptual Model for Studying Social Welfare Policy Comparatively, J of Soc Work Educ, 32, 1 (Winter 96): 101-113; coauth, "Private Social Welfare Expenditures: The Mirror Welfare State," Encyclopedia of Social Work (97): 274-281; auth, "The Social Work

and Politics Initiative: A Model for Increasing Political Content in Social Work Education," J of Community Practice, (99): 6, 3; auth, "Protection, Prizes or Patrons? Explaining the Origins and Maintenance of Human Services Interest Groups," J of Sociol and Soc Welfare, 26, 4 (Dec 99): 115-136; auth, "Making a Difference: Human Service Interest Group Influence on Social Welfare Program Regulations," J of Sociol and Soc Welfare (forthcoming); auth, "Human Services Interest Groups in Four States: Lessons for Effective Advocacy," J of Community Practice (forthcoming); coauth, "Reliability and Validity in Qualitative Research," in Bruce Thyer, ed, Handbook of Social Work Research Methods (forthcoming). **CONTACT ADDRESS** Dept Soc Work, Univ of Texas, Arlington, Box 19129, Arlington, TX 76019-0001. **EMAIL** rhoefer@utarlg.uta.edu

HOFMANN, STEFAN G.
PERSONAL Born 12/15/1964, Bietigheim, Germany, m, 1999, 1 child **DISCIPLINE** PSYCHOLOGY **EDUCATION** Univ Marburg, BS, 88; MS, 90; PhD, 93. **CAREER** Vis scholar, Stanford Univ, 91-93; asst prof, Univ Dresden, 93-94; res sci, SUNY Albany, 94-96; res asst prof to asst prof, Boston Univ, 96-. **HONORS AND AWARDS** Young Investigator Award, 98-00; First Indep Res Support and Transition Award, Nat Inst of Mental Health, 98; Young Investigator Award, Nat Alliance for Res on Schizophrenia and Depression; DAAD Dissertation Fel, Stanford Univ, 91. **MEMBERSHIPS** Acad of Cognitive Therapy; Am Psychol Asn; Am Psychol Soc; Am Asn for the Adv of Sci; Anxiety Disorders Asn of Am; Asn for the Adv of Beh Therapy; Soc for a Sci of Clinic Psychol; Soc of Clinic Psychol. **RESEARCH** Anxiety disorders; Psychotherapy; Emotions; Psychophysiology; Philosophy of science. **SELECTED PUBLICATIONS** Co-auth, "Psychophysiological differences between subgroups of social phobia," J of Abnormal Psychol, (95): 224-231; co-auth, "Conditioning theory: A model for the etiology of public speaking anxiety?" Beh Res and Therapy, (95): 567-571; co-auth, "Pretreatment attrition in a comparative treatment outcome study on panic disorder," Am J of Psychiat, (98): 43-47; auth, "Relationship between panic and schizophrenia," Depression and Anxiety, (99): 101-106; auth, "Introducing the grandmother test into psychological science," J of Theoretical and Philosophical Psychology, (99): 167-176; co-auth, "Why do personality disorders change? Possible explanations from cognitive and psychodynamic models," Psychiat Annals, (99): 725-729; auth, "Treatment of social phobia: Potential mediators and moderators," Clinical Psychol, (00): 717-725; co-auth, "An instrument to assess self-statements during public speaking: Scale development and preliminary psychometric properties," Beh Therapy, (00): 499-515; co-auth, From social anxiety to social phobia: Multiple perspectives, Allyn and Bacon, 01. **CONTACT ADDRESS** Dept Psychol, Boston Univ, 648 Beacon St, 6th Floor, Boston, MA 02215. **EMAIL** shofmann@bu.edu

HOFSTRA, WARREN R.
PERSONAL Born 05/12/1947, New York, NY, m, 1979, 2 children **DISCIPLINE** EARLY AMERICAN HISTORY, SOCIAL, MATERIAL CULTURE **EDUCATION** Washington Univ, BA, 69; Boston Univ, MA, 74; Univ Virginia, PhD, 85. **CAREER** Proj dir, 86-; instr, 76-85; asst prof, 85-90; assoc prof, 90-95; Shenandoah Univ, prof, 95-. **HONORS AND AWARDS** DuPont Fel; Vir Found Hum, res Fel; Ben Belchic Awd; MESDA Res Fel; Mednick Fel; James R and Mary B Wilkins Awd; NEH, 92, 94; Mellon Fel. **MEMBERSHIPS** OAH; AHA; SHA; SHS; VHS; ASEH; VAF. **RESEARCH** Early American social and cultural history; material culture; landscape. **SELECTED PUBLICATIONS** Auth, "Ethnicity and Community Formation on the Shenandoah Valley Frontier, 1730-1800." in Diversity and Accommodation: Essays on the Cultural Composition of the Virginia Frontier, ed. Michael J Puglisi (Knoxville: Univ Tenn Press, 97); ed, George Washington and the Virginia Backcountry, Madison House (Madison, Wis, 98); auth, "'The Extension of His Majesties Dominions': The Virginia Backcountry and the Reconfiguration of Imperial Frontiers." J Am Hist 84 (98): 1281-1312; auth, Epilogue: Interdisciplinary Dialogues on the Southern Colonial Backcountry, 1893-97." In The Southern Colonial Backcountry: Interdisciplinary Perspectives on Frontier Communities, ed. David C Crass, Richard D Brooks, Steven Smith, Martha Zierden (Knoxville: Univ Tenn Press, 98); auth, A Separate Place: The Formation of Clarke County, Virginia, White Post Virginia, 1986, Madison House (Madison Wis), 99; coauth, "Native American Settlement within the Middle and Upper Drainage of Opequon Creek, Frederick County, Virginia," Quart Bul Archeo Soc Vir 54 (99): 154-65; coauth, "'A Murder. . of Horrible and Savage Barbarity': The Death of Robert Berkeley and the Burden of Race in the Southern Past,." J South Hist 65 (99): 41-76; auth, "Reconstructing the Colonial Environment of the Upper Chesapeake Watershed," in Discovering the Chesapeake: The History of a Watershed Ecosystem, ed. Philip D Curtin (Baltimore: Johns Hopkins Univ Press, forthcoming); co-ed, After the Backcountry: Rural Life in the Great Valley of Virginia, 1800-1900, Univ Tenn Press (Knoxville), forthcoming; auth, "From Farm to Mill to Market: The Historical Archaeology of an Emerging Grain Economy in the Shenandoah Valley of Virginia," in After the Backcountry: Rural Life in the Great Valley of Virginia, 1800-1900, ed. Kenneth E Koons, Warren R Hofstra (Knoxville: Univ Tenn Press, forthcoming). **CONTACT ADDRESS** Dept Social, Behavioral Science, Shenandoah Univ, 1460 University Dr, Winchester, VA 22601. **EMAIL** whofstra@su.edu

HOGE, DEAN R.
PERSONAL Born 05/27/1937, New Knoxville, OH, m, 1965, 2 children **DISCIPLINE** SOCIOLOGY, RELIGIOUS STUDIES **EDUCATION** Ohio State Univ, BA, 60; Harvard Divinity Sch, BD, 64; Harvard Univ, PhD, 70. **CAREER** Instr/Asst Prof, Princeton Theol Sem, 69-74; Assoc Prof/Prof, Cath Univ of Am, 74-. **HONORS AND AWARDS** Distinguished Book Awd, for "Vanishing Boundaries," Soc for the Sci Study of Relig, 94. **MEMBERSHIPS** Am Sociol Asn, Soc for the Sci Study of Relig, Relig Res Asn. **RESEARCH** Sociology of religion and churches. **SELECTED PUBLICATIONS** Auth, Converts, Dropouts, Returnees: A Study of Religious Change Among Catholics, US Cath Conf, 81; auth, The Future of Catholic Leadership: Responses to Priest Shortage, Sheed and Ward, 87; coauth, Vanishing Boundaries: The Religion of Mainline Protestant Baby Boomers, Westminster/John Knox Press, 94; coauth, Money Matters: Personal Giving in American Churches, Westminster/John Knox Press, 96; coauth, Laity, American and Catholic: Transforming the Church, Sheed and Ward, 96. **CONTACT ADDRESS** Dept Sociol, Catholic Univ of America, 620 Michigan Ave, Washington, DC 20064-0002. **EMAIL** hoge@cua.edu

HOLDEN, GEORGE W.
PERSONAL Born 09/26/1954, New Haven, CT, m, 1983, 3 children **DISCIPLINE** PSYCHOLOGY **EDUCATION** Yale Univ, BA, 77; Univ NC, MA, 82; PhD, 84. **CAREER** Instr, Univ Tex, 84-85; From Asst Prof to Prof, Univ Tex, 85-. **MEMBERSHIPS** SRCD, APS, APSAC. **RESEARCH** Parent-child relationships, family violence. **SELECTED PUBLICATIONS** Auth, Parents and the Dynamics of Child Rearing, Westview Pr (Boulder, CO), 97; coauth, Children Exposed to Marital Violence: Theory, Research and Applied Issues, APA Pr (Washington, DC), 98; coauth, "The Co-Occurrence of Spouse and Physical Child Abuse: A Review and Appraisal," J of Family Psychol 12 (98): 578-599; coauth, "Immediate Contextual Influences on Maternal Behavior: Environmental Affordances and Demands," J of Environ Psychol 18 (98): 387-398; coauth, "Protective Orders and Domestic Violence: Risk Factors for Re-Abuse," J of Family Violence 14 (99): 205-226; coauth, "The Instrumental Side of Corporal Punishment: Parents' Reported Practices and Outcome Expectancies," J of Marriage and the Family 61 (99): 971-981; coauth, The Handbook of Family Measurement Techniques, Vol 3: Instruments, Sage Publ (Newbury Park, CA), 00; coauth, The Handbook of Family Measurement Techniques, Vol 2: Abstracts, Sage Publ (Newbury Park, CA), 00. **CONTACT ADDRESS** Dept Psychol, Univ of Texas, Austin, Austin, TX 78712. **EMAIL** holden@psy.utexas.edu

HOLLOWAY, RALPH L.
PERSONAL Born 02/06/1935, Philadelphia, PA, m, 1959, 3 children **DISCIPLINE** ANTHROPOLOGY **EDUCATION** Univ N Mex, BS, 59; Univ Calif, PhD, 64. **CAREER** Asst Prof to Full Prof, Columbia Univ, 64-. **HONORS AND AWARDS** Guggenheim Fel, 73; Fel, NYAS, 77; Fel, AAS, 69; Phi Beta Kappa, 92; Phi Kappa Phi; Who's Who; Who's Who in the East; Dictionary of Intl Biography; Am Men & Women of Sci. **MEMBERSHIPS** AAAS, AAPA, Soc Neurosci, NYAS. **RESEARCH** Evolution of brain and behavior, The fossil record of human, Evolution of brain mechanisms. **SELECTED PUBLICATIONS** Auth, "Extreme measures of SK 1585 brain endocast: the endocranial capacities of robust australopithecines revisited," Am Journal Psys Anthro, (00): 181-182; auth, "Carotid canal as a predictor of cranial capacity in great apes," Am Journal Phys Anthro, (99): 249; auth, "The brain-face interface: Does brain size correlate with facial dimensions?," am Journal Phys anthro, (99): 98; auth, "did Australopithecines have inflated brains?," am Journal Phys anthro, (99): 155; auth, "When did sex differences in the human brain evolve? An examination of the brain's major hemispheric pathway in macaques," Soc Neuroscience, (99): 105; auth, "Hominid brain volume," Science, (99): 283; auth, "Human-like pattern of hemispheric asymmetry in planum parietale of chimpanzees," Soc Neuroscience, 98; auth, "Anatomic expression Heschl's gyrus and planum temporale asymmetry in great apes, lesser apes and Old World Monkeys," soc Neuroscience, 98; auth, "Relative size of the human corpus callosum redux: Statistical smoke and mirrors?," Behavioral and Brain Sciences, (98): 333-335; auth, " When did sexual dimorphism appear in the brain's hemispheric highway?," am Journal Phys anthro, (98): 114. **CONTACT ADDRESS** Dept Anthropol, Columbia Univ, 2960 Broadway, New York, NY 10027.

HOLSEY, LILLA G.
PERSONAL Born 08/26/1941, San Mateo, FL **DISCIPLINE** EDUCATION **EDUCATION** Hampton Institute, BS 1963; FL State University, MS 1971, PhD 1974. **CAREER** East Carolina Univ, assoc prof home economics, 74-; FL State Univ, graduate rsch asst, 71, 73; Gainesville High School, home economics teacher, 70-72; Lincoln High School, 64-70. **HONORS AND AWARDS** Ford Foundation felllowship 1973-74; Danforth associate 1977; charter mem Putnam Co Educ Hall of Fame Palatha FL. **MEMBERSHIPS** Natl & Amer Home Econ Assns; Amer & Vocational Assn; NC Consumer Assn; Bethel AME Church; bd trustees Alpha Kappa Alpha; Kappa Delta Pi & Omicron Nu Honor Society; Phi Kappa Delta. **CONTACT ADDRESS** East Carolina Univ, 1000 E Fifth St, Greenville, NC 27858.

HOLTER, MARK CLARK
PERSONAL Born 07/07/1960, Minneapolis, MN, m, 1994, 1 child **DISCIPLINE** SOCIAL WORK **EDUCATION** Univ Minn, BA, 87; Columbia Univ, MS, 90; PhD, 98. **CAREER** Sen Res Assoc, Center for Poverty Univ Mich, 97-98; Asst Prof, Univ Mich, 98-. **RESEARCH** Mental Health Services; Homelessness. **CONTACT ADDRESS** Sch Soc Work, Univ of Michigan, Ann Arbor, 105 S State St, Ann Arbor, MI 48109. **EMAIL** holter@umich.edu

HOLTZ, BARRY
PERSONAL Born Boston, MA, m, 1985, 2 children **DISCIPLINE** JEWISH EDUCATION AND STUDIES **EDUCATION** Tufts Univ, BA; Brandeis Univ, PhD. **CAREER** Vis prof, Hebrew Univ; co-dir, Melton Res Ctr; assoc prof, Jewish Theol Sem; lect, 92nd Street Y, New York. **SELECTED PUBLICATIONS** Auth, Back to the Sources: Reading the Classic Jewish Texts, Simon and Schuster 84; Finding Our Way: Jewish Texts and the Lives we Lead Today, Schocken, 90; The Schocken Guide to Jewish Books, 92; coauth, Your Word is Fire: The Hasidic Masters on Contemplative Prayer, Jewish Lights Press. **CONTACT ADDRESS** Jewish Theol Sem of America, 3080 Broadway, New York, NY 10027. **EMAIL** baholtz@jtsa.edu

HONEY, MAUREEN
PERSONAL Born 10/25/1945, Memphis, TN **DISCIPLINE** AMERICAN STUDIES, WOMEN'S STUDIES **EDUCATION** Mich State Univ, BA, 67; MA, 70; PhD, 79. **CAREER** Instr, Mich State univ, 77-79; from asst prof to prof, Univ Nebr, 79-. **HONORS AND AWARDS** Distinguished Teaching Awd, 91. **MEMBERSHIPS** Am Studies Asn, Am Culture Asn, Edith Wharton Soc, Melus. **RESEARCH** Women in World War II, American Women's Literature, Harlem Renaissance, Popular Fiction (1890-1930). **SELECTED PUBLICATIONS** Auth, Creating Rosie the Riveter: Class, Gender, and Propaganda During World War II, Univ Mass Press, 84; auth, Shadowed Dreams: Women's Poetry of the Harlem Renaissance, Rutgers Univ Press, 89, 96, & 99; auth, Breaking the Ties that Bind: Popular Stories of the New Woman, 1915-1930, Univ Okla Press, 92 & 98; auth, "Introduction," in The Job by Sinclair Lewis (NE: Univ Nebr Press, 94); ed, Bitter Fruit: African American Women in World War II, Univ Mo Press, 99; co-ed, Texts and Contexts of the Harlem Renaissance: A Multi-Genre Anthology, forthcoming. **CONTACT ADDRESS** Dept English, Univ of Nebraska, Lincoln, PO Box 880333, Lincoln, NE 68588-0333. **EMAIL** mhoney1@unl.edu

HOOD, MANTLE
DISCIPLINE ETHNOMUSICOLOGY **EDUCATION** Univ Calif, MA, BA; Univ Amsterdam, PhD. **CAREER** Prof emer, UCLA; vis prof; adj prof-. **HONORS AND AWARDS** Sr fel, NEH; Fulbright fel; Ford Found fel; former pres, soc ethnomusicology. **MEMBERSHIPS** Soc for Ethnomusicology. **RESEARCH** Indonesian music. **SELECTED PUBLICATIONS** Publ, twenty books and book chapters as well as over sixty articles in scholarly journals and encyclopedias. **CONTACT ADDRESS** Dept of Mus, West Virginia Univ, Morgantown, PO Box 6009, Morgantown, WV 26506-6009.

HOPKINS, DIANNE MCAFEE
PERSONAL Born 12/30/1944, Houston, TX, m, 1982, 1 child **DISCIPLINE** EDUCATION **EDUCATION** Fisk University, Nashville, TN, BA, 1966; Atlanta University, Atlanta, GA, MSLS, 1967; Western Michigan University, Kalamazoo, MI, EdS, 73; Univ of Wis-Madison, PhD, 1981. **CAREER** Houston Independent School District, Houston, TX, librarian, 67-71; Dept of Education, Michigan, Lansing, MI, school library consultant, 72-73; West Bloomfield Schools, West Bloomfield, MI, high school librarian, 73-74; University of Michigan, Ann Arbor, MI, school library consultant, 74-77; Wisconsin Dept of Public Instr, Madison, dir, school library bureau, 77-87; University of Wisconsin-Madison, asst professor, 87-92, associate prof, 92-99; prof, 99-. **HONORS AND AWARDS** Recipient, US Dept of Education Grant, 1989; Beta Phi Mu International Library Fraternity, 1967; Phi Delta Kappa, 1980; Exceptional Performance Awd, Wisconsin Dept of Public Instr, 1982; Winner, ALISE Research Awd, 1992; Winner, Distinguished Service Awd, American Association of School Librarians; Co-principal Investigator, Natl Library Power Evaluation, Dewitt Wallace-Readers Digest Fund, 1994-00. **MEMBERSHIPS** Executive committee, educators of school library media specialists, 1988-91, member, editorial board, school library media quarterly, 1988-91, chair, AASL White House conference, 1986-92, American Assn of School Librarians; member, ALA presidents White House conference task force, American Library Assn, 1990-92; chair, local arrangement committee ALISE national conference, Assn for Library and Information Science Education, 1990-91; ALA Intellectual Freedom Comm, 1991-; AASL Vision Comm for New Natl Guidelines, 1995-98; Intellectual Freedom Honor Roll, 99-; Am Libr Asn; Am Civil Liberties Union; WEMA; Wisconsin Libr Asn. **RESEARCH** Intellectual freedom in schools; school library media program

development. **SELECTED PUBLICATIONS** Auth, "School Library Media Centers and Intellectual Freedom," in Intellectual Freedom Manuel, 5th ed (Chicago, Am Libr Asn, 96), 268-281; auth, "The School Library Media Specialist and Intellectual Freedom During the Twentieth Century," in The Emerging School Library Media Program: Historical Perspectives and Issues (Englewood, CO, Libraries Unlimited, 98), 39-55; auth, "Toward a Conceptual Path of Support for School Library Media Specialists With Challenges," School Library Media Quarterly Online (98); coauth, Lessons From Library Power: Enriching Teaching and Learning, Libraries Unlimited (Englewood, CO), 99; auth, "The School Library Collection: An Essential Building Block to Teaching and Learning," School Libraries Worldwide 502 (99): 1-15; coauth, "Student Learning Opportunities Summarize Library Power," School Libraries Worldwide 502 (99): 97-110. **CONTACT ADDRESS** School of Library and Information Sciences, Univ of Wisconsin, Madison, 600 N Park St, Helen C White Building, Madison, WI 53706. **EMAIL** DHopkins@facstaff.wisc.edu

HOPKINS, JOHN ORVILLE
PERSONAL Born 01/27/1930, Missoula, MT **DISCIPLINE** EDUCATION **EDUCATION** Gonzaga U, BA 1956, MA 1957; Columbia U, MPhil, PhD 1976; Columbia Univ Rsrch Prof, prep kndergrad educ 1977-78. **CAREER** State Univ of NY, prof, 76-77; MARC Public Educ Assn, educ dir, 70-74; Bd of Educ Baltimore, asst supt, 68-69; Fed Civil Rights Officer for Educ, 65-67; Amer Philos Assn, parish priest, teacher, 62-64. **HONORS AND AWARDS** Columbia Univ Pub Speaking Awds Univ MT, Seattle U, Gonzaga U, Elks, Rotary Club. **MEMBERSHIPS** Am Assn of Sch Adminstrs; NAACP; Assn fcor Study of Black Religion; Minority Parents Assn; African Studies Assn; corporate bds MD Day Care Council; dir S African Rsrch Progm. **CONTACT ADDRESS** 420 W 118th St 1318, New York, NY 10027.

HORNER, DAVID T.
DISCIPLINE PSYCHOLOGY **EDUCATION** Univ CA, Santa Cruz, BA, 81; Indiana Univ, PhD, 89. **CAREER** Instr, Indiana Univ, 87-89; asst prof, Truman State Univ, 89-92; asst prof, Univ Wisc, Oshkosk, 92-97, assoc prof, 97-. **HONORS AND AWARDS** Vis Res, Inst for the Study of Human Capabilities, summer 91; vis scholar, Indiana Univ, summers 92-93; Wisc teaching Fel, 99-2000. **MEMBERSHIPS** Am Psychol Soc; The Psychonomic Soc; Tactile Res Group; Midwestern Psychol Asn; Coun of Teachers of Undergraduate Psychol. **RESEARCH** Perceptual and cognitive factors influencing how humans process tactile information. **SELECTED PUBLICATIONS** Auth, with J. C. Craig, "A Comparison of Discrimination and Identification of Vibrotactile Patterns," Perception & Psychophysics, 45, 21-302 (89); auth, "The Effects of Complexity on the Perception of Vibrotactile Patterns," Perception & Psychophysics, 49, 551-562 (91); auth, "The Effects of Complexity on the Perception of Vibrotactile Patterns Presented to Separate Fingers," Perception & Psychophysics, 52, 201-210 (92); auth, "The Effect of Location on the Discrimination of Spatial Vibrotactile Patterns," Perception & Psychophysics, 57, 463-474 (95); auth with K. D. Robinson, "Demonstrations of the Size-Weight Illusion," Teaching of Psychology, 24 (3), 195-197 (97); auth, "Demonstrations of Color Perception and the Importance of Contours," Teaching of Psychology, 24 (4), 268-269 (97); auth, "The Effect of Shape and Location on Temporal Masking of Spatial Vibrotactile Patterns," Perception & Psychophysics, 59, 1255-1265 (97); auth, with K. R. Stetter and L. I. McCann, "Adding Structure to Unstructured Research Courses," Teaching of Psychology (97); auth, "Perceptual Processing at Adjacent Locations on a Single Finger: Masking and Response Competition," Perception & Psychophysics (in press). **CONTACT ADDRESS** Dept Psychol, Univ of Wisconsin, Oshkosh, 899 Algoma Blvd, Oshkosh, WI 54901. **EMAIL** horner@uwosh.edu

HOROWITZ, IRVING LOUIS
PERSONAL Born 09/25/1929, New York, NY, m, 1979, 2 children **DISCIPLINE** SOCIOLOGY **EDUCATION** CCNY, BSS, 51; Columbia Univ, MA, 52; Buenos Aires Univ, PhD, 57. **CAREER** Prof, Rutgers Univ, 69-. **HONORS AND AWARDS** Fel, Brandeis Univ, 58; Harold D Lasswell Awd, Ben Gurion Unvi; Lifetime Achievement Awd, Inter Univ Sem. **MEMBERSHIPS** AAAS; AAUP, USIA; Am Polit Sci Asn; Nat Asn Scholars; Authors Guild; Ctr for Study the Pres; Intl Soc Polit Psychol; Soc Intl Devel. **SELECTED PUBLICATIONS** Auth, Social Science and Public Policy in the United States, 77; auth, Dialogues on American Politics, 79; auth, Taking Lives: Genocide and State Power, 79; auth, Beyond Empire and Revolution, 82; auth, C. Wright Mills: An American Utopian, 83; auth, Winners and Losers, 85; auth, Communicating Ideas, 87; auth, Daydreams and Nightmares, 90; auth, The Decomposition of Sociology, 93; auth, Behemoth: Main Currents in the History and Theory of Political Sociology, 99. **CONTACT ADDRESS** Dept Sociol, Rutgers, The State Univ of New Jersey, New Brunswick, PO Box 5072, New Brunswick, NJ 08903. **EMAIL** ilh@transactionpub.com

HOROWITZ, MICHAEL M.
DISCIPLINE ANTHROPOLOGY **EDUCATION** Oberlin Col, BA, Hon, 55; Columbia Univ, MA, 59; PhD, 59. **CAREER** Prof, Anthro, Binghamton Univ, 61-; Dir Inst, Devel Anthro, 76-. **HONORS AND AWARDS** Keynote Speaker Proposal 21, Tokyo, 96; Distinguished Lecturer, Pakistan Soc of Devl Ecib, 95; Elizabeth Colson Lecturer, Oxford Univ, 91; Fulbright Sr Res Scholar, Bergen Univ, 66-67; Phi Beta Kappa; Sigma XI; Woodrow Wilson fellow; Soc Sci Res Council Fellow; Columbia Univ Fellow. **MEMBERSHIPS** Amer Anthro Assoc; Soc for Applied Anthro; Amer Fed of Teacher (AFL-CIO) Intl Comm on the Anthro of Food; Amer Civil Liberties Union; African Studies Assoc. **RESEARCH** Soc and Env Sustainable Eco Devel; Human Rights; The Soc of Pastoralism; The Soc of Riparian Peoples; Africa; Southwest Asia; South Asia; SE Asia. **SELECTED PUBLICATIONS** Devel-Induced Food Insecurity in the Middle Senegal Valley, Michael M Horowitz and Muneera-Salem Murdock, GeoJournal 30(2) 179-184, 93; Large Dams and Small People Producer director writer, senior anthropological advisor; An Inst for Devel Anthro Production, 93; Awarded screenings at Rencontre Medias Nord-Sud, Geneva March 93; WSKG Public Television, 94; Les Barrages de la Controverse; M Salem-Murdock,M Niasse J Magistro, M Horowitz et al; Paris: L'Harmattan, 94; Ethenicity and Socioeconomic Vulnerability in Pakistan, Forou Jowkar, Michael M Hororwitz et al, Binghamton NY Inst for Devel Anthro, 95; Environmental Film Festival in the Nation's Capital, 96; Soc of Wetland Sci, 96; "On Not Offending the Borrower: (Self?)-Ghettoization of Soc Sci at the World Bank," Devel Anthro 14(1-2):1-12, 96; The Sustainability of Anthro and Devel, Keynote Address to Proposal 21, Tokyo, 96; The Green Revolution, In The Dicitionary of Anthropology, Thomas J Barfield, ed, Oxford Blackwell Publishers, 97; Environment and Society in the Lower Mekong Basin: A Landscaping Review of the Literature, Pamela McElwee and Michael M Horowitz Binghamton NY Inst for Devel Anthro for Oxfam America 98; Devel Anthro (forthcoming). **CONTACT ADDRESS** Dept of Anthro, SUNY, Binghamton, Binghamton, NY 13902-6000. **EMAIL** mhorowi@binghamton.edu

HOSKINS, BILLIE
PERSONAL Born Lake Charles, LA, m, 1966, 2 children **DISCIPLINE** SOCIOLOGY **EDUCATION** Southern Univ, BS, 64; Iowa State Univ, MS, 65. **CAREER** Instr, Wis State Univ, Stevens Point, 65-68; assoc prof, Galveston Col, 68-98, adjunct prof, 98-. **HONORS AND AWARDS** Chairperson for convention meetings, bd of dirs, Rosenberg Lib, Galveston, Partnership for Better Living. **MEMBERSHIPS** Tex Community Col Teachers Asn. **CONTACT ADDRESS** Dept Soc & Behav Sci, Galveston Col, 4015 Ave Q, Galveston, TX 77550.

HOSSAIN, ZIARAT
PERSONAL Born 02/12/1960, Dhaka, Bangladesh, m, 1995 **DISCIPLINE** PSYCHOLOGY **EDUCATION** Jahangirnagar Univ, MSc 84; Univ Manitoba, MA, 88; Syracuse Univ, PhD, 92. **CAREER** Postdoctoral Fel, Univ of Miami Med Sch, 92-94; Asst prof, Fort Lewis Col, 94-. **HONORS AND AWARDS** Special Merit Awd, Fort Lewis Col, 97; Nomination for Featured Scholar, 99. **MEMBERSHIPS** Am Psychol Asn, Soc for Res in Child Develop. **RESEARCH** Parent-child interactions across cultures, impact of western civilization on indigenous cultures. **SELECTED PUBLICATIONS** Coauth, "Postraumatic stress, depression and social support among college students after Hurricane Andrew, " J of Col Student Develop 36-2 (95): 152-161; coauth, "Father involvement in childcare and household wok in common-law low income dual-earner and single-earner Jamaican families, " J of Appl Developmental Psychol 16 (95): 35-52; coauth, "Touch among children at nursery school, " Early Child Develop and Care 126 (96): 101-110; coauth, "Depressed mothers' touching increases infants' positive affect and attention in still-face interactions," Child Develop 67 (96): 1780-1792; coauth, "Family socialization in an East Indian village in Guyana: A focus on fathers," in Caribbean Families: Diversity Among Ethic Groups, ed. J. Roopnarine and J. Brown (Greenwich, CT: Ablex Publ, 97), 57-83; coauth, "Fathers caregiving in low income African-American and Hispanic-American families," Early Develop and Parenting 6 (97): 73-82; coauth, "An ecosystemic analysis of agrarian and urban societies in India and Bangladesh," Proceedings of the Am Asoc of Behave and Soc Sci 1 (98); coauth, "Fathers participation in childcare within Navajo Indian families," Early Child Develop and Care 154 (99): 63-74; coauth, "Blood pressure symptoms are reduced by massage therapy," J of Bodywork and Movement Therapies 4 (00): 31-38; coauth, "Sustainable lifestyles of the Ladakhis in India: An ethnographic study," Indian Psychol Rev (in press). **CONTACT ADDRESS** Dept of Psychology, Fort Lewis Col, 1000 Rim Dr, Durango, CO 81381. **EMAIL** hossainz@fortlewis.edu

HOURCADE, JACK
PERSONAL Born 01/12/1953, New Orleans, LA, d, 1 child **DISCIPLINE** EDUCATION **EDUCATION** Univ La Lafayette, BA, 75; Univ Ariz, MEd, 75; Univ Mo, PhD, 79. **CAREER** Asst Prof, Eastern Ky Univ, 79-82; Asst Prof, La Tech Univ, 82-87; Prof, Boise State Univ, 87-. **HONORS AND AWARDS** Researcher of the Year, La Tech Univ, 86; Who's Who of Emerging Leaders in Am, 90; Who's Who in the W, 96; Who's Who in Am W, 97; Who's Who Among America's Teachers, 00. **MEMBERSHIPS** Coun for Exceptional C. **RESEARCH** Professional collaboration, selection of technology for students with disabilities. **SELECTED PUBLICATIONS** Coauth, Cooperative teaching: Rebuilding the schoolhouse for all students, PRO-ED (Austin, TX), 95; coauth, "Degree of involvement in young children with cerebral palsy," Phys Disabilities: Educ and Related Serv 14-2 (96): 33-59; coauth, "Let us not talk falsely now, for the hour is getting late: An acknowledgement of Realpolitik," Phys Disabilities: Educ and Related Serv 15-1 (96): 7-11; coauth, "Family-centered assistive technology assessment," Intervention in Sch and Clinic 32 (96): 104-112; coauth, "Cooperative teaching: Pictures of possibilities," Intervention in Sch and Clinic 33 (97): 81-85, 89; coauth, "Family and cultural alert! Consideration in assistive technology assessment," Teaching Exceptional C 30 (97): 40-44; coauth, "Family issues and assistive technology needs: A sampling of state practices," J of Special Educ Technol 13 (97): 27-43; coauth, "Women at the top: Why are so few women in university administration?," Nat Soc Sci J 9 (98): 37-44; coauth, "The importance of structured computer experiences for young children with and without disabilities," J of Early Childhood Educ (in press); coauth, "The importance of training in assistive technology for parents of students with disabilities," Special Educ Technol Practice (in press). **CONTACT ADDRESS** Dept Teacher Educ, Boise State Univ, 1910 Univ Dr, Boise, ID 83725-0399. **EMAIL** jhourca@boisestate.edu

HOUSE, JAMES S.
PERSONAL Born 01/27/1944, Philadelphia, PA, m, 2 children **DISCIPLINE** SOCIOLOGY **EDUCATION** Havermont Col, BA, 65; Univ Mich, PhD, 72. **CAREER** Instr to assoc prof, Duke Univ, 70-78; assoc res sci, assoc prof, Univ Michigan, 78-82; prof, 82-; ch, 86-90; dir, 91-. **HONORS AND AWARDS** Guggenheim Fel; Elect Mem, SRA; Elect Mem, AAAS; Elect Mem, AAAS; Elect Mem, IMNAS. **MEMBERSHIPS** ABMR; ASA; SPSSI; SER. **RESEARCH** Social psychology; social structure and personality; psychosocial factors and health; aging and health. **SELECTED PUBLICATIONS** Coauth, "SES differentials in health by age and alternative indicators of SES," J Aging Health 8 (96): 359-388; coauth, "Income dynamics and adult mortality in the US, 1972-1989," Am J Pub Health 87(97): 1476-1483; coauth, "Socioeconomic factors, health behaviors, and mortality: Results from a nationally-representative prospective study of US adults," J Am Med Asn 279 (98):1703-1708; coauth, "Gender and the socioeconomic Gradient in Mortality," J Health Soc Behav 40 (99): 17-31; coauth, "Volunteering and Mortality Among Older Adults: Findings From a National Sample," J Geron Soc Sci 54 (99): 173-180; coauth, "Socioeconomic inequalities in health: Integrating individual-, community-, and societal-level theory and research," in Handbook of Social Studies in Health and Medicine, eds. Gary Albrecht, Ray Fitzpatrick, Susan Scrimshaw (London: Sage Pub, 00); coauth, "Socioeconomic Inequalities in Health: An Enduring Sociological Problem," in Handbook of Medical Sociology, eds. Chioc Bird, Peter Conrad, Alan Fremont (Upper Saddle River, NJ: Prentice Hall, 00). **CONTACT ADDRESS** Dept Sociology, Univ of Michigan, Ann Arbor, 500 South State St, Ann Arbor, MI 48109. **EMAIL** jimhouse@umich.edu

HOVANEC, EVELYN ANN
PERSONAL Born 12/23/1937, Uniontown, PA **DISCIPLINE** ENGLISH, FOLKLORE, HISTORY AND LORE OF COAL MINERS **EDUCATION** Duquesne Univ, BEd, 62, MA, 66; Univ Pittsburgh, PhD, 73. **CAREER** Teacher social studies & English, Pittsburgh pub jr high schs, 62-66; ASSOC prof English, PA State Univ, Fayette, 66-85 and 92-00, dir Acad Aff, PA State, McKeesport 85-92. **HONORS AND AWARDS** PSF Awd for Pub Svc, 94; PSM Awd for Svc, 89; PSF Awd for Teach Excel, 97; PSF Min Stu Org Fac Awd, 98. **MEMBERSHIPS** Nat Coun Teachers English; Col English Asn; MLA. **RESEARCH** Mining literature and lore; mythology; Henry James. **SELECTED PUBLICATIONS** Auth, 3 poems, Earth & You, 72; coauth, Making the humanities human, WVa Rev Educ Res, fall 73; auth, Horses of the Sun (2 poems), In: Cathedral Poets II, Boxwood, 76; coauth, Patch/Work Voices: The Culture & Lore of a Mining People, Harry Hoffman, 77; auth, Coal culture & communities, Pa Oral Hist Newslett, 77; The Sea (poem), In: Strawberry Saxifrage, Nat Soc Publ Poets, 77; coauth, Making the Humanities Human, West VA Review of Educ Res 1, 46-47, 73; auth, A Mythological Approach to Tomorrow, Assoc of Teach Educ Review 3, 78; auth, Reader's Guide to Coal Mining Fiction and Selected Prose Narratives, Bul of Biblio, 41-57, Sept, 86; auth, Marie Belloc Lowndes, An Encyclopedia of British Women Writers, Garland, 297-298, 88. **CONTACT ADDRESS** Pennsylvania State Univ, Fayette, PO Box 519, Uniontown, PA 15401-0519. **EMAIL** eah2@psu.edu

HOVENDICK, KELLY B.
PERSONAL Born 12/18/1970, Hanover, PA, m, 1996, 1 child **DISCIPLINE** HISTORY; ANTHROPOLOGY; LIBRARY SCIENCE **EDUCATION** E NM Univ, BS, 94; Univ Az, MA, 99. **MEMBERSHIPS** Amer Libr Assoc **RESEARCH** Gender & libr sci; technophobia. **CONTACT ADDRESS** E.S. Bird Libr, Syracuse Univ, Reference Dept, Room 210, Syracuse, NY 13244-2010. **EMAIL** kbhovend@library.syr.edu

HOVEY, JOSEPH
PERSONAL Born 10/16/1963, Los Angeles, CA, s **DISCIPLINE** PSYCHOLOGY **EDUCATION** Univ Calif, BA, 89; Univ Mich, MA, 93; PhD, 97. **CAREER** Instr and clinical In-

ternship, Univ Mich, 92-97; Psychotherapist, Univ Toledo, 97-; Lecturer, Univ Mich, 00-; Asst Prof, Univ Toledo, 97-. **HONORS AND AWARDS** Who's Who in Am: 2001; Who's Who in Sci and Engineering: 2000-2001; Intl Biographical Ctr 2000 Outstanding Scientists of the 20th Century. **MEMBERSHIPS** Intl Asn for Suicide prevention, Soc for the Psychol Study of ethnic Minority Issues, Am Asn of suicidology, Am foundation for Suicide Prevention, The Migrant clinicians network, Am Psychol Asn. **RESEARCH** Depression and suicide among immigrants; Acculturative stress and mental health; Psychological functioning of migrant farmworkers; suicide prevention within the community; Attitudes towards immigration; ethnic identity and discrimination. **SELECTED PUBLICATIONS** Auth, "Acculturative stress, depression, and suicidal ideation among Mexican immigrants," cultural Diversity and Ethnic Minority psychology, 00; auth, "Acculturative stress, depression, and suicidal ideation among Central American immigrants," suicide and Life-Threatening Behavior, 00; auth, "Proposition 187 reexamined: Attitudes toward immigration among California voters," current Psychology, 00; auth, "Psychosocial predictors of acculturative stress in Mexican immigrants," The Journal of Psychology, 00; auth, "Acculturative stress, anxiety, and depression among Mexican immigrant farmworkers in the Midwest United States," Journal of Immigrant Health, 00; auth, "Psychosocial predictors of depression among Central American immigrants," Psychological Reports, 00; auth, "Psychosocial predictors of acculturative stress in Central American immigrants," Journal of Immigrant Health, Vol I, (99): 187-194; auth, "The moderating influence of social support on suicidal ideation in a sample of Mexican immigrants," Psychological Reports, (99): 78-79; auth, "Religion and suicidal ideation in a sample of Latin American immigrants," psychological Reports, (99): 171-177; auth, "Acculturative stress, depression, and suicidal ideation among Mexican-American adolescents: Implications for the development of suicide prevention programs in schools," psychological Reports, (98): 249-250. **CONTACT ADDRESS** Dept Psychol, Univ of Toledo, 2801 W Bancroft St, Toledo, OH 43606. **EMAIL** jhovey@utoledo.edu

HOWARD, JOHN ROBERT
PERSONAL Born 01/24/1933, Boston, MA, m **DISCIPLINE** SOCIOLOGY **EDUCATION** Brandeis Univ, BA 1955; NYork Univ, MA 1961; Stanford Univ, PhD 1965; J Du Pace Univ 1985. **CAREER** Univ of OR, asst prof, 65-68; Rutgers Univ, assoc prof, 69-71; State Univ of NY, dean & prof, 71-80, State Univ of NY, prof of sociology, 71-; atty in private practice, 86-. **HONORS AND AWARDS** Publ Lifestyles in the Black, WW Norton 1969; The Cutting Edge, J B Lippincott Publ 1974; Urban Black Politics, Annals of the Am Acad 1978; various articles. **MEMBERSHIPS** Bd mem United Way of Westchester 1976-78; bd of advs Inst for Urban Design 1978-; vice pres Soc for the Study of Social Problems 1978-79; bd mem Street Theater Inc 1978-80; bd Friends of the Nueberger Museum 1982-85. **CONTACT ADDRESS** Sociology Dept, SUNY, Col at Purchase, Lincoln Ave, Purchase, NY 10577.

HOWELL, J. SUSAN
PERSONAL Born 08/07/1962, Evansville, IN, m, 1982, 2 children **DISCIPLINE** SOCIOLOGY **EDUCATION** Cammpbellsville Col, BS, 82; Univ Louisville, MeD, 88; EdD, 95. **CAREER** Asst prof, Austin Peay State Univ, 93-94; adj prof, 94-95; asst prof, 95-99; assoc prof, Campbellsville Univ, 99-. **MEMBERSHIPS** APA. **RESEARCH** Children of divorce; psychology of religion. **SELECTED PUBLICATIONS** Coauth, "Family functions and children's postdivorce adjustment," Am J Orthopsychiatry (92): 613-617; coauth, "The effect of pre-group training on members' level of anxiety," J Spec Group Work (93): 109-114; coauth, "Assessing the effect of live theater on adolescents' attitudes toward pregnancy," Intl J Cog Edu Media (93):122-131; coauth, "Gender and age differences in child adjustment to parental separation," J Div Remarr 27 (97): 141-158. **CONTACT ADDRESS** Dept Social Science, Campbellsville Univ, Campbellsville, KY 42718. **EMAIL** showell@campbellsvil.edu

HRABOWSKI, FREEMAN ALPHONSA, III
PERSONAL Born 08/13/1950, Birmingham, AL, m, 1 child **DISCIPLINE** EDUCATION **EDUCATION** Hampton Inst, BA 1970; Univ of IL, MA 1971, PhD 1975. **CAREER** Univ of IL at Urbana-Champaign, math instr, 72-73, admin intern, 73-74, asst dean, 74-76; AL A&M Univ Normal, assoc dean, 76-77; Coppin State Coll Baltimore, dean arts & scis div, 77-81, vice pres academic affairs, 81-87; Univ of MD, Baltimore County, vice provost, 87-90, exec vice president, 90-92, interim pres, 92-93; Univ of Maryland, Catonville, pres, 93-. **HONORS AND AWARDS** Scholarship for Study Abroad Amer Univ Cairo Egypt 1968-69; Phi Delta Kappa, Univ of IL at Urbana-Champaign 1971; Outstanding Alumni Awd, Hampton Univ, Baltimore Chapter; Outstanding Community Service Awd, Tuskegee Univ. **MEMBERSHIPS** Alpha Phi Alpha; Hampton Inst, sr class pres, 1969-70; bd of trustees; evaluator, Middle States Assn of Coll and Schools; Baltimore Equitable Society; Unity of MD Medical Systems; bd mem: Amer Coun on Educ, Baltimore Gas & Electric Co, Baltimore Comm Foundation, Ctr Stage, Greater Baltimore Comm, Joint Ctr for Political & Economic Development, McCormick & Co, Mercantile Safe Deposit & Trust Co, Merrick & France Foundation, Maryland High-Technology Coun.; American Assoc of Colleges & Universities, Citizen's Scholarship Foundation of America, Education Commission of the States. **SELECTED PUBLICATIONS** Co-author, Beating the Odds, 1998. **CONTACT ADDRESS** Univ of Maryland, Baltimore County, 1000 Hilltop Circle, Baltimore, MD 21250. **EMAIL** hrabowski@umbc.edu

HUACO, GEORGE
PERSONAL Born 12/21/1927, Oakland, CA, m, 1978, 2 children **DISCIPLINE** SOCIOLOGY **EDUCATION** Univ Calif, Berkeley, BA, 54; PhD, 63; Univ Calif, Los Angeles, MA, 59. **CAREER** Asst prof, Yale Univ, 63-69; assoc prof, SUNY Buffalo, 69-71; prof, Univ New Mexico, 71-. **RESEARCH** Marx, sociobiology, sociology of high culture, sociological theory. **SELECTED PUBLICATIONS** Auth, The Sociology of Film Art, NY Basic Books (65), Japanese trans, Tokio: Yuhikaku Ltd (85); auth, "On Ideology," ACTA Sociologica, Civ. No. 4, Helsinki, Finland (71); auth, "Ideology and Literature," New Literary Hist, IV, Univ VA (72-73); auth, "Review Essay of Alexander Cockburn, 'Idle Passion: Chess and the Dance of Death," The Sociol Quart 17 (winter 76); auth, "The Novel and Novelists of the Mexican Revolution," Humboldt J of Social Relations, V, No. 2 (spring/summer 78); auth, "Toward a Sociology of Western Philosophy," in Henrika Kuklick and Elizabeth Long, eds, Knowledge and Society: Studies in the Sociology of Culture, JAI Press Vol. 5 (84); auth, "Ideology and General Theory: The Case of Sociological Functionalism," Comparative Studies in Society and History 28:1 (Jan 86); auth, Marx and Sociobiology, U. P. A. (99). **CONTACT ADDRESS** Dept Sociol, Univ of New Mexico, Albuquerque, SSCI-1072, Albuquerque, NM 87131-0001. **EMAIL** georgeh@unm.edu

HUANG, ZHEN
PERSONAL Born 12/21/1951, Shanghai, China, m, 1986, 1 child **DISCIPLINE** LANGUAGE EDUCATION **EDUCATION** East China Normal Univ, BA, 76; MA, 82; Hofstra Univ, PhD, 91. **CAREER** Lecturer, East China Normal Univ, 78-86; Adj Instructor, Hofstra Univ, 88-90; Instructor to Assoc Prof, Suffolk Cmty Col, 90-. **HONORS AND AWARDS** Intl Who's Who of Prof Educators, 00; Who's Who Among Asian Am, 95-96. **MEMBERSHIPS** Intl Reading Asn. **RESEARCH** Language Acquisition and Language Learning; Learning Processes and Theories. **CONTACT ADDRESS** Dept Reading, Suffolk County Comm Col, Ammerman, 533 Col Rd, Selden, NY 11784-2851. **EMAIL** huangz@sunysuffolk.com

HUBER, R. JOHN
PERSONAL Born 10/26/1940, Cleveland, OH, m, 1966, 3 children **DISCIPLINE** PSYCHOLOGY **EDUCATION** Kent State Univ, BA, 62; Univ Vt, MA, 65; Univ NN, PhD, 70. **CAREER** Inst SUNY Plattsburgh, 65-67; Asst Prof, Skidmore Col, 70-74; Assoc Prof, Prof, Chair, Meredith Col, 74-. **HONORS AND AWARDS** Danforth Fel. **MEMBERSHIPS** Am Psychol Asn, Eastern Psychol Asn, N Am Soc for Adlerian Psychology, Am Psychol Soc. **RESEARCH** Personality theory Cadler - Emphatic and Co-operative behavior, History of psychology. **SELECTED PUBLICATIONS** Coauth, Cornerstones of Psychology; Publ in J of Individual Psychology. **CONTACT ADDRESS** Dept Psychology, Meredith Col, 3800 Hillsborough St, Raleigh, NC 27067. **EMAIL** hubertj@meredith.edu

HUBER, TONYA
PERSONAL Born 02/28/2958, Lackawanna, NY **DISCIPLINE** EDUCATION **EDUCATION** Altoon Campus, LAS, 79; Pa State Univ, BS, 82; MEd, 85; PhD, 90. **CAREER** Assoc prof, Wichita State Univ, 90-. **HONORS AND AWARDS** Howard Soule Grad Fel, Phi Delta Kappa, 89; Excellence in Teaching Awd, Wichita State Univ, 94; Serv Awd, Nat Asn for Multicultural Educ, 90-98. **MEMBERSHIPS** Am Educ Res Assoc; Assoc of Teacher Educ; Holmes Partnership; Nat Assoc of Multicultural Educ; Phi Kappa Phi. **RESEARCH** Educational Equity, Interracial Relationships, Cultural Foundations in Education. **SELECTED PUBLICATIONS** Auth, Teaching in the diverse classroom: Learner-centered activities that work, Nat Educ Serv, (Bloomington, IN), 93; coauth, "We are all related": COE and community collaboration to explore Native American Contributions to this World", Assoc of Teacher Educators, 94; auth, "The Underlying assumptions of a teacher preparation program for diverse student populations: A call for the return to American Expectations of Democracy", Assoc of Teacher Educators, (94): auth, "Social and Multicultural Foundations of Education, Wichita State University, a program review", Making connections between multicultural and global education; Teacher educators and teacher education programs, AACTE, (Washington, DC, 96): 102-103; coauth, "From traditional teacher education to culturally responsible pedagogy: Moving a graveyard", Meeting the Challenge of Diversity in Teacher Education, ed J.E. King, SUNY Pr, (NY, 97): 129-145; auth, "Of pigs and wolves at the OK Corral: Or the merging alternative paradigm and the Construction of Knowledge", Annual Editions Multicultural Education 97/98, ed F. Schultz, Dushkin/McGraw-Hill, (97): 56-59; auth, "Grahame Greene", Billy Mills", Elizabeth W. Peratrovich", Magills Choice: American Indian biographies, Salem Pr, (Pasadena, CA), 99; auth, Multicultural planning to maximize learning: Creating quality learning experiences (QLEs), Caddo Gap Pr, (San Francisco, CA) 00. **CONTACT ADDRESS** Dept Curric and Instr, Wichita State Univ, 1845 Fairmount St, Wichita, KS 67260-0001. **EMAIL** huber@twsu.edu

HUBERTY, CARL J.
PERSONAL Born 11/14/1934, Lena, WI, m, 1966, 4 children **DISCIPLINE** EDUCATIONAL PSYCHOLOGY **EDUCATION** Univ Wisc, Stevens Point, BS, 56, Madison, MS, 58; Univ Iowa, PhD, 69. **CAREER** High school math teacher, 56-64; asst prof, Univ Wisc, Oshkosh, 65-66; asst prof, Univ Ga, 69-2000. **HONORS AND AWARDS** Outstanding student-athlete, Wisc State Univ-Stevens Point, 56; Certificate for participation, GERA, 89; Certificate, Evaluation Trainer for Ga SDOE, 89; col nominee for Univ System Regents prof, 90; col nominee for UGA Res Prof, 91, 92; Outstanding Alumnus, Sch of Ed, Univ Wisc-Stevens Point, 95; Nominee for Fel of the Am Statistical Asn, 95, 95; Int Man of the Year, Int Biographical Centre, Cambridge, England, 98, 99; UGA Col of Ed Fac Res Awd, 98; Int Man of the Millenium, 99; Outstanding People of the 20th Century, 99; Fel, Nat Acad for Ed Res, 99; Outstanding Intellectual of the 20th Century, 99, 2000; Outstanding Scholar of the 20th Century, 99. **MEMBERSHIPS** ASA, AERA. **RESEARCH** Multivariate methods, project evaluation. **SELECTED PUBLICATIONS** Auth, Applied Discriminate Analysis, New York: Wiley (94, 95, 98); coauth with S. O. Olejnik, J. Li, and S. Supattathum, "Multiple testing and statistical power with modified Bonferroni procedures," J of Behav and Ed Statistics, 22 (97): 389-406; coauth with R. W. Kamphaus, C. DiStephano, and M. D. Petoskey, "A typology of teacher rated child behavior for a national U. S. sample," J of Abnormal Child Psychology, 25 (97): 453-463; coauth with L. L. Lowman, "Discriminate analysis in higher education research," in J. C. Smart, ed, Higher education: Handbook of theory and research, vol XIII, New York: Agathon Press (98); coauth with E. J. Davis, "Evaluation of a state critical thinking skills training program," Studies in Ed Evaluation, 24 (98): 45-69; coauth with H. J. Keselman, L. Lix, S. Olejnik, R. A. Cribbie, B. Donahue, R. K. Kowalchuk, L. L. Lowman, M. D. Petroskey, J. C. Kelelman, and J. R. Levin, "Statistical practices of educational researchers: An analysis of their ANOVA, MANOVA, and ANCOVA Analyses," Rev of Ed Res, 68 (98): 350-386; coauth with C. J. Pike, "On some history regarding statistical testing," in B. Thompson, ed, Advances in social science methodology, vol 5, Greenwich, CT: JAI Press (99); coauth with M. D. Petoskey, "Use of multiple correlation analysis and multiple regression analysis," J of Vocational Ed Res, 24 (99): 15-43; coauth with R. W. Kamphaus, M. D. Petoskey, A. H. Cody, E. W. Rowe, and C. R. Reynolds, "A typology of parent rated child behavior for a national U. S. sample," The J of Child Psychology and Psychiatry, 40 (99): 607-616; coauth with M. D. Petoskey, "Multi variate analysis of variance and covariance," in H. E. A. Tinsley & S. D. Brown, eds, Handbook of applied multi variate statistics and mathematical modeling," New York: Academic Press (2000); auth, "Judgement in quantitative research," The Mathematics Educator, 10 (2000): 5-10. **CONTACT ADDRESS** Dept ed Psych, Univ of Georgia, 325 Aderhold Hall, Athens, GA 30602-7343. **EMAIL** chuberty@coe.uga.edu

HUDAK, THOMAS JOHN
PERSONAL Born 01/31/1945, South Bend, IN **DISCIPLINE** ANTHROPOLOGY **EDUCATION** Univ Wis-Madison, BA, 67; MA, 74; Univ Mich, PhD, 81. **CAREER** Asst prof, Univ Ky, 81-88; assoc prof, prof, Ariz State Univ, 88-. **HONORS AND AWARDS** Fulbright Gnt; NSF Gnt. **MEMBERSHIPS** AAS; AOS; Siam Soc; TESOL. **RESEARCH** Languages and literatures of Southeast Asia, esp Thai and Indonesia. **SELECTED PUBLICATIONS** Ed, William J GedneyÛs Central Thai Dialects: Glossaries, Texts, and Translations, Michigan Papers on South and Southeast Asia 43 (Ann Arbor: Cen South and Southeast Asian Studies, Univ Mich), 95; ed, William J GedneyÛs The Lue Language: Glossaries, Texts, and Translations, Michigan Papers on South and Southeast Asia 44 (Ann Arbor: Cen South and Southeast Asian Studies, Univ Mich), 96; ed, William J GedneyÛs Tai Dialect Studies: Glossaries, Texts, and Translations, Michigan Papers on South and Southeast Asia 45 (Ann Arbor: Cen South and Southeast Asian Studies, Univ Mich), 97; ed, William J GedneyÛs Thai and Indie Literary Studies, Michigan Papers on South and Southeast Asia 46 (Ann Arbor: Cen South and Southeast Asian Studies, Univ Mich), 97; ed, Kam-English Dictionary, Prog Southeast Asian Stud (Tempe, AZ, AZ State Univ) 99. **CONTACT ADDRESS** Dept Anthropology, Arizona State Univ, PO Box 872402, Tempe, AZ 85287. **EMAIL** thomas.hudak@asu.edu

HUDSON, CHARLES M.
PERSONAL Born 12/24/1932, Monterey, KY, m, 1968, 2 children **DISCIPLINE** ANTHROPOLOGY **EDUCATION** Univ Kentucky, AB, 59; Univ N Carolina, PhD, 65. **CAREER** Asst prof, 64-68, assoc prof, 68-77, prof, 77-93, Franklin Prof, 93-, Univ Georgia, 64- . **HONORS AND AWARDS** GA Gov Awd in Hum, 88; James Mooney Awd, 91; Rembert W Patrick Awd, 94. **MEMBERSHIPS** Am Anthrop Asn; Am Soc Ethnohistory. **RESEARCH** Culture and history of the native people of the Southeastern US. **SELECTED PUBLICATIONS** Auth, Hudson, Charles, The Catawba Nation, Athens: University of Georgia Press, 70; auth, Hill, Jr., Samuel S., with Edgar T. Thompson, Ann Firor Scott, Charles Hudson, and Edwin S. Gaustad, 72, Religion and the Solid South, Nashville, New York: Abingdon Press; ed, Hudson, Charles, 75, Four Centuries of Southern Indians, Athens: University of Georgia Press; auth, Hudson, Charles, The Southeastern Indians, Knoxville: University of Tennessee Press, 76; ed, Hudson, Charles, Black Drink:

A Native American Tea, Athens: University of Georgia Press, 79; ed, Hudson, Charles, Ethnology of the Southeastern Indians: A Sourcebook, New York: Garland Publishing, Inc., 85; auth, Hudson, Charles, The Juan Pardo Expeditions: Exploration of the Carolinas and Tennessee, 1566-1568, with Documents Relating to the Pardo Expeditions Transcribed, Translated and Annotated by Paul E. Hoffman, Washington, D.C.: Smithsonian Institution Press, 90; auth, Milanich, Jerald and Charles Hudson, Hernando de Soto and the Indians of Florida, Gainesville: University Press of Florida, 93; ed, Hudson, Charles and Carmen Chaves Tesser, The Forgotten Centuries: Indians and Europeans in the American South, 1521-1704, Athens: University of Georgia Press, 94; auth, Hudson, Charles, Knights of Spain, Warriors of the Sun: Hernando de Soto and the South's Ancient Chiefdoms, Athens: University of Georgia Press, 97. **CONTACT ADDRESS** Dept of Anthropology, Franklin Col of Arts and Sciences, 250A Baldwin Hall, Jackson St., Athens, GA 30602-1619. **EMAIL** anthro@arches.uga.edu

HUDSON, CHRISTOPHER G.
PERSONAL Born 06/24/1949, Casper, WY, m, 1984, 2 children **DISCIPLINE** SOCIAL WORK **EDUCATION** Univ Chicago, BA, 72; MA, 74; Univ Ill, PhD, 83. **CAREER** Soc planner, Goldenrod Hills Comity Action Coun, 70-71; psych soc worker, NE Cmty Hosp, 74-75; soc worker, Bd of Educ Chicago, 75-76; Clinic soc worker, Jewish Fam and Cmty Service, 77-80; instr, Univ Ill, 80-82; asst prof, George Williams col, 83-86; asst prof, E Carolina Univ, 87; assoc prof to prof, Salem State Col, 87-. **HONORS AND AWARDS** Res of the Year Awd, Nat all for the Mentally ill of Mass, 99; Acad and Sch Achievement, Sale Col, 91; Who's Who Among Human Service Profess, 92-93; Fel, Nat Inst of Mental Health, 80-82. **MEMBERSHIPS** Nat Asn of Soc Workers, NE Mental Health Bd, Alliance for the Mentally Ill, Acad of Cert Soc Workers, Coun on Soc Work Educ. **RESEARCH** Mental health policy and financing, Homelessness, Managed care, Complex systems theory, Program evaluation. **SELECTED PUBLICATIONS** Auth, Dimensions of state Mental Health Policy, Praeger: New York, 90; auth, an Interdependency Model of Homelessness: The Dynamics of Social Disintegration, Edwin Mellen Press: Lewiston, 98; auth, "Estimating Homeless Populations through Structural Equation Modeling," Journal of Sociology and Social Welfare, (98): 136-154; auth, "At the Edge of Chaos: A New Paradigm for Social Work?", Journal of Social Work Education, (in press); auth, "System Reform in Public Mental Health: The Massachusetts Experience," Managed Care in Human Services, (99); auth, "Review of: From Poorhouses to Homelessness by David Rochefort," Health Affairs, (98): 239-240. **CONTACT ADDRESS** School of Soc Work, Salem State Col, 352 Lafayette St, Salem, MA 01970. **EMAIL** cghudson@mediaone.net

HUDSON, JAMES BLAINE, III
PERSONAL Born 09/08/1949, Louisville, KY, m **DISCIPLINE** EDUCATION **EDUCATION** Univ of Louisville, BS 1974, MEd 1975; Univ of Ky, EdD 1981. **CAREER** School of Educ Univ of Louisville, admin coord, 74-75; West Louisville Educ Prog Univ of Louisville, admin coord, 75-77, asst dir, 77-80, dir, 80-82; Univ of Louisville, assoc dir; Univ of Louisville Preparatory Div, assoc dir, 82-92; asst prof, Pan-African Studies, University of Louisville, 92-97; assoc prof, 98-; chair, Pan African Studies, 98-; assoc dean, 99-. **HONORS AND AWARDS** Nat Merit Schlar 1967; Haggin Fel Univ of K 1977-78; Black Fac/Staff Mem of the year, Univ of Louisville, 1982. **MEMBERSHIPS** Mem APGA, KPGA, ACPA 1976-; MENSA 1984-. **RESEARCH** African American history; education; race. **CONTACT ADDRESS** Pan-African Studies, Univ of Louisville, Louisville, KY 40292. **EMAIL** jbhuds01@gwise.louisville.edu

HUFF, DELORES J.
PERSONAL Born 05/27/1934, New York, NY, d, 2 children **DISCIPLINE** AMERICAN INDIAN EDUCATION, SOCIAL POLICY **EDUCATION** Tufts Univ, BA, 72; MA, 73; Harvard Univ, EdD, 78. **CAREER** Dir of Educ, Boston Indian Center, 69-73; principle, Pierre Indian Learning Center, 75-77; prof, San Diego State Univ, 77-78; prof, Chico State Univ, 78-85; prof, Calif State Univ at Fresno, 85-. **HONORS AND AWARDS** Whitney Fel, 70; Univ Calif, Los Angeles, post doctoral fel, 84; teaching excellence Awd, Calif State Univ at Fresno, 97; delegate, White House Conf on Indian Educ. **MEMBERSHIPS** Nat Indian Educ Asn, Calif Indian Educ Asn. **RESEARCH** Educational planning & economic development. **SELECTED PUBLICATIONS** Auth, A Thumbnail Sketch of American Indian History, Calif State Univ at Chico, 82; auth, The Tribal Ethic. The Protestant Ethic and American Indian Economic Development, UCLA Indian Studies Res Center, 87; auth, "Indian Brand, White Image," The Pygmalion Effect on Indian Education, Univ of Genoa, 92; auth, "J. Edgar Hoover and the Indians," European J of Am Indian Studies (93); auth, "On Becoming a Mensch or a Mentor," Teaching in a Multicultural University, Sage Pub, 94; auth, "Wilma Mankiller. The Unforeseen Legacy of the Federal Indian Relocation Program," Women in American Indian Culture, Possao Univ Press (Opporto, Portugal), 96; auth, "To Live Heroically--Institutional Racism and American Indian Education, SUNY Press (97). **CONTACT ADDRESS** Dept Ethnic Studies, California State Univ, Fresno, 2225 E San Ramon Ave, Fresno, CA 93740-8029.

HUFF, TOBY E.
PERSONAL Born 04/24/1942, Portland, ME, m, 1989, 2 children **DISCIPLINE** SOCIOLOGY **EDUCATION** NE Univ, AB, 65; Northwestern U, MA, 67; New Sch for Soc Res, PhD, 71. **CAREER** Asst to full Prof, 71, 81, Univ Mass, Dartmouth; Founder & Dir, Ctr for Policy Analysis, Univ Mass, 84-86; Chancellor Prof, 9/98. **HONORS AND AWARDS** Postdoc Fellow at Univ Calif Berkeley, 76-77; Inst for Adv Stud, Princeton, 78-79. **MEMBERSHIPS** Am Sociol Asn; Hist of Sci Soc; Mid E Stud Asn; Int Soc for Comp Stud of Civilization. **RESEARCH** Comparative historical sociology; science in the Muslim world; women in the Islamic world; comp sociology of law; Globalization and the Internet. **SELECTED PUBLICATIONS** Ed, On the Road to Modernity: Conscience, Science and Civilizations, Rowman & Littlefield, 81; auth, Max Weber and the Methodology of the Social Sciences, Transaction Books, 84; auth, The Rise of Early Modern Science: Islam, China, and the West, Cambridge Univ Press, 93, 95; auth, Science and the Public Sphere: Comparative Institutional Developments in Islam and the West, Soc Epistem, A J of Knowledge, Cult, and Soc Policy, 11:1, 25-27, 97; co-ed, Max Weber and Islam, Transaction Books, 98. **CONTACT ADDRESS** Dept Sociol & Anthrop, Univ of Massachusetts, Dartmouth, 285 Old Westport Rd, North Dartmouth, MA 02747-2350. **EMAIL** thuff@umassd.edu

HUGHES, CARL D.
PERSONAL Born Indianapolis, IN, m **DISCIPLINE** EDUCATION **EDUCATION** WV State Coll Inst, BS 1942; Wharton Sch of Finance Univ of PA, MA 1943; Christian Theol Sem, BD 1957; Christian Theol Sem, MA 1958; Centrl Bapt Theol Semin of IN, DD 1975; Christian Theol Sem, MDiv 1972; IN Univ Sch of Law Wayne State Univ & Univ of Detroit, Post Grad Studies. **CAREER** Mt Zion Bapt Ch Indianapolis, ministers asst, 52; Second Bapt Ch Lafayette, 52-56; St John Missionary Bapt Ch, 56-60; Christian Educ Met Bapt Ch Detroit, dir, 60-61; Bethel Bapt Ch East Detroit, pastor, 61; Hughes Enterprise Inc, vice pres treas; Detroit Christian Training Cntr, former dean; Bus Educ Detroit Pub Sch, former tchr; Ch Bldr & Bus Educ Detroit Pub Sch, dept hd; Calvary Dist Assn Detroit, former instr; Wolverine State Conv SS & BTU Cong MI, former instr; Nat Bapt SS & BTU Congress, former instr; Central Bible Sem, former instr. **HONORS AND AWARDS** Received First John L Webb Awd Nat Bapt Conv 1948; **MEMBERSHIPS** Membership com YMCA; membership Com NAACP; former mem Grand Bd Dir Kappa Alpha Psi Nat Coll Frat; Mason; budget com Nat Negro Bus League; treas StEmma Military Acad Parent Assn of Detroit; chmn bd of trustees Todd-Phillips Children Home of the Wolverine State Missionary Bapt Conv Inc; chmn of Finance Pastors' Div of the Nat Bapt Congress of Christian Edn. **SELECTED PUBLICATIONS** Auth, The Church Orgnzd For A Meaning Ministry; Financing the Local Church Property. **CONTACT ADDRESS** Bethel Baptist Church East, 5715-33 Holcomb, Detroit, MI 48213.

HUGHES, KATHY L.
PERSONAL Born 02/12/1953, Jenkins, KY, s **DISCIPLINE** SOCIOLOGY **EDUCATION** Morehead State Univ, BSW, 76; MA, 77. **CAREER** Assoc prof, Henderson Community Col, 77-. **HONORS AND AWARDS** Teacher of the Year Awd, Pi Gamma Mu. **MEMBERSHIPS** Pi Gamma Mu. **CONTACT ADDRESS** Dept Soc and Behav Sci, Henderson Community Col, 2660 S Green St, Henderson, KY 42420. **EMAIL** kathy.hughes@kctcs.net

HUMBLE, JEANNE
PERSONAL Born 10/07/1947, Lexington, KY, d **DISCIPLINE** SOCIOLOGY **EDUCATION** Univ Ky, MA, 70; PhD, 84. **CAREER** Assoc Prof, Lexington Cmty Col, 90-. **HONORS AND AWARDS** Nat Sci Foundation Grad Fel, 67-70; Outstanding Sociol Grad, 67. **MEMBERSHIPS** ASA; SSS; ASK. **RESEARCH** Medical Sociology and Cultural Anthropology. **CONTACT ADDRESS** Dept Soc Sci, Lexington Comm Col, Oswald Bldg, Lexington, KY 40506-0235. **EMAIL** jshumb1@pop.uky.edu

HUME, WENDELIN M.
PERSONAL Born 02/04/1961, St Louis Park, MN, m, 1980, 3 children **DISCIPLINE** SOCIOLOGY, CRIMINAL JUSTICE **EDUCATION** Black Hills State Col, BS, 87; Sam Houston State Univ, MA, 91; PhD, 00. **CAREER** Teaching Asst, Sam Houston State Univ, 87-88; Asst Prof, Univ ND, 91-. **HONORS AND AWARDS** Outstanding Academic Book Awd, Encycl of Am Prisons; Who's Who Among Am Teachers, 96-98. **MEMBERSHIPS** Midwestern Criminal Justice Assoc, Assoc of Am Indian and Alaska Native Profs, Drug Policy Found. **RESEARCH** Victimization issues, gender equity, native American crime issues, drug laws. **SELECTED PUBLICATIONS** Auth, "1988 Texas Crime Poll Report on Experience with and Performance of the Texas Criminal Justice System," Survey Res Prog (88); auth, "1989 Texas Crime Poll Report," Survey Res Prog (89); coauth, Texas Jails: Law and Practice, Sam Houston Pr (Huntsville, TX), 90; coauth, "Texas Crime Poll Report," Survey Res Prog (91); coauth, Texas Juvenile Law and Practice, Sam Houston Pr (Huntsville, TX), 91; auth, "A Difference in Perceptions: The Final Report of the North Dakota Commission on Gender Fairness in the Courts," North Dakota Law Rev, vol 72, no 4 (96): 1112-1344; auth, "The Reliability of Drug testing," New Frontiers in Drug Policy (91): 317-322; auth, "Change Name for a Better Atmosphere," Grand Forks Herald, p 2b (97); auth, "The Interstate Compact Agreement," The Encycl of Am Prisons, Garland Publ Co, 96. **CONTACT ADDRESS** Dept Sociol, Univ of No Dakota, PO Box 8050, Grand Forks, ND 58202-8050. **EMAIL** whume@badlands.nodak.edu

HUNNICUTT, BENJAMIN K.
DISCIPLINE PHYSICAL EDUCATION **EDUCATION** Univ NC, BA, 67; MA, 72; PhD, 76. **CAREER** Asst Prof to Full Prof, Univ Iowa, 75-. **HONORS AND AWARDS** Men of Achievement 16th ed., Cambridge England; Intl Authors and Writers Who's Who 93-99; Carol E. Gordon and Mary Lou Enberg Distinguished Lecturer, Wash State Univ, 94; Old Gold Fel, Univ Iowa, 79. **MEMBERSHIPS** NRPA, Am Asn for State and Local History, Soc for the Reduction of Human Labor, SPRE, NTRS, Org of Am Historians, Iowa Parks and Rec Asn, Intl Platform Asn. **SELECTED PUBLICATIONS** Auth, Kellogg's Six-Hour Day; Temple Univ Press, 96; auth, Work Without End: Abandoning Shorter Hours for the Right to Work, Temple Univ Press, 88; auth, "Leisure and Play, Still the Basis of Culture, Recent Developments in Cultural Anthropology ad History," Leisure Science, (98): 143-148; auth, "The Pursuit of Happiness," In Context, 94; auth, "La Izuierda y el Futuro del Trabajo," El Socialismo del Futuro, 93; auth, "Lazy Americans," Society for the Reduction of Human Labor Newsletter 93; auth, "In Aller Gemutlichkeit," Society for the Reduction of Human Labor Newsletter 93; auth, "Child Labor," Society for the Reduction of Human Labor Newsletter 93; auth, "More Leisure: Japan's National Goal," Society for the Reduction of Human Labor Newsletter 93; auth, "El Futuro Del Trabajo," Society for the Reduction of Human Labor Newsletter 93; auth, "Senator Eugene McCarthy and the Iowa Caucus," Society for the Reduction of Human Labor Newsletter 93. **CONTACT ADDRESS** Dept Phys Ed, The Univ of Iowa, 105 Field House, Iowa City, IA 52242. **EMAIL** Benjamin-Hunnicutt@uiowa.edu

HUNT, BARBARA ANN
PERSONAL Born Aberdeen, MS, d **DISCIPLINE** WOMEN'S STUDIES **EDUCATION** Bennett Coll Greensboro NC, BA 1948-52; Syracuse U, MSLS 1952-54; MS Univ for Women, MA 1969-73; Univ of IL, CAS 1971-73; Northwestern University, PhD, 1988. **CAREER** MS Univ for Women, dir curr lab, 77-79; AL A&M Univ Huntsville, asst prof, 74-77; AL A&M University, acting dean, 75-76; Bennett Coll Greensboro, head librn, 67-73; Dist 65 Evanston IL, librn cataloger, 61-66; Morgan State Coll, Baltimore MD, asst librn, 55-57; Rust Coll Holly Springs MS, head librn, assoc prof, 54-55; S Assn of Coll & Schools, consult 68; Alabama State Univ, dir of communications, 83-85; Univ of Mississippi, African-American Novel Project, co-dir, dir, 88-91; Knoxville Col, Division of Arts & Humanities, head, 93. **HONORS AND AWARDS** Cerf Lib Admin Dev Prog Univ of MD Coll Pk; University Fellowship, Northwestern University; Janet Green Flwshp, Nrthwstrn Univ 1980; Minority Flwshp St of MS 1979-81; Ford Found & Flwshp 1970-73; Minority Grant Univ of IL 1972; cadetship Syracuse Univ NY 1952-54. **MEMBERSHIPS** Mem bd of dir Wesley Found MS Univ for Women 1979-; mem bd of trustees Millsaps Coll Jackson MS 1979-; coord Wesley Found St James Meth 1979-; cert lay asso United Meth Ch; co-chrprsn Local United Negro Coll Fund 1978. **CONTACT ADDRESS** Div Arts and Humanities, Knoxville Col, Knoxville, TN 37921.

HUNT, RICHARD M.
PERSONAL Born 10/16/1926, Pittsburgh, PA, m, 1955, 3 children **DISCIPLINE** HISTORY, SOCIOLOGY **EDUCATION** Yale Univ, BA, 49; Columbia Univ, MA, 51; Harvard Univ, PhD, 60. **CAREER** Sr Lectr Social Studies & Univ Marshal, Harvard Univ, Vice Chair, Am Coun on Ger, New York; founding chair, Am Russian Young Artists Orch. **MEMBERSHIPS** AHA. **RESEARCH** Nazi German history; 20th century European intellectual history; contemporary sociological theory. **SELECTED PUBLICATIONS** Auth, Surviving the Swastika--Scientific-Research in Nazi Germany, J Interdisciplinary Hist, Vol 0026, 95; The Logic of Evil--The Social Origins of the Nazi Party, 1925-1933, J Interdisciplinary Hist, Vol 0028, 97. **CONTACT ADDRESS** Harvard Univ, Marshal's Office, Wadsworth Home, Cambridge, MA 02138. **EMAIL** marshal@harvard.edu

HUNTER, ALLAN
PERSONAL Born 07/05/1955, United Kingdom, d **DISCIPLINE** PSYCHOLOGY, PHILOSOPHY **EDUCATION** Oxford Univ, St. John's Col, BA, 76; MA, 78; PhD, 83. **CAREER** Prof, Curry Col, 86-. **HONORS AND AWARDS** Surrey Co Scholar; Stratosch Scholar, **MEMBERSHIPS** Asn for Psychological Type. **RESEARCH** Joseph Conrad, Writing for Self Exploration. **SELECTED PUBLICATIONS** Auth, "Some Unpublished Letters by Conrad to Arthur Symons, " Conradiana xviii: 183-198; auth, "Edmund Gosse: Four Unpublished Letters," Notes and Queries xxxiv: 179-184; auth, "Three Letters and a poem by Hardy," Notes and Queries xxxiv: 53-54; auth, "An Unpublished Letter by H.G. Wells," Notes and Que-

ries xxxiv: 54-55; rev, of "A Portrait in Letters: Correspondence to and about Conrad," by ed. J.H. Stape and O.Knowles, Notes and Queries xliv: 137-138; rev, of "The Collected Letters of Joseph Conrad," by J. Conrad, ed. Karl and Davies, Notes and Queries xliv: 418-419; auth, "Writing as a Therapeutic Tool," in A Closer Look, ed. Adelizzi and Goss (Milton: CC Press, 95); auth, Joseph Conrad and the Ethics of Darwinism, Croom Helm (London, NY, Canberra), 83,85; auth, The Therapeutic Uses of Writing, Nova Sci and Kroshka Books (NY), 97, reprinted as Sanity Manual, 99; auth, Life Passage: Writing Exercises for Self-Exploration, Nova Sci and Kroshka Books (NY), forthcoming. **CONTACT ADDRESS** Dept Humanities, Curry Col, 1071 Blue Hill Ave, Milton, MA 02186-2302.

HUNTER, LAURIE SULLIVAN
PERSONAL Born 09/28/1967, Milwaukee, WI, m, 1998 **DISCIPLINE** PSYCHOLOGY **EDUCATION** Univ Ala, Huntsville, BA, 90; MA, 91; Univ Ala, Birmingham, PhD, 96. **CAREER** Asst prof of Psychology, Francis Marion Univ, 97-. **HONORS AND AWARDS** Psi Chi; Pi Gamma Mu. **MEMBERSHIPS** Soc for Res on Child Develop, Am Psychol Asn, Am Psychol Soc, Am Prof Soc Against Abuse of Children, Southeastern Psychol Asn. **RESEARCH** Developmental psychology, recognition of emotional expressions, child sexual abuse incidence and treatment issues, interpersonal violence issues, prevention and intervention for children with developmental disabilities, and statistical methods/research design. **SELECTED PUBLICATIONS** Coauth with S. W. Kirkpatrick and P. M. MacDonald, "Interpretation of facial expression in sexually abused and non-abused girls," J of Child Sexual Abuse, 4, 1 995): 45-61; coauth with P. M. MacDonald and L. A. Kirkpatrick, "Production of facial expressions of emotion in preschool children," Perceptual and Motor Skills, 82 (96): 76-78; coauth with S. W. Kirkpatrick, F. E. Bell, C. Johnson, and J. Perkins, "Interpretation of facial expressions of emotion: The influence of eyebrows," Genetic, Social, and General Psychology Monographs, 122, 4 (96): 405-424; coauth with P. M. MacDonald and S. W. Kirkpatrick, "Schematic drawings of facial expressions for emotional recognition and interpretation," Genetic, Social, and General Psychology Monographs, 122, 4 (96): 373-388; auth, S. W. Kirkpatrick, "Facial interpretation and component consistency," Genetic, Social, and General Psychology Monographs, 122, 4 (96): 389-404. **CONTACT ADDRESS** Dept Psychol and Sociol, Francis Marion Univ, PO Box 100547, Florence, SC 29501. **EMAIL** lhunter@fmarion.edu

HURH, WON MOO
PERSONAL Born 09/24/1932, Choong-Nam, Korea, m, 1963, 3 children **DISCIPLINE** SOCIOLOGY, ETHNOLOGY **EDUCATION** Monmouth Col, Ill, BA, 60; Univ Heidelberg, Germany, PhD, 65. **CAREER** Asst prof and chair, Monmouth Col, 65-69; asst to assoc prof, Western Ill Univ, 69-72; assoc prof, Trinity Univ, 72-74; assoc prof to prof, Western Ill Univ, 74-. **HONORS AND AWARDS** Magna cum laude, Dr Phil, Universitat Heidelberg, 65; Presidential Merit Awds and Fac Excellence Awds, 77- 78, 83-84, 85-86, 90-91, 93-94; Outstanding Fac Awd for Res, Western Ill Univ; Distinguished Fac Lect, 99-2000; Nat Inst of Mental Health res, 75-76, 79-80, 86-88. **MEMBERSHIPS** Am Sociol Asn, Midwest Sociol Soc, Asn Asian Studies, Asn Asian Am Studies, Korean Sociol Asn, Nat Res Center on Asian Am Mental Health. **RESEARCH** Asian Americans, sociology of personality. **SELECTED PUBLICATIONS** Coauth with Kwang C. Kim, Korean Immigrants in America: A Structural Analysis of Ethnic Confinement and Adhesive Adaptation, Cranbury: NJ: Fairleigh Dickinson Univ Press (84); coauth with Kwang C. Kim, "The 'Success' Image of Asian Americans: Its Validity, Practical and Theoretical Implications," Ethnic and Racial Studies, 12 (89): 513-537; coauth with Kwang C. Kim, "Religious Participation of Korean Immigrants in the United States," J for the Sci Study of Relig,29(90): 19-34; auth, "The 1.5 Generation Phenomenon: A Paragon of Korean-American Pluralism," Korean Culture, 11 (90): 21-31; coauth with Kwang C. Kim, "Adaptation Stages and Mental Health of Korean Male Immigrants in the U. S.," Int Migration Rev, 24 (90): 456-479; coauth with Kwang C. Kim, "Correlates of Korean Immigrants' Mental Health," The J of Nervous and Mental Disease, 178 (90): 703-711; auth, Personality in Culture and Society: An Interdisciplinary and Cross-Cultural Approach, Dubuque, Iowa: Kendall/Hunt (94, 97, 2000); auth, The Korean Americans, Westport, CT: Greenwood Press (98). **CONTACT ADDRESS** Dept Anthopol & Sociol, Western Illinois Univ, University Cir, Macomb, IL 61455.

HURLEY, JAMES
PERSONAL 3 children **DISCIPLINE** MARRIAGE; FAMILY THERAPY **EDUCATION** Harvard Univ, BA; Westminster Seminary, M.Div, Cambridge Univ, PhD; Florida State Univ, PhD. **CAREER** Dept ch; prof. **HONORS AND AWARDS** Gold Medallion awd as the Evangel Bk Yr, Man and Woman in Bibl Perspective; clinical supervisor, amer assn for marriage and family therapy. **MEMBERSHIPS** Bd mem, Miss Assn for Marriage and Family Therapy; Pastoral Counseling Inst; Pres-elect Mississippi Ass-fr Marriage & Family Therapy. **RESEARCH** New Testament, theology, and counseling. **SELECTED PUBLICATIONS** Auth, Man and Woman in Biblical Perspective. **CONTACT ADDRESS** Dept of Marriage and Family Therapy, Reformed Theol Sem, Mississippi, 5422 Clinton Blvd, Jackson, MS 39209-3099. **EMAIL** jhurley@rts.edu

HUTCHINSON, DOROTHY STAUSS
PERSONAL Born 08/07/1960, Milford, CT, m, 1986, 3 children **DISCIPLINE** PSYCHIATRY **EDUCATION** Bowdoin Col, AB, 82; Boston Univ, MS, 85, ScD, 96. **CAREER** Adjunct asst prof, Sargent Col of Health & Rehabilitation Sciences, Boston Univ, 87-, Dir of services, The Recovery Center, 99-; principle investigator, The Impact of Rehabilitation Introduction Group on Vocational Rehabilitation, 98-; principle investigator, Experimental and Innovative Training of State Vocational Rehabilitation Counselors, 98-. **HONORS AND AWARDS** MS and ScD with Distinction, Boston Univ. **MEMBERSHIPS** Nat Coun of Rehabilitation Educators, Nat Rehabilitation Asn, Int Asn of Psychosocial Rehabilitation Services. **RESEARCH** Wellness in mental health, women's issues in mental health, recovery from mental illness. **SELECTED PUBLICATIONS** Auth, "Promoting Wellness in Rehabilitation and Recovery-A call to action," Community Support Network News, 2, 2 (96); auth, A Descriptive Study of Two Selected Lifestyle Components: Physical Activity and Nutritional Habits in Persons with Psychiatric Disabilities: Their Readiness to Change, Univ of Mich Diss Services, Ann Arbor, Mich (96); coauth with R. Salafia, Employment Success and Satisfaction: A Seminar Series Guide, The Center for Psychiatric Rehabilitation, Sargent Col of Health and Rehabilitation Sciences, Boston Univ, Mass (97); coauth with K. Danley and K. MacDonald-Wilson, The Choose-Get-Keep Approach to Employment Supports: Operational Guidelines, The Center for Psychiatric Rehabilitation, Sargent Col of Health and Rehabilitation Sciences, Boston Univ, Mass (98); coauth with L. Spaniol and M. Koehler, La Recuperacion: libro Practico. Estrategias practicas para personasa con enfermedades psiquiatricas que conducen a enfrentar mejor la vida y a crear seutido de poder intemo. Centro De Rehabilitacion Psiquiatrica, The Center for Psychiatric Rehabilitation, Sargent Col of Health and Rehabilitation Sciences, Boston Univ, Mass (98); coauth with K. Danley and M. Restrepo-Toro, Career Planning and Curriculum for people with Psychiatric Disabilities. Instructor Guide and Reference Handbook, The Center for Psychiatric Rehabilitation, Sargent Col of Health and Rehabilitation Sciences, Boston Univ, Mass (98); coauth with G. Skrinar and C. Cross, ":The effects of physical exercise on persons with psychiatric disabilities," Psychosocial Rehabilitaion J, 22, 4 (99): 351-361; coauth with M. Farkas, "Rehabilitation-Oriented Case Management," in Case Management in Rehabilitation (forthcoming); coauth with C. Gagne, "A journey from self-neglect to self-care and wellness," in P. Ridgeway & C. Rapp, The Recovery Paradigm, Univ of Kans (forthcoming). **CONTACT ADDRESS** Dept Rehabilitation Counseling, Boston Univ, University Rd, Boston, MA 02215. **EMAIL** dorih@bu.edu

HUTCHINSON, GEORGE
PERSONAL Born 12/19/1938, Albuquerque, NM, m **DISCIPLINE** EDUCATION **EDUCATION** California State Univ Los Angeles, BS 1969, MS 1971; United States International Univ, PhD 1977; National University, San Diego, California, Post Doctoral Law 1988. **CAREER** California State Univ, Assoc Dean Educ Support Serv, 86-; Sand Diego State Univ, asst prof dept of recreation, 73-79, asst dean, 74-77 assoc dean, 78-81, college of professional studies and fine arts, Assoc Prof, Dept of Recreation, 79-, Dir Student Outreach Serv Dir, 81-. **HONORS AND AWARDS** Honorary Mem US Navy ROTC Selection Bd Chief of Naval Opers Washington DC 1979-82; Distinguished Alumna San Diego Comm Leadership Develop 1980; Honorary Member Phi Kappa Phi San Diego State Univ 1980-86; Letter of Commendation, Mayor, City of San Diego, 1989; Proclamation, Board of Supervisors, 1990; Resolution, Assemblyman Chacon 75th District, 1990; San Diego Urban League, Letter of Commendation, 1991; National Black Child Dev Inc, Certificate of Appreciation, 1992; San Diego Housing Commission, Proclamation, 1992. **MEMBERSHIPS** Mem Advisory Council for Minority Officer Recruiting US Navy 1977-; mem at large Industry Educ Council Greater San Diego 1980-; mem Phi Kappa Phi; mem bd dirs Amer Cancer Society 1984-; mem Athletic Adv Comm 1985-; mem Senate Comm Minority; mem CA Academic Partnership Program 1985-; mem Naval Reserve Officers Assn, Navy League of the US; member, San Diego Chapter, Urban League; member, State Bar of California, 1988-; president, Boy Scouts of America Explorers Division, 1988-. **SELECTED PUBLICATIONS** Publications including "Trends Affecting Black Recreators in the Professional Society," California Parks and Recreation Society Magazine 1981; Role of Higher Educ in Educational Reform of Adolescents 1988; Meeting the Challenge of Technology 1988. **CONTACT ADDRESS** Student Outreach Serv, San Diego State Univ, San Diego, CA 92182-0777.

HY, LE XUAN
PERSONAL Born 02/25/1957, Vietnam, m, 1992, 4 children **DISCIPLINE** PSYCHOLOGY **EDUCATION** St. Louis Univ, BA, BS, 82; Washington Univ, MA, 84; PhD, 86; George Washington Univ, Post Doct, 93-99. **CAREER** Asst prof, Rockhurst Univ, 86-88; asst prof, Wash Univ, 88-90; eval, US Gen Acct Off, 90-94; couns, 94-96; sr eval, 94-99; asst prof, Seattle Univ, 99-. **HONORS AND AWARDS** Samuel Beck Awd, Soc Personality Assess Univ Chicago; Minority Fel, APA. **MEMBERSHIPS** Mem, Strategic Planning Team, Mercer Island School Dist; Mem, Minority Stud Achieve Oversight Comm; Mem, Fairfax County Pub School Diversity Training Adv Coun; APA; AEA; Soc Psychological Study of Social Issues. **SELECTED PUBLICATIONS** Co-ed, Ego strength and ego development: Assessment and application, Psychol Desk Ref, Oxford Univ Press (NY), 98; coauth, Other uses of the Washington University Sentence Completion Test, ed. J Loevinger, Tech Found Measuring Ego Development, Eribaum (Hilsdale, NJ) 98; coauth, Testing and revising the rules for obtaining total protocol ratings for 36-item and 18-item forms, ed. J Loevinger, Tech Found Measuring Ego Development, Eribaum (Hillsdale, NJ) 98; auth, How to use the sentence completion test in translation, ed. J Loevinger, Tech Found Measuring Ego Development, Eribaum (Hillsdale, NJ) 98; auth, Excel macros for handling sentence completion test data, ed. J Loevinger, Tech Found Measuring Ego Development, Eribaum (Hillsdale, NJ) 98; auth, Managing sentence completion test data, ed. J Loevinger, Tech Found Measuring Ego Development, Eribaum (Hillsdale, NJ) 98. **CONTACT ADDRESS** Dept Psychology, Seattle Univ, 901 12th Ave, Seattle, WA 98122. **EMAIL** hyl@seattleu.edu

HYATT, SUSAN BRIN
DISCIPLINE ANTHROPOLOGY **EDUCATION** Grinnell Col, BA, 76; Univ Mich, MA, 80; Univ Mass, PhD, 96. **CAREER** Asst Prof, Temple Univ, 96-. **HONORS AND AWARDS** Fac Summer Res Grant, Temple Univ, 97; Fac Grant-in-Aid Res Grant, Temple Univ, 97-98; Richard Carley Hunt Fel, 99; Fel, Nat Sci Found, 99-00. **MEMBERSHIPS** AAA, SANA, SAW, SUA, SFA. **RESEARCH** Poverty, welfare, housing, gender, urban social movements. **SELECTED PUBLICATIONS** Auth, "Poverty and the Medicalization of Motherhood," in Sex, Gender and Health (Cambridge: Cambridge UP, 99), 94-117; auth, "Pollard, Tessa and Susan B Hyatt: Gender and Health: Integrating Biological and Social Perspectives," introduction to Sex, gender and Health (Cambridge: Cambridge UP, 99), 1-17; auth, "Caulkins, D Douglas and Susan B Hunt: Using Consensus Analysis to Measure Cultural Diversity in Organizations and Social Movements," in Field Methods, vol 1, no 1 (99), 5-26; auth, Sex, Gender and Health, Cambridge UP, 99; auth, "The Volunteering Poor: Neoliberal Governance and the Erasure of Poverty," in New Poverty Studies (New York: NY UP,00). **CONTACT ADDRESS** Dept Anthrop, Temple Univ, 1115 W Berks St, Philadelphia, PA 19122. **EMAIL** shyatt@nimbus.temple.edu

I

IATRIDIS, DEMETRIUS S.
PERSONAL Born 02/11/1923, Munich, Germany, m, 1954, 4 children **DISCIPLINE** SOCIAL WORK **EDUCATION** Wash and Jefferson Col, BA, 49; Univ Pittsburgh, MSW, 51; Bryn Mawr Col, PhD, 54. **CAREER** VP for res, Doxiadis Assoc, 59-66; prof, Athens Tech Inst, 59-66; VP, Athens Center of Ekistics, 60-66; res prof to dept chair, Boston Col, 66-. **MEMBERSHIPS** World soc of Ekistics, Nat Asn, of Soc Workers, Am Asn of Univ Prof, Am Orthopsychiatric Asn, Worl Furture Soc, Engandiner Kollegium, Coun on Soc Work Educ, Greek Asn of Soc Workers, Greek Soc of Soc Planners and So Res. **SELECTED PUBLICATIONS** Auth, Social Justice and the Welfare State in Central and Eastern: The Impact of Privatization, London, (in press); auth, "The social Justice contexts of Privatization," in social Justice and the Welfare state in Central and Eastern Europe: The Impact of Privatization, London, (in press); auth, "State Social Welfare: Global Perspectives," in Social Work at the Millenium, New York, (in press); auth, "Critical Social Policy," in Handbook of Social Policy, Berkeley, 00; auth, "A Global Approach to Privatization," in Privatization in Central and Eastern Europe: Perspectives and Approaches, London, 98; auth, "Implications of Critical Social Policy," Social Work, 51, (98): 119-140; auth, Privatization in Central and Eastern Europe: Perspectives and Approaches, London, 98; auth, "Policy Practice," Encyclopedia of Social Work, 95; auth, Social Policy: Institutional context of Social Development and Human Services, Pacific Grove, 94; auth, auth, Social Policy Planning: Theory and Practice, Athens, 90; auth, Social Planning and policy Alternatives in Greece: Income Support and AFDC, 80; auth, Housing the Poor in Suburbia: Public Policy at the Grass Roots, New York, 74. **CONTACT ADDRESS** Grad School of Soc Work, Boston Col, Chestnut Hill, 140 Commonwealth Ave, Chestnut Hill, MA 02467.

ICARD, LARRY D.
PERSONAL Born 08/04/1949, Lenoir, NC, s **DISCIPLINE** SOCIAL WORK **EDUCATION** Johnson C. Smith Univ, Charlotte, NC, BA; WVa Univ, Morgantown, MSW; Columbia Univ, DSW. **CAREER** Public Welfare Worker, State Dept of Public Welfare, Dallas, Tex, 72-73; instr, Univ Wisc, Superior, 75-76; proj dir, Minority Services Proj, Central District Mental Health Center, Clarksburg, WVa, 78-80; asst prof, WVa Univ, Morgantown, 76-80; acting dir, Sch of Soc Work, Univ of Cincinnati, summer 82, asst prof and chairperson, Baccalaureate prog, 80-87, assoc prof, 87-93; assoc prof of Social Work, Interim Dir of PhD Prog, Sch of Soc Work, Univ Washington, Seattle, 93-. **HONORS AND AWARDS** Minority Fel Awd, Nat Inst of Mental Health, Coun on Social Work Educ, 89. **RESEARCH** HIV prevention among African-Americans; service

needs of sexual minorities. **SELECTED PUBLICATIONS** Auth, "Assessing the Strengths and Needs of African American Gays: A Multidimensional Perspective," J of Gay & Lesbian Soc Services (96); coauth with S. Sohng, "Cultural Imperatives for Practice in Sexual Problems with Korean Men," J of Gay & Lesbian Soc Services (96); coauth with P. S. Nutrius, "The Loss of Self in Coming Out: Special Risks for African American Gays and Lesbians," J of Personal and Interpersonal Loss, 1, 29 (96): 29-47; coauth with M. Spearmon and Jackson Curry, "BSW Programs in Black Colleges; Building on the Strengths of Tradition," J of Soc Work Educ (96); auth, "Does Reliance on diagnostic labels help clients more than it hurts them? Yes," in E. Gambrill and R. Pruger, eds, Controversial Issues in Social Work Ethics, Boston: Allyn & Bacon (96); coauth with E. C. Hernades-Zamora, M. S. Spencer, and R. Catalano, "Designing & Evaluating Strategies to Recruit African Americans for AIDS/HIV Interventions: Targeting the Black Family," Ethnicity & Disease (97); coauth with J. F. Longres and M. Spencer, "The Effect of Minority Status on Distress Among Children and Adolescents," Soc Service Rev, Vol 25, 1/2, (99); coauth with T. Jones and S. Wahab, "Empowering Lesbian and Bisexual Women of Color," in L. Gutierrez & E. Lewis, eds, Empowering Women of Color, Columbia Univ Press (99); auth, "Community Practice: Theory and Skills for Social Workers by David A. Hardcastle, Stanley Wenocur, and Patrick R. Powers, Social Work, 44, 2, .191 (99); coauth with M. S. Spenser and T. Harachi, " Measuring Ethnic Identity among Monoracial and Multiracial Early Adolescents,": J of Adolescents (in press). **CONTACT ADDRESS** Sch of Soc Work, Univ of Washington, 4101 15TH Ave NE, JH-30, Seattle, WA 98195. **EMAIL** icardl@u.washington.edu

IDLEBURG, DOROTHY

PERSONAL Born 08/17/1951, Tunica, MS, m, 1972, 3 children **DISCIPLINE** SOCIOLOGY, GERONTOLOGY **EDUCATION** Jackson State Univ, BA, 75; MA, 76; Wash Univ, MSW, 79; PhD, 82. **CAREER** Asst Prof, Jackson State Univ, 84-89; Prof, Tougaloo Col, 89-97; Prof, Alcorn State Univ, 97-. **HONORS AND AWARDS** Who's Who Among Am Teachers; Who's Who in the S and Southwest; Personalities of the S; Postdoctoral Fel, 95; Deleg to the White House Conf on Aging. **MEMBERSHIPS** Asn for Gerontology and Human Develop in HBCUs, NASW, Mid S Soc Asn. **RESEARCH** Long term care and caregiving, violence in the academic environment, older women and issues of diversity, health care. **SELECTED PUBLICATIONS** Auth, "Elderly Women: Issues of Diversity," Voices of African-Am Women on the Issues, Nat Coun of Negro Women (96); auth, "The Color Line," The Philadelphia Tribune Suppl (99), 18. **CONTACT ADDRESS** Dept Soc Sci, Alcorn State Univ, 1000 Alcorn Dr, Alcorn State, MS 39096-7500.

IMAMURA, SHIGEO

PERSONAL Born 08/14/1922, San Jose, CA, m, 1963 **DISCIPLINE** LINGUISTICS, ENGLISH AS A SECOND LANGUAGE **EDUCATION** Matsuyama Univ Commerce, Dipl, 43; Univ Mich, Ann Arbor, BA, 53, MA, 64. **CAREER** Teacher supvr English as second lang, Ehime State Bd Educ, Japan, 49-55; asst prof, Ehime Univ, Japan, 55-61, assoc dir English teaching inst, 56-61; asst prof English as second lang, Mich State Univ, 61-62; asst prof, Ehime Univ, 62-63; asst prof, 63-64, dir English lang ctr, 64-73, Assoc Prof English as a Second Lang, Mich State Univ, 66-, Dir Spec Progs, English Lang Ctr, 78-, Dir, Konan-Ill Ctr, Kobe, Japan, 77-78. **MEMBERSHIPS** Nat Asn Foreign Student Affairs; Asn Teachers English as Second Lang; Teachers English to Speakers Other Lang. **RESEARCH** Pronunciation and grammar in teaching English as a second language; teaching Japanese as a second language, especially grammar; inter-cultural understanding. **SELECTED PUBLICATIONS** Coauth, Readings from Samuel Clemens, 69 & Readings on American Society, 69, Blaisdell; auth, Basic knowledge for Studies in the United States, Kenkyusha, Tokyo, 72; Teaching of English in the Middle East and Indonesia, 72 & Cultural interference in language learning, 73, English Lang Educ Coun Bull, Tokyo; International Understanding and the Teaching of English, Lang Educ Coun Tokyo, 74. **CONTACT ADDRESS** English Lang Ctr, Michigan State Univ, East Lansing, MI 48824.

INCE, ELIZABETH

PERSONAL Born 09/28/1970, New York, NY, m, 2000 **DISCIPLINE** PSYCHOLOGY **EDUCATION** Richard Stockton Col, BA, 92; Univ Toledo, MA, 95; PhD, 00. **CAREER** Instr to Asst Prof, Richard Stockton Col, 98-. **HONORS AND AWARDS** Res and Professional Development Grant, Richard Stockton Col, 00; Grant, Richard Stockton Col, 99; Grant, Office of Intl Studies Univ Toledo, 98. **MEMBERSHIPS** Am Psychol Soc, Cognitive Sci Soc, Eastern Psychol Asn, Am Psychol Asn **RESEARCH** Right and Left Hemisphere Asymmetric for Perception and Language Acquisition Processing. **SELECTED PUBLICATIONS** Co-auth, The metacontrol of word knowledge acquisition, forthcoming; **CONTACT ADDRESS** Dept Soc & Beh Sci, Richard Stockton Col, PO Box 195, Pomona, NJ 08240. **EMAIL** incee@stockton.edu

INGERSOLL, RICHARD

PERSONAL Born Wilmington, DE, m, 1992, 2 children **DISCIPLINE** SOCIOLOGY **EDUCATION** Univ Pa, PhD, 92; MA. **CAREER** High School Social Studies Teacher, 80-86; Research Fellow, U.S. Dept of Educ, 91-93; Research Scientist, American Institutes of Research, 93-95; Asst Prof, Dept of Sociology, Univ of Georgia, 95-. **HONORS AND AWARDS** Richard B. Russell Excellence in Teaching Awd, Univ of Georgia, 99, Sandy Beaver Excellence in Teaching Awd, College of Arts and Sciences, Univ of Georgia, 98, Finalist, Am Sociological Asn Annual Dissertation Awd, 93, Recipient, Doctoral and Post-Doctoral Fellowships, from the National Science Foundation/U.S. Dept of Edu/American Educ Research Asn Joint Program, 91-92 and 92-93, E. Digby Baltzell Awd for Dissertation, Dept of Sociology, Univ of Pennsylvania, 92, Braverman Awd, Society for the Study of Social Problems, 90-91, Honorable Mention, for second place, 92, Candace Rogers Awd, from the Eastern Sociological Society, Dean's Scholar, Univ Awd for outstanding academic achievement, Univ of Pennsylvania, 92, Magna Cum Laude, Univ of CA. **MEMBERSHIPS** American Sociological Assoc, American Educ Research Assoc, Society for the Study of Social Problems, Southern Sociological Society, Academy of Management, American Statistical Assoc. **RESEARCH** The organization of elementary and secondary schools, Teacher's work and the teaching occupation, Educ Policy. **SELECTED PUBLICATIONS** Auth, "Loosely Coupled Organizations Revisited," Research in the Sociology of Organizations 11 (93): 81-112; auth, "Organizational Control in Secondary Schools," Harvard Educational Review 64 (94): 150-172; auth, "Teacher's Decision-Making Power and School Conflict," Sociology of Educ (96): 159-176; auth, "The Recurring Myth of Teacher Shortages," Teacher's College Record 99 (97): 41-45; auth, "The Problem of Out-of-Field Teaching," Phi Delta Kappan 79 (98): 773-76; auth, "The Problem of Underqualified Teachers in American Secondary Schools," Educational Researcher, 2(99): 26-37; auth, "Understanding The Problem of Teacher Quality in American School," Education Statistics Quarterly 1 (99): 1 (99): 14-18, auth, "Teacher Turnover, Teacher Shortages and the Organization of Schools, Center for the Study of Teachning and Policy, Univ of Washington, 99; auth, "Teacher Assessment and Evaluation: a Sociological Perspective,"In Educations and Sociology: An Encyclopedia, ed. By D. Levinson, P. Cookson and A. Sadovnik (Washington, DC: Taylor and Francis) forthcoming, 00; auth, "The Status of Teaching as a Profession," In Schools and Society: a Sociological Perspective, ed. By Jeanne Ballantine and Joan Spade, Wadsworth Press, 00. **CONTACT ADDRESS** Dept Sociology, Univ of Georgia, Baldwin Hall, Athens, GA 30602. **EMAIL** ingersol@arches.uga.edu

INGRAM-WALLACE, BRENDA

PERSONAL Born Youngstown, OH, m, 1995, 1 child **DISCIPLINE** PSYCHOLOGY **EDUCATION** Youngstown State Univ, BA, 83; Miami Univ, MA,86; PhD, 89. **CAREER** Assoc Prof, Albright Col, 89-. **HONORS AND AWARDS** United Methodist Exemplary Teaching Awd. **MEMBERSHIPS** APA; ABPsi; Psi Chi; AACC. **RESEARCH** Body Image; Racial Identity. **CONTACT ADDRESS** Dept Psychol, Albright Col, PO Box 15234, Reading, PA 19612. **EMAIL** brendai@alb.edu

INMAN, M. L.

PERSONAL Born 01/23/1965, Davenport, IA, m **DISCIPLINE** PSYCHOLOGY **EDUCATION** IA State Univ, 87; Univ IA, MA, 89, PhD, 92. **CAREER** Asst prof, Trinity Univ, 92-97; assoc prof, Hope Col, 99-. **MEMBERSHIPS** APA, SPSP, MPA, SWPA. **RESEARCH** Prejudice and discrimination. **SELECTED PUBLICATIONS** Coauth with R. S. Baron, C. F. Kao, and H. Logan, "Negative Emotion and Superficial Social Processing, " Motivation and Emotion, 16 (4), 323-345 (92); coauth with A. J. Reichl and R. S. Baron, "Do We Tell Less Than We Know or Hear Less Than We Are Told? Exploring the Teller-Listener Extremity Effect," J of Experimental Soc Psychol, 29, 528-550 (93); coauth with R. S. Baron, H. Logan, J. Lilly, and M. Brennan, "Negative Emotion and Message Processing," J of Experimental Soc Psychol, 30, 181-201 (94); coauth with R. S. Baron, "The Influence of Prototypes on Perceptions of Prejudice," J of Personality and Soc Psychol, 70 (4), 727-739 (96); coauth with R. S. Baron, J. OP. David, and B. M. Brunsman, "Why Listeners Hear Less Than They Are Told: Attentional Load and the Teller-Listener Extremity Effect," J of Personality and Soc Psychol, 72(4), 826-836 (97); coauth with J. Huerta and S. Oh, "Perceiving Discrimination: The Role of Prototypes and Norm Violation," Social Cognition (Trinity Graduates) (Dec 98). **CONTACT ADDRESS** Dept Psychol, Hope Col, 137 E 12th St, Holland, MI 49423. **EMAIL** inman@hope.edu

INSIGNARES, HARRIETTE B.

PERSONAL Born 10/24/1943, Savannah, GA, d, 4 children **DISCIPLINE** EDUCATION, ENGLISH **EDUCATION** Fisk Univ, BA, 64; Univ Wis, MST, 72; George Peabody Col, PhD, 80. **CAREER** Acad coun, Univ Wis, 70-72; asst cen dir, instr, 73-77; instr, Meharry Col, 75-76; instr, Geo Peabody Col, 76-77; instr, Am Baptist Col, 77-79; asst prof, Univ Tenn, 77-79; assoc prof, 80-88; prof, 88-; prog coord, 95-98. **HONORS AND AWARDS** Wis Leadershp Grant; Ford Fel; Sylvia Wilson Mem Fel; ASNE Fel; API Fel; Freedom Forum Fel; Outstand Teach Awd; David Eshelman Outstand Lead Awd; Trailblazer Awd; Adj Gen Dist Patriot Awd and Med; Poet of Merit Plaque and Med. **MEMBERSHIPS** Phi Beta Kappa; SPJ; NABJ; GKHS; Theta Alpha Phi; Pi Kappa Delta; ISP; Consortium of Doctors. **RESEARCH** Writing literacy; African-American rhetoric. **SELECTED PUBLICATIONS** Auth, Genesis, 76; auth, Juba's Folk Games: A Collection of Afo-American Children's Games; coauth, "Black Liberation and Legitimation: Rejection of the Mask," Writers Circle Mag, 75; auth, A Salute to the Heroes of Desert Storm; auth, "Tennessee Volunteers is No Idle Boast," Quill; auth, "Family Tree," in Last Goodbyes, Nat Lib of Poetry; auth, "No Unknown Soldiers," in America At the Millennium: Best Poets, Best Poems of the 20th Century; auth, "Sloe Gin," Old Hickory Rev; auth, "Blacks and the Bicentennial: A Response," Fisk Univ Herald; auth, "Gentle Georgian," Congressional Rec; auth, "Earth Sister," Trolley; auth, "A Juju of Their Own," Tenn Speech Comm J. **CONTACT ADDRESS** Dept Communications, Tennessee State Univ, 3500 John A Merritt Blvd, Nashville, TN 37209-1500. **EMAIL** hinsignare@aol.com

IRIZARRY, MARIA A.

PERSONAL Born 10/20/1943, Yabucoa, PR, w, 1970, 2 children **DISCIPLINE** EDUCATION **EDUCATION** Teachers Col, Columbia Univ, Ed.D, 77; Teachers Col, Columbia Univ, M.Ed, 73; Teachers Col, Columbia Univ, MA, 72; Univ Puerto Rico, BA.Ed, 65. **CAREER** Dean Col Education, Univ of Puerto Rico in Rio Piedras (UPR), 99-; Assoc Dean, Col of Education, Univ of Puerto Rico in Rio Piedras, 98-99; Thirty five years experience as ESL professor, 65-; Prof, Graduate School of Education, Col of Education UPR, 85-; Director, Department of Education, Saced Heart Univ (SHU), Santurce, PR, 82-84; Project Director Bilingual Teacher Training Program SHU, 80-82; Professor ESL, SHU, 77-84; Assoc Asst Superintendent, Newsard, New Jersey, 75-77. **HONORS AND AWARDS** 25th Anniversary Silver Plate as PRTESOL past president; Plaque as Keynote Speaker at Puerto Rico Southern TESOL Annual Conference; Medal as Distinguished Puerto Rican Educator in the Area of Bilingual Education. **MEMBERSHIPS** Teachers' Assoc of Puerto Rico; International TESOL; Puerto Rico TESOL; National Association. **RESEARCH** Second Language Acquisition; Bilingual Education; Foreign and Second Language Teaching of Bilingual Education; National Geographic Society; NEA; Phi Delta Kappa; Asociacion Graduados UPR **SELECTED PUBLICATIONS** Auth, "Puerto Ricans coming from the United States mainland: Their impact on the system, by Irizarry, M.A., NABE News, 3, (5); auth, "The attitutdes of permanent and migrant Puerto Ricans determined by language usage, Puerto Rican Migration: The Return Flow, La Migracion Puertorriueria, by Irizarry, M.A., An Annotated Bibliography by Pauita Vivo por the National Institute of Education in Washington, D.C., 82; auth, "Review of literature of functions of English and needs assessment," by Irizarry, M.A., Rio Piedras, PR: Inter-American Univ, 87; auth, "The teaching of English in Puerto Rico: The earl stage, TESOL-GRAM, 14 (1), 5; auth, "English teachers: Scapegoats for Puerto Rico's English language dilemma," by Irizrry, M.A. & Vega, N., TESOL-GRAM, 4, (1), 13, 97; auth, "Literary treasure, Ponce, PR: Editorial Centro Padagogico," by Irizarry, M.A., 98; auth, "Evaluacion del Proyecto para formar un ciudadano bilingue," by Irizarry, M.A., Gonzalez, E., & Vazuez, J., pedagogia, 33, 73, 99; **CONTACT ADDRESS** Dept Education, Univ of Puerto Rico, Rio Piedras, PO Box 23302, Rio Piedras, PR 00931. **EMAIL** mirizarr@waldenu.edu

IRSCHICK, EUGENE FREDERICK

PERSONAL Born 08/15/1934, Kodaikanal, m, 1998, 5 children **DISCIPLINE** HISTORY, ANTHROPOLOGY, PHILOSOPHY **EDUCATION** Gettysburg Col, AB, 55; Univ Pa, AM, 59; Univ Chicago, PhD(hist), 64. **CAREER** Instr Indian civilization & Carnegie Corp teaching internship, Univ Chicago, 60-61; asst prof hist, 63-69, assoc prof, 69-78, Prof Hist, Univ Calif Berkeley, 78-, Am Inst Indian Studies grant, 67-68 & 79; Fulbright res fel, Institute for the International Exchange of Persons, 80. **HONORS AND AWARDS** Walmull Prize, 69. **MEMBERSHIPS** Asn Asian Studies; Am Hist Asn; Am Philosophical Soc, 82; Humanities Institute, 85; Am Institute of Indian Studies, 85-6; Fulbright, Institute for the International Exchange of Persons, 89; Fulbright, Institute for the International Exchange of Persons, 93; Am Institute of Indian Stud, 93; Fulbright-Hays Fel, 96. **RESEARCH** South Asian history; social change; peasant culture and economy; critical stud, postcolonialism. **SELECTED PUBLICATIONS** Auth, "Peasant Survival Stratagies and Rehearsals for Rebellion in Eighteenth Century South India," Peasant Studies, Vol. 9:4, (82): 215-241; auth, "Gandhian non-violent Protest," Economic and Political Weekly, (86): 1276-1285; auth, Tamil Revivalism in the 1930s, Madas: Crea, 86; auth, "Order and Disorder in Colonial South India," Modern Asian Studies, (89): 459-492; auth, Dialogue and History: Constructing South India, 1795-1895, Berkeley: Univ of Calif Press, 94; auth, The Nation and its Fragments--Colonial and Postcolonial Histories, Int Hist Rev, Vol 0017, 95; Gandhi,Mahatma--Nonviolent Power in Action, J Interdisciplinary Hist, Vol 0026, 95; Caste, Nationalism and Communism in South-India, Malabar, 1900-1948, J Interdisciplinary Hist, Vol 0027, 96; Hindu Nationalists in India--The Rise of the Bahratiya-Janata Party, J Church and State, Vol 0038, 96; The Origins of Industrial Capitalism in India--Business Strategies and the Working Classes in Bombay, 1900-1940, J Interdisciplinary Hist, Vol 0027, 97. **CONTACT ADDRESS** Univ of California, Berkeley, 3229 Dwinelle MC2550, Berkeley, CA 94720. **EMAIL** irschick@socrates.berkeley.edu

IRVIN, DEBORAH M.
DISCIPLINE BEHAVIORAL DISORDERS, SPECIAL EDUCATION **EDUCATION** Temple Univ, BA; Univ Nebr, Omaha, MS; Univ Nebr, Lincoln, PhD. **CAREER** Career counr, career placement serv, 88-91, instr, 91-95, asst prof, Univ Nebr, Omaha, 95-. **RESEARCH** Illegal and legal chemical substance use among adolescent populations. **SELECTED PUBLICATIONS** Auth, Substance Abuse in Adolescents: Implications for At-risk Youth, Spec Serv in Sch, 1. **CONTACT ADDRESS** Univ of Nebraska, Omaha, 60th & Dodge Sts, Kayser Hal, Omaha, NE 68182-0054.

IRVINE, MARGOT ELISABETH
PERSONAL Born 05/28/1969, New Haven, CT, m, 1992, 2 children **DISCIPLINE** WOMAN'S STUDIES, FRENCH **EDUCATION** Univ Toronto, BA, 92; MA, 93; PhD, 00. **CAREER** Asst prof, Univ Toronto, 00-. **HONORS AND AWARDS** SSHRC Awd, 97-99; Ont Grad Study Fel 94-96; Univ Toronto Fel, 99-00; Senior Doct Teaching Assocshp. **MEMBERSHIPS** MLA; Women in Fr; 19th-centruy Fr Studies; SERN; CWSA. **RESEARCH** Nineteenth century French women's writing. **CONTACT ADDRESS** Humanities Soc Sci Dept, Univ of Toronto, 130 St George St, Roberts Library 14th Fl, Toronto, ON, Canada M5S 3H1. **EMAIL** mirvine@chass.utoronto.ca

ISAAC, LARRY
PERSONAL Born 06/12/1949, Cleveland, OH, m, 1969, 2 children **DISCIPLINE** SOCIOLOGY **EDUCATION** Indiana Univ, PhD. 79. **CAREER** Prof, Fla State Univ, 78-. **HONORS AND AWARDS** Nat Inst of Mental Health Fel, 75-77; Moore Awd, ASA, 90; ASA/NSF Awd, 90; NSF Dissertation Endowment Awd; Vice Pres of Southern Sociol Soc; NEH Summer Awd. **MEMBERSHIPS** Am Sociol Asn; Soc for the Study of Social Problems; Southern Sociol Soc. **RESEARCH** Social Movements; Labor; Comparative-Historical Methods; Social Change; Political Sociology. **SELECTED PUBLICATIONS** Auth, Transforming Localities: Reflections on Time, Causality, and Narrative in Contemporary Historical Sociology, Hist Methods, 97; Class Conflict, Encycl of Violence, Peace, and Conflict, 98; coauth, Introduction to Time-Series Analysis; Quality of Quantity in Comparative-Historical Analysis: temporally Changing Wage Labor Regimes in the United States and Sweden, in The Comparative Political Economy of the Welfare State: New Methodologies and Approaches, 94; Analyzing Historical Contingency With Formal Methods: The Case of the 'Relief Explosion' and 1968, in Sociol Methods and Res, 94; Regimes of Power and the Power of Analytic Regimes: Explaining US Military Procurement Keynesianism as Historical Process, Hist Methods, 97; Degradation of Labor, cultures of Co-Operation: Braverman's 'Labor', Lordstown, and the Social Factory, in Rethinking the Labor Process: The Braverman Legacy and Beyond, 99; Temporally Recursive Regression and Social Historical Inquiry: An Example of Cross-Movement Militancy Spillover, in Int Rev of Soc Hist, 98. **CONTACT ADDRESS** Dept of Sociology, Florida State Univ, Tallahassee, FL 32306. **EMAIL** lisaac@garnet.acns.fsu.edu

IUTCOVICH, MARK
PERSONAL Born 07/17/1929, Rumania, m, 1970, 2 children **DISCIPLINE** SOCIOLOGY **EDUCATION** Univ Buchares, Rumania, Lecentiate, 50; Univ Man, MA, 62; Case Western Reserve Univ, PhD, 70. **CAREER** Asst prof, Col of Mount St Joseph, 64-65; asst prof, Xavier Univ, 66-67; assoc prof to prof, Edinboro Univ Of Pa, 67-; Dir of Res, Keystone Univ Res Corp, 80-. **HONORS AND AWARDS** Canada Fel, 63-65; Cert for Exceptional Acad Serv, Commonwealth of Pa, 77; Marquis Who's Who, 77-78, 79-80; Notable Am Awd, Am Biographical Inst, 78-79; Who's Who Worldwide, 94-95; Alex Boros Awd, Soc of Appl Sociol, 97. **MEMBERSHIPS** Pa State Educ Assoc; Am Sociol Assoc; AAUP; Market Res Assoc; N Central Sociol Assoc; Pa Sociol Assoc; Soc for Appl Sociol. **RESEARCH** Evaluation Research, Organizational Research and Marketing Research. **SELECTED PUBLICATIONS** Coauth, "Just for Fun: Alcohol and the College Student", Chemical Dependencies: Behav and Biomedical Issues 4.3 (82); auth, "Industrialization, Women's Burden and Consequences of Mental Disturbances", Soc Towards the Year 2,000: The Sociol Galaxy, Pa Sociol Soc, (83); auth, "Establishing a Consulting/Research Firm: The Nitty Gritty", J for Appl Sociol (85); coauth, "The Politics of Evaluation Research: A Case Study of Community Development Block Grant Funding for Human Services in Evaluation and Program Planning, Vol 10, (87); coauth, Consulting as a Sociologist, Praeger Pub, 87; coauth, "Assessment of the Transportation Needs of Pennsylvania's Elderly Population", J of Appl Gerontology 12, (88); auth, ""The Sociology of Success", J of Appl Sociol 5, (88); auth, "The Society of Applied Sociology: What is your Future?", The Useful Sociologist, Vol 16, (95); ed, Social Insight: Knowledge at Work, Soc for Appl Sociol, 96; auth, An Immigrant's Journey, Rivercross Pub, 97. **CONTACT ADDRESS** Dept Sociol and Anthrop, Edinboro Univ of Pennsylvania, 219 Meadville St, Edinboro, PA 16444-0001. **EMAIL** marki@kurc.org

IVANOFF, ANDRE
PERSONAL Born 10/08/1955, Cuba, NY, m, 1980, 2 children **DISCIPLINE** SOCIAL WORK **EDUCATION** Univ Ndak, BS, 76; Univ Wash, MSW, 78; PhD, 85. **CAREER** Asst prof, SUNY, 85-88; asst to assoc prof, Columbia Univ, 88-. **RESEARCH** Suicidal behaviors in jail and prison populations, Dialectical behavior therapy in forensic and criminal justice populations. **SELECTED PUBLICATIONS** Auth, "Impulsive self-injury: Dialectical behavior therapy," in Self-Injurious Behaviors: Assessment and Treatment, Washington, (forthcoming); auth, "Dialectical behavior therapy," in Handbook of Personality Disorders, New York, (in press), auth, "Suicide and suicidal behavior," in Handbook of Social Work Practice with Vulnerable Populations, 2nd ed, New York, (in press); auth, "Reduction of low response rates in interview surveys of poor African-American families," Journal of Social Service Research, (99): 41-60; auth, "Stages of change among incarcerated women," Addictive Behavior, (98): 384-394; auth, "Assessing the World Health Organization's Alcohol Use Disorder Identification test among incarcerated women," Journal of Offender Rehabilitation, (98): 71-89; auth, "Clinical risk factors associated with parasuicide in prison," International Journal of Offender Therapy and Comparative Criminology, (96): 135-146; auth, "Clinical risk factors associated with parasuicide in prison," International Journal of Offender Therapy and Comparative Criminology, (96): 135-146; auth, "Fewer reasons for living when you're thinking about killing yourself: The Brief Reasons for Living Inventory," Psychopathology and Behavioral Assessment, (94): 1-13; auth, Involuntary Clients in Social Work Practice: A Researched-Based Approach, New York, 94 **CONTACT ADDRESS** School of Soc Work, Columbia Univ, 2960 Broadway, New York, NY 10027. **EMAIL** ami2@columbia.edu

IVES, EDWARD DAWSON
PERSONAL Born 09/04/1925, White Plains, NY, m, 1951, 3 children **DISCIPLINE** FOLKLORE; ORAL HISTORY **EDUCATION** Hamilton Col, AB, 48; Columbia Univ, MA, 50; Ind Univ, PhD, 62. **CAREER** Instr English, Ill Col, 50-53; lectr English, City Col New York, 53-54; from instr to assoc prof English, 55-67, assoc prof, 67-70, PROF FOLKLORE, UNIV MAINE, ORONO, 70-99, Coe res fund grant & Guggenheim fel, 65-66; lectr, NY State Hist Asn; Sem Am Cult, Cooperstown, NY, 67; assoc ed, J Am Folklore, 68-73; dir, Northeast Arch of Folklore & Oral Hist, 72-; folk arts panelist, Nat Endowment Arts, 77-80; ed, Northeast Folklore; LLD Univ Prince Edward Is, 86; Litt D, Mem Univ Nfld, 96. **HONORS AND AWARDS** Marius Barbeau Medal, Can Fol Stud Asn, 91. **MEMBERSHIPS** Am Folklore Soc; Can Folk Studies Asn; Can Folk Music Coun; Northeast Folklore Soc; Oral Hist Asn. **RESEARCH** All aspects of the folklore of the Northeast; the authorship of folksongs; oral history. **SELECTED PUBLICATIONS** Auth, Twenty-one folksongs from Prince Edward Island, Northeast Folklore, 63; Larry Gorman: The Man Who Made the Songs, Ind Univ, 64; coauth, Folksongs and Their Makers, Bowling Green Univ, 70; auth, Lawrence Doyle: Farmer poet of Prince Edward Island, Maine Studies, 71; Argyle boom, Northeast Folklore, 76; Joe Scott: The Woodsman Songmaker, Univ Ill, 78; The tape-recorded interview, 80; George Magoon and the Down East Game War, Univ Ill, 85; Folksongs of New Brunswick, Goose Lane, 89; The Bonn of Earl of Murray: The Man, The Murder, The Ballad, Univ Ill, 97; auth, Drive Dull Care Away, Folksongs from Prince Edward Island, Island Studies (Prince Edward Island), 99. **CONTACT ADDRESS** Rual Route 1, Box 535, Bucksport, ME 04416. **EMAIL** sandy_ives@umit.maine.edu

IWAMASA, GAYLE
DISCIPLINE PSYCHOLOGY **EDUCATION** Univ Calif, BA, 86; Purdue Univ, MS, 88; PhD, 92. **CAREER** Postdoctoral Fel, Univ Calif, 92-93; Asst Prof, Ball State Univ, 93-96; Asst Prof, Okla State Univ, 96-99; Asst Prof, Univ Indianapolis, 99-. **HONORS AND AWARDS** Early Career Awd, Asian Am Psychol Asn, 99; Fac Assoc of the Year, Okla State Univ, 99; Certificate of Appreciation, Sienan Sen citizen's Ctr, 98; Rock of Inspiration Awd, Okla State Univ, 98; Hurly Goodall distinguished Fac Awd, Ball State Univ, 96; Teacher of the Week, Ball State Univ, 95; Who's Who of am Women, 94-96; Dissertation Awd, Am Psychol Asn, 93; dissertation Awd, Am Psychol Asn, 91; Purdue foundation Fel, Purdue Univ, 91; am Psychol Asn Minority Fel, 86-89. **MEMBERSHIPS** Am Psychol Asn, Am Psychol Soc, Asian Am Psychol Asn, Asn for the Advancement of Beh Therapy. **RESEARCH** Multicultural mental health across the lifespan; current research emphasizes an emic approach to examining the conceptualization of psychological disorders among Asian Americans, with a specific focus on depression, anxiety, and personality disorders; Additional research interests include assessment of acculturation and ethnic identity; Women's issues and clinical training and research mentoring. **SELECTED PUBLICATIONS** Auth, "Cognitive-behavioral therapy with ethnic minority adolescents: Therapist perspectives," Cognitive and Behavioral practice, in press; auth, "Japanese American older adults' conceptualization of anxiety," Journal of Clinical Gerontology, in press; auth, "Are personality disorder criteria ethnically biased?: A cardsort analysis," Cultural Diversity and Ethnic Minority Psychology, in press; auth, "Depression and anxiety among Asian American elderly: A review of the literature," Clinical Psychology Review, (99): 343-358; auth, "The Geriatric depression Scale and Japanese American older adults," Clinical Gerontologist, (98): 13-54; auth, "Conceptualizing anxiety and depression: The Japanese American older adult perspective, " Clinical Gerontologist, (98): 77-93; auth, "Acculturation of Japanese Americans: Utility of the SL-ASIA with a community sample," Asian American and Pacific Islander Journal of Health, (98): 25-34; auth, "Behavior therapy and cultural diversity: Is there a Commitment?," The Behavior Therapist, (99): 193; auth, "Behavior therapy and Asian Americans: Is there a commitment?," The Behavior Therapist, (99): auth, "Connectedness," in Key Words in Multicultural Interventions: A dictionary, Greenwood Press, 99 **CONTACT ADDRESS** Dept Psychol, Univ of Indianapolis, 1400 E Hanna Ave, Indianapolis, IN 46227. **EMAIL** giwamasa@uindy.edu

IZAWA, CHIZUKO
PERSONAL Born Tokushima, Japan, m, 1973, 2 children **DISCIPLINE** PSYCHOLOGY **EDUCATION** Univ Tokyo, BA, 60; Stanford Univ, MA, 62; PhD, 65. **CAREER** Asst Prof, San Diego State Univ, 65-67; Postdoctoral Fel, Univ Calif, 67-68; Asst Prof, SUNY, 68-72; Assoc Prof to Full Prof, Tulane Univ, 72-. **HONORS AND AWARDS** Fel, am Psychol Asn; Fel, Am Psychol Soc; Fel, Western Psychol Asn. **MEMBERSHIPS** Am Psychol Asn, Am Psychol Soc, Psychnomic Soc, Psychometric Soc, Asian Am Psychol Soc, Soc for Math, Psychol. **RESEARCH** Learning, Memory, cognition, Cross-cultural Psychology, Psychology of Women and Minority, Effects of TV Viewing on children, Mathematical information Processing, and Health issues. **SELECTED PUBLICATIONS** Auth, Current issues in cognitive processes: The Tulane Flowerree Symposium on Cognition, Erlbaum Pub, 89; auth, Cognitive Psychology Applied, Erlbaum Pub, 93; auth, On human memory: Evolution, progress, and reflections on the 30th Anniversary of the Atkinson-Shiffrin model, Erlbaum Pub, 99; auth, "Introduction to the applied cognitive psychology Symposium, Kyoto International Congress of Applies Psychology," in Cognitive Psychology Applied, Erlbaum Pub, 93; auth, "Power behind the scenes: Hidden effects of test trials unveiled," in Cognitive Psychology Applied, Erlbaum Pub, 93; auth, "Reducing racial discrimination on the 50th anniversary of the atomic bomb," Satsuki: Essays for the 35th Anniversary of the Women Alumni Association of the University of Tokyo, (96): 56; auth, "Unmasking Japan: Myths and realties about the emotions of the Japanese by David Matsumoto, Stanford, Calif: Stanford University Press," Journal of Asian Studies, (97): 504-506; auth, "Efficiency in acquisition and short-tem memory: Study-Test-Rest presentation programs and learning difficulty," in On human memory: Evolution, progress and reflections on the 30th Anniversary of the Atkinson-Shiffrin model, Erlbaum Pub, 99; auth, "On human memory: A brief introduction," in On human memory: Evolution, progress and reflections on the 30th Anniversary of the Atkinson-Shiffrin model, Erlbaum Pub, 99; auth, "Total time and efficient time management: In search of optimal learning and retention via study-test-rest presentation programs," American Journal of Psychology, (00): 125-165. **CONTACT ADDRESS** Dept Psychol, Tulane Univ, 6823 St Charles Ave, New Orleans, LA 70118.

J

JACKS, JULIA ZUWERINK
PERSONAL Born 01/11/1966, MI, m, 1996, 3 children **DISCIPLINE** PSYCHOLOGY **EDUCATION** Univ Wisconsin Madison, PhD, 95. **CAREER** Asst prof, Univ North Carolina, 5 years. **HONORS AND AWARDS** Wayne F Placek Invst Dev Awd. **MEMBERSHIPS** APA; SEPA; SPSP; SSSP; MPA. **SELECTED PUBLICATIONS** Coauth, "Prejudice with and without compunction," J Pers Soc Psych 60 (91): 817-830; coauth, "Self-directed vs. other-directed affect as a consequence of prejudice-related discrepancies," J Person Soc Psych 64 (93): 198-210; coauth, "Prejudice and guilt: The internal struggle to overcome prejudice," in Psychology and culture, eds. W J Lonner, R S Malpass (Needham Hts, MA: Allyn and Bacon, 94); coauth, "Prejudice and prejudice reduction: Classic challenges, contemporary approaches," in Social cognition: Impact on social psychology, eds. PO Devine, D L Hamilton, TM Ostrom (San Diego, CA: Acad Press, 94); coauth, "Prejudice toward Blacks: With and without compunction?," Basic and App Soc Psych 18 (96): 131-150; coauth, "Attitude importance and resistance to persuasion: It's not just the thought that counts," J Person Soc Psych 70 (96): 931-944; coauth, "Attitude importance, forewarning of message content, and resistance to persuasion," Basic App Soc Psych 22 (00):19-29. **CONTACT ADDRESS** Dept Psychology, Univ of No Carolina, Greensboro, PO Box 26164, Greensboro, NC 27412-6164. **EMAIL** jrjacks@uncg.edu

JACKSON, AGNES MORELAND
PERSONAL Born 12/02/1930, Pine Bluff, AR, m **DISCIPLINE** EDUCATION **EDUCATION** Univ Redlands, BA, cum laude, 1952; Univ of WA, MA, 1953; Columbia Univ, PhD, 1960. **CAREER** Spelman Col, instructor, 53-55; Col of Basic Studies, Liberal Arts, Boston Univ, instructor, asst prof, 59-63; CA State Univ LA, asst & assoc prof, 63-69; Pitzer Col,

The Intercollegiate Dept of Black Studies, English prof, 69-. **HONORS AND AWARDS** United Church of Christ Danforth Grad Fellowship 1952-59; So Fellowships Fund Awd 1955; Society for Values in Higher Ed Cross-Disciplinary Post-Doctoral Fellowship; Distinguished Service Awd Univ of the Redlands Alumni Assn 1973. **MEMBERSHIPS** Society for Values in Higher Educ Central Committee 1971-74; bd of dirs 1985-88, Modern Lang Assn; AAUP; Amer Assn of Univ Women; Danforth Assn Prog 1971-; adv counc & panels/symposia at various English & other professional society meetings; bd of trustees 1981-85, 1985-89, pres 1983-84 Pomona Unified School District; nominating committee 1981-84, 1987-90 bd of dir 1984-86, 1988 Spanish Trails Girl Scout Council; Phi Beta Kappa Univ of Redlands 1982-. **CONTACT ADDRESS** English Dept, Pitzer Col, Claremont, CA 91711.

JACKSON, ANDREW
PERSONAL Born 02/02/1945, Montgomery, AL, m **DISCIPLINE** PSYCHOLOGY **EDUCATION** Yale Univ, Study Prog 1966; Univ of Nairobi Kenya, Ed 1969-70; Univ of CA, MA Ed, Psych 1970, MA 1972, PhD Soc 1974. **CAREER** Desegregation Inst Emergency School Aid Act, consult 1977; Fisk Univ, adj prof 1978-; US Dept of Labor, hbc faculty fellow 1980; Natl Assoc for Equal Oppty in Higher Ed, consult 1981; TN State Univ, prof of soc 1973-. **HONORS AND AWARDS** Delegate Crisis of Black Family Summit NAACP 1984. **MEMBERSHIPS** Pres Assoc of Social & Behavioral Scientists Inc 1983-84; mem Ed Bd Jrnl of Soc & Behavioral Sci 1984-; chairperson, bd of dir Sankofa Dance Theatre1984-; mem Amer Soc Assoc, Amer Acad of Political & Soc Sci, Southern Soc Assoc, Amer Assoc of Univ Prof, Kappa Alpha Psi, Islamic Ctr Inc; life mem Assn of Social and Behavioral Scientists Inc. **SELECTED PUBLICATIONS** Article "Illuminating the Path to Community Self-Reliance" Journal of Soc & Behavioral Sci 1984; Textbook Sci of Soc, 1985; article "Apartheid, the Great Debate and Martin Luther King Jr" The AME Church Review Jan-March 1985. **CONTACT ADDRESS** Professor of Sociology, Tennessee State Univ, 3500 John A Merritt Blvd, Nashville, TN 37203.

JACKSON, CHARLES C.
PERSONAL Born 02/21/1949, m, 1985, 2 children **DISCIPLINE** EDUCATON **EDUCATION** Wayne State Univ, BA, 76; Univ Cincinnati, MEd, 82; EdD, 88. **CAREER** Northern Ky Univ, 89-96; Assoc Prof, Augusta State Univ, 96-. **HONORS AND AWARDS** Alpha Phi Alpha. **MEMBERSHIPS** Am Educ Studies Asn, Phi Delta Kappa, Asn of Supervision and Curriculum Development, Southern Conf on African American Studies. **RESEARCH** Desegregation; Multicultural studies; Affirmative action; Civil rights; African American history. **SELECTED PUBLICATIONS** auth, "The Multicultural Education War," in The African Presence in Black America, Univ Kans, 00; auth, "Education and racial/ethnic Relations," Education Reform, Salem Press, 99; auth, "Speaking of Washington and Dubois," in Booker T. Washington: Interpretative Essays, forthcoming; auth, "The Immediate Years of the Brown Case," in African Americans: Their History, Custom Pub, 98; auth, "The state of African American society in the 1980's," in African Americans: Their History, Custom Pub, 98; auth, "Learning disorders and families," in Ready Reference: Family Life, Salem Press, Inc, 98; auth, "March on Washington,: in The Encyclopedia of North American History, Salem Press, 97; auth, "Civil Disobedience," in The Encyclopedia of Civil Rights in America, Salem Press, 96; auth, "Affirmative Action," in Ready Reference: American Justice, Salem Press, 95; auth, "Busing," in Ready Reference: American Justice, Salem Press, 95. **CONTACT ADDRESS** Dept Clinical & Professional Studies, Augusta State Univ, 2500 Walton Way, Augusta, GA 30904. **EMAIL** cjackson@aug.edu

JACKSON, JAMES S.
PERSONAL Born 07/30/1944, Detroit, MI, m, 1979, 2 children **DISCIPLINE** PSYCHOLOGY **EDUCATION** Mich State Univ, BS, 66; Univ Toledo, MA, 70; Wayne State Univ, PhD, 72. **CAREER** Assoc Prof, Univ Mich, 88-. **HONORS AND AWARDS** Harold R. Johnson Diversity Service Awd, Univ, MI, 00; Dist Visiting Prof, All-Univ Coun on Aging Univ MN, 95; Fogarty Sen Intl Fel, 93; Robert W. Kleemeier Awd Res, Gerontol Soc of Am, 94. **MEMBERSHIPS** APA; APS; AAAS; APSA; ABP; European Asn of Experimental Soc Psychol; European Cmty Studies Asn; GSA; Intl Soc of Political Sci. **RESEARCH** International Dimensions of Racism; Ethnic Minorities; Mental Health Services; Human Development & Family Studies; Research Design & Methodology; Health & Aging. **SELECTED PUBLICATIONS** Co-auth, "Skin tone and racial identity among African Americans: A theoretical and research framework," in Advances in African American psychology, (Cobb and Henry Pub, 99), 191-214; co-auth, "Perceptions of discrimination: The stress process and physical and psychological health," in Social stressors, personal and social resources, and their mental health consequences, 99; co-auth, "Racial attitudes, gender roles, and athletic identity in the adjustment of first-year black and white intercollegiate athletes," in A sporting chance: The role of youth sport in urban settings, Univ MN Press, 99; co-auth, "Traditional and contemporary prejudice and urban whites' support for affirmative action," Social Problems, (00): 503-527; co-auth, "The contribution of hope to the quality of life among aging African Americans,"

The Intl Journal of Aging and Human Development, (00): 35-51; co-auth, "Race/ethnicity and the year 2000 census: Recommendations for African American and other black populations in the United States," Am Journal of Publick Health, 00; co-auth, "Unfair treatment, neighborhood effects, and mental health in the Detroit metropolitan area," Journal of Health and Social Behavior, in press; co-auth, "The use of coping strategies and breast cancer survival: Results from the black/white cancer survival study," Am Journal of Epidemiology, in press; auth, "Older Black Americans," in The encyclopedia of aging, Springer Pub Co, in press; auth, "Changes Over the Life-Course in Productive Activities: Black and White Comparisons," in Productive aging: Perspectives and research directions, Johns Hopkins Univ Press, in press. **CONTACT ADDRESS** Dept Psychol, Univ of Michigan, Ann Arbor, 525 E Univ Ave, Ann Arbor, MI 48109. **EMAIL** jamessj@umich.edu

JACKSON, JOSEPH HOLLISTER
PERSONAL Born 10/13/1912, Springfield, VT, m, 1941, 1 child **DISCIPLINE** PHILOSOPHY, PSYCHOLOGY **EDUCATION** Middlebury Col, AB, 35; Brown Univ, MA, 37, PhD(philos), 40. **CAREER** Personnel dir, Columbia Broadcasting Syst, Inc, 44-50; training dir, Am Electric Power Co, 50-54; publ dir, Soc Advan Mgt, 54-55; managing ed, Ronald Press Co, 55-60; consult ed sci, Encycl Americana, 60-64; writer, Sci Fortnightly & Dateline in Sci, Richard Sigerson, 64-65; ed-in-chief, Investigating the Earth, Houghton, 65-67; instr philos, New Sch Social Res, 66-67; asst prof, Univ Conn, 68-72; Res & Writing, 72-, Nat Sci Found fel, Conn Res Found, 68-69; proj ed, Earth Sci Curriculum Proj, Nat Sci Found, 65-67; WRITER HARVARD PHYSICS PROF, 68-. **MEMBERSHIPS** Am Philos Asn; AAAS. **RESEARCH** Ethics; motivation; developmental and social psychology. **SELECTED PUBLICATIONS** Auth Pictorial guide to the Planets, 65, 3rd ed, 81 & coauth, Pictorial Guide to the Moon, 69, 3rd ed, 73, Crowell; Spaceship Earth-Earth Sciences, Houghton, 73, 2nd ed, 80; contribr, Psychology 73/74, Dushkin, 73; auth, Measurement of ethical values, Perceptual & Motor Skills, 36: 1075-1088; coauth, Investigating Behavior, Harper, 76; Infant Culture, Crowell, 78. **CONTACT ADDRESS** 57 Attawan Ave, Niantic, CT 06357.

JACKSON, PAMELA A.
PERSONAL Born 02/10/1958, Bristol, TN, m, 2000, 1 child **DISCIPLINE** PSYCHOLOGY **EDUCATION** Univ Ky, PhD, 89. **CAREER** Assoc Prof, Radford Univ. **RESEARCH** Animal Cognition; Neurobiology of Learning and Memory. **SELECTED PUBLICATIONS** Co-auth, "Memory for duration: Role of hippocampus and medial prefrontal cortex," Neurobiology of Learning and Memory, (98): 328-348; co-auth, "Impaired place learning and unimpaired cue learning in hippocampal-lesioned pigeons," Behavioral Neuroscience, (97): 963-975; co-auth, "Effects of Ibogaine on sensory-motor function, activity, and spatial learning in rats," Pharmacology, Biochemistry, and Behavior, (95): 103-190; co-auth, "Rats do show primacy and recency effects in memory for lists of spatial locations: a reply to Gaffan," Animal Learning & Behavior, (94): 214-218; auth, "Continuous recognition of spatial and nonspatial stimuli in hippocampal-lesioned rats," Behavioral and Neural Biology, (93): 107-119; co-auth, Prospective and retrospective memory processes in pigeons' performance on a successive delayed matching-to-sample task," Learning and Motivation, (93): 1-22; co-=auth, "Neurobiology of an attribute model of memory; role of prefrontal cortex," in Learning and Memory: Behavioral and Biological Substrates,92. **CONTACT ADDRESS** Dept Psychol, Radford Univ, PO Box 6946, Radford, VA 24142. **EMAIL** pjackson@runet.edu

JACKSON, ROBERT MAX
DISCIPLINE SOCIOLOGY **EDUCATION** Univ Mich, BA, 71; Univ Calif, MA, 74; PhD, 81. **CAREER** From Asst Prof to Assoc Prof, NYork Univ, 81-. **RESEARCH** Gender inequality, stratification, economy and society, theory, research methods. **SELECTED PUBLICATIONS** Coauth, Networks and Places, Free Pr (Glencoe, ILL), 77; auth, The Formation of Craft Labor Markets, Acad Pr (New York), 84; auth, Destined for Equality: The Inevitable Rise of Women's Status, Harvard UP (Cambridge), 98; auth, The Subordination of Women, Cambridge UP (Cambridge), forthcoming. **CONTACT ADDRESS** Dept Sociol, New York Univ, 269 Mercer St, New York, NY 10003. **EMAIL** robert.jackson@nyu.edu

JACOBS, JANIS E.
PERSONAL Born 03/26/1954, Lincoln, NE, m, 1980, 1 child **DISCIPLINE** CHILD DEVELOPMENT **EDUCATION** Colorado State Univ, BS, 77; Univ Mich, MA, 83; PhD, 87. **CAREER** Asst prof, Univ Neb, 86-93; assoc prof, 93-96; assoc prof, PaState Univ, 96-; vice pres admin, 99-. **HONORS AND AWARDS** Aaron Hinsdale Awd; Rackham Grad Predoc Fel; Willard C Olsen Awd. **MEMBERSHIPS** SRCD; SRA; APA; AERA. **RESEARCH** Parental influences on achievement motivation in middle childhood and adolescence; gender differences in achievement. **SELECTED PUBLICATIONS** Coauth, "Consultant choice: A comparison between abortion and other decisions," J Adole Res 11 (96): 235-260; coauth, "Retrospective reports of the family of origin environment and the transition to college," J Coll Student Devel 38 (97): 49-61; coauth, "The role of age, experience, and situational factors in the drink-

ing and driving decisions of college students," J Youth Adole 27 (98): 493-511; coauth, "The career plans of science-talented rural adolescent girls," Am Edu Res J 35 (98): 681-704; coauth, "Gender-role socialization in the family: A longitudinal approach," in The developmental social psychology of gender, eds. T Eckes, HM Trautner (Mahwah, NJ: Erlbaum, in press); coauth, "Parents, task values, and real life achievement choices," in Intrinsic motivation, eds. C Sansone, J Harackiewicz (San Diego, CA: Academic Press, in press); auth, "Developmental Changes in Thinking About the Social World: Implications for Cheating," Am Edu, in press. **CONTACT ADDRESS** Office of the President, Pennsylvania State Univ, Univ Park, 201 Old Main, University Park, PA 16802. **EMAIL** jej6@psu.edu

JACOBS, MARK D.
PERSONAL Born 04/02/1947, Paris, France, m, 1969, 2 children **DISCIPLINE** SOCIOLOGY **EDUCATION** Columbia Univ, BA, 68; Univ Chicago, PhD, 87. **CAREER** Asst to assoc prof, George Mason Univ, 85-; founding director PhD Prog in Cultural Studies, George Mason Univ, 92-99. **MEMBERSHIPS** Am Sociol Asn. **RESEARCH** Sociology of Culture, Sociological theory, Urban sociology. **SELECTED PUBLICATIONS** Auth, Screwing the System and Making It Work: Juvenile Justice in the No-Fault Society, Univ of Chicago Press, 90; auth, "'Not on a Friday or Saturday Night:' Performance Anxieties of a College Arts Audience," Journal of Arts Management, Law, and Society, (99): in press; auth, "Against Closure: Amplifying the Semantic Richness of the Section's Culture," culture, (99); auth, "the End of Liberalism in the Administration of Social Casework," Administration and Society, (86): 7-27. **CONTACT ADDRESS** Dept Sociol & Anthropol, George Mason Univ, Fairfax, 4400 Univ Dr, Fairfax, VA 22030. **EMAIL** mjacobs@gmu.edu

JACOBS, NORMAN G.
PERSONAL Born 02/28/1924, New York, NY, m, 1956, 2 children **DISCIPLINE** SOCIOLOGY **EDUCATION** Col of the City of NYork, BS, 43; Harvard Univ, AM, 50; PhD, 51. **CAREER** Asst prof to prof, Univ Kans, 62-65; prof, Univ Ill, Urbana-Champaign, 65-89; adjunct prof, Davidson Col, 89-; lect, Taiwan Normal Univ, 55-57; res sci, Am Univ, 57-59; Community Develop Adv, Fars province, Iran, 59-61; Fulbright prof, Prasarnmitr & Thammasat Univ, Bangkok, Thailand; res prof, Keio Univ, Tokyo, 68-69. **HONORS AND AWARDS** Fulbright Sr Res, Korean Inst Buddhist Studies, Seoul, 75. **MEMBERSHIPS** Pali Text Soc; Dai Nippon Soc, Netherlands; Int Soc Japanese Philately; Indian Sociol Soc. **RESEARCH** Asian societies in historical perspective, comparative studies. **SELECTED PUBLICATIONS** Coauth, Japanese Coinage, NY, (53), revised ed, (72); auth, The Origin of Modern Capitalism and Eastern Asia, Hong Kong Press, 58, reprint, Octagon Books (81); auth, The Sociology of Development: Iran as an Asian Case Study, NY, (66); Modernization without Development: Thailand as an Asian Case Study, NY (71); auth, "Max Weber, The Theory of Asian Socioty, and the Study of Thailand, Sociol Quart (autumn 71); auth, "Patrimonialism, Feudalism, and Far Eastern Development," in Technology and Social Change in East Asia, Iowa State Univ (73); auth, "The Institutional Roots of Korean Character," in Wild Asters, Explorations in Korean Thought, Culture and Society, ed by Ronald Morse, Washington, DC (86). **CONTACT ADDRESS** Dickinson Col, FAS Mail Center, Carlisle, PA 17013.

JACOBS, RUTH
PERSONAL Born 11/15/1924, Boston, MA, d, 2 children **DISCIPLINE** SOCIOLOGY **EDUCATION** Boston Univ, BS, 64; Brandeis Univ, MA, 66; PhD, 69. **CAREER** Prof, Boston Univ, 69-82; Prof and Dept Chair, Clark Univ, 82-87; Prof, Regis Col, 87-. **RESEARCH** Gerontology; Gender. **SELECTED PUBLICATIONS** Auth, Women Who Touched My Life: A Memoir, 96; auth, Button, Button, Who Has the Button?, 96; auth, Be An Outrageous Older Woman - A R.A.S.P. (Remarkable Aging Smart Person), 97; auth, Older Women: Surviving and Thriving, 97; auth, The ABCs of Aging, 00. **CONTACT ADDRESS** Dept Sociol, Regis Col, Massachusetts, 235 Wellesley St, Weston, MA 02493.

JACOBSON, CARDELL K.
PERSONAL Born 09/14/1941, UT, m, 4 children **DISCIPLINE** SOCIOLOGY **EDUCATION** Brigham Young Univ, BS, 66; Univ NC at Chapel Hill, MA, 69, PhD, 71. **CAREER** Prof, Brigham Young Univ, 85-. **HONORS AND AWARDS** Univ Res Prof, Central Mich Univ, 79-80; Alcuin Fel in General Educ, Brigham Young Univ, 98-2001. **MEMBERSHIPS** Am Sociol Asn, Soc for the Scientific Study of Relig. **RESEARCH** Race and ethnic relations, social psychology, sociology of religion. **SELECTED PUBLICATIONS** Ed, Racial and Ethnic Families in the United States, New York: Garland Pubs (95); auth, "Denominational and Racial and Ethnic Differences in Fatalism," Rev of Religious Res, 41 (99): 9-20; coauth with Tim B. Heaton and Kimberly Holland, "Persistence and Change in Childless Intentions," J of Marriage and the Family, 61 (99): 531-539; coauth with Jeffrey C. Chin, "Attributional Style and Racial Prejudice: A Preliminary Study," in James A. Holstein and Gale Miller, eds, Perspectives on Social Problems, Vol 11, Stamford, Ct: JAI Press (99); coauth with Tim B. Heaton and

Bruce A. Chadwick, Statistical Handbook on Racial Groups in America, Phoenix: Oryx (2000); coauth with Tim B. Heaton, "Intergroup Marriage: An Analysis of Opportunity Structures," Sociological Inquiry (forthcoming); coauth with Jeffrey C. Chin, "Religion, Religiosity, and Attribution of Responsibility," Res in the Soc Scientific Study of Relig, Vol 11 (forthcoming). **CONTACT ADDRESS** Dept Sociol, Brigham Young Univ, Provo, UT 84602.

JACOBSON, RODOLFO

PERSONAL m, 1944, 4 children **DISCIPLINE** LINGUISTICS, BILINGUAL EDUCATION **EDUCATION** Univ Panama, AB, 52; Univ Mich, MA, 64, PhD(ling), 66. **CAREER** Teacher, Escuela Prof, Panama, 52-62; instr English as foreign lang, English Lang Inst, Univ Mich, 65, lectr, 65-66; assoc prof English, State Univ NY Col Cortland, 66-69, prof English & dir English socioling prog, 69-74; Prof Ling, Univ Tex, San Antonio, 74-, Consult, Ministry Educ, Panama, 60-62; lectr, Am Univ Beirut & Am Univ Cairo, 73; consult, United Independent Sch Dist, Laredo, Tex, 75-79; dir, Title VIII Training fel, demonstration proj, 77-; interpreter & examr, Adm US Courts, Washington, DC, 80-81. **MEMBERSHIPS** Teachers English to Speakers Other Lang; Nat Asn Bilingual Educ; Int Sociol Asn; Ling Asn Southwest; Am Educ Res Asn. **RESEARCH** Sociolinguistics; Spanish language varieties and use; methods in bilingual instruction. **SELECTED PUBLICATIONS** Auth, Incorporating sociolinguistic norms into an EFL program, TESOL Quart, 76; La reinvindicacion de parole, Estudios Filol, 76; The social implications of intrasentential codeswitching, in: Chicano Scholarship (the New Scholar), 77; Anticipatory embedding and imaginary content, in: Swallow VI Proc, 78; Semantic compounding in the speech of Mexican American bilinguals, in: Bilingualism & Bilingual Educ, 79; Beyond ESL: The teaching of content other than language arts in bilingual education, Southwest Educ Development Lab, Austin, Tex, 79; Can bilingual teaching techniques reflect bilingual community behavior?, in: Bilingual Educ and Public Policy, Ypsilanti, Mich, 79; Can and should the Laredo experiment be duplicated elsewhere?, in: NABE Proc, 81. **CONTACT ADDRESS** 14222 Golden Woods, San Antonio, TX 78285.

JAIMES-GUERRERO, MARIANA

PERSONAL Born 09/10/1946, Mesa, AZ, s, 2 children **DISCIPLINE** AMERICAN HISTORY, HIGHER EDUCATION AND PUBLIC POLICY **EDUCATION** AZ State Univ, BA, 71, MA, 78, EdD, 90. **CAREER** Vis prof, Cornell Univ, Soc for the Humanities, 91-92; vis prof, School of Justice Studies, AZ State Univ, 94-95; Assoc Prof, Women's Dept, Humanities Col at San Francisco State Univ, 95-. **HONORS AND AWARDS** Humanities fel, Australian Nat Univ, 96; Humanities fel, Cornell Univ, Soc for the Humanities, 91-92. **MEMBERSHIPS** Amer Academy Relig; World Philos Congress; Native Amer Methodist Assoc. **RESEARCH** Indigenous perspectives and experiences; Native women and cancer control res; impact of peoples, cultures, and ecology. **SELECTED PUBLICATIONS** Auth, The State of Native America, SEP, 92; numerous articles in academic journals; several works in progress; brd, Aboriginal Voices; reviewer brd, Journal of American Indian Education, CIE at ASU, Tempe, AZ. **CONTACT ADDRESS** College of Humanities, San Francisco State Univ, 1600 Holloway Ave., Room 363, San Francisco, CA 94132. **EMAIL** guerrero@athena.sfsu.edu

JALATA, ASAFA

PERSONAL Born 12/13/1954, Oromia, m, 1985, 2 children **DISCIPLINE** SOCIOLOGY **EDUCATION** BSW, 78; MS, 85; MA, 87; PhD, 90. **HONORS AND AWARDS** Grad Fel Awd; Travel Awd. **MEMBERSHIPS** Oromo Studies Asn; African Studies Asn. **RESEARCH** Oromo Studies; African American Studies; Global Studies. **SELECTED PUBLICATIONS** Auth, Oromia & Ethiopia: State Formation and Ethnonational Conflict, 1868-1992, Lynne Rienner Pub, 93; auth, "African American Nationalism, Development, and Afrocentricity: Implications for the Twenty-first Century," in Molefi Kete and Afrocentricity: In Praise and Criticism, (Winston-Derek Pub Group, 95), 153-174; auth, "Poverty, Powerlessness and the Imperial Interstate System in the Horn of Africa," in Disaster and Development in the Horn of Africa, (Macmillan, 95), 31-75; auth, "Oromo Nationalism and Ethiopian Reaction," in Oromo Nationalism and the Ethiopian Discourse, (Red Sea Press, 98), 1-26; auth, "The Struggle for Knowledge: The Case of Emergent Oromo Studies," in Oromo Nationalism and the Ethiopian Discourse, (Red Sea Press, 98), 253-290; auth, "The Impact of a Racist US Foreign Policy on the Oromo National Struggle," Journal of Oromo Studies, (99): 49-89; auth, "Two Liberation Movements Compared: The Cases of the Southern Sudan and Oromia," Social Justice: A Journal of Crime, Conflict & World Order, forthcoming; auth, "US-Sponsored Ethiopian Democracy and State Terrorism," Autopsy of Terror: Human Rights and Democracy in the Horn of Africa, forthcoming. **CONTACT ADDRESS** Dept Sociol, Univ of Tennessee, Knoxville, 1345 Circle Park, Knoxville, TN 37996-0001. **EMAIL** ajalata@utkux.utcc.utk.edu

JALONGO, MARY

PERSONAL Born 01/30/1950, Pittsburgh, PA, m, 1977 **DISCIPLINE** EDUCATION **EDUCATION** Univ Detroit, BA, 71; Oakland Univ, MAT, 72; Univ Toledo, PhD, 78. **CAREER** Instr, Univ of toledo, 77-78; asst prof to prof, Ind Univ, 78-. **HONORS AND AWARDS** Who's Who in the World, 95; Kappa Delta Pi Beta Famma Chapter Awd, 98; Who's Who Among Am Teachers, 99; Outstanding Am, 99. **SELECTED PUBLICATIONS** Coauth, The arts in young children's lives: Aesthetic experiences in early childhood, Allyn & Bacon (Boston), 97; coed, Major trends and issues in early childhood: Challenges, controversies, and insights, Teachers Col Pr, (NY), 97; coauth, The college learner: Reading, studying, and attaining academic success, Prentice Hall (Upper Saddle River, NJ), 97; coauth, "Creating caring communities in classrooms: Advice from an intervention specialist", Childhood Educ 75.2 (98): 83-89; coauth, "National public school pre-kindergarten: Issues and future Trends", Dimensions of Early Childhood 26.3-4, (99): 3-11; coauth, "But, what's wrong with letter grades? Responding to parents' questions about alternative assessment", Childhood Educ 75.3 (99): 130-135; ed, Resisting the pendulum swing: Informed perspectives on education controversies, Assoc for Childhood Educ Int, (Olney, MD), 99; coauth, Exploring your role: A practitioner's introduction to early childhood education, Prentice Hall (Englewood Cliffs, NJ), 00; auth, Early childhood language arts: Meeting diverse literacy needs through collaboration with families and professionals, Allyn & Bacon (Boston), 00; coauth, Creative expression and play in early childhood, Merrill/Prentice Hall (forthcoming). **CONTACT ADDRESS** Prof Studies in Educ Dept, Indiana Univ of Pennsylvania, Indiana, PA 15701-0001.

JAMES, ALICE

PERSONAL Born 03/23/1949, Oxford, OH **DISCIPLINE** ANTHROPOLOGY **EDUCATION** Bucknell Univ, BA, 71; Penn State Univ, MA, 74; PhD, 83. **CAREER** Assoc Prof, Shippensburg Univ, 88-99; Sen Res Assoc, PaState Univ, 93-94; Vis Res Fel, Nat Soc Sci Res Center, 97-98; Prof, Shippensburg Univ, 99-. **HONORS AND AWARDS** Phi Kappa Phi, 99; Teaching Fel, SSHE, 89-90; Outstanding Women Teacher, Penn State, 94; Nat Sci Foundation Grant. **MEMBERSHIPS** Am Anthropol Asn, Population Asn of Am, Mod Greek Studies Asn, Penn Asn of Teaching Scholars. **RESEARCH** Greece, The Caribbean, Small population demography, Fertility, Family, Household, Refugee populations, Marriage patterns and mate choice. **SELECTED PUBLICATIONS** Auth, "Use of House and Space: Public and Private Family Interaction on Chios, Greece," in House Life: Space, Place and Family in Europe, Berg Publishers, (99): 205-220; auth, "Family in Cross Cultural Perspective," in Teaching About Families, Washington, (96): 87-91; auth, "Fertility Patterns in a Bastardy Prone sub-Society," Journal of Quantitative Anthropology, (91): 227-241; auth, "Modernization and Household Formation on St. Bart, F.W.I. : Continuity and Change," Human Ecology, (90): 457-474; auth, "Culturally Irregular Reproductive Choices in a Population Isolate," in approche pluri-disciplinaire des isolats humains, Paris, (90): 331-338; auth, "Isonymy and Mate Choice on St. Bart, French West Indies: computer Simulations of Random and Total Isonymy," Human Biology, (83): 297-303; auth, "Estimation of Random Isonymy," Annals of Human Biology, (83): 295-298; auth, "Inheritance, Demographic Structure, and Marriage: A Cross-cultural Perspective," Journal of Family History, (82): 289-298. **CONTACT ADDRESS** Dept Sociol, Shippensburg Univ of Pennsylvania, 1871 Old Main Dr, Shippensburg, PA 17257. **EMAIL** ajames@ship.edu

JAMES, DAVID L.

PERSONAL Born 09/01/1955, Detroit, MI, m, 1977, 3 children **DISCIPLINE** EDUCATION **EDUCATION** Western Mich Univ, BA, 77; Central Mich Univ, MA, 79; Wayne State Univ, EdD, 98. **CAREER** Dir Admis, Siena Heights Col, 80-86; Dir Admiss, Univ Mich-Flint, 86-96; Dean of Acad and Student Services, Oakland Community Col, 96-. **HONORS AND AWARDS** Magna cum laude, Western Mich Univ, 77. **RESEARCH** Humor in teaching. **SELECTED PUBLICATIONS** Auth, A Heart Out of This World (poems), Carnegie Mellon Univ (84); auth, Do Not Give Dogs What is Holy (poems), March Street Press (94). **CONTACT ADDRESS** Chief Academic Dean, Oakland Comm Col, 7350 Cooley Lake Rd, Waterford, MI 48327. **EMAIL** dljames@occ.cc.mi.us

JAMES, DAVID PHILLIP

PERSONAL Born 09/02/1940, Greenville, NC, m **DISCIPLINE** EDUCATION **EDUCATION** Elizabeth City State Univ, NC, BS, 1962; Georgetown Univ, Washington, DC, MA, 1971; Nova Univ, Fort Lauderdale, FL, EdD 1978. **CAREER** Pitt Co NC, teacher/coach, 62-63; Clarke Co VA, social sci teacher/coach, 63-67; Washington, DC Public Schools, Social Science teacher/coach, 67-71; Prince George's Community Coll, educ admin, 71-, dean of educational development and extension centers & special programs, currently. **HONORS AND AWARDS** Outstanding Teacher of the Year, Washington, DC Public Schools, 1971; Phi Alpha Theta Intl Awd, History, Georgetown Univ, 1971; 1st Black Assoc Dean, Prince George's Community Coll, 1979; Honored Graduate, Elizabeth City State Coll, NC, 1962; Honored as the Outstanding Admin, Prince George Community Coll, 1988; Honorable Mention Recipient, Maryland Assn for Higher Educ as Outstanding Educator, 1989; Named Project Dir of the Black & Minority Student Retention Programs, Prince George's Community Coll, 1988. **MEMBERSHIPS** Part-time consultant, self-employed, 1978-; Student Retention; mem, Natl Council Community Serv & Continued Educ, 1973-; mem, Adult Educ Assn, 1978-; mem, Amer Assn for Higher Educ, 1982. **SELECTED PUBLICATIONS** Auth, "Black Issues in Higher Education," 1988, "Increasing the Retention Rates of Black & Minority Students Through Mentoring & Tutorial Services at Prince George's Community College," 1989. **CONTACT ADDRESS** Dean, Prince George's Comm Col, 301 Largo Rd, Largo, MD 20772.

JAMES, ELRIDGE M.

PERSONAL Born 03/23/1942, Eunice, LA, m **DISCIPLINE** EDUCATION **EDUCATION** Grambling State U, BS 1966; Wayne State U, MEd 1969; MI State U, PhD 1973. **CAREER** NE LA Univ, mem grad faculty, asst prof sec & coun educ, 75-76; Quachia Parish Bd of Educ, asst prof & clinical prof, 74-; Grambling State Univ, assoc prof, 73-74; MI State Univ, graduate asst, 72; Great Lakes Steel Corp, indus instructor, 69-70; Ecorse HS, teacher, 68-70; CJ Miller Elementary School; Great Lakes Steel Corp, dir educ, 68-70; Ford Motor Co, supvr, 66-68. **HONORS AND AWARDS** Dean's list of outstanding grads MI State U. **MEMBERSHIPS** LA Indsl Arts Assn; Am Vocat Assn; LA Assn Pub Sch Adult Edn; So Assn for Counselor Educ & Supervision; LA State Reading Council; Assn Supr & Curriculum Devel; mem Phi Delta Kappa; Scottish Rite Mason King Solomon's Lodge; Omega Psi Phi. **SELECTED PUBLICATIONS** Wrote several articles & books for Grambling Coll. **CONTACT ADDRESS** Sec Coun Educ, Northeast Louisiana Univ, Monroe, LA 71202.

JAMES, H. RHETT

PERSONAL Born 12/01/1928, Baltimore, MD, m **DISCIPLINE** EDUCATION, THEOLOGY **EDUCATION** VA Union U, AB 1950; Our Lady of the Lake Coll, MEd 1951; VA Union U, MDiv 1957; TX Christian U, MTh 1961; Harvard Univ Inst of Mgt, 1974; Univ ofIN, Memphis Univ Insts on on Mgt-Commun Servs 1974-75; Univ of TX at Arlington, PhD 1974. **CAREER** Urban Affairs & Community Devel Center, asst prof of soc sci, assoc dir of devel, dir; New Careers for the Handicapped Program Bishop Coll TX, dir, 62-; New Hope Baptist Church TX, pastor, 58-; VA Union Univ, instructor, 55-58; San Antonio School System St Phillips Jr Coll, instructor, 50-55. **HONORS AND AWARDS** Goals for Dallas Commun Serv Aw; OIC Commun Serv Aw; Urban Leag Disting Serv Aw; NKOK Radio Sta Commun Serv Aw; Big Bros Commun Serv Aw; Disting Serv Aw Urban Leag; Trail Blazers Aw; Dllas City Counc Serv Aw. **MEMBERSHIPS** Educ com chmn Dallas NAACP 1961; pres Dallas NAACP 1962; bd of dir TX Counc of Chs; del Pres Com on Equal Employ Opportun; fdr, 1st pres Dallas Frontiers Internat; pres Dallas Dem Men; bd mem Family Guid Ctr; bd mem Am Civ Lib Union; ret bd mem Dallas Urban Leag; bd mem TX Assn of Devlpng Colls 1970-74; bd mem City of Dallas; mem Am Mensa Soc; bd mem N Dallas Am Cancer Soc; mem So Histl Assn; mem Am Assn of Univ Profs; bd mem Am Bapt Conv Chs of the S; mem Sigma Pi Phi & Kappa Alpha Psi Frat. **CONTACT ADDRESS** New Hope Baptist Church, 5002 S Central Expressway, Dallas, TX 75215.

JAMESON, ELIZABETH

DISCIPLINE WESTERN AMERICA, U.S. SOCIAL, WOMEN'S HISTORY **EDUCATION** Univ Mich, PhD. **CAREER** Assoc prof, Univ NMex. **RESEARCH** Women's and gender history; labor history. **SELECTED PUBLICATIONS** Auth, Building Colorado: The United Brotherhood of Carpenters and Joiners in the Centennial State, 84; coed, The Women's West, 87. **CONTACT ADDRESS** Univ of New Mexico, Albuquerque, Albuquerque, NM 87131.

JANELLE, CHRISTOPHER M.

PERSONAL Born 05/05/1968, Boston, MA, m, 1992, 2 children **DISCIPLINE** SPORT PSYCHOLOGY **EDUCATION** Miami Univ, Oh, BA, 91; Springfield Col, Mass, MS, 93; Univ Fla, PhD, 97. **CAREER** Asst prof, Dir of Performance Psychology Lab, Univ of Fla. **HONORS AND AWARDS** Elected to the Am Acad of Distinguished Students, 96; Nominated for Univ of Fla Grad Student Teaching Excellence Awd, 97; Recipient of the Univ of Fla Presidential Recognition for Outstanding Achievement, 97; nominated for Univ of Fla Col of Health and Human Performance Teacher of the Year, 98-99; Recipient of Univ of Fla Presidential Recognition for productivity, 99. **MEMBERSHIPS** Am Psychol Asn; Asn for the Advancement of Applied Sport Psychol; North Am Soc for the Psychol of Sport and Physical Activity; Am Alliance for Health, Physical Educ, Recreation, and Dance; Int Soc of Sport Psychol. **SELECTED PUBLICATIONS** Coauth with D. A. Barba, S. G. Frehlich, L. K. Tennant, and J. H. Cauraugh, "Maximizing feedback effectiveness through attentional cueing and self-regulation," Res Quart for Exercise and Sport, 68, 4 (97): 269-279; coauth with R. N. Singer, A. M. Williams, S. G. Frehlich, S. J. Radlo, D. A. Barba, and L. Bouchard, "New frontiers in visual research: An exploratory study in live tennis situations," Res Quart for Exercise and Sport, 69 (98): 290-296; coauth with R. N. Singer and A. M. Williams, "External distraction and attentional narrowing: Visual search evidence," J of Sport and Exercise Psychol, 21 (99): 70-91; coauth with T. W. Kaninski and M. Murray, "College football injuries: Physical self-perception as a predictor," Int Sports J, 3 (99): 93-102; coauth with R. N.

Singer, "Determining sport expertise: From genes to supremes," Int J of Sports Psychol, 30 (99): 117-150; coauth with J. P. Brunelle and L. K. Tennant, "Controlling competitive anger among male soccer players," J of Applied Sport Psychol, 11 (99): 283-297; auth, "Ironic mental processes in sport: Implications for sport psychologists," The Sport Psychol, 13 (99): 201-220; coauth with C. H. Hillman, R. J. Apparies, and B. D. Hatfield, "To shoot or not to shoot? A psychphysiological profile of peak performance preparatory states," Biological Psychol, 52 (2000): 71-83; coauth with J. H. Cauraugh, "Attentional considerations in the sport of tennis," in K. Davids, ed, Interceptive actions, E & FN Spon (in press); coauth with R. N. Singer, "Sport Psychology in the United States," in R. Lidor, ed, World sport psychology sourcebook, 3rd ed, Champaign, Il: Human Kinetics (in press). **CONTACT ADDRESS** Dept of Exercise and Sport Scis, Univ of Florida, 132-E Florida Gym, Gainesville, FL 32611. **EMAIL** cjanelle@hhp.ufl.edu

JANELLI, ROGER L.
PERSONAL Born 09/21/1943, New York, NY, m, 1970 **DISCIPLINE** ANTHROPOLOGY, FOLKLORE **EDUCATION** Univ Penn, MBA, 67; MA, 73; MS, 74; PhD, 75. **CAREER** Prof, Ind Univ, 75-; res fel, Univ Tok, 00. **MEMBERSHIPS** AAA; AAS; KCAS; AFS. **RESEARCH** Social and cultural change; East Asia; popular religion. **SELECTED PUBLICATIONS** Auth, Making Capitalism, Stanford, 93; auth, Anthropology of Korea, Japanese Nat Museum Ethno (Osaka), 98. **CONTACT ADDRESS** Folklore, Ethnomusicology, Indiana Univ, Bloomington, 504 North Fess Ave, Bloomington, IN 47408-3822.

JANG, SUNG JOON
PERSONAL Born 03/12/1957, Seoul, Korea, m, 1986, 4 children **DISCIPLINE** SOCIOLOGY **EDUCATION** SUNY, Albany, MA, 89; PhD, 92. **CAREER** Asst prof, Oh State Univ, 92-00; assoc prof, Louisiana State Univ, 00-. **MEMBERSHIPS** ASA; ASC. **RESEARCH** Sociology of crime and deviance; juvenile delinquency. **SELECTED PUBLICATIONS** Coauth, "Clinical Risk Factors Associated with Parasuicide in Prison." Intl J Offen Ther Comp Crim 40 (96): 135-146; coauth, "Self-Esteem, Delinquent Peers, and Delinquency: A Test of the Self-Enhancement Thesis." Am Soc Rev 63 (98): 587-599; coauth, "A Test of Reciprocal Causal Relationships among Parental Supervision, Affective Ties, and Delinquency." J Res Crime Delinq 34 (97): 307-336; auth, "Age-Varying Effects of Family, School, and Peers on Delinquency: A Multilevel Modeling Test of Interactional Theory." Crim 37 (99): 643-685; coauth, "Urban Families and Adolescent Mental Health." Soc Work Res 23 (99):15-27; coauth, "Escaping from the Crime of Inner Cities: Church Attendance and Religious Salience Among Disadvantaged Youth." Just Quart, forthcoming; coauth, "Neighborhood Disorder, Fear, and Mistrust: The Buffering Role of Social Ties with Neighbors." Am J Comm Psych, forthcoming. **CONTACT ADDRESS** Dept Sociology, Ohio State Univ, Columbus, 190 N Oval Mall, Columbus, OH 43210. **EMAIL** jang.11@osu.edu

JANKOWSKY, KAREN HERMINE
DISCIPLINE WOMEN'S STUDIES **EDUCATION** Wash Univ, St. Louis, BA 78; MA 81; PhD 86. **CAREER** Vis Lectr, Univ Wash-Seattle, 86-87; Vis Asst Prof, Univ Wis-Madison, 87-88; Asst Prof, Univ Wis-Madison, 88-94; Vis Asst Prof, Wayne State Univ, 94-95; Asst Prof, Wayne State Univ, 95-98. **HONORS AND AWARDS** Hon Res Fel, Women's Studies Res Cen, Univ Wis Madison,99, 01; Res Fel, Alexander von Humboldt Found, Free Univ Berlin, Ger, 97, 99; Res Stip, Grad Sch, Wayne State Univ, 97, 98; Res Stip Col of Lib Arts Wayne State Univ, 97, 98; Sum Res Sup, Hum Cen, Wayne State Univ 97; Sum Res Sup, Col of Urban, Labor, and Metro Affairs, Wayne State Univ, 97, 95. **RESEARCH** Histories of writing women, citizenship, literary and cultural theory, semiotics. **SELECTED PUBLICATIONS** Auth, "Unsinn/anderer Sinn/ neuer Sinn: Zur Bewegung im Denken von Christa, Wolfs Kassandra uber den Krieg und die Heldengesellschaft," Ed Philo und Sozial 15 (89, 91); auth, "Foregrounding Foreignness in Teaching German Unification: Video as a Tool for Processing Interviews with Berliners in a Study-Abroad Course," AQFL 24 (92): 23-29; auth, "Canons Crumble Just Like Walls: Discovering the Works of GDR Women Writers," in Cultural Transformations in Germany: American and German Perspectives, ed. F. Eigler and P. Pfeiffer (Columbia: Camden House, 93), 102-116; auth, "German Literature Contested: The 1991 Ingeborg Bachmann Prize Debate, 'Cultural Diversity,' and Emine Sevgi zdamar," Ger Qtly (97): 261-276; auth, "Other Germanies - Questioning Identity," in WomenÛs Literature and Art, ed. W. C. Love, Postmodern Culture Series (Albany: U of NY, 97); ed, "Christa Wolf," in Woman Writers in German Speaking Countries (Westport: Greenwood, 97): 485-499. **CONTACT ADDRESS** 2244 Commonwealth Ave, Madison, WI 53705.

JARVIE, IAN CHARLES
PERSONAL Born 07/08/1937, South Shields, England, m, 1962, 2 children **DISCIPLINE** PHILOSOPHY, ANTHROPOLOGY **EDUCATION** Univ London, BS, 58, PhD(philos), 61. **CAREER** Lectr philos, Univ Hong Kong, 62-66; chmn dept, 76-79, PROF PHILOS, YORK UNIV, 67-. **MEMBERSHIPS** Royal Anthrop Inst; Brit Soc Philos Sci; Soc Cinema Studies. **RESEARCH** Philosophy of the social sciences; anthropological theory; movies. **SELECTED PUBLICATIONS** Auth, The Postwar Economic Foreign Policy of the American Film Industry: Europe 1945-1950 in David Ellwood and Rob Kroes eds., Hollywood in Europe, Experiences of Cultural Hegemony, Amsterdam: VU University Press, (1994): pp. 154-75; auth, The Justificationist Roots of Relativism, and "Reply" in Charles M. Lewis, ed., Relativism and Religion, London: Macmillan, (1995): pp. 52-70 and 125-28; auth, Popper, Sir Karl, in Edward Craig, ed., The Routledge Encyclopedia of Philosophy, London: Routledge, Volume 7, (1998), pp. 533-40; auth, Free Trade as Cultural Threat: American film and tv exports in the post-war period, in Geoffrey Nowell-Smith and Steven Ricci, eds., Hollywood and Europe, Economics, Culture, National Identity 1948-95, London: BFI, (1998), PP. 34-46; auth, Creativity, in Michael J. Kelly, ed., Encyclopedia of Aeshetics, New York: Oxford Unviersity Press, Volume I, pp. 456-59; auth, Popper's Contribution to the Social Sciences, in a volume of lectures to be published in Vienna; auth, National Cinema: A Theoretical Assessment, in a volume edited by Matte Hjort and Scott Mackenzie, Cinema and Nation: Interdisciplinary Approaches to Nationalism and Nation Identity, Routledge; auth, Working Rationality and the Reasonable of Dogmatism in David Johnson and Christina Erneling, eds., The Mind as Scienticic Object: Brain and Culture, Oxford University Press. **CONTACT ADDRESS** Dept of Philos, York Univ, 4700 Keele St, S428 Ross Bldg, Toronto, ON, Canada M3J 1P3. **EMAIL** jarvie@yorku.ca

JARVIS, GILBERT ANDREW
PERSONAL Born 02/13/1941, Boston, MA, m, 1963, 2 children **DISCIPLINE** FOREIGN & SECOND LANGUAGE EDUCATION **EDUCATION** St Norbert Col, BA, 63; Purdue Univ, West Lafayette, MA, 66, PhD(foreign lang educ), 70. **CAREER** Teacher French & English, Mineral Point High Sch, Wis, 63-65; instr French & educ, Purdue Univ, 65-70; from asst prof to prof, 70-76, prof Foreign & Second Lang Educ, Ohio State Univ, 76-, chmn Humanities Educ, 80-86, chmn, Educational studies, 87-95, dir, English as a Second Language Programs, 95-00. **HONORS AND AWARDS** NY State Nat Foreign Language Leadership Award, 81. **MEMBERSHIPS** Am Coun Teaching Foreign Lang; Am Educ Res Asn. **RESEARCH** Foreign language learning and curricula development and measurement. **SELECTED PUBLICATIONS** Ed, Review of Foreign Language Education, Nat Texbk, Vols V, VI, VII & VIII, 73, 74, 75 & 76; coauth, Connaitre et se Connaitre, 76, Passeport pour la France & Vivent les Differences, 77, Invitation, 79, 84, 88, 93; Holt; Invitation Essentials, 91, 95; Invitation au monde francophone, 00. **CONTACT ADDRESS** English as a Second Language Programs, Ohio State Univ, Columbus, Columbus, OH 43235. **EMAIL** Jarvis.3@osu.edu

JASPER, JAMES M.
PERSONAL Born 09/30/1957, Washington, DC, m, 1996 **DISCIPLINE** SOCIOLOGY **EDUCATION** Harvard, BA, 79; Univ Calif Berkeley, MA, 81; PhD, 88. **CAREER** NYork Univ, 86-96; Columbia Univ, 97; Princeton Univ, 97, 99-00. **RESEARCH** Politics, Culture, History. **SELECTED PUBLICATIONS** Auth, Nuclear Politics: Energy and the State in the United States, Sweden, and France, Princeton Univ Press (Princeton), 90; coauth, The Animal Rights Crusade: The Growth of a Moral Protest, The Free Press (NY), 92; coauth, "Recruiting Strangers and Friends: Moral Shocks and Social Networks in Animal Rights and Antinuclear Protest," Soc Prob 42-4 (Nov 95): 401-420; coauth, "Interests and Credibility: Whistleblowers in Technological Conflicts," Soc Sci Infor 35-3 (Sept 96): 565-589; auth, "The Emotions of Protest: Affective and Reactive Emotions in and around Social Movements," Sociol Forum 13-3 (Sept 98): 397-424; coauth, "Caught in a Winding, Snarling Vine: the Structural Bias of Political Process Theory," Sociol Forum 14-1 (Mar 99): 27-54; auth, "Nostalgie: Verdammung der Gegewart, Kontrolle der Zukunft," Lettre International 47 (Dec 99): 74-81; auth, Restles Nation: Starting Over in America, Univ of Chicago Press (Chicago), 00; co-ed, Social Movements: Classical and Contemporary Readings, Blackwell (Cambridge, Mass, 01). **CONTACT ADDRESS** Dept Sociol, Princeton Univ, 2-N-1 Green Hall, Princeton, NJ 08544-0001. **EMAIL** jmjasper@juno.com

JASSO, GUILLERMINA
PERSONAL Born 07/22/1942, Laredo, TX, s **DISCIPLINE** SOCIOLOGY **EDUCATION** Our Lady of the Lake Col, BA, 62; Univ Notre Dame, MA, 70; Johns Hopkins Univ, PhD, 74. **CAREER** Asst prof, Columbia, 74-77; spec asst to commissioner, INS, 77-79; director of res, US Select commission on Immigration & Refugee Policy, 79-80; asst prof, Univ Mich, 80-82; assoc prof to prof, Univ Minn, 82-87; prof, Univ Iowa, 87-91; prof, New York Univ, 91-. **HONORS AND AWARDS** Johns Hopkins soc of scholars, 94; Sociol Res Asn, Fel, Ctr for Adv Study, 99-00. **MEMBERSHIPS** Am Sociol Asn, Population Asn of Am, Am Econ Asn, Am Statistical Asn. **RESEARCH** Theory, Justice, Migration, Theoretical and empirical methods. **SELECTED PUBLICATIONS** Auth, "The New Immigrant Survey Pilot: Overview and New Findings about US Legal Immigrants at Admission," Demography, (00): 127-138; auth, "How Much Injustice is There in the World? Two New Justice Indexes," American Sociological Review, (99): 133-168; auth, "Methods for Empirical Justice Analysis: Part I. Framework, Models, and Quantities," Social Justice Research, (97): 393-430; auth, "Double Standards in Just Earnings for Male and Female Workers," Social Psychology Quarterly, (97): 66-78; auth, "Probing the Character of Norms: A Factorial Survey Analysis of the Norms of Political Action," American Sociological Review, (97): 947-964; auth, The New Chosen People: Immigrants in the United States, Russell Sage: New York, 90; auth, "Methods for the Theoretical and Empirical Analysis of Comparison Processes," Sociological Methodology, (90): 369-419; auth, "Whom Shall We Welcome? Elite Judgments of the Criteria for the Selection of Immigrants," American sociological Review, (88): American sociological Review, (88): 919-932; auth, "Principles of Theoretical Analysis," Sociological Theory, (88): 1-20; auth, "Marital Coital Frequency and the Passage of Time: Estimating the Separate Effects of Spouses' Ages and Marital Duration, Birth and Marriage Cohorts, and Period Influences," American Sociological Review (85): 224-241. **CONTACT ADDRESS** Dept Sociol, New York Univ, 269 Mercer St, New York, NY 10003. **EMAIL** jasso@nyu.edu

JEDLICKA, DAVOR
PERSONAL Born 08/03/1945, Dubrovrik, Croatia **DISCIPLINE** SOCIOLOGY, SOCIAL PSYCHOLOGY **EDUCATION** Univ HI, PhD, 75; Tex Women's Univ, PhD, 99. **CAREER** Asst prof, Univ of Ga, 76-82; assoc prof to prof, Univ of Tex Tyler, 82-. **HONORS AND AWARDS** Fulbright-Hays Awd, Yugoslavia, 79-80. **MEMBERSHIPS** Am Sociol Assoc; Nat Coun on Family Relations; Grove Conf. **RESEARCH** Study of serial monogamy, Marital therapy on the Internet. **SELECTED PUBLICATIONS** Auth, "Opportunities, Information Networks and International Migration Streams" Social Networks 1 (Feb 79):277-284; auth, "Sex Inequality in Marriage and Work", Sociolosky Pregled 13.3 (79):89-93; auth, "Suicide and Adaptation to Aging", Aging Int 6.2 (79):23; auth, "A Test of Psychoanalytic Theory of Mate Selection" Jour of Social Psychol, (Dec 80:292-299; auth, "Formal Mate Selection networks in the United States", Family Relations 30 (April 80): 199-203; auth, "Automated Go-Betweens: Mate Selections of Tomorrow", Family Relations 30 (July 81):373-376; auth, "Indirect Parental Influence on Mate Choice", Jour of Marriage and the Family, (Feb 84):65-70; coed, Family, Society and the Individual, Harper and Row Pub (NY), 91; auth, "Ethnic Consistency in Remarriage", Family Perspective 25.3 (91):237-245; auth, "the Role of the Higher Education in Reduction of Interethnic Tensions", Napredak 140.4 (99):417-424. **CONTACT ADDRESS** Dept Soc Sci, Univ of Texas, Tyler, 3900 University Blvd, Tyler, TX 75799-0001. **EMAIL** davor45@yahoo.com

JEFFERSON, JOSEPH L.
PERSONAL Born 11/08/1940, Pensacola, FL, m **DISCIPLINE** EDUCATION **EDUCATION** TX Southern Univ, BA, 1968, MA, 1971; OH State Univ, PhD, 1974. **CAREER** Vocational Guidance Houston, counselor 1971; TX Southern Univ, admin asst to dean coll of arts & sciences dir inst; TX Southern Univ, assoc dir Office of Inst Research, prof Col of Educ. **HONORS AND AWARDS** Recip Grad Fellow TX So Univ 1970-71; Acad Year Inst Study Grant 1972-73 OH State U. **MEMBERSHIPS** Mem Am Educ & Research Assn; Phi Delta Kappa; Assn for Inst Research; Am Counseling Assn; TX Counseling Assn; Kappa Alpha Psi Frat; Houston Jr Chamber of Commerce; Houston Lion's Club. **CONTACT ADDRESS** 3100 Cleburne, Houston, TX 77004.

JENKINS, CAROL A.
PERSONAL Born 03/01/1945, Kearny, NJ, s **DISCIPLINE** SOCIOLOGY **EDUCATION** Malone Col, BA, 68; Chicago Grad Sch Theol, MA, 69; Western Mich Univ, MA, 72; Kans State Univ, PhD, 86. **CAREER** Asst prof, Tabor Col, Hillsboro, Kans, 78-82; instr, Kans State Univ, Manhattan, Kans, 82-85; assoc prof, Biola Univ, LaMirada, Calif, 85-92; vis scholar, Va Tech Univ, 92; prof, Glendale Community Col, Ariz, 92-; vis scholar, Iowa State Univ, 98-99. **HONORS AND AWARDS** Listed in: Who's Who of Women Execs (90), Who's Who in the West (90, 98) , Who's Who of Emerging Leaders in Am (92), Who's Who of Am Women (92, 93, 96), Who's Who in Am Ed (93), Who's Who Among Am's Teachers (96, 98); Alpha Kappa Delta, 86; granted tenure, Biola Univ, LaMirada, Calif, 92; granted tenure, Glendale Community Col, Ariz, 97. **MEMBERSHIPS** Am Sociol Asn, Rural Sociol Soc, Midwest Sociol Soc, Alpha Kappa Delta. **RESEARCH** Pedagogical issues in the multicultural college classroom, rural religious/ethnic family farm issues. **SELECTED PUBLICATIONS** Auth, "Educating for Equity: Challenges, Choices, and Changes," Fac Dialogue, Portland, Ore: J of the Inst for Christian Leadership, Vol 9 (fall87): 53-68; coauth with D. Bainer, "Common Instructional Problems in the Multicultural Classroom," J on Excellence in Col Teaching, Vol 2 (91): 77-88; coauth with D. Bainer, "Educating for Equity: Issues and Strategies for Effective Multicultural Instruction," chapter in Lee, Nieves, Allen, Ethnic-Minorities and Evangelical Christian Colleges, Lanham, Md: Univ Press Am (92): 259-289; coauth with D. Kratt, "Sociological Foundations of Multicultural Religious Education," chapter in B. Wilkerson, ed Multicultural Religious Education, Religious Ed Press (97); coauth with C. Rakowski, Rural Sociology-Teaching About the Complexities and Diversities of Contemporary American Rural Life, Am Sociol Asn Teaching Resources Center, Washington, DC (2000). **CONTACT ADDRESS** Dept Soc Sci-Sociology, Glendale

Comm Col, Arizona, 6000 W Olive Ave, Glendale, AZ 85302. **EMAIL** carol.jenkins@gcmail.maricopa.edu

JENNINGS, ROBERT RAY
PERSONAL Born 11/15/1950, Atlanta, GA **DISCIPLINE** SOCIOLOGY **EDUCATION** Univ of Ghana Legon West Africa, Charles Merrill Scholar 1971; Morehouse Coll, BA, Sociology, 1972; Atlanta Univ, MA, Educ Psych, 1974; GA State Univ Sch of Educ, Certificate in Gifted Educ 1975; Univ of GA, Certificate in Adult Basic Educ, 1978; Atlanta Univ, Educ Specialist in Interrelated Learning, 1979; Doctorate, Admin, 1982. **CAREER** Atlanta Univ, asst to dir of public relations, 73; Atlanta Public Sch, Hoffman reading coord 1973-76; Literacy Action Inc Atlanta, reading consultant 1974-75; Reading Learning Ctr Inc East Point, dir 1975-79; Atlanta Public Schs, tchr of the gifted 1976-79; Atlanta Univ, consultant dean's grant proj 1979-80; Atlanta Area Tech Sch, part-time prof 1979-84; Equal Employ Comm US Govt, equal oppor specialist 1979-82; Morris Brown Coll Atlanta, assoc prof 1982-84; US Equal Employment Oppor Commn, Atlanta Dist, official commn rep office of dir 1982-84, Washington, employee devel specialist 1984-85; asst vice pres, devel & placement, Atlanta Univ, 85-88; Norfolk State Univ, vice pres of development, 88-91; Albany State University, vp for institutional advancement, 91-97; North Carolina Agricultural and Technical State University, vice chancellor for Development and University Relations and CEO for the Foundation, 97-. **HONORS AND AWARDS** Outstanding Achievement Awd, Economic Opportunity Atlanta 1972; Outstanding Serv Awd Atlanta Inquirer Newspaper 1972; Director's Awd Frederick Douglass Tutorial Inst Morehouse Coll 1972; Outstanding Serv Awd Student Natl Educ Assn, 1972; Awd of Excellence Student Mississippi Teacher's Assn, 1972; WSB TV & Radio Fellow 1975; Teacher of the Year Home Park School Atlanta 1976; Awd of Excellence Wm Finch Sch PTA, 1976; Appreciation Awd for Outstanding Leadership SM Inman Sch PTA 1976; Outstanding Chapter Mem of the Yr Atlanta Univ 1979; Best of Service Awd Frank Lebby Stanton Sch Atlanta 1979; Alumnus of the Yr Atlanta Univ 1980; Special Serv Awd, Council for Exceptional Children, Atlanta, 1981; Special Serv Awd, Natl Bd of Dirs, Atlanta Univ Alumni, 1981; Phi Delta KappaPrssional Fraternity in Educ, 1982; cited by Atlanta Journal & Constitution Newspaper as one of Atlanta's Most Outstanding Volunteers, 1982; Outstanding Serv Awd, United Way of Metro Atlanta, 1984; First Recipient Leadership Awd in Educ, Delta Sigma Theta Sor, 1986; Outstanding Atlantan, 1986. **MEMBERSHIPS** Pres, Atlanta Univ Natl Alumni Assn, 1979-81; mem, bd of dirs, Exodus Right-to-Read Program Adult Literacy Prog, 1980; bd of advisors, Volunteer Atlanta, 1980-84; parlimentarian Council for Exceptional Children Atlanta Area Chap 1980-81; bd of dirs, Parents Anonymous of GA, 1981-84; bd of trustees, Atlanta Univ 1981-85; founder and editor-in-chief Alumni Update of Leadership Atlanta 1982-; Self-Study Evaluation Comm, Morris Brown Coll, 1983-84; bd of dirs, Planned Parenthood, 1983-87; exec bd, Leadership Atlanta 1986-87; vice pres, Council for Advancement of Public Black Colleges & Universities, 1989-; NAACP Education Legal Advisory Board, chairman, 1987-; Leadership Albany, 1992-93; Southwest Georgia Comprehensive Health Institute, board of directors, 1992-; Community Relations Council and Turner Job Corp, Inc, Albany GA, mem board of directors, 1996-98; American Lung Assn, Albany Chap, mem board of directors, 1994-; West End Church of Christ, mem, 1988-; American Assn for Higher Educ, 1988-; American Biographical Inst, honorary mem, bd of advisors, 1987-; Council for the Advancement & Support of Education, 1984-; Phi Delta Kappa, 1982-. **CONTACT ADDRESS** No Carolina Agr and Tech State Univ, Greensboro, NC 27411.

JENSEN, KATHARINE
DISCIPLINE 17TH AND 18TH CENTURY LITERATURE, WOMEN'S WRITING, FEMINIST THEORY **EDUCATION** Columbia Univ, PhD, 88. **CAREER** Assoc prof, La State Univ. **SELECTED PUBLICATIONS** Auth, Male Models of Feminine Epistolarity, Writing the Female Voice, 88; The Inheritance of Masculinity and the Limits of Heterosexual Revision, 18th Century Life, 92; Writing Love: Letters, Women, and the Novel, 95. **CONTACT ADDRESS** Dept of Fr Grad Stud, Louisiana State Univ and A&M Col, Baton Rouge, LA 70803.

JENSEN, KATHERINE RUTH
PERSONAL Born 05/05/1946, Deadwood, SD, m, 1982, 4 children **DISCIPLINE** SOCIOLOGY **EDUCATION** Carleton Col, BA, 68; Univ Wis, MA, 74, PhD, 77. **CAREER** Teacher, Many Farms High Sch, 69-71; instr, Navajo Community Col, 71-72; lectr and teaching asst, Univ Wisc, 76-77; lectr to prof, Univ Wyo, 77-, Assoc Dean, Col of Arts and Scis, 88-91, Dir, Int Studies, 95-98; fac, Acad of Int Economic Affairs, Ministry of Economic Affairs, Republic of China, summers of 96-98. **HONORS AND AWARDS** Presidential Scholar, 64; Nat Merit Scholar, 64-68; Carleton Mortarboard, 67; Fulbright Teaching Asst to India, 68 (declined); Univ Wisc E. B. Fred Fel, nonresident scholar, 73-76; Consortium for Int Develop Training Assistantship to Egypt, 86; Univ Wyo Mortarboard Top prof, 87; Fulbright Summer Sem in Egypt, Am Univ in Cairo, 89; UW London Sem, Spring 95. **SELECTED PUBLICATIONS** Coauth, "Gambling on the Lure of Historic Preservation: Community Transformation in Rocky Mountain Mining Towns," J of the Community Develop Soc, Vol 26, No 1 (95); auth, "Getting to the Third World: Agencies as Gatekeepers," in Women, International Development, and Politics: The Bureaucratic Mire, ed. Kathleen Staudt (Temple, 89, 2nd ed, 97); coauth, "Builder, Retailer, Restorer: Three Women from Three Generations in Lead-Deadwood's Formation and Preservation," Small Town, Vol 29, No 1 (98); coauth, "Gambling as a Community Development Quick Fix in Four Rocky Mountain Gold Mining Towns," Annals of the Am Acad of Political and Soc Scis, Vol 556 (March 98); auth, "Residential and Household Poverty on the Wind River Indian Reservation," Executive Summaries of Working Papers published by the JCPR, Vol 1, No 8; coauth, The Last Gamble: Betting on the Future in Four Rocky Mountain Mining Towns, Univ Ariz Press (98). **CONTACT ADDRESS** Dept Sociol, Univ of Wyoming, PO Box 3293, Laramie, WY 82071. **EMAIL** cowgirl@uwyo.edu

JINDRA, MICHAEL
PERSONAL Born 06/29/1962, Manitowoc, WI, m, 1997, 1 child **DISCIPLINE** ANTHROPOLOGY, SOCIOLOGY, RELIGION **EDUCATION** Univ Wis Madison, ABA, 84; MA, 91; PhD, 97. **CAREER** Prof, Bethany Luterhan Col, 97-; dir, Ylvisakor Center for Personal and Pub Responsibility, 99-. **MEMBERSHIPS** Am Anthrop Assoc. **RESEARCH** Religion and popular culture, Africa, public policy. **SELECTED PUBLICATIONS** Auth, "Star Trek Fandom as a Religious Phenomenon", Sociol of Relig, 55.1 (94): 27-51; auth, "Star Trek to Me is a Way of Life: Fan Expressions Star Trek Philosophy", in Star Trek and Sacred Ground: Essays on Star Trek, Religion and Popular Culture, eds Jennifer Porter and Carcee McLaren, SUNY Pr, 99; auth, "It's About Faith in Our Future: Star Trek Fandom as Cultural Religion", in Religion and Popular Culture in America, eds Jeffrey Mahan and Bruce Forbes, Univ of Calif Pr, 00. **CONTACT ADDRESS** Dept Soc Sci, Bethany Lutheran Col, 700 Luther Dr, Mankato, MN 56001. **EMAIL** mjindra@blc.edu

JOFFE, JUSTIN M.
PERSONAL Born 10/29/1938, Johannesburg, South Africa, d, 4 children **DISCIPLINE** PSYCHOLOGY **EDUCATION** Univ of the WitWatersrand, BA, 59; Hons, BA, 60; MA, 62; London Univ, PhD, 65. **CAREER** Lecturer, Birmingham Univ, 65-67; Postdoctoral Res Fellow, Stanford U. School of Medicine, 67-69; Asst, Assoc, Professor, Univ of Vermont, 69-; Chair, Dept of Psychology, 92-00. **HONORS AND AWARDS** Fulbright Res. Scholar, 84-85; Visiting Res. Scientist, 80-81. **MEMBERSHIPS** British Psychological Society Fellow. **RESEARCH** Mental Disorder and its prevention. **SELECTED PUBLICATIONS** Auth, "Prenatal determinants of behavior," by Joffe, J.M., Oxford: Pergamon Press; ed, " Primary prevention of psychopathology, Vol. 1: The Issues," by Albee, G.W. and Joffe, J.M., Hanover, NH: University Press of New England, 77; ed, "The issues: An overview of primary prevention, by Albee, G.W. and Joffe, J.M, 81; ed, "Prevention through political action and social change," by Joffe, J.M. and Albee, G.W., Hanover, NH: University Press of New England; ed, "Facilitating infant and early childhood development," by Bond, L.A. and Joffe, J.M., Hanover, NH: University Press of New England; ed, "Readings in primary prevention of psychopathology: Basic concepts, by Joffe, J.M., Albee, G.W., and L.D. Kelly, Hanover, NH: Univ Press of New England; ed, "Prevention, powerlessness, and politics: A book of readings," Newbury Park, CA: Sage Publications; ed, "The present and future of prevention, In honor of George W. Albee," by Kesler, M., S.E. Goldston, and Joffe, J.M., Newbury Park, CA: Sage Publications. **CONTACT ADDRESS** Dept Psychology, Univ of Vermont, Dewey Hall, Burlington, VT 05405-0001. **EMAIL** jjoffe@zoo.uvm.edu

JOHANNESEN, RICHARD LEE
PERSONAL Born 08/14/1937, Davenport, IA, 2 children **DISCIPLINE** ENGLISH EDUCATION **EDUCATION** Augustana Col, Ill, BA, 59; Univ Kans, MA, 60, PhD(speech), 64. **CAREER** Instr speech, Univ Kans, 61-62; from instr to asst prof, Ind Univ, Bloomington, 64-71; assoc prof, 72-77, prof Commun Studies, Northern Ill Univ, 77-, dept chair, 88-96. **MEMBERSHIPS** Nat Comm Assoc. **RESEARCH** Contemporary theories of rhetoric; rhetorical criticism; ethical problems in communication. **SELECTED PUBLICATIONS** Ed, Ethics and Persuasion, Random, 67; co-ed, Language is Sermonic: Richard M Weaver on the Nature of Rhetoric, La State Univ, 70; ed, Contemporary Theories of Rhetoric, Harper, 71; auth, "The Jeremiad and Jenkin Jones," Communication Monographs, June 85; auth, "Collaborative Writing Interactions in One Ninth-Grade Classroom" Journal of Educational Research, 94, 334-344; auth, The Emerging Concept of Communication as Dialogue, Quart J Speech, 12/71; Ethics in Human Communication, Waveland Press, 4th ed, 96; auth, "Dilemmas of Fidelity: Qualitative Research in the Classroom," Invited chapter in Ethics and Representation in Qualitative Studies of Literacy, Urbana, IL: ncte, 96: 77-94; auth, "The Influence of Coauthoring on the Writing Process," Journal of Teaching Writing, 96, 65-79; auth, "Letters of Intent: Collaborative Self-Study as Reform in Teacher Education" in The Heart of the Matter: Teacher Education Reform Perspectives and Possibilities, Caddo Gap Press, 98: 81-99; auth, "Creating Literacy Communities: High School/University Partnership," English Journal 88.1, 98; co-ed, Contemporary American Speeches, Kendall-Hunt, 8th ed, 97, updated 9th ed., 00; articles, "Becoming Multicultural Supervisors: Lessons from a Collaborative Field Study" Journal of Curriculum and Supervision, 16.1, 00, 28-47; **CONTACT ADDRESS** Dept of Communication, No Illinois Univ, De Kalb, IL 60115-2825. **EMAIL** rjohannesen@niu.edu

JOHANNINGMEIER, ERWIN
PERSONAL Born 12/18/1937, St Louis, MO, m, 1982, 2 children **DISCIPLINE** EDUCATION **EDUCATION** Wash Univ, AB, 60; Wash Univ, MA, 64; Univ Ill, PhD, 67. **CAREER** Prof, Univ S Fla, 80-. **HONORS AND AWARDS** Travel Grant, Int Standing Conf Hist Educ, 94; Travel Grant, Int Standing Conf Hist Educ, 95; Travel Grant, Int Standing Conf Hist Educ, 96; Travel Grant, Int Standing Conf Hist Educ, 97; Phi Delta Kappa. **MEMBERSHIPS** AERA, AESA, AES. **SELECTED PUBLICATIONS** Auth, "Wychowanie publiczne w Stanash Zjednoconych," in Prace z Historii Oswiaty I Wychowania, IV (Krakow, Poland: Wydawnicwo Naukowe WSP, 94); coauth, "Schooling in Changing Societies: Historical and Comparative Perspectives," Pedagogica Hist (98); coauth, "Dropping Out and the Military Metaphor for Schooling," Hist of Educ Quart, vol 39, no 2 (99); coauth, "Educational Reform in International Perspective: Past, Present and Future," Polish Acad of Sci (00); auth, "Criticism and Reform: Education and Schooling in the United States 1942-1983," in Educ Reform in Int Perspective: Past, Present and Future (Krakow, Poland: Polish Acad of Sci, 00); auth, "The Training of Educational Researchers," J of Exper Educ (forthcoming); auth, "Family Circle," St James Encycl of Pop Cult (forthcoming); auth, Woman's Day," St James Encycl of Pop Cult (forthcoming). **CONTACT ADDRESS** Dept Educ, Univ of So Florida, 4202 Flowler Ave, Tampa, FL 33620-7750. **EMAIL** johannin@tempest.coedu.usf.edu

JOHANSON, DONALD C.
PERSONAL Born 06/28/1943, Chicago, IL, m, 1988, 1 child **DISCIPLINE** ANTHROPOLOGY **EDUCATION** Univ IL, BA, 66; Univ Chicago, MA, 70, PhD, 74. **CAREER** Teach, Case Western Res Univ, 72-76; adj prof, Kent State and Case Western Univ, 78-81; prof, Stanford, Univ, 83-89; prof, Ariz State Univ, 97-. **HONORS AND AWARDS** San Francisco Exploratorium Awd, 86; Who's Who in Am, Int Who's Who, 87; In Praise of Reason Awd, CSICOP, 91; Dist Alumni Awd, Univ of IL, 95; Anthrop in the Media Awd, Am Anthrop Assoc. **MEMBERSHIPS** Exploers Club; Am Assoc for the Advan of Sci; Calif Acad of Sci; Royal Geog Soc; Am Assoc of Physical Anthrop; Soc of Vertebrate Paleontology. **RESEARCH** Human origins. **SELECTED PUBLICATIONS** Coauth, Lucy: The Beginnings of Humankind, Simon and Schuster (NY), 81; coauth, Blueprints: Solving the Mystery of Evolution, Little, Brown, (NY), 89; coauth, Lucy's Child: The Discovery of a Human Ancestor, William Morrow (NY) 89; coauth, Journey from the Dawn: Life with the World's First Family, Villard Books (NY), 90; coauth, Ancestors: In Search of Human Origins, Villard Books, (NY), 94; coauth, From Lucy to Language, Simon & Schuster (NY), 96; coauth, "Late Pliocene Homo and Oldowan Tools from the Hadar Formation (Kada Hadar Member), Ethiopia, J of Human Evolution 31, (96): 549-561; coauth, "The Crescent of Foramina in Australopithecus afarensis and Other Early Hominids", Am J of Physical Anthrop 101 (96): 93-99; coauth, "Systematic Assessment of a Maxilla of Homo From Hadar, Ethiopia", Am J of Physical Antrhop 103, (97): 235-262; coed, Ecce Homo, Electra, (Milan, Ital), 99. **CONTACT ADDRESS** Dept Anthrop, Arizona State Univ, PO Box 872402, Tempe, AZ 85287. **EMAIL** johanson.iho@asu.edu

JOHNS, ADRIAN
PERSONAL Born, Britain, m, 1992 **DISCIPLINE** SOCIOLOGY **EDUCATION** Cambridge, PhD, 92. **CAREER** Sr res fel, Caltech, 94; prof, Univ Calif San Diego, 99-. **RESEARCH** History of science, **SELECTED PUBLICATIONS** Auth, The Nature of the Book, Univ Chicago Press (98). **CONTACT ADDRESS** Dept Sociol, Univ of California, San Diego, 9500 Gilman Dr, La Jolla, CA 92093.

JOHNSON, ALICE K.
PERSONAL Born 03/18/1950, Mitchell, SD, m, 1995, 9 children **DISCIPLINE** SOCIOLOGY **EDUCATION** Dakota Wesleyan Univ, BSW, 85; Washington Univ in St Louis, MSW, 87; Washington Univ in St Louis, PhD, 90. **CAREER** Assoc prof, Case Western Res Univ, 19-00; prof, Univ of Ill at Chicago, 00-. **HONORS AND AWARDS** Nat Winner for MSW Fac, INFLUENCE, 98. **MEMBERSHIPS** ACOSA, INFLUENCE, Phi Kappa Phi, IFSW. **RESEARCH** Homelessness, low income housing, community practice. **SELECTED PUBLICATIONS** Auth, "Homelessness," Encycl of Soc Work 19th Ed (Washington, DC: NASW Press, 95): 1338-1346; coauth, "Teaching family policy and advocacy: A policy-practice course for direct practice students," J of Soc Work Educ 33(3) (97): 433-444; coauth, "A profile of the nonprofit sector in Romania," Voltas 8(3) (97): 303-322; coauth, "The Romania-US connection: A civil society partnership," in Beyond Prince and Merchant: Citizen Participation and the Rise of Civil Society, ed. J. Burbridge (NY: Pact Publ, 97): 143-160; coauth, "No home, no family: Homeless children in rural Ohio," Human Serv in the Rural Environ 19(2/3) (97): 9-13; auth, "Seminar in International Social Work," in Global Perspectives in Soc Work Educ, eds. L.M. Healy & Y.W. Asamoah (Alexandria, VA:

Council on Soc Work Educ, 97): 23-44; auth, "Homelessness," Encycl of Soc Work 19th Ed(rev) (Washington, DC: NASW Press, 97); auth, "The revitalization of community practice: Characteristics, competencies, and curricula for community-based services," J of Community Practice 5(3) (98): 37-62; auth, "Globalization from below: The use of the Internet to internationalize social work education," J of Soc Work Educ 35(3) (99): 377-393; auth, "Working and non-working women: Becoming homeless in the context of work education," AFFILIA: J of Women & Soc Work 14(1) (99): 42-77. **CONTACT ADDRESS** Mandel Sch of Appl Soc Sci, Case Western Reserve Univ, 10900 Euclid Ave, Cleveland, OH 44106. **EMAIL** akj3@po.cwru.edu

JOHNSON, CHRISTOPHER J.
PERSONAL Born 07/07/1949, Fort Madison, IA, m, 1991, 2 children **DISCIPLINE** SOCIOLOGY **EDUCATION** Univ Denver, BA, 71; Univ N Iowa, MA, 76; Iowa State Univ, PhD, 81. **CAREER** Teaching asst, Univ Northern Iowa, 74-75; part-time instr, Area II Community Col, 77; part-time instr, Drake Univ, 78 & 79; from asst prof to prof, Northeast La Univ, 81-. **HONORS AND AWARDS** Researcher of the Year, Northeast La Univ, 84 & 88; appointed to Governor's Long-Term Care Task Force, 97-98; Distinguished Fel in Gerontology, Asn for Gerontology in Higher Educ, 97. **MEMBERSHIPS** Alpha Kappa Delta, Gerontology Soc of Am, Clinical Sociol Asn, Asn for Gerontology in Higher Educ. **RESEARCH** Oral History Research, Ethnicity and Aging, Long-Term Care, Community-Based Care, Dementia Care. **SELECTED PUBLICATIONS** Coauth, Practical Sociology: Applications for the 90's, Harper and Row, 96; co-ed, How Different Religions View Death and the After Life, Charles Press (Philadelphia, PA), 98; auth, "Alzheimer's Wings in Nursing Facilities," in Annual Editions: Aging, 98-99, ed. Harold Cox (98), 184-186; auth, "The Eden Alternative: An Evolving Paradigm for Long Term Care," The Southwest J on Aging 14.2 (98): 133-136; auth, "Seeking Sources of Private Funding," in What Works, A.G.H.E. Press (99); coauth, Death and Dying Bibliography, A.G.H.E. Press, 99. **CONTACT ADDRESS** Dept Sociol & Soc Work, Northeast Louisiana Univ, 700 University Ave, Monroe, LA 71209-9000. **EMAIL** igjohnson@ulm.edu

JOHNSON, DON HANLON
DISCIPLINE PSYCHOLOGY **EDUCATION** Gonzaga Univ, MA, 62; Univ Santa Clara, MA, 69; Yale Univ, PhD, 71. **CAREER** Asst prof, Loyola Univ; assoc prof, Antioch Univ; prof, New Col of Calif, prof, Cal Inst Integral Studies. **RESEARCH** The nature and efficacies of body practices cross-cultural. **SELECTED PUBLICATIONS** Ed, Bone, Breath and Gesture: Practices of Embodiment, CIIS, North Atlantic Books, 95; auth, "The Hidden Body", N Calif Chapter of the Am Dance Therapy Newsletter (Winter 96-97); ed, Groundworks: Narratives of Embodiment (Berkeley: CIIS/N Atlantic Books, 97); auth, "Der Weg des leibes: Eine Kurze Geschichte der somatischen Bewegung", in Korpererfahrungen: Anregungen zur Selbstheilung, ed H. Milz and M.V. von Kibed, (Zurich: Walter Verlag), 98; coed, The Body in Psychotherapy: Inquiries in Somatic Psychology, CIIS/N Atlantic Books, 98; auth" The Methodological Cultivation of Tactile Intricacy in Nine Schools of Integrative Bodywork: A Challenge to Research Design", in The Biolog Basis for Mind-Body Interactions, ed Emeran A. Mayer and Clifford Saper, Elsevier Science Pr, 99; auth; "Body Practices and Consciousness: A Neglected Link" Jour of Anthrop of Consciousness, 00; auth, "Subjectivity in Western Integrative Bodyworks", in Encycl of the Scientific Study of Subjectivity: Cognition, Psychiat, and Neuroscience, ed Aaron Mishara, (Dordrecht: Kluwer Acad Pr), 00; auth, "Sitting, Writing, Listening, Speaking, Yearning: Practices of Alienation or Engagement", Body Movements: Pedagogy, Politics and Social Change, Univ of NC, 00. **CONTACT ADDRESS** Dept Psychology, California Inst of Integral Studies, 1453 Mission St, San Francisco, CA 94103. **EMAIL** donj@ciis.edu

JOHNSON, ERIC L.
PERSONAL Born 06/15/1956, Lansing, MI, m, 1979, 2 children **DISCIPLINE** PSYCHOLOGY **EDUCATION** Mich State Univ, PhD, 92. **CAREER** Assoc prof, Northwestern Col, 91-00; assoc prof, Southern Baptist Theol Sem, 00-. **MEMBERSHIPS** Am Psychol Soc, Am Psychol Asn, Christian Asn for Psychol Studies. **RESEARCH** Early adult development, Wisdom, Christian spirituality and therapy. **SELECTED PUBLICATIONS** Ed, Psychology and Christianity: Four Views, 00; auth, "A postmodern reconstruction of psychotherapy: Orienteering, religion, and the healing of the soul," Psychotherapy, (99): 1-13; auth, "Growing in wisdom in christian community: Toward measures of christian postformal development," Journal of Psychology and Theology, (98): 365-381; auth, "Some Contributions of Augustine to a Christian Psychology," Journal of Psychology and Christianity, (98): 293-305; auth, "Whatever happened to the human soul/ a brief, Christian genealogy of a psychological term," Journal of Psychology and Theology, (98): 16-28; auth, "Playing games and living metaphors: The incarnation and the end of gender," Journal of the Evangelical Theological Society, (97): 271-285; auth, "The call of wisdom: Adult development within Christian community, Part I: The crisis of modern theories of post-formal development," Journal of Psychology and Theology, (96): 88-95; auth, "The call of wisdom: Adult development within christian community, Part I: the crisis of modern theories of post-formal development," Journal of Psychology and Theology, (96): 88-95; auth, "The call of wisdom: Adult development within Christian community, Part II: Toward a conventional constructivist model of post-formal development," Journal of Psychology and theology, (96): 96-103. **CONTACT ADDRESS** Dept Psychol, Northwestern Col, Minnesota, 3003 Snelling Ave N, Saint Paul, MN 55113.

JOHNSON, HARRIETTE C.
PERSONAL Born 07/10/1936, Cambridge, MA, m, 1990, 2 children **DISCIPLINE** SOCIAL WORK **EDUCATION** Smith Col, BA, 57; MSW, 59; Rutgers Univ, PhD, 76. **CAREER** Caseworker, Yale Univ School of Med, 59-61; Director, Crisis Consultation Center, 69-71; Caseworker, Bureau of child Guidance, 75; Asst Prof to Assoc Prof, Adelphi Univ, 78-87; Assoc Prof to Prof, Univ Conn, 87-. **RESEARCH** Child/adolescent mental health, Parent/professional collaboration, Neurobiological foundations of behavior. **SELECTED PUBLICATIONS** Auth, "Borderline Personality Disorder," in Adult Psychopathology, 2nd ed, New York, 99; auth, "Neurological disorders," in adult Psychopathology, 2nd ed, New York, 99; auth, "The biological bases of psychopathology," in Adult Psychopathology, 2nd ed, New York, 99; auth, Psyche, Synapse and Substance: The Role of Neurobiology in Emotions, Behavior, cognition, and Addiction for Non-Scientists, Greenfield, MA, 99; auth, "Social Workers' Views of Parents with Mental and emotional disabilities," Families in Society, (98): 173-187; auth, "Professional beliefs about parents of children with mental and emotional disabilities: a cross-discipline comparison," Journal of Emotional and Behavioral Disorders, (97): 149-161; auth, "Telemonitoring in mental health services to youth: Enhanced roles for parents?," Health Care Review, (96): 13-14; ed, child Mental Health in the 1990s: Curricula for Graduate and Undergraduate Professional Education, Washington, 93; ed, Government Money for Everyday People, Garden City, NY, 82. **CONTACT ADDRESS** Dept Soc Work, Univ of Connecticut, Hartford, 85 Lawler Ave, West Hartford, CT 06117. **EMAIL** hjohnson@shaysnet.com

JOHNSON, LEROY
DISCIPLINE EDUCATION **CAREER** Miles College, Birmingham, AL, Pres/Chancellor, currently. **CONTACT ADDRESS** Miles Col, Birmingham, AL 35208.

JOHNSON, MARION L.
PERSONAL Born 07/24/1937, Haskell, TX, m, 1959, 5 children **DISCIPLINE** EDUCATION **EDUCATION** Abilene Christian Univ, BS, 59; Baylor Univ, MEd, 60; Univ Tex, EdD, 66; Colo State Univ, MEd, 86; PhD. **CAREER** Prof, Southeastern La Univ, 66-80; prof, Colo State Univ, 80-. **HONORS AND AWARDS** Outstanding Young Educator Awd, 66; Jaycees Outstanding Young Men of Am, 67; Leaders in Educ, 74; Who's Who in Education, 85; Who's Who in Society, 88. **MEMBERSHIPS** Phi Delta Kappa. **RESEARCH** Education policy, cognitive development, skill acquisition. **SELECTED PUBLICATIONS** Auth, "Stages and Transitions in cognitive Development", J of Thought 23.3, 95; coauth, "Tensile strength comparison of athletic tapes", J of Indus Tech 16.1, 99. **CONTACT ADDRESS** Dept Exercise Sci, Colorado State Univ, Fort Collins, CO 80525-0001. **EMAIL** johnson@cahs.colostate.edu

JOHNSON, RHODA E.
PERSONAL Born 11/14/1946, Bessemer, AL, m, 1968, 2 children **DISCIPLINE** WOMEN'S STUDIES **EDUCATION** Tuskegee Institute, Tuskegee, AL, BS, 1968; University of Michigan, Ann Arbor, MI, AM, 1970; University of Alabama, Tuscaloosa, AL, PhD, 1980. **CAREER** University of Michigan, Ann Arbor, MI, student research asst, 69-70; Tuskegee Institute, Tuskegee, AL, instructor, 70-77, asst prof, 77-81, assoc prof, dir of MARC, 82-85; University of Alabama, Tuscaloosa, AL, visiting prof, acting dir, 85-86, assoc prof, chair, 86-92; assoc prof, 92-. **HONORS AND AWARDS** Minority Access to Research Careers Grant, ADAMHA, 1982-85; Higher Education Component Grant, Southern Education Foundation, 1980-81; Poverty and Mental Health in the Rural South, CSRS/USDA, Carver Foundation, 1978-83. **MEMBERSHIPS** Member, steering committee, 21st Century Leadership Movement, 1989-; bd member, National Voting Rights Museum, 1994-; bd member, National Register Review Bd, Alabama Historical Commission. **RESEARCH** Health and empowerment. **SELECTED PUBLICATIONS** Ed, Women's Studies in the South, Kendall/Hunt, 91. **CONTACT ADDRESS** Dept of Womens Studies, Univ of Alabama, Tuscaloosa, Box 870272, Tuscaloosa, AL 35487-0272. **EMAIL** rjohnson@tenhoor.as.ua.edu

JOHNSON, ROBERT C.
PERSONAL Born 08/27/1945, Richmond, VA **DISCIPLINE** EDUCATION **EDUCATION** Lincoln Univ, BA 1967; Institut D'Etudes Francaises France 1967; MAT 1969; MA 1974; Washington Univ, PhD 1976; Washington Univ, BS 1984. **CAREER** Lincoln Univ Foreign Lang Lab, student dir 1964-67; Washington Univ, lectr 1969-71; Educ Cntr of E St Louis, dir 1969-72; Fontbonne Coll, lectr 1971; Inst Black Studies St Louis, dir educ 1971; Washington Univ, asst prof 1971-84; Grambling State Univ, assoc prof 1984-. **HONORS AND AWARDS** Numerous publ appearances/addresses/publications in field; 1st Intl Black Merit Acad Awd 1973; World Future Soc; Amer Assn for the Advancement of Sci; Eval Network; African Heritage Studies Assn; Outstanding Young Men in Amer 1974, 1977; Men of Achievement 1977; Comm Ldrs & Noteworthy Amer 1977; numerous scholarships/fellowships/grants. **MEMBERSHIPS** Numerous consultantships in field; mem Amer Assn for Higher Educ 1973-, Amer Assn Univ Profs 1971-, Assn for the Study of Afro-Am Life & Hist 1970-, Educators to Africa Assn 1972-, Natl & Reg Assn African-Am Educators 1969-72, Phi Delta Kappa 1969-; bd dirs Trainers Tchr Trainers Prog 1969-71; spl serv Washington Univ 1970-71; Inst Black Studies 1970-; Educ Center of E St Louis 1972-; mem So IL Univ Citizens Adv Com 1970-72; Comp Educ Comm 1970; E St Louis Model Cities Planning Com 1969-71; Afro-Am Studies Curriculum Adv Com 1972; St Louis Com on Africa 1970-; UN Assn 1973-. **CONTACT ADDRESS** Dept of Educ, Master's Col and Sem, PO Box 91322, Newhall, CA 91322.

JOHNSON, ROGER N.
PERSONAL Born 04/22/1939, Dayton, OH, m, 1968, 2 children **DISCIPLINE** PSYCHOLOGY **EDUCATION** Swarthmore Col, BA, 61; Univ Conn, MA, 62, PhD, 66. **CAREER** Univ Mass, 65; Amherst Coll, 65-68; Tufts Univ, 68-71; Rampao Col, 71- ; Univ Jyvaskyla, 79; New Sch for Soc Res, 80-82; Richmond Coll, 88. **HONORS AND AWARDS** Who's Who in Am; Who's Who in the East; am Men and Women of Sci; Who's Who in Writers, Editors & Poets; Who's Who of Int Auth and Writers; Int Dir of Distinguished Leadership; Int Dict of Contemporary Achievement; Fulbright Fel, 79. **MEMBERSHIPS** APA; Int Soc for Research on Aggression; Eastern Psych Asn; Int Soc for Political Psychology. **SELECTED PUBLICATIONS** Auth, Aggression in Man and Animals, Missouri, 96; Bad News Revisited, Peace and Conflict, 96. **CONTACT ADDRESS** Ramapo Col of New Jersey, Mahwah, NJ 07430. **EMAIL** rjohnson@ramapo.edu

JOHNSON, RONALD C.
PERSONAL Born 07/18/1927, Duluth, MN, w, 1954, 3 children **DISCIPLINE** PSYCHOLOGY **EDUCATION** Univ Minn, BA, psychology, 49, PhD, child development; Denver Univ, MA, sociol, 50. **CAREER** Instr, Univ Minn, 56-57; asst to assoc prof, San Jose State Coll, 57-62; assoc prof, 62-65, prof, 70-93, prof emeritus, 93-, Univ Hawaii; assoc prof, Univ Colorado, 65-70; dir, Behavioral Biology Lab, 72-93. **HONORS AND AWARDS** Distinguished Sci Contribution Awd, Hawaii Psychol Assn, 95; Dobzhansky Awd, Behavior Genetics Assn, 97. **MEMBERSHIPS** Amer Assn Advancement Sci; Amer Psychol Soc; Behavior Genetics Assn; Soc Study Social Biol. **RESEARCH** Human viability; behavior genetics; ethology; psychometrics. **SELECTED PUBLICATIONS** Coauth, "Intergroup Similarities in Judgments of Psychiatric Symptom Severity," Cultural Diversity and Mental Health, vol 3, no 1, 97; coauth, "Kinship and the Quest for Wealth and Power in the Punjab, 1839-1845," Evolution and Human Behavior, 97; coauth, "Active Phenotypic Assortment in Mate Selection," Social Biology, vol 44, 97; coauth, "Depressive Symptomatology among Filipino-American Adolescents," Cultural Diversity and Mental Health, vol 4, no 1, 98; coauth, "Prediction of Major Depression and Dsythymia from CES-D Scores among Ethnic Minority Adolescents," Journ Amer Acad Child and Adolescent Psychiatry, vol 37, no 5, 98. **CONTACT ADDRESS** 23 Kalaka Pl, Kailua, HI 96734.

JOHNSON, RONALD MABERRY
PERSONAL Born 10/15/1936, Kansas City, MO, m, 1965, 3 children **DISCIPLINE** AMERICAN SOCIAL & CULTURAL HISTORY **EDUCATION** Col Emporia, BA, 61; Univ Kans, MA, 65; Univ Ill, Urbana, PhD(Am social & intellectual hist), 70. **CAREER** Asst prof Afro-Am hist, Cleveland State Univ, 69-72; asst prof urban & Afro-Am hist, 72-76, assoc prof Am Hist, Georgetown Univ, 76-86, prof Am Hist, Georgetown, 86-, dir Am Studies, 79-85, 89-. **MEMBERSHIPS** ASA; AHA; Orgn Am Historians. **RESEARCH** Social and cultural history; history of race relations; educational history. **SELECTED PUBLICATIONS** Auth, Schooling the Savage: Andrew S Draper and Indian Education, Phylon, 3/74; coauth, Forgotten Pages: Black Literary Magazines in the 1920s, J Am Studies, 12/74; auth, Politics and Pedagogy: The 1892 Cleveland School Reform, Ohio Hist, autumn 75; Captain of Education: Andrew S Draper, 1848-1913, Societas, summer 76; Black History and White Students: Broadening Cultural Horizons, Negro Educ Rev, 1/77; coauth, Away from Acommodation: Radical Editors and Protest Journalism, J Negro Hist, 10/77; Propaganda and Aesthetics: Literary Politics of Afro-American Magazines in the Twentieth Century, Univ Mass Press, 79, rev ed, 92. **CONTACT ADDRESS** Dept of Hist, Georgetown Univ, 1421 37th St N W, Washington, DC 20057-0001. **EMAIL** johnson2@gusun.georgetown.edu

JOHNSON, RONALD WILLIAM
PERSONAL Born 07/29/1937, Rockford, IL, 1 child **DISCIPLINE** HISTORY OF ART, PSYCHOLOGY **EDUCATION** Calif State Univ, San Diego, AB, 59; MA, 63; Univ Calif, Berkeley, MA, 65, PhD, 71. **CAREER** Asst prof art hist, Univ Iowa, 70-73; prof art hist, Humboldt State Univ, 74-. **HONORS AND AWARDS** Nat Defense Travelling Fel, 67; Kress Fel, 69-

70; Nat Endowment for the Humanities Summer Seminar, 76; Nat Endowment for the Humanities Summer Seminar, 80; President's Merit Awd, (H.S.U.), 85. **MEMBERSHIPS** Col Art Asn Am. **RESEARCH** Late 19th and early 20th century art history. **SELECTED PUBLICATIONS** Auth, Picasso's Old Guitarist and the Symbolist Sensibility, Artforum XIII, 12/74; Dante Rossetti's Beata Beatrix and the New Life, Art Bull, 12/75; Poetic Pathways to Dada: Marcel Duchamp and Jules Laforgue, 5/76, Picasso's Parisian Family and the Saltimbanques, 1/77, Vincent van Gogh and the Vernacular: His Southern Accent, 6/78, Arts Mag; Picasso's Demoiselles d'Avignon and the Theatre of the Absurd, 10/80 & Whistler's Musical Modes: Symbolist Symphonies, 4/81, Arts Mag; auth, "The Early Picasso & Spanish Literature," National Gallery, Washington, DC, 96. **CONTACT ADDRESS** Humboldt State Univ, 1 Harpst St, Arcata, CA 95521-8299. **EMAIL** rwj1@axe.humboldt.edu

JOHNSON, RONNIE J.
PERSONAL Born 12/09/1956, Springhill, LA, m, 1963 **DISCIPLINE** CHRISTIAN EDUCATION **EDUCATION** Southern Ark Univ, BS, 79; Baptist Missionary Assoc Theol Sem, MDiv, 83; Tex A&M Univ, Commerce, MS, 85; PhD, 94. **CAREER** Prof, Baptist Missionary Assoc Theol Sem, 90-. **MEMBERSHIPS** NAPCE. **RESEARCH** General Education and Ministry with Older Adults. **SELECTED PUBLICATIONS** Auth, "Parade of Love", E Tex Christian Monthly (96): 5; auth, "When to Say I Told You So", E Tex Christian Monthly, (96): 18; auth, "Don't Wear Protective Clothing When Handling God's Word", E Tex Christian Monthly, (96): 7; auth, Facing the Crises of Life Teacher's Guide, Baptist Pub House, (Texarkana), 96; auth, Knowing and Doing God's Will, Baptist Pub House, (Texarkana), 96; auth, Patterns for Prayer, Baptist Pub House, (Texarkana), 97; auth, The Parables of Jesus, Baptist Pub House, (Texarkana), 98; auth, Making Disciples, Baptist Pub House, (Texarkana), 98; auth, Social Issues in the Minor Prophets, Baptist Pub House, (Texarkana), 99; auth, Social Issues in the Minor Prophets Teacher's Guide, Baptist Pub House, (Texarkana), 99. **CONTACT ADDRESS** Dept Theol, Baptist Missionary Association Theol Sem, 1530 E Pine St, Jacksonville, TX 75766-5407.

JOHNSON, SHERI L.
DISCIPLINE PSYCHOLOGY **EDUCATION** Salem Col, BA, 82; Univ Pittsburgh, MS, 86; PhD, 92. **CAREER** Teaching Fel, Univ Pittsburgh, 89-90; Asst Prof, Brown Univ, 93-95; Asst Prof, Univ Miami, 95-. **HONORS AND AWARDS** Young Investigator Awd, Nat Alliance for Research, 91; Max and Jennie Bassell Awd, 85. **MEMBERSHIPS** Am Psychol Asn, Asn for Clinical Psychosocial Res, Soc for Res on Psychopathol, Asn for the Advancement of Beh Therapy. **SELECTED PUBLICATIONS** Co-auth, "Acceptance and Denial Coping are Associated with Medication Adherence in Bipolar Disorder," Journal of Affective Disorders, in press; co-auth, "Do personality traits predict depressive and manic symptoms?," Journal of Affective Disorders, in press; co-auth, "Sequential Interactions in the Marital Communications of Depressed Me and Women," Journal of Consulting and Clinical Psychology, (00): 4-12; co-auth, "Social support and self-esteem predict changes in bipolar depression but not mania," Journal of Affective Disorders, in press; co-ed, Stress, Coping and Depression: Proceedings of the fifteenth Annual Stress and coping Conference, Lawrence Erlbaum Pub, 00; co-auth, "Psychosocial approaches to bipolar disorder," Current Opinion in Psychiatry, (00): 89-72; co-auth, "Predictors of child outcome in families with a depressed parent: An application of hierarchical linear modeling," in Stress, Coping and Depression: Proceedings of the Fifteenth Annual Stress and Coping Conference, Lawrence Erlbaum Pub, 00; co-auth, "Family influences on alcohol and substance abuse, in Sourcebook on Substance Abuse: Etiology, Epidemiology, Assessment, and Treatment, Allyn and Bacon, 99; auth, "Review of Interpersonal Psychotherapy for Dysthymic Disorder," Contemporary Psychology, (99): 252-253. **CONTACT ADDRESS** Dept Psychol, Univ of Miami, PO Box 248185, Miami, FL 33124.

JOHNSON, STEVE
PERSONAL Born 01/05/1954, Clovis, NM, m, 1976, 2 children **DISCIPLINE** PSYCHOLOGY **EDUCATION** Abilene Christian Univ, BA, 76; MMFT, 83; Univ Nebr, PhD, 84. **CAREER** Sr Clinical Caseworker, Jewish family and Children's Serv, El Paso Tex, 85-86; Instr, El Paso Community Col, 88-89; Adj Fac, Park Col, Ft Bliss, Tex, 88-90; Family Therapist, El Paso Child Guidance Center Tex, 89-91; Family Therapist, Jewish family and Children's Serv, El Paso Tex, 91-93; Adj Fac, Webster Univ Ft Bliss Tex, 88-95; From Adj Fac to Asst Prof, Univ of Tex at El Paso, 88-; Family Therapist, El Paso Child Guidance Center Tex, 94-; Pvt Practice in Marriage and Family Ther, Family Coun Serv of El Paso Tex, 85-. **MEMBERSHIPS** Am Asn for Marriage and Family Ther, Am Coun Asn, Tex Coun Asn, Chi Sigma Lota Coun and Prof Hon Soc Int. **SELECTED PUBLICATIONS** Coauth, "Teaching family relationships through interactive television," Family Perspective 18 (84): 111-115; coauth, "The impact of economic stressors on rural and urban family relationships," in Family Strengths 6, ed. R. Williams et al (Lincoln, NE: Univ of Nebr, 85); coauth, "The use of interactive television in live supervision," Tex Coun Asn J 25 (97): 11-18; coauth, "Factors associated with assigning students to behavioral classrooms," J of Educ Res 91 (97): 123-126; coauth, "Precipitating variables and Post-Traumatic Stress Disorder among battered Hispanic women: A pilot study," Tex Coun Asn J 27 (99): 23-31. **CONTACT ADDRESS** Dept Educ Psychology, Univ of Texas, El Paso, 500 W Univ Ave, El Paso, TX 79968-0001.

JOHNSON, THOMAS E.
PERSONAL Born 06/19/1948, Denver, CO, m, 1982, 3 children **DISCIPLINE** PSYCHOLOGY **EDUCATION** MIT, BSc, 70; Univ Wash, PhD, 75. **CAREER** Res assoc, Cornell Univ, 75-77; res assoc to fel, Univ Colo, 77-82; asst prof, Univ Calif, 82-88; assoc prof, Univ Colo, 88-95. **HONORS AND AWARDS** Gates Found Scholar, 70; NIH Predoc Fel, 72; USPHS Postdoc Fel, 79; USPHS Young Investigator Awd, 82; Fel, Am Fed of Aging Res, 86; Fel, Gerontol Soc of Am, 86; Res Career Develop Awd, USPHS, 92; Glenn Found Fel, 90; Busse Res Awd, Intl Asn for Gerontol, 93; Res Scientist Develop Awd, Nat Inst on Alcohol Abuse and Alcoholism, 94; Who's Who in Am, 96; Ellison Med Found Sen Scholar, 98. **MEMBERSHIPS** Am Aging Asn; Am Asn for the Adv of Sci; Am Fed for Aging Res; Beh Genetics Asn; Genetics Soc of am; Gerontol Soc of Am; Intl Mammalian Genome Soc; Intl Soc for Biomed Res on Alcoholism; Res Soc on Alcoholism. **RESEARCH** Genetics of Aging; Genetics of Alcohol Action. **SELECTED PUBLICATIONS** Auth, "Increased life span of age-1 mutants in Caenorhabditis elegans and lower Gompertz rate of aging," Science (90): 908-912; co-auth, "Mortality rates in a genetically heterogeneous population of Caenorhabditis elegans," Science (94): 668-671; co-auth, "Thermotolerance of a long-lived mutant of Caenorhabditis elegans," J Gerontol Bio Sci, (94): B270-B276; co-auth, "Genetic analysis of aging: Role of oxidative damage and environmental stresses," Nat Genetics, (96): 25-34; co-auth, "Mapping quantitative trait loci specifying hermaphrodite survival or self-fertility in the nematode Caenorhabditis elegans," Genetics (96): 801-817; co-auth, "Confirmation of quantitative trait loci for ethanol sensitivity in long-sleep and short-sleep mice," Gen Res, (97): 92-99; co-auth, "Life extension and stress resistance stress in Caenorhabditis elegans modulated by the tkr-1 gene," Curr Biol, (98): 1091-1094. **CONTACT ADDRESS** Dept Psychol, Univ of Colorado, Boulder, Campus Box 345, Boulder, CO 80309-0345. **EMAIL** johnson@colorado.edu

JOHNSON, WILLIE J.
PERSONAL Born 06/02/1953, Detroit, MI, m, 4 children **DISCIPLINE** COMMUNICATION, EDUCATION **EDUCATION** Hamline Univ, BA, 75; Univ Minn, MA, 80; PhD, 96. **CAREER** Instr, Normandale Community Col, 82-. **HONORS AND AWARDS** Fulbright Scholar; McKnight Fel; SPAN Fac Adv, Univ of Minn; Alpha Kappa Alpha Golden Apple Excellence in Educ Awd; Student Support Serv Fac Awd; Normandale Community Col Found Fac Awd; Distinguished Fac Awd. **MEMBERSHIPS** NEA; Educ Minn; Minn Community Col Fac Assoc. **RESEARCH** Minorities in Higher Education, Cross-Cultural Adoption, Intercultural Communication, Ethics in Education. **SELECTED PUBLICATIONS** Auth, "Being First Sometimes Too Heavy a Burden", St. Paul Pioneer Pr, June 99; auth, "Bringing 4-H to Chicago Was One Unusual Way Whites Have Done the Right Thing", St. Paul Pioneer Pr, Aug 99; auth, "Being a Person of Color Means Being Constantly On Your Guard, St. Paul Pioneer Pr, Sept 99; auth, "It's Time to Relearn Manners and Respect For Our Fellow Human Beings", St. Paul Pioneer Pr, Nov 99; auth, "Emotional Cost of Submerging Identity Is High", St. Paul Pioneer Pr, Nov 99; auth, "Christian Chauvinism Blocking Out Goodwill", St. Paul Pioneer Pr, Dec 99; auth, "Sometimes Love Isn't Enough: The Voices of Some Adult Korean Adoptees in Minnesota", Korean Am Hist Soc; Dec 99; auth, "For New Year, Resolve to be Agent of Change", St. Paul Pioneer Pr, Jan 00; auth, "The Loathsome 'N' Word: Time Young African Americans Quit Using It", St. Paul Pioneer Pr, Feb 00; auth, "Dive Into State's Cultural Kaleidoscope", St. Paul Pioneer Pr, Mar 00. **CONTACT ADDRESS** Dept Speech and Theatre, Normandale Comm Col, 9700 France Ave S, Minneapolis, MN 55431-4309.

JOHNSTON, BARBARA J.
PERSONAL Born 03/09/1929, Minneapolis, MN, s **DISCIPLINE** SOCIOLOGY **EDUCATION** Macalester Col, BA; Univ NC, MA; Univ Minn, PhD. **CAREER** Asst prof of Sociol, Macalester Col; adjunct prof of Sociol, Univ Md; asst prof of Sociol, St Olaf Col; prof of Sociol, Chair, North Hennepin Community Col; res assoc and principal investigator, St Paul-Ramsey Community Mental Health Center and Dept of Psychiatry; res consult and dir of ed progs, Unity Settlement Asn. **HONORS AND AWARDS** Minn Prof of Year Council Advancement, Support of Ed, 91; 1st Annual Awd Outstanding Contributions for Teaching, Sociols of Minn State, 89; Human Relations Commission Human Rights Awd, 91; Fac Mem of Year, Minn State Bd Community Cols, 94; Distinguished Sociol Awd, Sociols of Minn, 99. **MEMBERSHIPS** Am Sociol Asn, Midwest Sociol Soc, Commission on Women in Profession, Undergrad Ed Endowment, Sociols of Minn, Sociols for Women in Soc, Regional Midwest Sociols for Women in Soc; Minn Women in Higher Ed. **RESEARCH** Family violence, problem youth, alienation, women in politics, evaluation research. **CONTACT ADDRESS** Dept Sociol, No Hennepin Comm Col, 7411 85th Ave N, Brooklyn Park, MN 55445. **EMAIL** bjohnsto@nh.cc.mn.us

JOHNSTON, NORMAN
PERSONAL Born 08/05/1921, Marion, MI, s **DISCIPLINE** SOCIOLOGY **EDUCATION** Cent Mich Univ, BA, 43; Univ Chicago, AM, 51; Univ Penn, PhD, 58. **CAREER** Sociologist, Ill State Penitentiary system, 48-51; Res Assoc, Univ Penn, 60-62; Visiting Assoc Prof, Univ Mo, 68-69; Prof to Prof Emeritus, Beaver Col, 62-. **HONORS AND AWARDS** CASE Prof of the Year, Beaver Col, 92; Lindbach Distinguished Teaching Awd, Beaver Col, 63; Fulbright Scholar, Londong, 58-59. **RESEARCH** Criminology; Prison architecture & history of prison architecture. **SELECTED PUBLICATIONS** Auth, Forms of Constraint: A History of Prison Architecture, Univ IL Press, 00; auth, "A Complete but Very, Very Short History of Prison Architecture," Criminal Justice Matters, (96): 24; auth, Eastern State Penitentiary: Crucible of Good Intentions, Univ Penn Press, 94. **CONTACT ADDRESS** Dept Sociol & Anthropol, Beaver Col, 450 S Easton Rd, Glenside, PA 19038.

JOHNSTON, WILLIAM
DISCIPLINE SOCIAL AND CULTURAL CHANGE **EDUCATION** Elmira Col, BA, Harvard Univ, MA, PhD. **CAREER** Wesleyan Univ. **SELECTED PUBLICATIONS** Auth, The Modern Epidemic: A History Of Tuberculosis In Japan. **CONTACT ADDRESS** Wesleyan Univ, Middletown, CT 06459. **EMAIL** wjohnston@wesleyan.edus

JOHNSTONE, D. BRUCE
PERSONAL Born 01/13/1941, Minneapolis, MN, m, 1965 **DISCIPLINE** HIGHER AND COMPARATIVE EDUCATION **EDUCATION** Harvard Col, BA, 63; Harvard Univ, MAT, 64; Univ Minn, PhD, 69. **CAREER** Vice Pres for Admin, Univ of Pa, 74-79; Pres, State Univ Col at Buffalo, 79-88; Chancellor, State Univ of NY, 88-94; Prof, SUNY Buffalo, 94-. **HONORS AND AWARDS** Evans-Young Humanitarian Awd, Urban League of Buffalo, 94; Distinguished Service Awd, Nat Asn of Student Financial Aid Adminrs; Col Coun Medal, Buffalo State Col, 94; Chancellor Norton Medal, Univ at Buffalo, 94; Honorary doctorates: Towson State Univ, 95, D'Youville Col, 95; Calif State Univ at San Diego, 97; Distinguished Alumni Awd, Univ of Minn Sch of Educ Medaille Col Awd, 97; ed bds: J of Educ Finance, J of Student Retention in Higher Educ, Higher Educ in Europe. **MEMBERSHIPS** Asn for the Study of Higher Educ, Comparative and Int Educ Soc, Am Asn for Higher educ. **RESEARCH** Higher education finance, governance, and policy in both American and international-comparative perspectives. **SELECTED PUBLICATIONS** Auth, "The Productivity of Learning," J for Higher Educ Management, (summer/fall 95): 11-17; auth, "Starting Points: Fundamental Assumptions Underlying the Principles and Policies of Federal Financial Aid to Students," in Financing Postsecondary Education: The Federal Role, Washington, DC: US Dept of Educ (95): 77-83; auth, "Public and Private Partnerships: Leveraging Private Giving With Public Policies and Public Revenues," in Mary Kay Murphy, ed, The Advancement President and the Academy: Profiles in Institutional Leadership, Phoenix: Oryx Press (97): 66-75; auth, "Academic Leadership in the United States," in Madeline Greene, ed, Transforming Higher Education: Views from Leaders Around the World, Phoenix: Oryx Press (97): 134-149; auth, "Patterns of Finance: Revolution, Evolution, or More of the Same?," The Rev of Higher Educ, 21:3 (spring 98): 254-255; auth, "Management and Leadership Challenges of Multicampus Systems," in Jerry Gaither, ed, The Multicampus System: Perspectives on Practice and Prospects, Sterling, Va: Stylus Press (99); auth, "Financing Higher Education: Who Should Pay?," in Philip G. Altbach, Robert O. Berdahl, and Patricia J. Gumport, eds, American Higher Education in the Twentieth Century: Social, Political, and Economic Challenges, Baltimore: Johns Hopkins Univ Press (99); auth, "The Future of the University: Reasonable Predictions, Hoped-For Reforms, or Technological Possibilities?," in Mary Taylor Huber, ed, What Kind of University?, London: Open Univ Press (99); auth, "The Special Ethicality of the Academy," review essay of Academic Duty by Donald Kennedy, The Political University by Robert Rosenzweig, and All the Essential Half-Truths of Higher Education by George Dennis O'Brien, The Rev of Higher Educ, vol 23, no 2 (fall 2000): 229-236; auth, "The Challenge of Planning in Public," Planning for Higher Educ, vol 28 (winter 99-2000): 57-64. **CONTACT ADDRESS** Dept Educ Leadership & Policy, SUNY, Buffalo, Baldy Hall, PO Box 601000, Buffalo, NY 14260-1000. **EMAIL** dbj@acsu.buffalo.edu

JOLLEY, JERRY
PERSONAL Born 02/09/1945, Murray, UT, m, 1971, 2 children **DISCIPLINE** SOCIOLOGY **EDUCATION** Univ Ut, BA, 69; Univ Ut, MA, 71; Univ Ut, PhD, 75. **CAREER** Student Teacher, Skyline High Sch, 69; Teaching Asst, Univ Ut, 70; Instr, Kansas State Teachers Col, 70-72; Teaching Fel, Univ Ut, 72-75; Spec Instr, Brigham Young Univ, 74-75; From Asst Prof to Prof, Lewis Clark State Col, 75-. **HONORS AND AWARDS** Grant, Asn for the Humanities in Idaho, 83. **MEMBERSHIPS** AHII, ASA, ASC, ACJS, ACA, ICA, NSSA, WPACJE, ISA. **RESEARCH** Deviance and control, social problems, criminology, corrections, sociology of religion, social change. **SELECTED PUBLICATIONS** Auth, "Shock Incarceration Bootcamps: Idaho and the U S," Nat Sol Sci J, vol 9, no 2 (97): 45-55; auth, "Off The Mark: The Media Portrayal of the Arrasmith Double Murder Case," Nat Soc Sci Perspec-

tives J, vol 13, no 3 (98); auth, "Failure of Confidence: Deviance and Crime by Society's Trusted Professionals," (99). **CONTACT ADDRESS** Dept Sociol, Lewis-Clark State Col, 500 8th Ave, Lewiston, ID 83501.

JONES, CARROLL J.
PERSONAL Born 06/29/1944, Hays, KS, m, 1963, 2 children **DISCIPLINE** EDUCATION **EDUCATION** Univ Ariz, BA, 66; MEd, 70; Kans State Univ, PhD, 83. **CAREER** Asst Prof, Assoc Col of Cent Kans, 85-86; Asst Prof, Fayetteville State Univ, 86-88; Assoc Prof and Div Dir, Methodist Col, 88-89; Assoc Prof, Lander Col, 89-91; Manager, Fac Co-ord, City Col of Chicago-Europe, Wiesbaden Germany, 92; Assoc Prof, Lauder Univ, 93-96; Assoc Prof, State Univ of W Ga, 96-97; Assoc Prof, Clarke Col, 98-. **HONORS AND AWARDS** Poet Laureate, Washburn Univ, 78; Service to the Univ Awd, Fayetteville State Univ, 87; Nominated, Grawemeyer Awd in Educ, Univ Louisville, 93; Delta Kappa Gamma Soc Intl; Who's Who in Am, 00, 01. **MEMBERSHIPS** Am Asn of Col for Teacher Educ; Learning disabilities Asn; Phi Delta Kappa; Kappa Delta Pi; Coun of Exceptional Children; Intl Asn for Spec Educ; Delta Kappa Gamma Soc Intl **RESEARCH** Gifted students with special needs; Curriculum-based assessment; Portfolio assessment. **SELECTED PUBLICATIONS** Auth, Social and Emotional Development of Exceptional Students, Handicapped and Gifted, Springfield, 92; auth, Case Studies of Mildly Handicapped Students: Learning Disabled, Mildly Mentally Retarded and Behavior Disordered, Springfield, 92; auth, Case Studies of Severely/Multihandicapped Students, Springfield, 93; auth, Introduction to the Nature and Needs of Students with Mild disabilities: Mental Retardation, Behavior Disorders, Learning disabilities, Springfield, 96; auth, Curriculum-Based Assessment: The Easy Way, Springfield, 98; auth, Curriculum Development for Students with Mild disabilities: Academic and Social Skills for Writing Includion IEPs, Springfield, 00. **CONTACT ADDRESS** Dept Educ, Clarke Col, 1550 Clarke Dr, Dubuque, IA 52001. **EMAIL** cjones@keller.clarke.edu

JONES, JERRY
PERSONAL Born 09/11/1944, Charleston, WV, m, 1985, 2 children **DISCIPLINE** EDUCATION **EDUCATION** WV State Col, 72; WV Col Grad Studies, 74; VPI, 78. **CAREER** Supt of Schools, WV, 84-87, 93-95; prof, Univ of Charleston 98-. **MEMBERSHIPS** Southern Res Assoc. **RESEARCH** Self concept and creativity. **SELECTED PUBLICATIONS** Coauth, Postive Creativity, TM Pub, (Brentwood, TN), 90; coauth, Adviser, Advisee Program, Cambridge Pr, (Charleston), 99. **CONTACT ADDRESS** Dept Educ, Univ of Charleston, 2300 MacCorkle SE, Charleston, WV 25304.

JONES, JOHN F.
PERSONAL Born 03/29/1929, Dublin, Ireland, m, 1974, 2 children **DISCIPLINE** SOCIOLOGY **EDUCATION** National Univ of Ireland, BA 53; Univ Michigan, MSW 66; Univ Minnesota, MAPA, PhD, 68. **CAREER** Univ of Minnesota-Duluth, dean/prof, 71-76; Chinese Univ of Hong Kong, dir/ch, 76-87; Univ of Denver, dean/prof, 87-96, prof, 96-. **HONORS AND AWARDS** Inter Univ Consortium for Intl Development Founders Awd. **MEMBERSHIPS** IUCISD; CSWE **RESEARCH** Intl soc development; community development; training. **SELECTED PUBLICATIONS** Auth, New Training Design for Local Social Development, with T. Yogo, Nagoya, United Nat Cen for Reg Dev, 95; Call To Competence: Child Protective Services Training and Evaluation, et al, Englewood, CO, Amer Hum Assoc, 95; Glossary of Social Work Terms in Chinese and English, with Wang Shek, Hong Kong, Chinese Univ Press, 90. **CONTACT ADDRESS** Graduate Sch of Social Work, Univ of Denver, 2148 South High St, Denver, CO 80208. **EMAIL** jojones@du.edu

JONES, MICHAEL OWEN
PERSONAL Born 10/11/1942, Wichita, KS, m, 1964, 1 child **DISCIPLINE** AMERICAN FOLKLORE, FOLK ART; TECHNOLOGY; FOLK MEDICINE **EDUCATION** Univ Kans, BA, 64; Ind Univ, MA, 66, PhD(folklore and Am studies), 70. **CAREER** Actg asst prof, 68-70, asst prof, 70-75, assoc prof, 75-81, Prof Folkloristics & Hist, Univ Calif, Los Angeles, 81-, Consult & reviewer, Nat Endowment for Humanities, 79- **MEMBERSHIPS** Am Folklore Soc; Am Studies Asn; Popular Cult Asn; Soc Anthrop of Work. **RESEARCH** Organizational folklore; folk art and aesthetics; folk belief and custom; food symbolism and customs. **SELECTED PUBLICATIONS** Coed, Inside organizations, 88; ed, Putting Folklore to Use, 94; auth, 'Spirits in the Woods, the Chainsaw Art of Skip Armstrong', J Amer Folklore, Vol 0107, 94; 'Traditions in Clay C.J. and Cleater Meaders', J Amer Folklore, Vol 0107, 94; The 1995 Archer Taylor Memorial Lecture, Why Make Folk Art, Western Folklore, Vol 0054, 95; coauth, Folkloristics: An Introduction, 95; auth, Studying organizational symbolism, 96. **CONTACT ADDRESS** Folklore & Mythol Ctr, Univ of California, Los Angeles, 1037 Grad Sch Mgt, Los Angeles, CA 90024. **EMAIL** mojones@humnet.ucla.edu

JONES, PHILLIP ERSKINE
PERSONAL Born 10/26/1940, Chicago, IL, m **DISCIPLINE** EDUCATION **EDUCATION** Univ of IL, BS 1963; Univ of IA, MA 1967, PhD 1975. **CAREER** Chicago Youth Ctrs, group work counselor 1963-64; Flint Comm Schs, secondary tchr phys ed 1967-68; Univ of IA, dir special support serv 1970-75, asstvice pres & dir affirmative action asst prof of counselor educ 1975-78, assoc dean of student serv & asst prof of counselor educ 1978-83, dean of student serv & asst prof of counselor educ 1983-89, associate vice president of academic affairs & dean of students, 89-97, vice pres for student services and dean of students, 97-. **HONORS AND AWARDS** Rep US Ethnic Professional Exchange Prog to W Germany; Sister Cities Intl; Carl Duisberg-Gesellschaft; and Instut fur Auslandsbeziehungen; proceedings of the 1972 ACT Invitational Conf Iowa City. **MEMBERSHIPS** Mem IA City Human Relations Comm 1972-74; chair IA City Human Relations Comm 1974-75; human relations training sessions IA City Fire Dept 1985; field reader for spec serv prog US Office of Educ 1980-87; human relations workshop Dept of Correction Serv Session 1981; reentry workshop for tchrs IA City Sch Dist; consul redevelopment of training prog for Educators in USOE; field reader for grad & professional oppor progs US Office of Educ 1978; consul HUD. **SELECTED PUBLICATIONS** Special Educ & Socioeconomic Retardation, J for Spec ducators, Vol 19 No 4 1983; "Student Decision Making, When and How"; College/Career Choice, Right Student Right Time Right Place. **CONTACT ADDRESS** Vice President for Student Services, Univ of Iowa, Rm 114 Jessup Hall, Iowa City, IA 52242.

JONES, TERRY L.
PERSONAL Born 11/22/1954, Columbus, OH, m, 1986, 1 child **DISCIPLINE** ANTHROPOLOGY **EDUCATION** Univ Calif, Santa Cruz, BA, 78; Sonoma State Univ, MA, 82; Univ Calif, Davis, MA, 89; PhD, 95. **CAREER** Asst prof, Calif Poly State Univ, 98-. **MEMBERSHIPS** Soc for Am Archaeol; Reg of Prof Archaeol. **RESEARCH** New World Prehistory, California Archaeology, Maritime Adaptations. **SELECTED PUBLICATIONS** Rev, of "Early Hunter-gatherers of the California Coast", by Jon Erlandson, Am Antiquity 62 (97): 161-162; coauth, "Climatic Consequences or Population Pragmatism?: A Mid-Holocene Prehistory of the Central California Coast", Mid Holocene Hunter-Gatherers of the California Coast, ed M. Glassow and J.M. Erlandson, Univ of Calif, 97; auth, "Lakes and Estuaries Reconsidered: A Comment on Lacustrine Intensification in the southern Santa Clara Valley, California", J of Calif and Great Basin Anthrop 19 (97): 281-288; rev, of "Diversity and Complexity in Prehistoric Maritime Societies: A Gulf of Maine Perspective", by Bruce J Borque, J of Field Archaeol 25 (98): 115-116; coauth, "Late Holocene Sea Temperatures along the central California Coast", Quarternary Res 51, (99): 74-82; coauth, "Environmental Imperatives Reconsidered: Demographic Crisis in western North America during the Medieval Climatic Anomaly", Current Anthrop 40 (99): 137-156; coauth, "The Milling Stone Horizon Revisited: New Perspectives from northern and central California", J of Calif and Great Basin Anthrop 21 (99): 65-93; coauth, "Archaeological Investigations at the Point Bennett Pinniped Rookery on San Miguel Island, California", Proceedings of the Fifth Calif Islands Symposium, ed David Browne, Kathryn Mitchell and Henry Chaney, U.S. Minerals Management Serv, (forthcoming); coauth, "Transholocene Marine Mammal Exploitation on San Clemente Island, California: A Tragedy of the Commons Revisited", J of Anthrop Archaeol (forthcoming). **CONTACT ADDRESS** Dept Soc Sci, California Polytech State Univ, San Luis Obispo, 1 Grand Ave, San Luis Obispo, CA 93407. **EMAIL** tljones@calpoly.edu

JORDAN, ABBIE H.
PERSONAL Born Wilcox County, GA, m **DISCIPLINE** EDUCATION **EDUCATION** Albany State Coll, BS 1949; Atlanta Univ, MA 1953; Univ of GA, PhD, 1979. **CAREER** Tuskegee Inst, instr; Atlanta Univ Complex, instr of reading; Jr HS Ben Hill Cty, principal; Veterans School, principal, instr; GA-SC Read Conf, org & dir; Savannah Morning News, ed-op columnist; Savannah State Coll Reading Inst, founder; US Office of Education (EPDA). **HONORS AND AWARDS** Outstanding Teacher of the Year 1973; featured in Essence Mag 1976; Novelet "Ms Lily" 1977; authored numerous articles; featured in Atlanta Constitution Journal, June 1988; Jet, Sept 28, 1992, Oct 5, 1992. **MEMBERSHIPS** Consultant in reading for the Southeastern Area of the US; mem adv comm IRA Resol Comm 1974-; exec sec/treasurer Savannah Hospital Authority 1975-; mem adv comm GA Hist Found 1974-80, Telfair Art Acad 1975-80, Basic Ed & Reading 1977-78; mem, exec bd NAACP 1977-83; coord/founder of the Society of Doctors Inc 1986-; founder/director, The Consortium of Doctors, Ltd, 1989. **CONTACT ADDRESS** Consortium of Doctors Ltd, PO Box 20402, University System, Savannah, GA 31404.

JORDAN, CATHELEEN
PERSONAL Born 06/01/1947, Kansas City, MO, m, 1999, 3 children **DISCIPLINE** SOCIAL WORK **EDUCATION** Univ Houston, BA, 73; Univ Tex, MS, 79; Univ Cal, PhD, 86. **CAREER** Teach, res asst, Univ Cal, Berk, 81-83; instr, Dana Col, 83-84; vis asst prof, Univ Tex, Arling, 85-86; asst prof, 86-91; assoc prof, 91-95; prof, 95-. **HONORS AND AWARDS** Who's Who in Am Women, Exec's and Prof, Fac SW, Hum Ser Prof; Fernando Torgeson Awd. **MEMBERSHIPS** SSWR; NASW; CSWE; SSSA. **SELECTED PUBLICATIONS** Coauth, Clinical assessment: Quantitative and Qualitative methods, Lyceum Books (Chicago), 95; coauth, Introduction to family social work, Peacock Pub (Itasca, IL), 99; coauth, Family Practice: Brief Systems Methods for Social Work, Brooks/Cole (Pacific Grove, CA), 99; coauth, "Social work response to mental illness," in Social work: Issues and opportunities in a challenging profession, eds. D Dinitto, A McNeese (Boston: Allyn and Bacon, 97); coauth, "Developing measuring instruments," in Social work research and evaluation, ed. Richard Grinnell (Itasca, FL: Peacock, 97); coauth, "Qualitative assessment: A methodological review," in Constructivism in practice: Methods and challenges, eds. C Franklin, PA Nurius (Milwaukee, WI: Families Intl, 98); coauth, "Assessment in managed care: The clinical utility of models and methods," in Social work processes, eds. B Compton, B Galloway (Pacific Grove, CA: Brooks/Cole, 99); coauth, "Competency-based treatment for persons with marital discord," in Structuring change, ed. Kevin Corcoran (Chicago, IL: Lyceum Books, 00); coauth, "Reliability and validity in quantitative measurement," in Handbook of social work research methods, ed. B Thyer (Sage Pub, 00). **CONTACT ADDRESS** Dept Social Work, Univ of Texas, Arlington, PO Box 19129, Arlington, TX 76019-0001.

JORDAN, EDDIE JACK, SR.
PERSONAL Born 07/29/1927, Wichita Falls, TX, w **DISCIPLINE** EDUCATION **EDUCATION** Langston Univ, BA 1948; IA Univ, MA 1949; State Univ of IA, MFA 1956; IN Univ, MS 1973, DEd 1975. **CAREER** Claflin Univ, chmn dept of art 1950-Army; Allen Univ, chmn dept of art 1954-56; Langston Univ, chmn dept of art 1956-61; Southern Univ at NO, chmn dept of art 1961-. **HONORS AND AWARDS** Rec'd 44 awds in local regional & natl competition; Sculpture Awd Rhode Island Natl, Philbrook Museum in OK, Walker ARt Ctr MN, Gibbs Art Museum SC, Carnegie Inst Pgh; 2 sculptures as a first of Blacks purchased for IN Museum 1974; Delta Phi Delta Natl Hon Art Frat. **MEMBERSHIPS** Natl co chmn Comm for Devel of Art in Negro Colls 1962-; pres, adm bd Bethany United Ch 1968-80; mem comm Phi Delta Kappa Inc 1980-81; pres bd of dirs Natl Conf of Artists 1983-; sec treas New Orleans Ctr of Creative Arts 1983-; life mem NAACP; life mem Alpha Phi Frat Inc; life mem, National Conference of Artists. **CONTACT ADDRESS** Art Dept, So Univ, New Orleans, 6400 Press Dr, New Orleans, LA 70126.

JORDAN, J. SCOTT
PERSONAL Born 10/08/1962, Aurora, IL, m, 1985, 1 child **DISCIPLINE** PSYCHOLOGY **EDUCATION** Northern Ill Univ, BA, 85, MA, 88, PhD, 91. **CAREER** Asst prof, St Xavier Col, Chicago, 91-92; Alexander von Humboldt Post-Doctoral Fel, Univ of Ulm, Germany, 92-93; asst prof, St Xavier Univ, 93-95, assoc prof, 95-; Vis Scholar, Max Planck Inst for Psychol Res, Munich, Germany, 98-99. **HONORS AND AWARDS** Phi Kappa Phi; The Nat Dean's List, 84-85; Alexander Von Humboldt Post-doctoral Fel, 92-93; Who's Who Among America's Teachers, 98; Outstanding Young Americans, 98; Invited Scholar, Max Planck Inst for Psychol Res, 98-99. **MEMBERSHIPS** Psychonomic Soc; Midwestern Psychol Soc; Asn for the Sci Study of Consciousness; Soc for Chaos Theory in Psychol and the Life Scis. **RESEARCH** Spatial perception and action. **SELECTED PUBLICATIONS** Coauth, "The Phantom Array: A peri-saccadic illusion of visual direction," The Psychol Record, 48 (98): 21-32; auth, "Recasting Dewey's critique of the reflex-arc concept via a theory of anticipatory consciousness: Implications for theories of perception," New Ideas in Psychol, 16, 3 (98): 165-187; ed, Modeling consciousness across the disciplines, Lantham, Md: Univ Press of Am, Inc (99); auth, "Cognition and spatial perception: Production of output or control of input?," in G. Aschersleben, J. Muessler, and T. Bachmann, eds, Cognitive contributions to the perception of spatial and temporal events, North Holland: Elsevier (99): 69-90; coauth, "The role of perceptual anticipation in the localization of the final position of a moving target," Manuscript submitted; auth, ""Utilizing intra- and inter-trial complexity to assess executive coordination of action-control systems," Manuscript submitted. **CONTACT ADDRESS** Dept Psychol, Saint Xavier Univ, 3700 W 103rd St, Chicago, IL 60655. **EMAIL** jordan@sxu.edu

JORDAN, KARIN B.
PERSONAL Born 07/26/1958, Hannover, Germany, m, 1981 **DISCIPLINE** EDUCATION **EDUCATION** Colo Christian col, BA, 87; Rollins col, MA, 89; Univ GA, PhD, 92. **CAREER** Sen instr to asst prof, Univ Colo, 94-. **HONORS AND AWARDS** Outstanding Teaching Awd, 99. **MEMBERSHIPS** Am Asn for Marriage & Family Therapy, Int Family Therapy Asn, Am Coun Asn. **RESEARCH** Programmed distance writing, Clinical supervision, Therapy techniques/strategies. **SELECTED PUBLICATIONS** Auth, "Programmed distance writing divorce adjustment for children: A single case study," family Therapy, (in press); auth, "Family art therapy: the joint family holiday drawing," The Family Journal, (in press); auth, "Programmed writing: an enhancement to traditional talk therapy," Family Therapy, (99)L 149-155; auth, "Live supervision for the beginning counselor in practicum: Crucial for quality counseling and avoiding litigation," Family Therapy, (99): 81-86; auth, "A writing exercise to explore dreams," Journal of Family Psychotherapy, (99): 75-77; auth, "The tape of the mind program: A single case study," Journal of Family Psychotherapy, (99): 13-25; auth, "The child, adolescent, and family support network: Providing ongoing services for mentally ill children,

adolescents, and their families, and training for student therapists," Family Therapy, (99): 51-55; auth, "Revising the ethics code of IAMFC-- A training exercise for counseling psychology and counselor education students," the Family Journal, (99): 170-175; auth, "The Cultural experiences and identified needs of the ethnic minority supervisee in the context of Caucasian supervision," Family Therapy, (98): 181-187. **CONTACT ADDRESS** School of Educ, Univ of Colorado, Denver, PO Box 173364, Denver, CO 80217. **EMAIL** drkbjordan@cs.com

JORDAN, ROSAN
PERSONAL Born 05/16/1939, Fort Worth, TX, m, 1970 **DISCIPLINE** FOLKLORE, WOMEN'S AND GENDER STUDIES **EDUCATION** Ind Univ, PhD, 75. **CAREER** Assoc prof, La State Univ; bk rev ed, Southern Folklore, 86-92; ed bd, Revista de Investigaciones Folkloricas, 87-. **HONORS AND AWARDS** Centennial Awd, Am Folklore Soc, 89; Lynwood Montell Prize, Southern Folklore, 92. **MEMBERSHIPS** Exec bd, La Folklore Soc, 81-; nominating comt, Am Folklore Soc, 93-96; Exec Bd, Am Folklore Soc, 99-01. **RESEARCH** Folklore; women's and gender studies. **SELECTED PUBLICATIONS** Auth, "Ethnic Identity and the Lore of the Supernatural," Journal of American Folklore, 75; auth, "Tension and Speech Play in Mexican-American Folklore," in And Other Neighborly Names: Social Process and Cultural Image in Texas Folklore, U of Texas Press, 81; auth, Folklore and Ethnicity: Some Theoretical Considerations, in, Louisiana Folklife: A Guide to the State, 85; Louisiana Folk Crafts: An Overview; Louisiana Folklife: A Guide to the State, 85; The Vaginal Serpent and Other Themes from Mexican-American Women's Lore, in Women's Folklore, Women's Culture, 85; Not into Cold Space: Zora Neale Hurston and J. Frank Dobie as Holistic Folklorists, Southern Folklore, 92; 'In This Folk-Lore Land': Race, Class, Identity, and Folklore Studies in Louisiana, J of Am Fo lklore, 96; coauth, Louisiana Traditional Crafts, 80; Comentarios Acerca del Folklore de una Elite Colonial, Cuadernos Inst Nac de Antropologia, 91; coed, Women's Folklore, Women's Culture, 85. **CONTACT ADDRESS** Dept of Eng, Louisiana State Univ, Baton Rouge, LA 70803-5001. **EMAIL** enrosan@lsu.edu

JORDEN, CRYSTAL W.
PERSONAL Born 08/15/1942, South Grove, CA, m, 1964, 2 children **DISCIPLINE** SPORT PSYCHOLOGY **EDUCATION** Univ Calif, Santa Barbara, BA, 64, MA, 70. **CAREER** Teacher, Physical Ed, Santa Barbara District High School, 64-72; assoc prof, Dept of Kinesiology, Westmont Col, 72-, chair, 88-98. **HONORS AND AWARDS** Instr: Portable swimming experience for disadvantaged student, 64 & 66; Dir, Cataline Private Camp, 65; Rhythmic instr, Federally funded progs for learning impaired, 67; elected District Coor of Physical Ed for S. B. Schools-Secondary, 71; elected mem, Delta Kappa Gamma-ed org honorary, 73; Assoc athletic dir, sat on district executive comm, 83-86; Cited Recommended for Public Service before the Santa Barbara Bd of Supervisors, 84; Chair, Dept of Kinesiology, Westmont Col, 88-98. **MEMBERSHIPS** Am Asn for Health, Physical Ed, Recreation, & Dance; Calif Asn of H., P. E., Recreation and Dance; Am Asn for Supervision of Curriculum Develop; Calif Asn for Supervision of Curriculum develop; N. A. I. A. **RESEARCH** Applied learning theory, cross-cultural issues in Kinesiology and sport, women in sport. **SELECTED PUBLICATIONS** Auth, "Physical Education a Multifaceted Discipline;" auth, "Practicums: Exciting and Invaluable." **CONTACT ADDRESS** Dept Physical Ed, Westmont Col, 955 La Paz Rd, Santa Barbara, CA 93108. **EMAIL** jorden@westmont.edu

JOSEPH, ALFRED
PERSONAL Born 09/13/1955, Columbus, OH, m, 1989, 3 children **DISCIPLINE** SOCIAL WORK **EDUCATION** Ohio State Univ, BA, 79; MSW, 89; PhD, 95. **CAREER** Planner, Franklin W. C Serv, 89-91; Asst Prof, Miami Univ Ohio, 94-. **MEMBERSHIPS** NASW, CSWE, SSSP. **RESEARCH** Tracking, Social Work in Schools, Poverty. **SELECTED PUBLICATIONS** Auth, "Partnership Programs: Is There a Relationship Between Self-Esteem and Academic Performance in African-American Schoolchildren?," Soc Work in Educ 14-3 (92): 185-189; coauth, "Tracking: A child welfare issue?," in Expanded Partnership for Vulnerable Children, Youth and Families, ed. K. Hooper-Briar and H. Lawson (Washington, DC: Coun on Soc Work Educ, 96), 121-132; coauth, "School-linked comprehensive services: promising beginnings, Lessons Learned, and Future Challenges," in Community Building: Renewal, Well-Being, and Shared Responsibility, ed. P. Ewalt, E. Freeman, and D. Poole (Washington, DC: NASW Press, 97), 343-354; coauth, "Drug Wars and Racial Sentencing Disparities," BCR Reports 9-2 (97): 8-9; coauth, "School-Linked Comprehensive services: Promising Beginnings, Lessons Learned, and Future Challenges," Soc Work in Educ 19-3 (97): 136-148; coauth, "Tracking: A form of educational neglect?," Soc Work in Educ 20-2 (98): 110-120; auth, "The impact of tracking: An Examination of Outcomes," J of Poverty 1-2 (98): 1-21; coauth, "Institutional Racism and Sentencing Disparities for Cocaine Possessions," J of Poverty 3-4 (99): 1-17. **CONTACT ADDRESS** Dept Family Studies and Soc Work, Miami Univ, 500 E High St, Oxford, OH 45056. **EMAIL** JosephAL@muohio.edu

JOSEPH, CHERYL
PERSONAL Born 04/20/1948, Detroit, MI, s **DISCIPLINE** SOCIOLOGY **EDUCATION** Wayne State Univ, BA, 76; PhD, 85; Univ Detroit, MA, 77. **CAREER** Prof, Col Notre Dame, 88-. **MEMBERSHIPS** Am Sociol Asn, Am Humanist Soc. **RESEARCH** Sociological Theory, Service-Learning, Animal-Human Bond. **SELECTED PUBLICATIONS** Auth, Effects of Hypnotherapy on Test Anxiety in Adult Learners; auth, From Hitler to Hip-Hop: Fifty Years of Sociological Theory. **CONTACT ADDRESS** Dept Sociol, Col of Notre Dame, 1500 Ralston Ave, Belmont, CA 94002. **EMAIL** cjoseph@cnd.edu

JOU, JERWEN
PERSONAL Born 09/22/1945, China, m, 1974, 2 children **DISCIPLINE** PSYCHOLOGY **EDUCATION** Nat Chengchi Univ, BA, 69; Fujen Univ, MA, 75; East Tex State Univ, MS, 80; Kans State Univ, PhD, 90. **CAREER** Asst prof, Ga Southern Univ, 90-93; asst prof, Univ Tex, Pan American, 95-96, assoc prof, 96-. **HONORS AND AWARDS** Res grant, Nat Inst of Health for Minority Biomedical Res Support, 95-98; educator in Tex Hall of Fame, 96; Who's Who in Am Teachers, 96. **MEMBERSHIPS** Am psychol Soc, The Psychonomic Soc. **RESEARCH** Human memory, judgement and decision making. **SELECTED PUBLICATIONS** Auth, "The development of comprehension of double negation in Chinese children," J of Experimental Child Psychol, 45 (88): 457-471; coauth with M. H. Birnbaum, "A theory of comparative response times and difference judgements," Cognitive Psychol, 22 (90): 184-210; coauth with R. J. Harris, "Event order vs. syntactic structure in recall of adverbial complex sentences," J of Psycholinguistic Res, 19 (90): 21-42; coauth with R. J. Harris, "Processing inflections: Dynamic processes in sentence comprehension," J of Experimental Psychol: Learning, Memory, and Cognition, 17 (91): 1082-1094; coauth with R. J. Harris,"The effect of divided attention on speech production," Bull of the Psychonomic Soc, 30 (92): 301-304; auth, "Reading inflectionally incongruent texts: Automatic and strategic processes in language performance," J of Psycholinguistic Res, 21 (92): 365-382; coauth with J. Shanteau, "The gestalt and dynamic processes in decision making," Behav Processes, 33 (95): 305-318; coauth with J. Shanteau and R. J. Harris, "An information processing view of framing effects: The role of causal-schemas in decision making," Memory & Cognition, 24 (96): 1-15; auth, "Why is the alphabetically middle letter in a multiletter array so hard to determine? Memory processes in linear-order information processing," J of Experimental Psychology: Human Perception and Performance, 23 (97): 1743-1763; coauth with J. W. Aldridge, "Memory representation of alphabetic position and interval information," J of Experimental Psychol: Learning, Memory, and Cognition, 25 (99): 680-701. **CONTACT ADDRESS** Dept Psychol, Univ of Texas, Pan American, 1201 W University Dr, Edinburg, TX 78539. **EMAIL** jjou@Panam.edu

JOY, DONALD MARVIN
PERSONAL Born 08/20/1928, Gray County, KS, m, 1948, 2 children **DISCIPLINE** CURRICULUM DEVELOPMENT; EDUCATIONAL PSYCHOLOGY; ENGLISH **EDUCATION** Cent Col, AA, 47; Greenville (IL) Col, BA, 49; Asbury Sem, BD, 54; Ind Univ, PhD, 69. **CAREER** Pastoral Min, 49-51 & 54-58; public school music, 49-51; Exec ed Free Methodist Church NA, 58-71; prof Human Develop Fam Studies, Asbury Sem, 71-98; dir, Ctr for the Study of the Family, 98-; Phi Beta Kappa. **HONORS AND AWARDS** Outstanding Christian Educator of the Year, Nat Assoc Prof Christian Educ, 99. **MEMBERSHIPS** Assoc Prof & Res in Relig Educ; Nat Assoc Prof Christian Educ. **RESEARCH** Moral development; consicience formation; spiritual direction. **SELECTED PUBLICATIONS** Becoming A Man!, Ventura:Regal, 90; Men Under Construction, Victor Chariot, 93; Women at Risk, with Dr. David Hager, Bristol House Ltd, 93; Celebrating the New Woman in the Family, Bristol House Ltd, 94; Risk-Proofing Your Family, US Ctr for World Mission, 95; Re-Bonding: Preventing and Restoring Broken Relationships, Evangel Publ House, 96; Bonding: Relationships in the Image of God, Evangel Publ House, 96; Beyond Adolescence! Hope for Teens and Families, Asbury Theol Sem, 96; How to Use Camping Experiences in Religious Education: Transformation Through Christian Camping, Relig Educ Press, 98; auth, Empower Your Kids to Be Adult: A Guide for Parents, Ministers, and Other Mentors, Evangel Publ House, 00. **CONTACT ADDRESS** Ctr fo the Study of the Family, 600 N Lexington Ave, Wilmore, KY 40390. **EMAIL** rodojoy@juno.com

JOY, STEPHEN
PERSONAL Born 03/06/1958, Rochester, NY, m, 1995, 2 children **DISCIPLINE** PSYCHOLOGY **EDUCATION** Bowdoin Col, BA, 80; S Conn State Univ, BS, 88; Univ Conn, PhD, 00. **CAREER** Res Assoc, Yale Psychiat Inst, 87-90; clinical Psychol Assoc, Norwich Hospital, 92-94; Clinical Psychol Intern, Conn Valley Hospital, 94-95; Istructor to Asst Prof, Albertus Magnus Col, 89-. **HONORS AND AWARDS** State of Conn Univ Outstanding Scholar Awd. **MEMBERSHIPS** Am Psychol Asn, am Psychol Soc. **RESEARCH** Neuropsychological assessment, Psychopathology, Personality, Creativity. **SELECTED PUBLICATIONS** Auth, "Speed and Memory in WAIS-R-NI Digit symbol Performance among Healthy Older Adults," Journal of the International Neuropsychological Soc, 00; auth, "Quantifying qualitative features of Block Design performance among healthy older adults," Archives of Clinical Neuropsychology, 00; auth, "The need to be different predicts divergent production: Toward a social learning model of originality," Journal of Creative Behaviour, 00; auth, "Information Multiple choice among healthy older adults: Characteristics, correlates, and clinical implications," The Clinical Neuropsychologist, 99; auth, "Autism and Pervasive developmental disorders," Neuropsychiatry, 96; auth, "Language and cognition in Autism: An Overview, Neuropsychiatry, 96. **CONTACT ADDRESS** Dept Psychol, Albertus Magnus Col, 700 Prospect St, New Haven, CT 06511. **EMAIL** joy@laurel.albertus.edu

JOYCE, ROSEMARY A.
PERSONAL Born 04/07/1956, Lackawanna, NY, m, 1984 **DISCIPLINE** ANTHROPOLOGY, ARCHAEOLOGY **EDUCATION** Cornell Univ, AB, 78; Univ Ill, Urbana-Champaign, PhD, 85. **CAREER** Asst curator, 85-94, asst dir, 86-89, Peabody Museum, Harvard Univ; asst prof, 89-91, assoc prof, 91-94, anthrop, Harvard Univ; dir, Phoebe Hearst Museum of Anthropology, 94-99, assoc prof, anthrop, Univ Calif Berkeley, 94. **HONORS AND AWARDS** Resident fellowships: Bunting Inst, Radcliffe Coll, Harvard Univ, 92-93; Stanford Univ Center Study Behavioral Scis, 98 (deferred); Univ Calif Humanities Research Inst, spring 99; research grants: Getty Grant Program; Wenner-G Fren Found Anthrop Research; Heinz Charitable Fund; Nat Sci Foundation; Nat Endowment for the Humanities; Fulbright-Hays Prog, Fam SI. **MEMBERSHIPS** Soc Amer Archeol; Amer Anthrop Assn; Coun Museum Anthrop; Amer Assn Museums. **RESEARCH** Archaeology of Central America and Mesoamerica; the archaeology of gender; ceramic analysis; Maya writing; the anthropology of representation and identity; museum anthropology. **SELECTED PUBLICATIONS** Coauth, Encounters with the Americas: The Latin American Gallery of the Peabody Museum, 95; auth, "The Construction of Gender in Classic Maya Monuments," in Gender in Archaeology: Essays in Research and Practice, 96; co-ed, Women in Prehistory: North American and Mesoamerica, 97; co-ed, Social Patterns in Pre-Classic Mesoamerica, 98; auth, "Performing the Body in Prehispanic Central America," RES: Anthropology and Aesthetics, spring 98. **CONTACT ADDRESS** Dept Anthropology, Univ of California, Berkeley, Kroeber Hall, #3710, Berkeley, CA 94720-3710. **EMAIL** rajoyce@uclink.berkeley.edu

JUDD, CATHERINE
PERSONAL Born Berkeley, CA, 1 child **DISCIPLINE** BRITISH LITERATURE, WOMEN'S STUDIES **EDUCATION** Univ Calif, Santa Cruz, BA, 82; Univ Calif Berkeley, MA, 85; PhD, 92. **CAREER** Asst to assoc prof, Univ of Miami, 92-. **HONORS AND AWARDS** NEH Summer Fel, 94; Univ of Miami Res Fel, 95; Univ of Miami Fel, 98, 99. **MEMBERSHIPS** MLA; Interdisciplinary Nineteenth-Century Studies Assoc; Nineteenth-Century Studies Assoc; Univ of Miami Women's Studies Assoc. **SELECTED PUBLICATIONS** Auth, "Nine Oils or the Balm of Gilead: Nursing and Social Healing in Hard Times", Reading Hard Times, ed Murray Baumgarten, Dickens Proj Pr, (Santa Cruz, 89); auth, "Male Pseudonyms and Female Authority in Victorian England", Literature and the Marketplace: Nineteenth-Century British Publishing and Reading Practices, eds John O Jordan and Robert L Patten, Cambridge Univ Pr, (Cambridge, 95); rev art on illness and mortality in Victorian fiction, Nineteenth-Century Contexts 19.4 (96): 109-112; rev art on Victorian prostitution, Nineteenth-Century Contexts, 20.1 (97): 115-118; auth, Bedside Seductions: Nursing and the Victorian Imagination, 1830-1880, St Martin's Pr, (NY), 98. **CONTACT ADDRESS** Dept English, Univ of Miami, PO Box 248106, Miami, FL 33124-8106. **EMAIL** catjudd@umiami.ir.miami.edu

JULIA, MARIA C.
PERSONAL Born, Puerto Rico **DISCIPLINE** SOCIAL WORK **EDUCATION** Univ Puerto Rico, BA, 67; MSW, 69; Ohio State Univ, PhD, 81. **CAREER** Lecturer to Assoc Prof, Ohio State Univ, 84-. **HONORS AND AWARDS** Distinguished alumna of the Year, Ohio State Univ, 91; Success Stories Awd, Ohio State Univ, 92; Phi Beta Delta Honor Soc; Phi Kappa Phi Nat Honor Soc. **MEMBERSHIPS** Asn of Fac and Professional Women, Asn for Res on Non-Profit Org and voluntary Action, Colegio de Trabajadores sociales de Puerto Rico, Columbus Intl Prog, Coun on Soc Work Educ, global Awareness soc Intl, Intl Asn of Schools of Soc Work, Intl Coun on soc Welfare, Inter-Univ Consortium for Intl Soc Development; Nat Asn of Soc Workers, Ohio State Univ Alumni Soc, so for Transcultural Family relations, State of Ohio Licensed social Worker, women and Children Health Cooperative, women in International Development. **RESEARCH** International Social Development; Gender; Multiculturalism. **SELECTED PUBLICATIONS** Auth, Metodos de Investigacion Social Centifica (Social Research Methodology), forthcoming; auth, "empowerment in the Research curriculum: Is social Work Education Meeting the Challenge?," Journal of Teaching in Social Work, forthcoming; auth, "Acerca de la Educacion Interprofessional: Un Programa Innovador que Incluye el Trabajo social y Otras Profesiones de Servicios Humanos," Homines, forthcoming; auth, "Clitoridectomy, Excision, and Infibulation: Implications for Social Development," Social Development issues, forthcoming; auth, "The Transfer of Social Work Technology," Journal of Scientific Information, forthcoming; auth, Constructing Gender; Multicultural Perspectives in Working with Women,

Brooks Cole, 00; auth, "Poverty in Zambit - The People's Experience: What Next for civil Society and Socioeconomic Development?," Social Development issues, (99): 37-46; auth, "The Need for Cultural Considerations in Examining and facilitating Puerto Rican Financial Planning," Free Inquiry in Creative sociology, (99): 1-8; auth, "Ethnoracial Awareness in Intercountry Adoption," International Social Work, (99): 61-73; auth, "Student perceptions of Culture: An Integral Part of Social Work Practice," International Journal of Intercultural Relations, 99. **CONTACT ADDRESS** Col of Soc Work, Ohio State Univ, Columbus, 1947 College Rd, Columbus, OH 43210. **EMAIL** julia.1@osu.edu

JURKOWSKI, ELAINE
PERSONAL Born 10/04/1958, Winnipeg, MAN, Canada **DISCIPLINE** SOCIAL WORK **EDUCATION** Univ Manitoba, BSW, 80; MSW, 86; Univ Ill, PhD, 97. **CAREER** Asst Prof, Univ Windsor, 97-98; Asst Prof, Southern Ill, 98-. **HONORS AND AWARDS** For Stud Service Awd, Univ IL, 94; Who's Who in Student leadership, 95; Who's Who in Academia Intl, 97; Res Fel, Univ IL, 96-97; Reaching Fel Awd, S IL Univ, 98; Intl Women of the Year, Intl Biographical Centre, 99. **MEMBERSHIPS** Am Public Health Asn; IL Public Health Asn; Am Asn for Mental Retardation; IL Rural Health Asn; Coun on Soc Work Educ. **RESEARCH** Public health; Community planning for health and social services; Leadership; Citizen participation; Trends and issues in disability; International models for disability and health; The use of technology in teaching. **SELECTED PUBLICATIONS** Co-auth, "Evaluation of HIV Prevention and Self-Protection Training Programs," in HIV Infection and Developmental Disabilities, Pub Brookes Pub, 92; co-auth, "Affection, Love, Intimacy and Sexual Relationships," in Friendships and Community Connections between people with and without Developmental Disabilities, (Paul Brookes Pub Co, 93), 129-153; co-auth, "The Myths and Realities of Depression and Down Syndrome," in Living and Learning in the community, New York, 94; co-auth, "Trends in International Research, Chapter 14," in Handbook on Research for Social Work, Sage Pub, forthcoming; co-auth, "Assisted Living, Social Work Practice & The Elderly," in Social Work Practice and the Elderly, Toronto, forthcoming. **CONTACT ADDRESS** Dept Soc Work, So Illinois Univ, Carbondale, Southern Ill Union, Carbondale, IL 62901. **EMAIL** etjurkow@sju.edu

JUSCZYK, P. W.
PERSONAL Born 01/31/1948, RI, m, 1971, 2 children **DISCIPLINE** PSYCHOLOGY **EDUCATION** Brown Univ, BS, 70; Univ Penn, MA, 71; Univ Penn, PhD, 75 **CAREER** Asst to assoc prof, Dalhousie Univ, 75-80; assoc to prof, Univ Oregon, 80-90; prof, SUNY, 90-96; Johns Hopkins Univ, 96- **HONORS AND AWARDS** Sloane Fel, Univ Penn, 84; Fulbright Schola, Cath Univ; NIMH Senior Scientist Awd, 97-2002 **MEMBERSHIPS** Sigma Xi; Soc Res Child Develop; Acoustical Soc Amer; Amer Psychol Soc; Cognitive Sci Soc; Psychonomic Soc **RESEARCH** Psycholinguistics; Speech Perception; Infant Language Acquisition; Cognitive Development **SELECTED PUBLICATIONS** coauth, "18 month olds' sensitivity to relationships between morphemes: Interactions among relationships, frequency and processing," Proceedings of the 22nd Annual Boston University Conference on Language Development, Vol. 2, 98; coauth, "Talker-specificity and persistence of infants' word representations," Proceedings of the 22nd Annual Boston University Conference on Language Development, Vol. 1, 98; coauth, "American infant discrimination of Dutch and French word lists," Proceedings of the 21st Annual Boston University Conference on Language Development, Vol. 2, 97 **CONTACT ADDRESS** Dept Psychol, Johns Hopkins Univ, Baltimore, Ames Hall, Baltimore, MD 21218. **EMAIL** jusczyk@jhu.edu

JUSSIM, LEE
PERSONAL Born 12/02/1955, Brooklyn, NY, m, 1982, 3 children **DISCIPLINE** PSYCHOLOGY **EDUCATION** Univ Mass, BA, 81; Univ Mich, PhD, 87. **CAREER** From asst prof to prof, Rutgers Univ, 87-. **HONORS AND AWARDS** Dissertation Awd, Soc for Experimental Soc Psychology, 88; Gordon Allport Intergroup relations Prize, Soc for the Psychol Study of Soc Issues, 91; Fel, Soc for Personality and Soc Psychology, 96; Emerging Researcher Awd, NJ Psychol Asn, 96; Fel, Am Psychol Asn, 97; Fel, Soc for the Psychol Study of Soc Issues, 99. **MEMBERSHIPS** Am Psychol Asn, Soc of Experimental Soc Psychology, Soc for Personality and Soc Psychology, Soc for the Psychol Study of Soc Issues, Int Soc for Self and Identity. **RESEARCH** Social Cognition, Social Perception, Person Perception, Stereotypes, Prejudice, Discrimination, Self-fulfilling Prophecies and Interpersonal Expectancies, Motivation and Achievement, Self and Identity. **SELECTED PUBLICATIONS** Rev, of "Interpersonal Perception," Psychol Inquiry 7 (96): 265-272; coauth, "The nature of stereotypes II: A multiple-process model of evaluations," J of Applied Soc Psychol 26 (96): 283-312; coauth, "Social perception, social stereotypes, and teacher expectations: Accuracy and the quest for the powerful self-fulfilling prophecy," Advances in Experimental Soc Psychology 29 (96): 281-388; co-ed, Self and Identity: Fundamental Issues, Oxford Univ Press (New York), 97; coauth, "In search of the powerful self-fulfilling prophecy," J of Personality and Soc Psychology 72 (97): 791-809; coauth, "Teacher expectations," in Advances in Research on Teaching Volume 7, ed. J. Brophy (CT: JAI Press, 98), 1-48; coauth, "Do self-fulfilling prophecies accumulate, dissipate, or remain stable over time?," J of Personality and Soc Psychology 77 (99): 548-565; coauth, "Stigma and self-fulfilling prophecies," in Stigma, eds. T. Heatherton, R. Kleck, J. Hull, & D. Cioffi (NY: Guilford Press, forthcoming). **CONTACT ADDRESS** Dept Psychology, Rutgers Univ, 53 Ave E, Piscataway, NJ 08854-8040. **EMAIL** jussim@rci.rutgers.edu

K

KABATECK, GLADYS
PERSONAL Born 09/13/1935, Chicago, IL, m, 1958, 2 children **DISCIPLINE** STUDENT DEVELOPMENT **EDUCATION** Calif State Univ, BA, 57; BA, 82; MS, 87. **CAREER** Assoc prof, Glendale Community Col. **HONORS AND AWARDS** Nat Womens Hall of Fame; Who's Who of Am Women, 91-92; Soroptimist Int Awd, 92 **MEMBERSHIPS** Calif Assoc for Counseling and Develop; Calif Community Col Counselor Assoc; Am Assoc of Women in Community Junior Col; Am Assoc for Univ Women; Prof Org for Women in Re-Entry and Educ; Glendale Community Col Patrons Club; President's Advisory Board; BPW. **CONTACT ADDRESS** Dept Student Development, Glendale Comm Col, California, 1383 Opechee Way, Glendale, CA 91208.

KAGAN, JEROME
PERSONAL Born 02/25/1929, Newark, NJ, m, 1958, 1 child **DISCIPLINE** PSYCHOLOGY **EDUCATION** Rutgers Univ, BA, 50; Yale Univ, PhD, 54. **CAREER** Prof, Harvard Univ, 64-. **HONORS AND AWARDS** Phi Beta Kappa; Sigma Xi; Hofheimer Prize for Res, APA, 63; Fel, AAAS, 65; Fel, AAAS, 68-; Wilbur Lucius Cross Medal, Yale Univ, 82; Distinguished Scientist Awd, APA, 87; C Anderson Aldrich Awd, AAP, 93. **MEMBERSHIPS** Am Asn for the Advancement of Sci, Am Acad of Arts and Sci, NICHD, MBBI, ABA, SRCD. **RESEARCH** Children. **SELECTED PUBLICATIONS** Auth, Unstable Ideas, Harvard UP (Cambridge), 89; coauth, "Temperament and Allergic Symptoms," Psychosomatic Med 53 (90): 332-340; auth, "Yesterdays Premises, Tomorrows Promises," Develop Psychol 28 (92): 990-997; coauth, "Initial Reactions to Unfamiliarity," Current Directions (92): 171-174; auth, "Behavior, Biology and the Meanings of Temperamental Constructs," Pediatrics 90, no 3 (92): 510-513; auth, Galen's Prophecy, Basic Books (New York), 94; auth, Three Seductive Ideas, Harvard UP (Cambridge), 98. **CONTACT ADDRESS** Dept Psychol, Harvard Univ, William James Hall, Cambridge, MA 02138.

KAHF, MOHJA
PERSONAL Born 10/17/1967, Damascus, Syria **DISCIPLINE** WOMEN'S STUDIES, LITERATURE **EDUCATION** Douglass College/Rutgers Univ, BA, 88; Rutgers Univ, PhD, 94. **CAREER** Instr, Rutgers Univ, 94-95; asst prof, Univ Ark, 95-. **HONORS AND AWARDS** Pi Sigma Alpha, 87; Phi Beta Kappa, 88; Phi Beta Delta, 98. **MEMBERSHIPS** MLA, Middle E Studies Asn, Asn of Middle E Women's Studies, Radius of Arab-American Writers. **RESEARCH** Lit, Women's Studies. **SELECTED PUBLICATIONS** Auth, "Recognition Risky but Rewarding," Chicago Tribune (98); auth, "Huda Sha'rawi's Mudhakkirati: The Memoirs of the First Lady of Arab Modernity," Arab Studies Quart 20.1 (98): 53-82; auth, Western Representations of the Muslim Woman: From Termagant to Odalisque, Univ Tex Press (Austin, TX), 99; auth, "The Road to Damascus," PEN Int Bullet 49.2 (99): 75; rev, of "Wild Thorns," by Sahar Khalifeh, World Lit Today (00); auth, "Packaging Huda: Sha'rawi's Memoirs in the US Reading Environment," in The Politics of Reception: Globalizing Third World Women's Literature, eds. Amal Amireh and Lisa Suhair Majaj (NY: Garland Pub, 00); auth, "Braiding the Stories: Women's Eloquence in the Early Islamic Era," in Windows of Faith: Muslim Women's Scholarship and Activism, ed. Gisela Webb (NY: Syracuse Univ Press, 00); auth, "Politics and Erotics in Nizar Kabbani's Poetry: From the Sultan's Wife to the Lady Friend," World Lit Today 74.1 (forthcoming). **CONTACT ADDRESS** Dept English, Univ of Arkansas, Fayetteville, 338 Kimpel, Fayetteville, AR 72701-1201. **EMAIL** mkahf@comp.uark.edu

KAHN, MIRIAM
PERSONAL Born 03/30/1948, New York, NY, m, 1985, 1 child **DISCIPLINE** ANTHROPOLOGY **EDUCATION** Univ Wis, BA, 70; Bryn Mawr Col, MA, 74; PhD, 80. **CAREER** Adj Cur and Cur, Burke Museum, 86-99; From Asst Prof to Prof, Univ Wash, 86-. **HONORS AND AWARDS** NEH Fel, Pac Voices Exhibit Implementation Grant, 94-95; Fulbright Fel, 95; NEH Fel, 95-97; Grant, Nat Sci Found, 96-97; Royalty Res Grant, 97-98. **MEMBERSHIPS** CMA, ASAO. **RESEARCH** Place, tourism, French Polynesia, food, gender, Melanesia, museums and exhibits. **SELECTED PUBLICATIONS** Auth, "Heterotopic Dissonance in the Museum Representation of Pacific Island Cultures," Am Anthrop 97.2 (95): 324-338; auth, "Your Place or Mine: Sharing Emotional Landscapes in Wamira, Papua New Guinea," in Senses of Place (Santa Fe: Sch of Am Res, 96), 167-196; auth, "Chiefs Who Fall Down and Get Washed Out to Sea: The Limitation of Museum Objects in the Representation of Ethnographic Reality," in Soc Orgn and Cult Aesthetics: Essays in Hon of William Davenport (New York: UP of Am, 97), 113-127; auth, "Cultural Interpretation: 'Pacific Voices' Speak Up. The InterpEdge," Int J on Innovation, Technol and Cutting Edge Thought for Interpretive Commun (98); auth, "Applying Anthropology: Another View of Museum Exhibit Development," Anthropologica 41.2 (99); auth, "Tahiti Intertwined: Ancestral Land, Tourist Postcard and Nuclear Test Site," Am Anthropologist 102.1 (00); coauth, Pacific Voices, Wash UP (Seattle, WA), 00. **CONTACT ADDRESS** Dept Anthrop, Univ of Washington, PO Box 353100, Seattle, WA 98195-3100. **EMAIL** mkahn@u.washington.edu

KAHNE, HILDA
PERSONAL Born 04/27/1922, Melford, CT, m, 1956, 3 children **DISCIPLINE** SOCIOLOGY **EDUCATION** Univ Wisconsin, BA, 43; Harvard Univ, MA, 48; PhD, 53. **CAREER** Inst and asst prof, Wellesley Col, 48-58; res assoc, Harvard Sch of Public Health, 54-58; res assoc and asst dean, Radcliffe Inst, 66-77; prof, Wheaton Col, 77-92; prof, Heller Sch for Adv Study of Soc Policy, Brandeis Univ, 92-. **MEMBERSHIPS** Am Economics Asn **RESEARCH** Low Earning Workers, Single Mothers, Welfare, Training and Educators. **SELECTED PUBLICATIONS** Rev, Reassessment for a Changing Economy, Social Service Review, (94); auth, "Employment for the Low Income Elderly: Experiences from the Field" (York: Garland Press, 97); auth, "Social Policy and Self Sufficiency for Poor Single Mothers," Radcliffe Public Policy Institute, Work in America Series (99); auth, Kahne Course Syllabus selected for inclusion in American Sociological Assoc, Teaching Family Policy: A Handbook of Course Syllabi, 99; auth, Training and Education and Self-Sufficiency For Single Mothers, 00. **CONTACT ADDRESS** Dept Social Welfare, Brandeis Univ, 415 S St, Waltham, MA 02453. **EMAIL** kahne@brandeis.edu

KAISER, CHARLES F.
DISCIPLINE PSYCHOLOGY **EDUCATION** CUNY, BS, 64; MA, 67; Univ Houston, PhD, 73. **CAREER** Asst Prof to Full Prof, Col of Charleston, 72-; Adj Asst Prof, Med Univ SCar, 81-89; **HONORS AND AWARDS** NIMH Fel, Baylor Col, 66-70; Teaching Fel, Univ Houston, 66-72; Fac Res Committee Grant, 76., 87; Grant, SC Lung Asn, 77; Grant, Nat Hazards Res Ctr, 92-93, 98-99; Grant, F.I.P.S.E. 96; Who's Who in am; Who's Who of Emerging Leaders in Am; Intl Directory of Distinguished Leadership; Five Thousand Personalities of the World; Who's Who in am Educ; Who's Who Among Human Services Prof; am Men and Women of Sci; five Hundred Leaders of Influence; Man of the Year, 96; Who's Who in Medicine and Healthcare. **MEMBERSHIPS** Am Psychol Soc; Am Psychol Asn; SE Psychol Asn; Biofeedback Soc of Am; Asn for Applied Psychophysiol and Biofeedback; Biofeedback and Beh Med Soc of SC; SC Psychol Asn; Intl Stress Management Asn; Asn of Heads of Dept of Psychol. **SELECTED PUBLICATIONS** Co-auth, "Moral judgment and depression in gifted adolescents," in Expanding awareness of creative potentials worldwide, (Brain Talent-Powers Press, 90), 657-7661; co-auth, "Self-reported depression profiles in chronic pain and family practice patients," The Clinical Journal of Pain, (90): 271-275; co-auth, Hurricane Iniki: Psychological functioning following disaster, Boulder, 94; co-auth, "Hurricane Andrew: Psychological distress among shelter victims," International Journal of Stress Management, (95): 133-143; co-auth, Multiscore depression inventory for children (MDI-C) manual, Western Psychol Services, 96; co-auth, "A conservation of resources approach to a natural disaster; Sense of co9herence and psychological distress," Journal of social Behavior and Personality, (96): 459-476; co-auth, "Natural disasters and psychological adjustment: Implications of research for intervention efforts," Journal of Psychological Practice, (97): 113-127. **CONTACT ADDRESS** Dept Psychol, Col of Charleston, 66 George St, Charleston, SC 29424. **EMAIL** KaiserC@admin.CofC.edu

KALOF, LINDA E.
PERSONAL Born 12/17/1946, Norfolk, VA, 2 children **DISCIPLINE** SOCIOLOGY **EDUCATION** Univ Fla, BA, 75; Am Univ, PhD, 89. **CAREER** From Asst to Assoc Prof, State Univ of NYork Plattsburgh, 89-96; Assoc Prof, George Mason Univ, 96-. **MEMBERSHIPS** Human Sociol Rev. **RESEARCH** Social Psychology, Race, gender and nature. **SELECTED PUBLICATIONS** Coauth, "Values and Vegetarianism: An Exploratory Analysis," Rural Sociol 60 (95): 533-542; coauth, Evaluating Social Science Research, Oxford Univ Press (NY), 96; auth, "Understanding the Social Construction of Environmental Concern," Human Ecol Rev 4-2 (98): 101-105; coauth, "A Value, Belief, Norm Theory of Support for Social Movements: The Case of Environmentalism," Human Ecol rev 6-2 (99): 81-97; coauth, "Assessing the Social value of Programs: The Case of Sexual Assault Prevention," J of Col Student Develop 40-4 (99): 418-422; auth, "The Effects of Gender and Music Video Imagery on Sexual Attitudes," The J of Soc Psychol 139-3 (99): 378-385; coauth, "Social Psychological and Structural Influences on Vegetarian Beliefs," Rural Sociol 64-3 (99): 500-511; auth, "Stereotyped Evaluative Judgements and Female Attractiveness," Gender Issues 17-2 (99): 68-82; coauth, "The Animal Text: Message and Meaning in Television Advertisements, " The Sociol Quart 40-4 (99): 565-586; auth, "The Multi-Layered Discourses of Animal Concern," in Social Disclosure and Environmental Policy, ed. Helen Addams and

John Stropp (Edward Elgar Publishers, forthcoming). **CONTACT ADDRESS** Dept Sociol and Anthrop, George Mason Univ, Fairfax, 4400 Univ Dr, Fairfax, VA 22030. **EMAIL** lkalof@gmu.edu

KAMBEITZ, TERESITA
PERSONAL Born Richmond, SK, Canada **DISCIPLINE** RELIGIOUS EDUCATION **EDUCATION** St.Angela's Acad, ARTC, 57; tchrs col, 58-59; Univ Sask, BA, 69, BEd, 69; St Paul Univ, Ottawa, Theol, 69-70; St. Michael's Col, MRE, 76; Ont Inst Stud Educ, Univ Toronto, MEd, 86, PhD, 88. **CAREER** Tchr, various schs Sask, 59-64; princ/tchr, St. Patrick, Swift Current, Sask, 64-68; tchr, Holy Cross Sch, Saskatoon, 70-85; Dir Religious Educ, Newman Theol Col, Edmonton, 88-. **HONORS AND AWARDS** Peter Craigie Awd, Alta Tchrs Asn. **MEMBERSHIPS** Newman Theol Col; Alta Tchrs Asn; Asn Profs Res Relig Educ; Relig Educ Asn US & Can; Ursuline Congregation Prelate. **SELECTED PUBLICATIONS** Auth, Death and Dying, 79; auth, Health Hazards of So-Called Low-Radiation, 80; auth, Ursulines Remember, vol 1, 94, vol 2, 95. **CONTACT ADDRESS** Religious Education Program, Newman Theol Col, Edmonton, AB, Canada T5L 4H8.

KAMINSKI, PATRICIA
DISCIPLINE PSYCHOLOGY **EDUCATION** Harvard Univ, BA, 88; Colo State Univ, BS, 92; PhD, 95; Karl Menninger School Psychiatry, Post Doctoral Fel, 97. **CAREER** Instr, Colo State Univ, 91-93; vis asst prof to asst prof, Wittenberg Univ, 97. **HONORS AND AWARDS** Omicron Delta Kappa Awd for Excellence in Teaching, 98-99; Seligman Awd for Applied Achievements in applied Res in Psychol, 93; Exceptional Teacher, Col State Univ, 92. **MEMBERSHIPS** Am Psychol Soc, APA, Cincinnati Psychoanalytic Soc, Am Asn Univ Prof. **RESEARCH** Psychological attunement in dyads at high-risk and low-risk for abuse, Self-esteem and body-esteem in older adults, Body-esteem of college men, Effects of gingko biloba on cognitive functioning, Gender and leadership. **SELECTED PUBLICATIONS** Auth, "Introduction to the Parent-Child Interaction Assessment," Bulletin of the Menninger Clinic, (99): 413-428; auth, "Academic coping in college students self-reporting high and low symptoms of attention deficit hyperactivity disorder," Journal of College Student Development, (98): 484-493; auth, "A treatment for college women at risk for bulimia: A controlled evaluation," Journal of counseling and Development, (96): 288-294; auth, "Typical and optimal aging in women and men: Is there a double standard?" International Journal of Aging and Human Development, (95): 187-207; auth, PAS: Parental Attunement Scale, Topeka, 98; auth, PCIA: Parent-Child Interaction Assessment, Topeka, 97; auth, "Electrodermal activity in at-risk for abuse parents during interaction with their children," Child Abuse and Neglect, (forthcoming); auth, "The role of goal instability and maladaptive coping in academic procrastination," Journal of counseling and Development, (forthcoming); auth, "Using the story of cinderella to teach the major approaches to treatment and therapy," Journal of Human Service Education, (forthcoming). **CONTACT ADDRESS** Dept Psychol, Wittenberg Univ, PO Box 720, Springfield, OH 45501.

KANDO, THOMAS M.
PERSONAL Born 04/08/1941, Budapest, Hungary, m, 1973, 2 children **DISCIPLINE** SOCIOLOGY **EDUCATION** Univ MN, MA, 67, PhD, 69. **CAREER** Asst prof, Univ CA, Riverside, 72-73; assoc prof, PA State (main campus), 77-79; prof, CA State Univ, Sacremento, 79-. **HONORS AND AWARDS** Fulbright fel, 60-61; fel, Univ Amsterdam, 62-65; fel, Univ MN, 67; Merit Awds, CA State Univ, Sacramento, 85, 97. **MEMBERSHIPS** Am Sociol Asn; Phi Beta Kappa Honor Soc; Am Asn of Univ Profs (pres, local and statewide, 76-78); Int Sociol Asn; Int Committee on Sports Sociol. **RESEARCH** Sociol of marriage and sexuality; social psychology; sociol of leisure; criminology and deviance. **SELECTED PUBLICATIONS** Auth, L A Debate: Police are also Victims, Wall Street J, March 19, 91; Clintonomics, Int J on World Peace, summer 93; Eastern Europe: Prospects for Progress, Int J on World Peace, June 94; Interstellar Travel, Gold River Scene, spring 95; Postmodernism: Old Wine in New Bottles?, Int J on World Peace, Sept 96; The Family in Global Transition, Int J on World Peace, March 97; The Influence of the Family on the Formation of Selfhood, in Identity and Character: the Main Influence of Family and Society on Personality Development, N Pitrie, ed, PWPA Press, 98; numerous other scholarly articles, book reviews, and newspaper and magazine articles. **CONTACT ADDRESS** Dept of Sociol, California State Univ, Sacramento, Sacramento, CA 95819. **EMAIL** kandotom@csus.edu

KANEL, KRISTI L.
PERSONAL Born 03/12/1958, Minneapolis, MN, m, 1990, 1 child **DISCIPLINE** PSYCHOLOGY **EDUCATION** Univ Southern Calif, PhD, 91. **CAREER** Friendly Hills Medical Group; Co Mental Health; Private Practice-. **HONORS AND AWARDS** Jewell Plummer Cobb Awd for Diversity in Educ; Outstanding Prof of the Year, Human Serv Student Asn, 95, 96, 98. **MEMBERSHIPS** Cali Asn of Marital and Family Therapists. **RESEARCH** Mental Health Needs of Spanish Speaking Clients, Crisis Intervention, Pedagogy of teaching Counseling Skills. **SELECTED PUBLICATIONS** Auth, A Guide to Crisis Intervention; auth, Manual to Accompany: A Guide to Crisis Intervention; auth, The ABC Model of Crisis Intervention: A Formula for Understanding and Treating Crises; **CONTACT ADDRESS** Dept Human Serv, California State Univ, Fullerton, 800 N State Col, Fullerton, CA 92831. **EMAIL** Kkanel@fullerton.edu

KANIPE, ESTHER SUE
PERSONAL Born 03/22/1945, Rockingham, NC **DISCIPLINE** EUROPEAN & WOMEN'S HISTORY **EDUCATION** Univ NC, Greensboro, BA, 67; Univ Wis, MA, 70, PhD(hist), 76. **CAREER** Instr hist, Grinnell Col, 73-75; asst prof, Lawrence Univ, 75-76; asst prof, 76-82, Assoc Prof Hist, Hamilton Col, 82-, Nat Endowment for the Humanities fel hist, Brown Univ, 80-81; consult, Nat Endowment for the Humanities, 81-; prof of hist, Marjorie and Robert W. McEwen, 91. **MEMBERSHIPS** AHA; Soc French Hist Studies. **RESEARCH** Modern French social history; World War I. **SELECTED PUBLICATIONS** Auth, Women and Medicine in the French Enlightenment--The Debate Over Maladies Des Femmes, J Hist Sexuality, Vol 0004, 94. **CONTACT ADDRESS** Dept of Hist, Hamilton Col, New York, 198 College Hill Rd, Clinton, NY 13323-1292. **EMAIL** ekanipe@hamilton.edu

KANTOR, JOHN
PERSONAL Born 04/08/1946, Hungary, m, 1974, 1 child **DISCIPLINE** PSYCHOLOGY **EDUCATION** Alma White Col, BA, 71; Wichita State Univ, MSEd, 75; MBA, 83; Calif School Prof Psychol, PhD, 88. **CAREER** Personnel Res Psychol, US Navy; Assoc Prof, US Intl Univ, 91-. **RESEARCH** Leadership **CONTACT ADDRESS** Dept Psychol, United States Intl Univ, 10455 Pomerado Rd, San Diego, CA 92131. **EMAIL** jkantor@usiu.edu

KAPLAN, FRANCENE E.
PERSONAL Born 01/17/1961, Whittier, CA, m **DISCIPLINE** PSYCHOLOGY **EDUCATION** Orange Coast Col, AA, 81; Univ Calif, Santa Barbara, BA, 83; Calif State Univ, Long Beach, teaching credentials, 85; United States Int Univ, MA, 91; PhD, 95. **CAREER** Teacher, Coast High Sch/Huntington Beach Adult Sch. 84-; teacher, Cypress Community Col, 97-; United State Int Univ, 99-; teacher, Univ of Phoenix, 99-; psychologist, The Hope Inst, Costa Mesa, Calif, 95-. **HONORS AND AWARDS** Outstanding Academic Achievement Awd, United States Int Univ, 92, 95; Certificate of Recognition for Outstanding Volunteer Contribution and Dedication to the Community and the Health Care Agency, County of Orange, 95; Mem, Bd of Dir, Hope Inst, 97-. **MEMBERSHIPS** Am Psychol Asn, Nat Asn of Sch Psychologists, Am Acad of Health Care Providers, Calif Teachers Asn, Calif Consortium for Independent Study. **CONTACT ADDRESS** Dept Soc Sci, Cypress Col, 9200 Valley View, Cypress, CA 90630.

KAPLAN, LAURA DUHAN
DISCIPLINE FEMINIST PHILOSOPHY, PHILOSOPHY OF EDUCATION, PHILOSOPHY OF PEACE, PHENOMEN **EDUCATION** Brandeis Univ, BA, 80; Cambridge Col, MEd, 83; Claremont Grad Sch, MA, 87, PhD, 91. **CAREER** Assoc prof, coord, Women's Stud prog, Univ NC, Charlotte. **RESEARCH** Family life, from the perspective of existential phenomenology. **SELECTED PUBLICATIONS** Auth, Speaking for Myself in Philosophy, Philos and the Contemp World, 1:4, 94; My Mother the Mirror, The Trumpeter, 11:4, 94; Teaching As Applied Philosophy, Tchg Philos , 17:1, 94; Woman as Caretaker: An Archetype That Supports Patriarchal Militarism, Hypatia: A J of Feminist Philos, 9:2, 94; Persons and Mystery: Art, Conflict and Self-Knowledge, in Becoming Persons, ed, Robert N. Fisher, Oxford: App Theol Press, 94; The Parable of the Levite's Concubine, in From the Eye of the Storm: Regional Conflicts and the Philosophy of Peace, eds, Laurence F. Bove and Laura Duhan Kaplan, Rodopi, 95; Physical Education for Domination and Emancipation: A Foucauldian Analysis of Aerobics and Hatha Yoga, in Philosophical Perspectives on Power and Domination: Theories and Practices, eds, Laura Duhan Kaplan and Laurence F. Bove, Rodopi, 96; Devaluing Others to Enhance our Self-Esteem: A Moral Phenomenology of Racism, in Institutional Violence, eds, Robert Litke and Deane Curtin, Rodopi, 96; coauth, Paradigms for the Philosophy of Peace, in From the Eye of the Storm: Regional Conflicts and the Philosophy of Peace, eds, Laurence F. Bove and Laura Duhan Kaplan, Rodopi, 95; coed, From the Eye of the Storm: Regional Conflicts and the Philosophy of Peace, Rodopi, 95; Philosophical Perspectives on Power and Domination: Theories and Practices, Rodopi, 97. **CONTACT ADDRESS** Univ of No Carolina, Charlotte, Charlotte, NC 28223-0001. **EMAIL** ldkaplan@email.uncc.edu

KAPLOWITZ, HENRY L.
PERSONAL Born 02/12/1944, New Heaven, CT, m, 1965, 2 children **DISCIPLINE** PSYCHOLOGY **EDUCATION** Yeshiva Col, BA, 65; Yeshiva Univ, MA, 67; PhD, 77. **CAREER** From Instr to Full Prof, Kean Univ of NJ, 72-; Grad Prog Coordr - Psychology Dept Kean Univ, 76-. **HONORS AND AWARDS** Phi Delta Kappa; Phi Kappa Phi; Alpha Sigma Lambda;Teacher of the Year, Kean Univ; Grad Teacher of the Year, Kean Univ. **MEMBERSHIPS** Am Psychol Asn, Eastern Psychol Asn, Soc for the Psychol Studies of Soc Issues, Soc for Personality and Soc Psychology. **RESEARCH** Social Psychology of the classroom, student retention and attention, The Interaction of Personality Traits and Social Behavior. **SELECTED PUBLICATIONS** Coauth, "Learning to Learn (LTL): Offering the student academic behaviors that work," in The Culture of Learning, ed. V. M. Fitzsimons and M.L. Kelley (NY: Nat League for Nursing Press, 96), 49-60; coauth, "Developmental aspects of students' course selection," J of Educ Psychology 91 (99): 157-168; coauth, "A 'classic' revisited: Students' immediate and delayed evaluations of a warm/cold instructor," Soc Psychology of Educ 3 (99): 81-102; auth, "What is a freshman? Helping faculty relate to freshman culture," in Understanding Cultural Diversity: Culture, Curriculum and Community, ed. V. M. Fitzsimons and M.L. Kelley (Sudbury, MA: Jones and Bartlett/Nat League for Nursing, 00), 177-184. **CONTACT ADDRESS** Dept Psychology, Kean Col of New Jersey, 1000 Morris Ave, Union, NJ 07083. **EMAIL** hkaplowi@turbo.kean.edu

KAPOOR, JITENDRA M.
PERSONAL Born 12/29/1936, Lucknow, India, m, 1963, 2 children **DISCIPLINE** SOCIAL WORK **EDUCATION** LUCKNow Univ, BA; DPA, 58; DSW, 59; MSW, 59; PhD, 65. **CAREER** Practicum Supvr, LUCKNow Univ India, 59-64; Res Officer, NICD, Hyderabad, India, 66-67; Res Fel, Mich State Univ. 68-69; Asst/Assoc Prof, Ind Univ Purdue Univ, Sch of Soc Work, 69-. **HONORS AND AWARDS** Outstanding Soc Worker; Outstanding Educators of Am; Who's Who in Midwest; Who's Who Ind; Hon Citizen of Indianapolis; Outstanding Achievement in Field of Int Relations. **MEMBERSHIPS** Coun of Soc Work Educ, Nat Conf on Soc Welfare, Nat Asn of Soc Workers. **RESEARCH** Modernization and social change. **SELECTED PUBLICATIONS** Auth, Social Work Manpower Needs in Indiana," Ind Univ Sch of Soc Work, 74; coauth, Retention of Literacy, McMillan Publ of India, 75; auth, "Innovation in Social Work Education and Practice;" auth, "Study of Indiana University-Purdue University Staff Turnover," Ind Univ Sch of Soc Work, 78; coauth, "Field Learning Experiences;" auth, Educational technology and Social Work Education;" **CONTACT ADDRESS** Dept Soc Work, Indiana Univ-Purdue Univ, Indianapolis, 1100 W Michigan St, Indianapolis, IN 46202. **EMAIL** jkapoor@iupui.edu

KARON, BERTRAM PAUL
PERSONAL Born 04/29/1930, Taunton, MA, m, 3 children **DISCIPLINE** PSYCHOLOGIST **EDUCATION** Harvard Univ, BA 52; Princeton Univ, MA 54, PhD 57. **CAREER** Educational Testing Ser, res fel 52-55; Direct Analysis, intern 55-56; Princeton Univ, fel 56-57; Annandale NJ Reformatory, sr clin psychol 58; Phil Psych Hosp, res psycho 58-59, post doc fel 59-61; Private Prac PA 61-62; MI State Univ, asst prof 62-63, assoc prof 63-68, prof 68-; MI State Psychotherapy Proj Dir 66-81. **HONORS AND AWARDS** Psychoanal Publication Awd; Distg Psychoanal Awd; Raymon D Fowler Awd; MST Lectr Awd; Distg Practitioner; Fellow APA; Fell MPA; Fell Academy of Clinic Psychol. **MEMBERSHIPS** APA; MI PA; ASA; Soc PR; Mich Soc Clinic Gerontology; MPC; APP; Intl Symposium Psychotherapy of Schizophrenia, Center Study Psychiatry Psychology. **RESEARCH** Psychoanalysis, Psychotherapy, Schizophrenia. **SELECTED PUBLICATIONS** Video tape, The APA Psychotherapy Videotape Series: Effective Psychoanalytic Therapy of Schizophrenia and Other Severe Disorders, Washington DC, APA, 94; Ch by B P KARON, In Search of Truth, 95, How To Become A Schizophrenic: The Case Against Biological Psychiatry, Everett, WA Appolyer Press; Psychotherapy For Schizophrenia; Dynamic Therapies for Psychiatric Disorders, Axis I NY, Basic Books, 94; The Future of Psychoanalysis; A History of the Division of Psychoanalysis of the Amer Psychol Assn, Hillsdale NJ, Erlbaum; et al; BOOKS; Psykoterapi vid schizophrenia: Overstattning av qun zetterstrom, Stockholm, Wahlstrom & Widstrand, 85; Psychotherapy of Schizofrene: The Treatment of Choice, NY, Aronson; et al; ARTICLES; with M A Teiexeira, 95, Guidelines for the Treatment of Depression in Primary Care, and the APA response, Amer Psycho; 95, Becoming a First Rate Psychologist Despite Graduate Education, Prof Psychol: Res and Pract; 95, Provision of Psychotherapy under managed health care: A growing crisis and national nightmare, Prof Psychol: Res and Pract; et al. **CONTACT ADDRESS** Psychology Dept, Michigan State Univ, East Lansing, MI 48824. **EMAIL** karon@pilot.msu.edu

KARP, DAVID
DISCIPLINE SOCIOLOGY **EDUCATION** Univ Calif Berkeley, BA, 86; Univ Wash, MA, 91; PhD, 95. **CAREER** Res Sci, George Washington Univ, 96-98; assoc prof, Skidmore Col, 98-. **HONORS AND AWARDS** Smith Rchardson Found Grant, 97; Grant, Nat Inst of Justice, 97, 98; Grant, US Dept of Justice, 99; Grant, State of Vt Dept of Social and Rehab Serv, 99. **SELECTED PUBLICATIONS** Coauth, "The Community Justice Movement", Community Justice: An Emerging Field, ed David R. Karp, Rowman and Littlefield Pr, (98): 3-30; coauth, "Community Justice: An Essay", Correctional Management Quarterly 2 (98): 49-60; ed, Community Justice: An Emerging Field, Rowman and Littlefield, (Lanham, MD), 98; auth, "Zes uidagingen Voor rechtshandhaving in de Buurt", Christen Democratische Verkenningen 7, (99): 68-81; coauth, The Community Justice Ideal, Westview (Boulder, CO), 99; auth, "Values

Theory and Research", Encyclopedia of Sociology, ed Edgar Borgatta, MacMillan, (forthcoming); auth, "Sociological Communitarianism and the Just Community", Contemp Justice Rev, (forthcoming); auth, "Community Justice: Six Challenges", J of Community Psychol, (forthcoming); coauth, "Community Reparative Boards: Theory and Practice", Community and Restorative Justice: Cultivating Common Ground for Victims, Communities, and Offenders, eds Maria Schiff and Gordon Basemore, Anderson, (forthcoming); coauth, "Community Justice: A Conceptual Framework", Criminal Justice 2000: Changing Boundaries in Criminal Justice Organizations, Nat Inst of Justice (forthcoming). **CONTACT ADDRESS** Dept Anthrop and Sociol, Skidmore Col, 815 N Broadway, Saratoga Springs, NY 12866. **EMAIL** dkarp@skidmore.edu

KARP, STEPHEN A.

PERSONAL Born 08/28/1928, Brooklyn, NY, d, 3 children **DISCIPLINE** PSYCHOLOGY **EDUCATION** Brookly Col, BA 49; New Sch Soc Research, MA 52; NYork Univ, PhD 62. **CAREER** George Washington Univ, assoc prof to prof 69; Chief Psychol, Sinai Hosp Balt, Assoc Prof, John Hopkins Univ, 64-69; Univ NY, Dwntn Med Cen, instr 54-64. **MEMBERSHIPS** APA; Soc for Personality Assess; APS. **RESEARCH** Psychological Tests **SELECTED PUBLICATIONS** The Karp Objective Word Association Test KOWAT manual, Brooklandville MD, 98; Apperceptive Personality Tests, consolidated manual: child and adult brief versions, with D E Silber, R W Holmstrom, OH, IDS Pub Corp, 93; Outcomes of Thematic Apperception Test and Apperceptive Personality Test stories, with D E Silber, R W Holmstrom, V Banks, J Karp, Perceptual and Motor Skills, 92; Personality of rape survivors as a group and by relation to survivor to perpetrator, Journal of Clinical Psychology, 95; Personalities of women reporting incestuous abuse during childhood, Perceptual and Motor Skills, 95. **CONTACT ADDRESS** Dept Psychology, The George Washington Univ, Washington, DC 20052. **EMAIL** skarp@gwu.edu

KASHEFI, MAHMOUD

PERSONAL Born 11/10/1949, Iran, m, 1975, 2 children **DISCIPLINE** SOCIOLOGY **EDUCATION** Ind Univ, PhD, 89. **CAREER** Full Prof, Eastern Ill Univ, 84-. **HONORS AND AWARDS** Phd in Sociol scholar; Res Awd, Col of Sci, Eastern Ill Univ. **MEMBERSHIPS** Mid W Sociologists Asn, Ill Sociologists Asn, Am Sociol Asn. **RESEARCH** Social changes, Industrial Sociology. **SELECTED PUBLICATIONS** Rev, of "Khomeinism: Essays on the Islamic Republic," J of Politic Sociol 23-1(95); auth, "Automation and Deskilling," in Encyclopedia of Contemporary Social Science, ed. John K. Roth, Salem Press Publ Co, 96; auth, "Censorship in Iran," in Ready Reference: Censorship, ed. Kent R. Rasmussen. Salem Press Publ Co, 97; rev, of "McDonaldization of Society," Critical Sociol 23-1(97):132-136; rev, of "Socio-economic Source of Iranian Mysticism--Hallaj," Par Monthly J 13-7 (98); auth, "Work and the Family," in Reader Reference:Family Life, ed. Robert Michaels, Salem Press Publ Co, 98; auth, "Religious Apartheid in Islamic Republic of Iran," Monthly Par 15 (00):12-16. **CONTACT ADDRESS** Dept Sociol and Anthrop, Eastern Illinois Univ, 600 Lincoln Ave, Charleston, IL 61920. **EMAIL** cfMNK@EIU.edu

KASPER, LORETTA F.

PERSONAL Born 02/14/1951, Brooklyn, NY, m, 1973 **DISCIPLINE** COGNITIVE PSYCHOLOGY **EDUCATION** Brooklyn Col, BA, 72, MA, 75; Col Staten Island, BA, 80; Rutgers Univ, MS, 82, PhD, 85. **CAREER** Lectr, coordr, 83-88, Wagner Col; adj instr, Kean Col, New Jersey, 87-88; instr, adj asst prof, 87-92, Col Staten Island, from asst prof to assoc prof, 92-, Kingsborough Commun Col, CUNY. **HONORS AND AWARDS** New York State Regents Scholar, 68-72; Phi Beta Kappa, 72; Nat Honor Soc, 80; Rutgers Univ Fel, 82-83; Col Staten Island Alumni Hall of Fame, 88; Merit Awd Excellence Tchg, 89, Col Staten Island; Who's Who East, 94; PSC-CUNY-26 Grant, 95-96; Kingsborough Commun Col Grant, 96; PSC-CUNY-27 Grant, 96-97; CUNY Fac Development Colloquium Grant, 97; PSC-CUNY-29 Grant, 98-99; Kingsburough Performance Excellence Awd, 00; PSC-CUNY-30 Grant, 99-00; PSC-CUNY-31 Grant, 00-01. **MEMBERSHIPS** CUNY Asn Readers Educators; CUNY ESL Council; Int Consortium: NCTE; Int Reading Asn; Nat Council Tchrs English; NJ TESOL-BE, Inc; NYS TESOL; TESOL Int. **RESEARCH** Content-Based ESL instruction; technology in ESL instruction; metacognitive factors in second language acquisition; reading and writing as integrated skills. **SELECTED PUBLICATIONS** Auth, art, Writing, metacognition, and computer technology, 97; auth, Teaching English Through the Disciplines: Psychology, 97; auth, Interdisciplinary English, 98; auth, art, ESL writing and the principle of nonjudgmental awareness: Rationale and implementation, 98; auth, art, Interdisciplinary English and the Internet: Technology meets content in the ESL course, 98; auth, Content-Based College ESL Instruction, 00. **CONTACT ADDRESS** 2001 Oriental Blvd., Brooklyn, NY 11235. **EMAIL** lkasper@kbcc.cuny.edu

KATTAGO, SIOBHAN

PERSONAL Born 03/03/1966, New York, NY, m, 1992, 1 child **DISCIPLINE** SOCIOLOGY **EDUCATION** Wright State Univ, BA, 88; New Sch for Soc Res, MA, 93; PhD, 97. **CAREER** Adj Asst Prof, Gallatin School NYork Univ, 98-99; Teaching Fel, Eugene Lang Col, 99-. **HONORS AND AWARDS** Edith and Henry Johnson Memorial Commencement Awd, 97; DAAD Res Grant, Berlin, 96; Scholarship, Graduate Exchange Program, Johann Wolfgang-Goethe-Universitat Frankfurt, 92-93 **RESEARCH** Contemporary social and political thought, European intellectual history, collective memory, National identity, and contemporary German history. **SELECTED PUBLICATIONS** Auth, "Representing German Victimhood and Guilt: The Neue Wache and Unified German Memory,: in German Politics and Society, 98; auth, "Narrating the Histories of Buchenwald," in Constellations: an International Journal of Critical and Democratic Theory, 98; auth, "The Politics of Memory and Identity in Germany," Columbia Univ Press, 96; auth, "Judgment and Intersubjectivity in Kant and Habermas's Ethics," in Conference: A Journal of Philosophy and Theory, 95. **CONTACT ADDRESS** Eugene Lang Col, New Sch for Social Research, 65 W 11th St, New York, NY 10011-8662.

KATZ, JEFFREY S.

PERSONAL Born 10/30/1967, Boston, MA, m, 1995 **DISCIPLINE** PSYCHOLOGY **EDUCATION** Ithaca Col, BA, 89; Tufts Univ, MS, 96; PhD, 98. **CAREER** Lab technician to supvr, Oncolab Inc, 89-93; fel, Univ Tex, 98-00; asst prof, Auburn Univ, 00-. **HONORS AND AWARDS** Training Grant, Nat Inst of Health, 98-99; Nat Res Serv Awd, Nat Inst of Health, 99-00. **MEMBERSHIPS** Am Psychol Asn; Am Psychol Soc; Comparative Cognition Soc; Psychonomic Soc. **RESEARCH** Visual Search; Concept Learning; List Memory; Neural Mechanisms of Behavior; Object Perception; Pattern Recognition. **SELECTED PUBLICATIONS** Co-auth, "Pigeon perception and discrimination of rapidly changing texture stimuli," J of Experimental Psychol, (97): 390-400; co-auth, "Pigeon same/different concept learning with multiple stimulus classes," J of Experimental Psychol, (97): 417-433; co-auth, "Processes of visual cognition in the pigeon," in Perspectives on Fundamental Processes in Intellectual Functioning, Vol I, Ables, 98; co-auth, "Dynamic object perception by pigeons," J of Experimental Psychol, (99): 194-210; co-auth, "Pictorial same/differ categorical learning and discrimination in pigeons," Current Psychol of Cognition, (99): 805-843; co-auth, "Stimulus repetition effects on texture-based visual search by pigeons," J of Experimental Psychol, (00): 220-236; co-auth, "The multiplicity of visual search strategies in pigeons," in Perspectives on Fundamental Processes in Intellectual Functioning, Vol 2, Ables, in press. **CONTACT ADDRESS** Dept Psychol, Auburn Univ, 226 Thatch, Auburn, AL 36849. **EMAIL** katzjef@auburn.edu

KATZ, JENNIFER

PERSONAL Born 08/24/1972, Hollywood, FL, m, 2000, 1 child **DISCIPLINE** PSYCHOLOGY **EDUCATION** Univ Miami, BS, 93; Univ Ga, MS, 95; PhD, 98. **CAREER** Asst prof, WA State Univ, 98-. **HONORS AND AWARDS** Phi Beta Kappa, 93; Herbert Zimmer Res Scholar Awd, Univ GA, 95, 98; Univ Wide Fel, Awd, Univ GA, 97; Fel, Ctr for Family Res, Univ GA, 98; Initiation Res Grant, WA State Univ, 98, 99. **MEMBERSHIPS** Am Psychol Asn; Asn for the Advancement of Beh Therapy; Asn for Women in Psychol; **RESEARCH** Abnormal Psychology; Theories of Personality; Child Development; Close Relationships; Individual Assessment; Psychology of Women; Psychology of adjustment; Social Psychology; Abnormal Child Psychology; Psychology of Social issues; Human Sexuality; Marriage and Family Processes; Interpersonal Communication; Behavior Modification; Basic Helping Skills. **SELECTED PUBLICATIONS** Co-auth, "When does partner devaluation predict emotional distress? Prospective moderating effects of reassurance-seeking and self-esteem," Personal Relationship, (98): 409-421; co-auth, "Marital therapy in the treatment of depression: Toward a third generation of treatment and research," clinical Psychology Review, (98): 635-661; co-auth, "Contagious depression in dating couples," Journal of Social and Clinical Psychology, (99): 1-13; co-auth, "Harbingers of depressotypic reassurance-seeking: Negative life events, increased anxiety, and decreased self-esteem," Personality and Social Psychology bulletin, (990: 630-637; co-auth, "contagion of depressive symptoms and mood: Meta-analytic review and explanations from cognitive, behavioral, and interpersonal viewpoints," clinical Psychology: Science and Practice, (99): 149-164; co-auth, "Psychological abuse and depressive symptoms in dating women: Do different types of abuse have differential effects?," Journal of Family Violence, (99): 281-295; co-auth, "Be (re)assured: Excessive reassurance-seeking has (at least) some explanatory power regarding depression," Psychological Inquiry, (99): 305-308; co-auth, "Depression and excessive reassurance-seeking," Psychological Inquiry, (99): 269-278; co-auth, "Sexual desire discrepancies, relationship satisfaction, and sexual satisfaction in dating couples," Archives of Sexual Behavior, (99): 789-803; co-auth, "Personality features differentiate men from women with chronic bulimic symptoms," International Journal of Eating disorders, (00): 191-197. **CONTACT ADDRESS** Dept Psychol, Washington State Univ, PO Box 644820, Pullman, WA 99164-4820. **EMAIL** katzja@wsu.edu

KATZ, SANFORD NOAH

PERSONAL Born 12/23/1933, Holyoke, MA, m, 1958, 2 children **DISCIPLINE** LAW, BEHAVIORAL SCIENCES **EDUCATION** Boston Univ, AB, 55; Univ Chicago, JD, 58. **CAREER** Assoc prof law, Cath Univ Am, 59-64; prof, Univ Fla, 64-68; prof law, Boston Col, 68-, Darald and Juliet Libby Chair, 01-; lectr law & social work, Smith Col, 65-68; ed-in-chief, Family Law Quart, 71-; assoc law, Clare Hall, Cambridge Univ, 73; visiting fel All Souls Col, Oxford, 97. **HONORS AND AWARDS** Ford Found law fac fel, 64-65; Sterling Fel, Yale Law Sch, 63-64; dept Health, Educ & Welfare res grant, 66-78; Field Found res grant, 68-70; **MEMBERSHIPS** Am Bar Assn; Int Soc Family Law. **RESEARCH** Law and social work; family law. **SELECTED PUBLICATIONS** Auth, Judicial and Statutory Trends In The Law Of Adoption, Georgetown Law J, 62; auth, When Parents Fail: The Law's Response to Family Breakdown, Beacon, 71; ed, The Youngest Minority (2 vols), Am Bar Assn, 74; auth, Creativity in Social Work, Temple Univ, 75; coauth, Adoptions Without Agencies, Child Welfare League Am, 78; co-ed, Family Violence, 78; coauth, Marriage and Cohabitation in Contemporary Society, Butterworths, 81; auth, Child Snatching-The Legal Response to the Abduction of Children, Am Bar Assn, 81; auth, Cross Currents, Oxford Univ Press. **CONTACT ADDRESS** Law School, Boston Col, Newton Ctr, 885 Centre St, Stuart House F317, Newton, MA 02459. **EMAIL** sanford.katz.1@bc.edu

KATZMAN, DAVID MANNERS

PERSONAL Born 10/25/1941, New York, NY, m, 1965, 2 children **DISCIPLINE** AMERICAN STUDIES, ETHNIC STUDIES, AMERICAN HISTORY **EDUCATION** Queens Col, NYork, BA, 63; Univ Mich, Ann Arbor, PhD (hist), 69. **CAREER** Prof, 78-90, Prof and Chair Am Studies, Univ Kans, 90-, assoc dean, col lib arts & scis & dir honors prog, 80-87, Ford Found fel, 75-76; vis prof mod hist, Univ Col Dublin, Ireland, 76-77; assoc ed, Am Studies, 77-; Guggenheim fel, 79-80, vis prof eco hist, Univ Birmingham, Eng, 84-85, Ed Bd, Regents Press of Kansas, 83-86; dir, NEH Sumer Seminars for Col Teachers, 90, 92, 94, 96; dir and commissioner, Nat Commission on Social Stud, 88-92; elected member, Professional Comm., AHA, 88-91; contributing ed, Perspectives (AHA), 89-92, 95-97; vis prof Am Stud, Univ Tokushima, Japan, 94, vis prof hist & Am Studies, Hong Kong Univ, 95, NEH fel, 94-95; ed, Am Stud, 98-. **HONORS AND AWARDS** Certificate of Commendation, Am Asn State & Local Hist, 74; Philip Taft Labor History Prize, 79; Byron Caldwell Smith Award, Humanistic Scholarship, 80. **MEMBERSHIPS** AHA; Orgn Am Historians; Am Jewish Hist Soc; Immigrant Hist Soc; Am Studies Asn. **RESEARCH** Race and Ethnicity; African Am culture. **SELECTED PUBLICATIONS** Auth, Ann Arbor: Depression City, Mich Hist, 12/66; Black Slavery in Michigan, Midcontinent Am Studies J, fall 70; contribr, Perspectives in Geography II: Geography of the Ghetto, Northern Ill Univ, 72; auth, Before the Ghetto: Black Detroit in the Nineteenth Century, Univ Ill, 73; coauth, Three Generations in 20th Century America, Dorsey, 77, rev ed, 82; auth, Seven Days a Week: Women and Domestic in Industrializing America, Oxford Univ, 78 & Univ Ill, 81; coauth, A People & A Nation, Houghton Mifflin, 82, 86, 90, 94, 98; co-ed, Plain Folk: The Life Stories of Undistinguished Americans, Univ Ill, 82; co-ed, Technical Knowledge in American Culture, Univ Ala, 96; contr, La storia americana e le scienze sociali, Inst della Enciclopedia Italiana, 96; auth, A People & Nation, 01. **CONTACT ADDRESS** Dept of Hist, Univ of Kansas, Lawrence, Lawrence, KS 66045-0001. **EMAIL** dkatzman@ku.edu

KAUFFMAN, JAMES M.

PERSONAL Born 12/07/1940, Hannibal, MO, m **DISCIPLINE** EDUCATION **EDUCATION** Goshen Col, BS, 62; Washburn Univ, MEd, 66; Univ Kansas, EdD, 69. **CAREER** Asst prof, IL State Univ, 69-70; asst prof to prof, Univ of Va, 70-. **HONORS AND AWARDS** Outstanding Serv Awd, Midwest Symp for Leadership in Behav Disorders, 91; William Clay Parrish, Jr Prof of Educ, Univ of Va, 92-94; Res Awd, Coun For Exceptional Children, 94; W. Kuhn Barnett Awd, Coun for Exceptional Children, 95; Omicron Delta Kappa, 95; Raven soc, 97; Outstanding Fac Awd, Curry Sch of Educ Found, 97. **SELECTED PUBLICATIONS** Auth, "Commentary: Today's special education and its messages for tomorrow", J of Spec Educ 32, (99): 244-254; auth, "Comments on social development research in EBD", J of Emotional and Behav Disorders 7, (99): 189-191; auth, "How we prevent the prevention of emotional and behavioral disorders", Exceptional Children 65, (99): 448-468; auth, "The role of science in behavioral disorders", Behav Disorders 24, (99): 265-272; coauth, "Constructing habilitative environments for students with emotional or behavioral disorders: Conclusion to the special issue", Can J of Spec Educ 11.1 (99): 100-108; coauth, "Creating supportive environments for students with emotional or behavioral disorders", Effective School Practices 17.2 (99): 25-35; coauth, "Practice parameters for the assessment and treatment of children and adolescents with language and learning disorders", J of the Am Acad of Child and Adolescent Psych 37.10, (99): 46S-62S; coauth, "Cultural causes of rage and violence in children and youth", Reaching Today's Youth: the Community Circle of Caring J 4.2 (00): 54-59; auth, "The special education story: Obituary, accident report, conversion experience, reincarnation, or none of the above?", Exceptionality 8.1 (00): 61-71; coauth, "What's right about special education", Exceptionality 8.1 (00): 3-11. **CONTACT ADDRESS** Dept Curric and Instr, Univ of Virginia, 405 Emmet St, 235 Ruffner Hall, Charlottesville, VA 22903. **EMAIL** jmk9t@virginia.edu

KAUFMAN, DEBRA RENEE
PERSONAL Born 04/02/1941, Cleveland, OH, m, 1963, 2 children **DISCIPLINE** SOCIOLOGY, ANTHROPOLOGY **EDUCATION** Univ Mich, BA, 63, MA, 66; Cornell Univ, PhD, 75. **CAREER** Mellon Fel Sem Participant, Center for Res on Women, Wellesley Col, 83-84; assoc prof, Northeastern Univ, 81-86, Dir and Founder, of Women's Studies Prog, Col of Arts and Scis, 81-89; adv coun, Prog in Women's Studies, Princeton Univ, 83-88; vis res scholar, Murray Res Center, Radcliffe Col, 89-90; vis scholar, Brigham Young Univ, Jan-Mar 93; Dir, Women's Studies Prog, Northeastern Univ, 93-94, Matthews Distinguished Prof, 94-96, prof, 86-; vis scholar, Oxford Centre for Hebrew and Jewish Studies, Oxford Univ, England, March-June 97. **HONORS AND AWARDS** Matthews Distinguished Prof, 94-96; Achievement and Women nominated for C. Wright Mills Awd, Received Honorable Mention, 83; Phi Kappa Phi; Twenty-Third Annual Univ Lectureship, awarded the Robert D. Klein Lectureship, 87; nominated as conf participant, Am Coun on Educ Nat Identification Prog, 87; elected to membership, Nat Coun on Educ, Women in High Ed, Mass, 87; Am Asn of Relig grant, 93-94; invited contribur: The Reader's Companion to U.S. Women's History, Houghton Mifflin Co, 97, and Jewish Women in America: An Historical Encyclopedia, Routledge, Inc, 98; Phi Beta Delta Honor Soc for Int Scholars, 98; listed in: Int Who's Who of Professional and Business Women, Two Thousand Notable American Women, and Who's Who in American Women. **MEMBERSHIPS** Am Coun on Educ, Am Sociol Asn, Asn for Jewish Studies, Asn for the Sociol Study of Jewry, Eastern Sociol Soc, îhi Kappa Phi, Relig Res Asn, Sociols for Women in Soc, Soc Sci Study of Relig. **RESEARCH** Gender, feminist theory and methods, Jewish Studies. **SELECTED PUBLICATIONS** Coauth with Barbara Richardson, Achievement and Women: Challenging the Assumption, New York: The Free Press (82); ed, Public/Private Spheres: Women Past and Present, Northeastern Univ Customs Textbooks (89); auth, Rachel's Daughters: Newly Orthodox Jewish Women, Rutgers Univ Press (91, 2nd paperback ed, 93); auth, "Engendering Orthodoxy: Newly Orthodox Women and Hasidism," in New World Hasidism: Ethnographic Studies of Hasidic Jews, ed Janet Belcove-Shalin, SUNY Press: Albany, NY (95); auth, "Experiencing Hasidism: Newly Orthodox Women's Perspectives on Sexuality and Domesticity," in Women in Jewish Culture: An Active Voice, ed Maurie Sacks, Univ Ill Press: Urbana-Champaign, Ill (95); auth, "Rethinking, Reflecting and Rewriting: Teaching Feminist Methodology," J of Radical Educ and Cultural Studies, #181 (96): 165-174; auth, "The Holocaust and Sociological Inquiry: A Feminist Analysis," Contemporary Jewry, Vol 17 (96): 6-17; auth, "Gender and Jewish Identity among Twenty-Somethings in the United States," in Religion in a Changing World, ed Madeleine Cousineau, Greenwood Press (98); auth, "Embedded Categories: Identity among Jewish Young Adults in the United States," in Race, Class and Gender: Jewish American Perspectives, guest ed of the journal, Race, Class and Gender, Vol 6, No 3 (99). **CONTACT ADDRESS** Dept of Sociol and Anthropol, Northeastern Univ, 143 Ridge Ave, Newton Center, Boston, MA 02159. **EMAIL** dkaufman@nuhub.neu.edu

KAUFMAN, TERRENCE SCOTT
PERSONAL Born 06/12/1937, Portland, OR, d, 1 child **DISCIPLINE** ANTHROPOLOGY; LINGUISTICS **EDUCATION** Univ Chicago, AB, 59; Univ Calif, Berkeley, PhD(ling), 63. **CAREER** Asst prof ling, Ohio State Univ, 63-64; asst prof, Univ Calif, Berkeley, 64-70; Assoc Prof Anthrop, Univ Pitts, 71-80, Tech dir ling, Francisco Marroquin ling proj, Antigua, Guatemala, 71-79; prof, Anthrop, Univ Pitts, 80- . **MEMBERSHIPS** Ling Soc Am. **RESEARCH** Mayan synchronic and diachronic linguistics; comparative and historical linguistic method and theory; Romani linguistics. **SELECTED PUBLICATIONS** Auth, Teco: A new Mayan language, Int J Am Ling, 69; Tzeltal Phonology and Morphology, Univ Calif, 69; El proto Tzeltal-Tzotzil, Nat Univ Mex, 72; Areal linguistics and Middle America, In: Current Trends in Linguistics, Mouton, The Hague, 73; auth, A Decipherment of epi-Olmec Hieroglyphic Writing, Science, 93. **CONTACT ADDRESS** Dept of Anthrop, Univ of Pittsburgh, 3H01 WWPH, Pittsburgh, PA 15260. **EMAIL** topkat@pitt.edu

KAWEWE, SALIEW
PERSONAL Born 11/15/1949, Zimbabwe, s, 1 child **DISCIPLINE** SOCIAL WORK **EDUCATION** Univ Zambia, BSW, 74; Wash Univ, MSW, 79; St. Louis Univ, PhD, 85. **CAREER** Asst prof, SE La Univ, 85-88; asst prof, Central State Univ, 89; asst prof, James Madison Univ, 89-91; asst prof, Wichita State Univ, 91-096; assoc prof, S IL Univ Carbondale, 96-. **HONORS AND AWARDS** Meritorious Awd, Univ of Zambia, 79; Superior Acad Achievement, St. Louis Univ, 84; Beta Delta. **MEMBERSHIPS** SIUC; IEA/NEA; NASW; NWSA; ICSW; IUCISD; CSWE. **RESEARCH** Teaching social welfare policy, research and community practice, HIV/AIDS, Women and children. **SELECTED PUBLICATIONS** Auth, "Social welfare of indigenous peoples in Zimbabwe", in Social Welfare with Indigenous Peoples, eds J. Dixon and R. Scheurell (London: Routledge, 95), 276-311; auth, "Social-networking Zimbabwean families: An African traditional approach to waging a war against HIV/AIDS", Soc Develop Issues 18.2 (96):34-51; auth, "Population movements in Zimbabwe: Their implications for traditional and modern social security", New Global Develop: Jour of Int and Comparative Social Welfare XIII, (97):84-105; auth, "Black women in diverse academic settings: Gender and racial crimes of commission and omission in academia", in Black Women in the Acad Promises and Perils, ed L. Benjamin, (Gainesville: Univ of Fla Pr, 97), 263-269; auth, "Black women faculty; The dynamics of patriarchal meritocracy in the academy", in Black Women in the Acad Promises and Perils, ed L. Benjamin, (Gainesville: Univ of Fla Pr, 97), 246-251; auth, "The inability of the United Nations to reform world practices that endanger Third World Children", New Global Develop: Jour of Int and Comparative Social Welfare X1V, (98):46-61; coauth, "United Nations and the problem of women and children abuse in Third World nations", Social Justice 26.1 (99):78-98; coauth, "Education Policy and the future of sustainable development in Zimbabwe and Nigeria", Soc Develop Issues 21.1 (forthcoming); "auth, "The Impact of Gender Disempowerment on the Welfare of Zimbabwean Women and Children", Int Social Work Jour (forthcoming). **CONTACT ADDRESS** Dept Social Work, So Illinois Univ, Carbondale, 132 Wood Rd, Carbondale, IL 62901. **EMAIL** smkawewe@siu.edu

KAYE, HARVEY JORDAN
PERSONAL Born 10/09/1949, Englewood, NJ, m, 1973, 2 children **DISCIPLINE** HISTORY OF CULTURE **EDUCATION** Rutger Univ, BA, 71; Univ London, MA 73; La St Univ, PhD 76. **CAREER** Inst, hist & sociology, La St Univ, 74, 75; asst prof social sci, St. Cloud St Univ, 77-78; from asst prof to assoc prof, Univ Wisc, 78-86, Ben & Joyce Rosenberg Prof of Social Change & Develop & Dir, Ctr for Hist & Social Change, 86- . **HONORS AND AWARDS** Honors Res Student in Hist, Rutger Col, 70-71; Fel, La St Univ, 74-75 & 75-76; postdoctoral fel, Lilly Endowment, 78-79; Nat Endowment for the Humanities Fel, 81 & 83; Visiting Fel, Inst for Advanced Res in the Humanities, Univ Birmingham, Engl, 87; Ed & Executor, George Rude Lit Estate, 88-; Endowed Chair, Rosenberg Professorship, 90-; Bd of Dir, Wisc Hist Soc, 81-; Deutscher Memorial Lect, London Sch of Econ, 94; Teaching Awd, St. Cloud St Univ, 77-78; Awd for Excellence in Scholarship, UWGB Founders Assn, 85; Isaac Deutscher Memorial Prize, 93; scholarship, columbia univ, 77. **MEMBERSHIPS** Amer Historical Assn; Amer Studies Assn; Org of Amer Historians. **RESEARCH** Amer History; politics; ideas; intellectuals; critics and radicals. **SELECTED PUBLICATIONS** Auth, British Marxist Historians: An Introductory Analysis, Polity Press/ Blackwell, 84; auth, The Powers of the Past: Reflections on the Crisis and the Promise of History, Simon & Schuster & Univ Minn, 91; auth, The Education of Desire: Marxists and the Writing of History, Routledge, 92; auth, Why Do Ruling Classes Fear History? and Other Questions, St Martin's/Macmillan, 96; auth, Thomas Paine-A Young People's Biography, Oxford Univ, 99; ed History, Classes and Nation-States: Selected Writings of VG Kiernan, Polity Press/Blackwell, 88; ed Face of the Crowd: Selected Essays of George Rude, Simon & Schuster & Humanities Press, 88; ed, Poets, Politics and the People: Selected Writings of VG Kiernan, Verso, 89; co-ed, EP Thompson: Critical Perspectives, Polity Press & Temple Univ, 90; co-ed, American Radical, Routledge, 94; ed, Imperialism and Its Contradictions: Selected Writings of VG Kiernan, Routledge, 95; ed, Ideology and Popular Protest, Univ NCar, 95; series co-ed, American Radicals, Routledge, 92-98. **CONTACT ADDRESS** Dept of Social Change & Develop, Univ of Wisconsin, Green Bay, Green Bay, WI 54301. **EMAIL** kayeh@uwgb.edu

KAYE, HOWARD
PERSONAL Born 07/05/1951, Washington, DC, m, 1976, 2 children **DISCIPLINE** SOCIOLOGY **EDUCATION** Univ Pa, BA, 74, MA, 76; PhD, 81; Univ Chicago, MA, 75. **CAREER** Asst prof to prof, Franklin & Marshall Col, 82-. **HONORS AND AWARDS** Phi Beta Kappa. **MEMBERSHIPS** Am Sociol Assoc; Assoc for Politics and the Life Sciences. **RESEARCH** Sociological theory, Bioethics, Sociobiology. **SELECTED PUBLICATIONS** Auth, The Social Meaning of Modern Biology, Yale Univ Pr, (New Haven), 86; auth, "Are We the Sum of Our Genes?", Wilson Quarterly XVI.2, (92):77-84; auth, "Why Freud Hated America", Wilson Quarterly XVII.2 (93):118-25; auth, "Cultural Being or Biological Being: The Implications of Modern Biology" in Evolution and Human Values, ed R. Wesson and P.A. Williams, (Amsterdam: Rodopi, 95); rev, of "In the Belgian Chateau: The Spirit and Culture of A European Society in an Age of Change" By Renee C. Fox, Am Sociol 26, (Winter 95), 118-119; rev, of "Unifying Biology: The Evolutionary Synthesis and Evolutionary Biology" by Vassiliki Betty Smocovitis, Am Hist Rev 103 (June 98) 857-58; rev, of "Crossing Boundaries: Knowledge, Disciplinarites and Interdisciplinarities" by Julie Thompson Klein, Society 36 (Nov/ Dec 98), 84-85; auth, "The Return of the Repressed: Peter Gay's Bourgeois Experience", Society 36, (July/Aug 99), 90-93. **CONTACT ADDRESS** Dept Sociol, Franklin and Marshall Col, PO Box 3003, Lancaster, PA 17604. **EMAIL** h_kaye@acad.fandm.edu

KEARNS, EMILY
DISCIPLINE SOCIOLOGY **EDUCATION** Mimmack Col, BA, 83; Boston Col, MA, 86; PhD, 96. **CAREER** Dept Chair, Clarke Col, 97-. **HONORS AND AWARDS** Who's Who Among Am Teachers; Who's Who in the World. **MEMBERSHIPS** ASA, MSS. **RESEARCH** Gender; Culture; Ritual; Theory. **CONTACT ADDRESS** Dept Sociol, Clarke Col, 1550 Clarke Dr, Dubuque, IA 52001.

KEATEN, JAMES A.
DISCIPLINE INTERCULTURAL COMMUNICATION **EDUCATION** PA State Univ, PhD, 70. **CAREER** Prof, Univ Northern CO. **MEMBERSHIPS** Speech Commun Asn; Western States Commun Asn; Japanese Psychol Asn. **RESEARCH** Commun apprehension; cross-cultural commun. **SELECTED PUBLICATIONS** Coauth, Teaching people to speak well: Training and remediation of communication reticence, Hampton Publ Co, 95; Komyunikeishon fuan to wa nanika? [A definition of communication apprehension and related constructs], Hokuriku Daiguku Kiyo, 20, 96; Development of an instrument to measure reticence, Commun Quart, 45, 97; Communication apprehension in Japan: Grade school through secondary school, Int J of Intercultural Rel, 21, 97; Assessing the cross-cultural validity of the Personal Report of Communication Apprehension scale (PRCA-24), Japanese Psychol Res, 40, 98; Fundamentals of communication: An intercultural perspective, Kawashima Shotem, 98. **CONTACT ADDRESS** Univ of No Colorado, Greeley, CO 80639. **EMAIL** jkeaten@bentley.unco.edu

KEEFE, SUSAN E.
PERSONAL Born 12/01/1947, Spokane, WA, w, 1970, 1 child **DISCIPLINE** ANTHROPOLOGY **EDUCATION** UCSB, BA, 69; MA, 71; PhD, 74. **CAREER** Asst prof, Appalachian State Univ, 78-82, assoc prof, 82-87, prof, 87-, chair, 92-. **HONORS AND AWARDS** Woodrow Wilson Diss Fel, UCSB, 72-73; ASU Col of Arts and Scis, Outstanding Scholar Awd, 97; COUPI NSF grants in 82-83, 98-99. **MEMBERSHIPS** Am Anthropol Asn, Soc for Applied Anthropol. **RESEARCH** Ethnicity, medical anthropology. **SELECTED PUBLICATIONS** Coauth with Amado M. Padilla, Chican Ethnicity, UNM Press (87); ed, Appalchian Mental Health, UK Press (88); ed, Negotiating Ethnicity (89). **CONTACT ADDRESS** Depot Anthropol, Appalachian State Univ, 1 Appalachian State, Boone, NC 28608-0001. **EMAIL** keefese@appstate.edu

KEEN, CHERYL
PERSONAL Born 03/22/1952, Gary, IN, m, 1975, 1 child **DISCIPLINE** EDUCATION **EDUCATION** Bethany Col, BS, 73; Harvard Univ, EdM, 74; EdD, 81. **CAREER** Teacher, Cambridge, Mass Public Schs, 74-75; coord of the comt on int studies, Harvard Univ, 74-82; instr, Mass Bay Community Col, 75-76; fac member, Goddard Col, 76-81; teaching fel, Harvard Univ, 82-85; prof, Lesley Col Grad Sch, 81-88; Millicent Fenwick Res prof of Public Issues and Educ & co-dir, governor's sch on public issues and the future of NJ, Monmouth Col, 82-95; dean of fac, Antioch Col, 95-97; prof, Antioch Col, 97-. **MEMBERSHIPS** Nat Soc for Experiential Educ. **RESEARCH** Adolescence, Commitment to Common Good, Work-Based Learning. **SELECTED PUBLICATIONS** Coauth, "The Governor's School on Public Issues," Educ Leadership (90); auth, "Effects of an Intensive Program on Public Issues on Adolescents' Moral and Intellectual Development," in Combining Service and Learning, ed. Jane Kendall (Nat Soc for Experiential Educ, 90); ed, "There's no Place Like Homeless: A Simulation to Create Awareness, Monmouth Univ, 95; co-ed, "Education for the New Commons," Educ Week (96); coauth, Common Fire: Leading Lives of Commitment in a Complex World, Beacon Press (Boston, MA), 97. **CONTACT ADDRESS** Dept Self, Soc & Culture, Antioch Col, 795 Livermore St, Yellow Springs, OH 45387. **EMAIL** ckeen@antioch-college.edu

KEEN, J. ERNEST
PERSONAL Born 02/15/1937, Indianapolis, IN, m, 3 children **DISCIPLINE** PSYCHOLOGY **EDUCATION** Harvard Univ, PhD 63. **CAREER** Bucknell Univ, Psychologist/tchr 64. **HONORS AND AWARDS** Linbach Awd for Tchg. **RESEARCH** Psychopharmacology; drugs and society. **SELECTED PUBLICATIONS** Drugs Therapy and Professional Power, Praeger, 98. **CONTACT ADDRESS** Dept of Psychology, Bucknell Univ, Lewisberg, PA 17837. **EMAIL** keen@bucknell.edu

KEEN, MIKE F.
PERSONAL Born 08/14/1958, Tiffin, OH, m **DISCIPLINE** SOCIOLOGY **EDUCATION** Heidelberg Col, BA, 79; Univ Notre Dame, MA, 83; PhD, 85. **CAREER** Asst Prof to Assoc Prof and Dept Chair, Ind Univ, 89-. **HONORS AND AWARDS** President's Distinguished Teaching Awd, 94; Distinguished Teaching Awd, IN Univ, 93; Chancellor's Fel, UISB, 98-99. **MEMBERSHIPS** Am Sociol Asn; Intl Sociol Asn; AAUP. **RESEARCH** Social theory; History of Sociology; Society and Environment; Urban Society. **SELECTED PUBLICATIONS** Auth, "No One Above suspicion: Talcott arsons Under Surveillance," The American sociologist, (93(: 37-54; auth, "Teaching Qualitative Methods: A Face-to-Face encounter," Teaching Sociology, (96): 166-176; co-auth, "Cafe Kultur: The coffeehouses of Vienna," contemporary Review, (96): 24-32; co-ed, Eastern Europe in Transition: The Impact on Sociology, Greenwood Press, 94; co-ed, Sojologia Europy Srodkowo-Wschodniej: 1956-1990, Warszawa, 95; auth, Stalking the Sociological Imagination: FBI Surveillance of American Sociology, Greenwood Press, 99. **CONTACT ADDRESS** Dept Sociol, Indiana Univ, South Bend, PO Box 7111, South Bend, IN 46634. **EMAIL** mkeen@iusb.edu

KEESEY, RICHARD E.
PERSONAL Born 10/14/1934, York, PA, d, 1 child **DISCIPLINE** PSYCHOLOGY **EDUCATION** Dartmouth Col, AB, 56; Brown Univ, ScM, 58; PhD, 60. **CAREER** Asst Prof to Prof, Univ Wisc, 62-; Visiting Lecturer, Sydney Univ, 74. **MEMBERSHIPS** Intl Brain Res Org; Sigma Xi; Am Inst of Nutrition; N Am Soc for the Study of Obesity; Soc for the Study of Ingestive Beh **RESEARCH** Physiology of body energy regulation. **SELECTED PUBLICATIONS** Co-auth, "Fever and the acute elevation in whole-body thermogenesis induced by lateral hypothalamic lesions," Physiology and Behavior, (95): 237-243; co-auth, "Chronically-altered body protein levels following lesions of the lateral hypothalamus in rats," American Journal of Physiology: Regulatory, Integrative, and Comparative Physiology, (96): R738-R743; co-auth, "The specific locus and time course of the body protein adjustments produced in rats by lesions of the lateral hypothalamus," Physiology and Behavior, (96): 725-731; co-auth, "Growth hormone or insulin-like growth factor-I increase fat oxidation and decrease protein oxidation without altering energy expenditure in parenterally-fed rats," American Journal of Clinical Nutrition, (97): 1384-1390; co-auth, "Selective breeding for diet-induced obesity and resistance in Spregue-Dawley rats," American Journal of Physiology: Regulatory, Integrative, and Comparative Physiology, (97): R725-R730; co-auth, "Body weight set points: determination and adjustment," Journal of Nutrition, (97): 1875-1883; co-auth, "Defense of differing body weight set-points in diet-induced obese and resistant rats," American Journal of Physiology, (98): R412-R419. **CONTACT ADDRESS** Dept Psychol, Univ of Wisconsin, Madison, 1202 W Johnson St, Madison, WI 53706.

KEHOE, ALICE
PERSONAL Born 09/18/1934, New York, NY, d, 3 children **DISCIPLINE** ANTHROPOLOGY **EDUCATION** Barnard Col, BA, 56; Harvard Univ, PhD, 64. **CAREER** Asst Prof, Univ Neb, 65-68; Assoc Prof to Prof, Marquette Univ, 68-99; Adj Prof, Univ Wisc, 99-. **MEMBERSHIPS** Am Anthropol Asn; Soc for Am Archaeol. **RESEARCH** american archaeology; History of archaeology; First Nations of America. **SELECTED PUBLICATIONS** Auth, The Ghost Dance: Ethnohistory and Revitalization, New York, 89; co-ed, Powers of Observation: alternate Views in Archeology, Washington, 90; auth, "Points and Lines," in Powers of Observation: alternate Views in Archeology, (Washington, 90), 23-37; auth, North American Indians: A comprehensive Account, 2nd ed, Prentice-Hall, 92; auth, Humans, Introductory Anthropology Textbook, Routledge, 98; auth, The Land of Prehistory: A Critical History of American Archaeology, Routledge Press, 98; co-ed, Assembling the Past: Studies in the Professionalization of Archaeology, Univ NM Press, 99; auth, "Recognizing the Foundation of Prehistory," in Assembling the Past: Studies in the Professionalization of Archaeology, (Univ NM Press, 99), 53-68. **CONTACT ADDRESS** 3014 N Shepard Ave, Milwaukee, WI 53211-3436.

KEIL, CHARLES M. H.
PERSONAL Born 08/12/1939, Norwalk, CT, m, 1964, 2 children **DISCIPLINE** ANTHROPOLOGY, MUSIC **EDUCATION** Yale Univ, BA; Univ Chicago, MA, 64; PhD, 79. **CAREER** From asst prof to prof emer, Dept of Am Stud, SUNY Buffalo, 70- ; acting chemn, 78-89, 92, 94-95, Dir Undergrad Stud, 86-89, dir Grad Stud, 70-77, 79-82; vis prof, music, Univ Natal, 93; vis lectr, sociol of music, 82, 83. **HONORS AND AWARDS** Chicago Folklore Prize, co-winner, 80; Chicago Folklore Prize, 95; Woodrow Wilson Fel, 61-62; Ford Found Fel, 62-63; NIMH Fel, 63-64; Foreign Area Fel Prog, 65-67; Rockefeller Found Res Grant, 75; Guggenheim fel, 79-80. **SELECTED PUBLICATIONS** Auth, Urban Blues, Univ Chicago, 66; auth, Tiv Song: The Sociology of Art in a Classless Society, Univ Chicago, 79; coauth, Polka Happiness, Temple Univ, 92; co-ed, My Music, Wesleyan Univ, 93; coauth, Music Grooves: Essays and Dialogues, Univ Chicago, 94. **CONTACT ADDRESS** Dept of American Studies, SUNY, Buffalo, 1010 Clemens Hall, N Campus, Buffalo, NY 14260. **EMAIL** amsckeil@acsu.buffalo.edu

KEILLOR, ELAINE
DISCIPLINE BAROQUE AND CLASSICAL PERIODS, ETHNOMUSICOLOGY **EDUCATION** Univ Toronto, BA, MA, PhD. **CAREER** Lectr, York Univ, 75-76; instr, Queen's Univ, 76-77; asst prof, 77-82, assoc prof, 82-95, prof, Carleton Univ, 95-. **HONORS AND AWARDS** Chappell Medal, 58; Merit Awd, Fac Arts, Carleton Univ, 81; Canadian Women's Mentor Awd, 99; principal investigator, the can mus heritage soc; co-ch, another organized res unit. **MEMBERSHIPS** Can Musical Heritage; Am Musicol Soc; Int Musicol Soc; Soc Ethnomusicol; Can Univ Music Soc; Can Soc Traditional Music. **RESEARCH** Canadian music. **SELECTED PUBLICATIONS** Auth, monograph John Weinzweig and His Music: The Radical Romantic of Canada, 94; **CONTACT ADDRESS** Dept of Mus, Carleton Univ, 1125 Colonel By Dr, Ottawa, ON, Canada K1S 5B6. **EMAIL** elaine_keillor@carleton.ca

KEITH, REBECCA M.
PERSONAL Born 11/20/1954, KoKomo, IN, m, 1981, 2 children **DISCIPLINE** ANTHROPOLOGY **EDUCATION** Ball State Univ, BS, 89; MA, 94; PhD Cand. **CAREER** Adj Fac, Ind Univ KoKomo, 89-00; Instr, Ball State Univ, 90-00. **HONORS AND AWARDS** Charles R. Jenkins Awd, Nat Lambda Alpha Collegiate Hon Soc for Anthrop. **RESEARCH** Symbolic Anthropology, Native American Studies, American Culture, Development of Modern Anthropology, Human Evolution. **SELECTED PUBLICATIONS** Auth, Be There: The World of Outlaw's and the Community of Sprint Car Racing, Ball State Univ, 94. **CONTACT ADDRESS** Dept Anthrop, Ball State Univ, 2000 W Univ, Muncie, IN 47306-0002. **EMAIL** becca46936@aol.com

KELEMEN, DEBORAH A.
PERSONAL Born 07/03/1967, London, England **DISCIPLINE** PSYCHOLOGY **EDUCATION** Univ Manchester, BA, 88; Univ Ariz, MA, 96; PhD, 96. **CAREER** Postdoc Fel, Univ Calif Berkeley, 96-97; Asst Prof, Pa State Univ, 97-00; Asst Prof, Boston Univ, 00-. **HONORS AND AWARDS** Nat Inst of Health, 99-. **MEMBERSHIPS** Am Psychol Soc; Soc for Res in Child Develop; Cognitive Develop Soc. **RESEARCH** Cognitive Development with particular emphasis on conceptual development: the nature of children's and adults' concepts of the artificial and natural world; Conceptual constraints on intuitive and scientific theory-formation; Object categorization; Cross-cultural and individual differences in cognition. Also language development: conceptual and linguistic constraints on the acquisition of word meaning. **SELECTED PUBLICATIONS** Co-auth, "Domain-specific knowledge in simple categorization tasks," Psychonomic Bulletin & Rev, 94; co-auth, "Syntactic and conceptual factors in the acquisition of collective nouns," Proceedings of the Twenty-Sixth Annual Child Lang Res Forum, 95; co-auth, "Syntactic cues in the acquisition of collective nouns," Cognition, 95; auth, "Beliefs about purpose: On the origins of teleological thought," in The Descent of Mind, Oxford Univ Press, 99; auth, "The scope of teleological thinking in preschool children," Cognition, 99; auth, "Why are rocks pointy?: Children's preference for teleological explanations of the natural world," Develop Psychol, 99; auth, "Functions, goals and intentions: Children's teleological reasoning," Trends in Cognitive Sci, 99. **CONTACT ADDRESS** Dept Psychol, Boston Univ, 64 Cummington St, Boston, MA 02215. **EMAIL** dkelemen@bu.edu

KELLER, EVELYN FOX
PERSONAL Born New York, NY **DISCIPLINE** SCIENCE, SOCIOLOGY **EDUCATION** Brandeis Univ, BA, 57; Radcliffe Col, MA, 59; Harvard Univ, PhD, 63. **CAREER** Prof, Northeastern Univ, 82-88; Prof, Univ Calif, 88-92; Prof, Massachusetts Inst of Tech (MIT), 92-. **HONORS AND AWARDS** MacArthur Fel, 92-97; Alumni Achievement Awd, Brandeis Univ, 91; Achievement Awd, AAUW's Educ Found, 90; Distinguished Publ Awd, Asn for Women in Psychol. **MEMBERSHIPS** Asn for Women in Psychol, AAUW. **RESEARCH** History and philosophy of science; technology and society. **SELECTED PUBLICATIONS** Auth, Reflections on Gender and Science, Yale Univ Pr (New Haven, CT), 85; co-ed, Women, Science and the Body, Routledge, 89; co-ed, Conflicts in Feminism, Routledge, 90; co-ed, Keywords in Evolutionary Biology, Harvard Univ Pr, 92; auth, Secrets of Life, Secrets of Death: Essays on Language, Gender and Science, Routledge, 92; auth, A Feeling for the Organism: The Life and Work of Barbara McClintock, 2nd Ed, W.H. Freeman, 93; auth, Refiguring Life: Metaphors of Twentieth-Century Biology, Columbia Univ Pr, 95; co-ed, Feminism and Science, Oxford Univ Pr, 96; auth, The Century of the Gene, Harvard Univ Pr, forthcoming; auth, The Uses of Disunity: Models and Explanation in Developmental Biology, forthcoming. **CONTACT ADDRESS** Dept Sci & Sociol, Massachusetts Inst of Tech, 77 Massachusetts Ave, Cambridge, MA 02139-4301.

KELLER, ROBERT J.
PERSONAL Born 02/07/1952, Grand Forks, ND, s **DISCIPLINE** SOCIOLOGY **EDUCATION** Graduate Theol Union, PhD, 93. **CAREER** Author **MEMBERSHIPS** AAR; ASR. **RESEARCH** Cath social teaching; sociology-theology of work; the works of M.-D. Chenu, 20th century French Dominican). **CONTACT ADDRESS** 1815 Las Lomas NE, Albuquerque, NM 87106. **EMAIL** FBJK@juno.com

KELLER, ROBERT L.
PERSONAL Born 08/17/1945, Denver, CO, m, 1965, 1 child **DISCIPLINE** SOCIOLOGY, CRIMINOLOGY **EDUCATION** Univ Colo, BA, 68; Colo State Univ, MS, 70; Univ Mont, PhD, 76. **CAREER** Instr, Southwest Mo State Col, 70-71; instr, Univ Wis, 71-72; prof, Univ Southern Colo, 74-. **RESEARCH** Criminological Theory, Government Crime, UFO Coverup, Animal Mutilations. **SELECTED PUBLICATIONS** Auth, "From Cons to Counselors," Int J of Offender Therapy 37.1 (93); coauth & co-ed, Prison Crisis, Harrow and Heston, 95. **CONTACT ADDRESS** Dept Sociol & Anthrop, Univ of So Colorado, 2200 Bonforte Blvd, Pueblo, CO 81001. **EMAIL** keller@uscolo.edu

KELLEY, KARL NEAL
PERSONAL Born 02/25/1960, Richmond, VA, m, 1 child **DISCIPLINE** PSYCHOLOGY **EDUCATION** Va Commonwealth Univ, BS, 82; MS, 85; PhD, 87. **CAREER** From teaching asst to instr, Va Commonwealth Univ, 84-86; instr, Mary Washington Col, 86-87; vis asst prof, Univ Richmond, 87-88; vis asst prof, Randolph-Macon Col, 88; from asst prof to assoc prof, N Central Col, 88-. **HONORS AND AWARDS** Psi Chi Honor Soc, 81; Dissinger Teaching Awd for First Year Fac, N Central Col, 89; Dissinger Awd for Fac Scholar, 99; listed in Who's Who Amon America's Teachers, 00. **MEMBERSHIPS** Am Psychol Soc, Midwestern Psychol Asn, Nat Acad Advising Asn, Soc for Industrial/Organizational Psychologists, Soc for the Advancement of Soc Psychology, The Coun of Teachers of Undergraduate Psychology. **RESEARCH** Social Psychology Applied to Industrial/Organizational and Education Settings, Statistics and Methodologies for the Behavioral Sciences, Relationships among Science, Religion, Law, and Society, Assessment of self-concept, Personal & Organizational Issues Related to Work/Family/Leisure Time, Affective, behavioral, and cognitive consequenses of success and failure. **SELECTED PUBLICATIONS** Coauth, "Heuristic-based biases in estimations of personal contributions to collective endeavors," in What's Social About Social Cognition? Social Cognition Research in Small Groups, eds. J. L. Nye & A. Bower (CA: Sage Publ, 96); auth, "Academic probation: A theoretical model," Nat Acad Advising Asn J 16 (96): 28-34; ed, Perspectives: Industrial/Organizational psychology, Coursewise Publ (Madison, WI), 00. **CONTACT ADDRESS** Dept Psychology, No Central Col, PO Box 3063, Naperville, IL 60566-7063. **EMAIL** knk@noctrl.edu

KENNEDY, ELIZABETH
PERSONAL Born 05/05/1948, Rochester, NY, s, 1 child **DISCIPLINE** PSYCHOLOGY **EDUCATION** Broward Cmty Col, AA, 86; Fl Atlantic Univ, BA, 89; MA, 93; Phd, 98. **CAREER** Res Asst, Fla Atlantic Univ, 89-96; Instructor to Asst Prof, SE Okla State Univ, 96-. **HONORS AND AWARDS** Outstanding Student of the Year Awd, 86; Phi Kappa Phi, 88; Phi Kappa Phi Scholarship, FAU. **MEMBERSHIPS** APA; SRCD; PKP; Psi Chi; APS. **RESEARCH** Develpmental aspects of memory, cognition, juvenile development. **SELECTED PUBLICATIONS** Co-auth, "conflict and the development of antisocial behavior," in conflict in child and adolescent development, Cambridge, 92; co-auth, "A Two-Year Longitudinal Study of adult and Child Free-and Unbiased-Cued Recall," Regional congress of Psychol of Prof, Mexico City, 97. **CONTACT ADDRESS** Dept Psychol, Southeastern Oklahoma State Univ, Durant, OK 74701. **EMAIL** ekennedy@sosu.edu

KENNEDY, JOYCE S.
PERSONAL Born 06/15/1943, St. Louis, MO, d **DISCIPLINE** EDUCATION **EDUCATION** Harris Tchr Coll, AB 1965; St Louis U, MEd 1968; MI State U, PhD 1975. **CAREER** Coll of Arts & Sciences Governors State Univ, occupational educ coordinator, prof 1975-; Meramec Jr Coll, counselor 1971-74; Forest Park Jr Coll, counselor 1969-71; St Louis Job Corps Center for Women, counselor 1968-69; Carver Elementary School, teacher 1966-68. **HONORS AND AWARDS** Cert of Recognition for Outstanding Serv IL Guidance adn Personnel Assn 1977; Distinguished Prof Governors State Univ 1977; Outstanding Young Woman of Am Awd 1978. **MEMBERSHIPS** Mem Am Personnel and Guidance assn; mem IL Assn of Non-White Concerns; mem IL Guidance and Personnel Assn; keynote speaker Roseland Community Sch Graduation 1978; facilitator Career Awareness Workshop 1978; speaker Harvey Pub Library 1978; Urban Counseling Fellowship Nat Mental Health Inst MI State Univ 1972-74. **CONTACT ADDRESS** Col of Arts & Sciences, Governors State Univ, University Park, IL 60466.

KENNEDY, KENNETH ADRIAN RAINE
PERSONAL Born 06/26/1930, Oakland, CA, m, 1969 **DISCIPLINE** ANTHROPOLOGY **EDUCATION** Univ Calif-Berkeley, BA, 53, MA, 54, PhD, 62. **CAREER** PROF, ECOL & EVOLUTIONARY BIOLOGY, BIOL SCI, CORNELL UNIV, 64-. **MEMBERSHIPS** Am Asn Physical Anthrop; Am Anthropol Asn; AmAsn Advancement Sci; Am Acad Forensic Sci; Anthrop Soc India; Archaeol Inst Am; Asn South Asian Archaeolog West Europ; Indo-Pacific Prehist Asn; Inst Human Origins; Int Asn Human Biol; Nat Center Sci Edu; Northeast Forensic Anthrop Asn; Paleopath Asn **RESEARCH** Biological anthropology; Palaeoecology & palaeodemography; Human paleontology; Forensic anthropology; Palaeopathology. **SELECTED PUBLICATIONS** South Asia: India and Sri Lanka, Anthropol Prehist Inst Royal Sci Naturelles Belgique; Reconstruction of Life from the Skeleton, Wiley/Liss, 89; "The Wrong Urn," Commingling of Cremains in Mortuary Practices, Jour Forensic Sci, 96; "A Canine Tooth from the Siwaliks: First Recorded Discovery of a Fossil Ape," Human Evolution (99). **CONTACT ADDRESS** Sect Ecol & Systematics, Cornell Univ, Corson Hall, Ithaca, NY 14853. **EMAIL** KAK10@cornell.edu

KENNETT, DOUGLAS
PERSONAL Born 06/16/1967, Los Angeles, CA **DISCIPLINE** ANTHROPOLOGY **EDUCATION** Univ Calif, Santa Barbara, PhD, 98. **CAREER** Asst prof, anthrop, Calif State Univ, Long Beach. **MEMBERSHIPS** Am Anthrop Asn; Soc for Am Archaeol. **RESEARCH** Anthropological archaeology; evolutionary ecology; isotope geochemistry. **CONTACT ADDRESS** Dept of Anthropology, California State Univ, Long Beach, Long Beach, CA 90840. **EMAIL** dkennett@csulb.edu

KENNISON, SHELIA
PERSONAL Born 04/24/1967, Montgomery, WV, s **DISCIPLINE** PSYCHOLOGY **EDUCATION** Harvard Univ, AB, 89; Univ Mass, MS, 93; PhD, 95. **CAREER** Instr, Univ Mass, 92-95; postdoc fel, Univ Ill, 95-96; vis asst prof, 96; asst prof, Univ Okla, 96-. **HONORS AND AWARDS** NIH, 93, 95; NSF, 89; Harvard Schl; Agassiz Awd, 89. **MEMBERSHIPS** IRA; PSAM; MPA; Sigma Xi. **RESEARCH** Language comprehension; employing multiple methodologies; questionnaire methods, self paced reading and eye movement recording. **SELECTED PUBLICATIONS** Coauth, "Determinants of parafoveal preview benefit in high and low working memory capacity readers: Implications for eye movement control," J Exper Psych 21 (95): 68-81; auth, "The role of sentence context in processing temporarily ambiguous prepositional phrases," in Univ Of Mass Occasional Papers: Linguistics in the Laboratory, eds. M Dickey, S Tunstall (Amherst, MA: Graduate Linguistic Student Asn, 96): 289-301; auth, "The role of verb information in syntactic ambiguity resolution," in MIT Occasional Paners in Linguistics 9: Proceedings of the NELS 26 Sentence Processing Workshop, ed. C Schultze (Cambridge, MA: MIT Press, 96), 73-84; coauth, "Reading the words 'her', 'his', and 'him': Implications for parsing principles based on frequency and on structure," J Memory and Lang 36 (97): 276-292; coauth, "Comprehending referential expressions during reading: Evidence from eye tracking," Discourse Processes 24 (97): 229-252; auth, "American English usage frequencies for noun phrase and tensed sentence complement-taking verbs," J Psycholinguistic Res 28 (97): 165-177; auth, "Processing agentive 'by'-phrases in complex event and non event nominals," Linguistic Inquiry 30 (99): 502-508. **CONTACT ADDRESS** Dept Psychology, Univ of Oklahoma, 455 W Lindsey St, Norman, OK 73019-2000.

KERBER, JORDAN E.
PERSONAL Born 02/19/1957, Boston, MA, m, 1988, 2 children **DISCIPLINE** SOCIOLOGY, ANTHROPOLOGY **EDUCATION** Haverford Col, BA, 79; Brown Univ, MA, 81; PhD, 84. **CAREER** Vis Lectr, Bridgewater St Col, 85-86; Vis Asst Prof, Brown Univ, 88-89; From Asst Prof to Assoc Prof, Colgate Univ, 89-. **HONORS AND AWARDS** Grant, Am Asn for St and Local Hist, 88-89; Paul Garrison Fel, Colgate Univ, 91-92; Grant, Sloan Found, 92; Grant, John Ben Snow Found, 95-97; Grant, Oneida Indian Nat, 98, 99. **MEMBERSHIPS** SAA, CNEA, NYAC, NYSAA, MAS. **RESEARCH** Archaeology of the Iroquois, paleoenvironmental reconstruction, public educational programs, coastal archaeology. **SELECTED PUBLICATIONS** Auth, "Native American Treatment of Dogs in Northeastern North America," Archaeol of Eastern N Am, vol 25 (97): 81-96; auth, "Lambert Farm: Public Archaeology and Canine Burials Along Narragansett Bay," Case Studies in Archaeol, Harcourt Brace Col Publ (97); auth, "Coastal and Maritime Archaeology in New England: Current Research Issues and Future Directions," Conf on New Eng Archaeol Newsletter, vol 18 (99): 1-7; auth, "Interpreting Diverse Marine Shell Deposits of the Woodland Period in New England and New York: Interrelationships Among Subsistence, Symbolism and Ceremonialism," Northeast Anthrop, vol 57 (99): 57-68; rev, "At a Crossroads: Archaeology and First Peoples in Canada," Northeast Anthrop (00). **CONTACT ADDRESS** Dept Sociol & Anthrop, Colgate Univ, 13 Oak Dr, Hamilton, NY 13346. **EMAIL** jkerber@mail.colgate.edu

KERNS, VIRGINIA B.
PERSONAL Born 08/26/1948, San Diego, CA, m **DISCIPLINE** ANTHROPOLOGY **EDUCATION** Col William and Mary, BA, 70; Univ Ill, PhD, 77. **CAREER** Vis asst prof, Col of William and Mary, 77-78; asst prof, Va Polytech Inst, 78-83; indep consul, 84-85; asst prof to prof, Col of William and Mary, 85-. **HONORS AND AWARDS** Phi Beta Kappa Fac Awd, 88; Jefferson Teaching Awd, 89; Outstanding Awd, 91. **MEMBERSHIPS** Am Anthrop Asn, Asn for Feminist Anthrop. **RESEARCH** Life history and biography, gender, life course. **SELECTED PUBLICATIONS** Auth, "Learning the Land," in Julian Steward and the Great Basin: The Making of an Anthropologist, (Univ of Utah Press: Salt Lake City, 99); auth Women and the Ancestors: Black Carib Kinship and Ritual, Univ of Ill Press: Urbana, 97; co-ed, In Her Prime: New Views of Middle-Aged Women, Univ of Ill Press: Urbana, 92. **CONTACT ADDRESS** Dept Anthrop, Col of William and Mary, PO Box 8795, Williamsburg, VA 23187. **EMAIL** vbkern@facstaff.wm.edu

KERTZER, DAVID ISRAEL
PERSONAL Born 02/20/1948, New York, NY, m, 1970, 2 children **DISCIPLINE** ANTHROPOLOGY **EDUCATION** Brown Univ, BA, 69; Brandeis, PhD, 74. **CAREER** William Kenan Prof of Anthropology, Bowdoin Col, 89-92; PAUL DUPEE UNIV PROF, PROF OF ANTHROPOLOGY & HIST, BROWN UNIV, 92-. **HONORS AND AWARDS** Guggenheim fel; NEH fel; NSF fel; NIH fel; Center for Advanced Study in the Behavior Scis fel. **MEMBERSHIPS** PEN; Am Anthropological Asn; Soc Sci Hist Asn; Population Asn of Am; Int Union for the Sci Study of Population. **RESEARCH** European social history; politics and symbolism; anthropological population studies. **SELECTED PUBLICATIONS** Auth, Ritual, Politics, and Power, Yale Univ Press, 88; coauth, Family, Political Economy and Demographic Change, Univ Wisconsin Press, 89; auth, Sacrificed for Honor: Italian Infant Abandonment and the Polics of Reproductive Control, Beacon Press, 93; auth, Politics and Symbols: The Italian Communist Party and the Fall of Communism, Yale Univ Press, 96; The Kidnapping of Edgardo Mortara, Knopf, 97; co-ed, Aging in the Past: Demography, Society, and Old Age, Univ of Calif Press, 95; coed, Italian Politics, 1996, Il Mulino, 96; coed, Anthropological Demography: Towards a New Synthesis, Univ of Chicago Press, 97. **CONTACT ADDRESS** Dept of Anthropology, Brown Univ, Box 1921, Providence, RI 02912. **EMAIL** David_Kertzer@brown.edu

KETEKU, OHENEBA E.
PERSONAL Born 07/05/1949, Hollywood, CA, s **DISCIPLINE** SOCIOLOGY **EDUCATION** Univ Calgary, PhD, 81. **CAREER** asst prof, assoc prof, Univ Nairobi, 82-; vis schl, Temple Univ, 92-94; adj prof, Univ Hartford, 94-. **RESEARCH** African pre-history; human origins; slavery and Colonial America; the urban phenomenon. **SELECTED PUBLICATIONS** Auth, The History of Akwamu, Africa World Press, 86; auth, The Archaeology of Ghana, Africa World Press, 88; auth, Ethnocentrism: An African Royal Heritage, African World Press, 88; auth, Jurisprudence: De Legibus of Universality, Macmillan Pubs, 91; The Prince II: An African Royal Heritage, African World Press, 91. **CONTACT ADDRESS** Dept Sociology, Univ of Hartford, 200 Bloomfield Ave, West Hartford, CT 06117-1545.

KETT, JOSEPH FRANCIS
PERSONAL Born 03/11/1938, Brooklyn, NY, m, 1965, 2 children **DISCIPLINE** AMERICAN HISTORY, HISTORY OF EDUCATION **EDUCATION** Holy Cross Col, AB, 59; Harvard Univ, MA, 60, PhD (hist), 64. **CAREER** Instr hist, Harvard Univ, 65-66; from asst prof to assoc prof, 66-76, prof hist, Univ VA, 76-, mem panel on youth, President's Sci Adv Coun, 71-72, chair, hist dept, 85-90. **MEMBERSHIPS** Orgn Am Hist. **RESEARCH** American social and intellectual history; history of education. **SELECTED PUBLICATIONS** Auth, The Formation of the American Medical Profession, Yale Univ, 68; Adolescence and youth in nineteenth century America, J Interdisciplinary Hist, 71; Growing up in rural New England, 1800-1840, in: Anonymous Americans, Prentice-Hall, 72; Rites of Passage: Adolescence in America, 1790 to the Present, Basic Bk, 77; The perils of precocity, in: Turning Points, Univ Chicago Press, 78; The Adolescence of Vocational Education, Stanford Univ Press, 82; The Pursuit of Knowledge Under Difficulties: From Self Improvement to Adult Education in America, 1750-1990, Stanford Univ Press, 94; co-auth, The Enduring Vision: A History of the American People, Houghton Mifflin, 96; Dictionary of Cultural Literacy, 93. **CONTACT ADDRESS** Dept of History, Univ of Virginia, 1 Randall Hall, Charlottesville, VA 22903-3244. **EMAIL** jfk9v@virginia.edu

KEYS, CHRISTOPHER
PERSONAL Born New York, NY **DISCIPLINE** PSYCHOLOGY **EDUCATION** Oberlin Col, BA, 68; Univ Cincinnati, MA, 71; Phd, 73. **CAREER** Chair, 99-; Prof of Psychology and of Disability and Human Development, 89-; Assoc Prof of Psychology, 78-89; Asst Prof of Psychology, 73-78. **HONORS AND AWARDS** President, Society for Community Research and Action, 93-94; Fellow, Am Psychological Assoc; Chair, Council of Community Psychology Program Directors, 85-87. **MEMBERSHIPS** Amer Psychological Assoc; Amer Assoc in Mental Retardation; Midwestern Psychological Assoc. **RESEARCH** Empowerment of persons wit disabilities and their families. **SELECTED PUBLICATIONS** Auth, "Researching community Psychology: Issues of theory and Methods," by Tolan, P., Keys, C., Chertok, F., & Jason, L. Eds., Washington D.C.: American Psychological Association; auth, "Developing social competencies for recruiting help; An intervention with adjudicated male youths with disabilities," by Balcazar, F., & Keys, C., & Grarate, J., Rehabilitation and Special Education, 16, 237-246; auth, "Advocate development in developmental disabilities: A data-based conceptual model," Mental Retardation, 34, 341-351; auth, Using collaborative advocacy to foster intergroup cooperation: A joint insider-outsider investigation," Human Relations, 49, 701-733; auth, "The community living attitudes scale, mental retardation form: Development and psycometric properties, Mental Retardation, 34, 149-158; auth, "Awareness, action, and collaboration: How the self-advocacy movement is empowering for persons with developmental disabilities," Mental Retardation, 34, 312-319; auth, "Gender and relationship variables as predictors of sexual attraction in cross-sex platonic friendships between young heterosexual adults," Journal of Social and Personal Relationships, 14, 191-206. **CONTACT ADDRESS** Dept Psychology, Univ of Illinois, Chicago, 1007 W Harrison 1009, Chicago, IL 60607.

KEYS, PAUL
PERSONAL Born 03/21/1940, St Louis, MO, m, 1998, 2 children **DISCIPLINE** SOCIAL WORK **EDUCATION** St. Louis Univ, BS, 61; MSW, 71; Univ Wis Milwaukee, PhD, 83. **CAREER** Prof, CUNY, 83-94; assoc prof, PACE Univ, 84-94; assoc provost, prof, dean, SE Mo State Univ. **HONORS AND AWARDS** Fel, Wood Wilson Nat Found, 71; Martin Luther King, Jr. Fel, 71; Fel, Nat Urban League, 71; Outstanding Young Men of Am, 75; HEW Fel, 77; Omega Psi Phi Comm Serv Awd, Fla, 77; Council on Social Work Educ Minority Res Fel, 80; GARIO/Fulbright Sr Res Nissan Grant, 90-91; Alumni Distinguished Serv Awd, St. Louis Univ, 96. **MEMBERSHIPS** Nat Advisory Council, Nat Network for Social Work Managers; Prevent Child Abuse Mo; Comm Counseling Center of SE Mo; GARIAO/Fulbright Alumni Assoc; Emmett and Mary Doerr Center for Social Justice, Ed and Res; SE Mo Week and Seed, Inc. **RESEARCH** Public and non-profit management, C.E.O. and executive development, community and social development, public social policy. **SELECTED PUBLICATIONS** Coauth, New Management in Human Service, Nat Assoc of Social Workers, (Wash, DC), 88; auth, "Contemporary Trends in American Social Work", Annual Report of the Social Work Res Inst, 26 (92); coauth, "Performance Characteristics of American Mental Health, Social Services, and Corrections C.E.O.'s", Admin in Social Work 17 (93); ed, School Social Workers in the Multicultural Environment - New Roles, Responsibilities, and Educational Enrichment, Haworth Pr, NY), 94; auth, "Management by Walking Around" in Social Work Executive, 95; auth, "Managing for Quality" in Encycl of Social Work, 19th Ed (Wash, DC: Nat Assoc of Social Workers, 95); coauth, New Management in Human Service, Nat Assoc of Social Workers (Wash, DC), 95; auth, "American Management - the Long and Torturous Path from Theory X", Social Work Executive 13.1 (98); auth, "Beyond Skills: What Followers Expect from Leaders", Social Work Executive 13.2 (98):1; auth "The Betrayal of TQM in Western Management: Managed Health Care and Provider Stress", Jour of Family and Community Health, 21.2 (98). **CONTACT ADDRESS** Col Health and Human Services, Southeast Missouri State Univ, 1 Univ Plaza, Mail Stop 8000, Cape Girardeau, MO 63701.

KHOPKAR, ASHA D.
PERSONAL Born 11/10/1949, Gujrath, India, m, 1973, 2 children **DISCIPLINE** SOCIOLOGY **EDUCATION** Univ Pune, BA, 70; MA, 72; PhD, 82. **CAREER** Reader and Dept Chair, Fergusson Col, 74-94; Assoc Prof, Bennett Col, 95-. **MEMBERSHIPS** NC Sociol Asn; Indian Sociol Soc. **RESEARCH** Population studies; Fertility related to Status of Women; Economic Devlopment. **CONTACT ADDRESS** Dept Sociol & Soc Work, Bennett Col, 900 E Washington, Greensboro, NC 27401. **EMAIL** ashakhopkar@yahoo.com

KIAH, RUTH JOSEPHINE
PERSONAL Born 04/16/1927, Elkhart, IN, m, 1980 **DISCIPLINE** EDUCATION **EDUCATION** Wayne State University, Detroit, MI, BS, 1948, MEd, 1954, EdD, 1975. **CAREER** Mercy Col Reading Methods Course, instr, 66-67, consultant, 62-74, facilitator of change needs assessment trainer & problem analysis for school staff, 74-83; Detroit Public Schools, Office of Adult Cont Educ, coordinator, 67-72, dept of staff devel & tchr training, tchr corps coordinator, 72-; teacher, Detroit Public Schools MGT Academy, on camera teacher reading, 62-67, WTVS 56; administrative asst, 68-84; Wayne State University, Detroit, MI, executive director of Detroit Center for Professional Growth and Develpopment, 84-, adjunct associate professor, 85-. **HONORS AND AWARDS** Awd in recognition & of creativity pioneering spirit & serv to youth Womens Fellowship & Youth Ministry Plymouth United Ch of Christ Detroit 1971; Quarterly Publications Professional Development Programs with Thematic Inservice Modules 1984-; A Multi Faceted Approach to Staff Development and Its Relationship to Student Achievement 1975; Distinguished Contribution to Field Reading Instruction, Wayne County Reader Assn, 1988; Distinguished Alumna, Wayne State University, 1988; Outstanding Service Awd, Friends International Institute, 1990. **MEMBERSHIPS** Mem Women's Economic Club, 1982; board of directors, membership chairperson, secretary, 1978-91, Friends International Institute; board of directors Michigan Coalition of Staff Development and School Improvement 1987-92; board of directors Effective Instruction Consortium 1987-91; mem Assn of Supervisors and Curriculum, 1980-; mem Phi Delta Kappa, Wayne State University Chapter 1985-; executive board, Michigan Coalition for Staff Development and School Improvement, 1984-; faculty advisory/member, Phi Lambda Theta, 1986-. **SELECTED PUBLICATIONS** Author of several books. **CONTACT ADDRESS** Detroit Ctr for Prof Growth & Devel, Wayne State Univ, 114 College of Education, Detroit, MI 48202.

KIDWELL, R. JAY
PERSONAL Born 10/25/1958, Abilene, TX, m, 1981, 4 children **DISCIPLINE** PSYCHOLOGY **EDUCATION** Northern Ky Univ, BA, 85; Univ Cincinnati, MA, 89; Union Inst, PhD, 97. **CAREER** Assoc prof, Cincinnati Bible Col & Sem, 89-. **SELECTED PUBLICATIONS** Auth, Instinctive Archery Insists: Secret from Sports Psychology; various magazine articles on sports psychology. **CONTACT ADDRESS** Dept General Ed, Cincinnati Bible Col and Sem, 2700 Glenway Ave, Cincinnati, OH 45204. **EMAIL** Jay.Kidwell@cincybible.edu

KIERSTEAD, FRED P.
PERSONAL Born 03/14/1943, Red Bank, NJ, s **DISCIPLINE** EDUCATION **EDUCATION** Wideuer Univ, BA, 65; West Chester State Univ, MEd, 66; Univ Okla, PhD, 74. **CAREER** Special instr, Univ Okla, 72-74; sr educ officer, Ministry of Educ, Nigeria, 74-75; prof, Univ Houston, Clear Lake, 75-.

HONORS AND AWARDS PDK Outstanding Teacher Awd, Univ of Okla, 74; Outstanding Service Awd, Univ Houston, Clear Lake, 83; Fulbright Scholar, Egypt, 88; Awd of Merit, Southern Futures Soc, 96. **MEMBERSHIPS** POK, AESA, Southern Futures Soc, World Futures Soc, Soc of Philos and Hist of Educ. **RESEARCH** Future of education, ethics in teaching, philosophy of education. **SELECTED PUBLICATIONS** Coauth, The Ethical, Legal and Multicultural Foundations of Teaching, Madison, WI: Wm C. Brown Co (93); auth, "Cases #1, Case of Plagarism, " "Case #7, Grading Practices," and "Case #9, Quest for Tenure," in The Culture of Higher Education: A Case Study Approach, ed. J. Van Patten (NY: Univ Press Am, 96); auth, "Age-Free, Time-Free and Location-Free Education and the Need for Moral Dialogue," in J. Arters, ed, Creating Preferable Futures: For Whom?, Murfeesburo, TN: Southern Future Soc, Vol 19 (96); auth, "Tenure: An Ethical Retrospective and Prospective for University Faculty," in J. Van Patten, ed, Watersheds in Higher Education, Lewiston: Edwin Mellon Press (97); auth, "Are Our Schools Moral Wastelands?," in D. Snellgrove, ed, J of Educ Philos and Hist, Vol 48, No 1 (Spring 97); auth, "A Future of Tolerance, Patience and Compassion in Education," Southern Futures Soc J, Vol 20 (Nov 97); auth, "Teaching: What's the Moral?," J of Educ Philos and Hist, Vol 49, No 1 (Spring 98). **CONTACT ADDRESS** Dept Foundations of educ, Univ of Houston, Clear Lake, 2700 Bay area Blvd, Houston, TX 77058. **EMAIL** kierstead@cl.uh.edu

KIJNE, HUGO
PERSONAL Born 03/13/1951, Bussum, Holland, m, 1990, 1 child **DISCIPLINE** EDUCATION **EDUCATION** Delft Univ, PhD, 90. **CAREER** Admin dir CIBER, Rutgers Univ, 95-98; Director Div of Ext Educ Prog, Rutgers, 98-. **HONORS AND AWARDS** Res Scholar, Nat Org for Sci Res, 86. **MEMBERSHIPS** Am Management Asn, Univ Cont Educ Asn. **RESEARCH** Organizational theory; Organizational behaviour. **SELECTED PUBLICATIONS** Auth, Scientific Management, T.W. Taylor's Gift to the World?, Uluwer Academic Pub, 96. **CONTACT ADDRESS** Dir of Cont Educ, Rutgers, The State Univ of New Jersey, Newark, 180 Univ Ave, Newark, NJ 07102-1803.

KILPATRICK, THOMAS L.
PERSONAL Born 11/27/1937, Springville, TN, s **DISCIPLINE** HIGHER EDUCATION **EDUCATION** Vanderbilt Univ, PhD, 82 **CAREER** Asst educ librn, 64-75, Ill Librn, 75-1993; ACCESS SVCS LIBRN, 92-, SOUTHERN ILL UNIV, CARBONDALE. **HONORS AND AWARDS** Ill Asn Col, Res Librs Acad Librn Year, 98; MCB Univ Press Awd Exc, 97; SO Ill Univ Libr Aff Outstanding Fac Awd. **MEMBERSHIPS** ALA, Ill Lib Asn. **RESEARCH** Ill lit, libr resource sharing; libr computer applications. **SELECTED PUBLICATIONS** Auth, Illinois! Illinois! An Annotated Bibliography of Fiction: A Twenty-Year Supplement, 1976-1996; Ill State Libr, 98; auth, Microcomputers and Libraries: A Bibliographic Sourcebook, 1986-1989, Scarecrow Press, 90; co-auth, Cutting Out the Middle- Man: Patron-Initiated Interlibrary Loans, Library Trends 46, Oct 98; auth, A Critical Look at the Availability of Gay and Lesbian Periodical Literature in Libraries and Standard Indexing Services, Serials Rev 22, Winter 96; co-auth, Serial Cuts and Interlibrary Loan: Filling in the Gaps, Interlending & Document Supply 24, no 1, 96; auth, Tales of the Windy City, Libr J 120, June 95. **CONTACT ADDRESS** 106 S Mark Ct, Carbondale, IL 62901. **EMAIL** tkilpatr@lib.siu.edu

KIM, ELAINE
PERSONAL Born 02/26/1942, New York, NY, d, 1 child **DISCIPLINE** CULTURAL STUDIES **EDUCATION** Univ Pa, BA, 63; Columbia Univ, MA, 65; Univ Calif Berkeley, PhD, 76. **CAREER** Asst Prof to Prof and Assoc Dean, Univ Calif at Berkeley, 76-. **HONORS AND AWARDS** Fulbright Grant, 87-88; Rockefeller Fel, 92; Hon Doctorate in Humane Letters, Univ Mass, 95; Global Korea Awd, 98; 100 Most Influential Asian Am of the 1990s Awd, 99. **MEMBERSHIPS** Asian Immigrant Women Advocates; AAAS; ASA. **RESEARCH** Asian American Cultural Studies; Interracial Conflict and Collaboration; Literature and Visual Culture; Korean American History and Culture. **SELECTED PUBLICATIONS** Auth, "Home is Where the Han Is: A Korean American Perspective on the Los Angeles Upheavals," in Reading Rodney King/Reading Urban Uprising, Routledge, 93; co-ed, Writing Self, Writing Nation: Four Essays on Theresa Hak Kyung Cha's DICTEE, Third Woman Press, 94; co-ed, East to America: Korean American Life Stories, The New Press, 96; auth, "Bad Women: Asian American Visual Artists Hanh Thi Pham, Hung Liu, and Yong Soon Min," Feminist Studies, (96): 573-601; auth, "Korean American Literature," in An Interethnic companion to Asian American Literature, (Cambridge Univ Press, 97), 156-191; co-ed, Making More Waves: New Writing By Asian American Women, Beacon Press, 97; co-ed, "New formations, new questions: Asian American Studies, 97; co-ed, Dangerous Women: Gender and Korean Nationalism, Routledge, 98; co-ed, Korean American Cultural Production, 99. **CONTACT ADDRESS** Dept Ethnic Studies, Univ of California, Berkeley, 506 Barrows Hall, Berkeley, CA 94720-2570. **EMAIL** ehkim@uclink4.berkeley.edu

KIM, KWANG CHUNG
PERSONAL Born 06/02/1937, Seoul, Korea, m, 1972, 1 child **DISCIPLINE** SOCIOLOGY **EDUCATION** Yonsei Univ, BA, 61; Ind Univ, MA, 65; PhD,72. **CAREER** Prof, Western Ill Univ. **HONORS AND AWARDS** Res Grant, Nat Inst of Ment Health, 78-80; Res Grant, Nat Inst of Ment Health, 86-88. **MEMBERSHIPS** Am Sociol Asn. **RESEARCH** Korean and other Asian Americans: Their Experience in the United States. **SELECTED PUBLICATIONS** Ed, Koreans in the Hood: Conflict with African Americans, Johns Hopkins Univ Press, 99. **CONTACT ADDRESS** Dept Anthrop and Sociol, Western Illinois Univ, 332 S Wesley, Oak Park, IL 60302.

KIM-RENAUD, YOUNG-KEY
DISCIPLINE LANGUAGE, LINGUISTICS, & CULTURE **EDUCATION** Ewha Woman's Univ, BA, 63; Univ Calif at Berkeley, MA, 65; Inst des Professeurs de Francais a l'Etranger at Univ de Paris, Diploma in French, 66; Univ Haw, PhD, 74. **CAREER** Asst prog dir for Ling, U.S. Nat Sci Found, 78-79; vis lectr, Dept of E Asian Lang and Civilizations at Harvard Univ, 86-87; from asst professorial lectr to prof, The George Wash Univ, 83-. **HONORS AND AWARDS** Phi Kappa Phi, 75-; Fulbright Awds, 85, 94, & 97-98; Phi Beta Delta, 93; Achievement Awd, Int Asn of Korean Language Educ, 99. **MEMBERSHIPS** Ling Soc of Am, Int Circle of Korean Ling, Ling Soc of Korea, Korean Lang Asn, Korean Lang Soc, Int Asn for Korean Lang Educ, Asn for Asian Studies, The Asia Soc, The Korea Club, The Phonological Soc of Korea, The Fulbright Asn. **RESEARCH** Theoretical and Applied Linguistics (Phonology, Historical Linguistics, Sociolinguistics, Second Language Acquisition, Syntax, Language Pedagogy), Literary Translation: Intercultural Communication. **SELECTED PUBLICATIONS** Ed, King Sejong the Great: The Light of Fifteenth Century Korea, Int Circle of Korean Ling (Washington, DC), 92 & 97; ed, Theoretical Issues in Korean Linguistics, Ctr for the Study of Lang and Info at Stanford Univ, 94; ed, The Korean Alphabet: Its History and Structure, Univ of Haw Press (Honolulu, HI), 97; co-ed, "Creation and Re-Creation: Modern Korean Fiction and Its Translation," Sigur Center Asia papers 8 (00). **CONTACT ADDRESS** Dept Asian Lang & Lit, The George Washington Univ, 801 22nd St, NW, Washington, DC 20052. **EMAIL** kimrenau@gwu.edu

KIMBALL, GAYLE H.
PERSONAL Born 06/12/1943, Los Angeles, CA, s, 1 child **DISCIPLINE** SOCIOLOGY **EDUCATION** Univ Calif, Berkeley, BA; teaching credential, UCB; Univ Calif at Los Angeles, MA; UCSB, MA, PhD. **CAREER** History teacher, LA City Schs; part-time instr, CSU, Northridge; teaching asst, UCSB; prof of Women's Studies and Sociol, CSU, Chico; teacher and dir, Earth Haven: Center for Spiritual Enrichment. **SELECTED PUBLICATIONS** Auth, 21st Century Families: Blueprints for Family-Friendly Workplaces, Schools and Governments, Equality Press; auth, The Teen Trip: The Complete Resource Guide, Equality Press; auth, 50/50 Parenting, Lexington Books; 50/50 Marriage, Beacon Press; ed, Everything You Need to Know to Succeed After College, Equality Press; auth, How to Survive Your Parents' Divorce, Equality Press; ed, Women's Culture, Scarecrow Press; auth, The Religious Ideas of Harriet Beecher Stowe, Mellin Press. **CONTACT ADDRESS** Dept Women's Studies, California State Univ, Chico, 400 W 1st St, Chico, CA 95929-0001. **EMAIL** gkimball@csuchico.edu

KIMMEL, RICHARD H.
PERSONAL Born Dayton, OH **DISCIPLINE** ANTHROPOLOGY AND ARCHAEOLOGY **EDUCATION** Univ NC, anthrop, MA, 78. **CAREER** Archaeol, US Army Corps of Engineers. **MEMBERSHIPS** Soc for Hist Archaeol; Southeastern Archaeol Conf. **RESEARCH** Mid-Atlantic and southeast U.S. historical archaeology, ecology and climate. **SELECTED PUBLICATIONS** Papers, Notes on the Cultural Origins and Functions of Sub-Floor Pits, Hist Archaeol, 27, 3, 102-113, 93; Estimating Magnetic Anomaly Sampling Fractions in Underwater Archaeology: Resolving Funding and Date Limitations, Underwater Archaeol Proceedings: Soc for Hist Archaeol Conf, 90-93, 90; Mitigating the Federal Review Process: A Preliminary Formulation of Data Contexts for the Ecological Interpretation of Small Craft, Underwater Archaeol Proceedings: Soc for Hist Archaeol Conf, 64-70, 89; Introduction to the Symposium: Current Research and Management Perspectives on Confederate Maritime Trade, Underwater Archaeol Proceedings: Soc for Hist Archaeol Conf, 19, 85. **CONTACT ADDRESS** US Army Corps Engineers, Environmental Resources Branch, PO Box 1890, Wilmington, NC 28402-1890.

KING, C. RICHARD
PERSONAL Born 02/02/1968, Manhattan, KS, m, 1992, 2 children **DISCIPLINE** SOCIOLOGY **EDUCATION** Univ Kansas, BA, 90; MA, 92; Univ Ill, PhD, 96. **CAREER** Asst prof, Drake Univ, 96-. **MEMBERSHIPS** AAA; NAES; NASSS. **RESEARCH** Race; postcolonial studies; Native American; ethnic relations; cultural politics and representation. **SELECTED PUBLICATIONS** Auth, "Segregated Stories: The Colonial Contours of the Little Bighorn Battlefield National Monument," in Dressing in Feathers: Images of Native Americans in American Popular Culture, ed. S Elizabeth Bird (Boulder: Westview Press, 96), 167-180; auth, "The Siren Scream of Telesex: Speech, Seduction, and Simulation," J Popular Culture 30 (96): 91-101; auth, "Surrounded by Indians: The Exhibition of Comanche and the Predicaments of Representing Native American History," in Representing Native American History, The Public Historian 18 (96): 37-51; auth, "Choreographing Colonialism: Athletic Mascots, (Dis)Embodied Indians, and Euro American Subjectivities," Cultural Studies: A Research Annual 5 (00); ed, Dislocating Postcoloniality, Relocating American Empire, Univ Ill Press (Urbana), 00; auth, "Fighting Spirits: The Racial Politics of Sports Mascots," J Sport Social Issues (00); coauth, "Race, Power, and Representation in Contemporary American Sports," in Multiculturalism in the United States: Current Issues Contemporary Voices, eds. Peter Kivisto, Georgeanne Rundblad (Pine Forge Press, 00), 161-174; coauth, "Race, Ritual, and Remembrance Embodied: Manifest Destiny and the Symbolic Sacrifice of 'Chief Illiniwek'," in Exercising Power: The Making and Remaking of the Body, eds. Cheryl Cole, John W Loy, Michael A Messner (Albany: State Univ NY Press, 00). **CONTACT ADDRESS** Dept Sociology, Drake Univ, 2507 University Ave, Des Moines, IA 50311. **EMAIL** richard.king@drake.edu

KING, EDITH
PERSONAL Born 07/08/1930, Detroit, MI, m, 2 children **DISCIPLINE** SOCIOLOGY, EDUCATION **EDUCATION** Wayne State Univ, Detroit, EdD. **CAREER** Prof, Univ Denver, 66-. **HONORS AND AWARDS** Phi Beta Kappa; Phi Delta Kappa Res Awd, 92; Outstanding fac mem, Minority Affairs Recognition Awd, Univ Denver, 94; Am Sociol Asn, Nat Sociol Expert on Ed, 94; Res grants, Univ Denver: Office of Internalization, 93-99, 2000; Penrose Lib, Women's Lib Asn, 99; res proj, mem adv comt, 98-2000, coord further res, 2000. **MEMBERSHIPS** Am Sociol Asn, Am Ed Res Asn, Sisterhood is Global Inst, Phi Beta Kappa, Phi Delta Kappa, Comp and Int Ed Soc, Int Peace Res Asn. **RESEARCH** Multiethnic education, ethnic heritage studies, sociology of education, qualitative research methods, international/cross-cultural education. **SELECTED PUBLICATIONS** Auth, Teaching Ethnic Awareness, Scott Foresman (80); coauth with R. P. Cuzzort, Twentieth Century Social Thought, Holt, Rinehart and Winston (89), Chinese transl (94), 5th ed, Harcourt, Brace Pub (95); auth, Teaching Ethnic and Gender Awareness: Methods and Materials for the Elementary School: Kendall/Hunt Pub, Dubuque, Iowa (90); coauth with M. Chipman and Marta Cruz-Janzen, Educating Young Children in a Diverse Society, Allyn & Bacon (94), Instructor's Manual (94); auth, "Early Childhood Education and the Need for Peace-Building," Peace-Building, J of the Peace Ed Comn, Malta, vol 1, no 3, 12-13 (June 96); coauth with S. Nakanishi, "Gakko Soji-Students Cleaning Their Schools: A Curriculum for Social Education," Ed Practice and Theory, J. Nichlas Pub, Australia, vol 19, no 1, 3-13 (97), and in Ed and Society, ed Jos Zajda, James Nicholas Pub (98); auth, "The Hidden Aspects of Social Class in the Lives of Young Children," Ed and Soc, J. Nicholas Australia (June 97); coauth with Eisa Al Balhan, "Peace Education and the Lives of Kuwaiti Children," Multicultural Reaching, vol 16, no 2, 6-9 (spring 98); auth, "Entering the 21st Century: Educators Respond to a Questionnaire About Their Use of Communications Technology," submitted to Ed & Soc, James Nicholas Pubs, Melbourne, Australia (99); auth, Looking Into the Lives of Children: A Worldwide View, James Nicholas Pubs, Melbourne, Australia (99). **CONTACT ADDRESS** Sch Ed Sch Ed, Univ of Denver, 2450 S Vine St, Denver, CO 80210. **EMAIL** eking@du.edu

KING, ORA STERLING
PERSONAL Born 10/15/1931, Delta, AL, m, 1 child **DISCIPLINE** EDUCATION **EDUCATION** Spelman Coll, BA 1954; Atlanta Univ, MA 1969; Univ of Maryland, PhD, 1982. **CAREER** Atlanta Public Schools, teacher/instructional coord, 54-72; Federal City Coll, reading dept chair, 75-78; Univ of the District of Columbia, asst prof of educ, 78-81; Coppin State Coll, prof & dept chair of C&I, 81-88, dean Division of Education, 88-90, dean, Division of Education and Graduate Studies, 90-91, Prof of Education, Coord of Masters of Arts in Teaching, 91-; prof emeritus, 99. **HONORS AND AWARDS** Mem editorial adv bd Reading World Coll Reading Assn 1982-84; mem US Delegation to the People's Republic of China US China Scientific Exchange 1985; twenty articles published in educational journals 1979-92.received NAFEO Distinguished Alumni Awd, 1988; Fulbright Scholarship Recipient, Monrovia, Liberia, 1988. **MEMBERSHIPS** 1st vice pres Natl Alumnae Assn of Spelman Coll 1982-86; mem editorial adv bd Innovative Learning Strategies Intl Reading Assn 1985-86; pres Natl Alumnae Assn of Spelman Coll 1986-88; mem Alpha Kappa Alpha Iota Lambda Chap; president Columbia Chapter NAASC 1990-95. **SELECTED PUBLICATIONS** Published textbook Reading & Study Skills for the Urban College Student, Kendall/Hunt Publ 1984, 1988, 2nd ed. **CONTACT ADDRESS** Education, Coppin State Col, 2500 W North Ave, Baltimore, MD 21216.

KING, ROBERTA R.
PERSONAL Born 07/05/1949, CA, s **DISCIPLINE** MUSIC, MISSIOLOGY, ANTHROPOLOGY, ETHNOMUSICOLOGY **EDUCATION** Univ Calif Santa Barbara, BA, 72; Univ Ore, M Mus, 76, Fuller Theol Sem, MA, 82; PhD, 89. **CAREER** Lectr, Daustar Univ, Kenya, 78-99; ethnomusicologist, CBI Int, 82-99; Fuller Theol Sem, 00-. **HONORS AND AWARDS** David

Allen Hubbard Awd, Fuller Sem; Regent Scholar, Univ of Calif. **MEMBERSHIPS** Soc for Ethnomusicology. **RESEARCH** African music, Communication (intercultural), ethnomusicology, Anthropology. **SELECTED PUBLICATIONS** Auth, Pathways in Christian Music Communication, Fuller Theol Sem, (Pasadena, CA), 89; auth, A Time to Sing, Evangel Pub (Nairobi, Kenya), 99. **CONTACT ADDRESS** School of World Mission, Fuller Theol Sem, 135 N Oakland Ave, Pasadena, CA 91182-0001. **EMAIL** rking@fuller.edu

KINSELLA, SUSAN
PERSONAL Born 09/10/1955, PA, m, 1978, 2 children **DISCIPLINE** SOCIAL WORK **EDUCATION** Penn State Univ, BA; Marywood Univ, MSW; Fordham Univ, PhD. **CAREER** Col prof, 85-2000; coordr of Practicum Ed, Marywood Univ, 85-90; coordr of BS Sociology, Social Service emphasis, Ga Southern Univ, 99-. **MEMBERSHIPS** Nat Asn Social Workers, Nat Asn for Human Service Ed. **RESEARCH** Child and family. **SELECTED PUBLICATIONS** Coauth with Norma Feinberg, "Satisfaction with Day Care Services," Pa Dept of Public Welfare, Northeast Region (80); coauth with Terry Singer, "Continuing Education Model to Address the Needs of the Part-Time Social Work Education Missing Link--the Practicum Instructor," Topics, 3, 1 (86): 19-25; coauth with Joanne Whelley, "Hill Congregations Housing Survey," The Scranton Times (Jan 90); coauth with Roslyn Chernesky, "Administrative Models in Profit and Non-Profit Child Care Agencies," Child and Youth Care Quart (spring 90); auth, "The Relationship Between Cosmopolitan and Local Orientation and Job Competency of Child Protective Service Workers," Dissertation Abstracts (91); auth, "A Comparative Cross-Discipline Study of Traditional and Nontraditional College Students," The J of Col Students , 32, 4 (winter 98); auth of classroom materials and exercises pub in Instructor's Guide, Days in the Lives of Social Workers, L. Grobman, White Hat Commun, Harrisburg, Pa (99). **CONTACT ADDRESS** Georgia So Univ, Dept Anthropol & Sociol, PO Box 8052, Stateboro, GA 30460. **EMAIL** skinsell@gsix2.cc.gason.edu

KINTIGH, KEITH W.
PERSONAL Born 05/19/1951, Kansas City, MO, m, 1988, 1 child **DISCIPLINE** ANTHROPOLOGY **EDUCATION** Stanford Univ, BA, 74, MS, 74; Univ Michigan, PhD, 82. **CAREER** Assoc archeol, Ariz State Mus, Univ Ariz, 80-85; asst, assoc prof, anthrop, Univ Calif, Santa Barbara, 85-87; res assoc, Zuni Archeol Prog, 86- ; assoc and prof, Dept Anthrop, Ariz State Univ, 87- . **HONORS AND AWARDS** Pres recognition Awd, Soc for Am Archeol, 91, 95, 97. **MEMBERSHIPS** Am Anthrop Asn; Ariz Archeol and Hist Soc; Ariz Archeol Coun; Sigma Xi; Soc for Am Archeol. **SELECTED PUBLICATIONS** Coauth, Archaeological Settlement Pattern Data from the Chalco, Zochimilco, Ixtapalapa, Texcoco and Zumpango Regions, Mexico, Univ Mich, 83; auth, Settlement, Subsistence, and Society in Late Zuni Prehistory, Univ Ariz, 85; coauth, Demographic Alternatives: Consequences for Current Models of Southwestern Prehistory, in Gumerman, ed, Understanding Complexity in the Prehistoric Southwest, Addison Wesley, 94; coauth, Processes of Aggregation in the Prehistoric Southwest, in Gumerman, ed, Themes in Southwest Prehistory, Sch of Am Res Press, 94; auth, Chaco, Communal Architecture, and Cibolan Aggregation, in Wills, ed, The Ancient Southwestern Community: Methods and Models for the Study of Prehistoric Social Organizations, New Mexico, 94; auth, Contending with Contemporaneity in Settlemant Pattern Studies, Am Antiquity, 94; auth, A Test of the Relationship between Site Size and Population, Am Antiquity, 96; auth, Post-Chacoan Social Integration at the Hinkson Site, New Mexico, Kiva, 96; coauth, Archaeological Identification of Kin Groups Using Mortuary and Biological Data: An Example from the American Southwest, Am Antiquity, 96; coauth, Ceramic Seriation and Site Reoccupation in Lowland South America, Latin Am Antiquity, 96; coauth, Determining Gender and Kinship at Hawikku: A Reply to Corruccini, Am Antiquity, 98. **CONTACT ADDRESS** Dept of Anthropolgy, Arizona State Univ, MC 2402, Tempe, AZ 85287. **EMAIL** keith.kintigh@asu.edu

KINTSCH, WALTER
PERSONAL Born 05/30/1932, Romania, m, 1959, 2 children **DISCIPLINE** PSYCHOLOGY **EDUCATION** Univ Kans, MA, 57; PhD, 60. **CAREER** Teacher, Vorarlberg Austria, 51-55; asst prof to assoc prof, Univ Mo, 61-65; assoc prof, Univ Calif Riverside, 65-68; vis assoc prof, Stanford Univ, 67-68; vis sci, Max Planck Inst, Munich, 91-92; prof, Univ Colo, 68-. **HONORS AND AWARDS** Distinguished Sci Contribution Award, Am Psychol Asn, 92; Nat Acad of Educ, 92. **MEMBERSHIPS** Am Psychol Asn; Am Psychol Soc; Psychonomic Soc; Cognitive Sci Soc. **RESEARCH** Psychology of language. **SELECTED PUBLICATIONS** Co-auth, "Planning routine computing tasks: Understanding what to do," Cognitive Sci, (91): 305-342; co-auth, "A theory of word algebra problem comprehension and its implications for the design of learning environments," Cognition and Instruction, (92): 329-389; auth, "Text comprehension, memory, and learning," Am Psychol, (94): 294-303; co-auth, "Long-term working memory," Psychol Rev, (95): 211-245; co-auth, "Are good texts always better? Interactions of text coherence, background knowledge, and levels of understanding in learning from text," Cognition and Instruction, (96): 1-43; auth, Comprehension: A paradigm for cognition, Cambridge Univ Press, 98. **CONTACT ADDRESS** Dept Psychol, Univ of Colorado, Boulder, Campus PO Box 345, Boulder, CO 80309-0345. **EMAIL** wkintsch@psych.colorado.edu

KIPP, RITA
PERSONAL Born 04/04/1948, Wilburton, OK, m, 1969, 3 children **DISCIPLINE** ANTHROPOLOGY **EDUCATION** Univ Pittsburg, PhD, 76 **CAREER** Prof, Keyon Coll, 76-present. **HONORS AND AWARDS** Oden Professorship, 00-05. **MEMBERSHIPS** Asian Studies Assn; Amer Anthropological Assn. **RESEARCH** Cultural Anthropology; Religion; Ethnicity **SELECTED PUBLICATIONS** Co-ed, Indonesian Religions in Transition, Univ of AZ Press, 87; The Early Years of a Dutch Colonial Mission: The Karo Field, Univ of Mich Press, 90; Dissociated Identities: Ethnicity, Religion, and Class in an Indonesian Society, Univ of Mich Press, 93. **CONTACT ADDRESS** Dept of Anthropology and Sociology, Kenyon Col, Gambier, OH 43022. **EMAIL** kipp@kenyon.edu

KIPPER, DAVID A.
PERSONAL Born 03/24/1939, Tel-Aviv, Israel, m, 2 children **DISCIPLINE** PSYCHOLOGY **EDUCATION** Univ Durham, England, PhD, 69. **CAREER** Prof, Roosevelt Univ. **HONORS AND AWARDS** Past president of : Am Soc of Group Psychotherapy and Psychodrama; Div 49: Group Psychology and Group Psychotherapy, The Am Psychol Asn. **RESEARCH** Group psychotherapy, psychodrama, psychotherapeutic simulations. **SELECTED PUBLICATIONS** Auth, Psychotherapy through clinical role playing, New York: Brunner/Mazel (86); auth, Clinical role playing and psychodrama, Moscow: Kraas (93, in Russian, 96); ed, "New models of psychodrama: A theme series," The Int J of Action Methods: Psychodrama, Skill Training, and Role Playing, 50, 3 (97); co-ed, "Treating trauma survivors," The Int J of Action Methods: Psychodrama, Skill Training, and Role Playing, 51, 2 (98); coauth, "Action methods and the treatment of trauma survivors," The Int J of Action Methods: Psychodrama, Skill Training, and Role Playing, 51 (98): 43-46; auth, "Psychodrama and trauma: Implications for future interventions of psychodramatic role-playing modalities," The Int J of Action Methods: Psychodrama, Skill Training, and Role Playing, 51 (98): 113-121; auth, "L'affermarsi del role playing come forma di psicoterapia," Psychodrama Classico, 1 (99): 75-94; auth, "The changing character of psychodrama: What's next?," in D. Altimay, ed, Psikodrama grup psikoterapisi el kitabi (Handbook of psychodrama group therapy), Istanbul, Turkey: Sistem Yayincilik (in English and Turkish) (2000): 41-1010. **CONTACT ADDRESS** Sch of Psychol, Roosevelt Univ, 430 S Michigan Ave, Chicago, IL 60605. **EMAIL** kipperda@aol.com

KIRCH, PATRICK V.
PERSONAL Born 07/07/1950, Honolulu, HI, m **DISCIPLINE** ANTHROPOLOGY **EDUCATION** Pa Univ, BA, 71; Yale, M Philos, 74, PhD, 75. **CAREER** Affiliate Fac, Univ Hawaii, 79-84; archaeol, Bernice P Bishop Museum, 75-84; prof, Univ Washington, (dir, Burke Muiseum), 84-89; prof anthrop, Univ Calif, Berkeley, 89-; dir, 99-. **HONORS AND AWARDS** Nat Acad Sci, USA, 90; Am Acad Arts & Sci, 92; Fellow, Am Asn for the Advancement of Sci, 96; Carty Awd for the Advan of Sci (NAS), 97; Fellow, Calif Acad of Sci, 97; Fellow, Ctr for Advan Stud in the Behav Sci, 97-98; Am Philos Soc, 98; Staley Prize (Sch Am Res), 98; curator of oceanic archaeol, pa hearst museum of anthrop. **MEMBERSHIPS** AAAS; Am Anthrop Asn; Soc Am Archaeol; Pac Sci Assoc; Sigma Xi; Asn Field Archaeol; Polynesian Soc; Prehist Soc; New Zealand Archaeol Asn 2E. **RESEARCH** Archaeology. **SELECTED PUBLICATIONS** Co-auth, Anahulu: The Anthropology of History in the Kingdom of Hawaii, 92; auth, Legacy of the Landscape, Hawaii, 96; Historical Ecology in the Pacific Islands, Yale, 97; The Lapita Peoples: Ancestors of the Oceanic World, Blackwell, 97; auth, On the Road of the Winds, 00. **CONTACT ADDRESS** Dept of Anthrop, Univ of California, Berkeley, Berkeley, CA 94720.

KIRK, WYATT D.
PERSONAL Born 05/10/1935, Elgin, IL, m **DISCIPLINE** EDUCATION **EDUCATION** Western MI U, BA 1963; Western MI U, MA 1969; Western MI U, EdD 1973; Licensed Psycologist 1978; NBCC 1984. **CAREER** NC A&T State Univ Dept of Human Development & Services, chairperson; Benton Harbor HS, tchr 1963-67; Ft Custer Job Corps, counselor 1967-68; Kalamazoo Pub Sch, counselor 1967-68; Western MI U, counselor 1968-70; Kalamazoo Resources Devel Council, assistance to founder, dir 1968-69; Experimental Program toEmploy Ex-Consult & Drug Users Ford Motor Co Dearborn, consult 1969-71; In-Serv Training Program for Tchr Grand Rapids Pub Sch, consult 1970; Western MI U; assoc prof 1970-78; Staff Relations Kalamazoo Planned Parenthood, consult 1972; Basic Treatment Counseling Techniques for Minorities MI Probate Ct, consult 1975; NC A&T St Univ, professor/chairperson. **HONORS AND AWARDS** MI Personnel & Guidance Assn serv awd 1976; Faculty Research Grant for Scholarly & Creative Research 1977; Presidents Citation, the Natl Assn of Nonwhite Concerns in Personnel & Guidance 1977 & 1978; Assn Counselor Educ & Spvsn recognition awd for successful completion of the Accreditation Workshop Training 1979; grants awds Kalamazoo Fdn Doctoral Research, Grand Rapids Fnd, Title IV Desegregation Inst, Intern, Cmty-Based Alternatives, State of NC, Dept of Human Resources, Managerial Schlrshp Centerfor Creative Leadership, Greensboro, NC; several publications published & non-published. **MEMBERSHIPS** Pres elect Amer Assoc for Counseling Dev; Assn Counselor Educ & Sprvsn; MI Personnel & Guidance Assn; MI Coll Personnel Assn; MI and NC Assn for Non-White Concerns; NC Assn Counselor Educ & Supervision; NC Personnel & Guidance Assn; Assn of Black Psychologists; charter mem MI and mem Natl Alliance of Black School Educ; Kappa Alpha Psi Inc; vice pres NAACP; bd mem, treas Churches United Effort; Equal Empl for the Disadvantaged & Minority chrmn; bd of trustees for the Lift Fdn; Inter-Faith Housing Council bd of dir; Greater Kalamazoo Cncl vice chairperson; Kalamazoo Cnty Substance Abuse bd mem; Greater Kalamazoo United Way Allocation & Budget Committeel editorial bd Journal of Multicultural Counseling and Develop; chairperson NC Assoc for Counseling and-Develop; mem AMCD Comm. **CONTACT ADDRESS** No Carolina Agr and Tech State Univ, 212 Hodgin Hall, Greensboro, NC 27411.

KIRKHART, MATTHEW
PERSONAL Born 06/26/1965, Charleston, WV, d **DISCIPLINE** PSYCHOLOGY **EDUCATION** West Virginia Univ, BA, 87; MA, 91; Univ North Carolina, PhD, 97. **CAREER** Instr, Hih Poi Univ, 95-96; predoc int, Univ Florida, 96-97; asst prof, Loyola Col, 97-. **MEMBERSHIPS** AABT; MABA. **RESEARCH** Learning memory and cognition; adaptation to chronic illness; functional analysis of language; functional analytic psychotherapy; interpersonal psychotherapy. **SELECTED PUBLICATIONS** Auth, "Properties of verbal and nonverbal learning of persons exhibiting schizotypal cognitions," Clin Behav Anal (95): 8-9; auth, "The effects of schizotypal thinking on implicit and explicit learning," forthcoming; auth, The nature of declarative and nondeclarative knowledge in implicit and explicit learning, forthcoming. **CONTACT ADDRESS** Dept Psychology, Loyola Col, 4501 N Charles St, Baltimore, MD 21210. **EMAIL** mkirkhart@loyola.edu

KIRKPATRICK, SUSAN
PERSONAL Born 01/16/1942, Newcastle, WY, 1 child **DISCIPLINE** SPANISH LITERATURE, FEMINIST CRITICISM **EDUCATION** Univ Wyo, BA, 63; Cambridge Univ, MA, 65; Harvard Univ, PhD(comp lit), 72. **CAREER** Instr Span, Brandeis Univ, 70-71; asst prof Span Lit, 71-78, from assoc to prof Span Lit, Univ Calif, San Diego, 78-88. **HONORS AND AWARDS** Guggenheim Fellowship, 86-87. **MEMBERSHIPS** MLA; Int Asn Hispanists; Exec Council 93-96. **RESEARCH** Spanish nineteenth century literature; romanticism. **SELECTED PUBLICATIONS** Auth, From Octavia Santino to El yermo de las almas, Rev Hispanica Mod, Vol 37, 72-73; Tirano Banderas y la estructura de la historian Nueva Rev Filologia Hispanica, Vol 24, 76; Spanish romaniticism and the liberal project: The crisis of Larra, Studies Romanticism, Vol 16, 77; Larra: El laberinto inextricable de un romantics liberal, Gredos, Madrid, 77; The Ideology of Costumbrismo, Ideologies & Lit, Vol 2, No 7; auth, Las Romanticas: Women and Subjectivity in Spain, Univ Calif Pr (Berkeley), 89; auth, Antologia poetica de escritoras del siglo XIX, Castalia (Madrid), 92; On the threshold of the realist novel: Fernan Caballero, Publ Mod Lang Asn; Fantasy, Seduction and the Woman Reader: Rosalia de Castro's Novels, in The Politics/Poetics of Gender, ed. Lou Charnon-Deutsch and Jo Labanyi; New York, Oxford Univ Press, 95; auth, "Constituting the Subject: Race, Gender and Nation in the Early Nineteenth Century," in Culture and the State in Spain, ed. Tom Lewis and Francisco Sanchez (NYork: Garland Pr, 99). **CONTACT ADDRESS** Lit Dept, Univ of California, San Diego, 9500 Gilman Dr, La Jolla, CA 92093-5003. **EMAIL** skirkpatrick@ucsd.edu

KIRSCHENBAUM, HOWARD
PERSONAL Born 10/06/1944, New York, NY, m, 1988, 1 child **DISCIPLINE** EDUCATION **EDUCATION** New School Univ, BA, 66; Temple Univ, Med, 68; Temple Univ, Ed, 75. **CAREER** Pres, Values Associates, 91-97; Prof, Univ Rochester, 1997-. **HONORS AND AWARDS** George Walk Awd, Temple Univ, 80; Humanistic Educator of the Year Awd, Asn Humanistic Educ, 83; Who's Who in Am, 00. **MEMBERSHIPS** Educ Res Asn, Author's Guild, Nat Asn of Partners in Educ, Character Education Partnership. **RESEARCH** Values and education, school, family, community relations **SELECTED PUBLICATIONS** Auth, Wad-Ja-Get? The Grading Game in American Education, 71; Auth, Values Clarification, 72; Auth, Developing Support Groups, 78; Auth, Auth, On Becoming Carl Rogers, biography, 79; Auth, The Carl Rogers Reader, 89; Auth, One Hundred Ways to Enhance Values and Morality in Schools and Youth Settings, 95. **CONTACT ADDRESS** Dept Educ, Univ of Rochester, PO Box 270425, Rochester, NY 14627. **EMAIL** kirs@troi.cc.rochester, edu

KIRSHNER, DAVID
PERSONAL Born 04/29/1950, Montreal, QC, Canada, m, 1993, 2 children **DISCIPLINE** MATHEMATICS EDUCATION **EDUCATION** Concordia Univ, BA, 72; Univ British Columbia, MA, 77, EdD, 87. **CAREER** Asst prof, 87-93, assoc prof, La State Univ, 93-. **HONORS AND AWARDS** 8 doctoral

graduates; Chair of Ed Bd, J for Res in Mathematics Ed, 99-2000; Pres, North Am Chapter of the Int Group for the Psychol of Math Ed. **MEMBERSHIPS** J for Res in Mathematics Ed, North Am Chapter of the Int Group for the Psychol of Math Ed; Psychol of Math Learning. **SELECTED PUBLICATIONS** Auth, "A student centered approach to elementary mathematics education: Four models of instruction in the U. S.," in New Directions for Elementary Mathematics Education: Proceedings of the Association of Elementary Mathematics Education of Cheju Island (97); auth, "Accomplishments and prospects in the psychology of mathematics learning," J of the Korea Soc of Math Ed series D, 1, 1 (97): 13-23; auth, "The situated development of logic in infancy," in, Situated cognition: Social, semiotic, and psychological perspectives, coed with J. Whitson, Mahwah, NJ: Lawrence Erlbaum Assocs (97); coauth with J. Whitson, "Editor's Introduction," in Situated cognition: Social, semiotic, and psychological perspectives, coed with J. Whitson, Mahwah, NJ: Lawrence Erlbaum Assocs (97); coauth with P. K. Jeon, J. S. Pang, and S. S. Park, "Sociomathematical norms of elementary school classrooms: Crossnational perspectives on challenges of reform in mathematics teaching," final report to the res found of the Korea Nat Univ of Ed (98); coauth with J. Whitson, "Obstacles to understanding cognition as situated," Ed Res, 27, 8 (98): 22-28; coauth with J. Whitson, "Situated cognition," in D. A. Gabbard, ed, Knowledge and power in the global economy: Politics and rhetoric of school reform, Mahwah, NJ: Lawrence Erlbaum Assocs (2000); auth, "The structural algebra option revisited," in R. Sutherland and T. Rojano, eds, Algebraic processes and structure, Kluwer Academic Pub (in press); auth, "Exercises, probes, puzzles: A crossdisciplinary typology of school mathematics problems," J of Curric Theorizing, 16, 2 (in press); coauth with D. Simoneaux, "The interference of non-meaningful instruction on students' subsequent meaningful learning," J for Res in Math Ed (in press). **CONTACT ADDRESS** Dept Curric & Instr, La State Univ Baton Rouge, La State Union, Baton Rouge, LA 70803-0001. **EMAIL** dkirsh@lsu.edu

KISSEN, RITA
PERSONAL Born 11/22/1942, Far Rockaway, NY, m, 1990, 4 children **DISCIPLINE** TEACHER EDUCATION **EDUCATION** Cornell Univ, BA, 64; MA, 65; Univ Mass, PhD, 86. **CAREER** Teacher, Am Int Col, 69-75; teacher, Minnechaug Reg High School, 75-83; Wayne State Col, 83-87; Central Mich Univ, 87-90; Univ of Southern Maine, 90-. **HONORS AND AWARDS** Phi Beta Kappa, Cornell, 64. **MEMBERSHIPS** Am Educ Res Assoc; GLSEN; Pi Delta Kappa. **RESEARCH** Lesbian and gay issues in schools, multicultural education, conflict resolution, gender/women's studies. **SELECTED PUBLICATIONS** Auth, "Teaching Under Siege: Gay and Lesbian Educators in Colorado, Idaho and Oregon" in Open Lives, Safe Schools; Addressing Gay and Lesbian Issues in Education, ed Donovan r. Walling, Phi Delta Kappa Educ Found, 96; auth, "Gay and Lesbian Teachers: Forbidden to Care", in Caring in an Unjust World: Negotiating Borders and Boundaries in Schools, ed Deborah Eaker and Jane Van Galen, State Univ of NY Pr, 96; auth, The Last Closet: The Real Lives of Lesbian and Gay Teachers, Heinemann, 96; auth, "Children of the Future Age: Lesbian and Gay Parents Talk about School, in Queering Elementary Education: Advancing the Dialogue About Sexualities and Schooling, eds James t. Sears and Will Letts, Rowman & Littlefield, 99; auth, "Talking to Michelle: Mothering a Lesbian daughter", in Mother Daughter Communication: Voices from the Professions, eds Alice Deakins and Rebecca Bryant Lockridge, (forthcoming). **CONTACT ADDRESS** Dept Teacher Educ, Univ of So Maine, 500 Bailey Hall, Gorham, ME 04038. **EMAIL** kissen@maine.edu

KISTHARDT, WALTER E.
PERSONAL Born 05/13/1953, Hazleton, PA, m, 1976, 3 children **DISCIPLINE** SOCIOLOGY **EDUCATION** Elizabethtown Col, BA, 75; Univ Haw, MSW, 83; Univ Kans, PhD, 97. **CAREER** Res Assoc, Univ Kans, 85-97; Visiting Assoc Prof to Asst Prof, Univ Mo, 98-. **HONORS AND AWARDS** Finalist for Outstanding Doctoral Student, 97. **MEMBERSHIPS** Nat Asn of Soc Workers. **RESEARCH** Social Work and Mental Health. **CONTACT ADDRESS** Dept Sociol, Univ of Missouri, Kansas City, 5100 Rockhill Rd, Kansas City, MO 64110. **EMAIL** kisthardtw@umkc.edu

KITCH, SALLY L.
DISCIPLINE WOMENS STUDIES **EDUCATION** Emory Univ, PhD. **CAREER** Prof, Chair of Women's Studies, Ohio State Univ. **HONORS AND AWARDS** WEEA grant, US Dept of Ed, 76-78; Danforth Found Fel, 80-83; Woodrow Wilson Res Grant in Women's Studies, 83; Nat Women's Studies Asn-Univ of Ill Press Book Awd, 87; NEH Summer Inst, Tutts Univ, 88; Helen Hooven Santmyer Prize in Women's Studies, Ohio State Univ Press, 90; NEH Seminar in Feminist Literary Criticism, Penn State Univ, 91. **RESEARCH** Feminist theory and epistemology, cultural theory, utopian societies and utopianism, women's literature and feminist literary criticism. **SELECTED PUBLICATIONS** Coauth, The Source Book: An Inductive Approach to Composition, NY: Longman, (81); auth, Chaste Liberation: Celibacy and Female Cultural Status, Urbana: Ill Univ Press (89); auth, This Strange Society of Women: Reading the Letters and Lives of the Woman's Commonwealth, Columbus, OH: State Univ Press (93); co-ed with Carol Konek, Women and Careers: Issues and Challenges, Thousand Oaks, CA: Sge Pubs (94); auth, " 'What is the Matter that You Don't Write': Letters as Interdisciplinary Texts, Re-Visioning Knowledge and the Curriculum: Feminist Perspectives, ed Lisa Fine, et al, Mich State Press (97): 103-18; auth, "The Hom(m)osexual Economy and the Opaque Female Persona in the Fiction of Marguerite Yourcenar," Continental, Latin American, and Francophone Women Writers, 1988-1989, Vol 3, Lanham, Md: Univ Press Am, (97): 187-98; auth, "Of Motherlands and Foremothers: African American Women's Texts and the Concept of Relationship," Analyzing the Different Voice, ed Jerilyn Fisher and Ellen Silber, NY: Rowman & Littlefield (98): 141-65; coauth with Judith A. Allen, "Disciplines by Disciplines?: The Need For an Interdisciplinary Research Mission in/and for Women's Studies," Feminist Studies, 24.2 (summer 98): 275-99; auth, "Gender and Utopia: From Promise to Paradox," Critical Terms for Gender Studies, ed Gilbert Herdt and Catharine Stimpson, Univ Chicago Press (forthcoming); auth, On Higher Ground: From Utopianism to Realism in Feminist Thought and Theory, Univ Chicago Press (spring 2000). **CONTACT ADDRESS** Dept Womens Studies, Ohio State Univ, Columbus, 286 University Hall, Columbus, OH 43210.

KIVISTO, PETER J.
PERSONAL Born 11/17/1948, Ishpeming, MI, m, 1973, 2 children **DISCIPLINE** SOCIOLOGY **EDUCATION** Univ Mich, BA, 70; Yale Univ, MDiv, 73; New Sch for Soc Res, MA, 77; PhD, 82. **CAREER** Prof, Augustana Col, 82-. **HONORS AND AWARDS** Fullbright Fel, Center for Advanced Studies, Univ Iowa; Fel Democratic Studies. **MEMBERSHIPS** Am Sociol Asn, Soc for Study of Soc Prob, Midwest Sociol Soc. **RESEARCH** Race and ethnicity, theory, religion. **SELECTED PUBLICATIONS** Auth, Illuminating Social Life, Pine Forge Pr, 98; Auth, Key Ideas in Sociology, Pine Forge Pr, 98; Auth, Social Theory: Roots and Branches, Roxbury Pr, 00; Auth, Multiculturalism in the United States, Pine Forge Pr, 00. **CONTACT ADDRESS** Dept Sociol, Augustana Col, Illinois, 639 38th St, Rock Island, IL 61201. **EMAIL** sokivisto@augustana.edu

KLAHR, DAVID
DISCIPLINE PSYCHOLOGY **EDUCATION** MIT, SB, 60; Carnegie Inst Tech, MS, 75; Carnegie Mellon Univ, PhD, 68. **CAREER** Instr, Carnegie Inst of Tech, 64-66; instr to asst prof, Univ of Chicago, 66-69; assoc prof to prof, Carnegie Mellon Univ, 69-. **HONORS AND AWARDS** Ford Found Fel, 64-66; Grant, NIE, 78-81; Grants, Spencer Found, 84-88; Grants, Nat Sci Found, 86-88, 87; Grant, Mellon Found 89-94; Grants, NICHHD, 89-93, 95-99, 99-04; Grant, McDonnell Found, 96-01. **RESEARCH** Cognitive psychology, especially information processing analysis of cognitive development, problem solving instruction, scientific discovery in children and adults, instructional interventions in science. **SELECTED PUBLICATIONS** Ed, Cognition and instruction, Lawrence Erlbaum Assoc, (Hillsdale, NJ), 76; coauth, Cognitive development: An information processing view, Lawrence Erlbaum Assoc, (Hillsdale, NJ), 76; coed, Production system models of learning and development, MIT Pr, (Cambridge, MA), 87; coed, Complex information processing: The impact of Herbert A. Simon, Lawrence Erlbaum Assoc, (Hillsdale, NJ), 89; coauth, "Solving Induction Problems in Mathematics: Not-so-Trivial PURSUIT", Cognitive Sci, (99); coauth, "All Other Things being Equal: Children's Acquisition of the Control of Variables Strategy", Child Develop 70.5, (99): 1098-1120; coauth, "Studies of Scientific Discovery: Complementary Approaches and Convergent Findings", Psychol Bulletin 125.5 (99): 524-543; auth, Exploring Science: The Cognition and Development of Discovery Processes, MIT Pr, (Cambridge, MA), 00; coauth, "From Cognition to Instruction to Cognition: A Case Study in Elementary School Science Instruction", Designing for Science: Implications from Professional, Instructional, and Everyday Science, eds K. Crowley, C.D. Schunn, and T. Okada, Erlbaum (Mawah, NJ), (forthcoming); coauth, "Cognitive development and science education: Ships passing in the night or beacons of mutual illumination?", Cognition and Instructions: 25 years of progress, eds S.M. Carver and D. Klahr, Erlbaum, (Mawah, NJ), (forthcoming). **CONTACT ADDRESS** Dept Psychol, Carnegie Mellon Univ, 5000 Forbes Ave, Pittsburgh, PA 15213. **EMAIL** klahr@cmu.edu

KLATCH, REBECCA
PERSONAL Born, OH, m, 2 children **DISCIPLINE** SOCIOLOGY **EDUCATION** Univ Calif, BA, 75; Harvard Univ, MA, 80; PhD, 84. **CAREER** Reaching Fel, Harvard Univ, 79-84; Asst Prof, WA Univ, 84-87; Asst Prof to Assoc Prof, Univ Calif Santa Cruz, 87-92; Assoc Prof to Full Prof, Univ Calif San Diego, 92-. **HONORS AND AWARDS** Teaching Awd, Harvard Univ, 82, 83; Victoria Shuck Awd, Am Polit Sci Asn, 88; Fel, Am Asn of Univ Women, 89; Fel, Stanford Humanities Ctr, 89-90; Fel, Rockefeller Foundation, 90-91; Outstanding Prof, Kappa Alpha Theta, 98. **RESEARCH** Sociology of Gender; Social Movements; Qualitative Methods; Sociology of Culture; American Society; Sociology of Family. **SELECTED PUBLICATIONS** Auth, "Of Meanings and Masters: Political Symbolism and Symbolic Action," Polity, (88): 99-110; auth, "the Methodological Problems of studying a Politically Resistant Community," in Studies in Qualitative methodology Vol I, (JAI Press, 88), 73-88;' auth, "The Two worlds of women of the New Right," in Women, Politics and Change, Russell Sage Foundation, 90; auth, "Complexities of Conservatism: How Right-Wing Women Understand the World," in The Re-Centering of America: American Society in Transition, Univ CA Press, 91; auth, "Women of the New Right in the W.U.: Family, Feminism, and Politics," in Identity Politics and Women: Cultural Reassertions and Feminisms in International Perspectives, Westview Press, 93; auth, "The counterculture, the New Left, and the New Right," Qualitative sociology, 94; auth, "The Counterculture, the New Left, and the New Right," in Social Movements and Cultural Politics, Temple Univ Press, 95; auth, "Women and Right-wing Movements," in The Reader's companion to U.S. Women's History, Houghton Mifflin, 98; auth, Women of the New Right, Temple Univ press, 87; auth, A Generation divided: The new Left, The New right, and The 1960s, Univ CA Press, 99. **CONTACT ADDRESS** Dept Sociol, Univ of California, San Diego, 9500 Gilman Dr, La Jolla, CA 92093.

KLECK, ROBERT E.
PERSONAL Born 03/08/1937, Archbold, OH, m, 1959, 2 children **DISCIPLINE** PSYCHOLOGY **EDUCATION** Denison Univ, AB, 59; Stanford Univ, PhD, 63. **CAREER** Postdoc Fel; Stanford Univ, 63-64; asst prof, Williams Col, 64-66; asst prof, Dartmouth Col, 66-69; assoc prof, 69-75; vis res prof, Stanford Univ, 74-75; vis res sci, Maison des Sci de L'Homme, 89; vis schl, Univ Vir, 92-93; prof, Dartmouth Col, 75-; dept ch, 93-99. **HONORS AND AWARDS** Gen Motors Schl; Phi Beta Kappa; Danforth Fel; Sigma Xi; NSF Fel; APS Fel. **RESEARCH** Social psychology of stigma; interpersonal communication processes. **SELECTED PUBLICATIONS** Coauth, "The cues decoders use in attempting to differentiate emotion elicited and posed facial expressions," Euro J Soc Psychol 24 (94): 367-381; coauth, "Angle of regard: The effect of vertical viewing angle on the perception of facial expressions," J Nonverbal Behavior (94): 263-280; coauth, "Self-other perception of the intensity of facial expressions of emotion: Do we know what we show?" J Person Soc Psychol (95): 608-618; coauth, "Differentiating emotion elicited and deliberate emotional facial expressions," in What the face reveals: Basic and applied studies of spontaneous expression using the Facial Action Coding System, eds. P Ekinan, E Rosenberg (FACS), 271-286 (NY: Oxford Press, 97); coauth, "The relationship between the intensity of emotional facial expressions and observer's decoding," J Nonverbal Behavior 21 (98): 241-257; coauth, "The influence of expression intensity, gender, and ethnicity on judgments of dominance and affiliation," J Nonverbal Behavior, 99; coed, Stigma, Guilford Pub (NY), 99; coauth, " Issues in the stigma of physical disability," in Stigma, coed (NY: Guilford Pub, 99). **CONTACT ADDRESS** Dept Psychology, Dartmouth Col, 6207 Moore Hall, Hanover, NH 03755. **EMAIL** robert.e.kleck@dartmouth.edu

KLEDARAS, CONSTANTINE G.
PERSONAL Born 07/22/1934, Raleigh, NC **DISCIPLINE** SOCIOLOGY **EDUCATION** Duke Univ, BA, 56; UNC Chapel Hill, MSW, 60; Cath Univ Amer, DSW, 71. **CAREER** Dept super, Dorothea Dix Hosp, 60-67; fac assoc dean, E Carolina Sch Soc Wk, 71-94; dept chair, Campbell Univ, 94-. **HONORS AND AWARDS** 1st Doc Schl, NC Dept Ment Health, Outstand Dist Ser Awds; Soc Worker of the Year Awd, NASW. **MEMBERSHIPS** NASW; NC Soc Clin Soc Wk; MHA; KRIKOS. **RESEARCH** Mental health; nursing care; long term care. **CONTACT ADDRESS** Dept Social Work, Campbell Univ, PO Box 369, Buies Creek, NC 27506.

KLEE, CAROL A.
PERSONAL Born 09/06/1953, Royal Oak, MI, m, 1987, 1 child **DISCIPLINE** HISPANIC LINGUISTICS **EDUCATION** Col of Wooster, BA, 75; Univ of Tex Austin, MA, 80; PhD, 84. **CAREER** Lectr, Univ of IL Urbana, 83=85; asst prof to assoc prof, chair, Univ of Minn, 85-. **HONORS AND AWARDS** Nat Presby Scholar, 71-75; Tinker Field Res Grant, 85; Grant, Univ of Minn, 86, 88, 89, 94-96, 99, 00; Diploma in Recognition of Outstanding Serv, Univ of Minn, 92; Emma Birkmaier Awd, 97. **MEMBERSHIPS** Am Assoc of Appl Ling; Am Assoc of Teachers of Span and Port; AAUP; Am Assoc of Univ Supervisors, Coordinators and Directors of Lang Prog; MLA; AM Coun on the Teaching of For Lang; Minn Coun on the Teaching of Lang and Cult. **RESEARCH** Spanish Sociolinguistics, Quechua-Spanish language contact, the acquisition of Spanish as a second language, foreign language teaching and learning. **SELECTED PUBLICATIONS** Auth, "Spanish language contact in the Andes", Word 41 (90): 35-46; coauth, "Reconsidering the FL requirement: From seat-time to proficiency in the Minnesota experience", Problems Confronting Foreign Language Programs in the 1990's, ed Sally Sieloff Magnan, Heinle & Heinle (91): 55-69; ed, Sociolinguistics of the Spanish-speaking world: Spain, Latin America and the United States, Bilingual Rev Pr, (Tucson, AZ), 91; ed, Faces in a crowd: the individual learner in multisection courses, AAUSC Series on Issues in Lang Prog Direction, Heinle & Heinle, 94; coauth, "The expression of past reference in Spanish narratives of Spanish/Quechua bilingual speakers", Spanish in contact with other languages, ed Carmen Silva-Corvalan, Georgetown Univ Pr, (95): 52-70; auth, "The Spanish and Peruvian Andes: The influence of Quechua on Spanish Language structure", Spanish in contact: Studies in bilingualism, eds John B Jensen and Ana Roca, Cascadilla Pr, (96): 73-91; coauth, "The undergraduate foreign language immersion program in

Spanish at the University of Minnesota", Content-Based Instruction in the Foreign Language Classroom, ed Steven Stryker and Betty L Leaver, Georgetown Univ Pr, (97): 140-173; auth, "Communication as an Organizing Principle in the National Standards: Sociolinguistic Aspects of Spanish Language Teaching", Hispania 81, (98): 321-333; auth, "Foreign Language Instruction: Past, Present, and Future", Handbook of Undergraduate Second Language Education: ESL, Bilingual, and Foreign Language Instruction for a Multilingual World, ed Judith Rosenthal, Lawrence Erlbaum, 00; coed, The interaction of social and cognitive factors in second language acquisition, Proceedings of the 1999 Second Lang Res Forum, Cascadilla Pr, (Somerville, MA), (forthcoming). **CONTACT ADDRESS** Dept Span, Univ of Minnesota, Twin Cities, 9 Pleasant St SE, Minneapolis, MN 55455-0194. **EMAIL** klee@umn.edu

KLEIN, ROBERT H.
PERSONAL Born 11/04/1938, Seoul, Korea, m, 1980, 3 children **DISCIPLINE** EDUCATION **EDUCATION** Han'guk Univ, Korea, BA, 62; Vanderbilt Univ, BA, 64; MA, 65; PhD, 69. **CAREER** Assoc prof to prof, Western Wash Univ, 74-; chair, 94-97. **MEMBERSHIPS** Am Educ Studies Assoc; Assoc of Asian Am Studies; Assoc of Korean Polit Sci in N Am; Comparative and Int Educ Soc; Korean Am Hist Soc. **SELECTED PUBLICATIONS** Auth, Distinguished Asian Americans, A Biographical Dictionary, Greenwood Pr, (Westport, CT), 99; auth, Hyon Sun's Autobiography: Korea's Hidden Hero, Yonsei Univ Pr, (Seoul), 99; auth, To Helen, My Beloved Wife, Sohwa Pub, (Seoul), 99. **CONTACT ADDRESS** Dept Educ Found, Western Washington Univ, 516 High St, Bellingham, WA 98225-5946. **EMAIL** kimhchan@wwu.edu

KLIMES, RUDOLF
PERSONAL Born 01/09/1932, Sternberk, Czech Republic, m, 1954, 3 children **DISCIPLINE** EDUCATION **EDUCATION** Walla Walla Col, BA, 57; MA, 75; Ind Univ, EdS, 64; PhD, 64, Andrews Univ, MA, 77; McCormick Theol Sem, DMin, 81; Johns Hopkins Univ, MPH, 83. **CAREER** Lectr to president, Sahmyook Col, Korea, 60-69; president, Saniku Gakuin Col, Japan, 69-73; prof, Andrews Univ, 73-79; president Samyuk Col, Hong Kong, 86-89; prof, Korean Sahmyook Univ, 89-; dean, 92-. **HONORS AND AWARDS** Outstanding Serv Awd, Min of Educ, Korea, 69; Order of Civil Merit, Korea, 69. **SELECTED PUBLICATIONS** Auth, Solving Problems, Pacifica Inst, (Orangevale, CA), 90; auth, Curriculum Basics, Helpers Int, (Fulsom, CA), 90; auth, Research It, Pacifica Inst, (Orangevale, CA), 90; auth, "Comparison of Mind-Images Seen in Private Prayer in Pupils with High and Low Scores on a Faith Assessment", Korean Sahmyook Univ J, 91; auth, Survey It, Korean Sahmyook Univ, (Seoul), 91; auth, Trust Me, Korean Sahmyook Univ, (Seoul), 91; auth, Help One, Pacifica Inst, (Orangevale, CA), 91; auth, "Problem Classification in Counseling", Korean Sahmyook Univ J, 92; auth, Team Up, Pacific Inst, (Orangevale, CA); 92; auth, Learn Now, Korean Sahmyook Univ (Seoul), 93. **CONTACT ADDRESS** Dept Sci, Cosumnes River Col, 6699 Green Valley Rd, Placerville, CA 95667-8704.

KLITZKIE, LOURDES PALOMO
PERSONAL Born Agana, Guam **DISCIPLINE** EDUCATION, SPECIAL EDUCATION **EDUCATION** Univ Guam, BA, 70; Univ NMex, MA, 74; Utah State Univ, PhD, 79. **CAREER** Teacher TT, Elementary Classroom Teacher, Dept of Ed, Guam Public Schs, 70-71; Remedial Reading Teacher, Bernadlillo Sch District, NMex, 71-72, Teacher IV, Elementary Classroom Teacher, 72-74; Teacher IV, Elementary Classroom Teacher, Dept of Ed, Guam Public Schs, 74-76; asst prof, Col of Ed, Univ Guam, 79-86, assoc prof, Special Ed Dept, 87-93, full prof, Foundation, Ed Res & Human Services, Col of Ed, Univ Guam, 93-. **MEMBERSHIPS** Coun of Vocational Ed, Phi Delta Kappa, Univ of Guam Fedn of Teachers, Coun for Exceptional Children, Guam Fedn of Teachers, Am Asn of Mental Deficiency Ed Res Asn. **SELECTED PUBLICATIONS** Auth, "Multi-Ethnic Teacher-Pupil Classroom," International Association of Educational and Vocational Guidance, Manila, Republic of the Philippines, Bulletin (79): 89; auth, "Multi-Ethnic Teacher-Pupil Classroom Interaction," 4th annual Reading symposium, Ed Resources J (83): 10; auth, "Limited English Proficient, Bilingual, and Multicultural Special Education Students: Implications for Teacher and Service Delivery, " Internal J of Special Ed, Vol 9 (91); auth, "Training Teachers and Parents to Work Collaboratively in the Teaching and Training of Children with Disabilities," Issues in Special and Rehabilitation, Vol 8, No 1 (93): 17-22; auth, "Guam Caregivers Training Institute: Inclusion of Families and Children with Disabilities," A Publication of the Int Asn of Special Ed (95): 177. **CONTACT ADDRESS** Col of Ed, Univ of Guam, 303 University Dr, Mangilao, GU 96923.

KNAPP, RONALD G.
PERSONAL Born 08/15/1940, Pittsburgh, PA, m, 1968, 3 children **DISCIPLINE** CULTURAL GEOGRAPHY **EDUCATION** Stetson Univ, BA, 62; Univ of Pittsburgh, PhD, 68. **CAREER** SUNY exchange prof, Nanyang Univ, 71-72; asst prof, 68-71, assoc prof, 71-78, prof, 78-98, Distinguished prof, State Univ of NY, NEW PALTZ, 98-. **HONORS AND AWARDS** Woodrow Wilson Nat Fel, 62-63; ACLS/Mellon Found Postdoctoral Fel for Advanced Training in Chinese Studies, 78; Summer Seminar, 79, Fel, Nat Endowment for the Humanities, 84 & 94; Nat Geographic Soc Comt for Res and Exploration Grant, 87; Nat Geographic Soc Comt for Res and Exploration, 80; Chiang Ching-kuo Found, 96. **MEMBERSHIPS** Asn of Am Geographers; Asn for Asian Studies; Vernacular Archit Forum; Int Asn for the Study of Traditional Environments; NY Conf on Asian Studies. **RESEARCH** The cultural and historical geography of China, especially the frontier settlement and the evolution of cultural landscapes; Chinese vernacular architecture; Chinese folk symbols and household ornamentation. **SELECTED PUBLICATIONS** Auth, China's Traditional Rural Architecture, Univ of Hawaii Press, 86; auth, China's Vernacular Architecture, Univ of Hawaii Press, 89; auth, The Chinese House, Oxford Univ Press, 90; auth, Chinese Bridges, Oxford Univ Press, 93; auth, Popular Rural Architecture, Handbook of Chinese Popular Culture, Greenwood Pub Group, 94; auth, China's didactic landscapes: the folk tradition and the built environment, History and Culture of Vernacular Architecture, South China Univ of Tech, 95; auth, Chinese Villages as Didactic Texts, Landscape, Culture, and Power in Chinese Soc, Inst of East Asian Studies, Univ of Calif, 98; auth, The Shaping of Taiwan's Landscapes, Taiwan: A Hist 1600-1994, M.E. Sharpe, 98; auth, China's Living Houses: Folk Beliefs, symbols and Household Ornamentation, Univ of Hawaii Press, 99; auth, China's Walled Cities, Oxford Univ Press, 00; auth, China's Old Dwellings, Univ of Hawaii Press, 00. **CONTACT ADDRESS** Dept of Geography, SUNY, New Paltz, New Paltz, NY 12561-2499. **EMAIL** knappr@newpaltz.edu

KNEESHAW, STEPHEN
PERSONAL Born 10/04/1946, Tacoma, WA, m, 1969, 3 children **DISCIPLINE** AMERICAN HISTORY, HISTORY OF EDUCATION **EDUCATION** Univ Puget Sound, BA, 68; Univ Colo, Boulder, MA, 69; PhD, 71. **CAREER** Instr, Univ Colo, 71-72; asst to prof and chair, Col of the Ozarks, 72-; ed of Teaching Hist: A J of Methods, 76-. **HONORS AND AWARDS** Phi Alpha Theta; Mu Sigma Delta; Nat Man-of-the-Year for Sigma Nu Frat, 68; Who's Who in Am Cols and Univs, 68; Outstanding Educators in Am, 75; Outstanding Young Men of Am, 79, 82; NEH Fel in State and Community Hist, Newberry Lib, Chicago, 79; Vis Scholar, Univ Puget Sound, 82, 89; Distinguished Fac Awd, Col of the Ozarks, 85; nominee for CASE Nat Prof of the Year, 86; Wye Fel, Wye Fac Inst, 89; Who's Who Among Am Teachers, 94, 96, 98; West Point ROTC Fel in Military Hist, 96; Outstanding Americans, 97-98. **MEMBERSHIPS** Am Hist Asn, Org of Am Hists, Soc of Hists of Am Foreign Relations, Nat Comn for Hist Educ. **RESEARCH** 20th century American Diplomatic History, especially World War II and Vietnam, and history educations, including teaching methods and computer-based methods and materials. **SELECTED PUBLICATIONS** Auth, In Pursuit of Peace: The American Reaction to the Kellogg-Briand Pact, 1928-1929, New York: Garland Pub (91); auth, "Hugh Simons Gibson," in The Encyclopedia of U.S. Foreign Relations, Lakeview, Ct: Am Reference Pub Co (96); auth, "The Internet, Email, and the Environment," OAH Mag of Hist, 10 (96); auth, "Using Reader Response to Improve Student Writing in History," OAH Mag of Hist, 13 (99); auth, "Some Thoughts on American Education and on American Teachers," Teaching History, 24 (99); auth, "Teaching History at Twenty-Five Years," Teaching History, 25 (spring 2000); auth, "History Websites on the Internet and WWW," in The History Highway 2000 (2000); auth, "Teaching History with Technology," in History.Edu (2000). **CONTACT ADDRESS** Dept Humanities, Col of the Ozarks, Point Lookout, MO 65726. **EMAIL** kneeshaw@cofo.edu

KNIGHT, EILEEN Q.
PERSONAL Born 10/07/1948, Rockville Center, NY, w, 1975, 3 children **DISCIPLINE** EDUCATION **EDUCATION** Siena Hts Col, MI, BS, 69; DePaul Univ, MA, 75; Northwestern Univ, postgrad coun, 76; Univ IL, PhD, 92; Harvard Univ, post doc, 99. **CAREER** Teach, St Patrick, IL, 69-70; teach, Sci Rel, FL, 70-73; teach, Pace HS, FL, 73-74; teach, St Luke, River Forest, 75-76; chair, St Mich Parr, 80-84; instr, Felician Col, 84; instr; Gov State Univ, 85; gst lectr, Limerick Univ, IRE, 98; St Xavier Univ, IL, 85-. **MEMBERSHIPS** NCTM; ASCD; ICTM; Jean Piaget Soc. **SELECTED PUBLICATIONS** Coauth, "Meaning, Love and Self in the Classroom," Harvard Ed Rev (94); coauth, "Pre-service Teachers Sense of Themselves as Meaning Makers in Mathmatics," Teaching Edu 6 (94); auth, "Constructivist Mathmatics," Connections (99); auth, "Building Healthy Relationships," New World (99); auth, "Life in Schools: A Review," Connections (99). **CONTACT ADDRESS** Dept Education, Saint Xavier Univ, 3700 W 103rd Street, Chicago, IL 60655.

KNOKE, DAVID
PERSONAL Born 03/04/1947, Philadelphia, PA, m, 1970, 1 child **DISCIPLINE** SOCIOLOGY **EDUCATION** Univ Mich, BA, 69; Univ Chicago, MA, 70; Univ Mich, MSW, 71; PhD, 72. **CAREER** Asst prof, Ind Univ, 72-85; prof, Univ Minn, 85-. **MEMBERSHIPS** ASA. **RESEARCH** Organizations; social networks. **SELECTED PUBLICATIONS** Auth, Organizing for Collective Action, Aldine de Gruter, 90; auth, Political Networks, Cambridge Univ Press, 90; coauth, Statistics for Social Data Analysis, 3rd ed, Peacock, 94; coauth, Comparing Policy Networks, Cambridge Univ Press, 96; coauth, Organizations in America, Sage Pub, 96; coauth, Change at Work, Oxford Univ Press. **CONTACT ADDRESS** Dept Sociology, Univ of Minnesota, Twin Cities, 267 19th Ave S, 909 Social Sci Bldg, Minneapolis, MN 55455. **EMAIL** knoke@atlas.socsci.umn.edu

KOCEL, KATHERINE
PERSONAL Born 03/29/1946, Detroit, MI, m, 1993, 1 child **DISCIPLINE** PSYCHOLOGY **EDUCATION** Antioch Col, BA, 68; Univ Hawaii, PhD, 78. **CAREER** Res Psychol, UCLA 78-80; Instructor, Univ Haw, 91-93; Asst Prof, Jackson State Univ, 93-. **HONORS AND AWARDS** Distinguished Teacher of Psychology, 99; MS Psychol Asn; Outstanding Teaching Awd, 98. **MEMBERSHIPS** Am Asn for Adv of Sci; Am Psychol Asn; Am Psychol Soc; SE Psychol Asn; Sigma XI. **RESEARCH** Social development. **SELECTED PUBLICATIONS** Co-auth, "Early Field Experiences Influence the Attitudes of Preservice Teachers," Center for Excellence in Education Newsletter, 95; co-auth, "Alternative Approaches to the Evaluation of Education Reform," in MidSouth Educational Research Association Proceedings, (96): 42-43; co-auth, The Influence of Early Field Experiences on the Attitudes of Preservice Teachers, 96; co-auth, "Griffith, Goldsborough Sappington," in American national Biography, Oxford Univ Press, 99; co-auth, The Influence of Early Field Experiences on the attitudes of Preservice Teachers, 99; co-auth, "Interactions of gender and ethnicity on both sides of the managerial evaluation process," Papers of the 8th Annual Economic Research symposium, in press. **CONTACT ADDRESS** Dept Psychol, Jackson State Univ, 1400 Lynch St, Jackson, MS 39217. **EMAIL** johnk@ayrix.com

KOCH, CHRIS
PERSONAL Born 01/04/1965, Allentown, PA, m, 1988, 3 children **DISCIPLINE** PSYCHOLOGY **EDUCATION** Penn State Univ, BS, 87; Univ Ga, MS, 90; PhD, 93. **CAREER** Asst Prof to Assoc Prof, George Fox Univ, 93-. **HONORS AND AWARDS** Who's Who in Am Sci and Engineering, 99; Who's Who Among Am Teachers, 96; Psi Chi; Sigma Xi. **MEMBERSHIPS** Am Psychol Asn, Am Psychol Soc, Psychonomic Soc, W Psychol Asn, Cognitive Sci Soc, Am Statistical Asn. **RESEARCH** Examining the cognitive and perceptual processes associated with attention as well as the cognitive mechanisms responsible for attention and how attention can be properly assessed. **SELECTED PUBLICATIONS** Co-auth, "Experimental versus applied object recognition tasks and theory," Psychological Reports, in press; co-auth, "Influences of occlusion, color, luminance, and size on the perception of fragmented pictures," Perceptual & Motor skills, (00): 1033-1044; co-auth, "Perception of parental acceptance-rejection and satisfaction with life in women with Binge Eating Disorder," Journal of Psychology, (00): 23-36; co-auth, "Differences in mentoring across time and subfield of psychology: An exploratory study," Psychotherapy, in press; co-auth, "Documenting the benefits of undergraduate mentoring," Council on Undergraduate Research Quarterly, (00): 172-175; co-auth, "Using cluster analysis to examine individual differences in Stroop processing," Psycoloquy, (99): 25; co-auth, "The role of geons in object recognition across ages," Perceptual & Motor Skills, (99): 983-991; co-auth, "A web based tutorial with links to the Web for teaching statistics and research methods," Behavioral Research Methods, Instrumentation, & Computers, (99): 7-13; co-auth, "Integrating across the curriculum: An evaluation plan," Journal of Psychology and Theology, (98): 204-208. **CONTACT ADDRESS** Dept Soc Sci, George Fox Univ, 414 N Meridan St, Newberg, OR 97132. **EMAIL** ckoch@georgefox.edu

KODA, KEIKO
DISCIPLINE JAPANESE AND SECOND LANGUAGE ACQUISITION **EDUCATION** Univ Ill, PhD. **CAREER** Languages, Carnegie Mellon Univ. **SELECTED PUBLICATIONS** Auth, Second language reading research: Problems and possibilities. Applied Psycholinguistics, 94; Development of L2 word recognition, 94; Cognitive consequences of L1 and L2 orthographies, 95; L2 Word Recognition Research: A Critical Rev, Mod Lang Jour , 96, Cross-linguistic transfer of orthographic knowledge, 97; Cambridge Univ Press. **CONTACT ADDRESS** Carnegie Mellon Univ, 5000 Forbes Ave, Pittsburgh, PA 15213.

KOLODNY, ANNETTE
PERSONAL Born 08/21/1941, New York, NY **DISCIPLINE** AMERICAN LITERATURE, WOMENS STUDIES **EDUCATION** Brooklyn Col, BA, 62; Univ Calif, Berkeley, MA, 65, PhD(Am lit), 69. **CAREER** Asst prof English, Yale Univ, 69-70 and Univ BC, 70-74; admin coordr womens studies prog, Univ BC, 72-74; assoc prof English, Univ NH, 74-82; Univ BC Sr Res Grants, 70-; Can Coun sr res grant, 73-74; Mem Adv Bd, AM Lit, 74-; consult grants and fels, Can Coun, 77; Nat Endowment Humanities, 75-; fel study women soc, Ford Found, 75-76; Rockefeller found, 78-79; Guggenheim found, 79-80; Prof, Univ of Ariz. **HONORS AND AWARDS** Florence Howe Essay Prize, 79. **MEMBERSHIPS** MLA; Am Studies Asn; Can Asn Am Studies; Nat Womens Studies Asn. **RESEARCH** Early and contemporary American literature; women writers. **SELECTED PUBLICATIONS** Auth, Inventing a Feminist Discourse, Rhetoric and Resistance in Fuller, Margaret Woman

in the Nineteenth Century, New Literary Hist, Vol 0025, 94; Response to Hartman, Rome, New Literary Hist, Vol 0027, 96; 60 Minutes at the University of Arizona in the Polemic Against Tenure, New Literary Hist, Vol 0027, 96; auth, Failing the Future: A Dean books at Higher Education in the 20th Century, Duke Univ Pr, 98. **CONTACT ADDRESS** Comp Cult & Lit Studies, Univ of Arizona, 1239 N Highland, PO Box 210431, Tuscon, AZ 85721-0431.

KOME, PENNY J.
PERSONAL Born 11/02/1948, Chicago, IL **DISCIPLINE** WOMEN'S STUDIES **CAREER** RES ASSOC, CAN RES INST FOR THE ADVANCEMENT OF WOMEN. **HONORS AND AWARDS** Robertine Barry Prize, CRIAW, 84. **SELECTED PUBLICATIONS** Auth, Somebody Has To Do It: Whose Work is Housework?, 82; auth, The Taking of Twenty-Eight, 83; auth, Women of Influence: Canadian Women & Politics, 85; auth, Every Voice Counts, 89; auth, Working Wounded: The Politics of Musculoskeletal Injuries, 98; co-ed, Peace: A Dream Unfolding, 86. **CONTACT ADDRESS** 2319 Uxbridge Dr NW, Calgary, AB, Canada T2N 3Z7.

KONDITI, JANE
PERSONAL Born 01/14/1957, Kenya, m, 1972, 5 children **DISCIPLINE** LIBERAL ARTS, EDUCATION, ACCOUNTING **EDUCATION** Tex Wesleyan Univ, BBA; Tex Woman's Univ, MBA; Univ North Tex, PhD. **CAREER** Chairman, Accounting Dept; Academic Dean. **HONORS AND AWARDS** Started an accounting prog at Northwood Univ; Fac Excellence Awd; Elizabeth Armstrong Scholarship Awd; Who's who of Professionals; Professor of the Year, Northwood Univ. **MEMBERSHIPS** Nat Soc of Accountants. **RESEARCH** Women issues, education, children issues. **CONTACT ADDRESS** Chief Academic Dean, Northwood Univ, Texas, 1114 W Fm 1382, Cedar Hill, TX 75104. **EMAIL** konditi@northwood.edu

KONECNI, VLADIMIR J.
PERSONAL Born 10/27/1944, Belgrade, Yugoslavia, m, 1993, 2 children **DISCIPLINE** PSYCHOLOGY **EDUCATION** Second Belgrade Acad Gymnasium, 63; Univ Belgrade, BA, 69; Univ Toronto, MA, 71, PhD, 73. **CAREER** Asst prof, Univ Calif, San Diego, 73-78, assoc prof, 78-82, prof, 82-. **HONORS AND AWARDS** Univ Belgrade, BA, cum magna laude, 69; Guggenheim Fel, 79-80; DAAD Fel, 87; Academician (active mem), Int Informatics Acad, 93-. **MEMBERSHIPS** Am Psychol Soc, European Asn for Psychol and Law, Int Asn for Empirical Aesthetics. **RESEARCH** Social psychology (emotion, aggression, altruism), legal psychology, empirical aesthetics, methodology. **SELECTED PUBLICATIONS** Auth, "Altruism: Methodological and definitional issues," Sci (76): 194, 562; co-ed with E. B. Ebbesen, The criminal justice system: A social-psychological analysis, San Francisco: W. H. freeman (82); co-ed with R. M. Kaplan and R. W. Novaco, Aggression in children and youth, The Hague, The Netherlands: Martinus Nijhoff Pubs (84); auth, Social interaction and musical preference, in D. Deutsch, ed, The psychology of music, New York: Academic Press (82): 497-516, trans into Japanese, Nihimura Co Ltd (88); auth, "Portraiture: An Experimental study of the creative process," Leonardo, 24 (91): 325-328; auth, "Psychological aspects of the expression of anger and violence on the stage," Comp Drama, 25 (91): 215-241; coauth with E. B. Ebbensen, "Eyewitness memory research: Probative v. prejudicial value," Expert Evidence, 5, nos 1 & 2 (97): 2-28; auth, "The vase on the mantelpiece: The golden section in context," Empirical Studies of the arts, 15 (97): 177-207; coauth with E. B. Ebbesen and R. R. Hock, "Factors affecting simulated jurors' decisions in capital cases," Psychol, Crime, and Law, 2 (96): 269-197; auth, "Expression and meaning in 'Tasol': Hedonic effects of development vs. chance in resolved and unresolved aural episodes," Music Psychology, 14 (99): 102-123. **CONTACT ADDRESS** Dept Psychol 0109, Univ of California, San Diego, 9500 Gilman Dr, La Jolla, CA 92093. **EMAIL** vkonecni@ucsd.edu

KONEK, CAROL WOLFE
PERSONAL Born 01/06/1934, Meade, KS, 4 children **DISCIPLINE** WOMENS STUDIES, ENGLISH **EDUCATION** Univ Kans, BS, 60; Wichita State Univ, MA, 68; Univ Okla, PhD(admin), 77. **CAREER** Instr compos, 68-76, Asst Prof Womens Studies, Wichita State Univ, 70-; Proj dir, proj DELTA, Womens Educ Equity Act, Wichita State Univ, 76-78. **MEMBERSHIPS** Am Educ Asn; Nat Asn of Women Deans, Adminrs and Counr; Nat Womens Studies Asn. **SELECTED PUBLICATIONS** Auth, The Creation of Feminist Consciousness From the Middle Ages, Historian, Vol 0056, 94; Contemporary Western-European Feminism, Historian, Vol 0056, 94. **CONTACT ADDRESS** Dept of Womens Studies, Wichita State Univ, 1845 Fairmont St, Wichita, KS 67260-0001.

KOPP, CLAIRE
PERSONAL Born 07/08/1931, New York, NY, m, 1950, 3 children **DISCIPLINE** PSYCHOLOGY **EDUCATION** NY Univ, BS, Univ Southern Calif, MA, Claremont Grad Univ, PhD, 70. **CAREER** Lecturer, Calif State Polytech Univ, 68-69, lecturer, Calif State Univ, 70-73; asst res psychol to adj prof, Univ Calif, Los Angeles, 71-95; prof, Claremont Grad Univ, 95-. **HONORS AND AWARDS** Bureau of Educ for the Handicapped, 77-82; Spencer foundation, 80; Nat Inst for Handicap Res, 86-89; Nat Sci foundation, 87-90; NICHD, NIH 90-93; Smith-Richardson Foundation 90-91; NIDDR, Tech for Children with Orthopedic Disabilites, 95-00; Children's Hosp, Los angeles, 96-97; Grant foundation 97; Haynes foundation, 98; Commonwealth fund, 98. **MEMBERSHIPS** Soc for Res in Child Development, Am Psychol Asn, Am Psychol Soc, Intl Soc of Infancy Studies, Am Asn for the Adv of Sci. **RESEARCH** Self-regulation in young children, Emotion regulation, Applied developmental psychology. **SELECTED PUBLICATIONS** Auth, Appraisals of parenting, parent and child interaction, parenting styles, and children. An annotated bibliography, Commonwealth Fund: New York, (in press); auth, "Motivation revisited," Contemporary Psychology, 99; auth, "Self-Regulated, revisited, (forthcoming); auth, Self-Regulation: Developmentally delayed young children, (forthcoming); auth, "Emotional development during infancy," in Handbook of affective sciences, Oxford Univ Press, (forthcoming); auth, "Self-regulation," in International Encyclopedia of social and behavioral sciences, Elsvier Sci Ltd: Oxford, (forthcoming); auth, "Infancy research: A view from across the Atlantic," Contemporary Psychology, (98): 871; auth, "Graduate training changing once again," contemporary Psychology, (97): 1112-1113; auth, "Children's conflict tactics with mothers: A longitudinal investigation of the toddler and preschool years," Merrill-Palmer quarterly, 99; auth, "High risk environments and young children," in The Handbook of child and Adolescent Psychiatry Vol 1: Development and syndromes, New York, 97. **CONTACT ADDRESS** Dept Beh Sci, Claremont Graduate Sch, 170 E 10th St, Claremont, CA 91711-3955. **EMAIL** claire.kopp@cgu.edu

KOPPER, BEVERLY A.
PERSONAL Born 02/03/1954, Syracuse, NY, m, 1983, 1 child **DISCIPLINE** PSYCHOLOGY **EDUCATION** SUNY at Buffalo, BA, 75; MSSW, Univ Wis, 79; Iowa State Univ, MS, 86; PhD, 88. **CAREER** From Lectr to Assoc Prof, Univ Northern Iowa, 88-. **HONORS AND AWARDS** Outstanding Teacher Awd for Untenured Fac, Col of Soc And Behav Sci, Univ of Northern Iowa, 95. **MEMBERSHIPS** Am Psychol Asn, Iowa Psychol Asn, Western Psychol Asn, Nat Asn of Soc Work. **RESEARCH** Gender, Depression, Anger, Suicide, Anxiety, Infertility. **SELECTED PUBLICATIONS** Coauth, "The Beck Anxiety Inventory: Reexamination of factor structure and psychometric properties," J of Clinical Psychology 53 (97): 7-14; coauth, "factor structure and psychometric characteristics of the Beck Depression Inventory-II," J of Psychopathology and Behav Assessment 19 (97): 359-376; coauth, "Factor structure, reliability, and validity of the pain catastrophizing scale," J of Behav Med 20 (97): 589-605; coauth, "The Reasons for Living Inventory for Adolescents (RFL-A): Development and psychometric properties in a nonclinical sample," J of Clinical Psychology 54 (98): 1063-1078; coauth, "The positive and negative suicide ideation inventory: Development and validation," Psychol Reports 82 (98): 783-793; coauth, "The social phobia and social interaction anxiety scales: Evaluation of Psychometric Properties," J of Psychopathology and Behav Assessment 20 (98): 249-264; coauth, "Clinical utility of the MMPI-A content scales and Harris-Lingoes subscales in the asssessment of suicidal risk factors in psychiatric adolescents," J of Clinical Psychology 54 (98): 191-200; coauth, "Validation of the Adult Suicidal Ideation Questionnaire and the Reasons for Living Inventory in an adult psychiatric inpatient sample," Psychol Assessment (99); coauth, "The Multi-Attitude Suicide Tendency Scale: Further validation with adolescent psychiatric inpatients," Suicide and Life-Threatening Behavior (in press); coauth, "Why young people do not kill themselves: The Reasons for Living Inventory for Adolescents," J of Clinical Child Psychology (in press). **CONTACT ADDRESS** Dept Psychology, Univ of No Iowa, Cedar Falls, IA 50614-0001. **EMAIL** kopper@uni.edu

KOPYTOFF, IGOR
PERSONAL Born 04/16/1930, Mukden, China, w, 1 child **DISCIPLINE** ANTHROPOLOGY **EDUCATION** NW Univ, BA, 55; Univ Pa, MA, 58; NW Univ, PhD, 60. **CAREER** Instructor, Brown Univ, 60-62; Asst Prof to Prof, Univ Pa, 62-. **HONORS AND AWARDS** Ford Foundation Fel, 57-60; Nat Sci Foundation Grant, 69-71, 73; NEH Fel, 75-76; Guggenheim Fel, 84-85. **MEMBERSHIPS** Am Anthropol Asn; African Studies Asn; Royal Anthropol Inst; Intl African Inst. **RESEARCH** African Ethnology; Cultural Anthropology. **SELECTED PUBLICATIONS** Co-auth, "African Slavery as an Institution of Marginality," in Slavery in Africa: Historical and Anthropological Perspectives, (Univ WI, 77), 3-8; co-ed, Slavery in Africa: Historical and Anthropological Perspectives, Univ WI Press, 77; contrib, Beyond Chiefdoms, Cambridge Univ Press, 99. **CONTACT ADDRESS** Dept Anthropol, Univ of Pennsylvania, 325 Univ Museum, Philadelphia, PA 19104. **EMAIL** kopytoff@sas.upenn.edu

KORGEN, KATHLEEN
DISCIPLINE SOCIOLOGY **EDUCATION** Col of the Holy Cross, BA, 89; Boston Col, PhD, 97. **CAREER** Vis Lecturer, Framingham State Col, 93; Teaching Fel, Boston Col, 93-94; Vis Lecturer, Framingham State Col, 94; Teaching Fel, Boston Col, 94-96; Vis Lecturer, Framingham State Col, 96-97; Teaching Fel, Boston Col, 97; Instr, Stonehill Col, 97; Asst prof, Drury Col, 97-98; Asst Prof, William Paterson Univ, 98-. **HONORS AND AWARDS** Dissertation Fel, 96-97. **MEMBERSHIPS** Am Sociol Asn, Eastern Sociol Soc, Soc for the Study of Soc Problems. **RESEARCH** Racial identity of multiracial Americans; Inter-racial friendships; Race-ethnic relations; Stratification. **SELECTED PUBLICATIONS** Auth, "Mixed-Race Americans and Affirmative Action: From the One Drop Rule to the Pigmentation Rule," southeastern Sociological Review, forthcoming; auth, "Beyond a Multiracial America: Racial Demographics and Crime in the US Today," in Race and Crime, CourseWise Pub, forthcoming; auth, From Black to Biracial: Transforming Racial Identity Among Americans, Praeger pub, 99; auth, "Blackness and Whiteness: Legal Definitions of : United States," in Racial and Ethnic Relations in America, Salem Press, 99; auth, "Irish-African American Conflict," in Racial and Ethnic Relations in America, Salem press, 99; auth, "Hispanics: The New Irish in the American Criminal Justice System?" in Perspectives: Criminal Justice, CourseWise Pub, 99. **CONTACT ADDRESS** Dept Sociol, William Paterson Univ of New Jersey, 300 Pompton Rd, Wayne, NJ 07470. **EMAIL** korgenk@wpunj.edu

KOROM, FRANK J.
PERSONAL Born 12/15/1957, Kikinda, Yugoslavia, s **DISCIPLINE** FOLKLORE AND FOLKLIFE **EDUCATION** Univ Col, BA, 84; Univ Penn, MA, 87, PhD, 92. **CAREER** Postdoc fel, Smithsonian Inst, 92-93; adj lec, Santa Fe Commun Col, 94-98; cur, Museum of Int Folk Art, 93-98; asst prof, Boston Univ, 98- **HONORS AND AWARDS** Phi Beta Kappa, Univ Col, 84. **MEMBERSHIPS** All India Folklore Cong; Am Acad of Relig; Am Folklore Soc; Asn of Asian Stud; Folklore Fels of Finland; Int Asn for Tibetan Stud; Int Soc for Folk Narrative Res; Int Union of Anthrop and Ethnol Sci; Phi Beta Kappa. **RESEARCH** Hinduism; Islam; Buddhism; ritual, muth, folklore and material culture. **SELECTED PUBLICATIONS** Auth, "A Festive Mourning: Moharram in Trinidad," India Mag, 93; Report on a Planned Exhibit of Tibetan Material Culture in Diaspora," Asian Folklore Stud, 94; "Community Process and the Performance of Muharram Observances in Trinidad," Drama Rev, 94; "Memory, Innovation and Emergent Ethnicities: The Creolization of an Indo-Trinidadian Performance," Diaspora, 94; "Transformation of Language to Rhythm: The Hosay Drums of Trinidad," World of Music, 94; "Recycling in India: Status and Economic Realities," Recycled, Reseen, Reseen: Folk Art from the Global Scrap Heap, Abrams, 96; "Oral Canon Formation in a Bengali Religious Community," Suomen Anthrop, 96; "Place, Space and Identity: The Cultural, Economic and Aesthetic Politics of Tibetan Diaspora," Tibetan Culture in the Diaspora, Austrian Acad of Sci, 97; "Old Age Tibet in New Age America," Constructing Tibetan Culture: Contemporary Perspectives, 97; "Tibetans," American Immigrant Cultures: Builders of a Nation, Macmillan, 97; "Language, Belief and Experience in Bengali Folk Deity," Western Folklore, 97; "Editing Dharmaraj: Academic Genealogies of a Bengali Folk Deity," Western Folklore, 97; Oral Exegesis, Western Folklore, 97; "Foreword," The Art of Exile, Mus of New Mexico Pr, 98 **CONTACT ADDRESS** Dept of Religion, Boston Univ, 745 Commonwealth Ave., Boston, MA 02215. **EMAIL** korom@bu.edu

KOSTELANETZ, RICHARD
PERSONAL Born 05/14/1940, New York, NY **DISCIPLINE** AMERICAN CULTURE **EDUCATION** Brown Univ, AB, 62; Columbia Univ, MA, 66. **CAREER** Co-founder and president, Assembling Press, 70-82; Contrib Ed, NY Arts J, 80-; prog assoc thematic studies, John Jay Col Criminal Justice, 72-73; sr staff, Univ Indiana Writers Conf, 76; vis prof, Am Studies and English, Univ Tex, Austin, 77; co-ed, Precisely: A Critical Jour, 76-; Sole proprietor, Archaeol Editions, 78-. **HONORS AND AWARDS** Res and Writing, 62-; Guggenheim fel, 67-68; Pulitzer Fel, 65; Guggenheim Fel, 67; Best Books of 1976 by the American Inst of Graphic Arts, Nat Endowment for Arts grant, 76; Ludwig Vogelstein Foundation, 80; CCLM Editors Fel, 81; NEA Visual arts senior fel, 85; Fel, New Assoc of Sephardi/Mizrahi Artists and Writers Int, 00-02. **RESEARCH** Experimental literature, particularly in North America; arts and artists in America; criticism of avant- garde arts, particularly literature. **SELECTED PUBLICATIONS** Auth, Avant Garde American Radio Art, North Am Rev, Vol 0278, 93; Flood in a Novel in Pictures, Am Book Rev, Vol 0014, 93; The Roaring Silence in Cage, John, A Life, Notes, Vol 0049, 93; Caxon, Caxton, a Predating, A Definition, and a Supposed Derivation, Notes and Queries, Vol 0040, 93; Not Wanting to Say Anything About Cage, John 1912-92, Chicago Rev, Vol 0038, 93; Grrrh-hhh, Amn Book Rev, Vol 0014, 93; The Phenomenology of Revelation, Am Book Rev, Vol 0014, 93; Minimal Audio Plays, Western Hum Rev, Vol 0048, 94; It Too Shall Pass, Modern Languages Association Rev, Am Book Rev, Vol 0016, 94; Hysterical Pregnancy, North Am Rev, Vol 0279, 94; The Boulez-Cage Correspondence, Am Book Rev, Vol 0016, 95; Literary Video, Visible Language, Vol 0029, 95; Postmodern American Poetry in a Norton Anthology, Am Book Rev, Vol 0016, 95; Preface to Solos, Duets, Trios, and Choruses Membrane Future, Midwest Quart-A J Contemporary Thought, Vol 0037, 95; A Poetry-Film Storyboard in Transformations, Visible Lang, Vol 0030, 96; Anarchist Voices in an Oral-History of Anarchism in America, Am Book Rev, Vol 0017, 96; Interview With Schwartz, Tony, American Horspielmacher, Perspectives New

Mus, Vol 0034, 96; Conservative Subversion, Am Book Rev, Vol 0017, 96; Format And Anxiety, Am Book Rev, Vol 0017, 96; The Year of the Hot Jock and Other Stories, Am Book Rev, Vol 0019, 97; A Star in the Family, Am Book Rev, Vol 0019, 97; Newsreel, Am Book Rev, Vol 0019, 97; Jim Dandy, Am Book Rev, Vol 0019, 97; The File on Stanley Patton Buchta, Am Book Rev, Vol 0019, 97; Roar Lion Roar and Other Stories, Am Book Rev, Vol 0019, 97; The Steagle, Am Book Rev, Vol 0019, 97; The Winner of the Slow Bicycle Race, Am Book Rev, Vol 0018, 97; Willy Remembers, Am Book Rev, Vol 0019, 97; Foreign Devils, Am Book Rev, Vol 0019, 97; auth, Political Essays, Autonomedia, 99; auth, Thirty Years of Visible Writing, BGB, 00; auth, More On Innovative Music(ian)s, Fallen Leaf-Scarecrow, 01. **CONTACT ADDRESS** Prince St, PO Box 444, New York, NY 10013. **EMAIL** rkostelanetz@bigfoot.com

KOURVETARIS, GEORGE A.
PERSONAL Born 11/21/1933, Eleochriou, Arcondla, Greece, m, 1998, 3 children **DISCIPLINE** SOCIOLOGY **EDUCATION** Loyola Col, BS, 63; Roosevelt Univ, MA, 65; Northwestern Univ, PhD 69. **CAREER** Lectr, Northwestern Univ, 67-68; asst prof, Chicago City Col, 67; asst prof to prof, Northern Ill Univ, 69-. **HONORS AND AWARDS** Delta Tau Kappa; Who's Who in the Am Acad of Human Serv, 74; Heritage Awd, Greek Am Community Serv of Chicago, 87; Am Biographical Inst, 85; Contemporary Authors, 89; Awd, Hellenic Coun on Educ, Chicago, 91; Grant, Northern IL Univ, 76-77. **MEMBERSHIPS** Am Sociol Assoc; Mod Greek Studies Assoc; Southeast Europ Assoc; KRIKOS; Europ Community Studies Assoc. **RESEARCH** Political Sociology, Intergroup Relations, Social Inequality, Social Theory. **SELECTED PUBLICATIONS** Auth, First and Second Generation Greeks in Chicago: An Inquiry Into their Stratification and Mobility Patterns, Center for Soc Res, (Athens), 71; coauth, A Profile of Modern Greece: In Search of Identity, Clarendon Pr, (Oxford), 87; auth, Poetry: Nostalgias Kai Xenitias, Mauromatis and Co, (Athens), 92; coed, The Impact of European Integration: Political, Sociological, and Economic Changes, Greenwod Pub, (Westport, CT), 96; auth, Political Sociology: Structure and Process, Allyn and Bacon (Needham Heights, MA), 97; auth, "Continuity and Discontinuity of Greek Ethnicity in Anglo-Saxonic Countries in the 21st Century", Neos Kosmos (Australia), 97; auth, "The Dionysian and Apollonian Dimensions of Ethnicity: A Convergence Model", Nit Rev of Social 7.2, (97): 229-237; auth, "Studies on Greek Americans", East Europe Monographs 27.5, (98): 510-511; auth, Studies on Modern Greece and Politics, East Europe Monographs, 99; auth, "Sociology", Modern Greece: An Annotated Bibliography of Works Published in English from 1900 to 1995, Mod Green Studies Assoc, 99; auth, "Greek American Ethnicity", Our Multicultural Heritage: A Guide to America's Principal Ethnic Groups, ed Elliott R. Barman, Greenwood Pub (Westport, 99). **CONTACT ADDRESS** Dept Sociol, No Illinois Univ, 1425 W Lincoln Hwy, Dekalb, IL 60115. **EMAIL** yorgosk@sun.soci.niu.edu

KOVACS, EDNA M.
PERSONAL Born 04/27/1953, Chicago, IL, s **DISCIPLINE** EDUCATION **EDUCATION** Northwestern Univ Evanston, BA, 76; Univ Ill Chicago, MEd, 78; Union Grad Inst Cincinnati, PhD, 98. **CAREER** Lit artist, RACC, 88-01; Lit artist, Oreg, 92-01; vis scholar, Oreg Coun for the Humanities; adj prof, Lidfield Col, 01- ; lang arts specialist, Portland Public and Middle Schools, 01. **HONORS AND AWARDS** Grants, Reg Arts & Cult Coun. **MEMBERSHIPS** MLA, OSPA, OCTE. **RESEARCH** Multiple Intelligences, Multicultural Studies. **SELECTED PUBLICATIONS** Auth, Mandales, 93; auth, Writing Across Cultures, 94; auth, Aquarelles, 97; auth, Writing With Multiple. **CONTACT ADDRESS** 6131 SW 55 Dr, Portland, OR 97221-1604. **EMAIL** ekovacs319@aol.com

KOWALSKI, ROBIN MARIE
PERSONAL Born 05/23/1964, Anderson, SC, m, 1998, 2 children **DISCIPLINE** PSYCHOLOGY **EDUCATION** Furman Univ, BA, 85; Lake Forest Univ, MA, 87; Univ NC, PhD, 90. **CAREER** Prof, Western Carolina Univ, 1990-. **HONORS AND AWARDS** Phi Beta Kappa, Botner Superior Teaching Awd Winner, 99. **RESEARCH** Complaining, Teasing, aversive behaviors in close relationships. **SELECTED PUBLICATIONS** Auth, Social Anxiety (New York: Guilford), 95; auth, Aversive Interpersonal Behaviors (New York: Plenum), 97; auth, The Social Psychology of Emotional and Behavioral Problems (Washington, DC: American Psychological Assoc), 99; auth, Behaving Badly: Behaviors in Interpersonal Relationships (Washington DC: American Psychological Assoc), 00. **CONTACT ADDRESS** Dept Psychology, Western Carolina Univ, 1 University Dr, Cullowhee, NC 28723.

KPOSOWA, AUGUSTINE
PERSONAL Born 08/24/1959, Bo, Sierra Leone, m, 1991, 2 children **DISCIPLINE** SOCIOLOGY **EDUCATION** St Paul's Col, BA, 77; Univ Cincinnati, MA, 86; Ohio State Univ, PhD, 90. **CAREER** Asst prof, Wayne State Univ, 90-94; Assoc Prof, Univ Calif, 95-. **MEMBERSHIPS** Am Pub Health Asn, Am Sociol Asn. **RESEARCH** Social Epidemiology; Immigration; Political Instability. **CONTACT ADDRESS** Dept Sociol, Univ of California, Riverside, 900 Univ Ave, Riverside, CA 92521-0001. **EMAIL** augustine.kposowa@ucr.edu

KRAFT, WILLIAM F.
PERSONAL Born 07/08/1938, Pittsburgh, PA, m, 1967, 2 children **DISCIPLINE** PSYCHOLOGY **EDUCATION** Duquesne Univ, BA, 60; MA, 62; PhD, 65. **CAREER** Chief Psychol, Somerset State Hospital, 65-68; Chief Psychol, Dixmont State Hospital, 68-71; Prof, Carlow Col, 65-. **HONORS AND AWARDS** Outstanding Educator of Am. **MEMBERSHIPS** Am Psychol Asn; PA Psychol Asn; Psychol in Indep Practice; Psychol Interested in Religious Issues. **RESEARCH** Sexual Abstinence; The Structure and Dynamics of Fun; Achieving Acceptance; The Psychology of Caretaking; The Art of Being Kind. **SELECTED PUBLICATIONS** Auth, The Search for the Holy, Cathedral Pub, Co, 99; auth, The Normal Alcoholic, Alba House, 99; auth, Ways of the Desert, Haworth Press, 00. **CONTACT ADDRESS** Div Soc Sci, Carlow Col, 3333 5th Ave, Pittsburgh, PA 15213. **EMAIL** wkraft@carlow.edu

KRAMER, JOHN E.
PERSONAL Born 05/19/1935, Philadelphia, PA, m, 1958, 2 children **DISCIPLINE** SOCIOLOGY **EDUCATION** Dartmouth Col, AB, 56; George Wash Univ, MA, 61; Yale Univ, MA, 63, PhD, 65. **CAREER** Asst prof, Univ of Mo at St Louis, 65-68; assoc prof, 68-69, prof, 69-97, prof emeritus, SUNY Brockport, 97-. **RESEARCH** Sociology of literature; fiction about higher education. **SELECTED PUBLICATIONS** Auth, North American Suburbs, Glendessary, 72; The American College Novel, Garland Pub, 81; College Mystery Novels, Garland Pub, 83; coauth, Strategy and Conflict in Metropolitan Housing, Heinemann, 78; auth, Academe in Mystery and Detective Fiction, Scarecrow, 00. **CONTACT ADDRESS** Dept of Sociology, SUNY, Col at Brockport, Brockport, NY 14420. **EMAIL** jkramer@frontiernet.net

KRAMER, JOYCE MARIE
PERSONAL Born 05/15/1941, Sacramento, CA, w, 1964, 2 children **DISCIPLINE** SOCIAL WORK **EDUCATION** Univ Colo, BA, 63; Univ Wash, MA, 73; Univ NC, PhD, 80. **CAREER** Asst prof to prof, Univ of Minn, 80-. **RESEARCH** Sustainable Development, Health and Well-Being of 3rd and 4th World peoples, especially the indigenous peoples of North America and Africa. **SELECTED PUBLICATIONS** Auth, "Social Welfare within American Indian and Alaskan Native Communites", Social Welfare with Indigenous Peoples, eds John Dixon and Robert Sheurel, Routledge, (London), 95; coauth, "Ethnic Minorities, Health Care Systems, and Behavior", Health Psychol 14.7, (96); 641-646; coauth, "Sustainable Development and Social Development: Necessary Partners for the Future in the Reality of the New Global Economy", J of Sociol and Social Welfare XXIII.1, (96): 75-91; coauth, "Canadian-Chinese Collaboration on Sustainable Development Initiatives for Social and Technological Change", Soc Develop Issues 20.1 (98); coauth, "Sustainable Development in Civil and Structural Engineering Education - A Partnership of Necessity for the Twenty-First Century", Proceedings of the Int Symp on 21st Century Educ in Civil and Structural Engineering - Higher Educ of Civil and Structural Engineering: Facing the Challenge of the 21st Century, eds Chen Yiyhi and Lu Fengwu, China Arch and Bldg Pr, (Shanghai, China), (99): 52-58; auth, "Technical and Socio-economic Change for a Sustainable Future", Pakistan Engineer, (99): 17-27; coauth, "Health Practices and Health Care Systems Among Cultural Groups", Handbook of Gender, Culture and Health, eds R.M. Eisler and M. Hersen, Lawrence Erlbaum Assoc, 00; coauth, "Cultivating Sustainability in Cuba", Sustainable Communities Rev (forthcoming); coauth, "The AIDS Pandemic and the Sustainability of African Communities", Social Develop Issues 22.1 (forthcoming). **CONTACT ADDRESS** Dept Soc Work, Univ of Minnesota, Duluth, 10 University Dr, Duluth, MN 55812. **EMAIL** jkramer@d.umn.edu

KRANTZ, GROVER S.
PERSONAL Born 11/05/1931, Salt Lake City, UT, m, 1982 **DISCIPLINE** ANTHROPOLOGY **EDUCATION** Univ Minn, PhD, 70. **CAREER** Asst prof to prof emer, Wash State Univ, 68- . **HONORS AND AWARDS** Bd dir, Int Soc Cryptozoology. **MEMBERSHIPS** Int Soc Cryptozoology. **RESEARCH** Evolution; races; linguistics; sasquatch. **SELECTED PUBLICATIONS** auth, Big Footprints: A Scientific Inquiry into the Reality of Sasquatch, Boulder Johnson Bks, 92; auth, The Antiquity of Race, Student Bookstore, 94; auth, The Process of Human Evolution, 2nd Ed, Student Bookstore, 95; auth, Only a Dog, Hoflin Publ Co, 98. **CONTACT ADDRESS** 363 Gunn Rd, Port Angeles, WA 98362. **EMAIL** krantz@olypen.com

KRAUSE, CORINNE AZEN
PERSONAL Born 03/03/1927, Pittsburgh, PA, m, 1948, 4 children **DISCIPLINE** HISTORY, SOCIOLOGY **EDUCATION** Univ Mich, BA, 48; Carnegie-Mellon Univ, MA, 66; Univ Pittsburgh, PhD(hist), 70. **CAREER** Teacher, Chatham Col, Carnegie-Mellon Univ and Univ Pittsburg, Greensburg; proj dir, Women, Ethnicity, and Mental Health Oral Hist Study, Am Jewish Comt, 75-78; Res and Writing, 78-; Proj dir, Roots and Branches, exhibit Pittsburghs Jewish hist. **MEMBERSHIPS** Inst Res Hist; Orgn Am Historians; Am Jewish Hist Soc; AHA; Oral Hist Soc. **RESEARCH** Womens history in United States; United States Jewish history; Latin American history. **SELECTED PUBLICATIONS** Auth, "Mexico, Another Promised Land," Am Jewish Hist Qtly LXI (72): 325-341; auth, "Positivist Liberalism in Mexico," Jrnl of Inter-American Stud and Wrld Affairs LVIII (76): 475-494; auth, "Italian, Jewish, and Slavic Grandmothers in Pittsburgh: Their Economic Roles," Frontiers II, (77): 18-28; auth, "Urbanization Without Breakdown: Italian, Jewish, and Slavic Immigrant Women in Pittsburgh, 1900-1945," Jrn of Urban Hist (78): 291-306, reprinted in Immigrant Women, ed Maxine Schwartz Seller, (Philadelphia: Temple Univ Press, 81); auth, Isaac W. Frank, Idustrialist and Civic Leader, Historical Soc of Western Penn (Pittsburgh), 84; auth, Los Judios in Mexico: Una Historia con Enfasis en el Periodo de 1857 a 1930, Universidad Iberoamericana (Mexico), 87; auth, Refractories: The Hidden Industry, A History of Refractories in the United States, 1860 to 1985, Am Ceramic Soc (Cincinnati), 87; auth, Grandmothers, Mothers, and Daughters: Oral Histories of Three Generations of Ethnic American Women, Twayne Publishing Company (Boston), 91; auth, Immigrant Family Patterns in Demography, Fertility, Housing, Kinship, and Urban Life, Vol 11, of American Immigration and Ethnicity, J Am Ethnic Hist, Vol 0013, 94. **CONTACT ADDRESS** 7 Darlington Ct, Pittsburgh, PA 15217. **EMAIL** ckrause@bellatlantic.net

KRAYBILL, DONALD B.
DISCIPLINE SOCIOLOGY **EDUCATION** Temple Univ, PhD, 75. **CAREER** Prof, Elizabethtown Col, Pa, 71-96; Provost, Messiah Col, Pa, 96-00. **HONORS AND AWARDS** Best relig book. **RESEARCH** Anabaptist Groups - Amish, Mennonites, Hutterites. **SELECTED PUBLICATIONS** The Riddle of Amish Culture; Amish Enterprise; Mennonite Peacemaking; Mennonite Mutual Aid. **CONTACT ADDRESS** Office of the Provost, Messiah Col, Grantham, PA 17027. **EMAIL** Kraybill4@aol.com

KRESSEL, NEIL
PERSONAL Born 08/28/1957, Newark, NJ, m, 1991, 2 children **DISCIPLINE** PSYCHOLOGY **EDUCATION** Brandeis Univ, Ba, 78; MA, 78; Harvard Univ, MA, 81; PhD, 83. **CAREER** Instr, Harvard Univ, 79-83; private consulting practice, New York, 83-90; adj asst prof, New York Univ, 89-91; adj assoc prof, Stevens Inst of Tech, 89-94; asst prof to full prof, William Paterson Univ, 85-. **SELECTED PUBLICATIONS** Auth, Mass Hate: The Global Rise of Genocide and Terror, Plenum Press: New York, 96; auth, Political Psychology: Classic and Contemporary Readings, Paragon House: New York, 93. **CONTACT ADDRESS** Dept Psychol, William Paterson Col of New Jersey, 300 Pompton Rd, Wayne, NJ 07470. **EMAIL** kresseln@wpunj.edu

KRIESBERG, LOUIS
PERSONAL Born 07/30/1926, Chicago, IL, m, 1959, 2 children **DISCIPLINE** SOCIOLOGY **EDUCATION** Univ Chicago, PhB, 47; MA, 50; PhD, 53. **CAREER** Instructor, Columbia Univ, 53-56; Res Scholar, Univ Cologne, 56-57; Sen Fel to Res Assoc, Univ Chicago, 57-62; Assoc Prof to Prof, 62-97 **HONORS AND AWARDS** Phi Beta Kappa, 50; Marshall Field Fel, 50-51; Fel, Ford Res, 52-53; Fulbright Res Scholar, 56-57; Sen Fel, Univ Chicago, 57-58; I.P. Gellman Awd, E Sociol Soc, 81; Founders Awd, Soc for the Study of Soc Prob, 90; Chancellor's Citation, Syracuse Univ, 93; Annual Awd, Peace Studies Asn, 95; Distinguished Service Awd, NY State Sociol Asn, 99. **MEMBERSHIPS** Soc for the Study of Soc Problems; Am Sociol Asn; consortium on Peace Res Educ and Dev; E Sociol Soc; Intl Peace Res Asn; Intl Sociol Asn; NY State Sociol Asn; Intl Studies Asn; Intl Soc of Polit Psychol; Am Asn of Univ Prof; Inter-Univ Sem on Armed Forces and Soc; Peace Studies Asn. **RESEARCH** Conflict analysis and resolution; Inter-communal conflicts. **SELECTED PUBLICATIONS** Ed, Research in Social Movements, Conflicts and Change, Vol I, JAI Press, 78; Vol 2, 79; Vol 3, 80; Vol 4, 81; Vol 5, 83; Vol 7, 84; Vol 8, 85; Vol 10, 88; Vol 11, 89; Vol 12, 90; Vol 14, 92; co-ed, Intractable Conflicts and Their Transofrmation, Syracuse Univ Press, 89; co-ed, Timing the De-Escalation of International Conflicts, Syracuse Univ Press, 91; auth, International conflict Resolution: The U.S.-U.S.S.R. and Arab-Israeli Cases, Yale Univ Press, 92; auth, "Preventive Conflict Resolutio of Communal Conflicts," in Wars in the Midst of Peace: The International Politics of Ethnic Conflict, Univ Pittsburgh Press, 97; auth, Contructive Conflicts: From Escalation to Resolution, Rowman & Littlefield, 98; auth, "The Phases of Destructive Communal Conflicts and Proactive Solutions," in The International Politics of Ethnic Conflict: Prevention and Peacekeeping, Univ SC Press, 98; auth, "Paths to Varieties of Inter-Communal Reconciliation," in Conflict Resolution: Dynamics, Process and Structure, Ashgate, 99; auth, "On Advancing Truth and Morality in Conflict Resolution," Peace and Conflict Studies, (99): 7-19. **CONTACT ADDRESS** Dept Sociol, Syracuse Univ, 0 Maxwell, Syracuse, NY 13244-1090. **EMAIL** lkriesbe@mailbox.syr.edu

KRING, HILDA ADAM
PERSONAL Born 01/03/1921, Munich, Germany, m, 1946 **DISCIPLINE** FOLKLORE & FOLKLIFE, ENGLISH **EDUCATION** Millersville State Col, BS, 42; Univ Pittsburgh, MLitt, 52; Univ PA, PhD(folklore, folklife), 69. **CAREER** Teacher English, social studies & Ger, Salisbury Twp High Sch, Gap, PA, 42-46; teacher English, Westmont-Upper Yoder High

Sch, Johnstown, 46-47, Adams Twp High Sch, Sidman, 47-48 & Conemaugh Twp High Sch, Davidsville, 48-56; suprv, Slippery Rock State Col, 56-68; teacher, Slippery Rock Area Joint High Sch, 58-64 & 66-67; Prof English & Commun Arts, Grove City Col, 67-. **HONORS AND AWARDS** PA Teacher of the Year, 67; Florence E. MacKenzie Campus-Community Awd, 83; Mercer Co Medical Soc -Benjamin Rush Awd for Outstanding Community Service, 87; A. G. Sikorsky Awd-Leadership through Education -United Community Hospital, 92; Grove City Area Chamber of Commerce, 96; Daughters of the Am Revolution, Excellence in Community Service, 96. **SELECTED PUBLICATIONS** Auth, The Bird That Couldn't Sing (playette), Plays, 57; Another Approach to Poetry, English J, 1/61; The Mountain Wreath, Delta Kappa Gamma J, winter 65; Mary Goes Over the Mountain, PA Folklife, summer 70; The Harmonists: A Folk Cultural Approach, Scarecrow, 73; The Cult of St Walburga in Pennsylvania, PA Folklife, winter 74-75; The Many Faces of Teaching, Univ SC, 78; The Harmonist Kuche, 98. **CONTACT ADDRESS** Dept of English, 5 Kring Dr., Grove City, PA 16127.

KRISSMAN, FRED
DISCIPLINE ANTHROPOLOGY **EDUCATION** Univ Calif, BA, 84; MA, 88; PhD, 96. **CAREER** Instr, Calif State Univ, 89; Assoc, Univ Calif, 91-92; Instr, Univ Wash, 98; Instr, Calif State Univ, 98-. **HONORS AND AWARDS** Writers grant, Wenner-Gren Foundation, 00; Resident Scholar, Rockefeller Fel, 96-97; Res Fel, Univ Miami, 95-96; Writers grant, Urban Institute, 95; Res Fel, Univ Calif, 94-95; Res Fel, Wenner-Gren Foundation, 89-90. **MEMBERSHIPS** Am Anthropol Asn, Latin Am Studies Asn, Soc for Applied Anthropol. **RESEARCH** Immigration (Mexico to US), ethnicity. **SELECTED PUBLICATIONS** Auth, Comparing Apples and Oranges: US agribusiness strategies to recruit new immigrant workers, forthcoming; auth, Coming or Going?: Mexican farm workers in California, forthcoming; auth, "Immigrant Labor Recruitment: the personnel practices of US agribusiness and undocumented migration from Mexico," in Transformations: Immigration and Immigration Research in the US, forthcoming; auth, Cycles of Poverty in Rural California, forthcoming; auth, "Undocumented Mexicans in California: disenfranchising some of our best and brightest 21st century citizens," California Studies, forthcoming; auth, "Agribusiness strategies to divide the labor force by class, ethnicity, and legal status," in Race/Ethnicity/Nationality in the United States: toward the twenty-first century, Westview press, 99; auth, "California's Agricultural Labor Market: historical variations in the use of unfree labor, c. 1769-1994," in Free and Unfree Labor: the debate continues, 97; auth, "Cycles of Poverty in Farmersville and McFarland," in Poverty amid Prosperity: immigration and the changing face of rural California, 97; auth, "Californian Agribusiness and Mexican Farm Workers (1942-1992): a bi-national agricultural system of production/reproduction, Univ Calif press, 96; auth, "The Use of Networks to Supply New Immigrant Farm Workers to Californian Agribusiness," Culture and Agriculture, (96): 3-8. **CONTACT ADDRESS** Dept Anthropol, California State Univ, Northridge, 18111 Nordhoff St, Northridge, CA 91330-8200. **EMAIL** fred.krissman@csun.edu

KRISTOFCO, JOHN P.
PERSONAL Born Cleveland, OH, m, 3 children **DISCIPLINE** EDUCATION **EDUCATION** John Carroll Univ, BA, 70; Cleveland State Univ, MA, 76; Wright State Univ, Eds, 87; Ohio State Univ, PhD, 90. **CAREER** Asst dir, Commun Learning Ctr, Cuyahuga Community Col, 72-77; fac, 77-86; chair, Educ Svcs Div, 86-91, assoc dean, 91-97, Clark State Community Col; adj assoc prof, grad sch educ, Wright State Univ, 92-97; dean, Wayne Col, 97-. **HONORS AND AWARDS** Distinguished Grad Student in Educ Administration, Wright State Univ, 87; Fleshen Fel, Ohio State Univ, 90; Two-Yearl Col Administration of the Year in Ohio, 95. **RESEARCH** Educ and culture; educational leadership; contemporary poetry. **SELECTED PUBLICATIONS** Poetry and short stories published in over 40 publications. **CONTACT ADDRESS** Univ of Akron, 1901 Smucker Rd, Orrville, OH 44667. **EMAIL** jpkrist@uakron.edu

KRONENFELD, DAVID B.
PERSONAL Born 12/21/1941, Miami Beach, FL, m, 1964, 2 children **DISCIPLINE** ANTHROPOLOGY **EDUCATION** Harvard Univ, BA, 63; Stanford Univ, MA, 65; PhD, 69. **CAREER** Asst Prof to Prof, Univ Calif, 69-. **HONORS AND AWARDS** Fel, Yale Univ, 63-64; Fel, Nat Sci Foundation, 64-65, 65-66; Fel, Am Asn for the Adv of Sci, 83; Fel, Univ CA, 92. **MEMBERSHIPS** Am Anthropol Asn; Am Ethnol Soc; Am Asn for the Adv of Sci; Coun for General Anthropol; Current Anthropol; Ling Soc of Am; Royal Anthropol Inst; SW Anthropol Asn; Soc for the Anthropol of N AM; Soc for Cultural Anthropol; Soc for Linguistic Anthropol; soc for Psychol Anthropol; Soc for Urban Anthropol. **RESEARCH** Social anthropology; Kinship; Social organization; Ethnicity and stranger communities; Linguistic anthropology; Semantics; cognitive anthropology; Computer and mathematical applications; Culture as distributed cognition; Africa. **SELECTED PUBLICATIONS** Auth, "Fanti Kinship: Language, Inheritance and Kin groups," Arthropods, (91): 19-31; auth, "Goodenough vs. Fischer on Residence: a Generation Later," Journal of Quantitative Anthropology, (92): 1-21; co-auth, "Language, Nineteen

Eighty-Four and 1989," Language in Society, (94): 555-578; auth, "Stranger Communities and 'Sweetheart Dances'," Anthropos, ((8): 77-88. **CONTACT ADDRESS** Dept Anthropol, Univ of California, Riverside, 900 University Ave, Riverside, CA 92521-0001. **EMAIL** kfeld@citrus.ucr.edu

KRONENFELD, JENNIE JACOBS
PERSONAL Born 08/11/1949, Hampton, VA, m, 1970, 3 children **DISCIPLINE** SOCIOLOGY **EDUCATION** Univ NC, BA, 71; Brown Univ, MA, 76. **CAREER** Asst Prof to Assoc Prof, Univ Ala, 75-80; Assoc Prof to Prof, Univ SC, 80-90; Prof, Ariz State Univ, 90-. **MEMBERSHIPS** Am Sociol Asn; Am Pub Health Asn; P Sociol Soc; S Sociol Soc; Soc of Behav Med; Gerontol Soc of Am; Sociol for Women in Soc; Sigma Xi. **RESEARCH** Health care policy; Health behavior and preventive health behavior; Child health; Aging. **SELECTED PUBLICATIONS** Auth, Controversial Issues in Health Care Policy, Sage Press, 93; co-auth, Confronting Ethical Dilemmas in Research and Technology, Sage, 94; co-auth, "health, Illness and Healing in an Uncertain Era: challenges from and for Medical Sociology," J of Health and Soc Behav, 95; co-auth, "Unintentional Injury: A Major Health Problem for Young Children," J of Family and Econ Issues, 95; auth, The Changing Federal Role in U.S. Health Care Policy, Praeger, 97; auth, Protecting the Future: Schools and the Health of Children, Sage, 00; ed, Research in the Sociology of Health Care: Health Care Providers, Institutions and Patients, JAI, 00; ed, Health, Illness and the use of Care, JAI, 00. **CONTACT ADDRESS** Dept Sociol, Arizona State Univ, Box 872101, Tempe, AZ 85287-2101. **EMAIL** jennie.kronenfeld@asu.edu

KRUMHANSL, CAROL L.
PERSONAL Born 09/17/1947, Providence, RI, s **DISCIPLINE** PSYCHOLOGY **EDUCATION** Wellesley Col, BA, 69; Brown Univ, AM, 73; Stanford Univ, PhD, 78. **CAREER** Asst Prof, Rockefeller Univ, 78-79; Asst prof, Harvard Univ, 79-80; Asst Prof to Full Prof, Cornell Univ, 80-. **HONORS AND AWARDS** Distinguished Sci Awd, Am Psychol Asn, 83; Fel, Am Psychol Soc, 93; Member, Soc of Experimental Psychologists, 93; Fel, Center for Adv Study in the Beh Sci, 83-84, 93-94; Visiting Scientist, IRCAM Paris, 87-88; Fulbright Fel, Finland, 98; Pres, Soc for Music Perception and Cognition, 98-01. **MEMBERSHIPS** Psychonomic Soc, Am Psychol Soc, Soc for Music Perception and Cognition, European Soc for the Cognitive Sci of Music, Soc for Res in Psychol of Music and Music Educ, Intl Cooperative in Systematic and Comparative Musicology. **RESEARCH** Experimental psychology of the perception and cognition of music, focusing on pitch structures, rhythm, and musical timbre, using mathematical, cross-cultural, and developmental approaches. **SELECTED PUBLICATIONS** Auth, Music Perception. Encyclopedia of Psychology, 00; auth, "Rhythm and pitch in music cognition," Psychological Bulletin, (00): 159-179; auth, "Melodic expectancy in Finnish folk hymns: Convergence of behavioral, statistical, and computational approaches," Music Perception, (99): 151-196; auth, Hearing (human), infant's perception of music, McGraw-Hill, 99; auth, "Neo-Riemannian Transformations: Mathematics and Applications," Journal of Music Theory, (98): 265-281; auth, "Topic in music: An empirical study of memorability, openness, and emotion in Mozart's Quintet in C major and Beethoven's Strong quartet in A minor," Music Perception, (98): 119-134; auth, "An exploratory study of musical emotions and psychophysiology," Canadian Journal of Psychology, (98): 36-52; auth, "Can dance reflect the structural and expressive qualities of music? A perceptual experiment on Balanchine's choreography of Mozart's Divertimento No. 15," Musicae Scientiae, (97): 63-85; auth, "Effects of perceptual organization and musical form on melodic expectancies," in Music, Gestalt, and Computing: Studies in cognitive and systematic musicology, Berlin, 97; auth, "An experimental study of internalized interval standards of Javanese and Western musicians," Music Perception, (96): 95-116. **CONTACT ADDRESS** Dept Psychol, Cornell Univ, 211 Uris Hall, Ithaca, NY 14853. **EMAIL** clk4@cornell.edu

KRUMHOLZ, SUSAN
PERSONAL Born 12/10/1953, Trenton, NJ, m, 1996 **DISCIPLINE** SOCIOLOGY **EDUCATION** Keene State Col, BA, 75; Univ Puget Sound, JD, 78; Northeastern Univ, MS, 89; PhD, 00. **CAREER** Attorney, 78-89; Visiting Lecturer and Prog Coordinator, Univ Mass, 90-. **MEMBERSHIPS** Am Soc of Criminol, Acad of Criminal Justice Sci. **RESEARCH** Domestic Violence; Policing D.V.; Restorative Justices and D.V. **CONTACT ADDRESS** Dept Anthropol & Sociol, Univ of Massachusetts, Dartmouth, 285 Old Westport Rd, North Dartmouth, MA 02747.

KUBEY, ROBERT W.
PERSONAL Born 07/20/1952, Berkeley, CA, m, 1981, 2 children **DISCIPLINE** PSYCHOLOGY, BEHAVIORAL SCIENCE, HUMAN DEVELOPMENT **EDUCATION** Univ Calif, Santa Cruz, AB, 74; Univ Chicago, MA, 78, PhD, 84. **CAREER** Asst prof, 85-91, Assoc Prof Commun, 91-99, Assoc Prof Journalism and Media Studies, 99-; DIR, Center for Media Studies, DIR, Master's Prog Commun Info Stud, Rutgers Univ, 97-. **HONORS AND AWARDS** Conference Grant funding from Johnson & Johnson, Centers for Disease Control, National Cancer Institute; Discovery Channel; Res award, Sch Commun,

Rutgers Univ, 97-98; Annenberg Scholar, 93; Ctr Critical Analysis of Contemporary Cult fel, 86-87; fel, Nat Inst Mental Health, 84-85. **MEMBERSHIPS** Nat Commun Asn; Int Commun Asn; Asn Media Literacy. **RESEARCH** Media analysis, production and soc of culture; media literacy; psychol and polit impact of media. **SELECTED PUBLICATIONS** Co-auth, Television and the Quality of Life: How Viewing Shapes Everyday Experience, Lawrence Erlbaum Assoc, 90; ed, Media Literacy in the Information Age: Current Perspectives, in Information and Behavior, Vol 6, Transaction Publishers, 97; auth, Creating Television: Then and Now, Lawrence Erlbaum Assoc, forthcoming; auth, Obstacles to the Development of Media Education in the United States, J of Commun, 48, 98. **CONTACT ADDRESS** Center for Media Studies, Rutgers, The State Univ of New Jersey, New Brunswick, 4 Huntington St, New Brunswick, NJ 08901-1071. **EMAIL** kubey@scils.rutgers.edu

KUBOVY, MICHAEL
DISCIPLINE PSYCHOLOGY **EDUCATION** Hebrew Univ Jerusalem, BA, 65; PhD, 72. **CAREER** Vis asst prof, Univ of IL, 72-73; asst to assoc prof, Yale Univ, 72-78; assoc prof to prof, 78-79, 80-87; prof, Univ of Va, 87-. **HONORS AND AWARDS** NSF Grants, 83-86, 87-90; Fel, Am Psychol Assoc; Fel, Am Psychol Soc; Sr Fel, Univ of Va; Fel, Soc of Experimental Psychol; Cattell Fel, 98-99. **MEMBERSHIPS** Am Psychol Assoc; Psychonomic Soc; Am Psychol Soc; Assoc for Res in Vision and Ophthalmology. **SELECTED PUBLICATIONS** Coed, Perceptual Organization, Erlbaum, (Hillsdale, NJ), 81; auth, The psychology of perspective and renaissance art, Cambridge Univ Pr, (NY), 86; auth, The arrow in the eye: the psychology of perspective and Renaissance art, Muzzio (Padua), 92; auth, "Pleasures of the Mind", Well-being: The Foundations of Hedonic Psychology, eds D. Kahneman, E. Diener and N. Schwarz, Russell Sage Found (NY, 99): 134-154; coauth, "Perceiving transformations of space in perspective pictures", Perception & Psychophysics 61 (99): 456-467; auth, "Gestalt: From Phenomena to Laws", Perceptual Organization for Artificial Vision systems, ed K. Boyer and S. Sarkar, Kluwar Acad Pub, (Dordrecht, Netherlands, 00): 41-72; auth, "Visual aesthetics", Encyclopedia of Psychology, ed E. Kazdin, Oxford Univ Pr, (NY), (forthcoming); coauth, "Internalization: A metaphor we can live without", Brain & Behav Sci, (forthcoming), coauth, "Auditory and visual objects", Cognition (forthcoming). **CONTACT ADDRESS** Dept Psychol, Univ of Virginia, filmer Hall, Charlottesville, VA 22903-2477. **EMAIL** kubovy@virginia.edu

KUCAN, LINDA
PERSONAL Born 12/13/1948, Steubenville, OH, s **DISCIPLINE** EDUCATION **EDUCATION** WVa Univ, BA, 70; MA, 74; Carnegie Mellon Univ, BS, 79; Univ Pittsburgh, PhD, 98. **CAREER** VP, Macmillan Pub Co, 80-93; Res Asst, Univ Pittsburgh, 93-96; Asst Prof, Bethany Col, 97-. **HONORS AND AWARDS** Jean Slack Fel, Univ Pittsburgh, 96; Teacher of the Month, Bethany Col, 97; Richard B. Kenney Awd, 99. **MEMBERSHIPS** Am Educ Res Asn; Am Psychol Soc; Asn for Supervision and Curriculum Dev; Intl Reading Asn; Nat Coun of Teachers of Eng; Nat Reading Conf; OH Valley Lang Arts Coun; Teachers and Writers Collaborative; WV Lang Arts Coun; WV State Reading Asn; WV Writers, Inc. **SELECTED PUBLICATIONS** Auth, "The art of publishing illustrated tradebooks that have already been published," Language Arts, (94): 220-228; co-auth, "Four fourth graders thinking aloud: An investigation of genre effects," The Journal of Literacy Research, (96): 259-287; co-auth, "Thinking aloud and reading comprehension research: Inquiry, instruction, and social interaction," Review of Educational Research, (97): 271-299; co-auth, "Getting at the meaning," American Educator, (98): 66-71, 85; co-auth, "Engaging students in communicating their understanding as they construct it: A comparison of individual and group interactions with expository texts," forthcoming. **CONTACT ADDRESS** Dept Prof Studies, Bethany Col, West Virginia, RR 1, Bethany, WV 26032. **EMAIL** l.kucan@mail.bethanywv.edu

KUHLMANN, ANNETTE
DISCIPLINE SOCIOLOGY **EDUCATION** Univ Kans, MA, 82; PhD, 89; MA, 91; PhD, 98. **CAREER** Teaching Asst to Instructor, Univ Kans, 82-90; Prof, Univ Wisc, 94-. **HONORS AND AWARDS** Helen Waddle Roofe Summer Scholarship, 90; PEO Intl Peace Scholarship, 83-84; DAAD Scholarship, 80-81. **RESEARCH** Race and Ethnic Relations; Contemporary North American Indians; Social Inequalities; Gender; Social Theory; Crime and Criminology. **SELECTED PUBLICATIONS** Auth, "Collaborative Research Among the Kickapoo of Oklahoma," Human Organization, 92; auth, "American Indian Women of the Plains and Northern Woodlands," Mid-American review of sociology, 92; auth, "On the Critique of sociology - Herbert Marcuse," Mid-American Review of Sociology, 92; auth, "Tribes, States,· and stereotypes: Indian Gaming and Changing Political Relationships," forthcoming; auth, Bingo, Blackjack, and One-Armed Bandits in the Northwoods: Indian Gaming on the National, State, and Tribal Levels, forthcoming. **CONTACT ADDRESS** Dept Soc Sci, Univ of Wisconsin Ctr, Baraboo/Sauk County, 1006 Connie Rd, Baraboo, WI 53913. **EMAIL** akuhlman@uwc.edu

KULKOSKY, PAUL
PERSONAL Born 03/03/1949, Newark, NJ, m, 1978 **DISCIPLINE** PSYCHOLOGY **EDUCATION** Columbia Univ NY City, BA, 71; MA, 72; Univ Wash, PhD, 75. **CAREER** Res Assoc, Cornell Univ White Plains NY, 80-81; Instr, Cornell Univ White Plains NY, 81-82; Asst Prof to Prof, Univ Southern Colo, 82-; Chemn Dept Psychology, Univ Southern Colo, 88-91; Bd of Advisors Pueblo Zool Soc, 84-85, 88-91; Bd of Dir, Pueblo Zool Sol, 85-88; Editorial Consult to Publ, Consult Ed J of Neurotherapy. **HONORS AND AWARDS** Hon Affiliate Prof, Am Univ Wash, 77; Res Grant, NEH, 84-97; Staff Fel Nat Inst Alcohol Abuse and Alcoholism, 76-80; Phi Kappa Phi; Sigma Xi. **MEMBERSHIPS** AAAS, Consortium Aquariums, Univs and Zoos, Int Soc Biomedical Res on Alcoholism, Soc for Study of Ingestive Behavior, Colo-Wyo Acad Sci, Univ Southern Colo Club. **RESEARCH** Physiological psychology. **SELECTED PUBLICATIONS** Coauth, "Conditioned aversions induced by alcohol and lithium in rats selectively bred for ethanol sensitivity," Alcoholism: Clinical and Exp Res 19 (95): 945-950; coauth, "Glucagon produces delayed increase in drinking-associated food intake," Mod Psychol Studies 3(950: 29-35; coauth, "Angiotensisn II reduces alcohol intake and choice in water- or food-restricted rats," Alcohol 1113 (96): 359-363; auth, "Neuropeptidergic control of ethanol intake," Toxin Rev 15 (96): 341-351; coauth, "Psoralen-induced growth inhibition in Wister rats," Cancer Letters 114 (97): 159-160; coauth, "Mammalian toxicity of 5-methoxypsoralen and 8-methoxypsoralen, two compounds used in skin photochemotherapy," J of Natural Toxins 6 (97): 183-192; coauth, "Interaction of CCk and 8-OH-DPAT in the satiation of alcohol intake," Alcohol 16 (98): 305-309; coauth, "Neurofeedback in the treatment of addictive disorders," in Introduction to Quantitative EEG and Neurofeedback, ed. J.R. Evans and A. Abarbanel (San Diego, CA: Acad Press, 99), 157-179; coauth, "A novel group of ovarian toxicants: The psoralens," J of Biochemical and Molecular Toxicology 13-3/4 (99): 195-203; coauth, "Thyrotropin releasing hormone decreases alcohol intake and preferences in rats," Alcohol 20 (00): 87-91. **CONTACT ADDRESS** Dept Psychology, Univ of So Colorado, 2200 Bonforte Blvd, Pueblo, CO 81001. **EMAIL** kulkosky@uscolo.edu

KUNKEL, CHARLOTTE A.
PERSONAL Born 03/10/1966, St Cloud, MN **DISCIPLINE** SOCIOLOGY **EDUCATION** St. Cloud State Univ, MN, BA, 88; Univ Colo, Boulder, PhD, 95. **CAREER** Asst prof, Luther Col. **MEMBERSHIPS** ASA, MSS, IVSA, SSSI. **RESEARCH** Gender, race, stratification, visual sociology. **SELECTED PUBLICATIONS** Auth, "Meeting Women's Needs on the University Campus," Initiatives, J Nat Asn Women Ed, 56(2), 15-28 (94); coauth with Suzanne K. Leahy, "Human Sexuality," Teaching Sociology, vol 23, no 4, 424-426 (95); auth with Feminist Scholars in Sociology, "What's Wrong is Right: A Response to the State of the Discipline," Sociol Forum, vol 10, no 3, 493-498 (95); coauth with Joyce M. Nielson, "Gender, Residual Deviance, and Social Control," Deviant Behaviour, 19:339-360 (98); auth, "A Visual Analysis of Feminist Dress," The Meanings of Dress, eds Mary Lynn Damhorst, Kimberly A. Miller, and Susan O. Michelman, Faitchild Pubs: NY (99); coauth with Linda Boynton Arthur, "The Complexities of Feminist Bodies: Negotiating Engendered Space," in Paidnesis: J of Interdisciplinary and Cross-Cultural Studies, 2:1-15 (2000); coauth with Joyce McCarl Nielson and Glenda Walden, "Gendered Heteronormativity: Empirical Illustrations in Everyday Life," The Sociol Quart, 41(2) (May 2000); auth, "Starting a Women's Center," The Handbook for the College and University Women's Center, ed Sharon Davie, Greenwood Pub Group (forthcoming). **CONTACT ADDRESS** Dept Sociol & Anthropol, Luther Col, 700 Col Dr, Decorah, IA 52101.

KUNZ, GEORGE
PERSONAL Born 07/03/1934, Spokane, WA, m, 1974, 5 children **DISCIPLINE** PSYCHOLOGY **EDUCATION** Gonzaga Univ, BA, 60; Marquette Univ, MA, 64; Duquesne Univ, PhD, 75. **CAREER** Assoc prof, Seattle Univ, 71-. **HONORS AND AWARDS** Gaffney Chair, 88-91; Teacher of the Year, Seattle, 88; McGoldric Fel, 95-96. **RESEARCH** Philosophical foundations of psychology. **SELECTED PUBLICATIONS** Auth, The Paradox of Power and Weakness, SUNY Press, 98. **CONTACT ADDRESS** Dept Psychol, Seattle Univ, 901 12th Ave, Seattle, WA 98122. **EMAIL** gkunz@seattleu.edu

KUNZ, JENNIFER
PERSONAL Born 01/13/1967, Evanston, WY, s **DISCIPLINE** SOCIOLOGY **EDUCATION** Brigham Young Univ, PhD, 94. **CAREER** Asst Prof to Assoc Prof, W Tex A&M Univ, 93-. **HONORS AND AWARDS** Outstanding Prof Awd, W Tex A&M Univ; President's Teaching Fel, W Tex A&M Univ. **MEMBERSHIPS** ASA, NCFA, ISA, CFR. **RESEARCH** Family; Organization, Race and ethnicity; Gender. **SELECTED PUBLICATIONS** Auth, "Social Class differences in Response to Christmas Cards," Perceptual And Motor Skills, forthcoming; auth, "The Intergenerational Transmission of Divorce: A Nine Generation Study,: Journal of Divorce and Remarriage, forthcoming; auth, "Parental Divorce and Children's Interpersonal Relationships: A Meta-analysis," Journal of Divorce and Remarriage, forthcoming; auth, "Christmas Cards: A Study of Social class," in Sociology 2000 - The New Millennium, Hunt Pub, forthcoming; auth, "Introduction to Sociology," in Sociology 2000 - The New Millennium, Hunt Pub, forthcoming; auth, "Depression and Suicide in the Dark Months," Perceptual and Motor Skills, (97): 537-538; auth, "A Profile of Parental Homicide Against Children,: Journal of Family Violence, (96): 337-352; auth, "Divorce and Social Support," Journal of Divorce and Remarriage, (95): 111-119; auth, "The Impact of Divorce on children's Intellectual Functioning: A Meta-analysis," Family Perspective, (95): 75-101 **CONTACT ADDRESS** Dept Beh Sci, West Texas A&M Univ, 2501 4th Ave, Canyon, TX 79016-0002. **EMAIL** jkunz@mail.wtamu.edu

KUPERS, TERRY
PERSONAL Born 10/14/1943, Philadelphia, PA, m, 1982, 3 children **DISCIPLINE** PSYCHOLOGY **EDUCATION** Stanford Univ, BA, 64; Univ Calif at Los Angeles, MD, 68; MSP, 74. **CAREER** Asst prof, Charles Drew Med School 74-76; co-dir, richmond CMH Center, 79-81; prof, Wright Inst, 81-. **HONORS AND AWARDS** Alpha Omega Alpha, 68. **MEMBERSHIPS** Am Psychiat Assoc; Am Orthopsychiatric Assoc; Am Assoc of Community Psychiatrists. **RESEARCH** Psychotherapy, public mental health, gender studies and prisons. **SELECTED PUBLICATIONS** Auth, Public Therapy: The Practice of Psychotherapy in the Public Mental Health Clinic, Free Pr, 81; auth, Ending Therapy: The Meaning of Termination, NY Univ Pr, 88; auth, Revisioning Men's Lives: Gender, Intimacy and Power, Guilford, 93; auth, Prison Madness: The Mental Health Crisis Behind Bars and What We Must Do About It, Jossey Bass, 99. **CONTACT ADDRESS** Dept Psychol, Wright Inst, 2728 Durant Ave, Berkeley, CA 94704. **EMAIL** kupers@igc.org

KURZMAN, PAUL
PERSONAL Born 11/25/1938, New York, NY, m, 1965, 2 children **DISCIPLINE** SOCIAL WORK **EDUCATION** Princeton Univ, AB, 60; Columbia Univ, MS, 64; NY Univ, PhD, 70. **CAREER** Program Dir, Industrial Soc Welfare Cent Columbia Univ, 72-74; Prof, CUNY, 72-. **HONORS AND AWARDS** Exceptional Career Leadership Awd, Col Univ School of Soc Work, 97; Lifetime Prof Achievement Awd, Nat Asn of Soc Workers, 91; Employee Assistance Educ Awd, New York, 89; Founders Day Awd, New York Univ, 71; Dr. Martin E. Dworkis Memorial Awd, New York Univ, 70; Asn of the US Army Awd, 61; Distinguished Military Grad, Officer Candidate School, 60. **SELECTED PUBLICATIONS** Auth, Work and the Workplace: Implications for Social Work Policy and Practice, Columbia Univ Press, forthcoming; auth, "Bakalinsky's Conundrum: Should Social Workers Practice in the World of Work," Administration in Social Work, 99; auth, "Introduction," in Register of Clinical Social Workers, Washington, 99; auth, "Workplace Ethics: Issues for Human Service Professionals," in The Encyclopedia of Applied Ethics, Academic Press, 98; auth, "Managing Risk in Nonprofit Settings," in Skills for Effective Management of Nonprofit Organizations, Washington, 98; auth, "Professional Liability and Malpractice," in The Encyclopedia of Social Work, Washington, 95; auth, Psychosocial and Policy Issues in the World of Work, Families International Press, 95; ed, Work and Well-Being: The Occupational Social Work Advantage, NASW Press, 93; ed, Work, Workers and Work Organizations: A View from Social Work, Prentice-Hall, 82; ed, Labor and Industrial Settings: Sites for Social Work practice, Columbia Univ, 79. **CONTACT ADDRESS** School of Soc Work, Hunter Col, CUNY, 695 Park Ave, New York, NY 10021. **EMAIL** paul.kurzman@hunter.cuny.edu

KUTHER, TARA
PERSONAL Born 04/26/1972, New York, NY **DISCIPLINE** PSYCHOLOGY **EDUCATION** Fordham Univ, MA, 95; PhD, 98; Western CT State Univ, BA, 93. **CAREER** Asst Prof, Western CT State Univ, 89-. **HONORS AND AWARDS** Putting Children First Fel, Columbia Univ, 95; Presidential Scholarship, Fordham Univ, 93-98. **MEMBERSHIPS** American Psych Assoc, Society for Research on Adolescence, Society for Research on Child Development. **RESEARCH** Social Cognition and Risky Behavior, Adolescence and Young Adult, Ethics. **SELECTED PUBLICATIONS** Auth, Rational decision perspectives on alcohol consumption by youth: Revising the theory of planned behavior, Addictive Behaviors; auth, "Moral reasoning, perceived competence, and adolescent engagement in risky activity," Journal of Adolescence; auth, "Bridging the gap between moral reasoning and adolescent engagement in risky behavior, "Journal of Adolescence; auth, "Competency to provide informed consent in older adulthood," Gerontology and Geriatrics Education, 20 (1): 15-30; auth, "A developmental-contextual perspective on youth covictimization by community violence," Adolescence 34, 699-714; auth, "Victimization by community violence of young adolescents from a suburban city," Journal of Early Adolescent, 18 (1): 53-76; auth, Excerpted in Heath and Psychosocial Instruments Database; auth, "Integrating research ethics into the introductory psychology curriculum," Teaching of Psychology 24 (3): 172-175; Reprinted in Hartley, J & McKeachie, W 99, Teaching psychology: Readings from Teaching of Psychology, (Mahwah, NJ, Lawrence Erlbaum); auth, Ethical issues in longitudinal research with at-risk children and adolescents; auth, Research ethics: Fifteen cases and commentaries, ed. B. Schrag (Bloomington, IN), Assoc for Practical and Prof Ethics; auth, Referring and reporting research participants at risk: Views from urban adolescents, Child Development 67 (5): 2086-2100; Reprinted in Hertzig, M E, Farber, E A et all, 98, Annual progress in child psychiatry and child development, (Bristol, PA), 97, Brunner/Mazel, Inc; auth, Doctoral training in applied development psychology: Matching graduate education and accreditation standards to student need, career opportunity, and licensure requirements, Applied development science: Graduate training for diverse disciplines and educational settings, (Norwood, NJ), Ablex Publishing Corp. **CONTACT ADDRESS** Dept Psychology, Western Connecticut State Univ, 181 White St, Danbury, CT 06810. **EMAIL** kuthert@ucsu.edu

KUTULAS, JUDY
PERSONAL Born 02/22/1953, San Francisco, CA, m, 1986, 2 children **DISCIPLINE** US HISTORY, AMERICAN STUDIES, WOMENS STUDIES **EDUCATION** Univ Cal, BA, 75; Univ Calif at Los Angeles, MA, 77; PhD, 86. **CAREER** Loyola Univ, 86; Univ St Thomas, 87; asst, assoc prof, St Olaf, 89-. **HONORS AND AWARDS** ACLS Gnt; NEH Trv Gnt; Newberry Lib Fel. **MEMBERSHIPS** AHA; OAH; PCA; ASA. **RESEARCH** 20th Century American liberals and radicals; media; gender. **SELECTED PUBLICATIONS** Auth, The Long War: The Intellectual People's Front and Anti-Stalinism, 1930-1940, Duke Univ Press (95). **CONTACT ADDRESS** Dept History, St. Olaf Col, 1520 St Olaf Ave, Northfield, MN 55057-1574. **EMAIL** kutulas@stolaf.edu

KWIATKOWSKI, J.
PERSONAL Born 11/11/1971, Toledo, OH, s **DISCIPLINE** PSYCHOLOGY **EDUCATION** St Mary's Col, BA, 94. **CAREER** Interface designer, Andersen Cons, 94-96. **HONORS AND AWARDS** Who's Who Among Am Col Students, 94; St Mary's Outstanding Achievement in Psychol, 94; Outstanding Grad Student, Univ of Maine, 98-99. **MEMBERSHIPS** Am Psychol Assoc; Int Assoc of Empirical Aesthetics. **SELECTED PUBLICATIONS** Rev, Empirical Studies of the Arts: 1998; coauth, "The aesthetic merit of academic art", General psychology and psychology of arts and literature at the beginning of the third era, eds A. Fusco and R. Tomassoni, Angeli, (Milan), 98; coauth, "Creativity and speed of information processing", Empirical Studies of the Arts 17.2 (99): 187-196. **CONTACT ADDRESS** Dept Psychol, Univ of Maine, 5742 Little Hall, Orono, ME 04469-5742. **EMAIL** jkwiat61@maine.edu

KYLE HIGGINS, AMANDA
DISCIPLINE GENERAL AND SPECIAL EDUCATION; LEARNING DISABILITIES **EDUCATION** Univ NMex, BA, 73, MA, 78, PhD, 88. **CAREER** Coordr, spec educ undergrad prog, spec educ grad generalist prog, Univ Nev, Las Vegas. **HONORS AND AWARDS** University System and Nevada Board of Regents Salute to Higher Education Awd, 96, 98; Clarke County School District Bean of Light Awd, 96; College of Education Res Awd, 98. **MEMBERSHIPS** CEC; CLD; AERA; ASCD. **RESEARCH** Special Edcucation Technology; Reading; Alternative Methods of Providing teacher education; diversity issues in education. **SELECTED PUBLICATIONS** Coauth, "Computer-based multimedia and videodiscs: Uses in supporting content-area instruction for student with LD," Intervention in School and Clinic, 32 (97): 302-311; coauth, "A technology toolbook for science education," J of Sci for Persons with Disabilites, 1 (98): 2-13; coauth, "Delivering instruction via interactive television and videotape: Student achievement and satisfaction," J of Special Education Technol, 13 (98): 59-77; coauth, "Expanding the writing process with the World Wide Web," Teaching Execptional Children, 30 (98): 22-26; coauth, "Children who are homeless: Implications for educational diagnosticians," Special Services in the Schools 13 (98): 63-83; coauth, "Research-to-practice: Suggestions for educators," Intervention in School and Clinic 34 (99): 205-211, 223; coauth, "A new challenge for school counselors: Children who are homeless," Professional School Counseling, 3 (00): 162-171; coauth, "Health issues of Gay and Lesbian youth: Implications for Schools," J of Health Education, 31 (00): 28-36; coauth, "Forming and Benefiting from Educator Study Groups," Teaching Exceptional Children, 32 (00): 30-37. **CONTACT ADDRESS** Dept of Spec Educ, Univ of Nevada, Las Vegas, 4505 Maryland Pky, Las Vegas, NV 89154-3014. **EMAIL** higgins@nevada.edu

L

L'ABATE, LUCIANO
PERSONAL Born 09/19/1928, Brindisi, Italy, m, 1958, 2 children **DISCIPLINE** PSYCHOLOGY **EDUCATION** Tabor Col, BA, 50; Wichita State Univ, MA, 53; Duke Univ, PhD, 56. **CAREER** Prof emer, psychol, Ga State Univ. **HONORS AND AWARDS** "Family Psychologist of the Year 94" Division of Family Psychology; Am Psychol Asn. **MEMBERSHIPS** Am Psychol Asn; Am Asn Marriage & Family Ther. **RESEARCH** Computer assisted interventions; Programmed distance writing. **SELECTED PUBLICATIONS** Ed, Family Psychopathology: The Relational Roots of Dysfunctional Behavior, Guilford Press, 98; auth, "How Should a Theory of Personality Socialization in the Family Be Evaluated? Strategies of Theory Testing,"

Famiglia, Interdisciplinarita', Ricera: Rivista di Studi Familiari, 98; auth, "Increasing Intimacy in Couples Through Distance Writing and Face-to-Face Approaches," The Intimate Couple, 98; coauth, "The Forgotten Others: The Importance of Prevention With Couples and Families," The Family and Family Therapy in International Perspective, 98; ed, "Distance Writing and Computer-assisted Interventions," in Psychiatry and Mental Health, Greenwood Press, 01; auth, Beyond Psychotherapy: Programmed Writing and Structured Computer-Assisted Interventions, Greenwood Press (forthcoming); ed, Workbooks in Mental Health, Haworth Press (forthcoming). **CONTACT ADDRESS** Dept of Psychol, Georgia State Univ, Univ Plaza, Atlanta, GA 30303. **EMAIL** labate@gsu.edu

LA JEUNESSE, CHARLES A.
PERSONAL Born 06/10/1949, Phillipsburg, NJ, m, 1977, 2 children **DISCIPLINE** PSYCHOLOGY **EDUCATION** Univ Mo at Rolla, BS, 70; Univ Mo at Columbia, Med, 76; PhD, 79. **CAREER** From asst prof to prof, Col Misericordia, 79-; dir of counseling, Col Misericordia, 81-84. **HONORS AND AWARDS** Faculty Development Awd, 89-91. **MEMBERSHIPS** Am Psychol Asn, Soc for the Teaching of Psychol, Am Counseling Asn, Pa Psychol Asn, Asn for the Treatment of Sex Abusers. **RESEARCH** Program Evaluation, Teaching Pedagogy. **SELECTED PUBLICATIONS** Auth, "Ranking characteristics: A comparison of decision-making approaches," in 1987 Annual: Developing Human Resources (Univ Associates, 87); coauth, "Generalizing a predictor of male alcoholic treatment outcomes," The Int J of Addictions 23.2 (88): 183-205; auth, "Facilitating Inclusion: the role of learning strategies to support secondary students with special needs," Preventing School Failure 39.3 (95): 35-39. **CONTACT ADDRESS** Dept Behav Sci, Col Misericordia, 301 Lake St, Dallas, PA 18612. **EMAIL** clajeune@miseri.edu

LABIANCA, OYSTEIN S.
PERSONAL Born 09/10/1949, Kristiansand, Norway, m, 1972, 3 children **DISCIPLINE** ANTHROPOLOGY **EDUCATION** Andrews Univ, BA, 71; Loma Linda Univ, MA, 76; Brandeis Univ, PhD, 87; Cambridge Univ, Eng, Post-doc fel, 90. **CAREER** Assoc dir, Inst Archaeol, 81-, Andrews Univ; dir, Hinterland proj, 82-, Madaba Plains Proj, Jordan; res prof, dept beh sci, 91-, Andrews Univ. **HONORS AND AWARDS** NEH Res Grant, 79; NEH Fel, 89; NGS Res Grant, 97. **MEMBERSHIPS** Amer Antaro Assn; Soc Amer Archaeol; Amer Schls of Orient Res. **RESEARCH** Ancient and modern food systems **SELECTED PUBLICATIONS** Auth, Sedentarization and Nomadization: Food System Cycles at Hesban and Vicinity in Transjordan, Andrew Univ Press, 90; art, Food Systems Research: An Overview and a Case Study From Madaba Plains, Food & Foodways 4, 91; art, Residential Caves and Rock Shelters, Amer J of Anthrop 96:541, 92; auth, The Fluidity of Tribal Peoples in Central Transjordan: Four Millenia of Sedentarization and Nomadization on the Madaba Plains, Middle East - Unity & Diversity papers from the 2nd Nordic Conf on Middle East Stud, 93. **CONTACT ADDRESS** 4075 Lake Chapin Rd, Berrien Springs, MI 49103-9654. **EMAIL** labianca@andrews.edu

LACY, WILLIAM B.
PERSONAL Born 04/27/1942, Wellsville, NY, m, 2 children **DISCIPLINE** SOCIOLOGY, SOCIAL PSYCHOLOGY **EDUCATION** Cornell Univ, BS, 64; Colgate Univ, MA, 65; Univ Mich, MA, 71, PhD, 75. **CAREER** Asst Dean for Res and Asst Dir of the Experiment Station, Col of Agricultural Scis, Pa State Univ, 89-94; Assoc Dean-Cols of Agriculture and Life Scis, and Human Ecology, Cornell Univ, Dir, Cornell Cooperative Extension, 94-98; prof, Dept Rural Sociol, Cornell Univ, 98-99; Vice Provost, Univ Outreach and Int Progs, Univ Calif, Davis, 99-. **HONORS AND AWARDS** Fel, Am Asn for the Advancement of Sci, 90; Pres, Agriculture, Food, Human Values, 92-93; mem, President Clinton's Coun on Sustainable Develop, Sustainable Communities Task Force, Environmental Working Group, 94-95; mem, Bd of Trustees, Nat 4-H Coun, 96-98; chair, Nat Asn of State Univs and Land Grant Cols-Extension Comt on Org and Policy, 1998 Budget Comt, 96-98; Pres-elect, and Pres, Rural Sociol Soc, 97-99; Sr adv Comt, Res Competitiveness Prog, Am Asn for the Advancement of Sci, 97-99. **MEMBERSHIPS** Agriculture, Food, Human Values Soc; Am Asn for the Advancement of Sci; Am Sociol Asn; Community Develop Soc; Epsilon Sigma Phi; Gamma Sigma Delta; Int Rural Sociol Soc; Rural Sociol Soc. **RESEARCH** Sociology of science; sociology of agriculture and agricultural research (U.S. and international); organizational behavior/social psychology of organizations; sociology/social psychology of education and outreach. **SELECTED PUBLICATIONS** Coauth with L. Busch, J. Burkhardt, D. Hemken, J. Morega, T. Koponen, and J. Silva, Making Nature, Shaping Culture: Plant Biodiversity in Global Context, Lincoln, NE: Univ Nebr Press (95); auth, "Socioeconomic context and political strategies for U. S. public agricultural sciences," Sci and Public Policy, 22, 4 (95): 239-247; auth, "The global plant genetic resources system: A competition-cooperation paradox," Crop Sci, 35, 2 (95): 335-345; auth, "Research, extension and user partnerships: Models for collaboration and strategies for change," Agriculture and Human Values, 13, 2 (96): 33-41; auth, "Educating lifelong learners for the American food system," in W. Lockeretz, ed, Visions of American Agriculture, Ames, IA: Iowa State Univ Press (97); auth, "Impact 98: Cornell University Addresses Contemporary Issues, with D. Lund and F. Firebaugh, Report of the Colleges of Agriculture and Life sciences, Human Ecology and Cornell Cooperative Extension (97); auth, "Empowering communities: Revisiting democracy and globalization," Rural Sociol, 65, 1 (2000): 3-26; auth, "Agricultural biotechnology, policy and the fourth criterion," in M. Mehlman and T. M. Murray, eds, Encyclopedia of Biotechnology: Ethical, legal and Policy Issues, NY: John Wiley and Sons, Inc (forthcoming); auth, "Generation and commercialization of Knowledge: Trends, implications and models for public and private agricultural research and education," in S. Wolfe, ed, Knowledge, Generation and Transfer: Implications for Agriculture in the 21st Century (forthcoming). **CONTACT ADDRESS** Vice Provost, Univ Outreach & Int Progs, Univ of California, Davis, 577 Mrak Hall, One Shields Ave, Davis, CA 95616. **EMAIL** Wblacy@ucdavis.edu

LADERMAN, CAROL
PERSONAL Born 10/25/1932, Brooklyn, NY, m, 1953, 2 children **DISCIPLINE** ANTHROPOLOGY **EDUCATION** Columbia Univ, PhD, 77. **CAREER** Vis Lect, Yale Univ, 80-82; Assoc Prof, Fordham Univ, 82-90; Prof, Chemn, City Col CUNY, 90-. **HONORS AND AWARDS** Danforth Foun 72-75, 78; Soc Sci Res Counc, 75-78; NIMH, 75-78; NEH, 82-85, 87-90; Guggenheim Memorial Found, 87-88; Stirling Awd, 87: Rockefeller Found Resident Scholar Bellagio Ctr, 89; Smithsonian Inst, 90; Victor Turner Awd, 91. **RESEARCH** Cultural Anthropology, Medical Anthropology, Southeast Asia. **SELECTED PUBLICATIONS** Auth, Wives and Midwives: Childbirth and Nutrition in Rural Malaysia, Univ of Calif Press (Los Angeles and Berkeley), 83, 87; co-ed, Techniques of Healing in Southeast Asian, publ as Spec Issue of Soc Sci and Med 27-8 (Oxford: Pergamon Press, 88); auth, Taming the Wind of Desire: Psychology, Medicine and Aesthetics in Malay Shamanistic Performance, Univ of Calif Press (Los Angeles, Berkeley, and London), 91, 92; auth, Main Peteri: Malay Shamanism, Fed Museum J Monograph (Kuala Lumpur), 91; co-ed, The Performance of Healing, Routledge (NY), 96; auth, "The Poetics of Healing," in The Performance of Healing, ed. Carol Laderman and Marina Roseman (NY: Routledge, 96); auth, "The Limits of Magic," Am Anthropologist 99-2 (97): 331-341; auth, "Destructive Heat and Cooling Prayer: Malay Humoralism in Pregnancy, Childbirth, and the Postpartum Period," in The Daughters of Hariti: Childbirth and Female Healers in South and Southeast Asia, ed. Goeffrey Samuel and Santi Rozano (Gordon and Breach, 00); auth, "Magical Medicine," in collection ed. Sylvia Macros (00); auth, "Tradition and Change in Malay Medicine," in Healing Powers and Modernity: Traditional Medicine, Shamanism, and Science in Asian Societies, ed. Linda Connor and Geoffrey Samuel (Bergin and Garvey, 00). **CONTACT ADDRESS** Dept Anthrop, City Col, CUNY, 160 Convent Ave, New York, NY 10031. **EMAIL** zita@interport.net

LAGEMANN, ELLEN CONDLIFFE
PERSONAL Born 12/20/1945, New York, NY, m, 1969, 1 child **DISCIPLINE** AMERICAN AND WOMEN'S HISTORY **EDUCATION** Smith Col, AB, 67; Columbia Univ, MA, 68, PhD(hist and educ), 78. **CAREER** Asst prof, 78-81, Assoc Prof Hist and Educ, Teachers Col, Columbia Univ, 81-, Res Assoc, Inst Philos and Politics Educ, 78-. **HONORS AND AWARDS** Outstanding res award, Nat Soc of Fund Raising Executives for The Politics of Knowledge: The Carnegie Corporation, Philanthropy, and Public Policy, 89; Critics' Choice Award, Am Educational Studies Asn, for Private Power for the Public Good: A History of the Carnegie Found for the Advancement of Teaching; Outstanding Mentor Award, Spencer Found, 94. **MEMBERSHIPS** Hist Educ Asn; AHA; Orgn Am Historians; Coord Comt Women Hist Professions; Am Educ Res Asn. **RESEARCH** History of philanthropy; Twentieth century history of education; Contemporary education policy. **SELECTED PUBLICATIONS** Coed, Brown v. Board of Education: The Challenge for Today's Schools, Teachers Col Press, 96; auth, "From Discipline-Based to Problem-Centered Learning," in Education and Democracy: Reimagining Liberal Learning (Col Board, 97); auth, "A Subjective Necessity: Being and Becoming an Historian of Education," in Learning from Our Lives: Women, Research, and Autobiography (Teachers Col Press, 97); coed, Issues in Education Research: Problems and Possibilities, Jossey-Bass, 99; ed, Philanthropic Foundations: New Scholarship, New Possibilities, Indiana Univ Press, 99; auth, John Dewey's Defeat: The Problem of Scholarship in Education, Univ of Chicago Press (forthcoming). **CONTACT ADDRESS** Dept of Humanities and Social Sciences, New York Univ, 70 Washinton Square South, New York, NY 10012. **EMAIL** ec11@is.nyu.edu

LAGUERRE, MICHEL S.
PERSONAL Born, Haiti, s **DISCIPLINE** SOCIAL ANTHROPOLOGY **EDUCATION** Univ Quebec, BA, 71; Roosevelt Univ, MA, 73; Univ Ill Urbana, PhD, 76. **CAREER** Prof & member of exec comt of letters & sci, Univ Calif at Berkeley, 90-. **HONORS AND AWARDS** Barbara Weinstock Lectureship on the Morals of Trade, Univ Calif at Berkeley, 93-94. **MEMBERSHIPS** Am Soc Asn, Am Anthrop Asn. **RESEARCH** Information Technology, Urban Studies, Globalization, Diasporas. **SELECTED PUBLICATIONS** Auth, American Odyssey, Cornell Univ Pr, 84; auth, The Global Ethnopolis: Chinatown, Japantown, and Manslatown in American Society, Macmillan Pr, 00. **CONTACT ADDRESS** Dept Afro-American Studies, Univ of California, Berkeley, 664 Barrows Hall, Berkeley, CA 94720-2602. **EMAIL** mlaguerr@uclink4.berkeley.edu

LAMBERG-KARLOVSKI, CLIFFORD CHARLES
PERSONAL Born 10/02/1937, Prague, Czechoslovakia, m, 1959, 2 children **DISCIPLINE** ANTHROPOLOGY **EDUCATION** Dartmouth Col , BA, 59; Univ Pa, MA, 64; PhD, 65; Harvard Univ, AM, 70. **CAREER** Asst curator of Old World Archaeology, Peabody Museum, Harvard Univ, 64-69; asst prof, Harvard Univ, 64-69; asst prof, Franklin and Marshall College Lancaster Pa, 64-65; dir, Peabody Museum, Harvard Univ, 77-91; prof, Harvard Univ, 69-91; curator on Near Eastern Archaeol, Peabody Museum, Harvard Univ, 69-; Univ assoc, Columbia Univ NY, 71-; Stephen Phillips prof, 91-, Harvard Univ. **MEMBERSHIPS** Am Acad of Arts and Sci; Fel of the Soc of Antiquaries of Great Britain and Ireland; Soviet Acad of Sci; Istituto para Medio e Extremo Orient, Italian Acad Rome; AM Anthropol Asn; Am Asn for the Advancement of Sci; Am School of Oriental Res; Am School of Prehistoric Res; Am Inst of Iranian Studies; Archaeol Inst of Am; Sigma Xi Socl Am Inst of Archaeol Pakistan. **SELECTED PUBLICATIONS** Auth, Beyond the Tigris and Euphrates Bronze Age Civilizations, 96; numerous books, monographs and articles, 65-. **CONTACT ADDRESS** Peabody Museum, Harvard Univ, 11 Divinity Ave, Cambridge, MA 02138. **EMAIL** karlovsk@fas.harvard.edu

LAMBERT BRIGHAM YOUNG UNIV, MICHAEL J.
PERSONAL Born 07/17/1944, Salt Lake City, UT, m, 1961, 5 children **DISCIPLINE** PSYCHOLOGY **EDUCATION** Univ Ut, BS, 67; MS, 68; PhD, 71. **CAREER** Res Consultant, Human Affairs Intl, 95; Assoc Dir of Clinical Psychol Training to Prof, Brigham Young Univ, 82-. **HONORS AND AWARDS** Fel, Nat Inst of Health, 68-71; Maeser Res Awd, Brigham Young Univ, 98; Prof of the Year, Brigham Young Univ, 86-87. **MEMBERSHIPS** Am Psychol Asn, Western Psychol Asn, Soc for Psychotherapy Res, Utah Psychol Asn. **RESEARCH** Psychotherapy Research, Quality-management research. **SELECTED PUBLICATIONS** Auth, "Patient-focused research: Using patient outcome data to enhance treatment effects," Journal of Clinical and Consulting Psychology, in press; auth, "The impact of psychological interventions on medical offset: A meta-analytic review," Clinical Psychology: Science and Practice, (99): 204-220; auth, "A qualitative examination of borderline personality disordered patients: Interpersonal dynamics and underlying paradoxes," Journal of Personality Disorder, (99): 287-296; auth, "Are differential treatment effects inflated by researcher therapy allegiance? Could Clever Hans count?," Clinical Psychology: Science & Practice, (99): 127-130; auth, "The Outcome Questionnaire: A confirmatory factor analysis," Journal of Personality Assessment, (98): 248-262; auth, "Manual-based treatment and clinical practice: Hangman of life or promising development?," Clinical Psychology: Science and practice, (98): 391-395; auth, "What are the implications of psychotherapy research for clinical practice and training," Nordic Journal of Psychiatry, (98): 38-49; auth, "Outcome assessment: From conceptualization to implementation," Professional Psychology: Research and Practice, (98): 63-70; auth, "The reliability and validity of a short form of the Inventory of Interpersonal Problems," Journal of Psychoeducational Assessment, (98): 200-213; auth, "The problems and promise of psychotherapy research in a managed care setting," Psychotherapy Research, (97): 321-332; ed, Measuring patient changes in mood, anxiety and personality disorders: Toward a core battery, American Psychological Association Press; auth, Assessing Outcome in Clinical Practice, Allyn & Bacon, 96. **CONTACT ADDRESS** PO Box 25543, Provo, UT 84602. **EMAIL** michael_lambert@byu.edu

LAMPE, PHILIP
PERSONAL Born 07/25/1934, St Louis, MO, w, 1961, 3 children **DISCIPLINE** PHILOSOPHY, SOCIOLOGY **EDUCATION** Conception Sem, BA, 58; Southern Ill Univ, MA, 67; La State Univ, PhD, 73. **CAREER** Bi-Nat Cult Inst, Morelia, Michoacan, Mex, 60-65; Southern Ill Univ, Carbondale Community Develop Serv, 65-67; Teacher, Southwestern La Univ, 67-70; Univ of Incarnate Word, 70-. **MEMBERSHIPS** Soc for Sci Study of Relig: Southwest. **RESEARCH** Mexican Americans, Religion. **SELECTED PUBLICATIONS** Auth, "Adultery," in Family Life (Pasadena, CA: Salem Press, 98); co-ed, Our Changing Culture, Univ of Incarnate Word (San Antonio), 98; auth, "Culture & Change: An Introduction," in Our Changing Culture, ed. Philip Lampe and Roger Barnes (San Antonio: Univ of Incarnate Word, 98); auth, "Marriage & Sex or Sex & Marriage," in Our Changing Culture, ed. Philip Lampe and Roger Barnes (San Antonio: Univ of Incarnate Word, 98); auth, "Stereotypes," in Aging in America (Pasadena, CA: Salem Press, 99); auth, "Capital Punishment," in African American Encyclopedia (Pasadena, CA: Salem Press, 99); auth, "Chicano Movement," in The Sixties in America (Pasadena, CA: Salem Press, 99); co-ed, Violence in America, Univ of Incarnate Word (San Antonio), 99; auth, "Anatomy of Violence: An Introduction," in Violence in America, ed. Philip Lampe and Roger Barnes (San Antonio: Univ of Incarnate Word, 99); auth, "Violent to the Core," in Violence in America, ed. Philip Lampe and

Roger Barnes (San Antonio: Univ of Incarnate Word, 99). **CONTACT ADDRESS** Dept Sci, Univ of the Incarnate Word, 4301 Broadway, San Antonio, TX 78209.

LANCASTER, JANE FAIRCHILD
PERSONAL Born Hamilton, MS, m, 2 children **DISCIPLINE** EDUCATION, HISTORY **EDUCATION** MS State Univ, BS in educ, Sci, 66; MS Univ for Women, MA, 69; MS State Univ, PhD, 86. **CAREER** Amory HS, Amory MS, Teacher, Dept head, 69-73; MS State Univ, fel Teaching Asst, 81-86; Historian, Auth, 86-. **HONORS AND AWARDS** Grad fellowship, MS Univ for Women; Garner Fellowship and Grant, MS State Univ; Listed in Contemporary Authors, Who's Who in the South and Southwest, Outstanding Young Women of Am; Notable Am Women; Outstanding Scholars of the Twentieth Cen; Writers Dir; Peronalities of the South. **MEMBERSHIPS** Phi Alpha Theta; Southern Hist Asn; Organization Am Historians; Asn Univ Women; Oklahoma Historical Soc; Monroe County Historical Soc. **RESEARCH** Native Am Hist, USA **SELECTED PUBLICATIONS** Historical Dict of the Gilded Age, M E Sharp Inc, (in press); Removal Aftershock: The Seminole's Struggles to Survive in the West, 1836-1866, Univ TN Press, 94; William Tecumseh Sherman's Introduction to War, 1840-1842, Lesson for Action, Florida Historical Quarterly, 93; Nonhistorical article in Ostomy Quarterly, 92; Tallahassee Jail-In and Nashville Sit-ins, Encyclopedia of African Am Civil Rights from Emancipation to Present, Greenwood Press, 92; Hamilton: Take Your place in History as the First County Seat of Monroe, self pub, 75; Book Reviews, J Am Hist; J Southern Hist; J MS Hist; MS Quarterly; Florida Hist Quarterly; Notable American Women, 00; Outstanding Scholar of the Twentieth Century, 00; Writers Directory; Personalities of the South. **CONTACT ADDRESS** 40191 Hwy 373, Hamilton, MS 39746. **EMAIL** jafalan@yahoo.com

LANDON, MICHAEL LEE
DISCIPLINE ANTHROPOLOGY **EDUCATION** Okla Christian Col, BS, 79; Okla Christian Col, BA, 79; Harding Grad Sch Relig, MA, 83; Trinity Evangelical Divinity Sch, PhD, 97. **CAREER** Missionary, Sao Paulo, Brazil, 82-90; Minister, 94-99; Prof, Barclay Col, 99-. **HONORS AND AWARDS** Who's Who in Am Cols and Univs; Alpha Chi. **MEMBERSHIPS** Am Anthrop Asn, ASM, EMS. **RESEARCH** Latin American culture, poverty, liberation theology, missions. **SELECTED PUBLICATIONS** Auth, "A Missiological Interpretation of Amos 2:6-16: An Example of Theology on Edge," Christian Scholars Conf (96); auth, "An Underclass View of Churches," Pepperdine UP (98); auth, "The Psalms as an Example of and Paradigm for Missions," Harding UP (99); auth, "Community Development according to Nehemiah," Restoration Quart 42#1 (00): 47-51; auth, "The Psalms as a Paradigm for Missions," St Louis Christian Col Pr (00). **CONTACT ADDRESS** Dept Anthrop, Barclay Col, PO Box 288, Haviland, KS 67059-0288. **EMAIL** lanmi@barclaycollege.edu

LANER, MARY RIEGE
PERSONAL Born 12/09/1927, Chicago, IL, d **DISCIPLINE** SOCIOLOGY **EDUCATION** Univ Chicago, AB, 66; Univ NMex, MA, 69; Va Tech, PhD, 76. **CAREER** Instr, N Ariz Univ, 69-73; asst prof to prof, Ariz State Univ, 76-. **HONORS AND AWARDS** Faculty Appreciation Awd, 94. **MEMBERSHIPS** Int Soc for the Study of Personal Relationships, Nat Counc on Family Relations, pacific Sociol Assoc. **RESEARCH** Various aspects of courtship and marriage, an examination of wedding/commitment ceremonies, cohabitation motivators, bystander behavior in cases of observed violence. **SELECTED PUBLICATIONS** Auth, Dating: Delights, Discontents, and Dilemmas, Sheffield Publ Co, (Salem, WI), 95; auth, "Singles," Encycl of Marriage and the Family, ed D. Levinson, Macmillan (NY, 95): 670-674; coauth, "Egalitarian daters/Traditionalist dates," Jour of Family Issues 19.4, (98): 468-474; coauth, "Desired characteristics of spouses and best friends: Do they differ by sex and/or gender?" Sociol Inquiry 68.2, (98): 186-202; coauth, "Dating scripts revisited," Jour of Family Issues 21.4, (00): 488-500; auth, "Sex vs. Gender: A Renewed Plea," Sociol Inquiry 70.4, (00): 462-472; coauth, "The effects of sexual assault on sexual attitudes", Marriage and Family Rev 30.1/2, (00): 109-125; auth, "Courtship (revised)," Encycl of Sociol, ed E. Borgatta and R. Montgomery, Macmillan, (NY, 00): 483-490; auth, "Sexual Violence in Dating and Courtship," Encycl of Criminology and Deviant Behav, Taylor and Francis, (Bristol, PA, 01): 67-70; coauth, "Bystander attitudes toward victims of violence: Who's worth helping?" Deviant Behav 22.1, (01): 28-42. **CONTACT ADDRESS** Dept Sociol, Arizona State Univ, Tempe, AZ 85287. **EMAIL** mary.lander@asu.edu

LANG, GERHARD
PERSONAL Born 03/19/1925, Germany, m, 1951, 2 children **DISCIPLINE** PSYCHOLOGY **EDUCATION** City Col, New York, BS, 52, MA, 54; Columbia Univ, PhD, 58. **CAREER** Lectr, City Col of CUNY, NY, 54-58; assoc prof, Fairleigh Dickinson Univ, 58-94; prof, Montclair State Univ, 66-; res psychol, Bd of Examiners, Bd of Ed, New York, NY, 64-66; dir, USOE res projects, Title I Evaluator, 62-80; consult, NYC Bd of Ed; Clinical Experience: Psychol Clinic, Fairleigh Dickinson Univ, 61-64; NJ Center for Psychotherapy, 67-69; Coun and Psychotherapy Center, fair Lawn, NJ, 67-73; private practice, 71-; Horizon Behav Health Care Management Corp, 85-; Lakeview Convalescent Center, Wayne, NJ, 91-96. **HONORS AND AWARDS** Listed in: Am Men and Women of Sci, Who's Who in Am Ed, Leaders in Ed, Int Scholar's Directory, Who's Who in the East. **MEMBERSHIPS** Am Psychol Asn, Am Ed Res Asn, Nat Coun on Measurements in Ed. **SELECTED PUBLICATIONS** Author of 41 articles, reports, pamphlets, and two college textbooks. **CONTACT ADDRESS** Dept Psychol, Montclair State Univ, 1 Normal Ave, Montclair, NJ 07043.

LANGER, ELLEN J.
DISCIPLINE PSYCHOLOGY **EDUCATION** NY Univ, BA, 70; Yale Univ, PhD, 74. **CAREER** Asst Prof, City Univ NYork (CUNY), 74-77; From Assoc Prof to Prof, Harvard Univ, 77-. **HONORS AND AWARDS** Sloan Found Fel; Guggenheim Fel; James McKeen Cattel Awd; Fel, Am Psychol Asn; Fel, Am Psychol Soc; Fel, Am Asn for the Advancement of Sci; Fel, Comput and Soc; Fel, Soc for the Psychol Study of Soc Issues; Founders Day Awd; Psychol Awd, NY Univ; Phi Beta Kappa. **MEMBERSHIPS** Soc of Experimental Soc Psychol, APA, APS, AAAS, SPSSI, Am Asn of Applied & Preventive Psychol. **SELECTED PUBLICATIONS** Auth, The Power of Mindful Learning, Addison-Wesley Publ (Reading, PA), 97; coauth, "Horizontal Hostility: Relations Between Similar Minority Groups," J of Soc Issues 55-3 (99): 537-559; coauth, "Mindful and Masculine: Freeing Women Leaders from the Constraints of Gender Roles," J of Soc Issues (forthcoming); coauth, "Mindfulness Research and the Future," J of Soc Issues (forthcoming); coauth, Journal of Social Issues, Mindfulness: Theory and Application, forthcoming; coauth, You Are Therefore I Think, forthcoming; auth, Creating Choices: Health and Well Being, forthcoming. **CONTACT ADDRESS** Dept Psychol, Harvard Univ, 33 Kirkland St, William James Hall, Cambridge, MA 02138.

LANGSTON, DONNA HIGHTOWER
PERSONAL Born 07/14/1953, CA, s, 2 children **DISCIPLINE** WOMEN'S STUDIES **EDUCATION** Western Wash Univ, BA, 83; MA, 85; Univ Wash, PhD, 93, **CAREER** Teach asst, West Wash Univ, 84-85; instr, Pacific Lutheran Univ, 89; instr, Univ Wash, 85-89; asst prof, 89-94; assoc prof, 94-99; prof, 99-, Minn State Univ Mankato. **HONORS AND AWARDS** Teach Excel Awd, CSBS, MSUM, 98; Minn High Edu Bd Gnt, 95; MHS Res Gnt, 95; Fulbright, Costa Rica, 90; Loft Creat Non-Fic Awd, Minn, 90; Fac Res Gnt, MSUM, 91; Fac Improv Gnt, MSUM, 90, 97; Fel, Eng Speak Union, Eng, 87; Fel, Evergreen Legal Ser, 77; Wash State Gov Vol Awd, 77; Nat Merit Schl Finalist, Cal State Schl, 71. **SELECTED PUBLICATIONS** Auth, "Housing in Costa Rica: A Feminist Issue", Ethics and Critical Thinking (98); auth, "Feminisms, Civil Rights and Power," Race, Class, Gender (98); auth, "Who Am I Now?," in Laborers in the Knowledge Factory, eds. Elizabeth Fay, Michelle Tokarczyk (Univ Mass Press, Amherst, MA, 93); auth, "Anna Lewis: Born For Trouble", Negro History Bulletin 62 (00); Co-ed, Changing Our Power: An introduction to Women's Studies, Kendall Hunt Pub 88- 96, 2 ed, 7 printings; The Native American Encyclopedia, Wiley and Sons Inc, forthcoming; auth, "Tired of Playing Monopoly?," in Race. Class and Gender: An Anthology, eds. Patricia Hill Collins, Margaret Anderson (Wadsworth Pub, 00). **CONTACT ADDRESS** Dept Women's Studies, Minnesota State Univ, Mankato, PO Box 8400, Mankato, MN 56002-8400. **EMAIL** donna.langston@manakto.msus.edu

LANKFORD, GEORGE E.
PERSONAL Born 08/18/1938, Birmingham, AL **DISCIPLINE** FOLKLORE **EDUCATION** La St Univ, BA, 60; Princeton Theolog Sem, BD, 63; Ind Univ, PhD, 75. **CAREER** Instr to asst prof, Spring Hill Col, 66-67; asst prof, to Pauline M. & Brooks Bradley Prof, Lyon Col, 76- . **HONORS AND AWARDS** Ark Prof of the Year, 91 **MEMBERSHIPS** AFS, SAA, Ark Historical A, Ark Arch Soc, AAVP. **RESEARCH** Native American culture; Ozarks culture; iconography. **SELECTED PUBLICATIONS** Auth, A Documentary Study of Native American Life in the Lower Tombigbee Valley, Univ S Al, 83; Native American Legends, August House, 87; The Bates in Batesville, Ind Co Chronicle, 96; A brief History of Block 3, Old Town, Batesville, Ind Co Chronicle, 97; From Maryland to Batesville: The Hynson Brothers, Ind Co Chronicle, 98. **CONTACT ADDRESS** Lyon Col, 300 Highland Rd, Batesville, AR 72501. **EMAIL** lankford@cei.net

LARSEN, NICK
PERSONAL Born 07/23/1948, Canada **DISCIPLINE** SOCIOLOGY **EDUCATION** Simon Fraser Univ, BA, 79; MA, 82; Univ Manitoba, PhD, 91. **CAREER** Criminal Justice Coordr, Chapman Univ, 96-. **MEMBERSHIPS** Am Soc of Criminol, Acad of Criminal Justice Sci, Pac Sociol Asn. **RESEARCH** Law and Society, Legal and Criminal Justice Policy, Native American Law, Victimless Crimes. **SELECTED PUBLICATIONS** Auth "It's Time to Legalize Prostitution,"Policy Options 13-7 (92): 21-22; auth, "The Politics of Prostitution Control: Interest Group Politics in Four Canadian Cities," Int J of Urban and Regional Res 16-2 (June 92): 169-189; auth, "Canadian Prostitution Control Between 1914-1970: An Exercise in Chauvinist Reasoning," Can J of Law and Soc 7-2 (93): 137-156; ed, The Canadian Criminal Justice System: An Issues Approach to the Administration of Justice, Can Scholars Press (Toronto), 95; auth, "The Effect of Different Police Strategies on the Control of Street Prostitution," Can Public Policy XXI-1 (96): 40-55; auth, "The Limits of the Law: A Critical Examination of Prostitution Control in Three Canadian Cities," Hybrid: The Univ of Pa J of Law and Soc Change 3-1 (96): 19-42; auth, "The Politics of Law Reform: Prostitution Policy in Canada Between 1985 and 1995," in Law and Society: A Canadian Reader, ed. N. Larsen & B. Burtch (99), 6074; auth, "Prostitution: Deviant Activity or Legitimate Occupation?," in New Perspectives on Deviance: The Construction of Deviance in Everyday Life, ed. Lori Beaman (Toronto: Prentice Hall, 99), 50-66; auth, "Urban Politics and Prostitution Control: A Qualitative Analysis of a Controversial Urban Problem," Can J of Urban Res 8-1 (99): 28-46; coauth, Law in Society: Canadian Readings, Harcourt Brace (Toronto, Can), 99. **CONTACT ADDRESS** Dept Sociol, Chapman Univ, 333 N Glassell St, Orange, CA 92866. **EMAIL** nlarsen@chapman.edu

LARSON, CALVIN J.
PERSONAL Born 09/25/1933, Oakland, CA, m, 1959, 2 children **DISCIPLINE** SOCIOLOGY **EDUCATION** Univ Cal Berk, BA 56; San Jose State Univ, MS 60; Univ Oregon, PhD 65. **CAREER** Purdue Univ, asst prof, 65-70; Univ Vermont, assoc prof, 70-71; Univ Mass Boston, 71-. **RESEARCH** Soc Theory; crime and correction; family violence and deviant behavior. **SELECTED PUBLICATIONS** Auth, Crime, Justice and Society, with Gerald Garrett, Gen Hall Inc, 96; Pure and Applied Sociology Theory: Problems and Issues, Har Brace Jovanovich, 93; Child Abuse, Ready Ref Fam Life, Salem Press, 96; White-collar Crime, Encycl of Soc Issues, Salem Press, 96; Theory and Applied Sociology, Jour of Appl Soc, 95. **CONTACT ADDRESS** Dept of Sociology, Univ of Massachusetts, Boston, 100 Morrissey Blvd, Boston, MA 02125-3393. **EMAIL** larson@umbsky.cc.umb.edu

LARZELERE, R. E.
PERSONAL Born 04/03/1945, Greensburg, PA, m, 1972, 2 children **DISCIPLINE** PSYCHOLOGY **EDUCATION** Wabash Col, BA, 67; Georgia Tech, MS, 74; Penn State Univ, PhD, 79. **CAREER** Asst prof, hd Psych Dept; Bryan Col, 77-79; asst prof, Western Con Baptist Sem, 80-82; assoc prof, Rosemead Sch of Psych, Biola Univ, 82-90; dir behavioral health care res, Boys Town, 90-. **HONORS AND AWARDS** NIMH fel, 79-80, 88-89; Who's Who in the Midwest; Omicron Nu; Psi Chi. **MEMBERSHIPS** Am Psychol Asn; Soc for Res in Child Develop; Asn for Advan of Behavior Ther; Nat Coun on Family Relations; Am Scientific Affil. **RESEARCH** Stat anal and res methodology; parental discipline; eval and treatment of children in out-of-home placement. **SELECTED PUBLICATIONS** Auth, Should the Use of Corporal Punishment by Parents be Considered Child Abuse? No., in Debating Children's Lives, 94; coauth, The Effectiveness of Parental Discipline for Toddler Misbehavior at Different Levels of Child Distress, in Family Rel, 94; auth, Discipline, in Encyclopedia of Marriage and the Family, 95; coauth, Predictive Validity of the Suicide Probability Scale Among Adolescents in a Group Home Treatment, in J of Am Acad of Child and Adolescent Psychiat, 96; coauth, The Effects of Discipline Responses in Delaying Toddler Misbehavior Recurrences, Child & Family Behavior Therapy, 96; auth, A Review of the Outcomes of Parental Use of Nonabusive or Customary Physical Punishment, in Pediatrics, 96; coauth, Nonabusive Spanking: Parental Liberty or Child Abuse?, in Children's Legal Rights J, 97; auth, Effective vs. Counterproductive parental Spanking: Toward More Light and Less Heat, in Marriage and Family, 98; coauth, Punishment Enhances Reasoning's Effectiveness as a Disciplinary Response to Toddlers, in J of Marriage and the Family, 98; coauth, Two Emerging Perspectives of Parental Spanking, Archiv of Pediatric & Adolescent Med, 98; coauth, "Single-sample Tests for Many Correlations, in Psychological Bulletin, 77; coauth, "Methodology, In Handbook of marriage and the Family," 87; coauth, "Parental Management: Mediator of the Effect of Socioeconomic Status on Early Delinuency, in Criminology," 90; coauth, "Evaluation of the Effects of Sweden's Spanking Ban on Physical Child Abuse Rate: A Literature Review, in Psychological Reports," 99; auth, "Combining Love and Limits in Authoritative Parenting: A Conditional Sequence Model of Disciplinary Responses, in Parenthood in America," in press. **CONTACT ADDRESS** Youth Care Bldg, Father Flanagan's Boys Home, Boys Town, NE 68010. **EMAIL** larzelerer@boystown.org

LASSEK, YUN JA
PERSONAL Born 06/07/1941, Korea, 2 children **DISCIPLINE** PHILOSOPHY OF EDUCATION **EDUCATION** NYork Univ, PhD, 85 **CAREER** Adjunct prof, 93-94, Rosemont Col; managing dir, 93-94, 94- , program chair, The Board of Governors, The Greater Philadelphia Philosophy Consortium. **HONORS AND AWARDS** Boston Univ, Teaching Assistanship, 65-66; The first prize award in the Liberal Arts Col for the chung-Ang Univ Sch, 63-64. **MEMBERSHIPS** APA; SAAP **RESEARCH** Critical thinking; Perception and cognition; Visual arts education **SELECTED PUBLICATIONS** Auth,Ecology and the 18th century world view, Children: Thinking in Philosophy Proceedings of the 5th International Conf on Philosphy for Children, 92. **CONTACT ADDRESS**

415 Barclay Rd., Bryn Mawr, PA 19010. **EMAIL** 102165.3562@compuserve.com

LASSITER, ERIC
DISCIPLINE ANTHROPOLOGY **EDUCATION** Radford Univ Va, BS, 90; Univ NC, Chapel Hill, PhD, 95. **CAREER** Vis asst prof, Transylvania Univ, Lexington, Ky, 95-96; asst prof, Ball State Univ, 96-. **HONORS AND AWARDS** Cum Laude, Radford Univ, 90. **MEMBERSHIPS** Am Anthropol Asn, Soc for Ethnomusicology, Soc for Applied Anthropol. **RESEARCH** Ethnography, race and ethnicity, belief and worldview, folklore and community aesthetics, ethnomusicology, and Native American Studies. **SELECTED PUBLICATIONS** Auth, The Power of Song: A Collaborative Ethnography, Tucson: Univ Ariz Press (98). **CONTACT ADDRESS** Dept Anthropol, Ball State Univ, 2000 W Univ, Muncie, IN 47306-0435. **EMAIL** elassite@gw.bsu.edu

LASSITER, LUKE E.
PERSONAL Born 02/29/1968, Danville, VA, m, 1997 **DISCIPLINE** ANTHROPOLOGY **EDUCATION** Radford Univ, BS, 90; Univ NC, PhD, 95. **CAREER** Asst Prof to Assoc Prof, Ball State Univ, 96-. **MEMBERSHIPS** Am Anthropol Asn; Soc for Ethnomusicology; Soc for App Anthropol. **RESEARCH** Ethnographic Theory and Practice; Ethnomusicology; Folklore and Community Aesthetics; Belief and Worldview; Race and Ethnicity; Native American Studies. **SELECTED PUBLICATIONS** Auth, "Charlie Brown: Not Just Another Essay on the Gourd Dance," Am Indian Cult and Res J, 97; co-auth, "On Inherent Sovereignty: A Perspective from Billy Evans Horse, Kiowa Tribal Chairman," St Thomas L Rev, 97; auth, Power of Kiowa Song: A Collaborative Ethnography, Univ Ariz Press, 98; auth, "Who Am I? I Am the One Who Sits in the Middle: A Conversation with Billy Evans Horse, former Kiowa Tribal Chairman (1982-1986, 1994-1998)," Am Indian Quart, 99; auth, "Southwestern Oklahoma, the Gourd Dance, and Charlie Brown," Contemporary Native Am Cult Issues, 99; auth, "Authoritative Texts, Collaborative Ethnography, and Native American Studies," Am Indian Quart, 01; auth, "From Here On, I Will be Praying to You: Indian Churches, Kiowa Hymns, and Native American Christianity in Southwestern Oklahoma," Ethnomusicology, 01; auth, "From Reading Over the Shoulders of Natives to Reading alongside Natives, Literally: Toward a Collaborative and Reciprocal Ethnography," J of Anthropol Res, 01; co-auth, The Jesus Road: Kiowas, Christianity, and Indian Hymns, Univ Nebr Press, forthcoming. **CONTACT ADDRESS** Dept Anthropol, Ball State Univ, 3100 W Amherst, Muncie, IN 47304. **EMAIL** elassite@bsu.edu

LASSNER, PHYLLIS
PERSONAL Born 05/14/1936, New York, NY, m, 1972, 2 children **DISCIPLINE** GENDER STUDIES, WRITING **EDUCATION** Wayne State Univ, BA, 58; PhD, 83. **CAREER** Lectr, Univ of Mich, 80-93; sr lectr, Northwestern Univ, 93-. **HONORS AND AWARDS** Northwestern Univ Humanities Ctr Fel; Panhellenic Distinguished Teaching Awd. **MEMBERSHIPS** MLA, Modernist Studies Assoc, Soc for the Study of the Space Between 1914-1945. **RESEARCH** British women interwar and World War II writers, British women writers at the end of the Empire, Women's Writing of the Holocaust. **SELECTED PUBLICATIONS** Auth, Elizabeth Bowen, Macmillan, 90; auth, Elizabeth Bowen: A Study of the Short Fiction, GK Hall, 91; auth, British Women Writers of World War II, Macmillan, 98. **CONTACT ADDRESS** 2111 Orrington Ave, Evanston, IL 60201-2913. **EMAIL** phyllisl@northwestern.edu

LAUBSCHER, LESWIN
PERSONAL Born 11/02/1965, Cape Town, S Africa, m, 1999 **DISCIPLINE** PSYCHOLOGY **EDUCATION** Univ Wes Cap, BA, 89; Northwestern Univ, PhD, 95. **CAREER** Psych, Univ Western Cape, SA, 89-91; asst prof, Univ Western Cape, SA, 95-97; asst prof, Ill Sch Professional Psych, 97-. **HONORS AND AWARDS** Outstand Teach of Year. **MEMBERSHIPS** APA; IACCP; PASA. **RESEARCH** Cross-cultural; culture; social psychology of difference; racial/ethnic. **SELECTED PUBLICATIONS** Coauth, The impact of a college counseling program on economically disadvantaged gifted students and their subsequent college adjustment, Roeper Rev J Edu Gifted 18 (96): 202-206; coauth, "Climbing Kilimanjaro: The case for an African philosophy and psychology," Psych Bul 5(95): 1-l0; auth, "To sleep, perchance to dream: A psychobiography of Arthur Nortje," Psych Bull 6 (96): l6-24; coauth, "Story and the making of the self," in Contemporary issues in human development: A South African focus, eds. C de la Rey, N Duncan, T Shefer, A van Niekerk (Johannesburg: Intl Thomson Pub, 97). **CONTACT ADDRESS** Dept Psychology, Illinois Sch of Professional Psychology, Chicago, 20 S Clark St, Chicago, IL 60603.

LAUDUN, JOHN
DISCIPLINE FOLKLORE, LITERATURE **EDUCATION** La State Univ, BA, 86; Syracuse Univ, MA, 89; Ind Univ, PhD, 99. **CAREER** Asst prof, Univ of La Lafayette, 99-. **HONORS AND AWARDS** Jacob K Javitz Fel, 87-92; Delmore Schwartz Prize for Poetry, 89; MacArthur Scholar, 92-93. **MEMBERSHIPS** Am Folklore Soc, La Folklore Soc, MLA, Soc for Ling Anthrop. **RESEARCH** Material folk culture, folk life, folk art, verbal art. **SELECTED PUBLICATIONS** Auth, "Talking Shit in Reyne", La Folklore (99); auth, "The Poetrics of Vernacular Spaces," S Folklore 57.2 (00); auth, Louisiana Gumbos, forthcoming. **CONTACT ADDRESS** Dept English, Univ of Louisiana, Lafayette, Box 44691, Lafayette, LA 70504-0001. **EMAIL** laudun@louisiana, edu

LAUER, RACHEL M.
DISCIPLINE PSYCHOLOGY **EDUCATION** Mich State Univ, BA; Univ Connecticut, MA; New York Univ, PhD, 64. **CAREER** Train assoc, NTL, 54; instr, Columbia Univ, 54-55; lectr, CUNY, 56-60; sch psych, Valley Stream, 56-65; lectr, New School Uinv, 69-75; chf sch psych, BCG, 65-76; consul, PEA, 79-80; priv prac, 65-85; rep sch psych, NYSBPP, 80-85; adj prof, prof, Pace Univ, 74-; found dir, Straus TLC, 84-. **SELECTED PUBLICATIONS** Ed-in Ch, Straus Cen Forum, 91-; Ed-in-Ch, The Stylus; auth, "Reaching all disciplines with critical thinking," in Thinking critically, ed. K Johnson (Englewood, NJ: Inst Gen Semantics, 91); auth, "Critical thinking: Overview," in Developing sanity in human affairs, eds. S Kodish, R Holston (Westport, CT: Greenwood, 98); auth, "Integrating critical thinking and general semantics: An interactive panel," in Developing sanity in human affairs, eds. S Kodish, R Holston (Westport, CT: Greenwood, 98); auth, "How general semantics contributes to the understanding of violence," in Developing sanity in human affairs, eds. S Kodish, R Holston (Westport, CT: Greenwood, 98); auth, "Some basic ideas of general semantics," ETC 53(96); auth, "A meta-curriculum based upon critical thinking," ETC 53(96); auth, "Profile: Rachel Lauer, PhD," Network (97); auth, "Teaching psychology according to a quantum physics paradigm," ETC 55(98); auth, "A crisis for educators: An opportunity for service," ETC 56 (99); auth, Learners of the world, unite! (in progress). **CONTACT ADDRESS** Dept Psychology, Pace Univ, New York, 1 Lincoln Plaza, New York, NY 10023.

LAUGHLIN, JOHN C. H.
PERSONAL Born 09/05/1942, Asheboro, NC, m, 1965, 1 child **DISCIPLINE** HEBREW BIBLE STUDIES, NEAR EASTERN ANTHROPOLOGY AND PHILOSOPHY **EDUCATION** Wake Forest Univ, BA, Greek, 67; Southern Bapt Theol Sem, M Div, 71; PhD, 75. **CAREER** Pastor, Col Ave Bapt Church, Bluefield, WV, 75-76; asst prof relig, Hardin-Simmons Univ, Abilene, TX, 76-77; asst prof relig, Palm Beach Atlantic Col, West Palm Beach, Fla, 77-79; prof relig and cha, dept relig, Averett Col, Danville, Va, 79-. **MEMBERSHIPS** Nat Asn Bapt Prof of Relig; Amer Sch of Oriental Res; Soc of Bibl Lit; Bibl Archaeo Soc. **RESEARCH** Archaeology and the Bible; Near Eastern Archaeology; Biblical Studies. **SELECTED PUBLICATIONS** Articles, Mercer Dict of the Bible, 90; Capernaum from Jesus' Time and After, Bibl Archaeol Rev, 54-61, 90, 93; Joshua, Mercer Commentary on the Bible, 95; Israel and the Liberation of Canaan, Joseph A. Callaway's Faces of the Old Testament, Mercer Univ Press, 95; Digging Archaeology, The Bibl Illusr, fall, 97; Samaria the Strong, The Bibl Illusr, fall, 98; auth, Archaeology and the Bible, Routledge, 00. **CONTACT ADDRESS** Averett Col, 420 W. Main St., Danville, VA 24541. **EMAIL** laughlin@averett.edu

LAUMANN, EDWARD O.
PERSONAL Born 08/31/1938, Youngstown, OH, m, 1980, 4 children **DISCIPLINE** SOCIOLOGY **EDUCATION** Oberlin Col, AB, 60; Harvard Univ, AM, 62; PhD, 64. **CAREER** Asst prof, Univ of Mich, 64-69, assoc prof, 69-73; prof, Univ of Chicago, 73-,George Herbert Mead Distinguished Service prof of Sociol, 85-; Lectr, Management Development Sem, Univ of Chicago at Vail, Colo, July -Aug 89-94; co-chair, NAE/CBASSE Workshop on Adoption of Workplace Technologies, Woods Hole, MA, June 5-8, 88 and March 13-14, 89; Dir, Ogburn Stouffer Center for Population and Soc Orgn, Univ of Chicago, 94-, chair, Dept of Sociol, 97-. **HONORS AND AWARDS** Phi Beta Kappa, 59; Harvard Grad Nat Fel (four years); Phi Beta Kappa Vis Lectr, 95-96; Gordon J. Laing Awd, Univ of Chicago Press for Outstanding Book by Fac, 96. **MEMBERSHIPS** Am Sociol Asn, Am Asn for the Advancement of Sci, Int Sociol Asn, Sociol Res Asn. **SELECTED PUBLICATIONS** Coauth with John P. Heinz, Chicago Lawyers: The Social Structure of the Bar, NY: Russell Sage Found/Am Bar Asn (82); coauth with David Knoke, The Organizational State: Social Choice in National Policy Domains, Madison: Univ Wisc Press (87); coauth with Gerry Nadler, Designing for Technological Change: People in the Process, Washington, DC: Nat Acad of Engineering/Comn on Behav and Soc Sci and Educ (91); coauth with John P. Heinz, Robert Nelson, and Robert Salisbury, The Hollow Core: Private Interests in National Policy Making, Cambridge: Harvard Univ Press 993); coauth with John H. Gagnon, Robert T. Michael, and Stuart Michaels, The Social Organization of Sexuality, Chicago: Univ of Chicago Press (94); coauth with John H. Gagnon, Robert T. Michael, and Gina Kolata, Sex in America, NY: Little, Brown (94); coauth with Robert T. Michael, The Social Organization of Sexuality in the United States: Further Studies (in prep). **CONTACT ADDRESS** Dept Sociol, Univ of Chicago, 1126 E 59th St, Chicago, IL 60637. **EMAIL** ob01@midway.uchicago,edu

LAUNAY, ROBERT G.
PERSONAL Born 10/23/1947, New York, NY, m, 1971, 2 children **DISCIPLINE** ANTHROPOLOGY **EDUCATION** Columbia Univ, BA, 70; Univ Cambridge, PhD, 76. **CAREER** Supervisor, Univ Cambridge, 75-76; Asst Prof to Prof, Northwestern Univ, 76-. **HONORS AND AWARDS** Scholar Incentive Awd, 66-70; Albert Schweitzer Fel, 69; Phi Beta Kappa; Fel, Nat Sci Foundation; Euretta J. Kellett Fel; Amaury Talbot Prize, 92; Fel, Northwestern Univ, 94-95. **MEMBERSHIPS** Am Anthropol Asn; Am Ethnol Soc; Asn of Africanist Anthropol; African Studies Asn; Mande Studies Asn. **RESEARCH** West African ethnography; Trading diasporas; Anthropology of Islam; History of anthropological theory. **SELECTED PUBLICATIONS** Auth, Beyond the Stream: Islam and Society in an African Town, Univ CA Press, 92; auth, "The Power of Names: Illegitimacy in a Muslim community of cote d'Ivoire," in Situationg Fertility: Anthropology and Demographic Inquiry, (Cambridge Univ Press, 95), 108-129; auth, "Spirit Media: the electronic media and Islam among the Dyula of northern cote d'Ivoire," Africa, (97): 441-453; auth, "Knowledgeable Muslims," Reviews in Anthropology, (98): 379-391; co-auth, "The formation of an 'Islamic sphere' in French colonial West Africa," Economy and Society, (99): 497-519; auth, "Writes of Passage: the Cape of Good Hope in late seventeenth century narratives of travel to Asia," Journal of Asian and African Studies, in press; co-auth, "Beyond Mande Mory: Islam and Ethnicity in Cote d'Ivoire, in press. **CONTACT ADDRESS** Dept Anthropol, Northwestern Univ, 1810 Hinman Ave, Evanston, IL 60208-0809. **EMAIL** rgl201@nwu.edu

LAUTERBACH, DEAN
PERSONAL Born 09/13/1958, Milwaukee, WI, m, 1992, 1 child **DISCIPLINE** PSYCHOLOGY **EDUCATION** Univ Wis, Madison, BS, 84; Purdue Univ, MS, 88; PhD, 94. **CAREER** Staff Psychol Clement, Zablocki V.A. Medical Center, 94-95; adjunct fac mem, Carthage Col, 93-95; asst prof, Northwestern State Univ, 95-. **HONORS AND AWARDS** Indiana Crisis Resource Found, 90; Coun for Univ Res Incentive Awd, 96, 97, 98; La Bd of Regents Support Fund, Res and Develop Subprogram, 99; **MEMBERSHIPS** Am Psychol Asn, Am Psychol Soc, Int Soc for Traumatic Stress Studies, Midwestern Psychol Asn, Southeastern Psychol Asn,. **RESEARCH** Posttraumatic Stress Disorder; trauma related symptoms among African American and European American trauma survivors; the impact that trauma exposure has on the academic performance of college students. **SELECTED PUBLICATIONS** Coauth, "Three studies on the reliability and validity of a self-report measure of Posttraumatic Stress Disorder," Assessment, 3 (96): 17-25; coauth, "Psychometric properties of the civilian version of the Mississippi PTSD scale," J of Traumatic Stress, 10 (97): 499-514; coauth, Differences Between African Americans and European Americans in Trauma Exposure and Trauma-Related Symptolmology (manuscript submitted, 99); coauth, Relationship between trauma exposure and substance use in a sample of college students (manuscript submitted, 99); coauth, The home field advantage: Does it exist?." (manuscript submitted, 99); auth, Personality profiles of trauma survivors, (manuscript submitted, 99); auth, "Trauma among college students: Reasons to consider studying this population," Traumatic Stress Points, 13, 3 6 (99); coauth, "The relationship between personality variables, exposure to traumatic events and severity of posttraumatic stress symptoms," J of Traumatic Stress (in press). **CONTACT ADDRESS** Dept Psychol, Northwestern State Univ of Louisiana, Room 313 Bienvenu Hall, Natchitoches, LA 71497.

LAUZEN, MARTHA M.
DISCIPLINE GENDER AND MASS COMMUNICATION **EDUCATION** Univ IA, BA, MA; Univ MD, PhD. **CAREER** Comm, San Diego St Univ. **MEMBERSHIPS** Mem, ICA, Women in Film. **RESEARCH** Women in television and film. **SELECTED PUBLICATIONS** Auth, numerous articles on Women in television, Jour of Broadcasting and Electronic Media, Jour of Commun Inquiry, Mass Commun and Society and issues mgt and pub rel(s), Jour Pub Rel(s) Res; Mgt Commun Quart; Jour Quart. **CONTACT ADDRESS** San Diego State Univ, School of Commun, 5500 Campanile Dr, San Diego, CA 92182. **EMAIL** comments@sdsu.edu

LAVIN, DAVID E.
PERSONAL Born 09/28/1931, New York, NY, m, 1997, 3 children **DISCIPLINE** SOCIOLOGY OF EDUCATION **EDUCATION** New York Univ, PhD, 66. **CAREER** Res fel in social relations, Harvard U, 60-62; asst to assoc prof, Univ Pa, 62-70; Prof, City Univ Grad Sch and Lohman Col, 70- . **MEMBERSHIPS** Am Sociol Asoc; Eastern Sociol Asoc; Am Educ Res Asoc. **RESEARCH** Education and Social Inequality **SELECTED PUBLICATIONS** auth, Right vs. Privilege: Open Admissions Experiment at City University of New York, 81; Changing the Odds: Open Admissions and Life Chances of the Disadvantaged, 96. **CONTACT ADDRESS** Graduate Sch and Univ Ctr, CUNY, 250 Bedford Park Blvd W, Bronx, NY 10468. **EMAIL** dlavin@gc.cuny.edu

LAWLESS, ROBERT
PERSONAL Born 10/04/1937, Tulsa, OK **DISCIPLINE** ANTHROPOLOGY **EDUCATION** Northwestern Univ, BSJ, 59; Univ Philippines, MA, 68; New Sch Univ, PhD, 75. **CAREER**

From Asst Prof to Assoc Prof, Univ Fla, 76-92; Prof, Wichita State Univ, 92-. **HONORS AND AWARDS** Sigma Delta Chi; Phi Kappa Phi. **MEMBERSHIPS** Am Anthrop Asn. **RESEARCH** Sociocultural anthropology. **SELECTED PUBLICATIONS** Auth, Haiti's Bad Press: Origins, Development and Consequences, Schenkman (Rochester, VT), 92; auth, "Haitians," in Encycl of World Cult, vol 8: Middle Am and the Caribbean (Boston, MA: Hall, 95), 120-123; auth, "Religious Forces in Haiti," J of Third World Studies, 12 (95): 477-481: auth, "Haitians: From Political Repression to Chaos, in "Portraits of Cult: Ethnographic Originals, vol 2" S and Middle Am (Englewood Cliffs, NJ: Prentice-Hall, 97), 143-166; auth, "The History of Value-Norm Research in the Philippines: Its Significance for Peace," Human Peace and human Rights, 12 (99): 16-19. **CONTACT ADDRESS** Dept Anthrop, Wichita State Univ, 1845 Fairmount St, Wichita, KS 67260-0001. **EMAIL** lawless@twsuvm.uc.twsu.edu

LAWRY, JOHN
PERSONAL Born 05/26/1938, Pittsburgh, PA, d, 1 child **DISCIPLINE** PSYCHOLOGY **EDUCATION** St Charles Borromeo Sem, BA, 60; Duquesne Univ, MA, 65; Fordham Univ, PhD, 72. **CAREER** Prof Marymount Col, 65-. **HONORS AND AWARDS** Distinguished Service Awd,98. **MEMBERSHIPS** AAUP, Westchester Co Psych Asn. **RESEARCH** Developing more holistic approaches to college teaching especially the first year. **SELECTED PUBLICATIONS** Ed, College 101: A First Year Reader, McGraw-Hill, New York, 99; auth, May You never Stop Dancing: A Professor's Letter to his Daughter, St Mary's Press, 98; auth, "Defusing the Messages that Rob Students of their Intelligence," SKOLE the Journal of Alternative Education, (98): 86-91; auth, "Psychology Lessons from Two Japanese Novels: The Woman in the dunes and Snow country," Interdisciplinary Humanities, (94): 9-16; auth, guide to the History of Psychology, Univ Press of America, 91; auth, "Caritas in the Classroom: The Opening of the american Student's Heart," College Teaching, (90): 83-89. **CONTACT ADDRESS** Dept Beh Sci, Marymount Col, New York, 100 Marymount Ave, Tarrytown, NY 10591. **EMAIL** lawry@mmc.marymt.edu

LAWSON, CASSELL A.
PERSONAL Born 03/29/1937, Little Rock, AR, m, 1993, 6 children **DISCIPLINE** EDUCATION **EDUCATION** Langston Univ, BA, 59; Ind Univ, MSEd, 70; Univ Notre Dame, PhD, 74. **CAREER** Dir of Student Outreach & Minority Student Affairs, Notre Dame Univ, 73-74; asst prof, Univ of Mass at Amherst, 74-75; dir AIDP, Morgan State Univ, 74-78; Dean of Educ, Coppin State Col, 78-79; vpres acad affairs, Coppin State Col, 80-81; prof, Coppin State Col, 81-83; computs vpres, Erie Community Col, 83-86; exec dean, Wayne County Community Col, 86-90; vpres, Gateway Tech Col, 90-. **HONORS AND AWARDS** Basketball Scholar, Langston Univ, 55; Most Valuable Player, ADC, 63; Community Service Awd, Suburban Club, 67; Community Service Awd, Lambda Kappa Mu, 68; Nat Urban League Scholar Awd, 68; Outstanding young man of the Year Awd, Jaycees, 71; Rockefeller Fel AACMU Admin Internship, Ind State Univ, 75-76; listed in Who's Who in Black America, 77; Distinguished Alumni Citation of the Year Awd, NAFEO, 87-88; GMMA Admin of the Year, 91-92; WVA Admin of the Year, 96; Phi Delta Kappa Kistinguished Service to Educ Awd, 97; Sr Action Council Community Service Awd, 97. **MEMBERSHIPS** Nat Educ Asn, Am Personnel and Guidance Asn, Am Asn for Higher Educ, Md Educ Asn, Am Asn of Colleges for Teacher Educ, Nat Coun on Community Service and Continuing Educ, Nat Coun of Instructional Admin, Am Vocational Association/Wisconsin Vocational Asn. **RESEARCH** Quality Improvement. **SELECTED PUBLICATIONS** Coauth, "Quality Education: A View from the Top," Notre Dame J of Educ 2.3 (71): 221-232; auth, "Institutional Power: A View from the Top," Contemporary Educ (76): 223-240. **CONTACT ADDRESS** Community Campus, Gateway Tech Col, 3520 30th Ave, Kenosha, WI 53144-1690.

LAWSON-BRIDDELL, LOIS Y.
PERSONAL Born 01/10/1955, Philadelphia, PA, 4 children **DISCIPLINE** PSYCHOLOGY **EDUCATION** Temple Univ, BSW, 77; Rutgers Univ, MSW, 92; Capella Univ, PhD, 00. **CAREER** Investigator, U.S. Dept of Housing, 78-82; Admissions and Prof, Gloucester County Col, 85-. **HONORS AND AWARDS** Nat Soc Work Honor Soc. **RESEARCH** Women Issues; Depression; Study Skills of at-risk students. **CONTACT ADDRESS** Dept Lib Arts, Gloucester County Col, 1400 Tanyard Rd, Sewell, NJ 08080. **EMAIL** lbriddell@gccnj.edu

LAY, NANCY
PERSONAL Born 01/26/1938, Philippines **DISCIPLINE** ENGLISH AS A SECOND LANGUAGE **EDUCATION** Divine Word Univ, BS, 58; Columbia Univ, MA, 65; EdD, 71. **CAREER** Instr, New School, Jap/Am Inst, 67-70; lectr, City Col, 71-72; asst prof, 72-80; assoc prof, 81-88; prof, 88-; prof, Columbia, 93-94. **HONORS AND AWARDS** PSC-CUNY Grant, 96, 97; Ford Found Grant; APAWLI Grant; CAAC Ser Awd; Cit Woman of Year Awd; ASPIRA Awd. **SELECTED PUBLICATIONS** Auth, A Contrastive Guide to Teach English to Chinese Students, ERIC (City Coll), 91; auth, "Promotion and Tenure Review of ESL/Basic Skills Teachers," in Academic Advancement in Composition Studies, eds. Richard Gebhardt, Barbara GS Gebhardt (Lawrence Erlbaum, 97); auth, "English Teaching in Berlin, Germany: In Transition from East to West," TESOL EFL NL (93); auth, "ESL: Only For Asians?" AAHEC J (94); auth, "Guessing From Context," in New Ways in Teaching Vocabulary, ed. Paul Nation (TESOL Series, 94); auth, "Response Journals in the ESL Classroom: Windows to the World," J Teach Eng Two Yr Coll NCTE (95); auth, "Enhancing Vocabulary: Using Eyes and Minds As a Microscope," Coll ESL (95); auth, "That Will Make the Pelican Cannot Swallow the Fish: Translating from the First Language?" CASA NL (96); auth, "The Golden Orchid Sisters in Southern China," CUNY Alum (97). **CONTACT ADDRESS** Dept English, City Col, CUNY, 160 Convent Ave, New York, NY 10031-9101.

LAZREG, MARNIA
PERSONAL Born 01/10/1946, Algeria **DISCIPLINE** SOCIOLOGY **EDUCATION** Univ Algiers, BA; NY Univ, MA, 71; PhD, 74. **CAREER** Prof, CUNY Hunter Col, 88-. **HONORS AND AWARDS** Fel, Bunting Inst, Harvard Univ; Fel, Pembroke Centre, Brown Univ. **MEMBERSHIPS** Am Sociol Assoc. **RESEARCH** Development, Gender, International Relations. **SELECTED PUBLICATIONS** Auth, The Eloquence of Silence: Algerian Women in Question, Routledge; auth, "The Perils of Writing as A Woman on Women in Algeria", Feminist Studies; auth, The Emergence of Classes in Algeria, Westview Pr. **CONTACT ADDRESS** Dept Sociol, Hunter Col, CUNY, 695 Park Ave, New York, NY 10021.

LEAF, MURRAY J.
PERSONAL Born 06/01/1939, New York, NY, m, 1965 **DISCIPLINE** SOCIAL ANTHROPOLOGY **EDUCATION** Reed Col, BA, 61; Univ Chicago, MA, 63; PhD, 66. **CAREER** Asst prof, Pomona Col, 66-67; asst prof, Univ Calif, Los Angeles, 67-75; assoc prof to full prof, Univ Tex, 75-. **HONORS AND AWARDS** Tuition scholarship, Reed col, 60-61; tuition scholarship, Univ Chicago, 62-63; Fel of Soc Sci Res Coun, 63; NIMH Predoctoral Fel, 63-66; NIMH Supplementary Res grant, 64-66; Fac Res grants, Univ Caif, 68-69; Wenner-Gren Foundation res grant, 69-70; Junio fac Fel, Univ Calif, 70; Fac Res grant, Univ Calif, 72; NIMH Samll grant, 79; UT Dallas Fac Organized Res grant, 79-80; NEH Seminar, Amherst col, 86. **MEMBERSHIPS** Am anthropol as, Royal Anthropol Inst of Great Britain and Ireland, Am Ethnol Soc, Asn for Asian Studies. **RESEARCH** South Asia: politics, social organization, history and culture, particularly as they affect development, General: social theory, Historical of social theory including legal theory, Irrigation ociology, Irrigation and development, Law and development. **SELECTED PUBLICATIONS** Auth, Pragmatism and Development: The Prospect for Pluralist Transformation in the Third World, Bergen and Garvey: Westport, 98; auth, "Local Control Versus Technocracy: The Bangladesh Flood Response Study," Journal of International Affiars, (97): 180-200; auth, "Agriculture and Farming Systems," in The Encyclopedia of Cultural Anthropology, Henry Holt: New York, (96): 31-38; auth, "irrigation and authority in Rajasthan," Ethnology, (92): 115-132; auth, "Punjabi," in The Encyclopedia of World cultures, vol III: South Asia, Macmillan Pub Co: New York; auth, "The Punjab Crisis," Asian Survey, (85): 475-498; auth, Song of Hope: The Green Revolution in a Panjab Village, Rutgers Univ Press, 84; auth, "The Green Revolution and Cultural Change in a Panjab Village, 1965-1978," Economic Development and Cultural Change, (83): 227-270; auth, Man, Mind, and Science: A History of Anthropology, Columbia Univ Press: New York, 79; auth, Information and Behavior in a Sikh Village, Univ Calif Press: Berkeley, 72. **CONTACT ADDRESS** Dept Soc Sci, Univ of Texas, Dallas, PO Box 830688, Richardson, TX 75083-0688. **EMAIL** mjleaf@utdallas.edu

LEARY, JAMES PATRICK
PERSONAL Born 08/19/1950, Rice Lake, WI **DISCIPLINE** FOLKLORE, AMERICAN STUDIES **EDUCATION** Univ Notre Dame, AB, 72; Univ NC, MA, 73; Ind Univ, PhD(folklore), 77. **CAREER** Asst Prof Folklore, Univ KY, 77-. **MEMBERSHIPS** Am Folklore Soc; Maledilta Soc. **RESEARCH** Folk narrative; ethnic folklore; folklore of the upper midwest. **SELECTED PUBLICATIONS** Auth, Images of Loggers + Recent Videos on Historic Lumbering, J Amer Folklore, Vol 0106, 93. **CONTACT ADDRESS** Dept Folklore, Univ of Wisconsin, Madison, 1155 Observatory Dr, Madison, WI 53706-1319.

LEAVITT, FRED I.
PERSONAL Born 12/12/1940, Brooklyn, NY, m, 1964, 2 children **DISCIPLINE** PSYCHOLOGY **EDUCATION** Univ Mich, PhD, 68. **CAREER** Prof, Calif State Univ Hayward, 70-. **SELECTED PUBLICATIONS** Auth, Research Methods for Behavior Scientists, William C. Brown, 91; auth, Drugs and Behavior, third edition, Sage Pub, 95; auth, "Resolving Hempel's Raven Paradox", Philos Now, Winter 97; auth, Evaluating Scientific Research: Separating Fact from Fiction, Prentice-Hall (forthcoming). **CONTACT ADDRESS** Dept Psychol, California State Univ, Hayward, 25800 Carlos Bee Blvd, Hayward, CA 94542. **EMAIL** fleavitt@bay.csuhayward.edu

LEBLANC, ALBERT
PERSONAL Born 09/18/1942, Baton Rouge, LA, m, 1971 **DISCIPLINE** MUSIC EDUCATION **EDUCATION** Univ Illinois, MS 69, PhD 75; Louisiana State Univ, B Mus Ed 65. **CAREER** Michigan state Univ, prof 76-; Cemrel Inc, eval specialist, 73-76; Thibodaux LA, HS band dir, 65-70. **HONORS AND AWARDS** Mus Educ Nat Conf Sr res awd. **MEMBERSHIPS** MENC; SAH. **RESEARCH** Music listening preferences; music performance anxiety. **SELECTED PUBLICATIONS** Auth, Effects of style tempo and performing medium on children's music preference, in: Music edu research: An anthology from the Jour of Research in Music edu, ed, Harry E Price, Reston VA, MENC, 98; Effect of audience on music performance anxiety, coauth, Jour of res in Music Edu, 97; rev of, Experiencing music technology: Software and Hardware, by David Brian Williams, Peter Richard Webster, Music Edu Jour, 97; Building theory in music education: A personal account, Philo of Music Edu Rev, 96; Music style preferences of different age listeners, Jour of Res in Music Edu, 96; rev of, Music matters: A new philosophy of music education, by David J. Elliott, Music Edu Jour, 96; Differing results in research on preferences for music tempo, Perceptual and Motor Skills, 95; A theory of music performance anxiety, Quart Jour of Music teaching and Learning, 94. **CONTACT ADDRESS** School of Music, Michigan State Univ, East Lansing, MI 48824-1043. **EMAIL** aleblanc@pilot.msu.edu

LEE, JOHNG O.
PERSONAL Born 11/20/1948, Kyung-Buk, S Korea, m, 1974 **DISCIPLINE** RELIGIOUS, BIBLE EDUCATION **EDUCATION** Trinity Intl Univ, BA, 79; Southwestern Baptist Theo Sem, M Ed, 82; PhD, 90; Liberty Univ, MA, 94. **CAREER** Adj prof, Reformed Theol Sem, N Bap Sem, Canaan Theol Sem; asst prof, Univ Virginia; prof, Moody Bible Inst. **HONORS AND AWARDS** Deans Hon Roll; Who's Who Am Coll. **MEMBERSHIPS** NAPCE. **RESEARCH** Religious Biblical education. **SELECTED PUBLICATIONS** Auth, Major Educational Characteristics of Asian-American, Moody Press; auth, Global Cultures, Moody Press (forthcoming). **CONTACT ADDRESS** Dept Christian Education, Moody Bible Inst, 820 N Lasalle St, Chicago, IL 60610. **EMAIL** jlee@moody.edu

LEE, ROBERT E.
PERSONAL Born 11/08/1943, Los Angeles, CA, m, 1973, 2 children **DISCIPLINE** PSYCHOLOGY **EDUCATION** Princeton Univ, MA/PhD, 68; Wash and Lee Univ, AB, 95. **CAREER** Psychol, Veterans Admin, 69-76; Assoc Prof, Mich State Univ, 93-. **MEMBERSHIPS** Am Asn Marriage and Family Therapy, Am Psychol Asn, Nat Coun on Family Relations. **RESEARCH** Marriage and Family Therapy, Foster Care, Methodology. **SELECTED PUBLICATIONS** Ed, The Eclectic Trainer, Geist & Russell, 98; auth, "Clinical assessment using the Clinical Rating Scale (CRS): Thomas and Olson revisited," Journal of Marital and Family Therapy, in press; auth, "Managing the difficult ex-spouse," Family Advocate, in press; auth, "The factor structure of the Beavers Interactional Scales," Contemporary Family Therapy, (00): 81-90; auth, "Uncovering strengths of children of alcoholic parents," Contemporary Family Therapy, (98): 521-538; auth, "Combating foster care drift: An ecosystemic treatment model for neglect cases," Contemporary Family Therapy, (98): 351-370; auth, "The marital and family therapy examination program: A survey of participants," Journal of Marital and Family Therapy, (98): 127-134; auth, "The MSU/FTQ: Obtaining client feedback about theory-driven interventions," The Supervision Bulletin, (97): 2-3; auth, "A minimalist model for novice trainers," The International Connection, (97): 13-16; auth, "The national marital and family therapy examination program," Journal of Marital and Family Therapy, (97): 255-269. **CONTACT ADDRESS** Dept Family/ Child Ecol, Michigan State Univ, 107 Human Ecology, East Lansing, MI 48824. **EMAIL** boblee@msu.edu

LEE, SHOOU-YIH D.
PERSONAL Born 08/13/1961, Taiwan, 1 child **DISCIPLINE** SOCIOLOGY **EDUCATION** Nat Taiwan Univ, BS, 84; Nat Yang-Ming Univ, MS, 88; Univ Mich, PhD, 97. **CAREER** Manager/ Res Assoc, Taipei Veterans Gen Hosp Taiwan, 88-90; Res Assoc, Univ of Mich, 90-97; Asst Prof, Univ of Ill at Chicago, 97-. **HONORS AND AWARDS** Who's Who in the World; Who's Who in Am; Acad Excellence Awd, the Blue Cross and Blue Shield of Mich Found; Best Poster Awd, Asn for Health Serv Res; Best PhD Paper, Inst for Behavior and Appl Management. **MEMBERSHIPS** Am Sociol Asn, Acad of Management, Asn for Health Serv Res. **RESEARCH** Complex Organizations in Health Care, Medical Sociology, Health Policy. **SELECTED PUBLICATIONS** Auth, "Linking Acute and Long-Term Care: Hospitals' Involvement in Post-Acute Care," in 1999 Post-Acute Outcomes Sourcebook: A Guide to Methods, Measures and Strategies in Post-Acute Care (NY: Faulkner & Gray Inc, 98), 46-49; auth, "Trust between managers and physicians in community hospitals: The effect of power over hospital decisionmaking," J of Healthcare Management 43-5 (98): 397-415; auth, "Using CEO succession to integrate acquired organizations: A contingency analysis," Brit J of Management 9 (98): 181-197; auth, "Les Medicins Francais aux Etats-Unis et les Enjeux pour la France," Cahiers de Sociologie et Demographie Medicales 38-4 (98): 253-269; auth, "Do market-level hospital and physician resources affect small area variation in hospital use?," Med Care Res and Rev 56-1 (99): 94-117; auth, "Are there need-based geographical differences between international medical graduates and US medical

graduates in rural US countries," J of Rural Health 15-1 (99): 26-43; auth, "Variations in geographical distribution of foreign- and domestically-trained physicians in the United States: 'Safty nets' or 'surplus exacerbation'?," Soc Sci and Med 50 (99): 185-202; auth, "Managing hospitals in turbulent times: Do organizational changes improve hospital survival?," Health Serv Res 34-4 (99): 921-944; auth, "Consequences of organization change in U.S. hospitals," Med Care Res and Rev 56-3 (99): 227-276; auth, "International and US medical graduates in US cities," J of Urban Health (forthcoming). **CONTACT ADDRESS** Dept Sociol, Univ of Illinois, Chicago, 1007 W Harrison, Chicago, IL 60607. **EMAIL** sylee@uic.edu

LEE, YUEH-TING
PERSONAL Born 10/16/1963, China, m, 1988, 3 children **DISCIPLINE** PSYCHOLOGY **EDUCATION** Changsha Railway Univ, BA, 84; Beijing Normal Univ, MS, 86; SUNY, PhD, 91. **CAREER** Asst prof, Philadelphia Col, 91-94; assoc prof, Westfield State Col, 94-. **HONORS AND AWARDS** Who's Who Intl Biog; Outstand Comm Ser Awd; Excell Schlp Awd; Chun-Hui Found Grant; CAS and CNS Found Fel; Sci Direct Grant. **MEMBERSHIPS** AM; APA; APS; NAES; SCCR; SPSP; SPSSI; IACCP; ICP. **SELECTED PUBLICATIONS** Coauth, "Are Americans more optimistic than the Chinese?" Person Soc Psych Bull 23 (97): 32-40; coauth, "Descriptive and Prescriptive Beliefs About Justice: A Sino-US Comparison," Cross Cult 31 (97): 101-120; auth, "Fundamental Advances in Psychological Globalization and Revitalization," World Psychol 1 (96): 114-116; auth, A guide to teaching social Psychology across cultures, W H Freeman (NY), 98; coauth, "Cultural differences in economic growth," in Personality and person perception across cultures, eds. Y T Lee, C R McCauley, J Draguns (Mahwah, NJ: Lawrence Erlbaum Assoc Pub, 99); coauth, "Person perception across cultures," in Personality and person perception across cultures, eds. Y T Lee, C R McCauley, J Draguns (Mahwah, NJ: Lawrence Erlbaum Assoc Pub, 99); co-ed, Personality and Personality perception across cultures, Lawrence Erlbaum Assoc Pub (Mahwah, NJ), 99; coauth, "Why study personality in culture?" in Personality and person perception across cultures, eds. Y T Lee, C R McCauley, J Draguns (Mahwah, NJ: Lawrence Erlbaum Assoc Pub, 99); coauth, "Chinese-American differences: A Chinese view," in Personality and person perception across cultures, eds. Y T Lee, CR McCauley, J Draguns (Mahwah, NJ: Lawrence Erlbaum Assoc Pub, 99); coauth, "Social Perception and Stereotypes: Toward cross-cultural psychology," in Cross-Cultural and International Dimensions of Psychology, ed. UP Gielen, AL Comunian (Italy, Edizioni Lint Trieste Sri Pub, in press). **CONTACT ADDRESS** Dept Psychology, Westfield State Col, 577 Western Ave, Westfield, MA 01085. **EMAIL** ylee@foma.wsc.mass.edu

LEEDER, ELAINE
PERSONAL Born 07/07/1944, MA, s, 1 child **DISCIPLINE** SOCIOLOGY **EDUCATION** Northeastern Univ, BA, 67; Yeshiva Univ, MSW, 69; Univ Calif, MPH, 75; Cornell Univ, PhD, 85. **CAREER** Caseworker, Sheltering Arms Childrens Service, 69-70; Psych Soc Worker, Elmira Psychiatric Center, 72-73; Intake Worker, southern Tier Alcoholism Rehabilitation Service, 73-77; Coordinator of Soc Work Program, 77-; Assoc Prof to Prof and Chair, Ithaca Col, 92-. **HONORS AND AWARDS** NEH Summer Seminar, 96; Fulbright Scholar Awd, 94-95; Dana Res Awd, Ithaca Col, 93-94; Fulbright Seminar, 90; Dana Teaching Awd, Ithaca Col, 85-86; Sheltering Arms Childrens Service Fel, 68. **SELECTED PUBLICATIONS** Auth, We Are Family: A Global Journey Into the Family, McGraw Hill, in press; auth, "Anarchist Women 1920-1950: The Politics of Sexuality," Anarchist Studies, in press; auth, "Anarchism and Women: Historical and Comparative," Women's Studies Encyclopedia, in press; auth, "Reflections From a Mid-Life Lesbian Therapist," Women and Therapy, 96; auth, "Speaking Rich People's Words: Implications of a Feminist Class Analysis and Psychotherapy," Women and Therapy, 96; auth, "A Feminist Community Based Intervention Strategy," Psychological Interventions: A Guide to Strategies, 95; auth, "Violence at The Door: Treatment of Lesbian Batterers," Violence Against Women: An Interdisciplinary and International Journal, 95; auth, Treating Abuse in Families: A Feminist and Community Approach, Springer Pub Co, 94; auth, The Gentle General: Rose Pesotta, Anarchist and Labor Organizer, State Univ New York, 93. **CONTACT ADDRESS** Dept Sociol, Ithaca Col, 953 Danby Rd, Ithaca, NY 14850. **EMAIL** leeder@ithaca.edu

LEFKOVITZ, LORI HOPE
PERSONAL Born 05/06/1956, New York, NY, m, 1977, 2 children **DISCIPLINE** JEWISH WOMEN'S STUDIES **EDUCATION** Brandeis Univ, AB, 77; Brown Univ, MA, 80; PhD, 84. **CAREER** Asst prof to assoc prof, Kenyon Col, 86-96; prof, Reconstructionist Rabbinical Col, 96-. **HONORS AND AWARDS** Fel, Inst of Philadelphia Asn of Psychoanalysis; Woodrow Wilson Fel, 82; Golda Meir Fel, Hebrew Univ, 89. **MEMBERSHIPS** MLA, AJS. **RESEARCH** Narrative, Bible, Critical Theory, Victorian Literature. **SELECTED PUBLICATIONS** Auth, The Character of Beauty in the Victorian Novel, UMI Res Pr, 87; auth, "Eavesdropping on Angels," Gender and Judaism, ed Rudavsky, NYU Pr, (92); ed, Textual Bodies: Changing Boundaries of Literary Representation, SUNY Pr, 97; auth, "Inherited Holocaust Memories and the Ethics of Ventriloquism," Kenyon Rev, (98); coed, Shaping Losses: Cultural Memory and the Holocaust, Univ of Ill Pr, 01. **CONTACT ADDRESS** 636 Burnham Rd, Philadelphia, PA 19119-3510. **EMAIL** llefkovi@rrc.edu

LEFKOWITZ, JOEL M.
PERSONAL Born 10/17/1940, New York, NY, m, 1994, 2 children **DISCIPLINE** INDUSTRIAL-ORGANIZATIONAL PSYCHOLOGY **EDUCATION** Case Western Reserve Univ, PhD 65. **CAREER** CUNY Baruch Col, asst prof to prof, 65-; Head of PhD prog in I/O Psychology. **HONORS AND AWARDS** ABPP in I/O psychol. **MEMBERSHIPS** APA; APS; NY ACAD of SCI. **RESEARCH** Fair employment practices in industry. **SELECTED PUBLICATIONS** Coauth, "The shelflife of a test validation study: A survey of expert opinion," J of Business and Psychology, 97; coauth, "Potential sources of criterion bias in supervisor ratings used for test validation," J of Business and Psychology, 95; auth, "Sex-related differences in job attitudes and dispositional variables: Now you seem them. . . .," Acad of Mgmt J, 94; coauth, "Dimensions of biodata items and their relationships to item validity," J of Occupational and Organizational Psychology, 99. **CONTACT ADDRESS** Dept of Psychology, Baruch Col, CUNY, 17 Lexington Ave, PO Box G-1126, New York, NY 10010. **EMAIL** joel_lefkowitz@baruch.cuny.edu

LEHMANN, JENNIFER M.
PERSONAL Born Detroit, MI **DISCIPLINE** SOCIOLOGY, WOMEN'S STUDIES **EDUCATION** Grand Valley State Cols, BA, 80; SUNY, Buffalo, MA, 85, PhD, 89. **CAREER** Assoc prof, Univ Nebr, 89-. **MEMBERSHIPS** Am Sociol Asn, Midwest Sociol Soc, Int Sociol Asn. **RESEARCH** Theory, women's studies, cultural studies. **SELECTED PUBLICATIONS** Auth, "Durkheim's Response to Feminism: Prescriptions for Women," Sociol Theory, vol 8, 2 (fall 90); auth, "Durkheim's Women: His Theory of the Structures and Functions of Sexuality," Current Perspectives in Soc Theory, vol 11 (91); auth, "The Undecideability of Derrida/The Premature Demise of Althusser," Current Perspectives in Soc Theory, vol 13 (93); auth, Deconstructing Durkheim: A Post-Post-Structuralist Critique, NY and London: Routledge (June 93, paperback, June 95); auth, Durkheim and Women, Lincoln and London: Univ Nebr Press (June 94); auth, "Durkheim's Thoeries of Deviance and Suicide: A Feminist Reconsideration," Am J of Sociol, 10:4 (Jan 95); auth, "The Question of Caste in Modern Society: Durkheim's Contradictory Theories of Race, Class, and Sex," Am Sociol Rev, 60:4 (Aug 95); auth, "The Question of Caste in Modern Society: Durkheim's Contradictory Theories of Race, Class, and Sex," reprinted in The Living Legacy of Marx, Durkheim and Weber: Applications and Analyses of Classical Sociological Theory by Modern Social Scientists, ed by Richard Altschuler, Gordon Knot Books (98); ed, Current Perspectives in Social Theory, Elsevier Press. **CONTACT ADDRESS** Dept Sociol, Univ of Nebraska, Lincoln, 737 Oldfather Hall, PO Box 880324, Lincoln, NE 68588-0324. **EMAIL** JLehmann1@unl.edu

LEHMANN, TIMOTHY J.
PERSONAL Born 03/22/1949, Indianapolis, IN, m, 1980, 2 children **DISCIPLINE** PSYCHOLOGY **EDUCATION** Univ Fla, EdD, 74. **CAREER** Prof of psychology, Valencia Community Col, 75-. **HONORS AND AWARDS** Marriage and family therapist, mental health counr, prof, hostage negotiations/crisis management. **MEMBERSHIPS** Hypnosis Assn, Hostage Negotiators of Am. **RESEARCH** Crisis management, abnormal behavior. **SELECTED PUBLICATIONS** Auth, Hostage Negotiations; a Psychological Approach. **CONTACT ADDRESS** Dept Soc Sci, Valencia Comm Col, 1800 S Kirkman Ed, Orlando, FL 32811. **EMAIL** tlehmanngwmail@Valencia.cc.fl.us.

LEHRER, RICHARD
DISCIPLINE EDUCATIONAL PSYCHOLOGY **EDUCATION** Rensselaer Polytechnic Inst, BS, 73; Univ NYork, Albany, MS, 76; PhD, 83. **CAREER** Assoc Dir, Nat Center for Res in Mathematical Scis Educ, 92-96; Assoc Dir, Nat Center for Improving Student Learning and Achievement in Mathematics and Sci, 96-; prof, Univ of Wisc-Madison. **HONORS AND AWARDS** President's Distinguished Diss Awd, Univ NY, Albany, 83; Vilas Assoc, Univ of Wisc-Madison, 99. **MEMBERSHIPS** Am Asn for the Advancement of Sci, Am Educ Res Asn, Am Psychol Asn, Cognitive Sci Soc. **RESEARCH** Children's mathematical and scientific reasoning in the context of schooling with special emphasis on tools and notations for developing thought. **SELECTED PUBLICATIONS** Coauth, Designing learning environments for developing understanding of geometry and space," Mahwah, NJ: Lawrence Erlbaum Assocs (98); coauth with A. Jeong, "Reflective teaching of Logo," J of the Learning Scis, 8 (99): 245-288; coauth with C. Curtis, "Why are some solids perfect? Conjunctions and experiments by third graders," Teaching Children Mathematics, 12 (2000); coauth with E. Penner, "The shape of fairness," Teaching Children Mathematics (in press); coauth with L. Schauble, "The development of model-based reasoning," J of Applied Develop Psychol, 21, 1 (in press);coauth with L. Schauble, "Inventing data structures for representational purposes: Elementary grade students' classification models," Mathematical Thinking and Learning (in press); coauth with C. Jacobson, "Teacher appropriation and student learning of geometry through design," J for Res in Mathematics Educ, 30, 4 (in press); coauth, "Similarity of from and substance: Modeling material kind," in D. Klahr and S. Carver, eds, Cognition and instruction: 25 years of progress, Mahwah, NJ: Lawrence Erlbaum Assocs (in press); coauth, "Reconsidering the role of experiment in science education," in K. Crowley, C. Schunn, and T. Okada, eds, Designing for science: Implications from everyday, classroom, and professional settings, Mahwah, NJ: Lawrence Werlbaum Assocs (in press); coauth, "What's in a link? Student conceptions of the rhetoric of association in hypermedia composition," in S. Lajoie, ed, Computers as cognitive tools, vol 2, Mahwah, NJ: Lawrence Erlbaum Assocs (in press). **CONTACT ADDRESS** Ed Psychol, Univ of Wisconsin, Madison, 1025 W Johnson St, 316 Ed Sci Bldg, Madison, WI 53706. **EMAIL** rlehrer@facstaff.wisc.edu

LEIBO, STEVE
DISCIPLINE SOCIOLOGY **EDUCATION** Univ Calif, BA, 72; Univ Calif, MA, 74; Wash State Univ, PhD, 82. **CAREER** Instr, Wash State Univ, 79-81; Lectr, Union Col, 87; Lectr, Skidmore Col, 93; Lectr, State Univ NYork (SUNY), 86-; Prof, Russell Sage Col, 86-. **HONORS AND AWARDS** Fulbright Res Fel, 80; NEH Fel, Columbia Univ, 87-89; Fel, Semerad (Travel to India), 90; Fel, Columbia Univ and Japan Found, 96-97. **MEMBERSHIPS** AHA, AAS, FDC. **SELECTED PUBLICATIONS** Auth, International Conflict in the 20th-Century: A Study Guide, Regents Col Pr, 94; auth, "The Foochow Dockyard and the Origins of Chinese Self-Strengthening: The View from the French Archives," Mod China in Transition, Regina Books (95); auth, East Southeast Asia and the Western Pacific, Stryker-Post Publ, rev annual ed, 97; auth, East Southeast Asia and the Western Pacific, Stryker-Post Publ, rev annual ed, 98; auth, East Southeast Asia and the Western Pacific, Stryker-Post Publ, rev annual ed, 99. **CONTACT ADDRESS** Dept Sociol, Russell Sage Col, 140 New Scotland Ave, Albany, NY 12208-3425. **EMAIL** leibos@sage.edu

LEIGH, IRENE W.
PERSONAL Born 10/20/1944, London, England, s, 2 children **DISCIPLINE** PSYCHOLOGY **EDUCATION** Northwestern Univ, BS, 66; NY Univ, MA Rehabil Coun, 69; MA Psychology, 83; PhD, 86. **CAREER** Psychologist and Asst Dir, Lexington Center for Mental Health Serv, NYork City, 85-91; Assoc to Full Prof, Gallaudet Univ, 91-. **HONORS AND AWARDS** AG Bell Asn Scholar, 82; Berger Scholars Scholar, 81-82; Best presentation, Am Deafness and Rehabil Asn Conv, 97; Gallauder Res Inst Res Grants, 96, 97, 98. **MEMBERSHIPS** Am Psyhcol Asn, Am Deafness and Rehabil Asn. **RESEARCH** Depression, identity and socialization, maternal attachment, all related to deafness. **SELECTED PUBLICATIONS** Coauth, "Deaf/hearing cultural identity paradigms: Modification of the Deaf Identity Development Scale," J of Deaf Studies and Deaf Educ 3 (98): 319-338; coauth, "Parent bonding in clinically depressed deaf and hard of hearing adults," J of Deaf Studies and Deaf Educ 4 (99): 28-36; auth, "Book Review: We can hear and speak," Perspectives in Educ and Deafness (Mar/Apr 99): 18-19; coauth, "Minorities SIG Issues for 2000 and beyond," World Fed of the Deaf News 12-01 (Apr 99): 8-9; auth, "Inclusive education and personal development," J of Deaf Studies and Deaf Educ 4 (99): 236-245; auth, "CDIP Update," Rehabil Psychology News Div 22 APA 26-4 (Summer 99): 2; ed, Psychotherapy with deaf clients from diverse groups, Gallaudet Univ Press (Wash DC), 99; coauth, "Deaf therapists and the deaf community: How the twain meet," in Psychotherapy with deaf clients from diverse groups, ed. I.W. Leigh (Wash DC: Gallaudet Univ Press, 99); coauth, "Deaf culture definition," in Cross-cultural dictionary for psychotherapy, ed. J. Trible et al (Westport, CT: Greenwood Press, 99), 91-92; coauth, "Internship accessibility issues for deaf and hard of hearing applicant: No cause for complacency," Prof Psychology: Res and Practice (in press). **CONTACT ADDRESS** Dept Psychology, Gallaudet Univ, 800 Florida Ave NE, Washington, DC 20002. **EMAIL** irene.leigh@gallaudet.edu

LEIGHTON, PAUL S.
DISCIPLINE SOCIOLOGY, LEGAL STUDIES **EDUCATION** State Univ NY at Albany, BA, 86; Am Univ, MS, 90; PhD, 95. **CAREER** Asst Prof, Univ of San Francisco, 95-96; Adj Fac/Lectr, The Am Univ, 90-94, 96; Asst Prof, Eastern Mich Univ, 97-. **MEMBERSHIPS** Am Soc of Criminol, Acad of Criminal Justice Sci. **RESEARCH** Criminology, Penology, prison and social control, White collar, corporate and crimes of domination, Violence, hate, prejudice and genocide, Theory and public policy, Gender and race. **SELECTED PUBLICATIONS** Auth, "Industrialized Social Control," Peace Rev: A Transnational Quart 7-3/4 (Dec 95); coauth, "Black Genocide? Prelimanry Thoughts on the Plight of America's Poor Black Men," J of African Am Men 1-2 (95); coauth, "American Genocide?: The Destruction of the Black Underclass," in Collective Violence: Harmful Behavior in Groups and Government, ed. Craig Summers and Erik Markusen (Rowman & Littlefield, 99); auth, "Television Execution, Primetime 'Live'," The Justice Prof 12-2 (99): auth, "Migrant Labor in the Ivory Toweer: The Crossroads and Crapshoots of a New Professor," in Inside Jobs: A Realistic Guide to Criminal Justice Careers for College Graduates, ed. Stuart Henry, 2nd ed (Sheffield, WI: Salem, 00); coauth, Class, Race, Gender: The Social Realities of Justice in

America, Roxbury, 00; co-ed, Criminal Justice Ethics and Morality, Prentice-Hall, 01. **CONTACT ADDRESS** Dept Sociol and Anthrop, Eastern Michigan Univ, 712 Pray Harrold, Ypsilanti, MI 48197. **EMAIL** SOC_Leighton@online.emich.edu

LEITMA, GRANT
PERSONAL Born 05/31/1956, Washington, DC, m, 1980, 3 children **DISCIPLINE** PSYCHOLOGY **EDUCATION** Columbia Union Col, BA, 77; Cent Mich Univ, MA, 80; Ill Inst Dev Psychol, 87. **CAREER** Prof, Columbia Union Col, 82-. **HONORS AND AWARDS** Phi Alpha Theta, 77; Psi Chi, 88. **MEMBERSHIPS** APA **RESEARCH** Applied Research. **CONTACT ADDRESS** Dept Psychol, Columbia Union Col, 7600 Flower Ave, Silver Spring, MD 20912. **EMAIL** gleitma@cuc.edu

LEKI, ILONA
PERSONAL Born 12/24/1947, Dieburg, Germany **DISCIPLINE** FRENCH LITERATURE, ENGLISH AS A SECOND LANGUAGE **EDUCATION** Univ Ill, AB, 68, AM, 70, PhD(-French), 75. **CAREER** Instr English, Knox County Adult Educ, 74-76; instr, 76-80, Asst Prof English, Univ Tenn, 80-, Translr French, US Govt Joint Publ Res, 74-; sr ed fac publ, Univ Tenn, 75-77; asst prof French, Knoxville Col, 75-77. **MEMBERSHIPS** MLA;SAtlantic Mod Lang Asn; Am Asn Teachers Fr; Southern Comp Lit Asn; Alliance Francaise (treas, 77-78). **RESEARCH** French New Novel, particularly novels of Alain Robbe-Grillet; prose works of Henri Michaux; second language acquisition. **SELECTED PUBLICATIONS** Auth, Assessing 2nd-Language Writing in Academic Contexts, Coll Composition and Commun, Vol 0044, 93; Students Perceptions of Eap Writing Instruction and Writing Needs Across the Disciplines, Tesol Quart, Vol 0028, 94; Coping Strategies of Esl Students in Writing Tasks Across the Curriculum, Tesol Quart, Vol 0029, 95; Completely Different Worlds--Eap and the Writing Experiences of Esl Students in University Courses, Tesol Quart, Vol 0031, 97. **CONTACT ADDRESS** Univ of Tennessee, Knoxville, 502 Longview Rd Apt E, Knoxville, TN 37996.

LEMELLE, ANTHONY J.
PERSONAL Born 12/05/1952, Galveston, TX, s **DISCIPLINE** SOCIOLOGY **EDUCATION** Park Col, BA, 74; Calif State Univ, MA, 77; Univ Calif, PhD, 84. **CAREER** Reaching Asst to Instr, Univ Calif, 77-84; Asst Prof, Univ Minn, 84-86; Asst Dean and Lecturer, Gettysburg Col, 86-87; Asst Prof, La State Univ, 87-88; Vis Lecturer, Calif State Univ, 88; Asst Prof, Bradley Univ, 88-89; Vis Assoc Prof to Assoc Prof, Purdue Univ, 89-; Vis Assoc Prof, Bard Col, 99; Adj Instr, CUNY, 99. **HONORS AND AWARDS** Director's Travel Awd, Nat Inst on Drug Abuse, 99; Sen Fel, Nat Inst on Drug Abuse, 99; Travel Grant, Purdue Res Foundation, 97; Purdue Minority Fac Fel, 89; Outstanding Young Men in Am, 85; Pi Gamma Mu, Delta Tau Kappa, Clifford W. Sackett Memorial Scholarship, 73. **MEMBERSHIPS** Asn of Black Sociol, Am Sociol Asn. **RESEARCH** African American culture, Health and aging, Political Sociology. **SELECTED PUBLICATIONS** Auth, Black Male Deviance, Praeger Pub, 95; co-ed, Readings in the Sociology of AIDS, Prentice Hall, 99; auth, "Black Masculinity and Colorblind Juridical Ideology," in Introduction to Africana Studies, Kendall Hunt, forthcoming; auth, "Black Male Gay Youth, Internal Colonialism, and AIDS: Afrocentric Pedagogies for Effective Interventions," in Pedagogies of AIDS, forthcoming; auth, "The Other Cyborgs: African American Male Role and Feminist Theory," in Advances in Gender Research, JAI Press, 96; auth, "Black Underclass and Culture," in Leading Essays in African American Studies, Carolina Acad Press, 97; co-auth, "The Political Economy of Caregiving for People with AIDS," in The Political Economy of AIDS, Baywood Press, 97; auth, "Oliver C. Cox: Toward a Pan-Africanist Epistemology for Community Action," Journal of Black Studies, forthcoming; auth, "The Political Sociology of Black Masculinity and Tropes of Domination," Journal of African American Men, (95): 87-101; auth, "Killing the Author of Life; or, Decimating 'Bad Niggers'," Journal of Black Studies, (88): 216-231; auth, "Beyond Black Power: The Contradiction between Capital and Liberty," The Western Journal of Black Studies, (86): 70-76. **CONTACT ADDRESS** Dept Sociol & Anthropol, Purdue Univ, West Lafayette, West Lafayette, IN 47907.

LEMIEUX, GERMAIN
PERSONAL Born 01/05/1914, Cap-Chat, PQ, Canada **DISCIPLINE** HISTORY, FOLKLORE **EDUCATION** Univ Laval, BA, 35, MA, 56, PhD, 61; York Univ, LLD(hon), 77; Univ Ottawa, LittD(hon), 78; Univ Laurentienne, LittD(hon), 84. **CAREER** Prof, Col Sacre-Coeur, Sudbury, 41-44, 49-50, 51-53, 56-59; prof Univ Laurentienne, 61-65; prof, Univ Laval, 66-69; prof dep folklore, 70-80, dir, Center for Franco-ontarian Folklore, Univ Sudbury. **HONORS AND AWARDS** Prix Champlain, 73; Medaille Luc-Lacourciere, 80; Prix du Nouvel-Ontario, 83; Carnochan Awd, Ont Hist Soc, 83; mem, l'Ordre Can, 84; Medaille Marius-Barbeau, 86; mem, l'Ordre de l'Ontario, 92; commandeur, l'Ordre des Palmes, 96. **SELECTED PUBLICATIONS** Auth, Chansonnier franco-ontarien, 2 vols, 74, 76; auth, Les vieux m'ont conte, 33 vols, completee 91; ed, Les jongleurs du billochet, 72; ed, Le four de glaise, 82; ed, La vie paysanne (1860-1900), 82. **CONTACT ADDRESS** Dept of Folklore (French), Univ of Sudbury, 935 Ramsey Lake Rd, Sudbury, ON, Canada P3E 2C6.

LEMONCHECK, LINDA
PERSONAL Born 07/15/1954, Los Angeles, CA, m, 1984 **DISCIPLINE** PHILOSOPHY; FEMINIST THEORY **EDUCATION** Occidental Col, AB, 76; UCLA, MA, PhD, 81. **CAREER** Lctr, Occidental Col, 78-81, UCLA, 81-83, Calif State Univ, LongBeach, 81-83, 90-92, 94-96, USC 96 & 98-99. **HONORS AND AWARDS** Phi Beta Kappa; Women's Studies Awd, Calif State Univ, Long Beach, 93; Editor, Oxford Univ Press, 98-. **MEMBERSHIPS** Am Philos Asn; Soc Women Philos; Nat Coun Res Women. **RESEARCH** Feminist applied ethics, specifically womens sexual and reproductive issues: promiscuity, sexual preference and deviance, pornography and prostitution, sexual harassment and sexual violence, new reproductive technologies. **SELECTED PUBLICATIONS** Auth, Dehumanizing Women: Treating Persons as Sex Objects, Rowman & Littlefield, 85; auth, Loose Women. Lecherous Men: A Feminist Philosophy of Sex, Oxford Univ Press, 97; coauth, Sexual Harassment: A Debate, Rowman & Littlefield, 97; coedi, Sexual Harassment: Issues and Answers, Oxford Univ Pr, forthcoming. **CONTACT ADDRESS** 128 6th St., Seal Beach, CA 90740. **EMAIL** llemon@msn.com

LENAGHAN, DONNA D.
PERSONAL Born 07/28/1952, Atlanta, GA, m, 1982 **DISCIPLINE** EDUCATION **EDUCATION** Salem Col, BA, 76; Univ Md, MS, 84; Barry Univ, EdD, 90; EdS, 99. **CAREER** Asst Curriculum Dir, Rockhurst Col, 91-92; Assoc Prof, Open Col, 92-99; Assoc Prof, Barry Univ, 99-. **HONORS AND AWARDS** Who's Who Among Am Teachers, 98; Who's Who of Professionals, 97; Who's Who in Am Women, 97; Who's Who in the World, 96; Leadership Awd, Japan Soc, 93; Distinguished Leadership, 91; Achievement Awd, Am Red Cross Soc, 88; Golden Eagle for Interactive Video, 87; Hall of Fame Awd, Am Hist Archives, 87; Excellence Awd, Nat Hemophilia Foundation, 85. **MEMBERSHIPS** Am Asn for Adult and Cont Educ; Am Soc for Training & Dev; Asn of Supervision and Curriculum Dev; Am Asn for Univ Women; Intl Platform Asn; Intl Platform Asn. **RESEARCH** Teaching and learning; Educational technology; Multiple intelliences; Brain based learning; cognitive psychology; Train the trainer; Occupational socialization. **SELECTED PUBLICATIONS** Auth, Teaching for Learning: A Partnership Between Professor and Students, FL Asn of Community Col, 95; auth, "Balancing the SeeSaw Paradigm: Education and Training Priorities for 21st Century," in Educational Research Information Clearinghouse, 96; auth, "Educational Audit of 'Use of Force' and Train the Trainer Courses," Col of Criminal Justice Assessment Center for Correctional and Police Officers, 97; auth, Take AIM: Acknowledge and Individualize Your Multiple Intelligences, Multigogy Assoc, 97; auth, SUPER Learner, Center for Fac and Staff Dev, 97; auth, "Internet for the Intellect," 98; auth, Multiple Intelligences = Multiple Ways to be A Star, 98; auth, "Brave New World: A Good News Scenario for Educational Reform," Resources in Education, 99. **CONTACT ADDRESS** Dept Educ, Barry Univ, 11300 NE Second Ave, Miami Shores, FL 33161-6695. **EMAIL** dleaghan@mail.barry.edu

LEONARD, KAREN ISAKSEN
PERSONAL Born 12/04/1939, Madison, WI, w, 1962, 2 children **DISCIPLINE** ANTHROPOLOGY **EDUCATION** Univ of Wis, BA, 62; MA, 64, PhD, 69. **CAREER** Assoc of Center for South and Southeast Asian Studies, 67-68, visiting lectr, Univ of Mich, 68; lectr in hist, Univ of San Diego, 69; lectr in hist, 69, full-time lectr, Univ of Calif at San Diego, 70; Asst Prof Prog in comparative culture, 72-78, Assoc prof, Social relations 78-85, Prof Social relations, 85-87, Prof 88-, Dept of Antorop, Univ of Calif, Irvine; dir of Women's Studies, UCI, 78-79; visiting asst prof in Indian Hist, Univ of Va, 78; asst ed, J of Asian Studies, 78-80; ed comt, 83-87, mem of editorial comm., Univ of Calif Press, 83-87. **HONORS AND AWARDS** Phi Beta Kappa, Mortar Board, 62; Nat Defense Foreign Lang fels, 62-66; Ford Found fel, Univ of Chicago, 63; Res fel, Univ of Chicago, 67; Am Inst of Indian Studies Fac Res Fel, 70-71, 76, & 83; UCI Fac Fel, 73; grant, Innovative Training Funds for Women's Studies, 75; UC Instructional Improvement Grants for Women's Studies Core Corse, 76-77 & 77-78; SSRC Grant, 77; Fulbright Res Fel, Pakistan, 92-93; CAORC Smithsonian Grant, 95-96; Rupee grant from His Exalted Highness the Nizam's Charitable Trust, 95-96; Global Peace & Conflict Studies grant to Uzbekistan, 99. **MEMBERSHIPS** Reviewer for J of Asian Studies, Am Anthropologist, Amerasia J, Int Migration Rev, Am Ethnologist; referee for NSF Anthropology Prog, NEH, Oxford Univ Press, Univ of Calif Press, Univ of Chicago Press; referee for grants, Wenner-Gren Found. **SELECTED PUBLICATIONS** Auth, Social History of an Indian Caste: The Kayasths of Hyderabad, Oxford Univ Press, 78 & Longman, 92; auth, Making Ethnic Choices: California's Punjabi-Mexican-Americans, Temple Univ Press, 92 & 94; auth, The South Asian Americans, Greenwood Press, 97; auth, Finding One's Own Place: Asian Landscapes Re-Visioned in Rural California, in Culture, Power, Place: Explorations in Critical Anthropology, Duke Univ Press, 97; auth, Identities in the Diaspora: Surprising Voices, in Cultural Compass: Ethnographic Explorations of Asian America, Temple Univ Press, forthcoming; auth, Remembering/Claiming Homelands: California's Punjabi Pioneers, in Movement and Memory: The Mastery of Displacement in South Asian Experience 1800-1995, Univ of Iow Press, forthcoming. **CONTACT ADDRESS** Dept of Anthropology, Univ of California, Irvine, Irvine, CA 92697. **EMAIL** kbleonar@uci.edu

LEONARD, WILLIAM R.
PERSONAL Born 02/16/1959, Jamestown, NY, m, 1996 **DISCIPLINE** ANTHROPOLOGY **EDUCATION** Pa State Univ, BS, 80; Univ Mich, MA, 83; PhD, 87. **CAREER** Post-Doctoral Fel, Univ Ky, 87-89; asst prof, Univ of Guelph, 89-95, assoc prof, 95-96; asst prof, Univ of Fla, 96-98; assoc prof, Northwestern Univ, 98-. **HONORS AND AWARDS** Phi Sigma, 80; Gold Key Honor Soc, 80; Phi Beta Kappa, 81; Nat Scis & Engineering Res Coun of Can Four Year Res Grant, 94-98; Nat Geographic Soc Two Year Res Grant, 96-98; Wenner-Gren Found Conf Grant, 2000. **MEMBERSHIPS** Am Asn of Physical Anthropols, Am Anthropol Asn, Human Biology Asn, Am Inst of Nutrition/Am Soc for Clinical Nutrition. **RESEARCH** Human biology, biological anthropology. **SELECTED PUBLICATIONS** Coauth, "The central Siberian origin for native American Y-chromosomes," Am J of Human Genetics, 64 (99): 619-628; coauth, "Nutrition, thyroid function and basal metabolism of the Evenki of Central Siberia," Int J of Circumpolar Health, 58 (99): 281-295; coauth, "Ecological correlates of home range variation in primates: Implications for hominid evolution," in S. Binski and P. A. Garber, eds, On the Move: How and Why Animals Travel in Groups, Chicago: Univ of Chicago Press (2000); auth, "Human nutritional evolution (Ch 9)," in S. Stinson, B. Bogin, R. Huss-Ashmore, and D. O'Rourke, eds, Human Biology: An Evolutionary and Biocultural Approach, NY: Wiley-Liss (2000); coauth, "Basal metabolic adaptation of the Evenki reindeer herders of Central Siberia," Am J of Human Biology, 12 (2000): 75-87; coauth, "Caretakers, child care practices and growth failure in highland Ecuador," Medical Anthropol Quart, 14, 2 (in press); coauth, "The distribution of the 3' VNTR polymorphism in the human dopamine transporter gene (DAT1) in world populations," Human Biology (in press). **CONTACT ADDRESS** Dept Anthropol, Northwestern Univ, 1810 Hinman Ave, Evanston, IL 60208-0809.

LEROUX, JEFFREY
PERSONAL Born 07/13/1950, Denver, CO, d, 2 children **DISCIPLINE** PSYCHOLOGY **EDUCATION** Univ Oregon, BA, 72; Oregon State Univ, MED, 74; Univ CA, PhD, 87. **CAREER** Asst Prof, Scripps Col, 87-88; Asst Prof, Univ of Hawaii Hilo, 88-89; Lecturer, San Francisco State Univ, 89-00. **MEMBERSHIPS** APA **RESEARCH** Altruism, Empathy, Cross Cultural Personality, Buddhist Psychology. **SELECTED PUBLICATIONS** Auth, "The Psychological Screening Inventory as a predictor of predispositions to suicide at the Oregon State Hospital," Larsen, K.S., Garcia, D. & Langenberg, D. & LeRoux, J.A., Journal of Clinical Psychology, 39 (83): 100-103; auth, "Item analysis versus factor analysis in the development of unidimensional scales," The Journal of Social Psychology, 119 (83): 95-101; auth, "A study of same sex touching attitudes: scale development and personality predictors," The Journal of Sex Research, 20 (84): 264-278; auth, "Perception" book chapter in Matsumoto, D.R. People: Psychology from a Cultural Perspective, Brooks/Cole, Pacific Grove, 94; auth, "Cognition" book chapter in Matsumoto, D.R. People: Psychology from a Cultural Perspective, Brooks/Cole, Pacific Grove, 94; auth, "A Buddhist Approach to Relationship and Sexuality" book chapter in Sex and Relationships: An Anthology, J.P. Elia, ed., Kendall/Hunt (Dubuque), 99; auth, "auth, "Intercultural Adjustment Potential Scale (ICAPS) a new measure of the capacity to adjust to moving to the United States", Matsumoto, D & LeRoux, J.A., 00. **CONTACT ADDRESS** Dept Psychology, San Francisco State Univ, 1600 Holloway Ave, San Francisco, CA 94132. **EMAIL** leroux@sfsu.edu

LEROY CONRAD, ROBERT
DISCIPLINE EDUCATIONAL MINISTRY **EDUCATION** Concordia Sem, MDiv, STM; Wash Univ, MA; Princeton Sem, PhD. **CAREER** Dir, Extension Educ; prof. **HONORS AND AWARDS** Educ Comm ch, Commn for Church and Youth Agency Relationships. **SELECTED PUBLICATIONS** Auth, What Planners and Teachers Need to Know About Today's Adults, Lifelong Learning: A Practical Guide to Adult Education in the Church, Augsburg Fortress, 97. **CONTACT ADDRESS** Dept of Educational Ministry, Lutheran Sch of Theol at Chicago, 1100 E 55th St, Chicago, IL 60615.

LESIKIN, JOAN
DISCIPLINE ENGLISH TO SPEAKERS OF OTHER LANGUAGES **EDUCATION** Rutgers Univ, MFA, 70; Columbia Univ, PhD, 95. **CAREER** Asst prof & act dir, Acad ESL prog. **RESEARCH** Areas of sociology of education and res methodologies related to educational texts. **SELECTED PUBLICATIONS** Publ on res interest. **CONTACT ADDRESS** Dept of Language and Cultures, William Paterson Col of New Jersey, 300 Pompton Rd., Wayne, NJ 07470. **EMAIL** lesikinj@wpunj.edu

LESTER, DAVID
PERSONAL Born 06/01/1942, London, England, m, 1987, 1 child **DISCIPLINE** PSYCHOLOGY **EDUCATION** Brandeis Univ, PhD 68; Cambridge Univ, PhD, 91. **CAREER** Wellesley Col, asst prof 67-69; Suicide Prev Cen, Buff, dir res 69-71; Richard Stockton Col, prof 71-. **HONORS AND AWARDS**

Dublin Awd. **MEMBERSHIPS** Amer Assn of Suicidology. **RESEARCH** Thanatology; Suicide. **SELECTED PUBLICATIONS** Ed, Suicide 90, American Association of Suicidology, 90; auth, Psychotherapy for suicidal clients, Thomas, 91; auth, Questions and answers about murder, Charles, 91; ed, Suicide 91, American Association of Suicidology, 91, Braswell M, Van Voorhis P. Coorectional counseling, 2nd. Edition, Anderson, 92; auth, Why people kill themselves, 3rd. Edition, Thomas, 92; ed, Sucide 92, American Association of Suicidology, 91; ed., Suicide in Creative Women, Commack NY, Nova Sci, 93; Judy Garland, in: F N Magill ed, Great Lives from History: Amer Women, Pasadena, Salem 95; Amy Lowell, in: F N Magill ed, Great lives from hist: Amer Women, Pasadena, Salem, 95; The unconscious and suicide in literature, in" A A Leenaars D Lester eds, Suicide and the Unconscious, Northvale NJ, Jason Aronson, 96; auth, An Encyclopedia of Famouds Suicides, Commack NY, Nova Science, 96. **CONTACT ADDRESS** Psychology Program, Richard Stockton Col, Pomona, NJ 08240-0195. **EMAIL** lesterd@stockton.edu

LETT, JAMES W.
PERSONAL Born 09/25/1955, Augsburg, Germany, s **DISCIPLINE** ANTHROPOLOGY **EDUCATION** Col William and Mary, BA, 77; Univ Fla, MA, 80; PhD, 83. **CAREER** Instructor, Univ Fla, 80-82; Adj Prof, Barry Univ, 84; Adj Prof, Fla Inst of Technol, 86; Lecturer, Univ Ut, 89; Adj Prof, Fla Atlantic Univ, 90; Prof, Indian River Cmty Col, 86-. **HONORS AND AWARDS** Instructional Innovation Awd, 94, 98; Grant, IRCC Foundation, 92, 95; Excellence Awd for teaching, NISOD, 94; Outstanding Acad Book of the Year, 87-88; Newsmaker Awd of Excellence, 86; Fel, Inter-American Foundation, 79. **MEMBERSHIPS** Am Anthropol Asn; Am Asn of Univ Prof. **RESEARCH** Anthropological theory; Human evolution; Nature of reason; Religion and other irrational belief systems. **SELECTED PUBLICATIONS** Co-auth, "A Field Guide to Critical Thinking: Six Simple Rules to Follow in Examining Paranormal Claims," Skeptical Inquirer, (90: 153-160); auth, "Interpretive Anthropology, Metaphysics, and the Paranormal," Journal of Anthropological Research, (91): 305-329; auth, "Scientific Anthropology," in Encyclopedia of Cultural Anthropology, (Henry Holt and Co, 96), 1141-1148; auth, Science, Reason, and Anthropology: The Principles of Rational Inquiry, Rowan & Littlefield Pub, 97; auth, "The Persistent Popularity of the Paranormal," in Encounters with the Paranormal: Science, Knowledge, and Belief, (Prometheus Books, 98), 187-194; auth, "An Anthropologist on the Anchor Desk," in classics of Practicing Anthropology, 99; auth, "New Age Anthropology," Skeptical Inquirer, (00: 66. **CONTACT ADDRESS** Dept Soc Sci, Indian River Comm Col, 3209 Virginia Ave, Fort Pierce, FL 34981. **EMAIL** jlett@ircc.cc.fl.us

LEVIN, IRWIN P.
PERSONAL Born 10/16/1938, Providence, RI, m, 1963, 2 children **DISCIPLINE** PSYCHOLOGY **EDUCATION** Univ Calif, BA, 60; Univ Calif, MA, 63; Univ Calif, PhD, 65. **CAREER** From Asst Prof to Prof, Univ Iowa, 65-. **HONORS AND AWARDS** Fac Achievement Awd, Burlington Northern Found, 89; Collegiate Teaching Awd, Univ Iowa, 97; Regents Awd for Fac Excellence, 98; Hon Prog Fac Awd, 99; Sigma Xi. **MEMBERSHIPS** Psychonomic Soc, Midwestern Psychol Assoc, Judgement and Decision Making Soc, Assoc for Consumer Res, Europ Acad for Decision Making, APS. **SELECTED PUBLICATIONS** Coauth, Experimental Psychology: Contemporary Methods and Applications, Brown and Benchmark (Dubuque, IA), 95; coauth, "Movie Stars and Authors as Brand Names: Measuring Brand Equity in Experiential Products," in Advances in Consumer Res, XXIV (97), 175-181; coauth, "All Frames are not created Equal: A Typology and Critical Analysis of Framing Effects," Organizational Behav and Human Decision Processes, 76 (98): 149-188; auth, "Relating Statistics and Experimental Design: An Introduction," Quantitative Applications in the Soc Sci, no 07-125 (99); coauth, "Tennis, Anyone? Personality Correlates of Singles and Doubles Playing Preferences," Psi Chi J of Undergrad Res, 4 (99): 107-112; coauth, "Modeling the Role of Brand Alliances in the Assimilation of Product Evaluations," J of Consumer Psychol, 9 (00): 43-52. **CONTACT ADDRESS** Dept Psychol, Univ Iowa, 11 Seashore Hall E, Iowa City, IA 52242.

LEVIN, SHANA
DISCIPLINE PSYCHOLOGY **EDUCATION** Univ Calif, BA, 90; MA, 93; PhD, 96. **CAREER** Res Fel to Instr, Univ Calif, 96-98; Asst Prof, Claremont McKenna Col, 98-. **HONORS AND AWARDS** Nominated for Joseph A Gengerelli distinguished dissertation Awd, Univ Calif, Los Angeles, 96; Res Fel, Ctr for the Study of Soc and Politics, Univ Calif, Los Angeles, 95-98; Sigma Xi Grant, 95; Lady Davis Grad Fel, Hebrew Univ, 93-94; Univ Calif, Los Angeles, Alumni Fel, Univ Calif, Los Angeles, 91-93; UCB Univ Medal, Univ Calif, 90; Phi Beta Kappa, 90. **MEMBERSHIPS** Am Psychol Asn, Am Psychol Soc, Intl Soc of Polit Psychol, Soc for Personality and Soc Psychol, Soc for the Psychol Study of Soc Issues. **RESEARCH** Ethnic identification, Group dominance motives, Ideologies of group inequality, Perceived discrimination, Diversity in higher education, Intergroup attitudes in the United States and Israel. **SELECTED PUBLICATIONS** Auth, "Social dominance orientation and the legitimization of inequality across culture," Journal of Cross-cultural Psychology, in press; auth, "Legiti-

mizing ideologies: The social dominance approach," in The Psychology of Legitimacy: Emerging perspectives on ideology, justice, and intergroup relation, Cambridge Univ Press, in press; auth, "Social dominance orientation, antiegalitarianism, and the political psychology of gender: An extension and cross-cultural replication," European Journal of Social Psychology, (00): 41-67; auth, "Social psychological evidence on race and racism," in Compelling interest: Examining the evidence on racial dynamics in higher education, Stanford Univ, 99; auth, "Social dominance and social identity in the United States and Israel: Ingroup favoritism or outgroup derogation?," Political Psychology, (99): 99-126; auth, "Peering into the jaws of the beast: The integrative dynamics of social identity, symbolic racism, and social dominance," in Cultural divides: Understanding and overcoming group conflict, Russell Sage, 99; auth, "Theoretical, empirical, and practical approaches to intergroup conflict," Journal of Social Issues, (98): 629-639; ed, Understanding and resolving national and international group conflict, 98; auth, "Ethnic identity, legitimizing ideologies, and social status: A matter of ideological asymmetry," Political Psychology, (98): 373-404; auth, "Hierarchical group relations, institutional terror, and the dynamics of the criminal justice system," in Confronting racism: The problem and the response, Sage Pub, 98; auth, "The interface between ethnic and social system attachment: The differential effects of hierarchy-enhancing and hierarchy-attenuating environments," Journal of Social Issues, (98): 741-757; auth, "The interface between ethnic and national attachment: Ethnic pluralism or ethnic dominance?," Public Opinion Quarterly, (97): 102-133. **CONTACT ADDRESS** Dept Psychol, Claremont McKenna Col, 500 E 9th St, Claremont, CA 91711. **EMAIL** shana_levin@mckenna.edu

LEVINE, HILLEL
PERSONAL Born 05/28/1946, Flushing, NY, m, 1977, 3 children **DISCIPLINE** SOCIOLOGY **EDUCATION** Queens Col CUNY, BA, 65; New School for Soc Res, MA, 69; Jewish Theol Sem Am, MHL, 67; Harvard Univ, Cert Bus Admin, 80; Harvard Univ, MA, 72; PhD, 74. **CAREER** Assoc prof, Yale Univ, 77-81; prof, Boston Univ, 81-; vis prof, Tokyo Univ, 94; vis prof, Moscow State Univ, 92; vis prof, Jagiellonian Univ Cracow, 84-85. **RESEARCH** Human rights, Conflict resolution, comparative historical sociology, Jewish history. **SELECTED PUBLICATIONS** auth, In Search of Sugihara: The elusive Japanese Diplomat who risked his life to rescue 10,000 Jews from the Holocaust, The Free Press, 96; auth, The Death of an American Jewish community: a Tragedy of Good Intentions, The Free Press, 92; auth, Economic Origins of Anti-Semitism: Poland and Its Jews in the Early Modern Period, Yale Univ Press, 91; auth, "Between Social Legitimization and Moral Legitimacy in Military Commitment," Legitimacy and commitment in the Military, 90; auth, "Jews and Mercantilism," Zion, 88. **CONTACT ADDRESS** Dept Sociol, Boston Univ, 745 Commonwealth Ave, Boston, MA 02215-1401.

LEVINE, VICTORIA LINDSAY
PERSONAL Born 09/08/1954, Palo Alto, CA, m, 1982, 2 children **DISCIPLINE** ETHNOMUSICOLOGY, AMERICAN INDIAN STUDIES **EDUCATION** San Francisco State Univ, BMUS, BA, 77; MA, 80; Univ Ill Urbana, PhD, 90. **CAREER** W.M. Keck Foundation dir of the Hulbert Center for Southwestern Studies; Assoc prof, Colorado Col. **HONORS AND AWARDS** John D. & Catherine T. McArthur prof, 91-93; Am Council of Learned Soc Sr Fellow, 94-95; Ida Halpern Fellow and Awd, 99. **MEMBERSHIPS** Soc for Ethnomusicology; Col Music Soc; Soc for Am Music. **RESEARCH** Am Indian musics & cultures; Latino musics & cultures; Balinese music. **SELECTED PUBLICATIONS** Auth, pubs on Ethnomusicology, American Indian Musical Cultures, Music of the American Southwest, and Latino Music of the US; co-auth, book on Choctaw Indian Music; co-ed; Catalogue of Music in the Ruben Cobos Collection of New Mexican Folklore. **CONTACT ADDRESS** Music Dept, Colo Col, 14 E Cache La Poudre St, Colorado Springs, CO 80903. **EMAIL** vlevine@coloradocollege.edu

LEVY, EMANUEL
PERSONAL Born 02/04/1947, Israel, d **DISCIPLINE** SOCIOLOGY, CULTURAL FILM STUDIES **EDUCATION** Tel-Aviv Univ, BA, 71; MA, 73; Columbia Univ, MPhil, 75; PhD, 78. **CAREER** Assoc prof, CUNY and Columbia, 81-85; assoc prof, Wellesley Col, 86-89; ten prof, Ariz State Univ, 90-. **HONORS AND AWARDS** Nat Jewish Bk Awd; Fac Res Creat Awd; Who' Who in Am, World; Outstand People of 20th Century. **MEMBERSHIPS** NSFC. **RESEARCH** Film; popular culture; global cinema; mass communications. **SELECTED PUBLICATIONS** Auth, John Wayne: Prophet of the American Way of Life, 88, 99; auth, The History and Politics of the Oscar Awards, 86, 91; auth, Small-Town America in Film, 91; auth, George Cukor, Master of Elegance, 94; auth, Cinema of Outsiders: The Rise of American Independent Film, NYUP, 99; auth, Andrew Sarris: American Film Critic, forthcoming. **CONTACT ADDRESS** Dept Sociology, Arizona State Univ, West, PO Box 37100, Glendale, AZ 85306.

LEWELLEN, TED CHARLES
PERSONAL Born 06/26/1940, Redding, CA, m, 1985 **DISCIPLINE** CULTURAL ANTHROPOLOGY **EDUCATION**

Alaska Methodist Univ, BA, Philos/Comp Relig, 63; NYork Univ, MA, Anthrop, 73; Univ Colo, PhD, Cult Anthrop, 77. **CAREER** Vis asst prof, Anthrop, Tex Tech Univ, 77-78; asst prof to prof, Univ Richmond, 78- **HONORS AND AWARDS** Prof of the year, Omicron Delta Kappa, Univ of Richmond, 82; Distinguished Tchr, Mortarboard Leadership Soc, Univ of Richmond, 81. **MEMBERSHIPS** Am Anthrop Asn; World Acad Develop and Coop. **RESEARCH** Anthropology of globalization. **SELECTED PUBLICATIONS** Auth, "Holy and Unholy Alliances: The Politics of Catholicism in Revolutionary Nicaragua," J Church and State, 89; auth, "Individualism and Heirarchy: A Grid/Group Analysis of American Political Culture," Polar-Polit & Legal Anthrop Rev, 93; "Structures of Terror: A Systems Analysis of Repression in El Salvador," Human Rights and Third World Develop, 85; auth, "The U.S. and State Terrorism in the Third World," Terrible Beyond Endurance: Foreign Policy of State Terrorism, 88; auth, Political Anthropology, Bergin and Garvey, 92; auth, Dependency and Development: An Introduction to the Third World, Bergin and Garvey, 95. **CONTACT ADDRESS** Dept Soc and Anthrop, Univ of Richmond, Richmond, VA 23173. **EMAIL** tlewelle@richmond.edu

LEWIECKI-WILSON, CYNTHIA B.
DISCIPLINE WOMEN'S STUDIES **EDUCATION** Univ NMex, PhD, 90. **CAREER** Asst prof to assoc prof to prof, Miami Univ Ohio, 90-. **MEMBERSHIPS** MLA; NCTE. **RESEARCH** Compositure and rhetoric; women's studies; disability studies. **SELECTED PUBLICATIONS** Auth, Writing Against the Family: Gender in Lawrence and Joyce, Southern Ill Univ Pr, 94; auth, From Community to College: Reading and Writing Across Diverse Contexts, St Martin's Pr, 96; auth, Embodied Rhetorics: Disability in Language and Culture, Southern Ill Univ Pr, 01. **CONTACT ADDRESS** Dept Women's Studies, Miami Univ, Middletown, 4200 N University Blvd, Middletown, OH 45042-3458. **EMAIL** lewiecc@muohio.edu

LEWIS, DAN A.
PERSONAL Born 02/14/1946, Chicago, IL, m, 1992, 2 children **DISCIPLINE** EDUCATION **EDUCATION** Stanford Univ, BA, 68; Univ Calif at Santa Cruz, PhD, 80. **CAREER** From asst prof to prof, Northwestern Univ, 80-; assoc dir of Inst for Policy Res, Northwestern Univ, 87-90; chemn, Grad Prog of Sch of Educ and Social Policy at Northwestern Univ, 87-90; assoc dean of Sch of Educ and Soc Policy, Northwestern Univ, 90; vis scholar, Stanford Univ, 90-91; chemn, General Fac Comt of Executive Comt of Fac Senate, Northwestern Univ, 95-96; chemn, Fac Advisory Comt of Civic Educ Project, 98; dir of Undergrad Educ, Sch of Educ and Soc Policy at Northwestern Univ, 94-. **HONORS AND AWARDS** Dean's Awd for Innovative Teaching, Sch of Educ and Soc Policy at Northwestern Univ, 97; Excellence in Teaching Awd, Northwestern Alumni Asn at Northwestern Univ, 98. **SELECTED PUBLICATIONS** Contribur, The State Mental Patient and Urban Life, Charles C. Thomas (Springfield, IL), 94; coauth, Race and Educational Reform in the American Metropolis, State Univ NY Press (Albany, NY), 95; coauth, "Welfare Reform Efforts in Illinois," in Families, Poverty and Welfare Reform, ed. Lawrence B. Joseph (IL: Univ Ill Press, 99); auth, "The Costs of Violent Crime," in Encyclopedia of Violence in the United States, ed. Ronald Gottesman (NY: Charles Scribner's Sons, 99); coauth, "Person-Centered Policy Analysis," in Policy Analysis Methods, ed. Stuart S. Nagel (NY: Nova Sci Pub, 99); coauth, "Quality of Life of Persons with Severe and Persistent Mental Illness Living in an Intermediate Care Facility," Am J of Clinical Psychol (forthcoming). **CONTACT ADDRESS** Sch of Educ & Soc Policy, Northwestern Univ, 633 Clark St, Evanston, IL 60208-0001.

LEWIS, GEORGE H.
PERSONAL Born 10/18/1943, Houlton, ME, m, 1970, 1 child **DISCIPLINE** SOCIOLOGY **EDUCATION** Bowdoin Col, BA, 65; Univ Oregon, MA, 69, PhD, 70. **CAREER** Prof, sociology, Univ of the Pacific. **HONORS AND AWARDS** Distinguished fac awd, 84, distinguished fac res lec, 86, Univ of the Pacific; Eberhart Teacher/Scholar Awd, 90; Fishwick Awd, 91; bd of gov, am cult asn. **MEMBERSHIPS** Am Cult Asn; Pop Cult Asn; Pacific Sociol Asn. **RESEARCH** Popular culture; popular music; food and culture. **SELECTED PUBLICATIONS** Auth, Side Saddle on the Golden Calf: Social Structure and Popular Culture in America, Goodyear, 72; auth, Storm Blowing From Paradise: Social Protest and Oppositional Idealogy in Popular Hawaiian Music, in Pop Music, 91; auth, All that Glitters: Country Music in America, Popular, 93; auth, Shell Games in Vacationland: Homanus Americanus and the State of Maine, in Usable Pasts: Traditions and Group Expressions in N Am, Utah State Univ Pr, 97. **CONTACT ADDRESS** Sociology Dept, Univ of the Pacific, Stockton, Stockton, CA 95211. **EMAIL** glewis@uop.edu

LEWIS, LIONEL STANLEY
PERSONAL Born 07/29/1933, Ottawa, Canada, m, 1962, 2 children **DISCIPLINE** SOCIOLOGY **EDUCATION** Washington Univ, BA, 57; Cornell Univ, MA, 58; Yale Univ, PhD, 61. **CAREER** Asst prof, sociol, Univ Nev, 61-63; from asst prof to prof, sociol, SUNY Buffalo, 63-99; dir grad stud, 71-72, 94-96; chemn dept, 88-91; adj prof Higher Educ, SUNY Buffa-

lo, 73- ; prof, emer, 99-. **HONORS AND AWARDS** Phi Beta Kappa; Woodrow Wilson Fel, 57-58; Soc Sci Res Coun Fac Res Grant, 69-70; cited as auth of Outstanding Book on the Subject of Human Rights in 1994, Myers Ctr for Stud of Human Rights. **RESEARCH** Sociology of higher education. **SELECTED PUBLICATIONS** Auth, Scaling the Ivory Tower: Merit and Its Limits in Academic Careers, Johns Hopkins, 75; auth, Cold War on Campus: A Study of the Politics of Organizational Control, Transaction, 88; auth, The Cold War and Academic Governance, SUNY, 93; auth, Marginal Worth: Teaching and the Academic Labor Market, Transaction, 96; auth, When Power Corrupts, Transaction, 00. **CONTACT ADDRESS** Dept of Sociology, SUNY, Buffalo, 430 Park Hall, Buffalo, NY 14260. **EMAIL** soclsl@acsu.buffalo.edu

LEWIS, MARY R.
PERSONAL Born 10/12/1930, Montgomery, AL, s **DISCIPLINE** SOCIAL WORK **EDUCATION** Wesleyan Col, BA, 51; Univ Ala, MA, 52; Univ Denver, Master Soc Work, 61; Bryn Maur Col, PhD, 73. **HONORS AND AWARDS** Rotary Int Found Fel, London Sch of Economics & Political Sci, 52-53; Distinguished Achievement Alumnae Awd, Wesleyan Col, 76. **MEMBERSHIPS** Coun on Soc Work Educ, Nat Asn of Soc Workers, Licensed Master of Soc Worker & Advanced Clinical Practitioner. **RESEARCH** Social policies & services for children, youth & families--international perspectives. **SELECTED PUBLICATIONS** Auth, Integrating Services for Children at Risk: Denmark, France, Netherlands, Sweden, United Kingdom (England and Wales), Orgn for Economic Coop and Development, 96; coauth, "California, USA: Moving towards integration in America's 'Honeypot' State," in OECD: Services that work for our children and families at risk: A world overview, Orgn for Economic Coop and Development, 97; coauth, "Alberta, Canada: Radical change towards services integration," in OECD: Services that work for our children and families at risk: A world overview, Orgn for Economic Coop and Development, 97; coauth, "Portugal: Integrating services in the context of socio-economic change," in OECD: Services that work for our children and families at risk: A world overview, Orgn for Economic Coop and Development, 97; coauth, "Finland: A safety net approach to integrated services provision," in OECD: Services that work for our children and families at risk: A world overview, Orgn for Economic Coop and Development, 97; coauth, "Germany: The human service underpinnings of Europe's economic giant," in OECD: Services that work for our children and families at risk: A world overview, Orgn for Economic Coop and Development, 97; auth, "Professional social work education and service integration roles," in Children and families at risk: New issues in integrating services, Orgn for Economic Coop and Development, 98; auth, "The many faces of school social work: A research partnership, Soc Work in Educ 20.3 (98): 177-190. **CONTACT ADDRESS** Grad Sch of Soc Work, Univ of Houston, Houston, TX 77204-0001. **EMAIL** mrlewis@uh.edu

LEWIS, MEHARRY HUBBARD
PERSONAL Born 08/02/1936, Nashville, TN, m, 2 children **DISCIPLINE** COUNSELING, PSYCHOLOGY **EDUCATION** TN State Univ, BA 1959; TN State Univ, MS 1961; IN Univ, PhD 1971. **CAREER** IN Univ, NDEA fellow 1966-67; Student Activities Office IN Univ, frat affairs adv 1967-69, lecturer 1970, visiting asst prof 1970-72; Macon Cty Bd Ed, coord rsch & eval 1972-73; Natl Alliance of Black School Educators, dir rsch proj 1973-74; School of Educ, prof of educ, asst dean Tuskegee Inst, dir institutional rsch & planning 1974-84; MGMT Inc, pres, dir 1984-; Bullock County Bd of Education, sr counselor, currently. **HONORS AND AWARDS** Who's Who Among Students, 59; Nat Sci Foundation (Federal Government) Fel, 63; Outstanding Young Men of America, 72; President's Awd, Outstanding Service, Nat Alliance of Black School Educators, 74; Exchange Scholar, The Asn of Carribbean Universities, U.S. Dept of State, Phelps-Stokes Fund, 75; Who's Who Among Black Americans, 75-76; Phi Delta Kappa Nat Honorary in Educ, 76-78; Robert Russa Moton Res Fel, 78-79; Outstanding Service Awd, The Church of the Living God, the Pillar and Ground of the Truth, 79. **MEMBERSHIPS** Am Asn for Counseling and Development, Alabama Asn for Counseling and Development, Am Asn of Univ Professors, Nat Alliance of Black Sch Educators. **CONTACT ADDRESS** Bullock County Board of Education, PO Box 830384, Tuskegee, AL 36083-0384. **EMAIL** meharrylew@usa.net

LEY, RONALD
PERSONAL Born 10/19/1929, m, 1965, 1 child **DISCIPLINE** PSYCHOLOGY **EDUCATION** Univ Buffalo, BA, 51; Syracuse Univ, PhD, 63; postdoctoral training, Temple Univ Sch Medicine Inst in Behav Therapy, 71; Certified Psychologist, Univ State NYork, 72. **CAREER** Res asst, Univ Buffalo, 50-51; counselor and lectr, Univ Buffalo, 54-56; counselor and lectr, Utica Col of Syracuse Univ, 56-59; res asst, Syracuse Univ, 59-62; res dir, Madison Area Project, 62-63; asst prof, Northern Ill Univ, 63-64; asst prof, New Sch for Soc Res, 64-66; prof & res prof, State Univ NYork at Albany, 66-. **HONORS AND AWARDS** Pergamon Press J Awd, 87; listed in Dictionary of International Biography, 93-94; listed in Am Men and Women of Science; listed in Who's Who in the East, 93-94 & 96; listed in Who's Who in America, 94-00; listed in Who's Who in Science and Engineering, 94-95 & 96-97; listed in Men of Achievement, 94; Distinguished Psychologist Awd, Psychol Asn of Northeastern NY, 96; Fel, Am Psychol Soc; Fac Res Awd, State Univ NY at Albany, 96-97; Individual Development Awd, NYS/UUP Professional Development and Quality of Working Life Comt, 98. **MEMBERSHIPS** Am Psychol Asn, Am Psychol Soc, Am Statistical Asn, Asn for Applied Psychophysiology and Biofeedback, Asn for the Advancement of Behav Therapy, Author's Guild, Author's League of Am, Behav Therapy and Res Soc, Eastern Psychol Asn, Federation of Behav, Psychol, and Cognitive Sci, Int Soc for the Advancement of Respiratory Psychophysiology, New England Soc of Behav Analysis and Therapy, Psychol Asn of Northeastern NY, Psychonomic Soc, Psychophysiology in Ergonomics Div of Int Ergonomics Asn, Soc for Psychophysiological Res. **RESEARCH** Respiratory Psychophysiology, Learning/Motivation, Memory, History. **SELECTED PUBLICATIONS** Auth, Rumores de Espionaje: Wolfgang Kohler y los Monos en Tenerife, Univ de la Laguna Press, 95; coauth, "Pavlovian conditioning of hyperventilation, supplement to Psychophysiology 33 (96): 55; coauth, "End-tidal CO2 as a conditioned response in a Pavlovian conditioning paradigm," Biol Psychology (97); auth, "Pulmonary function and dyspnea/suffocation-fear theory of panic," J of Behav Therapy and Experimental Psychiatry 29 (98): 1-11; coauth, "Fractional end-tidal CO2 as an index of the effects of stress on math performance and verbal memory of test-anxious adolescents," Biol Psychology 49 (99): 83-94; auth, "The modification of breathing behavior: Pavlovian and operant control in emotion and cognition," Behav Modification 23 (99): 441-479; coauth, "Effects of workload demands on end-tidal PCO2 as an index of psychophysiological activity in computer operators," Biol Psychology (in press); coauth, "Loss of voluntary control of respiration during a dyspnea/suffocation panic attack precipitated by relaxation," Biol Psychology (in press); coauth, "Conditioned hyperventilation in test-anxious adults: Preliminary findings," Biol Psychology (in press). **CONTACT ADDRESS** Dept Educ Psychology, SUNY, Albany, 1400 Washington Ave, Albany, NY 12222-1000.

LI, JIAN
PERSONAL Born 10/17/1957, Sichuan, China, m, 1989, 1 child **DISCIPLINE** CULTURAL ANTHROPOLOGY **EDUCATION** SW China Normal Univ, BA, 83; Lock Haven Univ, MA, 93; Univ Kans, MA, 95; PhD, 00. **CAREER** Res assoc, Univ Missouri; assoc prof, Johnson Cnty Comm Coll. **HONORS AND AWARDS** Grad Stud Res Awd, Univ Kans. **MEMBERSHIPS** AAA; SAA. **RESEARCH** Cultural anthropology; tribal society; cultural change; agriculture; horticulture. **SELECTED PUBLICATIONS** Auth, Development and Tribal Agricultural Economy: A Yao Mountain Village In Northern Thailand, Human Org, 00. **CONTACT ADDRESS** Dept Humanities, Johnson County Comm Col, 12345 College Blvd, Overland Park, KS 66210. **EMAIL** jli@jccc.net

LI, PING
PERSONAL Born 12/22/1962, Hunan, China, m, 1992, 1 child **DISCIPLINE** PSYCHOLOGY **EDUCATION** Peking Univ, BA, 83; MA, 86; Univ Leiden, PhD, 90. **CAREER** Asst Prof, Chinese Univ of Hong Kong, 92-96; Asst Prof to Assoc Prof, Univ Richmond, 96-. **HONORS AND AWARDS** Who's Who in the World; Nat Sci Foundation Awd, 99-00; Human Frontier Sci Prog Res Fel, 90-92. **MEMBERSHIPS** Psychonomic Soc, Cognitive Sci Soc, Intl Neural Network Soc. **RESEARCH** Psycholinguistics; Language learning; Neural networks; Cognitive science. **CONTACT ADDRESS** Dept Psychol, Univ of Richmond, 28 Westhampton Way, Richmond, VA 23173. **EMAIL** pli@richmond.edu

LI, REBECCA
PERSONAL Born 02/09/1969, Hong Kong, China, m, 1999 **DISCIPLINE** SOCIOLOGY **EDUCATION** Chinese Univ Hong Kong, BSS,91; Univ Calif Riverside, PhD, 98. **CAREER** Asst prof, Col of NJ, 98-. **MEMBERSHIPS** Am Sociol Assoc; Pacific Sociol Assoc; E Sociol Soc. **RESEARCH** State breakdown, economic development, emotion. **SELECTED PUBLICATIONS** Coauth, The Next Step: A handbook for UCR teaching assistants, Univ of Calif, 96; auth, "Time Management", "Academic Dishonesty", "Tips for Teaching Problem-Solving Classes" in Training Teaching Asst: Materials for the Selection and Training of TA in Sociol Courses, ed Kenneth Allan and Melinda Messineo, ASA Teaching Resources Center, 97; coauth, "The Politics of Professionals in Five Advanced Industrial Societies" in Citizen Politics in Post-Industrial Societies, ed. Terry Nichols Clark and Michael Rempel (CO: Westview, 97); coauth, "The Continuing Tradition II: Conflict Theories in Historical-Comparative Sociology" in The Structure of Sociological Theory, ed Jonathan H. Turner (CA: Wadsworth, 97). **CONTACT ADDRESS** Dept Anthrop and Sociol, The Col of New Jersey, PO Box 7718, Ewing, NJ 08628. **EMAIL** lirebecc@tcnj.edu

LIAZOS, ALEXANDER
PERSONAL Born 04/12/1941, Albania, d, 2 children **DISCIPLINE** SOCIOLOGY **EDUCATION** Brandeis Univ, PhD, 70. **CAREER** Quinnipuge Col, Hamden, CT, 68-71; prof, Regis Col, 71-. **MEMBERSHIPS** Asn Humanist Sociol, New England Sociol Asn. **RESEARCH** Family, divorce. **SELECTED PUBLICATIONS** Auth, "The Poverty of the Sociology of Deviance: Nuts, Sluts, and Perverts," (72); auth, People First: An Introduction to Social Problems (82); Sociology: A Liberating Perspective (85). **CONTACT ADDRESS** Dept Sociol, Regis Col, Massachusetts, 235 Wellesley St, Weston, MA 02493.

LIBERMAN, KENNETH B.
PERSONAL Born 08/28/1948, Los Angeles, CA, s, 1 child **DISCIPLINE** SOCIOLOGY **EDUCATION** Pomona Col, 66; SUNY Old Westbury, BA, 68-70; Univ CA, MA, 76; PhD, 81. **CAREER** Tutor, Murdoch Univ, Perth, 75-76; Postdoctoral Fellow, Indiana Univ, 82-83; Asst Prof/Assoc/Prof/Prof, Univ of Oregon, 83-00. **HONORS AND AWARDS** Assoc Member, Australian Institute of Aboriginal & T.S. Islanders Studies Former Chair, Society for Phenomenology and the Human Sciences, Grants from Am Council of Learned Societies, Am Philosphical Society, Spencer Foundation, Am Inst. Of Indian Studies, Oregon Council for Humanities. **MEMBERSHIPS** Society for Phenomenology and Existentialism, Am Sociological Asn. **RESEARCH** Ethomnethodological studies of non-Western practices of reasoning, comparative philosophy. **SELECTED PUBLICATIONS** Auth, "The Hermeneutics of Intercultural Communication," Anthropological Linguistics 26 (84): 53-83; auth, Understanding Interaction in Central Australia, London: Routledge, 85; auth, "Decentering the Self: Two Perspectives form Philosophical Anthropology," in Arlene Dallery and Charles Scott (eds.), The Question of the Other (Albany:SUNY Press, 89), auth, "The Hermenuetics of Formal Analytics: The Case of Tibetan Philosophical Critcism," International Philosophical Quarterly 35 (95): 129-40; auth, "'Universal Reason's as a Local Organizational Method," Human Studies 19 (96): 289-301; auth, "Meaning Reflexivity: Gendlin's Contribution to Ethnomethodology," in David Michael Levin (ed.), Language Beyond Postmodernism (Evanston, IL: Northwestern Univ Press, 97), 252-67; auth, "Can Emptiness be Formulated?": A Debate from a Gelugpa Monastic Univ," The Tibet Journal 23 (98): 33-48; auth, "The Social Praxis of Communicating Meaning," Text 19 (99): 57-72; auth, "The Dialectics of Oppression: A Phenomenological Perspective," Philosophy Today 43 (99): 272-282; auth, "Ethnographic Practice and the Critical Spirit," in Lewis Carter (ed.), Reflexive Ethnography (Greenwich, CT: JAI Press), forthcoming. **CONTACT ADDRESS** Dept Sociology, Univ of Oregon, 1291 Unov of Oregon, Eugene, OR 97403. **EMAIL** liberman@darkwing.uoregon.edu

LIBEROPOULOS, MAURA H.
PERSONAL Born 03/23/1968, m, 1999 **DISCIPLINE** HEALTH EDUCATION **EDUCATION** SUNY, BS, 90; CUNY, MS, 95; Nova SE Univ, PhD, 00. **CAREER** Public Health Educator, NY State, 90-98; Adj Instructor to Instructor, Borough Manhattan Cmty Col, 92-. **MEMBERSHIPS** Am Asn for Health Ed; Am Asn for Health, Phys Ed, Recreation and Dance. **CONTACT ADDRESS** Dept Health, Borough of Manhattan Comm Col, CUNY, 199 Chambers St, New York, NY 10007. **EMAIL** liberopoulos@yahoo.com

LICHTENBERG, PHILLIP
PERSONAL Born 10/01/1926, Schenectady, NY, m, 1949, 4 children **DISCIPLINE** PSYCHOLOGY **EDUCATION** Case Western Reserve Univ, BS, 48, MA, 50, PhD, 52. **CAREER** Bryn Mawr Col, Mary Hale Chase Prof Emer, Soc Sci, Soc Wk, Soc research, 96-, Mary Hale Chase Prof Soc Sci, Soc Wk, Soc Research, 90-96, Professor, 68-90, Assoc Prof, 61-68; Co Director, Gestalt Therapy Institute, Phil, 83-; Assoc Soc Psych, Mental Health Research Unit, NY Dept Mental Hygiene, Syracuse, NY, 57-61; Clinical Asst Prof, Psychiatry, Dept of Psychiatry State Univ NY, Upstate Medical Cen, Syracuse, NY, 57-61; Research Psychologist, Inst for Psychosomatic Psychiatric Research and Training, Michael Reese Hosp, Chicago, Ill, 54-57; Research Consultant, Sonia Shankman Orthogenic School, Univ Chicago, 57; Research Asst Psychology Prof, Research Cen Human Relations, NY Univ, 52-54; Research Fellow, Clinical Psychology, Dept Soc Relations, Harvard Univ, 51-52. **HONORS AND AWARDS** Phi Beta Kappa, 48; Mary Hale Chase Professorship, 90. **MEMBERSHIPS** Am Psychol Asn; Penn Psychol Asn; Eastern Psychol Asn; Soc for the Psychol Study of Soc Issues; Am Asn Advancement Science; Am Asn Univ Profs; Am Orthopsychiatric Asn; Intl Soc Pol Psychol; Phil Soc Clinical Psychols; Gestalt Therapy Inst Phil; Soc Advancement Field Theory; Psychols Soc Responsibility; Social Work Action Alliance. **RESEARCH** Clinical Contributions to Social Change. **SELECTED PUBLICATIONS** Motivation for Child Psychiatry Treatment, Russell and Russell, 60; Psychoanalysis: Radical and Conservative, Springer, 69; Getting Even: Equalizing Law of Relationship, Univ Press Am, 88; Undoing the Clinch of Oppression, Peter Lang Pub, 90; Encountering Bigotry: Befriending, Projecting Persons in Everyday Life, Jason Aronson, 97. **CONTACT ADDRESS** 25 Lowry's Lane, Bryn Mawr, PA 19010-1402. **EMAIL** plichtenberg@erols.com

LICKONA, THOMAS E.
PERSONAL Born 04/04/1943, Poughkeepsie, NY, m, 1966, 2 children **DISCIPLINE** ENGLISH, PSYCHOLOGY **EDUCATION** Siena Col, BA, 64; Ohio Univ, MA, 65; State Univ NYork, Albany, PhD, 71. **CAREER** Prof, Educ, State Univ NY, Cortland, 70-; vis prof, Harvard Univ, Boston Univ, 78-79;

Dir, Ctr 4th, 5th R's, State Univ NY, Cortland, 94-. **MEMBERSHIPS** Character Education Partnership; Nat Asn Scholars; Soc of Cath Soc Scientists. **RESEARCH** Moral development, character education. **SELECTED PUBLICATIONS** Moral Development and Behavior, 76; Raising Good Children, 83; Educating for Character: How Our Schools Can Teach Respect and Responsibility, 91; Character Development in Schools and Beyond, 92; Sex, Love, and You: Making the Right Decision, 94. **CONTACT ADDRESS** Educ Dept, SUNY, Col at Cortland, Cortland, NY 13045. **EMAIL** C4n5RS@Cortland.edu

LIE, JOHN J.
DISCIPLINE SOCIOLOGY EDUCATION Harvard Univ, AB, 82; AM, 84; PhD, 88. **CAREER** Prof and Dept Head , Univ of Ill at Urbana - Champaign, 96-. **SELECTED PUBLICATIONS** Auth, Blue Dreams: Korean Americans and the Los Angeles Riots, Harvard Univ Press, 95; auth, Han Unbound: The Political Economy of South Korea, Stanford Univ Press, 98; auth, Multiethnic Japan, Harvard Univ Press, 00. **CONTACT ADDRESS** Dept Sociol, Univ of Illinois, Urbana-Champaign, 702 S Wright, Urbana, IL 61801. **EMAIL** j-lie@uiuc.edu

LIEBERMAN, PHILIP
PERSONAL Born 10/25/1934, Brooklyn, NY, m, 1957, 2 children **DISCIPLINE** COGNITIVE SCIENCE EDUCATION Mass Inst Technol, BSEE & MSEE, 58, PhD(ling), 66. **CAREER** Res asst elec eng, Mass Inst Technol, 56-58; phys scientist speech, Air Force Comn Res Labs, 58-67; assoc prof ling & elec eng, Univ Conn, 67-69, prof ling, 69-74; prof ling, Brown Univ, 74-, guest, inst ling, Mass Inst Technol, 67-70; mem staff ling, Haskins Lab, New York, 67-74; prof, George Hazard Crooker Univ, 86-97; Fred M. Seed Prof of Cognitive and Linguistic Sci, 97-. **HONORS AND AWARDS** Fel Am Asn for Advan of Sci (AAAS), 82; Guggenheim Fel, 82; Visiting NATO Prof, 82; Max-Plank Institit fur Psycholinguistik, Neimegen Lectures, 90; Distinguished Lectr, Academia Sinica, Taipei, 91. **MEMBERSHIPS** Acoust Soc Am; Ling Soc Am; MLA; fel Am Anthrop Asn; fel Am Asn Phys Anthrop. **RESEARCH** Speech production and perception; innate mechanisms and linguistic ability; evolution of linguistic ability. **SELECTED PUBLICATIONS** Auth, Intonation, Perception and Language, Mass Inst Technol, 67; Speech of Primates, Mouton, The Hague, 72; Phonetic Ability and Related Anatomy of the Newborn and Adult Human, Neanderthal Man & the Chimpanzee, Am Anthrop, 6/72; On the Origins of Language, Macmillan, 75; Speech Physiology & Acoustic Phonetics, Macmillan, 76; Biology and Evolution of Language, Harvard, 84; Uniquely Human, Harvard, 91; Eve Spoke: Human Language and Human Evolution, Norton, 98; The Functional Language System of the Human Brain, Harvard, 99. **CONTACT ADDRESS** Dept of Cognitive and Ling Sci, Brown Univ, Providence, RI 02912-1978. **EMAIL** Philip_Lieberman@Brown.edu

LIEBIG, PHOEBE
PERSONAL Born 12/28/1933, Cambridge, MA, s, 1 child **DISCIPLINE** GERONTOLOGY EDUCATION UCLA, BA, 55; MA, 56; Univ S Calif, PhD, 83. **CAREER** Sen Policy Analyst, AARP Pub Policy Inst, 86-88; Res Asst Prof to Assoc Prof, Univ S Calif, 89-. **HONORS AND AWARDS** Visiting Fel, Andrew Norman Institute on Aging; Hansen Family Asst Prof; Fel, UCLA; Fulbright Sen Scholar; AGHE Distinguished Teacher; Teacher of the Year, Andrus Gerontol Cent. **MEMBERSHIPS** Gerontol Soc of Am; Am Soc on Aging; W Polit Sci Asn; Asn for Public Police and Mgmt; Am Polit Sci Asn; Am Pub Admin Soc. **RESEARCH** Housing and services; State-level policies for the aged; Comparative policies for aged; Aging in India; Assistive technology and home modification. **SELECTED PUBLICATIONS** Co-ed, Housing frail elders: International policies, perspectives, and prospects, Johns Hopkins Univ Press, 95; co-auth, "The delivery of home modification and repair services," in Housing adaptations to meet changing needs: Research, policy, and programs," (Baywood, 96); co-auth, "Gerontechnology: The aging of rehabilitation," Rehabilitation Management (97): 100-102; auth, "Policy and political contexts of financing long-term care," in A secure old age: Practical approaches for financing long-term care, Springer, 97; auth, "Housing for the elderly: Intragenerational issues and perspectives," in The new aging policy, SUNY Press, 98; co-auth, "Ageism, disability and access to environmental interventions," Technology & Disability, (98): 69-84; auth, "Using home modifications to promote self-maintenance and mutual care: The case of old-age homes in India," Physical and Occupational Therapy in Geriatrics, (99): 79-99. **CONTACT ADDRESS** Sch Humanities, Univ of So California, 3715 McClintock Ave, Los Angeles, CA 9000-0191. **EMAIL** liebig@usc.edu

LIGHT, IVAN
PERSONAL Born 11/03/1941, Chicago, IL, m, 1966, 2 children **DISCIPLINE** SOCIOLOGY EDUCATION Univ CA, Berkeley, PhD 69. **CAREER** UCLA, Prof sociology, 69. **HONORS AND AWARDS** 4 Times NSF Grantee; Recipient "distinguished career achievement" Awd of the International Migration Section of the Am Sociological Asn, 00. **MEMBERSHIPS** ISA; ASA **RESEARCH** Immigration, entrepreneurship. **SELECTED PUBLICATIONS** Globalization, Vacancy

Chains, or Migration Networks? Immigrant Employment and income in Greater Los Angeles, 1970-190, ed by Don Kalb Marco van der Land, Bart van Steenbergen, Richard Staring and Nico Wilterdink, forthcoming, 99; Ethnic Entrepreneurs in America's Largest Metropolitan Areas, Journal of Urban Affairs, 98; The ethnic economy, NY Academic, forthcoming, with Steven Gold; Just Who Do You Think You Aren't? Society, 97. **CONTACT ADDRESS** Dept of Sociology, Univ of California, Los Angeles, Los Angeles, CA 90095. **EMAIL** light@soc.ucla.edu

LILENFELD, LISA
PERSONAL Born 11/01/1968, New York, NY, m, 1999 **DISCIPLINE** PSYCHOLOGY EDUCATION Cornell Univ, BS, 90; Univ Minn, PhD, 95. **CAREER** Asst Prof, Ga State Univ, 98-. **HONORS AND AWARDS** NIH Fel, W Psychiat Inst, 95-98. **MEMBERSHIPS** Acad for Eating Disorders; Am Psychol Asn; Anxiety Disorders Asn of Am; Asn for the Adv of Beh Therapy; Beh Genetics Asn; Eating Disorders Res Soc. **RESEARCH** Eating Disorders; Anxiety Disorders. **SELECTED PUBLICATIONS** Co-auth, "Referential thinking as an indicator of schizotypy: Scale development and initial construct validation," Psychological Assessment, (97): 452-463; co-auth, "Genetics and family studies of anorexia nervosa and bulimia nervosa," Bailliere's Clinical Psychiatry: International Practice and Research, (97): 177-197; co-auth, "Psychiatric disorders in women with bulimia nervosa and their first-degree relatives: Effects of comorbid substance dependence," International Journal of Eating Disorders, (97): 253-264; co-auth, "A controlled family study of restricting anorexia and bulimia nervosa: Comorbidity in probands and disorders in first-degree relatives," Archives of General Psychiatry, (98): 603-610; co-auth, "Alterations in serotonin activity and psychiatric symptomatology after recovery from bulimia nervosa," Archives of General Psychiatry, (98): 927-935; co-auth, "Genetic studies of anorexia and bulimia nervosa," in Neurobiology in the treatment of eating disorders, (John Wiley & Sons, 98), 169-194; co-auth, "Sexual abuse in eating disorder subtypes and control women: The role of comorbid substance dependence in bulimia nervosa," International Journal of Eating Disorders, (99): 1-10; co-auth, "Familial aggregation of eating disorders: Results from a controlled family study of bulimia nervosa," International Journal of Eating Disorders, (99): 211-215; co-auth, "A genome-wide search for susceptibility loci in anorexia nervosa: methods and sample description," Biological Psychiatry, in press; co-auth, "Genetic factors in anorexia nervosa and bulimia nervosa," in Feeding problems and eating disorders, Harwood Pub, in press. **CONTACT ADDRESS** Dept Psychol, Georgia State Univ, 33 Gilmer St, SE, Atlanta, GA 30303. **EMAIL** llilenfeld@gsu.edu

LILLIOS, KATINA
PERSONAL Born 12/07/1960, Salvador, Bahia, Brazil, m, 1995, 1 child **DISCIPLINE** ANTHROPOLOGY, SOCIOLOGY EDUCATION Boston Univ, BA, 82; Yale Univ, MA, 84; PhD, 91. **CAREER** Lectr, Tufts Univ, 1991; lectr, Brandeis Univ, 92; instr, Johns Hopkins Univ, 92-93; lectr, Hunter Col, 95; vis prof to asst prof, Ripon Col, 93-. **HONORS AND AWARDS** Sigma Xi, 88, 89; Wenner-Gren Found Grant, 89; Am Philos Soc Grant, 93, 94; Nat Science Found Res Grant, 94; Archaeol Inst of Am Grant, 99. **MEMBERSHIPS** Soc for Am Archaeol; Am Anthrop Assoc; Archaeol Inst of Am; Europ Assoc of Archaeol. **RESEARCH** Archaeology of Portugal and Spain, Complex Societies, Nationalism and Archaeology, Geoarchaeology, Material Culture Studies. **SELECTED PUBLICATIONS** Auth, "Regional settlement abandonment at the end of the Copper Age in the lowlands of west-central Portugal" in Abandonment of Settlements and Regions: Ethnoarchaeological and Archaeological Approaches, ed Catherine Cameron and Steven Tomka, (Cambridge: Cambridge Univ Pr, 93), 110-120; auth, "Agroal and the Early Bronze Age of the Portuguese lowlands", Actas dos Trabalhos de Antropologia e Etnologia 33 (93):261-281; ed, The Origins of Complex Societies in Late Prehistoric Iberia, Int Monographs in Prehistory, (MI), 95; auth, "The historiography of late prehistoric Portugal" in Origins of Complex Societies in Late prehistoric Iberia, Int Monographs in Prehistory, (MI), 95; auth, "Nationalism and Copper Age research during the Salazar Regime (1932-1974)" in Nationalism, Politics, and the Practice of Archaeology, eds Philips L. Kohl and Clare Fawcett, (Cambridge: Cambridge Univ Pr, 95), 57-69; auth, "Amphibolite tools of the Portuguese Copper Age (3000-2000 BC): a geoarchaeological study of prehistoric economics and symbolism", Geoarchaeology 12.2 (97): 137-163; auth, "Symbolic artifacts and spheres of meaning: groundstone tools from Copper Age Portugal" in Material Symbols: Culture and Economy in Prehistory, ed John Robb, Carbondale: Center for Archaeol Investigations (99):173-187; auth, "Objects of Memory: the ethnography and archaeology of heirlooms", Jour of Archaeol method and Theory 6.2 (99):235-262. **CONTACT ADDRESS** Dept Anthrop and Sociol, Ripon Col, PO Box 248, Ripon, WI 54971. **EMAIL** lilliosk@mail.ripon.edu

LINDAHL, CARL
PERSONAL Born 12/02/1947, Boston, MA **DISCIPLINE** FOLKLORE, ENGLISH, MEDIEVAL STUDIES EDUCATION Harvard Univ, BA, 71; Indiana Univ, Bloomington, MA, 76, PhD, 80. **CAREER** Asst prof, 80-86, assoc prof, 86-97, prof, 97- , English Dept, Univ Houston. **HONORS AND**

AWARDS Magna Cum Laude, 71; fel, Am Coun Learned Soc, 83; tchg excellence awd, 93; Alcee Fortier Awd, Am Folklore Soc, 96; fel, Virginia Found for Hum, 97; Lib of Cong Parsons Grant, 98; Founder and ed, World Folktale Library, Garland and Univ Pr Miss; editorial bd, Folklore; dist ed bd, Medieval Folklore. **MEMBERSHIPS** Am Folklore Soc; Folklore Soc, London; Int Soc for Contemp Legend Res; Int Soc for Folk Narrative Res; New Chaucer Soc; Nordic Inst of Folklore, **RESEARCH** Folk narrative; medieval literature; medieval folklore; American folklore. **SELECTED PUBLICATIONS** Auth, the Oral Undertones of Late Medieval Romance, in Oral Tradition in the Middle Ages, Medival and Renaissance Texts Series, 95; auth, Bakhtin's Carnival Laughter and The Cajun Country Mardi Gras, in Folklore, 96; ed, Outlaws and Other Medieval Heroes, Southern Folklore, 96; co-ed, Swapping Stories: Folktales from Louisiana, Mississippi, 97; co-auth, Cajun Mardi Gras Masks, Mississippi, 97; auth, the Presence of the Past in the Cajun Country Mardi Gras, in J of Folklore Res, 96; auth, Some Uses of Numbers, in J of Folklore Res, 97; auth, the Oral Aesthetic and the Bicameral Mind, in Gilgamesh: A Reader, Bolchazy-Carducci, 97; auth, the Power of Being Outnumbered, in La Folklore Miscellany, 97; auth, Chaucer and the Shape of Performance, in Critical Essays on Geoffrey Chaucer, GK Hall, 98; auth, Sir Gawain and the Green Knight, Robert Burns's 'Halloween,' and Myth in its Time, in telling Tales, Medieval Narratives and the Folk Tradition, St Martins, 98; coed, Medieval Folklore: An Encyclopedia of Myths, Legends, Tales, Beliefs, and Customs, ACB-CLIO, 00. **CONTACT ADDRESS** Dept of English, Univ of Houston, Houston, TX 77204-3012. **EMAIL** clindahl@uh.edu

LINDENFELD, FRANK
PERSONAL Born 03/04/1934, Vienna, Austria, m, 1984, 4 children **DISCIPLINE** SOCIOLOGY EDUCATION Cornell Univ, BA, 55; Columbia Univ, MA, 58; PhD, 61. **CAREER** Assoc Prof to Prof, Cheyney Univ, 74-88; Prof, Bloomsburg Univ, 88-. **HONORS AND AWARDS** Grant, Ctr for Rural PA, 92. **MEMBERSHIPS** Asn for Humanist Sociol; PACE of Philadelphia. **SELECTED PUBLICATIONS** Co-ed, From the Ground Up: Essays on Grassroots and Workplace Democracy by C. George Benello, South End Press, 91; co-ed, When Workers Decide: Workplace Democracy Takes Root in America, New Society Pub, 92; auth, "The cooperative commonwealth: an alternative to Corporate Capitalism and State Socialism," Humanity and Society, 97; co-auth, "Success and Failure of Worker Co-ops: The role of Internal and External Environment Factors," Humanity and Society, 97; auth, "Possibilities and Limits of U.S. Microenterprise Development for Creating good Jobs and Increasing the Incomes of the Poor," Humanity and Society, 98. **CONTACT ADDRESS** Dept Sociol , Soc Work & Criminal Justice, Bloomsburg Univ of Pennsylvania, 400 E 2nd St, Bloomsburg, PA 17815.

LINDGREN, C. E.
PERSONAL Born 11/20/1949, Coeburn, VA, s **DISCIPLINE** MEDIEVAL HISTORY, HISTORY OF EDUCATION EDUCATION Univ Miss, MEd, 77, EdS, 93; Coll of Preceptors, MPhil, 93; UNISA, DEd, 98. **CAREER** Dir, Delta Hills Educ Asn, 76-80; dir, Educ consultants of Oxford, 81-; chm, Hist & Phil of Educ, Greenwitch Univ, 98-; Dean, College of Arts and Humanities, 99-; Faculty Am Military Univ. **HONORS AND AWARDS** Robert A. Taft Fel; EDPA Fel; hon fel, World Jnana Sadhak Soc; assoc IIPS, knighthood, Order of Isnatias of Antioch (Catholic). **MEMBERSHIPS** Royal Soc Arts; Royal Asiatic Soc; Col of Preceptors; Royal Hist Soc; Am Acad Relig; Medieval Acad of Am; PSA; Hist of Ed Soc. **RESEARCH** Egyptology; medieval history; Qu Gong; metagogics; religion. **CONTACT ADDRESS** 10431 Hwy51, Courtland, MS 38620. **EMAIL** lindgren@panola.com

LINDNER, CARL MARTIN
PERSONAL Born 08/31/1940, Brooklyn, NY, 2 children **DISCIPLINE** AMERICAN LITERATURE AND CULTURE EDUCATION Univ Wis-Madison, PhD. **CAREER** Prof, Univ of WI, Parkside. **HONORS AND AWARDS** UW-Parkside Awd, Exellence in Res and Creative Act 96; Univ WI Regents Tchg Exellence Awd, 92; Stella C Gray Distinguished Tchg Awd, 90-91; Ragdale Found fel, 90; WI Arts Bd Creative Writing fel for Poetry, 80; Standard Oil Distinguished Tchr Awd, 69-70. **SELECTED PUBLICATIONS** Essays on, lit; publ approx 200 poems in var lit jour, 2 chapbks of poetry, Vampire & The Only Game; bk of poetry, Shooting Baskets in a Dark Gymnasium. **CONTACT ADDRESS** Dept of Eng, Univ of Wisconsin, Parkside, 900 Wood Rd, 218 Commun, PO Box 2000, Kenosha, WI 53141-2000. **EMAIL** carl.lindner@uwp.edu

LINDSAY, CINDY
PERSONAL Born 04/04/1956, Phoenix, AZ, s **DISCIPLINE** PSYCHOLOGY EDUCATION Univ Calif, PhD, 89. **CAREER** Asst Prof, Ind Univ, 87-91; Assoc Prof, Calif School of Professional Psychol, 91-. **HONORS AND AWARDS** Best Paper Awd, 95. **MEMBERSHIPS** Org Beh Teaching Soc, Acad of Management. **RESEARCH** Andean Shamanism; Energetic transformation; Alternative healing for individuals group and organizations. **CONTACT ADDRESS** Dept Organizational Psychol, California Sch of Professional Psychology, Los Angeles, 1000 S Fremont Ave, Alhambra, CA 91803. **EMAIL** shaman@loop.com

LINDSTROM, LAMONT
PERSONAL Born 05/11/1953, Oakland, CA, d, 3 children **DISCIPLINE** ANTHROPOLOGY **EDUCATION** Univ Cal Berkeley, AB, 75; MA, 76; PhD, 81. **CAREER** Prof, Univ Tulsa, 92-. **HONORS AND AWARDS** OHIRA Memorial Prize, 92. **MEMBERSHIPS** AAA; ASAO. **RESEARCH** Sociolinguistics; ethno history; Pacific studies. **SELECTED PUBLICATIONS** Auth, Knowledge and Power in a South Pacific Society, Smithsonian Inst Press, 90; coauth, Kava: The Pacific Drug, Yale Univ (New Haven), 92, reprinted, Kava: The Pacific Elixir: The Definitive Guide to its Ethnobotany, History, and Chemistry, Healing Arts Press (Rochester, VT), 97; auth, Cargo Cult: Strange Stories of Desire from Melanesia and Beyond, Univ Hawaii Press (Honolulu), 93; coauth, Culture, Custom, Tradition: Developing Cultural Policy in Melanesia, Inst Pacific Stud (Suva), 94; coauth, Languages of the World, Lincom Europa (Munich), 94; co-ed, Chiefs Today: Traditional Pacific Leadership and the Postcolonial State, Stan Univ Press (Stanford), 97; co-ed, Big Wok: Storian Blong Wol We Tu long Vanuatu, Inst Pac Stud (Suva); coauth, "Anthropologies New Cargo: Future Horizons," Ethnology 34 (95): 201-209; rev of "Seeking Personal Responsibility in Strange Places," Semiotica 111 (96): 173-182; auth, "Cultural Tourism in the Pacific," S Pac Stud 18 (97): 33-45; coauth, "Ungka the Gibbon and the Pearly Nautilus," J Pac Hist 33 (98): 5-27. **CONTACT ADDRESS** Dept Anthropology, Univ of Tulsa, 600 S College, Tulsa, OK 74104.

LINEHAN, MARSHA M.
PERSONAL Born 05/05/1943 **DISCIPLINE** PSYCHOLOGY **EDUCATION** Loyola Univ, BS, 68; MA, 70; PhD, 71. **CAREER** Lectr, Loyola Univ, 69-72; postdoctoral intern, Suicide Prevention and Crisis Service, Inc., 71-72; adj asst prof, State Univ Col at Buffalo, 72; postdoctoral fel, State Univ NYork Stony Brook, 72-73; adj asst prof, Inst of Pastoral Studies at Loyola Univ, 73-75; asst prof, The Catholic Univ of Am, 73-77; from asst prof to prof, Univ Wash, 77-; vis scientist, Cambridge Univ, 91. **HONORS AND AWARDS** Distinguished Contributions to the Practice of Psychol Awd, Am Asn of Applied and Preventative Psychol, 94; Am Psychol Asn Fel, Div of Clinical Psychol, 95; Stanton Lecture, Harvard Medical Sch, 95; Am Psychopathological Asn Fel, 96; Res Scientist Awd, Am Found for Suicide Prevention, 99; Louis I. Dublin Awd for Lifetime Achievement in the Field of Suicide, Am Asn of Suicidology, 99; Distinguished Contributions for Clinical Activities, Asn for the Advancement of Behav Therapy, 99. **MEMBERSHIPS** Asn for Advancement of Behav Therapy, Am Psychol Soc, Am Psychol Asn, Asn for Clinical Psychol Res, Int Asn for Suicide Prevention, Soc for Psychotherapy Res, Int Soc for the Improvement and Teaching of Dialectical Behavior Therapy, Am Psychopathological Asn, Am Asn for the Advancement of Sci. **SELECTED PUBLICATIONS** Coauth, Succeeding Socially, Lifecycle Pub, 83; auth, Cognitive Behavioral Treatment of Borderline Personality Disorder, Guilford Press, 93; auth, Skills Training Manual for Treating Borderline Personality Disorder, Guilford Press, 93; coauth, "Dialectical behavior therapy for patients with borderline personality disorder and drug-dependence," The Am J on Addictions 8 (99): 279-292; coauth, "Recognition of facial expressions of emotion ability among women with borderline personality disorder," J of Personality Disorders 13 (99): 329-344; auth, "The empirical basis of dialectical behavior therapy: Development of new treatments vs. evaluation of existing treatments," Clinical Psychology: Sci and Practice 7 (00): 113-119; coauth, "Therapeutic burnout among borderline personality disorder disordered clients and their therapists: Development and evaluation of two adaptations of the Maslach Burnout Inventory," Cognitive Behav Practice (in press). **CONTACT ADDRESS** Dept Psychol, Univ of Washington, PO Box 351525, Seattle, WA 98195-1525. **EMAIL** linehan@u.washington.edu

LINGER, DANIEL T.
PERSONAL Born 09/12/1946, Akron, OH **DISCIPLINE** ANTHROPOLOGY **EDUCATION** UCSD, PhD, 87. **CAREER** Assoc prof, Univ of Calif at Santa Cruz, 88-. **MEMBERSHIPS** Am Anthrop Asn, Soc for Cultural Anthrop, Soc for Psychol Anthrop, Am Ethnol Soc. **RESEARCH** Sociocultural anthropology, psychological anthropology, politics, identity, transactional experience, Brazil, Japan. **SELECTED PUBLICATIONS** Auth, Dangerous Encounters: Meanings of Violence in a Brazilian City, Stanford Univ Press (Stanford), 92; auth, "The Hegemony of Discontent," Am Ethnol 20 (93): 3-24; auth, "Has Culture Theory Lost Its Minds?" Ethos 22 (94): 284-315; auth, "Brazil Displaced: Restaurante 51 in Nagoya, Japan," Horizontes Antropologicos 5 (97): 181-203; auth, No One Home: Japanese-Brazilian Identities in Motion, Stanford Univ Press (Stanford), in press; auth, "Missing Persons: Methodological Notes on Japanese-Brazilian Identities," Estudios Interdisciplinarios de Am Latina e el Caribe (in press); auth, "The Identity Path of Eduard Mori," History in Person, Am Res Press, in press. **CONTACT ADDRESS** Dept Anthrop and Social Sci, Univ of California, Santa Cruz, 1156 High St, Santa Cruz, CA 95064.

LINKEY, HELEN E.
PERSONAL Born 09/26/1938, Toledo, OH, s **DISCIPLINE** PSYCHOLOGY **EDUCATION** Siena Heights Col, BS, 65; Bowling Green State Univ, MA, 69; Univ Detroit, MA, 77; Wayne State Univ, MA, 86; PhD, 90. **CAREER** Secondary School Teacher, 65-81; Teaching Asst, Wayne State Univ, 83-88; Asst Prof to Assoc Prof, Marshall Univ, 88-. **HONORS AND AWARDS** Nat Sci Foundation Summer Traineeship, Bowling Green State Univ, 66-69; Nat Inst of Metal Health Traineeship, Wayne state Univ, 82-83; Fac Development Awd, Marshall Univ, 90; Capital Area soc Psychol Asn Dissertation Competition winner, 991; Fac Development Awd, Marshall Univ, 91; Summer Res Grant, Marshall Univ, 94 Sigma Xi. **MEMBERSHIPS** Am Psychol Asn, Soc for the Sci Study of Relig, Soc for Personality and Soc Psychol, Midwestern Psychol Asn. **RESEARCH** Procedural and distributive fairness; Interpersonal influence; Religious behavior; Nonverbal behavior as a function of personality and situation; Attachment and individuation across the life span; Interpersonal influence; Procedural and distributive justice; conflict processes. **SELECTED PUBLICATIONS** Co-auth, "Need norm, demographic influences, social roles, and justice judgments," current Psychology, (98): 152-162; co-auth, "How to ruin a signshop," sings of the times, (93): 128-129; co-auth, :Dyad dominance composition effects, nonverbal behaviors, and influence," Journal of Research in Personality, (90): 206-215; co-auth, "dominance displays as indicators of a social success motive," in Power, dominance, and nonverbal behavior, (85): 109-128. **CONTACT ADDRESS** Dept Psychol, Marshall Univ, 400 Hal Greer Blvd, Huntington, WV 25755-0003. **EMAIL** linkey@marshall.edu

LINZEY, SHARON
PERSONAL Born 04/17/1949, San Diego, CA, s **DISCIPLINE** SOCIOLOGY **EDUCATION** Vanguard Univ, BA, 71; Ind Univ, MA, 79; MA, 82; PhD, 84. **CAREER** Assoc Prof, Seattle Pacific Univ, 85-92; Prof, Moscow State Univ, 92-94; Prof, Hope Intl Univ, 95-97; Prof, George Fox Univ, 97-. **HONORS AND AWARDS** Fulbright Scholar, Runmin Univ, 00; Alumni of the Year, Vanguard Univ; Edwin Sutherland Teaching Awd, Ind Univ, 84; Burlington Northern Awd, Seattle Pacific Univ, Fulbright Scholar, Univ Ryokyos, 89-90; Fulbright Scholar, Moscow State Univ, 93-94. **MEMBERSHIPS** ASA, PSA, Health Development Intl. **RESEARCH** Religion in Eastern Europe, Church-state relations in Russia. **SELECTED PUBLICATIONS** Auth, "Future of Religious Freedom in Russia," Kontinent Magazine, forthcoming; auth, "God in Russia: The Challenge of Freedom, Univ Press of America, 99; auth, "The 'real' reason for NATO's Actions?" The Kansas Christian, 99; auth, "Religion as politics in Russia," Christian Courier Reformed Weekly, (98): 12-13; auth, "West learns Yeltsin no champion of democracy, religious freedom," The Kansas Christian, (98): 8; auth, "The agony and exhilaration of Andrei," Christian Courier Reformed Weekly, (98): 10; auth, Directory of Indigenous Christian Organizations of the Former Soviet Union and East Central Europe, Berry Pub, 96; auth, "Catholic-Orthodox Relations in Russia," National Catholic Register, 96; auth, "Rethinking the Reasonableness of the Religious Right," Review of Religious Research, 95. **CONTACT ADDRESS** Dept Soc Sci, George Fox Univ, 414 N Meridan St, Newberg, OR 97132. **EMAIL** slinzey@georgefox.edu

LITTLE, ELIZABETH A.
PERSONAL Born 09/25/1926, Mineola, NY, m, 1953, 4 children **DISCIPLINE** ARCHAEOLOGY, ANTHROPOLOGY **EDUCATION** Wellesley Col, BA (Physics, Durant Scholar with high honors), 48; MIT, D Phil (Physics), 54; Univ MA, MA (Anthropology), 85. **CAREER** Nantucket Hist Asn Archaeological Field Dir, 76-77; coord, MA Hist Commission survey grant, 78-79, res dir, 79-84, curator of Prehistoric Artifacts, Nantucket Historical Association, 85-95; MA Archaeological Soc, trustee, 79-96, pres, 84-86, ed of the Bul of the MA Archaeological Soc, 86-96; res assoc, R S Peabody Museum of Archaeology, Philips Academy, Andover, MA; res fel, Archaeology, Nantucket Hist Asn. **HONORS AND AWARDS** Phi Beta Kappa, Sigma Xi, IBM fel, 47-54; Preservation Awds, MA Hist Commission, 79, 88. **MEMBERSHIPS** Soc for Am Archaeology; Soc for Archaeological Sciences. **RESEARCH** Radiocarbon dating; stable isotope studies of prehistoric diet; ethnohistory. **SELECTED PUBLICATIONS** Auth, Radiocarbon Age Calibration at Archaeological Sites of Coastal Massachusetts and Vicinity, J of Archaeological Science, 93; with Margaret J Schoeninger, The Late Woodland Diet on Nantucket Island and the Problem of Maize in Coastal New England, Am Antiquity, 95; Daniel Spotso: A Sachem at Nantucket Island, Massachusetts, circa 1691-1741, in Northeastern Indian Lives, 1632-1816, R S Grumet, ed, Univ MA Press, 96; Analyzing Prehistoric Diets by Linear Programming, with John D C Little, J of Archaeological Science, 97. **CONTACT ADDRESS** 37 Conant Road, Lincoln, MA 01773. **EMAIL** ealittle@alum.mit.edu

LITTLEJOHN, WALTER L.
PERSONAL Born 03/05/1932, Pine Bluff, AR, m **DISCIPLINE** EDUCATION **EDUCATION** BS 1954; MEd 1957; EdD 1966. **CAREER** Magnolia, AR, teacher 1954; Magnolia AR, principal 1965-58; Magnolia, AR, public school supt 1958-64; AM&N, prof 1966-74, dean of educ 1975-91, coordinator of graduate programs, 91-. **MEMBERSHIPS** Mem Phi Delta Kappa; Alpha Kappa Mu; life mem Omega Psi Phi Frat; Natl Educ Assn; past pres State Tchrn Assn. **CONTACT ADDRESS** Coord Grad Programs, Sch Educ, Univ of Arkansas, Pine Bluff, University Dr, Pine Bluff, AR 71601.

LIU, RUTH A.
PERSONAL Born 02/25/1945, Chung King, China, m, 1975, 2 children **DISCIPLINE** EDUCATION **EDUCATION** Union Col, BS, 66; Univ Calif, MS, 67; Univ Tenn, EdD, 97. **CAREER** Adj Prof, Southern Adventist Univ, 96-; Res Assoc, Univ Tenn, 98- **HONORS AND AWARDS** Outstanding Young Woman of Am, 76; Intl Biographical Dictionary, 73; Personalities of the West and Midwest, 71; Young Career Girl of the Year, Englewood, 66. **MEMBERSHIPS** Sigma Theta Tau, Phi Kappa Phi, Ga-Cumberland Conf of Seventh-day Adventists. **SELECTED PUBLICATIONS** Auth, "Educational and career expectations of Chinese-American College students," Journal of College Student Development, (98): 577-588; co-auth, "In search of community: Faculty assessment of its presence at three institutions," Community College Review, (97): 3-14; auth, "Doesn't anyone care?," Southern Tidings, 89; auth, "From Buddhism to Adventism," Southern Tidings, 89; auth, "Hope for that hopeless essay test," Journal of Nursing Education, 77 **CONTACT ADDRESS** Dept Educ & Psychol, Southern Adventist Univ, PO Box 370, Collegedale, TN 37315. **EMAIL** raliu@southern.edu

LIU, XIN
PERSONAL Born 06/26/1957, Beijing, m, 1 child **DISCIPLINE** ANTHROPOLOGY **EDUCATION** Shanxi Sch Econ and Finance, China, MA, 82; Renmin Univ Beijing, MSc, 85; Univ London, MA, 90; PhD, 95. **CAREER** Asst prof, UC Berkeley. **HONORS AND AWARDS** Asian Leadership Fel, Japan Found and the Int House of Japan, 98-99. **MEMBERSHIPS** Am Anthrop Asn. **RESEARCH** Anthropology of modern life with a particular interest in East Asia. **SELECTED PUBLICATIONS** Auth, In One's Own Shadow: An Ethnographic Account of the Condition of Post-reform Rural China, Univ of Calif Press, 00. **CONTACT ADDRESS** Dept Anthrop, Univ of California, Berkeley, 232 Kroeber Hall, Berkeley, CA 94720-3710. **EMAIL** xinliu@sscl.berkeley.edu

LIU, ZILI
PERSONAL Born Beijing, China, s **DISCIPLINE** PSYCHOLOGY **EDUCATION** Brown Univ, PhD, 94. **CAREER** Asst Prof, Rutgers Univ, 98-. **CONTACT ADDRESS** Dept Psychol, Rutgers, The State Univ of New Jersey, Newark, 180 Univ Ave, Newark, NJ 07102. **EMAIL** liu@psychology.rutgers.edu

LLOYD, CARL
PERSONAL Born 04/14/1952, Niles, MI, m, 1974, 3 children **DISCIPLINE** PSYCHOLOGY, SOCIAL WORK **EDUCATION** Columbia Christian Col, BA, 75; Eastern NM Univ, MA, 78; Ore State Univ, MS, 82; Univ T, PhD, 89; MSSW, 93. **CAREER** Prof, Dallas Bapt, Univ, 89-93; prof, Colo Christian Univ, 93-94; prof, George Fox Univ, 94-. **HONORS AND AWARDS** Who's Who in Am Professionals, 99; Who's Who of Am Teachers, 98; Fac of the Year Awd, 98. **MEMBERSHIPS** LMSW, LPC, LMFT, LCDC, AAMFT, NASW. **RESEARCH** Bioethics **CONTACT ADDRESS** Dept Soc Sci, George Fox Univ, 414 N Meridan St, Newberg, OR 97132. **EMAIL** clloyd@georgefox.edu

LLOYD, JENNIFER
PERSONAL Born 04/01/1939, United Kingdom, d, 2 children **DISCIPLINE** HISTORY, WOMEN'S STUDIES **EDUCATION** Cambridge Univ, BA, 61; Univ London, Post Graduate Certificate in Educ, 62; Cambridge Univ, MA, 66; State Univ NY at Brockport, MA, 87; Univ Rochester, PhD, 92. **CAREER** Asst prof & dir women's studies, State Univ NY at Brockport, 96-. **HONORS AND AWARDS** Eileen Power Prize, Gimton Col, 59; George Queen Awd for Teaching, Stat Univ NY at Brockport, 86 & 97; W. Wayne Dedman Awd, State Univ NY at Brockport, 86; Wilson S. Coates & Hilda M. Altschule Prize, Univ Rochester, 88 & 90. **MEMBERSHIPS** Am Hist Asn, Nat Women's Studies Asn, N Am Confr on British Studies, Berkshire Confr of Women's Historians. **RESEARCH** Nineteenth-Century British Women's History. **SELECTED PUBLICATIONS** Auth, "Cultivating Lilies: Ruskin and Women," J of British Studies, 95; auth, "Strains in the Ideas of Compasionate Marriage in Victorian England: The Failed Marriage of Effie Gray and John Ruskin," J of Women's Hist, 99. **CONTACT ADDRESS** Dept Hist, SUNY, Col at Brockport, 350 New Campus Dr, Brockport, NY 14410-2997. **EMAIL** jlloyd@brockport.edu

LLOYD, PAUL J.
PERSONAL Born 05/05/1941, Denver, CO, m **DISCIPLINE** PSYCHOLOGY **EDUCATION** Metropolitan State Col Colo, BA, 70; N Mex Highland Univ, MS, 72; St Louis Univ, PhD, 78. **CAREER** Instr to Prof and Dept Chair, Southeast Mo State Univ, 71-. **HONORS AND AWARDS** Fel, Am Psychol Asn; Excellency in Scholarship Awd, Southeast Mo State Univ; Outstanding Fac Service Awd, Southeast Mo State Univ, Distinguished Toastmasters Recognition; Rotary International Paul Harris Fel **MEMBERSHIPS** River Heritage Mural Asn, Cottonwood Residential Treatment Center, Cultural Exchange Network, Rotary Intl, Southeast Mo Coun of the Arts, Toastmasters Intl, Wally Byam Caravan Club Intl. **RESEARCH** Psychosocial factors related to health, fitness and longevity; Lifestyle enhancement; Consulting psychology; Organizational develop-

ment; Occupational stress management; The psychology major and career alternatives and program evaluation. **SELECTED PUBLICATIONS** Auth, "Managing the Bottom Line Via Managing Employee Stress," The Psychologist-Manager Journal; auth, "Evaluation of Preventive and Rehabilitative Exercise Programs." **CONTACT ADDRESS** Dept Psychol, Southeast Missouri State Univ, 1 Univ Plaza, Cape Girardeau, MO 63701.

LO, CELIA C.
PERSONAL Born 01/11/1961, Hong Kong, China, m, 1995 **DISCIPLINE** SOCIOLOGY **EDUCATION** Univ Ala, PhD, 93. **CAREER** Asst prof, Central Mich Univ, 93-96; asst prof, Univ Akron, 96-. **MEMBERSHIPS** Am Sociol Asn, Am Soc of Criminology. **RESEARCH** Alcohol and drug use, deviance, criminology, juvenile delinquency. **SELECTED PUBLICATIONS** Coauth with Carol Cassel, "Theories of Political Literacy," Political Behav, 19, 4 (97): 317-335; coauth with Denise L. Bissler, "Gender Differences in Reasons for Drinking and Not Drinking: Association with Drinking Levels and Alcohol Related Consequences," Free Inquiry in Creative Sociology, 26, 2 (98): 1-11; coauth with Gerald Globetti, "Gender Differences in Consequences of Alcohol Use among Adolescents," in Sociology of Crime, Law, and Deviance, vol 1, ed by Jeffery T. Ulmer, Greenwich, CT: JAI (98); coauth with Gerald Globetti, "Gender Differences in the Drinking Patterns of American and Hong Kong Adolescents: A Cross-Cultural Study," Int J of Comp Sociol, 40, 3 (99): 307-331; coauth with Richard C. Stephens, "Drugs and Prisoners: Treatment Needs upon Entering Prison," Am J of Drug and Alcohol Abuse, 26, 2 (2000): 229-245; coauth with Gerald Globetti, "Gender Differences in Drinking Patterns among Hong Kong Chinese Youth: A Pilot Study," Substance Use and Misuse, 35, 8 (2000): 157-166; coauth with Gerald Globetti, "Alcohol and Crime," Encyclopedia of Criminology and Deviant Behavior (2000); coauth with Gerald Globetti, "Teenage Alcohol and Drug Abuse," in Extraordinary Behavior: Case Studies in the Unusual," ed by Dennis L. Peck and Norman Dolch, Westport, CT: Greenwood Pub Co (2000); auth, "The Impact of First Drinking and Differential Association on Collegiate Drinking," Sociol Focus (forthcoming); coauth with Gerald Globetti, "Gender Differences in Alcohol Beliefs and Usual Blood-Alcohol Concentration," J of Child and Adolescent Substance Abuse (forthcoming); auth, "Timing of Drinking Initiation: A Trend Study Predicting Drug Use among High School Seniors," J of Drug Issues (forthcoming). **CONTACT ADDRESS** Dept Sociol, Univ of Akron, 302 Buchtel Mall, Akron, OH 44325-0002. **EMAIL** Lo@uakron.edu

LOCKE, DON C.
PERSONAL Born 04/30/1943, Macon, MS **DISCIPLINE** EDUCATION **EDUCATION** TN A&I State Univ, BS 1963, MEd 1964; Ball State Univ, EdD 1974. **CAREER** South Side HS, social studies teacher 1964-70; Wayne HS, school counselor 1971-73; Ball State Univ European Program, asst prof 1974-75; NC State Univ, asst/assoc prof/prof 1975-89, dept head 1987-93; Director, NCSU Doctoral Program at the Asheville Graduate Center, 93-; Dir, Asheville Graduate Center, 00-. **HONORS AND AWARDS** Summer Fellow Center for Advanced Study in Behaviorial Sciences 1979, 1992; ACA Professional Development Awd, 1996. **MEMBERSHIPS** Mem Alpha Phi Alpha Fraternity Inc; mem New Bern Ave Day Care Center Bd, 1978-86; pres NC Counseling Assoc 1979-80; chairperson S Region Branch ACA 1983-84; mem Carroll Comm Schools Advisory Council 1984-87, ex director, 1987-1991; chairperson NC Bd of Registered Practicing Counselors 1984-87; Pres Asn for Counselor Educ & Supervision 00-01; pres Southern Association for counselor Educ and Supervision 1988-89, member board dir, Asheville -Buncombe United Way, 1997-. **SELECTED PUBLICATIONS** Co-author "Psychological Techniques for Teachers"; author Increasing Multicultural Understanding; author or co-author of more than 50 articles in professional journals. **CONTACT ADDRESS** Dir, Ash Grad Center 123, 143 Karpen Hall, CPO 2140, Asheville, NC 28804. **EMAIL** dlcoke@unca.edu

LOCKE, RALPH PAUL
PERSONAL Born 03/09/1949, Boston, MA, m, 1979, 2 children **DISCIPLINE** MUSICOLOGY, MUSIC, HISTORY, SOCIOLOGY **EDUCATION** Harvard Univ, BA, 70; Univ Chicago, MA, 74, PhD, 80. **CAREER** Prof, Eastman School Music, 75-. **HONORS AND AWARDS** ASCAP Deems Taylor Awd, 92, 96, and 99. **MEMBERSHIPS** Am Musicol Soc; Sonneck Soc Am Music. **RESEARCH** Music and society; Music and gender; Music in France & Italy; Music patronage in the US; Musical exoticism and Orientalism. **SELECTED PUBLICATIONS** Auth Music, Musicians, and the Saint-Simonians, Univ Chicago Press, 86; Paris: Centre of Intellectual Ferment (1789-1852), Man & Music: The Early Romantic Era, Between Revolutions: 1789 and 1848, Prentice-Hall, 91; What Are These Women Doing in Opera? En travesti: Women, Gender Subversion, Opera, Columbia Univ Press, 95; Cultivating Music in America: Women Patrons and Activists since 1860, Univ Cal Press, 97; Constructing the Oriental 'Other': Saint-Saens's Samson et Dalila, The Work of Opera: Genre, Nationhood, and Sexual Difference, Columbia Univ Press, 97; The French Symphony: David, Gounod, and Bizet to Saint-Saens, Franck, and Their Followers, The Nineteenth-Century Symphony, Schirmer Books, 97; Cutthroats and Casbah Dancers, Muezzins and Timeless Sands: Musical Images of the Middle East, The Exotic in Western Music, NE Univ Press, 98; Musicology and/as Social Concern: Imagining the Relevant Musicologist, Oxford Univ Press, 98; Auth, Musical Exoticism and Orientalism: Problems for the Worldly Critic, Edward Said and the Work of the Critic, Duke Univ Press, 00. **CONTACT ADDRESS** Eastman Sch of Music, 26 Gibbs St, Rochester, NY 14604-2599. **EMAIL** RLPH@MAIL.ROCHESTER.EDU

LOCKMAN, PAUL
PERSONAL Born 06/12/1945, Pittsburgh, PA, s **DISCIPLINE** SOCIOLOGY **EDUCATION** Ind Univ PA, BA, 69; Univ NH, MA 76; Univ Colo Boulder, PhD, 84; Eastern NMex Univ, MA, 95. **CAREER** Assoc prof, Eastern NMex Univ. **MEMBERSHIPS** Western Soc Sci Assoc. **RESEARCH** Criminal Justice, Black Humanities. **CONTACT ADDRESS** Dept Sociol, Eastern New Mexico Univ, Portales, 1500 S Ave K, Portales, NM 88130. **EMAIL** paul.lockman@enmu.edu

LOESSIN, JONATHAN K.
PERSONAL Born 09/10/1960, Columbus, TX, m, 1994, 4 children **DISCIPLINE** BEHAVIORAL SCIENCES **EDUCATION** Sam Houston State Univ, BS, 82; MA, 84; TX AM Univ, ABD, 86. **CAREER** Lect, Univ LA Monroe, 86-89; instr, Wharton County Jr Col, 89-. **HONORS AND AWARDS** Guest Lect, Univ Port Elizabeth, S Africa, 94; Keynote Spkr, TX Ger Conven, 99; Ed Y2K Proceed, ASSR. **MEMBERSHIPS** ASSR; SW Comm Rel Stud. **RESEARCH** Religious studies; social theory; counterrevolutionary movements. **SELECTED PUBLICATIONS** Auth, "de Maistre and the Divine", in The Year 2000 Proceedings of the ASSR (Dallas, 2000); auth, "Ecce Spiritus", in A Voyage to Remember, National Lib of Poetry, 96. **CONTACT ADDRESS** Dept Social Sci, Wharton County Junior Col, 911 Boling Hwy, Wharton, TX 77488. **EMAIL** wcjcsociology@hotmail.com

LOEWEN, JAMES W.
PERSONAL Born 02/06/1942, Decatur, IL, d, 2 children **DISCIPLINE** SOCIOLOGY **EDUCATION** Carleton Col, BA, 64; Harvard, PhD, 68. **CAREER** Tougaloo Col, assoc prof, sociol, 68-75; Univ VT, prof, sociol, 75-97, emeritus 97-; Catholic Univ Am, vis prof, 97-. **HONORS AND AWARDS** Lillian Smith Awd, best S non fict; Sydney Spivack Awd, inter grp rel; Am book Awd; Oliver Cox Awd, anti racist schol. **MEMBERSHIPS** ASA; AS; A.H.A. **RESEARCH** Race relations; Am hist; Stand Test. **SELECTED PUBLICATIONS** Lies My Teacher Told Me: Everything Your High School History Text Book Got Wrong, NY, The New Press, 95; The Mississippi Chinese: Between Black and White, Prospect Hts IL, Waveland Press, 88; auth, Lies Across America; What Ourt Historic Sites Get Wrong, NY, the New Press, 99; **CONTACT ADDRESS** Life Cycle Inst, Catholic Univ of America, Washington, DC 20064. **EMAIL** jloewen@zoo.uvm.edu

LOLLAR, LADDIE H.
PERSONAL Born 06/04/1930, South Greenfield, MO, m, 1959, 3 children **DISCIPLINE** PSYCHOLOGY **EDUCATION** SW Mo State Univ, BS, 51; Univ Mo, MEd, 56; PhD, 68. **CAREER** Teacher, School of the Osage, 51-57; Counselor, Univ Mo, 57-61; Prof, Bethel Col, 61-. **HONORS AND AWARDS** Teacher of the Year, Bethel Col; Outstanding Board Member Awd, Carroll County Developmental Ctr, 91-92, 98-99; Who's Who among Am Teachers, 98, 00. **MEMBERSHIPS** Am Psychol Asn, SE Psychol Asn, Tenn Psychol Asn, Am Asn of Univ Prof, Phi Delta Kappa. **RESEARCH** Counseling Psychology; Education Psychology. **CONTACT ADDRESS** Dept Soc Sci, Bethel Col, Tennessee, 325 Cherry Ave, McKenzie, TN 38201. **EMAIL** lollarl@bethel-college.edu

LONDON, CLEMENT B. G.
PERSONAL Born 09/12/1928, m **DISCIPLINE** EDUCATION **EDUCATION** City Clg City Univ of NYork, BA 1967, MA 1969; Tchr Clg Columbia Univ NYork, EdM 1972, EdD 1973. **CAREER** Toco & Morvant EC Elem Schs Trinidad-Tobago Sch Systm Trinidad, W Indies, asst prncpl 1953-60; St Augustine Parochial Sch Brooklyn, NY, tchr 1960-61; Harlem Hosp Sch of Nrsng New York City, sec/registrar 1963-66; Development & Training Ctr Distrbtv Trades Inc NYC, instr math & engl 1967-70; Crossroads Alternative HS East 105th St NYC, assc prncl dean stdnt 1970-71; Tchr Clg Columbia Univ NYC, grad asst & instrctnl asst 1971-73; Intermediate Sch 136 Manhattan NYC, substitute tchr math 1974; Fordham Univ at Lincoln Center, Graduate School of Educ, asst prof of educ 1974-82, assoc prof of educ 1982-91, professor of education, currently. **HONORS AND AWARDS** Project Real, Special Recognition, Awd for Outstanding Quality, 1983; Toco Anglican Elementary School, Clement London Day, Celebrant, 1977; Salem Community Service Council of New York City, 1981. **MEMBERSHIPS** Natl Alliance Black Sch EDUCATIONs 1975; Editorial Bd College Student Journal, editor Curriculum for a Career Ed & Dev Demonstration Proj for Youth 1978; editorial consultant Natl Council Negro Women 1978; Assn Teacher Educators 1979; summer chmn Div Curriculum & Teaching 1979; bd elders Council of Mwamko Wa Siasa Educ Institute 1980; Natl Sch Bd Assn 1980-; Org Amer Historians 1980; Assn Caribbean Studies 1980-; Amer Assn for Advancement of Humanities 1980; American Academy Political & Social Sci 1980-; rprtr bd dir Kappa Alpha Psi 1980-; faculty secretary Sch of Educ Fordham Univ 1981; Journal of Curiculum Theorizing 1982-; dir Project Real, 1984; bd dir Solidaridad Humana 1984; faculty adv, exec comm memPhi Delta Kappa; Kappa Delta Pi; adv bd, curriculum consultant La Nueva Raza Half House program; bd mem African Heritage Studies Assn; Schomburg Corp., Center for Research in Black Culture, board member, 1992-; ALL Bereavement Center, Ltd, bd mem, 1996-. **SELECTED PUBLICATIONS** Author, numerous research publications & professional activities including: On Wings of Changes, 1991; Through Caribbean Eyes, 1989; Test-taking Skills: Guidelines for Curricular & Instructional Practices, 1989; A Piagetian Constructivist Perspective on Curriculum, 1989; "Multicultural Curriculum Thought: A Perspective," 1992; "Multicultural Education and Curriculum Thought: One Perspective," 1992; "Curriculum as Transformation: A Case for the Inclusion of Multiculturality," 1992; "Afro-American Catholic School NYC", Black EDUCATION in the Univ Role as Moral Authority Clg Stdnt Jrnl Monograph 18(1 Pt 2), Career Ed for Educational Ldrs, A Focus on Decision Making 1983, "Crucibles of Caribbean Conditions, Factors of Understanding for Teachg & Learng Caribbean Stdnts Am Ed Settings" Jrnl of Caribbean Studies, 2&3, p 182-188, Autumn/Winter 1982; "Career & Emplymnt, Critical Factors in Ed Plng," African-American Jrnl Res & Ed, 1981; "Black Women of Valor," African Heritage Studies Assn Nwsltr, p 9, 1976; "Conf Call, The Caribbean & Latin Am," WABC Radio, 3 hr brdcst, 1979-80; 2 video-taped TV appearances: Natl TV Trinidad, W Indies, featuring emotionally oriented issues, 1976-77; Parents and Schools: A sourcebook, Garland Publishings, Inc, 1993; A critical perspective of multiculturality as a philosophy for educational change, Education, 114(3), p 368-383, 1994; Three Turtle Stories, New Mind Productions, Inc, 1994; Linking cultures through literacy: A perspective for the future, In NJ Ellsworth, CN Hedley and AN Baratta (Eds), Literacy: A redefinition, Lawrence Erlbaum Associates, 1994; Queens Public Access Television, discussing Fordham University Graduate School of Education and its leadership role in Language, Literacy, and Learning, 1994. **CONTACT ADDRESS** Graduate Sch Educ, Fordham Univ, 113 W 60th St, New York, NY 10023-7478. **EMAIL** london@mary.fordham.edu

LONECK, BARRY MARTIN
PERSONAL Born 12/05/1954, Erie, PA, m, 1977, 4 children **DISCIPLINE** SOCIAL WELFARE **EDUCATION** Case Western Res Univ, BA, 76; MS, 78; PhD, 85. **CAREER** Adj Instructor, Case Western Res Univ, 86-88; Asst Prof to Assoc Prof, SUNY, 89-. **HONORS AND AWARDS** Nat Res Service Awd, Nat Inst on Alcohol Abuse and Alcoholism, 78-80; Grant Awd, Nat Inst on Alcohol Abuse and Alcoholism, 76-78; Who's Who Among Human Service Professionals, 92-93; Who's Who in Am, 00; Who's Who in the World, 00. **MEMBERSHIPS** Acad of Cert Soc Workers; Nat Asn of Soc Workers; United Univ Prof. **SELECTED PUBLICATIONS** Auth, "Getting persons with alcohol or other drug problems into treatment: Teaching the Johnson Intervention in the practice curriculum," Journal of Teaching in Social Work 11, (95): 31-48; co-auth, "Stress and outcome in the alcoholism intervention: A preliminary investigation," Alcoholism Treatment Quarterly 13, (95): 33-42; co-auth, "A comparison of the Johnson Intervention to four other methods of referral to outpatient treatment," The American Journal of Drug and Alcohol Abuse 22, (96): 233-246; co-auth, "The Johnson Intervention and relapse during outpatient treatment," The American Journal of Drug and Alcohol Abuse 22, (96): 363-375; co-auth, "Using a focus group of clinicians to develop a research project on therapeutic process for clients with dual diagnoses," Social Work 42, (97): 107-111; auth, "How particular social environments affect alcoholics," in Advances in bioethics: Values, ethics, and alcoholism, (JAI Press, 97), 171-205; co-auth, "Substance use disorders: Module for Human Behavior in the Social Environment," in Getting Persons with Alcohol and Other Drug Problems into Treatment: Teaching the Window of Opportunities Meta-protocol in the General Social Work Practice Curriculum, Albany, 98; co-auth, "An empirical model of therapeutic process for clients with dual disorders in a psychiatric emergency room," Social Work Research, forthcoming; co-auth, "Engaging and retaining clients from a diverse population in alcohol and other drug treatment," Families in Society, forthcoming. **CONTACT ADDRESS** Sch of Soc Welfare, SUNY, 1400 Washington Ave, Albany, NY 12222-1000.

LONEWOL, TED
PERSONAL Born 03/31/1948, Carnegie, OK, m, 1973, 3 children **DISCIPLINE** EDUCATION **EDUCATION** Emporia State Univ, BS, 74; MS, 75; Ariz State Univ, MEd, 80; Univ Okla, PhD, 98. **CAREER** Teacher, Cherokee High Sch; principal, Powhattan Pub Sch; principal, Apache Pub Sch; admin, Kiowa Tribe of Okla; recruiter, Univ of Okla; chair, Southwestern Indian Polytech Inst. **CONTACT ADDRESS** Dept Gen Educ, Southwestern Indian Polytech Inst, PO Box 10146, Albuquerque, NM 87184. **EMAIL** tlonewol@sipi.bia.edu

LONG, ADA
DISCIPLINE EIGHTEENTH-CENTURY LITERATURE AND WOMEN'S LITERATURE **EDUCATION** Stanford, BA, 67; SUNY, PhD, 76. **CAREER** Dir, Univ honors prog, Univ AL. **SELECTED PUBLICATIONS** Auth, Off the Map:

Selected Poems of Gloria Fuertes; Stepping Out: An Introduction to the Arts; A Handbook for Honors Directors. **CONTACT ADDRESS** Univ of Alabama, Birmingham, 1400 University Blvd, Birmingham, AL 35294-1150.

LONG, LYNN LANDIS
PERSONAL Born 01/02/1949, Orlando, FL, m, 2 children **DISCIPLINE** EDUCATION **EDUCATION** Wesleyan Col, AB, 70; Rollins Col, MA, 81; Univ Fla, EdS, 87; Univ Fla, PhD, 91. **CAREER** Instr, Valencia Community Col, 79-80; Teaching Asst, Univ Fla, 88-89; Vis Instr, Rollins Col, 89-91; From Assoc Prof to Prof, Stetson Univ, 89-. **HONORS AND AWARDS** Outstanding Young Women of Am Awd, 82; Chi Sigma Iota; Outstanding Alumni Awd, Rollins Col, 89. **MEMBERSHIPS** AAMFT, ACA, IAMFC, CDTF. **RESEARCH** Treatment for abusive families, suicide prevention, working with adolescents, dynamics of family therapy. **SELECTED PUBLICATIONS** Coauth, "Child Custody Arrangements - Application of the Best Interests Standards," Fla Family Law Reporter 9-4 (89); coauth, "The Use of the Mock Trial as an Instructional Method," Counsr Educ and Supervision 34 (94): 58-67; coauth, "The Use of the Reflecting Team as an Instructional Strategy in Counselor Education," Counsr Educ and Supervision 33 (94): 210-218; coauth, Counseling and Therapy for Couples, Brooks-Cole Publ (Pacific Grove, CA), 98. **CONTACT ADDRESS** Dept Educ, Stetson Univ, De Land, 421 N Woodland Blvd, Deland, FL 32720. **EMAIL** llong@stetson.edu

LONG, SUSAN O.
PERSONAL Born 04/25/1951, Chicago, IL, m, 1973, 2 children **DISCIPLINE** SOCIOLOGY **EDUCATION** Univ Mich, AB, 73; Univ Ill, AM, 75; PhD, 80. **CAREER** Lectr, 80-81, 84-87, asst prof, 89-94, assoc prof, 94-, prof, 00-, John Carroll Univ. **HONORS AND AWARDS** ABE Fel; NEH Gnt; AAS Gnt; Fulbright -Hays Fel; NSF Gnt; NDFL Fel; Phi Beta Kappa; Phi Kappa Phi. **MEMBERSHIPS** AAA; AAS; ASBH. **RESEARCH** Culture and end-of-life decision making; care giving of the elderly; gender and family; Japanese society and culture. **SELECTED PUBLICATIONS** Auth, "Nurturing and Femininity: The Impact of the Ideal Of Caregiving in Postwar Japan," in Re-Imaging Japanese Women, ed Ann Imamura (Berkeley: Univ Cal Press, 96); coauth, "Caring for the Bedridden Elderly: Ideals, Reality, and Social Change in Japan," in Aging: Asian Concepts and Experiences Past and Present, eds. Susan Formanek, Sepp Linhart (Vienna: Osterreichische Akademie der Wissenschaften, 97); auth, "Becoming a Master Physician," in Learning in Likely Places, ed. John Singleton (Cambridge: Cambridge Univ Press, 98); coauth, "Husbands and Sons in the United States and Japan: Cultural Expectations and Caregiving Experiences," J Aging Studies 3 (99): 241-267; auth, "Family Surrogacy and Cancer Disclosure in Japan," J Palliative Care 15 (99): 31-42; ed, "Lives in Motion: Composing Circles of Self and Community in Japan," Cornell East Asia Series (99); coauth, "Passages, Personal Passages, and Reluctant Passages: Notes on Investigating Cancer Disclosure Practices in Japan," J Med Humanities 21 (00): 3-13; coauth, "Gender and Elder Care: Social Change and the Role of the Caregiver in Japan," Soc Sci Japan J 3 (00): 21-36; auth, "Caring for the Elderly in Japan and the US: Practices and Policies, Routledge (00); auth, "Living Poorly or Dying Well: Decisions about Life Support and Treatment Termination for American and Japanese Patients," J Clinical Ethics (forthcoming). **CONTACT ADDRESS** Dept Sociology, John Carroll Univ, 20700 Carroll Univ, Cleveland, OH 44118. **EMAIL** long@jcu.edu

LONGACRE, WILLIAM A., II
PERSONAL Born 12/16/1937, Hancock, MI, s **DISCIPLINE** ANTHROPOLOGY **EDUCATION** Univ Ill, BA, 59; Univ Chicago, MA, 62; PhD, 63. **CAREER** Asst prof to prof and dept head, Univ Ariz, 64-. **HONORS AND AWARDS** Woodrow Wilson Fel, Center for Adv Study, 72-73; Fel, Adv of Sci, 91. **MEMBERSHIPS** Am Anthropol Asn; Soc for Am Archaeol; AAS; Sigma Xi; Am Ceramics Soc. **RESEARCH** Archaeology and ethnoarchaeology; Southwest USA and Philippines and SW China **SELECTED PUBLICATIONS** Auth, "Standardization and Specialization: What's the Link?" in Pottery and People, (Univ Ut Press, 99), 44-58; auth, "Why did the BAE Hire an Architect?" J of the Southwest, (99): 350-369; auth, Pottery Making Villages in SW China, 99; co-auth, "I Want to Buy a Black Pot!" J of Archaeol Method and Theory, (00): 273-293; auth, "Exploring Prehistoric Social and Political Organization in the American Southwest," J of Anthropol Research, (00): 287-300. **CONTACT ADDRESS** Dept Anthropol, Univ of Arizona, 1009 E S Campus Dr, Bldg 30, Tucson, AZ 85721-0030. **EMAIL** longacre@u.arizona.edu

LOOSER, DEVONEY K.
PERSONAL Born 04/11/1967, St Paul, MN, m, 1996 **DISCIPLINE** ENGLISH, WOMEN'S STUDIES **EDUCATION** Augsburg Col, BA, 89; SUNY Stony Brook, PhD, 93. **CAREER** Instr to asst to dir, SUNY, 89-93; asst prof, Ind State Univ, 93-98; asst prof, Univ of Wis, 98-00; vis asst prof, Ariz State Univ, 00-01; asst prof, La State Univ, 01-. **HONORS AND AWARDS** NEH Fel, 97; William Andrews Clark Mem Libr Fel, 97. **MEMBERSHIPS** MLA, Am Soc for Eighteenth Century Studies, Jane Austen Soc of NA, NA Soc for the Study

of Romanticisim, Nat Women's Studies Assoc. **RESEARCH** British women writers, feminist theory, histories of aging, historiography, Jane Austen. **SELECTED PUBLICATIONS** Ed, Jane Austen and Discourses of Feminism, St. Martin's Pr, 95; coed, Generations: Academic Feminists in Dialogue, Univ of Minn Pr, 97; auth, British Women Writers and the Writing of History, 1670-1820, Johns Hopkins Univ Pr, 00. **CONTACT ADDRESS** Dept English, La State Univ, Baton Rouge, LA 70803-5001. **EMAIL** devoney@mac.com

LOPATA, HELENA Z.
PERSONAL Born 10/01/1925, Poznan, Poland, w, 1946, 2 children **DISCIPLINE** SOCIOLOGY **EDUCATION** Univ Ill, BA, 46, MA, 47; Univ Chicago, PhD, 54. **CAREER** Asst Prof to Assoc Prof, Roosevelt Univ, 65-69; Prof Sociology, 69-97, Sr Prof Sociology, Loyola Univ Chicago, 97-, Dept Chair, 70-72, Dir, Ctr Comp Study Soc Roles, 72-; Vis Prof, Univ Southern Calif, 75; Vis Prof, Univ Minn, 80; Vis Prof, Boston Col, 82; Short-Term Vis Prof, Univ Guelph, 87; Landgrove Distinguished Vis Prof, Univ Victoria, 96. **HONORS AND AWARDS** Fac Mem of the Year, Loyola Univ Chicago, 75; Mieczyslaw Haiman Awd for Sustained Scholarship Effort in the Field of Polish American Studies, Polish Am Hist Asn, 87; Distinguished Schol Awd, Family Div Soc Study Soc Roles, 89; Burgess Awd, Nat Coun Family Relations, 90; Distinguished Career Awd, Section on Aging, Am Sociol Asn, 92; Distinguished Career Awd, Soc Study Symbolic Interaction, 93; co-recipient, Bronislaw Malinowski Awd of the Polish Inst Arts & Sci in Am, 95; Honorary Doctor of Science, Univ Guelph, 95. **MEMBERSHIPS** Int Sociol Asn; Int Sociol Inst; Int Gerontol Soc; Am Sociol Asn; Gerontol Soc Am; Soc Study Social Problems; Soc Study Symbolic Interaction; Sociol Women Soc; Nat Coun Family Relations; Midwest Sociol Soc; Polish Inst Arts & Sci Am; Polish Sociol Inst; Midwest Coun Social Res Aging. **RESEARCH** Cosmopolitan community of scholars; occupations and professions; widowhood; changing roles of American women. **SELECTED PUBLICATIONS** Ed, Widows: The Middle East, Asia and the Pacific, vol 1, Widows: North America, vol 2, Duke Univ Press, 87; co-ed, Friendship in Context, JAI Press, 90; Polish Americans, Second, Revised Edition, Transaction, 94; auth, Circles and Settings: Role Changes of American Women, State Univ NY Press, 94; auth, Current Widowhood: Myths and Realities, Sage, 96; series ed, Research on the Interweave of Social Roles. Renamed: Current Research on Occupations and Professions, JAI Press; co-ed, Unusual Occupations, vol II of Current Research on Occupations & Professions, JAI Pr, 00. **CONTACT ADDRESS** Sociology Dept, Loyola Univ, Chicago, 6525 N. Sheridan Rd., Chicago, IL 60626. **EMAIL** helenaZL@aol.com

LOPES, WILLIAM H.
PERSONAL Born 10/25/1946, Providence, RI, m **DISCIPLINE** EDUCATION **EDUCATION** Providence Coll, BA 1967; Univ of CT, MA 1972; Univ of RI, MBA; Univ of CT, PhD Educ Admin 1976. **CAREER** McAlister Middle Sch, vice principal 1972-74; RI Col, instr 1974-, exec asst to pres 1977-. **HONORS AND AWARDS** RI Educator of the Yr; IBA of RI; Phi Kappa Phi Hon Soc; other grants awds. **MEMBERSHIPS** Pub ASCD Annual Bulletin 1970; trustee Providence Public Library; bd dir OIC RI; bd dir RI Grp Health Assn; EPDA Fellow 1970-72; sev art in prof journals; doctoral dis felshp Univ of CT. **CONTACT ADDRESS** Rhode Island Col, 600 Mount Pleasant Ave, Providence, RI 02908.

LOPREATO, JOSEPH
PERSONAL Born 07/13/1928, Italy, d, 2 children **DISCIPLINE** EVOLUTIONARY SOCIOLOGY, ANTHROPOLOGY **EDUCATION** Univ of Conn, BA, 56; Yale Univ, PhD, 60. **CAREER** Asst prof, Univ of Mass, 60-62; res scholar, Univ of Rome, 62-64; assoc prof, Univ of Conn, 64-66; assoc prof, 66-68; prof, Univ Tex, Austin, 68-98; chmn, Dept of Sociology, Univ of TX, Austin, 69-72; assoc ed, Am Sociological Review, 69-73; assoc ed, Social Forces, 87-90. **HONORS AND AWARDS** Fulbright Res Scholar to Italy, 62-64 & 74; Soc Sci Res Coun Fac Res Fel, 63-64; Nat Sci Found Res Fel, 65-68; Univ of Tx Fac Res Fel, 73-74, spring 84 & spring 93; Italy's Guido Dorso 1992 Award for the U.S.A. **MEMBERSHIPS** Human Behavior and Evolution Soc; Int Soc for Human Ethology; Int Sociological Asn; European Sociobiological Soc; Nat Comt, U.S.A. Bicentennial, The Italian Contribution, 75-76; Steering Comt, Coun for European Stud, Columbia Univ, 77-81. **RESEARCH** Ethnic assimilation; the evolution of gender roles; social inequality; the evolution of religion; politics and the economy; fertility; mortality. **SELECTED PUBLICATIONS** Auth, Italian Made Simple, 59; Peasants No More, 67; Italian Americans, 70; Class Conflict and Mobility: Theories and Studies of Class Structure, 72; The Sociology of Vilfredo Pareto, 75; Human Nature and Biocultural Evolution, 84; Evoluzione e Natura Umana, 90; Crisis in Sociology: The Need for Darwin, 99; Numerous Contributions to Scholarly Journals in Several Languages. **CONTACT ADDRESS** Dept of Sociology, Univ of Texas, Austin, 1801 Lavaca St, Austin, TX 78701. **EMAIL** lopreato@mail.la.utexas.edu

LORD, GEORGE F.
PERSONAL Born Houston, TX **DISCIPLINE** SOCIOLOGY **EDUCATION** Christopher Newport Col, BA, 77; La State

Univ, MA, 79; PhD, 83. **CAREER** Asst Prof, Memphis State Univ, 82-84; Asst Prof, Dennison Univ, 84-85; Res Manager, Ohio Dept of Mental Health, 85-87; Assoc Prof and Dir, Univ Mich, 87-98; Assoc Prof and Chair, Pittsburgh State Univ, 98-00; Chair, Ark State Univ, 00-. **MEMBERSHIPS** S Sociol Soc; Am Sociol Asn. **RESEARCH** Sociology of Labor Markets; Sociology of Work and Work Organization; Social Stratification; sociology of Labor. **SELECTED PUBLICATIONS** Auth, "Growth Ideology in a Period of Decline," Social Problems, 92. **CONTACT ADDRESS** Dept Sociol, Arkansas State Univ, State University, AR 72467. **EMAIL** glord@mail.astate.edu

LORD-MAES, JANIECE
DISCIPLINE PSYCHOLOGY, EDUCATION **EDUCATION** Univ Az, PhD. **CAREER** 12 years post doctorate; developed the Mental health component of a "state of the arts" prog to facilitate learning for seriously emotionally disabled children. **HONORS AND AWARDS** Post doctoral work in brain mapping laboratories, Golden Key Awd; Awded honors for work done on the Navajo Indian Reservation Public Schools; Awded financial benefits for program development in Tucson, Az Public School; various certificates and consultations. **MEMBERSHIPS** APA, MyKid, Spec Ed Admin. **RESEARCH** Neuropsychology and learning, brain behavior correlates, brain injury in children. **SELECTED PUBLICATIONS** Auth, published chapter in Erin Bufer, ed Children with Brain Injury; several articles in the area of neuropsychology and learning. **CONTACT ADDRESS** Dept Special Ed, Univ of Arizona, PO Box 210069, Tucson, AZ 85721-0069.

LOVE, BARBARA
PERSONAL Born 04/13/1946, Dumas, AR **DISCIPLINE** EDUCATION **EDUCATION** AR AM & N, BA 1965; Univ of AR, MA 1967; Univ of MA, PhD, EdD 1972. **CAREER** Univ of MA Amherst Campus, assoc prof; Fellowship House, exec dir; Kansas City, teacher 1969-70; Center for Urban Educ, Univ of MA, grad asst 1970-71, instructor 1971-72, asso prof, chmn. **HONORS AND AWARDS** Leadership Found Scholarship 1965-66; Jr League Awd 1967. **MEMBERSHIPS** Mem Phi Delta Kappa 1974; Nat Alliance Black Sch Educators 1973; Am Educ Studies Assn 1974; Panel Am Women 1968-70; Urban Coalition Task Force on Educ 1968-70; comm rep Nat Tchrs Corps 1969-70; tast force Nat Alternative Schs Prgm 1971-73. **CONTACT ADDRESS** Univ of Massachusetts, Amherst, Furcolo Hall, Amherst, MA 01002.

LOVE, JAMES
PERSONAL Born 08/05/1945, Timpson, TX, m **DISCIPLINE** SOCIOLOGY **EDUCATION** Lamar Univ, BA, 66; Univ Tex, JD, 69. **CAREER** Asst Prof, Lamar Univ, 76-. **MEMBERSHIPS** Tex Bar Asn, ACJS. **RESEARCH** Law, hate crimes, sexual orientation legislation. **CONTACT ADDRESS** Dept Sociol, Lamar Univ, Beaumont, PO Box 10026, Beaumont, TX 77710. **EMAIL** lovejj@hal.lamar.edu

LOVELACE, EUGENE A.
PERSONAL Born 07/27/1939, Montour Falls, NY, m, 2 children **DISCIPLINE** PSYCHOLOGY **EDUCATION** SUNY Binghamton, BA, 60; Univ Iowa, MA, 63; PhD, 64. **CAREER** Asst to assoc prof, Univ of Va, 64-85; prof, Alfred Univ, 85-. **HONORS AND AWARDS** USPHS Fel, NASA Predoctoral Fel; White House Conf on Aging, 81; Nat Res Serv Awd, nat Inst of Aging, 81-82. **MEMBERSHIPS** Am Psychol Soc; Psychonomic Soc; Eastern Psychol Assoc. **RESEARCH** Metamemory, Cognition and Aging. **SELECTED PUBLICATIONS** Coauth, "Decision times for alphabetic order of letter pairs", J of Exp Psychol 88, (71): 258-264; coauth, "Free associations of older adults to single words and to conceptually related word triads", J of Gerontology 37, (82): 432-437; coauth, "Structure and process in alphabetic retrieval", J of Exp Psychol: Learning, Memory and Cognition 9, (83): 462-477; auth, "Metamemory: Monitoring future recallability during study", J of Exp Psychol: Learning, Memory and Cognition 10, (84): 756-766; coauth, "Prediction and evaluation of memory performance by young and old adults", J of Gerontology 40, (85): 192-197; ed, Aging and cognition: Mental processes, self-awareness, and interventions, Elsevier Sci Pr, (Amsterdam, Holland), 90; coauth, Research Methods and Statistics: An integrated approach, Harcourt Brace Pub, (Fort Worth, TX), 00. **CONTACT ADDRESS** Dept Psychol, Alfred Univ, 1 Saxon Dr, Alfred, NY 14802. **EMAIL** flovelace@alfred.edu

LOX, CURT L.
PERSONAL Born 11/10/1967, Harbor City, CA, m, 1991, 1 child **DISCIPLINE** SPORT PSYCHOLOGY **EDUCATION** Univ Calif, BA, 89; Miami Univ, MS, 91; Univ Ill, PhD, 94. **CAREER** Asst prof, N Ill Univ, 94-96; Asst Prof to Assoc Prof, S Ill Univ, 96-. **MEMBERSHIPS** Am Col of Sports Medicine; Am Psychol Asn; N Am Soc for the Psychol of Sport and Phys Activity; Soc of Beh Medicine. **SELECTED PUBLICATIONS** Co-auth, "Enhancing exercise adherence in middle-aged males and females," Preventive Medicine, (94): 498-506; co-auth, "Self-efficacy and intrinsic motivation in exercising older adults," Journal of applied Gerontology, (94): 355-370; co-auth, "Physique anxiety and exercise in middle-aged adults," Journal of Gerontology, (95): 229-235; co-auth, "Physical training effects on acute exercise-induced feeling states in HIV-1-

positive individuals," Journal of Health Psychology, (96): 235-240; co-auth, "Self-esteem and coping responses of athletes with acute versus chronic injuries," Perceptual and Motor Skills, (98): 1402; co-auth, "Tennis racket head-size comparisons and their effect on beginning college players' achievement and self-efficacy," Journal of Teaching in Physical Education, (98): 453-467; co-auth, "Determinants of physical activity in a sedentary, obese female population," Journal of Sport and Exercise Psychology, (98): 218-224; co-auth, "The impact of pulmonary rehabilitation on self-efficacy, quality of life, and exercise tolerance," Rehabilitation Psychology, (99): 1-14; co-auth, Skills, Drills, and Strategies for Volleyball, Holcomb Hathaway Pub, 00. **CONTACT ADDRESS** Dept Kinesiol, So Illinois Univ, Edwardsville, 1021 Vadalabene Center, PO Box 1126, Edwardsville, IL 62026-1126. **EMAIL** clox@siue.edu

LU, MIN-ZHAN
PERSONAL Born 02/06/1946, Shanghai, China, m, 1984, 1 child **DISCIPLINE** CULTURAL AND CRITICAL STUDIES **EDUCATION** Univ Pittsburgh, PhD. **CAREER** Assoc prof, 89, Drake Univ. **HONORS AND AWARDS** Mina P Shaughnessy Awd; Endowment Professor of the Humanities. **MEMBERSHIPS** NCTE **SELECTED PUBLICATIONS** Auth, feminist and post colonial theory in rel pedag; educ non-mainstream col students; fiction. **CONTACT ADDRESS** Drake Univ, University Ave, PO Box 2507, Des Moines, IA 50311-4505. **EMAIL** min.zhan.lu@drake.edu

LU, ZHONG-LIN
PERSONAL Born 11/19/1967, Hubei, China, m, 1990, 2 children **DISCIPLINE** PSYCHOLOGY **EDUCATION** Univ Sci and Tech China, BS, 89; NY Univ, MS, 91; PhD, 92. **CAREER** Asst res, Univ of Calif Irvine, 92-96; asst prof, Univ of Southern Calif, 96-. **HONORS AND AWARDS** Fel, Univ of Sci and Tech of China, 86; Grant, China-US Physica Examination Application; Meyer Fel, NY Univ, 89; Fel, NY Univ, 91; Dean's Diss Fel, NY Univ, 91. **MEMBERSHIPS** Am Physics Soc; ARVO; Soc for Math Psychol, Psychonomics Soc. **RESEARCH** Computational and psychophysical study of visual motion, texture, and attention, visual memory systems, perceptual learning, computer image processing. Neurophysiological and neuromagnetic study of sensory and attentional processes. Visual neural networks. Brain Imaging. **SELECTED PUBLICATIONS** Coauth, "Mechanisms of perceptual learning", Visual Res 39, (99): 1075-1088; coauth, "Second-order reversed phi", Perception and Psychophysics, (99): 1075-1088; coauth, "Measuring the amplification and the spatial resolution of visual attention", "Invariance between subjects of brain-wave representations of language", "Invariance of brain-wave representations of simple visual images and their names", and, "Perceptual motion standstill from rapidly moving chromatic displays", Proceedings of the Nat Acad of Sci, 96, (99); coauth, "Attention mechanism for multi-location first-and second-order motion perception", Vision Res 40, (00): 173-186; coauth, "Noise exclusion in spatial attention", Psychol Sci, (forthcoming); coauth, "Mechanisms of perceptual attention in precuing of location", Vision Res, (forthcoming); coauth, "Spatial attention: Different mechanisms for central and peripheral cues?", J of Exp Psychol: Human Perception and Performance (forthcoming). **CONTACT ADDRESS** Dept Psychol, Univ of So California, 3620 McClintock Ave, Los Angeles, CA 90089-1061. **EMAIL** zhonglin@rcf.usc.edu

LUBIN, BERNARD
PERSONAL Born 10/15/1923, Washington, DC, m, 1957 **DISCIPLINE** PSYCHOLOGY **EDUCATION** George Wash Univ, BA, 52; MA, 53; Penn State Univ, PhD, 58. **CAREER** From staff psychologist to chief psychologist, Ind Univ Medical Ctr, 58-62; from instr to assoc prof, Ind Univ Sch of Medicine, 58-67; dir of psychology services, Dept of Mental Health, 62-63; dir, div of res and training, Dept of Mental Health, 63-67; dir of div of psychology, Greater Kans City Mental Health Found, 67-74; prof, Univ Mo Sch of Medicine, 67-74; clinical prof, Univ Tex Health Sciences Ctr, 74-76; clinical prof, Baylor Univ Sch of Medicine, 74-76; prof, Univ Houston, 74-76; dir of clinical training, Univ Houston, 74-76; prof, Univ Mo at Kans City, 76-; res prof, UMKC Inst, 76-; chemn of Dept of Psychology, Univ Mo at Kans City, 76-83; dir doctoral prog in community psychology, Univ Mo at Kans City, 76-84; clinical prof, Univ Kans Medical Ctr, 86-. **HONORS AND AWARDS** N. T. Veatch Awd, Univ Mo at Kans City, 81; Fac Res Fel, Univ Mo at Kans City, 84; Fac Commuity Service Fel, Univ Mo at Kans City, 85; Curators' Professorship, Univ Mo, 88; U.K.C. Fac Fel, Univ Mo at Kans City, 94; Distinguished Sr Contribur in Counseling Psychology, 95; Harry Levinson Awd for Excellence in Consultation, 96; Richard Wilkinson Awd for Distinguished Contributions to Psychology, 97. **MEMBERSHIPS** Am Psychol Asn, Am Psychol Soc, Am Asn for the Advancement of Sci, NTL Inst, Am Group Psychotherapy Asn, Psi Chi, Midwestern Psychol Asn, Ind Psychol Asn, World Federation for Mental Health, Confr on Psychologist Directors and Consultants in State, Inter-American Congress of Psychol, Int Coun of Psychol, Houston Psychol Asn, Mo Psychol Asn, Coun of Directors of Grad Psychology Programs. **SELECTED PUBLICATIONS** Auth, "The psychological dimension in personal injury cases," in Establishing Damages in Catastrophic Injury Litigation, ed. J. O. Ward and K. V. Krueger (AZ: Lawyers and Judges Pub Co., 94), 35-40; coauth, Homelessness in America 1893-1992: An Annotated Bibliography, Greenwood Press (Westport, CT), 94; coauth, Answers to most Frequently Asked Questions About Organization Development, Sage Pub Co. (Newbury Park, CA), 95; coauth, Research in Professional Consultation and Consultation for Organizational Change: An Annotated Bibliography 1974-1995, Greenwood Press (Westport, CT), 97; coauth, Response to Disaster: Psychosocial, Community, and Ecological Approaches, Taylor & Francis (Washington, DC), 99; coauth, Mental Health Services in Criminal Justice System Settings: A Selectively Annotated Bibliography 1970-1997, Greenwood Press (Westport, CT), 99; coauth, Multiple Affect Adjective Check List--Revised, EdITS (San Diego, CA), 99. **CONTACT ADDRESS** Dept Psychol, Univ of Missouri, Kansas City, 5319 Holmes St, Kansas City, MO 64110.

LUBINSKI, DAVID
PERSONAL Born 12/29/1953, Minneapolis, MN, m, 1999 **DISCIPLINE** PSYCHOLOGY **EDUCATION** Univ Min, BA, 81; PhD, 87; Univ Ill, postdoc fel, 87-89. **CAREER** Vis asst prof, Univ Ill, 89-90; asst prof, Iowa State Univ, 90-94; assoc prof, 94-98; assoc prof, Vanderbilt Univ, 98-. **HONORS AND AWARDS** Eva O Miller Fel; Dist Fel; Mensa Awd for Res Excell, 90, 91, 94, 99; AERA Res Excell Awd; George A Miller Awd; Dist Sci Awd; Templeton Awd; Who's Who Am. **MEMBERSHIPS** AERA; APA; APS; ISSID; NAGC; SMEP. **SELECTED PUBLICATIONS** Co-ed, Assessing individual differences in human behavior: New methods, concepts, and findings, Consulting Psych Press (Palo Alto, CA), 95; co-ed, Intellectual Talent: Psychometric and social issues, John Hopkins Univ Press (Baltimore), 96; coauth, "Our future leaders in science: Who are they? Can we identify them early?" in Talent Development, eds. N Colangelo, SG Assouline Dayton, OH: Oh Psych Press, 99); auth, "Assessing individual differences in human behavior: Sinking shafts at a few critical points," Annual Rev Psychol 51 (00): 405-444; auth, "Conceptualizations of Intelligence: Review of Jean Khalfa's "What is intelligence?" Am Sci 84 (96): 86-87; coauth, "Validity of assessing educational-vocational preference dimensions among intellectually talented 13 year olds," J Counsel Psychol 45 (98): 436-453; coauth, "DNA pooling and dense marker maps: A systematic search for genes for cognitive ability," NeuroReports 10 (99): 843-848; coauth, "DNA pooling identifies QTLs for general cognitive ability in children on chromosome 4," Human Molecular Genetics 8 (99): 915-922; coauth, "Assessing vocational preferences among gifted adolescents adds incremental validity to abilities: A discriminate analysis of educational outcomes over a 10-year interval. Journal of Educational Psychology 9 (99): 777-786; coauth, "States of excellence," American Psychologist 55 (99): 137-150; coauth, "Sex differences in mathematical reasoning ability: Their status 20 years later," forthcoming; coauth, "Men and woman at promise for scientific excellence: They are not as different as you might think," forthcoming; coauth, "Top 1 in 10,000: A 10-year follow up of the profoundly gifted," forthcoming. **CONTACT ADDRESS** Dept Psychology, Human Development, Vanderbilt Univ, Box 512, Nashville, TN 37203. **EMAIL** david.lubinski@vanderbilt.edu

LUCAS, WAYNE L.
PERSONAL Born 01/06/1947, Joliet, IL, m, 1969, 2 children **DISCIPLINE** SOCIOLOGY **EDUCATION** Iowa State Univ, BS, 69; MS, 72; PhD, 76. **CAREER** Asst prof, Univ Missouri, 76-82; assoc prof, 82-. **HONORS AND AWARDS** Phi Kappa Phi, Alpha Kappa Delta, Hon Soc; Who's Who World, Midwest, Am. **MEMBERSHIPS** ACJS; MCJA; ASC; SSSP. **RESEARCH** Substance abuse prevention; drug treatment intervention for offender populations; correction programs and policies. **SELECTED PUBLICATIONS** Auth, "Research Note on Compliance with Guidelines for Protection of Human Subjects," J Alcohol Drug Edu 25 (80): 33-37; auth, "Changes in Social and Attitudinal Dimensions of Marijuana Abstainers: 1969-1976, " J Drug Issues (81): 399-414; auth, "Perceptions of the Volunteer Role," J Offender Coun, Serv Rehab 12 (8): 141-146; coauth, "Profiles of Drug Use and Attitudes Among Young Adolescents," J Child Adoles Substance Abuse 4 (95): 41-60; coauth; "The Impact of Drug Education and Prevention Programs: Disparity Between Impressionistic and Empirical Assessments," Evalu Rev 21 (97): 589-613. **CONTACT ADDRESS** Dept Sociology, Univ of Missouri, Kansas City, 5100 Rockhill Rd, Kansas City, KS 64110.

LUCKEY, EVELYN F.
PERSONAL Born 04/30/1926, Bellefonte, PA, d **DISCIPLINE** EDUCATION **EDUCATION** Central State Univ, 1945; OH State Univ, BA, BsEd, English, Psych 1947, MA English 1950, PhD Ed 1970. **CAREER** Columbus Public Schools, teacher 1957-66, evaluation asst 1965-67; OH State Univ, asst prof 1971-72; Columbus Public Schools, exec dir 1972-77, asst supt 1977-90; Otterbein Col, Westerville, OH, asst prof, 90-. **HONORS AND AWARDS** Outstanding Educator Awd Alpha Kappa Alpha 1978; Woman on the Move Moles 1978; Woman of the Year Omega Psi Phi 1980; Distinguished Kappan Awd Phi Delta Kappa 1981; Disting Alumnae Awd OH State Univ 1982; Certificate of Honor City of Columbus 1984; YWCA Woman of Achievement Awd 1987, 1991; United Negro College Fund Eminent Scholar, 1990. **MEMBERSHIPS** Mem Amer Assoc of School Admin 1977-, Adv Bd of Urban Network of No Central Reg Ed Lab 1985-90, Assoc for Suprv & Curriculum Devel 1972-93, Natl Alliance of Black School Ed 1978-, Central OH Mktg Council 1984-89, Bd of Planned Parenthood of Central OH 1984-87; trustee, pres Bd of Public Libr of Columbus & Franklin Cty 1973-89; member, Links, Inc, 1988-; trustee, pres, board, Columbus Metropolitan Library, 1973-89; trustee, Central Ohio Marketing Council, 1984-89. **CONTACT ADDRESS** Otterbein Col, Westerville, OH 43081.

LUDEWIG, LARRY M.
PERSONAL Born 10/21/1946, Houston, TX, m, 1970, 2 children **DISCIPLINE** SOCIOLOGY **EDUCATION** Tex A & M Univ, BA, 70, MEd, 75, PhD, 79. **CAREER** Admin, Tex A & M Univ, 73-75; asst dean/registrar, Southern Ark Univ, 75-77; assoc dean of students, Angelo State Univ, 77-79; dean of students, Lamar Univ, 79-80, assoc vice pres for student affairs and dean of students, 80-84; prof, Kilgore Col, 88-. **HONORS AND AWARDS** NASPA ed bd (Journal); nominated for Outstanding Teacher of the Year, 92-93; Who's Who Among Am's Teachers, 2000. **MEMBERSHIPS** TCCTA, APA. **RESEARCH** Study skills (collegiate). **SELECTED PUBLICATIONS** Auth, "Student Perceptions of Instructor Behaviors," The Teaching Prof, vol 7, no 4, Magna Pubs (April 93); auth, "10 Worst Student Behaviors," The Teaching Prof, vol 8, no 5, Magna Pubs (May 94); auth, "Students, professors point out each other's irritating behaviors," Recruitment and Retention, vol 8, no 7, Magna Pubs (July 94); auth, "10 Worst Student Behaviors," Advising Tips, SUNY Inst Tech at Utica/Rome, Sch of Bus and Public Management (fall 94); auth, "Ten Commandments for Effective Study skills," pub in S. Farmer, J. Gustafson, and C. Poziemski, Making the Grade in College: Learned Strategies for Success, 2E Harper Collins, NY (95, 97); auth, "Ten Commandments for Effective Study Skills," pub in Writing and Speaking at USU, ed C. Hirschi (permission granted 4/25/1995); auth, "Students' Pet Peeves: Student Perceptions of Antithetical Instructor Behaviors," in a book by D. Larry Crumbley, KPMG Peat Marwick Prof, La State Univ (permission granted 11/12/1996); auth, "Students, professors Point Out Each Other's Irritating Behaviors," in "Seeing Through a Professor's Eyes," Va Commonwealth Univ (forthcoming). **CONTACT ADDRESS** Dept Social & Behav Sci, Kilgore Col, 1100 Broadway, Kilgore, TX 75662. **EMAIL** ludewigl@kilgore.cc.tx.us

LUDLOW, JEANNIE
PERSONAL Born 06/02/1961, Fountain County, IN, p, 1995, 1 child **DISCIPLINE** AMERICAN CULTURE STUDIES **EDUCATION** Bowling Green State Univ, PhD, 92. **CAREER** Instr, 90-98; prof, 98-, Bowling Green State Univ. **HONORS AND AWARDS** Diss Res Fel; Shankin Awd, Res Excel. **MEMBERSHIPS** NWSA; ASA; MMLA. **RESEARCH** Cultural studies approaches to various aspects of American Women's lived experiences and cultural expressions. **SELECTED PUBLICATIONS** Auth, "Working (In) the In-Between: Poetry, Criticism, Interrogation and Interruption," SML: Studies in American Indian Literatures (94); auth, "Priorities and Power: Adjuncts in the Academy," Thought & Action (98); auth, "Seaming Meanings: Wendy Rose, Diane Glancy and Carol Sanchez Writing In Between," forthcoming. **CONTACT ADDRESS** American Culture Studies, Bowling Green State Univ, 910 N Main St, Bowling Green, OH 43402-1819. **EMAIL** jludlow@bgnet.bgsu.edu

LUECKEN, LINDA
DISCIPLINE PSYCHOLOGY **EDUCATION** Univ NC, MA, 92; Duke Univ, PhD, 98. **CAREER** Res asst prof, Univ Vt, 98-00; asst prof, Ariz State Univ, 00-. **MEMBERSHIPS** Am Psychol Asn; Soc for Beh Med; Am Heart Asn; Vt Cancer Center. **SELECTED PUBLICATIONS** Co-auth, "Suppression of the development of adjuvant arthritis by a conditioned aversive stimulus," Brain, Beh and Immunity, (91): 64-73; co-auth, "Evidence for the involvement of beta-adrenergic receptors in conditioned immunomodulation," J of Neuroimmunology, (92): 209-220; co-auth, "Psychosocial correlates of job strain in a sample of working women," Archives of Gen Psychiat, (97): 543-548; co-auth, "Relationship of mood ratings and neurohormonal responses during daily life in employed women," Intl J of Beh Med, (97): 1-16; co-auth, "Stress in employed women: Impact of marriage and children at home on neurohormone output and home strain," Psychosomatic Med, (97): 352-359; auth, "Childhood attachment and loss experiences affect adult cardiovascular and cortisol function," Psychosomatic Med, (98): 765-772; auth, "Attachment and loss experiences during childhood are associated with adult hostility, depression, and social support," J of Psychosomatic Res, (00): 85-91; auth, "Parental caring and loss during childhood and adult cortisol responses to stress," Psychol and Health, (00): 841-851. **CONTACT ADDRESS** Dept Psychol, Arizona State Univ, MC 1104, Box 871104, Tempe, AZ 85287. **EMAIL** Linda.Luecken@asu.edu

LUESCHEN, GUENTHER
PERSONAL Born 01/21/1930, Oldenburg, Germany, m, 1989, 3 children **DISCIPLINE** SOCIOLOGY **EDUCATION** Univ Grae, Austria, 59; post-doc, Univ Mich, 60-61. **CAREER** Prof, Univ Ill, 66-89; prof, Univ Dusseldorf, Germany, 90-95; prof, Univ Ala of Birmingham, 95-. **HONORS AND AWARDS** Federal Medal of Merit 1st Class, Germany, 89; Hon D, Univ Jyvashyla, Finland, 90; advised 22 PhD's; conducted 10 major

res projects on family, health, sport, theory. **MEMBERSHIPS** Am Sociol Asn, Ger Sociol Asn. **RESEARCH** Health, family, sport, Epistemology. **SELECTED PUBLICATIONS** Twenty books authored, coauthored, or edited; 130 articles in journals and independent pubs. **CONTACT ADDRESS** Dept Sociol, Univ of Alabama, Birmingham, 1530 3rd Ave S, Birmingham, AL 35294-0001.

LUIBHEID, E.
DISCIPLINE WOMEN'S STUDIES **EDUCATION** Hampsire Col, BA, 86; Univ Mass Boston, in ESL Studies, 92; Univ Cal/Berkeley, 98. **CAREER** Asst Prof, Ethnic Studies and American Culture Studies, Bowling Green State Univ, 99-. **HONORS AND AWARDS** Postdoctoral Fellow; Humanities Research Institute, Univ of Calif Irvine, Fall 98. **MEMBERSHIPS** Amer Studies Assoc. **RESEARCH** Post-1965 immigration to the US; Immigrant, refugee, & transnational women; Intersections of race, sexuality, immigration, & nation; Contemporary Irish emigration. **SELECTED PUBLICATIONS** Auth, "Obvious Homosexuals and Homosexuals Who Cover Up: The Organization of Lesbian and Gay Exclusion in US Immigration," Radical America 26:2, October, 96. auth, "Irish Immigrants in the United States Racial System," In Jim MacLaugh, ed., Location and Dislocation in Irish Society: Mutlidisciplinary Essays on Emigration and Irish Identities," Cork, Ireland: Univ College Cork Press, 97; auth, "The 1965 Immigration and Nationality Act: An End to Exclusion?" Positions: East Asia Cultures Critiue 5:2, fall 97. Auth, "The Nod and The Wink: White Solidarity Within Irish Immigrants in the USA," In Ethel Crowley and Jim MacLaughlin, eds., Under The Belly of The Tiger: Class, Race, Identity and Culture in Global Ireland, Dublin, Ireland: Irish Reporter Publications, 97; auth, "Looking Like a Lesbian: The Organization of Sexual Monitoring at the US-Mexico Border," Journal of the History of Sexuality, 8:3, Spring 98; auth, "Queer Circuits: The Construction of Lesbian and Gay Identities Through Emigration," In Ronit Lentin, ed., Emerging Irish Identities, Dublin: Trinity College, 00; auth, Eithne Luibheid and Sasha Khokha, "Linking the Struggles of Queers and Immigrants," In Steve Schacht, ed., Coalition Building/Radical Alliances (n.d.); auth, "The Pink Tide: Narrating Ireland's Lesbian and Gay Migrations," Under review. **CONTACT ADDRESS** Dept Ethnic Studies, Bowling Green State Univ, 1001 E Wooster St, Bowling Green, OH 43403-0001.

LUMIN, BERNARD
PERSONAL Born 10/15/1923, Washington, DC, m, 1957 **DISCIPLINE** PSYCHOLOGY **EDUCATION** PA State Univ, PhD, 58; George Washington Univ, MA, 53; BA, 52. **CAREER** Prof Dept of Psychol, 76-; City Chm Dept Psychol, 76-83; Univ MO-Kansas, Dir Clin Training, Dept of Psychol, 74-76; Univ of Houston, Dir of Psychol, 67-74; Greater Kansas City Mental Health Found. **HONORS AND AWARDS** Curators Prof, Univ of MO, 88; N T Veatech Awd for Res and Creative Activity, 81; Unic MO-Kansas City; Listed in Who's Who in the World; Who's Who in Amer. **MEMBERSHIPS** Amer Psychol Assoc; Amer Assoc for the Advacement of Sci. **RESEARCH** Measurement and Mgt of Mood. **SELECTED PUBLICATIONS** Ecological and community approaches to disaster response, Washington DC, forthcoming; Taylor & Fracis, Hanson P G & Lubin B, Answers to most frequently asked questions about organization development Newbury Park CA, Sage Publishing Co, 95; Psychological Aspects of Disaster, NY, Wiley and Sons, 89; Psychological Dimension in Personal Injury Cases, Estalblishin damages in catastrophic injury litigation, pp35-40, Tucson AZ Lawyers and Judges Publ, 94; The mental health of incaracerated persons, Greenwood Press, fprthcoming; Multiple Affect Adjective List-Revised 3rd ed, San Diego CA Edits, 98; Research in professional consultation and consultation for organizational change: An annotated bibilography, Grenwoood Press, 74-95. **CONTACT ADDRESS** Dept Psychol, Univ of Missouri, Kansas City, Kansas City, MO 64110. **EMAIL** Lubin@cctr.umkc.edu

LUNDELL, TORBORG LOVISA
PERSONAL Born Stockholm, Sweden, 1 child **DISCIPLINE** COMPARATIVE LITERATURE, FOLKTALE **EDUCATION** Univ Calif, Berkeley, PhD(comp Lit), 73. **CAREER** Assoc 69-70, Act ass prof 70-72; lectr, 72-73, asst prof, 73-77, Assoc Prof Swed, Univ Calif, Santa Barbara, 77-83, prof 84-. **MEMBERSHIPS** Soc Advan Scand Studies; Philol Asn Pacific Coast; C G Jung Found Anal Psychol. **SELECTED PUBLICATIONS** Auth, Gender Related Biases in the Type and Motif Indexes as a Aaron and Thompson in Fairy Tales and Society, ed. R. Boehipeimen, 86; auth, Lars Ahlin, Fairytale Mathers, 90; auth, Canada in Sweden, Scand Studies, 99. **CONTACT ADDRESS** Dept of Ger and Slavic Lang, Univ of California, Santa Barbara, 552 University Rd, Santa Barbara, CA 93106-0001.

LUNDGREN, AMY
PERSONAL Born 08/26/1948, Denver, CO, m, 1968, 2 children **DISCIPLINE** PSYCHOLOGY **EDUCATION** BA, 93; MA Psychology, 95; MA Theol, 98; Fuller Grad Sch Psychology, PhD, 99. **CAREER** Instr, Santa Monica Col, 96-; Post Doctoral Fel, For the Child - A Child Trauma Treatment Agency, 99-. **HONORS AND AWARDS** Psi Chi Distinguished Scholar Awd, 93. **MEMBERSHIPS** APA. **RESEARCH** Couple Assessment, Psychotherapy outcome, Trauma treatment. **SELECTED PUBLICATIONS** Auth, The Love Power Questionnaire: An Outcome Measure, forthcoming. **CONTACT ADDRESS** Dept Behav Sci, Santa Monica Col, 1900 Pico Blvd, Santa Monica, CA 90405.

LUNDY, DUANE
PERSONAL Born 12/09/1968, Brantford, Canada, m, 1999 **DISCIPLINE** PSYCHOLOGY **EDUCATION** Univ Toronto, BS, 92; Lakehead Univ, MA, 94; Univ Louisville, PhD, 98. **CAREER** Asst prof, psychology, Limestone Col, 98-. **RESEARCH** Social psychology (interpersonal attraction, humor). **SELECTED PUBLICATIONS** Coauth with J. Tan and M. R. Cummingham, "Heterosexual romantic preferences: The importance of humor and physical attractiveness for different types of relationships," Personal Relationships 5 (98): 311-325. **CONTACT ADDRESS** Dept Soc & Behav Sci, Limestone Col, 1115 Col Dr, Gaffney, SC 29340. **EMAIL** dlundy@saint-limestone.edu

LURIE, ALISON
PERSONAL Born 09/03/1926, Chicago, IL, m, 1996, 3 children **DISCIPLINE** CHILDREN'S LITERATURE, FOLKLORE **EDUCATION** Radcliffe Col, AB, 47. **CAREER** Lectr Eng, 69-73, adj assoc prof, 73-76, assoc prof, 76-79, Prof Eng, Cornell Univ, 79-, Frederic J Whiton Prof Am Lit, Cornell Univ, Yaddo Found fel, 63, 64 & 66; Guggenheim fel, 65; Rockefeller Found fel, 67. **HONORS AND AWARDS** New York State Cultural Coun Found Grant (CAPS), 72-73; Am Ac Arts & Lett Awd, Fiction, 84; Pulitzer Prize, Fiction, 85; Radcliffe Col Alumnae Recognition Awd, 87; Prix Femina Etranger, 89 **MEMBERSHIPS** MLA; Aaup; Children's Lit Asn; Pen Club; Author's Guild. **SELECTED PUBLICATIONS** Auth, Love and Friendship, Macmillan, 62; The Nowhere City, Coward McCann, 65; Imaginary Friends, 67, Coward McCann; Real People, 69 & The War Between the Tates, 74, Random House; V R Lang: Poems and Plays, with Memoir by Alison Lurie, Random House, 75; co-ed, The Garland Library of Children's Classics (73 vols), Garland Publ, 76; auth, Only Children, Random House, 79; Clever Gretchen and Other Forgotten Folk Tales, Crowell, 80; The Heavenly Zoo, Farrar Strauss, 81; The Language of Clothes, Random House, 81; Foreign Affairs, Random House, 84; The Truth abut Lorin Jones, Little Brown, 88; Don't Tell the Grownups: Subversive Children's Literature, Little Brown, 90; Women and Ghosts, Doubleday, 94; The Last Resort, Holt, 98; ed, The Oxford Book of Modern Fairy Tales. **CONTACT ADDRESS** Eng Dept, Cornell Univ, 252 Goldwin Smith Hall, Ithaca, NY 14853-0001. **EMAIL** al28@cornell.edu

LUSTIG, MYRON W.
DISCIPLINE INTERCULTURAL COMMUNICATION **EDUCATION** Univ Wis, PhD. **CAREER** Comm, San Diego St Univ; ed, Commun Reports; assoc ed, W Jour Commun. **MEMBERSHIPS** NCA, WSCA **RESEARCH** Interpersonal and Intercultural Communication. **SELECTED PUBLICATIONS** Auth, Intercultural Competence: Interpersonal Communication Across Cultures, 99. **CONTACT ADDRESS** School of Commun, San Diego State Univ, 5500 Campanile Dr, San Diego, CA 92182-4561. **EMAIL** rlustig@mail.sdsu.edu

LUTKE, DEBI REED
PERSONAL Born 04/01/1950, Monett, MO, m, 1973 **DISCIPLINE** SOCIOLOGY **EDUCATION** Pittsburgh State Univ, BS, 75; Central State Univ, MEd, 80; Okla State Univ, PhD, 93. **CAREER** Adj Faculty, Okla State Univ, 87-96; Adj Faculty, Univ of Sci and Art, 95; Assoc Prof, Cottey Col, 96-. **HONORS AND AWARDS** Larry Perkins Scholarship Awd, 91; Scholar in Sociol, 90; Teacher of the Year, 99; Merit Awd, 99; Lillian Corley Awd, 00'; Who's Who Among Am Teachers, 00. **MEMBERSHIPS** ASA, SWS, SSSA, MSA, MSSA, SAC. **RESEARCH** Religious social movements; Osa Johnson. **CONTACT ADDRESS** Dept Soc Sci, Cottey Col, 1000 W Austin, Nevada, MO 64772. **EMAIL** dlutke@cottey.edu

LUZBETAK, LOUIS JOSEPH
PERSONAL Born 09/19/1918, Joliet, IL **DISCIPLINE** LINGUISTIC ANALYSIS, CULTURAL ANTHROPOLOGY **EDUCATION** Divine Word Sem, BA, 42; Pontif Gregorian Univ, STL, 46, JCB, 47; Univ Fribourg, PhD(anthrop), 51. **CAREER** Prof anthrop, ling and missiology, Divine Word Sem, Ill, 51-52, 56-58; lectr and summer asst prof appl anthrop, Cath Univ Am, 60-65; exec dir, Ctr Appl Res in Apostolate, Washington, DC, 65-73; pres, Divine Word Col, Iowa, 73-78; Ed, Anthropos, Int Rev Ethnology and Ling, 79-, Dir, Anthropos Inst, St Augustin bei Sieberg, WGer, 51-; Ford Found fel, 52-54; cult anthrop and ling field work, New Guinea, 52-56; lectr appl anthrop, Ctr Intercult Formation, Cuernavaca, Mex, 60-65; Ctr for Intercult Commun, Cath Univ PR, 60-65; rector, Divine Word Col, DC, 68-73; Walsh-Price fel, Ctr Mission Studies, Maryknoll, NY, 78-79. **HONORS AND AWARDS** Pierre Charles Awd, Fordham Univ, 64. **MEMBERSHIPS** Fel Am Anthrop Asn; Cath Anthrop Asn (vpres, 61-62, pres, 62-69); Ling Soc Am; Soc Appl Anthrop; Am Soc Missiology (pres, 75-76). **SELECTED PUBLICATIONS** Auth, The Church and Cultures: New Perspectives in Missiological Anthropology, Orbis, 95. **CONTACT ADDRESS** 1985 Waukegan Rd, PO Box 6067, Techny, IL 60082-6067.

LYMAN, R. LEE
PERSONAL Born 01/13/1951, Dayton, WA, m, 1974, 2 children **DISCIPLINE** ANTHROPOLOGY **EDUCATION** WA State Univ, BA, 72, MA, 76; Univ WA, PhD, 82. **CAREER** Asst prof, OR State Univ, 82-86; asst prof, 86-89, assoc prof, 89-95, prof, Univ MO-Columbia, 95-. **RESEARCH** North Am archaeology; zooarchaeology. **SELECTED PUBLICATIONS** Auth, Vertebrate Taphonomy, Cambridge Univ Press, 94; sr ed with M J O'Brien and R C Dunnell, American Culture History: Fundamentals of Time, Space, and Form, Plenum Press, 97; The Rise and Fall of Culture History, sr author with M J O'Brien and R C Dunnell, 97; White Goats, White Lies: The Abuse of Science in Olympic National Park, Univ UT Press, 98; James A Ford and the Growth of Americanist Archaeology, co-auth with M J O'Brien, Univ MO Press, 98; Seriation, Superposition, and Interdigitation: A History of Americanist Graphic Depictions of Cultural Change, Am Antiquity, sr auth with S Wolverton and M J O'Brien, 98; Basic Incompatabilities between Evolutionary and Behavioral Archaeology, Am Antiquity, co-auth with M J O'Brien and R Leonard, 98; Measuring Late Quaternary Ursid Dimunition in the Midwest, Quaternary Res, co-auth with S Wolverton, 98; The Goals of Evolutionary Archaeology: History and Explanation, Current Anthropol, in press, sr auth with M J O'Brien, 98; numerous other publications, several forthcoming. **CONTACT ADDRESS** Dept of Anthropology, Univ of Missouri, Columbia, 107 Swallow Hall, Columbia, MO 65211. **EMAIL** lymanr@missouri.edu

LYNCH, OWEN
PERSONAL Born 01/04/1931, New York, NY, s **DISCIPLINE** ANTHROPOLOGY **EDUCATION** Fordham Univ, AB, 56; Columbia Univ, PhD, 66. **CAREER** Asst to assoc prof, SUNY Binghamton, 66-73; prof, NY Univ, 74-. **MEMBERSHIPS** Am Anthrop Assoc; Am Ethnological Assoc; Assoc for Asian Studies, Indian Sociol Soc. **RESEARCH** Dalits in India, Urban Anthropology, Pilgrimage, Cultural Construction of Emotions, Globalization. **SELECTED PUBLICATIONS** Auth, "The social construction of emotion in India" and "The Mastram: emotion and the person among Mathura's Chaubes", Divine Passions: The Social Construction of Emotion in India, ed Owen M. Lynch, Univ of Calif Pr, (Berkeley, 90): 3-34, 91-115; auth, "Jatavs", Encyclopedia of World Cultures, ed David Levinson, G K Hall, (Boston, 91): 67-80; auth, "Stratification, inequality: India", Guide to Asian Case Studies in the Social Sciences, ed Myron Cohen, M.E. Sharpe, (Armonk, NY, 92): 67-80; auth, "Urban anthropology, postmodernism and perspectives", City and Society, (94): 35-52; auth, "Urban anthropology: An Agenda for the end of the millennium", Anthrop Newsletter 37.5 (96): 50; auth, "Contesting and contested self-identities: Mathura's Chaubes", Narratives of Agency: Self Making in China, India and Japan, ed Wimal Dissanayake, Univ of Minn Pr, (Minneapolis, 96): 74-103; auth, "Dalit Buddhism: the liberate Bodh Gaha Movement", Dalit Int Newsletter 3.1 (98): 10-11; auth, "Sujata's Vahini (Army): Dalit Buddhist women and self emancipation", Women Changing Contemporary Buddhism, ed Ellison Findly, Wisdom Publications (00). **CONTACT ADDRESS** Dept Anthrop, New York Univ, 25 Waverly Pl, New York, NY 10003. **EMAIL** owen.lynch@nyu.edu

LYON, JANET W.
PERSONAL Born 10/30/1954, Springfield, MA, m, 1985, 2 children **DISCIPLINE** ENGLISH, LITERATURE, WOMEN'S STUDIES **EDUCATION** Yale Univ, New Haven, RN, 75; Trinity Col, BA, 82; Univ Vir, MA, 84; PhD, 92. **CAREER** Assoc prof, Univ Ill, 99-01; assoc prof, Penn State Univ, 01-. **HONORS AND AWARDS** Campus Wide Teaching Awd, Col Wide Teaching Awd, Univ Ill, 99. **MEMBERSHIPS** MLA; MSA; SDS. **RESEARCH** British modernism; feminist theory; women's literature; modern studies; disability studies. **SELECTED PUBLICATIONS** Auth, Manifestoes: Provocations of the Modern, Cornell UP, 99. **CONTACT ADDRESS** English Dept, Penn State Univ, 813 W Forester Ave, State College, PA 16801.

M

MACDONALD, DON
PERSONAL Born 03/24/1950, Dowagrac, MI, m, 1981, 3 children **DISCIPLINE** PSYCHOLOGY **EDUCATION** Univ Tex at Austin, BA, 72; Ind Univ, MS, 73; Mich State Univ, PhD, 84. **CAREER** Teacher, Shelton View School, 75-76; teaching asst, Mich State Univ, 76-79; staff psychol, House of Commons, 77-79; prof, Seattle Pac Univ, 80-. **HONORS AND AWARDS** Mental Health counselors Awd, 89; Fac Res Grant, 86, 89, 99; Dept of Health Service Awd, 93; Fac Awd, 96. **MEMBERSHIPS** Christian Asn of Psychol Studies, Am Psychol Asn, Soc for the Study of Psychol and W Theol. **RESEARCH** Epistemology and ontology of psychology, Ethics and law. **SELECTED PUBLICATIONS** Auth, Social and psychological foundations of education, Ginn: Lexington, 86; auth, "What kind of counselors do clients really prefer?" New Jersey Journal of Professional Counseling, 86; auth, "Characteristics of counselors and therapists in three professional associations," Oregon Counseling Journal, (89): 22-25; auth, "Philoso-

phies that underlie models of mental health counseling: More than meets the eye," Journal of Mental Health Counseling, (91): 379-392; auth, "Confidentiality and the duty to report suspected child abuse: A recent case study," Journal of Psychology and Theology, (93): 119-126; auth, "Counseling and the law: A cross-cultural perspective," Journal of counseling and Development, (in print). **CONTACT ADDRESS** Dept Graduate Psychol, Seattle Pacific Univ, 3307 3rd Ave W, Seattle, WA 98119. **EMAIL** eieio@spu.edu

MACDONALD, JANE
PERSONAL Born 06/12/1950, Brooklyn, NY, m, 1973, 1 child **DISCIPLINE** EDUCATION **EDUCATION** Georgian Court Col, BA, 71; Kean Univ, MA, 75; Nova SE Univ, PhD, 84. **CAREER** Teacher, Toms River Reg Schools, 71-00; Adj Instructor, Ocean County Col, 99-; Instructor, Brookdale Cmty Col, 99-00. **HONORS AND AWARDS** NEA Hilda Moehling Fel; Who's Who in the World; Who's Who of Am Women; Disney Am Teacher Awd Nominee; Dictionary of Intl Biography. **MEMBERSHIPS** Asn FOR Supervision and Curriculum; Phi Delta Kappa, Alpha Delta Kappa, Nat Educ Asn, NAFE. **RESEARCH** Parenting; Professional Staff Development; Curriculum Standards. **CONTACT ADDRESS** Dept Humanities, Ocean County Col, PO Box 2001, Toms River, NJ 08754-2001. **EMAIL** djmacassoc@aol.com

MACDONALD, MARGARET READ
PERSONAL Born 01/21/1940, Seymour, IN, m, 1965, 2 children **DISCIPLINE** FOLKLORE; CHILDREN'S LITERATURE **EDUCATION** Ind Univ, AB, 62, PhD, 79; Univ Wash, Seattle, MLS, 64; Univ Hawaii, MEdEc, 68. **CAREER** Children's Specialist, 64-72, Childrens Lbn, 77-, King Co Lib System, Seattle, Wash; Vis Lecturer, Univ Wash, Seattle, 75-79, 96-. **HONORS AND AWARDS** Fulbright Schol, 95-96; Nat Storytelling Asn Leadership Awd, 98. **MEMBERSHIPS** Am Folklore Soc; Am Library Asn; Nat Storytelling Asn; Int Bd on Books for Youth; Soc of Children's Book Writers & Illustrators. **RESEARCH** Personal narrative; performance theory; the folktale. **SELECTED PUBLICATIONS** Auth, The Storyteller's Sourcebook: A Subject, Title, and Motif Index to Folklore Collections for Children, Gale, 82; auth, Scipio, Indiana: Threads from the Past, Ye Galleon, 88; auth, The Folklore of World Holidays, Gale, 91; auth, The Storyteller's Start-up Book: Finding, Learning, Performing, and Using Folktales, Aug Hse, 93; auth, Scipio Storytelling: Talk in a Southern Indiana Community, Univ Press of Am, 96; ed, Thai Tales: Folktales of Thailand by Supaporn Vathanaprida, Libraries Unltd, 94; auth, Traditional Storytelling Today: An International Sourcebook, Fitzroy Dearborn, 99. **CONTACT ADDRESS** 11507 NE 104th, Kirkland, WA 98083. **EMAIL** margmacd@kcls.org

MACDONALD, MARYELLEN
DISCIPLINE PSYCHOLOGY, LINGUISTICS, AND THE NEUROSCIENCE PROGRAM **EDUCATION** Univ Calif, Los Angeles, PhD, 86. **CAREER** Assoc prof, Univ Southern Calif. **RESEARCH** Human language comprehension; Speech production & its relationship to comprehension; role of working memory in language processing; decline of language processing abilities in patients with Alzheimer's Disease. **SELECTED PUBLICATIONS** Coauth, The lexical nature of syntactic ambiguity resolution, Psycholog Rev, 101, 94; ed, Lexical representations & sentence processing, Hove, Sussex, UK: Psychology Press, Publ simultaneously as Issues 2-3 jour Lang and Cognitive Processes, 97. **CONTACT ADDRESS** Dept of Linguistics, Univ of So California, University Park Campus, Los Angeles, CA 90089-2520. **EMAIL** mcm@gizmo.usc.edu

MACDONALD, WILLIAM L.
PERSONAL Born 12/02/1963, Columbus, OH, m, 1993, 2 children **DISCIPLINE** SOCIOLOGY **EDUCATION** Bowling Green State Univ, PhD, 92. **CAREER** Asst Prof, 92-98, Assoc Prof Sociol, Ohio State Univ at Newark, 98-. **HONORS AND AWARDS** Young Schol in Am Relig, 97-98; Newark Schol Achievement Awd, Ohio State Univ. **MEMBERSHIPS** Am Sociol Asn; Soc Scientific Study Relig; Southern Sociol Soc; Nat Coun Family Relations. **RESEARCH** Religion; family; social movements; voluntary euthanasia; science. **SELECTED PUBLICATIONS** Coauth, Remarriage, Stepchildren, and Marital Conflict: Challenges to the Incomplete Institutionalization Hypothesis, J Marriage and the Family, 95; auth, The Effects of Religiosity and Structural Strain on Reported Paranormal Experiences, J Scientific Study Relig, 95; coauth, Parenting Stepchildren and Biological Children: The Effects of Stepparent's Gender and New Biological Children, J Family Issues, 96; auth, Situational Factors and Attitudes toward Voluntary Euthanasia, Soc Sci & Med, 98; The Difference Between Blacks' and Whites' Attitudes toward Voluntary Euthanasia, J Scientific Study Relig (forthcoming). **CONTACT ADDRESS** Sociology Dept, Ohio State Univ, Newark, Newark, OH 43055. **EMAIL** macdonald.24@osu.edu

MACHARIA, KINUTHIA
PERSONAL Born 03/12/1956, Kenya, w, 1982, 2 children **DISCIPLINE** SOCIOLOGY **EDUCATION** Univ Nairobi, BA, 80; Univ Calif, MA, 86; PhD, 89. **CAREER** Asst Prof, Harvard Univ, 90-95; Asst Prof, Am Univ, 95-. **HONORS AND AWARDS** Ghadi Smarak Nithoi Prize. **MEMBER-**

SHIPS ASA, African Studies Asn. **RESEARCH** Urban sociology, development, informal economy. **SELECTED PUBLICATIONS** Auth, Social and Political Dynamics of the Informal Economy in African Cities, Univ Pa Pr, 97. **CONTACT ADDRESS** Dept Sociol, American Univ, 4400 Mass Ave NW, Washington, DC 20016. **EMAIL** kmachar@american.edu

MACKEY, RICHARD A.
DISCIPLINE SOCIAL WORK **EDUCATION** Merrimack Col, AB, 57; Cath Univ Am, MSW, 59; DSW, 66. **CAREER** Asst prof to prof, Boston Col, 66-. **HONORS AND AWARDS** Outstanding Professionals in Human Serv, 88-93; Diplomat in Clinical Soc Work, 93; Who's Who in the East, 94-95; Who's Who in Med and Health Care, 95-99; Contemporary Authors, 98-00. **MEMBERSHIPS** Nat Assoc of Soc Workers; Acad of Cert Soc Workers; Nat Reg of Clinical Soc Workers; LICSW. **SELECTED PUBLICATIONS** Auth, Ego Psychology and Clinical Practice, Gardner Pr, (NY), 85; coauth, "Personal Psychotherapy and the Development of a Professional Self", Families in Soc: J of Contemp Human Serv 75.8 (94): 490-498; coauth, Lasting Marriages: Men and Women Growing Together, Praeger Pub, (Westport, CT), 95; coauth, Gay and Lesbian Couples: Voices from Lasting Relationships, Praeger Pub, (Westport, CT), 97; coauth, "Marital conflict management: gender and ethnic differences", Social Work: J of the Nat Assoc of Soc Workers 43.2 (98): 128-141; coauth, "Adaptation in lasting marriages: A multi-dimensional prospective", Families in Soc: J of Contemp Human Serv, (99); coauth, "Conflict management styles of spouses in lasting relationships, Psychotherapy: Theory/Research/Practice (forthcoming); coauth, "Satisfaction in the lasting relationships of heterosexual and same sex relationships", (forthcoming); coauth, "Psychological intimacy in the lasting relationships of heterosexual and same sex relationships", (forthcoming). **CONTACT ADDRESS** Sch of Soc Work, Boston Col, Chestnut Hill, 140 Commonwealth Ave, Chestnut Hill, MA 02467. **EMAIL** mackey@bc.edu

MACKINNON, PATRICIA L.
DISCIPLINE LIBERAL ARTS, GENERAL EDUCATION, INTERDISCIPLINARY STUDIES **EDUCATION** Univ CA, Irvine, BA; Univ CA, Santa Cruz, PhD. **CAREER** Instr, UCLA, Stanford Univ, Clarkson Univ, St Lawrence Univ, Univ CA, Davis; asst prof Hum, Golden Gate Univ. **SELECTED PUBLICATIONS** Auth of articles in medieval and renaissance studies. **CONTACT ADDRESS** Golden Gate Univ, San Francisco, CA 94105-2968.

MADRIL, JIM
PERSONAL Born 05/19/1944, Tucson, AZ, s, 2 children **DISCIPLINE** BEHAVIORAL SCIENCES **EDUCATION** Univ Az, BA, 65; Calif State San Diego, MSW, 67; Univ Az, EdD, 89. **CAREER** Asst clinical prof, Grad Sch of Social Work, Ariz State Univ, 79-81; Mem, Governors Coun on Developmental Disabilities, 85-; head, Dept Behav Sci, Cochise Col, 96-. **HONORS AND AWARDS** Teach 13 different behav sci courses; vice-pres, Western Regional Org for Human Services Ed, 99-. **MEMBERSHIPS** Am Psychol Soc, Nat Asn of social Workers, Nat Org for Human Services Eds. **RESEARCH** Pathology (emotions). **SELECTED PUBLICATIONS** Auth, "On Depression," US/Mexico Border Health Conf VII Pub on Proceedings of Conference VII (80); auth, Human Services Student Field Manual (94); auth, Introduction to Pathosology: Psychological Study of Emotions (99); auth, Introduction to Pathosology: Sociological Study of Emotions, 2000. **CONTACT ADDRESS** Dept Math & Sci, Cochise Col, Sierra Vista, 901 N Columbo, Sierra Vista, AZ 85635.

MADSEN, CAROL CORNWALL
PERSONAL Born Salt Lake City, UT **DISCIPLINE** AMERICAN AND WOMEN'S HISTORY **EDUCATION** Univ Utah, BA, 51; PhD, 86. **CAREER** Prof of Hist; Res Historian, Joseph Fielding Smith Inst for LDS Hist, Brigham Young Univ, 80-. **RESEARCH** Women in American history; women in Western American history; women in Mormon history. **SELECTED PUBLICATIONS** Auth, Sisters and Little Saints, A History of the Primary, 78; auth, In Their Own Words, Women and the Story of Nauvoo, 92; auth, Battle for the Ballot; Women Suffrage in Utah, 97; auth, Journey to Zion, Voices from the Mormon Trail, 97. **CONTACT ADDRESS** Smith Inst for Latter Day Saints Hist, Brigham Young Univ, 123 KMB, Provo, UT 84602. **EMAIL** carol_madsen@byu.edu

MAGDOL, LYNN
DISCIPLINE SOCIOLOGY **EDUCATION** Univ Wisc, PhD, 95. **CAREER** Asst prof, SUNY Buffalo Sociol Dept, 96-. **MEMBERSHIPS** Am Sociol asn, Nat Coun on Family Relations, Eastern Sociol Soc. **RESEARCH** Family, social networks, social support, mobility and immigration, couple relations. **SELECTED PUBLICATIONS** Coauth with T. E. Moffitt, A. Caspi, D. L. Newman, J. Fagan, and P. Silva, "Gender Differences in Partner Violence in a Birth Cohort of 21-Year-Olds: Bridging the Gap between Clinical and Epidemiological Approaches," J of Consulting and Clinical Psychol (97); coauth with T. E. Moffitt, A. Caspi, and P. Silva, "Hitting Without a License: Testing Explanations for Differences in Partner Abuse Between Young Adult Daters and Cohabitors," J of Marriage and the Family (98); coauth with T. E. Moffitt, A. Caspi,

and P. Silva, "Developmental Antecedents of Partner Abuse: a Prospective-Longitudinal Study," J of Abnormal Psychol (98); auth, "The People You Know: The Impact of Residential Mobility on Mothers' Social Network Ties," J of Personal and Social Relationships (2000). **CONTACT ADDRESS** Dept Sociol-Park Hall, SUNY, Buffalo, PO Box 604140, Buffalo, NY 14260-0001. **EMAIL** magdol@acsu.buffalo.edu

MAGLIOCCO, SABINA
PERSONAL Born 12/30/1959, Topeka, KS, d **DISCIPLINE** ANTHROPOLOGY **EDUCATION** Brown Univ, BA, 80; Ind Univ, MA, 83; PhD, 88. **CAREER** Vis asst prof, Dept of Anthropol, Univ Calif, Berkeley, 95-96; asst prof, Dept of Anthropol, Calif State Univ, Northridge, 97-. **HONORS AND AWARDS** Fulbright-Hayes Doctoral Res Grant, Italy, 85; Fulbright Post-Doctoral Res Grant, Italy, 89; Hewlett Awd, Univ of Wisc, 90; The Chicago Folklore Prize, 94; John Simon Guggenheim Memorial Fel, 96. **MEMBERSHIPS** Am Anthropol Asn, Am Folklore Soc. **RESEARCH** Ritual, festival and religion; occultism and "new" religions; narrative; ethnic/regional/national identity issues; gender; oppositionality; cultural studies and critical theory; Mediterranean, contemporary US. **SELECTED PUBLICATIONS** Auth, The Two Madonnas: the Politics of Festival in a Sardinian Community, Lang (93); auth," Playing with Food: the negotiation of Identity in the Ethnic Display Event by Italian-Americans in Clinton, Indiana," Studies in Italian American Folklore, ed by Luisa Del Giudice, Ut State Univ Press (93): 107-126, reprinted in Barbara G. Shortridge and James R. Shortridge, ed, A Taste of American Place, NY: Rowman & Littlefield (98): 145-162; auth, "Ritual is My Chosen Art Form: The Creation of Ritual as Folk Art Among Contemporary Pagans," Magical Religions and Modern Witchcraft, ed by James Lewis, SUNY Press (96): 93-119; coauth with Holly Tannen, "The Real Old-Time Religion: Towards an Aesthetic of Neo-Pagan Song," Ethnologies, 20/1 (98): 175-201. **CONTACT ADDRESS** Dept Anthropol, California State Univ, Northridge, 18111 Nordhoff St, Northridge, CA 91330-8244. **EMAIL** sabina.magliocco@csun.edu

MAGUIRE, LAMBERT
PERSONAL Born 10/26/1946, Chicago, IL, m, 1971, 2 children **DISCIPLINE** SOCIAL WORK **EDUCATION** Loyola Univ, BS, 68; Univ Chicago, MA, 71; Univ Mich, MA, 76; Univ Mich, PhD, 79. **CAREER** Commissioned Off, US Public Health Serv, 71-74; Asst Prof, 79-85; Assoc Prof, 85-90; Prof, Univ Pittsburgh, 94-. **HONORS AND AWARDS** NIMH Fel, Univ Chicago. **MEMBERSHIPS** Nat Asn of Soc Workers, Coun on Soc Work Ed, Acad of Cert Soc Workers. **RESEARCH** Social support systems and networks in mental health. **SELECTED PUBLICATIONS** Auth, "Peer Review in Community Mental Health," Community Mental Health J, (3)3 (78); auth, "The Interface of Social Workers with Personal Networks," Social Work with Groups, (3)3 (80); coauth, "The Use of Networks in Social Welfare: Jumping on the Bandwagon," Social Welfare Forum, Columbia Univ Pr (82); auth, "Networking for Self-Help: An Empirically Based Guideline," in Tactics and Techniques in Community Practice, 2nd ed (IL: Peacock Publ, Itasca, 84); auth, "Networks of the Chronically Mental Ill: A Project Description," Western Pa Group Psychotherapy Soc Newsletter, Dec (85); auth, "Creating Ties and Maintaining Support: Networking and Self-Help," in Alzheimer's Disease: Problems, Prospects and Perspective, (NY: Plenum Publ, 87); coauth, "A Comparison of Extended and Traditional Master's of Social Work Students: A Repeated Measures Analysis," J of Ed for Soc Work, vol 23, 1, Winter (87); auth, "Brief Interventions with Adolescents," in Casebook of Brief Psychotherapies, (NY: Plenum Publ, 93); auth, Social Support Systems in Practice: A Generalist Approach, NASW Pr (Wash, D.C.), 93; auth, Social Work Practice Beyond Generalist, Brooks/Cole Publ Co (Monterey, Calif), forthcoming. **CONTACT ADDRESS** Dept Soc Work, Univ of Pittsburgh, 2201 Cathedral/Learn, Pittsburgh, PA 15260. **EMAIL** burt+@pitt.edu

MAHDI, AKBAR
PERSONAL Born Rey, Iran, m, 1978 **DISCIPLINE** SOCIOLOGY **EDUCATION** Nat Univ Iran, BA, 75; Mich State Univ, MA. 78; PhD, 83. **CAREER** Liason Coordr for the Middle E, Am Sociol Asn, 85-96; Pres, Mich Sociol Asn, 87-88; Exec Dir, The Center for Iranian Res and Analysis, 93-95; Instr, Mich State Univ, 82-83; Assoc Prof, Adrian Col, 83-91; Vis Assoc Prof, Central State Univ, 91-92; Assoc Prof, Ohio Wesleyan Univ, 93-. **HONORS AND AWARDS** Exellence in Teaching Citation Awd, Mich State Univ, 83; The Sears Found Teaching Excellence and Campus Leadership Awd, Adrian Col, 90; Teaching Excellence Awd, Mich Sociol Asn, 90; Marvin E. Olsen Serv Awd, Mich Sociol Asn, 94. **MEMBERSHIPS** Am Sociol Asn, N Central Sociol Asn, Middle Eastern Studies Asn, Soc for Iranian Studies, Center for Res and Analysis of Iran. **RESEARCH** Middle East, Islam, Iran, Development, Gender, Political Economy. **SELECTED PUBLICATIONS** Coauth, Sociology in Iran, Jahan Book Co (Bethesda, MD), 92; auth, "The Case of Incorporating Middle East into the Curricula," W Va Sociol Rev 1-1 (Spring 95); auth, "Reconstructing Gender in Post-Revolutionary Iran: Transcending the Revolution?," Middle E Insight 11-5 (July/Aug 95); auth, "Civil Society in the Islamic Republic," CIRA Bul 11-3 (Spring 96); auth, "Commentary on Pre-Capitalist Iran: A Theoretical History," Cri-

tique: J of Critical Studies of the Middle E 8 (Spring 96); auth, "Determinants of Adaptations for Second Generation Iranians," CIRA Bul 13-1 (Mar 97); auth, "Ethnic Identity among Second-Generation Iranians in the United States," Iranian Studies 31-1 (Winter 98); auth, Iranian Culture, Civil Society, and Concern for Democracy, Javan Publ (Can), 98; auth, "The Student Movement in the Islamic Republic of Iran," J of Iranian Res and Analysis 15-2 (Nov 99); auth, "Trading Places: Changes in Gender Roles within the Iranian Immigrant Family," Critique: J of Critical Studies of the Middle E 15 (Fall 99). **CONTACT ADDRESS** Dept Sociol and Anthrop, Ohio Wesleyan Univ, 61 S Sandusky St, Delaware, OH 43015. **EMAIL** aamahdi@cc.owu.edu

MAHMOUDI, KOOROS M.
PERSONAL Born 06/15/1945, Mashhad, Iran, m, 1987, 2 children **DISCIPLINE** SOCIOLOGY **EDUCATION** Utah State Univ, BS; MS; PhD, 73. **CAREER** Lecturer to Asst Prof, Ind Purdue Univ, 71-77; Lecturer, San Diego State Univ, 78-81; Asst Prof to Prof & Chair, Northern Ariz Univ, 81-. **HONORS AND AWARDS** Fulbright Prog, US Office of Educ, India, 80; Alpha Kappa Delta; Fel, Utah State Univ, 70-71; Who's Who among Student in Am Col and Univ, 65-66; NAU Organized Res Grant, 86; Who's' Who Among Am Teachers, 96. **MEMBERSHIPS** Pac Sociol Asn, Population Asn of Am, Soc for Intercultural Educ, Training and Res, Intl Sociol Asn, Population Ref Bureau, Intl Asn for Impact Assessment. **RESEARCH** Sociological theory, Demography, Principles of sociology, Social organization, Human ecology, Macro sociology, Applied sociology, Methods of demographic analysis, Social problems, Sustainable communities. **SELECTED PUBLICATIONS** Auth, "NAFTA, The Environment, and Immigration: A Research Agenda," Proceedings of the International Environmental Association, (99): 62-72; auth, "Ecological Design: Peace with the Environment," International Journal of Humanities and Peace, (99): 55-58; auth, "Sustainability and the Role of Impact Assessment in Ecological Design," Proceedings of the International Association for Impact Assessment, (99): 1-13; auth, "Social Control and Moral pragmatism: The Role of Impact Assessment," Proceedings of the International Association for Impact Assessment, (98): 1-12; ed, Sociological Inquiry, 6th ed, Kendall/Hunt Pub Co., 97; auth, "Living in Harmony with Nature," International Journal of Humanities and Peace, (97): 48-51; ed, Sociological Inquiry: A Humanistic Perspective, 4th ed, Kendall/Hunt Pub Co., 87; auth, Sociological Inquiry: A Humanistic Perspective, rev 3rd ed, Kendall/Hunt Pub Co., 84; auth, Sociological Inquiry: A Humanistic Perspective, 3rd ed, Kendall/Hunt Pub Co., 81. **CONTACT ADDRESS** Dept Sociol, No Arizona Univ, PO Box Nau, Flagstaff, AZ 86011-001.

MAHONEY, DANIEL F.
PERSONAL Born 10/22/1964, Lancaster, PA, m, 1994, 1 child **DISCIPLINE** HEALTH, PHYSICAL EDUCATION **EDUCATION** Va Tech, BS, 87; WVa Univ, MS, 90; Oh State Univ, PhD, 95. **CAREER** Vis asst prof, Univ Okla, 94-95; asst prof and program dir, Univ of Louisville, 95-. **HONORS AND AWARDS** Magna cum laude, Outstanding Student-Col of Business, Va Tech, 87; GPA of 4.00, WVa Univ, 90; GPA, 3,98, Ohio State Univ, 95. **MEMBERSHIPS** North Am Soc for Sport Management. **RESEARCH** Fan behavior, ethics and cheating in sport, resource distribution in college athletics. **SELECTED PUBLICATIONS** Coauth with A. Moorman, "The impact of attitudes on the behavioral intentions of professional basketball fans," Sport management Rev, 2,(99): 43-66; coauth with R. Madrigal and D. R. Howard, "The effect of self-monitoring on behavioral and attitudinal loyalty towards athletic teams," Int J of Sport marketing and Sponsorship, 1 (99): 146-167; auth, "Collective reaction to injustice in intercollegiate sport: Injustice to women and student athletes as test cases," J of Sport & Soc Issues, 23 (99): 328-352; coauth with M. Nakazawa, D. C. Funk, and S. Hirakawa, "Segmenting J. League spectators based on length of time as a fan," Sport Marketing Quart, 8, 4 999): 55-65; coauth with R. Madrigal and D. R. Howard, "BIRGing and CORFing behaviors by sport spectators: High self-monitoring versus low self-monitors," Int Sports J, 4, 1 (2000); coauth with D. R. Howard and R. Madrigal, "Using the psychological commitment to team (PCT) scale to segment sport consumers based on loyalty," Sport Marketing Quart (in press); coauth with M. Nakazawa, S. Hirakawa, M. A. Hums, J. Togari, and Y. Nakatsuka, "Female spectators in J. League," The Japanese J of Sport Industry (in press); coauth with M. Nakazawa, A. M. Moorman, and S. Hirakawa, "The relationship between stadium size & location and spectator characteristics: Implications for marketing strategies," Int Sports J (in press); coauth with T. C. Greenwell, A. L. Geist, J.S. Jordan, and D. L. Pastore, "Characteristics of NCAA conference codes of ethics," Int J of Sport Management (in press); coauth with J. Fink and D. Pastore, "Ethics in Intercollegiate Athletics: An Examination of NCAA Violations and Penalties-1952-1997," Prof Ethics j (in press). **CONTACT ADDRESS** Dept Health, Physical Educ, Univ of Louisville, 2301 S 3rd St, Louisville, KY 40292-2001.

MAIDA, LORI
PERSONAL Born 08/23/1954, Bronx, NY, m, 1980, 2 children **DISCIPLINE** SOCIOLOGY **EDUCATION** Drew Univ, BA, 76; Boston Univ, MA, 78; Fordham Univ, PhD, 87. **CAREER** Asst Prof, Westchester Community Col, 87-93; From Asst to Assoc Prof, Concordia Col, 93-. **HONORS AND AWARDS** Fac Awd, Student Govt Asn, Concordia Col, 96. **MEMBERSHIPS** ASA. **RESEARCH** Societal and interpersonal violence. **SELECTED PUBLICATIONS** Auth, "Emotional Intelligence," Fours Mag (99). **CONTACT ADDRESS** Dept Sociol, Concordia Col, New York, 171 White Plains Rd, Bronxville, NY 10708.

MAJERES, RAYMOND L.
PERSONAL Born 07/24/1942, Wilmont, MN, m, 1967, 1 child **DISCIPLINE** PSYCHOLOGY **EDUCATION** Mankato State Col, BA, 64; Univ Nebr, PhD, 70. **CAREER** Intern, Coun and Testing Center, Stanford Univ, 67-68; Post Doctoral Educ Testing Serv, Princeton, NJ, 70-72; Asst Prof to Prof, Western Ill Univ, 72-. **HONORS AND AWARDS** Outstanding Res Awd, Col of Arts and Sci, Western Ill Univ, 96; Who's Who Among Am Teachers, 97, 98; Phi Kappa Phi; Sigma Xi. **MEMBERSHIPS** Am Psychol Soc, Midwestern Psychol Asn, **RESEARCH** Cognitive Psychology/Developmental Psychology. **SELECTED PUBLICATIONS** Auth, "The combined effects of stimulus and response conditions on the delay in identifying the print color of words," J of Exp Psychology 102 (74): 868-874; auth, "Sex differences in clerical speed: Perceptual encoding versus verbal encoding," Memory and Cognition 5 (77): 468-476; coauth, "Children's spontaneous use of real-world information in problem solving," J of Genetic Psychology 144 (84): 89-97; auth, "Sex differences in comparison and decision processes when matching strings of symbols," Intelligence 14 (90): 357-370; auth, "Sex differences in phonological processes: Speeded matching and word reading," Memory and Cognition 27 (99): 246-253. **CONTACT ADDRESS** Dept Psychology, Western Illinois Univ, 1 University Circle, Macomb, IL 61455. **EMAIL** Ray_Majeres@ccmail.wiu.edu

MAKEPEACE, JAMES
PERSONAL Born 01/11/1946, Stoneham, MA, m, 3 children **DISCIPLINE** SOCIOLOGY **EDUCATION** St John's Univ, BA, 70; Washington State Univ, MA, 73; PhD, 75. **CAREER** Prof, St John's Univ, 79-. **HONORS AND AWARDS** Outstanding Teacher Awd, Danforth Foundation. **MEMBERSHIPS** Am Sociol Asn, Nat Coun Family Relations, Am Asn Beh and Soc Sci. **RESEARCH** Family violence. **SELECTED PUBLICATIONS** Ed, Perspectives, Journal of Am Asn Beh and Soc Sci. **CONTACT ADDRESS** Dept Sociol, St. John's Univ, Collegeville, MN 56321. **EMAIL** jmakepeace@csbsju.edu

MAKEREC, KATHERINE
PERSONAL Born 04/15/1960, Sudbury, ON, Canada, m **DISCIPLINE** PSYCHOLOGY **EDUCATION** Laurentian Univ, BA, 85; York Univ, MA, 90; York Univ, PhD, 95. **MEMBERSHIPS** Am Psychol Asn, Am Psychol Soc, Can Soc for Brain, Behavior and Cognitive Sci. **SELECTED PUBLICATIONS** coauth, "Electroencephalograph Validation of Temporal Lobe Signs Inventory in a Normal Population," J of Res in Personality 34 (90): 323-337; coauth, "University Females are More Fearful and Males are More Egocentric: Possible Implications for Vocational Pursuits and Response to Crisis," Perceptual and Motor Skills, 70 (90): 1297-1298; coauth, "Psychometric Differentiation of Men and Women by the Personal Philosophy Inventory," J of Personality and Individual Differences, 12 (91): 1267-1271; coauth, "Differential Effects of Wave Form and the Subjects' Possible Temporal Lobe Signs Upon Experiences During Cerebral Exposure to Weak Intensity Magnetic Fields," J of Bioelectricity, 10 (91): 141-148; coauth, "The Sensed Presence and Verbal Meaningfulness as Temporal Lobe Signs: Factor Analytic Verification of the Muses?" Brain and Cognition, 20 (92): 217-226; coauth, "Reinforcement Generalization as Interaction Between Processes Rather Than Events: Absence of Schedule-Induced Hyperdipsia in Rats with Histories of Minimal Food-Water Contiguity," Perceptual and Motor Skills, 77 (93): 751-754; coauth, "Complex Partial Epileptic-Like Signs as a Continuum from Normals to Epileptics: Normative Data and Clinical Populations," J of Clinical Psychology, 49 (93): 33-45; coauth, "Bilingual Men but not Women Display Verbal Memory Weakness but not Figural Memory Differences Compared to Monolinguals," Personality and Individual Differences, 15 (93): 531-536; coauth, "An FMRI Analysis of Sex and Laterality Effects in 3-D Mental Rotation," Society of Neuroscience Abstracts, 2 (97): 2113; coauth, "Functional MRI of 3-D Mental Rotation: A Clinical Study," Neuroimage, 7(4) (98): 65. **CONTACT ADDRESS** Dept Psychol, William Paterson Univ of New Jersey, 300 Pompton Rd, Wayne, NJ 07470-2103. **EMAIL** makareck@wpunj.edu

MAKWARD, CHRISTIANE PERRIN
PERSONAL Born 01/06/1941, Hyeres, France, m, 1960, 2 children **DISCIPLINE** FRENCH LITERATURE, WOMEN'S STUDIES **EDUCATION** Sorbonne, Lic es Lett, 63, DLit, 74; Univ Dakar, DES, 65. **CAREER** From asst lectr to lectr French lang & lit, Univ Ibadan, Nigeria, 62-67; lectr French lit, Univ Wis, 68-69 & 74-75; lectr, Univ Que-Rimouski, 76-77; asst prof, 77-80, assoc prof French, prof French, 96-, Pa State Univ, 80-96, Ed, Breff, Pa State Univ, 76-. **MEMBERSHIPS** MLA; Am Asn Teachers Fr; Women's Caucus Mod Lang; Asn Int Femmes Ecrivians; Asn Amis Cerisy-la-Salle. **RESEARCH** Contemporary French literature; psychoanalysis; stylistics. **SELECTED PUBLICATIONS** Auth, Mallarme and Ricardou: Echoes, 73, Claude Simon: Earth, Eros and Death, 74 & Interview with Helene Cixous, 76, Sub-Stance; La critique feministe: Elements d'une problematique, Revue Sci Humanies, Lille, 12/77; auth, Aspects of bisexuality in Claude Simon's works, In: Blinded Orion, Bucknell Univ; Structures du silence/du delire: Marguerite Duras/Helene Cixous, Poetique, Paris; Nouveau regard sur la critique feministe, Revue de l'Univ d'Ottawa, Vol 50, No 1; Colette and signs, In: Colette, The Woman, The Writer, Pa State Univ Press, 81. **CONTACT ADDRESS** Dept of French, Pennsylvania State Univ, Univ Park, 316 Burrowes Bldg, University Park, PA 16802-6203. **EMAIL** cjm9@psu.edu

MALAND, CHARLES J.
PERSONAL Born 09/21/1949, Albert Lea, MN, m, 1973, 1 child **DISCIPLINE** AMERICAN CULTURE **EDUCATION** Augsburg Col, BA, 71; Univ Mich, MA, 72; PhD, 75. **CAREER** Lake Forest Col, 76-78; asst prof, 78-83; assoc prof, 83-90; prof, 90-, Univ Tenn. **HONORS AND AWARDS** AFI, Rockefeller Found Sem; Lilly Found Fel; Fulbright Fel; Hodges Teach Awd; AA Outstand Teach Awd. **MEMBERSHIPS** ASA; SCS; IAMHIST. **RESEARCH** American film and its relationship to American culture. **SELECTED PUBLICATIONS** Auth, American Visions: The films of Chaplin, Ford, Capra and Welles, 1936-1941, 71; rev, ed, Frank Capra, 95; auth, Chaplin and American Culture: The Evolution of a Star Image, 89. **CONTACT ADDRESS** Dept English, Univ of Tennessee, Knoxville, 1345 Circle Park, Knoxville, TN 37996-0001.

MALIN, JO E.
PERSONAL Born 09/25/1942, St Louis, MO, 2 children **DISCIPLINE** WOMEN'S STUDIES **EDUCATION** Washington Univ, AB, 64; Ind Univ, MA, 68; Binghamton Univ, PhD, 95. **CAREER** Proj dir, coordinatory, assoc dir, Binghamton Univ, 97-. **MEMBERSHIPS** MLA, Autobiography Soc. **RESEARCH** Women's Autobiographies, Feminist Theory, Personal Narratives, Women and Solitude. **SELECTED PUBLICATIONS** Auth, "A Dissertation in Cyberspace," Education at a Distance, (97); auth, The Voice of the Mother: Embedded Maternal Narratives in Twentieth Century Women's Autobiographies, S Ill Univ Pr, 00; coed, HERSPACE: Women, Writing, Solitude, S Ill Univ Pr, forthcoming. **CONTACT ADDRESS** Scholars Prog, SUNY, Binghamton, PO Box 6000, Binghamton, NY 13902-6000.

MALM, WILLIAM P.
PERSONAL Born 03/06/1928, LaGrange, IL, m, 1954, 3 children **DISCIPLINE** ETHNOMUSICOLOGY **EDUCATION** Northwestern Univ, BA, 49, MM, 50; Univ Calif, Los Angeles, PhD, 59. **CAREER** Instr music, Univ Ill, 50-51; instr, US Naval Sch Music, 51-52; lectr, Univ Calif, Los Angeles, 57-60; from asst prof to assoc prof, 60-66, PROF MUSIC, UNIV MICH, ANN ARBOR, 66-94, Am Coun Learned Soc grant, 63; sr fel, Cult Learning Inst, EAst-West Ctr, Hawaii, 73; Ernest Bloch prof music, Univ Calif, Berkeley, 80; dir, Stearns Collection, 81-94; Univ of Haw, 00. **HONORS AND AWARDS** Henry Russel Awd, 65; Koizumi Fumio Prize, 93. **MEMBERSHIPS** Soc Ethnomusicol (pres, 77-79); Soc Asian Music; Asn Asian Studies; Int Folk Music Coun. **RESEARCH** Japanese music; holography; computer data banks in organology. **SELECTED PUBLICATIONS** Auth, Comparative Musicology and Anthropology of Music--Essays on the History of Ethnomusicology, Music and Letters, Vol 0074, 93; auth, Music Cultures of the Pacific, Near East and Asia, Prentice-Hall, 3rd ed, 96; auth, Japanese Traditional Music and Musical Instrument, Kodansua, 00. **CONTACT ADDRESS** 1530 Cedar Bend Dr, Ann Arbor, MI 48105. **EMAIL** malm@umich.edu

MALONE, MARTIN J.
PERSONAL Born 05/26/1950, New Brunswick, NJ, m, 1972, 2 children **DISCIPLINE** SOCIOLOGY **EDUCATION** NY Univ, BA, 72; S IL Univ, MA, 76; Ind Univ, PhD, 85. **CAREER** Asst prof to prof, Mount St. Mary's Col, 85-, chair, 95-. **HONORS AND AWARDS** ASA Grant; ACLS Grant, 81; Choice Outstanding Book of the Year. **MEMBERSHIPS** Am Sociol Assoc; Soc for the Study of Symbolic Interaction; Alpha Kappa Delta. **RESEARCH** Sociology of language, social theory, sociology of the body, sociology of emotions. **SELECTED PUBLICATIONS** Auth, "Small disagreements: Character contests and working consensus in informal talk", Symbolic Interaction 17 (94):107-27; coauth, "Conflicting demands in writing response groups", Writing Instr 14, (95):77-88; auth, "How to do things with friends: Altercasting and recipient design", Res on Lang and Social Interaction 28 (95):147-170; auth, "Semiotics" in The encyclopedia of cultural Anthrop, eds D. Levinson and M. Ember, Henry Holt (96):1150-54; auth, Worlds of Talk: the Presentation of Self in Everyday Conversation, London: Polity Pr, 97. **CONTACT ADDRESS** Dept Sociol, Mount Saint Mary's Col and Sem, 16300 Old Emmitsburg, Emmitsburg, MD 21727. **EMAIL** malone@msmary.edu

MALONEBEACH, EILEEN
DISCIPLINE GERONTOLOGY, FAMILY STUDIES **EDUCATION** Penn State Univ, PhD, 91. **CAREER** Asst prof, Univ Ala, 91-95; assoc prof, Central Mich Univ, 95-00. **MEMBER-**

SHIPS GSA, ASA, NCFR. **RESEARCH** Aging, Family Caregiving, Intergenerational Relations. **SELECTED PUBLICATIONS** Coauth, "Conflict, well-being and depression: Young adults in intergenerational caregiving and noncaregiving families," Korean J of Res in Gerontology 7 (98): 5-16; coauth, "Testing the fit between cognitively impaired elders and selected Video Respite Tapes," The J of Gerontological Nursing 25 (99): 17-21; coauth, "Making a place for young mothers in the university: Perspectives of professionals, young mothers, and university mothers," Mich J of Counseling and Development (99); coauth, "Home delivered mental health services for aged rural home health care recipients," J of Applied Gerontology (99); coauth, "Intergenerational solidarity: Norms, affection and association in caregiving and noncaregiving families," Korean j of Res in Gerontology 8 (99): 5-16; coauth, "Critical events in the Women's identity development: Lessons for the course in human development," Family Sci (00). **CONTACT ADDRESS** Dept of Human Environmental Studies, Central Michigan Univ, 220 Wightman Hall, Mount Pleasant, MI 48859. **EMAIL** e.malonebeach@cmich.edu

MALPASS, LESLIE FREDERICK
PERSONAL Born 05/16/1922, Hartford, CT, m, 1946, 4 children **DISCIPLINE** PSYCHOLOGY **EDUCATION** Syracuse Univ, BA, 47, MA, 49, PhD, 52. **CAREER** Asst to assoc prof, Southern Ill Univ, 52-60; visiting prof, Univ of Fla, 59-60; prof, chmn, Behavioral Sci, Univ of South Fla, 60-65; post-doctoral fel, UNC-Chapel Hill, 62-63; prof of Psychology, 65-74, 74-87, dean, Col of Arts & Sci, 65-68, VP, Acad Affairs, 68-74, Va Tech; pres emeritus, Western Ill Univ. **HONORS AND AWARDS** Honorary Doctorate in Humanities, Carl Sandburg Col, 74. **MEMBERSHIPS** Am Psychol Asn; Asn of Higher Ed; Nat Asn of State Univ/Land Grand Cols. **RESEARCH** Learning-bright, normal, retarded children (awards from Kennedy Found and more). **SELECTED PUBLICATIONS** Auth, nine books and 30-plus scholarly articles including: Individual Behavior, McGraw-Hill, 65; Social Behavior, McGraw-Hill, 66; Chapter 19, Handbook of Mental Deficiency, McGraw-Hill; What's Past is Prologue, Western Ill Univ Press, 88. **CONTACT ADDRESS** 4 Garber Ct, Durham, NC 27705. **EMAIL** lesswinn@aol.com

MAMALI, CATALIN
PERSONAL Born 11/10/1945, Bucharest, Romania, m, 1970 **DISCIPLINE** PSYCHOLOGY **EDUCATION** Univ Bucharest, MS, 68; PhD, 76. **CAREER** Asst prof, Institutul Politchnic Bucuresti, 75-81; assoc prof, Kirkwood community col, 92-93; prof, Mount Mercy Col, 93-94; prof, St. Francis Univ, 96-97; prof, Loras Col, 96-. **HONORS AND AWARDS** Ful Fel, Univ Iowa, 90-90. **MEMBERSHIPS** Am Psychol Soc, Intl Network for Personal Relationships, European Asn of Experimental Soc Psychol, Soc for the Psychol Study of Soc Issues, Soc of Reversal Psychol, Soc for Personality and Soc Psychol. **RESEARCH** Motivation, Interpersonal cognitive processes (interpersonal understanding, social maps, networks, the dialectic observer/observed), Dynamics of questioning and answering processes during the life-span development, Interpersonal communication (mainly the epistolary behavior), Participative techniques in psycho-social research, Non-violent values, attitudes, behaviors, Narrative psychology. **SELECTED PUBLICATIONS** Auth, The Gandhian Mode of Becoming, Gujarat Vidyapith: Ahmedabad, 98; auth, "Interpersonal relationships in totalitarian societies," Communication in Personal Relationships Across Cultures, New Delhi, 96; auth, "Correspondence et dialogue virtuel," La Lettre a La Croissee de L'Individuel et du social, Paris, 94; auth, "The societal issues: a dynamic transdisciplinary field," European Bulletin of social Psychology, (99): 11-13; auth, "Manifeste sincornice and celebrari anapoda," Psihologia Sociala, Buletinul Laboratorului de Psihologie Sociala, (98): 148-153. **CONTACT ADDRESS** Dept Psychol, Loras Col, 1450 Alta Vista St, Dubuque, IA 52001.

MANEKER, JERRY S.
PERSONAL Born 04/12/1940, New York, NY, m, 1962, 2 children **DISCIPLINE** SOCIOLOGY **EDUCATION** New York Univ, BA; MA; PhD. **CAREER** Prof, Cal State Univ, Chico, 70-. **MEMBERSHIPS** ASA; PSA. **RESEARCH** Religion; deviant behavior. **SELECTED PUBLICATIONS** Auth, "Understanding Christianity: Biblical Studies for Effective Living, Sociological Essays (http://www.csuchico.edu/~jmaneker/) **CONTACT ADDRESS** Dept Sociology, California State Univ, Chico, 400 West 1st Street, Chico, CA 95929-0001.

MANES, AVERELL
PERSONAL Born 08/06/1961, Syracuse, NY, s **DISCIPLINE** SOCIOLOGY **EDUCATION** McGill Univ, BA, 83; Syracuse Univ, MA, 86; PhD, 91. **CAREER** Adj Asst Prof and Instr, Syracuse Univ, 85-91; Asst Prof, Wash St Univ, 91-93; From Assoc Prof to Prof, Western Ct St Univ, 93-. **HONORS AND AWARDS** Prof of the Year, Arts and Sci, 97; Res Grant, Western Ct St Univ, 98; Travel Grant, Western Ct St Univ, 00. **MEMBERSHIPS** AAUP, AAUW, APSA, CREN, CPRE, CES, NACM, NIDR, SPDR. **RESEARCH** Comparative politics, world governments, economies and cultures, comparative communist systems, Russian government and politics, conflict resolution. **SELECTED PUBLICATIONS** Coauth, "The Use of Mediation on the Great Peace March," Breakthrough (94); auth, "The Pieds-noirs: A case Study in the Persistence of Subcultural Distinctiveness," UP of Am, 99; auth, "Managing Emotion in Conflict," forthcoming. **CONTACT ADDRESS** Dept Sociol, Western Connecticut State Univ, 181 White St, Danbury, CT 06810. **EMAIL** manes@wcsu.ctstateu.edu

MANNING, CHRISTEL
PERSONAL Born 11/11/1961, Long Beach, CA, m **DISCIPLINE** SOCIOLOGY OF RELIGION **EDUCATION** Tufts Univ, BA, economics (Magna cum laude), 84; Univ CA, Santa Barbara, MA, relig studies, 91, PhD, relig studies, 95. **CAREER** Teacher, Social Studies, Noble and Greenough School, 86-89; lect, Elderhostel, Santa Barbara, 94; instr, dept of philos and relig, Hollins Col, 94-95; Asst Prof, Dept of Philos and Religious Studies, Sacred Heart Univ, 95-. **HONORS AND AWARDS** Omnicron Delta Epsilon (Int Honor Soc in Economics), 84; Phi Beta Kappa, 84; Distinguished Scholars fel, 89-90; CA State grad fel, 91-92, 92-93; nominated for UCSB Outstanding Teaching Asst Awd, 94; Thomas O'Day Awd for the Study of Religion and Soc, 94; Soc for the Scientific Study of Religion, Res Awd, 94. **MEMBERSHIPS** Am Academy Relig; Asn for Soc of Relig; Soc for the Scientific Study of Relig, Nat prog chair, 97; Governing Coun of SSSR, 99. **RESEARCH** Gender and religion; fundamentalism; new religions. **SELECTED PUBLICATIONS** Auth, Review of Margaret Lamberts Bendroth, Fundamentalism and Gender, J for the Scientific Study of Religion 33.3, 94; Cultural Conflicts and Identity: Second Generation Hispanic Catholics in the United States, with Wade Clark Roof, Social Compass, 94; Embracing Jesus and the Goddess: Towards a Reconceptualizing of Conversion to Syncretistic Religion, in Magical Religion and Modern Witchcraft, ed by James Lewis, State Univ NY Press, 95; Review of Miriam Therese Winter, Defecting in Place: Women Claiming Responsibility for Their Own Spiritual Lives, J for the Scientific Study of Relig, 96; Women in a Divided Church: Liberal and Conservative Catholic Women Negotiate Changing Gender Roles, Sociology of Relig, 97; Review of Martin Marty & Scott Appleby, Fundamentalisms Comprehended, Review of Relig Res, 97; Women in New Religious Movements, in Encyclopedia of Women and World Religions, ed by Serinity Young, Macmillan, forthcoming, 98; Return to Mother Nature: The Politics of Paganism in America and Western Europe, in The Encyclopedia of Politics and Religion, ed by Robert Wuthnow, Congressional Quart Books, forthcoming, 98; God Gave Us the Right: Conservative Catholic, Evangelical Protestant, and Orthodox Jewish Women Grappel with Feminism, Rutgers Univ Press, 99; Conversations Among Women: Gender as a Bridge between Religious and Ideological Cultures, in Reflexive Ethnography: Remembering for Whom We Speak, ed by Lewis Carter, JAI Press, forthcoming, 99; auth, Sex & Religion, forthcoming, 02. **CONTACT ADDRESS** Dept Philos & Relig Studies, Sacred Heart Univ, 5151 Park Ave., Fairfield, CT 06432. **EMAIL** manningc@sacredheart.edu

MANNING, JEAN BELL
PERSONAL Born 08/14/1937, LaMarque, TX, m **DISCIPLINE** EDUCATION **EDUCATION** Bishop Col, BA (hon student Valedictoria Scholarship) 1958; Univ of N Tex, MEd 1964, EDd 1970. **CAREER** Douglas HS Ardmore OK, instr 1958-60; Reading Lab Jarvis Coll Hawkins TX; instr & dir 1961-64; TX So Univ Houston, vis prof 1964-65; Douglas HS OK, instr 1964-65, 65-67; Univ of Liberia, Liberia, W Africa, prof of English 1973-74; Paul Quinn Col Waco TX, chmn dept educ 1970-73, 74-78; Langston Univ OK, assoc prof/dir resources 1978-86, vice pres for acad affairs 1986-. **HONORS AND AWARDS** Women of the Year in Waco, Tex, 78, and by the Langston/Coyle BPW, 98 **MEMBERSHIPS** Nat Asn of Deans and Registrars; NEA; Phi Delta Kappa; NAACP; Nat Prog Coordr of the Links, Inc; Alpha Kappa Alpha; Who's Who in Am Higher Educ, Who's Who in Black Am; Outstanding African Am Women. **CONTACT ADDRESS** Langston Univ, PO Box 907, Langston, OK 73050.

MANNING, PETER K.
PERSONAL Born 09/27/1940, Salem, OR, d, 3 children **DISCIPLINE** SOCIOLOGY **CAREER** Vis Prof, Univ Victoria, 68, Portland State Univ, 76, Purdue Univ, 77, SUNY Albany, 82, MIT Sloan Sch, 82, Univ Mich, 93. **HONORS AND AWARDS** Pi Gamma Mu Soc Sci Hon; NDEA Fellow, Duke Univ, 62-64; NSF Summer Fellow, Duke, 63, 64; Alumni Citiation, Williamette Univ, 81; Vis Fellow, Wolfson Col, Oxford, 81, 82; Fellow, Balliol Col, Oxford, 82-83; Res Fellow, Wolfson Col, Oxford, 84-86; Beto Lecturer, Sam Houston State Univ, 90; Bruce W Smith Awd, ACJS, 94; OW Wilson Awd, ACJS, 97. **CONTACT ADDRESS** Dept Sociol, Michigan State Univ, 201 Berkey Hall, East Lansing, MI 48824-1111.

MANTYH, MARK R.
PERSONAL Born 10/04/1947, Milwaukee, WI **DISCIPLINE** SOCIOLOGY **EDUCATION** Univ Wis, BA, 82; MA, 89, PhD, 94. **CAREER** Assoc lectr, Univ of Wisc, 93; assoc lectr, Marquette Univ, 93-94; lectr, Univ of Wis Milwaukee, 94-. **MEMBERSHIPS** Midwest Sociol Soc; Wis Sociol Assoc. **RESEARCH** Social Change, Third World Development, Social Movements, Criminology, Juvenile Delinquency, Urban Sociology, Organizations. **SELECTED PUBLICATIONS** Auth, The Bureaucratization of Indigent Defense, Urban Res Center, Univ of Wis, 94; auth, "Political Process and the Creation of the Office of State Public Defender in Wisconsin", Sociol Imagination, (Winter 97); auth, "Development Dilemmas Associated With Dependency: The Case of Jamaica", Sociol Imagination (Spring 98). **CONTACT ADDRESS** Dept Sociol, Univ of Wisconsin, Milwaukee, PO Box 413, Milwaukee, WI 53201.

MARCUS, PAUL
PERSONAL Born 02/26/1953, New York, NY, m, 1987, 2 children **DISCIPLINE** CLINICAL PSYCHOLOGY **EDUCATION** Univ London, PhD, 80. **CAREER** Psychologist and psychoanalyst. **MEMBERSHIPS** APA, Amer Col of Forensic Psychology. **RESEARCH** Trauma, Ethnic conflict, Child custody. **SELECTED PUBLICATIONS** Auth, Autonomy in the Extreme Situation: Bruno Bettelheim, the Nazi Concentration Camps and the Mass Society, Praeger, 98; Co-ed, Psychoanalytic Versions of the Human Condition: Philosophies of Life and Their Impact on Practice, New York Univ, 98. **CONTACT ADDRESS** 115 Wooleys Ln, Great Neck, NY 11023.

MARGOLIS, GARY
PERSONAL Born 05/24/1945, Great Falls, MT, m, 1975, 2 children **DISCIPLINE** SOCIOLOGY **EDUCATION** Middlebury College, BA; SUNY Buffalo, PhD. **CAREER** Middlebury College, assoc prof, dir Cen for Counseling and Human Rel. **HONORS AND AWARDS** Robert Frost Fell; VT Counc Arts Gnt; Bread Loaf Winter's Conf. **SELECTED PUBLICATIONS** Auth, The Day We Still Stand Here Falling Awake, in: College Student Psychotherapy: Dev Opportunities. **CONTACT ADDRESS** Carr Hall, Middlebury Col, Middlebury, VT 05753. **EMAIL** margolis@middlebury.edu

MARGOLIS, MAXINE LUANNA
PERSONAL Born 08/02/1942, New York, NY, m, 1970, 1 child **DISCIPLINE** ANTHROPOLOGY **EDUCATION** New York Univ, BA, 64; Columbia Univ, PhD, 70. **CAREER** ASST PROF, 70-74, ASSOC PROF, 74-83, PROF, 84-, UNIV OF FL, 84. **HONORS AND AWARDS** Fulbright Senior Res/Lectr, Rio de Janeiro, 97. **MEMBERSHIPS** Am Anthropological Asn; Latin Am Studies Asn. **RESEARCH** Gender roles; transnational migration; Brazilian immigrants. **SELECTED PUBLICATIONS** Auth, Little Brazil: An Ethnography of Brazilian Immigrants in New York City, Princeton Univ Press, 94; auth, An Invisible Minority: Brazilian Immigrants in New Yo rk City, Allyn & Bacon, 98; auth, Brazilians and the 1990 United States Census: Immigrants, Ethnicity and the Undercount, Human Org, 95; auth, Transnationalism and Popular Culture: The Case of Brazilian Immigrants in the United States, J of Popular Culture, 95; auth, Brazilians, Encycl of Am Immigrant Cultures, Macmillan, 97; auth, "We Are Not Immigrants: Contested Categories Among Brazilians in New York City and Rio de Janeiro," General Anthropology Division, Am Anthropological Asn, 98; co-ed, Science, Materialism, and the Study of Culture: Readings in Cultural Materialism, Univ Pres of FL; auth, True to Her Nature: Changing Advice to American Women, Waveland Press, 00; auth, "Some Political Dimensions of Transnationalism: The Brazilian Case, Network, 00. **CONTACT ADDRESS** Dept of Anthropology, Univ of Florida, PO Box 117305, Gainesville, FL 32611. **EMAIL** maxinem@anthro.ufl.edu

MARIOTTI, ARLEEN
DISCIPLINE READING, LANGUAGE ARTS AND EDUCATIONAL MEASUREMENT **EDUCATION** Univ FL, BA, 70, MEd, 71; Univ S FL, PhD, 82. **CAREER** Assoc prof, Univ of Tampa. **MEMBERSHIPS** Phi Delta Kappa; Kappa Delta Pi. **SELECTED PUBLICATIONS** Coauth, text Linking Reading Assessment to Instruction: An Application Worktext for Elementary Classroom Teachers, 2nd ed, 97. **CONTACT ADDRESS** Dept of Educ, Univ of Tampa, 401 W. Kennedy Blvd, Tampa, FL 33606-1490.

MARKERT, JOHN P.
PERSONAL Born 11/04/1945, Lancaster, PA, m, 1980 **DISCIPLINE** SOCIOLOGY **EDUCATION** Univ S Fla, MA, 75; MA, 79; Vanderbilt Univ, MA, 83; PhD, 84. **CAREER** Founder/exec dir, Alternative Human Services, 69-74; dir soc services, Medfield Psychiatric ctr, 74-81; principal/ sr. consult, The Markert Res Group, 85-90; assoc prof, Cumberland Univ, 90-. **MEMBERSHIPS** Am Sociol Asn, Southern Sociol Asn. **RESEARCH** Medici Social Issues. **SELECTED PUBLICATIONS** Auth, "Pornography," in Encyclopedia of Contemporary Social Issues (Marshal Cavandish Corp, 95), 1234-1238; auth, "Parental Assessment of Education: Research Insights," Educ Forum 62.2 (97): 153-159; auth, "Sexual Harassment and the Communication Conundrum," Gender Issues Volume 17 (99): 34-52; auth, "Installing Circuit Breakers: Mechanisms to Avoid Sexual Harassment in the Workplace," Sociol Practice: A J of Clinical and Applied Sociol Volume 1 (99): 19-43; auth, "Sing a Song of Drug Use-Abuse: Drug Lyrics in Popular Music--From the Sixties through the Nineties," Sociol Inquiry (forthcoming). **CONTACT ADDRESS** Dept Sociol, Cumberland Univ, 1 Cumberland Square, Lebanon, TN 37087. **EMAIL** jmarkert@bellsouth.net

MARKIDES, KYRIACOS
PERSONAL Born 11/19/1942, Nicosia, Cyprus, m, 1972, 2 children **DISCIPLINE** SOCIOLOGY **EDUCATION** Youngstown Univ, BS, 64; Bowling Green State Univ, MA, 66; Wayne State Univ, PhD, 70. **CAREER** Asst prof, Univ Maine, 72-77, assoc prof, 77-85, prof, 85-. **MEMBERSHIPS** Am Sociol Asn. **RESEARCH** Religion, and peace. **SELECTED PUBLICATIONS** Auth, The Rise and Fall of the Cyrus Republic, New Haven: Yale Univ Press (77); auth, The Magnus of Strovolos: The Extraordinary World of a Spiritual Healer, London: Routledge & Kegan Paul (85), republished by Penguin; auth, Homage to the Sun: The Wisdom of the Magnus of Strovolos, London: Routledge & Kegan Paul (87), republished by Penguin; auth, Fire in the Heart: Healers, Sages and Mystics, New York: Paragon House (90), republished by Penguin; auth, Riding With the Lion: In Search of Mystical Christianity, New York: Viking (95), Penguin (96). **CONTACT ADDRESS** Dept Sociol, Univ of Maine, Orono, ME 04469-0001. **EMAIL** markides@maine.edu

MARKLEY, ROBERT
PERSONAL Born 12/06/1940, Los Angeles, CA, m, 1964, 2 children **DISCIPLINE** PSYCHOLOGY **EDUCATION** Redlands Univ, AB, 62; Univ Alberta, MSc, 65; PhD, 70. **CAREER** Instructor, Tex Christian Univ, 67-70; Asst Prof to Prof, Fort Hays State Univ, 70-. **MEMBERSHIPS** APA; APS, Psychonomic Sco. **CONTACT ADDRESS** Dept Psychol, Fort Hays State Univ, 600 Park St, Hays, KS 67601. **EMAIL** rmarkley@fhsu.edu

MARKOFF, JOHN
PERSONAL Born 03/19/1942, New York, NY, m, 1995, 1 child **DISCIPLINE** SOCIOLOGY **EDUCATION** Columbia Col, BA, 62; Johns Hopkins, PhD, 72. **CAREER** Prof, sociol, hist, polit sci, Univ Pittsburgh. **HONORS AND AWARDS** Pinkney Prize, Soc for Fr Hist Stud, 97, 99; co-winner Sharlin Prize, Soc Sci Hist Asn; Distinguished Scholarly Pub Award, Am Sociol Asn; election to Sociol Res Asn; Chancellor's Distinguished Res Award, Univ of Pittsburgh. **RESEARCH** Social movements; democracy; French Revolution. **SELECTED PUBLICATIONS** Coauth, Democrats and Technocrats: professional Economists and Regime Transitions in Latin America, in Can J of Develop Stud, 93; auth, Frontier Societies, in Encycl of Soc Hist, 94; auth, Violence, Emancipation and Democracy: The Countryside and the French Revolution, in Am Hist Rev, 95; auth, The Great Wave of Democracy in Historical Perspective, Cornell Univ, 95; auth, Waves of Democracy: Social Movements and Political Change, Pine Forge Pr, 96; auth, The Abolition of Feudalism: Peasants, Lords and Legislators in The French Revolution, Penn St Univ Pr, 97; auth, Peasants Help Destroy an Old Regime and Defy a New One: Lessons from (and for) the Study of Social Movements, in Am J of Sociol, 97; auth, Really Existing Democracy: Latin America in the 1990s, New Left Review, 97; coauth with Shapiro, Revolutionary Demands: A Content Analysis of the Cahiers de Doleances of 1789, Stanford, 98; auth, "Where and When Was Democracy Invented"?, Comparative Studies in Soc and Hist 41, 99. **CONTACT ADDRESS** Dept of Sociology, Univ of Pittsburgh, Pittsburgh, PA 15260. **EMAIL** jm2@pitt.edu

MARKOVSKY, BARRY
PERSONAL Born 04/03/1956, Framingham, MA, m, 1987, 1 child **DISCIPLINE** SOCIOLOGY **EDUCATION** Univ MA, BA, 78; Stanford Univ, PhD, 83. **CAREER** Asst Prof to Prof, Univ IA, 83-. **HONORS AND AWARDS** Scholar Awd, Univ IA, 94-98; Nat Sci Foundation Fel, OH State Univ, 90; Exceptional Teachng Awd, Univ IA, 89-9; Fel, Nat Inst of Mental Health, Stanford Univ, 88-89; Old Gold Jr Fel, Univ IA, 84, 85, 87; Nat Res Service Awd, Stanford Univ, 83; Nat Sci Foundation Fel, 78-81; Phi Beta Kappa, 78. **MEMBERSHIPS** Am Sociol Asn; Intl Network for Social Network Analysis; Skeptics Soc. **RESEARCH** Small group processes (status, power, justice, decision-making), Social networks; Social judgment; Social perceptions; Computer simulation; Social/psychophysiology; Theoretical methods. **SELECTED PUBLICATIONS** Co-ed, Advances in Group Processes, Vol 11, JAI Press, 94; co-ed, Advances in Group Processes, Vol 12, JAI Press, 95; co-ed, Advances in Group Processes, Vol 13, JAI Press, 96; co-ed, Advances in Group Processes, Vol 14, JAI Press, 97; co-auth, "Evaluating heterodox theories," Social Forces, (97): 511-525; co-auth, "Power and influence: a theoretical bridge," Social Forces, (97): 571-603; co-auth, "Power in exchange networks: critique of a new theory," American Sociological Review, (97): 833-837; auth, "Social network conceptions of group solidarity," in The Problem of Solidarity, Gordon and Breach, 98; co-auth, "Group processes and IQ," American Journal of Sociology, (98): 195-228; co-auth, "An automated approach to theoretical analysis of difficult problems," in Network Exchange Theory, Greenwood Pub, 99. **CONTACT ADDRESS** Dept Sociol, The Univ of Iowa, Iowa City, IA 52242-1401. **EMAIL** barry-markovsky@uiowa.edu

MARLOWE, FRANK
PERSONAL Born 04/17/1954 **DISCIPLINE** ANTHROPOLOGY **EDUCATION** Univ Texas, BA, 78; Univ Calif at Los Angeles, MA, 84; MFA, 87; PhD, 97. **CAREER** Archeo, CAS, 78-79; instr, writ, IIS, 80-81; film mkr, Univ Calif, Los Angeles, 81-87; assoc prof, West Coast Univ, 87-96; lectr, Univ Calif, Los Angeles, 97-98; lectr, Cal State Univ, 97-98; lectr, Univ California SB, 98; asst prof, Harvard Univ, 98-. **HONORS AND AWARDS** Jack Nicholson Scnwting Awd, 85; Sam Goldwyn Scnwting Awd, 86; David L Wolper Flm Awd, 87; NSF Gnt 96, 99; Leakey Found Gnt; Diss Fel; Macarthur Found Gnt; HBESC Postdoc Awd. **MEMBERSHIPS** HBES; AAA. **RESEARCH** Hunter-gatherers; behavioral ecology; mating system. **SELECTED PUBLICATIONS** Auth, " Why the Hadza are still hunter-gatherers," in Ethnicity, Hunter-gatherers, and the "Other": Association or Assimilation?, ed. S Kent, in press; auth, The evolution of morality, Zygon, in press; auth, "The patriarch hypothesis: An alternative explanation of menopause,: Hum Nat 11 (00):27-42; auth, "Showoffs or providers?: The parenting effort of Hadza men," Evol Hum Behav 20 (99): 391-404; auth, Sharing among Hadza hunter-gatherers, Evol Coop, in press; auth, Paternal care and the human mating system, Behav Processes, in press; coauth, Preferred waist-to-hip ratio and ecology, Person Indiv Diff, in press; auth, Dictators and ultimatums in an egalitarian society of hunter-gatherers, the Hadza of Tanzania, Exper Econ Trad Soc, in press; coauth, "Hunter-gatherer divorce rates and the paternal investment theory of human pair-bonding," in Human Behavior Adaptation: An Anthropological Perspective, eds. L Cronk, N Chagnon, W Irons (NY: Elsevier, in press) **CONTACT ADDRESS** Dept Anthropology, Harvard Univ, 11 Divinity Ave, Peabody Museum, Cambridge, MA 02138. **EMAIL** fmarlowe@fas.harvard.edu

MARRIOTT, MC KIM
PERSONAL Born 02/01/1924, St Louis, MO, w, 1946, 4 children **DISCIPLINE** ANTHROPOLOGY **EDUCATION** Univ Chicago, PhD, 55. **CAREER** Teaching Asst, Univ Chicago, 49-50; Res Asst, Univ Calif, 53-55; From Asst Prof to Prof, Univ Chicago, 55-. **HONORS AND AWARDS** Nat Scholar, Harvard Univ, 41-43; Fel, Ctr for Advanced Study in the Behav Sci, 61-62; LJ & HM Quantrell Awd for Excellence in Undergrad Teaching, Univ Chicago, 63; Lewis Henry Morgan Lect, Univ Rochester, 67; RP Chanda Centenary Medalist, the Asiatic Soc, 97. **MEMBERSHIPS** Am Coun of Learned Soc and Soc Sci Res, Am Anthrop Assoc, Royal Anthrop Soc of Gr Brit & Ireland, Am Assoc for the Advancement of Sci, Assoc for Asian Studies. **RESEARCH** Society and culture of civilians. **SELECTED PUBLICATIONS** Auth, The Feast of Love," in Krishna: Myths, Rites and Attitudes (Honolulu: East-West Ctr Pr, 66), 200-212; coauth, "Caste Systems," Encycl Britannica Macropaedia, 3 (74): 982-991; auth, "Constructing an Indian Ethnosociology," Contributions to Indian Soc, 25 (89): 1-39; ed, India Through Hindu Categories, Sage Publ (London, UK), 90; auth, "India Without Hindu Categories" j of the Am Orient Soc, 118 (98): 377-380; auth, "The Female Family Core Explored Ethnosociologically," Contributions to Indian Soc, 32 (98): 279-304. **CONTACT ADDRESS** Dept Anthrop, Univ of Chicago, 1126 E 59th St, Chicago, IL 60637. **EMAIL** mmarriot@midway.uchicago.edu

MARSH, CLIFTON
PERSONAL Born 07/10/1946, Los Angeles, CA, d, 1 child **DISCIPLINE** SOCIOLOGY, AFRICAN AMERICAN STUDIES **EDUCATION** Calif State Univ, Long Beach, BA; MA; Syracuse Univ NY, PhD. **CAREER** Prof, Calif State Univ Long Beach, Univ of Va, Va Commonwealth Univ, Va Union Col, Col of NJ, SUNY, Univ of the Virgin Islands, Morris Brown Univ. **HONORS AND AWARDS** Dean's Awd for Outstanding Scholar and Res; Res Awd, Bureau of Libr, Museums and Archeol Serv; NEH. **MEMBERSHIPS** Am Sociol Assoc; Nat Counc of Black Studies; Southern Sociol Assoc. **RESEARCH** The Nation of Islam, Social Movements, Homelessness, Domestic Violence, Sexual Assault, Caribbean Studies. **SELECTED PUBLICATIONS** Auth, Hartford County Homeless and Shelter Survey, Housing and Shelter in a Community in Transition, Univ Pr of Am, 66; auth, The Danish Virgin Islands: A Socio-Historical Analysis of the Emancipation of 1848 and the Labor Revolt of 1878; Wyndham Hall Pr, 84; auth, From Black Muslims to Muslims: The Transition from Separatism to Islam. 1930-1980, Scarecrow Pr, 85. **CONTACT ADDRESS** Dept Soc Sci, Morris Brown Col, 643 Martin Luther King Dr NW, Atlanta, GA 30314-4140.

MARSHALL, ALICIA A.
DISCIPLINE HEALTH COMMUNICATION **EDUCATION** Purdue Univ, PhD. **CAREER** Asst prof, Texas A&M Univ. **HONORS AND AWARDS** National Inst Health grant; US Army Dept grant. **SELECTED PUBLICATIONS** Publ in, Health Commun; Commun Monographs; Acad Med; J Gen Internal Med; contribur, Health Communication and the Disenfranchised; Integrated Approaches to Communication Theory and Research; Case Studies in Health Communication. **CONTACT ADDRESS** Dept of Speech Communication, Texas A&M Univ, Col Station, College Station, TX 77843-4234.

MARSHALL, LINDA
PERSONAL Born 05/07/1949, Amarillo, TX, m, 1995, 1 child **DISCIPLINE** SOCIOLOGY, SOCIAL WORK **EDUCATION** Tex Tech Univ, BA; Univ Tex at Arlington, MSSW, 80; Tex Womens Univ, PhD, 93. **CAREER** Protective Serv Worker, Adoption Worker, Tex Dept Human Resources, 72-75; Instr, Coun Women's Prog, Amarillo Col, 80-81; Asst Prof, W Tex State Univ, 81-86; Vis Asst Prof, Univ of Tex at Arlington, 91-92; Prog Dir, Soc Work Prog, Univ of Tex at Arlington, 95-; Asst Prof, Univ of Tex at Arlington, 92-. **HONORS AND AWARDS** Robert Touluse Scholar, Outstanding Grad Student; Soc Worker of the Year, Amarillo NASW, 86. **MEMBERSHIPS** NASW, BPD, CSWE, Southwestern Soc Sci Asn, Licensed Soc Worker Tex. **RESEARCH** Domestic Violence. **SELECTED PUBLICATIONS** Auth, The Protective Order Experience, Cummings & Hataway Publ, 00. **CONTACT ADDRESS** Dept Sociol and Soc Work, Texas Woman's Univ, PO Box 415887, Denton, TX 76204. **EMAIL** F_2Marshall@twu.edu

MARSHALL, SUZANNE G.
PERSONAL Born 11/18/1947, Augusta, GA, m, 1973, 3 children **DISCIPLINE** WOMENS STUDIES **EDUCATION** Univ Ga, BS; Okla State Univ, MS; UCLA, MA; PhD **CAREER** Assoc Prof, Calif State Univ, 87-. **HONORS AND AWARDS** Advancement to Candidacy Awd, Univ CA, 96-97. **MEMBERSHIPS** ITAA; AAFCS. **RESEARCH** Women's leadership. **SELECTED PUBLICATIONS** Auth, "Apparel retail sales training: A comparisons by store type," Monument CO, 95; auth, "Her way: Leading companies, creating cultures," Proceeding, Monument CO, 96; auth, "Their way: Leading companies, influencing culture" Dissertation Abstracts International, 97; auth, Instructor's Manual": Individuality in clothing selection and personal appearance: A guide for the Consumer 5th ed, Prentice hall, 00; co-auth, Individuality in clothing selection and personal appearance: A guide for the Consumer, Prentice Hall, 00. **CONTACT ADDRESS** Dept Family & Consumer Sci, California State Univ, Long Beach, 1250 N Bellflower, Long Beach, CA 90840-0001.

MARSHALL-BRADLEY, TINA
PERSONAL Born 03/24/1962, Ft Dix, NJ, m, 1983, 2 children **DISCIPLINE** EDUCATION **EDUCATION** Col Charl, BS, 83; Nova SE Univ, MS, 87; Iowa State Univ, PhD, 92. **CAREER** Teach, Bam HS, 83-85; adj instr, Daytona Beach CC, 87-89; adj instr, Bethel CC, 86-89; tech, Volusia PS, 85-89; dir, ISMEP, 89-92; acad adv, Iowa State Univ, 89-92; asst prof, Nor State Univ, 92-95; asst prof, S Car State Univ, 95-99; asst prof, Citadel, 99-. **HONORS AND AWARDS** ASEE Fac Fel; Fulbright Fel; USDA Gnt; CDF Gnt; Gov Dist Prof Awd; Teach of Year, 98; Profess Ser Awd; ASEE Fel; Who's Who in Edu; Outstand Yg Women Am, 94. **MEMBERSHIPS** MDI; USSC; UGECC; NSF; MWS; MITYC; EMSP; AACTE; ASCD; NCATE; Phi Delta Kappa. **SELECTED PUBLICATIONS** Coauth, Can teacher educators effect eternity too? J Vir Asn Teach Edu (93); coauth, "Starting from ground zero: Integrating technology in education programs," Soc Info Tech Teach Edu 9 (98): 52-55; coauth, "A theoretical analysis of effective education programs," Teach Edu J SC (99): 86-88. **CONTACT ADDRESS** Dept Education, The Citadel, The Military Col of So Carolina, 171 Moultrie St, Charleston, SC 29409.

MARSHOOD, NABIL
PERSONAL Born 10/30/1950, Israel, m, 1976, 2 children **DISCIPLINE** SOCIOLOGY **EDUCATION** Hebrew Univ, BA, 73; MA, 77; Columbia Univ, PhD, 87. **CAREER** From Assc Prof to Prof, Hudson County Community Col, 86-. **HONORS AND AWARDS** US Inst for Peace Grant; NJ Coun for the Humanities: Relig Pluralism Grant; Fac Senate Excellence Awd, Hudson County Community Col. **MEMBERSHIPS** Nat Soc Sci Asn, Am Sociol Asn. **RESEARCH** Culture, religion, rare ethnic relations (sociological perspective). **SELECTED PUBLICATIONS** Auth, "Aspects of the Rehabilitation of Handicapped Persons in East Jerusalem," Soc Security 22 (81): 92-98; coauth, "Ethics Differential in Foster Care Placement," Soc Work Res and Abstracts 19-3 (83): 41-45; auth, "Community Adjustment of Chronic Psychiatric Patients: Dropouts vs. non-Dropouts," Soc Work Res and Abstracts 23-3 (87): 336; auth, "Assessment of Field Placement," ERIC #JC930363 (93); rev, "Psychology, Adjustment, and Everyday Living," (93); co-ed, The Sociological Outlook: A Text with Readings, by Reid Luhman (Collegiate Press, 97); auth, "Community College Administration and Faculty Scholarship: A Pilot Study," Community Col Rev 23-1 (95): 51-62; auth, Palestinian Teenage Refugees and Immigrants Speak Out, Rosen Publ Group, 97; rev, of "Race, Ethnicity, Gender, and Class: The Sociology of Group Conflict and Change," by Joseph F. Healey (98), coauth, Everyday Sociology, Star Point Press, 98. **CONTACT ADDRESS** Dept Soc Sci, Hudson County Comm Col, 25 Journal Sq, Jersey City, NJ 07306. **EMAIL** marshoodn@aol.com

MARSON, STEPHEN
PERSONAL Born 03/02/1951, Columbus, OH, m, 1982, 1 child **DISCIPLINE** SOCIOLOGY **EDUCATION** Ohio Dominican Col, BA, 74; Ohio State Univ, MSW, 76; NC State Univ, PhD, 91. **CAREER** Intake, Alcoholic Rehab Unit St Anthony Hospital, 74-76; Case manager, Vita Treatment Center, 76-77; Instr, Pembroke State Univ, 77-80; Private Practice, 78-; Asst Prof to Assoc Prof, Pembroke state Univ, 80-96; Prof and Dir of Soc Work Prog, Univ NC, 96-. **HONORS AND AWARDS** Certificate of appreciation, UNCP's campus Asn, 98; Outstanding Young Men of Am, 97; Certificate of appreciation, Nat Asn of soc Workers, 97; Honor Soc of agriculture, 83;

Intl Sociol Honor soc, 82. **MEMBERSHIPS** Acad of Certified Soc Workers, Am Sociol Asn, Asn of Baccalaureate Soc Work Program Dir, Certified Master Soc Work, Coun on Soc Work Educ, Nat Asn of Soc Workers, Nat Committee Gerontology in Soc Work Educ, Nat Org of Forensic Soc Work, Rural Soc Work Caucus, Sex Information and Educ Coun, Soc for the Sci Study of Sex, Sociol Grad Student Asn, Soc of Soc Work and Res, Southern Gerontology Soc. **RESEARCH** Technology, Gerontology, Human Sexuality, Law. **SELECTED PUBLICATIONS** Co-auth, "Ethical interaction in cyberspace for social work practice," Advances in Social Work, in press; co-auth, "The social/demographic dimensions of misidentification: Implications for social work and law," the Journal of Law and Social Work, in press; auth, "Uncovering UnCover," The New Social Worker, (9): 23-24, 28; auth, "Major uses of the Internet for social workers: a brief report for new users," Arete, (98): 21-28; co-auth, "A selective history of the Internet technology and social work," Computer in Human Services, (97): 35-49; co-auth, "The first social worker," The New Social Worker, (96): 11; co-auth, "Therapy on the Internet: Current Trends and Implications, Part III," North Carolina Social Worker Newsletter, (96): 2,6-7; co-auth, "Therapy on the Internet: Confidentiality as a misnomer, Part II," North Carolina Social Worker Newsletter, (96): 2, 6-7; co-auth, "Therapy on the Internet: Internet culture and values, Part I," North Carolina Social Worker Newsletter, (96): 2, 7. **CONTACT ADDRESS** Dept Sociol, Univ of No Carolina, Pembroke, PO Box 1510, Pembroke, NC 28372.

MARTASIAN, PAULA J.
PERSONAL Born 04/25/1959, Providence, RI, m, 1987, 2 children **DISCIPLINE** PSYCHOLOGY **EDUCATION** Univ RI, BA, 81; MA, 88; PhD, 89. **HONORS AND AWARDS** N Eng Psychol Asn Fel, RI, 81; Carpenter's Prize, Univ RI, 81; Suma Cum Laude, Phi Kappa Phi, Kappa Delta Pi Psychol Club Advisor Apprec Awd, 99; Fac Recognition Awd for Teaching Excellence, 98; Honors Prof Apprec Cert, 96. **MEMBERSHIPS** Am Psychol Asn, Am Psychol Soc, Foundation for Biomedical Res. **RESEARCH** Psychology of Learning, Teaching of Psychology. **SELECTED PUBLICATIONS** Auth, "Students' beliefs about animal researchers as a function of Researcher's Gender," Psychological Reports, (97): 803-811; auth, "A preliminary resolution of the retention of distributed vs. massed response prevention in rats," Psychological Reports, (93): 1367-1377; auth, "Retention of massed vs. distributed response prevention treatments in rats and a revised training procedure," Psychological Reports, (92): 339-355; auth, "Handicap parking: The social reasons for its abuse," Journal of Police and Criminal Psychology, (90): 23-25; auth, Test item bank for statistical reasoning for behavioral sciences, Allyn & Bacon: Boston, 96. **CONTACT ADDRESS** Dept Psychol, Salve Regina Univ, 100 Ochre Point Ave, Newport, RI 02840. **EMAIL** martasip@alve.edu

MARTHALER, BERARD LAWRENCE
PERSONAL Born 05/01/1927, Chicago Heights, IL **DISCIPLINE** RELIGIOUS EDUCATION **EDUCATION** Pontif Fac Theol, San Bonaventura, Rome, STL, 52, STD, 53; Univ Minn, MA, 56, PhD(ancient hist), 68. **CAREER** Instr church hist, Assumption Sem, 53-61; asst prof theol, Bellarmine Col, Ky, 61-63; asst prof relig educ, 63-67, assoc prof and head dept, 67-72, pres, 74-75, Prof Relig Educ, Cath Univ Am, 73, Chmn Dept, 74-. Exec ed, the Living Light, 72-; Prof Emeritus, Cath Univ am, 98-. **HONORS AND AWARDS** Professed member of Order Affairs, Minor Conventual Ordained Rome, 52; Benemerenti from Pope John Paul II, 88; Johannes Quasten Medal, 98. **MEMBERSHIPS** Col Theol Soc (vpres, 68-70); Am Acad Relig; Asn Prof and Researchers Relig Educ (pres, 74-75); Cath Theol Soc Am; Relig Educ Asn. **RESEARCH** Religious education as socialization. **SELECTED PUBLICATIONS** Auth, The Creed: The Apostolic faith in Contemporary Theology, 93; auth, The Catechism Yesterday and Today: The Evolution of a Genre, 95. **CONTACT ADDRESS** Dept of Relig and Relig Educ, Catholic Univ of America, Washington, DC 20064.

MARTIN, JANE ROLAND
PERSONAL Born 07/20/1929, New York, NY, m, 1962, 2 children **DISCIPLINE** PHILOSOPHY, EDUCATION **EDUCATION** Radcliffe Col, AB, 51; Harvard Univ, M Ed, 56; Radcliffe Col, PhD, 61. **CAREER** From assoc prof philos to prof emerita, Univ MA, Boston, 72-. **HONORS AND AWARDS** Hon doct: Univ of Umea, Sweden; Salem St Univ, MA; Guggenheim fel, 87; NSF, 84; Bunting, inst fel, 81. **MEMBERSHIPS** APA; Philos of Ed Soc; Soc for Women in Philos; Am Ed Res Asn. **RESEARCH** Philos of ed; feminist theory and philos. **SELECTED PUBLICATIONS** Auth, Reclaiming a Conversation: The Ideal of the Educated Woman, Yale Univ Press, 85; auth, Science in a Different Style, Am Philos Quart, 25, 88; auth, Idealogical Critique and the Philosophy of Science, Philos of Science, 56, 89; auth, The Schoolhome: Rethinking Schools for Changing Families, Harvard Univ Press, 92; auth, Changing the Educational Landscape: Philosophy, Women, and Curriculum, Routledge, 94; auth, Methodological Essentialism, False Difference, and Other Dangerous Traps, Signs, 19, 94; auth, Aerial Distance, Esotericism, and Other Closely Related Traps, Signs, 21, 96; auth, Bound for the Promised Land: the Gendered Character of Higher Education, Duke J of Gender Law & Pol, 4, 97; auth, Coming of Age in Academe: Rekindling Women's Hopes and Reforming the Academy, Raitledge, 00. **CONTACT ADDRESS** 8 Gerry's Landing Rd, Cambridge, MA 02138. **EMAIL** mlmartin@bu.edu

MARTIN, MICHAEL T.
PERSONAL Born 09/13/1947, New York, NY, 1 child **DISCIPLINE** PSYCHOLOGY **EDUCATION** CUNY, BA, 70; Columbia Univ, MA, 71; EdM, 72; Univ Mass, PhD, 79. **CAREER** Instr, Kans State Univ, 79; Asst Prof, Univ Washington, 79-81; Prof and Chair, Calif State Univ, 83-89; Vis Prof, Princeton Univ, 85-88; Prof, Wayne State Univ, 90-97. **HONORS AND AWARDS** LASA Awd of Merit, Latin Am Studies Asn, 89; Mellon foundation Grant, Princeton Univ, 90; President's Bonus Awd, Wayne State Univ, 93; Fac Res Grant, Bowling Green State Univ. **RESEARCH** Race/ethnic and Diaspora studies; Film studies; Sociology of development; Transnational migration; Documentary video production. **SELECTED PUBLICATIONS** Ed, New Latin American Cinema. Vol I: Theory, Practices, and Transcontinental articulations, Wayne State Univ press, 97; ed, New Latin American Cinema. Vol II: Studies of National Cinemas, Wayne State Univ press, 97; ed, Cinemas of the Black Diaspora: Diversity, Dependence and Oppositionality, Wayne State Univ Press, 95; ed, Studies of Development and Change in the Modern World, Oxford Univ Press, 89; auth, "Fortress Europe and Third World Immigration in the Post-Cold War Global Context," Third World Quarterly, (99): 821-837; auth, "The Unfinished Social Practice of the New Latin American Cinema: Introductory Notes," in The New Latin American Cinema: Origins, Trajectory and Development, Wayne State Univ Press, 97; auth, "Filmmaking, the State, and Social Relations in Brazil: An Interview with Suzana Amaral," in The New Latin American Cinema: Origins, Trajectory and Development, Wayne State Univ, 97; auth, "Framing the Black in Black Diasporic Cinemas," in Cinemas of the Black Diaspora: Diversity, Dependence, and Oppositionality, Wayne State Univ Press, 95. **CONTACT ADDRESS** Dept Ethnic Studies, Bowling Green State Univ, 1001 E Wooster St, Bowling Green, OH 43403-0001. **EMAIL** mtmart@bgnet.bgsu.edu

MARTIN, RANDY
DISCIPLINE SOCIOLOGY; POLICY STUDIES **EDUCATION** Univ Calif Berkeley, BA, 79; Univ Wis Madison, MS, 80; CUNY Grad Cen, PhD, 84. **CAREER** Asst prof to assoc prof to prof to dept chmn, Pratt Inst, 89-00; prof to assoc dean, NYork Univ Sch Arts, 00-. **HONORS AND AWARDS** Inst Prof, Distinguished Teacher, 94; HRI Fel, Univ Calif, 93. **MEMBERSHIPS** Co-ed, Social Text, ed col, 84-; co-ed, Socialism and Democracy, 90-98. **RESEARCH** Writing a book, Financialization of Daily Life for Temple UP. **SELECTED PUBLICATIONS** Auth, Performance or Political Art: The Embodied Self, Bergen/Garvey, 90; auth, Socialist Ensembles: Theater and State in Cuba and Nicaragua, Minn UP, 94; auth, On Your Marx: Relinking Socialism and the Left, Univ Minn Pr, 01; auth, Critical Mover: Dance Standing in Theory and Politics, Duke UP, 98; ed, Chalk Lines: The Politics Of Work in the Managed University, Duke UP, 99; co-ed, Sportcult, Minn UP, 99; co-ed, "Globalization?" Soc Text (99). **CONTACT ADDRESS** Sch of Art, New York Univ, 721 Broadway, New York, NY 10003. **EMAIL** randy.martin@nyu.edu

MARTINEZ, ELIZABETH COONROD
PERSONAL Born 06/03/1954, Austin, TX **DISCIPLINE** LATIN AMERICAN LITERATURE & CULTURE **EDUCATION** Portland State Univ, 83 BA; NYork Univ, MA, 91; Univ NM in Albuquerque, PhD, 95. **CAREER** Journalist; prof, Mod Langs & Lits, Sonoma St Univ. **HONORS AND AWARDS** Poynter Institute Summer Fel for Journalism Teachers, 95; SSU Summer Res Fel, 98, 99; NEH Summer Institute on "The Maya World", 00. **MEMBERSHIPS** MLA, AATSP, NACCS, Letras Femeninas, MALCS. **RESEARCH** 20th century and colonial Latin Am narrative, indigenous studies, cultural and gender studies. **SELECTED PUBLICATIONS** Auth, Henry Cisneros: Mexican-American Leader, 93; Sor Juana Ines de la Cruz: A Trail-blazing Thinker, 93; Edward James Olmos: Mexican-American Actor, 94; Coming to America: The Mexican-American Experience, 95; auth, "Before the Boom: Latin Am Revolutionary Novels of the 1920s," Lanham, MD: Univ Press of Am, 01. **CONTACT ADDRESS** Dept of Modern Lang & Lit, Sonoma State Univ, 1801 E. Cotati Ave., Rohnert Park, CA 94928-3609. **EMAIL** elizabeth.martinez@sonoma.edu

MARTINEZ, JACQUELINE M.
DISCIPLINE SEMIOTICS, PHENOMENOLOGY, FEMINIST THEORY, INTERCULTURAL COMMUNICATION **EDUCATION** Southern Ill Univ, PhD, 92. **CAREER** Asst prof, Purdue Univ. **SELECTED PUBLICATIONS** Auth, Radical Ambiguities and the Chicana Lesbian; Body Topographies on Contested Lands, in Spoils of War: Women of Color, Cultures, Revolutions, 97; coauth, Signifying Harassment: Communication, Ambiguity, and Power, Human Stud, 95. **CONTACT ADDRESS** Dept of Commun, Purdue Univ, West Lafayette, 1080 Schleman Hall, West Lafayette, IN 47907-1080. **EMAIL** martinez@purdue.edu

MARTINEZ, THOMAS
PERSONAL Born 12/01/1949, Pomona, CA, m, 1973, 3 children **DISCIPLINE** PSYCHOLOGY **EDUCATION** Mount San Antonio Jr Col, AA, 70; Calif State Univ, BA, 72; MS, 73; Univ Mich, MA, 76; PhD, 79. **CAREER** Prof, Pepperdine Univ, 77-; Director of Latino Services, San Fernando Valley Community Mental health Center, 79-85; Exec Director, El Centro de Amistad, Inc, 85-96; Instr, Cambridge Grad School, 89; Grad Program Director, Pepperdine Univ, 83-86; Director of Program Development, el Centro de Amistad Inc, 96-. **HONORS AND AWARDS** Opportunity Awd Fel, Univ Mich, 72-74; Ford Foundation Fel, Univ Mich, 74-77; Recognition for Service, Congressman Gary Hart, 90. **MEMBERSHIPS** Wellness Foundation Cancer Support Project, Latino Children Coalition, Los Angeles Commission for Children, Youth and Families, Mexican-American Educ Commission, Nat Asn of Hispanic Psychol, Coalition of Spanish Speaking Mental Health and Human Services Org, Ethnic Minority Mental Health Task Force, Nat Coun of Schools of Professional Psychol. **SELECTED PUBLICATIONS** Auth, Family Violence with Latino Families, Los Angeles, 96; auth, "The Relationship Between Violence, Social Support, and Self Blame in Battered Women," Journal of Interpersonal Violence, (96): 221-223; auth, Children's Issues: Health/Mental health, 96; auth, "Jealousy and Romantic Attachment in Maritally Violent and Nonviolent Men," Journal of Interpersonal Violence, (95): 473-486. **CONTACT ADDRESS** Dept Soc Sci, Pepperdine Univ, 24255 Pacific Co Hwy, Malibu, CA 90263. **EMAIL** Martinez@pepperdine.edu

MARX, JONATHAN I.
PERSONAL Born 12/27/1959, m, 1984, 2 children **DISCIPLINE** SOCIOLOGY **EDUCATION** Emory Univ, BA; MA, 82; Indiana Univ, PhD, 89. **CAREER** Assoc prof, Winthrop Univ, 89-. **HONORS AND AWARDS** High Honors Magna Cum Laude; Outstand Jr Prof, Winthrop Univ, 94-95; Phi Kappa Phi Outstand Teach Awd, 96-97. **RESEARCH** Education, gift exchange. **SELECTED PUBLICATIONS** Coauth, Grandmother's House We Go: Health and School Adjustment of Children Raised Solely By Grandparents, The Gerontologist 35 (95), 386-394; coauth, Day-Care and the Incidence of Otitis Media in Young Children, Otolaryngology--Head and Neck Surgery (95), 695-699; auth, Mona Lisa, Mona Lisa Men Have Named You: Smiles as Social Facts, Teaching Sociology vol 23 (95), 274-279; coauth, ""Successful Job Search and Informal Networks," in Women and Work: A Reader, eds. Paula J Dubeck and Kathryn Borman (New Brunswick: Rutgers Univ Press, 97), 312-314; coauth, "The Consequences of Informal Job Finding for Men and Women," Acad Management Rev vol 40, (97): 967-987; coauth, "Moving On: Residential Mobility and Children's School Lives," Sociology of Education, vol 71 (98): 111-129; coauth, "The Grandparent Grandchild Caregiving Gradient: Hours of caring for Grandchildren and its Relationship to Grandparent Health" The Southwestern J on Aging, vol 14, no 2 (98): 31-39; coauth, "The Physical, Mental, and Social Health of Custodial Grandparents," in Grandparenting Raising Grandchildren: Theoretical, Empirical, and Clinical Perspectives, eds. Robin Goldberg-Glen, Bert Hayslip, Jr. (Thousand Oaks, CA, Springer Press, 99); coauth, "Physical Health of Custodial Grandparents," in To Grandmother's House We Go and Stay: The Issues, Needs, and Policy Affecting Grandparents Raising Grandchildren, ed. Carol Cox (Thousand Oaks, CA, Springer Press, 99); coauth, "Who Cares? Grandparenting/Grandchild Households," J Women and Aging (99): vol 11, issue 1. **CONTACT ADDRESS** Dept Sociology, Winthrop Univ, 701 W Oakland Ave, Rock Hill, SC 29733-0001. **EMAIL** marxj@winthrop.edu

MASI, DALE A.
PERSONAL Born, NY, m **DISCIPLINE** SOCIAL WORK **EDUCATION** Cath Univ, DSW, 65; Post Doctoral, AAUN. **CAREER** Ad Prof/Prof, Univ of Md. **HONORS AND AWARDS** Rhoda Saran Awd Int Soc Work; Alumna of the Year, Mt St. Vincent, 91; Fulbright Scholar to Hong Kong and Italy. **MEMBERSHIPS** NASW, EAPA, EASNA, Fulbright Asn. **RESEARCH** Employee Assistance Evaluation. **SELECTED PUBLICATIONS** Coauth, "Selecting a Substance Abuse Professional," MRO Update (Apr 95): 1-3; coauth, "The Role of A Payor Advisory Board in Managed Mental Health Care: The IBM Approach," Admin and Policy in Mental health 22-6 (July 95): 581-595; auth, "The Evaluation of Employee Assistance Programs (EAPs) and Its Application to Managed Behavioral Care," in Employee Assistance Practice in Twenty-first Century, ed. Nan Van Den Bergh (NY: Springer Press, 95); ed, International Employee Assistance Anthology, Performance Resource Press (Detroit, MI), 96; auth, "Evaluation of Employee Assistance Programs (EAPS)," Res on Soc Work Practice 7-3 (July 97): 378-390; auth, "The Role of Employee Assistance Programs in Managed Behavioral Healthcare," in Technical Assistance Series of the Center for Health Serv on Managed Behav Healthcare, SAMHSA, US Public Health Serv, US Dept of Health and Human Serv (Feb 98); auth, Shrink to Fit, Health Commun Inc (Deerfiled Beach, FL), 98; auth, Productivity Lost: Alcohol and Drugs in the Workplace, LRP Publ (Palm Beach, FL), 99; coauth, "Utilization of Telephone and Face-to-Face Consultation," Employee Assistance Res Supplement; coauth, "Quantifying Quality: Findings From Clinical Reviews," Employee Assistance Quart (Fall 01). **CONTACT ADDRESS** Dept Soc Work, Univ of Maryland, Baltimore, 525 W Redwood St, Baltimore, MD 21201. **EMAIL** Masi.Rsrch@aol.com

MASON, DONNA S.
PERSONAL Born 01/15/1947, Mount Vernon, NY, m, 1973 **DISCIPLINE** EDUCATION **EDUCATION** Howard Univ, BA, 1969, MEd, 1972; Univ of Maryland, Colllege Park, AGS, 1975, PhD, 1987. **CAREER** District of Columbia Public Schools, classroom teacher, building resource teacher, computer camp teacher, computer curriculum writer, computer teacher trainer, computer education instructor/lab coordinator, 69-. **HONORS AND AWARDS** Electronic Learning's, Educator of the Decade, 10 Who Made A Difference Awd, 1991; Washington Post, Agnes Meyer Outstanding Teacher Awd, 1991; Learning Magazine/Oldsmobile, Professional Best Teacher Excellence Awd, 1991; Apple Computer, Thanks to Teachers Awd, 1990; Business Week, Awd for Innovative Teaching, 1990; University of MD Distinguished Alumni Awd, 1995; Freedom Foundation at Valley Forge Awd, 1995. **MEMBERSHIPS** Maryland Instructional Computer Coordinators Assn; Univ of Maryland Alumni Assn; International Society for Technology in Education; Special Interest Group for Computing Coordinators. **SELECTED PUBLICATIONS** US Office of Education, Christa McAuliffe Fellowship, 1988, 1994; IBM/Classroom Computer Learning, Teacher of the Year for the District of Columbia, 1988; The Cafritz Foundation, Cafritz Foundation Teacher Fellowship, 1988; The Washington Post, The Washington Post Mini-Grant Award, 1986; "A Teacher's Place To Work and Learn," Teaching & Computers 1986; "Multimedia Applications in the Curriculum: Are Schools Preparing Students for the 21st Century?" NASSP Curriculum Report, 1997; "Display Word Processing Terms" The Computing Teacher, 1986; "Ten Computers-One Thousand Students" Sigcc Bulletin for Computing Coordinators, 1987; "Factors that Influence Computer Laboratory Use in Exemplary Junior High/Middle schools in the District of Columbia" UMI's Dissertation Abstracts, 1988. **CONTACT ADDRESS** Alice Deal Junior High Sch, Fort Drive & Nebraska Ave, NW, Room 201, Washington, VT 20016-1886.

MASQUELIER, ADELINE M.
PERSONAL Born 07/06/1960, Mulhouse, France, d, 3 children **DISCIPLINE** ANTHROPOLOGY **EDUCATION** Univ NC, Chapel Hill, BA, 80; S.I.U., Carbondale, MA, 84; Univ Chicago, PhD, 93. **CAREER** Instr, Univ of Chicago, 90-91; vis asst prof, Notre Dame, 93; asst prof, Tulane Univ, 93-98, assoc prof, 99-. **HONORS AND AWARDS** Univ Tuition Fel, Univ of Chicago, 85-87; U. S. Dept of Educ Fel, 87; summer fel, Tulane Univ Comt on Res, 94; Tulane Lilly Endowment Teaching Fel, 94-95; Tulane Univ Newcomb Found Grants, 94, 95, 96, 98, 99; Grant from the Cultural Services of the French Embassy in the United States in collaboration with Gaurav Desai and Madeline Dobie, 98. **MEMBERSHIPS** African Studies Asn, Am Ethnological Asn, Am Anthropol Asn. **RESEARCH** Sub-Saharan cultures and history; issues of gender; medicine and religion in Africa. **SELECTED PUBLICATIONS** Auth, "Tied Bodies, Lost Money: A Moral Physiology of Power, Production, and Consumption," in Africa und das Andere: Alteritat und Innovation, Albert Wirz and Heike Schmidt, eds, Muenster and Hamburg: Lit Verlag (98); auth, "The Medium is the Message: Teaching Africa Through Music, " in Great Ideas for Teaching About Africa, Misty L. Bastian and Jane Parpart, eds, Boulder, Colo: Lynne Rienner Pubs (99); auth, "The Invention of the Anti-Tradition: Dodo Spirits in Southern Niger," in Spirit Possession, Modernity, and Power in Africa, Heinke Behrend and Uta Luig, eds, Madison, Wisc: Univ of Wisc Press (99); auth, "Debating Muslims, Disputing Practices: Struggles for the Realization of an Alternative Moral Order in Niger," in Civil Soc and the Political Imagination in Africa: Critical Perspectives, John L. and Jean Comaroff, eds, Chicago: Univ of Chicago Press (99); auth, "Hausa States," in Encarta Africana, Kwame Anthony Appiah and Henry Louis Gates, Jr, eds, Microsoft Corp (99); auth, " 'Money and Serpents: Their Remedy is Killing', The Pathology of Consumption in the Mawri Imagination," Cultural Anthropol, 15, 1 (2000): 1-45; auth, "Prayer Has Spoiled Everything": Possession, Power, and Identity in an Islamic Town of Niger, Durham, NC: Duke Univ Press (forthcoming). **CONTACT ADDRESS** Dept Anthropol, Tulane Univ, 1021 Audubon St, New Orleans, LA 70118. **EMAIL** amasquel@mailhost.tcs.tulane.edu

MATHER, PATRICIA L.
PERSONAL Born Glen Ridge, NJ **DISCIPLINE** PSYCHOLOGY **EDUCATION** Univ Iowa, BA, 72; Purdue Univ, MS, 75; PhD, 79. **CAREER** Ten assoc prof, Utica Col, Syracuse Univ, 79-86; ten assoc prof, Northeaster Ill Univ, 86-90; priv prac, 89-95; assoc prof, Ill Cen Col, 95-. **HONORS AND AWARDS** Dist Teach Awd; Who's Who in Human Ser Prof, Am Women, Am Teach. **MEMBERSHIPS** AAWCC; APS; ACCH. **RESEARCH** At-risk college students; teaching techniques; effective communication between physicians and cancer patients. **SELECTED PUBLICATIONS** Rev of, "Take this book to the hospital with you: A consumer's guide to surviving your hospital stay," by C.B. Inlander & E. Weiner, Children's Health Care (88): 126-127; auth, "Educating preschoolers about health care," Childhood Edu (88): 94-100; coauth, "Genetic factors in the ontogeny of spoken language: Evidence from monozygotic and dizygotic twins," J Child Lang (89): 553-559; coauth, "Student workbook in early childhood education: Practicum and student teaching Manual used in senior practicum and student teaching seminars, Northeastern Ill Univ 89; coauth, "Therapeutic Play activities for hospitalized children," Mosby Year Book (St. Louis), 92; auth, "New year's resolutions," Family Business Relationships (93): 10-11. **CONTACT ADDRESS** Dept Social Science, Illinois Central Col, 1 College Dr, Peoria, IL 61635-0002.

MATHES, EUGENE W.
PERSONAL Born 10/11/1941, Pella, IA, m, 1985, 3 children **DISCIPLINE** PSYCHOLOGY **EDUCATION** Central Col, BA, 66; IA State Univ, MS, 68; PhD, 73. **CAREER** Prof, W Ill Univ, 73-. **HONORS AND AWARDS** Teacher of the Year, Col of Arts & Sci, 98-99 **MEMBERSHIPS** Asn for Humanistic Psychol; Midwestern Psychol Asn; Soc for the Sci Study of Relig; Soc of the Sigma Xi. **RESEARCH** romantic love and jealousy **SELECTED PUBLICATIONS** Auth, "Jealousy and romantic love. A longitudinal study," Psychological Reports, (86): 885-886; co-auth, "Reik's complementarity theory of romantic love," The Journal of Social Psychology, (85): 321-328; co-auth, "Antiques: Does age enhance the value of an object?," Psychological Reports, (87): 957-958; auth, "The ultimate good: survival of the individual and society," Psychological Reports, (87): 1001-1002; auth, "Rational suicide: A test of the prescriptions of Epicurus concerning suicide," Psychological Reports, (90: 307-310; auth, "Dealing with romantic jealousy by finding a replacement relationship," Psychological Reports, (91): 1001-1102; auth, "a cognitive theory of jealousy," in The psychology of jealousy and envy, Guilford Press, 91; auth, Jealousy: The psychological data, Univ Press of Am, 92; auth, "Behavior genetics and a horse's show performance," Psychological Reports, (93): 530; co-auth, "Jealous aggression: Who is the target, the beloved or the rival?," Psychological Reports, (93): 1071-1074. **CONTACT ADDRESS** Dept Psychol, Western Illinois Univ, 1 University Circle, Macomb, IL 61455. **EMAIL** Eugene_Mathes@ccmail.wiu.edu

MATHEWS, GARY
PERSONAL Born 04/04/1944, Cincinnati, OH, s, 4 children **DISCIPLINE** SOCIAL WORK **EDUCATION** Univ Cincinnati, BA, 66; Wayne State Univ, MSW, 68; Western Mich Univ, PhD, 89. **CAREER** Prof, Western Mich Univ, 76-2000. **HONORS AND AWARDS** Who's Who; White House Conf on Families, 81; Bd of Dirs, Coun on Soc Work Ed, 92-94; managing ed, J of Sociol and Soc Welfare, 91-97. **MEMBERSHIPS** AAUP. **RESEARCH** Evaluation research. **SELECTED PUBLICATIONS** Guest ed with Thomas Holmes and Merl C. Hokenstad, Special Issue: International Mental Health, J of Sociol and Soc Welfare (June 91); coauth with William Brady, Dennis Heinonen, Robert Lathers, Danelle Pross, and Michael Schlinz, "Strategies and Techniques for the Home-Based Family Counselor: A Survey," Practice (fall 91): 1-4; coauth with Thomas Holmes, "Innovations in Cross-cultural Social Work Education," Arete, 18, 1 (93): 43-47; auth, "Social Workers and Political Influence," reprinted in Gonzalez-Ramos, Social Welfare Programs and Policies, Ginn Press (94); rev of Katherine Tyson's New Foundations for Scientific Social and Behavioral Research, in the J of Sociol and Soc Welfare, XXI, 4 (94): 177-178; auth of editorial, J of Sociol and Soc Welfare, XXII, 3 (94): 4; coauth with Kenneth Reid and Peggy Solow Liss, "My Partner is Hurting: Group Work With Male Partners of Adult Survivors of Sexual Abuse," Soc Work with Groups, 18, 1 (95); coauth with Michi Rose, "Internal Family Systems Therapy: Managing Personal Anger," Proceedings, Int Soc for the Systems Scis, APM, Budapest, Hungary (96); coauth with Reid and Liss, "My Partner is Hurting" in Galinsky and Schopler, eds, Support Groups: Current Perspectives on Theory and Practice, NY: Haworth Press (96); coauth with Susan Weinger and Marion Wijnberg, "Ethical Decision-Making in Field Education: Promise, Pretension, or Practice?" J of Sociol & Welfare, 24, 2 (97). **CONTACT ADDRESS** Dept Soc Work, Western Michigan Univ, 1201 Oliver St, Kalamazoo, MI 49008.

MATHEWS, SPENCER R.
PERSONAL Born 08/24/1939, Norfolk, VA, m, 1965, 2 children **DISCIPLINE** PSYCHOLOGY **EDUCATION** Univ Va, PhD, 67. **CAREER** Assoc Prof, Converse Col, 67-. **MEMBERSHIPS** SC Psychol Asn; SE Asn for Beh Analysis; Nat Asn of Scholars. **RESEARCH** Experimental Analysis of Behavior; Early Behavioral Intervention in Autism. **CONTACT ADDRESS** Sept Psychol, Converse Col, 580 E Main St, Spartanburg, SC 29302. **EMAIL** spencer.mathews@converse.edu

MATHIOT, MADELEINE
PERSONAL Born 06/11/1927, Saulxures-sur-Moselotte, France, m, 1960, 1 child **DISCIPLINE** LINGUISTICS, ANTHROPOLOGY **EDUCATION** Georgetown Univ, BS, 54, MS, 55; Cath Univ Am, PhD(anthrop), 66. **CAREER** Asst prof anthrop, Univ Calif, Los Angeles, 67-69; assoc prof ling, 69-74, Prof Ling & Anthrop, State Univ NY Buffalo, 74-, Dir, Ctr Studies Cult Transmission, 74- **MEMBERSHIPS** Am Anthrop Asn; Ling Soc Am; Semiotic Soc Am. **RESEARCH** Lexicology; ethnosemantics; face-to-face interaction. **SELECTED PUBLICATIONS** Auth, An Approach to the Cognitive Study of Language, 68 & A Papago Dictionary of Usage, vol 1, 73, vol 2, 78, Ind Univ; ed, Approaches to the Analysis of Face-to-Face Interaction, Semiotica, 78; Ethnolinguistics: Boas, Sapir, Whorf Revisited, Mouton, 79; A meaning based theory of face to face interaction, Int J Soc Ling (in prep). **CONTACT ADDRESS** Dept Ling, SUNY, Buffalo, Buffalo, NY 14260. **EMAIL** mathiotm@acsu.buffalo.edu

MATHURA, CLYDE
PERSONAL Born 02/05/1938, Tobago, Trinidad, d, 2 children **DISCIPLINE** PSYCHOLOGY **EDUCATION** Univ Miami, Coral Gables, BA, 70; Univ Nebr Lincoln, MA, 73; PhD, 75. **CAREER** Fac, Howard Univ Hosp; Chair of Psychology Dept, Coppin State Col; Dean of Arts and Sci, Coppin State Col. **RESEARCH** Developing Brain, Minority Mental Health. **SELECTED PUBLICATIONS** Coauth, "Frequency of Schizophrenia and Depression in Black, In-patient Population," J of the Nat Med Asn 72-9 (80): 851-856; coauth, "Phencyclidine (PCP): Effects of Serum Testosterone and Luteinizing Hormone Concentration in rats," Res Comm Sub Abuse 4-3 (83): 193-199; coauth, "Effects of Maternal Geophagia in Infants and Juvenile rats," J of the Nat Med Asn 75-9 (83): 895-902; coauth, "The Treatment of Multi-Cultural Patient Population," Hosp and Community Psychiat 35-4 (84): 372-376; coauth, "Effects of Chronic Trypthohan Loading on Serotonin Levels in Neonatal Rat Brain," J of Med Asn 78-7 (86): 654-647; coauth, "Improving the Relationship Between the White Psychotherapist and the Black Patient," in Monograph Ser, Howard Univ Press, 86; coauth, "Social Factors in Diagnosis and Treatment," in Handbook of Health and Mental Disorders Among Blacks in America, ed. Dorothy Ruiz (Wesport, Ct: Greenwood Press, 90); coauth, "Ethnic and Cultural Factors in Psychiatric Diagnosis and Treatment," in Handbook of Health and Mental Disorders Among Blacks in America, ed. Dorothy Ruiz (Wesport, Ct: Greenwood Press, 90); coauth, "Psychology," In Head and Neck Oncology: Diagnosis, Treatment, and Rehabilitation, ed. E.M. Myers (Mass: Little Brown & Co, 91); coauth, "Genetic Factors in Conditioned Tolerance to the Analgesic Effects of Etonitazene," Pharmacology, Biochemistry and Behav 45(93). **CONTACT ADDRESS** Dean, Arts and Sci, Coppin State Col, 2500 W N Ave, Baltimore, MD 21216. **EMAIL** cmathura@coppin.edu

MATTHEWS, G.
PERSONAL Born 07/02/1959, Edinburgh, United Kingdom, m, 1999 **DISCIPLINE** PSYCHOLOGY **EDUCATION** Univ Cambridge, England, BA, 80, PhD, 86. **CAREER** Lect, Aston Univ, 85-89; res fel, Univ of Wales Inst Sci & Technol, 84-85; Univ of Cincinnati, 86-. **HONORS AND AWARDS** Passingham Prize, 80; British Psychol Soc Book Awd, 98. **MEMBERSHIPS** Human Factors and Ergonomics Soc, Psychonomic Soc, Int Asn for Applied Psychol. **RESEARCH** Personality, stress, emotion, performance, cognitive science. **SELECTED PUBLICATIONS** Coauth with A. Wells, Attention and emotion: A clinical perspective, Hove: Erlbaum (94); ed, Cognitive science perspectives on personality and emotion, Amsterdam: Elksevier Sci (97); coauth with I. Deary, Personality traits, Cambridge: Cambridge Univ Press (98); auth, "Personality and skill: A cognitive-adaptive framework," in P. L. Ackerman P. C. Kyllonen and R. D. Roberts, eds, The future of learning and individual differences research: Processes, traits, and content, Washington, DC: Am Psychol Asn (99); coauth with K. Gilliland, "The personality theories of H. J. Eysenck and J. A. Gray: A comparative review," Personality and Individual Differences, 26 (99): 583-626; coauth with A.Wells, "The cognitive science of attention and emotion," in T. Dalgeish & M. Power, eds, Handbook of cognition and emotion, New York: Wiley (99); coauth with D. R. Davies and R. B. Stammers, Human performance: Cognition, stress and individual differences, London: Routledge (2000); auth, "Levels of transaction: A cognitive science framework for operator stress," in P. A. Hancock and P. A. Desmond, eds, Stress, workload and fatigue, Mahwah, NJ: Lawrence Erlbaum (2000); coauth with V. L. Schwean, S. E. Campbell, D. H. Saklofske, & A. A. R. Mohammed, "Personality, self-regulation and adaptation: A cognitive-social framework," in M. Boekarts, P. R. Pintrich & M. Zeidner, eds, Handbook of self-regulation, New York: Academic (2000); coauth with A. Wells, "Attention, automaticity and affective disorder," Behavior Modification, 24 (2000): 69-93. **CONTACT ADDRESS** Dept Psychol, Univ of Cincinnati, PO Box 210376, Cincinnati, OH 45221-0376. **EMAIL** matthegd@email.uc.edu

MATTHEWS, JACK
PERSONAL Born 06/17/1917, Winnipeg, MB, Canada, m, 1942, 2 children **DISCIPLINE** COMMUNICATION & PSYCHOLOGY **EDUCATION** Heidelberg, AB, 38; Ohio Univ, MA, 40, PhD, 46 **CAREER** Asst Dir, 46-48, Purdue Univ; Asst Prof, Prof, 48-88, Univ of Pittsburgh **HONORS AND AWARDS** Dr Sci, Heidelberg **MEMBERSHIPS** Am Phychol Assoc; Speech Assoc of Am **RESEARCH** Speech Pathology; Social Psychology **SELECTED PUBLICATIONS** Auth, The Speech Communications Process, Scott, Foresmans; The Emeritus Professor: Old Rank-New Meaning, George Washington U Press & ASHE; The Professions of Speech-Language Pathology in Human Communications Disorders, McMillan; Communication Disorders in the Mentally retarded, Appleton Century Crofts **CONTACT ADDRESS** Verona, PA 15147-3851. **EMAIL** jmatthws@pitt.edu

MATTIS, SARA
PERSONAL Born 04/10/1968, Providence, RI, m, 1996 **DISCIPLINE** PSYCHOLOGY **EDUCATION** Dartmouth Col, BA, 90; Va Polytech Inst and State Univ, MS, 93; PhD, 97. **CAREER** Res assoc and dir, Boston Univ, 96-98; staff psychol and admin, Dana Group Assoc, 98-99; clin psychol, private prac-

tice, 01-; res asst prof, Boston Univ, 97-. **HONORS AND AWARDS** Phi Beta Kappa; Finalist, Am Psychol Asn Section on Clin Child Psychol Stud Res Awd; FIRST Awd Grant, NIMH, 98. **MEMBERSHIPS** Am Psychol Asn; Asn for Adv of Beh Therapy; Anxiety Disorders Asn of Am; Mass Psychol Asn. **RESEARCH** The assessment and treatment of anxiety disorders in children and adolescents, with a particular emphasis on the prevalence, associated symptomatology, and treatment of panic in a young population. **SELECTED PUBLICATIONS** Co-auth, "Panic in children and adolescents: Normative and clinical studies," Australian Psychol, (94): 14-17; co-auth, "Panic in children and adolescents: A review," J of Child Psychol and Psychiat, (94): 113-134; co-auth, "Relationship between risk and protective factors, developmental outcome, and the home environment at 4 years-of-age in term and preterm infants," in Children in poverty: Research, health care, and policy issues, (Garland Press, 95), 197-227; co-auth, "Nonclinical panic attacks in adolescents: Prevalence, symptomatology, and associated features," Beh Change, (96): 171-183; co-auth, "Panic in children and adolescents: A developmental analysis," in Advances in clinical child psychology, (Plenum Press, 97), 27-74; co-auth, "Children's cognitive responses to the somatic symptoms of panic," J of Abnormal Child Psychol, (97): 47-57; co-auth, "A Developmental adaptation of panic control treatment for panic disorder in adolescence," Cognitive and Beh Practice, 900): 253-261; co-auth, "Nonclinical panic attacks in late adolescence: Prevalence and associated psychopathology," J of Anxiety Disorders, in press; co-auth, "Panic disorder and anxiety in adolescence," in Parent, adolescent, and child training skills series," Brit Psychol Soc, in press; co-auth, "School refusal and separation anxiety disorder," in Clinical behavior therapy: Adults and children, John Wiley & Sons, Inc, in press. **CONTACT ADDRESS** Dept Psychol, Boston Univ, 64 Cummington St, Boston, MA 02215. **EMAIL** smattis@bu.edu

MATTISON, WILLIAM H.
PERSONAL Born 01/16/1937, Aberdeen, MS, m, 1959, 2 children **DISCIPLINE** HISTORY, PSYCHOLOGY **EDUCATION** Itawamba Jr Col, AA, 56; Miss State Univ, BS, 58; M Ed, 61; MSS, 65; EDS, 67; Uniiv Sarasota, PhD, 71. **CAREER** Instr, Zama High School, 58-59; instr, Jane-Macon Jr High School, 59-63; instr, Amory Middle School; 63-64; dir, Amory city School; 64-71; dir, Itawamba Community Col, 71-79; instr, Itawamba Community Col, 79-. **HONORS AND AWARDS** DAR Hist Nat Awd. **MEMBERSHIPS** Miss Hist Soc; MAE; NEA; Monroe County Hist Soc; Patriotic Order Sons of Am; Sons of Confederate Veterans; Sons of Am Revolution; Bonnie Blue Soc; Mil Order of Stars and Bars, Amory Fine Arts Coun. **RESEARCH** Regional/local history in the areas of Civil War, Revolutionary War, Railroad History, Native-American History. **CONTACT ADDRESS** Dept Soc Sci, Itawamba Comm Col, 602 W Hill St, Fulton, MS 38843-1022.

MAUSER, AUGUST J.
PERSONAL Born 06/01/1936, Valparaiso, IN, m, 1980, 2 children **DISCIPLINE** EDUCATION **EDUCATION** Ind State Univ, BS, 58; Ind Univ, MA, 62; PhD, 68. **CAREER** Asst Prof, Ind Univ, 64-68; Assoc Prof, Ind State Univ, 68-72; Prof, Northern Ill Univ, 72-81; Prof and Chair, Univ S Fla, 81-. **HONORS AND AWARDS** Outstanding Young Men in Am Awd, US Jaycees, 71; Outstanding Young Hoosier Educ Awd, IN Jaycees, 70-71; Caleb Mills Distinguished Teaching Awd, IN State Univ, 72; Golden Services Awd, WCGS, 96. **MEMBERSHIPS** CEC; CLD; CCBD; CASE; MR; TED; TAG; LDA/ACLD; Orton Dyslexia Soc; Nat Asn of Gifted Children; Soc for Learning Disabilities; TASH; IRA; ATE; PEN. **RESEARCH** Career Choice influences on special education; Parents of pre-K handicapped children's perceptions of professionals; Managing disruptive children in the schools. **CONTACT ADDRESS** Dept Spec Educ, Univ of So Florida, 4202 Fowler Ave, Tampa, FL 33620. **EMAIL** mauser@tempest.coedu.usf.edu

MAUSS, ARMAND
PERSONAL Born 06/05/1928, Salt Lake City, UT, m, 1951, 8 children **DISCIPLINE** HISTORY; SOCIOLOGY **EDUCATION** Sophia Univ, Tokyo, BA, 54; Univ CA Berkeley, MA, 57, PhD, 70. **CAREER** Inst, 63-67, Diablo Valley coll; assoc prof, 67-69, Utah State Univ; prof, 69-99, Washington State Univ. **HONORS AND AWARDS** Ed, Journal for the Scientific Study of Religion, 89-92; pres, Mormon History Assn, 97-98; Chipman Awd for best book (MHA), 94; Arrington Career Awd, (MHA), 94. **MEMBERSHIPS** Soc for the Scientific Study of Religion; Assn for the Sociology of Religion; Religion Research Assn; Mormon History Assn; Mormon Social Science Assn. **RESEARCH** Sociology of Religion; deviant behavior and social problems **SELECTED PUBLICATIONS** Auth, Neither White nor Black: Mormon Scholars Confront the Race Issue in a Universal Church, Signature Books, Salt Lk City, 84; The Angel and the Beehive: The Mormon Struggle with Assimilation, Univ of Ill Press, 94; Marketing for Miracles: Mormonism in the Twenty-First Century, Dialogue: A Journal of Mormon Thought, Spring 96; The Impact Of Feminism and Religious Involvement on Sentiment toward God, Review of Religious Research, March 96; In Search of Ephraim: Tradition Mormon Conceptions of Lineage and Race, Journal of Mormon History, Spring 99. **CONTACT ADDRESS** 7 Springwater, Irvine, CA 92604-4660. **EMAIL** almauss@home.com

MAXWELL, DAVID LOWELL
DISCIPLINE ANATOMY AND PHYSIOLOGY OF SPEECH AND HEARING **EDUCATION** Southern IL Univ, BS, MS, PhD. **CAREER** Emerson Col. **MEMBERSHIPS** Boston Naval Hosp; Depart Behav Neurology Eunice Kennedy Shriver Ctr, Mass Gener Hospital; Craniofacial Study Gp; Harvard Med Sch; Boston Univ Medic Sch; Boston Univ Grad Sch Dental Med; Instit Correction Facial Deformities; Univ Hospital; New England Med Ctr; Cognitive Behav Assessment Unit Douglas Thom Clinic. **SELECTED PUBLICATIONS** Auth, Research and Statistical Meghods in Communication Disorders, Maxwell & Satake, 97; Theory of Probability for Clinical Diagnostic Testing, Satake & Maxwell, 93. **CONTACT ADDRESS** Emerson Col, 100 Beacon Street, Boston, MA 02116-1596.

MAY, JILL P.
PERSONAL Born 08/23/1943, Rocky Ford, CO, m, 1967, 2 children **DISCIPLINE** CHILDREN'S LITERATURE, LIBRARY EDUCATION **EDUCATION** Wis State Univ-Eau Claire, BA, 65, Univ Wis-Madison, Msls, 66. **CAREER** Vis asst prof, 70-75, asst prof, 75-82, assoc prof, 82-91, prof, Children's Lit, Purdue Univ, 91- ; **HONORS AND AWARDS** Nat Endowment for the Humanities, Ind Libr Asn, 79; ed, Ind Libraries: A Quart J, 80-82; Pub Ch, Children's Lit Asn, 83-89; vpres, Children's Lit Asn, 88-89; Mod Lang Asn, Children's Lit Div Ch, 87-88. **MEMBERSHIPS** Children's Lit Asn; MLA; NCTE; Col Engl Asn. **RESEARCH** Historical children's literature; film in children's literature; minority children's literature. **SELECTED PUBLICATIONS** Auth, Feminism and Childrens Literature, Fitting 'Little Women' Into the American Literary Canon, Cea Critic, vol 0056, 94; auth, Children's Literature and Critical Theory: Reading and Writing for Understanding, Oxford Univ Pr, 95; auth, Theory and Textual Interpretation--Childrens Literature and Literary Criticism, J Midwest Mod Lang Asn, vol 0030, 97. **CONTACT ADDRESS** Lit & Lang Dept, Purdue Univ, West Lafayette, 4168 LAEB, West Lafayette, IN 47907-1968. **EMAIL** jillmay@purdue.edu

MAYERS, MARVIN K.
PERSONAL Born 10/25/1927, Canton, OH, m, 1952, 2 children **DISCIPLINE** ANTHROPOLOGY, LINGUISTICS **EDUCATION** Wheaton Col, BA, 49; Fuller Theol Sem, Mdiv, 52; Univ Chicago, MA, 58; PhD, 60. **CAREER** Field Dir, Bd of Dir, SIL Calif, 60-61; Field Res in Ling and Soc Anthrop, SIL, Guatemala, Caif, 53-65; Prof, Wheaton Col, 65-74; Chair, Dept of Sociol and Anthrop, Wheaton Col, 68-74; Adj Prof, Univ of Tex Arlington, 74-82; Dir, Tex SIL Dallas, 76-82; Assoc Coordr for Res in Anthrop in the Inst of Ling Tex, 89-93; Prof/Prof Emeritus, Biola Univ, 82-89, 92-; Founding Dean, Dean Emeritus, Grad Sch of Intercultural Studies, Biola Univ, Calif, 83-89, 92-. **HONORS AND AWARDS** NSF Grant, 58; OAS Grant, 59-60; Teacher of the Year, Wheaton Col, 67; Christianity Confronts Culture named among 30 most significant books in Protestant Christian Mission, 96; Who's Who in Am Educ, 80-. **MEMBERSHIPS** Am Anthrop Asn. **RESEARCH** Latin America, Cross-Cultural Communication. **SELECTED PUBLICATIONS** Auth, Pocomchi Texts, The Univ of Okla and SIL (Norman, OK), 58; ed, Languages of Guatemala, Mouton (The Hague), 65; ed, Love Goes on Forever, Zondervan (Grand Rapids), 72; coauth, Reshaping Evangelical Higher Education, Zondervan (Grand Rapids), 72; auth, A Look At Filipino Lifestyles, Int Mus of Cultures (Dallas, Tex), 80, 84; coauth, Ministering Cross-Culturally, Baker Books (Grand Rapids), 86, in Korean, 89, in Ger, 91; coauth, Cultural Anthropology, Zondervan (Grand Rapids), 79, 87, Spanish Ed, 97; auth, Christianity Confronts Culture, 74, 88, in Korean, 88; co-ed, Nucleation in Papua New Guinea Cultures, Int Mus of Cultures, (Dallas, Tex), 88; auth, A Look at Latin American Lifestyles, 4th ed, Int Mus of Cultures (Dallas, Tex), 90. **CONTACT ADDRESS** Dept Arts and Sci, Fla Gulf Coast Univ, 19501 Treeline Ave S, Fort Myers, FL 33965-0001.

MAYPOLE, DONALD E.
PERSONAL Born 07/07/1934, Boise, ID, m, 1964, 2 children **DISCIPLINE** SOCIAL WORK **EDUCATION** Boise Jr Col, AA, 54; ID State Col, BS, 57; Univ Wisc, MSSW, 61; Univ Minn, 79. **CAREER** Assoc Prof, Univ N IA, 79-86; Assoc Prof to Prof, Univ Minn, 86-. **HONORS AND AWARDS** Prof Achievement Awd, ID State Univ, 90. **MEMBERSHIPS** Nat Asn of Soc Workers; Coun on Soc Work Educ; MN Coun on Soc Work Educ; Fulbright Alumni Asn. **SELECTED PUBLICATIONS** Auth, "Alcohol control: Issues in taxing, production and distribution," The International Journal of the Addictions, (91): 1013-1018; auth, "Some cross-cultural perspectives in caring for the chronically mentally ill," Chinese Journal of Foreign Science, (92): 160-163; co-auth, "The American and Portuguese generalist social work degrees at the masters level: Models for emerging social work education programs," Issues in Social Work Education, (93): 92-106; auth, "The cross-cultural exchange of development and evaluation of programs for drug education," International Social Work, (95): 287-298. **CONTACT ADDRESS** Dept Soc Work, Univ of Minnesota, Duluth, 10 University Dr, Duluth, MN 55812. **EMAIL** maypo@discover-net.net

MAZUMDAR, RINITA
PERSONAL Born 10/11/1959, Calcutta, India, m, 1987, 1 child **DISCIPLINE** PHILOSOPHY, ETHICS, WOMEN'S STUDIES **EDUCATION** Calcutta Univ, BA; Brock Univ, MA; Univ Mass, PhD. **CAREER** Inst, St Phillips Coll; adj prof, Univ NMex, Valencia. **HONORS AND AWARDS** Fel, Brock Univ, Canada; **MEMBERSHIPS** APA; NWSA. **RESEARCH** Ethics, political philosophy, feminist theory. **SELECTED PUBLICATIONS** Auth, Karma and Utilitarianism, S W Philos Soc; auth, Women and Hindu Rights, NWSA, 99. **CONTACT ADDRESS** Dept Womans Studies, Univ of New Mexico, Albuquerque, Albuquerque, NM 87131-0001. **EMAIL** rinita@nmt.edu

MAZUMDAR, SANJOY
DISCIPLINE SOCIAL ECOLOGY **EDUCATION** Indian Inst Technol, B Arch, 71; Mass Inst Technol, M Arch AS, 81; MCP, 81; PhD, 89. **CAREER** Instr, MIT, 82; lectr, Northeastern Univ, 86; asst prof, Univ Calif, Irvine, 88-94, assoc prof, 94-. **HONORS AND AWARDS** National Awd, Nat Asn of Students of Architecture, Chandigarh, India, 70; Urban Design Nat Competition by D.D.A., with Susan Goel & Assocs, 72; NEA Grant, 79; UCI Cultural Diversity Grant,, 89-90; UCI Fel, 89-90; Cultural Diversity Grant, UCI, 92; Social Ecology Assocs Awd, 94; Order of the Omega Fac Recognition Awd, 91, 97; Humanities Res Inst Fel, 99; Who's Who Worldwide, Platinum Ed, 92-. **MEMBERSHIPS** EDRA, Cultural Aspects of Design, IASTE. **RESEARCH** Cultures and physical environments; organizational culture and physical environments; ethnic groups and enclaves; prof organization in architecture and planning; social and cultural aspects of environmental design; planning and architecture. **SELECTED PUBLICATIONS** Coauth, "Sacred Space and Place Attachment," J of Environmental Design, 13, 3 (Sept 93): 231-242; auth, "Cultural Values in Architectural Education: An Example form India," J of Architectural Planning, 46, 4 (May 93): 230-238; coauth, "Intergroup Social Relations and Architecture: Vernacular Architecture and Issues of Status, Power, and Conflict," Environment and Behavior, 29, 3 (May 97): 374-421; coauth, "Religious Traditions and Domestic Architecture: A Comparative Analysis of Zoroastrian and Islamic Houses in Iran," J of Architectural and Planning Res, 14, 2 (Autumn 97): 181-208; coauth, "Ritual Lives of Muslim Women: Agency in Practice," J of Ritual Studies, 13, 2 (99): 58-70; coauth, " 'Women's Significant Spaces': Religion, space and community," J of Environmental Psychol, 19, 2 (June 99): 159-170; coauth, "Stadium Sightlines and Wheelchair Patrons: A Case Study in Implementation of the ADA," Res in Soc Sci and Disability, vol 1, Ch 9 (2000); coauth, "Creating a Sense of Place: The Vietnamese and Little Saigon," J of Environmental Psychol (in press); coauth, "Rethinking Public and Private Space: Religion and women in Muslim society," J of Architectural and Planning Res (in press); coauth, "Silent Resistance: A Hindu Child Widow's Lived Experience," in Arvind Sharma and Katherine K. Young, eds, The Annual Rev of Women in World Religions,, vol VII (in press). **CONTACT ADDRESS** Sch of Social Ecology, Univ of California, Irvine, Irvine, CA 92697-7075.

MBABUIKE, MICHAEL C.
PERSONAL Born 08/15/1943, Nigeria, m, 1981, 6 children **DISCIPLINE** LITERATURE, ANTHROPOLOGY **EDUCATION** Univ Nigeria, BA, 71; Univ Sorbonne, Paris, MA, 73; D Lit, 75. **CAREER** Prof, City Univ NYork, Hostos Comm Col, 86-. **HONORS AND AWARDS** Dist Merit Awd, UNN Alumnus, 98; Dist Lead Awd, NYASA, 99. **MEMBERSHIPS** ASA; ALA; NYASA. **RESEARCH** Literature; anthropology and the dispossessed. **SELECTED PUBLICATIONS** Auth, Poems of Memory Trips (98), vol 1; auth Poems of Memory Trips (99), vol 2. **CONTACT ADDRESS** Dept Humanities, City Univ NY, Hostos Comm Col, 475 Grand Concourse, Bronx, NY 10451-5307.

MC GRANE, BERNARD
PERSONAL Born 08/23/1947, New York, NY, d, 1 child **DISCIPLINE** SOCIOLOGY, ANTHROPOLOGY, PHILOSOPHY **EDUCATION** New York Univ, PhD, 76; Fairfield Univ, BA, 69. **CAREER** Assoc Prof, Chapman Univ, 89-; Lecturer, UC Irvine, 85-; Lecturer, Univ Calif, Los Angeles, 83-85. **RESEARCH** Buddhist Sociology; Ethnomethodology; Media Studies. **SELECTED PUBLICATIONS** Auth, "This Book is Not Required, An Emotional Survuval Guide for Students," Pine Forge Press, 99; auth, "The UN-TV and the 10MPH car, Experiments in Personal Freedom and Everyday Life," Small Press, 94; auth, "Beyond Anthropology: Society and the Other," Columbian Press, 89; auth, "Videos: The Ad and the Id-Sex, Death and Advertising, Univ of Calif, 92; auth, "The Ad and the Ego," California Newsreel, 96. **CONTACT ADDRESS** Dept Sociology, Chapman Univ, 333 N Glassell St, Orange, CA 92866-1011. **EMAIL** mcgrane@chapman.edu

MC GUIRE, PATRICK
PERSONAL Born 07/13/1953, Gouvernor, NY, m, 1985, 2 children **DISCIPLINE** SOCIOLOGY **HONORS AND AWARDS** Scholarly Achievement Awd, Am Sociol Asn Marxist Section, 94. **MEMBERSHIPS** Am Sociol Asn. **RESEARCH** Economic Sociology, Electric Industry History, Social Theory. **SELECTED PUBLICATIONS** Coauth, "Thomas

Edison and the Social Construction of the Early Electric Utility Industry in America," in Explorations in Economic Sociology, ed. Richard Swedberg (NY: Russell Sage Press, 93), 213-246; co-ed, From the Left bank to the Mainstream: Historical Debates and Contemporary Research in Marxist Sociology," General Hall Publ (NY), 94; auth, "The Nonpartisan League and Social Democracy in the U.S.: Social Networks, Class Power, State Occupancy, and Embedded Class Biases," Polit Power and Soc Theory 9 (95): 61-87; coauth, "The Making of An Industry: Electricity in the United States," in The Law of the Markets, ed. Michelle Callon (NY: Basil Blackwell, 99), 147-173; co-ed, Toward a Second Dimension: A Sociological Reader, 2nd ed, Kendall/Hunt Publ (Dubusque), 99. **CONTACT ADDRESS** Dept Sociol and Anthrop, Univ of Toledo, 2801 W Bancroft St, Toledo, OH 43606. **EMAIL** Patrick.McGuire@utoledo.edu

MC LEOD, ANN M.
PERSONAL Born 03/03/1939, New York, NY, w, 1990 **DISCIPLINE** PSYCHOLOGY, ARCHAEOLOGY **EDUCATION** Bennett Jr Col, AA, 59; Lindenwood Col, BA, 61; Wash Univ, MA, 64; NY State Univ, MS, 65. **CAREER** Asst to Dir, Villa Mercede, Bellosqurda, Florence, Ital, 65-67; Dir of Admis, Psychometrists, Learning Disabilities Specialist, Allen Stevenson New York City, 67-70; Sch Psychol, Polk Community Col, 70-71; Prof, Polk Community Col, 71-00. **HONORS AND AWARDS** Teacher of the Year, Polk Community Col, 73; Awd for salvaging documents, books, T.U. documentary "Angels in the Mud", Florence, Ital, Psi Beta. **MEMBERSHIPS** Archaeol Club, Psi Beta Nat Honors Soc, AM Univ Professors, Am Psychol Asn, Portrait Painters of Am. **RESEARCH** Archaeology: NAG Hammadi, Dead Sea Scrolls, Jewish revolt 66 AD, Abnormal Psychology: Bi Polar, Paranoia, Minoan, Mycenean, Troy. **SELECTED PUBLICATIONS** Auth, Excavations: Graves A and B Myceneacn Culture (Mycenae Greece), 63, 64; Salvaging documents, Libr in Florence, Ital, 66, 67. **CONTACT ADDRESS** Dept Arts, Letters and Soc Sci, Polk Comm Col, 3425 Winter Lake Rd, Lakeland, FL 33803.

MC MASTER, MICHELE
DISCIPLINE PSYCHOLOGY, COMMUNICATION **EDUCATION** Knox Col, BA, 71; Governors State Univ, MA, 75; MA, 89; Union Institute, PhD, 99. **CAREER** Educator, Tinley Park Mental Health Ctr, 71-78; Coordinator of Out-Patient Psychiatric Svcs, 79-90; Dir of Women's Svcs, 81-82; Psychotherapist, 82-94; Univ Lecturer, Governors State Univ, 92-. **HONORS AND AWARDS** Who's Who in the Human Services, Who's Who of America's Teachers, 94-95; Who's Who of America's Teachers, 96-97; Fac Appreciation Awd; Fac Appreciation Awd; Who's Who of America's Teachers, 98-99; Who's Who of Am Women, 99-00; Who's Who of Am Women, 00-01. **MEMBERSHIPS** Jean Gebser Society. **RESEARCH** Intrapersonal Communication, Consciousness, Learning. **SELECTED PUBLICATIONS** Auth, "Alternative Intercultural Learning," Proceedings of the 26th Annual Third World Conference; auth, "An Intrapersonal System View of Communication," Doctoral dissertation, The Union Institute, 99; auth, "Study Guide (for the correspondence for Concepts in Human Communication), 92-. **CONTACT ADDRESS** Dept Liberal Arts, Governors State Univ, 1 Univ Pkwy, Park Forest, IL 60466. **EMAIL** gmmcmast@govst.edu

MCBEATH, MICHAEL K.
DISCIPLINE PSYCHOLOGY **EDUCATION** Brown Univ, BA, 77; Univ Calif, MS, 79; Stanford Univ, PhD, 90; NASA, Ames Res Center, Post Doc, 90-92. **CAREER** Res engineer, Washington Univ, St. Louis, Mo, 80-85; res engineer, NASA-Ames Res Center, Moffett Field, CA, 86-90, res assoc, 90-92; asst prof, Kent State Univ, 92-98; asst prof, Ariz State Univ, 98-. **HONORS AND AWARDS** Who's Who in Sci and Engineering, 94; Nat Eye Inst Young Investigator, ARVO travel Awd, 94; Sigma Xi, 95; Advisor of the Semester Finalist, Kent State Ohffice of Campus life, 95, 96; Innovative Teaching Awd, Kent Psi Chi Psychol Honor Soc, 96. **SELECTED PUBLICATIONS** Coauth with D. M. Schaffer and M. K. Kaiser, "How baseball outfielders determine where to catch fly balls," Science, 268(5210), 569-573 (95); coauth with D. M. Schaffer and M. K. Kaiser, "Play ball," Sci, 268 (5218), 1681-1685 (95); coauth with J. G. Neuhoff, "The Doppler Illusion: the perception of rising pitch with falling frequency," J of Experimental Psychol: Human Perception and Performance, 22(4), 970-985 (96); coauth with D. M. Schaffer and M.K. Kaiser,"On catching fly balls," Sci, 273(5272), 256-259 (96); coauth with K. Morikawa, "Forward-facing motion biases for rigid and nonrigid biologically likely transformations," Perceptual & Motor Skills, 85, 1187-1193 (97); ed with J. H. Banks, G. M. Shreve, and S. B. Fountain, Cognitive Processes in Translation and Interpreting, Thousand Oaks:Sage (97); coauth with D. J. Schiano and B. Tversky, "Three dimensional bilateral symmetry assumed in judging figural identity and orientation," Psychol Sci, 8(3), 217-223 (97); coauth with J. G. Neuhoff, "Overcoming naïve mental models in explaining the Doppler shift: An illusion creates confusion," Am J Physics, 65(7), 618-622 (97); coauth with J. G. Neuhoff and W. C. Wanzie, "Dynamic Frequency change influences loudness preception: A central analytic process," J of Experimental Psychol: Human Perception and Performance, 25(4), 1050-1059 (99); coauth with K. W. Chambers, D. J. Schiano, and E. Metz, "Tops are more salient than bottoms," Perception & Psychophysics, 61(4), 625-635 (99). **CONTACT ADDRESS** Dept Psychol, Arizona State Univ, PO Box 871104, Tempe, AZ 85287. **EMAIL** m.m@asu.edu

MCBRIDE, PAUL WILBERT
PERSONAL Born 05/23/1940, Youngstown, OH, m, 1962, 3 children **DISCIPLINE** UNITED STATES HISTORY, ETHNIC STUDIES **EDUCATION** Youngstown State Univ, BA, 63; Kans State Univ, MA, 65; Univ Ga, PhD(hist), 72. **CAREER** Instr hist, Augusta Col, 67; asst prof, 70-74, assoc prof Hist, Ithaca Col, 74-, Dana Teaching fel, 82. **MEMBERSHIPS** Orgn Am Historians; Immigration Hist Asn; Hist Educ Asn. **RESEARCH** Twentieth-century United States history; United States ethnic history; Italian American studies. **SELECTED PUBLICATIONS** Auth, The co-op industrial education experiment, Hist Educ Quart, summer 74; Culture Clash: Immigrants and Reformers 1880-1920, R & E Res Assocs, 75; Peter Roberts and the YMCA Americanization Program, Pa Hist, 4/77; Daniel Bell and the permissive society, summer 77, Occas Rev; Manipulated schools, manipulated history, Hist Educ Quart, spring 79; Masters of their fate, J Ethnic Studies, 11/79; The solitary Christians: Italian Americans and their church, 12/81 & Reflections on dreams and memories, summer 82, Ethnic Groups. **CONTACT ADDRESS** Dept of History, Ithaca Col, Ithaca, NY 14850-7002. **EMAIL** McBride@Ithaca.edu

MCCANN, HAROLD G.
PERSONAL Born 01/10/1942, Hoboken, NJ, m, 5 children **DISCIPLINE** SOCIOLOGY **EDUCATION** Allegheny Col, BA 64; Princeton Univ, MA, 66; PhD, 74. **CAREER** Act asst prof, Univ Cal, 67-69; asst prof, Univ New Mex, 70-73; lectr, Princeton Univ, 69-70, 90; res assoc prof, Tulane Univ, 95-96; asst prof, assoc prof, 74-, Univ Vermont. **RESEARCH** Social stratification; fertility in developing countries. **SELECTED PUBLICATIONS** Coauth, Population and Housing Estimates, Vermont, 1998, Ver Dept Health (Burlington), 99; coauth, Population and Housing Estimates, Vermont, 1997, Ver Dept Health (Burlington), 98; coauth, Population and Housing Estimates, Vermont, 1996, Ver Dept Health (Burlington), 97; coauth, "State Corporations and Mixed Economies: A Brief Introduction," West Behav Sci Inst (82); coauth, "The reliability of reporting of contraceptive behavior in DHS calendar data: evidence from Morocco", Stud Fam Plan (97); coauth, "Detecting induced abortions from reports of pregnancy terminations in DHS calendar data," Stud Fam Plan 27 (96): 36-43; coauth, "Assessing the effects of monetized food aid on reproductive behavior in rural Honduras," Eval Prog Planning 22 (99): 399-411; coauth, "The effects of monetized food aid on reproductive behavior in rural Honduras," Pop Res Policy Rev 17 (98): 305-328. **CONTACT ADDRESS** Dept Sociology, Univ of Vermont, 31 S Prospect St, Burlington, VT 05405-1704. **EMAIL** mccann@200.uvm.edu

MCCARTHY, JOSEPH M.
PERSONAL Born 10/02/1049, Lynn, MA, m, 1966, 4 children **DISCIPLINE** EDUCATION **EDUCATION** St. John's Sem, AB, 61; Boston Col, AM, 68; PhD, 72. **CAREER** Lectr, Boston Col, 71-73; asst prof to prof, Suffolk Univ, 73-. **HONORS AND AWARDS** Hearn Scholar, 59-61; Hearn Fel, 61-63; St. Meinrad Prize, 63. **MEMBERSHIPS** AHA; Cath Hist Assoc; New England Hist Assoc; Northwest Popular Culture Assoc; Soc for Romanian Studies; Soc for Medieval and Renaissance Philos. **SELECTED PUBLICATIONS** Auth, "Ecclesiology in the Letters of St. Ignatius of Antioch", Am Benedictine Rev XXII.3, (Sept 71): 319-325; auth, "Humanistic Emphases in the Educational Thought of Vincent of Beauvais", Studien und Texte zur Geistsgeschichte des Mittelalters 20, E.J. Brill (Cologne), 76; auth, Guinea-Bissau and Cape Verde Island: A Comprehensive Bibliography, Garland (NY), 77; auth, An International List of Articles on the History of Education, Published in Non-Educational Serials, 1965-74, Garland, (NY), 77; ed, Benedict Joseph Fenwick, Memoirs to Serve for the Future Ecclesiastical History of the Diocese of Boston, US Cath Hist Soc, (Yonkers), 78; auth, Pierre Teilhard de Chardin: A Comprehensive Bibliography, Garland (NY), 81; auth, "Intercultural Dimensions of Vincent de Beauvais's Writings: Some Preliminary Considerations,", Vincent of Beauvais Newsletter VIII (83): 6-10; auth, "New Directions in the Teaching of Creativity", Creativity and Liberal Learning: Problems and Possibilities in American Education, ed David G. Tuerck, Ablex (Norwood, NJ), (87): 167-181; auth, Innovation in Late Medieval Educational Thought: Vincent of Beauvais, Ramon Lull and Pierre Dubois, ERIC Clearinghouse on Soc Sci/Soc Studies Educ, (Bloomington, IN), 93; auth, The Russell Case: Academic Freedom vs Public Hysteria, ERIC Clearinghouse on Higher Educ, (Washington, DC), 94. **CONTACT ADDRESS** Dept Educ, Suffolk Univ, 8 Ashburton Pl, Boston, MA 02108-2701. **EMAIL** jmccarth@acad.suffolk.edu

MCCARTHY, WILLIAM
DISCIPLINE SOCIOLOGY **EDUCATION** Univ Guelph, Canada, HBA, 80; Univ W Ontario, Bed, 81; Univ Toronto, MA, 84, PhD, 90. **CAREER** Asst prof, Univ Victoria, 89-94, assoc prof, 94-98; assoc prof, Univ Calif, Davis, 98-. **HONORS AND AWARDS** Michael J. Hindelang Outstanding Book on Crime Awd, Am Soc of Criminology, 98; C. Wright Mills Outstanding Book on Social Problems Awd, Soc for the Study of Social Problems, 98; Soc Sci and Humanities Res Coun Grant, 90, 94, 98; Finalist for the Kathleen Gregory Klein Awd, Women's Caucus Popular Culture-Am Culture Asn, 99; Dept of Justice, Canada, Grant, 2000. **SELECTED PUBLICATIONS** Auth, "The Attitudes and Actions of Others: Testing Sutherland's Theory of Differential Association," British J of Criminology, 36 (96): 135-51; coauth, Mean Streets: Youth Crime and Homelessness, Cambridge Univ Press, 97, paperback, 98; coauth, "Anomie, Social Capital and Street Crime," in The Future of Anomie Theory, eds. Nikos Passas and Robert Agnew (MA: Northeastern Univ Press, 97), 73-90; coauth, "La theorie du capital social et la renouveau du paradigm des tensions et des opportunities en criminologie sociologique,--Social Capital Theory and the Renewal of a Strain and Opportunity Paradigm in Sociological Criminology," Sociologie et Societes, 30 (98): 145-58; coauth, "Uncertainty, Cooperation and Crime: Understanding the Decision to Co-offend," Social Forces, 77 (98): 155-84; coauth, "In the Company of Women: Structure and Agency in a Revised Power-Control Theory of Gender and Delinquency," Criminology, 37 (99): 761-788. **CONTACT ADDRESS** Dept Sociol, Univ of California, Davis, 1 Shields Ave, Davis, CA 95616-8701.

MCCAULEY, TERITA
PERSONAL Born 12/28/1953, Chicago, IL, m, 1990, 3 children **DISCIPLINE** EDUCATION, SPECIAL EDUCATION **EDUCATION** Univ Mo, BS, BS, Univ Kans, MS, Doctor Ed. **CAREER** 24 years teaching experience, Palmyra Mo Public Schs; Archdiocese of Chicago, Ill; Kansas City, Mo Public Schs; Coastal Carolina Univ, Morris Col. **HONORS AND AWARDS** Distinguished Prof of the Year, Coastal Carolina Univ, 93-94; Who's Who Among Am Eds, 93-94; Who's Who Among Int Eds, 99-2000. **MEMBERSHIPS** NEA, SAEOPP, SCEOPP, NAACP, SCEA. **RESEARCH** Juvenile male incarceration alternatives. **CONTACT ADDRESS** Dept Ed, Morris Col, 100 W Col St, Sumpter, SC 29150. **EMAIL** teritag@hotmail.com

MCCLAIN, ANDREW BRADLEY
PERSONAL Born 11/12/1948, Akron, OH **DISCIPLINE** EDUCATION **EDUCATION** Univ of Akron, Akron, OH JD 1984-88; Kent State Univ Kent, OH, M Ed 1976-78; Univ of Akron Akron, OH, BA 1966-70. **CAREER** Akron Bd of Educ, English teacher, 70-73; Western Reserve Acad, dir upward bound, 73-87; The Univ of Akron, dir upward bound, 87; Western Reserve Academy, Hudson, OH, dir Upward Bound, 73-87; Univ of Akron, dir pre college programs, 88, Dir of Academic Achievement Programs, currently; Private Practice, Atty. **HONORS AND AWARDS** Fellowship Natl Assoc of Independent Schools 1982; Fellowship Inst for Educational Leadership 1982-; Ohio Assn of Educational Opportunity Program Personnel OAEOPP, James Rankin Awd, 1990. **MEMBERSHIPS** Consultant A Better Chance 1975-86; dir School Scholarship Serv 1979-84; consultant Mid-South Assoc of Independent Schools 1981-83, Marquette Univ 1984; mem former dir and pres state chap MAEOPP; mem NAACP; consultant, Natl Council of Educational Opportunity Assn, (NCEOA); parlamentarian, NCEOA, 1993-94; treasurer, Education Foundation Mid American Assn, Educ Opportunity Probram Personnel (MAEOPP), 1992-95; mem, African Amer Male Commission, 1989-. **CONTACT ADDRESS** Academic Achievement Program, Univ of Akron, Gallucci Hall 112, Akron, OH 44325-7908.

MCCLAIN, SHIRLA R.
PERSONAL Born 02/04/1935, Akron, OH, m, 1957 **DISCIPLINE** EDUCATION **EDUCATION** Univ of Akron, Akron OH, BS, 1956, MS, 1970, PhD, 1975. **CAREER** Akron Public School, Akron OH, teacher and supervisor, 56-76; Kent State University, Kent OH, prof of education, 76-87; Walsh University, North Canton OH, prof of education, 87-; asst director of teacher preparation, 90-. **HONORS AND AWARDS** Achievement award, Akron Urban League, 1975; distinguished black alumna award, Black Alumna Assoc of Univ of Akron, 1986; lifetime achievement award, Black United Students, Walsh College, 1988; distinguished educator award, Multicultural Education Special Interest Group of the Assn of Teacher Educators, 1989; Akron Grassroots Activist Awd, University of Akron's Afro-American Studies, 1991; Alumni Honor Awd for Excellence in Professional Achievement, Univ of Akron, 1994; Inducted into the Consortium of Doctors, Savannah GA, 1994. **MEMBERSHIPS** Mem, Assn of Teacher Educators, 1984-87, 1989-; mem, Univ of Akron Black Cultural Center advisory board, 1987. **SELECTED PUBLICATIONS** Author of numerous monographs, book chapters, and reviews. **CONTACT ADDRESS** Professor of Education, Walsh Univ, 2020 Easton St N W, Farrell Hall 212, Canton, OH 44720.

MCCLARTY, WILMA KING- DOERING
PERSONAL Born 07/21/1939, w, 1962, 2 children **DISCIPLINE** ENGLISH, ENGLISH EDUCATION **EDUCATION** Andrews Univ BA, 61, MA, 62; Univ MT, DEduc, 68. **CAREER** Asst prof Eng & educ, Southwestern Union Col, 68-72; assoc prof, 72-80, Prof Eng & Chmn Dept, Southern Adventist University, 80-; Coord, Seventh-day Adventist Sec Sch Eng

Tchrs Conv, Southern Missionary Col, 73. **MEMBERSHIPS** NCTE. **SELECTED PUBLICATIONS** Auth, Why are you so peculiar?, Rev & Herald, 8/71; Open-minded or just empty headed, J Adventist Educ, 2-3/72; Urgency (poem), Ministry, 2/72. **CONTACT ADDRESS** Dept of Eng, So Adventist Univ, PO Box 370, Collegedale, TN 37315-0370. **EMAIL** wmclarty@southern.edu

MCCLELLAND, PATRICIA
PERSONAL Born 06/06/1945, Kansas City, MO, m, 1965, 2 children **DISCIPLINE** SOCIAL STUDIES, EDUCATION **EDUCATION** BA, 63; MA, 80; Ed Spec, 86; PhD, 93. **CAREER** Assoc Prof, Park Col, 94-; Dir of Educ Prog, Park Col, 94-; Dean of Grad Studies, Park Col, 98-00. **HONORS AND AWARDS** Who's Who Among Am Teachers, 96, 00. **MEMBERSHIPS** Phi Lambda Theta, Phi Delta Kappa, Nat Coun of Soc Studies, Asn Curric and Supervision Develop, Mo Asn for Col Teacher Educ. **CONTACT ADDRESS** Univ Educ, Park Col, 8700 N W River Pk, Parkville, MO 64152. **EMAIL** pmcclelland@mail.park.edu

MCCLENNEN, JOAN
PERSONAL Born 12/27/1945, Paterson, NJ, w **DISCIPLINE** SOCIAL WORK **EDUCATION** Pa State Univ, BS, 69; Fla State Univ, MSW, 80; Univ Southern Fla, PhD, 90. **CAREER** Asst prof, Southwest Mo State Univ, 95-. **RESEARCH** Child Abuse, Domestic Violence, Elderly Abuse, Same-gender Domestic Violence, Women's Issues, Program Evaluation and Research, and Macro-practice. **SELECTED PUBLICATIONS** Coauth, "Use of social services by African-American families: A Multivariate Analysis", Family therapy 24.1 (97): 39-53; coauth, "Cultural change through quality process management", Col Student J 31.1 (97): 51-68; coed, A professional's guide to understanding gay and lesbian domestic violence: Understanding practice interventions, Edwin Mellen Pr, (Lewiston, NY), 99; auth, "Family health and family violence", Family health in social work practice, eds J.T. Pardeck and F. Yuen, Auburn House, (Westport, CT), 99; auth, "Forward", "Lesbian partner abuse: Toward a Better understanding", "Prevailing theories on same-gender partner abuse: Proposing the feminist social-psychological model", and "Future directions for practice interventions with same gender partner abuse", A Professional's guide to understanding gay and lesbian domestic violence: Understanding practice interventions, eds J.C. McClennen and J.F. Gunther, Edwin Mellen Pr, 99; coauth, "Lesbian partner abuse scale", Res for Soc Work Practice (forthcoming). **CONTACT ADDRESS** Dept Soc Work, Southwest Missouri State Univ, Springfield, 901 S National, Springfield, MO 65804.

MCCLOSKEY, MICHAEL
PERSONAL Born 07/13/1941, New Orleans, LA, m, 1970, 2 children **DISCIPLINE** SOCIOLOGY **EDUCATION** Univ Scranton, AB, 65; Loyola Univ, MA, 69; PhD, 74; Catholic Theol Union, MDiv, 87. **CAREER** Asst Prof, Benedictine Univ, 70-74; Prof, Truman Col, 74-. **HONORS AND AWARDS** Arthur J. Schmitt Fel, 69; Loyola Centennial Medallion and Grad Medal, 70; Finalist, Chicago City Pub Service Awd, 98. **MEMBERSHIPS** Am Sociol Asn; Asn for Sociol of Relig; Relig Res Asn; Midwest IL Sociol Soc; Soc for Sci Study of Relig. **RESEARCH** Sociology of Religion. **CONTACT ADDRESS** Dept Soc Sci, Truman Col, 1145 W Wilson Ave, Chicago, IL 60640. **EMAIL** mmccloskey@ccc.edu

MCCLUNG, PHIL
PERSONAL Born 07/01/1947, Pakersburg, WV, m, 1979, 2 children **DISCIPLINE** PSYCHOLOGY **EDUCATION** W Va Univ, MS, 73; W Va Univ, CAS, 83; W Va Univ, EdD, 93. **CAREER** Dir Student Assistance, 75-89; Prof, W Va Univ, 89-. **HONORS AND AWARDS** Who's Who Among Am Teachers; Who's Who in the South and Southwest; Outstanding Young Man of Am. **MEMBERSHIPS** APA, WVCA, WVCDA. **RESEARCH** Mental illness. **SELECTED PUBLICATIONS** Auth, Assessing General Education: Selection and Implementation of an Instrument to Satisfy Internal and External Constituencies, 95. **CONTACT ADDRESS** Dept Soc Sci, West Virginia Univ, Parkersburg, 300 Campus Dr, Parkersburg, WV 26101. **EMAIL** philwvup@hotmail.com

MCCLURE, KIMBERLEY A.
DISCIPLINE PSYCHOLOGY **EDUCATION** Univ Tex, BS, 89; MA, 94; PhD, 98. **CAREER** Asst Instructor, Univ Tex, 95-97; Adj Instructor, El Paso Cmty Col, 98; Asst Prof, W Ill Univ, 98-. **HONORS AND AWARDS** NE Optimist Club Scholarship Awd, Univ TX, 85-89; Patricia Roberts-Harris Fel, Univ TX, 91-93; Conference Presentation Awd, Am Psychol Asn, 96. **MEMBERSHIPS** Am Psychol-Law Soc; Am Psychol Soc; Psi Chi; Midwestern Psychol Asn; W Psychol Asn. **SELECTED PUBLICATIONS** Co-auth, "Suggestions for improving interviews in child protection agencies," Child Maltreatment, (96): 223-230; co-auth, "Repeated postevent questioning can lead to elevated levels of eyewitness confidence," Law and Human Behavior, (96): 629-653; co-auth, "Adolescent and adult mothers' perceptions of hazardous situations for their children," Journal of Adolescent Health, (96): 227-231; co-auth, "A lay perspective on the accuracy of eyewitness testimony," Journal of Applied Social Psychology, (990: 52-71; co-auth, "Recognition instructions and recognition practice can alter the confidence-response time relationship for eyewitnesses," Journal of Applied Psychology, in press. **CONTACT ADDRESS** Dept Psychol, Western Illinois Univ, 1 University Circle, Macomb, IL 61455. **EMAIL** Kim_McClure@ccmail.wiu.edu

MCCLURE, WESLEY CORNELIOUS
DISCIPLINE EDUCATION **CAREER** Virginia State University, Petersburg, VA, president; Lane College, Pres, 92-. **CONTACT ADDRESS** Lane Col, 545 Lane Ave, Jackson, TN 38301-4598.

MCCORD, BETH K.
PERSONAL Born 04/16/1968, Van Wert, OH, 2 children **DISCIPLINE** ANTHROPOLOGY **EDUCATION** Ball State Univ, BA, 90; MA, 94. **CAREER** Staff Archaeol to Asst Dir, Ball State Univ, 90-. **MEMBERSHIPS** Coun for the Conservation of Ind Archaeol; Ind Acad of Sci. **RESEARCH** Midwestern U.S.: Prehistory, Ceramics, Ceremonial sites, Bioarchaeology, Site formation processes. **SELECTED PUBLICATIONS** Auth, "Hopewell Panpipes," Midcontinental J of Archaeol, 92; auth, "An Archaeological Assessment of Three Unique Woodland Sites in Henry Co., Indiana," Archaeol Res Management Serv, 98; auth, "The New Castle Site Revisited," Archaeol Res Management Serv, 99; co-auth, "A Survey of Collections: an Archaeological Evaluation of Eight Earthworks in Eastern Indiana," Archaeol Res Management Serv, 00; co-auth, "The Morell-Sheets Site: Refining the Albee Phase," Ind Archaeol, in press. **CONTACT ADDRESS** Dept Anthropol, Ball State Univ, Muncie, IN 47306. **EMAIL** bmccord@gw.bsu.edu

MCCRACKEN, BLAIR
PERSONAL Born 11/12/1963, Los Angeles, CA, d, 1 child **DISCIPLINE** PSYCHOLOGY **EDUCATION** George Wash Univ, BA, 57; Columbia Univ, 65; Calif School Prof Psychol, PhD, 89. **CAREER** Teaching Fel, Northeastern Univ, 79-80; Assoc Prof, Col of Notre Dame, 91-. **HONORS AND AWARDS** Fac Development Awd, Col of Notre Dame; distinguished service Awd, San Francisco Psychol Asn,; Who's Who in Govt, 77' Who's Who in the East, 80; Who's Who in Am, 80; Who's Who in the West, 82. **MEMBERSHIPS** Am Psychol Asn, Calif State Psychol Asn, Psi Chi Nat Psychol Honor Soc. **RESEARCH** Long term memory; cross paradigmatic approach. **SELECTED PUBLICATIONS** auth, "The Symbolic Dimension of Long Term Memory," Dissertation, 89; auth, "The Essential Enigma"; . **CONTACT ADDRESS** Dept Counseling Psychol, Col of Notre Dame, 1500 Ralston Ave, Belmont, CA 94002. **EMAIL** mccracken@cnd.edu

MCCUMMINGS, LEVERNE
PERSONAL Born 10/28/1932, Marion, SC, m **DISCIPLINE** EDUCATION **EDUCATION** St Augustine's, BA 1960; Univ of PA, MSW 1966; Ohio State Univ, PhD 1975. **CAREER** Competency Certification Bd, Bd of Health & Human Svcs, Futures Think Tank, chmn, 81-82; Natl Conf of Grad Deans/Dirs & Off Soc Work Progs, pres, 82-85; Cheyney Univ of PA, Pres, currently. **HONORS AND AWARDS** Outstanding Educators Awd Univ of KY 1971; Recognition Awd NASW Sixth Biennial Prof Symposium 1980; Distinguished Alumni Awd Univ of PA 1980; Recognition Awd Council of Intl Prog 1981; Institute for Educational Management, Harvard University, l989. **CONTACT ADDRESS** Cheyney Univ of Pennsylvania, Cheyney, PA 19319.

MCDOWELL-LOUDAN, ELLIS
PERSONAL Born 07/13/1938, Rome, GA, m, 1975, 2 children **DISCIPLINE** ANTHROPOLOGY **EDUCATION** The Am Univ, Wash DC, PhD, 72. **CAREER** Prof, SUNY Col Cortland, 72-. **HONORS AND AWARDS** Fel, Am Anthrop Asn; Fel, NY State Arhaeol Asn. **MEMBERSHIPS** Am Anthrop Asn, NYSAA, NYAC, COPA, Soc for Am Archaeol. **RESEARCH** Native American Archaeology, Ethnology, Research Methods, CRM. **SELECTED PUBLICATIONS** Ed, Coauth, Research Frontiers in Anthropology, by C.R. Ember and M. Ember (Englewood Cliffs: Prentice Hall, 94); ed, William M. Beauchamp Chapter Special Publication, 6-1 (Fall 94), 7-1(Spring 95); rev, of "Woven by the Grandmothers: Nineteenth -Century Navajo Textiles for the National Museum of the American Indian, 1996," ed. Eulalie H. Bonar, Otsiningo Circle Premier Issue (Winter 97); rev, of "The Living Tradition of Yup'ik Masks: Agayuliyararput, Our Way of Making Prayer," by Anne Fienup-Riordan, Otsiningo Circle 2 (Summer 97); auth, "Obituary: Hans Hoffmann: Professor of Anthropology, SUNY Binghamton," Otsiningo Circle 2 (Summer 97); rev, of "Kegginaqut, Kangiit-llu: Our Way of Making Prayer: Yup'ik Masks and Stories They Tell," ed. Anne Fienup-Riordan, transl. Marie Meade, Otsiningo Circle 2 (Summer 97); rev, of "Reading Beyond Words: Contexts for Native History," ed. S.H. Jennifer Brown and Elizabeth Vibert, Otsiningo Circle 3 (Winter 98); rev, of "Cornplanter Chronicles, Volume One 1733-1775: A Tale of the Legendary Seneca Chieftain," Otsiningo Circle 4 (Summer 98); auth, "Ste. Marie de Gannentaha Living History Museum: A Review," Otsiningo Circle 4 (Summer 98); auth, "Archaeology and the Law," in An Introduction to Archaeology in Central New York (Syracuse: William M. Beauchamp Chapter, NYSAA, Committee Authorship, 98). **CONTACT ADDRESS** Dept Sociol and Anthrop, SUNY, Col at Cortland, PO Box 2000, Cortland, NY 13045. **EMAIL** loudane@snycorva.cortland.edu

MCGAHAN, JOSEPH R.
PERSONAL Born 11/05/1953, New York, NY, m, 1983, 1 child **DISCIPLINE** PSYCHOLOGY **EDUCATION** Nassau Community Col, AA, 73; SUNY, BA, 75; Yeshiva Univ, MS, 78; Univ Okla, PhD, 88. **CAREER** Prof, Univ La, 89-. **RESEARCH** The effects of subtle linguistic variations on reasoning; eye contact as a function of familiarity, gender, and competition vs. cooperation; attraction and dominance relative to eye contact as an independent variable; Parallels between facial characteristics associated with the perceptions of threat and seduction. **SELECTED PUBLICATIONS** Auth, "The equivalence of contingency structure for intuitive covariation judgments about height, weight, and body fat," Journal of Psychology, in press; auth, The effect of imaginary sexual stimulation on the perceived covariation between freedom and responsibility: A preliminary study," Journal of Psychology, in press; auth, "The association between need for cognition and judgments in height, weight, and body fat covariation, in press; auth, Intuitive covariation assessment of the illusory correlation, in press; auth, "dominance and visual interactions between college classmates," Southeastern Psychological Asn conf, 00; auth, "New technology for recording human gaze and mutual gaze," Southwestern Psychological Asn, 00. **CONTACT ADDRESS** Dept Psychol, Northeast Louisiana Univ, 700 Univ Ave, Monroe, LA 71209-9000. **EMAIL** psmcgahan@ucm.edu

MCGARVA, ANDREW R.
PERSONAL Born 11/07/1968, Buffalo, NY, s **DISCIPLINE** PSYCHOLOGY **EDUCATION** Univ NH, PhD, 97. **CAREER** Asst Prof, Dickinson State Univ, 97-. **HONORS AND AWARDS** Sigma X. **MEMBERSHIPS** APA. **RESEARCH** Driver aggression, rumor transmission, risk behavior. **SELECTED PUBLICATIONS** Coauth, "Approval Motivation and Sexual Daydreaming," The J of Genetic Psychol, 154 (93): 383-388; coauth, "The Perception of Social and Nonsocial Contingencies" J of Soc Behav and Personality, 12 (96): 433-451; coauth, "Provoked Drive Aggression and Status: A Field Study," J of Transp Res, F1 (forthcoming). **CONTACT ADDRESS** Dept Soc Sci, Dickinson State Univ, 291 Campus Dr, Dickinson, ND 58601. **EMAIL** amcgarva@eagle.dsu.nodak.edu

MCGEE, PATRICK
DISCIPLINE CULTURAL STUDIES, POSTCOLONIAL THEORY **EDUCATION** Univ Calif, Santa Cruz, PhD, 84. **CAREER** Prof, La State Univ. **HONORS AND AWARDS** Fulbright grad res grant for Fr, 82-83; NEH summer stipend, 88; LSU res coun summer grant, 92, 94. **RESEARCH** Modernism (Joyce); Shakespeare; film; African-American literature. **SELECTED PUBLICATIONS** Auth, Telling the Other: The Question of Value in Modern and Postcolonial Writing, 92; The Politics of Modernist Form, or, Who Rules the Waves?, in Mod Fiction Stud, 92; Decolonization and the Curriculum of English, Race, Identity, and Representation in Educ, 93; When Is a Man Not a Man? or, The Male Feminist Approaches 'Nausicaa,' in Joyce in the Hibernian Metropolis, 96; Ishmael Reed and the Ends of Race, 97; Cinema, Theory, and Political Responsibility in Contemporary Culture, 97. **CONTACT ADDRESS** Dept of Eng, Louisiana State Univ and A&M Col, 212T Allen Hall, Baton Rouge, LA 70803. **EMAIL** pmcgee@unixl.sncc.lsu.edu

MCGEE, REECE JEROME
PERSONAL Born 10/19/1929, St. Paul, MN, m, 1978, 3 children **DISCIPLINE** SOCIOLOGY **EDUCATION** Univ Minn, BA, 52, MA, 53, PhD, 56 **CAREER** Asst prof, 56, Humboldt St Col; res assoc, 57, Univ Minn; asst prof, 57-61, assoc prof, 61-64, Univ Texas Austin; vis assoc prof, 64-65, prof, 65-67, Macalester Col; prof, master tchr, 67-94, prof emeritus, 94-, dept head, sociology & anthropology, 87-92, Purdue Univ. **CONTACT ADDRESS** Dept of Sociology & Antropol, Purdue Univ, West Lafayette, Stone Hall 1365, West Lafayette, IN 47907-1365.

MCGILVRAY, DENNIS B.
PERSONAL Born 08/16/1943, Palo Alto, CA, m, 1973, 3 children **DISCIPLINE** ANTHROPOLOGY **EDUCATION** Reed Col, BA, 65; Univ Chicago, MA, 68; Univ Chicago, PhD, 74. **CAREER** Asst Prof, Univ Santa Clara, 72-73; Asst Lect, Univ Cambridge, 73-78; Mellon Fel, Cornell Univ, 78-80; Assoc Prof, Univ Colorado, 80-. **HONORS AND AWARDS** Stirling Awd, Am Anthrop Asn, 87. **MEMBERSHIPS** Am Anthrop Asn, Royal Anthrop Inst, Am Ethnological Soc. **RESEARCH** Cultural anthropology of South Asia, Tamil culture, visual anthropology. **SELECTED PUBLICATIONS** Auth, "Dutch Burghers and Portuguese Mechanics: Eurasian Ethnicity in Sri Lanka," Comparative Studies in Society and History 24 (82): 235-263; Auth, "Mukkuvar Vannimai: Tamil Caste and Matriclan Ideology in Batticaloa, Sri Lanka," in Caste Ideology and Interaction (Cambridge Univ Pr, 82):34-97; Auth, "Paraiyar Drummers of Sri Lanka: Consensus and Constraint in an Untouchable Caste," American Ethnologist 10 (83): 97-115; Auth, "households in Akkaraipattu: Dowry and Domestic Organization Among the Matrilineal Tamils and Moors of Sri Lanka," in Society from the Inside Out: Anthropological Perspectives on the South Asian Household (New Delhi, Newbury Park, and London: Sage, 89): 192-235; Auth, "Tamils and Muslims in the Shadow of War: Schism or Continuity?" South Asia 20 (97):

239-253; Auth, "Arabs, Moors, and Muslims: Sri Lankan Muslim Ethnicity in Regional Perspective," Contributions to Indian Sociology 32 (98): 433-483. **CONTACT ADDRESS** Dept Anthrop, Univ of Colorado, Boulder, PO Box 233, Boulder, CO 80309-0233. **EMAIL** dennis.mcgilvray@colorado,edu

MCGOWAN, MARCIA PHILLIPS
PERSONAL Born 03/27/1943, Holyoke, MA, m, 1964, 2 children **DISCIPLINE** FEMINIST CRITICISM **EDUCATION** Conn Col, BA; Rutgers Univ, MA, PhD. **CAREER** Eng Dept, Eastern Conn State Univ **HONORS AND AWARDS** Phi Beta Kappa. **SELECTED PUBLICATIONS** Coed, Claribel Alegria and Central American Literature, Oh Univ Press, 94; articles on works of Edith Wharton (Conn Review) and Claribel Alegria; auth, Letras Femeninas. **CONTACT ADDRESS** Eastern Connecticut State Univ, 83 Windham Street, Willimantic, CT 06226. **EMAIL** mcgowan@ecsu.ctstateu.edu

MCGUIRE, WILLIAM J.
PERSONAL Born 02/17/1925, New York, NY, m, 1954, 3 children **DISCIPLINE** PSYCHOLOGY **EDUCATION** U.S. Army, 43-46; Fordham Col, BA, 49; Fordham Univ Grad Sch, MA, 50; Louvain Univ, 50-51; Yale Univ, PhD, 54; SSRC Advanced Inst on Mathematics for Soc Scientists, 55; SSRC Inst on Computer Simulation Cognition, 63. **CAREER** SSRC Postdoctoral Fel, Univ Minn, 54-55; from instr to asst prof, Yale Univ, 55-58; from asst prof to assoc prof, Univ Ill, 58-61; from assoc prof to prof, Columbia Univ, 61-67; prof, Univ Calif at San Diego, 67-70; prof, Yale Univ, 70-; dept of psychology chemn, Yale Univ, 71-73. **HONORS AND AWARDS** Phi Beta Kappa, Fordham Col; Fulbright Scholar, Univ Louvain, 50-51; Fels, Yale Univ, 51-54; SSRC Postdoctoral Fel, Univ Minn, 54-55; Am Psychol Asn Vis Scientist, 61 & 65-67; Annual Socio-Psychol Awd, Am Asn for the Advancement of Sci, 63; General Electric Found Awd, 63, 64, & 66; Fel, Ctr for Advanced Study in the Behav Sci at Stanford, 65-66; Guggenheim Fel, London Sch of Economics, 70-71; NIMH Sr Postdoctoral Fel, London Sch of Economics, 70-71; Distinguished Scientific Contribution Awd, Am Psychol Asn, 88; William James Fel, Am Psychol Soc; Honorary Degree, Eotvos Lorand Univ, 90; Distinguished Scientist Awd, Soc of Experimental Soc Psychology, 92; Harold D. Lasswell Awd, Int Soc of Political Psychology, 99. **MEMBERSHIPS** Am Psychol Asn, Am Sociol Asn, Am Asn of Public Opinion Res, Am Asn for the Advancement of Sci, Sigma Xi, Am Marketing Asn, Acad of Behav Medicine Res, Int Commun Asn, Am Psychol Soc, European Asn of Experiment Soc Psychology, British Psychol Soc, Int Soc of Polit Psychol, Int Asn of Applied Psychology. **RESEARCH** Social and Personality Psychology, Cognitive Psychology. **SELECTED PUBLICATIONS** Coauth, "Enhancing self-esteem by directed thinking tasks: Cognitive and affective positivity asymmetries," J of Personality and Soc Psychology 70 (96): 1117-1124; auth, "Going beyond the banalities of bubbapsychology: A perspectivist social psychology," in The Message of Social Psychology, eds. A. Haslam & C. MacGarty (UK: Blackwell Publ, 97), 221-237; auth, "Creative hypothesis generating in psychology: some useful heuristics," Annual Rev of Psychology 48 (97): 1-30; auth, Constructing Social Psychology: Creative and Critical Processes, Cambridge Univ Press (New York, NY), 99; auth, "Consistency theory," in Encyclopedia of Psychology, ed. A. E. Kazdin (DC: Am Psychol Asn & Oxford Univ Press, 99); auth, "Standing on the shoulders of ancients: Consumer research, persuasion, and figurative language," J of Consumer Res (00); auth, "Psychology's dialectical evolution by means of shifting resolutions of its antinomies," Rassegna di Psicologia (forthcoming); auth, "After a half-century of election studies: Whence, where, and whither?," in Election Studies, eds. Elihu Katz & Yael Warshel (NY: Westview Press, forthcoming). **CONTACT ADDRESS** Dept Psychology, Yale Univ, PO Box 208205, New Haven, CT 06520. **EMAIL** william.mcguire@yale.edu

MCHENRY, HENRY M.
PERSONAL Born 05/19/1944, Los Angeles, CA, m, 1966, 2 children **DISCIPLINE** ANTHROPOLOGY **EDUCATION** Univ Calif, Davis, BA, 66; Harvard Univ, PhD, 72. **CAREER** Prof, Univ Calif, Davis, 71-, chair, Dept Anthropol, Univ Calif, Davis, 84-88. **HONORS AND AWARDS** Phi Beta Kappa; Fel, Calif Acad of Sci; Univ Calif Davis Prize for Teaching and Scholarly Achievement. **MEMBERSHIPS** Am Anthropol Asn, Am Asn Physical Anthropols, Vertebrate Paleontological Soc, Soc for the Study of Evolution. **RESEARCH** Paleoanthropology; human evolution. **SELECTED PUBLICATIONS** Auth, "Human evolution," in Encyclopedia of Human Biology, 2nd ed, Vol 4, New York: Academic Press (97): 539-599; coauth, "Trait list bias and a reappraisal of early hominid phylogeny," J of Human Evolution, 34 (98): 109-113; auth, " 'Mrs. Ples' now and then," South African J of Sci, 93 (98): 165; coauth, "Body proportions in Australopithecus afrensis and A. Africanus and the origin of the genus Homo," J of Human Evolution, 35 (98): 1-22; co-ed, Primate Locomotion: Recent Advances, New York: Plenum Pub (98); auth, "Fossils and reconstructing the origins and evolution of taxa-introduction," in Primate Locomotion: Recent Advances, E. Strasser, J. Fleagle, A. Rosenberger, and H. M. McHenry, eds, New York: Plenum Pub (98): 333-336; coauth, "Limb lengths in Australopithecus and the origin of the genus Homo," South African J of Sci, 94 (98): 447-450; rev of Function, Phylogeny, and Fossils: Miocene Hominoid Evolution and Adaptations, Int J of Primatiology, 18 (98): 1053-1056. **CONTACT ADDRESS** Dept Anthropol, Univ of California, Davis, 1 Shields Ave, Davis, CA 95616. **EMAIL** hmmchenry@ucdavis.edu

MCKAY, DIANE L.
PERSONAL Born Milwaukee, WI **DISCIPLINE** WOMAN'S STUDIES **EDUCATION** Duke Univ, AB, 87; AM, 00; PhD, 01. **CAREER** Instr, Duke Univ, 91-. **HONORS AND AWARDS** Women's Study Grad Inst Awd, 97. **MEMBERSHIPS** MLA; ASA. **RESEARCH** 20th-century American literature; American studies; cultural studies; modernism; women's and gender studies. **SELECTED PUBLICATIONS** Auth, "Margo St James," in Significant Contemporary American Feminists: A Biographical Sourcebook, ed. Jennifer Scanlon (CT: Greenwood Pr, 99). **CONTACT ADDRESS** 200 E 94th St, Apt 311, New York, NY 10128. **EMAIL** dmckay@alumni.duke.edu

MCKEACHIE, WILLIAM M.
PERSONAL Born 08/24/1921, Clarkston, MI, m, 1942, 2 children **DISCIPLINE** PSYCHOLOGY **EDUCATION** Mich State Normal Col, BS, 42; Univ Mich, PhD, 49. **CAREER** Teaching Fel to prof, Univ of Mich, 46-. **HONORS AND AWARDS** LLD, E Mich Univ, Univ of Cincinnati; DHL, Shawnee State Univ; LittD, Hope Col; ScD, NW Univ, Denison Univ, Alma Col. **MEMBERSHIPS** Am Psychol Assoc; Am Ed Res Assoc; British Psychol Soc. **RESEARCH** Learning and teaching in colleges and universities. **SELECTED PUBLICATIONS** Coauth, "Judgments of ingroups and outgroups by members of three denominations in the United States and Poland", Jour of Psychology and Christianity (93):225-235; coauth, "Reliability and predictive validity of the Motivated Strategies for Learning Questionnaire (MSLQ), Ed and Psychol Measurement (93):801-813; auth, "Critical elements in training university teachers", The Int Jour for Ed Dev (97):67-74; coauth, "Individual differences in students' retention of knowledge and conceptual structures learned in university and high school courses: The case of test anxiety", Appl Cognitive Psychol, (97):507-526; auth, "Student ratings: The validity of use", Am Psychol (97):1218-1225; coauth, "Assessment and modification of flexibility of cognitive structures created in university courses", Contemp Ed Psychol 23 (98):209-232; auth, "Teaching Tips: Strategies, Research, and Theory for College and University Teachers", Houghton-Mifflin (Boston), 99. **CONTACT ADDRESS** Dept Psychology, Univ of Michigan, Ann Arbor, 525 E Univ Ave, Ann Arbor, MI 48109. **EMAIL** billmck@umich.edu

MCKEEN, WILLIAM
PERSONAL Born 09/16/1954, Indianapolis, IN, d, 3 children **DISCIPLINE** HISTORY; MASS COMMUNICATION; EDUCATION **EDUCATION** Indiana Univ, BA, 74, MA, 77; Univ OK, PhD, 86. **CAREER** Educator, 77-; Prof and ch, jour dept, Univ Florida. **HONORS AND AWARDS** Various teaching Awds **MEMBERSHIPS** Pop culture asn; SO book critics cir; AJHA; asn for edu in journ and mass comm. **RESEARCH** Pop cult; journ hist; music. **SELECTED PUBLICATIONS** Rock and Roll is Here to Stay, 00; Literary Journalism, 00; Tom Wolfe, 95; Bob Dylan: A Bio-Bibliography, 93; Hunter S Thompson, 91; The Beatles: A Bio-Bibliography, 90. **CONTACT ADDRESS** Univ of Florida, 2089 Weimer Hall, Gainesville, FL 32611. **EMAIL** wmckeen@jou.ufl.edu

MCKENNA, MARY OLGA
DISCIPLINE EDUCATION, HISTORY **EDUCATION** Mt St Vincent Univ, BA, 47; Boston Col, Mass, MA, 57, PhD, 64; Univ London, ALE, 77; Univ PEI, LLD, 90. **CAREER** Sch tchr, 39-61; super educ, Archdiocese Boston, 61-64; Prof Emer Educ, Mt St Vincent Univ 64-86; congregational hist, Sisters Charity, Halifax, 86-. **MEMBERSHIPS** Am Conf Relig Women; Can Cath Hist Asn; Can Soc Stud Educ. **SELECTED PUBLICATIONS** Auth, Micmac by Choice: An Island Legend, 90; auth, Paradigm Shifts in a Women's Religious Institution: The Sisters of Charity, Halifax, 1950-79, in CCHA Hist Studs 61, 95. **CONTACT ADDRESS** Dept of Educ, Mount Saint Vincent Univ, Halifax, NS, Canada B3M 3J5.

MCKINLEY, NITA MARY
PERSONAL Born 03/05/1953, Pearsall, TX **DISCIPLINE** PSYCHOLOGY, WOMEN'S STUDIES **EDUCATION** Univ Tex at Austin, BA, 74; Univ Wis, PhD, 95. **MEMBERSHIPS** Soc for the Psychol of Women; Asn for Women in Psychol; Am Psychol Asn. **SELECTED PUBLICATIONS** Co-auth, "The Objectified Body Consciousness Scale," Psychol of Women Quart, 96. **CONTACT ADDRESS** Dept Psychol, Allegheny Col, Dept Psychol, Meadville, PA 16335.

MCLANAHAN, SARA S.
PERSONAL Born 12/27/1940, Tyler, TX, m, 1982, 3 children **DISCIPLINE** SOCIOLOGY **EDUCATION** Univ Houston, BA, 74; Univ Tex, Austin, MA, 76, PhD, 79. **CAREER** NIMH Postdoctoral Fel, Dept Psychiatry, Univ Wisc, 79-81, asst prof, dept of Sociol, Univ of Wisc, 81-86, assoc prof, 86-89, prof, 89-92; prof of Sociol and Public Affairs, Princeton Univ, 90-, Dir, Center for Res on Child Wellbeing, Princeton Univ, 96-. **HONORS AND AWARDS** Hogg Found Fel, Univ Tex, Austin, 77-78; Univ Fel, Univ Tex, Austin, 77-78; Reuben Hill Awd for Outstanding Paper, Nat Coun on Family Relations, 87, 88; Vis Fac Fel, Russell Sage Found, 89; Romnes Fac Fel, Grad Sch, Univ Wisc, 89; NIH, Soc Sci and Population Study Section, 92-96; Finalist for Best Book of Current Interest, Growing Up With a Single Parent, Los Angeles Times, 95; Goode Distinguished Book Awd for Growing Up With a Single Parent, Family Section of Am Sociol Asn, 95; Duncan Distinguished Book Awd for Growing Up With a Single Parent, Population Section of Am Sociol Asn, 96; Nat Fel, Prog in Inequality and Social Policy, Harvard Univ, 98-2001. **MEMBERSHIPS** Population Asn of Am, Am Sociol Asn, Sociol Res Asn, **RESEARCH** Family demography, stratification, and social policy; poverty and family policy. **SELECTED PUBLICATIONS** Coauth with Irwin Garfinkel, Daniel Meyer, and Judith Seltzer, "Introduction" and "Conclusion," in I. Garfinkel, S. McLanahan, D. Meyer, and J. Seltzer, eds, Fathers Under Fire: The Revolution in Child Support Enforcement, NY: Russell Sage Found (98); coauth with Erin Kelly, "The Feminization of Poverty: Past and Future," in Janet Chafetz, ed, Handbook of the Sociology of Gender, NY: Plenum Pub Corp (99); auth, "Father Absence and the Welfare of Children," in Mavis Hetherington, ed, Coping with Divorce, Single Parenting, and Remarriage: A Risk and Resiliency Perspective, Mahwah, NJ: Lawrence Erlbaum Assocs, Inc Pubs (99); coauth with Anne Case and Lin I-fen, "How Hungry is the Selfish Gene?" Nat Bureau of Economic Res, Inc, Working paper 7401, Cambridge, MA (99); coauth with Anne Case and Lin I-fen, "Household Resource Allocation in Stepfamilies: Darwin Reflects on the Plight of Cinderella," Am Economic Rev: Papers and Proceedings, 89, 2 (99): 234-238; coauth with Hongxin Zhao, Jeanne Brooks-Gunn and Burt Singer, "Studying the real child rather than the ideal child: Bringing the person into developmental studies," in L. R. Bergman and R. Cairns, eds, Developmental Science and the Holistic Approach, Mahwah, NJ: Lawrence Erlbaum Assocs Inc Pubs (99); coauth with Anne Case and Lin I-fen, "How Hungry is the Selfish Gene? Evidence from Two Cultures," Economic J (99); coauth with Connie Gager and Dana Glei, "Preparing for Parenting: Who's Ready, Who's Not?" Chapter 3 in Neal Halfon, Mark Schuster and Kathryn Taafe Young, eds, The Health and Social Conditions of Young Children in American Families," The Commonwealth Fund (99); coauth with Irwin Garfinkel and Jeanne Brooks-Gunn, "One of Three Births: Research and Policy Implications of Unwed Parenthood for Family Relationships," Child Development (special issue), New Directions for Child Development in the Twenty-First Century (99); auth, "Family, State and Child Wellbeing," Annual Rev (forthcoming). **CONTACT ADDRESS** Dir, Center for Research on Child Wellbeing, Princeton Univ, 21 Prospect Center, Princeton, NJ 08544-2091. **EMAIL** mclanaha@princeton.edu

MCLAUGHLIN, ANDREE NICOLA
PERSONAL Born 02/12/1948, White Plains, NY **DISCIPLINE** LITERATURE, WOMEN'S STUDIES **EDUCATION** Cornell Univ, BS 70; Univ of MA-Amherst, Med, 71, EdD, 74. **CAREER** Medgar Evers College/CUNY, asst prof/project dir 1974-77, chairperson 1977-79, dean of administration and assoc prof, 79-82, planning coord of Women's Studies Rsch & Develop 1984-89, professor of Humanities, 86-; University of London Institute of Education, distinguished visiting scholar, 86; Hamilton Col, Jane Watson Irwin Visiting Prof of Women's Studies, 89-91; Medgar Evers College/CUNY, prof of literature & language/prof of interdisciplinary studies, 92-, Office of International Women's Affairs, director, 96-. **HONORS AND AWARDS** Natl Endowment for the Humanities Fellow, 1976, 1979, 1984, 1989, 1993; 25 articles published; Amer Council on Educ, Fellow in Acad Admin, 1980-81; Andrew W Mellon Fellow, CUNY Graduate School & Univ Center, 1987; **MEMBERSHIPS** Bd mem, Where We At, Black Women Artists, 1979-87; mem Natl Women's Studies Assoc 1980-84, Amer Assoc of Univ Profs 1982-; founding intl coord, Intl Resource Network of Women of African Descent, 1982-85, founding mem Sisterhood in Support of Sisters in South Africa 1984-; adv bd mem Sisterhood of Black Single Mothers 1984-86; founding intl coordinator, International Cross-Cultural Black Women's Studies Inst, 1987-; chair, Editorial Bd, Network: A Pan African Women's Forum (journal), 1987-91; mem, Policy & Publication Comm, The Feminist Press, CUNY, 1988-99. **SELECTED PUBLICATIONS** Co-editor, Wild Women in the Whirlwind: Afra-American Culture & the Contemporary Literary Renaissance, Rutgers Univ Press, 1990; Author, Double Dutch, poetry, 1989; author, "Black Women's Studies in America," 1989; author, "Urban Politics in the Higher Education of Black Women," 1988; author, "The International Nature of the Southern African Women's Struggles," 1988; author, "Unfinished Business of the Sixties: Black Women on the Front Line," 1990; author, "Black Women, Identity and the Quest for Humanhood and Wholeness," 1990; author, Through the Barrel of Her Consciousness: Contemporary Black Women's Literature and Activism in Cross Cultural Perspective, 1994. Susan Koppelman Book Award for Best Edited Feminist work in Popular/American Culture Studies, 1990; author The Impact of the Black Consciousness and Women's Movements on Black Women's Identity: Intercontinental Empowerment, 1995. **CONTACT ADDRESS** Medgar Evers Col, CUNY, 1650 Bedford Ave, Brooklyn, NY 11225. **EMAIL** mclaughlin@mec.cuny.edu

MCLEAN, ATHENA H.
PERSONAL Born 01/12/1948, McKeesport, PA, m, 1970, 2 children **DISCIPLINE** ANTHROPOLOGY **EDUCATION** Temple Univ, BA, 77; PhD, 90; Univ Pittsburgh, MA, 80. **CAREER** Sr Assoc, The Acadia Inst, Bar Harbor, ME, 95-96; asst prof, Central Mich Univ, Mount Pleasant, Mich, 97-. **HONORS AND AWARDS** Nat Inst of Mental Health Res Grant, 93-94; Invited participant with honorarium to symposium, "Understanding/Dealing with the Mentally Ill in Western Cultures," Berlin, Germany, June 2-4, 1994. **MEMBERSHIPS** Am Anthropol Asn, Soc for Medial Anthropol, Soc for the Anthropol of North Am, Gerontological Soc of Mich, Asn for Anthropol and Gerontology. **RESEARCH** Anthropology of medicine, aging, dementia and institutionalization, community mental health, political economy of health. **SELECTED PUBLICATIONS** Auth, "Empowerment and the Psychiatric Consumer/Ex-Patient Movement in the United States: Contraindications, Crisis, and Change," Soc Sci and Medicine , 40, 8 (95): 1053-71; coauth with Margaret Perkinson, "The Head Nurse as Key Informant: How Beliefs and Institutional Pressures Can Structure Dementia Care," in The Culture eof Long Term Care: Nursing Home Ethnography, J Neil Henderson ands Maria Vesperi, eds, Westport, Ct: Bergin & Harvey (95); combined book rev of The Anthropology of Medicine: From Culture to Method, 3rd ed, Lola Romanucci-Ross, Daniel Moerman and Laurence Tancredi, eds, and The Cultural Context of Health, Illness and Medicine, Martha Loustaunau and Elisa Sobo, Medical Anthropol Quart, 13, 4 (99): 510-511; auth, "Power in the Nursing Home: the Case of a Special Care Unit," Medical Anthropology (forthcoming); auth, "From Ex-Patient Alternatives to Consumer Options: Consequences of Consumerism for Psychiatric Consumers and the Ex-Patient Movement," Int J of Health Services (forthcoming). **CONTACT ADDRESS** Dept Sociol & Anthropol, Central Michigan Univ, 100 W Preston Rd, Mount Pleasant, MI 48859-0001. **EMAIL** Athena.H.McLean@cmich.edu

MCLEAN, MABLE PARKER
PERSONAL Born Cameron, NC, w **DISCIPLINE** EDUCATION **EDUCATION** Barber Scotia Coll; Johnson C Smith U; Howard U; NW U; Cath Univ of Am; Inst for Educ Mgmt Harvard Univ 1972; Johnson C Smith U, LHD 1976; Rust Coll, LHS 1976; Coll of Granada, LlD; Barber-Scotia, Pedu. **CAREER** Barber-Scotia Coll, prof of educ and psychology, coordinator of student teaching 1969-71, chairman dept of elementary educ 1970-71, dean of Col 1971-74, apptd interim president 1974, apptd acting president of Col 1974, apptd president of the Col 1974-. **HONORS AND AWARDS** 7 Honorary Degrees; numerous awds and citations among which are Johnson C Smith Alumni Outstanding Achievement Awd 1977; Disting Alumna Awd 1977; Alumna of the Year Johnson C Smith Univ 1980; Dedicated Service Citation-Consortium on Rsch Training 1982; Disting Service Awd Grambling State Univ 1984; Presidential Scroll for devotion to higher educ by promoting achievement of excellence 1986. **MEMBERSHIPS** Mem Assn for Childhood Edn; Assn for Student Teaching; Nat & St NC Assn for Supr & Curriculum Devel; St Coun on Early Childhood Edn; Delta Kappa Gamma Soc of Women Edn; NC Adminstrv Women in Edn; Am Assn of Univ Adminstr; Nat Coun of Adminstrv Women in Edn; mem exec com Metrolina Lung Assn; Dem Women's Org of Cabarrus Co; Alpha Kappa Alpha Sorority Inc; elder John Hall Presb Ch; elected bd of dir Children's Home Soc of NC; past pres United Presb Women's Org of John Hall United Presb Ch; pres Presidents Roundtable of UPC USA; bd dir NAFEO; mem United Bd for Coll Develop; mem United Way of Cabarrus Co; mem exec com NC Assn of Independent Colleges & U; mem exec com NC Assn of Colleges & U. **CONTACT ADDRESS** Barber-Scotia Col, Concord, NC 28025.

MCLEOD, STEPHEN G.
DISCIPLINE HIGHER EDUCATION, ENGLISH LITERATURE **EDUCATION** Pensacola Col, AA, 69; Univ W Fla, BA, 71; Vanderbilt Univ, MA, 73; Nova Southeastern Univ, EdD, 92. **CAREER** Adj instr, St Leo Col Military Educ Prog, 84-92; adj instr, Pensacola Jr Col, 91-; grad prog admin, Nova Southeastern Univ, 94-. **HONORS AND AWARDS** Outstanding dissertation, Nova Southeastern Univ; Professional Development Awd (four times), St Leo Col; Chapter 1419 Res Awd, Phi Delta Kappa. **MEMBERSHIPS** Two-year Col English Asn, Nat Coun of Teachers of English, Phi Delta Kappa. **RESEARCH** Writing across the curriculum, assessing writing, the writing process, interdisciplinary connections. **SELECTED PUBLICATIONS** Auth, "A Possible Source of the 'Broken Jaw' Image in T. S. Eliot's 'The Hollow Men,'" Yeats-Eliot Rev 9 (88): 69-71; auth, "The Eve of Rosh Hashanah," TYCA-Southeast J 30.2 (97): 26. **CONTACT ADDRESS** Dept Liberal Arts, Pensacola Junior Col, 5555 W Hwy 98, Pensacola, FL 32507-1015. **EMAIL** mcleod@bellsouth.net

MCMILLAN, CAROL
PERSONAL Born 05/21/1944, Berkeley, CA **DISCIPLINE** ANTHROPOLOGY **EDUCATION** Univ Colo, BA, 66; Univ Calif Berkeley, MA, 72; SUNY Buffalo, MA, 78; PhD, 82. **CAREER** Instr, Wenatchee Valley Col N, 83-. **HONORS AND AWARDS** Sigma Xi; SUNY Grant, 80; Juan Comas Prize, 82; Willard B Elliot Awd, 82. **MEMBERSHIPS** Sigma Xi; AAAS; Am Anthrop Assoc; Animal Behav Soc; Am Zoological Soc; Am Soc of Primatologists. **RESEARCH** Primate behavior. **SELECTED PUBLICATIONS** Auth, "Genetic differentiation of female lineages in rhesus macaques on Cayo Santiago", Am J Phys Anthrop 50, (79): 461-462; auth, "The possibility of selection as a factor in the patterning of genetic distances between matrilineages of rhesus macaques on Cayo Santiago, Am J Phys Anthrop 52, (80): 251-252; auth, "Preliminary evidence for the importance of context as a variable in rhesus dominance displays", Proceeds of the third Annual Conf on Communicative Behav, SUNY Pr, (80): 66-68; auth, "Synchrony of estrus in macaque matrilines at Cayo Santiago", Am J Phys Anthrop 54, (81): 251; coauth, "Interlineage genetic differentiation among rhesus macaques on Cayo Santiago", Am J Phys Anthrop 56, (81): 305-312; auth, "Lineage-Specific Mating: Does it exist?", The Cayo Santiago Macaques, eds R Rawlins and M Kessler, SUNY Pr, (Albany, 86). **CONTACT ADDRESS** Dept Gen Educ, Wenatchee Valley Col N, PO Box 2058, Omak, WA 98841. **EMAIL** cmcmillan@wvcmail.ctc.edu

MCMULLEN, MIKE
PERSONAL Born 10/14/1965, Fremont, NE, m, 1989, 1 child **DISCIPLINE** RELIGION; SOCIOLOGY **EDUCATION** Emory Univ, PhD, 95 **CAREER** Asst prof Sociol, Univ Houston, 95- **HONORS AND AWARDS** Univ Houston Res Awd, 96, 97; SSSR Res Awd, 94; RRA Res Awd, 94; Emory Grad Tchg Awd, 93. **MEMBERSHIPS** Amer Acad Relig; Amer Sociol Assoc; Assoc Sociol Relig; Soc Sci Study Relig **RESEARCH** Baha'I Faith; Religious Denominations; Religion and Peace Issues; Conflict Resolution and Mediation. **SELECTED PUBLICATIONS** The Religious Construction of a Global Identity: The Baha'i Faith in Atlanta, Rutgers Univ, forthcoming; bk rev, Sacred Acts, Sacred Space, Sacred Time, by John Walbridge, Jour Baha'I Studies, forthcoming; bk rev, The Origins of the Baha'i Community of Can, 1889-1948, by Will C Van den Hoonaard, Soc Relig, 97. **CONTACT ADDRESS** Dept of Sociology, Univ of Houston, Clear Lake, 2700 Bay Area Blvd, Box 203, Houston, TX 77058. **EMAIL** mcmullen@cl.uh.edu

MCNAIRY, FRANCINE G.
PERSONAL Born 11/13/1946, Pittsburgh, PA **DISCIPLINE** EDUCATION **EDUCATION** Univ of Pittsburgh, BA, Sociology, 1968, MSW, 1970, PhD, Comm, 1978. **CAREER** Allegheny Co Child Welfare Servs supvr & soc worker, 70-72; Comm Action Regional training, tech asst specialist, 72; Clarion Univ of PA, assoc prof/counselor 1973-82, coord of academic devel & retention 1983, dean of acad support serv & asst to the acad vice pres, 83-88; West Chester Univ, Assoc Provost, 88-. **MEMBERSHIPS** Presenter Natl Conf on the Freshmen Yr Experience Univ of SC 1982-86; advisor Clarion Univ Black Student Union 1973-; vice chair Clarion Co Human Resources Develop Comm 1983-86; presenter, Intl Conf on the First Year Experience England, 1986, Creative Mgmt in Higher Educ, Boston 1986; consultant, Univ of NE, Briar Cliff Coll, Marshall Univ 1986; St Lawrence Coll 1984, Wesleyan Coll 1983; mem, PA Advisory Bd to ACT; member, AAHE; member, National Assn of Black Women in Higher Education. **SELECTED PUBLICATIONS** Publications "Clarion Univ Increases Black Student Retention"; co-authored "Taking the Library to Freshman Students via Freshman Seminar Concept" 1986, "The Minority Student on Campus" 1985. **CONTACT ADDRESS** West Chester Univ of Pennsylvania, 151 E O Bull Center, West Chester, PA 19383.

MCNAMARA, DENNIS
PERSONAL Born 03/11/1945, s **DISCIPLINE** SOCIOLOGY **EDUCATION** St Louis Univ, BA, 69; Fordham Univ, MA, 74; Jesuit School Theol, MDiv, 76; STM, 77; Harvard Univ, PhD, 83. **CAREER** Asst Prof, Sogang Univ, Seoul, 77-78; Post-doc Res School, Univ Calif, 83-84; Co-chair of Korea Seminar of the Adv Area Studies Program, Foreign Service Inst US Dept of State, 86-; Asst Prof to Dept Chair, Georgetown Univ, 84-. **HONORS AND AWARDS** Fulbright Res Prof, Sophia Univ, Tokyo, 99; Fulbright Res Prof, Thammasat Univ Bangkok, 99; Fulbright-Hayes Res Prof, Sogang Univ Seoul, 92; Nat Sci Foundation Res School, Sophia Univ Tokyo, 91-92; Fulbright Res Scholar, Sogang Univ, Seoul, 87-88. **MEMBERSHIPS** Council on Foreign Relations, Intl Sociol Asn, Intl Studies Asn, Am Political Sci Asn, Am Sociol Asn, Asn for Asian Studies. **RESEARCH** Political economy of East and Southeast Asia; Between Militaries and markets - Societal Bases for Asian Regional Cooperation; Theories of Economy and Society, Korean Society, Japanese society. **SELECTED PUBLICATIONS** Auth, Corporatism and Korean Capitalism, Routledge Press, 99; auth, "Global Adjustment in Korean Textiles," Creativity and Innovation Management, (99): 48-56; auth, Trade and Transformation in Korea, 1876-1945, Westview Press, 96; auth, Textiles and Industrial Transition in Japan, Cornell Univ Press, 95; auth, "Corporatism and Cooperation among Japanese Labor," Comparative Politics, Vol 28, (96): 379-398. **CONTACT ADDRESS** Dept Sociol, Georgetown Univ, PO Box 571037, Washington, DC 20057-1037. **EMAIL** Mcnamard@georgetown.edu

MCNEELY, R. L.
PERSONAL Born Flint, MI **DISCIPLINE** SOCIOLOGY **EDUCATION** Eastern Mich Univ, BA, 68; Univ Mich, MSW, 70; Brandeis Univ, PhD, 75; Marquette Univ, JD, 94. **CAREER** Instr, Edmonds Comm Col, 74; instr, Simmons Col, 74-75; vis prof, Fla Intl Univ, 82-83; vis prof, Univ New Orleans, 89-90; asst prof, Univ Wis-Milwaukee, 75-82; prof, 82-. **HONORS AND AWARDS** Milwaukee Man Distinct, 87; MUL Vol Awd, 88; ACE Fel, 88-89; Law Schol Awd, Marquette Univ, 92-93, 93-94; Res Fel, Geront Soc Am, 90. **MEMBERSHIPS** State Bar, WI; Thomas E Fairchild Soc. **RESEARCH** Job satisfaction in the human services; work/family balancing programs; work-related family violence. **SELECTED PUBLICATIONS** Coauth, "The Demographics of Aging," in Services to The Aging and Aged: Public Policies and Programs, ed. PH Kim (CT: Garland Pub, 94), 3-16; coauth, "Quality Circles, Human Service Organizations, and the Law," Administration in Social Work (97), 65-71; coauth, "Rational Emotive Behavior Therapy in the Death and Dying Process of Aged African Americans and Latinos," J of Human Behavior in the Social Env (98), 305-321; coauth, "Ethnicity, Gender, Earnings, Occupational Rank, and Job Satisfaction in the Public Social Services: What Do the Workers Say?" in Workplace Diversity: Issues and Perspectives, ed. A Daly (Lanham, MD, NASW Press, 98), 144-165; coauth, "Is Domestic Violence a Gender Issue, or a Human Issue?," J of Human Behavior in the Social Env (98). **CONTACT ADDRESS** School of Social Welfare, Univ of Wisconsin, Milwaukee, PO Box 413, Milwaukee, WI 53201. **EMAIL** rlmatty@execpc.com

MCNEIL, WILLIAM KINNETH
PERSONAL Born 08/13/1940, Canton, NC **DISCIPLINE** AMERICAN FOLKLORE AND HISTORY **EDUCATION** Carson-Newman Col, BA, 62; Okla State Univ, MA, 63; State Univ NYork, Oneonta, MA, 67; Ind Univ, PhD(Am folklore), 80. **CAREER** Historian, Off State Hist, Albany, NY, 67-70; adminr & folklorist, Smithsonian Inst, 75-76; FOLKLORIST, OZARK FOLK CTR, 76-, Adv & consult, Fr Cult Proj, Old Mines, Mo, 78-80; bd mem, Nat Coun Traditional Arts, 79-; chief consult, Echoes of Ozarks, 82. **MEMBERSHIPS** Am Folklore Soc; Am Asn State & Local Hist; Ozark States Folklore Soc; Southern Folklore Soc. **RESEARCH** American music, particularly 19th century popular and 20th century country; American theater; American folklore, particulary folklore of the Southern mountains. **SELECTED PUBLICATIONS** Auth, The autograph album custom: A tradition and its scholarly treatment, Keystone Folklore, spring 68; A Schoharie County songster, NY Folklore Quart, 3/69; We'll make the Spanish grunt: Popular songs about the sinking of the Maine, J Popular Cult, summer 69; Mrs F-Little Joe: The multiple personality experience and the folklorist, Ind Folklore, 71; coauth, American proverb literature, Folklore Forum, 71; auth, Syncopated slander: The Coon Song 1890-1900, Keystone Folklore, spring 72; Appalachian folklore scholarship, Appalachian J, spring 77; James Athearn Jones: Pioneer American folklorist, In: Folklore on Two Continents: A Festschrift for Linda Degh, 81. **CONTACT ADDRESS** PO Box 500, Nature View, AR 72560.

MCNEILL, DAVID
PERSONAL Born 12/21/1933, Santa Rosa, CA, m, 1957, 2 children **DISCIPLINE** PSYCHOLINGUISTICS **EDUCATION** Univ Calif, Berkeley, AB, 53, PhD(psychol), 62. **CAREER** Res fel, Ctr Cognitive Studies, Harvard Univ, 63-65; from asst prof to assoc prof psychol, Univ Mich, 65-68; Prof Behav Sci & Ling, Univ Chicago, 69-, Guggenheim Found fel, 73-74; mem, Inst Advan Studies, 73-75. **MEMBERSHIPS** Ling Soc Am; Am Asn Advan Sci. **RESEARCH** Psychological processes involved in the use of language; comparison of gestures for language; development of gesture in children. **SELECTED PUBLICATIONS** Auth, Abstract Deixis, Semiotica, vol 0095, 93. **CONTACT ADDRESS** Dept of Behav Sci, Univ of Chicago, Chicago, IL 60637.

MCNICOL, SHARON-ANN
PERSONAL Born 10/06/1958, Trinidad, m, 1979, 1 child **DISCIPLINE** PSYCHOLOGY **EDUCATION** NY Univ, BA, 81; Columbia Univ, MA, 82; Hofstra Univ, MA, 84; Hofstra Univ, ME, 85; Hofstra Univ, PhD, 86. **CAREER** From Assoc Prof to Prof, Howard Univ, 97-. **HONORS AND AWARDS** Outstanding Young Woman of Am, 86; Mayoral Awd, Town of Hempstead, 93; Outstanding Serv Awd, St Johns Univ, 96; Provost Acad Excellence Awd, Howard Univ, 97; Eric Williams Educ Achievement Awd, 98; The Achievement Awd, Caribbean Bus, 99. **MEMBERSHIPS** APA, NCPA, CSA. **SELECTED PUBLICATIONS** Coauth, Assessing Intelligence: Applying a Bio-Cultural Model, Sage Publ (CA), 98; coauth, "Ethnocultural Perspectives on Child-Rearing Practices in the Caribbean," Int Soc Work, vol 42, no 1 (98): 89-97; coauth, "African American Education and the Ebonics Issues," J of Negro Educ, vol 67, no 1 (99): 2-4; coauth, "Psychoeducational Assessment Issues and Ebonics," J of Negro Educ, vol 67, no 1 (99): 16-23; coauth, "Introduction," in A Test Rev Guide for Bilingual Children: Cognitive Assessment (PA: Lincoln UP, 99), ix-xi; coauth, "A Bio-Ecological Approach to Cognitive Assessment," in A Test Rev Guide for Bilingual Children: Cognitive Assessment (PA: Lincoln UP, 99), 147-157; coauth, A Test Review Guide for Bilingual Children: Cognitive Assessment, Lincoln Univ Pr (PA), 99; coauth, Assessment and Culture: Cognitive, Achievement, Vocational, Visual-Motor, Personality and Linguistic Competencies, Int UP (CT), 99; coauth, Women and Politics: Fear of Leadership, Greenwood Publ Group (CT), forthcoming. **CON-**

TACT ADDRESS Dept Psychol, Howard Univ, 2400 6th St NW, Washington, DC 20059-0002.

MCNUTT, JAMES CHARLES

PERSONAL Born 08/10/1950, Denison, TX, m, 1971, 2 children **DISCIPLINE** AMERICAN STUDIES, FOLKLORE **EDUCATION** Harvard Univ, BA, 72; Univ Tex, Austin, MA, 77, PhD(Am civilization), 82. **CAREER** Asst instr Am studies, Univ Tex, Austin, 80-82; res assoc, Univ Tex, San Antonio; asst prof, Thomas More Col. **MEMBERSHIPS** Am Studies Asn; Am Folklore Soc. **RESEARCH** Regionalism. **SELECTED PUBLICATIONS** Auth, Mark Twain and the American Indian: Earthly realism & heavenly idealism, Am Indian Quart, 8/78; John Comfort Fillmore: A student of Indian music reconsidered, Am Music. **CONTACT ADDRESS** Dept of Hist, Thomas More Col, 333 Thomas More Pkwy, Crestview Hills, KY 41017. **EMAIL** james.mcnutt@thomasmore.edu

MCNUTT, PAULA M.

PERSONAL Born 03/12/1955, Denver, CO, s **DISCIPLINE** HEBREW BIBLE, ANTHROPOLOGY AND ARCHAEOLOGY **EDUCATION** Univ Colorado, BA, 78; Univ Montana, MA, 83; Vanderbilt Univ, PhD, 89. **CAREER** Prof, Canisius Col, 87-. **HONORS AND AWARDS** NEH Fel for Col Tchr, 94-95. **MEMBERSHIPS** Amer Acad Relig; Soc Bibl Lit, Cath Bibl Asn, Amer Sch Oriental Res, Archaeol Inst Amer **RESEARCH** Social world of ancient Israel; social roles and statuses of artisans; religion and technology. **SELECTED PUBLICATIONS** Reconstructing the Society of Ancient Israel, Libr of Ancient Israel Series, Louisville, Westminster John Knox Press, 99; The Kenites, the Midianites, and the Rechabites as Marginal Mediators in Ancient Israelite Tradition, Semeia 67, p 109-132, 94; coauth with James W. Flanagan, David W. McCreery and Khair Yassin, Preliminary Report of the 1993 Excavations at Tell Nimrin, Jordan, Ann of the Dept of Antiquities of Jordan, XXXVIII, pp 205-244, 94; Kenites, P. 407 in The Oxford Companion to the Bible, Bruce M. Metzger and Michael D. Coogan eds, Oxford Univ Press, 93; The Development and Adoption of Iron Technology in the Ancient Near East, Proceedings: The Eastern Great Lakes Bibilical Society, 12, pp 47-66, 92; The African Ironsmith as Marginal Mediator: A Symbolic Analysis, Journ of Ritual Studies, 5/2, pp 75-98, 91; The Forging of Israel: Iron Technology, Symbolism, and Tradition in Ancient Society, The Social World of Biblical Antiquity Series, 8, Sheffield, Almond Press, 90; Sociology of the Old Testament, pp 835-839, Mercer Dict of the Bible, Macon, GA, Mercer Univ Press, 90; Egypt as an Iron Furnace: A Metaphor of Transformation, pp 293-301, Society of Biblical Literature 1988 Seminar Papers, David J. Lull ed, Atlanta, Schol Press, 88; Interpreting Ancient Israel's Fold Traditions, Journ for the Study of the Old Testament, 39, pp 44-52, 87. **CONTACT ADDRESS** Canisius Col, 2001 Main St., Buffalo, NY 14208. **EMAIL** mcnutt@canisius.edu

MCPHERSON, MILLER

DISCIPLINE SOCIOLOGY **EDUCATION** Vanderbilt, PhD, 73. **CAREER** Dept of Sociol, Univ of Arizona, Tuscon. **HONORS AND AWARDS** Nat Sci Found grant, 81, 82-84, 84-86, 89-91, 93-96, 94-96. **MEMBERSHIPS** Am Sociol Asn, AAAS, INSA. **RESEARCH** Organizations, associations, social networks, quantitative sociology. **SELECTED PUBLICATIONS** Coauth with O. Galle and W. Gove, "Population Density and Pathology: What are the Relationships for Man?," Science, 7 (April 72): 136-153, reprinted in Issues in Social Ecology: Human Milieus, NY: Nat Press Books (74), reprinted in Comparative Urban Structure, Heath Books (74); coauth with T. Rotolo, "Diversity and Change: Modelling the Social Composition of Voluntary Groups," Am Sociol Rev 996); coauth with Bruce H. Mayhew, Tomas Rotolo, and Lynn Smith-Lovin, "Sex and Ethnic Heterogeneity in Face-to-Face Groups in Public Places: An Ecological Perspective on Social Interaction," Social Forces (96); coauth with D. Cress, "Competition and Commitment in Voluntary Groups," Sociological Perspectives (97); coauth with Lynn Smith-Lovin and Allison Munch, "Gender, Children, and Social Contact: The Effects of Childbearing for Men and Women," Am Sociol Rev (97); auth, "Modelling Change in Fields of Organizations: Some Simulatin Results," in Daniel Ilgen and Charles Hulin, eds, Computational Modelling of Behavioral Processes in Organizations, Am Psychol Asn Press (98). **CONTACT ADDRESS** Dept Sociol, Univ of Arizona, PO Box 210027, Tuscon, AZ 85721-0027.

MCRAE, MARY B.

PERSONAL Born 01/26/1948, NC, d, 1 child **DISCIPLINE** PSYCHOLOGY **EDUCATION** Teachers Col, Columbia Univ, EdD, 87. **CAREER** Asst prof, Hunter Col; assoc prof Applied Psychol, NYU. **HONORS AND AWARDS** Goddard Awd for Jr Fac, NYU, 93-94; Post-doctoral fel, Inst Soc Res, prog for res in Black Ams, Univ Mich, 96-97. **MEMBERSHIPS** Am Psychol Asn, Am Coun Asn, Asn of Black Psychols. **RESEARCH** Groups and systems-influences of race, class, and ethics identity. **SELECTED PUBLICATIONS** Auth, "The influence of sex role stereotypes on personnel decisions of Black managers," J of Applied Psychol, 79 (94): 306-309; auth, "Interracial group dynamics: A new perspective," J of Specialists in Groups, 19 (94): 168-174; auth, "Sex bias in hiring decisions of African American managers," in J. McAdoo, ed, Monograph of the Thirteenth Conf on Empirical Res in Black Psychol, Lansing, MI: MI State Univ (95); coauth with D. Noumair, "Race and gender in group research," African Am Res Perspectives, Inst of Soc Res, Univ of Mich (spring 97); coauth with P. M. Carey and Roxanna Anderson-Scott, "Black churches as therapeutic systems: A group process perspective," J of Health and Ed, 25 (98): 778-789; auth, "I'm living in fear for my black men," Daily News (Jan 14, 98); coauth with L. Suzuki, "End Social Promotion? Holding back doesn't work," Daily News (Feb 22, 99); auth, "NYC Black churches as organized healing systems," in T. Carnes and A. Karpathakis, eds, New York Glory: Religions in the City, New York: New York Univ Press (in press); coauth with D. A. Thompson and S. Cooper, "Black churches as therapeutic groups," J of Multicultural Coun and Develop, 27 (99): 207-220. **CONTACT ADDRESS** Dept Applied Psychol, New York Univ, New York, NY 10003. **EMAIL** mm13@152.nyu.edu

MCSPADDEN, LUCIA

PERSONAL Born 02/14/1934, NJ, m, 1961, 3 children **DISCIPLINE** CULTURAL ANTHROPOLOGY; CULTURAL FOUNDATIONS OF EDUCATION **EDUCATION** Univ CA, Davis-BA, 56; Univ Nebraska, MA, 68; Univ Utah, PhD, 78, PhD, 89. **CAREER** Supervision of Doctor of Ministry and Master of Arts candidates, 88-94, CA and San Francisco Theological Seminary; adjunct prof, 89-94, Pacific Sch of Religion; researcher and consultant, 90-92, United Methodist Committee on Relief; organizer and principal investigator, From Token to Colleague, an inter-denominational team funded by the Fund for Theological Education to research barriers to multi-ethnic/racial/immigrant inclusiveness in United Methodist, American Baptist and Roman Catholic denominations in Northern California and to develop training models to overcome such barriers, 91-93; coordinator seminary intern study cluster, 92-93, Fund for Theological Education; project dir, 94, Negotiations between UNHCR and the Eritrean government for Repatriation of Eritrean Refugees; principal investigator, 96, Eritrea: NGOs and Repatriation (in process); sr res fel, Life & Peace Institute, 98-; Principal Investigator, United Methodist Church, 99-. **HONORS AND AWARDS** General Bd of higher Education and Ministry, United Methodist Church, Res Grant; Swedish International Development Agency, Res Grant; Rockefeller Found, Res Grant; Fund for Theological Education Res Grant; Phi Beta Kappa, Univ of Calif; Phi Kappa Phi, Univ of Calif; Prospective Teacher Fel, Univ of Nebr; Graduate Res Competitive Fel, Univ of Utah. **MEMBERSHIPS** Phi Beta Kappa Honorary; Phi Kappa Phi Honorary; Soc foro Christian Ethics; Am Academy of Relig; International Peace Res Asn; Am Anthropoogical Asn; Comt for Human Rights, Am Anthrop Asn, co-ch; Comt on Refugee Issues, Am Anthrop Asn, founding member; Nat Asn for Practicing Anthrop; International soc for Intercultural Education, Teaching, and Res; International Asn for the Study of Forced Migration, founding member; International Refugee Res and Advisory Panel, refugee Studies Programme, Oxford Univ; Soc for Applied Anthrop; Soc for Applied Anthrop, ch and founder; Soc for Applied Anthrop, Policy Comt. **RESEARCH** Forced migration; social place theory; ethnicity; applied anthropology, development; non-government organization; anthropology of religion; peace research. **SELECTED PUBLICATIONS** Auth, "Generating the Political Will for Protecting the Rights of Refugees," in The Future of the United Nations System, ed. C.F. Alger, (Tokyo: UN Univ Press, 98): 282-314; auth, "NGOs and Repatriation: leaders or led?," New Routes, vol. 3, No. 1, (98): 3-6; auth, "Power and Contradictions in Repatriation; Negotiations for the Return of 500,000 Eritrean Refugees," in The End of the Refugee Cycle? Refugee Repatriation and Reconsturction, eds, K. Koser and R. Black, (Oxford: Berghahn Press, 98): 69-84; auth, "Assessing Essential Qualities of Communities: Eritrean Refugees' Resistance and Return," in Negotiating Power and Placec at the Margins: Selected Papers on Refugees and Immigrants, Vol. VIII, eds, J. Lipson and L.A.McSpadden, (Washington, D.C.: American Anthropological Asn, 99): 75-104; co-ed, Negotiating Power and Place at the Margins: Selected Papers on Refugees and Immigrants, Vol. VII, Washington, D.C.: American Anthrop Asn, 99; auth, "Refugees in the Horn of Africa: An Endangered People," in Endangered Peoples of Africa, ed, Robert Hitchcock, (London: Greenwood Press, 00); coauth, "Human Rights and Complex Emergencies," in Anthropology and Complex Emergencies (Tentative Title), ed. Holly Williams, (Arlington, Virginia: National Asn for Practicing Anthropology, 00); auth, Negotiating a Conflicted Refugee Repatriation: UNHCR and the Eritrean Government, Uppsala, Sweden: Life & Peace Institute, 00; auth, "Introduction," in Reaching Reconciliation: Churches in the transitions to democracy in Eastern and Central Europe, ed. Lucia Ann McSpadden, (Uppsala, Sweden: Life & Peace Institute, 00); auth, Reaching Reconciliation: Churches in the transitions to democracy in Eastern and Central Europe, Uppsala, sweden: Life & Peace Institute, 00. **CONTACT ADDRESS** 66 Sandpoint Dr, Richmond, CA 94804. **EMAIL** lmcspad@igc.org

MCVEIGH, FRANK J.

PERSONAL Born 06/10/1931, Hi-Nellz, NJ, m, 1991, 2 children **DISCIPLINE** SOCIOLOGY **EDUCATION** Lasalle Univ, BA, 57; Loyola Univ, MA, 63; St John's Univ, PhD, 70; Marywood Univ, MSW, 85. **CAREER** Prof, Muhlenberg Col, 83-. **MEMBERSHIPS** Soc for the Study of Soc Problems; Nat Asn of Soc Workers. **RESEARCH** Sociology of business and industry; Aging and elderly; Race relations; The family. **SELECTED PUBLICATIONS** Auth, The changing American Family; auth, Social Indicators of Racial Progress; auth, Social Welfare System of Germany; co-auth, Modern Social Problems, Holt, Rinehart & Winston, 78; auth, Brief History of Social Problems, 01. **CONTACT ADDRESS** Dept Sociol & Anthropol, Muhlenberg Col, 2400 W Chew St, Allentown, PA 18104.

MCWHORTER, KATHLEEN T.

PERSONAL Born 10/10/1944, Buffalo, NY, m **DISCIPLINE** EDUCATION **EDUCATION** State Univ NYork at Buffalo, BA, 65; EdM, 68; PhD, 78. **CAREER** Instr, State Univ Col at Buffalo, 69-71; prof, Niagara County Community Col, Sanborn, NY, 71-. **MEMBERSHIPS** Nat Asn of Developmental Educators, Nat Coun of Teachers of English, Col Reading and Learning Asn, Col Reading Asn, New England Reading Asn, New York State Learning Skills Asn, Textbook Authors Asn. **RESEARCH** Developmental writing, developmental reading, learning and study skills. **SELECTED PUBLICATIONS** Auth, College Reading and Study Skills, NY: Longman (80, 83, 86, 89, 92, 96, 98); auth, Efficient and Flexible Reading, NY: Longman, 83, 87, 92, 96, 99; auth, Guide to College Reading, NY: Longman (86, 89, 93, 96, 2000); auth, Study and Thinking Skills in College, NY: Longman (88, 92, 96, 2000); auth, Academic Reading, NY: Longman (90, 94, 98); auth, The Writer's Express, Boston: Houghton (93, 97); auth, The Writer's Guide, Boston: Houghton (97); auth, The Writer's Selections, Boston: Houghton (97, 2000); auth, The Writer's Compass, Boston: Houghton (95, 99); auth, Successful College Writing, Bedford/St Martins (2000). **CONTACT ADDRESS** Dept Humanities, Niagara County Comm Col, 3111 Saunders Settlement Rd, Sanborn, NY 14132. **EMAIL** ktmcw@aol.com

MCWILLIAMS, ALFRED E., JR.

PERSONAL Born 02/03/1938, Wewoka, OK, m **DISCIPLINE** EDUCATION **EDUCATION** CO State Coll, BA 1959, MA 1960; Univ No CO, PhD 1970. **CAREER** Denver Public School CO, teacher, counselor & admin asst 1960-68; Proj Upward Bound Univ No CO, dir 1968-70; Univ No CO, asst dean-special educ & rehabilitation 1970-72; Fed of Rocky Mt States Inc, consultant & career educ content coord 1972-76; Univ No CO, dir personnel AA/EEO 1976-79, asst vice pres admin serv personnel 1979-82; Univ of CO, asst to vice pres for admin 1982-84; Atlanta Univ, vice pres for admin 1984-85; Atlanta Univ, dean, School of Educ, 85-87; GA State Univ, professor, educational policy studies, 87-, coordinator, educational leadership program, 95-. **HONORS AND AWARDS** Appreciation Awd Natl Brotherhood of Skiers 1979; Leadership Styles & Management Strategies, Management Education, series at Atlanta Univ, 1986; Review of KA Heller, et al Placing Children in Special Education: A Strategy for Equity, Natl Academy Press, 1987. **MEMBERSHIPS** Chmn/co-founder Black Educators United 1967-68; asst prof 1970-72, assoc prof educ 1976-82 Univ of No CO; bd mem CO Christian Home Denver 1977-; sec 1977-, chmn 1980-84 Aurora CO Career Serv Comm; bd mem Natl Brotherhood of Skiers 1978-79; mem 1978-, bd mem 1980-85 Amer Assn of Univ Admin; mem 1978-, Gov Lamm appointed chmn 1980-84 CO Merit System Council; council mem 1978-, chmn elect 1981-82 (EEO) Coll & Univ Personnel Assn; mem Am Soc for Personnel Admin 1979-; cons, trainer Natl Center for Leadership Development Atlanta Univ 1979-80; cons, trainer Leadership Develop Training Prog Howard Univ 1981-82; mem, Rotary Club of West End Atlanta, 1984-87, 1989-; mem & army committeeman, Greater Atlanta Chapter reserve Officers Assn of US, 1985-; mem & chairman ofbd of dir, APPLE Corps, 1986; mem, Professional Journal Committee, Assn of Teacher Educators, 1987-; member, Amer Assn for Higher Education, 1989-; member, Assn for Supervision and Curriculum Development, 1989-; Amer Assn of Univ Professors, 1995-. **CONTACT ADDRESS** Educ Policy Studies, Georgia State Univ, University Plaza, Atlanta, GA 30303.

MCWORTER, GERALD A.

PERSONAL Born 11/21/1942, Chicago, IL, d **DISCIPLINE** SOCIOLOGY **EDUCATION** Ottawa Univ, BA Soc & Philosophy, 1963; Univ of Chicago, MA, 1966, PhD, 1974. **CAREER** Ottawa Univ Dept of Philosophy, teaching asst, 62-63; Univ of Chicago Natl Opinion Research Center, research asst, asst study dir, 63-67; Fisk Univ Center for Afro-Amer Studies, asst prof of sociology, 67-68; Inst of the Black World, asst prof of sociology, 67-68; Fisk Univ, asst prof, assoc prof of sociology & Afro-Amer studies, 69-75, dir, Afro-Amer Studies Program, 69-75; Univ of Illinois at Chicago, assoc prof of Black studies, 75-79; Univ of Illinois at Urbana-Champaign, assoc prof of sociology & Afro-Amer studies, 79-87, dir Afro-Am Studies & Research Program, 79-84; Twenty-First Century Books & Publications, sr editor, currently; State Univ of New York at Stony Brook, assoc prof of Africana studies, currently. **MEMBERSHIPS** Founder & dir, Cooperative Research Network in Black Studies, 1984-; ed bd, Malcolm X Studies Newsletter, 1987-, Afro Scholar Newsletter, 1983-, Western Journal of Black Studies, 1983-, Black Scholar, 1969-; founder, chair, Org of Black Amer Culture, 1965-67 **CONTACT ADDRESS** SUNY, Stony Brook, Stony Brook, NY 11794.

MEADOW, PHYLLIS W.
DISCIPLINE PSYCHOANALYSIS **EDUCATION** Univ Md, BA, 46; Theodor Reik Inst, Cert in Psychoanalysis, 62; NYork Univ, PhD, 69. **CAREER** Instr, Perkins Inst for the Blind, 48-49; adjunct assoc prof and prof, Long Island Univ, 64-73; fac, Calif Grad Inst, 74-76; fac, Philadelphia Sch of Psychoanalysis, 76-77; Dean of Res Studies, Center for Modern Psychoanalytic Studies, 93-, prof, 71-; prof, Boston Grad Sch of Psychoanalysis, 73-, Pres and Exec Dir, 79-. **HONORS AND AWARDS** Dir and Founder, Ctr for Modern Psychoanalytic Studies, 71-79; Pres, Boston Ctr for Modern Analytic Studies at Los Angeles, 90-92. **MEMBERSHIPS** Soc of Modern Psychoanalysts, Am Psychol Asn, Theodor Reik Psychoanalytic Inst, Nat Psychol Asn for Psychoanalysis. **RESEARCH** Preverbal/destructive aggression. **SELECTED PUBLICATIONS** Coauth with Hymn Spotnitz, Treatment of the Narcissistic Neuroses, Northvale, NJ: J. Aronson (95); auth, "Selected Theoretical and Clinical Papers of Phyllis W. Meadow," monograph, Modern Psychoanalysis, NY: Center for Modern Psychoanalytic Studies (96); auth, "A Reply to Mackay," Modern Psychoanalysis, Vol 21, 1 (96): 31-37; auth, "Psychoanalysis: An open system of research," Modern Psychoanalysis, Vol 21, 2 (96): 359-380; auth, "Is Psychoanalysis a science?," Modern Psychoanalysis, Vol 21, 2 (96): 335-358; auth, "Issues in psychoanalytic research," Modern Psychoanalysis, Vol 21, 2 (96): 309-333; auth, "Breaking taboos in group analysis," Modern Psychoanalysis, Vol 21, 2 (96): 267-292; auth, " Psychoanalysis and Violence," Modern Psychoanalysis, Vol 22, 1 (97): 3-15; auth, "What do infants want?," Modern Psychoanalysis, Vol 22, 2 (97): 137-143; coauth with Charles Lemert, The New Psychoanalysis (in prep). **CONTACT ADDRESS** President, Boston Grad Sch of Psychoanalysis, 158 Beacon St, Brookline, MA 02446.

MEADOWS, EDDIE
PERSONAL Born 06/24/1939, LaGrange, TN, m, 1996 **DISCIPLINE** ETHNOMUSICOLOGY, JAZZ STUDIES **EDUCATION** Tenn State Univ, BA; Univ Ill, MS; Mich State Univ, PhD; Univ Calif, postdoc stud; study at Univ of Ghana. **CAREER** Vis prof, Univ Calif, Berkeley; vis prof, Univ Ghana, W Africa; vis prof, UCLA; vis prof, Mich State Univ; prof, grad adv, San Diego State Univ, School of Music and Dance. **HONORS AND AWARDS** Martin Luther King distinguished vis profship, MI State Univ; Meritorious Performance and Prof Promise awards, San Diego State Univ. **MEMBERSHIPS** Jazz Educrs; Soc for Ethnomusicology; African Studies Asn. **RESEARCH** African-American music; Jazz studies. **SELECTED PUBLICATIONS** Auth, Afro-America Music, 76; auth, Theses and Dissertations on Black and American Music, 80; auth, Jazz Reference and Research Materials, 81; auth, Jazz Research and Performance Materials: A Select Annotated Bibliography, 95; coed, California Soul: Music of African Americans in the West, Univ of Calif Press, 98. **CONTACT ADDRESS** Sch Mus and Dance, San Diego State Univ, 5500 Campanile Dr, San Diego, CA 92182. **EMAIL** meadows@mail.sdsu.edu

MEANA, MARTA
PERSONAL Born 12/01/1957, Madrid, Spain, m, 1998 **DISCIPLINE** PSYCHOLOGY **EDUCATION** McGill Univ, BA, 81, MA, 86, BA, 91, PhD, 96. **CAREER** Asst prof, Dept of Psychol, Univ Nevada, Las Vegas. **HONORS AND AWARDS** McGill Univ: Fac Scholar, 90, James McGill Awd, 90, Univ Scholar, 91, Soc Scis Res grant, 93, Soc Scis Travel Awd, 94, Post-Grad Students Soc Travel Awd, 94, Dean's Honor List Diss Awd, 96; Fel, Nat Scis and Engineering Res Coun, summer 91; Am Psychol Asn Student Travel Awd, 94; Med Res Coun of Can Studentship, 92-95; Fred Lowry Awd, Univ of Toronto Sch of Med, 97; William Morris Awd for Excellence in Teaching, Col of Liberal Arts, UNLV, 2000. **MEMBERSHIPS** Am Psychol Asn, Health Psychol Div (APA), Div of the Psychol of Women (APA), Int Asn for the Study of Pain, Nat Vulvodynia Asn, Int Acad for Sex Res, Soc for Sex Therapy and Res. **SELECTED PUBLICATIONS** Rev of Breast Cancer: A Psychological Treatment Manual, ed S. Haber, Gen Hosp Psychiatry, 19:4 (97): 303-304; coauth with D. S. Stewart, S. Abbey, and K. M. Boydell, "What makes women tired? A community sample," J of Women's Health, 7, 1 (98): 69-76; coauth with Y. M. Binik, S. Khalife and D. Cohen, "Affect and Marital Adjustment in Women's Rating of Dyspareunic Pain," Can J of Psychiatry, 43:4 (98): 381-385; auth, "The meeting of pain and depression: Co-morbidity in women," Can J of Psychiatry, 43, 9 (98): 893-899; auth, "Is dyspareunia primarily a sexual dysfunction or a pain disorder?," (comment) Medical Aspects of Human Sexuality, 1, 6, 10 (98); coauth with S. D. Pruitt and T. R. Dresselhaus, "Opinoid Therapy for Chronic Pancreatitis: Controlling aberrant use through behavioral management," Gen Hosp Psychiatry, 21 (99): 137-140; coauth with I. Binik, S. Khalife and D. Cohen, "Psychosocial Correlates of Pain Attributions in Women with Dyspareunia," Psychosomatics, 40: 6 (99): 497-502; coauth with B. Crawford and D. Stewart, "Treatment decision making in mature adults: Gender Differences," Health Care for Women Int, 21 (2000): 91-104; coauth with D. E. Stewart, "Pain: Adding to the affective burden," in Pain and Mood Disorders in Women, eds, M. Steiner, K. A. Yonkers, and E. Ericsson, London: Martin Dunitz (in press); rev of Psychological Mechanisms of Pain and Analgesia by Donald D. Price, J of Nervous and Mental Disease (in press). **CONTACT ADDRESS** Dept Psychology, Univ of Nevada, Las Vegas, 4505 Maryland Pkwy, Las Vegas, NV 89154. **EMAIL** meana@nevada.edu

MEDHI, ABBAS
PERSONAL Born 07/01/1950, Iraq, s **DISCIPLINE** SOCIOLOGY, ANTHROPOLOGY **EDUCATION** Baghdad Univ, BA, 74; Bath Univ, MA, 82; Ohio State Univ, PhD, 87. **CAREER** Lectr, The Ohio State Univ, 87-88; prof, Univ Minn, 91-97; prof, St Cloud State Univ, 89-. **HONORS AND AWARDS** Grad Asn Awd, The Ohio State Univ, 87; Distinguished Teacher Awd, St Cloud State Univ, 90 & 91; Outstanding Teaching Awd, Student Senate, 91. **MEMBERSHIPS** Acad of Management Asn, Human Resource and Organizational Behav Asn, Int Acad of Management and Accounting Asn, Am Sociol Asn, The Sociol of Work and Occupation Group, St Cloud Chamber of Commerce, St Cloud Human Rights Comn, Study Group of the Int Industrial Relations Asn, Soc for Advancement of Socio-economic Asn, Minn Int Ctr, United Nations Asn of Minn. **SELECTED PUBLICATIONS** Auth, "Problems of Industrial Development in Iraq," Al-Sinaa 6 (75); auth, "Economic Development of the Labor Market in Iraq," Int J of Manpower 4 (83); rev, of "The Iraqui Economy Under Saddam Hussein: Development or Decline," Middle E Policy J (95); auth, "What the U.S. Can Do to Help End the Suffering," Washington Report on Middle E Affairs (99); auth, "Beyond the Big Stick," Azzaman J (99); auth, "Toward a Realistic American Policy on Iraq," Azzaman J (99); auth, "Doing Business Cross Culture," Trend Magazine (99). **CONTACT ADDRESS** Dept Sociol & Anthrop, St. Cloud State Univ, 720 4th Ave S, Saint Cloud, MN 56301. **EMAIL** amehdi@stcloudstate.edu

MEHIEL, RONALD
PERSONAL Born 07/10/1950, Vienna, Austria, m, 1982, 4 children **DISCIPLINE** PSYCHOLOGY **EDUCATION** Univ Washington, BS, 82; PhD, 88. **CAREER** Asst Prof to Prof and Chair, Shippensburg, Univ, 88-. **MEMBERSHIPS** Phi Kappa Phi, Soc for the Study of Ingestive Beh, E Psychol Asn, Coun on Undergrad Res, Comparative Cognition Group, Psychonomic Soc, Beh Neurosci and Comparative Psychol. **RESEARCH** Motivation; Hunger; Flavor preference learning; Control of food intake, Hedonics. **SELECTED PUBLICATIONS** Auth, "Hedonic shifts in rats: A physiological model for learned flavor preferences based on calories," in Hedonics of Taste, Lawrence Erlbaum, 91; auth, "Try it, you'll like it," Scholars, (93): 34-38; auth, "The effects of maloxone on flavor-calorie preference learning indicate involvement of opioid reward systems," The Psychological Record, (96): 435-450; auth, "The Psychological Hedonism of Robert C Bolles," in The legacy of Robert C Bolles, Lawrence Erlbaum, 96. **CONTACT ADDRESS** Dept Psychol, Shippensburg Univ of Pennsylvania, 1871 Old Main Dr, Shippensburg, PA 17257. **EMAIL** rmehie@ship.edu

MEINDL, RICHARD S.
PERSONAL Born 11/22/1947, Chicago, IL, m, 1975, 1 child **DISCIPLINE** ANTHROPOLOGY **EDUCATION** Mass, PhD, 79. **CAREER** Grad Fac, Kent State Univ, 86-; Prof, Chemn of Dept of Anthrop, Kent State Univ, 91-. **MEMBERSHIPS** AAPA. **RESEARCH** Biological Anthropology, Populations Genetics, Statistics. **SELECTED PUBLICATIONS** Coauth, "Eukaryote mutation and the protein clock," Yearbk of Phys Anthrop 16 (72): 18-30; auth, "Family Formation and health in 19th century Franklin County, Massachusetts," in Genealogical Demography, ed. B. Dyke and W. Morrill (NY: Acad Press, 80); auth, "A selective advantage for cystic fibrosis heterozygotes," AJPA 74 (87): 39-45; coauth, "Relative dental development in hominoids and its failure to predict somatic growth velocity," AJPA 86 (91): 113-120; coauth, "The comparative senescent biology of the hominoid pelvis," in Integrating Archaeological Demography, ed. R.R. Paine (Carbondale: Southern Ill Univ Press, 97); coauth, "Recent advances in methods and theory in paleodemography," Ann Rev Anthrop 27 (98): 375-399. **CONTACT ADDRESS** Dept Anthrop, Kent State Univ, PO Box 5190, Kent, OH 44242-0001. **EMAIL** rmeindl@kent.edu

MEISSE, TOM
DISCIPLINE GEOGRAPHY, SOCIOLOGY **EDUCATION** Wayne State Univ, PhD. **CAREER** Adj Prof, Eastern Mich Univ; Adj Prof, Univ of Detroit; Dir of Res, US Dept of Housing Urban Develop, Mich. **HONORS AND AWARDS** Smithsonian Fel; Departmental Secretarial Citation. **RESEARCH** Urban studies, Entrepreneurship, Economic development, US, Middle East, Caribbean. **CONTACT ADDRESS** Dept Sociol, Univ of Detroit Mercy, PO Box 19900, Detroit, MI 48219.

MELANCON, DONALD
PERSONAL Born 11/12/1939, Franklin, LA, m **DISCIPLINE** EDUCATION **EDUCATION** Southern Univ, BS, 1963; Univ of IL, MEd 1971, PhD 1976. **CAREER** Kankakee Sch Dist, cent off adminstr 1971-72, sch psychol couns 1970; St Anne HS, tchr 1964-70; MO, tchr 1963; Nympum Mini-bike Prgm YMCA, consult 1972; Pembroke Consol Sch Dist, 72; Opport Ind Ctr, 72; Kankakee Boys Camp, 72; UofIL, lab trainer 1972; Ofc of Edn,1979; Union Grad Sch, 79; St Ann Sch Bd of Educ 1976; Kankakee Sch Dist, elem sch prin; Lemoyne-Owen Col, professor, 94-. **HONORS AND AWARDS** Sel Phi Delta Kappa-Hon Soc in Edn; Bicent Declar for Serv to Cub Sct 1976; Ebony Esteem Aw 1976; Men of prgss Outst Edecator Awd 1978. **MEMBERSHIPS** Bd of dir Kankakee Drug Abuse; Old Fair Pk Day Care; Kankakee Cult Prgm; YMCA Exten Dept; Cub Sct Mstr; Appt by Gov of IL Reg Manpwr Comm for CETA; mem NEA; IL Educ Assn; Humanist Assn; Sch Bd Assn of IL; Kankakee Co Adminstr Assn. **SELECTED PUBLICATIONS** "As Students See Things" IL Educ Assn Jour 1969; "Staff Dev on a Shoestring" IL Princ Journl 1973; "A System Apprch to Tension Monit & Tension Reduct in an Educ Setting" Journl of Rsrch in Educ 1973; "Model for Sch Commun Relat" Phi Delta Kappan 1974. **CONTACT ADDRESS** LeMoyne-Owen Col, Memphis, TN 38126.

MENDOZA, LOUIS
DISCIPLINE LITERATURE, CULTURAL STUDIES, GENDER STUDIES **EDUCATION** Univ TX at Austin, MA, PhD. **CAREER** Taught at Univ Houston-Downtown & Brown Univ, asst prof, Univ TX San Antonio. **RESEARCH** Cult studies; contemp lit theory; Chicano/a lit and film; ethnic studies; gender studies; post-colonial lit and theory. **SELECTED PUBLICATIONS** Publ on, computer pedagogy, border lit, poetry of Sara Estela Ramirez and Raul Salinas; ed, East of the Freeway. **CONTACT ADDRESS** Col of Fine Arts and Hum, Dept of English, Univ of Texas, San Antonio, 6900 N Loop 1604 W, San Antonio, TX 78249. **EMAIL** lmendoza@utsa.edu

MENDOZA, RUBEN
PERSONAL Born 06/18/1956, Frenchcamp, CA, m, 1990, 1 child **DISCIPLINE** ANTHROPOLOGY **EDUCATION** Calif State Univ, BA, 78; Univ Ariz, MA, 80, PhD, 92. **CAREER** Curatorial Asst, Ariz State Museum, 88-90; Asst prof, Univ Colo, 91-95; Assoc Prof to Dir, Calif State Univ, 95-. **HONORS AND AWARDS** Fel, NEH Summer Fellowships, 86; Fel, El colegio de Mexico, 83; Bicentennial Committee Awd, San Juan Bautista, 97; Hispanic Spotlight Awd, Denver, 94; Denver Committee of Honor, Denver Art Museum, 94; Dissertation Fel, Ford Foundation, 90-91; Nat Hispanic Scholarship fund Scholar, 81, 82, 87; Grad Student competition Awd, Southwestern anthropol Asn, 75. **MEMBERSHIPS** Calif Missions Foundation, Asn of Latina & Latino Anthropol, Am Anthropol Asn, Soc for Calif Archaeol. **RESEARCH** Spanish Colonial and Mexican Era archaeology and ethnohistory; Hispanic material culture in North America; Mesoamerican and southwestern archaeology and ethnohistory; Non-Western science and technology; Precolonial African civilizations; Visual anthropology and documentary photography; Multimedia educational courseware development; Museum Anthropology; California Missions. **SELECTED PUBLICATIONS** Auth, "El Tajin," in Encyclopedia of the ancient World, Salem Press, in press; auth, "Atlatl (Olmec Spearthrower; 1200-900 b.c.e.)," in Encyclopedia of the ancient World, Salem Press, in press; auth, "Chenes," in The Oxford Encyclopedia of Mesoamerican Cultures, Oxford Univ Press, in press; auth, "Jade and Greenstone," in The Oxford Encyclopedia of Mesoamerican Cultures, Oxford Univ Press, in press; auth, "Mesoamerican Chronology: Periodization," in The Oxford encyclopedia of Mesoamerican Cultures, Oxford Univ Press, in press; auth, "Transportation," The Oxford encyclopedia of Mesoamerican Cultures, Oxford Univ Press, in press; auth, "Mission San Gabriel," in America's Historic Sites, Salem Press, in press; auth, "Mission San Juan Capistrano," in America's Historic Sites, Salem Press, in press; auth, "Tribal Warfare," in Magill's Guide to Military History, Salem Press, in press; auth, "Zulu Wars of empire (1817-1879)," in Magill's Guide to Military History, Salem Press, in press. **CONTACT ADDRESS** Dept Soc & Beh Sci, Calif State Univ, 100 Campus Center, Seaside, CA 93955.

MENJARES, PETE
PERSONAL Born 11/11/1955, Los Angeles, CA, m, 1 child **DISCIPLINE** EDUCATION **EDUCATION** southern Calif Col, BA, 87; Calif State Univ, MA, 92; Univ Southern Calif, 97. **CAREER** Director of Educ, Assemblies of God church, 80-88; Teacher, CW Nimitz Middle School, 88-94; Res Asst, Univ southern Calif, 93-97; Lecture to Assoc Prof and Dept Chair, 94-. **HONORS AND AWARDS** Fel, Exec Leadership Development Inst, 00; Who's Who Amongst Am Teachers, 98; Fel, Office of Bilingual Educ and Minority Lang Affairs, 94-97; Scholarship, Calif New Teacher Project, 91-92; Scholarship, Assemblies of God Minister, 84-87; Dean's List, Southern Calif Col, 82-87. **MEMBERSHIPS** Northeastern Educ Res Asn, Calif Coun on the Educ of Teachers. **RESEARCH** The integration of faith and learning into the practice of teaching and its implications for the development, leadership, and evaluation of educational programs in culturally and linguistically diverse settings. **SELECTED PUBLICATIONS** Auth, differentiated learning, 00; auth, "Team games in the secondary language arts classroom," in Strategies for hope. Claremont Reading conference 63rd Yearbook, 99; auth, "The Development and construct Validation of a Spanish Version of a Self-Concept Scale for Middle School Hispanic Students from Families of Low Socioeconomic Levels," The Spanish Journal of Psychology, (00): 53-62; auth, Interrelationships Among Academic Self-Concept, Acculturation and English Proficiency, 97. **CONTACT ADDRESS** Dept Educ, Biola Univ, 13800 Biola Ave, La Mirada, CA 90639-0001. **EMAIL** pete_menjares@peter.biola.edu

MERCADO, JUAN CARLOS
DISCIPLINE CULTURAL STUDIES **EDUCATION** Univ Comahue, BS; Queens Col, MA; CUNY, PhD. **CAREER** Eastern Stroudsburg Univ PA **HONORS AND AWARDS** NEH grant. **SELECTED PUBLICATIONS** Auth, Esteban Echeverrea: Building a Nation: The Case of Echeverrea. **CONTACT ADDRESS** East Stroudsburg Univ of Pennsylvania, 200 Prospect Street, East Stroudsburg, PA 18301-2999.

MERRIFIELD, WILLIAM R.
PERSONAL Born 09/28/1932, Chicago, IL, m, 1952, 4 children **DISCIPLINE** LINGUISTICS, ANTHROPOLOGY **EDUCATION** Wheaton Col, Ill BA, 54; Cornell Univ, MA, 63, PhD(cult anthrop), 65. **CAREER** Ling consult in Mex, 62-74, coordr anthrop res in Mex, 65-69, coordr ling res in Mex, 65-59, 72-74, dir sch, Univ Okla, 74-77, Int Coordr Anthrop and Commun Develop, Summer Inst Ling, 72-, Dir, Mus Anthrop, Tex, 74-, Vis asst prof ling, Univ Wash, 65-72; vis prof anthrop, Wheaton Col, 71-72; Adj Prof Ling, Univ Tex, Arlington, 74-; adj prof anthrop, Univ Okla, 75-77, adj prof ling, 77. **MEMBERSHIPS** Am Anthrop Asn; Ling Soc Am; Am Sci Affiliation; Am Asn Mus; Ling Asn Can and US. **RESEARCH** Cultural and applied anthropology; social organization; theory of grammar. **SELECTED PUBLICATIONS** Auth, Linguistic Theory and Grammatical Description Joseph, Je, Lan, Vol 70, 94. **CONTACT ADDRESS** Summer Inst of Ling, 7500 Camp Wisdom Rd, Dallas, TX 75236.

MERRY, SALLY E.
PERSONAL Born 12/01/1944, PA, m, 1967, 2 children **DISCIPLINE** ANTHROPOLOGY **MEMBERSHIPS** Am Anthropol Asn; Law and Society Asn. **SELECTED PUBLICATIONS** Auth, Urban Danger, Temple Univ Press (81); auth, Getting Justice and Getting Even, Univ Chicago Press (90); auth, Colonizing Hawaii, Princeton Univ Press (2000). **CONTACT ADDRESS** Dept Anthropol, Wellesley Col, 106 Central St., Wellesley, MA 02481. **EMAIL** smerry@wellesley.edu

MERTENS, THOMAS R.
PERSONAL Born 05/22/1930, Ft Wayne, IN, m, 1953, 2 children **DISCIPLINE** BIOLOGY, GENETICS EDUCATION **EDUCATION** Ball State Univ, BS, 52; Purdue Univ, MS, 54, PhD, 56. **CAREER** Res Assoc, Univ Wisc, 56-57; Ball State Univ, Asst Prof Biol, 57-62, Assoc Prof, 62-66, Prof, 66-93, Distinguished Prof, 88-93, Distinguished Prof Emeritus, 93-. **HONORS AND AWARDS** Fellow, Am Asn for the Adv of Sci, 82; Distinguished Svc to Sci Educ, 87; Nat Sci Tchrs Asn; Hon member, Nat Asn of Biol Thcrs; McGuffey Awd in Life Sci, Texts Acad Auths Asn. **MEMBERSHIPS** AAAS; Nat Asn of Biol Tchrs (pres 85); Nat Sci Tchrs Asn; Genetics Soc of Am. **RESEARCH** Genetics education; plant cytology/genetics. **SELECTED PUBLICATIONS** Co-auth, Genetics Laboratory Investigations, Prentice Hall, 10th ed, 95, 11th ed, 98; co-auth, Tradescantia: A Tool for Teaching Meiosis, The Am Biol Tchr, 59:5, 300-304, 5/97. **CONTACT ADDRESS** Dept of Biology, Ball State Univ, 4501 N. Wheeling Ave., 9B-4, Muncie, IN 47304-1277.

MESLER, MARK A.
PERSONAL Born 03/23/1949, Niagara Falls, NY, m, 1983, 2 children **DISCIPLINE** SOCIOLOGY, PHARMACOLOGY **EDUCATION** Memphis State Univ, BA, 76, MA, 78; Univ Conn, PhD, 85. **CAREER** Asst prof, Concord Col, Athens, WV, 86-90; asst prof, Mass Col of Pharmacy and Health Sci, 90-94, assoc prof, 94-2000. **HONORS AND AWARDS** BA cum laude, Memphis State Univ, 76. **MEMBERSHIPS** Am Sociol Asn, Eastern Sociol Asn, Asn for Death Ed Coun. **RESEARCH** Hospice care, professionalization of pharmacy (theory-symbolic interaction & medical sociology). **SELECTED PUBLICATIONS** Auth, "Negotiated order and the clinical pharmacist: The ongoing process of structure," Symbolic Interaction, 12 (89): 139-157; auth, "Boundary encroachment and task delegation: Clinical pharmacists on the medical team," Sociol of Health and Illness, 13 (91): 310-331, reprinted in Kathy Charmaz & Debra A. Paterniti, eds, Health, Illness, & Healing: Society, Social Context, and Self, Los Angeles, CA: Roxbury Pub (99); auth, "The philosophy and practice of patient control in hospice: The dynamics of autonomy versus paternalism," Omega, 30 (95): 173-189; auth, "Negotiating life for the dying: Hospice and the strategy of tactical socialization," Death Studies,19 (95): 235-255; coauth with P. J. Miller, "Incarnating heaven: Making the hospice philosophy mean business," Sociol and Soc Welfare, 23 (96): 31-49; coauth with E. Krypat, "Models of Patient Care," in Introduction to Health Care Delivery: A Primer for Pharmacists, R. L. McCarthy, ed, Aspen Pub (98); auth, "Volunteering to be Mortal," J of Medical Humanities, 19 (98): 39-49; coauth with P. J. Miller, "Hospice and Assisted Suicide: The Structure and Process of an Inherent Dilemma," Death Studies, 24 (2000): 135-155. **CONTACT ADDRESS** Dept Arts & Sci, Massachusetts Col of Pharmacy and Allied Health Sciences, 179 Longwood Ave, Boston, MA 02115. **EMAIL** mmesler@mcp.edu

MESSINGER, SHELDON L.
PERSONAL Born 08/26/1925, Chicago, IL, m, 1947, 2 children **DISCIPLINE** SOCIOLOGY **EDUCATION** UCLA, PhD, 69 **CAREER** Res Sociologist, Ctr for the Study of Law and Soc, Univ Calif Berkeley, 61-70; prof and dean, School of Criminology, Univ Calif Berkeley, 70-77; prof, School of Law, Univ Calif Berkeley, 77-91; prof emeritus, Univ Calif Berkeley, 91-; Chair, Council of Univ of CA Emeritt Association, 00-01. **HONORS AND AWARDS** President's Awd, Western Society of Criminooogy Chair-Elected, Council of Univ of CA, Emeritt Associations, 99-00.A. McGee Awd for Outstanding Contributions to Criminal Justice Research, Am Justice Inst; Awd of Merit, Calif Bureau of Criminal Statistics; award for Outstanding Contributions to the Field of Criminology, Western Soc of Criminology; fel, Inst of Criminology, Univ Cambridge; fel, Ctr for Advanced Study in Behavioral Sciences; fel, Soc Sci Res Council. **MEMBERSHIPS** Asn for Criminal Justice Res. **RESEARCH** Health insurance, especially for elderly; experiences with chronic illness, especially among elderly. **CONTACT ADDRESS** School of Law, Univ of California, Berkeley, Berkeley, CA 94720. **EMAIL** slm@uclink.berkeley.edu

MESTELLER, JEAN C.
DISCIPLINE AMERICAN LITERATURE, AMERICAN STUDIES, WOMEN WRITERS **EDUCATION** Lynchburg Col, BA; Univ Va, MA; Univ Minn, PhD 78. **CAREER** Instr, Univ Minn; Ill State Univ; prof, 78-. **HONORS AND AWARDS** Sally Ann Abshire Awds (3). **RESEARCH** Nineteenth-century popular fiction and the working girl. **SELECTED PUBLICATIONS** Auth, Romancing the Reader: From Laura Jean Libbey to Harlequin Romance and Beyond. **CONTACT ADDRESS** Dept of Eng, Whitman Col, 345 Boyer Ave, Walla Walla, WA 99362-2038. **EMAIL** mastellerj@whitman.edu

METRESS, SEAMUS
PERSONAL Born 08/25/1933, Southampton, NY, m, 1974 **DISCIPLINE** SOCIOLOGY, ANTHROPOLOGY **EDUCATION** Univ Notre Dame, BS, 55; Columbia Univ, MS, 57; Ind Univ, PhD, 71. **CAREER** Prof, Clarion State Col, 66-69; Prof, Univ Toledo, 69-. **HONORS AND AWARDS** Outstanding Teacher, Univ Toledo, 71; Master Teacher, Univ Toledo, 91-93; Doermann Distinguished Lect, Univ Toledo, 97. **MEMBERSHIPS** Am Anthrop Asn, Am Catholic Hist Soc, Irish-American Cultural Inst, Can Assoc for Irish Studies, Am Conf on Irish Studies, Celtic League Int Dublin, Center for the Study of Am Catholicism, Catholic Hist Soc, Immigration Hist Soc, Catholic Hist Soc of Philadelphia. **RESEARCH** Irish-American experience, conflict in Northeast Ireland. **SELECTED PUBLICATIONS** Auth, Outlines in Irish History, Connolly Books (Detroit, MI), 95; auth, The American Irish and Irish Nationalism: Sociohistorical Introduction, Scarecrow Pr (Lanham, MA), 95; coauth, The Great Starvation: An Irish Holocaust, Am Ireland Ed Found (Stoney Point, NY), 96; auth, "British Racism and Its Impact on Anglo-Irish Relations," in Race and Other Misadventures (Nelson Hall, 96), 50-63; auth, "The Irish Americans: From Frontier to the White House," in Multiculturalism Today (Begin-Garvey, 97), 131-144; auth, "The Great Starvation in Ireland 1845-1853: A Biocultural Perspective," The Rev 33,1 (97): 39-51; auth, "John Devoy: An Irish Rebel," Am Irish Newsletter (97); auth, "The Irish American Experience," Bonded Shores 4,1 (97): 4-7; auth, The Irish in Canada, Great Lakes Irish Study, no 2, 98; auth, The American Irish and the Growth and Development of the Catholic Church, Univ Notre Dame Pr, 98. **CONTACT ADDRESS** Dept Sociol & Anthrop, Univ of Toledo, 4625 Paisley Rd, Toledo, OH 43615.

METTLIN, CONNIE
PERSONAL Born 08/21/1951, Waterloo, IA, m, 1993, 6 children **DISCIPLINE** PSYCHOLOGY **EDUCATION** Univ Iowa, BA, 84; MSW, 87. **HONORS AND AWARDS** Who's Who in Am Women; Who's Who in Mental Health Professions **MEMBERSHIPS** NASW, LISW, ACSW. **RESEARCH** Aging. **CONTACT ADDRESS** Dept Soc Sci, Kirkwood Comm Col, PO Box 2068, Cedar Rapids, IA 52406. **EMAIL** cml5167@cedarnet.org

METZ, BRENT E.
PERSONAL Born 09/12/1964, St Joseph, MI **DISCIPLINE** ANTHROPOLOGY **EDUCATION** Western Mich Univ, BA, 86; Univ Mich, MA, 89; SUNY Albany, PhD, 95. **CAREER** Vis Prof, Western Mich Univ, 95; Central Conn Univ, 95-96; Vis Prof, Grinnell Col, 96-98; Vis Prof, Temple Univ, 98-00; Asst prof, Monmouth Col Ill, 00-. **MEMBERSHIPS** Am Anthrop Asn, Latin Am Studies Asn, Guatemala Scholars Network. **RESEARCH** Political economy, Central America, Indigenous peoples. **SELECTED PUBLICATIONS** Auth, "The Dynamics of Culture and Law: Anglo Domination of Mexican Migrants in Michigan," Mich Sociol Rev 4 (90): 33-45; coauth, "An Expression of Cultural Change: Invisible Converts to Protestantism among the Highland Guatemala Mayas," Ethnol 30 (91): 325-338, coauth, "Invisible Converts to Protestantism in Highland Guatemala," in Crosscurrents in Indigenous Spirituality: Interface of Maya, Catholic and Protestant Worldviews, ed. Guillermo Cook (Leiden: E.J. Brill, 97), 61-80; auth, "Without Nation, Without Community: The Growth of Maya Nationalism Among Ch'orti's of Eastern Guatemala," J of Anthrop Res 54-3 (Fall 98). **CONTACT ADDRESS** Dept Antrhop, Temple Univ, 1115 W Berks St, Philadelphia, PA 19122.

MEWHORT, DOUG J. K.
PERSONAL Born 01/14/1942, Toronto, ON, Canada, m, 1985, 1 child **DISCIPLINE** PSYCHOLOGY **EDUCATION** Univ Toronto, BA, 64; Univ Waterloo, MA, 65; PhD, 68. **CAREER** Asst prof to prof, Queen's Univ, 68-. **HONORS AND AWARDS** Fel, CPA. **MEMBERSHIPS** Soc for Math Psychol; Am Psychol Asn; Can Psychol Asn; Psychonomic Soc; Cognitive Sci Soc; C3.ca; Can Soc for Brain Beh and Cog Sci. **RESEARCH** Human memory; Cognition; Computational modeling. **SELECTED PUBLICATIONS** Co-auth, "Serial recall of tachistoscopic letter strings," in Relating theory and data: Essays in honor of Bennet B. Murdock, (Erlbaum, 91(, 425-443; co-auth, "Representation and selection of relative position," J Experimental Psychol, (93): 488-516; co-auth, "On serial recall: A critique of chaining in TODAM," Psychol Rev, (94): 534-538; co-auth, "Modeling lexical decision and word naming as a retrieval process," Can J Experimental Psychol, (99): 306-315; co-auth, "The extralist-feature effect: A test of item matching in short-term recognition memory," J Experimental Psychol, (00): 262-284; co-auth, "The power law repealed: The case for an exponential law of practice," Psychonomic Bulletin and Rev, (00): 185-207. **CONTACT ADDRESS** Dept Psychol, Queen's Univ at Kingston, Queen's Univ, Kingston, ON, Canada K7L 3N6. **EMAIL** doug@ebbinghaus.psyc.Queensu.ca

MEYERS, BARTON
PERSONAL Born 09/04/1936, Washington, DC, m, 1977, 4 children **DISCIPLINE** PSYCHOLOGY **EDUCATION** George Washington Univ, BA, 58; Univ Mich, MA, 59, PhD, 63. **CAREER** Asst prof to prof, Brooklyn Col, 63-; Univ Mich, USPHS Postdoctoral Fel, Dept Pharmacology, Medical School, 62-63. **HONORS AND AWARDS** Phi Beta Kappa; Sigma Xi; Univ Mich, USPHS Postdoctoral Res Fel, 60-62; Bette Zeller Prof in Public Policy and Admin, 95-97. **RESEARCH** Defense against aerial attack in the Third World, intelligence and nature vs. nurture. **SELECTED PUBLICATIONS** Auth, "Disaster study of war," Disasters 15:318-330 (91); auth, "Defense against aerial attack in El Salvador, J of Political and Military Sociol, 22:327-342 (94); auth, "The Bell Curve: An exercise in social Darwinism," Sci and Soc 60:195-204 (96); auth, "The CUNY wars," Soc Text 51: 119-130 (97); auth, "In defense of CUNY," Radical Teacher, 53:33-37 (98), reprinted in Martin, Randy ed, Chalk Liones: The Politics of Work in the Managed University, Durham, NC: Duke Univ Press, 236-248 (98). **CONTACT ADDRESS** Dept Psychol, Brooklyn Col, CUNY, 2900 Bedford Ave, Brooklyn, NY 11210.

MEYERS, DIANA TIETJENS
DISCIPLINE ETHICS, FEMINIST THEORY, SOCIAL AND POLITICAL PHILOSOPHY **EDUCATION** Univ Chicago, AB, philosophical psychol, 69; City Univ New York Grad Center, MA, philosophy, 76, PhD, philosophy, 78. **CAREER** Visiting asst prof, State Univ New York Stony Brook, 78-79; asst prof, Government Dept , Cornell Univ, , 79-85; asst prof, Montclair State Coll, 85-87; assoc prof, 87-90, prof, 90-, Univ of Connecticut Storrs. **HONORS AND AWARDS** Univ Fellowship, 76-77; graduate fellow, res, 77-78; humanities faculty res grant, summer, 90; general educ development grant, 81; grant, Exxon Educ Found, 84-85; Rockefeller Residency Fellowship, Center for Philosophy and Public Policy (declined), 85-86; fellowship, ACLS/Ford Found, 86; Career Devel Grant, Montclair State Coll, 86-87; Special Achievements Awds, 90, 94, major res grants, 91, 93, Provost's Fellowship, spring 93, Univ Conn; Rockefeller Found Study Center at Bellagio, Italy, residency, summer 93; Who's Who in the East, 86-; Intl, Who's Who of Women, 86-; Who's Who of Amer Women, 98; Who's Who in America, 00. **MEMBERSHIPS** Ex officio member, Comt Status Women 92-97, chair, Eastern Div Program Comt, 94-96, Amer Philosophical Assn; treas, New York Group, 97-, natl hq, Exec Comt, 80-84, 91-95, exec sec, 84-91, Soc Philosophy and Public Affairs; co-chair, 87-, Women's Studies Exec Bd, Women's Studies Curriculum Courses Comt, 91-, chair, Grad Placement Comt, 96-, sexual harassment officer, 94-, Dept of Philosophy, Women's Studies/Psychol Search Comt for the Dir of Women's Studies, 97-, Univ Conn; Member Comt Status of Women, 00-. **RESEARCH** Philosophy of law; applied ethics. **SELECTED PUBLICATIONS** Ed, Feminist Social Thought: A Reader, 97; auth, "Inalienable Rights: A Denfense (Columbia UP); Self, Society, and Personal Choice (Columbia UP); Subjection and Subjectivity (Routledge); Gender in the Mirror (Oxford UP, forthcoming). **CONTACT ADDRESS** Dept of Philosophy, Univ of Connecticut, Storrs, Storrs, CT 06269-2054. **EMAIL** diana.meyers@uconn.edu

MEYERS, THOMAS J.
PERSONAL Born 12/16/1952, Doylestown, PA, m, 1976, 3 children **DISCIPLINE** SOCIOLOGY **EDUCATION** Goshen Col, BA, 75; Boston Univ, MA, 78; PhD, 83. **CAREER** Asst prof, Goshen Col, 83-85; assoc prof, 86-91, prof, 94-. **HONORS AND AWARDS** Lilly Grant, 99. **RESEARCH** Amish, African Studies. **SELECTED PUBLICATIONS** Auth, "Education and Schooling", The Amish and the State, ed Donald Kraybill, Johns Hopkins Univ Pr, (93): 87-108; auth, "Social Change in The Amish Communities of Northern Indiana", Internal and External Perspectives on Amish and Mennonite Life 4: Old and New World Anabaptists Studies on the Language, Culture, Society and Health of the Amish and Mennonites, eds, J. Dow, W. Enninger and J. Raith, Univ of Essen & Iowa State

Univ, (94): 10-20; auth, "The Old Order Amish: To Remain in the Faith or to Leave", Mennonite Quarterly Rev LXVIII.3 (94): 378-395; auth, "Lunch Pails and Factories", The Amish Struggle with Modernity", eds D.B. Kraybill and M.A. Olsham, Univ Pr. Of New England, (94): 165-181; auth, "The Amish Division: A Review of the Literature", Les Amish: origine et particularismes 1693-1993, ed L. Hege and C. Wiebe, Assoc Fr d'Hist Anabaptiste-Mennonite, (96): 72-93. **CONTACT ADDRESS** Dept Sociol and Anthrop, Goshen Col, 1700 S Main St, Goshen, IN 46526. **EMAIL** tomjm@goshen.edu

MICCO, MELINDA
DISCIPLINE ETHNIC STUDIES **EDUCATION** Univ Calif at Berkeley, BA, 90, MA, 92, PhD, 95. **CAREER** Asst prof; Mills Col, 93-. **RESEARCH** American Indian history and literature; mixed race identity studies. **SELECTED PUBLICATIONS** Auth, Tribal Recreations: Buffalo Child Long Lance and Black Seminole Narratives, in Lit Stud E and W, Vol 16, Univ Hawai'i & E-W Ctr, 98; Racial Identity in the New Millenium: Black and Indian Communities, Nat Asn for Ethnic Stud, Inc, Fresno, 98; Isolation Of and Demands on Native American Faculty, Amer Indian/97 Alaska Native Prof Asn Conf, Lawrence, 97; Tribal Re-Creations: Buffalo Child Long Lance and Black Seminole Narratives, for the panel: Changing Paradigms: The Ethnic Self and Its Transvestisms, Multi-Ethnic Lit US, Honolulu, 97; Experiment in Domesticity: Native Women in Missionary and Boarding Schools, Western Soc Sci Asn, Oakland, 95; African Americans and American Indians: Historical Significance and Present Realities, Western Soc Scie Asn, Albuquerque, 94; co-ed, Pretending To Be Me: Ethnic Transvestism and Cross-Writing, Univ Ill Press, Encycl Amer Indian, African Americans and Amer Indians, Boston: Houghton Mifflin; 95. **CONTACT ADDRESS** Dept of Ethnic Studies, Mills Col, 5000 MacArthur Blvd, Oakland, CA 94613-1301. **EMAIL** melinda@mills.edu

MIDDLETON, RICHARD TEMPLE, III
PERSONAL Born 01/17/1942, Jackson, MS, m **DISCIPLINE** EDUCATION **EDUCATION** Lincoln Univ of MO, BS 1963, MEd 1965; Univ of Southern MO, EdD 1972. **CAREER** Tougaloo Coll, instructor of educ 1967-70; Jackson State Univ, asst & assoc prof 1970-76, dir student teaching 1976-97; Episcopal priest, 95-. **HONORS AND AWARDS** Woodrow-Wilson King Fellowship Doctoral Study 1969; selected as mem of leadership, Jackson MS Chamber of Commerce 1987-88. **MEMBERSHIPS** Bd mem Ballet Mississippi 1983-85, Security Life Ins Co 1985; pres Beta Gamma Boule Sigma Pi Phi Frat 1985-87; bd mem Opera/South Co 1986-90, Catholic Charities 1986-90; vice pres Mississippi Religious Leadership Conference 1988-89; mem Natl Executive Council The Episcopal Church 1987-88; vice chairman, Jackson, MS Planning Board, 1990-94; NCATE Board of Examiners. **CONTACT ADDRESS** Dir of Student Teaching, Jackson State Univ, 1400 JR Lynch St, Jackson, MS 39217.

MIELENZ, CECILE C.
DISCIPLINE PARENT EDUCATION **CONTACT ADDRESS** Dept Soc Sci, Shoreline Comm Col, 16101 Greenwood Ave, Seattle, WA 98133. **EMAIL** cmielenz@ctc.edu

MIKA, JOSEPH JOHN
PERSONAL Born 03/01/1948, MeKees Rocks, PA, m, 3 children **DISCIPLINE** LIBRARY EDUCATION **EDUCATION** Univ Pitts, BA, 69, MLS, 71, PhD, 80. **CAREER** Asst librn & instr, Ohio State Univ, 71-73; asst librn & asst prof, Johnson State Col, 73-75; grad asst, tchg fel School Libr & Info Sci, Univ Pitts, 75-77; asst dean, assoc prof libr sci, Univ S Miss, 77-86, dir libr & info sci prog 86-94, Prof, 94- , Wayne State Univ; Co-Ed Jour Educ Libr & Info Sci, 95- . **HONORS AND AWARDS** Served to Col. U.S Army Reserve; Decorated DSM; Army Res Comp Achiev Medal; Meriterious Svc Medal; Army Commendation Medal. **MEMBERSHIPS** Phi Delta Kappa. **SELECTED PUBLICATIONS** Articles to prof jour. **CONTACT ADDRESS** Libr & Info Sci Prog, Wayne State Univ, 106 Kresge Library, Detroit, MI 48202. **EMAIL** aa2500@wayne.edu

MIKHAIL, MONA
PERSONAL Born, Egypt, s **DISCIPLINE** MODERN ARABIC LITERATURE, GENDER STUDIES **EDUCATION** Univ Mich, PhD, 73. **HONORS AND AWARDS** PEN Prize for Translation; Translation Prize, Columbia Univ. **MEMBERSHIPS** MESA; Am Res Cent in Egypt Ara Am Univ Grad; Middle E Studies Asn. **RESEARCH** Arabic comparative Literature; Gender/Women Studies. **SELECTED PUBLICATIONS** Auth, Images of Arab Women Fact and Fiction, Three Continents Press, 79; auth, Studies in the Short Fiction of Idris and Mahfouz, NYU Press, 92. **CONTACT ADDRESS** Dept Near East Lang & Lit, New York Univ, 50 Washington Square S, New York, NY 10012-1018. **EMAIL** mnml@is.nyu.edu

MIKLOWITZ, DAVID J.
PERSONAL Born 07/18/1957, Pasadena, CA, s, 1 child **DISCIPLINE** PSYCHOLOGY **EDUCATION** Univ Calif at Los Angeles, PhD, 85. **CAREER** Prof, Univ of Colo, 89-. **HONORS AND AWARDS** Postdoctoral Fel, Univ Calif, Los Angeles, 85-88; Outstanding Publ, Am Asn for Marital and Family Ther. **MEMBERSHIPS** Am Psychol Asn. **RESEARCH** Adult psychopathology and families. **SELECTED PUBLICATIONS** Coauth, Bipolar Disorder: A Family-Focused Treatment Approach, Guilford Press (NY), 97. **CONTACT ADDRESS** Dept Psychology, Univ of Colorado, Boulder, Box 345, Boulder, CO 80309-0345. **EMAIL** miklow@psych.colorado.edu

MILBURN, MICHAEL A.
PERSONAL Born 07/22/1950, Palo Alto, CA, m, 1976, 3 children **DISCIPLINE** PSYCHOLOGY **EDUCATION** Stanford Univ, AB, 72; Harvard Univ, PhD, 78. **CAREER** Asst prof, UMB, 79-85; assoc prof, 85-92; prof, 92-. **HONORS AND AWARDS** Chan Dist Teach Awd, UMB, 98; Alfred E Freedman Awd, ISPP, 93; Fel, Shorenstein Cen, Harvard Univ, 93. **MEMBERSHIPS** ISPP. **RESEARCH** Political psychology; health; sexuality. **SELECTED PUBLICATIONS** Auth, Persuasion and Politics: The Social Psychology of Public Opinion, Brooks-Cole/Wadsworth (Pacific Grove, CA), 91; coauth, The Politics of Denial, MIT Press (Cambridge), 96; coauth, "CYBERPSYCH: Resources for psychologists on the Internet," Psychological Science 6 (95): 203-211; coauth, "Childhood punishment, denial, and political attitudes," Political Psych 16 (95): 447-478; coauth, "Patients' health as a predictor of physician and patient behavior in medical visits: A synthesis of two studies," Medical Care 34 (96): 1205-1218; coauth, "Adwatch: Covering campaign ads," in Politics and the Press, ed. P. Nords (Boulder, CO: Lynne Rienner Pub), 97; coauth, "Why are sicker patients less satisfied with their medical care? An analysis of two studies," Health Psycho 17 (98): 1-6; coauth, "Illness and satisfaction with medical care," Current Directions in Psychological Science 8 (99): 96-99; coauth, "Homeopathic treatment of mild traumatic brain injury: A randomized, double-blind placebo-controlled clinical trial," J Head Trauma Rehab 14 (99): 521-542; coauth, "The Socialization of Authoritarianism," in S Rippl, New Perspectives on Authoritanianism, 00. **CONTACT ADDRESS** Dept Psychology, Univ of Massachusetts, Boston, 100 Morrissey Blvd, Boston, MA 02125. **EMAIL** michael.milburn@umb.edu

MILES, DOROTHY D.
PERSONAL Born 03/17/1937, Akron, OH, m, 1961, 1 child **DISCIPLINE** EDUCATION **EDUCATION** Univ Akron, BA, 59; Bradley Univ, MA, 69; Alfred Univ, Spec, 73; Univ Conn, PhD, 91. **CAREER** Director, Hillyer Col, 86-91; director& adj prof, Univ of Hartford, 91-94; asst prof, Saint Louis Univ, 94-. **MEMBERSHIPS** NASP, CEC, MASP. **RESEARCH** Special Education, Assessment. **SELECTED PUBLICATIONS** Auth, "Why Principals Succedd: Comparing Principal Performance to National Professional Standards", Education Research Service Spectrum, (in press); auth, "AIDS: Special Concern to Special Educators", Physical Disabilities: Education and Related Services, (in press). **CONTACT ADDRESS** Dept Educ, Saint Louis Univ, 3750 Lindell Blvd, McGannon Hall, Saint Louis, MO 63108. **EMAIL** miles2@slu.edu

MILLER, BERNICE JOHNSON
PERSONAL Born Chicago, IL, m **DISCIPLINE** EDUCATION **EDUCATION** Roosevelt Univ Chicago IL, BA; Chicago Teachers Coll, MA 1965; CAS Harvard Univ Grad School of Ed, 1968-69, EdD 1972; Harvard Univ Grad School of Ed, 1972. **CAREER** Chicago Bd of Ed, teacher elem & hs 50-66; The New School for Children Inc, headmistress 66-68; Jackson Coll, assoc dean 68-70; Radcliffe, instr, 70-73; Harvard Grad School of Ed, assoc dir 71-75; Boston Public Schools Lucy Stone School, principal 77-78; Boston Public Schools, sr officer, 78-84; Harvard Grad School, dir high tech rsch proj , 83-84; City Coll of Chgo, Pres, currently. **HONORS AND AWARDS** Educator's Awd Boston 350th Anniv of Boston MA 1980; Educator of the Year Urban Bankers Ed Awd Boston 1982; Woman of the Year Awd Assoc of Mannequins 1984; Woman in Ed Business & Professional Women Boston & Vicinity 1984; Freedom Awd Roosevelt Univ 1985; Disting Alumni of Chicago State Univ NABSE 1985; Outstanding Achievement Awd in Educ YWCA 1986; Minority Networking Org of Focus & Seana Mag Serv Awd 1986. **MEMBERSHIPS** Bd mem, Children's World Day Care Ctr Boston 1972-84, Blue Cross/Blue Shield Boston, United Way; trustee, Brigham's & Women's Hosp Med Found; mem 1968-84, pres, United Commun Plng Corp 1983-85; bd mem, Chicago Metro History Fair Bd; mem, Mayor's Commiss on Women. **CONTACT ADDRESS** City Cols of Chicago, Harold Washington Col, President, 30 E Lake St, Chicago, IL 60601.

MILLER, DONALD
DISCIPLINE SOCIOLOGY OF RELIGION **EDUCATION** Univ Southern Calif, BA, 68; USC, MA, 72, PhD, 75. **CAREER** Firestone prof; Univ Southern Calif, 75-. **RESEARCH** Sociology of religion; religion and social change in America; religion and community organizing/development; genocide. **SELECTED PUBLICATIONS** Auth or coauth, bk(s), Survivors: An Oral History of the Armenian Genocide, Univ Calif Press, 93; Homeless Families: The Struggle for Dignity, Univ Ill Press, 93; Writing and Research in Religious Studies, Prentice Hall, 92 & The Case for Liberal Christianity, Harper & Row, 81. **CONTACT ADDRESS** Dept of Religion, Univ of So California, University Park Campus, Los Angeles, CA 90089. **EMAIL** demiller@bcf.usc.edu

MILLER, ERIC D.
PERSONAL Born 09/05/1972, New York, NY, m, 1998, 1 child **DISCIPLINE** PSYCHOLOGY **EDUCATION** Oberlin Col, BA, 94; Univ IA, PhD, 99 **CAREER** Res Asst, Oberlin Col, 92-94; Res Asst, Univ IA, 97-99; Asst Prof, Kent State Univ, 99-. **HONORS AND AWARDS** Outstanding Teaching Asst Awd, Univ IA, 97; Scholarly Presentation Travel Grant, IA Student Govt, 98; Travel Grant, Univ IA Grad Stud Senate, 98; Travel Grants, Univ IA, 97, 98. **MEMBERSHIPS** Am Psychol Asn; Intl Soc for the Study of Personal Relationships; Midwestern Psychol Asn; Am Psychol Soc. **SELECTED PUBLICATIONS** Co-auth, "Toward a unified system of social and personal motivation," Psychological Inquiry, (96): 231-234; auth, "About this issue," Journal of Personal and Interpersonal Loss, (98): 5-6; auth, "It's not that easy to let go: Living with loss," Contemporary Psychology, (98): 64-65; co-auth, "Forever utopia," Contemporary Psychology, (98): 286-287; co-auth, "Making Sense of the Nonsensical: Understanding Hitler," contemporary Psychology, (98): 856-857; co-auth, "Toward a psychology of loss," Psychological Science, (98): 429-434; co-auth, "New directions in loss research," in perspectives on loss: A sourcebook, (Washington, 98), 3-20; co-auth, "Introduction: Toward a field of work on loss and trauma," in Loss and trauma: General and close relationship perspective, Bruner/Mazel, in press. **CONTACT ADDRESS** Dept Psychol, Kent State Univ, 400 E 4th St, East Liverpool, OH 43920. **EMAIL** emiller@kenteliv.kent.edu

MILLER, JAMES BLAIR
PERSONAL Born 08/02/1916, Mt Vernon, OH, m, 1943, 3 children **DISCIPLINE** CHRISTIAN EDUCATION, PRACTICAL THEOLOGY **EDUCATION** Bethany Col, WVa, AB, 38; Yale Univ, BD, 41; Ind Univ, EdD(educ), 55. **CAREER** Pastor, First Christian Church, Plymouth, Pa, 41-44; instr relig, Bethany Col, WVa, 44-51; asst prof Christian educ, 51-55, prof, 55-80, Emer Prof Christian Educ, Christian Theol Sem, 80-, Pastor, Mem Church, Bethany, WVa, 44-51; consult educ dept, United Christian Missionary Soc, 62-63; chmn prof and res sect, Div Christian Educ, Nat Coun Churches, 62; mem curric and prog coun, Christian Churches, 64-68 and Comn Christian Educ, Am Asn Theol Schs, 65-67. **MEMBERSHIPS** Asn Professors and Researchers in Relig Educ; Asn Christian Church Educators. **RESEARCH** Theological foundations for Christian education; history of education; learning theory. **SELECTED PUBLICATIONS** Auth, Our Church's Story, 60 & coauth, Basics for Teaching in the Church, 68, Christian Bd Publ. **CONTACT ADDRESS** Christian Theol Sem, 1000 W 42nd St, Indianapolis, IN 46208.

MILLER, LAURA L.
PERSONAL Born 07/26/1967, Springfield, IL **DISCIPLINE** SOCIOLOGY **EDUCATION** Univ Redlands, BA, 89; Northwestern Univ, MA, 91; PhD, 95. **CAREER** Asst prof, Univ Calif, 96-. **HONORS AND AWARDS** Phi Bet Kappa, 89; Phi Alph Theta, 89; Postdoctoral Fel, Harvard Univ, 97. **MEMBERSHIPS** Am Sociol Asn, Unter-university Seminar on Armed Forces and Soc. **RESEARCH** Military Sociology, Social Inequality, Qualitative Methodology. **SELECTED PUBLICATIONS** Auth, "Fighting for a Just Cause: soldiers' Attitudes on Gays in the Military," in Gays and Lesbians in the Military: Issues, Concerns, and Contrasts, New York, (94): 69-85; auth, "Humanitarians or Warriors? Race, Gender and Combat Status in Operation Restore Hope," Armed Forces and Society (95): 615-637; auth, "Not Just Weapons of the Weak: Gender Harassment as a Form of Protest for Army Men," Social Psychology Quarterly, (97): 32-51; auth, "Do Soldiers Hate Peacekeeping? The Case of Preventive Diplomacy Operations in Macedonia," Armed Forces & Society, (97): 415-450; auth, "Feminism and the Exclusion of Army Women from Combat," Gender Issues, (98): 33-64; auth, "From Adversaries to Allies: Relief Workers' Attitudes Toward the U.S. Military," Qualitative Sociology, (99): 181-197. **CONTACT ADDRESS** Dept Sociol, Univ of California, Los Angeles, PO Box 951551, Los Angeles, CA 90095-1551. **EMAIL** llmiller@ucla.edu

MILLER, MARA
DISCIPLINE WOMEN'S VOICES AND IMAGES OF WOMEN IN JAPANESE ART **EDUCATION** Yale Univ, PhD, 87. **CAREER** Emory Univ. **SELECTED PUBLICATIONS** Auth, The Garden as an Art. **CONTACT ADDRESS** Dept of Art, William Jewell Col, 500 College Hill, Liberty, MO 64068-1896.

MILLER, NAOMI F.
DISCIPLINE ANTHROPOLOGY **EDUCATION** Univ MI, BA 72, MA 73, PhD 82. **CAREER** Visiting Asst Prof, Washington Univ, St. Louis, 84-86; Research Specialist, Applied Sci Ctr for Archaeology, 87-97; Senior Research Scientist, Univ PA Museum, 97-present. **RESEARCH** Ancient environment and land use systems (especially in the Near East); complex societies (especially their economic base) **SELECTED PUBLICATIONS** Auth, Bulletin of the American Schools of Oriental Research, The Aspalathus Caper, 95; Current Anthropology, Seed Eaters of the Ancient Near East, 96; MASCA Research Papers in Science and Archaeology, Farming and Herding along the Euphrates: Environmental Constraint and Cultural Choice (Fourth to Second Millennia B.C.), 97; Paleorient, The Macro-

botanical Evidence for Vegetation in the Near East, c. 18000/16000 bc to 4000 bc, 97. **CONTACT ADDRESS** Museum Applied Science Center for Archaeology, Univ of Pennsylvania, 33rd and Spruce Sts, Philadelphia, PA 19104. **EMAIL** nmiller0@sas.upenn.edu

MILLER, ROBERT D.
PERSONAL Born 09/04/1941, Chapel Hill, NC, d **DISCIPLINE** PSYCHIATRY **EDUCATION** Davidson Col, BS, 64; Duke Univ, PhD, 72, MD, 73. **CAREER** Clin assoc in psych, 76-78, Duke Univ Medical Ctr; clin asst prof, 78-81, clin assoc prof, 81-82; lect, law, 82-91, clin assoc prof of psych, 83-90, clin prof, 90-91, Univ Wis; clin assoc prof of psych, 84-91, Med Col of Wis; prof of psych, dir91-, Univ Co Health Sci Ctr; lect in law, 93-98, adj prof, law, 98, Univ Denver Col of Law; staff psych, 76-78, John Umstead Hosp, Butner, NC; dir, 78-80,, Eastern Admissions Unit, dir, 80, Adult Admissions Unit, dir, res trng, 80-82; co-dir, 80-82, Duke Univ/John Umstead Psychiatric Residency Prog; trng dir, 82-91, Forensic ctr, Mendota Mental Health Inst, Madison; ch psych, 91-95, Co Dept of Corrections; dir of res and ed, 93-, Inst for Forensic Psychiatry, Co Mental Health Inst At Pueblo; Consul, 95-, Co Dept of Corrections. **HONORS AND AWARDS** Phi Eta Sigma, 60; Phi Beta Kappa, 63; Sigma Xi, 71; Manfred S. Guttmacher Awd, Am Psychiatric Asn, 89, 90; listed in The Best Doctors in America, 94, 98; Manfred S. Guttmacher Awd, Am Psychiatric Asn Honorable Mention, 95. **MEMBERSHIPS** APA; Am Orthopsych Asn; NC Neuroscis Soc; Am Group Psycother Asn; NC Neuropsych Asn; WI Psych Asn; CO Psych Asn; Southeastern Group Psycother Asn; NC Group Behavior Soc; Am Acad of Psych & the Law; The Hastings Ctr, assoc member; Int Acad of Law & Mental Health; Am Acad of Forensic Scis, Psychiatry & Behavioral Sci Sect; Am Acad of Psych & Law, Midwest Chap; Wis St Med Soc; Am Bd of Forensic Psych. **SELECTED PUBLICATIONS** Auth, Involuntary Civil Commitment of the Mentally Ill in the Post-Reform Era, Charles C. Thomas, 87; coauth, Hypnosis and Dissimulation, Clin Asses of Malingering & Deception, Guilford Press, 88; auth, The US. Supreme Court Looks at Voluntariness and Consent, Int J of Law & Psychiatry, 94; coauth, Mental Health Screening and Evaluation Within Prisons, Bul of the Am Acad of Psych & Law, 94; coauth, Psychiatric Stigma in Correctional Facilities, Bul of the Am Acad of Psych & Law, 94; auth, Abolition of the Insanity Defense in the United States, Int Bul of Law & Mental Health, 94; auth, Involuntary Commitment to Outpatient Treatment, Principles & Practice of Forensic Psychiatry, Chapman & Hall, 94; coauth, Law & Mental Health Professionals: Wisconsin, APA, 95; auth, The Continuum of Coercion: Constitutional and Clinical Considerations in the Treatment of Mentally Disordered Persons, Univ Denver Law Rev, 97; auth, The Forced Administration of Sex-Drive Reducing Medications to Sex Offenders: Treatment or Punishment?, Psychol, Pub Pol & Law, in press; auth, Advance Directives for Psychiatric Treatment: A View from the Trenches, Psychol, Pub Pol & Law, in press; auth, Coerced Treatment in the Community, Psychiatric Clinics of North America, in Press. **CONTACT ADDRESS** Dept Psychiat, Univ of Colorado, Denver, 4200 E 9th Ave, Denver, CO 80220-3700.

MILLER, SHARON L.
PERSONAL Born 08/18/1952, India, s **DISCIPLINE** SOCIOLOGY **EDUCATION** Grand Valley State Univ, BA, 77; McCormick Theol Sem, 84; Univ Notre Dame, MA, 94, PhD, 99. **CAREER** Vis asst prof, Hope Col, 98-00; asst prof, St Mary's Univ, 00- . **HONORS AND AWARDS** David Dodge Mem Teaching Awd, 94 & Moore Diss fel, 97, Univ Notre Dame. **MEMBERSHIPS** Soc Sci Studenty Relig; Relig Res Asn; Asn Sociol Relig. **RESEARCH** Sociology of religion, Religious non-profits. **SELECTED PUBLICATIONS** Co-ed, The Financing of American Religion, Alta Mira Press, (99). **CONTACT ADDRESS** Dept Sociol & Soc Work, Hope Col, PO Box 112, Douglas, MI 49406. **EMAIL** millers@Hope.edu

MILLER, SHEILA D.
PERSONAL Born 07/02/1950, Richmond, VA, s **DISCIPLINE** SOCIAL WORK **EDUCATION** Norfolk State Univ, BA, 72; Univ Penn, MSW, 74; Howard Univ, DSW, 84. **CAREER** Social wkr, Hosp Univ Pa, 73-77; asst prof, 77-84; assoc prof, 84-94; prof, 94-, Norfolk Univ. **HONORS AND AWARDS** Who' Who Am Teach, 96, 00. **MEMBERSHIPS** CSWE; NASW; NABSW. **RESEARCH** Health, illness and disability; rehabilitation; mental health; substance abuse. **SELECTED PUBLICATIONS** Coauth, "Social Work Practice in a Black Community-Based Teaching Hospital," in Social Work Practice and Health Care Settings, Can Scholars Press, 2nd ed (94); auth, "Increasing the Adjustment Success of the Disabled African-American," J Health Soc Policy 5 (93); auth, "Patients Perceptions of Their Adjustment of Disability and Social Support in a Community-Based Teaching Hospital," Equal to the Challenge: Bureau Educational Res (86). **CONTACT ADDRESS** Dept Social Work, Norfolk State Univ, 700 Park Ave, Norfolk, VA 23540.

MILLER, STUART J.
PERSONAL Born 11/24/1938, Ann Arbor, MI, m, 1973, 3 children **DISCIPLINE** SOCIOLOGY **EDUCATION** Ohio State Univ, BS, 60; MA, 66; PhD, 71. **CAREER** From asst prof to prof, Wash & Jefferson Col, 67-. **HONORS AND AWARDS** Distinguished Prof, Wash & Jefferson Col. **MEMBERSHIPS** AAUP. **RESEARCH** Juvenile Victimization, Juvenile Justice. **SELECTED PUBLICATIONS** Coauth, Juvenile Justice in America, Prentice-Hall, 94 (1st ed), 98 (2nd ed), & forthcoming (3rd ed). **CONTACT ADDRESS** Dept Sociol, Washington and Jefferson Col, 60 S Lincoln St, Washington, PA 15301. **EMAIL** smiller@washjeff.edu

MILLER, SUSAN P.
PERSONAL Born Cheyenne, WY, M **DISCIPLINE** LEARNING DISABILITIES; LEARNING STRATEGIES, EDUCATIONAL ADMINISTRATION **EDUCATION** Univ Fla, PhD. **CAREER** Prof, Univ Nev, Las Vegas. **HONORS AND AWARDS** SIM Leadership Awd, 00; Nevada Prof of the Year, 98-99. **MEMBERSHIPS** Council for Exceptional Children; Council for Learning Disabilites. **RESEARCH** Math Strategies for students with Learning Disabilities. **SELECTED PUBLICATIONS** Auth, Perspectives on mathematics instruction, in Deshler, D, Ellis, E S, & Lenz, B K, Teaching adolescents with learning disabilities (2nd ed), Love Publ Co, 96; coauth, Strategic Math Series, Edge Enterprises, 91-94; auth, Validated practices for teaching mathematics to students with learning disabilities: A review of literature, Focus on Exceptional Children, 31, 1, 98. **CONTACT ADDRESS** Dept of Spec Educ, Univ of Nevada, Las Vegas, 4505 Maryland Pky, P O Box 453014, Las Vegas, NV 89154-3014. **EMAIL** millersp@nevada.edu

MILLER, THOMAS W.
PERSONAL Born 02/07/1943, Rochester, NY, m, 1967, 2 children **DISCIPLINE** PSYCHOLOGY **EDUCATION** St. John Fisher Col, BS, 65; Univ Scranton, MS, 67; SUNY, PhD, 71. **CAREER** Prof, Univ of Ky, 81; prof, Univ of Lexington, 81-; prof, Murray State Univ, 96-. **HONORS AND AWARDS** Great Teacher Awd, Univ of Ky, 92; Master Teacher Awd, Univ of Ky, 94; Distinguished Serv Awd, Am Psychol Assoc, 95; RHR Int Awd for Excellence in Consultation, Am Psychol Assoc, 96. **MEMBERSHIPS** Am Psychol Assoc; Am Assoc of Applied Sport Psychol; Am Col of Sports Med. **RESEARCH** Post Traumatic Stress Disorder, Character Education, Telehealth. **CONTACT ADDRESS** Dept Educ Leadership, Murray State Univ, 1 Murray St, Murray, KS 42071. **EMAIL** tom.miller@coe.murraystate.edu

MILLER-JONES, DALTON
PERSONAL Born 07/06/1940, St. Louis, MO, m **DISCIPLINE** PSYCHOLOGY **EDUCATION** Rutgers Univ, BA & BS, 62; Tufts Univ, MS, 65; Cornell Univ, PhD, 73. **CAREER** Cornell Univ Africana Studies, lecturer & rsch assoc 1969-73; Univ of Mass/Amherst, asst prof 1973-82; Williams Coll, Henry Luce assoc prof 1982-84; City Univ of New York Grad School, Assoc Prof, 84-; prof, Portland State Univ, 91-. **HONORS AND AWARDS** NSF & Office Education Fellowships 1966-69; NSF 1972; Carnegie Corp New York Grant 1972-73; articles and book chapters on Black children's language & thought in J of Black Studies and Academic Press 1979-84. **MEMBERSHIPS** Adjunct prof & fellow Inst Comparative Human Cognition Rockefeller Univ, NY 1974-76; member Soc for Rsch in Child Dev 1978-; empirical rsch consultant in Black psychology for New York Board of Ed, Am Can Co & Black community organizations 1980; Jean Piaget Society 1981-; Amer Psych Assn 1982-; Amer Ed Rsch Assn 1981-. **RESEARCH** Impact of culture on development and learning and reasoning, especially for African American children, identity and learning. **SELECTED PUBLICATIONS** Coauth, "Teacher interactions with strong and weak speakers of nonstandard English during reading instruction," Contemporary Educational Psychology, 14 (89): 280-312; auth, "Culture and testing, ed Rogoff, Culture and Development," American Psychologist, 44 (89): 360-366; auth, "Informal reasoning in inner-city children," Informal Reasoning in Education, (107-130), Lawrence Erlbaum Associates, 90; auth, Proficiency-based admissions standards: University school collaboration, Journal Higher Education, Hikkaida Univ, special ed, 39-49, 97. **CONTACT ADDRESS** Dept of Psychology, Portland State Univ, 317 Cramer Hall, PO Box 751, Portland, OR 97207-0751. **EMAIL** millerjonesd@pdx.edu

MILLER-PERRIN, CINDY
PERSONAL Born 02/26/1962, McKeesport, PA, m, 1985, 2 children **DISCIPLINE** PSYCHOLOGY **EDUCATION** Pepperdine Univ, BA, 83; Wash State Univ, MS, 87; PhD, 91. **CAREER** Instr, Wash State Univ, 88-89; instr, Seattle Pacific Univ, 90; asst prof, Pepperdine Univ, 92-96; assoc prof, 96-. **HONORS AND AWARDS** Sigma Xi Hon Soc; Psi Chi Hon Soc; Alpha Chi Hon Soc; Phi Eta Sigma; Outstand People 20th C; Seaver Res Grant, 93, 94, 96, 99; Outstand Am; Who's Who in Am, West, Women, Am Women; APA Dist Res Awd; Sigma Xi SRS Grant; WSU Outstand Women Awd. **MEMBERSHIPS** APA; WPA; ISPCA; CURWPA; AOA; APSAC; CPSAC; CUPP. **RESEARCH** Child maltreatment; clinical child psychology. **SELECTED PUBLICATIONS** Coauth, "Reactions to childhood sexual abuse: Implications for post-traumatic stress disorder," in Posttraumatic stress disorder: Assessment, differential diagnosis and forensic evaluation, ed. CL Meek (Sarasota, FL: Profess Res Exchange, 90); coauth, "Sexually Abused and No-abused children's conceptions of personal body safety," Child Abuse Neg 14 (90): 99-112; coauth, Preventing child sexual abuse: sharing the responsibility, Univ Neb Press (Nebraska), 92; coauth, "When life support is questioned early in the care of patients with cervical-level quadriplegia," New Eng J Med 328 (93): 506-509; coauth, Family violence across the lifespan, Sage Pub (Thousand Oaks, CA), 97; auth, "Sexually abused children's conceptions of sexual abuse: A preliminary analysis and comparison across ages," J Child Sexual Abuse 2 (98): 1-22; coauth, Child maltreatment: An introduction, Sage Pub (Thousand Oaks, CA), 99. **CONTACT ADDRESS** Dept Social Science, Pepperdine Univ, 24255 Pacific Co Hwy, Malibu, CA 90263. **EMAIL** cperrin@pepperdine.edu

MILNER, JOSEPH O'BEIRNE
PERSONAL Born 06/18/1937, m, 1963, 3 children **DISCIPLINE** ENGLISH, EDUCATION **EDUCATION** Davidson Col, AB, 59; Univ NC, Chapel Hill, MA, 65, PhD, 71. **CAREER** Instr Eng, NC State Univ, 65-66; instr, Univ NC, Chapel Hill, 68-69; asst prof, 69-80, Assoc Prof Eng & Educ, Wake Forest Univ, 80, Ed, NC Eng Tchr, 72-; consult, Winston-Salem-Forsyth County Schs, 73. **HONORS AND AWARDS** Chair, English Educators; NCTE. **MEMBERSHIPS** MLA; Aaup; Southeastern Mod Lang Asn. **RESEARCH** Am lit, 1960-1973. **SELECTED PUBLICATIONS** Auth, "Bridging English," Prentice Hall; auth, "Webs and Wardrobes University Press of America; auth, "Developing Teachers University Press of America. **CONTACT ADDRESS** Dept of Eng, Wake Forest Univ, PO Box 7266, Winston-Salem, NC 27109. **EMAIL** milner@wfu.edu

MINER, MADONNE
DISCIPLINE AMERICAN LITERATURE AND WOMEN'S STUDIES **EDUCATION** SUNY, Buffalo, PhD, 82. **CAREER** Prof, ch, dept Eng, TX Tech Univ, 97-. **SELECTED PUBLICATIONS** Auth, Insatiable Appetites: Twentieth-Century American Women's Bestsellers, 84. **CONTACT ADDRESS** Texas Tech Univ, Lubbock, TX 79409-5015. **EMAIL** M.Miner@ttu.edu

MINOR-EVANS, LESLIE
PERSONAL Born Seattle, WA, m, 7 children **DISCIPLINE** PSYCHOLOGY **EDUCATION** Univ Wash, BA, 82; Univ Calif at Irvine, MA, 90; PhD, 95. **CAREER** assoc prof, Central Ore Community Col, 92-; adj prof, Linfield Col, 96-; adj prof, Univ Ore, 00-. **HONORS AND AWARDS** Listed in Who's Who in America's Teachers, 95; Golden Shovel Awd, 95; Judy Roberts Awd, 95. **MEMBERSHIPS** Western Psychol Asn, Am Psychol Asn, Pacific Sociol Asn. **RESEARCH** Social Psychology: work & family behavior. **SELECTED PUBLICATIONS** Coauth, Human Relations: Strategies for Success, Mirror Press & Richard D. Irwin Publ Co. (Boston, MA), 95; coauth, Working with People: A Human Relations Guide, Richard D. Irwin Publ Co. & Times Mirror Higher Educ Group, Inc. (Boston, MA), 96. **CONTACT ADDRESS** Dept Soc Sci, Central Oregon Comm Col, 2600 NW College Way, Bend, OR 97701.

MITCHELL, WILLIAM P.
PERSONAL Born 08/30/1937, Brooklyn, NY, m, 1998, 2 children **DISCIPLINE** ANTHROPOLOGY **EDUCATION** Brooklyn Col, BA, 61; Univ Pitt, PhD, 72 **CAREER** Freed prof Soc Sci, Monmouth Univ, 86-; prof Anthropology, Monmouth Univ, 78-; res assoc Anthropology, Universidad Catolica, 83, 96 **HONORS AND AWARDS** NY Acad Sci Fel; Intl Representative of Regional Assoc of Displaced People of Central Area of Peru, 96; Peace Maker of Year, Monmouth People for Peace and Disarmament, 95; Magna cum laude, Brooklyn Col; Phi Beta Kappa and Sigma Xi, Brooklyn Col, 61 **MEMBERSHIPS** Amer Anthropolog Assoc; NY Acad Sci; Sigma Xi; Phi Beta Kappa **RESEARCH** War and Peace; Social Evolution; Andes; Migration **SELECTED PUBLICATIONS** Auth, Peasants on the Edge: Crop, Cult, and Crisis in the Andes, Univ Tex, 91; auth, Picturing Faith: The Huntington Quechua Pictographic catechism, Huntington Free Library, forthcoming; ed, Irrigation at High Altitudes: The Social Organization of Water Control Systems in the Andes, Amer Anthropolog Assoc, 94 **CONTACT ADDRESS** Dept Hist/Anthropology, Monmouth Univ, 400 Cedar Ave, West Long Branch, NJ 07764. **EMAIL** mitchell@mondec.monmouth.edu

MITTAL, SUSHIL
PERSONAL Born 03/04/1967, ON, Canada, m, 1996, 2 children **DISCIPLINE** RELIGION, ANTHROPOLOGY, SOUTH ASIAN STUDIES **EDUCATION** McGill Univ, BA, 90; Carleton Univ, MA, 93; Univ Montreal, PhD, 98. **CAREER** Vis asst prof, Univ Fla, 98-99; asst prof, Millikin Univ, 99-. **HONORS AND AWARDS** Millikin Univ Fac Summer Res Grant, 00; Millikin Univ Merit Awd, 00; Am Acad of Relig Individual res grant, 99-00; Soc sci and Humanities res coun of Canada Doctoral Fel, 93-97; Nominated for fac teaching Awd, Univ Fla, 98-99. **MEMBERSHIPS** Am Acad of Relig. **RESEARCH** Comparative history of religions, Hindu civilization, Hindu theories of social and human sciences, Mahatma Gandhi, Occidentalism, Structure, logic and meaning of Hindu worldviews. **SELECTED PUBLICATIONS** Ed, International Journal of Hindu Studies, Quebec: World Heritage Press, 97-. **CONTACT ADDRESS** Dept Relig, Millikin Univ, 1124 W Main St, Decatur, IL 62522-2084. **EMAIL** smittal@mail.millikin.edu

MIYAMOTO, JOHN M.
PERSONAL Born 03/16/1947, Seattle, WA, s **DISCIPLINE** PSYCHOLOGY **EDUCATION** Harvard Col, BA, 69.Univ Mich, MA, 78; PhD, 85. **CAREER** From acting asst prof to assoc prof, Univ of Wash, 84-. **MEMBERSHIPS** Am Psychol Soc, Soc for Judgment and Decision Making, Soc for Mathematical Psychol, Soc for Medical Decision Making, The Psychonomic Soc. **RESEARCH** Psychology of Preference, Utility, and Value, Inductive Reasoning, Medical Utility Analysis, Conjoint Measurement Models of Judgment. **SELECTED PUBLICATIONS** Coauth, "Risk adjustment of markov process models: Importance in individual decision making," Medical Decision Making 17 (97): 340-350; coauth, " The zero condition: A simplifying assumption in QALY measurement," Management Sci 44 (98): 839-849; auth, " Quality-adjusted life years (QALY) untility models under expected utitlity and rank-dependent utility assumptions," J of Mathematical Psychol 43 (99): 201-237; coauth, "Are actions regretted more than inactions?" Orgn Behavior and Human Decision Processes 78 (99): 232-255; auth, "Utility assessment under expected utility and rank dependent utility assumptions," in Decision making in health care: Theory, psychology, and applications, eds. G.B. Chapman & F. Sonnenberg (NY: Cambridge Univ Press, 00). **CONTACT ADDRESS** Psychol, Univ of Washington, PO Box 351525, Seattle, WA 98195-1525. **EMAIL** jmiyamot@u.washington.edu

MO, SUCHOON S.
PERSONAL Born 04/19/1932, Nagoya, Japan, m **DISCIPLINE** PSYCHOLOGY **EDUCATION** Univ Penn, PhD. **CAREER** Prof of Psychol, Univ Southern Colo. **SELECTED PUBLICATIONS** Auth, "On reversal of temporality of human cognition and dialectical self," J of Mind and Behav, 11 (90): 37-46. **CONTACT ADDRESS** Dept Psychol, Univ of So Colorado, 2200 Bonforte Blvd, Pueblo, CO 81001.

MOBERG, DAVID OSCAR
PERSONAL Born 02/13/1922, Montevideo, MN, m, 1994, 4 children **DISCIPLINE** SOCIOLOGY **EDUCATION** Bethel Jr Col, AA, 42; Seattle Pacific Col, AB, 47; Univ Wash, MA, 49; Univ Minn, PhD, 52. **CAREER** US army, 42-46; student-pastor, Sylvan Way Bapt Church, Bremerton, Wash, 46-48; assoc instr, sociol, Univ Wash, 48-49; instr to prof, sociol, Bethel Col, St Paul, Minn, 49-68; Fulbright lectr, sociol, State Univ Groningen, Netherlands, 57-58; sr Fulbright lectr, sociol of relig, Muenster Univ, Ger, 64-65; Marquette Univ, chair, dept of sociol and anthrop, 68-77, prof, sociol, 68-91, prof emer, 91-. **HONORS AND AWARDS** Alumnus of the year, Bethel Col and Sem, 76; Alpha Kappa Delta, 48; Pi Gamma Mu, 54; Fulbright lectr, H. Paul Douglass Lectr, Relig Res Asn, 86; Inaugual Kellogg Gerontology Lectr, Southwestern Baptist Theol Sem, 87; Inaugural lectr, Frederick Alexander Shippey lectures in the sociol of christ, Drew Univ Theol Sch, Madison, NJ, oct, 88. **MEMBERSHIPS** Am Soc Affiliation; Am Soc Assn; Assn for the Sociology of Religion; Gerontological Soc of Am; Midwest Sociological Soc; Religious Research Assn; Soc for the Scientific Study of Religion; Wisconsin Sociological Assn. **RESEARCH** Spirituality; Religion; Aging. **SELECTED PUBLICATIONS** Auth, Religion and Aging, Gerontology (NY), Springer, 97; auth, Honoring Older Parents, Decision, 98; auth, The Great Commission and Research, Perspectives on Science & Christian Faith, 99; auth, Woman of God: An Assessment of the Spirituality of Women in the Lutheran Church--Missouri Synod, St. Louis, MO: Lutheran Women's Missionary League, 99; co-ed, Research in the Social Scientific Study of Religion (Greenwich, CT), JAI Press, 89-00; auth, Assessing and Measuring Spirituality, Journal of Adult Development, in press; ed, Aging & Spirituality, Haworth Pastoral Press, 00. **CONTACT ADDRESS** 7120 W. Dove Ct., Milwaukee, WI 53223. **EMAIL** domoberg@juno.com

MOFTAKHAR, HOSSEIN
PERSONAL Born 02/28/1936, Tehran, Iran, m, 1975, 3 children **DISCIPLINE** PSYCHOLOGY **EDUCATION** Calif State Univ, BA, 70; MA, 71; Okla State Univ, EdD, 74. **CAREER** Prof, Chapman Univ, 84-89; Prof, Calif State Univ, 96-. **HONORS AND AWARDS** Govt of Iran Scholarship, 72-74. **RESEARCH** Cross-cultural communication. **SELECTED PUBLICATIONS** Auth, "Ten easy Steps to Research Design," Sacramento, 99; auth, "A Handbook for Career Development and employment," Intl Refugee assistance Program, Sacramento, 86; auth, "a comparative Study of Blacks, Whites & Chicanos Self and Other perception and of violence and discrimination," Calif State Univ, Press, 83; auth, "Multicultural Education: A Cross-cultural Training approach," Intl Journal of Intercultural Relations, (82): 217-219; auth, "Iranian-American Perceptions and cultural Frames of Reference," A communication Lexicon for Cultural Understanding, Washington D., 79; auth, "An Introduction to Research Methodology," Nat University, Tehran, 78. **CONTACT ADDRESS** Dept Soc & Beh Sci, Sacramento City Col, 3835 Freeport Blvd, Sacramento, CA 95822. **EMAIL** hosseinm@aol.com

MOGHADAM, VALENTINE M.
PERSONAL Born 09/17/1952, Tehran, Iran, s **DISCIPLINE** SOCIOLOGY **EDUCATION** Univ Waterloo, Ontario, Can, BA, 78; Am Univ, Wash, DC, MA, 82, PhD, 86. **CAREER** Sr res fel, UNU/WIDER (Helsinki, Finland), and coordr of the Res Prog on Women and Development, 90-95; consult to UN and CAORC fel, 96; Dir, Women's Studies and Assoc Prof of Sociol, Ill State Univ, Normal, 96-. **HONORS AND AWARDS** Fulbright, Indo-Am Fel Prog, Advanced Res in India, 90-91 (declined); Modernizing Women selected as a Choice Outstanding Academic Book for 93-94; Coun of Am Overseas Res Ctrs, Grant and Fel for Regional Res, Fall 96; Ill State Univ: Res Initiative Awd, 98-99, Univ Res Grant, 99-2000, Team Excellence Awd, 99-2000. **MEMBERSHIPS** Am Sociol Asn, Int Sociol Asn, Am Political Sci Asn, Asn for Women in Develop, Soc for Int Develop, Middle East Studies Asn, Center for Iranian Res and Analysis, Asn for Middle East Women's Studies. **RESEARCH** Sociology of gender, gender and development, social change/social movements, sociology and political economy of the Middle East and North Africa, Iran, Afghanistan, globalization, women and employment, women and development in the Middle East and North Africa, women's organizations and transnational feminist networks, revolutions and social movements. **SELECTED PUBLICATIONS** Auth, Modernizing Women: Gender and Social Change in the Middle East, Boulder, CO: Lynne Rienner Pubs (93); auth, Women, Work, and Economic Reform in the Middle East and North Africa, Boulder, CO: Lynne Rienner Pubs (98); coauth, "Middle East Politics and Women's Collective Action: Challenging the Status Quo," Social Politics: Int Studies in Gender, State, and Society, vol 6, no 3 (fall 99): 273-291; auth, "Population, Urbanization, and the Challenges of Underemployment and Poverty," Understanding the Middle East, ed by Deborah Gerner, Lynne Rienner (99): 239-262; auth, "Gender and Economic Reforms: A Framework for Analysis and Evidence from Central Asia, the Caucasus, and Turkey," in Feride Acar and Ayse Ayata, eds, Gender and Identity Construction, Leiden: Brill Pubs (2000); auth, "Transnational Feminist Networks: Collective Action in an Era of Globalization," Int Sociol, vol 15, no 1 (March 2000); auth, "Economic Restructuring and the Gender Contract: A Case Study of Jordan," in Marianne Marchland and Anne Sisson Runyan, eds, Gender and Global Restructuring: Sightings, Sites, and Resistances, London and New York: Routledge (2000): 99-115. **CONTACT ADDRESS** Dept Sociol and Anthropol, Illinois State Univ, Normal, IL 61790-4260. **EMAIL** vmmogha@ilstu.edu

MOHAMED, A. RAFIL
PERSONAL Born 10/29/1969, Washington, DC, s **DISCIPLINE** SOCIOLOGY **EDUCATION** Univ Calif, Irvine, PhD, 00. **CAREER** Asst Prof, Univ of San Diego, 99-. **MEMBERSHIPS** ASA, Law and Soc, Am Soc of Criminol. **RESEARCH** Sociology of law, Urban Sociology, Everyday resistance. **CONTACT ADDRESS** Dept Sociol, Univ of San Diego, 5998 Alcala Park, San Diego, CA 92110. **EMAIL** rmohamed@acusd.edu

MOLFESE, DENNIS L.
PERSONAL Born 03/18/1946, Tulsa, OK, m, 1971, 2 children **DISCIPLINE** PSYCHOLOGY **EDUCATION** OK City Univ, BA, 69; Penn St Univ, MS, 70, PhD, 72. **CAREER** Asst prof, 72-76, assoc prof, 76-80, Southern IL Univ; res assoc, Yerkes Regional Primate Res Center Emory Univ; prof, Dept of Pediatrics Physiology Behavioral & Social Sciences School of Med, 80, chmn Behavioral & Social Sciences, School of Med, 92-, Southern IL Univ. **HONORS AND AWARDS** Phi Kappa Phi Outstanding Scholar, 97; Univ Outstanding Scholar, 90; Southern IL Univ Sigma Xi Kaplan Res Awd for Significant Contributions in Child Psychology, 87; vis res Scientist Univ of Konstanz West Germany, 73, 75, 81. **MEMBERSHIPS** APA; Sigma Xi; Midwestern Psychol Asn; Phi Kappa Phi; Soc for Neuroscience; Acoustical Soc of Amer; Psychonomic Soc; Aerospace Med Asn; Intl Neuropsychological Soc; Amer Psychol Soc; Soc for Res in Child Dev; New York Academy of Science; The Belgian Soc of Electromyography and Clinical Neurophysiology. **RESEARCH** Development changes in the neurophysiological correlates of linguistic and cognitive processes; predicting cognitive and linguistic skills from infancy; brain-language relationships in language trained chimpanzees; cognitive functions in head injured adults; factors underlying lateralization of language and cognitive functions; phonological and semantic confusions by aphasics; electrophysiological techniques to assess hearing abilities in infants; and children, neural network applications to neuropsychology. **SELECTED PUBLICATIONS** Coauth, Known Versus Unknown Word Discrimination In 12 Month Old Human Infants, Dev Neuropsychology 3-4, 93; coauth, Predicting Long-Term Development From Electrophysiological Measures Taken At Birth, Human Behavior and Brain Development, Guilford Press, **CONTACT ADDRESS** Psychiatry of SIUSOM, So Illinois Univ, Sch of Medicine, Mail Code 9642, Springfield, IL 62794. **EMAIL** molfese@siu.edu

MOLLENKOTT, VIRGINIA RAMEY
PERSONAL Born 01/28/1932, Philadelphia, PA, m, 1954, 1 child **DISCIPLINE** ENGLISH, WOMEN'S STUDIES **EDUCATION** Bob Jones Univ, BA, 53; Temple Univ, MA, 55; NYork Univ, PhD, 64. **CAREER** Chmn, Shelton Col, 55-63; chmn, Nyack Col, 63-67; prof to emer, William Paterson Col, 67-97-. **HONORS AND AWARDS** Founder Day Award, 63; Andiron Award, 64. **MEMBERSHIPS** MLA; WIFP; MSA. **RESEARCH** Gender; religion; sexuality. **SELECTED PUBLICATIONS** Auth, Adamant and Stone Chips: A Christian Humanist Approach to Knowledge, 67; auth, In Search of Balance, 69; ed, Women of Faith of Dialogue, 87; auth, Godding: Human Responsibility and the Bible, 87; auth, Speech, Silence, Action: The Cycle of Faith, 87; auth, Women, Men and the Bible, 77, 88; auth, Is the Homosexual My Neighbor? A Positive Christian Response, 78, 94; auth, Sensuous Spirituality: Out from Fundamentalism, 92; auth, The Divine Feminine: Biblical Imagery of God as Female, 83, Ger 85, Fr 90, Ital 93; auth, Omnigender: A Trans-Religious Approach, 01. **CONTACT ADDRESS** 11 Yearling Trl, Hewitt, NJ 07421-2510. **EMAIL** jstvrm@warwick.net

MONNETT, JOHN
PERSONAL Born 05/21/1944, Kansas City, MO, m, 1973, 1 child **DISCIPLINE** EDUCATION, HISTORY **EDUCATION** Univ Kan, BS, 67; San Jose State Univ, MA, 71; Univ N Col, PhD, 80. **CAREER** Prof, Cochise Univ, 71-77; assoc dean, Comm Col Den, 81-86; prof, Metro State Col, 86-. **HONORS AND AWARDS** Outstand Fac Mem, Cochise, 74. **MEMBERSHIPS** WHA; CAL. **RESEARCH** Western history. **SELECTED PUBLICATIONS** Auth, A Rocky Mountain Christmas: Yuletide Stories of the West, Pruett Pub, 88, 93, 99; auth, Cutthroat and Campfire Tales: The Flyfishing Heritage of the West, Pruett Pub, 90; auth, Colorado Profiles: Men and Women Who Shaped the Centennial State, Cordillera Press, 90, 94; auth, The Battle of Beecher Island and the Indian War of 1867-1869, Univ Press Col, 92; auth, Tragedy at Cheyenne Hole: Lieutenant Austin Henely and the Sappa Creek Massacre, Univ Press Col, 99; auth, Tell Them We are Going Home: The Odyssey of the Northern Cheyenne, Univ Okla Press, forthcoming. **CONTACT ADDRESS** Dept History, Metropolitan State Col of Denver, PO Box 173362, Denver, CO 80217-3362. **EMAIL** jmonnett@aol.com

MONTEIRO, THOMAS
PERSONAL Born 10/06/1939, New York, NY, d **DISCIPLINE** EDUCATION **EDUCATION** Winston-Salem State University, Winston-Salem, NC, BS, 1961; Queens Col City Univ NYork, MA, 1966; Fordham University, NYork, professional diploma, 1968-69, PhD, 1971-74. **CAREER** Board of Education, New York, NY, teacher, 61-68, district curriculum director, 69-70; Brooklyn College of the City Univ of New York, New York, NY, prof, 70-85, Chairperson, Dept of Educ Admin and Supervision, Dir, The Principal's Center at Brooklyn Coll, 85-. **HONORS AND AWARDS** Congressional Achievement Awd, Congressman Floyd Flake, 1990; Outstanding Educator Awd, Success Guide George Fraser, Editor, 1991; Educator of the Year Awd, New York Association of Black Educators, 1988; Educational Leadership Awd, Council of Supervisors and Administrators of New York, 1991; Awd of Excellence, New York, Alliance of Black School Educators, 1988. **MEMBERSHIPS** President, New York Jamaica Branch, NAACP, 1977, 1978; education co-chairperson, New York State, NAACP, 1976-1980. **CONTACT ADDRESS** Sch of Education, Brooklyn Col, CUNY, Ave H & Bedford Ave, Brooklyn, NY 11210.

MONTEJO, VICTOR
PERSONAL Born 10/09/1951, Guatemala, m, 3 children **DISCIPLINE** ANTHROPOLOGY **EDUCATION** Guatemla - BA; SUNY Albany, MA; Univ Conn, PhD. **CAREER** Asst prof, Bucknell Univ, 93; asst prof, Univ of Mont, 96; assoc prof, Univ of Calif Davis. **MEMBERSHIPS** AAA; LASA. **RESEARCH** Maya culture, indigenous literatures, indigenous knowledge, human rights. **SELECTED PUBLICATIONS** Auth, Testimony: Death of a Guatemalan Village, 87; auth, the Bird Who Cleans the World and Other Mayan Fables, 91; auth, Popol Virh: Sacred book of the Mayas, 99; auth, Voices from Exile, Okla Pr, 99. **CONTACT ADDRESS** Dept Am Indian Studies, Univ of California, Davis, 1 Shields Ave, Davis, CA 95616-5270. **EMAIL** vmontejo@ucdavis.edu

MOODY, CHARLES DAVID, SR.
PERSONAL Born 08/30/1932, Baton Rouge, LA, m **DISCIPLINE** EDUCATION **EDUCATION** Central State Univ, BS Biology 1954; Chicago Tchrs Coll, MA Sci Ed 1961; Univ of Chicago, Cert Adv Study 1969; Northwestern Univ, PhD Ed Admin1971. **CAREER** Mentally Handicapped Chicago Schs, tchr of educable 1959-62; Dist #143 1/2 Posen-Robbins IL, tchr of sci & soc studies 1962-64; Sch Dist #65 Evanston, asst principal 1964-68; Sch Dist #147, supt 1968-70; Urban Fellows TTT Prog North WU, instr 1979-70; Div of Educ Specialist Univ MI, chmn 1973-77; Proj for Fair Admn Student Disc Univ MI, dir 1975-80; Univ MI, prof educ SOE 1970-, dir prog for educ oppor 1970-87, dir ctr for sex equity in schs 1981-87, vice provost for minority affairs 1987-. **HONORS AND AWARDS** Awd of Respect Washtenaw Comm Coll Ann Arbor MI 1984; Dr of Laws Degree Central State Univ 1981; Comm Leader Awd Ann Arbor Veterans Admn Med Ctr 1980; Professional of the Yr Awd Ann Arbor Chap of Natl Assn of Negro Businesses & Professional Women Inc 1979; Charter Inductee, Central State Univ, Wilberforce OH 1989. **MEMBERSHIPS** Fndr/ex bd NABSE 1970-; pres/fndr CD Moody & Assocs Inc 1981-; bd dirs Ann Arbor NAACP 1983-85; bd dirs NITV. **CONTACT ADDRESS** Vice Provost for Minority Affairs, Univ of Michigan, Ann Arbor, 503 Thompson St, 3052 Fleming Admin Building, Ann Arbor, MI 48109-1340.

MOORE, GWEN L.
PERSONAL Born 04/29/1944, Orange, NJ, m, 1977, 2 children **DISCIPLINE** SOCIOLOGY **EDUCATION** Bucknell Univ, AB, 66; New York Univ, MA, 71; PhD, 77. **CAREER** Vis Asst Prof, SUNY Brockport, 78-80; vis asst prof, SUNY Albany, 80-82; assoc prof, Russel Sage Col, 82-88; assoc prof, Univ Albany, 88-. **HONORS AND AWARDS** Fulbright Res Fel, Germany, 86-87. **MEMBERSHIPS** Am Sociol Asn, Eastern Sociol Soc, Intl Polit Sci Assoc. **RESEARCH** Political Sociology, Gender Inequality, Social Networks. **SELECTED PUBLICATIONS** Ed, Gendering Elites: Economic and Political Leaders in Twenty-Seven Societies, Macmillan, 99; auth, "Women in elite positions: Insiders or outsiders?", Sociological Forum 3, (88): 566-585; auth, "Structural Determinants of Men's and Women's Personal Networks", American Sociological Review, (90): 726-735; auth, "Gender and Informal Networks in State Government", Social Science Quarterly 73, (92): 46-61; auth, "Gender and Authority: A Cross-National Study", Social Science Quarterly 77, (96): 273-288. **CONTACT ADDRESS** Dept Sociol, SUNY Albany, 1400 Washington Ave, Albany, NY 12222-1000. **EMAIL** g.moore@albany.edu

MOORE, MELANIE
PERSONAL Born 03/23/1960, Norfolk, VA, s **DISCIPLINE** SOCIOLOGY **EDUCATION** Penn State Univ, BA, 81; Univ Ga, MA, 83; Univ Washington, PhD, 91. **CAREER** Post-Doctoral Fel, Indiana Univ, 91-93, assoc prof, 93-. **HONORS AND AWARDS** Phi Beta Kappa; Favorite Prof, Univ Northern Colo, 94, 96; Teaching Excellence Awd, Univ Northern Colo, 97. **MEMBERSHIPS** Am Sociol Asn, Nat Women's Studies Asn. **RESEARCH** Am Sociol Asn, Nat Women's Studies Asn. **SELECTED PUBLICATIONS** Auth, "Paper topics for family," in G. Macheski, K.S. Lowney, and T. Meyers, eds, Teaching About Family: A Collection of Syllabi, Projects, and Class Materials, Washington, DC: Am Sociol Asn (96): 196-198; auth, "Course syllabi for research methods," in K. P. Mulvey, ed, Research Methods Courses: Syllabi, Assignments, and Projects, Washington, DC: Am Sociol Asn (97); auth, "Student resistance to course content: Reactions to the gender of the messenger," Teaching Sociol, 25 (97): 128-133; coauth with Richard Trahan, "Evaluating a reading about gender: Does sex of author matter?" Psychological Reports, 82 (98): 247-253; rev of Richard A. Mackey, Bernard A. O'Brien, and Eileen F. Mackey's Gay and Lesbian Couples: Voices from Lasting Relationships, J of Marriage and the Family, 60 (98): 1042-1043; rev, Mary B. Harris' School Experiences of Gay and Lesbian Youth, SSSP Rev, 29 (98): 47-48; rev, Anne Haas Dyson's Writing Superheroes: Contemporary Childhood, Popular Culture, and Classroom Literacy, Contemporary Sociol, 27 (98): 276-277; coauth with Philip Blumstein and Pepper Schwartz, "The power of motherhood: A contextual evolution of family resource," Free Inquiry in Creative Sociol, 26 (98): 1-7; coauth with Richard Trahan, "Tenure status and grading practices," Sociol Perspectives, 41 (98): 775-781; auth, "Value structures and priorities of three generations of Japanese Americans," Sociol Spectrum, 19 (99): 119-132. **CONTACT ADDRESS** Dept Sociol, Univ of No Colorado, 501 20th St, Greeley, CO 80639-0001. **EMAIL** mmoore@bentley.unco.edu

MOORE, SALLY F.
PERSONAL Born 01/18/1924, New York, NY, m, 1951, 2 children **DISCIPLINE** ANTHROPOLOGY **EDUCATION** Barnard Col, BA, 43; Columbia Law School, LLB, 45; Columbia Univ, PhD, 57. **CAREER** Assoc attorney, Spence Hotchkiss, Parker and Duryea, 45-46; staff attorney, War Dept, Nuremberg Trials, 46; dept asst, Dept of Anthropology, Columbia Univ, 50-52; asst prof, 63-65, part-time lectr in the Law School, 70-75, prof on Anthrop, 70-77, chemn, Anthrop Section, Dept of Sociology and Anthrop, Univ of Southern Calif, 72-77; res assoc, Univ Col, Univ of East Africa, 68-69; res assoc, Univ of Dar es Salaam, 73-74; vis prof, Dept of Anthrop, Yale Univ, 75-76; prof of Anthrop, Univ of Calif, 77-81; VIS PROF OF LAW AND ANTHROP, 78, DEAN OF GRAD SCHOOL OF ARTS AND SCI, 85-89, PROF OF ANTHROP, HARVARD UNIV, 81-; consult, A.I.D., U.S. State Dept, 91-96. **HONORS AND AWARDS** Ansley Prize, Columbia Univ, 57; Post-doctoral res scholar, 67-68; res grant, Soc Sci Res Coun, 68-69; Dart Awd for Innovative Teaching, 71; res grant, Nat Sci Found, 72-75 & 79; honorary res fel, Dept of Anthropology, Univ of London, 73-; co-chair, Wenner Gren Conf, 74; award for creativ scholar and res, Assoc of U.S.C, 75; honorary membership, Iota Chapter, Phi Beat Kappa, Radcliffe, 83-; res grant, Wenner Gren Found, 83; Barnard Col Medal of Distinction, Columbia Univ, 87; Guggenheim Fel, 94; Huxley Memorial Medallist and Lectr for 1999, Coun of Royal Anthrop Inst of Great Britain and Ireland, 97. **MEMBERSHIPS** Bar of the State of NY; Am Anthrop Asn; Royal Anthrop Inst of Great Britain and Ireland; Int African Inst, London; African Studies Asn; Asn of Social Anthropologists; Law and Soc Asn; Comn of Folk Law and Pluralism; Am Acad of Arts and Sci; Am Ethnological Soc; Asn for Legal and Political Anthrop; Asn for Africanist Anthrop. **SELECTED PUBLICATIONS** Auth, Anthropology and Africa: Changing Perspectives on a Changing Scene, The Univ of Va Press, 94; Law in Unstable Settings: The Dilemma of Migration, Focaal, 94; Imperfect Communications, Understanding Disputes: The Politics of Argument, Berg Pub, 95; Introduction to O.F. Raum's Chaga Childhood, 96, Int African Inst, 96; Doctrine as Determinism, Rechthistorisches J, 96; Post-socialist Micropolitics: Kilimanjaro 1993, Int African Inst, 96; Concerning Archie Mafeje's Reinvention of Anthropology and Africa, Codesria Bulletin, 96; Archie Mafeje's Prescriptions for the Academic Future, Af Sociological Rev, 98; Cusomary Law, Encyclo of Africa, Simon and Schuster, 98. **CONTACT ADDRESS** Harvard Univ, 350 William James Hall, Cambridge, MA 02138. **EMAIL** moore@wjh.harvard.edu

MOOTRY, RUSSELL
PERSONAL Born 06/17/1947, Helena, GA, m, 1974, 2 children **DISCIPLINE** SOCIOLOGY **EDUCATION** B Community Col, BA, 73; Barry Univ, MA, 76; Howard Univ, PhD, 82. **CAREER** Tenured Prof, Interim Chemn of Div of Soc Sci, Bethune Cookman Col. **HONORS AND AWARDS** Excellence in Res and Community Serv, Bethune Cookman Col; Presidential Citation, NAFEO. **RESEARCH** Black achievement, Social Systems. **SELECTED PUBLICATIONS** Auth, Black Diamonds Profile of Successful Blacks in a Small Southern Community; auth, "Approaching the 21st Century: The Period After Affirmative Action." **CONTACT ADDRESS** Dept of Soc Sci, Bethune-Cookman Col, 640 Dr Mary Rd, Daytona Beach, FL 32114. **EMAIL** mootryr@cookman.edu

MORAWSKA, EWA
PERSONAL Born 04/18/1949, Cracow, Poland, m **DISCIPLINE** SOCIOLOGY **EDUCATION** Warsaw Univ, MA, 72, MA, 73; Boston Univ, PhD, 76. **CAREER** Lectr, Poznan Univ, 77; res prof, Polish Acad of Scis, Western Inst, 76-78, Warsaw, 78-80; Am Coun of Learned Socs Postdoctoral Fel and lectr, Carnegie-Mellon Univ, 79-81; Andrew Mellon Postdoctoral Fel, Univ Pittsburgh, 81-82; Univ Center for Int Studies Assoc, Univ Pittsburgh, 82-84; lectr, Univ Pittsburgh, 82-84; asst prof to prof, Dept Sociol, Univ Pa, 84-, assoc prof to prof, Dept Hist, Univ Pa, 88-. **HONORS AND AWARDS** Res Fel, NEH, 81; Res Fel, Am Coun of Learned Socs, 85; John Simon Guggenheim Fel, 87-88; Fel, The Ctr for Advanced Study in the Behavioral Scis, Stanford, 93-94; Awds for Insecure Prosperity: Small-town Jews in Industrial America, 1890-1940: Leeds Prize in Urban Anthropol, 97, Theodore Saloutos Awd, 97; The Alfred Jurzykowski Cultural Found Awd, 97; The European Univ Fel, European Forum on Int Migrations, Florence, Italy, 97-98. **MEMBERSHIPS** Am Sociol Asn, Soc Sci Hist Asn, Immigration Hist Soc, The Balch Inst for Ethnic Studies, Am Jewish Hist Soc. **RESEARCH** (Im)Migration/Ethnicity; urban and community sociology; East European societies; historical sociology. **SELECTED PUBLICATIONS** Coauth, " 'Cultural Pluralism' in Historical Sociology: Recent Theoretical Directions," in The Sociology of Culture, ed Diana Crane, Basil Blackwell (94): 45-90; auth, Insecure Prosperity: Jews in Small-town Industrial America, 1880-1940, Princeton Univ Press (96); coauth, "Moving Europeans: Contemporary Migrations in a Historical Perspective," in Global History and Migrations, ed Wang Gungwu, Westview Press (97): 23-61; auth, "An Historical Ethnography in the Making: A (Self-) Reflexive Account," Historical Methods, ed Larry Isaac (winter 97): 58-70; auth, "A Historical Turn in Feminism and Historical Sociology: Convergences and Difference," Social Politics (spring 98): 39-47; auth, "International Migration and the Consolidation of Democracy in Post-communist East Central Europe: A Problematic Relationship in a Historical Perspective," in Alex Pravda and Jan Zielonka, eds, Democratic Consolidation in Eastern Europe: International and Transnational Factors, London: Routledge (forthcoming). **CONTACT ADDRESS** Dept Sociol, McNb 113, Univ of Pennsylvania, 3718 Locust Walk, Philadelphia, PA 19104. **EMAIL** emorawsk@sas.upenn.edu

MOREHEAD, JOSEPH HYDE
PERSONAL Born 01/30/1931, New York, NY, m, 1966, 1 child **DISCIPLINE** LIBRARY EDUCATION **EDUCATION** Univ Calif-Berkeley, BA, MA, MLS, EdD, 73. **CAREER** Prof, Sch Info Sci & Policy, Univ Albany, 70-. **HONORS AND AWARDS** Phi Beta Kappa, Trinity Col, Hartford, CT, 51; Salutatorian, Honors in English, Trinity Col, 52; Sustained Superior Performance Award, U.S. Civil Service Commission, U.S. Dept of the Air Force, London, 61; Haggin Fel, Univ of KY, 63-64; First recipient, CIS/GODORT/ALA Documents to the People Award, 77; first recipient, Outstanding Alumnus Award, Univ of KY Col of Libr and Information Sciences, 84; Who's Who in the East, 86-87; James Bennet Childs Award, GODORT, Am Libr Asn, 89; Isadore Gilbert Mudge-R.R. Bowker Award, Am Libr Asn, 96. **MEMBERSHIPS** Am Libr Asn. **RESEARCH** Access to governmentt information as a First Right Amendment. **SELECTED PUBLICATIONS** Auth, Theory and Practice in Library Education: The Teaching-Learning Process, Libr Unlimited (Littleton, CO), 80; auth, Introduction to United States Public Documents, 3rd ed, Libr Unlimited, 83; auth, Essays on Public Documents and Government Policies, Haworth Press (NY), 86; auth, Introduction to United States Government Information Sources, 6th ed, Libr Unlimited, 99; more than 170 articles. **CONTACT ADDRESS** Sch Info Sci & Policy, SUNY, Albany, Albany, NY 12222. **EMAIL** jhm@albany.edu

MOREHOUSE, RICHARD
PERSONAL Born 05/21/1941, La Crosse, WI, m, 1967, 1 child **DISCIPLINE** PSYCHOLOGY **CAREER** Drug Educ Coord, CESA 4, 73-74; Educ Consult, CESA 4, 75-77; Project Dir, Cooperative Educ Servs Agency, 77-80; Dir of Cooperative Educ, Viterbo Col, 80-85; Teacher, Aquinas High School, 69-70; Faculty Asst, Univ of Wis, La Crosse, 72-73; Instr, Univ of Wis, La Crosse, 73-80; Adjunct Faculty, St Francis Medical Center, 88-93; Adjunct Asst Prof, St Mary's Col, 86-89; Adjunct Prof, St Mary's Univ, 96-; Vis Professor, Univ of Turku, 90; Vis Scholar, Texas Wesleyan Univ, 93-94; Asst Prof, Viterbo Col, 85-88; Assoc Prof, Viterbo Col, 87-93; Chair, Viterbo Col, 95-99; Prof, Viterbo Col, 93-. **HONORS AND AWARDS** Burlington Northern Fac Achievement Awd, 89. **MEMBERSHIPS** American Psychological Assoc, Am Psyc Society, ASCD, Am Ed Res Assoc, Morehouse, R. & Vestal, L., 1991, 1994. **RESEARCH** Classroom discussion, Teacher training, Belief Systems, Who's Who in America, 96-97, Who's Who in American Educ, 96-97, Who's Who in the World, 97-98. **CONTACT ADDRESS** Dept Psychology, Viterbo Col, 815 S 9th St, La Crosse, WI 54601. **EMAIL** remorehouse@viterbo.edu

MORELAND, RAYMOND T., JR.
PERSONAL Born 03/12/1944, Baltimore, MD, m, 1980 **DISCIPLINE** PASTORAL THEOLOGY AND PSYCHOLOGY **EDUCATION** Randolph-Macon Col, BA, 66; Wesley Theological Sem, M Div, 70, D Min, 73; St Mary's Sem & Univ-Ecumenical Inst, MA, 91; Graduate Theol Found, PhD, 97. **CAREER** Pastor for 29 years in MD and WV; taught course of study at Wesley Theol Sem for 3 years; Academic Policy Committee, Ecumenical Inst of Theol, St Mary's Sem and Univ; currently exec dir, MD Bible Soc. **HONORS AND AWARDS** Who's Who in Am Colleges and Universities; Nat Preaching Fel, 71. **MEMBERSHIPS** AAR; Soc of Biblical Lit; Academy of Parish Clergy; Alban Inst, AGO; Asn for Relig and Intellectual Life; Network of Biblical Storytellers. **RESEARCH** Carl Jung's influence on Biblical hermeneutics; the thinking of Joseph Campbell on myth and the Bible. **SELECTED PUBLICATIONS** Auth, thesis abstract on The Beloved Journey-Psychospiritual Study of Persons Living, Struggling and Dying of HIV-AIDS-Sharing the Practice, J of the Academy of Parish Clegy; several book reviews for the Academy. **CONTACT ADDRESS** 9731 Hall Rd, Frederick, MD 21701-6736. **EMAIL** agape@erols.com

MORGAN, GORDON D.
PERSONAL Born 10/31/1931, m, 1957, 4 children **DISCIPLINE** SOCIOLOGY **EDUCATION** Arkansas AM N Col, BA, 53; Univ Arkansas, MA, 56; Washington State Univ, PhD, 63. **CAREER** Res asst; Columbus Univ, 63-65; assoc prof, Lincoln Univ, Mo, 65-69; Prof, Univ Ark, 69-00. **HONORS AND AWARDS** Russell Sage Gnt; AM Coll Gnt; Ford Found Gnt; HEH. **MEMBERSHIPS** ASBS. **RESEARCH** Teaching; Africa; Caribbean. **SELECTED PUBLICATIONS** Auth, Tilman C Cothran: Second Generation Sociologist, Wyndham Hall (Bristol, IN), 95; auth, Toward an American Sociology: Questioning the European Constraint, Praeger (Westport, CT), 97. **CONTACT ADDRESS** Dept Sociology, Univ of Arkansas, Fayetteville, 211 Old Main St, Fayetteville, AR 72701.

MORGAN, HARRY
PERSONAL Born 06/06/1926, Blenheim, VA, s, 2 children **DISCIPLINE** EDUCATION **EDUCATION** New York Univ, BS, 49; Univ Wisc, MSW, 67; Univ Mass, EdD, 70. **CAREER** Head Start Director, Neighborhood Prog, 64-66; Coordinator, Bank State Col, 68-70; Prof, Ohio Univ, 70-72; Prof, Syracuse Univ, 72-84; Prof, State Univ W Ga, 84-. **HONORS AND AWARDS** Ford Fel, Phi Delta Kappa. **MEMBERSHIPS** AERA, Am Psychol Soc, Nat Asn for the Educ of Young Children, Nat Asn of Soc Workers, Nat Head Start Asn. **RESEARCH** Sociology of Education; Social Distance, Middle School Social Experiences, The future of Head Start Graduates. **SELECTED PUBLICATIONS** Auth, The Imagination of Early childhood Education, Bergin & Garvey, 99; auth, "Institutional language of control: Race, class, and gender issues," Trotter Review, 98; auth, Cognitive Styles and Classroom Learning, Praeger Publishers, 97; auth, "An analysis of multiple intelligences," Roeper Review, (96): 263-269; auth, Historical Perspectives on the Education of Black Children, Praeger Publishing, 95; auth, "Legal and Illegal Drug use in high schools," The Journal of Educational Research, (95): 301-308; auth, "Race preference studies: A critique of methodology," Western Journal of African-American Studies, 91. **CONTACT ADDRESS** Dept Early Childhood Educ, State Univ of West Georgia, 1601 Maple St, Carrollton, GA 30117. **EMAIL** hmorgan@westga.edu

MORGAN, KATHRYN L.
PERSONAL Born Philadelphia, PA, 1 child **DISCIPLINE** HISTORY, FOLKLORE **EDUCATION** VA State Col, BA, 46; Howard Univ, MA, 52; Univ Pa, MA, 68, PhD, 70. **CAREER** Asst prof folklore, Univ Del, 71-72; Assoc Prof to prof emer Hist & Folklore, Swarthmore Col, 72-, Guest lectr, Bryn Mawr Col, 71-73 & Haverford Col, 71-73; consult, Smithsonian Inst, 73-; assoc, Danforth Found. **HONORS AND AWARDS** Swarthmore's First African-American Prof. **MEMBERSHIPS** Am Folklife Soc, Am Soc Ethnohist, Oral Hist Asn, National Council of Black Studies, African American Folklore Association, National Afrocentric Inst, Philadelphia Folklore Project . **RESEARCH** Folklife history; Black studies. **SELECTED PUBLICATIONS** Contribr, Mother Wit from the Laughing

Barrel Caddy Buffers: Legends of a Middle Class Negro Family in Philadelphia, Prentice-Hall, 73; In Search of the Miraculous, Bryn Mawr Col, 73; auth, Jokes among urban Blacks, In: Black Folk, 73; auth, Social Distance From Jews In Russia And Ukraine, Slavic Review, Vol 0053, 1994. **CONTACT ADDRESS** Swarthmore Col, 500 College Ave, Swarthmore, PA 19081-1390. **EMAIL** kmorgan1@swarthmore.edu

MORGAN, LYLE W., II
PERSONAL Born 04/05/1947, Fremont, NE **DISCIPLINE** ENGLISH EDUCATION **EDUCATION** Doane Col, AB; M. Ed., Fla State Christian Col, MEd; Wayne State Col, MAE, MSE; University Nebr, PhD. **CAREER** Prof. **HONORS AND AWARDS** Fcollp, Col of Teachers, UK. **MEMBERSHIPS** NCTE, CCCC, KATE. **RESEARCH** Late 19th and early 20th Century British fiction, Thomas Haizdn. **SELECTED PUBLICATIONS** Auth, The Homeopathic Treatment of Sports Injuries, 86; Homeopathic Medicine and Emergency Care, 90; Treating Sports Injuries the Natural Way, 84; Homeopathy and Your Child, 92; articles on bk censorship; bk rev(s). **CONTACT ADDRESS** Dept of Eng, Pittsburg State Univ, 1701 S Broadway St, Pittsburg, KS 66762. **EMAIL** lmorgan@pittstate.edu

MORI, BARBARA L.
PERSONAL Born 12/19/1946, Brooklyn, NY **DISCIPLINE** HISTORY, SOCIOLOGY **EDUCATION** Hofstra Univ, BA, 67; Univ HI, MA, 79; MA, 83; PhD, 88. **HONORS AND AWARDS** James Shigeta Awd, 79; FLAS, 80; Chado Scholar, Urasenke Found, 83-85; Res Scholar, Japan Found, 85-86; Pacific and Asian Scholar, 85-86; Affirmative Action Fac Dev, 88, 90, 91, 93, 94; Field Res Fel, 91; Grant, Calif Fac State, 94; Grant, Calif Poly Plan Fac Develop Prog, 96. **MEMBERSHIPS** Am Sociol Assoc; Assoc for Asian Studies; Calif Sociol Assoc; HI sociol Assoc; Int House of Japan; Soc for Women in Soc; Nat Women's Studies Assoc; Nat Orgn of Women; ASPAC; Phi Beta Delta; Int Center for Asian Studies; Can Asian Studies Assoc; Soc for the Sci Study of Relig. **RESEARCH** Traditional arts in Asian Societies, women's higher education in China, Korea and Japan, Buddhist studies, Asian immigration to the United States. **SELECTED PUBLICATIONS** Auth, "Japanese Women in Chado: Accommodations in a Male Dominated Profession", Midwest Feminist Papers 6, (Apr 86): 50-52; auth, "The Tea Ceremony: A Ritual in Transition", Gender & Soc 5.1, (91): 86-97; auth, Americans Studying the Traditional Japanese Art of the Tea Ceremony: The Internationalizing of a Traditional Art, Mellen Res Univ Pr, (San Francisco), 92; rev, of "The Japanese Woman" by Sumiko Iwao, Jof Asian Studies, 53.1 (Feb 94): 206-208; auth, "Traditional Arts as Leisure Activities for Contemporary Japanese Women", in Re-Imaging Japanese Women, ed Anne Imamura, Univ of Calif Pr, (Berkeley), 96; rev, of "Empire of Schools: Japan's Universities and the Molding of a National Power Elite", by Robert Cutts, Educ About Asia, Asian Studies Found J3.2 (Fall 98): 67-68, 70; rev, of "May Fourth women Writers: Memoirs", by Janet Ng and Janice Wickeri, Educ About Asia, Asian Studies Assoc J3.1 (spr 98): 66; rev, of "Sweet and Sour: One Woman's Chinese Adventure, One Man's chinese torture", by Brooks Robards and Jim Kaplan, Educ in Asia, Asian Studies Assoc J,4.2 (Fall 98): 50-52; auth, "On the Japanese Tea Culture", Jof Hanzhong Teachers Col, (98): 62-66; auth, Stand! Race and Ethic Relations, Coursewise Publishers, 99. **CONTACT ADDRESS** Dept Soc Sci, California Polytech State Univ, San Luis Obispo, 1 Grand Ave, San Luis Obispo, CA 93407-9000. **EMAIL** bmori@calpoly.edu

MORRIS, BONNIE J.
PERSONAL Born 05/14/1961, Los Angeles, CA, s **DISCIPLINE** HISTORY, WOMEN'S STUDIES **EDUCATION** Am Univ, BA, 83; SUNY Binghamton, MA, 85, PhD, 90. **CAREER** Adjunct lectr, Binghamton Univ, 87-89; asst prof, Calif state Univ, Chico, 89-90; res assoc and vis scholar, Harvard Divinity Sch, 90-91; vis lectr, Northeastern Univ, 91-92; asst prof, Semester at Sea, Univ Pittsburgh, fall 93; asst prof, St Lawrence Univ, 92-94; asst prof, Northern Ky Univ, fall 95; vis asst prof, George Washington Univ, 94-99. **HONORS AND AWARDS** Rosa M. Colecchio Awd, SUNY Binghamton, 87; vis fel, Dartmouth Col, 89; winner, Millennium Inst int think-tank competition, 97; Who's Who in Am Women, 99-2000; George Washington Univ's Trachtenberg Teaching Prize, 97-99; nominated for a 1999 Lambda Literary Awd. **MEMBERSHIPS** Am Hist Asn, Mensa, Women's Sports Found. **RESEARCH** U.S. women's history, colonial era to present: work, wartime, ethnic identity, politics; feminist movements--Western and global--from radical subcultures to anti-feminist backlash; women's music; lesbian history; Jewish women; women's sports. **SELECTED PUBLICATIONS** Auth, The High School Scene in the Fifties: Voices From West L.A., Greenwood (97); auth, Lubavitcher Women in America: Identity and Activism, SUNY Press (98); auth, Eden Built by Eves: The Culture of Women's Music Festivals, Alyson (99); auth, "Teaching the Virtue of Women's Sports," Washington Times (March 15, 99); auth, Girl Reel: Growing Up at the Movies, Coffee House Press (spring 2000); coauth, Radical Harmonies: The Story of the Women's Music Movement, Univ Ill Press (2002). **CONTACT ADDRESS** Women's Studies Prog, The George Washington Univ, Funger Hall 506, Washington, DC 20052. **EMAIL** drbon@gwu.edu

MORRIS, KENNETH EARL
PERSONAL Born 03/19/1955, Baltimore, s, 1 child **DISCIPLINE** SOCIOLOGY **EDUCATION** Ind Univ, BS, 76; Stanford Univ, AM, 77; Univ Ga, PhD, 83. **CAREER** Instructor at various colleges and universities. **HONORS AND AWARDS** NEH summer fel, 87, 94, 97. **RESEARCH** Social thought. **SELECTED PUBLICATIONS** Auth, Bonhoeffer's Ethic of Discipleship, 86; Jimmy Carter, American Moralist, 96. **CONTACT ADDRESS** 187 Chattooga Ave., Athens, GA 30601. **EMAIL** kemorris@arches.uga.edu

MORRIS, ROBIN K.
DISCIPLINE PSYCHOLOGY **EDUCATION** Portland State Univ, BS, 84; Univ Mass, MS, 87; Univ Mass, PhD, 90. **CAREER** Res Asst, Neurological Sci Center, Good Samaritan Hosp, Portland, OR, 83-84; Instr, Univ Mass, 88; Res Asst, Univ Mass, 84-90; Asst Prof, Univ SC, 90-96; Vis Res Schol, Univ Glasgow, 97-98; Assoc Prof, Univ SC, 96-. **HONORS AND AWARDS** Mortar Bd Excellence in Teaching Awd, 96; Outstanding Fac Mem, 96-97. **MEMBERSHIPS** Am Psychol Asn, Am Psychol Soc, Psychonomic Soc. **RESEARCH** Perceptual and language processing in skilled reading, eye movements as measure of cognitive processing. **SELECTED PUBLICATIONS** Coauth, "Lexical Ambiguity and Fixation Times in Reading," J of Memory & Lang, 27 (88): 429-446; coauth, "Eye Movement Guidance in Reading: The Role of Parafoveal Letter and space Information," J of Exp Psychol: Human Perception & Performance, 16 (90): 268-282; coauth, "Eye Movements in Skilled Reading: Implications for Developmental Dyslexia," in Vision and Visual Dyslexia, Macmillan (90): 233-242; auth, "Sentence Context Effects on Lexical Access," in Eye Movements and Visual Cognition, Springer-Verlag (92): 317-332; auth, "Lexical and Message Level Sentence Context Effects on Fixation Times in Reading," J of Exp Psychol: Learning, Memory & Cognition, 20 (94): 92-103; coauth, "Multiple Lexical Codes in Reading: Evidence from Eye Movements, Naming Time and Oral Reading," J of Exp Psychol: Learning, Memory and Cognition, 21 (95): 1412-1429; coauth, "Eye Movements and Lexical Ambiguity Resolution: Effects of Prior Encounter and Discourse Topic," J of Exp Psychol: Learning, Memory and Cognition, 21 (95): 1186-1196; coauth, "Focus as a Contextual Priming Mechanism," Memory & Cognition, 26 (98): 1313-1322; coauth, "Phonology is Used to Access Word Meaning During Silent Reading: Evidence from Lexical Ambiguity Resolution," in Reading as a Perceptual Process (Elsevier Sci Publ, 00); coauth, "Lexical Processing and Text Integration of Function and Content Words: Evidence from Priming and Eye Fixations," Memory & Cognition (forthcoming). **CONTACT ADDRESS** Dept Psychol, Univ of So Carolina, Columbia, Columbia, SC 29225-0001. **EMAIL** morrisr@sc.edu

MOSELEY, MICHAEL EDWARD
PERSONAL Born 03/29/1941, Dayton, OH, m, 1963, 1 child **DISCIPLINE** ANTHROPOLOGY, ARCHAEOLOGY **EDUCATION** Univ Calif, Berkeley, BA, 63; Harvard Univ, MA & PhD(anthrop), 68. **CAREER** From instr to assoc prof anthrop, Harvard Univ, 68-76, asst cur SAm archaeol, 70-76; Assoc Cur Mid & S AM Archaeol & Ethnol, Field Mus of Natural Hist, 76-. **MEMBERSHIPS** Soc Am Archaeol. **RESEARCH** The development of agriculture and the functioning of pre- industrial cities in the New World. **SELECTED PUBLICATIONS** Coauth, Twenty-Four Architectural Plans of Chan Chan, Peur, Peabody Mus, 74; auth, The Maritime Foundations of Andean Civilization, Cummings, 75; contribr, Social and technological management in dry lands, Westview, 78; coauth, Peru's Golden Treasures, Field Mus of Natural Hist, 78; Preagricultural coastal civilization in Peru, Carolina Biological, 78. **CONTACT ADDRESS** Field Mus of Natural History, Chicago, IL 60605.

MOSES, CLAIRE G.
PERSONAL Born 06/22/1941, Hartford, CT, m, 1966, 2 children **DISCIPLINE** WOMENS STUDIES **EDUCATION** Smith Col, AB, 63; George Wash Univ, MPhil, 72; PhD, 78. **CAREER** Asst prof lectr hist, George Washington Univ, 71-76; chair & prof Women's Studies, Univ MD, 77-; ed, Feminist Studies, 77-. **HONORS AND AWARDS** Joan Kelly Mem Prize, 86; Women Legislators of the State of MD, 86. **MEMBERSHIPS** Am Hist Asn, Nat Womens Studies Asn, Soc for French Hist Studies, Conf Group of Women in Hist, Phi Beta Kappa. **RESEARCH** Women's history in 19th century France; feminist theory; feminist history (intellectual, political, global). **SELECTED PUBLICATIONS** Auth, U.S. Women in struggle, Univ Ill Press, 95; auth, Feminism, socialism, and French Romanticism, Ind Univ Press, 93; auth, French Feminism in the Nineteenth Century, State Univ New York Pres, 84; auth, "French Utopians: The Word and the Act," in Six Feminist Waves: Languages of Feminism in Modern History, London, 97; auth, "Utopian Socialists and Women," in Women's Studies Encyclopedia Vol 3, Greenwood Press, 92; auth, "Equality and Difference in Historical Perspective: A Comparative Examination of the Feminisms of French Revolutionaries and Utopian Socialists," in Rebel Daughters: Women and the French Revolution, New York, 92; auth, "A Look at the Future: The Legacy of the Eighteenth Century," in French Women and the Age of Enlightenment, Bloomington, 84; auth, "Made in America: French Feminism in the American Academy," Feminist Studies 24, (98); auth, "Debating the Present/Writing the Past: Feminism in French History and Historiography," Radical History Review 52, (92): 79-94; auth, "Saint-Simonian Men/Saint-Simonian Women: The Transformation of Feminist Thought in 1830s' France," Journal of Modern History 54, (82): 240-267. **CONTACT ADDRESS** Dept Womens Studies, Univ of Maryland, Col Park, 2101 Woods Hall, College Park, MD 20742-7416. **EMAIL** cm45@umail.umd.edu

MOSIG, YOZAN DIRK
PERSONAL Born 04/15/1943, Berlin, Germany, m, 1965, 3 children **DISCIPLINE** PSYCHOLOGY **EDUCATION** E NM Univ, BA, 66; Univ Fla, MA, 69; PhD, 74. **CAREER** Grad Asst to Interim Instructor, Univ Fla, 66-71; Asst Prof, Ga Southwestern Col, 71-77; Prof, Univ Neb, 77-. **HONORS AND AWARDS** Robert Bloch Scholarship Awd, N Eng Lovecraft Soc, 97; Pratt-Heins Scholarship Awd, Univ NE, 98. **MEMBERSHIPS** Japan Sibelius Soc. **RESEARCH** Psychology of Zen Buddhism; Psychology of Music (Sibelius). **SELECTED PUBLICATIONS** auth, "The enlightenment of Zen," U.S.K.A. Forum, (94): 2-5; auth, "The Teachings of the Buddha," Sokushin Jobutsu: International Journal of Mushindokai Studies, (94): 20-21; auth, "Erwachen," Tenshin, (95): 17-20; auth, "The Buddha and his Teachings," U.S.K.A. Forum, (95): 2-8; auth, "What is the Buddha?," U.S.K.A. Forum, (96): 2-3; auth, "Lovecraft, Buddhism, and Quantum Reality," in Mosig at Last: A Psychologist Looks at H.P. Lovecraft, Necronomicon Press, 97; auth, "Zen Buddhism," in Personality theories: an introduction, 5th ed, Houghton Mifflin, 98; auth, "Life in a Zen Monastery," in Instructor's Guide for Barbara Engler's Personality theories: An introduction, 5th ed, Houghton Mifflin, 98; auth, "Revised test question & list of resources for chapter 17 in Instructor's Guide for Barbara Engler's Personality theories: An introduction, 5th ed, Houghton Mifflin, 98; auth, "The Archetypal Power of Sibelius," Intl Conf on Jean Sibelius, 00. **CONTACT ADDRESS** Dept Psychol, Univ of Nebraska, Kearney, 905 W 25th St, Kearney, NE 68847. **EMAIL** mosigy@unk.edu

MOSKOS, CHARLES C.
PERSONAL Born 05/20/1934, Chicago, IL, m, 1966, 2 children **DISCIPLINE** SOCIOLOGY **EDUCATION** Princeton Univ, BA, 56; Univ Calif, LA, PhD, 63. **CAREER** Assoc prof, Northwestern Univ, 66; Prof, Soc, Northwestern Univ. **MEMBERSHIPS** Am Soc Asn; Am Polit Asn; Inter-Univ Sem Armed Forces & Soc **RESEARCH** Military Sociology; Greek Americans **SELECTED PUBLICATIONS** "Humanitarians or Warriors?: Race, Gender, and Combat Status in Operation Restore Hope," Armed Forces & Soc, 95; "Affirmative Action in the Army: Why it Works," The Aff Action Debate, 96; "The Army's Success," Double Exposure: Poverty and Race in America, 97; "Civil-Military Relations After the Cold War," Civil-Mil Relations in Post-Communist States, 97; "Black Leadership and Racial Integration: Army Lessons for American Society," Raceand& Ethnic Relations in the US: Readings for the 21st Century, 98. **CONTACT ADDRESS** Dept Sociol, Northwestern Univ, Evanston, IL 60208. **EMAIL** c-moskos@nwu.edu

MOSS, ROGER W.
PERSONAL Born 01/31/1940, Zanesville, OH, m, 1981, 2 children **DISCIPLINE** CULTURAL HISTORY **EDUCATION** Univ Delaware, PhD 72; Ohio Univ, MA 66, BSed 63. **CAREER** Athenaeum of Philadelphia, exec dir 68-00; Univ Penn, adj prof 81-00; Univ Maryland, lectr 67-68; Univ Delaware, lectr 66-68. **HONORS AND AWARDS** NEH; NEA; Joel Polsky prize, ASID, 89. **MEMBERSHIPS** RSA; SAH; HSP. **RESEARCH** American architecture and hist preservation. **SELECTED PUBLICATIONS** Auth, Historic Houses of Philadelphia, Phil, UPP, 98; Philadelphia Victorian: The Building of the Athenaeum, Phil, The Athenaeum, 98; Paint in America, ed, NY, John Wiley & Son, 94; The American Country House, NY, Henry Holt & Co, 90; auth, Lighting for Historic Buildings, John Wiley & Son (New York), 88; auth, Victorian Exterior Decoration, henry Holt (New York), 87; auth, Victorian Interior Decoration, Henry Holt (New York), 86; auth, Biographical Dictionary of Philadelphia Architects, 1700-1930, G.K. Hall (Boston), 85; auth, Century of Color, Watkins Glen (New York), 81. **CONTACT ADDRESS** Athenaeum of Philadelphia, 219 S. Sixth St, Philadelphia, PA 19106. **EMAIL** rwmoss@pobox.upenn.edu

MOTIFF, JAMES P.
PERSONAL Born 09/03/1943, Green Bay, WI, m, 1981, 1 child **DISCIPLINE** PSYCHOLOGY **EDUCATION** St Norbert Col, BS, 65; Univ S Dak, MA, 67; PhD, 69. **CAREER** Asst prof, Hope Col, 69-71; assoc prof, 72-85; dept ch, 89-97; prof, 85-. **HONORS AND AWARDS** Dist Achiev Awd; Outstand Edu of Am; Kelly Danen Dist Alum Awd; Delta Epsilon Sigma; Am Men of Sci; Who's Who in Am, Midwest. **MEMBERSHIPS** BSM; Sigma Xi; Psi Chi; CUPD. **RESEARCH** Health psychology; physiological psychology; clinical psychology. **SELECTED PUBLICATIONS** Co-rev of, "Healing Through Stress Management," Holland Sentinel (85); coauth, "Physiological Psychology: The Sensory Homunculus," an Activities Handbook for the Teaching of Psychology vol 2, APA (87); coauth, "Difficult Situations, Difficulties with Faculty Members," ADFL Bulletin (94): 26-30; coauth, "Learning While

Serving in a Psychology Internship," Mich J Comm Ser Learn 1 (94): 70-76. **CONTACT ADDRESS** Dept Psychology, Hope Col, 35 E 12th St, Holland, MI 49422-9000. **EMAIL** motiff@hope.edu

MOUNT, GEORGE
PERSONAL Born 09/03/1941, Longview, TX, m, 2 children **DISCIPLINE** PSYCHOLOGY **EDUCATION** Univ Tex, BA, 67; Univ North Tex, MS, 69; PhD, 71. **CAREER** Asst prof, East Cen State Col, 71-72; instr, Mountain View Col, 72-; adj asst prof, Univ Tex, 75-; priv prac, 98-. **MEMBERSHIPS** APA; TPA; DPA; NSSA; ASCH; SPCP; NAN. **SELECTED PUBLICATIONS** Auth, Effective Parenting Strategies, Prac Innov Press (Dallas, TX), 94; auth, "Assessing and Coping with Violent Behavior," J Crisis Neg (95): 69-71; coauth, "Workplace Violence," Tex Police J 43 (95): 11-16; coauth, "Evaluating Mental Status-A Guide for Polygraph Examiners," Am Asn Police Polygraphists (97): 60-67. **CONTACT ADDRESS** Dept Social Science, Mountain View Col, 4849 W Illinois, Dallas, TX 75211.

MOXLEY, ROBERT L.
PERSONAL Born 03/06/1937, Jacksonville, FL, m, 1965, 2 children **DISCIPLINE** SOCIOLOGY **EDUCATION** Fla State Univ, BS, 61; Springfield Col, MEd, 62; Cornell Univ, PhD, 70. **CAREER** Asst prof to prof, NC State Univ, 70-. **HONORS AND AWARDS** Fulbright Lecturer, Brazil, 79; Excellence in Instruction Awd, RSS, 90; Awd for Outstanding Accomplishments in Teaching, SRSA, 93; Sigma Iota Rho. **MEMBERSHIPS** Am Sociol Assoc; Rural Sociol Soc; Sigma Iota Rho; Int Rural Sociol Soc; Community Develop Soc. **RESEARCH** Community Organization, Problems and theories of development, International Development. **SELECTED PUBLICATIONS** Coauth, "Is Locality Differentiation a Unidimensional Phenomenon?", Southern Rural Sociol 5.1 (87): 17-40; coauth, "Reviewing Papers for the Social Sciences: Recurrent Problems and Suggestions for Improving the Evaluation Process", Family Sci Rev 2.2 (89): auth, "Comparative Community Structure: Organizational Solidarity, Social Rigidity, Political Competitiveness and Population", Res in Community Sociol II, (92): 171-186; auth, "U.S. Rural Drug Abuse Research Needs and Research Policy", Drugs and Society 7 (92): 117-139; coauth, "New Directions In Integrated Pest Management (IPM) Technology Transfer: Research on Peanut Farmers, Attitudes and Socioeconomic Impacts", Res Report 92-01, Univ of Ga, 92; coauth, "The Economic Impact of Peanut CRSP in Jamaica: Performance of CARDI/PAYNE Cultivar", Res Report 92-02, Univ of Ga, 93; coauth, "Socioeconomic Impacts of Peanut CRSP Graduate Training Efforts", Res Report 94-01, Univ of Ga, 94; coauth, "Dimensions of Farm Commodity Production: Horses, Strawberries and Why", Southern Rural Sociol 11.1 (95): 44-59; auth, "Community Solidarity, Political Competitiveness, and Social Rigidity: Relationships with Social and Health Services", Rural Sociol 60.2 (95): 310-332; coauth, "Peanut CRSP Human Resource Development", Impacts and Scientific Advances Through Collaborative Research on Peanut, ed James H. Williams, Univ of Ga, 97. **CONTACT ADDRESS** Dept Sociol and Anthrop, No Carolina State Univ, Box 8107, Raleigh, NC 27695-0001.

MTIKA, MIKE M.
PERSONAL Born 06/25/1954, Mzimba, Malawi, m, 1979, 3 children **DISCIPLINE** SOCIOLOGY **EDUCATION** Univ Malawi, BS, 78; Reading Univ, MS, 80; Wash State Univ, PhD, 98. **CAREER** Agr Exten Off, Malawi, 78-79; Res Off, Malawi, 80-83; Marketing Off, Malawi, 83-86; Proj Coordr, World Vision; 88-91; Tech Svc Dir, World Vision, 87-88; Oper Dir, World Vision, 88-91; Dev Ed, Dev Ed Proj, 91-93; Res Asst, TA, Wash State Univ, 93-95; TA, Wash State Univ, 96-98; asst prof, Univ of Alaska Anchorage, 98-. **HONORS AND AWARDS** Alexandra A. Smick Scholar, 93; Univ of Wis Summer Inst for African Scholars Awd, 95; Wash State Univ Summer Grad Res Asst Awd, 95; Rockefeller Found African Diss Res Awd, 95; Ann Madsen De Pew Mem Scholar, 96, Mellon Fel Res Awd, 00. **MEMBERSHIPS** Am Sociol Assoc; Rural Sociol Soc. **RESEARCH** Specializes in sociology of community and development processes, social stratification and political sociology. Research interest is in how people and communities draw upon their social capital to deal with problems they experience and to develop their communities. **SELECTED PUBLICATIONS** Auth, The Role of Evaluation and Action Research in Extension Media Productions, Training for Agriculture, Rome: the Food and Agricultural Organization, 83; coauth, Continuity and Change in Food Consumption in Washington and Japan, Wash State Univ IMPACT Center Report: Information Series 78, 94; coauth, Land-Grant Univ Agr and Nat Resources Res: Perceptions and Influence of External Interest Groups, Wash State Univ: Col of Agr and Home Econ Res Bull XB1031, 94; Auth, Social and Cultural Relations in Econ Action: The Embeddedness of Food Security in Rural Malawi Amidst The AIDS Epidemic, (forthcoming). **CONTACT ADDRESS** Dept Sociol, Univ of Alaska, Anchorage, 3211 Providence Dr, Anchorage, AK 99508-8198.

MUELLER, CLAUS
PERSONAL Born 07/23/1941, Berlin, Germany, m, 1984, 2 children **DISCIPLINE** SOCIOLOGY, MEDIA **EDUCATION** Univ of Cologne, BA (equiv), 64; New Schl for Soc Res, MA, 60, PhD, 70; CEP Inst dEtudes Politiques, Paris, 77. **CAREER** Sr Part, Media Resource Assoc, 75-85; Pres, Intl Film and TV Exchange Inc, 85-, curator, New York Screening Days, 86-; Adv, 89/95-, Assoc Prof, 76-80, Dir, 85-, Hunter Col, CUNY. **HONORS AND AWARDS** Brd Mem/Off, Intl Film and TV Exchange, NY Film/video Coun; election to Am Council on Germany; Fulbright Scholar, 95. **MEMBERSHIPS** New York Film and Video Coun, Assoc of Independent Video and Film Prof, Carnegie Coun on Intl Relation, New York Film/Video Coun, Intl Radio and TV Soc **RESEARCH** International Communications; information and the class structure; contemporary documentaries. **SELECTED PUBLICATIONS** Auth, The Politics of Communicaiton, Oxford Univ Press, 74, Japanese ed, 76, German ed, 75; auth, Development Communication in the USA, Media Sup and Develop Comm in a World of Change, Bad Honnef: 95; The Refracted Mirror, Intl Jour of Group Tensions, 96; The Cologne Medien Forum, Change Ahead for the Berlinale, Germany's WDR, The Independent, 99, Inside Havana, The Independent, 00; The Ind, 98; US Films at the 2000 Berlinale, Indiwire Third World Television Access to US Media, F Naumann Found, 89. **CONTACT ADDRESS** 420 East 64th W2H, New York, NY 10021. **EMAIL** cmueller@hunter.cuny.edu

MUGA, DAVID
DISCIPLINE SOCIOLOGY **EDUCATION** Univ Calif Berkeley, BS, 64; MA Inst Tech, MS, 66; Univ Goteborg Sweden, PhD, 77. **CAREER** Instructor, Univ Goteborg, Sweden, 76-77; Instructor, Olympic Cmty Col, 87-91; Dir of Ethnic Student Center, W WA Univ, 91-92; Prof, Skagit Valley Col, 92-. **HONORS AND AWARDS** Exception Fac Awd, Skagit Valley Col, 97-98; Who's Who Among Am Teachers, 96-00. **MEMBERSHIPS** Am Sociol Asn; Pacific Sociol Asn. **RESEARCH** Stratification. **CONTACT ADDRESS** Dept Soc Sci, Skagit Valley Col, 2405 Col Way, Mount Vernon, WA 98273. **EMAIL** muga@skagit.ctc.edu

MULGREW, JOHN
PERSONAL Born 01/02/1936, New York, NY, d, 2 children **DISCIPLINE** PSYCHOLOGY **EDUCATION** Fla State Univ, PhD, 71. **CAREER** Teacher, New York Board of Educ, 64-69; Assoc Dir, Coun and Psychol Service Center, 71-73; Prof, Appalachian State Univ, 71-. **MEMBERSHIPS** Am Acad of Psychotherapists; Am Asn of Marriage and Family Therapists; Am Group Psychotherapy Asn; Asn for the Advancement of Gestalt Therapy; Atlanta Group Psychotherapy Soc; Am Board of Prof Psychol. **SELECTED PUBLICATIONS** Auth, "Evolving," Voices: The Art and Science of Psychotherapy, (93): 13; auth, "Some Considerations for Students Who Wish to Become Psychotherapist," Voices: The Art and Science of Psychotherapy, (96): 84; auth, "Intervision," Voices: The Art and Science of Psychotherapy, (96): 91-92; co-auth, "Dreams Without Interpretation," Voices: The Art and Science of Psychotherapy, (96): 47-53; co-auth, "A Systems Dialectical Model of Supervision: A Symbolic Process," Contemporary Family Therapy, 99. **CONTACT ADDRESS** Dept Human Development, Appalachian State Univ, 1 Appalachian State, Boone, NC 28608-0001.

MUNDY, PETER
PERSONAL Born 05/13/1954, Trinidad, m, 1986, 1 child **DISCIPLINE** PSYCHOLOGY **EDUCATION** Univ Miami, PhD, 81. **CAREER** Asst Clinical prof, Univ Calif, Los Angeles, 86-91; assoc prof, Univ Miami, 91-96, prof, 96-, Dir, Child and Development Div, 00-. **HONORS AND AWARDS** NSRA Postdoctoral Fel, Univ Calif, Los Angeles, Neuropsychiatric Inst, 81-83; UAP Postdoctoral Fel, Univ Calif, Los Angeles NPI, 83-85. **MEMBERSHIPS** Am Psychol Asn, Am Psychol Soc, Soc for Res in Child Development, Int Soc for Infant Studies. **RESEARCH** The development of social competence in typical and atypical infants and children. **SELECTED PUBLICATIONS** Coauth, "Social and non-social factors in the Childhood Autism Rating Scales," J of Autism and Related Disorders, 29 (99): 303-313; coauth with J. Stella, "Joint attention, social orienting, and nonverbal communication in autism," in A. Weatherby and B. Prizant, eds, Autism spectrum disorders: A transactional development perspective, Baltimore, Md: Paul Brookes (2000); coauth, "Fourteen month cortical activity and different infant joint attention skills," Developmental Psychobiology, 36 (2000); coauth with R. Neal, "Neural plasticity, joint attention and autistic developmental pathology," in L. M. Glidden, ed, International Review of Research in Mental Retardation, Vol 23, NY: Academic Press (2000); coauth, "Atypical vocal development in young children with autism," J of Autism and Related Disorders (in press); coauth, "Individual differences in infant skills as predictors of child-caregiver joint attention and language," Social Development (in press); coauth, "Responding to joint attention across the 6- to 24-month age period and early language acquisition," J of Applied Developmental Psychol (in press). **CONTACT ADDRESS** Dept Psychol, Univ of Miami, 5665 Ponce De Leon Blvd, Coral Gables, FL 33124. **EMAIL** pmundy@miami.edu

MUNOZ, CARLOS, JR
PERSONAL Born 08/25/1939, El Paso, TX, m, 1977, 5 children **DISCIPLINE** ETHNIC STUDIES **EDUCATION** Los Angeles City Col, AA, 64; Calif State Univ, BA, 67; Claremont Grad Sch, PhD, 73. **CAREER** Instr, Calif State Univ, 68-69; lectr, Pitzer Col, 69-70; asst prof, Univ Calif Irvine, 70-76; prof to prof emeritus, Univ Calif Berkeley, 76-. **HONORS AND AWARDS** Who's Who Among Hispanic Am; Who's Who of Ed, Writers and Poets; Dr, Martin Luther King, Jr, Cesar Chavez and Rosa Parks Award, Univ Mich, 96; Scholar of the Year Award, Nat Asn of Chicana and Chicano Studies, 99; Gustavus Myers Book Award, 90. **MEMBERSHIPS** Nat Asn for Chicana/Chicano Studies; Am Polit Sci Asn; Am Hist Asn; Soc for Am Baseball Res. **RESEARCH** Racial and ethnic politics; Social movements; History of the 1960s; Latino experience in major league baseball. **SELECTED PUBLICATIONS** Auth, "Coalition Politics in San Antonio and Denver," in Racial Politics in American Cities, 90; auth, "Latinos and the Democratic Party," in The Democrats Must Lead, 92; auth, "Reclaiming our Heritage," in without Discovery: A Native Response to Columbus, 92; auth, "The Militant Challenge: The Chicano Generation," in Beyond 1848: Readings in the Modern Chicano Hist Experience, 93; auth, "Chicano Protest Politics in the 60s," in Peoples of Color in the American West, 94; auth, "The Quest for Paradigm," in Latinos and Education, 97. **CONTACT ADDRESS** Dept Ethnic Studies, Univ of California, Berkeley, 506 Barrows Hall, No 2570, Berkeley, CA 94720-2570. **EMAIL** cmjr@uclink4.berkeley.edu

MUNSON, HENRY LEE
PERSONAL Born 11/01/1946, New York, NY, m, 1971, 4 children **DISCIPLINE** ANTHROPOLOGY **EDUCATION** Columbia Col, BA 70; Univ Chicago, MA 73, PhD. **CAREER** Univ CA, Santa Barb, vis lectr 80-81; Univ ME, asst prof 82-88, assoc prof 88-94;prof 94-, chair 98. **HONORS AND AWARDS** Woodrow Wilson Fell; John D and Catherine T MacArthur Gnt. **MEMBERSHIPS** AAA; Middle East Stud Assn. **RESEARCH** Relig and polit, Comp Relig. **SELECTED PUBLICATIONS** Religion and Power in Morocco, Yale Univ Press, 93; Islam and Revolution in the Middle East, Yale Univ Press, 88; The House of S Abd Allah, Yale Univ Press, 84 **CONTACT ADDRESS** Dept of Anthrop, Univ of Maine, Orono, ME 04469. **EMAIL** henry_munson@umit.maine.edu

MURDOCK, GWENDOLYN K.
PERSONAL Born Denver, CO **DISCIPLINE** PSYCHOLOGY **EDUCATION** Univ Colo, BA, 72; MA, 81; Ga Inst Tech, PhD, 83. **CAREER** Adj Fac, George Mason Univ, 84-85; Adj Prof, Univ of DC, 84-85; Asst Prof to Full Prof, Mo Southern State Col, 85-. **HONORS AND AWARDS** Outstanding Teacher Awd, MO Southern Foundation, 91. **MEMBERSHIPS** Animal Behavior Soc; Am Soc of Mammalogists; Sigma Xi. **RESEARCH** Bovid social behavior: bison, sable antelope. **SELECTED PUBLICATIONS** Co-auth, "Observations of Maternal-Infant Interactions in a Captive Herd of Sable Antelope (Hippotragus niger)," Zoo Biology, (83); 215-224; co-auth, "Behavioral Study of a Small Bison Herd at Prairie State Park," Proceeding of the Tenth North Am Prairie Conf, 86; co-auth, "Small Bison Herd Utilization of and Impact on Tall Grass Prairie," Proceedings of the Eleventh North Am Prairie Conf, (88): 243-245. **CONTACT ADDRESS** Dept Psychol, Missouri So State Col, 3950 Newman Rd, Joplin, MO 64801. **EMAIL** murdock_g@mail.mssc.edu

MURNION, PHILIP JOSEPH
PERSONAL Born 03/01/1938, New York, NY **DISCIPLINE** SOCIOLOGY **EDUCATION** Columbia Univ, MA, PhD, Theol. **CAREER** Priest **CONTACT ADDRESS** 309 Elizabeth St, New York, NY 10012.

MURRAY, ED
PERSONAL Born 08/22/1937, Cleveland, OH, m, 1973, 2 children **DISCIPLINE** PSYCHOLOGY **EDUCATION** Bromeo Sem, PhB, 59; St. Mary Sem, MDiv, 63; Kent State Univ, MA, 72; Universidad Inca Garcicesco De La Vega, PhD, 93. **CAREER** Asst prof, Kent State Univ, 77-. **HONORS AND AWARDS** Grant, State of Ohio; Int Who's Who, 96. **MEMBERSHIPS** AAUP; Phi Delta Kappa. **RESEARCH** Depression, Anxiety and Adolescent Identity, Role Playing. **SELECTED PUBLICATIONS** Auth, "Effectiveness of ingratiation tactics in a cover letter on mail questionnaire response", Psychonomic Science 26, (72): 349-351; auth, "Race vs. Belief as determinants of attraction in a live interaction setting", J of Experimental Res in Personality 6, (72): 162-168; auth, "Race vs Belief as determinants of attraction in a group interaction context", Memory and Cognition 1, (73): 41-46; auth, "The Relationship between religious beliefs and attending the fear-provoking religiously oriented movie The Exorcist", Omega, 76; auth, "Bystander intervention in a mild need situation", Bull of the Psychonomic Soc 2, (76): 133-135; auth, "The effect of interviewer's race and sex on the responses of white policemen", J of Crime and Justice, Jan 79. **CONTACT ADDRESS** Dept Soc Sci, Kent State Univ, 3325 W 13th St, Ashtabula, OH 44004.

MURRAY, JOSEPH L.
PERSONAL Born 05/25/1960, Evergreen Park, IL, s **DISCIPLINE** EDUCATION **EDUCATION** Quincy Col, BA/BS, 82; Ohio Univ, MEd, 84; Mich State Univ, PhD, 91. **CAREER** Teacher, Special Education Lake County, 82-83; grad assoc, Ohio Univ, 83-84; residence hall director, Saint Martins Col,

84-87; staff advisor, Mich State Univ, 87-91; deputy director student services, Thomas cooley Law School, 91-94; asst prof, Bucknell Univ, 94-. **HONORS AND AWARDS** Am Col Personnel Asn; Annuit Coeptis Awd, 91. **MEMBERSHIPS** ACPA, NASPA, ASCD. **RESEARCH** Employee training and development, moral reasoning, student leadership in higher education. **SELECTED PUBLICATIONS** Auth, Training for Student Leaders Rev ed, Dubuque, 98; auth, Training for Student Leaders, Dubuque, 94; auth, "The Student activities interest questionnaire: Relating Holland's vocational theory to student involvement," Journal of College Student Retention, (in press); auth, "The teacher belief inventory: Measuring the theoretical and practical orientations of preservice teachers," Education, (in press); auth, "The effects of training on resident assistant job performance," Journal of College Student Development 40, (99): 744-747. **CONTACT ADDRESS** Dept Educ, Bucknell Univ, Lewisburg, PA 17837.

MURRAY, MABEL LAKE
PERSONAL Born 02/24/1935, Baltimore, MD, m, 1968 **DISCIPLINE** EDUCATION **EDUCATION** Coppin State Teachers Coll, Baltimore MD, BS, 1956; Loyola Coll, Balitmore MD, MED, 1969; Virginia Polytechnic Institute, Blacksburg VA, Case, 1978-81, EdD, 1982. **CAREER** Baltimore City Public Schs, teacher, 56-68; Prince Georges County Public Schs, reading specialist, 68-70; Proj KAPS, Baltimore MD, reading coordr, 70-72; Univ of MD, reading coordr, 72-76; Johns Hopkins Univ, adjunct prof, 72-76; Carroll County Public Schs, supervisor, 76-87; Sojourner Douglass Col, Baltimore MD, prof, beginning 1987-, supervisor, Student Teaching, currently; NAACP Educ Dept, nat coordr NTE; Sojourner-Douglass Col, Human Growth Dev, coord, currently. **HONORS AND AWARDS** Designed curriculum material for two sch systems, 1968-72; Conducted numerous workshops, 1969-89; Guest speaker at variety of educ/human relations activities, 1969-89; Outstanding Educator, State of MD Intl Reading Assn, 1979; Guest Lectr, Baltimore City Schs Spec Educ, 1979; Developed reading prog for state mental hospital, 1981; Mayor's Citation, 1982; Serv Awd, Baltimore City Chapter, Delta Sigma Theta, 1983; Mem of Congressman Louis Stokes Committee on Black Health Issues, 1989. **MEMBERSHIPS** Mem, Delta Sigma Theta Sorority, 1972-; Baltimore County Alumnae Chapter, Delta Sigma Theta; advisor, Lambda Kappa and Mu Psi Chapters, Delta Sigma Theta; consultant, Piney Woods School, 1984-89; commission chair-instruction, Nat Alliance of Black School Educators, 1987-96; exec bd, Nat Alliance of Black School Educators, 1987-; consultant, AIDS Project MSDE, 1988; consultant, Dunbar Middle School, 1989; consultant, Des Moines Iowa Schools; Nat Coun on Educating Black Children; pres, Md Coun of Deltas; nat pres, Pinochle Bugs Soc and Civic Club; nat treas, The Societas Doctas; Baho Chap, The Soc. **CONTACT ADDRESS** Dept Chmn Human Growth & Dev, Sojourner-Douglass Col, 500 N Caroline St, Baltimore, MD 21205. **EMAIL** mabeldst@hotmail.com

MURRAY, PAUL
DISCIPLINE SOCIOLOGY **EDUCATION** Fla State Univ, PhD. **CAREER** Prof, Siena Col, 79-. **MEMBERSHIPS** Am Sociol Asn. **RESEARCH** Race relations, Social Movements, Civil Rights. **SELECTED PUBLICATIONS** Auth, The Civil Rights Movements: References and Resources, G.K. Hall, 93. **CONTACT ADDRESS** Dept Sociol, Siena Col, 515 Loudonville Rd, Loudonville, NY 12211. **EMAIL** murray@siena.ued

MURRAY, S. B.
PERSONAL Born 08/22/1961, Glasgow, Scotland **DISCIPLINE** SOCIOLOGY **EDUCATION** N Ariz Univ, BS, 84; Univ Cal, Santa Cruz, MA, 88; PhD, 95. **CAREER** Asst prof, San Jose Univ, 98-. **RESEARCH** Families in modern society; sociology of gender; child care workers; violence in families; social psychology; qualitative research methods. **SELECTED PUBLICATIONS** Auth, "The Unhappy Marriage of Theory and Practice: An Analysis of a Battered Woman's Shelter," Nat Women's Stud Asn J 1 (88): 75-92; auth, "We All Love Charles: Men in Child Care and the Social Construction of Gender," Gender and Soc 10 (96): 368-385; auth, "Its Safer This Way: The Subtle and Not-So-Subtle Exclusion of Men in Child Care," in Subtle Sexism: Current Practices and Prospects for Change, eds. NV Benokraitis, JR Feagin (NY: Sage, 97); auth, "Child Care Work: Intimacy in the Shadow of Family Life," Qualitative Soc 21 (98): 149-168; auth, "Getting Paid in Smiles: The Gendering of Child Care Work," Symbolic Interaction 23 (00). **CONTACT ADDRESS** Dept Sociology, San Jose State Univ, 1 Washington Sq, San Jose, CA 95192-0001. **EMAIL** julsue@aol.com

MURRAY, STEPHEN O.
PERSONAL Born 05/04/1950, St. Paul, MN **DISCIPLINE** SOCIOLOGY **EDUCATION** James Madison Col, BA, 72; Univ AZ, MA, 75; Univ Toronto, PhD, 79; Univ CA, Berkeley, post-doctoral study, 80-82. **CAREER** Res dir, El Instituto Obregon, 82-. **HONORS AND AWARDS** Theory Development award, Int Gay Academic Union, 82; Academy for the Study of Male Homosexualities, 95; Ong Iotek Awd, Taiwan Found, 95. **MEMBERSHIPS** Am Anthropology Asn; Am Sociol Asn. **RESEARCH** Ethnology of sexuality; science of studies. **SELECTED PUBLICATIONS** Auth, Theory Groups in the Study of Language in North America: A Social History, John Benjamins, 94; Taiwanese Society, Taiwanese Culture, with Keelung Hong, Univ Press of Am, 94; Latin American Male Homosexualities, Univ NM Press, 95; American Gay, Univ Chicago Press, 96; Angkor Life, Bangkok: Bua Luang, 96; Islamic Homosexualities, with Will Roscoe, NY Univ Press, 97; Boy Wives and Female Husbands: Studies in African Homosexualities, with Will Roscoe St Martin's Press, 98; American Sociolinguistics: A Social NetworkHistory, John Bemjamins, 98; Homosexualities, Univ Chicago Press, 00. **CONTACT ADDRESS** El Instituto Obregon, 1360 De Haro, San Francisco, CA 94107. **EMAIL** som1950@hotmail.com

MURSTEIN, BERNARD I.
PERSONAL Born 04/29/1929, Vilnius, Lithuania, m, 1954, 2 children **DISCIPLINE** PSYCHOLOGY **EDUCATION** Col of City of NYork, BSS, 50; Univ Miami, MS, 51; Univ Tex, PhD, 55. **CAREER** Endowed Ch, May Buckley Sadowski Prof Psychology, Conn Col, 94-; chairperson Dept Psychology, Conn Col, 76-79; 90-91; Fulbright Prof, Institut de Psychologie, Universite de Louvain, 68-69; prof Psychology, Conn Col, 65-. **HONORS AND AWARDS** Amer Psycholog Assoc Convention Invited Address, 91; Honored in Twentieth Century Psychologists series, October 1987 issue of Papeles Psicologos del Colegio; George I Alden Trust Acad Bus Integration Prog Grant, 82; Mellon Grant, 78, 80; Ntl Sci Found Grant, 70; Ntl Sci Found Grant Consultant; Editorial Consultant to various psychological journals; Amer Psychol Fel, 63, 77, 93; ABPP Diplomate in Clinical Psychol, 61; Soc for Projective Techniques Fel, 59; US Pub Health Fel Stipend, 54-55. **MEMBERSHIPS** Amer Psychol Assoc; Soc for Personality Assessment; Ntl Council on Family Relations; Intl Council of Psychologists; Intl Soc for Study of Interpersonal Relationships. **SELECTED PUBLICATIONS** Auth, The psychology of investment, Conn Col Mag, 98; coauth, Gender differences in love, sex, and motivation for sex, Psychol Reports, 98; auth, On exchange theory, androcentrism, and sex stereotypy, Psychol Reports, 97; coauth, "Paranoia assessment with the SIS-II: In a college student sample, Jour of Projective Psychol and Mental Health, 96. **CONTACT ADDRESS** Dept of Psychology, Connecticut Col, 270 Mohegan Ave., Box 5581, New London, CT 06320-4196. **EMAIL** bimur@conncoll.edu

MUSTO, DAVID F.
PERSONAL Born 01/08/1936, Tacoma, WA, m, 1961, 4 children **DISCIPLINE** HISTORY, PSYCHOLOGY **EDUCATION** Univ Wash, BA, 56, MD, 63; Yale Univ, MA, 61. **CAREER** Spec asst to dir, Nat Inst Mental Health, 67-69; from asst prof to assoc prof hist & psychiat, 69-78, sr res scientist, Child Study Ctr, 78-80, Lectr Hist & Am Studies, Yale Univ, 78-, Prof Psychiat, Child Study Ctr & Prof Hist Med, 81-, Head, Sect Hist & Social Policy, Child Study Ctr & Bush Ctr, 81-, Residency psychiat, Yale Univ, 64-67; vis asst prof, Johns Hopkins Univ, 68-69; fel, Drug Abuse Coun, 72-73; consult, Nat Comn Marijuana & Drug Abuse, 72-73; prog dir, Nat Humanities Inst, 77-78; hist consult, President's Comn Ment Health, 77-78; mem US deleg, UN Comn Narcotic Drugs, 78 & 79; mem, White House Strategy Coun, Off Pres US, 77-81; mem, Nat Coun Smithsonian Inst, 81-; mem panel on alcohol policy, Nat Res Coun, 78-81. **HONORS AND AWARDS** William Osler Medal, Am Asn Hist Med, 60; Edward Kremers Awd, Am Inst Hist Pharmacy, 74. **MEMBERSHIPS** AHA; Am Psychiat Asn; Am Asn Hist Med. **RESEARCH** History of the family; application of psychology to history; history of drug control in America. **SELECTED PUBLICATIONS** Coauth, Strange encounter, Psychiatry, 868; auth, Youth of John Quincy Adams, Proc Am Philos Soc, 869; The American Disease: Origins of Narcotic Control, Yale Univ, 73; coauth, Historical perspectives on mental health and racism in the United States, In: Racism and Mental Health, Univ Pittsburgh, 73; Whatever happened to community mental health?, Pub Interest, spring 75; Continuity Across Generations, Smithsonian Inst Press, 79; Temperance and prohibition in America, In: Alcohol and Pubic Policy, Nat Acad Press, 81; Adams family, Proc Mass Hist Soc, 82; Drugs And Narcotics in History - Porter,r, Teich,m, J of Interdisciplinary History, Vol 0028, 1997. **CONTACT ADDRESS** Child Study Ctr, Box 90015. **EMAIL** david.musto@yale.edu

MUTISYA, PHILLIPH
PERSONAL Born 09/22/1950, Kenya, m, 1987, 4 children **DISCIPLINE** EDUCATION **EDUCATION** Univ Mass, MEd, 84; Univ Mass, EdD, 89. **CAREER** Assoc Prof, Fayetteville State Univ, 91-. **HONORS AND AWARDS** Back Student Board Serv Awd, NC St Univ, 90; Teacher of the Year, NC St Univ, 96; Teacher of the Year, Fayetteville St Univ, 98-99. **MEMBERSHIPS** ASBS, UCI, NAME, NCCSS, SAPES. **RESEARCH** Diversity and character education. **SELECTED PUBLICATIONS** Auth, "Demythologization and Demystification of African Initiation Rites: A Positive and Meaningful Educational Aspect Heading for Extinction," J of Black Studies, Temple UP, vol 27, no 1 (96); coauth, "Who are We? Building a Knowledge Base About Different Ethnic, Racial and Cultural Groups in America: A Self-Study and a Workshop Facilitator's Guide," in African-Americans (F Toms/A Hobbs, 97); auth, Developing Diversity Modules Across the Curriculum, Sch of Educ Newsletter, Fayetteville UP, 97. **CONTACT ADDRESS** Dept Educ, Fayetteville State Univ, 1200 Murchison Rd, Fayetteville, NC 28301. **EMAIL** pmutisya@uncfsu.edu

MUUSS, ROLF EDUARD HELMUT
PERSONAL Born 09/26/1924, Tating, Germany, w, 1953, 2 children **DISCIPLINE** EDUCATIONAL PSYCHOLOGY, MINOR CLINICAL PSYCHOLOGY **EDUCATION** Univ Maryland Law School and Anne Arundel Community Col, State Level Hearing Officer Training Prog, 80; Univ IL, Urbana, PhD, 57; Western Maryland Col, Westminster, MD, Med, 53-54; Teachers Col, Columbia Univ, NYork, 52; Central Missouri State Col, Warrensburg, MO, 51-52; Univ Hamburg, Germany, 51; Padagogische Hochschule, Flensburg, Teaching Diploma, 49-51; People's High School, Sigtuna, Sweden, 48-49. **CAREER** Prof Emer, Goucher Col, Towson, MD, 95-; State Level Hearing Officer (Spec Edu Hearings) for the State of Maryland, 80-95; Chair, Sociology and Anthropology, Goucher Col, Towson, MD, 83-85; Dir Spec Edu, Goucher Col, Towson,MD, 77-92; Chair, Dept edu, Goucher Col, Towson, MD, 72-75; Full Prof, Goucher Col, Towson, MD, 64-95; Assoc Prof, Goucher Col, Towson, MD, 59-64; Research Asst Prof, State Univ Iowa, IA, 57-59; Grad Asst, Univ Illinois, Urbana, IL, 54-57; Houseparent, Child Study Cen, Baltimore, MD, 53; Sub Principal and Teacher, Flensburg, Germany, 52-53; Teacher Trainee, Office of Edu, Washington, DC, 51-52; Public School Teacher, Sudtondern, Germany, 45-46. **HONORS AND AWARDS** Holder of the Elizabeth C Todd Distinguished Professorship, (honorary chair with fin support for research), 80-85; Goucher Col Awd for Distinguished Scholarship, 79; Andrew Mellon Foundation Grant for Faculty Development, 76-77; Mary Williams Fellowship in the Social Services, 72, 73. **MEMBERSHIPS** Soc for Research on Adolescence; Soc for Research in Child Development; Am Psychol Asn, (Fellow in div 7 and 15); Am Psychol Soc (Fellow); Maryland Psychol Asn (Treasurer 71-73); Baltimore Psychol Asn (VP 70-71); Phi Delta Kappa; Kappa Delta Pi (chapter VP 56-57). **RESEARCH** Adolescent development; Theories of Adolescence; Adolescent Problem Behavior. **SELECTED PUBLICATIONS** Theories of Adolescence, Random House, NY, 1st ed 62, 2d ed 68, 3d ed 75, 4th ed 82, 5th ed 88, 6th ed with McGraw-Hill, 96, trans into Dutch, German, Hebrew, Italian, Japanese, Portuguese, Spanish; Adolescent Behavior and Society: A Book of Readings, Random House, NY, 1st ed 71, 2d ed 75, 3d ed 80, 4th ed 80, 4th and 5th eds, with McGraw-Hill, NY, 5th ed 99; First Aid for Classroom Discipline Problems, Holt Rinehart & Winston, 62, trans Portuguese; Grundlagen der Jugendpsychologie, Hansiche Verlagsanstalt, Lubeck, Germany; More than 100 scientific papers and research articles in medical, psychol, edu, journals in USA, Eng, Ger, Switz, Swed. **CONTACT ADDRESS** 1540 Pickett Rd, Lutherville, MD 21093-5822. **EMAIL** rmuuss@goucher.edu

MYERS, CHARLES BENNETT
PERSONAL Born 06/08/1939, Columbia, PA, m, 1959, 3 children **DISCIPLINE** TEACHER EDUCATION; SOCIAL STUDIES EDUCATION **EDUCATION** Pa State Univ, BS, 61; George Peabody Col Teachers, MA, 63, PhD, 68. **CAREER** Hist teacher, Jr High Sch, Pa, 61-62; teacher demonstration sch, Peabody Col, 64; asst prof educ & hist, Rider Col, 65-68; soc sci specialist, Speedier Proj, Palmyra, Pa, 68-70; Prog develop specialist, Teacher Educ Alliance Proj, Tenn, 68-70; from asst prof to assoc prof, 70-78, prof hist & soc sci educ, George Peabody Col, 78-79, dir, Progs for Educ Youth, 74-79; mem bd dir, Nat Coun for Social Studies, 76-81; adminr, Ctr Econ & Soc Studies Educ, 77-79; prof social studies educ, George Peabody Col, Vanderbilt Univ, 79-86; chmn, dept teaching and learning, 79-86; assoc dean for academic affairs, Vanderbilt Univ, 89-92. **MEMBERSHIPS** Nat Coun Social Studies; NEA; Asn Pvt Enterprise Educ (secy-treas, 78-79, vpres, 79-80, pres, 80-81); Am Edu Res Asn; Am Asn of Col for Teacher Edu; Nat Coun for the Accred of Teacher Educ; Soc Sci Cons; Phi Delt Kap; Kap Delt Pi; Pi Gam Mu; Phi Alph Thet; Phi Kap Phi. **RESEARCH** Teacher education and learning; school reform; accreditation of teacher education institutions and programs. **SELECTED PUBLICATIONS** Auth, The Environmental Crisis, Prentice-Hall, 72, coauth 2nd ed, 76; ed and coauth, Taba Program in Social Science, Addison-Wesley, 73-75; coauth, Peope, Time, and Change, 83; coauth, An Introducation to Teaching and Schools, Holt, Rinehart, and Winston, 90; coauth, The Professional Educator: A New Introduction to Teaching and Schools, Wadsworth, 95; coauth, A Student Study Guide for the Professional Educator: A New Introduction to Teaching and Schools, Wadsworth, 95; coauth, Re-Creating Schools: Places Where Everyone Learns and Likes It, Crowin, 98. **CONTACT ADDRESS** Peabody Col, Vanderbilt Univ, Peabody Col Sta, PO Box 330, Nashville, TN 37203-2402. **EMAIL** charles.b.meyers@vanderbilt.edu

MYERS, ELWIN R.
PERSONAL Born 10/31/1952, Turlock, CA, m, 1990, 1 child **DISCIPLINE** BUSINESS EDUCATION **EDUCATION** Univ S Calif, BA, 74; MS, 75; Calif State Univ at Sacramento, MA, 77; Ariz State Univ, PhD, 83. **CAREER** Assoc prof, Howard Payne Univ, 83-88; assoc prof, Tex A & M Univ at Corpus Christi, 88-. **HONORS AND AWARDS** Phi Beta Kappa. **MEMBERSHIPS** Asn for Business Commun. **RESEARCH** Business Communication, Management. **CONTACT ADDRESS** Dept Humanities, Texas A&M Univ, Corpus Christi, 6300 Ocean Dr, Corpus Christi, TX 78412-5503. **EMAIL** emyers@falcon.tamucc.edu

MYERS, ERNEST R.
PERSONAL Born Middleton, OH, m **DISCIPLINE** PSYCHOLOGY **EDUCATION** Howard Univ, BA, 62; MSW, 64; Union Inst, PhD, 76. **CAREER** Asst to Prof and Chair, Univ D.C, 72-. **HONORS AND AWARDS** White House Fel, St. Elizabeth's Hosp, 63; Scholar of the Year Awd, Nat Asn of Black Psychol, 81; Fel, Am Psychol Asn, 95; Outstanding Alumni Awds, Howard Univ, 82; Outstanding Alumni Awds, Union Inst, 96. **MEMBERSHIPS** Asn of Black Psychol, Am Psychol Asn, Asn of Soc Workers. **RESEARCH** Entrepreneurial mental health services, Nontraditional social support systems and networking, Employee motivation and organizational analysis, Vietnam veteran readjustment, Higher education and University-community relations, Community impact studies and multi-cultural employee-employer relations, intercultural relations. **SELECTED PUBLICATIONS** Auth, Challenges of a Changing America: Perspectives on Immigration & Multiculturalism, Austin &Winfield, 94; auth, The Community Psychology Concept: Integrating Theory. Education and Practice in Psychology. Social Work and Public Administration, Univ Press of Am, 80; auth, Race and Culture in the Mental Health Service Delivery System, Univ Press of Am, 81; auth, An Exploratory Study of An Urban University-Interface prototype, Fed City Col Press, 71. **CONTACT ADDRESS** Dept Psychol, Univ of D.C., 4200 Conn N W, Washington, DC 20008.

MYERS, LENA WRIGHT
PERSONAL w **DISCIPLINE** SOCIOLOGY **EDUCATION** Tougaloo Coll, BA Sociology; MI State Univ, MA Sociology & Anthropology 1964, PhD Sociology & Social Psychology 1973. **CAREER** Utica Jr Coll, instructor of soc & psych 1962-68; Washtenaw Comm Coll, asst prof of psychology 1968; Center for Urban Affairs MI State Univ, urban rsch 1970-73; Jackson State Univ, prof of sociology 1973-?; prof, Ohio Univ. **HONORS AND AWARDS** State of MS House of Rep Concurrent Resolution No 70 Commendation 1981; Disting Amer Awd 1981. **MEMBERSHIPS** Mem of comm on status of women in sociology Amer Sociol Assoc 1974-77; rsch/consul TIDE 1975-78; pres Assn of Social/Behavioral Scientists Inc 1976-77; rsch/consul KOBA 1979-80; mem bd of dirs Soc for the Study of Social Problems 1980-83; rsch/consul Natl Sci Foundation 1983; pres Assn of Black Sociologists 1983-84. **RESEARCH** Social psychology; deviant behaviour; theory. **SELECTED PUBLICATIONS** Auth, "Black Male Socialization: A Broken Silence With Empirical Evidence," Challenge 7.3 (96); auth, "Systematic Oppression or Family Structure: Voices in Retrospect," National Journal of Sociology 11.1,2 (97); auth, Black Male Socialization Revisited in the Minds of Respondents, JAI Press, Inc (Stanford, CT), 98; auth, "The Academic Pendulum and Self-Esteem of African American Males," Perspectives (00): 74-78; auth, "Black Male Socialization: A Symbolic Interactionist Perspective," National Social Science Perspectives Journal 16.2 (00); auth, "Realities of Academe for African American Women," Women in Higher Education 9.4 (00). **CONTACT ADDRESS** Dept of Sociology & Anthropology, Ohio Univ, Athens, OH 45701. **EMAIL** myersle@ohio.edu

MYRICK, HOWARD A., JR.
PERSONAL Born 06/22/1934, Dawson, GA, m, 1955 **DISCIPLINE** EDUCATION **EDUCATION** Florida A&M University, Tallahassee, FL, BS, 1955; University of Southern California, Los Angeles, CA, MA, 1966, PhD, 1967. **CAREER** Corp for Public Broadcasting, Washington, DC, director of research, 77-82; Clark-Atlanta University, Atlanta, GA, professor, 82-83; Howard University, Washington, DC, chairman, radio/tv/film dept, 83-89. **HONORS AND AWARDS** Legion of Merit, Dept of Defense, 1977; Distinguished Graduate, Florida A&M University, 1989; Soldier's Medal, Republic of China, 1969. **MEMBERSHIPS** Editorial board, National Academy of Television Arts & Sciences, 1989-91; chairman, commission on minorities, Broadcast Education Association, 1988-90; board of directors, International Association of Knowledge Engineers, 1988-91; consultant, National Telecom and Info Agency, 1986-90; board of experts, National Endowment for the Arts, 1988-91. **CONTACT ADDRESS** Dept of Radio, Television and Film, Temple Univ, #15 Annenberg Hall, Philadelphia, PA 19122.

N

NA'ALLAH, ABDUL-RASHEED
PERSONAL Born 12/21/1962, Ilorin, Nigeria, m, 1995, 2 children **DISCIPLINE** LITERATURE, FOLKLORE **EDUCATION** BA in English and Education. **CAREER** Teacher, Ilorin School Board--Nigeria, 81-84; lectr, Univ of Ilorin, 89-94; prof, Western Ill univ, 98-. **HONORS AND AWARDS** Gold Key Recognition Awd, Univ of Alberta, 98; Charles Noble Awd, Province of Alberta, 98; Province of Alberta G. Fel, Univ of Alberta, 99. **MEMBERSHIPS** African Lit Asn, African Studies Asn, Int Comparative Lit Asn, Writer's Guild of Alberta. **RESEARCH** Comparative Oral Traditions, Multiculturalism (Africa & New World Societies), African & African American Traditions, Sociolinguistics. **SELECTED PUBLICATIONS** Auth, Introduction To African Oral Literature, 91; auth, Ogoni's Agonies, 98; auth, Almajiri, forthcoming; auth, People's poet, forthcoming. **CONTACT ADDRESS** Dept Afro-American Studies, Western Illinois Univ, 1 University Cir, Macomb, IL 61455-1367. **EMAIL** a-naallah@wiu.edu

NABOKOV, ISABBELLE
PERSONAL Born 06/18/1956, Paris, France, d, 1 child **DISCIPLINE** ANTHROPOLOGY **EDUCATION** Univ Calif Berkeley, BA, 86; PhD, 95. **CAREER** Asst prof, Princeton Unv. **RESEARCH** Sonon India, religion, folklore, performance narrative, experience. **SELECTED PUBLICATIONS** Auth, Religion Against the Self: An Ethnography of Tamil Rituals, Oxford Univ Pr, 00. **CONTACT ADDRESS** Dept Anthrop, Princeton Univ, 100A Aaron burr Hall, Princeton, NJ 08544-0001. **EMAIL** inabokov@princeton.edu

NAG, MONI
PERSONAL Born 04/01/1925, India, m, 1964, 1 child **DISCIPLINE** ANTHROPOLOGY; PUBLIC HEALTH; POPULATION; STATISTICS **EDUCATION** Calcutta Univ, M.SC, 46; Yale Univ, MA, 59, Yale Univ, PhD, 61 **CAREER** Adjunct prof Anthropol, Columbia Univ, 76-; senior assoc, Population Council, 76-92 **HONORS AND AWARDS** Fyfe Scholar, Scottish Church Col Calcutta, 42-44; Fulbright Travel Grant, 57-61; Brady, Boies Fel, Yale Univ, 57-58; Univ Fel, Yale Univ, 58-59; Boies Fel, Yale Univ, 59-60; Fel from Committee of Res on Sex, National Res Coun, 60-61 **RESEARCH** Statistics; Anthropology; Population; Health. **SELECTED PUBLICATIONS** Auth, Sexual Behavior and AIDS in India, Vikas, 96; auth, "Sexual behaviour in India with risk of HIV/AIDS transmission," Health Transmission Rev; coauth, Listening to Women Talk about Their Health: Issues and Evidence from India, Har-Anand, 94 **CONTACT ADDRESS** 260 Garth Rd., 5E5, Scarsdale, NY 10583-4051. **EMAIL** mn1925@yahoo.com

NAGAR, RICHA
PERSONAL Born 09/21/1968, Lucknow, India, m, 1993, 1 child **DISCIPLINE** WOMEN'S STUDIES, GEOGRAPHY **EDUCATION** Lucknow Univ, BA, 86; Punc Univ, MA, 89; Univ Minn, PhD, 95. **CAREER** Asst prof, Univ Colo, 95-97; asst prof, Univ Minn, 97-; adj asst prof, Univ Minn, 99-. **HONORS AND AWARDS** McKnight Land Grant; NSF Grant; Macarthur Fel. **MEMBERSHIPS** AAG; IGU. **RESEARCH** Gender; identity; communal politics; activism and development; politics. **SELECTED PUBLICATIONS** Auth, "I'd Rather be Rude than Ruled,Û Gender, Place, and Communal Politics among South Asian Communities in Dar es Salaam," Women's Stud Intl Forum 23 (00); auth, "Religion, Race and the Debate over Mut' a in Dar es Salaam," Feminist Studies, 26 (00); auth, "Communal Discourses, Marriage, and the Politics of Gendered Social Boundaries among South Asian Immigrants in Tanzania," Gender, Place and Culture 5 (98): 117-139, reprinted in Gender and Migration, eds. Katie Willis, Brenda Yeoh, The International Library Of Studies On Migration, series ed. Robin Cohen (Cheltenham: Edward Elgar Pub, 00); coauth, Contesting Social Relations in Communal Places: Identity Politics Among Asians in Dar es Salaam," in Cities of Difference, eds. Ruth Fincher, Jane Jacobs (NY: Guilford Press, 98): 226-251; auth, "The Making of Hindu Communal Organizations, Places and Identities in Postcolonial Dar es Salaam," Environment and Planning D: Society and Space 15 (98): 707-730; auth, "Communal Places and the Politics of Multiple Identities: The case of Tanzanian Asians," Ecumene: J Environ, Culture, Meaning 4 (98): 3-26; auth, "Exploring Methodological Borderlands Through Oral Narratives," in Thresholds in Feminist Geography, eds. John Paul Jones III, Heidi J Nast, Susan M Roberts (Lanham, Maryland: Rowman and Littlefield, 98): 203-224; auth, "The South Asian Diaspora in Tanzania: A History Retold," Comparative Studies of South Asia, Africa and the Middle East: J Polit Cult Econ 16 (96): 62-80. **CONTACT ADDRESS** Dept Women's Studies, Univ of Minnesota, Twin Cities, 224 Church St, Minneapolis, MN 55455.

NAGY, KAROLY
PERSONAL Born 05/24/1934, Nyiregyhaza, Hungary, m, 1988, 2 children **DISCIPLINE** SOCIOLOGY **EDUCATION** Rutgers Univ, BA, 62; New Sch ofr Soc Res, MA, 66, PhD, 70. **CAREER** Teacher, pub sch, Hungary, 54-56; counr, supvr, NJ Rehab Commn, New Brunswick, 62-68; lect, Rutgers Univ, 66-94; assoc prof to prof, chair, Middlesex Co Col, 68-82, prof, 82-. **HONORS AND AWARDS** Lajos Kassak Awd Magyar Muhely, 76; Geza Barczi Awd Anyanyelvi Konferencia, 81; Imre Nagy Plaque Pres of Hungarian Republic, 93; Merit Order Rep of Hungary, 99. **MEMBERSHIPS** Am Sociol Asn, Int P. E. N., World Coun of Hungarian Profs, Friends of Hungarian Higher Ed Found, Am Asn for the Study of Hungarian Hist, Am Hungarian Eds Asn, Int Asn of Hungarian Lang and Culture, Hungarian Alumni Asn. **SELECTED PUBLICATIONS** Auth, Tanitsunk magyarul, Puski, NY (77); auth, Magyar szigetvilkagban ma es holnap, Puskli, NY (84); auth, Szigetmagyarsag es szolidaritas, Corvin, Montreal (88); coed, Istvan Bibo: Democracy, Revolution, Self-Determination, Selected Writings, Social Sci Monographs, Boulder, Colo, Atlantic Res and Pubs, NJ (91); auth, Kuldetesben, Madach, Pozsony (96). **CONTACT ADDRESS** Dept Hist & Soc Behav, Middlesex County Col, PO Box 3050, Edison, NJ 08818.

NAIL, PAUL R.
PERSONAL Born 07/07/1952, Kansas City, MO, m, 1978, 3 children **DISCIPLINE** PSYCHOLOGY **EDUCATION** Southwestern Okla State Univ, BS, 74; MEd, 78; MS, 78, Tex Christian Univ, PhD, 81. **CAREER** Res Fel, Inst of Behav Res, Tex Christian Univ, 78-80; Prof, Southwestern Okla State Univ, 80-. **HONORS AND AWARDS** Robert S. Tyler, Outstanding Psychology Student Awd, Southwestern Okla State Univ, 78; Fel, Oxford Soc of Scholars, Oxford Univ, UK, 00. **MEMBERSHIPS** Soc for Personality and Soc Psychology, Midwestern Psychol Asn, Southwestern Psychol Asn. **RESEARCH** Social influence, Conformity, Minority influence, Prejudice, Dissonance Theory, Coalition formation. **SELECTED PUBLICATIONS** Coauth, "A demonstration of the reformulated diamond model of social response," J of Soc Behav and Personality 5 (90): 711-722; coauth, "Social influence and the diamond model of social response: Toward an extended theory of information influence," Brit J of Soc Psychology 31 (92): 171-187; coauth, "Contagion: A theoretical and empirical review and reconceptualization," Genetic, Social and General Psychology Monographs 119 (93): 235-284; coauth, "An analysis and restructuring of the diamond model of social response," Personality and Soc Psychology Bul 19 (93): 106-116; coauth, "Coalition preference as a function of expected values in a tetradic weighted majority game," Basic and Appl Soc Psychology 16 (95): 109-120; coauth, "The effectance versus the self-presentational view of reactance: Are importance ratings influenced by anticipated surveillance?," J of Soc Behav and Personality 11 (96): 573-584; coauth, "A New model of interpersonal influence," J of Soc Behav and Personality 13 (98): 715-733; coauth, "Self-affirmation theory: An update and appraisal," in Cognitive dissonance: Progress on a pivotal theory in social psychology, ed. E. Harmon-Jones and J. Mills (Wash, DC: Am Psychol Asn, 99); coauth, "On the distinction between behavioral contagion, conversion conformity, and compliance conformity," N Am J of Psychology 1 (99): 87-94; coauth, "Proposal on Four-Dimension Model of Social Response," Psychol Bul (in press). **CONTACT ADDRESS** Dept Psychology, Southwestern Oklahoma State Univ, Weatherford, 100 Campus Dr, Weatherford, OK 73096. **EMAIL** nailp@swosu.edu

NASH, JUNE C.
DISCIPLINE ANTHROPOLOGY **EDUCATION** Barnard Col, BA, 48; Univ Chicago, MA, 53, PhD, 60. **CAREER** Yale Univ, asst prof, 63-68; NYU, assoc prof, 69-72; City Col CUNY, prof, distinguished prof, 72-. **HONORS AND AWARDS** C. Wright Mills Awd, AAA Distinguished Svc Awd. **MEMBERSHIPS** AAA, AES, LASA, Sigma Phi. **RESEARCH** Latin America; Industry; Artisan Prosecution; Indigenous social organization. **SELECTED PUBLICATIONS** Auth, J. C. Nash, In the Eyes of the Ancestors: Belief and Behavior in a Maya Community, New Haven: Yale University Press, 70; auth, J. C. Nash, We Eat the Mines and the Mines Eat Us: Dependency and Exploitation in Bolivian Tin Mining Communities, New York: Columbia University Press, 79; auth, J. C. Nash, From Tank Town to High Tech: The Clash of Community and Industrial Cycles, Albany: SUNY Press; auth, J. C. Nash, ed. Crafts in the World Market: The Impact of International Exchange on Middle American Artisans, Albany: SUNY Press, 93; auth, J. C. Nash, "The Fiesta of the Word: Radical Democracy in Chiapas, Mexico," American Anthropologist, Vol. 99 (2), 97. **CONTACT ADDRESS** Dept of Anthropology, New York Univ, New York, NY 10031. **EMAIL** junenash@midway.uchicago.edu

NASH, PEGGY
PERSONAL Born 06/23/1949, Ft Myers, FL, d, 2 children **DISCIPLINE** PSYCHOLOGY **EDUCATION** Fla Atlantic Univ, MA, 72; EdD, 78. **CAREER** Sr Prof, Broward Community Col, 72-. **HONORS AND AWARDS** Teacher of the Year, State of Fla - Carnegie Found. **MEMBERSHIPS** APA, Am Psychotherapist Asn. **RESEARCH** Biofeedback. **SELECTED PUBLICATIONS** Auth, Essentials of Psychology, Bernstein and Nash, 99. **CONTACT ADDRESS** Dept Soc and Behav Sci, Broward Comm Col, 1000 Coconut Creek Blvd, Pompano Beach, FL 33066.

NATALICIO, DIANA
PERSONAL Born 08/25/1939, St Louis, MO **DISCIPLINE** LINGUISTICS, ENGLISH AS SECOND LANGUAGE **EDUCATION** St, Louis Univ, BS, 61; Univ Tex, Austin, MA, 64; PhD, 69. **CAREER** Res assoc eval res, Ctr Commun Res, 70-71; asst prof ling & mod lang, 71-73, chmn mod lang & assoc prof, 73-77, assoc dean lib arts, 77-79, Prof Ling & Mod Lang, Univ Tex, El Paso, 77- & Dean Lib Arts, 80-84, vp, acad aff, 84-88, pres, 88-. **HONORS AND AWARDS** Harold W. McGraw Jr. Prize in Educ; Torch of Liberty Awd; Conquistador Awd for Outstand Svc to Citizens of El Paso; El Paso Women's Hall of Fame; Humanitarian Awd; Fulbright scholar, Rio de Janeiro, Brazil; Gulbenkian fel, Lisbon, Portugal. **MEMBERSHIPS** Nat Sci Bd; NASA Adv Cnl; US-Mexico Comm for Educ and Cultural Exchange; Nat Act Cnl for Minorities in Engineering; Coun for Aid to Education; Nature Conservancy of Tex. **RESEARCH** Language acquisition; bilingualism; language testing. **SELECTED PUBLICATIONS** Coauth, A comparative study of English pluralization by native and nonnative English speakers, Child Develop, 71; auth, Sentence repetition as a language assessment technique: Some issues and applications, Bilingual Rev/La Rev Bilingue, 77; coauth, The Sounds of Children, Prentice-Hall, 77 & 81; contribr, Theory & Practice or Early Reading, Lawrence Earlbaum Assoc, 79; auth, Repetition and dictation as language testing techniques,

Mod Lang J, 79; contribr, Festschrift in Honor of Jacob Ornstein: Studies in General and Sociolinguistics, Newbury House, 80; coauth, Some characteristics of word classification in a second language, Mod Lang J, 82. **CONTACT ADDRESS** Off of President, Univ of Texas, El Paso, El Paso, TX 79968-0500. **EMAIL** dnatlicio@utep.edu

NATH, PAMELA S.
PERSONAL Born 06/05/1963, Pittsburgh, PA, s **DISCIPLINE** PSYCHOLOGY **EDUCATION** Univ Dayton, BS, 85; Univ Notre Dame, MA, 88; PhD, 91. **CAREER** Adj prof, Wright State Univ, 91-93; psychol, Bluffton OH, 96-; assoc prof, Bluffton Col, 96-. **MEMBERSHIPS** APA; APSAC. **SELECTED PUBLICATIONS** Coauth, "Predicting and Understanding Development Delay of Children of Adolescent Mothers: A Multidimensional Approach," AM J Mental Deficiency 92 (87): 40-56; coauth, "Passing the Baton," in 101 Favorite Family Therapy Interventions, eds. TS Nelson, TS Trepper (Hawthorne Press, 92). **CONTACT ADDRESS** Dept Psychology, Bluffton Col, 280 W College St, Bluffton, OH 45817. **EMAIL** nathp@bluffton.edu

NATHAN, MITCHELL J.
PERSONAL Born 11/14/1962, New York, NY, m, 2000 **DISCIPLINE** PSYCHOLOGY **EDUCATION** Univ Colo, PhD, 91. **CAREER** Postdoctoral, Univ Pittsburgh, 91-93; sr res sci, Vanderbilt Univ, 93-95; asst prof, Univ Colo, 95-. **HONORS AND AWARDS** James S. McDonnell Post-doctoral Awd, 91-93; James S. McDonnell Found Grants, 95-97, 98-2000. **MEMBERSHIPS** AERA, NCTM, Nat Acad of Sci, Cognitive Sci Soc. **RESEARCH** Student mathematical cognition, teacher cognition, educational technology. **SELECTED PUBLICATIONS** Coauth, "Less can be more: Unintelligent tutoring based on psychological theories and experimentation," in S. Vosniadou, E. De Corte, & H. Mandl, eds, Technology -based Learning Environments: Psychological and Educational Foundations, NATO ASI Series F, Computer and Systems Sciences, Vol 137, NY: Springer Verlag (95): 183-192; coauth with Cognition and Technology Group at Vanderbilt, "Looking at technology in context: A framework for understanding technology and educational research," in D. C. Berliner & R. C. Calfee, eds, Handbook of Educational Psychology, NY: MacMillan (96): 807-840; auth, "The impact of theories of learning on learning environment design," Intelligent Tutoring Media, 2, 3 & 4 (98): 135-160; coauth, "An investigation of teachers' beliefs of students' algebra development," Cognition and Instruction, 18 (2000): 2; coauth, "Moving beyond teachers' intuitive beliefs about algebra learning," Mathematics Teacher, 93 (2000): 3; coauth, "Teachers' and researchers' about the development of algebraic reasoning," J of Res in Mathematics Educ, 31 (2000): 3. **CONTACT ADDRESS** Sch of Educ, Univ of Colorado, Boulder, Box 249, Boulder, CO 80309-0249. **EMAIL** mitch.nathan@colorado.edu

NAYLOR, LARRY L.
PERSONAL Born 03/14/1940, Corning, NY, m, 1998, 4 children **DISCIPLINE** ANTHROPOLOGY **EDUCATION** State Univ New York, BS, 62, MS, 68; S Ill Univ, PhD, 74. **CAREER** Asst Prof, Univ Alaska, 74-78; dept dir, Univ of North Texas, 78-83; dir, chair, assoc prof, 83-86; assoc prof, 86-90; dir, chair, assoc prof, 90-93; assoc prof, 94-97; prof, 97-. **HONORS AND AWARDS** Who's Who Edu; Top Prof' Awd; Spec Recog Awd; Off Dean Stud; Outstand Teach Awd; Outstand Service; "Larry L Naylor" Outstanding Student Anthropology Awd established in my name for dedicated service as Inst Dir and exceptional ability as teacher by the Fac of the Inst Anthro Univ of North Texas. **MEMBERSHIPS** AAA; SAA; AAAS; NYAS. **SELECTED PUBLICATIONS** Auth, Anthropology, in the Yearbook of Science and the Future, Encyc Britannica, Inc (92-97); coauth, Interactive Study Guide for Anthropology: User's Guide Version 2, Harcourt Brace Jovanovich (96); auth, Culture Change: An Introduction, Bergin & Garvey (Westport), 96; ed, Cultural Diversity in the United States, Bergin & Garvey (Westport), 97; auth, American Culture: Myth and Reality of a Culture of Diversity, Bergin & Garvey (Westport) 98; ed, Issues and Problems of Culture Diversity in the United States, Bergin & Garvey (Westport), 99. **CONTACT ADDRESS** School Community Service, Univ of No Texas, PO Box 311340, Denton, TX 76203. **EMAIL** naylor@scs.cmm.unt.edu

NAYLOR, NATALIE A.
PERSONAL Born 08/20/1937, Peekskill, NY, s **DISCIPLINE** AMERICAN HISTORY, WOMEN'S STUDIES, LONG ISLAND HISTORY **EDUCATION** Bryn Mawr Col AB, 59; Columbia Univ, MA, 62, EdD, 71. **CAREER** Res asst, Nat Bur Econ Res, 59-62; teacher social studies, Tuckahoe High Sch, 62-65; from instr hist & found educ to prof emerita, Hofstra Univ, 68-00; dir, Long Island Studies Inst, Hofstra Univ, 86-00. **HONORS AND AWARDS** Teaching Fel Am Hist, New College, Hofstra Univ, 76-. **MEMBERSHIPS** Am Educ Studies Asn; Orgn Am Historians; Am Studies Asn. **RESEARCH** History of education; women and education; Long Island history. **SELECTED PUBLICATIONS** Auth, The antebellum College movement: A reappraisal of Tewksbury's Founding of American Colleges and Universities, Hist Educ Quart, fall 73; Paul Monroe, In: Dict of American Biography, Supplement Four, Charles Scribner's Sons, 74; The theological seminary in the configuration of American higher education: The antebellum years, Hist Educ Quart, spring 77; Horace Mann, In: American Renaissance in New England Vol I, In: Dict of Literary Biography, Gale Res, 78; Hilda Taba In: Notable American Women: Modern Period, Belknap Press, 80; coauth, Teaching Today and Tomorrow, Charles E Merrill, 81; auth, "Mary Steichen Calderone" and "Emma Hart Willard," in Women Educators in the United States 1820-1993, ed. Maxine Schwartz Seller, (Westport: Greenwood Pr, 94) 86-94, 525-535; ed, Nassau County Historical Society Journal, 96-; auth, "The 'Encouragement of Seminaries of Learning': The Origins and Development of Early Long Island Academies," Long Island Historical Journal, 12 (fall 99): 11-30; co-ed, Nassau County: From Rural Hinterland to Suburban Metropolis, Empire State Books/Long Island Studies Inst (Interlaken, NYork), 00; **CONTACT ADDRESS** 496 Clarendon Road, Uniondale, NY 11553. **EMAIL** nucnzn@hofstra.edu

NEELY, MARGERY A.
PERSONAL Born 01/13/1934, Springfield, MO, s, 4 children **DISCIPLINE** PSYCHOLOGY **EDUCATION** SW Mo State Univ, AB, 55; Univ Mo, MEd, 68; PhD, 71. **CAREER** Assoc Prof to Prof, Kans State Univ, 71-. **HONORS AND AWARDS** Intl Leadership Recognition, Asn Coun Educ & Supervision, 99; Outstanding Scientists of the 20th Century, Cambridge, 00. **MEMBERSHIPS** Am Psychol Asn; Am Coun Asn. **RESEARCH** Measurement instruments; Processes in counseling; Diversity; Career Development. **SELECTED PUBLICATIONS** Co-auth, "Effects of leadership training during wilderness camping," small Group Behavior, (87): 266-280; co-auth, A parent's work is never done, New Horizon Press, 87; co-auth, "Two adaptable and reliable data-collection measures: Goal Attainment Scaling and the Semantic Differential," The Counseling Psychologist, (88): 261-271; co-auth, A parent's work is never done, New Horizon Press, 89; co-auth, "Exploring critical incidents in high school counseling," The School Counselor, (89): 179-185; auth, Quality interviews with adult students and trainees: A communications course in student personnel and in-service training, Charles C Thomas, 92; co-auth, Where jobs are advertised 2nd ed, Kansas Careers, 92; auth, "Single parents and family dynamics," Proceedings of the Conference - Counseling in the 21st Century in the Pacific Rim Countries, Singapore, 93; co-auth, "Conflict resolution: An Overview for classroom managers," International Journal of Educational Management, (93): 4-8; co-auth, Counseling single parents: A cognitive-behavioral approach, 00. **CONTACT ADDRESS** Dept Psychol & Coun, Kansas State Univ, 369 Bluemont Hall, Manhattan, KS 66506. **EMAIL** maneely@ksu.edu

NEFF, HECTOR
PERSONAL Born 12/19/1952, Los Angeles, CA, m, 1984, 2 children **DISCIPLINE** ANTHROPOLOGY **EDUCATION** Stanford Univ, AB, 75; Univ Calif, MA, 79; PhD, 84. British Coun Archaeol Study Tour to Northern Ireland, 93; completed MIT Center for Materials Res in Archaeol and Ethnology Summer Inst Course, 84; trainee in neutron activation analysis and statistical modeling, Brookhaven Nat Lab, 10/82-12/82. **CAREER** Archaeologist, Center for Archaeol Studies, 80-84 & 85-86, asst res archaeologist, Mesoamerican Res Center, Univ of Calif, 86-90; programmer/analyst, Univ of San Francisco, 84-85; postdoctoral fel, res collaborator & consult database programmer, Conservation Analytical Lab, Smithsonian Inst, 86-90; res scientist, 90-93, Sr Res Scientist, MO Univ Res Reactor, 93-; adjunct asst prof, anthropology, 90-97, Adjunct Assoc Prof, Anthropology, Univ of MO, Columbia, 97-. **HONORS AND AWARDS** UCSB Humanities Grant, 81; postdoctoral fel, 86 & 87, res opportunity fund grant, Smithsonian Inst, 87, 88, & 89; NSF Grants, 89, 91, 95, 96, & 99-2000; grant, Univ Houston-Clear Lake, 90 & 92; Weldon Springs Fund, 91, fac res grant, 91, res board grant, Univ Mo, 94; British Council Grant, 93; grant, Nat Park Service, 93 & 94; **MEMBERSHIPS** Soc for Am Archaeol; Am Anthropological Asn; Asn for Field Archaeol. **RESEARCH** Archaeological Method and Theory, Mesoamerican Archaeology, Quantitative Methods, Ceramic Analysis, Neutron Activation Analysis, Southwest Archaeology, paleoenvironmental reconstruction, orgins/agriculture. **SELECTED PUBLICATIONS** Coauth, Methodology of Comparison in Evolutionary Archaeology, Rediscovering Darwin: Evolutionary Theory in Archaeol Explanation, 97; The Evolution of Anasazi Ceramic Production and Distribution: Compositional Evidence from a Pueblo-III Site in South-Central Utah, J of Field Archaeol, 97; A Reassessment of the Acid-Extraction Approach to Compositional Characterization of Archaeological Ceramics, Am Antiquity, 96; The Current State of Nuclear Archaeology, J of Radioanalytical and Nuclear Chemistry, 95; A Ceramic Compositional Perspective on the Formative to Classic Transition in Southern Mesoamerica, Latin Am Antiquity, 94; auth, The Development of Plumbate Ceramic Ware in Southern Mesoamerica, JOM, 95; RQ-mode Principal Components Analysis of Ceramic Compositional Data, Archaeometry, 94; Theory, Sampling, and Technical Studies in Archeological Pottery Analysis, Am Antiquity, 93. **CONTACT ADDRESS** Research Reactor, Univ of Missouri, Columbia, Columbia, MO 65211. **EMAIL** neffh@missouri.edu

NEGREY, CYNTHIA
PERSONAL Born Cleveland, OH **DISCIPLINE** SOCIOLOGY **EDUCATION** Bowling Green State Univ, BS, 75, MA, 77; Mich State Univ, PhD, 88. **CAREER** Instr, Ohio Northern Univ, Ada, 78-82; asst prof, Univ Louisville, 88-94, assoc prof, 94-; Study Dir, Inst for Women's Policy Res, Washington, DC, 99-2000. **MEMBERSHIPS** Am Sociol Asn. **RESEARCH** Working time/work schedules, contingent work, occupational gender segregation, economic restructuring. **SELECTED PUBLICATIONS** Coauth with Richard Child Hill, "Deindustrialization in the Great Lakes," Urban Affairs Quart, 22, 4 (87): 580-597; coauth with Richard Child Hill, "Deindustrialization and Racial Minorities in the Great Lakes Region," in The Reshaping of America: Social Consequences of the Changing Economy, ed by D. Stanley Eitzen and Maxine Baca Zinn, Englewood Cliffs, NJ: Prentice-Hall (89): 168-178; auth, Gender, Time, and Reduced Work, Albany, NY: State Univ of NY Press (93); coauth with Mary Beth Zickel, "Industrial Shifts and Uneven Development: Patterns of Growth and Decline in U.S. Metropolitan Areas," Urban Affairs Quart, 30, 1 (94): 27-47; auth, "Urban Economy," in Handbook of Research on Urban Politics and Policy in the United States, ed by Ronald K. Vogel, Westport, CT: Greenwood Pub Group, Inc (97); coauth with Mary Beth Zickel and Jeanne M. Fenn, "Industrial Restructuring and Regional Household Income Growth," Regional Studies, 32, 2 (98): 103-111; coauth with Carmen Sirianni, "Working Time as Gendered Time," Feminist Economics, 6, 1 (March 2000); auth, "The Missing Feminist Revolution in Sociology Revisited," in Elizabeth Macnabb, ed, Transforming the Disciplines, Binghamton, NY: Haworth Press (forthcoming). **CONTACT ADDRESS** Dept Sociol, Univ of Louisville, Lutz Hall, Louisville, KY 40292. **EMAIL** negrey@iwpr.org

NEIGHBORS, IRA
PERSONAL Born 10/10/1946, Los Angeles, CA, s **DISCIPLINE** SOCIAL WORK **EDUCATION** Univ Calif at Los Angeles, MSW, 83; Howard Univ, DSW, 94. **CAREER** Asst prof, Cal State Univ, 95-99; assoc prof, Southern Univ, 99-. **HONORS AND AWARDS** Pres Awd, Calif, 99. **MEMBERSHIPS** Nat Org of Forensic Social Work, Nat Asn of Black Soc Workers, Nat Asn of Social Workers. **RESEARCH** Forensic Social Work, Developmental Disabilities, African American Men in Criminal Justice. **SELECTED PUBLICATIONS** Auth, Forensic Social Work: The Interface between Social Work and Law, 00; auth, Satisfaction with Police among African American Men in San Bernardino & Riverside Counties, 97; auth, Education & Labor: Correlates of Satisfaction with Police among African American Men, 96. **CONTACT ADDRESS** Dept Soc Work, So Univ, New Orleans, 6400 Press Dr, New Orleans, LA 70126. **EMAIL** ineighbo@csusb.edu

NEIHOFF, ARTHUR H.
PERSONAL Born 12/30/1921, Indianapolis, IN, 1 child **DISCIPLINE** ANTHROPOLOGY **EDUCATION** BA, IN Univ, 49; PhD Columbia Univ, 57. **CAREER** Milwaukee Museum-Curator, 51-59; WS State Dept Comm Develop, 59-61; Univ Wisc, 62-64; Univ Washington, 64-70; Calif State Univ, LA, 70-90, Retired 91. **HONORS AND AWARDS** Fullbright 51-52, India. **MEMBERSHIPS** Am Anthro Assoc; PMA **RESEARCH** Humankind-in all places, all times. **SELECTED PUBLICATIONS** Auth, "On Becoming Human," The Hominid Press, (96), 420; auth, "Take over: How Eeroman Changed the World," , Hominid Press, (96), 250; auth, "On Being a Cultural Animal," The Hominid Press, (97), 310; An Anthropologist Under the Bed, The Hominid Press, (99), 400. **CONTACT ADDRESS** 31765 Rockinghorse, Escondido, CA 92026. **EMAIL** neihoff@accessl.net

NEISLER, OTHERINE JOHNSON
PERSONAL Born St Louis, MO, d, 2 children **DISCIPLINE** EDUCATION **EDUCATION** Brandeis Univ, BA, 72; Fairfield Univ, MA, 91; Syracuse Univ, PhD, 94. **CAREER** Teacher, Farifield Univ, 90-91; Grad Assoc, Syracuse Univ, 91-94; Asst Prof, Boston Col, 94-. **HONORS AND AWARDS** Holmes Scholar, 93--94; African Am Fel, 93; Best Fel, 90-91; Constance Weinman Scholarship, 93. **MEMBERSHIPS** ASCD, AECT, NSTA, AERA, NERA, ISPP, NCSS. **RESEARCH** Diversification of schools of education, Development of sociopolitical attitudes and the relationship of those attitudes to young adult citizenship behaior, Qualitative research methods including participant observation and large roup self-study. **SELECTED PUBLICATIONS** Auth, "Socialization, promotion and tenure of Holmes Scholars: A 10-year study," The Professional Educator, in press; auth, "Seeking Social Justice: A Teacher Education Faculty's Self Study," in Transforming Social Inquiry, Transforming Social Action, Kluwer Academic Pub, 00; auth, "The assessment of psychosocial and educational issues: Impact on Learning," in Interprofessional Collaboration: School and social service partnerships, Greenwod Publ, 99; auth, "Socio-Educational Realities of the Twenty-first Century: A Need for Change," in Interprofessional Collaboration: School and social service partnerships, Greenwood Pub Group, 99; auth, "Cultural Influences and Iteractions in the ESL Classroom," Educational Considerations, (99): 19-24; auth, "Seeking Social Justice: A Teacher Education Faculty's Self-Study," Journal of Leadership in Education, (99): 229-253; auth, "Standards-based Instruction for the Inclusive Social Studies Classroom," The Docket, (98): 5-11; auth, "Learning Standards, Black teachers and Multicultural education: Overcoming racism and classism in education," Educational Policy, (98): 318-328; auth, "Integrating mission into the life of institutions," in

Conversations in Excellence, (97): 39-56; auth, Teaching and learning the Caribbean heritage: A resource guide for educators, Boston, 96. **CONTACT ADDRESS** Dept Educ, Boston Col, Chestnut Hill, 140 Commonwealth Ave, Chestnut Hill, MA 02467. **EMAIL** otherine.neisler@yale.edu

NELKIN, DOROTHY
PERSONAL Born 07/30/1933, Boston, MA, m, 1952, 2 children **DISCIPLINE** SOCIOLOGY **EDUCATION** Cornell Univ, BA, 54. **CAREER** New York Univ, Prof 88; Prof, 64-88, Cornell Univ. **HONORS AND AWARDS** Bernal Prize; Guggenheim Fel; AAAS Fel; National Academy of Sciences Institute of Medicine. **RESEARCH** Science and society; Biotechnical, genetics, law. **SELECTED PUBLICATIONS** Auth, Controversy: The Politics of Technical Decisions; Science as Intellectual Property; The Creation Controversy; Workers at Risk; Selling Science:" How the Press Covers Science and Technology; coauth; A Disease of Society: The Cultural Impact of AIDS, coauth; Dangerous Diagnostics: The Social Power of Biological Information, The DNA Mystic: coauth, The Gene as a Cultural Icon. **CONTACT ADDRESS** 269 Mercer St Room 440, New York, NY 10003. **EMAIL** dorothy.nelkin@nyu.edu

NELSON, CHARLES A.
PERSONAL Born 03/07/1953, Flushing, NY, m, 1981, 1 child **DISCIPLINE** DEVELOPMENTAL PSYCHOLOGY **EDUCATION** McGill Univ, BA, 75; Univ Wisconsin, MS, 76; MS, 77; Univ Kansas, PhD, 81. **CAREER** Proj asst, Univ Wisc, 75-76; res asst, 76-78; predoc train, Univ Kansas, 78-81; postdoc fel, Univ Minn, 81-83; asst prof, Purdue Univ, 83-86; asst prof, Univ Minn, 86-88; assoc prof, 88-93; dir grad stud, 93-98; prof, 93-. **HONORS AND AWARDS** Who's Who in Am, World; Joseph P Kennedy Awd; MacArthur FRN Mem; APS Fel; Dist McKnight Prof. **MEMBERSHIPS** AAAS; APS; ISIS; SN; SRCD; SPR; OECD; NASI Liaison to Integ Sci Early Child Dev. **SELECTED PUBLICATIONS** Coauth, Brian, Mind, and Behavior, Worth Pub (NY), in press, 3rd ed; coauth, "Electrophysiological studies II: Evoked potentials and event-related potentials," in Textbook of Pediatric Neuropsychiatry, eds. CE Coffey, RA Brumback (Am Psych Press: Washington, DC, 98), 331-356; coauth, "Discrimination and categorization of facial expressions of emotion during infancy," in Perceptual Development: Visual, Auditory, and Language Perception in Infancy, ed. AM Slater (Univ Coll London Press: London, UK, 98), 287-309; coauth, "Neurobiology of Fetal and Infant Development: Implications for Infant Mental Health," in Handbook of Infant Mental Health, ed. CH Zeanah (Guilford Press: NY, 00); auth, "The neurobiological bases of early intervention," in Handbook of early childhood intervention, eds. JP Shonkoff, SJ Meisels (Cambridge Univ Press: Cambridge, MA, 00) 2nd ed; coauth, "Neurodevelopmental assessment of cognitive function using the Cambridge Neuropsychological Testing Automated Battery (CANTAB): Validation and Future Goals," in Functional Neuroimaging in Child Psychiatry, eds. M Ernst, J Rumsey (Cambridge Press: UK, in press); ed, Threats to Optimal Development: Integrating Biological, Psychological, and Social Risk Factors. The Minnesota Symposia on Child Psychology, Lawrence Erlbaum (NJ), 94; ed, Basic and Applied Perspectives on Learning, Cognition, and Development. Minnesota Symposia on Child Psychology, Lawrence Erlbaum (NJ), in press; ed, The Effects of Early Adversity on Neurobehavioral Development. Minnesota Symposia on Child Psychology, Lawrence Erlbaum (NJ), in press; co-ed, Handbook of Developmental Cognitive Neuroscience. MIT Press (Cambridge, MA), in press; auth, "Neural Plasticity and Human Development: The Role of Early Experience in Sculpting Memory Systems," Dev Sci 3 (00): 115-136; coauth, "Functional Neuroanatomy of Spatial Working Memory in Children," Dev Psychol 36 (00): 109-116; auth, "Change and Continuity in Neurobehavioral Development," Infant Behav Dev (in press). **CONTACT ADDRESS** Institute Child Development, Univ of Minnesota, Twin Cities, 51 East River Rd, Minneapolis, MN 55455. **EMAIL** canelson@tc.umn.edu

NELSON, DOROTHY J. SMITH
PERSONAL Born 06/24/1948, Greenville, MS, s **DISCIPLINE** EDUCATION **EDUCATION** Tufts University, BA, 1970, MEd, 1971; Southern Illinois University at Carbondale, PhD, 1981. **CAREER** Southern Illinois University at Carbondale Office of Student Development, coordinator of student development, 79-81; Mississippi Valley State University, assistant vice pres for academic affairs & director academic skills parlor, 71-. **HONORS AND AWARDS** Clark Doctoral Scholar Awd for Research, Southern Illinois University, 1981; NAACP, Education Awd, 1981; Education Achievement Awd, Progressive Art & Civic Club, 1982; Outstanding Young Woman of America, 1979-. **MEMBERSHIPS** Board, NAACP, 1982-84; Post Doctoral Academy of Higher Education, 1979-; financial sec, Les Modernette Social Club, 1981-; International Reading Assoc, 1985; Southern Illinois University Alumni Assoc; Concerned Educators of Black Students; Southeast Regional Reading Conference; Alpha Kappa Alpha; Progressive Art and Civic Club, Mississippi Reading Assoc, Natl Assoc of Develop Educators, Mississippi Assoc of Develop Educators. **CONTACT ADDRESS** Director, Student Counseling, Mississippi Valley State Univ, 14000 Highway 82 W #7232, Itta Bena, MS 38941-1400.

NELSON, JUDITH C.
PERSONAL Born 09/17/1938, Elmhurst, IL, w, 1989 **DISCIPLINE** SOCIAL WORK **EDUCATION** Univ Neb, BA, 60; Columbia Univ, MSSW, 62; DSW, 73. **CAREER** Lectr, Hunter Col, 71-73; asst prof, 73-75; asst prof, Univ Chicago, 75-78; assoc prof, Univ Ill, 78-84; priv prac, NY, IL, 71-; prof, Univ Ill, 84-. **MEMBERSHIPS** CSW; ACSW; AOA; NASW. **RESEARCH** Qualitive and single-system methodologies; mental health and couple practice. **SELECTED PUBLICATIONS** Auth, Communication Theory and Social Work Practice, Univ Chicago Press (Chicago), 80; auth, Treatment: An Integrative Approach, Prentice Hall (Englewood Cliffs NJ), 83; auth, Couple Treatment: Assessment and Intervention, Jason Aronson (Northvale NJ), 98; auth, "Single-Case Research and Traditional Practice: Issues and Possibilities," In Advances in Clinical Practice Research, eds. Lynn Videka-Sherman, William J. Reid (Silver Spring MD: Nat Asn of Social Wkrs, 90); auth, "Varieties of Narcissistically Vulnerable Couples: Dynamics and Practice Implications," Clinical Soc Work J 223 (90): 59-70; auth, "Testing Practice Wisdom: Another Use for Single-System Research," J Soc Ser Res 18 (93): 65-82, a chapter, in Single-System Designs in the Social Services: Issues and Options for the 90's, ed. Martin Bloom (NY: Haworth Press, 93); auth, "One Partner Impaired: Implications for Couple Treatment," Family Therapy 21(94):185-196; auth, "Ethics, Gender, and Ethnicity in Single-Case Research and Evaluation," J Soc Ser Res 18 (94):139-152. **CONTACT ADDRESS** College of Social Work, Univ of Illinois, Chicago, 1040 W Harrison St, Chicago, IL 60612. **EMAIL** judnel@uic.edu

NELSON, RANDOLPH A.
DISCIPLINE CONTEXTUAL EDUCATION **EDUCATION** Gustavus Adolphus Col, BA; Lutheran Sch Theol, MDiv, 68; Univ Chicago Divinity Sch, MA, 70, PhD, 78. **CAREER** Instr, Lutheran Sch Theol, 69-71; act dean of stud (s), Lutheran Sch Theol, 71-73; asst to the dir, Lutheran Sch Theol, 73-75; asst prof, 75; Melvin A. Hammarberg prof, 82-. **HONORS AND AWARDS** Scholar, Bavarian State Government; Fulbright Travel grant; Lutheran Brotherhood Grad Stud grant; pastor, resurrection lutheran church, 68-75; 5 **SELECTED PUBLICATIONS** Auth, Making Faithful Choices: How Do I Decide?, Cross Signs, 93. **CONTACT ADDRESS** Dept of Contextual Education, Luther Sem, 2481 Como Ave, Saint Paul, MN 55108. **EMAIL** rnelson@luthersem.edu

NELSON, RANDY J.
PERSONAL Born 01/31/1954, Detroit, MI **DISCIPLINE** PSYCHOLOGY **EDUCATION** Univ Calif, Berkeley, AB, 78; MA, 80; PhD, 83; PhD, 84. **CAREER** Asst prof, Johns Hopkins Univ, 86-91, assoc prof, 91-96, prof, 96-; Prog Dir, Physiology and Behavior Prog, Integrative Biology and Neuroscience Div, Nat Sci Found, Arlington, Va, 95-96, Prog Dir, Neuroendocrinology Prof, 98; **HONORS AND AWARDS** Phi Beta Kappa, 78; Psi Chi, 78; Nat Inst of Mental Health Pre-Doctoral Traineeship, 81-83; Distinguished Teacher, Univ Calif, 81-82, 82-83; Nat Inst of Health Post-Doctoral Fel, 84-86; Sigma Xi, 85; James A. Shannon Awd, Nat Cancer Inst, 92-94. **MEMBERSHIPS** Am Asn for the Advancement of Sci, Am Soc of Mammalogists, Animal Behavior Soc, Soc for Behavioral Neuroendocrinology, Soc for Neurosci, Soc for the Study of Biological Rhythms, Soc for the Study of Reproduction. **SELECTED PUBLICATIONS** Auth, An Introduction to Behavioral Endocrinology, Sinauer Assocs: Sunderland, MA (95); auth, "Psico-endocrinologia: Las Bases Hormonales de la Conducta, Ariel: Barcelona (96); auth, An Introduction to Behavioral Endocrinology, 2nd ed, Sinauer Assoc: Sunderland, MA (2000); coauth, Seasonal Patterns of Stress, Immune Function, and Disease, Cambridge Univ Press: NY (2000); coauth, "Aggression in knockout mice," Inst of Laboratory Animal Resources J (in press); coauth, "Seasonal fluctuations of stress," in Encyclopedia of Stress, ed by George Fink, Academic Press: NY (in press); coauth, "Influence of nitric oxide on neuroendocrine function and behavior," in Biology of Nitric Oxide, ed by L. Ignarro, Academic Press: NY (in press); coauth, "Short photoperiod reduces vascular endothelial growth factor (VEGF) in the testes of white-footed mice (Peromyscus Ieucopus), Am J of Physiology (in press). **CONTACT ADDRESS** Dept Psychol, Johns Hopkins Univ, Baltimore, 3400 N Charles St, Baltimore, MD 21218. **EMAIL** rnelson@jhu.edu

NELSON, WANDA LEE
PERSONAL Born 11/16/1952, Franklin, LA, m, 2 children **DISCIPLINE** EDUCATION **EDUCATION** Grambling State Univ, BA 1973; Ball State Univ, MA 1975; Natl Cert Counselor 1984; Louisiana State Univ, Ed S 1985; Northern Illinois Univ DeKalb Il Ed.D 1989. **CAREER** Bicester Amer Elem School, England, learning specialist 1974-76; Summer Enrichment Program LSUE, music teacher 1984; LSUE, counselor; Northern Illinois Univ, counselor & minority programs coordinator, 85-89; Univ of Texas, Austin TX, asst dean of students 1989-92; aaoc dean of students, 92-95, Executive Director University Outreach Centers, 95-. **HONORS AND AWARDS** Magna Cum Laude Grambling State Univ 1973; President's Awd Little Zion BC Matrons, Opelousas, LA 1985; Alpha Kappa Mu Honor Society, Grambling State Univ; Kappa Delta Pi Honor Society, Northern Illinois Univ 1988; Best Advisor of the Year, 1989; Alpha Golden Image Awd, Northern ILL Univ; Outstanding Educator, Texas Employees Retirement System, 1991; African-American Faculty/Staff of the Year, 1995; Pan-Hellenic Image Awd, Univ of Texas; Leadership Austin Class, 1997-98; Governor's Executive Development Program, 1998. **MEMBERSHIPS** Advisor Awareness of Culture, Ed & Soc Student Club 1978-85; Anti-Grammateus Epsilon Alpha Sigma Chap, 1979-80; organized Mu Upsilon Chap, 1992; Basileus Alpha Kappa Sigma, Chapter 1994-; life mem, Sigma Gamma Rho Sorority, Inc; Jack and Jill of America Inc, 1996-; advisor, Innervisions Gospel Choir, Univ of Texas, 1993-95; advisor, Zeta Nu Chap, 1984-89; life member Grambling State Univ Alumni Assn; member Amer Assn for Counseling & Dev; American Assn of Higher Education; Amer college Personnel Assn. **CONTACT ADDRESS** University Outreach Ctrs, Univ of Texas, Austin, 600 W 24th St, Austin, TX 78705. **EMAIL** wnelson@mail.utexas.edu

NEMZOFF, RUTH
PERSONAL Born 12/10/1940, Boston, MA, m, 1964, 4 children **DISCIPLINE** GOVERNMENT, GENDER ISSUES **EDUCATION** Columbia Univ, Barnard Col, BA, 62; MA, 64; Harvard Univ, EdD, 79. **CAREER** Lectr, Rivier Col, 79; vis res scholar, Wellesley Center for Res, Wellesley Col, 91-93; adjunct asst prof, Regis and Lesley Cols, 91-93; vis scholar, Women Studies, Brandeis Univ, 97-98; adjunct assoc prof, Govt, Bentley Col, 93-, Gender Issues Coordr, 96-. **HONORS AND AWARDS** Phi Delta Kappa; Who's Who in Am Politics; New Hampshire Coun for Better Schools Awd for Outstanding Innovative Progs; Regional Wise Awd, Outstanding Contribution to Enlarging Opportunities for Women; "Hers" Program at Management Inst for Women in Higher Educ at Wellesley Col, Wellesley. **MEMBERSHIPS** Nat Asn Jewish Legislators, Nat Orgn of Women, Nashua Asn for Retarded Citizens, Nat and Mass Women's Political Caucuses, Women's Action for New dirs, Hadassah. **RESEARCH** Gender issues in Jewish education. **SELECTED PUBLICATIONS** Auth, "Ignoring the Mothers Voice: Sex Bias in Individual Education Plans," in AAUW, eds, "Classroom on the Campus: Focusing on the 21st Century" (95); coauth, "A Tale of Two Professions: Women in Business and Politics," Business and the Contemporary World, vol 7, no 3 (95); coauth, "The Greening of Advertising: A Twenty-five year Look at Environmental Advertising," J of Marketing Theory and Practice (winter 96): 20; coauth, "Derech Eretz in the Classroom: Gender Issues in Classroom Management Conference Proceedings," Conference Proceeding: Exploring Issues of Gender and Jewish Day School Education, Brandeis Institute for Community and Religion and Cohen Center for Modern Jewish Studies, Brandeis Univ (97): 23-29. **CONTACT ADDRESS** Dept Govt, Bentley Col, 175 Forest St, Waltham, MA 02452. **EMAIL** rnemzoff@bentley.edu

NERSESSIAN, NANCY
DISCIPLINE COGNITIVE SCIENCES **EDUCATION** Case Western Reserve Univ, PhD. **CAREER** Prof, Ga Inst of Technol; ser ed, Sci and Philos bk ser, Kluwer Acad Publ. **MEMBERSHIPS** Gov bd, Philos of Sci Asn. **RESEARCH** The role of imagery, analogy, and thought experimenting in conceptual change. **SELECTED PUBLICATIONS** Auth, Faraday to Einstein: Constructing Meaning in Scientific Theories, Kluwer Acad Publ, 84, 90; How do scientists think? Capturing the dynamics of conceptual change in science, in Cognitive Models of Science, R Giere, ed, Minn Stud in Philos of Sci 15, Univ Minn Press,91; Constructing and Instructing: The role of 'abstraction techniques' in developing and teaching scientific theories, in Philosophy of Science, Cognitive Science, and Educational Theory and Practice, R Duschl & R Hamilton, eds, SUNY Press, 92; In the theoretician's laboratory: thought experimenting as mental modeling, PSA 92, Vol 2, D Hull, M Forbes, K Okruhlik, eds, 93. **CONTACT ADDRESS** Sch of Lit, Commun, & Cult, Georgia Inst of Tech, Skiles Cla, Atlanta, GA 30332. **EMAIL** nancyn@cc.gatech.edu

NESS, GAYL DEFORREST
PERSONAL Born 03/19/1929, Los Angeles, CA, m, 1955, 4 children **DISCIPLINE** SOCIOLOGY **EDUCATION** Univ Calif Berkeley, MA, 57; PhD, 61. **CAREER** Asst prof Sociology, 64-66, Assoc prof Sociology, 66-72, prof Sociology, 72-96, Prof Emer, 96-, Univ Mich, 64- . **HONORS AND AWARDS** Univ Mich Fac Governance Award, 95. **MEMBERSHIPS** Am Soc Assoc; Am Assoc Asian Studies; Pop Assoc Am. **RESEARCH** Population, Development, and Environment, Especially in Asia. **SELECTED PUBLICATIONS** coauth, Population-Environment Dynamics: Ideas and Observations, Univ Mich Press, 93; "People, Parks, and Biodiversity, People, Parks, and Biodiversity," Am Assoc Advan Sci, 95; World Population Growth, The Global Environ: Science, Technology and management, Scand Sci Press, 96; Population and Strategies for National Sustainable Development: A guidebook to assist environmental planners in dealing with population issues, Earthscan Press, 97; Environment for People: Building Bridges for Sustainable Development, UNFPA, 97; auth, Five Cities: Modeling Asian Urban Population Environment Dynamics, Oxford Univ Press of Singapore, 00. **CONTACT ADDRESS** Dept of Sociology, Univ of Michigan, Ann Arbor, 3012 Literature, Science, & the Arts Building, Ann Arbor, MI 48109-1382. **EMAIL** gaylness@umich.edu

NESS, SALLY A.
PERSONAL Born 10/29/1959, Washington, DC **DISCIPLINE** CULTURAL ANTHROPOLOGY **EDUCATION** Univ Washington, PhD 87. **CAREER** Univ Cal Riverside, assoc prof 93-. **HONORS AND AWARDS** SSRC S E Asia Adv Res Gnt. **MEMBERSHIPS** AAA **RESEARCH** Philippine studies; tourism; dance. **SELECTED PUBLICATIONS** Auth, Body Movement and Culture: Kinesthetic and Visual Symbolism in a Philippine Community, Philadelphia PA, Univ Penn Press, 92. **CONTACT ADDRESS** Dept of Dance, Univ of California, Riverside, Riverside, CA 92521.

NEU, JOYCE
PERSONAL Born 08/27/1950, Torrance, CA, s **DISCIPLINE** ANTHROPOLOGY **EDUCATION** Univ Colo, BA, 72; Univ S Calif, MA, 80; PhD, 85. **CAREER** Adj Assoc Prof, Emory Univ, 93-; Sen Assoc Dir, Conflict Resolution Program, The Carter Center, 92-. **HONORS AND AWARDS** Fulbright Lecturer, Poland, 87; USA Acad Expert, Estonia, 96. **MEMBERSHIPS** Am Asn of Applied Ling, Intl Soc of Polit Psychol, Ling Soc of Am, Speech Comm Asn, Teachers of English to Speakers of Other Lang. **RESEARCH** Conflict prevention and resolution, Medication, Discourse analysis. **SELECTED PUBLICATIONS** Co-ed, Speech acts across cultures: Challenges to communication in a second language, 96; auth, "Interpersonal dynamics in international conflict resolution," Natural Conflict Resolution, Univ Calif Press, forthcoming,; auth, "Eminent third party mediation: The Carter Center intervention in Bosnia," forthcoming; auth, "A methodology for conflict prevention: The case of Estonia," The Carter Center, 99; auth, "Reconciliation: saying what we mean and meaning what we say," OSCE Bulletin, (97): 5-6; auth, "An analysis of language use in negotiations: The role of context and content," in The discourse of business negotiation, Berlin, 95. **CONTACT ADDRESS** Dept Anthropol, Emory Univ, 1364 Clifton Rd NE, Atlanta, GA 30322-0001. **EMAIL** ccjn@emory.edu

NEUGEBOREN, BERNARD
PERSONAL Born 10/10/1924, New York, NY, m, 1977, 3 children **DISCIPLINE** SOCIAL WORK **EDUCATION** Brooklyn Col, BA, 46; Western Reserve Unvi, MS, 51; Brandesi Univ, PhD, 69. **CAREER** Prof, Rutgers Univ, 67-. **MEMBERSHIPS** Nat Assoc of Soc Work; Coun on Soc Work Educ. **RESEARCH** Organizational behavior, social work administration. **SELECTED PUBLICATIONS** Auth, Organization, Policy and Practice in Human Services, 91; auth, Environmental Practice in Human Services, Haworth, Pr, 96. **CONTACT ADDRESS** Dept Soc Work, Rutgers, The State Univ of New Jersey, New Brunswick, PO Box 5058, New Brunswick, NJ 08903. **EMAIL** drbgn@aol.com

NEVILLE, GWEN K.
PERSONAL Born 03/23/1938, Taylor, TX, m, 1975, 3 children **DISCIPLINE** ANTHROPOLOGY **EDUCATION** Mary Baldwin Col, BA, 59; Univ of Fla, MA, 68, PhD, 71. **CAREER** Asst prof to assoc prof, Emory Univ, 71-79; assoc prof to full prof, Southwestern Univ, 79-. **HONORS AND AWARDS** Phi Beta kappa; William Carrington Finch Awd, Southwestern univ; NEH fellowships. **MEMBERSHIPS** Am Anthrop Asn; Am Ethnological Soc; Soc for the Anthrop of Europe; Soc for Cultural Anthrop. **RESEARCH** Symbolic anthropology; ritual; religion; family; Scotland; USA. **SELECTED PUBLICATIONS** Auth, Kinship and Pilgrimage: Rituals of Reunion in American Protestant Culture, Oxford Univ Press, 87; The Mother Town: Civic Ritual, Symbol, and Experience in the Scottish Borders, 94. **CONTACT ADDRESS** Dept of Sociology and Anthropology, Southwestern Univ, University Ave., Georgetown, TX 78626.

NEWMAN, J. R.
PERSONAL Born 03/26/1954, Chicago, IL, m, 1995, 1 child **DISCIPLINE** ANTHROPOLOGY, ARCHAEOLOGY **EDUCATION** Triton Col, AA, 74; Grinnell Col, BA, 76; Southern Methodist Univ, MA, 84, PhD, 97. **CAREER** Archaeologist, Southern Methodist Univ, 78-87; archaeologist, U.S. Army Corps of Engineers, 87-00. **HONORS AND AWARDS** Certificate of Appreciation, Office of the Secretary of Defense, 90; Achievement Medal for Civilian Service, 92; Design & Environmental Excellence Awd, 93, Commendations, 89, 90, 91, & 92, Certificate of Achievement, 90, 91, Dept of Army; Fort Burgwin Res Fel, 81 & 82; Grant, Inst for the Study of Earth and Man, 83 & 85; Weber Grant, 87, multiple small grants, 82-85, Southern Methodist Univ. **MEMBERSHIPS** Soc of Professional Archaeologists; Register of Professional Archaeologists; Tx Archeological Soc; Soc for Am Archaeology; Coun of Tx Archeologists. **RESEARCH** Lithic sourcing & analysis; Lithic economic procurement patterns & use; statistical analysis; cultural resources management. **SELECTED PUBLICATIONS** Contributing auth, Shoreline Survey of Lewisville Lake, Denton County, Texas, 1986, Univ of North Tx, 90; auth, A Cultural Resources Survey of the Proposed Central Distribution Center (CDC) Construction Site and Sanitary Landfill Area at the Red River Army Depot, Bowie County, Texas, U.S. Army Corps of Engineers, 88; coauth, An Archeological Inventory of a Proposed Incinerator Construction Site at the Louisiana Army Ammunition Plant, Webster Parish, Louisiana, U.S. Army Corps of Engineers, 88; auth, A Cultural Resources Survey of Proposed Actions Related to Test Area Expansions, Longhorn Army Ammunition Plant, Harrison County, Texas, U.S. Army Corps of Engineers, 88; auth, Initial Notes On the XRF Sourcing of Northern New Mexico Obsidians, Journal of Field Archaeol, Boston Univ, 85; auth, Initial Notes On the X-ray Flourescence Characterization of the Rhyodacite Sources of the Taos Plateau, New Mexico, Archaeometry, Oxford Univ, 87; auth, The Effects of Source Distance on Lithic Material Reduction Technology, J of Field Archaeology, 94; auth, Task Selection of Lithic Raw Materials in the Northern Rio Grande Valley, New Mexico, Bulletin of the Tx Archaeological Soc, 99. **CONTACT ADDRESS** CESWF-EV-EC, U.S. Army Corps of Engineers, PO Box 17300, Fort Worth, TX 76102-0300. **EMAIL** jay.r.newman@swf.usace.army.mil

NEWTON, ESTHER
PERSONAL Born 11/28/1940, New York, NY **DISCIPLINE** ANTHROPOLOGY **EDUCATION** Univ Mich, BA, 62; Univ Chicago, MA, 64, PhD, 68. **CAREER** Assoc Prof, Prof, 72 to 93-, SUNY Purchase; Asst Prof, 68-71, Queens College. **HONORS AND AWARDS** Ruth Benedict Prize; Gustavus Meyer Prize. **MEMBERSHIPS** AAA **RESEARCH** Gay and Lesbian History and Culture. **SELECTED PUBLICATIONS** Auth, Cherry Grove, Fire Island: Sixty Years in America's First Gay and Lesbian Town, Boston, Beacon Press, 93; coauth, Womenfriends, NY, Friends Press, 76; Dick(less) Tracys' and the Homecoming Queen: Lesbian Power and Representation In Gay Male Cherry Grove, in: Ellen Lewin, ed, Inventing Lesbian Cultures in America, Beacon Press, 96; My Best Informant's Dress: The Erotic Equation in Fieldwork, in: Cultural Anthropology, 93, reprinted in Ellen Lewin and Wm Leap, eds, Out In the Field: Reflections of Lesbian and Gay Anthropologists, Urbana IL, U of IL Press, 94; auth, Margaret Mead Made Me Gay: Personal Essays, Public Ideas, Duke Univ Press (Durham), 00. **CONTACT ADDRESS** Division of Social Science, SUNY, Col at Purchase, 735 Anderson Hill Rd, Purchase, NY 10577. **EMAIL** newton@purchase.edu

NEWTON, PETER M.
PERSONAL Born 12/15/1942, Oakland, CA, m, 2 children **DISCIPLINE** PSYCHOLOGY **EDUCATION** Univ WA, BS, 64; Columbia Univ, PhD, 69. **CAREER** Instructor, Columbia Univ, 68-69; Asst Prof, Yale Univ, 70-76; Assoc Prof, Univ WA, 77; Visiting Lecturer, Univ Calif, 78-79; Dean, Assoc Prof to Prof Emeritus, The Wright Inst, 79-. **HONORS AND AWARDS** Diplomate in Clinical Psychol, Am Bd of Prof Psychol, 89; Teacher of the Year, Univ CA, 78-79; Fel, Branford Col, 71-76; Fel, Nat Inst of Mental Health, 64, 65, 67. **MEMBERSHIPS** Am Psychol Asn; Intl Soc for the Psychoanalytic Study of the Org; Nat Register of Health Service Providers in Psychol. **RESEARCH** Adult development; Psychological biography; Psychoanalysis; Group and organizational dynamics. **SELECTED PUBLICATIONS** Auth, Freud: From Youthful Dream to Mid-Life Crisis, Guilford Press, 95; co-auth, Unorthodox Freud: The View From the Couch, Guilford Press, 96; auth, "A Last Word," Psychoanalytic Books, (96): 447-451; auth, "Reply to Holt," Psychoanalytic Books, (96): 295-298; co-auth, "Reply to Makari," International Journal of Psycho-Analysis, (98): 1003-1004; auth, "Trivializing the mentor relationship," Legal Week, 99; co-auth, "In Kaplan," in The Comprehensive Textbook of Psychiatry, Williams & Wilkins, 99; co-auth, Developmental Studies of Women Writers, forthcoming. **CONTACT ADDRESS** Dept Psychol, The Wright Inst, 2728 Durant Ave, Berkeley, CA 94704.

NICHOLSON, ROBERT A.
PERSONAL Born 03/13/1954, Memphis, TN, d, 4 children **DISCIPLINE** PSYCHOLOGY **EDUCATION** Rhodes Col, BA, 78; Univ Tex, Austin, PhD, 86. **CAREER** Asst prof, Dept Psychol, Univ Tulsa, 86-92, assoc prof, 92-. **HONORS AND AWARDS** Phi Beta Kappa, BA, 78; Univ Tex, Austin, PhD, 86. **MEMBERSHIPS** Am Psychol Asn, Am Psychol-Law Soc. **RESEARCH** Forensic assessment (assessment of legal competencies, assessment of malingering and defensiveness); coercion in psychiatric treatment. **SELECTED PUBLICATIONS** Auth, "Forensic assessment," in R. Roesch, S. Hart, & J. R. P. Ogloff, eds, Psychology and Law: The State of the Discipline, New York: Plenum (99); coauth with R. M. Bagby, T. Buis, H. Radovanovic, & B. J. Fidler, "Defensive responding on the MMPI-2 in family custody and access evaluations," Psychol Assessment, 11 (99): 24-28; coauth with J. F. Edens, N. G. Poythress, & R. K. Otto, "Effects of state organizational structure and forensic examiner training on pre-trial competence assessments," J of Behav Health Services and Res, 26 (99): 140-150; auth, "Test Review: The Malingering Probability Scale," Am Psychol-Law Soc News, 19 (99): 8-14; auth, "The effects of coerced psychiatric hospitalization and treatment," in J. P. Morrissey & J. Monahan, eds, Research in Community and Mental Health, Vol 10: Coercion in Mental Health services: International Perspectives, Stamford, Ct: JAI Press (99); coauth with N. G. Poythress, R. K. Otto, J. F. Edens, R. J. Bonnie, J. Monahan, & S. K. Hoge, MacArthur Competence Assessment Tool-Criminal Adjudication (MacCAT-CA) Professional Manual, Odessa, Fl: Psychol Assessment Resources (99); coauth with L. J. Porkorny and R. Shull, "Dangerousness and disability as predictors of psychiatric patients' legal status," Behav Scis and the Law, 17 (99): 253-267; coauth with R. M. Bagby, "Differential diagnosis with the MMPI-2 Clinical, Content, and Personality Psychopathology Five Scales," MMPI/MMPI-2 News and Profiles (2000); coauth with S. Norwood, "The quality of forensic psychological assessments, reports, and testimony: Acknowledging the gap between promise and practice," Law and Human Behavior, 24 (2000): 9-44; coauth with R. M. Bagby, T. Buis & J. R. Bacchiochi, "Can the MMPI-2 validity indicators successfully detect depression feigned by experts?" Assessment (in press). **CONTACT ADDRESS** Dept Psychology, Univ of Tulsa, Lorton Hall 307C, Tulsa, OK 74104.

NIELSEN, MICHAEL
PERSONAL Born, UT, m, 1985, 1 child **DISCIPLINE** PSYCHOLOGY **EDUCATION** Southern Ut Univ, BA, 86; Northern Ill Univ, MA, 90; PhD, 92. **CAREER** Vis lectr, Lake Forest Col, 93; asst prof, Ga Southern Univ, 93-00. **HONORS AND AWARDS** Travel Awd, Ga Southern Univ, 97; Special Initiatives Grant Winner, Ga Southern Univ, 99. **MEMBERSHIPS** Soc for the Sci Study of Relig, Am Psychol Asn, Mormon Soc Sci Asn. **RESEARCH** Psychology of Religion. **SELECTED PUBLICATIONS** Coauth, "Further examination of religious conflict and religious orientation," Rev of Relig Res 36 (95): 369-381; auth, "Operationalizing religious orientation: Iron rods and compasses," J of Psychol: Interdisciplinary and Applied 129 (95): 485-494; auth, "H-Comp: A program to calculate information complexity," Behavior Res Methods, Instruments, & Computers 28 (96): 483-485; coauth, "An alternative view of religious complexity," The Int J for the Psychol of Relig 7 (97): 23-35; coauth, The transmission of norms regarding group decision rules," Personality and Soc Psychol Bull 23 (97): 516-525; auth, "An assessment of religious conflicts and their resolutions," J for the Sci Study of Relig 37 (98): 181-190; auth, "Descriptions of religious experience using trait and affect adjectives," Psychol Reports (in press). **CONTACT ADDRESS** Dept Psychol, Georgia So Univ, PO Box 8041, Statesboro, GA 30460. **EMAIL** mnielsen@gasou.edu

NIELSON, KRISTY A.
PERSONAL Born 12/11/1964, Inglewood, CA **DISCIPLINE** PSYCHOLOGY **EDUCATION** Calif State Univ, Long Beach, BA, 87; Southern Ill Univ, MA, 90, PhD, 93; Univ Calif, Irvine, Post-Doctoral, 93-96. **CAREER** Instr, The Learning Center, Santa Ana, Calif, 85-86; substitute preschool teacher, St Peter Lutheran Sch, Santa Ana, 85-86; res asst, Dept of Cummun Disorders, CSULB, 85-88, undergrad teaching asst, 86-87; res asst, Southern Ill Univ, Carbondale, 88-92, lectr, 91-92; Neuropsychology Intern, Alzheimer's Disease Res Center, Univ Calif, Irvine, 92-95; Postdoctoral Fel, Inst for Brain Aging and Dementia, Univ Calif, Irvine, 92-96; lectr, Psychobiology Dept, Univ Calif, Irvine, 96; asst prof, Dept Psychology, Marquette Univ, 96-; asst clinical prof, Dept of Psychiatry and Behav Med, Medical Col of Wisc, 98-; Dir, Foley Center for Aging and Development, Dept of Psychiatry and Behav Med, Med Col of Wisc, 98-. **HONORS AND AWARDS** Outstanding Undergrad, Communicative Disorders, summa cum Laude, CSULB, 86-87; Doctoral Diss Res Awd, Southern Ill Univ Carbondale, 91-92; Outstanding Diss Awd, Southern Univ Carbondale, 94; Fac Scholar Awd, Psychol Dept, Marquette Univ, 97-98; Mistress of Ceremonies, 40th Annual Honors Convocation, Col of Arts and Scis, Marquette Univ, 98; listed in: Who's Who Among America's Teachers, Who's Who Millennium Ed, and Who's Who Among Am Women. **MEMBERSHIPS** Phi Kappa Phi, Am Asn for the Advancement of Sci, The Planetary Soc, Am Psychol Soc, Soc for Neuroscience, Women in Neuroscience, Alzheimer's Asn of SE Wisc, Sigma Xi, Am Psychol Asn, Am Asn of Univ Profs, Org for Human Brain Mapping. **RESEARCH** Cognitive neuroscience, psychobiology, cognitive psychology, neuropsychology, psychology of aging. **SELECTED PUBLICATIONS** Coauth with J. Nolan, N. Berchtold, C. Sandman, R. Mulnard, and C. Cotman, "Apolipoprotein-E genotyping of diabetic dementia patients: Is diabetes rare in Alzheimer's disease?" J of the Am Geriatrics Soc, 44 (96): 897-904; coauth with B. J. Cummings and C. W. Cotman, "Constructional apraxia in Alzheimer's disease correlates with neuritic neuropathy in occipital cortex," Brain Res, 74, 1-2 (96): 284-293; coauth with J. I. Victoroff and D. Mungsas, "Caregiver and clinician assessment of behavior disorders: The California Dementia Behavior Questionnaire," Int Psychogeriatrics, 9, 2 (97): 155-174; coauth with T. Satou, B. J. Cummings, E. Head, F. F. Hahn, M. W. Milgram, P. Valezquez, D. Cribbs, A. Tenner, and C. W. Cotman, "The progression of B-amyloid deposition in the frontal cortex of the aged canine," Brain Res, 774 (97): 35-43; coauth with C. A. Sandman, R. A. Mulnard and C. W. Cotman, "Non-insulin-dependent diabetes mellitus and Alzheimer's disease: Reply," J of the Am Geriatrics Soc, 45 (97): 654-655; coauth with J. I. Victoroff and W. J. Mack, "Psychiatric complications of dementia: Impact on caregivers?," Dementia and Geriatric Cognitive Disorders, 9 (98): 50-55; coauth with D. A. Czech and K. K. Laubmeier, "Chronic administration of propranolol impairs inhibitory avoidance retention in the mouse," Neurobiology of Learning and Memory, 71 (99): 248-257; coauth with H. Gravan, S. L. Langenecker, E. A. Stein and E. A. Rao, "Event-related fMRI of inhibitory control reveals lateralized prefrontal activation differences between healthy young and older adults," Brain and Cognition (in press); coauth with L. A. Stone, "Physiological response to arousal and impaired emotional expression in alexithymia," Psychotherapy and Psychosomatics (in press); coauth with D. A. Czech and K. K. Laubmeirer, "Chronic administration of propranolol impairs

Morris water maze retention in the mouse," Neurobiology of Learning and Memory (in press). **CONTACT ADDRESS** Dept Psychol, Marquette Univ, PO Box 1881, Milwaukee, WI 53201. **EMAIL** Kristy.Nielson@Marquette.edu

NIENONEN, JACK E.
PERSONAL Born 01/08/1952, Duluth, MN, m, 1990, 3 children **DISCIPLINE** SOCIOLOGY **EDUCATION** Concordia Col, BA, 74; Mich State Univ, MA, 77; PhD, 82. **CAREER** Teaching Asst to Instructor, MI State Univ, 74-80; Asst Prof, Augustana Col, 83-84, 86-89; Visiting Asst Prof, Cornell Col, 85-86; Asst Prof to Assoc Prof, Univ SDak, 89-. **HONORS AND AWARDS** Excellence-in-Teaching Awd, 99. **MEMBERSHIPS** Am Sociol Asn; Soc for the Study of Soc Problems; Midwest Sociol Soc; Asn for Humanist Sociol; Mid-South Sociol Asn; Great Plains Sociol Asn. **RESEARCH** The race relations problematic in American sociology; The sociology of knowledge. **SELECTED PUBLICATIONS** Auth, "Some Observations on the Problem of Paradigms in Recent Racial and Ethnic Relations Texts," Teaching Sociology, (93): 271-286; auth, "The Role of the State in the sociology of Racial and Ethnic Relations: Some Theoretical considerations," Free Inquiry in Creative Sociology, (95): 27-38; auth, "The Race Relations Problematic in American Sociology: A Case Study and Critique," The American Sociologist, (97): 15-54; auth, "Deconstructing Cultural Pluralism," sociological Spectrum, (99): 401-419. **CONTACT ADDRESS** Dept Soc & Beh Sci, Univ of So Dakota, Vermillion, 414 E Clark St, Vermillion, SD 57069. **EMAIL** jniemone@usd.edu

NIKELLY, ARTHUR G.
DISCIPLINE PSYCHOLOGY **EDUCATION** Roosevelt Univ, Chicago, BA 54, MA 55; Univ Ottawa CA, PhD 59. **CAREER** Univ IL Health Cen, assoc prof clin psychol 59. **MEMBERSHIPS** APA; IPA; NA Soc of Adlerian Psychol. **SELECTED PUBLICATIONS** Cultural Babel: The challenge of immigrants to the helping professions, Cultur Div and Mental Health, 97; Alternatives to the androcentric bias of personality disorders, Clinical Psychol and Psychotherapy; Drug Advertisements and the medicalization of unipolar depression in women, Health Care for Women Intl, 95; Alcoholism: Social as well as Psycho-medical problem: the missing big picture, Journal of Alcohol and Drug Education, 94. **CONTACT ADDRESS** Univ of Illinois, Urbana-Champaign, Urbana, IL 61801.

NILSEN, ALLEEN PACE
PERSONAL Born 10/10/1936, Phoenix, AZ, m, 1958, 3 children **DISCIPLINE** ENGLISH EDUCATION AND LINGUISTICS **EDUCATION** Brigham Young Univ, BA, 58; Am Univ, MEd, 61; Univ Iowa, PhD(English, ling), 73. **CAREER** Instr English, Eastern Mich Univ, 66-67; teacher, Am Int Sch Kabul, Afghanistan, 67-69: instr English, Eastern Mich Univ, 69-71; asst prof educ, Univ Northern Iowa, 71-73; assoc prof, 73-80, Prof English, Ariz State Univ, 80- **HONORS AND AWARDS** Rewey Belle Inglis Awd, Natl Coun of Tchrs of English, 90; Nicholas J. Silvaroli Awd, 94 for Outstanding Contribution to Literacy in Arizona. **MEMBERSHIPS** Nat Coun Teachers English; Membership in International Soc of Humor Studies (ISHS), Pres, 01; MLA. **RESEARCH** Sexism as shown in language; children's and adolescent literature; humor scholarship. **SELECTED PUBLICATIONS** Coauth, Pronunciation Contrasts in English, Simon & Schuster, 71; auth, Sexism in English: A feminist view, In: Female Studies VI: Closer to the Ground, Feminist Press, 72; coauth, Semantic Theory: A Linguistic Perspective, Newbury House, 75; ed & coauth, Sexism and Language, Nat Coun Teachers English, 77; Five factors contributing to the unequal treatment of females in picture books, Top News, spring 78; coauth, Language Play: An Introduction to Linguistics, Newbury House, 78; auth, Living Language, Allyn & Bacon, 99; co-auth, Encyclopedia of 20th Century American Humor, Oryx 00; ; coauth, Literature for Today's Young Adults, 6th ed, Longman, 01. **CONTACT ADDRESS** Dept of English, Arizona State Univ, PO Box 870302, Tempe, AZ 85287-0302. **EMAIL** Alleen.Nilsen@asu.edu

NIMBARK, ASHAKANT
PERSONAL Born 01/20/1934, Bhoringda, India, d, 3 children **DISCIPLINE** SOCIOLOGY **EDUCATION** New School Univ, PhD, 67. **CAREER** Prof, Dowling Col, 79-. **HONORS AND AWARDS** Excellence in Teaching, Outstanding scholar, Outstanding Faculty. **MEMBERSHIPS** Am Sociol Asn, Intl Sociol Asn, E Sociol Soc, Asn of Asian Studies, Asia Soc. **RESEARCH** Mass media and society, Sociology of the future, Comparative (global) sociology, South Asia. **SELECTED PUBLICATIONS** Auth, Debating Points: Mass media and Society, (forthcoming); auth, New York Glory, (in press). **CONTACT ADDRESS** Dept Soc Sci, Dowling Col, 150 Idle Hour Blvd, Oakdale, NY 11769. **EMAIL** nimbarka@dowling.edu

NISHI, SETSUKO MATSUNAGA
PERSONAL Born 10/17/1921, Los Angeles, CA, m, 1944, 5 children **DISCIPLINE** SOCIOLOGY **EDUCATION** Wash Univ, AB, 44; MA, 44; Univ Chicago, PhD, 63. **CAREER** Prof, CUNY Brooklyn Col, Grad Cen, 65-; Principal Investigator at CLPEF, Nat Study, 98-. **HONORS AND AWARDS** Phi Beta Kappa; Dean's Honor List; Mortar Bd Awd; Alpha Kappa Delta; Sigma Chi; AAUW Fel; Japan Found Fel; NIMH Fel; MARC Fel; John H Whitney Fel; PSC CUNY Fac Res Awd; CLPEF Awd; SPSS Awd; Julius Rosenwald Fund. **MEMBERSHIPS** ASA; ESS; SSSP. **RESEARCH** Institutionalized discrimination; long term sequelae of Wartime incarceration of Japanese families. **SELECTED PUBLICATIONS** Auth, "Asian Americans at the Intersection of International and Domestic Tensions," ch 7 in Across the Pacific: Asian Americans and Globalization, ed. Evelyn Hudehart (Philadelphia: Temple UP, 99); auth, "Japanese Americans," Ch 5 in Asian Americans: A Survey of Ethnic Groups, ed. Pyong Gap Min (Newberry Park, CA: Sage, 94); auth, "Restoration of Community in Chicago Resettlement," Japanese Am Nat (99); auth, "Asian Americans and the Myth of the 'Good Minority,"' in "The United States in the 1990's, Autrement (92); auth, "Perceptions and Deceptions: Contemporary Views of Asian Americans," in A Look Beyond the Model Minority Image: Critical Issues in Asian America, ed. Grace Yun (NY: Minority Rights Group, U. S.A., Inc, 89); coauth, "The Status of Asian Americans in the Health Care Delivery System in New York," NYS J Med 85 (85): 153-158. **CONTACT ADDRESS** Dept Sociology, Brooklyn Col, CUNY, 2901 Bedford Ave, Brooklyn, NY 11210.

NITSCHE, RICHARD
PERSONAL Born 09/28/1939, Cleveland, OH, d, 1 child **DISCIPLINE** ENGLISH, ENGLISH AS A SECOND LANGUAGE, CHINESE **EDUCATION** Oh State Univ, BA, 66; PhD, 77; Nat Taiwan Univ, MA. **CAREER** Instr, Youngstown State Univ, 69-75; asst prof, prog dir, Monterey Inst Intl Stud, 77-80; lectr, Tianjin Univ, China, 80-81; instr, Monterey Peninsula Univ, 81-. **HONORS AND AWARDS** Rockefeller Gnt; Geraldine R Dodge Found Gnt; Fulbright Gnt. **MEMBERSHIPS** CLTA; CFLP. **SELECTED PUBLICATIONS** Auth, Situational Exercises in Cross-Cultural Awareness, Chas Merrill Pub (77); auth, Becoming Fluent in English, Kendall/Hunt pub, (73). **CONTACT ADDRESS** Dept Humanities, Monterey Peninsula Col, 980 Fremont St, Monterey, CA 93940. **EMAIL** rnitsche@hotmail.com

NJOKU, JOHN
PERSONAL Born, Nigeria, m, 1960, 2 children **DISCIPLINE** SOCIOLOGY, ANTHROPOLOGY **EDUCATION** Mich State Univ, BS, 56; New Sch Univ, MA, 60; PhD, 74. **CAREER** Agr Economist, Ministry of Agr, 61-62; Prov Adminr, Biafra Emergency Food Prod, 67-70; Prof, Touro Col, 79-. **HONORS AND AWARDS** Leadership Awd, Nigerian Student Union, 60; Author Awds, New York Nat Local Writers, 90-91; Long Service Awd, Touro Col, 93; Onyehi Found Awd, Nigeria Community of the US, 94; Ed Accomplishment Awd, 98; Touro Col Alumni Investment Awd, 99. **MEMBERSHIPS** African Studies Asn, Nigerian Studies Asn. **RESEARCH** Tradition and change in Africa, Old Jewish settlement in West Africa. **SELECTED PUBLICATIONS** Auth, Dictionary of Igbo Names, Culture and Proverbs, Univ Pr of Am (Wash, D.C.), 77; Auth, The World of African Women, Scare Crow Pr (NJ), 80; Auth, Malthusianism, An African Dilemma, Hunger, Starvation and Drought in Africa, Scare Crow Pr (NJ), 90; Auth, Short Stories of the Traditional People of Nigeria, African Folks Back Home, Edwin Mellen Pr (NY), 95; Auth, "African Childhood! Poor Social and Economic Environments," (Edwin Mellen Pr, 95); Auth, "Identity with Nigerian Clergy," Nigerian Studies, 97; Auth, African Wild Missiles, Poems of Nature, Culture and Cosmology, Jay Publ (NY), 98; Auth, "Remembering the Irish Missionaries in Igbo Land, Development of Christianity in Nigeria," (Jay Publ, 00). **CONTACT ADDRESS** Dept Sociol and Antrop, Touro Col, New York, 27 W 23rd St, #33, New York, NY 10010.

NOEL, MELVINA
PERSONAL Born 07/27/1951, Portsmouth, VA, s **DISCIPLINE** EDUCATION **EDUCATION** Tidewater Cmty Col, AA, 92; AA, 81; Hampton Univ, BS, 73; Old Dominion Univ, MS, 75; George Washington Univ, DEd, 00. **CAREER** Instructor, Commonwealth Col; Instructor, Thomas Nelson Cmty Col. **HONORS AND AWARDS** Who's Who Among Am Teachers, 00; Teacher of the Quarter, Commonwealth Col, 93; Speech Teacher of the Year, VA Speech Comm Asn, 80. **MEMBERSHIPS** Asn of Literary Scholars and Critics; VA Cmty Col Asn. **RESEARCH** Adult learners and student services. **SELECTED PUBLICATIONS** Auth, "Affirmative Action in Higher Education: Three Approaches to the Issue," Eric Digest, (97): 780; auth, "The Keys to Successful Learning," Sufism: The Science of the Soul, Vol 2, 99. **CONTACT ADDRESS** Dept Humanities, Thomas Nelson Comm Col, PO Box 9407, Hampton, VA 23670-0407. **EMAIL** melvina777@aol.com

NOICE, HELGA
PERSONAL Born 12/26/1939, Pyritz, Germany, m, 1970 **DISCIPLINE** COGNITIVE PSYCHOLOGY **EDUCATION** Florida Atlantic Univ, BA, 81, MA, 84; PhD, Rutgers Univ, 88. **CAREER** Res asst, Fla Atlantic Univ, 82-84; tchg asst, Rutgers Univ, 84-88; instr, Rutgers Univ, summers, 85-88, visiting asst prof, Fla Atlantic Univ, fall 88-summer 89; asst prof, Augustana Col, 89-96; assoc prof, Augustana Col, 96-; assoc prof, Elmhurst Col. **HONORS AND AWARDS** Who's Who in Sci and Eng, 96; Phi Kappa Phi; Sigma X1. **MEMBERSHIPS** Cognitive Sci Soc; Psychonomics; Am Psychol Soc; Midwestern Psychol Asn; Intl Asn for the Empirical Study of Lit; Soc for Text and Discourse; Soc of Appl Res in Mem and Cognition. **RESEARCH** Mental representation; Text comprehension; Cognition and emotion; Human memory, esp memory training for older adults. **SELECTED PUBLICATIONS** Coauth, "Verbatim retention of theatrical scripts by means of character analysis," in S. Toetoesy de Zepetnek & Irene Sywenky, The systemic and empirical approach to literature and culture as theory and application, (Edmonton, Alberta: Univ of Alberta, 97), 485-504; coauth, "Effort and active experiencing as factors in verbatim recall," Discourse Processes 23 (97): 51-69; coauth, Expertise of professional actors: A cognitive view, NJ: Lawrence Erlbaum Associates, 97; coauth, "Improving memory in older adults by instructing them in professional actors' learning strategies," Applied Cognitive Psychology 13 (99): 315-328; coauth, "Theatrical training for older adults," in P. Perrig-Chiello, H.B. Staehelin, & W.J. Perrig, Well-being, health and cognitive competence, (Bern, Switzerland: Verlag Paul Haupt), 99; coauth, "Long-term retention of theatircal roles," Memory 7 (99): 357-382; coauth, "Effects of enactment by professional actors at encoding and retrieval," Memory 8 (00): 353-363; coauth, "Two approaches to learning a theatrical script," in U. Neisser & I.R. Hyman, Jr. Memory observed: Remembering in natural contexts, (New York: Worth Publishers, 00); coauth, "Very long-term recall and recognition of well-learned material," Applied Cognitive Psychology, in press; coauth, "Learning dialogue with and without movement," Memory & Cognition, in press. **CONTACT ADDRESS** Dept. of Psychology, Elmhurst Col, 190 Prospect Ave, Elmhurst, IL 60126-3296. **EMAIL** helgan@elmhurst.edu

NOLAN, MARY
PERSONAL Born 01/17/1944, Chicago, IL, 2 children **DISCIPLINE** MODERN EUROPEAN & WOMEN'S HISTORY **EDUCATION** Smith Col, BA, 66; Columbia Univ, MA, 69, PhD, 75. **CAREER** Asst prof, Harvard Univ, 75-80; from Asst Prof to Assoc Prof, 80-92, prof hist, NY Univ, 92-. **RESEARCH** Modern German history; comparative working-class history. **SELECTED PUBLICATIONS** Auth, Social policy, economic mobilization and the working class in the Thrid Reich: A review of the literature, Radical Hist Rev, No 39, 77; Proletarischer anti-feminismus, Frauen und Wissenschaft Courage, Verlag, 77; coauth, The social democratic reform cycle in Germany, Polit Power & Social Theory, 81; auth, Social Democracy and Society: Working-class Radicalism in Dusseldorf, 1890-1920, Cambridge Univ Press, 82; The Historikenstreit & Social History, New Ger Critique 44, 88; Housework Made Easy: The Taylorized Housewife in Weimar Germany's Rationalized Economy, Feminist Studies, Fall 90; Vision of Modernity: American Business & The Modernization of Germany. Oxford, 94; Is Liberalism Really the Answer?, Int Labor & Working Class Hist 46, 94; Anti-Fascism Under Fascism: German Vision & Voices, New Ger Critique, 96. **CONTACT ADDRESS** Dept Hist, New York Univ, 53 Washington Square S, New York, NY 10003-4556. **EMAIL** mn4@is2.nyu.edu

NOONBERG, AARON R.
PERSONAL Born 05/26/1950, Baltimore, MD, s **DISCIPLINE** PSYCHOLOGY **EDUCATION** Kent State Univ, PhD, 85. **CAREER** Adj asst prof, Johns Hopkins Univ, 92-. **MEMBERSHIPS** Soc of Behav Med; Am Acad of Pain Management; Int Acad of Behav Med, Counseling and Psychotherapy. **RESEARCH** Pain, forensic psychology. **SELECTED PUBLICATIONS** Coauth, Biofeedback: Clinical Applications in Behavioral Medicine, Prentice Hall, (NJ), 80. **CONTACT ADDRESS** Dept Psychol, Johns Hopkins Univ, Baltimore, 3400 N Charles St, Baltimore, MD 21218.

NORCROSS, JOHN C.
PERSONAL Born 08/13/1957, NJ, m, 2 children **DISCIPLINE** PSYCHOLOGY **EDUCATION** Rutgers Univ, BA, 80; Univ RI, MA, 81; PhD, 84. **CAREER** Asst prof to prof, Univ of Scranton, 85-. **HONORS AND AWARDS** Athenaeum Honor Soc, 78; Psi Chi, 78; Jack D. Krasner Mem Awd, 92; Univ of Scranton Prof of the Year, 92; Pa Prof of the Year, Carnegie Found, 92. **MEMBERSHIPS** Am Psychol Assoc; Assoc for the Advan of Psychol; AAUP; Eastern Psychol Assoc; Pa Psychol Assoc; Psi Chi; Soc for Psychotherapy Res; Am Assoc of Applied and Preventive Psychol; Am Evaluation Assoc. **RESEARCH** Clinical psychology, psychotherapy, self-help, behavior change. **SELECTED PUBLICATIONS** Coauth, Changing for good, William Morrow, (NY), 94; coauth, Insider's guide to graduate programs in clinical and counseling psychology, 97/97 edition, 98/99 edition, 00/01 edition; Guilford, (NY), 96-; coed, Psychologists' desk reference, Oxford Univ Pr, 98, coauth, Systems of psychotherapy: A transtheoretical analysis, Brooks/Cole (Pacific Grove, CA), 98; auth, "Treating anger in psychotherapy". In Session 55.3 (99): 275-379; coauth, Leaving it at the office: Understanding and alleviating the distress of conducting psychotherapy, Guilford (NY), (forthcoming). **CONTACT ADDRESS** Dept Psychology, Univ of Scranton, Scranton, PA 18510-4596. **EMAIL** norcross@uofs.edu

NORRIS, DEBORAH OLIN
PERSONAL Born 03/24/1957, Bethesda, MD, m, 1982, 3 children **DISCIPLINE** PSYCHOLOGY **EDUCATION** The Colo Col, BA, 79; Am Univ, MA, 84; PhD, 88. **CAREER** Adjunct

prof, Georgetown Univ Medical Center, 91-94; adjunct prof, The American Univ, 84-, asst to the Dean of Students, 84-86; Neurotoxicologist, U.S. Environmental Protection Agency, Office of Pollution Prevention and Toxics, Risk Assessment Div, Washington, DC, 97-. **HONORS AND AWARDS** Phi Kappa Phi; Sigma Xi; Who's Who in Women; Nat Sci Found Fel, 74; Dept of Veteran's Affairs, Performance Awd, 92; Montgomery Co Dept of Family Resources Awd, 95; U.S.E.P.A. Bronze Medal for Commendable Service, 96; U.S.E.P.A./OPPT Mission Awd, 97. **MEMBERSHIPS** Am Asn of Univ Women. **SELECTED PUBLICATIONS** Coauth, "Facing the needs for collaboration between the art historian and the art conservator," Collections (91); coauth, "Effects of milacemide, a glycine prodrug, on ethanol's antiseizure efficacy," Pharmacology Biochemistry and Behavior, 41, 2 (92): 263-266; coauth, "Paradoxical effect of flurazepam," Pharmacology, Biochemistry and Behavior, 42, 1 (92): 517-518; coauth, "Reduction of Flurazepam's antiseizure efficacy persists after stress," Pharmacology, Biochemistry and Behavior, 42, 4 (92): 681-684; coauth, "Glycinergic interventions potentiate the ability of MK-801 to raise the threshold voltage for tonic hindlimb extension in mice," Pharmacology, Biochemistry and Behavior, 43, 1 (92): 609-612; coauth, "A glycinergic intervention restores the stress-induced reduction in the antiseizure efficacy of MK-801 and Flurazepam," Clinical Neuropharmacology, 19, 2 (94): 161-165. **CONTACT ADDRESS** Dept Psychol, American Univ, 4400 Mass Ave NW, Washington, DC 20016.

NORTON-HAWK, MAUREEN

PERSONAL Born 07/06/1949, MA, w, 2 children **DISCIPLINE** SOCIOLOGY **EDUCATION** Mary Wash Col, BA, 83; Va Commonwealth, MS, 87; Univ Ala, MS, 88; Northeastern Univ, PhD, 94. **CAREER** Lectr, Northeastern Univ, 89-; asst prof, Suffolk Univ, 96-. **HONORS AND AWARDS** Ctr on Alcohol Studies Summer Fel, Rutgers Univ, 82; Sigma Omega Chi, 83; mem, Am Sociol Asn Honors Prog, 91; Res Fel, Ctr Alcohol and Addiction Studies, Brown Univ, 94-96. **MEMBERSHIPS** Am Sociol Asn, Law and Soc Asn, Soc for the Study of Soc Problems, Eastern Sociol Soc, Am Soc of Criminol, Acad of Criminal Justice Scis, Va Alcoholism and Drug Abuse Counselors, Nat Asn of Forensic counselors. **SELECTED PUBLICATIONS** Auth, "Unintended Consequences: Maternal Substance Abuse," Drug Use in America: Social and Cultural Perspectives, P. Venturelli, ed (94): 315-321; auth, "How Social Policies Make Matters Worse: The Case of Maternal Substance Abuse," J of Drug Issues, 24, 3 (summer 94); auth, "Prevalence of Drug Use in Pregnancy: Assessment, Critique and Policy Implications," J Drug Issues 27, 3 (97): 447-462; auth, "The Framingham Eight," Encyclopedia of Women and Crime (forthcoming spring 2000); auth, "Career of a Crisis: Cocaine Babies and the Interrelationship of Professional, Political and Ideological Forces," J of Drugs and Soc (forthcoming); auth, "The Counterproductive Aspects of Anti-Prostitution Laws," Women and Crime (under revision). **CONTACT ADDRESS** Dept Sociol, Suffolk Univ, 8 Ashburton Pl, Boston, MA 02108. **EMAIL** mhawks@acad.suffolk.edu

NORWOOD, MARGARET M.

PERSONAL Born New York, NY, m, 1994, 2 children **DISCIPLINE** PSYCHOLOGY **EDUCATION** Brown Univ, AB, 86; Univ Va, MEd, 87; PhD, 91. **CAREER** Psychotherapist, Hampton Va, 92-94; Counselor, Newport Va, 94-96; Prof, Thomas Nelson Cmty Col, 96-. **CONTACT ADDRESS** Dept Bus & Soc Sci, Thomas Nelson Comm Col, PO Box 9407, Hampton, VA 23670. **EMAIL** drpeg@hotmail.com

NUCHO, AINA O.

PERSONAL Born Riga, Latvia, w, 1951 **DISCIPLINE** SOCIAL WORK **EDUCATION** St. Olaf Col, BA, 50; Bryn Mawr Col, MSS, 57; PhD, 66. **CAREER** From Asst Prof to Prof, Sch of Soc Work, Univ of Md, 66-. **HONORS AND AWARDS** Distinguished Fel, Am Soc for Study of Psychopathology of Expression, 93; Short Term Travel Grant, Int Res and Exchanges Bd, 94, 95. **MEMBERSHIPS** Am Art Ther Asn, Asn for the Advancement of Baltic Studies, Nat Asn of Soc Work. **RESEARCH** Art Therapy, Imagery, Stress Management. **SELECTED PUBLICATIONS** Auth, The Psychcybernetic Model of Art Therapy, Charles C Thomas (Springfiled, IL), 87; auth, Stree Management: The Quest for Zest, Charles C Thomas (Springfiled, IL), 88; auth, Spontaneous Creative Imagery: Problem-Solving and Life-Enchancing Skills, Charles C Thomas (Springfiled, IL), 95; coauth, Stresa Menedzements: Parvaresana un Profilakse, AGB Publ (Riga, Latvia), 98; coauth, Maksla un Pasatklasme, AGB Publ (Riga, Latvia), 99. **CONTACT ADDRESS** Dept Soc Work, Univ of Maryland, Baltimore, 525 W Redwoond St, Baltimore, MD 21201.

NULL, ELISABETH M.

PERSONAL Born 12/01/1942, Worcester, MA, 2 children **DISCIPLINE** FOLKLORE, HISTORY, LIBRARY SCIENCE **EDUCATION** Sarah Lawrence Col, BA; MA; Yale Univ 85; MPhil, 89; Univ of Pa, MA, 86; Cath Univ of Am, MLIS, 95. **CAREER** Librarian, ed, digital content provider, Lib of Congress, 95-98; guest lectr, Georgetown Univ, 91-98; writer, cybrarian, Rural Sch Community Trust, 99-; co-chair, Washington Folk Festival, 99-00. **MEMBERSHIPS** Am Folklore Soc. **RESEARCH** American musical life and cultural history. **SELECTED PUBLICATIONS** Reviews in Journal of Am Folklore, New York Folklore Quarterly, New England Quarterly; produced ethnographic recordings, Green Linnet Records; edited digitized historical collections, Lib of Congress. **CONTACT ADDRESS** 706 Bonifant Street, Silver Spring, MD 20910-5534. **EMAIL** elisabeth.null@tcs.wap.org

NUNIS, DOYCE BLACKMAN, JR.

PERSONAL Born 05/30/1924, Cedartown, GA **DISCIPLINE** HISTORY, EDUCATION **EDUCATION** BA, UCLA, 47; MS in Ed, USC,50; M Ed, USC, 52; PhD Hist, USC,58. **CAREER** Univ Southern Cal, Prof Emer, 89-, Hist Prof, 68-89, Assoc Prof, 65-68; UCLA, Assoc Prof, Edu, Assoc Research Hist, Office Oral Hist, 64-65, Asst Prof, Ed Hist, 61-64, Lectr, Hist Edu, 60-61; El Camino Col, Instr, 56-59; Los Angeles City Col, Instr, 52-57; Univ Southern Cal, Lectr, 53-56, Teaching Asst, Dept Am Civilizations Institutions, 51-53. **HONORS AND AWARDS** Huntington Library, Fel, 60; Guggenheim Found, Fel, 63-64; Fel Cal Hist Soc, 81; Am Philos Soc, Fel, 81; Benemerinti Medal, pontifical honor, 84; Henry R Wagner Mem Awd, CHS, 88; Fel Hist Soc of S Calif, 90; Knight Commander St Gregory, pontifical honor, 94; Distinguished Emer Awd, USC, 94; Order Isabel la Catholica, Spanish Govt., 95; Doyce B Nunis Jr Awd, est by the Historical Soc Southern Cal to honor 37 yrs as editor of its pub, Southern California Quarterly, 96; Oscar Lewis Awd, 98; five distinguished teaching awards, USC. **RESEARCH** Hist of Am West; California; Los Angeles; Hist of Medicine. **SELECTED PUBLICATIONS** Southern California Local Hist: A Gathering of the Writings of W W Robinson, ed, 93; From Mexican Days to the Gold Rush, ed, 93; Tales of Mexican California by Antonio Coronel, ed, 94; Land Policy and Land Use in Southern California, ed, 94; The St Francis Dam Disaster Revisited, ed, 95; Women in the Life of Southern California, ed, 96; Hispanic California Revisited: Essays by Francis F Guest, ed, 96; El Presidio de San Francisco: A History Under Spain and Mexico, 1776-1846, ed, 96; Mission San Fernando Rey de Espana: A Bicentennial Salute, 97. **CONTACT ADDRESS** 4426 Cromwell Ave, Los Angeles, CA 90089-0034.

NUNNALLY, DAVID H., SR.

PERSONAL Born 10/16/1929, Athens Clarke Co, GA, m **DISCIPLINE** EDUCATION **EDUCATION** Union Bapt Inst; Tuskegee Inst; Atlanta U; Univ of GA; Gov State U, MS; Loyal Univ of Chicago, PhD. **CAREER** Kennedy-Ing Coll, counselor; teacher; Jr HS counselor; HS counselor; residential counselor; Sutdent Personnel Ser, dir; Comm Adult HS, asst dir; athletic coach; employment counselor; camp counselor; Georgia Dome, personnel asst. **HONORS AND AWARDS** BSA Outstanding Male Tchr Am Tchr Assn 1964; Martin Luther King Hum Rel Awd Eta Iota Lambda Chap 1970; Man of Yr Eta Iota Lambda Chap & GA Alpha Phi Alpha 1970. **MEMBERSHIPS** Mem PTA; AFT; NEA; Phi Delta Kappa; VFW; APGA; IGPA; ICPA; GAE; past dir Dist IX Assn of Educators; past mem Assn of Educ Bd of Dir; Chicago Hghts Ldrshp Forum; founder Athens Chap Ita Iota Lambda; mem Lions Intl Club; Alpha Phi Alpha; Masonic Lodge; sponsor Comm Ser Club; troop scout master. **CONTACT ADDRESS** 3394 Charlemagne Dr, Decatur, GA 30034.

O

O'BIRECK, GARY M.

PERSONAL Born 06/21/1953, Welland, ON, Canada, m, 1998, 3 children **DISCIPLINE** SOCIOLOGY **EDUCATION** York Univ, North York, Ont, Can, PhD, 94. **CAREER** Brock Univ, St Catherines, Ont, 94-95; Lakehead Univ, Thunder Bay, Ont, 95-96; SUNY Potsdam, 96-. **HONORS AND AWARDS** Teaching Awds: Brock Univ, Lakehead Univ, SUNY Potsdam. **RESEARCH** Troubled youth, criminal justice, deviance, popular culture, victimology. **SELECTED PUBLICATIONS** Auth, " A Canadian Metropolitan Police Force: An Exploratory Case Study Into Application, Training and Advancement Procedures: Subcultural Perspectives," in K. McCormick and L. Visano, eds, Understanding Policing, Toronto: Can Scholars' Press (92); auth, "Getting' Tall": Cocaine Use Within a Subculture of Canadian Professional Musicians: An Ethnographic Inquiry, Toronto: Can Scholars' Press (93); auth, "Preppies and Heavies in Bigtown: Comparative Secondary School Experiences," in G. M. O'Bireck, ed, Not a Kid Anymore: Canadian Youth, Crime, and Subcultures, Toronto: Nelson Canada (96); auth, "Ya Gotta Walk That Walk and Talk That Talk: Youth Subcultures and Gang Violence," in G. M. O'Bireck, ed, Not a Kid Anymore: Canadian Youth, Crime, and Subcultures, Toronto: Nelson Canada (96); ed, Not a Kid Anymore: Canadian Youth, Crime, and Subcultures, Toronto: Nelson Canada (96); auth, "Towards and Understanding of the Typical Arsonist: Revisiting and Synthesizing Sociological, Criminological and Psychological Perspectives in Research," "Gumshoes and Rats: Power, Coercion, and Information Exchange," and "The NoMoS MC: Concentrated Career Criminality by the Age of Eighteen," in G. M. O'Bireck, ed, Insights of Human Social Life: Sociological Perspectives and Analyses, Toronto: Canadian Scholars' Press (2000); ed, Insights of Human Social Life: Sociological Perspectives and Analyses, Toronto: Canadian Scholars' Press (2000); auth, An Introduction to Deviance, Conformity and Social Control, Toronto: Canadian Scholars' Press (2000). **CONTACT ADDRESS** Dept Sociol, SUNY, Col at Potsdam, 44 Pierrepont Ave, Potsdam, NY 13676. **EMAIL** obirecgm@potsdam.edu

O'BRIEN, JEAN

PERSONAL Born 08/17/1950, Berlin, NH, m, 1981, 2 children **DISCIPLINE** SOCIOLOGY **EDUCATION** Univ Mass Amhers, BS; MS; PhD, 81. **CAREER** Prof, Kings Col, 84-. **HONORS AND AWARDS** Psi Chi; Delta Epsilon Sigma; John H.A. Whitman Distinguished Service Prof. **MEMBERSHIPS** APA; APS; SIOP; SHRM. **RESEARCH** Self-esteem, humor, gender studies, family and work issues. **SELECTED PUBLICATIONS** Coauth, "Variations in Trait-Anxiety and Achievement Motivation of College Students as a Function of Classroom Seating Position", J of Exp Educ 61.3 (93); coauth, "Subliminal Psychodynamic Activation", in MacLaboratory for Psychology (3rd Ed) Student Laboratory Manual, eds D. Chute and R. Daniel, Brooks/Cole Pub Co., (Pacific Grove, CA), 94; coauth, "Self-Esteem and Health-Related Behaviors in College Students and Their Parents", Psi Chi J of Undergraduate Res, 96; coauth, "The Sophomore-Junior Diagnostic Project" in Assessment in Practice, eds T. Banta, J. Lund, K. Black and F. Oblander, Jossey-Bass Pub, (San Francisco, CA), 96; coauth, "Perception of a Model's Self-Esteem as a Function of Observer Self-Esteem and Model's Duration of Eye Contact", Psychol Record, 98. **CONTACT ADDRESS** Dept Human Res Management, King's Col, 133 N River St, Wilkes-Barre, PA 18711. **EMAIL** jpobrien@kings.edu

O'CONNELL, DANIEL C.

PERSONAL Born 05/20/1928, Sand Springs, OK, s **DISCIPLINE** EXPERIMENTAL PSYCHOLOGY **EDUCATION** St Louis Univ, AB, 51; St Louis Univ, AM, 53; St Louis Univ, PhL, 52; St Louis Univ, STL, 60; Univ Illinois, PhD, 63 **CAREER** Prof, Georgetown Univ, 90-98; chmn, Dept Pyschol, 91-96; visiting prof, Georgetown Univ, 86, 89, 90; dir, Graduate Prog Cognitive Pyschol, Loyola Univ, 85-89; prof, Loyola Univ, 80-90, 98- **HONORS AND AWARDS** Georgetown Univ Grad School Grant, 97; Georgetown Univ Fac Grant, 91; Humboldt-Stiftung Grant to Germany, 90, 91; Fulbright Fel, Univ Kassel, 79-80; Alpha Sigma Nu Ntl Jesuit Honor Soc, 75; Phi Beta Kappa, 74 **MEMBERSHIPS** Amer Psychol Soc; Amer Psychol Assoc; Midwestern Psychol Assoc; Missouri Psychol Assoc; Illinois Psychol Assoc; Southwestern Psychol Assoc; Eastern Psychol Assoc; Psychonomic Soc; Soc Scientific Study Relig; Amer Assoc Advancement Sci; Amer Assoc Univ Professors **RESEARCH** Psycholinguistics; Temporal Organization of Speech **SELECTED PUBLICATIONS** Coauth, "Theoretical ideals and their violation: Princess Diana and Martin Bashir in the BBC interview," Pragmatics, 97; coauth, "Language use and time," KODIKAS/CODE, 96; coauth, "Language use and dialogue from a psychological perspective," Der Dialogbegriff am Ende des 20. Johrhunderts, 96 **CONTACT ADDRESS** Pyschol Dept, Loyola Univ, Chicago, 6525 N Sheridan Rd, Chicago, IL 60626. **EMAIL** doconn1@luc.edu

O'DAY, EDWARD FRANCIS

PERSONAL Born 04/27/1925, Portsmouth, VA, m, 1961, 5 children **DISCIPLINE** PSYCHOLOGY **EDUCATION** Univ of Florida, PhD 56, MA 54, BS 52. **CAREER** San Diego State Univ, prof, assoc prof, asst prof, 57-86. **HONORS AND AWARDS** Phi Beta Kappa; Phi Beta Phi **CONTACT ADDRESS** Apt# 8093, Livingston, TX 77351-9330.

O'DELL, CYNTHIA D.

PERSONAL Born 02/14/1963, Hellbron, Germany, m, 1991, 2 children **DISCIPLINE** PSYCHOLOGY **EDUCATION** Univ SCar, BS, 85; Emory Univ, MA, 90; PhD, 93. **CAREER** Asst Prof, Ind Univ NW, 95-. **HONORS AND AWARDS** Phi Beta Kappa, 85; ARNO Young Invest Travel Awd, 91. **MEMBERSHIPS** Sigma Xi. **RESEARCH** Development of haptic exploration; Achievement motivation. **SELECTED PUBLICATIONS** Co-auth, "A Vision screening program for use in profoundly retarded populations," Mental Retardation, (93): 154-160; auth, Psychology P316: Psychology of Childhood and Adolescence, A Learning Guide, UN Univ Press, 94; co-auth, "The development of stereoacuity in infant rhesus monkeys," Vision Research, (97): 2675-2684; auth, "A longitudinal assessment of stereoacuity development," Perception, (97): 755-796; auth, Psychology P316: Psychology of Childhood and Adolescence, A Learning Guide 2nd ed, UN Univ Press, 97; auth, Psychology P316: Psychology of Childhood and Adolescence, A Learning Guide 3rd ed, UN Univ Press, 00; co-auth, "Examining memory phenomena through flashbulb memories," Teaching of Psychology, in press; auth, "Yong children's haptic object recognition of shape and texture," Perception and Psychophysics, forthcoming; co-auth, "The normal development of acuity in rhesus monkeys," Investigative Ophthalmology and visual Science, forthcoming; auth, "A longitudinal examination of the development of stereoacuity," Vision Research, forthcoming. **CONTACT ADDRESS** Dept Psychol, Indiana Univ, Northwest, 3400 Broadway, Gary, IN 46408. **EMAIL** codell@iunhaw1.iun.indiana.edu

O'DELL, EARLENE R.
PERSONAL Born 11/09/1940, Bristol, TN, m, 1962, 2 children **DISCIPLINE** ANTHROPOLOGY **EDUCATION** Va Intermont Col, BA 75; E Tenn State Univ, MA, 79; post grad work, Colo State Univ, 93; post grad work, E Tenn State Univ, 95-97. **CAREER** From grad asst to adj instr & researcher, E Tenn State Univ, 78-79; from instr to assoc prof, Northeast State Tech Community Col, 79-. **HONORS AND AWARDS** Alpha Kappa Delta; Pi Gamma Mu; listed in Who's Who Among America's Teachers, 94 & 00. **MEMBERSHIPS** Am Anthrop Asn, Coun on Nutritional Anthrop, Soc for Anthrop in Community Cols. **RESEARCH** Regional Studies, Culture and Foodways. **SELECTED PUBLICATIONS** Auth, "Teaching Anthropology in a Tennessee Cow Pasture," Teaching Anthrop: SACC Notes (97); auth, "The Flavour of Home: A Southern Appalachian Family Remembers, The Overmountain Press, 00. **CONTACT ADDRESS** Dept Humanities & Soc Sci, Northeast State Tech Comm Col, PO Box 246, Blountville, TN 37617. **EMAIL** odell@preferred.com

O'DONNELL, KIM
PERSONAL Born 06/05/1965, Brooklyn, NY, m, 1990, 3 children **DISCIPLINE** PSYCHOLOGY **EDUCATION** New York Univ, BA, 87; Temple Univ, PhD, 95. **CAREER** Psychol Fel, Yale Univ, 92-94; staff psychol, Elmcrest Psychiatric Inst, 94-97; chemn, Naugatuck Valley Com Tech Col, 97-. **HONORS AND AWARDS** Presidential Scholar, New York Univ, 83-87. **MEMBERSHIPS** Am Psychol Asn **RESEARCH** Adolescence; autonomy develop; substance abuse; personality disorders. **SELECTED PUBLICATIONS** Coauth, art, Discrepancies between perceptions of decision making and behavioral autonomy, 91; coauth, art, Toddler language and play in the second year: Stability, covariation and influences of parenting, 92. **CONTACT ADDRESS** Naugatuck Valley Comm-Tech Col, 750 Chase Pky, Waterbury, CT 06708. **EMAIL** kodonnell@nvctc5.commnet.edu

O'LEARY, VIRGINIA
PERSONAL Born 07/03/1943, Washington, DC, m, 1 child **DISCIPLINE** PSYCHOLOGY **EDUCATION** Chatham Col, BA, 65; Wayne State Univ, MA, 67; PhD, 69. **CAREER** Sr res assoc, Wayne State Univ, 69-70; asst prof, assoc prof, Oakland Univ, 70-80; admin, APA, 78-81; dept exec off, APA, 81-84; vis assoc prof, Georg Wash Univ, 85-86; vis assoc prof, Boston Univ, 86-87; vis scholar, Radcliffe Col, 87-89; sr res fel, Mass Inst, 89-90; prof, chmn, Ind State Univ, 90-94; prof, chmn, Auburn Univ, 94-. **HONORS AND AWARDS** Outs Young Wom Am, 76; AWP, Dist Pub Awd, 78, 85; APA, Comm on Women in Psych Leader Cit Awd, 90. **MEMBERSHIPS** Mortar Bd; APA; APS; AWP; SESP; Acad of Manag. **RESEARCH** Women and achievement; resilience and thriving; cross cultural psychology. **SELECTED PUBLICATIONS** Auth, "The Hawthorne effect in reverse: Trainee orientation for hard core unemployed women," J Appl Psych 56 (72): 491-494; auth, "Some attitudinal barriers to occupational aspirations in women: A review of the literature on women in management," Psych Bullet 81 (74): 809-826; co-auth, "Sex as an attributional fact," in Nebraska Symposium on Motivation, ed. T. Sondergegger (NE: Univ Neb Press, 85); auth, Toward understanding women, Brooks/Cole (Monterey, CA), 77; co-ed, Women, gender and social psychology (Hillsdale, NJ: Erlbaum and Associates, 85); co-ed, Storming the tower: Academic women around the world (London: Routledge, 90); co-auth, "Resilience and thriving in response to challenge: An opportunity for a paradigm shift in women's health" Women's Health: Res on Gender, Behav and Pol 1 (95): 121-142; co-auth, "Models of life change and post traumatic growth" in Post-traumatic growth; Theory and research on change in the aftermath of crisis, eds. R. Tedeschi, C. Parks, L. Calhoun (Hillsdale, NJ: Erlbaum, 98); co-auth, " Leadership" in Encyclopedia of Gender, ed. J. Worell (San Diego: Academic Press, forthcoming). **CONTACT ADDRESS** Psych Dept, Auburn Univ, 226 Thatch, Auburn, AL 36849. **EMAIL** olearvi@mail.auburn.edu

O'REILLY, RANDALL C.
PERSONAL Born 03/01/1967, Denver, CO, s **DISCIPLINE** PSYCHOLOGY **EDUCATION** Harvard Univ, AB, 89; Carnegie Mellon Univ, MS, 92; PhD, 96. **CAREER** Asst prof, Univ Colo Boulder, 97-. **HONORS AND AWARDS** Excellence in Teaching Award, CU Neurosci Club, 99; Fel, MIT, 96-97; Fel, Off of Naval Res, 90-93. **MEMBERSHIPS** Am Psychol Asn; Am Psychol Soc; Cognitive Neurosci Soc; Cognitive Sci Soc. **RESEARCH** Specialization of function in and interactions between hippocampus, prefrontal cortex, and posterior neocortex in learning, memory, attention and controlled processing; Visual object recognition in biological systems; Computational and formal models of the biological bases of cognition (computational cognitive neuroscience). **SELECTED PUBLICATIONS** Co-auth, "Dissociated overt and covert recognition as an emergent property of a lesioned neural network," Psychol Rev, (93): 571-588; co-auth, "Hippocampal conjunctive encoding, storage, and recall: Avoiding a tradeoff," Hippocampus, (94): 661-682; co-auth, "Why there are complementary learning systems in the hippocampus and neocortex: Insights from the successes and failures of connectionist models of learning and memory,: Psychol Rev, (95): 419-457; co-auth, "A computational approach to prefrontal cortex, cognitive control, and schizophrenia: Recent developments and current challenges," Philos Transactions of the Royal Soc, (96): 1515-1527; auth, "Biologically plausible error-driven learning using local activation differences: The generalized recirculation algorithm," Neural Computation, (96): 895-938; auth, "Six principles for biologically-based computational models of cortical cognition," Trends in Cognitive Sci, (98): 455-462; co-auth, "Computational principles of learning in the neocortex and hippocampus," Hippocampus, (00): 389-397; auth, "Generalization in interactive networks: The benefits of inhibitory competition and Hebbian learning," Neural Computation, (forthcoming); co-auth, "Conjunctive representations in learning and memory: Principles of hippocampla and cortical function," Psychol Rev, (forthcoming). **CONTACT ADDRESS** Dept Psychol, Univ of Colorado, Boulder, 345 UCB, Boulder, CO 80309-0345. **EMAIL** oreilly@psych.colorado.edu

OATES, JOHN F.
PERSONAL Born 12/12/1944, Colwyn Bay, United Kingdom, s **DISCIPLINE** ANTHROPOLOGY **EDUCATION** Univ Col London, BSc, 66; Univ London, PhD, 74. **CAREER** Res asst, Univ Nigeria, 66-67; teacher, Woodhouse Grammar Sch, 68-69; editorial adviser, Reader's Digest Asn, 69-70; adj res assoc, Rockefeller Univ, 72-73; group head, Life Sciences Group, Mitchell Beazley Multimedia, 73-74; postdoctoral fel, Rockefeller Univ, 75-76; res assoc, Rockefeller Univ, 77-78; vis researcher, Physiological Lab at Univ Cambridge, 78; from asst prof to prof, Hunter Col of City Univ NY, 78-. **HONORS AND AWARDS** NERC res studentship, Univ Col London, 67; USPHS-NIMH res grant, 76; CUNY PSC-BHE Awd, 79; PSC-CUNY Awd, 80, 82, 84, 88, 90, 92, 95, & 97; CUNY Scholar Incentive Awd, 82; Nat Sci Found grant, 82-84 & 85-87; People's Trust for Endangered Species, 93. **MEMBERSHIPS** Am Soc of Primatologists, Asn for the Study of Animal Behav, Asn for Tropical Biol, Int Primatological Soc, Primate Soc of Great Britain, Soc for Conservation Biol, Zoological Soc of London. **SELECTED PUBLICATIONS** Co-ed, Colobine Monkeys: Their Ecology, Behaviour and Evolution, Cambridge Univ Press, 94; auth, African Primates: Status Survey and Conservation Action Plan, IUCN, 96; coauth, "Primate studies at Kakum," in Facing the Storm: Five Years of Research In and Around Kakum National park, Ghana, ed. B. Bailey, (DC: Conservation Int, in press); auth, Myth and Reality in the Rain Forest: How Conservation Strategies are Failing in West Africa, Univ Calif Press, in press; coauth, "New information on the loud calls of black-and-white colobus monkeys, and a reappraissal of their phylogenetic and functional significance," in Old World Monkeys, eds. P. Whitehead and C. Jolly, Cambridge Univ Press (in press); coauth, "African primate communities: determinants of structure and threats to survival," in Primate Communities, eds. J. G. Fleagle, C. Janson, and K. Reed, Cambridge Univ Press (in press). **CONTACT ADDRESS** Dept Anthrop, Hunter Col, CUNY, 695 Park Ave, New York, NY 10021. **EMAIL** joates@hejira.hunter.cuny.edu

OBOLER, REGINA
PERSONAL Born 01/15/1947, Baltimore, MD, m, 1968, 2 children **DISCIPLINE** ANTHROPOLOGY **EDUCATION** Temple Univ, PhD, 82. **CAREER** Supervisor, Swarthmore Col, 82-84; Visiting Asst Prof, Kutztown Univ, 84-88; Asst Prof to Assoc Prof, Ursinus Col, 88-. **MEMBERSHIPS** Am Anthropol Asn, Asn for Feminist Authors, Asn for Africanist Authors, Nat Women's Studies Asn. **RESEARCH** East African pastoralism; Gender; Social change; New and small religions (US) - Neo-paganism. **SELECTED PUBLICATIONS** Auth, Women, Power & Economic Change: The Nandi of Kenya, Stanford Univ Press, 85; auth, The House-Property Complex in African Social Organization - Africa, (94): 342-358; auth, "Whose Cows Are They, Anyway?" Human Ecology, 96; auth, "Is the Female Husband a Man?: Woman/Woman Marriage Among the Nandi of Kenya," Ethnology, (80): 69-88. **CONTACT ADDRESS** Dept Sociol & Anthropol, Ursinus Col, 601 E Main St, Collegeville, PA 19426.

OBRINGER, STEPHEN
PERSONAL Born 09/27/1944, Buffalo, NY, m, 1978, 3 children **DISCIPLINE** EDUCATION, SPECIAL EDUCATION **EDUCATION** Jacksonville Univ, BA, 67; Miss State Univ, MEd, 69; EdD, 72. **CAREER** Teacher, Duval Co Sch Syst, 67-70; Supvr, Spec Educ, Noxubee Sch Syst, 70-71; From Grad Asst to Prof, Miss State Univ, 71-. **HONORS AND AWARDS** Phi Delta Kappa; Fel, Univ Ariz, 85; Outstanding Res Awd, 86; Outstanding Teaching Awd, Miss State Univ, 94. **MEMBERSHIPS** CEC. **RESEARCH** Disabled students. **SELECTED PUBLICATIONS** Coauth, "A Search for Variables Affecting Underidentification of Behavior Disordered Students," J of Behav Disorders, 12 3 (88): 169-174; auth, "The Story of Pedro," Disability and Rehabil J, 1 3 (88): 22-23; auth, "Survey of Perceptions of School Psychologists of the Stanford-Binet IV," Diagnostique 13 2-4 (88): 120-122; coauth, "Rural School - Community Partnerships: We Take Care of Our Own," Rural Spec Educ Quart 13 1 (94): 46-50; coauth, "Eligibility Criteria for Learning Disabilities: An Administrative Case Study," Diagnostique 23 2 (97): 77-86; auth, "Review of Research and Conceptual Literature on the Use of Botox with Individuals with Cerebral Palsy and Related Services," Phys Disabilities: Educ and Related Serv 18 2 (00). **CONTACT ADDRESS** Dept Educ, Mississippi State Univ, 310 Allen Hall, PO Box 9705, Mississippi State, MS 39762. **EMAIL** sjo1@ra.msstate.edu

OETTING, JANNA B.
PERSONAL Born 01/15/1964, Seward, NE, m, 1991, 2 children **DISCIPLINE** CHILD LANGUAGE **EDUCATION** Augustana Col, BA, 86; Univ Kans, MA, 88, PhD, 92. **CAREER** Asst Prof, 92-98, Assoc Prof, La State Univ, 98-. **HONORS AND AWARDS** Nat Asn Am Bus Clubs Student Schol, 87; Colmery O'Neil Veteran's Admin Student Traineeship, 87; Sertoma Student Schol, 87; Dept Speech-Lang-Hearing Grad Clinician Awd, Univ Kans, 88; Kappa Kappa Gamma Student Rehab Schol, Nat Office, 88; Dept Speech-Lang-Hearing Grad Res Awd, Univ Kans, 89; Scheifelbush Grad Student Res Awd, Univ Kans, 92; recipient of numerous research grants and student training grants. **MEMBERSHIPS** Omicron Delta Kappa; Phi Kappa Phi; Am Speech-Lang-Hearing Asn, 88; Soc Res Child Development; Sigma Xi; Int Asn Study Child Lang; La Speech-Lang-Hearing Asn; Int Clinical Phonetics and Ling Asn; Coun Exceptional Children. **RESEARCH** Child language acquisition; language impairments in children; linguistic diversity/dialect. **SELECTED PUBLICATIONS** Coauth, Frequency of input effects on SLI children's Word Comprehension, J Speech & Hearing Res, 94; Quick incidental learning (QUIL) of words by school-age children with and without a language impairment, J Speech & Hearing Res, 95; Past tense marking by children with and without specific language impairment, J Speech, Lang, & Hearing Res, 97; "Identifying language impairmentin the context of dialect," Clinical Ling & Phonetics, 99; auth, "Children with SLI use Syntactic cues to Learn Verbs", J Speech, Lang & Hearing Res (00); auth, "Nonmainstream dialect and SLI", J of Speech, Lang & Hearing Res, (in press). **CONTACT ADDRESS** Louisiana State Univ and A&M Col, M&DA Bldg, Rm 163, Baton Rouge, LA 70803-2606. **EMAIL** cdjanna@lsu.edu

OGLES, ROBERT M.
DISCIPLINE SOCIAL PSYCHOLOGICAL EFFECTS OF MASS COMMUNICATION CONTENT, HISTORY OF MASS **EDUCATION** Univ Wis, PhD, 87. **CAREER** Assoc prof, Purdue Univ. **RESEARCH** History of mass communications. **SELECTED PUBLICATIONS** Auth, Getting Research Out of the Classroom and Into the Newspaper, Col Media Rev, 91; MTV: Music Television in R.G. Picard (ed), The Cable Network Handbk, 93; coauth, Question Specificity in Studies of Television's Contributions to Viewers' Fear and Perceived Probability of Criminal Victimization", Mass Commun Rev, 93. **CONTACT ADDRESS** Dept of Commun, Purdue Univ, West Lafayette, 1080 Schleman Hall, West Lafayette, IN 47907-1080. **EMAIL** rogles@sla.purdue.edu

OGLESBY, JAMES ROBERT
PERSONAL Born 05/30/1941, m **DISCIPLINE** EDUCATION **EDUCATION** SC State Coll, BS 1966; Univ of Missouri-Columbia, MEd 1969, PhD 1972. **CAREER** Jefferson Jr High School, classroom teacher; Univ of Missouri-Columbia, graduate research asst, 69-70, graduate teaching asst, 70-71, coord of space & facilities and asst prof of educ, 72-74, asst prof of educ and asst provost for admin, 74-80, asst prof of educ and dir facilities utilization, beginning 80, Asst to the Chancellor; Prog Dir, Div of Educ Syst Reform, Nat Sci Found. **HONORS AND AWARDS** grant received, Boone County Comm Serv Council (to partially fund a building addition for Columbia Day Care Corp), City of Columbia (to fund a summer youth employment prog titled CARE). **MEMBERSHIPS** Guest lecturer for educ courses Univ of MO-Columbia 1972-; bd dirs Columbia Day Care Corp 1973-; mem Bd of Educ Columbia MO 1974-; mem MO State Teacher's Assn 1974-; mem, 1976-, pres, 1989, Natl Sch Bds Assn; MO School Bd Assn 1977- (holding various positions and serving on numerous bds in both assocs); sec Bd of Trustees Columbia Coll 1978-; mem Ambassador Club 1982-; comm develop consultant on Educ and Politics for Minneapolis MN; consultant Task Force on Governance-Natl Sci Foundation; consultant site visitor Secondary Sch Recognition Program US Dept of Educ. **SELECTED PUBLICATIONS** Published material includes "Education for the Twenty First Century," Natl Science Foundation Comm on Public Educ 1983. **CONTACT ADDRESS** Div of Educ Syst Reform, National Sci Foundation, 4201 Wilson Blvd, Arlington, VA 22230. **EMAIL** joglesby@nsf.gov

OGUNSEITAN, OLADELE
PERSONAL Born 04/04/1961, Ilesa, Nigeria, m, 1994, 2 children **DISCIPLINE** HEALTH SCIENCES **EDUCATION** Univ Ife, Nigeria, BSc, 80; MSc, 82; Univ Tenn, PhD, 88; MPH, Univ Calif, 98; Cert Intl Health, 98. **CAREER** Asst Res Prof to Assoc Prof, Univ Calif, 90-; Fac Fel, Harvard Univ, 99-00. **HONORS AND AWARDS** Nat Youth Service Cert, Nigeria, 80; Am Asn for the Advancement of Sci Enrichment Awd, 87-88; Am Inst for Biol Sci Enrichment Awd, 87; Intl Inst for Educ Step Awd, Washington, 87; Sci Alliance Awd, Univ Tenn, 86, 87, 88; Wesley Foundation Peace Prize, Tenn, 88; Fac Career Dev Awd, Univ CA, 91, 96; Josiah Macy Jr Res Fel, Woods Hole, MA, 99. **MEMBERSHIPS** NY Acad of Sci; Sigma Xi; Am Soc for Microbiol; Genetics Soc of Am; Intl Soc for the Arts, Sci and Technol; Soc for Industrial Microbiol; Am Public Health Asn. **RESEARCH** Environmental health. **SELECTED PUBLICATIONS** Auth, "Protein profile variation in cultivated and native freshwater microorganisms exposed to chemical environmental pollutants," Microbial Ecology 31 (96): 291-304; auth, "Removal of caffeine in sewage by Pseudo-

monas putida: Implications for water pollution index," World Journal of Microbiology and Biotechnology 12 (96): 251-256; auth, "Direct extraction of catalytic proteins from natural microbial communities," Journal of Microbiological Methods 28 (97): 55-63; co-auth, "Tetranucleotide frequencies in microbial genomes," Electrophoresis 19 (998): 528-535; auth, "Protein method for investigating mercuric reductase gene expression in aquatic environments," Applied and Environmental Microbiologhy 64 (98): 695-702; co-auth, "Gender differences in the perception of genetic engineering applied to human reproduction," Social Indicators Research, in press; co-auth, "Mocrobial aminolevulinate dehydratase as a biosensor of lead (Pb) bioavailability in contaminated environments," Soil Biology and Biochemistry, in press; co-auth, "The aminolevulinate dehydratase of Vibrio alginolyticus is resistant to lead (Pb)," Biological Bulletin 197 (99): 283-284; co-auth, "The origin of adaptive mutants in mercury-resistant cultures of Pseudomonas aeruginosa, forthcoming; co-auth, "Microbial community proteomics," in Environmental Molecular Microbiology: Protocols and Applications, in press. **CONTACT ADDRESS** Dept Social Ecol, Univ of California, Irvine, Irvine, CA 92697-0001. **EMAIL** oaogunse@uci.edu

OHIWEREI, GODWIN

PERSONAL Born 08/15/1956, Ibadan, Nigeria, m, 1995, 2 children **DISCIPLINE** SOCIOLOGY **EDUCATION** Dillard Univ, BA, 80; Southern Univ, MA, 80; La State Univ, Phd, 89. **CAREER** Prof, NJ City Univ. **HONORS AND AWARDS** EOF Fac Inst, NJ Inst for Collegiate Teaching & Learning, 94; Scholarship The NJ Project, Drew Univ, 91; Nat Endowment for the Humanities, Univ Wis, 90; Nat Council for Black Studies, Ind Univ, 89. **MEMBERSHIPS** Am Sociol Asn, Asn of Third World Studies, African Studies Asn, Nat Council for Black Studies, Comparative and Intl Educ Soc, nat Asn, for Multicultural Educ. **SELECTED PUBLICATIONS** Co-ed, Urban Issues, New York, 97; ed, Developing Strategies for Excellence in Urban Education, Nova Sci Pub; auth, "Third World Women and the Politics of Feminism," ABAFAZI, 92; auth, "Third World Women and the Politics of Feminism," Women's Studies International Forum, 92; auth, "Restructuring African Economies: Impediments to Privatization," The Horn Review, 92; auth, "Blacks: Physically Superior and Mentally Inferior?," The Metro Forum, 89; auth, "New Wave of Racism in the 1980's," The Metro Forum, 89; auth, "Afrocentricity as an Intellectual Exercise," The Metro Forum, 90. **CONTACT ADDRESS** Dept Sociol, New Jersey City Univ, 2039 Kennedy Blvd, Jersey City, NJ 07305.

OHNUKI-TIERNEY, EMIKO

PERSONAL Born Kobe, Japan **DISCIPLINE** ANTHROPOLOGY **EDUCATION** Tsuda Col, BA, 57; Wayne State Univ, ME, 60; Univ Wisc, MS, 64; PhD, 64. **CAREER** Instructor, Marquette Univ, 68; Visiting Lecturer to Asst Prof, Beloit Col, 70-76; Asst Prof to Prof, Univ Wisc, 77-. **HONORS AND AWARDS** NEH Fel, 99-00; Fel, Harvard Univ, 93; NSF Grant, Stanford, 88-89; NEH Grant, 86-87; Guggenheim Fel, 85-86; HI Romnes Fac Awd, 82. **MEMBERSHIPS** Am Acad of Arts and Sci; Am Anthropol Asn; Royal Anthropol Inst of Great Britain and Ireland; Asn of Soc Anthropol of the Commonwealth. **RESEARCH** Sociolcultural anthropology; Nationalism/totalitarian ideology; Anthropological history. **SELECTED PUBLICATIONS** Auth, The Ainu of the Northwest Coast of Southern Sakhalin, New York, 74; auth, Illness and Healing among the Sakhalin Ainu: A Symbolic Interpretation, Cambridge Univ Press, 81; auth, Illness and Culture in Contemporary Japan: An Anthropological View, Cambridge Univ Press, 84; auth, The Monkey as Mirror: Symbolic Transformations in Japanese History and Ritual, Princeton Univ Press, 87; ed, Culture Through Time: Anthropological Approaches, Stanford Univ Press, 90; auth, Rice as Self: Japanese Identities Through Time, Princeton Univ Press, 93. **CONTACT ADDRESS** Dept Anthropol, Univ of Wisconsin, Madison, 1180 Observatory Dr, Madison, WI 53706. **EMAIL** eohnukit@facstaff.wisc.edu

OLINER, SAMUEL P.

PERSONAL Born 03/10/1930, Poland, m, 1955, 3 children **DISCIPLINE** SOCIOLOGY **EDUCATION** Brooklyn Col, BA, 57; San Francisco State Univ, MA, 65; Univ Calif Berkeley, PhD, 73. **CAREER** Prof to Dept Chair, Humboldt State Univ. **HONORS AND AWARDS** Scholar of the Year Awd, 90. **MEMBERSHIPS** ASA; PSA. **RESEARCH** Altruism; Genocide; Racism and antisemitism. **SELECTED PUBLICATIONS** Auth, The Altruistic Personality: Rescuers of Jews in Nazi Europe, Free Press, 92; auth, Embracing the Other: Philosophical, Psychological, and Historical Perspectives on Altruism, New York Univ Press, 92; co-ed, To ward a Caring Society: Ideas into Action, Praeger, 95; auth, Who Shall Live: The Wilhelm Bachner Story, Acad Chicago Pub, 96; auth, Race Ethnicity and Gender: A Global Perspective, Hunt Pub, 97. **CONTACT ADDRESS** Dept Sociol, Humboldt State Univ, 1 Harpst St, Arcata, CA 95521-4957. **EMAIL** spo1@axe.humboldt.edu

OLITZKY, KERRY M.

PERSONAL Born 12/22/1954, Pittsburgh, PA, m, 1977, 2 children **DISCIPLINE** EDUCATIONAL DEVELOPMENT **EDUCATION** Hebrew Union Col, DHL, 85; Hebrew Union Col, MAHL, 80; Univ S Fla, BA, 74; MA, 75. **CAREER** Vpres, Wexner Heritage Found, 98-99; Ntl Dean of Adult Jewish Learning, Hebrew Union Col, 96-98; Ntl Dir of Res & Educ Development, Hebrew Union Col, 84-97; Dir Grad Studies Prog, Hebrew Union Col, 84-97; executive dir, Jewish Outreach Inst, 00-. **HONORS AND AWARDS** Listed in: Dir of Amer Scholars, Man of the Year, Intl Dir of Distinguished Leadership, Contemporary Auths, Intl Man of Year, Intl Who's Who of Intellectuals, Dict of Intl Biography, Men of Achievement, Who's Who in Relig, Who's Who Among Young American Prof, Who's Who Among Human Services Prof, Who's Who in the East, Who's Who in Amer Educ; Amer Jewish Archives Res & Travel Grant. **MEMBERSHIPS** Advisor, Jewish Alcoholics, Chemically Dependent Persons, and Significant Others Council; Inter-Relig Proj Advisory Council Member, Felician Col; Jrnl of Psychology and Judaism former Special Ed; Shofar Magazine former Exec Ed; Jrnl of Ministry in Addiction and Recovery Ed Board; Jewish Educ News Ed Board; Assoc of Reform Zionist of Amer; Ntl Assoc Temple Educ; Central Conf of Amer Rabbis; UAHC Older Adults Committee; Gerontology Soc of Amer; Committee on Jewish Fam; Joint Commission on Jewish Educ; Assoc for Supervision and Curriculum Develop; Ntl Interfaith Coalition on Aging; Amer Soc on Aging; Assoc of Jewish Studies. **SELECTED PUBLICATIONS** Grief in Our Seasons: A Mourner's Companion for Kaddish, Jewish Lights Pub, 98; Jewish Spiritual Guidance, Jossey-Bass Pub, 97; Rediscovering Judaism: A Course of Study for Adult Bar/Bat Mitzvah, KTAV Pub, 97; The American Synagogue: A Historical Dictionary, Greenwood Pr, 96. **CONTACT ADDRESS** Jewish Outreach Inst, 1270 Broadway, Suite 609, New York, NY 10001. **EMAIL** kolitzsky1@joi.org

OLMSTED, JANE

PERSONAL 3 children **DISCIPLINE** AMERICAN LITERATURE, WOMEN'S STUDIES **EDUCATION** Bowling Green State Univ, BFA; Univ Louisville, MA; Univ Minn, PhD. **CAREER** Prof **RESEARCH** Women Writers. **SELECTED PUBLICATIONS** Auth, The Pull to Memory and the Language of Place in Paule Marshall's The Chosen Place, The Timeless People, and Praisesong for the Widow, African Am Rev, 97; auth, "The Uses of Blood in Leslie Maronon Silko's 'Almanac of the Dead,'" Contemporary Literature, fall 99; auth, "Black Moves, White Ways, Every Body's Blues: Langston Hughes' The Way of White Folks," in Black Orpheus (NY: Garland, 99). **CONTACT ADDRESS** Western Kentucky Univ, 1 Big Red Way, Bowling Green, KY 42101. **EMAIL** jane.olmsted@wku.edu

OLNEY, MARJORIE F.

PERSONAL Born 05/14/1955, Buffalo, NY, s **DISCIPLINE** COMMUNITY HEALTH **EDUCATION** Syracuse Univ, MS, 92; PhD, 95. **CAREER** Asst prof, Univ Ill, 97-. **HONORS AND AWARDS** M.J. Neer Res Grant, 97-98, 00-01. **MEMBERSHIPS** Am Asn on Mental Retardation, Am Asn of Univ Prof, Am Public Health Asn, Am Rehabilitation Coun Asn, Asn for Persons in Supported Employment, Ill Chap of the asn for Persons in Supported Employment, Soc for Disability Studies, TASH. **RESEARCH** Inclusion & accommodation of individuals with disabilities. **SELECTED PUBLICATIONS** Auth, "A controlled study of facilitated communication using computer games," in Contested words, contested science, New York, 97; auth, "The situation of women with developmental disabilities: Implications for practitioners in supported employment," Journal of Applied Rehabilitation Counseling, (98): 3-8; auth, "Proactive lifestyle planning: a way to enhance life choices for injured persons," Journal of Forensic Vocational Assessment, (99): 22-30; auth, "The roles of support staff in the lives of individuals with sever disabilities," Journal of Rehabilitation Administration, (99): 249-257; auth, "The anatomy of commitment: An in vivo study," Mental Retardation, (in press); auth, "Working with autism and other social-communication disorders," Journal of Rehabilitation, (in press). **CONTACT ADDRESS** Dept Cmty Health Professions, Univ of Illinois, Urbana-Champaign, Champaign, IL 61820. **EMAIL** olney@uiuc.edu

OLZAK, SUSAN

PERSONAL Born 12/27/1947, Chicago, IL, m, 1984, 1 child **DISCIPLINE** SOCIOLOGY **EDUCATION** Stanford Univ, PhD, 78. **CAREER** Yale Univ; Cornell Univ; Univ of Ga; prof, Stanford Univ. **SELECTED PUBLICATIONS** Coed, Competitive Ethnic Relations, Academic Pr, (Orlando, FL), 86; coauth, "Ethnic Conflicts and the Rise and Fall of Ethnic Newspapers", Am Sociol Rev 56 (91): 458-474; auth, The Dynamics of Ethnic Competition and Conflict, Stanford Univ Pr, 92; coauth, "Interracial Exposure and Antibusing Activity in Contemporary Urban America", Am J of Sociol 100 (94): 196-214; coauth, "Deprivation and Race Riots: An Extension of Spilerman's Analysis", Social Forces 74 (96): 931-961; coauth, "Poverty, Segregation, and Race Riots, 1960-1993", Am Sociol Rev 61 (96): 590-613; coauth, "Racial Conflict and Protest in South Africa and the United States", European Sociol Rev 14 (98); auth, "Ethnic Protest in Core and Periphery States", Ethnic and Racial Studies 21, (98): 187-217; coauth, "Comparative Methods and Event Analysis: Black Civil Rights Protest in the United States and South Africa", Acts of Dissent: New Developments of the Study of Protest, eds Dieter Rucht, Ruud Koopmans and Friedhelm Neidhardt, Sigma Pr, (forthcoming); auth, Globe Dynamics of Ethnic Mobilization. **CONTACT ADDRESS** Dept Sociol, Stanford Univ, Bldg 120, Stanford, CA 94305.

OMATSEYE, JIM

PERSONAL Born 07/31/1946, Warri, Nigeria, m, 1972, 4 children **DISCIPLINE** PHILOSOPHY, EDUCATION **HONORS AND AWARDS** Vis Fulbright Scholar, Univ of Ky, Ky State Univ 85-86; Vis Prof, Fla International Univ, 94. **MEMBERSHIPS** Am Educ Studies Asn, Mid S Educ Res Asn. **RESEARCH** Phenomenology of Schooling and Education, Multicultural Education. **SELECTED PUBLICATIONS** Auth, "Moral Education: A Saga of Nigeria's Ethical Revolution," in PEAN Yearbook: 1st Education. The Teaching of Moral Values in Nigerian Education, ed. J.A. Akinpelu, Philos of Educ Asn in Nigeria, 84; auth, "Between Development and Educational Policy," J of Educ in Developing Areas, Univ of Port Harcourt (Jan 85); auth, "Philosophy and Education Policy," in J or Educ Policy and J of Educ Studies 1,2, Univ of Jos (88); auth, "Wazobia and Democratic Pluralism," NJEP, Philos of Educ Asn of Nigeria, 91; coauth, "Pre-School and Primary Education in Nigeria," in History and Organization of School and Primary Education - A New International Reference Book, Sch of Early Childhood Educ, Ryerson Polytech Inst Toronto, Ontario, Can, 91; auth, "Towards An Integrated Philosophy of Teacher Education," The Nigerian Teachers, Nat Comn on Col Educ, 94. **CONTACT ADDRESS** Dept Educ Admin, Eastern Kentucky Univ, 521 Lancaster Ave, Richmond, KY 40475. **EMAIL** eduomats@acs.euk.edu

OMOSUPE, EKUA RASHIDA

PERSONAL Born 08/29/1951, Yazoo, MI, m, 1999, 3 children **DISCIPLINE** ENGLISH, WOMEN'S STUDIES **EDUCATION** Univ Colo Colorado Springs, BA, 85; Univ Calif Santa Cruz, MA, 89; PhD, 97. **CAREER** prof, Cabriello Col, 92-. **HONORS AND AWARDS** Cert of Honor, Univ of Calif, Santa Cruz, 97; Who's Who Among am Col Teachers, 98; Santa Cruz County Ethnic Arts Awd, 00; Teacher, Friend, Mentor Awd, Aptos, CA, 00. **MEMBERSHIPS** MLA, Santa Clara Alliance of Black Educators. **RESEARCH** Gay and Lesbian Studies, Cultural Studies, Gender Studies, African American Literature. **SELECTED PUBLICATIONS** Auth, "Differences," Jour of Feminist cult Studies 3.2, (Providence, RI: Brown, 91; auth, From Wedded Wife to Lesbian Lives, Spinsters Aunt Lute Books, (Oakland, CA), 95; auth, Legacy, 97; auth, Quarry West, Collected Poetry Publ, Univ of Calif Santa Cruz, 97. **CONTACT ADDRESS** 21 San Tomas Way, Watsonville, CA 95076. **EMAIL** makua@cruzio.com

ONYEKWULUJE, ANNE B.

PERSONAL Born 07/10/1957, Hutto, TX, m, 1991, 4 children **DISCIPLINE** SOCIOLOGY **EDUCATION** Univ Nebr, Lincoln, PhD, 95. **CAREER** Asst prof of sociol, Western Ky Univ. **HONORS AND AWARDS** ASA Minority Fel; Fac grant Awd; Nat Soc Sci Honor Soc; Nat Sociol Honor Soc; Nat Mathematics Honor Soc; Nat Oral Interpretation Honor Soc. **MEMBERSHIPS** ASA. **RESEARCH** Developing the diversity of adolescents' concept of self. **SELECTED PUBLICATIONS** Coauth with Keith D. Parker, "African-Americans' Perceptions of Violent Crime: A Multivariate Analysis," The Western J of Black Studies, Vol 15, No 3 (fall 19); coauth with Keith D. Parker, "The Influence of Demographic and Economic Factors on Fear of Crime Among African Americans," The Western J of Black Studies, Vol 16, No 3 (fall 92); coauth with Keith D. Parker and Komanduri S. Murty, "African Americans' Attitudes Toward the Local Police: A Multivariate Analysis," J of Black Studies, Vol 25, No 3 (Jan 95); auth, "Multiculturalism, Diversity, and the Impact Parents and Schools Have on Societal Race Relations," The Sch Community J, Vol 8, No 2 (fall/winter 98); auth, "Adult Role Models: Needed Voices for Adolescents Multiculturalism, Diversity, and Race Relations," The Urban Rev, 31:4 (Dec 99); auth, "Multiculturalism: Connecting Race, Class, and Gender to African American Females' Critical Consciousness," (under review); auth, "Black Female Family Heads and Black Male Offspring: Understanding the Effects of Modeling," (in progress); auth, "Race, Class, and Action: Adolescents Redefining Difference," (in progress); auth, "The Global Self and Multiculturalism: A Necessity for the Survival of Humankind," (in progress). **CONTACT ADDRESS** Dept Sociol, Western Kentucky Univ, 1 Big Red Way St, Bowling Green, KY 42101. **EMAIL** anne.onyekwuluje@wku.edu

OPPENHEIMER, MARTIN

PERSONAL Born 07/24/1930, Soest, Germany **DISCIPLINE** SOCIOLOGY **EDUCATION** Templ Univ, BS, 52; Columbia Univ, MA, 53; Univ PA, PhD, 63. **CAREER** Chair, Dept of Sociol & Anthropol, Lincoln Univ, PA, 68-70; assoc prof, Rutgers Univ, 70-. **HONORS AND AWARDS** Fulbright Fels, 82, 98; bd of dirs, Critical Sociol. **MEMBERSHIPS** Eastern Sociol Soc, Am Asn Univ Profs. **RESEARCH** Political sociology, social inequality. **SELECTED PUBLICATIONS** Auth, White Collar Politics, Monthy Rev Press (85); auth, The Sit-In Movement of 1960, Carlson Pub, Inc (89); ed with Rhonda Levine and Martin Murray, Radical Sociologists and the Movement, Temple Univ Press (91); auth, "Rechter Extremismus in den USA," Perspektiven, Univ Frankfurt #28 (summer 96); auth, "Footnote to the Cold War: The Harvard Russian Research Center," Monthly Rev, v 48, no 11 (April 97); auth, "Sociology," in Encyclopedia of the American Left, Oxford Univ Press (98); auth, "Right-Wing Extremism in Germany," New Politics, v VII #2 (winter 99); auth, The State in Modern Society, Promethus/Humanities Press (2000). **CONTACT ADDRESS** Dept Sociol,

Rutgers, The State Univ of New Jersey, New Brunswick, PO Box 5072, New Brunswick, NJ 08903.

ORELLANA, SANDRA
PERSONAL Born 03/06/1941, Fredricksburg, VA, d **DISCIPLINE** ANTHROPOLOGY **EDUCATION** Univ Calif, Los Angeles, BA, 63; MA, 65; MA, 69; PhD, 76. **CAREER** Asst prof to prof, Calif State Univ, Domingues Hills, 73-; instr Univ Calif, Los Angeles, 74-86; res assoc, Cotsen Inst of Archaeol, Univ Calif, Los Angeles, 98-. **HONORS AND AWARDS** Mabel Wilson Richards Teaching Fel, 67-68; Cora Black Fund Grant, 71; Del Amo Found Fel, 77; Res Grant, Am Philos Soc, 79; CSU Res Grant, 80; SBS Dean's Awd for Outstanding Scholar, 88-89. **MEMBERSHIPS** Am Anthrop Assoc; ARCE; Costume Soc; Cotsen Inst of Archaeol, Nat Space Soc; Planetary Soc; Soc for Hist of Tech. Soc for Am Archaeol; Space Tourism Soc. **RESEARCH** Egyptian and Ancient Mayan costume, machine technology, space industrialization. **SELECTED PUBLICATIONS** Auth, "Prehispanic Tzutujil Society", "Postconquest Tzutujil Society" and "Precolumbian Medicine in Highland Guatemala", Historia General de Guatemala, Vol I and II, Guatemala; auth, "Early Medicinal Herbals from Mexico and Guatemala", Katunob, 91; auth, "The Mayas", Columbus Encyclopedia, Simons & Schuster, 92; auth, "Ethnohistory of the Pacific Coast: Prehispanic and Colonial Life in Guatemala and Mexico", Labyrinthos, 95; rev, "Mayan Folklores" by James Sexton, Univ of Okla Pr, 99; auth, Machines and Prime Movers: Technological Development and Social Change From Hellenistic Greece to the End of the Twenty-First Century, (forthcoming); auth, "Female costume in the Usumacinta Region in the Late Classic Period", Ancient Mesoamerica (forthcoming); auth, "Pyramids and Sphinx" and "Palenque", Encyclopedia of the Ancient World, Salem Pr, (forthcoming); **CONTACT ADDRESS** Dept Anthrop, California State Univ, Dominguez Hills, 1000 E Victoria St, Carson, CA 90747-0005. **EMAIL** sorellana@dhvx20.csudh.edu

ORENSTEIN, GLORIA FEMAN
PERSONAL Born New York City, NY, d, 2 children **DISCIPLINE** GENDER STUDIES AND COMPARATIVE LITERATURE **EDUCATION** NYork Univ, PhD. **CAREER** Assoc prof, Univ Southern Calif. **RESEARCH** Feminist Scholar on a Spiritual Quest. **SELECTED PUBLICATIONS** Auth, The Theater of the Marvelous: Surrealism and The Contemporary Stage; The Reflowering of the Goddess; Multi-Cultural Celebrations: Betty La Duke Paintings 1972-1992; co-ed, Reweaving The World: The Emergence of Ecofeminism; coauth, The Women's Salon for Literature in New York, 75-85; auth, The Women of Surrealism. **CONTACT ADDRESS** Col Letters, Arts & Sciences, Univ of So California, University Park Campus, Los Angeles, CA 90089. **EMAIL** orenstei@usc.edu

ORING, ELLIOTT
PERSONAL Born 04/20/1945, New York, NY **DISCIPLINE** ANTHROPOLOGY **EDUCATION** Queens Col, NY, BA, 66; Indiana Univ, MA, 68, PhD, 74. **CAREER** Asst prof, Calif State Univ, Los Angeles, 71-76, assoc prof, 76-80, prof, 80-. **HONORS AND AWARDS** Woodrow Wilson Fel, Soc of Fels of the Am Folklore Soc, Folklore Fel of the Finnish Acad of Sci and Letters, Stirling Awd for Contributions to Psychological Anthropology. **MEMBERSHIPS** Am Folklore Soc, Am Anthropol Asn, Int Soc for Humor Studies, Calif Folklore Soc. **RESEARCH** Folklore, humor, cultural symbolism. **SELECTED PUBLICATIONS** Auth, Israeli Humor: The Content and Structure of the Chizbat of the Palmah, Albany: State Univ of New York Press (81); auth, The Jokes of Sigmund Freud: A Study in Humor and Jewish Identity, Philadelphia: Univ Pa Press (84), 2nd ed, Northvale, NJ: Jason Aronson (97); ed, Humor and the Individual, Los Angeles: Calif Folklore Soc (84); ed, Folk Groups and Folklore Genres: An Introduction, Logan, UT: Utah State Univ Press (86); ed, Folk Groups and Folklore Genres: A Reader, Logan: Utah State Univ Press (89); auth, Jokes and Their Relations, Lexington: Univ Press Ky (92). **CONTACT ADDRESS** Dept Anthropol, California State Univ, Los Angeles, 5151 State Univ Dr, Los Angeles, CA 90032. **EMAIL** eoring@calstatela.edu

ORLANS, HAROLD
PERSONAL Born 07/29/1921, New York, NY, m, 1982, 3 children **DISCIPLINE** ANTHROPOLOGY, EDUCATION **EDUCATION** City Col NYork, BS, 41; Yale Univ, PhD, 49. **CAREER** Sec chmn, NSF, 54-59; sr fel, Brookings Inst, 60-73; sr res assoc, NAPA, 73-83; special asst, US Comm Civil Rights, 83-86; writer, editor, 86-. **HONORS AND AWARDS** SSRC; Fulbright Fel. **MEMBERSHIPS** AHA; MLA; AAAS. **RESEARCH** Higher education; social knowledge; T. E. Lawrence. **SELECTED PUBLICATIONS** Auth, Stevenage, 52; auth, Effects of Federal Programs on Higher Education, 62; auth, The Use of Social Research in Federal Domestic Programs, 67; auth, Science Policy and the University, 68; auth, The Non-Profit Research Institute, 72; auth, Contracting for Knowledge, 73; auth, Private Accreditation and Public Eligibility, 75; auth, Adjustment to Adult Hearing Loss, 85; Lawrence of Arabia, 93; auth, T. E. Lawrence, 02. **CONTACT ADDRESS** 8202 Kenfield Ct, Bethesda, MD 20817-3147. **EMAIL** horlans@erols.com

ORNSTEIN, ALLAN
PERSONAL Born Pittsburgh, PA, 3 children **DISCIPLINE** EDUCATION **EDUCATION** CCNY, BA, 62; Brooklyn Col, MA, 65; NYU, MA, 67, EdD, 70. **CAREER** Prof, St. Johns Univ; consultant-60 higher ed & govt agencies. **HONORS AND AWARDS** Fulbright Hayes Scholar. **RESEARCH** Curriculum, teaching, administration. **SELECTED PUBLICATIONS** Auth, Foundations of Education, 7th ed, Boston: Houghton Mifflin (2000); auth, Strategies for Effective Teaching, 3rd ed, Boston: McGraw-Hill (2000); auth, Educational Administration, 3rd ed, Belmont, CA: Wadsworth (2000). **CONTACT ADDRESS** Dept Curric & Instr, Loyola Univ, Chicago, 1041 Ridge Rd, Wilmette, IL 60091.

ORTNER, SHERRY B.
DISCIPLINE ANTHROPOLOGY **EDUCATION** Bryn Mawr Col, AB, 62; Univ Chicago, MA, 66, PhD, 70. **CAREER** Lectr, 69-70, vis fel, 70-71, Princeton Univ; fac, Sarah Lawrence Col, 71-77; assoc prof, 77-84, prof anthropol, 84-95, chair anthropol, 86-89, prof women's stud, 88-95m, Sylvia L Thrupp prof anthropol & women's stud, 92-94, Univ Mich; prof anthropol, Univ Calif, Berkeley, 94-96; PROF ANTHROPOL, COLUMBIA UNIV, 96-. **CONTACT ADDRESS** Dept of Anthropol, Columbia Univ, 1200 Amsterdam Ave, New York, NY 10027. **EMAIL** sbo3@columbia.edu

ORTON, ARLENE
PERSONAL Born 02/24/1956, Chisholm, MN, s **DISCIPLINE** EDUCATION **EDUCATION** Hibbing Cmty Col, AA, 76; Pillsbury Bapt Bible Col, BS, 80; Central Bapt Theol Sem, MA, 84; Bob Jones Univ, EdD, 93. **CAREER** Prof, Pillsbury Bapt Bible Col, 90-. **MEMBERSHIPS** MAFAA. **RESEARCH** Christian School Principals/Administrators. **CONTACT ADDRESS** Dept Educ, Pillsbury Baptist Bible Col, 315 S Grove Ave, Owatonna, MN 55060. **EMAIL** aaorton@ll.net

OSBORNE, RANDALL E.
PERSONAL Born 09/13/1962, Ft Wayne, IN, m, 1985, 1 child **DISCIPLINE** SOCIOLOGY, BEHAVIORAL SCIENCE **EDUCATION** Ind Univ, BA, 85; Univ Tex, PhD, 90. **CAREER** Vis Asst Prof, Luther Col, 89-90; Asst Prof, Phillips Univ, 90-92; Assoc Prof, Ind Univ, 92-. **HONORS AND AWARDS** Helen Lees Awd for Excellence in Teaching, 96; Teaching Excellence Recognition Awds, 97-99. **MEMBERSHIPS** Coun for Teachers of Undergraduate Psychol, Midwestern Psychol Assoc, APS, APA. **RESEARCH** Biased first impressions, self-concept and self-esteem development and enhancement, personality processes. **SELECTED PUBLICATIONS** Coauth, "The Effects of Motivation and Need for Cognition on Recovery from Biased First Impressions," Int J of Psychol, vol 31, nos 3&4 (91); auth, "You Are What You Think: The Perpetuating Nature of Self-Esteem," Proceedings of the Ind Acad of Sci, 104 (96): 235-241; auth, Self: An Eclectic Approach, Allyn & Bacon (Needham Heights, MA), 96; coauth, "Different I's of Different Beholders: Self-Monitoring and the Categorization of Self and Others," Psi Chi J of Undergraduate Res, 3 (98): 56-68; coauth, A Critical Thinking and Study Guide to Accompany "Lifespan Development - 2nd Edition" by Helen Bee, Longman Publ, 98; coauth, "Student Effects of Service-Learning: Tracking Change Across a Semester," Mich J of Community Serv Learning, 5 (98): 5-13; coauth, "Undergraduate Students: An Untapped Resource," in Proceedings of the 11th Annual Conf on Undergraduate Teaching of Psychol: Ideas and Innovations (98); coauth, Case Analyses for Abnormal Psychology: Learning to Look Beyond the Symptoms, Psychol Pr, 00; coauth, Instructor's Manual for Critical Issues in Lifespan Development, 00; coauth, Critical Issues in Lifespan Development: Issues and Examples for the Helping Professions, Allyn & Bacon (Needham Heights, MA), forthcoming. **CONTACT ADDRESS** Dept Sociol & Behav Sci, Indiana Univ, East, 2325 Chester Blvd, Richmond, IN 47374. **EMAIL** reosborn@indiana.edu

OSTER, JUDITH
DISCIPLINE COMPOSITION AND ENGLISH AS A SECOND LANGUAGE TEACHING **EDUCATION** Case Western Reserve Univ, BA, MA, PhD. **CAREER** English, Case Western Reserve Univ. **HONORS AND AWARDS** Dir, Writing Ctr. **SELECTED PUBLICATIONS** Auth or ed, Toward Robert Frost: The Reader and the Poet; From Reading to Writing: A Rhetoric and Reader. **CONTACT ADDRESS** Case Western Reserve Univ, 10900 Euclid Ave, Cleveland, OH 44106.

OSTERBERG, SUSAN
PERSONAL Born Baltimore, MD, m, 1 child **DISCIPLINE** ARTS EDUCATION **EDUCATION** The Roycemore Sch, 62; Northwestern Univ, BS, 66; Southern Ill Univ, MS, 67; Univ Houston, EdD, 80. **CAREER** Adj prof, Univ Houston, 67-72 & 84-; consult, Houston Independent Sch District, 67-83; teacher, Grissom Elementary Sch, 67-70; teacher, Nina Vance Alley Theatre, 70-85; ed, Opera Cues Magazine, 72-74; res, NEA, 79; arts educator, Am Asn of Univ Women, Int Commun Agency and Sierra Leone Asn of Univ Women, 81. **HONORS AND AWARDS** Zeta Phi Eta, 67-; listed in World Who's Who of Women, 79-85 & 99-00; Notable Women of Tex, 84-85; Woman of the Year, 94-95 & 97-00;listed in Strathmore's Who's Who, 98-99; listed in Two Thousand Notable Am Women, 99; 2000 Millennium Medal of Honor, 99-00; listed in 2000 Outstanding Intellectuals of the 20th Century, 00-01; Outstanding people of the 20th Century, 00-01. **RESEARCH** Arts Education, Gender Communication, Business Communication. **SELECTED PUBLICATIONS** Auth, "Behavioral Objectives in Creative drama," The J of Educ Res (69); auth, Bumper Snickers, I.E. Clark Pub, 78; auth, "Survey of Support for Educational Training and Development by NEA, 1976-1978," Nat Endowment for the Arts (79); auth, "A Study of 1976-1978 Allocation and Use of NEA Grants in Arts Training, Education and Career Development," Nat Endowment for the Arts (79); auth, "A Survey of Arts Administration/Theatre Management programs at the Graduate and Undergraduate Levels in Colleges and Universities in the United States, 1980," Theatre News (81); auth, "Theatre Management/Arts Administration Programs: A Profile," Theatre News (81); auth, "The Arts Are Good for Business," Theatre News (83); auth, A Test for Those Who Quest the Best Bequest, 00. **CONTACT ADDRESS** Dept Arts & Humanities, Univ of Houston, 1 Main Street # 1048 South, Houston, TX 77002-1014. **EMAIL** eosterberg@aol.com

OTHS, KATHRYN S.
PERSONAL Born 10/22/1959, Cincinnati, OH, m, 1992 **DISCIPLINE** ANTHROPOLOGY **EDUCATION** Stanford Univ, BA, 82; Case Western Reserve Univ, MA, 85; PhD, 91. **CAREER** Instr, CWRU, 89-90; Asst Prof to Assoc Prof, Univ Ala, 90-. **HONORS AND AWARDS** Pancoast Travel Fel Awd, 87; Inter-Am Foundation Fel Grant, 88; Nat Sci Foundation Grant, 88; Res Grants Committee Awd, Univ Ala, 93; First Awd, NICHHD, 92-97. **MEMBERSHIPS** Am anthropol Asn, Soc for Applied Anthropol, Soc for Med Anthropol, Soc for the Anthropol of Work, council on the Anthropol of Reproduction. **RESEARCH** Medical decision-making, Reproductive health, Domestic violence, Health beliefs and practices cross-culturally, International health, Chronic illness especially musculoskeletal disorders, Alternative healers, South American populations especially Andean and Brazilian, US populations. **SELECTED PUBLICATIONS** Auth, "A prospective study of psychosocial job strain and birth outcomes," Am Journal of Public Health, forthcoming; auth, Partner influence on unwanted pregnancy, in press; auth, "Social status and food preferences in southeast Brazil," in Contemporary Cultures and Societies of Latin America, 3rd ed, forthcoming; auth, "Seeking early care: The role of prenatal advocates," Medical Anthropology Quarterly, in press; auth, "Debilidad: A biocultural assessment of an embodied Andean illness," Medical Anthropology Quarterly, (99): 286-315; auth, "Assessing variation in health status in the Andes: A biocultural model," Social Science and Medicine, (98): 1017-1030; auth, "Cultural determinants of health behavior," in Handbook of Health Behavior Research, Vol. 1: Determinants of Health Behavior: Personal and Social, Plenum Press, 97; auth, "Ecological and macrolevel influences on illness in northern Peru: Beyond the international health paradigm," in Society, Health and Disease: Transcultural Perspectives, Prentice Hall, 96. **CONTACT ADDRESS** Dept Anthropol, Univ of Alabama, Tuscaloosa, PO Box 870210, Tuscaloosa, AL 35487-0154.

OTTENBERG, SIMON
PERSONAL Born 06/06/1923, New York, NY, m, 1986 **DISCIPLINE** CULTURAL ANTHROPOLOGY **EDUCATION** Univ Wis, Madison, BA (anthropology), 48; Northwestern Univ, PhD (anthropology), PhD, 57. **CAREER** Instr, anthropol, Univ Chicago, 54; instr, anthropology, WA State Col, 54-55; instr to prof, Univ WA, 55-90, Emeritus prof, 90-. **HONORS AND AWARDS** Guggenheim fel, 70-71; NSF grant, 59-60; Social Science res Coun fel, 51-53, 62-63; NEH fel, 78-79; Honorary D of Lit, Univ Nigeria, 92; Leadership award, Arts Coun of the African Studies Asn, 92; Regents fel, Smithsonian Inst, 93-94. **MEMBERSHIPS** Am Anthropological Asn; African Studies Asn; Royal Anthropological Inst. **RESEARCH** Traditional and contemporary African art, ethnicity, change. **SELECTED PUBLICATIONS** Auth, Boyhood Rituals in an African Society: An Interpretation, Univ WA Press, 89; Seeing With Music: The Lives of 3 Blind African Musicians, Univ WA Press, 96; New Traditions from Nigeria: Seven Artists of the Nsukka Group, Smithsonian Inst Press, 97. **CONTACT ADDRESS** 2317 22nd Ave E, Seattle, WA 98112-2604. **EMAIL** otten@homer.u.washington.edu

OTTERBEIN, KEITH F.
PERSONAL Born 05/24/1936, Warren, PA, m, 1965, 1 child **DISCIPLINE** ANTHROPOLOGY **EDUCATION** Pa State Univ, MA, 58; Univ Pa, AM, 60; Univ Pittsburgh, PhD, 63. **CAREER** Asst Prof, Am Univ, 63-64; Asst Prof, Univ Kans, 64-66; Asst Prof to Prof, SUNY, 67-. **MEMBERSHIPS** Am Anthropol Asn, Soc for Cross-cultural Res, Am Ethnol Soc, Asn for Polit and Legal Anthropol, Buffalo Soc of Nat Sci, Buffalo and Erie County Hist Soc, Warren County Hist Soc, Niagara County Hist Soc, Old Fort Niagara Asn. **RESEARCH** Political anthropology: Warfare, Feuding, Crime, Caribbean: Bahamas, West Africa and American South; social structure: family organization, folk housing, architecture, Comparative research. **SELECTED PUBLICATIONS** Auth, When War Began, Westview Press, forthcoming; auth, "Crime," in The Encyclopedia of Cultural Anthropology, New York, 96; auth, "Feuding," in The Encyclopedia of Cultural Anthropology, New York, 96; auth, "The Origins of War," Critical Review, (97): 251-277; auth, "Clan and Tribal Conflict," Encyclopedia

of Violence, Peace, and Conflict, 99; auth, "War," in Reader's Guide to the Social Sciences, 00; auth, "The Killing of Captured Enemies: A Cross-cultural Study," Current Anthropology, in press; auth, "Dueling," Martial Arts in International Perspective: An Encyclopedia, forthcoming. **CONTACT ADDRESS** Dept Anthropol, SUNY, Buffalo, PO Box 610005, Buffalo, NY 14261-0005.

OUSLEY, CHARLES
PERSONAL Born 08/09/1938, Picher, OK, m, 1973, 1 child **DISCIPLINE** SOCIOLOGY **EDUCATION** Univ Okla, BA, 74; Golden Gate Univ, MS, 76; Pac Western Univ, PhD, 89. **CAREER** Chief of Police, Seminole St Col PD, 92-97; Dir and Prof, Seminole St Col, 89-. **HONORS AND AWARDS** Who's Who in Am Law Enforcement, 76; Distinguished Serv Medal, OSBI, 78; Grad Gold Key Awd, Am Criminal Justice Asn, 97. **MEMBERSHIPS** ACJA, OPOA. **RESEARCH** All areas of law enforcement. **SELECTED PUBLICATIONS** Auth, Wyoming Law Enforcement Officers Killed in the Line of Duty 1878-1985; auth, Law Enforcement's Responsibilities in Investigating Incidents of Child Abuse; auth, Postal Security Officer Defensive Tactics. **CONTACT ADDRESS** Dept Sociol, Seminole State Col, PO Box 351, Seminole, OK 74818. **EMAIL** ousley_b@ssc.cc.ok.us

OVERBECK, T. JEROME
PERSONAL Born 11/21/1946, Cincinnati, OH, s **DISCIPLINE** LITURGICAL THEOLOGY, COUNSELING PSYCHOLOGY **EDUCATION** Loy Univ, AB, 70; Xavier Univ, M Ed, 72; Jes Sch Theol, M Div, 74; ThM, 75; STL, 82; Grad Theol Union, PhD, 83. **CAREER** Liturgist, Loy Univ, 83-. **HONORS AND AWARDS** Fac Fel, Univ Cal; Who's Who, Midwest, Religion; Alpha Epsilon Delta; W Daniel Conroyd Awd; Outstand Ser to Stud Awd; Excell in Teach Awd; Golden Key Hon Soc; Fav Fac Mem Recog, 97, 98; Dist Fac, 92, 93; Dir Am Schls; Alpha Sigma Nu. **MEMBERSHIPS** ACA; ASCA; AJL; LC; NAAL; SL. **RESEARCH** How culture impacts the warp people formulate their myth and ritual. **SELECTED PUBLICATIONS** Auth, "The Cross," "Sacred Vessels," "Eucharistic Chapel, ""Reconciliation Room," in The New Dictionary on Sacramental Worship (Collegeville: Liturgical Press, 90); auth, "Theses on Art and Environment for Christian Worship Space," Mod Lit 18 (91): 20-23; auth, Liturgical consultant for Come, Follow Me, Benzinger Pub (Mission Hills, CA), 91; auth, "Building and Renovating a Church: Well Begun Is More Than Half Done," Mod Lit 19 (92): 14-16; auth, "The Way We Pray," Loyola (95): 16-19; auth, "How Sacred Is Your Sacred Space?" Mod Lit 25 (98): 6-8; auth, Ancient Fonts Modern Lessons, Liturgy Training Pub (Chicago), 98; coauth, "Unhealthy Attitudes: Colleges Try to Make Student Care A More Popular Subject," Chic Tribune, Edu Today 5 (00): 18; coauth, Preparing a Catholic Wedding: Contemporary Parables, forthcoming. **CONTACT ADDRESS** Dept Theology, Loyola Univ, Chicago, 6526 N Sheridan Rd, Chicago, IL 60626-5344.

OVERMIER, J. BRUCE
PERSONAL Born 08/02/1938, Queens, NY, 1 child **DISCIPLINE** PSYCHOLOGY **EDUCATION** Kenyon Col, AB, 60; Bowling Green State Univ, MA, 61; Univ Pa, PhD, 65. **CAREER** Prof of psychol, Univ Minn, 65-; ed, Learning & Motivation, 73-76; consulting ed, J of Experimental Psychol, 71-74, 88-; assoc ed, Am Psychol, 93-; assoc ed, J of Int Psychol, 94-97. **HONORS AND AWARDS** Fulbright-Hayes Fel, 80; Fogarty Sr Fel, 84; James McKeen Cattell Fel, 85; Norwegian Marshall Fel, 87; Scholar of the Col, Univ Minn, 89; Pres, APA Behav Neurosci, 90-91; Pres, APA Experimental Psychol, 92-93; Pres, Pavlovian Soc, 96; Pres, Minn Soc of Sigma Xi, 96; Doc of Sci (hon), 90; Sigma Xi Nat Distinguished Lect, 99-2000. **MEMBERSHIPS** Am Psychol Asn, Am Psychol Soc, Nat Academy of Sci, Psychonomic Soc. **SELECTED PUBLICATIONS** Auth, "Psychological determinants of when stressors stress," in D. H. Hellhammer, I. Florin, & H. Weiner, eds, neurobiological Approaches to Human Disease, Hans Huber (88); coauth with R. Murison, "Parallelisms among stress effects on ulcer, immunosupression, and analgesia: Commonality of mechanisms?," J of Physiobiol (Paris), 87 (93): 253-259; coauth with M. P. McDonald, E. E. Dahl, P. Mantyh, and J. Cleary, "Effects of exogenous-beta-amyloid on memory," Behav & Neural Biol, 62 (94): 60-67: coauth with B. Joseph & T. I. Thompson, "Equivalence relations and differential outcomes in adults with Prader-Willi syndrome," Am J of Mental Retardation,101 (97): 374-386; coauth with V. M. LoLordo, "Learned Helplessness," in W. O'Donohue, ed, Learning and Behavior Therapy, Ch. 17, Allyn & Bacon (97); coauth with D. R. Linden and L. M. Savage, "General learned irrelevance: A Pavlovian analog to learned helplessness," Learning & Motivation, 28 (97): 230-247; coauth with M. P. McDonald, "Present Imperfect: A critical review of animal models of the mnemonic impairments in Alzheimer's disease," Neurosci & Behav Revs, 22 (98): 99-120; coauth with R. Murison, "Animal models reveal the 'psych' in the psychosomatics of peptic ulcer," Current Directions in Psychol Res, 6 (97): 180-184; coauth, "Psychoneuroimmunology: The final hurdle," Integrative Physiological and Behav Sci, 33 (98): 137-140; coauth with L. K. Langley, D. S. Knopman & M. M. Prod'homme, "Inhibition and habituation: Preserved mechanisms of attentional selection in aging and Alzheimer's Disease," (98). **CONTACT ADDRESS** Dept Psychology, Univ of Minnesota, Twin Cities, 75 E River Rd, N-128 Elliott Hall, Minneapolis, MN 55455.

OVERSTREET, CHARLES
PERSONAL Born 04/04/1955, Wichita, KS, s, 3 children **DISCIPLINE** PSYCHOLOGY **EDUCATION** Univ Tex, BS, 80; MS, 84; PhD, 90. **CAREER** Director Adult Psychiatry, St Joseph Hosp, 90-94; Prof, Tarrant County Col, 95-. **HONORS AND AWARDS** Excellence in Teaching Awd, Univ Tex. **MEMBERSHIPS** Am Psychol Asn, Am Asn of Marriage and Family Therapists. **RESEARCH** Family violence. **CONTACT ADDRESS** Dept Beh Sci, Tarrant County Junior Col, 5301 Campus Dr, Fort Worth, TX 76119. **EMAIL** covers@dl.tccd.net

OZORAK, ELIZABETH WEISS
PERSONAL Born 06/12/1957, Tacoma Park, MD, m, 1 child **DISCIPLINE** PSYCHOLOGY **EDUCATION** Wesleyan Univ, BA, 78; Harvard Univ, MA, 83, PhD, 87. **CAREER** Assoc prof of Psychology, chair, Dept of Psychol, Allegheny Col. **HONORS AND AWARDS** Phi Beta Kappa, 77; Psi Chi, 90. **MEMBERSHIPS** APS; NSEE; SSSR. **RESEARCH** Religious beliefs, practices and commitment; religious identity. **SELECTED PUBLICATIONS** Auth, Social and Cognitive Influences on the Development of Religious Beliefs and Commitment in Adolescence, J for the Scientific Study of Relig, 28, 89; The Power, But Not the Glory: How Women Empower Themselves Through Religion, J for the Scientific Study of Relig, 35, 96; Women's Faith and Women's Lives: The Connections Between Psychology and Theology, Explorations, 14, 96; In the Eye of the Beholder: A Social-Cognitive Model of Religious Belief, in B Spilka & D McIntosh, eds, The Psychology of Religion: Theoretical Approaches, Westview, 96. **CONTACT ADDRESS** Dept of Psychology, Allegheny Col, 520 N Main St, Meadville, PA 16335. **EMAIL** eozorak@allegheny.edu

P

PACHECO, PAUL J.
PERSONAL Born 09/25/1961, Salt Lake City, UT, m, 1998, 4 children **DISCIPLINE** ANTHROPOLOGY **EDUCATION** Univ Utah, BS, 83; Ohio State Univ, MA, 85; PhD, 93. **CAREER** Adj Prof, Kent State Univ, 94-99; Asst Prof, SUNY, 99-. **HONORS AND AWARDS** Ohio Hist Preservation Awd, 93; US Senate Page, 77. **MEMBERSHIPS** Soc for Am Archaeol, Ohio Archaeol Coun. **RESEARCH** Hopewell/Middle Woodland; Late prehistoric cultures of Eastern woodlands, settlement and social change. **SELECTED PUBLICATIONS** Ed, Ohio Hopewell Community Organization, Kent State Univ Press, 97; co-auth, "A Community Model of Ohio Hopewell Settlement," in Ohio Hopewell Community Organization, Kent State Univ Press, 97; auth, "The Legacy of the Moundbuilders: An Overview of Early and Middle Woodland Archaeology in the Licking River Basin," in Vanishing Heritage: The Story of Archaeology in Licking county, 92; co-auth, "A Laterally Hafted Ohio Hopewell Bladelet from Dow Chemical #2," Ohio Archaeologist, (92): 12-15; auth, "Ohio Hopewell Settlement Patterns: An Application of the Vacant Center Model to Middle Woodland Period Intracommuity Settlement Variability I the Upper Liking River Drainage," Ohio State Univ, 93; ed, A View From the Core: A Synthesis of Ohio Hopewell Archaeology, Ohio Archaeol Couno, 96; auth, "Ohio Hopewell Regional Settlement Patterns," in A View From the Core: A Synthesis of Ohio Hopewell Archaeology, Ohio Archaeol Coun, 96; co-auth, "Variation in the Limb bones of Terminal Late Archaic Populations of Ohio," Midcontinental Journal of Archeology, (99): 247-271. **CONTACT ADDRESS** Dept Anthropol, SUNY, Col at Geneseo, 1 College Circle, Geneseo, NY 14454. **EMAIL** pacheco@geneseo.edu

PADILLA, YOLANDA C.
PERSONAL Born 02/17/1957, Adrian, MI, m, 1983, 2 children **DISCIPLINE** SOCIOLOGY **EDUCATION** Univ Tex, BA, 79; MS, 80; Univ Mich, MA, 90; PhD, 92. **CAREER** From Fac Assoc to Assoc Prof, Univ Tex, 95-. **HONORS AND AWARDS** Psi Chi; Phi Alpha; Rackham Merit Doctoral Fel, Univ Mich, 88-92. **MEMBERSHIPS** CSWE, ALSWE, ASA, SSSP, NACCS. **RESEARCH** Population studies with focus on Latino social stratification and social mobility and the implications for all aspects of social well being and social welfare policy, social work and Latino studies with an emphasis on poverty and immigration, the design of human services for multicultural populations, social welfare policy analysis, social services administration and community development. **SELECTED PUBLICATIONS** Auth, "The Influence of Family Background on the Educational Attainment of Latinos," New Eng J of Public Policy, 11:2 (96): 1-12; auth, "Participation Patterns of Persons with Disabilities in Welfare-to-Work Programs," SCI Psychosocial Process, 10:3 (97): 81-88; auth, "Considering the Explanations for the Poor Labor Market Outcomes of Mexican Immigrants," Reflexiones 1997: New Directions in Mex Am Studies, 1 (98): 109-132; coauth, "Inter-Agency Collaboration in an International Setting," Admin in Soc Work, 22:1 (98): 65-81; auth, "A Study of Latino Internal Migration in the Context of the Socioeconomic Life Cycle," Latino Studies J, 9:2 (99): 45-73; coauth, "Community-Based Research in Policy Planning: A Case Study--Addressing Poverty in the U S-Mexico Border Region," J of Community Practice, 6:4 (99): 1-22; coauth, "Variations in the Process of Earnings Attainment Among Mexican Immigrants and Natives," Hisp J of Behav Sci (forthcoming); auth, "The Social Ecology of Child Development in the Mexican American Population: Current Theoretical and Empirical Perspectives," J of Human Behav in the Soc Environ (forthcoming). **CONTACT ADDRESS** Dept Sociol, Univ of Texas, Austin, 1925 San Jacinto Blvd, Austin, TX 78712. **EMAIL** ypadilla@mail.utexas.edu

PAGE, JOHN BRYAN
PERSONAL Born 10/27/1947, Charlotte, NC, m, 1976, 1 child **DISCIPLINE** ANTHROPOLOGY **EDUCATION** Univ Fla, BA, 69; Univ North Carolina, MA, 71; Univ Fla, PhD, 76. **CAREER** res assoc prof, Univ Miami, 85-92; assoc dir, Bio Stud AIDS, 87-91; dept dir, Bio Stud AIDS, 91-92; res prof, dept psychia, 92-93; prof, anth/psychia, 93-; dept ch, 99-. **MEMBERSHIPS** AAA; SAA; Phi Mu Alpha. **RESEARCH** Street based drug use; HIV/AIDS; immigration; development. **SELECTED PUBLICATIONS** Coauth, "AIDS, IV Drug Use, and the Federal Agenda," in Handbook on Drug Control in the United States ed. JA Inciardi (Westport, CT: Greenwood Press, 90), 267-282; coauth, "The Risk of Exposure to HIV contaminated needles in shooting galleries," in The American Drug Scene, ed. Karen McElrath (Roxbury Press, 95), 277-283; coauth, "Homeless Adults and Crack," in The American Pipe Dream, eds. DD Chitwood, JE Rivers, JA Inciardi (NY: Harcourt Brace Coll Pub, 96), 104-114; coauth, "Medication therapy among intravenous drug users (IDUs) with HIV infection," AIDS Patient Care 10 (96): 101-110; coauth, "Cognitive correlates of chronic cannabis use in Costa Rican Men," Archives Gen Psych 53 (96):1051-1057; coauth, "HIV Counseling for Haitian Women: Culturally Sensitive Approaches," Health Edu Behavior 24 (97):736-745; coauth, "Skills for HIV Risk Reduction: Evaluation of Recall and Performance in Injecting Drug Users," Substance Use and Misuse 32 (97): 229-247; auth, "Needle Exchange and Reduction of Harm: An Anthropological View," Med Anthro 18 (97):1-21; coauth, "Use of Needles and Syringes in Miami and Valencia: Observations of High and Low Availability," Med Anthro Quart (98). **CONTACT ADDRESS** Dept Anthropology, Univ of Miami, PO Box 248106, Miami, FL 33124. **EMAIL** bryan.page@miami.edu

PAGE, PATRICIA
PERSONAL Born 11/11/1923, Melrose, MA **DISCIPLINE** SOCIOLOGY; RELIGIOUS EDUCATION **EDUCATION** Smith Coll, AB 45; Harvard Graduate School of Education, EdM, 74; NYork Univ, PhD, 86 **CAREER** Dir of Christian Education Episcopal Church Parishes in North Carolina and Maine 46-55; Chaplain, Episcopal Church Smith Coll, 55-63; Advisor in Christian Education Dioces of Zamia, 63-73; Dir, Natl Inst Lay Training New York, 75-80; Prof Educ and Dir of Continuing Educ, Church Divinity Sch of the Pacific, 80-89. **HONORS AND AWARDS** Honorary Doctor of Divinity, 89; Nat Network of Lay Professionals at the Episcopal Church Ruth Schmidt Awd. **MEMBERSHIPS** Assoc of Profs and Researchers in Religious Educ; Network of Lay Profs of the Episopal Church; Ministry in Daily Life **RESEARCH** Adult Religions Educ; History of Episcopal Church Women; Theology and practice of ministry. **SELECTED PUBLICATIONS** All God's People Are Ministers, Augsburg Press, 93. **CONTACT ADDRESS** 715 Shepherd St., Durham, NC 27701. **EMAIL** pnpage@juno.com

PAGE, ROGER A.
PERSONAL Born 03/01/1947, Flint, MI **DISCIPLINE** PSYCHOLOGY **EDUCATION** Mich State Univ, BS, 69; Ohio State Univ, MA, 73; PhD, 75. **CAREER** Prof, Ohio State Univ, 75-. **HONORS AND AWARDS** Clark Hull Awd, 99; Outstand Schl Awd, OSU, 93. **MEMBERSHIPS** APA; ASCH. **RESEARCH** Hypnotic after effects; measuring hypnotic susceptibility. **SELECTED PUBLICATIONS** Auth, "Longitudinal evidence for the sequentiality of Kohlberg' s stages of moral judgment in adolescent males," J Genetic Psychol 139 (81): 3-9; auth, " An attempt to induce lower moral hypnotic and task-motivated age regression," J of Psychol 122, (88): 119-131; coauth, "The Rapid Induction Susceptibility Scale," Psychology: A Journal of Human Behavior 26 (89): 49-55; auth, "Clark Hull and his roll in the study of hypnosis," Am J Hypnosis 34 (92): 178-184; coauth, "What do reports of hypnotic experiences tell us? "Contemporary Hypnosis 11 (94): 121-130; auth, "Is differential item difficulty specific to hypnosis?" Am J Clinical Hypnosis 36 (94): 258-265; auth, "Mental imagery, hypnotizability, differential item difficulty, and context effects, " Am J of Clinical Hypnosis 41 (98): 162-167; auth, "Identifying hypnotic sequelae: The problem of attribution," Am J Clinical Hypnosis 41 (99): 316-318. **CONTACT ADDRESS** Dept Social Sci, Ohio State Univ, Lima, 4240 Campus Dr, Lima, OH 45804. **EMAIL** page.6@osu.edu

PAILLIOTET, ANN WATTS
PERSONAL Born 10/10/1955, Long Beach, CA, s **DISCIPLINE** EDUCATION, ENGLISH **EDUCATION** Col Santa Fe, BS; Syracuse Univ, MS, 92, PhD, 95. **CAREER** Asst prof

of Educ, Whitman Col, Wall Walla, Wash, 95-. **HONORS AND AWARDS** Grad Doctoral Fel, Syracuse Univ, 3 year Awd; Nat Reading Conf Grad Res Awd; Grad Convocation Speaker, Sch of Educ, Syracuse Univ; Masters Thesis Awd, Syracuse Univ Gad Sch; Syracuse Univ Sch of Educ Res Apprenticeship Awd; Whitman Col 1999 Ball Advising Awd; Nat Sci Found Grant; Col Composition and Commun Citation for Outstanding Classroom Practice. **MEMBERSHIPS** Am Educ Res Asn, Assembly on Media Arts, Asn of Teacher Educators, Nat Coun of Teachers of English, Nat Media Educators, Phi Delta Kappa, American Mensa Ltd, Nat Alliance for Media Arts and culture, WORD (Washington Int Reading Asn). **RESEARCH** Media literacy, technology, preservice teacher education. **SELECTED PUBLICATIONS** Auth, "Deep Viewing: Intermediality in Teacher Education," in Intermediatality: The Teachers' Handbook of Critical Media Literacy, L. Semali and A. Watts Pailliotet, eds, Westview/Harper Collins (98): 31-51; co-ed with L. Semali, Intermediatality: The Teachers' Handbook of Critical Media Literacy, L. Semali and A. Watts Pailliotet, eds, Westview/Harper Collins (98); coauth, "Preparing the Post-Formalist Practitioner: Pitfalls and Promises," in J. Kincheloe & S. Steinberg, eds, Prethinking Intelligence: Confronting psychological assumptions about teaching and learning, Routledge (99): 165-88; coauth, "Standards of Complexity in Preservice education," in The Encyclopedia of Educational Standards, Joe L. Kincheloe, Shirley R. Steinberg, and Dan Weil, eds, Garland (forthcoming); coauth, "Intermediality: Path to Critical Media Literacy," The Reading Teacher (forthcoming); coauth, "Recommended Print and Electronic Resources for Teaching about Media and Technology in the K-12 Classroom," Reconceptualizing Literacy in the Media Age, JAI/ABLEX/Elsevier Press (forthcoming); auth, "Reconceptulaizing Literacy in the Media Age: The 4 I's of Media Literacy," Reconceptualizing Literacy in the Media Age, JAI/Ablex/Elsevier Press (forthcoming); co-ed, Reconceptualizing Literacy in the Media Age, JAI/Ablex/Elsevier Press (forthcoming); invited section ed, Reading On-Line: "New Literacies," 99-2002. **CONTACT ADDRESS** Dept Educ, Whitman Col, 122 Maxey Hall, Walla Walla, WA 99362. **EMAIL** pailliaw@whitman.edu

PAINTER, LORENE H.
PERSONAL Born 08/16/1932, Catabwa Co, NC, m, 1950, 2 children **DISCIPLINE** EDUCATION **EDUCATION** Lenour-Rhyne Col, AB, 53; Appalachain State Univ, MA, 57; Univ NC at Greensboro, EdD, 80. **CAREER** Teacher, Taylorsville Sr High Sch, 53-54; teacher, Col Park Jr High, 54-59; From Instr to Full Prof, Lenoir-Rhyne Cp; Hickory NC, 59-. **HONORS AND AWARDS** Scholar Grants, Lutheran Church in Am, 75; Delta Kappa Gamma NC State Scholar Recipient for Grad Study, 78; Who's Who in AM Educ; Who's Who in Am Women. **MEMBERSHIPS** DKG, Asn for Supervision and Curric Develop, Am Asn for Col and Teacher Educ. **RESEARCH** Secondary Innovations, Middle School Education, Character/values Education, Reading and Writing in Content Areas. **SELECTED PUBLICATIONS** Auth, Guide to Secondary Student teaching, Manual of practicum assignments unique to Lenoir-Rhyne Col, revised annually, 64-95; auth, "From Machiavelli to Martians: The Challenge of Department Chairmanship," NC English Teacher (Spring 68); auth, "A Short Course in Compassion: Learning About Human Nature Through Reading," Bul of Delta Kappa Gamma Int (Spring 73); auth, "The Role of the Supervising Teacher," ERIC Microfiche, 74; auth, "Social-Emotional Impact of Selected English Curricula on Secondary Students," ERIC Microfiche, 77; auth, "Developing Competent Cooperating Teachers: A Challenge to Teacher Education," Col and Univ Teaching (Winter 79); auth, "Teaching English Language and Study Skills to the Vietnamese," NC English Teacher (Fall 79). **CONTACT ADDRESS** Dept Educ, Lenoir-Rhyne Col, 743 6th St N E, Hickory, NC 28601.

PALEN, J. JOHN
PERSONAL Born 02/24/1939, Dubuque, IA, m, 1962, 3 children **DISCIPLINE** SOCIOLOGY **EDUCATION** Univ Notre Dame, BA, 61; Univ Wis, MA, 63; PhD, 67. **CAREER** Vis Prof, Nat Univ Singapore, 82-83; Asst to Full Prof, Univ Wis; Prof, Va Commonwealth Univ; Dept Chair, Va Commonwealth Univ, 86-92. **HONORS AND AWARDS** Distinguished Scholar Awd, Virginia Commonwealth Univ Col, 94; Distinguished Fulbright Lecturer, Univ Calgary, 97-98; USIA Univ Program, va commonwealth Univ, 94; Fulbright Foundation, Taiwan, 92; Nat Sci Foundation, Singapore, 85; Grant, Rockefeller foundation, Singapore, 85; Grant, United Nations fund for Population Activities, 85. **MEMBERSHIPS** Am Sociol Asn, Population Asn of Am, Urban Affairs Asn. **RESEARCH** Urban sociology, Urban ecology, Population. **SELECTED PUBLICATIONS** Auth, Social Problems for the Twenty-first Century, New York, 00; auth, "Suburbanization," in Encyclopedia of Housing, Thousand Oaks, 98; auth, The Urban World, 5th ed., New York, 97; auth, "Some comparisons between Taiwan and the United States," in The Urban Society of Taiwan, Taiwan, 97; auth, "The Suburban Revolution," sociological Focus, 96; auth, The Suburbs, New York, 95; auth, Gentrification, Dislacement, and Neighborhood Revitalization, New York, 85; auth, City Scenes: Problems and Prospects, 2nd ed., Boston, 81; auth, Social Problems, New York, 79; auth, Urban America, New York, 72. **CONTACT ADDRESS** Dept Sociol & Anthropol, Virginia Commonwealth Univ, Box 842040, Richmond, VA 23284. **EMAIL** jpalen@saturn.vcu.edu

PALLEY, HOWARD A.
PERSONAL Born 03/22/1936, New York, NY, m, 1961, 2 children **DISCIPLINE** SOCIAL WORK **EDUCATION** Brooklyn Col, BA, 57; Yeshiva Univ, MS, 59; Syracuse Univ, PhD, 63. **CAREER** Grad teaching asst, Syracuse Univ, 59-61; asst prof, Paterson State Col, 62-65; asst prof, Univ Wis at Milwaukee, 65-66; assoc prof, Adelphi Univ, 66-70; grad fac member, Univ Md, 71-; vis prof, Hebrew Univ, 78; vis scholar, Brookdale Inst of Gerontology and Adult Human Behav, 85; vis prof, Hadassah-Hebrew Univ, 85; Fulbright vis prof, Chung-Ang Univ, 90; from assoc prof to prof, Univ Md, 70-. **HONORS AND AWARDS** Nat Ctr for Educ in politics Fel, 61-62; Ford Fac Res Fel, 64; Nat Sci Found Grant, 65; Res Grant, Bureau of Family Services, 67; Res Grant, Univ of Md, 73 & 74; Sabbatical Grant, Univ Md, 78; World Health Orgn Fel, 84; Sabbatical Grant, Univ Md, 85 & 93-93; DRIF Grant, Univ Md, 87-88 & 90-92; Nat Inst on Aging Travel Grant, 89; Fulbright Res Awd, 90; Geriatrics and Gerontology Educ and Res Prog Grant, Univ Md, 93-95; listed in Who's Who in the East, 97-99. **MEMBERSHIPS** Am Asn of Univ Professors, Am Political Sci Asn, Coun on Soc Work Educ, Nat Asn of Soc Workers, Pi Sigma Alpha, Policy Studies Orgn. **RESEARCH** Social Policy Analysis, Comparative Social Policy, Social Policy and Health Care, Long-Term Care Policy. **SELECTED PUBLICATIONS** Coauth, Urban American and Public Policies, D. C. Heath (Lexington, MA), 77; auth, "A Survey of the Service Needs of Caregivers of Alzheimer's Disease Patients in Maryland's Capital Area," Am J of Alzheimer's Disease 11 (96): 20-24; coauth, "Work, Welfare and the Attack on the Welfare State," Scandinavian J of Soc Welfare 5 (96): 238-248; coauth, "The Development of Social policy for the Elderly in Japan," Soc Service Rev 71 (97): 360-381; coauth, "The Impact of Having a Child with Developmental Disabilities on the Family in Taiwan," Soc Development Issues 20 (97): 35-52; coauth, "The Regulatory Process, The Food and Drug Administration, and the Silicone Breat Implant controversy," Health and Soc Policy 11 (99): 1-20; coauth, "Rethinking a Women's Health Agenda," Women and Politics (00); auth, "An Essay Review Comparing the U.S. and Canadian health Systems," Health and Soc Policy 11 (00): 79-85. **CONTACT ADDRESS** Dept Social Work, Univ of Maryland, Baltimore, 525 W Redwood St, Baltimore, MD 21201. **EMAIL** hpalley@ssw.umaryland.edu

PALMER, ROBERT L., II
PERSONAL Born 03/01/1943, Tuscaloosa, AL, m, 1990 **DISCIPLINE** EDUCATION **EDUCATION** Indiana University, Bloomington, IN, BS, 1969, MS, 1973; State University of New York at Buffalo, Buffalo, NYork, PhD, 1979. **CAREER** State University College at Buffalo, Buffalo, NY, counselor education opportunity prog, 72-74, asst dir educational opportunity program, 73-74; State Univ of NY at Buffalo, asst vice pres of student affairs, 74-82, assoc provost, 82-87, Provost of Student Affairs, 87-. **HONORS AND AWARDS** Outstanding Service Awd, Buffalo Urban League, 1989; Buffalo Black Achievers Awd, Buffalo 1840 Enterprise Inc, 1985; Outstanding Leadership Awd, University at Buffalo Campus Ministry, 1985; Awd of Excellence, United Way of Buffalo & Erie County, 1989; Human Relations Awd, Buffalo NAACP, 1988. **MEMBERSHIPS** Co-chair, United Negro College Fund, Buffalo & Western New York Campaign, 1989-; board of directors, Coordinated Care, 1989-; chairman, board of directors, Buffalo Urban League, 1987-90; member, board of directors, Buffalo Area Engineering Awareness, 1982-; member, The Western New York Health Science Consortium Minority Manpower Task Force for Minorities, 1989-. **CONTACT ADDRESS** SUNY, Buffalo, 542 Capen Hall, Buffalo, NY 14260.

PALMER, STUART
PERSONAL Born 04/29/1924, New York, NY, m, 1946, 1 child **DISCIPLINE** SOCIOLOGY **EDUCATION** Yale Univ, BA, 49, MA 51, PhD, 55. **CAREER** Instr, Univ NH, 55-58; from prof to prof emeritus, Univ NH, 64-; from dean to dean emritus of Col of Liberian Arts, Univ NH, 82-. **HONORS AND AWARDS** Phi Beta Kappa; Sigma Chi. **MEMBERSHIPS** Amer Sociological Assoc; NY Acad of Sci. **RESEARCH** Criminology; Social institutions. **SELECTED PUBLICATIONS** Auth, A Study of Murder, 60; auth, The Prevention of Crime, 72; auth, Role Stress, 81; auth, The Universities Today, 98. **CONTACT ADDRESS** Dept of Sociology and Anthropology, Univ of New Hampshire, Durham, PO Box 904, Durham, NH 03824.

PAMBOOKIAN, HAGOP S.
PERSONAL Born 12/18/1932, Kerek-Khan, Turkey **DISCIPLINE** PSYCHOLOGY **EDUCATION** Am Univ Beirut, BA, 57; Columbia Univ, MA, 63; Univ Mich, PhD, 72. **CAREER** Teacher, Armenian Evangel Col, 57-60; teacher Melkonian Educ Inst, Cyprus, 60-61; instr, Adirondack Comm Col, 64-66; asst prof, SUNY Col Potsdam, 66-70; asst prof, Marquette Univ, 74-78; assoc prof, Elizabeth City State Univ, 80-85; prof, Shawnee State Univ, 87-. **HONORS AND AWARDS** Fulbright Fel, USSR, 78-79; Grant, Ohio Humanities Coun, 90; Paul Swaddling Awd, OEA, 97. **MEMBERSHIPS** Am Psychol Assoc; Int Coun of Psychol; Nat Assoc for Armenian Studies and Res, Phi Delta Kappa. **RESEARCH** International Psychology, inter-cultural communication, parent-child relations. **CONTACT ADDRESS** Dept Soc Sci, Shawnee State Univ, 940 - 2nd St, Portsmouth, OH 45662. **EMAIL** HPambookian@shawnee.edu

PAOLETTI, JO
DISCIPLINE AMERICAN CULTURE **EDUCATION** Syracuse Univ, BS, 71; Univ RI, MS, 76; Univ MD, PhD, 80. **CAREER** Am Stud Dept, Univ Md **RESEARCH** 1970s unisex trends, on-line exhibition and publ. **SELECTED PUBLICATIONS** Co-auth, Conclusion" in Men and Women: Dressing the Part, Smithsonian Inst Press, 89; The Children's Department,Men and Women: Dressing the Part, Smithsonian Inst Press, 89; auth, Little Lord Fauntleroy and His Dad, Hope and Glory, 91; The Value of Conversation in Teaching and Learning, Essays on Teaching, Univ Md IBM-TQ Project, 97; The Gendering of Infants' and Toddlers' Clothing in America, The Material Culture of Gender/The Gender of Material Culture, Winterthur Mus, 97. **CONTACT ADDRESS** Am Stud Dept, Univ of Maryland, Col Park, 4210 Underrwood St, University Park, MD 20782. **EMAIL** jp4@umail.umd.edu

PARETTE, HOWARD P.
PERSONAL Born 07/09/1952, Pine Bluff, AR, s **DISCIPLINE** ELEMENTARY, EARLY, AND EXCEPTIONAL CHILD EDUCATION **EDUCATION** Univ Ark, BSE, 76; ME, 79; Univ Ala, EdD, 82. **CAREER** Asst prof, La Tech Univ, 82-84; res assoc, Univ of Ark for Med Scis, 88-89; asst prof, Univ of Ark at Little Rock, 89-93; assoc prof, Southeast Mo State Univ, 93-97, prof, 97-2000. **HONORS AND AWARDS** Ark Traveler, 96; Who's Who Among America's Teachers, 96, 98; Outstanding Researcher, 98; web pages in all courses developed since 97; invited contribur to thematic journals; textbook reviewer; developing on-line courses for Masters and undergraduate programs; facilitating portfolio implementation. **MEMBERSHIPS** Coun for Exceptional Children (MRDD, TAM, DEC, DCLD). **RESEARCH** Assistive technology applications and children with disabilities across cultures. **SELECTED PUBLICATIONS** Co-ed with S. L. Judge, Assistive technology for young children with disabilities: A guide to providing family-centered services, Cambridge, MA: Brookline (98); co-ed with A. VanBiervliet, J. W. Reyna, and D. Heisserer, Families, cultures, and augmentative and alternative communication (AAC), A multimedia instructional program for related service personnel and family members [online], http://ctsl.semo.edu/parette/homepage/database.pdf; coauth with A. VanBiervliet, "Family views," in H. P. Parette and A. VanBiervliet (CD-ROM), Families, Cultures, and AAC, Little Rock, AR: Southeast Mo State Univ and Univ of Ark for Medical Scis (99); coauth with M. J. Brotherson, and M. B. Huer, "Respecting family values and cultures," in H. P. Parette and A. VanBiervliet (CD-ROM), Families, Cultures, and AAC, Little Rock, AR: Southeast Mo State Univ and Univ of Ark for Medical Scis (99); auth, "Transition planning with families across cultures," Career Development for Exceptional Individuals, 22, 2 (99): 213-231; coauth with T. I. Senz, A. Iglesias, and M. B. Huer, "Culturally and linguistically diverse preschoolers' verbal and nonverbal requests," Commun Disorders Quart, 21, 1 (99): 39-49; coauth with J. J. Hourcade and M. B. Huer, "Family and cultural alert! Considerations in assertive technology assessment," in John J. Hirschbuhl, ed, Annual Editions. Educating Exceptional Children, Guilford, CT: Duskin Pub Group (2000/2001); coauth with M. J. Brotherson and M. B. Huer, "Giving families a voice in augmentative and alternative communication decision-making," Education and Training in Mental Retardation and Developmental Disabilities (June 2000; coauth with C. Kemp, "Barriers to minority parent involvement in assistive technology (AT) decision-making processes," Educ and Training in Mental Retardation and Developmental Disabilities (Dec 2000); coauth with J. J. Hourcade, "Assistive technology training for parents of students with disabilities," Special Education Technology Practice (in press); coauth with J. J. Hourcade and G. Heiple, "The importance of structured computer experiences for young children with and without disabilities," Early Childhood educ J (in press). **CONTACT ADDRESS** Dept Elem, Early, & Exceptional Child Educ, Southeast Missouri State Univ, One Univ Plaza, Cape Girardeau, MO 63701-4799. **EMAIL** pparette@semovm.semo.edu

PAREZO, NANCY JEAN
PERSONAL Born 01/08/1951, Buffalo, NY, m, 1982 **DISCIPLINE** ANTHROPOLOGY **EDUCATION** Univ Arizona, PhD 81, MA 76; Miami Univ, BA cum laude, 73. **CAREER** Prof, Amer Indian Stud and Anthro, 91-; Univ Arizona, Bureau Ethnic Research, grad res asst, Dept Land Architecture, inst, Women's Studies Faculty, aff fac mem, Dept of Anthropology, grad res asst/assoc, grad tchg asst, inst, ethnologist, dir, lect, assoc res prof, res prof, 74 to 92-; AZ BD Regents, loaned exec 90-91; AZ State Museum, assoc curator, curator 85 to 90; Ntl Sci foun, assoc prog dir 87-88; UA Women's Stud Fac, aff fac mem, 85-; Prima Comm Col, inst, 83, 79-81; Smithsonian Inst Ntl Museum Nat Hist, inst 81-82; Prima Coll, inst 79-81; AZ State Museum, res 76; Miami Univ, lab tech, tchg asst, student register 70-73; Musee de'Etat Luxembourg, ceramic rest 71-72. **HONORS AND AWARDS** D'Arcy McNickle Ind Voices Fel; Post doc Fel Smithsonian; Weatherhead Res Sch; Sigma Xi schshp; UZ Grad schshp; Miami U Alum schshp; NPA schshp;

NYS Regent schshp; 10 Wenner-Gren Foun Gnts; APSR Gnt; 3 NEH Fel; Comins Fel; et al. **MEMBERSHIPS** Coun Preservation of Anthro Records; NICCP; CMA; Phi Beta Kappa; AAA; WFA; AES; SAA; HAC; AAAS; AEA; SFA; AAM; HAN; AAUW. **SELECTED PUBLICATIONS** Auth, Bureau of American Ethnology, in: The History of Science in the United States: An Encycl, ed Marc Rothenberg, NY, Garland Pub, in press; Matilda Coxe Stevenson, in: American National Biography, eds John A. Garraty, Mark C. Carnes, NY, ACLS and Oxford Press, 99; Community Motherhood and Health: Issues in Lesbian; Gay Life, in: Reviews in Anthropology, 00; Paths of Life: American Indians of the Southwest and Northern Mexico, co-ed, Tucson, Univ AZ Press, 96; Preserving the Anthropological Record, co-ed, 2nd ed, NY, Wenner-Gren Foun AR, 95; Hidden Scholars, Women Anthrop and the Native American Southwest, ed, Albuquerque, Univ N Mexico Press, 93; Indian Chic: The Denver Art Museum's Indian Style Show, coauth, Amer Ind Art Mag, 97; Matthews and the Discovery of Navajo Dry Paintings, in: Washington Matthews, Studies of Navajo Culture, eds, Katherine Spencer Halpern, Susan Brown McGreevy, Albuquerque, U of N Mexico Press, 97; Southwestern Art Worlds, Jour of Southwest, 96; Indian Trade Blankets, coauth, artiFACT, 97; Wealth Concealed, coauth, Common Ground, 96; Southwest Native Amer Painting, Southwest Native Amer Metalwork, Southwest Native Amer Dress and Adornment, Southwest Native Amer Carving and Sculpture, in: Dictionary of Art, London, Macmillan, 96; Painting a Local Landscape, rev of High Art Down Home, An Economic Anthropology of a Local art Market, by Stuart Plattner, Current Anthrop, 98; et al. **CONTACT ADDRESS** Dept of American Indian Studies, Univ of Arizona, American Indian Studies, Tucson, AZ 85721. **EMAIL** parezo@u.arizona.edu

PARIS, GINETTE
PERSONAL Born 03/05/1946, Montreal, QC, Canada, m, 1980, 2 children **DISCIPLINE** PSYCHOLOGY **SELECTED PUBLICATIONS** Auth, Le Reveil Des Difux, Editions De Mortagne (Montreal, Can), 80; auth, La Renaissance D'aphrodite, Editions Boreal Express (Montreal, Can), 86; auth, Pagan Meditations, Spring Publications (Dallas, Texas), 86; auth, Pagan Grace, Spring Publications, (Dallas, Texas), 90; auth, The Sacrament Of Abortion, Spring Publications (Dallas, Texas), 92; auth, Mythology: CD Rom Encyclopedia Of Greek And Roman Mythology, forthcoming. **CONTACT ADDRESS** Dept Psychology, Pacifica Graduate Inst, 249 Lambert Rd, Carpenteria, CA 93013. **EMAIL** paris@silcom.com

PARKER, JACQUELINE
PERSONAL Born 06/03/1934, Yuba City, CA, s **DISCIPLINE** SOCIAL WORK **EDUCATION** Univ Calif Berkeley, BA, 59; MSW, 61; PhD, 72. **CAREER** Assoc Prof, Radford Univ. **HONORS AND AWARDS** Who's Who of Am Women.; Travel Grants; Prog Activity Grants. **MEMBERSHIPS** Nat Asn of Soc Workers; Coun on Soc Work Educ; Friends of Schlesinger Library; Oral Hist Asn. **RESEARCH** Collective Oral History; Mainline Church. **SELECTED PUBLICATIONS** Auth, "Women at the helm: Succession Politics at the Chilren's Bureau, 1912-1968", Social Work, (94): 557-559; co-auth, "Julia Lathrop and the Children's Bureau: The emergence of an institution," Social Service Review, (81): 60-77; auth, "Tax Reform," in Social Work Speaks: Policy Statements of the NASW, 97. **CONTACT ADDRESS** Dept Soc Work, Radford Univ, PO Box 6958, Radford, VA 24142. **EMAIL** jk3parker@aol.com

PARKER, SIDNEY BAYNES
PERSONAL Born 07/13/1922, Jamaica, West Indies, m, 1978 **DISCIPLINE** EDUCATION **EDUCATION** Mico Teachers' College, attended, 1941-43; Howard University, BS, MA, 1949, MDiv, 1953; Geneva Theological College, EdD, 1970; LaSalle University, LLB, 1970. **CAREER** Excelsior High School, teacher, 44-45; St Michael's Episcopal Church, vicar, 53-57; Leland College, instructor, 53-57; Trinity Episcopal Church, rector, 57-70; Newark Public School System, instructor, 60-70; St Mary's Anglican Church, interim rector, 67; St Philip's Episcopal Church, rector, 70-78; St Gabriel's Episcopal Church, Vicar, 70-; Edward Waters College, Prof, 76-. **HONORS AND AWARDS** Howard University, Homiletic Awd, 1952; City of Jacksonville, Mayor's Awd, 1979; University of North Florida, Achievement Awd, 1990. **MEMBERSHIPS** Montclair Mayor's Committee, president, 1969-70; Diocese of Florida Standing Committee, 1976-79; Jacksonville Library, bd of trustees, 1987-. **CONTACT ADDRESS** St. Gabriel Episcopal Church, 5235 Moncrief Rd W, Jacksonville, FL 32209.

PARKER, SUE T.
PERSONAL Born 01/01/1938, Seattle, WA, m, 1997, 1 child **DISCIPLINE** ANTHROPOLOGY **EDUCATION** Univ Calif, BA, 66; MA, 69; PhD, 73. **CAREER** Asst Prof to Full Prof, Sonoma State Univ, 71-. **HONORS AND AWARDS** Fullbright Res Fel, Italy, 86. **MEMBERSHIPS** Am Asn Advancement of Sci; Am Asn Phys Anthropol; Am Anthropol Soc; Jean Piaget Soc. **RESEARCH** Evolution of Cognitive Development in Primates. **SELECTED PUBLICATIONS** Auth, Piaget's Sensorimotor Series in an Infant Macaque: The Organization of Nonstereotyped Behavior in the Evolution of Intelligence, Univ CA, 73; auth, 'Language' and Intelligence in Monkeys & Apes: A Developmental Approach, Cambridge Univ Press, 90; co-ed, Self-Awareness in Animals and Humans, Cambridge Univ Press, 94; co-ed, Naming Our Ancestors: An Anthology of Hominid Taxonomy, Waveland Press, 94; co-ed, Reaching into Thougth: The Minds of Great Apes, Cambridge Univ Press, 96; co-auth, Origins of Intelligence: The Evolution of Cognitive Development in Monkeys, Apes and Humans, Johns Hopkins Univ Press, 99; co-ed, The Mentalities of Gorillas and Orangutans in Comparative Perspective, Cambridge Univ Press, 99; co-ed, Brains, Bodies, and Behavior: The Evolution of Development, Sch of Am Res Press, in press. **CONTACT ADDRESS** Dept Anthropol, Sonoma State Univ, 1801 E Cotati Ave, Rohnert Park, CA 94928. **EMAIL** parker@sonoma.edu

PARMAN, SUSAN
PERSONAL Born 08/17/1945, CT, m, 1972, 1 child **DISCIPLINE** ANTHROPOLOGY **EDUCATION** Antioch Col, BA, 67; Rice Univ, PhD, 72. **CAREER** Prof, Calif State Univ Fullerton, 93-; Chair Dept of Anthrop, Calif State Univ Fullerton, 96-. **HONORS AND AWARDS** Grant, Nat Sci Found; Fel, Soc of Antiquarians of Scotland; Sigma Xi. **MEMBERSHIPS** Am Anthrop Soc, Soc for the Anthrop of Europe. **RESEARCH** Anthropology of Europe/Scotland, History & Anthropology, Cartography, islands, dremas, and salt. **SELECTED PUBLICATIONS** Auth, "George and Louise Spindler and the issue of Homogeneity and Heterogeneity in American Cultural Anthropology," in The Psychoanalytic Study of Society, Vol 17: Essays in Honor of George D. and Louise A. Spindler, ed. L. Bruce Boyer and Ruth Boyer (Hillsdale, NJ: The Analytic Press, 92), 29-43; rev, of "Dreaming: Anthropological and Psychological Interpretations," ed by Barbara Tedlock, AM Anthropologist 95-3 (93): 733; auth, "The Future of European Boundaries: A Case Study," in Cultural Change and the New Europe: Perspectives on the European Community, ed. Thomas M. Wilson and M. Estellie Smith (Westview Press, 93), 189-202; rev, of "Inside European Identities," cd by Sharon Macdonald, Am Anthropologist 96-3 (94): 743-744; auth, "$1 Million Definition of Science in Anthropology," Anthrop Newsletter 36-7 (95): 36-37; auth, "William Robertson Smith and American Anthropology: Science, Religion, and Interpretation," in William Robertson Smith: Essays in Reassessment, ed. William Johnstone (England: Sheffield Publ, 95), 264-271; auth, "Common Ground and Common Good: Four-Field Anthropology Along the Margins of Europe," in Aegean Strategies: Studies of Culture and Environment on the European Fringe, ed. P Nick Kardulias and Mark T. Shutes (Savage, MD: Rowman and Littlefiled Publ Inc, 97), 293-298; ed, Europe in Anthropological Imagination, Prentice Hall (NJ), 98; rev, of "Missing Persons: A Critique of Personhood in the Social Sciences," by Mary Douglas and Steven Ney, Anthrop Quart 72-2 (99): 99-100; auth, "Making the Familiar Strange: The Anthropological Dialogue of George and Louise Spindler," in Fifty Years of Anthropology and Education, ed. George D. Spindler (Lawrence Erlbaum Associates, 99). **CONTACT ADDRESS** Dept Anthrop, California State Univ, Fullerton, 800 N State Col, Fullerton, CA 92831. **EMAIL** sparman@fullerton.edu

PASLEY, B. KAY
PERSONAL Born 05/21/1948, Vancouver, WA, s **DISCIPLINE** HUMAN DEVELOPMENT, FAMILY STUDIES **EDUCATION** La Univ de Granada, 68-69; Calif State Univ at Fresno, BA, 70; Ind Univ, MS, 72; EdD, 74. **CAREER** vis lectr, Central Wash Univ, 77; asst prof, Calif Stat Univ at Sacramento, 73-77; asst prof, Wash State Univ, 77-83; asst prof & dir of Early Childhood Lab, Univ Ky, 83-85; vis assoc prof, Univ Tenn, 86-90; from assoc prof to prof, Colo State Univ, 86-91; from assoc prof to prof, Univ NC at Greensboro, 91-; interim assoc dean for res and grad studies of sch of human environmental sci, Univ NC at Greensboro, 97-98; dir grad studies of human development and family studies, Univ NC at Greensboro, 98-; editor-elect, Family Relations, 00-. **HONORS AND AWARDS** Ruth Griswald Scholar Awd for Outstanding Acad Performance, Ind Univ, 71; Outstanding Fac of the Year, Wash State Univ, 81; Recognition for support to Adult Students with Learning Differences, Colo State Univ, 88; listed in Nat Distinguished Service Registry, 89; Career Enhancement Awd, Colo State Univ, 89; Summer Excellence Res Awd, Univ NC at Greensboro, 92. **MEMBERSHIPS** Groves Confr on Marriage and the Family, Nat Coun on Family Relations, Soc for Res in Adolescence, Stepfamily Asn of Am. **SELECTED PUBLICATIONS** Coauth, "Successful stepfamily therapy: Clients' perspectives," J of Marital and Family Therapy 22 (96): 319-333; coauth, "Fathers' parenting role identity and father involvement in nondivorce and divorced," J of Family Issues 17 (96): 26-45; coauth, "Thinking about the sexes: The relation between cognitions and gender stereotyping," Am J of Family Therapy 26 (98): 189-202; coauth, "Are adopted children and their parents at greater risk for negative outcomes?," Family Relations 47 (98): 237-241; auth, "Does living in a stepfamily increase the risk of delinquency in children?," Stepfamilies 18.4 (98): 1, 3; coauth, "Fathering after divorce in Israel and the U.S.," J of Divorce and Remarriage 31.1-2 (99): 55-82; auth, "Views of stepfamily life from the older generation," Stepfamilies 18.5 (99): 5, 7; coauth, "Explaining marital stability: An identity disruption model," J of Soc and Personal Relationships (in press); coauth, "The relationship of gender role beliefs, negativity, distancing and marital instability," The Family J (in press); coauth, "Family boundary ambiguity, marital status, and youth adjustment," J of Early Adolescence (in press). **CONTACT ADDRESS** Dept Human Development & Family Studies, Univ of No Carolina, Greensboro, PO Box 26170, Greensboro, NC 27402-6170. **EMAIL** kay_pasley@uncg.edu

PATTERSON, H. ORLANDO L.
PERSONAL Born 05/05/1940, Jamaica, m, 1995, 2 children **DISCIPLINE** SOCIOLOGY **EDUCATION** Univ Col of W Indies, BS, 62; UCWI, London, Honors External; London Sch of Econ: Sociol, PhD, 65. **CAREER** John Cowles Prof of Soc, Harvard Univ, 71-. **HONORS AND AWARDS** AM, Harvard Univ, 71; Dr of Humane Letters, Trinity Col, 92; UCLA Medal, 92; Walter Channing Cabot Fac Prize, Harvard, 97. **MEMBERSHIPS** Am Acad of Arts & Sci; Am Sociol Asn. **RESEARCH** Race relations (contemporary); historical sociology; freedom & slavery. **SELECTED PUBLICATIONS** Auth, Freedom in the Making of Western Culture, Basic Books, 91; auth, About Freedom, Earth Stars & Writers, Lib of Cong, 93; auth, The New Puritanism, Salmagundi, 94; auth, The Crisis of Gender Relations in the African American Community, Race, Gender, and Power in America, Oxford Univ Press, 94; auth, For Whom the Bell Curves, The Bell Curve Wars, Basic Books, 95; auth, The Ordeal of Integration: Progress and Resentment in America's Racial Crisis, Counterpoint/Civitas, 97; auth, Rituals of Blood: Redefining the Color Line in Modern America, Counterpoint/ Civitas, (in press), 98. **CONTACT ADDRESS** Dept Sociol, Harvard Univ, 33 Kirkland St, Cambridge, MA 02138. **EMAIL** op@wjh.harvard.edu

PATTERSON, MILES L.
PERSONAL Born 01/17/1942, Palatine, IL, m, 1972, 1 child **DISCIPLINE** PSYCHOLOGY **EDUCATION** Loyola Univ, BS, 64; Northwestern Univ, MA, 66; PhD, 68. **CAREER** Asst Prof of Psychology, Univ Mo, St Louis, 69-74; Assoc Prof of Psychology, Univ Mo, St Louis, 74-79; Prof of Psychology, Univ Mo, St Louis, 79-; Chairperson, Univ Mo, St Louis, 82-85; Editor, J of Nonverbal Behavior, 86-91. **HONORS AND AWARDS** UM-St Louis Chancellor's Awd for Research and Creativity, 90, Fellow of the Am Psychological Assn. **MEMBERSHIPS** Am Psychological Assn, Am Psychological Society, Society of Experimental Social Psychology, International Communication Assn. **RESEARCH** Nonverbal communication, social interaction. **SELECTED PUBLICATIONS** Auth, Social behavior and social cognition: A parallel process approach, in J.L. Nye & A.M. Brower eds., What's social about social cognition? Social cognition research in small groups, Sage Publications (Thousand Oaks, CA), 96; auth, Social and communicative anxiety: A review and meta-analysis, in B.R. Burleson eds., Communication Yearbook 20, Sage Publications (Thousand Oaks, CA), 97; auth, Parallel processes in nonverbal communication, in M.T. Palmer, & G. Barnett eds., Progerss in communication science: Theory and research in mutual influence, Ablex Publishers (Greenwich, CT), 98; auth, The evolution of a parallel process model of nonverbal communication, in P. Philipott, R. Feldman, & E Coats eds., The social context of nonverbal behavior, Cambridge Univ Press (Cambridge), 99; auth, Toward a comprehensive model of nonverbal communication, in W.P. Robinson & H. Giles eds., Handbook of language and social psychology, Wiley & Sons (Chichester, UK). **CONTACT ADDRESS** Dept Psychology, Univ of Missouri, St. Louis, 8001 Natural Bridge, Saint Louis, MO 63121. **EMAIL** miles_patterson@umsl.edu

PATTI, RINO J.
PERSONAL Born 09/07/1936, New Orleans, LA, m, 1959, 2 children **DISCIPLINE** SOCIAL WORK **EDUCATION** San Diego State Univ, AB; Univ Southern Calif, MSW; DSW. **CAREER** Assoc to prof, Univ of Wash, 67-88; prof, dean, Univ of Southern Calif, 88-97. **HONORS AND AWARDS** NASW Presidential Awd; Margaret Driseou - Florence Clerenger Prof. **MEMBERSHIPS** Nat Assoc fo Soc Workers; Coun on Soc Work Educ. **RESEARCH** Human service organizations, management of non-profit social agencies. **SELECTED PUBLICATIONS** Coed, Change From Within, Temple Univ Pr, 80; auth, Social Welfare Administration: Managing Social Programs in a Developmental Context, Prentice-Hall, 83; coed, Managing for Service Effectiveness in Social Welfare, Haworth Pr, 89; coauth, "Utilization of Research in Administrative Practice", Research Utilization: a Decade of Practice, eds A. Grasso and I. Epstein, Haworth Pr, 92; auth, "Building Influence and Autonomy for Social Work Programs", The Administration of Social Work Education Programs: The Roles of Deans and Directors, ed F. Raymond, Nat Assoc of Dean Directors, (95): 117-126; coauth, "Factors Influencing Priorities in Hospital Social Work Departments: A Director's Perspective", Social Work in Health Care 26.1 (97); ed, The Handbook of Social Welfare Management, Sage Pub, 00. **CONTACT ADDRESS** Sch of Soc Work, Univ of So California, 669 W 34th St, Los Angeles, CA 90089-0067. **EMAIL** rpatti@usc.edu

PATTNAYAK, SATYA R.
PERSONAL Born 06/02/1956, Puri, India, s **DISCIPLINE** SOCIOLOGY **EDUCATION** Jawaharlal Nehru Univ, MA, 78, MPhil, 79; Vanderbilt Univ, MA, 85, MA, 87, PhD, 90. **CAREER** Asst prof, Villanova Univ, 90-96, assoc prof, 97-. **HONORS AND AWARDS** Consultant to the World Bank, 95. **MEMBERSHIPS** Am Sociol Asn, Am Political Sci Asn, Latin

Am Studies Asn. **RESEARCH** Political economy, development, social movements. **SELECTED PUBLICATIONS** Auth, Explaining Differential Levels of Industrial Growth: A Cross-National study of Foreign Capital and State Efficacy in Asia and Latin America, 1965-1985, Univ Mich Diss Services, Ann Arbor, Mich (91); ed, Organized Religion in the Political Transformation of Latin America, Univ Am Press, Lanham, Md (95); coauth with D. Shai, "Mortality Rates as Indicators of Cross-Cultural Development: Regional Variations in the Third World," J of Developing Socs, 11 (95): 252-262; auth, :Modernization, Dependency, and the State in Asia, Africa, and Latin America," Int J of Comp Sociol, 37 (96): 274-286; ed, Globalization, Urbanization, and the State, Univ Press Am, Lanham, Md (96); auth, "India: atolladero sociedad-Estado (State-Society Quagmire in India)," Estudios de Asia y Africa, XXIX, no 103 (97): 271-288; auth, "Globalization and Social Inequality: Latin America at a Cross-roads," J of Peace Studies, VI (99): 45-54; auth, "Growth Effects of Foreign Investment, Domestic Investment, and State Coercive Capacity," Int Studies, XXXVI, 4 (99): 339-353. **CONTACT ADDRESS** Dept Sociol, Villanova Univ, 800 E Lancaster Ave, Villanova, PA 19085. **EMAIL** satya.pattnayak@villanova.edu

PATTON, GERALD WILSON
PERSONAL Born 11/13/1947, Chattanooga, TN, m **DISCIPLINE** EDUCATION **EDUCATION** Kentucky State Univ, BA 1969; Western Illinois Univ, MA 1973; Univ of Iowa, PhD 1978. **CAREER** North Carolina State Univ, asst prof history 1978; Washington Univ, asst dean of graduate school of arts & science 1978-81; North Central Assn of Colleges & Schools, assoc dir, commission on institutions of higher eduction, currently. **HONORS AND AWARDS** Congressional Black Caucus Found Scholars lecturer 1984. **MEMBERSHIPS** Coordinator "St Louis A Policy Framework for Racial Justice, an Agenda for the 80's" sponsored by the Danforth Found 1984-85; chmn Educ Comm 100 Black Men of St Louis 1983-; chmn MO Comm of Black Studies 1984-. **SELECTED PUBLICATIONS** "War and Race, Black Officer in the Amer Military" 1981; **CONTACT ADDRESS** Commission on Institutions of Higher Education, North Central Association of Cols & Schools, 159 N Dearborn, Chicago, IL 60601.

PAUKETAT, TIMOTHY
PERSONAL Born 04/28/1961, Belleville, IL, m, 2 children **DISCIPLINE** ANTHROPOLOGY **EDUCATION** Southern IL Univ, MA, 86; Univ Mich, PhD, 91. **CAREER** Asst prof, Univ of Okla, 92-96; assoc prof, SUNY Buffalo, 96-98; assoc prof, Univ of IL, 98-. **MEMBERSHIPS** Soc for Am Archeol; Am Anthrop Assoc. **RESEARCH** Domination, community, identity, inequality. **SELECTED PUBLICATIONS** Auth, "The Foundations of Inequality within a Simulated Shan Community", J of Anthrop Archeol 15, (96): 219-236; auth, "Specialization, Political Symbols, and the Crafty Elite of Cahokia", Southeastern Archaeol 16, (97): 1-15; coed, Cahokia: Domination and Ideology in the Mississippian World, Univ of Nebr Pr, (Lincoln), 97; auth, "Refiguring the Archaeology of Greater Cahokia", J of Archaeol Res 6, (98): 45-89; coauth, "The Representation of Hegemony as Community at Cahokia", Material Symbols: Culture and Economy in Prehistory, ed J.E. Robb, Center for Archaeol Investigations, Southern Il Univ, (99): 302-317; auth, "Politicization and Community in the Pre-Columbian Mississippian Valley", The Archaeology of Communities" A New World Perspective, eds M.A. Canuto, and J. Yaeger, Routledge, (Oxford), 00; auth, "The Tragedy of the Commoners", Agency in Archaeology, ed M.A. Dobres and J. Robb, Routledge, (Oxford), 00; auth, "Practice and History in Archaeology: An Emerging Paradigm", Anthrop Theory 1, (00). **CONTACT ADDRESS** Dept Anthrop, Univ of Illinois, Urbana-Champaign, 607 S Mathews Ave, Urbana, IL 61801. **EMAIL** pauketat@uiuc.edu

PAZMINO, ROBERT W.
PERSONAL Born 06/15/1948, Brooklyn, NY, m, 1969, 2 children **DISCIPLINE** RELIGIOUS EDUCATION: CURRICULUM AND TEACHING **EDUCATION** Gordon-Conwell Theol Sem, M Div; Teachers Col, Columbia Univ in coop with Union Sem, Ed D. **CAREER** Asst prof of Christian Education, Gordon-Conwell Theol Sem, 81-86; assoc prof, 86-90, prof of relig ed, 90-96, Valeria Stone prof of Christian Education, Andover Newton Theol School, 96-. **HONORS AND AWARDS** Phi Beta Kappa; Psi Chi; Phi Eta Sigma; Phi Alpha Chi; Nat Dean's List; Hispanic Doctoral fel of the Fund for Theol Ed. **MEMBERSHIPS** North Am Professors of Christian Education. **RESEARCH** Theol foundations of Christian education. **SELECTED PUBLICATIONS** Auth, Principles and Practices of Christian Education: An Evangelical Perspective, Baker, 92, trans, Editorial Caribe, 95; Foundational Issues in Christian Education: An Introduction in Evangelical Perspective, Baker, 88, 2nd ed, Baker, 97; Latin American Journey: Insights for Christian Education in North America, United Church Press, 94; By What Authority Do We Teach? Sources for Empowering Christian Educators, Baker, 94; Nurturing the Spiritual Lives of Teachers, in The Christian Educator's Handbook on Spiritual Formation, eds Kenneth O Gangel and James C Wilhoit, Victor Books, 94; Designing the Urban Theological Education Curriculum, in The Urban Theological Education Curriculum: Occasional Papers, eds, Eldin Villafane and Bruce Jackson, CUTEEP, 96, Christian Ed J, fall 97; review of Jesuit Education and Social Change in El Salvador by Charles D Beirne in J of Res on Christian Ed 5, fall 96; Basics of Teaching for Christians: Preparation Instruction and Evaluation, Baker, 98; numerous other publications. **CONTACT ADDRESS** Andover Newton Theol Sch, 210 Herrick Rd, Newton, MA 02459-2243. **EMAIL** rpazmino@arts.edu

PEASE, JOHN
PERSONAL Born 03/08/1936, Grand Rapids, MI, d, 2 children **DISCIPLINE** SOCIOLOGY **EDUCATION** Mich State Univ, PhD, 68; Mich State Univ, MA, 63; Western Mich Univ, 60, BS. **CAREER** Asst Prof, Univ of Maryland, 67-71; Assoc Prof, Univ of Maryland, 71-. **HONORS AND AWARDS** Who's Who Among America's Teachers; Phi Kappa Phi; Alpha Kappa Delta; Omicron Delta Kappa; Mortar Board; Alpha Kappa Delta; Alpha Lambda Delta; Phi Eta Sigma; Who's Who in the World; and two dozen campus teaching Awds. **MEMBERSHIPS** American Sociological Assoc; Eastern Sociological Society; District of Columbia Sociological Society. **SELECTED PUBLICATIONS** Auth, "The Student-faculty Ratio in Graduate Programs of Selected Departments of Sociology: A Supplement to the Janes Report," (with Abraham D. Lavender and Richard A. Mathers,) The American Sociologist, VI (February, 1971), 29-30; auth, "Toward Complete Equality? Soviet Views on the Future of Inequality" (with Janet S. Schwartz), International Review of Modern Sociology, III, September, 73, 141-151; auth, "Sociology and Social Life," (with Raymond W. Mack), 5th ed, (New York): D. Van Nostrand Company, 73, xxii+561, auth, "Use of the General Social Survey Data and Cross-tabulation Programs in Teaching Data Analysis," (with David L. Kruegel), High School Behavioral Science, III, Fall, 75, 30-33; auth, "Association for Whom? The Regionals and the American Sociological Association," (with Barbara Hetrick), The American Sociologist, XII, (February, 77), 42-47; auth, "An Historical Sketch of the Relationship between the Regional Sociological Societies and the American Sociological Association, 34-77," (with Barbara Hetrick), ASA Footnotes, V, (May, 77), 9-10; auth, "Historical Notes on the First Regional Sociological Society," (with Barbara Hetrick and Richard A. Mathers), Sociological Forum, I (Fall, 78), 87-93; auth, "Sociology and the Sense of the Commoners," The American Sociologist, XVI, November 81, 257-271; auth, "Professor Mom: Woman's Work in a Man's World," Sociological Forum, VIII, March, 93, 133-139; auth, "Want Ads and Jobs for the Poor: A Glaring Mismatch," (with Lee Martin), Sociological Forum, XII (December, 97), 545-564. **CONTACT ADDRESS** Dept Sociology, Univ of Maryland, Col Park, 2112 Art-Sociology Bldg, College Park, MD 20742-1315. **EMAIL** jpease@socy.und.edu

PECORINO, PHILIP ANTHONY
PERSONAL Born 10/10/1947, New York, NY, m, 1968, 1 child **DISCIPLINE** PHILOSOPHY, PSYCHOLOGY **EDUCATION** Boston Col, BA, 69; Fordham Univ, MA, 70, PhD, 80. **CAREER** From Instr to Assoc Prof, 72-88, Prof Philos, City Univ New York, 88-. **MEMBERSHIPS** Am Asn Philos Teachers (vpres, 80-82, pres, 82-84); Community Col Humanities Asn (Eastern vpres, 81-83); Am Philos Asn; Soc Study Process Philos; AILACT. **RESEARCH** Critical reasoning; applied ethics; metaphysics and scientific inquiry. **SELECTED PUBLICATIONS** Auth, The midwife's trickery, Vol 3, No 2 & Philosophy and interdisciplinary studies, Vol 4, No 3, Aitia; Nursing ethics, technical training and values, Process, Vol VI, No 2; Evil as direction in Plotinus, Philos Res Arch, 82; ed, Perspectives on Death and Dying, Ginn Publ Co, 2nd ed, 82; coauth, Philosophy and science fiction, in The Intersection of Philosophy and Science Fiction, Greenwood Press, 88. **CONTACT ADDRESS** Social Sci Dept, Queensborough Comm Col, CUNY, 22205 56th Ave, Flushing, NY 11364-1497. **EMAIL** ppecorino@qcc.cuny.edu

PEDERSEN, DARHL M.
PERSONAL Born 10/12/1935, Orem, UT, s, 1 child **DISCIPLINE** PSYCHOLOGY **EDUCATION** Brigham Young Univ, BS, 57; MS, 58; Univ Ill, PhD, 62. **CAREER** Teaching Asst, Univ Il, 58-61; Asst Prof to Prof and Dept Chair, Brigham Young Univ, 62-. **HONORS AND AWARDS** NSF Summer Fel, 62; Honorable Mention Awd, Am Inst for Res, 62. **MEMBERSHIPS** Phi Kappa Phi; Psi Chi; Soc of the Sigma Xi; AAUP; Soc for the Sci study of Relig. **RESEARCH** Environmental Psychology: Psychological privacy, personal space, route selection factors, classroom seat selection, environmental competence; sport Psychology: athlete distress and performance, sport participation and gender identification, perceptions of high risk sports: Personality: centrality model for levels of self-identity; sex role behaviors, fear of success motivation. **SELECTED PUBLICATIONS** Auth, "A factorial comparison of privacy questionnaires," social Behavior and Personality, (96): 249-262; auth, "Perceived traits of male and female athletes," Perceptual and Motor Skills, (97): 547-550; auth, "Psychological functions of privacy," Journal of Environmental Psychology, (97): 147-156; auth, "Factors in route selection," Perceptual and Motor Skills, (98): 999-1006; auth, "Characteristics related to centrality of spiritual self-identity," Perceptual and Motor Skills, (98): 1359-1368; auth, "Validating a centrality model of self-identity," Social Behavior and personality, (99): 73-86; auth, "Model for types of privacy by privacy functions," Journal of Environmental Psychology, (99): 397-405. **CONTACT ADDRESS** Dept Psychol, Brigham Young Univ, PO Box 25543, Provo, UT 84602. **EMAIL** darhl_pedersen@byu.edu

PENG, KAIPING
PERSONAL Born 09/16/1962, Hunan, China, m, 1988, 2 children **DISCIPLINE** PSYCHOLOGY **EDUCATION** Beijing Univ, China, BS, 83; Univ Mich, PhD, 97. **CAREER** Teaching Fellow, Dept of Psychology, Beijing Univ, China, 83-87; Lecturer in Psychology, Dept of Psychology, Beijing Univ, China, 87-89; Asst Prof, Dept of Psychology, UC-Berkeley, 97-. **HONORS AND AWARDS** American Cultures Fellow, Ctr of Am Cultures, UC-Berkeley, 98/99, Regent's Junior Fac Research Fellow, UC-Berkeley, 98, Junior Fac Career Development Awd, UC-Berkeley, 97-98, The Excellence in Research Awd, Beijing Univ, China, 88, The Outstanding Teaching Awd, Beijing Univ, China, 87. **MEMBERSHIPS** American Psychological Assoc, American Psychological Society. **RESEARCH** Cultural and Social Psychology, culture and cognition. **SELECTED PUBLICATIONS** Auth, Extroversion, neuroticism and psychoticism of some school-age children in Beijing, Acta Psychological Sinica, 17 (85): 250-256; auth, A brief introduction to sociometry, Journal of Peking Univ (Philosophy and Social Science), 113 (86): 119-125; auth, Chinese value orientation among univ students, Acta Psychologica Sinica, 21 (89): 149-155; auth, Americans & Chinese: Passage to Differences, by F. Hsu, Huaxia Press, Beijing, 89; auth, Psychological testing: Theories and Practice, Huaxia Press, Beijing, 89; auth, Culture and cause: American and Chinese attributions for social and physical events, Journal of Personality and Social Psychology 67 (94): 949-971; auth, Causal understanding acreoss domains and cultures, In D. Sperber, D. Premack and A. Premack eds., Causal Cognition: A multidisciplinary debate, Clarendon Press, Oxford, (95): 577-614; auth, Validity problems comparing value across cultures and possible solutions, Psychological Methods 2 (97): 329-344; auth, Seld-organization and social organization: American and Chinese constructions, in T.Tyler, Kramer, R., & John, O. eds., The psychology of the social self, Laurence Erlbaum and Assoc (98): 193-222; auth, Culture, dialectics, and reasoning about contradiction, American Psychologist 54 (99): 741-754. **CONTACT ADDRESS** Dept Psychology, Univ of California, Berkeley, 3210 Tolman Hall, Berkeley, CA 94720-1600. **EMAIL** kppeng@socrates.berkeley.edu

PENNER, MERRILYNN J.
PERSONAL Born 12/09/1944, New York, NY, s **DISCIPLINE** MATH; PSYCHOLOGY **EDUCATION** Harvard Univ, BA, 66; Univ Calif San Diego, PhD, 70. **CAREER** Adjunct prof Dept Surgery, Univ Md Med School, 95-; adjunct prof, Univ Md, 81-; prof, Univ Md, 80-; assoc prof, Univ Md, 76-80; asst prof, Hunter Col NY, 74-76; res Psychologist, Bell Telephone Lab, 73-74. **HONORS AND AWARDS** Ntl Inst of Health, Tinnitus, idiotones and spontaneous otoacoustic emissions Grant, 2000; Ntl Inst of Health, Tinnitus in patients with sensorineural hearing loss Grant, 85, 90, 96; Ntl Inst of Health, Res and Career Devop Grant, 77-82; Ntl Inst of Health & Ntl Sci Found Grant, 78-83; Ntl Inst Health, Temporal processing of auditory stimuli Grant, 75-78; Univ Md Distinguished Fac Res Fel Awd, 92-93; Univ Md Semester Res Awd, 90-91; Burroughs-Wellcome Res Travel Grant, 90. **MEMBERSHIPS** Psychonomic Soc; Ntl Acad Sci Committee on Hearing & Bioacoustics; Amer Specch & Hearing Assoc; Acoustical Soc Amer; Amer Psycholog Soc; Amer Assoc Advancement Sci. **RESEARCH** Auditory Perception; Auditory Psychophysics; Temporal Factors in Information Processing; Acoustic Emissions; Mathematical Models of Human Information Processing; Speech Perception; Tinnitus. **SELECTED PUBLICATIONS** Coauth, Prevalence of spontaneous otoacoustic emissions in adults revisited, Hearing Res, 97; auth, Rating the annoyance of synthesized tinnitus, Intl Tinnitus Jrnl, 96; auth, The emergence and disappearance of one subject's spontaneous otoacoustic emissions, Ear & Hearing, 96 **CONTACT ADDRESS** Dept Psychology, Univ of Maryland, Col Park, College Park, MD 20742. **EMAIL** oceanvac@cts.com

PENNIX, PAMELA R.
PERSONAL Born 01/22/1950, Washington, DC, m, 1995, 3 children **DISCIPLINE** BEHAVIORAL SCIENCE **EDUCATION** Bennett Col, BA, 72; Coppin State Col, MS, 75; Howard Univ, MSW, 88; DSW, 94. **CAREER** Asst prof, Bowie State Univ, 96-. **HONORS AND AWARDS** Outstand Ser and Leadership. **MEMBERSHIPS** CSWE; ACA. **RESEARCH** Mothers in prison; domestic violence; child development. **SELECTED PUBLICATIONS** Auth, "An Analysis of Mothers in Prison," Am Corr J (99). **CONTACT ADDRESS** Dept Behavioral Science, Bowie State Univ, 14000 Jericho Park, Bowie, MD 20715. **EMAIL** prpg@erols.com

PENROD, STEVEN D.
DISCIPLINE PSYCHOLOGY; LAW **EDUCATION** Yale Col, BA; Harvard Univ, JD; PhD. **CAREER** Vis prof, Law and Psychol, Univ of Minn, 88-89; prof of Law, Univ of Minn, 89-96; dir, Conflict and Change Ctr, Univ of Minn, 91-95; prof of Psychol Program, Univ of Nebr, 95-01; Gallup prof, Univ of Nebr, 99-00. **HONORS AND AWARDS** Yale Col: Political Science Honor Soc; Harvard Law School: Taft Scholarship; Harvard Univ: Nat Sci Found Dissertation Res Grant: Law and

Social Sciences; Co-winner of Soc for the Psychol Study of Social Issues Dissertation Awd, 80; Soc for Experimentl Social Psychol Dissertation Awd, 80; Cattell Dissertation Awrd, 80; Second Prize Am Psychol Asn Diision 13 Meltzer Res Awd, 81; Am Psychol Asn Distinguished Scientific Awd for and Early Career Contribution to Applied Psychology, 86; Davis Professorship in Law, Univ of Minn, 94-95; Gallup Professorship, Univ of Nebr, 99-00. **MEMBERSHIPS** Soc for the Psychol Study of Social Issues; Soc for Experimental Social Psychol; Textbook Authors Asn; International Asn of Conflict Management; Psychonomic Soc; Midwestern Psychol Asn; Law & Soc Asn; International Asn for Applied Psychol; European Asn of Psychology and Law; Am Sociological Asn; Am Psychology-Law Soc; Am Psychol Soc; Am Psychol Asn. **RESEARCH** Jury decsionmaking, eyewitness reliability, media effects, Alternative dispute resolution. **SELECTED PUBLICATIONS** Auth, pubs on eyewitness reliability and jury decisionmaking. **CONTACT ADDRESS** Psychol Dept, John Jay Col of Criminal Justice, CUNY, 899 Tenth Ave, New York, NY 10019. **EMAIL** spenrod@unlinfo.unl.edu

PEOPLES, VERJANIS ANDREWS
PERSONAL Born 08/08/1955, Monroe, LA, m, 1975 **DISCIPLINE** EDUCATION **EDUCATION** Grambling St University, BS, 1976, MS, 1978; Kansas St University, PhD, 1990. **CAREER** Bienville Parish School System, teacher, 76-79; Grambling St Univ, lab school, teacher, 79-88, College of Education, prof, 89-91; Southern Univ, College of Educ, prof, 91-92, asst dean, 92-95, Interim Dean, 95-. **HONORS AND AWARDS** Teacher of the Year, Grambling Lab School, 1989. **MEMBERSHIPS** LA Association of Teacher Educators, 1996; Association of Teacher Educators, 1996; Association for Supervision & Curriculum Dev, 1996; LA Alliance for Education Reform, 1996; LA Council for Teacher Education, 1996; American Association of Colleges for Teacher Education, 1996. Created proposal for Teachers Alumni As-Partners Program (TAAP); Instituted "First Class Teachers Program;" Dev Partnership programs with surrounding parishes. **SELECTED PUBLICATIONS** Published article, "Restoring Human Dignity: A Model for Prevention & Intervention;" Published chapter, "Teacher Preparation Programs at Historically Black Colleges." **CONTACT ADDRESS** Dept of Curriculum and Instruction, So Univ and A&M Col, PO Box 9983, Baton Rouge, LA 70813.

PERDUE, CHARLES L.
PERSONAL Born 12/01/1930, DeKalb Co., GA, m, 1954, 4 children **DISCIPLINE** FOLKLORE **EDUCATION** North Ga Coll, 48-49; Santa Rosa Jun Coll, 53; Univ Calif-Berkeley, AB, Geol, 55-59; Univ Penn, MA, Folklore, MA, 67-68, PhD, 68-71. **CAREER** Engg writer, Convair astronautics, Vandenberg Air Force Base, CA, 59-60; Geol, Branch Mineral Class, US Geol Survey, 60-67; asst prof, Eng, Univ Va, 71-76; assoc prof, Univ Va, 76-92; PROF, ENG & FOLKLORE, 92-. **HONORS AND AWARDS** Ntl Oral Hist Assoc Awd, 97 **MEMBERSHIPS** Am Folklore Soc; Middle Atlantic Folklife Asn; Nat Coun Traditional Arts; Va Folklore Soc **SELECTED PUBLICATIONS** "The Madison County, Virginia FSA Photographs of Arthur Rothstein," Madison County Bicentennial Commission, 93; foreward, The Negro in Virginia, John F. Blair Publ, 94; coauth, "Shenandoah Removals," The Appalachian Trail Reader, Oxford Univ Press, 96; coauth, "An Abiding Haven," Virginia Cavalcade, 97; coauth, "Talk About Trouble: The Virginia Writers' Project," Virginia Cavalcade, 97; "What Made Little Sister Die?: The Core Aesthetic and Personal Culture of a Traditional Singer," Western Folklore, 95; coauth, Talk About Trouble: A New Deal Protrait of Virginians in the Great Depression," Univ North Carolina Press, 96. **CONTACT ADDRESS** Dept Anthro, Univ of Virginia, P O Box 400120, Charlottesville, VA 22904-4120. **EMAIL** clp5a@virginia.edu

PERLSTADT, HARRY
DISCIPLINE SOCIOLOGY **EDUCATION** Univ Mich, BA, 63; PhD, 73; MPH, 79. **CAREER** Int exec dir, Mich Pub Hlth Inst, 93; instr to full prof, Mich State Univ, 68-. **HONORS AND AWARDS** Alex Boros Awd; Phi Beta Delta; Apprec Cert for Teach; Advocate of Year Awd. **MEMBERSHIPS** APHA; ASA; SAS. **RESEARCH** Evaluation of community and school based health and prevention programs. **SELECTED PUBLICATIONS** Coauth, "Trends in Medical and Nursing Education: Faculty Attitudes on Multi-Professional Training," in Research in the Sociology of Health Care, ed. Jennie Jacobs Kronenfeld (Greenwich, CT: JAI Press, 96); coauth, "An Overview of Citizen Participation in Health Planning: Lessons Learned from the Literature," Nat Civic Rev 87 (98): 347-367; auth, "Accreditation of Sociology Programs: A Bridge to a Broader Audience," Can J Soc 23 (98): 195-207; coauth, "Leadership Behaviors for Successful University-Community Collaborations to Change Curricula," Acad Med 74 (98): 1227-1237; coauth, "When (Not If) Evaluation Flexibility is Desirable: Examples from the CPHPE Initiative," Evaluation and the Health Professions 22 (99): 325-341.; coauth, "Citizen Participation in Health Planning: A Case Study of Changing Delivery Systems," in Research in the Sociology of Health Care, ed. Jennie Jacobs Kronenfeld (Greenwich, CT: JAI Press, 99). **CONTACT ADDRESS** Dept Sociology, Michigan State Univ, 316 Berkeley Hall, East Lansing, MI 48824.

PERROTT, DAVID R.
PERSONAL Born 12/06/1942, Salem, OH, m, 1976, 1 child **DISCIPLINE** PSYCHOLOGY **EDUCATION** Kent State Univ, PhD, 68. **CAREER** Prof, Calif State Univ, 68-. **HONORS AND AWARDS** Acoust Soc of Am Gold Key Fel; Outstanding Prof, Calif State Univ, 86. **MEMBERSHIPS** Acoust Soc of Am, Psychonomic Soc. **RESEARCH** Evolutionary psychology, psychoacoustics. **CONTACT ADDRESS** Dept Psychol, California State Univ, Los Angeles, 5151 State Univ Dr, Los Angeles, CA 90032. **EMAIL** dperrot@calstatela.edu

PERRUCCI, ALISSA
DISCIPLINE PSYCHOLOGY **EDUCATION** Duquesne Univ, PhD, 99. **CAREER** adj prof, Duquesne Univ, 98-. **MEMBERSHIPS** APA. **RESEARCH** Gender, Feminine subjectivity, Sex work. **SELECTED PUBLICATIONS** Auth, "The Relationship between persona and self inexotic dancer's experience of privacy," Current Research in Occupations and Professions, (forthcoming); auth, "What's in a good moment: A hermeneutic study of psychotherapy values across levels of psychotherapy training," Psychotherapy Research, (99): 304-326. **CONTACT ADDRESS** Dept Psychology, Duquesne Univ, 600 Forbes Ave, Pittsburgh, PA 15282-0001. **EMAIL** aperrucci@hotmail.com

PERRY, ROBERT LEE
PERSONAL Born 12/06/1932, Toledo, OH, m **DISCIPLINE** ETHNOHISTORY **EDUCATION** Bowling Green St Univ, BA sociology 1959, MA sociology 1965; Wayne St Univ, PhD sociology 1978. **CAREER** Lucas Cnty Juv Ct Toledo, OH, probation counselor 1960-64, juvenile ct referee 1964-67; Detroit Inst Techn, asst prof 1967-70; Department of Ethnic Studies, Bowling Green State Univ Chmn, 70-; licensed professional counselor, 88; Ohio certified prevention consultant, 89-. **HONORS AND AWARDS** Sigma Delta Pi natl Spanish Hon Soc 1958; Alpha Kappa Delta Natl Soc Honor Soc 1976; $37,000 Grant, Dept HEW 1979; Post Doct Fellowship Amer Social Soc Inst for Soc Research UCLA 1980; Charles C Irby National Association of Ethnic Studies (NAES), Distinguished Service Awd, 1994. **MEMBERSHIPS** Consult Natl Inst of Law Enf and Crimin Just 1978-82; consult Div Soc Law and Econ Scis Natl Sci Found 1980; consult Children's Def Fund Task Force on Adoption Assist 1980; chair Status of Women & Minorities Comm N Cent Sociol Soc 1983-85; bd mem Citizens Review Bd Lucas Cnty Juv Ct Toledo, OH 1979-91; bd mem Inst for Child Advocacy Cleveland, OH 1981-85. **CONTACT ADDRESS** African American Studies Dept, Eastern Michigan Univ, 620 Pray Harrold, Ypsilanti, MI 48197.

PERSON, DAWN RENEE
PERSONAL Born 12/10/1956, Sewickley, PA, m, 1986 **DISCIPLINE** EDUCATION **EDUCATION** Slippery Rock Univ, BS Educ 1977, M Educ 1979; Teachers College, Columbia Univ, EdD, 1990. **CAREER** Slippery Rock Univ, human relations counselor, 78-79, minority affairs coord 79-80, advisor to black & intl students 80-81; CO State Univ, dir black student services, 81-85; Lafayette College, asst dean of academic services, 85-90; Teachers College, Columbia Univ, asst prof of higher educ, 90-97; Student Development in Higher Education, Assoc Prof. **HONORS AND AWARDS** Outstanding Black Achiever in Pennsylvania, Black Opinions, 1989; Service Awd, Lafayette College Alumni Chapter of Black Collegians, 1988; Excellence in Higher Education, Lafayette College Minority Students, 1990; Publication & Research in Minority Student Retention, Student Cultures, & Multicultural Issues in Higher Educ. **MEMBERSHIPS** Workshop facilitator Male/Female Relation 1978-; mem ACPA; mem NAACP Easton PA Chap 1985-87; mem Black Conference-Higher Educ PA 1986-87; NASPA; Leadership Lehigh Valley 1989-90. **CONTACT ADDRESS** Student Devt in Higher Educ, California State Univ, Long Beach, Bellflower Blvd, Ed Bu II, No. 214, Long Beach, CA 90840.

PERSON, WILLIAM ALFRED
PERSONAL Born 08/29/1945, Henderson, NC, m **DISCIPLINE** EDUCATION **EDUCATION** Johnson C Smith University, BA, 1963-67; University of Georgia, MEd, 1972-73, EdD, 1973-77. **CAREER** Wilkes City Board of Education, teacher, 67-72; University of Georgia, Grad Asst/Admin Asst, 73-77; Mississippi State Univ, asst prof, 77-80, assoc professor, 80-. **HONORS AND AWARDS** Two academic scholarships, 1963-65; Sigma Man of the Year, Phi Beta Sigma, 1979. **MEMBERSHIPS** Treasurer, Phi Delta Kappa, 1982-83; vice pres, Phi Beta Sigma, 1982-83; president, Phi Beta Sigma, 1983-; bd of directors, Starkville Kiwanis Breakfast Club, 1984-. **CONTACT ADDRESS** Mississippi State Univ, P O Box 6331, Mississippi State, MS 39762-6331.

PETCH-HOGAN, BEVERLY M.
PERSONAL Born 10/24/1940, Kent, OH, m, 1994, 1 child **DISCIPLINE** SPECIAL EDUCATION **EDUCATION** Baldwin Wallace Col, BS, 63; Tex A&M Univ, MEd, 82; PhD, 85. **CAREER** Asst prof, Hardin-Simmons Univ, 85-91; assoc prof to prof, SE MO State Univ, 91-. **HONORS AND AWARDS** Receipt of Title II Teacher Quality enhancement Grant. **MEMBERSHIPS** Phi Kappa Chi, Kappa Delta Pi, Asn, of Teacher Educ, Coun for Excep Child, Coun for learning disabilities. **RESEARCH** Teacher Work Sample Methodology. **SELECTED PUBLICATIONS** Auth, "Advocates vs. opponents: the inclusion debate continues," Kappa Delta Pi Record, 99; auth, "Moving toward excellence: A special education teacher preparation program," Small Special Education programs Caucus Monograph, 97; auth, "Classroom modifications for enhancing the effectiveness of the inclusion of students with disabilities, 97; auth, "Inclusive classroom management: Using preintervention strategies," Intervention in School and Clinic, (96): 172-176; auth, "The branching strategy for teaching mathematics," LD Forum, (95): 20-24; auth, "A performance based teacher evaluation system," International Conference Proceedings: Evaluation Faculty Performance: The State of the Practice II, 94. **CONTACT ADDRESS** Dept Elem & Spec Educ, Southeast Missouri State Univ, 1 Univ Plaza, Cape Girardeau, MO 63701. **EMAIL** bpetchhogan@semovm.semo.edu

PETERS, WILLIAM H.
PERSONAL Born 09/10/1933, Milwaukee, WI, m, 1956, 3 children **DISCIPLINE** CURRICULUM, INSTRUCTION **EDUCATION** Marquette Univ. BA, 56; univ Wis, MA, 65; EdD, 68. **CAREER** Prof, Univ Kentucky, 68-81; chair, 77-81; dept hd, Texas AM Univ, 81-90; prof, coord, 90-. **HONORS AND AWARDS** Who's Who Am edu; Who's Who S SE; Who's Who World; Men Achiev; Dict Intl Biog; Lead edu; Person South. **MEMBERSHIPS** AERA; NCTE; CEE. **RESEARCH** Secondary teacher education; English education. **SELECTED PUBLICATIONS** Auth, Guidelines for the Preparation of Teachers of English Language Arts, Nat Coun Teach of Eng (Urbana, IL), 96; ed, "Initiating a secondary professional development school: The Westfield high school Texas A&M University partnership," in Portraits of Twelve High School Partner Schools in the National Network for Educational Renewal, Cen Edu Renewal, Reflect on Pract Ser 3 (97); coauth, "A Collaborative Process," in Collaborations: English Education and English Studies, eds. D Appleman, A Fishman (Urbana, IL: Nat Coun Teach of Eng, in press); coauth, "Sensitivity issues in tracking school change," Plan Change 26 (95): 232-245; auth, "Prospective English teachers' thought processes and the English methods class," Eng Tex 26 (94): 42-47; auth, " A study of diverse teaching approaches to literature using RosenblattÛs Transactional Theory," Focus: Teaching English Language Arts 22 (96): 69-75; coauth, "Factors affecting school restructuring and change: Implications for teacher educators," Teach Edu Prac 14 (98): 43-53. **CONTACT ADDRESS** Dept Curriculum, Instruction, Texas A&M Univ, Col Station, College Station, TX 77843-0001. **EMAIL** wpeters@tamu.edu

PETLICHKOFF, LINDA M.
PERSONAL Born 09/25/1950, Dearborn **DISCIPLINE** SPORT PSYCHOLOGY **EDUCATION** Henry Ford Community Col, AA, 71; Mich State Univ, BS, 72; MA, 82; Univ IL, PhD, 88. **CAREER** Teacher, Anglo-Am School, Sweden, 76; asst prof to prof, Boise State Univ, 87-; adj grad, Idaho State Univ, 91-. **MEMBERSHIPS** Assoc for the Advan of Appl Sport Psychology. **RESEARCH** Children in sports. **SELECTED PUBLICATIONS** Coauth, "Psychological predictors of state anxiety and performance in age group wrestlers", Pediatric Exercise Science 3 (91):198-208; auth, "Youth sport participation and withdrawal: Is it simply a matter of FUN?", Pediatric Exercise Science 4 (92):5-10; auth, "Group differences on achievement goal orientations, perceived ability, and level of satisfaction during a season", Pediatric Exercise Science 5 (93): 12-24; auth, "Coaching children: Understanding the motivational process", Sport Science Rev 2.2 (93):48-61; auth, "Relationship of player status and time of season to achievement goals and perceived ability in interscholastic athletes", Pediatric Exercise Science 5 (93):242-252; auth, "Response", Pediatric Exercise Science 6, (94):102-103; auth, "Dropping out of sport: Speculation versus reality" in Sport science int - Psychosocial problems in elite sports, ed D. Hackfort, (Frankfurt: Lang, 94) 60-87; auth, "Introductory Philosophy: Developing the appropriate objectives in sport", Coaching Focus 27 (94):3-4; auth, "Dropout dilemma in youth sports" in the child and the adolescent athlete: The encyclopaedia of sports medicine, ed O. Bar-Or, (Oxford: Blackwell Scientific, 95), 418-430; coauth, "The relationship of belt rank to self-esteem and ego in Taekwondo", Jour of Martial Arts Studies 4, (99):201-225. **CONTACT ADDRESS** Dept Kinesiology, Boise State Univ, 1910 University Dr, Boise, ID 83725-1710. **EMAIL** lpetlic@boisestate.edu

PETRAGLIA, MICHAEL
PERSONAL Born 10/06/1960, New York, NY, m, 1994 **DISCIPLINE** ANTHROPOLOGY AND ARCHAEOLOGY **EDUCATION** Univ NYork, BA, anthrop, 82; Univ Nmex, anthrop, MA, 84, PhD, 87. **CAREER** Dir, Cultural Resources Dept, Parsons, 88-; res, Nat Mus of Natural Hist; Smithsonian Inst, 88-. **HONORS AND AWARDS** Postdoctoral fel, Smithsonian Inst. **MEMBERSHIPS** Soc for Amer Archaeol; Amer Anthrop Asn. **RESEARCH** Early human behavior; Hunter-gatherers; Lithic technology; Site formation. **SELECTED PUBLICATIONS** Co-ed, Early Human Behavior in Global Context: the Rise and Development of the Lower Paleolithic Record, London, Routledge Press, 98; coauth, The Old World Paleolithic Collections of the National Museum of Natural History, Smithsonian Inst, Smithsonian Press, 98; coauth, The Prehistory of Lums Pond: The Formation of a Woodland Site in Delaware, vols I and II, Del Dept of Transp Archaeol Series,

98; co-ed, The Lower Paleolithic of India and its Bearing on the Asian Record, in Early Human Behavior in Global Context: the Rise and Diversity of the Lower Paleolithic Record, London, Routledge Press, 98; coauth, Upper Paleolithic Collections from the Salat Valley of Pyrenean France, 98; coauth, Specialized Occupations on Kettle Creek, a Tributary of the West Branch of the Susquehanna, Archaeol of Eastern N Amer, 98; coauth, Assessing Prehistoric Chronology in Piedmont Contexts, N Amer Archaeol, 17, 37-59, 96; coauth, Immunological and Microwear Analysis of Chipped-stone Artifacts from Piedmont Contexts, Amer Antiquity, 61, 127-135, 96; coauth, Prehistoric Occupation at the Connoquenessing Site, an Upland Setting in the Upper Ohio River Valley, Archaeol of Eastern N Amer, 24, 29-57, 96; auth, Reassembling the Quarry: Quartzite Procurement and Reduction along the Potomac, N Amer, Archaeol, 15, 283-319, 94; coauth, Status, Technology, and Rural Traditions in Western Pennsylvania: Excavations at the Shaeffer Farm Site, Northeast Hist Archaeol, 23, 29-58, 94. **CONTACT ADDRESS** 4557 Sawgrass Ct., Alexandria, VA 22312. **EMAIL** petraglia.michael@nmnh.si.edu

PETRONE, SERAFINA
PERSONAL Born Thunder Bay, ON, Canada **DISCIPLINE** EDUCATION **EDUCATION** Univ Toronto, ATCM, 42; Univ Western Ont, BA, 51; Lakehead Univ, MA, 70; Univ Alta, PhD, 77. **CAREER** Tchr, rural, elementary, secondary, Tchrs Col, univ; Prof Emer, Lakehead Univ. **HONORS AND AWARDS** Can 125 Medal, 92; Order Ont, 92; Excellence Tchg, Lakehead Univ, 89; Citizens of Exceptional Achievement Awd, Thunder Bay, 81, 84, 89; Hon Chief, Tibaajimowowinan Kaabaabaamaawadoonany, Gatherer of Legends and Stories. **MEMBERSHIPS** Can Coun; Can Fedn Univ Women; Thunder Bay Regional Arts Coun. **SELECTED PUBLICATIONS** Auth, Selected Short Stories of Isabella Valancy Crawford, 75; auth, the Fairy Tales of Isabella Valancy Crawford, 77; auth, First People, First Voices, 83; auth, Northern Voices, 88; auth, Breaking the Mould: A Memoir, 95. **CONTACT ADDRESS** Lakehead Univ, Thunder Bay, ON, Canada P7B 5E1.

PETTIGREW, THOMAS FRASER
PERSONAL Born 03/14/1931, Richmond, VA, m, 1956, 1 child **DISCIPLINE** SOCIOLOGY **EDUCATION** Univ Va, BA, 52; Harvard Univ, Ma, 55; PhD, 56. **CAREER** Asst Prof, Univ NC, 56-57; Prof, Harvard Univ, 57-80; Prof, Univ Amsterdam, 86-91; Prof, Univ Calif, 80-. **HONORS AND AWARDS** Kurt Lewin Awd, Soc for the Psychol Study of Soc Issues, 87; Fac Res Awd, Univ Calif, 89; Fel, Rockefeller Found, 91; Norman Munn Distinguished Scholar Awd, The Flinders Univ of S Australia, 97; Distinguished Serv Awd, Soc for the Psychol Study of Soc Issues. **MEMBERSHIPS** APA, ASA, Assoc of Exp Soc Psychol, Soc for the Psychol Study of Soc Issues. **RESEARCH** Intergroup relations. **SELECTED PUBLICATIONS** Auth, How to Think like a Social Scientist, Harper Collins (New York, NY), 96; auth, "Personality and Social Structure: Social Psychological Contributions," in Handbk of Personality Psychol (San Diego, CA: Acad Pr, 97), 417-438; auth, "Responses to the New Minorities of Western Europ," Annual Rev of sociol, 24 (97): 77-103; auth, "Intergroup Contact Theory," Annual Rev of Psychol, 49 (98): 65-85; auth, "Countering Convenient Fictions," J of Applied Behav Sci, 34 (98): 431-434; auth, "Sociological Analyses Confront Fashionable Racial Fallacies," Sociol Forum, 14 (99): 181-188; auth, "Applying Social Psychology to International Social Issues," J of Soc Issues, 54 (99): 663-675; auth, "Systematizing the Predictors of Prejudice," in Racialized Politics: The Debate About Racism in America (Chicago, IL: Univ Chicago Pr, 00), 280-301. **CONTACT ADDRESS** Dept Sociol, Univ of California, Santa Cruz, 524 Van Ness Ave, Santa Cruz, CA 95060.

PHELPS, BRADY
PERSONAL Born 05/01/1959, Seca Springs, ID, s **DISCIPLINE** PSYCHOLOGY **EDUCATION** Utah State Univ, BS, 83; MS, 86; PhD, 92. **CAREER** Instr, Utah State Univ, 86-90; Vis Lecturer, Univ MD, 90-91; Asst Prof to Assoc Prof, SD State Univ, 92-. **HONORS AND AWARDS** Intl Behaviorol Asn Basic Res Awd, 94; New Idea Instructional Grant, SD State Univ, 95. **MEMBERSHIPS** Asn for Behav Analysis, Am Psychol Asn, Sigma Xi. **RESEARCH** Behavioral pharmacology, Gambling. **SELECTED PUBLICATIONS** Auth, "Dissociative disorders: The relevance of behavior analysis," The Psychological Record, in press; auth, "Memory rehabilitation techniques with the brain-injured," in Contemporary issues in behavior therapy: Improving the human condition, New York, (96): 123-136; auth, "And then there wer none. A Review of S.J. Gould's Eight Little Piggies," Behaviorology, (95): 161-164; auth, "Of critics and constraints. A Review of S.B. Klein's Contemporary learning theories: Instrumental conditioning theory and the impact of biological constraints on learning," Behaviorology, (94): 81-83; auth, "Factors predisposing drug abuse," Journal of Psychology and the Behavioral Sciences, (93): 61-72; auth, "Sundown syndrome: Is it reflected in the use of PRN medications for nursing home residents?," The Gerontologist, (93): 756-761; auth, "Subliminal tapes: How to get the message across," The Skeptical Inquirer, (92): 282-286; auth, "A comparison of response patterns under fixed-, variable-, and random-ratio schedules," Journal of theExperimental analysis of Behavior, (87): 395-406; auth, Analysis of behavior: Basic processes, 4th ed, Lexinton, 87. **CONTACT ADDRESS** Dept Psychol, So Dakota State Univ, 1 Sd State Univ, Brookings, SD 57007-0002. **EMAIL** brady_phelps@sdstate.edu

PHILLIPS, JULIE
PERSONAL Born 06/27/1968, Great Britain, m, 1995 **DISCIPLINE** SOCIOLOGY **EDUCATION** Univ Pa, BA, 90; MA Sci, 90; MA, 94; PhD, 98. **CAREER** Asst Prof, Rutgers Univ, 99-. **HONORS AND AWARDS** Phi Beta Kappa, 90; William Penn Fel, 93-97. **MEMBERSHIPS** ASA, PAA, ASC. **RESEARCH** Demography, criminology, urban sociology. **SELECTED PUBLICATIONS** Auth, Causes of Death that Contribute to the Racial Mortality Differential in the United States 1970-1989, Univ Pa Pr, 94; auth, "Variation in African-American Homicide Rates: An Assessment of Potential Explanations," Criminol 35,4 (97): 527-559; coauth, "The New Labor Market: Immigrants and Wages After IRCA," Demography 36,2 (99): 233-246. **CONTACT ADDRESS** Dept Sociol, Rutgers, The State Univ of New Jersey, New Brunswick, PO Box 5072, New Brunswick, NJ 08903. **EMAIL** japhill@rci.rutgers.edu

PHILLIPS, PETER
PERSONAL Born 12/09/1947, Sacramento, CA, m, 2000, 1 child **DISCIPLINE** SOCIOLOGY **EDUCATION** Santa Clara Univ, BA, 70; Calif State Univ, MA, 74; Univ Calif Davis, MA, 91; PhD, 94. **CAREER** Assoc prof, Sonoma State Univ, 94-. **HONORS AND AWARDS** Firecracker Book Awd, 97. **MEMBERSHIPS** Pacific Sociol Assoc. **RESEARCH** Media, Elites, Political Soc. **SELECTED PUBLICATIONS** Auth, Censored 1997 - The News That didn't Make the News, Seven Stories Pr, 97; auth, censored 1998 - the News that Didn't Make the News, Seven Stories Pr, 98; auth, censored 1999- The News that Didn't Make the News, Seven Stories Pr, 99; auth, Project Censored: Progressive Guide to Alternative Media and Activism, Seven Stories Pr, 99; auth, Censored 2000, 25 Most Censored New Stories, Seven Stories Pr, 00. **CONTACT ADDRESS** Dept Sociol, Sonoma State Univ, 1801 E Cotati Ave, Rohnert Park, CA 94928. **EMAIL** peter.phillips@sonoma.edu

PHILLIPS, ROMEO ELDRIDGE
PERSONAL Born 03/11/1928, Chicago, IL, m **DISCIPLINE** MUSIC EDUCATION **EDUCATION** Chicago Conservatory Coll, MusB 1949; Chicago Musical Coll, MusM 1951; Eastern MI Univ, MA 1963; Wayne State Univ, PhD 1966. **CAREER** Chicago IL Public Schools, teacher 1949-55; Detroit MI Public Schools, teacher 1955-57; Inkster MI Public Schools, teacher 1957-66; Kalamazoo Coll, chmn dept of educ 1974-86, tenured prof of educ/music 1968-93, prof emeritus, 93-; Portage MI, city councilman, 91-. **HONORS AND AWARDS** Invited by the govt of the Republic of Nigeria West Africa to be a guest to the World Festival of Black and African Art 1977; Omega Psi Phi Leadership Awd 1982; Committee of Scholars for the Accreditation of MI Colls 1982-84; Kalamazoo NAACP Appreciation Awd 1982; Fulbright Scholar to Liberia West Africa 1984-85; **MEMBERSHIPS** Mem Amer Assoc of Coll for Teacher Educ, Music Educators Natl Conf, MI Sch Vocal Assoc, Assoc for Supervison & Curriculum Develop, MI Assoc for Supervision & Curriculum Develop, MI Assoc for Improvement of Sch Legislation, Natl Alliance of Black School Educators, Natl Assoc of Negro Musicians, Phi Delta Kappa, Kappa Alpha Psi; conductor AfraAmerican Chorale. **SELECTED PUBLICATIONS** article; 2 book reviews; chapters contributed to or credit given in 6 books. **CONTACT ADDRESS** Prof Emeritus, Kalamazoo Col, 1200 Academy, Kalamazoo, MI 49006.

PHINNEY, JEAN S.
PERSONAL Born 05/12/1933, Princeton, NJ, m, 1965, 2 children **DISCIPLINE** PSYCHOLOGY **CAREER** Ta, Univ Calif, Los Angeles, 72; lect, Cal State, Long Bch, 72-73; post doc res, Univ Calif, Los Angeles, 73-75; lect, Santa Monica Col, 75; lect, Cal State, Fullerton, 75-76; act asst prof, Univ Calif, Los Angeles, 76-77; asst prof, CSULA, 77-81; vis res fel, Univ Bristol, England, 82-83; assoc prof, CSULA, 81-86; prof, CSULA, 86-. **HONORS AND AWARDS** Who's Who Amer; Phi Beta Kappa. **MEMBERSHIPS** APA; Soc Res Child Devel. **RESEARCH** Ethnicity, ideality, culture, adolescence. **SELECTED PUBLICATIONS** Auth, "Ethnic identity in adolescents and adults: A review of research," Psychological Bulletin 108 (90): 499-514; auth, "At the interface of cultures: Multiethnic/multiracial high school and college students," J Social Psychology 136 (96): 139-158; coauth, "Reasoning about intergroup relations among Hispanic and Euro-American adolescents," J Adolescent Res 11(96): 304-322; auth, "When we talk about American ethnic groups, what do we mean?" American Psychologist 51 (96): 918-927; coauth, "Ethnic and American identity as predictors of self-esteem among African American, Latino, and White adolescents," J Youth Adolescence 26 (97): 165-185; coauth, "Intergroup attitudes among ethnic minority adolescents: A causal model," Child Development 68 (97): 955-969; coauth, "Cultural values and intergenerational value discrepancies in immigrant and non-immigrant families," Child Development 71 (00): 2; auth, "Ethnic identity," in Encyclopedia of Psychology, ed. A. Kazdin (Washington, DC: Am Psychol Assoc, 00); auth, "Ethnic identity," in International encyclopedia of the social and behavioral sciences, eds. N Smelser, P Baltes (Oxford, UK: Elsevier Science Ltd, in press). **CONTACT ADDRESS** Dept Psychology, California State Univ, Los Angeles, 5151 State Univ Dr, Los Angeles, CA 90032. **EMAIL** jphinne@calstatela.edu

PIAN, RULAN CHAO
PERSONAL Born 04/20/1922, Cambridge, MA, m, 1945, 1 child **DISCIPLINE** ETHNO-MUSICOLOGY **EDUCATION** Radcliffe Col, BA, 44, MA, 46, PhD, 60. **CAREER** Tchng asst Chinese, 47-58, instr, 59-61, lectr, 61-74, prof East Asian lang, civilizations, and of music, 74-92, Harvard Univ; Yenching Inst grant travel & res Orient music in Japan, Hong Kong, Taiwan & Korea, 58-59; Am Coun Learned Socs-J D Rockefeller III Fund travel & res grant Peking opera, US, Asia & Europe, 65-66; NEH grant res abroad, 78-79; vis prof, music, 75, 78-79, 82, 94, Chinese Univ Hong Kong; vis prof, 90-, Inst Lit Natl Tsing Hua Univ Taiwan; vis prof, 92-, Schl Human Natl Central Univ Taiwan. **HONORS AND AWARDS** Caroline I Wilby Prize, Radcliffe Col, 60; Otto Kinkeldey Awd, Am Musicol Soc, 68; Radcliffe Grad Soc Medal, 80; Academician, Acad Sinica Taiwan ROC, 90. **MEMBERSHIPS** Am Musicol Soc; Soc Ethnomusicol; Intl Musicol Soc; Soc for Asian Music; Assn for Asian Stud; Int Coun for Trad Music; Chinese Lang Tchrs Assn; Assn for Chinese Music Res. **RESEARCH** Chinese modern language; Chinese music history; interpretation of Sonq dynasty musical sources; present day Chinese musical dramatic and narrative arts. **SELECTED PUBLICATIONS** Auth, A Syllabus for the Mandarin Primer, 61; auth, Sonq Dynasty Musical Sources and Their Interpretation, Harvard Univ, 67; auth, The Function of Rhythm in the Peking Opera, The Musics of Asia, Nat Music Coun Philippines-UNESCO Nat Comn Philippines, 71; auth, Aria Structural Patterns in the Peking Opera, 71; auth, Text Setting with the Shipyi Animated Aria, Words and Music, the Scholar's View: A Medley of Problems and Solutions, Harvard Univ, 72; auth, Modes, Transposed Scales, Melody Types and Tune Types, Proc 12th Cong Int Musicol Soc; auth, Transcription and Study of the Medley Song, The Courtesan's Jewel Box, Chinoperl Papers, Vol 9, No 10, Cornell Univ. **CONTACT ADDRESS** Dept of East Asian Lang & Civilizations, Harvard Univ, 2 Divinity Ave, Cambridge, MA 02138. **EMAIL** thhpian@aol.com

PICCHI, DEBRA
PERSONAL Born 03/13/1953, Japan, m, 1989 **DISCIPLINE** BEHAVIORAL SCIENCES **EDUCATION** SUNY, Undergrad, 75; Univ Fla, PhD, 82. **CAREER** From Mem Fac to Prof, Franklin Pierce Col, 82-. **HONORS AND AWARDS** Fac Mem of the Year, Franklin Pierce Cool, 88-89; Outstanding Fac Mem of the Year, Franklin Pierce Cool, 94-95. **MEMBERSHIPS** Am Anthrop Assoc., Soc for Applied Anthrop. **RESEARCH** Brazilian Indians, ecology. **SELECTED PUBLICATIONS** Auth, "Introduction," J of S Am Indians (98); auth, The Bakairi Indians of Brazil: Politics, Ecology and Change, Waveland Publ (Prospect Hills, IL), 00. **CONTACT ADDRESS** Dept Behav Sci, Franklin Pierce Col, Crestview Hall, PO Box 60, Rindge, NH 03461-0060. **EMAIL** picchids@fpc.edu

PICHUGIN, VALENTINA
PERSONAL Born 02/26/1960, Russia, m, 1991, 1 child **DISCIPLINE** RUSSIAN SLAVIC LANGUAGES, LITERATURE, CULTURE, FOLKLORE **EDUCATION** Omsk State Univ, Rus, MA, 85; Inst Acad Sci, Rus, PhD, 90. **CAREER** Asst prof, Fla State Univ, 93-. **HONORS AND AWARDS** FSU Res Gnt; FSU Teach Awd; FSU Res Gnt. **MEMBERSHIPS** AATSEEL; AAASS; MLA; SCSS; BASEEL. **RESEARCH** Russian linguistics (synchrony and diachrony); pre-19th century literature; folklore; culture; film. **SELECTED PUBLICATIONS** Auth, Deverbatives with Suffix -k(a), in Russian Language (from 11th to 17th century), Hermitage Pub (Tenafly) 98; auth "Russian Surnames in the Seventeenth Century: Sociolinguistics Aspect," Palaeoslavic 5 (97): 347-357; auth, "Neumatic Designations in Old Russian Chant," Palaeoslavic 6 (98): 314-330. **CONTACT ADDRESS** Dept Modern Languages, Florida State Univ, PO Box 3061540, Tallahassee, FL 32306-1540.

PIERCE, THOMAS B.
DISCIPLINE MENTAL RETARDATION **EDUCATION** Univ NMex, PhD, 89. **CAREER** Dept chair, Univ Nev, Las Vegas. **HONORS AND AWARDS** Lilly Fong Distinguished Prof, 95; pres, Div of Legal Proc and Advocacy, Am Asn on Ment Retardation, 96-98. **SELECTED PUBLICATIONS** Auth, Teaching functional skills to people with developmental disabilities, Korean Inst of Spec Educ, Nov, 95; coauth, Effects of self-determined, data-determined and supervisor-determined goals on student teacher behavior, Prof Educ, 17 (2), 95; The state of special education leadership training and college and university faculty: What we know and what we don't, Tchr Educ and Spec Educ, 18, 96. **CONTACT ADDRESS** Dept of Spec Educ, Univ of Nevada, Las Vegas, 4505 Maryland Pky, Las Vegas, NV 89154-3014. **EMAIL** pierce@nevada.edu

PIERCY, EARL
PERSONAL Born 09/14/1947, Santa Paula, CA, m, 1984, 1 child **DISCIPLINE** SOCIOLOGY **EDUCATION** San Francisco State Univ, MA, 76; Cornell Univ, PhD, 82. **CAREER** Instructor, City Col of San Francisco, 82-90; Dean, Calif Inst for Adv Studies, 90-92; Instructor to Prof, Truckee Meadows

Cmty Col, 92-. **MEMBERSHIPS** AAUP, Am Sociol Asn. **RESEARCH** Environmental Sociology. **CONTACT ADDRESS** Dept Soc Sci, Truckee Meadows Comm Col, 7000 Dandini Blvd, Reno, NV 89512. **EMAIL** piercy_earl@tmcc.edu

PIERMAN, CAROL J.
PERSONAL Born 10/16/1947, Lima, OH, s **DISCIPLINE** WOMENS STUDIES **EDUCATION** Institut de Touraine, Certificat, 67; Bowling Green State Univ, BA, 69; MFA, 72; PhD, 80. **CAREER** Teaching Asst to Teaching Fel, 70-80; Vis Asst Prof, Southern Ill Univ, 81-86; Asst Prof to Assoc Prof and Dept Chair, Univ Ala, 89-. **HONORS AND AWARDS** Res Grant, Univ Ala, 96, 94, 91; Poetry Fel, Ill Arts Coun, 86; Fiction Fel, Ill Arts Coun, 85; Devine Fel in Poetry, Bowling Green State Univ, 72. **MEMBERSHIPS** Poets and Writers, SE Women's Studies Asn. **RESEARCH** 20th Century American literature and culture. **SELECTED PUBLICATIONS** Auth, Sweet Franchise, forthcoming; auth, The Age of Krypton, Univ Press, 89; auth, The Naturalized Citizen, New Rivers Press, 81; auth, Returning Light, forthcoming; auth, Passage, Madeira Press, 77; auth, "Cal Ripken and the Condition of Freedom: Theme and Variation on the American Work Ethic," NIN: A Journal of Baseball History and Social Policy Perspective, forthcoming; auth, "A Fantastic Way of Life," in Over West: Selected Writings of Frederick Eckman, National Poetry Foundation, (99): 192-199; auth, "You Can Go Fly a Kite," The MacGuffin, , (97): 102-105; auth, "An Air of Gaiety and Zest," The Iowa Review, (94): 153-160. **CONTACT ADDRESS** Dept Women's Studies, Univ of Alabama, Tuscaloosa, PO Box 870272, Tuscaloosa, AL 35487-0154.

PIERSON, STEVEN J.
PERSONAL Born 02/05/1950, IL, m, 1979, 2 children **DISCIPLINE** EDUCATION, MUSIC **EDUCATION** Univ Ill, BA, 72; MS, 74; Wheaton Col, MA, 83; Trinity Int Univ, PhD, 98. **CAREER** Acad Dean, Nordiska Bibelinstitutet, 77-92; Wheaton Col, Col Du Page, Trinity Int Univ, 96-. **HONORS AND AWARDS** Wedell Awd for Scholar in Educ, Trinity Int Univ. **MEMBERSHIPS** Asn for the Advanc of Baltic Studies, N Am Asn for Prof of Christian Educ. **RESEARCH** Baltic Singing Culture. **SELECTED PUBLICATIONS** Auth, "De Vanligaste Fragorna och Studierktorns Svar," ("The Most Common Questions and Answers from the Academic Dean"), Nymark (Winter 91): 3; auth, "NMI och des Profil," ("Nordiska Bibelinstitutet and Its Profile"), Nymark (Summer 91): 4; auth, "Cures for Performance Nerves," The Instrumentalist (Mar 98): 62-68; auth, "Laulsime End Vabaks: Muusikaline Tegevus Ja Selle Areng Eesti Kristlaste Seas," ("We Sang Ourselves Free: Musical Experience and Development among Estonian Christians"), Teater Muusika Kino (Dec 98): 23-28; auth, "Misjoniajaloo Iuhiulevaade," ("Missions History"), Oleviste (Aug/Sep 94): 7; auth, "Sweden," "Ansgar," "The Baltics," "Latvia," "Lithuanian," "Dialogue," "Sociology of Music," in The Evangelical Dictionary of Missions, ed. Scott Moreau (Grand Rapids, MI: Baker Book House, 99); auth, "A Nation Than Sang Itself Free," Christianity Today (Oct 25, 99): 99. **CONTACT ADDRESS** Dept Humanities and Fine Arts, Col of DuPage, 425 22nd St, Glen Ellyn, IL 60137-6784. **EMAIL** Pierstevj@aol.com

PIETSCH, PAUL ANDREW
PERSONAL Born 08/08/1929, New York, NY, m, 1950, 4 children **DISCIPLINE** ANATOMY, BIOLOGY, & PHILOSOPHY **EDUCATION** Syracuse Univ, AB, 54; Univ of Pa, PhD, 60. **CAREER** Instr in nursing, School of Nursing, Univ of Pa, 59; instr in anatomy, The Bowman Gray School of Medicine, Wake Forest Col, 60-61; asst prof of anatomy, School of Medicine, School of Dentistry and the Grad School, SUNY, 61-64; senior res molecular biologist, Biochemical Res Lab, The Dow Chemical Co, 64-70; assoc prof, 70-78, chair, Dept of Basic Health Sci, School of Optometry, 75-83, prof, 78-94, prof emer, 94-, Ind Univ. **HONORS AND AWARDS** Medical Journalism Awd, AMA, 72; res featured on 60 Minutes, 73; 14 teaching awards, 73-94. **MEMBERSHIPS** Am Asn of Anatomists; AAAS; Soc Dev Biol (emeritus); Am Federation of Teachers; Am Asn of Univ Profs; Sci Handicapped Asn. **RESEARCH** Neurosciences: memory; developmental biology: regeneration; science journalism: publishing on the World Wide Web. **SELECTED PUBLICATIONS** Auth, Shufflebrain, Houghton-Mifflin, 81; auth, The Mind of a Microbe, Sci Digest, 83; auth, The Effects of Retinoic Acid on Mitosis During Tail and Limb Regeneration in the Axolotl Larva, Ambystoma mexicanum, Roux's Arch Dev Biol, 87; coauth, C.W. Vision and the Skin Camouflage Reactions of Ambystoma Larvae: the Effects of Eye Transplants and Brain Lesions, Brain Res, 85; coauth, The Dermal Melanophore of the Larval Salamander, Ambystoma tigrinum, Cytobios, 92; coauth, Phototaxic Behavior and the Retinotectal Transport of Horseradish Perxidase (HRP) in Surgically Created Cyclopean Salamander Larvae (Ambystoma), Neuroscience Res, 93. **CONTACT ADDRESS** School of Optometry, Indiana Univ, Bloomington, Bloomington, IN 47405-3680. **EMAIL** pietsch@indiana.edu

PIGG, KENNETH E.
DISCIPLINE DEVELOPMENT SOCIOLOGY **EDUCATION** Cornell Univ, PhD, 76. **CAREER** Assoc prof, Univ Ky, 75-83; extension prog dir and assoc dean, Univ Mo, 83-87; assoc prof, Univ Mo, 87- . **RESEARCH** Community development; program evaluation **CONTACT ADDRESS** Univ of Missouri, Columbia, 204 Sociology Bldg., Columbia, MO 65211. **EMAIL** piggk@missouri.edu

PIGOTT, RUTH
PERSONAL Born 11/09/1934, Sac City, IA, s **DISCIPLINE** SOCIOLOGY **EDUCATION** Iowa State Univ, MS, 74; Univ Neb, PhD, 85. **CAREER** Asst to assoc prof, Univ Ne, 74-. **MEMBERSHIPS** Midwest Sociol Soc. **RESEARCH** Family, Women's Studies, Work. **SELECTED PUBLICATIONS** Auth, "Living, Loving and Laboring: Sexual Division of Labor and Durkhumian Functionalism," in Perspectives on Social Problems, (92): 255-274. **CONTACT ADDRESS** Dept Sociol, Univ of Nebraska, Kearney, 905 W 25th St, Kearney, NE 68847.

PINCH, TREVOR J.
PERSONAL Born 01/01/1952, Lisnaskea, N. Ireland, m, 1992, 2 children **DISCIPLINE** SOCIOLOGY, SCIENCE AND TECHNOLOGY STUDIES **EDUCATION** Bath Univ, UK, PhD, 82. **CAREER** Lectr, Dept of Sociology, York Univ, UK, 83-90; prof, Dept of Sci and Technol Stud, Cornell Univ, 90- . **HONORS AND AWARDS** Merton Prize, Am Sociol Asn, 95. **MEMBERSHIPS** ASA; SHOT; HSS. **RESEARCH** Sociology of science and technology, sound technologies and the synthesizer. **SELECTED PUBLICATIONS** Coauth, The Golem: What Everyone Should Know about Science, Cambridge, 94, 2d ed,98; co-ed, The Handbook of Science and Technology Studies, Sage, 95; coauth, The Golem at Large: What You Should Know about Technology, Cambridge, 98; auth, The Hard Sell: The Language and Lessons of Street-Wise Marketing, HarperCollins, 96. **CONTACT ADDRESS** Dept of Science and Technology Studies, Cornell Univ, Clark Hall 622, Ithaca, NY 14853. **EMAIL** TJP2@cornell.edu

PIOTROWSKI, THADDEUS M.
PERSONAL Born 02/10/1940, Poland, m, 1971, 3 children **DISCIPLINE** SOCIOLOGY, POLISH HISTORY **EDUCATION** St Francis Col, BA, 63; Univ Penn, MA, 71; PhD, 73. **CAREER** Prof, Univ NH, 72-. **HONORS AND AWARDS** Outstanding Assoc Prof Awd, Univ NHamp; Fac Scholar Awd, Univ NH; Carpenter Professorship Awd, Univ NH; Cultural Achievement Awd, Am Council for Polish Culture; Literary Awd, Polish Sociol-Cultural Ctr London; Perennial Wisdom Awd, Monuments Conservancy of New York. **MEMBERSHIPS** Am Sociol Asn, Polish Inst of Arts and Sci of Am. **RESEARCH** East Central Europe, Poland, Holocaust. **SELECTED PUBLICATIONS** Auth, Genocide and Rescue in Wolyn: Recollections of the Ukrainian Nationalist Ethnic Cleansing Campaign Against the Poles During World War II, McFarland, 00; auth, Poland's Holocaust: Ethnic Strife, Collaboration with Occupying Forces, and Genocide in the Second Republic, 1918-1947, McFarland, 98; auth, Vengeance of the Swallows: Memoir of a Polish Family's Ordeal Under Soviet Aggression, Ukrainian Ethnic Cleansing and Nazi Enslavement, and Their Emigration to America, McFarland, 95; auth, Ukrainian Integral Nationalism: Chronological Assessment and Bibliography, Toronto, 97; auth, Polish-Ukrainian Relations During World War II: Ethnic Cleansing in Volhynia and Eastern Galicia, Toronto, 95. **CONTACT ADDRESS** Dept Science, Univ of New Hampshire, Manchester, 220 Hackett Hill Rd, Manchester, NH 03102. **EMAIL** thaddeus@cisunix.unh.edu

PISACRETA, RICHARD J.
PERSONAL Born 06/19/1946, New York, NY, m, 1981, 2 children **DISCIPLINE** PSYCHOLOGY **EDUCATION** City Univ NYork, BA, 73; Adelphi Univ, MA, 76; PhD, 79. **CAREER** Asst prof, Ferris State Univ, 80-83, assoc prof, 84-88, prof, 89-. **HONORS AND AWARDS** MAGB Teaching Awd; Humboldt Scholarship Awd. **MEMBERSHIPS** APA, Psychonomic Soc. **RESEARCH** Animal and human cognition. **SELECTED PUBLICATIONS** Coauth with A. Auerbach, Instructor's manual and test bank for Auerbach, The World of Work, Chicago, Il: Brown and Benchmark (96); auth, "Transfer of oddity-from-compound samples in the pigeon: Some assembly required," Behavior Analyst, 37 (96): 103-124; coauth with R. T. Kellogg, The Best Test Preparation for the Graduate Record Examination (GRE) Psychology Test, 4th ed, Piscataway, NJ: REA (97); auth, "Superstitious behavior and response stereotypy prevent the emergence of efficient rule governed behavior in humans," Psychol Record, 48 (98): 251-274. **CONTACT ADDRESS** Dept Soc Sci, Ferris State Univ, 820 Campus Dr, Big Rapids, MI 49307. **EMAIL** Richard.J.Pisacreta@Ferris.edu

PITTS, VERA L.
PERSONAL Born 01/23/1931, Wichita, KS, w **DISCIPLINE** EDUCATION **EDUCATION** Mills Coll, AA 1950; NC Berkeley, BA 1953; Sacramento State Univ, MA 1962; MI State Univ, PhD 1969. **CAREER** Stockton Unified School Dist, teacher, counselor, admin 1954-65; City Coll NY, asst prof 1967-69; Palmer Handwriting Co, consult 1975-; CA State Univ Hayward, prof, dept chair ed admin 1969-; program mgr, Dept of Educ, 86-87; assoc supt, Oakland Unified School District 1987-88; Oakland Public Schools, Oakland, CA, interim supt, 89; Natl Hispanic Univ, San Jose, CA, provost, 90-91. **HONORS AND AWARDS** Mott Fellowship Natl Awd MI 1965-67; Danforth Assoc Found 1974-; Vstg Professorships Univ Houston, Univ MI, Pepperdine Univ 1974-; Rockefeller Postdoctoral Fellowship 1978-80; Natl Faculty Exchange to US Dept of Ed 1986-87. **MEMBERSHIPS** Mem bd dir League of Women Voters 1975-; mem Western Assoc Accrediting Teams 1975-; pres San Mateo Br Amer Assoc Univ Women 1976-77; vice pres CA State Div Amer Assoc Univ Women 1978-82; mem Foster City Ed Facilities Comm 1983; counselor Univ of CA Alumni Assoc 1979-83; Natl Urban League Ed Adv Comm 1979-; dir-at-large Natl Council Admin Women in Ed 1982-; Phi Delta Kappa 1982-85; Pacific School of Religion Bd of Trustees, 1989-; Rotary Intl, 1988-. **CONTACT ADDRESS** Dept Chair, California State Univ, Hayward, 25800 Carlos Bee Blvd, Hayward, CA 94542.

PLASCAK-CRAIG, FAYE D.
PERSONAL Born 01/13/1945, CO, m, 1988, 2 children **DISCIPLINE** PSYCHOLOGY **EDUCATION** Ind Univ, BA, 81; PhD, 88; Purdue Univ, MS, 83. **CAREER** Instr, Marian Col, 83-84, asst prof, 84-87, assoc prof, 87-91, prof, 91-. **HONORS AND AWARDS** Res Awd, Purdue Univ, 83; Reviewer for Teaching of Psychol J, 97-; Teaching Awd, Marian Col, 90. **MEMBERSHIPS** APA, MPA, Sigma Phi Alpha. **RESEARCH** Self concept, student retention, program assessment. **SELECTED PUBLICATIONS** Coauth with R. List, "The effects of dress and gender in a simulated job interview," J of Psychol and the Behav Scis, 5 (90): 55-64; coauth with F. Norton, "The effects of information presentation on rape blame," J of Psychol and the Behav Scis, 6 (91): 127-134; coauth with M. Poynter, "Is the Pygmalion Effect still occurring in the 1990's?," J of Psychol and the Behav Scis, 6 (91): 147-152; coauth with D. Wetzel, "The priming effects of parental divorce on relational attitudes," Modern Psychol Studies: A J of Undergrad Res, 1 (92): 48-52; auth, "A research-based retention case study for an urban liberal arts college," in D. Hossler and J. Bean, eds, Strategic Enrollment Management: A Handbook, San Francisco: Jossey-Bass Pubs (92). **CONTACT ADDRESS** Dept Psychol, Marian Col, 3200 Cold Springs Rd, Indianapolis, IN 46222.

PLATT, GERALD M.
PERSONAL Born 02/13/1933, Brooklyn, NY, s, 2 children **DISCIPLINE** SOCIOLOGY **EDUCATION** Brooklyn College, BA 55, MA 57; Univ Cal LA, PhD 64. **CAREER** Univ Cal LA, inst 61-63; Harvard Univ, lect 64-70; Univ Mass, assoc prof 70-74; John Hopkins Univ, vis assoc prof 73; London Sch Econ Pol Sci, acad vis 77; Univ Cal Santa Cruz, vis prof 78; Univ Cal LA, vis prof 79-80; Univ Mass, prof 74-. **HONORS AND AWARDS** NSF Fel; Carnegie Corp Fel; SSRC Fel; NIH Fel; Inst ASH Fel; Albert Einstein Fel **MEMBERSHIPS** ASA; ESS **RESEARCH** Social movements; social change; the Amer Civil Rights Movement, 1954-1970. **SELECTED PUBLICATIONS** Auth, Race and Gender Discourse Strategies: Creating Solidarity and Framing the Civil Rights Movement, coauth, Social Prob, 98; Correspondents' Images of Martin Luther King Jr: An Interpretive Theory of Movement Leadership, coauth, in: Constructing the Social, eds Theodore R. Sarbin John I. Kitsues, Sage Pub, 94, reprint Leadership : Classical Contemporary and Critical Approaches, ed Keith Grint, Oxford, OUP, 97; Religion Ideology and Electoral Politics, Society, 88, reprint, in: Cultural Wars in Amer Politics: Crit Revs of a Popular Myth, ed, Rhys H. Williams, NY, Aldine De Gruyter, 97; Multiple Images of a Charismatic: An Interpretive Concept of Martin Luther King Jr's Leadership, coauth, in: Self Collected Behavior and Society: Essays Honoring the Contributions of Ralph H Turner, eds, Gerald M Platt Chad Gordon, Contemp Stud in Sociol, Theoretical and Empirical Monos, Greenwich CT, JAI Press, 94. **CONTACT ADDRESS** Dept of Sociology, Univ of Massachusetts, Amherst, Thompson Hall, Amherst, MA 01003. **EMAIL** platt@soc.umass.edu

POGATSHNIK, LEE WOLFRAM
PERSONAL Born 10/12/1955, Camden, NJ, m, 1975, 2 children **DISCIPLINE** PSYCHOLOGY **EDUCATION** Univ Minn, BA, 77; Cornell Univ, PhD, 83. **CAREER** Lecturer, E Conn State Univ, 83-85; Instructor, S Ill Univ, 89-. **HONORS AND AWARDS** Teaching Recognition Awd, SIVE, 99; Grad Thesis Res Awd, Cornell Univ, 80. **MEMBERSHIPS** Am Psychol Soc; Psi Chi. **RESEARCH** Interaction of Gender Development and Math/Science Education. **CONTACT ADDRESS** Dept Psychol, So Illinois Univ, Edwardsville, Edwardsville, IL 62026-1121. **EMAIL** lpogats@sive.edu

POLISCHUK, PABLO
DISCIPLINE PASTORAL COUNSELING, PSYCHOLOGY **EDUCATION** Univ Calif, BA; SF State Univ, MA; Fuller Theol Sem, MA, PhD. **CAREER** Adj prof, S Calif Col; Fuller Theol Sem; instr, Harvard Med Sch; prof, Gordon-Conwell Theol Sem, 80-. **HONORS AND AWARDS** Ch psychologist, Chelsea Health Ctr; dir, Willowdale Ctr for Psychol Svc. **SELECTED PUBLICATIONS** Auth, Depression and its Treatment; The Therapeutic Counseling; Dotting the I's. **CONTACT ADDRESS** Gordon-Conwell Theol Sem, 130 Essex St, South Hamilton, MA 01982.

POLK, ROBERT L.
PERSONAL Born 05/08/1928, Chicago, IL, d **DISCIPLINE** EDUCATION **EDUCATION** Doane Coll, BA 1952; Hartford Theol Sem, MDiv 1955; Doane Coll, Hon Dr of Div 1971; Huston-Tillotson, Hon Dr of Div 1984. **CAREER** 1st Congregational Church Berthold ND, pastor 1955-57; YMCA Minot ND, youth prog coord 1957-60; Riverside Church, minister to youth 1960-66; Dillard Univ New Orleans, dean of chapel & dean of students 1966-68; Riverside Church, minister of urban affairs 1969-76; Edwin Gould Serv for Children, exec dir 1976-80; Council of Churches City of NY, exec dir, 80-88; City Coll of New York, City Univ of New York, Acting Vice Pres External Relations & Community Affairs, 88-. **HONORS AND AWARDS** Distinguished Service Awd, Black Christian Caucus Riverside Church 1983; Sam Levinson Memorial Awd, Jewish Community Relations Council, New York City 1984. **MEMBERSHIPS** Chmn CUNY Constr Fund; Mayor's Comm of Religious Leaders, Assoc Black Charities, Hole-in-the-Wall-Gang Camp Inc; New York City Bd of Educ, Capital Task Force on Construction & Renovation of Public Schools; New York State Dept of Educ Interfaith Educ Advisory Council to the Commr of Educ; Governor's Comm on Scholastic Achievement; Health Watch Advisory Bd. **CONTACT ADDRESS** External Relations & Community Affairs, City Col, CUNY, 138th St & Convent Ave, A-2050, New York, NY 10031.

POLL, CAROL
PERSONAL Born 01/19/1942, w **DISCIPLINE** SOCIOLOGY **EDUCATION** Hunter Col, BA, 65; MA, 70; Univ Center of the city of NYork, PhD, 78. **CAREER** Adj Asst Prof, Queens Col, 87-91; Assoc Prof, Fashion Institute of Technol, 80-. **HONORS AND AWARDS** Avalon Group Awd, SUNY, 98; chancellor's Awd for Excellence in Teaching, SUNY, 98; Outstanding Fac Advisor Recognition Awd, Fashion Inst Of Technol, 92. **MEMBERSHIPS** Am Sociol Asn, Am Educ Res Asn, Asn for the Soc Sci Study of Jewry, Eastern Sociol Soc, Oral Hist Asn, Oral Hist in the Mid-Atlantic Region, Soc for the Study of Disability, Sociol for Women in Soc. **RESEARCH** Sociology of Teaching; Sociology of Jewry; Oral History as a Research Technique **SELECTED PUBLICATIONS** Auth, "The Jewish Community in America: It is the Safest of Times and the Most Dangerous of Times," in Jewish Identity in the Postmodern Age, Paragon House, 99; auth, "Priced Out of the Marital market: The Case of the Single Achieving Jewish Women," Current Research: Proceedings, (98): 213-227; auth, "Term Paper: An Analysis of a Family," in Teaching About Families: A Collection of Syllabi, Projects, & Class Materials, Washington, 97; auth, "More that Reading books: Using Oral Histories in Courses in Race and Ethnic Relations," Teaching Sociology, (95): 145-149; auth, "Beyond 'The Stand and Deliver' Model of Teaching Sociology: Strategies for Teaching Students with Learning Disabilities," Current Research, 94; auth, "Good IDEA Gone Wrong: The Need to Rework the 'Individuals with Disabilities Education Act'; for Children," Sociological Practice Review, (92): 203-211; rev, of "Critical Choices: Applying Sociological Insight in Your Life, Family, and Community," by Scott Sernau, Journal of the American Sociological Association, 98; rev, of "Anti-Semitism, Misogyny, and The Logic of Cultural Difference: Casare Lombroso and Matilde Serao," by Nancy Harrowitz, Jewish Book World, 94; rev, of "Minorities: The New Europe's Old Issue," Institute for East West Studies, 95. **CONTACT ADDRESS** Dept Soc Sci, Fashion Inst of Tech, 227 W 27th St, New York, NY 10001-5902. **EMAIL** profpoll@aol.com

POLLACK, BONNIE N.
DISCIPLINE PSYCHOLOGY **EDUCATION** Univ Mich, MA, 92; MS, 94; PhD, 96. **CAREER** Asst Prof, Univ NC at Charlotte, 96-. **HONORS AND AWARDS** Lyman Porter Awd for Best Doctoral Student Paper, 92; Jr Fac Summer Fel, 97. **MEMBERSHIPS** APA, AOM, SIOP. **RESEARCH** Organizational Psychology. **SELECTED PUBLICATIONS** Auth, "Hierarchical Linear Model and the 'unit of analysis' problem," Group Dynamics; auth, "The impact of the sociophysical environment in. . .," People, Places, and Public Policy. **CONTACT ADDRESS** Dept Psychology, Univ of No Carolina, Charlotte, 9201 Univ City, Charlotte, NC 28223. **EMAIL** bonnienp@email.uncc.edu

POLLACK, ROBERT
PERSONAL Born 06/26/1927, New York, NY, m, 1948, 3 children **DISCIPLINE** PSYCHOLOGY **EDUCATION** CUNY, BS, 48; Clark Univ, MA, 50, PhD, 53. **CAREER** Lect, Univ of Sydney, 53-61; special res fel, Columbia Univ, 61; deputy dir res, Inst for J Res; prof, Univ Ga, 69-96, prof emeritus, 96-. **HONORS AND AWARDS** Hugo G. Beigrl Awd , Soc for the Sci Study of Sexuality; originated graduate courses in perceptual development, perceptual aging, human sexual behavior, art and eroticism, developmental theory; developed grad specialty in human sexuality; grad progs in developmental and experimental psychol. **MEMBERSHIPS** Am Psychology Asn, Am Assoc for the Advancement of Sci. **RESEARCH** A developmental approach to human sexual behavior. **SELECTED PUBLICATIONS** Coed with M. J. Brenner, The experimental psychology of Alfred Binet, NY: Springer Pub Co (69, 74); auth, "Perceptuo-cognitive performance in the aged," in S. Wapner and B. Kaplan, eds, Toward a Holistic Developmental Psychology, NY: Erlbaum (83); coauth with T. Stanford, "Configurational color vision tests: The inaction between aging and the complexity of figure-ground segregation," J of Gerontology, 39 (84): 568-571; coauth with A. Raj, "Factors predicting High-Risk Sexual Behavior in Heterosexual College Females," J of Sex & Marital Therapy, 21 (95): 213-224; coauth with Lara Blackford and Shannon Doty, "Differences in Subjective Sexual Arousal in Heterosexual, Bisexual, & Lesbian Women," Can J of Human Sexuality, 5 (96): 157-167; coauth with T. J. Corley, "Sex role ideology: do changes in the stereotypical depiction of a Lesbian couple effect heterosexuals' attitudes towards Lesbianism?," J of Homosexuality, 32 (96): 1-18; coauth with S. F. Pearson, "Female Response to sexually explicit films," J of Psychol and Human Sexuality, 9 (97): 73-87. **CONTACT ADDRESS** Dept Psychol, Univ of Georgia, Ga Ave, Athens, GA 30602. **EMAIL** bpollack@arches.uga.edu

POLLARD, DIANE S.
PERSONAL Born 10/31/1944, Richmond, VA, m **DISCIPLINE** EDUCATION **EDUCATION** Wellesley Coll, BA 1966; Univ of Chicago, MA 1967, PhD 1972. **CAREER** Roosevelt Univ, instructor 1969-72; Univ of WI, asst prof 1972-76, assoc prof 1976-, assoc prof of educ psychology & dir ctr for study of minorities & disadvantaged 1979-85; prof, 93-. **HONORS AND AWARDS** AERA/SIG Research on Women & Education, Willystine Goodsell Awd, 1996; Faculty Distinguished Public Service Awd, 1993. **MEMBERSHIPS** Mem Amer Educ Rsch Assn 1972-; mem Assn of Black Psychologists 1973-; mem Eta Phi Beta Inc 1978-; mem Soc for the Psychological Study of Social Issues; mem Alpha Kappa Alpha, Inc. **SELECTED PUBLICATIONS** Author: "A Profile of Black Professional Women in Educ, Psychology and Sociology"; "Perceptions of Black Parents Regarding the Socialization of their Children"; "Against the Odds: A Profile of Academic Achievers from the Urban Underclass," Journal of Negro Education, 1989; "Patterns of Coping in Black School Children;" Motivational Factors Underlying Achievement; book chapter, Black Women, Interpersonal Support and Institutional Change in Changing Education: Woman as Radicals and Conservators; "Reducing the Impact of Racism on Students," in Educational Leadership, 1990; "Toward a Pluralistic Perspective on Equity," WEEA Digest, 1992; co-author, book, Gender and Achievement, 1993; "Perspectives on Gender & Race," Educational Leadership, 1996; "Race, Gender & Educational Leadership," Educational Policy, 1997. **CONTACT ADDRESS** Educ Psych, Univ of Wisconsin, Milwaukee, Milwaukee, WI 53201.

POLOMA, MARGARET MARY
PERSONAL Born 08/27/1943, Los Angeles, CA, d **DISCIPLINE** SOCIOLOGY **EDUCATION** Case Western Reserve Univ, PhD, 70. **CAREER** Prof emer, sociol, Univ Akron, Oh, 70-; visiting prof, grad relig and sociol, Southern Calif Col, Costa Mesa, 97-. **MEMBERSHIPS** Soc for the Sci Study of Relig; Relig Res Asn; Asn for the Sociol of Relig. **RESEARCH** Sociology of Religion, Spirituality and Health; Pentecostal/charismatic movement; Prayer. **SELECTED PUBLICATIONS** Coauth, with John C. Green, James L. Guth & Corwin E. Smidt, The Politics of Protestant Preachers, Univ Ks Press, Lawrence, Ks, 97; monogr, The Toronto Report, Terra Nova Publ, Wiltshire, UK, 96; jour articles, Routinization and Reality: Reflections on Serpents and the Spirit, Intl Jour for the Psychol of Relig, 8, 101-105, 98; coauth, with Lynette F. Hoelter, The Toronto Blessing: A Holistic Model of Healing, Jour for the Sci Study of Relig, vol 37, no 2, 258-273, fall, 98; The Spirit Movement in North America at the Millennium: From Azusa Street to Toronto, Pensacola and Beyond, Jour of Pentecostal Theol, 12, 83-107, 98; The Toronto Blessing: Charisma, Institutionalization, and Revival, Jour for the Sci Study of Relig, vol 36, no 2, 257-271, jun, 97; Charisma, Institutionalization and Social Change, Pneuma, Jour of the Soc for Pentecostal Studies, vol 17, no 2, 245-253, fall, 95. **CONTACT ADDRESS** 2872 Silver Lake Blvd., Silver Lake, OH 44224. **EMAIL** mpoloma@uakron.edu

POLVINO, GERALDINE J.
PERSONAL Born 07/23/1941, Rochester, NY, s **DISCIPLINE** PHYSICAL EDUCATION **EDUCATION** State Univ NYork, Brockport, BS, 63; Eastern Ky Univ, Richmond, MA, 66; Univ Iowa, PhD, 70. **CAREER** Retired Head Coach, Volleyball, Eastern Ky Univ Division I Program, 66-97; certified coach-instr, Fedn Int Volleyball and United States Volleyball Asn Coaching Accreditation Prog; prof, Physical Educ, Eastern Ky Univ. **HONORS AND AWARDS** Ohio Valley Conf Coach of the Year, 81-86, 88, 90; First female Coach-Instr of the Fedn Int Volleyball, Rome, Italy, 82; Ohio Valley Conf All Time Volleyball Coach Awd, 88; inducted into the Hall of Fame, State Univ of NY at Brockport, 89; Eastern Ky Univ Hall of Distinguished Alumni, 91; recognized for 600 wins by the Am Volleyball Coaches Asn, 95; Nat Asn for Girls and Women in Sports, Pathfinder Awd, 97; Disney Sports Student Internship, 98-99; assoc ed, In t J Volleyball Res, 98-; bd of dirs, United States Volleyball Asn, 96-2000; United States Volleyball Asn Awds and Recognition Chair, 96-2000; Nat Asn Girls and Women in Sports, Vollleyball Rules Chair, 97-2000 **MEMBERSHIPS** North Am Soc for the Psychol of Sport and Physical Activity; Am Alliance for Health, Physical Educ, Recreation, and Dance; United State Volleyball Asn. **SELECTED PUBLICATIONS** Auth, "Concentrate," USA Coaching Accreditation Manual (98); auth, "Funding for Collegiate Volleyball," Coaching Volleyball (90); auth et al, Volleyball's Cadre Collection, Vol II, Volleyball Support Syndicate (90); coauth with Terry Lawton, "Interactive Behavior Between Coach and Official," Coaching Volleyball (97); coauth with Terry Lawton, "Unlimited Substitution," Coaching Volleyball (97); auth, Nat Asn Girls and Women's Sport, Volleyball Rule Book (98, 99). **CONTACT ADDRESS** Dept Physical Educ, Eastern Kentucky Univ, 521 Lancaster Ave, Richmond, KY 40475.

POMPER, PHILIP
PERSONAL Born 04/15/1936, Chicago, IL, m, 3 children **DISCIPLINE** HISTORY, RUSSIAN HISTORY AND PSYCHOHISTORY **EDUCATION** Univ Chicago, BA; MA; PhD; Wesleyan Univ, MAAE. **CAREER** Wesleyan Univ. **HONORS AND AWARDS** Assoc ed, History and Theory. **SELECTED PUBLICATIONS** Auth, Peter Lavroc and the Russian Revolutionary Movement, 72; auth, Sergei Nechaev, 79; auth, The Structure Of Mind In History, 85; ed, Trotsky's Notebooks, 1933-1935, 86; auth, Lenin, Trotsky, and Stalin: The Intelligentsia and Power, 90; auth, The Russian Revolutionary Intelligentsia, 2nd ed., 93; coed, History and Theory: Contemporary Readings, 98. coed, World History: Ideologies, Structures, and Identities, 98. **CONTACT ADDRESS** Wesleyan Univ, Middletown, CT 06459-0002. **EMAIL** ppomper@wesleyan.edu

PONDER, FRED T.
PERSONAL Born 03/06/1940, Coosa County, AL, m, 1987, 1 child **DISCIPLINE** PSYCHOLOGY, EDUCATION **EDUCATION** Univ Ala, EdS, 71; Univ N Tex, PhD, 87. **CAREER** Fayetteville State Univ, NC, 82-84; Texas A & M Univ Kingsville Tex, 95-. **MEMBERSHIPS** APA, Am Coun Asn. **RESEARCH** Addictions. **SELECTED PUBLICATIONS** Auth, "The Quest for a Better Search," Black Issues in Higher Educ 15-20 (Nov 98): 144; auth, "The 1998 Conventional Toronto," PHP News (Fall 98). **CONTACT ADDRESS** Dept Educ, Texas A&M Univ, Kingsville, 700 Univ Blvd, MSC 196, Kingsville, TX 78363. **EMAIL** Fred.Ponder@tamuk.edu

POPENOE, DAVID
PERSONAL Born 10/01/1932, Los Angeles, CA, m, 1959, 2 children **DISCIPLINE** SOCIOLOGY **EDUCATION** Antioch Univ, AB, 54; Univ of Pa, MCP, 58; PhD, 63. **CAREER** Asst to Full Prof, Rutgers Univ, 61-; Soc & Behav Sci Dean, Rutgers Univ, 88-97. **HONORS AND AWARDS** Sr Fulbright Res Scholar; Vis Fulbright Lectr in Greece, Isreal, Spain; Am Counc of Learned Soc Fel; Am Scand Found Fel; Govnt of Sweden Fel; Rutgers Univ Res Coun Fel. **MEMBERSHIPS** Nat Fatherhood Initative, Civil Soc Project, Parenting Project, Howard Center for Family, Relig, and Soc, Duquesne Family Inst Coun on Families (co-ch 92-96). **RESEARCH** Family and community life in modern societies. **SELECTED PUBLICATIONS** Ed, The Urban-Industrial Frontier, 69; co-ed, Neighborhood, City and Metropolis, 70; auth, The Suburban Environment: Sweden and the United States, 77; auth, Private Pleasure, Public Plight: Am Metropolitan Community Life in Comparative Perspective, 85, 89; co-ed, Housing and Neighborhoods, 87; auth, Disturbing the Nest: Family Change and Decline in Modern Societies, 88; auth, Life Without Father: Compelling New Evidence that Fatherhood and Marriage are Indispensable for the Good of Children and Society, 96, 99; co-ed, Promises to Keep: Decline and Renewal of Marriage in Am, 96; auth, Sociology , col textbook, 11 ed, 71-00. **CONTACT ADDRESS** Dept Sociol, Rutgers, The State Univ of New Jersey, New Brunswick, PO Box 5072, New Brunswick, NJ 08903. **EMAIL** dpopenoe@rci.rutgers.edu

PORTER, CURTISS E.
PERSONAL Born 12/29/1939, Braddock, PA, d **DISCIPLINE** EDUCATION **EDUCATION** Univ Pgh, BA; Univ Pgh, PhD. **CAREER** Univ Pittsburgh, chmn dept of black comm educ research & devel; DBCERD/PITT, asso dir 1969-72; DBCERD-PITT, dir program devel 1972-74. **MEMBERSHIPS** Chmn Reg 3 Nat Counc of Black Studies; consult Def Race Rels Inst; spl guest 6th Pan African Congress; mem Commn on Educ & Rsrch African Heritage Studies Assn; exec bd Nat Coun of Black Studies; mem Assn for the Study of Afro-Am Life & Hist; part Kuntu Writers Workshop; fdr Black Horizons Theatre; fdr Black Action Soc; mem Adv EST; mem EST Hunger Proj Com. **CONTACT ADDRESS** 3804 Forbes Ave, Pittsburgh, PA 15260.

PORTER, DAVID B.
PERSONAL Born 06/17/1949, Lexington, KY, m, 1971, 2 children **DISCIPLINE** BEHAVIORAL SCIENCE **EDUCATION** USAF Acad, BS, 71; Univ Calif, MS, 72; Oxford Univ, DPhil, 86. **CAREER** Prof, USAF Acad, 86-. **HONORS AND AWARDS** Distinguished Grad, 71. **MEMBERSHIPS** APS, Am Assoc. of Higher Educ. **RESEARCH** Creativity, learning organizations, leadership. **SELECTED PUBLICATIONS** Auth, "Computer Games: Paradigms of opportunity," Behav Roes Methods, Instruments and Comput, 27 (95): 229-234; auth, United States Air Force Academy Educational Outcomes Assessment Working Group, Phase II, Final Report, (USAF Acad, CO), 97; auth, "Educational Outcomes Assessment: The Good, The Bad and the Ugly," Adult Assessment Forum: J of Qual Management in Adult Centered Educ, 8 (98); coauth, "Reflections on Accreditation, Assessment and Accountability,"

Assessment and Accountability Forum, 9 (99): 3-4, 15, 19; coauth, "The Toothless Bathing Beauty and the T-Test," Teaching Statistics (forthcoming). **CONTACT ADDRESS** Dept Behav Sci, United States Air Force Acad, 2304 Cadet Dr, United States Air Force Academy, CO 80840. **EMAIL** david.porter@usafa.af.mil

PORTER, JACK NUSAN
PERSONAL Born 12/02/1944, Rovno, Ukraine, d, 2 children **DISCIPLINE** SOCIOLOGY **EDUCATION** Univ Wisconsin, BA 67; Northwestern Univ, MA PhD, 67-71. **CAREER** Harvard Univ, res assoc 82-84; The Spencer Group, pres 84-; Spencer Sch of RE, exe dir 86-; Spencer Inst for Bus & Soc, 84-; Boston Univ, asst prof 89-90, vis lect 87-88; Bryant Col, vis lect 91; Adj Prof Soc, Univ Mass at Lowell. **HONORS AND AWARDS** John Atherton Fel; Nom Natl Jewish Bk Awd; Who's Who in America; vp assoc of genocide scholars; advisory bd cen for comparative genocide; ed bd of the encycl of genocide; ntl steering comm black fam stud. **MEMBERSHIPS** PEN; Harvard Club; ASA; Bnai Brith Realty Lodge; AAAS. **SELECTED PUBLICATIONS** Auth, The Jew as Outsider: Historical and Contemporary Perspectives: Collected Essays; Genocide and Human Rights: A Global Anthology; Jewish Partisans: A Documentary of Jewish Resistance in the Soviet Union; Jews in Cults; Kids in Cults; Handbook of Cults, Sects and Alternative Religious Groups; The Sociology of Jewry; Women in Chains: A Source Book on the Agunah; Sexual Politics in Nazi Germany: The Persecution of the Homosexuals. **CONTACT ADDRESS** The Spencer Inst, 35 Webster St, Apt 4, West Newton, MA 02465-1859. **EMAIL** jacksonnusan@aol.com

PORTER, SAMUEL C.
PERSONAL Born 09/25/1952, Eugene, OR, d, 1 child **DISCIPLINE** RELIGION; SOCIOLOGY OF RELIGION AND CULTURE IN THE US **EDUCATION** Emory Univ, PhD, 96. **CAREER** Instr, Univ OR, 98-. **HONORS AND AWARDS** Graduate fellowships, tuition scholarships, Emory Univ. **MEMBERSHIPS** Am Academy of Relig; Asn for the Sociology of Relig; Soc for the Scientific Study of Relig; Asn of Religious Res. **RESEARCH** Sociology of religion and culture; religion in the US; history and theory of religion; morality and society; religion and ecological politics. **SELECTED PUBLICATIONS** Auth, Review, The Future of Religion: Secularization, Revival, and Cult Formation, by Rodney Stark and William Sims Bainbridge, in the J for the Am Academy of Relig 54, 86; submission under review, The Paufre Northwest Forest Debate: Bringing Religion Back In?, Worldviews: Environment, Culture, and Religion, ed, Clare Palmer, Univ Greenwich, 98. **CONTACT ADDRESS** Dept of Sociology, Univ of Oregon, 1291 Univ of Oregon, Eugene, OR 97403-1291. **EMAIL** sporter@oregon.uoregon.edu

PORTES, PEDRO R.
PERSONAL Born 06/19/1950, Havana, Cuba, m, 1977, 1 child **DISCIPLINE** PSYCHOLOGY **EDUCATION** Univ Iowa, BS, 72; Nova Univ, MS, 77; Fla State Univ, PhD, 82. **CAREER** Prof, Univ Louisville, 82-. **HONORS AND AWARDS** Fulbright Awd, Peru, 87-88; Fulbright Awd, Colombia, 96; President's Distinguished Research Fac Awd, 98; Who's Who. **MEMBERSHIPS** AERA, Soc for Res on Identity Formation. **RESEARCH** Educational policy re: Group-based Inequality; Cultural psychology; Family interaction and Cognitive development; Cultural influences on educational achievement; Children's divorce adjustment. **SELECTED PUBLICATIONS** Auth, "Cultural Differences in Self-Esteem: Ethnic Variations in the adaptation of Recent Immigrant Asian Adolescents," in Issues in Counseling Asian and Pacific Islanders, Nova Pub, 99; auth, Chapter in The Academic Achievement of Minority Students, Univ Press of Am, in press. **CONTACT ADDRESS** Dept Educ Psychol, Univ of Louisville, 2301 S 3rd St, Louisville, KY 40292-2001. **EMAIL** prport01@louisville.edu

POTTER, ELIZABETH
DISCIPLINE WOMEN'S STUDIES **EDUCATION** Agnes Scott Col, Atlanta, BA, 69; Rice Univ, Houston, MA, 73, PhD, 74. **CAREER** Alice Andrews Quigley prof; Mills Col, 92-. **HONORS AND AWARDS** AESA's Critic's Choice awd, 93. **RESEARCH** Gender and science; intersections of feminism and epistemology; philosophy. **SELECTED PUBLICATIONS** Auth, Underdetermination Undeterred, in Feminism, Science and the Philosophy of Science, Kluwer Acad Publ, 96; Good Science and Good Philosophy of Science, in Synthese, Vol 104, 95; ethodological Norms in Traditional and Feminist Philosophy of Science, in PSA 94, Vol 2, 95; Locke's Epistemology and Women's Struggles, in Modern Engendering: Critical Feminist Essays in the History of Western Philosophy, SUNY Press, 94; coauth, Gender and Epistemic Negtiation, Elizabeth Potter, When Feminisms Intersect Epistemology; coed, Feminist Epistemologies, Routledge, 93. **CONTACT ADDRESS** Dept of Women's Studies, Mills Col, 5000 MacArthur Blvd, Oakland, CA 94613-1301. **EMAIL** epotter@mills.edu

POTTS, D. MALCOLM
DISCIPLINE SOCIOLOGY **EDUCATION** St Catherine's Col, UK, MBb, 62; Sidney Sussex Col, UK, PhD, 65. **CAREER** Fel, Sidney Sussex Col, 64-67; med doc, IPPF, London, 68-78; pres, CEO, Fam Hlth Intl, 78-90; Bixby prof, Univ Cal, Berkeley, 92-. **MEMBERSHIPS** ZSL; APHA; PAA. **SELECTED PUBLICATIONS** Coauth, Ever Since Adam and Eve: The Evolution of Human Sexuality, UP (Cambridge), 99; coauth, Queen Victoria's Gene, Suttons (Eng), 95; coauth, Natural Human Fertility: Social and Biological Determinants, Macmillan (London), 88; auth, "The Unmet Need for Family Planning," Sci Am 282 (00): 70-76; auth, "Sex and the Birth Rate: Human biology, demographic change, and access to fertility regulation," Population and Devel rev 23 (97): 1-39; coauth, "Abortion and fertility regulation," Lancet 347 (96): 1663-1668. **CONTACT ADDRESS** Sch Public Health, Univ of California, Berkeley, 140 Warren Hall, Berkeley, CA 94720-7360. **EMAIL** potts@socrates.berkeley.edu

POUNCEY, ALICE
PERSONAL Born 07/09/1939, Lauderdale, MS, m, 1959, 3 children **DISCIPLINE** PSYCHOLOGY **EDUCATION** Jones Jr Col, AA, 59; Univ Southern Miss, MS, 61; Livingston Univ, MS, 68; **CAREER** Instr, Jr High Sch Soc Studies, 61-63; Instr, High Sch Home Econ and Psychol, 63-. **HONORS AND AWARDS** Outstanding Fac Awd, 93; Eccc Instructor of the Year Awd, 94; Who's Who among Am Teachers, four years. **MEMBERSHIPS** Miss Prof Ed, Miss Asn Women in Higher Ed, MJC Fac Asn, Eccc Fac Asn. **CONTACT ADDRESS** Dept Bus and Soc Sci, East Central Comm Col, PO Box 121, Decatur, MS 39327. **EMAIL** apouncey@eccc.cc.ms.us

POWELL, LYDIA C.
PERSONAL Born 03/26/1953, Oxford, NC, m, 1979, 2 children **DISCIPLINE** EDUCATION **EDUCATION** Wake Forest Univ, BA, 75; NCar Central Univ, MA, 84. **CAREER** Prof to Prog Head, Vance-Granville Cmty Col, 79-. **MEMBERSHIPS** NCCCSPA. **CONTACT ADDRESS** Dept Gen Educ, Vance Granville Comm Col, PO Box 917, Henderson, NC 27536. **EMAIL** powell@admin.vgcc.cc.nc.us

POWER, MARY
DISCIPLINE IRISH AND WOMEN'S LITERATURE **EDUCATION** Univ Wis, PhD, 67. **CAREER** Instr, Univ NMex, 67-. **RESEARCH** James Joyce. **SELECTED PUBLICATIONS** Auth, Molly Bloom and Mary Anderson: The Inside Story, Europ Joyce Stud, 90. **CONTACT ADDRESS** Univ of New Mexico, Albuquerque, Albuquerque, NM 87131. **EMAIL** rejoyce@unm.edu

POYTHRESS, N. G.
PERSONAL Born 04/01/1947, Birmingham, AL, d **DISCIPLINE** CLINICAL PSYCHOLOGY **EDUCATION** Univ TX at Austin, PhD, 77. **CAREER** Psychologist, Ctr for Forensic Psychiat, 77-82; Psychologist, Taylor Hardin Secure Med Facil, 82-90; prof, Univ South FL, 90-. **MEMBERSHIPS** Fel, Am Psychological Asn. **RESEARCH** Psychology and law. **SELECTED PUBLICATIONS** Auth, "The competence-related abilities of women criminal defendants," J of the Am Acad of Psychiatry and the Law 26 (98): 215-222; auth, auth, "Psychometric properties of the MacArthur Competence Assessment Tool-Criminal Adjudication (MacCAT-CA)," Psychological Assessment 10, (98): 435-443; auth, Prediction of dangerousness and release decision-making, In V.B. Van Hasselt & M. Hersen, eds, Handbook of Psychological Approaches with Violent Criminal Offenders: Contemporary Strategies and Issues, New York: Kluwer Acad/Plenum, 99; auth, "Effects of state organizational structure and forensic examiner training on pretrial competence assessments," J of Behavioral Health Services & Research 26 (99): 140-150; auth, "Identifying inmates at risk for disciplinary infractions: A comparison of two measures of psychopathy," Behavioral Sciences and the Law 17 (99): 435-443; auth, Construct validity of the Psychopathic Personality Inventory in a correctional sample, J of Personality Assessment 74, (00): 262-281; auth, C. Commentary on "The Mental State at theTime of the Offense Measure," J of the Am Acad of Psychiatry and the Law 28, (00): 29-32; auth, "Mental health courts: A workable proposition? Psychiatric Bulletin 25 (01): 5-7; auth, Procedural justice in the context of civil commitment: An analogue study," Behavioral Sciences and the Law 18 (01): 731-740. **CONTACT ADDRESS** Dept of Mental Health Law and Policy, Univ of So Florida, 13301 Bruce B Downs Blvd, Tampa, FL 33612-3899. **EMAIL** poythres@mirage.fmhi.usf.edu

PRADES, JOSE ALBERT
PERSONAL Born 11/01/1929, Valencia, Spain, m, 1971 **DISCIPLINE** SOCIOLOGY OF RELIGION **EDUCATION** Cath Univ Louvain, lic econ, 57, lic soc sci, 63, PhD(soc sci), 65. **CAREER** Asst soc sci, Cath Univ Louvain, 65-70; asst prof sociol relig, Cath Inst Paris, 70-71; vis prof, 71-74, Prof Sociol Relig, Univ Que, Montreal, 74-, Dir Dept Relig, 78-, Mem, Coun Sci Res, Spain, 65-; Conf Learned Socs, Can, 71- **MEMBERSHIPS** Fr-Can Asn Advan Sci. **RESEARCH** Contemporary industrial society; ultimate concerns and social class in Canada today. **SELECTED PUBLICATIONS** Auth, Valeurs Religieuses En Milieu Urbain, Social Compass, 66; La Cociologie De La Religion Chez Max Weber, Nauwelaerts, Louvain, 69; Sur Le Concept De Religion, Relig Studies, 73; Renouveau Communantaire Et Utopie Autogestionnaire, In: Renouveau Communantaire Au Quebec, Ed Fides, 74. **CONTACT ADDRESS** Dept of Relig, Univ of Quebec, Montreal, C P 8888, Montreal, QC, Canada H3C 3P8. **EMAIL** prades.jose_a@uqam.ca

PRAETZELLIS, ADRIAN
PERSONAL Born London, England, m, 1975, 2 children **DISCIPLINE** ANTHROPOLOGY **EDUCATION** Univ Calif Berkeley, PhD. **CAREER** Assoc prof, Sonoma State Univ, 92-. **RESEARCH** Historical archaeology, local history, cultural resources management. **CONTACT ADDRESS** Dept Anthrop, Sonoma State Univ, 1801 E Cotati Ave, Rohnert Park, CA 94928. **EMAIL** adrian.praetzellis@sonoma.edu

PRAHLAD, SW. ANAND
DISCIPLINE POETRY AND FOLKLORE **EDUCATION** UCLA, PhD, 91. **CAREER** Assoc prof; adj fac, anthropology dept and Black Studies Prog. **HONORS AND AWARDS** Grants to work on the production of multimedia packages for classroom instr. **MEMBERSHIPS** Inst for African Diasporan Literatures and Languages. **SELECTED PUBLICATIONS** Auth, Hear My Story and Other Poems, Berkeley Poets Workshop, 82; Under His Own Vine and Fig Tree: A Theory of Contextual Meaning in African-American Proverb Speech Acts, Univ Miss Ptes, 96; auth, African-American Proverbs in Context, UP of Miss, 96. **CONTACT ADDRESS** Dept of English, Univ of Missouri, Columbia, 306 Tate Hall, Columbia, MO 65211. **EMAIL** FollyD@missouri.edu

PRANZARONE, GALDINO F.
PERSONAL Born 05/09/1942, Chicago, IL, m, 1997, 1 child **DISCIPLINE** PSYCHOLOGY **EDUCATION** Loyola Univ Chicago, BS Psychology, 66; Peabody Col Vanderbilt Univ, MA Psychology, 68; Peabody Col Vanderbilt Univ, PhD Psychology, 72. **CAREER** Prof of Psychology at Roanoke Col, Salem VA, 72-. **MEMBERSHIPS** Amer Assoc for Advancement of Science; SIEECUS; Amer Assoc of Sex Educators; Counselor & Therapists; Society for the Scientific Study of Sexuality. **RESEARCH** Study of Sexuality, Love map theory of John Money; Paraphilias; Pornography. **SELECTED PUBLICATIONS** Auth, "Money & Pranzarone Development of the Paraphilias in Childhood and Adolescence," Psychiatric Clinics of North America, 93. **CONTACT ADDRESS** Dept Psychology, Roanoke Col, 221 College Lane, Salem, VA 24153.

PRELL, RIV-ELLEN
PERSONAL Born 10/15/1947, Los Angeles, CA, m, 1970, 2 children **DISCIPLINE** AMERICAN STUDIES, JEWISH STUDIES, ANTHROPOLOGY **EDUCATION** Univ S Calif, BA; Univ Chicago, MA; PhD. **CAREER** From assoc prof to prof of Am Studies, Univ Minn, Twin Cities. **HONORS AND AWARDS** Phi Beta Kappa; Nat Jewish Bk Awd, 89. **MEMBERSHIPS** ASA; ASSJ; JSA. **RESEARCH** Ethnicity, 20th century American Jews, ritual, religion. **SELECTED PUBLICATIONS** Auth, Fighting to Become Americans: Jews, Gender and the Anxiety of Assimilation; auth, Prayer and Community: The Hauura in American Judaism; coed, Interpreting Women's Lives: Personal Narratives and Feminist Theory. **CONTACT ADDRESS** Dept Am Studies, Univ of Minnesota, Twin Cities, 72 Pleasant St SE, 203 Scott Hall, Minneapolis, MN 55455. **EMAIL** prell001@tc.umn.edu

PRENTICE, ALISON
PERSONAL Born Wilmington, DE **DISCIPLINE** EDUCATION, HISTORY **EDUCATION** Smith Col, BA, 55; Univ Toronto, MA, 58, PhD, 74. **CAREER** Tch, hist, Bishop Strachan Sch, 55-57; tchg asst, hist, Univ Toronto, 58-59; tchr, Harbord Col Inst, 59-61, 63; tchg asst, Univ Toronto, 64-67; lectr, asst prof, York Univ, 72-73; assoc prof, 75-83, Prof History & Philos, Ont Inst Srud Educ, Univ Toronto, 83-, found head, Ctr Women's Studs, 83-85. **SELECTED PUBLICATIONS** Auth, the School Promoters: Education and Social Class in Mid-Nineteenth Century Upper Canada, 77; coauth, Schooling and Scholars in Nineteenth Century Ontario, 88; coauth, Gender and Education in Ontario: An Historical Reader, 91. **CONTACT ADDRESS** Dept of Theory & Policy Stud in Educ, OISE, Univ of Toronto, Toronto, ON, Canada M5S 1V6. **EMAIL** aprentice@oise.on.ca

PRESSEAU, JACK R.
PERSONAL Born 11/16/1933, Curtisville, PA, m, 1955, 4 children **DISCIPLINE** RELIGIOUS EDUCATION **EDUCATION** IN State Tchr(s), Col PA, BS, 55; Pittsburgh-Xenia Sem, MDiv, 58; Presby Sch Christian Educ, MCE, 59; Univ Pittsburgh, PhD, 65. **CAREER** Assoc pastor, North Presby Church, Elmira, NY, 59-62; studies asst relig educ, Univ Pittsburgh, 63-65; assoc prof relig & psychol, 65-69, prof psychol, 69-75, counselor, 72-75, Prof Relig, Presby Col, SC, 69-98, retired, 98. **RESEARCH** Faith development; recruiting and training for church vocations. **SELECTED PUBLICATIONS** Auth, I'm Saved, You're Saved--Maybe, John Knox Press, 77; Gospel illustrations: What's memorable may be irrelevant, Duke Divinity Sch Rev, winter 78; Life maps, Harvard Educ Rev, 11/80; Tradition, trends, and tomorrow, Presby Survey, 9/81; Pendulum swings and pre-ministerial preparation, The Presby Outlook, 4/12/80; Teach-niques, John Knox Press, 82. **CONTACT ADDRESS** Rt 2, Box 327, Clinton, SC 29325-2865.

PRESSER, HARRIET B.
PERSONAL Born 08/29/1936, New York, NY, d, 1 child **DISCIPLINE** SOCIOLOGY **EDUCATION** George Washington Univ, BA, 59; Univ NC, MA, 62; Univ Calif, PhD, 69. **CAREER** Lecturer, Univ Sussex, 67-68; Staff Assoc, Population Council, 68-69; Vis Lecturer, Rutgers Univ, 69-74; Asst to Assoc Prof, Columbia Univ, 69-76; Prof, Univ Md, 76-. **HONORS AND AWARDS** Outstanding Woman on Campus, Univ Md, 99; Hero of the School of Public Health, Columbia Univ, 98; Distinguished Alumni Scholar of the Year, George Washington Univ, 92; Who's Who in Am, Who's Who of Am Women, Resident Scholar, Rockefeller foundation, 00; distinguished Fac Res Fel, Univ Md,93-94 **MEMBERSHIPS** Population Asn of Am, Am Sociol Asn, Am Public Health Asn **SELECTED PUBLICATIONS** Ed, Women's Empowerment and Demographic Processes: Moving Beyond Cairo, Oxford Univ Press, in press; auth, Toward a 24-Hour Economy, forthcoming; auth, "Nonstandard Work Schedules and Marital Instability," Journal of Marriage and the Family, (00): 93-110; auth, "Nonstandard Employment Schedules Among American Mothers: The Relevance of Marital Status," in Work and Family: Research Informing Policy, Sage Pub, (00): 97-130; auth, "Toward a 24-Hour Economy," Science, (99): 1178-1179; auth, "The State Bonus to Reward a Decrease in 'Illegitimacy': Flawed Methods and Questionable Effects," Family Planning Perspectives, (99): 142-147; auth, "Toward a 24-Hour Economy: The US Experience and Implications for the Family," in Challenges for Work and Family in the 21st Century, 98; auth, "Decapitating the US Census Bureau's 'Head of Household': Feminist Mobilization in the 1970s," Feminist Economics, (98): 147-160; auth, "Demography, Feminism, and the Science-Policy Nexus," Population and Development Review, (97): 295-331; auth, "The Work Schedules of Low-Educated American Women and Welfare Reform," Monthly Labor Review, (97): 25-34. **CONTACT ADDRESS** Dept Sociol, Univ of Maryland, Col Park, 2112 art-Sociology, College Park, MD 20742-0001. **EMAIL** presser@socy.umd.edu

PRIBRAM, KARL H.
PERSONAL Born 02/25/1919, Vienna, Austria, m, 1960, 5 children **DISCIPLINE** PSYCHOLOGY **EDUCATION** Univ Chicago, BS, 38; MD, 41. **CAREER** Prof Emeritus, Stanford Univ, 59-89; Prof, Radford Univ, 89-; Distinguished Res Prof, Georgetown Univ, 99-. **HONORS AND AWARDS** NIH Lifetime Res Career Awd, 89; Realia Honor, Inst for Adv Philos Res, 93; First Neural Network Leadership Awd, 94; Computing Anticipatory Systems Awd, Belgium 99; Vize Prize, 99; Med of Consciousness Res, 99. **MEMBERSHIPS** AAAS; AAUP; AMA; AMNH, AAA; APS; IBNS; NYAS; SEP; Soc for Neuroscience. **RESEARCH** Brain Science. **SELECTED PUBLICATIONS** Auth, Brain and Perception; auth, Languages of the Brain; auth, Plans and the Structure of Behavior. **CONTACT ADDRESS** Dept Psychol, Radford Univ, PO Box 6946, Radford, VA 24142.

PRICE, SALLY
PERSONAL Born 09/16/1943, Boston, MA, m, 1963, 2 children **DISCIPLINE** ANTHROPOLOGY **EDUCATION** Harvard Univ, AB, 65; Johns Hopkins, PhD, 82. **CAREER** Prof, Col of William & Mary. **HONORS AND AWARDS** Alice and Edith Hamilton Prize. **RESEARCH** Art, Museums, Gender, Caribbean. **SELECTED PUBLICATIONS** Auth, Maroon arts: Cultural Vitality in the African Diaspora, Beacon Press, 99; co-auth, Enigma Variations, Harvard Univ Press, 95; auth, Co-Wives and Calabashes 2nd ed, Univ Mich Press, 93; co-ed, Stedman's Surinam: Life in an Eighteenth-Century slave society, Johns Hopkins Univ Press, 92; co-auth, Equatoria, Routledge Pub, 92; co0auth, Two Evenings in Saramaka, Univ Chicago Press, 91; auth, Primitive Art in civilized Places, Univ Chicago Press, 89. **CONTACT ADDRESS** Dept Anthropol, Col of William and Mary, PO Box 8795, Williamsburg, VA 23187-8795. **EMAIL** rixsal@wm.edu

PRICE, TANYA Y.
PERSONAL Born Cincinnati, OH **DISCIPLINE** SOCIOLOGY **EDUCATION** Miami Univ, AB, 85; Ind Univ, MA, 88; PhD, 94. **CAREER** Assoc instr to vis asst prof, 88-94; vis asst prof, Southern IL Univ, 94-93; asst prof, Univ of Miss, 98-. **HONORS AND AWARDS** Fel, Ind Univ, 85-87; Fel, Confessional Black Caucus Found, 90-91; US Dept of Educ For Lang Fel, 92; Elliott Lieber Awd for Outstanding Student Teaching 93; Grant, Southern IL Univ, 97. **MEMBERSHIPS** Am Anthrop Assoc; Assoc of Black Anthrop; Wash Assoc of Practicing Anthrop. **RESEARCH** Race and racism, policy, African Diaspora, African American Culture. **SELECTED PUBLICATIONS** Auth, "Ms Datin Paduka Ruby Lee", Resolution, Congressional Record, (90): E3474; auth, "Archibald W Singham", Resolution, Congressional Record, (91): E2161; auth, "Learning the Ropes, One Year in the Life of a Congressional Staffer", Practicing throp (Jan 98); auth, "White Public Spaces in Black Places: The Social Reconstruction of Whiteness in Washington, DC", Urban Anthrop 27.3-4, (99): 301-344. **CONTACT ADDRESS** Dept Sociol, Univ of Missouri, Kansas City, 5100 Rockhill Rd, Kansas City, MO 64110. **EMAIL** priceta@umkc.edu

PRICE-SPRATLEN, TOWNSAND
PERSONAL Born Bellingham, WA **DISCIPLINE** SOCIOLOGY **EDUCATION** Univ Wash, BS, 85; MA, 90; PhD, 93. **CAREER** Instr, Pa State Univ, 94-95; asst prof, Ohio State Univ, 95-. **HONORS AND AWARDS** Grant, ASA/NSF Fund, 96; Grant, Ohio State Univ, 97. **SELECTED PUBLICATIONS** Auth, "Negotiating Legacies: Audre Lorde, W.E.B. DuBois, Marlon Riggs and Me", Harvard Educ Rev 66 (96): 216-230; auth, "Leaps of an Unjust Faith: Missing Links in the Causes of Labor Force Participation", Measured Lies: The Bell Curve Examined, eds, J.L. Kinchloe, S.R. Steinberg and A.D. Gressom III, St. Martins Pr, 96; coauth, "On Ways of Thinking About and Measuring Neighborhoods: Implications for Studying Context and Developmental Outcomes for Children, Neighborhood Poverty: Policy Implications in Studying Neighborhoods, Vol 2, eds, J. Brooks-Gunn, G.J. Duncan and J. Lawrence Aber, Russell Sage, (NY), 97; coauth, "Through the Eyes of Children: An Ethnographic Perspective on Neighborhoods and Child Development", Minn Symp on Child Psychol, Vol 29, ed A. Masten, Erlbaum (NJ, 98); auth, "Between Depression and Prosperity? Changes in the Community Context of Historical African American Migration", Soc Forces 77 (98): 515-540; coauth, "The Geography of Homelessness in the United States, Pop Res and Policy Rev, 99; auth, "Gendered Ethnogenesis and the Great Migration: African American Women's Depression Era Migration", Gender, Race and Class 6, (99): 147-170; auth, "Living For the City: African American Community Development and Depression Era Migration", Demography 36, (99): 553-568; auth, "Nurturing Images, Whispering Walls: Identity Intersections and Empowerment in the Academic Workplace, Queer Theory, Pedagogy and Cultural Practices, eds S. Talburt and S.R. Steinberg, Peter Lang Pub, (NY), 00; auth, "Safe Among Strangers: Queer Reflections on the Million Man March", The Greatest Taboo, ed D. Constantine-Simms, Alyson Pub, (forthcoming). **CONTACT ADDRESS** Dept Sociol, Ohio State Univ, Columbus, 190 N Oval Mall, Columbus, OH 43210. **EMAIL** TPS+@osu.edu

PRIMOUS, DIANELLA
PERSONAL Born 02/03/1943, Greenwood, MA, d, 2 children **DISCIPLINE** SOCIOLOGY **EDUCATION** Tougaloo Col, BS, 65; Univ Ill Chicago, MS, 67; Chicago State Univ, MS in Criminal Justice, 78; NOVA Univ, EdD, 81. **CAREER** Res Asst, Univ of Ill, 65-66; Resident Asst, Univ of Ill, 66-67; Teacher, Chicago City Col, 69-. **MEMBERSHIPS** Acad of Criminol, Am Sociol Asn. **RESEARCH** Marriage and Family. **CONTACT ADDRESS** Dept Soc and Behav Sci, Malcolm X Col, 1900 W Van Buren St, Chicago, IL 60612.

PRINS, HARALD E.
PERSONAL Born 09/01/1951, Alphen a/d Rijn, Netherlands, m, 1985 **DISCIPLINE** ANTHROPOLOGY **EDUCATION** Univ Nymegen, Netherland, Cand, 72, Drs, 76; Parsons School Design, NY, Certificate Filmmaking, 80; New School for Social Res, PhD, 88. **CAREER** Asst prof, Univ Nijmegen, Netherlands, 76-78; Dir res & develop, Asn Aroostook Indians, 81-82; staff anthropol, Aroostook Band of Micmacs, 82-90; vis lect, Bowdoin Col, ME, 86-88; vis prof, SALT Inst for Documentary Film Studies, 90; vis asst prof, Colby Col, ME, 88-89; prof anthropol, Kans State Univ, 90-. **HONORS AND AWARDS** Aroostook Micmac Indian Service Awd, 82; Native Rights Expert Witness, US Congress, 90, Can Provincial Court, 99-2000; ed bd mem, Maine Hist, 91-; jury Baxter Awd, Maine Hist Soc, 91-; int observer, Presidential Elections, Paraguay, 93; Conoco Awd for Outstanding Undergraduate Teaching, Kans State Univ, 93; hon mention for film "Wabanaki: A New Dawn," 96; finalist, Margaret Mead Awd, Soc Applied Anthropol, 92, 97; jury, SVA Ethnographic Film & Video Festival, 98; ed bd mem, Am Anthropol, 97-2000; vis anthropol ed, Am Anthropol, 97-2000; pres, Soc for Visiual Anthropol, 99-2001. **MEMBERSHIPS** Am Anthropol Asn, Soc for Visual Anthropol, Am Soc for Ethnohistory, Soc for Latin Am Anthropol. **RESEARCH** Cultural anthropology, ethnohistory, ethnographic film, indigenous peoples, North Central South America. **SELECTED PUBLICATIONS** Auth, "Cornfields at Meductic: Ethnic and Territorial Reconfigurations in Colonial Acadia," Man in the Northeast, 44: 55-72 (92); auth, "To the Land of the Mistigoches: American Indians Traveling to Europe in the Age of Exploration," Am Indian Culture and res J, 17(1): 175-95 (93); coed with E. Baker, et al, American Beginnings: Exploration, Culture and Cartography in the Land of Norumbega, Lincoln: Univ Nebr Press (96); auth, "Turmoil on the Wabanaki Frontier, 1524-1678," in Maine: The Pine Tree State from Prehistory to Present, ed by R. Judd, et al, Orono: Univ Press of Maine (95); auth, The Mi'kmag: Resistance, Accomodation, and Cultural Survival, Ft. Worth: Harcourt Brace Col Pubs (96); auth, "Tribal Network and Migrant Labor: Mi'kmag Indians as Seasonal Workers in Aroostook's potato Fields (1870-1980)," in Native Americans and Wage Labor: Ethnohistorical Perspectives, ed by A. Littlefield and M. Knack, Norman: Univ of OK Press, (96); auth, "Chief Rawandagon alias Robin Hood: Native 'Lord of Misrule' in the Maine Wilderness," in Northeastern Indian Lives, 1632-1816, ed by R. Grumet, Amherst: Univ Mass Press (96); auth, "The Paradox of Primitivism: Native Rights and the Problems of Imagery in Cultural Surviival Films," Visual Anthropol, 9: 243-266 (97); auth, "Eine Handuoll Asche: Uberlegungen zu 'Traurige Tropen'," in Wegmarken: Eine Bibliothek der Ethnologischen Imagination, ed by R. Kapfer, et al, Wuppertal: Peter Hammer Verlag (98); auth, "Chief Big Thunder (1827-1906): The Life of a Penabscot Trickster,": Maine Hist, 37(3): 140-158 (98). **CONTACT ADDRESS** Dept Sociol & Anthropol, Kansas State Univ, 207 Waters Hall, Manhattan, KS 66506. **EMAIL** prins@ksu.edu

PRUITT, ANNE SMITH
PERSONAL Born Bainbridge, GA, m, 5 children **DISCIPLINE** EDUCATION **EDUCATION** Howard Univ, BS (cum laude), 1949; Teachers Coll Columbia Univ, MA 1950, EdD 1964. **CAREER** Howard Univ, counselor 50-52; Hutto HS, dir of guidance 52-55; Albany State Coll, dean of students, 55-59; Fisk Univ, dean of students, 59-61; Case Western Reserve Univ, prof of educ, 63-79; OH State Univ, assoc dean grad school, 79-84, assoc provost, 84-86, dir Center for Teaching Excellence, 86-94, prof of Educ Policy and Leadership, 79-95; Council of Graduate Schools, dean in residence, 94-96, Scholar in Residence, 96-. **HONORS AND AWARDS** Outstanding Alumnus Howard Univ 1975; Amer Council on Educ Fellow 1977-78; honorary degree DHum Central State Univ 1982; Named one of America's Top 100 Black Business & Professional Women, Dollars & Sense Magazine 1986; Ohio State Univ Distinguished Affirmative Action Awd 1988; Amer Coll Personnel Assn Senior Scholar Awd 1989, Dipolmate, 1996; Phi Beta Delta Honor Soc for Intl Scholars 1989. **MEMBERSHIPS** Mem Alpha Kappa Alpha Sor; mem Links Inc; consultant Women's Job Corps creation Pres Lyndon Johnson's War on Poverty 1964; mem bd of trustees Cleveland Urban League 1965-71; consultant Southern Regional Educ Bd 1968-81; mem Bd of Trustees Central State Univ 1973-82; moderator Mt Zion Congregational Church 1975-78; Research Task Force Southern Educ Found 1978-87; mem Adv Comm US Coast Guard Acad 1980-83; Amer Assn for Counseling and Devel; sec, Journal bd mem, pres-elect, pres 1976-77, 1st Black, Amer Coll Personnel Assn; Amer Educ Research Assn; Amer Assn for Higher Educ; Amer Assn of Univ Professors; mem Columbus, OH, Mayor's Task Force on Private Sector Initiatives 1986-88, bd of trustees, Case Western Reserve Univ 1987-; member, board of directors, Columbus Area Leadership Program, 1988-92; member, Columbus 1992 Education Committee, 1988-92; co-chairperson, Ohio State Univ United Way Campaign, 1990-91; member, National Science Foundation, Committee on Equal Opportunities in Science and Engineering, 1989-95; coordinator, CIC Alliance for Success Planning Committee, 1989-90; Black Women's Agenda, pres, 1998-. **CONTACT ADDRESS** Scholar in Res, Council of Graduate Schools, One Dupont Circle NW, Ste 430, Washington, DC 20036-1173. **EMAIL** apruitt@cgs.nche.edu

PRUITT, DEAN
PERSONAL Born 12/26/1930, Philadelphia, PA, m, 1959, 3 children **DISCIPLINE** PSYCHOLOGY **EDUCATION** Oberlin Col, BA, 52; Yale Univ, MS, 54; PhD, 57. **CAREER** Asst to Assoc Prof, Univ of Del, 61-66; Assoc to Distinguished Prof, State Univ of NYork at Buffalo, 66-. **HONORS AND AWARDS** Phi Beta Kappa; Sigma Xi; Harold D. Lasswell Awd for Distinguished Scientific Contrib to Polit Psychology, Int Soc of Polit Psychology; Lifetime Achievement Awd, Int Asn for Conflict Management; Wilhelm Wundt Awd, NY State Psychol Asn. **MEMBERSHIPS** Am Psychol Asn, Am Psychol Soc, Int Asn for Conflict Management. **RESEARCH** Social conflict, Bargaining, Mediation. **SELECTED PUBLICATIONS** Auth, Negotiation behavior, Acad Press (NY), 81; coauth, Mediation research: The process and effectiveness of third-party intervention, Jossey-Bass (San Francisco), 89; coauth, Negotiation in social conflict, Open Univ Press (Buckingham, England), and Brooks/Cole (Pacific Grove, CA), 93; coauth, Social conflict: Escalation, stalemate and settlement, McGraw-Hill (NY), 94; coauth, "A brief history of Oslo talks," Int Negotiation 2 (97): 177-182; auth, "Ripeness theory and Oslo talks," Int Negotiation 2 (97): 237-250; coauth, "Escalation as a reaction to persistent annoyance," Int J of Conflict Management 8 (97): 252-270; auth, "Social conflict," in Handbook of social psychology, ed. D.T. Gilbert, S.T. Fiske, and G. Lindzey (NY: McGraw-Hill, 98), 4th ed vol 2 470-503; auth, "Alternative dispute resolution," and "Conflict resolution," in Encyclopedia of Psychology (in press); auth, "Mediator behavior and success in negotiation," in Mediation in international relations, ed. J. Bercovitch (NY: St. Martin's Press, in press). **CONTACT ADDRESS** Dept Psychology, SUNY, Buffalo, Park Hall, PO Box 604110, Buffalo, NY 14260-0001. **EMAIL** dpruitt@acsu.buffalo.edu

PSATHAS, GEORGE
PERSONAL Born 02/22/1929, New Haven, CT, m, 1951, 3 children **DISCIPLINE** SOCIOLOGY **EDUCATION** Yale Univ, BA, 1950; Univ Michigan, MA, 51; Yale Univ, PhD, 56; New England School Photography, MA 78-79 **CAREER** Emeritus prof, Boston Univ, 97-; editor-in-chief, Human Studies, 78-; guest prof, Institute Human Sciences, Vienna, April 96; visiting prof, Manchester Univ, March 96; prof Sociology, Boston Univ, 68- **HONORS AND AWARDS** Postdoctoral fel, National Inst Mental Health, 61-62; Science Faculty Prof Develop Awd, National Sci Found 78-79; Fulbright Grant, 82; British Academy for Res in Gt Brit, 95-96 **MEMBERSHIPS** Amer Sociol Assoc; Eastern Sociol Soc; Amer Assoc Univ Professors; Int Visual Sociol Assoc; Soc Phenomenol Existential Philos; Soc Phenomenol Human Sci **RE-**

SEARCH Social Interaction; Phenomenological Sociology; Qualitative Methods; Ethnomethodology; Visual Sociology **SELECTED PUBLICATIONS** "On Zaner's Methods for Becoming an Ethicist," Human Studies, 98; On multiple realities and the world of film," Sociol Aspect Lit, 97; "Phenomenology in Sociology in the United States," Encycl Phenomenol, 97; co-ed, Alfred Schultz Collected Papers, Kluwer, 96; ed, "Ethnomethodology: Discussions and Contributions," Human Studies, 95 **CONTACT ADDRESS** Dept Sociol, Boston Univ, 100 Cummington St., Boston, MA 02215. **EMAIL** Geops1@bu.edu

PULLEN, DANIEL J.
PERSONAL Born 05/19/1954, Pittsburg, KS **DISCIPLINE** CLASSICAL ARCHAEOLOGY; ANTHROPOLOGY **EDUCATION** Univ Kans, BA, 76; Indiana Univ, MA, 78,PhD, 85. **CAREER** Administrator, Sardis Expedition, Harvard Univ Art Museums; asst prof, classics dept, 88-93, assoc prof, 93- , FL State Univ. **HONORS AND AWARDS** Univ Teaching Awd, FL State Univ, 98. **MEMBERSHIPS** Archaeological Institute of Am; Soc for Amer Archaeology; **RESEARCH** Classic studies Aegean Prehistory; Classical Archaeology; Complex Societies **SELECTED PUBLICATIONS** Auth, Modelling Mortuary Behavior on a Regional Scale: A Case Study from Mainland Greece in the Early Bronze Age, Beyond The Site: Regional Studies in the Aegean Area, 94; auth, A lead seal from Tsoungiza Hill, Ancient Nemea, and Early Bronze Age Sealing Systems, American Journal of Archaeology, 94; auth, Artifact and Assemblage: The Finds from a Regional Survey of the Southern Argolid, Greece, vol I: The Prehistoric and Early Iron Age Pottery and the Lithic Artifacts, 95. **CONTACT ADDRESS** Dept of Classics, Florida State Univ, Tallahassee, FL 32306-1510.

PURCELL, TREVOR W.
PERSONAL Born 06/26/1945, Jamaica, d, 1 child **DISCIPLINE** ANTHROPOLOGY **EDUCATION** Brooklyn Col, BA, 75; Johns Hopkins Univ, PhD. **CAREER** Asst Prof, Reed Col, 82-88; Assoc Prof, Univ S Fla, 92-. **HONORS AND AWARDS** NSF Res Grant, 98-99; Wenner Gren Res Grant, 93-96; Ford Foundation Fel, 75-79. **MEMBERSHIPS** Am Anthropol Asn; Caribbean Studies Asn; Soc for Applies Anthropol. **RESEARCH** Caribbean societies; Diaspora; Indigenous knowledge in development; Social theory. **SELECTED PUBLICATIONS** Auth, Banana Fallout: Class, Color and Culture among West Indians in Costa Rica, UCLA Press, 93. **CONTACT ADDRESS** Dept Afro-Amer Studies, Univ of So Florida, 4202 E Fowler Ave, Tampa, FL 33620-9951. **EMAIL** purcell@chuma1.cas.usf.edu

PURKEY, WILLIAM WATSON
PERSONAL Born 08/22/1929, Shenandoah, VA, m, 1951, 2 children **DISCIPLINE** EDUCATION **EDUCATION** Univ Va, Bs, 57; MEd, 58; EdD, 64. **CAREER** Teacher, Public Schools Chatham, NJers, 58-61; Asst Prof to Prof, Univ Fla, 64-76; Prof, Univ NCar, 76-. **HONORS AND AWARDS** Instructor Excellence, Univ FL; Teaching Awd, Standard Oil foundation; Outstanding Teacher Awd, Omicron Delta Kappa; John McGovern Awd; Professional Development Awd; Alumni Teaching Excellence Awd; Board of Governors Awd for Excellence in Teaching. **MEMBERSHIPS** AERA; ASCD; ACA. **RESEARCH** Invitational theory; Human motivation; Self-concept theory **SELECTED PUBLICATIONS** Auth, Inviting School Success; auth, The Inviting School Treasury; auth, Invitational Counseling; auth, What Students Say to Themselves: Internal Dialogue and School Success, Corwin Press **CONTACT ADDRESS** Dept Coun and Educ Dev, Univ of No Carolina, Greensboro, PO Box 26171, Greensboro, NC 27412-5001. **EMAIL** wwpurkey@uncg.edu

PUTSCHE, LAURA
DISCIPLINE ANTHROPOLOGY **EDUCATION** Univ Wash, BA, BS, 81; Wash State Univ, MA, 85; PhD, 93. **CAREER** Assoc prof, Univ of Idaho, 93-. **HONORS AND AWARDS** Alumni Asn Awd for Fac Excellence. **MEMBERSHIPS** Am Anthrop Assoc; Soc for Latin Am Anthrop; Sigma Xi; Idaho Acad of Science. **RESEARCH** Indigenous peoples of South America, particularly Amazonia, cultural ecology; indigenous peoples. **SELECTED PUBLICATIONS** Auth, "Changes in Frontier Development and the New Indian Resistance in Brazil", Humboldt Jour of Social Relations 19.2 (93): 131-156; auth, "The Dynamics of State Expansion and Indian Resistance in Brazil" in Race, Ethnicity and Gender: A Global Perspective, eds. Samuel Oliner and Philip Gay, Kendall/Hunt (97):179-195; auth, "A Reassessment of Resource Depletion, Market Dependency, and Culture Change on a Shipibo Reserve in the Peruvian Amazon" Human Ecology 28.1, 00. **CONTACT ADDRESS** Dept Sociol and Anthrop, Univ of Idaho, PO Box 441110, Moscow, ID 83844-1110. **EMAIL** putsche@uidaho.edu

PYLE, RALPH
PERSONAL Born 09/22/1953, Bryn Mawr, PA, m, 1996 **DISCIPLINE** SOCIOLOGY **EDUCATION** Villanova Univ, BA, 87; Purdue Univ, MA, 89; PhD, 95. **CAREER** Lect, Univ Nev, 95-96; Lect, Univ Nev, 96-97; Vis Asst Prof, Mich State Univ, 97-. **MEMBERSHIPS** Relig Res Assoc. **RESEARCH** Religion, social stratification, race and ethnicity. **SELECTED PUBLICATIONS** Coauth, "Persistence and Change in the Protestant Establishment 1930-1992," Soc Forces 74 (95): 157-175; auth, Persistence and Change in the Protestant Establishment, Praeger (Westport, CT), 96: coauth, "Forward to the Past," in Religion, Mobilization and Soc Action (Westport, CT: Praeger, 98); coauth, "Public Religion and Economic Inequality," in The Power of Relig Publics (Westport, CT: Praeger, 99). **CONTACT ADDRESS** Dept Sociol, Michigan State Univ, 316 Berkey Hall, East Lansing, MI 48824. **EMAIL** ralph.pyle@ssc.msu.edu

Q

QUAYTMAN, JOYCE A.
PERSONAL Born 11/04/1944, Tacoma, WA, d, 1 child **DISCIPLINE** PSYCHOLOGY **EDUCATION** Cal State Univ Northridge, BA, 73; Pepperdine Univ, MA, 75; Cal Grad Sch, PhD, 92. **CAREER** Perm lect, Univ La Paz, MX; lect, CSUC, Butte Comm Col, Univ San Francisco; priv pract, marr/fam thera; clin psychol. **HONORS AND AWARDS** Pres, Psych Clin, USSR, 89; Bech Clin, 89. **MEMBERSHIPS** AAMFT. **RESEARCH** Domestic violence; substance abuse; addictions; systems theories. **SELECTED PUBLICATIONS** Auth, "Violent Families: Cross Generational Transmission of Events in the Cycle of Abuse," Doct Diss, Library Congress, (WA, DC), 92. **CONTACT ADDRESS** Dept Psychology, California State Univ, Chico, 2240 St George Lane, Ste 4 & 5, Chico, CA 95926. **EMAIL** mkbooks@mkbooks.com

QUICKEL, KIM
PERSONAL Born 06/05/1958, Lafayette, IN, m, 1992, 4 children **DISCIPLINE** PSYCHOLOGY **EDUCATION** Calif State Univ Long Beach, BA, 79; MA, 82. **CAREER** Prof, Community Col, Orange Coast and Saddleback, 84-; Therapist, 84-. **MEMBERSHIPS** Calif Asn of Marriage and Family Therapists, Anorexia Nervosa and Assoc Disorders. **RESEARCH** Eating Disorders. **CONTACT ADDRESS** Dep Soc and Behav Sci, Saddleback Col, 2800 Marguerite Pky, Mission Viejo, CA 92692.

QUINN, JAMES F.
PERSONAL Born 08/31/1955, Cheverly, MD, m, 1987 **DISCIPLINE** SOCIOLOGY **EDUCATION** Fla Int Univ, BA; Univ Miami, MA, 83; La State Univ, PhD, 86. **CAREER** Assoc prof of Addictions and Criminal Justice (joint appt), Univ of North Tex. **HONORS AND AWARDS** Frederick M. Threshen Awd for Innovative Gang Res, 94. **RESEARCH** Drugs, corrections, rehabilitation, offender behavior, criminal justice policy. **SELECTED PUBLICATIONS** Coauth with Richard Enos, Clifford m. Black, and John E. Holman, Alternative Sentencing: Electronically Monitored Correctional Supervision, Bristol, IN: Wyndham Press (92); coauth with John E. Holman, Criminology: Applying Theory, West: St Paul, MN (92); coauth with Bill Downs, "Predictors of Gang Violence: The Impact of Drugs and Guns on Police Perceptions in Nine States," J of Gang Res, 2, 3 (spring 95): 15-27; coauth with John E. Holman, Criminal Justice: Principles and Perspectives, West: St Paul, MN (96); auth, Corrections: A Concise Introduction, Waveland Press, Prospect Heights, Il (99); auth, "Community Participation in the Parole Process: Texas' Community Participatory Councils," Corrections Management Quart, 3, 2 (spring 99): 77-83; auth, "The Complex Intertwining of Drugs and Crime," in The Encyclopedia of Criminology and Deviant Behavior, Clifton Bryant, ed-in-chief, London: Taylor & Francis (forthcoming 2000). **CONTACT ADDRESS** Sch of Community Service, Univ of No Texas, PO Box 310919, Denton, TX 76203-0919. **EMAIL** quinn@scs.cmm.unt.edu

QUINSEY, VERNON L.
PERSONAL Born 10/10/1944, Flin Flon, MAN, Canada, m, 1992, 5 children **DISCIPLINE** PSYCHOLOGY **EDUCATION** Univ N Dak, BSc, 66; Univ Mass Amherst, MSc, 69; PhD, 70. **CAREER** Teaching fel, Smith Col, 69-70; postdoc fel, Dalhousie Univ, 70-71; psychologist to dir, Penetanguishene Mental Health Centre, 71-84; vis scientist, Philippe Pinel Inst Montreal, 84-86; assoc prof, Univ Toronto, 86-88; prof, Queen's Univ, 88-. **HONORS AND AWARDS** Significant Achievement Awd, Asn for the Treatment of Sexual Abusers, 94; Sen Res Fel, Ont Mental Health Found, 97-03. **MEMBERSHIPS** Can Psychol Asn; Am Psychol Soc; Am Psychol Asn; Human Beh and Evolution Soc; Intl Acad of Sex Res; Asn for the Treatment of Sexual Abusers; Beh and Brain Sci; Assoc of the Soc for Evolutionary Analysis in Law. **RESEARCH** Prediction, modification, and management of antisocial and violent behavior; Applied decision making; Program development and evaluation; Sexual preference assessment; Sex offenders; Forensic/correctional psychology; Evolutionary explanations of sexual and aggressive behaviors. **SELECTED PUBLICATIONS** Co-auth, "Evolutionary perspectives on sexual offending," Sexual Abuse, (95): 301-315; co-auth, "Proximal antecedents of eloping and reoffending among mentally disordered offenders," J of Interpersonal Violence, (97): 794-813; co-auth, The criminal recidivism process, Univ Cambridge Press, 97; co-auth, Violent offenders: Appraising and managing risk, am Psychol Asn, 98; co-auth, Assessment of sexual offenders against children, rev ed, Sage, 01; co-auth, "Evidence of a taxon underlying serious antisocial behavior in Boys," Criminal Justice Behavior, in press. **CONTACT ADDRESS** Dept Psychol, Queen's Univ at Kingston, 50 Arch St, Kingston, ON, Canada K7L 3L6. **EMAIL** quinsey@psyc.queensu.ca

QUIVIK, FREDRIC L.
PERSONAL Born 08/10/1949, Northfield, MN, m, 1971 **DISCIPLINE** HISTORY, SOCIOLOGY OF SCIENCE **EDUCATION** Univ Pa, PhD, 98 **CAREER** Archit hist, 82-90; Consulting Hist Tech, 94-. **MEMBERSHIPS** Soc Ind Archeol; Soc Hist Tech; Soc Archit Historians. **RESEARCH** Hist tech; Am West, 19th, 20th cent especially hist of metallurgical engg. **SELECTED PUBLICATIONS** Auth, The Industrial Landscape of Butte and Anaconda, in Images of an American Land, Univ NM, 97. **CONTACT ADDRESS** 2830 Pearl Harbor, Alameda, CA 94501. **EMAIL** fquivik@lmi.net

R

RAABE, PHYLLIS H.
PERSONAL Born 04/17/1941, Philadelphia, PA, d, 2 children **DISCIPLINE** SOCIOLOGY **EDUCATION** Pa State Univ, BA, 63; MA, 68; PhD, 73. **CAREER** Asst prof, Loyola Unv, 69-75; project leader, Tulane Univ, 79-80; asst prof, Univ of New Orleans, 81-. **HONORS AND AWARDS** Fulbright-Hays Seminar, Czechoslovakia, 91; Grant, LA Ctr for Women and Govt. **MEMBERSHIPS** Am Sociol Assoc; Sociol for Women in Soc; Int Soc for Work Options. **RESEARCH** Women, work and family, Alternative Work Arrangements, Policies that Promote Work-Family Integration and Gender Equality. **SELECTED PUBLICATIONS** Auth, "Constructing Pluralistic Work and Career Arrangements", in the Work-Family Challenge: Rethinking Employment, eds Suzan Lewis and Jeremy Lewis, Sage, 96; auth, "Work-Family Policies for Faculty: How 'Career and Family-Friendly' is Academe?, in Academic Couples, eds Marianne Ferber and Jane Loeb, Univ of IL Pr, 97; auth, "Women, Work and Family in the Czech Reputlis - and Comparisons with the West", Community Work & Family 1.1. (98); auth, "Being a Part-time Manager: One Way to Combine Family and Career, in Challenges for Work & Family in the 21st Century, eds Dana Vannoy and Paula Dubeck, Aldine de Gruyter, 98; auth, "Women and Gender in the Czech Republic and Cross-National Comparisons", Czech Sociol Rev, VII.2 (99). **CONTACT ADDRESS** Dept Sociol, Univ of New Orleans, 2000 Lakeshore Dr, New Orleans, LA 70148-0001. **EMAIL** praabe@uno.edu

RAAJPOOT, UZZER A.
PERSONAL Born 08/08/1947, Pakistan, m, 1979, 2 children **DISCIPLINE** SOCIOLOGY **EDUCATION** Punjab Univ, BA, 66; MA, 69; Univ Ore, MA, 87; PhD, 91. **CAREER** Res Asst, Pakistan Inst of Develop Econom, 73-75; Staff Demographer, Pakistan Inst of Develop Econom, 75-82; Teaching Asst, Univ Ore, 83-86; Grad Student Teacher, Univ Ore, 86-90; Prof, Univ Tex, 91-. **MEMBERSHIPS** Population Assoc of Am. **RESEARCH** Demography, statistics. **SELECTED PUBLICATIONS** Auth, "Estimation of Net Currently Married Life Within the Reproductive Period of Females in Pakistan," Pakistan Develop Rev vol xiv, no 1 (75); auth, "Change and Differentials in the Women's Knowledge of, Attitude Towards and Practice of family Planning in Pakistan During the 60's," Pakistan Develop Rev, vol xlv, no 3 (75); auth, "Change and Differentials in the Men's Knowledge of, Attitude Towards and Practice of Family Planning in Pakistan," Res Report, no 100, Pakistan Inst of Develop Econom (77); auth, "Differentials in Cumulative Fertility by Education of Mother," Res Report no 112, Pakistan Inst of Develop Econom (80); auth, "Correlates of Birth Intervals: Fresh Evidence from the World Fertility Survey Data," Int J of Contemp Sociol, vol 32, no 1 (95); auth, "An Investigation into the Spacing of Births Among a Sample of Ever-Married Women," Soc Sci J, Col 33, no 1 (96); auth, "Multicultural Demographic Development: Current and Future Trends," in The Handbk of Multi-Cult Ment Health: Assessment and Treatment of Diverse Pop (00). **CONTACT ADDRESS** Dept Sociol, Univ of Texas, Pan American, 1201 W University Dr, Edinburg, TX 78539. **EMAIL** raajpoot@panam.edu

RACHLIN, HOWARD C.
PERSONAL Born 03/10/1935, New York, NY, m, 1961, 1 child **DISCIPLINE** PSYCHOLOGY **EDUCATION** Cooper Univ, BME, 57; New School Univ, MA, 63; Harvard Univ, 65. **CAREER** Asst prof, Harvard Univ, 65-69; SUNY Stony Brook, MA, 69-. **RESEARCH** Choice, self-control, gambling. **SELECTED PUBLICATIONS** Auth, Behavior and Mind, Oxford Univ Pr, 94; auth, The Science of Self-Control, Harvard Univ Pr, 00. **CONTACT ADDRESS** Dept Psychology, SUNY, Stony Brook, 1000 Nicolls Rd, Stony Brook, NY 11794-0002.

RADOSH, MARY F.
PERSONAL Born 02/11/1953, Corning, NY, m, 1978, 4 children **DISCIPLINE** SOCIOLOGY **EDUCATION** SUNY, BA, 76; S Ill Univ, MA, 78; PhD, 83. **CAREER** Prof, Western Ill

Univ, 84-; dir Women Studies, 95-. **HONORS AND AWARDS** Outstand Wk Woman of Ill; Outstand Teach Awd; Who's Who of Am Women, Teach, Women, Prof Women, Am Coll Stud; CDLET Awd; NUCEA Awd; Outstand Teach Awd, CAS; Fac Excell Awd; 88, 92, 94, 95; Outstand Yg Women of Am 85, 87; Diss Fel, SIU. **MEMBERSHIPS** ASC. **RESEARCH** Women and crime. **SELECTED PUBLICATIONS** Co-ed, The Past, Present and Future of American Criminal Justice, General Hall (NY), 96; coauth, Introduction to Criminology, Wadsworth (Belmont, CA), 99; coauth, "Gender, Social Character, Cultural Forces and the Importance of Love: Erich Fromm's Theories Applied to Patterns of Crime." in Erich Fromm and Critical Criminology: Beyond the Punitive Society, eds. Kevin Anderson, Richard Quinney (Urbana, IL: Univ Ill Press, in press); coauth, "Midwifery," in Ready Reference Women's Issues, ed. Margaret McFadden (Pasadena, CA: Salem Press, 99); co-ed, "Contemporary Corrections in the United States," in The Past, Present and Future of American Criminal Justice, General Hall (NY), 96; co-ed, "A Sociological Introduction to Criminal Justice," in The Past, Present and Future of American Criminal Justice, General Hall (NY), 96; coauth, "Pay Inequity at a Midwestern University: A Case Study of Faculty Protest," Sociol Imagination 32 (95): 44-56; auth, "Women and Crime in the United States: A Marxian Explanation," in Female Criminality: The State of the Art, ed. Concetta Culliver (Garland Pub: Hamden, CT, 93). **CONTACT ADDRESS** Dept Sociology, Anthropology, Western Illinois Univ, 1 University Circle, Macomb, IL 61455. **EMAIL** mf_radosh@wiu.edu

RAFERTY, ADRIAN E.
PERSONAL Born 07/22/1955, Dublin, Ireland, m, 1980, 2 children **DISCIPLINE** SOCIOLOGY **EDUCATION** Trinity Col, BA, 76; MSc, 77; Univ de Paris VI, Diplome d'Etudes Approfondies, 78; Docteur de troisieme cycle, 80. **CAREER** Lectr, Trinity Col, 80-86; assoc prof to prof, Univ of Wash, 86-. **HONORS AND AWARDS** Grants, Nat Sci Found, 86-88, 92-94; NICHD Grant, 90-92; Grant, Office of Naval Res, 95-01; Grant, Nat Ctr for Res on Statistics and Environ, 97-99; Grant, EPA, 96-01. **MEMBERSHIPS** Am Statistical Assoc; Am Sociol Assoc; Inst of Math Statistics; Royal Statistical Soc; Int Sociol Assoc. **RESEARCH** Bayesian model selection, Spatial statistics and image analysis, Cluster analysis and mixture models, Inference for deterministic simulation models, Statistical methods for sociology, demography, marine mammal research, and environemntal risk assessment. **SELECTED PUBLICATIONS** Ed, Sociological Methodology, 1996, 1997, 1998, Basil Blackwell, (Cambridge, MA), 96-98; auth, "Family structure and social mobility", Soc Forces 75, (97): 1319-1339; coauth, "Bayesian model averaging in proportional hazard models: assessing stroke risk", J of the Royal Statistical Soc, 46 (97): 433-448; coauth, "A note on the Dirichlet process prior in Bayesian non-parametric inference with partial exchangeability", Statistics and Probability Letters 36, (97): 69-83; coauth, "A proposed stock assessment method and its application to bowhead whales, Balaena mysticetus", Fishery Bull 97, (144-152; coauth, "Linear flaw detection in woven textiles using model-based clustering", Pattern Recognition Letters 18, (97): 1539-1548; coauth, "How many clusters? Which clustering methods? Answers via model-based cluster analysis", Computer J 41, (98): 578-588; coauth, "Three types of gamma ray bursts", Astrophysical J 508 (98): 314-327; coauth, "Bayesian morphology: Fast unsupervised Bayesian image analysis", J of the Am Statistical Assoc 94.2 (forthcoming); coauth, "Family structure, educational attainment and socioeconomic success: Rethinking the Pathology of Matriarchy", Am J of Sociol (forthcoming); coauth, "Comparing explanations of fertility decline using event history models and unobserved hetergeneity", Sociol Methods and Res, (forthcoming). **CONTACT ADDRESS** Dept Sociol, Univ of Washington, PO Box 353340, Seattle, WA 98195-3340. **EMAIL** raftery@stat.washington.edu

RAINER, JACKSON P.
PERSONAL Born 11/15/1954, Tifton, GA, m, 1978 **DISCIPLINE** PSYCHOLOGY **EDUCATION** Fla State Univ, BA, 76; Ga State Univ, MEd, 80; PhD, 86. **CAREER** Assoc Prof, Gardner Webb Univ, 97-. **HONORS AND AWARDS** Outstanding Grad Student, Ga State Univ, 85; Outstanding Young Men in Am, 82; Omicron Delta Kappa, Gold Key Honor Soc, Kappa Kappa Psi, Psi Chi Honor Soc. **MEMBERSHIPS** Am Psychol Asn, Am Acad of Psychotherapists, SE Psychol Asn, Ga Psychol Asn, NC Psychol Asn, Healthcare Financial Management Asn. **SELECTED PUBLICATIONS** auth, "Compassion fatigue: when caregiving hurts," in Innovations in Clinical Cractice, Ccholastic Res Press, in press; auth, "Columbine masacre should sound an alarm - and a call to action," Asheville Citizen Times, (99): 8A; auth, "Colorado shootings everybody's crisis, Hendersonville Times - News, (99): 5D; auth, "Colorado tragedy a reflection all of us," The Corest City Daily Courier, (99): 12A; auth, "Everybody's cirsis: the impact of the CO shootings," Charlotte Observer, (99): 27A; auth, "Everybody's cirsis: the impact of the school shooting in Littleton, CO," The Shelby Star, (99): 9A; auth, "Everybody's crisis: Littleton," Tryon Daily Bulletin, (99): 22-23; auth, "Some see death as the only outlet," The Shelby Star, (99): 4A; auth, "Final rights: caring for people in the last phases of life," in Innovations in Clinical Practice, Scholastic Res Press, 99; auth, "Life and loss: living and dying in the fmaily system," in Innovations in Clinical Practice, Scholastic Res Press, 99. **CONTACT ADDRESS** Dept Psychol, Gardner-Webb Univ, Box 7251, Boiling Springs, NC 28017.

RAINS, G. DENNIS
PERSONAL Born 03/11/1946, San Jose, Costa Rica, m, 1973, 2 children **DISCIPLINE** PSYCHOLOGY **EDUCATION** St Johns Col, BA, 69; New Sch for Soc Res, MA, 76; Cornell Univ, PhD, 81. **CAREER** Sen Staff Psychol, Friends Hospital, 81-89; Prof, Kutztown Univ, 89-. **MEMBERSHIPS** Am Psychol Asn; Intl Neuropsychol Soc. **RESEARCH** Frontal Lobes and Human Behavior. **CONTACT ADDRESS** Dept Psychol, Kutztown Univ of Pennsylvania, Kutztown, PA 19530.

RAJAGOPAL, ARVIND
DISCIPLINE CULTURAL STUDIES, MASS MEDIA, POSTCOLONIAL STUDIES **EDUCATION** Madras, BF, 81; Univ of Ky, MA, 84; Univ of Calif, Berkeley, PhD, 92. **CAREER** Asst prof, Purdue Univ. **HONORS AND AWARDS** Eli Sagan Awd, Univ of Calif, 90; Univ of Calif, Berkeley, Departmental Fel, 90-91; Rockefeller Fel, Univ of Chicago, 93; Amer Inst of Indian Studs Sr Fel, 93-94, 96-97; Macarthur Found Fel for Res and Writing on Peace and Int Coop, 96-97; Sawyer Fel, Int Inst, Univ of Mich, 96-97; NYork Univ challenge Grant, 99-00. **RESEARCH** Political economy of culture, social theory, contemporary South Asia, globalization. **SELECTED PUBLICATIONS** Auth, "Communalism and the Consuming Subject," Econ & Polit Weekly Vol 31, No 6 (96): 341-348; auth, "Mediating Modernity: Theorizing Reception in a Non-Western society," Commun Rev Vol 1, no 4 (96): 441-469; auth, "Hindu Immigrants in the US: Imagining Different Communities?" Bulletin of Concerned Asian Scholars (97): 51-65; auth, "Advertising, Politics and the Sentimental Education of the Indian Consumer," Visual Anthrop Rev Vol 14, No 2 (98/99): 14-31; auth, "Communities Imagined and Unimagined: Contemporary Indian Variations on the Public Sphere," Discourse: J for the Theoret Study of Media & Cult Vol 21, No 2 (99): 48-84; auth, "Thinking through emerging markets: brand logics and the cultural forms of political society in India," Social Text 60 (Fall 99): 131-149; auth, "Hindu Nationalism in the US: Changing Configurations of Political Practice," Ethnic & Racial Studies Vol 23, No 3 (00), 67-96. **CONTACT ADDRESS** Dept of Cult & Commun, New York Univ, Sch of Education, East Bldg 7th Fl, 239 Greene St, New York, NY 10003. **EMAIL** arvind.rajagopal@nyu.edu

RALEY, R. KELLY
PERSONAL Born, TX **DISCIPLINE** SOCIOLOGY **EDUCATION** Univ Tex, BA, 89; Univ Wisc, MS, 91, PhD, 94. **CAREER** Res asst, Center for Demograohy and Ecology, 89-92; Carolina Population Center, Res Assoc, 96-97; Asst prof, Univ Tex, Austin, 97-. **HONORS AND AWARDS** Ctr for Demography and Ecology Predoctoral Trainee, Univ Wisc, Madison, 92-94; Carolina Population Ctr, Postdoctoral Fel, 94-96; Summer Res Awd, Univ Tex, Fac Develop Prog, 98. **MEMBERSHIPS** Am Sociol Asn, Population Asn Am, Southern Demographic Asn. **RESEARCH** Family demography, stratification, race and ethnicity. **SELECTED PUBLICATIONS** Auth, "Black-White Differences in Kin Contact and Exchange Among Never Married Adults," J of Family Issues, 16(1): 77-103 (95); coauth with Larry Bumpass, "Redefining Single-Parent Families: Cohabitation and Changing Family Reality," Demography, 32(1): 97-109 (95); coauth with Larry Bumpass and James Sweet, "The Changing Character of Stepfamilies: Implications of Cohabitation and Nonmarital Child Bearing," Demography, 32:425-436 (95); coauth with Carol Roan, "Intergenerational Contact and Coresidence: A Longitudinal Analysis of Adult Children's Response to Mother's Widowhood," J of Marriage and the Family (96); auth, "A Shortage of Marriageable Men? A Note on the Role of Cohabitation in Race Differences in Marriage," Am Sociol Rev, 61: 973-983 (96); coauth with Ronald R. Rindfuss, "Intergenerational Contact in the United States and Japan," in K. O. Mason, N. O. Tsyua and M. K. Choe, eds, The Changing Family in Comparative Perspective: Asia and the U. S., Honolulu, HI: East-West Center (98); coauth with Ronald R. Rindfuss, "The effect of respondent's kinship position on reported levels of intergenerational contact: USA and Japan," Population Res and Policy Rev, 18(3): 279-298 (99); coauth with Stephen Russell and Carol Patterson, "Is Cohabitation Replacing Marriage? A Comparative Study of the United States, Canada, and Great Britain," Acta Demographica (forthcoming); coauth with Kathleen Mullan Harris and Ronald R. Rindfuss, "The Quality and Comparability of Child Care Data in U. S. Surveys, Soc Sci Res (forthcoming); auth, "Recent Trends in Marriage, Cohabitation, and Sexual Relationships," in Linda Waite, Christine Bachrach, Michelle Hindin, Elizabeth Thomson, and Arland Thornton, eds, Ties That Bind: Perspectives on Marriage and Cohabitation, Hawthorne: Aldine de Gruyter (forthcoming). **CONTACT ADDRESS** Dept Sociol, Univ of Texas, Austin, 336 Burdine, Austin, TX 78712-1088.

RALLIS, HELEN
PERSONAL Born 03/20/1960, Johannesburg, South Africa **DISCIPLINE** EDUCATION **EDUCATION** Rhodes Univ, SAfrica, BA Phychical Educ, 80; Univ Witwatersrand, Safrica, BA, 81; Univ Miami Fla, MA, 84; Pa State Univ, PhD, 89. **CAREER** Assoc Prof, Univ of Minn Duluth, 89-. **HONORS AND AWARDS** Horace T. Morse Awd for Outstanding Contrib to Undergraduate Educ; Univ of Minn Acad of Distinguished Teachers. **MEMBERSHIPS** ASCD, PDK, AACE. **RESEARCH** Technology in Education, Instructional Methods. **CONTACT ADDRESS** Dept Educ, Univ of Minnesota, Duluth, 10 Univ Dr, Duluth, MN 55812.

RAMAGE, JEAN C.
DISCIPLINE COUNSELING, SCHOOL PSYCHOLOGY **EDUCATION** Univ Oregon, BA; Univ Cal, Berkeley, MA; PhD. **CAREER** Asst prof, Univ Oregon, 71-73; assoc prov, Univ Mass, 73-75; exec mgr, NASP, 76-85; asst dean, prof, dir, San Diego State Univ, 75-89; dir, APA, 88-89; dean, prof, James Madison Univ, 89-91; dean, prof, Cal State, San Bernardino, 91-94; prof, 95-; dean 95-98; Univ Nebraska, Kearney. **HONORS AND AWARDS** Recog Cert, Cal St Assem; Christa McAuliffe Awd; ATE Apprec Awd; Sandra Goff Awd; NASP Hon Life Mem; Outstand Teach Awd; Outstand Prof Leadshp Awd; NSF Fel; NIMH Fel. **MEMBERSHIPS** AACTE; CACTE; VACTE; APA; ATE; SCATE; NATE; VATE; CASP; NAPSO; NASP; NCATE; NEA; Phi Kappa Phi; Phi Delta Kappa; TECSCU. **SELECTED PUBLICATIONS** Auth, "Restructuring teacher education," Renaissance Group NL 1(93); ed, "Teacher Education as an All Community Responsibility: A Proposal for the Restructuring of Teacher Education in California," SCATE, 93; ed, "Restructuring of teacher education in California," Issues Teach Edu (94); ed, "Teacher education as an all community responsibility: A proposal for restructuring California teacher education," SCATE (San Diego, CA), 94; auth, "University view of rural education," Neb Cen Rural Edu Sm Sch NL (95); auth, "Restructuring teacher education to reflect the professional development continuum," in The Dynamic Interaction of Higher Education, Teacher Education and School Reform, ed. D Else (95): 155-157; coauth, "Multicultural education: A 21st century paradigm," in Handbook of Research on Teacher Education, ed. J Sikula (NY: Macmillan, 96); auth, "Nebraska Council on Teacher Education: 50 years of success," Platte Valley Rev (forthcoming); co-ed, "Regulation of Teacher Education," in ATEIMCTE Commission on Regulation of Teacher Education (Washington, D.C.; AACTEIATE, forthcoming); auth, "Organizational Policies of the Nebraska Council on Teacher Education," a book for ATEIMCTE Commission on Regulation of Teacher Education (Washington, D.C.: MCTEIATE, forthcoming). **CONTACT ADDRESS** College of Education, Univ of Nebraska, Kearney, Kearney, NE 68849-1255. **EMAIL** ramagej@unk.edu

RAMIREZ, PAUL
PERSONAL Born 05/15/1951, New York, NY, s **DISCIPLINE** PSYCHOLOGY **EDUCATION** CUNY, BA, 73; NY Univ, MA, 76; CUNY, 80; MPhil, 87; PhD, 90. **CAREER** Instr, Fiorello LaGuardia Community Col, 75-76; fac, CUNY, 77-81; adj fac, Hunter Col, CUNY, 82-; assoc prof, Long Island Univ, 93-. **HONORS AND AWARDS** Nat Sci Found Fel, 78-81; Psi Chi, 85; Sigma Xi, 90; Nat Inst of Mental Health Res Awd, 92-93; PEW Fac Develop Awd, 93-94; CUNY Alumni Achievement Awd, 99. **MEMBERSHIPS** Am Psychol Assoc; Int Neuropsychological Soc; NY Neuropsychology Group; Assoc for Applied Psychophysiology and Biofeedback; Int Reading (Disabilities) Assoc. **RESEARCH** Behavioral Neurology, Psychiatric Phenomenology, Psychopharmacology, Psychophysiology, Cross-Cultural Issues. **SELECTED PUBLICATIONS** Auth, "Cultural awareness and mental health", Hispanic Outlook in Higher Educ 6, (95): 17-18; coauth, "Cognitive deficits in affective disorders and schizophrenia", Am J of Psych 152.2 (95): 303; coauth, "Pharmacologic treatment of delusional disorders", Psych Clinics of N Am 18.2 (95): 379-391; coauth, "Managed Care and the therapeutic Community Psychologist", Time Effective Treatment: Psychotherapy in The Era of Rational Care, eds L.K.W. Berg and M.G. O'Leary, GCMH (Albany, NY), 96; coauth, "The Use of the Positive and Negative Syndrome Scale (PANSS) in Clinical Practice", J of Practical Psych & Behav Health 4, (98): 157-162; coauth, The Informant Questionnaire for the Positive and Negative Syndrome Scale (IQ-PANSS), Multi-Health Systems Pub, (Toronto), 99; coauth, "Rethinking Medication Prescribing Practices in an Inner-City Hispanic Mental health Clinic", J of Practical Psych & Behav Health, (99); coauth, "Psychostimulants in the treatment of adults with psychosis and attention deficit disorder" and "EEG biofeedback training in the treatment of attention deficit disorder in adults: A viable augmentation to traditional medical intervention?", Adult Attention Deficit Disorder: Brain Mechanisms and Life Outcomes, eds J. Wasserstein, L. Wolf and F.F. LeFever, NY Acad of Sciences, (00); coauth, 'Outcome assessment in the treatment of serious mental illness", Outcome Measurement in Psychiatry: A Critical Review, eds, L. Sederer, T. Burt and W. Ishak, Am Psych Pr, (00). **CONTACT ADDRESS** Dept Psychol, Long Island Univ, Brooklyn, 1 University Plaza, Brooklyn, NY 11201. **EMAIL** pramirez@liu.edu

RAMSAY, CAROL
PERSONAL Born 01/29/1939, Nashville, AR, s **DISCIPLINE** PSYCHOLOGY **EDUCATION** Centenary Col, Shreveport, La, BA, 71; Northeast La Univ, Monroe, MS, 75. **CAREER** Psychological examiner, state of Ark, 76-; 17 years as a therapist at mental health centers; instr, Univ Ark Community Col Hope, 95-. **HONORS AND AWARDS** Psychological

internship, Ark State Hospital, 73. **RESEARCH** Brain wave patterns, cognitive psychology. **CONTACT ADDRESS** Dept Soc Sci, Univ of Arkansas, PO Box 140, Hope, AZ 71802.

RAMSEY, PATRICIA G.

PERSONAL Born 01/05/1946, New York, NY, m, 1979, 2 children **DISCIPLINE** PSYCHOLOGY, EDUCATION **EDUCATION** Middlebury Col, BA, 67; San Fran State Univ, MA, 73; Univ Mass, EdD, 78. **CAREER** Asst prof, Ind Univ, 78-79; asst prof, Wheelock Col, 79-84; asst prof, Mount Holyoke Col, 84-88; assoc prof, 88-94; prof, 94-. **MEMBERSHIPS** AERA; NAEYC; SRCD. **RESEARCH** Early development of racial attitudes; young children's peer relations. **SELECTED PUBLICATIONS** Auth, Teaching and Learning in a Diverse World: Multicultural Education for Young Children, Teach Coll Press (NY), 87; coauth, Multicultural Education: A Resource Book, Garland Press (NY), 89; auth, Making Friends in School: Promoting Early Peer Relationships, Teach Coll Press (NY), 91; auth, Teaching and Learning in a Diverse World, Teach Coll Press (NY), 2nd ed; co-ed, In Their Own Way: How Teachers Become Anti-Bias Educators, Redleaf Press (MN), 99; rev, Fostering Children's Social Competence: The Teacher's Role, Early Childhood Res Quart 13 (98): 373-376; coauth, "Early Childhood Multicultural, Anti-Bias Education in the 1990s: Toward the 21st Century," in Approaches to Early Childhood Education, eds. JL Roopnarine, JE Johnson (NY: Macmillan Pub Co, 93), 275-294; auth, "Diversity and Play: Influences of Race, Culture, Class and Gender," in Play From Birth to Twelve: Contexts, Perspectives, and Meanings (NY: Garland Press, 98), 23-33; auth, "Changing Social Dynamics in Early Childhood Classrooms," Child Development 66 (95): 764-773; auth, "Research in Review: Growing Up with the Contradictions of Race and Class," Young Children 50 (95): 18-22; auth, "Successful and Unsuccessful Entries in Pre-schools," J Applied Devel Psychol 17 (96): 135-150. **CONTACT ADDRESS** Dept Psychology Education, Mount Holyoke Col, 50 College St, South Hadley, MA 01075. **EMAIL** pramsey@mtholyoke.edu

RANDOLPH, MICKEY M. K.

PERSONAL Born 03/15/1958, Augusta, GA, m **DISCIPLINE** PSYCHOLOGY EDUCATION Col Charleston, BA, 80; Univ SC, MA, 85; PhD, 87. **CAREER** Prof, Western Carolina Univ, 88-. **HONORS AND AWARDS** Super Teacher Awd, 92. **MEMBERSHIPS** Nat Assoc of Sch Psychol, Southeastern Psychol Assoc, Sigma X. **RESEARCH** Domestic violence, effects on children **SELECTED PUBLICATIONS** Coauth, "Intrafamilial Child Sexual Abuse," Soc-Emotional Assessment and Intervention, 5 (89): 8-13; auth, "Adolescent Suicide," Psychol Newsletter for High Sch Teachers, 5 (90); auth, "The Long-Term Consequences of Father-Daughter Incest," Educ Resources Information Ctr, CG022549 (90); auth, "Child Witnesses of Domestic Violence," The Communique, 21 (93): 20-22; auth, "Behavioral and Emotional Characteristics of Children Who Witness Parental Violence," Family Violence and Sexual Assault Bull, 9 (93): 23-27; coauth, "Laterality Effects in Cherokee and Anglo Children," J of Genetic Psychol, 155 (94): 123-124; coauth, "Child Sexual Abuse: An Evaluation of a Teacher Training Program," Sch Psychol Rev, 23 (94): 485-495; coauth, "Behavioral and Emotional Characteristics of Children Who Witness Parental Violence," Sociol Abstracts (95); coauth, "Working Effectively with Handicapped Children and Their Families," The NC J of Teacher Educ, 8 (96): 38-51; coauth, "Children with Hemophilia," in A Practitioner's Handbk of Health Related Disorders in Children, Am Psychol Asn (Wash, DC), 98. **CONTACT ADDRESS** Dept Psychol, Western Carolina Univ, 1 University Dr, Killian Bldg, Cullowhee, NC 28723. **EMAIL** randolph@wca.edu

RAO, K. VANINADHA

DISCIPLINE SOCIOLOGY EDUCATION Viknam Univ, MS, 78; Univ Western Ont, PhD, 87. **CAREER** Notestein Fel, Princeton Univ, 87-88; from Asst to Assoc Prof, Bowling Green State Univ, 89-. **MEMBERSHIPS** Int Union for the Study of Pop, Am Sociol Asn, Indian Asn for Study of Pop. **SELECTED PUBLICATIONS** Auth, "Asian Indians in United States", Demog India, 97. **CONTACT ADDRESS** Dept Sociol, Bowling Green State Univ, 1001 E Wooster St, Bowling Green, OH 43403-0001. **EMAIL** kvrao@bgnet.bgsu.edu

RAO, NAGESH

DISCIPLINE INTERCULTURAL COMMUNICATION EDUCATION Univ of Southern Miss, MS; Mich State Univ, PhD, 94. **CAREER** Asst prof, Univ Md; asst prof, Oh Univ . **HONORS AND AWARDS** Outstanding Teacher Award, Univ of Md; Outstanding Teacher of the Year Award, Univ of NMex; Pew Teaching Leadership Award; Excellence in Teaching Award, Int Commun Asn. **RESEARCH** Intercultural communication, health communication, role of emotion in creating attitude and behavior change, entertainment-education. **SELECTED PUBLICATIONS** Coauth, "Communication and Community in a City Under Seige: The AIDS Epidemic in San Francisco," Commun Res 22 (95). **CONTACT ADDRESS** School of Interpersonal Commun, Ohio Univ, Athens, OH 45701. **EMAIL** rao@ohio.edu

RAOUL, VALERIE

PERSONAL Born Shrewsbury, England **DISCIPLINE** FRENCH AND WOMEN'S STUDIES **EDUCATION** Girton Col, Univ Cambridge, BA, 63, MA, 68; London Sch Econ, Dip Social Admin, 64; McMaster Univ, MA, 71, PhD, 78. **CAREER** Tchr, McMaster Univ, Univ Toronto, Ryerson Polytechnic Univ, 70-79; dept Fr, 79-, head dept, 91-96, Prof Univ British Columbia, 92-, dir, Ctr Res Women's Studs & Gender Rels 96-. **MEMBERSHIPS** Asn Prof Fr Can Univs; Asn Can Que Lits; CFH; Asn Chs Fr Depts Can Univs; **SELECTED PUBLICATIONS** Auth, The French Fictional Journal: Fictional Narcissism/Narcissistic Fiction, 79; auth, Distinctly Narcissistic: Diary Fiction in Quebec, 94; co-ed, The Anatomy of Gender: Women's Struggle for the Body, 88. **CONTACT ADDRESS** Dept of French, Univ of British Columbia, 1896 E Mall, Vancouver, BC, Canada V6T 1Z1. **EMAIL** valraoul@interchange.ubc.ca

RASHOTTE, LISA SLATTERY

PERSONAL Born 05/22/1970, Hinsdale, IL, 1 child **DISCIPLINE** SOCIOLOGY EDUCATION Univ Ariz, PhD, 98. **CAREER** Asst prof, Univ NC, 98-. **HONORS AND AWARDS** Curr and Instructional Dev grant, Univ NC, 99; Jun Feac Fel, Univ NC, 99; Nat Sci Foundation Doctoral Dissertation Improvement grant, 97; Soc and Beh Sci Res Instit, Ariz, 97. **MEMBERSHIPS** Am Sociol Asn, S Sociol Soc. **RESEARCH** Social psychology, Small groups. **SELECTED PUBLICATIONS** Auth, "Who Benefits from Being bold: the Interactive Effects of Task Cues and status Characteristics on Influence in Mock Jury Groups," Advances in Group Processes, (97): 235-255; auth, "The Use of Videotape in Studying emotions," Sociology of Emotions Section Newsletter, American Sociological, 94. **CONTACT ADDRESS** Dept Anthropol & Sociol, Univ of No Carolina, Charlotte, 9201 Univ City, Charlotte, NC 28223. **EMAIL** lrashott@email.uncc.edu

RASMUSSEN, S. J.

PERSONAL Born 05/19/1949, Chicago, IL, m, 1986 **DISCIPLINE** ANTHROPOLOGY EDUCATION Univ of Chicago, MA, 72; Indiana Univ, PhD, 86. **CAREER** Prof, Dept of Anthrop, Univ of Houston, 90- . **HONORS AND AWARDS** Fulbright Fel; Social Sci Res Coun. **MEMBERSHIPS** Am Anthrop Asn; Af Stud Asn. **RESEARCH** Anthropology of religion; gender; life cycle and aging. **SELECTED PUBLICATIONS** Auth, Joking in Researcher-Resident Dialogue: Ethnography of Hierarchy amoung Tuareg, in Anthropological Q, 93; auth, Speech by Allusion: Voice and Authority in Tuareg Verbal Art, in J of Anthrop and Humanism, 93; auth, The Head Dance, Contested Self, and Art as a Balancing Act in Female Possession among the Tuareg, in Africa: J of the Internatl African Inst, 94; auth, The Poetics of Childhood and Politics of Resistance in Tuareg Society, in Ethos, 94; auth, Female Sexuality, Social Reproduction, and Medical Intervention: Kel Ewey Tuareg Perspectives, in Culture, Medicine, and Psychiatry, 94; auth, Zarraf, A Tuareg Women's Wedding Dance, in Ethnology, 95; auth, Art as Process and Product: Patronage and Change in Tuareg Smith/Artisan Roles, in Africa: J of Internatl African Inst, 95; auth, Spirit Possession and Personhood among the Kel Ewey Tuareg, Cambridge Univ Pr, 95; auth, The Tuareg, in HRAF Encycl of World Cultures, 96; auth, Matters of Taste: Food, Eating, and Reflections on 'the Body Politic' in Tuareg Society, in J of Anthrop Res, 96; auth, Tuareg Tent as Field Space and Cultural Symbol, in Anthrop Q, 96; auth, Knowledge and Power amoung the Tuareg, in Oral Tradition, 96; auth, The Tuareg, in Eastwood Encycl of Cultures and Daily Life, 97; auth, African Myth and Cosmology, in Scribner Encycl of African South of the Sahara, 97; auth, Between Ritual, Theatre, and Play: Blacksmith Praise at Tuareg Marriage, in J of Am Folklore, 97; auth, Gender and health Care: The Case of Tuareg Women in Niger, in the Political Economy of Health Care in Sub-Saharan Africa, 97; auth, The Poetics and Politics of Tuareg Aging: Life Course and Personal Destiny in Niger, Northern Ill Univ Pr, 97. **CONTACT ADDRESS** Dept of Anthropology, Univ of Houston, McElhinney Hall, Houston, TX 77204-5882. **EMAIL** srasmussen@uh.edu

RASMUSSON, D. X.

PERSONAL Born 06/01/1965, Cleveland, OH, s **DISCIPLINE** PSYCHOLOGY EDUCATION Augusta Col, BA, 87; Univ Ga, MS, 89; PhD, 92. **CAREER** Res Fel, Johns Hopkins Univ, 92-95; Res Fel, Nat Inst on Aging, 95-98. **HONORS AND AWARDS** Graduate Teaching Excellence Awd, Univ Ga, 95; Intramural Res Training Awd, Nat Inst on Aging, 95; Grant, Calif State Univ, 99. **MEMBERSHIPS** Gerontonlogical Soc of Am, Intl Neuropsychological Soc. **RESEARCH** Health; Aging; Cognition; Dementia; Medical Marijuana **SELECTED PUBLICATIONS** Coo-auth, "CT Measurement of the suprasellar cistern predicts rate of decline in Alzheimer's disease," Journal of the International Neuropsychological Soc, (96): 345-350; co-auth, "Apo-E Genotype and Verbal Deficits in Alzheimer's Disease," The Journal of Neuropsychiatry and Clinical Neuroscience, (96): 335-337; co-auth, "Predicting rate of decline in probable Alzheimer's disease," Brain and Cognition, (96): 133-147; co-auth, "Prospects for computerized memory training in normal elderly: Effects of practice on explicit and implicit memory tasks," Applied Cognitive Psychology, (96): 211-223; co-auth, "Accuracy o clinical diagnosis of Alzheimer's disease and clinical features of patients with non-

Alzheimer's neuropathology," Alzheimer Disease and Associated Disorders, (96): 180-188; co-auth, "Improving memory in community elderly through group-based and individualized memory training," in Interactions in Basic and Applied Memory Research, Lawrence Erlbaum, 97; co-auth, "Memory improvement tapes: How effective for older adults?," Aging, Neuropsychology, and cognition, (97): 304-311; co-auth, "Effects of age and dementia on the Trail Making Test, The Clinical Neuropsychologist, (98): 313-319; auth, "A study of the efficacy of a comprehensive memory enhancement program I healthy elderly persons," Psychiatry Research, (98): 183-195; auth, "Effects of three types of memory training in normal elderly," Aging, Neuropsychology, and Cognition, (99): 56-66. **CONTACT ADDRESS** Dept Human Development, California State Univ, Hayward, 25800 Carlos Bee Blvd, Hayward, CA 94542. **EMAIL** xeno@csuhayward.edu

RATCLIFF, DONALD

PERSONAL Born 04/06/1951, Pomeroy, OH, m, 1978, 3 children **DISCIPLINE** EDUCATIONAL PSYCHOLOGY EDUCATION Spring Arbor Col, BA, 73; Mich State Univ, MA, 75; Univ Ga, EdS, 86; PhD, 95. **CAREER** Assoc prof, Toccoa Falls Col, 82-; temp asst prof, Univ Ga, 95-96. **HONORS AND AWARDS** Fac Scholar of the Year, 92; Fac Develop in Ga Grant, 94-95; Who's Who in Religion, Who's Who in Educ. **MEMBERSHIPS** Christian Asn for Psychol Studies, North Am Prof of Christian Educ. **RESEARCH** Qualitative research methods, research of children, children's spirituality. **SELECTED PUBLICATIONS** Auth, "Counseling parents of the mentally retarded," J of Psychol and Theol (90); auth, "Baby faith: Infants, toddlers, and religion," Relig Educ (92); auth, "How Children Understand Religious Concepts," Relig and Public Educ (92); coauth, Bruised and Broken: Understanding and Healing Psychological Problems, Baker Books (92); auth, "Stages of Spiritual Development: Crisis Experiences in the Christian Life," Christian Educ J (93); coauth, Complete Guide to Volunteers in Religious Education, Relig Educ Press (93); coauth, Child-Rearing and Personality Development, Baker Books (93); co-ed, Handbook of Family Religious Education, Relig Educ Press (95); ed, Psychological Foundations," in Barbara Wilkerson, Multicultural Religious Education, Relig Educ Press (98); coauth, Raising Your Child from Birth to Age Twelve, Spire Books (99). **CONTACT ADDRESS** Dept Psychol, Toccoa Falls Col, Toccoa Falls, GA 30598. **EMAIL** dratclif@toccoafalls.edu

RATHNAM, MAHADEV

DISCIPLINE EDUCATION EDUCATION Nizam Col, BA, 53; Osmania Univ, BEd, 57; Karnataka Univ, MEd, 61; Asbury Theol Sem, MRE, 66; George Peabody Col, MA, 67; George Wash Univ, EdD, 75. **CAREER** Prof, Univ DC, 71-94; Adj Prof, George Wash Univ, 95-. **HONORS AND AWARDS** Ten Year Serv Awd, George Wash Univ; 23 Year Recognition Awd, Univ DC, 95. **RESEARCH** Curriculum and instruction, multicultural education and international education. **SELECTED PUBLICATIONS** Auth, Multicultural Education: An Overview and Implications for School and Society: Consortium of Southern Colleges for Teacher Education, 80; auth, "Stay Close to Students," Higher Educ, vol 7, no 5 (90); auth, "Basic Principles of Idea Curriculum and Instruction," Perspectives in Educ, vol 12, no 1 (96). **CONTACT ADDRESS** Dept Educ, The George Washington Univ, 2134 G St NW, Washington, DC 20052-0001. **EMAIL** mrathnam@erols.com

RAUCH, ALAN

DISCIPLINE CULTURAL STUDIES OF SCIENCE EDUCATION Rutgers Univ, PhD, 89. **CAREER** Assoc ch, assoc prof, Ga Inst of Technol; bk rev ed, Configurations: A J of Lit, Sci, and Technol, Johns Hopkins UP. **RESEARCH** The dissemination of knowledge in the 19th century. **SELECTED PUBLICATIONS** Ed, The Mummy! A Tale of the Twenty-Second Century (1827), Univ Mich Press, 94; coed, One Culture: Essays in Science and Literature, Univ Wis, 87. **CONTACT ADDRESS** Sch of Lit, Commun & Cult, Georgia Inst of Tech, Skiles Cla, Atlanta, GA 30332. **EMAIL** alan.rauch@lcc.gatech.edu

RAVER-LAMPMAN, SHARON

PERSONAL Born 02/18/1948, Yokosuka, Japan, m, 1979, 1 child **DISCIPLINE** EDUCATION EDUCATION Univ S Fla, BA, 72; Vanderbilt Univ, MA, 73; EdS, 74; Univ S Fla, PhD, 85. **CAREER** Res Asst, George Peabody Col, 72-74; Adj Prof, Dominican Col, 75; Instr, Santa Rosa Junior Col, 74-79; Intl Consultant, Intl Institute for the Child, 83; Adj Prof to Res Assoc, Univ of S Fla, 84-85; Asst Prof, Old Dominion Univ, 85-91; Fulbright Scholar, Palasky Univ, 93-94; Assoc Prof to Prof, Old Dominion Univ, 91-. **HONORS AND AWARDS** Fulbright Scholar, Calcutta, 99; Outstanding Fac Member, Old Dominion Univ, 97; Tonelson Awd for Excellence in Teaching, Service and Research, Old dominion Univ, 94-95; Teaching/Cultural Exchange, Univ Allepo, 95; Fulbright Scholar, Palasky Univ, 93-94; Certificate of appreciation, Coun for Exceptional Children, 93; Fac Scholar Awd, Old Dominion Univ, 88, 90-92; Distinguished Res in Educ Awd, Va Educational Res Asn, 87; Certificate of Appreciation, Pinellas County School, 84; Outstanding Educator Awd, Pinellas County school Board, 83. **MEMBERSHIPS** Va Institutions of Higher Educ Coun for the

Early Educ of Children with Disabilities, Coun for Exceptional Children, Va Early Intervention Network, Intl Asn in Spec Educ, State Coalition of Spec Educ Prog, Asn of Va Infant Programs, Asn for Retarded Citizens Respite Care Cooperative Program **RESEARCH** Early intervention for disabled children (0-6 yrs). **SELECTED PUBLICATIONS** Auth, Intervention Strategies for Infants and Toddlers with Special Needs: A Team approach, Prentice-Hall Pub Co, 99; auth, Strategies for Teaching At-Risk and Handicapped Infants and Toddlers: A Transdisciplinary Approach, Macmillan Pub co, 91; auth, "A special report on training," Manovikas Kendra Annual Report (1998-99), (00): 33-34; auth, "An interactive interview with Sharon Raver-Lampman: How can family-centered practices help families in Hampton Roads?," Cox Interactive media, 98; auth, "Programs for children with multiple handicaps in the United States: What does this mean in the 90s?," Specialni Pedagogika, (98): 37-42; auth, "Special Education in the Czech Republic," The International Journal of Special Education, (97): 16-23; auth, "Special education in the Czech Republic; Where it is and where it would like to go," The Journal of the International Association of Special Education, (97): 47-56; auth, "Coping in young children," Journal of Early Intervention, (96): 58-359; auth, "Family-centered practices in early childhood special education: What are they and why use them?," TAC-5 Network News, 95; auth, "Grandparents as a source of support for parents of children with disabilities: A brief report," mental Retardation, (95): 248-50. **CONTACT ADDRESS** Dept Early Chldhd, Spec Educ, Old Dominion Univ, Norfolk, VA 23529. **EMAIL** sraverla@odu.edu

RAYMOND, FRANK B.
PERSONAL Born 12/18/1939, Apex, NC, m, 1964, 1 child **DISCIPLINE** SOCIAL WORK **EDUCATION** Wake Forest Univ, BA, 62; Univ NC, Chapel Hill, 65; Tulane Univ, PhD, 71. **CAREER** Prof, Col of Soc Work, Univ SC, 72-79, acting dean and prof, 79-80, Dean and Prof, 80-. **HONORS AND AWARDS** Phi Beta Kappa, 62; Amoco Found Outstanding Teaching Awd, 79; Soc Worker of the Year, SC Chapter of Nat Asn of Soc Workers, 81, 84; Distinguished Service Awd, SC Bd of Soc Work Examiners, 84; Outstanding Achievement Awd, SC Asn of Sch Soc Workers, 89; Affirmative Action Awd, USC Black Fac and Staff Asn, 90; State/Univ Interdisciplinary Collaboration Proj Awd for Exemplary Collaboration, Am Psychiatric Asn, 95; Outstanding Alumnus Awd, Sch of Soc Work, Tulane Univ, 97; Outstanding Alumnus Awd, Sch of Soc Work, Univ NC, 98. **MEMBERSHIPS** Inter-Univ Consortium for Int Soc Development, Coun on Soc Work Educ, Global Awareness Soc Int, SC Chapter of the Nat Asn of Soc Workers. **RESEARCH** Social work education administration, corrections, social work consultation and hospital social work. **SELECTED PUBLICATIONS** Coauth, "Enhancing the Preparation of Social Workers for Rural Mental Health Settings through a Public/Academic Consortium," Rural Community Mental Health (April 98); auth, "Should There Be a Moratorium on the Development of Social Work Programs?," in J on Soc Work Educ (spring/summer 98); co-ed with L. Ginsberg and D. Gohagan, Computers in Human Services, "Information Technologies: Teaching to Use--Using to Teach," Binghamton, NY: Haworth Press, Inc (98); coauth, "Developing international education partnerships," in J of Global Awareness (May 98); coauth, "Enhancing the preparation of social workers for rural mental health settings through a public/academic consortium," in Rural/Community Mental Health, 24 (5) (summer 99); auth, "Delivering distance education through technology: A pioneer's experience," in Campus-wide Information Systems, MCB Univ Press, West Yorkshire, England (in press); coauth, "Building an international student body, in J of Global Awareness (May 99). **CONTACT ADDRESS** Dept Social Work, Univ of So Carolina, Columbia, Columbia, SC 29225-0001. **EMAIL** frank.raymond@sc.edu

REAGAN, MARY JANE
PERSONAL Born 08/27/1921, Brainerd, MN, d, 1 child **DISCIPLINE** EDUCATION **EDUCATION** Univ Minn, PhD, 68. **CAREER** Dir Remedial Reading Ctr, Minneapolis,MN Public Sch Sys. **MEMBERSHIPS** Am Philos Asn **SELECTED PUBLICATIONS** Auth, Getting It Right for K-12 Schooling, Huntington House, 98. **CONTACT ADDRESS** 1917 Pinehurst Ave., Saint Paul, MN 55116-1340.

REAVES, BENJAMIN FRANKLIN
PERSONAL Born 11/22/1932, New York, NY, m, 1955 **DISCIPLINE** EDUCATION **EDUCATION** Oakwood Coll Huntsville AL, BA, 1955; Andrews Univ, MA, M Div; Chicago Theological Seminary. **CAREER** MI Conference of Seventh-Day Adventist, pastor, 56-68; Westside Hospital, Chicago IL, counselor, 68-72; Andrews Univ, Berrien Springs MI, youth pastor, 72-73, assoc prof, 73-77; US Army, instr for homeletics, 77-85; Oakwood Coll, Huntsville AL, Pres, 85-. **HONORS AND AWARDS** Distinguished Alumnus Awd, Oakwood Coll, 1973; Teacher of the Year, Oakwood Coll, 1983; Music Humanitarian Awd, Oakwood Coll, 1984; Outstanding Leadership Awd, Oakwood Coll, 1986; **MEMBERSHIPS** Mem, Advisory Board of Andrews Univ; mem, Advisory Board of Loma Linda Univ; mem, United Negro College Fund; mem, Natl Assn for Equal Opportunity in Higher Educ; mem, Council for the Advancement of Private Colleges in AL; mem, Huntsville Chamber of Commerce Board; mem, Vision 2000; mem, Rotary club; mem, Urban Ministries Program; board of directors, UNCF; Chicago Sunday Evening Club, speaker. **SELECTED PUBLICATIONS** Author of articles in numerous journals such as: Message, The Review and Herald, Ministry, The Adventist Laymen, Collegiate Quarterly, South African Signs of the Times. **CONTACT ADDRESS** Oakwood Col, Oakwood Road, Huntsville, AL 35896.

RECK, DAVID
PERSONAL Born 01/12/1935, Rising Star, TX, m, 1968, 2 children **DISCIPLINE** ETHNOMUSICOLGY; COMPOSITION **EDUCATION** Univ of Houston, BM, 58; Univ of Texas, MM, 59; Wesleyan Univ, PhD, 84. **CAREER** Prof, Amherst Col, 74-. **HONORS AND AWARDS** Guggenheim fel. **RESEARCH** Music of South India **SELECTED PUBLICATIONS** Coauth, Worlds of Music, 97; auth, Music of the Whole Earth, 97. **CONTACT ADDRESS** Dept of Music, Amherst Col, Amherst, MA 01002. **EMAIL** dbreck@amherst.edu

RECKMEYER, WILLIAM J.
PERSONAL Born 06/17/1948, Riverside, CA, m, 1969, 3 children **DISCIPLINE** ANTHROPOLOGY **EDUCATION** Randolph-Macon Col, BA, 70; Am Univ, MA, 73; PhD, 82. **CAREER** Adj prof to Prof, San Jose State Univ, 77-. **HONORS AND AWARDS** Kellogg Nat Leadership Fel, 88-; Salzburg Fel, 95, 97, 98. **RESEARCH** Leadership; Systems science; National strategy; Elder care; Strategic change. **CONTACT ADDRESS** Dept Anthropol, San Jose State Univ, 1 Washington Square, San Jose, CA 95162-0001. **EMAIL** reckmeyer@aol.com

REDIEHS, ROBERT E.
PERSONAL Born 06/10/1933, Hinsdale, IL, m, 1958, 3 children **DISCIPLINE** PSYCHOLOGY **EDUCATION** Concordia Theol Sem, MDiv, 59; STM, 70; Univ Edinburgh, PhD, 71. **CAREER** Asst prof, Concordia Col, 71-73; asst prof, Judson Col, 73-75; instr, Danville Area Community Col, 75-. **HONORS AND AWARDS** Lectr, Col and REs Inst, Madras India, 62. **MEMBERSHIPS** Am Psychol Soc; Am Psychol Assoc; Soc for the Sci Study of Relig. **RESEARCH** Psychology of Religion. **SELECTED PUBLICATIONS** Auth, Confession and absolution; a study of their significance for pastoral counseling, 70. **CONTACT ADDRESS** Dept Lib Arts, Danville Area Comm Col, 2000 E Main St, Danville, IL 61832. **EMAIL** rediehs@dacc.cc.il.us

REED, DAISY FRYE
PERSONAL Born Washington, DC, d **DISCIPLINE** EDUCATION **EDUCATION** DC Teachers Coll, BS 1953-56; George Washington Univ, MA 1957-61; Teachers Coll Columbia Univ, MEd, EdD 1973-75; Loyola Univ, MRE, 1992-94. **CAREER** Washington DC Publ Schools, teacher 1956-73; Teachers Coll Columbia Univ, asst prof, dir of teacher corps proj 1975-76; Publ School Syst VA, consult; State Department of Education, consultant; School of Ed VA Commonwealth Univ, professor, 76-. **HONORS AND AWARDS** Innovation Awd DC Publ Schools Washington; Minority Student Scholarship Teachers Coll Columbia Univ; Reise-Melton Awd for Promoting Cross-Cultural Understanding, Virginia Commonwealth University, 1990-91; Outstanding Service Awd, 1991-92; Outstanding Teacher Awd, 1994-95; Phi Kappa Phi; Bd of Visitors, teaching fellow, 1998-2000. **MEMBERSHIPS** President, Assn of Teacher Educatorss in Virginia, 1988-91; ATE, 1978-; Phi Delta Kappa; Zeta Phi Beta Sorority, 1955-. **SELECTED PUBLICATIONS** Co-Author: Classroom Management for the Realities of Today's Schools; Author of book chapter in J Wood's Mainstreaming; articles published in Action in Teacher Education; NASSP Journal; Middle School Journal; research studies: Resilient At-Risk Children; Teaching in Culturally Diverse Classrooms; Overage & Disruptive Students in the Middle School. **CONTACT ADDRESS** Sch Educ, Virginia Commonwealth Univ, Box 842020, Richmond, VA 23284-2020.

REED, T. V.
DISCIPLINE CULTURAL THEORY, CONTEMPORARY AMERICAN FICTION, AND THE 1960S **EDUCATION** Univ Calif, Santa Cruz, PhD. **CAREER** Assoc prof & dir Amer Stud, Washington State Univ. **RESEARCH** Various art forms as they have helped to shape social movement cultures from the Civil Rights era to the 1990s. **SELECTED PUBLICATIONS** Auth, Fifteen Jugglers, Five Believers: Literary Politics and the Poetics of American Social Movements, 92. **CONTACT ADDRESS** Dept of English, Washington State Univ, 1 SE Stadium Way, PO Box 645020, Pullman, WA 99164-5020. **EMAIL** reedtv@wsu.edu

REED, WILLIAM
PERSONAL Born 11/26/1945, Williamston, NC, m, 1996, 1 child **DISCIPLINE** PSYCHOLOGY **EDUCATION** NC A&T Univ, BS, 70; Hampton Univ, MA, 71; Atlanta Univ, PhD, 86. **CAREER** Asst prof, Selma Univ; adj asst prof, Univ of NC; adj asst prof, Winston Salem State Univ; prof, St Leo Col; assoc prof, NC Agr and Tech Inst; assoc prof, Albany State Univ. **HONORS AND AWARDS** Psi Chi; Pi Lambda theta; Kappa Delta Phi; Phi Delta Kappa; Outstanding Achievement Awd, Alpha Phi Alpha; Outstanding Freshment Acad Advisor, NC A&T State Univ, 93-94, 94-95. **MEMBERSHIPS** Assoc for the Advan of Psychol; Am Psychol Assoc; Am Psychol Soc; Southeastern Psychol Assoc; Nat Board for Certified Coun. **RESEARCH** Health psychology, Biofeedback. **SELECTED PUBLICATIONS** Auth, "Parenting", Morehouse Sch of Med Community Health Unit Newsletter 1.2 (85); coauth, "Consumer Education Training Manual", Grant Pub, 85; auth, "Becoming A New Parent", Morehouse Sch of Med Community Health Unit Newsletter 2.1 (86); coauth, "Campus Daddies: Unwed Fathers Takes on Responsibilities of Babies and Books", Black Issues of Higher Educ 95. 12.17; coauth, "Panelists Challenge Men to Fight Violence", Greensboro (Oct 95); coauth, "Differential Gender Effects of Exposure to Rap Music on African American Adolescents Acceptance of Teen Dating Violence", Sex Roles 35; auth, "Study Skills the Key to Student Success", Kendall/Hunt Pub, (Dubuque, Iowa), 96; coauth, "Perceptual Ambiguity, and Target Intoxication: Assessing the effects of factors that moderate perceptions of sexual harassment", J of Appl Soc Psycho 27.14 (97); auth, Practicum Handbook for Psychology, Family Life Educ Consultant Pub, (Albany, GA), 99; auth, "The Art of Peer Tutoring", Ethics and Critical Thinking J, 99. **CONTACT ADDRESS** Dept Psychol, Sociol and Soc Work, Albany State Univ, 504 College Dr, Albany, GA 31705. **EMAIL** wmreed@asurams.edu

REEDER, GLENN D.
PERSONAL Born 08/04/1949, Chicago, IL, m, 1979, 1 child **DISCIPLINE** PSYCHOLOGY **EDUCATION** Univ Calif, PhD, 77 **CAREER** Assoc Prof to Prof, Ill State Univ, 81-. **HONORS AND AWARDS** Outstanding Col Researcher, IL State Univ, 87; Erskine Fel, Univ of Canterbury, 93. **MEMBERSHIPS** Am Psychol Soc; Am Psychol Asn; Soc of Experimental Soc Psychol; European Asn of Experimental Soc Psychol; Midwestern Psychol Asn. **RESEARCH** Person Perception; Stigma of HIV/AIDS; Social Cognition. **SELECTED PUBLICATIONS** Co-auth, Collective and individual representations of HIV/AIDS stigma, Lawrence Erlbaum, 93; auth, "Trait-behavior relations in dispositional inference," personality and Social psychology Bulletin, (93): 586-593; auth, "Dispositional inferences of ability: content and process," Journal of Experimental Social Psychology, (97): 171-189; co-auth, "Activity and similarity in safer-sex workshops led by peer educators," AIDS Education and Prevention, (97): 77-89; co-auth, "School psychologists and full-service schools: Partnerships with medical, mental health, and social services," School psychology Review, (97): 603-621; co-auth, "the self-serving bias in relational context," Journal of Personality and Social Psychology, (98): 378-386; co-auth, "A social psychological analysis of HIV-related stigma: A two factor theory," American Behavioral Scientist, (99): 1193-1211; co-auth, "African-American volunteers carrying an HIV prevention message: Selective communication," AIDS Education and prevention, (99): 436-449; co-auth, "Attitudes toward persons with HIV/AIDS: Linking a functional approach with underlying process," in Why we evaluate: Functions of attitudes, (Lawrence Erlbaum, 00), 295-323; co-auth, "Narcissism and comparative self-enhancement strategies," Journal of Research in Personality, in press. **CONTACT ADDRESS** Dept Psychol, Illinois State Univ, 1 Campus, PO Box 4620, Normal, IL 61790-4620.

REESE, HAYNE W.
PERSONAL Born 01/14/1931, Comanche, TX, m, 1967, 4 children **DISCIPLINE** PSYCHOLOGY **EDUCATION** Univ Texas at Austin, BA, 53; MA, 55; State Univ Iowa, PhD, 58. **CAREER** Asst Prof, 58-62; Assoc Prof, 62-66; Prof, State Univ of New York at Buffalo, 66-68; Centennial Prof Psychology, West Virginia Univ, 68-70; Vis Prof, Univ of Iowa, 72; Univ of Hawaii, 75; Southwest China Normal Univ, 97-00. **MEMBERSHIPS** Assoc for Behavior Analysis, Intl Society for the Study of Behavioral Development, Psychonomic Society, American Psychological Society, Society for Research in Child Development, Eastern Psychological Assoc, American Assoc for the Advancement of Science, American Assoc o Univ Prof, Society of the Sigma Xi. **RESEARCH** Life-span psychological development. **SELECTED PUBLICATIONS** Auth, Soviet psychology and behavior analysis: Philosophical similarities and substantive differences. Behavioral Development (Newsletter of the Development & Behavior Special Interest Group of the Association for Behavior Analysis, 5 (95): 2-4; ed, Advances in child development and behavior, Academic Press (San Diego, CA) 26 (96); auth, How is physiology relevant to behavior analysis? The Behavior Analyst, 19 (96): 61-70; auth, A Belated response to Moxley. The Behavior Analyst, 20 (97): 43-47; auth, Counterbalancing and other uses of repeated-measures Latin-square designs: Analyses and interpretations. Journal of Experimental Child Psychology, 64 (97): 137-158; auth, The life-span developmental program at WVU, West Virginia Univ Dept of Psychology Alumni Newsletter, (98); auth, Utility of group methodology in behavior analysis and developmental psychology, Mexican Journal of Behavior Analysis, (98); ed, Advances in child development and behavior, San Diego , CA, Academic Press 27 (99); auth, Explanation is not description, Adult Development Bulletin, 8 (99): 3-7; auth, The first life-span conference. Mexican Journal of Behavior Analysis 24 (99): 39-68. **CONTACT ADDRESS** Dept Psychology, West Virginia Univ, Morgantown, PO Box 6040, Morgantown, WV 26506. **EMAIL** hreese@wvu.edu

REGELSKI, THOMAS ADAM
PERSONAL Born 05/04/1941, Goshen, NY, m, 1993 **DISCIPLINE** MUSIC EDUCATION **EDUCATION** State Univ Col, Fredonia, BM (Music Ed), 58; Columbia Univ, MA (Choral and Vocal Music), 63; State Univ Col, Fredonia graduate studies, 63-64; OH Univ, Athens, PhD (Comparative Arts), 70. **CAREER** Public schools, New York City, 62-63; central schools, Bemus Point, NY, 63-65; public schools, Middletown, NY, 65-66; School of Music, State Univ Col, Fredonia, 66-68; OH Univ at Athens and Zanesville, 68-70; School of Music, State Univ Col, Fredonia, NY, 70-; vis prof, Aichi Univ, Nagoya, Japan, 84-85; assoc in ed, Harvard Univ, fall 91. **HONORS AND AWARDS** Kappa Delta Pi, SUNY Fredonia, 62; cum laude, SUNY Fredonia, 62; Dean Earl C Siegfred Awd, OH Univ, 70; Phi Kappa Phi, OH State Univ, 70; Outstanding Educators of Am, 73-74; Distinguished Prof Awd and rank, SUNY Board of Trustees, 83; vis teaching and res scholar, Aichi Univ , Nagoya, Japan, 84-85; vis scholar, Philos of Ed Res Center, Harvard Graduate School of Ed, fall 91; Kasling Awd for Senior res, SUNY Fredonia 99; Fulbright Awd as lecturer, Sibelius academy of Music, Helsinki Finland, 00. **RESEARCH** Philos of music; philos of ed; sociol of music; sociol of ed. **SELECTED PUBLICATIONS** Auth, Action Research and Critical Theory: Empowering Music Teachers to Professionalize Praxis, Bul of the Coun for Res in Music Ed, no 123, winter 94-95; Scientism in Experimantal Music Research, Philos of Music Ed Rec, vol 4, no 1, spring 96; Taking the Art of Music for Granted: A Critical Sociology of the Aesthetic Philosophy of Music, in Critical Reflections on Music Education, ed L R Bartel and D J Elliott, Univ of Toronto, Can Music Ed Res Center, 96; Action for Change in Music Education-Guiding Ideals of the MayDay Group, with J T Gates, Univ Buffalo, postion paper of the May-Day Group, fall 96 (www.members.aol.com/jtgates/maydaygroup/); Critical Theory as a Basis for Critical Thinking in Music Education, in Studies in Music from the Univ of Western Ontario, vol 17, 98; A Prolegomenon to a Praxial Theory of Music and Music Education, Finnish J of Music Ed, vol 1 no 1, fall, 96, reprinted and expanded in Can Music Educator vol 38, no 3, spring 97; A Critical Pagmatism of Creativity for General Music, General Music Today, vol 10, no 3, spring 97; Action Learning: Curriculum as and for Praxis, Proceedings of the Charles Fowler Conference on Arts Education, Univ MD, College Park, May 97; Critical Theory and Praxis: Professionalizing Music Education, MayDay Group, web page(see above); The Aristotelian Bases of Music and Music Education, The Philos of Music Ed Rev, spring 98; numerous other publications. **CONTACT ADDRESS** School of Music, SUNY, Col at Fredonia, Mason Hall, Fredonia, NY 14063. **EMAIL** regelski@cecomet.net

REGNEY, GABRIELLE
PERSONAL Born 09/09/1966, Burlington, VT, s **DISCIPLINE** COMPOSITION, GENDER STUDIES **EDUCATION** Univ Conn Storrs, BA, 89; Hunter Col, MA, 92; CUNY, PhD, 00. **CAREER** Asst prof, Mercer County Community Col, 96-00; asst prof, Bronx Community Col, 00-. **HONORS AND AWARDS** Honors Scholar, Univ Conn, 89. **MEMBERSHIPS** CLAGS, Acad of Am Poets, MLA, Col Eng Assoc, Nat Assoc of Women's Studies. **RESEARCH** Semiotics, modern poetry, pre-Christian culture, biography, gender, feminist theory, American Literature. **SELECTED PUBLICATIONS** Auth, "Asphodel Out of the Grave - HD's Novel Trilogy," Jour of Imagism, 01. **CONTACT ADDRESS** 1755 Highview Lane, Upper Black Eddy, PA 18972. **EMAIL** gregney@ptd.net

REGOLI, ROBERT M.
PERSONAL Born 08/25/1950, Pittsburg, PA, m, 1972, 2 children **DISCIPLINE** SOCIOLOGY **EDUCATION** Wash State Univ, BS, 71; Wash State Univ, MA, 72; Wash State Univ, PhD, 75. **CAREER** Asst Prof, Ind State Univ, 75-77; Asst Prof, Texas Christian Univ, 77-81; Prof, Univ Colo, 81-. **HONORS AND AWARDS** Fel, Acad of Criminal Justice Sci. **MEMBERSHIPS** ACJS, NASSS. **RESEARCH** Crime and deviants in collectibles. **SELECTED PUBLICATIONS** Auth, Criminal Justice, Prentice-Hall (Englewood Cliffs, NJ), 96; auth, Delinquency in Society, 4th ed, McGraw-Hill (New York), 00. **CONTACT ADDRESS** Dept Sociol, Univ of Colorado, Boulder, PO Box 327, Boulder, CO 80309-0327. **EMAIL** regoli@spot.colorado.edu

REID, JOEL OTTO
PERSONAL Born 05/17/1936, Newark, NJ **DISCIPLINE** SOCIOLOGY **EDUCATION** New York University School of Education, BS, 1959; Montclair State College, MA, 1965; Claremont Graduate School, Claremont, CA, PhD, 1973. **CAREER** Elizabeth Public School System, Elizabeth, NJ, teacher; White Plaines High School, counselor, teacher, 62-65; White Plaines Board of Education, professional recruiter, 65-67; National Teachers Corps, Migrant University, Southern California, teacher, leader, 67-68; Claremont Graduate School, staff member, 71-72; Social Science Department, professor, 78; Pasadena City Col, dean of continuing education, 68-78, professor of social science, 78-. **HONORS AND AWARDS** Two year Scholarship to College; Kiwanis Rotary Club Scholarship; Valley Settlement House Scholarship, West Orange, NJ; Womens Aux Scholarship, West Orange, NJ. **MEMBERSHIPS** Pasadena Education Association; Pasadena City College Faculty Association; NEA; Los Angeles Co Adult Education Adminstrators Association; chairman, Eval Com for Western Associations Schools & Colleges, 1969, 1970, 1974; board of directors, Urban League Com for Educ Fund Dr; Fair Hsg Com of Westchester Co, New York; Am Friends Ser Com on Hsg, Pasadena; counseled Neighborhod Youth Center; worked with economically educationally deprived areas; lectured at educational, civic, & religious organizations; consultant to schools, pvt groups & Comm agencies. **CONTACT ADDRESS** Social Science Dept, Pasadena City Col, 1570 E Colorado Blvd, Pasadena, CA 91106.

REIGSTAD, RUTH
PERSONAL Born 04/24/1923, Minneapolis, MN **DISCIPLINE** CLINICAL PHYSICAL THERAPY, HISTORY OF ENGLISH, SCIENCE **EDUCATION** St Olef Coll, BA, 45; Univ Minn, RTP, 47. **CAREER** Consultant, Wash State Health Dept, 41-73; clin phys therapist, 47-61; volunteer activities. **HONORS AND AWARDS** Stipends for Post Grad Study, UCLA, USC, NYU; Children's Bureau; US Public Health. **MEMBERSHIPS** Public Health Asn; Am Phys Therapy Asn; Am Acad of Rel; AF Asn. **RESEARCH** Correlations between studies of science and religion; Early childhood development. **CONTACT ADDRESS** Box 4237, Tacoma, WA 98438-0001.

REILICH, EILEEN
PERSONAL Born 03/22/1956, Sacramento, CA, s **DISCIPLINE** EDUCATION **EDUCATION** Univ Id, BS, 80; Wash State Univ, PhD, 96. **CAREER** Teacher, South San Francisco School district, 85-89; Teacher, Clarkston School District, 89-90; Res Assoc, Washington State Univ, 90-95; Instr, Col of Educ, 95-96; Asst Principal, Sand Point Middle School, 96-97; Asst Prof, Saint Martin's Col, 97-. **HONORS AND AWARDS** Deans List, Univ Idaho, 79-80; Teaching Asst, Col of Educ Washington State Univ, 95; George B. Brain Scholarship, 95-96; Nominated for Harriet B. Rigas Awd, 95. **MEMBERSHIPS** ASCD, NSTA, WSTA, NARST, AERA, AAAS **RESEARCH** Instructional improvement, Science methods. **SELECTED PUBLICATIONS** Auth, "A morphometric study of bone marrow megakaryocytes in foals infected with equine infectious anemia virus," Vet Path, in press; auth, "A primary production deficit in the thrombocytopenia of equine infectious anemia, forthcoming **CONTACT ADDRESS** Dept Educ & Phys Educ, Saint Martin's Col, 5300 Pacific Ave SE, Lacey, WA 98503.

REILLY, MICHAEL S.
PERSONAL Born 12/29/1946, San Diego, CA, m, 1966, 2 children **DISCIPLINE** EDUCATION **EDUCATION** Union Inst, BA, 85; Nat Univ, MA, 89; Walden Univ, PhD, 95. **CAREER** Dir of Educ, Horizon Christian Schools, 84-88; Supt of School, Maranatha Christian Schools, 89-93; prof, S Calif Univ, 93-96; Dir of Acad Affairs, Art Inst of Calif, 96-; Instr, Univ of Phoenix, 98-. **HONORS AND AWARDS** 2000 Outstanding Scientists of the 20th Century; Who's Who in the West, 00-01. **MEMBERSHIPS** Soc for Human Res Management; Doctorate Assoc of NY Educators. **RESEARCH** Human performance in organizations and worksite wellness. **SELECTED PUBLICATIONS** Auth, "The responsibility of parents in the education process", Good News Etc., 14, 92; auth, "The value of a college education", Calif Christian Times 23.6, 93; auth, "Worksite Wellness", Abundant Health Rev 1.1, 97; auth, "A matter of stress", Abundant Health Review 2.1, 97; auth, "Repetitive stress injury: It's more common than you think", Abundant Health Rev 3.1 (97). **CONTACT ADDRESS** Dept Gen Educ, Art Inst of So California, 10025 Mesa Rim Rd, San Diego, CA 92121.

REINBERG, RICHARD
PERSONAL Born 11/04/1947, Norfolk, VA, m, 1978, 2 children **DISCIPLINE** ANTHROPOLOGY **EDUCATION** Univ Calif, AB, 69; Univ Chicago, MA, 71; PhD, 74. **CAREER** Instr, Roosevelt Univ, 74; Asst Prof to Prof, Kent State Univ, 74-. **HONORS AND AWARDS** Sigma Xi Sci Honorary, 94; Kent Res Group, 93; Kent State Univ PEW Campus Round Table, 93; NEH summer stipend, 91; Travel grant, Am Coun of Learned Soc, 88. **MEMBERSHIPS** AAA, ASAO, CSAS, Polynesian Soc, AAUP **RESEARCH** Cultural anthropology, Pacific Islands, Native North Americans. **SELECTED PUBLICATIONS** Auth, Oral History of a Polynesian Outlier: Texts and Translations from Anuta, Solomon Islands, Univ Calif, 93; auth, "Politics of Culture in the Pacific Islands," Ethnology, (95): 89-209; ed, Seafaring in the contemporary Pacific Islands: Studies in Continuity and Change, Northern Ill Univ Press, 95; ed, Leadership and Change in the Western Pacific: Essays in Honor of Sir Raymond Firth, London, 96; auth, Oral Traditions of Anuta: A Polynesian Outlier in the Solomon Islands, Oxford Univ Press, 98; auth, "Christian Polynesians and pagan spirits: Anuta, Solomon Islands," Journal of the Polynesian Society, (95): 267-301; auth, "Outer islanders and urban resettlement in the Solomon Islands: The case of Anutans on Guadalcanal," Journal de la Society des Oceanistes, (96): 207-217; auth, "Righting wrongs on Anuta," Pacific Studies, in press; "Motiki-tiki the Trickster and the Creation of Anuta," Journal of Hawaiian and Pacific Folklore, in press. **CONTACT ADDRESS** Dept Anthropol, Kent State Univ, PO Box 5190, Kent, OH 44242-0001. **EMAIL** rfeinber@kent.edu

REITER, HENRY H.
PERSONAL Born New York, NY **DISCIPLINE** PSYCHOLOGY **EDUCATION** NY Univ, BA, 57; Hofstra Univ, MA, 59; St John's Univ, PhD, 63. **CAREER** Instr to assoc prof, Psychology Dept, Long Island Univ/ C. W. Post Campus, 69-. **HONORS AND AWARDS** Psi Chi Nat Honor Soc, 58; Community Leaders Am, 70; Who's Who in the East, 70, 94; Who's Who in Am, 75; vice pres, bd of dirs, Nassau Ctr for the Emotionally Disturbed, Inc, Woodbury, NY, 70's; Who's Who in Sci & Engineering; Who's Who Registry, 98-99; Int Who's Who of Professionals, NC, 98; Diplomate status: Forensic Evaluation (99), Behavioral Med (81), and Professional Psychotherapy (82). **MEMBERSHIPS** APA, NCPA, NYSPA, Law Psych Soc. **RESEARCH** Foreign and sports psychology. **SELECTED PUBLICATIONS** Auth, "Personality correlates of Left-handedness," The Mankind Quart, 26(3-4):271-275 (86); coauth with A. Kirsch, "Relative Influence of Income, Occupation, and Appearance on Rater Judgments," Indian Psychol Rev, 31, 1-3 (86); coauth with F. Hornberger, "Personality traits of junk and non-junk food eaters," As J Psychol & Ed, 21 (6), (88); auth, "Personality profile of crisis center volunteers," As J Psychol & Ed, 21(9), (88); coauth with F. Goldstein and M. E. Vezza, "Personality differences between allergic and non-allergic college students," As J of Psychol and Ed, 21 (4), (88); coauth with M. Ulrich and D. Roddini, "Seasons, Climate and Weather: Effects on Human Behavior," Int J Behav Sci (89); auth, "The Psychology of Winning," Sports Strategy and Performance Report (March 89); coauth with L. Rubin and L. Bitondo, "Note on the Relationship Between Personality and Horticultural Interests," Int J Behav Sci, 1(2), 9-11 (90); coauth with C. Lang, "Relationship Between the Dial-R-Test and MR Test," Ind J Psychol Issues, 1(1), 26-27 (93); auth, "Psychosomatic implications of hypoglocemia," IJPI, 4(2) (96). **CONTACT ADDRESS** Dept Psychol, Long Island Univ, C.W. Post, 720 Northern Blvd, Greenvale, NY 11548.

REITZ, CHARLES
PERSONAL Born 03/10/1946, Buffalo, NY, m, 1987, 2 children **DISCIPLINE** PHILOSOPHY OF EDUCATION **EDUCATION** Canisius Col, BA, 68; SUNY Buffalo, PhD, 83. **CAREER** Prof philos, Kansas City Commun Col, 87- . **HONORS AND AWARDS** Tchg awards, 90, 00. **MEMBERSHIPS** APA; Soc for Ger-Am Stud. **RESEARCH** Critical theory of society and education. **SELECTED PUBLICATIONS** Auth, Art, Alienation and the Humanities: A Critical Engagement with Herbert Marcuse, SUNY, 00. **CONTACT ADDRESS** 2 East 58th St, Kansas City, MO 64113. **EMAIL** creitz@toto.net

REITZ, MIRIAM
PERSONAL Born 12/25/1935, Canada, w, 1985 **DISCIPLINE** SOCIAL WORK **EDUCATION** School of Soc Scv Admin, Univ Chicago, PhD, 82; MA, 62. **CAREER** Independent practice of therapy and consultation re family relationships, 89-present, Part-time Sr staff member at CFS/FIC, Inst of psych, NW Memorial Hosp and Medical School, Coordinator of Consult and Comm Ser CFS/FIC, 82-86; Part-time staff member CFS/FIC, 76-82; Edith Abbott Teaching Fellow at the School of Soc Scv Admin, Univ Chicago, 79-80; Dir of Prof Edu, Family Inst of Chicago, 73-76; Assoc Dir, Prof Edu, FIC, 72-73; Chief Soc Worker, 68, Commun Family Svc and Mental Health Center, LaGrange IL, 66-72. **MEMBERSHIPS** Natl Assoc of Soc Worker; IL Soc for Clin Soc Work; Clin Member Amer Assoc for Marriage and Family Therapy; Amer Family Therapy Academy; Alumni Assoc The Family Inst of Chicago. **SELECTED PUBLICATIONS** Reitz, Miriam and Watson, Kenneth W, Adoption and the Family System: Strategies fo Treatment, Guilford Publ, 92; Reitz, Miriam, The Groundswell of Change in Adoption Requires Anchoring by Resarch, forthcoming, Journal of Child & Adolescnt Social Work, 99. **CONTACT ADDRESS** 401 East Illinois St., Ste 320, Chicago, IL 60611.

REMINICK, RONALD A.
PERSONAL Born 03/10/1938, Washington, DC, s, 5 children **DISCIPLINE** ANTHROPOLOGY **EDUCATION** Kent State Univ, BA, 62; Univ Chicago, PhD, 73. **CAREER** Cleveland State Univ, 70-; Addis Ababa Univ, 93-95. **HONORS AND AWARDS** Fulbright Fel, Ethiopia, 93-95. **MEMBERSHIPS** Am Anthropol Asn, Soc for Psychol Anthropol. **RESEARCH** Psychology; Anthropology; Ethiopia. **SELECTED PUBLICATIONS** Auth, "Amhara Evil Eye Belief," Ethnology, 74; auth, "Symbolic Significance of ceremonial Defloration among the Amhara of Ethiopia," American Ethnologist, 76; auth, "Sport of Buhe among the Manze Amhara of Ethiopia," sport and culture 84; auth, "Transaction and Meaning: directions in the anthropology of Exchange and Symbolic Behavior," Journal of Psychoanalytic Anthropology, 82; auth, "Comparing Methodologies and emerging Data of Long term studies on emotion, Stress, and retardation," Reviews in Anthropology, (91): 225-234; auth, "Challenging Paths of Research in Theoretical and applied Psychological Anthropology," Reviews in Anthropology, (96): 77-84; auth, Theory of Ethnicity, Univ Books of am, 83; auth, Black Ethnicity: Culture, Social Organization, and Personality, Kendall-Hunt Pub, 88; auth, Evolution of an Urban African Cultural Landscape. A study of Addis Ababa, Ethiopia, forthcoming; auth, Introduction to the Peoples and cultures of Ethiopia, forthcoming. **CONTACT ADDRESS** Dept Anthropol, Cleveland State Univ, 1983 E 24th St, Cleveland, OH 44115. **EMAIL** rreminick@hotmail.com

RENDON, MARIE E.
PERSONAL Born 07/23/1947, Worland, WY, m, 1990 **DISCIPLINE** EDUCATION **EDUCATION** Augustana Col, BS, 69; Colo State Univ, MS, 79; PhD, 81. **CAREER** Instr, S Dak School for the Deaf, 69-71; Instr, Colo School for the Deaf, 71-75; Freelance Interpreter, Spokane, 75-76; Educator, School for the Deaf and the Blind, Colo, 76-78; Grad Asst Colo State Univ, 78-81; Asst Exec Dir, Nev Adv Coun for Vocational Technical Educ, 80-81; Consultant, Nat project on Career Educ, 80-84; Asst Prof, Ore State Univ, 81-85; Rehabilitation counselor, Mike Stipe and Assoc, 85-86; Lecturer, San Francisco State Univ, 87-90; Asst Dir, Univ of Calif Center on Deafness, 90-92; Instr, Spokane Falls Cmty Col, 92-. **HONORS AND AWARDS** Grad Leadership Development program, Colo State Univ, 78-81; distinguished Service Awd, Ore Vocational Asn, 84; special needs membership Awd, 86; Outstanding Service Provider, Ore Vocational Asn of Vocational Special Needs, 85; Phi Delta Kappa, 89-91; Vocational Technical Educator contributor of the Year, Washington State Coun, 94; Who's Who Among Am Teachers, 96. **MEMBERSHIPS** Registry of Interpreters for the Deaf; Am Sign Lang Teachers Asn; Washington Asn of Occupational Educ; Washington State Asn of the Deaf. **RESEARCH** Body Language and its implications for interpreters; Vocal inflections/interpreters and processing of information. **SELECTED PUBLICATIONS** Auth, American Sign Language Workbook, I; II, III; auth, ASL Interpreting I, II, III; auth, Transliteration Workbook I, II; auth, Voicing Workbook, I; auth, Deaf Culture Workbook I; auth, Deaf Culture Workbook for Long distance Learners; auth, Introduction to Interpreting; auth, Introduction to Interpreting, Long distance learning; auth, Human Services practicum manual for Social Services, Chemical Dependency and Interpreter Training. **CONTACT ADDRESS** Dept Soc Sci, Spokane Falls Comm Col, 3410 W Fort Wright Dr, Spokane, WA 99224-5204. **EMAIL** marier@sfcc.spokane.cc.wa.us

RESICK, PATRICIA A.
DISCIPLINE PSYCHOLOGY **EDUCATION** Ken State Univ, BA, 72; Univ Georgia, MA, 74; PhD, 76. **CAREER** Prof, 87-; dir, CTR, 92-; co-dir, NVAWPC, 98-00; Univ Missouri. **HONORS AND AWARDS** Chanc Awd, 95; Pres Awd, 92; Cura Prof, 99. **MEMBERSHIPS** AABT; APA; Metro St Louis Sex Assau Tsk Fce; MOVA; ISTSS. **RESEARCH** Violence against women; post traumatic stress disorders. **SELECTED PUBLICATIONS** Coauth, Cognitive processing therapy for rape victims: A treatment manual, Sage Pub (Newbury Park, CA(, 93; auth, Stress and Trauma, Psychol Press Erlbaum (London, Eng), forthcoming; coauth, "General memory functioning at pre and post treatment in female rape victims with posttraumatic stress disorder," in Trauma and Memory, eds. LM Williams, VL Banyard (Thousand Oaks, CA: Sage Pub, 98); coauth, "Cognitive-behavior intervention," in Handbook of Posttraumatic Stress Disorders, ed. DJ Miller (NY: Plenum Pub, forthcoming); coauth, "Empirically based therapy for posttraumatic stress disorder," in Effective Interventions in Mental Health: Cognitive Behavior Therapy Introduced (NZ: Cen Inst Tech, 99); coauth, "Group treatment of sexual assault survivors," in Group treatments for posttraumatic stress disorders: Conceptualization, themes, and processes, eds. BH Young, DD Blake (Phila, PA: Brunner/Mazel, 99); coauth, " Parent child interactions: Habituation and desensitization effects," J Clin Child Psychol 8 (79): 69-71; coauth, "Child maltreatment intervention: Directions and issues," J Soc Iss 35 (79): 140-160. **CONTACT ADDRESS** Dept Psychology, Univ of Missouri, St. Louis, 8001 Natural Bridge, Saint Louis, MO 63121. **EMAIL** resick@umsl.edu

RESTIVO, SAL
PERSONAL Born 09/22/1940, Brooklyn, NY, s, 2 children **DISCIPLINE** SOCIOLOGY **EDUCATION** City Col of NYork, BA, 65; Mich State Univ, MA, 66, PhD, 71. **CAREER** Instr, Mich State Univ, 67-70; instr to asst prof, Wellesley Col, 70-72; asst prof and Dir of the Grad Prog in Sociol, Univ of Hartford, 72-74; asst to assoc prof, Dept of Anthropol and Sociol, and Center for the Study of the Human Dimensions of Sci and Technol, Rensselaer Polytech Univ, 74-82, prof, 83-, Dir of Grad Progs in STS, 88-90. **HONORS AND AWARDS** Fel, Res Inst for the Study of Man, 64; NDEA Fel in Comparative Social Structures, Mich State, 65-68; Phi Kappa Phi, 67; Nat Sci Found Fel, Mich State, 68-70; NEH Fel, 85-86; NEH Summer grant, 87; Belgian Nat Res Found Prof, spring 95. **MEMBERSHIPS** Soc for Social Studies of Sci. **RESEARCH** The sociology of mathematics; social theory of mind, AI, & robotics; sociology of religion; general theory of erotics. **SELECTED PUBLICATIONS** Co-ed with C. K. Vanderpool, Comparative Studies in Science and Society, C. E. Merrill, Columbus (74); auth, The Social Relations of Physics, Mysticism, and Mathematics, S. Reidel, Dordrecht (83, Pallas paperback, 85); auth, The Sociological Worldview, B. Blackwell, Oxford (91), Swedish ed pub by Bokforlaget Korpen, Goteborg, Sweden (95); auth, Mathematics in Society and History, Kluwer Academic Pubs, Dordrecht (92); co-ed with J. P. Van Bendegem and Roland Fischer, Math Worlds: Philosophical and Social Studies of Mathematics and Mathematics Education, SUNY Press, Albany (93); auth, Science, Society, and Values: Toward a Sociology of Objectivity, Lehigh Univ Press, Bethlehem, Pa (94); co-ed with Jennifer Croissant, Degrees of Compromise: Industrial Interests and Academic Values, SUNY Press, Albany (2000). **CONTACT ADDRESS** Dept Sci & Technol Studies, Rensselaer Polytech Inst, 110 8th St, Troy, NY 12180. **EMAIL** restis@rpi.edu

RETTIG, SALOMON
PERSONAL Born 04/20/1923, Berlin, Germany, d, 2 children **DISCIPLINE** PSYCHOLOGY **EDUCATION** Temple Univ, BA, 53; Ohio State Univ, MA, 53; PhD, 56. **CAREER** Ohio State Univ Scholar, 53-54; teaching asst, OH State Univ, 54-56; res assoc, Columbus Psychiatric Inst and Hospital, 56-66; instr to prof, OH State Univ, 56-67; attending psychologist, New York Hospital, 75-84; adjunct prof, Cornell Univ Medical Col, 75-84; prof, Hunter Col, CUNY, 67-, chair, 69-75; vis prof, ANS Inst, Patna, India, 74; vis prof, Tel-Aviv Univ, Israel, 66; member and founder of Kibbutz Givoth Said, Israel. **HONORS AND AWARDS** Res grants, Nat Inst Mental Health, 62; CUNY, 68; Nat Science Found, 75; CUNY, 81; Who's Who in America, 37th and 38th eds; Am Men of Science; Dict of Int Biography; Int Scholars' Directory. **MEMBERSHIPS** Am Psychol Asn; Am Sociol Asn; Am Assoc for the Advancement of Science. **RESEARCH** Philosophy of science in psychology; small groups (group therapy); ethical decision making. **SELECTED PUBLICATIONS** Auth, The discursive social psychology of evidence: creating symbolic reality, NY: Plenum Press (90); auth, "On discursive evidence," in R. Rieber & W. A. Stewart, eds,"The language scientists as an expert witness: issues in forensic linguistics, " Annals of the New York Acad of Science, 606, 65-72 (90); coauth with G. Bavasso and J. Jacobs, "Changes in moral values over three decades, 1958-1988," Youth and Society, 22, 468-481 (91); auth, "Freedom of movement among blue collar workers," J of Social Distress and the Homeless, 2, 23-34 (91); auth, "Can relating the past disclose the future?" J of Mind and Behavior, 14, 133-144 (93); coauth with S. Rich-Kelly, "An art-historical view of social disintegration," J of Social Distress and the Homeless, 2, 223-237 (93); auth, "Creative dialects via dichotic listening," Int J of Group Tensions, 25, 189-206 (95); coauth with D. Latendresse and M. Smith, "Black Identity: The O. J. Simpson Case," J of Social Distress and the Homeless, 5, 273-303 (96); coauth with D. Latendresse & M. Smith, "Black Identity: Response to our viewers," J of Social Distress and the Homeless, 5, 327-334 (96); coauth with G. Bovasso, "The self reference effect in perceptual judgements by individuals and groups," Perceptual and Motor Skills (in press). **CONTACT ADDRESS** Dept Psychol, Hunter Col, CUNY, 695 Park Ave, New York, NY 10021.

RHOADES, VANCE
PERSONAL Born 04/18/1956, Vicksburg, MS, m, 1978, 2 children **DISCIPLINE** PSYCHOLOGY **EDUCATION** Copiah-Lincoln Community Col, AA, 76; Univ Southern Miss, BS, 78, MS, 79; Ga Southern Univ, EdS, 88. **CAREER** Assoc prof, Brewton Parker Col, 79-; adjunct asst prof, Tift Col, 80-86; adjunct instr, Mercer Univ, 86-88. **HONORS AND AWARDS** Phi Theta Kappa Scholarship to Univ of Southern Miss; Psychology Awd, Psi Chi Mem; Dean's Scholar each term in col; AA (special honors) and BS (honors); Teacher of the Year, Brewton-Parker Col, 80, 84, 87, 90; State Composite Bd approved licensed prof coun supervisor, 93; Service Awd from Educational Testing Service, 94; Achievement Awd from the Col Bd of Ed Testing Service, 99. **MEMBERSHIPS** Am Coun Asn, Am Psychol Soc, Baptist Asn for Student Affairs, Ga Licensed Prof Coun Asn. **SELECTED PUBLICATIONS** College textbook reviews- 9 texts, "A Systemic Resident Assistant Training Program ," manual for Brewton-Parker Col. **CONTACT ADDRESS** Dept Soc & Behav Sci, Brewton-Parker Col, PO Box 2084, Mount Vernon, GA 30445. **EMAIL** prhoades@cybersouth.com

RHOADS, LINDA S.
PERSONAL Born 02/22/1949, Harrisburg, PA, m, 1969, 2 children **DISCIPLINE** HISTORY OF THE BOOK, WOMEN'S HISTORY **EDUCATION** Simmons Col, BA, 71; Univ of Chicago, MA; ABD. **CAREER** Managing ed, Critical Inquiry, 74-77; asst ed to co-ed, New England Quart, 81-. **MEMBERSHIPS** Paul Revere Mem Asn, Mass Hist Soc, Col Soc of Mass, New England Women's Diaries Proj, Am Studies Asn, MLA. **RESEARCH** History of the Book, Women's History. **SELECTED PUBLICATIONS** Ed, Tradition and Innovation: Reflections on Northeastern University's First Century, Northeastern Univ, 98; auth, Amelia Peabody: A Biographical Study, 98; auth, Lt Col Ruby Winslow Linn: Doubling a Life of Service, 01. **CONTACT ADDRESS** Mass Hist Soc, 1154 Boylston St, Boston, MA 02215. **EMAIL** lrhoads@masshist.org

RICE, BERRY
PERSONAL Born 03/23/1940, Birmingham, AL, m, 1962, 2 children **DISCIPLINE** ELEMENTARY EDUCATION, NURSING; DIVINITY **EDUCATION** Univ Ala, BSED, 61; Med Col Ga, BNursing, 89; Interdenominational Theol Ctr, MDiv, 96. **CAREER** Reg Nurse, Athens Reg Med Ctr, 89- . **HONORS AND AWARDS** Theta Phi; Briggs NT scholar awd; nurs hon soc. **MEMBERSHIPS** Ga Nurses Asn; Soc Bibl Studs. **RESEARCH** Prayer, Judaic and Christian; Healing. **CONTACT ADDRESS** Athens Regional Medical Ctr, 386 Milledge Cir, Athens, GA 30606. **EMAIL** price@negia.net

RICHARDS, CONSTANCE S.
PERSONAL Born 09/18/1948, Columbus, OH, s **DISCIPLINE** ENGLISH, WOMEN'S STUDIES, BLACK STUDIES **EDUCATION** Ohio State Univ, BA, 90; MA, 92; PhD, 96. **CAREER** Lectr, Ohio State Univ, 96-; adj asst prof, Ohio Wesleyan Univ, 97-. **MEMBERSHIPS** Nat Womens Studies Assoc, Mod For Lang Assoc. **RESEARCH** Global/TransNational Women's Literature. **SELECTED PUBLICATIONS** Auth, On the Winds and Waves of Imagination: Transnational Feminism and Literature, (Garland, NY), 00. **CONTACT ADDRESS** Ohio Wesleyan Univ, 3550 Olentangy Blvd, Columbus, OH 43214-4023. **EMAIL** richards.5@osu.edu

RICHARDS, STEPHEN C.
PERSONAL Born 08/15/1951, Cleveland, OH **DISCIPLINE** SOCIOLOGY, CRIMINOLOGY **EDUCATION** Univ Wis, BS, 86; MA, 89; Iowa State Univ, PhD, 92. **CAREER** Assoc Prof, Northern Ky Univ. **MEMBERSHIPS** Am Sociol Asn, Am Soc for Criminol, Acad of Criminal Justice Sci. **SELECTED PUBLICATIONS** Auth, The Sociological Significance of Tattoos, 95; auth, The Structure of Prison Release, 95. **CONTACT ADDRESS** Dept Sociol and Anthrop, No Kentucky Univ, Newport, KY 41099-0001.

RICHARDSON, BRIAN C.
PERSONAL Born 11/18/1941, Amsterdam, NY, m, 3 children **DISCIPLINE** CHRISTIAN EDUCATION **EDUCATION** Campbell Univ, BA; Southwestern Baptist Theol Sem, MA, PhD. **CAREER** Prof, ch, Biblical Stud Div, Bryan Col; Basil Manly, Jr. prof, S Baptist Theol Sem. **HONORS AND AWARDS** Outstanding Ed of Am. **MEMBERSHIPS** NAPCE, YME. **RESEARCH** Youth. **SELECTED PUBLICATIONS** Auth, Christian Education: Foundations for the Future, Moody Press. **CONTACT ADDRESS** Sch Christian Edu and Leadership, So Baptist Theol Sem, 2825 Lexington Rd, Louisville, KY 40280. **EMAIL** brichardson@sbts.edu

RICHARDSON, CORDELL
PERSONAL Born 11/10/1946, Pittsburgh, PA, m **DISCIPLINE** EDUCATION **EDUCATION** Lincoln U, BS 1968; Univ of Pitts, MS 1970, PhD 1974. **CAREER** Carnegie Mellon U, conslr asst dir & dir of upwrd bnd dir of Stud servs; Exclnc Prgm PUSH, natl dir. **MEMBERSHIPS** Mem Omega Psi Phi Frat; Am Soc for Engr Educs; Am Prpsychl Rsrch Fnd; Prince Hall Masons. **CONTACT ADDRESS** 5000 Forbes, Pittsburgh, PA 15213.

RICHARDSON, LAUREL
PERSONAL Born 07/15/1936, Chicago, IL, m, 1980, 5 children **DISCIPLINE** SOCIOLOGY **EDUCATION** Univ Chicago, BA, 56; Univ Colorado, PhD, 63. **CAREER** Asst prof, Dept Sociology, Calif State Univ Los Angeles, 62-64; asst prof, Dept Sociology, Denison Univ, 65-70; post-doctoral fellow, Coll Medicine, Natl Inst Health, 64-65, visiting asst prof, Dept Sociology, 69-70, asst prof, Dept Sociology, 70-74, assoc prof, Dept Sociology, 74-77, prof, Dept Sociology, 78-94, prof emerita, Dept Sociology, 93-, Graduate Prof of Women's Studies, Dept Sociology, 88-, visiting prof, Cultural Studies Program, Educ Policy and Leadership, Coll Educ, 95-, Ohio State Univ. **HONORS AND AWARDS** Visiting Distinguished Prof, New Mexico State Univ, 94; fellow, Natl Endowment for Humanities, declined; grant, co-recipient, Ohio Dept Health, "Impact of Rape Educ Strategies on Coll Students, 87-88; NIMH grant, 77; NSF Pre-doctoral fel, 60-63; Cooley award for best book of 98. **MEMBERSHIPS** Amer Sociological Assn; North Central Sociological Assn; Soc Study Symbolic Interaction; Natl Women's Studies Assn; Sociologists Women in Soc. **RESEARCH** Qualitative methodology; gender; contemporary theory; feminist theory; interpretive studies; science studies; sociology of knowledge. **SELECTED PUBLICATIONS** Auth, **CONTACT ADDRESS** Dept of Sociology, Ohio State Univ, Columbus, 190 N. Oval Mall, Columbus, OH 43210. **EMAIL** Richardson.9@osu.edu

RICHARDSON, MILES E.
PERSONAL Born 01/22/1932, Palestine, TX, m, 1959, 3 children **DISCIPLINE** ANTHROPOLOGY **EDUCATION** Stephen F Austin, BS, 57; Tulane Univ, PhD, 65. **CAREER** Asst Prof to Assoc Prof, Ind Univ of Pa, 63-65; Asst Prof to Prof, 65-. **HONORS AND AWARDS** Vis Scholar, Univ NC, 95; Nixon Fel, Whittier Col, 88; Vis Scholar, Tex Univ, 87; Vis Scholar, Princeton Univ, 80. **MEMBERSHIPS** Soc for Humanistic Anthropol, Southern Anthropol Soc, Sigma XI, Phi Kappa Phi; Asn of Am Geog, Am Anthropol Asn. **SELECTED PUBLICATIONS** Auth, Cry Lonesome and Other Accounts of the Anthropologist's Project, State Univ of New York Press, 90; ed, Place: Experience and Symbol, Geoscience Pub, 84; ed, The Human Mirror, Louisiana State Univ Press, 74; auth, San Pedro, Colombia: Small Town in a Developing Society, Holt, Rinehart and Winston, 86; auth, "Clarifying the Dark in Black Christs: The Play of Icon, Narrative, and Experience in the Construction of Presence," in Yearbook of the Conference of Latin Americanist Geographers, 95; auth, "The Poetics of a Resurrection: Re-Seeing 30 Years of Change in a Colombian Community and in the Anthropological Enterprise," American Anthropologist, (98): 11-21; auth, "Place, Narrative, and the Writing Self: The

Poetics of Being in The Garden of Eden," The Southern Review, (99): 330-337; auth, "Being-in-Christ and the Social Construction of Death in Spanish America and in the American South: An Anthropologist's Project," forthcoming. **CONTACT ADDRESS** Dept Anthropol & Geog, La State Univ, Baton Rouge, LA 70803-0001. **EMAIL** gamile@lsu.edu

RICHARDSON, RICHARD C., JR.
PERSONAL Born 09/10/1933, Burlington, VT, m, 1954, 3 children **DISCIPLINE** EDUCATION **EDUCATION** Castleton State Col, BS, 54; Mich State Univ, MA, 58; Univ Tex, PhD, 63. **CAREER** Comn Off, US Marine Corps Res, 54-57; res asst, Mich State Univ, 58; instr Soc Stud & Counr, Vermont Col, 58-61; Dean Stud Pers Serv, Meramec Commun Col, 63-64; Dean of Instr, Forest Pk Commun Col, 64-67; founding pres, Northampton County Area Commun Col, 67-77; prof & chr Dept Higher & Adult Educ, 77-83, Assoc dir, Nat Ctr Postsecondary Goverance & Fin Res Ctr, 85-90, Prof Div Ed Ldr & Policy Stud, 84-99, prof emer, 99-, Ariz State Univ; prof of Higher Ed, NYork Univ, 99-. **HONORS AND AWARDS** Distinguished grad award, Col Educ Univ Texas-Austin, 82; distinguished serv award, Am Asn Commun & Jr Col, 84; res of Year Awd, Col Educ Ariz State Univ, 88 & 93. Hon Litt.D, Lafayette Col, 72. **MEMBERSHIPS** AERA; ASHE; AACC; Acad Mgt; AAUP **RESEARCH** Access and equity; higher education governance; state higher education policy issues. **SELECTED PUBLICATIONS** Auth, Achieving Quality and Diversity: Universities in a Multicultural Society, Macmillan, 91; coauth, Creating Effective Learning Environments: State Policy and College Learning, 93; coauth Overcoming the Effects of Apartheid in South African Universities, The Rev of Higher Educ, 96; State Structures for the Governance of Higher Education: A Comparative Study, Calif Higher Educ Policy Ctr, 97; Designing State Higher Education Systems For a New Century, Oryx Press, 98; auth, Designing State Higher Education Systems for a New Century, ACE/Oryx Press, 99; auth, Systemic Change in Higher Education, WICHE, 99; coauth, "Policy Environments and System Design: Understanding State Governance Structures," The Rev of Higher Educ, 99. **CONTACT ADDRESS** 7-13 Washington St #2A, New York, NY 10003. **EMAIL** richard.richardson@nyu.edu

RICHARDSON, WILLIAM
DISCIPLINE MARRIAGE; FAMILY THERAPY **EDUCATION** Georgia State Univ, PhD. **CAREER** Prof; prof therapist. **HONORS AND AWARDS** Clinical dir, Ctr for Marriage and Family Therapy at RTS. **MEMBERSHIPS** Clinical mem, clinical supvr, Amer Assn of Marriage and Family Therapy. **RESEARCH** Parenting skills; ethical and legal issues in psychotherapy. **SELECTED PUBLICATIONS** Auth, Train Up A Child: A Christian Parent's Handbook, re-release as Loving Obedience, Northfield Press. **CONTACT ADDRESS** Dept of Marriage and Family Therapy, Reformed Theol Sem, Mississippi, 5422 Clinton Blvd, Jackson, MS 39209-3099. **EMAIL** brichardson@rts.edu

RICHTER, MAURICE N.
PERSONAL Born 05/21/1930, New York, NY **DISCIPLINE** SOCIOLOGY **EDUCATION** Bard Col, BA, 53; Univ Chicago, MA, 54; PhD, 62. **CAREER** Assoc Prof, State Univ of NYork at Albany, 66-. **HONORS AND AWARDS** Outstanding Acad Book for "Technology and Social Complexity," Choice, 83. **MEMBERSHIPS** Am Sociol Asn. **RESEARCH** Sociology of Science and Technology, Social Change. **SELECTED PUBLICATIONS** Auth, The Autonomy of Science: An Historical and Comparative Analysis, Schekman (Cambridge, MA), 81, Chinese ed, Chinese Acad of Sci (Beijing), 82; auth, "University Scientists As Enterpreneurs," Society 23 (86): 81-83, and in Academic Labor Markets and Careers, ed. David Breneman and Ted Youn (Falmer Press, Stanford Ser in Public Policy, 88); auth, "After Forty-five Years: Ogburn's Predictions Concerning Aviation Re-examined," Technology in Society 13 (91): 317-325; auth, Technology and Social Complexity, SUNY Press (Albany, NY), 92, Korean ed, in Lucky Polymer Technology 27-32 (93-95); auth, "Evolution: Biological, Social, and Cultural, in Encyclopedia of Sociology (Macmillan, NY), 93. **CONTACT ADDRESS** Dept Sociol, SUNY at Albany, 1400 Washington Ave, Albany, NY 12222-1000.

RICKERT, EDWARD J.
PERSONAL Born 07/24/1936, Houston, TX, m, 1975, 2 children **DISCIPLINE** PSYCHOLOGY **EDUCATION** Univ NM, BA, 60; MS, 63; PhD, 68; Univ Alabama, MPH, 86. **CAREER** Res asst, UNM, 63-67; asst prof, Cal State Univ, 67-71; assoc prof, UAB, 71-98; adj assoc prof, Univ SC, 98-. **HONORS AND AWARDS** Phi Kappa Phi; Soc Sigma Xi; Univ Fel, UNM; Am Men Women Sci; Men of Achiev; Who's Who Front Sci; Who's Who S SW. **MEMBERSHIPS** AAVP; RMPA; APS; ASA; ISPP. **RESEARCH** Nature of memory deficits in early stage Alzheimer's disease. **SELECTED PUBLICATIONS** Coauth, "Different HIV risk profiles in samples of college students and homeless persons," Psychol Rep (96): 1123-1132; coauth, "Relationships among child abuse, date abuse, and psychological problems," J Clinical Psychol 53 (97): 1-11; coauth, " Misunderstanding or rape? Student evaluations of actual and hypothetical examples of saying 'No' to sex," Violence Against Women: An international and interdisciplinary J 23 (98): 322-333; coauth, "Early stage Alzheimer's Disease disrupts encoding of contextual Information," Aging, Neuro Cog 5 (98): 73-81; auth, "Authoritarianism and economic threat: Implications for political behavior," Polit Psychol 9 (98): 707-720; coauth, "Self-efficacy in overweight individuals with binge eating disorder," Obesity Research 1 (99): 552-555; auth, "Two-process learning theory," in Encyclopedia of Psychology and neuroscience, eds. WF Craighead, C Nemeroff (New York: John Wiley and Sons), in press. **CONTACT ADDRESS** Dept Psychology, Univ of So Carolina, Columbia, 414 Barnwell Hall, Columbia, SC 29208.

RIDGEL, GUS TOLVER
PERSONAL Born 07/01/1926, Poplar Bluff, m **DISCIPLINE** EDUCATION **EDUCATION** Lincoln Univ, BS, 1950; Univ of MO, Columbia, MO, MA, 1951; Univ of Wis, Madison, PhD, 1956. **CAREER** Fort Valley State Coll, Ft Valley, GA, head dept of business, 52-58; Wiley Coll, Marshall, TX, dean academic affairs, 58-60; Kentucky State Univ, Frankfort, KY, dean, School of Business, 60-84; Central State Univ, Wilberforce, OH, vice pres, academic affairs, 72-74; Southern Univ, Baton Rouge, vice pres of academic affairs, beginning, 85; Kentucky State Coll, Vice Pres of Admin Affairs, currently. **HONORS AND AWARDS** Univ of Missouri-Columbia, The Gus T Ridgel Minority Graduate Fellowship, 1988. **MEMBERSHIPS** Advisory bd, Republic Savings Bank, 1983-86; mem of LA Univ, Marine Consortium Council, 1986-. **CONTACT ADDRESS** So Univ and A&M Col, J S Clark Admin Bldg, 3rd Fl, Baton Rouge, LA 70813.

RIEGNER, ELIZABETH JANE
PERSONAL Born 03/09/1944, PA, d, 3 children **DISCIPLINE** PSYCHOLOGY **EDUCATION** Methodist Hosp School Nursing, RN, 66; Millersville Univ, BSEd, 68; W Chester Univ, MS, 77; Fla State Univ, PhD, 96. **CAREER** Lic Mental Health Counselor, 77-; Reg Nurse, 66-; Faculty, Daytona Beach Col, current. **MEMBERSHIPS** Am Asn Marriage & Fam Therapists; Intl Asn Play Therapy; Nat Acad Cert Mental Health Coun. **RESEARCH** Holistic Health; Mind-Body Connection; Humor and Health. **CONTACT ADDRESS** Dept Arts, Daytona Beach Comm Col, 3959 S Nova Rd, Port Orange, FL 32124. **EMAIL** ejriegner@aol.com

RISO, LAWRENCE P.
PERSONAL Born 02/27/1965, Queens, NY, m, 1999 **DISCIPLINE** PSYCHOLOGY **EDUCATION** State Univ NY at Buffalo, BA, 87; State Univ NY at Stony Brook, PhD, 94. **CAREER** Res Fel, Univ of Pittsburgh, 94-96; Instr, Univ of Pittsburgh, 96-. **HONORS AND AWARDS** Inst of Mental Health Grant. **MEMBERSHIPS** Am Psychol Asn. **RESEARCH** Depressive Disorders, Cognitive Therapy, Personality Disorders. **SELECTED PUBLICATIONS** Auth, "Psychiatric disorders: Problems of boundaries and comorbidity," in Basic Issue in Psychopathology, ed. C.G. Costello (NY: Guilford, 93); coauth, "DSM-III-R dysthymnia: Antecedents and underlying assumptions," in Progress in Experimental Personality and Psychopathology Research Vol 16, ed. L.J. Chapman, J.P. Chapman, and D.C. Fowles (NY: Springer, 93); coauth, "Family study of early-onset dysthymnia: Mood and personality disorders in relatives of outpatients with dysthymnia and episodic major depression, and normal controls," Archives of Gen Psychiatry 52 (95): 487-496; coauth, "The subaffective-character spectrum subtyping distinction in primary early-onset dysthymnia: A Clinical and family study, " J of Affective Disorders 38 (96): 13-22; coauth, "Understanding the comorbidity between early-onset dysthymnia and unstable personality disorders: A family study," Am J of Psychiatry 153 (96): 900-906; coauth, "Convergent and discriminant validity of perceived criticism from spouses and family members," Behav Ther 27 (96): 129-137; coauth, "Reply to: The comorbidity between personality and systhymnic disorder - Historical and conceptual issues," Am J of Psychiatry 154 (97): 1039-1040; coauth, "Comorbidity between dysthymnic and major depressive disorders: A family study analysis," J of Affective Disorders 42 (97): 103-111; coauth, "A prospective test of criteria for response, remission, relapse, recovery, and recurrence in depressed patients treated with cognitive behavior therapy," J of Affective Disorders 43 (97): 131-142; coauth, "A family study of outpatients with borderline personality disorder and no history of mood disorder," J of Personality Disorders (in press). **CONTACT ADDRESS** Dept Psychology, Georgia State Univ, 30 Decatus St, Atlanta, GA 30303.

RITTENHOUSE, ROBERT K.
PERSONAL Born 02/05/1946, Port Orchard, WA, m, 1987, 3 children **DISCIPLINE** PSYCHOLOGY, DEAF EDUCATION **EDUCATION** Ill Col, BA, 68; Canisius Col, MSEd, 69; Univ Ill, PhD, 77. **CAREER** Teacher, Minn Sch for the Deaf, 69-71; state dir of deaf-blind, 71-74; res fel, Univ Ill, 74-77; prof & dir of deaf educ, Ill State Univ, 77-87; prof & dir of deaf educ, Univ Ark, 87-. **HONORS AND AWARDS** Outstanding Alumni Awd, Univ Ill, 95; Fulbright, 99; Excellence Awds in res, teaching, service, and leadership, Univ Ark. **MEMBERSHIPS** Coun on Educ of the Deaf, NEA. **RESEARCH** Cognition and Metaphor for the Deaf, Early Deafness Intervention. **SELECTED PUBLICATIONS** Coauth, The Full Inclusion of Persons With Disabilities in American Society, Network Pub (Levin, New Zealand), 95; auth, Metaphor Stories for Deaf Children, Butte Pub (Hillsboro, OR), 98; coauth, The Electronic Classroom: Using Technology to Create a 21st Century Classroom, Butte Pub (Hillsboro, OR), 00; auth, Deaf Education at the Dawn of the 21st Century: Old Challenges, New Directions, Butte Pub, Inc. (Hillsboro, OR), 00. **CONTACT ADDRESS** Dept Teacher Educ, Univ of Arkansas, Little Rock, 2801 S University Ave, Little Rock, AR 72204-1000.

RITTS, VICKI
PERSONAL Born 07/20/1958, St Louis, MO, m, 1979 **DISCIPLINE** PSYCHOLOGY **EDUCATION** Univ Mo, BA, 88; S Ill Univ, MA, 90; Univ Mo, PhD, 94. **CAREER** Instructor, St Louis Cmty Col, 89-94; Instructor, S Ill Univ, 90-94; Instructor to Assoc Prof, St Louis Cmty Col, 94-. **HONORS AND AWARDS** Outstanding Instructor Awd, Phi Theta Kappa, 97, 98; Who's Who among am Teachers, 98; MCCA's Fac Innovation of the Year 98; Teacher of the Year, Montage's (Campus Newpaper), 99; Intl Who's Who of Prof and Business Women, 00; Two Thousand Notable Am Wome, 00; Who's Who Among Am Teachers, 00 **MEMBERSHIPS** Am Psychol Asn; Midwest Psychol Asn; Coun of Teachers of Undergrad Psychol; MO NEA; MO Cmty Col Asn; Am Asn of Women in Cmty Col; Intl Asn of Cross-Cultural Psychol; Soc for Cross Cultural Res. **RESEARCH** Gender; Culture; Social Anxiety; and Physical Attractiveness. **SELECTED PUBLICATIONS** Co-auth, "College students' attitudes toward adult material and the legal rental of adult videos," College Student Journal (91): 440-450; co-auth, "Expectations, impressions, and judgments of physically attractive students: A Review," Review of Educational Research, (92): 413-426; co-auth, "Six ways to improve your nonverbal communication," Teaching for Success, (93): 6-7; co-auth, "Nonverbal teaching tips," Intervention: In School and Clinic, (94): 133; co-auth, "Verification and commitment in marital relationships: An exploration of self-verification theory in community college students," Psychological Reports, (95): 385-386; co-auth, "Nonverbal communication in correctional education," Journal for Juvenile Justice and Detention Services, (96): 12-14; co-auth, "Multicultural nonverbal behavior in the correctional classroom," Journal for Juvenile Justice and Detention Services, (96): 64-66; co-auth, "Effects of social anxiety and action identification on impressions and thoughts in interaction," Journal of Social and Clinical Psychology, (96): 19+1-205; co-auth, "Social and communicative anxiety: A meta-analysis," Communication Yearbook, 97; co-auth, "Verification and commitment in marital relationships: An exploration of self-verification theory in community college students," in Stand! Contending Ideas and Opinions in Social Psychology, Coursewise, 98. **CONTACT ADDRESS** Dept Beh Sci, St. Louis Comm Col, Meramec, 11333 Big Bend Rd, Saint Louis, MO 63122.

RITZER, GEORGE
PERSONAL Born 10/14/1940, New York, NY, m, 1964, 2 children **DISCIPLINE** SOCIOLOGY **EDUCATION** CCNY, BA, 62; Univ MI, MBA, 64; Cornell Univ, PhD, 68. **CAREER** Asst prof, Tulane Univ, 68-70; Assoc prof, Univ Kansas, 70-74; prof, Univ of Maryland, 74-present. **HONORS AND AWARDS** Fulbright-Hays Fel; Distinguished Scholar-Teacher; Teaching Excellence Awd; Fel in Residence Russian Acad of Sci. **MEMBERSHIPS** Amer, Eastern, Southern Sociological Soc **RESEARCH** Sociological theory, sociology of consumption. **SELECTED PUBLICATIONS** Auth, The McDonaldization of Society, 93, 96 (revised edition); co auth, McDisneyization and Post-Tourism: Complementary Perspectives on Tourism in Touring Cultures: Transformations in Travel and Theory, 97; Fast Food, in Gotterspeisen, 97; McDonaldization and Globalization, The Student's Companion to Sociology, 97; Postmodern Social Theory, 97; The McDonaldization Thesis: Extensions and Explorations, 98; Enchanting a Disenchanted World: Revolutionizing the Means of Consumption, forthcoming. **CONTACT ADDRESS** Dept. of Sociology, Univ of Maryland, Col Park, College Park, MD 20740. **EMAIL** ritzer@bss1.umd.edu

RIVERS, ELIAS LYNCH
PERSONAL Born 09/19/1924, Charleston, SC, m, 1945, 3 children **DISCIPLINE** SPANISH **EDUCATION** Yale Univ, AB, 48, MA, 50, PhD(Span), 52. **CAREER** Instr Span, Yale Univ, 51-52; from instr to asst prof, Dartmouth Uol, 52-62; prof, Ohio State Univ, 62-64; prof, Johns Hopkins Univ, 64-78; Prof Span & Comp Lit, State Univ NY, 78-, Howard fel, 56-57; Guggenheim fel, 59-60; Fulbright res grant, Madrid, 64-65; Nat Endowment for Humanities res grant, 67-68, 70-71 & 81-82, sem dir, 75-76. **HONORS AND AWARDS** MA, Dartmouth Col, 62. **MEMBERSHIPS** MLA; Am Asn Teachers Span & Port; Asoc Int Hispanistas (secy-gen, 62-80). **RESEARCH** Renaissance poetry in Spain; oral and written styles of composition. **SELECTED PUBLICATIONS** Auth, Francisco de Aldana, Poesias, Espasa-Calpe, 57; Thirty-Six Spanish Poems, Houghton, 57; Garcilaso de la Vega, Obras Completas, Ohio State Univ, 64; Nature, art and science in Spanish poetry of the Renaissance, Bull Hisp Studies, 67; ed, Hijos de la Ira, Labor Barcelona, 70 & English translr, Children of Wrath, Johns Hopkins Univ, 70; Spanish Renaissance & Baroque Poetry, Scribners, 72; auth, Talking and writing in Don Quixote, Thought, 76. **CONTACT ADDRESS** Dept of Hisp Studies, SUNY, Stony Brook, Stony Brook, NY 11794.

ROBBINS, PAUL RICHARD
PERSONAL Born 10/27/1930, Washington, DC, d **DISCIPLINE** SOCIAL PSYCHOLOGY **EDUCATION** Univ Chicago, BA, 50; Columbia Univ, PhD, 59. **CAREER** Res asst, NIMH, 55-58; res psychol, USPHS, 59-62; dir consult proj, Ca Dept Health, 62-65; psychol School Med George Wash Univ, 66-72; Psychol Private Practice, 75-96. **HONORS AND AWARDS** Fel Columbia Univ. **MEMBERSHIPS** Am Psychol Asn **RESEARCH** Issues relating to personality and clinical psychology ie coping behaviors, dreams, and depression. **SELECTED PUBLICATIONS** auth Adolescent Suicide, Understanding Depression, The Psychology of Dreams, McFarland & Co NC; Medieval Summer, Branden Press. **CONTACT ADDRESS** 8401 Park Crest Dr, Silver Spring, MD 20910.

ROBBINS, RICHARD H.
PERSONAL Born 05/19/1922, New York, NY, m, 1994, 2 children **DISCIPLINE** SOCIOLOGY **EDUCATION** Brooklyn Col, BA, 46; Washington State Univ, MA, 48; Univ Ill, PhD, 58. **CAREER** Instr, Wellesley Col, 54-58; asst prof to prof, Wheaton Col, 58-67; prof, Univ Mass, Boston, 67-90, chair, 67-71, emeritus, 90-; lect, Curry Col, 94-2000. **HONORS AND AWARDS** Fulbrights, 49-50, 62-63; Guggenheim, 74-75; Nat Endowment Humanities, 80, 83. **MEMBERSHIPS** Am Soc Asn, Eastern Sociol Asn, North England Sociol Asn. **RESEARCH** Racial and ethnic religion, sociology of education, political sociology. **SELECTED PUBLICATIONS** Auth, Sidelines Activist, Univ Miss Press (96); articles in Notable American Black Males (Gale); American National Biography (Oxford); and Racial and Ethnic Relations (Salem Press). **CONTACT ADDRESS** Dept Behav Sci, Curry Col, 1071 Blue Hill Ave, Milton, MA 02186.

ROBBINS, SUSAN P.
PERSONAL Born 08/15/1948, Brooklyn, NY, s **DISCIPLINE** SOCIAL WORK **EDUCATION** Borough Manhattan Community Col, AA, 72; Hamline Univ, St Paul, Minn, BA, 74; Univ Minn, MSW, 76; Tulane Univ, PhD, 79. **CAREER** Asst prof, New Orleans Consortium Dept of Soc Work, Dominican Col, New Orleans, La, 77-80; adjunct instr, Univ Tex Health Sci Center, Houston, 92-97; Tex Dept of Protective Services Training Inst, 95-; private practice, Houston, 80-; asst prof to assoc prof and Dean, Univ Houston, 80-. **HONORS AND AWARDS** Manhattan Community Col: Valedictorian, Dean's Awd, Liberal Arts Awd, Phi Beta Kappa Awd, Phi Theta Kappa, 72; Hamline Univ: Alpha Kappa Delta, Pi Gamma Mu, Kappa Phi, 74; Univ Minn: Phi Kappa Phi, 76; Fel, Nat Inst of Mental Health, 76-78; Outstanding Young Woman of Am, 81; Outstanding Fac Awd, Univ Houston, 88, 93; Curriculum Infusion Awd, Univ Houston, 92; Nat Fac Excellence Awd, Univ Continuing Educ Asn, 98; Regional Continuing Educ Fac Awd, Univ Continuing Educ Asn, 98. **MEMBERSHIPS** Nat Asn of Soc Workers, Coun on Soc Work Educ, Bertha Capen Reynolds Soc, Asn for Community Org and Soc Admin, Southern Sociol Asn, Phi Kappa Phi. **RESEARCH** Theories of human behavior, juvenile delinquency, cults, satanic ritual abuse, recovered memories of abuse, false allegations, mediation. **SELECTED PUBLICATIONS** Auth, "Sidebar: Children's memory: The benefits of scientific knowledge," Families in Society: The J of Contemp Human Services, 78, 6 (97); auth, "Cults (update)," in Encyclopedia of Social Work, 19th ed on CD ROM, Washington, DC: Nat Asn of Soc Workers Press (97); coauth, Contemporary human behavior theory: A critical perspective for social work, Boston: Allyn and Bacon (98); auth, "Book review oversimplified complexities of recovered memory (Letter to the Editor)," Families in Society: The J of Contemp Human Services, 79, 2 (98); auth, "The social and cultural context of satanic ritual abuse allegations," J of Issues in Child Abuse Allegations, 10 (98); guest ed, Families in Society: The J of Contemp Human Services, Special Focus Issue on Knowledge Building, 80, 4 (99); coauth, "Ideology, theory, and social work practice," Families in Society: The J of Contemp Human Services, 80, 4 (99). **CONTACT ADDRESS** Grad Sch of Soc Work, Univ of Houston, Houston, TX 77204-0001. **EMAIL** Srobbins@UH.edu

ROBERTS, BARBARA A.
PERSONAL Born Riverside, CA **DISCIPLINE** HISTORY, WOMEN'S STUDIES **EDUCATION** Simon Fraser Univ, BA, 72, MA, 76; Univ Ottawa, PhD, 80. **CAREER** Vis prof, 80-82, lectr, Univ Winnipeg, 82-83; asst prof, Univ Sask, 83-84; asst prof, Concordia Univ, 87-88; assoc prof, 89-92, Prof Women's Studies, Athabaska Univ 92-. **MEMBERSHIPS** Bd dir, Can Res Inst Advan Women; Voice of Women. **SELECTED PUBLICATIONS** Auth, Whence They Came: Deportation from Canada 1900-35, 88; auth, A Decent Living: Women in the Winnipeg Garment Industry, 91; auth, Strategies for the Year 2000: A Women's Handbook, 95; auth, A Reconstructed World: A Feminist Biography of Gertrude Richardson, 96. **CONTACT ADDRESS** Dept of Women's Studies, Athabasca Univ, Athabasca, AB, Canada TOG 2RO. **EMAIL** barbara@cs.athabaska.ca

ROBERTS, BRYNDIS WYNETTE
PERSONAL Born 09/04/1957, Sylvania, GA, s **DISCIPLINE** EDUCATION **EDUCATION** Wesleyan Coll, Macon, GA, AB (magna cum laude), 1978; Univ of GA, Athens, Ga, JD (cum laude), 1981. **CAREER** State Law Dept, Atlanta, GA, asst attorney general, 81-87; Univ of GA, Athens, GA, Vice Pres for Legal Affairs, 87-. **HONORS AND AWARDS** Business & Professional Women Young Careerist, DeKalb Business & Professional Women, 1985; Outstanding Woman Law Student, GA Assn of Women Lawyers, 1981. **MEMBERSHIPS** Mem, Classic City Pilot Club, 1991-92, sec, School & College Law Section, State Bar, 1988-89; mem, National Association of College & University Attorney's, 1987-92, 1986-, chairman, 1986-87; mem, GA State Board of Accountancy, 1988-; Wesleyan Board of Trustees, 1991. **CONTACT ADDRESS** Legal Affairs, Univ of Georgia, 310 Old College, Athens, GA 30602.

ROBERTS, KEITH A.
PERSONAL Born 01/30/1949, Columbus, OH, m, 1969, 3 children **DISCIPLINE** SOCIOLOGY **EDUCATION** Muskingum Col, BA, 62; Boston Univ ThM, 72; PhD, 76. **CAREER** From Asst to Full Prof, Boroling Green State Univ, 76-91; Hanover Col, 91-. **HONORS AND AWARDS** Dempster Scholar, 74-75; OATYC Ohio Teacher of the Year Awd, 87; NCSA Distinguished Contrib to Teaching, 93; NCSA Distinguished Serv Awd, 97. **MEMBERSHIPS** Am Sociol Asn, N Central Sociol Asn, Social Sci Study of Relig, Asn for Sociol of Relig, Rel Res Asn. **RESEARCH** Scholarship of Teaching, Sociology of Religion, Religion and Bigotry. **SELECTED PUBLICATIONS** Auth, "Toward a Generic Concept of Counter-Culture," Sociol Focus (Apr 78): 111-126; auth, "Requisite Conditions for the Formation and Viability of a Counter-Cultural Community," Sociol Spectrum (Dec 83): 371-394; auth, "Sociology in General Education Curriculum: A Cognitive Structuralist perspective," Teaching Sociol (Oct 86): 207-215; auth, "A Sociological Overview: Mental Health Implications of Religio-Cultural Megatrends in the United States," in Religion and Prevention in Mental Health: Research, Vision, and Action, ed. Kenneth Pargament, Kenneth Maton, and Robert Hess (NY: Haworth, 92); auth, "Ritual and the Transmission of a Cultural Tradition: An Ethnographic Perspective," in Beyond Establishment: Protestant Identity in a Post-Protestant Age, ed. Jackson Carroll and Wade Clark Roof (Louisville: John Knox Press, 93); auth, "Toward a Sociology of Writing," Teaching Sociol (Oct 93): 317-324; coauth, Writing in the Undergraduate Sociology Curriculum: A Guide for Teachers, ASA Teaching Resources Center (Washington DC), 93; auth, Religion in Sociological Perspective, Wadsworth Publ Co (Belmont, CA), 95. **CONTACT ADDRESS** Dept Sociol, Hanover Col, PO Box 108, Hanover, IN 47243. **EMAIL** robertak@hanover.edu

ROBERTS, MICHAEL C.
PERSONAL Born 01/16/1951, Waynesville, MO, m, 1973, 2 children **DISCIPLINE** PSYCHOLOGY **EDUCATION** Univ Mo, BA, 73; Purdue Univ, MS, 74; PhD, 78. **CAREER** Asst Prof to Full Prof, Univ Ala, 78-91; Prof and Director, Univ Kans, 91-. **HONORS AND AWARDS** Diplomate in Clinical Psychol, Am Board of Professional Psychol, 98; Lee Salk Distinguished Service Awd, 93; Fel, Am Psychol Soc, Fel, Am Psychol Asn. **MEMBERSHIPS** Am Psychol Asn. **SELECTED PUBLICATIONS** Auth, Managing managed care, Plenum Press, 97; ed, Beyond appearances: a new look at adolescent girls, Washington, DC, 99; auth, "Psychotherapy with children and families," in Handbook of psychological change, (00): 500-519; auth, "The collaboration of a university and state mental health agency: A curriculum for improving services for children," Professional Psychology, (90): 69-71; auth, "Vale dictum: An editor's view of the field of pediatric psychology and its journal," Journal of Pediatric Psychology, (92): 785-805; auth, "Promotion and prevention in America: still spitting on the sidewalk," Journal of Pediatric Psychology, (94): 267-281; auth, "Models for service delivery in children's mental health: common characteristics," Journal of clinical Child Psychology, (94): 212-219; auth, "A model for training psychologists to provide services for children and adolescents," Professional Psychology: Research and Practice, (98): 293-299; auth, "Innovations in Specialty Training: The clinical Child Psychology Program at the University of Kansas," Professional Psychology: Research and Practice, (98): 394-397; auth, "Future issues in pediatric psychology: Delphic survey," Journal of clinical Psychology in Medical Setting, (00): 5-15. **CONTACT ADDRESS** Dept Psychol, Univ of Kansas, Lawrence, 1 Univ Kans, Lawrence, KS 66045-1500. **EMAIL** mroberts@ukans.edu

ROBERTS, MICHAEL J.
PERSONAL Born 02/21/1967, Mountain View, CA, m, 1993 **DISCIPLINE** SOCIOLOGY **EDUCATION** San Jose State Univ, BA, 92; New School for Soc Res, PhD, 94; CUNY, MPhil, 98. **CAREER** Adj instr, San Jose State Univ, 91-92; res asst to adj instr, CUNY, 94-97; adj instr, Long Island Univ, 97-; adj instr, CUNY 98-. **HONORS AND AWARDS** Phi Alpha Theta; Gorostorday Schol, San Jose State Univ, 93; Fel, CUNY, 95-99. **SELECTED PUBLICATIONS** Auth, "Between Agency and Structure and the Deconstruction of American Exceptionalism: A Critical Review of the Works of Christine Stansell and Sean Wilentz", Passports, San Jose State Univ, 92; auth, "Re-reading Marx and Nietzsche", Rethinking Marxism 8.1, (95); auth, "Rethinking the Postmodern Perspective in Sociology", Sociol Quarterly 41.4, (forthcoming). **CONTACT ADDRESS** Dept Sociol, Queens Col, CUNY, 6530 Kissena Blvd, Flushing, NY 11367. **EMAIL** roberts914@cs.com

ROBERTS, ROBIN
DISCIPLINE WOMEN'S STUDIES, AMERICAN STUDIES **EDUCATION** Univ Pa, PhD, 85. **CAREER** Prof, La State Univ. **HONORS AND AWARDS** Russell B. Nye Awd, Popular Cult Asn, 87; Kathleen Gregory Klein Awd, Popular Cult Asn, 90. **RESEARCH** Popular culture; music videos; Star Trek. **SELECTED PUBLICATIONS** Auth, A New Species: Gender and Science in Science Fiction, 93; Sisters in the Name of Rap: Rapping for Women's Lives, Black Women in Am, 94; Ladies First: Queen Latifah's Afrocentric Feminist Music Video, African Am Rev, 94; It's Still Science Fiction: Strategies of Feminist Science Fiction Criticism, Extrapolation, 95; Ladies First Women in Music Videos, 96; Anne McCaffrey: A Critical Study, 96. **CONTACT ADDRESS** Dept of Eng, Louisiana State Univ and A&M Col, 212H Allen Hall, Baton Rouge, LA 70803. **EMAIL** rrobert@unix1.sncc.lsu.edu

ROBERTSON, PATRICIA
PERSONAL Born Rochester, NY **DISCIPLINE** BEHAVIORAL SCIENCE **EDUCATION** BA, 75; MSW, 80; MA, 98; PhD, 00. **CAREER** Prof, Calif Baptist Univ, 93-. **HONORS AND AWARDS** Intl Who's Who; Who's Who in Am. **MEMBERSHIPS** AAUW, NACSW, APA. **RESEARCH** Conflict resolution models, social effects of medical environment on medical care delivery, cross-cultural competencies, women in academic settings, academic standards in psychology graduate studies. **CONTACT ADDRESS** Dept Behav Sci, California Baptist Col, 8432 Magnolia Ave, Riverside, CA 92504.

ROBINSON, ANDREW
PERSONAL Born 02/16/1939, Chicago, IL **DISCIPLINE** EDUCATION **EDUCATION** Chicago State U, BA 1966; Roosevelt U, MA 1970; Northwestern U, PhD 1973. **CAREER** Univ of KY, asst prof, asso dir Cntr for urban educ 1975-; Chicago City Colls, adminstr 1974-75; Urban & Ethnic Edn, Asst dir; Pub Inst Chicago, supt 1973-74; Chicago Urban League, educ dir 1970-73; Univ IL, visiting instr 1972-73; Chicago Pub Schs, tchr 1966-69. **MEMBERSHIPS** Mem Phi Delta Kappa; Am Assn Sch Adminstrs; Am Assn of Tchr Edn; Nat Alliance Black Sch Educators; Prog Planning Comm Am Assoc of Coll Tchr Edn. **CONTACT ADDRESS** Col of Educ Asst Dean, Univ of Kentucky, Lexington, KY 40506.

ROBINSON, RUTH
PERSONAL Born 12/17/1949, Chicago, IL **DISCIPLINE** EDUCATION **EDUCATION** No IL Univ DeKalb, BA Elem Educ 1971; Pacific Oaks Coll, MA Child Develop 1974; Univ of CA Berkeley, PhD 1980. **CAREER** Pacific Oaks Coll & Children's School, faculty/head teacher 1972-73; Harold E Jones Child Study Center, teacher 1976-77; CA State Polytechnic Univ, lectr 1974-75, 77-78; IN State Univ, asst prof, assoc prof early childhood educ, asst dean school of educ 1984-. **HONORS AND AWARDS** Grad Minority Fellowship UC Berkeley 1977-79; Doctoral Fellowship Carnegie Corp 1975-76; Collective Monologues I Toward a Black Perspective in Educ Stage Seven Inc Pasadena CA 1976. **MEMBERSHIPS** Curriculum consult Merced Co Region III Child Develop & migrant Child Care Prog 1978; curriculum consult Oakland Comm Sch 1975-76; mem Natl Assn Educ of Young Children 1979-; bd of dir Stage Seven Inc Black Perspective in Early Childhood Educ 1973-80. **CONTACT ADDRESS** Indiana State Univ, Statesman Towers West, Terre Haute, IN 47809.

ROBINSON, WILLIAM I.
PERSONAL Born 03/28/1959, New York, NY, m, 1985, 2 children **DISCIPLINE** SOCIOLOGY **EDUCATION** Univ NM, MA, 92; PhD, 94. **CAREER** Adj Prof, Univ NMex, 94-96; Asst Prof, Univ Tenn, 96-98; Asst Prof, NMex State Univ, 98-. **HONORS AND AWARDS** Outstanding Book Awd, Gustavus Myers Ctr, 87; PEWS Awd, Am Sociol Asn, 97; Globe of the Month Recipient, Ctr for Intl Prog NM State Univ, 99; Finalist, Distinguished Pub Awd, Am Sociol Asn, 99; Who's Who in Am, 00. **MEMBERSHIPS** Am Sociol Asn; Latin Am Studies Asn; Intl Studies Asn. **RESEARCH** Globalization; Political Economy; Development; Political Sociology; Central and Latin America; Transnationalism. **SELECTED PUBLICATIONS** Auth, A Faustian Bargain: U.S. Intervention in the Nicaraguan Elections and american Foreign Policy in the Post Cold War Era, Westview Press, 92; auth, Promoting Plyarch: Globalization, U.S. Intervention, and Hegemony, Cabmridge Univ Press, 96; auth, "Global Capitalism and the Oromo Liberation Struggle: Theoretical Notes on W.S. Policy Towards the Ethiopian Empire," Journal of Oromo Studies, (97): 1-46; auth, "(Mal)development in Central America: Globalization and Social Change," Development and Change, (98): 467-497; auth, "Beyond Nation-State Paradigms: Globalization, Sociology, and the Challenge of Transnational Studies," sociological Forum, (98): 561-594; auth, "Latin american and Global Capitalism," Race and Class (98): 111-131; co-auth, "The Find de Siecle Debate: Globalization as Epochal Shift," Science and Soceity, (99): 41-67; auth, "Latin America in the Age of Inequality: Confronting the New 'Utopia'," International Studies Review, (99): 41-67; auth, "Toward a Global Ruling Class?: Globalization and the Transnational Capitalist Class," Science and Society, 00; auth, "Neo-Liberalism, the Global Elite, and the Guatemalan Transition: A Critical Macrosocial Analysis," Journal of Inter-American and World Affairs, 00. **CONTACT**

ADDRESS Dept Sociol & Anthropol, New Mexico State Univ, PO Box 30001, Las Cruces, NM 88003. **EMAIL** wirobins@nmsu.edu

ROBY, PAMELA A.
PERSONAL Born 11/17/1942, Milwaukee, WI, d **DISCIPLINE** SOCIOLOGY **EDUCATION** Denver Univ, BA, 63, Syracuse Univ, MA, 66; NYork Univ, PhD, 71. **CAREER** George Washington Univ, asst prof, 70-71; Branders Univ, asst prof, 71-73; Univ of Cal SC, assoc prof, prof, dir soc doc prog, chrmn dept soc, 73-. **HONORS AND AWARDS** ACLS/ITG, UofC Innov in Tchg Awd, Andrew W. Mellon fel, NSF Dissert Fel **MEMBERSHIPS** SSSP, SWS, PSA, ISA, ASA, ESA. **RESEARCH** Soc of leadership; gender and emotion. **SELECTED PUBLICATIONS** Women in the Workplace, Schenkman Pub Co, 81; The Poverty Establishment, ed, Prentice-hall, 74, Child Care - Who Cares? Foreign and Domestic Infant and Early Childhood Development Policies, ed, Basic Books 73; The Future of Inequality, coauth, Basic Books, 70; art, Becoming a Shop Steward: Perspectives on Gender and Race in Ten Trade Unions, in: Labor Studies Jour, 95; Becoming an Active Feminist Academic: Gender, Class, Race and Intelligence, in: Individual Voices, Collective Visions: Fifty Years of Women in Sociology, Temple Univ Press, 95. **CONTACT ADDRESS** Dept of Sociology, Univ of California, Santa Cruz, Santa Cruz, CA 95064. **EMAIL** roby@cats.ucsc.edu

ROBYN, ELISA
PERSONAL Born 01/25/1955, Los Angeles, CA, m, 1987 **DISCIPLINE** EDUCATIONAL PSYCHOLOGY **EDUCATION** Northern Ariz Univ, BS, 76; Univ Calif at Santa Barbara, MA, 80; Univ Colo at Boulder, PhD, 91. **CAREER** Lectr, Arapaho Community Col, 86-87; adj, Colo Mountain Col, 89-; adj prof, Regis Univ, 94-; chair, Rocky Mountain Col of Art and Design, 97-; assoc academic dean, Rocky Mountain Col of Art and Design, 99-. **MEMBERSHIPS** Am Asn of Higher Ed, Nat Asn of Women in Educ. **RESEARCH** Ecology of leadership, tribal metaphors. **SELECTED PUBLICATIONS** Auth, "Through Their Eyes," Taplight 4 (91); auth, "War At Home," Taplight 5 (91); auth, "Leaving Old Patterns," Taplight 6 (91); auth, "Playing With Passion," Taplight 3 (92); auth, "Lawsuit Lessons: A Modern Witch Trial," Woman's Way 2 (94): 17; auth, "The Call of the Quest," Women's Way 1 (95): 18; auth, "Seven Traits of Successful Step-Mothers," Divorce Today (98). **CONTACT ADDRESS** Dept General Educ, Rocky Mountain Col of Art & Design, 6875 E Evans Ave, Denver, CO 80224-2329. **EMAIL** erobyn@rmcad.edu

ROCCA, AL M.
PERSONAL Born 05/08/1949, Brooklyn, NY, m, 1970, 2 children **DISCIPLINE** HISTORY, EDUCATION **EDUCATION** San Jose City Col, AA, 70; San Jose State Univ, BA, 72; San Jose State Univ, Elem Teach Cred, 73; San Jose State Univ, MA; Univ Calif at Davis, PhD. **CAREER** History Teacher, Sequoia Middle School, Redding, CA, 77-92; History Instr, Shasta Col, 80-; Assoc Prof of Education & History, Simpson Col, 92-. **HONORS AND AWARDS** Numerous local and state teaching Awds including outstanding history teacher by the Native Daughters of the Golden West. **MEMBERSHIPS** California Council for the Social Studies; National Council for the Social Studies; California Council on the Education of Teachers; Assoc for Supervision and Curriculum Development. **RESEARCH** Integration of geography into historical studies; building in the American West. **SELECTED PUBLICATIONS** Auth, "The Shasta Boomtowns: Community Building in the New Deal Era 93; "America's, Shasta, 1995. **CONTACT ADDRESS** Dept Arts & Sciences, Simpson Col, California, 2211 Coll View Dr, Redding, CA 96003-8601. **EMAIL** arocca@simpsmca.edu

ROCHA, CYNTHIA
PERSONAL Born 08/16/1960, Alton, IL, s, 1 child **DISCIPLINE** SOCIAL WORK **EDUCATION** Univ Tex, BA, 87; MSW, 91; Univ St Louis, PhD, 94. **CAREER** High School Teacher, Round Rock, 88-89; Director, Counseling Services Austin, 89-91; Program Consultant, 91-99; Asst Prof, Univ Tenn, 94-. **HONORS AND AWARDS** Award, Nat Committee for Educating Students, 98. **MEMBERSHIPS** ACOSA, CSWE. **RESEARCH** Working Poor, Health Insurance Status, Dislocated Worker Well-Being. **SELECTED PUBLICATIONS** Auth, "Evaluating experiential teaching methods in a policy practice course: The case for service learning to increase political participation," Journal of Social Work Education, (00): 53-64; co-auth, "Closing time: Workers' last call," Journal of applied Research and Public Policy, (990: 65-68; co-auth, "A Comparison Study of Access to Health Care under a Medicaid Managed Care Program," Health and Social Work, 99; auth, "Teaching Family Policy through a Policy Practice Framework," Journal of Social Work Education, (97): 433-444; auth, "The Working Poor," in Encyclopedia of Social Work, NASW Press, 97; auth, "Factors that contribute to Economic Wellbeing in Female Headed Households," Journal of Social Service Research, 97; auth, "Use of health insurance in county funded clinics: Issues for health care reform," Health and social Work, (96): 16-22; co-auth, "Predictors of permanent housing for sheltered homeless families," families in Society: Journal of contemporary Human Services, (96): 50-57; co-auth, "Research on homeless families: are they the same as the urban Poor?," Journal of Sociology and Social Welfare, (95): 5-22. **CONTACT ADDRESS** Dept Soc Work, Univ of Tennessee, Knoxville, 1345 Circle Park, Knoxville, TN 37996-0001. **EMAIL** crocha@utk.edu

ROCHEDECOPPENS, PETER
PERSONAL Born 05/24/1938, Vevey, Switzerland, p **DISCIPLINE** SOCIOLOGY **EDUCATION** Columbai Univ, BS, 65; Fordham Univ, MA, 66; PhD, 72; Univ Montreal, MSW, 78. **CAREER** Teaching Asst to Instructor, Fordham Univ, 65-69; Assoc Prof to Full Prof, E Stroudsburg Univ, 70-; Adj Prof, McGill, 98-00; Fac Member, Humanistic Psychol Inst, 75-83; Editor, Llewellyn Pub, 85-89. **HONORS AND AWARDS** Phi Beta Kappa; Alpha Delta Kappa; Woodrow Wilson Fel; Woodrow Wilson Intern; Who's Who in the East; Who's Who in Am; Who's Who in the World; Knight Commander of Malta. **MEMBERSHIPS** NY Acad of Sci; Am Sociol Asn; Am Orthopsychiat. **RESEARCH** Spirituality and the unfoldment of spiritual consciousness; Holistic health. **SELECTED PUBLICATIONS** Auth, The Divine Light and Fire, Divine Light and Love, Element Books, 92; auth, The Sociological Adventure: A Holistic Perspective, Kendall-Hunt, 96; auth, Comment rester sain dans un monde malade, Les vitamines d'amour, 98. **CONTACT ADDRESS** Dept Sociol & Anthropol, East Stroudsburg Univ of Pennsylvania, 200 Prospect St, East Stroudsburg, PA 18301. **EMAIL** proche@esu.edu

RODKIN, PHILIP C.
PERSONAL Born 03/03/1968, New York, NY, m, 1999 **DISCIPLINE** HUMAN & CHILD DEVELOPMENT **EDUCATION** Univ Chicago, BA, 88; Harvard Univ, MA, 91; PhD, 94. **CAREER** Postdoc fel, Univ North Carolina, 94-96; act asst dir, 97-98; adj fac, 98-; vis asst prof, Duke Univ, 96-. **HONORS AND AWARDS** Phi Beta Kappa; DBH, Dept Hon, Univ Chic. **MEMBERSHIPS** AERA; SRCD. **RESEARCH** Group processes in childhood and early adolescence; development of aggressive and antisocial behavior; ethnicity and intergroup relations in childhood and early adolescence; social integration of children with mild disabilities; methodology and statistical analysis of longitudinal data. **SELECTED PUBLICATIONS** Coauth, "Antisocial and prosocial correlates of classroom social positions: The social network centrality perspective," Soc Devel 5 (96): 174-188; auth, "A developmental, holistic, future-oriented behaviorism: Kuo's The Dynamics of Behavior Development revisited," Contem Psych 41 (96): 1085-1088; coauth, "The social integration of students with mild disabilities in general education classrooms: Peer group membership and peer-assessed social behavior," Elem Sch J 99 (98): 167-185; coauth, "Phenomena regained: From configurations to pathways in longitudinal research," in Methods and models for studying the individual, eds. RB Cairns, L Bergman, J Kagan (Thousand Oaks, CA: Sage, 98); coauth, "New directions in developmental research: Models and methods," in New perspectives on adolescent risk behavior, ed. R Jessor (NY: Cambridge Univ Press, 98); coauth, Social networks and peer-assessed problem behavior in elementary classrooms: Students with and without disabilities. Remedial and Special Education. 20 (99): 244-256; coauth, Teacher-assessed behavioral configurations, peer-assessments, and self-concepts of elementary students with mild disabilities. Journal of Special Education. 33 (99): 66-80; coauth, "Can current methods of pathonormal inference tell us anything about modularity?," Behavi Brain Sci 22 (99): 571-572; coauth, "Heterogeneity of popular boys: Antisocial and prosocial configurations," Devel Psych 36 (00): 14-24. **CONTACT ADDRESS** Dept Psychology, Duke Univ, PO Box 90086, Durham, NC 27708. **EMAIL** rodkin@duke.edu

RODRIGUEZ, CLARA
PERSONAL Born 03/29/1969, New York, NY, m, 2 children **DISCIPLINE** SOCIOLOGY **EDUCATION** CUNY, BA; Cornell Univ, MA; Wash Univ, PhD. **CAREER** Vis Fel, Yale Univ, 92; Vis Scholar, Russell Sage Foundation, 93-94; Sen Fel, Smithsonian Institution, 98; Vis Prof, Columbia Univ, 99; Prof, Fordham Univ, 81-. **HONORS AND AWARDS** Alumnis Asn Plaque, Fordham Univ, 91; Star Awd, New York, 92; Profile, New York Daily News, 92; Leadership in Educational Excellence Awd, Nat Soc of Hispanic MBAs, 95; Distinguished Prize in Soc Sci, Instituto de Puerto Rico, 97; Centennial Historian of the City of New York, New York. **MEMBERSHIPS** Am Sociol Asn. **RESEARCH** Labor market issues and policy, Media, Race and ethnicity, Education, Latinas/os in the United States. **SELECTED PUBLICATIONS** Auth, Changing Race: Latinos, the Census, and the History of Ethnicity in the United States, New York Univ Press, in press; auth, Latin Looks: Latina and Latino Images in the Media, Westview Press, 97; auth, Historical Perspectives on Puerto Rican Survival in the United States, Markus Wiener Publishers, 96; co-ed, Hispanics in the Labor Force: Issues and Policies, Plenum Press, 91; auth, Puerto Ricans: Born in the USA, Boulder, Westview Press, 89. **CONTACT ADDRESS** Dept Soc Sci, Fordham Univ, 113 W 60th St, New York, NY 10023-7404.

RODRIGUEZ, JUAN A.
PERSONAL Born 09/20/1946, Santiago, Dominican Republic, m, 1972, 2 children **DISCIPLINE** SECOND LANGUAGE ACQUISITION **EDUCATION** Univ St Thomas, BA, 70; Sam Houston State Univ, MA, 72; Tex Tech Univ, grad studies, 72-76; Union Inst, PhD, 80. **CAREER** Part-time instr, Tex Tech Univ, 72-73; prof, Pontifica Univ Catolica Madre y Maestra, 73-74; prof & part-time adminr, Chaffey Col, 76-. **HONORS AND AWARDS** Teaching Fel, Tex Tech, 72-73; listed in Who's Who Amongst Hispanic-Americans; listed in Personalities of America. **MEMBERSHIPS** CATSOL. **RESEARCH** Minority Higher Education, Second Language Acquisition. **SELECTED PUBLICATIONS** Auth, English for Legalization and Living in the USA, 88; auth, The English Language Through Cognitive Code, 91. **CONTACT ADDRESS** Sch of Arts & Humanities, Chaffey Col, 5885 Haven Ave, Alta Loma, CA 91737-3002. **EMAIL** drjarod@hotmail.com

RODRIGUEZ, SYLVIA
PERSONAL Born 08/16/1947, Taos, NM, s **DISCIPLINE** ANTHROPOLOGY **EDUCATION** Barnard Col, BA, 69, Stanford Univ, MA, PhD, 81. **CAREER** Instr to Asst Prof, Carleton Col, 77-81, Asst Prof, UCLA, 83-88, Asst Prof, 88-92, Assoc Prof, 92- , Univ NMex. **HONORS AND AWARDS** Edward Spicer Award, Jour SW, 90, Webb-Smith Essay Competition, 93, Fulbright Guest Pro, 93-94, 99-00, Snead-Wertheim Lectr, Univ New Mexico, 96-97, Chicago Folklore Prize, 97, Border Reg Libr Asn Book Award, 97. **MEMBERSHIPS** Am Anthrop Asn, Am Ethnol Soc, Cult Anthrop Asn, Asn Lat Anthrop, Am Folklore Soc, Sm Stud Asn. **RESEARCH** Interethnic Rel, Ethnicity, Ethnic identity, particularly in US-Mexico borderlands, upper Rio Grande Valley, Tourism, Land and water issues. **SELECTED PUBLICATIONS** Auth, "Land, Water, and Ethnic Indentity in Taos," In C. Biggs & J. Van Ness eds, Univ of new Mexico Press, 87; auth, "Art, Tourism and Race Relations in Taos: Toward A Sociology of the Art Colony," Journal of Anthropological Research, 89; auth, "Applied Research on Land and Water in New Mexico: A Critique, "Journal of the Southwest, 90; auth, "Ethnic Reconstruction in Contemporary Taos," Journal of the Southwest, 90; auth, "The Taos Pueblo Matachines: Ritual Symbolism and Interethnic Relations," American Ethnologist, 91; auth, The Hispano Homeland Debate Revised," Perspectives in Mexican American Studies, 92; auth, "Art as Racial Inscription," Radical Folk, Winter, 92-93; auth, "Defended Boundaries, Precarious Elites: The Arroyo Seco Matachines Dance, " Journal of American Folklore, 94; auth, "The Tourist Gaze, Gentrification, and the Commodification of Subjectivity in Taos," R. Francaviglia & D. Narrett eds., Essay on the Changing Images of the Southwest, Texas A&M Press, 94; auth, "Saying Nothing: John Cage and Henry David Thoreau's Aesthetics of Co-Existence," Tijdschrift voor Musiektheorie, 98. **CONTACT ADDRESS** Anthropology Dept, Univ of New Mexico, Albuquerque, Albuquerque, NM 87131.

ROEDER, BEA
PERSONAL Born 11/08/1941, Pasadena, CA, m, 1966, 2 children **DISCIPLINE** LITERATURE, FOLKLORE, MYTHOLOGY **EDUCATION** Univ Calif Santa Barb, BA, 63; Univ Calif Berk, MA, 65; Univ Calif LA, PhD, 84. **CAREER** Part time fac, Univ Colo, Univ Denver, Colo Col, Pike Peak Comm Col, 75-98; state folklorist, CCA, 79-. **HONORS AND AWARDS** NEA, NEH, 88, 90-91, 93, 96, 97, 00; IAC and UCLA Grants, 79, 80; UCLA Res Asstshp, 78-79; Berkeley TA, 64-65; Woodrow Wilson Fel, 63. **MEMBERSHIPS** AFS; AWSF. **RESEARCH** Coloradan folklore; Southwestern cultures; Lakota and Latino studies; folk medicine and narrative; dance. **SELECTED PUBLICATIONS** Auth, Chicano Folk Medicine from the Greater Los Angeles Area, Univ Calif Pr, Berkeley, 88; co-auth, "Los Dias," Mono Hisp New Year's Tradition, 95; co-auth, Ties that Bind: Coloradan Folk Arts in the Classroom, 97. **CONTACT ADDRESS** 10 Ridge Rd, Colorado Springs, CO 80904-1145. **EMAIL** bearoeder@yahoo.com

ROEDIGER, HENRY L.
PERSONAL Born 07/24/1947, Roanoke, VA, m, 1982, 2 children **DISCIPLINE** PSYCHOLOGY **EDUCATION** Washington & Lee Univ, BA, 69; Yale Univ, PhD, 73. **CAREER** Asst prof, 73-76, assoc prof, 78-82, prof, 82-88, Purdue Univ; vis asst prof, 76-78, vis assoc prof, 81-82, Univ Toronto; prof psych, Rice Univ, 88-96; prof, chemn dept, 96-, James S. McDonnell Dist Univ prof psych, 98-, Washington Univ. **HONORS AND AWARDS** NSF res fel, 67-69; Magna Cum Laude, 69; Phi Beta Kappa; Yale Univ fel, 72-73; Guggenheim fel, 94-95; fel, Canadian Psychol Asn; fel, Am Psychol Soc; fel, Am Psychol Asn; fel, AAAS; pres*, div 3, Am Psychol Asn, 2000-2001; elected, Soc of Exp Psychol. **MEMBERSHIPS** AAAS; Am Psychol Asn; Am Psychol Soc; Can Psychol Asn; Cognitive Neuroscience Soc; Coun of Grad Dept of Psychol; False Memory Syndrome Found, Sci Advisory Bd; Memory Disorders Res Soc; Sigma Xi; Soc for Applied Res in Memory and Cognition; Soc for Neuroscience; Psychonomic Soc. **RESEARCH** Human learning and memory; cognitive psychology; retrieval processes in memory; implicit memory; cognitive illusions. **SELECTED PUBLICATIONS** Co-ed Varieties of Memory and Consciousness: Essays in Honour of Endel Tulving, Erlbaum, 89; coauth, Psychology, 4th ed, West, 96; co-ed, Readings in Psychology, West, 97; coauth, Experimental Psychology: Understanding Psychological Research, 6th ed, West, 97; coauth, Research Methods in Psychology, 6th ed, Brooks-Cole, 98. **CONTACT ADDRESS** Dept of Psychology, Washington Univ, One Brookings Dr, PO Box 1125, Saint Louis, MO 63130-4899. **EMAIL** roediger@artsci.wustl.edu

ROESCH, RONALD
PERSONAL Born 05/25/1947, Montclair, NJ, m, 1976, 4 children **DISCIPLINE** PSYCHOLOGY **EDUCATION** Arizona State Univ, BS, 71; Univ of IL, PhD, 77. **CAREER** Dir, Simon Fraser Univ, 78-86; assoc prof, Simon Fraser Univ, 80-84; prof of Psychol, Simon Fraser Univ, 84-; dir, Simon Fraser Univ, 91-. **HONORS AND AWARDS** Consul Psych Res Awd, Amer Psychol Assoc, 77; Social Issues Dissertation Awd, Soc Psychol Stud of Soc Issues, 77; Cert of Merit, ABA Gavel Awd Comp, 82; Pres APLS (Div 41 of APA) 93-94. **MEMBERSHIPS** Fel, CPA; Fel, APA, APLAS **RESEARCH** Law and Psychology; mentally disordered offenders. **SELECTED PUBLICATIONS** Co-ed, Family violence: Perspectives on treatment, research, and policy, Burnaby, B.C.: British Columbia Family Violence Institute, 90; co-ed, International perspectives on mental health research in the criminal justice system, International Journal of Law and Psychiatry, 18, 95; coauth, The impact of Canadian Criminal Code changes on assessments of fitness to stand trial and criminal responsibility, Canadian Journal of Psychiatry, 42, (97): 509-514; coauth, Training in law and psychology: Models from the Villanova conference, Am Psychologist, 52, (97): 1301-1310; coauth, The Fitness Interview Test, Burnaby, BC: Mental Health, Law, and Policy Institute, Simon Fraser Univ, 98; coauth, Fitness to stand trial: Characteristics of remands since the 1992 Criminal Code amendments, Canadian Journal of Psychiatry, 43, (98): 287-293; coauth, Defining and assessing competency to stand trial, in Handbook of forensic psychology, (NY: Wiley, 98): 327-349; coauth, Jail and prison inmates, in Comprehensive clinical psychology: Applications in diverse populations, eds. I. B. Weiner & A. K. Hess, (Oxford: Elsevier, 98): 85-104; coauth, The assessment of crriminal responsibility: Current controversies, in Handbook of forensic psychology, (NY: Wiley, 98): 379-408; co-ed, Psychology and law: The state of the discipline, NY: Kluwer Academic/Plenum, 99. **CONTACT ADDRESS** Prof, Dept of Psychol, Simon Fraser Univ, Burnaby, BC, Canada V5A 1S6. **EMAIL** ronald_roesch@sfu.ca

ROGERS, JACK E.
PERSONAL Born 12/13/1957, Stillwater, OK, m, 1991, 4 children **DISCIPLINE** SPEECH COMMUNICATION, SOCIOLOGY **EDUCATION** La State Univ, PhD, 94. **CAREER** Assoc prof, Southern Univ, 86-95; Asst Prof, Univ of TX at Tyler, 96-. **HONORS AND AWARDS** Pres, Int Debat Asn. **MEMBERSHIPS** NCA, SSCA, CEDA, IPDA. **RESEARCH** Debate; forensics. **SELECTED PUBLICATIONS** Auth, A Community of Unequals: An Analysis of Dominant and Subdominant Culturally Linked Perceptions of Participation and Success within Intercollegiate Competitive Debate, Contemporary Argumentations & Debate: The J of the Cross-Examination Debate Asn, 97; A Critique of the Lexis/Nexis Debate: What's Missing Here?, The Southern J of Forensics, 96; Interrogating the Myth of Multiculturalism: Toward Significant Membership and Participation of Afrian Americans in Forensics, The Forensic of Pi Kappa Delta, 95; The Minority Perspective: Toward the Future Forensics Participation of Historically Black College and Universities, Proceedings from the Pi Kappa Delta Development Conf, 95; Constructing the Deconstruction: Toward the Empowerment of Women and Minorities in Forensics, Pi Kappa Delta Nat Development Conf, 95; What do they have that I haven't got? Comparison Survey Data of the Resources and Support Systems of Top CEDA Programs and Directors, CEDA Yearbook, 91. **CONTACT ADDRESS** Univ of Texas, Tyler, 3900 University Blvd, Tyler, TX 75799.

ROGERS, OSCAR ALLAN, JR.
PERSONAL Born 09/10/1928, Natchez, MS, m **DISCIPLINE** EDUCATION **EDUCATION** Tougaloo Coll, AB (Summa Cum Laude) 1950; Harvard Divinity Sch, STB 1953; Harvard Univ, MAT 1954; Univ of AR, EdD 1960; Univ of Washington, Postdoctoral study 1968-69. **CAREER** Natchez Jr Coll, dean/registrar, 54-56; AR Baptist Coll, pres, 56-59; Jackson State Univ, dean of students/prof of social science, 60-69, dean of the grad school, 69-84; Claflin Coll, pres; Oklahoma City University, DHL, 92; Claflin College, Pres, 84-94. **MEMBERSHIPS** Pastor Bolton-Edward United Methodist Church 1961-84; dir Orangeburg Chamber of Commerce 1987-90. **SELECTED PUBLICATIONS** "My Mother Cooked My Way Through Harvard With These Creole Recipes," 1972; "Mississippi, The View From Tougaloo," 1979. **CONTACT ADDRESS** Claflin Col, 400 College Ave, Orangeburg, SC 29115.

ROGLER, LLOYD H.
PERSONAL Born 07/21/1930, Puerto Rico, m, 1986, 2 children **DISCIPLINE** SOCIOLOGY **EDUCATION** Univ Iowa, BS, 51; MA, 52; PhD, 57. **CAREER** Assoc prof, Yale Univ, 64-68; prof, Case Western Univ, 68-74; Dir, Hispanic Res Center, Fordham, 77-90; Albert Schweitzer Univ Prof, Fordham Univ, 74-. **HONORS AND AWARDS** Fel, Hubert Humphrey Chair of Internationally Renowned Scholars, Macalester Col, St Paul, Mn, 72; Alber Schweitzer Prof in the Humanities, 74-; Distinguished Alumni Achievement Awd, Univ Iowa, 81; Doctor of Humane Letters, honoris causa, John Jay Col of Criminal Justice, 91; Sci Awd, Inst de Puerto Rico, 95; Simon Bolivar Awd, Am Psychiatric Asn, 96. **MEMBERSHIPS** Am Sociol Asn, Am Psychol Asn. **RESEARCH** Culture and psychiatric diagnosis, human migrations, medical sociology, social change. **SELECTED PUBLICATIONS** Coauth with A. B. Hollingshead, Trapped: Families and Schizophrenia, New York: Wiley (65); auth, Migrant in the city: The life of a Puerto Rican action group, New York: Basic Books (72); auth, "Framing research on culture in psychiatric diagnosis: The case of the DSM-IV," Psychiatry, 59 (96): 145-155; auth, "Research on mental health services for Hispanics: Targets of Convergence," Cultural Diversity and Mental Health, 2 (96): 145-156; auth, "Making sense of historical changes in the Diagnostic and Statistical Manual of Mental Disorders: Five propositions," The J of Health and Soc Behav, 38 (97): 9-20; auth, "Implementing cultural sensitivity in mental health research: Convergence and new directions Parts I, II, and III," Psychline, 3, Vols 1, 2, and 3 (99); auth, "Methodological sources of cultural insensitivity in mental health research," Am Psychol, 54 999): 424-433; coauth with P. J. Guarnaccia, "Research on culture-bound syndromes: New directions," Am J of Psychiatry, 156 (99): 1322-1327. **CONTACT ADDRESS** Dept Sociol & Anthropol, Fordham Univ, 441 E Fordham Rd, Bronx, NY 10458-5149. **EMAIL** rogler@fordham.edu

ROJAHN, JOHANNES
PERSONAL Born 05/23/1948, Vienna, Austria, d, 2 children **DISCIPLINE** PSYCHOLOGY, PSYCHIATRY **EDUCATION** Univ Vienna, grad studies, 71-76, Doctoral prog, 75-76, PhD, 76; Univ North Carolina, Chapel Hill, Fulbright-Hays res fel, 76-77; Phillips-Universitat, Marburg, privatdozent, 83. **CAREER** Res ast, Murdoch Center, North Carolina, 76-77; postdoctoral res fel, Div for Disorders of Development and Learning, Univ of North Carolina, Chapel Hill, 77-78; res assoc, Biological Scis Res Center, Univ North Carolina, Chapel Hill, 78-79; asst prof, Phillips-Univ, Marburg, Germany, 79-84; asst prof, Univ Pittsburgh Sch of Med, Western Psychiatric Inst & Clinic, 84-87; assoc prof, Ohio State Univ, 87-95, full prof, 95-. **HONORS AND AWARDS** Fulbright-Hays Post-Doctoral Res Fel, 76-77; res fel, Biological Scis Res Ctr, UNC Chapel Hill, 77-79, 81; Heisenberg Fel, 3 year career development Awd from the German Heisenberg Found, 85; tenure, Ohio State Univ, Dept of Psycho, July 1, 89; listed in Am Men and Women of Sci, since 90; Fel, Am Psychol Asn, since 99. **MEMBERSHIPS** Am Psychol Asn, Am Asn on Mental Retardation, Am Acad on Mental Retardation, Asn for the Advancement of Behavior Therapy, Deutsche Gesellschaft fur Psychol, Deutsche Gesellschaft fur Verhaltensmedizin und Verhaltensmodifikation, Sigma Xi. **RESEARCH** Psychopathology and severe behavior problems in mental retardation, emotional development and mental retardation. **SELECTED PUBLICATIONS** Coauth with M. B. DeWitt and M. G. Aman, "Effects of reinforcement contingencies on performance of children with mental retardation and attention problems," J of Developmental and Physical Disabilities, 9 (97): 101-115; coauth with S. R. Schroeder and R. M. Reese, "Reliability and validity of instruments for assessing psychotropic medication effects on self-injurious behavior in mental retardation," J of Autism and Developmental Disorders, 27 (97): 89-102; coauth with M. G. Aman, R. A. Kern, P. Osborne, R. Tumuluru, and V. del Medico, "Fenfluramine and methylphenidate in children with mental retardation and borderline IQ: Clinical effects, Am J on Mental Retardation, 101 (97): 521-534; coauth with M. J. Tasse and P. Sturmey, "The Stereotyped Behavior Scale for adolescents and adults with mental retardation," Am J on Mental Retardation, 102 (97): 137-146; coauth with V. J. Warren, "Emotion recognition as a function of social competence and depressed mood in individuals with intellectual disability," J of Intellectual Disability Res, 41 (97): 469-475; coauth with M. J. Tasse and D. Morin, "Self-injurious behavior and stereotypes," in T. H. Ollendick and M. Hersen, eds, Handbook of Child Psychopathology, 3rd ed, New York: Plenum Press (98): 307-336; coauth with J. M. Shultz and M. G. Aman, "Psychometric evaluation of a measure of cognitive decline in elderly people with mental retardation," Res in Developmental Disabilities, 19 (98): 63-71; coauth with M. J. Tasse, M. G. Aman, and R. A. Kern, "Developmental Disabilities," in R. T. Ammerman & J. V. Campo, eds, Handbook of Pediatric Psychology and Psychiatry, Vol 1, Boston: Allyn & Bacon, (98): 199-226; coauth with J. Zsambok and D. Hammer, "Put Your Money Where Your Mouth Is: A Comparison Between a Direct and an Indirect Measure of Attitude Toward Community Integration," Am J on Mental Retardation, 104 (99): 88-92; coauth with S. T. Matlock and M. J. Tasse, "The Stereotyped Behavior Scale: Psychometric properties and norms," Res in Developmental Disabilities (in press). **CONTACT ADDRESS** Nisonger Center, Ohio State Univ, Columbus, 1581 Dodd Dr, Columbus, OH 43210-1205. **EMAIL** rojahn.1@osu.edu

ROLLINS, JUDITH
PERSONAL Born Boston, MA, s **DISCIPLINE** AFRICANA STUDIES, SOCIOLOGY **EDUCATION** Howard Univ, BA, 70; MA, 72; Brandeis Univ, PhD, 83. **CAREER** Asst prof, 84-89; assoc prof, 89-92, Simmons Coll; assoc prof, 92-95; prof, 95-; Wellesley Coll. **HONORS AND AWARDS** Jessie Barnard Awd, ASA, 87. **MEMBERSHIPS** ASA; SSSP. **RESEARCH** Social psychology of domination; women's studies. **SELECTED PUBLICATIONS** Auth, "Between Women: Domestics and Their Employers," Temple Univ Press (85); auth, "All is Never Said: The Narrative of Odette Harper Hines," Temple Univ Press (95); auth, "Part of a Whole: The Interdependence of the Civil Rights Movement With Other Social Movements," Phylon 1 (86); auth, "Ideology and Servitude" in At Work in Homes: Domestic Work in World Perspective, eds. Roger Sanjek, Shellee Colen, Am Ethno Soc Monograph 3 (90); auth, "Housing Civil Rights Workers," J Women's Hist 5 (93); auth, "Feminism and Parasitism," Abafazi 1 (91); auth, "Entre Femmes: Les Domestiques et Leurs Patronnes," Actes de la Recherche en Sci Soc 84 (90). **CONTACT ADDRESS** Dept Africana, Sociology, Wellesley Col, 106 Central St, Wellesley, MA 02481. **EMAIL** jrollins@wellesley.edu

ROMANOWSKI, WILLIAM D.
PERSONAL Born 08/02/1954, m, 1977, 2 children **DISCIPLINE** AMERICAN CULTURE STUDIES **EDUCATION** Ind Univ Pa, BA, 76; Youngstown State Univ, MA, 81; Bow Gr State Univ, PhD, 90. **CAREER** Min, CCO, 76-88; grad asst, Bowling Green State Univ, 86-88; vis fac fel, Calvin Col, 88-89; assoc prof, 92-96; prof, 96-. **HONORS AND AWARDS** Thomas F Staley Dist Schl, 91-; Peter J Steen Awd, 88; CCCS Res Fel, 88; Christ Today Crit Choic Awd; CC Alum Res Gnt; CC Res Fel, 93, 98, 00; Billy Graham Res Gnt; Who's Who in Midwest; CCA Res Gnt, 94, 95; CCC Schl Gnt, 00. **RESEARCH** American pop culture; film; religion. **SELECTED PUBLICATIONS** Auth, Pop Culture Wars: Religion and the Role of Entertainment in American Life, InterVar Press (Downers Grove, IL), 96; coauth, Dancing in the Dark: Youth, Popular Culture and the Electronic Media, Eerdmans Pub (Grand Rapids, Mich), 91; coauth, Risky Business: Rock in Film, Trans Bks (New Brunswick), 91; auth, Evan gelicals and Popular Music: The Contemporary Christian Music Industry," in Religion and Popular Culture in America, eds. Jeffrey H Mahan, Bruce Forbes (LA: Univ Cal Press, 00): 105-24; auth, "Boycotts, Baptists, and NYPD Blue," Theol News Notes (97): 14-17; " 'Take Your Girlie to the Movies': Dating and Entertainment in Twentieth-Century America," in Religion, Feminism and the Family, eds. Ann Cair, Mary Stewart Van Leeuwen (The Family, Religion, and Culture, eds. Don S Browning, Ian S Evison, Philadelphia: Westminster John Knox Press, 96); auth, "'You Talkin' to Me?': The Christian Liberal Arts Tradition and the Challenge of Popular Culture," in Keeping Faith: Embracing the Tensions in Christian Higher Education (Grand Rapids, MI: Eerdmans, 96); auth, "John Calvin Meets the Creature from the Black Lagoon: The Christian Reformed Church and the Movies 1928-1966," Christ Schol Rev 25 (95): 47-62; auth, "The Joys Are Simply Told: Calvin Seerveld's Contribution to the Study of Popular Culture," in Pledges of Jubilee: Essays on the Arts and Culture in Honor of Calvin G Seerveld, eds. Lainbert Zuidervarrt, Henry Luttikhuizen (Grand Rapids, Mich: Eerdmans, 95). **CONTACT ADDRESS** Dept Communication Arts Sciences, Calvin Col, 3201 Burton St S, Grand Rapids, MI 49546-4301. **EMAIL** romw@calvin.edu

ROMNEY, A. KIMBALL
PERSONAL Born 08/15/1925, Rexberg, ID, m, 1945, 5 children **DISCIPLINE** SOCIOLOGY, ANTHROPOLOGY **EDUCATION** Brigham Young Univ, BA, 47: MA, 48: Harvard Univ, PhD, 56. **CAREER** Asst Prof, Univ of Chicago, 55-56; from Asst to Assoc Prof, Stanford Univ, 57-66; Dir of Anthrop Res, Stanford Univ, 60-65; Prof, Harvard Univ, 66-68; Dean of Sch of Soc Sci, Univ of Calif, Irvine, 69-71; Prof, Univ of Calif Irvine, 68-. **HONORS AND AWARDS** Fel, Ctr for Advan Study in the Behav Sci, 56-57; Fel, Am Nat Acad of Arts and Sci. **MEMBERSHIPS** Nat Acad of Sci. **RESEARCH** Cognitive and quantitative behavioral models. **SELECTED PUBLICATIONS** Coauth, "Correspondence analysis as a multidimensional scaling technique for non-frequency similarity matrices," in Visualization of Categorical Data, ed. Joerg Blasius and Michael Greenacre (San Diego: Acad Press, 98), 329-345; coauth, "Towards a Theory of Culture as Shared Cognitive Structures," Ethos 26 (98): 314-337; coauth, "Developmental patterns in the cytoarchitecture of the human cerebral cortex from birth to six years evaluated by correspondence analysis," Proceedings of the Nat Acad of Sci 95 (98): 4023-4028; auth, "Measuring cognitive universals and cultural particulars, " Behav and Brain Sci 21 (98): 586-587; coauth, "Cultural Census Theory," in MIT Encyclopedia of Cognitive Sciences, Robert A. Wilson and Frank C. Keil (99), 208-209; coauth, "Cognitive Aspects of step-terms in American kinship," Am Anthropologist 101 (99): 374-378; auth, "Cultural consensus as a statistical model," Current Anthrop 40 (99): S103-S115; coauth, "Methods for the study of inter- and intra-cultural variability: the universality of the semantic structure of emotion terms," Am Anthropologist 101 (99): 529-546; coauth, "Statistical Methods for Characterizing Similarities and Differences between Semantic Domains," Proceedings of the Nat Acad of Sci 97 (00): 518-523; coauth, "Systemic Culture Patterns as Basic Units of Cultural Transmission and Evolution," Cross-Cult Res (forthcoming). **CONTACT ADDRESS** Dept of Anthrop, Univ of California, Irvine, Irvine, CA 92697-0001. **EMAIL** akromney@uci.edu

RONAN, GEORGE F.
PERSONAL Born 12/13/1953, Salem, MA, m, 1997, 2 children **DISCIPLINE** PSYCHOLOGY **EDUCATION** Salem State Col, BA, 79; Fairleigh Dick Univ, MA, 82; PhD, 85. **CAREER** Dir clin Train, Cen Mich Univ; ed, Behavioral Therapist. **MEMBERSHIPS** APA, AABT. **RESEARCH** Violence; problem solving. **SELECTED PUBLICATIONS** Coauth, "Personal Problem-Solving System for scoring TAT responses: Preliminary reliability and validity data," J Personality Assess 61 (93): 28-40; coauth, "Personal problem-Solving Scoring of

the TAT: Sensitivity to training, " J Personality Assess 64 (95): 119-131; coauth, "Personal problem-Solving scoring of TAT responses: Known-groups validation," J Personality Assess 67 (96): 641-653; auth, "Fresh faces and fresh formats," Behavior Thera 22 (99): 165-66; auth, "From the editor," Behavior Thera 22 (99): 1-2; auth, "Musings of a New Year resolutionist," Behavior Thera 23 (00): 1-2; coauth, "An examination of attitudes and behaviors presumed to mediate partner abuse, " J Interpersonal Violence (in press); coauth, Practitioners guide to depression, Kiuwer Pub (Norwell, MA), in press; coauth, "Measuring Patient Symptom Change on Rural Psychiatry Units: Utility of the Symptom Checklist-90 Revised," J Clinical Psych (in press). **CONTACT ADDRESS** Dept Psychology, Central Michigan Univ, 100 W Preston Rd, Mount Pleasant, MI 48859-0001. **EMAIL** george.f.ronan@cmich.edu

ROOF, WADE CLARK
DISCIPLINE SOCIOLOGY **EDUCATION** Univ NC, PhD, 71. **CAREER** Asst prof, prof, Univ Mass; J.F. Rowny Prof, relig & soc, Univ Calif, Santa Barbara. **MEMBERSHIPS** Soc Sci Stud of Relig. **RESEARCH** Religion **SELECTED PUBLICATIONS** Auth, A Generation of Seekers: the Spiritual Journeys of the Baby Boom Generation, Harper San Francisco, 93; auth, Spiritual Marketplace: Baby Boomers and the Remaking of American Religion, Princeton Univ Press, 99. **CONTACT ADDRESS** Dept Religious Studies, Univ of California, Santa Barbara, Santa Barbara, CA 93106. **EMAIL** wcroof@humanities.UCSB.edu

ROOME, DOROTHY M.
PERSONAL Born Johannesburg, South Africa, m, 3 children **DISCIPLINE** WOMEN'S STUDIES, MEDIA STUDIES **EDUCATION** Univ Ariz, MA, 94; Univ Natal, Durban, PhD, 98. **CAREER** Managing ed, Critical Arts: A J of Cultural Studies, 95-98; lectr/consult, Varsity Col, Durban, 97-98; lectr, Univ Natal, Durban, South Africa, 95-98; adjunct fac/instr, Essex Community Col, Baltimore, Md, fall 98; adjunct fac/instr, Univ Md Baltimore County, spring 99, fall 99; adjunct fac/instr, Univ Ariz, summer 99; adjunct fac/instr, Towson Univ, Baltimore, Md, 98-2000. **HONORS AND AWARDS** Mem, Gender Studies Initiative to establish a department at Univ Natal campus, 95-96; mem, Development Support Commun, a res group involved in formulating commun policy within a multicultural context in South Africa, sponsored by the Human Services Res Coun, 96-97; Centre for Sci Development Scholar, PhD, 96, 97; mem, Ed Bd for Critical Arts: A J of Cultural Studies, 99. **MEMBERSHIPS** Nat Commun Asn, African Coun for Commun Ed, Int Asn Media & Commun Res, Comn on the Status of Women (Univ Ariz), Univ Ariz Child Care Steering Comt. **RESEARCH** Reception analysis for "Homicide, Life Everlasting "(2000), made-for-tv film; women's issues discussed during reception analysis. **SELECTED PUBLICATIONS** Auth, Introduction to "Culture and Media" in Critical Arts: A J for Cultural Studies, 2, 1 (95): auth, "Transformation ands Cultural Reconciliation: 'Simunye', a Flexible Model," in Critical Arts: A J of Cultural Studies, 11, 1 (97); co-theme ed with Ruth Teer-Tomaselli, for "Identity and Popular Culture," in Critical Arts, 11, 1 (97); auth, "Global versus Local: Audience-as-public in South African Situation Comedy," in the Int J for Cultural Studies, 2, 3 (Dec 99); auth, "Humour as 'Cultural Reconciliation' in South African Situation Comedy: Suburban Bliss and Multicultural Viewers," in the J for Film and Video (April 2000). **CONTACT ADDRESS** Dept Women's Studies & Electronic Media & Film, Towson State Univ, 8000 York Rd, Baltimore, MD 21252-0001.

ROOSEVELT, ANNA C.
PERSONAL Born 05/24/1946, Glen Cove, NY, s **DISCIPLINE** ANTHROPOLOGY **EDUCATION** Stanford Univ, BA, 68; Columbia Univ, MA, 74; Columbia Univ, PhD, 77. **CAREER** Cur, Mus of the Am Indian, 75-85; Guest Cur, Am Mus Natural Hist, 85-91; Cur, Am Mus Natural Hist, 91-; Prof, Univ Ill, 94-. **HONORS AND AWARDS** Nat Sci Found Fel, 87-90; MacArthur Fel, 88-93; Nat Endowment Humanities Fel, 91-93; Phi Beta Kappa, 93-94; Bettenderf Medal, 96; Order of Rio Branco Awd, 97; NEH Fel, 97; Soc Women Gold Medal, 99. **MEMBERSHIPS** Am Acad of Arts and Sci. **RESEARCH** America, Central Africa, tropical forests and savannas, hunter-gatherers, complex societies. **SELECTED PUBLICATIONS** Auth, Ancient Lakes, Their Cultural and Biological Diversity, Kenobi Publ, 99; auth, "The Maritime-Highland-Forest Dynamic and the Origins of Complex Society," in Hist of the Native Peoples of the Americas. South Am, Part 1 (New York: Cambridge UP, 99), 264-349; auth, "Ancient Hunter-Gatherers of South America," in Cambridge Univ Encycl of Hunter-Gatherers (Cambridge: Cambridge UP, 99), 86-92; auth, "The Role of Floodplain Lakes in Human Evolution in Amazonia and Beyond," in 1999 under books and monographs (99), 87-100; auth, "The Development of Prehistoric Complex Societies: Amazonia, a Tropical Forest," for Complex Politics in the Ancient Tropical World (99): 13-14. **CONTACT ADDRESS** Dept Anthrop, Univ of Illinois, Chicago, 1007 W Harrison St, Chicago, IL 60607.

ROSA, EUGENE A.
PERSONAL Born 09/20/1941, Canandaiqua, NY, d **DISCIPLINE** SOCIOLOGY **EDUCATION** Rochester Inst Technol, BS, 67; Syracuse Univ, MA, 75, PhD, 76; Stanford Univ, Postgrad Certificate. **CAREER** NSF Postdoctoral Fel for Energy Studies and Teaching Asst, Stanford Univ, 76-77; NIMH Postdoctoral Fel for Neurobiobehavioral Res and instr, Stanford Univ, 77-78; vis prof, The London Sch of Economics and Political Sci, 78; asst prof to the Edward R. Meyer Distinguished Prof in Natural Resource and Environmental Policy, Washington State Univ, 78-2000. **HONORS AND AWARDS** Maxwell Fel; Herbert H. Lehman Fel; Fel, Ctr for Advanced Study in the Behavioral Scis; Distinguished Contribution Awd, Section on Environment and Technol, Am Sociol Asn; Edward R. Meyer Distinguished Professorship in Natural Resource and Environmental Policy, Washington State Univ, 96, reappointed 99. **MEMBERSHIPS** Am Asn for the Advancement of Sci, Am Sociol Asn, Sigma Xi, New York Academy of Scis, Soc for Risk Analysis. **RESEARCH** Environmental and Technological Risks, Global Environmental Change, Theory. **SELECTED PUBLICATIONS** Co-ed, Public Reactions to Nuclear Waste: Citizens' Views of Repository Siting, Durham, NC: Duke Univ Press (93); auth, "Cross-National Trends in Aggregate Consumption, Societal Well-Being and Carbon Releases," in Environmentally Significant Consumption: Research Directions, The Nat Res Coun/Nat Acad of Scis, Washington, DC: Nat Acad Press (97): 100-109; coauth with Thomas Dietz, "Environmental Impacts of Population and Consumption," in Environmentally Significant Consumption: Research Directions, The Nat Res Coun/Nat Acad of Scis, Washington, DC: Nat Acad Press (97): 92-99; coauth with Thomas Dietz, "Climate Change and Society: Speculation, Construction, and Scientific Investigation," Int Sociol, 13 998): 421-455; auth, "Old-Fashioned Hypertext: Comments on the Commentary of Ravetz and Funtowicz," J of Risk Res, 1 (98): 111-115; coauth, "Decision Analysis and Rational Action," in Steve Raynor and Elizabeth L. Malone, eds, Human Choice & Climate Change, Vol 3 , Tools for Policy Analysis, Columbus, Oh: Battelle Press (98): 141-215; coauth, "The Rational Actor Paradigm in Risk Theories: Analysis and Critique," in Maurie J. Cohen, ed, Risk in the Modern Age: Social Theory, Science, and the Environment, London: Macmillan (99); coauth with Donald L. Clark, Jr, "Historical Routes to Technological Gridlock: Nuclear Technology as Prototypical Vehicle," Res in Soc Problems and Public Policy, 7 (99): 21-57; auth, "The Quest to Understand Society and Nature: Looking Back, But Mostly Forward," Soc and Natural Resources, 12 (99): 371-376. **CONTACT ADDRESS** Dept Sociol, Washington State Univ, PO Box 644020, Pullman, WA 99164-4020. **EMAIL** rosa@wsu.edu

ROSEN, LAWRENCE
PERSONAL Born 12/09/1941, Cincinnati, OH, s **DISCIPLINE** ANTHROPOLOGY **EDUCATION** Brandeis Univ, BA, 63; Univ Chicago, MA, 65; PhD, 68; JD, 74. **CAREER** Prof, Princeton Univ, 78; adj prof, Columbia Univ, 79-. **HONORS AND AWARDS** John D. and Catherine M. MacArthur Awd, Guggenheim Fel; Inst for Advan Study; Fel, Wolfson Col, Oxford; Princeton Distinguished Teaching Awd. **MEMBERSHIPS** NC Bar; U.S. Supreme Court. **RESEARCH** Anthropology of the Muslim world, rights of indigenous peoples, cultural theory. **SELECTED PUBLICATIONS** Ed, The American Indian and the Law, Transaction Books, 78; coauth, Meaning and Order in Moroccan Society, Cambridge Univ Pr, 79; auth, Bargaining For Reality: The Construction of Social Relations in a Muslim Community, Univ of Chicago Pr, 84; auth, The Anthropology of Justice: Law as Culture in Islamic Society, Cambridge Univ Pr, 89; ed, Other Intentions: Cultural Concepts and the Attributions of Inner States, School of Am Res Pr, 95; auth, The Justice of Islam: Comparative Perspectives on Islamic Law and Society, Oxford Univ Pr, 00. **CONTACT ADDRESS** Dept Anthrop, Princeton Univ, 100A Aaron Burr Hall, Princeton, NJ 08544-0001. **EMAIL** lrosen@princeton.edu

ROSENBERG, BRUCE
PERSONAL Born 07/27/1934, New York, NY, m, 1981, 4 children **DISCIPLINE** ENGLISH; FOLKLORE **EDUCATION** Hofstra Univ, BA, 55; Pa State Univ, MA, 62; Ohio State Univ, PhD, 65. **CAREER** Instr English, Univ Wis-Milwaukee, 62; asst prof, Univ Calif, Santa Barbara, 65-67 & Univ Va, 67-69; prof English & comp lit, Pa State Univ, 69-77; prof to prof emer English lit & American Civilization, Brown Univ, 77-. **HONORS AND AWARDS** Am Coun Learned Soc fel, 67-68; James Russell Lowell Prize, 70; Nat Endowment for Humanities fel, 72-73; Guggenheim fel, 82-83. **MEMBERSHIPS** MLA; Folklore Fel Int; Am Folklore Soc. **RESEARCH** Middle English literature; folklore; comparative literature. **SELECTED PUBLICATIONS** Auth, Annus Mirabilis distilled, PMLA, 6/64; Wandering Angus & Celtic renaissance, Philol Quart, fall 67; Lord of the fire Flies, Centennial Rev, winter 67; ed, The Folksongs of Virginia, Univ Va, 69; auth, The Art of the American Folk Preacher, Oxford Univ, 70; co-ed, Medieval Literature and Folklore Studies, Rutgers Univ, 71; auth, Custer and the Epic of Defeat, Penn State, 75; The Code of the West, Ind Univ, 82; The Neutral Ground, 94. **CONTACT ADDRESS** Dept English, Brown Univ, Box 1892, Providence, RI 02912-1892. **EMAIL** bruce_rosenberg@brown.edu

ROSENBERG, JACK L.
PERSONAL Born 09/11/1932, San Diego, CA, m, 1994, 5 children **DISCIPLINE** PSYCHOLOGY **EDUCATION** Univ Calif Berkeley, BA, 54; Col Physician & Surgeons, DDS, 58; Calif Scho Professional Psychology, PhD. **CAREER** Assoc prof, Univ Calif San Francisco; assoc prof to post grad instr Univ Pacific Dental School. **HONORS AND AWARDS** Golden Pen Awd,72; Pioneer in Field 99. **MEMBERSHIPS** ADA, AHP, APA. **RESEARCH** Somatic Psychotherapy. **SELECTED PUBLICATIONS** Auth, Total Orgasm, Random House, 73; auth, Body, Self and Soul, 85; auth, The Intimate Couple, 96. **CONTACT ADDRESS** Rosenberg Kitaen Inst, 1107 Abbot Kinney Bil, Venice, CA 90291.

ROSENBLATT, JAY
PERSONAL Born 11/18/1923, New York, NY, w, 1948, 2 children **DISCIPLINE** PSYCHOLOGY **EDUCATION** NY Univ, BA, 48; MA, 50; PhD, 53. **CAREER** Adj asst prof, NY Univ, 57-58; assoc res specialist, Rutgers Univ, 59-65; assoc prof to prof, Rutgers Univ, 65-87; Daniel S. Lehrman Prof, 87-. **HONORS AND AWARDS** Sigma Psi Nat Lectr, 72-73; Lindback Awd for Res; Kenneth Craik Lectr, Cambridge, 87; Hon Degree, Goteborg Univ, Sweden, 87; Merit Awd, NIMH, 95; Hon Degree, Nat Educ at Distance, Spain, 97. **MEMBERSHIPS** Am Psychol Assoc; Int Soc for Develop Psychol; Soc for Behav Neuroeudocrenology. **SELECTED PUBLICATIONS** Coauth, "Estrogen implants in the medial preoptic area stimulate maternal behavior in male rats", Horm Behav 33 (98): 23-30; coauth, "Microinfusion of cocaine into the medial preoptic area or nucleus accumens transiently impairs maternal behavior in the rat", Behav Neurosci 113 (99): 377-390; coauth, "Estrogen implants in the lateral habenula do not stimulate the onset of maternal behavior in female rats", Horm Behav 35, (99): 71-80; coauth, "First and second order maternal behavior related afferents of the lateral habenula", NeuroReport 10, (99): 883-887; coauth, "Induction of c-Fos and FosB-like immunoreactivity reveals neuropopulations involved in pup-mediated maternal behavior differentially in juvenile and adult rats", J Comp Neuro 416 (00): 45-78; auth, "Medial Preoptic area (MPOA) neurons differentially affect non-hormonally mediated display of maternal behavior in 27- and 60-day old rats", Behav Neurosci (forthcoming); coauth, "Prolactin (PRL) may act together with other factors to facilitate maternal behavior in rabbits", J Neuroendocrin (forthcoming); coauth, "The differential effect of the anxiolytic agent 8-OH-DPAT during lactation is independent of pup withdraw and maternal behavior (forthcoming); coauth, "Combined C-Fos and 14C-2-Deoxyglucose analysis of maternal behavior in the rat: Evidence of site-specific excitatory and inhibitory synaptic relationships, British Res, (forthcoming). **CONTACT ADDRESS** Dept Psychol, Rutgers, The State Univ of New Jersey, Newark, 101 Warren St, Newark, NJ 07102. **EMAIL** jzr@psychology.rutgers.edu

ROSENTHAL, BETH
PERSONAL Born, NY, m, 3 children **DISCIPLINE** SOCIAL WORK **EDUCATION** Queens Col, BA, 63; Adelphi Univ , MSW, 80; DSW, 86. **CAREER** Asst prof to assoc prof, York Col CUNY, 93-; assoc prof, Grad School CUNY, 00-. **HONORS AND AWARDS** Nat Inst Health Res grant, 00. **MEMBERSHIPS** Soc for Social Work and Res, Coun on Social Work Educ, Nat Asn of Social Workers, Bertha Capen Reynolds Soc. **RESEARCH** Community violence, High school dropout, Adolescents. **SELECTED PUBLICATIONS** Auth, "Exposure to community violence and trauma symptoms in late adolescence," Adolescence, (in press); auth, "Who is at risk? Differential exposure to recurring community violence," Tulane Studies in social Welfare, (in press); auth, "Psychological health among diverse undergraduate students in an urban public college," Journal of American College Health, (in press); auth, "Psychosocial correlates of dropout: An integrated review of the literature," Children & Youth Services Review, (98): 413-433; auth, "Social support and 10th graders' plans for staying in school," The High School Journal, (96): 298-304; auth, "The influence of social support on school completion among Haitians," Social Work in Education, (95): 30-39; auth, "Upper middle class support for family allowances," Journal of sociology and social Welfare, (93): 81-91; auth, "Graduate social work students' beliefs about poverty and attitudes toward the poor," Journal of Teaching in social Work, (93): 107-121; auth, "Anxiety and performance in an MSW research and statistics course," Journal of Teaching in Social Work, (92): 75-85; auth, "Student factors affecting performance in an MSW course in research and statistics," Journal of Social Work Education, (92): 77-84. **CONTACT ADDRESS** Dept Soc Sci, York Col, CUNY, 9420 Guy Brewer Blvd, Jamaica, NY 11451-0001. **EMAIL** rosenthal@york.cuny.edu

ROSENTHAL, HOWARD
PERSONAL Born St Louis, MO, m, 1987, 2 children **DISCIPLINE** PSYCHOLOGY **EDUCATION** Florissant Valley Community Col, AA, Univ MO, St Louis, BA, MEd, 76, EdD, 81. **CAREER** Prof, prog coord, Human Services, St Louis Community Col at Florissant, 94-; private practice therapist. **HONORS AND AWARDS** State of MO, Wayne B. McClelland Achievement Awd, 87; St Louis Community Col Hall of Fame Instr, 88; Emerson Excellence in Teaching Awd, 98. **MEMBERSHIPS** ACA, NBCC, CCMHC. **SELECTED PUBLICATIONS** Auth, Encyclopedia of Counseling (93); auth, Before You See Your First Client (97); auth, Favorite Counseling and Therapy Techniques (98); auth, Favorite Counseling and Therapy Homework Assignments (2000). **CONTACT ADDRESS** Dept Soc Sci, St. Louis Comm Col, Florissant Valley, 3400 Pershall Rd, Saint Louis, MO 63135.

ROSENTHAL, MARILYNN M.
PERSONAL Born 05/10/1930, Detroit, MI, d, 2 children **DISCIPLINE** SOCIOLOGY, BEHAVIORAL SCIENCES **EDUCATION** Wayne State Univ, BA, 52; Univ Mich, MA, 65; PhD, 76. **CAREER** Asst prof, Univ Mich, Dearborn, 76-82, assoc prof, 82-88, prof, 88-; vis prof, Sociol Dept, Columbia Univ, Summer 96, 97. **HONORS AND AWARDS** Hopwood Writing Awd, Univ Mich, 70; Danforth Grad Fel for Women, 70-75; Rackham Grad Fel, 70-71; Univ Mich Fac Recognition Awd, 92; Baxter Awd Distinguished Submission, European Health Care Management Asn, Celle, Germany, July 95; Distinguished Fac Res Awd, Univ Mich Dearborn, 98; Distinguished Fac Awd, Mich Asn of Governing Bodies, April 99; Nominated for the Baxter Awd by the Open Univ Press for the European Health Management Asn, July 2000. **MEMBERSHIPS** Int Sociol Asn, Int Soc for Health Care Quality Assurance, Am Public Health assn, Am Sociol Asn, Women's Res Club of the Univ of Mich. **RESEARCH** Medical mishaps; professional regulation and self-regulation; comparative medical malpractice systems, comparative physician manpower policy, Swedish health policy. **SELECTED PUBLICATIONS** auth, The Incompetent Doctor: Behind Closed Doors, Open Univ Press, England (Jan 95); coauth with Troyan Brennan, MD, "Medical Malpractice Reform: The Current Proposals," J of General Internal Medicine (95); auth, "The Incompetent Doctor," Nordisk Medicin (Jan 95); auth, "Managed Care Revolution in the USA," Swedish Med J (winter 96); auth, "Regulating Medical Work," British Medical J, No 7094 (May 31, 97): 1633; coauth with Linda Mulcahy, "Beyond blaming and perfection: a multi-dimensional approach to medical mishap," Ch 1 in Medical Mishaps: Pieces of the Puzzle, Open Univ Press, England (98); co-ed with Linda Mulcahy, PhD and Sally Lloyd-Bostock, PhD, LLB, Medical Mishaps: Pieces of the Puzzle, Open Univ (Dec 98); co-ed with Max Heirich, PhD, Health Policy: Understanding Our Choices from National Reform to Market Forces, Westview Press (98); auth, editorial: "What Do We Know About Medical Mishaps?," Swedish Medical J (fall 99); auth, "Medical Uncertainty, Medical Collegiality and Improving Quality of Care," invited chapter in Sociological Research, Kronefield ed, Vol 16, JAI Press (99). **CONTACT ADDRESS** Dept Behav Sci, Univ of Michigan, Dearborn, 4901 Evergreen Rd, Dearborn, MI 48128. **EMAIL** mmrosent@umich.edu

ROSENTHAL, NAOMI
DISCIPLINE SOCIOLOGY, HISTORY **EDUCATION** Univ Chicago, BA, 63; London Sch Econ, MScEcon, 66; SUNY, PhD, 76. **CAREER** From Instr to Prof, State Univ NYork (SUNY), 75-. **HONORS AND AWARDS** Res Grant, Nat Sci Found, 81-84; Nat Endowment Humanities Fel, 95-96; Grants, United Univ PDQWL, 87, 89, 99. **MEMBERSHIPS** ASA, SWS, NSF. **RESEARCH** Gender, historical sociology, social movements. **SELECTED PUBLICATIONS** Auth, "Social History and 19th Century Women: A Review Essay," CHOICE (87): 67-77; auth, "Centrality Analysis for Historians," Hist Methods Quart, vol 20, no 2 (87): 53-62; coauth, "Spontaneity and Democracy in Social Movements," in Int Soc Movement Res: Organizing for Change, vol 2 (JAI Pr, 89), 1-17; coauth, "Social Movements and Network Analysis: A Case Study of 19th Century Women's Reform in New York State," Collective Behav and Soc Movements (93): 157-167; coauth, "Structural Tensions in the Nineteenth Century Women's Movement," Mobilization 2:1 (97): 21-46; auth, Spinsterhood and Womanly Possibilities in the Twentieth Century, SUNY Pr (Albany, NY), forthcoming. **CONTACT ADDRESS** 116 Jones Ave, Port Jefferson, NY 11777. **EMAIL** rosenthaln@soldvb.oldwestbury.edu

ROSNER, STANLEY
PERSONAL Born 07/06/1928, Yonkers, NY, m, 1955, 4 children **DISCIPLINE** PSYCHOLOGY **EDUCATION** New School for Social Research, Phd, 56. **CAREER** Clinical Psycologist-Private Practice. **HONORS AND AWARDS** Outstanding contribution to state Psychological Affairs; American Psychological Assoc. **MEMBERSHIPS** American Psychological Assoc; CT Psych Assoc; National Academy of Neuropsychology; Int Society Neuropsych. **RESEARCH** Psychoanalysis. **SELECTED PUBLICATIONS** Ophthalmology, optometry and learning difficulties, J. Learning Disabilities,1(8) p17-19, 68; Opthalmology, optometry and learning disabilities, J. Pediatric Opthalmomogy, p82-85; Emotional aspects of intensive care, J. Contemporary Psychotherapy, 6(1), p62-66, 72; Some aspects of marriage and divorce in Israel, Interaction 3(1), with Tamar Cohen, 80; Further considerations of the internalization process, Dynamic Psychhtherapy,1(2) p149-158, 83; Analytic neutrality, stimulus ambiguity and the projective hypothesis, Dynamic Psychotherapy 6(1) p51-54, 88; Pine's Four Psychologies of Psychoanalysis and the Rorschach Psychoanalysis and Psychotherapy 8(2) p103-118, 90. **CONTACT ADDRESS** Counseling and Psychotherapy Group, 1305 Post Rd., Fairfield, CT 06430. **EMAIL** srosner@snet.net

ROSNOW, RALPH LEON
PERSONAL Born 01/10/1936, Baltimore, MD, m, 1963 **DISCIPLINE** PSYCHOLOGY **EDUCATION** BS, Univ MD, 53-57; MA, George Wash Univ, 57-58; PhD Experimental Soc Psychol, Am Univ, 60-62. **CAREER** Asst Prof of Cumm Res Boston Univ, 63-67; Assoc Prof, 67-70, Prof Psychol, Temple Univ, 70-82, Thaddeus L Boltonj Prof of Psychol, 82-; Dir Div of Soc & Org Psychol; Vis Prof of London School Of Econ & Poli Sci, 73; Vis Prof Psychol, Harvard Univ, 74, 88-89. **HONORS AND AWARDS** Fel of AAAS, APA, APS; James McKeen Cattell Fel in Applied Arts; APS; Psi Chi Distinguished Lectr EPA; APA Invited Address in Gn Psychol Div. **MEMBERSHIPS** Am Assoc for the Advan of Sci; Am Psychol Assoc Div 1,2,5,8,24; Comm on Standards in Res Ch; Am Psychol Soc EPA; Soc of Experimental Soc Psychol. **RESEARCH** How people imbue events, situations, or personal experiences with surplus meaning; epistemological found of soc psychology, certain complexities of ethical dilemmas and methodological artifacts in res with human participants; statis procedures for addressing focused questions; and corelational indices of effect sizes. **SELECTED PUBLICATIONS** Coauth, The Volunteer Subject, Wiley, 75; coauth, Rumor and Gossip: The Social Psychology of Hearsay, Elsevier, 76; auth, "Paradigms in Transition: The Methodology of Social Inquiry," Oxford Univ Press, 81; coed, Contextalism and Understanding in Behavior Science: Implications for Research and Theory, Praeger, 86; coauth, Essentials of Behavioral Research Methods and Data Analysis," McGraw-Hill, 91; coauth, People Studying People: Artifacts and Ethics in Behavioral Research, W. H. Freeman, 97; coauth, Beginning Behavioral Research: A Conceptual Primer, Prentice Hall, 99; coauth, Contrasts and Effect Sizes in Behavioral Research: A Correlational Approach, Cambridge University Press, 00; coauth, Writing Papers in Psychology: A Student Guide, Wadsworth, 01. **CONTACT ADDRESS** 177 Biddulph Rd., Radnor, PA 19087-4506. **EMAIL** rrosnow@nimbus.ocis.temple.edu

ROSS, CHRISTOPHER F. J.
PERSONAL Born 06/17/1946, London, England, s, 1 child **DISCIPLINE** PSYCHOLOGY OF RELIGION **EDUCATION** Univ Durham, BA, 67; Univ Edinburgh, MSc, 69; Univ Calany, PhD, 73. **CAREER** Assoc Prof **HONORS AND AWARDS** Citation in Outstanding Young Men of Amer, 77. **MEMBERSHIPS** Clinical Psychologist, 69-71; clinical supervisor, 80-82, **RESEARCH** Relig and psychol issues; psychol and spiritual; dev; psychotherapy and spiritual direction; psychological type and spirituality; mysticism and spirituality; philosophical aspects of interdisciplinary studies in relig and the social sciences; relig and social change; the peace movement; new relig movements. **SELECTED PUBLICATIONS** Auth, The Intuitive Function and Religious Orientation, Journal of Analytical Psychology, 92; auth, Orientation to Religion and the Feeling Function in Jung's Personality Typology, Studies in Religion, 92; auth, Type Patterns Among Members of the Anglican Church: Comparisions with Catholics, Evangelicals and Clergy, Journal of Psychological Type, 93; auth, Type Patterns among Catholics: A Study of Four Anglophone Congregations with Comparisons to Protestants, Francophone Catholics and Priests, Journal of Psychological Type, 95; co auth, Relationship of Jungian Psychological Type to Religious Orientation and Spiritual Practices, International Journal for the Psychology of Religion, 97; auth, Experiencing Mother Meera, Canadian Woman Studies, 97; coauth, The Perceiving Function and Christian Spirituality: Distinguishing between Sensing and Intuition, Pastoral Sciences, forthcoming. **CONTACT ADDRESS** Dept of Relig and Culture, Wilfrid Laurier Univ, 75 Univ Ave W, Waterloo, ON, Canada N2L 3C5. **EMAIL** cross@wlu.ca

ROSS, PETER A.
PERSONAL Born 03/05/1954, Canada, m, 1984, 2 children **DISCIPLINE** EDUCATION, PSYCHOLOGY **EDUCATION** Univ Fla, PhD, 88. **CAREER** Part-time fac member, Mercer Univ; dir & founder of Children's Evaluation & Counseling Associates Practice. **HONORS AND AWARDS** Ga Sch Psychologist, 92; named one of the top five sch psychologists in the nation, 93. **MEMBERSHIPS** Nat Asn of Sch Psychologists, Ga Professional Counselors Asn. **RESEARCH** Human Motivation, Learning, Behavior Management. **SELECTED PUBLICATIONS** Auth, Understanding Today's Child: Parent and Teacher Guide for Children's Success at Home and School, CECA, 94; coauth, "Curriculum-Based Writing Fluency Assessment of Attention Deficit Hyperactivity Disordered and Normal Children," Reading and Writing Quart: Overcoming Learning Difficulties Volume 11 (95): 201-208; auth, Practical Guide to Discipline and Behavior Management for Teachers and Parents, Behav Health Res Press/Manisses Commun, 95; auth, New Approaches to Problem Behavior: A practical guide to discipline and behavior management for parents and teachers 2nd edition, Manisses Commun Group, Inc., 99. **CONTACT ADDRESS** Dept Educ, Mercer Univ, Cecil B. Day, 3001 Mercer University Dr, Atlanta, GA 30341. **EMAIL** peterross5@aol.com

ROSS, ROBERT J. S.
PERSONAL Born 02/01/1943, New York, NY, m, 2 children **DISCIPLINE** SOCIOLOGY **EDUCATION** Univ Mich, BA, 63; Univ London, Post-Graduate Studies, 63-64; Univ Chicago, MA, 66; PhD, 75. **CAREER** Exec Dir, New Univ Confr, 68-69; res assoc, Univ of Mich, 69-72; from asst prof to prof, Clark Univ, 72-; dept chemn, Clark Univ, 75-78, 80-81, 85-86, & 93-99; dir, Intl Studies Stream, 00-. **HONORS AND AWARDS** Phi Beta Kappa; Honorary Woodrow Wilson Fel, 63-64; Hoopes Awd, Harvard Univ, 91; listed in Who's Who in the E, Who's Who in Educ, and Who's Who Among Am Teachers. **MEMBERSHIPS** Am Sociol Asn, Eastern Sociol Soc, Soc for the Study of Soc Problems **RESEARCH** Urban and Regional Studies, Political Economy of Development and Public Policy, Political Sociology, Globalization. **SELECTED PUBLICATIONS** Auth, "Global capitalism and labor at the end of history," Socialism and Democracy 19 (Fall/Winter 95-96); auth, "Your Father's Oldsmobile," Boston Rev 21 (96): 9; auth, "A Sea of Sweatshops," Peaceworks (97); auth, "Women and Sweatshops, Women and money vol. 1 no. 11 (97): 15-18; auth, "Immigration Restriction--a sweatshop nonsolution," An Academic Search for Sweatshop Solutions: Conference Proceedings, Marymount Univ (Arlington, VA), 98; auth, "The New Sweatshops in the United States: How New, How Real, How Many, and Why?" Global Labor Standards and the Apparel Industry: Can we regulate global production, Harvard Univ, 98. **CONTACT ADDRESS** Dept Sociol, Clark univ, 950 Main St, Worcester, MA 01610. **EMAIL** rross@clarku.edu

ROSS, STEPHANIE A.
DISCIPLINE AESTHETICS, FEMINISM **EDUCATION** Smith Col, BA, 71; Harvard Univ, MA, 74, PhD, 77. **CAREER** Assoc prof, Univ Mo, St Louis. **HONORS AND AWARDS** UMSL summer res fel, 78; NEH summer sem, 80; Weldon Spg grant, Univ Mo, St Louis, 81; UMSL summer res fel, 84; trustee, Am Soc for Aesthet, 86-89; Huntington Libr NEH fel, 89; fel, Yale Ctr for Brit Art, 90; Univ Mo Res Bd grant, 94; NEH summer inst, 95. **MEMBERSHIPS** Am Philos Asn; Am Soc for Aesthet; Soc for Women in Philos. **RESEARCH** Misguided marriage. **SELECTED PUBLICATIONS** Auth, Conducting and Musical Interpretation, Brit J of Aesthet, Vol 36, No 1, 96. **CONTACT ADDRESS** Univ of Missouri, St. Louis, Saint Louis, MO 63121.

ROSSI, JOSEPH S.
PERSONAL Born 02/22/1951, Providence, RI, m, 1981 **DISCIPLINE** PSYCHOLOGY **EDUCATION** RI Col, BA, 75; Univ RI, MA, 80; PhD, 84. **CAREER** Instructor, Univ RI, 78-81; Instructor, RI Col, 78-82; Instructor, Univ RI, 82-83; Adj Assoc Prof, Roger Williams Cancer Center, 91-94; Visiting Instructor, Conn Col, 92; Prof, Univ RI, 85-. **HONORS AND AWARDS** Citation Paper Awd, 93, 94, 95; Alumni Honor Roll Awd, RI Col, 92; Fac Merit Awds, 87, 88, 89; Fel, Univ RI, 78-79, 79-80; RI State Scholarship, 69-7-, 73-74, 74-75. **MEMBERSHIPS** Am Asn for the Adv of Sci; Am Asn for App and Preventive Psychol; Am Psychol Asn; Am Public Health Asn; E Psychol Asn; Psychometric Soc; Soc Beh Medicine; Soc of Multivariate Experimental Psychol. **RESEARCH** Transtheoretical Model of Behavioral Change; Stages of Change; Health Promotion and Disease Prevention; Sun Exposure; Smoking Cessation; Addictive Behaviors; Exercise; Diet; Diabetes Self Management; HIV risk; Radon Gas. **SELECTED PUBLICATIONS** Co-auth, "Stage of regular exercise and health-related quality of life," Preventive Medicine, (99): 349-360; co-auth, "Testing a model of situational self-efficacy for safer sex among college students: Stage of change and gender-based differences," Psychology and Health, (99): 467-486; co-auth, "Dietary applications of the stages of change model," Journal of the American Dietetic Association, (99): 673-678; co-auth, "Transtheoretical individualized multimedia expert systems targeting adolescents' health behaviors," Cognitive and Behavioral Practice, (99): 144-153; co-auth, "Stages of change across ten health risk behaviors for older adults," The Gerontologist, (99): 473-482; co-auth, "Development of a pregnancy-tailored decisional balance measure for smoking cessation," Addictive Behaviors, (99): 795-799; co-auth, "Stages of change and the intake of dietary fat in African-American women: Improving stage assignment using the Eating Styles Questionnaire," Journal of the American Dietetic Association, (990: 1392-1399; co-auth, "Health behavior models," in SPM Handbook of health assessment tools, (Pittsburgh, 99), 83-93; co-auth, "Concepts and theoretical models," in Coronary heart disease and risk factor management: A nursing perspective, (Orlando, 99), 47-69; auth, "How often are our statistics wrong? A statistics class exercise," in Handbook of demonstrations and activities in the teaching of psychology. Vol I: Introductory, statistics, research methods, and history, (Lawrence Erlbaum Assoc, 00), 101-105. **CONTACT ADDRESS** Dept Psychol, Univ of Rhode Island, Kingston, RI 02881. **EMAIL** jsrossi@uri.edu

ROTHSTEIN, WILLIAM G.
PERSONAL Born 02/26/1937, Waterbury, CT, s **DISCIPLINE** SOCIOLOGY, ANTHROPOLOGY **EDUCATION** MIT, BS, 59; Univ Minn, MA, 61; Cornell Univ, PhD, 65. **CAREER** Prof, Univ Md, 66-. **MEMBERSHIPS** Am Asn for the Hist of Med, Am Sociol Soc. **RESEARCH** American medical history, medical sociology. **SELECTED PUBLICATIONS** Auth, American Physicians in the Nineteenth Century (72); Auth, American Medical Schools and the Practice of Medicine (87); Ed, Readings in American Health Care (95). **CONTACT ADDRESS** Dept of Sociol and Anthrop, Univ of Maryland, Baltimore, 1000 Hilltop Cir, Baltimore, MD 21250-0002. **EMAIL** rothstei@umbc.edu

ROUSE, DONALD E.
PERSONAL Born 05/30/1932, Philadelphia, PA, m **DISCIPLINE** EDUCATION **EDUCATION** BS; MS; MEd; PhD Educ Admin. **CAREER** New Teacher's Elementary & Second-

ary Coordinator, Intergroup Educ, teacher/consultant; principal; assoc prof educ; educ consultant; Elementary Summer School Program, original instructor; Adult Educ Germany, instructor; New Teachers Clinic, coordinator; reading consultant; Urban Centers, dir. **HONORS AND AWARDS** W Philadelphia Comm Awd 1972; Landreth Man Yr Awd 1971; St Thomas Church Awd; Schoolmen's Club 1986. **MEMBERSHIPS** PSEA; NEA; Amer Assn of Univ Profs; Coll Grad Council; Natl AAU; Phi Delta Kappa; Philadelphia Assn of School Admins; bd dir Tribune Charities; Interested Negroes Inc; Am Assn, Afro-Amer Educators; NAACP; Masons; Amer Found Negro Affairs. **CONTACT ADDRESS** Dir, Urban Center, Cheyney Univ of Pennsylvania, Philadelphia, PA 19139.

ROWE, BRUCE M.
PERSONAL Born 08/30/1945, Los Angeles, CA, m, 1978, 2 children **DISCIPLINE** PHYSICAL ANTHROPOLOGY **EDUCATION** Univ Calif, BA, 67; Univ Calif, MA, 69. **CAREER** Prof, LA Pierce Col, 70-. **HONORS AND AWARDS** Golden Apple Awd Excellence in Teaching, 77-80, 82; Alpha Gamma Sigma. **MEMBERSHIPS** AAA, AAPA, SACC. **RESEARCH** Evolutionary theory. **SELECTED PUBLICATIONS** Coauth, Instructor's Manual to Accompany Physical Anthropology--The Core, 2nd Ed, McGraw-Hill, 98; auth, The College Survival Guide: Hints and References to Aid Col Students, 4th Ed, Brook-Cole Publ, 98; coauth, Instructor's Manual to Accompany Physical Anthropology, 7th Ed, 00; coauth, Study Guide to Accompany Physical Anthropology, McGraw-Hill, 00; coauth, Physical Anthropology, 7th Ed, McGraw-Hill, 00. **CONTACT ADDRESS** Dept Physics, Los Angeles Pierce Col, 6201 Winnetka Ave, Woodland Hills, CA 91371-0002. **EMAIL** anthrorowe@aol.com

ROWE, DAVID C.
PERSONAL Born 09/27/1949, Montclair, NJ, m, 1974, 1 child **DISCIPLINE** PSYCHOLOGY AND BEHAVIORAL GENETICS **EDUCATION** Harvard Univ, AB, 72; Univ Colo, PhD, 77. **CAREER** Asst prof, Oberlin Col, 77-82; assoc prof, Univ Okla, 82-88; full prof of family studies, Univ Ariz, 88-. **HONORS AND AWARDS** Magna Cum Laude, Harvard Univ, 72. **MEMBERSHIPS** Behavior Genetics Asn; Amer Psychol Soc. **RESEARCH** Behavioral genetics; Molecular genetics of behavior. **SELECTED PUBLICATIONS** Auth, Genes, environment, and psychological development, ed A. Campbell & S. Muncer, The social child, London, UCL Press, 98; coauth, with E. van den Oord, An examination of genotype-environment interactions for academic achievement in an U. S. longitudinal survey, Intelligence, 25, 205-228, 97; with S. Losoya, S. Callor & H. H. Goldsmith, The origins of familial similarity in parenting: A study of twins and adoptive siblings; Develop Psychol, 33, 1012-1024, 97; auth, Genetics, temperament and personality, ed R. Hogan, J. A. Johnson & S. R. Briggs, Handbook of Personality Psychology, pp 367-386, NY, Acad Press, 97; Genetik und sozialisation: Die grenzen der erziehung, Beltz: Psychologie Verlags Union, Ger transl of The Limits of Family Influence, 97; book rev, Born to rebel: Birth order, family dynamics, and creative lives, by Frank J. Sulloway, Evolution and Human Behavior, 18, 1-7, 97; coauth, with J. L. Rodgers, Poverty and behavior: Are environmental measures nature and nurture?, Develop Rev, 17, 358-375, 97; with T. Vazsonyi & D. J. Flannery, No more than skin deep: Ethnic and racial similarity in development process, reprinted ed N. BaNikongo, Leading essays in Afro-American studies, NY, IAAS Publ, 97; with J. L. Rodgers, Poverty and behavior: A response to a critique of a critique of a special issue, Develop Rev, 17, 394-406, 97; with D. Kandel, In the eye of the beholder? Parental ratings of externalizing and internalizing symptoms, Jour of Abnormal Child Psychol, 25, 265-275, 97; auth, A place at the policy table? Behavior genetics and estimates of family environmental effects on IQ, Intelligence, 24, 133-158, 97; Group differences in developmental processes The exception or the rule?, Psychol Inquiry, 8, 218-222, 97; coauth, with A. T. Vazsonyi & A. J. Figueredo, Mating effort in adolescence: Conditional or alternative strategy, Personality and Individual Differences, 23, 105-115, 97; Are parents to blame? A look at The Antisocial Personalities, Psychol Inquiry, 28, 251-260, 97. **CONTACT ADDRESS** Univ of Arizona, Campus Box 210033, Tucson, AZ 85721. **EMAIL** dcr091@ag.arizona.edu

ROWLETT, RALPH M.
PERSONAL Born 10/11/1934, Richmond, KY, d, 3 children **DISCIPLINE** ANTHROPOLOGY **EDUCATION** Marshall Univ, BA, 56; Sorbonne, Univ De Paris, non-degree student, 64; Harvard Univ, PhD, 68. **CAREER** Teaching fel, Harvard, 61-62; instr, Univ Mo-Columbia, 65-68; asst prof, 68-70, assoc prof, 70-75, Prof of Anthropology, Univ Mo-Columbia, 75-. **HONORS AND AWARDS** Marshall Univ, BA, summa cum laude, 56; Chevalier, Grand Duchy of Luxembourg, 76; NSF grants, 73, 74-83; Kappa Delta Prof of the Year, 84; Mo Humanities Coun Speaker's Bureau, 88-; Romanian Acad of Sci, 96; IREX grant, 97-98. **MEMBERSHIPS** Am Anthropol Asn, Soc for Am Archaeol, Sigma Xi. **RESEARCH** Old World archaeology (especially Iron Age of W. Eurasia), archaeological methos and theory. **SELECTED PUBLICATIONS** Auth, "Detecting Political Units in Archaeology: An Iron Age Example," in Archaeological Approaches to Cultural Identity, ed by Stephen Shennan, Routledge: London (95); auth, "North Gaulish and North Baltic Forms on the Gundestrup Cauldron," Proceedings of the Harvard Celtic Colloquium, 13 (95): 166-182; auth, "Hypothesis Testing by Structuraliste Analysis (abstract)," Proceedings of the Society for American Archaeology, annual meeting (95); auth, "Did Ancient Celts Hunt Wild Boar?," Proceedings of the Harvard Celtic Colloquium, 14 (96); auth, "A Case of Iron Age Sabotage (abstract)," Proceedings of the Soc for Am Archaeol, annual meeting, Nashville (97); auth, "Differential Skeletal Preservation in the Mound Cemetary at Celic-Dere in Northern Dobrogea," Proces se Symposium Int sur les Rites Fumeraires, 3 (98); auth, "Demographic Factors in La Tene Marnian Social and Cultural Development (abstract)," Proceedings of the Am Anthropol Asn, annual meeting, Chicago (98): auth, "The Cultural Context Producing the Renowned Golden Celtic Warrior Fibula (abstract), Proceedings of the Soc for Am Archaeol, annual meeting, Chicago (99); auth, "Fire Use," Sci, 284 (99): 74; coauth with Robert B. Graber and Michael Davis, "Friendly Fire," Discovering Archaeol, 1 (99): 82-89; auth, "Comment on 'The Raw and the Stolen: Cooking and the Ecology of Human Origins'," Current Anthropol, 40 (99): 584-585. **CONTACT ADDRESS** Dept Anthol, Univ of Missouri, Columbia, 107 Swallow Hall, Columbia, MO 65211-1440. **EMAIL** rowlettr@missouri.edu

ROY, WILLIAM G.
PERSONAL Born Rochester, NY, m **DISCIPLINE** SOCIOLOGY **EDUCATION** Emory Univ, BA, 68; Univ Mich, PhD, 77. **CAREER** Asst to Full Prof, Univ Calif Los Angeles. **HONORS AND AWARDS** Distinguished Contribution to teaching, Am Sociol Asn, 99. **SELECTED PUBLICATIONS** Coauth, "Centrality, Dominance, and Interorganizational Power in a Network Structure: Interlocking Directorates Among American Railroads, 1886-1905," J of Math Sociol 12 (86): 127-137; auth, "Time, Place, and People in History and Sociology: Boundary Definitions and the Logic of Inquiry," Soc Sci Hist 11(87): 53-62; coauth, "Interlocking, Directorates and Communities of Interest Among American Railroad Companies, 1905," The Am Sociol Rev 53 (88): 368-379; auth, "Functional and Historical Logics in Explaining the Rise of the American Industrial Corporation," Comp Soc Res 12 (90): 19-44; auth, "The Organization of the Corporate Class Segment of the American Capitalist Class at the Turn of this Century, " in Bringing Class Back, ed. Scott G. McNall, Rhonda F. Levine, and Rick Fantasia (Boulder, Colo: Westview Press, 91), 139-163; coauth, "Corporate law and the Organization of Property in the U.S.: The Origin and Institutionalization of New Jersey Corporation Law," Politics and Soc 24 (96): 111-136; coauth, A Guide to Writing Sociology Papers, St. Martin's Press, 97; auth, Socializing Capital: The Rise of the Large Industrial Corporation in America, Princeton Univ Press, 97; coauth, "How Many Logics of Collective Action?," Theory and Soc 28 (99): 203-237; auth, Making Societies: The Rise of the World We Live In, Pine Forge Press, forthcoming. **CONTACT ADDRESS** Dept Sociol, Univ of California, Los Angeles, PO Box 951551, Los Angeles, CA 90095-1551. **EMAIL** billroy@soc.ucla.edu

RUBEL, ARTHUR J.
PERSONAL Born 08/29/1924, Shanghai, China, m, 1 child **DISCIPLINE** ANTHROPOLOGY **EDUCATION** Univ North Carolina, Chapel Hill, Phd, 62; Univ Chicago, MA, 56; Mexico City Col, BA. **CAREER** Prof, Dept Family Medicine, and Dept Anthropology, UCI, 84-94; Prof of Anthropology, MSU, 74-84. **HONORS AND AWARDS** Pres, Society for Medical Anthropology. **MEMBERSHIPS** Amer Anthropological Assoc; Society for Medical Anthropology; Society for Applied Anthropology. **SELECTED PUBLICATIONS** Auth, "Susto, a Folk Illness," by Rubel AJ, O'Nell CW, Ardon RC, University of California Press: Los Angeles and Berkeley, 84; auth, "A Methodology for Cross-Cultural Ethnomedical Research," by Browner CH, Ortiz de Montellano B, Rubel, AJ, Current Anthropology, 88, 29, 5: 681-702; auth, "Narrativas Chinantecas," as written by Florentino Lopez Lopez, by Rubel AJ, Oaxaca: GADE, A.C., 89; auth, "La Enfermedad Popular de Susto," Interciencia: 90, 15: 278-86; auth, "The Study of Latino Folk Illnesses," Medical Anthropology 93, 15, 2:209-213; auth, "Recommended Core Curriculum Guidelines on Culturally Sensitive and Competent Health Care," by Like, RC, Steiner, RP, and Rubel, AJ, Family Medicine, 96, 27: 291-297; auth, "Antropologia de la Salud en Oaxaca," by Rubel, AJ and C.H. Browner, Oaxaca, Perspectives Anthropologicas, Alteridades 9, 17, enero-junio, 99: 85-94; **CONTACT ADDRESS** Dept Anthropology, Univ of California, Irvine, Irvine, CA 92697-0001. **EMAIL** arubel@uci.edu

RUBENSTEIN, JOSEPH H.
PERSONAL Born 10/05/1936, New York, NY, m, 1968, 2 children **DISCIPLINE** SCIENCE EDUCATION **EDUCATION** NY Univ, BA, 60; MS, 64, PhD, 69. **CAREER** Asst prof to assoc res sci, NYork Univ, 67-71; Director, Open Court Pub, 72-79; prof, Coker Col, 84-; chair, 84-98. **MEMBERSHIPS** NCTM; NSTA; NY Acad of Sci; Sigma Xi. **RESEARCH** Science Education, Mathematics Education. **SELECTED PUBLICATIONS** Coauth, "Real Math", K-8 Mathematics Series, Open Court Pub, 84-95; coauth, Math Explorations and Applications, SRA Div of McGraw Hill, 98-99; coauth, Real Science", K-6 Sci Series, SRA Div of McGraw Hill, 99. **CONTACT ADDRESS** Dept Educ, Coker Col, 300 E Col Ave, Hartsville, SC 29550-3742. **EMAIL** jrubinstein@coker.edu

RUBIN, LINDA J.
PERSONAL Born 04/01/1960, Kansas City, MO **DISCIPLINE** PSYCHOLOGY **EDUCATION** Univ Kans, Lawrence, BS, 84, MS, 87, PhD, 92. **CAREER** Staff counr, Univ Kans, Lawrence, 87-89; adjunct Fac, Kansas City Kansas Community Col, 88-89; vis psychol fac, Johnson Co Community Col, Overland Park, Kans, 90-91; staff psychol, Veterans Affairs Medical Center, Des Moines, Iowa, 92; staff psychol, Osawatomie State Hosp, Kans, 93; assoc prof, Tex Woman's Univ, Denton, 93-. **HONORS AND AWARDS** Beta Gamma Sigma Awd for Outstanding Academic Achievement in Business Admin, 83; Kans Psychol Asn Grad Paper Competition, First Place, 90, Second Place, 90; Summer Fel Awd for Academic Excellence, 89; Who's Who Among America's Teachers, 96; Outstanding Grad Teacher Awd, Col of Arts and Scis, Tex Woman's Univ, 96-97; Mary Mason Lyon Awd for Distinguished Fac, Tex Woman's Univ, 98; Phi Kappa Phi, 99; Who's Who in Medicine and Healthcare, 2000-2001. **MEMBERSHIPS** Am Psychol Asn, Dallas Soc for Psychoanalytic Psychol, Interdisciplinary Psychoanalysis Consortium, Dallas Psychol Asn, Tex Coun on Family Violence. **SELECTED PUBLICATIONS** Coauth, "Sexual harassment in academia: Individual differences in student reporting behaviors," Initiatives: J of the Nat Asn of Women in Educ, 57 (96): 37-45; auth, "Childhood sexual abuse: Whose memories are faulty?," The Counseling Psychol, 24 (96): 140-143; auth, "Childhood sexual abuse: False accusations of "false memories?," Prof Psychol: Res and Practice, 27 (96): 447-451; coauth, "Sexual harassment of students by professional psychology educators: A national survey," Sex Roles, 37 (97): 753-771; coauth, "Statistics lessons from the study of mate selection," Teaching of Psychol, 25 (98): 221-224; coauth, "Definitional research on African American women and social/sexual interactions in academia," Psychol of Women Quart, 23 (99): 813-817; coauth, "The Minnesota Multiphasic Personality Inventory-2, post-traumatic stress disorder, and women domestic violence survivors," Prof Psychol: Res and Practice (in press); coauth, Sexual boundary violations: A continuum of misconduct (under review). **CONTACT ADDRESS** Dept Psychol & Philos, Texas Woman's Univ, PO Box 425470, Denton, TX 76204. **EMAIL** LRubin@twu.edu

RUBINSTEIN, ROBERT L.
PERSONAL Born 01/03/1951, Brooklyn, NY, m, 1980, 2 children **DISCIPLINE** SOCIOLOGY **EDUCATION** Bryn Mawr Col, PhD, 78. **CAREER** Res, Philadelphia Geriatric Center, 80-97; prof, Univ Md Baltimore, 97-. **HONORS AND AWARDS** Fel, Gerontological Soc of Am. **MEMBERSHIPS** GSA **RESEARCH** Old age and aging. **SELECTED PUBLICATIONS** Coauth, Old Souls: Aged Women, Poverty and the Experience of God, Springer, 00. **CONTACT ADDRESS** Dept Sociol, Univ of Maryland, Baltimore, 1000 Hilltop Circle, Baltimore, MD 21250-0002. **EMAIL** daphnisr@aol.com

RUBY, JAY W.
PERSONAL Born 10/25/1937, Oak Park, IL, m, 1980, 3 children **DISCIPLINE** ANTHROPOLOGY **EDUCATION** Univ Calif, Los Angeles, BA, 60, MA, 62, PhD, 70. **CAREER** Lectr, Univ Calif, Santa Barbara, 64-65, Davis, 65-67; instr, Temple Univ, 67-69, asst prof, 69-70, tenured, 73, assoc prof, 77-94, full prof, 94-. **HONORS AND AWARDS** Wenner Gren Found grant, 69-71, 80-81; Nat Sci Found grant, 72; NEA grants, 76, 78, 80, 80-81; NEH grants, 82-84, 84-85; Pa Coun on the Humanities grant, 83; Pa Humanities Coun, 89, 92; Pa Museum and Hist Comn, 91, 92, 93, 94; co-dir, Advanced Sem in Visual Anthropol, Sch of Am Res, Santa Fe, 94; summer fel, Temple, 95; grant-in-aid, Temple, 95-96; summer fel, grant-in-aid, res incentive Awd, Temple Univ, 99. **MEMBERSHIPS** Am Anthropol Asn, Comn on Visual Anthropol, Int Films Sem, Soc for Visual Anthropol, Visual Sociol Asn, Univ Film and Video Asn, Soc for Cinema Studies. **SELECTED PUBLICATIONS** Ed, The Films of John Marshall, NY: Gordon & Breech (92); auth, "Who Can Image Whom?," Media & Culture: The Newsletter for the Va Center for Media and culture, 1,2 (93): 8-11; auth, "The Moral Burden of Authorship in Ethnographic Film," Visual Anthropol Rev, 11, 2 (95): 1-6; auth, "Visual Anthropology," Encyclopedia of Cultural Anthropol (95); auth, Secure the Shadow: Death and Photography in America, Cambridge: MIT Press (95); auth, "Objectivity Revisited- A Book Review Essay," Am Anthropol, vol 98, no 2 (96): 7-9; auth, "Third Voice Films. In The Documentary: Strangely Compelling," M. Delofski and J. Mills, eds, Media Int Australia, No 82 (96): 12-18; auth, The World of Francis Cooper: Nineteenth Century Pennsylvania Photography, Penn State Press (99); compiled with Linda A. Ries, Directory of Pennsylvania Photographers, 1839-1900, Harrisburg: Pa Museum and Hist Comn (99); auth, Picturing Culture: Essays on Film and Anthropology, Chicago: Univ Chicago Press (in press). **CONTACT ADDRESS** Dept Anthropol-Galdfelter, Temple Univ, 1115 W Berks St, Philadelphia, PA 19122.

RUDGE, DAVID W.
PERSONAL Born 11/29/1962, Syracuse, NY, s **DISCIPLINE** SCIENCE EDUCATION **EDUCATION** Duke Univ, BS, 86; Univ Pittsburgh, MS, 90; Univ Pittsburgh, MA, 92; Univ Pittsburgh, PhD, 96. **CAREER** Lectr, philos, Tex A&M Univ, 96-97; temp asst prof, philos, Iowa State Univ, 97-99. **HONORS AND AWARDS** London Visiting Scholars fel, Centre for the Philos of the Natural and Soc Sci, London Sch of Econ and Polit

Sci, summer, 97; Intl Res Travel Assistance grant, Office of the Asst Provost for Intl Prog, Tex A&M Univ, spring, 97; Pew teaching leadership award, fall, 93. **MEMBERSHIPS** Am Philos Asn; Central States Philos Asn; Hist of Sci Soc; Intl Soc for the Hist, Philos & Soc Studies of Bio; Philos of Sci Asn; Sigma Xi. **RESEARCH** Experiments in evolutionary biology; H. B. D. Kettlewell. **SELECTED PUBLICATIONS** Article, Classroom Videotaping: A Protocol for Camera Operators and Consultants, Jour of Grad Teaching Asst Develop, 2, 3, 113-123, 95; co-auth, article, Structure, Function and Variation in the Hindlimb Muscles of the Margarornis Assemblage, Annals of the Carnegie Mus, 61, 207-237, 92; co-auth, article, The Phylogenetic Relationships of the Margarornis Assemblage, Condor, 94, 760-766, 92; coauth, "Structure, Function, and Variation in the Hisdlimb Muscles of the Margarornis Assemblage, (Aves: Passeriformes: Furnariidae)," Annals of the Caranegie Museum 61, (92): 207-237; auth, "Classroom Videotaping: A Protocol for Camera Operators and Consultants," The Journal of Graduate Teaching Assistant Development, 2, (95): 113-123; auth, "A Bayesian Analysis of Strategies in Evolutionary Biology," Perspectives on Science 6, (98): 341-360; auth, "Taking the Peppered Moth with a Grain of Salt" Biology and Philos 14, (99): 9-37; auth, "The Complementary Roles of Observation and Experiment: Th. Dobzhansky's Genetics of Natural Populations IX and XII" History and Philosophy of the Life Sciences 22, (00): 165-184; auth, "Does Being Wrong Make Kettlewell Wrong for Science Teaching?" Journal of Biological Education, 35, (00): 5-11; book rev, Scientific Thinking by Robert M. Martin, Philos in Rev/Comptes rendus philos, 17, 5, 350-352, 97; auth, . **CONTACT ADDRESS** Department of Sci Studies, Western Michigan Univ, 3134 Wood Hall, Kalamazoo, MI 49008-5033. **EMAIL** david.rudge@wmich.edu

RUDMAN, MASHA
PERSONAL Born 01/16/1933, New York, NY, w, 1953, 3 children **DISCIPLINE** EDUCATION **EDUCATION** Hunter Col, AB, 53; MS, 56; Univ Mass EdD, 70. **CAREER** Teacher, New York City, 53-63; lecturer, Hunter Col, 64; literary reviewer, WFCR, 66-70; prof, Univ Mass, 65-. **HONORS AND AWARDS** School of Educ Outstanding Teacher of the Year, 99; Who's Who in Am Educ, 93-94; Celebrate Literacy Awd, Pioneer Valley Reading Coun, 89; Distinguished Teachers Awd, 88; Nat Endowment for the Humanities, 83; Hum Fel, Univ Mass, 83; Fel Grant, Noyes Foundation, 82-83; Sch of Educ Alumni Asn Awd, 81; Departmental Growth grant, 81; Distinguished Teacher Awd, Univ Mass, 72; Fac Res Grant, 68-69. **SELECTED PUBLICATIONS** Auth, Children's Literature: An Issues Approach, 4th ed, Lawrence Erlbaum Assoc: New York, forthcoming; auth, Mirrors, Windows and Doors: Critical Reflections on Multicultural Childre's Literature, Lawrence Erlbaum Assoc: New York, forthcoming; auth, "Building community and Character Through Service Learning," Classroom Leadership, (99): 4-5; assoc ed, Multicultural Children's Literature Catalog, The New Press: New York, 97; auth, Children's Literature: An Issues Approach, 3rd edition, Longman, 95; auth, "Is That Book Politically Correct? Truth and Trends in Historical Literature for Young People: An Educator Speaks," Journal of Youth Services in Libraries, (94): 164-172; auth, Children's Literature: Resource for the Classroom 2nd ed, Christopher Gordon, 93; auth, Books to Help Children Cope with Separation and Loss 4th ed, Bowker, 93; auth, "Confronting History: Holocaust Books for Children," in The New Advocate, (91): 163-177; auth, From Mother Goose to Judy Blume, The Hume Corporation, 89. **CONTACT ADDRESS** School of Educ, Univ of Massachusetts, Amherst, 226 Furcolo Hall, Amherst, MA 01003-3035. **EMAIL** rudman@educ.umas.edu

RUNCO, MARK
DISCIPLINE CHILD, ADOLESCENT STUDIES **EDUCATION** Claremont Men's Col, BA, 79; Grad Sch, MA, 81; PhD, 84. **CAREER** Asst prof, assoc prof, Univ Haw, 83-87; vis assoc prof, Pitzer Col, 89; assoc prof, Cal State Univ, 87; vis sch, Univ Bergen, 92; chf curator, Milken Found, 94; prof, Cal State Univ, 91-. **HONORS AND AWARDS** Hughes Aircraft Res Awd; Spencer Found Grant; CEF Awd; Outstand Ser Awd; Outstand Scholar Awd; NAGC Early Scholar Awd; APA Fel. **MEMBERSHIPS** APA; IAEA; NAGC; Phi Eta Sigma. **SELECTED PUBLICATIONS** Auth, "Tension, adaptability, and creativity," in Affect, creative experience, and psychological adjustment, ed. SW Russ (Philadelphia, PA: Taylor & Francis, 99); auth, "Creativity need not be social," in Social creativity, eds. A Montuori, R Purser (Cresskill, NJ: Hampton, 99); auth, "Misjudgment of creativity," In Encyclopedia of creativity, co-ed. Steven Pritzker (San Diego, CA: Academic Press, 99); auth, "Time for creativity," in Encyclopedia of Creativity, co-ed. Steven Pritzker (San Diego, CA: Academic Press, 99); coauth, "The history of creativity research," In Handbook of human creativity, ed. RS Sternberg (NY: Cambridge UP, 99); coauth, "Economic and investment theories of creativity," in Encyclopedia of creativity, co-ed. Steven Pritzker (San Diego, CA: Academic Press, 99); coauth, "Enhancement of creativity," In Encyclopedia of creativity, co-ed. Steven Pritzker (San Diego, CA: Academic Press, 99); coauth, "Deviance and creativity," in Encyclopedia of creativity, co-ed. Steven Pritzker (San Diego, CA: Academic Press, 99); coauth, "Understanding how creative thinking skills, attitudes, and behaviors work together: A causal process model," J Creative Behavior (in press); coauth, "Developmental trends in the evaluative and divergent thinking of children," Creativity Res J (in press); auth, "Cognition and creativity: A review of Creative thought: An investigation of conceptual structures and processes," Contemporary Psychology (in press); ed, Critical creative processes, Hampton Press (Cresskill, NJ), in press; coauth, "Parents' personality and the creative potential of exceptionally gifted boys," Gifted Child Quart (in press). **CONTACT ADDRESS** Dept Psychology, California State Univ, Fullerton, Bldg EC105, PO Box 6868, Fullerton, CA 92634.

RUNDBLAD, GEORGANNE
PERSONAL Born 01/17/1960, St Charles, IL, m, 1989, 1 child **DISCIPLINE** SOCIOLOGY **EDUCATION** Ill State Univ, BS, 82; MS, 86; Univ Ill, PhD, 93. **CAREER** Lecturer to assoc prof, Ill Wesleyan Univ, 92-. **HONORS AND AWARDS** Phi Kappa Phi. **MEMBERSHIPS** Am Sociol Asn, Ill Sociol Asn, Intl Asn for Visual Sociol, Midwest Sociol Asn, Midwest Sociol for Women in Soc, Sociol for Women in Soc. **RESEARCH** Women and Men Working in Sex-nontraditional Work, Occupational Sex Segregation, Visual Sociology. **SELECTED PUBLICATIONS** Auth, Multiculturalism in the United States: Current Issues, Contemporary Voices, Pine Forge Press: Thousand Oaks, 00; auth, "Multicultural America in the Post-Civil Rights Era," Multiculturalism in the United States: Current Issues, Contemporary Voices, 00; auth, "Addressing Social Problems, Focusing on Solutions: The Community Exploration Project," Teaching Sociology, (98): 330-340; auth, "Strategies and Techniques for Multicultural Teaching in Undergraduate Courses," Multicultural Prism: Voices from the Field, (96): 151-167; auth, "Exhuming Women's Duties in the Care of the Dead," Gender and Society, (95): 173-192; auth, "A Politics of Anatomy: Women's Work Roles in Early Undertaking," Perspectives on Social Problems, (94): 173-194; auth, "Feminism and the construction of knowledge," Speculations on a Subjective Science, (90): 53-55. **CONTACT ADDRESS** Dept Sociol, Illinois Wesleyan Univ, PO Box 2900, Bloomington, IL 61702. **EMAIL** grundbl@titan.iwu.edu

RUPP, GARY
DISCIPLINE COUNSELING **EDUCATION** Georgia State Univ, MEd, PhD. **CAREER** Assoc prof, Reformed Theol Sem, 91-. **RESEARCH** Clinical psychology. **SELECTED PUBLICATIONS** Coauth, Enrichment: Skills Training on Family Life; contrib, Jour of Commun Psychol. **CONTACT ADDRESS** Dept of Counseling, Reformed Theol Sem, Florida, 1231 Reformation Dr, Oviedo, FL 32765. **EMAIL** grupp@rts.edu

RUPP, LEILA J.
PERSONAL Born 02/13/1950, Plainfield, NJ **DISCIPLINE** HISTORY, WOMEN'S STUDIES **EDUCATION** Bryn Mawr Col, AB, 72, PhD(hist), 76. **CAREER** Vis lectr hist, Univ Pa, 76-77; asst prof, 77-82, assoc prof, 82-87, prof, Ohio State Univ, 87-. **HONORS AND AWARDS** Ohio Acad of Hist Outstand Tchg Awd **MEMBERSHIPS** Berkshire Conf Women Historians; AHA; OHA **RESEARCH** Women's history; hist of sexuality. **SELECTED PUBLICATIONS** Auth, Mobilizing Women for War: German and American Propaganda, 1939-1945, Princeton Univ, 78; co-ed, Nazi Ideology Before 1933: A Documentation, Univ Tex, 78; coauth, Survival in the Doldrums: The American Women's Rights Movement, 1945 to the 1960s, Oxford Univ, 87; auth Wolrds of Women: The Making of an International Women's Movement, Princeton Univ, 97; auth, A Desired Past: A Short Hist of Same-Sex Love in Am, Chicago Univ, 99. **CONTACT ADDRESS** 230 W 17th Ave, Columbus, OH 43210-1361. **EMAIL** rupp.1@osu.edu

RUSCIO, J.
PERSONAL Born 05/02/1971, Pittsfield, MA, m, 1997 **DISCIPLINE** PSYCHOLOGY **EDUCATION** Asst prof, Elizabethtown Col, 98-. **CAREER** Brandeis Univ, PhD, 98. **MEMBERSHIPS** Am Psychol Soc, Am Psychol Asn, Soc for Personality & Soc Psychol. **RESEARCH** Human judgement and decision making, classification of psycopathology. **SELECTED PUBLICATIONS** Coauth with T. M. Amabile, "How does creativity happen?," in N. Colangelo & S. G. Assouline, eds, Talent Development, vol 3, Dayton OH: Psychol Press (96); coauth with D. Whitney and T. M. Amabile, "Looking inside the fishbowl of creativity: Verbal and behavioral predictors of creative performance," Creativity Res J, 11(3):243-263 (98); auth, "The perils of post-hockery," Skeptical Inquirer, 22(6): 44-48 (98); auth, "Gatekeeping, compensation, and fallibility," Am Psychol, 53(5):568-569 (98); auth, "Information integration in child welfare cases: An introduction to statistical decision making," Child Maltreatment, 3(2): 143-156 (98); auth, "Applying what we have learned: Understanding and correcting biased judgement," Psycoloquy, 9(69)(1998); auth, "Statistical models and strong inference in social judgement research," Psycoloquy, 10(27)(1999); auth, "Informing the comtinuity controversy: A taxometric analysis of depression, J of Abnormal Psychol (in press); auth, "Risky business: Vividness, availability, and the media paradox," Skeptical Enquirer, 23 (in press): auth, "The role of complex thought in clinical prediction: Social accountability and the need for recognition," J of Consulting and Clinical Psychol, 68(1) (in press). **CONTACT ADDRESS** Dept Psychol, Elizabethtown Col, 1 Alpha Dr, Elizabethtown, PA 17022.

RUSSELL, DIANA ELIZABETH H.
PERSONAL Born 11/06/1938, CapeTown, South Africa, d **DISCIPLINE** SOCIOLOGY **EDUCATION** PhD, 70, MA, 67, Harvard Univ; Postgraduate Diploma London School of Econ and Poli Sci, Soc Sci and Admin; Univ of Capetown South Africa, Psychol, BA, 58. **CAREER** Asst Prof, 69-75, Assoc Prof, 75-83, Prof Emerita Soc, Mills Col Oakland, CA, 91-present; Prof Soc, 83-91; Res Assoc Inst of Criminol, Univ Capetown, SAfrica, 92-93; Writer, Res, Intl, Consul and Pub Speaker, 91-92; Res Assoc Univ Capetown, South Africa, 91; Writer, Res, Intl Consul and Pub speaker, 94-. **HONORS AND AWARDS** Mostyn Lloyd Memorial Prize, 61; C. Wright Mills Awd, 86; Pioneer Awd, 88; Outstanding Book on human rights, 90. **RESEARCH** Sexual assault, pornography, sexual violence of all kinds, women in SAfrica. **SELECTED PUBLICATIONS** Russell, D E H, Dangeous Relationshops: Pornography, Misogyny, and Rape, Newbury Park CA, Sage Publications, Revised expanded ed of Against Pornography: The Evidence of Harm, Berkeley, CA, Russell Publications, 94; Russell, D E H, Behind Closed Doors in White South Africa: Incest Survivors Tell Their Stories, Basingstoke, Hampshire, UK, Macmillan Press, 97; Russell, D E H, Incestuous Abuse: Itls Long-Term Effects, Pretoria, South Africa: The Human Sciences, Research Council Publishers, 95; Russell, D E H, Against Pornography: The Evidence of Harm, Berkeley, CA, Russell Publications, 94; Numerous more publications. **CONTACT ADDRESS** Div Soc Sci, Mills Col, 5000 MacArthur Blvd, Oakland, CA 94613. **EMAIL** russell@mills.edu

RUSSO, DONALD T.
PERSONAL Born 04/05/1943, New York, NY, d, 1 child **DISCIPLINE** RELIGIOUS EDUCATION AND RELIGIOUS STUDIES **EDUCATION** Cathedral Col, Brooklyn, NYork, BA, Philos, 64; Gregorian Univ, Rome, theol, STB, 66, STL, 75; New York Univ, PhD, relig educ, 84. **CAREER** Tchr, relig and latin, Xaverian High Sch, Brooklyn, NY, 73-; asst prin for supv, Xaverian High Sch, Brooklyn, NY, 75-77; adjunct lectr, relig dept, Syracuse Univ, 79-; adjunct asst prof, develop reading, NY City Tech Col, Brooklyn, NY, 73-. **HONORS AND AWARDS** Who's Who among students in Amer Univ, 77-78; Educr of the Yr, Asn of Tchrs of NY, 86; Educr of the Yr, Xaverian Brothers Sponsored Sch, 95; Who's Who among Amer Tchrs, 98, 00. **MEMBERSHIPS** Amer Acad of Relig; Amer Class Leag; Asn of Prof and Res in Relig Educ; Asn for Supv and Curric Develop; Class Asn of the Empire State; Nat Cath Educ Asn; NY Metro Asn of Develop Educ; NY State Asn of Foreign Lang Tchrs; Relig Educ Asn of the US and Can. **RESEARCH** Religion and American culture; Religious education and ecumenism. **SELECTED PUBLICATIONS** Auth, Twenty-five Years of Religious Education in Catholic High Schools, PACE 25, Professional Approaches for Christ Educ, Mar, 96; auth, A Response to Dykstra: Youth and the Language of Faith, Relig Educ, 81, 188-193, 86; book rev, Ministries, James Dunning, Relig Educ, Summer, 81. **CONTACT ADDRESS** 7100 Shore Rd., Brooklyn, NY 11209. **EMAIL** drussodr@aol.com

RUSSO, NANCY FELIPE
PERSONAL Born 05/03/1942, Oroville, CA, m, 1974 **DISCIPLINE** PSYCHOLOGY **EDUCATION** Yuba Col, AA, 63; Univ Calif Davis, BA, 65; Cornell Univ, PhD, 70. **CAREER** Assoc res scientist, Am Inst for Res, 69-70; asst prof, Am Univ, 70-71; asst prof, Richmond Col, 71-73; asst prof, Am Univ, 73-74; staff assoc to spec asst , APA, 74-76; health scientist admin, NIH, 76-77; admin off, APA, 77-85; prof to dir and regents prof, Ariz State Univ, 85-. **HONORS AND AWARDS** Publication Awd, Asn for Women in Psychol, 65-79; Fel, Am Psychol Soc; APA Distinguished Vis Prog, 84-90; Recognition Awd, Psychology of Women, 85; Distinguished Leadership Citation, APA, 86; Distinguished Publication Awd, AWP, 88; Robert A. Morris Mem Distinguished Lectr, Univ Nebr, 89; Distinguished Service Awd, APA, 90; Distinguished Career Awd, Asn for Women in Psychol, 91; Heritage Awd, APA, 92; Distinguished Fac Achievement Awd, Ariz State Univ, 92; Carolyn Wood Sheriff Awd, APA, 93; Wash EdPress Book Awd, 94; Awd for Distinguished Contributions to Psychol in the Pub Interest, APA, 95. **MEMBERSHIPS** APA; Soc for the Study of Soc Psychol; Soc for the Psychol Study of Soc Issues; Soc for the Study of Population and Environ Psychol; Soc for the Study of the Psychol of Women; Soc for the Psychol Study of Ethnic Minority and Cross-Cultural Psychol. **RESEARCH** Gender and sex roles particularly with regard to the self, unwanted childbearing, violence, and health (physical and mental), education, and careers; Hispanic women's issues; ethnic minority issues. **SELECTED PUBLICATIONS** Co-ed, Women and depression: Risk factors and treatment issues, Washington, APA, 90; co-ed, Women in psychology: A biobibliographical sourcebook, Greenwood Press, 90; co-ed, Women's Heritage in Psychology: Origins, Development, and Future Directions, Cambridge Univ Press, 91; co-auth, No safe haven: Male violence against women at home, at work, and in the community, Am Psychol Asn, 94; co-auth, "Why is abortion such a controversial issue in the United States," in The New Civil War: The Psychology, Culture, and Politics of Abortion, (Washington, 98), 25-60; co-auth, "Understanding the relationship of violence against women to unwanted pregnancy and its resolution," in The New Civil War: The Psychology, Culture, and Politics of Abortion, (Washington, 98), 211-234; co-auth, Psychology: Behavior in Context, W.W. Norton, 98; co-auth,

"Rape: A Global Health Issue," in Women's Health: Contemporary International Perspectives, (London, 00), 129-141; co-auth, "The Socio-Political Context of Abortion and its Relationship to Women's Mental Health," in Women's Health: Contemporary International Perspectives, (London, 00), 431-449. **CONTACT ADDRESS** Dept Psychol, Arizona State Univ, MC 1104, Tempe, AZ 85287-1104. **EMAIL** nancy.russo@asu.edu

RYAN, KEVIN
PERSONAL Born 10/07/1932, Mt. Vernon, NY, m, 1964, 3 children **DISCIPLINE** EDUCATION **EDUCATION** Univ Toronto, BA, 55; Stanford Univ, MA, 60; Harvard Univ, PhD, 66. **CAREER** Teacher, Suffern High Sch, 59-63; Instr, Naval Officers Candidate Sch, 63; Supvr Intern Teachers, 63-64, Coordr Supvrs, 64-66, Instr & Fac Resident, Stanford Univ, 65-66; Alfred North Whitehead Fel, Harvard Univ, 70-71; Sr. Study Dir, Nat Opinion Res Ctr, 73-75; Vis Prof, Harvard Univ, 73-74; Asst Prof, 66-68, Assoc Prof , Univ Chicago, 68-75; Sr. Fulbright Hayes Schol, Ministry Educ, Lisbon, Portugal, 80; Prof Educ, Ohio State Univ, 75-82, Assoc Dean Prog Development, Col Educ, 75-78; Prof, Sch Educ, 82-, Dir, Ctr Advancement Ethics & Character, Boston Univ, 89-. **HONORS AND AWARDS** Wall Street Journal Awd, Columbia Univ, 62; Alfred North Whitehead Fel, Harvard Univ, 70-71; Certificate of Recognition, Am Asn Col for Teacher Educ, 75; Fulbright-Hayes Sr. Schol, 80; Distinguished Service Medal, Univ Helsinki, 80; Boston Univ Schol-Teacher Awd, 89-90; Outstanding Teacher Educr Awd, Asn Teacher Educ, 90. **MEMBERSHIPS** Character Educ Partnership; Am Educ Res Asn; Asn Supervision & Curriculum Development; Asn Teacher Educr; Phi Delta Kappa; Nat Soc Study Educ; Network Educ Excellence. **RESEARCH** Character and moral education; teacher education. **SELECTED PUBLICATIONS** Coauth, Lenses on Teaching, Holt/Dryden/Saunders, 89, 2nd ed, 94; co-ed, The Art of Lo Loving Well, Boston Univ, 90; ed, The Roller Coaster Year: Accounts of First Year Teachers, Harper Collins, 91; coauth, Reclaiming Our Schools: A Handbook for Teaching Character, Academics and Discipline, Macmillan, 93, 2nd ed, Prentice Hall/Merrill, 97; Building Character in Schools, Jossey-Bass (in press 98); author of numerous other publications. **CONTACT ADDRESS** School of Education, Boston Univ, 127 Commonwealth Ave., Boston, MA 02167. **EMAIL** kryan@bu.edu

RYANG, SONIA
PERSONAL Born 01/10/1960, Japan, s, 1 child **DISCIPLINE** ANTHROPOLOGY **EDUCATION** Univ York, MPhil, 87; Cambridge Univ, MPhil, 91; PhD, 95. **CAREER** Asst Prof, Johns Hopkins Univ, 97-. **HONORS AND AWARDS** Res Fel, Australian Nat Univ, 95-97. **MEMBERSHIPS** Assoc of Am Anthrop. **RESEARCH** Love and romance, ideology. **SELECTED PUBLICATIONS** Auth, North Koreans in Japan, Westview Pr, 97; ed, Koreans in Japan, Routledge, 00. **CONTACT ADDRESS** Dept Anthrop, Johns Hopkins Univ, Baltimore, 3400 N Charles St, Baltimore, MD 21218.

RYCHLAK, JOSEPH F.
DISCIPLINE CLINICAL PSYCHOLOGY **EDUCATION** OH State Univ, PhD (clinical psychology), 57. **CAREER** Asst prof psychol, FL State Univ, 57-58; asst prof psychol, WA State Univ, 58-61; assoc & full prof, St Louis Univ, 61-69; full prof, Purdue Univ, 69-83, interim head psychol dept, 79-80; Maude C Clarke prof Psychol, Loyola Univ of Chicago, 83-99. **HONORS AND AWARDS** Donald Biggs-Gerald J Pine Awd for Outstanding Scholarly Contribution to Counseling and Values, 88. **MEMBERSHIPS** Fel, Am Psychol Asn; fel, Am Psychol Soc. **RESEARCH** Agency in human behavior, learning, and memory. **SELECTED PUBLICATIONS** Auth, Artificial Intelligence and Human Reason: A Teleological Critique, Columbia Univ Press, 91; Logical Learning Theory: A Human Teleology and Its Empirical Support, Univ NE Press, 94; In Defense of Human Consciousness, Am Psychol Asn Press, 97. **CONTACT ADDRESS** Dept of Psychology, Loyola Univ, Chicago, 6526 N Sheridan Rd, Chicago, IL 60626. **EMAIL** jrychlak@luc.edu

RYU, JAI
PERSONAL Born 10/17/1941, Seoul, Korea, m, 1971, 2 children **DISCIPLINE** SOCIOLOGY **EDUCATION** Seoul Nat Univ, BA, 64; Univ MN, MA, 69; PhD, 72. **CAREER** Res asst, Univ Minn, 66-67; asst prof, Calif State Fullerton, 70-71; asst prof, Loyola Univ, 71-76; Fulbright prof, Seoul Nat Univ, 82-83; assoc prof, Loyola Col, 76-84; prof, 84-; census coord, City Baltimore, 88-90; spec asst, Baltimore Mayor, 89-. **HONORS AND AWARDS** SH Found Grant, 85; Fulbright-Hays Awd, 82; US-HUD Grant, 77. **MEMBERSHIPS** ASA; PAA; AAS; KAA; KSA. **RESEARCH** Sociology theory; race/ethnic relations; demography. **SELECTED PUBLICATIONS** Auth, Residential Segregation of Blacks in Metropolitan America, 83. **CONTACT ADDRESS** Dept Sociology, Loyola Col, 4501 N Charles St, Baltimore, MD 21210. **EMAIL** jryu@loyola.edu

S

SAARI, CAROLYN
PERSONAL Born 10/30/1939, Jersey City, NJ **DISCIPLINE** SOCIAL WORK **EDUCATION** Vassar Col, AB, 61; Simmons Col, SM, 64; Smith Col Sch for Soc Work, PhD, 73. **CAREER** Prof, Loyola Univ, 80-. **HONORS AND AWARDS** Distinguished Career Awd, Simmons Col, 93; Alpha Sigma Nu; Distinguished Practitioner, Nat Acad of Practice. **MEMBERSHIPS** IL Coun for Soc Work; Coun on Soc Work Educ; Nat Assoc of Soc Work; Infant Mental Health Assoc; Soc for the Exploration of Psychotherapy Integration. **SELECTED PUBLICATIONS** Auth, Clinical Social Work Treatment: How Does it Work?, Gardner Pr, (NY), 86; auth, The Creation of Meaning in Clinical Social Work, Guilford Pr, (NY), 91; auth, "The Concept of Projective Identification; A Narrative Critique", Smith Col Studies in Soc Work 66, (95): 3-16; auth, "An Integrationist Perspective on Resistance in Psychotherapy", In Session: Psychotherapy in Practice 2 (96): 67-76; auth, "Collaboration Between Psychoanalysis and Social Work Education", Fostering Healing and Growth: A Psychoanalytic Social Work Approach, eds Jean Sanville and Joyce Edward, Jason Aronson (NY, 96): 404-415; auth, "Relationship Factors in the Creation of Identity: A Psychodynamic Perspective", Constructing Realities: Meaning-Making Perspectives for Psychotherapists, eds Hugh Rosen and Kevin Kuehlwein, Jossey-Bass, (San Francisco, 96): 141-165; auth, The Environment in Theory and Psychotherapy, Columbia Univ Pr, (forthcoming). **CONTACT ADDRESS** Dept Soc Work, Loyola Univ, Chicago, 820 N Michigan Ave, Chicago, IL 60611.

SABARATNAM, LAKSHMANAN
PERSONAL Born 10/27/1946, Colombo, Sri Lanka, m, 1986, 2 children **DISCIPLINE** SOCIOLOGY **EDUCATION** Univ Sri Lanka, BA, 74; Univ Washington, MA, 79, PhD, 84. **CAREER** Asst to assoc prof, Davidson Col, 86-2000. **HONORS AND AWARDS** Mellon Found, Fulbright, Am Philos Soc, Rotary Found, Nat Endowment for Humanities. **MEMBERSHIPS** Sociol Soc, Am Acad of Rel. **RESEARCH** Ethnic conflict. **SELECTED PUBLICATIONS** Rev of Sri Lanka: The Invention of Enmity, by David Little, in "Ethnic and Racial Studies, vol 19, 206-207 (Jan 96); auth, "Motifs, Metaphors, and Mythomoteurs: An exploration of Medieval Ethnicity in South Asia," Nations and Nationalism, vol 3, no 3, 397-426 (97); auth, "Cultural Division of Labour in British Ceylon 1911 to 1921," J of Commonwealth and Post-Colonial Studies, vol 5, (1), 100-109 (97); auth, "The Sri Lanks Tamil Revolt and Civil War (1983-present)," in Encyclopedia of Political Revolutions, ed Jack Goldstone, Congressional Quarterly, (98); auth, "Games Politicians Play: The BC Pact and Sri Lankan Political Culture," Independent Times, vol 1 (7), 16-21 (Oct 98); auth, "Two Games in Sri Lankan Politics" and "Threats in Political Games: The Deceber 19th Proposals," Thamiz Thendral, vol 10, 62-65, 66-67 (Aug 98). **CONTACT ADDRESS** Dept Sociol, Davidson Col, PO Box 1719, Davidson, NC 28036.

SABAT, STEVEN
PERSONAL Born 11/12/1948, New York, NY, s, 1 child **DISCIPLINE** PSYCHOLOGY **EDUCATION** Queens Col, BA, 69; MA, 72; CUNY, PhD, 76. **CAREER** Adj Lecturer, Baruch Col, 72-73; Res Fel, Mt Sinai Hospital, 72-73; Asst Prof to Assoc Prof and Prog Dir, Georgetown Univ, 75-. **HONORS AND AWARDS** Alpha Sigma Nu; Edward B. Bunn Awd, Georgetown Univ, 88, 95; Who's Who among Am Teachers, 94, 98. **SELECTED PUBLICATIONS** Co-auth, "The Alzheimer's disease sufferer as a semiotic subject," Philosophy, Psychiatry, and Psychology, (94): 145-160; co-auth, "Extralinguistic communication compensates for the loss of verbal fluency: A case study of Alzheimer's disease," Language and communication, (97): 341-351; auth, "Voices of Alzheimer's disease sufferers: A call for treatment based on personhood," The Journal of Clinical Ethics, (98): 38-51; co-auth, "Positioning and the recovery of social identity," in Positioning Theory: Moral Contexts of Intentional Action, (Oxford, 98), 87-101; auth, "Facilitating conversation with an Alzheimer's disease sufferer through the use of indirect repair," in Language and communication in Old Age: Multidisciplinary Perspectives, (Garland Press, 99), 115-131/ co-auth, "Intact use of politeness strategies in the discourse of Alzheimer's disease sufferers," Language and communication, (99): 163-180. **CONTACT ADDRESS** Dept Psychol, Georgetown Univ, PO Box 571001, Washington, DC 20057-1001. **EMAIL** sabats@gunet.georgetown.edu

SADLER, WILBERT L., JR.
PERSONAL Born Atlanta, GA, m **DISCIPLINE** EDUCATION **EDUCATION** Paine Coll, BS 1970; Morgan State Univ, MS 1972; Boston Univ, EdD 1981; Univ of Pennsylvania, Post Doctorate study 1981; Columbia Univ, post doctorate study, 1988. **CAREER** Morgan State Coll, instructor, 70-74; Boston Univ, grad asst, 74-76; Livingstone Coll, asst prof, 76-82; Winston-Salem State Univ, assoc prof, 82-92, Prof, 92-. **HONORS AND AWARDS** Natl Endowment for Humanities Fellowship; Published 2 books, 5 articles; member, Alpha Upsilon Alpha, National Reading Honor Society, 1989-90; member, Phi Delta Kappa, National Education Honor Society, 1989-90. **MEM-BERSHIPS** Mem Pinehurst Comm Club 1976-; mem Salisbury Rown Symphony Guild; mem Optimist Club; mem Assn of Coll & Univ Profs; NAACP; life mem, Alpha Upsilon Alpha (Read Honor Society), NC College Read; Coll Reading Assn, Intl Reading Assn, Alpha Kappa Mu Hon Soc; mem Beta Mu Lambda, Alpha Phi Alpha Frat Inc. **CONTACT ADDRESS** Education Dept, Winston-Salem State Univ, Martin Luther King Jr Dr, Winston-Salem, NC 27101.

SADRI, AHMAD
PERSONAL Born 11/17/1953, Tehran, Iran, s **DISCIPLINE** SOCIOLOGY **EDUCATION** Univ Tehran, BA, MA. **CAREER** Asst prof, 88-95, assoc prof, Lake Forest Col, 95-. **HONORS AND AWARDS** William L Dunn Awd, excel teach; Lake Forest Shclsp. **MEMBERSHIPS** ASA; Middle Eastern Inst, Univ Chicago. **RESEARCH** Sociology of religion, politics; study of civilizations. **SELECTED PUBLICATIONS** Max Weber's Sociology of Intellectuals, NY, Oxford Press, 94; Reason Freedom Democracy in Islam: Essays By Abdolkarim Soroush, NY, Oxford Univ Press, 99, trans, ed, intro, co auth Mahmoud Sadri; Civilization Imagination Ethnic Coexistence IN: Handbook of Interethnic Coexistence, Cotinuum Press, 98; Searchers: The New Iranian Film, Brochure of Chicago Film Festival, 97; The Making of Foreign Policy in the United States, Round Table Discussion, The Middle East Quarterly, 98; many more articles and publications. **CONTACT ADDRESS** Lake Forest Col, Dept Sociology Anthropology, Lake Forest, IL 60045. **EMAIL** sadri@lfc.edu

SADRI, MALMOUD
PERSONAL Born 11/17/1953, Tehran, Iran, s **DISCIPLINE** SOCIOLOGY **EDUCATION** New School Univ, 88. **CAREER** Assoc Prof, Tex Woman's Univ. **HONORS AND AWARDS** Who's Who in America, 99; Service Recognition, Tex Woman's Univ, 97; Who's Who among Am Teachers, 96; Alvin Johnson Fel, New School for Social Res, 81-82Schoarship, Farabi Univ, 78-81; Study Scholarship, Univ Tehran, 70-76. **MEMBERSHIPS** ASA, MESA. **RESEARCH** Sociology of religion; Sociology of culture; Theory. **SELECTED PUBLICATIONS** Auth, "Good News About Modernity,: in The Living Legacy of Marx, Durkheim & Weber, vol II: Applications and Analysis of classical Theory by Modern Social Scientists, Godian Knot Books, 00; trans, "Eshortation of the Faithful and Purification of the Nation or Islam's View concerning the nature of Government," by Mohammad Hossein Naini, in Modernist Islam: A Sourcebook, Oxford Univ Press, 00; auth, Reason, Freedom, and Democracy in Islam: the Essential Writings of Abdolkarim Soroush, Oxford Univ Press, 99; auth, "Intercultural Understanding: Max Weber and Leo Strauss," in The Living Legacy of Marx, Durkheim & Weber,: Applications and Analysis of Classical Sociological Theory by Modern Social Scientists, Godian Knot Books, 98; trans, of "Islam and Liberty," by Mehdi Bazargan, in Liberal Islam, Oxford Univ Press, 98; auth, "Selective Saliency of Ascriptive and Achieved Status in Organically Solidary Societies," in Durkheim's division of Labor 1893-1993, Presses Universitaires de France, 93; contrib auth, " Hosseinieh Ershad, Hojjatieh, Halabi," in Encyclopedia Iranica, Columbia Univ Press, 00; auth, "Occidentalism: Images of the West," in Contemporary sociology, 96; auth, "Common Good, ayatollah Khomeinie, Amitai Etzioni," in The encyclopedia of Modern Social Issues, Salem Press, 96; auth, "Doppelganger: Twins' disruption of the Assumptions of constancy and Uniqueness of Self in Everyday Life," symbolic Interaction , 94. **CONTACT ADDRESS** Dept Sociol & Soc Work, Texas Woman's Univ, PO Box 425887, Denton, TX 76204.

SAFRAN, JOAN
PERSONAL Born 10/05/1951, NJ, m, 1974, 2 children **DISCIPLINE** EDUCATION **EDUCATION** Conn Col, BA, 73; Rutgers Univ, ME, 75; Univ Va, PhD, 80. **CAREER** Assoc Prof, Ohio Univ, 95-. **HONORS AND AWARDS** Grant, Va State Dept of Educ, 80; Grant, Ohio Univ Res Comt, 82; Grant, Ohio State Dept of Educ, 98-99. **MEMBERSHIPS** APA, Coun for Children with Behav Disorders, Coun for Exceptional Children. **RESEARCH** Asperger's Syndrome, mentoring, effective teacher training, teaching educational psychology. **SELECTED PUBLICATIONS** Coauth, "What Disturbs Students? An Examination of Age and Gender Differences," J of Spec Educ, 28 (94): 138-148; coauth, "Native American Youth: Meeting Their Needs in a Multicultural Society," J of Humanistic Educ and Develop, 33 (94): 50-57; coauth, "Intervention Assistance Programs and Pre-Referral Teams: Directions for the Twenty-First Century," Remedial and Spec Educ, 17 (96): 363-369; coauth, "Communication and Mainstreaming: Translating the Behavioral Consultation Research into Effective Practices," Reading and Writing Quart: Overcoming Learning Difficulties, 12 (96): 77-90; coauth, "Pre-Referral Consultation and Intervention Assistance Teams Revisited: Some New Food for Thought," J of Educ and Psychol Consultation, 8 (97): 93-100. **CONTACT ADDRESS** Dept Educ, Ohio Univ, Athens, OH 45701. **EMAIL** safranj@ohio.edu

SAFRAN, STEPHEN P.
PERSONAL Born New York, NY, m, 1974, 2 children **DISCIPLINE** SPECIAL EDUCATION **EDUCATION** Univ Virginia, PhD, 80. **CAREER** Prof, Oh Univ, 80-. **HONORS AND**

AWARDS Who's Who, Intl. **MEMBERSHIPS** Council for Exceptional Children. **RESEARCH** Asperger Syndrome; school behavior and discipline; disability portrayal in the media. **SELECTED PUBLICATIONS** Coauth, "What disturbs students? An examination of age and gender differences," J Spec Edu 28 (94): 138-148; coauth, "Peers' perceptions of emotional and behavioral difficulties: what are students thinking?" J of Emotional and Behavioral Disorders 3 (95): 66-75; coauth, "Communication and mainstreaming: Translating the behavioral consultation research into effective practices," Reading and Writing Quarterly: Overcoming Learning Difficulties 12 (96) 77-90; coauth, "Peripheral consultation and intervention assistance teams revisited: Some new food for thought," J of Edu Psychol Consult 8 (97): 93-100; auth, "The first century of disability portrayal in film: An analysis of the literature," J of Spec Edu 31 (98): 467-479; coauth, "The social validity of level systems, " BC J of Spec Edu 21 (98): 112-127; auth, "Disability portrayal in film: Reflecting the past, directing the future," Exceptional Child 64 (98): 227-238; coauth, "Using movies to teach students about disabilities," Teaching Exceptional Child 32 (00): 44-47; coauth, "Cooperative learning and social stories: Effective social skills strategies for reading teachers," Reading and Writing Quarterly: Overcoming Learning Difficulties (in press). **CONTACT ADDRESS** Dept Teacher Edu, Ohio Univ, Athens, OH 45701. **EMAIL** safran@ohio.edu

SAGARIA, MARY ANN D.
DISCIPLINE EDUCATION **EDUCATION** Penn State Univ, BA, 69; Univ Miami, MEd, 71; Penn State Univ, EdD, 80. **CAREER** Asst Prof to Assoc Prof and Dept Director, Ohio State Univ, 84-; Faculty Director, Internship Prog at Lancaster Univ, Lancaster England, 95-. **HONORS AND AWARDS** Prof Development Awd, Va Soc Sci Asn, 83; Hilda Dais Awd, Nat Asn for Women Dearns, 89; Fulbright Res Awd, Indonesia, 90-91. **SELECTED PUBLICATIONS** Auth, "Constructions of Feminism in Unequal Relationships: A Personal Account from a North American in a Cross-Cultural Household," NWSA Journal, (00): 100-118; auth, "Internal Meanings and Markers of College and University Community Service," Metropolitan Universities, (99): 29-42; auth, "Feminists at Work: Collaboration Among Women Faculty," Review of Higher Education, (97): 79-101; auth, "Career Patterns of Athletic Directors: Challenging the Conventional Wisdom," Journal of Sports Management, (94): 14-26; auth, "University Staffing Decisions to Hire or Promote," International Journal of Educational Management, (92): 20-31; auth, "Administrative Promotion: The Structuring of Opportunity Within a University," Review of Higher Education, (91): 91-121; auth, "Recruiting, Advancing and Retaining Minorities in Student Affairs: Moving From Rhetoric To Results," NASPA Journal, (91): 105-120; auth, "The Situation of Women in Research Universities in the United States: Within the Inner Circles of Academic Power," in Women's Higher Education in Comparative Perspective, Kleiwer Acad Pub, 91; auth, "Thriving at Home: Developing a Career as an Insider," in Administrative Careers and the Marketplace, Jossey-Bass, 90. **CONTACT ADDRESS** Dept Educ Policy Studies, Ohio State Univ, Columbus, 29 W Woodruff, Columbus, OH 43210. **EMAIL** sagaria.1@osu.edu

SAGINI, MESHACK
PERSONAL Born 11/30/1944, Kisii, Kenya, m, 1973, 4 children **DISCIPLINE** EDUCATION ADMINISTRATION, HISTORY **EDUCATION** West Indies, BEd, 79; Andrews, MA, 82; MSU, PhD, 87. **CAREER** Elementary school teacher, 67; high school deputy principal, 71-75; Col lecturer, 89-97; asst prof to res prof, Langston Univ, 98-. **HONORS AND AWARDS** Excellence in Teaching, Am Pol Sci Asn, 97; Excellence in Res and teaching, Langston Univ, 97. **MEMBERSHIPS** OK Pol Sci Asn, am Pol Sci Asn, MAAAS, Ok League of Pol Sci, African Professionals Asn. **RESEARCH** Organizational behavior, Public policy, Africans in higher education. **SELECTED PUBLICATIONS** Auth, The African and the African-American University: a Historical and Sociological Analysis, Univ Press of America, 96. **CONTACT ADDRESS** Dept Soc Sci & Humanities, Langston Univ, PO Box 157, Langston, OK 73050-0728. **EMAIL** mmsagini@lunet.edu

SAIEDI, NADER
PERSONAL Born 03/21/1955, Tehran, Iran, m, 1992 **DISCIPLINE** SOCIOLOGY **EDUCATION** Pahlavi Univ, Shiraz, MS, 78; Univ Wis Madison, PhD, 83. **CAREER** Asst prof, Univ Calif, Los Angeles, 84-85; asst prof, Vanderbilt Univ, 85-86; prof, Carleton Col, 86-. **RESEARCH** Social Theory, Baha'i studies, Middle East, stratification. **SELECTED PUBLICATIONS** Auth, The Birth of Social Theory, Univ Pr of Am, 93; auth, Logos and Civilization, univ Pr of Ma, 00. **CONTACT ADDRESS** Dept Sociol and Anthrop, Carleton Col, 1 N College St, Northfield, MN 55057. **EMAIL** nsaiedi@carleton.edu

SAILES, GARY
PERSONAL Born 09/15/1951, Albany, NY, m, 1992, 1 child **DISCIPLINE** SPORT SOCIOLOGY **EDUCATION** Univ Minn, PhD. **CAREER** Assoc prof, Chicago State Univ, 76-85; asst prof, Univ Del, 85-89; assoc prof, Indiana Univ, 89-. **HONORS AND AWARDS** Outstanding Young Am; Who's Who in Am Educ; Teaching Excellence Awd, Indiana Univ; Teaching Excellence Awd, USPTA. **MEMBERSHIPS** North American Soc for the Sociol of Sport. **RESEARCH** Sport sociology: race and sport. **SELECTED PUBLICATIONS** Auth, Tennis Drills for Coaches and Athletes, Chicago State Univ: Chicago, Ill (84); auth, Winning Tennis Drills, Brown Pubs: Dubuque, Iowa (91); auth, Mental Training for Tennis, Kendall/Hunt Pubs: DuBuque, Iowa (95); auth, "A Comparison of Professional Sports Career Aspirations Among College Athletes," Academic Athletic J, 11:2 (96): 20-28; auth, "Betting Against the Odds: An Overview of Black Sports Participation," J of African American Men, 2:2/3 (97): 11-22; auth, The African American Athlete: Contemporary Themes, Transaction Pubs: Rutgers, NJ (98); auth, "The African American Athlete: Social Myths and Stereotypes," in Racism in College Sports II, eds. Dana Brooks and Ron Althouse (WV: Fitness Technologies, 99). **CONTACT ADDRESS** Sch of Health Phys Educ, Indiana Univ, Bloomington, 1025 E 7th St, Bloomington, IN 47405. **EMAIL** gsailes@indiana.edu

SAITZ, ROBERT LEONARD
PERSONAL Born 07/09/1928, Boston, MA, m, 1962, 1 child **DISCIPLINE** ENGLISH AS SECOND LANGUAGE, LINGUISTICS **EDUCATION** Boston Univ, BA, 49; Univ Iowa, MA, 50; Univ Wis, PhD(English ling), 55. **CAREER** Instr English, Univ Wis, 57-59; asst prof, Southern Ill Univ, 59-60; coord, English as second lang, Fulbright grant, Colombia, 60-62; from asst prof to assoc prof, 62-72, Prof Ling & English As Second Lang, Boston Univ, 72-, Consult English as second lang, Boston & New Bedford schs, 67; Fulbright lectr, Univ Seville, 69-70. **MEMBERSHIPS** Ling Soc Am; Nat Asn Foreign Student Affairs; Teachers English to Speakers Other Langs. **RESEARCH** Old English syntax; second language learning; kinesics. **SELECTED PUBLICATIONS** Coauth, Selected Readings in English, Winthrop, 72; Handbook of Gestures, Mouton, The Hague, 72; Ideas in English, Winthrop, 74; Advanced Reading & Writing, Holt, 78; Challenge, Winthrop, 78; Stimulus, Little Brown, 83; Contemporary Perspectives, Little Brown, 84; Points Wkbks, Addison-Wesley, 86; Milestones, Little Brown, 87; Short Takes, Addison-Wesley, 93, Workout in English, Prentic-Halle, 98. **CONTACT ADDRESS** Dept of English, Boston Univ, 236 Bay State Rd, Boston, MA 02215-1403. **EMAIL** bsaitz@bu.edu

SALAMON, SONYA
PERSONAL Born 11/01/1939, Pittsburgh, PA, m, 1960, 2 children **DISCIPLINE** ANTHROPOLOGY **EDUCATION** Carnegie Mellon Univ, BFA, 61; Univ of Calif at Berkeley, MA, 65; Univ of Ill at Urbana-Champaign, PhD, 74. **CAREER** Acting Dept Head, Human Development and Ffamil Ecology, 80-81, Grad Prog Coord, Divisoin of Human Development and Family Studies, 81-88 & 91-93, Asst to Full Prof, 74-, Dept of Human and Community Development, Univ of ILL Urbana-Champaign. **HONORS AND AWARDS** Postdoctoral fel coun for European Studies/DAAD, German Acad Exchange Prog, 74-75; assoc, Center for Advanced Study, 80-81, Paul A. Funk Recognition Award, Univ of Ill, 98; Rural Sociological Soc Policy fel, 88-89; Ameritech res fel, 88-89; visiting scholar, Economic Res Service U.S. Dept of Agriculture, 88-89 & 95-96. **MEMBERSHIPS** Am Anthropological Asn; Rural Sociological Soc; Ill Coun on Family Relations; Soc for Applied Anthropology; Nat Coun on Family Relations. **RESEARCH** Rural Mobile Home Parks **SELECTED PUBLICATIONS** Auth, Ethnic Communities and the Structure of Agriculture, Rural Sociology, 85; auth, Prairie Patrimony: Family, Farming and Community in the Midwest, Univ of NC Press, 92; auth, Culture and Agricultural Land Tenure, Rural Sociology, 93; coauth, Share and Share Alike: Inheritance Patterns in Two Illinois Farm Communities, J of Family Hist, 88; coauth, Territory Contested through Property in a Midwestern Post-Agricultural Community, Rural Sociology, 94; Family Factors Affecting Adoption of Sustainable Farming Systems, J of Soil and Water Conservation, 97; coauth, Is Locally Led Conservation Planning Working? A Farm Town Case Study, Rural Sociology, 98; coauth, "Mobile Home Park on the Prairie: a New Rural Community corm, Rural Soc, 01. **CONTACT ADDRESS** Dept of Human and Community Development, Univ of Illinois, Urbana-Champaign, 905 S Goodwin Ave, Urbana, IL 61801. **EMAIL** ssalamon@uiuc.edu

SALAMONE, FRANK A.
PERSONAL Born 03/26/1939, Rochester, NY, m, 1977, 7 children **DISCIPLINE** SOCIOLOGY **EDUCATION** St John Fisher, BA, 61; Univ Rochester, MA, 66; SUNY, Buffalo, PhD, 73. **CAREER** Prof, ch, Iona Col, 81-. **MEMBERSHIPS** NYSASA; NYSSS; ASA; AAA. **RESEARCH** Africa; Italian-American popular culture. **SELECTED PUBLICATIONS** Auth, Bridges to Humanity: Anthropological Narratives of Friendship, Waveland Press (Prospect Hts, IL), 95; auth, The Fulbright Experiences in Nigeria, Coll Will and Mary (Williamsburg, VA), 95; auth, Who Speaks for the Yanomami, Coll Will and Mary (Williamsburg, VA), 95; auth, Art and Leisure, ABC-CLIO, 99; auth, New Directions in Anthropology and Theology, Univ Press (Lanham, MD), 97; auth, "Children's Games as Mechanisms for Easing Ethnic Interaction in Ethically Heterogeneous Communities: A Nigerian Case," in International Encyclopedia of Anthropology, ed. SM Channa (NEW Delhi: Vedams Books, 98); auth, Readings in Introductory Sociology, Whittier Press (Long Beach), 99; coauth, "Images of Main Street: Disney World and the American Adventure," J Am Cult 22 (99): 27-34; auth, "Afigbo, A E," in Encyclopedia of Historians and Historical Writing (Chicago: Fitzroy Dearborn, 99); auth, "The Vatican," in Encyclopedia of National Cultures, ed. Melvin Ember (NY: Macmillan, 00); auth, "Italy," in Encyclopedia of National Cultures, ed. Melvin Ember (NY: Macmillan, 00). **CONTACT ADDRESS** Dept Sociology, Iona Col, 715 North Ave, New Rochelle, NY 10801.

SALEKIN, RANDALL T.
PERSONAL Born 08/20/1966, BC, Canada, m, 1994, 1 child **DISCIPLINE** PSYCHOLOGY **EDUCATION** Simon Fraser Univ, Burnaby, British Columbia, BA, 93; Univ N Tex, MS, 95, PhD, 98. **CAREER** Asst prof, Fla Int Univ, 98-. **HONORS AND AWARDS** Challenge 90 Project Awd, 90; Vancouver Health and Sci Found Grant, 91; Metrocrest Scholar Awd, 93; UNT Clinical Forensic Scholar Awd, 94, 95; UNT Outstanding Grad Student in Psychol Awd, 97; FIU Grant-In-Aid Awd, 98, 2000. **MEMBERSHIPS** Am Psychol Asn, Am Psychol-Law Soc, Clinical Psychol. **RESEARCH** Forensic psychology. **SELECTED PUBLICATIONS** Coauth, "Convergent validity of the Personality Assessment Inventory: A study of emergency referrals in a correctional setting," Assessment, 5 (98): 3-12; coauth, "Psychopathy and recidivism among female inmates," Law and Human Behavior, 22 (98): 109-128; coauth, "Validation of the Millon Multiaxial Inventory for Axis II Disorders: Does it meet the Daubert standard?," Law and Human Behavior, 23 (99): 425-443; coauth, An investigation of the Psychopathy Checklist--Screening Version: An examination of criteria and subcritieria, Assessment (in press); coauth, "Toward effective treatment and release of NGRI patients: Current knowledge and future directions," in J. B. Ashford, B. D. Sales, and W. Reid, eds, Treating adult and juvenile offenders with special needs, Washington, DC: Am Psychol Asn (in press); coauth, "Prototypical analysis of antisocial personality disorder: An insiders perspective," Criminal Justice and Behavior (in press). **CONTACT ADDRESS** Dept Psychol, Florida Intl Univ, 3000 NE 151st St, North Miami, FL 33181. **EMAIL** salekin@fiu.edu

SALLEE, ALVIN L.
PERSONAL Born 01/19/1950, Albuquerque, NM, m, 1971, 3 children **DISCIPLINE** SOCIAL WORK **EDUCATION** Phillips Univ, BA. **CAREER** Instr, Southwest Tex State Univ, 74-76; Asst Prof, to Full Prof and Director of Family Preservation Inst, N Mex State Univ, 76-. **HONORS AND AWARDS** N Mex NASW President's Awd, 91; Nat Asn of Soc Workers; Soc Worker of the Year, Soc Workers of Southern N Mex, 90-91; Dona Ana Program Unit NASW; Professional Soc Worker of the Year, 86; Outstanding Young Men of Am, 85; Nat Asn of Soc Workers, ACBSW Review Committee. **MEMBERSHIPS** Am Asn of Board of Soc Work Examiners, Am Humane Asn, Nat Asn of Deans and Directors, Nat Asn of Family-based Services, N Mex State Chapter NASW, Nat Asn of Soc Workers, N Mex Coun Mental Health Services Task Force, Am Indian Law Center, N Mex Family Policy Task Force. **RESEARCH** Adoption, foster Care, Family Preservation, Information and Referral **SELECTED PUBLICATIONS** Auth, Child Welfare: Clinical Theory and Practice, Eddie Bowers Pub, 99; auth, Social work practice: Bridges to change, Allyn & Bacon, 94; auth, Study guide for social work practice; Bridges to change, Allyn & Bacon, 93; auth, Listen to our children: Clinical theory and practice (2nd ed), Hunt Pub, 92; auth, Listen to our children: Clinical theory and practice, Hunt Pub, 86; auth, "The role of families," Family Preservation Journal, 98; auth, "Family Preservation: Collaboration and Teamwork," Family Preservation Journal, 97; auth, "The Impact of Welfare Reform on families," Family Preservation Journal, 97; auth, "The Impact of Welfare Reform on Families," Family Preservation Journal, 96; auth, "What's Good for families," Family Preservation Journal; auth, "Child Welfare Reform Litigation: Achieving Substantial Compliance," Journal of Law and Social Work, (96): 14-24. **CONTACT ADDRESS** Dept Soc Work, New Mexico State Univ, PO Box 30001, Las Cruces, NM 88003. **EMAIL** asallee@nmsu.edu

SALLIS, CHARLES
DISCIPLINE SOUTHERN HISTORY AND ETHNIC AND CULTURAL DIVERSITY **EDUCATION** Univ Ky, PhD. **CAREER** Prof & past dept ch and past dir, Heritage Prog; fac, Millsaps Col, 68-; past tutor, Brit Stud Prog, Oxford Univ, 5 summers sessions. **HONORS AND AWARDS** Millsaps Distinquished prof, 73; 2 Nat Endowment for the Humanities fel(s); Southern Reg Council's Lillian Smith awd, 75. **SELECTED PUBLICATIONS** Coauth, Mississippi: Conflict and Change. **CONTACT ADDRESS** Dept of History, Millsaps Col, 1701 N State St, Jackson, MS 39210. **EMAIL** salliwc@okra.millsaps.edu

SALZWEDEL, KENNETH D.
PERSONAL Born 11/06/1932, Columbus, WI, m, 1957, 3 children **DISCIPLINE** PSYCHOLOGY **EDUCATION** Univ Wisc, BS, 54; Univ Ky, MS, 61; Univ Wisc, PhD, 70. **CAREER** Instr, Ind Central Univ, 54-60; instr to prof, Univ Wisc-Whitewater, 62-. **HONORS AND AWARDS** Honored for his efforts with students, res presentation at Nat Conf; 3 times elected as a Fac to membership in the Blue Key Honors Soc; Phi Kappa Phi, 82; chair, dept of Psychol, Univ Wisc-

Whitewater; res in Hardy Harlow's private lab, chair, Nat Honors Coun, res comt; Dir, Univ Wisc-Whitewater Honors prog for three years. **MEMBERSHIPS** Am Psychol Asn, Am Asn of behav Therapy, Nat Honors Coun. **RESEARCH** Alzheimer's disease, perfectionism, math education problems. **SELECTED PUBLICATIONS** Auth, "The effects of academic materials on controlling attention of emotionally disturbed childres," Children's Treatment Center Report (69); coauth with R. A. Schaller, "Using recognition and recall measures to evaualte the stimulus imagery effect in associative learning," J of General Psychol, 101, 55-63 (79); coauth with S. T. Hartley, "Behavioral writing for an autistic-like child," Academic Therapy, 16, 101-110 (80); auth, "Socrates and the other disciplines," The Nat Honors Report, 19, no 2, 19 (88); auth, "Teaching by the discourse method: VII: A review with a view," The Nat Honors Report, 19, no 3, 15-17 (88); auth, "Science and mathematics education at the collegiate level: How are we doing?," The Nat Honors Report, 21, 25-26 (90); coauth with C. J. Randall, "Honors students as "Prometheans," Forum for Honors, 20, 29-34 (90). **CONTACT ADDRESS** Dept Psychol, Univ of Wisconsin, Whitewater, 800 W Main, Whitewater, WI 53190. **EMAIL** salzwedk@uwwvax.uww.edu

SAMARASINGHE, VIDYAMALI

DISCIPLINE GENDER AND DEVELOPMENT, POPULATION AND MIGRATION ISSUES **EDUCATION** Univ Ceylon, BA; Camridge Univ, PhD. **CAREER** Prof, Am Univ. **RESEARCH** Southeast Asia, tea plantation women in Sri Lanka; income inequalities among farming communities; and female adolescent food allocation patterns in Sri Lanka. **SELECTED PUBLICATIONS** Co-ed, Women at the Crossroads: A SriLankan Perspective, Vikas, 90; Women at the Center: Gender and Development Issues for the 1990's, Kumarian, 93. **CONTACT ADDRESS** American Univ, 4400 Massachusetts Ave, Washington, DC 20016.

SAMEROFF, ARNOLD

DISCIPLINE PSYCHOLOGY **EDUCATION** Univ Mich, BS, 61; Yale Univ, PhD, 65. **CAREER** Asst to prof, Univ of Rochester, 67-78; prof, Univ of IL Chicago, 78-86; prof, Brown Univ 86-92; prof, Univ of Mich, 92-. **HONORS AND AWARDS** NIMH Fel, 62, 65-67; Fel, AAAS; Fel, Am Psychol Assoc; W.T. Grant Found Lectr, 84; NIMH Res Sci Awd, 94-99. **MEMBERSHIPS** Am Psychol Assoc; AAAS; AAUP; World Assoc of Infant Mental Health; Int Soc for Infant Studies; Int Soc for Study of Behav Develop; Soc for Res in Child Develop; Soc for Res on Adolescence. **SELECTED PUBLICATIONS** Coed, The five to seven year shift: The age of reason and responsibility, Univ of Chicago Pr, 96; coauth, Managing to make it: Urban families and adolescent success, Univ of Chicago Pr; coed, Handbook of Developmental Psychopathology, Plenum (NY), 00; coauth, The stories that families tell: Narrative coherence, narrative interaction, and relationship beliefs, Monographs of the Soc for Res in Child Develop, 257.64.2 (Blackwell Pub), 99; coauth, "Transactional regulation: The developmental ecology of early intervention", Early Intervention: A Handbook of Theory, Practice, and Analysis, eds S.J. Meisels, and J.P. Shonkoff, Cambridge Univ Pr, (00); auth, "Ecological perspectives on developmental risk", WAIMH Handbook of Infant Mental Health: Vol 4. Infant Mental Health Groups at Risk, eds J.D. Osofsky and H.E. Fitzgerald, Wiley (NY, 00); coauth, "Models of development and ecological risk", Handbook of Infant Mental H'ealth, ed C.H. Zeanah, Guilford, (NY, 00): 3-19; coauth, "Transactional regulation: The developmental ecology of early intervention", Early Intervention: A Handbook of Theory, Practice and Analysis, eds S.J. Meisels and J.P. Shonkoff, Cambridge Univ Pr, 00; auth, "Developmental systems and psychopathology", Develop and Psychopathology (forthcoming); coauth, "Observing families through the stories that they tell: A multidimensional approach", Family observational coding systems: Resources for systematic research, eds P. Kerig and K. Lindahl, LEA, (forthcoming). **CONTACT ADDRESS** Dept Psychol, Univ of Michigan, Ann Arbor, 525 E University Ave, Ann Arbor, MI 48109. **EMAIL** sameroff@umich.edu

SANCHEZ, MARY ANN M.

PERSONAL Born 04/09/1963, Redwood Falls, MN, m, 1989 **DISCIPLINE** PSYCHOLOGY **EDUCATION** Duke Univ, BA, 85; Univ Notre Dame, MA, 92; PhD, 96. **CAREER** Instr to prof, Pima Cmty Col, 96-. **MEMBERSHIPS** Am Psych Asn. **RESEARCH** Health Psychology, Cancer and Social Support. **SELECTED PUBLICATIONS** Auth, Assessment of Self-efficacy and coping with cancer: Development and validation of the Cancer Behavior Inventory, (in press); auth, Facor structure of the Psychosocial Adjustment to Illness Scale (Self-Report) for persons with cancer, (forthcoming); auth, Perceptions of coping behaviors by persons with cancer and medical staff, (forthcoming); auth, Toward a model of social support for the cancer patient, 93. **CONTACT ADDRESS** Dept Human Sci, Pima Comm Col, 2202 W Anklam Rd, Tucson, AZ 85709-0001.

SANDHU, DAVA S.

PERSONAL Born 03/03/1943, Sarhali, India, m, 1974, 4 children **DISCIPLINE** PSYCHOLOGY **EDUCATION** Doctor Counselor, Mississippi State, 84; Specialists Degree in English,

Univ Mississippi, 79; Master Education, Delta State Univ, MS, 70; Master Arts, (English) Punjab Univ, India, Bachelor Teaching, Pujab Univ, India. **CAREER** Asst, Assoc, Prof, Chair of the Dept, Univ of Louisville, 91-; Asst Prof Choctaw Central High School, Guidance Counselor, 82-89. **HONORS AND AWARDS** 2000 Alumnus of the Year Awd, Mississippi State Univ, Multicultuural Teaching Awd, 00; Multicultural Research Awd, Univ of Louisville, Asn on Multicultural Counseling and Development, 00. **MEMBERSHIPS** Amer Counseling Assoc; Amer Educational Research Assoc; Amer School Counseling Assoc. **RESEARCH** School Counseling; Multicultural Counseling; Career Counseling. **SELECTED PUBLICATIONS** Auth, "Learning Styles," Sandhu, D.S., Journal of Accelerative Learning and Teaching, 21, 96: 1-95; auth, "The invisible minority: Counseling Asian Americans," Sandhu, D.S., Counseling Today, 40, 97, 1, 21-22; auth, "Asian and Pacific Islander Americans," Sandhu, D.S., Journal of Multicultural Counseling and Development, 25, 97: 3-88; auth, "Counselors need to take a more proactive role in prejudice prevention," Sandhu, D.S., & Aspy, C.B., Counseling Today, 39, 97: 14 & 22; auth, "An acculturative stress scale for international students: A practical approach to stress measurement," Sandhu, D.S., & Asrabadi, B.R., In C.P. Zalaquett and R.J. Wood (eds.), Evaluating stress: A book of resources, V.2. 98: 1-33, Lanham, MD & London: The Scarecrow Press, Inc; auth, "Empowering women for equity: A counseling approach," Aspy, C.B., & Sandhu, D.S., Alexandria, VA: Washington, DC; autth, "Asian and Pacific Islander Americans: Issues and concerns for counseling and psychotherapy," Sandhu, D.S., Commack, NY: Nova Science Publishers; auth, "Assessment of spirituality: psychometric characteristics of selected instruments," Stanard, R.P., Sandhu, D.S., & Painter, L.C., Journal of Counseling and Development, Implications for counseling and psychotherapy, 00; auth, " ethnocultural background of Asian Indian Americans and substance abuse treatment," Sandhu, D.S., & Malik, R., In S.L.A. Straussner, Ed., Ethnic minorities and drug abuse, New York: Guilford, 00; auth, "Violence in American shools: A practical guide for Counselors," Sandhu, D.S., & Aspy, C.B., Alexandria, VA: American Counseling Association, 00. **CONTACT ADDRESS** Dept of Educational & Counseling Psychology, Univ of Louisville, School of Education, Rm 230, Louisville, KY 40292. **EMAIL** daya.sandhu@louisville.edu

SANDIFORD, KEITH

PERSONAL Born Barbados, WI **DISCIPLINE** EIGHTEENTH CENTURY BRITISH LITERATURE, THE NOVEL, CULTURAL STUDIES **EDUCATION** Univ Ill, Urbana-Champaign, PhD, 79. **CAREER** Prof, La State Univ. **HONORS AND AWARDS** NEH Research Fel, 87; LSU Col of Arts and Sciences Manship Summer Grant for Faculty Research, 93; LSU Research Grand, summer 86. **MEMBERSHIPS** Am Soc for Eighteenth Century Studies, South Central Soc for Eighteenth Century Studies, Group for Early Modern Cultural Studies. **RESEARCH** Slavery, Anti-Slavery, Sugar and Colonial Commodities, Hybridity, Genre and Colonial Text Formation. **SELECTED PUBLICATIONS** Auth, "Paule Marshall's Praisesong for the Widow: The Reluctant Heiress, Or Whose Life is it Anyway?," Black American Literature Forum, 86;auth, ' Images of the African in his Literature from Renaissance to Enlightenment," essay in Daniel Droixhe and Klaus H. Keifer, Images de L African de l Antiquite au Xxe Siecle,(Frankfurt: Verlag Peter Lanf, 87; auth, Measuring the Moment: Strategies of Protest in Eighteenth-Century Afro-English Writing, 88; auth, " Inkle and Yarico: The Construction of Alterity from History to Literature," Nieuwe West-Indische Gids, 90; auth, Gothic and Intertextual Constructions in Gloria Naylor's Linden Hills, Arizona Quaterly, 91; auth, "Rochefort's History: The Poetics of Collusion in a Colonizing Narrative," Papers in Language and Literature, 93; auth, " Our Caribs are not Savages: The Use of Colloquy in Rochefort's Natural and Moral History of the Carribby-Islands, " Studies in Western Civilization, 93; auth, Mónk Lewis and the Slavery Sublime: The Agon of Romantic Desire in the Journal" Essays in Literature 23:1, (96): 84-98; auth, " Sugar Slaves and Machines: An Economy of Bodies in Colonizing Narratives," Synthesis, 98; auth,The Cultural Politics of Sugar, Cambridge Univ Press,00. **CONTACT ADDRESS** Dept of Eng, Louisiana State Univ and A&M Col, 212V Allen Hall, Baton Rouge, LA 70803. **EMAIL** ksandif@lsu.edu

SANDOVAL, DOLORES S.

PERSONAL Born 09/30/1937, Montreal, PQ, Canada **DISCIPLINE** EDUCATION **EDUCATION** Institute of Chicago, art, 1956-58; University of Michigan, BSD, 1958-60; Indiana Univ, MS, 1968, PhD, 1970; Harvard University Institute for Educational Management, IEM, 1975. **CAREER** University of Vermont, assoc prof of education, 71-, Middle East studies, cochair, 94-, assistant to the president for human resources, 72-77; State University College at Buffalo, assoc prof, 70-71; Author/Illustrator of "Be Patient Abdul,", Margaret McElderry Books, 96; Paintings and photography of Africa, Middle East & Latin America exhibited in Europe, Canada and USA, 87-; Represented by program Corp. of America, 94; consultant on Race Relations & Diversity Programming. **HONORS AND AWARDS** Elected Democratic candidate for Congress from VT, 1990; Primary candidate, 1988; President's Fellow, Rhode Island School of Design, 1981, mem board of trustees, 1976-82; University Senate, University of VT, chair, 1981-82; Fellowship Challenges to Unity: The European Community, 1995, Maastricht, 1995; Fellow, University of New Mexico College of Fine Arts National Arts Project, Daring To Do It, 1993-94; Malone Alumni Fellow to Jordan, Israel, Palestine and Syria, summer, 1991; Malone Fellow in Arab and Islamic Studies in Tunisia, summer, 1989; Awd from Black American Heritage Foundation, NYC for Contributions to Duke Ellington Concert & Speech Series, 1989-92; Fellow, National Endowment for the Humanities Summer Institute on African & African-American Culture, 1987. **MEMBERSHIPS** Partners of the Americas, Vermont/Honduras, president, 1997-, vice pres, 1994-96, board member, 1992-; Sister Cities, Burlington, (VT) Arad (Israel & Bethlehem), board member, 1995-96; Public Access Government TV, Channel 17 (VT), board member, 1991-95. **CONTACT ADDRESS** Univ of Vermont, Burlington, VT 05405-0001.

SANDOVAL, JONATHAN H.

PERSONAL Born 10/05/1942, Hayward, CA, m, 1982, 1 child **DISCIPLINE** EDUCATION, PSYCHOLOGY **EDUCATION** Univ Calif, AB, 64; MA, 66; PhD, 69. **CAREER** Lectr, Univ Calif Berkeley, 69-73; asst prof to prof, Univ Calif Davis, 71-. **HONORS AND AWARDS** Sandra Goff Memorial Awd, Calif Asn of Sch Psychol, 00. **MEMBERSHIPS** Am Psychol Assoc; Am Orthopsychiatric Assoc; Nat Assoc of Sch Psychol; Am Educ Res Assoc; Phi Delta Kappa; Calif Assoc of Sch Psychol; Soc for the Study of Sch Psychol; Am Acad of Sch Psychol. **RESEARCH** Prevention of School Failure, Training of Education Professionals, Issues in Applied Measurement, Promotion of Mental Health in Schools. **SELECTED PUBLICATIONS** Coauth, "Community-based Service Integration: Family Resource Center Initiatives", Integrated services for children and families: Opportunities for psychological practice, APA, (97); auth, "Neuromuscular Diseases", Health-related disorders in children and adolescents: A guidebook for understanding and educating, ed L. Phelps, APA (98: 463-473; coed, Test Interpretation and Diversity: Achieving equity in psychological assessment, APA (Washington), 98; coauth, "Mainstreaming children with a neuromuscular disease: A map of concerns", Exceptional Children 65, (99): 353-366; coauth, Estrategias para el Maestro en el manejo de ninos hiperactivos, Psciologia, (Venezuela), (forthcoming); auth, "Examining the role of culture in educational assessment", Asian American Mental Health: Assessment, theories and methods, eds K.S. Kurasaki, S. Okazaki, and S. Sue, Kluwer (forthcoming). **CONTACT ADDRESS** Dept Educ, Univ of California, Davis, 1 Shields Ave, Davis, CA 95616. **EMAIL** jhsandoval@ucdavis.edu

SANDOZ, CHARLES JEFFREY

PERSONAL Born 10/08/1953, Opelousas, LA, m, 1984, 3 children **DISCIPLINE** PSYCHOLOGY **EDUCATION** La State Univ, BS, 75; Tex Woman's Univ, MA, 88; Temple Univ, PhD, 95. **CAREER** Teaching Asst, Tex Woman's Univ, 85-88; Adj Prof, Cumberland Cty Col, 91; Adj Prof, Camden Cty Col, 90-95; Adj Prof, La State Univ, 95-; Instructor, Univ La, 98-. **HONORS AND AWARDS** Am Red Cross Cert of Recognition, 88; Diplomate, Am Psychotherapy Asn, 99; Who's Who in Exec and Prof, 00. **MEMBERSHIPS** Am Psychotherapy Asn; Am Col of Coun; Am Asn of Christian Coun; LA Coun Asn; LA Mental Health Coun Asn; Am Coun Asn; Am Mental Health Coun Asn. **SELECTED PUBLICATIONS** Auth, "Wounded Healer: A Portrait of a Physician with Alzheimer's Disease," Activities, Adaptation & Aging, (97): 21-26; co-auth, Alzheimer's Disease Learning Enhancement Resources, 97; auth, "The Effects of Parental Alcoholism upon Locus of Control and Intimacy of Recovering Alcoholics," Alcoholism Treatment Quarterly, (98): 91-99; co-auth, "The AA Home Group Effect," Journal of Ministry in the Addiction, (98): 57-63; auth, "The Effects of AA's 12 Step Program on Self Differentiation," Journal of the Louisiana Counseling Assoc, (99): 31-39; auth, "Exploring the Spiritual Experience of the Twelve Steps of Alcoholics Anonymous," Journal of Ministry in the Addiction, (99): 99-107; auth, "The Spiritual Experience in Recovery: A closer look," Journal of Ministry in the Addictions, (99): 53-59; auth, "Prometheus as a Model for Alcoholism Recovery," Context: Journal of the ACC, 99; auth, "Alcoholism Recovery: A Mythic, Psychological and Spiritual Path," Counselor Magazine, 00; auth, "Behavioral Strategies: Building Systems," ERIC Pub, 00. **CONTACT ADDRESS** Dept Psychol, Univ of Louisiana, Lafayette, Box 43131, Lafayette, LA 70504-001. **EMAIL** sandoz@louisiana.edu

SANDY, LEO

PERSONAL Born 08/29/1943, Lowell, MS, m, 1965, 2 children **DISCIPLINE** EDUCATION **EDUCATION** Univ Mass, BA, 70; Boston Univ, EdM; EdD. **CAREER** Prof, Ribier Col, 84-96; assoc prof, Plymouth State Col, 96-. **HONORS AND AWARDS** Who's Who Among Am Teachers; Who's Who in Am Educ; Who's Who in Staff Develop Serv for Pub and Private Sch. **MEMBERSHIPS** Pi Lambda Theta; Assoc of Supr and Curric Develop; Phi Delta Kappa; Peace Studies Assoc; Veterans for Peace. **RESEARCH** College pedagogy, parenting, humor dervelopment. **SELECTED PUBLICATIONS** Auth, "Violence in America: Its Contributors", Insight 1.1 (92): 59-64; auth, "Parent Education: An Ounce of Prevention", Insight 1.2 (94): 45-51; auth, "A Definition of Peace", Insight 1.2 (94): 117-122; auth, "Human Development: Two Steps Forward, One Step Back", Insight 3, (96): 187-194; auth, "JROTC: The Antithesis of Education" Veterans for Peace J 38, (97): auth,

"Good Schools", Phi Delta Kappa Newsletter, Plymouth State Col, (97): auth, "The Effective Teacher", Phi Delta Kappa Newsletter, Plymouth State Col, (98): auth, "Creating a Culture of Peace: Notes from the Hague Appeal for Peace, May 1999, TESOL Matters, (99); auth, "The Permeable Classroom", J on Excellence in Col Teaching 93, (forthcoming); auth, "Faculty Development Regarding Pedagogy: Faculty Perceptions at New Hampshire Colleges and Universities", J of Staff, Program and org Develop (forthcoming). **CONTACT ADDRESS** Dept Educ, Plymouth State Col of the Univ System of New Hampshire, 17 High St, Plymouth, NH 03264. **EMAIL** lsandy@mail.plymouth.edu

SANSONE, FRANK A.
PERSONAL Born 10/23/1942, Baltimore, MD, m, 1987, 2 children **DISCIPLINE** SOCIAL WORK **EDUCATION** Towson Univ, BS, 65; W Va Univ, MSW, 76; Va Commonwealth Univ, PhD, 93. **CAREER** Instr, Allegheny Col, 67-68; Adj instr, Hamot Hospital School of Nursing, 68-70; Instr, PaState Univ, 68-70; Towson Univ, BS, 65; Va Commonwealth Univ, MSW, 76; PhD, 93; Asst Prof, Univ W Fla, 93-. **HONORS AND AWARDS** Grant, Nat Inst of Mental Health, 72-74; Grant, Law Enforcement Assistance Administration, 77-78; Grant, Nat Commission for Employment Policy, 88-89; Grant, Nat Commission for Employment Policy, 89-90; Grant, UWF Small Grants program, 98; Pace Awd, 96; Who's Who among Am Teachers; Distinguished Teaching Awd, Univ W Fla, 94. **MEMBERSHIPS** Phi Alpha Nat Soc Work Honor Soc, Pi Gamma Mu Nat Soc Sci Honor Soc. **RESEARCH** Social support theory; Support networks, Welfare to work and job training policy. **SELECTED PUBLICATIONS** Auth, "Assets Group Model: Empowerment through Investment Clubs," in Strengthening Resiliency through Group Work, forthcoming; auth, "BSW Faculty Workload and Scholarship Expectations for Tenure," Journal of Baccalaureate Social Work, forthcoming; auth, "Trauma of children in a Residential Wilderness Treatment Program," Traumatology, (98): 1-13; auth, "Social Support's Contributions to Reduced Welfare Dependency: Program outcomes of long term welfare recipients," Journal of Sociology and Social Welfare, (98): 105-126; auth, "A follow-up Evaluation of a Program for long Term AFDC Recipients: The Relationship of Case Management and Social Support to Reduced Welfare Dependency, 97. **CONTACT ADDRESS** Div of Soc Work & Aging Studies, Univ of West Florida, 11000 Univ Pkwy, Pensacola, FL 32514-5751. **EMAIL** fsansone@uwf.edu

SANTANA, DEBORAH BERMAN
DISCIPLINE ETHNIC STUDIES **EDUCATION** San Francisco State Univ, BA, 86; Univ Calif, Berkeley, MA, 89, PhD, 93. **CAREER** Asst prof; field and archival research on commun power and sustainable develop, funded by the Fac Res Awd Prog, SUNY-Albany, 94; ciriacy-wantrup postdr fel, Univ Calif, Berkeley, 94-95; res to create a curric on develop and the env, Title VI grant from the US Dept Educ, 93-94. **HONORS AND AWARDS** Current Reviews for Acad Libraries Outstanding Acad Bk award, 97; founding mem, 98 gp, 94-. **MEMBERSHIPS** Asn of Am Geographers; Latin Am Studies Asn; Puerto Rican Studies Asn. **RESEARCH** Sustainable development; Labor; trade; migration; env; political ecology of natural resources; population; development policies; historical legacy of racism and colonialism; race; class; gender and the env; local responses to global processes; latin America; African diaspora in the Americas; US current and former Pacific Island possessions; US communities of color. **SELECTED PUBLICATIONS** Auth, Kicking off the bootstraps: env, develop, and commun power in PR, ser Society, Env, and Place, Tucson: Univ Ariz Press, 96; Geographers, colonialism, and development strategies: the case of PR, Spec issue on env racism, In Urban Geog 17:5, 96; El desarrollo economico, la lucha ambiental y el podereo comunitario en PR, In Homines 17:2, 94; Colonialism, resistance, and the search for alternatives: the enval movement in PR, In Race, Poverty and the Env VI:1, 94; bk chap, Envalism and the charge of genocide, USA on trial: the int tribunal on indigenous and oppressed peoples, Chicago: Ed Coque, 96; auth, "Puerto Rico's Operation Bootstrap: Colonist Roots of a persistent model for development," Revista Geografica, No. 124 (98); auth, "No Somos unicos: The Status question from Manila to San Juan," Centro 11:1 (99); auth, "The Western Lands of Vieques: community revival or colonial land grab?" Que Ondee Sola 28:9 (00). **CONTACT ADDRESS** Dept of Ethnic Studies, Mills Col, 5000 MacArthur Blvd, Oakland, CA 94613-1301. **EMAIL** santana@mills.edu

SANTILLI, NICHOLAS R.
PERSONAL Born 03/08/1957, Cleveland, OH, m, 1981, 2 children **DISCIPLINE** PSYCHOLOGY **EDUCATION** Univ Toledo, BA, 79; MeD, 82; Catholic Univ Am, PhD, 86. **CAREER** Adj asst prof, Mt Vernon Col, 84-86; vis asst prof, Augustana Col, 86-87; asst prof, Millersville Univ, 87-88; vis asst prof, John Carroll Univ, 89-92; asst prof, 92-; ch, 95-; assoc prof, 98-. **HONORS AND AWARDS** Fac Dev Fel; Ameritech Found Grant; Graeul Fac Fel. **MEMBERSHIPS** APS; Jean Piaget Soc; SRCD; SRA; NAHPN; NSEE. **SELECTED PUBLICATIONS** Coauth, "Enhancing moral growth: Is communication the key?" Adolescence 27 (92): 145-160; coauth, "Development of athletes' conceptions of sport officials' authority," J Sport Exercise Psychol 14 (94): 392-404; coauth, "Sex differences in perceptions of spousal abuse," in Handbook of Gender Research, ed. R Crandall, J Soc Behav Personality 11 (96): 229-238; coauth, "John Carroll University: A model for assessing student impact," in Establishing Universities as citizens: Towards the scholarship of engagement, ed. M Romman (Indianapolis, IN: Indiana Campus Compact, 98); coauth, "What Factors Sustain School-Initiated Professional Development for Deep Understanding?" Teaching and Teacher Education, in press; coauth, "Measuring individuation in late adolescence: The Adolescent Individuation Measure," J Soc Behav Personality, forthcoming; coauth, "Parental indicators of children's psychosocial functioning," J Soc Behav Personality, forthcoming; coauth, "Children's perceptions of social rule violations: Could God make a wrong a right?" forthcoming. **CONTACT ADDRESS** Dept Psychology, John Carroll Univ, 20700 N Park Blvd, Cleveland, OH 44118. **EMAIL** santilli@jcu.edu

SARBIN, THEODORE R.
PERSONAL Born 05/08/1911, Cleveland, OH, w, 1949, 3 children **DISCIPLINE** PSYCHOLOGY **EDUCATION** Ohio St Univ, BA, 36; Western Reserve Univ, MA, 37; Ohio St Univ, PhD, 41. **CAREER** Counr, 38-41, Univ Minn; post doc fel, 41-43, SSRC, Univ Chicago; supvr psychol, 43-44, Illinois St; indep practice, 44-49; clin psychol, 46-69, Veterans Admin; prof, psychol & criminol, 49-69, Berkley, 69-76, Santa Cruz, emer prof, 76-90, Univ Calif; res psychol, 87-98, Security Res Ctr, Monterey CA. **HONORS AND AWARDS** Sr Fulbright award, Oxford Univ, 61-62; fel, John Simon Guggenheim Found, 65-66; fel, Ctr for Advance Stud, Wesleyan Univ, 68-69; Clement Staff Essay Awd, Psychoanalytic Rev, 71; fel, Ctr for Hum, Wesleyan Univ, 75; APA, div 30 Awd for dist contr to Scientific Hypnosis, 93; Am Psychological Asn Division 8 Henry A Murray Awd (Society for Personality and Social Psychology); Am Psychol Asn Division 24 Awd for Distinguished Theoretical and Philosophical Contributions to Psychology. **MEMBERSHIPS** Fel Amer Psychol Asn; Fel Amer Psychol Soc; Am Sociol Asn. **RESEARCH** Narrative stud; emotional life; deviance; imagining. **SELECTED PUBLICATIONS** Co-ed, Varieties of Scientific Contextualism, Context Press 93; auth, The Narrative as a Root Metaphor for Contextualism, Ibid, 93; auth, Whither Hypnosis? A Rhetorical Analysis, Contemp Hypnosis, 93; auth, Steps to the Narratory Principle: an Autobiographical Essay, Life & Story: Autobiographies for a Narrative Psychology, Greenwood, 93; co-ed, Constructing the Social, Sage Pub, 94; auth, Prologue to Constructing the Social, Ibid, 94; art, Dissociation: State, Trait, or Skill, Contemp Hypnosis, 94; co-ed, Citizen Espionage: Studies in Trust and Betrayal, Praeger, 94; auth, A Criminological Theory of Citizen Espionage, Ibid, 94; art, On the Belief That One Body May Be Host to Two or More Personalities, Intl J of Clin & Exper Hypnosis, 95; art, A narrative approach to "Repressed Memories", J of Narrative & Personal Hist, 95; art, Emotional Life, Rhetoric, and Roles, J of Narrative & Personal Hist, 95; auth, Deconstructing Stereotypes: Homosexuals and Military Policy, Out in Force: Sexual Orientation and the Military, Univ Chicago Press, 96; art, The Poetics of Identity, Theory & Psychol, 97; art, On the Futility of Psychiatric Dagnostic Manuals (DSMs) and the Return of Personal Agency, Applied & Prev Psychol, 97; art, Multiple Personality Disorder: Fact or Artifact?, Current Opinion in Psych, 97; art, Hypnosis as a Conversation: Believed-in imaginings, Contemp Hypnosis, 97; coauth, Conventional and Unconventional Narratives of Emotional Life, in Emotions in Psychopathology: Theory & Res, Oxford Univ Press, 98; coauth, Nontraditional Ways of Classifying Mental Disorders, Encycl of Mental Health vol 1, Acad Press, 98; coauth, The Narrative Construction of Emotional Life, What Develops in Emotional Development? Plenum Press, 98; co-ed, Believed-in Imaginings: The Narrative Construction of Reality, APA, 98; auth, Believing and Imagining: A Narrative Perspective, Ibid, 98; auth, The Poetic Construction of Reality and Other Explanatory Categories, Ibid, 98; auth, The social construction of truth, Journal of Theorectical and Philosophical Psychology, 18 (98): 144-150. **CONTACT ADDRESS** 25515 Hatton Rd, Carmel, CA 93923. **EMAIL** trs85@aol.com

SARLES, HARVEY BURTON
PERSONAL Born 07/12/1933, Buffalo, NY, m, 1956, 2 children **DISCIPLINE** CULTURAL STUDIES, COMPARATIVE LITERATURE **EDUCATION** Univ Buffalo, BA, 54; MA, 59; Univ Chicago, PhD, 66. **CAREER** Mathematician, Cornell Aeronaut Lab, 55-56; res asst Ling, Univ Chicago, 60-61; asst prof Anthrop & Ling, Sch Med, Univ Pittsburgh, 62-66; from assoc prof to prof Anthrop, Univ Minn, Minneapolis, 66-88; Leverhulme vis fel ethnoling, Univ Sussex, 70-71; consult, Allegheny County Ment Health/Ment Retardation, 73-74; vis prof Ling, State Univ NYork, Buffalo, 74; vis prof Sci, Tech & Soc, Cornell Univ, 79; prof Cult Studies & Comp Lit, Univ Minn, 92-. **HONORS AND AWARDS** Invited Speaker, Univ Chicago Anthrop Dept 50th Anniversary, 79. **MEMBERSHIPS** MLA. **RESEARCH** Pragmatism; cultural critique; teaching as dialogue; language and human nature. **SELECTED PUBLICATIONS** Auth, Language and Human Nature, Univ Minn, 85; auth, Teaching As Dialogue, Univ Press of Am, 93; auth, "Ethology and the Philosophy of Language," in Handbuch Sprachphilosophie, ed. M. Dascal et al (Berlin: De Gruyter, 95); auth, "Essentialism and Evolutionism in the Nature of Language: The Biology of Language," in The Biology of Language, ed. Stanislaw Puppel (Amsterdam: John Benamins, 95); Toward an Anthropology of the Ordinary: Seeing with New Lenses, In Ethics and Cultural Diversity, ed, L Olive, Univ Nacional Autonoma de Mexico, publishing in Spanish, 95; Is Life But a Dream? The World as Text or Text as the World, Religious Humanism: vol XXX, nos 1-2, 96; The Emergent University, Humanism Today, vol 11, 97; auth, Nietzschecs Prophecy: The Crisis in Meaning, Humanity Press, 01. **CONTACT ADDRESS** Univ of Minnesota, Twin Cities, 9 Pleasant St. SE, 350 Folwell Hall, Minneapolis, MN 55455. **EMAIL** sarle001@tc.umn.edu

SARNOFF, SUSAN
DISCIPLINE SOCIAL WORK **EDUCATION** Adelphi Univ, DSW, 94. **CAREER** Asst prof and grad chair, Ohio Univ Dept of Soc Work. **HONORS AND AWARDS** Rita Paprin Scholar. **MEMBERSHIPS** CSWE, NASW. **RESEARCH** Technology, ethics, victim compensation. **SELECTED PUBLICATIONS** Auth, Paying for Crime, Praeger (96). **CONTACT ADDRESS** Dept Soc Work, Ohio Univ, Morton Hall 522, Athens, OH 45701. **EMAIL** sarnoff@ohio.edu

SASS, LOUISE A.
PERSONAL Born 01/10/1949, New York, NY, m, 2 children **DISCIPLINE** PSYCHOLOGY **EDUCATION** Harvard Col, BA, 70; Univ Calif, PhD, 79. **CAREER** Lecturer to Instr, Harvard Med School, 87-86; Asst Prof, Holy Cross Col, 79-83; Asst Prof to Prof, Rutgers Univ, 83-. **HONORS AND AWARDS** Inst for Advanced Study, Princeton, 82-83; NEH Fel, 82-83; Fel, NYU, 86-; Fel, World Economic Forum , 00. **MEMBERSHIPS** Am Psychol Asn, Am Asn for the Advancement of Sci, NY Acad of Sci, World Fed for Mental Health, Asn for the Advancement of Philos and Psychiat, Inst for Hist of Psychiat. **RESEARCH** Schizophrenia, schizoid conditions, and related disorders; Modernism and postmodernism; dilemmas of the modern self; Philosophy of psychology and of psychoanalysis. **SELECTED PUBLICATIONS** Auth, Madness and Modernism: Insanity in the Light of Modern Art, Literature, and Thought, Basic Books, 92; auth, The paradoxes of Delusion: Wittgenstein, Schreber, and the Schizophrenic Mind, Cornell Univ Press, 94; co-ed, Hermeneutics and Psychological Theory: Interpretive Approaches to Personality, Psychopathology and Psychotherapy, Rutgers Univ Press; auth, "The Catastrophes of heaven,": Modernism, Primitivism, and the Madness of Anonin Artaud," Modernism/Modernity, (96): 73-92; auth, "Schizophrenia, Self-consciousness, and the Modern Mind," Journal of Consciousness Studies, (98): 543-565; auth, "The Borderline Personality," The New York Times Magazine, (82): 66-67; auth, "Anthropology's Native Problems: Revisionism in the Field," Harper's Magazine, (86): 49-57; auth, "Ambiguity is of the Essence: The Relevance of Hermeneutics for Psychoanalysis," in Psychoanalytic Versions of the Human Condition and Clinical Practice, New York Univ Press, 98; auth, "A Fugitive Condition: The rise and fall of a convenient mental disorder, 99. **CONTACT ADDRESS** Dept Psychol, Rutgers, The State Univ of New Jersey, PO Box 6836, Piscataway, NJ 08855. **EMAIL** LouisSass@aol.com

SASSEN, SASKIA
PERSONAL Born 01/05/1949, The Hague, Netherlands, m, 1 child **DISCIPLINE** SOCIOLOGY, POLITICAL ECONOMY **EDUCATION** Univ Notre Dame, Ind, PhD, 74; Post-Doctorate, Center for Int Affairs, Harvard Univ, 74-75. **CAREER** Prof, Queens Col and The Grad Sch, CUNY, NY, 76-88; prof, Columbia Univ, 85-98; prof, Univ Chicago, 98-; res fel, Am Bar Found, 98-. **HONORS AND AWARDS** Fels and res grants from Ford, Tinker, Russell Sage, Reuson, and other founds; Distinguished Profs and Endowed Lectureships at various institutions (Clark, SUNY-Binghampton, Inst for Advanced Studies Vienna, Univ of Toronto Law Sch, etc.; Resident Scholar, The Ctr for Advanced Behav Studies, The Russel Sage Found, The Woodrow Wilson Ctr for Scholars, The Ctr for Int Studies of Harvard Univ, etc. **MEMBERSHIPS** ASA, APSA, ISA. **RESEARCH** The global economy, cities, immigration, digitilization, the state and globalization. **SELECTED PUBLICATIONS** Auth, Migranten, Siedler, Fluchtlinge: Von der Massenauswanderung zur Festung Europa, Frankfurt: Fiuscher Verlag (96, English, The New Press, 99, Italian, Fetrinelli, 99); auth, "The New Centrality: The Impact of Telematics and Globalization," in W. S. Saunders, et al, eds, Reflections on Architectural Practices in the Nineties, Princeton Architectural Press (96): 206-218; auth, "New Employment Regimes in Cities: Impacts on Immigrant Workers," New Community, Vol 22, no 4 (Oct 96): 579-594); auth, "Toward a Feminist Analytics of the Global Economy," Indiana J of Global Legal Studies, Vol 4, No 1 (fall 96): 7-41; auth, Losing Control? Sovereignty in an Age of Globalization, The 1995 Columbia Univ Schoff Memorial Lectures, New York: Columbia Univ Press (96); auth, Globalization and Its Discontents, New York: New York Press (98); auth, "The De-Nationalization of Time and Space," invited contrib, Millenial Issue of Public Culture (forthcoming 2000); auth, invited contrib, Millenial Issue of The Annals of the British Asn of Geogs (forthcoming 2000); auth, "Immigration policy in a global economy," invited contrib, Millenial Issue of The Annals of the Am Acad of Arts and Scis (forthcoming 2000); auth, "The Global City" Theoretical and Methodological Elements," invited contrib, Milleneial Issue of the British J of Sociol (forthcoming 2000). **CONTACT ADDRESS** Soc Sci Bldg, Univ of Chicago, 1126 E 59th St, Chicago, IL 60637. **EMAIL** ssassen@midway.uchicago.edu

SATLER, GAIL R.
PERSONAL Born 08/19/1951, New York, NY, s DISCIPLINE SOCIOLOGY EDUCATION Stony Brook Univ, BA, 72; Queens Col, CUNY, MA, 76; Grad Center, CUNY, PhD, 85. CAREER Asst prof, Hobart & William Smith Cols, 84-85; instr, Nassau Community Col, 91-94; adj asst to assoc prof, Hofstra Univ, 86-. HONORS AND AWARDS Presidential Res Awd, Hofstra Univ, 98. MEMBERSHIPS Am Sociol Assoc; Food Scholars. RESEARCH Urban design. SELECTED PUBLICATIONS Auth, Frank Lloyd Wright's Living space: Architecture's Fourth Dimension, Northern IL Univ Pr, 99; auth, "Taking a Global View: placing rather than replacing cultures and conceptions of building in the architecture of Frank Lloyd Wright", J of Archit Educ 53.1, (99); auth, ""Restaurants: Tasting the Global Economy", Cities A to Z, ed Steve Pile, Routledge (forthcoming). CONTACT ADDRESS Dept Soc Sci, Hofstra Univ, 211 Roosevelt Hall, 130 Hofstra Univ, Hempstead, NY 11549-1300.

SATO, TORU
PERSONAL Born 05/31/1967, Beirut, Lebanon, m, 1994 DISCIPLINE PSYCHOLOGY EDUCATION Kwanseigakuin Univ, BA, 91; York Univ, MA, 93; PhD, 99. CAREER Instr, Morehead State Univ, 98-99; Asst Prof, Morehead State Univ, 99-. HONORS AND AWARDS Doctoral Feel, Soc SCI and Humanities Roes Coun of Can, 96-97. MEMBERSHIPS Am Psychol Assoc. RESEARCH Personality and cross-cultural psychology. SELECTED PUBLICATIONS Auth, "Type I and Type II Error in Multiple Comparisons," J of Psychol, 130 (96): 293-302; coauth, "Vulnerability Factors in Depression: The Facets of Sociotropy and Autonomy," J of Psychopathology and Behav Assessment, 19 (97): 41-62; auth, "Seasonal Affective Disorder and Phototherapy: A Critical Review," Professional Psychol: Roes and Practice, 28 (97): 164-168; coauth, ""Agency and Communion: The Relationship Between Therapy and Culture," Cult Diversity and Ment Health, 4 (98): 278-290; coauth, "The Relationship Between Collective Self-Esteem and Self-Construal in Japan and Canada," J of Soc Psychol, 139 (99): 426-435; auth, "Seasonal Affective Disorder," in Encycl of Human Emotions (NY: MacMillan, forthcoming); auth, "Family Allocentrism Scale," in Handbk of Psychol Tests (Wales, UK: Edwin Mellen Pr, forthcoming). CONTACT ADDRESS Dept Psychol, Morehead State Univ, 150 University Blvd, Morehead, KY 40351.

SAULNIER, CHRISTINE F.
PERSONAL Born 11/13/1950, Medford, MA, d, 1 child DISCIPLINE SOCIAL WORK EDUCATION Mich State Univ, BS, 80; Boston Univ, MA, MSW, 85; Univ Calif, Berkeley, PhD, 94. CAREER Prog dir, QMRP, East Middlesex Residential Progs for the Mentally Retarded, Melrose, MA, 84-86; soc worker, Perkins Sch for the Blind, 86-88; dir soc services, Quigley Mem Hosp/Sloldier's Home, Chelsea, MA, 88-89; asst prof, SUNY Buffalo, 94-97, chair, 97; asst prof, Boston Univ, 97-. HONORS AND AWARDS Fac develop Awd for curriculum innovation using tech, Boston Univ Sch of Social Work; res for two projects funded by the Community and Difference Group, Baldy Ctr for Law and Social Policy; Certificate of Appreciation, Iroquois Job Corps; listing, Who's Who Online; NIH, Alcohol Res training grant, 92-94; Fel, Boston Univ Sch of Social Work; Mich State Univ, grad "with honor"; Lansing Community Col, grad "summa cum laude"; Univ Calif, Berkeley: Regents Fel, Provost's Res Fund Awd. MEMBERSHIPS Asn for the Advan of Social Work with Groups, Coun Social Work Ed, Nat Asn Social Workers, Nat Lesbian and Gay Health Asn. RESEARCH The needs of women, particularly those with alcohol and drug problems; current thinking among feminist scholars; research on social work education. SELECTED PUBLICATIONS Auth, "Twelve Steps for everyone? Lesbians in Al-Anon," in T. Powell, ed, Understanding Self-Help Organizations: Frameworks and Findings, Newbury Park, CA: Sage (94); auth, Feminist theories and social work: Approaches and applications, Binghamton, NY: Haworth Press (96, paperback, 99); auth, "Alcohol problems and marginalization: Social group work with lesbians," Soc Work with Groups, 20(3), 37-59 (97); auth, "Prevalence of suicide attepts and suicidal ideation among lesbian and gay youth," J of Gay & Lesbian Soc Services, 8(3), 51-68 (98); auth, "Choosing a provider: A community survey of what is important to lesbians," Families in Soc, 80(3), 254-262 (99); auth, "Policy practice: Training direct service social workers to get involved," J of Teaching in Social Work, 20(1/2) (in press); auth, "Incorporating feminist theory into social work: Group work practice examples," Soc Work with Groups, 23(1) (in press); auth, "Deciding who to see: Lesbians discuss their preferences in physical and mental health care providers," Soc Work (in press); auth, "A preliminary dimension analysis of women-specified alcohol intervention programs: A study of specialized services in Western New York," Substance Use & Misuse, 35 (in press); auth, "Feminist theories," in N. Coady and P. Lehmann, eds, Theoretical perspectives in direct social work practice: An eclectic-generalist approach, NY,NY: Springer (in press). CONTACT ADDRESS Sch Social Work, Boston Univ, 264 Bay State Rd, Boston, MA 02215. EMAIL cfsauln@bu.edu

SAUNDERS, GEORGE R.
PERSONAL Born 02/14/1946, CA, m, 1994, 2 children DISCIPLINE ANTHROPOLOGY EDUCATION Claremont Mc-Kenna Col, BA, 67; Univ Calif San Diego, MA, 72; PhD, 91. CAREER Asst to full prof, Lawrence Univ, 77-. MEMBERSHIPS Am Anthropol Asn, Soc for Anthropol of Europe, Soc for Psych Anthropol, Soc Lin Anthropol. RESEARCH Religion, Italy, India. SELECTED PUBLICATIONS Auth, "Un appuntamento mancato: Ernesto de Marino e l'antropologia statunitense," in Ernesto de Martino nella cultura europea, (98): 35-38; auth, "The Magic of the south: Popular Religion and elite Catholicism in Italian Ethnology," in Italy's Southern Question: Orientalism in One Country, (98): 177-202; auth, "L'etnocentrismo critico e l'etnologia di Ernesto de Martino," Ossimore: Periodico di antropologia e scinze umane, (95): 59-74; auth, "The Crisis of Presence in Italian Pentecostal Conversion," American Ethnologist, (95): 324-340; auth, "Critical Ethnocentrism and the Ethnology of Ernesto De Martin," American Anthropologist, (93): 875-893; auth, "Ernesto De Marino," International Dictionary of Anthropologists, (91); auth, "Politica e religione a Valbella (Cuneo)," Religioni e Societa, (91): 123-137; ed, Culture and Christianity: The dialects of Transformation, Westport, 88. CONTACT ADDRESS Dept Anthropol, Lawrence Univ, PO Box 599, Appleton, WI 54912-0599. EMAIL george.r.sauners@lawrence.edu

SAUNDERS, MAUDERIE HANCOCK
PERSONAL Born 06/13/1929, Bartlesville, OK DISCIPLINE EDUCATION EDUCATION Langston Univ Langston OK, BA 1947; Univ of OK Norman, MEd 1950; Univ of OK, PhD education & Psychology, 1961; Univ of Chicago, 1965. CAREER Howard Univ, coordr special educ prof of educ 79-, chemn & prof of educ psychoednl studies dept 76-79, prof dir special educ 1974-76; Howard Univ Center for the Study of Handicapped Children, asst dir 1973-74; Eastern Il Univ Charleston IL, prof 1970-73; WV State Coll Inst, prof 1966-70; Minot State Coll Minot ND, prof 1963-66; So Univ Baton Rouge, asso prof 1960-62; OK City Public Schools, visiting counselor school psychology 1950-59; Child Serv State Dept of Welfare Minot ND, psychol 1963-66; WV State Dept Mental Health, psychology consultant 1966-70; WV St Dept of Health. HONORS AND AWARDS Listed in black OK res guide Archives of OK 1950; first black wom to rec PhD Univ of OK Norman 1961. MEMBERSHIPS Mem Am Psychol Assn 1961-; mem Alpha Kappa Alpha 1972; sponsor Chartered Chap Eta Gamma East IL campus 1972; spons Charter Chap #253 Counc of Except Child Howard Univ 1976. SELECTED PUBLICATIONS "Teach the Educ Mental Retard Reading" Curr The Pointer 1964; outst W Virginians 1969; analys of cult diff Jour of Negro Educ 1970, and other publications. CONTACT ADDRESS Professor of Education, Howard Univ, 2400 6th St, NW, Washington, VT 20059.

SAVELSBERG, JOACHIM
PERSONAL Born 03/29/1951, Ahlen, Germany, m, 1986, 2 children DISCIPLINE SOCIOLOGY EDUCATION Univ Cologne, BA, 75; MA, 78; Univ Trier, PhD, 82. CAREER Instr & Res Sci, Univ Trier, 78-82; Res Fel, Johns Hopkins Univ, 82-83; Res Sci, Univ Bremen, 83-86; Asst Prof, Univ Minn, 89-94; Assoc Prof, Univ Minn, 94-. HONORS AND AWARDS John F. Kennedy Fel, Harvard Univ, 86; Summer Grant, Univ Minn, 91; Andrew W. Mellen Grant, Univ Minn, 91; Distinguished Book Awd, Am Soc of Criminology, 95; Outstanding Fac Awd, Univ Minn, 99. MEMBERSHIPS ASA, Am Soc of Criminology, Law and Soc Assoc, Soc for the study of Soc Probs. RESEARCH Social conditions of crime and punishment, comparative macro-sociology. SELECTED PUBLICATIONS Auth, "Gun Control in Germany," NY Law Sch J of Int and Comparative Law, vol 15, nos 2&3 (95): 259-263; auth, "Struwwelpeter at One Hundred and Fifty: Norms, Control and Discipline in the Civilizing Process," The Lion and the Unicorn, vol 20, no 2 (96): 181-200; auth, "Controlling Violence: Criminal Justice, Society and Lessons from the US," Crime, Law and Soc Change, 30 (98): 185-203; auth, "Knowledge, Domination and Criminal Punishment Revisited: Incorporating State Socialism," Punishment and Soc, vol 1, no 1 (99): 45-70; auth, "Linking Mean Streets with Adverse Structures," Theoret Criminology, vol 4, no 2 (00); auth, "Contradictions, Law and State Socialism," Law and Soc Inquiry, vol 25, no 4 (forthcoming). CONTACT ADDRESS Dept Sociol, Univ of Minnesota, Twin Cities, 267 19th Ave S, 909 Social Services Bldg, Minneapolis, MN 55455. EMAIL savelsbg@soc.umn.edu

SAVONA, JEANNELLE
PERSONAL Born 07/31/1929, Bordeaux, France DISCIPLINE WOMENS STUDIES EDUCATION Bordeaux Univ, Dip d'Etudes; Doct d'Universito. CAREER Lectr, Univ Leicester, 55-56; lectr, Univ St Andrews, 57-59; Fulbright instr, Stephen's Col, 61-63; lectr, asst prof to assoc prof to Brock prof, Trinity Col Univ Toronto, 63-. HONORS AND AWARDS IWS Hon Mem. MEMBERSHIPS MLA; CAUCTF. RESEARCH Women's studies; French theater; lesbian and gay studies. SELECTED PUBLICATIONS Auth, Jean Genet, Macmillan Pr; auth, Theatralite Ecriture et Mise en Scene; auth, Le Juif Dans le Roman American Contemporary, Dieder. CONTACT ADDRESS 100 Quebec Ave, Apt 1711, Toronto, ON, Canada M6P 4B8. EMAIL jsavona@class.utoronto.ca

SAWYER, WILLIAM GREGORY
PERSONAL Born 11/06/1954, Columbus, OH, s DISCIPLINE EDUCATION EDUCATION Eastern MI Univ, Ypsilanti, MI, 72; Mount Union Coll, Alliance, OH, BA, 76; Eastern New Mexico Univ, Portales, NM, MA, 78; Univ of North TX, Denton, TX, PhD, 86. CAREER Amarillo Coll, Amarillo, TX, communication instructor, 78-80; Univ of North TX, Denton, TX, teaching fellow, 80-83, hall dir, 83-85, coordinator of interculture services, 85-86, asst dean of students, 86-88, assoc dean of students, 88-90, dean of students, 90-; Fla Gulf Coast Univ, Chief Student Affairs Officer & Dean of Students, 95-. HONORS AND AWARDS "Top Prof," Mortar Bd Honors Society, 87-92; Outstanding Contributions to the Minority Community, TX Woman's Univ; Outstanding Service to the African Community, The Progressive Black Student Org; The Texas Awd for Outstanding Vision and Leadership in Education. MEMBERSHIPS Pres, TX Assn of Coll & Univ Personnel Administrators, 91-92, pres elect, 90-91, vice pres, 89-90, minority comm chair, 87-89; mem, TX Assn of Black Professionals, 88-92; Texas State Sickle Cell Foundation, board member; Minority Caucus Advisor Unit, 85-; Progressive Black Student Organization, University of North Texas, advisor, 85-. CONTACT ADDRESS Student Services, Florida Gulf Coast Univ, Roy E. McTarnaghan Hall for Student Services 137, Fort Myers, FL 33908. EMAIL GSAWYER@FGCU.EDU

SAXBY, WILLIAM R.
DISCIPLINE PSYCHOLOGY EDUCATION Univ Vermont, BA, 72; Fullerton Theol Sem, MA, 78; Univ Vermont, PhD, 81. CAREER Res asst, ABETS, 72-75; teach asst, 75-78; instr, 74-78; vis asst prof, 80-82; Univ Vermont; asst prof, Nyack Col, 92-95; adj prof, 92-; ch, 95-97; dept hd, 94-; assoc prof, 95-98; prof, 98-. HONORS AND AWARDS USPHS/NIAAA Res Fel; Heublein Found Fel; Who's Who in Am Teach. SELECTED PUBLICATIONS Coauth, "Effects of Marihuana and Alcohol in Humans After Self Determined Dosing in a Social Setting," in Marihuana, ed. D Harvey (Oxford: IRL Press, 85) CONTACT ADDRESS Dept Psychology, Nyack Col, 1 South Blvd, Nyack, NY 10960. EMAIL saxbyw@nyack.edu

SCANLON, JENNIFER
PERSONAL Born 12/23/1958, New York, NY DISCIPLINE WOMENS STUDIES EDUCATION SUNY, BS, 80; Univ Del, MA, 82; Binghamton Univ, MA, 86; PhD, 89. CAREER Asst prof to prof, Plattsburgh State Univ, 89-. HONORS AND AWARDS Phi Eta Sigma, 92; Chancellors Awd, 96; Fulbright Schol, Trinidad and Tobago, 98-99. MEMBERSHIPS OAH; ASA; AHA; NWSA. RESEARCH Women and popular and consumer culture, feminist pedagogy. SELECTED PUBLICATIONS Auth, "Educating the Living, Remembering the Dead: The Montreal Massacre as Metaphor", Feminist Teacher 8.2 (94): 75-79; auth, "Culturally Diverse or Culturally Divisive: Entering the Debate on Multicultural Education", Diversity 3 (95): 9-17; auth, Inarticulate Longings: The Ladies' Home Journal, Gender and the Promises of Consumer Culture, Routledge, (NY) 95; coauth, American Women Historians, 1700s-1990s: A Biographical Dictionary, Greenwood (Westport, CT), 96; auth, "Empathy Education: Teaching About Women and Poverty in the Introductory Women's Studies Classroom", Radical Teacher 48 (96): 7-10; auth, "Material, Girls: Women and Popular Culture in the 20th Century", Radical Hist Rev 66, (96): 172-183; ed, Significant Contemporary American Feminists: A Biocritical Sourcebook, Greenwood Pr, (Westport, CT), 99; ed, Gender and Consumer Culture Reader, NY Univ Pr, (NY), 00. CONTACT ADDRESS Dept Womens Studies, SUNY, Col at Plattsburgh, 101 Broad St, Plattsburgh, NY 12901.

SCHAEFER, CHARLES
PERSONAL Born 11/15/1933, m, 1967, 2 children DISCIPLINE PSYCHOLOGY EDUCATION Fordham Univ, PhD, 67. CAREER Prof, Fairleigh Dickinson Univ, 85-. MEMBERSHIPS APA. RESEARCH Play and play therapy. SELECTED PUBLICATIONS Coauth, Clinical Handbook of Anxiety Disorders in Children and Adolescents, Jason Aronson, 95; coauth, Family Play Therapy, Jason Aronson, 94; coauth, The Quotable Play Therapist, Jason Aronson, 94; coauth, Handbook of Play Therapy, John Wiley, 94; auth, Clinical Handbook of Sleep Disorders in Children, Jason Aronson, 95; auth, Words of Wisdom for Parents, Jason Aronson, 96; auth, Toilet Training Without Tears, Penguin Putnam, 97; auth, Favorite Play Therapy Techniques, Jason Aronson, 97; coauth, The Playing Cure: Individualized Play Therapy for Specific Childhood Problems, Jason Aronson, 97; auth, Handbook of Parent Training, John Wiley, 98; auth, Selective Mutism: Advances in Treatment, Jason Aronson, 99; co-ed, Helping Parents Solve Their Children's Behavior Problems, Jason Aronson, 98; coauth, How to Talk to Teens about Really Important Things, Jossey-Bass Pub, 99; auth, Innovative Psychotherapy Techniques in Child & Adolescent Therapy, John Wiley, 99; auth, Psychotherapy Groups for Children: Adapting Group Processes for Specific Problems, Jason Aronson, 99. CONTACT ADDRESS Dept Psychology, Fairleigh Dickinson Univ, Teaneck-Hackensack, 1000 River Rd, Teaneck, NJ 07666.

SCHARF, BERTRAM
PERSONAL Born 03/03/1931, New York, NY, m, 1965, 2 children DISCIPLINE EXPERIMENTAL PSYCHOLOGY

EDUCATION Harvard, PhD. CAREER Prof of Pschology, Northeastern Univ, 58-98, res prof, Emeritus, 98-. HONORS AND AWARDS Fel, ASA, 71, AAAS, 76; Distinguished Service Awd of MA Sp Hearing Asn, 77; Fechner Medal, ISP, 95. MEMBERSHIPS Acoust Soc Am; Int Soc Psychophysics (ISP). RESEARCH Hearing, auditory attention. SELECTED PUBLICATIONS Co-auth with M Floentine and C H Meiselman, Critical Band in Auditory Lateralization, Sensory Processes, 76; auth, Loudness, in E C Carterette and M P Friedman, eds, Handbook of Perception, vol 4, Hearing, 78; Loudness Adaptation, in J V Tobias & E D Schuber, eds, Hearing Research and Theory, vol 2, 83; with S Quigley, C Aoki, N Peachey, and A Reeves, Focused Auditory Attention and Frequency Selectivity, Perception and Psychophysics, 42, 87; with A Chays & J Magnum, The Role of the Olivocochlear Bundle in Hearing: Sixteen Case Studies, Hearing Res, 103, 97. CONTACT ADDRESS Dept of Psychology, Northeastern Univ, 413 MU, Boston, MA 02115-5096. EMAIL scharf@neu.edu

SCHARFF, LAUREN F.
PERSONAL Born 05/31/1966, Austin, TX, m, 1998, 1 child DISCIPLINE PSYCHOLOGY EDUCATION Univ Tex, BA, 87; MA, 89; PhD, 92. CAREER Teaching Asst to Instr, Univ Tex, 87-92; Asst Prof to Assoc Prof, Stephen F Austin State Univ, 93-. HONORS AND AWARDS SFA President's Lagniappe Awd, 98; Teaching Excellence Awd, Col of Liberal Arts; John Wallace Dallenbach Fel, 89; Emma F Clark Fel, 90. MEMBERSHIPS Asn for Res in Vision and Opthalmol; Optical Soc of Am, Psychonomic Soc, Sigma Xi, Am Asn of Univ Women. RESEARCH Visual search, Depth perception, Readability of text displays. SELECTED PUBLICATIONS Auth, "Discriminability measures for predicting readability of text on textured backgrounds," Optics Express, (00):P 81-91; auth, "Discriminability Measure for Predicting Readability," in Human Vision and Electronic Imaging, 99; auth, "Readability of computer displays as a function of color, saturation, and background texture," in Engineering Psychology and Cognitive Ergonomics Vol. 4, 99; auth, "Decreases in critical disparity gradient with eccentricity may reflect size-disparity correlation," Journal of the Optical Society of America, (97): 1205-1212; auth, "Steropsis at isoluminance in the absence of chromatic aberrations," Journal of the Optical society of America, (92): 868-876. CONTACT ADDRESS Dept Psychol, Stephen F. Austin State Univ, 1936 North St, PO Box 13046, Nacogdoches, TX 75961. EMAIL lscharff@sfasu.edu

SCHEFF, THOMAS
PERSONAL m, 1986, 3 children DISCIPLINE SOCIOLOGY EDUCATION Univ or Ariz, BS, 50; Univ Calif Berkeley, PhD, 60. CAREER Asst Prof, Univ of Wis, Madison, 59-64; from Prof to Emer Prof, Univ Calif Santa Barbara, 65-. HONORS AND AWARDS Award for Lifetime Achievement, Soc for Appl Sociol, 99. MEMBERSHIPS Am Sociol Asn, Pac Soc Asn, Int Soc for Res on Emotions. SELECTED PUBLICATIONS Auth, Microsociology, 90; coauth, Emotions and Violence, 91; auth, Bloody Revenge, 94; Social Bond, and Human Reality, 97. CONTACT ADDRESS Dept Sociol, Univ of California, Santa Barbara, Santa Barbara, CA 93106. EMAIL scheff@sscf.ucsb.edu

SCHEFFT, BRUCE K.
PERSONAL Born 08/21/1952, Milwaukee, WI, m, 1995, 3 children DISCIPLINE PSYCHOLOGY EDUCATION Univ Wis Milwaukee, BS, 75; Univ Ill, Med, 78; Univ Wis Milwaukee, NS, 80; PhD, 83. CAREER From Asst to Assoc Prof, Univ of Cincinnati, 89-; Dir, Neuropsychology Prog, Univ of Cincinnati, 91-; Dir, Neuropsychology Clinic, Univ of Cincinnati, 91-. HONORS AND AWARDS Summer Fac Res Fel Prog, Univ of Cincinnati, 98. MEMBERSHIPS Int Neuropsychological Soc, Nat Acad of Neuropsychology. RESEARCH The application of self-regulatory methods to patients with neurobehavioral disorders. SELECTED PUBLICATIONS Coauth, "The role of self-regulation therapy with the brain-injured patient," in Clinical Neuropsychology: Theoretical foundations for practitioners, ed. M. Maruish and J.A. Moses (NY: Lawrence Erlbaum, 97), 237-282; auth, "Neuropsychology: Integration without confusion. Review of Clinical Neuropsychology; Behavioral and Brain Science," Contemp Psychology 42 (97): 249-250; coauth, "Recovery in pediatric injury: Is Psychostimulant medication beneficial?," J of Head Trauma Rehabil 13 (98): 73-81; coauth, "The effects of olfactory stimulation on the vigilance performance of individuals with brain injury," J of Clinical and Experimental neuropsychology 20 (98): 227-236; coauth, "The neurologic validity of the Wisconsin Card Sorting Test (WCST) with a pediatric population," J of the Int Neuropsychological Soc 4 (98): 29; coauth, "Retrieval deficits in patients with medically intractable temporal lobe epilepsy: An information processing perspective," J of the Int Neuropsychological Soc 5 (99): 122; coauth, "Directed forgetting deficits in patients with temporal lobe epilepsy: An information processing perspective," J of the Int Neuropsychological Soc 5 (99): 227-236; coauth, "Effects of experimentally-induced emotional states on frontal lobe cognitive task performance," J of the Int Neuropsychologia 37 (99): 677-683; coauth, "Diagnostic sensitivity and specificity of the Boston Naming Test and the M. A. E. Visual Naming Test in epilepsy surgery candidates," J of the Int Neuropsychological Soc 6 (00): 198; coauth, "The neurologic validity of the Wisconsin Card

Sorting test with a pediatric population, " The Clinical Neuropsychologist (in press). CONTACT ADDRESS Dept Psychology, Univ of Cincinnati, PO Box 210367, Cincinnati, OH 45221-0376. EMAIL Bruce.Schefft@uc.edu

SCHEIFFELE, EBERHARD
PERSONAL Born 09/10/1959, Wehr, Germany, s DISCIPLINE PSYCHOLOGY, THEATRE ARTS EDUCATION Universitat Freiburg, Germany, 82; Univ TX, Austin, MA, 85; Univ Calif, Grad cert, 91, PhD, 95. CAREER Tchng asst, 82-83, Univ Freiburg; tchng asst, 84-85, Univ TX; tchng asst, 84-85, Univ Mich; tchng asst, 85-87, 89-90, 92, 95, grad stud instr, logic, 87-88, knowledge & its limits, 89, Univ Calif, Berkeley; tchng asst, 91, Univ Calif, Santa Cruz; tchng asst, guest presenter, Psychodrama/role playing for Hum Int, guest presenter, Dynamic Med for Psychol of Conscious, 98-, West Chester Univ; Adjunct Prof of Psychol, West Chester, Pa, 00-. HONORS AND AWARDS Myrtle L. Judkins Mem Schol, 93-94; Wheeler Fel, 85-86; UC Berkeley; German Exchan Fel, Univ TX, Austin MEMBERSHIPS Amer Sc of Group Psychotherapy & Psychodrama; Assn for Theatre in Higher Ed; Intl Fed for Theare Res; Amer Soc Theatre Res; Natl Assn for Drama Therapy; Amer Phil Assn; Amer Psychol Assn; Natl Ed Assn. RESEARCH Psychodrama, spontaneity & improvisation; theatrical theories & influences of Jacob Levy Moreno. SELECTED PUBLICATIONS Coauth, Proof by Mathematical Induction, Discov Geometry Tchrs Res Book, Key Curr Press, 77; auth, Writing a Logic Puzzle, Discov Geometry Tchrs Res Book, Key Curr Press, 97; art, The Theatre of Truth, Res in Drama Ed, 97; art, Therapeutic Theatre and Spontaneity: Goethe and Moreno, J of Group Psychotherapy, Psychodrama & Sociometry, 96. CONTACT ADDRESS Group in Logic and Methodology of Sci, Univ of California, Berkeley, Berkeley, CA 94720. EMAIL scheiffe@math.berkeley.edu

SCHIFF, FREDERICK
PERSONAL s DISCIPLINE SOCIOLOGY AND COMMUNICATION EDUCATION Reed College, BA, 64; UCLA, MA, 65, PhD, 70. CAREER Assoc Prof comm, 89-, Univ Houston; Asst Prof, 86-89, Univ Dayton; Asst Prof, 70-75, Wash Univ. HONORS AND AWARDS NIMH; NSF; Nat Science Found, 00-02; Am Newspaper Publishers: Ideological Management and Class Bias in the News; One of 21 grants in sociology in 00. MEMBERSHIPS ASA; AEJMC; NSA; ICA; MESA. RESEARCH Media Corp; News Content; Ideology. SELECTED PUBLICATIONS Auth, "The Lebanese Prince: The Aftermath of the Continuing Civil War: Journal of South Asian and Middle Eastern Studies, 12:3, (89): 7-36; auth, "Brazilian Film and Military Censorship: Cinema Novo, 1964-1974," Historical Journal of Film, Radio and Television, 12:4, (93): 487-512; auth, "Deconstructing Attitude Structure in Public Opinion Studies," Critical Studies in Mass Communication, 11:3, (94): 287-297; auth, "Ethical Problems in Advising Theses and Dissertations," Journalism and Mass Communication Educator, 51:1, (96): 23-35; auth, "The Dominant Ideology and Brazilian Tabloids: News Content in Class-Targeted Newspapers," Sociological Perspectives 39:1, (96): 175-206; auth, "The Associated Press: Its Worldwide Staff and American Interests," International Communication Bulletin, 31:3-4, (96): 3-9; auth, "How Public Opinion is Perceived and Produced by U.S. Newspaper Publishers," Javnost, The Public: Journal of the European Institute for Communication and Culture, 4:2, (97): 71-90; auth, "Nude Dancing: Scenes of Sexual Celebration in a Contested Culture," Journal of Am Culture, 2:4, (99): 9-16. CONTACT ADDRESS 701 Welch St, Houston, TX 77006-1307. EMAIL fschiff@uh.edu

SCHIFFER, MICHAEL B.
PERSONAL Born 10/04/1947, Winnipeg, MAN, Canada, m, 1968, 2 children DISCIPLINE ANTHROPOLOGY EDUCATION UCLA, BA, 69; Univ Ariz, MA, 72; PhD, 73. CAREER Asst archaeol, Ark Archaeol Survey, 73-75; asst prof to prof, Univ Ariz 75-. HONORS AND AWARDS Cugnot Awd of Distinction, Soc of Automotive Hist, 95; Outstanding Fac Advisor Awd, Univ Ariz, 94; Res Fel, Bakken Libr and Museum, Minn, 00; Sen Fel, Dibner Inst for the Hist of Sci and Technol, MIT, 01. MEMBERSHIPS Am Asn for the Adv of Sci; Am Anthropol Asn; Soc for Am Archaeol; Soc for Hist Archaeol; Soc for the Hist of Technol; S Ariz Clay Artists. RESEARCH Anthropological and archaeological theory; Technology and society; Human communication; SELECTED PUBLICATIONS Auth, The Portable Radio in American Life, Univ Ariz Press, 91; auth, Technological Perspectives on Behavioral Change, Univ of Ariz Press, 92; co-auth, Taking Charge: The Electric Automobile in America, Smithsonian, 94; auth, Behavioral Archaeology: First Principles, Univ of Ut Press, 95; co-auth, The Material Life of Human Beings: Artifacts, Behavior, and Communication, Routledge Press, 99; ed, Social Theory in Archaeology, Univ of Ut Press, 00; ed, Anthropological Perspectives on Technology, Univ of N Mex Press, 01. CONTACT ADDRESS Dept Anthropol, Univ of Arizona, 1009 E S Campus Dr, Tucson, AZ 85721-0030. EMAIL Schiffer@u.arizona.edu

SCHLENKER, BARRY R.
PERSONAL Born 02/21/1947, Passaic, NJ, m, 1972, 2 children DISCIPLINE PSYCHOLOGY EDUCATION Univ

Miami, AB 69; United States International Univ, San Diego, MA, 70; State Univ New York at Albany, PhD, 72; Summa Cum Laude, AB, 69. CAREER Prof of Psychology, Univ of Florida, 80-; Dir of Social Psychology Program, Univ of Florida, 84-97; Prof of Clinical and Health Psychology, Univ of Florida, 76-; Prof of Marketing, Univ of Florida, 77-; Assoc Prof of Psychology, Univ of Florida, 76-80; Asst Prof of Psychology, Univ of Florida, 72-76. HONORS AND AWARDS Research Scientist Dev Awd, National Institute of Mental Health, 79-83; Fellow, Am Psychological Assoc; Fellow, Am Psychological Society, Fellow, Society for the Psychological Study of Social Issues; Fellow, Society for Personality and Social Psychology; Teacher of the Year Awd, College of Liberal Arts and Sciences, 95; Outstanding Teacher, Teaching Improvement Program Awd, Univ of Florida, 94; Teacher of the Year Awd, Psi Chi honor society, 96; Anderson Scholar Fac Honoree, 96; National Science Foundation Predoctoral Fel, 70-72. MEMBERSHIPS American Psychological Assoc; American Psychological Society; Society for Personality and Social Psychology; Society for the Psychological Study of Social Issues; Society of Experimental Social Psychology, Southeastern Psychological Assoc. RESEARCH Impression management and Self-presentation; Self and Identity; Personal Responsibility and Accountability. SELECTED PUBLICATIONS Auth, "Interpersonal processes involving impression regulation and management," Annual Review Psychology 43, 133-168; auth, "The triangle model of responsibility", Psychological Review 101, 632-652; auth, "Personal responsibility: Application of the Triangle Model", ed. L. L. Cummings and B. Staw, Research in Organizational Behavior 19 (97): 241-301; (Greenwich, Connecticut: JAI Press); auth, " Beneficial impression management: Strategically controlling information to help friends. Journal of Personality and Social Psychology 76, 559-73; auth, "The strategic control of information: Impression management and self-presentation in daily life, ed. A. Tresser, , R. Felson, and J. Suls, Perspectives on self and identity (Washington, DC: American Psychological Assoc). CONTACT ADDRESS Dept Psychology, Univ of Florida, PO Box 112250, Gainesville, FL 32611. EMAIL schlenkr@psych.ufl.edu

SCHLENKER, JON A.
PERSONAL Born 09/17/1946, Takoma Park, MD, m, 1969, 3 children DISCIPLINE SOCIOLOGY EDUCATION Muhlenberg Col, AB, 68; Univ S Miss, MA, 72; MA, 74, Univ S Maine, MS 80; Berne Univ CAGS, 99; PhD, 00. CAREER Instr, Jones County Jun Col, 70-74; prof, Univ Maine, 75-. HONORS AND AWARDS Who's Who in Am, 00; Who's Who among Am Teachers, 94,96,98,00; Outstanding Educ of Am, 74-75. MEMBERSHIPS Nat Col Hon Coun, NE Reg of nat Col & Honors Coun. RESEARCH Higher Education, Adult Education, Distance Education. SELECTED PUBLICATIONS Coauth, In the Public Interest: The Quilian Conservatory Corps in Maine, 88; coauth, The Choctaws: cultural Evolution of a Native American Tribe, 80. CONTACT ADDRESS Dept Soc & Beh Sci, Univ of Maine, Augusta, 46 Univ Dr, Augusta, ME 04330-9488. EMAIL jons@maine.edu

SCHLESINGER, YAFFA
PERSONAL Born 04/24/1925, Israel, w, 1949, 2 children DISCIPLINE SOCIOLOGY EDUCATION NYU, BS, 63; MA, 64; PhD, 75. CAREER Asst prof Stern Col, 67; Hunter Col, 67-. HONORS AND AWARDS Who's Who. RESEARCH Sociology of Art; sociology of the family; sociology of inequality. SELECTED PUBLICATIONS Auth, An Interview with My Grandparent, McGraw Hill, 98. CONTACT ADDRESS Dept Sociology, Hunter Col, CUNY, 695 Park Ave, New York, NY 10021.

SCHLEWITT-HAYNES, LORA D.
PERSONAL Born 07/26/1967, Springfield, IL, m, 1997 DISCIPLINE PSYCHOLOGY EDUCATION E Ill Univ, BA, 89; Univ Louisville, MA, 92; PhD, 97. CAREER Instructor, Univ Louisville, 92-95; Asst Prof, Univ N Colo, 95-. MEMBERSHIPS RMPA; APS. RESEARCH Cognition and Development: Attention; Achievement Motivation Theories of Intelligence. CONTACT ADDRESS Dept Psychol, Univ of No Colorado, 501 20th St, Greeley, CO 80639-0001. EMAIL ldschle@bentley.unco.edu

SCHMID, CAROL L.
PERSONAL Born 12/11/1946, Santa Barbara, CA, m, 1969, 1 child DISCIPLINE SOCIOLOGY EDUCATION Univ California, BA, 69; McMaster Univ, MA, 76; PhD, 78; Duke Univ, MLS, 86; North Carolina Central Univ, JD, 91. CAREER Vis schl, Free Univ, Trie Univ, Brandeis Univ, Fordham Univ, Univ Toronto, Duke Univ, 77-79; vis asst prof, Univ Oregon, 79-82; prof, Guil Tech Com Col, 82-. HONORS AND AWARDS NEH Fel; NEH Res Gnt; Can Emb Fac Res Gnt; Ger Acad Res Gnt; Fulbright Fel; NSF Gnt: ASA Gnt; GTCC Excell Teach. MEMBERSHIPS ABA; ASA; CCES; LS; NCBA; NCSA; SSSP; SWS; SCCS; SSS; WPSA. RESEARCH Multilingualism and Multiculturalism in Canada, Switzerland and the United States; Immigration and Emigration in Canada, the United States, and Germany; Public policy and periphery groups in North America and Western Europe, Comparative Social Problems including Crime, Health, and Sex Roles, Comparative Nationalism and Identity, Comparative Public Policy (including

emerging language, legal and human rights issues). **SELECTED PUBLICATIONS** Auth, "Quebec in the 1970s-80s: Submerged Nation or Canadian Fringe?" in Political Sociology and the State, ed, Richard Braungart (NY: JAI, 90); auth, "Women in the Green Party: The Uneasy Alliance of Feminism and Ecology." in Women and Protest, eds. Rhoda Lois Blumberg, Guilda West (Cambridge: Oxford Univ Press, 90); auth, "The Changing Status of Women in the United States and Canada," in Continuity and Change in Marriage and Family, ed. Jean E. Veevers (Toronto: Holt, Reinhart and Winston of Can, 91); auth, "Language Rights and the Legal Status of English-only Laws in the Public and Private Sector," NC Cen Law J 20 (92):65-91; "Soiled Identities: Anti-Foreigner Political Violence, Structural Location and Social Action in Contemporary Germany," Can J Sociol 20 (95); auth, "The New Immigrant Communities in the United States and the Ideology of Exclusion," Res Comm Soc 6 (96): 39-67; auth, "Between the Lines: Reconciling Diversity and Standard English," in Language Ideologies: Critical Perspectives on the Official English Movement, ed. Roseann Dueflas Gonzalez, (Urbana: Scholars' Press, 99); auth, The Politics of Language: Conflict Identity, and Cultural Pluralism in Comparative Perspective, Oxford Univ Press, forthcoming. **CONTACT ADDRESS** Dept Sociology, Guilford Tech Comm Col, PO Box 309, Jamestown, NC 27282. **EMAIL** schmidc@gtcc.cc.nc.us

SCHNEIDER, MARELEYN
PERSONAL Born 05/28/1945, New York, NY, s **DISCIPLINE** SOCIOLOGY **EDUCATION** CUNY, BA, 67; MS, 76; MA, 84; Fordham Univ, PhD, 88. **CAREER** Adj instr, Fordham Univ, 88; adj instr, Yeshiva Col, 88; adj asst prof, Azr Grad Inst, 89, 92; adj prof, Lehman Col, 00; assoc prof, Yeshiva Col, 92-. **HONORS AND AWARDS** SAA Fel; Appoint, Jewish Wom Thnk Tank; Who's Who in, World, Among Am, Am Women, Who of Women, the East. **MEMBERSHIPS** ASR; CAJE; SAA; SSSR; WUJS. **RESEARCH** Jewish education; Jewish women; death and dying; Jewish folklore. **SELECTED PUBLICATIONS** Coauth, The Jewishness Quotient of Jewish Day School Graduates: Studying the Effect of Jewish Education on Adult Jewish Behavior, Azrieli Grad Inst (NY), 94; Coauth, Far-Reaching Effects of Extensive Jewish Day School Attendance: The impact of Jewish Education on Adult Jewish Behavior and Attitudes, Azrieli Grad Inst (NY), 94; coauth, Fortifying and Restoring Jewish Behavior: The interaction of Home and School, Azrieli Grad Inst (NY), 94; auth, Jewish Censorship, in Ready Reference: Censorship, Salem Press (Pasadena, CA), 97; auth, Wills, in Encyclopedia of Social Issues, Marshall Cavendish (Tarrytown), 97; auth, "Yenti Redux: Orthodox Jewish Women Openly Involved in Torah Study," in New York Glory: Religions in the City, eds. A Karpathakis, A Carnes (NY: NY Univ Press, 97); auth, Asei Toratekha Keva: Make the Study of Torah a Regular Practice," in History of the Reform Movement in the United States, ed. D Kaplan (Chicago: Routledge Press, in press). **CONTACT ADDRESS** Dept Social and Behavioral Science, Yeshiva Univ, 500 West 185th St, BH1308, New York, NY 10033. **EMAIL** mschneid@ymail.yu.edu

SCHNEIDER, MARK A.
DISCIPLINE SOCIOLOGY **EDUCATION** Univ Chicago, BA, 66; MA, 68; Yale Univ, PhD, 85. **CAREER** Lect, Yale Univ, 85-89; Lect, Princeton Univ, 89-90; Lect, Univ Mich, 90-94; Asst Prof, Southern Ill Univ, 94-. **MEMBERSHIPS** ASA, Soc for Soc studies of Sci. **RESEARCH** Sociology of science. **SELECTED PUBLICATIONS** Auth, Culture and Enchantment, Univ Chicago Pr, 93; auth, "Sacredness, Status and Bodily Violation," Body & Soc, 2, (96): 75-92; auth, "Social Dimensions of the Epistemological Disputes: The Case of Literary Theory," Sociol Perspectives, 40 (97): 243-263; coauth, "Olfactory Sexual Inhibition and the Westermarck Effect," Human Nature, 11 (00): 65-91. **CONTACT ADDRESS** Dept Sociol, So Illinois Univ, Carbondale, Southern Ill Union, Mailcode 4524, Carbondale, IL 62901.

SCHOEN, JILL
PERSONAL Born 11/28/1945, Aberdeen, SD, m, 1965, 4 children **DISCIPLINE** COUNSELING, HUMAN RESOURCE DEVELOPMENT **EDUCATION** Northern State Univ, BS, 68; MS, 77; Univ SDak, EdD, 91. **CAREER** From asst prof to assoc prof, SDak State Univ, 93-98; asst prof, Moorhead State Univ, 98-00. **HONORS AND AWARDS** Outstanding Grad, Univ SDak, 91; Outstanding Service Awd, SDak State Univ; SDCA Mary Lark Humanitarian Awd, 98. **MEMBERSHIPS** ACA, AQA, ACES, NCACES, Chi Sigma Iota. **RESEARCH** Gerontology, Populations with Special Needs. **SELECTED PUBLICATIONS** Coauth, "Teaching diagnosis in counselor education training, The Dakota Counselor 3 (96): 18-20; coauth, "Multiple roles of CHRD graduate students," The Dakota Counselor 4 (97): 24-27; auth, Special considerations when providing mental health services for persons with mental retardation, SDak State Univ (Brookings, SD), 97; rev, of "Cultural Diversity and Social Skills Instruction," Counseling Today (Aug 97); rev, of "Social Action: A Mandate for Counselors," Counseling Today (July, 98); rev, of "Consumer's Guide to Psychiatric Drugs," Counseling Today (July 99). **CONTACT ADDRESS** Dept Counseling, Moorhead State Univ, 1104 7th Ave S, Moorhead, MN 56563-0002.

SCHOFIELD, JANET W.
PERSONAL Born 05/08/1946, Newark, NJ, m, 1968, 3 children **DISCIPLINE** PSYCHOLOGY **EDUCATION** Radcliffe Col, BA, 68; Harvard Univ, MA, 69; PhD, 72. **CAREER** Asst prof to prof, Univ of Pittsburgh, 74-. **HONORS AND AWARDS** Phi Beta Kappa; Phi Eta Sigma; Allport Intergroup Relations Prize. **MEMBERSHIPS** Am Psychol Soc; Am Psychol Assoc; Soc for Experimental Soc Psychol **RESEARCH** Race Relations, Computer and Internet Use in Schools. **SELECTED PUBLICATIONS** Auth, Black and white in school: Trust tension or tolerance?, Teachers Col Pr, 89; auth, Computers and classroom culture, Cambridge Univ, Pr, (NY), 95; auth, "Causes and consequences of the colorblind perspective", Multicultural education: Issues and Perspectives, eds JA Banks and CA McGee Banks, Allyn and Bacon, (97): 251-271; coauth, "The Internet in school: A case study of educator demand and its precursors", Culture of the Internet, ed S Keisler, Erlbaum (Mahwah, 97): 361-381; coauth, "Educational reform and professional development", Mathematics teachers in transition, ed E Fennema and BS Nelson, Erlbaum, (Mahwah, 97): 283-308; coauth, "Bringing the Internet to Schools: A case study of educational and technical professionals' collaboration for change", Info Soc, (00): coauth, "Female voices in virtual reality: Drawing young girls into an on line world", Building virtual communities: Learning and change in cyberspace, ed KA Renninger and W Shumar, Cambridge Univ Pr, (NY, 00); coauth, "When and how school desegregation improves intergroup relations", Handbook of Social Psychology, eds R Brown and S Gaertner, Blackwell, (NY, 00). **CONTACT ADDRESS** Dept Psychol, Univ of Pittsburgh, 3939 O'Harra St, 517 LRDC, Pittsburgh, PA 15260. **EMAIL** schof+@pitt.edu

SCHUDSON, MICHAEL
PERSONAL Born 11/03/1946, m, 1982, 3 children **DISCIPLINE** SOCIOLOGY **EDUCATION** Swarthmore Col, BA, 69; Harvard, PhD, 76. **CAREER** Asst prof, Univ Chicago, 76-80; assoc to full prof, Univ Cal San Diego, 80-; Guggenheim fel, MacArthur Prize fel. **MEMBERSHIPS** Am Sociol Asn; Int Commun Asn; Orgn Am Hist. **RESEARCH** US political culture; News media; History of communication. **SELECTED PUBLICATIONS** Discovering the News, Basic, 78; Advertising, The Uneasy Persuasion, Basic, 84; Watergate in American Memory, Basic Books, 92; The Power of News, Harvard, 95; The Good Citizen, Free Press, 98. **CONTACT ADDRESS** Dept of Communication, Univ of California, San Diego, La Jolla, CA 92093-0503. **EMAIL** mschudson@ucsd.edu

SCHULZ, RENATE A.
PERSONAL Born 02/24/1940, Lohr/Main, Germany, d, 1 child **DISCIPLINE** GERMAN STUDIES, SECOND LANGUAGE ACQUISITION **EDUCATION** Mankato State Coll, BS, 62; Univ Co, MA, 67; Oh State Univ, PhD, 74. **CAREER** Asst prof, Otterbein Col, 74-76; asst prof, SUNY, Buffalo, 76-77; asst, assoc prof, Univ AR, 77-81; prof Univ AZ, 81-. **HONORS AND AWARDS** Creative Tchg Awd, 84 Univ Az; ACTFL's Florence Steiner Awd, 93; Verdienstkreuz erster Klasse, 90, Federal Republic Germany; J. William Fulbright Fel, 97. **MEMBERSHIPS** AAAL; AATG; ACTFL; MLA; ATTF; AATSP; TESOL; Az Foreign Lang Asn. **RESEARCH** Second language acquisition; foreign language learning and teaching; testing and evaluation; foreign language teacher development. **SELECTED PUBLICATIONS** Co-auth, Im Kontext: Lesebuch zur Landdskunde, Holt, Rinehart, and Winston, 90; auth, "Second Language Acquistion Theories and Teaching Practice: How Do They Fit?," Modern Lang Jour, 91; "Profile of the Profession: Results of the 1992 AATG Membership Survey," Unterrichtspraxis, 93; co-auth, "Beer, Fast Cars, and . . .: Stereotypes Held by US College-Level Students of German," Unterrichtspraxis, 95; auth, "Focus on Form in the Foreign Language Classroom: Students and Teachers Views on Error Correction and the Role of Grammar," For Lang Annals, 96. **CONTACT ADDRESS** Dept of German Studies, Univ of Arizona, Tucson, AZ 85721-0067. **EMAIL** schulzr@u.arizona.edu

SCHUMAN, ELLIOTT PAUL
DISCIPLINE PSYCHOLOGY **EDUCATION** U.S. Naval Acad, BS, 49; Columbia Univ, MA, 55; PhD, 58. **CAREER** Lectr to asst to dean and counselor, Columbia Col, 55-58; lectr, counselor, Brooklyn Col, 58-60; adjunct asst prof, LIU, 60-62, asst prof to prof, 62-; coord grad prog, Long Island Univ, 84-; faculty, Mid Manhattan Inst Modern Psychoanalysis, 92-; psychologist, Morningside Mental Hygiene Clinic, 60-66; psycotherapist, Community Guidance Service, NY, 62-69, supr, 69-87; psychoanalyst, Theodore Reik Consultation Center, 66-69, teaching analyst, 69-; faculty, Am Inst for Psychotherapy and Psychoanalysis, 72-73, Center for Modern Psychoanalytic Studies, 73-, Nat Psychol Asn for Psychoanalysis, 74, Inst for Expressive Ananysis, 80-81, Inst for Modern Psychoanalysis, 81-86; supervisor, Mt. Sinai Hosp, 79-. **HONORS AND AWARDS** Sigma Xi; Phi Del;ta Kappa; Kappa Delta Pi; Fel, Found for Economic Ed. **MEMBERSHIPS** AAAS, APA, AAUP, NY State Psychol Asn, NY Acad of Science, NY Soc Clinical Psychologists, E Psychol Asn, Soc Projective Techniques, Nat Asn for Advancement of Psychoanalysis, Coun Nat Register Health Service Providers in Psychol, Am Group Psychotherapy Asn, Am Acad Psychotherapists, NY Soc for Ericksonian Psychotherapy and Hypnosis, Asn Family and Conciliation Cts. **SELECTED PUBLICATIONS** Auth, Guide for Evaluation of Instruction, Navy Dept, 58; many articles in professional journals. **CONTACT ADDRESS** Dept Psychol, Long Island Univ, Brooklyn, 1 University Plaza, Brooklyn, NY 11201.

SCHUMM, WALTER R.
PERSONAL Born 01/09/1951, Bethesda, MD, m, 1979, 7 children **DISCIPLINE** FAMILY STUDIES **EDUCATION** Col William and Mary, BS, 72; Kans State Univ, MS, 76; Purdue Univ, PhD, 79. **CAREER** Asst prof to prof, Kans State Univ, 79-. **HONORS AND AWARDS** Moran Mem Res Awd, Am Home Econ Assoc, 90; Awd, Col of Human Ecol, KSU, 97. **MEMBERSHIPS** Nat Coun on Family Relations. **RESEARCH** Military Families, Premarital Preparation/Counseling, Religion and Family Life, Research Methodologies Used with Familes. **SELECTED PUBLICATIONS** Coauth, Sourcebook of family theories and methods: a contextual approach, Plenum, NY, 93; auth, "Non-marital sexual behavior," Handbook of child and adolescent sexual problems, ed G.A. Rekers, MacMillan (Lexington, MA, 95): 381-423; auth, "Trends in homeschooling in a Midwestern community," Psychological Reports 82, (98): 364-366; coauth, "Treating prisoners humanely," Military Rev LXXVIII.1, (98): 83-93; coauth, "Measurement in family studies," Handbook of Marriage and the Family, eds M. Sussman, S.K. Steinmetz and G. Peterson, Plenum, (99); auth, "Satisfaction," Encyclopedia of Human Emotions, Vol 2, ed D. Levinson, J.J. Ponzetti, Jr., and P.F. Jorgensen, (NY: MacMillan, 99); coauth, "The Desert Fax: Calling Home from Somalia," Armed Forces and Soc 25.3, (99): 509-521; coauth, "Marriage preparation programs: a literature review," Family Jour 8, (00): 133-142; coauth, "Soldiers at risk for individual readiness or morale problems during a six-month peacekeeping deployment to the Sinai," Psychol Reports 87, (00): 623-633; coauth, "Providing family support during military deployments," The Military Family, eds J.A. Martin, L.N. Rosen and L.R. Sparacino, Greenwood Publ Co, (CT: Westport), in press. **CONTACT ADDRESS** Sch of Family Studies and Human Serv, Kansas State Univ, 1700 Anderson Ave, Manhattan, KS 66506-1403. **EMAIL** schumm@humec.ksu.edu

SCHUNN, C.
PERSONAL Born 04/02/1969, Kitchener, ON, Canada, m, 1996, 1 child **DISCIPLINE** PSYCHOLOGY **EDUCATION** McGill Univ, BS, 90; Carnegie Mellon Univ, PhD, 95. **CAREER** Postdoctorate Assoc, Carnegie Mellon Univ, 95-98; Asst Prof, George Mason Univ, 98-. **HONORS AND AWARDS** JW McConnell Awd, McGill Univ, 88; Natural Sci and Engineering Res Coun Undergrad Summer Res Awd, 89; Boris Muskatov Prize, McGill Univ, 89; Major Hiram Mills Medal, McGill Univ, 90; Natural Sci and Engineering Res Coun Undergrad Summer Res Awd, 90; Natural Sci and Engineering Res Coun Grad Fel, 90-92; Best Student Proposal Awd, Tex A&M Univ, 95. **MEMBERSHIPS** Cognitive Sci Soc, Psychonomic Soc, APS, APA, Am Assoc for the Advancement of Sci. **RESEARCH** Psychology of scientific reasoning, strategy selection and decision making, individual variability and development in complex cognition, computational and quantitative modeling, categorization and causal reasoning. **SELECTED PUBLICATIONS** Coauth, "Priming, Analogy and Awareness in Complex Reasoning," Memory & Cognition, 24 (96): 271-284; coauth, "Task Representations, Strategy Variability and Base-Rate Neglect," J of Exp Psychol: Gen, 128 (99): 107-130; coauth, "The Generality/Specificity of Expertise in Scientific reasoning," Cognitive Sci, 23 (99): 337-370; coauth, "Bringing Together the Psychometric and Strategy Worlds: Predicting Adaptivity in a Dynamic Task," in Cognitive Regulation of Performance: Interaction of Theory and Application, Attention and Performance XVII (99): 315-342; coauth, "Discovery Processes in a More Complex Task," in Exploring Science: The Cognition and Development of Discovery Processes (Cambridge: MIT Pr, 00), 161-199; coauth, Designing for Science: Implications from Professional, Instructional and Everyday Science, Erlbaum (Mahwah, NJ), forthcoming. **CONTACT ADDRESS** Dept Psychol, George Mason Univ, Fairfax, 4400 University Dr, Fairfax, VA 22030. **EMAIL** cschunn@gmu.edu

SCHUSTER, MARILYN R.
PERSONAL Born 09/23/1943, Washington, DC **DISCIPLINE** FRENCH, WOMEN'S STUDIES **EDUCATION** Mills Coll, BA, Fr, 65; Yale Univ, PhD, Fr Lang & Lit, 73. **CAREER** Instr, Sonoma Sate Col, 67; tchg assoc, Yale Univ, 67068; instr, Yale Summer Lang Inst, 70; instr, Fordham Univ-Lincoln Center, 70-71; from isntr to prof Fr & women's stud, Smith Col, 71-; dean, Smith Col, 81-83; dir, Women's Stud Prog, Smith Coll, 86-87; assoc dean of faculty, Smith Col, 87-90; ch, Fr dept, Smith Col, 92-95. **MEMBERSHIPS** MLA; NWSA. **RESEARCH** 20th century women's fiction in France & England; gay/lesbian/queer studies **SELECTED PUBLICATIONS** Coed, Women's Place in the Academy: Transforming the Liberal Arts Curriculum, Rowman & Allanheld, 85; Marguerite Duras Revisited, MacMillan publ, 93; "The Gendered Politics of Knowledge: Lessons from the US," Asian Women, 96; "Inscribing a Lesbian Reader, Projecting a Lesbian Subject: A Jane Rule Diptych," The Jour of Homosexuality, Gay & Lesbian Lit Since World War II: His & Memory, 98; Passionate Communities: Reading Lesbian Resistance in Jene Rule's Fiction, NYork Univ Pr, 99. **CONTACT ADDRESS** Neilson Libr, Smith Col, Northampton, MA 01063. **EMAIL** mschuste@smith.edu

SCHUYLER, ROBERT L.
PERSONAL Born 09/13/1941, New Haven, CT, s **DISCIPLINE** ANTHROPOLOGY **EDUCATION** Univ Az, BA, 64; Univ Calif, Santa Barbara, MA, 68; PhD, 74. **CAREER** City Univ of New York, 70-79; Univ Pa, 80-. **HONORS AND AWARDS** Pres, Soc for Hist Anthropol, 82. **MEMBERSHIPS** Soc for Hist Anthropol, Am Anthropol Asn. **RESEARCH** Anthropology, historical archaeology, history of anthropology and archaeology. **SELECTED PUBLICATIONS** Auth, "Cultural Contact in Evolutionary Perspective," Ch 4, Studies in Culture Contact: Interaction, Culture Change and Archaeology, ed James G. Cusick, Southern Ill Press (97); auth, "History of Historical Archaeology," Bull of the Hist of Archaeol, 8, 2 (98): 7-17; auth, "Comments on 'Historical Archaeology in the Next Millenium: A Forum'," Hist Archaeol, 33, 2 (99): 66-70; rev of Anders Andrean, "Between Artifacts and Texts: Historical Archaeology in Global Perspective," Am Anthropologist, 101, 4 (99): 1-2; auth, "The Centrality of Post Medieval Studies to General Historical Archaeology," Ch 2, in Geoff Egan and R. L. Michael, eds, Old and New Worlds, Oxbow Books, London (99). **CONTACT ADDRESS** Dept Anthropol- Univ Museum, Univ of Pennsylvania, 3260 South St, Philadelphia, PA 19104. **EMAIL** schuyler@sas.upenn.edu

SCHWARTZ, DOUGLAS W.
PERSONAL Born 07/29/1929, Erie, PA, m, 1950, 3 children **DISCIPLINE** ANTHROPOLOGY **EDUCATION** Univ Ky, BA, 50; Yale Univ, PhD, 55. **CAREER** Dir, Mus Anthrop, Univ Ky, 56-67; asst prof to prof, Univ Ky, 56-67; Acad Asst to Pres, Univ Ky, 63-64; Pres & CEO, Sch of Am Res, 67-01. **HONORS AND AWARDS** Hon Dr of Letters, Univ NMex, 81; Hin Dr of Letters, Univ Ky, 89; Dist Service Award, Soc for Am Archaeol, 90; Dist Service Award, Am Anthrop Asn, 92. **MEMBERSHIPS** Witter Bynner Foundation for Poetry, Inc (bd member); Am Anthrop Asn, Long Range Planning Committee; Pres, Jane Goodall African Wildlife Institute, 86-88; ch, Sec of Interior's Advisory Bd on Nat Parks, 78; Pres, Witter Bynner Found for Poetry, 77-91; Pres, Soc for Am Archaeol, 73-74; Bd Member, 1st Nat Bank of Santa Fe, 95-; ch, Harvard Univ visiting comm, Peabody Museum, 98-. **RESEARCH** Southwestern U.S. archaeol and the nurturing of genius: a Charles Darwin case study. **SELECTED PUBLICATIONS** Auth, North American Archaeology in Historic Perspective, Warsaw, 67; auth, Conceptions of Kentucky Prehistory, A Case Study in the History of Archaeology, Univ of KY Press, 68; ed and auth, Creativity in the Classroom Context, Univ, KY, 79-93; auth, On the Edge of Splendor: Exploring the Grand Canyon's Human Past, SAR Press, 89; forward, The Pottery of Arroyo Hondo Pueblo, New Mexico, SAR Press, 93; forward, The Architecture of Arroyo Hondo Peublo, New Mexico, SAR Press, 93; forward, The Men Who Made Kentucky's Past, Ky Archaeol, Univ Ky Press, 96; auth, Introduction to Kidder's Introduction to Southwestern Archaeology, Yale Univ Press, 00; auth, The Colonizing Experience: A Cross-Cultural Perspective, Un Calif Press. **CONTACT ADDRESS** Sch of American Research, PO Box 2188, Santa Fe, NM 87504-2188. **EMAIL** dws@sarsf.org

SCHWARTZ, MILDRED A.
PERSONAL Born Toronto, ON, Canada **DISCIPLINE** SOCIOLOGY **EDUCATION** Univ Toronto, BA, 54; MA, 56; Columbia Univ, PhD, 65. **CAREER** Prof to Prof Emeritus, Univ Ill, 69-. **HONORS AND AWARDS** Thomas Enders Fel; Assoc Fel, Ctr for Great Plains Studies; Can Stud Sen Fel. **MEMBERSHIPS** ASA; APSA; CPSA; IPSA; ISA; SSHA; ACSUS; MPSA. **RESEARCH** Political sociology; Political parties; Organizations; Social movements. **SELECTED PUBLICATIONS** Auth, "Party Organization as a Network of Relations: The Republican Party of Illinois," in How Political Parties Work, (Praeger Press, 94), 75-101; auth, "Regions and Regionalism in Canada," in Politics, Society, and Democracy: Comparative Studies, (Westview Pub, 95), 141-157; auth, "NAFTA: Where Are We Going," in NAFT NOW! The Changing Political Economy of North America, (Univ Press of Am, 95), 77-88; auth, "Canada," in The Encyclopedia of Democracy Vol I, (Washington, 95), 157-163; auth, "Canadian Policy Studies in Comparative Perspective," in Policy Studies in Canada: The State of the Art, (Univ Toronto Press, 96), 346-355; auth, "Boundary Problems in Political Organizations," Journal of Organizational Change Management, (96): 43-55; auth, "Cross-Border Ties Among Protest Movements: The Great Plains Connection," Great Plains Quarterly, (97): 119-130; auth, "Democracy and Agrarian Socialism," Extensions: A Journal of the Carl Albert Congressional Research and Studies Center, (98): 18-21; auth, "NAFTA and the Fragmentation of Canada," The American Review of Canadian Studies, (98): 11-28. **CONTACT ADDRESS** Dept Sociol, Univ of Illinois, Chicago, 1007 W Harrison 4112, Chicago, IL 60607. **EMAIL** mildred@uic.edu

SCHWARTZ, NORMAN B.
PERSONAL Born 02/13/1932, New York, NY, m, 1955, 4 children **DISCIPLINE** ANTHROPOLOGY **EDUCATION** Col of the City of NY, BS, 58; Univ of Pa, MS, 60; PhD, 68. **CAREER** Instr to asst prof, Middlebury Col, 62-68; asst prof to prof, Univ of Del, 68-; chair, Univ of Del, 72-77. **HONORS AND AWARDS** Phi Beta Kappa; George Leib Harrison Fel. **MEMBERSHIPS** Am Anthrop Assoc; Soc for Applied Anthrop; Guatemla Scholars Network; Anthrop Study Group on Agrarian Systems; Soc for Latin Am Anthrop. **RESEARCH** Conservation: forestry, fishing and horticulture systems, regional development, conflict resolution, montoring and evaluation methods, Geo area - mesoamerica. **SELECTED PUBLICATIONS** Auth, "Would You Like to Know How We (Used to) Do It? Becoming Modern in Peten, Guatemala", in The Fragmented Present: Mesoamerican Societies Facing Modernization, ed R. Gubler and U. Hostettler, Acta Mesoamerica 9, (95): 161-168; auth, "Re-Privatization and Privation: Traditional and Contemporary Land Tenure Systems in Peten, Guatemala", Mesoamerica 29, (95):215-232; coauth, "Itzaj Maya", in Encycl of World Cultures: Middle Am and the Caribbean, Vol 8, ed J. Dow and R.V. Kemper, (NY: HRAF and Hall-Macmillan, 95), 132-135; coauth, "Community Consultation, Sustainable Development and the Inter-American Development Bank: A Concept Paper", (Washington DC: Inter-Am Develop Bank, 96); coauth, "San Andres: Su Origen e Importancia Dentro del Contexto petenero", La Revista San Andres 1:10, 96; coauth, IDB Resources Book on Participation, Inter-Am Develo Bank, (Washington, DC), 96; auth, "Traditional Practices and Conservation of Forests in Peten, Guatemala", in Thirteen Ways of Looking at a Tropical Forest, ed J. Nations, C. Rader and I.Q. Neubauer, Conservation Int, (99):14-19; coauth, "The Influence of Fish Culture Technology, Extension Methodology, and Socioeconomics on the Success of Fish Culture on Limited-Resource Farms in Guatemala and Panama: An Ex-Post Evaluation, Aquanews 14.2 (99):10-11; auth, "San Benito: Estereotipos Socioculturales, Nooch Naj Cultunich; Revista Cultural de San Benito 29, (99):7-18. **CONTACT ADDRESS** Dept Anthrop, Univ of Delaware, 15 Orchard Ave, Newark, DE 19716. **EMAIL** nbsanth@udel.edu

SCHWARTZ, PEPPER J.
PERSONAL Born 05/11/1945, Chicago, IL, m, 2 children **DISCIPLINE** SOCIOLOGY **EDUCATION** Washington Univ, BA, 67; MA, 68; Yale Univ, MPhil, 70; PhD, 74. **CAREER** Teaching Asst, Yale Univ, 69-70; Asst Prof to Full Prof, Univ Washington, 72-. **HONORS AND AWARDS** Consultant, Nat Mtg with Surgeon General on Sexual Policy for the US, 99; Fel, Soc for the Sci Study of Sex, 95; Awd, Intl Women's Forum, 94; Matrix Awd in Educ, women in Comm, 92; Nat Mortar board alumni Achievement Awd, 91; Outstanding Young Men and Women of the Future, Seattle Chamber of Commerce, 78; Grant, Ctr for disease control, 85-87; Nat Sci Foundation Grant, 77-80; Russell Sage foundation, grant, 75; Innovative Teaching Grant, Univ Washington, 74-075; Res Grant, Univ Washington, 72-73. **MEMBERSHIPS** Intl Women's Forum; The Diet; Yale Club. **RESEARCH** Marriage and the Family; Gender; Human Sexuality; Qualitative Methodologies. **SELECTED PUBLICATIONS** Auth, The Gender of Sexuality, Pine Forge Press, 98; auth, Peer Marriage: How Love Between Equals Really Works, The Free Press, 94; auth, "Identity Acquisition and Affinity Groups," Qualitative Sociology as Everyday Life, 99; auth, "Stage Fright or Disciplinary Death Wish? Sociology in the Mass Media," Contemporary Sociology, 98; auth, "The Possibilities of Peer Marriage," The Responsive Community, 98; auth, 210 Questions for Parents to Ask Kids/201 Questions for Kids to Ask Parents, Avon Books, 00; auth, What I Learned About Sex: What America's Sex Educators, Counselors, and Therapists Want You to Know, Berkeley-Putnam, 98; auth, The Great Sex Weekend, Perigee-Putnam, 98; auth, "Bisexuality," Sexual Health, 97; auth, "Teasing: When Words Cut Deep," Family Life, 97. **CONTACT ADDRESS** Dept Sociol, Univ of Washington, PO Box 353340, Seattle, WA 98195-3340. **EMAIL** couples@u.washington.edu

SCHWEER, KATHRYN
PERSONAL Born 06/23/1938, Lincoln, NE, m, 1959, 3 children **DISCIPLINE** PSYCHOLOGY, NURSING **EDUCATION** Univ Iowa, BSN, 61; MA, 71; PhD, 75. **CAREER** Asst/Assoc Prof, Univ of Iowa, 71-80; Chairperson, Dept of Nursing Educ, Coe Col, Cedar Rapids, Iowa, 80-87; Dean, Sch of Nursing, Mankato State Univ, 87-94; Prof and Dean of Acad Affairs, Allen Col, Waterloo, Iowa, 94-. **HONORS AND AWARDS** Fifth District Nurse of the Year; Edith Ruppert Awd-Iowa Nurses Asn, Sigma Theta Tau Int; Virginia Handerson Fel; Phi Delta Kappa; Pi Lambda Theta. **MEMBERSHIPS** Iowa/Am Nurses Asn. **RESEARCH** Health Communities, Nursing Education. **SELECTED PUBLICATIONS** Auth, "Obesity in Childhood and Adolescence: The Role of the School Nurse," Sch Nurse Magazine (Mar 80); coauth, Author's Guide to Journals in Nursing and Related Fields, Haworth Press (NY), 82; auth, "Lessons from Nursing's Historians: A Tribute to Teresa E. Christy, Ed.D., F.A.A.N. (1927-1982)," Image XIV-3 (Oct 82):66; coauth, "Children of Alcoholic Parents: Identification and Intervention," Children's Health Care (Mar 86); co-ed, Building Healthy Communities: The Challenge of Health Care in the 21st Century, Allyn & Bacon (NY), 00. **CONTACT ADDRESS** Chief Acad Dean, Allen Col of Nursing, 1825 Logan Ave, Waterloo, IA 50703. **EMAIL** admin@sbtek.net

SCHWEIGERT, FRANCIS J.
PERSONAL Born 12/29/1950, Ladysmith, WI, m, 1976, 4 children **DISCIPLINE** EDUCATIONAL POLICY AND ADMINISTRATION **EDUCATION** Macalester Col, BA, 73; Col of St. Thomas, MA, 80; Col of St. Catherine, MA, 88; Univ Minn, PhD, 97. **CAREER** Dir Relig Ed, Church of St Alphonsus, Brooklyn Center, Minn, 88-94; Dir of Adult Formation, Church of St. Joan of Arc, Minneapolis, 94-96; guest tchr, St. Paul Public Schools, 97- ; independent consult, instr, 88- ; adj fac, Col of St. Catherine, Hamline Univ, United Theol Sem, Univ Minn, Univ St. Thomas, 88-; community liaison, Northwest Area Found. **MEMBERSHIPS** Am Acad Relig; Am Cath Philos Asn; Am Educ Res Asn; Asn for Moral Ed; Philos of Educ Soc. **RESEARCH** Moral education; theory and practice of restorative justice; social ethics; community organization and leadership; Church ministries and religious education; Catholic pastoral theology. **SELECTED PUBLICATIONS** Auth, Faith Formation Futures, The Living Light, 93; auth, Small Christian Communities: An Invitation to Discipleship, Evangelization Update, 98; auth, Learning the Common Good: Principles of Community- Based Moral Education in Restorative Justice, J of Moral Educ, 99; auth, Undoing Violence: Restorative Justice Versus Punitive Justice, Chicago Stud, 99; auth, "Underlying Principles: The Spirituality of the Circle," Full Circle, vol. 3: 2, (99): 2-4; auth, "Learning the Common Good: Principles of Community-Based Moral Education in Restorative Justice," Journal of Moral Education, Vol. 28:2, (99): 163-183; auth, "Undoing Violence: Restorative Justice Versus Punitive Justice," Chicago Studies, vol. 38:2, (99): 207-227; auth, "Moral Education in Victim Offender Conferencing," Criminal Justice Ethics, Vol. 18: 2, (99): 29-40; auth, "Mending the Moralnet: Moral Education in Strenthening Personal and Family Networks," Journal of Res and Dev in Education, Vol. 33: 2, (00): 74-84; auth, "Solidarity and Subsidiarity: Complementary Principles of Community Development," Journal of Social Philosophy, (in press). **CONTACT ADDRESS** Dept of Philosophy, Univ of St. Thomas, Minnesota, 332 Minnesota St, Ste 1201-E, Saint Paul, MN 55101. **EMAIL** schwe015@tc.umn.edu

SCHWEIKER, WILLIAM F.
PERSONAL Born 07/05/1939, Philadelphia, PA, m, 1996, 3 children **DISCIPLINE** SOCIOLOGY **EDUCATION** WVU, BA; Univ Minn, MA, PhD. **CAREER** Assoc prof, WVU, 67-72; prof , Calif Univ of Pa, 72-2000. **MEMBERSHIPS** ASH, RRI. **RESEARCH** Violence in the media. **SELECTED PUBLICATIONS** Auth, How to Snap the Shackles of Society; auth, Evaluation Research: A Family Connections Project. **CONTACT ADDRESS** Dept Soc Sci, California Univ of Pennsylvania, PO Box 46, California, PA 15419. **EMAIL** scweiker@cup.edu

SCHWEIKER-MARRA, KAREN
PERSONAL Born 08/08/1948, Englewood, NJ, m, 1994, 7 children **DISCIPLINE** EDUCATION **EDUCATION** West VA Univ, BS, 71; West Va Univ, MA, 79; West Va Univ, EdD, 94. **CAREER** Teacher, Monongalia Co Public Schs; Prof, Frostburg State Univ, 98-. **HONORS AND AWARDS** West Va Humanities Grant; West Va State Mini-Grants, 2; NASA Grant, Bell Atlantic Grants, 6; Golden Apple Awd, 91; Who's Who in America, Teachers, 94, 95, 96-99; Who's Who in America, Women, 95-96, 96-99. **MEMBERSHIPS** Eastern Ed. **RESEARCH** Writing, technology, at-risk students, school culture, teacher change. **SELECTED PUBLICATIONS** Auth, Suggestions for Involving Parents in Primary Grade Activities, Monongalia Co Bd of Ed, 79; auth, "The Principal's Role in Affecting a Change in School Culture," Ed Res Serv Spectrum 13 (3) (95): 3-11; auth, "Three English Teachers in Search of Answers: Issues of Ownership and Authorship," Alliance of Calif Univ and Western Pa English Teachers' J, Univ Calif Pr, (97); auth, "Issues of Ownership and Authorship," English J 86 (6) (97): 16-26; auth, Investigating the Effects of Prewriting Activities on Writing Performance and Anxiety of At-Risk Students," Reading Psychol (forthcoming). **CONTACT ADDRESS** Dept Ed, Frostburg State Univ, 101 Braddock Rd, 108 Frampton Hall, Frostburg, MD 21532-1099.

SCHWEIZER, KARL W.
PERSONAL Born 06/30/1946, Mannheim, Germany, m, 1969, 1 child **DISCIPLINE** SOCIOLOGY **EDUCATION** Univ Waterloo, BA, 69; MA, 70; Cambridge Univ, MA, PhD, 76. **CAREER** Prof, Bishops Univ, 76-86; Prof, NJ Inst Technol, 86-. **HONORS AND AWARDS** Adelle Mellen Awd, 90; NJ Writers Awd, 93; Fel, Royal Hist Soc. **RESEARCH** Military and diplomatic history, history of science, historiography. **SELECTED PUBLICATIONS** Auth, Cobbett in His Times (London), 90; auth, Frederick the Great, William Pitt and Lord Bute: Anglo-Prussian Relations 1756-1763 (New York), 91; auth, William Pitt: Earl of Chatham (New York), 93; auth, The Art of Diplomacy, (London) 94; auth, Francois de Callieres: Diplomat and Man of Letters (Lewiston, NY), 95; auth, Partners in Blood: The Gray/Snyder Murder Case, forthcoming. **CONTACT ADDRESS** Dept Sociol, New Jersey Inst of Tech, 323 M L K Blvd, Newark, NJ 07102-1824.

SCHWIEDER, DOROTHY ANN
PERSONAL Born 11/28/1933, Presho, SD, m, 1955, 2 children **DISCIPLINE** IOWA & WOMAN'S HISTORY **EDUCATION** Dakota Wesleyan Univ, BA, 55; Iowa State Univ, MA, 68; Univ Iowa, PhD, 81. **CAREER** Instr Am govt, Dakota Wesleyan Univ, 60-62; instr, 69-81, Asst Prof Am Hist, Iowa State Univ, 81- **MEMBERSHIPS** Orgn Am Hist; AAUP; Am Asn Univ Women. **RESEARCH** Communitarian studies; woman's economic history and ethnic history. **SELECTED PUBLICATIONS** Coauth, A paradox of change in the life

style of Iowa's old order Amish, Int Rev Mod Sociol, spring 76; contribr, Reader's Encycl of the American West, Thomas Crowell, 77; Labor roles of Iowa farm women, Proceedings Nat Archives Conf, 4/77; coauth, The Granger Homestead project, Palimpsest, 9-10/77; The Beachy Amish in Iowa: A case study, Mennonite Quart Rev, winter 77; Frontier brethern, Mont Mag Western Hist, winter 78; Italian-Americans in Iowa's coal camps, Annals of Iowa, spring, 82; Early exploration and settlement, In: Iowa's Natural Heritage, 82. **CONTACT ADDRESS** Dept of Hist, Iowa State Univ of Science and Tech, Ames, IA 50010.

SCOBIE, INGRID WINTHER
PERSONAL Born 01/02/1943, Bloomington, IN, 4 children **DISCIPLINE** AMERICAN & WOMEN'S HISTORY **EDUCATION** Brown Univ, BA, 64; Univ Rochester, MA, 65; Univ Wis, PhD(Am hist), 70. **CAREER** Vis lectr hist, Princeton Univ, 75; sr Fulbright Hays prof, Univ El Salvador & Nat Inst Teacher Training, Buenos Aires, 76; lectr US hist & res assoc, Univ Calif, San Diego, 77-79 & 81-82; Asst Prof US Hist, Tex Woman's Univ, 82-, Ed & interviewer, Regional Oral Hist Off, Bancroft Libr, Univ Calif, Berkeley, 77-81; panelist & reviewer, Nat Endowment for Humanities, 79-, res grant, 81-84; Eleanor Roosevelt Inst grant, 80; Am Philos Soc grant, 80. **MEMBERSHIPS** AHA; Orgn Am Historians; Oral Hist Asn; Nat Coun Pub Hist. **RESEARCH** California; legislative activity; 20th century social and political history, especially women in politics. **SELECTED PUBLICATIONS** Auth, Las distintas interpretaciones del progresivismo norteamericano como resultado de la vision historica de sus autores, In: Actas de las Terceras Jornadas de Investigacion de la Historia y Literatura Rioplatense y de los Estados Unidos, Mendoza, Argentina, 70; Jack B Tenney and the parasitic menace: Anti-communist legislation in California, 1940-49, Pac Hist Rev, 5/74; Helen Gahagan Douglas and her 1950 senate race with Richard M Nixon, Southern Calif Hist Quart, spring 76; Ella Reeve Bloor, In: Dict of American Biography, suppl 5, 77; Family and community history through oral history, Pub Historian, summer 79. **CONTACT ADDRESS** Dept of Hist & Govt, Texas Woman's Univ, P O Box 425889, Denton, TX 76204-5889.

SCOTT, BONNIE KIME
PERSONAL Born 12/28/1944, Philadelphia, PA, m, 1967, 3 children **DISCIPLINE** ENGLISH, WOMEN'S STUDIES **EDUCATION** Wellesley Col, BA, 67; Univ NC, Chapel Hill, MA, 69, PhD(Eng), 73. **CAREER** Asst prof, 75-80, assoc, 80-86, prof Eng, Univ DE, 86-; dir grad stud in Eng; Fac res grants Eng, Univ DE, 76, 81, 87, 95, 00. **HONORS AND AWARDS** DE Outstanding young woman, Outstanding Young Women Am, 77. **MEMBERSHIPS** MLA; Am Conf Irish Studies; James Joyce Found; VA Wolf Soc; Soc for the Study of Narrative Lit. **RESEARCH** Women's studies; modernism; James Joyce; Irish lit. **SELECTED PUBLICATIONS** Auth, Joyce and Feminism. Indiana, 84; auth, James Joyce, Humanities, 87; ed and contribur, New Alliances in Joyce Studies: "Whan it's Aped to Foul a Delfian," Delaware, 88; ed and contribur, The Gender of Modernism, Indiana, 90; auth, Refiguring Modernism, 2v, Indiana, 95; co-ed, Images of Joyce: Papers of the 12th International James Joyce Symposium, 2v, Colin Smyth, 98; ed and contribur, The Selected Letters of Rebecca West, Yale, 00. **CONTACT ADDRESS** Dept of English, Univ of Delaware, Newark, DE 19716. **EMAIL** bscott@udel.edu

SCOTT, ELLEN
DISCIPLINE SOCIOLOGY **EDUCATION** Williams Col, BA, 82; New Sch for Soc Res, MA, 90; Univ Calif at Davis, MA, 92; PhD, 97. **CAREER** Asst prof, Kent State Univ, 97-. **MEMBERSHIPS** ASA, SSP, SWS. **RESEARCH** Welfare, Welfare Reform, Race, Organizations, Gender. **SELECTED PUBLICATIONS** Auth, "How to Stop the Rapists? A Question of Strategy in Two Rape Crisis Centers," Soc Problems 40.3 (93): 343-361; auth, "Creating Partnerships for Change: alliances and betrayals in the racial politics of two feminist organizations," Gender & Soc 12.4 (98); auth, "From Race Cognizance to Racism Cognizance: dilemmas in anti-racist activism," in Feminism and Anti-Racism: International Struggles, eds. Kathleen Blee and France Winddance Twine (NY: New York Univ Press, forthcoming). **CONTACT ADDRESS** Dept Sociol, Kent State Univ, PO Box 5190, Kent, OH 44242-0001. **EMAIL** ekscott@kent.edu

SCOTT, JAMES J.
PERSONAL Born 05/09/1948, Dunkirk, NY, m, 1974, 3 children **DISCIPLINE** HEALTH AND PHYSICAL EDUCATION **EDUCATION** Erie County Tech Inst, AS; Findley Univ, BS; Colo State Univ, MSEd; Mich State Univ, PhD. **CAREER** Prof, Fitness Center Coord, Jackson Community Col, 80-, consult stress management and wellness, 80-, dept chair, 82-92; Metro dir, Cardiovascular Health and Fitness, Columbus YMCA, 78-80; physical dir, Findlay YMCA, 74-78. **HONORS AND AWARDS** Outstanding Grad Student, 74; Outstanding Citizen Finalist, 88; developed on on-line wellness course; initiated instructional skill workshop and prog on campus for faculty. **SELECTED PUBLICATIONS** Coauth, Teaching a Joy, ASCD (98). **CONTACT ADDRESS** Dept Health, Physical Ed, Jackson Comm Col, 2111 Emmons Rd, Jackson, MI 49201. **EMAIL** jim_scott@jackson.cc.mi.us

SCOTT, JOHN SHERMAN
PERSONAL Born 07/20/1937, Bellaire, OH, m, 1982 **DISCIPLINE** ETHNIC STUDIES **EDUCATION** SC State U, BA 1961; Bowling Green U, MA 1966; PhD 1972. **CAREER** Bowling Green State Univ OH, prof ethnic studies & resident-writer beginning 1970, prof emeritus, currently; director, Ethnic Cultural Arts Program. **HONORS AND AWARDS** Governor's Awd for the Arts, State of Ohio, 1990; produced play (TV), CURRENTS, 1991, produced docu-drama (TV), Hats & Fans, 1991, PBS. **MEMBERSHIPS** Consultant Toledo Model Cities Prog 1969-72; consult Toledo Bd Edn; mem NY Dramatists League 1971-; Speech Comm Assn 1966-73; Eugene O'Neill Memorial Theatre Center 1970-; Frank Silvera Writer's Wrkshp 1973-. **SELECTED PUBLICATIONS** Pub articles Players Black Lines; plays performed, Off-Broadway, NYC; Ride a Black Horse, Negro Ensemble Company 1972; Karma and The Goodship Credit, Richard Allen Center 1978-79. **CONTACT ADDRESS** Prof of Ethnic Studies & Resident-Writer, Bowling Green State Univ, Shatzel Hall, Bowling Green, OH 43402.

SCOTT, KIERAN
PERSONAL Born 08/28/1942, County Cavan, Ireland, m, 1988 **DISCIPLINE** RELIGION, EDUCATION **EDUCATION** Columbia Univ, PhD, 78. **CAREER** Fordham Univ NY. **MEMBERSHIPS** AAR, CTS, APRRE, REA **RESEARCH** Church edu; ecclesiology; adult edu; youth ministry, ministerial theology. **SELECTED PUBLICATIONS** Coauth, Perspectives on Marriage, Oxford Press; auth, Perspectives on Marriage, Oxford Press, 00. **CONTACT ADDRESS** 115 Cornell Ave, Hawthorne, NJ 07506. **EMAIL** kieranscott@yahoo.com

SCOTT, OTIS L.
PERSONAL Born 12/27/1941, Marion, OH, m, 1963, 3 children **DISCIPLINE** ETHNIC STUDIES **EDUCATION** University of MD & Eastern Washington State College, Cheney, WA; Central State College, Wilberforce, OH; California State University, Sacramento, BA, 1971, MA, 1973; Union Graduate School, Cincinnati, OH, PhD, 1982. **CAREER** California State University, Sacramento, CA, professor, 74-. **HONORS AND AWARDS** Co-Project Director, Beyond the Canon, 1990-; CSUS Exceptional Merit Awd, 1984. **MEMBERSHIPS** Member, National Conference of Black Political Scientists, 1989-; member, National Council for Black Studies, 1979-; member, National Association of Ethnic Studies, 1985-; member, Sacramento Area Black Caucus, 1974-; National Association for Ethnic Studies, 1996-98, pres, 1998. **SELECTED PUBLICATIONS** Author, The Veil: Perspectives on Race & Ethnicity in the US, West Publishing Co, 1994; co-author, Teaching From A Multicultural Perspective, Sage, 1994; author, "Lines, Borders and Corrections," Kendall Hunt, 1997; Journal article, Ethnic Studies Past and Present Explorations in Ethnic Studies Vol 11, No 2, 1988; Journal article, Coping Strategies of Women in Alice Walkers Novels Explorations in Ethnic Studies, Vol 10, No 1, 1987. **CONTACT ADDRESS** Ethnic Studies Department, California State Univ, Sacramento, 6000 J St, Sacramento, CA 95819. **EMAIL** scottol@csus.edu

SCOTT, ROXANNA
PERSONAL Born 03/22/1945, Detroit, MI, d, 2 children **DISCIPLINE** PSYCHOLOGY **EDUCATION** NY Univ, BS, 73; MA, 75; PhD, 77. **CAREER** Asst prof, acting chair, Bennett Col, 97-; adj instr, NC A & T. **MEMBERSHIPS** Am Psychol Soc; Am Psychol Assoc; SE Psychol Assoc. **RESEARCH** Self-esteem, coping, intrinsic religious motivation. **SELECTED PUBLICATIONS** Coauth, The Black Church as a Therapeutic Process: Health Education and Behavior, 98. **CONTACT ADDRESS** Dept Psychology, Bennett Col, 900 E Washington, Greensboro, NC 27401. **EMAIL** roxmscott@aol.com

SCOTT, VANN
PERSONAL Born 05/11/1969, Charlotte, NC, s **DISCIPLINE** PSYCHOLOGY **EDUCATION** Univ NC, AB, 91; GA S Univ, MA, 93; NC State Univ, PhD, 98. **CAREER** Asst prof, Armstrong Atlantic State Univ, 97-. **MEMBERSHIPS** Am Psychol Soc, Am Psychol Asn, SE Psychol Asn. **RESEARCH** Rumination, Stress, emotions, Non-verbal communication, Stereotyping and attitudes. **SELECTED PUBLICATIONS** Auth, "The development of a trait measure of ruminative thought," Personality and Individual Differences, (99): 1045-1056. **CONTACT ADDRESS** Dept Soc & Beh Sci, Armstrong Atlantic State Univ, 11935 Abercorn St, Savannah, GA 31419. **EMAIL** scottvan@mail.armstrong.edu

SCOTT, WILLIAM RICHARD
PERSONAL Born 12/18/1932, Parsons, KS, m, 1955, 3 children **DISCIPLINE** SOCIOLOGY **EDUCATION** Parsons Jr Coll, AA, 52; Univ Kansas, BS, 54, MA, 55; Univ Chicago, PhD, 61. **CAREER** Asst prof, Stanford Univ, 60; vice ch, Soc, SU, 68-72; ch, Soc, SU, 72-75; vis sr res, nat Ctr Health Servs Res, Dept Health Educ & Welfare, 75-76; dir, Stanford Ctr Orgs Res, 88-96; adj prof, Public Pol & Admin, Univ Tromso, Norway, 91-92; vis prof, Copenhagen Bus Sch, 92; vis prof, Kellogg Grad Sch Mgt, Northwestern Univ, 97; PROF, STANFORD UNIV, SOC. **HONORS AND AWARDS** Institute of Medicine, National Academy of Sciences, 75-; Distingished Scholar Awd, Management and Organizational Theory Division, Academy of Management, 88; Fellow, Center ofr Advanced Study in the Behavioral Sciences, 89-90; Richard D. Irwin Awd for Scholarly Contributions to Mangement, Academy of Management, 96; Honorary Doctorate in Economics and Business Administration, Copenhagen Business Schoo, 00. **MEMBERSHIPS** Am Soc Asn; Acad Mgt; Macro-Org Behav Soc; Soc Res Asn; Inst Medicine; Nat Academy of Sciences. **RESEARCH** Effects of institutional facets of environments on organizations; Structure & performance of public & nonprofit organizations. **SELECTED PUBLICATIONS** Institutions and Organizations, Sage; coauth, Organizational Environments: Ritual and Rationality, Sage, 92; ed, Organisational Sociology, Dartmouth Publ, 94; co-edr, Institutional Environments and Organizations: Structural Complexity and Individualism, Sage, 94; The Institutional Construction of Organizations: International and Longitudinal Studies, Sage 95; Organizations: Rational,Natural and Open Systems, Prentice Hall, 98; coauth, Institutional Change and Healthcare Organizations: From Professional Dominance to Managed Care, U of Chicago Press, 00; auth, Institutions and Organizations, 2nd ed, Sage, 01. **CONTACT ADDRESS** Dept Sociol, Stanford Univ, Stanford, CA 94305. **EMAIL** scottwr@leland.stanford.edu

SEAL, ROBERT
PERSONAL Born 05/31/1962, Charlottesville, VA, s **DISCIPLINE** EDUCATION **EDUCATION** Col William and Mary, AB, 84; MEd, 87; EdS, 89; EdD, 91. **CAREER** Sen res assoc, Seton Hall Univ, 92-96; asst dean, Stevens Inst of Tech, 96-97; exec asst to the provost & exec VP, William Paterson Univ, 97-. **MEMBERSHIPS** AIR, POD, AAHE, ACE. **RESEARCH** Faculty roles and responsibilities. **SELECTED PUBLICATIONS** Auth, The New Academic Generation: A Profession in Transformation, Johns Hopkins Univ Press: Baltimore, 98; auth, New Entrants to the Full-time Faculty of Higher Education Institutions, Nat Center for Educ Statistics: Washington, 98; auth, "Assessing student experiences in a workshop approach to academic and social integration: A preliminary study at two community colleges," Journal of Applied Research in the Community College, 96; auth, "Reforming the mathematics classroom: If it works for calculus, will it work for pre-calculus and college algebra?" UME Trends: News and Reports on Undergraduate Mathematics Education, 96; auth, "Review of Handbook of college Teaching: Theory and Applications, " Journal of Staff, Program, and Organization Development, 95; auth, "Nurturing Our Most Precious Resource: What We're Learning About Promoting Faculty vitality in Higher Education," Metropolitan Universities, 95; auth, "Vitalizing Senior Faculty," The Department Chair: A Newsletter for Academic Adminsitrators, Boston, 95. **CONTACT ADDRESS** Dept Curriculum & Instruction, William Paterson Col of New Jersey, 300 Pompton Rd, Wayne, NJ 07470. **EMAIL** sealr@wpunj.edu

SEARS, DAVID O.
PERSONAL Born 06/24/1935, IL, d, 3 children **DISCIPLINE** PSYCHOLOGY **EDUCATION** Stanford Univ, AB, 57; Yale Univ, PhD, 62. **CAREER** From asst prof to prof, Univ Calif at Los Angeles, 61-. **RESEARCH** Political Psychology, Racial Politics, Political Socialization. **SELECTED PUBLICATIONS** Auth, Tax Revolt, 86; auth, Political Cognition, 86; auth, Racialized Politics, 00. **CONTACT ADDRESS** Dept Psychology, Univ of California, Los Angeles, PO Box 951563, Los Angeles, CA 90095-1563.

SEATON, SHIRLEY SMITH
PERSONAL Born Cleveland, OH, m, 1965, 1 child **DISCIPLINE** MULTICULTURAL AFFAIRS **EDUCATION** Howard Univ, Washington DC, BA, 1947, MA, 1948; Case Western Reserve Univ, Cleveland OH, MA, 1956; Institute Universitario di Studi Europei, Turin, Italy, cert. advanced study, 1959; Univ of Akron, Akron OH, PhD, 1981; Beijing Normal Univ, Beijing, China, 1982; postdoctorate. **CAREER** Cleveland Board of Education, teacher, 50-58, asst principal, 59-65, principal, 66-76; US Government, Department of Education, educational specialist, 65; WEWS-TV, Cleveland OH, teacher, 63-67; Cleveland State Univ, adjunct prof, 77-85; Basics and Beyond Education Consultants, dir; John Carroll Univ, Assoc Dir, Multicultural Affairs, 89-. **HONORS AND AWARDS** Fulbright grant to Italy, 1959, and to China, 1982; Martin Luther King Outstanding Educator Awd, 1989; Outstanding Educator Awds, Cleveland City Cncl and Ohio State Legislature; Governor of Ohio, Martin Luther King Humanitarian Awd, 1992. **MEMBERSHIPS** Nat Alliance of Black School Educators, Nat Council for Social Studies, Nat Asn of Secondary School Principals, Asn for Supervision & Curriculum Development; pres, Metropolitan Cleveland Alliance of Black School Educators 1981-85; Coalition of 100 Black Women 1991-; Phi Delta Kappa 1979-; Fulbright Asn; board member, Western Reserve Historical Soc; board member, Retired and Senior Volunteer Program. **CONTACT ADDRESS** Multicultural Affairs, John Carroll Univ, 20700 N Park Blvd, University Heights, OH 44118. **EMAIL** sseaton664@aol.com

SECKINGER, DONALD SHERMAN
PERSONAL Born 02/01/1933, New York, NY, m, 1955, 3 children **DISCIPLINE** PHILOSOPHY & HISTORY OF EDUCATION **EDUCATION** Univ Calif, Los Angeles, AB, 54, MA, 56, EdD, 65. **CAREER** From asst prof to assoc prof educ,

Calif State Univ, Los Angeles, 64-70; assoc prof educ found, 70-77, Prof Educ Found, Univ Wyo, 77-, Vis lectr educ, Univ Calif, Los Angeles, 68-69. **MEMBERSHIPS** Fel Philos Educ Soc; Am Educ Studies Asn; fel Far Western Philos Educ Soc(-secy-treas, 74-77, vpres, 77 & pres, 78-). **RESEARCH** Philosophical anthropology; existential philosophy. **SELECTED PUBLICATIONS** Auth, Tombaugh,Clyde - Discoverer Of The Planet Pluto - Levy,D/, J Of The W, Vol 0032, 1993. **CONTACT ADDRESS** Dept of Educ Founds, Univ of Wyoming, Laramie, WY 82070.

SEELY, GORDON M.
PERSONAL Born 04/14/1930, San Mateo, CA, m, 1958, 2 children **DISCIPLINE** HISTORY OF EDUCATION **EDUCATION** Stanford Univ, AB, 51, MA, 54 & 58, PhD, 63. **CAREER** Teacher, High Schs & Jr Col, Calif, 54-55, 56-57, 59-60; from asst prof to assoc prof, 60-69, prof History, San Francisco State Univ, 69-. **RESEARCH** American social and intellectual history, especially education; California history. **SELECTED PUBLICATIONS** Ed, Education and Opportunity, Prentice-Hall, 1st ed, 71, 2nd ed, 75. **CONTACT ADDRESS** Dept Hist, San Francisco State Univ, 1600 Holloway Ave, San Francisco, CA 94132-1740. **EMAIL** evgor@worldnet.att.net

SEGAL, DAVID R.
PERSONAL Born 06/22/1941, New York, NY, m, 1966, 1 child **DISCIPLINE** SOCIOLOGY **EDUCATION** Binghamton Univ, BA, 62; Univ Chicago, MA, 63; PhD, 67. **CAREER** Asst prof, 66-71; assoc prof, 71-75, Univ Michigan; tec ch, ARI, 73-75; prof, Univ Maryland, 75-; cen dir, 95-. **HONORS AND AWARDS** Doc Hum Let, TSU; Dist Schl; Outstand Ser Medal. **MEMBERSHIPS** ASA; ISA; SSS; IUSAFS; DCSS. **RESEARCH** Military organization; Military manpower and personnel. **SELECTED PUBLICATIONS** Auth, The Postmodern Military, Ox Univ Press (00); Auth, "Who Chooses Military Service?," Mil Psych (00); auth, "Propensity to Serve in the US Military," Arm Force (99); auth, "Gender and the Propensity to Enlist in the US Military," Gend Issues (99). **CONTACT ADDRESS** Dept Sociology, Univ of Maryland, Col Park, College Park, MD 20742-0001. **EMAIL** dsegal@socy.umd.edu

SEGAL, MARILYN
PERSONAL Born 08/09/1927, Utica, NY, d, 5 children **DISCIPLINE** DEVELOPMENTAL PSYCHOLOGY **EDUCATION** Wellesley Col, BA; McGill Univ , BSc soc wk; Nova Univ, PhD, psychol. **CAREER** Boston City Hosp, casewkr, 50-51; Dir pre-sch and hd start cen, 65-70; Nova Southeastern Univ, asst prof, assoc prof, prof, dean, 70-98-. **HONORS AND AWARDS** Sentin Pub Awd winner, 97; Spirit of excell Awd; NSU outstand alumni; Chief Awd, FL Indep Col; Woman of the Year Awd. **MEMBERSHIPS** APA; FL Psychol Asn; Zero to Three; Nat Cen for Infants Toddlers and Family. **RESEARCH** Devel of play in typical children with autism; social interaction in yng childrn; infant toddler interactive play; play assment. **SELECTED PUBLICATIONS** Non-Structured Play Observations: Guidelines, benefits, caveats, M Segal N Webber in: New Visions for the Delvel Assess of Infants and Young Children, ed S Meisels E Fenichel, Zero to Three, Washington DC, 96; Creative Beginnings, Addison Wellesley Alt, Pub, CA, 95; Play Together Grow Together, Nova Univ, 93; several other pub and articles. **CONTACT ADDRESS** Family Center, Nova Southeastern Univ, Fort Lauderdale, 3301 College Ave, Fort Lauderdale, FL 33314. **EMAIL** segal@nova.edu

SEGAL, N. L.
DISCIPLINE PSYCHOLOGY **EDUCATION** Boston Univ BA 73; Univ Chicago ma 74, PhD 82. **CAREER** California State Univ Fullerton, prof 91-; MN Center for Twins Adoption Research, asst dir 82-91. **HONORS AND AWARDS** Dist alumni Boston U 90 **MEMBERSHIPS** APA; APS; ISTS; BGA **RESEARCH** Twin studies **CONTACT ADDRESS** Dept of Psychology, California State Univ, Fullerton, Fullerton, CA 92634.

SEGAL, STEVE P.
DISCIPLINE SOCIAL WELFARE **EDUCATION** Hunter Col, BA, 65; Univ Mich, MSW, 67; Univ Wisc, PhD, 72. **CAREER** Dir, Center for Self Help Res, Univ Calif, 90-; Dir, Mental Health and soc Welfare Res Group, Univ Calif, 73-; Prof, Univ Calif, 82-. **HONORS AND AWARDS** Sen Res and Lecture Fulbright Awd, Australia, 98-99; Harris Trust Awd, 88-89; Medal of Brescia, Italy, 87; Western European Regional Res Fulbright, 85-86. **MEMBERSHIPS** Am Psychol Asn, Am Social Asn, Nat Asn of Soc Workers/ACSW, Am Public Health Asn. **RESEARCH** Mental Health and Health Policy; Evaluation and Research Methodology; Psychiatric Epidemiology; Dangerousness and Grave Disability attributable to mental Disorder; Civil commitment; Homelessness; Self Help. **SELECTED PUBLICATIONS** Co-auth, "Social breakdown syndrome: Environmental and host factors associated with chronicity," Am Journal of Public Health, (72): 91-94; auth, "Research on the outcome of social work therapeutic interventions: A review of the literature," Journal of Health and Social Behavior, (72): 3-17; auth, "Outcome Measurement systems in Mental Health: A Program Prospective," in Outcomes Measurement in the Human Services, Washington, 97; auth, "Response to Fuller Torrey," Psychiatric Services, (97): 604; co-auth, "The Quality of Psychiatric emergency Evaluations," Breakthrough, (97): 17-30; co-auth, "Program Environments of Self-Help Agencies," Journal of Mental Health administration, (97): 49-61; co-auth, "Coping, catastrophic life events and disabling experiences among users of mental health self help agencies," Psychiatry in Medicine, (97): 350-351; co-auth, "Health Status of Long-term Users of Self Help Agencies," Health and social Work, (98): 45-52; co-auth, "Involuntary return to a psychiatric emergency service within twelve months," Psychiatric Services, (98): 1212-1217; auth, "The impact of managed care on the practice of psychotherapy, A review," Journal of Sociology and Social Welfare, (98): 186-188; auth, "Social Work in a Managed Care Environment," International Journal of Social Welfare, (990: 47-55 **CONTACT ADDRESS** Dept Soc Welfare, Univ of California, Berkeley, 120 Haviland Hall, Berkeley, CA 94720-7400. **EMAIL** spsegal@uclink4.berkeley.edu

SEIBERT-MCCAULEY, MARY F.
PERSONAL Born 06/21/1930, LA, w **DISCIPLINE** EDUCATION **EDUCATION** TN State Univ, BS 1952, MA 1961; Northwestern Univ, 1957; Vanderbilt, 1966, 1967, 1977; George Peabody Vanderbilt, PhD 1983. **CAREER** Future City Sch, teacher 1952-57; Roosevelt HS, English teacher 1957-62; Bruce HS, English teacher 1963-66; Dyersburg City High School, English teacher, 66-69; Dyersburg Comm Coll, assoc prof 1969-, chmn of English 1974-84; prof of English 1985, chmn of humanities 1976-84; Union City Ford, Lincoln Mercury, Union City, TN, part owner, 88-; Math Contracting Co, Dyersberg, TN, president, 77-90; Dyersburg State College, Dyersburg, TN, Humanities Dept, chair, professor of English, 69-94. **HONORS AND AWARDS** Outstanding Teacher Awd, TN Governor's Comm on Handicapped 1966; First Black Teacher Dyersburg HS & DSCC 1966-; Certificate Outstanding Educator of Amer 1975; Stipend Natl Endowment for Humanities 1976. **MEMBERSHIPS** Mem Delta Sigma Theta Sor 1951-; WDSG, first African-American disc-jockey, WJRO, 1953-57; pres NAACP Dyersburg Chap 1963-64; pres Math Inc Construction Co 1977-; mem 1st Woman Dyer Co Bd of Educ 1977-; bd mem Dyer Co Mentally Retarded Assn 1980-; bd mem Dyer Co Cancer Assn 1982-; mem Tabernacle Bapt Ch; real estate holdings; mem Kiwanis Club 1988-; 1st Black Dyersburg City Bd of Educ 1988-; 1st Black director, First Citizen National Bank, 1991; mem, Dyersburg Dyer County Modernization Committee, 1990; West Tennessee Habitat; director, Tennessee State Alumni; Board for Dyersburg Dyer County Crimstoppers, 1990-; Dyersburg Dyer County Consolidation Committee, 1993-94; Aurora Civic and Social Club. **SELECTED PUBLICATIONS** Wrote first dissertation on and with assistance from Alex Haley: Alex Haley: A Southern Griot, 1988; First African-American Jury Commissioner, 1994. **CONTACT ADDRESS** Chmn of Humanities, Dyersburg State Comm Col, Dyersburg, TN 38024.

SEIDENBERG, MARK
DISCIPLINE PSYCHOLOGY, LINGUISTICS, COMPUTER SCIENCE **EDUCATION** Columbia Univ, PhD, 80. **CAREER** Prof, Univ Southern Calif. **RESEARCH** Psycholinguistics, Neurolinguistics. **SELECTED PUBLICATIONS** Auth, Language Acquisition and Use: Learning and Applying Probabilistic Constraints, Sci, 275, 97; coauth, Evaluating Behavioral and Neuroimaging Data on Past Tense Processing, Language, 74, 98; Category Specific Semantic Deficits in Focal and Widespread Brain Damage: A Computational Account, J Cognitive Neuroscience 10, 98; Learning to Segment Speech Using Multiple Cues: A Connectionist Model, Language and Cognitive Processes 13, 98; On the Nature and Scope of Featural Representations of Word Meaning, J Experimental Psychology: Gen 126, 97; On the basis of Two Subtypes of Developmental Dyslexia, Cognition 58, 96. **CONTACT ADDRESS** Dept of Linguistics, Univ of So California, University Park Campus, Los Angeles, CA 90089. **EMAIL** marks@gizmo.usc.edu

SEIFMAN, ELI
PERSONAL Born 08/04/1936, Brooklyn, NY, m, 1990, 2 children **DISCIPLINE** EDUCATION **EDUCATION** Queens Col, CUNY, BA, 55, MS, 59; New York Univ, PhD, 65. **CAREER** Lect, 64-65, asst prof, 65-68, assoc prof, 68-71, asst prof, 71-75, prof, 75-, chair soc sci interdisc prog, 78-, dir, Center for Excellence & Innovation in Education, 88-, dist serv prof, 92- prof, 96-, SUNY, Stony Brook. **HONORS AND AWARDS** Phi Beta Kappa; Phi Alpha Theta; Kappa Delta Pi; The Royal Soc for Asian Affairs of Great Britain; Dante Medal, Long Island Chap, Amer Assoc of Teachers of Italian. **MEMBERSHIPS** Assoc for Asian Stud; Royal Soc for Asian Affairs; Nat Counc for the Soc Stud. **RESEARCH** Cont Chinese ed; soc stud teacher ed. **SELECTED PUBLICATIONS** Art, The Formation of China's Educational Policy for the 1990s: The Ten-Year program of the Eighth Five-Year Plan of the People's Republic of China, Proceedings of the 13th International Symposium on Asian Studies, 91; art, China: The Anti-Child Labor Regulations, Asian Thought & Society, Aug, 92; art, China, The Law for the Protection of Minors, Asian Thought & Society, Jan-Apr 92; art, The Law for the Protection of the Handicapped, Asian Thought & Society, Jan-Apr, 94; coauth, Chinese Education in the Decade of Socialist Modernization, Asian Thought & Society, Set-Dec, 96. **CONTACT ADDRESS** 11 Royalston Ln, Centereach, NY 11720-1414.

SEIGFRIED, CHARLENE
DISCIPLINE CLASSICAL AMERICAN PHILOSOPHY, 19TH-CENTURY PHILOSOPHY, FEMINIST PHILOSOPHY **EDUCATION** Loyola Univ, Chicago, PhD. **CAREER** Prof, Purdue Univ. **RESEARCH** Pragmatism and feminism. **SELECTED PUBLICATIONS** Published works in the areas of social and political philosophy, metaphysics, and aesthetics. **CONTACT ADDRESS** Dept of Philos, Purdue Univ, West Lafayette, 1080 Schleman Hall, West Lafayette, IN 47907-1080.

SEITZ, JAY
PERSONAL Born 01/08/1957, Princeton, NJ, s **DISCIPLINE** PSYCHOLOGY **EDUCATION** Rutgers Univ, AB, 78; New Sch Soc Res, MA, 81; CUNY, Grad Sch, PhD, 87. **CAREER** Chair, Adelphi Univ, Child Act Cen, 91-94; assoc clin prof, Adelphi UNIV, Derner Inst, 91-94; asst prof, Adelphi Univ, Sch Ed, 91-94; asst prof, Wagner Col, 94-96; adj asst prof, NYork Univ, 95-96; asst prof, CUNY, York Col, 96-. **HONORS AND AWARDS** Grad res assist, Grad Sch CUNY, 82-85; Scholar, Intl Summer Inst Semiotic Struct Stud Univ Toronto, 84; Univ Fel, Grad Sch CUNY, 85-86; Teach assist, Hunter Coll, 86-87; Durant Fel, St. Peter's Coll, 90; NYU Fac Assoc, 90, 95, 96; Fac Schol, Inst Rat-Emotive Ther, 92. **MEMBERSHIPS** Soc Res Child Devel; Jean Piaget Soc; NYAS; NYNG; EPA; APA; APS; AAAS; AAUP; AERA; NAEYC. **RESEARCH** Human learning/cognitive development in young children; development of sensorimotor intelligence; the role of brain systems and social deficits in autism; the effects of political and social institutions on human behavior. **SELECTED PUBLICATIONS** Auth, "The development of bodily-kinesthetic intelligence in children: Implications for education and artistry," Holistic Ed Rev (92); auth, "The development of aesthetic movement: Linkages to preschool education. J of Early Edu and Family Rev 5 (96), 7-9; auth, "The development of metaphoric understanding: Implications for a theory of creativity," Creat Res J 10 (97), 347-353; auth, "Metaphor, symbolic play, and logical thought in early childhood, Genetic, Social, and Gen Psychol Mono 123 (97), 373-391; auth, "Nonverbal metaphor: A review of theories and evidence," Genetic, Social, and Gen Psychol Mono 124 (98), 121-143; auth, "Political science and creativity," in The Encyc of Creat, eds. M A Runco, Pritzker (NY: Academic Press), 99; auth, "The bodily basis of thought," New Ideas in Psychology: An International Journal of Innovative Theory in Psychology 18, in press. **CONTACT ADDRESS** Dept Political Sci and Psychology, York Col, CUNY, 94-20 Guy Brewer Blvd, Jamaica, NY 11451-0001. **EMAIL** seitz@york.cuny.edu

SEIZER, SUSAN
DISCIPLINE ANTHROPOLOGY **EDUCATION** Columbia Univ, BA; Univ Chicago, MA; PhD, 97. **CAREER** Asst Prof, Scripps Col, 98-. **MEMBERSHIPS** AAA; ALA; ACA. **RESEARCH** Theater artists in South Asia; Stigma; Humor; Cultural anthropology. **SELECTED PUBLICATIONS** Auth, "Paradoxes of Visibility in the Field: Rites of queer passage in anthropology," Public Culture, (95): 73-100; auth, "Jokes, Gender, and Discursive Distance on the Tamil Popular Stage," American Ethnologist, (97): 62-90; auth, "Roadwork: Offstage with Special Drama Actresses in Tamilnadu, South India," Cultural Anthropology, 00; auth, "Gender Plays: sociospatial paradigms on the Tamil popular stage," Tamil Geographies: Constructions of Space in Tamilnadu, SUNY Press, forthcoming. **CONTACT ADDRESS** Dept Anthropol, Scripps Col, 1030 Columbia Ave, Claremont, CA 91711. **EMAIL** sseizer@scrippscol.edu

SENGSTOCK, MARY C.
PERSONAL Born 03/24/1936, Detroit, MI, m, 1988, 5 children **DISCIPLINE** SOCIOLOGY **EDUCATION** Washington Univ, St Louis, PhD; Univ Mich, MA; Univ Detroit, PhB. **CAREER** Prof Sociol, Wayne State Univ, 66-. **HONORS AND AWARDS** Wayne State Univ Bd of Governors Fac Recognition, 84; Wayne State Univ Col of Liberal Arts Teaching Excellence, 99; Chaldean Fed Cultural Awd, 99. **MEMBERSHIPS** Sociol Practice Asn, Comn on Applied & Clinical Sociol. **RESEARCH** Ethnic groups, Chaldean community, elder house, family violence, sociology of law. **SELECTED PUBLICATIONS** Auth, Chaldean Americans (82, 99); pubs in prof journals. **CONTACT ADDRESS** Dept Sociol, Wayne state Univ, 2247 F. A. B., Detroit, MI 48202. **EMAIL** marycay910@aol.com

SERA, MARIA D.
PERSONAL Born 12/17/1959, Havana, Cuba, m, 1990 **DISCIPLINE** CHILD DEVELOPMENT **EDUCATION** Ind Univ, BA, 82; PhD, 87. **CAREER** Instr, Univ Iowa, 87; asst prof, 87-89; asst prof, Univ Minn, 89-94; assoc prof, 94-. **MEMBERSHIPS** Psychonomic Soc; SRCD. **RESEARCH** The Role of language in cognitive development. **SELECTED PUBLICATIONS** Coauth, "Developing definitions of objects and events in English and Spanish speakers," Cognitive Dev 6 (91): 119-142; auth, "To Be or To Be: Use and acquisition of the Spanish copulas," J Memory Lang 31 (92): 408-427; coauth, Grammatical and conceptual forces in the attribution of gender by English and Spanish speaker," Cognitive Dev 9 (94): 261-292; coauth, "Ser Helps Speakers of Spanish Identify 'Real' Properties," Child Dev 68 (97): 820-831; coauth, "Language and Ontological Knowledge: The Contrast Between Objects and Events

made by English and Spanish Speakers," J Memory Lang 41 (99): 303-326. **CONTACT ADDRESS** Dept Child Development, Univ of Minnesota, Twin Cities, 51 E River Rd, Minneapolis, MN 55455.

SERELS, M. MITCHELL
PERSONAL Born 01/12/1948, New York, NY, m, 1979, 4 children **DISCIPLINE** PSYCHOLOGY; HISTORY **EDUCATION** Yeshiva Univ, BA, 67, MS, 70; Hunter Col, MA, 71; NYork Univ, PhD, 90. **CAREER** Assoc Dir, Jacob E Safea Inst of Sephardic Stud, Yeshiva Univ, 73-; Univ Dir of Foreign Stud Svcs, Yeshiva Univ, 92-99; Chair, Dept of Histiory, Berkely College. **HONORS AND AWARDS** Knighted, Caballero de order de Merito Civil, by King Juan Carlos I of Spain. **MEMBERSHIPS** Am Soc of Sephardic Stud; Nat Asn of Foreign Stud Advisors. **RESEARCH** Jews of Spanish origin; Morocco; W Africa. **SELECTED PUBLICATIONS** Auth, Sephardim and the Holocaust, NY, 94; auth, Historia de los Judios de Tanger, Caracos, 96; auth, Jews of Cape Verde: A Brief History, NY, 97; auth, Studies on the History of Portuguese Jews. **CONTACT ADDRESS** Berkeley Col, White Plains, 40 Red Oak Lane, White Plains, NY 10604. **EMAIL** mitchser@aol.com

SERPER, MARK R.
PERSONAL Born 05/18/1963, Brooklyn, NY, m, 1998 **DISCIPLINE** PSYCHOLOGY **EDUCATION** SUNY, PhD, 91. **CAREER** Asst Prof, NJ School of Medicine, 92-93; Assoc Prof, Hofstra Univ, 96-. **HONORS AND AWARDS** Gerald Klerman Awd, NARSAD, 98; Young Investigator's Awd, NIMH, 94. **MEMBERSHIPS** Am Psychol Asn, Soc of Biolog Psychiat. **RESEARCH** Schizophrenia; Cocaine addictions; Alcoholism. **SELECTED PUBLICATIONS** Co-auth, "Neurocognitive Deficits in Recently Abstinent Cocaine Abusing Schizophrenic Patients," Journal of Substance Abuse, in press; co-auth, "Cognitive functioning and Substance Use Disorders in Schizophrenia," in Cognition in Schizophrenia, Oxford Univ Press, in press; co-auth, "Practice-Related Improvement in Information Processing with Novel Antipsychotic Treatment," schizophrenia Research, in press; co-auth, Street Madness: Stemming the Rising Tide of Violence by the Mentally Ill, Intl Univ Press; in press; co-auth, "Learning and Memory Impairment in Cocaine Dependent and Comorbid Schizophrenic Patients,: Psychiatry Research, (00): 21-32; co-auth, "Emergency Presentation of Acute Cocaine Intoxication in Schizophrenia," Schizophrenia Bulletin, (99): 387-394; co-auth, "Social Support and Psychopathology in Homeless Patients Presenting for Emergency Psychiatric Treatment," Journal of Clinical Psychology, (99): 1127-1133; co-auth, Evaluating and Managing Suicidal and Violent Patients," in Toxicologic Emergencies, Appleton & Lange, 98; co-auth, "Ziprasidone: A Hew Highly Atypical Antipsychotc," Essential Psychopharmacology, (98): 463-485; co-auth, "Attentional And Clinical Neuroleptic Response in Schizophrenia: A Study with the Continuous Performance Test, "Cognitive Neuropsychiatry, 9(&): 51-56. **CONTACT ADDRESS** Dept Psychol, Hofstra Univ, 1000 Fulton Ave, Hempstead, NY 11550. **EMAIL** mark.serper@nyu.edu

SERVATY, HEATHER
PERSONAL Born 07/21/1970, Cambridge, MN, s **DISCIPLINE** PSYCHOLOGY **EDUCATION** Univ North Tex, PhD, 97. **CAREER** Asst prof, Rad Univ, 97-. **HONORS AND AWARDS** Rad Univ Seed Gnt; ADEC Gnt. **MEMBERSHIPS** APA; ADEC. **RESEARCH** Death and dying; grief and bereavement; aging. **SELECTED PUBLICATIONS** Coauth, Psychology of Aging: An annotated bibliography, Greenwood Press (Westport, CT), 95; coauth, "Levels of death anxiety in terminally ill persons: A cross validation and extension," Omega, 34 (96): 203-218; coauth, "Psychoneuroindocrinological indicators of stress and intellectual performance among older adults: An exploratory study," Exper Aging Res 22 (97): 393-401; coauth, "Death education and communication apprehension regarding dying persons," Omega 34 (96): 133-142; coauth, "Relationships Between Death Anxiety, Communication Apprehension with the Dying, and Empathy in Those Seeking Occupations as Nurses and Physicians," Death Stud 20 (96): 149-161; coauth, "Physiological indicators of stress and intellectual performance among anxious older adults," Edu Geron 23 (97): 477-487; coauth, "The impact of cortisol on practice-related gains in intelligence," Exper Aging Res 24 (98): 217-230; coauth, "A paradox of personal identity in Kierkegaard's Philosophical Fragments," in International Kierkegaard commentary: Philosophical fragments and Johanness Climacus, ed. RL Perkins (Macon, GA: Mercer, 94); coauth, "Factor structure of the communication apprehension with the dying scale," in End of life issues: Interdisciplinary and multidimensional perspectives, ed. B de Vries (NY: Springer, 99); coauth, "Age cohort differences in perceptions of funerals," in End of life issues: Interdisciplinary and multidimensional perspective, ed. B de Vries (NY: Springer, 99). **CONTACT ADDRESS** Dept Psychology, Radford Univ, PO Box 6946, Radford, VA 24142. **EMAIL** hservaty@runet.edu

SETTLES, ROSETTA HAYES
PERSONAL Born 11/16/1920, Little Rock, AR, m **DISCIPLINE** EDUCATION **EDUCATION** Wiley Coll, BA 1948; Harvard U, EdM 1951; Walden U, PhD 1977; Oakland U, Grad Study 1970; Summer Sch, Overseas Study 1971; Great Britain Sch, TourStudy 1973. **CAREER** Oakland Univ, asso prof 1969-; Garden City Public School, rdng supr 1967-, first black teacher 1967-; Clintondale Public School, rdng spec, clinician 1965-67; Little Rock, remedial rdng elem teacher 1945-56; Harvard Boston Summer School Prog, team teacher 1965; Summer School Prog, asst dir; Detroit Public School, rdng consultant 1972; Garden City Summer School Prog, prin, dir 1974. **HONORS AND AWARDS** Originator, sponsor Lena D Hayes Schlrshp Awd 1950; Harvard Univ Schlrshp 1951; Top Ten Outstndng Dunbar HS Alumni Nation 1973; Tribute Awd 1977; Top Ten Outstndng Dunbar HS Alumni Nat, Little Rock AR Conv 1979; **MEMBERSHIPS** Fdr org Nat Dunbar HS Alumni Reunion of Classes; vice pres Detroit Chap Dunbar High Alumni 1980-; mem Nat Bd of Dir Dunbar HS Alumni Assn 1977-; mem IRA; NCTE; MRA; del NEA; mem NAACP. **SELECTED PUBLICATIONS** Auth, "Reading & Rhythm" 1970. **CONTACT ADDRESS** 31753 Maplewood St, Garden City, MI 48135.

SEXTON, JAMES D.
PERSONAL m, 1 child **DISCIPLINE** ANTHROPOLOGY **EDUCATION** UCLA, BA 67, MA 71, PhD 73. **CAREER** Northern Arizona Univ, asst, assoc, prof, Regent's prof, 73 to 91-. **HONORS AND AWARDS** NAU Pres Awd for Tchg, Research and Service; NAU Phi Kappa Phi Faculty Scholar Awd. **MEMBERSHIPS** AAA; SWAA **RESEARCH** Latin Amer **SELECTED PUBLICATIONS** Auth, Heart of Heaven Heart of Earth, 99; Mayan Folktales, 92; Ignacio, 92; Campesino, 85; Son of Tecun Uman, 81; auth, Jaseno, 01. **CONTACT ADDRESS** Dept of Anthropology, No Arizona Univ, PO Box 15200, Flagstaff, AZ 86014-5200. **EMAIL** James.Sexton@nau.edu

SEYMOUR, JACK L.
PERSONAL Born 10/27/1948, Kokomo, IN, m, 1997, 2 children **DISCIPLINE** HISTORY AND PHILOSOPHY OF EDUCATION **EDUCATION** Ball State Univ, BS; Vanderbilt Divinity School, DMin & MDiv; George Peabody Col of Vanderbilt, PhD. **CAREER** Asst prof Church & Ministry, Vanderbilt Univ 74-78; Dir Field Educ, Chicago Theol Sem, 78-82; prof Christian Educ, assoc prof, asst prof, Scarritt Grad School, 82-88; prof Relig Educ, 88-, acad dean, 96-, Garrett-Evangelical Theol Sem, 88-. **RESEARCH** Theology of people of God; Ethnographic Research in education; Theological education. **SELECTED PUBLICATIONS** Coauth Educating Christians: The Intersection of Meaning, Learning, and Vocation, Abdington Press, 93; For the Life of a Child: The 'Religious' in the Education of the Public, Relig Educ, 94; Contemporary Approaches to Christian Education, Theological Perspectives on Christian Formation, W B Eerdmans, 96; The Ethnographer as Minister: Ethnographic Research in the Context of Ministry Vocations, Relig Educ, 96; Temples of Meaning: Theology and the People of God, Lib Relig Educ, 96; rev Essays on Religion and Education: An Issue in Honor of William Bean Kennedy, Relig Educ, 96; The Cry for Theology: Laity Speak about the Church, and The Cry for Theology: Laity Speak about Theology, PACE: Professional Approaches for Christian Education, 96; auth Mapping Christian Education: Approaches to Congregational Learning, Abingdon Press, 97; Thrashing in the Night: Laity Speak about Religious Knowing, Relig Educ, 97. **CONTACT ADDRESS** Garrett-Evangelical Theol Sem, 2121 Sheridan Rd, Evanston, IL 60201. **EMAIL** Jack-Seymour@garrett.edu

SHACKLEY, M. STEVEN
PERSONAL Born 05/13/1949, San Diego, CA, m, 1995, 1 child **DISCIPLINE** ANTHROPOLOGY **EDUCATION** San Diego State Univ, BA, 79, MA, 81; PhD, 90, Arizona State Univ. **CAREER** Tchg asst, anthrop, San Diego State Univ, 80-81; tchg asst, lectr, anthrop, 83-84, 85-86, Arizona State Univ; lectr archaeol, Calif State Univ, Fullerton, 87-91; adj asst prof, anthrop, San Diego State Univ, 89-90; fac memb Archaeol Res Facil, Univ Calif, Berkeley, 90- ; adj asst prof, anthrop, Univ Calif, Berkeley, 94-95; adj asst prod, anthrop, Univ Calif, Berkeley, 95-99; Research Prof, 00-; Dir of Archaeological XRF Laboratory, Univ CA, Berkeley. **HONORS AND AWARDS** Phi Beta Kappa; Regents Grad Acad Scholar, 84-86; ARCS Fel, 84-85; listed Who's Who in the West & Who's Who in Science and Engineering. **MEMBERSHIPS** AAAS; Geol Soc Am; Az Archaeol and Hist Soc; Int Asn for Obsidian Stud; Soc for Am Archaeol; Soc for Archaeol Sci; Soc for Calif Archaeol. **RESEARCH** Prehisory American Southwest and Northern Mexico, Archaeological Science-mateiral studies, Lithic Technology, Early Agriculture in the Southwest. **SELECTED PUBLICATIONS** Contribur, Current Issues and Future Directions in Archaeological Volcanic Glass Studies: An Introduction; contribur, Intrasource Chemical Variability and Secondary Depositional Processes in Sources of Archaeological Obsidian: A Case Study from the American Southwest; contribur, Factors Affecting the Energy-Dispersive X-Ray Fluorescence Analysis of Archaeological Obsidian; auth, Archaeological Obsidian Studies: Method and Theory, Plenum, 98. **CONTACT ADDRESS** Phoebe Hearst Museum of Anthropology, Univ of California, Berkeley, 103 Kroeber Hall, Berkeley, CA 94720-3712. **EMAIL** shackley@sscl.berkeley.edu

SHADE, BARBARA J.
PERSONAL Born 10/30/1933, Armstrong, MO, m **DISCIPLINE** EDUCATION **EDUCATION** Pittsburg St Univ Pittsburg KS, BS 1955; Univ of Wis Milwaukee, MS 1967; Univ of Wis Madison, PhD 1973. **CAREER** Univ of WI, asst prof dept Afro-am Studies 1975; Dane Co Head Start, exec dir 1969-71; Milwaukee WI Pub Schs, tchr 1960-68; Consult parent Devel Regn V, 73-75; Dept of Pub Instr WI, urban ed consult 1974-75; Univ of WI Parkside, assoc prof/chair div of educ; professor/dean, school of education. **HONORS AND AWARDS** Postdoctorial Fellow, Nat Endwmnt for Hmnties 1973-74. **MEMBERSHIPS** Mem Delta Sigma Theta Sor 1952-; mem Am Psychol Assn; bd pres St Mary's Hosp Med Cntr 1978; vice pres priorities Dane Co United Way 1979; mem Assoc of Black Psychologists, Amer Educ Rsch Assoc. **SELECTED PUBLICATIONS** Publ Jour of Psychol Jour of Social Psychol; Negro Educ Rvw; Review of Educational Rsch; Journal of Negro Educ; Journal of School Psychology. **CONTACT ADDRESS** Dean of Education, Univ of Wisconsin, Parkside, Kenosha, WI 53141.

SHADISH, W. R.
PERSONAL Born 03/11/1949, Brooklyn, NY, m, 1981 **DISCIPLINE** CLINICAL PSYCHOLOGY **EDUCATION** Santa Clara Univ, BA, 72; Purdue Univ, MA, 75, PhD, 78. **CAREER** Staff asst, State of Calif Legis, Joint Comt on the Master Plan for Higher Educ, 72; core staff therapist, Purdue Univ Psychol Svc Ctr, 75-77; intern, Memphis Clin Psychol Internship Consortium, 77-78; instr part-time, Dept of Psychol, Northwestern Univ, 79-81; post-doctoral res fel, Ctr for Health Svc and Policy Res, Northwestern Univ, 78-81; vis res assoc, Vanderbilt Inst for Pub Policy Studies, Vanderbilt Univ, 85-90; vis scholar, Inst for Policy Res, Northwestern Univ, spring quarter, 97; dir, Ctr for Appl Psychol Res, Dept of Psychol, Univ Memphis, 90-97; dir, res design and stat prog, Dept of Psychol, Univ Memphis, 87-; prof, Dept of Psychol, Univ Memphis, 90-. **HONORS AND AWARDS** Outstanding Res Publ Awd, Amer Asn for Marriage and Family Therapy, 94; Paul F. Lazarsfeld Awd for Eval Theory, Amer Eval Asn, 94; Outstanding Res Publ Awd, Amer Asn for Marriage and Family Therapy, 96; James McKeen Cattell Fund Sabattical Awd, 96-97; Pres elect, 96; pres, 97, past-pres, 98, Amer Eval Asn; Svc award, Amer Eval Asn, 93; bd of visitors eminent facul award, Univ Memphis, 95; distinguished res award, Univ Memphis, 88; Merit Facul award, Col of Arts and Sci, Univ Memphis, 91; SPUR award (Superior Performance in Univ Res), Univ Memphis, 87, 88, 90, 93, 94. **MEMBERSHIPS** Amer Asn for Appl and Preventive Psychol; Amer Eval Asn; Amer Psychol Asn; Amer Psychol Soc; Amer Stat Asn; Soc for Clin Trials. **RESEARCH** Experimental and Quasi-experimental design; Program evaluation; Meta-analysis. **SELECTED PUBLICATIONS** Co-ed, with E. Chelimsky, Evaluation for the 21st Century: A Handbook, Thousand Oaks, Calif, Sage Publ, 97; with D. L. Newman, M. A. Scheirer & C. Wye, Guiding Principles for Evaluators, San Francisco, Jossey-Bass, 95; with S. Fuller, The Social Psychology of Science, NY, Guilford Publ, 94; jour articles, Evaluation theory is who we are, Amer Jour of Eval, 19, 1-19, 98; with X. Hu, R. R. Glaser, R. J. Kownacki & T. Wong, A method for exploring the effects of attrition in randomized experiments with dichotomous outcomes, Psychol Methods, 3, 3-22, 98; with M. D. Stanton, Outcome, attrition and family-couples treatment for drug abuse: A meta-analysis and review of the controlled, comparative studies, Psychol Bulletin, 122, 170-191; with G. Matt, A. Novaro, G. Siegle, P. Crits-Christoph, M. Hazelrigg, A. Jorm, L. S. Lyons, M. T. Nietzel, H. T. Prout, L. Robinson, M. L. Smith, M. Svartberg & B. Weiss, Evidence that therapy works in clinically representative conditions. Jour of Cons and Clin Psychol, 65, 355-365, 97; with R. C. Klesges, S. E. Winders, A. W. Meyers, L. H. Eck, K. D. Ward, C. M. Hulquist & J. W. Ray, How much weight gain occurs following smoking cessation? A comparison of weight gain using both continous and point prevalence abstinence, Jour of Cons and Clin Psychol, 65, 286-291, 97. **CONTACT ADDRESS** Dept. of Psychology, Univ of Memphis, Memphis, TN 38152. **EMAIL** shadish@mail.psyc.memphis.edu

SHAIDIAN, HAMMED
PERSONAL Born 11/12/1959, Sari, Iran, m, 1994 **DISCIPLINE** SOCIOLOGY **EDUCATION** Hamline Univ, BA, 82; Brandeis Univ, MA, 86; PhD, 90. **CAREER** Asst Prof to Assoc Prof, Univ of Ill, 93-; Chair of Dept Sociol and Anthrop, Univ of Ill, -. **HONORS AND AWARDS** Univ Scholar, Univ of Ill, 96. **RESEARCH** Social Movements, Gender, Culture, Refugee and Migration Studies. **SELECTED PUBLICATIONS** Auth, "Islam, Politics, and Writing Women's History in Iran," J of Women's Hist 7-2 (95): 113-144; auth, "Iranian Exiles and Sexual Politics: Issue of Gender Relations and Identity," J of Refugee Studies 9-1 (96): 43-72; auth, "Woman and Clandestine Politics in Iran, 1970-85," Feminist Studies 23-1 (97): 7-42; auth, "The Politics of the Veil: Reflections on Symbolism, Islam and Feminism," Thamyris: Mythmaking from Past to Present 4-2 (97): 325-337; auth, "Political Activism, Feminism, and Exile," J of Iranian Res and Analysis 14-1 (98): 7-11; auth, "Islam's 'Others': Living Out(side) Islam," ISIM Newsletter 3 (July 99): 5; auth, "Saving the Savior," Sociol Inquiry 69-2 (99): 303-327; auth, "Gender and Sexuality among Iranian Immigrants in Canada," Sexualities 2-2 (99): 189-223; auth, "Sociology and Exile: Banishment and Tensional Loyalties," Current

Sociol 84-2 (00); auth, Coercion and Resistance: Gender in the Cultural Politics of the Iranian Revolution, Greenwood Publ (Westport, CT), 00. **CONTACT ADDRESS** Dept Sociol and Anthrop, Univ of Illinois, Springfield, PO Box 19243, Springfield, IL 62794. **EMAIL** shaidian.hhammed@uis.edu

SHAKINOVSKY, LYNN
DISCIPLINE 19TH- AND 20TH-CENTURY AMERICAN; BRITISH WOMEN WRITERS **EDUCATION** Witwatersrand, BA; Toronto, MA, PhD. **CAREER** Assoc Prof **RESEARCH** 19th and 20th century Am and British women writers, Emily Dickinson, feminist literary theory, psychoanalysis. **SELECTED PUBLICATIONS** Auth, The Return of the Repressed: Illiteracy and the Death of the Narrative in Hawthorne's The Birthmark; No Frame of Reference: The Absence of Context in Emily Dickinson's Poems; Hidden Listeners: Dialogism in the Poetry of Emily Dickinson; Emily Dickinson's Poem 293. **CONTACT ADDRESS** Dept of English, Wilfrid Laurier Univ, 75 University Ave W, Waterloo, ON, Canada N2L 3C5. **EMAIL** lshakino@wlu.ca

SHALE, RICK
DISCIPLINE FILM STUDY; POPULAR CULTURE **EDUCATION** Ohio esleyan Univ, BA, 69; Univ Mich, MA, 72, PhD, 76. **CAREER** Fac member, Youngstown State Univ, 76-. **HONORS AND AWARDS** Phi Beta Kappa; Phi Kappa Phi. **MEMBERSHIPS** Univ Film & Video Assoc; Popular Culture Asn; Col Eng Asn. **RESEARCH** Film study; screwball comedy; Hitchcock; screenwriting. **SELECTED PUBLICATIONS** Auth, Academy Awards: The Complete Categorical and Chronological Record, Greenwood Press, 93. **CONTACT ADDRESS** Dept of English, Youngstown State Univ, Youngstown, OH 44555-3415.

SHANKS, HERSHEL
PERSONAL Born 03/08/1930, Sharon, PA, m, 1966, 2 children **DISCIPLINE** ENGLISH LITERATURE; SOCIOLOGY; LAW **EDUCATION** Haverford Col, BA, 52; Colombia Univ, MA, 56; Harvard Law Sch, LLB, 56. **CAREER** Founder and ed, Bibl Archaeol Rev, 74-; ed, Bible Rev, Archaeol Odyssey, and Moment. **MEMBERSHIPS** ASOR; SBL; AOS; NEAS; ABA. **RESEARCH** Archaeol; Bible; Judaism. **SELECTED PUBLICATIONS** Ed, Understanding the Dead Sea Scrolls, Random Hse, 92; co-auth, The Rise of Ancient Israel, Biblical Archaeol Soc, 92; ed, Christianity and Rabbinic Judaism: A Parallel History of Their Origins and Early Development, Biblical Archaeol Soc, 92; auth, Jerusalem: An Archaeological Biography, Random Hse, 95; auth, The Mystery and Meaning of the Dead Sea Scrolls, Random Hse, 98. **CONTACT ADDRESS** Biblical Archael Soc, 5208 38th St, NW, Washington, DC 20015. **EMAIL** shanks@clark.net

SHAPIRO, LEWIS P.
DISCIPLINE PSYCHOLINGUISTICS **EDUCATION** Brandeis Univ, PhD, 87. **CAREER** Dir, Lang Processes Lab; ERP Lab Doctoral Program Executive Comt. **RESEARCH** Adult lang disorders. **SELECTED PUBLICATIONS** Auth, An introduction to syntax, Jour of Speech, Lang, and Hearing Res 40, 97; co-auth, Context effects re-visited, Sentence Processing: A Cross-Linguistic Perspective, Acad Press; How to milk a coat: The effects of semantic and acoustic information on phoneme categorization, Jour Acoustical Soc Am 103, 98; On-line examination of language performance in normal and neurologically-impaired adults, Amer Jour Speech-Lang Pathol, 98; Training wh-question productions in agrammatic aphasia: An analysis of lexical and syntactic properties, Brain and Lang, 98. **CONTACT ADDRESS** Dept of Commun Disorders, San Diego State Univ, 5500 Campanile Dr, San Diego, CA 92182. **EMAIL** shapiro@mail.sdsu.edu

SHARF, BARBARA F.
PERSONAL Born 03/27/1948, Philadelphia, PA, m, 1988 **DISCIPLINE** HEALTH COMMUNICATION, RHETORICAL ANALYSIS **EDUCATION** Univ Minn, PhD. **CAREER** Prof, Texas A&M Univ. **CONTACT ADDRESS** Dept of Speech Communication, Texas A&M Univ, Col Station, College Station, TX 77843-4234. **EMAIL** bsharf@tamu.edu

SHARF, RICHARD S.
PERSONAL Born 12/08/1939, Boston, MA, m, 1967, 2 children **DISCIPLINE** PSYCHOLOGY **CAREER** Assoc prof, Univ of Dela, 69-. **MEMBERSHIPS** Am Psychol Assoc; Am Coun Assoc. **RESEARCH** Career development **SELECTED PUBLICATIONS** Auth, Theories of psychotherapy and counseling: Concepts and Cases, Brooks/Cole, (Pacific Grove, CA), 96; auth, Applying career development theory to counseling, Brooks/Cole, (Pacific Grove, CA), 97; auth, Applying career development theory to counseling. Instructor's manual, Brooks/Cole, (Pacific Grove, CA), 97; auth, "Psychotherapy", Encarta Encycl, Microsoft, (Redmond, WA), 98; auth, Theories of psychotherapy and counseling: Concepts and Cases, 2nd edition, Brooks/Cole, (Pacific Grove, CA), 00; auth, Theories of psychotherapy and counseling: Concepts and Cases, 2nd edition, Student manual, Brooks/Cole, (Pacific Grove, CA), 00; auth, Theories of psychotherapy and counseling: Concepts and Cases, 2nd edition, Instructors manual, Brooks/Cole, (Pacific Grove, CA), 00. **CONTACT ADDRESS** Center for Coun and Student Develop, Univ of Delaware, Newark, DE 19716. **EMAIL** rsharf@udel.edu

SHARMA, MANOJ
PERSONAL Born 11/24/1963, New Delhi, India, m, 1991, 2 children **DISCIPLINE** PHYSICAL EDUCATION **EDUCATION** Ohio State Univ, PhD, 97. **CAREER** Supvr, Columbus Health Dept, 95-97; Asst Prof, Univ Neb, 97-. **HONORS AND AWARDS** Pride Awd, Ohio Public health Assoc., 97; William Oxley Thompson Awd, Ohio State Univ, 98, ETA Sigma Gamma. **MEMBERSHIPS** Am Public Health Assoc., Ohio Public Health Assoc., Am St Health Assoc. **RESEARCH** Theory based program planning a valuation, Freirian Praris **SELECTED PUBLICATIONS** Coauth, "The Voluntary Community Health Movement in India: A Strengths, Weaknesses, Opportunities and Threats (SWOT) Analysis," J of Advancement in Ed, 7 (96): 453-464; coauth, "Lessons for Health Promotion from Selected Community-Based Heart Disease Prevention Programs," The Health Educr, 28 (97): 21-26; coauth, "Impact of Expectant Fathers in Breast-Feeding Decision," J of the Am Dietetic Assoc., 97 (97): 1311-1313; auth, "Improving Interventions that Develop Problem-Solving Skills for Stress Management Among Children," Int J of Stress Management, 5 (98): 250-253; auth, "Evaluation of a Brief Intervention Based on Social Cognitive Theory to Develop Problem-Solving Skills Among Sixth Grade Children," Health Educ and Behav, 26 (99): 465-467; auth, Practical Stress Management: A Comprehensive Workbook for Promoting Health and Managing Change Through Stress Reduction, 2nd Ed, Allyn & Bacon (Boston, MA), 00. **CONTACT ADDRESS** Dept Phys Ed, Univ of Nebraska, Omaha, 6001 Dodge St, Omaha, NE 68182-0216. **EMAIL** manoj-sharma@unomaha.edu

SHARMA, R. N.
PERSONAL Born 10/22/1944, Punjab, India, m, 1972, 2 children **DISCIPLINE** LIBRARY AND INFORMATION SCIENCE; HIGHER EDUCATION; HISTORY **EDUCATION** Univ Delhi, BA, 63, MA, 66; N TX State Univ, MLS, 70; SUNY, Buffalo, PhD, 82. **CAREER** Asst librn, Col Ozarks, 70-71; ref librn, Colgate Univ, 71-81; head librn, Penn State Univ, Beaver Campus, 81-85; asst dir, Univ WI, 85-89; dir, Univ Evansville, 89-95; dir, WV State Col, 96-. **HONORS AND AWARDS** Who's Who Among Asian Am, 92-94; advisory bd, 94-98; Asian Lit; Humprhy/OCLC/Forest Press Awd, 97, ALA; chair, Am Librns Delegation to Palestine, 97; Am Librns Delegation to Northern Ireland, 97; Benjamin Franklin Awd, 98, Publishers Marketing Asn; Editor-in-Chief, Library Times International 84; President, Asian/American Libraries Association, 93-94. **MEMBERSHIPS** Am Libr Asn; Asn Col Res Libr; Int Relations Round Table; Indian Libr Asn; Asian/Pacific Am Librn Asn. **RESEARCH** International librarianship; history of libraries; library administration; reference services. **SELECTED PUBLICATIONS** Auth, "Indian Librarianship: Perspectives and Prospects," Kalayni 81; auth, Indian Academic Libraries and Dr. S. R. Ranganathan: A Critical Study, Sterling, 86; Ranganathan and the West, Sterling, 92; Research and Academic Librarians: A Global View, Resources in Education, 92; Changing Dimensions: Managing Library and Information Services for the 1990's: A Global Perspective, Ed Resources Infor Center, 94; Linking Asian/Pacific Collections to America, Educational Resources Infor Center, 95; auth, "Libraries and Education in Palestine, Near East and South Asia," Subcommittee/Internetional Relations/ALA, 99. **CONTACT ADDRESS** Drain-Jordan Library, West Virginia State Col, PO Box 1002, Institute, WV 25112-1002. **EMAIL** sharmarn@mail.wvsc.edu

SHARPES, DONALD KENNETH
DISCIPLINE EDUCATIONAL PSYCHOLOGY **EDUCATION** Gonzaga Univ, AB, 58, MA, 61; Stanford Univ, MA, 67; AZ State, PhD, 68. **CAREER** Technical Div Dir, US Dept of Education, Washington, DC, 68-73; assoc prof and dir, Ed progs VPI and SU, 73-78; prof of Graduate Education, Weber State Univ, 78-. **HONORS AND AWARDS** Hinckley Awd, Weber State, 96; UT Academy of Sciences, Arts and Letters (Best Paper), 97; **MEMBERSHIPS** Am Psychol Asn; Am Ed Res Asn; UT Academy of Sciences, Arts and Letters. **RESEARCH** Ed psychol; ed foundations; curriculum and instruction; ed policy. **SELECTED PUBLICATIONS** Auth, Special issue ed, Int Ed, Teacher Education Quart, winter 95; Preparing Youth for the Changing Work World, J of Pedagogics, 15 (2), 95; Higher Education Faces Deeper Cuts, Salt Lake Tribune, 9/28/95; Princess Pocahontas, Rebecca Rolfe (1595-1617), Am Indian Culture and Res J, 19 (4); review, Sexuality Education, a Guide for Educators, Canadian and Int Ed, 24 (1), 95; Defining a Multicultural Curriculum: The Anthropological Perspective, in The Dynamic Concept of Curriculum, Sharpes with A-L Leino, eds, Univ Helsinki Press, 95; The Dynamic Concept of Curriculum, Sharpes with A-L Leino, eds, Univ Helsinki Press, 95; Postmodern Philosophies and Educational Values, Proceedings, Mofet Inst, Ministry of Education, Culture & Sport, Israel, eds N Ephraty & R Lidor, 96; Skewed SAT Scores Give False Sense of Education, Salt Lake Tribune, 06/16/1996; The Manufactured Crisis, Educational Leadership, 53 (7), April 96; Educational Qualifications for Teachers in Former Soviet Republics, in W Bunder & K Rebel, eds, Teacher Education--Theoretical Requirements and Professsional Reality, Inst of Science Education, 97; Hong Kong Tentatively Steps Toward Chinese Control, Standard Examiner, 6/15/1997; Lindisfarne, Holy Island, Standard Examiner, 5/1/1997; China May Buy More Utah Goods, Salt Lake Tribune, 7/8/1997; China Looks

at Taiwan as the Ultimate Prize, Salt Lake Tribune, 6/22/1997; There's More to See in Macao Than Gaming Tables, Standard Examiner, 1/11/1998; A Study of Adolescent Self-Concept Among Han, Mongolian and Korean Chinese, with Xinbing Wang, Adolescence, 32, 98; Covering Hong Kong's Handover, Junction, serialized in V-II, nos 7, 8, 9, 98; Advanced Psychology for Teachers, McGraw Hill, forthcoming fall 98; numerous other publications, several works in progress. **CONTACT ADDRESS** College of Education, Weber State Univ, 1300 Univ Circle, Ogden, UT 84408.

SHARPS, MATTHEW J.
PERSONAL Born 11/11/1958, Denver, CO, m, 1995, 1 child **DISCIPLINE** PSYCHOLOGY **EDUCATION** Univ Colo, BA, 81; MA, 84; PhD, 86; Univ Calif, Los Angeles, MA, 82. **CAREER** Res scientist, Univ Colo, 86-88; Asst Prof, Univ Wyoming, 88-90; Prof, Calif St Univ, 90-. **HONORS AND AWARDS** Karl Muenzinger Psychol Awd, Univ Colo, 81; Phi Beta Kappa, 81; Sigma Xi, 86; Outstanding Young Men of Am Awd, 98; Prof of the Year, Calif St Univ, 98-99. **MEMBERSHIPS** APA, APS, WPA, AAUP, CCGG, ACFE. **RESEARCH** Memory and adult memory development, contextual reasoning, cognitive aspects of addiction and dependencies, developmental psychology. **SELECTED PUBLICATIONS** Coauth, "Visual Memory Support: An Effective Mnemonic Device for Older Adults," The Gerontologist, 36 (96): 706-708; auth, "Category Superiority Effects in Young and Elderly Adults," J of Genetic Psychol, 158 (97): 165-171; auth, "Spatial Memory in Young and Older Adults: Environmental Support and Contextual Influences at Encoding and Retrieval," J of Genetic Psychol, 159 (98): 5-12; coauth, "Auditory Imagery and the Category Superiority Effect," J of Gen Psychol, 125: 109-116; auth, "Attitudes of Young Adults Toward Older Adults: Evidence from the United States and Thailand," Educ Gerontology, 24: 655-660; coauth, "Relational Frameworks for Recall in Young and Older Adults," Current Psychol, 18: 254-271; coauth, "Spatial and Relational Frameworks for Free Recall in Young and Older Adults," Rev of Gen Psychol, 18: 241-253; coauth, "Gestalt Perspectives on Cognitive Science and Experimental Psychology," Rev of General Psychol (forthcoming). **CONTACT ADDRESS** Dept Psychol, California State Univ, Fresno, 5310 N Campus Dr, Fresno, CA 93740-8019. **EMAIL** matthew.sharps@csufresno.edu

SHAVER, PHILLIP R.
PERSONAL Born 07/07/1944, Iowa City, IA, m, 1966, 2 children **DISCIPLINE** PSYCHOLOGY **EDUCATION** Wesleyan Univ, BA, 66; Univ Mich, PhD, 70. **CAREER** Columbia Univ; NYU; Univ of Denver, SUNY Buffalo; Univ of Calif Davis. **HONORS AND AWARDS** Fel, Am Psychol Assoc; Fel, am Psychol Soc. **MEMBERSHIPS** APA; APS; SESP; Int Soc for Res on Emotion; Int Soc for the Study of Personal Relationships; Soc for Personality and Soc Pschol; Soc for the Psychol Study of Soc Issues. **RESEARCH** Human emotions, close interpersonal relationships. **SELECTED PUBLICATIONS** Coauth, "Methods of assessing adult attachment: do they converge?", Attachment theory and close relationships, eds J.A. Simpson and W.S. Rholes, Guilford Pr, (NY, 98): 25-45; coauth, "Dismissing avoidance and the defensive organization of emotion, cognition, and behavior", Attachment theory and close relationships, eds J.A. Simpson and W.S. Rholes, Guilford Pr, (NY, 98): 249-279; coauth, "Attachment styles and personality disorders: Their connections to each other and to parental divorce, parental death, and perceptions of parental caregiving", J of Personality 66 (98): 835-878; coauth, "Airport separations: A naturalistic study of adult attachment dynamics in separating couples", J of Personality and Soc Psychol 75, (98): 1198-1212; coauth, "Strategic behaviors in romantic relationship initiation", Personality and Soc Psychol Bulletin 25 (99): 707-720; coauth, "Measurement of adult attachment", Handbook of attachment: theory, research, and clinical applications, eds J. Cassidy and P.R. Shaver, Guilford Pr, (NY, 99): 434-465; coauth, "Loss and bereavement: Attachment theory and recent controversies concerning grief work and the nature of detachment", Handbook of attachment: Theory, research, and clinical applications, eds J. Cassidy and P.R. Shaver, Guilford Pr, (NY, 99): 735-759; coauth, "Imagined hunter-gatherers, happiness without a self, and the preference of neurotic individuals for immediate relief when frightened", Psychol Inquiry 10, (99): coauth, "Comparing measures of adult attachment: An examination of interview and self-report methods", Personal Relationships 7 (00): 25-43; coauth, "Attachment theory and caregiving", Psychol Inquiry 11 (00): 109-114. **CONTACT ADDRESS** Dept Psychol, Univ of California, Davis, 1 Shields Ave, Davis, CA 95616-8686. **EMAIL** prshaver@ucdavis.edu

SHAW, R. DANIEL
PERSONAL Born 11/19/1943, Seattle, WA, m, 1966, 3 children **DISCIPLINE** ANTHROPOLOGY **EDUCATION** Univ Ariz, BA, 67, MA, 68; Univ New Guinea, PhD, 75. **CAREER** Lectr, Clackamous Col, 68; lectr, Univ of Papua New Guinea, 73; lectr, Fuller Theol Sem, 80; vis scholar, Univ Washington, 74; asst prof, Fuller Theol Sem, 82-87, assoc prof, 87-92, prof, 92-, dir, Doctoral Studies, Sch of World Missions, 2000; Field experience: Anthropology: researcher, Health Concepts of the O'otham, Ariz, Health Progs Systems Center, 67; researcher, Culture and Language of the Samo, Papua New Guinea, 70-81; Int Anthropol Consult, 73-; Translation: Samo, PNG, Wycliffe

Bible Translators, 70-81. **HONORS AND AWARDS** Transculturation, placed on $200.00 book list Missiology, Asn of Evangelical Profs of Mission top ten books of the year, 88; Understanding Folk Religion placed on Int Bull of Missionary Res top fifteen books of the year, 99. **MEMBERSHIPS** Am Anthropol Asn, Am Literary Transls Asn, Am Soc of Missiologists, Asn for Soc Anthropols in Oceania, Australian Asn of Studies in Relig, Mission Aviation Fel, Pacific Studies Asn, Polynesian Soc. **RESEARCH** Melanesia; Papua New guinea; anthropology: research methods, social structure, anthropology of religion; translation: cultural issues/Hermeneutics, discourse analysis. **SELECTED PUBLICATIONS** Auth, Health Concepts & Attitudes of the Papago Indians, Tuscon: Health Progs Center (68); auth, "Kinship Studies in Papua New Guinea, Ukarumpa: Silprint (74, reprinted 76); auth, "Samo Social Structure: A Socio-Linguistic Approach to Understanding Interpersonal Relationships," Pt. Moresby: Univ Papua New Guinea (76); auth, Samo Mini-New Testament, Ukarumpa: Wycliffe Bible Translators (80); auth, Transculturation: The Cultural Factor in Translation, Pasadena: Wm. Carey Library (88); auth, Kandila: Samo Ceremonialism and Interpersonal Relationships, Ann Arbor: Univ Mich Press (90); auth, From Longhouse to Village: Samo Social Change, in Case Studies in Anthropology Series, George & Louise Spindler, eds, Fort Worth: Harcourt Brace (96); auth, "Samo House Styles and Social Change," in Rensel & Rodman, eds, Home in the Islands, Honolulu: Univ of Haw Press (97): 55-78; coauth with Paul Hiebert & Tite Tienou, Understanding Folk Religion: A Christian Response to Popular Beliefs and Practices, Grand Rapids: Baker (99); auth of several articles appearing in Evangelical Dictionary of World Mission, Grand Rapids: Baker (2000). **CONTACT ADDRESS** Sch of World Mission, Fuller Theol Sem, 135 N Oakland, Pasadena, CA 91182-0001. **EMAIL** danshaw@fuller.edu

SHAW, VICTOR
PERSONAL Born, China **DISCIPLINE** SOCIOLOGY EDUCATION Wuhan Univ, MA; Univ Hawaii, PhD, 94. **CAREER** Asst Prof, Calif State univ, 97-. **HONORS AND AWARDS** Winner Second Worldwide Competition for Young Sociol, Int Sociol Assoc, 94. **RESEARCH** Deviance, crimes, social control, organizational behavior. **SELECTED PUBLICATIONS** Auth, articles in Academic Journals; auth, Social Control in China: A Study of Chinese Work Units, Greenwood Publ Group, 96. **CONTACT ADDRESS** Dept Sociol, California State Univ, Northridge, 18111 Nordhoff St, Northridge, CA 91330-8318.

SHEAN, GLENN D.
PERSONAL Born 04/15/1939, New Orleans, LA, m, 1983, 2 children **DISCIPLINE** PSYCHOLOGY EDUCATION Univ Ariz, PhD, 66. **CAREER** Prof, Col of William and Mary, 66-00. **MEMBERSHIPS** Am Psychol Assoc. **RESEARCH** Psychopathology. **SELECTED PUBLICATIONS** Auth, "Gruesomeness, emotional attachment, and personal threat", J of Traumatic Stress 8.2 (95): 343-349; auth, "Depression, interpersonal style, and communication skills", J of Nervous and Mental Disease 183.7 (95): 485-587; coauth, "The values of student environmentalists", J of Psychol, 129.5 (95): 559-564; coauth, "Agoraphobia and relationships", J of Anxiety Disorders 10, (96): 477-487; auth, "Card sort performance and syndromes of schizophrenia, Genetic, Social (Clinical) and General Psychology Monographs 128, (97): 197-209; coauth, "Habituation of cognitive and physiological arousal and social anxiety", Behav Res and Therapy 35, (98): 1113-1122; coauth, "The effects of anxiety sensitivity and history of panic on reactions to stressors in a non-clinical sample", J of Behav Therapy and Experimental; Psych 29, (98): 279-288; auth, "Syndromes of schizophrenia and language dysfunction", J of Clinical Psych 55, (99): 233-240. **CONTACT ADDRESS** Dept Psychol, Col of William and Mary, PO Box 8795, Williamsburg, VA 23187.

SHEEHAN-HOLT, JAN
PERSONAL Born 10/24/1957, Aurora, IL, m, 1998, 2 children **DISCIPLINE** EDUCATIONAL PSYCHOLOGY EDUCATION Southern Ill Univ, Carbondale, BS, 81, MS, 90, PhD, 94. **CAREER** Asst prof, Northern Ill Univ, 94-99, asst chair/ asst prof, 99-. **HONORS AND AWARDS** Ill Beta Asn of Phi Beta Kappa, Book Awd for Outstanding Graduating Sr, 81; Charles L. Foot Achievement Awd for Superior Levels of Achievement, 81; Outstanding Res Awd, 94; Diss Res Awd, 94; Doctoral Fel, 94; External grant with M. C. Smith, Am Ed Res Asn, 96; chair, Measurement and res methodology div, Mid-Western Ed Res Asn, 99-2000; guest ed, Multiple Linear Regression Viewpoints, 99-2000. **MEMBERSHIPS** Am Ed Res Asn, Nat Coun on Measurement in Ed, Mid-Western Ed Res Asn, Am Psychol Asn. **RESEARCH** Research methodology and statistical techniques , research emphases in hierarchical linear modeling, analysis techniques for analysis of large-scale datasets, as well as adult literacy. **SELECTED PUBLICATIONS** Coauth with T. Han, "Hierarchical modeling techniques to analyze contextual effects: What happened to the aptitude by treatment design?," Mid-Western Ed Res, 9, 4-7 (96); coauth with K. B. Cole, L. R. Struyk, D. Kinder, and C. K. Kish, "Portfolio assessment: Challenges in secondary education," High Sch J, 80, 254-260 (97); coauth with C. K. Kish, K. B. Cole, L. R. Struyk, and C. K. Kish, "Portfolios in the classroom: A vehicle for developing reflective thinking," High Sch J, 80, 261-272 (97); coauth with

M. C. Smiyth, "Adults' reading practices and their associations with literary proficiencies," in M. C. Smith, ed, Literacy for the 21st century: Research, policy, practices, and the National Adult Literacy Survey, Westport, CT: Praeger (98); auth, "MANOVA simultaneous test procedures: The power and robustness of restricted multivariate contrasts," Ed and Psychol Measurement, 58, 861-881 (98); coauth with M. C. Smith, "Does basic skills education work? Some evidence from the National Adult Literacy Survey, Proceedings of the 40th Annual Adult Ed Res Conf, 303-306 (99); coauth with M. C. Smith, "Does basic skills education affect adults' proficiencies and reading practices?," Reading Res Quart (in press). **CONTACT ADDRESS** Dept Ed Psych, No Illinois Univ, 1425 W Lincoln Hwy, Dekalb, IL 60115. **EMAIL** jsheeham@niu.edu

SHEEHY, JOHN
PERSONAL Born 06/18/1925, Allegan, MI, m, 1968, 6 children **DISCIPLINE** PHILOSOPHY, THEOLOGY, SOCIOLOGY EDUCATION St Mary's, BA, 46; Catholic Univ Am, STL, 50; Notre Dame Univ, MA, 70. **CAREER** Management Development, Beth Steel Corp, 69-86; prof, Purdue Univ N Central Campus, 86-00; Priest. **HONORS AND AWARDS** Part-time Teacher of the Year, Purdue Univ N Central Campus, 99. **SELECTED PUBLICATIONS** Auth, Church's History of Injustice and Why This Priest Left, Univ Pr of Am, 99. **CONTACT ADDRESS** Dept Soc Sci, Purdue Univ, No Central, 1401 S US Hwy 421, Westville, IN 4631-9542. **EMAIL** jsheehy@purduenc.edu

SHELDON, KENNON
PERSONAL Born 08/17/1959, Williamsburg, VA, m, 1986, 3 children **DISCIPLINE** PSYCHOLOGY EDUCATION Univ Calif, PhD, 92. **CAREER** Vis Asst Prof, Univ Rochester, 93-97; Asst Prof, Univ Mo, 97-. **MEMBERSHIPS** Am Psychol Asn. **RESEARCH** Motivation, goals, well-being, creativity, personality development. **SELECTED PUBLICATIONS** Coauth, "Coherence and Congruence: Two Aspects of Personality Integration," J of Personality and Soc Psychol Bull, 24 (95): 531-543; coauth, "Pursuing Personal Goals: Skills Enable Progress, but not all Progress is Beneficial," Personality and Soc Psychol Bull, 24 (98): 546-557; coauth, "Not All Personal Goals are Personal: Comparing Autonomous and Controlled Reasons as Predictors of Effort and Attainment," Personality and Soc Psychol Bull, 24 (98): 546-557; coauth, "Goal striving, Need-Satisfaction and Longitudinal Well-Being: The Self-Concordance Model," J of Personality and Soc Psychol (99); coauth, "Personal Goals in Social Roles: Divergences and Convergences Across Roles and Levels of Analysis," J of Personality (forthcoming); coauth, "Personal Goals and Psychological Growth: Testing an Intervention to Enhance Goal-Attainment and Personality Integration," J of Personality (forthcoming); auth, "The Self-Concordance Model of Healthy goal-Striving: when Personal Goals Correctly Represent the Person," in Handbk of Self-Determination Theory, Univ Rochester Pr, (Rochester, NY), forthcoming. **CONTACT ADDRESS** Dept Psychol, Univ of Missouri, Columbia, 210 McAlester Hall, Columbia, MO 65211-0001. **EMAIL** sheldon@missouri.edu

SHENK, DENA
PERSONAL Born 02/22/1952, New York, NY, m, 1977, 2 children **DISCIPLINE** ANTHROPOLOGY EDUCATION SUNY, BA, 73; Univ Mass, MA, 76; PhD, 79. **CAREER** Asst Prof to Prof and Dir of Gerontol Prog, Dept Chair, St Cloud State Univ, 79-91; Prof, Univ NC, 91-. **HONORS AND AWARDS** Fel, Institute on Aging, 99; Fel, Gerontol Soc of am, 97; Fel, Asn for Gerontol in Higher Educ, 96; Phi Kappa Phi, 88; Merit Awd, St cloud State Univ, 84; Outstanding Young woman of 1982. **MEMBERSHIPS** Gerontol Soc of am, Health Care for Women Intl, Nat Coun on the aging, Nat women's Studies Asn, Southern Gerontol Soc, Am anthropol Asn, Am Asn of Retired Persons, am Soc on aging, Asn for anthropol and Gerontol, Asn for gerontol in Higher Educ. **RESEARCH** Anthropology of aging; Ethical issues in working with older adults; diversity in the aging experience including gender, culture and environment; social networks; Formal and informal supports for aging. **SELECTED PUBLICATIONS** Auth, "A Picture is worth.:the Use of Photography in Gerontological Research," Qualitative Gerontology, in press; auth, "Positive adaptations to aging in changing Environments," Journal of Cross-Cultural Gerontology, in press; auth, "Teaching About aging: Interdisciplinary and Cross-Cultural Perspectives, Asn for Gerontology in Higher Education, 99; auth, "Negating Identity: A Feminist Analysis of The social Invisibility of Older Lesbians," Journal of Women and Aging, 99; auth, Someone to Lend a Helping Hand: Women Growing Old in Rural Society, Gordon and Breach Pub, 98; auth, "Subjective Realities of Rural Older Women's Lives: a Case Study," Journal of Women and Aging, 98; auth, "Thriving Older African American Women: Aging after Jim Crow," Journal of Women and Aging, 98; auth, "Social Support Systems of rural Older women: A Comparison of the US and Denmark," in The Cultural Context of aging - worldwide perspectives, Greenwood Press, 97; auth, "Significant Relationships among Older women: Cultural and Personal constructions of Lesbianism," Journal of Women and Aging, 96; auth, Gender and Race through Education and political Activism: The Legacy of Sylvia Forman, Am Anthropological Asn, 95. **CONTACT ADDRESS** Dept Anthropol & Sociol, Univ of No Carolina, Charlotte, 9201 Univ City, Charlotte, NC 28223.

SHEPPERD, JAMES A.
PERSONAL Born 02/03/1961, Burnet, TX, m, 1995 **DISCIPLINE** PSYCHOLOGY EDUCATION S West Univ, BA, 83; Univ Texas, MA, 85; Univ Missouri, PhD, 88. **CAREER** Asst prof, Holy Cross Col, 88-92; asst prof, Univ Florida, 92-95; assoc prof, 95-; dir, 97-; vis assoc prof, LSC, Eng, 98. **HONORS AND AWARDS** Psi Chi Teach of Year Awd; Phi Beta Kappa Alum Awd; TIP Teach Awd; Edwin B Newman Nat Res Awd. **MEMBERSHIPS** APA; APS; MPA; SPA; SESP; SSSP; SASP. **RESEARCH** Self-esteem and identity regulation; motivation and productivity loss in groups. **SELECTED PUBLICATIONS** Coauth, "Constraints on excuse making: The deterring effects of shyness and anticipated retest," Person Soc Psych Bul 21(95): 1061-1072; auth, "Remedying motivation and productivity loss in collective settings," Curr Dir Psych Sci 4 (95): 131-134; coauth, "Abandoning unrealistic optimism: Performance estimates and the temporal proximity of self-relevant feedback," J Pers Soc Psych 70 (96): 844-855; rev of "The antecedents, consequences, and purpose of self-esteem," in Efficacy, Agency, and Self-Esteem, by Michael H. Kernis, Contem Psych (96); coauth, "Dispositional optimism as a predictor of health changes among cardiac patients," J Res Pers 30 (96): 517-534; coauth, "Probing suspicion among participants in deception research," Am Psych 51 (96): 651-652; coauth, "On the manipulative behavior of low Machiavellians: Feigning incompetence to 'sandbag' an opponent's effort," J Pers Soc Psych 12 997): 1448-1459; coauth, "Biases in the assessment of performance handicaps," J Soc Clin Psych 16(97): 420-439; coauth, "Bracing for the worst: severity, testing and feedback as moderators of the optimistic bias," Pers Soc Psych Bul 24 (98): 915-926; coauth, "Trait strength and the underestimation of validity," Pers Soc Psych Rev 3 999): 108-122; coauth, "Maladaptive image maintenance," in The social psychology of behavioral and emotional problems, eds. MR Kowalski, RM Leary (Washington, DC: APA press, 99); coauth, "Ascribing advantages to comparison targets," Basic App Soc Psych 21 (99): 103-117; coauth, "Social loafing and expectancy value theory," Pers Soc Psych Bul 215 (99): 1147-1158; coauth, "Bracing for Loss," J Pers Soc Psych (in press); auth, Social loafing and expectancy value theory," in Multiple Perspectives on the Effects of Evaluation on Performance: Toward an Integration, ed. SC Harkins (Kluwer Pub: NY, in press). **CONTACT ADDRESS** Dept Psychology, Univ of Florida, PO Box 112250, Gainesville, FL 32611. **EMAIL** shepperd@psych.ufl.edu

SHERIDAN, MARY
PERSONAL Born 08/05/1948, Pasadena, CA, w, 1969 **DISCIPLINE** SOCIOLOGY EDUCATION Northwestern Univ, BA, 69; Univ IL Chicago, MSW, 72; Univ HI Manoa, PhD, 85. **CAREER** Medical social worker, Univ of IL Hospital, Kapiolani Medical Center for Women and Children, Pali Momi Medical Center, Straub Found, 72-94; fac mem, HI Pacific Univ, 94-. **MEMBERSHIPS** Nat Assoc of Apnea Prof; Nat Assoc of Social Workers. **RESEARCH** Munchausen Syndrome by Proxy, infant apnea/SIDS. **SELECTED PUBLICATIONS** Coed, Munchausen Syndrome by Proxy, Lexington Pr, (Boston), 95; ed, The NAAP Handbook of Infant Apnea and Home Monitoring, Vol II, Nat Assoc of Apnea Professionals, (Waianae, HI, 96); auth, "Doing the Best They Can: The NAAP Workload Survey", Vol II, Nat Assoc of Apnea Professionals, (Waianae, HI, 96); coed, Second Japan-US Diabetes Epidemiology Training Course: Proceedings, Japan Diabetes Found Pub Series 5, 96; auth, "Our Efforts Make a Difference: Results of the NAAP Cooperative Survey", Neonatal Intensive Care 11.2 (98): 11; auth, "Risk Reduction to Prevent Sudden Infant Death Syndrome: Recommendations of Hawaii Physicians", HI Med J58 (99): 207; auth, "The Efficacy of Infant Apnea Home Monitoring. Part I: Does Monitoring Save Lives?, Neonatal Intensive Care 12.4 (99): 25; auth, The Efficacy of Infant Apnea Home Monitoring. Part II: Psychological Effects and Outcomes", Neonatal Intensive Care 12.5 (99): 25; coauth, Munchausen by Proxy: A Guide for Child Protective Personnel, (forthcoming). **CONTACT ADDRESS** Dept Arts and Sciences, Hawaii Pacific Univ, 1188 Fort St, Ste 430, Honolulu, HI 96813. **EMAIL** mserida@hpu.edu

SHERKAT, DARREN E.
PERSONAL Born 12/31/1965, Tulsa, OK, d, 1 child **DISCIPLINE** SOCIOLOGY EDUCATION Univ Tulsa, BA, 87; MA, 89, PhD, 91, Duke Univ. **CAREER** Asst Prof, 91-96, Assoc Prof, 96-, Vanderbilt Univ. **MEMBERSHIPS** Amer Sociological Assoc; Southern Sociological Assoc; Soc for the Scientific Study of Religion; Religious Research Assoc; Assoc for the Sociology of Religion; Intl Sociological Assoc. **RESEARCH** Sociology of religion; social movements; statistics and methods; contemporary sociological theory **SELECTED PUBLICATIONS** Coauth, Conservative Protestantism and Support for Corporal Punishment, American Sociological Review, 93; Theory and Method in Religious Mobility Research, Social Science Research, 93; The Political Development of Sixties Activists: Identifying the Influence of Class, Gender, and Socialization on Protest Protestantism, Social Forces, 94; Preferences, Constraints, and Choices in Religious Markets: An Examination of Religious Switching and Apostasy, 95; The Semi-Involuntary Institution Revisited: RegionalVariations in Church Participation Among Black Americans, Social Forces, 95; Auth, Embedding Religious Choices: Integrating Preferences and Social Constraints into Rational Choice Theories of Reli-

gious Behavior, Rational Choice Theory and Religion: Summary and Assessment, 97; Coauth, The Cognitive Structure of a Moral Crusade: Conservative Protestantism and Oppostion to Pornography, Social Forces, 97; Explaining the Political and Personal Consequences of Protest, Social Forces, 97; The Impact of Fundamentalism on Educational Attainment, American Sociological Review, 97; Auth, Counterculture or Continuity? Examining Competing Influences on Baby Boomers' Religious Orientations and Participation, Social Forces, 98. **CONTACT ADDRESS** Dept of Sociology, Vanderbilt Univ, Nashville, TN 37235. **EMAIL** sherkade@ctrvax.vanderbilt.edu

SHERMAN, SHARON R.
PERSONAL Born 04/16/1943, Toronto, ON, Canada, m, 1975, 1 child **DISCIPLINE** FOLKLORE **EDUCATION** Wayne State Univ, PhB, 65; Univ Calif at Los Angeles, MA, 71; Indiana Univ, PhD, 78. **CAREER** Lectr, Univ Calif, Los Angeles, 75-76; from asst prof to prof, Univ Ore, 76-, Dir of Folklore Prog, Univ Ore, 94-. **HONORS AND AWARDS** NEA grant; Fac Res grant; Vice pres, Calif Folklore Soc, 95-99; Rippey Teaching Innovation Awd, 99-2000. **MEMBERSHIPS** Am Folklore Soc, Calif Folklore Soc. **RESEARCH** Folklore; film and folklore; folklore & mythology; fieldwork; videography; popular culture. **SELECTED PUBLICATIONS** Auth, Chainsaw Sculptor: The Art of J. Chester "Skip" Armstrong," Univ Miss Press (95); auth, Documenting Ourselves: Film, Video, and Culture, Univ Ky Press (98). **CONTACT ADDRESS** Dept English, Univ of Oregon, 1286 Univ Ore, Eugene, OR 97403. **EMAIL** srs@oregon.uoregon.edu

SHERNOCK, STANLEY K.
PERSONAL Born 08/18/1947, San Francisco, CA, m, 1997, 2 children **DISCIPLINE** SOCIOLOGY **EDUCATION** Univ Calif, BA, 68; Ind Univ, MA, 71; Univ VA, PhD, 79. **CAREER** Instr to Asst Prof, Univ Wis, 78-82; Asst Prof, Nicolls State Univ, 82-85; Asst Prof to Prof, Norwich Univ, 85-. **HONORS AND AWARDS** Dana Category 1 Awd, Norwich Univ, 98; Dana Summer Res Fel, Norwich Univ, 98; Dana Summer Res Fel, Norwich Univ, 92; Dana Category 1 Awd, Norwich Univ, 90-91; Merit Awd, 88-90; Dana Summer Res Fel, Norwich Univ, 87; Dana Summer Res Fel, Norwich Univ, 86; Nicholls State Univ, 82; Special Merit Awd, Univ Wis, 80-81; Nat Endowment for the Humanities Summer Res Stipend, 80. **MEMBERSHIPS** Acad of Criminal Justice Sci, Am Soc of Criminol, NE Asn of Criminal Justice Sci, Am Sociol Asn. **RESEARCH** Police, Crime preention, Victimology, Governmental terror. **SELECTED PUBLICATIONS** Auth, "Education and Training: No Longer Just a Badge and a Gun," in Contemporary Policing, Butterworths-Heinemann, 97; auth, Correlates and Consequences of Police Officer Support for the Quasi-Military Stress Academy," Journal of Criminal and Police Psychology, (98): 45-57; auth, "The Differential Value of Work Experience Versus Pre-Serice Education and Training on Criticality Evaluations of Police Tasks and Functions," The Justice Professional, (98): 379-405; auth, "Police Solidarity," Encyclopedia of Police Science, (95): 619-624; auth, "Problematic Legitimacy and the Structuring of Reality Through Terror Under Stalinism," International ScienceSeminar on Stalinism: Regularity, Threat, Challenge; auth, auth, "The Effects of College Education on Police Attitudes," Journal of Criminal Justice Education, (92): 71-92; auth, "The Relationship Between Patrol Officers' Subcultural Perspecties on Autonomy and Isolation and Their Orientation Toward Police Ethical conduct," Criminal Justice Ethics, (90): 24-42; auth, "The Problem of Unplanned Terror in Repressive Movement-Regimes," State Organized Terror: The Case of Violent Internal Repression, (91): 169-207; auth, " An Empirical Examination of the Relationship between Police Solidarity & Community Orientation," Journal of Police Science & Admin, (88): 182-194; auth, "The Social Integration of Civilians in the Commuications Division of Police Organizations," Journal of Police Science & Administration, (87): 288-302; **CONTACT ADDRESS** Dept Soc Sci, Norwich Univ, Northfield, 158 Harmon Dr, Northfield, VT 05663. **EMAIL** sshernoc@Norwich.edu

SHERRADEN, MARGARET
DISCIPLINE SOCIAL WORK **EDUCATION** Belost Col, BA, 72; Univ Chicago, MA, 74; Washington Univ, PhD, 89. **CAREER** Asst Prof to Assoc Prof, Univ Mo, 89-. **RESEARCH** Social policy; Immigration; Community economic development **SELECTED PUBLICATIONS** Auth, "Social Policy in Latin America: Questions of Growth, Equality, and Political Freedom," Latin American Research Review, (95): 176-193; auth, "Development of Health Policy and Services for Rural Mexico," in Global Perspectives on Health Care, (Prentice Hall, 95), 122-140; co-auth, "Qualitative Research with an Understudied Population: In-Depth Interviews with Women of Mexican Descent," Hispanic Journal of Behavioral Sciences, (95): 452-470; co-auth, "Healthy Babies Against the Odds: Maternal Support and Cultural Influences among Mexican Immigrants," Families in Society, (96): 298-313; co-auth, "Poverty, Family Support, and Well Being of Children: Mexican Immigrant Women and Childbearing," Journal of Sociology and Social Welfare, (96): 27-54; co-auth, "Prenatal Care and Low Birth Weight: Evidence from a Qualitative Study with Mexican Immigrant Women," Journal of Medical Systems, (96): 337-358; co-auth, "The Great Flood of 1993: Response and Recovery in Five Communities," Journal of Community Practice, (97): 23-46; co-auth, "Culturally-Protective Health Practices: Everyday Pregnancy Care Among Mexican Immigrant Women," Journal of Multicultural Social Work, (97): 93-116; co-auth, "Women, Microenterprise and Family: Promises and Prospects," Women and Work, (99): 113-140; co-ed, Community Economic Development and Social Work, Haworth Press, 98. **CONTACT ADDRESS** Dept Soc Work, Univ of Missouri, St. Louis, 8001 Natural Bridge, Saint Louis, MO 63121. **EMAIL** sherraden@umsl.edu

SHERRICK, REBECCA LOUISE
PERSONAL Born 05/28/1953, Carthage, IL **DISCIPLINE** AMERICAN HISTORY, WOMEN'S STUDIES **EDUCATION** IL Wesleyan Univ, BA, 75; Northwestern Univ, PhD(hist), 80. **CAREER** Asst prof hist to provost, Carroll Col, 80-. **MEMBERSHIPS** AHA; Orgn Am Historians. **RESEARCH** Father-daughter relationship as a factor in identity formation; female friendships among late-Victorian women; autobiography and womens identity. **SELECTED PUBLICATIONS** Auth, Toward Universal Sisterhood, Women's Studies Int Forum, 9/82. **CONTACT ADDRESS** Dept Hist, Carroll Col, Wisconsin, 100 N East Ave, Waukesha, WI 53186-5593.

SHERRILL, CATHERINE ANNE
PERSONAL Born 02/26/1938, Houston, TX **DISCIPLINE** ENGLISH; EDUCATION **EDUCATION** Univ Texas, Austin, BA, 60, MA, 69; Univ Iowa, PhD, 81. **CAREER** Instr, 60-66, Houston Independent Sch Dist; teacher, 69-78, Col of Mainland; instr, prof English, E Tenn St Univ. **HONORS AND AWARDS** Fac mem of the Year from Panhellenic Asn, E Tenn State Univ, 89. **MEMBERSHIPS** Nat Coun of Teachers of English. **RESEARCH** Young people's literature; composition and rhetoric. **SELECTED PUBLICATIONS** Auth, Carlson, G.R. and Anne Sherrill, Varies of Readers: How We Come to Love Books, NCTE, 88; auth, Literature Is: Collected Essays of G. Robert Carlsen, U of Iowa Foundation, Auburn Univ East Tennessee State Univ, 94, articles and essays in books and professional journals. **CONTACT ADDRESS** Dept of English, East Tennessee State Univ, Johnson City, TN 37614. **EMAIL** sherrill@etsu.edu

SHERRILL, VANITA LYTLE
PERSONAL Born 02/23/1945, Nashville, TN, s **DISCIPLINE** EDUCATION **EDUCATION** Fisk U, BA 1966; Fisk U, MA 1971; Vanderbilt U, 1985. **CAREER** Volunteer State Comm Coll, instr/field supr 1973-; Vocational Diagnostic Component Nashville CE Program, coord 1973; Metro Health Dept, social worker consult 1971-72; TN State Planning Commn, research asst 1970-71; Hubbard Hosp MeHarry Med Center, asst proj adminstr 1966-69; Gerontology TN State U, instr 1977; Univ of TN, educ intern 1977; Vanderbilt Univ Com for the Behavioral Sci, review bd 1985; Dede Wallace Center, treas 1985; Samaritan Center, sec bd of dirs, 85; Nashville Urban League, bd of dirs 1985. **HONORS AND AWARDS** Grant Educ & Research Tour of W Africa Phelps-Stokes Found 1979; Commr Century III 1985; Charter Mem Leadership Nashville 1985. **MEMBERSHIPS** Mem Delta Sigma Theta Soc 1985; mem Intl Curr Devel Prog; mem Am Personnel & Guidance Assn; mem Am Psychol Assn; mem Nat Assn of Black Social Wkrs; mem Jack & Jill Inc Nashville Chap 1985; mem Hendersonville Chap of Links Inc 1985; bd of dirs Alive-Hospice 1985; bd of dirs Council of Comm Servs 1985. **CONTACT ADDRESS** Volunteer State Comm Col, Nashville Pike, Gallatin, TN 37066.

SHIFREN, KIM
DISCIPLINE PSYCHOLOGY **EDUCATION** Univ MD, BA, 88; Syracuse Univ, MA, 91; PhD, 93. **CAREER** Vis Asst Prof, Univ Fla, 93-96; Postdoctoral Fel, Univ Mich, 96-98; Asst Prof, Towson Univ, 98-. **HONORS AND AWARDS** Faculty Development and Res Grant, Towson Univ, 00; Nat Inst on Aging, 98; Seed Grant Prog, Ctr for Applied Cognitive Res on Aging, 97; Res Grant Awd, Syracuse Univ, 93; Student Travel Awd, Am Psychol Asn, 92. **MEMBERSHIPS** APA, GSA, EIA. **RESEARCH** Self-management of chronic illness, Personality and health risk behaviors. **SELECTED PUBLICATIONS** Ed, Medical information processing in aging patients: Cognitive and human factors perspectives, Mahwah, NJ, 99; auth, "Age, pain, and coping with rheumtoid arthritis," Pain, (99): 217-228; auth, "Do cognitive processes predict mental health in Rheumatoid Arthritis patients?," Journal of Behavioral Medicine, (99): 529-547; auth, "Judgments about Estrogen Replacement Therapy: The role of Age, Cognitive Abilities and Beliefs," Psychology and Aging, (99): 179-191; auth, "Personality counts for a lot: Predictors of mental and physical health of spouse caregivers in two disease groups," Journal of Gerontology: Psychological Sciences, (98): 73-85; auth, "Instrumental and expressive traits and eating attitudes: A replication across American and British students," Personality and Individual Differences, (98): 1-17; auth, "Structure and variation of mood in individuals with Parkinson's disease: A dynamic factor analysis," Psychology and Aging, (97): 328-339; auth, "Caregiving, personality and health," The Health Psychologiest, (97): 6-7, 26; auth, "Individual differences in the perception of optimism and disease severity: A study among individuals with Parkinson's disease," Journal of Behavioral Medicine, (96): 241-271; auth, "The relationship between instrumental and expressive traits, health behaviors, and perceived physical health," Sex Roles, (96): 841-864. **CONTACT ADDRESS** Dept Psychol, Towson State Univ, 8000 York Rd, Baltimore, MD 21252-0001. **EMAIL** kshifren@towson.edu

SHINER, REBECCA
PERSONAL Born 07/27/1968, Johnstown, PA, m, 1991, 1 child **DISCIPLINE** PSYCHOLOGY **EDUCATION** Haverford Col, BA, 90; Univ Minn, PhD, 98. **CAREER** Asst Prof, Colgate Univ, 99-. **HONORS AND AWARDS** Phi Beta Kappa, 85; Haverford Magna Cum Laude, 90; Grad Fel Univ of Minn, 92-93, 95-95, 96-97. **MEMBERSHIPS** Soc for Res in Child Develop, Am Psychol Asn, Am Psychol Soc. **RESEARCH** Personality Development. **SELECTED PUBLICATIONS** Coauth, "The Family environment of adolescents with lifetime depression: Associations with material depression history, " J of the Am Acad of Child and Adolescent Psychiat 37 (98): 1152-1160; auth, "How shell we speak of children's personalities in middle childhood?: A preliminary taxonomy," Psychol Bull 124 (98): 308-332; auth, "Linking childhood personality with adaptation: Evidence for continuity and change across time into late adolescence,"J of Personality and Soc Psychology 78 (00): 310-325. **CONTACT ADDRESS** Dept Psychol, Colgate Univ, 13 Oak Dr, Hamilton, NY 13346. **EMAIL** rshiner@mail.colgate.edu

SHIVELY, MARSHA L.
PERSONAL Born 05/01/1944, Fort Wayne, IN, d, 2 children **DISCIPLINE** EDUCATION **EDUCATION** MA; EdD; PhD. **CAREER** Ind Inst of Tech, 78-80; Ind Purdue Univ, 92-94; Ind Univ, 97-99; Ivy Tech Stae Col, 91-. **HONORS AND AWARDS** Phi Theta Kappa Good Teaching Awd, 93, 94; Glen Sample good Teacher, 96; Master Teacher Acad, Ivy Tech State Rep, 97-98. **MEMBERSHIPS** Sigma Tau Delta; Kappa Delta Pi; Phi Gama Mu; Midwest TYCA; NCTE; NEA; ASCD. **RESEARCH** Multiple learning styles, distance education, composition/tech, business writing. **SELECTED PUBLICATIONS** Auth, Teaching Tips, Nov 99; auth, "Learning Styles and Your Teaching", Ivy Leaf, Mar 00. **CONTACT ADDRESS** Dept Gen Educ, Ivy Tech State Col, Kokomo, PO Box 1373, Kokomo, IN 46903-1373. **EMAIL** mshively@ivy.tec.in.us

SHIVERS, JAY SANFORD
PERSONAL Born 07/07/1930, New York, NY, m, 1994, 1 child **DISCIPLINE** EDUCATION, RECREATIONAL SERVICE EDUCATION **EDUCATION** BS, IN Univ, 52; MA 53, Re Dir 55, NYork Univ; PhD, Univ Wis, 58. **CAREER** Coordr Nstl Rec and Park Assoc Dept Accreditation Univ Conn Baccalaureate Prog in Rec Scv Edu, with options in Natural Res Rec Mge and Therapeutic Rec, 91; Visiting Prof Wingate Inst, Israel, 76; Vis Prof Moorehead State Col, MN, 70; Vis Prof and Acting Ch Calif State Col, Hayward, 67; Asst Prof and Supvr of Rec Svc Edu, Assoc Prof, 67, Prof 70-, Prof Consul Keystone Training and Rehabil Inst Scranton, PA, 64-66. **HONORS AND AWARDS** Who's Who in Am Edu, Intl Dictionary of Biog, World Dictinary of Bio, Outstanding Am Edu, Contemporary Am Auth, Intl Dir of Auth, Natl Lit Awd from the Natl Rec and Park Assoc, Distinguishes Svc Awd, Natl Therapeutic Rec Soc. **MEMBERSHIPS** Natl Rec and Park Assoc, Int Playground Assock Intl Federation of Park and Rec Admin, Leisure Res Section Intl Sociol Assoc, Am Assoc Univ Prof Natl Consortium on Physical Edu and Rec for the Disabled. **SELECTED PUBLICATIONS** Auth, Introduction to Recreational Service, Charles C. Thomas, 93; auth, "Beware: The Doubters are Among Us" Editorial Bulletin of the Federation Internationale of Education Physique (FIEP) Vol. 62, No 3/4, 93; auth, "Physical Activity Through the Life Cycle," FIEP Bulletin, Vol. 64, 94-95; auth, The Story of Leisure, Human Kinetics, 97; auth, "Rehabilitation Using Adapted Aquatics, Bulletin of the Federation Internationale d'Education Physique (FIEP), Vol. 68, No. 3, (98): 26-30. **CONTACT ADDRESS** Dept of Kinesiology, Univ of Connecticut, Storrs, Gampel Pavilion, Unit 1110, Storrs, CT 06268. **EMAIL** jay.shivers@uconn.edu

SHMURAK, CAROLE B.
PERSONAL Born 04/19/1944, New York, NY, m, 1967, 1 child **DISCIPLINE** EDUCATION **EDUCATION** Mount Holyoke Col, BA, 65; Harvard Univ, MA, 66; Ind Univ, PhD, 74. **CAREER** Teacher, Dalton Schools, 67-71; dept chair, Miss Porter's School, 74-89; prof, Central Conn State Univ, 89-. **HONORS AND AWARDS** Phi Beta Kappa; USPHS Fel, Harvard; Univ Fel, Ind Univ. **MEMBERSHIPS** Am Educ Res Asn, Am Educ Studies Asn. **RESEARCH** Single sex schools, Gender equity. **SELECTED PUBLICATIONS** Auth, On Blue Creek farm, Smith & Kraus: Lyme, NH, (in press); auth, Matty's War, Smith & Kraus: NH, 99; auth, "Mary Lyon," in Historical dictionary of American education, (99): 220; auth, Voices of hope: Adolescent girls at single sex and coeducation schools, Peter Lang: New York, 98; auth, "Mary Lyon", in Historical dictionary of women's education, (98): 253-255; auth, "Mount Holyoke Seminary," in Historical dictionary of women's education, (98): 278-281; auth, "Emma Perry Carr," in Notable women in the physical sciences: A biographical dictionary, (97): 40-45; auth, "Anna Jane Harrison," Notable women in the physical sciences: A biographical dictionary, (97): 172-176; auth, "Cornelia M.Clapp," in Notable women in the life sciences: A biographical dictionary, (96): 75-78; auth, "Lydia W Shuttuck," in Notable women in the life sciences: A

biographical dictionary, (96): 354-359. **CONTACT ADDRESS** Dept Teacher Education, Central Connecticut State Univ, 1615 Stanley St, New Britain, CT 06053. **EMAIL** shmurack@ccsu.edu

SHOEMAKER, ALLEN L.
PERSONAL Born 12/26/1952, Grand Rapids, MI **DISCIPLINE** PSYCHOLOGY **EDUCATION** Univ Ill, PhD, 80. **CAREER** Regent Univ; Calvin Col. **SELECTED PUBLICATIONS** Author of several publications. **CONTACT ADDRESS** Dept Psychol, Calvin Col, 3201 Burton St E, Grand Rapids, MI 49546. **EMAIL** shoe@calvin.edu

SHOFFNER, MARIE F.
PERSONAL Born 10/06/1954, Roswell, NM **DISCIPLINE** COUNSELING, EDUCATION **EDUCATION** Col William and Mary, BS, 77; Univ Va, ME, 79; MEd, 90; PhD, 96. **CAREER** Counselor to Teaching Intern, Univ Va, 93-95; Asst Prof, Univ NCar, 96-. **HONORS AND AWARDS** Governor's Fel, Univ VA, 95-96; New Fac Grant Awd, 96; Excellence in Res Awd, Univ NC, 97, 98; Fel, Nat Centr for Educ Statistics, 98; GEMS 2000 Fel. **MEMBERSHIPS** Am Coun Asn; Asn of Coun Educ and Supervision; Am Sch Coun Asn; Asn for Assessment in Coun; Am Career Dev Asn; Multicultural Coun and Dev Asn; NC Coun Asn; NC Sch Acoun Asn; NC Asn for Assessment in Coun; Chi Sigma Iota. **RESEARCH** Talent Development; Career Development of Adolescents; Preparation of School Counselors; Career Development in Science, Mathematics, Engineering and Technology; Diverse Populations. **SELECTED PUBLICATIONS** Auth, "The role of school counselors in the transition to middle school," Middle Matters, (97): 6; co-auth, "The family debriefing model (FDM): An adpated critical incident stress debriefing for parents and older sibling suicide survivors," The Family Journal: Counseling and Therapy for Couples and Families, (99): 342-348; co-auth, "Careers in the Mathematical Sciences: The Role of the School Counselor," ERIC Digest, 99; co-auth, "Psychometric analysis of the Inviting School Safety Survey," Measurement and Evaluation in Counseling and Development, (99): 66-74; co-auth, "Facilitating student transitions," The Middle School Journal, in press; co-auth, "An Interactive Approach for Developing Interprofessional Collaboration: Preparing School Counselors," Counselor Educaiton and Supervision, forthcoming. **CONTACT ADDRESS** Dept Coun & Educ Dev, Univ of No Carolina, Greensboro, PO Box 26171, Greensboro, NC 27402-6171. **EMAIL** mfshoffn@uncg.edu

SHOW, DEAN R.
PERSONAL Born 10/18/1940, New Ulm, MN, m, 1963, 3 children **DISCIPLINE** ANTHROPOLOGY **EDUCATION** Univ Minn, BA, 62; Univ Ore, PhD, 66. **CAREER** Asst Prof, Univ of Maine at Orono, 66-69; from Asst Prof to Prof, SUNY Albany, 69-91; Chair of Anthrop Dept, SUNY Albany, 74-80, 89-91; Vis Prof, Univ de las Americas, Cholula, Mex, spring 78; Asoc/Acting Dean, Col of Soc and Behav Sci, SUNY Albany, 80-83; Prof, Head of Anthrop Dept, The Pa State Univ, 95-. **MEMBERSHIPS** Soc for Am Archaeol, Am Anthrop Asn, Soc of Sigma Xi, Am Soc for Ethnohistory, Northeast Anthrop Asn, NY Archaeol Coun, Archaeol Inst of Am, Union Internationale des Sci Prehistoriques et Protohistoriques, Iroquois Indian Museum, Am Asn for the Advancement of Sci, Europ Asn of Archaeol. **SELECTED PUBLICATIONS** Auth, The Iroquois, Basil Blackwell, 94; ed, Iroquois Medical Botany, by james Herrick, Syracuse Univ Press, 95; auth, Mohawk Valley Archaeology: The Collections, Univ at Albany for Archaeol Studies, and The Pa State Univ, 95; auth, Mohawk Valley Archaeology: The Sites, Univ at Albany for Archaeol Studies, and The Pa State Univ, 95; ed, In the Country of the Mohawks: Historical Narratives of a Native People, Syracuse Univ Press, 96; auth, "The Mohawks and Europeans: Cultural Exchange Amidst Conflict," in Transfers cultures et metissages Amerique/Europe XVIe-Xxe siecle, ed. Laurier Turgeon (Quebec: Le Presses de L'Universite Laval, 96): 271-277; auth, "More on Migration in Prehistory: Accommodating New Evidence in the Northern Iriquoian Case," AM Antiquity 61 (96): 791-796; auth, "The Architecture of Iroquois Longhouses," Northeast Anthrop 53 (97): 61-84; coauth, "The Mohawk Upper Castle Historic District National Historic Landmark," The Bull: j of NY State Archaeol Asn 114 (98): 32-44; auth, "Toward a New Understanding of Great Lakes Archaeology," in Taming the Taxonomy, ed. R. F. Williamson and C. M. Watts (Toronto: Eastenbooks, 99), 267-274. **CONTACT ADDRESS** Dept Anthrop, Pennsylvania State Univ, Univ Park, 409 Carpenter Bldg, University Park, PA 15802.

SHUMAN, R. BAIRD
PERSONAL Born 06/20/1929, Paterson, NJ **DISCIPLINE** ENGLISH, EDUCATION **EDUCATION** Lehigh Univ, AB, 51; Temple Univ, EdM, 53; Univ Vienna, cert, 54; Univ Pa, PhD, 61. **CAREER** Asst instr English, Univ Pa, 55-57; instr humanities, Drexel Inst Technol, 57-59: asst prof English, San Jose State Col, 59-62; from asst prof to prof educ, Duke Univ, 62-77; prof to prof emeritus englist & dir english educ, Univ Ill, Urbana-Champaign, 77-, dir freshman rhetoric, 79-, Lectr Am lit, Linz Sem Austrian Teachers, Austria, 53; univ scholar, Univ Pa, 56; vis lectr English, Moore Inst Art, 58; vis prof humanities, Philadelphia Conserv Music, 58-59, King Faisal Univ, Saudi Arabia, 78, 81, East Tenn State Univ, 80, Bread Loaf Sch English, Middlebury Col, 80; consult, Am Col Testing Prog & NC Dept Pub Instr, 75-, Kans State Col, Pittsburg, 80, Univ Ark, Little Rock, 80, Nat Univ Singapore, 81; exec ed, The Clearing House, 75-; contribr ed, Reading Horizons, 75-80; consult ed, Poet Lore, 76-, Cygnus, 78-, J Aethetic Ed, 78-82; ed, Speaking out column, The Clearing House, 76- **MEMBERSHIPS** MLA; NCTE; Int Asn Univ Prof English; Conf English Educ; Conf Col Comp & Commun. **RESEARCH** The teaching of writing and the teaching of reading; humanities education; educational drama. **SELECTED PUBLICATIONS** Auth, Signifying As A Scaffold For Literary Interpretation - The Pedagogical Implications Of An African-Am Discourse Genre, African Am Rev, 95. **CONTACT ADDRESS** Bos 27647, Las Vegas, NV 89126-1647. **EMAIL** rbaird@vegasnet.net

SHUMWAY, LARRY V.
PERSONAL Born 11/25/1934, Winslow, AZ, m, 1971, 6 children **DISCIPLINE** ETHNOMUSICOLOGY **EDUCATION** Brigham Young Univ, BA, 60; Seton Hall Univ, MA, 64; Univ Washington, PhD. **CAREER** Assoc Prof, Brigham Young Univ, 75-. **MEMBERSHIPS** Soc for Ethnomusicology; Natl Assoc for Humanities Education **RESEARCH** Music of Japan, Tonga, traditional USA **SELECTED PUBLICATIONS** Auth, Non-Western Humanities in the Undergraduate Curriculum: Developing an International Perspective, Interdisciplinary Humanities, 97; auth, Dancing the Buckles of Their Shoes in Pioneer Utah (bundled with CD recording including 7 of Mr. Shumway's fiddle tunes), BYU Studies, 97-98; auth, "Foundations of the Tradition: During Among the Mormon Pioneers," in Craig R. Miller, Social Dance in the Mormon West, with Craig R. Miller, (Salt Lake City: Utah Arts Coun, 00); auth, An Old-Time Utah Dance Party: Sheet Music and Dance Steps, Salt Lake City: Utah Arts Counc, 00. **CONTACT ADDRESS** Brigham Young Univ, JKHB 2007B, Provo, UT 84602. **EMAIL** larry_shumway@byu.edu

SIBALIS, MICHAEL
DISCIPLINE CULTURE; HISTORY OF MODERN FRANCE **EDUCATION** McGill, BA; Sir George Williams, MA; Concordia, PhD. **CAREER** Prof. **RESEARCH** Parisian labour movement from 1789 to 1834, the political police under Napoleon I, and the hist of sexuality in Modern France. **SELECTED PUBLICATIONS** Auth, "Andre Troncin, ouvrier (1802-1846): Une victime de la prison politique," 1848: Bulletin de la Societe d'histoire de la Revoution de 1848 et des Revolutions du XIXe siecle, 8, (91): 83-91; auth, "Prisoners by Mesure de haute police under Napoleon I: Reviving the Lettres de cachet," Proceedings of the Western Soc for French History 18, (91): 83-91; auth, "Un aspect de la legende noire de Napoleon Ier: Le mythe de l'enfemement d'opposants politiques comme fous," 'Revue de l'Institut Napoleon 156, (91): 8-24; auth, "La Cote-d'or, terre d'exil: Les residents sous surveillance pendant le Consulat et l'Empire," Annales de Bourgogne 64, (92): 39-51; auth, "Internal Exile in Napoleonic France, 1789-1815," Proceedings of the Western society for French Hist 20, (93): 189-98; auth, "Jan Czynski: Jalons pour la biographie d'un fourieriste de la Grande emigration polonaise," Cahiers Charles Fourier 6, (95): 58-85; auth, "The Regulation of Male Homosexuality in Revolutionary and Napoleonic France," in Homosexuality in Modern France, ed. Jeffrey Merrick and Bryant T. Ragan, (Oxford Univ Press: New York, 96): 80-81; auth, "Paris-Babylone/Paris-Sodome: Images of Homosexuality in the Nineteenth Century City," in Images of the City in Nineteenth-Century France, ed. John West-Sooby, (Boombana Publications: Mount Nebo, Queensland, Australia, 98): 13-22; auth, "The Parisian Tailors in 1848: The Association fraternelle des ouvriers tailleurs (The Atelier de Clichy)," in The Sphinx in the Tuileries and Other Essays in Modern French History: Papers Presented at the Eleventh George Rude Seminar, ed., Robert Aldrich and Martyn Lyons, (Univ of Sydney: Sydney, Australia, 99): 154-68; auth, "Paris," in Queer Sites: Gay Urban Histories since 1600, ed. David Higgs, (Routledge: London, 99): 10-37. **CONTACT ADDRESS** Dept of History, Wilfrid Laurier Univ, 75 University Ave W, Waterloo, ON, Canada N2L 3C5. **EMAIL** msibalis@mach1.wlu.ca

SICOLI, MARY L.
PERSONAL Born 11/15/1944, m, 1967, 2 children **DISCIPLINE** PSYCHOLOGY **EDUCATION** West Chester State Univ, BS, 66; MS, 73; Univ Wis, MS, 67; Bryn Mawr Col, PhD, 77. **CAREER** Prof, Cabrini Col, 74-. **HONORS AND AWARDS** Distinguished Col Teaching, Christian R & Mary F Lindback Foundation, 84; Who's Who among College Students, 65-66; Outstanding Young Women in Am, 80. **MEMBERSHIPS** Am Psychol Asn, Eastern Psychol Asn, Penn Psychol Asn, Campus Psychol Network, Kappa Delta Pi, Psi Chi, Delta Epsilon Sigma. **RESEARCH** Women musicians, Moral development, Altruism. **SELECTED PUBLICATIONS** Auth, "The Moral and Social Development of the Intellectually Gifted child," ERIC/CAPs, 79; auth, "Moral Development in the Second Grade Classroom: Educational Intervention and Mental Structure," Univ Southern Calif Press, 79; auth, "Moral Development: A Comparative Study of Male and Female College Students," Piagetian Theory and the Helping Professions, 80; auth, "The Grey World of the Gypsy Scholar," The Pennsylvania Professor, 79; auth, "A Comparative Study of the Moral Judgments of Adolescents Attending an Alternative and a Traditional High School," ERIC,ED, 81; auth, "Mid-Life Music: Mid-Life Message?," Popular Music and Society, 91; auth, "The Role of the Woman songwriter in Country Music,": Popular Music & Society, 94; auth, "Life Factors common to Women Who Write Popular Songs," Creativity Research Journal, (95): 265-276; auth, "Sisters in the Musical Ghetto," Women of Note Quarterly, 97. **CONTACT ADDRESS** Dept Psychol, Cabrini Col, 610 King of Prussia, Radnor, PA 19087. **EMAIL** m.l.corbin.sicoli@cabrini.edu

SIDELL, NANCY
PERSONAL Born 04/11/1958, Fremont, OH, m, 1980 **DISCIPLINE** SOCIAL WORK **EDUCATION** Kent State Univ, BA, 79; Bowling Green State Univ, MRC, 84; Case Western Reserve Univ, MSW, 90; Ohio State Univ, PhD, 98. **CAREER** Adj Prof, Bowling Green State Univ, 90-98; Adj Instr, Ohio State Univ, 97-98; Asst Prof, Mansfield Univ, 98-. **HONORS AND AWARDS** Outstanding Faculty-Student Mentor Outstanding Social Work Student of the Year, 99; Outstanding Service to the Soc Awd, Ohio Soc of Hosp Soc Workers, 93; Quality in Practice Awd, Ohio Hosp Asn, 93; President's Awd, Ohio Soc of Hosp Soc Workers, 90. **MEMBERSHIPS** Phi Eta Chi, Soc Work Club, Alpha Delta Mu, Nat Asn of Soc Workers, Soc of Hosp Soc Work Directors of the Am Hosp Asn. **SELECTED PUBLICATIONS** Auth, "Factors that explain marital happiness when a spouse lives in a nursing home: Married but living apart," Journal of Family Social Work, in press; auth, "The experience of community dwelling spouses of nursing home users: Marital satisfaction, coping and mental health," Clinical Gerontologist, in press; auth, Teaching legal research: A forgotten step in teaching legal issues, in review; auth, "The politics of Alzheimer's Special Care Units: Lessons to be learned from the demented?," Journal of Health and Social Policy, (98): 29-43; auth, "Easing transitions: Solution focused principles and the nursing home resident's family," Clinical Gerontologist, (97): 21-41; auth, "Adult adjustment to chronic illness: A review of the literature," Health and Social Work, (97): 5-11; auth, "The challenge of practice based research: A group approach," Social Work in Health Care, (96): 99-111; auth, "Social work in pediatric oncology: A family needs assessment," Social Work in Health Care, (95): 39-54; auth, "A Review of health care in Poland and the United States," in Columbus-Cracow Dialogues on East European Social Issues, 96; auth, "The experience of community dwelling spouses of nursing home users: Marital satisfaction, coping, and mental health," Clinical Gerontologist's Clinical Comment, (99): 57-60. **CONTACT ADDRESS** Dept Anthropol & Sociol, Mansfield Univ of Pennsylvania, Pine Crest, Mansfield, PA 16933.

SIEGEL, BRIAN V.
PERSONAL Born 07/14/1950, Milwukee, WI, d, 2 children **DISCIPLINE** ANTHROPOLOGY **EDUCATION** Univ Wis Madison, BA, 72; MA, 74, PhD, 83. **CAREER** TA, Univ of Wis, 74-76, 78; vis instr, Lawrence Univ, 80-81; instr to assoc prof, Furman Univ, 81-. **HONORS AND AWARDS** Phi Beta Kappa, 72; Fulbright-Hays Grant, 76, 85; NDEA Foreign Lang Fel, 72, 79; NEH Summer Inst, 85, 88, 92. **MEMBERSHIPS** Am Anthrop Assoc; African Studies Assoc; SE Reg Soc for African Studies; Archaeol Soc of SC; Soc for Hist Archaeol. **RESEARCH** Ethnicity, Race and Ethnic Relations, Political Economy of Social Change, History of Anthropology, African Studies (particularly Central and Southern Africa), and the Ethnohistory of the Lamba and the Central African Copperbelt. **SELECTED PUBLICATIONS** Auth, "Family and Kinship", Understanding Contemporary African, eds April A. and Donald L. Gordon, Lynne Rienner, (Bolder, CO, 92): 175-200; auth, "Chipimpi, Vulgar Clans, and Lala-Lamba Ethnohistory", Culture and Contradiction: Dialectics of Wealth, Power and Symbol, ed Hermine G. De Soto, Mellen Res Univ Pr, (San Francisco, 92): 273-293; auth, "Anthropology and the Science of Race", Furman Studies 38, (96): 1-21; coauth, Historical Dictionary of Zambia, Scarecrow Pr, (Metcheun, NJ/London), 98; auth, "Anthropology and the Science of Race, Perspectives on Social Problems, ed Robert P. McNamara, CourseWise, (boulder, 98): 105-12; rev, of "History, Power, Ideology: Central Issues in Marxism and Anthropology" by Donald L. Donham, Int J of African Hist Studies 32, (99): rev, of "African Christian Marriage", by Benezeri Kisembo, Laurenti Magesa and Aylward Shorter, African Book Pub Record 25, (99): 1. **CONTACT ADDRESS** Dept Sociol, Furman Univ, 3300 Poinsett Hwy, Greenville, SC 29613-1000.

SIEGEL, CAROL
PERSONAL Born 11/12/1952, Englewood, NJ, m, 1981, 0 child **DISCIPLINE** CULTURAL STUDIES, GENDER STUDIES **EDUCATION** Univ Calif at Berkeley, PhD. **CAREER** Prof, Washington State Univ. **RESEARCH** Feminist theory; Youth cultures; Modern British and Victorian Literature; Asian-American literature. **SELECTED PUBLICATIONS** Auth, D. H. Lawrence Among the Women: Wavering Boundaries in Women's Literary Traditions, 91; auth, Male Masochism: Modern Revisions of the Story of Love, 95; coed, spec issues of Genders: Eroticism and Containment, Forming and Reforming Identity, Sex Positives?, Bodies of Writing, Bodies in Performance, and The Gya 90s; auth, New Millennial Sexstyles, 00. **CONTACT ADDRESS** English and Cultural Studies, Washington State Univ, 14202 NE Salmon Creek Ave, Vancouver, WA 98626. **EMAIL** siegel@vancouver.wsu.edu

SIEGEL, PETER E.
PERSONAL Born 11/06/1953, Ann Arbor, MI, m, 1991, 2 children **DISCIPLINE** ANTHROPOLOGY AND ENTOMOLOGY **EDUCATION** Univ Del, BA, Anthrop, 78; Univ Del, AS, Entomology, 78; SUNY Binghamton Univ, MA, Anthrop, 81; SUNY Binghamton Univ, PhD, Anthrop, 92. **CAREER** Princ archeol, John Milner Asn; res assoc, Field Mus of Natural Hist; res assoc, Ctr de Invest Indigenas de Puerto Rico. **HONORS AND AWARDS** Heinz Family Found grant for archeol fieldwork in Latin Amer; Wenner-Gren grant for fieldwork in Puerto Rico; Natl Sci Found Diss Improvement grant. **MEMBERSHIPS** Soc Amer Archeol; Amer Anthrop Asn. **RESEARCH** Latin American Archeol; Eastern North America; Complex Society. **SELECTED PUBLICATIONS** Rev, The Indigenous People of the Caribbean, ed Samuel M. Wilson, Univ Press Fl, Gainesville, Latin Amer Antiquity, 9, 180-182, 98; auth, Ancestor Worship and Cosmology among the Tainos, Taino: Pre-Columbian Art and Culture from the Caribbean, ed Fatima Bercht, Estrellita Brodsky, John Alan Farmer and Dicey Taylor, pp 106-111, The Monacelli Press and El Museo del Barrio, New York, 97; An Interview with Irving Rouse, Current Anthrop, 37, 671-689; 96; Ideology and Culture Change in Prehistoric Puerto Rico: A View from the Community, Jour of Field Archaeol, 23, 313-333, 96; The Archaeology of Community Organization in the Tropical Lowlands: A Case Study from Puerto Rico, Archaeol in the Amer Tropics: Current Analytical Methods and Appln, ed Peter W. Stahl, pp 42-65, Cambridge Univ Press, Cambridge, 95; rev, The Archaeology of Pacific Nicaragua, Frederick W. Lange, Payson D. Sheets, Anibal Martinez and Suzanne Abel-Vidor, Univ Nmex Press, Albuquerque, The Latin Amer Anthrop Rev, spring 1993, 5, 1, 45-46, 95; auth, The First Documented Prehistoric Gold-Copper Alloy Artefact from the West Indies, Jour Archaeol Sci, 20, 67-79, 93; Saladoid Survivial Strategies: Evidence from Site Locations, Proceedings of the Intl Congress for Caribbean Archaeol, 14, 315-337, Barbados, 93. **CONTACT ADDRESS** John Milner Associates, 535 N Church St, West Chester, PA 19380. **EMAIL** psiegel@johnmilnerassociates.com

SILBER, DAVID E.
PERSONAL Born 09/19/1935, Detroit, MI, m, 1997, 3 children **DISCIPLINE** PSYCHOLOGY **EDUCATION** Wayne State Univ, BA, 58; Ohio Univ, MA, 60; Univ Mich, PhD, 65. **CAREER** From Asst Prof to Prof, George Washington Univ DC, 65-; Chair Dept Psychology, George Washington Univ DC, 91-96, 99-. **HONORS AND AWARDS** Fel, Soc Personality Assessment. **MEMBERSHIPS** Am Psychol Asn, Soc Personality Assessment. **RESEARCH** Assessment, Psychology of Crime. **SELECTED PUBLICATIONS** Coauth, "Relationship between the Appreciative Personality Test and verbal intelligence in a university sample," Psychology Reports 73 (93): 575-578; coauth, "Leadership pattern among undergraduate women on the Apperceptive Personality Test/Brief Adult," J of Soc Behav and Personality 9 (94): 63-68; coauth, "Prediction of depression with the Apperceptive Personality Test," J of Clinical Psychology 50 (94): 234-237; coauth, "Personality characteristics of incest survivors on the Draw-A-Person Questionnaire," J Personality Assessment 63 (94): 97-104; coauth, "Personality of rape survivors as a group and by type of perpetrator," J of Clinical Psychology 51 (95): 587-593; coauth, "Personalities of women reporting incestuous abuse during childhood," Perceptual & Motor Skills 81 (95): 955-965; coauth, "Incest survivors have different personality characteristics than non-assault persons," J of Soc Behav and Personality 13 (98): 437-450; coauth, "Views of men and women about personality characteristics associated with gender," in Studies of Objective/Projective Personality Tests Vol I, ed. S.A. Karp (Brooklandville, MD: Objective/Projective Personality Tests Inc, 99); coauth, "Word association patterns of women reporting earlier sexual abuse," n Studies of Objective/Projective Personality Tests Vol I, ed. S.A. Karp (Brooklandville, MD: Objective/Projective Personality Tests Inc, 99). **CONTACT ADDRESS** Dept Psychology, The George Washington Univ, 2035 H St NW, Washington, DC 20052-0001. **EMAIL** dsilber@gwu.edu

SILK, WILLIAM
PERSONAL Born 07/25/1941, Chicago, IL, m, 1982, 2 children **DISCIPLINE** CRIMINAL JUSTICE, CORRECTIONS, SOCIOLOGY **EDUCATION** Depaul Univ, BA, 69; Depaul Univ, MA, 74; Chicago State Univ, MS, 89; Nova Southeastern Univ, Doctor Public Administration Degree, 83. **CAREER** Adjunct Instr, Sociology Dept, Moraine Valley Community Col; Adjunct Instr, Criminal Justice and Corrections, City of Chicago Police Department, Sergeant of Police. **HONORS AND AWARDS** The National Dean's List, Eleventh Annual Edition, Volume II, 87-88, Educational Communication Inc.; Dept Commendation, Chicago Police Dept. **MEMBERSHIPS** Amer Academy for Professional Law Enforcement, Chicago, Illinois Chapter. **RESEARCH** Juvenile Delinquency, Criminal Activity. **SELECTED PUBLICATIONS** Auth, "Reducing the Rate of Juvenile Delinquency, Nova Southeastern Univ, Ft. Lauderdale, FLA; auth, "Juvenile Delinquency as a Learned Behavior," DePaul Univ, Chicago, Illinois. **CONTACT ADDRESS** Dept Social Science, Moraine Valley Comm Col, 10900 S 88th Ave, Palos Hills, IL 60465.

SILVA, CHRISTOPHER
PERSONAL Born 01/30/1962, Natick, MA, m, 1995, 1 child **DISCIPLINE** PSYCHOLOGY **EDUCATION** Trinity Col CT, BA, 84; Univ Conn, MA, 88; PhD, 90. **CAREER** Adj Asst Prof, Providence Col, RI, 90-92; Asst Prof, Hanover Col, Ind, 92-94; Postdoctoral Fel, Princeton Evaluation and Treatment Serv, NJ, 94-95; Asst Prof, Dickinson Col, Pa, 95-00. **HONORS AND AWARDS** Phi Beta Kappa, 84; Psi Chi, 84. **MEMBERSHIPS** Am Psychol Asn. **RESEARCH** Hypnotic Response, Fantasy Proheness, Dissociative Experiences, Intuitive thinking. **SELECTED PUBLICATIONS** Coauth, "Breaching hypnotic amnesia by manipulating expectancy," J of Abnormal Psychology 96 (87): 325-329; coauth, "The surreptitious observation design: An experimental paradigm for distinguishing artifact from essence in hypnosis," J of Abnormal Psychology 98 (88): 132-136; coauth, "Interpretive sets, expectancy, fantasy proneness and dissociation as predictors of hypnotic response," J of Personality and Soc Psychology 63 (92): 847-856; coauth, "A spectral analysis of cognitive and personality variables in hypnosis: Empirical disconfirmation of the two-factor model of hypnotic responding," J of Personality and Soc Psychology 69 (95): 167-175. **CONTACT ADDRESS** Dept Psychology, Dickinson Col, PO Box 1773, Carlisle, PA 17013.

SILVESTRI, ELENA M.
PERSONAL Born 06/11/1961, Hamilton, ON, Canada **DISCIPLINE** FRENCH, ENGLISH AS SECOND LANGUAGE **EDUCATION** McMaster Univ, BA, 84; Universite Rene Descartes, DEA, 85; doctorat en linguistique, 96. **CAREER** Lectr, instr, McMaster Univ, 92-97, 00; prof, Univ Regina, 97; asst prof, Yamaguchi Univ, 98-00; asst prof, McMaster Univ, 01-02, director, Int Lang and Cult Center, 00-. **HONORS AND AWARDS** Dalley Scholarship; Yates Scholarship; French Govt Book Prize; Swiss Govt Book Prize; 1st Prize, McMaster Univ Classics Contest. **MEMBERSHIPS** MLA, Can Ling Assoc. **RESEARCH** Bilingualism, Code-Switching, Conversational Analysis of bilingual interactions. **SELECTED PUBLICATIONS** Auth, "Choix de langues et roles discursifs dans une conversation familiale italo-canadienne," Plurilinguismes, no 1, (90): auth, "Personalized Profiles of Code-Switching," Europ Sci Found - Network on Code Switching and Lang Contact, (95); auth, "L'Alternance des langues dans une conversation familiale bilingue italo-canadienne," Presses Universitaires du Septentrion, (97); auth, "this is regular conversation . . .": Autocommentaires dans une conversation familiale bilingue," Plurilinguismes, no 14, (98). **CONTACT ADDRESS** Int Lang and Cult Centre, McMaster Univ, 65 Christopher Dr, Hamilton, ON, Canada L9B 1G6. **EMAIL** ilcc@canada.com

SIMMONS, BETTY JO
PERSONAL Born 05/09/1939, Amelia, VA, m, 1958, 2 children **DISCIPLINE** EDUCATION **EDUCATION** Longwood Col, BA; MS; Col William and Mary, PhD. **CAREER** Prof, Longwood Col, 66-. **HONORS AND AWARDS** Maude Glenn Raiford Awd for Teaching Excellence, 90; J.B. Fuqua Awd for Teaching Excellence, 94, 96, 98. **MEMBERSHIPS** Kappa Delta Pi; Phi Delta Kappa; Phi Kappa Phi. **RESEARCH** Beginning Teachers. **SELECTED PUBLICATIONS** Auth, "Videotaping and Teacher Self-evaluation", Educ Issues, 97; auth, "The Be-Attitudes of a Successful Teacher", New Teacher Advocate, (97): coauth, The Pros and Cons of School Uniforms", Va Educ J, (97): auth, "The Importance of Being Tested", Kappa Delta Pi Record, (98): auth, "Mentoring in Higher Education", Delta Kappa Gamma Bulletin, (98); coauth, "Assessing Multiple Intelligences", Educ Issues, (98); auth, "The Effects of Television Violence on Children", Early Childhood Educ (99); auth, "Creating Better Tests", Va Educ J, (99); auth, "Testing With A Capital T", Crucial Link (99); auth, "Making Better Tests", Educ Issues, (99). **CONTACT ADDRESS** Dept Educ, Longwood Col, 201 High St, Farmville, VA 23909-1801. **EMAIL** bjsimmon@longwood.lwc.edu

SIMMONS, LOUISE
PERSONAL Born 07/05/1949, Madison, WI **DISCIPLINE** SOCIAL WORK **EDUCATION** Univ Wisc, BA, 71; Univ Conn, MA, 80; MIT, PhD, 91. **CAREER** Lectr and Dir of Urban Semester Prog, Univ Conn, 80-98, asst prof and Dir of Urban Semester Prog, 98-. **HONORS AND AWARDS** Fraser Awd for Community Service, United Auto Workers, 90; Univ Conn Awd for Promoting Multi-Culturalism and Affirmative Action, 95; Emerging Scholar Awd, Asn of Community Orgn and Soc Admin, 2000. **MEMBERSHIPS** Urban Affairs Asn, Coun of Soc Work Ed, Asn of Community Orgn and Soc Admin, Asn of Col Schs of Planning. **RESEARCH** Urban politics, urban social movements, community organizing, welfare reform. **SELECTED PUBLICATIONS** Auth, "Organizational and Leadership Models in Community-Labor Coalitions," in Building Bridges: The Emerging Grassroots Coalition of Labor and Community, Jeremy Brecher and Tim Costello, eds, New York: Monthly Rev (90); coauth with Joan Fitzgerald, "From Consumption to Production: Labor Participation in Grassroots Movements in Pittsburgh and Hartford," Urban Affairs Quart, Vol 26, no 4 (June 91): 512-531; auth, Organizing in Hard Times, Temple Univ Press (94); auth, "Dilemmas of Progressive in Government: Playing Solomon in an Age of Posterity," Economic Develop Quart, Vol 10, No 2 (May 96): 159-171; auth, "The Battle for City Hall: What Is It We Fight Over," New England J of Public Policy, Vol 12, No 1 (fall/winter 96): 97-116; auth, "A New Urban Conservatism: The Case of Hartford, Connecticut," J of Urban Affairs, Vol 20, No 2 (97 Urban Conf Issue of the Urban Affairs J): 175-198; auth, "Community Labor Coalitions: A Well-Spring from Connecticut," Shelterforce: The J of Affordable Housing Strategies, issue No 101 (Sept/Oct 98); auth, "High Stakes: Casinos, Controversy and Community Cohesion: Examples from Connecticut," The J of Community Practice, Vol 7, no 2 (April 2000). **CONTACT ADDRESS** Sch of Soc Work, Univ of Connecticut, Hartford, 1798 Asylum Ave, West Hartford, CT 06117. **EMAIL** Louise.Simmons@uconn.edu

SIMMS, EVA-MARIA
PERSONAL Born 08/17/1959, Siegen, Germany, m, 1987, 2 children **DISCIPLINE** PSYCHOLOGY **EDUCATION** Gymnasium, Siegen, Ger, Abitur, 78; Phillips Univ Ger, 80; Univ Dallas, MA, 82; PhD, 88. **CAREER** Assoc Prof, Duquesne Univ, 87-; Dir Grad Studies in Human Develop, Duquesne Univ. **MEMBERSHIPS** SPEP. **RESEARCH** Phenomenology and Child Development, Psychology of Literature. **SELECTED PUBLICATIONS** Auth, "Die Dritte Frau: Rilke, Freud und das Todesproblem," in Das Bewusstein und das Unbewusste, ed. Heinz Weiss and Gerda Pagel (Wuerzburg: Koenigshausen u Neumann, 89); auth, "The Infant's Experience of the World: Stern, Merleau-Ponty and the Phenomenology of the Preverbal Self," The Humanistic Psychologist 21 (93): 27-40; auth, "Phenomenology of Child Development and the Postmodern Self: Continuing the Dialogue with Johson," The Humanistic Psychologist 22 (Summer 94): 228-235; auth, "Uncanny Dolls: Images of Death in Rilke and Freud," New Lit Hist 25-4 (Autumn 96): 663-667; auth, "In Destitute Times: Archetype and Existence in Rilke's 'Duino Elegies'," in Studies in Jungian Phenomenology, ed. R. Brooke (London: Routledge, 99). **CONTACT ADDRESS** Dept Psychology, Duquesne Univ, 600 Forbes Ave, Pittsburgh, PA 15282-0001. **EMAIL** simms@duq.edu

SIMON, GEORGIANNA
PERSONAL Born St Johns, MI **DISCIPLINE** EDUCATION **EDUCATION** Nazareth Col, AB, 65; E Mich Univ, MA, 70; Univ Mich, PhD, 77; Marygrove Col, MA, 85. **CAREER** Prof, coord, Marygrove Col, 77-. **HONORS AND AWARDS** Fulbright Schl, 89, 98; CMENAS & CREES, Grant; CID Grant; St John Hosp Bd Awd; Outstand Recog Awd; Who's Who in Midwest. **MEMBERSHIPS** AAUP; ASCD; DARTEP; MACUL; NCATE; MATE; MATCE; MACUL; MCTM; MCSS; MCTS; NCSS. **RESEARCH** Multisensory stimulation; multimedia critical thinking; informed decision making; proactive/planned action. **SELECTED PUBLICATIONS** Auth, "Integrating Computers into College Methods Courses," in Handbook for Preserviced Technology Training, Univ Mich Press; auth, "The Role of Educator in Arab Israel Conflict," FFF (Wash, DC); auth, "So You Want to Revise Your Social Science Program?" Mich Coun Soc Stud. **CONTACT ADDRESS** Dept Education, Marygrove Col, 8425 W McNichols Rd, Detroit, MI 48221. **EMAIL** gsimon@marygrove.edu

SIMON, HERBERT A.
PERSONAL Born 06/15/1916, Milwaukee, WI, m, 1937, 3 children **DISCIPLINE** PSYCHOLOGY **EDUCATION** Univ Chicago, AB, 36; PhD, 43. **CAREER** Asst Prof to Prof and Dept Chair, Ill Inst of Tech, 42-49; Prof to Dept Head and Assoc Dean, Carnegie Inst of Technol, 49-66, Richard King Mellon Univ Prof, Carnegie Mellon Univ, 66-. **HONORS AND AWARDS** Alfred Nobel Memorial Prize in Economics, 78; Nat Medal of Sci, 86; Procter prize, Sigma Xi, 80; James Madison Awd, Am Polit Sci Asn, 84; The Lord foundation Awd, 90; Am Psychol Asn Awd, 93; Dwight Waldo Awd, Am Soc of Public Admin, 95; Phi Beta Kappa, Sigma Xi. **MEMBERSHIPS** Am Acad of Arts and Sci, am Asn for the Advancement of Sci, Am Economic Asn, Am Psychol Asn, Am Sociol Soc, Econometric Soc, British Psychol Soc, Am Asn for Artificial Intelligence, Am Philos Soc, am Polit Sci Asn, Asn for computing Machinery, Artificial Intelligence in Medicine, Nat Acad of Sci. **SELECTED PUBLICATIONS** Auth, Models of Bounded Rationality: empirically Grounded Economic Reason vol 3, MIT Press, 97; auth, The Sciences of the Artificial 3rd ed, MIT Press, 96; auth, Models of My Life, MIT Press, 96; auth, Administrative Behavior 4th ed, The Free Press, 97; auth, Public Administration, Transaction Pub, 91; auth, Reason in Human Affairs, Stanford Univ Press, 83; auth, Scientific discovery: Computational Explorations of the Creative processes, 87; auth, Models of Thought: vol 1, 79; auth, Models of Thought: Vol II, 89; auth, Protocol Analysis: Verbal Reports as Data, MIT Press, 93; auth, Organizations, Blackwell, 93. **CONTACT ADDRESS** Dept Psychol, Carnegie Mellon Univ, 5000 Forbes Ave, Pittsburgh, PA 15213.

SIMONDS, PAUL E.
PERSONAL Born 12/19/1932, Ojai, CA, m, 1963, 1 child **DISCIPLINE** ANTHROPOLOGY **EDUCATION** Univ Cal Berkeley, BA, 54; MA, 59; PhD, 63. **CAREER** Instr, 62-63; asst prof, 63-67l; assoc prof, 67-75; prof, 75-; emer, 97-, Univ Oregon. **HONORS AND AWARDS** Pres, Univ Ore Sen, 94-96; Pres, IFS, 97. **MEMBERSHIPS** AAP; IAP; RAS; AAPA. **SELECTED PUBLICATIONS** Auth, The Social Primates, Harper and Row (NY), 74; auth, Sexuality, Evolution and Hu-

manity, Kendall-Hunt, 92. **CONTACT ADDRESS** Dept Anthropology, Univ of Oregon, 1218 Univ Oregon, Eugene, OR 97403. **EMAIL** simonds@oregon.uoregon.edu

SIMONTON, DEAN K.
DISCIPLINE PSYCHOLOGY **SELECTED PUBLICATIONS** Auth, "Creativity as variation and selection: Some critical constraints," in Critical creative processes, (Hampton Press, 00), 3-18; auth, "Creativity: Cognitive, developmental, personal, and social aspects," American Psychologist, (00): 151-158; auth, "Human creativity, cultural evolution, and niche construction," Behavioral and Brain Sciences, 00; auth, "Methodological and theoretical orientation and the long-term disciplinary impact of 54 eminent psychologists," Review of General Psychology, (00): 1-13; auth, "The positive repercussion of traumatic events: The life lessons of historic geniuses," PsychTalk, 00; auth, "Creative development as acquired expertise: Theoretical issues and an empirical test," Developmental Review, in press; auth, "Genius and giftedness: Same or different?," in International handbook of research and development of giftedness and talent, Pergamon Press, in press; auth, "Predicting presidential greatness: Equation replication on recent survey results," Journal of Social Psychology, in press; auth, "Psychohistory from a historiometric perspective," Clio's Psyche, in press; auth, "Talent development as a multidimensional, multiplicative, and dynamic process," Current Directions in Psychological Science, in press. **CONTACT ADDRESS** Dept Psychol, Univ of California, Davis, 1 Shields Ave, Davis, CA 95616.

SIMPSON, MARK E.
PERSONAL Born 07/29/1958, Saginaw, MI, s **DISCIPLINE** CHRISTIAN EDUCATION **EDUCATION** Spring Arbor Col, BA; Denver Conservative Baptist Sem, MACE; DePauw Univ, MA; Trinity Evangel Divinity Sch, PhD. **CAREER** Acad Doctorate Prog(s) coord, Trinity Evangel Divinity Sch; assoc dean, Nontraditional Edu, Col Liberal Arts, Trinity Intl Univ; assoc prof; assoc dean, Sch Christian Edu and Leadership; Gaines S. Dobbins assoc prof; assoc dean for doctoral studies, sch. . . **HONORS AND AWARDS** North Am Prof of CE (NAPCE) Cert of Recognition; Trinity Evangelical Divinity School Christian Service Awd. **RESEARCH** North Am Prof of Christian Education; Leadership, web-based education, simulation and discovery learning. **SELECTED PUBLICATIONS** Ed, NAPCE Newsletter; contrib, With an Eye on the Future: Development and Mission in the 21st Century; pub(s), Christian Edu Jour; Key To Christian Edu. **CONTACT ADDRESS** Sch Christian Edu and Leadership, So Baptist Theol Sem, 2825 Lexington Rd, Louisville, KY 40280. **EMAIL** msimpson@sbts.edu

SIMPSON, TERRY L.
DISCIPLINE EDUCATION **EDUCATION** Univ Tenn, BA, 73; MS, 78; Southwestern Baptist Theol Sem, MDiv, 84; Univ Tex A & M-Commerce, EdD, 90. **CAREER** Minister of Educ, Ridgecrest Baptist Church, Greenville, Tex, 80-86; Doctoral teaching asst, Dept of Secondary and Higher Educ, East Tex State Univ, 87-90; assoc prof of Secondary educ, Maryville Col, 90-, chair, 98-. **HONORS AND AWARDS** Who's Who Among America's Teachers, 96; Fel, Salzburg Sem, "The Social and Political Implications of the Internet," Austria, 98; Alumni Ambassador, Tex A & M-Commerce, April 99; Tenn State Bd of Examiners, Training to Evaluate Colleges and Universities in Tenn with Teacher Educ Programs, Feb 99. **MEMBERSHIPS** Kappa Delta Pi, Tenn Coun for the Soc Studies, Tenn Asn of Cols of Teacher Educ, Phi Delta Kappa. **SELECTED PUBLICATIONS** Auth, "Morality and the Social Studies: A Model for Addressing those Difficult Topics," Southern Soc Studies J, 21:1 (95): 65-73; coauth with M. J. Keith, "Maryville College & Secondary Educators: Linking Theory with Practice," in T. F. Warren, ed, Partnerships in Education: Schools and Colleges Working Together, The Univ Press of Am (96); auth, "From Appalachia to Texas and Back," Tenn Educ, 26 (97): 32-36; coauth with J. Brashears, "The Power of Human Touch," New Teacher Advocate, 7, 2 (99). **CONTACT ADDRESS** Dept Educ & Physical Educ, Maryville Col, 502 Lamar Alexander, Maryville, TN 37804. **EMAIL** simpson@maryvillecollege.edu

SIMS, TONI Y.
PERSONAL Born 08/26/1969, Monroe, LA, m, 1994, 3 children **DISCIPLINE** SOCIOLOGY **EDUCATION** NE La Univ, BA, 91; Grambling State Univ, MA, 93; Clark Atlanta Univ, PhD, 00. **CAREER** Instr, Grambling State Univ, 93-94; adj prof, DeVry Inst of Tech, 96-97; adj prof, Ga Perimeter Col, 96-. **SELECTED PUBLICATIONS** Auth, The Dynamics of Multicultural Education: A Study of Teacher and Student Attitudes, Wyndham Hall Press, 97. **CONTACT ADDRESS** Dept Soc Sci, Ga Perimeter Col, 555 N Indian Creek, Clarkston, GA 30021.

SINESHAW, T.
PERSONAL Born 03/16/1954, Addis Ababa, Ethiopia, d, 1 child **DISCIPLINE** SOCIOLOGY OF EDUCATION **EDUCATION** Addis Ababa Univ, BA, 71; Baylor Univ, MSEd, 85. **CAREER** Asst to assoc prof, Southeaster La Univ; assoc prof, Ramapo Col. **HONORS AND AWARDS** Fel, Rockefeller Found, 90-91; Fel, Union Col.f **MEMBERSHIPS** AERA;

AESA. **RESEARCH** Socio-cultural determination of learning and development. **SELECTED PUBLICATIONS** Auth, "Schooling and historical memories: The case of the battle of Adwa", Proceedings of the Centennial of the Battle of Adwa, Mich State Univ, (East Lansing, 96); auth, "Universalism vs particularism: Their expression in teacher education", Proceedings of the Nat Assoc of African Am Studies, ed Lemeul Berry, Jr, Univ Mich, (Ann Arbor, 96): 863-878; auth, "The land of the scribe and the thumb print: The sociology and politics of literacy in Ethiopia", Proceedings of the World Literacy Conference, Univ Of Pa, (96); auth, "The Ethiopian literacy canon: Ambitions and frustrations", Ethiopia in Broader Perspectives, eds K. Fukui, E. Kurmoto, and M. Shigeta, (Kyoto, Japan, 97): 506-521; auth, "The status of meta-narratives in the professionalization of teaching", J of Critical Pedagogy, 97. **CONTACT ADDRESS** Dept Soc Sci, Ramapo Col of New Jersey, 505 Ramapo Valley Rd, Mahwah, NJ 07430. **EMAIL** tsinesha@ramapo.edu

SINGELIS, THEODORE M.
PERSONAL Born 06/29/1949, Warren, OH, s **DISCIPLINE** PSYCHOLOGY **EDUCATION** Yale Univ, BA Psychology, 71; Univ Hawaii, MA, 92; Univ Hawaii, PhD, 95 **CAREER** Assoc prof, California State Univ, Chico, 95-98 **MEMBERSHIPS** Intl Assoc for Cross-Cult Psychol; Intl Communication Assoc **RESEARCH** Cultural Influences on Self; Intercultural Communication **SELECTED PUBLICATIONS** Coauth, "Unpackaging culture's influence on self-esteem and embarrassability: The role of self-construals," Jrnl Cross-Cultural Psychol; auth, Teaching about culture, ethnicity, and diversity: Exercises and planned activities," Sage; auth, "The context of intergroup communication," Jrnl Lang Soc Psychol, 96 **CONTACT ADDRESS** Dept Psychol, California State Univ, Chico, Chico, CA 95929. **EMAIL** tsingelis@csuchico.edu

SINGELMANN, PETER
PERSONAL Born 04/23/1942, Hamburg, Germany, m, 1969, 3 children **DISCIPLINE** SOCIOLOGY **EDUCATION** Univ Texas, PhD, 72. **CAREER** Prof, Univ Missouri Kansas City. **MEMBERSHIPS** ASA; LASA; RSA. **SELECTED PUBLICATIONS** Coauth, "Le fin de la reforme agraire et les nouvelles politiques agricoles au Mexique," in Le Mexique: De la reforme neoliberale a la contrerevolucion la presidencia de Carlos Salinas de Gortari, 1988-1994, eds. Henri Favre, Marie Lapointe (Paris: L'Harmattan, 97), 241-72; auth, 'Se gana poco, pero se queda algo': Liberalismo economico y los campesinos caleros en Nayarit," in Nayarit afin del milenlo, eds. Lourdes Pacheco Ladron de Guevara, E Heredia Quevedo (Univ Autonoma de Nayarit, 98), 31-56; auth, "The sugar industry in post-revolutionary Mexico: State intervention and private capital," Latin Am Res Rev 27 (93): 61-88; ed, The Mexican Cane Growers: Between Peasant Conquest and Capitalist Restructuring. Series on Transformation of Rural Mexico, UCSD Center for US-Mexican Studies (95); auth, "The closing triangle: Critical notes on a model for peasant mobilization in Latin America," in Essays on Mexico, Central and South America: Scholarly Debates from the 1950s to the 1990s, ed. Jorge I Dominguez (Hamden, CT: Garland, 95); auth, "Sugarcane cultivation, tradition and belated challenges of modernity," Culture & Agriculture 18 (96): 93-97. **CONTACT ADDRESS** Dept Sociology, Univ of Missouri, Kansas City, 5100 Rockhill Rd, Kansas City, MO 64110. **EMAIL** singelmannp@umkc.edu

SINGER, LAURIENNE
PERSONAL Born 08/04/1941, Pocatello, ID, d, 1 child **DISCIPLINE** PHYSICAL EDUCATION **EDUCATION** UCIA, BA, 68; MA, 70; Intermedia Found, 72-75. **CAREER** Dance therapy, Private Pract, 80-; dance spec, Univ Synagogue, 80-98; ;instr, Los Angeles City Col, 96-00-. **HONORS AND AWARDS** Inter generational Gnt; Co-recip, Rockefeller Gnt. **RESEARCH** Dance as a means of relaxation, meditation and dance therapy' empowerment; improvisional movement. **SELECTED PUBLICATIONS** Auth, Dance for People and Puppets, Puppetry J, 79. **CONTACT ADDRESS** Dept Physical Education, Los Angeles City Col, 855 N Vermont Ave, Los Angeles, CA 90029.

SINISI, CHRISTINA S.
PERSONAL Born 04/09/1964, Bethesda, MD, m, 1986, 2 children **DISCIPLINE** PSYCHOLOGY **EDUCATION** Hollins Col, BA, 86; Kans State Univ, MS, 88; PhD, 93. **CAREER** Teaching Asst to Instructor, KansU, 86-92; Instructor to Asst Prof, Ga S Univ, 92-94; Asst Prof, Charleston S Univ, 94-. **HONORS AND AWARDS** Who's Who Among Am Women, 00; Who's Who Among Am Teachers, 98; Sigma Xi; SW Soc for Res in Human Development, 92; KS State Univ Travel Awd, 90, 92; F. McGuigan Outstanding Res Awd, Hollins Col, 86; Who's Who Among Students in Am Univ, 86; Psi Chi; Phi Beta Kappa; Delta Kappa. **MEMBERSHIPS** SE Psychol Asn; Coun of Teachers of Undergrad Psychol' Am Psychol Asn; Asn for Res on Nonprofit Org and Voluntary Action; Soc for Res in Child Development; Am Psychol Soc **RESEARCH** Religiosity; Volunteerism; Reasons for Becoming Sexually Active. **SELECTED PUBLICATIONS** Co-auth, "Research findings in developmental psychology: common sense revisited," Teaching of Psychology, (88): 195-197; co-auth, "The initial validation of a liking of children scale," Journal of Personality Assessment, (90): 161-167; co-auth, "Perceived gender differences in

children's helpseeking," Journal of Genetic Psychology, (90): 451-460; co-auth, "Reations to a known rape victim: Role of subject's gender and personal experience with rape," Journal of Social Psychology, (91): 139-141; auth, "Examining the origins of planned helping behavior," SW Soc for Research in Human Development Newsletter, 91; co-auth, "The effect of kowing a rape victim on reactions to other victims," Journal of Interpersonal Violence, (92): 44-56; co-auth, "Liking of Children Scale," in Measures for Clinical Practice: A sourcebook, Vol 2, New York, 93; co-auth, "The role of critical experiences in moral development: Implications for 'justice/rights' and 'care/response' orientations," Basic and Applied Psychology, (95): 137-152; co-auth, "Factors affecting children's, adolescents' and young adults' perceptions of parental discipline," Journal of Genetic Psychology, (96): 411-424. **CONTACT ADDRESS** Dept Beh Sci, Charleston So Univ, PO Box 118087, Charleston, SC 29423. **EMAIL** csinisi@csuniv.edu

SINNOTT, JAN DYNDA
PERSONAL Born 06/14/1942, Cleveland, OH, p, 4 children **DISCIPLINE** PSYCHOLOGY **EDUCATION** St Louis Univ, BS, 64; Catholic Univ, MS, 73; PhD, 75. **CAREER** Prof, Towson Univ, 78-. **HONORS AND AWARDS** Fel, Am Psychol Soc; Fel, Am Psychol Asn; Univ Merit Awd; Fac Res Awd, Towson State Univ; Res Grant, Admin on Aging; Res Grant, Nat Inst on Aging; Fel, Nat Inst on Aging; Fel, Gerontol Soc of Am; Who's Who in Science and Medicine; Most Creative Prof Awd, Psi Chi Psychol Honors Soc, 97098. **MEMBERSHIPS** APA; APS; GSA; Asn for Women in Psychol; Asn for Humanistic Psychol; Psychol for Social Responsibility. **RESEARCH** Development of Postformal Thought; Midlife and Aging; Spirituality. **SELECTED PUBLICATIONS** Co-ed, Adult development: Models and methods in the study of adolescent and adult thought, Praeger Pub, 90; co-ed, Bridging paradigms: Positive development in adulthood and cognitive aging, Praeger Pub, 91; co-ed, Everyday memory and aging: Current research and methodology, Springer-Verlag, 91; ed, Interdisciplinary handbook of adult lifespan learning, Greenwood Pub, 94; co-auth, Reinventing the university: A radical proposal for a problem focused university, Ablex Pub, 96; auth, The development of logic in adulthood: Postformal thought and its applications, Plenum Pub, 98; ed, special Issue: Reinventing the university to foster adult development. Journal of Adult Development, 99. **CONTACT ADDRESS** Dept Psychol, Towson State Univ, 8000 York Rd, Baltimore, MD 21252-0001. **EMAIL** jsinnott@towson.edu

SIZEMORE, BARBARA A.
PERSONAL Born 12/17/1927, Chicago, IL, d, 1979, 6 children **DISCIPLINE** EDUCATION **EDUCATION** Northwestern Univ Evanston IL, BA 1947, MA 1954; Univ of Chicago IL, PhD 1979. **CAREER** Chicago Pub Schl Chicago IL, tchr, elem prin, hs prin dir of Woodlawn Exper Schl Proj 1947-72; Amer Assc of Schl Admin, assc sec 1972-73; Washington DC, supt of schls 1973-75; Univ of Pittsburgh, assc prof 1977-89, prof, 89-92; DePaul University, School of Education, dean, 92-98, prof emerita, 98-. **HONORS AND AWARDS** Honorary Doctor of Letters Central State Univ 1974; Honorary Doctor of Laws DE State Coll 1974; Honorary Doctor of Humane Letters Baltimore Coll of the Bible 1974; Honorary Doctor of Pedagogy, Niagara Univ, 1994; Northwestern Univ Merit Alumni Awd 1974; United Nations Assoc of Pittsburgh Human Rights Awd 1985; Racial Justice Awd, YWCA, 1995; The Ruptured Diamond: The Politics of the Decentralization of the DC Public Schools, Lanham, MD: Univ Press of America, 1981. **MEMBERSHIPS** Consult, Chicago Public Schools, 1992-; University of Alabama at Birmingham AL, 1992-; mem Delta Sigma Theta; Natl Alliance of Black Schl Educ; bd mem Journal of Negro Educ 1974-83. **CONTACT ADDRESS** School of Education, DePaul Univ, Chicago, IL 60614. **EMAIL** bas_60657@yahoo.com

SKAU, GEORGE
DISCIPLINE SOCIOLOGY **EDUCATION** Manhattan Col, BS, 59; Niagra Univ, MA, 61; St Johns Univ, PhD, 69. **CAREER** From Assoc Prof to Prof, Bergen Community Col, 70-. **HONORS AND AWARDS** Presidential Citation, Marist Col, 79; Mid Career Fel, Princeton Univ, 88-89; African-Am Hist Awd, Bergen Community Col, 92; Nat Collegiate Hon Grant, 93; Phi Alpha Theta; Distinguished Fac Scholar, Bergen Community Col, 95. **MEMBERSHIPS** ACIS. **RESEARCH** Northern Ireland peace agreement process. **SELECTED PUBLICATIONS** Co-ed, Power and the Presidency, Charles Scribner's Sons (New York), 76; auth, "Woodrow Wilson and the League of Nations," Festschrift (83); auth, "Honors Programs at Community Colleges," The ECCSSA J, vol 8, no 1 (93); **CONTACT ADDRESS** Dept Sociol, Bergen Comm Col, 400 Paramus Rd, Paramus, NJ 07652-1508.

SKIDELL, MYRNA
PERSONAL Born 08/22/1940, Brooklyn, NY, m, 1961, 3 children **DISCIPLINE** EDUCATION **EDUCATION** Brooklyn Col, BS, 61; Hofstra Univ, MA, 79; EdD 86. **CAREER** Assoc Prof, Nassau Community Col Garden City NY, 87-; Assessment Consult, 93-. **HONORS AND AWARDS** Newday in Educ, 86; Distinguished Fac Awd, 97. **MEMBERSHIPS** Int Reading Asn, NY Col Learning Skills Asn, Nat Asn for Devel-

opmental Educ. **RESEARCH** Assessment. **SELECTED PUB-LICATIONS** Coauth, The Main Idea: Reading to Learn, Allyne and Bacon, 96,99. **CONTACT ADDRESS** Dept Reading, Nassau Comm Col, 1 Education Dr, Garden City, NY 11530-6719. **EMAIL** skidelm@sunynassau.edu

SLAVIN, ROBERT EDWARD
PERSONAL Born 09/17/1950, Bethesda, MD, m, 1973, 3 children **DISCIPLINE** PSYCHOLOGY, SOCIAL RELATIONS **EDUCATION** Reed Col, BA, Psychol, 72; Johns Hopkins Univ, PhD, 75. **CAREER** Student tchr, Soc Stud, Aloha High Sch, 70-71; tchr, Aloha Children's center, 72-73; assoc res sci, Center Social Org Schs, Johns Hopkins Univ, 75-78; res sci, 78-85; dir, elem Sch Prog, Center Res Elem & Middle Schs, Johns Hopkins Univ, 85-90; prin res sci, Center Res Effective Schooling for Disadvantaged Students, Johns Hopkins Univ, 89-94; prin res sci & codir, Ctr for Soc Orgn of Schools, Johns Hopkins Univ, 94-; ch, Success for All Found, 97-. **HONORS AND AWARDS** Charles A. Dana award, 94; James Bryant Conant Award, Educ Comn of the States, 98; Outstanding Educr Award, Horace Mann League, 99; Hon Doctorate, Univ of Liege, Belgium, 99; Dist Service Award, Council of Chief State Schools Officers, 00. **MEMBERSHIPS** Am Educ Res Asn; Asn Supervision & Curric Dept; Int Asn Study of Coop in Educ **RESEARCH** School reform; Cooperative learning; Educational psychology; Research review; Students at risk. **SELECTED PUBLICATIONS** Coed, Preventing Early School Failure: Research , Policy, and Practice, Allyn & Bacon, 94; auth, Cooperative Learning: Theory, Research, and Practice, Allyne & Bacon, 95; coauth, Every Child, Every School: Success for All, Corwin, 96; auth, Education for All, Swets & Zeitlinger, 97; coauth, Show Me the Evidence: Proven and Promising Programs for Americas Schools, Corwin 98; auth, Educational psychology: Theory into practice, Allyn and Bacon, 6th ed, 00; coed, Success for All: Research and Reform in Elementary Education, Erlbaum, 01; coed, One Million Children: Success for All, Corwin, 01. **CONTACT ADDRESS** Ctr for Soc Orgn of Schools, Johns Hopkins Univ, Baltimore, 3003 N Charles St, Baltimore, MD 21218. **EMAIL** rslavin@csos.jhu.edu

SLIFE, BRENT D.
PERSONAL Born 12/07/1953, Ames, IA, m, 1976, 3 children **DISCIPLINE** PSYCHOLOGY **EDUCATION** Williams Jewell Col, BA, 76; Purdue Univ, MS, 77; PhD, 81. **CAREER** Asst Prof, Univ Santa Clara, 81-84; Asst Prof, Baylor Univ, 84-87; Dir, Baylor Univ, 86-88; Assoc Prof, Baylor Univ, 88-93; Dir, Baylor Univ, 91-93; Prof, Baylor Univ, 93-94; Prof, Brigham Young Univ, 94-. **HONORS AND AWARDS** Who's Who in Am; Who's Who Among Human Serv Professionals; David Ross Fel, Excellence in Teaching, Purdue Univ; Outstanding Theory Paper Awd, APA; Outstanding Res Prof, Baylor Univ; Teacher of the Year, Brigham Young Univ; Fel, APA; Circle of Achievement Awd, Baylor Univ. **MEMBERSHIPS** APA. **RESEARCH** Theoretical and philosophical underpinnings of psychology. **SELECTED PUBLICATIONS** Auth, "C.S. Lewis: Drawn by the Truth Made Flesh," in C.S. Lewis: The Man and His Message (UT: Bookcraft, 99), 20-37; coauth, "Beyond Objectivism and Relativism in Psychotherapy," Contemp Psychol 44,3 (99): 237-240; coauth, Methodological Pluralism: A Framework for Psychotherapy Research," J of Clin Psychol 55,12 (99): 1-13; auth, "The Significance of Theoretical Training for Critical Thinking," Resources in Ed, Sept ed (99); coauth, "Conceptions of Determinism in Racial Behaviorism: A Taxonomy," Behav & Philos 27 (99): 75-96; auth, "Theoretical Psychology," Encycl of Psychol, Oxford Univ Pr (00); coauth, "Modern and Postmodern Approaches to the Free Will/ Determinism Dilemma in Psychology," J of Humanistic Psychol 40, 1 (00): 80-108; coauth, "The Virtues of International Theoretical Discourse," Theory & Psychol 10,1 (00): 151-157; auth, Taking Sides: Clashing Views on Controversial Psychological Issues, 10th ed, McGraw-Hill/Dushkin (New York, NY), 00; auth, Instructor's Manual to Taking Sides: Clashing Views on Controversial Psychological Issues, 11th ed, McGraw-Hill/Dushkin (New York, NY), 00. **CONTACT ADDRESS** Dept Psychol, Brigham Young Univ, PO Box 25543, Provo, UT 84602. **EMAIL** brent_slife@byu.edu

SLOAN, TOD STRATTON
PERSONAL Born 07/06/1952, Washington, DC, d, 1 child **DISCIPLINE** PERSONALITY PSYCHOLOGY **EDUCATION** Univ MI, PhD (personality psychology). **CAREER** Asst prof, 82-89, assoc prof, Univ Tulsa, 89-. **HONORS AND AWARDS** Fulbright awards for Venezuela and Nicaragua. **MEMBERSHIPS** Int Soc for Theoretical Psychology; Am Psychol Asn. **RESEARCH** Social theory; psychoanalysis; modernization. **SELECTED PUBLICATIONS** Auth, Life Choices, Westview, 96; Damaged Life, Routledge, 96. **CONTACT ADDRESS** Dept of Psychology, Univ of Tulsa, Tulsa, OK 74104. **EMAIL** tod-sloan@utulsa.edu

SLOBIN, DAN ISAAC
PERSONAL Born 05/07/1939, Detroit, MI, d, 2 children **DISCIPLINE** PSYCHOLINGUISTICS **EDUCATION** Univ Mich, Ann Arbor, BA, 60; Harvard Univ, MA, 62, PhD(social psychol), 64. **CAREER** From asst prof to assoc prof, 64-72, Prof Psychol, Univ Calif, Berkeley, 72- ; res psychologist, Inst of Cognitive Stud and Inst of Human Develop; mem, 90- ,

chemn, 94- , Sci Council Max-Planck-Inst for Psycholinguistics. **HONORS AND AWARDS** Guggenheim fel, 84-85; NY Acad Sci award in behavioral sci, 86. **MEMBERSHIPS** Asn for Ling Typology; Int Asn of Cross-Cultural Psychol; Int Asn for Study of Child Lang; Int Cognitive Ling Asn; Ling Soc of Am; Int Pragmatics Asn; Soc for Study of Child Development; Turkish Stud Asn. **RESEARCH** Language and cognitive development in the child; linguistics; sign language. **SELECTED PUBLICATIONS** Auth, Psycholinguistics, Scott, Foresman, 71, 2nd ed, 79; auth, Cognitive Prerequisites for the Development of Grammar, in, Ferguson & Slobin, ed, Studies of Child Language Development, Holt, Rinehart & Winston, 73; auth, Crosslinguistic Evidence for the Language-Making Capacity, in Slobin, ed, The Crosslinguistic Study of Language Acquisition, vol, 2, Lawrence Erlbaum, 85; coauth, Relating Events in narrative: A Crosslinguistic Developmental Study, Lawrence Erlbaum, 94; coauth, Reference to Movement in Spoken and Signed Languages: Typological Considerations, Proc of Twentieth Annual Meeting of the Berkeley Ling Soc, 94; auth, From Thought and Language to Thinking for Speaking, in Gumperz, ed, Rethinking Linguistic Relativity, Cambridge, 96. **CONTACT ADDRESS** Dept of Psychology, Univ of California, Berkeley, 3210 Tolman Hall, #1650, Berkeley, CA 94720-1650. **EMAIL** slobin@cogsci.berkeley.edu

SLOBIN, KATHLEEN
PERSONAL Born 07/18/1942, Santa Ana, CA, d, 2 children **DISCIPLINE** SOCIOLOGY **EDUCATION** Pomona Col, BA, 64; Calif Col, MFA, 80; Calif State Univ, MPA, 84; Univ Calif, PhD, 91. **CAREER** Instr, Univ Calif, 91; Asst Prof to Assoc Prof, N Dak State Univ, 91-. **HONORS AND AWARDS** Teaching Awd, Apple Polisher, 97. 99; Anthony Fel, Univ Calif, 88, 89; Grad Stud Res, Univ Calif, 87. **MEMBERSHIPS** African Studies Asn, Am Anthropol As, Am Asn of Univ Prof, Am Sociol Asn, Mande Studies Asn, Midwest Sociol Asn, Soc for Soc Studies of Sci, Soc for Symbolic Interaction, Soc for the Study of Soc Problems, Sociol for Women in Soc. **RESEARCH** Health and Illness, Medical sociology, Africa Area Studies, Gender, Sociological and feminist theory, Qualitative methods--narrative. **SELECTED PUBLICATIONS** Auth, "Tracking the Imaginary, Post-colonial Subject in West Africa," Qualitative Inquiry, in press; auth, "Sobre la ritualizacion de ver a una nina quemada," Sybmbolic Interaction, (99): 33-52; auth, "Repairing Broken Rules: Care seeking Narratives for Menstrual problems in Rural Mali," Medical Anthropology Quarterly, (98): 363-383; auth, "Healing Through the Use of Symbolic Technolgies Among the Dogon of Mali," High Plains Applied Anthropology, (96): 136-143; auth, "Refugees in the Fargo Community: A Research Agenda," North Dakota Inst for Regional Studies, 96; auth, "Field Work and Subjectivity: On the Ritualization of Seeing A Burned Child," Symbolic Interaction, (95): 487-504. **CONTACT ADDRESS** Dept Sociol & Anthropol, No Dakota State Univ, PO Box 5075, Fargo, ND 58105. **EMAIL** slobin@plains.nodak.edu

SLOCUM, PATRICIA
DISCIPLINE PSYCHOLOGY **EDUCATION** Northern IL Univ, PhD. **CAREER** State of IL Dept of Mental Health, 70-74; Col of Du Page, 85-. **HONORS AND AWARDS** Outstanding Fac Awd, 97-98. **MEMBERSHIPS** Am Psychol Assoc. **RESEARCH** Cognitive science, Distance learning. **CONTACT ADDRESS** Dept Soc and Behav Sci, Col of DuPage, 425 - 22 St, Glen Ellyn, IL 60137. **EMAIL** slocum@cdnet.cod. edu

SLOMCZYNSKI, KAZIMIETZ M.
PERSONAL Born 05/10/1943, Warsaw, Poland, m, 1965 **DISCIPLINE** SOCIOLOGY **EDUCATION** Univ Lodz, MA, 65; Univ Warsaw, PhD, 71. **CAREER** Asst prof to prof, Inst of Sociol, Univ Warsaw, 79-89; Sr researcher, Polish Acad of Scis, 92-; prof, Ohio State Univ, 89-. **HONORS AND AWARDS** Ossowski Awd of the Polish Sociol Asn; Contribution to social stratification research and training programs. **MEMBERSHIPS** Am Sociol Asn, Int Sociol Asn. **RESEARCH** Social stratification, comparative sociology. **SELECTED PUBLICATIONS** Co-ed with Tadeusz Krauze, Social Stratification in Poland, Eight Empirical Studies, Armonk, NY: M. E. Sharpe (86); auth, "Social Structure and Mobility: Poland, Japan, and the United States, Methodological Studies, Warsaw: Inst of Philos and Sociol, Polish Acad of Scis (89); coauth with Melvin L. Kohn, "Social Structure and Self-Direction: A Comparative Analysis of the United States and Poland, with collaboration of Carrie Schoenbach, London: Basil Blackwell (93); coauth with Goldie Shabad, "Support for a Democracy and a Market Economy among Polish Students, Teachers, and Parents," in Richard C. Remy and Jacek Strzemieczny, eds, Building Civic Education for Democracy: Lessons from Poland, Bloomington: Nat Coun for Soc Studies (96); coauth with Bogdan W. Mach, "The Impact of Psychological Resources on Status Attainment: Poland, 1978-1980 and 1992-1993," Polish Sociol Rev, No 4, 116 (96): 337-352; coauth with Goldie Shabad, "Systemic Transformation and the Salience of Class Structure in East Central Europe," East European Politics and Societies, Vol 11 (winter 97): 155-189; coauth with Goldie Shabad, "Continuity and Change in Political Socialization in Poland," Comp Educ Rev, Vol 41, No 1 (97): 44-70; auth, "Formation of Class Structure under Conditions of Radical Social Change: An East European Experience," in Markku Kivinen, ed, The Kalamari Union: Middle

Class in East and West, Aldershot: Ashgate (98); coauth with Krystyna Janicka, Bogdan W. Mach, and Wojciech Zaborowski, Mental Adjustment to the Post-Communist System in Poland, Warsaw: IFIS Pubs (99); co-ed with Aleksandra Jasinska-Kania and Melvin L. Kohn, Power and Social Structure, Essays in honor of Wlodzimierz Wesolowski, Warsaw: Warsaw Univ Press (99). **CONTACT ADDRESS** Dept Sociol, Ohio State Univ, Columbus, 300 Bricker Hall, Columbus, OH 43210. **EMAIL** Slomczynski.1@osu.edu

SLOVENKO, RALPH
PERSONAL Born 11/04/1926, New Orleans, LA, m **DISCIPLINE** PSYCHIATRY **EDUCATION** Tulane Univ, BE, 48, LLB, 53, MA, 60, PhD(Psychiat, psycho-dynamics), 65. **CAREER** Law clerk, La Supreme Court, 53; prof law, Tulane Univ, 54-64, mem fac, psychiat, 60-65; prof psychiat & law, Menninger Found & Univ Kans, 65-67; assoc, Walter Hailey Law Firm, 67-69; Prof Law, Wayne State Univ, 69-, Ed, Am Lect Set Behav Sci & Law, Tulane Law Rev; consult, Group Advan Psychiat. **MEMBERSHIPS** Order of Coif; Am Psychol-Law Soc; assoc Am Acad Psychoanal; Southern Soc Philos & Psychol; Am Orthopsychiat Asn. **RESEARCH** Psychiatry and law; behavioral science and law. **SELECTED PUBLICATIONS** Auth, Psychotherapy, Confidentiality and Privileged Communication, 65 & ed, Sexual Behavior and the Law, 65, C C Thomas; auth, Security Rights, 66 & Handbook of Criminal Procedure, 67, Claitor's; co-ed, Motivations in Play, Games and Sports, C C Thomas, 67; auth, Psychiatry and Law, Little, 73; auth numerous journal articles; Psychiatry and Criminal Anlyability, Wiley, 95; Psychotherapy and Confidentiality, 98. **CONTACT ADDRESS** Law School, Wayne State Univ, 468 Ferry Mall, Detroit, MI 48202-3698.

SMITH, ANDREA L.
PERSONAL Born 08/15/1960, Tokyo, Japan, s **DISCIPLINE** SOCIOLOGY **EDUCATION** Wesleyan Univ, BA, 83; Univ Ariz, MA, 92; PhD, 98. **CAREER** Asst Prof, Lafayette Col, 99-. **HONORS AND AWARDS** Phi Beta Kappa, Wesleyan Univ, 83. **RESEARCH** Social Memory; Racism; Colonialism. **CONTACT ADDRESS** Dept Anthropol & Sociol, Lafayette Col, Easton, PA 18042. **EMAIL** smithal@lafayette.edu

SMITH, BARRY D.
PERSONAL Born 06/12/1940, Harford, PA, m, 1963, 2 children **DISCIPLINE** PSYCHOLOGY **EDUCATION** Pa State Univ, BS, 62; Bucknell Univ, MA, 64; Univ Mass, PhD, 67. **CAREER** Prof of Psychology, Univ of Md, 93-. **HONORS AND AWARDS** Fel, Int Org for Psychophysiology; Public Health Service Predoctoral Fel; Psi Chi; Pi Gamma Mu; Phi Kappa Phi; Am Men and Women of Sci; Contemporary Authors. **MEMBERSHIPS** Am Psychol Asn, Am Asn for the Advancement of Sci, Int Org for Psychophysiology. **SELECTED PUBLICATIONS** Auth, Psychology: Science and Understanding, NY: McGraw-Hill, Inc (98); coauth with V. Levine and J. Wilken, Instructor Manual to accompany Psychology: Science and understanding, NY: McGraw-Hill, Inc (98); auth, "The scientific crystal ball: Teaching the psychology of the future," APS Observer, 12, 5 (99): 14-15, 25; auth, "Tomorrow and tomorrow and tomorrow: Teaching the future of psychology," in APS, ed, Teaching Tips, Washington, DC: APS (99); coauth with D. Cranford, "Gender, cynical hostility, and cardiovascular function: Implications for differential cardiovascular disease risk?," Personality and Individual Differences (in press); coauth with K. Tola and M. Mann, "Caffeine and arousal: A biobehavioral theory of physiological, behavioral, and emotional effects," in B. S. Gupta, ed, Caffeine and Behavior: Current Views and Research Trends, CRC Press (in press); coauth with J. Wilken, K. Tola, and M. Mann, "Anxiety and arousal: Tests of a new six-system model," Int J of Psychophysiology (in press). **CONTACT ADDRESS** Dept Psychology, Univ of Maryland, Col Park, College Park, MD 20742.

SMITH, C. S.
PERSONAL Born 10/23/1960, PA, m, 1983, 3 children **DISCIPLINE** SOCIOLOGY **EDUCATION** Harvard, MA, PhD, 90. **CAREER** Dept Sociology, Univ NC. **MEMBERSHIPS** ASR; ASA; SSSR. **RESEARCH** Religion; social movements; Latin America. **SELECTED PUBLICATIONS** Auth, The Emergence of Liberation Theology: Radical Religion and Social Movement Theory, Univ Chicago Press, 91; Disruptive Religion: The Fare of Faith in Social Movement Activism, Routledge Pubs, 96; Resisting Reagan: The US Central America Peace Movement, Univ Chicago Press, 96; American Evangelicalism: Embattled and Thriving, Univ of Chicago Press, 98. **CONTACT ADDRESS** Dept of Sociol, Univ of No Carolina, Chapel Hill, Chapel Hill, NC 27599. **EMAIL** cssmith@email. unc.edu

SMITH, CAROL Y.
PERSONAL Born 07/04/1946, Dayton, OH, m, 1998, 2 children **DISCIPLINE** PSYCHOLOGY **EDUCATION** Ind Univ, BA; MSW; Fielding Inst, MS; Univ Wisc, PhD. **CAREER** Pres./CEO, C.Y.Smith & Assoc Inc; Owner/Director, Samuel Center for Psychological Services; Director, Masters Prog Concordia Univ. **HONORS AND AWARDS** Who's Who. **MEMBERSHIPS** Am Psychol Asn, Wisc Psychol Asn, Milwaukee Area Psychol Asn, Nat Med Asn. **RESEARCH** Celibacy and

married women. **CONTACT ADDRESS** Dept Soc Sci, Concordia Univ, Wisconsin, 12800 N Lake Shore, Mequon, WI 53097. **EMAIL** drcysmith@msn.com

SMITH, CHARLES F., JR.
PERSONAL Born 01/05/1933, Cleveland, OH, m, 2 children **DISCIPLINE** EDUCATION **EDUCATION** BS Ed, Bowling Green State Univ, 60; EdM, Kent State Univ, 63; CAS, Harvard Univ Graduate School of Education, 65; EdD, Michigan State Univ, 69. **CAREER** Military Service, Staff Sergeant, Medical Corps, 54-56; 5th Grade Teacher, Lorain, Ohio, 60-62; Academic Dir, Peace Corp Training Camp, Puerto Rico, 62-63; Teaching Fellow, Harvard Univ School of Education, 63-65; Asst Dir., Elementary Education, Flint Michigan, 65-66; Instructor, Michigan State Univ, 66-68; Boston College, 68-96; Assoc Prof of Education, Prof Emer-. **HONORS AND AWARDS** Danforth Assoc, 74; Visting Scholar, Univ of Michigan, 90; Atlanta Univ, 93; Yale Univ, 95; Phi Delta Kappa Emeritus, 98. **MEMBERSHIPS** Board of Dir, National Council for the Social Studies, 90-97; Am Assoc of College for Teacher Education; Am Assoc of Univ Prof; Am Assoc of Univ Prof; am Assoc of School Administrators; Assoc for Supervision and Curriculum Development; Department of Elementary School Principals; National Council for the Social Studies; Phi Delta Kappa. **CONTACT ADDRESS** Professor Emeritus, Education, Boston Col, Newton Ctr, 194 Parker St., Newton, MA 02459.

SMITH, CORRINE
PERSONAL Born 05/25/1945, Reading, PA, m, 1968, 2 children **DISCIPLINE** PSYCHOLOGY, EDUCATION **EDUCATION** Syracuse Univ, BA, 67; Temple Univ, MA, 69; Syracuse Univ, PhD, 73. **CAREER** Assoc prof to assoc dean, Syracuse Univ, 92-. **HONORS AND AWARDS** Syracuse Post Standard Women of Achievement Awd, Syracuse, 90; Syracuse Jewish Community Ctr Generation Awd, Syracuse, 98; Temple Adath Citizen of the Year Awd, 99. **MEMBERSHIPS** Coun for Except Children, Intl Sch Psychol Asn, Learning Disabilities Asn of Am, Nat Asn of Sch Psychol, Am Psychol Asn. **RESEARCH** Learning Disabilities. **SELECTED PUBLICATIONS** Auth, Learning disabilities: The interaction of learner, task, and setting 4th ed, Allyn and Bacon: Boston, 98; auth, Learning disabilities: A to Z. The complete parent's guide to learning disabilities from preschool to adulthood, The Free Press: New York, 97; auth, "Is your child ready to leave home?" Their World: National Center for Learning Disabilities, (00): 41-43; auth, "What parents can do to boost self-esteem in their children with learning disabilities," Their World: National Center for Learning Disabilities, (00): 108. **CONTACT ADDRESS** Dept Sp Educ, Syracuse Univ, Syracuse, NY 13244-0001. **EMAIL** crsmith@syr.edu

SMITH, DIANE M.
PERSONAL Born 03/22/1953, Lawrence, MA, m, 1995 **DISCIPLINE** EDUCATION, ENGLISH **EDUCATION** Univ of MA, MA, 98; Univ of So CA, BA, 81 **CAREER** Pub Svc libr, 93-, Bunker Hill Cmnty Col Lib; **MEMBERSHIPS** ALA; ACRL **RESEARCH** Infor Literacy **CONTACT ADDRESS** Library, Bunker Hill Comm Col, Boston, MA 02129-2925. **EMAIL** smith@noblenet.org

SMITH, ELEANOR JANE
PERSONAL Born 01/10/1933, Circleville, OH, m, 1972 **DISCIPLINE** EDUCATION **EDUCATION** Capital Univ, BSM 1955; Ohio St Univ, 1966; The Union Graduate School/UECU, PhD 1972. **CAREER** Board of Ed, Columbus, OH 2nd-6th grd tchr, 56-64; Board of Ed, Worthington OH 6 & 7th grd tchr, 64-69; Univ of Cinn, prof, Afro-Am Studies, 72-82; vice provost Faculty & Acad Affairs; Smith Coll, dean of institutional affairs, 88-90; William Paterson College, vice president for academic affairs and provost, 90-94; Univ of Wisconsin-Parkside, Chancellor, currently. **HONORS AND AWARDS** Historical Presentation, Black Heritage, History, Music & Dance written & produced 1972-; numerous publications; YWCA Career Women of Achievement 1983; Capital Univ, Alumni Achiev Awd 1986. **MEMBERSHIPS** Assoc of Black Women Historians, natl co-founder & co-director 1978-80; mem Natl Council for Black Studies 1982-88; mem Natl Assn Women in Education, 1986-; American Assn for Higher Education; American Council on Education; American Assn of State Colleges and Universities. **CONTACT ADDRESS** Univ of Wisconsin, Parkside, 900 Wood Rd, 2000, Kenosha, WI 53141-2000.

SMITH, G.
PERSONAL Born 08/16/1941, Colombia, d **DISCIPLINE** EDUCATION **EDUCATION** Penn State, PhD, 78. **CAREER** Educ Assoc, Delaware Dept of Educ. **HONORS AND AWARDS** Honorable Mention, 80; College of Educ Awd, 81; Nominee, Univ Awd, 82; Mortar Board Society Awd, 84; College of Continuing Educ Awd, 95. **MEMBERSHIPS** ADI, IRA **RESEARCH** Reading and Professional Development. **SELECTED PUBLICATIONS** Auth, Developing an external system of peer review for special populations,Unpublished manuscript, Univ of Delaware (Newark, DE), 84; Auth, Observer ereactivity under monitored and unmonitored analogue conditions, Journal of Psychoeducational Assessment 2 (84): 249-255; auth, Observer drift: A drifting definition, The Behavior Analyst, 9 (86): 127-128; auth, A reply to Goodman and Bond, Journal of Special Education 28 (94): 106-108; auth, Feasibility of determining the degree of correspondence among NCEO, Project PASS, and state outcome meaures. 17th Annual Report to Congress on the Implementation of IDEA (c1-5), Washington, DC: US Dept of Education, 95; auth, The impact of DI workshop training in the classroom, Effective School Practices, 16 (4), (97): 14-19. **CONTACT ADDRESS** Dept Education, Univ of Delaware, Univ Delaware, Newark, DE 19716. **EMAIL** gasmith@atsstate.de.us

SMITH, GARY
PERSONAL Born 10/12/1950, Franklin, PA, m, 1997, 5 children **DISCIPLINE** SOCIOLOGY **EDUCATION** Grove City Col, BA, 72; Gordon Conwell Theol Sem, M Div, 77; Johns Hopkins Univ, MA, 79, PhD, 81. **CAREER** Instr to prof, Grove City Col, 78-. **HONORS AND AWARDS** NEH Summer Sem, Princeton, 88; NEH Study Grant, 94, Vis Prof, Geneva Col, MA, 95-; Who's Who in Relig in Am; Who's Who Among Am Teachers. **MEMBERSHIPS** Conf on Faith and Hist. **RESEARCH** American religious history **SELECTED PUBLICATIONS** Ed, Building a Christian Worldview Vol 2: The Universe Society and Ethics, Presbyterian and Reformed (Phillipsburg, NJ), 88; ed, God and Politics: Four View on the Reformation of Civil Government, Presbyterian and Reformed (Phillipsburg, NJ), 89; auth, "Charles Sheldon's In His Steps in the Context of Religion and Culture in Late Nineteenth-Century America", Fides et Historia 22 (Summer 90):47-69; auth, "Walter Rauschenbusch and Christian Socialism", in Essays on Socialism, ed Louis Patsouras, (NY: Mellon Res Univ Pr, 92):267-98; auth, "Building the cooperative Commonwealth: Vida Scudder's Quest to Reconcile Christianity and Socialism", Anglican and Episcopal Hist 62 (Sep 93):397-428; auth, "Two Sides of the Evangelical Tradition: Presbyterian and Methodist theological Education, 1900-1920", in Theo Educ in the Evangelical Tradition, eds, D.G. Hart and R. Albert Mohler, Jr., (Grand Rapids: Baker Book House), 97; auth, "Calvinism and Politics" in The Encycl of Polit and Relig, Congressional Quarterly, 98; ed, Worldviews, Society, and Ethics: A Reader, Copley (Acton, MA, 99); auth, "Evangelicals Confront Corporate Capitalism: Advertising, Consumerism, Stewardship, and Spirituality, 1880-1930", In More Money, More Ministry: Money and Evangelical sin Recent Am Hist, eds Mark Noll and Larry Eskridge (Grand Rapids: Eerdmans, 00); auth, The Search for Social Salvation: Social Christianity and America, Lexington (Lanham MD), 00. **CONTACT ADDRESS** Dept Sociol, Grove City Col, 100 Campus Dr, Grove City, PA 16127-2101. **EMAIL** gssmith@gcc.edu

SMITH, GLENN R.
PERSONAL Born 07/14/1945, Topeka, KS, m **DISCIPLINE** EDUCATION **EDUCATION** Adams State Coll, BA 1968; Univ CO, MA 1971; Univ CO, PhD 1975. **CAREER** Community Coll Denver, instr; Met State Coll, asst dir financial aid; Urban Educ Prog, asst dir. **MEMBERSHIPS** Mem Am Educ Studies Assn; Black Eductors Denver; phi Delta Kappa; mem & Greater Park Hill; US Civil Serv Commn CU Fellowship Univ CO 1972-74. **CONTACT ADDRESS** 250 W 14 Ave, PO Box 375, Denver, CO 80204.

SMITH, GREGORY C.
PERSONAL Born 09/07/1951, Rochester, NY, m, 1992, 1 child **DISCIPLINE** HUMAN DEVELOPMENT **EDUCATION** SUNY Brockport, Ba, 73; Villanova Univ, MS, 79; Univ Rochester, EJD, 83. **CAREER** Res assoc, SUNY Albany, 85-91; assoc prof, Univ Md, 91-. **HONORS AND AWARDS** Fel, Gerontol Soc of Am. **MEMBERSHIPS** Gerontological Asn of Am, Am Psychol Asn. **RESEARCH** Psychology of Adult Development and Aging. **SELECTED PUBLICATIONS** Auth, "Family caregivers of the frail elderly," in Handbook of social work practice with vulnerable and resilient populations, Columbia Univ Press: New York; (in press): auth, "The effects of interpersonal and personal agency on perceived control and psychological well-being in adulthood," The Gerontologist, (in press); auth, Teaching Tips column, Division 20 Newsletter, American Psychological Association, 00; auth, "Prevention and promotion models of intervention for strengthening agin families," in Handbook of counseling and psychotherapy with older adults, John Wiley: New York, (99): 178-194; auth, "An interdisciplinary team research assignment for use in an Introduction to Gerontology course," Gerontology and Geriatrics Education, (99): 77-91; auth, "Using a cooperative learning strategy for promoting interprofessionalism in undergraduate education," in Essays in quality learning: Teacher's reflections on classroom practice, IBM Total Quality Project: College Park, MD, (98): 199-206; auth, "Older mothers who do not use day programs for their daughters and sons with mental retardation," Journal of Physical and Developmental Disabilities, (97): 153-173; auth, "The effects of offspring gender on older mothers caring for their sons and daughters with mental retardation," The Gerontologist, (97): 795-803; auth, "Aging families of adults with mental retardation: Patterns and correlates of service use, need, and knowledge," American Journal on Mental Retardation, (97): 13-26. **CONTACT ADDRESS** Dept Human Dev, Univ of Maryland, Col Park, 3304M Benjamin Bldg, College Park, MD 20742-1131. **EMAIL** 6580@umail.umd.edu

SMITH, JOANNE HAMLIN
PERSONAL Born 10/19/1954, Pittsburgh, PA, m, 1986 **DISCIPLINE** EDUCATION **EDUCATION** Edinboro Univ of Pennsylvania, Edinboro, PA, BS, 1972-76; Wichita State Univ, Wichita, KS, MEd, 1977-79; Kansas State University, Manhattan, KS, PhD, 1983-86. **CAREER** McPherson College, director of housing, assistant in student services, 76-86; Arizona State Univ, assistant director of residence life, 86-91; Southwest Texas State Univ, Director of Residence Life, 92-. **HONORS AND AWARDS** Women Helping Women Honoree, Soroptomist International, 1979; NASPA Region IV West Awd for Outstanding Contributions, 1978. **MEMBERSHIPS** Treasurer, president-elect, president, Arizona College Personnel Assn, 1986-91; Association of College & University Housing Officers, 1986-; American College Personnel Association, 1986-; Phi Delta Kappa, 1976-; Natl Bd of Certified Counselors, certified counselor, 1980-. **CONTACT ADDRESS** Residence Life, Southwest Texas State Univ, San Marcos, TX 78666.

SMITH, LAURENCE D.
PERSONAL Born 10/28/1950, Iowa City, IA, m, 1981 **DISCIPLINE** HISTORY OF PSYCHOLOGY **EDUCATION** Univ New Hampshire, PhD 83. **CAREER** Univ Maine, asst prof, assoc prof, 83 to 98-. **MEMBERSHIPS** HSS; CS; APA; APS **RESEARCH** History of psychology; philosophy of science; graphical data displays. **SELECTED PUBLICATIONS** Auth, Behaviorism and logical positivism: A reassessment of the alliance, Stanford, CA: Stanford Univ Press, 86; auth, On prediction and control: B.F. Skinner and the technological ideal of science, Am Psychologist, 47, (92): 216-223; co-ed with W. R. Woodward, B. F. Skinner and Behaviorism in American Culture, Beth PA, Lehigh Univ Press, 96; The role of data and theory in co-variation assessment: Implications for the theory-ladenness of observation, Coauth, Jour of Mind and Behav, 96; Behaviorism, in: R. Fox and J. Kloppenberg, eds, A companion to American thought, Cambridge MA, Blackwell, 95; coauth, Psychology without p values: Data analysis at the turn of the 19th century, Am Psychologist, 55, (00): 260-263; coauth, Scientific graphs and the hierarchy of the sciences: A Latourian survey of inscription practices, Social Studies of Science, 30, (00): 73-94. **CONTACT ADDRESS** Dept of Psychology, Univ of Maine, Orono, ME 04469. **EMAIL** ldsmith@maine.maine.edu

SMITH, LOUIS R.
PERSONAL Born 04/12/1945, Demopolis, AL, m, 1968, 3 children **DISCIPLINE** EDUCATION **EDUCATION** Birmingham Southern Col, BA, 67; Univ NC, MA, 69; Univ Ala, PhD, 88 **CAREER** Adj Prof, Livingston Univ, 84-85; Vis Fac, Univ Montevallo, 85-88; Vis Fac, Univ Ala, 87-88; Dir Student Development Center, Livingston Univ, 89; Adj Prof, Univ Ala, 94; Prof, Univ W Ala, 89-. **MEMBERSHIPS** Ala Asn for Counseling and Development, Southern Hist Asn, Ala Hist Asn, Sumter County Hist Asn, Phi Delta Kappa, Kappa Delta Pi, Ala Asn for Counselor Educ and Supervision, Ala Coun for Soc Studies, Southeast Coun for Soc Studies, Blue Key Nat Honor Soc, Omicron Delta Kappa, Phi Kappa Phi. **SELECTED PUBLICATIONS** Auth, "The Alaskan Boundary Dispute (1898-1903)," in The Encyclopedia of US Foreign Relations, Oxford Univ Press, 96; auth, "Andrew William Mellon," in The Encyclopedia of US Foreign Relations, Oxford Univ Press, 96; auth, "William Edward Dodd," in The Encyclopedia of US Foreign Relations, Oxford Univ Press, 96; auth, "The Dawes Plan," in The Encyclopedia of US Foreign Relations, Oxford Univ Press, 96; auth, "Anson Burlingame," in The Encyclopedia of US Foreign Relations, Oxford Univ Press, 96; auth, "Millard Fillmore," in The Encyclopedia of US Foreign Relations, Oxford Univ Press, 96; auth, "Ostend Manifesto," in The Encyclopedia of US Foreign Relations, Oxford Univ Press, 96; ed Cush: A Civil War Memoir, Livingston Press, 99; auth, "Sumter County, Alabama, and the Civil War," Alabama Review, 00. **CONTACT ADDRESS** Foundations & Sec Educ, Univ of West Alabama, 1 Col Dr, Livingston, AL 35470. **EMAIL** lsmith@univ.westal.edu

SMITH, MARSHALL L.
PERSONAL Born 09/13/1940, Toledo, OH, m, 1999, 3 children **DISCIPLINE** SOCIAL WORK **EDUCATION** Univ Mich, AB, 62; MSW, 63; SUNY, PhD, 73. **CAREER** Program Dir, YMCA Chicago, 63-68; SR Therapist, Crisis Center, Buffalo, 72-74; Asst Prof, SUNY, 74-76; Asst Prof to Full Prof, Rochester Inst Tech, 76-. **HONORS AND AWARDS** Outstanding Soc, NYSSWEA, 99; Outstanding Soc, BPD, 98. **MEMBERSHIPS** NASW; BPD; CSWE; AAUP; Phi Kappa Phi. **RESEARCH** Outcomes of Baccalaureate Social Work Education; Technology & Social Work. **SELECTED PUBLICATIONS** Co-auth, "How do BSW's and MSW's differ?", Journal of Baccalaureate Social Work, (95): 97-110; co-auth, "The use of the World Wide Web by undergraduate social work education programs," Journal of Baccalaureate Social Work, (97): 71-84; co-auth, "Follow the Yellow-Brick Information Superhighway: Using the Internet in the Classroom,", in The Electronic Classroom: Using Technology to Create a 21st Century Curriculum, (Omega Pub, 00), 86-102; co-auth, Baccalaureate Education Assessment Package: Exit Survey Questionnaire, Rochester, 00; co-auth, Baccalaureate Education Assessment Package: Alumni/ae Survey Questionnaire, Rochester, 00; co-auth, Baccalaureate Education Assessment Package: Employer Survey

OPSCAN Form, Rochester, 00; co-auth, Baccalaureate Education Assessment Package: Alumni/ae Survey OPSCAN Form, Rochester, 00; co-auth, Baccalaureate Education Assessment Package: Exit Survey OPSCAN Form, Rochester, 00; co-auth, Baccalaureate Education Assessment Package: Entrance Survey OPSCAN Form, Rochester, 00; co-auth, "Could Stevie Wonder read your web page?" in The New Social Workers Internet Handbook, White Hat Pub, 00. **CONTACT ADDRESS** Dept Soc Work, Rochester Inst of Tech, 3212 Eastman Bldg, Rochester, NY 14623. **EMAIL** docsmith@mail.rit.edu

SMITH, MICHAEL E.
PERSONAL Born 09/12/1953, Philippines, m, 1979, 2 children **DISCIPLINE** ANTHROPOLOGY **EDUCATION** Brandeis Univ, BA, 75; Univ Ill, MA, 78; PhD, 83. **CAREER** Asst Prof, Loyola Univ, 83-89; From Assoc Prof to Prof, State Univ NYork (SUNY), 91-. **MEMBERSHIPS** Soc for Am Archaeol, Am Anthrop Assoc. **SELECTED PUBLICATIONS** Auth, The Aztecs, Blackwell Publ (Oxford), 96; coauth, Aztec Imperial Strategies, Dumbarton Oaks (Wash, DC), 96; coauth, "A New Postclassic Chronology for Yautepec, Morelos," Ancient Mesoamerica, 7 (96): 281-298; coauth, "Excavations of Aztec Urban Houses at Yautepec, Morelos, Mexico," Latin Am Antiquity, 10 (99): 133-150; co-ed, The Ancient Civilizations of Mesoamerica: A Reader, Blackwell Publ (Oxford), 99; auth, "Aztec City-States," in City-State Cult in World Hist (Copenhagen: Publ of Royal Danish Acad, 00), 581-596. **CONTACT ADDRESS** Dept Anthrop, SUNY, 1400 Washington Ave, Albany, NY 12222-1000. **EMAIL** mesmith@csc.albany.edu

SMITH, PAUL M., JR.
PERSONAL Born 08/10/1920, Raleigh, NC, m, 1972 **DISCIPLINE** EDUCATION **EDUCATION** St Augustine's Coll, BA 1941; NC Central Univ, BLS 1947; Univ IL, MLS 1949; Indiana Univ, EdD 1957. **CAREER** Shepard High School, teacher, 41-42; Shaw University, assistant librarian, 47-48; Dillard University, head librarian/instructor, 50-53; Claflin College, head librarian, 54-55; A & T State University, chief librarian, 57-58; Albany State Coll, prof 1958-59; SC State Coll, prof 1959-60; NC Central Univ, prof 1960-69; Columbia Univ, adj prof 1969-70; Univ of Cincinnati, prof Afro-Amer Studies/prof psychology, professor emeritus. **HONORS AND AWARDS** Licensed Psychologist OH 1973-; publns in many nationally known journals. **MEMBERSHIPS** Mem Assn of Black Psychologists 1980-85. **CONTACT ADDRESS** Professor Emeritus, Univ of Cincinnati, Cincinnati, OH 45221.

SMITH, PRISCILLA R.
PERSONAL Born 10/27/1949, Pasadena, CA, s **DISCIPLINE** SOCIAL WORK **EDUCATION** Indiana Univ, BA, 72; Washington Univ, MSW, 80; Saint Louis Univ, PhD, 88. **CAREER** Asst prof, Southern Ill Univ at Edwardsville, 87-94; asst prof, Univ of Akron, Sch of Soc Work, 95-. **HONORS AND AWARDS** 1999 Int Honoree, Who's Who of Professional Business Women. **MEMBERSHIPS** Nat Asn of Soc Workers, Am Asn of Univ Women; Acad of Certified Soc Workers. **RESEARCH** Qualitative self-evaluation of practice, distance education, bisexuality, women. **SELECTED PUBLICATIONS** Coauth with W. J. Hutchison, J. J. Stretch, S. J. Anderman and J. Triegaard, "A profile of the emergency housing program in the City of St Louis," monograph (81); coauth with W. J. Hutchison and J. J. Stretch, "The Salvation Army Emergency Lodge in the City of St Louis--An impact study," monograph (82); coauth with W. J. Hutchison and J. J. Stretch, "An evaluative study of The Salvation Army Emergency Lodge in the City of St Louis, monograph (83); coauth with W. J. Hutchison and J. J. Stretch, "Multidimensional networking: A social response to the complex health and social service needs of homeless families and their children," monograph (85); coauth with W. J. Hutchison and J. J. Stretch, "Multidimensional networking: A social response to the complex health and social service needs of homeless families and their children," Social Work, (85): 427-431; coauth with H. R. Searight, "The family environments of children with school behavior problems," Psychological Reports, 60 (87): 1263-1266; coauth with H. R. Searight, "The homeless mentally ill: Overview, policy implications, and adult foster care as a neglected resource," Adult Foster Care J, 2 (88): 239-263; coauth with coauth with W. J. Hutchison and J. J. Stretch, "Social networking with homeless families," Chapter in Homelessness: A Prevention-oriented Approach, ed by R. Jahiel, Newbury Park, CA: Sage Pubs (92); auth, "How do we understand practice? A qualitative approach," Families in Society: The J of Contemporary Human Services, 79 (98): 543-550; coauth with N. W. Wingerson, "Blending Two Cultures: A Joint Distance Education Program," in Conference Proceedings of the Third Annual Technology Conference for Social Work Education and Practice, eds, G. M. Menon and N. K. Brown (99). **CONTACT ADDRESS** Sch of Soc Work, Univ of Akron, 525 S Martin St, Akron, OH 44325-8001. **EMAIL** psmith@uakron.edu

SMITH, RAYMOND T.
PERSONAL Born 01/12/1925, England, m, 1950, 3 children **DISCIPLINE** ANTHROPOLOGY **EDUCATION** Cambridge Univ, PhD, 54. **CAREER** Soc res off. Brit Gui Gov, 51-54; res fel, Univ West Indies, 54-59; vis prof, Univ California, 57-58; sr lectr, Univ Ghana, 59-60; prof; 61-62; sr lectr, Univ West Indies, 62-65; vis prof, McGi Univ, 64-65; prof, Univ W Indies, 66; prof, Univ Chicago, 66-95; ch, 75-85; dir, Univ West Indies/Ghana, 85-86; consul, 88; vis prof, Univ West Indies, 91; dept ch, Univ Chicago, 94-95; prof emer, 95-. **HONORS AND AWARDS** Guggenheim Fel; NSF Gnt, 75, 67; NIH Gnt; Commwlth Found Gnt; PCR Gnt; CSSRC Gnt. **MEMBERSHIPS** AAA. **SELECTED PUBLICATIONS** Auth, Kinship and Class in the West Indies: a genealogical study of Jamaica and Guyana, Cam Univ Press (Cambridge, MA), 88; auth, The Matrifocal Family: Power, Pluralism, and Politics, Routledge (NY), 96; auth, The Negro Family in British Guyana: Family Structure and Social Status in the Villages, Routledge and Kegan Paul (London), 98. **CONTACT ADDRESS** Dept Anthropology, Univ of Chicago, 1126 E 59th St, Chicago, IL 60637.

SMITH, ROY H.
PERSONAL Born 03/22/1945, Knoxville, TN, m, 1978, 2 children **DISCIPLINE** PSYCHOLOGY **EDUCATION** Univ Tenn, BS, 65; Univ Pa, PhD, 70. **CAREER** Asst Prof to Prof, Mary Washington Univ, 70-. **HONORS AND AWARDS** Merit Scholar; Phi Beta Kappa; NSF Fel. **MEMBERSHIPS** VA Psychol Asn; Am Psychol Soc; Beh Genetics Asn. **RESEARCH** Animal behavior and cognition; Evolution and domestication; Drug and alcohol abuse. **SELECTED PUBLICATIONS** Auth, A Curriculum for Alcohol Education, Univ Press of Am, 81; co-auth, "The Effects of Tactile Stimulation on Maternally Deprived albino Rat Pups," VA Soc Sci Journal, (91): 104-110; co-auth, "Predictors of alcohol abuse behaviors of undergraduates," Journal of Drug Education, (91): 159-166; co-auth, "Generalized Attraction: How Non-specific is the Arousal?," Journal of Psychology and the Behavioral Sciences, (91): 141-146; co-auth, "From Speaking Act to Natural Word: Animals, communication and Language," in Language: Introductory Readings, 5th ed, New York, 94; co-auth, "Signals, signs, and Words: From Animal communication to Language," in Language: Readings in Language and Culture, 6th ed, New York, 98; auth, Cognitive Neuroscience: an Introduction, Fitzpatrick Scientific press, 00. **CONTACT ADDRESS** Dept Psychol, Mary Washington Col, 1301 College Ave, Fredericksburg, VA 22401. **EMAIL** rhsmith@mwc.edu

SMITH, WALTER L.
PERSONAL Born 05/14/1935, Tampa, FL **DISCIPLINE** EDUCATION **EDUCATION** FL A&M Univ, BA Biology & Chem 1963, MEd Admin & Supv 1966; FL State Univ PhD Higher Ed Admin 1974. **CAREER** Natl Educ Assn, assoc regional dir for NEA 1969-70; FL Educ Assn, admin asst 1970, asst exec sec 1970-73; Hillsborough Comm Coll, collegium dir 1973, dean employee relations 1973-74, provost 1974; Roxbury Comm Coll, pres 1974-77; FL A&M Univ, prof, president 1977-85; Education Development in South Africa, international team leader; founding rector, Funda Comm Coll, South Africa currently; Univ of FL, Visiting Professor, currently. **HONORS AND AWARDS** Red-X Awd Cape Kennedy IBM Corp 1966; Scholarly Distinction Awd Natl Urban League 1974; Meritorious Serv Awd Amer Assoc State Colleges & Univs 1984; President's Awd, Natl Conf of Black Mayors; Jackson Memorial Awd Assoc of Classroom Teachers 1984; Fulbright Senior Scholar 1985; Congressional recognition for international leadership. **MEMBERSHIPS** Chairperson FL Supreme Ct Judicial Nominating Comm 1980-83; FL Supreme Ct Article V Comm 1983; chmn State Bd of Educ US Dept of Interior 1984; bd of dirs Natl Assoc for Equal Opportunity HE 1982-; bd dir Amer Assn of State Colleges and Univs; Urban League, chairman of the board. **CONTACT ADDRESS** Dept Ed Leadership, Univ of Florida, 258 Norman Hall, Gainesville, FL 32611.

SMITH, WILLIAM L.
DISCIPLINE SOCIOLOGY **EDUCATION** Loras Col, BA, 78; Marquette Univ, MA, 80; Univ Notre Dame, PhD, 84. **CAREER** Prof, Ga Southern Univ. **SELECTED PUBLICATIONS** Auth, Families and Communes: An Examination of Nontraditional Lifestyles, Sage Publ, 99. **CONTACT ADDRESS** Dept of Sociol and Anthrop, Georgia So Univ, PO Box 8051, Statesboro, GA 30460-8051.

SMITH-ROSENBERG, CARROLL
DISCIPLINE HISTORY & PSYCHIATRY **EDUCATION** Conn Col for Women, BA, 75; Columbia Univ, MA, 58; PhD, 68. **CAREER** Assoc prof, hist & psych, Univ Penn; PROF, HIST & WOMEN'S STUD, GRAD CH, AM CULT PROG, UNIV MICH. **MEMBERSHIPS** Am Antiquarian Soc **RESEARCH** Gender & class in 19th cent Am; Am identity & the US Constitution. **SELECTED PUBLICATIONS** Auth, "Sex as Symbol in Jacksonian America," Am Jour of Soc 84, 78; auth, "Davy Crockett as Trickster: Pornography, Liminality and Perversion in Victorian America," Jour of Contemp Hist 17, 82; auth, Disorderly Conduct; Visions of Gender in Victorian America, Alfred A. Knopf, 85; auth, "Domesticating Virtue: Coquettes and Rebels in Young America," in Literature and the Body, Johns Hopkins Univ Press, 88; auth, "Dis-covering the Subject of the Great Constitutional Discussion 1786-1789," Jour of Am Hist 79, 91; auth, "Subject Female: Engendering American Identity," Am Lit Hist, 93. **CONTACT ADDRESS** Prog in Am Culture, Univ of Michigan, Ann Arbor, 2402 Mason Hall, Ann Arbor, MI 48109-1027. **EMAIL** csmithro@umich.edu

SMITHERMAN, GENEVA
PERSONAL Born Brownsville, TN, m **DISCIPLINE** EDUCATION **EDUCATION** Wayne State University, BA, 1960, MA, 1962; University of Michigan, PhD, 1969. **CAREER** Detroit Public Schools, teacher, 60-66; Eastern Michigan University & Wayne State University, instructor, 65-71; Wayne State University, assistant professor; Afro-American studies, Harvard University, lecturer, 71-73; University of Michigan, adjunct professor, 73; Wayne State University, professor, 73-. **HONORS AND AWARDS** Dean's List of Honor Students, Wayne State University; University of Michigan, Pre-Doctoral Fellowship; Awd for Scholarly Leadership in Language Arts Instruction, 1980. **MEMBERSHIPS** National Council Teachers of English, 1979-82; Executive Committee Conference College Composition, 1971-73; chairman, Black Literature Section, Midwest Language Association, 1972; Modern Language Association Committee, Minorities, 1976-77; Oral History Committee, Afro Museum, 1967-68; judge, Scholastic Writing Awards Contest, 1975; advisory board, Ethnic Awareness Project, 1977-78; founding member, African-American Heritage Association, 1976. **CONTACT ADDRESS** English, Michigan State Univ, 201 Morrill Hall, East Lansing, MI 48824-1036.

SMORRA, MARY A.
PERSONAL Born 11/22/1948, West Long Branch, NJ, s **DISCIPLINE** EDUCATION **EDUCATION** Monmouth Univ, BS, 70; Rutgers Univ, EdM, 77; EdD, 81. **CAREER** Consultant, Rutgers Univ, 88-90; Facilitator, Univ Buffalo, 82-; Assoc Prof, Georgian Court Col, 90-. **HONORS AND AWARDS** Colleague, Creative Education Foundation; Phi Delta Kappa Honor Soc; Kappa Delta Pi Honor Soc. **MEMBERSHIPS** ASCD, ATE, **RESEARCH** Brain based learning, Multiple intelligences, Creativity. **SELECTED PUBLICATIONS** Auth, Using the Arts to Enhance Communication with Your Child, forthcoming; auth, "Using Mnemonics and Visual Imagery to Facilitate Critical Thinking," in Critical Thinking: Implications for Teaching and Teachers, 92; auth, "The Effect of Environment on Creative Thinking Test Performance," Journal for the Education of the Gifted, 83. **CONTACT ADDRESS** Dept Educ, Georgian Court Col, 900 Lakewood Ave, Lakewood, NJ 08701.

SNELL, JOEL C.
PERSONAL Born 07/15/1943, Omaha, NE, m, 1968, 2 children **DISCIPLINE** SOCIOLOGY **EDUCATION** Univ Omaha, BA, 66; Univ Neb, MA, 70; S Dak State Univ, PhD, 76. **CAREER** Asst Prof to Dept Head, Dana Col, 75-78; Assoc Prof to Prof, 78-; Res Fel, Arlington Inst, 91-. **HONORS AND AWARDS** Who's Who in Am; Dir of Environmental Sociol; Outstanding Young Am; Dir of Intl Biography; Personalities in Am; Governor of Iowa Awd; Outstanding Teacher, Kirkwood Community Col, 93; Awd, The Kirkwood Difference, 97. **SELECTED PUBLICATIONS** Auth, "Distance Learning, Web sites and Accreditation," College Student Journal, (99): 318-320; auth, "Surveys Validate Rigor of Distance Learning," Community College Week, (99): 5; auth, "One Size Does Not Fit all," Community College Week, (99): 5; auth, "21st Century Specter: No US Farms/Thought of barren Iowa is nightmarish: Let's fight it," The Gazette, April 99; auth, "Flaw in Pregnancy Report," Omaha World Herald, (99): 7; auth, "Idyllic setting in mid-city: Wonderful," The Gazette, July 99; auth, "Big Red brings Iowans the blues: Wait! Dust off those cliches/Visitors top scenario: Huskers harvest Hawks," The Gazette, Sept 99; auth, "Remember when white, heterosexual males sang love songs to hot cars?," The Gazette, Jan 99; auth, "Central City: Nearest Faraway Place," The Linn County Newsletter, March, 99; auth, "Subjective Gender Role Assessment Index for Use in College Classroom,: College Student Journal, (99): 513-514. **CONTACT ADDRESS** Dept Soc Sci, Kirkwood Comm Col, PO Box 2068, Cedar Rapids, IA 52406.

SNELL, WILLIAM, JR
PERSONAL Born 11/24/1950, Paris, TX, m **DISCIPLINE** PSYCHOLOGY **EDUCATION** Univ Tex at Austin, BS, 74; MA, 81; PhD, 83. **CAREER** Res asst, Univ Tex at Austin, 79-83; evaluation dir, Child, Inc., 82 & 83; evaluator of Head Start Prog, Child, Inc., 83; teaching asst, 83; statistician, Handicapped Minority Res Inst at Univ Tex at Austin, 83-85; fac member of Dept of Special Educ, Univ Tex at Austin, 84; res specialist II, Tex Dept of Human Resources, 86; strategic planner II, Tex Dept of Mental Health and Mental Retardation, 86; from asst prof to prof, Southeast Mo State Univ, 86-. **HONORS AND AWARDS** Dept of Psychol Merit Awd, Southeast Mo State Univ, 88-98; Teaching Enhancement Awds, Southeast Mo State Univ, 97; Col Res Merit Awd, Southeast Mo State Univ, 87-88; Outstanding Teacher-Scholar, Southeast Mo State Univ, 98-99. **MEMBERSHIPS** Am Asn of Univ Professors, Am Asn of Applied and Preventive Psychol, Am Psychol Soc, Asn for General and Liberal Studies, Soc of Personality Assessment, Phi Kappa Phi, Southwestern Psychol Asn, Int Soc for the Study of Personal Relationships, Soc for Southwestern Soc Psychol, Iowa Network on Personal Relationships, Midwestern Psychol Asn, Soc for the Psychological Study of Soc Issues, Soc for the Advancement of Soc Psychol, Soc of the Sci Study of Sex, Southern Soc for Philos and Psychol, Psychol Club and Psi Chi. **RESEARCH** Personality Psychology, Personality Disorders, Human Sexuality, Intimacy and Close Relationships, Health Psychology, Personality and Health. **SELECTED PUBLICA-**

TIONS Coauth, "Goldberg's bipolar measure of the big five personality dimensions: Reliability and validity," European J of Personality 10 (96): 1-17; coauth, "Sexual awareness: Contraception, sexual behaviors, and sexual attitudes," Sexual and Marital Therapy 13 (98): 191-199; coauth, "Coping in intimate relationships: Development of the Multidimensional Intimate Coping Questionnaire," J of Soc and Personal Relationships 16 (99): 133-144; auth, "The Sexual Relationship Scale," in Sexuality-related Measures: A Compendium, eds. W. L. Yarber and S. L Davis (Sage, in press); auth, "The AIDS Discussion Strategy Scale," in Sexuality-related Measures: A Compendium, eds. W. L. Yarber and S. L Davis (Sage, in press); coauth, "The Multidimensional Health Questionnaire," Am J of Health Behav (in press); coauth, "Personality disorders and contraceptive behavior in university women," J of Psychol and the Behav Sci 13 (in press); coauth, "Personality disorders and both clinical anger and depression," J of Psychol and the Behav Sci 13 (in press). **CONTACT ADDRESS** Dept Psychol, Southeast Missouri State Univ, 1 University Plaza, Cape Girardeau, MO 63701. **EMAIL** wesnell@semovm.semo.edu

SNIPES, MARJORIE M.
PERSONAL Born 07/25/1964, Charleston, SC, s **DISCIPLINE** ANTHROPOLOGY **EDUCATION** Col Will Mary, BA, 85; Univ Wis, MA, 89; PhD, 96. **CAREER** Adj prof, Col Will Mary, 94-97; asst prof, State Univ West Georgia, 98-. **HONORS AND AWARDS** Phi Beta Kappa. **MEMBERSHIPS** AAS; SAS; AAUP. **RESEARCH** Latin America; Andes; religion; human identity; political movements. **SELECTED PUBLICATIONS** Co-ed, Indigenous Perceptions of the Nation-State in Latin America, Studies in Third World Societies 56 (95): 13-46; auth, The "Gaze" of the State: School as Contested Territory in the Argentine Andes. Studies In Third World Societies 56 (95): 113-46; auth, When the Other Speaks: Animals and Place as Social Space in the Argentine Andes, Ann Arbor: UMI (97); auth, "Libritos y destinos en los Andes argentinos." Anthropologica, 16 (98): 277-290; coauth, "Early Behavioral and Temperamental Traits in Mother vs. Peer-reared Rhesus Monkeys," Primates 39 (98). **CONTACT ADDRESS** Dept Anthropology, State Univ of West Georgia, 1601 Maple St, Carrollton, GA 30117. **EMAIL** msnipes@westga.edu

SNODGRASS, JON
PERSONAL Born 07/27/1941, Colon, Panama **DISCIPLINE** SOCIOLOGY **EDUCATION** Univ MD, BA, 65, MA, 67; Univ Pa, PhD, 72; Reiss Davis Child Study Center, Los Angeles, Calif, PhD, 83. **CAREER** Asst prof to prof, Calif State Univ, 72-. **HONORS AND AWARDS** Licensed, Res Psychoanalyst, State of Calif; private practice psychotherapy and career counseling, So Pas, Calif. **SELECTED PUBLICATIONS** Auth, Follow Your Career Star: Career Quest Based on Inner Values, Kensington Pub Corp: NY (96); film Rev, "Life is Beautiful," On Course Mag (summer 99); auth, "On Becoming a Jedi Knight: Spiritual Wisdom in Star Wars," (in pub). **CONTACT ADDRESS** Depot Sociol, California State Univ, Los Angeles, 5151 State Univ Dr, Los Angeles, CA 90032. **EMAIL** jon@careerstar.com

SNOW, D. R.
PERSONAL Born 10/18/1940, New Ulm, MN, m, 1963, 3 children **DISCIPLINE** ANTHROPOLOGY **EDUCATION** Univ Minn, BA, 62; Univ Ore, PhD, 66. **CAREER** Teach asst, 65-66; asst prof, 66-69; asst prof, 69-72, assoc prof, 72-80, chair, dept anthrop, 74-80, PROF, ANTHROP, 80-95, 89-91, SUNY, ALBANY; assoc dean Soc & Beh Scis, 80-83, Act Dean Col Soc & Beh Scis, 83; vis prof, Univ Am, Mexico, 78; PROF, HEAD DEPT ANTHROP, PA STATE UNIV, 95-. **HONORS AND AWARDS** Awarded National Defense Edu Act Fellow for graduate study in anthropology, 62-65; naed Fratres in Facultate of Signum Laudis, Univ at Albany, SUNY, 78; elected fellow of the Am Assoc for the Advancement of Sci, 84; appointed mem of the NY St Brd for Historic preserv (v-chair, 87-95), 85-95; elected fellow of the NY St Archaeological Assoc, 88; presidential recognition awd, Soc for Am Archaeology, 94; cert of appreciation, Col of Arts and Sciences, Univ at Albany, SUNY.' **MEMBERSHIPS** Soc for Am Archaeology; Am Anthropological Assoc; Soc of Sigma Xi; Am Soc for Ethnohistory (pres, 78-79); NE Anthropological Assoc (pres, 84-86); NY Archaeological Council (pres, 87-89); Archaeological Inst of Am (pres of the central PA soc, 98-00); Union Internationale des Sciences Prehistoriques et Protohistoriques; Iroquois Indian Museum (trustee, 85-95); Am Assoc for the Adv of Sci (chair of anthropology section H, 99-00); European Assoc of Archaeologists; Am Assoc for the Adv of Sci (secretary of anthropology section H, 00-002). **RESEARCH** North American archaeology; Mesoamerican Archaeology; European archaeology; paleodemography; ethnihistory. **SELECTED PUBLICATIONS** Co-auth, Atlas of Ancient America, (NY), Facts on File, 86; auth, Archaeology of North American Indians, Chelsea Books, 89; auth, The Iroquois, Basil Blackwell, publisher, 94; ed, Iroquois Medical Botany, Syracuse Univ Press, 95; auth, Mohawk Valley Archaeology: The Collections, Univ at Albany Inst for Archaeological Studies, The Pennsylvania State Univ, 95; ed, In the County of the Mohawks: Historical Narratives of a Native People, Syracuse Univ Press. **CONTACT ADDRESS** Dept of Anthrop, Pennsylvania State Univ, Univ Park, 409 Carpenter Bldg, University Park, PA 16801. **EMAIL** drs17@psu.edu

SNYDER, DAVID W.
PERSONAL Born 03/21/1961, IN **DISCIPLINE** MUSIC EDUCATION **EDUCATION** Doctorate of music EDU , 96. **CAREER** Illinois state Univ, asst prof, 95-. **HONORS AND AWARDS** Teaching, Res, Ser Initiative Awds. **MEMBERSHIPS** CMS; MENC **RESEARCH** Teacher EDU ; pre-student teaching experience; classroom management. **CONTACT ADDRESS** Dept of Music, Illinois State Univ, Campus Box 5660, Normal, IL 61790. **EMAIL** dsnyder@ilstu.edu

SNYDER, KATHERINE ANN
PERSONAL Born 03/11/1970, Baltimore, MD, s **DISCIPLINE** PSYCHOLOGY **EDUCATION** WVa Wesleyan Col, BA, 92; Va Polytechnic Inst and State Univ, MS, 93; PhD, 96. **CAREER** Asst prof of Psychology, Shepherd Col. **HONORS AND AWARDS** Southwestern Col Integrative Studies Course Awd; WVa Wesleyan Col Class Key Awd; Sigma Iota Music Scholar Awd; Linthicum United Methodist Church Scholar, 88-94; MD Senatorial Scholar, 88-92; Basal Burns Memorial Psychol Scholar, 91-92; WVa Psychol Asn Undergrad Res Awd, 92. **MEMBERSHIPS** Am Psychol Asn, Eastern Psychol Asn, Cognitive Neurosci Soc, Fac for Undergrad Neuropsychol, Psi Chi, Phi Kappa Phi, Alpha Lambda Delta. **RESEARCH** The role of computer technology in the classroom; an assessment of verbal fluency as a function of mild to moderate depression. **SELECTED PUBLICATIONS** Coauth with R. S. Calef, M. C. Choban, and E. S. Geller, "Frequency of verbal transformations as a function of word presentation styles," Bull of the Psychonomic Soc, 30, 5 (92): 363-364; coauth with D. W. Harrison and W. J. Gorman, "Auditory affect perception in a dichotic listening paradigm as a function of verbal fluency classification," The Int J of Neurosci, 84 (96): 65-74; coauth with J. D. Alden, D. W. Harrison, E. Everhart, and K. A. Snyder, "Age differences in focused attention dichotic listening," (Manuscript accepted, 97); coauth with D. W. Harrison, "An affective auditory verbal learning test," The Archives of Clinical Neuropsychology (July 97); coauth with D. W. Harrison, "The Auditory Affective Learning Test," in J. Fabry, ed, The Rey Auditory Verbal Learning Test: A Primer (in prep, 98); coauth with D. W. Harrison and B. Shenal, "An affective auditory verbal learning test: Psychophysiological correlates," The Archives of Clinical Neuropsychology (99). **CONTACT ADDRESS** Dept Psychol, Shepherd Col, 218 White Hall, Shepherdstown, WV 25443.

SOARES, ANTHONY T.
PERSONAL Born 09/30/1923, MA, M, 2 children **DISCIPLINE** EDUCATIONAL PSYCHOLOGY **EDUCATION** Univ Ill, DEd, 62. **CAREER** PROF EDUC, Univ Bridgeport, 65-. **MEMBERSHIPS** AERA; APS; PDK; EERO; AAER; KDP; CPA; ASCD. **RESEARCH** Self perceptins, assessment, learning growth and develop. **SELECTED PUBLICATIONS** Self Perceptions Inventories, SPI; Apperception Inventories, API. **CONTACT ADDRESS** Univ of Bridgeport, University Ave, Bridgeport, CT 06602. **EMAIL** soares@bridgeport.edu

SODERSTROM, DOUG
PERSONAL Born 07/21/1941, Kansas City, MO, m, 1966, 1 child **DISCIPLINE** PSYCHOLOGY **EDUCATION** Kans State Univ, BS, 64; Colo State Col, MA, 66; Central Mo State Col, MS, 70; Utah State Univ, PhD, 76. **CAREER** Counr, Thief River Falls State Jr Col, 66-68; Instr, Edison Jr Col, Ft. Mayers, Fla, 69-70; Instr, Central Ore Community Col, Bend, Ore, 72-73; Counr, Fort Scott Community Col, Kans, 73-76; Counr, Kilgore Col, Tex, 76-78; Instr, Wharton Co Jr Col, Tex, 78-. **HONORS AND AWARDS** Who's Who Among Am Teachers; Who's Who in Medicine and Health Care. **MEMBERSHIPS** Tex Community Col Teachers Asn. **RESEARCH** Consensus and Conflict Between Psychology and Religion. **SELECTED PUBLICATIONS** Coauth, "Religious Orientation and Meaning in Life," J of Clinical Psychology 33-1 (Jan 77): 65-68; auth, "Religious Orientation and Meaning in Life," Psychologist Interested in Relig Issues, Div 36, Am Psychol Asn 1-1; auth, The Confessions of White Man, Nat Office for Black Cath, 92; auth, The Truth Less Told: Understanding Ourselves As We Really Are, self-publ, 95. **CONTACT ADDRESS** Dept Psychology, Wharton County Junior Col, 911 Boling Hwy, Wharton, TX 77488. **EMAIL** dougsoderstrom@yahoo.com

SOH, C. SARAH
PERSONAL Born 05/01/1947, Taegu, Korea, m **DISCIPLINE** ANTHROPOLOGY **EDUCATION** Sogang, Univ, BA, 71; Univ Haw, PhD, 87. **CAREER** Assoc prof, San Francisco State Univ, 94-. **HONORS AND AWARDS** Grant, East-West Ctr, 81-87; Fel, Nat Sci Found; Fel, Japan Found Fel, 97-98; Grant, John D. & Catherine T. MacArthur Found, 00-01. **MEMBERSHIPS** Am Anthrop Assoc. **RESEARCH** Gender, Social Inequality, Culture Change, Human Sexuality. **SELECTED PUBLICATIONS** Auth, Women in Korean Politics, Westview, 93. **CONTACT ADDRESS** Dept Anthrop, San Francisco State Univ, 1600 Hollway Ave, San Francisco, CA 94132. **EMAIL** soh@sfsu.edu

SOLOMON, BARBARA HOCHSTER
PERSONAL Born 09/25/1936, Brooklyn, NY, m, 1958, 2 children **DISCIPLINE** AMERICAN LITERATURE, WOMEN'S STUDIES **EDUCATION** Brooklyn Col, BA, 58; Univ Kans, MA, 60; Univ Pittsburgh, PhD(English), 68. **CAREER** Instr English, Doane Col, 60-62; adv to undergrads, Univ Pittsburgh, 63-65; instr, Temple Univ, 65-67; asst prof, 69-73, assoc prof, 73-80, PROF ENGLISH, IONA COL, 80- **MEMBERSHIPS** MLA **RESEARCH** The American heroine in nineteenth and twentieth century American literature. **SELECTED PUBLICATIONS** Ed, Short Fiction of Sarah Orne Jewett and Mary Wilkins Freeman, New Am Lib, 79; ed, Ain't We Got Fun: Essays, Lyrics and Stories of the Twenties, New Am Lib, 80; co-ed with Paula Berggren, A Mary Wllstonecraft Reader, New Am Lib, 83; ed, American Wives: Thirty Stories by Women, New Am Lib, 86; ed, American Families, New Am Lib, 89; ed, Other Voices, Other Vistas: Twenty-Five Non-Western Stories, New Am Lib, 92; ed, Herland and Selected Stories of Charlotte Perkins Gilman, New Am Lib, 92; ed, Rediscoveries: American Short Sotries by Women, 1832-1916, New Am Lib, 94; ed, Bernice Bobs Her Hair and Other Stories of F. Scott Fitzgerald, Dutton/Signet, 96; ed, Critical Essays on Toni Morrison's Beloved, Twayne, 98. **CONTACT ADDRESS** Dept of English, Iona Col, 715 North Ave, New Rochelle, NY 10801-1890.

SOLOMON, P.
PERSONAL Born 12/06/1945, Hartford, CT **DISCIPLINE** SOCIAL WORK **EDUCATION** Russell Sage Col BA 68; Case Western Reserve Univ MA 70 and PhD 78. **CAREER** From res assoc to dir, Action Res and Development, Commission on Mental Health, Federation for Community Planning, 78-88; res, Cleveland State Univ, Cleveland State Hospital, Cleveland Psychiatric Inst, 70-76; Univ Penn, prof School of Social Work 94-, School of Med prof Social Work in Psychiatry 95-; Allegheny Univ, adj prof psychiatry 94-97; Hahnemann Univ, sch med prof 88-94, dir Men Health Ser and Sys Res 88-94. **HONORS AND AWARDS** Outstanding People of the 20th Century, Dict of Intl Biography, Who's Who in the following, Amer Women, of Women, Medicine and Health Care, America, The World, Intellectuals, Prof and Business Women, Amer EDU , in the East, Finance and Industry; Evaluation of the Year, Ohio Program Evaluators Group, 87; First Place Res Awd, Soc for Social Work and Res, 97; Armin Loeb Awd, Int Asn of Psychosocial Rehabilitation Services, 99. **MEMBERSHIPS** Society for Social Work and Research; Intl Assoc of Psychosocial Rehab Serv **RESEARCH** Ser Delivery Sys of Severe Mental Illness and Families; Fam EDU and Psychiatric Rehab; Criminal Justice and Mental Health. **SELECTED PUBLICATIONS** Coauth, Psychiatric rehabilitation in practice, And over Med Pub, 93, New Developments in Psychiatric Rehabilitation: New directions for mental health serv, Jossey-Bass, 90; Consumer Providers in psychiatric rehabilitation, in: P. Corrigan, D. Giffort, Building Teams and Programs for Effective Psychiatric Rehabilitation, Jossey-Bass, in press; Evolution of service innovation for adults with severe mental illness. In: D. Biegal, A Blum, Innovation and Practice and Service Delivery across the Life Span, NY Oxford Press, in press; Families Coping with Mental Illness,: The Cultural Context, Jossy-Bass, 98; Recent Advances in Mental Health Research: Implications for Social Work Practice, NASW Press, 98. **CONTACT ADDRESS** School of Social Work, Univ of Pennsylvania, 3701 Locust Walk, Philadelphia, PA 19104. **EMAIL** solomonp@ssw.upenn.edu

SOMERS, CHERYL L.
PERSONAL Born 10/11/1970, Mt Clemens, MI, m, 1997, 1 child **DISCIPLINE** BEHAVIORAL EDUCATION **EDUCATION** Mich State Univ, BS, 92; Ball State Univ, MA, 93; PhD, 97. **CAREER** Asst Prof, Eastern Ill Univ, 96-98; Asst Prof, Wayne State Univ, 98-. **MEMBERSHIPS** Nat Assoc of Sch Psychologists, Midwestern Educ Res Assoc, Soc for Res on Adolescence, Mich Assoc of Sch Psychologists, Soc for Res in Child Develop. **RESEARCH** Adolescent sexuality, teen pregnancy prevention, parent-child-adolescent relationships, parenting approaches and styles. **SELECTED PUBLICATIONS** Coauth, "Birth Order and Family Size: Influences on Adolescent Achievement and Related Parenting Behaviors," Psychol Reports, 76 (95): 43-51; coauth, "My School is Like a Home: Using Metaphors to Assess Students' Attitudes Toward Parenting, Teaching and Schools," Psychol Reports 78 (96): 619-623; coauth, "Patterns of Parenting During Adolescence: Perceptions of Adolescents and Parents," Adolescence, 31(96): 369-381; coauth, "Student Perceptions of Parent-Adolescent Closeness and Communication About Sexuality: Relations with Sexual Knowledge, Attitudes and Behaviors," J of Adolescence (forthcoming); coauth, "Late Adolescents' Reactions to Three Types of Childhood Teasing: Relations with Self-Esteem and Body Image," Soc Behav and Personality, 28 (forthcoming). **CONTACT ADDRESS** Dept Behav Educ, Wayne State Univ, 5221 Gullen Mall, Detroit, MI 48202. **EMAIL** csomers@coe.wayne.edu

SORACI, SALVATORE
PERSONAL Born 04/30/1952, Yonkers, NY, m, 1980, 1 child **DISCIPLINE** PSYCHOLOGY **EDUCATION** Univ Fla, BA, 74; Vanderbilt Univ, PhD, 82. **CAREER** Res Scientist, Vanderbilt Univ, 84-93; Dir, Engineering Psychol Prog, Tufts Univ, 93-; Lecturer, Harvard Univ, 95-. **HONORS AND AWARDS** Phi Beta Kappa; Res Career Development Awd, NIH; New Investigator Res Awd, NIH. **MEMBERSHIPS** Psychonomic Soc; Human Factors and Ergonomics Soc; Am Psychol Soc. **RESEARCH** Cognitive Science; Memory; Mental Retardation. **SELECTED PUBLICATIONS** Co-auth, "Cognitive science

and the study of consciousness," Journal of Mathematical Psychology, 98; co-auth, "Facilitating visual attention," in Perspectives on fundamental processes in intellectual function, Ablex Pub, 98; co-auth, "The detection of interstimulus relations: A locus of intelligence-related differences," in Advances in cognition and education: contextual issues in research in intelligence, JAI Press, 98; co-ed, Perspectives on fundamental processes in intellectual functioning, Ablex Pub, 98; co-auth, "A multiple-process account of generation," Memory, (99): 483-508; co-auth, "Both sides now: Human symmetry detection," Journal of Mathematical Psychology, (99): 441-448; co-auth, "Detection of motion-defined forms: Evidence for modifiability," Intelligence, (99): 141-156; co-auth, "Cuing and encoding variability in generative processing," Journal of Memory and Language, (99): 541-559; co-auth, "From analog to digital: Teaching about criminal sentencing with technology," in Computer enhanced learning: vignettes of best practice from America's most wired campuses, Wake Forest Univ Press, in press; co-auth, "Aha" effects in the generation of pictures," Memory and Cognition, in press. **CONTACT ADDRESS** Dept Psychol, Tufts Univ, Medford, 520 Boston Ave, Medford, MA 02155. **EMAIL** ssoraci@tufts.edu

SOUHEAVER, HAROLD G.
PERSONAL Born 02/05/1957, Paragould, AR, d, 2 children **DISCIPLINE** PSYCHOLOGY **EDUCATION** Ark State Univ, BS, 86, MRC, 88; Southern Ill Univ, PhD, 93. **CAREER** Adjunct status, Col of Ed, Ark State Univ, 6 years; prof of psychol, East Ark Community Col, 7 years. **HONORS AND AWARDS** Doctoral Diss Res Awd recipient, SIU, 91; Who's Who Among America's Teachers, 98, 2000. **MEMBERSHIPS** Ark Asn of Two-Year Cols. **RESEARCH** Rehabilitation and special populations. **SELECTED PUBLICATIONS** Auth, "Use this system to check your parity level," Teaching for Success 8, 4 (96); coauth with J. J. Benshoff, W. R. Wright, and T. F. Rigger, "AIDS Knowledge among rehabilitative professionals," J of Rehabilitation, 62, 2 (96). **CONTACT ADDRESS** Dept Soc Sci, East Arkansas Comm Col, 1700 New castle Rd, Forrest City, AR 72335.

SOUTHERLAND, PETER
PERSONAL Born 05/29/1947, England **DISCIPLINE** RELIGIOUS STUDIES, ANTHROPOLOGY **EDUCATION** Univ London Sch Oriental and African Studies, MA, 76; Polytech Central London, BA Photography, 86; Oxford Univ, PhD, 99. **CAREER** Instr, La State Univ. **MEMBERSHIPS** Am Anthrop Asn. **RESEARCH** Architecture, Religion, Colonialism, Globalization, India, Benin. **SELECTED PUBLICATIONS** Auth, "Khash-Kanait Architecture," in Encyclopedia of Vernacular Architecture of the World, ed. Paul Oliver (Cambridge Univ Press, 97); auth, "In Memory of the Slaves: An African View of the Diaspora in the Americas," in Representation of Blackness and the Performance of Identity, ed. Jean Muteba Rahier (Greenwood Press, 99). **CONTACT ADDRESS** La State Univ, 1529 Moreland Ave, Baton Rouge, LA 70808. **EMAIL** psuther@lsu.edu

SOVEN, MARGOT
PERSONAL Born 10/18/1940, New York, NY, m, 1961, 3 children **DISCIPLINE** ENGLISH EDUCATION **EDUCATION** Univ Penn, PhD, 80. **CAREER** Prof, English dept, 81-, LaSalle Univ. **HONORS AND AWARDS** Instl Summer Grants; NEH Summer Seminar Grant **MEMBERSHIPS** MLA; NCTE **RESEARCH** The teaching of writing; Amer lit. **SELECTED PUBLICATIONS** Coauth, Writings from the Workplace Documents Models Cases, 96; auth, Write to Learn: A Guide to Writing Across the Curriculum, 96; auth, The Teaching of Writing in Middle & Secondary Schools, 98. **CONTACT ADDRESS** La Salle Univ, 1900 W Olney Ave, Philadelphia, PA 19141. **EMAIL** Soven@lasalle.edu

SPANO, RINA GANGEMI
PERSONAL Born 08/22/1948, Jersey City, NJ, m, 1971, 2 children **DISCIPLINE** SOCIOLOGY **EDUCATION** Caldwell Col, BA, 70; Montclair State Col, MAT, 75; MA, 82; Grad Sch and Univ Center, City Univ NYork, PhD, 91. **CAREER** Instr to prof, Caldwell Col, 79-97, Dir of Grad Studies, 97-98, Assoc Dean of Grad Studies, 98-. **HONORS AND AWARDS** Alpha Kappa Delta; World's Who's Who of Women; Who's Who in the East. **MEMBERSHIPS** Am Sociol Asn, Soc on Aging of NJ, Nat Org of Italian-Am Women, Nat Asn of Grad Admissions Profs, Nat Asn of Grad and Prof Students, NAWE: Advancing Women in Higher Educ. **SELECTED PUBLICATIONS** Auth, "Italian-American Children and Their Ethnic Peers at Play-1880-1930," in Italian -Americans in a Multicultural Society, eds Jerome Krase and Judith DeSena, NY: Forum Italicum (94): 142-152; auth, "Fascino e Bellezza: Advertisements in Italian and American Women's Magazines," Transociety (forthcoming); auth, "Play," in the Encyclopedia of Childhood, ed Barbara Katz Rothman and Donna King, NY: Holt (forthcoming). **CONTACT ADDRESS** Dept Sociol, Caldwell Col, 9 Ryerson Ave, Caldwell, NJ 07006. **EMAIL** rspano@caldwell.edu

SPATZ, K. CHRISTOPHER
PERSONAL Born 03/25/1940, Tyler, TX, m, 1961, 3 children **DISCIPLINE** PSYCHOLOGY **EDUCATION** Hendrix Col, BA, 62; Tulane Univ, MS, 64; PhD, 66. **CAREER** Instr to asst prof, Univ of the South, 66-69; assoc prof, Univ of Ark, 71-73; assoc prof to prof, Hendrix Col, 73-; chair, 76-80, 90-95. **HONORS AND AWARDS** NSF Fel, 68; NIMH Fel, 69-71; Ford Venture Fund Grant, 76. **MEMBERSHIPS** Am Psychol Soc; Coun of Teachers of Undergrad Psychol; Am Psychol Assoc. **SELECTED PUBLICATIONS** Auth, A laboratory manual for experimental psychology, Appleton-Century-Crofts, (NY), 70; auth, Instructors manual for a laboratory manual for experimental psychology, Appleton-Century-Crofts, (NY), 70; coauth, "Internal consistency of the Coopersmith Self-Esteem Inventory", Educ and Psychol Measurement 33, (73): 875-876; coauth, "Racial attitudes and self-esteem levels among Southeast Arkansas public school students", Educ Res in Ark 1971-72", Ark Dept of Higher Educ, (73); coauth, "Reminiscence: A rich source of individual differneces", J of Motor Behav 7 (75): 1-7; auth, Basic Statistics: Tales of Distributions, Brooks/Cole, (Pacific Grove, CA), 97; auth, "Study guide for basic statistics: Tales of distributions, Brooks/Cole, (Pacific Grove, CA), 97; auth, Instructors manual to accompany basic statistics: Tales of distributions, Brooks/Cole, (Pacific Grove, CA), 97. **CONTACT ADDRESS** Dept Psychol, Hendrix Col, 1600 Washington Ave, Conway, AR 72032.

SPEIDELL, TODD
PERSONAL Born 07/31/1957, Chicago, IL, m, 1990, 1 child **DISCIPLINE** THEOLOGY, ETHICS; PSYCHOLOGY **EDUCATION** Gordon Col, BA, 79; Fuller Theological Seminary, M Div, 83, PhD,86, Fuller Theological Seminary; New College Edinburgh, postdoctoral study, July 92, 95. **CAREER** Dir, of Extended Education and Adjunct prof, 87-89, Fuller Theological Seminary; assoc prof, 89-90, Knoxville Col; head of religious studies, 90- , Webb Sch of Knoxville. **MEMBERSHIPS** Karl Barth Soc of North America; Intl Bonhoeffer Soc. **RESEARCH** Theological ethics, theology and culture. **SELECTED PUBLICATIONS** Auth, The Incarnation as Theological Imperative for Human Reconciliation: A Christocentric Social Ethic, 86; Coed, Incarnational Ministry: The Presence of Christ in Church, Society, & Family, Essays in Honor of Ray S. Anderson, 90; auth, A Trinitarian Ontology of Persons in Society, Scottish Journal of Theology, 94; auth, I Want a Picture of God! The Chaplain's Craft, 94; auth, Confessions of a Lapsed Skeptic: acknowledging the Mystery and Manner of God, 00; auth, From Conduct to Character: A Primer in Ethical Theory, 00. **CONTACT ADDRESS** 1137 Farrington Dr., Knoxville, TN 37923. **EMAIL** todd_speidell@webbschool.org

SPENCER, PATRICIA
PERSONAL Born 10/29/1942, Galveston, TX, m, 1978, 2 children **DISCIPLINE** SOCIOLOGY **EDUCATION** Lamar Univ, BS, 65; Boston Univ, EdM, 73; Univ Tex, PhD, 80. **CAREER** Soc Work, Gallaudet Univ, 86-96; Assoc Prof, Gallaudet Univ, 96-. **HONORS AND AWARDS** Fulbright Sen Scholar, 99; Who's Who Among Am Teachers, 00. **MEMBERSHIPS** Soc for Res in Child Develop, Coun of Am Instr of the deaf. **RESEARCH** Child symbolic and social development, young deaf and hard of hearing children, cochlear implants. **SELECTED PUBLICATIONS** Coauth, "Maternal Sensitivity and the Visual Attentiveness of Children Who are Deaf," Early Develop and Parenting 5-4 (96): 213-223; coauth, "The Association Between Language and Symbolic Play: Evidence from Deaf Toddlers," Child Develop 67 (96): 867-876; coauth, "Play, Language and Maternal Responsiveness: A longitudinal Study of Deaf and Hearing Infants," Child Develop 67 (96): 3176-3201; coauth, "What Mothers do to Support Infant Visual Attention: Sensitivities to Age and Hearing Status," J of Deaf Studies and Deaf Educ 2-2 (97): 104-114; auth, "Every Opportunity: A Case Study of Hearing Parents and Their Deaf Child," in The Deaf Child in the Family and at Sch (Hillsdale, NJ: Erlbaum, 00); coauth, The Deaf Child in the Family and at School: Essays in Honor of Kathryn P Meadow-Orlans, Erlbaum Pr (Hillsdale, NJ), 00; coauth, "Word Learning Skills of Deaf Preschoolers: The Development of Movel Mapping and Rapid World Learning strategies," Child Develop (forthcoming). **CONTACT ADDRESS** Dept Sociol, Gallaudet Univ, 800 Florida Ave, Washington, DC 20002. **EMAIL** patriciaspencer@juno.com

SPIGNER, CLARENCE
PERSONAL Born 03/19/1946, Orangeburg, SC, m, 1994, 3 children **DISCIPLINE** SOCIOLOGY; PUBLIC HEALTH; SOCIAL BEHAVIORAL SCIENCES. **EDUCATION** Santa Monica Col, Santa Monica, CA, AA, soc studies, 1974-76; Univ of Calif, Berkeley, CA, AB, sociology, 1977-79, MPH, health, 1980-82, DrPH, health, 1983-87. **CAREER** Am Heart Asn, Marin, CA, evaluator, 81-82; Nat Health Serv, London, England, researcher/planner, 82-83; Univ of Calif, Berkeley, CA, fitness supvr, 83-86, teaching asst/post-doc/lectr, 84-88; Univ of Ore, Eugene, OR, asst prof, Assoc Prof, currently. **HONORS AND AWARDS** Phi Beta Kappa, Phi Beta Kappa Honor Soc, 1979-; Chancellor's Post-Doctoral Fel, Univ of Calif-Berkeley, 1987; Henrik Blum Distinguished Serv Award, Univ of Calif-Berkeley, 1987; Outstanding Fac Award, Office of Multicultural Affairs, Univ of Ore, 1990; Friars Sr Honor Soc, Univ of Ore, 1990. **MEMBERSHIPS** Bd mem, Womanspace, 1989-91; steering comt mem, Clergy and Laity Concerned, 1990-; Univ of Ore, Substance Abuse Advisory Bd, 1990-92, Affirmative Action Task Force, 1990-, Coun for Minority Educ, chair, 1990-91; Special Community for Minority fac-chair, 97-99. **RESEARCH** Community base research; race/ethnic relations; popular culture. **SELECTED PUBLICATIONS** Auth, "Explanations of Ethnic and Gender Differences in Youth Smoking: A Multi-site, Qualitative Investigation," Nicotine and Tobacco Research, 1 (99): S91-S98; auth, "Impact of School-based Teaching on Students' Opinions of Organ Donation and Transplantation," Transplant Proceedings 31 (99): 1086-1087; coauth, Teen Images of Smokers and Smoking, Public Health Reports, CDC/ASPH Supplement on Extramural Prevention Research, in press; coauth, Knowledge and Opinions about Organ Donation Among Urban High School Students: Pilot Test of a Health Education Program, Clinical Transplantation, in press; auth, African Americans, Democracy, and Biomedical and Behavioral Research: Contradictions and Consensus in Community-based Participatory Research? International Quarterly of Community Health Education, in press **CONTACT ADDRESS** Dept of Health Services, Univ of Washington, H692 Health Sciences Ctr, PO Box 357660, Seattle, WA 98195. **EMAIL** cspigner@u.washington.edu

SPILLMAN, LYNETTE P.
DISCIPLINE SOCIOLOGY **EDUCATION** BA, Australian Nat Univ, 82; MA, Univ Calif Berkeley, 85; PhD, 91. **CAREER** Sociol, Univ. Notre Dame **HONORS AND AWARDS** Vis fel, Res Sch of Soc Sci, Australian Nat Univ, spring, 98; Inst for Scholar in the Liberal Arts, Prep of New Course summer stipend, Found of Social Theory, 95; Inst for Scholar in the Liberal Arts, Travel grant, Book manuscript res, 94; Univ of Queensland, travel grant, 93; Univ Notre Dame Facul Res Prog award, 93; Lilly Endowment Tchg fel, 93; Chancellor's Dissertation year fel, Univ Calif Berkeley, 90; Eli Sagan prize, Sociol Dept, Univ Calif Berkeley; Outstanding grad student instr award, 87; Regents' fel, grad div, Univ Calif Berkeley, 83; Fulbright travel award, Australian-Amer Educ Found, 83; Quentin Gibson prize in Philos, Australian Nat Univ, 79. **MEMBERSHIPS** Soc Sci Hist Asn; Amer Sociol Asn; Amer Hist Asn. **RESEARCH** Cultural Sociology, comparative historical sociology, political sociology, economic sociology, social theory, nations, markets. **SELECTED PUBLICATIONS** Auth, Imagining Community and Hoping For Recognition: Bicentennial Celebrations in 1976 and 1988, Qual Soc, 17, 1, 3-28, 94; auth, Culture, Social Structure, and Discursive Fields, Current Perspectives in Soc Theory, 15, 129-54, 95; auth, How are Structures Meaningful? Cultural Sociology and Theories of Social Structure, Humboldt Jour of Soc Rel, spec issue, Recent Advances in Theory and Research in Social Structure, 22, 2, 31-45, 96; Neither the Same Nation Nor Different Nations: Constitutional Conventions in the United States and Australia, Comp Studies in Soc and Hist, 38, 1, 149-81, jan 96; auth, Nation and Commemoration: Creating National Identities in the United States and Australia, Cambridge and NY, Cambridge Univ Press, 97; auth, When Do Collective Memories Last? Founding Moments in the United States and Australia, Soc Sci Hist, 22, 4, 98; auth, "Enriching Exchanbe: Cultural Dimensions of Markets," Am J of Economics and Socioalogy, 58 (4), (99), 1-25; auth, "Australina Nationalism," Encycl of Nationalism, vol 2, Alexander Motyl, San Diego: Academic Press, (01), ed, Cultural sociology, Malden MA and Oxford, Blackwell, (02), auth, Self, Social structure, and Beliefs: Explorations in the sociological thought of Neil J. Smelser, Berkley: Univ of Cal Press, Forthcoming. **CONTACT ADDRESS** Dept of Sociology, Univ of Notre Dame, 810 Flanner Hall, Notre Dame, IN 46556-5639. **EMAIL** spillman.1@nd.edu

SPIVEY, MICHAEL
PERSONAL Born 10/22/1969, Atlanta, GA, m, 2000 **DISCIPLINE** PSYCHOLOGY **EDUCATION** Univ Santa Cruz, BA, 91; Univ Rochester, MA, 95; PhD, 96. **CAREER** Asst Prof, Cornell Univ, 96-. **HONORS AND AWARDS** Sloan Found Fel, 98. **MEMBERSHIPS** Cognitive Sci Soc. **RESEARCH** Psycholinguistics, visual perception, eye movements. **SELECTED PUBLICATIONS** Auth, "Proceedings of the Seventh Artificial Intelligence and Cognitive Science Conference," Univ Col of Dublin Pr (98); coauth, "The Categorical Perception of Consonants: The Interaction of Learning and Processing," in Proceedings of the Chicago Ling Soc (99); coauth, "Cross Talk Between Native and Second Languages: Partial Activation of an Irrelevant Lexicon," Psychol Sci, 10 (99): 281-284; coauth, "On Computational and Behavioral Evidence Regarding Hebbian Transcortical Cell Assemblies," Behav and Brain Sci, 22 (99): 302; auth, "Turning the Tables on the Turing Test: The Spivey Test," Connection Sci (forthcoming). **CONTACT ADDRESS** Dept Psychol, Cornell Univ, 211 Uris Hall, Ithaca, NY 14853. **EMAIL** spivey@cornell.edu

SPOKANE, ARNOLD R.
PERSONAL Born 05/22/1948, Rochester, NY, d, 2 children **DISCIPLINE** PSYCHOLOGY, EDUCATION **EDUCATION** Oh State Univ, PhD, 76. **CAREER** Prof of Education and Psychol, Lehigh Univ, 97-. **HONORS AND AWARDS** John Holland Awd, Am Psychol Asn, 87; AACD Res Awd, Am Asn for Couns and Devel, 89; Kathryn L. Hopwood/Mud A. Stewart Awd, Ohio State Univ, 89; Fel, Am Asn for Applied and Preventative Psychol, 94. **MEMBERSHIPS** Am Asn for Applied and Preventative Psychol, Pa Coun Asn, Soc for Vocational Psychol. **RESEARCH** Person-environment Interaction and Career Choice, Vocational Assessment and Intervention, Health Psychology. **SELECTED PUBLICATIONS** Coauth with A.

Decker, "Expressed and measured interests," in M. L. Savickas and A. R. Spokane, eds, Vocational interests: Their meaning, measurement, and counseling use, Palo Alto, CA: Davies Black (99); coauth with M. L. Savickas, Vocational interests: Their meaning, measurement, and counseling use, Palo Alto, CA: Davies Black (99); coauth with D. Ferrara, "Samuel H. Osipow's contributions to occupational mental health and the assessment of stress: The Occupational Stress Inventory," in F. Leong, ed, Contemporary models in vocational psychology, Hillsdale, NJ: Lawrence Erlbaum (in press); coauth with M. Catalano, "The Self-Directed Search: A theory-driven array of self-guiding career interventions," in E. Watkins & V. Campbell, eds, Testing in Counseling Practice, 2nd ed, Hillsdale, NJ: Lawrence Erlbaum (99). **CONTACT ADDRESS** Dept Educ and Human Services, Lehigh Univ, 111 Research Dr, Bethlehem, PA 18015. **EMAIL** ars1@lehigh.edu

SPRINGER, DAVID W.
PERSONAL Born 09/01/1968, Manhattan, NY, m, 1997 **DISCIPLINE** SOCIOLOGY **EDUCATION** Fla State Univ, BA, 90; Fla State Univ, MSW, 92; Fla State Univ, PhD, 97. **CAREER** Clinical Soc Worker, Univ Behav Center, 92-94; Asst Prof, Univ Tex, 97-. **HONORS AND AWARDS** Res Awd, Ohio St Univ, 98; Tex Exes Teaching Excellence Awd, Univ Tex, 98-99. **MEMBERSHIPS** NASW, Coun on Soc Work Ed, Soc for Soc Work and Res. **RESEARCH** Clinical intervention with adolescents and families, clinical assessment and applied measurement, psychometric theory, juvenile delinquency, intervention research. **SELECTED PUBLICATIONS** Auth, Social Work: Issues and Opportunities in a Challenging Profession, 2nd ed, Allyn & Bacon (Needham, Ma), 97; coauth, "Drug Abuse Prevention Programs," in Crime and the Justice System in America: An Encyclopedia, (Greenwood Publ Group, 97); coauth, "Treating Chemically Dependent Children and Adolescents," in Chemical Dependency: A Systems Approach, 2nd ed (Allyn & Bacon, 98): 213-228; coauth, "The Effects of an Abstinence-Based Sex Education Program on Middle School Students' Knowledge and Beliefs," Research on Social Practice, 9(1) (99): 10-24; coauth, "Operation of Juvenile Assessment Centers: Trends and Issues," J for Juvenile Justice and Detention Services, 14(1) (99): 45-62; Auth, "Adolescent Concerns Evaluation (ACE)," in Measures for Clinical Practice, Volume 1: Couples, Families and Children, 3rd ed, Free Pr (NY, 00). **CONTACT ADDRESS** Dept Sociol, Univ of Texas, Austin, Austin, TX 78712. **EMAIL** dwspringer@mail.utexas.edu

SROUFE, L. ALAN
PERSONAL Born 06/06/1941, Cincinnati, OH, m, 1978, 4 children **DISCIPLINE** CLINICAL PSYCHOLOGY, CHILD DEVELOPMENT **EDUCATION** Whittier Col, AB, 63; Univ Wis, MS, 65; PhD, 67. **CAREER** Asst prof, Inst of Child Develop, Univ Minn, 68-73, assoc prof, 73-76, prof, 76-. **HONORS AND AWARDS** William Harris Prof Awd, 890; Rosenberry Awd for Dedication to the Care of Children, Excellence in Teaching, Innovative Res & Scholarly Pursuits, Children's Hosp, Denver, Colo, April 94. **MEMBERSHIPS** Soc for Res in Child Develop. **RESEARCH** Attachment relationships, emotional development and developmental psychopathology. **SELECTED PUBLICATIONS** Coauth with E. Carlson, A. Levy, and B. Egeland, "Implications of attachment theory for developmental psychopathology," Develop and Psychopathol, 11 (99): 1-13; auth, Forward to Emotional Development: A Biosocial Perspective, Wadsworth Pubs: Belmont, CA (99); coauth with G. DeHart and R. Cooper, Child Development: Its nature and course, 4th ed, NY: McGraw-Hill (2000); coauth with S. Duggal, N. S. Weinfield, and E. Carlson, "Relationships, development, and psychopathology," in M. Lewis and A. Sameroff, eds, Handbook of developmental psychopathology, 2nd ed (in press); coauth with N. Weinfield and B. Egelund, "Attachment from infancy to young adulthood in a high risk sample: Continuity, discontinuity and their correlates," Child Development (in press); coauth with S. Warren and R. Emde, "Internal representations: Predicting anxiety from children's play narratives," J of the Am Acad of Child and Adolescent Psychiatry In press); coauth with S. Duggal, E. A. Carlson and B. Egeland, "Depressive Symptomatology in Childhood and Adolescence," Develop and Psychopathology (in press). **CONTACT ADDRESS** Inst of Child Development, Univ of Minnesota, Twin Cities, 51 E River Rd, Minneapolis, MN 55455.

ST CLAIR, MICHAEL
PERSONAL Born 08/02/1940, Jamaica, NY, m, 1974, 2 children **DISCIPLINE** PSYCHOLOGY **EDUCATION** Boston Col, BA, 64; Trinity Col, MA, 70; Boston Univ, PhD, 75; **CAREER** Prof psychol, Emmanuel Col. **MEMBERSHIPS** Am Psychol Asn, Mass Psychol Asn. **SELECTED PUBLICATIONS** Auth, Millenarian Movements in Historical Context, Garland Press (92); auth, Human Relationships and the Experience of God, Palmist Press (94); auth, Object Relations and Self Psychology: An Introduction, Brooks/Cole, 3rd ed (2000). **CONTACT ADDRESS** Dept Psychol, Emmanuel Col, Massachusetts, 400 Fenway, Boston, MA 02115. **EMAIL** StClair@emmanuel.edu

STACEY, JUDITH
PERSONAL Born 01/02/1945, Irvington, NJ, 1 child **DISCIPLINE** SOCIOLOGY **EDUCATION** Univ Mich, BA, 64; Univ Ill, MA, 68; Brandeis, PhD, 79. **CAREER** Asst Prof to Prof, Univ Calif, 79-97; Prof, Univ Southern Calif, 97-. **HONORS AND AWARDS** Jessie Bernard Awd, Am Sociol Asn, 85; Rockefeller Changing Gender Roles; ACLS Fel. **MEMBERSHIPS** ASA, SWS, Coun on Contemporary Families. **RESEARCH** Family change, Gay male kinship, Gender. **SELECTED PUBLICATIONS** Auth, In the Name of the Family: Rethinking Family Values in a Postmodern Age, Beacon Press, 96; auth, Brave New Families: Stories of Domestic Upheaval in Late Twentieth-Century America, Basic Books, 90; auth, Patriarchy and Socialist Revolution in China, Univ of Calif Press, 83; auth, And Jill Came Tumbling After: Sexism in American Education, 74; auth, "Is Academic Feminism an Oxymoron?," Signs, in press; auth, "Beyond the Tinkerbell Defense of Lesbian and Gay Parenting," Georgetown Journal of Gender and the Law, in press; auth, "The Handbook's Tail: Toward Revels or a Requiem for Family Diversity?," in Handbook of Family Diversity, Oxford Univ Press, 00; auth, "Ethnography Confronts the Global Village: A new Home for a New Century?," Journal of Contemporary Ethnography, (99): 687-697; auth, "Virtual Social Science and the Politics of Family Values," in New Locations: The Remaking of Fieldwork and the Critical Imperative at Century's End, 99; auth, "Virtual Truth with a Vengeance," Contemporary Sociology, 99. **CONTACT ADDRESS** Dept Sociol, Univ of So California, 3620 S Vermont Ave, Los Angeles, CA 90089-0259. **EMAIL** jstacey@usc.edu

STADTLANDER, LEANN (LEE) M.
PERSONAL Born 07/16/1954, New Brunswick, NJ, m, 1994, 3 children **DISCIPLINE** PSYCHOLOGY **EDUCATION** Oh State Univ, BS, 88; MA, 90; PhD, 93. **CAREER** Asst prof, Dept of Psychol, Montana State Univ, Bozeman, Mt, 93-. **HONORS AND AWARDS** Phi Kappa Phi, 88-; Psi Chi, 87-; Golden Key Nat Honor Soc, 88; Burns Telecommunications Fac Fel, 95; Montana Campus Compact Fac Fel, 99-2000. **MEMBERSHIPS** Am Psychol Asn, Psychonomic Soc, Sigma Xi. **RESEARCH** Lexical memory, object memory, cognitive aging. **SELECTED PUBLICATIONS** Auth, "A compilation of 800 orthographic word neighborhoods by frequency," Behavior, Research Methods, Instruments, & Computers, 29 (97): 636-644; auth, "Virtual instruction: Teaching an on-line graduate seminar," Teaching of Psychol, 25, 2 (98): 146-148; coauth with L. D. Murdoch and S. M. Heiser, "Visual and haptic influences on memory: Age differences in recall," Experimental Aging Res, 24 (98): 257-272; coauth with P. A. Allen, K. E. Groth, J. L. Pickle, and D. J. Madden, "Adult age variance in sentence utilization," Aging, Neuropsychology, and Cognition (in press). **CONTACT ADDRESS** Dept Psychol, Montana State Univ, Bozeman, W Kagy Ave, Bozeman, MT 59717-0001. **EMAIL** upyls@montana.edu

STAGE, SARAH J.
PERSONAL Born 02/18/1944, Davenport, IA, m, 1984, 1 child **DISCIPLINE** WOMEN'S STUDIES **EDUCATION** Univ Iowa, BA, 66; Univ Mass, MA, 67; Yale Univ, M Phil, 71; PhD, 75. **CAREER** Asst prof, 73-78; Williams Coll; asst prof, 79-82; assoc prof, 87-94; Univ Cal, Riverside; prof, 94-, Ariz State Univ. **HONORS AND AWARDS** Phi Beta Kappa. **RESEARCH** Women's history in US 20th century. **SELECTED PUBLICATIONS** Auth, Female Complaints: Lydia Pinkham and the Business of Women's Medicine, WW Norton (NY), 79, pb 81; coauth, The American Promise, St Martin's (Boston: Bedford), 98; co-ed, Rethinking Home Economics: Women and the History of a Profession, Cornell Univ Press (Ithaca), 97; coauth, The American Promise, St Martin's (Boston: Bedford), 00. **CONTACT ADDRESS** Dept Woman's Studies, Arizona State Univ, PO Box 37100, Glendale, AZ 85306. **EMAIL** sarah.stage@aus.edu

STAKE, JAYNE E.
PERSONAL Born 09/14/1944, New York, NY, m, 1969, 2 children **DISCIPLINE** PSYCHOLOGY **EDUCATION** Ariz State Univ, PhD, 74. **CAREER** Asst prof to prof, Univ of Miss St Louis, 74-. **HONORS AND AWARDS** Fel, Am Psychol Assoc; Fel, AARP. **MEMBERSHIPS** AARP; Am Psychol Assoc. **RESEARCH** Psychology of women. **SELECTED PUBLICATIONS** Coauth, "Trait self-esteem, positive and negative events, and event-specific shifts in self-evaluation and affect", J of Res in Personality 29, (95): 223-241; coauth, "The relation of instrumentality and expressiveness to self-concept and adjustment: A social context perspective", J of Soc and Clinical Psychol 15, (96): 167-190; coauth, "Evaluating sources of ego-threatening feedback: Self-esteem and narcissism effects", J of Res in Personality 30, (96): 483-495; auth, "Integrating expressiveness and instrumentality in real-life settings: A new perspective on the benefits of androgyny", Sex Roles 37, (97): 541-564; coauth, "Feminist pedagogy in theory and practice: An empirical investigation", J of the Nat Women Studies Assoc, 10, (98): 97-79; coauth, "Sexual harassment attitudes questionnaire", Handbook of Sexuality-Related Measures, eds, CM Davis et al, (98): 299-300; coauth, "The current state of sexual ethics training in clinical psychology: Issues of quantity, quality, and effectiveness", Prof Psychol: Res and Practice 30, (99): 302-311; coauth, "Putting feminist pedagogy to the test: The experience of women's studies from student and teacher perspectives", Psychol of Women Quarterly, (forthcoming). **CONTACT ADDRESS** Dept Psychol, Univ of Missouri, St. Louis, 8001 Natural Bridge, Saint Louis, MO 63121. **EMAIL** jayne_stake@umsl.edu

STALLKAMP, RAY H., III
PERSONAL Born 05/01/1953, Toledo, OH, d, 2 children **DISCIPLINE** PSYCHOLOGY **EDUCATION** Terra Tech Col, 89; 90; Lourdes Col, PhD, 97. **CAREER** Pres, Pathways Career Development, 99-; Assoc Prof, Tex Community Col, 90-. **HONORS AND AWARDS** Summa cum laude; Magna cum laude. **RESEARCH** Disabilities. **CONTACT ADDRESS** Dept Bus/Soc Sci & Humanities, Terra State Comm Col, 2830 Napoleon Rd, Fremont, OH 43420.

STAMPS, RICHARD B.
PERSONAL Born 11/10/1942, Oakland, CA, m, 1966, 5 children **DISCIPLINE** ANTHROPOLOGY **EDUCATION** Brigham Young Unvi, BA, 68, MA, 70; Mich State Univ, PhD, 75. **CAREER** Instr to prof, Anthropol and Chinese studies, Oakland Univ, 74-. **HONORS AND AWARDS** O. U. Fac Link Awd; Univ Teaching Excellence Teacher of the Year, 86; Mich Asn of Governing Bds of Cols and Univs Distinguished Fac Awd, 87. **MEMBERSHIPS** Asn Asian Studies, Mich Conf on Archael, Am Anthropol Asn, Soc Applied Anthropol. **RESEARCH** Anthropology, Chinese studies, archaeology. **SELECTED PUBLICATIONS** Coauth with T. F. Chung and T. C. Huang, "Paleoecological Study of Taiwan," Taiwania, vol 18, no 2, 179-193 (73); auth, "An Archaeological Survey of the P'uli Basin, West Central Taiwan, Republic of China," in Reports of Archaeological Investigation in the Choshui and Tatu River Valleys of West Central Taiwan, K. C. Chang, ed, Academia Sinica, Taipei, Taiwan (77); auth, "Jar Burials from the Lobusbussan Site, Orchid Island (Botel Tobago)," Asian Perspectives, vol 23, no 2, 181-192 (80); coauth with Richard L. Zurel, "A Pilot Survey of the Archaeological Resources of Oakland County, Michigan," Mich Hist Div, Oakland Univ (80); auth, "Accountability in Archaeology-Who Owns the Bones?," reprinted in the J of Northern Luzon, vol XIV, no 1 2, 114-120 (July 83-Jan 84); coauth with Nancy Wright, "Thomas Edison's Boyhood Years: A Puzzle," Mich Hist, vol 70, no 3, 36-43 (May/June 86); coauth with Bruce Hawkins, et al, Report of the Preliminary Excavations at Fort Gratiot 1814-1876 in Port Huron, Michigan, Oakland Univ Odyssey Monograph Series #2 (89); coauth with Bruce Hawkins, Nancy Wright, et el, Search for the House in the Grove, Port Huron, MI: Cultural Dynamics (94). **CONTACT ADDRESS** Dept Anthropol & Sociol, Oakland Univ, Rochester, MI 48309. **EMAIL** stamps@oakland.edu

STANLEY, JAY
PERSONAL Born 12/14/1940, Charleston, WV, m, 1978, 1 child **DISCIPLINE** SOCIOLOGY, ANTHROPOLOGY **EDUCATION** Univ Tenn, BS, 62; Univ Tenn, MA, 63; Univ Md, PhD, 70. **CAREER** Instr, Univ Md, 66-70; Asst Prof, Mason Univ, 70-71; From Assoc Prof to Prof, Towson Univ, 71-. **HONORS AND AWARDS** Lit Hall of Fame, Lincoln Mem Univ, 88; Charles H Coates Commemorative Awd, Univ Md; Prof of the Year, Towson Univ, 89-90; Athletic Hall of Fame, Lincoln Mem Univ, 94; Phi Kappa Phi; Alpha Kappa Delta; Omicron Delta Kappa; Sigma Xi; Order of Omega; Who's Who in Am; Who's Who in Am Educ. **MEMBERSHIPS** Inter-Univ Seminar on Armed Forces and Soc. **SELECTED PUBLICATIONS** Co-ed, Challenges in Military Health Care: Perspectives on Health Status and the Provision of Care, Rutgers UP (New Brunswick, NJ), 93; auth, "Harold Lasswell and the Idea of the Garrison State," Soc, vol 33, no 6 (96); auth, "An Invitation to Revisit Harold D Lasswell's Garrison State," in Essays on the Garrison St (New Brunswick, NJ: Rutgers UP, 97; auth, Essays on the Garrison State, Rutgers UP (New Brunswick, NJ), 97; auth, "Societal Influences and Military Medicine," in Textbook of Military Med, Borden Inst Pr, forthcoming. **CONTACT ADDRESS** Dept Sociol & Anthrop, Towson State Univ, 8000 York Rd, Baltimore, MD 21252-0001. **EMAIL** stanley@towson.edu

STANLEY, JULIAN CECIL
PERSONAL Born 07/09/1918, Macon, GA, m, 1980, 1 child **DISCIPLINE** PSYCHOLOGY **EDUCATION** Ga So Univ, BS, 37; Harvard Univ, EdM, 1946; EdD, 50. **CAREER** Teacher, Fulton and West Fulton high schs, Atlanta, 37-42; instr, Newton Jr Col, 46-48; instr, Harvard Univ, 48-49; assoc prof, George Peabody Teacher's Col, 49-53; Prof, Univ of Wisconsin (Madison); 53-67; prof, Johns Hopkins Univ, 67- . **HONORS AND AWARDS** Phi Beta Kappa; Sigma Xi; Phi Delta Kappa; Social Sci Res Coun Inst Math for Soc Sci, Univ Mich, 55; Postdoctoral fel, Univ Chicago, 55-56; Fulbright res scholar, Univ Louvain, Belgium, 58-59; Center for Advanced Study in the Behavioral Sciences, 65-67; Fulbright lectr, New Zealand and Autralia, 74. **MEMBERSHIPS** AAAS; Am Statis Asoc; Am Psychol Soc; Am Educ Res Asoc; Nat Asoc for Gifted Children; AAUP; Psychometric Soc; Tenn Psychol Asoc. **RESEARCH** Intellectually Talented Youth. **SELECTED PUBLICATIONS** Co-ed with W.C. George and C.H. Solano, The Gifted and the Creative: A Fifty-Year Perspective, 77; ed, Educational Programs and Intellectual Prodigies, 78; co-ed with W.C. George and S.J. Cohn, Educating the Gifted: Acceleration and Enrichment, 79; co-ed with C.P. Benbow, Academic Precocity; Aspects of Its Develoment, 83; co-auth with K.D. and B. Hopkins, Educational and Psychological Measurement and Evaluation, 90. **CONTACT ADDRESS** Dept. of Psychology, Johns Hopkins Univ, Baltimore, 2701 N Charles St., Baltimore, MD 21218.

STANLEY, PAULA H.
PERSONAL Born 05/22/1952, Whiteville, NC, s **DISCIPLINE** EDUCATION **EDUCATION** Appalachian State Univ, BA, 74; M Ed, 75; Univ NC Greensboro, PhD, 91. **CAREER** Instr, Surrey Community Col, 75-87; asst to assoc prof, Radford Univ, 91-. **HONORS AND AWARDS** Chi Sigma Iota Outstanding Doctoral Student Awd; Outstanding Service Awd, Radford Col. **MEMBERSHIPS** Am Counseling Assoc; Am Educ Res Assoc; Internal Alliance for Invitation. **RESEARCH** Self-concept, self-talk, group therapy, clinical supervision. **SELECTED PUBLICATIONS** Corev, of "A review of Resilient adults: Overcoming a cruel past" by Gina O'Connell Higgins, Jour for the Prof Counselor 11, (96):93-96; coauth, "Depression or endocrine disorder?: What counselors need to know about hypothyroidism" Jour of Mental Health counseling 19 (97):268-276; coauth, "The inviting school treasury: 1001 ways to invite school success, (NY: Scholastic), 94; coauth, "One World View", The Values Realization Jour 19, (97):20-21; coauth, "The tie that binds: Understanding intergenerational conflict within a moral development framework", The Family Jour: Counseling and therapy for Couples and Families 6, (98):175-181; coauth, "Mentors of aging", The Values Realization Jour II (98):32-33; coauth, "Freak the Mighty: resilience and valiance in a literary friendship", in Using Literature to Help Troubled Teenagers Cope with Health Issues (CT: Greenwood, 00); coauth, "The self in psychotherapy", in Handbook of res and practice in humanistic psychotherapies, ed D. Cain (forthcoming); coauth, "Internal dialogue in theory and practice: The whispering self", in Self concept theory, res and practice: Int Perspectives, (forthcoming). **CONTACT ADDRESS** Dept Counselor Educ, Radford Univ, 801 Norwood St, Radford, VA 24142.

STANNY, CLAUDIA J.
PERSONAL Born 08/09/1950, Detroit, MI, m, 1970, 1 child **DISCIPLINE** PSYCHOLOGY **EDUCATION** Fla State Univ, BA, 76; MS, 78; PhD, 81. **CAREER** Asst Prof, Coe Col, 81-82; Lectr/Honorary Fel, Univ Wis Madison, 82-84; from Adj and Vis Fac to Asst Prof, Univ of W Fla, 85-. **HONORS AND AWARDS** BA Cum Laude,Phi Kappa Phi, Psi Chi. **MEMBERSHIPS** Am Psychol Asn, Psychronomic Soc, Soc for Appl Res in Memory and Cognition, Soc for Computers in Psychology, Midwestern Psychol Asn, Southwestern Psychol Asn, Southern Works in Memory. **RESEARCH** Everytime memory, applied memory (everyday memory). **SELECTED PUBLICATIONS** Coauth, "Short-term retention of pictorial stimuli as assessed by a probe recognition technique," J of Exp Psychology: Human Learning and Memory 4 (78): 55-565; coauth, "Directed attention and the recognition of pictures," Bull of the Psychonomic Soc 15 (80): 410-412; coauth, "The role of detail information in the recognition of complex pictorial stimuli," J of Gen Psychology 111 (84): 185-199; coauth, "Effects of processing tasks on the recognition of pictures," Bull of the Psychonomic Soc 23 (85): 116-118; coauth, "Clinical judgements regarding involuntary commitment: A comparison of mental health professions," J of Psychol Practice 5 (99): 32-38; coauth, "Effects of stress induced by a simulated shooting on the recall of police and citizen witness, " Am J of Psychology (in press). **CONTACT ADDRESS** Dept Psychology, Univ of West Florida, 11000 University Pkwy, Pensacola, FL 31514. **EMAIL** cstanny@uwf.edu

STANSBURY, JAMES P.
PERSONAL Born 05/26/1953, Los Angeles, CA, m, 1997, 1 child **DISCIPLINE** ANTHROPOLOGY **EDUCATION** Univ NM, BA, 75; MA, 86; Univ Ky, PhD, 96. **CAREER** Asst Prof, Univ Fla. **MEMBERSHIPS** AAA; SMA; CAN; AES; SFAA. **RESEARCH** Medical Anthropology; Latin America. **CONTACT ADDRESS** Dept Anthropol, Univ of Florida, PO Box 117305, Gainesville, FL 32611. **EMAIL** jstansbu@ufl.edu

STAPLES, ROBERT EUGENE
PERSONAL Born 06/28/1942, Roanoke, VA, d **DISCIPLINE** SOCIOLOGY **EDUCATION** LA Valley Coll, AA, 60; Calif State Univ-Northridge, AB, 63; San Jose State Univ, MA, 65; Univ Minn, PhD, 70. **CAREER** PROF, SOCIOL, UNIV CALIF-SAN FRAN, 72-. **MEMBERSHIPS** Nat Coun Family Relations; Asn Black Nurs Fac **RESEARCH** Family, Human sexuality. **CONTACT ADDRESS** Dept Sociol, Univ of California, San Francisco, Box 0612, San Francisco, CA 94143.

STAPLES, S. L.
PERSONAL Born 12/21/1948, Newburgh, NY, m, 1984, 2 children **DISCIPLINE** SOCIAL, BEHAVIORAL SCIENCES **EDUCATION** Drew Univ, BA, 70; Wash State Univ, PhD. **CAREER** Coordr, Overlook Mental Health, 77-80; Staff Psychol, Ulster Co Mental Health, 80-83; Adj Instr, Marist Col, 98-. **HONORS AND AWARDS** Salutatorian, FDR High School, 66; Cum Laudes, Drew Univ, 70 **MEMBERSHIPS** Am Psychol Asn, Eastern Psychol Asn. **RESEARCH** Environmental noise, impact of technology on librarian role definition. **SELECTED PUBLICATIONS** Auth, "Human Response to Environmental Noise: Psychological Research and Public Policy," Am Psychologist (96): 143-150; Auth, "Public Policy and Environmental Noise: Modeling Exposure or Understanding Effects," Am J of Public Health, 87 (97): 2063-2067; Auth, "Comments on: Effects of Aircraft Overflights on Wilderness Recreationists," J of the Acoustical Soc of Am, 104 (98): 1726-1728; Auth, Disturbance from Noise near a Developing Airport: Perceived Risk or General Annoyance," Environment and Behavior, 31 (99): 692-710; Moving Down the Information Highway: Librarian Decision-Making about Electronic Information Services" (forthcoming). **CONTACT ADDRESS** Dept of Soc and Behav Sci, Marist Col, 290 North Rd, Poughkeepsie, NY 12601.

STAROSTA, WILLIAM J.
PERSONAL Born 05/23/1946, Oconomowoc, WI, m, 1967, 1 child **DISCIPLINE** INTERCULTURAL COMMUNICATION **EDUCATION** Indiana Univ, AM, 70, PhD, 73. **CAREER** Univ of Va, asst prof, 72-78; Howard Univ, grad prof, 78-. **HONORS AND AWARDS** Fulbright diss. fel; Am Inst of Indian Studies fel; Wis-Berkeley Year-in-India scholar; held professional office in regional and national socs. **MEMBERSHIPS** Nat Commun Asn; Eastern Commun Asn; World Commun Asn; Intl. Commun Asn. **RESEARCH** Ethnic conflict; Third Culture; Multiculturalism; Interethnic and intercultural communication; Culture and rhetoric. **SELECTED PUBLICATIONS** Coauth, Foundations of Intercultural Communication; ed, The Howard Jour of Communs; co-ed, comm in Global Society **CONTACT ADDRESS** Dept of Human Communication Studies, Howard Univ, 3015 Rosemoor Ln., Fairfax, VA 22031. **EMAIL** wstarosta@howard.edu

STARR, PAUL D.
PERSONAL Born 08/02/1942, Bismarck, ND, m, 1972, 2 children **DISCIPLINE** SOCIOLOGY **EDUCATION** Univ Pac, BA, 65; Univ Calif, MA, 70; Univ Calif, PhD, 72. **CAREER** Lect, Univ Calif, 71-72; Asst Prof, Am Univ Beirut, 72-75; From Asst Prof to Assoc Prof, Auburn Univ, 75-84; Vis Assoc Prof, Am Univ Cairo, 82-84; Prof, Auburn Univ, 85-. **HONORS AND AWARDS** Phi Beta Kappa; Alpha Kappa Delta; Miss-Ala Sea Grant, 81-82; Res Grant, Am Univ Cairo, 83; Vis Fel, Univ Sussex, 83; Who's Who in the Southwest, 84; Teaching Awd, Am Univ Cairo, 84; Vis Scholar, Oxford Univ, 94; Who's Who in Am, 87, 94; Pew Fac Fel, Harvard Univ, 94-95; Instructional Tech Grant, Auburn Univ, 99; Breeden Fel for Teaching Innovation, 96-98, 99-00. **MEMBERSHIPS** Am Assoc of Univ Profs, Am Soc Assoc, Assoc for Third World Studies, Int Soc Assoc. **RESEARCH** Comparative sociology, sociological social psychology. **SELECTED PUBLICATIONS** Auth, "Historical Time: Modern Industrial Society in Perspective," in Tech for Teaching Soc Concepts (Wash, DC: Am Soc Assoc, 95); auth, "Labeling Theory: Stereotyping," in Tech for Teaching Soc Concepts (Wash, DC: Am Soc Assoc, 95); auth, "The Social Sciences: Special Visions," in Soc, Cult and the Environ (NY: Am Heritage Inc, 96-97, 99); auth, "Status and Role," in Soc, Cult and the Environ (NY: Am Heritage Inc, 96-97, 99). **CONTACT ADDRESS** Dept Sociol, Auburn Univ, Auburn, AL 36849. **EMAIL** starrpd@auburn.edu

STAUDER, JACK
PERSONAL Born 03/02/1939, Pueblo, CO, d, 1963, 2 children **DISCIPLINE** ANTHROPOLOGY **EDUCATION** Harvard Col, BA, 62; Cambridge Univ, PhD, 68. **CAREER** Lect, Harvard Univ, 68-71; asst prof, Northeastern Univ, 71-73; prof, Univ Mass, Dartmouth, 73-. **MEMBERSHIPS** Am Anthopol Asn. **RESEARCH** Cultural ecology, family, ranching and environmental issues, morality and values. **SELECTED PUBLICATIONS** Auth, The Majangir: Cultural Ecology of a Southwest Ethiopian People. **CONTACT ADDRESS** Univ of Massachusetts, Dartmouth, 285 Old Westport Rd, North Dartmouth, MA 02747. **EMAIL** jstauder@umassd.edu

STEADMAN, LYLE B.
PERSONAL Born 09/06/1934, Pasadena, CA, d, 4 children **DISCIPLINE** ANTHROPOLOGY **EDUCATION** Occidental Col, BA, 56; UCLA, MA, 64; Australian Nat Univ, PhD, 71. **CAREER** Asst prof, Ariz State Univ, 71-. **HONORS AND AWARDS** UCLA Fel; Australian Nat Univ Fel. **MEMBERSHIPS** Human Behav and Evolution Soc. **RESEARCH** Evolution and Human Behavior, particularly religious and kinship behavior. **SELECTED PUBLICATIONS** Co-auth, "Visiting Dead Ancestors: Shamans as Interpreters of Religious Traditions," Zygon, (94): 173-189; co-auth, "The Human Breast and the Ancestral Reproductive Cycle: A Preliminary Inquiry into Breast Cancer Etiology using Modern Darwinian Theory," Human Nature, (95): 197-220; co-auth, "Religion as an Identifiable Traditional Behavior Subject to Natural Selection," J of Soc and Evolutionary Systems, (95): 149-164; co-auth, "The Universality of Ancestor Worship," Ethnology, (96): 63-76; coauth, "Myths as Instructions from Ancestors: The Example of Oedipus," Zygon, (97): 341-350; co-auth, "Human Kinship as a Descendant-Leaving Strategy: A Solution to an Evolutionary Puzzle," J of Soc and Evolutionary Systems, (97): 39-51. **CONTACT ADDRESS** Dept of Anthropol, Arizona State Univ, MC 2402, Tempe, AZ 85287.

STEELE, CLAUDE MASON
PERSONAL Born 01/01/1946, Chicago, IL, m **DISCIPLINE** PSYCHOLOGY **EDUCATION** Hiram College, BA, 1967; Ohio State University, MA, 1969, PhD, 1971. **CAREER** University of Utah, assistant professor, 71-73; University of Washington, assistant professor, 73-85; prof, 85-87; prof, Univ of Mich, 87-91; prof, Stanford Univ, 91-; dept chair, 97-. **HONORS AND AWARDS** Dissertation Year Fel, 70-71; Fel, Ctr for Advanced Study in the Behavioral Sciences, 94-95; Cattell Fac Fel, 94-95; Deans's Teaching Awd, Stanford Univ, 95; Elected to The Am Acad of Arts and Sciences, 96; Lucie Stern Prof in the Soc Sciences, Stanford Univ, 97; winner of the Gordon Allport Prize in Soc Psychology, 97; Elected to The National Acad of Educ, 98. **MEMBERSHIPS** Am Psychological Asn, Am Psychological Soc, Soc of Experimental Soc Psychology, Soc of Personality and Soc Psychology. **RESEARCH** Self-evaluative processing, The role of self-evaluation and identification in the school achievement of black Americans and women in natural sciences, role of alcohol and drug use in self-regulation processes and social behavior, compliance behavior and its mediation. **SELECTED PUBLICATIONS** Auth, A threat in the air: How stereotypes shape the intellectual identities and performance of women and African Americans, American Psychologist 52 (97): 613-629; coauth, The effects of stereotype threat on the standardized test performance of college students, In E. Aronson, Readings about the social animal, 8th ed, New York, Freeman, 98; auth, Stereotyping and its threat are real, American Psychological 53 (98): 680-681; auth, Social Stigma, The handbook of social psychology, McGraw Hill, 98; auth, Stereotype threat and the test performance of academically successful African Americans, Black-White test score gap, Brookings Institution Pr, 98; auth, When white men can't fo math: Necessary and sufficient factors in stereotype threat, Jouranl of Experimental Social Psychology 35 (99): 29-46; auth, Stereotype threat and women's math performance, Journal of experimental Social Psychology 35 (99): 4-28; auth, The mentor's dilemma: Providing critical feedback across the racial divide, Personality and Social Bulletin 25 (99): 1302-1318; auth, The psychological predicament of women on welfare. Cultural divides: Understanding and overcoming group conflict, Russell Sage Foundation, New York, 99; auth, Thin ice: " Stereotype threat" and black college students, The Atlantic Monthly 284 (2) (99): 44-47, 50-54, **CONTACT ADDRESS** Psychology, Stanford Univ, Building 420, Stanford, CA 94305. **EMAIL** steele@psych.stanford.edu

STEFFEN, TOM
PERSONAL Born 09/05/1947, Goshen, IN, m, 1967, 3 children **DISCIPLINE** INTERCULTURAL STUDIES **EDUCATION** Dallas Bible Col, BS, 84; Biola Univ, MA, 87; DMiss, 90. **CAREER** Assoc prof, Biola Univ, 91-. **HONORS AND AWARDS** Award of Excellence in Scholar, Biola Univ, 99; Listed in Who's Who Among America's Teachers, 00. **MEMBERSHIPS** Evangelical Missiological Soc. **RESEARCH** Narrative, Church Development. **SELECTED PUBLICATIONS** Auth, Passing the Baton: Church Planting that Empowers, Ctr for Orgn & Ministry Development (La Habra, CA), 93 & 97; auth, Reconnecting God's Story to Ministry: Crosscultural Storytelling at Home and Abroad, Ctr for Orgn & Ministry Development (La Habra, CA), 96; auth, "Global Implications of Western Education on the Antipolo/Amduntug Ifugao," Int J of Frontier Missions 15.2 (98): 97-105; auth, "Flawed Evangelism and Church Planting," Evangelical Missions Quart 34.4 (98): 428-435; auth, Business as Usual in the Missions Enterprise?, Ctr for Orgn & Ministry Development (La Habra, CA), 99. **CONTACT ADDRESS** Sch of Intercultural Studies, Biola Univ, 13800 Biola Ave, La Miranda, CA 90639-0002.

STEIGER, THOMAS L.
DISCIPLINE SOCIOLOGY **EDUCATION** Univ FL, BA, 80; Virginia Tech, MS, 82; Univ IL, Urbana, PhD, 88. **CAREER** Asst, assoc, Ind State Univ, 87-93; act assoc dean, Col AS, ISU, 93-95; assoc prof, Ind State Univ, 95-; dept dir, Ind State Univ, 99-. **MEMBERSHIPS** ASA; SSSP; MSS; NCSA. **RESEARCH** Work; gender; political economy. **SELECTED PUBLICATIONS** Co-ed, Rethinking the Labor Process, SUNY (99); coauth, "Gender and Employment in the Services Sector, Social Problems 42 (95): 91-123; coauth, "Affirmative Action and the "Level Playing Field": Comparing Perceptions of Own and Majority Job Advancement Opportunities," The Prison J (970: 313-334; auth, "Forms of the Labor Process and Labor's Share of Value," in Rethinking the Labor Process, co-ed. Mark Wardell, Peter Meiksins (SUNY Press, 99); coauth, "Creating Diversity in Social Stratification Courses: The 'Virtual Salon'," Critical Sociology (in press). **CONTACT ADDRESS** Dept Sociology, Indiana State Univ, 210 N 7th St, Terre Haute, IN 47809-0002. **EMAIL** soteig@scifac.indstate.edu

STEIL, JANICE M.
PERSONAL Born 03/01/1941, Fall River, MA, m, 1970, 2 children **DISCIPLINE** PSYCHOLOGY **EDUCATION** Univ Mass, BA, 62; Boston Univ, EdM, 65; Columbia Univ, PhD, 79. **CAREER** Project coord, Nat Comn on Resources for Youth, 71-73; res sci, NYork State Division of Substance Abuse, 78-79; asst prof to prof, Adelphi Univ, 79-. **HONORS AND AWARDS** Adelphi Univ Fac Res Grant, 80; Adelphi Fac Merit Awd for Outstanding Scholar, 86 & 90; Adelphi Univ Fac Res Grant, 87, Provosts Awd, Adelphi Univ. **MEMBERSHIPS** Am Psychol Asn, Am Psychol Soc, Int Soc for the Study of Personal Relationships, Int Network on Personal Relationships, Scholar in Residence Catalyst. **SELECTED PUBLICATIONS** Auth, "Maritial equality: It's relationship to the well-being of husbands and wives," The Sage Series on Close Rela-

tionships, Sage, 97; coauth, "Maritial equality: What does it mean?" J of Family Issues 3 (98): 227-244; auth, "Change and resistance to change in contemporary marriage," Close Relationships: A Sourcebook, 00; auth, "'His' and 'Her' Marriage," The Encyclopedia of Gender, Plenum Press, forthcoming; auth, "The Family at the Millenium," Psychol of Women Quart (forthcoming). **CONTACT ADDRESS** Dept Psychol, Adelphi Univ, 1 S Ave, Garden City, NY 11530.

STEIN, KAREN F.
PERSONAL Born 07/01/1941, Brooklyn, NY, d, 2 children **DISCIPLINE** ENGLISH, WOMEN'S STUDIES **EDUCATION** Brooklyn Col, BA, 62; Pa State Univ, MA, 66; Univ Conn, PhD, 82. **CAREER** Prof of English and Women's Studies, Univ of Rhode Island, 68-. **HONORS AND AWARDS** Graduated cum laude, Brooklyn Col, 62; Phi Beta Kappa; Woman of the Year, Asn of Academic and Prof Women, URI, 93; Can Govt Fac Enrichment Grant, 94; URI Found Summer Res Grant, 97; Champlin Found Grant; "Women, Science and Engineering Curricular Project," Am Asn of Cols and Univs, Second Tier Team Member; Development of "Women and the Natural Sciences," participant in FIPSE grant to bridge the humanities and science. **MEMBERSHIPS** AAUP, PBK, Margaret Atwood Soc, Toni Morrison Soc. **RESEARCH** Margaret Atwood, the Gothic, contemporary American poetry. **SELECTED PUBLICATIONS** Auth, "Speaking in Tongues: Margaret Laurence's A Jest of God as Gothic narrative," Studies in Can Lit, 20.2 (winter 95): 74-95; auth, "The Handmaid's Tale: Margaret Atwood's Modest Proposal," Can Lit, 148 (spring 96): 57-73; auth, Margaret Atwood Revisited, Twayne (99); auth, "Films of the Frankenstein Myth: Children of an Angry God," for Gary Harmon, ed, Film and Gender: Myth, Power and Change (with W. Brownell), Popular Press (forthcoming). **CONTACT ADDRESS** Dept English, Univ of Rhode Island, 60 Upper Col Rd, Kingston, RI 02881-2000. **EMAIL** karen_s@uri.edu

STEINMILLER, GEORGINE
PERSONAL Born 08/16/1948, IL, m, 2 children **DISCIPLINE** SPECIAL EDUCATION **EDUCATION** Cart Col, BA, 70; N Ill Univ, MS, 72; Univ Iowa, PhD, 85. **CAREER** Instr, Kirkwood CC, 82-84; asst prof, Arkansas Col, 84-87; prof, Henderson State Univ, 87-. **HONORS AND AWARDS** Who's Who AM Edu, Am Coll Univ's; Rockefeller Gnt; Fac Dev Gnt; Fac Res Gnt; Presch Spec Ed Gnt; YOUS Gnt; Margin Excell Gnt. **MEMBERSHIPS** CEC; ATE; NRERC; ACRSE; Alpha Psi Omega. **SELECTED PUBLICATIONS** Coauth, The Child With a Learning Disability of ADHD: A Manual for Nurses, NASN, 97; auth, ACRES, San Antonio, TX, 97; coauth, The Politics of Higher Education: Perspectives For Minorities in the 21st Century, Res Edu (93); coauth, "Youth Opportunities Unlimited: The Results of a Three Year Study," Am Coun Rur Spec Edu (93); coauth, "Alliance In Humanities," Am Coun Rur Spec Edu (93); coauth, "Academic Alliances: You Can Do It, Too," Am Coun Rur Edu (94); coauth, Creating a climate for change: Issues and challenges for the 21st Century, South Fut Proceed (94); auth, Review of Mentoring Student Teachers, Teach Edu Spec Edu 9 (96): 84-85. **CONTACT ADDRESS** Dept Special Education, Henderson State Univ, PO Box 7862, Arkadelphia, AR 71999-0001.

STELTENKAMP, MICHAEL F.
PERSONAL Born 11/14/1947, Detroit, MI, s **DISCIPLINE** PHILOSOPHY, ANTHROPOLOGY **EDUCATION** Univ Detroit, BA, 70; Ind Univ, MA, 71; Loyola Univ Chicago, MDiv; Mich State Univ, PhD. **CAREER** Chair of Soc Sci Dept, Red Cloud Indian Sch, Pine Ridge SD, 71-74; Adj Prof, Saginaw Valley State Univ, Mich, 86-90; Mus Curator, Prof, Bay Mills Community Col, May Mills Reservation, Brimley, Mich; Assoc Prof, Wheeling Jesuit Univ, WVa. **HONORS AND AWARDS** Alpha Sigma Nu Nat Book Awd, 94. **MEMBERSHIPS** Soc of Jesus (Jesuits) of Cath Church, Am Anthrop Asn. **RESEARCH** Native North America, World Religions, Religious Movements Today. **SELECTED PUBLICATIONS** Auth, The Sacred Vision: Native-American Religion and Its Practice Today, Paulist Press, 83; auth, Black Elk: Holy Man of the Oglala, Univ of Okla Press, 93. **CONTACT ADDRESS** Dept Relig and Philos, Wheeling Jesuit Univ, 316 Washington Ave, Wheeling, WV 26003-6243. **EMAIL** mfs@wju.edu

STENNIS-WILLIAMS, SHIRLEY
DISCIPLINE EDUCATION **EDUCATION** Jackson State Univ, BS, 58; Peabody Coll of Vanderbilt Univ, MA, 64, EdD, 72; Harvard Management Development Program, 90. **CAREER** Jackson State Lab School, teacher, 58-59; Chicago Public Schools, teacher 59-64; Peabody Coll of Vanderbilt Univ, teaching assistant 64-66; Univ of WI Oshkosh, asst prof, 66-72, coord of field experience, 75-83, assoc prof, 72-83, prof, 82-85, asst vice chancellor, 85-91; Senior System Academic Planner, Dean of Educ, 92-; dean ed, Southeast Missouri State Univ. **HONORS AND AWARDS** Natl Defense Education Act Doctoral Fellowship 1963-66. First African-American asst prof, assoc prof and coordinator of field experience at the Univ of Wisconsin, Oshkosh. **MEMBERSHIPS** Midwest Human Relations Asn, 82-83; Am Asn for Higher Educ, Black Caucus. **CONTACT ADDRESS** Col of Education, Southeast Missouri State Univ, One Univ Plaza, MS 5500, Cape Girardeau, MO 63701. **EMAIL** sstenniswilliams@semovm.semo.edu

STEPAN-NORRIS, JUDITH
PERSONAL Born 07/03/1957, Los Angeles, CA, m, 1979, 3 children **DISCIPLINE** SOCIOLOGY **EDUCATION** Univ Calif, Los Angeles, BA, 79; MA, 81; PhD, 88. **CAREER** Asst prof to assoc prof and chair, Univ of Calif Irvine, 90-. **HONORS AND AWARDS** Distinguished Scholar Awd, Am Sociol Assoc, 92, 96; Distinguished Asst Prof Awd for Res, UCI, 97; Inaugural labor Studies Awd, 97. **MEMBERSHIPS** ASA; SSSP. **RESEARCH** Labor and labor Movements, Political Sociology. **SELECTED PUBLICATIONS** Coauth, "Union Democracy, Radical Leadership, and the Hegemony of Capital, Am Sociol Rev 60, (96): 829-50; coauth, "Insurgency, Radicalism, and Democracy in America's Unions", Soc Forces 75, (96): 1-32; coauth, Talking Union, Univ of IL Pr, (Urbana and Chicago), 96; auth, "The Integration of Workplace and Community Relations at the Ford Rouge Plant, 1930s - 1940s", Polit Power and Soc Theory 11, (97): 3-44; auth, "The Making of Union Democracy", Soc Forces 76 (97): 475-510; auth, "Strangers to Their Own Class?", Sòciol Inquiry 68, (98): 329-353; coauth, Left Out!, Cambridge Univ Pr, (forthcoming). **CONTACT ADDRESS** Dept Sociol, Univ of California, Irvine, 3151 Social Science Plaza, Irvine, CA 92697-0001.

STEPHANIDES, MARIOS
DISCIPLINE SOCIOLOGY **EDUCATION** Wayne State Univ, BA, MA, PhD. **CAREER** Prof, Spalding Univ, 82-. **HONORS AND AWARDS** Nominated for Student Outstanding Teacher Awd, 93. **MEMBERSHIPS** KY Sociol Asn; Mod Greek Studies Asn; S Sociol Asn. **SELECTED PUBLICATIONS** Auth, "The Greek Community in Louisville," The Filson Quarterly, 81; auth, "Are We To Forget the Armenian Holocaust," Courier-Journal, 86; auth, "Correlates of Life Satisfaction Among Older Greek American and Aging Widows Living in a Retirement Home," The Gerontologist, (87): 74; auth, "Older Greek Americans: A Case Study of a Retirement Home in St. Louis," Modern Greek Studies Yearbook, (89): 227-240; auth, The Greeks in Detroit: Authoritatianism, R & E Research Pub, 75; auth The History of the Greeks in Kentucky, Mellen Press, 00. **CONTACT ADDRESS** Dept Humanities & Soc Sci, Spalding Univ, 851 S 4th St, Louisville, KY 40203. **EMAIL** Zoumberos@aol.com

STEPHENS, WILLIAM RICHARD
PERSONAL Born 01/02/1932, Ashburn, MO, m, 1952, 3 children **DISCIPLINE** AMERICAN SOCIAL & EDUCATIONAL HISTORY **EDUCATION** Greenville Col, BS, 53; Univ Mo, Columbia, MEd, 57; Wash Univ, EdD, 64. **CAREER** Assoc prof, Greenville col, 57-61; assoc prof, Ind State Univ, 64-70; prof, Ind Univ, Bloomington, 70-71; vpres & dean fac, 71-77, pres, 77-93, Greenville Col; retired as Pres Emeritus, 93; dir of Pres Fel Inst, 95-; senior advisor, Council for Christian Colleges and Univ. **HONORS AND AWARDS** Awd of Merit, Nat Voc Guid Assn, 73; Distinguished Alumnus Awd, Greenville Col, 81. **MEMBERSHIPS** Hist Educ Soc; Philos Educ Soc. **RESEARCH** Social and intellectual sources of American educational theory and systems, 1885-1920; progressive and reform values in American public education, 1890-1920. **SELECTED PUBLICATIONS** Coauth, Jesse Hewlon, Educ Forum, 11/67; Schools and wars, Teachers Col J, 5/67; The junior high school, a product of reform values, 1890-1920, 11/67, Teachers Col J; Social Reform and the Origins of Vocational Guidance, 1890-1925, Nat Voc Guid Assn, 70; coauth, Education in American Life, Houghton, 71; auth, Careers in Criminal Justice, 99. **CONTACT ADDRESS** Greenville Col, 321 8th St NE, Washington, DC 20002. **EMAIL** wstephen@greenville.edu

STERN, FRANCES MERITT
PERSONAL m **DISCIPLINE** PSYCHOLOGY **EDUCATION** Newark State Col, BA, 60, MA, 62; New York Univ, PhD, 72. **CAREER** Assoc Prof, Dept of Psychology, Kean Col of New Jersey, 69-; Licensed Practicing Psychologist, 80-; Dir, Inst for Behavioral Awareness, 73-. **HONORS AND AWARDS** Founder's Day Awd, NYU; Who's Who of Am Women; Who's Who in The East; temple univ school of medicine, dept of psychiatry, 76-80. **MEMBERSHIPS** APA; Asn for the Advancement of Behavior Therapy; NJ Psychol Asn; Am Soc for Training and Development. **RESEARCH** Test anxiety; stress reduction; behavioral modification. **SELECTED PUBLICATIONS** Coauth, Wash Away Stress-and Find the Gold in Gritty Situations, Veterinary Economics, 96; How Do You Handle a Stress Carrier?, Managing Stress in a Jewish Family, 94; Need for Achievement: Jewish love of Learning or Reflection of a Test-Crazed Society?, Jewish Family, 94; Taking the Angst Out of Test Anxiety, NJEA Rev, 94 Mind Trips to Help You Lose Weight, Playboy Press, 76; Stressless Selling, Prentice-Hall, 81; Stressless Selling-Revised Edition, Amacom, 90; Turning Visions Into Reality & Mind Over Body, Mind Over Matter, Time-Life Books, 88; auth, How to Live With Psychology and Maybe Learn to Like It, I.I.I., 72. **CONTACT ADDRESS** Inst for Behavioral Awareness, 810 Springfield Ave, Springfield, NJ 07081. **EMAIL** flashtrst@aol.com

STERNBERG, ROBERT
PERSONAL Born 12/08/1949, Newark, NJ, m, 2 children **DISCIPLINE** PSYCHOLOGY **EDUCATION** Yale, BA, 72; Stanford Univ, PhD, 75. **CAREER** Prof, Yale Univ. **HONORS AND AWARDS** Distinguished Sci Awd for an Early Contrib to Psychology, Am Psychol Asn; Boyd R. McCandless Young Sci Awd, Am Psychol Asn; Palmer O. Johnson Awd; Sylvia Scribner Awd; Res Rev Awd; Outstanding Book Awd, Am Educ Res Asn; Cattell Awd, Soc of Multivariate Exp Psychology; Distinguished Contrib Awd, Nat Asn for Gifted C; James McKeen Cattell Awd, Am Pyshcol Soc; Distinguished Lifetime Contrib to Psychology Awd, Conn Psychol Asn; Int Awd, Asn of Portuguese Psychologists; Guggenheim Fel; Nat Sci Found Grad Fel; Phi Betta Kappa. **MEMBERSHIPS** Am Psychol Asn, Am Acad of Arts and Sci, Am Asn for Advan of Sci, Am Psychol Soc. **RESEARCH** Trairchic Theory of Intelligence, Triangular Theory of Love, Theory of Mental Self-Government, Investment Theory of Creativity. **SELECTED PUBLICATIONS** Auth, Beyond IQ; auth, Cupid's Arrow; auth, Metaphors of Mind; coauth, Defying the Crowd; auth, Thinking Styles; auth, Successful Intelligence; auth, Love is a story; auth, In Search of the Human Mind; auth, Pathways to Psychology; auth, Cognitive Psychology. **CONTACT ADDRESS** Dept Psychology, Yale Univ, PO Box 208205, New Heaven, CT 06520.

STEVENS, JOYCE W.
PERSONAL Born 03/15/1936, St Louis, MO, d, 2 children **DISCIPLINE** SOCIAL WORK **EDUCATION** Loyola Univ, BS, 60; MSW, 64; DSW, 93. **CAREER** Counselor, Univ Ill, 73-74; Fac Advisor, Chicago State Univ, 74-75; Instr, Univ Chicago, 79-82; Coordinator and Psychosocial Therapist, Michael Reese Hospital, 74-91; Clinical Consultant, St. Philip Neri Parish, 89-91; Adj Instr, Loyola Univ, 90-92; Asst Prof, Boston Univ, 93-; Coordinator Dual Degree Program, Boston Univ, 97-. **HONORS AND AWARDS** Negro Stud Undergrad Study, 54; Fel, Cook County Dept Public Aid, 62-64; NIMH Minority Clinical Fel, 87-89; Ill Consortium for Educ Opportunity Fel, 90-93; Bertha Capen Reynolds Fel, Smith Col, 91-92; Who's Who among African Am 98-99; Black Admin in Child Welfare Scholars Awd, 97; Family Res Consortium Sem Inst, San Antonio, 97; Fac Fel, W.K.Kellogg Foundation, 95; Louise Frey Fund, Boston Univ, 94. **MEMBERSHIPS** Soc for Soc Work Res, coun on Soc Work Educ, Mass Acad of Clinical Soc Workers, Nat Asn, of Soc Workers. **RESEARCH** Adolescent development, Adolescent pregnancy among pregnant and nonpregnant African American late-aged female adolescents to better understand how blocked opportunities contribute to premature childbearing. **SELECTED PUBLICATIONS** Auth, "Creating collaborative partnerships: clinical intervention research in an inner-city middle school," social Work in Education, (99): 151-162; auth, "Early coital behavior and substance use among African American female adolescents," African American Research Perspectives, (98): 35-39; auth, "A question of values in social work practice: Working with the strengths of inner city Blackgirls," Families in Society, (98): 288-296; auth, "Opportunity, outlook and coping in poor urban African American late age female adolescent contraceptors," smith Studies, (97): 456-475; auth, "African American female adolescent identity development," Child Welfare, (97): 145-174; auth, "Adulthood status negotiation among poor urban black pregnant and nonpregnant late age adolescent females," Journal of Applied Social Science, (95): 39-50. **CONTACT ADDRESS** Dept Soc Work, Boston Univ, 264 Bay State Rd, Boston, MA 02215.

STEVENS, ROBERT
PERSONAL Born 03/15/1952, Trenton, NJ, m, 2 children **DISCIPLINE** PSYCHOLOGY, **EDUCATION** Bucknell Univ, BA, 74; Univ Ill, MS, 79; PhD, 83. **CAREER** Post-Doctoral Fel, LRDC Univ of Pittsburgh, Pa, 83-84; Res Scientist, Center for Soc Orgn of Schools, Johns Hopkins Univ, Baltimore Md, 84-91; Asst to Assoc, Pa State Univ, Univ Park Pa, 91-. **HONORS AND AWARDS** Col of Educ Awd for Excellence in Undergraduate Teaching, Univ of Ill, 83; Outstanding Fac Awd, Col of Educ, Pa State Univ, 95. **MEMBERSHIPS** Am Educ Res Asn, Am Psychol Asn, Div 15. **RESEARCH** Effective instruction in Reading, Cognitive Psychology applied to instruction. **SELECTED PUBLICATIONS** Coauth, "Teaching functions," in Handbook of research on teaching, ed. M.C. Wittrock (NY: Macmillan, 86); auth, "The effects of strategy training on the identification of the main idea of expository passages," J of Educ Psychology 80 (88): 21-26; coauth, "Cooperative learning and mainstreaming," in Perspectives on the integration of atypical students in regular education settings," ed. J. Lloyd, A. Repp and N. Singh (Sycamore, IL: Sycamore Press, 91); coauth, "Effects of cooperative learning and direct instruction in reading comprehension strategies on main idea identification," J of Educ Psychology 83 (91): 8-16; auth, "Using cooperative learning in literacy instruction: Theory, research, and application," in Literacy: A Redefiniton, ed. N. Ellsworth, C. Headley, and A. Baratte (Hillsdale, NJ: Erlbaum Associates, 94), 127-158; coauth, "Effects of a cooperative learning approach in reading and writing on academically handicapped and nonhandicapped students," Elementary Sch J 95 (95): 241-260; coauth, "The Cooperative Elementary School: Effects on students' achievement, attitudes, and social relations," Am Educ Res J 32 (95): 321-351; coauth, "Accommodating student heterogeneity in mainstreamed clementary classrooms through cooperative learning," in Issues in educating students with disabilities, ed. J.W. Lloyd, E. Kameenui, and D. Chard (Hillsdale, NJ: L. Erlbaum Associates, 97), 221-238; ed, Teaching in American School, Prentice Hall (Columbus, OH), 99; coauth, "Elementa-

ry education, " in Encyclopedia of Psychology, ed. A. Kazdin (NY: Oxford Univ Press), 00. **CONTACT ADDRESS** Dept Educ Psychology and Spec Educ, Pennsylvania State Univ, Univ Park, 227 Cedar Bldg, University Park, PA 16802. **EMAIL** rjs15@psu.edu

STEVENSON, CATHERINE BARNES
PERSONAL Born 05/23/1947, Chicago, IL, m, 1970 **DISCIPLINE** VICTORIAN LITERATURE, WOMEN'S STUDIES **EDUCATION** Manhattanville Col, BA, 68; NYork Univ, MA, 69, PhD(English), 73. **CAREER** Asst prof, Bryant Col, 75-77; ASST PROF ENGLISH, UNIV HARTFORD, 78-, Ed, Victorian Studies Bull, 78- **MEMBERSHIPS** Northeast Victorian Studies Asn; MLA; Tennyson Soc. **RESEARCH** Victorian poetry; women's travel writing; 19th century novel. **SELECTED PUBLICATIONS** Auth, The aesthetic function of the weird seizures in Tennyson's The Princess, Victorian Newsletter, 74; Tennyson's mutability canto: Time, memory, and art in The Princess, Victorian Poetry, 75; Druids, Bards, and Tennyson's Merlin, Victorian Newsletter, 79; Tennyson's Dying Swan: Mythology and the definition of the poet's role, Studies in English Lit, 80; Swinburne and Tennyson's Tristram, Victorian Poetry, 81; How it struck a contemporary: Tennyson's Lancelot and Elaine and Pre-Raphaelite art, Victorian Newsletter, 81; The shade of Homer exorcises the ghost of De Quincey: Tennyson's The Lotos-Eaters, Browning Inst Studies, 82; Victorian Women Travellers to Africa, G K Hall, 82; *Pub What Must Not Be Said, North And South And The Problem Of Womens Work, Victorian Lit And Culture, Vol 19, 91. **CONTACT ADDRESS** Dept of Literature, Univ of Hartford, 380 W Mountain Rd, West Simsbury, CT 06092. **EMAIL** stevenson@mail.hartford.edu

STEVENSON, MICHAEL R.
PERSONAL Born Brazil, IN **DISCIPLINE** PSYCHOLOGY **EDUCATION** Purdue Univ, BA, 79, MS, 81, PhD, 84. **CAREER** Instr/teaching asst, Purdue Univ, 80-84; asst prof, Ball State Univ, 84-89, assoc prof, 89-95, prof, 95-, Dir and Founder, Diversity Policy Inst, Ball State Univ, 97-. **HONORS AND AWARDS** Am Psychol Asn Div Two Teaching Awd, 84; Fulbright Sr Scholar, Am-Indonesian Exchange Found, 93-94; Mallone fel, Nat Coun on U. S. -Arab Relations, 97; Am Psychol Asn Sr Congressional fel, 95-96; Fel, Am Psychol Asn, Div 2, Div 44, 2000; Am Coun on Ed Fel, 2000-2001. **MEMBERSHIPS** Am Psychol Asn, Soc for the Sci Study of Sexuality. **RESEARCH** Diversity, public policy, gender, sexuality, HIV/AIDS, Anti-Gay prejudice, parental absence. **SELECTED PUBLICATIONS** Auth, "Sexuality, public policy and the 104th Congress," J of Psychol and Human Sexuality, 10, 1 (98): 1-13; auth, "Unwanted childhood sexual experience questionnaire," in C. M. Davis, W. L. Yarber, R. Bauserman, G. Shreer, & S. L. Davis, eds, Handbook of Sexuality-Related Measures, Thousand Oaks, CA: Sage (98); auth, "Reconciling sexual orientation," in G. G. Brannigan, A. R. Allgeier & E. R. Allgeier, eds, The Sex Scientists, New York: Harper Collins (98); auth, "Asia, Southeast," "Gender roles," and "Heterosexual men," in R. A. Smith, ed, Encyclopedia of AIDS: A Social, Political, Cultural, and Scientific Record of the Epidemic, Chicago: Fitzroy Dearborn (98); auth, "Sex education," and "U. S. Congress," in G. E. Haggerty, ed, The Encyclopedia of Gay Histories and Cultures," New York: Garland (99); auth, "Sexual victimization: Responses of the U. S. Congress," in M. Paludi, ed, The Psychology of Sexual Victimization: A Handbook, Westport, CT: Greenwood (99); auth, "Public policy and sexuality in midlife: Obstacles and impediments," in J. Bancroft & S. Sanders, eds, Sexuality in Midlife, Bloomington, IN: Indiana Univ Press (in press); auth, "Conceptualizing diversity in sexuality research," M. W. Wiederman & B. E. Whiley, Jr, eds, Handbook for Conducting Research on Human Sexuality, Mahwah, NJ: Erlbaum (2000). **CONTACT ADDRESS** Dept Psychol, Ball State Univ, 2000 W Univ, Muncie, IN 47306-0002. **EMAIL** 00mrstevenso@bsu.edu

STEWART, CISLEY P.
PERSONAL Born 05/18/1937, St. Andrew, Jamaica, d, 2 children **DISCIPLINE** EDUCATION **EDUCATION** City Col, City Univ of NY, BA, 67; MS, 70; Columbia Univ, Teachers Col, MA, 77; Walden Univ, PhD, 95. **CAREER** Initiating Acad Dir, S.E.E.K., Hunter Col, CUNY; assoc consult, Res and Educ, J.A.M.A.L., Jamaica; ordained non-denominational clergywoman; assoc prof, SUNY, Suffolk County Community Col, Eastern Campus. **HONORS AND AWARDS** Women in Am's Awd, 97; Asn Black Women Outstanding Advisors Awd, 97; On-line teaching cert, Walden Inst, 01. **MEMBERSHIPS** Asn of Black Women in Higher Educ; Community Col Gen Educ Asn; ABHWEI; Community Col, CCGEA. **RESEARCH** Motivation, learning, and psychology of success; on-line teaching; problem-based teaching; gaming and interactive teaching; increasing persistence through unlearning "learned helplessness." **SELECTED PUBLICATIONS** Auth, The Effect of Instruction in Reading Upon Mathematical Performance, 95; auth, Optimizing Student Success: Unlearning "Learned Helplessness," 99; **CONTACT ADDRESS** Humanities, Suffolk County Community Col, 2 Speonk Riverhead Rd, Riverhead, NY, 10 11901-3433.

STEWART, CISLEY P.
DISCIPLINE EDUCATION **CAREER** Assoc prof, SUNY-Suffolk Cty Commun Col. **RESEARCH** Problems developmental educaiton students experience in reading mathematics; problem-based teaching; gaming and interactive teaching; increasing persistence through unlearning 'learned helplessness;' online teaching. **CONTACT ADDRESS** Suffolk County Comm Col, Eastern, Selden, NY 11784.

STEWART, MAC A.
PERSONAL Born 07/07/1942, Forsyth, GA, m **DISCIPLINE** EDUCATION **EDUCATION** Morehouse Coll, BA 1963; Atlanta Univ, MA 1965; The Ohio State Univ, PhD 1973. **CAREER** Jasper County Training School, teacher/counselor 1963-64; Crispus Attucks HS, teacher 1965-66; Morehouse Coll, dir of student financial aid 1966-70; The Ohio State Univ, asst dean 1973-75, assoc dean 1975-90, acting dean, 90-91, dean 1991-. **HONORS AND AWARDS** Distinguished Affirmative Action Awd The Ohio State Univ 1984; Outstanding Alumni Awd Hubbard School 1986; Distinguished Service Awd, Negro Educational Review, 1992; Frederick D Patterson Awd, United Negro College Fund, 1992. **MEMBERSHIPS** Consultant KY State Univ 1978; mem bd dirs Buckeye Boys Ranch 1979-85; mem bd dirs Bethune Center for Unwed Mothers 1980-83; consultant Wilberforce Univ 1980; faculty mem Ohio Staters Inc 1982-91; consultant The Ohio Bd of Regents 1986; consultant, US Department of Education, 1990; consultant, Temple University, 1991; board of trustees, Columbus Academy, 1991-; consultant, Virginia Commonwealth University, 1992; mem Amer Personnel and Guidance Assoc, Amer Coll Personnel Assoc, Natl Assoc of Student Personnel Administrators, Mid-Western Assoc of Student Financial Aid Administrators, Alpha Kappa Delta Natl Hon Sociological Soc, Phi Delta Kappa Natl Hon Educ Frat, Phi Kappa Phi Natl Honor Soc, Amer Assoc of Higher Educ; bd mem, Human Subjects Research Committee Children's Hospital. **CONTACT ADDRESS** Dean, Ohio State Univ, Columbus, 154 W 12th Ave, Columbus, OH 43210.

STEWART, MARY W.
PERSONAL Born 01/11/1945, Compte Jeune, NC **DISCIPLINE** SOCIOLOGY **EDUCATION** Univ Nev Reno, BA, 66; PhD, 73; Temple Univ, MA, 68. **CAREER** Asst prof to assoc prof, Univ of Miss Kansas City, 74-89; assoc prof, Univ of Nev Reno, 89-. **MEMBERSHIPS** Am Sociol Assoc; Pacific Sociol Assoc; W Psychol Assoc; Sociol for Women in Soc; W Soc Sci Assoc. **RESEARCH** Violence and Gender, Social Psychology and Gender, Deviance, Family Violence. **SELECTED PUBLICATIONS** Auth, "The Redefinition of Incest: From Sin to Sickness", Family Sci Rev 4.1-2, 91; auth, "Images of Women in Advertising, 1945-1985, Vogue" in Images of Women in the Arts and Mass Media, Mellen, 93; auth, "Health Care and Homelessness: Is Health Care Enough?", Nev Pub Affairs Rev, Alan Bible Center for Appl Res, 93; auth, Sociology: A Down to Earth Approach; Annotated Instructors Manual, Allyn & Bacon, 95; coauth, "A Study of Shared Definitions of Reality in Rape Cases", Feminist Legal Studies, Aug 96; auth, Silicone Spills: Breast Implants on Trial, Praeger Pr, 97; rev, of "Science on Trial", by Marcia Angell, Am Judicature Soc, 80.4, 97; auth, To The Moon: Violence Against Women in Cultural and Social Context, Greenwood Pr, 00. **CONTACT ADDRESS** Dept Sociol, Univ of Nevada, Reno, N Virginia Ave, Reno, NV 89557-0001. **EMAIL** mary@scs.unr.edu

STIEGLITZ, ROBERT R.
PERSONAL Born 04/14/1943, Bershad, Ukraine, m, 1975, 2 children **DISCIPLINE** ANTHROPOLOGY, ARCHAEOLOGY **EDUCATION** City Col of NYork, BA, 67; Brandeis Univ, MA, 69; PhD, 71. **CAREER** Chemn, Hebraic Studies Dept, Rutgers Univ, Newark, NJ, 81-84; Vis Prof, Jewish Theol Sem of NY, 95-98; Assoc Prof, Rutgers Univ, Newark, NJ, 83-. **HONORS AND AWARDS** Archaeol Inst of Am Fel. **MEMBERSHIPS** Am Sch of Orient Res, Archaeol Inst of Am, Israel Explor Soc, Hellenic Inst of Marine Archaeol. **RESEARCH** Biblical Archaeology, Ancient Seafaring, West-Semitic Epigraphy. **SELECTED PUBLICATIONS** Coauth, Phoenicians on the Northern Coast of Israel, Haifa: Necht Museum, Univ of Haifa, 93; auth, "The Minoan Origin of Tyrian Purple," Bibl Archaeologist 57 (94): 46-54; auth, "Stratonos Pyrgos - Migdal Sar - Sebastos: History and Archaeology," in Caesarea Maritima: A Retrospective after Two Millennia, ed. A. Raban and K. G. Holum (Leiden: Brill, 96), 593-608; auth, "Ptolemy IX Soter II Lathyrus on Cyprus and the Coast of the Levant," in Res Maritima: Cyprus and the Eastern Mediterranean from Prehistory to Late Antiquity, CAARI Monograph Ser Vol I, ed. S Swiny et al (Atlanta: Scholar's Press, 97), 301-306; coauth, Illustrated Dictionary of Bible Life and Times, Reader's Digest (NY), 97; auth, "The Phoenician-Punic Menology," in Boundaries of the Ancient Near Eastern World: A Tribute to Cyrus H. Gordon, ed. M. Lubetski et al (Sheffield: Sheffield Acad Press, 98), 211-221; auth, "A Late Byzantine Reservoir and 'Piscina' at Tel Tanninim, " Israel Explor J 48 (98): 54-65; auth, "Phoenician Ship Equipment and Fittings," in Tropis V: International Symposium on Ship Construcion in Antiquity, ed. H. Tzalas (Athens: Hellenic Inst for the Preserv of Nautical Tradition, 99), 409-420; auth, "Straton's Tower and Demetrias again: one town or two?," in Caesare Papers 2, ed. K. G. Holum et al (Portsmouth, RI: JRA, 99), 359-360. **CONTACT ADDRESS** Classical and Modern Languages and Literatures Dept, Rutgers, The State Univ of New Jersey, Newark, 175 Univ Ave., Newark, NJ 07102-1814. **EMAIL** stieglit@andromeda.rutgers.edu

STILES, WILLIAM B.
PERSONAL Born 01/29/1944, Seattle, WA, m **DISCIPLINE** PSYCHOLOGY **EDUCATION** Oberlin Col, Oh, BA, 66; Univ Calif, Los Angeles, MA, 68; PhD, 72. **CAREER** Instr, Univ of NC, Chapel Hill, 71-72, asst prof, 73-79; assoc prof, Miami Univ, Oxford, Ohio, 79-85, Dir of Psychol Clinic, 86-91, prof, 85-; vis asst prof, Univ of NC, Chapel Hill, summer of 80 and 81; vis res, Univ of Sheffield, United Kingdom, 84-85, summers of 87, 89, and 91, NIH Fogarty Sr Int Fel, 92-93, special appt, Jan-Aug 95; honorary prof res fel, Univ Leeds, United Kingdom, summer 96, May 97; vis prof, Univ of Joensuu, Finland, June-Aug 97; vis scholar, Massey Univ, Palmerston North, New Zealand, May-Aug 82, May-Aug 90, July-Aug 99. **MEMBERSHIPS** Soc for Psychotherapy Res, Am Psychol Soc, Am Psychol Asn, Midwestern Psychol Asn, Person-Centered Asn, Sigma Xi, Soc for the Exploration of Psychotherapy Integration, Soc for Personality and Social Psychol. **RESEARCH** Verbal interaction in psychotherapy and medical interviews; assimilation of problematic experiences in psychotherapy; impact of psychotherapy sessions; development of interpersonal relationships; qualitative and narrative research methods. **SELECTED PUBLICATIONS** Auth, "Evaluating qualitative research," Evidence-Based Mental Health, 2 (99): 99-101; auth, "Signs and voices in psychotherapy," Psychotherapy Res, 9 (99): 1-21; auth, "Suppression of CBA voices: A theoretical note on the psychology and psychotherapy of depression," Psychotherapy, 36 (99): 268-273; coauth with R. Agnew-Davies, "Brief alliances [rev of The therapeutic alliance in brief psychotherapy, by J. D. Safran and J. C. Muran, eds], Contemporary Psychology: APA Review of Books, 44 (99): 392-394; coauth with L. Honos-Webb and L. M. Knobloch, "Treatment process research methods," in P. C. Kendall, J. N. Butcher, and G. N. Holmbeck, eds, Handbook of research methods in clinical psychology, NY: Wiley (99); coauth with L. Honos-Webb and J. A. Lani, "Some functions of narrative in the assimilation of problematic experiences," J of Clinical Psychol, 55 (99): 1213-1226; coauth with L. Honos-Webb and J. A. Lani, "Discovering markers of assimilation stages: The fear of losing control marker," J of Clinical Psychol, 55 (99): 1441-1452; coauth with L. Honos-Webb, M. Surko, and L. S. Greenberg, "Assimilation voices in psychotherapy: The case of Jan," J of Coun Psychol, 46 (99): 448-460; coauth with S. Macran and J. A. Smith, "How does personal therapy affect therapists' practice?" J of Coun Psychol, 46 (99): 419-431; coauth with S. Varvin, "Emergence of severe traumatic experiences: An assimilation analysis of psychoanalytic therapy with a political refugee," Psychotherapy Res, 9 (99): 381-404; coauth with J. M. G. Williams and D. A. Shapiro, "Cognitive mechanisms in the avoidance of painful and dangerous thoughts: Elaborating the assimilation model," Cognitive Therapy and Research, 23 (99): 285-306. **CONTACT ADDRESS** Dept Psychol, Miami Univ, 500 E High St, Oxford, OH 45056. **EMAIL** stileswb@muohio.edu

STILWELL, WILLIAM E., III
PERSONAL Born 07/28/1936, Cincinnati, OH, m, 1969, 2 children **DISCIPLINE** COUNSELING; PSYCHOLOGY **EDUCATION** Dartmouth, AB, 58; San Jose State Univ, MS, 66; Stanford, PhD, 69. **CAREER** Dept of Mental Hygiene, San Mateo Cty, 66-68; Am Inst of Res, Palo Alto, Calif, 67-69; Prof, Col of Educ, Univ Ky, 69-. **HONORS AND AWARDS** VP, Counseling & Human Dev, 80-82.Coun of Clnical Psychol Prog Outstanding Service, 98. **MEMBERSHIPS** APA; AERA; AAAPP; ROA. **RESEARCH** Human services delivery evaluation; teletherapy; internet in human sci. **SELECTED PUBLICATIONS** Co-auth, Psychology for teachers and students, McGraw-Hill, 81; co-auth, Social work education: Accessible to the handicapped?, J of Educ for Soc Work, 20, 43-50, 84; co-auth, Taming the beast: A comprehensive model for the implementation of microcomputers in education, Educ, 104, 377-384, 84; co-auth, A model for recruitment and retention of minority students in teacher preparation programs, J of Tchr Educ, 39:1, 14-18, 88; co-auth, Internet training programs: A college of education response, Reading Improvement, 34, 106-113, 97. **CONTACT ADDRESS** 1919 Williamsburg Rd, Lexington, KY 40504-3013. **EMAIL** westil3@pop.uky.edu

STIMPSON, CATHARINE R.
PERSONAL Born 06/04/1936, Bellingham, WA **DISCIPLINE** CONTEMPORARY LITERATURE, WOMEN'S STUDIES **EDUCATION** Bryn Mawr Col, AB, 58; Cambridge Univ, BA, 60, MA, 65; Columbia Univ, PhD(English), 67. **CAREER** From instr to asst prof, 63-73, assoc prof, Columbia Univ, 73-80; prof English, Rutgers Univ, 80-, mem, Nat Emergency Civil Liberties Comt; ed, SIGNS: J Women in Cult & Soc, 74-80; Nat Humanities Inst fel, 75-76; consult, Nat Inst Educ, 78-80; dir, Rutgers Inst for Res Women; chemn, Mass Bd Scholarship, Res & Educ. **MEMBERSHIPS** MLA; PEN. **RESEARCH** Post-modern literature; women and literature; relationship of revolution to literature. **SELECTED PUBLICATIONS** Auth, J R R Tolkien, Columbia Univ, 69; ed, Women and the Equal Rights Amendment, 72 & Discrimination Against Women, 73, Bowker; Class Notes, Times Bks, 78 & Avon, 79. **CONTACT ADDRESS** GSAS Dean's Office, New York Univ, 6 Washington Square N, Rm 12, New York, NY 10003-6668. **EMAIL** catharine.stimpson@nyu.edu

STITT, J. MICHAEL
DISCIPLINE FOLKLORE, MEDIEVAL LITERATURE **EDUCATION** Pa State Univ, BA, 73; Ind Univ, MA, 75, cert, 78, PhD, 81. **CAREER** Instr, Ind Univ-Purdue Univ, 79-81; asst prof, 81-91, assoc prof, 91-, interim dir, freshman compos, 91-92, Univ Nev, Las Vegas; ed bd, J Medieval Folklore. **HONORS AND AWARDS** Grant, Nevada Humanities Council, 82; University Research council grant, 83, 86, 88; sr Fulbright lectr, Univ Sofia, 97. **MEMBERSHIPS** Nev State Bd Geog Names. **RESEARCH** Bulgarian folk music and dance. **SELECTED PUBLICATIONS** Auth, Conversational Genres at a Las Vegas '21' Table, Western Folklore 45, 86; Beowulf and The Bear's Son. Epic, Saga, and Fairytale in the Northern Germanic Area, Albert B Lord Monogr Ser, Garland, 92; coauth, A Type and Motif Index of Early American Almanac Narrative, Greenwood, 91. **CONTACT ADDRESS** Dept of Eng, Univ of Nevada, Las Vegas, 4505 Maryland Pky, PO Box 455011, Las Vegas, NV 89154. **EMAIL** stitt@nevada.edu

STITZEL, JUDITH GOLD
PERSONAL Born 03/23/1941, New York, NY, m, 1961, 1 child **DISCIPLINE** ENGLISH, WOMEN'S STUDIES **EDUCATION** Barnard Col, BA, 61; Univ Wis, MA, 62; Univ MN, PhD, 68. **CAREER** Asst prof, 68-72; dir writing laboratory, 69-73; assoc prof, 72-79, coor and dir Center for Women's Stud 80-92, prof eng and women's studies, WVA Univ, 92-98, Assoc, Danforth Found, 75-82; WVA deleg NCent Women's Studies Asn, 79. **HONORS AND AWARDS** Phi Beta Kappa; Case Silver Medalist; National Prof of the Year. **MEMBERSHIPS** Nat Women's Studies Asn. **RESEARCH** Lit criticism; pedag; women's studies; Creative non-fiction. **SELECTED PUBLICATIONS** Auth, The uses of humor, Doris Lessing Newslett, 77; Morning cycle, Colo Quart, autumn, 79; Humor and survival in the works of Doris Lessing, Regionalism and the Female Imagination, 4: 61-69; Reading Doris Lessing, Col English, 40: 498-504; Toward the new year, Trellis, summer 79; Challenging curricular assumptions: Teaching, learning women's literature from a regional perspective, She who laughs firt, Stepping Off the Pedetal-Academic Women in the South, MLA, 82; auth, Reshaping the Introductory womens studies course: Dealing Upfront with Anger, Resistance and Reality (wit Ardeth Dery), Feminist Teacher, 6, 1 (Summer 91), 29-33. **CONTACT ADDRESS** 449 Devon Rd, Morgantown, WV 26505. **EMAIL** jstitzel@wvu.edu

STOCKWELL, EDWARD G.
PERSONAL Born 06/11/1933, Newbury Port, MA, m, 1956, 3 children **DISCIPLINE** SOCIOLOGY **EDUCATION** Harvard Univ, AB, 55; Univ Conn, MA, 57; Brown Univ, PhD, 60. **CAREER** Population Analysts, US Bureau of the Census, 60-61; Asst Prof to Prof, Univ Conn, 61-71; Prof, Bowling Green State Univ, 71-. **HONORS AND AWARDS** Population Coun Fel, 59-60. **MEMBERSHIPS** Population Asn of Am. **RESEARCH** General population trends. **CONTACT ADDRESS** Dept Sociol, Bowling Green State Univ, 1001 E Wooster St, Bowling Green, OH 43403-0001. **EMAIL** estockw@bgnet.bgsu.edu

STOFFREGEN, THOMAS
PERSONAL Born 07/15/1957, Cincinnati, OH, m, 1994, 1 child **DISCIPLINE** PSYCHOLOGY **EDUCATION** Oberlin Col, BA, 75; Cornell Univ, PhD, 84. **CAREER** Assoc Prof, Univ Cincinnati, 90-. **HONORS AND AWARDS** Univ Res Coun Grant, Univ Cincinnati, 91, 92; Fac Achievement Awd, Univ Cincinnati, 95; Who's Who, 00. **MEMBERSHIPS** Intl Soc for Ecol Psychol; Am Psychol Soc; Am Psychol Asn; Psychonomic Soc; Sigma Xi; Human Factors and Ergonomics Soc. **RESEARCH** Perception and action. **SELECTED PUBLICATIONS** Co-auth, "Postural stabilization for the control of touching," Human Movement Science, (99): 795-817; co-auth, "Interaction between task demands and surface properties in the control of goal-oriented stance," Human Movement Science, (99): 31-47; co-auth, "Perceiving affordances for another person's actions," Journal of Experimental Psychology: Human Perception & Performance, (99): 120-136; co-auth, "Postural coordination modes considered as emergent phenomena," Journal of Experimental Psychology, (99): 1284-1301; co-auth, "Postural stabilization of looking," Journal of Experimental Psychology, (99): 1641-1658; co-auth, "On the nature and evaluation of fidelity in virtual environments," in Psychological issues in the design and use of virtual environments, Lawrence Erlbaum Assoc, 00; co-auth, "Postural instability and motion sickness in a fixed-base flight simulator," Human Factors, 00; auth, "Affordances and events: Theory and research," Ecological Psychology, (00): 93-107; auth, "Affordances and events," Ecological Psychology, (00): 1-28; co-auth, "On specification and the sense," Behavioral and Brain Sciences, in press. **CONTACT ADDRESS** Dept Psychol, Univ of Cincinnati, PO Box 210376, Cincinnati, OH 45220-0376. **EMAIL** stoffrta@email.uc.edu

STOKES, H. BRUCE
PERSONAL Born 06/14/1950, Auburn, CA, m, 1970, 2 children **DISCIPLINE** ANTHROPOLOGY **EDUCATION** Calif State Univ, BA; Univ Calif, MA; PhD. **CAREER** Prof, Calif Baptist Univ, 84-; Chair Behav Sci Div, Calif Baptist Univ, 95-98; Chair, Div of Behav and Natural Sci, Calif Baptist Univ, 98-. **HONORS AND AWARDS** Fac Member of the Year, 90; Distinguished Prof of the Year, 99. **MEMBERSHIPS** Am Anthrop Asn, Soc for Psy Anthrop. **RESEARCH** Anthropology. **SELECTED PUBLICATIONS** Transl Committee, New American Standard Bible, The Lockman Found (Brea, CA), 95; auth, "The Role of Gentiles in the Messianic Movement," Kesher: J of the Union of Messianic Jewish Congregations (97); auth, "Messianic Jewish Life: The Role of Gentiles in Messianic Judaism;" auth, "Sex and Religion: A Culture History," Kesher: J of the Union of Messianic Jewish Congregations, 99; coauth, Integration of the Behavioral Sciences and Theology: a systematic and relational approach, Express Yourself Press (NY), 99. **CONTACT ADDRESS** Div of Behav and Natural Sci, California Baptist Col, 8432 Magnolia Ave, Riverside, CA 92504. **EMAIL** drstokes@aol.com

STOKES, SANDRA M.
DISCIPLINE EDUCATION, WOMEN'S STUDIES **EDUCATION** Univ Bridgeport, BA, 69; Fairfield Univ, MA, 73; Kent State Univ, PhD, 89. **CAREER** Assoc prof of Educ, Univ of Wis at Green Bay, 95-, chair, Women's Studies, 94-97, 2000-2003, Dir of Clinical Experiences in Educ, 97-200. **HONORS AND AWARDS** Univ Fel Recipient, Kent State Univ, 88; Outstanding Teaching Awd, Kent State Univ, Grad Student Awd, 88; Who's Who in Am Educ, 89-95. **MEMBERSHIPS** ADD Partnership of Ohio, Am Asn on Mental Retardation, Asn for Childhood Educ Int, Coun on Learning Disabilities, Int Reading Asn, Nat Coun of Teachers of English, Phi Delta Kappa. **SELECTED PUBLICATIONS** Auth, "Teacher education methods: Practice, not perfection," The Reading Prof, 17, 1 (94): 43-50; auth, "Teach the teachers, educators say," Flight Sch Business News, 2, 24 (96): 186-187; auth, "Developing a curriculum for Native American students using Native American values," The Reading Teacher, 50, 7 (97): 576-584; auth, "Empowering students with learning disabilities through language experience," in O. Nelson and W. Linek, eds, Practical classroom applications of language experience: Looking back and looking forward, Boston: Allyn & Bacon (98); auth, "A partnership for creating a multicultural teaching force: A model for the future," Multicultural Educ, 7, 1 (99): 8-12; auth, "Creating a sense of power through family resource centers," in A. Statham and K. Rhoades, eds, Proceedings of the Twenty-third Univ of Wisc System Statewide Women's Studies Conf, Madison, Wisc (99); co-ed with S. M. Stokes, Stand! Education, Madison, WI: CourseWise, Inc (99); auth, "Teachers as researchers: Changing the paradigm," WSRA J (in press); auth, "The role of the reading teacher in fostering resilience among at-risk students," WSRA J (in press); coauth with J. L. Simmons, "Creating a model of teacher education for the twenty-first century," J of Reading Educ (in press). **CONTACT ADDRESS** Dept Educ,, Univ of Wisconsin, Green Bay, 2420 Nicolet Dr, 416 Wood Hall, Green Bay, WI 54311. **EMAIL** STOKESS@gbms01.uwgb.edu

STOLBA, SOHEIR
PERSONAL Born 04/24/1945, Egypt, m, 1967, 3 children **DISCIPLINE** SOCIAL, BEHAVIORAL SCIENCE **EDUCATION** Cairo Univ, BA, 66; Sacramento State Univ, MA, 72; Teaching Credential, 73; Univ CA, MA, 74; PhD, 78. **CAREER** Training Advisor, Checchi & Co, 80-81; President, Project Implementation and Training Assoc, 96-; President, International Health and Development Assoc, 92-; Faculty Member, Am River Col, 87-. **HONORS AND AWARDS** The Patron's Awd for "Best Teacher Awd". **MEMBERSHIPS** Am Anthroplogy Asn, Medical Anthropology Asn, Applied Anthropogy Asn. **RESEARCH** Gender, Women's Health and Development. **SELECTED PUBLICATIONS** Rev, "Nubians in Egypt: Peaceful People," by Robert Fernea, Ethnohistory 20 (73); auth, "Copts and Muslims in Egypt," published in Muslim-Christian Conflicts: Economic, Political and Social Origins, ed. S. Joseph, and Barbara Pillsbury, Westview, Boulder, 78; auth, "She is No Stranger: The Traditional Midwife in Egypt," The Journal of Medical Anthropology,5 (81); auth, An Outline of Cultural Anthropology, Burgess, 83; rev, "Bitter Pills" by Donald Warwick, Medical Anthropology Quarterly, 15 (84); auth, "Food Classification and Diets of Young Children in Rural Egypt," Social Science and Medicine, 25 (87): 401-404; auth, Family Planning Modules for Yemen, 87; auth, "Indigenous Institutions and Adaptation to Famine: The case of Western Sudan," published in African Food Systems in Crisis, ed. R. Huss-Ashmore and S. Katz, Gordon and Breach, 89; auth, Academic Skills Manual, 89; auth, Oral Rehydration: Expanded Bibliography, 90. **CONTACT ADDRESS** Dept Social and Behavioral Science, American River Col, 4700 College Oak Dr, Sacramento, CA 95841. **EMAIL** sstolba@aol.com

STOLL, SHARON
PERSONAL Born 12/06/1946, Wadsworth, OH, m, 1981, 2 children **DISCIPLINE** PHYSICAL EDUCATION **EDUCATION** Col of the Ozarks, BS, 68; Kent State Univ, MEd, 70; PhD, 80. **CAREER** Asst Prof to Assoc Prof, Univ ID, 80-90; Visiting Prof, Lewis Clark State Col, 93; Visiting Prof, US Military Acad, 93-94; Prof, Univ ID, 90-. **HONORS AND AWARDS** Phi Kappa Phi, 87; Dist Fac, Univ ID, 89; Teaching Awd of Merit, Univ ID, 92; Ethics Fel, Univ RI, 93; Distinguished Service Awd, ID Asn of Health, 93. **MEMBERSHIPS** PSSS; ID Asn of Health, Phys Ed, Recreation and Dance; N Am Soc for Sport Hist; AAHPERD; ACSM. **RESEARCH** Sportsmanship; Character education; Moral education ; Sport philosophy. **SELECTED PUBLICATIONS** Auth, "Principled Thinking. Curriculum Guide, Center for ETHICS Pub, 98; co-auth, Sport Ethics: Applications for Fair Play, McGraw Hill, 99; auth, Who Cares? A Primer for Elementary Education Students, Center for ETHICS, 99; auth, "Moral Reasoning: What is it and How it is Best Accomplished in the Classroom and Gymnasium," in Physical Education, Sports, and Wellness: Looking to God as We Look at Ourselves, (Dordt Col Press, 99), 249-264; co-auth, "HIV, sport, and gamesmanship," in HIV/AIDS in sports: Impact, issues, and challenges, (Human Kinetic Press, 99), 83-94; auth, "Mirabel Vinson," in Encyclopedia of World Sport: From Ancient Times to the Present, (Oxford Univ Press, 99); auth, "Beatrice Loughran," in Encyclopedia of World Sport: From Ancient Times to the Present, (Oxford Univ Press, 99); co-auth, "Irving Jaffee," in Encyclopedia of World Sport: From Ancient Times to the Present, (Oxford Univ Press, 99); co-auth, Sport Ethics: Applications for Fair Play, McGraw Hill, 99. **CONTACT ADDRESS** Dept Health, Phys Ed, Univ of Idaho, 375 S Line St, Moscow, ID 83844-0001. **EMAIL** sstoll@uidaho.edu

STONE, GERALD L.
PERSONAL Born 08/25/1941, Glendale, CA, m, 1963, 2 children **DISCIPLINE** PSYCHOLOGY **EDUCATION** Univ Calif, Los Angeles, BA, 63; Princeton Theol Sem, BD, 66; Mich State Univ, MA, 70; PhD, 72. **CAREER** Psychologist, St. Thomas Psychiatric Hospital, Ont, Can, 72-76; asst prof, Univ Western Ont, 72-76, assoc prof, 77-79; assoc prof and coordr, Counseling Psychol, Univ Iowa, 79-81, prof and coordr (79-83), 81, acting dir, Clinical Services and Training, Univ Coun Service, 84, Dir, Univ Coun Service, 85-. **HONORS AND AWARDS** All Univ Res Awd, 70, 71; Phi Kappa Phi, Mich State Univ, 72; Old Gold Fel, 80, 81; Staff Excellence Awd, 93. **MEMBERSHIPS** Nat Col Personnel Asn, Am Educ Res Asn, Am Psychol Asn, Asn of Univ and Col Coun Center Dirs, State Licensed Psychologist (Iowa), State Health Service Provider (Iowa). **RESEARCH** Mental health policy in higher education, university counseling centers in higher education. **SELECTED PUBLICATIONS** Coauth with V. L. Stamler, Faculty-student sexual involvement: Issues and interactions, Thousand Oaks, CA: Sage (98); coauth with B. D. Johnson, E. M. Altmier and L. B. Berdahl, "The relationship of demographic factors, locus of control, and self-efficacy to successful nursing home adjustment," The Gernotologist, 38 (98): 209-216; auth, "Inventory of learning Processes-R," in J. C. Impara and B. S. Plake, The thirteenth mental measurements yearbook, Lincoln, NE: Univ Nebr Press (98); auth, "A handbook for psychotherapy supervision: A sign of importance and progress [Review of Handbook of Psychotherapy supervision]," Contemporary Psychology, 43 (98): 567; coauth with A. Badura, "Factors influencing counseling centers staff's perceptions of treatment difficulty in relation to student childhood sexual abuse," J of Col Student Psychotherapy, 31 (98): 15-38; coauth with D. P. Pope-Davis and B. J. Vandiver, "White racial identity attitude development: A psychometric examination of two instruments," J of Coun Psychol, 46 (99): 70-79; coauth with V. J. Keffala, "Role of HIV serostatus, relationship status of the patient, homophobia, and social desirability of the psychologist on decisions regarding confidentiality," Psychol and Health, 14 (99): 567-584; coauth with K. M. Vespia, "Counseling psychology students and professionals: Scientist and practitioner orientations and work environments," J of Col Student Psychotherapy, 14 (99): 23-41; coauth with K. M. Vespia and J. E. Kanz, "The relevance of vocational psychology in a multicultural workplace: Exploring issues of race/ethnicity and social class," in D. Pope-Davis and H. L. K. Hardin, eds, Multicultural counseling in 2000, Sage (in press); coauth with P. P. Heppner, J. M. Casas, and J. Carter, "The maturation of counseling psychology: Multifaceted perspectives, 1978-98," in S. D. Brown and R. W. Lent, eds, Handbook of counseling psychology, 3rd ed (in press). **CONTACT ADDRESS** Dept Psychol Foundations, The Univ of Iowa, 361 Lindquist Ctr N, Iowa City, IA 52242.

STONE, RUTH J.
PERSONAL Born 01/01/1949, Tuscumbia, AL, d, 1 child **DISCIPLINE** PSYCHOLOGY **EDUCATION** Univ N Ala, BS, 70; Univ N Ala, MA, 75; Vanderbilt Univ, EdD, 85. **CAREER** Adj Instr, Vanderbilt Univ, 81-83; Adj Prof, Univ N Ala, 85-87; Prof, Northwest-Shoals Community Col, 84-. **HONORS AND AWARDS** Int Poet of Merit, 99; Phi Delta Kappa. **MEMBERSHIPS** AEA, NEA. **RESEARCH** Human behavior, human development. **SELECTED PUBLICATIONS** Auth, 5 Easy Steps to Good Cursive Writing: Children's Moments. **CONTACT ADDRESS** Dept Soc Sci, Northwest-Shoals Comm Col, PO Box 2545, Muscle Shoals, AL 35662.

STORER, NORMAN WILLIAM
PERSONAL Born 06/08/1930, Middletown, CT, m, 1975, 2 children **DISCIPLINE** SOCIOLOGY **EDUCATION** Univ KS, BA, 52, MA, 56; Cornell Univ, PhD, 61. **CAREER** Instr-asst prof, Harvard Univ, 60-66; staff assoc, Soc Sci Res Coun, New York City, 66-70; prof, Baruch Col, CUNY, 70-88; prof Emeritus, 89- , Community Serv: Mem, San Diego Hate Crimes Mgt Team, 95- ; Citizen Volunteer, San Diego Sheriff's Dept, 93- ; Column ed., San Diego Writer's Monthly, 94-96. **HONORS AND AWARDS** Phi Beta Kappa, 52; Sigma Xi, 95. **MEMBERSHIPS** AAAS. **RESEARCH** Sociology of science;

academic organization; domestic violence. **SELECTED PUBLICATIONS** Auth, The Social System of Science, Holt, Rinehart & Winston, 66; ed, The Sociology of Science: Theoretical and Empirical Investigation, by Robert K Merton, Univ Chicago Press, 73; auth, Focus on Society: An Introduction to Sociology, Addison-Wesley, 2nd ed, 80; The Teaching Relationship: A Hypothesized Model and Its Consequences, in Mid-American Review of Sociology, vol 14, no 1-2, winter 90; The Department of Sociology and..: The Significance of Disciplinary Purity on American Campuses, in Gale Miller, ed, Studies in Organizational Sociology: Essays in Honor of Charles K Warriner, JAI Press, 91; How Alcohol Affects DV Calls, in Law Enforcement Quart, Nov 93-Jan 94; Domestic Violence in Suburban San Diego, with William D Flores, Conimar Press, 94. **CONTACT ADDRESS** 1417 Van Buren Ave, San Diego, CA 92103-2339. **EMAIL** mwstorer@peoplepc.com

STOTT, DEBORAH
PERSONAL Born 06/11/1942, Minneapolis, MN **DISCIPLINE** WOMEN'S STUDIES, ART HISTORY **EDUCATION** Wellesley Col, BA, 64; Columbia Univ, Phd, 75. **CAREER** Assoc prof. **HONORS AND AWARDS** Fel, Bunting Inst of Radcliffe Col, 83; fel, Am Academy in Rome, 80. **MEMBERSHIPS** Col Art Asn; Renaissance Soc; Sixteenth Century Studies Soc; Italian Art Soc; Asn of Textual Art Historians. **RESEARCH** European and Italian art history; history and imagery of early modern women; history of women artists. **SELECTED PUBLICATIONS** Auth, The Sculpture of Andrea and Nino Pisano (rev), 86; auth, Optical Corrections in the Sculpture of Donatello (rev), 87; auth, Style and Theory in Italian Renaissance Reliefs, Cambridge, 83; auth, Fatte a sembianza di pittura: Jacopo Sansovino's Bronze Reliefs in San Marco, Art Bulletin, 82; auth, Jacques Lipchitz and Cubism, Garland, 78; auth, Outstanding Dissertations in the Fine Arts, Garland, 78. **CONTACT ADDRESS** School of Arts and Humanities, Univ of Texas, Dallas, P.O. Box 830688, Richardson, TX 75083-0688. **EMAIL** stott@utdallas.edu

STRAND, VIRGINIA
PERSONAL Born 06/23/1948, New Rochelle, NY, s **DISCIPLINE** SOCIAL WORK **EDUCATION** McAlester Col, BA, 70; Cath Univ Sch Soc Work, MSW, 75; Columbia Univ Sch Soc Work, DSW, 86. **CAREER** Asst prof to assoc prof, Fordham Univ, 88-. **HONORS AND AWARDS** NASW Soc Worker of the Year, Westchester County, 86. **MEMBERSHIPS** Nat Asn of Soc Workers, Am Orthopsych Asn. **RESEARCH** Mental health and Child welfare. **SELECTED PUBLICATIONS** Auth, The assessment and treatment of family sexual abuse. Play therapy with children in crisis, Guilford Press: NY, 99; auth, The impact of race and ethnicity on treatment of the mother in the incest family in E Congress. Multi cultural perspectives in working with families, Springer Pub: NY, 96; auth, "Single parents: direct practice," Encyclopedia of social work, Silver Springs, 95. **CONTACT ADDRESS** Dept Soc Service, Fordham Univ, 113 W 60th St, New York, NY 10023. **EMAIL** strand@fordham.edu

STRASSBERG, BARBARA
PERSONAL Born 08/22/1945, Krakow, Poland, 2 children **DISCIPLINE** SOCIOLOGY **EDUCATION** MA, 67, 70, PhD, 75, Jagiellonian Univ, Cracow, Poland; post-doct stud, Univ Chicago, 77-78. **CAREER** Lectr, Teachers Col, Cracow, 70-72; asst prof, 72-76, assoc prof 78-84, Jagiellonian Univ; hon fel, 84-86, vis scholar, 87, Univ Chicago; lect, Triton Col, 85, 86, Univ Chicago, 86, Coll of Du Page, 86- , De Paul Univ, 89, Columbia Col, 90, 91; asst prof, 91-94, assoc prof, 94- , Aurora Univ. **HONORS AND AWARDS** F. Zananiecki Awd of the Polish Acad of Sci for The Church in the Process of Assimilation of Polish Americans, 85; Who's Who in the Midwest, 94; World Who's Who of Women, 95; Who's Who of Am Women, 95. **MEMBERSHIPS** Am Asn Univ Women; Midwest Sociol Soc; Illinois Sociol Asn; Soc for Sci Study of Jewry; Am Sociol Asn; Illinois Sociol Asn; Asn for Sociolog of Relig; Soc for Sci Study of Relig. **SELECTED PUBLICATIONS** Auth, "The Origins of the Polish National Catholic Church," PNCC Stud, 86; "Polish Catholicism in Transition," ed. Gannon,World Catholicism in Transition, Macmillan, 88; "Changes in Religious Culture in Post-World War II Poland," Sociol Analysis, 88; trans, Malinowski, Coral Gardens, Polish Scientific Pub, 85; Magic, Science and religion, Polish Scientific Pub, 85; Polish Americans, Ossolineum, 85; The Polish National Catholic Church in Relation to Modern Theological Ecumenical and Social Issues, Kosciol Polskokatolicki, 84. **CONTACT ADDRESS** Dept of Sociology, Aurora Univ, Aurora, IL 60605. **EMAIL** bstrass@admin.aurora.edu

STRATTON, JOHN RAY
PERSONAL Born 03/12/1935, Sandwich, IL, m, 1957, 2 children **DISCIPLINE** SOCIOLOGY **EDUCATION** Univ IL, BA, 57, MA, 69, PhD, 63. **CAREER** Instr, Bradley Univ, Peoria, IL, 61-64; asst prof, 64-68, assoc prof, Univ IA, 68-; vis asst prof, San Diego State Univ, summer 67. **HONORS AND AWARDS** NIMH, 66; Univ IA Old Gold Awd, summer 68; US Dept of Justice, Office of Law Enforcement Assistance, 68, 69; NSF Dissertation grants, two in 73; IA Dept of Social Services grants, two in 80; IA Criminal and Juvenile Justice Agency Quick Stop Evaluation, 84; Governors Volunteer Awd, 84; Outstanding Citizen Awd, IA Correctional Asn, 87; Correctional Center, 6th Judicial District, dedicated in honor of Dr Stratton, 92; Distinguished Service Awd, Midwest Psychoil Sco, 94l; SROP Distinguished Mentor Awd, Commitee on Inst Cooperation, 95. **MEMBERSHIPS** Midwest Sociol Asn. **RESEARCH** Corrections; sexual assault. **SELECTED PUBLICATIONS** Ed, with Robet Leger, Sociology of Corrections, Wiley & Sons, 77; auth, with David A Parton and Michael Shanahan, The Use of Discretion in Prison Discipline Committees, Am J of Criminal Justice, 12:1, fall 87; auth, with David A Parton and Mark Hansel, Measuring Crime Seriousness: Lessons from the National Survey of Crime Severity, British J of Criminology, 91; numerous other publications. **CONTACT ADDRESS** Dept of Sociol, The Univ of Iowa, Iowa City, IA 52246. **EMAIL** JohnStratton@blue.weeg.UIowa.edu

STRAUS, LAWRENCE G.
DISCIPLINE ANTHROPOLOGY **EDUCATION** Univ Chicago, AB, 71; AM, 72; PhD, 75. **CAREER** Asst to Full Prof and Dept Chair, 75-. **HONORS AND AWARDS** Fel, Nat Sci foundation; Fel, Nat Geog Soc, Fel, L.S.B. Leakey Foundation. **MEMBERSHIPS** SC Am Archeol, Am Anthropol Asn, IWOUA, UISPP, Societe Prehistorique Francoise, societe Prehistorigne de l'ariege-Pyrenees. **RESEARCH** Stone age prehistoric archeology/paleoanthropology, Western Europe (Spain, Portugal, France, Belgium), Upper Paleolithic, Middle Paleolithic, Mesolithic, Neolithic, hunter gatherers, lithics, fauna, paleoenivronments, caves/rockshelters, site formation processes. **SELECTED PUBLICATIONS** Auth, Le Trou Magrite, Eraul, Liege, 95; auth, Humans at the end of the Ice Age, Plenum Press, 96; auth, La Grotte du Bois Laiterie, Eraul, Liege, 97; auth, "As the world warmed: Human adaptations Across the Pleistocene-Holocene Boundary," Quaternary International, 98; auth, L'Abri du Pape, Eraul 88, Liege, 99; auth, "An American in stone age Spain: Homenaje de sus alumnos al Prof L.G. Freeman, jar, 00; auth, Out of Africa in the Pleistocene, Quaternary Intl, in press. **CONTACT ADDRESS** Dept Anthropol, Univ of New Mexico, Albuquerque, Albuquerque, NM 87131-0001. **EMAIL** lstraus@unm.edu

STRAUS, MURRAY A.
DISCIPLINE SOCIOLOGY **EDUCATION** Univ Wis, BA, 48; MS, 49; PhD, 56. **CAREER** Lectr, Univ of Ceylon, 49-52; asst prof, Wash State Univ, 54-47; asst prof, Univ of Wis, 57-59; assoc prof, Cornell Univ, 59-61; prof, Univ of Minn, 61-68; prof, Univ of NH, 68-. **HONORS AND AWARDS** Ernest W. Burgess Awd, 77; Awd for Contributions to Teaching, ASA, 79; Awd for Distinguished Contributions, NH Psychol Soc, 93; Research Career Achievement Awd, Am Prof Soc on the Abuse of Children, 94. **SELECTED PUBLICATIONS** Coauth, Handbook of Family Measurement Techniques, Sage, 90; coauth, Physical Violence in American Families: Risk Factors and Adaptations to Violence in 8,145 Families, Transaction Books, 90; coauth, Beating The Devil Out of Them: Corporal Punishment in American Families, Lexington/Jossey Bass, 94; coauth, Understanding Partner Violence, Nat Coun on Family Relations, 95; coauth, Stress, Culture and Aggression, Yale, 95; auth, "Spanking by Parents - Some ideas on Measurement and Analysis of a Neglected Risk Factor for Serious Mental health Problems, Behav Measurements Letter 15.2 (98): 3-8; coauth, "Impulsive Corporal Punishment by Mothers and Antisocial Behavior and Impulsiveness of Children", Behav Sci and the Law 16, (98): 353-374; auth, "The Controversy Over Domestic Violence by Women: A Methodological, Theoretical, and Sociology of Science Analysis", Violence in Intimate Relationships, eds X. Arriaga and S. Oskamp, Sage, (Thousand Oaks, Ca), 99; coauth, "Corporal punishment by American parents: National data on prevalence, chronicity, severity, and duration, in relation to child, and family characteristics", Clinical Child and Family Psychol Rev 2.2 (99): 55-70. **CONTACT ADDRESS** Dept Sociol, Univ of New Hampshire, Durham, 125 Technology Dr, Durham, NH 03824.

STRAUSER, DAVID
PERSONAL Born 09/04/1968, Wautosa, WI, m, 1990, 3 children **DISCIPLINE** COUNSELING **EDUCATION** Univ Wis Madison, BS, 90; MS, 91; PhD, 95. **CAREER** TA to asst prof, Univ of Memphis 93-. **HONORS AND AWARDS** NCRE Early Career Awd, 97; Certificate of Distinguished Serv, Alliance for Rehabil Coun, 99. **MEMBERSHIPS** Am Coun Assoc; Am Rehabil Coun Assoc; Nat Rehabil Assoc. **RESEARCH** Work, Personality, Career Development, Vocational Behavior. **SELECTED PUBLICATIONS** Coauth, "The role of self-efficacy and locus of control in job readiness training programs", Work 10, (98): 243-249; coauth, "A model of rehabilitation counseling case conceptualization", Rehabil Educ 12 (98): 181-192; coauth, "Applications of self-efficacy theory to college students with disabilities", J of Appl Rehabil Coun 29, (98): 25-30; coauth, "Planning strategies in disability management", Work 10, (98): 261-270; coauth, "Applications of self-efficacy to the transition from school to work", J of Vocational Rehabil 11 (98): 125-132; coauth, "Horizontal expansion of the role of the rehabilitation counselor", J of Rehabil 65.1 (99): 4-9; coauth, "Reconceptualizing the work personality", Rehabil Coun Bull 42, (99): 290-301; coauth, "Job readiness self-efficacy and work personality: A comparison of trainee and instructor perceptions", J of Vocational Rehabil (forthcoming); coauth, "The relationship between the sense of coherence to life satisfaction for students with disabilities", Rehabil Coun Bull (forthcoming). **CONTACT ADDRESS** Dept Coun, Univ of Memphis, 3706 Alumni St, Memphis, TN 38152-0001.

STRAUSSNER, SHULAMITH LALA
PERSONAL Born, Poland, m, 1969, 2 children **DISCIPLINE** SOCIAL WORK **EDUCATION** City Col NY, BA, 69; Fordham Univ, MSW, 72; Columbia Univ, DSW, 86. **CAREER** Asst prof to prof, NYork Univ, 85-. **HONORS AND AWARDS** Psi Chi; NIMH Grant, 79-80; Fel, Inst for Rational-Emotive Behav, 96; grant, NYS Addiction Tech Transfer Ctr, 98-99; Human Resources and Serv Admin/AMERSA Grant, 99-01. **MEMBERSHIPS** Acad of Certified Soc Workers; AAAS; AMERSA; Coun on Soc Work Educ; Employee Assistance Prof Assoc; Nat Assoc of Soc Workers; Soc of Clinical Soc Workers. **RESEARCH** Addictions, Mental health in the workplace. **SELECTED PUBLICATIONS** Coed, Psychosocial Issues in the Treatment of Alcoholism, Haworth Pr, (NY), 85; ed, Occupational Social Work Today, Haworth, Pr, 90; ed, Clinical Work with Substance Abusing Clients, Guilford Pr, (NY), 93; coed, Children in the Urban Environment: Linking Social Policy and Clinical Practice, Charles C Thomas, (Springfield, IL), 96; coed, Gender and Addictions: Men and Women in Treatment, Jason Aronson, (Northvale, NJ), 97; auth, "Gender issues in addictions: An overview", Gender and Addictions: Men and Women in Treatment, eds S Straussner and E Zelvin, Jason Aronson, (Northvale, 97); auth, "Group treatment with substance abusing clients: a model of treatment during the early phases of outpatient group therapy", Innovative approaches to group treatment with substance abusers, ed LD McVinney, Haworth Pr, (NY, 97); ed, Ethnocultural Issues in the Treatment of Addictions, Guilford, (NY), (forthcoming); auth, "The Referral Process", Addiction Technology Transfer Center Counselor Manual, Univ of Haw, (forthcoming); coauth, "Brief treatment of substance abusers", Handbook of Brief Treatment, eds B Dane, C Tosone and A Wolfson, Jason Aronson, (Northvale, NJ), (forthcoming). **CONTACT ADDRESS** Sch of Soc Work, New York Univ, 1 Washington Sq N, New York, NY 10003. **EMAIL** lala.straussner@nyu.edu

STRAWSER, SHERRI C.
DISCIPLINE SCHOOL PSYCHOLOGY, ASSESSMENT IN SPECIAL EDUCATION, LEARNING DISABILITIES **EDUCATION** Univ Utah, PhD, 85. **CAREER** Dir, except children's serv, Univ Nev, Las Vegas. **HONORS AND AWARDS** Educ of the Yr, State Asn for Retarded Citizens of Utah, 90; fed res grant, US Dept of Educ; fed trng pers prep grant, US Dept of Educ; Utah Ctr of Excellence grant, Off of Econ Develop of Utah. **SELECTED PUBLICATIONS** Auth, Assessment and identification practices, in W. N. Bender, ed, Learning disabilities: Best practices professionals, Andover Med Publ, 93; coauth, Assessment of subtypes of learning disabilities: A practical approach to diagnosis and intervention, Spec Serv in Sch, 6 (1/2), 90. **CONTACT ADDRESS** Dept of Spec Educ, Univ of Nevada, Las Vegas, 4505 Maryland Pky, Las Vegas, NV 89154-3014. **EMAIL** strawser@nevada.edu

STREET, RICHARD L., JR.
DISCIPLINE HEALTH COMMUNICATION **EDUCATION** Univ Tex, PhD. **CAREER** Prof, Texas A&M Univ; res prof, Col Med, Texas A&M Univ. **HONORS AND AWARDS** Col Liberal Arts Distinguished Tchg Awd, Former Students Asn Texas A&M Univ. **SELECTED PUBLICATIONS** Co-ed, Health Promotion and Interactive Technology; contribur, Talk of the Clinic: Explorations in the Analysis of Medical and Therapeutic Discourse; Communication and Health Outcomes; Handbook of Interpersonal Communication; Applied CommunicationTheory and Research. **CONTACT ADDRESS** Dept of Speech Communication, Texas A&M Univ, Col Station, College Station, TX 77843-4234. **EMAIL** r-street@tamu.edu

STRICKLAND, DOROTHY S.
PERSONAL Born 09/29/1933, Newark, NJ, m, 1955 **DISCIPLINE** EDUCATION **EDUCATION** Kean Coll, BS; NYork Univ, MA, PhD, 51-55; NYork Univ, MA, 56-58, PhD, 67-71. **CAREER** Kean Coll, prof 1970-80; NY Univ, adj prof; Jersey City State Coll, asst prof; Learning Disability Spec E Orange, teacher, reading consultant; Teachers Coll Columbia Univ, prof of Educ 1980-; Rutgers University, prof (state prof of reading) 1990; Teachers College, prof 1980-90. **HONORS AND AWARDS** Woman of the Year Zeta Phi Beta 1980; Natl Rsch Awd Natl Council Teachers English 1972; Founders Day Recognition NY Univ 1971; Outstanding Teacher Educ Reading, Intl Reading Assn, 1985; Awd for Outstanding Contribution to Ed, Natl Assn of Univ Women, 1987; emerging literacy, Intl Reading assn, 1989; admin & supvr, reading programs, Teachers Coll Press, 1989; Elected Reading Hall of Fame, International Reading Assn, 1990; Distinguished Alumni Awd, New York University, 1990; Outstanding Alumni Awd, Kean College of NJ, 1990; National Council of Teachers of English Awd for Research; Rewey Bell Inglis Awd as Outstanding Woman in English Education; Recipient, IN Univ Citation, Outstanding Contributions to Literacy, 1998. **MEMBERSHIPS** Teacher, East Orange, NJ, 1955-61; reading specialist, East Orange, NJ, 1961-66; Jersey City State Coll, Jersey City, NJ, 1966-70; bd of dir Natl Council Teachers English; Educ advisory bd Early Years Magazine; chmn Early Childhood Educ; mem Journal

Reading Instructor, Websters New World Dictionary, commission Sprint Magazine; pres Intl Reading Assoc 1978-79; mem Natl Comm Ed Migrant Children; trustee, Research Found, Natl Council Teachers English, 1983-86. **SELECTED PUBLICATIONS** Author, editor, or co-editor, Language Literacy and the Child, Process Reading and Writing: A Literature Based Approach, Emerging Literacy: Young Children Learn to Read and Write, The Administration and Supervision of Reading Programs, Educating Black Children: America's Challenge, Family Storybook Reading, Listen Children: An Anthology of Black Literature, Families: An Anthology of Poetry for Young Children; Publications: Literacy Instruction in Half Day and Full Day Kindergartens, Newark, DE Intl Reading Assn, Morrow LM, Strickland, DS, & Woo, D, 1998; Teaching Phonics Today, Newark, DE, Intl Reading Assn, Strickland DS, 1998. **CONTACT ADDRESS** Professor of Reading, Rutgers, The State Univ of New Jersey, New Brunswick, 10 Seminary Place, New Brunswick, NJ 08903.

STRICKLAND, JOHNYE
DISCIPLINE WOMEN WRITERS **EDUCATION** Univ Ark, PhD. **CAREER** English and Lit, Univ Ark **SELECTED PUBLICATIONS** Auth, Vietnamese Refugees in America: Expectations and Realities, SW Asian Soc Newsl; Huy Luc and Phan Tung Mai: Prize Winning Vietnamese Writers, S Central Mod Lang Asn Bull; Oral History in the College Classroom, Oral Hist Rev; The Position of Women--Teachers and Students, Col Comm & Composition; Two Hundred Years of Law and Liberty, Ark Lawyer. **CONTACT ADDRESS** Univ of Arkansas, Little Rock, 2801 S University Ave., Little Rock, AR 72204-1099. **EMAIL** jestrickland@ualr.edu

STRIEBY, H. REID
PERSONAL Born 10/05/1934, Chicago, IL, m, 1992, 2 children **DISCIPLINE** PSYCHOLOGY **EDUCATION** Univ Chicago, BA, 53, MS, 62; Fielding Inst, PhD, 74; Center for Behav Psychotherapy, Post-Doctoral Internship, 76, 78. **CAREER** Lectr, Ill Inst of Technol, Chicago, 58-60; Res Analyst, Nat Opinion Res Center, Univ Chicago, 58-60; Sr Res Analyst, Market Facts, Inc, Chicago, Ill, 62-64; assoc res dir, Ted Bates Adverstising Agency, NYC, 64-70; adjunct prof of psychol, New Sch for Soc Res, NYC, 77-78; Private Practice, Psychotherapy, New York City, 78-94; ed consult, Dept of Preventative Med, Montefiore Med Center, 87-91; prin investr, Health Force: Women Agaginst AIDS, 89-94; prin investr, BCC/AIDS Street Outreach Prog, BCC, 90-94; proj dir, Bronx Tech Prep Prog, BCC, 93-; proj dir, Federal Sch-to-Work Prog, BCC, 94-; Co-dir, Environ Tech Prog, BCC, 97-; Prof, Psychology, Bronx Community Col, 70-. **HONORS AND AWARDS** Coordr, Allied Health Comt, Bronx Community Col, 89-99; Honoree, Med Soc of NY, 93; Chair, Psycho-Social Service Sub-Comt, CUNY Task Force on Health Care Profs, 94-95; Co-chair, NY State Dept of Ed Task Force for Integration of Tech Prep and School-to-Work Progs in NYC, 95-96; Adv Bd and Steering Comt, Bronx Ed Alliance, 97-; Honoree and found mem, Health Force: Women Against AIDS, 96; Principal Investigator: Health Force: Women Against AIDS, and AIDS Street Outreach Prog; Proj Dir, School-to-Work Prog, Tech Prep Prog; Univ Honoree for Recipients of major institutional grants for teaching and public service, CUNY, 93-94, 99-2000; Chair PSY-CUNY, Univ Comt on Res Awds in Psychol, 97-; Delegate, Conf Study Tour in South Africa, Nat Ctr for Urban Partnerships, Aug 98; Co-dir, Environ Technol Prog, 98; Nat Sci Fel, 99. **MEMBERSHIPS** Partnership for Environ Technol Ed, NY City Acad of Sci, Union of Concerned Sci, Am Psychol Asn, Am Public Health Asn, Unitarian Universalists Asn, CUNY Acad for the Humanities and Scis. **SELECTED PUBLICATIONS** Auth, "How to Prepare and Receive a Federal Work-to-School Grant, " NY State Tech Prep Newsletter, Vol 1, No 1 (Jan 95); auth, "High Spirits in Highbridge: BCC's School-to-Work Program," CUNY Matters, Newsletter for the City University of New York (summer 95); auth, "A Re-evaluation of School-to-Work Employment Opportunities for high school youth," Vol 1 , No 1 (March 99). **CONTACT ADDRESS** Environ Technol Prog, Bronx Comm Col, CUNY, Butler Hall, Room 201, 181st & University Ave, Bronx, NY 10453. **EMAIL** faheychem@aol.com

STRIER, KAREN
DISCIPLINE ANTHROPOLOGY **EDUCATION** Swarthmore Col, BA, 80; Harvard Univ, MA, 81; PhD, 86. **CAREER** Asst prof, Beloit Col, 87-89; asst prof to prof, Univ of Wis Madison, 89-. **HONORS AND AWARDS** Presidential Young Investigator Awd, 89-94. **MEMBERSHIPS** AAAS; AAA; AAPA; Animal Behav Soc. **RESEARCH** Primate behavioral ecology and conservation. **SELECTED PUBLICATIONS** Auth, Faces in the Forest: The Endangered Murquis Monkey of Brazil, Oxford Univ Pr, 92, Harvard Univ Pr, 99; auth, Primate Behavior Ecology, Allyn and Bacon, 00. **CONTACT ADDRESS** Dept Anthropology, Univ of Wisconsin, Madison, 1180 Observatory Dr, 5240 Soc Sci Bldg, Madison, WI 53706. **EMAIL** kbstrier@facstaff.wisc.edu

STROMBERG, PETER G.
PERSONAL Born 10/28/1952, Minneapolis, MN, m, 1992, 2 children **DISCIPLINE** ANTHROPOLOGY **EDUCATION** Purdue Univ, BS, 70; BA, 74; Stanford Univ, PhD, 81. **CAREER** Assoc Prof, Univ Tulsa, 92-. **HONORS AND AWARDS** Bicentennial Swedish-Am Exchange Fund Fel, 86; Am-Scandinavian Found Res Fel, 86; Nat Endowment Humanities Fel, Univ Tulsa, 91; Fac Summer Develop Awd, Univ Tulsa, 92; Outstanding Teacher Awd, Univ Tulsa, 99. **MEMBERSHIPS** AAA, NAA, AES, SPA. **RESEARCH** Contemporary culture, addiction. **SELECTED PUBLICATIONS** Auth, Language and Self-Transformation: A Study of the Christian Conversion Narrative, Cambridge UP (Cambridge), 93; auth, "Theories of the Transcendent," Rev in Anthrop 27 (98): 303-316; auth, "The 'I' of Enthrallment," Ethos (99); auth, Enthralled: Symbolic Perfection in the Culture of Advertising and Entertainment, Cambridge UP (Cambridge), forthcoming. **CONTACT ADDRESS** Dept Anthrop, Univ of Tulsa, 600 S College, Tulsa, OK 74104. **EMAIL** peter-stromberg@utulsa.edu

STRONG-BOAG, VERONICA
PERSONAL Born 07/05/1947, Scotland **DISCIPLINE** HISTORY, WOMEN'S STUDIES **EDUCATION** Univ Toronto, BA, 70; Carleton Univ, MA, 71; Univ Toronto, PhD, 75. **CAREER** Hist/Women's Stud School, dept hist, Trent Univ, 74-76; Concordia Univ, 76-80; dept hist & women's stud prog, Simon Fraser Univ, 80-91; dir, Ctr Res Women's Stud & Gender Rel, 91-97, Prof Educational Studies, Univ BC, 91-. **HONORS AND AWARDS** John A. Macdonald Prize, Can Hist Asn **MEMBERSHIPS** Can Hist Asn (pres, 93-93) **RESEARCH** Women's History Family and Education Canadian History Gender. **SELECTED PUBLICATIONS** Co-ed, Rethinking Canada, (Toronto: Copp clark, Pitman, 91), 455; co-ed, british colubmia reconsidered: Essays on Women in B.C., (Vancouver Press Gang), 92; auth, "A History of the Canadian Peoples: 1867 to the Present," vol 2, (Tornonto: Copp Clark Pitman, 93), 2 chap; auth, "Janey Canuck: Women in Canada Between Two World Wars, 1919-1939," CHA Hist Booklet, 94; auth, Their Side of the Story: Women'sw Vioces from Ontario Suburbs, 1945-1960, (Toronto: Univ of Toronto Press, 95); auth, "Too Much and Not Enough-- The Pradox of Power for Feminnist Adaemics Working with Community Feminist on Issues Related to Violence," Violence: A Collectgive Responsibility, (Ottawa: Soc Sci Fed of Can, 95); auth, "Chapter 11 B.C. Society in th 20th Century," the Pacific Provice, (Vancover: Douglas & McIntyre, 96); co-auth, "Constructing Canada: An Intoduction," in Painting the Maple: Essays on Race, Gender and the Construction of Canada, (Vancouver: UBC Press, 98); auth, "A Red Girl's Reasoning: E. Pauline Johnson constructs the New Nation," in Painting the Maple, (Vancouver: UBC Press, 98); auth, "What Women's Space?: Changing Suburbs: Foundation, Form and Function, (London: E & FNSPON, 99). **CONTACT ADDRESS** Dept Educ Stud, Univ of British Columbia, 2125 Main Mall, Vancouver, BC, Canada V6T 1Z4. **EMAIL** veronica.strong-boag@ubc.ca

STUBBS, JANET C.
PERSONAL Born 05/18/1949, New York, NY, m, 1971, 2 children **DISCIPLINE** PSYCHOLOGY **EDUCATION** Univ Mass, BS, 71; Univ Mich, MA, 72; PhD, 81. **CAREER** Asst Prof, Bridgewater St Col, 78-84; Clinical Psychol, 86-; From Assoc Prof to Prof, Salem St Col, 90-. **HONORS AND AWARDS** Col Citation for Meritorious Serv, Salem St Col, 87; Phi Kappa Phi, 87-; Bronze Medal, CASE, 88. **MEMBERSHIPS** APA, NEPA. **RESEARCH** Transitional roles for women. **SELECTED PUBLICATIONS** Auth, "The Role of the Psychologist," in Soc Work with Abused and Neglected Children (New York: Free Pr, 81); auth, "Interviewing the Child," in Protecting Children Through the Legal Sys (Washington: Am Bar Asn, 81); auth, "Questioning Children," in Guardian Ad Litem Handbk, 2nd Ed (Madison, WI: St Bar of Wis, 97). **CONTACT ADDRESS** Dept Psychol, Salem State Col, 352 Lafayette St, Salem, MA 01970. **EMAIL** janet.stubbs@salem.mass.edu

STUBER-MCEWEN, DONNA
PERSONAL Born 12/12/1954, Kansas City, MD, m, 1999 **DISCIPLINE** PSYCHOLOGY **EDUCATION** Kans State Univ, PhD. **CAREER** Assoc prof, Friends Univ, 96-. **HONORS AND AWARDS** Master's Thesis accepted in grad student res competition at the 7th Int Congress of Personal Construct Psychol, May 87; Founded The Mid America Psychol Conf for Community & Jr Cols, 92; Psi Beta Nat Coun: South Central Regional vice-pres, 92-93, Nat Pres-Elect, 93-94, Nat Pres, 94-95, Nat Past Pres, 95-96; "Research Through the Curriculum" model prog, North Central Mo Col, featured in APA Monitor, Oct 95; listed in Who's Who in Am Teachers, 96, 98; Outstanding Recent Grad Awd, The Teachers' Col, Emporia State Univ, 98. **MEMBERSHIPS** Am Psychol Soc, Asn for Psychol & Ed Res in Kans, Coun of Teachers of Undergraduate Psychol, Great Plains Behavioral Res Asn, Southwestern Psychol Asn. **RESEARCH** College and university response to emotionally disturbed students, jury dynamics, student/faculty rapport. **SELECTED PUBLICATIONS** Auth, "The bell curve: A return to Social Darwinism?" Psi Beta Newsletter, 15, 2 (spring 95): 2,4; coauth with M. Dannells, "Responding to behaviorally and emotionally disturbed students: Assessment and intervention practices," Col Student J, 30 (96): 287-293; auth, "Innovative community college teaching methods: Research through the curriculum," (Report No CG026961) East Lansing, MI: Nat Center for Res on Teacher Learning (ERIC Document Reproduction Service No 395230) (96); coauth with J. Ruddman, R. Hailstorks, & R. Nesmith, How to host a psychology conference at your college: A model from the Psi Beta National Office," www and hard copy, URL: http://www.lemoyne.edu/ORTP/; auth, "Professional development (Part I): Career decisions," Psi Beta National Newsletter, 19, 1 (fall 99): 2-3; auth, "Professional development (Part II): Developing as a professional," Psi Beta National Newsletter, 19, 3 (winter 2000); auth, "Professional development (Part III): How to be both marketable and happy," Psi Beta Nat Newsletter (in press); auth, "Professional development (Part II): Building Your Credentials," Psi Beta National Newsletter, 20, 1 (in press): 1, 4-5; auth, "Professional development (Part III): To be, or not be marketable AND happy," Psi Beta National Newsletter (in press); coauth with J. Rudmann, "How to develop and implement a psychology career course at your college: A model from the National Office of Psi Beat (Teaching Resources), WWW and hard copy, URL: Http://www.ivc.cc.ca.us/PSIBETA/ (in press, web site in progress). **CONTACT ADDRESS** Dept Psychol, Friends Univ, 2100 W University, Wichita, KS 67213. **EMAIL** mcewen@friends.edu

STUCK, MARY FRANCES
PERSONAL Born 09/23/1949, Kenton, OH, p **DISCIPLINE** SOCIOLOGY **EDUCATION** Oh State Univ, BS, 71; Syracuse Univ, MS, 72; MA, 81; PhD, 85. **CAREER** Instructor, Syracuse Univ, 83; Adj Fac to Full Prof, SUNY-Oswego, 85-. **HONORS AND AWARDS** Phi Kappa Phi, 82; Alpha Kappa Delta, 82; Chancellor's Awd, SUNY, 91; Who's Who of Am Women, 93; PDQWL Experienced Fac Dev Awd, SUNY, 94, 95. **MEMBERSHIPS** Nat Women's Sport Foundation. **SELECTED PUBLICATIONS** Ed, Issues in Diversity: Voices of the Silenced, Copley, 90; auth, Adolescent Worlds: Drug Use and Athletic Activity, Praeger, 90; auth, "Sexism in Computer Clip Art," in Rethinking the Roles of Technology in Education, (Univ TX, 93), 95-97; auth, "Philanthropy or Marketing: Major Computer Corporations' Efforts to Place Computers into the Public Schools," in Rethinking the Roles of Technology in Education, (Univ TX, 93), 98-100; ed, Structures and Processes of Inequality, Copley, 94; auth, "Gay and Lesbian Studies Programs," in Encyclopedia of Multiculturalism, (Salem Press, 94), 758-760; auth, "Conflict Perspectives of Deviance," in Survey of Social Science; Sociology, (Salem Press, 94), 334-339; auth, "Deviance: Analysis and Overview," in Survey of Social Science: Sociology, (Salem Press, 94), 525-531; auth, "The Lesbian Experience: An Analysis," in Lesbians in Academia: Degrees of Freedom, (Routledge Pub, 97), 210-220; ed, Structures and Processes of Inequality 2nd ed, Copley; 97. **CONTACT ADDRESS** Dept Sociol, SUNY, Oswego, 7060 State Rte 104, Oswego, NY 13126. **EMAIL** Stuck@oswego.edu

STUCKEY, PRISCILLA F.
PERSONAL Born 03/21/1957, OH, s **DISCIPLINE** GENDER AND RELIGIOUS STUDIES **EDUCATION** Grad Theol Union, PhD, 97 **CAREER** Development Editor **HONORS AND AWARDS** Young Scholars Awd, 95. **MEMBERSHIPS** Natl Women's Studies Asn, Am Acad of Religion. **SELECTED PUBLICATIONS** Auth, Light Dispels Darkness: Gender, Ritual and Society in Mozart's The Magic Flute, 95. **CONTACT ADDRESS** 3060 Butters Dr, Oakland, CA 94602. **EMAIL** pstuckey@california.com

STUDZINSKI, RAYMOND JAMES
PERSONAL Born 04/18/1943, Detroit, MI **DISCIPLINE** RELIGION, PSYCHOLOGY **EDUCATION** St Meinrad Col, BA, 66; IN Univ, MA, 73; Fordham Univ, PhD(theol), 77. **CAREER** Asst prof theol, St Meinrad Sch Theol, 73-77; fel, Menninger Found, 79-81; asst prof relig, 81-85, assoc prof relig, Cath Univ Am, 85-. **MEMBERSHIPS** Soc Sci Study Relig; Relig Res Asn. **RESEARCH** Psychology of religion; contemporary spirituality; spiritual direction. **SELECTED PUBLICATIONS** Spiritual Direction and Midlife Development, Chicago: Loyola Univ Press, 85. **CONTACT ADDRESS** Relig Dept, Catholic Univ of America, 620 Michigan Ave N E, Washington, DC 20064-0002. **EMAIL** studzinski@cua.edu

STUKAS, ARTHUR A.
PERSONAL Born 10/28/1967, New York, NY, s **DISCIPLINE** PSYCHOLOGY **EDUCATION** Col Williams & Mary, BA, 89; Univ Minn, PhD, 96. **CAREER** Asst Prof, Univ Northern Colo, 98-. **MEMBERSHIPS** SPSP, SPSSI, APS, APA. **RESEARCH** Volunteerism, behavioral confirmation, prejudice and stereotyping, health psychology. **SELECTED PUBLICATIONS** Coauth, "Interpersonal Processes: The Interplay of cognitive Motivational and Behavioral Activities in Social Interaction," Annual Rev of Psychol 50 (99): 273-303; coauth, "Parental Helping Models, Gender and Service-Learning," J of Prev and Intervention in the Community 18 (1/2) (99): 5-18; coauth, "Post-Traumatic Stress Disorder in Heart Transplant Recipients and Their Primary Family Caregivers," Pshycosomatics 40 (99): 212-221; coauth, "Potential Bone Marrow Donors and Their Spouses: The Effects of Volunteerism on Distress Levels," J of Applied Soc Psychol 29 (1) (99): 1-22; coauth, "The Effects of 'Mandatory Volunteerism' on Intentions to Volunteer," Psychol Sci 10 (1) (99): 59-64. **CONTACT ADDRESS** Dept Psychol, Univ of No Colorado, 501 20th St, Greeley, CO 80639-0001. **EMAIL** aastuka@bentley.unco.edu

STURGEON, NOEL A.
DISCIPLINE WOMENS STUDIES EDUCATION Bard Col, BA, 79; Univ Calif, PhD, 91. CAREER Assoc prof, Wash State Univ, 97-; vis assoc prof, Univ of Calif, 97-98; vis Scholar, Murdoch Univ, Australia, 99; vis prof, JFK Inst for N Am Studies, Free Univ, Berlin, 00. HONORS AND AWARDS Susan Armitage Fac Awd, 92-93; Rockefeller Fel, Rutgers Univ, 94-95 MEMBERSHIPS Am Studies Assoc; Nat Women's Studies Assoc. RESEARCH Ecofeminist Natures: Race, Gender, Feminist Theory and Political Action. SELECTED PUBLICATIONS Auth, "Positional Feminism, Ecofeminism, and Radical Feminism Revisited", Am Philos Newsletter of Feminism and Philos (93); auth, "Theorizing Movements: Direct Action and Direct Theory" in Cultural Politics and Social Movement's, eds M. Darnovsky, B. Epstein, R. Flacks (PA: Temple Univ Pr, 95); rev, of "Earthcare: Women and the Environment", by Carolyn Merchant, Environ Hist 2.3 (July 97); ed, "Intersections of Environmentalism and Feminism", Frontiers: A Jour of Women Studies 18.2 (Aug 97); auth, Ecofeminist Natures: Race, Gender, Feminist Theory and Political Action, Routledge, 97; auth, "The Nature of Race: Discourses of Racial Difference in Ecofeminism", in Ecofeminism: Women, Nature, Culture, ed. Karen J. Warren (IN: Ind Univ Pr, 97); auth, "Environmentalism/Feminism: Construction Translations" in Transitions, Environments, Translations: Feminisms in Int Politics, eds JW. Scott, C. Kaplan and D. Keats (NY: Routledge, 97); auth, "Ecofeminist Appropriations and Transnational Environmentalisms" in Identities: Global Studies in Culture and Power, ed Peter Brosius (99); auth, "The Power is Yours, Planeteers! Environmentalism in Children's Popular Culture After the Cold War", Cultural Studies, (forthcoming). CONTACT ADDRESS Dept Womens Studies, Washington State Univ, PO Box 644007, Pullman, WA 99164-4007. EMAIL sturgeon@wsu.edu

STURGES, JAMES W.
DISCIPLINE BEHAVIORAL SCIENCE EDUCATION Univ Ala, PhD, 94. CAREER Asst prof, Univ Miss, 94-98; asst prof, Cal State Polytech Univ Pomona. MEMBERSHIPS Am Psychol Assoc; Assoc for the Advan of Behav Therapy. RESEARCH Health promotion. SELECTED PUBLICATIONS Coauth, "Psychophysiological disorders" in Clinical handbook of anxiety disorders in children and adolescents, ed A.R. Eisen, C.A. Kearney and C.D. Schaefer, (NJ: Jason Aronson, 95), 383-411; coauth, "Pediatric psychology", in An introd to clinical psychol, ed L.A. Heiden and M. Hersen, (NY: Plenum, 95), 361-379; coauth, "Preventative health psychology from a developmental perspective: An extension of protection motivation theory", Health Psychol 15 (96):158-166; auth, "Practical use of technology in professional practice", Prof Psychol: Res and Practice 29 (98):183-188; coauth, "In vivo systematic desensitization in a single-session treatment of a child's elevator phobia", Child and Family Behav Therapy 20, (98):55-62. CONTACT ADDRESS Dept Behav Sci, California State Polytech Univ, Pomona, 3801 W Temple Ave, Pomona, CA 91768. EMAIL jwsturges@csupomona.edu

STURM, CIRCE
PERSONAL Born 07/24/1967, Houston, TX, m, 1993 DISCIPLINE ANTHROPOLOGY EDUCATION Univ Tex, BA, 91; Univ Calif, MA, 94; PhD, 97. CAREER Teaching Asst, Univ Calif, 93-96; Adj Asst Prof to Prof, Univ Okla, 92-. HONORS AND AWARDS Grant, Nat Sci Foundation, 92-96; Fel, Univ CA, 92-96; Travel Grants, Univ OK, 97, 98. MEMBERSHIPS Race and ethnicity; Identity politics; Native American studies (North American emphasis); Mesoamerica (Maya culture); Ideology, hegemony and subjectivity; Race/class/gender systems; Anthropological linguistics; Indigenous languages and writing systems. SELECTED PUBLICATIONS Auth, "Hieroglyphic Writing and Maya Cultural Activism," in Maya Cultural Activism: (Re)Making History, (Univ TX Press, 96), 114-130; auth, "Blood Politics, Racial classification and Cherokee National identity: The Trials and Tribulations of the Cherokee Freedman," in confounding the Color Line: Native American-African American Relations in Historical and Anthropological Perspective, (98): 230-258; rev, of "Indians in the Making: Ethnic relations and Indian Identities around Puget Sound," by Alexandra Harmon, (Univ CA Press, 98), forthcoming; auth, Blood Politics: Racial Hybridity and Identity in the Cherokee Nation of Oklahoma, (Univ CA Press, forthcoming. CONTACT ADDRESS Dept Anthropol, Univ of Oklahoma, 900 Asp Ave, Norman, OK 73019-4050. EMAIL circe@ou.edu

SUAREZ-ARAUZ, NICOMEDES
PERSONAL Born 08/24/1946, Beni, Bolivia, m, 1975, 2 children DISCIPLINE INTERCULTURAL STUDIES EDUCATION Univ Tampa, BS, BA, 71; Ohio Univ, PhD, 76. CAREER Prof, Univ Catolica, Boli, 76-78; prof, Simo Rock Bard Col, 79-84; sr lectr, Smith Col, 88-. HONORS AND AWARDS Bolivia's Nat Premio Ed Franz Tamayo; Mellon Gnt; Found, Co-ed, Amaz Lit Rev. MEMBERSHIPS ALTA; LASA; MLA; NECLAS. SELECTED PUBLICATIONS Auth, Amnesis: The Art of the Lost Object, Lascaux Pub (NY), 88; co-ed, Coded Encounters: Writing , Gender, and Ethnicity in Colonial Latin America; auth, Loen: Amazonia/Amnesia/America, Fondo Mun de Cult (Santa Cruz, Bolivia), 97; auth, Edible Amazonia, Crosscult Comm, 00; ed, Literary Amazonia: An Anthology of Writing from the Amazon Region, forthcom-

ing. CONTACT ADDRESS Dept Spanish, Portuguese, Smith Col, 98 Green St, Northampton, MA 01063-1000.

SUDZINA, MARY
PERSONAL Born 06/09/1948, New Brunswick, NJ, m, 1970, 2 children DISCIPLINE EDUCATION EDUCATION Va Commonwealth, BS, 70; Villanova Univ, MA, 74; Temple Univ, PhD, 87. CAREER Teacher and chair, Special Interest Group in AERA, 95-; assoc prof, Univ of Dayton, 88-; exec dir of Project 30 Alliance, Univ of Dayton, 99-. HONORS AND AWARDS Res Awd, Unv of Dayton School of Educ, 94 & 00; Star Professor Awd, UD Educ Fraternity, 97; Service Awd, Mid-Western Educ Res Asn, 98; High Merit, Univ of Dayton Sch of Educ, 90, 95, &98; Dean's Special Awd of Merit, Univ of Dayton Sch of Educ, 99. MEMBERSHIPS AERA, ATE, MWERA, WACRA, AACTE, Project 30, Omicron Delta Kappa. RESEARCH Case-based teaching and learning, distance learning and teaching with technology, failure in student teaching, and educational reform and leadership in institutions of higher education. SELECTED PUBLICATIONS Auth, "Case study as a constructivist pedagogy for teaching educational psychology," Educ Psychol Rev, 9.2 (97): 199-218; coauth, "Mentor or tormentor: The role of the cooperating teacher in student teacher success or failure," Action in Teacher Educ 18.4 (97): 199-218; auth, Case Study Applications for Teacher Education: Cases of Teaching and Learning in the Content Areas, Allyn & Bacon (Boston, MA), 99; auth, "Educating competent and confident individuals: Revisiting Earl Kelley's fully functioning self," in Perceiving, Behaving, Becoming: A New Focus for Education, ed. H. Jerome Freiberg (VA: Asn for Supervision and Curriculum Development, 99); auth, "Organizing instruction for case-based teaching," in Education for Democracy: Case-method Teaching and Learning, eds. R.F. McNergney, E.R. Duchame, & M.K. Ducharme (NJ: Erlbaum, 99). CONTACT ADDRESS Dept Teacher Educ, Univ of Dayton, 300 College Park, Dayton, OH 45469-0525. EMAIL sudzina@udayton.edu

SUGGS, ROBERT CHINELO
PERSONAL Born 12/23/1943, Newport, RI, m DISCIPLINE EDUCATION EDUCATION Barrington Coll, BA 1967; State Univ of NYork at Albany, MS 1971, EdD 1979. CAREER Dept of Counselor Ed State Univ, asst prof 1972-80; Comm Bible Church, pastor 1974-80; Dept of Counselor Ed Millersville Univ, adjunct asst prof 1982-85; Psychophysiological Clinic Univ of MD, clinical asst prof 1983-85; Crossroads Counseling Assocs, therapist 1983-; Christian Assoc of Psych Studies, newsletter editor 1983-; Messiah Coll, assoc prof of psychology, professor of psychology, director of personnel, 86-; Cornerstone College, vp for academic affairs. HONORS AND AWARDS Doctoral fellow State Univ of NY at Albany 1971-73; outstanding teacher Messiah Coll 1981; Named to Top 500 High School Basketball Players in the US Dell Mag 1963. CONTACT ADDRESS Cornerstone Col, Vice President for Academic Affairs, Grand Rapids, MI 49505.

SUINN, RICHARD MICHAEL
PERSONAL Born 05/08/1933, Honolulu, HI, m, 1958, 4 children DISCIPLINE PSYCHOLOGY EDUCATION Ohio State Univ, BA, 55; Stanford Univ, PhD, 59. CAREER Counselor, Stanford Counseling Center, 58; asst prof, Whitman Col, 59-64; res assoc, Stanford Medical School, 64-66; assoc prof, Univ of Hawaii, 66-68; PROF OF PSYCHOLOGY, COLO STATE UNIV, 68-99; Emeritus Prof, 00-. HONORS AND AWARDS Honorary Doctor, Humane Letters, Calif Sch of Prof Psychol; Who's Who in Am; Career Contribution to Ed and Training, Am Psychol Asn. MEMBERSHIPS Am Psychol Asn; Asn for Advancement of Behavior Therapy; Board of Professional Psychology. RESEARCH Behavior therapy; stress management. SELECTED PUBLICATIONS Auth, Anxiety Management Training: A Behavior Therapy, Plenum, 90; auth, The Seven Steps to Peak Performance, Hans Huber Pubs Inc, 86; auth, Psychology in Sports: Methods and Applications, Burgess Pub Co, 90; auth, Fundamentals of Behavior Pathology, John Wiley & Sons, 70 & 75; coauth, The Innovative Medical-Psychiatric Therapies, Univ Park Press, 76; auth, The Innovative Psychological Therapies: Critical and Creative Incidents, Harper & Row, 75; auth, The Predictive Validity of Projective Measures, C.C. Thomas, 69. CONTACT ADDRESS Dept Psychol, Colorado State Univ, Fort Collins, CO 80523. EMAIL suinn@lamar.colostate.edu

SUKHOLUTSKAYA, MARA
PERSONAL Born 09/04/1950, Karaganda, Kazhastan, d, 2 children DISCIPLINE ENGLISH, SECOND LANGUAGE ACQUISITION EDUCATION Kiev State Univ Linguistics, Ukraine, BA, MA, 72, EdD, 87. CAREER Teacher, Secondary Sch No 80, Kiev, Ukraine, 72-84; asst prof, Kiev State Univ of Linguistics, 87-91, head, laboratory of Primary Foreign Langs Educ; asst prof of Foreign Langs and Lit, East Central Univ, Ada, Okla, 96-. HONORS AND AWARDS Ada Rotary Educator of the Month, May 96; Who's Who in the South and Southwest, 97; George Platt Awd, Outstanding Teacher of Russian in Okla, 98; Proj coordr, "Leadership in Languages," U.S. Dept of Educ and State Dept of educ, 96-99; Pres, Okla Coun of Teachers of Russian,96-; Bd of Dirs, Okla Foreign Lang Asn, 96-; Bd of Dirs, Southwest Conf on Language Teaching, 98-

2001; founder and chair, Central Asn of Russian Teachers of Am, 98-. MEMBERSHIPS Okla Coun of Teachers of Russian, Okla Foreign Lang Asn, Southwest Conf on Language Teaching, Central Asn of Russian Teachers of Am. RESEARCH Second language acquisition and Russian culture. SELECTED PUBLICATIONS Auth, Method Guide for Teaching English, German and Spanish at Special Foreign Language Schools, Kiev: Radyanska Shkola (90); auth, Method Guide for Initial Teaching of English to Junior Graders, Kiev (90); auth, "Music in English Classes in the First Grade," Pochatkova Shkola, No 2 (91); auth, "Humanizing Role of Puppets in Teaching Foreign Languages," Pochatkova Shkola, No 9-10 (92); auth, Speak and Read Essential Ukranian I, Heinle & Heinle Enterprises, Inc, Concord, Mass (93); rev of E. Daum and W. Schenk, A Dictionary of Russian Verbs, NY: Hippocrene (95), in Modern Lang J, Vol 80, No 1 (spring 96): 124; rev of Thomas Karras, A Concise English-Russian Phrase Book, Columbus, Ohio: Slavica (95), in Modern Lang J, Vol 80, No 4 (winter96): 557-558; rev of Emily Tall and Valentina Vlasikova, Let's Talk About Life: A Integrated Approach to Russian Conversation, NY: Wiley (96), in Modern Lang J, Vol 81, No 1 (spring 97): 140-141; rev of Lidija Iordanskaja and Slava Paperno, A Russian-English Collocational Dictionary of the Human Body, Columbus, Ohio: Slavica (96), in Modern Lang J, Vol 81, No 3 (fall 97): 434; rev of Derrek Offord, Using Russian: A Guide to Contemporary Usage, NY: Cambridge Univ Press (96), in Modern Lang J (forthcoming). CONTACT ADDRESS Dept English & Langs, East Central Univ, 1100 E 14th St, Ada, OK 74820-6915. EMAIL msukholu@mailclerk.ecok.edu

SULLINS, DONALD PAUL
PERSONAL Born 08/21/1953, Washington, DC, m, 1985, 3 children DISCIPLINE SOCIOLOGY EDUCATION Wheaton Col, BA, 73; Oral Roberts Univ, MDiv, 81; Va Theol Sem, Anglican Studies Cert, 83; Catholic Univ Am, MA, 95; PhD, 98. CAREER Teacher, Md, 74-79; Analyst, GEICO Ins, 81-82; Rector, Episcopal Church in Baltimore, 82-89; Principal, St. Timothy's School, 89-92; Res Asst, 92-93; Rector, Sunderland Md, 94-98; Visiting Asst Prof to Asst Prof, Catholic Univ of Am, 98-. SELECTED PUBLICATIONS Auth, "Switching Close to Home: Volatility or Coherence in Protestant Affiliation Patterns?", Social Forces, (93): 399-419; auth, "Getting Coherent about Coherence: A Rejoinder to McKinney and Roof," Social Forces, (94): 757-759; auth, "Clergy Early Retirement: Long-term Benefit or One-time Boon?," The Living Church, 96; auth, "Why Not Orthodoxy?," Salve! 98; auth, "Organizational Indicators of Religious Groups: An Alternative Classification," Review of Religious Research, 98; auth, "Catholic/Protestant Trends on Abortion: Convergence and Polarity," Journal for the Scientific Study of Religion, (99): 354-369; auth, "Of Angels, Soldiers and Priests," The Military Chaplain, (99): 5; co-auth, "Lectures in Technology and Culture," Catholic Univ Honors Program, forthcoming. CONTACT ADDRESS Life Cycle Inst, Catholic Univ of America, 620 Michigan Ave NE, Washington, DC 20064. EMAIL sullins@cua.edu

SULLIVAN, DEBORAH A.
PERSONAL Born 10/31/1947, Boston, MA DISCIPLINE SOCIOLOGY EDUCATION Univ Mass Amherst, BS, 76; Univ Calif Irvine, MS, 70; Duke Univ, MA, 72; PhD, 76. CAREER Assoc Prof, Ariz State Univ, 76-. MEMBERSHIPS Am Sociol Asn; Population Asn of Am; Am Public Health Asn; Sociol for Women in Soc. RESEARCH Health care occupations; Medicalization; Health care policy; Social epidemiology. SELECTED PUBLICATIONS Auth, "Cosmetic Surgery: Market Dynamics and Medicalization," in Research in the Sociology of Health Care, Vol 10, (93): 97-115; auth, Cosmetic Surgery: The Cutting Edge of Commercial Medicine in America, Rutgers Univ Press, 01. CONTACT ADDRESS Dept Sociol, Arizona State Univ, 2705 W Oakland St, Chandler, AZ 85224. EMAIL Deborah.Sullivan@asu.edu

SULLIVAN, G. SHARON
PERSONAL Born 09/22/1947, Austin, TX, s DISCIPLINE EDUCATION EDUCATION Maryville Col, BA, 69; W Ky Univ, MA, 82; Purdue Univ, PhD, 93. CAREER Visiting Instructor, Purdue Univ, 90; Asst Prof to Assoc Prof and Div Chair, Brescia Univ, 93-. HONORS AND AWARDS Outstanding Dissertation Awd, Purdue Univ; Phi Kappa Phi; Phi Kappa Theta. MEMBERSHIPS CEC; CLD; KATE; LDA RESEARCH Interventions with learning disabilites; Instructional technology. SELECTED PUBLICATIONS Co-auth, "The effect of mnemonic reconstruction of spatial learning," Learning Disability Quarterly, (92): 154-162; auth, Program offerings for out-of-school adults with learning disabilities, Purdue Univ, 92; co-auth, "Improving reasoning and recall: The differential effects of elaborative interrogation and mnemonic elaboration," Learning Disability Quarterly, (93): 233-240; co-auth, "Promoting relational thinking skills: Elaborative interrogation for students with mild disabilities," Exceptional Children, (94): 450-457; co-auth, "Social competence of individuals with learning disabilities," in Advances in Learning and Behavioral disabilities, (JAI Press, 94), 177-213; co-auth, "Reasoning and remembering: coaching students with learning disabilities to think," The Journal of Special Educ, (95): 310-322; co-auth, "What if? .You imagine," Momentum, (96): 56-57; auth, "Stick to your guns," in A company of women, (Triumph Books, 96), 25-54; co-auth, Technology Curriculum Guide, Owensboro, 97; **CON-**

TACT ADDRESS Dept Soc and Beh Sci and Educ Studies, Brescia Col, 717 Frederica St, Owensboro, KY 42301. **EMAIL** sharons@brescia.edu

SULLIVAN, KIERAN
PERSONAL Born 10/11/1967, San Diego, CA, m, 1993 **DISCIPLINE** PSYCHOLOGY **EDUCATION** Loyola Marymount Univ, BA, 90; Univ Calif, Los Angeles, MA, 92, PhD, 97. **CAREER** Asst prof, Santa Clara Univ, 97-. **HONORS AND AWARDS** Christopher Scholar, Loyola Marymount Univ, 89; Presidential Scholar, Loyola Marymount Univ, 86-90; Psi Chi, 88, Alpha Sigma Nu, 89; Univ Honors Prog, Loyola Marymount Univ, 86-90; Outstanding Grad, Psychol, Loyola Marymount Univ, 90; Univ Fel, Univ Calif, Los Angeles, 92; Shepard Ivory Franz Distinguished Teaching Awd, 95; Nat Res Service Awd, 94-96; Kaiser Found Res Grant, 96-97; Thomas Terry Res Grants, Santa Clara Univ, 98, 98-99, 99. **MEMBERSHIPS** Asn for the Advancement of Behavior Therapy, Soc for Prevention Research, Am Psychol Asn, Western Psychol Asn. **RESEARCH** Prevention of couple distress and divorce, couples therapy. **SELECTED PUBLICATIONS** Coauth, "Preventing marital dysfunction: The primacy of secondary strategies," The Behavior Therapist, 19 (95): 33-35; coauth, "Social support in marriage: An analysis of intraindividual and interpersonal components," in G. R. Pierce, B. Lakely, I. G. Sarason, and B. R. Sarason, eds, Soureebook of Theory and Research on Social Support and Personality, Plennum (97); coauth, "Are premarital prevention programs reaching couples at risk for marital dysfunction?," J of Consulting and Clinical Psychol, 65 (97): 24-30; coauth, "Couples therapy," in H. S. Friedman, ed, The Encyclopedia of Mental Health, Academic Press (98): 595-606; coauth, "Social support in marriage: Translating research into practical applications for clinicians," The Family J, 6 (98): 263-271; coauth, "Implementation of Empirically Validated Interventions in Managed Care Settings: The Premarital Relationship Enhancement Program (PREP)," Professional Psychology: Research and Practice (in press). **CONTACT ADDRESS** Dept Psychol, Alumni Sci Bldg 200, Santa Clara Univ, Santa Clara, CA 95053. **EMAIL** ksullivan@scu.edu

SURI, KUL BHUSHAN
PERSONAL Born 04/05/1943, Lahore, India, m, 1978, 2 children **DISCIPLINE** SOCIAL WORK **EDUCATION** Univ Maryland, PhD, 89. **CAREER** Porf, Dela State Univ. **HONORS AND AWARDS** Fulbright fel, India. **RESEARCH** Population policy, Child welfare. **SELECTED PUBLICATIONS** Auth, In The Concept of Karma & Social Work Considerations, J Soc Work, (95); auth, Locust of Control-A Reptoir for Social Workers, Scand J Soc Workers, 98. **CONTACT ADDRESS** Dept Soc Work, Delaware State Univ, 1200 N Dupont Highway, Dover, DE 19901.

SUSSMAN, ROBERT W.
PERSONAL Born 07/04/1941, Brooklyn, NY, m, 1972, 2 children **DISCIPLINE** ANTHROPOLOGY **EDUCATION** UCLA, BA, 65; MA, 67; Duke Univ, PhD, 72. **CAREER** .Asst Prof, CUNY, 71-73; Asst to Full Prof, WA Univ, 73-/ **MEMBERSHIPS** Am Asn Adv of Sci; Am Anthropol Asn, Am Asn Phys Anthropol. **RESEARCH** Primate Ecology. **SELECTED PUBLICATIONS** Ed, The Biological Basis of Human Behavior, Simon and Schuster Custom Pub, 97; Ed, The Biological Basis of Human Behavior, A Critical Review, Prentice Hall, 99; auth, Primate Ecology and Social Structure, Vol. I: Lorises, Lemurs and Tarsiers, Pearson Custom Pub, 99; co-auth, "Natural disasters and primate populations: the effects of a two-year drought on a naturally occurring population of ringtailed lemurs in southwestern Madagascar," Intl Journal Primatol, (99): 69-84; co-auth, "The ecology and social behavior of the ringtailed lemur," Evolutionary Anthropology, (99): 120-132; auth, "Piltdown Man: The father of American field primatology," in Primate Encounters: Models of Science, Gender and Society, (Univ Chicago Press, 00), 85-103; auth, Primate Ecology and Social Structure, Vol. 2: New World Monkeys, Pearson Custom Pub, 00; co-auth, "Adaptive array of the Madagascar lemurs revisited," in Primatology and Anthropology into the Third Millennium, (Wiley Press, forthcoming). **CONTACT ADDRESS** Dept Anthropol, Washington Univ, 1 Brookings Dr, Saint Louis, MO 63130. **EMAIL** rwsussma@artsci.wash.edu

SUSSMAN, STEPHAN
PERSONAL Born 08/17/1945, New York, NY, m **DISCIPLINE** PSYCHOLOGY **EDUCATION** Cooper Union, BS, 66; Mass Inst Technol, MS, 67; Univ Fla, MA, 70; PhD, 77. **CAREER** Prof, Santa Fe Community Col. **MEMBERSHIPS** Nat Soc Sci Asn, SEPA, Am Psychol Asn, Human Sci Res Conf, Coun of Teachers of Undergrad Psychol, Pi Tau Sigma Honor Soc. **CONTACT ADDRESS** Dept Soc Sci, Santa Fe Comm Col, Florida, 3000 NW 83rd St, Gainesville, FL 32606. **EMAIL** stephan.sussman@santafe.cc.fl.us

SUTHERLAND, KAY
PERSONAL Born 04/24/1942, Washington, DC, m, 1978, 2 children **DISCIPLINE** ANTHROPOLOGY **EDUCATION** Univ Tex Austin, BA, 63; MA, 67; Univ Ill Urbana, PhD, 73. **CAREER** Instr, El Paso Community Col, 71-78; Asst Prof, Southwest Tex State Univ, San Morces, Tex, 82-85; Assoc Prof, St. Edward's Univ Austin Tex, 88-. **MEMBERSHIPS** Am Rock Art Res Asn, El Paso Archit Soc. **RESEARCH** Rock art research. **SELECTED PUBLICATIONS** Auth, Spirits from the South, El Paso Archit Soc, 96; auth, "Rock Paintings at Hueco Tanky State Historical Park," Tex Parks and Wildlife, 95. **CONTACT ADDRESS** Dept Soc and Behav Sci, St. Edward's Univ, 3001 S Congress Ave, Austin, TX 78704. **EMAIL** kays@admin.stedwards.edu

SUTTER, LESLIE E.
PERSONAL Born 11/08/1960, Traverse City, MI, s **DISCIPLINE** PHILOSOPHY, EDUCATION **EDUCATION** CSUDH, MA, 86; Univ Berne, PhD, 91; Columbia Pacific Univ, D.A. (Hon.), 91, Univ Sarasota, EdD, 01. **CAREER** Adj prof, Edison Col, 94-; prof, Int Col, 97-; co-chair, Lib Arts, 00-, chair Lib Arts, 00; chair, Interdisciplinary studies; 00; asst dean, Social Sciences and Humanities, 01. **HONORS AND AWARDS** Non-resident scholar, Univ Berne, 93; prof of the year, Int col, 98, 00; Fulbright nominee to Republic of Moldova, 01. **MEMBERSHIPS** Am Hist Asn; APA; ASPCP; APPA. **RESEARCH** Existentialism; logical positivism; immigration questions. **SELECTED PUBLICATIONS** Auth, Joy of Catholic Paganism, Rustte Press, 87; auth, Swiss Emigration Agencies, UMI, 91; auth, Philosophy and Religion, McGraw-Hill, 97; auth, Logic for Beginners, Int. Press, 00. **CONTACT ADDRESS** Intl Col, 2655 Northbrooke Dr., Naples, FL 33919. **EMAIL** lsutter@internationalcollege.edu

SWANK, ERIC W.
DISCIPLINE SOCIOLOGY **EDUCATION** San Diego State Univ, BA, 88; Ohio State Univ, MA, 92; PhD, 98. **CAREER** Asst Prof, Morehead State Univ, 96-. **MEMBERSHIPS** ASA, Peace Studies Asn, Soc for the Study of Soc Probs. **SELECTED PUBLICATIONS** Auth, "The Ebbs and Flows of Gulf War Protests," J of Polit and Military Sociol, 25 (97): 211-231; coauth, "Institutional Racism and Media representations," Sociol Imagination, 34 (97): 105-128; auth, "The Social Backgrounds of Gulf War Protesters," J for the Study of Peace and Conflict, 11 (98): 21-29; auth, "Bill Clinton, Big Business and Welfare Reform: The Class and Political Loyalties of Clinton's Domestic Advisors," J of Poverty, 2 (98): 1-25; auth, "Who Do You Trust? Determining the Credibilities of Newspapers that Cover Protest Mobilizations," Res of Soc Movements, Conflict and Change (00). **CONTACT ADDRESS** Dept Sociol, Morehead State Univ, 150 University Blvd, Morehead, KY 40351. **EMAIL** e.swank@morehead-st.edu

SWANSON, LOUIS E.
PERSONAL Born 09/03/1949, Durham, NC, m, 1981, 2 children **DISCIPLINE** SOCIOLOGY **EDUCATION** St Andrews Presby Col, BA, 71; NC State Univ, MTech, 75; Pa State Univ, PhD, 82. **CAREER** Asst prof to prof, Univ of Kans, 82-97; prof, chair, Colo State Univ, 97-. **HONORS AND AWARDS** Kellogg Nat Leadership Fel, 88; Fel, Nat Ctr for Food and Agriculture Policy, 88-89; Awd, Prof Excellence, Am Agr Econ Assoc, 93; SWCSA President's Citation for Excellence, 95. **MEMBERSHIPS** Rural Sociol Soc. **RESEARCH** Agriculture Structure, Agriculture Environmental Policy, Rural Development and Community Policy. **SELECTED PUBLICATIONS** Coauth, "Determinants of farmer's satisfaction with farming and with life", Southern Rural Sociol 9.1 (92): 45-70; coauth, "Stewardship Values: Still Valid for the 21st Century?", Choices, (92): 20-25; coauth, Rural Communities: Legacy and Social Change, Westview Pr, (Boulder, CO), 92; coauth, "Sacred Cows and Hot Potatoes: Agrarian Myths in Agricultural Policy, Westview Pr, (Boulder, CO), 92; coauth, "Still Going: Recent Debates on the Goldschmidt Hypotheses", Rural Sociol 58.2 (93): 277-288; coauth, "Critical Sociology: A Theoretical Alternative for Rural Sociology", Int J of the Sociol of Food and Agr 2, (93): 143-158; coed, Agriculture Policy and the Environment: Iron Fist or Open Hand, Soil and Water Conserv Soc Pr, 94; coauth, "African Americans in Southern Rural Regions: The Importance of Legacy", Rev of Black Polit Econ 22, (95): coauth, "To cross the Rubicon: The college of agriculture and rural development dilemma", Southern Rural Sociol 13.1 (98): 19-40; auth, "Rural Opportunities: Minimalist Policy and Community-Based Experimentations", Policy Studies J, (forthcoming). **CONTACT ADDRESS** Dept Sociol, Colorado State Univ, Fort Collins, CO 80523-0001. **EMAIL** swansonl@lamar.colostate.edu

SWARTZ, BENJAMIN K., JR
PERSONAL Born 06/23/1931, Los Angeles, CA, m, 1966, 2 children **DISCIPLINE** ANTHROPOLOGY **EDUCATION** LA City Col, AA, 52; UCLA, BA, 54; MA, 58; Univ Ariz, PhD, 64. **CAREER** Curator and Res Assoc, Klamath County Museum, 59-62; Asst Prof to Assoc Prof, Ball State Univ, 64-72; Vis Sen Lectr, Univ Ghana, 70-71; Prof, Ball State Univ, 72-; Vis Prof, Univ Yaounde, 84-85. **HONORS AND AWARDS** Fel, Luso-Am Develop Found, 95; Fel, Ball State Univ-Yaounde Univ Exchange Prog, 84; Sigma Xi; Lambda Alpha. **MEMBERSHIPS** Am Asn for the Adv of Sci; Soc for Am Archaeol; Am Committee for the Study of Petroglyphs and Pictographs; Am Committee for the Preservation of Archaeol Collections; Coun for the Conservation of Ind Archaeol; Ind Acad of Sci. **RESEARCH** Archaeology: history, taxonomic analysis, methods (North America, West Africa); Petroglyphs: recording standards, information systems (Great Basin, USA and global). **SELECTED PUBLICATIONS** Co-ed, Rock Art and Posterity, AURA, 91; co-auth, "Space, Place and Territory in Rock Art Interpretation," Rock Art Res, 94; auth, "An Investigation of the Portuguese Government," Rock Art Res, 97; auth, "Middle Woodland Figurines from the Mann Site, Southwest Indiana," New World Figurine Project, Vol 3, 01. **CONTACT ADDRESS** Dept Anthropol, Ball State Univ, 805 W Charles St, Muncie, IN 47305. **EMAIL** 01bkswartz@bsuvc.bsu.edu

SWEENEY, THOMAS JOHN
PERSONAL Born 08/25/1936, Akron, OH, m, 5 children **DISCIPLINE** EDUCATION **EDUCATION** Univ Akron, BA, 59; Univ Wisc, MS, 60; Ohio St Univ, PhD, 64 **CAREER** Commd 2nd lt, through grades to capt, 58-66, U.S. Army; tchr, 58-61, Ohio St Pub schls; instr, 61-63, Ohio St Univ; couns, 63-64, S.W. City schls, Grove City OH; prof, 64-72, Univ SC; prof, 72-, Ohio Univ; couns, 69-86, Gen Electric Found; prof emer, 72-, Ohio Univ. **HONORS AND AWARDS** ACA Dist Svc Awd, 84; Dist Legis Svc Awd, 86; Stripling Excel Awd, 92; Couns Vision & Innov Awd, 98. **MEMBERSHIPS** ACA; Asn Couns Edn & Supervision; Chi Sigma Iota **SELECTED PUBLICATIONS** Auth, Adlerian Counseling, 98; auth, prod, telecourse series, Coping with Kids, 78. **CONTACT ADDRESS** Ohio Univ, McCracken Hall, Athens, OH 45701.

SWENSEN, CLIFFORD HENRIK
PERSONAL Born 11/25/1926, Welch, WV, m, 1948, 5 children **DISCIPLINE** CLINICAL PSYCHOLOGY **EDUCATION** Univ Pitts, BS, 49, MS, 50, PhD, 52. **CAREER** Clin psychol, V A, 52-54; asst to assoc prof, Univ Tenn, 54-62; assoc prof to Prof, Purdue Univ, 62-; vis prof, Univ Bergen (Norway), 76-77 & 83-84; vis prof Univ Fla, 68-69; distinguished sci lectr, APA/NSF, 69; Fulbright res/lectr, 76-77. **HONORS AND AWARDS** Gordon A Barrows Mem Awd for Distinguished Contrib to Psychol, 90; Presidential Citation, Am Psych Asn, 99. **MEMBERSHIPS** Am Psychol Asn; Am Psychol Soc; Soc Personality Assessment; Am Asn Appl & Prev Psychol; Midwstrn Psychol Asn; Ind Psychol Asn. **RESEARCH** Clinical psychology; Clinical gerontological psychology; Marriage and family psychology; Interpersonal relations. **SELECTED PUBLICATIONS** coauth Stage of religious faith and reactions to terminal cancer, Jour Psychol & Theol, 93; A guide for adjunctive psychological treatment for cancer pain patients, Innovations in clinical practice: a sourcebook, 93; auth Older individuals in the family, The handbook for developmental family psychology and psychopathology, John Wiley & Sons, 94; coauth Time spent together and relationship quality: long-distance relationships as a test case, Jour of Soc & Personal Relationships, 95; auth Case 3: Janet and Bill, A spiritual strategy for counseling and psychotherapy, Am Psychol Asn, 97. **CONTACT ADDRESS** Dept of Psychol Sci, Purdue Univ, West Lafayette, West Lafayette, IN 47907. **EMAIL** cswensen@psych.purdue.edu

SWENSON, ELIZABETH V.
DISCIPLINE PSYCHOLOGY **EDUCATION** Cleveland State Univ, JD, 85; Case Western Reserve Univ, PhD, 74. **CAREER** Prof, John Carroll Univ, 74-. **HONORS AND AWARDS** Phi Beta Kappa; Fel, Am Psychol Asn. **MEMBERSHIPS** Am Psychol Assoc; Am Psychol Soc. **RESEARCH** Ethics, teaching psychology. **SELECTED PUBLICATIONS** Auth, "Behavioral science and the negligent child", Jour of Psychiat and Law 12, (84):385-397; auth, "Legal Liability for a patient's suicide.", Jour of Psychiat and Law 14 (86):409-434; auth, "A content-oriented practicum in pediatric psychology", in Handbook on Student Develop: Advising, Career Develop and Field Placement, ed M.E. Ware and R. Millard, (NJ: Lawrence Erlbaum Assoc, 87); auth, "What about a career in law", in Is Psychology the Major for You?, ed P.J. Woods, (Wash: Am Psychol Assoc), 87; auth, "The psychology major as preparation for legal studies and the legal profession", in Is Psychol for Them? A Guide to Undergraduate Advising, ed P.J. Woods, (Wash: Am Psychol Assoc, 88); coauth, Writing Letters of Recommendation for Students: How to Protect Yourself from Liability, Div Two, Am Psychol Assoc, 91: auth, "An ADR activity for a legal environment course", Focus on Law Studies - Am Bar Assoc Comm on Col and Univ Legal Studies, 9.2 (94):4; auth, "Student v Instructor: Higher Education Law in the Trenches", Teaching of Psychol 22, (95):169-172; auth, "Applications of the APA Ethics Code to the Training of School Psychologists in the Classroom", Trainers' Forum 16.2 (98):12-14; auth, "Revising the Ethics Code for Psychologists to Approach the Challenges of the Next Millennium", Ohio Psychol 45.1, (98):32-33; auth, "The Insanity Trial of Hamlet: A Teaching Activity", in Activities Handbook on the Teaching of Psychol, ed L.T. Benjamin, Jr., Am Psychol Assoc, (99):355-358; auth, "Using Negotiation and Mediation to Resolve Disputes", Psychol Teacher Network 12 (00):12-14. **CONTACT ADDRESS** Dept Psychology, John Carroll Univ, 20700 N Park Blvd, Cleveland, OH 44118. **EMAIL** swenson@jcu.edu

SWIDERSKI, SUZANNE M.
PERSONAL Born 06/05/1965, Milwaukee, WI, s **DISCIPLINE** EDUCATIONAL PSYCHOLOGY, ENGLISH **EDUCATION** BA, 87; MA, 90; M Ed, 93. **CAREER** Asst coord, St Norbert Col, 87-88; grad tutor, Loyola Univ, 88-89; instr, 89-90; coord, 90-91; coun, 92-93; fac, Heartland Comm Col, 93-

95; asst prof, Loras Col, 95-. **HONORS AND AWARDS** NEH; Who's Who in Midwest, Am, World; Outstand People 20th Century. **MEMBERSHIPS** MCLCA; MWCA; NADE; NCTE; NWCA. **RESEARCH** Faculty development; teaching and learning; tutor training. **SELECTED PUBLICATIONS** Ed, contrb bibliographer, Tutor Training: An Annotated Bibliography of Theories, Principles, and Practices from 1989-1996 (MCLCA, 96); contr bibliogr, Annotated Research Bibliographies in Developmental Education: Tutoring (NCDE, 96); contr bibliogr, Conference on College Composition and Communication Bibliography of Composition Rhetoric, 95-98, 90-92, 88; rev of, "The Writing Center Resource Manual," Writing Lab NL (98): 12-13. **CONTACT ADDRESS** Dept English, Loras Col, 1450 Alta Vista St, Dubuque, IA 52001-4327.

SYLER, ELEANOR G.
PERSONAL Born 12/06/1933, Johnetta, KY, m, 1953, 2 children **DISCIPLINE** PSYCHOLOGY **EDUCATION** Evanger Univ, BA, 77; Southwest Missouri State Univ, MA, 78; Nova Southeastern Univ, EdD, 90. **CAREER** Adj Prof, Southwest Baptist Univ - Springfield Center, 87-90; Fac Mem, Evangel Univ, 77-. **HONORS AND AWARDS** Who's Who of Am Students, 76; Graduate Cum Laude, Evangel Univ, 76; Who's Who in Am Educ, 87; Who's Who in Am Educators, 94; Who's Who of Am Teachers, 98; Outstanding Educator Awd, Midwest Regional Asoc for Developmental Educ, 94; Cert of Appreciation, Nat Asoc for Developmental Educ, 96; Editor's Choice Awd for Outstanding Achievement in Poetry, Nat Libr of Poetry, 97; Gov Awd for Excellence in Teaching,98. **MEMBERSHIPS** Nat Asn for Developmental Educ, Midwest Regional Asn for Developmental Educ, Missouri Writer's Guild, Ozark's Writer's League. **RESEARCH** Teaching and learning techniques for under-achieving students. **SELECTED PUBLICATIONS** Auth, "1994: Performing and Evaluating Presentations of Chapter Material," Collaborative Learning: Sourcebook II, Nat Center of Post-Secondary Teaching, Learning and Assessment, Pa State Univ; auth, "M-O-T-I-V-A-T-E", Christian Educ Counsr, Gospel Publ House (96); auth, "Accommodations or Just Good Teaching? Strategies for Teaching College Students with Disabilities," Grenwood Publ (96). **CONTACT ADDRESS** Dept Behav Sci, Evangel Col, 1111 N Genstone, Springfield, MO 65802. **EMAIL** esyler@evangek.edu

SYLVAS, LIONEL B.
PERSONAL Born 05/10/1940, New Orleans, LA **DISCIPLINE** EDUCATION **EDUCATION** Southern Univ, BS 1963; Univ of Detroit, MA 1971; Nova Univ, EdD 1975. **CAREER** Ford Motor Co, indust rsch analy 1967-69, ed training spec 1969-71; Miami Dade Comm Coll, assoc acad dean 1971-74; Miami Dade Comm Coll, asst to pres 1974-77; Northern VA Comm Coll, Campus Provost. **HONORS AND AWARDS** Outstanding Educator Miami Dade Comm Coll 1975. **MEMBERSHIPS** Consult Southern Assoc of Coll & Schools Eval Team 1974-; mem advisory bd Black Amer Affairs, Natl School Volunteer Prog 1974-78; pres Southern Reg Couns 1977-88; field reader for Titles III & IV Office of Educ 1979-; mem advisory bd Amer Red Cross 1982-; consult advisory group VA Power Co 1983-87; panelist on the VA Commission of the Arts; mem Constitution Bicentennial Commiss VA. **CONTACT ADDRESS** No Virginia Comm Col, 15200 Neabsco Mills Rd, Woodbridge, VA 22191-4006.

SZEMAN, IMRE J.
PERSONAL Born 07/26/1968, Calgary, AB, Canada, M, 1996, 1 child **DISCIPLINE** ENGLISH, CULTURAL STUDIES **EDUCATION** Queens Univ, BA, 90; Univ Western Ont, MA, 93; Duke Univ, PhD, 98. **CAREER** Asst to assoc prof, McMaster Univ, 99-. **HONORS AND AWARDS** Gold Medal, Queen's Univ, 90; For Govt Award, Int Coun for Can Studies, 91; SSHRC Fel, 92-96, 97-99, 01-04; James B Duke Fel, 93-97; Myra and William Waldo Boone Fel, 97-98; John Charles Polanyi Prize, 00. **MEMBERSHIPS** MLA, Marxist Lit Group, Am Studies Asn, Am Comp Lit Asn. **RESEARCH** Critical and Cultural Theory, Globalization, Postcolonial Literature and Theory, Film, Contemporary visual Culture, History of Literary and Aesthetic Theory. **SELECTED PUBLICATIONS** Auth, "The Persistence of the Nation: Interdisciplinarity and Canadian Literary Criticism," Essays on Can Writing, (99); ed, Materializing Canada, Essays on Can Writing, (99); coed, Pierre Bourdieu: Fieldwork in Culture, Rowman and Littlefield, 00; auth, "The Rhetoric of Culture: Some Notes on Magazines, Canadian Culture and Globalization," Jour of Can Studies, (00); AUTH, "Belated of Isochronic?: Canadian Writing, Time and Globalization," Essays on Can Writing, (00); ed, Learning From Seattle, Rev of Educ/Pedagogy/Cult Studies, 01; auth, "Plundering the Empire: Globalization, Cultural Studies and Utopia," Rethinking Marxism, (01); auth, Zones of Instability: Literature, Postcolonialism and the Nation, Johns Hopkins Univ Pr, (forthcoming); coed, Anglophone Literatures and Global Changes, S Atlantic Quart, (forthcoming). **CONTACT ADDRESS** McMaster Univ, 1280 Main St W, Hamilton, ON, Canada L8S 4L9. **EMAIL** szeman@mcmaster.ca

T

TABORN, JOHN MARVIN
PERSONAL Born 11/07/1935, Carrier Mills, IL, m **DISCIPLINE** PSYCHOLOGY **EDUCATION** Southern IL Univ, BS 1956; Univ of IL, MA 1958; Univ of MN, PhD 1970; Harvard Business Sch, Mgmt Certificate 1971. **CAREER** Minneapolis Public Schools, psychologist, 66-70; Univ of MN, youth development consultant, 71-73; J Taborn Assocs Inc, Pres, 79-; Univ of MN, Assoc Prof, 73-. **HONORS AND AWARDS** Bush Leadership Fellow 1970; Monitor of the Year Monitors Minneapolis 1980. **MEMBERSHIPS** Mem Natl Assoc of Black Psychologists 1970-; professional mem Amer Psychological Assoc 1972-; consultant State of MN 1973-82; bd of dirs Minneapolis Urban League 1974-80; consultant Honeywell Inc 1981-84; mem Sigma Pi Phi Frat 1983-; consultant Natl Assoc Black Police 1984-, State of CA Education 1986-. **SELECTED PUBLICATIONS** Numerous scholarly publications. **CONTACT ADDRESS** Univ of Minnesota, Twin Cities, 808 Social Science Bldg, Minneapolis, MN 55455.

TAKOOSHIAN, HAROLD
PERSONAL Born 11/21/1949, New York, NY, w, 1 child **DISCIPLINE** PSYCHOLOGY **EDUCATION** CCNY, BA, 71; CUNY, PhD, 79. **CAREER** Assoc Prof, Fordham Univ, 78-. **HONORS AND AWARDS** Gulbenkian Foundation Fel, 71-73; NIMH Urban Trainee, 72-73; NYS Regents Scholar, 66-71; U.S. Fulbright Scholar, U.S.S.R., 87-88. **MEMBERSHIPS** Psi Chi Nat Honor Soc; Am Sociol Asn; Soc Indsl and Org Psychol; Am Evaluation Asn. **RESEARCH** Development of standardized scales; Use of field experiment to study social issues. **CONTACT ADDRESS** Dept Soc Sci, Fordham Univ, 113 W 60th St, New York, NY 10023.

TALLEY, WILLIAM B.
PERSONAL Born 09/22/1955, Sumter, SC, m, 1993 **DISCIPLINE** EDUCATION **EDUCATION** South Carolina State, BS, 1976, MS, 1978; Southern Illinois Univ, PhD, 1986 . **CAREER** State of South Carolina, counselor, trainee, 76-78, vocational rehab coun selor, 78-80, disability examiner, 80-82; State of Louisiana, LSU, educator, 86-88; PSI Inc, counselor, 88-90; Univ of Maryland, Eastern Shore, educator, dir of rehabilitation services; Coppin State College, asst prof, currently. **MEMBERSHIPS** Natl Rehab Assn, 1978-; Amer Asn of Counseling & Devt, 1982-; NAACP , 1973-; Alpha Phi Alpha, vp, Delta Omicron Lambda Chapter, 1994-; Univ of MD-E astern Shore Faculty Assembly, chair, 1993-; MD Rehab Counseling Assn, chair, m em comm, 1994-; Assn of Black Psychologists, 1988-; Amer Personnel & Guidance A ssn, 1984-; Natl Assn of Certified Hypnotherapists, 1988-; MD Rehab Assn, 1990- ; numerous other past and present memberships. **SELECTED PUBLICATIONS** Certified Rehabilitation Counselor; Nationally Certified Counselor; License d Professional Counselor; Publications: The Predictors of Case Outcome for Clie nts in a Private Rehabilitation Program in Illinois, Dissertation Abstracts Int l, 1982; The Predictors of Case Outcome for Clients in Private Rehabilitation: An Illinois Study, The Journal of Private Sector Rehabilitation, 1988. **CONTACT ADDRESS** Coppin State Col, 2500 W North Ave, Baltimore, MD 21216.

TANG, MEI
DISCIPLINE EDUCATIONAL PSYCHOLOGY **EDUCATION** Univ Wisc, PhD, 96. **CAREER** Asst prof, Univ Cincinnati, 97-. **MEMBERSHIPS** Am Coun Asn, Am Psychol Asn, Asn of Coun Ed and Supervision, Nat Career Development Asn. **RESEARCH** Career development, multicultural counseling. **SELECTED PUBLICATIONS** Coauth with N. A. Fouad, "Caught in two worlds: Jessica Chang from a cross-cultural perspective," Career Development Quart, 46 (97): 155-160; coauth with N. A. Fouad and P. L. Smith, "Asian Americans career choices: A pathmodel to examine the factors influencing choices," J of Vocational Behav, 54 (99); 142-157; coauth with R. K. Conyne, F. R. Wilson, and K. Shi, "Cultural differences in group work: A US-Chinese task group comparison," Group Dynamics: Theory, Research and Practice, 3 (99): 40-50; coauth with R. K. Conyne and F. R. Wilson, "Evolving lessons from group work involvement in China," J for Specialists in Group Work (in press); coauth with N. Fouad, "The magnitude of the acculturation and its impact on Asian Americans' career development," in D. S. Sanhu, ed, Asian American & Pacific Islander American: Issues and Concerns for counseling and Psychotherapy, New York: Nova Pubs (99); coauth with E. P. Cook, "Understanding relationship and career issues of middle school girls," in P. O'Reilly, E. Penn & D. deMarrais, eds, Educating young adolescent girls, Hillsdale, NJ: Lawrence Erlbaum (in press); coauth with N. Fouad, "Vocational Inventories," in B. Bolton, ed, Handbook of Measurement and Evaluation in Rehabilitation, 3rd ed, Paul Brookes Pub (in press); coauth with F. T. L leong, "A cultural accommodation approach to career assessment with Asian Americans," in D. Kurasaki, ed, Asian American Mental Health: Assessment Theories and Methods, Dordrecht, The Netherlands: Kluwer Acad Pubs (in press). **CONTACT ADDRESS** Dept Sch Psych & Counseling, Univ of Cincinnati, PO Box 210002, Cincinnati, OH 45221-0001. **EMAIL** mei.tang@uc.edu

TANG, SHENGMING
PERSONAL Born 09/05/1951, Shanghai, China, m, 1981, 1 child **DISCIPLINE** SOCIOLOGY **EDUCATION** East China Normal Univ, BA, 82, MA, 85; Univ Nebr-Lincoln, PhD, 92. **CAREER** Lectr, East China Normal Univ, 85-88; asst prof, Kenyon Col, 92-93; assoc prof, Western Ill Univ, 93-. **HONORS AND AWARDS** Outstanding Teaching Asst Awd, Univ Nebr-Lincoln, 92. **MEMBERSHIPS** Am Sociol Asn. **RESEARCH** Research methods, marriage and the family, education, Chinese society. **SELECTED PUBLICATIONS** Auth, "Official Corruption in Developing Economy: The Case of People's Republic of China," Humanity and Soc, 20, 2 (96): 58-71; coauth with Jiping Zuo, "Profile of College Examination Cheaters," Col Student J, 31, 3 (97): 340-346; auth, "The Timing of Home-Leaving: A Comparison of Early, On-Time, and Late Home Leavers," J of Youth and Adolescence, 26, 1 (97): 13-23; auth, "Repeated Home Leaving Behavior of American Youth," J of Comparative Family Studies, 28, 1 (97): 147-159; auth, "From Social Control to Disorganization: Official Corruption in China," Soc and Economic Studies, 46, 1 (97): 135-147; auth, Practical Approaches to Social Research, Shanghai, China: LiXin Pub House (98, in Chinese); auth, "Student Evaluation of Teachers: Effects of Grading at College Level," J of Res and Develop in Ed, 32, 2 (99): 83-88; auth, "Cooperation or Competition: A Comparison of American and Chinese College Students," The J of Psychol, 133, 4 (99): 413-423; coauth with Jiping Zuo, "Breadwinner Status and Gender Ideologies of Men and Women Towards Family Roles," Sociol Perspectives (2000); auth, "Dating Attitudes and Behaviors of American and Chinese College Students," Soc Sci J (2000). **CONTACT ADDRESS** Dept Anthropol & Sociol, Western Illinois Univ, 1 Univ Cir, Macomb, IL 61455. **EMAIL** mfst@wiu.edu

TANNER, HELEN HORNBECK
PERSONAL Born 07/05/1916, Northfield, MN, w, 1940, 3 children **DISCIPLINE** ETHNOHISTORY **EDUCATION** Swarthmore Col, AB, 37; Univ Fla, MA, 49; Univ Mich, PhD, 61. **CAREER** Vis lectr, Univ of Mich, 65; lectr, Univ of Mich Extensin Service, 74; acting dir, D'Arcy McNickle Ctr for Am Indian Hist, 84-85; res assoc, 81-95; sr res fel, 95-. **HONORS AND AWARDS** Am Asn of Univ Women, Nat Fel, 58-59; Grant form NEH for, Atlas of Great lakes Indian History,", 76; Recipient, Illinois Hist Soc Book Award, 87; Recipient, Erminie Wheeler-Voegelin Award from the Am Soc of Ethnohistory for best book in the filed published previous year, 88; Independent Scholar Fel from the Nat Endowment for the Humanities, 89; Travel Grant, Am Ocun for Learned Societies, 90. **MEMBERSHIPS** Can Cartographic Asn; Conf Latin Am Historians; Am Soc Ethnohist; Soc Hist Discoveries; Am Soc Ethnohist (pres, 82-). **RESEARCH** Indian history of Great Lakes; Spanish borderlands; historical cartography. **SELECTED PUBLICATIONS** Auth, Zespedes in East Florida, 1784-1790, (Coral Gables: Univ of Miami Press, 63; auth, The Ojibwas: A Critical Bibliography, Bloomington & London, Indiana Univ Press, 76; auth, "The Glaize in 1792, a Composite Community," in American Encounters, ed. James Merrell and Peter Mancall, (New York and London: Routledge Press, 00); reprint from Ethnohistory, vol. 25, no. 1, (78): 15-38; ed, Atlas of Great Lakes Indian History, Norman: Univ of Oklahoma Press, 87; auth, The Ojibwas, New York: Chelsea House Publishing Co., 92; coauth, "The Ojibwa-Jesuit Debate at Walpole Island, 1844," Ethnohistory, vol. 41, no. 2, 94; co-ed, "The Career of Joseph La Frane Coureur de Bois in the Upper Lakes," The Fur Trade Revisited: Selected Papers of the Sixth Fur Trade Conference in Mackinc Island 1991, (East Lansing, and Mackinac Island: Michigan State Univ and Mackinac Island Commission, (94): 171-188; ed, The Settling of North America, New York: Macmillan Books, 95; auth, "History vs. The Law: Proccessing Indians in the American Legal System," Univ of Detroit Mercy Law Review, Vol. 76, No. 3, 99; auth, "The Mille Lacs Band and the Treaty of 1855," in Fish in the Lakes, Wild Rice, and Gme in Abundance, (East Lansing, Mich State Univ Press, 00). **CONTACT ADDRESS** Newberry Library, 5178 Crystal Dr, Beulah, MI 49617.

TANSEY, CHARLOTTE
PERSONAL Born Montreal, PQ, Canada **DISCIPLINE** EDUCATION **EDUCATION** Univ Montreal, BA, 43; McGill Univ, MA, 48. **CAREER** Ch, publicity, Newman Club McGill Univ, 47-48; found dir/sec, 45-48, registrar, 48-66, acad VP, 62-81, Pres/Dir Studs, Thomas Moore Institute, 81-. **HONORS AND AWARDS** Citizen of the Year Awd, Montreal Citizenship Coun, 75; LLD Concordia Univ, 85; DL Burlington Col, Vermont, 95. **MEMBERSHIPS** Can Fedn Hum; Asn Continuing Higher Educ; Nontraditional Educ Comt. **SELECTED PUBLICATIONS** Auth, The Assumptions of Adult Learning in Culture, 57; auth, Other Voices, Other Classrooms, in Can Forum, 68; auth, Creativity and Method: Essays in Honor of Bernard Lonergan, 81; auth, Liberal Arts in the Post Classical World, in Temoignages: Reflections on the Humanities, 93. **CONTACT ADDRESS** Pres & Dir of Studies, Thomas Moore Inst, 3405 Atwater Ave, Montreal, QC, Canada H3H 1Y2.

TAPIA, ELENA
DISCIPLINE SECOND LANGUAGE ACQUISITION **EDUCATION** IN Univ, PhD. **CAREER** Eng Dept, Eastern Conn State Univ **SELECTED PUBLICATIONS** Areas: cognitive demand and writing assessment, second lang learners acquiring

conceptual metaphors, psycholinguistic factors influencing second lang writers. **CONTACT ADDRESS** Eastern Connecticut State Univ, 83 Windham Street, Willimantic, CT 06226. **EMAIL** TAPIAE@ECSU.CTSTATEU.EDU

TARR, ZOLTAN
PERSONAL Born, Hungary **DISCIPLINE** SOCIOLOGY, HISTORY **EDUCATION** Univ Ill, PhD, 74. **CAREER** CUNY; New School; Rutgers Univ. **HONORS AND AWARDS** Two Fullbright fel; two NEH fel. **MEMBERSHIPS** ASA; APSA; AHA. **RESEARCH** Intellectual history; history of European Jewry. **SELECTED PUBLICATIONS** Auth and coeditor, ten books, fifty articles. **CONTACT ADDRESS** 134 West 93rd St., #5-B, New York, NY 10025.

TARTTER, VIVIEN
PERSONAL Born 06/13/1952, Flushing, NY, m, 1972, 2 children **DISCIPLINE** PSYCHOLOGY **EDUCATION** Brown Univ, BA, 73; MA, 75, PhD, 77. **CAREER** Asst to assoc prof, Rutgers Univ, 79-88; prof, CUNY City Col, 91. **HONORS AND AWARDS** Phi Beta Kappa; Sigma Xi; Fogarty Sr Int Fel, 87; NSF, NIH Grant Awdee; Performance Excellence Awd, City Col, 97. **MEMBERSHIPS** AAS; Acoustical Soc of Am; Psytonomic Soc; Am Psychol Assoc. **RESEARCH** Psychology of language, reading acquisition, speech perception, cognitive psychology. **SELECTED PUBLICATIONS** Auth, Language Processes, Holt Rinehart & Winston, 86; coauth, "Vowel perception strategies of normal-hearing subjects and Nucleus multichannel and 3M/House cochlear implant patients", J of the Acoustical Soc of Am 92, (92): 1269-1283; coauth, "Speech changes following re-implantation from a single-channel to a multichannel cochlear implant", J of the Acoustical Soc of Am (92): 1310-1323; coauth, "Some acoustic effects of listening to noise on speech production", J of the Acoustical Soc of Am, 94, (93): 2437-2440; coauth, "Hearing smiles and frowns in chest and whisper registers", J of the Acoustical Soc of Am 96, (94): 2102-2107; coauth, "Lexical processing of visually and auditorily presented nouns and verbs: Evidence from reaction time and N400 priming data", Cognitive Brain Res 6, (97): 121-134; auth, Language Processing in Atypical Populations, Sage Pub, 98; Language and Its Normal Processing, Sage Pub, 98. **CONTACT ADDRESS** Dept Psychol, City Col, CUNY, 160 Convent Ave, New York, NY 10031. **EMAIL** vickyt@aol.com

TARVER-BEHRING, SHARI
PERSONAL Born 09/11/1954, SD, m, 1974, 3 children **DISCIPLINE** EDUCATIONAL PSYCHOLOGY **EDUCATION** Univ SDak, Vermillion, BS, 76; Marquette Univ, MS, 81; Univ Wis, Madison, PhD, 86. **CAREER** Assoc prof, Dept of Educ Psychol and Coun, Calif state Univ, Northridge, 91-, co-coordr, Sch Coun Prog. **HONORS AND AWARDS** Numerous grants; Outstanding Young Professional Woman, 97. **MEMBERSHIPS** Am Psychol Asn, Am Asn for Coun & Develop, Calif Asn of School Psychologists, Calif Psychol Asn. **RESEARCH** Multicultural consultation. **SELECTED PUBLICATIONS** Auth, "White women's identity and diversity: Awareness from the inside out,", Feminism and Psychol, 4, no 1 (94); coauth with Rosemary Tom-Gelinas, "School consultation with Asian American children and families," Calif Sch Psychologist, 1 (96): 13-20; coauth with M. E. Spagna and J. Sullivan, "School counselors as change agents toward full inclusion," Ariz Coun J, 21 (96): 50-57; coauth with M. E. Spagna, "The school counselor and full inclusion for children with special needs," The Sch Coun, 1 (98): 51-56; coauth with C. L. Ingraham, "Culture as a central component to consultation: A call to the field," J of Educ and Psychol Consult, 9 (98): 57-72; coauth with M. E. Spagna, "Counseling with exceptional children," in A. Vernon, ed, In Counseling Children and Adolescents, Denver, Co: Love Pub (99); coauth with B. Ericson, "When divorce comes to class," in J. Kaywell, ed, Current Issues in Secondary Education, Westport, Conn: Greenwood Pub (99). **CONTACT ADDRESS** Dept Educ Psychol & Coun, California State Univ, Northridge, 18111 Nordhoff St, Northridge, CA 91330-8265.

TAUB, EDWARD
PERSONAL m **DISCIPLINE** PSYCHOLOGY **EDUCATION** Brooklyn Col, BA, 53; Columbia Univ, MA, 59; New York Univ, PhD, 69. **CAREER** Res Asst, Columbia Univ, 56; Res Asst, Jewish Chronic Disease Hosp, 57-60; Res Assoc, Jewish Chronic Disease Hosp, 60-68; Dir, Inst for Behav Res, 68-83; Assoc Dir, Inst for Behav Res, 79-83; Vis Prof, CUNY, 84-85; Prof, Univ Ala, 86-; Vis Prof, Univ Tuebingen, 93-; Sen Sci, Univ Ala, 95-; Vis Prof, Univ Konstanz, 95-. **HONORS AND AWARDS** Pioneering Res Contrib Awd, 84; Guggenheim Fel, 83-85; Distinguished Res Awd, Biofeedback Soc of Am, 88; Fel, Am Psychol Asn; Fel, AAAS; Fel, Soc Behav Med; Fel, Am Psychol Soc; William James Fel Awd, Am Psychol Soc, 97; Carolyn and William Ireland Awd for Distinguished Scholar, UAB, 97; Distinguished Scholar Awd, Asn Psychophysiology & Biofeedback, 98. **MEMBERSHIPS** Am Psychol Asn, AAAS, Soc Behav Med, Am Psychol Soc. **RESEARCH** Neurological rehabilitation, behavioral neuroscience, biofeedback. **SELECTED PUBLICATIONS** Coauth, "Effects of Motor Restriction of an Unimpaired Upper Extremity and Training on Improving Functional Tasks and Altering Brain/Behaviors," in Imaging and Neurologic Rehabilitation (NY: Demos Publ, 96), 133-154; coauth, "Plasticity of Plastici-

ty? Perceptual Correlates of Reorganization are Stable in Extent but not in Pattern," Brain, 119 (97): 1213-1219; coauth, "Cortical Reorganization and Phantom Phenomena in Congenital and Traumatic Upper Extremity Amputees," Exp Brain Res, 117 (97): 161-164; coauth, "Constraint-Induced Movement Therapy: A New Approach to Treatment in Physical Rehabilitation," Rehabil Psychol, 43 (98): 152-170; coauth, "Changed Perceptions in Braille Readers," Nature, 391 (98): 134-135; coauth, "Motor Cortex Plasticity During Constraint-Induced Movement Therapy in Chronic Stroke Patients," Neurosci Lett, 250 (98): 5-8; coauth, "Reorganization of Primary Auditory Cortex in Tinnitus," Proc Nat Acad Sci, 95 (98): 10340-10343; coauth, "Alteration of Digital Representations in Somatosensory Cortex in Focal Hand Dystonia," NeuroReport, 9 (98): 3571-3575; coauth, "A Constraint-Induced Movement Therapy for Focal Hand Dystonia in Musicians," The Lancet, 353 (00): 42; coauth, "Coherence of Gamma-Band EEG Activity as a Basis for Associative Learning," Nature, 397 (99): 434-436; coauth, "A Spelling Device for the Paralyzed," Nature, 398 (99): 297-298. **CONTACT ADDRESS** Dept Psychol, Univ of Alabama, Birmingham, 1300 University Blvd, CH 415, Birmingham, AL 35294-0001.

TAUB, RICHARD P.
PERSONAL Born 04/16/1937, New York, NY, w, 1961, 2 children **DISCIPLINE** SOCIOLOGY **EDUCATION** Univ Mich, BA, 59; Harvard Univ, PhD, 66. **CAREER** Asst Prof, Brown Univ, 65-69; Asst Prof, Univ Chicago, 69-. **HONORS AND AWARDS** Woodrow Wilson Fel, Harvard Univ, 59; Quantrell Awd for Teaching, Univ Chicago, 75-. **MEMBERSHIPS** ASA, Rural Sociol Assoc. **SELECTED PUBLICATIONS** Coauth, Paths of Neighborhood Change, Univ Chicago Pr (Chicago, IL), 84; auth, Community Capitalism, Bus Sch Pr (Boston, MA), 88; coauth, Entrepreneurship in India's Small-Scale Industries, The Riverdale Co (Riverdale, MD), 89; auth, "What if Everyone Had a Job," Core Issues in Comprehensive Community Building Initiatives, Chapin Hall Ctr for Children (96); auth, "Making the Adaptation Across Cultures and Societies: A Report on an Attempt to Clone the Grameen Bank in Southern Arkansas," J of Develop Entrepreneurship (98). **CONTACT ADDRESS** Dept Sociol, Univ of Chicago, 5845 S Ellis, Chicago, IL 60637.

TAVANI, NICHOLAS J.
PERSONAL Born 06/22/1925, Camden, NJ, m, 1951, 3 children **DISCIPLINE** SOCIOLOGY **EDUCATION** Temple Univ, AB, 51; Reformed Episcopal Sem, BD; Univ Md, MA, 65; PhD, 69. **CAREER** Asst Prof, George Mason Col, 69-71; Visiting Scholar, Evangel Univ, 72-73; Assoc Prof, George Mason Univ, 71-; Adj Prof, Trinity Sem. **HONORS AND AWARDS** Bausch and Lomb Honorary Sci Awd; Dr. William H. Seip Awd; Pi Gamma Mu; Seminary Awd; Alpha Kappa Delta; Dissertation Fel, Univ MD; Commendation in the Congressional Record, 71; Phi Kappa Phi; Order of the Golden Shield, Evangel Univ; CAS Dean's Awd, George Mason Univ, 90. **MEMBERSHIPS** Am Sci Affiliation; Christian Sociol Asn; Am Asn of Christian Coun; The Soc for Pentecostal studies; Nat Coun on Family Relations. **SELECTED PUBLICATIONS** Co-auth, An Evaluation of Two Driver Improvement Programs Using Group Discussion Techniques: Final Report of Group Dynamics Study of Driver Attitudes, George Washington Univ, 67; auth, "Supplement to Final Report of Group Dynamics Study," Drive Beh Res Prof, George Washington Univ, 67; auth, Group Size and Frequency of Interaction as Criteria for Differentiating Student Participation in Sparetime Activities, 69; auth, "The Challenge of Social Pollution," Campus Ambassador Magazine, (70): 2-6; auth, "Silent Assassin," Gospel Publishing House, 71; auth, "Marriage, Divorce and Remarriage," VISTA, 73; auth, "Making Our Society Whole," CAM, 79; co-auth, "Family Management and Walking with God," VISTA, 80; auth, "Clinical Sociology," in Clinical Sociology Courses; Syllabi, Exercises, and Annotated Bibliography, (Washington, 84); co-auth, "George Mason University Drug/Alcohol Survey: final Report and Recommendations, 87. **CONTACT ADDRESS** Dept Sociol & Anthropol, George Mason Univ, Fairfax, 4400 Univ Dr, Fairfax, VA 22030. **EMAIL** njitavani@gmu.edu.com

TAYLOR, CHARLES AVON
PERSONAL Born Baltimore, MD, m, 1982 **DISCIPLINE** EDUCATION **EDUCATION** Univ of Maryland, Baltimore MD, BA, 1973; Johns Hopkins Univ, Washington DC, 1976; Loyola Univ of Chicago, Chicago IL, EdD, 1984. **CAREER** Univ of Maryland, Baltimore MD, counselor, resident life dept, 71-73; Univ of Kentucky, Minority Affairs Accreditation Team, consultant, 75; Catonsville Community Coll, Catonsville MD, student activities specialist, 73-76; Loyola Univ of Chicago, Chicago IL, asst dean of students, 76-86, instructor in counseling, psychology, and higher education, 83-88, instructor in African American studies, 84-88; Chicago State Univ, Chicago IL, dean of student development, 86-88; Kellogg Community Coll, Battle Creek MI, Vice Pres for Student Services, 88-. **HONORS AND AWARDS** Advisor of the Year, Loyola Univ of Chicago, 1980; Community Leadership Awd, Neighborhood Housing Services of Chicago, 1984; Black & Hispanic Achievers of Industry Awd, YMCA of Metropolitan Chicago, 1984; Outstanding Citizens Awd, Chicago Junior Assn of Commerce & Industry, 1986. **MEMBERSHIPS** Chmn, education

committee, NAACP of Battle Creek MI; exec bd mem, Michigan Assn of Community Coll Student Personnel Administrators; American Association for Higher Education, AAHE Black Caucus; Battle Creek Area Urbn League; Parent Teachers Association, River Side Elementary, Lakeview School District PTA, Battle Creek, MI; National Council on Student Development, A Council of the American Association of Community and Junior Colleges; American Association for Counseling and Development; National Association of Student Personnel Administrators; American College Personnel Association; ACU-I Region 8 Representative Committee on Minority Programs; John Hopkins Alumni Assocation; Battle Creek Community Foundation. **CONTACT ADDRESS** Student Services, Kellogg Comm Col, 450 North Ave, Battle Creek, MI 49017.

TAYLOR, CHRISTOPHER C.
PERSONAL Born 12/03/1946, New Britain, CT, m, 1994 **DISCIPLINE** ANTHROPOLOGY **EDUCATION** Yale Univ, BA, 68; Univ Paris, MA, 79; Univ Virginia, PhD, 88. **CAREER** Mellon instr, Univ Chicago; asst prof UAB, 91-96; assoc prof, 96-. **HONORS AND AWARDS** Final Herskovits Awd. **MEMBERSHIPS** AAS; AES; ASA; MAS. **RESEARCH** Africa; Rwanda; symbolic anthrop; body; violence; culture. **SELECTED PUBLICATIONS** Auth, Milk, Honey, and Money: Changing Concepts in Rwandan Healing, Smithsonian Inst Press, 92; auth, Sacrifice as Terror: the Rwandan Genocide of 1994, Berg Press, 99; co-transl, Rwanda 1994: Le Sacrifice et la Terreur, Editions Octares (Toulouse, France), 00; auth, "Rwandan Society and its Environment," Federal Res Div Area Handbook, Rwanda and Burundi, 90; auth, "The Harp that Plays by Itself," Medical Anthropology 13 (91): 99-119; auth, "The Harp that Plays by Itself," Anthropological Approaches to the Study of Ethno medicine, ed, M Nichter (Gordon & Breach, 92); auth, "Cosmology and Change in Rwanda," Societes d'Afrique et de SJDA Newsletter, 94; auth, "A Gendered Genocide: Tutsi Women and Hutu Extremists in the 1994 Rwanda Genocide," Political and Legal Anthropology Rev 22 (99): 42-54; rev of, Histoire d'une famine: Rwanda 1927-1930 crise alimentaire entre tradition et modernite, by Anne Cornet, Intl J Afri Hist Stud (98); rev of, "The United Nations and Rwanda 1993-1996," by the United Nations, Intl J Afri Hist Stud (98). **CONTACT ADDRESS** Dept Anthropology, Univ of Alabama, Birmingham, 1530 3rd Ave S, Birmingham, AL 35294-0001. **EMAIL** ctaylor@uab.edu

TAYLOR, CINDY
DISCIPLINE AMERICAN LITERATURE, WOMEN IN LITERATURE, SOUTHWESTERN LITERATURE **EDUCATION** Univ ID, BA, 77, MA, 79; Univ MN, PhD, 93. **CAREER** Asst prof, Univ of Southern Co. **RESEARCH** 20th century Am lit; women in lit; western lit; native Am lit; lit; environment. **SELECTED PUBLICATIONS** Auth, "Coming to Terms with the Image of the Mother in The Stone Angel," New Perspectives on Margaret Laurence, ed. Greta Coger (New York: Greenwood Press, 96); auth, "Claiming Female Space: Mary Austin's Western Landscapes," in The Big Empty: Essays on the Land as Narrative, ed. Leonard Engel (Alburquerque: Univ of New Mexico Press). **CONTACT ADDRESS** Dept of Eng, Univ of So Colorado, 2200 Bonforte Blvd, Pueblo, CO 81001-4901. **EMAIL** Ctaylor@meteor.uscolo.edu

TAYLOR, HOWARD F.
PERSONAL Born 07/07/1939, Cleveland, OH, m, 1963, 1 child **DISCIPLINE** SOCIOLOGY **EDUCATION** Yale, PhD 1966; Yale, MA 1964; Hiram Coll, AB 1961. **CAREER** Princeton Univ, prof 1973; Syracuse Univ, 68-73; IL Inst of Tech, 66-68; Natl Acad of Scis, cons. **HONORS AND AWARDS** Various grants; President's Distinguished Teaching Awd. **MEMBERSHIPS** NAAS; Am Sociol Assn; E Sociol Soc; Am Assn of Univ Profs; Assn of Black Sociologists. **RESEARCH** race and Ethnic Relations, Educational Inequality, Sociol Psychology. **CONTACT ADDRESS** Sociol Dept, Princeton Univ, Wallace Hall, Princeton, NJ 08544. **EMAIL** 0756353@princeton.edu

TAYLOR, JAMES COLERIDGE
PERSONAL Born 12/21/1922, Henderson, NC, m, 1982 **DISCIPLINE** EDUCATION **EDUCATION** Maryland University, European Div, BA, 1958, BS, 1963; Boston University, Boston, MA, MA, 1966; USC, Los Angeles, CA, PhD, 1972-73; International Inst of Human Rights, Strasbourg, France, 1973-75. **CAREER** US Army Medical Service, hospital administrator, 43-68; Monterey Peninsula College, Monterey, CA, division chairman, 70-71; University of Maryland, European Div, lecturer, 72; assistant director, 73-74. **MEMBERSHIPS** President, NAACP, Monterey, CA, Branch 1968-70; vice-president, UNA, NAACP Monterey, CA, Branch, 1969-71; Representative, Baha'i Intl Community, Human Rights Commission, Geneva, Switzerland, 1978, 1987; member, United Nations Assn Human Rights Committee, London, 1984-90; member, Univ of Maryland, Speakers Bureau, Europe; member, NCOBPS, APSA: Amer Academy Pol & Soc Scientist, ASALH. **CONTACT ADDRESS** Lecturer, Univ of Maryland, Col Park, Box 2187, New York, NY 09238.

TAYLOR, JENNIFER F.
PERSONAL Born San Francisco, CA **DISCIPLINE** PSYCHOLOGY **EDUCATION** Univ Calif, BA, 82; Calif State Univ, MPA, 88; Washington State Univ, MEd, 97; PhD, 99. **CAREER** Worker to Coordinator of Student Affairs, Univ Calif, 82-92; Career Counselor, Univ Calif, 89-92; Staff Psychologist, Humboldt State Univ, 98-. **HONORS AND AWARDS** Leroy C Olsen Scholarship, Washington State Univ, 93; Lawrence J Peter Scholarship, Washington State Univ, 93. **MEMBERSHIPS** APA. **RESEARCH** Multicultural Counseling and Education; Counseling Process. **CONTACT ADDRESS** Dept Psychol, Humboldt State Univ, 1 Harpst St, Arcata, CA 95521. **EMAIL** jft7002@axe.humboldt.edu

TAYLOR, LINDA L.
PERSONAL Born 12/09/1948, Ft Dodge, IA, s **DISCIPLINE** ANTHROPOLOGY **EDUCATION** Grossmont Col, AA, 76; San Diego State Univ, BA, 78; Wash Univ, St Louis, MA, 80, PhD, 86. **CAREER** Sessional instr, Univ Calgary, 88-89, adjunct asst prof, 89-90; adjunct asst prof, Fla Atlantic Univ, Boca Raton, 91-; res asst prof, Univ Miami, Coral Gables, 88-93, asst prof, 93-98, assoc prof, 99-; Behavioral Primatologist, Specific Pathogen Free Rhesus Monkey Breeding Center, Univ Miami, Miami, 89-93. **HONORS AND AWARDS** Phi Kappa Phi; Phi Beta Kappa; Sigma Xi, Grant-in Aid-of-Res, 82-83; Nat Sci Found, 83-85; Who's Who of Am Women, 91-96; James W. McLamore Summer Awd, Univ Miami, 97; Excellence in Teaching Awd, Univ Miami, 97; Innovative Teaching and Res, Univ Miami, 97; Gen Res Support Awd, Univ Miami, 97-98. **MEMBERSHIPS** Am Asn of Physical Anthropologists, Am Soc of Primatologists, Int Primatological Soc, Sigma Xi, Asn of Zoos and Aquariums, Fla Acad of Sci. **SELECTED PUBLICATIONS** Coauth, "The population genetics of the Mauritian macaques: an example of the founder-flush phenomenon," Am J of Anthropol, 96 (95): 133-141; auth, "The Importance of Kinship in the Management of Ring-tailed Lemurs (Lemur catta)," Regional Conference Proceedings of the American Association of Zoological Parks and Aquariums (95): 467-472; coauth, "Predation on an evening bat (Nycticeius sp.) by squirrel monkeys (Saimiri sciureus) in South Florida," The Florida Scientist, 60, 2 (97): 112-117; coauth, "Dietary preferences of an urban troop of squirrel monkeys in South Florida," in Regional Conference Proceedings of the American Association of Zoological Parks and Aquariums (97): 166-171; auth, "Promoting species typical behavior in Coquerel's sifakas (Propithecus verreauxi coquereli)," Regional Conference Proceedings of the Association of Zoos and Aquariums (98): 599-603. **CONTACT ADDRESS** Dept Anthropol, Univ of Miami, PO Box 248106, Miami, FL 33124-2005. **EMAIL** LTAYLOR@miami.edu

TAYLOR, LUCIEN
PERSONAL Born 01/10/1966, Liverpool, United Kingdom **DISCIPLINE** ANTHROPOLOGY **EDUCATION** Univ Cambridge, BA, 88; Univ Southern Calif, MA, 92; Univ Calif, Berkeley, PhD, 00. **CAREER** Asst prof, Univ of Colo, 98-. **HONORS AND AWARDS** Keasbey Bursar, 88; Haynes Found Fel, 89-90; Mellon Fel, 92; Simpson Fel, 94-5; Phoebe Hearst Bannister Fel, 95-96; Irving and Jean Stone Fel, 97-98; Grad Coun for Art and Humanities Grant, 99; IMPART Fel, 00. **RESEARCH** Anthropology and Intellectuals, Visual Anthropology, Cognitive Science. **SELECTED PUBLICATIONS** Ed, Visualizing Theory: Selected Essays from VAR, Routledge, 94; auth, "Iconophobia: How Anthropology Lost It At The Movies", Transition 69, (96); coauth, "Rethinking Ethnographic Film: A Conversation with David and Judith MacDougall", Am Anthrop 98 (96): 2; coauth, "Cross-Cultural Filmmaking: A Handbook for Making Documentary and Ethnographic Films and Videos, Univ of Calif Pr, 97; ed, Transcultural Cinema, and other Essays by David MacDougall, Princeton Univ Pr, 98; auth, "Creolite Bites", Transition 75, 98; auth, "Visual Anthropology is Dead! Long Live Visual Anthropology1", Am Anthrop 100 (98): 2; auth, "Joseph Zobel: From Sugar Cane Alley to Senghor's Senegal", Transition (forthcoming); auth, "Taking Leave of Your Lebenswelt", Aesthetics and Politics in the African Diaspora, ed B Jules-Rosette, Gordon & Breach, (forthcoming); auth, Creolite: The Anatomy of a Paracolonial Literary Movement, (forthcoming). **CONTACT ADDRESS** Dept Anthrop, Univ of Colorado, Boulder, Box 233, Boulder, CO 80309-0203. **EMAIL** lucien.taylor@colorado.edu

TAYLOR, SUSAN L.
DISCIPLINE WOMEN'S STUDIES, COMPOSITION **EDUCATION** Univ S Fla, BA, magna cum laude, 86; Fla State Univ, MA, 90, PhD, 94. **CAREER** Grad tchg asst, 87-93, vis instr, Fla State Univ, 93-94; lectr, 94-95, dir, Writing Ctr, 94-95, asst dir, freshman compos, 94-97, asst prof, 95-, dir, compos, Univ Nev, Las Vegas, 97-. **HONORS AND AWARDS** Eng Dept Excellence in Tchg Awd, 92, Univ Excellence in Tchg Awd, Fla State Univ, 93; State of Nev award for Distance Lrng, 96, 97. **MEMBERSHIPS** NCTE. **RESEARCH** Textbook selection. **SELECTED PUBLICATIONS** Auth, Time and Timelessness in Frank Waters' People of the Valley and Isak Dinesen's "The Blank Page," Stud in Frank Waters, 95; For a Good Time Type http://www.geekgirl.com.au/, Electronic Bk Rev, 96; Babes, BluBlockers, and Broncos, geekgirl, 96. **CONTACT ADDRESS** Dept English, Univ of Nevada, Las Vegas, PO Box 455011, Las Vegas, NV 89154-5011. **EMAIL** taylors@nevada.edu

TAYLOR, VERTA
PERSONAL Born 01/15/1948, Jonesboro, AR **DISCIPLINE** SOCIOLOGY **EDUCATION** Ohio State Univ, PhD 76, MA 71; Indiana State Univ, BA 70. **CAREER** Ohio State Univ, asst prof, assoc prof, prof, 76 to 97-, co-dir Disaster Res Cen 76-78, grad fac 80 to 98-, act dir WS 84-85. **HONORS AND AWARDS** Dist Tchr; Grad Tchg Awd; Mentoring Awd; Fem Lectr. **MEMBERSHIPS** ASA; SSSP; NASA; SWS. **RESEARCH** Gender; Social movements; Women's studies; Gay and lesbian studies. **SELECTED PUBLICATIONS** Auth, Rock-a-by Baby: Feminism Self-Help and Postpartum Depression, NY, Routledge, 96; auth, Survival in the Doldrums: The American Women's Rights Movement, 1945-1960's, NY, Oxford Univ Press, 87; auth, Feminist Frontiers IV: Rethinking Sex Gender and Society, co-ed, NY, McGraw Hill, 97; Women's Self Help and the Reconstruction of Gender: The Postpartum Support and Breast Cancer Movements, coauth, Mobilization: An Intl Jour, 96; auth, Identity Politics as High Risk Activism: Career Consequences for Lesbian Gay and Bisexual Sociologists, Social Problems, 95; auth, Women's Culture and Lesbian Feminist Activism: A Reconsideration of Cultural feminism, coauth, Signs: Jour of Women in Culture and Soc, 93. **CONTACT ADDRESS** Dept of Sociology, Ohio State Univ, Columbus, 190 North Oval Hall, Columbus, OH 43210. **EMAIL** vat@ohstsoca.sbs.ohio-state.edu

TE, JORDAN
PERSONAL Born 07/23/1929, Leeds, England, 3 children **DISCIPLINE** EDUCATIONAL PSYCHOLOGY **EDUCATION** Indiana Univ, EdD, 55. **CAREER** Dean, Grad School, Assoc Vice Chancellor for Acad Affairs, Curators' Prof, Univ of MO, 68-. **HONORS AND AWARDS** Royal Soc. Hlth-research prize, 81. **RESEARCH** Longitudinal research; Victorian Ireland and England. **SELECTED PUBLICATIONS** Auth, The Degeneracy Crisis and Victorian Youth, State Univ of NY Press, 93; auth, The Arrow of Time: Longitudinal Study and its Applications, Genetic, Social, and General Psychol Monographs, 94; auth, Ireland and the Quality of Life: The Famine Era, Mellen Press, 97; auth, The First Decade of Life Vol 1 & 2, Mellen Press, 97; auth, Ireland's Children: Stress, Quality of Life, and Child Development in the Famine Era, Greenwood Press, 98; The Census of Ireland 1821-1911: General Reports and Extracts (Three volumes), Mellen Press, 98; auth, Victorian-Edwardian Child-Savers and Their Culture: A Thematic Appraisal, Mellen Press, 98; auth, A Weighted Index of Quality of Life for Irish Children: 1841, 1851, & 1861, Soc Indicators Res, 96; auth, An Almighty Visitation of Providence: The Irish Famine 1845-1849, J of the Royal Soc of Health, 97; auth, Questioning the Predictive Validity of Historical Quality of Life Measures: The IREQUAL Index, Int Test Comn Newsletter, 97; A Century of Irish Censuses 1812-12911, New Hibernia Rev, 97; auth, Quality of Life in Victorian Ireland, New Hibernia Review, 00; auth, A Seventeen Year Prospective Study of Adolescents Vocational Knowledge, Journal of Vocational Behavior, 00; auth, Down's Essay and Nineteenth Century Science, Mental Retardation, 00. **CONTACT ADDRESS** 2361 Broadmont Ct., Chesterfield, MO 63017. **EMAIL** tkjor@aol.com

TEC, NECHAMA
PERSONAL Born 05/15/1931, Poland, m, 1950, 2 children **DISCIPLINE** SOCIOLOGY **EDUCATION** Columbia Univ, BS, 54; MA, 55; PhD, 63. **CAREER** Prof, Univ Conn, 74-. **HONORS AND AWARDS** Sen Res Fel, US Holocaust Museum Washington, 97; NEH, 91-92; First Prize for Holocaust literature, World Federation of fighters, Partisans and Concentration Camp Inmates in Israel, 95; Scholar-in-Residence, Intl Inst for Holocaust Res, 95; Intl Ann Frank Spec Recognition Prize, 94. **MEMBERSHIPS** Authors Guild, PEN, Alumni Asn. **RESEARCH** Holocaust, History. **SELECTED PUBLICATIONS** Auth, Defiance: The Bielski Partisans, Oxford Univ Press, 93; auth, "A Glimmer of Light," in the Holocaust and the Christian World, forthcoming; auth, "The Heroine of Minsk," in History of Photography, (99): 322-330; auth, "Denial of Jewish Heroism," Lessons and Legacies; forthcoming; auth, "Between Two Worlds," Literature and Belief, (98): 15-26; auth, "Jewish Resistance in Eastern Europe," Holocaust Encyclopedia, forthcoming; auth, "Righteous Among Nations," Holocaust Encyclopedia, forthcoming; auth, "Diaries and Oral History: Reflections on Methodological Issues in Holocaust Research," in Individualization in the Holocaust, forthcoming; auth, "Reflections on Rescuers," in The Holocaust and History: On the Known the Disputed and the Reexamined, 98; auth, "Women Among the Forest Partisans," in Women in the Holocaust, 98. **CONTACT ADDRESS** Dept Sociol, Univ of Connecticut, 1 Univ Place, Stamford, CT 06901.

TEDESCHI, JAMES
PERSONAL Born Coatesville, PA **DISCIPLINE** PSYCHOLOGY **EDUCATION** Univ Miami, AB, 56; Univ Miami, MS, 58, Univ Mich, PhD, 60. **CAREER** Prof, State Univ NYork (SUNY), 70-. **HONORS AND AWARDS** One of 30 Outstanding Citizens, St of Fla Kennedy Mem, 64; Outstanding Teacher Awd, Univ Miami, 67; Outstanding Educ of Am, NEA, 74-75; Fel, Japanese Soc for the Promotion of Sci, 97; Fulbright Sen Fel, 00. **MEMBERSHIPS** SESP, APA, JSPS. **SELECTED PUBLICATIONS** Coauth, "Violence, Aggression and Coercive Actions," APA (Washington, DC), 94; coauth, "Limitations of Laboratory Paradigms for Studying Aggression," Aggression and Violent Behav: A Rev J, 1 (96): 163-177; auth, "A Social Interactionist Interpretation of Motives for Youth Violence," in Nebr Symp on Motivation (Lincoln, NE: Univ Nebr Pr, 97); coauth, "A Further Comment on the Construct Validity of Laboratory Aggression Paradigms: A Response to Giancola and Chermack," Aggression and Violent Behav: A Rev J, 4 (99). **CONTACT ADDRESS** Dept Psychol, SUNY, 1400 Washington Ave, Albany, NY 12222-1000. **EMAIL** jtedeschi@global2000.net

TEMPLER, DONALD I.
PERSONAL Born 08/26/1938, Chicago, IL **DISCIPLINE** PSYCHOLOGY **EDUCATION** Washington Univ, postdoct fel, 68-69; Univ Louisville, predoct, 64-65; Ohio Univ, BA, 60; Bowling Green Univ, MA, 61; Univ Kentucky, PhD, 67. **CAREER** Dept dir, Western State Hosp, 65-67; asst prof, Western Kentucky Univ, 67-68; ch psychol, Carrier Clinic, 69-73; dir, Pleasant Grove Hosp, 73-74; ch psychol, Waterford Hosp, 74-75; priv pract, Louisville Kentucky, 75-78; core fac, Cal Sch Psychol, 78-. **HONORS AND AWARDS** PAF, Psychol of the Year; MPA Res Awd, 69; **MEMBERSHIPS** APS; APA; AAAPP. **SELECTED PUBLICATIONS** Coauth, Death Anxiety, Hemisphere Pub (NY), 86; co-ed, Preventable Brain Damage: Brain Vulnerability and Brain Health, Springer (NY), 92; coauth, Bisocial Psychopathology: Epidemiological Perspectives, Springer (NY), 93; coauth, Chronicity Suffering and Acceptance in Mental Health, Laser Quill Press (Fresno), in press; auth, Common Sense in Psychodiagnostics, Laser Quill Press (Fresno), 98; coauth, "Maternal support for sexually abused children," The Archives: Res and Applied Psychol 1 (99): 18-22; coauth, "Indirect attempt to change death attitude: negative findings and associated relationships, Omega 37 (98): 203-214; coauth, "California psychology licensing exam pass rates of graduates of accredited and unaccredited programs," Cal Psychol (in press); coauth, "The dimensions of psychiatric disorders: A compilation of factor analytic studies," Online J Psychology (in press); rev, "Homosexual Molestation Form," in Sexuality Related Measures: A Compendium, eds. CM Davis, WH Yarber, GS Bauserman, SL Davis, Sage Pub (Thousand Oaks), 99. **CONTACT ADDRESS** Dept Psychology, California Sch of Professional Psychology, Fresno, 5130 E Clinton Way, Fresno, CA 93727.

TENNYSON, ROBERT
PERSONAL Born 08/19/1941, Culver City, CA, m, 1987, 2 children **DISCIPLINE** PSYCHOLOGY **EDUCATION** BYU, BA, 64; Cal State Univ, MA, 66; MA, 68; BYU, PhD, 71. **CAREER** Prof, Fla State Univ, 71-74; prof, Univ Minn, 74-. **HONORS AND AWARDS** Fulbright Res Schl, 81; Fellow APAB, 88; Bk of the Yr, Asn Ed Comm and Tech, 95. **MEMBERSHIPS** AERA. **RESEARCH** Human learning and cognition, educational technology. **SELECTED PUBLICATIONS** Auth, "Defining the core competencies an instructional developer," J Courseware Eng 1 (98): 31-36; coauth, "Complexing theory: Inclusion of the affective domain in an interactive learning model for instructional design," Ed Tech 38 (98): 7-12; coauth, "System dynamics technologies and future directions in instructional design," J Struct Learn Intell Sys 13 (98): 89-101; auth, "Instructional development process and ISD4 methodology," Perf Improv 38 (99): 19-27; auth, "Goals for automated instructional systems: Analysis of content," J Struct Learn Intell Sys 13 (99): 215-226; auth, "Research foundations for instructional design: Introduction and overview", in Instructional design: International Perspectives vol 1: Theory and research, coeds. F Schott and S Dijkstra (Hillsdale NJ: Erlbaum, 97), 177-182; coauth, "Learning theory foundations for instructional design", in International Perspectives vol 1: Theory and research, coeds. F Schott and S Dijkstra (Hillsdale NJ: Erlbaum, 97), 177-182; coauth, "Instructional systems development", in Performance improvement interventions: Methods for organizational learning vol 2, eds. PJ Dean and DE Ripley (Wash DC: The Intl Soc Perm Improv, 98), 64-106; coauth, "Computers in education and school psychology: The existing and emerging technology knowledge base supporting interventions with children," in Handbook of school psychology 3rd ed, eds. CR Reynolds and TB Gutkin (NY: Wiley and Sons, 99), 885-906; coed. Handbook of research on educational communications and technology, Asn Ed Comm Tech, (Washington, DC), 97; coed. Instructional design: International perspectives vol 1: Theory and research, Erlbaum (Hillsdale, NJ), 97; coed. Instructional design: International perspectives vol 2: Solving instructional design problems, Erlbaum (Hillsdale, NJ), 97. **CONTACT ADDRESS** Ed Psychology, Univ of Minnesota, Twin Cities, 178 Pillsbury Dr S E, 204 Burton Hall, Minneapolis, MN 55455. **EMAIL** rtenny@umn.edu

TERRELL, MELVIN C.
PERSONAL Born 10/05/1949, Chicago, IL, s **DISCIPLINE** EDUCATION **EDUCATION** Chicago State Univ, BSEd 1971; Loyola Univ of Chicago, MEd 1974; Southern Illinois Univ at Carbondale, PhD 1978; Inst for Educ Mgmt Harvard Univ, Post-Doctoral Study/Mgmt Devel Program summer 1986; Univ of Virginia Annual Summer Professional Dept Workshop Educ Mgmt Strategies, 1987; Natl Assn of Student Personnel Admin, Richard F Stevens Inst, 1989; Amer Council on Educ, Fellow, Florida State Univ, 1993-94. **CAREER** Kennedy-King Coll Chicago, student devel specialist, counseling instructor 1973-

75; Eastern New Mexico Univ, coordinator/counselor of black affairs & asst prof ethnic studies 1977-78; Chicago State Univ, project director/asst professor of education, 78-79; Univ of Arkansas at Monticello, dir learning devel center 1979-80; Univ of Wisconsin-Oshkosh, dir multicultural educ center 1981-85; Univ of Toledo, dir of minority affairs & adjunct asst prof 1985-88; Northeastern Illinois Univ, full professor of counselor education, 88-, vice president for student affairs, 88-; Illinois State Univ, visiting prof, summer 1991. **HONORS AND AWARDS** Outstanding Admin, Univ of Toledo 1985, 1986, Administrator of the Year, 1986-88; recipient of a Ford Foundation Grant on Cultural Diversity, co-principal investigator, 1992-94; Identified as an Exemplary Leader in "Effective Leadership in Student Services," written by Linda M Clement & Scott T Rickard, Jossey-Bass, 1992. **MEMBERSHIPS** Past Vice chmn of educ comm NAACP Toledo Branch 1985-88; educ bd Natl Assoc of Student Personnel Admin Journal 1986-89 on Leadership Educ, 1986-; chair educ comm Alpha Phi Alpha 1986-88; natl chmn, Ethnic Minority Network, Natl Assn of Student Personnel Assn, 1988-90; vice chmn, Amer Assn of Higher Educ, 1989; chmn, Amer Assn of Higher Educ, Black Caucus Exec, 1991-93; life mem, Alpha Phi Alphi Fraternity, Inc; evaluation team mem, Middle States Assn of Colls & Univs; consultant evaluator, North Central Assn of Colleges & Universities, 1988-; member, National Assn of Student Personnel Administrators; past natl coord, Minority Undergraduate Fellows Program, Natl Assn of Student Personnel Admini, 1994-98; chair, exec comm, Ill Comm on Blacks Concerned in Higher Ed (ICBCHE), 1995-. **SELECTED PUBLICATIONS** "Diversity, Disunity and Campus Community," National Association of Student Personnel Administrators Monograph, 1992; Source of funding for minority student programming and its implications; Fund raising and development for student affairs; "Developing Student Government Leadership," New Directions for Student Services Monograph, Summer, 1994; author, "From Isolation to Mainstream, An Institutional Committment" 1987; co-author, Model Field Based Program in Multicultural Educ for Non-Urban Univs 1981, "Multicultural Educ Centers in Acad Marketplace" 1987; author, Racism: Undermining Higher Education, 1988; editor, NASPA Journal Series on Cultural Pluralism, 1988; Scott Goodnight Award for Outstanding Performance of a Dean, 1990; co-editor, From Survival to Success: Promoting Minority Student Retention, 1988; **CONTACT ADDRESS** Vice Pres for Student Affairs/Public Affairs & Professor of Counselor Education, 5500 N St Louis Ave, Rm B-104, Chicago, IL 60625.

TERRELL, NATHANIEL E.
PERSONAL Born 01/21/1960, Oklahoma City, OK, m, 1984, 2 children **DISCIPLINE** SOCIOLOGY **EDUCATION** Univ Cen Okla, BA, 86; MA, 88; Iowa State Univ, PhD, 93. **CAREER** Adj prof, Des Moines CC, 92-94; asst prof, 94-99, chair, 98-, Emporia State Univ. **HONORS AND AWARDS** OSA Awd, 85, 87, 88; Acad Achiev Awd, 88; Who's Who Teach; Outstand Young Am. **MEMBERSHIPS** Alpha Kappa Delta; Intl Soc Honor Soc; MSS; SSSA. **RESEARCH** Criminology and homelessness. **SELECTED PUBLICATIONS** Coauth, "The Black Intelligence Test of Cultural Homogeneity," Sci Tech Action Line, ISU (90): 16-17; auth, "Street Life: Rape and Assaults Among Homeless and Runaway Adolescents," Youth and Soc 28 (97):267-290; auth, "A Means For Re-Integrating African Americans Convicted of Non-Violent Crimes," J Offender Rehab 27 (98):25-35; coauth, "Readings is Deviant Behavior: Classic and Contemporary," Harcourt Brace, forthcoming. **CONTACT ADDRESS** Dept Sociology & Anthrop, Emporia State Univ, 1200 Commercial St, Box 4022 - RH 118, Emporia, KS 66801. **EMAIL** terrelln@emporia.edu

TERRERO, IRENE
PERSONAL Born 03/12/1938, Venezuela, D, 2 children **DISCIPLINE** NEUROPSYCHOLOGY, NEUROLINGUISTICS **EDUCATION** Kendall Col, AA, 70; George Washington Univ, BA, 72; Northwestern Univ, MA, 74; Univ Paris, Doctorate, 83. **CAREER** Clinical Dir, Clinica de Lenguaje IT, Clinica de Idiomas IT, 74-00; res assoc, Gallandet Univ, 84-94; res assoc, Int Cendie Universidad Metropolitana, 89-98. **HONORS AND AWARDS** Phi Beta Kappa; Gallandet Univ, Res Awd Nomination; Ministry of Educ, Special Educ Honors, 90, 00. **MEMBERSHIPS** ASHA, AAUW, George Sand Lit Assoc. **RESEARCH** Linguistics, Languages, Neurlinguistics, Hearing Impaired, Special Education, Bilingual Education and Development. **CONTACT ADDRESS** 13895 Folkstone Cir, Wellington, FL 33414-7738. **EMAIL** ireneterrero@hotmail.com

TERRY, JAMES L.
PERSONAL Born 09/12/1949, Terre Haute, IN **DISCIPLINE** LIBRARY SCIENCE; SOCIOLOGY **EDUCATION** Long Island Univ, MLS, 90; Purdue Univ, PhD, 88. **CAREER** Libr, Assoc Curator, New York Univ, 90-. **HONORS AND AWARDS** Louis Schneider Memorial Awd for Outstanding Dissertation, 88. **MEMBERSHIPS** Amer Libr Assoc; Amer Sociological Assoc. **RESEARCH** Political economy of information technology; information literacy; sociology of work and labor **SELECTED PUBLICATIONS** Auth, Authorship in College and Research Libraries revisited: Gender, Institutional Affiliation, Collaboration, College and Research Libraries, 96; auth, Automated Library Systems: A History of Constraints and Opportunities, Advances in Librarianship, 98. **CONTACT AD-**

DRESS Bobst Library, New York Univ, 70 Washington Sq S, New York, NY 10012. **EMAIL** terryj@elmer4.bobst.nyu.edu

TERRY, WILLIAM S.
PERSONAL Born Long Island, NY **DISCIPLINE** PSYCHOLOGY **EDUCATION** Fairfield Univ, BA, 71; Yale Univ, MS, 73; PhD, 76. **CAREER** From Asst Prof to Prof, Univ NC, 76-. **HONORS AND AWARDS** Undergrad Fel, New England Psychol Asn, 70. **MEMBERSHIPS** APA, Psychonomic Soc. **RESEARCH** Psychological research on learning and memory. **SELECTED PUBLICATIONS** Auth, "Retroactive Interference Effects of Surprising Reward Omission on Serial Spatial Memory," J of Exper Psychol: Animal Behav Processes, 22 (96): 472-479; auth, Learning and Memory: Basic Principles, Processes and Procedures, Allyn and Bacon, 00. **CONTACT ADDRESS** Dept Psychol, Univ of No Carolina, Charlotte, 9201 University City, Charlotte, NC 28223. **EMAIL** wsterry@email.uncc.edu

TESMER, FLOYD S.
PERSONAL Born 10/20/1947, Grand Island, NE, m, 1994 **DISCIPLINE** EDUCATION **EDUCATION** Univ Neb, BA, 71; MA, 72; PhD, 76. **CAREER** Asst Prof, Univ Neb, 74-76; Asst Prof, Southeastern Univ, 76-87; Asst Prof, Shenandoah Univ, 80-83; Prof, Strayer Univ, 85-. **HONORS AND AWARDS** Nat Athletic Scholarship Soc, 66; Phi Delta Kappa, 87; Alpha Chi scholarship, 96; Who's Who Among Am's Teachers, 94,96; Outstanding Service Awd, Strayer Univ, 98; Prof of the Year, Strayer Univ, 99. **MEMBERSHIPS** Phi Delta Kappa, Univ Neb Alumni Asn. **RESEARCH** Scientific method and Criminal behavior. **SELECTED PUBLICATIONS** Auth, Sociology of Development: A Study of Africa, Asia, and Latin America, Rev ed, Simon & Schuster, 95. **CONTACT ADDRESS** Dept Gen Educ, Strayer Univ, 11551 Nuckols Rd, Ste D, Glen Allen, VA 23059-5565.

TETTAH, JOSHUA
PERSONAL Born 11/07/1953, Ayikuma, Ghana, m, 1989, 1 child **DISCIPLINE** SOCIOLOGY **EDUCATION** Huntington Col, BS, 80; Univ Wisc, MA, 82; Am Univ, PhD, 98 **CAREER** Lecturer, Messiah Col, 96-; Adj Prof, Elizabethtown Col, 99-. **RESEARCH** Cultural Sociology; Globalization; Developing Societies; Race and Ethnicity; Stratification; Social Policy. **CONTACT ADDRESS** Dept Beh Sci, Messiah Col, Grantham, PA 17027.

TEWS, REBECCA
PERSONAL Born 09/06/1968, West Allis, WI, s **DISCIPLINE** PSYCHOLOGY **EDUCATION** St. Petersburg Jr Col, AA, 88; Wis Lutheran Col, BA, 90; Middle Tenn State Univ, MA, 94; Marguette Univ, PhD, 99. **CAREER** Lectr, Wis Lutheran Col, 95-97; Lectr, Univ of Wis Oshkosh, 97-98; Asst Prof, Undergraduate Field Placement Dir, Condordia Univ Wis, 95-. **HONORS AND AWARDS** Concordia Residential Scholar, 86; Schivan Acad Scholar, 89; Psi Chi Nat Hon Soc, 94; Marguette Acad Scholar, 94, 95. **RESEARCH** Factors in Attraction, Dating and Mating, Video Game Play: Behavior, Connection with Jungian Symbols and Social Impact. **SELECTED PUBLICATIONS** Auth, "Archetypes on Acid: Video Games and Culture," in Video Games in Culture, ed. M.J.P. Wolf (in press). **CONTACT ADDRESS** Dept Soc Sci, Concordia Univ, Wisconsin, 12800 N Lake Shore, Mequon, WI 53097. **EMAIL** Rebecca.Tews@cuw.edu

THAKUR, PARSRAM S.
PERSONAL Born 10/05/1937, Guyana, South Africa, m, 1989, 3 children **DISCIPLINE** PSYCHOLOGY **EDUCATION** Wisc State Univ, BS, 64; North Colo Univ, MA, 65; New York Univ, PhD, 75. **CAREER** Univ Guyana, 67-70; City Univ, La Guardia, 70-78; Community Col of RI, 78-. **HONORS AND AWARDS** Teaching Merit. **MEMBERSHIPS** Asn for Supervision and Curriculum Services. **RESEARCH** Religion, psychology, law. **SELECTED PUBLICATIONS** Auth, Psychology Trivia (99); auth, Hindu Names and Meanings (99). **CONTACT ADDRESS** Dept Psychol, Comm Col of Rhode Island, 1762 Louisquissett, Lincoln, RI 02865.

THARP, LOUIS
PERSONAL Born 03/05/1938, Miami, FL, m, 1996, 1 child **DISCIPLINE** PSYCHOLOGY, PHILOSOPHY **EDUCATION** Yale Univ, BA, 60; Claremont Grad Univ, MA, 67; PhD, 74. **CAREER** Prof, Long Beach City Col, 67-; Dir of Online Learning, 99-. **HONORS AND AWARDS** Yale Debate Asn Excellence Awd. **RESEARCH** Online learning in the Third World. **SELECTED PUBLICATIONS** Coauth, Letters to an Unborn Child, Harper & Row, 74; auth, Winning by Quitting, Synergy Pr, 00. **CONTACT ADDRESS** Dept Soc Sci, Long Beach City Col, 4901 E Carson St, Long Beach, CA 90808-1706. **EMAIL** louistharp@earthlink.com

THAW, KURT A.
PERSONAL Born 04/01/1965, Salisbury, MD, m, 1990, 3 children **DISCIPLINE** PSYCHOLOGY **EDUCATION** Ga Southern Univ, BS, 87; Fla State Univ, MS, 91; PhD, 94; Univ Va, Postdoc, 94; Cornell Univ, Postdoc, 97. **CAREER** Grad Instr,

Fla State Univ, 91-94; Vis Asst Prof, Sweet Briar Col, 96-97; Asst Prof, Millsaps Col, 98-. **HONORS AND AWARDS** Pilot Grant, NY Obesity Res Ctr, 00; Summer Res Grant, Millsaps Univ, 99; NIH Pilot Grant, NY Obesity Res Grant, 98-99; Res Grant, Jeffress Memorial Trust, 97-98; Res Grant, Cornell Univ Med Col, 97-98; Scholarship Grant, DuPont Minority Res, 97; Res Grant, Jeffress memorial Trust, 96-97; Res Grant, Sweet Briar col, 96; Training Grant, Univ Va, 94-96; Prof of the Year, Sweet Briar Col, 97; Excellence in Teaching Awd, Sweet Briar Col, 97; Joseph Grosslight Teaching Awd, 93. **MEMBERSHIPS** soc for Neurosci, Asn, for chemoreception Sci, Soc for the Study of Ingestive Beh, Phi kappa Phi, Psi-Chi. **RESEARCH** Ingestive behavior, Taste physiology, Gastrointestinal peptides, Satiety signals in the rat, Immune factors and feeding, Taste threshold testing, Development of the taste system, Regeneration of the taste system. **SELECTED PUBLICATIONS** Auth, "Emergence of altered central anatomy during development of sodium-restricted and control rats," Behavioral Neuroscience, 99; auth, "Behavioral taste responses of developmentally NaCl restricted rates," Behavioral Neuroscience, in press; auth, "Mammalian Bombesin-like peptides extend the intermeal interval in freely feeding rats," Physiology and Behavior, (98): 425-428; auth, "Orosensory response to fat is modified by intestinal fat infustion," Appetite, 98; auth, "Changes in taste threshold over the life span of the Sprague-Dawley rat," Chemical Senses, (96): 189-193. **CONTACT ADDRESS** Dept Psychol, Millsaps Col, 1701 N State St, Jackson, MS 39210. **EMAIL** thawak@millsaps.edu

THEODORATUS, ROBERT JAMES
PERSONAL Born 06/24/1928, Bellingham, WA, m, 1962, 3 children **DISCIPLINE** SOCIO-CULTURAL ANTHROPOLOGY **EDUCATION** Wash State Univ, BA, 50; Univ Wash, MA, 53, PhD, 61. **CAREER** Res anal, HRAF, 61-62; asst prof Anthropology, Sacremento State Col, 62-66; assoc prof, 66-80, Prof Anthropology, 80-; Col State Univ, 66-; Phi Beta Kappa, 50; Phi Kappa Phi, 50. **MEMBERSHIPS** Am Anthrop Assoc; Royal Anthrop Inst; Polynesian Soc; Spc Folk Life Stud. **RESEARCH** Immigrant ethnic cultures in North America; Ethnology of Europe; Comparative religion; Folk religion; Food; Culture. **SELECTED PUBLICATIONS** Auth Europe: A selected Ethnographic Bibliography, HRAF Press, 69; A Greek Community in America: Tacoma, Washington, Sacremento Anthrop Soc, 71; Patterns in Welsh Culture, Studies in Modern British Society, Az State Univ, 80; Orcadians, Shetlanders, Welsh, Encyclo World Cult, 92; British Isles, Encyclo Cult Anthrop, Henry Holt, 96; Shamanism in the Columbia-Fraser Plateau Region, Ancient Traditions: Shamanism in Central Asia and the Americas, Univ Press Col, 94. **CONTACT ADDRESS** Robert James Theodoratus, 3349 Oregon Trail, Fort Collins, CO 80526-4206.

THIBAULT, EDWARD
PERSONAL Born Syracuse, NY, d, 2 children **DISCIPLINE** SOCIOLOGY **EDUCATION** LeMoyne Col, BS, 62; SUNY, EdM, 65; MA, 66; Syracuse Univ, PhD, 71. **CAREER** Teacher to Dept Chair, Albert Einstein HS, 65-68; Asst Prof to Prof and Dept Chair, SUNY, 70-. **HONORS AND AWARDS** Who's Who in the East, 99; Awd, NY State Sociol Asn, 92; Awd of Merit, NYS Probation Officers Asn, 79; Ford Foundation Grant, 64-65. **SELECTED PUBLICATIONS** Auth, "Juvenile Delinquency Texts: What We Want and What We Get," Criminal Justice Educator, 90; auth, "Corrections/Penology Texts: What We Want and What We Get," Criminal Justice Educator, 90; auth, "Constitutional Revision," Criminal Justice Educator, 90; auth, "The Blue Milieu: Police as a Vocational Subculture," in Issues in Policing: New Perspectives, Autumn House Pub, 92; auth, Security Officer's Handbook, Municipal Police Pub, 94; co-auth, "From Friends to Lovers and Lovers to Friends," Loving More Magazine, 98; auth, "The Great Training Robbery: Again and Again," Criminal Justice Educator, 98; auth, Proactive Police Management Instructor's Manual, Prentice-Hall, 98; co-auth, Proactive Police Management, Prentice-Hall, 98. **CONTACT ADDRESS** Dept Sociol &Anthropol, SUNY, Oswego, 7060 State Route 104, Oswego, NY 13126. **EMAIL** DrThibaul@aol.com

THOMAS, JAY
PERSONAL Born 07/02/1951, Portland, OR, m, 1974, 3 children **DISCIPLINE** PSYCHOLOGY **EDUCATION** Portland State Univ, BS, 74; Univ Akron, MA, 76; PhD, 81. **CAREER** Asst prof, Ball State Univ, 79-81; vis asst prof, Rice Univ, 81-82; Senior Consult, NUS Corp, 82-84; principal, J.C. Thomas & Assoc, 84-98; Dir, Pacific Univ, 98. **HONORS AND AWARDS** Diplomat, Indust & Organ Psychol, Am Board of Prof Psychol. **MEMBERSHIPS** Soc for Indust & Org Psychol; Am Psychol Soc; Am Psychol Assoc; Am Statistical Assoc. **RESEARCH** Outcomes of psychological interventions, job stress, mental health in the work place. **SELECTED PUBLICATIONS** Coauth, "The relationship between specific mental ability measures to quality and quantity performance on a clerical job sample", Jour of Bus and Psychology 11, (96):35-42; coauth, "Randomized controlled trials are relevant to routine clinical practice", ADAA Reporter 10, 99; coauth, "Use of cognitive, emotive and behavioral interventions in rational emotive behavioral therapy when clients lack emotional insight", Jour of Rational-Emotive and Cognitive Behav Therapy 17 (99):201-209; coauth, "Cognitive-Behavior therapy of OCD in private

practice", Jour of Anxiety Disorders (forthcoming). **CONTACT ADDRESS** School OF Prof Psychology, Pacific Univ, 511 SW 10th Ave, 4th Fl, Portland, OR 97205. **EMAIL** thomajc@pacificu.edu

THOMAS, KATHERINE
PERSONAL Born 07/15/1940, Nashville, TN, m, 1961, 6 children **DISCIPLINE** HIGHER EDUCATION, COMPARATIVE LITERATURE **EDUCATION** St Louis Univ, AB, 61; Fordham univ, MA, 63; Pa State Univ, DEd, 81. **CAREER** Instr & grant writer, Ga Col, 87-92; assoc prof, Southeast Community Col, 94-. **HONORS AND AWARDS** Woodrow Wilson Fel, Fordham Univ, 61-63; NEH Fel, Univ of Ariz, 96; Univ of Ky Community Col Leadership Acad, 96-97. **MEMBERSHIPS** Ky Philol Asn, Int Asn of Caribbean Studies, Two Year Col English Asn. **RESEARCH** Caribbean Women's Literature, Classical Studies. **SELECTED PUBLICATIONS** Auth, "Mythic Archetypes in Casona's Le dama del alba," Text & Presentation 14 (93); auth, "Jocasta and Pertho: The Persuasive Voice in Oedipus Tyramos," Ky Philol Rev (99); auth, "Caribbean Women's Voices Speak to Two-Year College Students," Teaching English in the Two Year Col (99). **CONTACT ADDRESS** Dept Humanities, Southeast Community Col, 700 College Rd, Cumberland, KY 40823-1046.

THOMAS, SIDNEY C.
PERSONAL Born 04/23/1954, Long Beach, CA, d, 2 children **DISCIPLINE** EDUCATION **EDUCATION** Calif State Univ, BA, 76; Univ Rochester, MS, 91; PhD, 93. **CAREER** Instr, Univ Rochester, 89-92; From Asst Prof to Assoc. Prof, Univ Rochester, 92-99; Assoc. Prof, Univ Maine, 99-. **HONORS AND AWARDS** Cert of Awd for Invaluable Serv to the Am Counseling Assoc., 94; Summer Fac Roes Grant, 00. **MEMBERSHIPS** Psychol for the Ethical Treatment of Animals, Nat Assoc. for Poetry Therapy, Am Coun Assoc., Assoc. for Humanistic Educ and Develop, Maine St Counrs Assoc. **SELECTED PUBLICATIONS** Auth, "A Sociological Perspective on Contextualisms," J of Coun and Develop, vol 74, no 6 (96): 529-536; auth, "On Understanding the Processes of Peer Rejection: The Potential Contributions of Labeling Theory," The St Community J, vol 7, no 2 (97): 77-86; auth, "Context and Individualism: Critical Issues for Contextualist Counselors," Int J for the Advancement of Counseling, vol 19 (97): 101-110; auth, "The Soul of a Teacher," J of Maine Educ, vol XIV (98): 6-7; auth, "A Critical Social Interactionism for School Counselors," in Counseling and the Therapeutic State, Aldine de Gruyter Publ, 99; auth, "So Much Has Happened," Nat Assoc. of Poetry Therapy Chapter Book, 00 . **CONTACT ADDRESS** Dept Educ, Univ of Maine, 5766 Shibles Hall, Orono, ME 04469-5766.

THOMPSON, BECKY
PERSONAL Born 06/22/1959, Logan, UT **DISCIPLINE** SOCIOLOGY **EDUCATION** UCSC, BA, 83; Brandeis Univ, PhD, 91. **CAREER** Assoc Prof, Simmons Col. **HONORS AND AWARDS** Rockefeller Fel, NEH Fel, AAVW Fel, Ford Fel, Pol Res Assocs Fel. **RESEARCH** Race, social justice, qualitative methods. **SELECTED PUBLICATIONS** Auth, Names We Call Home: Autobiography of Racial Identity; Auth, A Hunger So Wide and So Deep, (Minnesota) 94; Auth, Mothering Without a Compass: White Mother's Love, Black Son's Courage, (Minnesota) 00; Auth, A Promise and A Way of Life: White Antiracist Activism, Univ Minnesota Pr (forthcoming). **CONTACT ADDRESS** Dept Sociol, Simmons Col, 300 Fenway, Boston, MA 02115.

THOMPSON, ROGER MARK
PERSONAL Born 07/15/1942, Oakland, CA, m, 1967, 10 children **DISCIPLINE** LINGUISTIC, SOCIOLINGUISTICS, TESL **EDUCATION** Brigham Young Univ, BA, 66, MA, 68; Univ Tex, Austin, PhD(Ling), 71. **CAREER** Prog specialist teaching English as Foreign Lang, Int Off, Univ Tex, Austin, 68-71; asst prof, 71-76, assoc prof English & Ling, Univ Fla, 76-, ed, Southern Folklore Quart, 72-75; vis prof Universidad de las Americas, Cholula, Puebla, Mexico, 82-83. **HONORS AND AWARDS** Fulbright Travel Grant/Hungary, 90; Fulbright Scholar, Philippine Depart of Ed, Culture and Sports, 96-97. **MEMBERSHIPS** Ling Soc Am; Am Dialect Soc; Teachers of English to Speakers of Other Lang; Am Asn Applied Ling. **RESEARCH** Bilingualism; second language acquisition; English as a second language. **SELECTED PUBLICATIONS** Coauth, Cakchiquel Basic Course, Brigham Young Univ, Vol I, 69; auth, Mexican American language loyalty and the validity of the 1970 census, Int J Sociol Lang, 74; The decline of Cedar Key: Mormon stories in North Florida and their social function, Southern Folklore Quart, 75; Mexican-American English: Social correlates of regional pronunciation, Am Speech, 75; Language planning in frontier America, Lang Problems & Lang Planning, 82; Linguistics Studies in Honor of Bohdan Saciuk, West Lafayett IN: Learning Systems, 97; Why can't they take a hint? The negative in spoken English, ACELT Journal, 97. **CONTACT ADDRESS** Dept of English, Univ of Florida, 4008 Turlington Hall, PO Box 117310, Gainesville, FL 32611-7310. **EMAIL** rthompso@english.ufl.edu

THOMPSON, SANNA J.
PERSONAL Born 02/18/1955, Logan, UT, m, 1995, 5 children **DISCIPLINE** SOCIAL WORK EDUCATION **EDUCATION** Weber State Univ, BS, 92; Wash Univ, MSW, 93; PhD, 98. **CAREER** Asst prof, Sch of Soc Work, State Univ of New York at Buffalo, 98-. **HONORS AND AWARDS** Nat Dean's List recipient, 88-92; Presidential Scholar for Academic Achievement, 89-92; Psychol Outstanding Grad of the Year, 92; Mary Uke's Scholar in Soc Work, 92. **MEMBERSHIPS** Coun on Soc Work Educ, Nat Asn of Soc Workers, Soc for Soc Work Res, Medical Outcomes Trust, Am Public Health Asn. **RESEARCH** Runaway and homeless youths. **SELECTED PUBLICATIONS** Coauth with W. F. Auslander and D. Dreitzer, "Patient satisfaction: Impact on adherence and medical outcomes," Practical Diabetology, 15, 2 (96): 8-13; coauth with C. S. North, D. E. Pollio, E. M. Smith, D. Ricci, E. M. Smith, and E. L. Spitznagel, "A comparison of clinical and structured interview diagnosis in a homeless mental health clinic," Community Mental Health J, 33, 6 (97): 531-543; coauth with D. E. Pollio, C. S. North, W. Paquin, and E. L. Spitznagel, "Predictors of achieving stable housing in a mentally ill homeless population," Psychiatric Services, 48, 4 (97): 528-530; coauth with C. S. North, D. E,. Pollio, E. M. Smith, D. Ricci and E. L. Sopitznagel, "A comparison of homeless and nonhomeless attenders of an urban mental health clinic," Soc Psychiatry and Psychiatric Epidemiology, 32 (97): 236-240; coauth with W. F. Auslander, D. Dreitzer, N. White and J. Santiago, "Disparity in health status and disparity between African American and Caucasian youths with diabetes: Family and community contexts," Diabetes Care, 20, 10 (97): 1569-1575; coauth with W. F. Auslander and D. Dreitzer, "Mothers' satisfaction with medical care: Relationship to medical outcomes in children with diabetes," Health and Soc Work, 22, 3 (97): 190-199; coauth with C. S. North, D. E. Pollio, E. L Spitzngel, and E. Smith, "The associations of psychiatric diagnosis with weather conditions in a large urban homeless sample," Soc Psychiatry and Psychiatric Epidemiology, 33 (98): 206-210; coauth with W. F. Auslander and D. Dreitzer, "Mothers' satisfaction with medical care: Perceptions of racism, family stress, and medical outcomes in children with diabetes," in P. Ewalt, E. Freeman, A. Fortune, D. Poole, and S. Witkin, eds, Multicultural Issues in Social Work, Washington, DC: NASW Press (99); coauth with D. E. Pollio and L. Bitner, "Predictors of outcomes for adolescents using runaway and homeless youth services," J of Human Behav and the Soc. Environment, 3, 1 (2000); coauth with D. E. Pollio and C. S. North, "Agency-based tracking of difficult-to-follow populations: Runaway and homeless youth programs," Community Mental Health J (in press); coauth with W. F. Auslander and N. H. White, "Influence of family structure on glycemic control in youths with diabetes," Health and Soc Work (in press). **CONTACT ADDRESS** Sch of Soc Work, SUNY, Buffalo, 685 Baldy Hall, Buffalo, NY 14260-1050. **EMAIL** sthompsn@acsu.buffalo.edu

THOMPSON, SPENCER K.
PERSONAL Born 06/08/1945, Soda Springs, ID, m, 1972, 3 children **DISCIPLINE** PSYCHOLOGY **EDUCATION** Brigham Young Univ, BS, 69; UCLA, MA, 71; PhD, 73. **CAREER** Asst Prof to Assoc Prof, Univ Tex, 74-. **MEMBERSHIPS** SWSRHD; SRCD; APS; SWPA. **RESEARCH** Socialization Processes in Developmental Psychology. **SELECTED PUBLICATIONS** Auth, "Gender labels and early sex-role development," Child Development, (75): 339-347. **CONTACT ADDRESS** Dept Beh Sci, Univ of Texas, Permian Bason, 4901 E Univ, Odessa, TX 79762. **EMAIL** thompson_s@utpd.edu

THOMPSON, VETTA L.
PERSONAL Born 09/07/1959, B'ham, AL, m, 4 children **DISCIPLINE** PSYCHOLOGY **EDUCATION** Harvard/Radcliffe Col, BA, 81; Duke Univ, MA, 84; PhD, 88. **CAREER** Asst/Assoc Prof, Univ of Mo St. Louis, 89-; Coordr Black Studies, Univ of Mo St. Louis, 95-. **HONORS AND AWARDS** Elizabeth Carey Aggassi Cert of Merit, Radcliffe Col, 81; Golden Key Hon Soc, 97; Distinguished Serv Awd, Mental Health Asn of greater St. Louis, 98; Who's Who in Medicine and Health Care 1st ed; Who's Who in the Midwest 26th ed. **MEMBERSHIPS** Am Psychol Asn, Am Ortho-Psychiatirc Asn, Mo State Committee of Psychologists. **RESEARCH** African American Identity, African American Mental Health, Impact of Discrimination. **SELECTED PUBLICATIONS** Coauth, "Attitudes of African American adults toward treatment in cases of rape," Community Mental health J 28 (92): 531-536; auth, "Educating the African American community on organ donations," J Nat Med Asn 85 (93): 17-19; coauth, "Attitudes of African American adults toward treatment in cases of child sexual abuse," J of Child Sexual Abuse 2 (93): 5-19; coauth, "An evaluation of two culture specific instruments," The Western J of Black Studies 18 (94): 179-184; auth, "Socialization to race and race relations in African American families," The J of Black Psychology 20-2 (94): 175-188; auth, "The empirical characteristics of the Multidimensional Racial Identification Scale," J of Res in Personality 29 (95): 208-222; auth, "Sociocultural Influences on African American Racial Identification," J of Appl Soc Psychology 25 (95): 1411-1429; auth, "Perceived experiences of racism as stressful life events," Community Mental Health J 32 (96): 223-233; auth, "Factors Affecting African American Racial Identity Salience and Racial Group Identification," The J of Soc Psychology 139 (99): 748-761; coauth, "The Jefferson bank Demonstrations: Historical Lessons in Racial Consciousness, Activism, and Organization," J of Res Asn of Minority Prof 4 (00): 81-93. **CONTACT ADDRESS** Dept Psychology, Univ of Missouri, St. Louis, 8001 Natural Bridge, Saint Louis, MO 63121. **EMAIL** Vthompson@umsl.edu

THOMPSON, WILLIAM
PERSONAL Born 10/20/1950, Tulsa, OK, m, 1972, 2 children **DISCIPLINE** SOCIOLOGY **EDUCATION** Northeastern State Univ, BA, 72; Southwest Missouri State Univ, MS, 74; Oklahoma State Univ, PhD, 79. **CAREER** Vis Instr, Univ of Tulsa, 79; Asst Prof to Prof, Emporia State Univ, 79-89; Dept Chair, Emporia State Univ, 84-89; Prof, Texas A & M Univ - Commerce, 89-; Dept Head, Dept Sociol and Criminal Justice Texas A & M Univ - Commerce, 89-94; Dir of Univ Studies, Texas A & M Univ - Commerce, 99-. **HONORS AND AWARDS** Alpha Kappa Delta; Phi Alpha Theta; Phi Kappa Phi; Distinguished Fac Teaching Awd, Tex Asn of Col Teachers, 92-93; Distinguished Fac Awd, E Tex State Univ (Tex A&M - Commerce), 94; Distinguished Alumni Awd, Northeastern State Univ, 97. **MEMBERSHIPS** Am Sociol Asn, Southwestern Sociol Asn. **RESEARCH** Qualitative Studies. **SELECTED PUBLICATIONS** Auth, Society in Focus, 3rd ed, Longman, 99; auth, Juvenile Delinquency, 4th ed, Allyn and Bacon, 99. **CONTACT ADDRESS** Dept Sociol and Criminal Justice, Texas A&M Univ, Commerce, PO Box 3011, Commerce, TX 75429. **EMAIL** wt@tamu-commerce.edu

THORNTON, JERI
PERSONAL Born 03/20/1952, Tulsa, OK, d, 3 children **DISCIPLINE** EDUCATION, ENGLISH **EDUCATION** Univ Central Okla, BA, 85; MA, 87. **CAREER** From grad teaching asst to adj english prof, Univ of Okla, 87-93; dir of the Learning Ctr at Okla State Univ, 93-. **HONORS AND AWARDS** Delta Pi Honor Soc; Alpha Chi Honor Soc; Teaching Fel, Univ of Central Okla, 86-87; Outstanding English Grad Student, 87; Teaching Fel, Univ of Okla, 87-91; listed in Who's Who in Am Colleges and Universities, 91; Phi Theta Kappa; State-Wide Awd for Excellence (to The Learning Ctr), Okla Asn for the Improvement of Developmental Educ, 98; Outstanding Advisor, Phi theta Kappa, 99; listed in Who's Who Among America's Teachers, 00. **MEMBERSHIPS** Okla Global Educ Consortium, Okla Asn for the Improvement of Developmental Educ, Okla Asn of Community Col, Okla Asn of Instnl Res. **RESEARCH** English, Philosophy, Humanities, and Film. **SELECTED PUBLICATIONS** Auth, "The Learning Center: TLC for Students," Innovations Abstracts 17 (95); auth, "My Old House," What's Hot! (97); auth, "For the Love of it: Shakespeare and Love," What's Hot! (97). **CONTACT ADDRESS** Dept Humanities, Oklahoma State Univ, Oklahoma City, 900 N Portland Ave, Oklahoma City, OK 73107-6120. **EMAIL** tjeri@osuokc.edu

THORP, JOHN P.
DISCIPLINE ANTHROPOLOGY **EDUCATION** Univ Notre Dame, 64, Holy Cross Col, Washington, DC, 68; Univ Chicago, MA, 73, PhD, 78. **CAREER** Vis prof, Univ Notre Dame, 78-79; asst prof, Saint Mary's Col, 79-87; res assoc, Memorial Hosp, South Bend, Ind, 88-89; Dept Head, Ferris State Univ, 89-. **HONORS AND AWARDS** Ferris State Univ fac and cirriculum develop proj, 93-. **MEMBERSHIPS** Am Anthropol Asn, Asn Asian Studies, Am Ethnol Soc. **RESEARCH** South Asia, Islam, Hinduism, religion and culture, politics and religion. **SELECTED PUBLICATIONS** Auth, "Sacramental Food Transactions among South Asian Muslims and Hindus," in Traditions in Contact and Change, eds Peter Slater, et al, 481-501, Wwaterloo, Ont: Wlifrid Laurier Univ Press and Atlantic Highlands, NJ: Humanities Press (83); auth, "Culturally Relevant Socioeconomic Categories of Rural Landholders in Bangladesh," South Asian Anthropol, 4(2): 83-92 (83); ed, with M. M. Khan, Bangladesh: Society, Politics, and Bureaucracy, Dhaka: Center for Admin Studies, and Riverdale, MD: The Riverdale Co (84); auth, "Bangladesh, Bangladesh!--A Review Article," J of Asian Studies 45, 789-796 (86); ed, Women, Development, Devotionalism, and Nationalism: Bengal Studies 1985, East Lansing, MI: Asian Studies Center, Mich State Univ (86); auth, "The Social Drama of Factional Feuding in Rural Bangladesh," South Asian Anthropol 7:47-56 (86); auth, "Sheikh Mujibur Rahman, a Cyclone, and the Emergence of Bangladesh," South Asia Res 7(2): 143-167 (87); auth, "Alternative Practitioners and Rural Health Care," in Rural Health Nursing, ed Angeline Bushy, 79-92, Newbury Park, CA: Sage Pubs (91); auth, "Modern Health Care in Kenya," in The Pharmaceutical Corporate Presence in Developing Countries," eds Lee Travis & Oliver Williams, 229-264, Notre Dame, IN: Notre Dame Press (93); auth, "Genocide in Bangladesh," in Encyclopedia of Genocide, 15-16, ed Israel W. Charny, Santa Barbara, CA: ABC-CLIO (99). **CONTACT ADDRESS** Dept Soc Sci, Ferris State Univ, 820 Campus Dr, ASC 2108, Big Rapids, MI 49307. **EMAIL** thorpj@ferris.edu

THORSON, JAMES A.
PERSONAL Born 10/08/1946, Chicago, IL, m, 1966, 2 children **DISCIPLINE** GERONTOLOGY **EDUCATION** Northern Ill Univ, BS, 67; Univ NC, MEd, 71; Univ Ga, EdD, 75. **CAREER** Asst Prof, Univ Ga, 75-77; From Assoc. Prof to Prof, Univ Neb, 77-. **HONORS AND AWARDS** Feel, Gerontologi-

cal Soc of Am; Awd for Distinguished Roes, Univ Neb, 91. **MEMBERSHIPS** Gerontological Soc of Am. **RESEARCH** Coping and adaptation in later life. **SELECTED PUBLICATIONS** Auth, Aging in a Changing Society, Wadsworth Publ (Belmont, CA), 95; coauth, "Women, Aging and Sense of Humor," Humor: The Int J of Humor Roes, 9 (96): 169-186; auth, "Qualitative Thanatology," Mortality, 1 (97): 177-190; coauth, "Age Differences in Death Anxiety Among African-American Women," Psychol Reports, 83 (98): 1173-1174; coauth, Geriatric Respiratory Care, Delmar Pr (Albany, NY), 98; auth, "Religion and Anxiety," in Handbk of Relig and Ment Health (San Diego, CA: Academic Pr, 98), 147-160; coauth, "Methodological Note on the Use of the CES-D with Older Samples," Psychol Reports. 85 (99): 823-824; coauth, "Developmental Aspects of Death Anxiety and Religion," in Perspectives on Spiritual Well-Being and Aging (Springfield, IL: Charles C Thomas, 00), 143-158; auth, Aging in a Changing Society, 2nd Ed, Brunner/Mazel (Philadelphia, PA), 00. **CONTACT ADDRESS** Dept Gerontology, Univ of Nebraska, Omaha, 6001 Dodge St, Omaha, NE 68182-0002. **EMAIL** jthorson@unomaha.edu

THROCKMORTON, E. WARREN
PERSONAL Born 01/26/1957, Portsmouth, OH, m, 1977, 3 children **DISCIPLINE** PSYCHOLOGY **EDUCATION** Cedarville Col, BA, 79; Central Mich Univ, MA, 82; Ohio Univ, PhD, 92. **CAREER** Out-patient therapist, Baptist Family Services, 79-84; Program Coordinator, Athens county Juvenile Court, 85-86; Director, Throckmorton & Associates, 84-93; Clinical Coordinator, Medical Center Psychiatric Associates, 93-94; Behavioral Healthcare Consultant, Grove City, 94-; Assoc Prof and Director of Col Counseling, Grove City Col, 94-. **HONORS AND AWARDS** Counselor's Nat Distinguished Service Registry, 90-92; Professional Service Awd, Am Mental Health Counselors Asn, 92; Counselor of the Year Awd, Ohio Mental Health Counselor's Asn, 92; Special Awd of Merit, Scioto County Children's Services Board, 92; Who's Who in the East, 96-97; George E Hill Distinguished alumni Awd, Ohio Univ, 98. **MEMBERSHIPS** Am Mental Health Counselors Asn, Am Counseling Asn. **RESEARCH** Homophobia, Sexual orientation and counseling, Pre-therapy information, Managed behavioral healthcare. **SELECTED PUBLICATIONS** Auth, "Insurance, Health and Mental Health," Encyclopedia of Psychology 2nd Ed, Baker Books, 99; auth, "Managed care," Encyclopedia of Psychology 2nd ed, Baker Books, 99; auth, "Health maintenance organization," Encyclopedia of Psychology 2nd ed, Baker Books, 99; auth, "Licensing," Encyclopedia of Psychology 2nd ed, Baker Books, 99; auth, "Responding to students who request help to modify sexual orientation," Visions: American Association of College counseling Newsletter, (98): 283-304; auth, "Efforts to modify sexual orientation: A review of outcome literature and ethical issues," Journal of Mental health Counseling, (98): 283-304; auth, "Managed care: The times they are a-changin'." Journal of Psychology and Christianity, 98; auth, "Managed care: 'It's like deja-vu, all over again'," Journal of Psychology and Christianity, 98; auth, "Sunrise Evaluation Report," Penn Dept of Occupational Licensing, 97; auth, "Mental health counselors and third party reimbursement," in Foundations of Mental Health Counseling 2nd ed, Springfield, 97. **CONTACT ADDRESS** Dept Psychol, Grove City Col, 100 Campus Dr, Grove City, PA 16127. **EMAIL** ewthrockmorton@gcc.edu

THUMIN, FRED J.
PERSONAL Born 01/09/1928, St Louis, MO, m, 1994, 3 children **DISCIPLINE** MANAGEMENT, PSYCHOLOGY **EDUCATION** Washington Univ, BA, 51; MA, 56; PhD, 57. **CAREER** Assoc prof, Washington Univ, 61-66; prof, Univ Missouri, 97-. **HONORS AND AWARDS** APA Fel; IOP Diplomate; MPA Past Pres. **MEMBERSHIPS** APA; Sigma Xi; Beta Gamma Sigma. **RESEARCH** Psychology tests and measurements; employee selection. **SELECTED PUBLICATIONS** Coauth, "Relationship between the Thumin Test of Mental Dexterity and the WAIS," Perceptual & Motor Skills 57 (83): 599-603; coauth, "Faking behavior and gender differences on a new personality research instrument," Consulting Psychol J 45 (93):11-22; auth, "Predictor validity as related to criterion relevance, restriction of range, and ethnicity," J Psychol 127 (93): 553-563; auth, "Correlations for a New Personality Test with Age, Education, Intelligence, and the MMPI-2,' Perceptual and Motor Skills 79 (94): 1383-1389; coauth, "Corporate values as related to occupation, gender, age, and company size," J Psychol 129 (95):389-4OO; coauth, "Toward Harmonization: A cross-cultural empirical study examining managerial values of accountants from four countries," J Global Bus (95): 51- 64; auth, "A comparison of the MMPI and MMPI-2 among job applicants," Consult Psychol J: Res Pract (00). **CONTACT ADDRESS** Dept Psychology, Univ of Missouri, St. Louis, 8001 Natural Bridge, Saint Louis, MO 63121. **EMAIL** thumin@umsl.edu

THURBER, KARL T.
PERSONAL Born 06/12/1941, New York, NY, m, 1965, 1 child **DISCIPLINE** EDUCATION **EDUCATION** Rochester Inst Technol, BS, 63; Univ Pittsburgh, MBA, 64; Auburn Univ, MPA, 88; Univ Ala, DPA, 92. **CAREER** Off, US Air Force, 64-86; Adj Instr, Troy State Univ, 93-. **HONORS AND AWARDS** Pi Sigma Alpha; Gamma Epsilon Tau. **MEMBER-**

SHIPS APSA, Ala Polit Sci Asn. **RESEARCH** Public administration, political science, public policy. **SELECTED PUBLICATIONS** Auth, "The Air Force's Experience with Matrix Management," Defense Management J 14 (78): 16-21; auth, "Big, Little, Littler: Synthesizing Hatch Act-Based Political Activity Legislation Research," Rev of Public Personnel Admin XIII (93): 38-51. **CONTACT ADDRESS** Dept Arts & Sci, Troy State Univ, PO Box 4419, Montgomery, AL 36103-4419. **EMAIL** kthurber@mindspring.com

THURMAN, ALFONZO
PERSONAL Born 10/24/1946, Mayfield, KY, m **DISCIPLINE** EDUCATION **EDUCATION** Univ of Wisconsin-LaCrosse, BS 1971, Univ of Wisconsin-Madison, MA 1973, PhD 1979. **CAREER** Univ of Wisconsin-Whitewater, coordinator minority affairs, 71-75; Univ of Wisconsin-Oshkosh, dir academic devel program, 75-80; Northern Illinois Univ, dir special projects, 80-84, asst to the provost, 84-87, Assoc Dean, Coll of Educ, Prof, Ed Policy Studies, 87-. **HONORS AND AWARDS** Outstanding Leadership Awd ILAEOPP 1985; **MEMBERSHIPS** Pres Illinois Assn of Educ Opportunity Program 1983-84; chairman DeKalb Human Relations Comm 1983-86; Parliamentarian Mid-America Assn of Educ Opportunity Programs, 1989-90; bd of dirs, IL Assn of Colleges of Teacher Education. **SELECTED PUBLICATIONS** Author: "Establishing Special Services on Campus" (chapter) IN Handbook of Minority Student Services, "Policy Making, Higher Education's Paradox" (article) in Thresholds 1986; Leadership of the Governing Board and Central Administration: Providing the Policy and Budgetary Framework for Incorporating Multicultural Elements into College and University Curriculum, co-authored with Carol Floyd, chapter, 1991; Trio Programs: A Proposal for Accrediting Programs Designed to Increase Underrepresented Groups in Higher Education, chapter, 1993. **CONTACT ADDRESS** Col of Educ, No Illinois Univ, Graham Hall 321, De Kalb, IL 60115.

TICHI, CECELIA
DISCIPLINE AMERICAN LITERATURE, WOMEN'S STUDIES **EDUCATION** UCLA, Davis, PhD. **CAREER** William R Kenan Jr Prof Eng, Vanderbilt Univ. **SELECTED PUBLICATIONS** Auth, New World, New Earth: Environmental Reform in American Literature from the Puritans through Whitman, 79; Shifting Gears: Technology, Literature, Culture in Modernist America; Electronic Hearth: Creating an American Television Culture, 91; High Lonesome: The American Culture of Country Music, 94. **CONTACT ADDRESS** Vanderbilt Univ, Nashville, TN 37203-1727.

TIESSEN, PAUL
DISCIPLINE GENDER POLITICS IN FILM; BRITISH MODERNISM **EDUCATION** WLU, BA; Alberta, MA, PhD. **CAREER** Prof **RESEARCH** British and Canadian modernism, film-and-literture studies cultural/media studies, Malcolm Lowry, Wyndham Lewis, Dorothy Richardson, Marshall McLuhan. **SELECTED PUBLICATIONS** Auth, and Apparently Incongruous Parts: The Worlds of Malcolm Lowry, Scarecrow Press, 90; The Letters of Malcolm Lowry and Gerald Noxon, 1940-1952 , UBC Press, 88; The Cinema of Malcolm Lowry: A Scholarly Edition of Lowry's Tender is the Night, UBC Press, 90; The 1940 Under the Volcano , MLR Editions Canada, 94; Co-ed, Joyce/Lowry: Critical Perspectives, UP of Kentucky, 97. **CONTACT ADDRESS** Dept of English, Wilfrid Laurier Univ, 75 University Ave W, Waterloo, ON, Canada N2L 3C5. **EMAIL** ptiessen@wlu.ca

TIMBERLAKE, CONSTANCE HECTOR
PERSONAL Born St John, NB, Canada, m **DISCIPLINE** EDUCATION **EDUCATION** Syracuse Univ, Doctorate in Educ Admin, 1979; MS; BA (cum laude); NYS, cert. **CAREER** Syracuse Univ, assoc prof Col Human Develop; Syracuse Sch Dist, chief counselor & admin ABE prog; Neighborhood Ctr, exec dir; Syracuse Pub Sch Dist, commiss of educ; Adolescent Pregnancy Prevention Program, project dir, 87-. **HONORS AND AWARDS** Citations, Meritorious Srvs 1972, March Wash 1963, Ldrshp Agway 1974; Jefferson Awd, WTVH-TV/Amer Inst for Public Service, 1989. **MEMBERSHIPS** NY Sch Brds Assc; mem Prog Com; Central NY Sch Bd Inst mem planning com; AERA; AAUP; Syracuse Prof Women; HEW Task Force Social Justice Natl Literacy Volunteers Amer; Human Rights Comm of Syracuse & Onondaga Co; vice pres Syracuse NAACP; v chrprsn Coalition Quality Educ; v chrprsn Onondaga Urban League Guild; Natl Org Women; Adv Bd Onondaga Comm Clge; Neighborhood Health Ctr adv council; Metr Ch Bd Human Srv Com; Fair-Employ Review Bd Onondaga Co; PEACE Head Start Self-Evaluation & Performance Stand Improvement Plan; exec mem Black Political Caucus; numerous vol srvs; trust Pi Lambda Theta Inc; pres elect NYS Council Family Relations Council; mem SUNY at Oswego Adv Council Oswego NY; pres, New York State Council on Family Relations, 1988-89; honoraryadvisory bd mem, For Kids Sake, 1987; mem & program dir, Syracuse Boys Club of Syracuse; vice chair, Syracuse Univ Black & Latino Faculty Org, 1986-89. **SELECTED PUBLICATIONS** Author of 30 journal articles & reviews, 1974-; more than 20 media presentations & documentaries, 1980-. **CONTACT ADDRESS** Chair Child Family Comm Study, Syracuse Univ, 201 Slocum Hall CFCS Dept, Syracuse, NY 13244-5300.

TING, SIU-MAN R.
PERSONAL Born 08/17/1959, Hong Kong, m, 1987, 1 child **DISCIPLINE** EDUCATION **EDUCATION** Chinese Univ Hong Kong, BA, 81; Biola Univ, MA, 89; Univ Iowa, PhD, 95. **CAREER** Counselor, Univ Wise, 94-95; Asst Prof, NC State Univ, 95-. **HONORS AND AWARDS** Distinguished Scholar, NC Col Personnel Asn, 98; Scholar, Nat Asn of Col Admission Counseling, 98; Who's Who in Am, 01. **MEMBERSHIPS** Am Col Personnel Asn, Am Coun Asn, Nat Asn of Student Personnel Admin, NC Col Personnel Asn. **RESEARCH** Academic success and student retention, Career counseling. **SELECTED PUBLICATIONS** Auth, "Predicting academic performance for first-year engineering students," International Journal of engineering education, in press; auth, "An application of repeated structured groups enhancing college first-year students' success," Journal of College Student Development, in press; auth, "The renewed commitment program: An intervention for academically at-risk college freshmen," North Carolina Journal of College Student Development, in press; auth, "Non-Cognitive variables in predicting academic success of college students," North Carolina Journal of College Student Development, in press; auth, "Career development of women in student affairs," The College Student Affairs Journal, (99): 92-101; auth, "The Career Key: Helping middle school students world wide," The Meridian, (99): online www.ncsu.edu/meridian/jan99/career; auth, "First-year academic success: A prediction combining cognitive and psychosocial variables for Caucasian and African American students," Journal of College Student Development, (98): 599-610; auth, "Predicting first-year grades and retention of college students of first-generation and low income families," Journal of College Admission, (98): 14-23; auth, "ExCEL: Excellence-Commitment-and-Effective-Learning Group: An intervention program for academically high-risk students," The National Academic Advising Association Journal, (98): 48-51; auth, "A comparison of student services in the United States and Hong Kong," in Compendium of Papers presented at the Second Annual International Symposium on Student Services, (98): 81-88. **CONTACT ADDRESS** Dept Educ, No Carolina State Univ, Box 7801, Raleigh, NC 27695-0001. **EMAIL** raymond_ting@ncsu.edu

TIRYAKIAN, EDWARD A.
PERSONAL Born 08/06/1929, Bronxville, NY, m, 1953, 2 children **DISCIPLINE** SOCIOLOGY **EDUCATION** Princeton Univ, BA, 52; Harvard Univ, MA, 54; PhD, 56. **CAREER** Instr to asst prof, Princeton Univ, 56-57; lecturer, Harvard univ, 62-65; Assoc prof, Duke Univ, 65-67; prof, Duke Univ, 67-. **HONORS AND AWARDS** Summa cum laude, Phi beta Kappa, Princeton; docteur honoris causa Univ Paris V; fellow, Ctr for Adv Stud in the Behavioral Sci, 97-98; ch, dept sociol & anthrop, duke univ, 69-72; dir of int stud, 88-91. **MEMBERSHIPS** Int Sociol Asn; Am Soc for the Stud of Relig (past pres); Int Asn of French-speaking Sociol (AISLF, past pres); Am Sociol Asn; Eastern Sociol Soc; Southern Sociol Soc. **RESEARCH** Sociology of religion; comparative nationalism; sociological theory. **SELECTED PUBLICATIONS** Ed, The 100th Anniversary of Durkheim's Division of Labor in Society, Sociol Forum, 9, 1, 3/94; Revisiting Sociology's First Classic: The Division of Labor in Society and its Actuality, Sociol Forum, 9, 3-16, 3/94; auth, Collective Effervescence, Social Change and Charisma: Durkheim, Weber, and 1989, Int Sociol, 10, 269-81, 9/95; auth, Three Metacultures of Modernity: Christian, Gnostic, Chthonic, Theory Culture & Society, 13, 99-118, 2/96; auth, The Wild Cards of Modernity, Daedalus, 126, 147-81, Spring 97. **CONTACT ADDRESS** Dept of Sociol, Duke Univ, Box 90088, Durham, NC 27708-0088. **EMAIL** durkhm@soc.duke.edu

TOBY, RONALD P.
PERSONAL Born 12/06/1942, White Plains, NY, m, 1987 **DISCIPLINE** HISTORY, ANTHROPOLOGY **EDUCATION** Columbia Univ, BA, 65, MA, 74, PhD, 77. **CAREER** Preceptor, 72-73, Columbia Univ; lectr, 77-78, Univ Calif Berkeley; asst prof to prof, dept head, 78-, Univ Il Urbana-Champaign; vis prof, 84-85, Keio Univ; vis prof, 95-96, Kyoto Univ; prof, Tokyo Univ, 00-. **HONORS AND AWARDS** Fulbright-Hays Fel, 74-76, 84-85; Univ Scholar Univ Il, 86-89; LAS Faculty Fel, 87-88; Nat Endow for the Human Sr Fel, 88-89; Japan Found Prof Fel, 89-90; Toyota Found Res Grant, 89-91; JSPS Sr Res Fel, 93; Nat Endow for the Humanities Summer Res Fel, 94. **MEMBERSHIPS** Amer Hist Asn; Asn for Asian Stud; Early Modern Japan Group; Chosen Gakkai(Korean Stud Asn); Int Soc for Ryukyuan Stud. **RESEARCH** Ethinicity & identity, cultural hist & international relations. **SELECTED PUBLICATIONS** Auth, State and Diplomacy in Early Modern Japan: Asia in the Development of the Tokugawa Bakufu, Stanford, 91; co-auth, Gyoretsu to misemono (Parades & Entertainments), Asahi Shinbunsha, 94; auth, " On the appearance of the " Hairy barbarian": ideas of Other and imagination of the foreign in early-modern Japan," A history of Japan at the boundary, Yamakawa shuppan, 97; auth, Imagining and Imaging 'Anthropos' in Early-modern Japan, Visual Anthrop Rev, 98; auth, Gazing at 'Man': the Early-Modern Japanese Imaginary and the Birth of a Visual Anthropology, Wanami world history, Iwanami Shoten, 99; auth, From 'sangoku' to 'bankoku': The Iberian Irruption and Japanese cosmology, Mare Liberum, forthcoming. **CONTACT ADDRESS** Dept of History, Univ of Illinois, Urbana-Champaign, 309 Gregory Hall, 810 S Wright St, Urbana, IL 61801. **EMAIL** rptoby@uiuc.edu

TODD, ALEXANDRA
PERSONAL Born 04/18/1946, Scotland, m, 1988, 1 child DISCIPLINE SOCIOLOGY EDUCATION Univ Calif, BA, 76; MA, 77; PhD, 82. CAREER Instr, San Diego State Univ, 79-81; Asst Prof to Prof and Dept Chair, 82-. HONORS AND AWARDS Intl Who's Who of Professional and Business Women, 88; Gerald R. Ford Foundation Grant, 90; Phi alpha Theat, 91. MEMBERSHIPS Intl Sociol Asn, Am Sociol Asn, Sociol for Women in Soc, Nat Writers' Union. RESEARCH Women's studies; Film studies; Medical sociology. SELECTED PUBLICATIONS Auth, Double Vision: An East-West Collaboration for Coping With Cancer, Univ Press of New England, 94; auth, Intimate Adversaries: Cultural Conflict Between Doctors and Women patients, Univ Penn press, 89; auth, Gender and discourse: The Power of Talk, Ablex Pub, 88; auth, The Structure of Discourse and Institutional Authority: Law, Medicine, Education, Ablex Pub, 86; auth, "Miscommunication and the case of Maria M," Peace Review, (99): 237-242; auth, "When She was Mad: Angry Women on Film," in The Image of America, (99): 204-219; auth, "Different Realities: autobiography and Medical Care," in Auto/Biography, Vol 4, 96; auth, "Big Guns and Gentle Healers: combining Eastern and Western remedies for Coping with Cancer," Aesclepian Chronicles, 95. CONTACT ADDRESS Dept Sociol, Suffolk Univ, 8 Ashburton Pl, Boston, MA 02108.

TOHIDI, NAYEREH E.
PERSONAL Born 09/24/1957, Tehran, Iran, m, 1974 DISCIPLINE EDUCATIONAL PSYCHOLOGY & SOCIOLOGY EDUCATION Univ Tehran, BS, 75; Univ Ill Champaign-Urbana, MA, 78, PhD, 83. CAREER Vis lectr & res assoc, Harvard Divinity School, 93-94; vis scholar & res fel Hoover Inst, Stanford Univ, 94-95; adj prof, UCLA, 95-97; asst prof, Calif State Univ, Northridge, 97-; HONORS AND AWARDS Fulbright prof USSR, 91-92; Postdr fel, Stanford Univ, 94-95. MEMBERSHIPS Mid E Studies Asn; W Sociol Asn; Amer Acad Relig. RESEARCH Women and gender in Muslim societies; Islamist Movements; Women and development in the Middle East; Islam and nationalism in the newly independent republics of Central Asia and the Caucasus (Azerbaijan in particular). SELECTED PUBLICATIONS Auth, Memoirs of Baku: An Oral History of a Woman Writer, Iran Nameh, 93; auth, Immigrant Iranians and Gender Relations: Irangeles: Iranians in Los Angeles, Univ Calif Press, 93; A Review of the Events in the Field, Central Asia Monitor, 94; Gender, Religion, and National Identity in Azerbaijan, Central Asia and Caucasia Rev, 94; Cultural and Political Dimensions of Development in Azervaijan: the Quest for Identity, Int Affairs, 94; Modernization, Islamization, and Gender in Iran, Gender and National Identity: Women and Politics in Muslim Societies, Oxford Univ Press, 94; Fundamentalist Backash and Muslim Women in the Bejing Conference, Canadian Women Studies, 96; Soviet in Public, Azeri in Private: Gender, Islam, and Nationalism in Soviet and Post-Soviet Azerbaijan, Womens Studies Int Forum, 96; Feminism, Demokracy ve Islamgarayi, Ketabsara, 96; auth, The Intersection of Gender, Ethnicity and Islam in Azerbaijan, Nationalities Papers, 97; Islamic Feminism: A Democratic Challenge or a Theocratic Ploy? Knakash, 97; coed, Women in Muslim Societies: Diversity Within Unity, Lynne Rienner Publ, 98; auth, "Gender and National Identity in Past-Soviet Azerbaijan: A Regional Perspective" in Gender and Identity Construction: Women of Central Asia, the Caucasus and Turkey, ed F. Acar & A.G. Ayata (Boston: Brill, 99). CONTACT ADDRESS Womens Studies Dept, California State Univ, Northridge, 18111 Nordhoff St, Northridge, CA 91330-8251. EMAIL ntohidi@humnet.ucla.edu

TOLEN, W. CHRISTOPHER
PERSONAL Born 11/29/1966, Santa Fe, NM, m, 1994, 3 children DISCIPLINE PSYCHOLOGY EDUCATION Brigham Young Univ, BA, 92; Pepperdine Univ, MA, 95; Calif Sch Prof Psychol, MA, 97; PhD, 99. CAREER Adj Prof, Citrus Col, 98-; Psychologist, Young Children's Day Treatment, Pacific Clinics, 99-. MEMBERSHIPS Am Psychol Asn; Los Angeles Cty Psychol Asn. RESEARCH Development of Identity and Self-esteem in children of alcoholics/drug addicted parents. CONTACT ADDRESS Dept Beh Sci, Citrus Col, 1000 W Foothill Blvd, Glendora, CA 91741.

TOMASKOVIC-DEVEY, BARBARA A.
DISCIPLINE SOCIOLOGY EDUCATION Manhattanville Col, BA, 79; Boston Univ, PhD, 88. CAREER Adj Lecturer, NCSU, 84; Exec Officer, SWS, 91-93. MEMBERSHIPS Am Sociol Asn; S Sociol Soc; Sociol for Women in Soc. RESEARCH Gender; Family; Sociology of Childhood; Inequality. CONTACT ADDRESS Dept Sociol & Anthropol, No Carolina State Univ, Box 8107, Raleigh, NC 27695-0001.

TOMS-ROBINSON, DOLORES C.
PERSONAL Born 12/26/1926, Washington, DC, m DISCIPLINE EDUCATION EDUCATION Howard Univ, BS cum laude 1947, MS 1948; Univ of MI, PhD 1957; Univ of IL Inst for Study of Mental Retardation, post doctoral study 1956-57. CAREER Univ of UT, rsch child psychology, 57-58; Jarvis Christian Coll, dir of psychol testing 1960-62; Jackson State Coll, dir fresh studies 1962-64; TX So Univ, prof of psychology 1964-70; Central MI Univ, chmn 1974-76, prof 1970-. MEM-

BERSHIPS Mem Council for Exceptional Children; NEA; Phi Delta Kappa. CONTACT ADDRESS Professor, Counseling & Special Education, Central Michigan Univ, Rowe Hall 208, Mount Pleasant, MI 48859.

TOROSYAN, ROBEN
PERSONAL Born 01/10/1968, Istanbul, Turkey, s DISCIPLINE PSYCHOLOGY EDUCATION New York Univ, BA, 91; MA, 96; Columbia Univ, M Phil, 98; PhD, 00. CAREER Asst dir, adj lectr, Pace Univ, 96-. HONORS AND AWARDS Hellenic Times Schlp; Nat Deans Lst; UMA Schlp; Cons Armen Rel Soc Schlp; Gallatins Dean Schlp; Garabed Zambak Mem Fund; Armen Miss Asn Am Schlp; APS Schlp; Dean Fac Res Gnt; Dolores Zohrab Liebmann Doc Fel; MENSA Schlp; McGill Univ Fac Awd; Gulbenkian Awd. MEMBERSHIPS SCTPLE; Kappa Delta Pi; PODNHE; SRAD; PES; IGS; AAUP; CCCUN; APC. SELECTED PUBLICATIONS Auth, "Undecidability in quantum physics, chaos theory and deconstruction: Implications for politics, ethics and society," in Developing sanity in human affairs, eds. S Kodish, R Holston (Westport, CT: Greenwood Pub, 98); auth, "How can I use technologies without getting overwhelmed?" in Connections, eds. D Robinson, M Zeigler (Needham Heights, MA: Simon & Schuster Cust Pub, 98); auth, "Applying learning to life: A theoretical framework in context," ETC 56 (99): 1-22; rev of, A Brief History of Everything, by K Wilber, New Ideas In Psych 18 (00); rev of, Chaos Theory in Psychology, eds. F D Abraham, A R Gilgen, New Ideas In Psych (00); auth, "Want a Friendly Cultural Briefing on Things Armenian?" Armen Report Intl (98). CONTACT ADDRESS Straus Thinking and Learning Center, Pace Univ, New York, 41 Park Row, New York, NY 10038-1598. EMAIL torosyan@pace.edu

TORRECILLA, JESUS
DISCIPLINE CULTURAL IDENTITY AND COLLECTIVE IMITATION, MARGINALITY, TIME AND POWER EDUCATION Univ Southern Calif, LA, PhD, 91. CAREER Asst prof Span, grad adv, La State Univ. RESEARCH Spanish peninsular literature-18th to 20th centuries. SELECTED PUBLICATIONS Auth, La imitaci?n colectiva: modernidad vs. autenticidad en la literatura espa?ola, Gredos, 96; coed, Raz?n, tradici?n y modernidad: Revision de la Ilustraci?n hisp?nica, Tecnos, 96. CONTACT ADDRESS Dept of Spanish and Portuguese, Univ of California, Los Angeles, 405 Highland Ave, PO Box 951361, Los Angeles, CA 90095-1361. EMAIL torrecil@humnet.ucla.edu

TORRES, LOUIS
PERSONAL Born 01/22/1938, Orange, NJ, m, 1987 DISCIPLINE PSYCHOLOGY, ENGLISH EDUCATION Rutgers Univ, BA, 60; Teachers Coll, Columbia Univ, 71. CAREER Teacher, Franklin School, NY City, 67-69; teacher, Indian Hills High School, NJ, 69-80; managing dir, William Carter Dance Ensemble, NY City, 80-82; teacher, Am Renaissance School, NY, 81-84; founder, ed, publ, Aristos, 82-91; co-ed, Publ, Aristos, 92-. MEMBERSHIPS Am Philos Asn; Am Soc for Aesthetics; Asn of Literary Scholars and Critics; Asn for Art Hist. RESEARCH Philosophy of Art. SELECTED PUBLICATIONS Auth, The New Dawn of Painting, ARISTOS, 86; The Child as Poet: An Insidious and Injurious Myth, Aristos, 88; Jack Schaefer, Teller of Tales, Aristos, 96; Jack Schaefer, Encycl of Frontier and Western Fiction, forthcoming; coauth, Ayn Rand's Philosophy of Art: A Critical Introduction, Aristos, 91-92; What Art Is: The Esthetic Theory of Ayn Rand, Open Court, 00. CONTACT ADDRESS Aristos, Radio City Station, PO Box 1105, New York, NY 10101.

TOSCANO, PETER
PERSONAL Born 04/27/1950, Worcester, MA, m, 1973, 2 children DISCIPLINE PSYCHOLOGY EDUCATION Clark Univ, BA, 72; SUNY Stony Brook, PhD, 76. CAREER Asst prof, Univ Mass, 84-; assoc prof, Assumption Col, 98-. HONORS AND AWARDS Phi Betta Kappa. MEMBERSHIPS Am Psychol Assoc; Mass Psychol Assoc; Assoc for the Advan of Behav Theory; Nat Register of Health Care Providers in Psychol. RESEARCH Child Maltreatment, Adoption, Child and Adolescent Psychopathology. SELECTED PUBLICATIONS Auth, "Child Maltreatment: Psychosocial Considerations", Diagnostic Imagery of Child Abuse, ed P. Kleinman, Mosby 98. CONTACT ADDRESS Dept Psychol, Assumption Col, PO Box 15005, Worcester, MA 01615. EMAIL ptoscano@assumption.edu

TOWNSEND, DAVID J.
PERSONAL Born 11/07/1946, Freeport, IL, m, 1968, 2 children DISCIPLINE PSYCHOLOGY EDUCATION Univ Mich, MA, 68; Wayne State Univ, MA, 71; PhD, 72. CAREER Asst Prof to Prof, Montclair State Col, 72-; Visiting Assoc Prof, Columbia Univ, 84-85; HONORS AND AWARDS Nat Sci Foundation, Principal Investigator, Montclair State Col, 79-81, 82-85; Who's Who in Sci and Engineering, 81; Distinguished Scholar Awd, Montclair State Col, 91-92. SELECTED PUBLICATIONS Co-auth, "A model of human response to workload stress," Bulletin of the Psychonomic Soc, (90): 547-550; co-auth, "The use of higher-level constraints in monitoring for a change in speaker demonstrates functionally-distinct levels of representation during discourse comprehension," Language and

Cognitive Processes, (91): 49-77; co-auth, "The emperor's psycholinguistics," Journal of Psycholinguistic Research, (98): 261-284; co-auth, "Lexical processing and familial handedness," Brain and Language, in press; co-auth, "Levels of representation during sentence comprehension interact with monitoring tasks," Journal of Psycholinguistic Research, in press. CONTACT ADDRESS Dept Psychol, Montclair State Univ, 1 Normal Ave, Montclair, NJ 07043. EMAIL townsend@mail.montclair.edu

TOWNSLEY, ELEANOR R.
PERSONAL Born 07/16/1967, Brisbane, Australia, m, 1995 DISCIPLINE SOCIOLOGY EDUCATION Univ Queensland, Australia, BA, 88; Univ Calif, Los Angeles, MA, 90; PhD, 96. CAREER Teaching Asst, Univ Calif, Los Angeles, 90-95; Lectr, Univ Calif, Los Angeles, 95; Vis Lectr, Rice Univ Houston, 95-96; Asst Prof, Mount Holyoke Col, 96-. MEMBERSHIPS ASA, TASA, ESS, SSSP, AAUP. RESEARCH Intellectuals, genders, states and elites, Eastern Europe, Methods. SELECTED PUBLICATIONS Auth, Making Capitalism Without Capitalists, Verso, 98; auth, "Husbands and Wives' Reporting Contributions," Gender and Society (98). CONTACT ADDRESS Dept Sociol and Anthrop, Mount Holyoke Col, 50 Col St, South Hadley, MA 01075.

TRAPP-DAIL, ROSA LEE
PERSONAL Born 12/19/1942, Bishopville, SC, m DISCIPLINE EDUCATION EDUCATION Madonna Coll, BA 1965; Univ of MI, EdS 1970; E MI, MA 1969; Univ of MI, PhD 1973. CAREER Univ of MI, teacher, training coord, lecturer 1970-71; Natl Inst Mental Health, dept of HEW fellow 1971-72; Dept of HEW, soc sci res analyst 1972-74; Howard Univ Center for Study of Handicapped Children & Youth, dir 1978-81; DC Parent Child Center, exec dir 1981-82; Howard Univ, assoc prof. HONORS AND AWARDS Participant DHEW Fellowship Prgm 1971-72; Awded $100,000 Title I Preschool Eval Contract DC Pub Sch 1975-76; elected Outstanding Young Women of AmerPrgm 1976; publ "Cognitive & Perceptual Devel in Low SES Minority Urban Children, Preschool Prgm Impact" Abstracts Soc for Res in Child Devel 1977; Awded approx $300,000 by USDOE Office of Sp Ed for Interdisciplinary Model for Parent and Child Training Project IMPACT 1978-81. MEMBERSHIPS Mem bd dir Dist Hghts Youth Club 1975; mem Soc for Res in Child Dev 1976-77; mem adv bd Early & Periodic Screening Diag & Treatment Prog Natl Child Day Care Assn 1976-77; consult Natl Educ in res proposal & prgm devel; sr collaborator Inst for Child Devel & Family Life; vice pres for Health Aff Howard Univ; 3 year mem bd dir Day Care & Child Devel Coun of Amer; mem Soc for Res in Child Devel; Natl Assn for Educ of Young Children; Amer Ed Res Assn; Natl Coun for Black Child Devel. CONTACT ADDRESS Howard Univ, 2400 6th St NW, Washington, DC 20059-0002.

TRAVER, HOLLY A.
PERSONAL Born Amsterdam, NY, m, 1998 DISCIPLINE PSYCHOLOGY EDUCATION State Univ NY at Albany, PhD, 99. CAREER Res Assoc/Adj Prof, Rensselaer Polytech Inst, 98-. HONORS AND AWARDS Res Awd. Am Soc for Training and Develop, 97; Who's Who Among America's Teachers. MEMBERSHIPS Am Psychol Asn, Am Psychol Soc, Soc for Indust and Orgn Psychology. RESEARCH Technology in the Classroom, Sexual Harassment, Affirmative Action. SELECTED PUBLICATIONS Coauth, "A Meta-analysis of the relations among training criteria," Personnel Psychology 50 (97): 341-358, and Air Force Materiel Command, Air Force Res Lab, Human Effectiveness Directorate (98). CONTACT ADDRESS Dept Philos, Psychology and Cognitive Sci, Rensselaer Polytech Inst, 110 8th St, Troy, MY 12180. EMAIL traveh@rpi.edu

TRAVIS, FRED
PERSONAL Born 07/05/1950, Binghamton, NY, m, 1976, 3 children DISCIPLINE PSYCHOLOGY EDUCATION Cornell Univ, BS, 76; Maharishi Univ Mgmt, MS, 86; PhD, 88. CAREER Director, Maharishi Univ of Mgmt, 90-; assoc dean, 95- assoc prof, 97-; chair, 98-. HONORS AND AWARDS Who's Who in Am Sch and Col, 85. MEMBERSHIPS Soc for Psychophysiological Res; Soc for Neuroscience; Am Psychol Assoc. SELECTED PUBLICATIONS Coauth, "Electrophysiological correlates of higher states of consciousness during sleep in long-term practitioners of the Transcendental Meditation program", Sleep 20, (97): 102-110; coauth, "Maharishi Vedic Psychology Brings Fulfillment to the Aspirations of Twentieth-Century Psychology", Mod Sci and Vedic Sci 7, (97): 241-268; coauth, "Autonomic Patterns during Respiratory Suspensions: Possible Markers of Transcendental Consciousness", Psychophysiology 34, (97): 39-46; auth, "CNV rebound and distraction effects before and after a TM session", Psychophysiology 34 (98): S89; auth, "Cortical and Cognitive Development in 4th, 8th and 12th Grade Students: The Contribution of Speed of Processing and Executive Functioning to Cognitive Development", Biological Psychol 48, (98): 37-56; coauth, "Effects of distracting stimuli on CNV amplitude and reaction time", Int J of Psychophysiology 31, (98): 45-50; coauth, "EEG and Autonomic Patterns during Eyes-Closed Rest and Transcendental Meditation Practice: The Basis for a Neural Model

of TM Practice", Consciousness and Cognition 8 (99): 302-318; coauth, "Distinct Phenomenological and Physiological Correlates of Consciousness Itself", Int J of Neuroscience 100 (00): 77-89; auth, "Transcendental Meditation technique", Encyclop of Psychol and Neuroscience, (forthcoming). **CONTACT ADDRESS** Dept Psychol, Maharishi Univ of Mgt, 1000 N 4th St, Fairfield, IA 52557-0001. **EMAIL** ftravis@mum.edu

TREADWELL, THOMAS
PERSONAL Born 10/16/1937, Norwalk, CT, d, 3 children **DISCIPLINE** PSYCHOLOGY **EDUCATION** Univ Charleston, BA, 62; Univ Bridgeport, MA, 64; Temple Univ, EdD, 81. **CAREER** Instr, York Col, 64-67; asst dean, Pa State Univ, 67-68; asst prof, West Chester State Univ, 69-71; asst prof, Antioch Grad Sch, 71-72; ch psychol, Comm Life Ser, 72-75; assoc prof, West Chester State Univ, 76-90; prof, 91-; clin assoc, Univ Pa, 97-. **HONORS AND AWARDS** David A Kipper, Schl Awd; ETA Sigma Gamma. **MEMBERSHIPS** APA; EPA; AHP; ASGPSP; PPA; DVSGP; DVSGPPS. **SELECTED PUBLICATIONS** Coauth, A Manuel for Sociometry and Use of Graph Plot, West Chester Univ (PA), 95; rev, Evaluating Human Resource Development, ed. Udai Pareek, Personal Psychology, forthcoming; auth, "Group Psychotherapy and the Internet: A Discussion List for Group Psychotherapists," Psychodrama Network News (98); auth, "New Technologies," Psychodrama Network News (98); auth, "Sociometry Publications," Psychodrama Network News (96); coauth, "Spontaneity Scale: Reliability and Validity," J Group Psycho Psychodrama Sociometry 48 (97); coauth, "Collaborative Teaching Over the Internet," J Manage Edu (98); coauth, "Perceived Cohesiveness and Sociometric Choice in Ongoing Groups," Intl J Action Methods, Psychodrama, Skill Training, Role Playing 50 (98): 122-137. **CONTACT ADDRESS** Dept Psychology, West Chester Univ of Pennsylvania, 700 S High St, West Chester, PA 19383-0001. **EMAIL** ttreadwe@albie.wcupa.edu

TREHUB, ARNOLD
PERSONAL Born 10/19/1923, Malden, MA, m, 1950, 3 children **DISCIPLINE** PSYCHOLOGY **EDUCATION** Boston Univ, PhD, 54. **CAREER** Res pyschol, dir of res, VA Medical Center, Northampton, Ma, 54-82; ADJUNCT PROF OF PSYCHOL, UNIV OF MASS AT AMHERST, 71-. **MEMBERSHIPS** Soc for Neuroscience; NY Acad of Sci; AAAS. **RESEARCH** Brain mechanisms of cognition. **SELECTED PUBLICATIONS** Auth, "Neuronal Models for Cognitive Processes: Networks for learning, perception and imagination," Journal of Theoretical biology 65, (77), 141-169; auth, "Neutonal model for stereoscopic vision," Journal of Theoretical Biology 71, (78), 479-486; auth, "Associative sequential redall in a sypnaptic matrix," Journal of Theoretical Biology, 79; auth,"Neuronal model for episodic learning and temporal routing of memory," Cognition and Brain Theory 6, (83), 483-497; auth, The Cognitive Brain, MIT Press, 91; auth, " Sparse Coding of Faces in a Neuronal Model: Interpreting Cell Population Response in Object Recognition," Neural--Network Models of Cognition, Elsevier Science, (97). **CONTACT ADDRESS** Dept of Psychology, Univ of Massachusetts, Amherst, Amherst, MA 01003. **EMAIL** trehub@psych.umass.edu

TREVISAN, CAREY
PERSONAL Born 05/29/1948, Newark, NJ, d, 2 children **DISCIPLINE** PSYCHOLOGY **EDUCATION** Wilmington Col, BA, 70; Seton Hall Univ, MEd, 73; Rutgers Univ, ABD, 82. **CAREER** Asst dir admissions/records, Ocean County Col, 73-78, assoc dir, 78-82, dir, 82-. **HONORS AND AWARDS** Outstanding Sr Student, NC, 70; Who's Who Among Students in Am Univs and Cols, 70; Who's Who Among Greek Fraternities and Sororities, 69; Who's Who in Am Education, 94-95; certified in rational-emotive therapy from Albant Ellis Inst. **MEMBERSHIPS** OCPLA, MSACANOA, NJACAC, many others. **RESEARCH** Psychotherapy. **CONTACT ADDRESS** Dept Soc Sci, Ocean County Col, PO Box 2001, Toms River, NJ 08754. **EMAIL** ctrevisan@ocean.cc.nj.us

TREVIZO, DOLORES
PERSONAL Born 01/05/1965, Hanford, CA, m, 1991, 2 children **DISCIPLINE** SOCIOLOGY **EDUCATION** UCLA, PhD, 98. **CAREER** Asst Prof, Occidental Col, 98-. **RESEARCH** Social Movements; Race/ethnics **CONTACT ADDRESS** Dept Sociol, Occidental Col, 1600 Campus Rd, Los Angeles, CA 90041. **EMAIL** dtrevizo@oxy.edu

TRICARICO, DONALD
PERSONAL Born New York, NY, m, 2 children **DISCIPLINE** SOCIOLOGY **EDUCATION** Forham Univ, BS, 70; New Sch for Soc Res, MA, 72; PhD, 80. **CAREER** Bronx Community Col, 73-75; Jersey City State Col, 75-77; prof, Queensborough/CUNY, 77-. **HONORS AND AWARDS** Visceglia Awd (AIHA), 1986. **MEMBERSHIPS** Am Sociol Asn, Am Ital Hist Asn, Am Asn Univ Profs. **RESEARCH** Ethnicity, youth culture, urban community, Italian American culture. **SELECTED PUBLICATIONS** Auth, The Italians of Greenwich Village: The Social Structure and Transformation of an Ethnic Community, Center for Migration Studies (84); auth, "The Greenwich Village Italian Neighborhood: The Emergence and Eclipse of an Ethnic Communal Form" in Italian Americans: New Perspective in Italian Immigration and Ethnicity, ed L. Thomasi (Center for Migration Studies, 85); auth, "In a New Light: Italian-American Ethnicity in the Mainstream," in The Ethnic Enigma, ed P. Kivisto (Balch Inst Press, 89); rev of "Militants and Migrants " by D. Gabaccia in J of Ethnic Hist (winter 90); rev of "Monte Carmelo: An Italian-American Community in the Bronx," by A. LaRuffa, J of Ethnic Studies (fall 91); auth, "Guido: Fashioning an Italian American Youth Style," J of Ethnic Studies (spring 91); auth, " Contemporary Italian-American Ethnicity: Into the Mainstream," in Italian Americans: The Search for a Usable past, eds P. Canistraro and R. Juliani (Center for Migration Studies, 88; also in Resource Reader for the Italian American Heritage Curriculum, NY State Education Dept, 93); auth, "Personals Ethnicity: Finding Italian Americans in Newspaper Dating Advertisements," Forum Italicum (summer 94); auth, "Italian Americans," in The Encyclopedia of New York City's Ethnic Groups, ed by K. T. Jackson (Yale Univ Press, 95); auth, "Labels and Stereotypes," in Encyclopedia of Italian Americans, ed by La Gumina, et al (Garland Press, 2000). **CONTACT ADDRESS** Dept Social Sciences, Queensborough Comm Col, CUNY, 22205 56th Ave, Bayside, NY 11364.

TRIGILIO, JO
DISCIPLINE PHILOSOPHY; WOMEN'S STUDIES **EDUCATION** Marietta Col, BA, 83; Univ Oregon, MA, 93, PhD, 96. **CAREER** Vis instr, 97-98, Calif St Univ, Chico; asst prof, 98-, Bentley Col. **HONORS AND AWARDS** Phi Beta Kappa **MEMBERSHIPS** Soc for Women in Phil; Soc for Advan of Am Phil; Nat Women' s Studies Asn. **RESEARCH** Feminist theory; feminist epistemology; Amer phil. **CONTACT ADDRESS** 15 Bay State Ave., #1, Somerville, MA 02144-2114. **EMAIL** jtrigilio@bentley.edu

TRIPODI, TONY
PERSONAL Born 11/30/1932, Sacramento, CA, m, 1998, 2 children **DISCIPLINE** SOCIAL WORK **EDUCATION** Sacramento City Col; Univ Calif, Berkeley, AB, 54, MSW, 58; Columbia Univ, DSW, 63. **CAREER** Asst prof, Columbia Univ, 63-65; asst prof, Univ Calif, Berkeley, 65-66; assoc prof to prof, dean, Univ MI, 66-87; assoc dean and prof, Univ Pittsburgh, 87-95; assoc dir, coordr of PhD prog, prof, Fla Int Univ, 92-95; dean and prof, Col of Social Work, Ohio State Univ, 95-. **HONORS AND AWARDS** Phi Theta Kappa; Phi Theta Kappa Scholarship for Highest Grade Point Average at Sacramento City Col; Phi Kappa Phi; Calif Scholar Fedn; Three scholars, Univ Calif , Berkeley, 51-54; two fels, Columbia Univ, 60-62; Fulbright-Hays Awd, Italy; res grants, Nat Inst Mental Health, Nat Sci Found; Int Who's Who of Professionals; Dictionary of Int Biog. **MEMBERSHIPS** Soc Soc Work and Res, Nat Inst of Soc Workers, Coun on Soc Work Ed. **RESEARCH** Program evaluation, social research methodology. **SELECTED PUBLICATIONS** Coauth with B. Blythe and S. Brian, Direct Practice Research in Human Service Agencies, Columbia Univ Press (94); auth, A Primer on Single-Subject Design for Clinical Social Workers, Nat Asn of Soc Workers (94); coauth with A. Ivanoff and B. Blythe, Social Work Practice with Involuntary Clients, Aldine (94); coed with M. Potocky-Tripodi, New Directions in Social Work Practice Research, Nat Asn of Soc Workers (99); coed. J of Soc Work Res and Eval: An Int Pub, Springer Pub Co, first issue, Vol 1 No 1 (spring 2000); auth, "The Contemporary Challenge in Evaluating Social Services-An International Perspective: The 1999 Peter Hedge Memorial Lecture, Hong Kong," J of Soc Work Res and Eval: An Int Pub, vol 1, no 1 (2000). **CONTACT ADDRESS** Col Soc Work, Ohio State Univ, Columbus, 1947 Col Rd, Columbus, OH 43210. **EMAIL** tripodi.5@osu.edu

TRIPP, LUKE S.
PERSONAL Born 02/06/1941, Atoka, TN, m, 1989, 3 children **DISCIPLINE** COMMUNITY STUDIES **EDUCATION** Wayne State Univ, BS, 66; Univ Mich, MA, 74; PhD, 80. **CAREER** Sem leader, Wayne State Univ, 68; teacher, Santa Maria Educ Center, 69-70; Instr, Wayne County Col, 71-72; Dir, Univ of Mich, 77-80; vis asst prof, Univ of IL, 81-82; asst prof, Southern Il Univ, 82-89; prof, St. Cloud State Univ, 89-. **HONORS AND AWARDS** Who's Who Among Black Americans, 87; Int. Dir of Distinguished Leadership, 88; Marcus Garvey Peace and Liberation Awd, 88; Mary B. Craik Awd for Equality and Justice Awd, 90; Distinguished Teacher Awd, St. Cloud State Univ, 90; Outstanding Fac Awd, St Cloud State Univ, 91; Outstanding Work as Human Rights Activist Awd, St. Cloud State Univ, 92; Awd for Outstanding Work in Human Rights, 93; Professor of the Year, St Cloud State Univ, 93; 96; Awd, Student Coalition Against Racism, 93; Awd for Contributions and Service to the Students of Color and Department of Minority Student Prog, St Cloud Statre Univ, 95. **MEMBERSHIPS** Am Assoc of Behav and Soc Sci; IL Counc for Black Studies; Nat Counc for Black Studies; Soc of Ethnic and special Studies. **RESEARCH** Black radicalism and student activism, and the various influences of Afro-American culture on American culture. **SELECTED PUBLICATIONS** Auth, "Black Students, Ideology, and Class", Afro-Scholar Working Paper Series 9 , Univ of IL, (83): 1-55; auth, "Community Leadership and Black Former Student Activists of the 1960s", Western J of Black Studies 10.2 (86): 86-89; auth, Black Student Activists: Transition to Middle Class Professionals, Univ Pr of Am, (Lanham, MD), 87; auth, "Race Consciousness Among African-American Students, 1980s", Western J of Black Studies 15.3 (91): 159-168; auth, "The Political Views of Black Students During the Reagan Era", Black Scholar 22.3 (92): 45-52; auth, "The Intellectual Roots of the Controversy around Cultural Diversity and Political Correctness", Western J of Black Studies 18.4 (94): 227-230; auth, "Blacks in America: American Mythology and Miseducation", Oppression and Social Justice: Critical Frameworks, ed J. Andrezjewski, Simon & Schulster, (Needham Heights, MA, 96): 316-321; auth, "Celebrating Diversity Through Community Events, Minnesota Cities 82.11, (Nov 97): auth, "Emphasizing Critical thinking In Studying Race, Class, And Gender", Excellence in Teaching, St Cloud State Univ, Vol 4, (Sept 98). **CONTACT ADDRESS** Dept Community Studies, St. Cloud State Univ, 720 4th Ave S, Saint Cloud, MN 56301-4442. **EMAIL** ltripp@stcloudstate.edu

TRIPP, MICHAEL
PERSONAL Born 01/30/1950, Ypsilanti, MI, s **DISCIPLINE** PSYCHOLOGY **EDUCATION** Mich State Univ, BA, 70; Univ Calif, MSW, 72; PhD, 81 **CAREER** Asst Prof, Tuskegee Inst, 76-80; Res Specialist, Allied Health Services Training and Res Assoc, 78-85; Counselor, Detroit Job Corps, 82-84; Res Coordinator, Sickle Cell Detection and Information Center, 84-89; Dir, Children's Aid Society, 87-88; Adj Asst Prof, Madonna Univ, 91-92; VP Res and Development, 89-; Assoc Prof, St Cloud State Univ, 92-. **HONORS AND AWARDS** Teacher of the Year, Kappa Delta Pi Nat Honor Soc, 99, Fac Ctr for Teaching Excellence Advisory Committee, 95-96; Fac Ctr for Teaching Excellence Director Search Committee; Alpha Delta Mu. **MEMBERSHIPS** MCAN, African Am in Minn Higher Educ Coun, Nat Asn of Soc Workers. **RESEARCH** Juvenile delinquency; Race relations and The pedagogy of Socratle methods to promote critical thinking about human relation problems and ethical issues. **SELECTED PUBLICATIONS** Auth, "Educational Issues Concerning African-American People," in Developing a Teaching Style, Methods for Elementary School, Harper Collins, 00. **CONTACT ADDRESS** Dept Hum Rel, St. Cloud State Univ, 720 4th Ave S, Saint Cloud, MN 56301. **EMAIL** tripp@stcloudstate.edu

TRIX, FRANCES
PERSONAL Born 08/17/1948, Bellefonte, PA, m, 1977, 1 child **DISCIPLINE** ANTHROPOLOGY **EDUCATION** Univ Mich, BA Near Eastern Languages & Literature, 70, Middlebury Col, 66-68; Univ Mich, MA Near Eastern Languages & Literature, 72; Univ Mich, MA Linguistics, 76; Univ Mich, PhD Linguistics, 88. **CAREER** Vis Asst, Prof of Linguistics, Univ of Michigan, 88-89; Vis Asst, Research Scientist, Center for Middle Eastern and North African Studies, 89-90; Asst Prof of Anthropology, Wayne State Univ, Univ of Michigan, 90-96; Assoc Prof of Anthropology, Wayne State Univ, 97-. **HONORS AND AWARDS** Woodrow Wilson Fellow, 70; IREX Fellow, Univ of Prishtina, Yugoslavia, 87-88; Distinguished Fac Honors Convocation Awd, Mich. Asn of Governing Bds of State Univ 95. **MEMBERSHIPS** Amer Anthropological Assoc; Middle East Studies Assoc; International Pragmatics Assoc. **RESEARCH** Discourse Analysis; Islam; Albanians. **SELECTED PUBLICATIONS** Auth, "Spiritual Discourse: Learning with an Islamic Master," Philadelphia: Univ of Penn Press, 93; auth, "The Stamboul Alphabet of Shemsetting Sami Bey: Precursor to Turkish Script Reform," International Journal of Middle Eastern Studies, 31:2, 99, 255-272; auth, "Women's Voices & Experiences of the Hill/Thomas Hearings," American Anthropologist, 100:1, 98, 32-40; auth, "Blessing Cars: A Classic Sufi Play on Ritual in Immigrant America," Journal of Ritual Studies, 10:2, 97, 109-130; auth, "The Resurfacing of Islam in Albania," The East European Quarterly, XXVIII:4, 95, 533-49. **CONTACT ADDRESS** Dept Anthropology, Wayne State Univ, 137 Manoogian, Detroit, MI 48202. **EMAIL** ftrix@umich.edu

TROPE, YAACOV
PERSONAL Born 06/18/1945, m, 1965, 3 children **DISCIPLINE** PSYCHOLOGY **EDUCATION** Tel Aviv Univ, BA, 70; Univ Mich, Ann Arbor, MA, 72, PhD, 74. **CAREER** Lect, Hebrew Univ of Jerusalem, 74-79, sr lect, 79-84, assoc to prof, 84-89; vis assoc prof, Univ Toronto, 79-80; vis assoc prof, Univ Mich, 80; vis assoc prof, NYork Univ, spring 83; vis prof, Princeton Univ, 83; prof, NYork Univ, 90-; assoc ed, J of Experimental Soc Psychol, 94-98; ed bd, J of Personality and Soc Psychol and J of Experimental Soc Psychol. **HONORS AND AWARDS** Soc of Experimental Soc Psychol Diss Awd, 75; Fulbright Awd, 80; numerous other grants andawards. **MEMBERSHIPS** APA, SESP, Israeli Psychol Asn, Israeli Soc for Experimental Soc Psychol. **RESEARCH** Motivation and cognition. **SELECTED PUBLICATIONS** Coauth with E. T. Higgins,"Dispositional inference from behavior," NY: Sage Pubs (93); coauth with T. Alfieri, "Effortfulness and flexibility of dispositional inference processes," J of Personality and Soc Psychol, 73, 662-674 (97); coauth with E. Pomerantz, "Resolving conflicts among self-evaluative motives: The role of positive experiences in overcoming defensiveness," Motivation & Emotion, 22, 53-72 (98); coauth with N. Liberman, "The role of feasibility and desirability considerations in near and distant future decisions," J of Personality and Soc Psychol, 75, 5-19 (98); auth, "Dispositional bias in person perception: A hypothesis-testing perspective," in J. Cooper & J. M. Darley, eds, Attribution processes, person perception, and social interaction: The legacy of Ned Jones, Am Psychol Asn Press (98); coauth with

E. T. Higgins and J. Kwon, "Augmenting and undermining interest from combining activities: The role of choice in activity engagement theory," J of Experimental Soc Psychol, 35, 285-307 (99); coauth with R. Gaunt, "A dual-process model of overconfidant attributions," in S. Chaiken & Y. Trope, eds, Dual process theories in social psychology, NY: Guilford Press (99); coauth with S. Chaiken, "Dual-process theories in social psychology," NY: Guilford Press (99); coauth with M. Ferguson, "Wishful thinking: When preferences influence inferences," in J. Bargh, ed, Uncovering the mysteries of social life, Washington, DC: APA press (2000); coauth with R. Hassin, "Facing the face," J of Personality and Soc Psychol (2000). **CONTACT ADDRESS** Dept Psychol, New York Univ, 6 Washington Pl, New York, NY 10003. **EMAIL** Trope@psych.nyu.edu

TROYER, LISA L.
PERSONAL Born 08/29/1961, Seattle, WA **DISCIPLINE** SOCIOLOGY **EDUCATION** Univ Washington, BA, 89; Stanford Univ, MA, 90; PhD, 95. **CAREER** Res Asst to Lecturer, Stanford Univ, 90-95; Asst Prof, Univ Iowa, 95-. **HONORS AND AWARDS** Dissertation Improvement Awd, Nat Sci Foundation, 93; Howard B Woolston Awd, Univ Washington, 89; Graduate Student Fel, Stanford Univ, 89-90, Dept Teaching Awd, Stanford Univ, 93; Best Interdisciplinary Paper, Western Decision Sci Inst, 94; Best Theoretical Paper, Western Decision Sci Inst, 94; Collegiate Teaching Awd, Univ Iowa, 99. **MEMBERSHIPS** Alpha Kappa Delta, Phi Beta Kappa, Am Sociol Asn, Decision Sci Inst, Intl Soc of Political Psychol. **RESEARCH** Group dynamics, Group Decision making, Social influence, Work design. **SELECTED PUBLICATIONS** Auth, "Who's the Boss? A Role-Theoretic Analysis of Customer Work," Work and Occupations, forthcoming; auth, "Effects of member Status on the Exchange of Information in an Interorganizational Decision-Making Team," in Advances in the Interdisciplinary Study of Work Teams, Vol 7, JAI Press, forthcoming; auth, "Institutional Logics and Group Environments: Toward an Open System Perspective on Group Processes," in Advances in Group Processes, Vol 16, JAI Press, 99; auth, "Social Structure and the duration of Social Acts," Social Psychology Quarterly, (99): 83-95; auth, "Judging the Consequences of Evaluation by Others in Status Heterogeneous Groups: Biases in the Microlevel Heuristics of Group Information Exchange," in Advances in Group Processes, Vol 15, JAI Press, 98; auth, "Whose Expectation Matter? The Relative Power of First-and Second- Order Expectations in Determining Social Influence," American Journal of Sociology, (97): 692-732; ed, Advances in Group Processes, Vol 14, JAI Press, 97; auth, "Parenting Styles, Adolescents' Attributions, and Educational Outcomes in Nine Heterogeneous High Schools," Child Development, (97): 507-529; auth, "Effects of Experimenter-Inserted Negative Evaluations on Idea Generation and Information Exchange in Computer-Mediated Groups," 1998 Proceedings, 98; auth, "Negative Evaluation and Innovativeness in Group Decision Making: Insights for GDSS Development from a Social Risk Framework," 1996 Proceedings. **CONTACT ADDRESS** Dept Sociol, The Univ of Iowa, 140 Seashore Hall W, Iowa City, IA 52242.

TRUSTY, JERRY
PERSONAL Born 12/18/1949, MS, m, 1977, 2 children **DISCIPLINE** COUNSELING **EDUCATION** Miss State Univ, PhD. **CAREER** Asst Prof, Univ Ala, 92-94; Asst Dean and Prof, Tex A & M, 94-. **HONORS AND AWARDS** Res Awd, Tex Coun Asn, 95. **MEMBERSHIPS** ACA, AERA, ASGW, ASCA, NCDA. **RESEARCH** Adolescents' educational and career development; Parental influences on adolescents. **SELECTED PUBLICATIONS** Auth, "Relationship of high-school seniors' religious perceptions and behavior to educational, career, and leisure variables," Counseling and Values, (99): 30-39; auth, "Effects of eighth-grade parental involvement on late adolescents' educational expectations," Journal of Research and Development in Education, (99): 224-233; auth, "Lost talent: predictors of the stability of educational expectations across adolescence," Journal of Adolescent Research, (99): 359-382; auth, "Teachers' perception and nomination of fifth-grade Hispanic and Anglo students," Journal of Research and Development in Education, (9): 113-123; auth, "Relationships among dogmatism, family ideology, and religiosity in master's level counseling students," Counseling and Values, (98): 70-77; auth, "Parents' transmission of educational goals to their adolescent children," Journal of Research and Development in Education, (98): 53-65; auth, "Family influences on educational expectations of late adolescents," Journal of Educational Research, (98): 260-270; auth, "Relationship of high-school seniors' perceptions of parental involvement and control to seniors' locus of control," Journal of Counseling and Development, (97): 375-384; auth, "Chaos and Christianity: a response to Butz and a Biblical alternative," Counseling and Values, (97): 88-96; auth, "Predictors of parents' involvement in their teens' career development," Journal of Career Development, (97): 189-201. **CONTACT ADDRESS** Dept Counseling, Texas A&M Univ, Commerce, PO Box 3011, Commerce, TX 75429. **EMAIL** Jerry_Trusty@tamu.commerce.edu

TUMMINIA, DIANA
DISCIPLINE SOCIOLOGY **EDUCATION** San Diego State Univ, BA, 84; MA, 87; Univ Calif at Los Angeles, PhD, 95. **CAREER** Sacramento State Univ, 95-. **MEMBERSHIPS** Am Sociol Asn, Pacific Sociol Asn, Calif Sociol Asn, Asn for Sociol of Relig. **RESEARCH** Social Construction of Reality, Religion, Theory, Gender, Race, Social Class. **SELECTED PUBLICATIONS** Coauth, "California Space Goddess: The Mystagogue in a Flying Saucer Group, in Twentieth-Century World Religious Movements in neo-Weberian Perspective, ed. William Swatos, Jr. (Edwin Mellen Press, 92); coauth, "Space Magic, Techno-Animism, and the Cult of the Goddess in A Southern Californian UFO Contactee Group: A Case Study of Millenarianism," Syzygy: J of Alternative Relig and Culture 1.2 (92): 159-172; auth, "Hard Work, Luck, and Uncontrollable Variables: A Guide to Getting into Graduate School," Sociol Practice Rev 3.1 (92): 37-41; coauth, "Unarius: Emergent Aspects of an American Flying Saucer Group," in The Gods Have Landed: New Religions from Other Worlds, ed. James R. Lewis (NY: State Univ NY Press, 95), 85-104; auth, "How Prophecy Never Fails: Interpretive Reason in a Flying-Saucer Group," Sociol of Relig 59.2 (98): 157-170; auth, "An Annotated Film Guide for Race, Gender, and Social Class," in Race, Gender, and Class in Sociology: Toward an Inclusive Classroom, ed. Ambert Belkhir (DC: Am Sociol Asn, 99); auth, "From Rumor to Postmodern Myth: A Sociological Study of the Transformation of Flying-Saucer Rumor," in Alien Gods: New Religions from Outer Space, ed. James R. Lewis (NY: Prometheus Books, 00); auth, "How Prophecy never Fails," in Alien Gods: New Religions from Outer Space, ed. James R. Lewis (NY: Prometheus Books, 00). **CONTACT ADDRESS** Dept Sociol, California State Univ, Sacramento, 6000 J St, Sacramento, CA 95819. **EMAIL** diana.tumminia@csus.edu

TURK, AUSTIN T.
PERSONAL Born 05/28/1934, Gainesville, GA, m, 1985, 2 children **DISCIPLINE** SOCIOLOGY **EDUCATION** Univ Georgia, BA, 56; Univ Kentucky, MA, 59; Univ Wisconsin, PhD, 62. **CAREER** Instr to Prof of Sociology, Indiana Univ, 62-74; Prof of Sociology, Univ of Toronto, 74-88; American Sociology Assoc, 75-76; Pres, North Central Sociological Assoc, 76-77; Trustee, Law and Society Assoc, 82-85; Chair, Section on Criminology, Prof of Sociology, Univ of CA, 89-94. **HONORS AND AWARDS** Phi Beta Kappa, Paul Tappan Awd, 89, President's Awd, 99, Western Society of Criminology, Fellow, 78, Am Society of Criminology. **MEMBERSHIPS** Academy of Criminal Justice Sciences, American Society of Criminology, American Sociological Assoc, Law and Crime and Justice, Sociolegal Society Assoc Studies, Social Conflict. **SELECTED PUBLICATIONS** Auth, Criminality and Legal Order, Rand McNally (Chicago), 69; auth, Political Criminality, The Defiance and Defense of Authority, Sage Publications (Beverly Hills), 82; auth, "Law, Power, and Social Change," ed. Craig Calhoun and George Ritzer, Sociology, McGraw-Hill 1 (93): 293-313; auth, "Transformation Versus Revolutionism and Reformism: Policy Implications of Conflicet Theory", ed. Hugh D. Barlow, 15-27, Crime and Public Policy: Putting Theory to Work, Westview Press (Boulder, CO), 95; auth, "Oklahoma City Bombing", ed. Ronald Gottesman, 490-492; Violence in American: An Encyclopedia, New York: Charles Scribner's Sons, 99. **CONTACT ADDRESS** Dept Sociology, Univ of California, Riverside, 900 Univ Ave, Riverside, CA 92521-0001. **EMAIL** austin.turk@ucr.edu

TURKEWITZ, GERALD
PERSONAL Born 02/25/1933, New York, NY, m, 1955, 4 children **DISCIPLINE** PSYCHOLOGY **EDUCATION** CUNY, BA, 55; MS, 57; NY Univ, PhD, 67. **CAREER** From Res Assoc to Asst Prof, Einstein Col of Med, 61-; From Assoc Prof to Prof, CUNY, 71-. **HONORS AND AWARDS** Sigma X. **MEMBERSHIPS** APS, ISIS, ISD, PSRCD. **RESEARCH** Intersensory functioning, development of hemispheric specialization, role of sensory limitations for the organization of brain and behavior. **SELECTED PUBLICATIONS** Coauth, "Asymmetric Headturning to Speech and Nonspeech in Human Newborns," Develop Psychobiol 29 (96): 205-218; coauth, "Prenatal Experience and Neonatal Responsiveness to Vocal Expressions of Emotion," Develop Psychobiol 35 (99): 204-214; coauth, "The Talking Face: Effects of Concurrent Speech on Hemispheric Lateralization of Face Recognition," Develop Neuropsychol 16 (99): 254-271; auth, "Cerebral Asymmetry of Emotions and its Relationship to Olfaction in Infancy," Laterality (forthcoming). **CONTACT ADDRESS** Dept Psychol, City Col, CUNY, 695 Park Ave, New York, NY 10021.

TURLEY, ALAN
PERSONAL Born 07/01/1967, Orange, CA, m, 1999 **DISCIPLINE** SOCIOLOGY **EDUCATION** Univ Tex, BA, 90; MA, 93; PhD, 97. **CAREER** Instructor, Austin Cmty Col, 95-98; Analyst, Tex Workforce Commission, 98-99; Asst Prof, SUNY Brockport, 99-. **HONORS AND AWARDS** Outstanding Achievement Awd, AISD Mentor prog; Differential Tuition Scholarship, 94, 95, 96; Mike Hogg Res Assistanceship, 96. **MEMBERSHIPS** SW Soc Sci Asn; Am Fed of Musicians. **RESEARCH** Music and Urban Issues; Urban Sociology; Race and Ethnic; Sociology of Culture and Sociology of Music **SELECTED PUBLICATIONS** Auth, "The Ecological and Social Determinants of the Production and Standardization of Jazz in New Orleans, c. 1900," Journal of the International Review of the Aesthetics and Sociology of Music, 95; auth, Expert Opinion for section concerning "Sunbelt Migration and the effect on Austin Music," Social Science Interactive Text with CD Rom, 96; rev, of "8-Ball Chicks," by Gini Sikes in Social Science Quarterly, 00; auth, Music and the City: A History of Austin's Music Scene, Silver Phoenix Pub, 00. **CONTACT ADDRESS** Dept Sociol, SUNY, Col at Brockport, 350 New Campus Dr, Brockport, NY 14420. **EMAIL** aturley@brockport.edu

TURNBAUGH, WILLIAM A.
PERSONAL Born 06/01/1948, Williamsport, PA, m, 1974 **DISCIPLINE** ANTHROPOLOGY **EDUCATION** Lycoming Col, BA, 70; Harvard Univ, PhD, 73. **CAREER** Curator of Archaeol, Lycoming Co Mus, PA, 68-70; teaching fel, Harvard Univ, 71-72, res asst, Peabody Mus, 73-74; asst to assoc prof, Univ RI, 74-83; dir, Univ RI Bicentennial Mus, 75-76; coord Anthropol, Univ RI, 80-83; rev ed, PA Archaeol, 81-94; assoc ed, Hist Archaeol, 86-; prof, Univ RI, 83-. **HONORS AND AWARDS** Phi Kappa Phi; Sigma Xi; Phi Alpha Theta; BA, summa cum laude, valedictorian, 70; Fel, Explorers Club; "Archey" Awd, Soc PA Archaeol, 67; Congressman Robert F. Rich Merit Scholar, 67-70; Woodrow Wilson Fel, 70-71; Nat Sci Foun Fel, 70-73; Teaching Excellence Nominee, Univ RI, 81; Distinguished Alumni Recognition, Lycoming Col, 87; J. Alden Mason Awd, Soc PA Archael, 88. **MEMBERSHIPS** Registry of Prof Archaeol, Soc Hist Archaeol, Soc Am Archaeol, Soc PA Archael. **RESEARCH** American archaeology and prehistory, ethnohistory, Native American craft arts. **SELECTED PUBLICATIONS** Auth, Man, Land, and Time: Cultural Prehistory and Demographic Patterns of North-Central Pennsylvania, Evansville, IN: Unigraphic Press (75, rev ed, 77); auth, The Material Culture of RI-1000, A Mid-17th Century Narragansett Indian Burial Site in North Kingstown, Rhode Island, Kingston, RI: Univ of RI (84); auth, R. F. D. Country! Mailboxes and Post Offices of Rural America, by Bill and Sarah Thornbrook (pennames), foreword by Postmaster General Preston Tisch, West Chester, PA: Schiffer Pub (88); coauth with S. Turnbaugh, The Nineteenth-Century Collector: A Rhode Island Perspective, Peace Dale, RI: Mus of Primitive Art and Culture, distributed by Univ PA Press (91); coauth with Sarah Peabody Turnbaugh, Indian Jewelry of the American Southwest, West Chester , PA: Schiffer Pub (88, rev ed, 95); coauth with Sarah Peabody Turnbaugh, Indian Baskets, Exton, PA: Schiffer Pub, in coollaboration with Peabody Mus, Harvard Univ (86, rev ed, 86); coauth with R. Jurmain, H. Nelson and L. Kilgore, Understanding Physical Anthropology and Archaeology, Belmont, CA: West/Wadsworth (81, 84, 87, 90, 93, 96, 99); coauth with S. Turnbaugh, Basket Tales of Grandmothers: American Indian Baskets in Myth and Legend, Peace Dale, RI: Thornbrook, distributed by Univ Wash Press 999). **CONTACT ADDRESS** Dept Sociol & Anthropol, Univ of Rhode Island, 10 Chafee Rd, Kingston, RI 02881. **EMAIL** wtu4496u@postoffice.uir.edu

TURNBULL, BARBARA
PERSONAL Born 03/22/1962, Ont, Canada, s **DISCIPLINE** EDUCATIONAL PSYCHOLOGY **EDUCATION** Univ British Columbia, PhD, 97. **CAREER** Asst prof, Ed Statistics and Measurement, Rutgers Univ. **HONORS AND AWARDS** Dir, Ctr for Prog Evaluation, Rutgers, The State Univ of NJ. **MEMBERSHIPS** Am Ed Res Asn, Am Evaluation Asn, Can Evaluation Soc. **RESEARCH** Participatory prog evaluation, teacher participation in school decision making. **SELECTED PUBLICATIONS** Auth, "Cognitive style and ability in art related tasks," Ed Insights, 1, 1 (92): 60-66; coauth with C. Meszaros, "Reliability and validity of the school tour effectiveness measure: A measure of teacher perceptions of the effectiveness of a school tours program," Visual Arts Res, 23, 1 (97): 151-157; auth, "Factors Affecting Consumer Confidence," Insurance Corporation of British Columbia, Dept of Res Services (May 98); auth, "An Evaluation of the Student Worksafe Program," Workers' Compensation Bd of British Columbia, Division of Res and Evaluation (June 98); auth, "Effects of Community Service for Adjudicated Youth," New Jersey Dept of Ed Division of Student Services, Office of Educational Support Services and Interagency Initiatives (Jan 99); auth, "Model of Collaboration: Reader's Digest and Tall Tree Library Initiative," Reader's Digest (June 99); auth, B. Erlichson and M. Goertz, "Implementing Whole School Reform in New Jersey: Year one in the first cohort," Dept of Public Policy and Center for Govt Services Edward J. Bloustein School of Planning and Public Policy, Rutgers, the State Univ of New Jersey (Aug 99); coauth with G. Camilli, "End-of-Course Evaluation Questionnaire," Nat Transit Inst, Rutgers, The State Univ of New Jersey (Aug 99); auth, "The mediating effect of participation efficacy on evaluation use," Evaluation and Program Planning, 22, 2 (99): 131-140. **CONTACT ADDRESS** Grad Sch of Ed, Rutgers, The State Univ of New Jersey, New Brunswick, 10 Sem Pl, New Brunswick, NJ 08901-1183. **EMAIL** turnbull@rci.rutgers.edu

TURNER, EDITH
PERSONAL Born 06/17/1921, Ely, United Kingdom, w, 1943, 5 children **DISCIPLINE** ANTHROPOLOGY **EDUCATION** Univ Va, MA, 80; Col Wooster, Honorary Doctor Humanities, 00. **CAREER** Dir of Comparative Symbology Inc., 71-; co-ed, Primavera Women's Lit Mag, 74-76; lectr, Univ Va, 84-; head consultation team, Circle of Life book and exhibition, 91. **HONORS AND AWARDS** Res Grant, Wenner-Gren Found, 85 & 88. **MEMBERSHIPS** Alaska Anthrop Asn, African Studies Asn, Am Ethnol Soc, Soc of Humanistic Anthrop, Soc of Anthrop of Consciousness, Anthrop of Relig Sect. **SELECTED PUBLICATIONS** Auth, Image and Pilgrimage in Christian Culture: Anthropological Perspectives, 78; auth, The Spirit

and the Drum, 87; auth, Experiencing Ritual: A New Interpretation of African Healing, 92; auth, The Hands Feel It: Healing and Spirit Presence Among the Inupiat of Northern Alaska, 96. **CONTACT ADDRESS** Dept Anthrop, Univ of Virginia, 1 Brook Hall, Charlottesville, VA 22901.

TURNER, JONATHAN H.
PERSONAL Born 09/07/1942, Oakland, CA, m, 1971, 3 children **DISCIPLINE** SOCIOLOGY **EDUCATION** Univ Cal, BS, 65; Cornell Univ, MA, 66; PhD, 68. **CAREER** Dist prof, Univ Cal, Riverside, 32 years. **HONORS AND AWARDS** ACRL Choice Awd; AAAS Fel. **MEMBERSHIPS** ASA. **RESEARCH** Theoretical sociology; stratification; emotions; evolution; social institutions. **SELECTED PUBLICATIONS** Auth, Sociology: Concepts and Uses, McGraw Hill (NY), 93; coauth, American Ethnicity: A Sociological Analysis of the Dynamics of Discrimination, McGraw Hill (NY), 98; auth, Macrodynamics: Toward a Theory on the Organization of Human Populations, Rutgers Univ Press (New Brunswick), 95; auth, The Institutional Order: Economy, Polity, Law, Kinship, Religion, and Education in Evolutionary and Comparative Perspective, Longman (London and NY), 97; auth, On the Origins of Human Emotions: A Sociological Inquiry into the Evolution of Human Affect, Stanford Univ Press, 00; auth, "The Neurology of Emotions: Implications for Sociological Theories of Interpersonal Behavior," in Mind, Brain and Society: Toward a Neurosociology of Emotions, eds D Franks, TS Smith (Stamfort, CN: Jai Press, 99); coauth, "Herbert Spencer," in International Encyclopedia of Sociological Thought, eds, NJ Smelser, PB Bates (NY: Pergamon, in press); auth, "Must Sociological Theory and Practice Be So Far Apart," Sociological 41 (98): 244-58; auth, "Some Elementary Principles of Geo-politics and Geo-economics," EuropAmerica: J Euro Am Stud 28 (98): 41-71; auth, "Toward a General Sociological Theory of Emotions," J Theory Soc Behav 29 (99): 133-162; auth, "Auguste Comte and Herbert Spencer on Positivism," in Handbook of Sociological Theory, eds. G Ritzer, B Smart (London: Sage, 00); auth, "The Formation of Social Capital," in Social Capital: A Multifaceted Perspective, eds. P Dasgupta, I Serageldin (Washington, DC: World Bank Press, 00); auth, "A Sociological Theory of the Economy," in The Socio-economics of Long-term Evolution: Advances in Theory Complex Modeling, and Methodology, eds. K S Althaler, M Lehmann-Waffesnschmid, K H Mueller (NY: Fakultas Verlag Press, in press). **CONTACT ADDRESS** Dept Sociology, Univ of California, Riverside, 900 University Ave, Riverside, CA 92521-0001. **EMAIL** jonathan.turner@ucr.edu

TURNER, STEPHEN
PERSONAL Born 03/01/1951, Chicago, IL, m, 1990, 2 children **DISCIPLINE** SOCIOLOGY; PHILOSOPHY **EDUCATION** AB, 71, AM, 71, AM, 72, PhD, 75, Univ Missouri-Columbia. **CAREER** Visiting prof, 82, Notre Dame; Visiting Prof, 85, Virginia Poytech Inst; Visiting Prof, 87, Boston Univ; Asst Prof to Graduate Res prof, Univ South Florida, 75-; ch, Dept of Philos, 00-. **HONORS AND AWARDS** NEH Fel, 91-92; Fel, Swedish Collegium for Advanced Studies in the Social Sciences, 92 & 98; Honorary Visiting Prof, Univ Manchester, 96. **RESEARCH** History of social thought; philosophy of social science; science studies **SELECTED PUBLICATIONS** Auth, Sociological Explanition as Translation, 80; coauth, Max Weber and the Dispute over Reason and Value, 84; auth, The Search for a Methodology of Social Science: Durkheim, Weber, and the Nineteenth Century Problem of Cause, Probability, and Action, Boston Studies in Philosophy of Science, 86; Coauth, The Impossible Science: An Institutional Analysis of American Sociology, 90; Max Weber: The Lawyer as a Social Thinker, 94; Auth, The Social Theory of Practices: Tradition, Tacit Knowledge, and Presuppositions, 94. **CONTACT ADDRESS** Dept of Philosophy, Univ of So Florida, Tampa, FL 33620. **EMAIL** turner@chuma.cas.usf.edu

TURNER, TERENCE S.
PERSONAL Born 12/30/1935, Philadelphia, PA, m, 1980, 2 children **DISCIPLINE** ANTHROPOLOGY **EDUCATION** Harvard Col, BA, 57; Univ Calif Berkeley, MA, 59; Harvard Univ, PhD, 65. **CAREER** Asst prof Anthrop, 66-68, Prof Anthrop, Cornell Univ, 99- ; asst prof , 68, prof , 82-98, Univ Chicago. **HONORS AND AWARDS** Forman lectr, Royal Anthrop Inst, 92; Solon T Kimball Awd, Am Anthrop Soc, 98. **MEMBERSHIPS** Am Anthrop Asn; Am Ethnol Soc; Royal Anthrop Inst Gr Brit & Ireland; Asn Soc Anthrop Gr Brit & Commonwealth; Soc Cult Anthrop; Soc Lat Am Anthrop; Soc des Am; Associacao Brasileir a de Antropologia. **RESEARCH** Comparative social organization; kinship; political systems; cultural and symbolic forms ; Marxist social theory and political economy; semiotics and literary theory; visual anthropology and indigenous media; rights of indigenous peoples; human rights as anthropological issue; political and cultural aspects of interethnic contact. **SELECTED PUBLICATIONS** Auth, Indigenous Rights vs Neo-Liberal Developmentalism in Brazil, Dissent, 96; Social Complexity and Recursive Hierarchy in Indigenous South American Societies, Structure, knowledge, and representation in the Andes, Jour Steward Anthrop Soc, 97; Il sacro come alienzzione della coscienza sociale: riti e cosmologia dei Cayapo, Culture e religioni indigine in Americhe, Trattato di Antropologia del Sacro, Editoriale Jaca Book, 97; coauth, Universal Human rights versus Cultural Relativity, Jour Anthrop Res, 97; Human Rights, human difference, and anthropology's contribution to an emancipatory cultural politics, Jour Anthrop Res, 97; Indigenous rights, environmental protection and the struggle over forest resources in the Amazon: the case of the Brazilian Kayapo, Earth, air, fire and water: the humanities and the environment, Univ Mass Press, 98; The poetics of play: ritual clowns, masking and performative mimesis among the Kayapo, The play of gods and men: Essays in Play and Performance,Lit Verlag, 98; Mineral extraction by and for indigenous Amazonian Communities: Gold Mining by the Walapi and Kayapo, Mining, Oil, Environment, People and Rights in the Amazon, 98. **CONTACT ADDRESS** 115 Eddy St., Ithaca, NY 14850. **EMAIL** tst3@cornell.edu

TURNER, WIN
PERSONAL Born 10/31/1943, New Haven, CT, m, 2 children **DISCIPLINE** SOCIAL WORK **EDUCATION** Lake Forest Col, BA, 66; DePaul Univ, MA, 69; Brandeis Univ, PhD, 87. **CAREER** Asst prof, Wilkes Col, 71-75; adj prof, Simmons Col Sch of Soc Work, 85-, res assoc, Harvard Med Sch, 88-91; instr, Harvard Med Sch, 90-98; adj lectr, Univ of Mass, 95; adj prof, Univ of Maine, 98-. **HONORS AND AWARDS** Res Fel, DePaul Univ, 67; NIH traineeship, Syracuse Univ, 68-71; NIMH Traineeship, Brandeis Univ, 84-87; Grant, Harvard Med Sch, 91-93. **RESEARCH** Substance abuse, schizophrenia and Native American studies. **SELECTED PUBLICATIONS** Coauth, "Assessing homeless mentally ill persons for permanent housing: Screening for safety", Community Mental Health J 32.3 (96): 275-288; coauth, "Self-report and observer measures of substance abuse among homeless mentally ill persons, in the cross section and over time", J of Nervous and Mental Disease 184.11 (96): 667-672; coauth, "Housing persons who are homeless and mentally ill: Independent living or evolving consumer households?, Mentally Ill and Homeless: Special Programs for Special Needs, eds, W. Breakey and J. Thompson, Gordon and Breach Pub, India, (97); coauth, "Neuropsychological Function in Homeless Mentally Ill Individuals", J of Nervous and Mental Disease 185.1 (97): 3-12; coauth, "Sex differences in olfactory identification and Wisconsin Card Sorting performance in Schizophrenia: Relationship to attention and verbal ability", Biol Psych 42, (97): 104-115; coauth, "The effects of increasing resource demand on vigilance performance in adults with schizophrenia or developmental attention/learning disorders: A preliminary study", Schizophrenia Res 34. 1-2, (98): 101-112; coauth, "Predicting homelessness after rehousing: A longitudinal study of mentally ill adults", Psych Serv 51.5 (99): 674-679; coauth, "Feasibility of multidimensional substance abuse treating matching: Automating the ASAM patient placement criteria", Drug and Alcohol Res, 55. 1-2, (99): 35-43; coauth, "Independent living or staffed group homes for homeless mentally ill adults: Client outcomes in a randomized trail", Am J of Pub Health, (forthcoming); coauth, "Effects of housing interventions on neuropsychologidal function in homeless mentally ill individuals", Am J of Psych, (forthcoming). **CONTACT ADDRESS** Dept Soc Work, Univ of Maine, Orono, ME 04469-0001. **EMAIL** win.turner@umit.maine.edu

TUTTLE, RUSSELL H.
PERSONAL Born 08/18/1939, Marion, OH, m, 1968, 2 children **DISCIPLINE** ANTHROPOLOGY **EDUCATION** Oh State Univ, BSc, 61; MA, 62; Univ Calif, Berkeley, PhD, 65. **CAREER** Instr, asst prof, assoc prof, and prof, Univ of Chicago, 64-; exec comt mem, Assoc Cols of the Midwest Tanzania Prog, 98-2000. **HONORS AND AWARDS** Phi Beta Kappa; Medallion of the College de France, 95; Rockefeller Found, NSF and Wenner-Gren Found Grants to support a Bellagio Conf, 95; named Patron of the Tanzania Asn of Archaeols and Palaeanthropols, March 95; Nat Geographic Soc, 98. **MEMBERSHIPS** Am Anthropol Asn, Am Asn for the Advancement of Sci, Am Asn of Physical Anthropols, Am Soc of Primatologists, Int Primatological Soc, Soc of Sigma Xi. **SELECTED PUBLICATIONS** Ed with S. Matano, H. Ishida and M. Goodman, Topics in Primatology, vol 3, Evolutionary Biology, Reproductive Endocrinology and Virology, Tokyo, Tokyo Univ Press (92); auth of forward, revision, and references, in Hands by J. R. Napier, Princeton Univ Press, NJ (93); film, composed and directed by R. H. Tuttle and William Harms, Windows to the Past as Doors to the Future, Media Process Group, Chicago, with special assistance of John Paterson (96); coauth with B. Hallgrinsson and J. V. Basmajian, "Electromyography, Elastic Energy and Knuckle-walking: a Lesson in Experimental Anthropology," in The New Anthropology, D. Lindburg and S.C. Strum, eds, Prentice-Hall, Englewood Cliif, NJ (99): 32-41; auth, "Physical Anthropology," Encyclopedia Britannica, Encyclopedia Britannica, Inc, Chicago. Il (2000); auth, "Hominids," in Encyclopedia of Paleontology, Ronald Singer, ed, Fitzroy Dearborn, Pubs, Chicago (in press); coauth, "Hominoid heels," Proceedings of the XVth Congress of the Int Primatological Soc, Kuta Bali, Indonesia, Aug 4, 1994 (in press); auth, "Fossils, Phylogenies and Feelings: Can Evolutionary Biology Contribute to the Great Ape Project?," in Great Apes and Humans at an Ethical Frontier, eds, B. B. Beck, T. S. Stoinski, A. Arluke, M. Hutchins, T. L. Maple, B. Norton, A, Rowan, and B. F. Stevens, Smithsonian Inst Press, Washington, DC (in press). **CONTACT ADDRESS** Dept Anthropol, Univ of Chicago, 1126 E 59th St, Chicago, IL 60637. **EMAIL** r-tuttle@uchicago.edu

TWENEY, RYAN D.
PERSONAL Born 12/30/1943, Detroit, MI, m, 2 children **DISCIPLINE** PSYCHOLOGY **EDUCATION** Univ Chicago, BA, 66; Wayne State Univ, MA, 69, PhD, 70. **CAREER** Prof, Bowling Green State Univ, 70-. **HONORS AND AWARDS** Vis Assoc Prof, Salk Inst, 76; Fulbright Res Fel, UK, 89. **MEMBERSHIPS** Cognitive Sci Soc; Psychomic Soc. **RESEARCH** Cognitive Basis of Scientific Thinking, History of Science, History of Psychology. **SELECTED PUBLICATIONS** Auth, "A framework for the cognitive psychology of science", in Psychology of science and metascience, eds B. Gholson, A. Houts, R.A. Neimeyer and W. Shadish, Cambridge Univ Pr, (89): 342-366; coed, Faraday's 1882 "Chemical Notes, Hints, Suggestions, and Objects of Pursuit", Science Mus and Peter Peregrinus, Ltd. (London), 91; auth, "Stopping time: Faraday and the scientific creation of perceptual order", Physis: RevistaInternazionale di Storia Della Scienza, 29 (92): 149-164; auth, "Inventing the field: Michael Faraday and the creative engineering of electromagnetic field theory", in Inventive minds: Creativity in Technology, eds D. Perkins and R. Weber, Oxford Univ Pr (NY, 92): 31-47; auth "Jonathan Edwards and determinism", J for the Hist of the Behav Sci 33, (97): 365-380; coed, The great catalog of the C.H. Stoelting Company, 1930-1937, Scholars Facsimiles and Reprints (Delmar, NY), 97; coauth, "Artifactual power curves in forgetting", Memory & Cognition 25, (97): 724-730; coauth, "The practice of mathematics and science: From calculus to the clothesline problem", in Rational Models of Cognition, eds M. Oaksford and N. Chater, Oxford Univ Pr, (98): 415-438; auth, "Toward a Cognitive Psychology of Science: Recent Research and its Implications" Current Directions in Psychol Sci 7, (99): 150-154; auth, "Toward a general theory of scientific thinking" in Designing for Science: Implications from Professional, Instructional, and Everyday Science, eds K. Crowley, C.D. Schunn and T. Okada, Erlbaum (Mahway, NJ) (forthcoming). **CONTACT ADDRESS** Dept Psychol, Bowling Green State Univ, 1001 E Wooster St, Bowling Green, OH 43403-0001. **EMAIL** tweney@bgnet.bgsu.edu

TY, ELEANOR R.
PERSONAL Born 10/11/1958, Manila, Philippines, m, 1982, 3 children **DISCIPLINE** ENGLISH, WOMEN'S STUDIES **EDUCATION** Univ Toronto, BA, 81; McMaster Univ, MA, 82; PhD, 88. **CAREER** Asst prof, McMaster Univ, 89-90; asst prof, Brock Univ, 90-91; asst prof to prof, Wilfrid Laurier Univ, 91-. **HONORS AND AWARDS** Wilfrid Laurier Fel, 93; SSHRCC Res Grant, 94-97, 00-02; Grace Anderson Fel, 96. **MEMBERSHIPS** MLA, Assoc for Asian Am Studies, Can Soc for 18th Century Studies, Am Soc for 18th Century Studies. **RESEARCH** Narratives by Asian Canadian and Asian American Authors, Late Eighteenth Century Fiction, Feminist Theory and Women's Writing, Diasporic, Ethnic, and Minority Children. **SELECTED PUBLICATIONS** Auth, Unsex'd Revolutionaries: Five Women Novelists of the 1790s. Theory and Cult Series, Univ of Tor Pr, 93; ed, The Victim of Prejudice, by Mary Hays, 1799, Broadview Pr, (Peterborough and Lewiston, NY), 94; ed, Memoirs of Emma Courtney by Mary Hays 1796, Oxford World's Classics, (Oxford), 96; auth, Empowering the Feminine: The Narratives of Mary Robinson, Jane West, and Amelia Opie, 1796-1812, Univ of Toronto Pr, 98. **CONTACT ADDRESS** Dept English, Wilfrid Laurier Univ, Waterloo, ON, Canada N2L 3C5. **EMAIL** ety@wlu.ca

TYKOT, ROBERT
PERSONAL Born 06/30/1961, New York, NY, m, 1989, 2 children **DISCIPLINE** ANTHROPOLOGY **EDUCATION** Tufts Univ, BS, 83; MA, 84; Harvard Univ, MA, 93; PhD, 95. **CAREER** Teaching Asst, Tufts Univ, 82-87; Res Asst to Laboratory Manager, Harvard Univ, 87-96; Lecturer, Univ Mass, 95-96; Asst Prof, Univ S Fla, 96-. **HONORS AND AWARDS** USF Presidential Young Fac Awd, 98. **MEMBERSHIPS** Am Anthropol Asn; Archaeol Inst of Am; Asn for the Study of Marble and Other Stones in Antiquity; Etruscan Foundation; European Asn of Archaeol; Harvard Archaeol Soc; Inst for Nautical Archaeol; Intl Asn for Obsidian Studies; Sigma Xi; Soc for Am Archaeol; Soc for Archaeol Sci. **RESEARCH** Archaeological science; Mediterranean prehistory; Sardinia; Malta; Italy **SELECTED PUBLICATIONS** Auth, Sardinia in the Mediterranean: A Footprint in the Seas. Studies in Sardinian Archaeology Presented to Miriam S. Balmuth, Sheffield Acad Press, 92; auth, "Obsidian Procurement and Distribution in the Central and Western Mediterranean," Journal of Mediterranean Archaeology, (96): 39-82; auth, "The Geological Source of an Obsidian Ear from the Museum of Fine Arts, Boston," Revue d'Egyptologie, (96): 177-179; auth, "Characterization of the Monte Arci Obsidian Sources," Journal of Archaeological Science, (97): 467-479; auth, "New Directions in Central Mediterranean Obsidian Studies," Antiquity, (97): 1000-1006; auth, "Mediterranean Islands and Multiple flows: The Sources and Exploitation of Sardinian Obsidian," in Method and Theory in Archaeological Obsidian Studies, (98): 67-82; auth, Sardinian and Aegean Chronology: Towards the Resolution of Relative and Absolute Dating in the Mediterranean, Oxbow Books, 98; auth, "Isotopic Source Determination of Greek and Roman Marble Sculptures in the Museum of Fine Arts, Boston: Recent Analyses," in Archeomareriaux. Marbrew et autres roches, Bordeaux, 99; auth, "Islands in the Stream: Stone Age Cultural Dynamics in Sardinia and Corsica," in Social Dynamics of the Prehistoric Central Mediterranean, (Univ London, 99), 67-82; auth,

Social Dynamics of the Prehistoric Central Mediterranean, Univ London, 99. **CONTACT ADDRESS** Dept Anthropol, Univ of So Florida, 4202 Fowler Ave, Tampa, FL 33620. **EMAIL** rtykot@chuma1.cas.usf.edu

TYLER, GERALD DEFOREST
PERSONAL Born 02/28/1946, Louisa Co, VA, d, 2 children **DISCIPLINE** EDUCATION **EDUCATION** Norfolk State Univ, BS (honors) 1977, MA (highest honors) 1983; Old Dominion Univ, pursuing PhD 1983. **CAREER** Dalmo Sales Co, salesman 1964-66; US Marine Corps, admiral's orderly 1966-69; Tidewater Regional Transit System, bus oper 1969-77; Elizabeth City State Univ, spec asst to chancellor 1977-84; Norfolk State Univ, Dir of Univ Relations, 84-. **HONORS AND AWARDS** Safe Driving Awd for operating 32 passenger bus free of accidents while employed at TRT 1969-77; Certificate of Appreciation UNCF New York 1979; Outstanding Boxer Awd USMC; First Awd Cert as Asst Head Coach for ECSU's Lady Vikings Softball Team 1980-81; NCSEA Inc Employee of the Year Awd 1981-82; Awd for Outstanding Leadership Unselfish and Dedicated Serv rendered as Sr Class Advisor 1982-84. **MEMBERSHIPS** Mem, NAACP, 1979-; Adv ECSU Student Chap NAACP 1980-84; mem NC State Employees Assn Inc 1980-84; pres Prof Business Assn 1980-81; alternate delegate 35th Annual NCSEA Convention Comm 1980-81; mem S Humanities Conf 1980-82; chmn NC State Employees Assoc Inc 1981-82; mem Greater Bibleway Temple 120 Club 1981; 1st vice pres Pasquotank Co Branch NAACP 1981-84; mem NCSEA Inc Area 24 Exec Bd 1981-84; adv ECSU Sr Class 1981-84; 1st vice chmn Pasquotank Co Voting Precinct 3B 1981-82; mem NCSEA Inc Bd of Governors 1981-82; chmn NCSEA Inc Area 24 1981-82; bd mem Gov's FOTC Assn 1982-84; bd mem Albemarle Develop Auth 1982-84; head adv ECSU Sr Class 1982-84; mem NCSEA Inc State Organ Study Comm 1982-83; mem Pasquotank Co Voting Precinct 3B 1983-84; mem Pasquotank Co Improvement Assn 1983-84; mem New Towne Civic League 1984-86; mem Tidewater Media Prof Assn 1984-89; bd mem New Towne Civic League 1984-86; mem VA Social Sci Assn 1984-94; mem Virginia Assn of Printing, Publications & Public Relations, 1986-; bd mem, Miss Black Virginia Pageant, 1986-88; mem bd of advisors, Miss Collegiate African American Pageant, 1989-93; mem board of directors, Tidewater Charter, American Red Cross, 1990-92; Hampton Roads Black Media Professionals, 1990-; The Council for the Advancement and Support of Education District III, board of directors and nominating committee, 1993-95. **CONTACT ADDRESS** University Relations, Norfolk State Univ, Wilson Hall, Ste 340, Norfolk, VA 23504. **EMAIL** gtyler@nsv.edu

TYLER, STEPHEN
PERSONAL Born 05/08/1932, Hartford, IA, m, 1962, 1 child **DISCIPLINE** ANTHROPOLOGY **EDUCATION** Simpson Col, BA, 57; Stanford Univ, MA, 62; PhD, 64. **CAREER** Asst prof, Univ Cal at Davis, 64-67; assoc prof, Tulane Univ, 67-70; prof, Rice Univ, 70-. **HONORS AND AWARDS** Fulbright Fel. **RESEARCH** Cognitive anthropology; postmodernism; Dravidian Languages. **SELECTED PUBLICATIONS** Auth, Cognitive Anthropology, 69; auth, India: An Anthropological Perspective, 73; auth, Roya: A Dravidian Language, 68; auth, The Said and the Unsaid, 78; auth, The Unspeakable, 88. **CONTACT ADDRESS** Dept Linguistics, Rice Univ, 6100 Main St, Houston, TX 77005-1827. **EMAIL** styler@rice.edu

U

UGGEN, CHRIS
PERSONAL Born 05/29/1964, St Paul, MN, m, 1986, 2 children **DISCIPLINE** SOCIOLOGY **EDUCATION** Univ Wisc, BA, 86; MS, 90; PhD, 95. **CAREER** Systems Analyst, Priv Industry Coun, 87-88; Teaching Asst, Univ Wisc, 89-95; Asst Prof, Univ Minn, 95-. **HONORS AND AWARDS** Outstanding Fac Awd, Col of Liberal Arts Student Board, 99; Cavan Young Scholar Awd, am Soc of Criminol, 00; Fel, Soros Foundation Open Soc Inst, 00; Jr Scholar Awd, Intl Soc of Criminol, 98. **MEMBERSHIPS** Am Sociol Asn, Am Soc of Criminol. **RESEARCH** Crime, Law and Deviance; Organizations and Work; Life Course; Methods and Statistics. **SELECTED PUBLICATIONS** Auth, "Crime and Class," in International Encyclopedia of the Social and Behavioral Sciences, forthcoming; auth, "Class, Gender, and Arrest: An Intergenerational Analysis of Workplace Power and Control," Criminology, forthcoming; auth, "Alcohol and Employment in the Transition to Adulthood," Journal of Health and Social Behavior, forthcoming; auth, "Work as a Turning Point in the Life Course of Criminals: A Duration Model of Age, Employment, and Recidivism," American Sociological Review, forthcoming; auth, "Career Jobs, Survival Jobs, and Employee Deviance: A Social Investment Model of Workplace Misconduct," The Sociological Quarterly, (00): 245-263; auth, "Predictors of Desistance among Sex Offenders: The Interaction of formal and Informal Social Controls," Justice Quarterly, (00): 401-428; auth, "Men and Women of Elite Law Firms: Reevaluating Kanter's Legacy," Law and Social Inquiry, (00): 41-68; co-auth, "Prevention of Juvenile Delinquency," in Encyclopedia of Crime and Justice, forthcoming; co-auth, "The Endogeneity of legal Regulation: Grievance procedures as Rational Myth," American Journal of Sociology, (99): 406-454; co-auth, "Volunteerism and Arrest in the Transition to Adulthood," Social Forces, (99): 331-362. **CONTACT ADDRESS** Dept Sociol, Univ of Minnesota, Twin Cities, 267 19th Ave S, Minneapolis, MN 55455. **EMAIL** uggen@atlas.socsci.umn.edu

UHDE, ANNA P.
PERSONAL Born 01/22/1947, West Chester, PA, 3 children **DISCIPLINE** EDUCATION **EDUCATION** Univ Georgia, Ed.D, 88; Univ. Georgia, Ed.S, 76; Univ Georgia, MSHE, 71; Univ Delaware, BSEd, 69. **CAREER** Part-time Faculty, Piedmont Col, 96-; Kindergarten teacher, Clark Co. School System, 82-; instr in Child Development, Univ of Georgia, 81-82; instr in Child Development, Athens Area Technical Insitute, 73-76. **HONORS AND AWARDS** Nominated Invent America Teacher of the year, 95; Best Demonstration of concepts learned with lightspan lightspan partnership, 95; Representative People to People program in Bejing China, 93; Representative in governors conference in Education, 93; Warren J. Findley Outstanding Dissertation of the year Kappa Deltta Pi honor Society; Teacher of Excellence Foundation for Excellence in Education, 89; Teacher of the Year Alps Road Elementary School, 85; Comprehensive school Reform Demonstration Grant, 99; Teacher Mini-Grant Foundation for Excellence in Education, 98; Science in the Classroom-Carrier Transicold, 98; Pay for Performance co-author, 94 7 96. **MEMBERSHIPS** Georgia Association of Teacher Educators. **RESEARCH** Math Anxiety in Adults, Adult Education, Early Childhood. **SELECTED PUBLICATIONS** Auth, "A Study of the Athens-Clark County authorities, boards, and commissions," by Uhde, A.P. (ed.), 99; auth, "Making mathematics come Alive, by Brown, A.H. & Uhde, A.P., Proceedings for Adult Education Research Conference, Vancouver, Canada, 00. **CONTACT ADDRESS** Dept Education, Piedmont Col, PO Box 10, Demorest, GA 30535. **EMAIL** auhde0147@aol.com

ULANOV, ANN BELFORD
PERSONAL Born 01/01/1938, Princeton, NJ, m, 1968, 4 children **DISCIPLINE** DEPTH PSYCHOLOGY, CHRISTIAN THEOLOGY **EDUCATION** Radcliffe Col, BA, 59; Union Theol Sem, MDiv, 62, PhD, 67. **CAREER** From instr to assoc prof psychiat and relig, Union Theol Sem, 66-74; Psycho-Therapist, 65-; prof psychiat and relig, union theol sem, 74-, Res psychotherapist, Inst Relig and Health, 62-65; bd mem, C G Jung Training Ctr, 71 **MEMBERSHIPS** Am Asn Pastoral Counr; C G Jung Found Anal Psychol; Int Asn Anal Psychol; Nat Accreditation Asn and Exam Bd Psychoanal; Am Theol Soc. **RESEARCH** Feminine psychology; religion and the unconscious; the witch archetype. **SELECTED PUBLICATIONS** Auth, The Golden Ass of Apuleius--the Liberation of the Feminine in Man, Parabola-Myth Tradition Search for Meaning, Vol 0018, 93; Exploring Sacred Landscapes--Religious and Spiritual Experiences in Psychotherapy, Jour Rel and Health, Vol 0033, 94; The Work of Loewald, Hans, an Introduction and Commentary, Jour Rel and Health, Vol 0033, 94; Leaving My Fathers House--A Journey to Conscious Femininity, Jour Rel and Health, Vol 0033, 94; A Womans Identity, Jour Rel and Health, Vol 0033, 94; Object Relations Therapy, Jour Rel and Health, Vol 0033, 94; Projective and Introjective Identification and the Use of the Therapists Self, Jour of Rel and Health, Vol 0033, 94; Envy--Further Thoughts, Jour Rel and Health, Vol 0034, 95; Sacred Chaos--Reflections on God Shadow and the Dark Self, Jour Rel and Health, Vol 0034, 95; The Mystery of the Conjunctio--Alchemical Images of Individuation, Jour Rel and Health, Vol 0034, 95; In Gods Shadow--The Collaboration of White, Victor and Jung,C.G., Jour Rel and Health, Vol 0034, 95; Protestantism and Jungian Psychology, Jour of Rel and Health, Vol 0035, 96; A Meeting of Minds--Mutuality in Psychoanalysis, Jour of Rel and Health, Vol 0035, 96; Tillich, Paul First--A Memoir of the Harvard Years, Jour Rel and Health, Vol 0036, 97; Always Becoming--An Autobiography, Jour Rel and Health, Vol 0036, 97; Practicing Wholeness, Jour of Rel and Health, Vol 0036, 97. **CONTACT ADDRESS** Union Theol Sem, New York, 3041 Broadway at 121st St, New York, NY 10027.

ULMER, JEFFERY T.
PERSONAL Born 03/02/1966, Harrisburg, PA, m, 1994, 1 child **DISCIPLINE** SOCIOLOGY, ANTHROPOLOGY **EDUCATION** Susquehanna Univ, BA, 88; Pa State Univ, MA, 90; PhD, 93. **CAREER** Grad Asst, Pa State Univ, 88-92; Roes Asst, Pa Crime Comn, 90; Instr, Pa State Univ, 92-94; Roes Assoc., Pa State Univ, 93-94; Asst Prof, Purdue Univ, 94-00; Assoc. Prof, Pa State Univ, 00-. **HONORS AND AWARDS** Lindback Scholar's Day Awd for Undergrad Roes, Susquehanna Univ, 88; Univ Scholar, Susquehanna Univ, 85-88. **MEMBERSHIPS** ASA, Am Soc of Criminology, Midwest Sociol Soc, Soc for the Study of Symbolic Interaction, Soc for the Study of Soc Problems. **RESEARCH** Sociology of crime and deviance, sociology of criminal justice and law, sociology of corrections, sociological theory, social psychology, integrating qualitative and quantitative methods, race and ethnicity. **SELECTED PUBLICATIONS** auth, "The Organization and Consequences of Social Pasts in Criminal Courts," The Sociol Quart, 36 (95): 901-919; coauth, "Court Communities Under Sentencing Guidelines: Dilemmas of Formal Rationality and Sentencing Disparity," Criminology, 34 (96): 306-332; coauth, "A Processional Order Approach to Studying Sentencing Guidelines: Contexts, Activities and Consequences," Applied Behav SCI Rev, 5 (97): 81-100; auth, Social Worlds of Sentencing: Court Communities Under Sentencing Guidelines, State Univ NY Pr (Albany, NY), 97; coauth, "The Use and Transformation of Formal Decision Making Criteria: Sentencing Guidelines, Organizational Contexts and Case Processing Strategies," Soc Problems, 45 (98): 248-267; ed, Sociology of Crime, Law and Deviance, vol 1 (Greenwich, CT: JAI Pr, 98); coauth, "The Contributions of an Interactionist Approach to Research and Theory on Criminal Careers," Theoretical Criminology, 3 (99): 95-124; ed, Sociology of Crime, Law and Deviance, vol 2, JAI Pr (Greenwich, CT), forthcoming. **CONTACT ADDRESS** Dept Sociol & Anthrop, Pennsylvania State Univ, Univ Park, 211 Oswald Tower, University Park, PA 16802.

UNNITHAN, N. PRABHA
PERSONAL Born 09/13/1952, Malaysia, m, 1982, 2 children **DISCIPLINE** SOCIOLOGY **EDUCATION** Karnatak Univ, BSc, 74; Univ Saugar, MA, 76; Univ Neb, PhD, 83. **CAREER** Instr, Univ of Neb, 83; asst prof, E Tex State Univ, 84-87; asst prof to prof, Colo State Univ, 87-. **HONORS AND AWARDS** Dr Ganesram Mukharya Gold Medal, 76; Regents Fel, Univ of Neb, 80; Six Happold Awds, 80-83; Grant, E Tex State Univ, 86; Grant, Colo State Univ, 88, 91; Grant, Res and Develop Ctr for the Advan of Student Learning, 97, 98. **MEMBERSHIPS** Acad of Criminal Justice Sci; Am Soc of Criminol; SW Assoc of Criminal Justice; Am Sociol Assoc; Western Soc Sci Assoc; Indian Soc of Criminol. **SELECTED PUBLICATIONS** Coauth, The Currents of Lethal Violence: An Integrated Model of Suicide and Homicide, SUNY Pr, 94; coauth, "Rhetoric and Policy Realities in Developing Countries: Community Councils in Jamaica, 1972-1980, J of Applied Behav Sci 31, (95): 65-79; coauth, "A Method for Distinguishing Gang Homicides from Non-Gang Homicides", Int Assoc of Law Enforcement Intelligence Analysists J 9 (95); 27-32; coauth, "Determinants of Privatization Levels in Developing Countries", Soc Sci Quarterly 77, (96): 134-144; auth, "Child homicide in Developed Countries", Int Rev of Victimology 4 (97): 313-326; coauth, "Child Homicide and the Economic Stress Hypothesis: A Research Note", Homicide Studies 1 (97): 281-290; auth, "Malayalam Speakers", American Immigrant Cultures: Builders of a Nation, ed David Levinson, Macmillan Ref, (NY), 97; coauth, "Wife Burning: Cultural Cues for Lethal Violence Against Women Among Asian Indians in the US", Violence Against Women 5 (99): 641-653; coauth, "Training in community Policing: A Suggested Curriculum", Policing 23, (00). **CONTACT ADDRESS** Dept Sociol, Colorado State Univ, 1 Colorado State, Fort Collins, CO 80523-001. **EMAIL** prabha@lamar.colostate.edu

UNRAU, YVONNE A.
DISCIPLINE SOCIAL WORK **EDUCATION** Univ Lethbridge, Alberta, BA, 87; Univ Calgary, Alberta, BSW, 88, MSW, 90; Univ Ut, Salt Lake City, PhD, 95. **CAREER** Instr, Univ Calgary, Alberta, 91-92; lectr, Univ Utah, 92-93; instr to assoc prof, Univ Calgary, 93-98; asst prof, Dept Soc Work, Ill State Univ, Normal, 99-. **HONORS AND AWARDS** With Kathy Wehrmann, Teaching-Learning Development grant, Ctr for the Advancement of Teaching, Ill State Univ, 99; Supplemental Travel for Teaching Prog grant, Ctr for Advancement of Teaching, Ill State Univ, 99-2000; First-Year Fac Summer Teaching Inst grant, The Ctr for the Advancement of Teaching, Ill State Univ, 99. **MEMBERSHIPS** Asn of Baccalaureate Soc Work Prog Dirs, Nat Asn of Soc Workers, Soc for Soc Work Res. **RESEARCH** Program design and evaluation; research methods and statistical applications in social work; service delivery systems in child welfare; services to vulnerable children and families. **SELECTED PUBLICATIONS** Auth, "Defining the black box of family preservation services A conceptual framework for service delivery," Community Alternatives, 7, 2 (95): 49-62; auth, "Selecting a data collection method and a data source," in Richard M. Grinnell, Jr, ed, Social work research and evaluation: Quantitative and qualitative approaches, 5th ed, Itasca, Il: F. E. Peacock Pubs (97): 3458-472; auth, "Predicting use of child welfare services after intensive family preservation services," Res on Soc Work Practice, 7, 1 (97): 202-215; coauth, "Understanding and interpreting polytomaous logistic regression," Res on Soc Work Practice, 8, 2 (98)" 223-235; coauth, Introduction to Social Work Research, Itasca, Il: F. E. Peacock Pubs, Inc. (98); coauth, Program evaluation for social workers: A quality improvement approach for the social services, 2nd ed, Needham Heights, MA: Allyn and Bacon (98); coauth, "Family group conferencing in child welfare: Lessons from a demonstration project," Families in Society (in press). **CONTACT ADDRESS** Dept Soc Work, Illinois State Univ, 309 Rachel Cooper, Campus Box 4650, Normal, IL 61790-4650. **EMAIL** yaunrau@ilstu.edu

URBINA, SUSANA P.
PERSONAL Born 01/20/1946, Lima, Peru **DISCIPLINE** PSYCHOLOGY **EDUCATION** Mary Manse Col, BA, 66; Fordham Univ, MA, 68; PhD, 72. **CAREER** Asst Prof to Full Prof, Univ of N Fla, 76-. **HONORS AND AWARDS** Sigma Xi, 69; Postdoctoral fel, Univ of Nebr Med Ctr, 81-82; Outstanding Young Women of Am. **MEMBERSHIPS** Am Pyshcol Asn, 73-, Soc for Personality Assessment, 81-; Am Psychol

Soc, 97-. **RESEARCH** Individual Differences - Assessment Instruments. **SELECTED PUBLICATIONS** Coauth, "Intelligence: Knowns and Unknowns," Am Psychologist 51 (96): 77-101; auth, Study Guide: Psychological Testing, 7th ed, Prentice Hall (Upper Saddle River, NJ), 97; auth, Instructor's Manual for Psychological Testing, 7th ed, Prentice Hall (Upper Saddle River, NJ), 97; coauth, Psychological Testing 7th ed, Prentice Hall (Upper Saddle River, NJ), 97; auth, "Review of the Balanced Emotional Empathy Scale," in Thirteenth Mental Measurements Yearbook (Lincoln, NE: Buros Inst, 98), 78-79; auth, "Review of the Insight Inventory," in Thirteenth Mental Measurements Yearbook (Lincoln, NE: Buros Inst, 98), 509-510; auth, "Nature versus Nature: The End of the Debate?," rev, of Intelligence, heredity, and environment, Contemp Psychology 43 (98): 639-640; auth, "The Past Revisited: Black and White Thinking about Race and Tests," rev, of Psychological Testing of American Minorities: Issues and Consequences, 2nd ed, Contemp Psychology 44 (99): 51-52; auth, "Review of Jesness Inventory," in Fourteenth Mental Measurements Yearbook (Lincoln, NE: Buros Inst, in press); auth, "Review of the Hand Test," in Fourteenth Mental Measurements Yearbook (Lincoln, NE: Buros Inst, in press). **CONTACT ADDRESS** Dept Psychology, Univ of No Florida, 4567 St. Johns Blf S, Jacksonville, FL 32224. **EMAIL** surbina@unf.edu

URDAN, TIMOTHY C.
PERSONAL Born 01/12/1964, Berkeley, CA, m, 1997 **DISCIPLINE** PSYCHOLOGY, EDUCATION **EDUCATION** Univ Berkeley, BA, 86; Harvard, EdM, 88; Univ Mich, PhD, 94. **CAREER** Asst prof, Emory Univ, 94-96; asst prof, Santa Clara, Univ, 96-. **MEMBERSHIPS** AGRA, APA, SRA. **RESEARCH** Motivation, Adolescents, Education. **SELECTED PUBLICATIONS** Auth, "Academic self handicapping and performance goals: A further examination," Contemporary Educational Psychology, (in press); auth, "Contextual influences on motivation and performance: An examination of achievement goal structures," in Proceeding of the International Conference on the Application of Psychology to the Quality of Learning and Teaching, (in press); auth, " Interpreting messages about motivation in the classroom: Examining the effects of achievement goal structures," Advances in Motivation and Achievement, Stamford, 99; auth, "Perceiving high or low home-school dissonance: Longitudinal effects on adolescent emotional and academic wellbeing," Journal of Research on Adolescence, (99): 441-467; auth, "Early adolescence: A review of the literature," Collected Papers from the OERI Conference on Adolescence: Designing Developmentally Appropriate Middle Schools, (99): 19-52; auth, "The development and validation of scales assessing students' achievement goal orientations," contemporary Educational Psychology, (98): 113-131; auth, "The Role of Classroom Goal Structure in Students' Use of Self-Handicapping," American Educational Research Journal, (98): 101-122. **CONTACT ADDRESS** Dept Psychology, Santa Clara Univ, 500 El Camino Real, Santa Clara, CA 95053-0001. **EMAIL** turdan@scu.edu

USISKIN, ZALMAN
PERSONAL Born 01/01/1943, Chicago, IL, m, 1979, 2 children **DISCIPLINE** EDUCATION **EDUCATION** Univ Ill, BS, 63; BS, 63; Harvard Univ, MAT, 64; Univ Mich, PhD, 69. **CAREER** Math Teacher, Niles W High Sch, 64-66;Vis Prof, Univ Ga, 80; Asst Prof, Univ Chicago, 69-74; Assoc Prof, Univ Chicago, 74-82; Prof, Univ Chicago, 82-. **HONORS AND AWARDS** Max Beberman Awd, Ill Coun of Teachers of Math, 81; Distinguished Lect, Asn for Supv and Curric Develop, 90; Glen Gilbert Nat Leadership Awd, Nat Coun of Math Proj, 94; Centennial Lect, Western Ill Univ, 99. **MEMBERSHIPS** Nat Coun of Teachers of Math, Math Assoc of Am, Nat Coun of Supervrs of Math, Ill Coun of Teachers of Math, Metro Math Club of Chicago and Vicinity, Sch Sci and Math Assoc, Nat Soc for the Study of Educ, Assoc for Superv and Curric Develop, Phi Delta Kappa. **RESEARCH** All aspects of mathematics education, with particular emphasis on matters related to curriculum, instruction and testing, the selection and organization of content, the teacher and learning of mathematics, international mathematics education and educational policy. **SELECTED PUBLICATIONS** Auth, "Why is Algebra Important to Learn?" Am Educ (95); coauth, "Rethinking the First Two Years of High School Mathematics: The University of Chicago School Mathematics Project," Math Teacher (95); auth, "Mathematics as a Language," in Communication in Mathematics: The 1996 Yearbk of the Nat Coun of Teachers of Mathematics (Reston, VA: NCTM, 96); auth, "Doing Algebra in Grades K-4," Teaching Children Math (97); Auth, "Applications in the Secondary School Mathematics Curriculum: A Generation of Change," Am J of Educ (97); auth, "On the Relationships Between Mathematics and Science in Schools," J of Math and Sci: Collab Explor (97); ed, "Reforming the Third R: Changing the School Mathematics Curriculum, Spec Issue," Am J of Educ (97); auth, "Paper and Pencil Algorithms in a Calculator/Computer Age," in Algorithms in Sch Math: The 1998 Yearbk of the Nat Coun of Teachers of Math (Reston, VA: NCTM, 98); auth, "The Mathematically Promising and the Mathematically Gifted," in Developing Mathematically Promising Students (Reston, VA: NCTM, 99); ed, Developments in School Mathematics Around the World, vol 4, Nat Coun of Teachers of Math Pr (Reston, VA), 99; **CONTACT ADDRESS** Dept Educ, Univ of Chicago, 5835 Kimbark Ave, Chicago, IL 60637. **EMAIL** z-usiskin@uchicago.edu

V

VALENTINE, P. V.
PERSONAL Born 07/24/1953, Greenville, MS, d, 3 children **DISCIPLINE** SOCIAL WORK **EDUCATION** Fla State Univ, PhD, 97. **CAREER** Asst prof, Univ Ala, Birmingham. **HONORS AND AWARDS** Nat Dissertation Awd. **MEMBERSHIPS** NASW, SSWR, CSWE. **RESEARCH** Assessing and treatment of traumatic events, especially as they relate to incarceration, substance abuse, domestic violence, and teen violence. **SELECTED PUBLICATIONS** Auth, "The etiology of addiction," in Chemical Dependency: A Systems Approach, eds. C. A. McNeese & D. DiNitto (Boston: Allyn & Bacon, 98), 20-31; coauth, "The stress-crisis continuum: Its application to domestic violence," in A. Roberts, ed, Battered Women and Their Families, 2nd ed, NY: Springer Pub Co (98): 29-57; auth, "Chapter 12: Traumatic Incident Reduction Approach," in C. Figley, ed, Brief Treatments in Traumatology, Philadelphia: Taylor & Francis (in press); auth, "An application of crisis intervention to situational crises frequently experienced by adult survivors of incest," in A. Robert, ed, Crisis Intervention Handbook, 2nd ed, NY: Oxford Univ Press (in press); auth, "Fight and flight instincts as they relate to violence," Encyclopedia of Violence in the United States (in press); auth, "Traumatic Incident Reduction of Traumatized Women Inmates, I: Dimensions of Research and Practice," J of Offender Rehabilitation, 31, 1 (in press); auth, "Traumatic Incident Reduction of Traumatized Women Inmates, II: Maria's Story," J of Offender Rehabilitation, 31, 1 (in press); auth, "Traumatic Incident Reduction (TIR): Brief, Intense Treatment for Battered Women," Crisis Intervention and Time-limited Treatment, 5, 2 (in press); coauth, "Evaluating Traumatic Incident Reduction (TIR) Therapy with female inmates: A randomized controlled clinical trial," Research on Social Work Practice (in press). **CONTACT ADDRESS** Dept Public Service, 339 Ullman Bldg, Univ of Alabama, Birmingham, 1212 University Blvd, Birmingham, AL 35294-3350.

VALIANTE, GIOVANNI
PERSONAL Born 04/11/1971, CT, s **DISCIPLINE** EDUCATIONAL PSYCHOLOGY **EDUCATION** Univ Fla, BA, 94; MA, 95; Emory Univ, PhD candidate for 2001. **CAREER** Schoolteacher, Park Springs Elementary, 95, Logan Run Middle School, 96; instr, Community Educ Prog, 96; instr, Emory Univ, 99, invited lectr, 2000, instr, Emory Univ, 2000-. **HONORS AND AWARDS** Couns of the Year, Pine Crest Summer Camp, summer 93, 94; Fla Educ Res Coun Grants, 94; Teacher of the Year nominee, Palm Beach County, Loggers Run Middle School, 96-97; 1st Place, Gender Issues Category, Southeastern Psychol Asn Comt on Equality of Prof Opportunity; Harold E. Mitzel Awd, Helen Dwight Reid Educ Found, 97; Nat Acad of Educ/Spenser Found Postdoctoral Fel, 98-99. **MEMBERSHIPS** Am Educ Res Asn, Am Psychol Asn, Southeastern Psychol Asn, Ga Educ Res Asn, Nat Asn for Invitational Educ. **RESEARCH** Self-efficacy, motivation and self-beliefs, sports and educational psychology. **SELECTED PUBLICATIONS** Coauth with F. Pajares, "Influence of writing self-efficacy beliefs on the writing performance of upper elementary students," J of Educ Res, 90 (97): 353-360; coauth with F. Pajares, "Grade level and gender differences in the writing self-beliefs of middle school students," Contemporary Educ Psychol, 24 (99): 390-405; coauth with F. Pajares, "The Inviting/Disinviting Index: Instrument validation and relation to motivation and achievement," J of Invitational Theory and Practice, 6 (99): 28-47; coauth with F. Pajares, "Writing goals of middle school students: relation to motivation constructs, achievement, gender, and gender orientation," Contemporary Educ Psychol (under review). **CONTACT ADDRESS** Div of Educ Studies, Emory Univ, 1784 N Decatur Rd, Atlanta, GA 30322. **EMAIL** gvalian@emory.edu

VAN BEVEREN, TOOSJE T.
PERSONAL Born 12/13/1941, Utrecht, Netherlands, m, 1991, 1 child **DISCIPLINE** HUMAN DEVELOPMENT **EDUCATION** S Methodist Univ, BA, 83; MA, 88; Univ Tex, PhD, 96. **CAREER** Develop psychologist, Univ of Tex, 90-; **MEMBERSHIPS** TAIMH **RESEARCH** Effects of pre and/or postnatal drug exposure on child development **SELECTED PUBLICATIONS** Coauth, "Levels of Thinking", Personality and Soc Pyschol Bull 16, (90):743-757; coauth, "Use of Sevoflurane during elective cesarean birth: A Comparison of Isoflurane and spinal anesthesia" Anesthesia and Analgesia 81 (95):90-95; coauth, "Placental transfer of selected substances of abuse", Sem in Perinatology 20 (96):147-153; coauth, "Effects of prenatal cocaine-exposure and postnal environment on child development", Am Jour of Human Biology (forthcoming). **CONTACT ADDRESS** Dept Human Develop, Univ of Texas, Dallas, PO Box 830688, Richardson, TX 75083. **EMAIL** tvanbe@mednet.swmed.edu

VAN DAM, DEEDEE
PERSONAL Born 02/05/1950, New York, NY, m, 1978, 2 children **DISCIPLINE** SOCIAL WORK **EDUCATION** Columbia Univ, MSW, 73. **CAREER** Adj Fac and Assoc Director of Counseling, Catholic Univ. **MEMBERSHIPS** NASW, ACSW, AASECT, Soc for Sex Therapy & Res, Am Asn of Ex Educator, Coun and Therapists. **RESEARCH** Sexual dysfunctions. **CONTACT ADDRESS** Dept Soc Welfare, Catholic Univ of America, 620 Mich Ave NE, Washington, DC 20064-0002.

VAN DE WALLE, ETIENNE
PERSONAL Born 04/19/1932, Namur, Belgium, m, 1956, 4 children **DISCIPLINE** SOCIOLOGY **EDUCATION** UC Louvain, LLD, 56; UC Louvain, NA, 57; UC Louvain, PhD, 73. **CAREER** Roes, Princeton Univ, 62-73; Prof, Univ Pa, 74-. **MEMBERSHIPS** Population Assoc. of Am, IUSSP. **RESEARCH** Historical demography, African demography. **SELECTED PUBLICATIONS** Auth, The Female Population of France in the Nineteenth Century, Princeton Univ Pr, 74; ed, Mortality and Society in Sub-Saharan Africa, Clarendon Pr (Oxford), 92; coauth, "Fatal Secrets and the French Fertility Transition," Population and Develop Rev, 21, no 2 (95): 261-279; coauth, "A Review of the Demographic Literature on the Status and the Condition of Women in Sub-Saharan Africa," in Women's Position and Demographic Change in Sub-Saharan Africa, IUSSP, Liege (95): 389-403; coauth, "Sexual Initiation and the Transmission of Reproductive Knowledge," Health Transition Rev, Suppl 6 (96): 61-68; auth, "Flowers and Fruits: Two Thousand Years of Menstrual Regulation," J of Interdisciplinary Hist, 28, no 2 (97): 183-203. **CONTACT ADDRESS** Dept Sociol, Univ of Pennsylvania, 3718 Locust Walk, Philadelphia, PA 19104-6298. **EMAIL** etienne@pop.upenn.edu

VAN DEN BERGHE, PIERRE L.
PERSONAL Born 01/20/1933, Lubumbashi, Congo **DISCIPLINE** SOCIOLOGY; ANTHROPOLOGY **EDUCATION** Stanford Univ, BA, 52; MA, 53; Harvard Univ, MA, 59; PhD, 60. **CAREER** Asst Prof, Wesleyan Univ, 62-63; Assoc Prof, SUNY, 63-65; Assoc Prof to Prof Emeritus, Univ WA, 65-. **RESEARCH** Ethnic and Race Relations; Social Stratification; Sociobiology; Kinship; Political Sociology; Age and Sex Differentiation; Tourism; Genocide Geographical specialization: Sub-Saharan Africa and Latin America. **SELECTED PUBLICATIONS** Auth, South Africa, A Study in Conflict, Wesleyan Univ Press, 65; auth, Race and Racism, A Comparative Perspective, New York, 67; auth, Man in Society: A Biosocial View, New York, 75; auth, Human Family Systems: An Evolutionary View, New York, 79; auth, The Ethnic Phenomenon, New York, 81; auth, Stranger in their Midst, Univ Press of Colo, 89; auth, The Quest for the Other: Ethnic Tourism in San Cristobal, Mexico, Univ WA Press, 94. **CONTACT ADDRESS** Dept Sociol, Univ of Washington, PO Box 353340, Seattle, WA 98195-3340. **EMAIL** pllvdb@u.washington.edu

VAN DER SLIK, JACK RONALD
PERSONAL Born 12/14/1936, Kalamazoo, MI, m, 1963, 3 children **DISCIPLINE** POLITICAL SCIENCE AND EDUCATION **EDUCATION** Calvin College, BA, 58; Western Michigan Univ, MA; Michigan State Univ, 67 MA, PhD. **CAREER** Instructor, Michigan State Univ, 67, Asst Prof to Assoc Prof, Southern Illinois Univ 67-78, Visiting Assoc Prof, Calvin College, 72-73, Academic Dean, Trinity Christian College, 78-81, Assoc Dean of Liberal Arts, Carbondale 75-78, Prof, Sangamon State Univ since 95, named Univ of Illinois at Springfield 81-98, emeritus to present. **HONORS AND AWARDS** Pi Sigma Alpha-political science honorary society, life member, Biography in Contemporary Authors, Listed in Who's Who in the Midwest; Who's Who Among Teachers 96. **MEMBERSHIPS** Amer Political Sci Assoc; Academy of Political Sci; Midwest Political Sci Assoc; Policy Studies Assoc; Christians in Political Sci. **RESEARCH** Amer national and state politics; Illinois politics; legislatures; religion and politics. **SELECTED PUBLICATIONS** Almanac of Illinois Politics, Institute for Public Affairs, editor, 90, 92, 94, 96, 98; Politics in the Amer States and Communities, A Contemporary Reader, Allyn & Bacon, 96; One for All and All for Illinois: Representing the Land of Lincoln in Congress Institute for Public Affairs, 95; Lawmaking in Illinois: Legislative Politics,People and Processes, 86; Amer Legislative Processes New York: Thomas Y. Crowell Co, 77; Clinton and the New Convenant: Theology Shaping a New Politics or Old Politics in Religious Dress?, Journal of Church and State, forthcoming; The Democratization of Legislative Politics in Korea, Korea Journal 37, No 4 p39-64, Doh C. Shin and Van Der Slik, 97; Contrain Congressional Behavior: Bipartisan Cooperation in the Illinois Delegation, Illinois Political Sci Review 2, no 1, p5-19, 96; A Polemic on Educ Reform in the Amer States, Social Indicators Research 27, no 3, p205-220, Doh C. Shinn and Van Der Slik, 92. **CONTACT ADDRESS** Dept of Political Studies, Univ of Illinois, Springfield, PO Box 19243, Springfield, IL 62794-9243. **EMAIL** jbvds@gate.net

VAN DYKE, ANNETTE
PERSONAL Born 11/09/1943, Sacramento, CA, d, 2 children **DISCIPLINE** WOMEN'S STUDIES **EDUCATION** Whitworth Col, BA, 70; Eastern Wash Univ, MA, 72; Univ Minn, PhD, 87. **CAREER** Instr, Bemidji State Univ, 78-81; Instr, Univ Minn, 81-87; Instr, Normandale Community Col, 87-88; Assoc Dir, Univ Cincinnati, 88-90; Asst Prof, Denison Univ, 90-93; Assoc Prof, Univ Ill, 93-. **HONORS AND AWARDS** Grant, Bemidji State Univ, 80; Am Studies Fel, Univ Minn, 85; Travel Grant, Univ Cincinnati, 90; Grant, Denison Univ, 91-92;

Curriculum Awds, Univ Ill, 95, 98; Fac Scholar Recognition Awds, Univ Ill, 94-99. **MEMBERSHIPS** Nat Women's Studies Asn, MLA, MELUS, MMLA, Native Am Lit Asn, Soc for the Study of Am Women Writers, ALA. **RESEARCH** Women's studies, native Am women writers, multicultural Am women's literature, women's spirituality. **SELECTED PUBLICATIONS** Auth, The Search for a Women-Centered Spirituality, 92; auth, Hooded Murder, 96; auth, "Paula Gunn Allen, June Arnold and Beth Brant," in Feminist Writers (96); auth, "From Big Green Fly to the Stone Serpent: Following the Dark Vision in Silko's Almanac of the Dead," Sail (98); auth, "Goddess Religion," Encycl of Lesbian Hist & Cult, 99; auth, "Of Vision Quests and Spirit Gaurdians: Female Power in the Novels of Louise Erdrich," in The Chippewa Landscape of Louise Erdrich (99); auth, "Dorothy Allison," Ref Guide to Am Lit (00). **CONTACT ADDRESS** Dept Women's Studies, Univ of Illinois, Springfield, PO Box 19243, Springfield, IL 62794-9243. **EMAIL** vandyke.annette@uis.edu

VANCE, CYNTHIA LYNN
PERSONAL Born 03/31/1960, Norwalk, CA, s **DISCIPLINE** PSYCHOLOGY **EDUCATION** Univ Ore, BS, 82; Univ Wisc, MS, 87; PhD, 91. **CAREER** Asst Prof to Assoc Prof, Piedmont Col, 93-98; **HONORS AND AWARDS** Who's Who in Am; Who's Who in Medicine and Healthcare; Who's Who in Sci and Engineering; Who's Who in the South and SW, Who's Who in the World; Who's Who of Am Women. **MEMBERSHIPS** Am Psychol Asn; SE Psychol Asn; Nat Col Honors Coun. **RESEARCH** Learning. **CONTACT ADDRESS** Dept Soc Sci, Piedmont Col, PO Box 10, Demorest, GA 30535. **EMAIL** cvace@piedmont.edu

VANDE KEMP, HENDRIKA
PERSONAL Born 12/13/1948, Voorthuizen, The Netherlands, s **DISCIPLINE** PSYCHOLOGY **EDUCATION** Hope Col, BA, 71, Univ of Mass, MS, 74; PhD, 77. **CAREER** Instr to prof, Fuller Theol Sem, 76-. **HONORS AND AWARDS** Community Building Awd, Fuller Theol Sem, 90; William Bier Awd, Am Psychol Assoc, 90; Fel, Am Psychol Assoc, 89; C. Davis Weyerhaeuser Awd for Excellence, Fuller theol Sem, 96; John Templeton Found Awd, 96. **MEMBERSHIPS** CHEIRON; Am Psychol Assoc; Am Assoc for Marriage and Family Therapy; Assoc for the Study of Dreams. **RESEARCH** History of psychology, with emphasis on psychology and religion; interpersonal psychology; family psychology; dream interpretation. **SELECTED PUBLICATIONS** Coauth, "How students learn integration: Replication of the Sorenson (1997a) model", Jour of Psychol and Theol 26 (99):340-350; coauth, "Humanistic psychology and feminist psychology" in Humanistic and Transpersonal Psychology: Historical and biographical sourcebook, ed D. Moss, (NY:Greenwood, 99), 125-144; auth, "Diana Baumrind: researcher and critical humanist" in Humanistic and transpersonal psychology: Historical and biographical sourcebook, ed D. Moss, (NY: Greenwood, 99), 249-259; auth, "Commentary: religion in the psychology of personality, Jour of Personality 67 (99):1195-1207; auth, "Grieving the death of a sibling or the death of a friend", Jour of Psychol and Christianity 18, (99):354-366; auth, "Lord Peter Wimsey in the novel. commedy of manners: Courtesy, intimacy, and the courage to be", The Lamp-Post 23.3 (99):11-23. **CONTACT ADDRESS** Grad School of Psychology, Fuller Theol Sem, 135 N Oakland, Pasadena, CA 91182-0001. **EMAIL** hendrika@fuller.edu

VANN, BARBARA H.
PERSONAL Born 06/19/1952, Birmingham, AL, d, 1 child **DISCIPLINE** SOCIOLOGY **EDUCATION** Univ Ala, BA, 74; E Tenn State Univ, MA, 79; Univ Ariz, PhD, 87. **CAREER** Assoc prof, Loyola Col, 94-. **HONORS AND AWARDS** Alpha Kappa Delta, Pi Gamma Mu; Florence Hemley Schneider Awd, 87; Grant, Dept of Human Res, Md, 88; Loyola Col Diversity Leadership Awd, 92; Grant, Loyola Col, 96, 98, 99; Grant, Baltimore City Dept of Soc Serv, 97. **MEMBERSHIPS** AAUW; ASA; MSSA; NAWCHE; NSEE; SSSI; SWS; SSA; Invisible Col. **RESEARCH** Gender, race and class. **SELECTED PUBLICATIONS** Coauth, "Politics and Pedagogy: The Creation of a Gender Studies Minor at a Jesuit College", Transformations, 3.2 (92): 47-55; coauth, "Cross-cultural Constancy of Reported Dream Use in Hawaii", Haw Med J 52.2 (92): 44-46; auth, "Child Care Needs of Welfare Recipients in Maryland's Welfare Reform Program", J of Sociol and Soc Welfare 20.2 (93): 69-88; coauth, "Reported Association of Stress and Dreaming: Community Background Levels and Changes with Disaster (Hurricane Iniki)", Dreaming 5.1 (95): 43-50; auth, "Sociology and Service Learning at Loyola College", Service Learning Across the Disciplines: Approaches and Perspectives, ed Ilona M. McGuiness, Loyola Col, 96; coauth, "Star Gazing: A Socio-cultural Approach To The Study Of Dreaming About Media Figures", Commun Quarterly 45.3, (97): auth, "Service Learning as Symbolic Interaction", Cultivating the Sociological Imagination: Concepts and Models for Service-learning in Sociology", eds J Ostrow, G Nessner and S Enos, Am Assoc for Higher Educ, (Washington, DC), 99. **CONTACT ADDRESS** Dept Sociol, Loyola Col, 4501 N Charles St, Baltimore, MD 21210. **EMAIL** bvann@loyola.edu

VANSINA, JAN
PERSONAL Born 09/14/1929, Antwerp, Belgium, m, 1954, 1 child **DISCIPLINE** AFRICAN HISTORY & ANTHROPOLOGY **EDUCATION** Univ Leuven, PhD(mod hist), 57. **CAREER** Resrchr, Inst Cent African Res, Belgium, 52-60, dir ctr, 57-60; vis lectr, Univ Lovanium, Leopoldville, 57-59; vis lectr, Northwestern Univ, 62-63; vis prof, Univ Lovanium Kinshasha, 66-67, prof, 71; vis prof, Univ Pa, 82; vis prof, Paris Sorbonne, 84-85; assoc prof, 60-64, prof, 64-73, 75-77, Vilas Res and JD MacArthur Prof, Univ Wis-Madison, 77- . **HONORS AND AWARDS** Quinquennial Prize, 67; Herskovits Prize, African Studies Asn, 67 . **MEMBERSHIPS** Fel African Studies Asn; Royal Acad Overseas Sci, Belgium; AHA; Int African Inst; Int Soc Folk Narrative Res. **RESEARCH** General social anthropology; African history; techniques and methods in culture history. **SELECTED PUBLICATIONS** Auth, Catastrophe and Creation--The Transformation of an African Culture, Jour African Hist, Vol 0034, 93; Ethnography and the Hist Imagination, Intl Jour African Hist Stud, Vol 0026, 93; Bantu Roots--French and English, Intl Jour African Hist Stud, Vol 0026, 93; History Making in Africa, Intl Jour African Hist Stud, Vol 0027, 94; Africa and the Disciplines--The Contribution of Research in Africa to the Social-Sciences and the Humanities, Intl Jour African Hist Stud, Vol 0027, 94; History in Popular Songs and Dances--The Bemba Cultural Zone of Upper Shaba Zaire--French, Jour African Hist, Vol 0035, 94; Valleys of the Niger--French, Jour African Hist, Vol 0036, 95; New Linguistic Evidence and the Bantu Expansion, Jour African Hist, Vol 0036, 95; Iron, Gender, and Power--Rituals, of Transformation in African Societies, Amer Hist Rev, Vol 0100, 95; African Masterworks in the Detroit-Institute-of-Arts, Jour African Hist, Vol 0038, 97; South-Pacific Oral Traditions, Jour Interdisciplinary Hist, Vol 0027, 97. **CONTACT ADDRESS** 2810 Ridge Rd, Madison, WI 53705.

VARACALLI, JOSEPH A.
PERSONAL Born 01/14/1952, Jersey City, NJ, m, 1988, 3 children **DISCIPLINE** SOCIOLOGY **EDUCATION** Rut Col, BA, 73; Univ Chi, MA, 75; Rut Univ, PhD, 80. **CAREER** Teach asst, Rut Univ, 75-78; adj prof, dir, Hud Cty CC, 78-81; instr, asst prof, assoc prof, act ch, asst dir, prof, Nass CC, SUNY, 81-. **HONORS AND AWARDS** Dante Aligheri Schlp Awd; Mellon Found Fel; NEH; Sab, NCC; Fac Ach Awd. **MEMBERSHIPS** SCSS; AIHS; FCS. **RESEARCH** Catholicism and social science; Catholics and political life; Italians and religion. **SELECTED PUBLICATIONS** Auth, Toward the Establishment of Liberal Catholicism in America, Univ Press Am (Lanham, MD), 83; auth, The Catholic and Politics in Post World War II America: A Sociological Analysis, Soc Catholic Social Sci (St Louis), 95; auth, Bright Promise, Failed Community: Catholics and the American Public Order, Lexington Books (Lanham, Maryland), 00; co-ed (in chief), The Catholic Social Science Review, vol 4, 99; co-ed, The Saints in the Lives of Italian Americans: An Interdisciplinary Investigation, Forum Italicum, Filibrary Series (Stony Brook, NY), 99; co-ed, The Italian-American Experience: An Encyclopedia, Garland Press (NY), 00; auth, "Catholicism, American Culture, and Monsignor George A Kelly: Reflections of and on a True Catholic Sociologist," Cath Soc Sci Rev 4 (99); auth, "Sharing or Secularizing Catholic Social Teaching?: A Reflection on the USCC Statement, Sharing Catholic Social Teaching: Challenges and Directions," Cath Soc Sci Rev 4 (99); auth, "Don Luigi Sturzo" in The Italian-American Experience: An Encyclopedia, Garland Press (NY), 00; auth, "Saints" in The Italian-American Experience: An Encyclopedia, Garland Press (NY), 00. **CONTACT ADDRESS** Dept Sociology, Nassau Comm Col, 1 Education Dr, Garden City, NJ 11530. **EMAIL** jjttlv@aol.com

VARALLO, SHARON
DISCIPLINE INTERPERSONAL COM, FAMILY AND GENDER COMMUNICATION **EDUCATION** PhD, OH State Univ, MA, Univ of NC, Chapel Hill, BA, Col of William and Mary. **CAREER** Comm, Cleveland St Univ. **SELECTED PUBLICATIONS** Co-auth, Dialectic of Difference: A Thematic Analysis of Intimates' Meanings for Differences, Interpretive Approaches to Interpersonal Communication, 94; auth, Family Photos: A Generic Critique, Rhetorical Criticism: Exploration and Practice, 96. **CONTACT ADDRESS** Commun Dept, Cleveland State Univ, 83 E 24th St, Cleveland, OH 44115.

VARDERI, ALEJANDRO
PERSONAL Born 01/17/1960, Caracas, Venezuela, d **DISCIPLINE** SPANISH, GENDER STUDIES **EDUCATION** Univ Central de Venezuela, BA, 84; Univ Ill, MA, 88; NY Univ, PhD, 95. **CAREER** Teaching Asst, Univ Ill, 85-88; From Instr to Assoc Prof, Bor of Manhattan Community Col, 93-. **HONORS AND AWARDS** Latino Recognition Awd, 88; Pennfield Fel, NY Univ, 93; BMCC Fac Develop Grant, 97; Res Awd, CUNY, 96, 98. **MEMBERSHIPS** AIH, LCI, ILI, MLA, NACH. **RESEARCH** Spanish and Latin American literature and film, gender studies. **SELECTED PUBLICATIONS** Auth, "Marco Antonio Ettedgui: A Profile," Latin Am Writers on Gay and Lesbian Themes, Greenwood Pr (94): 151-153; auth, Severo Sarduy y Pedro Almodovar: del barroco al kitsch en la narrativa y el cine postmodernos, Pliegos (Madrid, Spain), 96; auth, Anatomia de una seduccion: Reescrituras de lo femenino, Acad Nat de la Hist (Caracas, Venezuela), 96; auth, "Luis Lopez Alvarez: Literatura e identidad en Venezuela," Alba de Am, vol 16, no 30-31 (98): 365-369; auth, "Nueva York en Lorca," Verbigracia: El Universal (98): 2-3; auth, "Pasion y resurreccion del cuerpo de Marco Antonio Ettedgui," Verbigracia: El Universal (99); auth, "A La Recherche d'Isabel I Maria," in Voices and Visions: The Words and Works of Merce Rodoreda (Selinsgrove: Susquehanna UP, 99), 208-223; auth, Amantes y reverentes, Red Int del libro (Santiago de Chile), 99. **CONTACT ADDRESS** Dept Lang, Borough of Manhattan Comm Col, CUNY, 119 Chambers St, New York, NY 10007-1044. **EMAIL** avarderi@bmcc.cuny.edu

VARGAS, JULIE S.
PERSONAL Born 04/28/1938, Minneapolis, MN, m, 1962, 2 children **DISCIPLINE** BEHAVIOROLOGY **EDUCATION** Harvard Univ, AB, 60; Columbia Univ, MA, 62; Univ Pittsburgh, PhD, 69. **CAREER** Elementary school teacher, New York City and Monroeville, PA, 60-62; res assoc, Am Inst for Res, 62-64; res asst, Univ Pittsburgh, 64-66; fac member to prof, WV Univ, 66-. **HONORS AND AWARDS** Vis Scholar, Dept of Psychology, Harvard Univ, 93. **MEMBERSHIPS** Asn for Behavior Analysis; Sigma Xi; Int Behaviorology Soc; Phi Delta Kappa. **RESEARCH** Instructional design; verbal behavior; life and work of B F Skinner. **SELECTED PUBLICATIONS** Auth, Writing Worthwhile Behavioral Objectives, Harper & Row, 73; Behavioral Psychology for Teachers, Harper & Row, 77; with B M Stewart, Teaching Behavior to Infants: A Manual for Childcare Workers and Parents, Charles C Thomas, 90; with D Shanley, Academic Skills, in W O'Donohue and Leonard Krasner, eds, Handbook of Psychological Skills Training, Allyn and Bacon, 95; with E A Vargas, B F Skinner and the Origins of Programmed Instruction, in L D Smith and W R Woodward, eds, B F Skinner and Behaviorism in American Culture, Associated Univ Presses, 96; From Aircrib to Walden Two: B F Skinner as Social Inventor, in J P Cautela and W Ishaq, eds, Contemporary Issues in Behavior Therapy,: Improving the Human Condition, Plenum, 96; Problems in Vargas, J, Contributions of Verbal Behavior to Instructional Technology, The Analysis of Verbal Behavior, 15, 98; Commentary: Several other publications. **CONTACT ADDRESS** Dept of Educational Psychology, West Virginia Univ, Morgantown, Box 6122, Morgantown, WV 26506. **EMAIL** JVargas2@wvu.edu

VAUGHAN, STEPHANIE L.
PERSONAL Born 09/14/1955, Albuquerque, NM **DISCIPLINE** SOCIAL WORK **EDUCATION** Trinity Univ, BA, 77; Univ Tex, MSSW, 80. **CAREER** Social Worker, Child Protective Services, 80-85; Consultant, 85-89; Asst Prof to Assoc Prof, NMex State Univ, 89-. **HONORS AND AWARDS** Who's Who in the West, 88; Service Awd, NASW, 94; Donald C. Rousch Teaching Excellence Awd, 99. **MEMBERSHIPS** Soc Workers of S NM; Nat Asn of Soc Workers. **CONTACT ADDRESS** Dept Soc Work, New Mexico State Univ, PO Box 30001, Las Cruces, NM 88003. **EMAIL** stvaughn@nmsu.edu

VAZSONYI, ALEXANDER T.
PERSONAL Born 10/16/1964, Traverse City, MI **DISCIPLINE** FAMILY STUDIES **EDUCATION** Grand Valley State Univ, BS, 89; Univ Ariz, MS, 93; PhD, 95. **CAREER** Asst to assoc prof, Auburn Univ, 96-. **HONORS AND AWARDS** Acad Achievement Awd, Merit Awd, Northwestern Mich Col, 86; Cowden Scholar, Univ of Ariz; Gamma Sigma Delta; Int Fac Develop Grant, Auburn Univ, 96; Res Grant, Auburn Univ, 99. **MEMBERSHIPS** ASC; APA; NCFR; SRA; SRCD; ISSBD. **RESEARCH** Adolescent Development and Problem Behaviors, Etiology of Delinquent Behaviors and Delinquency, School-Work Nexus, Cross-national Comparative Method, Youth Violence Prevention and Program Evaluation. **SELECTED PUBLICATIONS** Coauth, "Peacebuilders: A theoretically driven, community-based model for early violence prevention", Am J of Preventative Med 12 (96): 91-100; coauth, "Caucasian and Hispanic early adolescent substance use: Parenting, personality, and school adjustment", J of Early Adolescence 16.1 (96): 71-89; auth, "Family socialization and delinquency: The United States and Switzerland", Europ J on Criminal Policy and Res 4.2 (96): 81-100; coauth, "Mating effort in adolescence: Conditional or alternative strategy", Personality and Individual Differences 23.1 (97): 105-115; coauth, "Early adolescent delinquent behaviors: Associations with family and school domains", J of Early Adolescence 17.3 (97): 271-293; coauth, "Adolescent apprentices in Germany: Job expectations, adult attachments, and delinquency attitudes", J of Adolescent Res, 13.3 (98): 254-271; coauth, "Who are they with and what are they doing? Delinquent behavior, substance use, and early adolescents' after-school time", Am J of Orthopsychiatry 69.2, (99): 247-253; coauth, "The utility of child self reports and teacher ratings in classifying official delinquency status", Studies on Crime and Crime Prevention 8.2 (99): 225-244; coauth, "Attachment and emotion: Predicting differential coping strategies in late adolescence", J of Youth and Adolescence 28.5 (99): 545-562; coauth, "Family processes and deviance: A comparison of apprentices and non-apprentices", J of Adolescent Res (forthcoming). **CONTACT ADDRESS** Dept Family Life and Develop, Auburn Univ, 284 Spidle Hall, Auburn, AL 36849. **EMAIL** vazsonyi@humsci.auburn.edu

VELICER, WAYNE F.
PERSONAL Born 03/04/1944, Green Bay, WI, m, 1981, 2 children **DISCIPLINE** PSYCHOLOGY **EDUCATION** Wisc State Univ, BS, 66; Purdue Univ, MS, 69; PhD, 72. **CAREER** Co-Dir, Cancer Prevention Res Cent Univ RI, 89-; Prof, Univ RI, 82-; Visiting Prof, Univ New South Wales, 94; Visiting Prof, Univ Limburg, 93. **HONORS AND AWARDS** One of 50 Highest Impact Authors in Psychol; Fel, Am Psychol Asn, Div 5; Fel, Am Psychol Asn, Div 38; Grant, NCI, 97-00; Grant, NIH/NAID, 98-01; Grant, NIAA, 99-03; Grant, PI, 99-00; Grant, NCI, 00-05; Grant, NIAA, 00-05. **MEMBERSHIPS** Am Asn of Univ Prof; Am Psychol Asn; Am Public Health Asn; Am Statistical Asn; Classification Soc; E Psychol Asn; Psychometric Soc; Soc of Beh Medicine; Soc for Clinical Trials; Soc for Multivariate Experimental Psychol; Soc for Res on Nicotine and Tobacco. **SELECTED PUBLICATIONS** Co-auth, "Time series analysis for prevention and treatment research," in The Science of Prevention: Methodological Advances from Alcohol and Substance Abuse Research, (Am Psychol Asn, 97), 211-249; co-auth, "Expert system interventions for smoking cessation and prevention," in GesundheitlichesRisikoverhalten im Jugenalter: Theoretische Konzeptionen und die Evaluation von Praentionsprogrammen, 98; co-auth, "Construct Explication through Factor or Component Analysis: A Review and Evaluation of Alternative Procedures for Determining the Number of Factors or Components," in Problems and Solutions in Human Assessment: Honoring Douglas Jackson at Seventy, 00; co-auth, "Health Behavior models," in SPM Handbook of Health Assessment Tools, Pittsburgh, 99; co-auth, "Expert systems for motivating health behavior change, in Beyond Advice: Changing Behavior in Health Organizations, Sage Pub, 99; co-auth, "Das Transtheoretische Modell--Eine Ubersicht (The Transtheoretical Model- -An Overview)," in Motivation for Behavior Change--Research and application of the Transtheoretical Model, (Freiburg: Lambertus, 99), 17-44; co-auth, "Predictions for the future of the Transtheoretical Model," Motivation for Behavior Change--Research and application of the Transtheoretical Model, (Freiburg: Lambertus, 99), 229-248; co-ed, Research Methods in Psychology, John Wiley & Sons, in press; co-ed, Research Methods in Psychology, in press. **CONTACT ADDRESS** Cancer Prevention Res Cent, Univ of Rhode Island, 2 Chafee Rd, Kingston, RI 02881. **EMAIL** velicer@uri.edu

VELTING, DREW
PERSONAL Born 09/20/1961, New Hyde Park, NY, m **DISCIPLINE** PSYCHIATRY **EDUCATION** Columbia Univ, BA, 83; SUNY, MA, 92; PhD, 95. **CAREER** Res Fel , Columbia Univ, 96-97; Asst Prof, Ball State Univ, 97-99; Asst Prof, Columbia Univ, 99-. **HONORS AND AWARDS** Grant, Am Foundation for Suicide Prevention, Viola Bernard Res Awd, Columbia Univ, 96; Res Fel, NIMH, 95-97. **MEMBERSHIPS** Am Asn of Suicidology, Task Force on Suicide Assessment, Am Psychol Asn, Asn for Advancement of Beh Therapy. **SELECTED PUBLICATIONS** Co-auth, "MACI personality scale profiles of depressed, adolescent suicide attempters: A pilot study," Journal of Clinical Psychology, in press; auth, "Suicidal ideation and the five-factor model of personality," Personality and Individual Differences, (990: 943-952; auth, "Personality and negative expectancies: Trait structure of the Beck Hopelessness Scale," Personality and Individual Differences, (990: 913-921; co-auth, "Parent-victim agreement in adolescent suicide research," Journal of the American Academy of Child & Adolescent Psychiatry, (98): 1161-1166; co-auth, "Asking adolescents to explain discrepancies in self-reported suicidality," Suicide and Life-Threatening Behavior, (98): 187-196; co-auth, "Auditory ERPs during rhyme and semantic processing: Effects of reading ability in college students," Journal of Clinical and Experimental Neuropsychology, (97): 1-18; co-auth, "Suicide Contagion," in Annual Review of Suicidology, 1997, Guilford Press, 97; co-auth, "Predicting three mood phenomena from factors and facets of the NEO-PI," Journal of Personality Assessment, (97): 165-172; co-auth, "Comorbidity and suicidality," in Treatment strategies for Patients with Psychiatric Comorbidity, Wiley Press, 97; co-auth, "Late cognitive brain potentials, phonological and semantic classification of spoken words, and reading ability in children," Journal of Clinical and Experimental Neuropsychology, (96): 161-177. **CONTACT ADDRESS** Dept Child Psychiat, Columbia Univ, New York, NY 10032.

VERBIT, MERVIN F.
PERSONAL Born 11/24/1936, Philadelphia, PA, m, 1965, 4 children **DISCIPLINE** SOCIOLOGY **EDUCATION** Univ Pa, AB, 58, AM, 61; Columbia Univ, PhD, 68. **CAREER** Instr to prof of Sociol, Brooklyn Col of the City Univ of New York; Dir, CUNY/Brooklyn Col Prog for Study in Israel; vis appointments at Bar Ian Univ, Hebrew Univ, Tel Aviv Univ, Yeshiva Univ, Jewish Theol Sem of Am, City Col; Dir, Interuniversity Fel Prog in Jewish Studies, 86-; Academic Dir, Mandell L. Berman Inst--North Am Jewish Data Bank, 98-. **HONORS AND AWARDS** Am Profs for Peace in the Middle East, Nat Chemn, 86-89, vice-chemn, 69-86; Fel, Jerusalem Ctr for Public Affairs, 78-, Secy-treas, 82-86; SEFER--The Moscow Ctr for University Teaching of Jewish Civilization, member, Int Advisory Coun, 97-; listed in: Who's Who in Am Jewry, Who's Who in World Jewry, Who's Who in Israel and Jewish Personalities Abroad. **MEMBERSHIPS** Joint Authority for Jewish Zionist Educ Commissioner; Am Zionist Youth Found; United Jewish Appeal-Federation of Greater New York Bd of Trustees; Nat B'nai B'rith Hillel Comn; United Jewish Appeal; Fedn of Jewish Philanthropies of NY; Anti-Defamation League of B'nai B'rith; Inst for Jewish Life; Am Jewish Congress; Coun of Jewish Fedns; Jewish Asn for Col Youth; Zionist Academic Coun; Asn for the Social Scientific Study of Jewry; Center for Jewish Community Studies. **RESEARCH** Sociology of religion, contemporary Jewry. **SELECTED PUBLICATIONS** Auth, "Is the Morality of Political Communities the Same as the Morality of Individuals?--Yes and No," in Daniel J. Elazar, ed, Morality and Power: Contemporary Jewish Views, Lanham: Univ Press of Am (90): 129-33; auth, "Content and Company: Jewish Identity and Choice of Friends among American Jewish University Students," in Menachem Mor, ed, Jewish Assimilation, Acculturation, and Accommodation, Lanham: Univ Press of Am (92): 246-61; auth, "Judaism in the 21st Century," contribution to a symposium in Menachem Mor, ed, Jewish Assimilation, Acculturation, and Accommodation, Lanham: Univ Press of Am (92): 304-12; auth, "Images of the Movements: Perceptions of American Jewish University Students," in Menachem Mor, ed, Jewish Sects, Religious Movements, and Political Parties, Omaha: Creighton Univ Press (92): 287-300; auth, "Intermarriage in the United States," in Encyclopedia Judaica Decennial Book 1983-1992, Jerusalem: Peter Pub House Ltd (94): 57-64; rev article, "Religion Timeless and Timely," on A Jewish Quest for Religious Meaning by Norman E. Frimer, in Tradition, Vol 30, No 3 (spring 96): 86-92; auth, "Zionism Today--Its Permanent Principles and Current Challenges," as chemn of the New York Sem in Zionist Thought and its Drafting Comt (97). **CONTACT ADDRESS** Dept Sociol, Brooklyn Col, CUNY, 2901 Bedford Ave, Brooklyn, NY 11210. **EMAIL** Mverbit@brooklyn.cuny.edu

VERSCHOOR, CHARLES V.
PERSONAL Born 06/25/1943, Sassenheim, Netherlands **DISCIPLINE** PSYCHOLOGY **EDUCATION** Old Dominion Col, BS, 65; Univ Georgia, MS, 67; Univ Miami, PhD, 81. **CAREER** Prof, Miami Dade Comm Col, 32 years. **HONORS AND AWARDS** Outstand Surv Awd. **MEMBERSHIPS** UFMDCC. **CONTACT ADDRESS** Dept Education, Psychology, Miami-Dade Comm Col, 11011 S W 104th St, Miami, FL 33176. **EMAIL** verschoor2@aol.com

VICK, LAURA G.
PERSONAL Born 12/07/1947, Whiteville, NC, m, 1968, 3 children **DISCIPLINE** ANTHROPOLOGY **EDUCATION** Univ NC at Chapel Hill, PhD, 77. **CAREER** Univ NC at Chapel Hill, 72-90 & 98-99; Univ NC at Greensboro, 84-90; from assoc prof to prof, Peace Col, 90-00. **HONORS AND AWARDS** Phi Beta Kappa, 70; NDEA Title IV Scholar, 70-; McCormick Teaching Awd, 95. **MEMBERSHIPS** Int Primatological Soc, Am Soc of Primatology, Mexican Asn of Primatology, Am Asn of Physical Anthropologists. **RESEARCH** Behavior/Conservation, Prosimians, Spider monkeys. **SELECTED PUBLICATIONS** Auth, Conserving monkeys and Mayans: initiation of a conservation/primatological project in Mexico, Southeastern Confr of Latin Am Studies (Chapel Hill, NC), 93; coauth, "Ecology and behavior of spider monkeys (Ateles Geoffrey) at Punta Laguna, Mexico," Am J of Primatology 36.2 (95): 160; coauth, "Poco a poco--steps toward spider monkey conservation in Mexico's Yucatan Peninsula, 1995 Chimpanzoo Confr (Tucson, AZ), 95; coauth, "Feeding opportunism, social organization, and breeding peaks in spider monkeys (Ateles geoffroyi) at punta Laguna, Mexico," Int Primatological Society/American Soc of Primatology Congress (Madison, WI, 96; coauth, "Changes in Behavior in Free-Ranging Lemur catta Following Release in a Natural Habitat," Am J of Primatology 47.1 (99): 15-28. **CONTACT ADDRESS** Dept Hist & Soc Sci, Peace Col, 15 E Peace St, Raleigh, NC 27604. **EMAIL** lvick@peace.edu

VICTOR, JEFFERY
PERSONAL Born 10/01/1941, New York, NY, m, 1965, 1 child **DISCIPLINE** SOCIOLOGY **EDUCATION** State Univ NYork, PhD, 74. **CAREER** Instr to prof, Jamestown Comm Col, 65-. **HONORS AND AWARDS** Chanc Teach Excell Awd; H L Mencken BK Awd. **MEMBERSHIPS** ISCLR; ASA. **RESEARCH** Sociology of deviant behavior; contemporary legends. **SELECTED PUBLICATIONS** Auth, Human Sexuality: A Social Psychological Approach, Prentice-Hall (Englewood, NJ), 80; auth, Satanic Panic: The Creation of a Contemporary Legend, Open Ct Press (Chicago, IL), 93; auth, "Hexanjagd! Eine Analyse der Satanismus-Hysterie," in Argumente und Kritik, eds. M Shermer, B Maidhof-Christig, L Traynor (IBCDK Verlag: Berlin, Ger, 96); auth, "The Future of Religion: The Next 50 Years," Humanist 56 (96): 20-22; auth, "Pseudo-Science in Psychotherapy," Skeptic (96): 101-103; auth, "Satanister og Syndebukker, "Humanist 96 (96); auth, "Moral Panics and the Social Construction of Deviant Behavior: A Theory and Application to the Case of Ritual Child Abuse," Sociol Persp 41 (98): 541-566; auth, "Social Construction of Satanic Ritual Abuse and the Creation of False Memories," in De Rivera, eds. J De Rivera, Theodore Sarbin, The Narrative Construction of Reality (98); auth, "The Spread of Satanic Cult Rumors, " in Science, Knowledge and Belief, ed. Kendrick Frazier (Prometheus Press, 98) **CONTACT ADDRESS** Dept Social Science, Jamestown Comm Col, PO Box 20, Jamestown, NY 14702. **EMAIL** victorjs@jccw22.cc.sunyjcc.edu

VIOLAS, PAUL CONSTANTINE
PERSONAL Born 05/04/1937, Rochester, NY, m, 1957, 4 children **DISCIPLINE** HISTORY OF EDUCATION **EDUCATION** Univ Rochester, BA, 59, MA, 66, EdD 69. **CAREER** Teacher US hist, Canandaigua Acad, 59-66; Prof Hist of Educ, Univ Ill, 68-; Assoc Dean, 82-; Assoc ed, Educ Theory, 70-. **MEMBERSHIPS** Hist Educ Soc. **RESEARCH** History of urban education United States; history of working class; class consciousness. **SELECTED PUBLICATIONS** Auth, Fear and freedom, Educ Theory, winter 70; The indoctrination debate & the Great Depression, Hist Teacher, 5/71; coauth, Roots of Crisis, Rand McNally, 73; auth, The Training of the Urban Working Class, Rand McNally, 78; Reflections on theories of human capital, skills, training and vocational education, Educ Theory, spring 82; co-ed, Readings in American Public Schooling, Ginn, 82. **CONTACT ADDRESS** Univ of Illinois, Urbana-Champaign, 375 Educ Bldg, Urbana, IL 61801.

VOIGT, DAVID QUENTIN
PERSONAL Born 08/09/1926, Reading, PA, m, 1951, 2 children **DISCIPLINE** HISTORY, SOCIOLOGY, ANTHROPOLOGY **EDUCATION** Albright Col, BS (history), 48; Columbia Univ, MA (Am hist), 49; Syracuse Univ, PhD (Hist, Socl Sci), 62. **CAREER** Teacher, state of NY, social studies, 50-56; assoc prof hist and social science, Millerville State Univ, PA, 56-63; assoc prof, sociology & anthroplogy, Muskingum Col, New Concord, OH, 63-64; prof of sociology & anthropology at Albright Col, Reading, PA, 64-95, prof Emeritus, 96-. **HONORS AND AWARDS** Winner of Lindback Distinguished Teaching Awd; Alumnus of the Year, Milton Hershey School, PA, 93. **MEMBERSHIPS** PA Sociol Soc (past pres); Am Anthropol Asn; Am Sociol Asn; Soc for Am Baseball Res (past pres); North Am Soc for Sports Hist. **RESEARCH** Am baseball studies--author of seven books on Am major league baseball; leisure in AM; Civil War hist. **SELECTED PUBLICATIONS** Auth, Thenk God for Nuts, in The Perfect Game, Marl Alvarez, ed, Dallas, TX, 93; The History of Major League Baseball, in 3rd ed of Total Baseball, 93; The League That Failed, Scarecrow Press of MD, 98. **CONTACT ADDRESS** Dept of Sociol, Albright Col, Reading, PA 19603.

VON BORSTEL, FEDERICO
PERSONAL Born 02/22/1950, Mexico, m, 1979, 1 child **DISCIPLINE** EDUCATION **EDUCATION** Univ Minn, BA, 72; Allende Inst, MA, 74; Univ of Americas, MA, 77; Univ Toronto, PhD, 82. **CAREER** Prof, 74-79, Metropolitan Univ; dir, planning & devel, 82-83, IberoAmerican Univ; chief acad off, 82-83, Univ Baja Calif; coord, Latin Amer rel, 84-86, assoc/adj prof, 86-97, dir, 86-89, career devel, dir, 84-89, So Bay Reg Ctr, US Intl Univ; principal, 89-99, Ed Planning & Devel Corp, San Diego, CA; prof, chmn, lib stud, dir res, 94-99, New School Architecture; executive vice-president, Newschool of Architecture, 98-00. **HONORS AND AWARDS** Fulbright Scholar. **RESEARCH** Educational planning, productive education, curriculum development. **CONTACT ADDRESS** 13527 Mountainside Dr, Poway, CA 92064. **EMAIL** executivevbe@newschoolarch.edu

VON EYE, ALEXANDER A.
PERSONAL Born 09/16/1949, Leipzig, Germany, m, 1973, 3 children **DISCIPLINE** PSYCHOLOGY **EDUCATION** Univ Munich, BA, 71; Univ Trier, MA, 74; PhD, 76. **CAREER** Res asst prof, Univ of Trier, Germany, 74-77; asst prof, Univ of Erlangen, 77-81; sr res scientist, Max Planck Inst, Berlin, Germany, 81-85; prof, PaState, 85-93; prof, Mich State Univ, 93-. **HONORS AND AWARDS** Summer fel, Stanford, 84; Biography in Who's Who in the World; Res Awd, Penn State, 90; mem of Scientific Comt, CIMAF Conferences, 96, 98, 2000; Fel, APA Div 5. **MEMBERSHIPS** APA, APS, ASA, Biomedical Soc, German Psychol Soc. **RESEARCH** Analysis of categorical data, longitudinal data, computational statistics, cognitive development. **SELECTED PUBLICATIONS** Coauth with R. AbuSabha, H. Smickilas-Wright, W. Harkness, and C. Achterberg, & G. Jensen,, "Reproducibility of food frequency questionnaire: diet and cognition," Am J of Clinical Nutrition, 65 (97): 1315 (abstract); auth, "Kognitive Komplexitat-Messung und Validitat, Zeitschrift fur differentielle und diagnostische Psychologie, 21 (99): 81-96; auth, "Standard and non-standard log-linear models for analyzing change in categorical variables," in R. K. Silbereisen & A. von Eye, eds, Growing up in times of social change, Berlin: de Gruyter (99): 225-244; coauth with L. P. Juang and J. P. McKinney, "The goodness-of-fit in autonomy timetable expectations between Asian-American late adolescents and their immigrant parents," Int J of Behav Develop, 23 (99): 1023-1048; coauth with J. V. Lerner and R. M. Lerner, "Modeling reciprocal relations at the level of manifest categorical variables," Multiciencia, 3 (99): 22-51; coauth with C. M. Ohannessian, R. M. Lerner and J. V. Lerner, "Does self-competence predict gender differences in adolescent depression and anxiety?," J of Adolescence, 22 (99): 379-411; auth, "Mit 65 in den Ruhestand?," Junge Gemeinde, 151 (99): 6-7; coauth with K. L.Clark, R. AbuShaba, and C. Achterberg, "Text and graphics: Manipulating nutrition brochures to maximize recall," Health Educ Res Theory and Practice, 14 (99): 555-564; coauth with E. Gutierrez-Pena, "A Bayesian approach to Configural Frequency Analysis, J of Mathematical Sociol, 24 (99)Z: 1-024; coauth with C. Spiel and G. Bohn, "Content analysis of an object sorting test of cognitive complexity," Int J of

Educ Res, 31 (99): 687-698. **CONTACT ADDRESS** Dept Psychol, Michigan State Univ, 119 Snyder, East Lansing, MI 48824-1117. **EMAIL** voneye@msu.edu

VON KELLENBACH, KATHARINE
PERSONAL Born 05/18/1960, Stuttgart, Germany, m, 1991, 2 children **DISCIPLINE** FEMINISM AND RELIGION **EDUCATION** Gymnasium Munich, Abitur, 79; Kirchliche Hochschule Berlin, Colloquiuum, 81; Georg August Univ Gottingen; Temple Univ, MA, 84, PhD, 90. **CAREER** Teaching Asst to Instr, Temple Univ, 85-88; Vis Lectr, Lehigh Univ, Spring 89; Vis Asst Prof, Lehigh Univ/Muhlenberg Col/Moravian Col (joint appointment), 90-91; Asst Prof Religion, St. Mary's Col of Md, 91-; Assoc Prof Religion, St. Mary's College, 00-. **HONORS AND AWARDS** DAAD Schol, Ger Acad Exchange Service, 83-84; Coolidge Colloquium, Cambridge, Mass, 86; Charlotte W. Newcombe Fel, 89-90; Fac Development Grants, St. Mary's Col, 91-98; ACLS Fellowship, 00-01; DAAD Study Visit Grant. **MEMBERSHIPS** Am Acad Relig; Soc Values in Higher Educ; Europ Soc Women Theol Res. **RESEARCH** Women and religion; Holocaust studies; Jewish-Christian relations. **SELECTED PUBLICATIONS** Auth, Anti-Judaism in Feminist Religious Writings, Schol Press, 94; God Does Not Oppress Any Human Being: The Life and Thought of Rabbi Regina Jonas, Leo Baeck Institute: Yearbook XXXIX, 94; Overcoming the Teaching of Contempt, Feminist Companion to the Bible, Sheffield Acad Press, 97; Reproduction and Resistance During the Holocaust, Women and the Holocaust, Univ Am Press (forthcoming); co-ed, Zwischen-Rame: Deutsche Feministische Theologinnen im Ausland, 00; author of numerous articles and other publications. **CONTACT ADDRESS** Dept Philosophy and Religious Studies, St. Mary's Col of Maryland, Saint Mary's City, MD 20686-0000. **EMAIL** kvonkellenbach@osprey.smcm.edu

VOSPER, JIM M.
PERSONAL Born 03/29/1947, Centralia, WA, s **DISCIPLINE** HISTORY, EDUCATION, PHILOSOPHY **EDUCATION** Saint Martin's Col, BA, 68; Univ Nebr, Lincoln, MA, 73, PhD, 76. **CAREER** Part-time instr, Centralia Col, 77-; part-time instr, South Puget Sound Community Col, 84-. **HONORS AND AWARDS** McNair Scholar Mentor, 96. **MEMBERSHIPS** Am Fedn of Teachers, Nat Educ Asn. **RESEARCH** Pacific Northwest history, educational history, religion in history. **SELECTED PUBLICATIONS** 19 biographical sketches for the three volume Biographical Dictionary of American Educators, 78. **CONTACT ADDRESS** Dept Humanities & Soc Sci, Centralia Col, 600 W Locust St, Centralia, WA 98531-4035. **EMAIL** jvosper@centralia.ctc.edu

VOSS, RICHARD W.
PERSONAL Born 08/27/1950, Philadelphia, PA, m, 1977 **DISCIPLINE** SOCIAL WORK, PASTORAL COUNSELING **EDUCATION** St Fidelis Col, BA, 73; Fordham Univ, MSW, 77; Wash Theol Union, Silver Spring, Md, MTS, 86; Loyola Col, PhD, 90. **CAREER** Asst prof, Neumann Col, Aston, Pa, 89-93; clinical work consult with Apogee, Inc, Long Term Care Div, King of Prussia, 95-97; Private Practice, Clinical Soc Work and Pastoral Counseling and Organizational Leadership Consultant, Glenmoore, Pa, 86-; appointed to prof staff, Villa St John Vianney Hospital, A Psychiatric Center for Healing, Downington, Pa, 95-99; asst prof, West Chester Univ of Pa, Dept of Soc Work, 96-. **HONORS AND AWARDS** Recipient of The Monsignor John O'Grady Awd, Nat Conf of Cath Charities, 84; Who's Who in Relig, 92-93; Who's Who Among Human Service Profs, 92-93; Certificate of Appreciation, Project Aware, Delaware Correctional Ctr, Smyrna, 98; President's Citation for Devoted Service, The Greater West Chester Sunrise Rotary Club, June 99; Certificate for Participation in Sponsored Progs Activities in the 98-99 Academic Year, Office of Grad Studies and Sponsored Res, West Chester Univ. **MEMBERSHIPS** Nat Asn of Soc Workers, Coun on Soc Work Educ, Am Asn of Pastoral Counselors. **RESEARCH** Alternative approached to healthcare and social work practice; traditional Lakota philosophies of help and healing; cultural competency; cross-cultural education, and issues in male development. **SELECTED PUBLICATIONS** Auth, "Two Wolves," and "Earthdance," in Ecotherapy: Healing ourselves, healing the earth, Howard Clinebell, Minneapolis, Mn: Fortress Press (96): 226, 225; auth, "Beyond the telescope of gender-polemics: Need for a wide angle lens in pastoral vision," Guest Editorial, J of Pastoral Care, Vol 51, 2 (summer 97): 133-137; rev of Pastoral Theology's & Pastoral Psychology's Contributions to helping heal a violent world," Michael Cordner, ed, Kurakarta, Indonesia: The International Pastoral Care Network for Social Responsibility and DABARA (96), J of Pastoral Care, Vol 51, 4, (97): 470-473; coauth, Wo'lakol kiciyapi: Traditional philosophies of helping and healing among the Lakotas. Toward a Lakota-centric practice of Social Work, J of Multicultural Social Work, Vol 7 1/2 (99): 73-93; ed, Select Readings. Topical Seminar in Social Work: Contemporary Issues in Indian Country, West Chester Univ, SSI Bookstore (May 5, 99); coauth, "Tribal and shamanic-based social work practice: A Lakota perspective," Social Work, Vol 44, 3 (May 99): 228-241; coauth, "Native American Medicine," Fundamentals of Complementary and Alternative Medicine, M. Micozzi, ed, St Louis, Mo: Mosby, Inc (in press); coauth, "Native American Medicine: Traditional Healing Practices of the Lakota Sioux," Doctors' Advise on Alternative Medicine, M. Micozzi, ed, Newton, Ma: Integrative Medicine Communications (in press). **CONTACT ADDRESS** Undergrad Dept Soc Work, West Chester Univ of Pennsylvania, McCoy Center, South Campus Dr, West Chester, PA 19383. **EMAIL** rvoss@wcupa.edu

VUCHINICH, RUDOLPH E.
PERSONAL Born 12/27/1949, Cumberland, MD **DISCIPLINE** PSYCHOLOGY **EDUCATION** Ind State Univ, BS, 73; Vanderbilt Univ, MA, 77; PhD, 78. **CAREER** Asst prof, Univ of Fla, 79-86; assoc prof, Wayne State Univ, 86-89; prof, Auburn Univ, 89-. **HONORS AND AWARDS** Fel, Vanderbilt Univ, 76-78; Outstanding Young Men of Am, 80; Who's Who in the S and SW, 82; Who's Who in Med and Health Care, 98; Grant, Auburn Univ, 98-99; Grant, Nat Inst on Alcohol Abuse and Alcoholism, 97-02. **MEMBERSHIPS** Am Psychol Soc; Southeastern Assoc for behav Analysis; Assoc for Behav Analysis; Soc of Psychol in Addictive Behav; Assoc for the Advan of Behav Therpay; Am Psychol Assoc. **SELECTED PUBLICATIONS** Coauth, "Behavioral economics", J of the Exp Analysis of Behav 64, (95): 257-262; coauth, "Alcoholic relapse, life events, and behavioral theories of choice: A prospective analysis", Exp and Clinical Psychopharmacology 4 (96): 19-28; auth, "Addiction as choice? Yes! As melioration? Maybe, maybe not", Behav and Brain Sci 19, (97): 597-598; coauth, "Does the repeated gambles procedure measure impulsivity in social drinkers?", Exp and Clinical Psychopharmacology 5, (97): 157-162; coauth, "Hyperbolic temporal discounting in social drinkers and problem drinkers", Exp and Clinical Psychopharmacology 6, (98): 292-305; coauth, "Temporal discounting and drinking in the laboratory and natural environment", Pharmacology, Biochemistry and Behav 61, (98): 158; auth, "Impulsiveness, temporal discounting, and alcohol abuse", Behav Pharmacology 10, (99): coauth, "Reliability of a measure of temporal discounting", Psychol Record, (forthcoming); auth, "Behavioral momentum and behavioral economic metaphors for excessive consumption", Behav and Brain Sci (forthcoming); coed, Reframing health behavior change with behavioral economics, Lawrence Erlbaum Assoc, (Mahweh, NJ), (forthcoming). **CONTACT ADDRESS** Dept Psychol, Auburn Univ, Auburn, AL 36849. **EMAIL** vuchire@mail.auburn.edu

W

WACHTEL, DAVID
PERSONAL Born 10/25/1943, Springfield, OH, m, 1983, 2 children **DISCIPLINE** SOCIOLOGY **EDUCATION** State Univ NY at Buffalo, BA, 69; MS, 76; PhD, 83; Univ Ky, MA. **CAREER** Instr, Erie County Sheriff's Dept Law Enforcement Training Acad, 74-76; adj instr, Law Enforcement Academy of the Navajo nation, 76-81; dir of Law Enforcement Training Acad & Criminal Justice Prog, Western NMex Univ, 76-81; instr, Western NMex Univ, 76-81; adj instr, Douglas Police Training Acad, 77-80; asst prof, Univ of Ala in Birmingham, 81-83; asst prof, Central State Univ, 83-94; adj instr, Law Enforcement Training Acad of Eastern Ky Univ, 85-; adj instr, Lexington Police Dept, 85-; instr, Lexington Community Col, 89-; Area Coord, Lexington Community Col, 90-. **SELECTED PUBLICATIONS** Auth, "An Historical Look at the BIA Police on the Reservations," Am Indian J 5 (80); auth, "Peyotism: It's Ritual, History and Legality," Wassaja/The Indian Historian 94 (80); auth, "Peyotism," Am Indian J, 3 (80); auth, "Indian Law Enforcement," Indians and Criminal Justice, Osmun publishers (Totowa, NJ), 82; auth, "The Navajo Police Officer: An Analysis of Their Traditionality and Assimilation," Quart J of Ideology 4 (87). **CONTACT ADDRESS** Dept Soc Sci, Lexington Community Col, 230 Maloney Bldg, Lexington, KY 40506-0235. **EMAIL** dwach1@pop.uky.edu

WADE, JENNY
PERSONAL Born 03/12/1952, Rowe, NY, m, 1991 **DISCIPLINE** PSYCHOLOGY **EDUCATION** TX Christian Univ, BA, 74; Fielding Inst, CA, MA, 91; PhD, 94. **CAREER** Prod mgr, Dresser Ind, TX, 74-79; mgr, Hanis Corp. TX, 79-85; dir, EAC, NY, 85-86; consul, NY, 86-90; dir, Integra Inc, PA, 90-93; pron, Cen Adv Human Stud, PA, 93-97; chair, Inst Trans Psychol, 98-; co-dir, Learn Collab, CT, 98-; prin, Res Adv, CA, 98-. **MEMBERSHIPS** SAC; SMN; ATP; SRAD; APPH; INS. **RESEARCH** Consciousness studies. **SELECTED PUBLICATIONS** Auth, "Physically transcendent awareness: A comparison of the phenomenology of consciousness before birth and after death," J Near-Death Stud 16 (98): 249-276; auth, "The phenomenology of near-death consciousness in past-life regression therapy: A pilot study," J of Near-Death Stud 17 (98): 31-54; auth," Mind and science: The impact of the new physics on psychology and the behavioral sciences," Am Asn Behav Social Sci J (98): 52-65; auth," Meeting God in the flesh: Spirituality in sexual intimacy," ReVision 21 (98): 35-41; auth, "Idealizing the Cartesian-Newtonian Paradigm as Reality: The Impact of New-Paradigm Physics on Psychological Theory," in Idealization VIII: Modeling in psychology, eds. J Brzezinski, T Maruszewski (Amsterdam-Atlanta, GA: Rodopi), 98; auth," The Love That Dares Not Speak Its Name, in Transpersonal Knowing: Exploring the Horizon of Consciousness, eds. T Hart, P L Nelson, K Puhakka (Albany, NY: State Univ NY Press), in press. **CONTACT ADDRESS** Dept Psychology, Inst of Transpersonal Psychology, 744 San Antonio Ave, Palo Alto, CA 94303.

WAELTI-WALTERS, JENNIFER
PERSONAL Born, England **DISCIPLINE** FRENCH AND WOMEN'S STUDIES **EDUCATION** Univ London, BA, 64, PhD, 68. **CAREER** Instr, Univ de Paris, 67-68; Prof French to Prof Emer, Univ Victoria, 68-, ch Fr dept, 79-84, instr, 79-, dir women's studs, 88-95. **HONORS AND AWARDS** Prize Best Work Pub French, Asn Profs de Francais des Univs Can, 89; Community Awd, Univ Victoria, 93. **MEMBERSHIPS** Can Fedn Hum; Hum Asn Can; Can Res Inst Advan Women; Can Asn Women's Studs; Sr Women Acad Admins Can. **SELECTED PUBLICATIONS** Auth, Fairytales and the Female Imagination, 82; auth, Jeanne Hyrvrard: Theorist of the Modern World, 96; coauth, Feminisms of the Belle Epoque, 94. **CONTACT ADDRESS** Women's Studies Dept, Univ of Victoria, PO Box 3045 Stn CSC, Victoria, BC, Canada V8W 3P4.

WAGNER, DAVID
PERSONAL Born 01/31/1950, Brooklyn, NY, m, 1980 **DISCIPLINE** SOCIAL WORK **EDUCATION** Columbia Univ, BA, 72; MSW, 76; Univ Mass, MLS, 80; Univ New York, PhD, 88. **CAREER** Assoc prof, asst prof, Univ Southern Maine, 88-; lectr, asst dir, Columbia Univ, 85-88; proj dir, AFSCME, 83-84; adj fac, Cornell Univ, LRC, 83-86 and Hofstra Univ Inst App Soc Sci, 84-85; org dir, RWDS U, AFL-CIO, 82-83; mgr, Ser Empl Intl Union, AFL-CIO, 78-80, 80-82; chair, prof, Univ Southern Maine. **HONORS AND AWARDS** C Wright Mills, Bk Awd; NEPCA Bk Awd. **SELECTED PUBLICATIONS** Auth, What's Love Got to do with it? A Critical Look at America, The New Press, Chanty, 00; auth, The New Temperance: The American Obsession with Sin and Vice, Westview, 97; auth, Checkerboard Square: Culture and Resistance in a Homeless Community, Westview, 93; auth, Quest for a Radical Profession: Social Service Careers and Political Ideology, Univ Press of Am, 90. **CONTACT ADDRESS** Dept Social Work, Univ of So Maine, 96 Falmouth St, Portland, ME 04104.

WAGNER, ROY
PERSONAL Born 10/02/1938, Cleveland, OH, d, 2 children **DISCIPLINE** MEDIEVAL HISTORY, CULTURAL ANTHROPOLGY **EDUCATION** Harvard Col, AB, 61; Univ Chicago, AM, 62, PhD, 66. **CAREER** Asst prof, South Ill Univ, 66-68; assoc prof, Northwest Univ, 68-74; Prof, Univ VA, 74-. **MEMBERSHIPS** Am Anthrop Asn **RESEARCH** Myth, cultural & religious conceptualization; Holographic world perspectives in Melanesia. **SELECTED PUBLICATIONS** The Curse of Souw, Chicago Press, 67; Habu, Chicago, 72; Lethal Speech, Cornell, 78; The Invention of Culture, Chicago Press, 81; Asiwinarong, Princeton, 86. **CONTACT ADDRESS** Dept Anthrop, Univ of Virginia, Brooks Hall, Charlottesville, VA 22903.

WAITE, LINDA J.
PERSONAL Born 10/25/1947, Ann Arbor, MI, m, 1974, 2 children **DISCIPLINE** SOCIOLOGY **EDUCATION** Univ Mich, MA, 69; PhD, 76. **CAREER** Demographer, Census B, 74-76; asst, Univ IL, Urbana, 76-80; sociol, Rand Corp, 80-91; assoc dir, 83-91; codir, 89-91; dir, 90-91; res assoc, 91-; comm chair, Univ Chicago, 91-95; res assoc, NORC/Univ Chicago, 91-; dir, 94-; co-dir, Cen Parents, Children, Work, 97-; prof, Univ Chicago, 91-. **HONORS AND AWARDS** Coun, ASA, 96-99; Pres, PAA, 95; Duncan Awd, ASA, 93; SRA. **MEMBERSHIPS** ASA; GSA; NCFR; PAA. **RESEARCH** The family; working families; aging. **SELECTED PUBLICATIONS** Coauth, " At Risk on the Cusp of Old Age: Living Arrangements and Functional Status Among Black, White, and Hispanic Adults," J Gerontol: Soc Sci 54 (99): 136-144; coauth, "Interrelated Family-building Behaviors: Cohabitation, Marriage, and Non-marital Conception," Demography (99); coauth, "The Case for Marriage," Doubleday (forthcoming); co-ed, "Ties that Bind: Perspectives on Marriage and Cohabitation, Aldine de Gruyter (forthcoming); coauth, "Emotional Satisfaction and Physical Pleasure in Sexual Unions: Time Horizon, Sexual Behavior and Sexual Exclusivity," J Marriage Family (00); coauth, "Trends in Men's and Women's Well-Being in Marriage," in Ties that Bind: Perspectives on Marriage and Cohabitation, coed. Aldine de Gruyter (00); auth, "Cohabitation: A Communitarian Perspective," in Strengthening American Marriages: A Communitarian Perspective, eds. in MK Whyte (contributions D Browning, W Doherty) Rowman and Littlefield (00); coauth, "Emotional and Physical Satisfaction with Sex in Married, Cohabiting and Dating Sexual Unions: Do Men and Women Differ?" in Studies on Sex, eds. E Laumann, R Michael (Univ Chicago Press, 00); coauth, "The Rise of the Dual-Worker Family: 1963-1997," in Women and Work in the Twentieth Century, eds. R Hertz, N Marshall (Univ CA Press, 00); auth, "The Negative Effects of Cohabitation," Responsive Community (00). **CONTACT ADDRESS** Dept Sociology, Univ of Chicago, 1126 E 59th Street, Chicago, IL 60637.

WAKEFIELD, JOHN F.
PERSONAL Born 01/28/1952, Chicago, IL, m, 1985, 2 children **DISCIPLINE** EDUCATION **EDUCATION** Univ Ill,

AB, 74; PhD, 81. **CAREER** Asst Prof, E Ill Univ, 81-82; Asst Prof to Full Prof, Univ N Ala, 82-. **HONORS AND AWARDS** Who's Who in Am Educ. **MEMBERSHIPS** Am Educ Res Asn; Text and Acad Authors. **RESEARCH** Creative thinking; Career development; Pedagogy. **SELECTED PUBLICATIONS** Auth, Creative thinking: Problem-solving skills and the arts orientation, Ablex Corp, 92; auth, "Problem finding and empathy in art," in Problem finding, problem solving, and creativity, (Ablex Corp, 94), 99-115; auth, Educational psychology: Learning to be a problem solver, Houghton Mifflin, 96; auth, "The development of creative thinking and critical reflection: Lessons from everyday problem finding," in Critical creative processes, (Hampton Press, 00), 253-272 **CONTACT ADDRESS** Dept Educ, Univ of No Alabama, 2 Univ N AL, Box 5046, Florence, AL 35632-0001. **EMAIL** jwakefie@unanov.una.edu

WALDNER-HAUGRUD, LISA
PERSONAL Born 08/20/1963, Willman, MN, 3 children **DISCIPLINE** SOCIOLOGY **EDUCATION** Mankato State Univ, BA, 85; MA, 87; Iowa State Univ, PhD, 92. **CAREER** Assoc prof, Univ of Houston-Downtown, 93-. **HONORS AND AWARDS** Res Excellence Awd; Teaching Excellence Awd, Iowa State Univ; Enron Teachin Excellence Awd, Houston. **MEMBERSHIPS** Am Sociol Asn, Nat coun of Family Relations. **RESEARCH** Sexual coercions, AIDS Knowledge, Domestic violence, Gay and lesbian issues, Political participation, Hate crimes. **SELECTED PUBLICATIONS** Auth, "Sexual Coercion in India: An exploratory analysis using demographic variables," Archives of Sexual Behavior (99): 759-774; auth, "Ethnic and sex differences in university students' knowledge of AIDS, fear of AIDS, and homophobia," Journal of Homosexuality, (99): 117-133; auth, "Coming out to parents: Perceptions of family relations, perceived resources, and identity expression as predictors of identity disclosure for gay and lesbian adolescents," Journal of Homosexuality, (99): 83-100; auth, "Sexual aggression in gay and lesbian relationships: A review of the literature and methodological critique," Aggression and Violence; auth, "Victimization and perpetration in gay and lesbian relationships: Gender Differences explored," Violence and Victims; auth, "Homosexual identity expression among lesbian and gay adolescents: An analysis of perceived structural associations, (96): 313-333; auth, "Male and female sexual victimization in dating relationships: Gender differences in coercion techniques and outcomes," Violence and Victims, (95): 125-136; auth, "Sexual coercion on dates: It's not just rape," Update on Law-Related Education, (95): 15-18; auth, "Variables associated with agricultural scientists' work alienation and publication productivity," Scientometrics, (93): 261-282. **CONTACT ADDRESS** Dept Soc Sci, Univ of Houston, 1 Main St, Houston, TX 77002. **EMAIL** waldnerL@dt.uh.edu

WALFORD, GERALD
PERSONAL Born 08/14/1937, Sudbury, ON, Canada, d **DISCIPLINE** PHYSICAL EDUCATION **EDUCATION** Univ NDak, BS, 61; Ithaca Col, MS, 65; Univ Md, PhD, 88. **CAREER** Instructor, Prince George's Cmty Col; Asst Prof, Dalhousie Univ; Asst Prof, E Stroudsburg Univ; Coach, Univ Wisc; Assoc Prof, Alice Lloyd Col. **MEMBERSHIPS** N Am Soc for Psychol of Sport and Phys Activity; PGA; Can PGA; Golf Coaches Asn of Am; Am Hockey Coaches Asn; Can Hockey Coaches Asn; Halifax Cent Lacrosse Asn. **RESEARCH** Proprioceptive and Visual Feedback on Learning the Golf Putt and Golf Pitch; Creating Power to the Baseball Swing; Learning Baseball Skills through Kinesthetic Feedback; Books on advanced strategies and drills for ice hockey; High speed photography of hockey fundamentals; Interval training program for ice hockey; Plasma Beta-Endorphin Response and Mood Alteration in Young and Old Males Following a Graded Exercise Test. **SELECTED PUBLICATIONS** Auth, Ice Hockey: An Illustrated Guide for Coaches, Ronald Press, 71; auth, Hockey Coaching, Masters Press, 93; auth, Hockey Skills and Drill Book, Masters Press, 93; auth, The Tao of Teaching - The Teaching Experience, American Press, 95. **CONTACT ADDRESS** Dept Soc Sci & Educ, Alice Lloyd Col, 100 Purpose Rd, Pippa Passes, KY 41844. **EMAIL** geraldwalford@alc.edu

WALKER, ALAN CYRIL
PERSONAL Born 08/23/1938, Leicester, United Kingdom, m, 1975, 1 child **DISCIPLINE** ANTHROPOLOGY **EDUCATION** Cambridge Univ, BA, 62; London Univ, PhD, 67. **CAREER** Lecturer, Makerere Univ Col, 65-69; Lecturer, Univ Nairobi, 69-72; Assoc Prof, Harvard Univ, 72-78; Prof, Johns Hopkins Univ, 78-95; Prof, Pa State Univ, 95-. **HONORS AND AWARDS** Guggenheim Fel, 86; MacArthur Fel, 88; Fel, Royal Soc, 99; Intl Foundation Prize, 98. **MEMBERSHIPS** Am Acad of Arts & Sci. **RESEARCH** Primate and Human Evolution. **CONTACT ADDRESS** Dept Anthropol, Pennsylvania State Univ, Univ Park, 409 Carpenter Bldg, University Park, PA 16802. **EMAIL** axw8@psu.edu

WALKER, CONNIE
PERSONAL Born 04/28/1933, Baltimore, MD, m, 1958, 4 children **DISCIPLINE** PHYSICAL EDUCATION, ENGLISH EDUCATION **EDUCATION** Wheaton Col, BA, 55; Olivet Nazarene Univ, MA Edu, 89; MA, 91. **CAREER** Phy ed, HS, 55-90; teach, HS, 90-93; adj prof, prof, Olivet Nazarene Univ, 93-. **MEMBERSHIPS** Phi Beta Kappa. **RESEARCH** Adult education; adult learning patterns; multiple learning styles. **SELECTED PUBLICATIONS** Auth, Triathlon Training Manual for Master Athletes, forthcoming. **CONTACT ADDRESS** Dept Communication, Olivet Nazarene Univ, PO Box 592, Kankakee, IL 60901-0592. **EMAIL** cwalker@olivet.edu

WALKER, DEWARD E.
PERSONAL Born 08/03/1935, Johnson City, TN, m, 1959, 6 children **DISCIPLINE** ANTHROPOLOGY **EDUCATION** Univ Ore, BA; PhD. **CAREER** Prof, Univ Colo, 69-. **HONORS AND AWARDS** Fel, Am Anthropol Asn, 65; Fel, Soc for Applied Anthropol, 65-98; Appreciation Awd, Pawnee Tribe of Oklahoma, 89; Nat Awd, Bureau of Land Management, 89; Boulder's Choice Awd, Univ CO, 94; Omer C. Stewart Memorial Awd, 94; **MEMBERSHIPS** Am Anthropol Asn; Soc for Applied Anthropol. **RESEARCH** Native Americans of western North America. **SELECTED PUBLICATIONS** Auth, "Kutenai at Bonners Ferry," in Native America in the Twentieth Century: An Encyclopedia, Garland Pub, 94; auth, "Coeur d'Alene," in Native America in the Twentieth Century: An Encyclopedia, Garland Pub, 94; auth, "Nez Perce," in Native America in the Twentieth Century: An Encyclopedia, Garland Pub, 94; auth, "Confederated Tribes of the Umatilla Indian Reservation," in Native America in the Twentieth Century: An Encyclopedia, Garland Pub, 94; auth, "Confederated Tribes of the Colville Reservation," in Native America in the Twentieth Century: An Encyclopedia, Garland Pub, 94; auth, "A Revisionist View of Julian Steward from the Northern Great Basin," Univ UT Press, in press; auth, Nez Perce Coyote Tales, Univ OK Press, in press; auth, Plateau Volume: HNAI, U.S. Govt Printing, in press. **CONTACT ADDRESS** Dept Ethnic Studies, Univ of Colorado, Boulder, PO Box 339, Boulder, CO 80309-0339. **EMAIL** walkerde@spot.colorado.edu

WALKER, GAIL
DISCIPLINE PSYCHOLOGY **EDUCATION** Okla State Univ, BA, 74; MS, 76; PhD, 78. **CAREER** Asst Prof, Marian Col, Found-du-Lac, Wis, 78-80; Cook Co Office of Special Educ, Chicago Ill, 80-81; From Asst Prof to Prof, Alfred Univ, 81-. **HONORS AND AWARDS** 8 Bi-Annual Excellence in Teaching Awds, 84-99; Citizen Ambassador to USSR, 89; Int Dir of Distinguished Leadership, 90; Sears Found Excellence in Teaching and Campus Leadership Awd, 91; Independent Col Fund of NY Teaching Excellence Awd, 93-99; Who's Who Among America's Teachers, 96, 98, 99; Outstanding Americans, 98. **MEMBERSHIPS** Found of Thanatology, Crisis Prevention Inst, Asc for Death Educ and Coun, Int Critical Incident Stress Found. **SELECTED PUBLICATIONS** Auth, "Crisis-care in critical incident debriefing," J of Death Studies, 14-2 (90): 121-133; auth, "Completed suicide sequelae," Asn of Death Educ and Coun: The Forum 4-IXX (93): 7-8, 14-15; auth, "Completed suicide sequelae," in Annual editions: Death, dying, and bereavement, ed. G.E. Dickson, M.R. Leming, and A.C. Mermann (Guilford, CT: Dushkin Publ Co, 94); auth, "Critical incident stress management," Jet Ink IX-2 (97): 4-6; auth, "The right to die: Healthcare workers' attitudes compared with a national public poll," Omega 35-4 (97): 339-345; auth, "Secular eschatology: Beliefs about afterlife," Omega (in press). **CONTACT ADDRESS** Dept Psychology, Alfred Univ, Saxon Dr, Alfred, NY 14802. **EMAIL** fwalkerg@alfred.edu

WALKER, T. B.
PERSONAL Born 05/21/1940, Utica, NY, m, 1988, 5 children **DISCIPLINE** LAW, SOCIOLOGY **EDUCATION** Princeton Univ, BA, 62; Univ Denver, JD, 67, MA, 69. **CAREER** Asst prof of Law, McGeorge Sch Law, Univ of the Pacific, 69-70; vis assoc prof of law, Univ of Toledo, 69-70; assoc prof of law, Indiana Univ, 70-71; Assoc prof to prof of law, Univ Denver, 71- . **HONORS AND AWARDS** Magna Cum Laude, 62, 67; Order of St. Ives; listed Who's Who in Am and Best Lawyers in Am Since 1987; ed-in-chief, family law q, 83-92. **MEMBERSHIPS** Fel, Am Acad of Matrimonial Lawyers; founding fel, Int Acad of Matrimonial Lawyers; ABA. **RESEARCH** Legal rights of children and the lawyer's role. **SELECTED PUBLICATIONS** Co-auth, Family Law in the Fifty States: An Overview, in Family Law Q, 85-93; auth, Family Law From A to Z: A Primer on Divorce, in Family Advocate, 90. **CONTACT ADDRESS** 6601 S University Blvd, Ste 200, Littleton, CO 80121. **EMAIL** TBWalker10@aol.com

WALKER, VALAIDA SMITH
PERSONAL Born Darby, PA, d **DISCIPLINE** EDUCATION **EDUCATION** Howard University, Washington, DC, BS, 1954; Temple University, Philadelphia, PA, MED, 1970, EdD, 1973. **CAREER** Temple Univ, Philadelphia, PA, Prof, 74-, chairperson, 80-83, assoc dean, 83-84, assoc vice provost, 84-90, vice provost, 87-90, Vice Pres for Student Affairs, 90-01. **HONORS AND AWARDS** Chapel of the Four Chaplains Service Awd; Special Educator of the Year, Sigma Pi Epsilon Delta, 1983. **MEMBERSHIPS** Former member, President's Commission on Mental Retardation; past president, American Association on Mental Retardation; PA Advisory Board on Special Education; William Penn Adult Community School Advisory Board, 1976-; Knoll/Shaffer Bi-Partisan Commission, 1989-; exec advisor, Caribbean Association on Mental Retardation. **CONTACT ADDRESS** Student Affairs, Temple Univ, Conwell Hall, 4th Fl, Philadelphia, PA 19122.

WALKER, WILLARD
PERSONAL Born 07/29/1926, Boston, MA, m, 1952, 2 children **DISCIPLINE** ANTHROPOLOGY, LINGUISTICS **EDUCATION** Harvard Univ, AB, 50; Univ Ariz, MA, 53; Cornell Univ, PhD (gen ling), 64. **CAREER** Res assoc, Univ Chicago Carnegie Cross-Cult Educ Proj, Tahlequah, Okla, 64-66; From asst prof to assoc prof anthrop, 66-77, prof Anthrop, 77-89; prof emeritus, 89-, Wesleyan Univ. **MEMBERSHIPS** Southern Anthropological Soc; SSILA. **RESEARCH** North American Indian languages; ethnology of North America; native writing systems. **SELECTED PUBLICATIONS** Auth, The Proto-Algonquians, Peter Ridder (Lisse), 75; auth, "Cherokee" in Studies in Southeastern Indian Languages (Univ Ga, 75); auth, "Zuni Semantic Categories," in Handbook of North American Indians, Vol 9 (Smithsonian Inst, 79); auth, "Cherokee Curing and Conjuring, Identity and the Southeastern Co-Tradition," in Persistent Peoples (Univ Az, 81); auth, "Wabanaki Wampum Protocol," Papers of the Fifteenth Algonquian Conference, Carelton Univ (Ottowa, 84); auth, "Literacy, Wampums, the Gud Buk and How Indians in the Far Northeast Read," Anthropological Linguistics (84); auth, "Creek Curing in Academe," in General and Amerindian Ehtnolinguistics in Rememberance of Stanley Newman, Moutou de Guryter, 89; coauth, The Early History of the Cherokee Syllabary, Ethnohistory, 93; auth, "Native Writing Systems," in Handbook of North American Indians, Vol 17 (Smithsonian Inst, 96); auth, "The Wabauaki Confederacy," in Special Issue in Honor of D. Frank T. Siebert, Maine Historical Quarterly (98). **CONTACT ADDRESS** Dept of Anthrop, Wesleyan Univ, Middletown, CT 06457. **EMAIL** wbwalker@kyud,com

WALLACE, WALTER L.
PERSONAL Born 08/21/1927, Washington, DC, s, 3 children **DISCIPLINE** SOCIOLOGY **EDUCATION** Columbia Univ, BA, 54; Atlanta Univ, MA, 55; Univ of Chicago, PhD, 63. **CAREER** Instr, Spelman Col, 55-57; assoc study dir, Nat Opinion Res Center, 60-62; instr to prof, Northwestern Univ, 62-71; vis adjunct prof, Columbia Univ, 69-71, 79-80; Staff Sociologist, Rusell Sage Found, 69-77; prof, Princeton Univ, 71-. **HONORS AND AWARDS** Vis scholar, Russell Sage Found, 68-69; fellow, Center for Advanced Study in the Behavioral Sciences, 74-75. **MEMBERSHIPS** Am Sociol Asn, Sociol Res Asn. **RESEARCH** Sociological theory; ethnicity, "race," and nationality in human society. **SELECTED PUBLICATIONS** Auth, Student Culture, 66; ed and introduced, Sociological Theory, 69; auth, The Logic of Science in Sociology, 71; auth, Principles of Scientific Sociology, 83; auth, A Weberian Theory of Human Society, 94; auth, The Future of Ethnicity, Race, and Nationality, 97. **CONTACT ADDRESS** Dept Sociology, Princeton Univ, 2-N-1 Green Hall, Princeton, NJ 08544-0001. **EMAIL** Wwallace@Princeton.edu

WALLERSTEIN, IMMANUEL
PERSONAL Born 09/28/1930, New York, NY, m, 1964, 3 children **DISCIPLINE** SOCIOLOGY **EDUCATION** Columbia Univ, BA, 51, MA, 54, PhD, 59. **CAREER** Columbia Univ, 58-71; prof, McGill Univ, 71-76; distinguished prof, Binghamton Univ, 76-99 (emer); senior res scholar, Yale Univ, 00-. **HONORS AND AWARDS** Honorary degrees, Univ Paris, 76, York Univ, 95, Univ Libre du Bruxelles, 96, Univ Nac Aut de Mexico, 98; mem, Am Acad of Arts and Sci, 98; **MEMBERSHIPS** African Studies Asn (president 72-73); Am Sociol Asn; Int Soc Asn (president, 94-98); Eco Hist Asn. **RESEARCH** Hist capitatism; modern-world system; structures of knowledge **SELECTED PUBLICATIONS** Auth, The Modern World-System, 3 vol, 74, 80, 89; Unthinking Social Science, 91; After Liberatism, 95; Utopistics: Or Historical Choices for the 21st Century, 98. **CONTACT ADDRESS** Dept of Sociol, Yale Univ, P.O. Box 208265, New Haven, CT 06520-8625. **EMAIL** immanuel.wallerstein@yale.edu

WALSH, JOSEPH A.
PERSONAL Born 12/23/1944, Evergreen Park, IL, m, 1966, 4 children **DISCIPLINE** SOCIOLOGY **EDUCATION** Loyola Univ, BS, 67; Loyola Univ, MSW, 69; Univ Ill, PhD, 78. **CAREER** Prof, Loyola Univ, 83-96; Dean, Loyola Univ, 96-. **HONORS AND AWARDS** NAWS: First Prof Paper Awd, 72; Fulbright Schol Awd, 98. **MEMBERSHIPS** NASW, Coun on Soc Work Ed, NCA, Comn on Higher Ed. **RESEARCH** Primary prevention, violence in the work place, organizational development, child welfare. **SELECTED PUBLICATIONS** coauth, "Murder in the Workplace: A Comparison of Corporate Response Models," EAP Digest July-Aug (87): 34-37, 66-69; Auth, "Reflections on Burnout and Values in the Social Service Profession," Social Casework 68 May (87): 279-284; Auth, "Clinician to Supervisor: Essential Ingredients for Training," Social Casework 71 Feb (90): 82-87; Auth, "Secondary Prevention: Clinical Treatment," in Dimensions of State Mental Health Policy, ed. Hudson, C * Cox, A., (NY. 90); coauth, "Using External Consultants in Social Service Agencies," Families in Society 71 May (90): 291-295; coauth, "The Clinical Doctorate: Developmental Milestones," Arete 16 summer (91):51-62; auth, "Should Doctoral Level Graduates in Social Work Be as Well Trained in Research as Those in Allied Disciplines?" in Controversial Issues in Social Work Research, ed. W. Hudson and P. Nurius (Boston: Allyn & Bacon, 94). **CONTACT ADDRESS** Dept Sociol, Loyola Univ, Chicago, 820 N Mich Ave, Chicago, IL 60611. **EMAIL** jwalsh3@luc.edu

WALSH, ROGER
PERSONAL Born BRISBANE, AUSTRALIA **DISCIPLINE** PSYCHIATRY **EDUCATION** Univ Queensland, MD 70, PhD 73. **CAREER** Univ Calif Irvine, Prof of Psychiatry, Philosophy, Anthropology. **RESEARCH** Transpersonal Psychology; Comparative Religion; Asian Psychologies and Philosophies; Meditation. **SELECTED PUBLICATIONS** Auth, Paths Beyond Ego: The Transpersonal Vision, co-ed, NY, Tarcher and Putnam. **CONTACT ADDRESS** Dept of Psychiatry, Univ of California, Irvine, Irvine, CA 92697. **EMAIL** Brlallie@uci.edu

WALTERS, GLENN D.
PERSONAL Born 09/21/1954, Trenton, NJ, m, 1976, 2 children **DISCIPLINE** COUNSELING PSYCHOLOGY **EDUCATION** Lebanon Valley Col, BA, psychol, 76; Indiana Univ of Penn, MA, clin psychol, 78; Texas Tech Univ, PhD, coun psychol, 82. **CAREER** Chief, psychol svc, US Disciplinary Barracks, 83-84; adjunct facul, St. Mary Col, 84-85; psychol svc, US Penitentiary, 84-90; psychol cons, Tirrell and Assoc, 85-90; psychol svc, Fed Correctional Inst, 90-92; adjunct facul, Chestnut Hill Col, 95-; adjunct facul, Penn State Schuylkill, 92-; psychol svc, Fed Correctional Inst, 92-. **HONORS AND AWARDS** Anderson-Swenson Scholar Awd, Texas Tech Univ, 78-79; Hea Prof Scholar Prog, US Army, 79-81; lic psychol, State of Penn, 90-; Drug Abuse Prog Psychol of the Year, Fed Bur of Prisons, 92; Info, Policy and Pub Affairs Div award for Outstanding contrib to res, Fed Bur of Prisons, 94, 98; assoc ed, Criminal Justice and Behavior, 92-; assoc ed, Intl Jour of Offender Therapy and Comp Criminol, 89-; cons ed, Jour of Mind and Behavior, 99-. **RESEARCH** Genetics of crime and alcohol; Outcome expectancies for crime, alcohol, and gambling; Effective interventions for crime and addictive behaviors; Development of an integrated theory of human behavior and intervention (Lifestyle Theory). **SELECTED PUBLICATIONS** Auth, "The Lifestyle Criminality Screening Form: Psychometric Properties and Practical Utility," Jour of Offender Rehabil, 27 (98): 9-23; auth, Changing Lives of Crime and Drugs: Intervening with the Substance Abusing Criminal Offender, Chichester, England, 98; auth, The Addiction Concept: Working Hypothesis or Self-fulfilling Prophesy, Allyn & Bacon (Boston), 99; auth, "Human Survival and the Self-Destruction Paradox: An Integrated Theoretical Model," Jour of Mind and Behavior 20 (99): 57-78; auth, "Psychotherapy Integration: Contributions from Lifestyle Theory," Jour of Psychotherapy Integration 8 (99): 147-159; auth, "Short-Term Outcome of Inmates Participating in the Lifestyle Change Program," Criminal Justice and Behavior 26 (99): 322-337; auth, "Behavioral Self-Control Training for Problem Drinkers: A Meta-analysis of Randomized Control Studies," Behavior Therapy 31 (00): 135-149; auth, Beyond Behavior: Construction of an Overarching Psychological Theory of Lifestyles, Praeger (Westport, CT), 00; auth, "Disposed to Aggress?: In Search of the Violence-prone Personality," Agression and Violent Behavior: A Review Journal 5 (00): 177-190; auth, "Spontaneous Remission from Alcohol, Tobacco, and Other Drug Abuse: Seeking Quantitative Answers to Qualitative Questions," American Journal of Drug and Alcohol Abuse 26 (00): 443-460. **CONTACT ADDRESS** Psychology Services, Federal Correctional Inst, Schuylkill, PO Box 700, Minersville, PA 17954. **EMAIL** gwalters@bop.gov

WALTERS, HUBERT EVERETT
PERSONAL Born 04/27/1933, Greenville, NC, d **DISCIPLINE** MUSIC **EDUCATION** NC Central Univ, BA 1951-55; vA State Univ, 1959; E Carolina Univ, MM 1963-65; Boston Univ, DMA (pending) 1969-; Boston University, School of Theology, pursing MDiv. **CAREER** TX Coll Tyler, TX, chrmn dept of Music 1965-66; Shaw Univ Raleigh, NC, asst prof Music 1966-69; Harvard Univ, lctr on Black Music 1970-74; Goddard Coll VT, lecturer on Black Music 1971-73; Boston State Coll, asst proj of Music 1971-82; Boston Coll, lecturer on Black Music 1982-; Univ of MA-Boston, asst prof of Music 1982-. **HONORS AND AWARDS** LO Kelly Awd Excell in Music NC Central Univ 1955; mem Pi Kappa Lambda; Natl Music Honor Soc; Martin Luther King, Jr flwshp Awd from Woodrow Wilson Fdn 1969. **MEMBERSHIPS** V pres NC State Music Teachers 1963; mem Music Educators Natl Conf; mem Amer Choral Dir Assoc; Omega Psi Phi Frat; deacon Emmanuel Bapt Church; minister, Worship at Peoples Baptist Church, Boston MA. **CONTACT ADDRESS** Univ of Massachusetts, Boston, Harbor Campus Columbia Pt, Boston, MA 02125. **EMAIL** hubert.walters@umb.edu

WALTERS, RONALD GORDON
PERSONAL Born 04/23/1942, Sacramento, CA, m, 1965, 1 child **DISCIPLINE** AMERICAN SOCIAL & CULTURAL HISTORY **EDUCATION** Stanford Univ, AB, 63; Univ CA, Berkeley, MA, 65, PhD, 71. **CAREER** Actg instr hist, Univ CA, Berkeley, 67-68; from instr to asst prof, 70-75, assoc prof, 75-81, prof hist, Johns Hopkins Univ, 81-, Nat Endowment for Humanities younger humanist fel, 74-75; Rockefeller Found hum fel, 77-78. **MEMBERSHIPS** Southern Hist Asn; AHA; Orgn Am Historians. **RESEARCH** Am reform movements; sexual attitudes and behavior; popular entertainment. **SELECTED PUBLICATIONS** Ed, Primers for Prudery: Sexual Advice to Victorian America, Prentice-Hall, 73; The Antislavery Appeal: American Abolitionism After 1830, Johns Hopkins Univ, 76; American Reformers: 1815-1860, Hill & Wang, 78, rev ed, 97; Signs of the times: Clifford Geertz and historians, Social Res, autumn 80; Popular Culture, In: Encyclopedia of the United States in the Twentieth Century (Kutler, ed), Scribner's, 96; ed, Scientific Authority in Twentieth-Century America, Johns Hopkins Univ, 97. **CONTACT ADDRESS** Dept Hist, Johns Hopkins Univ, Baltimore, 3400 N Charles St, Baltimore, MD 21218-2680. **EMAIL** rgw1@jhu.edu

WALTON, ELAINE
PERSONAL Born 09/14/1944, St George, UT, m, 1987, 4 children **DISCIPLINE** SOCIAL WORK **EDUCATION** Brigham Young Univ, BS, 66; MSW, 86; Univ Ut, PhD, 91. **CAREER** Asst prof, Ohio State Univ, 91-95; asst prof, Brigham Young Univ, 95-97, assoc prof, 97-. **HONORS AND AWARDS** Maurice Warshaw Scholar, Univ of Ut, 88; Outstanding Grad Teacher of the Year, Col of Soc Work, Ohio State Univ , 93; Honorable Mention Awd for published Res, Awded by the Soc for Soc Work and Res, 98; principle investigator for two Federally funded and two state funded res projs. **MEMBERSHIPS** CSWE, NASW, NAFBS, AASWG, SSWR, AHA, Fac Women's Asn-Brigham Young Univ. **RESEARCH** Family strengthening programs in the child welfare system. **SELECTED PUBLICATIONS** Co-ed with R. Davis and P. Sandau-Beckler, Empowering families: Papers from the ninth annual conference on family -based services, Riverdale, IL: Nat Asn for Family-Based Services; auth, Early provision of family preservation services to enhance child protective investigative and assessment decisions: The evaluation of an experimental model, Final Report, Grant pursuant to Bid #CG6055, Dept of Human Services, Div of Child and Family Services, Salt Lake City, Ut (98);auth, "In-home family-focused reunification: A six-year follow-up of a successful experiment," Soc Work Res, 22 (98): 205-214; auth, "Forgiveness as a therapeutic intervention: A model for LDS psychotherapists," J of the Asn of Mormon Coun and Psychotherapists, 23 (98): 71-95; coauth with C. Smith, "The genogram: A tool for assessment and intervention in child welfare," J of Family Soc Work, 3, 3 (99): 3-20; coauth with F. Dodini, "Intensive in-home family-based services: Reactions from consumers and providers," Family Preservation J, 4, 2 (99): 39-51; auth, "Combining child protective investigations with family preservation services: The evaluation of an experimental model," Res on Soc Work Practice (in press); auth, "Methods of social work with families," J Socionomia (in press); coauth with J. Roby, K. Harrison, C. Y. Roby, D. Spangler, and N. Stallings, "Preventing and healing from abuse," in D. Dollahite, ed, Strengthening Marriage and Family: Proclamation principles and scholarship, Salt Lake City, Ut: Bookcraft (in press). **CONTACT ADDRESS** Sch of Soc Work, Brigham Young Univ, 223 KMB, Provo, UT 84602. **EMAIL** elaine_walton@byu.edu

WANG, GUANG-ZHEN
DISCIPLINE SOCIOLOGY **EDUCATION** Univ Wisc-Platteville, MS, 92; Univ North Tex, PhD, 96. **CAREER** Asst prof, Russell Sage Col, 96-97; asst prof, gender studies coordr, Univ Ark, Little Rock, 97-. **HONORS AND AWARDS** Honorary Citizen of the City of Dubuque, Iowa, 91; Who's Who Among Students in Am Univs and Cols, 95; recipient of the Hiram J. Friedsam Awd for Outstanding Grad Student, 95; recipient of the David H. Malone Awd presented to exceptional student, 96. **RESEARCH** Women's reproductive health and reproductive rights, population, quantitative methodology. **SELECTED PUBLICATIONS** Auth, "Cai, Wen-mei, A Chinese Woman Sociologist," in Women in Sociology: Past and Present, New York: Whittier Pubs, Inc (97); coauth with Vijayan K. Pillai, Women's Reproductive Rights in Developing Countries, Ashgate Pubs Ltd, England (99); coauth with Vijayan K. Pillai, "Women's Reproductive Rights, Modernization, and Family Planning Programs in Developing Countries: A Causal Model," in Int J of Comp Sociol, Vol XL, 2 (99): 270-292; coauth with Vijayan K. Pillai, "Social Structural Model of Women's Reproductive Rights: A Cross National Study of Developing Countries," The Can J of Sociol, Vol 24, 2 (99): 255-281; coauth with Vijayan K. Pillai, "Women's Reproductive Rights and Social Equality," The Soc Sci J, Vol 36, 2 (99): 459-567; coauth with Vijayan K. Pillai, "Reproductive Rights in Developing Countries: An Assessment of Regional Variations," Mich Sociol Rev, Vol 13(99): 10-27. **CONTACT ADDRESS** Dept Sociol, Univ of Arkansas, Little Rock, 2801 S Univ Ave, Little Rock, AR 72204. **EMAIL** gxwang@ualr.edu

WAPNER, SEYMOUR
PERSONAL Born 11/20/1917, Brooklyn, NY, m, 1946, 2 children **DISCIPLINE** PSYCHOLOGY **EDUCATION** NYork Univ, AB, 39; Univ Mich, AM, 40; PhD, 43. **CAREER** Instructor and Tech Asst, Univ Rochester, 43-46; Asst Prof, Brooklyn Col, 46-48; Assoc Prof to Prof, Clark Univ, 48-. **MEMBERSHIPS** Am Asn for the Adv of Sci; Am Asn of Univ Prof; Am Psychol Asn; E Psychol Asn; MA Psychol Asn; N Eng Psychol Asn; Phi Beta Kappa; Psychonomic Soc; Sigma Xi; Soc for Psychol Study of Soc Issues; Soc for Res in Child Development; Coun on Undergrad Res. **RESEARCH** Developmental psychology; Environmental psychology; Perception and other cognitive processes **SELECTED PUBLICATIONS** Co-auth, "Linking organizational behavior and environmental psychology. Relations between environmental psychology and allied fields," Environment and Behavior, (95): 73-89; co-auth, "Relations between environmental psychology and allied fields," Environment and Behavior, (95): 100=108; co-auth, "Environmental psychology and health. Relations between environmental psychology and allied fields," Environment and Behavior, (95): 90-99; auth, "Toward integration: Environmental psychology in relations to other subfields of Psychology," Environment and Behavior, (95): 9-32; co-auth, "Age and gender differences in the nature, meaning, and function of cherished possessions for children and adolescents," Journal of Experimental Child Psychology, (96): 340-377; co-auth, "Cross-cultural differences in processes underlying sequential cognitive activity," Japanese Psychological Research, (96): 90-96; auth, "Restructuring of a complex person-in-environment system: The relocation of a university," MERA Journal, (96): 11-19; co-ed, History of developmental psychology in autobiography, Westview Press, 96. **CONTACT ADDRESS** Dept Psychol, Clark Univ, 950 Main St, Worcester, MA 01610. **EMAIL** swapner@clarku.edu

WARD, JEANNETTE P.
PERSONAL Born 06/19/1932, Oahu, HI, s, 2 children **DISCIPLINE** PSYCHOLOGY **EDUCATION** Birmingham-Southern Col, BA, 63; Vanderbilt Univ, PhD, 69. **CAREER** NSF Res. Asst, Iowa State Univ, 62; NSF Res. Asst, Vanderbilt Univ, 63; NASA Fellow, Vanderbilt Univ, 63-66; NIH Res. Fellow, Vanderbilt Univ, 66-67; Asst Prof, Memphis State Univ, 67-73; NIH Res. Fellow, Duke Univ, 70-71; Assoc Prof, Memphis State Univ, 73-76; Prof, The Univ of Memphis, 77-98. **HONORS AND AWARDS** Woodrow Wilson Fellow, Woodrow Wilson Scholarship Foundation, 63, Phi Beta Kappa Member, Phi Beta Chapter, Birmingham-Southern College, 63, Sigma Xi Member, Vanderbilt Univ, 66, MSU Sigma Xi Research Awd, 85, MSU SPUR Awd, Memphis State Univ, 88, Fellow, Am Psych Asn, 94, President-Elect, International Society for Comparative Psych, 96-98, President, International Society for Comparative Psych, 98-00. **RESEARCH** Biopsychology, primate behavior, laterality. **SELECTED PUBLICATIONS** Auth, "Analysis of lateralized components of feeding behavior in the ring-tailed lemur," Journal of Comparative Psychology 109 (95): 27-33; auth, "Relative efficiency of preferred and nonpreferred patterns of lateralized foraging in the gentle lemur," American Journal of Primatolgoy 36 (95): 71-77; auth, "Laterality in African and Malagasy prosimians, in L. Alterman, G. Doyle, & K. Izard (eds.), Creatures of the dark: The nocturnal prosimians (New York: Plenum (95): 293-309; auth, "An analysis of birth sex ratio bias in captive prosimian species, American Journal of Primatology 38 (96): 303-314; auth, "An assessment of temperment and problem-solving in the small-eared bushbaby (Otolemur garnettii), Journal of Comparative Psychology110 (96): 377-385; auth, "Origins and functions of laterality: Interactions of motroic systems, Laterality 2 (97): 279-303; auth, "Origins and functions of laterality: Interactions of motoric systems, in J. Fagot, L. Rogers, J. Ward, B. Bulman-Fleming, & W. Hopkins (eds.), Hemispheric specialisation in animals and humans, Hove (UK): Psychology Press Ltd (97): 280-303; auth, "Unexpected conservation of the X-linked color vision gene in nocturnal prosimians: Evidence from two bush babies, Journal of Molecular Evolution 45 (97): 610-618; auth, "Handedness in animals, in G. Greenberg & M. Haraway (eds.), Encyclopedia of Comparative psychology, New York: Garland Publishing Co, 98; auth, "Handedness, footedness, and language laterality: Evidence from Wada testing, Laterality 3 (98): 1-8. **CONTACT ADDRESS** Dept Psychology, Univ of Memphis, 3706 Alumni St, Memphis, TN 38152-0001. **EMAIL** j.ward@mail.psyc.memphis.edu

WARD, THOMAS W.
PERSONAL Born Syracuse, NY, 2 children **DISCIPLINE** ANTHROPOLOGY **EDUCATION** Univ Calif at Los Angeles, PhD, 87. **CAREER** Instr, Univ Southern Calif, 97-. **MEMBERSHIPS** SWAA, AAA. **RESEARCH** Urban Anthropology, Psychological and Medical Anthropology, Urban Gangs. **CONTACT ADDRESS** Dept Anthrop, Univ of So California, 3502 Trousdale Pky, Los Angeles, CA 990089-0007. **EMAIL** tww@usc.edu

WARNER, DENNIS A.
PERSONAL Born 04/27/1940, Idaho Falls, ID, m, 1962, 4 children **DISCIPLINE** EDUCATION **EDUCATION** Brigham Young Univ, BS, 64; Univ Ore, MS, 66; PhD, 68. **CAREER** From Asst Prof to Prof, Wash St Univ, 68-. **HONORS AND AWARDS** Phi Delta Kappa; Milton H Erickson Awd, 95; Henry Guze Awd, 96; Fac Excellence Awds, Wash St Univ, 97, 98; Fel, APA, 00; Who's Who in the West; Who's Who in Am; Who's Who in Am Educ. **MEMBERSHIPS** APA. **RESEARCH** Learning and instruction, assessment of student learning, hypnosis. **SELECTED PUBLICATIONS** Coauth, "Effects of Hypnosis on the Immune Response: B-Cells, T-Cells, Helper and Suppresser Cells," Am J of Clinical Hypnosis, 38.2 (95): 71-79; coauth, "Hypnosis Enhances Recall Memory: A Test of Forced and Non-Forced Conditions," AM J of Clinical Hypnosis, 40.4 (98): 297-305; coauth, "Brief Hypnosis Substitutes for Alprazolam Use in College Students: Transient Experiences and Quantitative EEG Responses," Am J of Clinical Hypnosis, 41.3 (99): 262-268; coauth, "Cortical Event Related Potentials Show the Structure of Hypnotic Suggestions is Crucial," Int J of Clinical and Exper Hypnosis, 47.1 (99): 5-22; coauth, "The Efficacy of Barabasz Alert Hypnosis and Neurotherapy on Attentiveness, Impulsivity and Hyperactivity in Children with ADHD," The Child Study J (forthcoming). **CON-**

TACT ADDRESS Dept Educ, Washington State Univ, PO Box 642114, Pullman, WA 99164-2114. **EMAIL** dawarner@mail.wsu.edu

WARNER, R. STEPHEN
PERSONAL Born 12/07/1941, Oakland, CA, m, 1979, 2 children **DISCIPLINE** SOCIOLOGY **EDUCATION** Univ Calif Berkeley, PhD, 72. **CAREER** Asst prof Sociology, Sonoma State Col, 67-78; actg asst prof, Univ Calif Berkely, 69-70; lectr to asst prof Sociology, Yale Univ, 70-76; asst prof to Prof of sociology, Univ ILL Chicago, 76-. **HONORS AND AWARDS** Guggenheim fel, 74-75; NEH, 91-92; Inst Advanced Study, 88-89 **MEMBERSHIPS** Am Sociol Asn; Asn for Sociol Relig; Soc for Sci Study Relig. **RESEARCH** Comtemporary American religion. **SELECTED PUBLICATIONS** Auth, New Wine in Old Wineskins, Univ Calif Press, 88; auth, A Work in Progress Toward a New Paradigm for the Sociological Study of Religion in the United States, Am Jour Sociol, 93; The Place of the Congragation in the American Religious Configuration, New Perspectives in the Study of Congragations, Am Congregations, Univ Chicago Press, 94; The Metropolitan Community Churches and the Gay Agenda: The Power of Pentecostalism and Essentialism, Sex, Lies, and Sanctity: Religion and Deviance in Contemporary North America, JAI Press, 95; Religion, Boundaries, and Bridges: The 1996 Paul Hanly Furfey Lecture, Sociol Relig, 97; Approaching Religious Diversity: Barriers, Byways, and Beginnings, Sociol Relig, 98; coed Gatherings in Disapora: Religious Communities and the New Immigration, Temple Univ Press, 98. **CONTACT ADDRESS** Sociology Dept M/C 312, Univ of Chicago, 1007 W Harrison, Chicago, IL 60607-7140. **EMAIL** rswarner@uic.edu

WARREN, DONALD R.
PERSONAL Born 09/27/1933, Waco, TX, m, 1957, 3 children **DISCIPLINE** HISTORY OF EDUCATION **EDUCATION** Univ Tex, BA, 56; Harvard Univ, ThM, 60; Univ Chicago, PhD (hist educ), 68. **CAREER** Prog dir social serv, Cambridge Neighborhood House, 56-60; dean students tutorials and social issues, College House, 60-62; dir studies adult educ, Ecumenical Inst, 62-64; asst prof hist and philos educ, Chicago State Univ, 65-69; assoc prof, Univ Ill, Chicago, 69, head dept policy studies, 70-79; Prof and Chmn Dept Educ Policy, Planning and Admin, Univ MD, College Park, 79-; Consult educ res, US Office Educ, 71-73; consult educ policy and hist educ, Holt, Rinehart, and Winston Inc, 72-79; chmn, Task Force Acad Stand, Am Educ Studies Asn, 76-78; Assoc ed, Educ Theory, 76-69; bd scholars, Potomac Educ Resources, 80-. **MEMBERSHIPS** Am Educ Studies Asn (pres, 75-76); Am Educ Res Asn (secy, 74-76); Ctr Study Democratic Inst; AHA; Hist Educ Soc. **RESEARCH** History of American education; history of federal education policy; education policy. **SELECTED PUBLICATIONS** Auth, Run for Office, Trial, Vol 29, 93. **CONTACT ADDRESS** Dept of Educ Policy Planning and Admin, Univ of Maryland, Col Park, College Park, MD 20742.

WARREN, JOSEPH DAVID
PERSONAL Born 04/02/1938, New York, NY, d **DISCIPLINE** EDUCATION **EDUCATION** North Carolina A&T Univ, Greensboro NC, BS 1969; Brandeis Univ, Waltham MA, MA 1973, PhD 1983. **CAREER** United Planning Org, Washington DC, dir of comm organization, 65-67; Policy Management System, New York NY, natl VISTA training coordinator, 67-69; Brandeis Univ, Waltham MA, exec dir of Upward Bound, 70-74; Commonwealth of Massachusetts, Boston MA, asst sec of educational affairs, 75-79; Northeastern Univ, Boston MA, urban asst to president 1979-82, dir of community affairs 1982-90, associate professor of African-American Studies, 90-. **HONORS AND AWARDS** MA Black Achievers Awds; Phi Kappa Phi Society Awd; First Annual MA Affirmative Action Awd; award for minority business from Gov of MA; Awd for Youth Service from Mayor of Boston; created & directed univ-based academy for pre-high schools; created & directed special higher educ opportunity for public housing residents; chaired Blue Ribbon Panel on Racial Incident, Newton MA; lead devel of MA business set-aside program. **MEMBERSHIPS** Pres, Devel & Training Associates; chair, Industrial Sites Devel Assn, Boston Mayor's Minority Business Advisory Council, MA Human Resource Center; mem, United Way of Greater Boston, Roxbury Multi-Service Center; trustee, Emmanual Coll. **CONTACT ADDRESS** Dept of African-Am Studies, Northeastern Univ, 132 Nightingale Hall, Boston, MA 02115. **EMAIL** jwarren@lynx.neu.edu

WARREN, MORRISON FULBRIGHT
PERSONAL Born 12/06/1923, Marlin, TX, s **DISCIPLINE** EDUCATION **EDUCATION** Ariz State Univ, BA, 48; MA, 51; EdD, 59. **CAREER** Phoenix Elem School Dist 1, teacher, 48-53, principal, 53-68; Ariz State Univ, Explt Progs Col Ed, dir, 68-84, prof emer, 84-. **HONORS AND AWARDS** Named one of four Outstanding Young Men of Phoenix Jr C of C 1958; Recipient of Natl Conference of Christians and Jews, Human Relations Awd w/Sandra O'Connor, (Western Region, Arizona). **MEMBERSHIPS** Mem 1966-70, vice mayor 1969, Phoenix City Council; pres Fiesta Bowl 1981-; life mem NEA; dir 1st Interstate Bank of AZ NA 1981-86; bd of dir Samaritan Health Svc until 1992, AZ Publ Svc, until 1994; State Bd of Education, Arizona, 1991-94; Far West Regional Laboratory for Educ, Res and Service, 1992-95. **CONTACT ADDRESS** Col of Education, Arizona State Univ, PO Box 870211, Tempe, AZ 85287.

WARREN, STANLEY
PERSONAL Born 12/18/1932, Indianapolis, IN **DISCIPLINE** EDUCATION **EDUCATION** Indiana Central Coll, BS 1959; Indiana Univ, MAT 1964; Indiana Univ, EdS; Indiana Univ, EdD 1973. **CAREER** DePauw Univ, dir black studies prof educ; Indianapolis Publ Sch, tchr admin; Indiana-Purdue Univ; Indiana Univ; Indiana Commn for Humanities, assoc; DePauw Univ, assoc dean. **MEMBERSHIPS** Fellowship & Grant, Carnegie; Wingspread; Eli Lilly; NSF; Natl Def Educ Act; John Hay; NEH; State Ethnic Studies Advisory Council; bd mem, Indiana Historical Society. **CONTACT ADDRESS** DePauw Univ, Asbury Hall, Greencastle, IN 46135.

WASHINGTON, EARL MELVIN
PERSONAL Born 06/22/1939, Chicago, IL, m **DISCIPLINE** EDUCATION **EDUCATION** Western MI Univ, BA 1963, MA 1968; Univ of MI, 1971; Western MI Univ EdD. **CAREER** Cleveland Public Schools, teacher 1963-68; Kalamazoo Valley CC, instructor 1968-70; Western MI Univ, asst prof communications 1975-82, assoc prof communications, dir black faculty devel prog 1982-, asst dean 1984-, associate professor, communications; The Institute for the Study of Race and Ethnic Relations, director, consultant, workshop presenter. **HONORS AND AWARDS** 2nd vice pres Kalamazoo PTA; various articles publ in communication, educ and communication quartery and black issues in higher education 1980-; press/publ dir Kalamazoo Metro Branch NAACP 1984-84; vice pres 100 men of Kalamazoo 1983-85; papers presented including at Natl Assn for Equal Oppty; Phi Kappa Phi. **MEMBERSHIPS** Knappen Voight Co, consultant 1977; Kalamazoo Valley Int Schl Dist, consultant 1979; WMU, dir blk college prog 1984. **SELECTED PUBLICATIONS** Several papers presented; co-author, College: The First Two Years. **CONTACT ADDRESS** Western Michigan Univ, 2020 Friedmann Hall, Kalamazoo, MI 49008.

WASHINGTON, MARY L.
DISCIPLINE SOCIOLOGY **EDUCATION** Johns Hopkins Univ, MA, 92; PhD, 97. **CAREER** Asst prof, Lehigh Univ, 96-. **MEMBERSHIPS** Am Sociol Assoc; Assoc of Black Sociol; Sociol for Women in Soc. **RESEARCH** Historical sociology, social construction of race and gender, sociology of U.S. census, mixed-race households, population and government statistics. **CONTACT ADDRESS** Dept Sociol and Anthrop, Lehigh Univ, 681 Taylor St, Bethlehem, PA 18015. **EMAIL** maw9@lehigh.edu

WASHINGTON, MICHAEL HARLAN
PERSONAL Born 09/25/1950, Cincinnati, OH, 3 children **DISCIPLINE** EDUCATION **EDUCATION** Raymond Walters Col, AA, 71; Univ of Cincinnati, BS, 73, MeD, EdD, 84. **CAREER** Univ of Cincinnati, learning skills specialist 74-79; Northern Ky Univ, learning skills specialist 79-80, dir of Afro-Amer Studies program 86-, assoc prof of history 80-. **HONORS AND AWARDS** Staff Developement grant, KY Council on Higher Educ 1979, 1980; Outstanding Professor of the Year, Northern Kentucky Univ, Professor of the Year, 1996; Raymond Walters College, Distinguished Alumni Awd, Raymond Walters College, 1996. **MEMBERSHIPS** Consultations Office of In-Service Educ No KY University 1980; United Christian Ministeries and Black Campus Ministries, University of Cincinnati 1980-81; University of Cincinnati Medical Ctr 1980; No KY Univ Div of Continuing Educ 1980-81; Inservice Tchr Training, Southwestern Business Coll 1982; Diocesan Secondary Social Studies Tchr, Thomas Moore Coll 1982; KY Assoc of Teachers of History 1981-; Black History Archives Comm 1985-; Phi Alpha Theta 1985-; Minority Students Retention Scholarship, No KY University, founder, 1986; African-American Studies Prog, No KY University, founder, 1986. **SELECTED PUBLICATIONS** Auth, poem "On Time," publ in American Poetry Anthology, 1986; author of book "Academic Success & the College Minority Student," 1986; co-author, "Undoing Racism," 1997. **CONTACT ADDRESS** Dir Afro American Studies Prog, No Kentucky Univ, 429B Landrum, Highland Heights, KY 41076. **EMAIL** washington@nku.edu

WASHINGTON, ROBERT ORLANDA
PERSONAL Born 02/08/1935, Newport News, VA, m, 1955 **DISCIPLINE** EDUCATION **EDUCATION** Hampton Institute, Hampton, VA, BS, 1956; Marquette University, Milwaukee, Wis, MA, 1966; University of Missouri, Columbia, MO, MS, 1968; Brandeis University, Waltham, MA, PhD, 1973. **CAREER** Greenleigh Assoc, New York, NY, sr research assoc, 68-72; University of Wisconsin-Milwaukee, Milwaukee, WI, assoc dean, 72-76; Ohio State University, Columbus, OH, dean, 76-82; University of Illinois, Champaign-Urbana, IL, dean, 82-86; Social Policy Research Group, Boston, MA, pres, 86-88; University of New Orleans, vice chancellor, 88-93, professor, currently; co-editor, Journal of Planning Education and Research. **HONORS AND AWARDS** Outstanding Teacher of the Year, 1975; Phi Kappa Phi, 1992; NDEA Fellow, 1968. **MEMBERSHIPS** Member, National Assn of Social Worker, 1976-90; commissioner, Council on Social Work Education Commission on Accreditation, 1978-81; Association of Collegiate Schools of Planning; URban Affairs Association. **CONTACT ADDRESS** Professor, College of Urban & Public Affairs, Univ of New Orleans, Lakefront Campus, New Orleans, LA 70148.

WATERMAN, THELMA M.
PERSONAL Born 06/10/1937, Hartford, CT, d **DISCIPLINE** EDUCATION **EDUCATION** Hartford Coll for Women, Hartford CT, AA 1969; Trinity Coll, Hartford CT, BA 1971; Yale Univ Divinity School, MDiv 1978. **CAREER** Proof oper bank 1956-57; dept store salesgirl 1959-61; Headstart Prog, teacher aide 1964-67; Trinity Coll, resident counselor of grad & undergrad students; City Hartford, teacher 1971; coll admin 1971-; Office of Community Affairs, Connecticut Coll, dir; New Haven Boys and Girls Club, New Haven CT, admin, 84-85; United Way of Southeastern Connecticut, Gales Ferry CT, assoc exec dir, 85-. **HONORS AND AWARDS** Delta Sigma Theta Sorority Awd, 1965; citationist, Lane Bryant Annual Awds Competition, 1965; Rudolph Haffner Awd for Community Service, Hartford Coll for Women, 1969; Samuel S Fishzoln Awd, Trinity Coll, 1971; Community Service Recognition, Norwich Branch NAACP, Norwich CT, 1980; Martin Luther King Jr Community Service Awd, Club Cosmos, New London CT, 1980; Certificate, Connecticut Advisory Council on Vocational and Career Education, 1985; Martin Luther King Jr Community Service Awd, Club Cosmos, New London, CT, 1980. **MEMBERSHIPS** Conducted leadership training sessions, community leaders devel manpower prog, workshops, seminars, conf prog evaluation; co-organizer of 1st public housing proj pre-school ctr 1963; group counselor, Parker Memorial Ctr Hartford 1967-68; counselor, Drop Outs Anonymous Hartford 1967-69; comm rep, Hartford Bd of Educ 1970; vice pres, Dwight School PTA Hartford 1970-71; pres, POWER Hartford 1970-71; bd mem, OIC 1972; United Way 1972; Connecticut Talent Asst Coop 1973-76; Southeastern Connecticut Youth Serv 1973-74; Info & Referral Agency 1974-77; vice pres, Black Seminarians 1974-75; Yale Univ Divinity School Comp Youth Serv 1972-75; Catholic Charities 1971-74; Educ Task Force Model City 1972-75; Minority Navy Wives Scholarship Comm 1972-74. **CONTACT ADDRESS** United Way of Southeastern Connecticut, Gales Ferry, CT 06335.

WATERS, MARY C.
PERSONAL Born 11/18/1957, Bronx, NY, m, 1993, 2 children **DISCIPLINE** SOCIOLOGY **EDUCATION** Johns Hopkins Univ, BA, 78; Univ Calif at Berkeley, MA, 81; MA, 83; PhD, 86. **CAREER** From asst prof to Harvard Col Prof of Sociol, Harvard Univ, 86-. **HONORS AND AWARDS** Grant, Nat Inst of Health; grant, Russell Sage Found; grant, Mellon Found; grant, Ford Found; grant, Rockefeller Found; grant, William T. Grant Found; Russell Sage Found Vis Fel, 91-92; Guggenheim Fel, 93-94. **MEMBERSHIPS** Am Sociol Asn, Population Asn of Am. **RESEARCH** Race and Ethnic Relations, Immigration. **SELECTED PUBLICATIONS** Auth, Black Identities: West Indian Immigrant Dreams and American Realities, The Russell Sage Found & Harvard Univ Press, 99; auth, "Explaining the Comfort Factor: West Indian Immigrants Confront American Race Relations," in Race, Class and Culture: Whites and Blacks in America, ed. Michele Lamont (IL: Univ Chicago Press, 99), 64-96; auth, "Immigrant Dreams and American Realities: The Causes and Consequences of the Ethnic Labor Market in American Cities," Work and Occupations 26.3 (99): 352-364; auth, "Sociology and the Study of Immigration," Am Behav Scientist 42.9 (99): 1264-1267; auth, "West Indians and African Americans at Work: Structural Differences and Cultural Stereotypes," in Immigration and Opportunity: Race, Ethnicity and Employment in the United States, eds. Frank Bean and Stephanie Bell Rose (Russell Sage Press, 99); auth, "Multiple Heritage Families in the United States: Patterns and Puzzles in Identity Choices," in We Are a People: Narrative and Multiplicity in Constructing Ethnic Identity, eds. Paul Spickard and W. Jeffrey Burroughs (Temple Univ Press, 00). **CONTACT ADDRESS** Dept Sociol, Harvard Univ, 530 William James Hall, 33 Kirkland St, Cambridge, MA 02138. **EMAIL** mcw@wjh.harvard.edu

WATERS, SHARON
PERSONAL Born 07/04/1945, Alamo, GA, m, 1963, 3 children **DISCIPLINE** EDUCATION **EDUCATION** Wake Forest Univ, BA, 73; Valdosta State Univ, MA, 77; NCar State Univ, EdD, 96. **CAREER** Dept Chair, Edgecombe Cmty Col, 85-. **HONORS AND AWARDS** Total Quality Trainer; NC Cmty Col Leadership; Inst for Sen Admin. **MEMBERSHIPS** NCCCSPA; NC Soc Asn; Phi Kappa; Sigma Phi. **RESEARCH** Older Students. **CONTACT ADDRESS** Dept Soc Sci, Edgecombe Comm Col, 2009 W Wilson, Tarboro, NC 27886. **EMAIL** waterss@edgecombe.cc.nc.us

WATKINS, PHILIP C.
PERSONAL Born 08/28/1957, Portland, OR, m, 1985, 3 children **DISCIPLINE** PSYCHOLOGY **EDUCATION** Univ Oregon, BA, 80; Louisiana State Univ, MA, 87; PhD, 91. **CAREER** Assoc prof, Eastern Washington Univ, 90-. **HONORS AND AWARDS** Deans Schl, 97. **MEMBERSHIPS** APA; APS. **RESEARCH** Memory bias in depression; gratitude; subjective well being. **SELECTED PUBLICATIONS** Coauth, "Equivalence of items on the Mini-Mental State," Archives

Clinical Neuropsychol 4 (89): 381-384; coauth, "Unconscious memory bias in depression: Perceptual and conceptual processes," J Abnormal Psychol; coauth, "Mood-congruent memory in depression: Emotional priming or elaboration?" J Abnormal Psychol 101 (92): 581-586; coauth, "Unconscious mood-congruent memory bias in depression," J Abnormal Psychol 1 (96): 34-41; coauth, "Prospective assessment of late-luteal dysphoria," J Psychopathology and Behavioral Assess 11(90): 249-259. **CONTACT ADDRESS** Dept Psychology, Eastern Washington Univ, M/S 94, Cheney, WA 99004. **EMAIL** philip.watkins@mail.ewu.edu

WATSON, DWIGHT C.
PERSONAL Born 12/14/1961, Sumter, SC, s **DISCIPLINE** EDUCATION **EDUCATION** Univ SCar, BA, 83; MA, 85; NCar State Univ, EdD, 94. **CAREER** Teacher, Wake County Schools, 87-94; Asst Prof, Campbell Univ, 94-96; Asst Prof, Hamline Univ, 96-. **HONORS AND AWARDS** Teacher of the Year, Wake Cty, 91; AILACTE Scholar Awd, 99; Eisenhower Grant, 99; Environmental Educ Grant, 00. **MEMBERSHIPS** AACTE; IRA; ASCD; NCTE; ACEI; Am Asn of Col of Teacher Educ; Asn of Supervision & Curriculum Dev. **RESEARCH** Literacy development; Conflict resolution; Portfolio assessment; Service learning. **SELECTED PUBLICATIONS** Auth, "Conflict resolution as curriculum: A definition, description, and process for integration in core curricula," The School Counselor, (96): 345-373; auth, "Expecting the best . . . Getting the most," Hamline Review, (97): 38-42; auth, "A look at portfolios: Process to product," AILACTE Views and News, (97): 11-14; auth, "Hamline University and Hancock Elementary School: The history of a collaborative partnership," Hamline Review, (98): 51-66; auth, "Literacy development: An integrated approach," AILACTE Views and News, (98): 8-9; auth, "A collaborative partnership: Where college begins in kindergarten," AILACTE Views and News, (99): 14-16. **CONTACT ADDRESS** Dept Educ, Hamline Univ, 1536 Hewitt Ave, Saint Paul, MN 55104. **EMAIL** dwatson@gw.hamline.edu

WATSON, JACK B.
PERSONAL Born 01/15/1954, Tyler, TX, m, 1978, 2 children **DISCIPLINE** SOCIOLOGY **EDUCATION** Univ La Monroe, BA; Tex Christian Univ, MA; Univ N Tex, PhD. **CAREER** Asst prof, Miss Col, 81-91; from asst prof to assoc prof, Stephen F. Austin State Univ, 91-. **HONORS AND AWARDS** Outstanding Alumni, 97. **MEMBERSHIPS** Nat Soc for Experiential Educ, Mid-South Sociol Asn. **RESEARCH** Service-learning, Gerontology, Volunteerism. **SELECTED PUBLICATIONS** Auth, "Service-learning and Elder care," New Horizons, 97; auth, "Alcohol Use and the Elderly: A Durkheimian Model," Southwest J on Aging, 93. **CONTACT ADDRESS** Sociol Anthrop, Stephen F. Austin State Univ, PO Box 13047, Nacogdoches, TX 75961. **EMAIL** jwatson@sfasu

WATSON, MARY ANN
PERSONAL Born 01/27/1944, OH, m, 1978, 3 children **DISCIPLINE** PSYCHOLOGY **EDUCATION** Grove City Col, BA, 66; Univ Pittsburgh, MA, 67; PhD, 69. **CAREER** Asst prof, Community Col of Philadelphia, 69-70; clinical psychol, Navaho and Hopi Reservations, 70-72; res assoc, The Johns Hopkins Univ Sch of Med, Psychohormonal Res Unit, 72-73; res assoc, Univ Colo Health Scis Center, 73-77; vis prof, Univ Colo, 79-82; vis prof, Univ of Denver, 86-88; vis prof, St Thomas Theol Sem, spring 93 & 95; clinical psychol, licensed by the Colo State Bd of Psychol Examiners, 75-; asst prof, Metropolitan State Col of Denver, 74-78, assoc prof, 78-82, prof, 82-. **MEMBERSHIPS** Colo Psychol Asn. **RESEARCH** Female circumcision/slavery; Indian cuastoms; videos for educational prrograms. **SELECTED PUBLICATIONS** Coproducer with A. Dahms, Videocases in Human Sexuality, Boston: McGraw-Hill (96); coauth with A. Dahms, Instructor's Manual to Accompany Videocases in Human Sexuality, Boston: McGraw-Hill (96); Coproducer with A. Dahms, Videocases in Human Develoment, Boston: McGraw-Hill (98); coauth with A. Dahms, S, Montgomery, and D. Fanatia, Instructor's Manual to Accompany Videocases in Human Development, Boston: McGraw-Hill 998); coproducer with R. K'okul, Rites of Passage: Videocases of Traditional African Peoples, Englewood Cliffs, NJ: Prentice Hall (99); coauth with S. Montgomery, Instructor's Manual to Accompany Rites of Passage: Videocases of Traditional African Peoples, Englewood Cliffs, NJ: Prentice Hall (99); auth, "Psychology of Sexuality," in D. Spender and C. Kramarae, eds, Routledge International Encyclopedia of Women's Studies, New york, NY: Routledge (2000); coauth with A. H. Thobhani, "Introduction: Why Kenya?," in M. A. Watson, Modern Kenya: Social Issues and Perspectives, Lanham, Md: Univ Press Am (2000); auth, "Rites of Passage: Birthing, Naming, Coming of Age, Marriage, Elderhood, Widowhood, Death," in in M. A. Watson, Modern Kenya: Social Issues and Perspectives, Lanham, Md: Univ Press Am (2000); ed, Modern Kenya: Social Issues and Perspectives, Lanham, Md: Univ Press Am (2000). **CONTACT ADDRESS** Dept Psychol, Metropolitan State Col of Denver, PO Box 173362, Denver, CO 80217. **EMAIL** watsonm@mscd.edu

WATSON, WILBUR H.
PERSONAL Born 04/14/1938, Cleveland, m **DISCIPLINE** SOCIOLOGY **EDUCATION** Kent St U, BA 1964, MA 1966; Univ of PA, PhD 1972. **CAREER** Temple Univ Phila, asst prof of Soc 1973-; Rutgers Coll, asst prof of Soc 1970-74; Cheyney St Coll, asst prof of soc 1969-70; Kent St Univ, instr 1966-68; Lincoln Univ, instr 1966-68. **HONORS AND AWARDS** Numerous flwshps & awards. **MEMBERSHIPS** Mem Am Soclgcl Assn; Soc for Study of Soc Problems; Assn of Black Soclgsts; Assn for Study of African Am Life & Hist; Assn of Soc & Behvrl Scientests; mem bd govs Ctr for Rsrch on Acts of Man Univ of PA 1969-70; chmn steering com Proj-Learn;Exprmntl Elem Sch 1970-71; steering com Nat Black Alliance for Grad Level Ed 1972-74; cnsltng rsrch soclgst Stephen Smith Geriatric Ctr Philadelphia 1972-; founding ed The Black Soclgst 1975-. **SELECTED PUBLICATIONS** Author of "Hum Aging & Dying" (with RJ Maxwell) 1977; "Stress & Old Age" 1980; other Publications. **CONTACT ADDRESS** Department of Sociology, Temple Univ, Philadelphia, PA 19122.

WATT, NORMAN F.
PERSONAL Born 05/26/1935, Richmond, IN, m, 1958, 3 children **DISCIPLINE** PSYCHOLOGY **EDUCATION** Northwestern Univ, BA, 57; Oh State Univ, MA, 60; PhD, 62. **CAREER** Asst Prof to Lecturer, Harvard Univ, 64-70; Assoc Prof to Prof, Univ Mass, 70-78; Prof, Univ Denver, 78-. **HONORS AND AWARDS** Fel, Univ Munich, 58; U.S. Public Health Service Fel, OH State Univ, 59; NIMH Fel, Swiss Fed Inst of Tech, 63; Ford Intl Res Fel, goettingen Germany, 67. **MEMBERSHIPS** Am Psychol Soc; Soc for Res in Psychopathol; Soc for Res in Childhood Dev; Soc for Life Hist Res in Psychopathol; Am Asn for Adv and Prevention in Psychol **RESEARCH** Longitudinal study of schizophrenia; Personality and intellectual development; Emotional vulnerability in adolescence; Psychological development of public school children, especially ethnic minorities; financial planning and institutional change in universities; Head start; Early head start; child care; Welfare reform. **SELECTED PUBLICATIONS** Co-auth, "Death of a parent as an etiological factor in schizophrenia," American Journal of Orthopsychiatry, (79): 465-473; co-auth, "Toward longitudinal conceptions of psychiatric disorder," in Progress in experimental personality research, vol 9, (Academic Press, 79), 199-283; co-auth, the abnormal personality, 5th ed, Wiley, 81; co-auth, "Social, emotional and intellectual functioning at school among children at high risk for schizophrenia," Journal of Consulting and Clinical Psychology, *82): 171-181; co-ed, children at risk for schizophrenia: A longitudinal perspective, Cambridge Univ press, 84; auth, "Risk research in schizophrenia and other major psychological disorders," in A decade of progress in primary prevention, (N Eng Univ Press, 86), 115-153; co-auth, A psychological study of educational attainment among Hispanics, Denver, 87; co-auth, "Academic performance in children of divorce: Psychological resilience and vulnerability," Psychiatry, (91): 268-280; co-auth, "The science of prevention: A conceptual framework and some directions for a national research program," American Psychologist, (93): 1013-1022; co-auth, "The Life course of psychological resilience: A phenomenological perspective on deflecting life's slings and arrows," Journal of Primary Prevention, (95): 209-246. **CONTACT ADDRESS** Dept Psychol, Univ of Denver, 2155 S Race St, Denver, CO 80210. **EMAIL** nwatt@du.edu

WATTS, ANNE WIMBUSH
PERSONAL Born 01/01/1943, Grambling, LA, m, 1967 **DISCIPLINE** EDUCATION **EDUCATION** Grambling State University, BS, 1962; University of Wisconsin, MA, 1964; Atlanta University, MA, 1966; Georgia State University, PhD, 1982. **CAREER** Grambling State University, instructor, 64-65; Jackson State University, instructor, 65-66; Atlanta University, instructor, 66-67; Spelman College, visiting professor, 91; Morehouse College, class dean, professor, 67-, director, summer academy, 91-. **HONORS AND AWARDS** Phi Beta Kappa Honor Society, honorary member, 1992; Grambling State University Hall of Fame, inducted member, 1991; Golden Key National Honor Society, 1992; NAFEO Distinguished Alumni Awd, nominated by GSU, 1990. **MEMBERSHIPS** National Cancer Institute Advisory Committee, chairperson of curriculum committee, 1988-90; National Black Political Action Forum, consultant, 1987-89; Alpha Kappa Alpha Sorority, Inc, internat consultant, 1991-; Atlanta Job Corps Center, advisory committee, 1992-; National Council of Negro Women, 1990-; 100 Women of Atlanta, internat pub editor, 1988-. **SELECTED PUBLICATIONS** The Litteratus, founder and editor, 1984-; Three Voices, 1988; M J: Modern Job, 1991, 1992. **CONTACT ADDRESS** Dean, Professor, Director of Summer Academy, Morehouse Col, 830 Westview Dr, Atlanta, GA 30314.

WATTS, LINDA K.
PERSONAL Born 06/26/1954, Columbus, OH, m, 1999 **DISCIPLINE** ANTHROPOLOGY **EDUCATION** SUNY Buffalo, BA, 76; MA, 79; Ariz State Univ, PhD, 92. **CAREER** Asst prof to assoc prof, Univ of Colo, 93-. **HONORS AND AWARDS** Grants, Ariz State Univ, 84-85, 85; Wenner-Gren Found Grant, 86-87; Nat Sci Found Grant, 87; Colo Springs Comm on Res and Creative Works Grant, 94-96. **RESEARCH** Southwest Native American languages/cultures/social organization, Cultural mdoels, traditional Native American cultural models of substance dependency and recovery. **SELECTED PUBLICATIONS** Auth, "Prosidic Analysis of the Speech of an Elderly Lady", LACUS Forum 1978, eds Wolfgang Wolf and Paul L Garvin, Hornbeam Pr, (Columbia, NC, 79): 230-234; coauth, "How the Rabbit Relinquished Control: Noun Ranking, Ergativity, and Sociolinguistic Relativity in the Southwest Chain of Being", The Lang of Native America, ed Amy Zaharlick, (81): 152-160; auth, "Zuni Family Values and Household-Group Values: A Revisionist Cultural Model of Zuni Social Organization", J of Anthrop Res 53.1 (97); coauth, "A Native American-Based Cultural Model of Substance Dependency and Recovery", Human Org 56.1 (97); coauth, "Some Considerations from Pueblo Languages and Social Organization for Tracing Ancestral Pueblo Cultural Affiliations", Affiliation Conf on Ancestral Peoples of the Four Corners Region, Nat Park Serv, (99): 139-146; auth, "Applying Cultural Models to Native American Substance Dependency Research", Am Ind Cult and Res J, (forthcoming); auth, The Social Semiotics of Relational Terminology at Zuni Pueblo, Edwin Mellen Pub, (Lewiston, NY), (forthcoming). **CONTACT ADDRESS** Dept Anthrop, Univ of Colorado, Colorado Springs, PO Box 7150, Colorado Springs, CO 80933-7150. **EMAIL** lkwatts@uccs.edu

WAUGH, BUTLER HUGGINS
PERSONAL Born 05/09/1934, Pittsburgh, PA, m, 1953, 6 children **DISCIPLINE** FOLKLORE, ENGLISH **EDUCATION** Washington & Jefferson Col, AB, 55; IN Univ, PhD, 59. **CAREER** Instr Eng, Univ KS, 59-61; from asst prof to assoc prof, Univ FL, 61-70; exec asst to pres, 69-70, dean col arts & sci, 70-76, prof eng, FL Int Univ, 70, Coordr hum & fine arts, State Univ Syst FL, 68-69. **MEMBERSHIPS** Am Folklore Soc; MLA; S Atlantic Mod Lang Asn. **RESEARCH** Mod Brit and Am poetry; comp folktale study; structural analysis of traditional lit. **SELECTED PUBLICATIONS** Auth, Negro tales of John Kendry, Midwest Folklore, 58; The child and the snake in North America, Norveg, 60; Deep and surface structure, SAtlantic Bull, 68. **CONTACT ADDRESS** Col Arts & Sci, Florida Intl Univ, 1 F I U South Campus, Miami, FL 33199-0001. **EMAIL** waugh@fiu.edu

WAUGH, CHARLES G.
PERSONAL Born 07/18/1943, Philadelphia, PA, m, 1968, 2 children **DISCIPLINE** COMMUNICATIONS AND PSYCHOLOGY **EDUCATION** Syracuse Univ, BS, 65; MA, 69; Kent State Univ, PhD, 82. **CAREER** Asst debate coach, teaching asst, Syracuse Univ, 665-66; instr, Ithaca Col, 67-69; teaching fel, Kent State Univ, 69-71; asst prof, Univ Maine at Augusta,71-78; Chairman, Div of Soc Sci, Univ Maine at Augusta, 74-76; pres fac assembly, Univ Maine at Augusta, 77-78; assoc prof, Univ Maine at Augusta, 78-81; prof, Univ Maine at Augusta, 81-; vp fac assembly, Univ Maine at Augusta, 97-98. **HONORS AND AWARDS** Unit citation, USCG, 66. **RESEARCH** Social interaction and influence; popular culture; mass media; Maine studies; Civil War. **SELECTED PUBLICATIONS** Coed, The Best Maine Stories, Lance Tapley, 86; co-compiled, Science Fiction and Fantasy Series and Sequels: Vol. 1, Garland Press, 86; co-compiled, Western Series and Sequels: A Reference Guide, Garland Press, 86; coed, Science Fiction: The Science Fiction Research Association Anthology, Harper & Row, 88; co-compiled, Women Writers: From Page to Screen: A Guide to the Literary Sources of British and American Feature Films, Garland Press, 90; coed, Wife or Spinster: Stories by Nineteenth Century Women, Yankee Books, 91; coed, A Distant War Comes Home: Maine in the Civil War, Down East, 96; coed, The Women's War in the South: Recollections and Reflections of the American Civil War, Cumberland House, 99; coed, The Price of Freedom: Slavery and the Civil War, Vols 1 &2, Cumberland House, 00; coauth, coed, Let's Talk: A Cognitive-Skills Approach to Interpersonal Communication, Kendal-Hunt, 01. **CONTACT ADDRESS** 5 Morrill St, Winthrop, ME 04364.

WAUTISCHER, HELMUT
PERSONAL Born 06/15/1954, Klagenfurt, Austria **DISCIPLINE** PHILOSOPHY, PSYCHOLOGY **EDUCATION** Karl-Franzens Univ, Graz Austria, PhD, 85. **CAREER** Concurrent lectr, San Diego State Univ, 88-91; CSU Long Beach, 89-92; vis asst prof, Humboldt State Univ, 92-94; Universitatslektor, Univ Klagenfurt Austria, 95-97; concurrent lectr, Sonoma State Univ 95-. **HONORS AND AWARDS** Fulbright, 81; Executive Bd SAC, 91-; Executive Bd COPS, 97-. **MEMBERSHIPS** Am Philos Asn; Amer Anthropol Asn; Soc for the A nthropol of Consciousness; Council of Philos Soc; Karl Jasper Soc; Osterreichische Gesellschaft Fur Philosophie. **RESEARCH** Consciousness Studies; Philosophical Anthropology. **SELECTED PUBLICATIONS** Auth, Dreaming 'On Love and Awareness' Dialogue and Humanism, 94; ed, Anthropology of Consciousness, 94; Tribal Epistemologies: Essays in the Philosophy of Anthropology, 98; auth, "Tribal Epistemlogies: Essays in the Philosophy of Anthropology," Ashgate Publishing, 98; auth, "Ontology of Consciousness: A Modern Synthesis," forthcoming; auth, "The Path to Knowledge, in V.M. Pivojev, ed. Bachtin and the Problem of Methodology for Humanitarian Knowledge," forthcoming; auth, "Bewufstseinsforschung in interkultureller Diskussion," Polylog 3, 99, 111-112; auth, "Pathways to Knowledge," in H. Wautischer, ed. Tribal Epistemologies, 3-14, Ashgate Publ., 98; auth, "Reason and Awareness in Ethics," Querying the Philosphers Desire for Safety through Reasoning," Journal of Ethical Studies, 95, 2-17; auth, "Dreaming and the Cognitive Revolution," Guest Editorial, Anthropology of Consciousness, 5/3 94, 1-2; auth, "On Love and Awareness," Dialogue and Humanism IV/2-3 94, 31-40. **CON-**

TACT ADDRESS Dept of Philosophy, Sonoma State Univ, 1801 E Cotati Ave, Rohnert Park, CA 94928-3609. EMAIL wautisch@sonoma.edu

WAVERING, MICHAEL J.
PERSONAL Born 03/10/1947, Quincy, IL, m, 1974 **DISCIPLINE** CURRICULUM AND INSTRUCTION **EDUCATION** Qunicy Univ, BS, 69; Indiana Unv, MAT, 71; Univ Iowa, PhD, 79. **CAREER** Graduate Asst, Univ of Iowa, 76-79; Assoc Prof, Eastern Univ, 79-84; Assoc Prof, Univ of Ark, 84-. **HONORS AND AWARDS** Research Awd, Univ of AR, College of Educ and Health Professions, 91. **MEMBERSHIPS** Am Asn for the Advancement of Science, Phi Delta Kappa, National Asn for Research in Science Teaching, National Science Teachers Asn. **RESEARCH** Cognitive Development, Development of Philosophies of Teaching and Science, Piaget's Theory, History and Philosophy of Science. **SELECTED PUBLICATIONS** Auth, Order of attainment of the mental structures for five of Piagets logical, infralogical and formal tasks, with Linda J. Kelsey and Bruce Perry, Journal of Genetic Psychology, 148 (87): 279-288; auth, Logical reasoning necessary to make line graphs, Journal of Research in Science Teaching, 26 (89): 373-379; auth, Inservice teacher's opinions of teacher preparation programs, with William Klingele and La Vonne Walter, Capstone Journal of Education, 3 (89): 11-20; auth, Crisis: Underepresentation of females and minority students in mathematics and science classes in public secondary schools, Eastern Kentucky Univ Educational Review 14 (92): 11-18; auth, Cognitive development of young adolescents, in M. Wavering (ed.), Educating young adolescents: Life in the middle (New York: Garland Publishing, 95), 111-130; auth, Science: A way of knowing: Part of an Arkansas Science Crusade module, Little Rock, AR: Arkansas Dept of Higher Educ, 95; auth, The Biographical Encyclopedia of Scientists, ed. R. Olson (New York: Marshall Cavendish Corp), 414-418; auth, In Translating and using research for improving teacher education in science and mathematics: The final report from the OERI-funded Chautauqua ISTEP research project, ed., Janet Robinson and Robert Yager, U.S. Dept of Educ, 98. **CONTACT ADDRESS** Curriculum & Inst 200 Grad, Univ of Arkansas, Fayetteville, Fayetteville, AR 72701. **EMAIL** wavering@comp.wark.edu

WAXMAN, CHAIM I.
PERSONAL Born 03/26/1941, New York, NY, m, 1962, 3 children **DISCIPLINE** SOCIOLOGY **EDUCATION** Yeshiva Univ, BA, 63; MHL, 66; New Sch for Soc Res, MA, 65; PhD, 74. **CAREER** Asst prof, Central Conn State Col, 65-72; asst prof, Brooklyn Col, 72-75; from assoc prof to prof, Rutgers Univ, 78-. **HONORS AND AWARDS** Bernard Revel Award, Yeshiva Univ. **MEMBERSHIPS** Am Sociol Asn, Eastern Sociol Soc, Soc for the Sci Study of Relig; Asn for the Sociol of Relig, Asn for Jewish Studies, Asn for Israel Studies, World Union of Jewish Studies. **RESEARCH** Religion, Ethnicity, Jews, Judaism, Israel, Society. **SELECTED PUBLICATIONS** Auth, The Stigma of Poverty, 77 & 83; auth, America's Jews in Transition, 83; auth, American Aliya, 89; coauth, Historical Dictionary of Zionism, 00; auth, Jewish Baby Boomers, 00; Historical Dictionary of Zionism, Scarecrow Press, 00; Jewish Baby Boomers: A Communal Perspective, State Univ of New York Press, 00. **CONTACT ADDRESS** Dept Sociol, Rutgers Univ, 54 Joyce Kilmer Ave, Piscataway, NJ 08854-8045. **EMAIL** waxmanci@rci.rutgers.edu

WAXMAN, SANDRA R.
DISCIPLINE PSYCHOLOGY **EDUCATION** Univ Pa, BS, 76; PhD, 85; Johns Hopkins Univ, MA, 81. **CAREER** Asst prof to assoc prof, Harvard Univ, 86-92; assoc prof, Northwestern Univ, 92-97, prof, 97-. **HONORS AND AWARDS** Doctoral Fel, Am Asn of Univ Women, 85-86; The John D. and Catherine T. MacArthur Found, Post-doctoral Fel, Harvard Univ, 86; The Spenser Found and The Nat Acad of Educ, Res Fel, 89; Boyd R. McCandless Young Scientist Awd Nominee, APA Div 7, 90; Wender-Lewis Res and Teaching Prof, Northwestern Univ, Col of Arts and Scis, 94-96; Am Psychol Asn, Div 7 Fel, 98. **SELECTED PUBLICATIONS** Coauth, "Words and gestures: Infants' interpretations of different forms of symbolic reference," Child Develop, 69, 2 (98): 295-308; coauth, "Conceptual organization," in W. Bechtel and G. Graham, eds, A Companion to Cognitive Science, Oxford, England: Blackwell (98): 167-175; coauth, "Object naming at multiple hierarchial levels: A comparison of preschools with and without word-finding deficits," J of Child Lang, 25, 2 (98): 419-430; coauth, "Preschoolers' acquisition of novel adjectives and the role of basic-level kind," in A. Greenhill, eds, Proceedings of the 22nd Boston Univ Conf on Lang Develop, Somerville, MA: Cascadilla Press (98); auth, "Specifying the scope of 13-month-olds' expectations for novel words," Cognition, 70, (99): B35-B50; auth, "The dubbing ceremony revisited: Object naming and categorization in infancy and early childhood," in D. L. Medin and S. Atran, eds, Folkbiology, Cambridge, MA: MIT, Pres/Bradford Books (99): 233-284; coauth, "Basic level object categories support the acquisition of novel adjectives: Evidence from preschool-aged children," Child Development (in press). **CONTACT ADDRESS** Dept Psychol, Northwestern Univ, 2029 Sheridan Rd, Evanston, IL 60208-2710. **EMAIL** s-waxman@nwu.edu

WEASMER, JERIE
PERSONAL Born 12/28/1949, Clinton, IA, m, 1985, 4 children **DISCIPLINE** ENGLISH COMPOSITION STUDIES; ENG TEACHER PREPARATION; LITERACY **EDUCATION** Upper IA Col, BA, 71; Univ IA, MA, 88, Purdue Univ, PhD, 96. **CAREER** Eng Dept, Eastern Ill Univ **HONORS AND AWARDS** Univ Achievement in Contribution Award for Teaching, Res, & Serv, 98-99; Best Practices in Teaching Award, 97-98; HECA Grant, PIE21 96-97. **MEMBERSHIPS** Nat Coun Teachers Engl; Ill Asn Teachers Eng IL; Asn Teacher Educators; IL Philol Asn. **RESEARCH** Building teaching efficacy; teacher retention; interdisciplinary teaching. **SELECTED PUBLICATIONS** Auth, The Changemakers: Teachers as Active Agents for Change, Midwest Association of Teacher Educators Conference Proceedings, 96; coauth, A.M. Formative Assessment in Teacher Preparation, Clearing House, 97; Teaching is a Team Sport: Enhancing Collegial Roles, Kappa Delta Pi Record, 97; coauth, Teacher Preparation: A Revision Process Fostered by Formative Assessment, The Clearing House, 97; coauth, Teaching is a Team Sport: Enhancing Collegial Roles, Kappa Delta Pi Record, 97; coauth, Beat Burnout!: Strategies for Remaining Professionally Stimulated, Teaching Elementary Physical Education, 98; coauth, I Think I Can: The Role of Personal Teaching Efficacy in Effecting Change, The Clearing House, 98; auth, Collaborative Efforts toward Change: Infusing Technology into an American Literature Curriculum, Midwest Association of Teacher Educators Conference Proceedings, 98; coauth, Technology Partnership in Teaching and Learning, Eastern Education Journal 27, 98; coauth, Facilitating Success for New Teachers, Principal 78, 98; auth, Collaboration in Cyberspace, MATE Conference Proceedings, 99; coauth, Integrated Learning: Greater Than the Sum of Its Parts, Teaching Elementary Physical Education, 99; coauth, Programs in Practice: Peer Partnering for Change, Kappa Delta Pi Record, 36, 99; coauth, Preventing Baptism by Fire: Fostering Growth in New Teachers, The Clearing House, 00; coauth, At Center Stage: Strategies for Shifting Classroom Ownership, Middle School Journal, 00; coauth, Special Issue on Career Stages, The Clearing House: A Journal of Educational Strategies, Issues, and Ideas, forthcoming; coauth, Maintaining Job Satisfaction: Engaging Professionals as Active Participants, The Clearing House: A Journal of Educational Strategies, Issues, and Ideas, forthcoming; auth, A Gift of Time: Career History of a Prime Time Teacher, The Clearing House: A Journal of Educational Strategies, Issues, and Ideas, forthcoming; coauth, Who's the Boss: Affording Students Agency, Kappa Delta Pi Record, forthcoming. **CONTACT ADDRESS** Eastern Illinois Univ, 600 Lincoln Ave, Charleston, IL 61920-3099. **EMAIL** cfjrw1@eiu.edu

WEATHERBY, GEORGIE ANN
PERSONAL Born 11/16/1954, Bellingham, WA, s **DISCIPLINE** SOCIOLOGY **EDUCATION** Western Wash Univ, BA, 79; Western Wash Univ, MA, 84; Univ Wash, PhD, 90. **CAREER** Asst Prof, Gonzaga Univ, 96-. **HONORS AND AWARDS** Students Choice Awd Teaching Excellence, Wash St Univ, 90-91; Phi Beta Kappa, Wash St Univ, 92; Commendation, Pac Soc Asn, 97-99; Who's Who Among Am Teachers, 00. **MEMBERSHIPS** ASA, AFW, NIJ, ACJS, AAUP. **RESEARCH** Gender, deviance, religion, law and justice. **SELECTED PUBLICATIONS** Co-ed, The Power of Gender in Religion, McGraw-Hill (New York), 96; coauth, Handbook for Committee Chairs, Pac Soc Asn, 97; coauth, "Television News Coverage of the Police: An Exploratory Study From A Small Town Locale," J of Contemp Criminal Justice, vol 15, no 2 (99): 171-190; coauth, "Crime Stories as Television News: A Content Analysis of National, Big City and Small Town Newscasts," J of Criminal Justice and Pop Cult, vol 7, no 1 (99): 1-14; coauth, "Television Commercial Content: Religion Versus Science and Professional Expertise," Sociol Focus, vol 32, no 4 (99): 413-425; coauth, "Violence, Morality and Television Commercials," Sociol Spectrum, vol 20, no 1 (00): 121-143; coauth, "The Coverage of School Shootings on National Network Television Newscasts," (forthcoming). **CONTACT ADDRESS** Dept Sociol, Gonzaga Univ, 502 E Boone Ave, Spokane, WA 99258-0001. **EMAIL** weatherb@gonzaga.edu

WEBB, ROBERT C.
PERSONAL Born 11/14/1932, Brooklyn, NY, m **DISCIPLINE** PSYCHOLOGY **EDUCATION** Middlebury Col, AB, 55; Brown Univ., MA, 62; Tufts Univ, PhD, 69. **CAREER** Air group Intelligence Officer, US Naval Reserve, 56-59; instr, Wheaton Col, 62-65; asst prof, Suffolk Univ, 66-69, assoc prof, 69-73, prof, 73-, chair, Dept Psychol, 78-82, acting chair, 87-88. **HONORS AND AWARDS** Danforth Found Teacher Grant, 65-66. **MEMBERSHIPS** Soc for Consumer Psychol, Eastern Psychol Asn, Visitor Studies Asn. **RESEARCH** Visitor studies (museum visitors), the nature of visitors, the nature of their visit; the psychology of the consumer; classical conditioning in advertising; affect in advertising; affect as the core of emotion. **SELECTED PUBLICATIONS** Auth, "Creativity: The Need for Definition," in D. Tuerck, ed, Creativity and Liberal Learning, Norwood, NJ: Ablex (87); auth, "The Relevance of the Consumer Behavior Literature, " in D. Thompson, A. Benefield, and S. Bitgood, eds, Visitor Studies: Theory, Research, and Practice, Vol 6, Jacksonville, AL: The Visitor Studies Asn (94); auth, "Comparing High-involved and Low-involved Visitors: A Review of the Consumer Behavior Literature," in M. Wells and R. Loomis, eds, Visitor Studies: Theory, Research, and Practice, Vol 9, Jacksonville, AL: The Visitor Studies Asn (97); auth, textbook: The Psychology of the Consumer and Its Development: An Introduction, NY: Plenum (99). **CONTACT ADDRESS** Dept Psychol, Suffolk Univ, 8 Ashburton Pl, Boston, MA 02108. **EMAIL** rwebb@acad.suffolk.edu

WEBB, RUTH H.
DISCIPLINE CLASSICAL AND BYZANTINE RHETORIC AND EDUCATION **EDUCATION** Oxford Univ, MA, 86; London, PhD, 92. **CAREER** Asst prof, Princeton Univ. **RESEARCH** Literary narrative in late antique texts. **SELECTED PUBLICATIONS** Areas: Byzantine education, female entertainers,rhetorical ekphrasis. **CONTACT ADDRESS** Princeton Univ, 1 Nassau Hall, Princeton, NJ 08544. **EMAIL** rhwebb@princeton.edu

WEBB-JOHNSON, GWENDOLYN
PERSONAL Born 11/01/1954, Clarksdale, MS, d, 2 children **DISCIPLINE** EDUCATION **EDUCATION** Knox Col, BA, 75; Northeastern Ill Univ, MA, 84; Ill State Univ, EdD, 94. **CAREER** Lecturer and Grad Asst, Ill State Univ, 93-94; Asst Prof, Tex A&M Univ, 94-98; Asst Prof, Univ Tex, 98-. **HONORS AND AWARDS** Bookfellow Awd in Poetry, 75; Outstanding Teacher Awd, PACE, 88; Gwendolyn Cafritz Teaching Fel, 88; Teaching Awd, Washington, 88; McHenry Fel, IL State Univ, 91; Fel, ICEOP, 91-93; Teaching Awd, TX A&M Univ, 96; Dearn's Fel, Univ TX, 99. **MEMBERSHIPS** Am Asn of Col of Teacher Educ; Am Educ Res Asn; Asn for Teacher Educ; Coun for Exceptional Chilren; Black Caucus of Sp Educators; Coun for Children with Beh Disordrs; Intl Asn of Sp Educ; Kappa Delta Pi; Nat alliance of Black Sch educators; TX Alliance of Black Sch Educators; Nat Asn for Multiculutral Educ; Nat Coun for Negro Women. **RESEARCH** Teacher education; Special education; Multicultural education; Curriculum and Instructional development; Recruitment and retention of culturally divers students in higher educaiton; Parental/Family involvement. **SELECTED PUBLICATIONS** Co-auth, "Cultural contexts, the seriously emotionally disturbed classification and African American learners," in Effective education of African American exceptional learners, (Austin, 95), 153-188; co-auth, "Self-concept development: an effective tool for behavior management," in Managing problem behaviors: Perspectives for general and special educators, (Kendall/Hunt, 95), 155-172; auth, "My emerging Destiny: Mentoring from an African American Perspective," in Breaking the circle of one: Redefining mentorship in the lives and writings of educators, (Peter Lang, 97), 3-19; co-auth, "instructional racism in American schools: A call for culturally responsive pedagogy," in Educators healing racism, (Reston, 99), 49-66; auth, "Cultural Contexts: Confronting the overrepresentation of African American learners in special education," in Behavioral intervention: Principles, models, and practices, (Brookline Pub, 99), 449-464; co-auth, "Embracing students of color in the graduate school experience: The mentoring approach," Nat Asn of Student Affairs Professionals Journal, (990: 47-55; co-auth, "Review of the McIntrye assessment of culture," Multiple Voices, (99): 37-47; co-auth, "African American faculty balancing the triumvirate," Nat Asn of Student Affairs Professionals Journal, (00): 46-65; co-auth, affirming all children and youth: The oral tradition as an integral part of classroom interactions, Joy Pub, in press. **CONTACT ADDRESS** Dept Sp Educ, Univ of Texas, Austin, George I. Sanchez Bldg 408A, Austin, TX 78712. **EMAIL** gwebbj@mail.utexas.edu

WEBBER, RANDALL C.
PERSONAL Born 11/28/1961, Oak Ridge, TN, s **DISCIPLINE** HISTORY; RELIGIOUS STUDIES, SOCIOLOGY **EDUCATION** Furman Univ, BA, 82; Southern Baptist Theological Seminary, MDiv, 85, PhD, 89. **CAREER** Manuscript editor, 87-89, Paradigms; asst ed, 89-92, Univ MI; dir, emergency housing, Salvation Army, 92- ; proprietor, Webber Church Consulting, 97- . **HONORS AND AWARDS** Who's Who in Bibl Studies and Archaeol, 93. **MEMBERSHIPS** Soc of Bibl Lit; Am Acad of Bereavement; Nat Bd of Cognitive Behavioral Therapists. **RESEARCH** Early Christianity; Grief; Politics. **SELECTED PUBLICATIONS** Auth, Successful Grief and Chronic Homelessness: Is There a Relationship? Grief Work, 95; auth, Kentucky Reader Proposes Ethics Code for Churches, Baptist Today, 95; auth, Reader-Response Analysis of the Epistle of James, 96; auth, An Idealistic Reading of the Apocalype, 99. **CONTACT ADDRESS** 325 E Kentucky St, Louisville, KY 40203-2709. **EMAIL** rcwbbb@juno.com

WECHSLER, HENRY
DISCIPLINE PUBLIC HEALTH **EDUCATION** Wash and Jefferson Col, Ab, 53; Harvard Univ, MA, 55; PhD, 57. **CAREER** Res asst, Res asst to Res Fel, Harvard Univ, 53-58; Res Assoc and asst prof, Clark Univ, 58-59; res soc psychol, Mass Mental Health Center, 59-65; res assoc, Harvard Med Sch, 60-66; res assoc, Harvard Sch Public Health, 63-66; lecturer, Harvard Univ, 69-70; vis lecturer, Boston Univ, 67-71; lecturer, Harvard Med Sch, 70-73; lecturer, Simmons Col Sch of Social Work, 69-79; adj prof, Boston Univ Sch of Public Health, 79-80; adj prof, simmons col Sch of social Work, 80-84; director, Col Alcohol Studies Prog Harvard School of Public Health, 92-.

HONORS AND AWARDS Washington and Jefferson Col, Summa cum laude, Phi Beta Kappa; Harvard Foundation for Adv Study Fel, 53-54; Harvard Univ Res Fel, 54-55; US Public Health Service Post-doctoral Res Fel, 57. **MEMBERSHIPS** Am Psychol Asn, Am sociol Asn, Am Public Health Asn, Mass Psychol Asn, Mass Public Health Asn. **RESEARCH** Alcohol and drug abuse among college students and youth, Prevention of substance abuse and related problem behaviors among college students, Public policy towards youthful alcohol abuse. **SELECTED PUBLICATIONS** Auth, "Community solutions to community problems - Preventing adolescent alcohol use," Am J Public Hlth, (96): 923-925; auth, "Correlates of college student marijuana use: Results of a US national survey," Addiction, (97): 571-582; auth, "Binge drinking, tobacco, and illicit drug use and involvement in college athletics," Journal Am Col Health, (97): 195-200; auth, "Binge drinking among college students: A comparison of California with other states," Journal American College Health, (97): 273-277; auth, "Price, tobacco control policies and smoking among young adults," Journal Health Econ (97): 359-373; auth, "Predictors of smoking among US college students," American Journal Public Health, (98): 104-107; auth, "Changes in binge drinking and related problems among American college students between 1993 and 1997: Results of the Harvard School of Public Health College Alcohol Study," Journal American College Health, (98); auth, "Increased levels of cigarette use among college students: A cause for national concern," JAMA, (98): 1673-1678; auth, "College alcohol use: a full or empty glass?", JACH (99): 247-252; auth, "Guns at College," JACH (99): 7-12. **CONTACT ADDRESS** Dept Health and Soc Beh, Harvard Univ, 677 Huntington Ave, Boston, MA 02115. **EMAIL** hwechsle@hsph.harvard.edu

WEHRLI, MARY BRENT
PERSONAL Born 03/17/1942, Los Angeles, CA, m, 1963, 2 children **DISCIPLINE** SOCIOLOGY **EDUCATION** Univ Calif at Los Angeles, BA, 64; MSW, 84. **CAREER** Exec dir, SCITCA, 86-93; fld liaison, fac, Univ Calif, Los Angeles, School Pub Pol Social Res, 93-; co-prod TV show, Lawson Live. **HONORS AND AWARDS** CRECEN, 87; SCECIT, 90; Barbara Boxer, 91; Soc Wkr of the Year, NASW, 98; Daniel E Koshland Awd, 99. **MEMBERSHIPS** CSWE; NASW; SWAA; SAJE; CLUE. **CONTACT ADDRESS** School Soc Welfare, Univ of California, Los Angeles, PO Box 951656, Los Angeles, CA 900095-1656. **EMAIL** mbwehrli@ucla.edu

WEI-ARTHUS, HUIYING
PERSONAL Born 08/39/1957, Beijing, China, 1 child **DISCIPLINE** SOCIOLOGY **EDUCATION** Sichnan Intl Studies Univ, BA, 81; SUNY, MA, 86; MA, 89; PhD, 94. **CAREER** Asst Prof to Assoc Prof, Weber State Univ, 95-. **MEMBERSHIPS** Am Sociol Asn; Pacific Sociol Asn; W Conf of Asian Studies Asn; SW Asn of Asian Studies. **RESEARCH** Organizational Studies; Work; China. **SELECTED PUBLICATIONS** Auth, "The Massive Unemployment in Present-Day China," Journal of SWAS, 99; auth, Neo-Patrimoniolism in Urban Work Units, Mellen Press, forthcoming. **CONTACT ADDRESS** Dept Sociol & Anthropol, Weber State Univ, 3750 Harrison Blvd, Ogden, UT 84408-0001. **EMAIL** hweiarthus@weber.edu

WEIGERT, ANDREW
PERSONAL Born 04/08/1934, New York, NY, m, 1967, 2 children **DISCIPLINE** SOCIOLOGY **EDUCATION** St. Louis Univ, BA, 58; PhL, 59; MA, 60; Woodstock Col, BTh, 64; Univ Minn, PhD, 68. **CAREER** Asst prof to prof, Univ Notre Dame, 65-. **HONORS AND AWARDS** Grant, NSF, 69. **MEMBERSHIPS** Soc for Study Symbolic Interaction; Soc for Sci Study Relig. **SELECTED PUBLICATIONS** Coauth, Society and Identity, 86; auth, Mixed Emotions, SUNY Press, 91; auth, Society and Identity, Cambridge Univ Press, 91; coauth, "Vital Realism and Sociology: A Metatheoretical Grounding in Mead, Ortega, and Schultz," Sociol Theory, 93; auth, "Lawn of Weeds," The Am Sociologist, 94; auth, "Jose Ortega y Gasset on Life and Meaning: Ultimate Reality and Meaning, 95; coauth, "Multiplicity and Dialogue in Social Psychology: An Essay in Metatheorizing," Jour for the Theory of Soc Behav, 95; auth, "Definitional and Responsive Meanings: A Median look at Landscapes and Droughts," Jou for the Theory of Soc Behav, 97; auth, Self, Interaction, and Natural Environment, 97. **CONTACT ADDRESS** Dept Sociol, Univ of Notre Dame, 325 O'Shaugnessy Hall, Notre Dame, IN 46556. **EMAIL** weigert1@nd.edu

WEIMER, JOAN MYERS
PERSONAL Born 03/12/1936, Cambridge, MA, m, 1971, 3 children **DISCIPLINE** AMERICAN LITERATURE, WOMEN'S STUDIES, NON-FICTION WRITING **EDUCATION** Tufts Univ, AB, 57; Rutgers Univ, New Brunswick, MA, 64, PhD, 70. **CAREER** From instr to assoc prof, 68-82, prof eng, Drew Univ, 82, Vis scholar, Ctr Res Women, Stanford Univ, 78, 87; Vis scholar, Univ AZ, 96; Consulting ed, Legacy; Proj dir, State of NJ grant, 84-86; Producer/moderator, Women in the Center and Why They Belong There, 13-part television series, 83-84. **HONORS AND AWARDS** Phi Beta Kappa, 56; John H McGinnis Awd, Southwest Rev, 77; Semi-finalist, Nat Play Awd Competition of Nat Repertory Theater, 80; Res and travel grants, Drew Univ, 90-98. **MEMBERSHIPS** NJ Project on Curriculum Integration (mem, Advisory board); Central NJ/Masaya, Nicaragua Friendship City Project (corrdinating comt, 85; leader of delegation to Nicaragua, 1/87); Madison Area Chap Amnesty Int (co-founder, secy), 76-82; Westfield Area Comt for Hum Rights 63-66. **RESEARCH** Memoir; feminist criticism of lit; relationship between roles of mothers and polit repression and torture; machismo. **SELECTED PUBLICATIONS** Co-ed (with David R Weimer), Literature of America, America, 7 vol, McDougal, Littell, 73; The Belly Dancer and the Virgin: Mythic Women in Modern Egypt, Southwest Rev, winter 76; Magic in Brazil, North Am Rev, winter 76; The Mother, the Macho, and the State, Int Jour Women's Studies, 1/78; Co-auth (with David Weimer), Ready About, orig play, 78; Co-auth (with David Weimer), Pyramid, orig play, 79; The Story Tellers, orig play, 80; Mythic Parables of Female Power: Inanna, Demeter and Persephone and the Sleeping Beauty, Anima, fall 86; Women, Artists as Exiles in the Stories of Constance Fenimore Woolson, Legacy, fall 86; Individuation and Intimacy: Eleusis and the Sleeping Beauty, Anima, fall 88; Ed, Women Artists: Women Exiles: Miss Grief and Other Stories by Constance Fenimore Woolson, Rutgers Univ Press, 88; The Admiring Aunt and the Proud Salmon of the Pond: Constance Fenimore Woolson's Struggle with Henry James, In: Critical Essays on Constance Fenimore Woolson (Cheryl Torsney, ed), G K Hall, 92; But I'm Not Writing Fiction! And Other Autobiographical Fictions, Soundings, fall 93; Back Talk: Teaching Lost Selves to Speak, Random House, 94 and Univ Chicago Press, 95; Co-auth (with Phyllis Paullette), Back Talk, orig play, 95; Intimate Knowing: A Tale of a Haunted Biographer, Belles Lettres, summer 95; Life Stand Still Here, In: The Writer's Journal (Sheila Bender, ed), Dell 96. **CONTACT ADDRESS** Dept of Eng, Drew Univ, 36 Madison Ave, Madison, NJ 07940-1493. **EMAIL** jweimer@drew.edu

WEINBERG, MARTIN
PERSONAL Born 01/23/1939, Albany, NY, m, 1964, 2 children **DISCIPLINE** SOCIOLOGY **EDUCATION** St. Lawrence Univ, BA, 60; Univ Mass, MA, 61; Northwestern Univ, PhD, 65. **CAREER** Rutgers Univ, 65-68; Ind Univ, 68-. **HONORS AND AWARDS** Phi Beta Kappa; Int Distinguished Sci Achievement Awd, Soc for the Sci Study of Sexuality. **MEMBERSHIPS** Am Sociol Asn, Soc for the Sci Study of Sci Problems, Soc for the Sci Study of Sex, Int Acad of Sex Res. **RESEARCH** Human Sexuality. **SELECTED PUBLICATIONS** Coauth, Dual Attraction; coauth, Sexual Preference; coauth, Homosexualities; coauth, Male Homosexuals; coauth, Deviance: The Interactionist Perspective; coauth, The Study of Social Problems; coauth, The Spilution of Social Problems. **CONTACT ADDRESS** Dept Sociol, Indiana Univ, Bloomington, 1020 E Kirkwood Ave, Bloomington, IN 47405. **EMAIL** weinberm@indiana.edu

WEINSTEIN, DEENA A.
PERSONAL Born New York, NY **DISCIPLINE** SOCIOLOGY **EDUCATION** Purdue Univ, PhD, 71. **CAREER** Prof, De Paul Univ, 79-. **RESEARCH** Rock, popular music; sociology theory; popular culture. **SELECTED PUBLICATIONS** Auth, Heavy Metal: A Cultural Sociology, Macmillan (Lexington, NY), 91; coauth, Postmodern(ized) Simmel, Routledge (London), 93; coauth, "George Simmel," in Perspectives (NY: McGraw Hill, 97) ; coauth, "Netgame Cameo," in Digital Delirium, eds. Arthur Kroker Marilouise Kroker (NY: St Martins Press, 97), 159-164; auth, "The History of Rock's Past Through Rock Covers," in Mapping the Beat: Popular Music and Contemporary Theory, eds. Thomas Swiss, John Sloop, Andrew Herman (Malden, MA: Blackwell, 98), 137-151; auth, "Art vs. Commerce: Deconstructing a (Useful) Romantic Illusion in Stars Don't Stand Still in the Sky: Music and Myth, eds. Karen Kelly, Evelyn McDonnell (NY: NY univ Press, 99), 56-69; auth, "Knockin' the Rock," (NY: McGraw Hill, rev 99), Primus Series; auth, "Youth," in Popular Music and Culture, eds. Bruce Horner, Thomas Swiss (Malden, MA: Blackwell, 99), 101-110; auth, "Chicago Music: Third in a series of articles in anticipation of the 1999 ASA Annual Meeting in Chicago," Footnotes 27 (99): 1,10. **CONTACT ADDRESS** Dept Sociology, DePaul Univ, 2320 N Kenmore Ave, Lincoln Park, Chicago, IL 60614. **EMAIL** dweinste@condor.depaul.edu

WEISMAN, AMY GINA
PERSONAL Born 06/22/1966, Severn, MD, s **DISCIPLINE** PSYCHOLOGY **EDUCATION** Univ Md, BA, 88; Univ S Calif, MA, 91; Univ S Calif, PhD, 94. **CAREER** Teacher, El Colegio de Espana, 87-89; Teaching Asst, Univ S Calif, 89-92; Asst Prof, Univ Mass, 96-. **HONORS AND AWARDS** Phi Kappa Phi; Training Fel, Nat Inst Ment Health, 92-93; Fel, Nat Inst Ment Health, 94-96; Fac Travel Awds, Univ Mass, 97-99. **MEMBERSHIPS** APA, APS, WPA, IACCP. **RESEARCH** Family factors related to the onset and course of schizophrenia, bipolar disorder and medical illness, attribution theory, minority mental health issues, cross-cultural psychology. **SELECTED PUBLICATIONS** Coauth, "An Attributional Analysis of Emotional Reactions to Schizophrenia in Mexican and Anglo Cultures," J of Applied Soc Psychol 27 (97): 224-245; coauth, "Evaluation of Therapist Competence and Adherence to Behavior Family Management with Bipolar Patients," Family Process 37 (98): 107-121; coauth, "Expressed Emotion, Attributions and Schizophrenia Symptom Dimensions," J of Abnormal Psychol 107 (98): 355-359; coauth, A Comparison of Psychiatric Symptoms Between Anglo-Americans and Mexican-Americans with Schizophrenia," Schizophrenia Bull (forthcoming); coauth, Controllability Perceptions and Reactions to Symptoms of Schizophrenia: A Within Family Comparison of High-EE and Low-EE Relatives," J of Abnormal Psychol (forthcoming); coauth, Difficulty in Implementing a Family Intervention for Bipolar Disorder: The Predictive Role of Patient and Family Attributes," Family Process (forthcoming); coauth, "Understanding Patients' Perceptions of their Relatives' Expressed Emotion" New Springer (forthcoming). **CONTACT ADDRESS** Dept Psychol, Univ of Massachusetts, Boston, 100 Morrissey Blvd, Boston, MA 02125-3393. **EMAIL** amy.weisman@umb.edu

WEISS, GREGORY L.
PERSONAL Born 08/19/1949, Canton, OH, m, 1989 **DISCIPLINE** SOCIOLOGY **EDUCATION** Wittenberg Univ, BA, 71; Purdue Univ, MS, 72; PhD, 75. **CAREER** Asst prof to prof, Roanoke Col, 75-. **HONORS AND AWARDS** Exemplary Teaching Awd, Roanoke Col; Outstanding Prof Awd, Roanoke Col; Sociol Scholar Awd, Va Soc Sci Asn; Outstanding Service Awd, Free Health Clinic, Roanoke Col. **MEMBERSHIPS** Am Sociol Assoc; Am Assoc for Higher Educ; S Sociol Soc; Am Pub Health Assoc; **RESEARCH** Ethical Issues in Life-sustaining Treatment, Theoretical Models Explaining Health Behavior, Role of Assessment in Higher Education. **SELECTED PUBLICATIONS** Coauth, "Health Value and Gender in Predicting Health Protective Behavior" , Women and Health 19, 92; auth, "Public Attitudes Toward Surrogate Motherhood, Mich Sociol Rev 6.6, 92; coauth, "Participation of Sociologists at Two-Year and Four-Year Colleges in the American Sociological Association", Am Sociol, 25.3, 94; coauth, The Sociology of Health, Healing, and Illness, Prentice-Hall (Englewood Cliffs, NJ), 94; coauth, "Gender and the Development of Health Protective Behavior Among College Students", Annual Res in the Sociol of Health Care, 14, 96; auth, "Attitudes of College Students About Physician-Assisted Suicide", Death Studies 20.6, 96; coauth, "The Development of Health Protective Behaviors Among College Students", Jour of Behav medicine, 19.2, 96; coauth, Handbook for Teaching Medical Sociology, Am Sociol Assoc Teaching Res Center (Wash, DC), 98; rev, of "The Sociology of Dying and Bereavement" by Clive Seale, Contemporary Sociol 28.4 (99); coauth, "The Do-Not-Resuscitate Decision: The Context, Process, and Consequences of NDR Orders", (forthcoming). **CONTACT ADDRESS** Dept Sociol, Roanoke Col, 221 College Lane, Salem, VA 24153. **EMAIL** weiss @roanoke.edu

WEITZER, RONALD
DISCIPLINE SOCIOLOGY **EDUCATION** Univ Calif, Santa Cruz, BA, 75; Univ Calif, Berkeley, MA, 78, PhD, 85. **CAREER** Prof, Sociol Dept, George Washington Univ. **RESEARCH** Policing and race, the sex industry, policing in North Ireland. **SELECTED PUBLICATIONS** Auth, Transforming Settler States: Communal Conflict and Internal Security in Northern Ireland and Zimbabwe, Univ Calif Press (90); auth, Policing Under Fire: Ethnic Conflict and Police-Community Relations in Northern Ireland, SUNY Press (95); auth, "Race, Class, and Perceptions of Discrimination by the Police," Crime & Delinquency (99); auth, "Citizens' Perceptions of Police Misconduct: Race and Neighborhood Context," Justice Quart (99); auth, "White, Black, or Blue Cops?: Race and Citizens' Assessments of Police Officers," J of Criminal Justice (2000); auth, "Racialized Policing: Residents' Perceptions in Three Neighborhoods," Law and Sco Rev (2000); auth, "Deficiencies in the Sociology of Sex Work," Sociol of Crime, Law, and Deviance (2000); auth, "Prostitutes' Rights Groups," Encyclopedia of Criminology and Deviant Behavior, Vol 2 (2000); auth, "Prostitution Control in America," Crime , Law, and Social Change (2000); auth, Sex for Sale: Prostitution, Pornography, and the Sex Industry, Routledge (2000). **CONTACT ADDRESS** Dept Sociol, The George Washington Univ, 2035 H St N W, Washington, DC 20052-0001. **EMAIL** weitzer@gwu.edu

WELLER, ROBERT P.
PERSONAL Born 12/08/1953, Philadelphia, PA, m, 1979, 2 children **DISCIPLINE** ANTHROPOLOGY **EDUCATION** Yale Univ, BA, 74; Johns Hopkins Univ, PhD, 80. **CAREER** Asst Prof, Duke Univ, 80-86; Asst Dean for Study Abroad, Duke Univ, 86-90; Res Assoc, Inst for the Study of Econ Cult, Boston Univ, 90-; Assoc Prof/Prof, Boston Univ, 90-. **MEMBERSHIPS** Am Anthrop Asn, Asn for Asian Studies. **RESEARCH** Culture and economic change, Religion, Civil Associations, China, Taiwan. **SELECTED PUBLICATIONS** Co-ed, Power and Protest in the Countryside: Studies of Rural Unrest in Asia, Europe and Latin America, Duke Univ Press, 82, 89; co-ed, Symposium on Hegemony and Chinese Folk Ideologies, Special Issue of Mod China, 87; auth, Unities and Diversities in Chinese Religion, Macmillan Press and Univ of Wash Press, 87; auth, Resistance, Chaos and Control in China, Macmillan Press and Univ of Wash Press, 94; co-ed, Unruly Gods: Divinity and Society in China, Univ of Hawaii Press, 96; coauth, "Culture, Gender and Community in Taiwan's Environmental Movement," in Environmental Movements in Asia, ed. Arne Kalland and Gerard Persoon (London: Curzon, 98), 83-109; auth, Alternate Civilities: Chinese Culture and the Prospects for Democracy, Westview, 99; auth, "Daoismums und die Moglichkeit einer chinesischen Zivilgesellschaft," in Dao in

China und in Westen: Impulse fur die oderne Gesellschaft, ed. Josef Thesing and Thomas Awe (Bonn: Bouvier, 99), 139-157; auth, "Identity and Social Change in Taiwanese Religion," in Taiwan: A New History, ed. Murray Rubenstein (Armonk, NY: M.E. Sharpe, 99), 339-365; auth, "From State-Owned Enterprise to Joint Venture: A Case Study of the Crisis in Urban Social Services," China J 43 (00): 83-99. **CONTACT ADDRESS** Dept Anthrop, Boston Univ, 232 Bay State Rd, Boston, MA 02215. **EMAIL** rpweller@bu.edu

WENDORF, D. FRED
PERSONAL Born 07/31/1924, TX, m, 1994, 6 children **DISCIPLINE** ANTHROPOLOGY **EDUCATION** Univ Ariz, BA, 47; Harvard Univ, MA, 50; PhD, 53. **CAREER** Henderson-Morrison Prof, Southern Methodist Univ, 64-. **HONORS AND AWARDS** Member, US Nat Acad of Sci; Distinguished Serv Awd, Soc for Am Archaeol, 90; John F. Seiberling Awd, Soc of Prof Archaeol, 90; Conserv Serv Awd, Dept of Interior, 87; Lucy Wharton Drexel Medal for Archaeol Achievement, 96. **MEMBERSHIPS** Soc for Am Archaeol. **RESEARCH** Prehistory of North East Africa. **SELECTED PUBLICATIONS** Auth, "From Under Desert Sands", Manual of Remote Sensing, ed J.T. Parry, Am Soc of Photogrammetry and Remote Sensing; coauth, "Prehistory of North Africa", Encyclop of Sub-Saharan Africa, ed J. Middleton, Charles Scribners Sons (NY); auth, "J. Desmond Clark", Archaeologists: A Biographical Encyclopedia, ed T. Murray, Garland (NY); coauth, "A Late Neolithic Megalith Complex in the Eastern Sahara: A Preliminary Report", Interregional Contacts in the Late Prehistory of Northeastern Africa, eds, L. Krzyzaniak and M. Kobusiewicz, Poznan Archaeol Museum and Polish Acad of Sci; coauth, "Prehistoric Egypt", Encyclop of Near Eastern Archaeology, ed E.M. Meyers, Oxford Univ Pr; auth, "Brew, John Otis (Jo)", Archaeology of Prehistoric North America: An Encyclopedia, ed G. Gibbon, Garland (NY); coauth, "A Survey of the Paleolithic" and "Wadi Kubbaniya", Archaeology of Ancient Egypt: An Encyclopedia, ed K. Bard, Garland (NY); coauth, "Middle Paleolithic Occupations at Bir Tarfawi and Bir Sahara East, Western Desert of Egypt", Environmental Change and Human Culture in the Nile Basic and Northern Africa Until the Second Millennium BC, eds L. Krzyzaniak and M. Kobusiewicz, Poznan Archaeol Museum and Polish Acad of Sci. **CONTACT ADDRESS** Dept Anthrop, So Methodist Univ, PO Box 750001, Dallas, TX 75275-0001. **EMAIL** fwendorf@mail.smu.edu

WENDORFF, LAURA C.
PERSONAL 1 child **DISCIPLINE** AMERICAN CULTURE **EDUCATION** Univ Wis, BA, 81; Univ Mich, MA, 84, PhD, 92. **CAREER** Tchg asst, Univ Mich, 83-84; asst prof, Univ Wis, 94-00; to assoc prof, 00-. **SELECTED PUBLICATIONS** Auth, Demonic Males: Apes and the Origins of Human Violence (rev), 98; Eric Heiden, Pierian, 88. **CONTACT ADDRESS** Dept of Humanities, Univ of Wisconsin, Platteville, 1 University Plaza, Platteville, WI 53818-3099. **EMAIL** wendorff@uwplatt.edu

WERNER, CYNTHIA
PERSONAL Born 07/24/1967, IL, s **DISCIPLINE** ANTHROPOLOGY **EDUCATION** Texas Christian Univ, BA, 89; Indiana Univ, MA, 93; PhD, 97. **CAREER** Vis asst prof, Univ Iowa, 97-98; vis asst prof, Pitzer Col, 98-00; asst prof, 00-. **HONORS AND AWARDS** SSRC Fel; Wenner-Gren Found Gnt, 95, 98; SSRC Diss Fel; SSRC Postdoc Fel; NCEEE Res Gnt. **MEMBERSHIPS** AAA; SEA; SAA; AES; PCCSIG. **RESEARCH** Post-Communist Societies: Central Asia; Kazakstan Economic Anthropology; Gift Exchange, Development, Markets, Consumption, Globalization Political Anthropology; Ethnonationalism; Democratization; Corruption. **SELECTED PUBLICATIONS** Auth, "A Preliminary Assessment of the Attitudes Toward the Privatization of Agriculture in Contemporary Kazakhstan," Cen Asian Sur 13 (94): 295-304; auth, "Women and the Art of Household Networking in Rural Kazakstan," Islam Quart 41 (97): 52-68; auth, "The Eighth Annual Nava'i Lecture. Marketing Gifts: The Dynamics of Change in a Kazak Village," Cen Asia Mon 6 (97): 1-7; auth, "Marriage, Markets and Merchants: Changes in Wedding Feasts and Household Consumption Patterns in Rural Kazakstan," Cult Agri (97): 6-13; auth, "Household Networks and the Security of Mutual Indebtedness in Rural Kazakstan," Cen Asian Surv 7 (98): 597-612; auth, "The Dynamics of Feasting and Gift Exchange in Rural Kazakstan," in Contemporary Kazaks: Social and Cultural Perspectives, ed. Ingvar Svanberg (London: Curzon Press, 99): 47-72; auth, "Gifts, Bribes and Development in Post-Soviet Kazakstan," Hum Org 59 (00): 11-22; auth, "Gifts, Bribes and Development in Post-Soviet Kazakstan," in Development Beyond the 20th Century: Critical Discussions in Economic Anthropology, ed. Jeffrey Cohen, Norbert Daunhauser (Lanham, MD: Univ Press Am,00). **CONTACT ADDRESS** Dept Anthropology, Pitzer Col, 1050 N Mills Ave, Claremont, CA 91711. **EMAIL** malika_cynny@yahoo.com

WERNER, SONIA S.
PERSONAL Born 07/02/1951, Abington, PA, m, 1976, 2 children **DISCIPLINE** PSYCHOLOGY **EDUCATION** W Conn Univ, BA, 74; Iowa State Univ, MS, 76; PhD, 79. **CAREER** Co-Dir, Corning Children's Center, 79-83; Instr, Corning Community Col and Alfred Univ, 83-90; Human Resource Profes-

sional, Corning, Inc, 90-95; Asst Prof, Bryn Athyn Col, 96-. **HONORS AND AWARDS** Outstanding Teacher, Corning Community Col, 90; Outstanding Individual Contributor, Corning, Inc, 94. **MEMBERSHIPS** APA, Nat Assoc for the Advancement of Young Children, Partnership for Serv Learning. **RESEARCH** Religion and psychology, assessing the development of college students after experiencing international service learning internships, social work, work satisfaction of employees in corporate and child care settings. **SELECTED PUBLICATIONS** Auth, "Measuring Work Satisfaction Among Child Care Employees," Child Care Infor Exchange (95); auth, "Flexible Work and Empowering Employees," The Advocate (95). **CONTACT ADDRESS** Dept Social Sci, Bryn Athyn Col, PO Box 717, Bryn Athyn, PA 19009. **EMAIL** sswerner@newchurch.edu

WERNET, STEPHEN P.
PERSONAL Born 09/13/1951, Ashland, MA, m, 1989, 4 children **DISCIPLINE** SOCIAL WORK **EDUCATION** Manhattan Col, BA, 73; Univ Conn, MSW, 82; Univ Tex, PhD, 88. **CAREER** Prof, Sch of Soc Service and Dept of Public Policy Studies, Col of Public Service, Saint Louis Univ, 95-. **HONORS AND AWARDS** Ctr for Social Justice Research and Education, Sch of Soc Service, Saint Louis Univ, grant, 99. **MEMBERSHIPS** Asn for Community Orgn and Soc Admin, Asn for Res on Nonprofit Organs and Voluntary Action, Am Asn of Univ Profs, Counc on Soc Work Educ, North Am Case Writers Asn, World Asn for Case Method Res and Application. **SELECTED PUBLICATIONS** Auth, "The Influence of Political Culture and Organizational Field Upon the Strategy and Structure of Nonprofit Social Service Organizations," Public Admin Quart, 20, 4 (97): 449-476; coauth, "The Role of the NonMSW Supervisor in Social Work Education," J of Teaching in Soc Work (99); auth, "Introduction to Managed Care in Human Services," Managed Care in Human Services, Lyceum Books (99); coauth, "Continuum of Care: A Strategy for Responding to Managed Care," in Stephen P. Wernet, ed, Managed Care in Human Services, Lyceum Books, Chicago, Ill (99); coauth, "Managed Psychcare: A Case Study," in Stephen P. Wernet, ed, Managed Care in Human Services, Lyceum Books, Chicago, Ill (99); ed, Managed Care in Human Services, Lyceum Books, Chicago, Ill (99); coauth, Cases in Macro Social Work Practice, Allyn & Bacon, Inc (2000). **CONTACT ADDRESS** Sch of Soc Sci, St. Louis Univ, 221 N Grand Blvd, Saint Louis, MO 63103. **EMAIL** wernetsp@slu.edu

WERTLIEB, DONALD
PERSONAL Born 02/22/1952, Washington, DC, m, 3 children **DISCIPLINE** PSYCHOLOGY **EDUCATION** Tufts Univ, BS, 74, MA, 75; Boston Univ, MA, 76, PhD, 78. **CAREER** Dir, Proj CoNECT, Tufts Univ, 81-84; lectr, Harvard Medical Sch, 84-89; res assoc, Harvard Sch of Public Health, 86-87; vis prof, Levin Center for Normal and Psychopathological Develop, Hebrew Univ, Jerusalem, 88; lectr to prof, Eliot-Pearson Dept of Child Study, Tufts Univ, 78-, Chair, 89-96, Dir, Center for Applied Child Develop, 89-96; res assoc prof, Tufts Univ Sch of Medicine, 92-. **HONORS AND AWARDS** Phi Beta Kappa, 73; Psi Chi Psychol Honor Student, 73; Carmichael Prize, 73; BS Summa cum laude, Tufts Univ, 74; NIMH Training Fel, Boston Univ, 74-76; Who's Who in the East; Who's Who: Professionals and Resources in Rehabilitation; Who's Who in the Behavioral Sciences; Who's Who in the Emerging Leaders in Am; Tufts Univ President's Recognition for Outstanding Fac Achievement, 96. **MEMBERSHIPS** Am Asn for Applied and Preventative Psychol, Am Asn of Univ Profs, Am Psychol Soc, Asn for the Advancement of Psychol, Mass Children's Lobby, Nat Coun on Family Relations, Psychologists for Soc Responsibility. **SELECTED PUBLICATIONS** Coauth, "The child with diabetes: Stress and coping in developmental perspective," in P. Costa & G. Vandenbos, eds, American Psychological Association Master Lectures: Psychological Aspects of Serious Illness, Washington, DC: APA (90): 61-101; coauth, "Self-perception and adolescent psychopathology: A clinical-developmental perspective," Am J of Orthopsychiatry, 64 (94): 293-300; coauth, "Doctoral education in applied child development," in C. Fisher, J. Murray, and I. Sigel, eds, Applied Developmental Science: Graduate Training for Diverse Disciplines and Educational Settings, NJ: Ablex (96): 121-141; auth, "Stress and coping, risk and resilience: Children and developmental trajectories," in A. Maney, ed, Social conditions, stress, resources and health," in A. Maney, ed, Social conditions, stress, resources and health, NIH (97). **CONTACT ADDRESS** Eliot-Pearson Dept of Child Development, Tufts Univ, Medford, 520 Boston Ave, Medford, MA 02155. **EMAIL** dwerlie@tufts.edu

WERUM, REGINA
PERSONAL Born 04/29/1966, Mainz, Germany **DISCIPLINE** SOCIOLOGY **EDUCATION** Hope Col, BA, 88; Ind Univ, MA, 90; Ind Univ, PhD, 95. **CAREER** Asst Prof, Emory Univ, 95-97; Proj Analyst, Microm GmbH, Duesseldorf, Germany, 97-98; Asst Prof, Emory Univ, 98-. **HONORS AND AWARDS** Fulbright Travel Grant, 87; MacArthur Found Fel, Ind Univ, 91; Spenser Found Fel, 93; Nat Acad of Ed Fel, 99; Nat Sci Found Grant Recipient, 00. **MEMBERSHIPS** Am Sociol Assoc, Southern Sociol Soc, Am Ed Res Assoc, Soc Sci Hist Assoc, Sociol for Women in Soc. **RESEARCH** Education, stratification, race/ethnic relations, social movements. **SE-LECTED PUBLICATIONS** Auth, "Sectionalism and Racial Politics," Social Sci Hist, 97; auth, "Tug-of-War: Political Mobilization and Access to Schooling in the Southern Racial State," Sociology of Ed, 99; auth, "Elite Control in State and Nation," Social Forces, 99. **CONTACT ADDRESS** Dept Sociol, Emory Univ, 1364 Clifton Rd, NE, Atlanta, GA 30322-0001. **EMAIL** rwerum@emory.edu

WESCOTT, ROGER WILLIAMS
PERSONAL Born 04/28/1925, Philadelphia, PA, m, 2 children **DISCIPLINE** LINGUISTIC ANTHROPOLOGY **EDUCATION** Princeton Univ, AB, 44 & 45, MA, 47, PhD(ling sci), 48; Oxford Univ, BLitt, 52. **CAREER** Ed & interviewer, Gallup Poll, 52; asst prof hist & human rels, Mass Inst Technol & Boston Univ, 53-57; assoc prof English & soc sci, Mich State Univ, 57-62, dir African lang prog, 59-62; prof anthrop & hist & chmn, Div Soc Sci, Southern Conn State Univ, 62-63; lectr sociol & anthrop, Wilson Col, 64-66; co-dir behav studies prog, 73-76, Prof Anthrop & Ling & Chmn Dept Anthrop, Drew Univ, 66-93, prof emer, 93-; Ford fel, Univ Ibadan, Nigeria, 55-56; foreign lang consult, US Off Educ, 61; West African Ling Surv grant, Ibadan, 61-62; consult ed, J African Lang, 62-; poetry ed, The Interpreter, 62-; ling fieldworker, Sierra Leone, 63; linguist, Bur Appl Social Res, Columbia Univ, 63-64; rev ed, Int Soc Comp Study Civilizations, 73-; pres prof humanities & soc sci, Colo Sch Mines, 80-81. **MEMBERSHIPS** Fel African Studies Asn; fel Am Anthrop Asn; fel AAAS; Int Ling Asn; Int Soc Comp Study of Civilizations. **SELECTED PUBLICATIONS** Auth, The Divine Animal: An Exploration of Human Potentiality, Funk, 69; coauth, A Pre-Conference Volume on Cultural Futurology, Am Anthrop Asn, 70; Human Futuristics, Univ Hawaii, 71; The Experimental Symposium on Comparative Futurology, Univ Minn, 71; auth, Traditional Greek conceptions of the future, In: The Experimental Symposium on Comparative Futurology, Univ Minn, 71; coauth, The Highest State of Consciousness, Anchor Bks, 72; auth, Seven Bini charms, Folklore Forum, 10/72; Metaphones in Bini and English, In: Studies in Linguistics in Honor of George L Trager, Mouton, The Hague, 73; Sound and Sense, Jupiter Press, 80. **CONTACT ADDRESS** 16-A Heritage Crest, Southbury, CT 06488-1370. **EMAIL** whilro@aol.com

WESSEL, THOMAS ROGER
PERSONAL Born 09/28/1937, Belmond, IA, m, 1964, 1 child **DISCIPLINE** AMERICAN HISTORY, ANTHROPOLOGY **EDUCATION** Iowa State Univ, BS, 63; Univ Md, MA, 68, PhD(hist), 72. **CAREER** Res asst hist, Smithsonian Inst, 65-68; asst prof, 72-75, head dept hist & philos, 79, Assoc Prof Hist, Mont State Univ, 75-79, Prof, Nat Endowment for Humanities fel anthrop, 73-74; Nat Prof, 80. **HONORS AND AWARDS** Res Achievement, Smithsonian Inst, 74. **MEMBERSHIPS** Agr Hist Soc; Orgn Am Historians; Western Hist Asn. **RESEARCH** American agricultural history; American Indian history. **SELECTED PUBLICATIONS** Auth, Prologue to the Shelterbelt, 1870-1934, J West, 68; Roosevelt and the Great Plains Shelterbelt, Great Plains J, 69; Agriculture and Iroquois hegemony in New York, 1604-1779, Md Historian, 70; A History of the Rocky Boy's Reservation, Bur Indian Affaris, 74; Agriculture, Indians and American history, Agr Hist, 76; Agriculture in the Great Plains, 1876-1930, Agr Hist Soc, 77; 4-H, An American Idea, 1900-1980, Nat 4-H Counc, 82; Centennial West - Essays On The Northern Tier States - Lang,Wl, Montana-The Magazine Of Western History, Vol 0043, 1993; The Northern-Cheyenne Indian Reservation, 1877-1900 - Svingen,Oj, Western Historical Quarterly, Vol 0025, 1994; Rooted In Dust - Surviving Drought And Depression In Southwestern Kansas - Rineykehrberg,P, Great Plains Quarterly, Vol 0016, 1996. **CONTACT ADDRESS** Dept of Hist, Montana State Univ, Bozeman, Bozeman, MT 59715.

WEST, HERBERT LEE, JR.
PERSONAL Born 05/04/1947, Warrenton, NC, m **DISCIPLINE** EDUCATION **EDUCATION** NC Central Univ, BA, 69; Univ of MN, MA, 72; PhD, 74. **CAREER** Teacher asst, Univ of Minnesota, 72; asst prof, Univ of Maryland Baltimore County, 74-80; asst prof, Howard University, 80-85; faculty intern, House Urban Devel, 80; advisor, Summer Work Program-Prince Georges County, Maryland; educator/admin, Howard County Bd of Education, 85- ; assoc prof, Villa Julie Col, 93-. **HONORS AND AWARDS** Ford Found Fel, 71; NEH Fellow Atlanta Univ, 78; Outstanding Teacher Univ of MD Baltimore Cty, 78, 79; Smithsonian Fellow Smithsonian Inst, 85; NEH Fellow Univ of NC, 83; Summer Fellow UMTA/Atlanta Univ, 84; Univ of Indiana guest lecturer, 88; NEH Fellow Columbia Univ, 89; Comga Graduate Fellowship Univ of Minnesota, 69; moderator, braodway show Sarifina, Kennedy Center, 90; NEW Fel, Emory Univ, 00. **MEMBERSHIPS** Mem NAACP, Triangle Geographers, Natl Council of Black Studies, Asn for the Study of Afro-Amer Life; Black Student Achievement Program, Howard County, Maryland. **CONTACT ADDRESS** Educator, Howard Cty Bd of Educ, 10910 Route 108, Ellicott City, MD 21043.

WESTERMEYER, JOSEPH JOHN
PERSONAL Born 04/08/1937, Chicago, IL, m, 1962, 7 children **DISCIPLINE** PSYCHOLOGY **EDUCATION** Notre Dame Univ and St Thomas Col 55-57, BS Biochem 59, MD

Medicine 61, MA Anthro 69, MPH Pub Health 70, PhD Psychiat/Anthro 70, Univ MN, NIDA-NIAAA Career Tchr/Res 74-77. **CAREER** Rotating Internship St Paul-Ramsey Hosp, 61-62; Gen Practive Payne Aven Medical Clin St Paul MN, 62-65; Deputy Chief Div Pub Health Agency Intl Devel Laos, 62-65; Memnrt Psychiat Staff Univ MN Hosp and Clin, 70-present; Prof and Chair Dept Psychiat and Behavioral Sci, Univ OK Health Sci Center OK 89-92; Residency in Psychiat /grad stud in Anthro/Pub Health 67-70, Univ MN, Chief of Psychiat MN VA Hosp; Prof Dept Psychiat, 92-. **HONORS AND AWARDS** AOA Hon Medical Soc, 61; Fel Am Anthro Asn, 76; Fel Am Asn of Family Practice, 76; Fel Am Psychiat Asn, 77; Who's Who in Am, 85-present; Fel Am Psychopathological Asn, 89; Fel Am Col Psychiat, 91; Best Drs Am, Alcoholism-Addictions Psychiat, Good Housekeeping, 93; Int Who's Who in Medicine, Cambridge UK, 94-; Int Who's Who Prof, Jacksonville NC, 95-. **MEMBERSHIPS** Am Acad Psychol in Alcoholism and Addictions; Am Anthro Assoc; Am Assoc for Advancement of Sci; Am Assoc of Soc Psychol; Am Col Psychol; Am Medical Assoc; Am Psychol Assoc; Am Pub Health Assoc; MN Council for Preventive Medicine; MN Psychol Assoc; OK Psychol Assoc; OK Medical Assoc; Soc of Biol Psychol; Soc for Traumatic Stress Studies. **RESEARCH** Substance abuse; psychiat disorder; treatemnt outcome of same; Cross cultural epidemiology of Psychiat disorder; diagnostic reliability/validity; methodology; theory. **SELECTED PUBLICATIONS** Westermeyer J, Neider J, Wetermeyer M, Culture Medicine Psychiatry 16(4): 519-529, 98; Westermeyer J, Cutural aspects of substance abuse and alcoholism, Assessment and Management; Psychiatric Clinics North America 18(3): 110-123, 96; Westermeyer J: Ethnic and cultural factors in dual disorder, Double Jeopardy: Chronic Mental Illness and Substance Abuse, eds, A D Lehman and L B Dixon, Univ Toronto Press, 95; Westermeyer J Bouafeuly-Kersey M, Her C: Hmong Children in Transcultural Child Development, eds, G Johnson-Powell and J Yamamoto, NY: John Wiley & Sons, 97; Westermeyer J: Cross-cultural aspects, Textbook of Substance Abuse, Vol(14) eds, M, Galanter and H D Kleber, Washington DC: American Press, in process. **CONTACT ADDRESS** 420 Delaware St. SE, Box 393 UMHC, Minneapolis, MN 55455. **EMAIL** weste010@email.umn.edu

WESTERN, BRUCE
PERSONAL Born 07/01/1964, Canberra, Australia, m, 3 children **DISCIPLINE** SOCIOLOGY **EDUCATION** Univ Queensland, Australia, BA, 87; Univ Calif Los Angeles, PhD, 93. **CAREER** Asst prof to assoc prof, Princeton Univ, 94-. **HONORS AND AWARDS** Cleary Prize, Univ of Queensland, 87; Hortense Fishbaugh Memorial Scholar, UCLA, 92-93; Chancellor's Dissertation Year Fel, UCLA, 92-93; Jean Monnet Fel, European Univ Inst, Florence, 95-96; vis scholar, Russell Gage Found, 99-2000. **MEMBERSHIPS** Am Sociol Asn, Am Statistical Asn, Am Political Sci Asn. **RESEARCH** Labor markets, social inequality, criminal justice methodology. **SELECTED PUBLICATIONS** Coauth, "The Penal System and the American Labor Market," Actes de la Reserche en Sciences Sociales, 124 (98): 27-35 (in French); coauth, ""How Unregulated is the U.S. Labor Market? The Penal System as a Labor Market Institution," Am J of Sociol, 104 (99): 1030-60; coauth, "Explaining the OECD Wage Slowdown: Recession or Labor Decline," European Sociol Rev, 15 (99): 233-49; coauth, "U.S. Earnings Inequality at the Close of the 20th Century," Annual Rev of Sociol, 25 (99): 623-57; auth, "Bayesian Analysis for Sociologists: An Introduction," Sociological Methods and Research, 28 (99): 7-34; auth, "Guest Editor's Introduction to Bayesian Methods in the Social Sciences," Sociol Methods and Research, 28 (99): 3-6; ed, Sociological Methods and Research, 28, 1 (99), special issue on "Bayesian Methods in the Social Sciences"; coauth, "Unions in Decline? What has Changed and Why," Annual Rev of Political Sci (forthcoming); coauth, "Crime Control American Style: the Emergence and Consequences of the U.S. War on Crime," in Criminal Justice in Transition: Criminal Policy Trends Into the New Millenium, ed by Penny Green and Andrew Rutherford, Oxford: Hart Pub (forthcoming); coauth, "Incarceration and Employment Inequality among Young Unskilled Men," Industrial and Labor Relations Rev (forthcoming). **CONTACT ADDRESS** Dept Sociol, Princeton Univ, 2-N-1 Green Hall, Princeton, NJ 08544-1010. **EMAIL** western@princeton.edu

WESTMAN, ALIDA S.
PERSONAL Born 10/16/1944, The Hague, Netherlands, d, 1 child **DISCIPLINE** PSYCHOLOGY **EDUCATION** Wash State Univ, BS, 66; MS, 68; Cornell Univ, PhD, 71. **CAREER** Asst prof to prof, Eastern Mich Univ, 72-. **HONORS AND AWARDS** Phi Beta Kappa; Phi Kappa Phi; Sigma Xi; Sigma Delta Epsilon; Psi Chi; HHS Fel; Eastern Mich Univ First Jr Fac Awd for Teaching and Commitment to Students, 77; Merit Awd, Univ of Mich, 81. **MEMBERSHIPS** Soc for the Sci Study of Relig; Am Psychol Assoc; Am Psychol Soc; Soc for Res on Child Develop. **RESEARCH** Perceptual and conceptual development, attitudes toward death and dying, psychology of religion. **SELECTED PUBLICATIONS** Coauth, "Relationships between learning styles and solutions based on analogies or background knowledge", Psychol Reports 77, (95): 1115-1120; coauth, "Social support desired vs received by high school students in or not in a delinquency prevention program", Psychol Reports 78, (96): 111-114; coauth, "Earliest memories and recall by modality involve recollections of different memories: memories are not amodal", Perceptual and Motor Skills 82, (96): 1131-1135; coauth, "Only visual impressions are almost always present in long-term memories, and reported completeness, accuracy, and verbalizability of recollections increase with age", Perceptual and Motor Skills 83, (96): 531-539; auth, "Religiosity correlates with failure to understand scientific methods and findings", Psychol Reports 80, (97): 161-162; coauth, "Lack of correlation's of sense-modality-oriented indices of learning styles with each other and with classroom tasks", Perceptual and Motor Skills 84, (97): 731-737; coauth, "The ESAD (Extension of Self and Attitude toward Death) was requested by and incorporated in the Behavioral Measurement Database Service of the National Library of Medicine of NIH, (97); coauth, "God-mediated control, religiousness, attributes of God and of the ideal religious life", Psychol Reports 84, (99): 585-586; coauth, "Relationship among assisted suicide and religiousness, resources available, denial of dying, and autonomy", Psychol Reports 85, (99): 1070-1076; coauth, "On perceived conflict between religion and science: the role of fundamentalism and right-wing authoritarianism", Psychol Reports, (forthcoming). **CONTACT ADDRESS** Dept Psychol, Eastern Michigan Univ, 537 Mark Jefferson Bldg, Ypsilanti, MI 48197. **EMAIL** psy_westman@online.emich.edu

WESTRA, MATTHEW R.
PERSONAL Born 06/26/1959, Kalamazoo, MI, m, 1989, 3 children **DISCIPLINE** PSYCHOLOGY **EDUCATION** Calif State Univ, Los Angeles, MS, 83. **CAREER** Supervising psychologist, Mass Dept of Mental Retardation, 89-90; instr, Longview Community Col, 90-. **HONORS AND AWARDS** Alpha Gamma Sigma Honor Soc, Psi Chi Psychol Honor Soc, BA with honors, MS with high honors. **MEMBERSHIPS** Coun of Teachers of Undergrad Psychol. **RESEARCH** Communication skills, parenting cross culturally, common sense. **SELECTED PUBLICATIONS** Auth, "Encounters with Oedipus Rex, " Full Time Dads, (Jan-Feb 95): 1, 14-15; auth, Active Communication, Pacific Grove, CA: Brooks/Cove (96). **CONTACT ADDRESS** Dept Soc Sci, Longview Comm Col, 500 Longview Rd, Lees Summit, MO 64081. **EMAIL** westra@longview.cc.mo.us

WEYLAND, KARIN
DISCIPLINE ANTHROPOLOGY, SOCIOLOGY **EDUCATION** Marlboro Col, BA, 91; New School for Social Research, MA, 93; PhD, 98. **CAREER** Adj Prof, Univ de Puerto Rico, 96-98; Asst Prof, Amherst Col, 98-. **HONORS AND AWARDS** Doctoral Writing Dean Fel, New School for Social Research, 95-96, Dissertation Research Fel, Organization of Am States, 95-96; Helen Safa Prize, Latin Am Studies Assoc, 00. **MEMBERSHIPS** Latin American Studies Assoc, 97-, American Sociological Assoc, 96-, International Visual Sociology Assoc, 92-, Institute for the Analysis of Contemporary Society, 92-. **RESEARCH** Research and teaching interests center around the issues of identity formation, border cultures, migration, gender and transnationalism with a special focus in the Hispanic Caribbean and Latino communities in the U.S. Also interested in visual sociology and the uses of photography and video-production in ethnographic research. **SELECTED PUBLICATIONS** Auth, "Donimicanness at the Crossroads: Surviving the Translocal Global Village,"; auth, "Hopscotch: A Cultural Review, ed. Ilan Stavans and Antonio Benitez Rojo, Duke Univ Press. **CONTACT ADDRESS** Dept Anthropology & Sociology, Amherst Col, Amherst College, PO Box 2226, Amherst, MA 01002-5000.

WHATLEY, MARK A.
PERSONAL Born, AL, m, 1996 **DISCIPLINE** PSYCHOLOGY **EDUCATION** Univ Ky, PhD, 98. **CAREER** Asst Prof, Valdosta State Univ, 98-. **HONORS AND AWARDS** Grant, Valdosta State Univ, 99; Outstanding Teaching Asst Awd, Univ KY, 98; Dissertation Res Awd, 97. **MEMBERSHIPS** Am Psychol Asn; Am Psychol Soc; Mid-west Psychol Asn; Soc for Personality and Soc Psychol **RESEARCH** Cross-cultural related behavior; Attribuition; Social influence; Victimization; Attractiveness; Just world beliefs. **SELECTED PUBLICATIONS** Co-auth, "Attributions of blame for female and male victims," Family Violence and Sexual Assault Bulletin, (92): 16-18; co-auth, "Gender differences in attributions of blame for male rape victims," Journal of Interpersonal Violence, (93): 502-511; auth, "For better or worse: The case of marital rape," Violence and Victims, (93): 31-41; auth, "Belief in a just world scale: Unidimensional or multidimensional?," Journal of Social Psychology, (93): 547-551; co-auth, "Effects of student academic ability on cognitive gains using reciprocal peer tutoring," Journal of Social Behavior and Personality, (94): 529-542; auth, "Victim characteristics influencing attributions of responsibility to rape victims: A meta-analysis," Aggression and Violent Behavior, (96): 81-95; co-auth, "The effect of a favor on public and private compliance: How internalized is the norm of reciprocity?," Basic and Applied Social Psychology, (99): 251-259; auth, "Secondary validation of the Global Belief in a Just World Scale," The Experimentalist, 00. **CONTACT ADDRESS** Dept Psychol & Guidance, Valdosta State Univ, 1500 N Patterson, Valdosta, GA 31698-0001. **EMAIL** mawhatle@valdosta.edu

WHEELER, JOHN
PERSONAL Born 04/05/1956, Washington, DC, d, 2 children **DISCIPLINE** EDUCATION **EDUCATION** Southern Ill Univ, PhD, 89. **CAREER** Asst Prof, Univ SDak, 89-94; Assoc Prof to Prof and Assoc Dean, Tenn Tech Univ, 94-. **HONORS AND AWARDS** Cert of Recognition in Teaching, TN Tech Univ Mortar Board Soc, 99; Nominated Prof of the Year, TN Tech Univ, 96. **MEMBERSHIPS** Coun for Exception Children; Asn for Beh Analysis; TN Asn for Beh Analysis. **RESEARCH** Applied behavior analysis; Children with moderte/severe disabilities; Systematic instruction. **SELECTED PUBLICATIONS** Co-auth, "Transition: An integrated model for pre-and in-service training of special education teachers," Journal of Career Development for Exceptional Individuals, (94): 145-158; co-auth, "Implementing supported employment in rural areas: Demographic variables affecting job development in South Dakota," rural special Educ Quarterly, (95): 20-23; co-auth, "Reducing challenging behavior through the modification of instructional antecedents," B.C. Journal of Special Education, (95): 4-14; auth, "The use of interactive focus groups to aid in the identification of perceived service and support delivery needs of persons with developmental disabilities and their families," Education and Training in retardation and Developmental Disabilities, (96): 294-303; co-auth, "A consultative model for the provision of behavioral supports to children with challenging behavior: Practical approaches for the development of school-based behavioral support teams," B.C. Journal of Special Education, (97): 5-16; co-auth, "The use of functional assessment procedures and individualized activity schedules in the treatment of autism: Recommendations for music therapists," Music Therapy Perspective, (97): 87-93; co-auth, "Using visual cues in the classroom for learners with Pervasive Developmental Disorders as a method for promoting positive behavior," B.C. Journal of special Education, (98): 64-73; co-auth, "Acquisition and generalization of photographic activity schedules and their effects on task engagement in a young child with autism in an inclusive pre-school classroom," Education and Training in Mental Retardation and Developmental Disabilities, 00; auth, "Principles of positive behavioral supports," in Inclusive early childhood education: Merging positive behavioral supports, activities-based intervention and developmentally appropriate practices, Delmar Pub, 00; auth, "Reducing challenging behavior in children with developmental disabilities through the modification of instructional practices in development disabilities, Pro-Ed, 98. **CONTACT ADDRESS** Dept Curriculum & Instrtuction, Tennessee Tech Univ, 1000 N Dixie Ave, Cookeville, TN 38505-0001.

WHEELER, KATHLEEN B.
DISCIPLINE EDUCATION **EDUCATION** Univ Neb, EdD, 96. **CAREER** Prof, York Col, 90-. **MEMBERSHIPS** ASCD, Nat Middle School Asn. **RESEARCH** Middle School transition (into and out of). **CONTACT ADDRESS** Dept Educ, York Col, Nebraska, 1125 E 8th St, York, NE 68467. **EMAIL** kbwheeler@york.edu

WHEELER, STANTON
PERSONAL Born 09/27/1930, Pomona, CA, m, 1951, 3 children **DISCIPLINE** SOCIOLOGY OF LAW **EDUCATION** Pomona Col, BA, 52; Univ Wash, MA, 56, PhD(sociol), 58. **CAREER** Acting instr, Univ Wash, 56-58; instr social rel, Harvard Univ, 58-60; Fulbright res scholar, Insts Sociol & Criminol, Univ Oslo, 60-61; asst prof social rel, Harvard Univ, 61-63; assoc prof sociol, Univ Wash, 63-64; sociologist, Russell Sage Found, 64-68; adj assoc prof sociol & law, 66-68, Prof Sociol & Law, Yale Law Sch, 68-, Mem, Russell Sage Found, 68-; fel, Ctr Advan Studies Behav Sci, 70-71; mem, Comt on Incarceration, 71-. **MEMBERSHIPS** Am Sociol Asn; Soc Studies Social Probs (pres-elect); Law & Soc Asn. **RESEARCH** Sociology of crime, deviance and incarceration; sociology of sport and leisure. **SELECTED PUBLICATIONS** Coauth, Socialization After Childhood: Two Essays, 66, auth, Deviant behavior, In: Sociology: An Introduction, 67, rev ed, 73 & coauth, Controlling Delinquents, 68, Wiley; auth, On Record: Files and Dossiers in American Life, Russell Sage Found, 69; Socialization in correctional institutions, In: Handbook of Socialization Theory and Research, Rand McNally, 69; The Prospects For Large-Scale Collaborative Research - Revisiting The Yale White-Collar Crime Research-Program, Law And Social Inquiry-Journal Of The American Bar Foundation, Vol 0018, 1993. **CONTACT ADDRESS** Russell Sage Prog, Yale Univ, PO Box 208215, New Haven, CT 06520-8215.

WHELCHEL, MARIANNE
DISCIPLINE AMERICAN LITERATURE AND WOMEN'S STUDIES **EDUCATION** LaGrange Col, BA; Purdue Univ, MA; Univ CT, PhD. **CAREER** Prof, Antioch Col. **HONORS AND AWARDS** NEH grant, 82-83. **RESEARCH** Alice Carr. **SELECTED PUBLICATIONS** Wrote on letters, jour(s), and oral testimony; publ on Adrienne Rich, and Alice Carr, a 1904 Antioch graduate who nursed in World War I and became internationally known for public health work in Greece during the 1920s. and 1930s. **CONTACT ADDRESS** Antioch Col, Yellow Springs, OH 45387.

WHITCHURCH, GAIL
PERSONAL Born 08/30/1952, Minneapolis, MN **DISCIPLINE** FAMILY STUDIES, COMMUNICATION STUDIES **EDUCATION** Univ Minn, BA, 74; MA, 81; Univ Del, PhD, 89. **CAREER** From asst prof to assoc prof, Indiana University--Purdue Univ Indianapolis, 93-. **HONORS AND AWARDS** Teaching Excellence Recognition Awd (Ind Univ Board of Trustees Awd), Ind Univ, 97 & 99. **MEMBERSHIPS** Nat Commun Asn, Nat Coun on Family Relations, Am Asn for Marriage and Family Therapy. **RESEARCH** Communication and families. **SELECTED PUBLICATIONS** Coauth, "Melding the objective and subjective sides of leadership: Behaviors and social judgments in decision-making groups," Commun Monographs 62 (95): 244-264; coauth, "Applied family communication research: Casting light upon the demon," J of Applied Commun Res 23 (95): 239-246; coauth, "Communication and emergent group leadership: Does content count?," Commun Res Reports 14 (97): 470-480; coauth, "Family Communication," in Handbook of Marriage and the Family, eds. M.B. Sussman, S.K. Steinmetz, & G.W. Peterson (NY: Plenum, 99), 687-704; coauth, "Big changes come with small packages: Communication processes in the transition to parenthood," in Case Studies in Interpersonal Communication: Processes and Problems, eds. D.O. Braithwaite & J.T. Wood (CA: ITP/Wadsworth, 00), 228-236; auth, "Violent critical incidents in four types of violent interspousal relationships," Marriage and Family Rev (in press). **CONTACT ADDRESS** Dept Commun, Indiana Univ-Purdue Univ, Indianapolis, 425 N University Blvd, Indianapolis, IN 46202-5140. **EMAIL** whig@iupui.edu

WHITE, CLOVIS L.
DISCIPLINE SOCIOLOGY **EDUCATION** Southeastern Mass Univ, BA, 75; SUNY Albany, MA, 77; Indiana Univ, PhD, 84. **CAREER** Asst prof, Univ Wisc, Madison, 84-88; asst prof, Oberlin Col, 88-2000. **MEMBERSHIPS** Am Sociol Asn. **RESEARCH** Race, social psychology. **CONTACT ADDRESS** Dept Sociol, Oberlin Col, 10 N Prof St, Oberlin, OH 44074. **EMAIL** Clovis.White@oberlin.edu

WHITE, DOUGLAS R.
PERSONAL Born Minneapolis, MN, m, 1970, 1 child **DISCIPLINE** ANTHROPOLOGY **EDUCATION** Univ Minn, PhD, 69. **CAREER** Asst prof, Univ of Pittsburgh, 69-72; assoc prof, 72-76; assoc prof, Univ Calif Irvine, 76-79; prof, Social Networks, Univ Calif Irvine, 82-; anthropology, social relations, Univ Calif Irvine, 89-; Univ Calif Intercampus Graduate Curriculum, 1995-; Institute for Mathematical Behavioral Science, Univ Calif Irvine, 1994-. **HONORS AND AWARDS** Am Fld Ser Schlshp, Madrid, 58-59; NSF Coop Fel, Univ MN, 63-64; CIC Trav Schl, MI, 64-65; Vis Fel, Columbia, 65-66; Predoc Fel, Nat Inst Mental Health, 64-67; Fel Cen Adv Stud, W Behavioral Sci Inst, 81-84; Distinguished Sr US Sci Awd, Alexander von Humboldt Found, 90-92; Bourse de Haute Niveau, Min Res Tech, Lab d'Analyse Sec et des Methodes App a la Soc, Paris, 91-92; Vis Fel, Univ Koln Leibritz Prog, Ger Res Soc, 96, 97, 98; Bourse de Haute Niveau, Univ Nanterre, Paris, pending. **MEMBERSHIPS** Fel AAA; Mem, Classification Society-No. American Branch, Society for Cross-Cultural Res; Pres Elect and Pres, Social Science Computing Association, 92-93; Found Gen Ed, World Cultures, 85-90; Mem, NSF Advisory Panel; Conference organizer: Urban Anthropology; Natural Decision Making; Social Networks; Cross-Cultural Research: Teleconferencing; Text Analysis; Research Methods; Approaches to Unified Social Science; Longitudinal Field Studies: Scholars Workstation; Social Science Computing (1995, UCS-DISDSC). **RESEARCH** Anthropology theory, Social networks/social org, Social Demography and Longitudinal Field Sites, Migration, Kinship and Marriage Networks, Gender, Exchange, Transnational Development and Community Change, Mathematical Anthropology and Computing, Comparative Historical Cross-Cultural Research, World Systems and Global Change, Urban Anthropology, Indian North America, Mesoamerica, Europe. **SELECTED PUBLICATIONS** Coauth, Foundations for Social and Biological Evolution, CDC Press, 93; coed, Kinship, Networks and Exchange, Cambridge University Press, 98; auth, "Statistical Entaiments and the Galois lattice," Social Networks 18 (98): 201-215; coauth, "Kinship Networks and Discrete Structure Theory: Applications and Implications," Social Networks 18 (96):267-314; coauth "Structures reticulaires de Ia pratique matrimoniale," L'Homme 139 (96): 59-85; auth, "Class, Property and Structural Endogamy: Visualizing Networked Histories," Theory and Society 25 (97): 161-208; auth, "Structural Endogamy and the graphe de parent~," Wlathimatique, Informatique et sciences humaines 137 (97): 107-125; coauth, "Kinship, Property and Stratification in Rural Java: A Network Analysis (98): 36-58; coauth, "Taking Sides: Marriage Networks and Dravidian Kinship in Lowland South America," in Transformations of Kinship, eds. Maurice Godelier, Thomas Trautmann, Franklin E. Tjon Sie Fat, Smithsonian Institution Press, 98; auth, "Elementary Simulation of Marriage Systems," J Aflificial Soc Social Simulation, 99; auth, "Networks, Cognition and Ethnography: Thomas Schweitzer Remembered," Connections 22 (99): 19-27. **CONTACT ADDRESS** Dept Anthropology, Univ of California, Irvine, Irvine, CA 92697-0001. **EMAIL** drwhite@uci.edu

WHITE, HELENE R.
PERSONAL Born 07/11/1949, Paterson, NJ, m, 1972 **DISCIPLINE** SOCIOLOGY **EDUCATION** Douglas Col, BA, 71; Rutgers Univ, MPhil, 75; PhD, 76. **CAREER** Res Assoc to Prof, Rutgers Univ, 75-. **HONORS AND AWARDS** Public Service Awd, New Jersey, 87; Fac Acad Service Increment, Rutgers Univ, 91, 93-99. **MEMBERSHIPS** Am Sociol Asn, Am Soc of Criminol. **RESEARCH** Alcohol and drug studies; Delinquency/Criminology; Medical sociology; Longitudinal research methods. **SELECTED PUBLICATIONS** Co-auth, "Developmental associations between substance use and violence," Development and Psychopathology, (99): 785-803; co-auth, "Developmental aspects of delinquency and internalizing problems and their association with persistent juvenile substance use between ages 7 and 18," Journal of clinical Child Psychology, (99): 322-332; auth, "Specific alcoholic beverages and physical and mental health among adolescents," Journal of Studies on alcohol, (990: 209-218; co-auth, "Adolescents at risk: Low socioeconomic status and early onset drug use in the US, in Global Drugs Law, Har-Anand Pub, 98; co-auth, "Adult outcomes of adolescent drug use: A comparison of process-oriented and incremental analyses, in New Perspectives on Adolescent Risk Behavior, Cambridge Univ Press, 98; co-auth, "Acute and long-term effects of drug use on aggression from adolescence into adulthood," Journal of Drug Issues, (98): 837-858; co-auth, "The relationship of cohabitation and mental health: A study of a young adult cohort," Journal of Marriage and the Family, (98): 124-136; co-auth, "Adolescents and HIV risk due to drug injection or sex with drug injectors in the United States," AIDS and adolescents, Harwood Acad Pub, 97; ed, Society, Culture and Drinking Patterns Reexamined, Rutgers Center of alcohol Studies, 91; co0ed, alcohol, Science and Society Revisited, Univ Mich Press, 82. **CONTACT ADDRESS** Dept Sociol, Rutgers, The State Univ of New Jersey, New Brunswick, PO Box 5072, New Brunswick, NJ 08903.

WHITE, JOSEPH
DISCIPLINE PSYCHOLOGY **EDUCATION** Ut State Univ, BS, 92; MS, 94; Tex Tech Univ, PhD, 97. **CAREER** Asst Prof, SDak State Univ, 97-. **MEMBERSHIPS** Nat Coun on Family Relations; Soc for Res on Adolescence; Soc for Res in Adult Dev; Soc for Res on Identity Formation. **RESEARCH** Life-span human development; Family contributions (e.g. fathering styles) to healthy psychosocial development; Adolescent and adult psychosocial development in relation to problematic behavior; Addiction and recovery. **SELECTED PUBLICATIONS** Co-auth, "Revised classification criteria for the Extended Objective Measure of Ego Identity Status," Journal of Adolescence, (94): 533-549; co-auth, "Identity styles of male inmates," Criminal Justice and Behavior, (96): 490-504; co-auth, "Predictors of attrition from an outpatient chemical dependency program," Substance Abuse, (98): 49-59; co-auth, "The Identity Style Inventory: A revision with a sixth grade reading level," Journal of Adolescent Research, (98): 223-245; auth, "Alcoholism and identity development: A theoretical integration of the least mature status with the typologies of alcoholism," Alcoholism Treatment Quarterly, (00): 1; co-auth, "Indicators of spiritual development in recovery from alcohol and other drug problems," Alcoholism Treatment Quarterly, (00): 3. **CONTACT ADDRESS** Dept Human Dev, So Dakota State Univ, Box 2275A, Brookings, SD 57007-0295. **EMAIL** Joseph_White@sdstate.edu

WHITE, LAWRENCE
PERSONAL Born 10/25/1953, San Rafael, CA, m, 1983, 2 children **DISCIPLINE** PSYCHOLOGY **EDUCATION** Whittier Col, BA, 75; Calif State Univ at Fresno, MA, 79; Univ Calif at Santa Cruz, PhD, 84. **CAREER** Prof, Beloit Col, 85-; vis prof, Portland State Univ, 87; vis prof, Calif School of Prof Psychology, 90. **HONORS AND AWARDS** ResGrant, Nat Inst of Mental Health, 87; Fulbright Scholar, Estonia, 97-98. **MEMBERSHIPS** Am Psychol Soc; Am Psychol-Law Soc; Midwestern Psychol Assoc; Soc for the Psychol Study of Social Issues. **RESEARCH** Reliability of witnesses, Capital punishment and capital trials. **SELECTED PUBLICATIONS** Coauth, "Energy conservation research of California's utilities: A meta-evaluation", Evaluation Review 8.2 (84):167-186; auth, "Attitudinal consequences of the pre-employment polygraph examination", Jour of Appl Social Psychol 14.4 (84):364-374; auth, "Juror decision-making in the capital penalty trial: An analysis of crimes and defense strategies", Law and Human Behav 11.2 (87):113-130; auth, "The mental illness defense in the capital penalty hearing", Behav Sciences and the Law 5.4 (87):411-421; coauth, "Effects of question repetition on the eyewitness testimony of children and adults", Developmental Psychology 27.6 (91):975-986; coauth, "Two years later: Effects of question repetition and retention interval on the eyewitness testimony of children and adults", Developmental Psychology 29.5 (93):844-853; coauth, "An overview of the death penalty and capital trials: History, current status, legal procedures, and cost", Jour of Social Issues 50.2 (94):1-18; coauth, "The death penalty in the United States", Jour of Social Issues 50.2 (94); coauth, "Tell me again and again: Stability and change in the repeated testimonies of children and adults" in Memory and Testimony in the Child Witness, eds M.S. Zarogoza, J.R. Graham, G.C.N. Hall, r. Hirschman and Y.S. Ben-Porath, (CA:Sage, 95) 24-43. **CONTACT ADDRESS** Dept Psychology, Beloit Col, 700 College St, Beloit, WI 53511.

WHITLEY, DAVID S.
PERSONAL Born 03/05/1953, Williams AFB, AZ, m, 1987, 1 child **DISCIPLINE** ANTHROPOLOGY, ARCHAEOLOGY **EDUCATION** UCLA, PhD, 82. **CAREER** Chiel Archaeologist, Inst of Archaeology, UCLA, 83-87; post-doc res fel, Archaeology dept, Univ of the Witwatersrand, 87-89; principle, WIS Consultants, 89-. **HONORS AND AWARDS** Special appreciation awards: CA Indian Found, 93; Simi Valley Hist Soc, 91; Canadian Tribal Coun, 89. **MEMBERSHIPS** Fel, Am Antropological Asn; Soc for Am Archaeology; Soc of Prof Archaeologists; Int Coun of Monuments and Sites. **RESEARCH** Western, northern Am archaeology; prehistoric religion; rock art; neuropsychology. **SELECTED PUBLICATIONS** Auth, New Light in Old Art: Recent Advances in Hunter-Gatherer Rock Art Research, co-ed with L L Loendorf, UCLA Inst of Archaeology, Monograph 36, 94; Guide to Rock Art Sites: Southern California and Southern Nevada, Mountain Press Pub Co, 96; Following the Shaman's Path, Maturango Museum, 98; Reader in Gender Archaeology, co-ed with K Hayes-Gilpen, Routledge, 98; ed, Reader in Archaeological Theory: Post-processual and Cognitive Approaches, Routledge, 98; Les Chamanes de Californie: Art Rupestre Amerindien de Californie, Editions du Seuil, in press; numerous other scholarly articles, book reviews, and other publications. **CONTACT ADDRESS** 447 Third St, Fillmore, CA 93015. **EMAIL** huitli@impulse.net

WHITNEY, RUTH
PERSONAL Born 03/08/1938, Quincy, IL, d **DISCIPLINE** RELIGION; WOMEN'S STUDIES **EDUCATION** Marquette Univ, BS; Catholic Univ Am, MA, PhD. **CAREER** Asst prof, relig, Rutgers Univ, 73-79; Adj fac, Women's Studies, Univ So Fla, 89- . **HONORS AND AWARDS** Alpha Sigma Nu. **MEMBERSHIPS** Am Acad Relig; Natl Women's Stud Asn. **RESEARCH** Women; religion; spirituality; psychology; politics. **SELECTED PUBLICATIONS** Auth, Feminism and Love: Transforming Ourselves and Our World, Cross Cultural, 98. **CONTACT ADDRESS** 700 14th Ave N, Saint Petersburg, FL 33701-1018. **EMAIL** whitneyra@aol.com

WHITTAKER, JOHN
DISCIPLINE PSYCHOLOGY OF RELIGION, THEORIES OF RELIGION, PHILOSOPHY OF RELIGION **EDUCATION** Yale Univ, PhD, 74. **CAREER** Prof Relig Stud, dir, Relig Stud prog, La State Univ. **RESEARCH** The philosophy of religion; D.Z. Phillips; Wittgenstein; Kierkegaard. **SELECTED PUBLICATIONS** Auth, Matters of Faith and Matters of Principle, Trinity UP, 81; The Logic of Religious Persuasion, Peter Lang, 91. **CONTACT ADDRESS** Dept of Philos & Relig Stud, Louisiana State Univ and A&M Col, 106 Coates Hall, Baton Rouge, LA 70803. **EMAIL** jwhitt1@lsu.edu

WHITTAKER, JOHN
PERSONAL Born 09/06/1953, Richland, WA, m, 1979, 1 child **DISCIPLINE** ANTHROPOLOGY **EDUCATION** Cornell Univ, BA, 75; Univ Ariz, MA, 79; PhD, 84. **CAREER** Lect, Grinnell Col, 84-89; Asst Prof, Grinnell Col, 89-94; Dept Ch, Grinnell Col, 97-99; Assoc Prof, Grinnell Col, 94-. **MEMBERSHIPS** Soc for Am Archaeol, Assoc of Iowa Archaeologists, Iowa Archaeol Soc, Am Comt for the Preserv of Archaeol Collections, Iowa State Hist Soc. **RESEARCH** Southwest United States prehistory, eight seasons excavation of Sinagua sites near Flagstaff, Arizona, lithic analysis and replicative experiment, other early technologies, ethnography of craftsmen, modern American flintknappers, anthropology and the American public. **SELECTED PUBLICATIONS** Coauth, "Sinagua Painted Armbands," Kiva 58 (92): 177-187; auth, Flintknapping: Making and Understanding Stone Tools, Univ Tex Pr (Austin, TX), 94; coauth, "Some Prehistoric Copper Flaking Tools in Minnesota," Wis Archaeologist, 77 (96): 3-10; auth, "A Cypriot Flintknapper and the Threshing Sledge Industry," Lithic Technol, 21 (96): 108-119; auth, "Reproducing a Bronze Age Dagger from the Thames: Statements and Questions," London Archaeologist, 8 (96): 51-54; auth, "Red Power Finds Creationism: Review of 'Red Earth, White Lies' by Vine Deloria, Jr," Skeptical Inquirer, 21 (97): 47-50; coauth, "Evaluating Consistency in Archaeological Typology and Classification," J of Archaeol Method and Theory, 5 (98): 129-164; coauth, Surviving Adversity: The Sinagua of Lizard Man Village, Univ Ut Pr (Salt Lake City, UT), 99; auth, "The Ethnoarchaeology of Cypriot Threshing Floors," J of Mediter Archaeology, 12 (99): 7-25; coauth, "Replicas, Fakes and Art: The Twentieth-Century Stone Age and its Effects on Archaeology," Am Antiquity, 64 (99): 203-214; **CONTACT ADDRESS** Dept Anthrop, Grinnell Col, PO Box 805, Grinnell, IA 50112.

WICKHAM-CROWLEY, TIMOTHY P.
PERSONAL Born 11/12/1951, Elizabeth, NJ, m, 1981 **DISCIPLINE** SOCIOLOGY **EDUCATION** Princeton Univ, AB, 73; Cornell Univ, MA, 75, PhD, 82. **CAREER** Vis prof, 83-84, Hamilton Col; vis prof, 84-86, Univ Rochester; asst prof, 86-92, assoc prof, 92-, Georgetown Univ. **HONORS AND AWARDS** NEH Fel, sum inst, 95. **MEMBERSHIPS** Latin Amer Stud Assn; Amer Sociol Assn; E Sociol Soc; Exec Cimt of Lat Am Studies Asn, 02-03. **RESEARCH** Latin Amer; revolution; development; theory. **SELECTED PUBLICATIONS** Art, The Rise (and Sometimes Fall) of Guerrilla Governments in Latin America, Sociol Forum 2, 87; auth, Winners, Losers, and Also-

rans: Toward a Comparative Sociology of Latin American Guerrilla Movements, Power & Popular Protest: Latin Amer Soc Movements, Univ Calif Press, 89; art, Understanding Failed Revolution in El Salvador: A Comparative Analysis of Regime Types and Social Structures, Politics & Soc 17, 89; art, Terror and Guerrilla Warfare in Latin America 1956-1970, Comparative Stud in Soc & Hist 32, 90; auth, Exploring Revolution: Essays on Latin American Insurgency and Revolutionary Theory, Armonk: Sharpe, 91; auth, Guerrillas and Revolution in Latin America: A Comparative Study of Insurgents and Regimes Since 1956, Princeton Univ Press, 92; art, A Qualitative Comparative Approach to Latin American Revolutions, Intl J of Comparative Soc 32, nos 1&2, 91; art, Elites, Elite Settlements and Revolutionary Movements in Latin America 1950-1980, Soc Science Hist 18, 94; art, Concerning Foxes and Hedgehogs: Tilly on State-Incited and State-Seeking Violence, Pol Powr & Soc theory, vol 9, JAI Press, 95; art, Structural Theories of Revolution, Theorizing Revolutions, Routledge, 97; co-ed, contrib, The Politics of Injustice in Latin American, Univ of Cal Pr, 02. **CONTACT ADDRESS** Dept of Sociology, Georgetown Univ, Box 571037, Washington, DC 20057. **EMAIL** Wickhamt@gunet.georgetown.edu

WIGGINS, JACQUELINE D.
DISCIPLINE MUSIC EDUCATION **EDUCATION** Univ IL, Ed D, 92. **CAREER** Public school music teacher, 72-94; coordinator of Music Ed, Oakland Univ, Rochester, MI, 94-. **MEMBERSHIPS** MENC; NASM; AERA. **RESEARCH** Creative process and connections to cognitive process. **SELECTED PUBLICATIONS** Auth, Children's Strategies for Solving Compositional Problems with Peers, J of Res in Music Ed, vol 42, no 3, 94; Teacher-Research in a General Music Classroom: Effects on the Teacher, Bul of the Coun for Res in Music Ed, no 123, winter 94/95; Building Structural Understanding: Sam's Story, The Quart J of Music-Teaching and Learning, vol 6, no 3, 96; with Karen Bodoin, Painting a Big Soup: Teaching and Learning in a Second Grade General Music Classroom, J of Res in Music Ed, vol 46, no 2, 98; auth, Composition in the Clasroom, MENC, 90; auth, Synthesizers in the Elem Music Classroom, MENC, 91; auth, Teaching for Musical Understanding, McGraw-Hill, 01. **CONTACT ADDRESS** Dept of Music, Theatre and Dance, Oakland Univ, Rochester, MI 48063. **EMAIL** jwiggins@oakland.edu

WIGGINS, ROBERT R.
PERSONAL Born 08/02/1939, Endicott, NY, m, 1962, 2 children **DISCIPLINE** SOCIOLOGY **EDUCATION** Baptist Bible Col, ThB, 64; Olivet Nazarete Col, BA, 66; Am Univ, MS, 70; Univ Tex, PhD, 87. **CAREER** Spec asst, US Board of Parole, 70-89; assoc prof, Liberty Univ, 89-92; assoc prof, 92-. **MEMBERSHIPS** Am Correctional Assoc; Am Probation and Parole Assoc; Am Soc of Pub Admin; Ohio Coun of Criminal Justice Educ; Acad of Criminal Justice Sci. **RESEARCH** Organization design and decision-making theory. **SELECTED PUBLICATIONS** Coauth, "Your Church Ministry: Planned Effort or Potluck", Cedarville Torch, 93; rev of "The Return of the Dangerous Classes" by Diana r. Gordon, "A Cultural Liberal's Analysis of Drug Prohibition" , in Fed Probation, 95; auth, "Principles of Biblical Leadership", Baptist Bulletin (96): auth, "Ten Ideas for Effective Managers", Fed Probation, 96; auth, "Sections on the topics: deterrence, goodtime, and sentence", Ready Reference: American Justice, US Parole Commission, Salem Pr, 96; rev, of "Poor Discipline: Parole and the Social Control of the Underclass" by Jonathan Simon, "The Power of Parole", in Fed Probation, 96; rev, of "Three Strikes and You're Out: Vengeance as Public Policy", eds, David Shichor and Dale K. Sechrest, "Three Strikes and You're In: America's Costly Shell Game", in Fed Probation, (June 97); rev of "Profitable Penalties: How to Cut Both Crime Rates and Costs" by Daniel Glaser, "Reflections on Crime Reduction and Punishment", in Fed Probation, (March 98); auth, Introduction to Corrections", Am Jails, (September 99). **CONTACT ADDRESS** Dept Hist and Soc Sci, Cedarville Col, PO Box 601, Cedarville, OH 45314.

WIINAMAKI, LIZABETH
PERSONAL Born 09/07/1955, Superior, WI, s **DISCIPLINE** SOCIAL WORK **EDUCATION** Univ Wis, BS, 76; Univ Okla, MSW, 94; Univ Tenn Knoxville, PhD, 97. **CAREER** Soc worker, Okla Dept of Human Res, 85-94; asst prof, Juniata Col, 97-. **MEMBERSHIPS** Acad of Crim Justice Sci. **RESEARCH** Victim-Offender Mediation Programs, Child Welfare Issues. **SELECTED PUBLICATIONS** Coauth, "The effects of anger control training on adolescent antisocial behavior", Res on Soc Work Practice 7.4 (97): 446-462; coauth, Participation in victim-offender mediation and reoffense: successful replications?", Res on Soc Work Practice (forthcoming); coauth, Participation in victim-offender mediation and the prevalence and severity of subsequent delinquent behavior (forthcoming). **CONTACT ADDRESS** Dept Sociol and Anthrop, Juniata Col, 1700 Moore St, Huntingdon, PA 16652. **EMAIL** wiinamaki@juniata.edu

WILCOX, RAND R.
PERSONAL Born 07/06/1946, Niagara Falls, NY, m, 1987, 2 children **DISCIPLINE** PSYCHOLOGY **EDUCATION** Univ Calif, BA, 68; MA, 76; PhD, 76. **CAREER** Sen Res Assoc, Univ Ca, 76-81; Asst Prof to Prof, Univ S Calif, 81-. **HONORS AND AWARDS** Thomas L. Saaty Awd, 83; Teaching Awd, USC; Fel, Royal Statistical Soc. **MEMBERSHIPS** Am Educ Res Asn; Am Statistical Asn; Inst of Mathematical Statistics; Psychometric Soc; Am Psychol Soc; British Psychol Asn; Royal Statistical Soc. **SELECTED PUBLICATIONS** Auth, "Some small-sample results on a bounded influence rank regression method," Communications in Statistics - Theory and Methods, (95): 881-888; auth, "Confidence intervals for the slope of a regression line when the error term has non-constant variance," Computational Statistics and Data Analysis, (96): 89-98; auth, "A review of some recent developments in robust regression," British Journal of Mathematical and Statistical Psychology, (96): 253-274; auth, "Some practical reasons for reconsidering the Kolmogorov-Smirnov test," British Journal of Mathematical and Statistical Psychology, (97); 9-20; auth, "A bootstrap modification of the Alexander-Govern ANOVA method, plus comments on comparing trimmed means," Educational and Psychological Measurement, (97): 655-665; auth, "The goals and strategies of robust methods," British Journal of Mathematical and Statistical Psychology, (98): 1-39; auth, "Reply to discussants of The goals and strategies of robust methods," British Journal of Mathematical and Statistical Psychology, (98): 55-62; auth, "Rank-based tests for interactions in a two-way design," computational Statistics and Data Analysis, (99): 275-284; auth, "Comments on Stute, Manteiga, and Quindimil," Journal of the American Statistical Association, (99): 659-660; auth, "Testing hypotheses about regression parameters when the error term is heteroscedastic," Biometrical Journal, (99): 411-426. **CONTACT ADDRESS** Dept Psychol, Univ of So California, 3620 McClintock Ave, Los Angeles, CA 90089-1061. **EMAIL** rwilcox@wilcox.usc.edu

WILDE, JERRY
PERSONAL Born 11/29/1962, La Crosse, WI, m, 1988, 2 children **DISCIPLINE** EDUCATION **EDUCATION** Univ Northern Iowa, EdS, 88; Marquette Univ, PhD, 93. **CAREER** Asst Prof, Ind Univ, 98-. **HONORS AND AWARDS** Henry O. Talle Awd for Acad Excellence. **MEMBERSHIPS** Eastern Educ Roes Assoc. **RESEARCH** Anger management in children, rational-emotive education **SELECTED PUBLICATIONS** Auth, "The Efficacy of Short-Term Rational Emotive Education: A Follow-up Evaluation," J of Cognitive Psychotherapy, 13 (99): 133-144; auth, Creative Strategies for Working with Oppositional and Defiant Children and Adolescents, Develop Resources (Chapin, SC), 99; coauth, Teaching Children Patience Without Losing Yours, LGR Publ (Richmond, IN), 99. Auth, An Educator's Guide to Difficult Parents, Kroshka Books (Commack, NY), forthcoming; auth, Surviving and Thriving in a Blended Family, William Neil Publ (Binghamton, NY), forthcoming. **CONTACT ADDRESS** Dept Educ, Indiana Univ, East, 2325 Chester Blvd, Richmond, IN 47374. **EMAIL** jwilde@indiana.edu

WILDMAN, LOUIS ROBERT
PERSONAL Born 11/15/1941, Portland, OR **DISCIPLINE** EDUCATION **EDUCATION** Lewis & Clark Col, AB, 63; Univ Portland, MEd, 64; Univ WA, EdD, 71. **CAREER** Prof & Co-ord, Calif State Univ. **HONORS AND AWARDS** Outstanding Service Awd, CA Asn of Prof of Educ Admin, 98. **MEMBERSHIPS** Nat Coun of Prof of Educ Admin. **RESEARCH** Instructional Leadership. **SELECTED PUBLICATIONS** Auth, Practical Understanding of the Percussion Section, Humphries, 64; auth, The University Community, Inst of Quality in Human Life, 74; auth, Hih School Graduation Competencies, Inst of Quality in Human Life, 74; auth, Teacher Evaluation: A Dialogue, Inst of Quality in Human Life, 75; auth, Economic Assumptions and the Future of Higher Education, Inst of Quality in Human Life, 76; auth, A Dialogue on the Selection of Educators, Inst of Quality in Human Life, 77; auth, Teacher Constructed Tests, Inst of Quality in Human Life, 77; auth, Studies in the Sociology of Music, Inst of Quality in Human Life, 81. **CONTACT ADDRESS** Dept Educ, California State Univ, Bakersfield, 9001 Stockdale Hwy, Bakersfield, CA 93311. **EMAIL** lwildman@csub.edu

WILDNER-BASSETT, MARY E.
PERSONAL Born 10/26/1952, Billings, MT, m, 1978, 3 children **DISCIPLINE** GERMAN STUDIES, SECOND LANGUAGE ACQUISITION **EDUCATION** E IL Univ, BA, 74; Univ Wis, Madison, MA, 78; Ruhr Univ, Bochum, Germany, PhD, 83. **CAREER** Asst prof, Univ Hamburg, 83-86; asst prof, 86-93, assoc prof, 93-, fac, 91-, Univ AZ. **HONORS AND AWARDS** Small Grant, 90-91, Diversity Action Coun Awd, 94-95, Hum Tchg Initiative Awd, 96-97, Univ AZ; Fulbright Sen Res full maintenance Awd, 93-94; Burlington Fac Excellence Tchg Awd, 93; Instructional Computing Grant, 94-95; Awd to attend Wakonse Tchg Conference, 95. **MEMBERSHIPS** AATG; ACTFL; AAUSC. **RESEARCH** Second language acquistion and teaching; interlanguage pragmatics; pragmatics of multiple literacies. **SELECTED PUBLICATIONS** Auth, Improving Pragmatic Aspects of Learners' Interlanguage, Gunter Narr Verlag, 84; Gesprachsroutinen und -strategien fur Deutsch als Alltags- und Wirtschaftssprache, Goethe Institut, 85; "Intercultural Pragmatics and Proficiency: Polite Noises for Cultural Appropriateness," Int Rev of Applied Ling, 94; "The Language Discovery Environment in the German Classroom of the 21st Century," Die Unterrichtspraxis, 94; "Intercultural Pragmatics and Metapragmatic Knowledge: Tapping the Source Using the Pragmatic Differential," Jour of Intensive Eng Studies, 97; auth, "Positionality, Cognition, and Complexity as Research Ideologies for Explorations in Interlanguage Pragmatics," in Cognitive Aspects of Foreign Language Learning and Teaching, ed. C. Riemer, Tubingen: Narr Verlag, 00. **CONTACT ADDRESS** Dept of German Studies, Univ of Arizona, ML 571, Tucson, AZ 85721. **EMAIL** wildnerb@u.arizona.edu

WILEY, JUNIPER
DISCIPLINE SOCIOLOGY **EDUCATION** PhD, UCSD, 88; Postdoctoral Fellow, Univ Calif at Los Angeles, 88-90. **CAREER** Assoc Prof, CSULB, 96-; Asst Prof, CSULB, 90-96. **RESEARCH** Cyberspace; Cybersexuality in Bondage (BDSM); Power Exchange Discipline/Sadomasochism. **SELECTED PUBLICATIONS** Auth, "Precarious Haven:" Westview Press, 96; auth, "Nobody is doing it: Cybersexuality as a Postmodern Narrative," Bodysociety Journal, 95, vol.1, no. 1, 145-162. **CONTACT ADDRESS** Dept Sociology, California State Univ, Long Beach, 1250 N Bellflower, Long Beach, CA 90840-0001. **EMAIL** jwiley@csulb.edu

WILKINS, LEONA B.
PERSONAL Born 02/09/1922, Winston-Salem, NC **DISCIPLINE** MUSIC EDUCATION **EDUCATION** NC Central Univ, BA 1941; Univ MI, MMus 1944, PhD 1971; Sorbonne Univ Paris, France, cert 1968. **CAREER** Raleigh NC, teacher 1942-44; St Louis, teacher 1952-55; Detroit, teacher 1955-64; Bluefield State, 44-45; Hampton Inst, 45-48; TN State Univ, 48-52; E MI Univ 1964-68; Temple Univ, 68-72; Northwestern Univ, assoc prof 1972-; Northwestern Univ, assoc prof emeritus, 88-; Trinity Episcopal Church, Chicago, IL, dir, children's music educ, 90-. **HONORS AND AWARDS** Consult Silver Burdett Music Series 1970-71. **MEMBERSHIPS** Mem Music Educ Conf; Intl Soc of Music Educators; Amer Assn of Univ Profs, Am Orff-Schulwerk Assn; Coll Music Soc; Alpha Kappa Alpha; mem Bicentennial Commn for MENC 1974-76; Comn for Revision of Natl Tchrs Exam for Music Educ 1974-75; consult IL State Arts Plan; Comn for Revision of Music Objectives for Natl Assessment of Educ Progress Task Force; Role of the Arts Comm USOE; MENC; consult Evanston Public School Dist 65. **CONTACT ADDRESS** Sch of Music, Northwestern Univ, Evanston, IL 60201.

WILKINSON, DORIS
PERSONAL Born Lexington, KY **DISCIPLINE** SOCIOLOGY **EDUCATION** Univ Ky, Ba, 58; Western Reserve, MA, 60; Case Western Reserve Univ, PhD, 68; post-doctoral study, Harvard Univ, 91. **CAREER** From assoc prof to prof, Macalester Col, 70-77; exec assoc, The Am Sociol Asn, 77-80; vis prof, Univ Va, 84-85; prof, Univ Ky, 85-. **HONORS AND AWARDS** Valedictorian; Phi Beta Kappa; AKD Outstanding Grad Student, Case Western Reserve Univ; Great Teacher Awd, Unv Ky, 92; Distinguished Arts and Sci Prof, 92; Distinguished Scholar Awd, 93. **MEMBERSHIPS** ASA, ESS, SSS, SSP, DCSS. **RESEARCH** Social Factors in Health, The African American Scientific, Intellectual, and Educational Heritage. **SELECTED PUBLICATIONS** Auth, "Reappraising the Race, Class, and Gender Education," 91; auth, "Gender and Social Inequality," 95; auth, "Integration Dilemmas," 96; auth, "American Families of African Descent," 97. **CONTACT ADDRESS** Dept Sociol, Univ of Kentucky, Lexington, KY 40506-0027.

WILLETO, AGELA A.
PERSONAL Born 11/03/1962, Los Angeles, CA, m, 1996 **DISCIPLINE** SOCIOLOGY **EDUCATION** Brigham Young Univ, BS, 84; Univ NC, MA, 90; PhD, 96. **CAREER** Asst Prof, Northern Ariz Univ, 95-. **HONORS AND AWARDS** Spencer Fel, 94-95. **MEMBERSHIPS** Am Sociol Asn, Pac Sociol Asn, Asn of Am Indians and Alaskan Native Profs. **SELECTED PUBLICATIONS** Auth, "Navajo Culture and Family Influences on Academic Success: Traditionalism is not a Significant Predictor of Achievements of Young Navajos," J of Am Indian Educ, Vol 38, No 2 (99); rev, "Resiliency in African-American Families," by H.I. McCuffin, E.A. Thompson, A.I. Thompson and J.A. Futrell for the J of Comparative Family Studies (forthcoming). **CONTACT ADDRESS** Dept Sociol, No Arizona Univ, PO Box 15300, Flagstaff, AZ 86011.

WILLEY, GORDON R.
PERSONAL Born 03/07/1913, Chariton, IA, m, 1938, 2 children **DISCIPLINE** ANTHROPOLOGY, ARCHAEOLOGY **EDUCATION** Univ AZ, AB, 35, AM, 36; Columbia Univ, PhD, 42. **CAREER** Sr anthropologist, Smithsonian Inst, 43-50; Bowdirch Prof of Archaeology, 50-87, prof Emeritus, Harvard Univ, 87-. **HONORS AND AWARDS** Litt D (honorary), Cambridge Univ, 77, Univ AZ, 81, Univ NM, 84; Gold Medal, Archaeol Inst of Am, 71; Huxley Medal, Royal Anthropol Inst, 84; Gold Medal, Society of Fantiquaries, London. **MEMBERSHIPS** Am Anthropol Asn; Soc for Am Archaeology; National Academy of Science; American Philosophical Soc. **RESEARCH** Mexican and Central American archaeology. **SELECTED PUBLICATIONS** Auth, Archaeology of the Florida Gulf Coast, Smithsonian Misc Colls, vol 113, Smithsonian Inst, 49; Prehistoric Settlement Patterns in the Viru Valley, Peru, Bul 155, Bureau of Am Ethnology, Smithsonian Inst, 53; Method and Theory in American Archaeology, with Phillip Phillips,

Univ Chicago Press, 58; Prehistoric Maya Settlements in the Belize Valley, with W R Bullard, J B Glass, and J C Gifford, Peabody Museum Papers, Harvard Univ, 65; An Introduction to American Archaeology: Vol I North and Middle America, 66, Vol II, South America, 71, Prentice-Hall; The Altar de Sacrificios Excavations: General Summary and Conclusions, Peabody Museum Papers, vol 64, no 3, Harvard Univ, 73; A History of American Archaeology, with J A Sabloff, Thames and Hudson, Ltd, and W H Freeman and Co, 74, 80, 93; New World Archaeology and Culture History: Collected Essays and Articles, republished with intro comments and annotations, Univ NM Press, 90; Excavations at Seibal, Department of Peten, Guatemala: General Summary and Conclusions, Memoirs, vol 17, no 4, Peabody Museum, Harvard Univ, 90; The Copan Residential Zone: Ceramics and Artifacts, with R M Leventhal, A A Demarest, and W L Fash, Jr, Papers Peabody Museum, vol 80, Harvard Univ, 94. **CONTACT ADDRESS** Peabody Museum, Harvard Univ, Cambridge, MA 02138.

WILLEY, PATRICK S.
PERSONAL Born 01/18/1946, Tulsa, OK, m, 1996 **DISCIPLINE** ANTHROPOLOGY **EDUCATION** Kans Univ, BA, 70; Pa State Univ, MA, 73; Univ Tenn, Knoxville, PhD, 82. **CAREER** Instr, W Tex State Univ; asst prof, Univ Tenn Knoxville, 75-89; prof, Calif State Univ Chico, 89-. **HONORS AND AWARDS** Phi Kappa Phi; Diplomate of Am Board of Forensic Anthrop. **MEMBERSHIPS** Am Assoc of Physical Anthrop; Am Acad of Forensic Sci; Sigma Xi Sci Res Soc. **RESEARCH** Skeletal Biology of Earlier Human Populations. **SELECTED PUBLICATIONS** Coauth, "The Bullets Buzzed Like Bees: Gunshot Wounds in Skeletons from the Battle of the Little Bighorn", Int J of Osteoarchaeology 6.1 (96): 15-27; coauth, "Oral Health of Seventh Cavalry Troopers: Dentitions from the Custer National Cemetery", J of the His of Dent 44.1 (96): 3-14; coauth, "Dental Fillings in Civil War Skulls: What Do They Tell Us?", J of the Am Dent Asoc 127 (96): 1671-1677; coauth, "Human Bone Mineral Densities and Survival of Bone Elements: A Contemporary Sample", in Forensic Taphonomy: The Postmortem Fate of Human Remains, eds William D. Haglund and Marcella H. Sorg, CRC Pr (Boca Raton, 97): 295-317; coauth, "Little Bighorn: Human Remains from the Custer National Cemetery", in Remembrance: Archaeology and Death, eds David a. Porter and Nicholas F. Belleton, Bergin and Garvey (Westport, CT, 97): 155-171; coauth, "Bone Mineral Density and Survival of Elements and Element Portions in the Bones of Crow Creek Massacre Victims", Am J of Physical Anthrop 104.4 (97): 513-528; coauth, "Dental Filling Materials in the Confederacy", J of the Hist of Dent 46.2 (98): 71-75; coauth, They Died with Custer: Soldiers' Remains from the Battle of the Little Bighorn, Univ of Oklahoma Pr, (Norman), 98; coauth, "Who's Buried in Custer's Grave?", J of Forensic Sci 44.3 (99): 648-657; coauth, "Clinkers on the Little bighorn Battlefield: In Situ Investigation of Scattered Recent Cremains", in Forensic Osteological Analysis: A Book of Case Studies, ed Scott Fairgrieve, C.C. Thomas, (Springfield, IL, 99): 129-140. **CONTACT ADDRESS** Dept Anthrop, California State Univ, Chico, Chico, CA 95929-0400. **EMAIL** pwilley@csuchico.edu

WILLIAMS, BRUCE
PERSONAL Born 07/03/1946, Saginaw, MI, d, 3 children **DISCIPLINE** SOCIOLOGY, ANTHROPOLOGY **EDUCATION** Wayne State Univ, PhB, 72; Univ Chicago, MA, 75; PhD, 79. **CAREER** Asst prof, Vanderbilt Univ, 79-86; assoc prof, Univ of Miss, 86-97; prof, Mills Col, 97-. **HONORS AND AWARDS** Fulbright Seminar, 89; Fulbright Awd, Egypt, Israel, 99. **MEMBERSHIPS** Am Sociol Assoc; Assoc of Black Sociol; Fulbright Assoc; Mid-South Sociol Assoc. **RESEARCH** Urban and rural social change and economic development and race and gender relations. African Americans and the American educational system. **SELECTED PUBLICATIONS** Auth, Black Workers in an Industrial Suburb: The Struggle Against Discrimination, Rutgers Univ Pr, 87; coauth, "Race, Gender and Poverty in the Rural South", in Rural Poverty in Am, ed Cynthia M. Duncan, Greenwood Pr, 92; coauth, Race and Economic Development in the Lower Mississippi Delta, Research Paper 15, Memphis State Univ, 92; auth "African Americans in the Rural South", in Rural Poverty: A Teaching Guide and Source Book, ed, Gene F. Summers, Rural Poverty Soc, 93; coauth, "African Americans in the Rural South: The Persistence of Race and Poverty", in The Am Country Side: Rural People and Places, ed Emery Castle, Univ of Kansas, 95; auth, "Industrial Suburbs", in Am Cities and Suburbs: An Encycl, ed Neil L. Shumsky, Garland, 98. **CONTACT ADDRESS** Dept Anthrop and Sociol, Mills Col, 5000 Macarthur Blvd, Oakland, CA 94613. **EMAIL** brucebw@mills.edu

WILLIAMS, CAROLYN CHANDLER
PERSONAL Born 01/13/1947, Maben, MS, m **DISCIPLINE** EDUCATION **EDUCATION** MS Valley State Univ, BA 1968; MS State Univ, MEd 1973, PhD 1975. **CAREER** Aberdeen Pub Schs, eng teach 1968-70; Oktibbeha Co Schs, eng teach 1970-71; Mary Holmes Coll, inst 1971-73; MS State Univ, inst 1974-75, asst prof 1975-78; assoc prof 1978-82; prof 1982-; Mississippi State Univ, Starkville, MS, administrative intern 1987. **HONORS AND AWARDS** Outstanding Univ Prof Assn of Univ Prof 1977; Outstanding Young Woman State Jaycees MS 1981; Outstanding Young Woman Starkville Jaycees local 1981; Outstanding Young Educator Phi Delta Kappa local 1982; Starkville Area Hall of Fame, Starkville Area Chamber of Commerce, 1990. **MEMBERSHIPS** Bd of dirs Mid South Educ Rsch Assn 1982-; pres, Midsouth Educational Research Assn, 1988-89; pres, Mississippi Reading Assn, 1990-91. **CONTACT ADDRESS** Prof of Instruction, Mississippi State Univ, PO Box 6331, Mississippi State, MS 39762.

WILLIAMS, DENNIS E.
PERSONAL Born 07/22/1934, Toledo, OH, m, 1956, 2 children **DISCIPLINE** CHRISTIAN EDUCATION **EDUCATION** Bob Jones Univ, BS, MA; N Ariz Univ, MA; Southwestern Baptist Theol Sem, MRE, PhD. **CAREER** Exec dir, Christian Ministries Convention, 84-94; prof, ch dept Edu Ministries and Admin, Denver Sem, 71-94; instr, King of Kings Col, Tel Aviv; Providence Theol Sem, Can; Caribbean Grad Sch Theol; Asian Grad Sch Theol; Asian Theol Sem, Philippines; dean, Sch Christian Edu and Leadership, prof, S Baptist Theol Sem, 94-. **HONORS AND AWARDS** Distinguished Educator award, Southwestern Baptist Rel Edu Assn. **SELECTED PUBLICATIONS** Auth, Volunteers For Today's Church: How To Recruit and Retain Workers; contrib, Leadership Handbook of Practical Theol; Christian Edu:Foundations For The Future; pub(s), Christian Edu Today; Christian Edu Jour; Key To Christian Edu; Leader Idea Bank; Small Gp Letter; Super Sunday Sch Sourcebook. **CONTACT ADDRESS** Sch Christian Edu and Leadership, So Baptist Theol Sem, 2825 Lexington Rd, Louisville, KY 40280. **EMAIL** celead@sbts.edu

WILLIAMS, DESSIMA
DISCIPLINE SOCIOLOGY **EDUCATION** Am Univ, MA, 85; PhD, 95. **CAREER** Assoc Prof, Brandeis Univ. **HONORS AND AWARDS** Am Acad of Arts and Sci; Am Anthropol Asn; Royal Anthropol Inst of Great Britain and Ireland; Asn of Soc Anthropol of the Commonwealth. **RESEARCH** Gender; Development; Iternational Relations; US-Caribbean Women's Leadership. **CONTACT ADDRESS** Dept Sociol, Brandeis Univ, 415 South St, Waltham, MA 02453. **EMAIL** dwilliams@brandeis.edu

WILLIAMS, EDDIE R., JR.
PERSONAL Born 01/06/1945, Chicago, IL, m, 1969 **DISCIPLINE** EDUCATION **EDUCATION** Ottawa University, Ottawa, Kansas, BA (highest honors), mathematics, 1966; Columbia University, PhD, mathematics, 1971. **CAREER** Northern Illinois Univ, assoc prof of mathematics, 70-91, assoc dir, operating budgets, 78-83, budget and planning, deputy dir, 83, dir, 83-85, asst vice pres, administrative affairs, vice pres, division of finance and planning, 85-96; Senior Vice Pres, Finance & Facilities, 96-. **MEMBERSHIPS** South Park Baptist Church, assistant pastor, director, youth activities, 1970-, senior pastor, 1997-; University Resource Advisory Committee; Presidential Commission on Status of Minorities; University Affirmative Action Committee, 1974-; American Mathematical Society. **CONTACT ADDRESS** No Illinois Univ, Lowden Hall, Rm 109, De Kalb, IL 60115.

WILLIAMS, JAMES HIAWATHA
PERSONAL Born 09/10/1945, Montgomery, AL, m, 1994 **DISCIPLINE** EDUCATION **EDUCATION** Los Angeles City Coll, Los Angeles CA, AA, 1967; California State Univ, Los Angeles CA, BA, 1973; Pepperdine Univ, Los Angeles Ca, MS, 1974; Washington State Univ, Pullman WA, PhD, 1983. **CAREER** California State Polytechnic Univ, Pomona CA, asst prof, 7-81, assoc dean & assoc prof, 80-85, dean of Coll of Arts & full prof, 88; Spokane Community College, Pres, currently. **HONORS AND AWARDS** Prism of Excellence Awd, Jerry Voorhis Claremont Democratic Club, 1986; Martin Luther King Jr Humanitarian Awd, Pomona Valley NAACP, 1987; Services to Youth, Claremont Area Chapter Links Inc, 1988. **MEMBERSHIPS** Mem, Phi Delta Kappa, 1977-; pres, Pomona Valley NAACP, 1984-86; mem, Phi Beta Delta, 1988-; National Association for Ethnic Studies, executive board member, 1988-, president, 1992-; Phi Kappa Phi, 1989-; pres-elect, Council of Colleges of Arts & Sciences, 1994. **CONTACT ADDRESS** Arapahoe Comm Col, PO Box 9002, Littleton, CO 80160-9002. **EMAIL** james.williams@arapahoe.edu

WILLIAMS, JOHN
PERSONAL Born 10/18/1935, Detroit, MI, m, 1994 **DISCIPLINE** PSYCHOLOGY **EDUCATION** St Mary's Sem, STM, 71; Pa State Univ, PhD, 76. **CAREER** Asst Specialist, Penn State, 71-76; Prof, Univ Wisc, 76-. **HONORS AND AWARDS** Annual Grad Fac Awd, Univ Wisc, 94. **MEMBERSHIPS** Am Orthopsychiat Asn, Am An for Marriage and Family Therapy, Nat Conf on Family Relations, Col Theol Soc, **RESEARCH** Development of Adult Moral Orientations, Psychology of hope and resilience, Profiles of Persons in Political conflict. **CONTACT ADDRESS** Dept Human Develop, Univ of Wisconsin, Stout, 129 K.E. Bldg, Menomonie, WI 54751-0790.

WILLIAMS, JOHN
PERSONAL Born 10/26/1938, Ordway, CO, m, 1980, 3 children **DISCIPLINE** EDUCATION **EDUCATION** Univ N Colo, BA, 59; MA, 60; PhD, 66; Fielding Inst, MA, 92; PhD, 94. **CAREER** Asst prof to prof, Univ of N Dak, 66-. **HONORS AND AWARDS** Sigma Xi Awd, Individual Excellence in Res, Univ N Dak, 79; Burlington N Awd for Excellence in Teaching and Fac Develop, Univ N Dak, 86. **MEMBERSHIPS** Am Statist Assoc; Am Psychol Assoc, Am Educ Res Assoc; Assoc for the Advan of Educ Res. **SELECTED PUBLICATIONS** Coauth, "clinical parameters and dietary intake of midwestern adolescent females", Adolescence 30 (95):881-889; coauth, Aging and cognition - Methodological differences in outcome", Experimental Aging Res 22, (96):219-244; auth, "Missing cells in developmental research", Midwest Educ Res 9.4 (96); auth, "Flashback: A Review", The Fourth Decade: A Jour of Res of the J.F. Kennedy Assassination 4.6 (97):14-17; auth, "Nightmare in Dallas", The Fourth Decade: A Jour of Res on the J.F. Kennedy Assassination 4.4 (97):21-26; auth, "Did Castro kill Kennedy? A Review", The fourth Decade: A Jour of Res on the J.F. Kennedy Assassination 5.4 (98):19-22; coauth, "Job satisfaction among rural physician assistants", the Jour of rural Health 14.2 (98):100-108; auth, "LBJ and the assassination conspiracies", JFK Deep Politics Quarterly 4.2 (99):25-28; auth, LBJ: A closer look: A review", The Fourth Decade: A Jour of Res on the J.F. Kennedy Assassination 6.4 (99):3-6. **CONTACT ADDRESS** Dept Found of Educ, Univ of No Dakota, Box 8158, Grand Forks, ND 58202. **EMAIL** jwilliam@plains.nodak.edu

WILLIAMS, JOYCE E.
PERSONAL Born 02/04/1937, Rockdale, TX, s **DISCIPLINE** SOCIOLOGY **EDUCATION** Mary Hardin-Baylor Col, BA, 58; Southern Methodist Univ, MA, 62; Wash Univ, PhD, 71. **CAREER** Soc Caseworker, Buckner Childrens Home, 58-62; Instr, Mary Hardin-Baylor Col, 62-65; Instr, Arlington State Col, 65-67; Teaching Asst, Wash Univ, 67-69; Asst to Assoc Prof, Univ Tex, 69-74; Asst to Assoc Prof, Trinity Univ, 74-80; Assoc Prof to Prof and Dept Chair, Tex Woman's Univ, 80-. **HONORS AND AWARDS** Dictionary of Intl Biography, World's Who's Who of Women, Contemporary Authors, 81; Distinguished Service Awd, Univ Mary Hardin-Baylor, 95; Women of Vision Awd, Tex Woman's Univ , 98; Who's Who in Am, 01. **MEMBERSHIPS** Am Sociol Asn, Soc for the Study of Soc Problems, Southwestern Soc Sci Asn, Southwestern Sociol Asn, Soc for Women in Sociol. **RESEARCH** Class, Ethnic, Gender Inequality, Women's Roles, Family violence. **SELECTED PUBLICATIONS** Auth, "Internment of Japanese Americans," The encyclopedia of Multiculturalism, 94; auth, "Education and academic achievement," the Latino Encyclopedia, 96; auth, "Color consciousness in the black community," the African American Encyclopedia, Supplement, 96; auth, "Domestic violence," Encyclopedia of Multiculturalism, Supplement, 98; auth, Homelessness in Denton: A Needs Assessment, 92; auth, "double Standard? TWU has reasons for all-woman status," Dallas Morning News, 95; auth, "Professional socialization: A Teaching-Scholar program at Texas Woman's University," in Training Teaching Assistants: Materials for the Selection and Training of Teaching Assistants in Sociology courses, 97; auth, "Community assessment Report: Denton County, Texas, 99; rev, of "Castles of Our conscience: Social Control and the American State," by William G Staples, Social Science Quarterly, 92; rev, of "Small victories," by Samuel G Freeman, International Journal of Comparative Family and Marriage, 94. **CONTACT ADDRESS** Dept Sociol & Soc Work, Texas Woman's Univ, PO Box 425887, Denton, TX 76204.

WILLIAMS, MELVIN D.
PERSONAL Born 02/03/1933, Pittsburgh, PA, m, 1958, 3 children **DISCIPLINE** ANTHROPOLOGY **EDUCATION** Univ Pittsburgh, PhD, 73. **CAREER** Adj Prof, Univ Pittsburgh, 79-82; Prof, Univ Md, 84-91; Prof, Univ Mich, 92-. **MEMBERSHIPS** African Studies Asn, Am Anthropol Asn, Am Asn for the Advancement of Sci, Am Asn of Univ Admin, Am Asn of Univ Prof, Am Ethnol Soc, Am Sociol Asn, Anthropol Soc of Washington, Asn for the Sociol of Relig. **SELECTED PUBLICATIONS** Auth, "Biophobia and the Human body," Journal of social and Evolutionary Systems, (96): 55-80; auth, "Biophobia, social Boundaries, and Racism," Journal of Social and Evolutionary Systems, (96): 171-186; auth, "Supremacy Narratives and Performances," Journal of Social and Evolutionary Systems, (96): 313-319; auth, "Racism," in Research Frontiers in anthropology: Ethnology, Linguistic Anthropology: The Study of social Problems, Vol 4, Simon and Schuster, 97; auth, "Race as Corporeal Denigration," anthropology Newsletter, (97): 6; auth, race for Theory, Praeger Pub, 98; auth, "an African American Experience," Journal of the Southern Conference for African American Studies, 98; auth, "Water, Power and human Nature, " JSES, (98): 7-18; auth, "Ethnographic Water: Observations at the riverside," The Griot, (99): 1-9; auth, The Black Experience I Middle-Class America, Mellen Press, in press **CONTACT ADDRESS** Dept Anthropol, Univ of Michigan, Ann Arbor, 500 South State St, Ann Arbor, MI 48109-1382.

WILLIAMS, NANCY M.
PERSONAL Born 06/15/1967, LaRochelle, France, s **DISCIPLINE** PHILOSOPHY, WOMEN'S STUDIES **EDUCATION** Winthrope Univ, BS, 89; Univ NC, Charlotte, BA, 93; Univ S Fla, MA, 97. **CAREER** Lectr, UNC Charlotte; lectr, Queens Coll. **MEMBERSHIPS** APA; NCPS; Feminist Ethics and Soc Theory; Intl Netwk Fem Appro Bioethics. **RESEARCH** Feminist Theory; feminism; 20th Cent continental philosophy; exis-

tentialism; history of philosophy; ancient and modern philosophy. **SELECTED PUBLICATIONS** Rev, "Justice for Here and Now, James Sterba (Cambridge, CUP, 98), Concerned Philos for Peace NL 19 (99): 18-20; auth, "Epilogue," in Globalizing Feminist Bioethics: Woman's Health Concerns Worldwide, in print. **CONTACT ADDRESS** Dept Philosophy, Univ of No Carolina, Charlotte, 9201 University City Blvd, Charlotte, NC 28223-0001. **EMAIL** nwilliam@email.uncc.edu

WILLIAMS, NUDIE EUGENE
PERSONAL Born 10/16/1936, Fairfield, AL, 1 child **DISCIPLINE** MINORITY AND AFRICAN HISTORY **EDUCATION** Clark Col, BS, 59; Okla State Univ, MA, 73, PhD(hist), 77. **CAREER** Instr, 76-77, Asst Prof Hist, Univ Ark, 77-, Coord Black studies, Univ Ark. **MEMBERSHIPS** Western Hist Soc; Southern Hist Asn; Orgn Am Historians; Asn Study Negro Life & Hist; Assoc Soc & Behav Sci. **RESEARCH** American minorities in the Southwest (Black lawmen); Black Western newspapers; West African comparative history. **SELECTED PUBLICATIONS** Auth, Cassius McDonald Barnes, governor of Oklahoma Territory, 1897-1901, Chronicles Okla, spring 75 & chap IV, In: Territorial Governors of Oklahoma, Okla Hist Soc, 75; A summary: Black newspapers in Oklahoma, 1889 to 1929, Okla Publ, 3/78; Black men who wore the star, The Chronicles of Oklahoma, Vol LIX, No 1; Black men who wore white hats: Grant Johnson, United States Deputy Marshall, Red River Valley Historical Rev, Vol V, No 3; Bass Reeves: Lawman in the Western Ozarks, Negro Hist Bull, Vol 42, No 2; A summary: Black newspapers in Oklahoma, 1889-1929, The Okla Publ, 678; Cassius McDonald Barnes, 1897-1901, Chronicles of Okla, Vol LII, No 1. **CONTACT ADDRESS** Main Campus, Univ of Arkansas, Fayetteville, Fayetteville, AR 72701-1202.

WILLIAMS, RHYS H.
PERSONAL Born 08/15/1955, Muncie, IN, s **DISCIPLINE** SOCIOLOGY **EDUCATION** Univ Mass Amherst, PhD, 88 **CAREER** Assoc prof, Southern Illinois Univ, present; visiting asst prof, Yale Divinity School, 92-94 **MEMBERSHIPS** Amer Socio Assoc; Soc Sci Study Relig; Soc Study Soc Prob **RESEARCH** Religion and American Politics **SELECTED PUBLICATIONS** Co-ed, Sacred Companies: Organizational Aspects of Religion and Religious Aspects of Organizations, Oxford, 98; Cultural Wars in American Politics: Critical Reviews of a Popular Myth, Aldine de Gruyter, 97; "Is America in a Culture War? Yes-No-Sort of." Christian Century, 97; "Politics, Religion, and the Analysis of Culture." Theory and Soc, 96 **CONTACT ADDRESS** Dept of Sociology, So Illinois Univ, Carbondale, m/c 4524, Carbondale, IL 62901-4524. **EMAIL** willrhys@siu.edu

WILLIAMS, ROBIN M.
PERSONAL Born 10/11/1914, Hillsborough, NC, m, 1939, 2 children **DISCIPLINE** SOCIOLOGIST **EDUCATION** NC State Col, BS, 33; MS, 35; Harvard Univ, MA, 39; PhD, 43. **CAREER** Prof to prof emeritus, Cornell Univ, 48-. **HONORS AND AWARDS** Nat Acad of Sci; Am Philos Soc; Career of Distinguished Scholarship; Am Sociol Asn, 90; commonwealth Awd for Distinguished Service, 88. **MEMBERSHIPS** Am Sociol Asn, am Acad Arts & Sci, Eastern Sociol Soc, Rural Sociol Soc. **RESEARCH** Ethnic relations, Conflict and conflict resolution. **SELECTED PUBLICATIONS** Auth, "The sociology of ethnic conflicts: comparative international perspectives," Annual Review of Sociology, (94): 49-79; co-ed, A Common Destiny: Blacks and American Society, Washington, 89; auth, "The American Soldier: An Assessment, Several Wars Later," Public Opinion Quarterly, (89): 153-174; auth, "Racial Attitudes and Behavior," in Surveying Social Life: Papers in Honor of Herbert Hyman, Wesleyan Univ Press, 88; auth, "The Use of Threats in US/USSR Relations," Research in Social Movements, Conflicts and Change, (86): 1-32; auth, "Individuals Welfare and Collective Dilemmas: Problems Without Solutions?" in Social Structure and Behavior: Essays in Honor of William Hamilton Sewell, 82; auth, "Structure and Process in Ethnic Relations: Increased Knowledge and Unanswered Questions," in Sociological Theory and Research: A Critical Approach, New York, 81; auth, "Competing Models of Multiethnic and Multiracial Societies: An Appraisal of Possibilities," in Major Social Issues: A Multidisciplinary View, New York, 78; auth, Mutual Accommodation: Ethnic Conflict and Cooperation, Univ Minn Press, 77. **CONTACT ADDRESS** Dept Sociol, Cornell Univ, 323 Uris Hall, Ithaca, NY 14853.

WILLIAMS, WENDY A.
PERSONAL Born 11/17/1958, San Diego, CA, m, 1995, 1 child **DISCIPLINE** PSYCHOLOGY **EDUCATION** San Diego State Univ, BA, 85; USCD, MA, 91; PhD, 94. **CAREER** Asst prof, Cen Wash Univ, 95-. **HONORS AND AWARDS** Fel, Univ of Otago, NZ, 95; Excellence in Teaching Awd, Cen Wash Univ, 96; Who's Who Among Am Teachers, 00. **MEMBERSHIPS** Assoc of Behav Analysts; NW ABA; W Psychol Assoc; Am Psychol Soc; Animal Behav Soc. **RESEARCH** Choice behavior under conditions of conflicting sources of behavior control, foraging-related choice, human memory, color perception and behavior. **SELECTED PUBLICATIONS** Coauth, "Choice and conditioned reinforcement", Jour of the Experimental Analysis of Behav 55 (91):177-188; auth, "Prechoice effects on foraging choice", Am Zoologist 34 (94):302; coauth, "Delay-reduction and optimal-foraging: Variable-ratio search in a foraging analogue", Jour of the Experimental Anal of Behav 61 (94):465-477; coauth, "Response-dependent prechoice effects on foraging-related choice", Jour of the Experimental Anal of Behav 61 (96):619-641; coauth, "Eleccion y forrageo optimo (choice and optimal foraging)" in Manual de analisis experimental del comportamiento, ed R. Ardila, Editorial Bibliotech Nueva (Spain, 98); coauth, "Sample frequency and sample duration as sources of stimulus control in delayed matching to sample" Behav Processes 46 (99):39-55. **CONTACT ADDRESS** Dept Psychology, Central Washington Univ, 400 E 8th Ave, Ellensburg, WA 98926.

WILSON, BEV J.
DISCIPLINE PSYCHOLOGY **EDUCATION** Calif State Univ, BA, 85; MA, 87; Univ Wash, PhD, 94. **CAREER** Asst Prof, Seattle Pac Univ, 98-. **HONORS AND AWARDS** Mortar Board Nat Sen Hon Soc Awd, 95-96; Mortar Board Top Prof Awd, 96-97; Grants, 92-93, 96-98. **MEMBERSHIPS** APA. **RESEARCH** Peer relationship difficulties in young children. **SELECTED PUBLICATIONS** Coauth, "Marital Interaction and Parenting," in Handbk of Parenting, vol 4, Applied and Practical Considerations of Parenting (Hillsdale, NJ: Lawrence Erlbaum, 95); coauth, "Attention-The Shuttle Between Emotion and Cognition: Risk, Resiliency and Physiological Bases," in Stress, Coping and Resiliency in Children and Families (Hillsdale, NJ: Lawrence Erlbaum, 96); coauth, "What Should be the Focus of Emotion Regulation? A Nonlinear Dynamic Mathematical Model of Children's Peer Interaction in Groups," J of Develop and Psychopathology (97): 421-452; coauth, "A Theory of Meta-Emotion: Parenting and Emotion Regulation," in Meta-Emotion: How Families Communicate Emotionally (Hillsdale, NJ: Lawrence Erlbaum, 97); coauth, "Meta-Emotion and Families," in Conflict and Closeness: The Formation, Functioning and Stability of Families (Hillsdale, NJ: Lawrence Erlbaum, 99); auth, "Entry Behavior and Emotion Regulation Abilities of Developmentally Delayed Boys," Develop Psychol 35 (99): 214-222. **CONTACT ADDRESS** Dept Psychol, Seattle Pacific Univ, 3307 3rd Ave W, Seattle, WA 98119-1997. **EMAIL** bjwilson@spu.edu

WILSON, CARTER
PERSONAL Born 12/27/1941, Washington, DC, s **DISCIPLINE** COMMUNITY STUDIES **EDUCATION** Harvard Univ, BA, 63; Syracuse Univ, MA, 66. **CAREER** Lectr, Harvard Univ, 66-69; Lectr, Tufts Univ, 69-72; From Asst Prof to Prof, Univ Calif, 72-. **HONORS AND AWARDS** Soc Sci Res Coun Awd, 94; Ruth Benedict Prize, SOGLA, 96. **RESEARCH** Maya people, Mexico, gay movements, family dynamics. **SELECTED PUBLICATIONS** Auth, Crazy February, 66; auth, On Firm Ice, 68; auth, I Have Fought the Good Fight, 69; auth, A Green Tree and a Dry Tree, 72; auth, Treasures on Earth, 81; auth, Hidden in the Blood, 95. **CONTACT ADDRESS** Dept Community Studies, Univ of California, Santa Cruz, 1156 High St, Santa Cruz, CA 95064-1077. **EMAIL** georgec@cats.ucsc.edu

WILSON, DAVID
PERSONAL Born 11/02/1954, Thomaston, AL, m, 1 child **DISCIPLINE** EDUCATION **EDUCATION** Tuskegee University, Tuskegee, AL, BS, 1977, MS, 1979; Harvard University, Cambridge, MA, EdM, 1984, PhD, 1987. **CAREER** Research & Development Institute of Philadelphia, Philadelphia, PA, project dir, 79-82; Kentucky State University, Frankfurt, KY, exec asst to vice pres for business affairs, 84-85; Woodrow Wilson National Fellowship Foundation, Princeton, NJ, 85-88; Rutgers University, Camden, NJ, assoc provost, 88-94; Auburn Univ, vp for univ outreach, assoc provost, currently. **HONORS AND AWARDS** Kellogg Fellow, WK Kellogg Foundation, 1988-92; Woodrow Wilson Fellow, Woodrow Wilson Natl Fellowship Foundation, 1984-85; One of America's Best and Brightest Young Business and Professional Men, Dollars and Sense Magazine, 1987; Certificate of Appreciation, Governor of Alabama, 1987; Certificate of Appreciation, Governor of Tennessee, 1988. **MEMBERSHIPS** Member, board of directors, Afro-American Historical & Cultural Museum, Philadelphia, PA, 1988-, Walt Whitman Association, Camden, NJ, 1988-, Princeton Ballet, 1988-, Optimist Club of Lower Bucks, Bensalem, PA, 1986-91; member, Alpha Phi Alpha Fraternity, Inc, 1975-. **CONTACT ADDRESS** VP for Univ Outreach, Auburn Univ, Auburn, AL 36849. **EMAIL** davidw@auburn.edu

WILSON, DICK
PERSONAL Born 09/18/1931, Estil, KY, m, 1955, 3 children **DISCIPLINE** PSYCHOLOGY **EDUCATION** Lincoln Christian Col, BA, 54; Christian Theol Sem, MDiv, 61; Butler Univ, MS, 64; Pepperdine Univ, MS, 78; US Intl Univ, PhD, 98. **CAREER** Prof and Dept Chair, Saddleback Col, 78-. **HONORS AND AWARDS** Theta Phi, Butler Univ, 64. **RESEARCH** Treatment affect of alcohol/drug/human services education; Successful drug court rehabilitation. **CONTACT ADDRESS** Div Soc & Beh Sci, Saddleback Col, 28000 Marguerite Pkwy, Mission Viejo, CA 92692. **EMAIL** dwilson@saddleback.cc.c2.us

WILSON, FRANK HAROLD
PERSONAL Born 10/06/1948, Washington, DC, m, 1984 **DISCIPLINE** SOCIOLOGY **EDUCATION** Howard Univ, BA, 71; Rutgers Univ, MA, 74; Univ Mich, PhD, 85. **CAREER** Instr, Lincoln Univ, Pa, 74-77; asst prof, Bowdoin Col, 85-88; asst prof, Univ Wisc, Milwaukee, 88-96, assoc prof, 96-. **HONORS AND AWARDS** Alpha Kappa Delta Sociol Honor Soc, 69; West African Heritage Sem; Univ fels, Rackham Grad Sch, 77-81; Rackham Diss grant, 82; post-doctoral fel, Ford Found, 93-94; Sr Chair, ASA comt on Public Understanding of Sociol, 88-; Exec comt, Asn of Afro-Am Hist and Life, 96-; Pres, Asn of Soc and Behav Sci, 99-2000. **MEMBERSHIPS** Stokes Found, Soc for Study of Soc Problems, Am Psychol Asn, Asn of Soc and Behav Scis, Asn of Black Sociols. **RESEARCH** Urban sociology, population, race and ethnic relations, sociological theory. **SELECTED PUBLICATIONS** Auth, "Concentrated Poverty, Housing Change, and Urban Redevelopment: Blacks in U.S. Cities, 1980-1990," Res in Community Sociol, JAI Press (95); auth, "Ebb Tide or Rising Tide: Changes in the Black Middle Class, 1980-90," in Rutledge Dennis, ed, The Black Middle Class. Res in Race and Ethnic Relations, JAI Press (95); auth, "For Whom Does the Bell Toll?: Meritocracy, the Cognitive Elite, and the Continuing Significance of Race in Post-Industrial America," J of Negro Ed (summer 96); auth, "Urban Redevelopment and the PostIndustrial City: The Persistence of Gentrification in American Central Cities, 1980-1990,: in Dennis Peck and J. Selwyn Hollingsworth, eds, Structural and Demographic Change, Greenwood (96); auth, Footsteps From North Brentwood: From Reconstruction to the Post-World War II Years, Washington, DC: Anacostia Mus of the Smithsonian Inst (97); auth, "Housing and Black Americans: The Persistent Significance of Race," in William Velez, ed, Race and Ethnicity in the United States: An Institutional Approach, Dix Hills: General Hall 998); rev of Fortress America: Gated Communities in the United States by Edward J. Blakely and Mary Gail Snyder, Contemporary Sociol (Jan 99); auth, Race, Class, and the Post-Industrial City: William Julius Wilson and the Promise of Sociology, SUNY Press (forthcoming); auth, "NeoConservatives, Black Conservatives, and the Retreat from Social Justice," The Crisis of the Negro Intellectual: A Tribute to Harold Cruse, New York: Morrow Pubs (forthcoming). **CONTACT ADDRESS** Dept Sociol, Univ of Wisconsin, Milwaukee, PO Box 413, Milwaukee, WI 53201. **EMAIL** chocchip@uwmi.edu

WILSON, JANELLE L.
PERSONAL Born 09/23/1968, Clare, MI, s **DISCIPLINE** SOCIOLOGY **EDUCATION** Mid Mich Cmty Col, AA, 88; Saginaw Valley State Univ, BA, 90; W Mich Univ, MA, 92; PhD, 95. **CAREER** Grad Rest Asst, W Mich Univ, 90-94; grad teaching assoc, W Mich Univ, 92-95; asst prof, Univ Minn, 95-. **HONORS AND AWARDS** Who's Who among America's Teacher, 98; Grad Teach Assoc, W Mich Univ, 92-95; Chair's Grad Stud Excellence Awd, W Mich Univ, 91-92, 94-95; Teaching Excellence Awd, W Mich Univ, 94; Alpha Chi; Phi Kappa Phi. **MEMBERSHIPS** am sociol Asn, Midwest, Sociol Soc, Saginaw Valley State Univ, Alumni Asn, W Mich Univ Alumni Asn. **RESEARCH** Generation X, Sociology of Nostalgia, The Self. **SELECTED PUBLICATIONS** Auth, "Remember When: A Consideration of the concept of Nostalgia," ETC: A Review of General Semantics, (99): 296-304; contrib, "Teaching Resources," Sociology: Exploring the architecture of Everyday Life, Pine Forge Press: Thousand Oaks,CA, 00; auth, "Individuals' Use of the Past: The Relationship Between Nostalgia and Identity," Reminiscence and Life Review Conference 1999: Selected Conference Papers and Proceedings, (99):153-157; auth, "Generation X: Who Are They? What of They Want?" Thought & Action XIV, (98): 9-18; auth, "Lost in the fifties: A Study of collected Memories," The Narrative Study of Lives, (97): 147-181; auth, "Past or Future> A Re-Formulation of Ortega's Question," A Review of General Semantics, (96): 152-169; auth, "Justify My Ideology: Madonna and Traditional Values," Popular Music and Society, (92): 75-84. **CONTACT ADDRESS** Dept Sociol & Anthropol, Univ of Minnesota, Duluth, 10 Univ Dr, Duluth, MN 55812. **EMAIL** jwilson2@d.umn.edu

WILSON, JANET
PERSONAL Born 01/01/1964, Riverside, CA, s **DISCIPLINE** SOCIOLOGY **EDUCATION** Univ Central Ark, BS, 86, MS, 87; Univ Nebr, PhD, 91. **CAREER** Vis asst prof, Univ Nebr, 91-91; asst prof, Univ Ark, 92-96; asst prof, Univ Central Ark, 96-. **HONORS AND AWARDS** Faculty Excellence Awd for Teaching, 96. **MEMBERSHIPS** Acad Criminal Justice Sci, Southwestern Asn Criminal Justice, Ark Anthropol & Sociol Asn. **RESEARCH** Victimology, domestic violence. **SELECTED PUBLICATIONS** Coauth with JoEtta A. Vernon, J. Allen Williams, Jr., and Terri Phillips, "Media stereotyping: Older women as minorities on prime time televison," J of Women and Aging,2(4), 55-68 (90); rev, of "Last one over the wall: The Massachusetts experiment in closing reform schools," Am J Criminal Justice, 16(1), 118-120 (91); coauth with Sheryl Grana, Helen Miller, and Michele Miller, "The contexts of housework and the paid labor force: Women's perceptions of the demand level of their work," Sex Roles, 28(5/6), 295-315 (93); coauth with D. Wayne Osgood, Patrick O'Malley, Jerald G. Bachman, and Lloyd D. Johnston, "Routine activities and individual deviant behavior," Am Sociol Rev, 61(4), 635--655

(96); coauth with Elaine Fox and Jeff Kamakahi, "Who is fighting fot the right to Die? Older women's participation in the Hemlock Society," Health Care for Women Int, 19(5), 1010-116 (98); coauth with Ronald J. Hy and David Huseman, "Grass roots support for a charter school system," Ark Bus and Econ Rev, 32(1), 6-21 (99); auth, Instructor's Resource Manual for Sheley's Criminology, 3rd ed, Belmont, CA: Wadsworth (99). **CONTACT ADDRESS** Dept Sociol, Univ of Central Arkansas, 201 Donaghey Ave, Conway, AR 72035-5003. **EMAIL** Jwilson@mail.uca.edu

WILSON, JANIE HAMN
PERSONAL Born 09/20/1963, Charleston, SC, m, 1989, 3 children **DISCIPLINE** PSYCHOLOGY **EDUCATION** Col Charleston, BS, 89; Univ SC, PhD, 94. **CAREER** Part-time instr, Univ of SC, 92-93; full-time instr, Columbia Col, 93-94; asst prof, Ga Southern Univ, 94-. **HONORS AND AWARDS** Fac Res Grant, Ga Southern Univ, 95, Fac Development Awds, Ga Southern Univ, 95, 97, 98; Nat Sci Found Instrument and Lab Improvement Prog grant, 97. **MEMBERSHIPS** Am Psychol Asn, Am Psychol Soc, Soc for Neurosci, Int Brain Res Org, Psi Chi Honor Org. **SELECTED PUBLICATIONS** Coauth with S. J. Kelly, "Play behavior: The effect of exposure to alcohol during development and involvement of opiods," Soc for Neurosci Abstracts, 17, 2 (91): 1505; coauth with S. J. Kelly, "The effect of early postnatal ethanol exposure on light-dark preference in preweanling rats," Soc for Neurosci Abstracts, 18, 2 (92): 1115; coauth with D. G. Campbell, P. J. Paradzinski, J. B. Appel, S. J. Kelly, and J. R. Coleman, "Effect of in utero cocaine exposure and developmental malnutrition on the rat auditory brainstem response," Asn for Res in Otolaryngology Abstract (93); coauth with S. J. Kelly, and M. A. Wilson, "Early postnatal alcohol exposure in rats: Maternal behavior and estradiol levels," Alcoholism: Clinical and Experimental Res, 19, 2 (95): 20A; coauth with S. J. Kelly, and M. A. Wilson, "Early postnatal alcohol exposure in rats: Maternal behavior and estradiol levels," Physiology & Behavior, 59, 2 (96): 287-293; auth, "Sample portfolios from across disciplines," in P. Seldin, ed, The Teaching Portfolio, 2nd ed, Bolton, MA: Anker Pub Co, Inc (97): 243-251; coauth with A. N. McFeeters, E. W. L. Smith, and M. E. Nielson, "Projected animal preferences in incarcerated and nonincarcerated men," Perceptual and Motor Skills, 86 (98): 250; coauth with J. D. Murray, "Can a psychology club be combined with a Psi Chi chapter?," Eye on Psi Chi, 3 (99): 20-21; coauth with K. W. Taylor, "Professor immediacy as behaviors associated with liking students," Teaching of Psychology (99, under review); coauth with S. A. Robertson, B. L. Young, "Prolactin levels in juvenile and adult rats following acute restraint and open field," Physiology & Behav (in press). **CONTACT ADDRESS** Dept Psychol, Georgia So Univ, PO Box 8041, Statesboro, GA 30460-8041. **EMAIL** JHWilson@GaSoU.edu

WILSON, PATRICIA I.
PERSONAL Born 06/07/1940, Belmont, NC, m, 1961, 2 children **DISCIPLINE** EDUCATION **EDUCATION** North Carolina A&T State University, Greensboro, NC, BS, 1961; University of Kentucky, Lexington, KY, MA, 1979, EdD, 1984. **CAREER** Morris Township Junior High, Morristown, NJ, teacher, 63-65; Roxbury High, Succasunna, NJ, teacher, 65-67; Morris Hills Regional High, Rockaway, NJ, teacher, 68-71; Central High, Joliet, IL, teacher, 72-73; Davenport West High School, Davenport, IA, teacher, 74-77; University of Kentucky, Lexington, KY, instructor, 79-81; Eastern Kentucky Univ, Richmond, KY, assistant professor, 81-85; University of Kentucky, Lexington, KY, assistant professor, 85-92; Alabama A&M University, associate professor, 92-. **HONORS AND AWARDS** President's Awd, ARMA, 1986-87; Outstanding Researcher Awd, A & M School of Business, 1994. **MEMBERSHIPS** President, Delta Pi Epsilon, 1988-90; president, Association of Records Managers Administrators, 1988-89; secretary/treasurer, Phi Delta Kappa, 1990-91, membership vice pres, 1991-92; secretary, Alabama Business Ed Assn, 1994-, pres elect, 1996-97; treasurer, Gamma Nu chapter, Delta Pi Epsilon, 1997-; president, Alabama Business Educator Assoc, 1998-; pres, Alabama Business Education Assn, 1998-00; editor, Southern Business Education Assn Newsletter, 1999-. **CONTACT ADDRESS** Alabama A&M Univ, PO Box 429, Normal, AL 35762. **EMAIL** aampiw01@aamu.edu

WILSON, RUDOLPH GEORGE
PERSONAL Born 06/17/1935, River Rouge, MI, m **DISCIPLINE** EDUCATION **EDUCATION** Los Angeles City Coll, AA, BA 1962, MA 1964; Washington Univ, PhD **CAREER** Southern Illinois Univ, assoc prof 1975-; Second Educ, lecturer 1969-72; Claremont High School, English teacher dept chmn 1964-69, master English teacher 1967-69; Juv Hall Couns 1961-63; Consult Affect Educ Drug Use & Abuse, Moral Educ, Val Educ, Ald Psychology, Methods of Teaching, Adult Educ, Flex Schedule, Humanistic Educ, Motiv of Reluctant Learner, English Educ, Supvr of Student Teachers, Teaching Learn Ctrs, Disc in the Sec Schools, Parent Effect Train, Transact Analy, Devel Teacher Compet; Southern IL Univ, dept chairperson curriculum instructor/prof, currently. **HONORS AND AWARDS** Teaching Excellence Awd 1971; Great Teacher Awd 1974; Danforth Leadership Awd; Danforth Fellow; Kimmel Leadership Awd; Martin Luther King Awd; St Louis American Outstanding Educator Awd. **MEMBERSHIPS** Mem Kappa Alpha Psi; funder, pres Southern IL Adoptive Parents Assn; bd mem Sr Citizens Inc; bd mem SW IL Area Agency on Aging; mem Edwardsville Dist 7 Bd of Educ 1972-; past pres Natl Assn for African Educ 1970-71; pres Faculty Sen, Southern IL Univ 1975-76; elected mem Pres Search Com, SIUE; vice pres Business Affairs Search Com; chmn Search Com for vice pres for student affairs. **SELECTED PUBLICATIONS** Auth, "Inner City Teaching Training Program" Office of Educ Journal 1972 **CONTACT ADDRESS** Professor, So Illinois Univ, Edwardsville, Box 1122, Edwardsville, IL 62026.

WILSON, WAYNE J.
PERSONAL Born 10/24/1932, Fort Smith, AK, d **DISCIPLINE** PSYCHOLOGY **EDUCATION** SMU, BA, 59; MA, 61; TCU, PhD, 65. **CAREER** Stephen F. Austin State Univ, 64-. **MEMBERSHIPS** Am Psychol Assoc. **RESEARCH** Aggression and humor **SELECTED PUBLICATIONS** Auth, Good murders and bad murders, (revised edition), Univ Pr of Am (Lanham, MD), 96; coauth, "Modus operandi of female serial killers", Psychol Reports, 82, (98):495-498; auth, The psychopath in film, Univ Pr of Am, (Lanham, MD), 99. **CONTACT ADDRESS** Dept Psychology, Stephen F. Austin State Univ, PO Box 4658 - SFA Station, Nacogdoches, TX 75962. **EMAIL** wwilson@sfasu.edu

WILSON, WILLIAM ALBERT
PERSONAL Born 09/23/1933, Tremonton, UT, m, 1957, 4 children **DISCIPLINE** FOLKLORE **EDUCATION** Brigham Young Univ, BA, 58, MA, 62; Ind Univ, PhD(folklore), 74. **CAREER** Instr English, Bountiful High Sch, 59-60; instr, Brigham Young Univ, 60-62, prof English & folklore, 67-78; instr English & folklore, Ind Univ, Ft Wayne, 66; PROF FOLKLORE, UTAH STATE UNIV, 78-, Vis prof, Univ Calif, Los Angeles, 68; bk rev ed, Western Folklore, 72-78, ed, 78-; dir, Utah State Univ Folklore Prog, 78-; Folk Arts panel mem, Nat Endowment for Arts, 80-. **HONORS AND AWARDS** Gustave O Arlt Humanities Awd, Coun Grad Schs US, 77. **MEMBERSHIPS** MLA; Am Folklore Soc; Mormon Hist Asn; Finnish Lit Soc. **RESEARCH** Finnish folklore; Mormon folklore; the history of folklore scholarship. **SELECTED PUBLICATIONS** Auth, Folklore and history: Fact amid the legends, Utah Hist Quart, 73; Herder, folklore and romantic nationalism, J Popular Cult, 73; The Kalevala and Finnish politics, J Folklore Inst, 75; Folklore and Nationalism in Modern Finland, Ind Univ Press, 76; The paradox of Mormon folklore, Brigham Young Univ Studies, 76; ed, Mormon folklore, Utah Hist Quart, Spec issue No 4, 76; auth, The evolutionary method in folklore theory and the Finnish method, Western Folklore, 76; On being human: The folklore of Mormon missionaries, Utah State Univ Press, 81. **CONTACT ADDRESS** 1140 E 50 South, Logan, UT 85321.

WILTENBURG, JOY
DISCIPLINE EARLY MODERN EUROPE AND WOMEN'S HISTORY **EDUCATION** Univ Rochester, BA; Univ Va, PhD, 84. **CAREER** Instr, Rowan Col of NJ. **RESEARCH** Social history, especially in early modern Germany and England. **SELECTED PUBLICATIONS** Published a book and several articles on social history in early modern Germany and England. **CONTACT ADDRESS** Rowan Univ, Glassboro, NJ 08028-1701.

WINBUSH, RAYMOND A.
PERSONAL Born 03/31/1948, Pittsburgh, PA, d, 3 children **DISCIPLINE** PSYCHOLOGY **EDUCATION** Oakwood Col, AB, 70; Univ Chicago, AM, 73; PhD, 76. **CAREER** Asst provost, Vanderbilt Univ, 90-95; director of Race Relations Inst, Fisk Univ, 95-. **HONORS AND AWARDS** Outstanding Teacher, Fisk Univ, 96; Leopold Senghor Awd, Nashville. **MEMBERSHIPS** Nat Coun for Black Studies. **RESEARCH** Racism, White supremacy, Identity formation in African adolescent. **CONTACT ADDRESS** Dept Psychol, Fisk Univ, 1000 17th Ave N, Nashville, TN 37208. **EMAIL** rwinbush@usit.net

WINFREE, L. THOMAS, JR
PERSONAL Born 12/02/1946, Wytheville, VA, m, 1969, 1 child **DISCIPLINE** SOCIOLOGY, CRIMINAL JUSTICE **EDUCATION** Univ Richmond, BA, 68; Va Commonwealth Univ, MS, 74; Univ Mont, PhD, 76. **CAREER** Vis instr, Univ NMex, 75-76; asst prof, East Tex State Univ, 76-79; asst prof to assoc prof, La State Univ, 79-87; assoc prof to prof, NMex State Univ, 87-. **HONORS AND AWARDS** Alpha Kappa Delta; Fel in Criminology and Deviant Behavior, Nat Inst of Mental Health; Who's Who in the South and Southwest; Who's Who in Am Law. **MEMBERSHIPS** Am Soc of Criminology, Acad of Criminal Justice Scis, Am Sociol Asn. **RESEARCH** Juvenile delinquency, youth gangs, American prison and jails. **SELECTED PUBLICATIONS** Co-ed, Expert Witnesses: Criminologists in the Courtroom, Albany, NY: State Univ of NY Press (87); coauth, Crime and Justice: An Introduction, 2nd ed, Chicago: Nelson Hall, Inc (92); coauth, Understanding Crime: Theory and Practice, Chicago: Nelson Hall, Inc (96); coauth, Contemporary Corrections: California: ITP/West/Wadsworth (98); coauth, Juvenile Justice, NY: McGraw-Hill (2000); coauth, "On classifying driving-whole-intoxicated offenders: The experiences of a city-wide D.W.I. Drug court," J of Criminal Justice, 28, 1 (2000): 1-9; coauth, "Exploring gang membership between Hispanic & youth in two southwestern cities," The Soc Sci J (forthcoming); coauth, "Drunk drivers, DWI 'drug court' treatment and recidivism: Who fails?," Justice Res and Policy (forthcoming). **CONTACT ADDRESS** Dept Criminal Justice, New Mexico State Univ, msc 3487, Las Cruces, NM 88003. **EMAIL** twinfree@nmsu.edu

WINGARD, EDWARD L.
DISCIPLINE EDUCATION **EDUCATION** Miami Univ, BS; MEd; Ohio State Univ, PhD. **CAREER** Prof. **SELECTED PUBLICATIONS** Auth, The Experience of Historically Black Colleges in Serving Diversely Prepared Students, 82; Annual Meeting, 81; Self-Study Report, National Council for Accreditation of Teacher Education, Central State Univ, 82. **CONTACT ADDRESS** Dept of Education, Union Inst, 440 E McMillan St, Cincinnati, OH 45206-1925.

WINKELMAN, MICHAEL
PERSONAL Born 11/27/1954, San Marcos, TX, m, 1990, 1 child **DISCIPLINE** ANTHROPOLOGY **EDUCATION** Rice Univ, BA, 76; Univ CA, PhD, 85. **CAREER** Dir ASU Ethnographic Field School, Ensenada, BC Mexico, 88-. **MEMBERSHIPS** Society for Applied Anthropology, American Anthropological Assoc. **RESEARCH** Shamanism, consciousness, traditional healing, cross-cultural, relations. **SELECTED PUBLICATIONS** Auth, Shamans, Priests and Witches: A Cross-cultural Study of Magico-religious Practitioners, Anthropological Research Papers (Tempe, AZ:Arizona State Univ) 92; auth, "Cultural Factors in Criminal Defense Proceedings", Human Organization 55 (96): 154-159; auth, Sacred Plants, Consciousness and Healing, Cross-Cultural and Interdisciplinary Perspectives, Yearbook of Cross-cultural Medicine and Psychotherapy, Berlin: Springer-Verlag, ed. Michael Winkelman and Walter Andritzy 96; auth," Altered States of Consciousness and Religious Behavior," In Anthropology of Religion: A Handbook of Method and Theory, ed. S. Glazier (Westport, Conn: Greenwood, 97), 393-428; auth, "Aztec Human Sacrifice:Cross-cultural Assessments of the Ecological Hypothesis," Ethnology 37 (98): 285-98; auth, Ethnic Relations in the US: A Sociohistorical Cultural Systems Approach, Eddie Bowers Publishing (Dubuque: Iowa), 98; auth, Ethnic Sensitivity in Social Work, Edddie Bowers Publishing, (Dubuque: Iowa), 99; auth, "Shamanistic Healers: A Cross-cultural Biopsychosocial Perspective, "In: Schenk, A. and Ratsch, C (eds.)" What is a Shaman? Shamans, Healers, and Medicine Men from a Western Point of View," (Berlin: VWB), 99; auth, "Cross-cultural Social Sexual Adaptations in Field Work: Perspectives from Mexican Field Settings, In Sex, Sexualtiy and the Anthropologist, ed. Fran Markowitz and Michael Ashkenazi (Champaign, Ill.: Univ of Ill. Press, 99), 75-91; auth, Shamanism: Ther Neural Ecology of Consciousness and Healing, Bergin and Garvey (Westport, CT), 00. **CONTACT ADDRESS** Dept Anthropology, Arizona State Univ, PO Box 872402, Tempe, AZ 85287. **EMAIL** michael.winkelman@asu.edu

WINSTEAD, ROY
PERSONAL Born 08/24/1950, Wilson, NC, m, 1973, 4 children **DISCIPLINE** EDUCATION **EDUCATION** Brigham Young Univ, EdD, 85; East Carolina Univ, MEd, 78; East Carolina Univ, BS, 72. **CAREER** Dean, School of Education, Brigham Young University, Hawaii, 95-; Chair, Elementary Education, Brigham Young University-Hawaii, 87-95; Supervisor of Mathematics and Science, Burke County Schools (NC); Math/Science Teacher, 6-8; Vice Principal, k-8; Pitt County Schools (NC), 76-78; Math Teacher, Greenville City Schools (NC); 72-76. **MEMBERSHIPS** Amer Educational Research. **RESEARCH** Teacher education issues; brain functions and learning. **SELECTED PUBLICATIONS** Auth, "The Brain Game: A Search for Understanding Intelligences," Laie, Hawaii: Brigham Young University, 95; auth, "Invitational Learning: A University Professor's Personal and Professional Reflections," Invitational Education Forum, v.16, n.2, September 95. **CONTACT ADDRESS** Dept Education, Brigham Young Univ, 55-220 Kulanui St, Laie, HI 96762. **EMAIL** winstear@byuh.edu

WINTER, DAVID G.
DISCIPLINE PSYCHOLOGY **EDUCATION** Harvard Univ, AB, 60; PhD, 67; Univ Oxford, BA, 62. **CAREER** Asst prof to prof, Wesleyan Univ, 67-88; teach fel, Harvard Univ, 64-66; vis lectr, 75-76; vis prof, 85; instr, Mass Inst Tech, 66; vis prof, Univ Amsterdam, 71-72; vis lectr, Col Holy Cross, 79; vis prof, Univ Mich, 87-88; vis prof, Peking Univ, 92; prof, Univ Mich, 88-. **HONORS AND AWARDS** Rhodes Schlp; Phi Beta Kappa; Sigma Xi; NIMH Predoc Fel; Guggenheim Fel. **MEMBERSHIPS** APA; APS; Soc Personology; ISPP. **SELECTED PUBLICATIONS** Auth, The contributions of David McClelland to personality assessment," J Personality Assess 71 (98): 129-14; auth, "Authoritarianism for the 21st Century," Contemp Psychol 43 (98): 825-826; rev of, Demythologizing an elite: American presidents in empirical, comparative, and historical perspective, Political Psychol 20 (99): 408-410; coauth, "History of modern personality theory and research," in Handbook of personality theory and research, ed. L Pervin, O John (NY: Guilford, 99); auth, "Linking personality and "scientific" psychology: The development of empirically derived Thematic Ap-

perception Test measures," in Evocative images: The Thematic Apperception Test and the Art of Projection, eds. L Gieser, M I Stein (Washington, DC: APA Books, 99); auth, "Assessment in the Oval Office," rev of Presidential personality and performance, by A L George, J L George, Contemp Psychol 44 (99): 371-373; auth, "Authoritarianism," in Encyclopedia of Psychology, ed. A F Kazdin (NY: Oxford Univ Press and Am Psychol Asn, in press); auth, "David Clarence McClelland," in Encyclopedia of Psychology, ed. A F Kazdin (NY: Oxford Univ Press and Am Psycho Asn, in press). **CONTACT ADDRESS** Dept Psychology, Univ of Michigan, Ann Arbor, 525 E University Ave, Ann Arbor, MI 48109.

WINTER, JERRY ALAN
PERSONAL Born 07/23/1937, Bronx, NY, m, 1964, 2 children **DISCIPLINE** SOCIOLOGY, SOCIAL PSYCHOLOGY **EDUCATION** BA, New York Univ, cum laude, 54-58; MA, Univ MI, 58-60; PhD, Univ MI, 60-64. **CAREER** Prof, Dept of Sociology, Connecticut College, 77-; Research Consultant, Dept of Research, Council of Jewish Federations, 90-91; Assoc Prof, Dept of Sociology, Connecticut College, 70-77; Asst Prof, Sociology Dept, Temple Univ, 68-70; Director, Research on Training for Metropolitan Ministry, Ministry Studies Board, 67-69; Asst Prof, Sociology Dept; Rutgers: The State Univ, 65-68; Instructor, Sociology Dept, The Univ of Michigan, 64-65; Editor, Contemporary Jewry, 92-97; Chair, Dept of Sociology, Conn College, 92-95; Fellow, NEH Summer Seminar, Yale Univ, 81; Acting Editor, MIMH Fellowship Program, Dept of Sociology, Temple Univ, 69-70. **HONORS AND AWARDS** Alpha Kappa Delta, Phi Beta Kappa, Psi Chi. **MEMBERSHIPS** Amer Sociological Assoc, Amer Assoc of Univ Prof, Religious Research Assoc, Assoc for the Sociological Study of Jewry. **SELECTED PUBLICATIONS** B. Lazerwitz, J. Winter, A Dashefskjy and E. Tabory, Jewish Choices: American Jewish Senominationalism, Albay NY, SUNY Press, 98; J. Winter Continues in the Sociology of Religion: Creed, Congregation and Community, NY, Harper and Row, 77; B. Lazerwitz, J.Alan Winter, A. Dashefsky and E. Tabory, A Study of Jewish Denominational Preferences: Summary Findings, American Jewish Year Book 97, 115-137, 97; Symbolic Ethenticity or Religion Among Jews in the US: A Test of Gansian Hypotheses, Review of Religious Research 37-233-247, 96; Not by Bread Alone: A National Replication and Refinement of a Study of Income, Identity and Household Composition and Jewish Involvement, Journal of Jewish Communal Service 69,75-81, 93; Jewish Giving and Strategies for Strengthening Campaigns, pp 361-377, In David M Gordis and Dorit P. Gary American Jewry: Portrait and Prognosis, Behrman House, 97. **CONTACT ADDRESS** Dept of Sociology, Connecticut Col, 270 Mohegan Ave, Box 5302, New London, CT 06320. **EMAIL** jawin@conncoll.edu

WINTER, JOHN ELLSWORTH
PERSONAL Born 10/26/1926, York, PA, m, 1982 **DISCIPLINE** PHILOSOPHY AND SOCIOLOGY **EDUCATION** Juniata Col, BA, 50; Villanova Univ, MA, 63; Temple Univ, 69. **CAREER** York Col, PA, 58-63; Clarion Univ, PA, 63-64; Millersville Univ, PA, 64-77, 78-94; Univ of Vienna, Austria, 77-78; prof emer, Millersville Univ, 95- . **HONORS AND AWARDS** Coleman Awd; Outstanding Tchr of Amer. **MEMBERSHIPS** AAUP; Foundation of Thanatology; APSCUF; PA Phil Assn; Am Phil Assn; Hobbes Assn; Kierkegaard Soc **RESEARCH** Philosophical anthropology; humor; political theory. **SELECTED PUBLICATIONS** The New American Scholar, Oregon St Univ, 63; A New Theory of Election to Public Office in America, Chicago, 98. **CONTACT ADDRESS** Millersville Univ of Pennsylvania, PO Box 1002, Millersville, PA 17551-0302.

WIRTH-CAUCHON, JANET
PERSONAL Born 03/08/1959, Lincoln Park, MI, m, 1982, 1 child **DISCIPLINE** SOCIOLOGY **EDUCATION** Western Mich Univ, BA, 81; Boston Col, PhD, 94. **CAREER** Teaching Fel, Boston Col, 90-92; Lectr, Bradford Col, 95; Asst Prof, Drake Univ, 95-. **HONORS AND AWARDS** Fac Grant, Drake Univ; Women's Studies Outstanding Fac Awd, Drake Univ. **MEMBERSHIPS** Soc for the Study of Soc Prob, MSS. **RESEARCH** Gender, cultural studies, identity and culture, women and mental health, feminist theory, contemporary social theory, the body and technology. **SELECTED PUBLICATIONS** Rev, Body Politics: Disease, Desire and the Family," SSSP Newsletter, vol 27, no 1 (96); auth, "Colonizing the Borderland: Deconstructing the Borderline in Psychiatry," in Perspectives in Soc Prob, vol 11 (JAI Pr, 99); auth, Borderlines: Women, Madness and Psychiatric Narrative, Rutgers UP, 00; auth, "A Dangerous Symbolic Mobility: Narratives of Borderline Personality Disorder," in Pathology and the Postmod: Mental Illness as Discourse and Experience (Sage Pr, 00). **CONTACT ADDRESS** Dept Sociol, Drake Univ, 2507 University Ave, Des Moines, IA 50311. **EMAIL** janet.wirth-cauchon@drake.edu

WISEMAN, MARY BITTNER
PERSONAL Born 08/21/1936, Philadelphia, PA, m, 1989, 1 child **DISCIPLINE** AESTHETICS; FEMINISM **EDUCATION** St John's Col, Md, AB, 59; Harvard Univ, AM, 63; Columbia Univ, PhD, 74. **CAREER** From Instr to Prof Philos, Brooklyn Col of the City University of New York, 72-98, Prof of Philos and Comparative Lit, Grad Sch of the City Univ of New York; Prof Emerita, 98-; Dep exec officer, Humanities Inst, Brooklyn Col, 81-83. **HONORS AND AWARDS** CUNY Research Grants; NEH Summer Stipend. **MEMBERSHIPS** Am Philos Asn; Am Soc Aesthet; Soc Women Philos; Col Art Asn. **RESEARCH** Philosophy of art; interpretation; theory of criticism. **SELECTED PUBLICATIONS** Auth, The Ecstasies of Roland Bartles, Routledge, 89; numerous articles in Am Philos Quart, Brit J of Aesthetics, J Aesthetics & Art Criticism, and others. **CONTACT ADDRESS** Dept of Philos, Brooklyn Col, CUNY, 4936 Curley Hill Rd., Doylestown, PA 18901. **EMAIL** hagold@aol.com

WITKIN-NEW HOLY, ALEXANDRA
PERSONAL Born 05/08/1963, Denver, CO, m, 2 children **DISCIPLINE** ETHNIC STUDIES **EDUCATION** Univ Calif-Berkeley, PhD, 97. **CAREER** Asst prof, Mont State Univ, 97-. **HONORS AND AWARDS** Am Coun of Learned Soc Contemplative Pract Fel, 98-99; Influential Teacher Award, Mont State Unv, 98; Phi Beta Kappa. **MEMBERSHIPS** AAR. **RESEARCH** Ethnic studies; Native American identities, lands, and religions. **SELECTED PUBLICATIONS** Auth, "Termination, Self-Determination, Zoning, and the Pinoleville Rancheria: The Governing Council of Pinoleville Indian Community vs. Mendocino County," 89; "To Silence a Drum: The Imposition of United States Citizenship on Native Peoples," 95; The Heart of Everything That Is: Paha Sapa, Treaties, and Lakota Identity, 98; "Black Elk and the Spiritual Significance of Paha Saps (the Black Hills)," 99. **CONTACT ADDRESS** Center for Native American Studies, Montana State Univ, Bozeman, 20186 Wils Hall, PO Box 172340, Bozeman, MT 59717-2340. **EMAIL** anewholy@montana.edu

WITT, IRVING M.
PERSONAL Born 09/12/1921, Stockton, CA, m, 1952, 2 children **DISCIPLINE** SOCIOLOGY **EDUCATION** Univ Calif Berkeley, BA, 42; Univ Chicago, MA, 48; Univ Calif Berkeley, PhD, 58. **CAREER** Instructor, City Col San Francisco, 50-51; Instructor, San Francisco State Univ, 52, 55-63; Prof to Prof Emeritus, Col of San Mateo, 63-. **HONORS AND AWARDS** Phi Beta Kappa. **MEMBERSHIPS** San Mateo Sen Citizens Comm. **RESEARCH** Aging. **SELECTED PUBLICATIONS** Auth, Guidebook to Sociology, St Martins Press. **CONTACT ADDRESS** Dept Soc Sci, Col of San Mateo, 1700 W Hillsdale Blvd, San Mateo, CA 94402.

WITTROCK, MERLIN CARL
PERSONAL Born 01/03/1931, Twin Falls, ID, m, 1953, 3 children **DISCIPLINE** EDUCATIONAL PSYCHOLOGY **EDUCATION** Univ of Mo, BS, 53; MEd, 56; Univ of Ill, PhD. 60. **CAREER** Asst prof, Univ of Calif, LA, 60-64; assoc prof, 64-67; Prof, 67-. **HONORS AND AWARDS** Outstanding Teacher of the Univ, Univ of Calif, LA, 90; UCLA Thorndike Awd for Outstanding Res. **MEMBERSHIPS** Am Psychol Asn; Am Educ Res Asn. **RESEARCH** Cognition; Learning; Teaching of reading, science, and math. **SELECTED PUBLICATIONS** Auth or Ed: Handbook of Research and Teaching; The Human Brain; The Brain and Psychology; Testing and Cognition; The Evaluation of Instruction; Taxonomy for Learning, Teaching, and Assessing, Longman Press, 01. **CONTACT ADDRESS** Grad Sch of Educ, Univ of California, Los Angeles, 3339 Moore Hall, Los Angeles, CA 90095. **EMAIL** wittrock@ucla.edu

WOJCIK, DANIEL
PERSONAL Born 12/21/1955, Detroit, MI **DISCIPLINE** ENGLISH; FOLKLORE **EDUCATION** BA, anthrop, Univ Calif Santa Barbara, 78; MA, folklore and myth, Univ Calif Los Angeles, 86; PhD, folklore and myth, Univ Calif Los Angeles, 92. **CAREER** Asst prof, 91-97, assoc prof, 97-, dept of eng, Univ Ore. **HONORS AND AWARDS** Amer Acad of Relig individual res grant, 96; summer res award, Office of Res and Sponsored Prog, Univ Ore, 95; Arnold Rubin award, Fowler Mus of Cultural Hist, Univ Calif Los Angeles, 90. **MEMBERSHIPS** Amer Acad of Relig; Amer Culture Asn; Amer Folklore Soc; Amer Studies Asn; Calif Folklore Soc; Intl Soc for Contemp Legend Res; Popular Culture Asn. **RESEARCH** Millennialist movements and apocalyptic beliefs; Contemporary American folklore; Popular culture; Subcultures and youth cultures; Body art; Popular religion. **SELECTED PUBLICATIONS** Auth, The End of the World As We Know It: Faith, Fatalism, and Apocalypse in America, NY Univ Press, 97; article, Embracing Doomsday: Faith, Fatalism, and Apocalyptic Beliefs in the Nuclear Age, Western Folklore, 55, no 4, 297-330, 96; article, Polaroids from Heaven: Photography, Folk Religion, and the Miraculous Image Tradition at a Marian Apparition Site, Jour of Amer Folklore, 109, no 432, 129-148, 96; auth, Punk and Neo-Tribal Body Art, Folk Art and Artists Series, Univ Press of Miss, 95. **CONTACT ADDRESS** English and Folklore Studies, Univ of Oregon, 1286 University of Oregon, Eugene, OR 97403-1286. **EMAIL** dwojcik@oregon.uoregon.edu

WOLACH, ALLEN H.
PERSONAL Born 05/14/1943, Chicago, IL, s **DISCIPLINE** PSYCHOLOGY **EDUCATION** Univ Ill, BA, 65; Roosevelt Univ, MA, 67; Univ NMex, PhD, 87. **CAREER** From Asst Prof to Prof, Ill Inst Tech, 70-. **HONORS AND AWARDS** Ill State Univ Scholar, 61-65, Sigma Xi. **MEMBERSHIPS** Psychonomic Soc, Rocky Mt Psychol Assoc, Midwestern Psychol Assoc. **RESEARCH** Learning, sequenced reinforcement, overtraining, contrast effects comparative, instrumentation, statistics and methodology. **SELECTED PUBLICATIONS** Auth, Journal Reference Assistance APA Style Documents: A Terminate and Stay Resident Program," Behav Res Methods: Instruments and Computers (93); auth, "Developing a Computer Program to Facilitate Language Training," Computers in Human Behav, 10 (94): 541-557; coauth, Writing Statistics Programs in Structured Basic, KNVHE (Chicago, IL), 97. **CONTACT ADDRESS** Dept Psychol, Illinois Inst of Tech, 3300 S Federal St, Chicago, IL 60616.

WOLF, MARYANNE
PERSONAL Born 10/25/1947, South Bend, IN, m, 1985, 2 children **DISCIPLINE** CHILD DEVELOPMENT, COGNITIVE NEUROSCIENCES **EDUCATION** St Mary's Col, BA, 69; Northwestern Univ, MA, 70; Harvard Univ, PhD, 79. **CAREER** Teach, Hawaii, Ind, 70-73; int, Chil Hosp Med Cen, 78; instr, Harvard Univ, 78; asst prof, Brandeis Univ, 79-80; res assoc, Vet Adm Hosp, 78-84; dir, Harvard Univ, 80-81; asst prof, Tuft Univ, 80-86; res sci, Harvard Univ, 92-; dir, Tuft Univ, 96-; assoc prof, 87-99; prof, 99-. **HONORS AND AWARDS** Radcliffe Fel; Livingston Fel; Dist Teach year Awd; APA Nat Teach excel Awd; Fulbright Fel; Alum Prof Ach Awd; Shannon Awd; Golden Key Hon Soc; Norman Geschwind Mem Lectr Awd; Alden Gnt; TFRAC Gnt; Stratford Found Gnt; Haan Found Gnt; NICHD Gnt. **MEMBERSHIPS** AAAS; APA; APS; CNS; IDA; INS; ISSBD; NECLA; NYACD; SSSR. **RESEARCH** Dyslexia; child development; cognitive neurosciences; reading. **SELECTED PUBLICATIONS** Coauth, "Naming-speed processes, timing, and reading: A conceptual review, "J Learn Disab (in press); coauth, "A brief history of time, phonology, and other dimensions of developmental dyslexia," in Brain Bases of Learning Disabilities; The Case of Reading Disabilities, eds. K Fischer, J Bernstein, F Benes, J Kagan, D Waber, M Wolf (in press); coauth, "The unique and combined contribution of naming speed and phonological processes in reading disability: A test of the Double-Deficit Hypothesis, Read Writ (in press); coauth, "The 'Double-Deficit Hypothesis' for the developmental dyslexias," J Edu Psych 91 (99): 1-24; coauth, "Retrieval-rate, Accuracy and Vocabulary Elaboration (RAVE) in reading-impaired children: A pilot intervention program," Dyslexia J Res Pract 5 (99): 1-27; coauth, "Relations between the K-Bit and the WISC-III in children with reading disabilities," J Intl Neuro Soc 5 (99); coauth, "Naming speed, processing speed, and reading in poor readers: A preliminary replication of Kail & Hall," J Intl Neur Soc (99); auth, "What Time may tell: Towards a new conceptualization of developmental dyslexia," Ann Dyslexia (99): 1-28. **CONTACT ADDRESS** Dept Child Development, Tufts Univ, Medford, 520 Boston Ave, Medford, MA 02155. **EMAIL** mwolf@emerald.tufts.edu

WOLFE, DAVID L.
PERSONAL Born 03/07/1939, Lock Haven, PA, m, 1962, 3 children **DISCIPLINE** ANTHROPOLOGY, THEOLOGY, PHILOSOPHY, PHILOSOPHY OF EDUCATION **EDUCATION** Wheaton Col, BA, 61, MA, 64; NYork Univ, PhD, 69. **CAREER** Inst to assoc prof of Philos, The Kings Col, NY, 63-70; asst to assoc prof of Philos, Wheaton Col, 70-74; assoc to prof of Philos, Gordon Col, 74-87; pastor, The Tunbridge Church, Tunbridge, VT, 87-. **MEMBERSHIPS** Am Philos Asn **RESEARCH** Religious epistemology' Philosophy of education; Philosophy of science. **SELECTED PUBLICATIONS** Auth Epistemology: The Justification of Belief, InterVarsity Press, 82; coed The Reality of Christian Learning, Christian Univ Press, 87; coed Slogans or Distinctives: Reforming Christian Education, Univ Press Am, 93. **CONTACT ADDRESS** Rivendell, 6 Wolfe Dr, Tunbridge, VT 05077. **EMAIL** rivendell5@juno.com

WOLFER, LOREEN T.
PERSONAL Born 12/04/1968, Allentown, PA, m, 1996 **DISCIPLINE** SOCIOLOGY **EDUCATION** Franklin and Marshall Col, BA, 91; Cornell Univ, MA, 93; PhD, 96. **CAREER** Vis prof, Dickinson Col, Carlisle, Pa, 94; instr, Rowan Col of NJ, 95-96; instr, Univ of Scranton, 96-97, asst prof, 97-. **HONORS AND AWARDS** Franklin and Marshall Chapter of Alpha Kappa Delta, 91; Franklin and Marshall Departmental Honors, 91; The Distinguished Honor Medal and Citation from the Nat Asn of Chiefs of Police and the Am Police Hall of Fame, 99. **MEMBERSHIPS** Am Sociol Asn, Am Sociol Asn Section on Educ, Am Sociol Asn Section on Children, Am Sociol Asn Section on the Family, Am Soc of Criminology, Pa Sociol Soc. **RESEARCH** Elderly and the fear of crime; community view of police; children's development; maternal employment practices; women in the workforce; crime and prevention. **SELECTED PUBLICATIONS** Coauth with D. P. Hayes and M. F. Wolfe, "Schoolbook Simplification and Its Relation to the Decline in SAT Scores," Am Educ Res J, Vol 33, No 2 (Sept 96); coauth with P. Moen, "Maternal Employment and Early Adult Transitions: Black and White Daughters' Schooling and Employment," J of Family Issues, Vol 17, No 4 (July 96); coauth with T. Baker, "Police Grantsmanship: A Case Study," The J of Police and Criminal Psychol, Vol 13, No 2 (98): 55-66; auth, "Parenthood and Marriage: Does Maternal Employment Influence the Timing of Adult Family Transitions for Daugh-

ters' from Different Economic Backgrounds?," Sociol Viewpoints, v 14 (98): 39-62; coauth with T. Baker and R. Zezza, "Problem-Solving Policing: Eliminating Hot Spots," The FBI Law Enforcement Bull (99); coauth with T. Baker, "Teaching Organized Crime: An Active Learning Approach," J of Criminal Justice Educ, Vol 11 (in press). **CONTACT ADDRESS** Dept Sociol/Criminal Justice, Univ of Scranton, Scranton, PA 18510. **EMAIL** wolferl2@epix.net

WOLFORD, R.
PERSONAL Born 12/01/1966, Salem, OR, m, 1988 **DISCIPLINE** SOCIOLOGY **EDUCATION** Sheperd Col, BASC, 95; Calif Univ PA, MA, 96. **CAREER** Hampshire Co Planner, WV, 97-2000; adjunct prof, Potomac State Col of LURU, 98-2000. **HONORS AND AWARDS** Vice pres, Phi Alpha Theta; Kappa Delta Pi. **RESEARCH** Civil war. **SELECTED PUBLICATIONS** Auth, The Role of the Bloomery Iron Furnace on the Village and District of Bloomery, Calif Univ of Penn (96). **CONTACT ADDRESS** Dept Soc Sci & Ed, Potomac State Col of West Virginia Univ, 101 Fort Ave, Keyser, WV 26726. **EMAIL** jrwolford@mountain.net

WOLOWITZ, HOWARD M.
PERSONAL Born 12/03/1931, New York, NY, m, 1952, 3 children **DISCIPLINE** PSYCHOLOGY **EDUCATION** CCNY, BA, 53; Univ Mich, MA, 59; PhD, 61. **CAREER** Lecture, E MI Univ, 58-61; Prof to Prof Emeritus, Univ MI, 63-; Visiting Prof, NYork Univ, 67. **HONORS AND AWARDS** NIMH Res Fel, 59-61; Distinguished Lecturer, Univ MI, 00. **MEMBERSHIPS** APA; MI Psychol Asn. **RESEARCH** Structural algorithm for personal problem solving and conflict resolution in Oreomo and cross-cultural applications; Analysis of nocturanal dreams as dramatic narrative data: formulating their role as paradigms of personal problem solving adaptations to inner conflict, external stress in psychopathology; Psychotherapy and index of mental health. **SELECTED PUBLICATIONS** Co-auth, "Contributions to psychohistory: XV: Structural characteristics as an index of mental health in Freud's. His patients and colleagues' manifest dreams," Perceptual & Motor Skills, (89): 811-819; co-auth, "Non-waking responses to waking stressors: Dreams and nightmares," Journal of Applied Social Psychology, (90): 199-226; auth, "Additional developments regarding manifest dream structure and function," Perceptual & Motor Skills, (98): 896-898. **CONTACT ADDRESS** Dept Psychol, Univ of Michigan, Ann Arbor, 525 E Univ Ave, Ann Arbor, MI 48109. **EMAIL** wolowitz@unmich.edu

WONG, BERNARD P.
PERSONAL Born 02/12/1941, China, m, 1973, 2 children **DISCIPLINE** ANTHROPOLOGY **EDUCATION** Univ Wisc, MA, 71; PhD, 74. **CAREER** Asst Prof to Assoc Prof, Univ Wisc, 74-86; Assoc Prof to Prof, San Francisco State Univ, 86-. **HONORS AND AWARDS** Ford Fel, 71-73; ford Dissertation Fel, 72-73; Res Grant, Nat Sci Foundation; NEH Fel, 80,m 86; Grants, Japanese Min of Educ. **MEMBERSHIPS** Am Anthropol Asn; Soc for Urban Anthropol **RESEARCH** Globalization; Tansnationla migration; Economic anthropology. **SELECTED PUBLICATIONS** Auth, "Social Stratification, Adaptive Strategies and the Chinese community of New York," Urban Life, 33-52; auth, "elites and Ethnic Boundary Maintenance," Urban anthropology, 001-025; auth, "A comparative study of the Assimilation of the Chinese in New York City and Lima, Peru," comparative Studies in Society and History, 335-358; auth, "The Role of Ethnicity in Enclave Enterprises: A Study of the Chinese Garment Factories in New York City," Human Organization, 120-131; auth, Chinatown: Economic Adaptation and Ethnic Identity of the Chinese, Harcourt Brace; auth, Patronage, Brokerage, Entrepreneurship and the Chinese Community of New York, AMS Press; auth, "Ethnicity and family Business: Chinese Family Firms in the San Francisco Bay Area," Family Business Review; auth, "Hong Kong Immigrants in San Francisco," in Reluctant Exiles? Migration from Hong Ko9ng and the New Overseas Chinese, M.E. Sharpe, 94; auth, "Anciens et Nouveaus Migrants chinois," Hommes & Migrations, 93; auth, Ethnicity and Entrepreneurship: The New Chinese Immigrants in the San Francisco Bay Area, Allyn And Bacon, 98. **CONTACT ADDRESS** Dept Anthropol, San Francisco State Univ, 1600 Holloway Ave, San Francisco, CA 94132. **EMAIL** bernardw@sfsu.edu

WONG, EUGENE F.
PERSONAL Born 12/10/1941, Boston, MA, m, 1998 **DISCIPLINE** SOCIOLOGY **EDUCATION** Univ Mass, BA, 72; Boston Col, MA, 74; Univ Denver, MA, 76; PhD, 79. **CAREER** Prof, Univ of Calif Irvine, 92-94; prof, Univ of Ark, 94-96; prof, Voorhees Col, 96-. **HONORS AND AWARDS** Nat Honor Soc; Martin Luther King Fel, 74-76; Res Stipends, Grad Sch of Int Studies, Univ of Denver, 77. **MEMBERSHIPS** Am Sociol Assoc; Southern Sociol Soc; Am Polit Sci Assoc; Assoc of Third World Studies. **RESEARCH** Socio-economic hierarchies and ethnic business enterprise, social imagery of ethnic groups in American Narrative film and the visual mass media, comparative minority group social pathologies, death and dying, widowhood and widowerhood and socio-sexual reintegration, genocide, auto-genocide, and mass murder, historical revisionism, holocaust denial groups, militia, survivalist, and racist para-military groups and movements. **SELECTED PUBLICATIONS** Coauth, "Current and Future Research at the Center on International Race Relations", Studies in Race and Nations, Univ of Denver, 74; auth, On Visual Media Racism: Asians in the American Motion Pictures, Arno Pr, NY Times, 78; auth, "Learned Helplessness: The Need for Self-Determination Among the Chinese American Elderly", J of Ethnic Studies, 8.2, (80); auth, "Asian American Middleman Minority Theory, The Constructional Framework of an American Myth", J of Ethnic Studies 13.1 (85); coauth, "Aaron Spelling", "Peter Fonda", "Friends", Encycl of Popular culture, Popular Pr, Bowling Green State Univ, 99; auth, "Race Relations Theory: An Overview", Racial and Ethnic Relations in America, Salem Pr, (Pasadena, 99). **CONTACT ADDRESS** Dept Soc Sci, Voorhees Col, 1411 Voorhees Rd, Denmark, SC 29042. **EMAIL** wong@voorhees.edu

WOOD, CORRINE SHEAR
PERSONAL Born 04/14/1925, Baltimore, MD, w, 4 children **DISCIPLINE** ANTHROPOLOGY **EDUCATION** Johns Hopkins Univ, BS, 59; Univ Calif, BS, 68; PhD, 73. **CAREER** Prof, Calif State Univ, 80-. **HONORS AND AWARDS** Phi Beta Kappa, 68; Fel, Nat Inst of Health, 70; 15th Annual Authors' Awd, Univ Calif, 80; Praxis Awd, honorable mention, App Anthropol Soc, 85; Outstanding Prof Awd, Calif State Univ, 84; Fel, Am Asn for Advancement of Sci, 84. **MEMBERSHIPS** Am Asn for the Advancement of Sci, Am Anthropol Asn, Am Public Health Asn, Am Women in Sci, Human Biol Coun, Occupational Safety and Health Committee, Orange County Health Planning Coun, Pan-Am Health Org, World Health Org, Soc for Med Anthropol, West Coast Nutrition Asn. **RESEARCH** Medical anthropology. **SELECTED PUBLICATIONS** Auth, Leprosy, The Next to Go, forthcoming; auth, Leprosy, An Annotated Bibliography, Mellen Pub, 97; auth, Human Sickness and Health: A Biocultural View, Mayfield Pub, 79; **CONTACT ADDRESS** Dept Soc Sci, Cabrillo Col, 6500 Soquel Dr, Aptos, CA 95003. **EMAIL** corinnesw@cs.com

WOOD, RICHARD L.
DISCIPLINE SOCIOLOGY **EDUCATION** Univ Calif, Davis, BA, 82; Graduate Theol Union, MA, 89; Univ Calif, Berkeley, MA, 91, PhD, 95. **CAREER** Staff assoc to Dir, Mexico Program, Center for Global Ed, Augsburg Col, Minn, 84-87; asst prof, Univ NMex, 96-. **HONORS AND AWARDS** Univ Calif Berkeley, Univ Fel, 89, Outstanding Grad Student Instr Awd, 92, Grad Res Fel, 92, Dora Garibaldi Fel, 93, Res Fel for "Discipleship and citizenship Project" at the Ctr for the Ethics and Social Policy, 93-95; Robert J. Mc Namara Awd, Asn for Sociol Rel, 94; Young Scholars of Am Rel, 97-99. **RESEARCH** Religion and political culture in America, policing and democratic life in America. **SELECTED PUBLICATIONS** Auth, "Religious Resources for Political Success in Three Congregations," Sociol of Rel, 55:4, 381-401 (Dec 94); auth, "Social Capital and Political Culture: God Meets Politics in the Inner City," Am Behav Sci, 40:5, 595-605 (March/April 97); auth, "Religious Culture and Political Action," Sociol Theory, 17:3, 307-332 (Nov 99); coauth with John Coleman, "Citizenship and Discipleship in Community Organizing," in Public Religion and Modern Citizenship by John Coleman, SJ, Univ Ill Press (forthcoming); auth, "Religion and Politics," in Religion in American Culture and Beyond, Prentice-Hall, Inc (forthcoming). **CONTACT ADDRESS** Dept Sociol, Univ of New Mexico, Albuquerque, 1915 Roma NE, SSCI #1103, Albuquerque, NM 87131-1166. **EMAIL** rlwood@unm.edu

WOODARD, FREDRICK
PERSONAL Born 01/29/1939, Kingfisher, OK, w **DISCIPLINE** EDUCATION **EDUCATION** Iowa Wesleyan College, Mt. Pleasant, IA, BA, 1961; University of Iowa, Iowa City, IA, MA, 1972, PhD, 1976. **CAREER** West High School, Davenport, IA, teacher, 61-66; Black Hawk Community College, Moline, IL, instructor, 67-69; Cornell College, Mt. Vernon, IA, instructor, 72-76; Univ of Iowa, Iowa City, IA, instructor, 73-76, asst prof, 76-79, assoc prof, 79-80, actg assoc dean of the Faculties, Office of Academic Affairs, 81-83, assoc dean of the Faculties, Office of the Vice Pres for Academic Affairs, 83-90, Assoc Vice Pres for Academic Affairs, 90-, Museum of Art, interim dir, 90-92; Univ of Calif at San Diego, visiting assoc prof, 80. **MEMBERSHIPS** Chair of session, Council on College Composition, 1975, 1977, 1981, 1983, 1985; chair of session, Midwest Modern Language Association, 1970, 1972, 1973, 1977-79, 1981-83; chair of session, National Council of the Teachers of English, 1985; member, American Library Association, 1980-; member, Modern Language Association, 1980-; committee member, Big 10 Academic Personnel Officers, 1985; committee member, Professional and Organizational Development Network in Higher Education, 1985-. **CONTACT ADDRESS** Office of Academic Affairs, Univ of Iowa, 111 Jessup Hall, Iowa City, IA 52242.

WOODDELL, GEORGE
PERSONAL Born 09/19/1953, Washington, DC, s, 3 children **DISCIPLINE** SOCIOLOGY **EDUCATION** Univ La, BA, 83; La State Univ, MA, 93; PhD, 99. **CAREER** Instr, Univ La, 94-. **HONORS AND AWARDS** Ben Kaplan Awd, Univ La; Fel, Univ Calif; Alumni Fel, La State Univ. **MEMBERSHIPS** Mid-South Sociol Asn. **RESEARCH** Environmental sociology, Minority groups, Crime. **SELECTED PUBLICATIONS** Auth, "Work Scheduling and The Construction of family disruption," Free Inquiry in Creative Sociology, forthcoming; auth, "Expert Informants and Relative Risk: A Methodology for Modeling Waterways," Risk Analysis, (98): 557-562; auth, "The Game of Poaching: Folk Crimes in Southwest Louisiana," Society and Natural Resources, (98): 25-38; auth, "Technological Change, Resource Management and Conflict: Commercial shrimping in Louisiana," Sociological Spectrum, (96): 472; auth, "Modeling the Mississippi: Oil spill Risk on Louisiana's Largest Waterway, 96; auth, "An Oil Resource Atlas for Louisiana, Baton Rouge, 95. **CONTACT ADDRESS** Dept Sociol & Anthropol, Univ of Louisiana, Lafayette, Box 40198, Lafayette, LA 70504-0001.

WOODLAND, CALVIN EMMANUEL
PERSONAL Born 11/03/1943, LaPlata, MD, s **DISCIPLINE** EDUCATION **EDUCATION** Morgan State Univ, BS 1965; Howard Univ, MA 1970; Rutgers Univ, EdD 1975; Southern California for Professional Studies, Psy D, 1997. **CAREER** MD Dept of Health & Mental Hygiene, music & rehab therapist 1966-70; Essex Co Coll, counselor/dir of educ advisement 1970-74; Morgan State Univ Sch of Educ, dir of teacher corps, assoc prof of educ asst dean 1974-81; Coppin State Coll, dir of spec svcs, acting dean of students 1981-82; Charles County Comm Coll, dean 1982-86; Northern Virginia Comm Coll, dean beginning 1986; vp of student dev, Bergen Comm Coll, vp of student services, currently. **HONORS AND AWARDS** HEW Fellow US Dept of Health, Educ Welfare 1976; ERIC Publications on Data Base as a Tool for Recruitment of Minority Students 1979, 85; Innovations in Counseling Psychology Book Review Journal of Contemporary Psychology 1979; Outstanding Achievement and Comm Serv Southern MD Chain Chap of Links 1986. **MEMBERSHIPS** Evaluator Middle States Assoc of Colleges & Schools 1979-; Amer Psychological Assoc, Amer Assoc for Counseling Dev, Amer Assoc of Rehab Therapists, Natl Commission for African-American Education; Health & Human Services Board for Volusia/Flagler Counties, children & family's service committee; Volusia/Flagler Counties, juvenile justice board. **CONTACT ADDRESS** VP Student Serivces, Bergen Comm Col, 400 Paramus Rd, Paramus, NJ 07652-1595.

WOODROFFE, ANNETTE
PERSONAL Born 05/18/1954, Barbados, West Indies, m, 1999 **DISCIPLINE** SOCIOLOGY **EDUCATION** Univ W Indies, BA, 79; Columbia Univ, MSW, 88; Univ Md, PhD, 93. **CAREER** Asst Prof, Wayne State Univ, 94-. **HONORS AND AWARDS** Recognition Awd, Baltimore City Coun, 93; Cert of Appreciation, Mich Region I HIV Prevention and Intervention Comprehensive Planning Comt, 97; Cert of Appreciation, Southwestern Mich HIV/AIDS Coun, 98. **RESEARCH** Interpersonal relationships between human service professionals, people with chronic or terminal diseases, HIV/AIDS, interpersonal relationships between friends and educational peers, ethical issues in relationships in human service delivery. **SELECTED PUBLICATIONS** Auth, "The Bajan Sunday School," in Every Day Life in Barbados: A Soc Perspective, Nation Publ Co (79); coauth, A Family-Centered Transagency Model for Drug-Exposed and HIV-Infected Children, 92; auth, "Considerations in Planning for the Care of Children Whose Mothers are HIV Symptomatic or have AIDS," The Skillman Ctr for Children, Col of Urban, Labor and Metropolitan Affairs, Wayne St Univ (97). **CONTACT ADDRESS** Dept Sociol, Wayne State Univ, 112 Cohn Bldg, Detroit, MI 48202.

WOODROW-LAFIELD, KARE
PERSONAL Born 10/14/1950, Fairfield, IL, m, 1991 **DISCIPLINE** SOCIOLOGY **EDUCATION** Univ Ill, Chicago, BA, 72; Univ Tenn, Knoxville, MA, 76; Univ Ill, Urbana, PhD, 84. **CAREER** Demographer, U.S. Census Bureau, 84-92; Sr Res Analyst, U.S. Comn on Immigration Reform, 94-95; Res Sci, Univ Tex, Austin, 95-96; asst to assoc prof, Miss State Univ, 96-. **HONORS AND AWARDS** Phi Beta Phi; BA, cum laude, Univ Ill, Chicago, 72; Mem, Mexico-U.S. Binational Migration Study, 95-97. **MEMBERSHIPS** Population Asn of Am, Am Sociol Asn, Am Statistical Asn, AAAS, et al. **RESEARCH** Demography, immigration, inequality. **SELECTED PUBLICATIONS** Auth, "An Analysis of Net Immigration in Census Coverage Evaluation," Population Res and Policy Rev, 14, 2 (95): 173-204; auth, "Emigration From the United States: Multiplicity Survey Evidence," Population Res and Policy Rev, 15, 2 (96): 171-199; auth, "To Dream of American Citizenship and Family Unification: The Long Welcome," Proceedings of the Social/Government Statistics Section, Am Statistical Asn, 1997 Joint Statistical Meetings, 11-19; auth, "Undocumented Residents in the United States in 1989-1990: Issues of Uncertainty in Quantification," Int Migration Rev, 32, 1 (98): 145-174; coauth with Frank D. Bean, Rodolfo Corona, and Rodolfo Tuiran, "Quantification of Migration Between Mexico and the United States," Migration Between Mexico and the United States: Binational Study, Vol 1, Thematic Chapters, Mexico-United States Binational Migration Study, Mexican Ministry of Foreign Affairs and U.S. Commission on Immigration Reform (98): 1-90; auth, "Estimating Authorized Immigration," and "Viewing Emigration at Century's End," Migration Between Mexico and the United States: Binational Study, Vol 2, Res Reports and Background Materials, Mexico-United States Bina-

tional Migration Study, Mexican Ministry of Foreign Affairs and U.S. Commission on Immigration Reform (98): 619-682, 683-694; auth, "Potential Sponsorship by IRCA-Legalized Immigrants," U.S. Commission on Immigration Reform, Washington, DC (98); auth, "Labor Migration, Family Integration, and the New America During the Twentieth Century," Chapter 2, Illegal Immigration in America: A Reference Handbook, David W. Haines and Karen E. Rosenblum, Greenwood Press (99): 13-26. **CONTACT ADDRESS** Dept Sociol, Mississippi State Univ, PO Box C, Mississippi State, MS 39762. **EMAIL** Woodrow_Lafield@Soc.MsState.Edu

WOODWARD, CAROLYN
DISCIPLINE THEORY, 18TH-CENTURY BRITISH LITERATURE, AND FEMINIST STUDIES **EDUCATION** Univ Wash, PhD, 87. **CAREER** Instr, Univ NMex, 87-. **RESEARCH** 18th-century cultural deviance and experimental fiction. **SELECTED PUBLICATIONS** Auth, 'My Heart S o Wrapt': Lesbian Disruptions in 18th-Century British Literature, Signs, 93; Who Wrote The Cry: a Fable for Our Times, 18th-Century Fiction, 96. **CONTACT ADDRESS** Univ of New Mexico, Albuquerque, Albuquerque, NM 87131. **EMAIL** woodward@unm.edu

WORRILL, CONRAD W.
PERSONAL Born 08/15/1941, Pasadena, CA, m **DISCIPLINE** EDUCATION **EDUCATION** George Williams Coll, BS 1968; Univ of Chicago, MA 1971; Univ of Wis, PhD 1973. **CAREER** Northeastern IL Univ Ctr for Inner City Studies Education, program coordinator. **HONORS AND AWARDS** Received numerous awds for community involvement; AKA Monarch Awds. **MEMBERSHIPS** Weekly columnist Chicago Defender 1983-, and other black newspapers in Chicago and around the country; chmn Natl Black United Front 1985-; bd mem IL Black United Fund 1985-; mem Chicago Housing Authority 1987-; talk show host WVON-AM, 1988-; Assn for Study of Classical African Civilizations; bd mem, Temple of the African Community of Chicago. **SELECTED PUBLICATIONS** Worrill's World Book of Newspaper columns/articles have appeared in numerous African Amer publications. **CONTACT ADDRESS** Ctr for Inner City Studies, Northeastern Illinois Univ, 700 E George H. Clements Blvd., Chicago, IL 60653. **EMAIL** c-worril@neiu.edu

WORTHAM, ANNE
PERSONAL Born 11/26/1941, Jackson, TN, s **DISCIPLINE** SOCIOLOGY **EDUCATION** Tuskegee Univ, BS, 63; Boston Col, PhD, 82. **CAREER** Adjunct asst prof, Wellesley Col, 82-83; asst prof, Kennedy Sch of Govt, Harvard Univ, 83-86; vis scholar, Hoover Inst, 86-89; asst prof, Washington & Lee Univ, 89-91; assoc prof, Ill State Univ, 91-. **HONORS AND AWARDS** Distinguished Alumni Citation of the Year Awd, Nat Asn for Equal Opportunity in Higher Ed, 87; Ill State Univ Res grant; Aspen Inst Scholar; John M. Olin Fac Fel; Earhart Postgrad Fel; Danforth Found Grad Fel; Earhart Found Grad Fel; Ludwig von Mises Humanities Fel; Inst for Humane Studies Fel. **MEMBERSHIPS** Am Sociol Asn, Midwest Sociol Soc, Ill Sociol Asn, Am Int Asn for Law and Soc Philos. **RESEARCH** Sociology of culture; history of ideas; race relations. **SELECTED PUBLICATIONS** Auth, The Other Side of Racism: A Philosophical Study of Black Race Consciousness, Columbus, Oh: Ohio State Univ Press (81); auth, "The Conservative Revolution That Wasn't: New Right Populism and the Preservation of New Deal Liberalism," in William J. Wilson, ed, American Sociological Association Presidential Volume on Public Policy 1990, Newbury Park, Ca: Sage Pubs (93); auth, "Black Victimhood: A 'Paradoxical Sequel' to Civil Rights," The World & I (April 93); auth, "Making Sense of the White Male Stigma of Not 'Getting It'," The World & I (Feb 94); auth of foreword to Civil Wrongs: What Went Wrong with Affirmative Action by Steven Yates, Inst for Contemporary Studies Press, San Francisco, Ca (94); auth, "Reason's Revenge on Sociology," Humanitas, Vol VIII, No 1 (95); auth, "Distorting the Dilemma," The World & I (Jan 96); auth, "America's Birth at Appomattox," The World & I (May 99); auth, "Behind the Walls of Segregation: Playing Cowboys," The World & I (Nov 99). **CONTACT ADDRESS** Dept Sociol-Anthrolpol, Illinois State Univ, Box 4660, Normal, IL 61790. **EMAIL** awortha@mail.ilstu.edu

WORTHEN, VAUGHN E.
PERSONAL Born 02/06/1956, Salt Lake City, UT, m, 1981, 4 children **DISCIPLINE** COUNSELING PSYCHOLOGY **EDUCATION** Brigham Young Univ, BS, 83; M Ed, 85; PhD, 94. **CAREER** Asst prof, Brigham Young Univ, 91-. **MEMBERSHIPS** Am Psychol Assoc; Nat Career Develop Assoc. **RESEARCH** Psychotherapy Supervision, Counseling Process and Outcomes, Career Counseling. **SELECTED PUBLICATIONS** Coauth, "Comparison of two IQ, conversion tables for the vocabulary-block design short form", Jof Clinical Psychol 44 (88): 950-952; coauth, "The parallel process in psychotherapy supervision", Prof Psychol: Res and Practice 20, (89): 329-363; coauth, "Comment on developmental models of supervision", Prof Psychol: Res and Practice 20, (89): 363; auth, Career exploration, Brigham Young Univ, 95; coauth, "a phenomenological investigation of "good" supervision events", Jof Counseling Psychol 43, (96): 25-34; coauth, "The meaning and blessings of family work", in Strengthening our families: An in-depth look at the proclamation on the family, ed, D.C. Dollahite, Bookcraft (Salt Lake City), 00. **CONTACT ADDRESS** Dept Student Develop, Brigham Young Univ, 2570 WSC, Provo, UT 84602. **EMAIL** vaughn_worthen@byu.edu

WORZBYT, JOHN C.
PERSONAL Born 09/09/1943, Auburn, NY, m, 1967, 2 children **DISCIPLINE** EDUCATION, COUNSELING **EDUCATION** SUNY, BS, 65; Univ Rochester, ME, 68; PhD, 71. **CAREER** Teacher, Union Springs Cent Schs, 65-67; Sch Counsr, W Genesee Public Schs, 70-72; From Coord to Prof, Ind Univ, 86-. **HONORS AND AWARDS** First Place Writing and Res Awd, Am Sch Coun Asn, 90; Fac Recognition Awd, Ind Univ, 92; Who's Who in the World, 12th ed, 95; Who's Who in the E, 95-96; Eminent Practitioner Awd, Pa Coun Asn, 97; Phi Delta Kappa. **MEMBERSHIPS** ACA, ASCA, PACES. **RESEARCH** School counseling, management of guidance services, counseling children. **SELECTED PUBLICATIONS** Coauth, Support Groups for Children, Accelerated Develop Pr (Muncie, IN), 96; auth, Caring Children Make Caring Choices, Pa Dept Educ (Harrisburg, PA), 98; auth, "Stop, Think and Go Decision-Making: A Matter of Driver and Traffic Safety (Module II)," in Pa Enhanced Driver Educ Curriculum Guide, PDE Publ (00). **CONTACT ADDRESS** Dept Educ, Indiana Univ of Pennsylvania, Indiana, PA 15705-0001. **EMAIL** jcworz@grove.iup.edu

WOSINSKA, WILHELMINA
PERSONAL Born, Poland, m, 1971, 3 children **DISCIPLINE** SOCIAL PSYCHOLOGY **EDUCATION** Univ Warsaw, Poland, BA, 65; Jagiellonian Univ, Poland, MA, 68; PhD, 76. **CAREER** Inst Dir, Univ Silesia, Poland, 75-80; dept chair, 75-90. **HONORS AND AWARDS** Merit Hon Mem, Polish Psychol Soc; UN Prog Sem Facilitator. **MEMBERSHIPS** PPA; EAESP. **RESEARCH** Psychology of social influence across cultures with an emphasis on organizational setting. **SELECTED PUBLICATIONS** Auth, Kierowanie ludzmi w swietle psychologi spolecznej (Leadership in the Organization from the Social Psychology Perspective) Katowice, Wydawnictwo Univ Slaskiego, 85; Auth, Psychologia niesprawiedliwosci interpersonalnej (Psychology of Interpersonal Injustice), Katowice, Wydawnictwo Univ Slaskiego, 89; co-ed, The Practice of Social Influence in Multiple Cultures, Lawrence Erlbaum Assoc, forthcoming. **CONTACT ADDRESS** Dept Social Psychology, Arizona State Univ, PO Box 37100, Glendale, AZ 85306. **EMAIL** wilhelmina@asu.edu

WRIGHT, ROBERT L.
PERSONAL Born 05/23/1920, Connersville, IN, m, 1944, 1 child **DISCIPLINE** LANGUAGES AND LITERATURES; FOLK SONG **EDUCATION** Defiance, BA, 43; Univ Minn, MA, 47; Columbia's Harvard, SU, 47-49; Teachers Col, EdD, 55; postdoc study, Stockholm, 57-58. **CAREER** Emer Prof Thought and Language, Mich State Univ; US Navy, active duty 43-46, 51-53 (from seamen to lieutenant-commander) **HONORS AND AWARDS** Mich State Univ Book Award; Swodish Gov't Fel, 57-58; Fel, Int Inst Arts and Letters, 61; MSU Bk Award, 63; Am Philosophical Soc grantee, 66-67, 69-70, 71-73; Huntington Lib Follow, 69; Fel, Am Antiquarian Soc, 74; Mich State Imov Distinguished Fac Award, 81; Doriance Col Alumni Achievement Award, 81. **MEMBERSHIPS** MLA; Am Folklore Soc; Canadian Folk Music Soc; Soc AAU; Scand in Study, etc. **RESEARCH** Ballads and songs, emigrant ballads. **CONTACT ADDRESS** 274 Oakland Dr., East Lansing, MI 48823-4747.

WRONG, DENNIS H.
PERSONAL Born 11/22/1923, Toronto, ON, Canada, m, 1966, 3 children **DISCIPLINE** SOCIOLOGY **EDUCATION** Columbia Univ **CAREER** Assoc prof, New School for Soc Res, 61-63; assoc prof, Brown Univ, 56-61; prof, New York Univ, 63-94. Emeritus prof, New York Univ, 94- **HONORS AND AWARDS** Guggenheim Fel, 84-85; Fel Wilson Cent for Int Scholars, 91-92 **MEMBERSHIPS** ASA; ESS **RESEARCH** Social Theory; Politics; Modern History **SELECTED PUBLICATIONS** Auth, The Problem of Order: What Unites and Divides Society, Harvard Univ 95; auth, The Modern Condition: Essays at Century's End, Stanford Univ, 98; auth, The Oversocialized Conception of Man, Transaction, 99. **CONTACT ADDRESS** 144 Drakes Corner Rd., Princeton, NJ 08540. **EMAIL** dhwrong@voicenet.com

WYNN, JEAN M.
PERSONAL Born 04/07/1940, Detroit, MI, m, 1966, 4 children **DISCIPLINE** ANTHROPOLOGY, PSYCHOLOGY **EDUCATION** Mercy Col Detroit, BS, 62; Univ Mich, MA, 66; Univ Connecticut, PhD, 91. **CAREER** Assist Prof of Anthropology & Psychology, Manchester Community Col, 93-; auth, Clinical Instr of Nursing, Capital Community Col, 81-90; Adjunct Prof, 86; Worked and established school for disabled, Penanq, Malaysia, U.S. Peace Corps, 66-68; Nurse, Tunisia, No. Africa, U.S. Peace Corps, 63-65. **HONORS AND AWARDS** Excellence in Teaching Awd, Manchester Community College, 96; Who's Who Among America's Teachers 96 and 98; Doctoral Dissertation Fel, 89-90; Univ of Connecticut Pre-Doctoral Fel, 86-88; Connecticut Research Foundation Summer Fel, 87; U.S. Federal Government Crippled and Impaired Fel, 65-66; Tri-County League of Nurses' Scholarship, 59-62; Mercy College of Detroit, Honor Scholarship, 58-59. **MEMBERSHIPS** Amer Psychological Society; Amer Anthropological Assoc. **RESEARCH** Medical Anthropology; Healing Styles Mental Well Being. **CONTACT ADDRESS** Dept Social Science, Manchester Comm-Tech Col, PO Box 1046, Manchester, CT 06045. **EMAIL** ma_wynn@commnet.edu

WYRICK, FLOYD I.
PERSONAL Born 05/26/1932, Chgo **DISCIPLINE** EDUCATION **EDUCATION** Chicago State U, BE 1954; DePaul U, MA 1963; Univ of IL, PhD 1972; Phi Delta Kappa; Kappa Delta Pi. **CAREER** Calumet HS Chicago Bd Educ, prin co-dir; Chicago Public School, teacher; Chicago City Coll; Northwestern Univ; Booz Allen & Hamilton, mgmt conselor; Adam & Assoc; Mitchell Watkins & Assoc. **MEMBERSHIPS** Mem Nat Alli of Black Sch Educ; Am Assn of Sch Adminstrs; Nat Assn of Scndry Sch Prins; Samuel B Stratton Educ Assn; mem Am Civil Libs Union; People Unit to Save Human; Alpha Phi Alpha Frat; Comm Fund of Metro Chgo. **CONTACT ADDRESS** 78131 S May St, Chicago, IL 60620.

WYSONG, EARL
PERSONAL Born 06/25/1944, Kokomo, IN, m, 1966, 2 children **DISCIPLINE** SOCIOLOGY, POLITICAL SCIENCE **EDUCATION** Indiana Univ, BS, 67; Ball State Univ, MA, 71; Purdue Univ, PhD, 90. **CAREER** Prof, Ind State Univ, Kokomo, 90-. **HONORS AND AWARDS** Claude Rich Teach Awd, 96; Teach Excell, 97, 98; IN Univ Fac Awd, 93; Co-nom, C Wright Mills Awd, 00; co-nom, NCSA Schol Achiev Awd, 00. **MEMBERSHIPS** IASS; SSSP; ASA; NCSA; MSS; SSSP. **RESEARCH** Social inequalities; class; work; organizations; healthcare; drug policies. **SELECTED PUBLICATIONS** Coauth, "Evaluating DARE: Drug Education and the Multiple Meanings of Success," Policy Studies Review 9 (90):727-747; coauth, "Truth and DARE: Tracking Drug Education to Graduation and As Symbolic Politics," Social Problems 41 (94): 501-25; coauth, "A Decade of DARE: Efficacy, Politics, and Drug Education," Sociological Focus 28 (95): 283-311; auth, "Professional Societies, Interorganizational Linkages and Occupational Health Policy Reform," Social Problems 39 (92): 201-218; auth, "Conflicting Agendas, Interests, and Actors in Disease Prevention Policy-Making: Business, Labor and The High Risk Act," Intern J Health Ser 23 (93): 301-322; coauth, "Influence Networks, Professional Societies, and occupational Health Policy," in Research in Politics and Society: The Political Consequences of Social Network, ed. Gwen Moore, J Allen Whitt (Greenwich, CT, JAI Press, 92), 189-218; auth, High Risk and High Stakes: Health Professionals, Politics, and Policy, Greenwood Press, (Westport, CT), 92; coauth, "Family Friendly Workplace Benefits: Policy Mirage, Organizational Contexts, and Worker Power," Critical Sociology 24 (98): 244-276; coauth, The New Class Society, Rowan and Littlefield (Lanham, MD), 99. **CONTACT ADDRESS** Dept Social and Behavioral Sci, Indiana Univ, Kokomo, PO Box 9003, Kokomo, IN 46904. **EMAIL** ewysong@iuk.edu

X

XIAO, HONG
PERSONAL Born, China, m, 2 children **DISCIPLINE** SOCIOLOGY **EDUCATION** Beijing Univ, BA, 82, MA, 84; Univ Conn, Storrs, MA, 89, PhD, 98. **CAREER** Knox Col, 95-97; instr, Monmouth Col, 98-99; asst prof, Central Washington Univ, 99-. **HONORS AND AWARDS** Midwest Fac seminar fel, Chicago Univ, 96, 97; Summer seminar fel from Nat Endowment of the Humanities, Columbia Univ, 99. **MEMBERSHIPS** Midwest Sociol Asn, Am Sociol Asn, Applied Sociol Asn. **RESEARCH** Family, stratification, gender, comparative sociology. **SELECTED PUBLICATIONS** Articles appearing in: J of Comparative Family Studies, 99; J of Human Values, 99; Gender and Society, 2000; Sociol Perspectives, 2000. **CONTACT ADDRESS** Dept Sociol, Central Washington Univ, 400 E 8th St, Ellensburg, WA 98926. **EMAIL** xiaoh@cwu.edu

XIE, XIAOLIN
PERSONAL Born 08/20/1963, Canton, China, m, 1988, 1 child **DISCIPLINE** PSYCHOLOGY, HUMAN ECOLOGY **EDUCATION** Univ Nebr-Lincoln, PhD, 94. **CAREER** Asst prof, Cameron Univ. **HONORS AND AWARDS** Who's Who Among Am's Teachers, 98, 2000. **MEMBERSHIPS** Nat Coun on Family Relations. **RESEARCH** Cross-cultural family studies. **SELECTED PUBLICATIONS** Coauth with L. Weinstein and C. Cleanthous, "Purpose in life, boredom, and volunteerism in a group of retirees, Psychol Reports, 76, 482 (95); coauth with L. Weinstein and W. Meredith, "Hotline in China: One way to help Chinese people," Psychol Reports, 78, 90 (96); coauth with R. Combs, "Older women's lives in coastal China," Asia Pacific J of Social Work, 6 (1), 62-80 (96); coauth with J. DeFrain and E. Millspaugh, "The psychological effects of miscarriage: A family system perspective," Families, Systems & Health, 14(3), 331-347 (96); coauth with J. DeFrain, W. Meredith, and R. Combs, "Family strengths as perceived by universi-

ty students and government employees in the People's Republic of China," Int J of Sociol of the Family, 26(2), 17-27 (autumn 96); coauth with S. Linn, "Gender differences in perceptions of family roles by Chinese university students," Perceptual and Motor Skills, 84, 127-130 (97); auth, "Scores on loneliness of Chinese, and American college students," Psychol Reports, 81, 317-318 (97); coauth with J. DeFrain, "Rural families in transition in the 1990s: An exploratory study in a brigade in central China," Asian Pacific J of Soc Work (98); coauth with J. Miller, M. Dzindolet, L. Weinstein, and C. Stones, "Faculty and students' views of teaching effectiveness in the United States, China and South Africa," J of Teaching Psychol (2000). **CONTACT ADDRESS** Dept Human Ecology, Cameron Univ, 2800 Gore Blvd, Lawton, OK 73505. **EMAIL** xiex@cameron.edu

Y

YABLONSKY, LEWIS

PERSONAL Born 11/23/1924, Irvington, NJ, s, 1 child **DISCIPLINE** SOCIOLOGY **EDUCATION** New York Univ, PhD, 58. **CAREER** Prof Sociol, Calif State Univ - Northridge, 63-. **HONORS AND AWARDS** CSU Bd Trustees Outstanding Prof Awd. **RESEARCH** Criminology. **SELECTED PUBLICATIONS** Auth, Criminology, HarperCollins, 90; Gangsters, NYU Press, 97; Juvenile Delinquency, 00. **CONTACT ADDRESS** 2311 4th St., #312, Santa Monica, CA 90405. **EMAIL** yablonsky@loop.com

YAGER, GEOFFREY

PERSONAL Born 10/30/1944, Schenectady, NY, m, 1993, 2 children **DISCIPLINE** COUNSELING **EDUCATION** State Univ NYork, Binghamton, BA, 66; State Univ NYork, Albany, MA, 67; Mich State Univ, PhD, 73. **CAREER** Asst prof, Univ of NDak, 73-75; Univ of Cincinnati, 75-, prof, 92-. **HONORS AND AWARDS** Distinguished Mentor Awd, Asn for Coun Educ and Supv, 94. **MEMBERSHIPS** Am Coun Assoc; Am Psychol Assoc; Am Educ Res Assoc; Assoc for Couns Educ and Supv. **RESEARCH** Counseling and values, video applications to counselor training. **SELECTED PUBLICATIONS** Auth, "A.C.A.'s proposed standards of practice and ethical standards", OH Coun Assoc Guidelines 20.2.6, 94; auth, "Multicultural issues in career development: Applications to school-to-work", OH State Univ, (Columbus, OH), 98; auth, Stressed - A Guidebook for Psychologists/Counselors, Educators, Families/ Individuals, Creative Therapy Associates, (Cincinnati, OH), 99. **CONTACT ADDRESS** Couns Prog, Univ of Cincinnati, PO Box 210002, Cincinnati, OH 45221-0002.

YAMAUCHI, JOANNE

DISCIPLINE CULTURAL DIVERSITY AND ASIAN PACIFIC AMERICAN ISSUES **EDUCATION** Goucher Col, BA; Columbia Col, MA, Northwestern Univ, PhD. **CAREER** Asst prof, Am Univ; consult, U.S. Govt Agencies, corp business. **HONORS AND AWARDS** Excellence Educ 2000; U.S. Pan Asian Chamber Com; Excellence Tchg; Multicultural Affairs Office, Am Univ; assoc ed, int & intercultural comm annual, int jour intercultural rels, jour applied comm. **MEMBERSHIPS** AT&T; NASA; Procter & Gamble; Am Coun Educ; Soc Intercultural Educa; Intercultural & Int comm commission Speech Comm Asn. **SELECTED PUBLICATIONS** Auth, Making a Difference Through ValuingDifferences; Asian Americans and the Glass Ceiling; Prejudice, Promotion,and Power in the Newsroom: A Survey of Asian American Broadcasters; Ass ed, International and Intercultural Commun Annual. **CONTACT ADDRESS** American Univ, 4400 Massachusetts Ave, Washington, DC 20016.

YAN, MARGARET M.

PERSONAL Born 09/11/1938, Amoy, Fujian, China, m, 1964, 1 child **DISCIPLINE** ANTHROPOLOGY, LINGUISTICS **EDUCATION** Nat Taiwan Univ, BA, 62; Cornell Univ, MA, 79. **CAREER** Asst prof, Univ of San Francisco, 73-74; lectr, Calif State Univ, 73-75; asst prof to prof, Ind Univ, 75-. **HONORS AND AWARDS** Fulbright-Hays Res Fel, 81-82; Pres, Chinese Teachers Assoc, 86-88; Grants, Ind Univ, 87, 88, 92, 95; grant, Academia Sinica, 93, 94. **MEMBERSHIPS** Ling Soc of Am; Chinese Lang Teachers Assoc; Chinese Lang Computer Soc; Int Assoc of Chinese Ling; Int Assoc for the Teaching Chinese as a Second Lang. **RESEARCH** Phonology, Chinese historical phonology, Chinese Dialectoloty, Anthropological/socio-linguistics, Taiwan Aboriginal Languages. **SELECTED PUBLICATIONS** Auth, "Historical Sound Changes as Criteria for the Classification of Fujian Dialects", A collected Volume on Sociocultural Studies on Taiwan and Fujian, eds Ying-chang chunag and Ying-hai Pan, Academica Sinica (Taiwan, 94): 257-283; coauth, Interactions I: A Cognitive Approach to Beginning Chinese, Ind Univ Pr, (Bloomington), 97; coauth, Workbook for Interactions I: A Cognitive Approach to Beginning Chinese, Ind Univ Pr, (Bloomington), 97; coauth, Interactions II: A Cognitive Approach to Beginning Chinese, Ind Univ Pr, (Bloomington), 97; coauth, Workbook for Interactions II: A Cognitive Approach to Beginning Chinese, Ind Univ Pr, (Bloomington), 97; coauth, Teacher's Manual for Interactions I-II, Ind Univ Pr, (Bloomington), 97; auth, "The Evolutionary Deverlopment of the MC *ri initial in the Dialects of Fujian and Taiwan", Proceedings of the 10th N Am Conf on Chinese Ling, Vol I, ed Chaofen Sun, Stanford Univ, (99): 74-89. **CONTACT ADDRESS** Dept E Asian Lang, Indiana Univ, Bloomington, 1011 E 3rd St, Bloomington, IN 47405-7005. **EMAIL** yan@indiana.edu

YANG, FENGGANG

PERSONAL Born 06/28/1962, Cangzhou, China, m, 1988, 2 children **DISCIPLINE** SOCIOLOGY; RELIGION; ETHNICITY **EDUCATION** Hebei Normal Univ, Shijiazhuang, China, BA, 82; Nankai Univ, Tianjin, China; MA, 92, PhD, 97, Catholic Univ of Amer. **CAREER** Lectr, Cangzhou Education Col, Hebei, China, 82-84; Asst Prof, People's Univ of China, 87-89; Research Assoc, Center for Immigration Research, Univ Houston, 97-. **HONORS AND AWARDS** Thomas V. Moore Doctoral Scholarship, 89-92; Research Awd for the Scientific Study of Religion, 93; Outstanding Graduate Student, Catholic Univ of Amer, 93 & 95; Teaching and Research Fel, People's Univ China, 94; Dissertation Fel, Univ of Illinois at Chicago, 94-95; Dissertation Fel, Louisville Inst of Protestantism and American Culture, 95-96; Postdoctoral Fel, Center for Immigration Research, 97-98; Research Fel, Center for Immigration Research, 99. **MEMBERSHIPS** Amer Sociological Assoc; Assoc for Sociology of Religion; Soc for the Scientific Study of Religion; Assoc for Asian Amer Studies; Assoc for Asian Studies; Amer Acad of Religion. **RESEARCH** Chinese American religions and cultures; Chinese religions and cultures; Diasporic identities; Immigrant assimilation and ethnic groups. **SELECTED PUBLICATIONS** Auth, Decree and Covenant: Different Notions of Law in Chinese and Western Societies, Cultural China, 96; A Sociological Comparison of Christianity and the Chinese Traditional Value System, Christian Culture Review, 96; Tension and the Healthy Development of Society, Economic Ethics and Chinese Culture, 97; auth, "The Chinese Gospel Church: The Sinicization of Christianity," pp. 89-107 in Religion and The New Immigrants: Continuities and Adaptions in Immigrant Congregation, edited by Helen Rose Ebaugh and Janet S. Chafetz, Walnut Creek, CA: AltaMira Press, 00; auth, "Hsi Nan Buddhist Temple: Seeking to Americanize," pp. 67-87 in Religion and The New Immigrants: Continuities and Adaptions in Immigrant Congregations, edited by Helen Rose Ebaugh and Janet S. Chafetz, Walnut Creek, CA: AltaMira Press, 00; "Chinese American Religions," pp. 113-115 in Encyclopedia of Contemporary American Religion, edited by Wade Clark Roof, New York: Macmillan Reference USA, 00; auth, Fengang Yang, "The Growing Literature of Asian American Religions: A Review of the Field," Journal of Asian American Studies, 00; auth, Fenggang Yang and Helen Rose Ebaugh, "Religion and Ethnicity among New Immigrants: The Impact of Majority/ Minority Status in Home and Host Countries," Journal for the Scientific Study of Religion, 01; auth, Fenggang Yang and Helen Rose Ebaugh, "Transformations in New Immigrant Religions and Their Global Implications," American Sociological Review, 01; auth, PRC Immigrants in the US: A Demographic Profile and an Assessment of their Integration in the Chinese American Community, The Chines Triangle of Mainland-Taiwan-Hong Kong: Comparate Institutional Analyses, 01. **CONTACT ADDRESS** Dept of Sociology, Univ of So Maine, Portland, ME 04104-9300. **EMAIL** fyang@usm.maine.edu

YBARROLA, STEVEN J.

PERSONAL Born 02/06/1955, Stockton, CA, m, 1982, 2 children **DISCIPLINE** ANTHROPOLOGY **EDUCATION** Bethel Col, BA, 85; Brown Univ, MA, 87; PhD, 95. **CAREER** Instr to assoc prof, Central Col, 91. **HONORS AND AWARDS** David Tutt Awd, Bethel Col, 84-85; Nat Sci Found Grant, 89-90; Res Grant, Min of Culture, Spain, 89-90; Huffman Awd, 95-96; Fantastic Fac Awd, 97-99. **MEMBERSHIPS** Am Anthrop Soc, Soc for the Anthrop of Europe. **RESEARCH** Inter-ethnic relations, culture change, research methods. **SELECTED PUBLICATIONS** Rev, of "The Unassimilated Greeks of Denver' by G. James Patterson, Bull of the Soc for Anthrop of Europe, 6.2 (92):13; rev, of "Investigating the Biological Foundations of Human Morality by James Hurd, Christian Scholars Rev, 97; auth, Competition and Ethnic conflict: the Dynamics of Native/Migrant Relations in the Peninsular Basque Country (forthcoming). **CONTACT ADDRESS** Dept Behav Sci, Central Col, Iowa, 812 University St, PO Box 085, Pella, IA 50219. **EMAIL** ybarrolas@central.edu

YEN, D. E.

PERSONAL Born 03/20/1924, Wellington, New Zealand, M, 1949, 2 children **DISCIPLINE** AGRICULTURE; ANTHROPOLOGY (PREHISTORY) **EDUCATION** Massey Agricultural Col, Univ of NZ, B Agr Sc, 47, M Agr Sc, 48; Auckland Univ NZ, D Sc, 75. **CAREER** Plant breeder, 48-53, Crop research div, dept sci and industry research, Lincoln, NZ; officer in charge of vegetable breeding, 54-66; enthnobotanist, dept anthrop, 66-80, Bishop Museum, Honolulu; prof, 80-90, Australian Natl Univ. **HONORS AND AWARDS** Fels, Australian Acad of Humanities; Linnean Soc; Foreign assoc, Natl Acad of Sci; Elsden Best Medal; Distinguished Economic Botanist, 92. **MEMBERSHIPS** Polynesian Soc; Soc for Economic Botany; Hakluyt Soc **RESEARCH** Origins of oceanic subsistence, agriculture **SELECTED PUBLICATIONS** Auth, Pacific Subsistence systems and Aspects of Cultural Evolution, A Community of Culture, 93; Kumara remains in Pit 0 at P5/288, The Archaeology of Pa Pouerua, Northland, New Zealand, 93; The development of Sahul agriculture with Australia as bystander, Antiquity 69, 95; Melanesian arboriculture: Historical perspecitves with emphasis on the genus Canarium, South Pacific Indigenous Nuts, 96. **CONTACT ADDRESS** Dept of Anthropol, Univ of Hawaii, Manoa, Honolulu, HI 96822.

YEN, SHU-CHEN

PERSONAL Born 12/16/1966, Taiwan, m, 1994, 1 child **DISCIPLINE** EDUCATION **EDUCATION** Tung-Hai Univ, BA, 90; Univ Mo, Med, 93; PhD, 98. **CAREER** Asst Instr, Univ Mo, 93-96; Asst Prof, Eastern Ill Univ, 98-. **HONORS AND AWARDS** Elizabeth Nelson Vemer Mem Minority Scholar, Univ Mo, 98; Sigma Xi, Eastern Ill Univ, 99. **MEMBERSHIPS** SRCD, NAEYC, AMS, ACEI, ILAECTE. **RESEARCH** Temperament, early childhood curriculum type and its influence on children's behavior. **SELECTED PUBLICATIONS** Auth, "Web Makes Montessori Album Accessible to All, Public Sch Montessorian," vol 12, no 2, 10 (00); auth, "Children's Temperament and Behavior in Montessori and Constructivist Early Childhood Programs," Early Educ and Develop (forthcoming); auth, "A Comparison of Children's Behavior in Montessori and Constructivist Preschools," The Open Forum, Montessori Educ Progs, Int (forthcoming). **CONTACT ADDRESS** Dept Educ, Eastern Illinois Univ, 600 Lincoln Ave, Charleston, IL 61920.

YETMAN, NORMAN ROGER

PERSONAL Born 01/10/1938, New York, NY, m, 1964, 2 children **DISCIPLINE** AMERICAN STUDIES, SOCIOLOGY **EDUCATION** Univ Redlands, BA, 60; Univ Pa, MA, 61, PhD(Am Civilization), 69. **CAREER** Instr sociol, Univ Redlands, 62-63; from asst prof to prof Am studies & sociol, 66-77; Chancellors Club Teaching Prof of Am Stud and Sociol, 92- , chmn Am studies, 73-81, 93-96, 00-, chair, Sociol, 86-89, Univ Kansas; Danforth assoc; Inst Southern Hist, Johns Hopkins Univ, sr res fel, 72-73; eval consult, Nat Endowment for Humanities, 75-76; Am spec, Dept State, 77, 82, 98; Fulbright prof, Odense Univ & Univ Copenhagen, 81-82. **MEMBERSHIPS** Am Sociol Asn; Orgn Am Historians; Am Studies Asn. **RESEARCH** Racial and ethnic relations; sociology of slavery; sociology of sport. **SELECTED PUBLICATIONS** Ed, Life Under the Peculiar Institution, 70 & Voices From Slavery, 70, Holt, reprint ed, Dover, 00; ed, Majority and Minority, Allyn & Bacon, 71, 75, 82, 85, 91, 99; coauth, Black Americans in sports, Civil Rights Digest, 72, 77; Family planning services and the distribution of Black Americans, Social Problems, 6/74; auth, The rise and fall of time on the cross, Rev Am Hist, spring 76; The Irish experience in America, In: Irish History and Culture, 76; coauth, Sociology: Experiencing a Changing Societies, Allyn & Bacon, 97. **CONTACT ADDRESS** American Studies Prog, Univ of Kansas, Lawrence, Lawrence, KS 66045-2117. **EMAIL** norm@falcon.cc.ukans.edu

YOCOM, MARGARET ROSE

PERSONAL Born 01/23/1948, Pottstown, PA **DISCIPLINE** FOLKLORE, ENGLISH LITERATURE **EDUCATION** Univ Pa, BA, 70; Univ Mass, Amherst, MA, 73; PhD, 80. **CAREER** Asst prof eng & folklore, George Mason Univ, 77-, consult folklife, Festival Am Folklife, Smithsonian Inst, 75-85; consult, Eskimo Heritage Prog of Nome, Alaska, 83-84; consult folklife, Rangeley Lakes Region Logging Mus, 84-. **MEMBERSHIPS** Am Folklore Soc; Oral Hist Asn; Mid Atlantic Folklife Asn (treas, 81-83); Northeast Folklore Asn. **RESEARCH** Family folklore and fieldwork; material culture; folk narrative; women's folklore. **SELECTED PUBLICATIONS** Auth, "Cut my teeth on a spud!, Rodney Richard, Mad Whittler from Rangeley, Maine," Chip Chats, 94; auth, "What is Culture? and Ethics from a Folklorist's Perspective," in Cultural Reporter: Reporter's Handbook (Tom Snyder Prod and Smithsonian Inst, 95); auth, "Marie Campbell," in American Folklore: An Encyclopedia (Garland Publ, 96) and in Notable American Women Folklorists (Am Folklore Soc, 97); auth, "Woodcarving," in American Folklore: An Encyclopedia (Garland Publ, 96); auth, The Yellow Ribboning of the USA: Contested Meanings in the Construction of a Political Symbol, Western Folklore, 96; auth, "Family Folklore," in Folklore: An Encyclopedia of Beliefs, Customs, Tales, Music, and Art (ABC-CLIO, 97); auth, " Women's Folklife," in Encyclopedia of New England Culture, (Yale Univ Press, forthcoming); auth, "If We Don't Joke With Each Other, We Won't Have No Fun, Will We? Storytelling in the Richard Family of Rangeley, Maine," in Traditional Storytelling Today (ABC-CLIO, 99); auth, Exuberance in Control: Dialogic Discourse in the Repertoire of Wood Carver and Storyteller William Richard, Northeast Folklore, 00; coauth, "Just Call Me Sandy, Son:" Poet Jeep Wilcox's Tribute to Sandy Ives, Northeast Folklore, 00. **CONTACT ADDRESS** Dept of Eng, George Mason Univ, Fairfax, 4400 University Dr, MSN 3E4, Fairfax, VA 22030-4444. **EMAIL** myocom@gmu.edu

YODER, JANICE

PERSONAL Born 12/31/1952, Reading, PA, m, 1981, 2 children **DISCIPLINE** PSYCHOLOGY **EDUCATION** SUNY, PhD, 79. **CAREER** Assoc prof, Webster Univ, 81-86; prof, Univ Wisc, 89-98; prof, Univ Akron, 98-. **HONORS AND AWARDS** Dist Teach Awd; Martine D Meyer Awd; Pres Elect, APA. **MEMBERSHIPS** APA; PW; SPSSI; APS; SESP; SPSP; EPA; MPA; SWS. **RESEARCH** Social psychology of women;

tokenism; workplace gender segregation and discrimination; norms of occupational appropriateness; feminist theory; women and power. **SELECTED PUBLICATIONS** Coauth, "When pranks become harassment: The case of African American women firefighters," Sex Roles 35 (96): 253-270; coauth, "Undergraduates regard deviation from occupational gender stereotypes as costly for women," Sex Roles 34 (96): 171-188; coauth, "'Outsider within' the firehouse: Subordination and difference in the social interactions of African American women firefighters," Gender Soc 11 (97): 324-341; reprint, in Gender culture and ethnicity: Current research about women and men, eds. LA Peplau, et al (Mountain View, CA: Mayfield, 99), 135-152); coauth, "Empowering token women leaders: The importance of organizationally legitimated credibility," Psychol Women Ouart 22 (98): 209-222; coauth, "Measuring sexist discrimination in the workplace: Support for the validity of the Schedule of Sexist Events," Psychol Women Ouart 22 (98): 487-491; auth, Women and gender: Transforming psychology, Prentice Hall (Upper Saddle River, NJ), (http ://www uakron. edu/psychology/faculty/textbook/Textbook.htm); coauth, "Adding feminist therapy to videotape demonstrations," Teach Psychol 27 (00): 56-57; auth, "Making work for women," in Issues in the Psychology of women: A textbook, eds. M Biaggio, M. Hersen (NY: Plenum, in press). **CONTACT ADDRESS** Dept Psychology, Univ of Akron, Akron, OH 44325-4301. **EMAIL** janyoder@uakron.edu

YOSHIOKA, MARIANNE R.
PERSONAL Born 10/15/1960, s, 2 children **DISCIPLINE** SOCIAL WORK **EDUCATION** Univ Western Ont, BA, 82; Univ Mich, MSW, 86; Fla State Univ, PhD, 95. **CAREER** Asst Prof, Columbia Univ, 95-. **HONORS AND AWARDS** Minority Res dissertation Grant, CSWE, 93; Minority Res Fel Awd, CSWE, 95; Dissertation Awd, 95; Fel, Okura Foundation Mental Health, 98. **RESEARCH** Addictions; Culturally appropriate practice; Domestic violence and Immigrant Women; Empirically based practice; HIV/STD prevention; Intervention Research; Marital and Family Therapy **SELECTED PUBLICATIONS** Co-auth, "Abstract of the Spouse Sobriety Influence Inventory," in Measures of clinical Practice: A Sourcebook 2nd ed, Free Press, 94; co-auth, "Abstract of the Spouse Enabling Inventory," in Measures of clinical Practice: A Sourcebook 2nd ed, Free Press, 94; co-auth, "Abstract of the Life Distress Inventory," in Measures of clinical Practice: A Sourcebook 2nd ed, Free Press, 94; co-auth, "An ethnography of couple and therapist experiences in reflecting team practice," Journal of Marital and Family Therapy, (94): 247-266; auth, "Measuring the assertive behavior of low income, culturally diverse women: Implications for culturally competent practice," Proceedings of the Eighth Nat Symposium on Doctoral Res in Soc Work, OH State Univ Press, 96; co-auth, "Spouse enabling of alcohol abuse: Assessment and modification," Journal of Substance Abuse, (96): 61-80; co-auth, "Measuring spouse sobriety influence," Issues in Substance Abuse: The Newsletter of the NASW Alcohol, Tobacco, and Other Drugs Section, 96; co-auth, "The development and implementation of a cognitive-based intervention aimed at culturally diverse women at risk for HIV/AIDS," International Quarterly of community Health Education, (97): 271-285; auth, "The use of developmental research methods to design culturally competent interventions," Journal of Multicultural Social Work, (990: 113-128; auth, "Substantive differences in the assertiveness of low income African American, Hispanic, and Caucasian women," Journal of Psychology, in press. **CONTACT ADDRESS** Dept Soc Work, Columbia Univ, 2960 Broadway, New York, NY 10027. **EMAIL** mry5@columbia. edu

YOUNG, ANDY
PERSONAL Born 09/20/1971, Atlantic City, NJ, m, 1995 **DISCIPLINE** SOCIOLOGY, PSYCHOLOGY **EDUCATION** Lubbock Christ Univ, BA, 93; Abilene Christ Univ, MS, 95; Texas Tech Univ, M Ed, 99. **CAREER** Instr, Lubbock Univ, 96-. **HONORS AND AWARDS** Dean's List; Who's Who. **MEMBERSHIPS** ACA. **RESEARCH** Counseling emergency workers; CISD. **CONTACT ADDRESS** Dept Sociology, Lubbock Christian Univ, 5601 West 19th St, Lubbock, TX 79407. **EMAIL** ayoungprof@aol.com

YOUNG, WILLIAM C.
PERSONAL Born 08/15/1951, Minneapolis, MN, s **DISCIPLINE** ANTHROPOLOGY **EDUCATION** Cornell Univ, BA, 72; Univ Calif at Los Angeles, MA, 75, PhD, 88. **CAREER** Book ed, Inst for Palestine Studies, Washington, DC, 89-91; Fulbright Lectr in Anthropol, Inst of Archaeol and Anthropol, Yarmouk Univ, Irbid, Jordan, 91-94; assoc prof, Ga Southern Univ, 94-. **HONORS AND AWARDS** Phi Beta Kappa, 72; grants from the Soc Sci Res Coun and Fulbright-Hays Comn for doctoral res, 77; Honorable Mention, Best Doctoral Diss in the Soc Scis Competition, Middle East Studies Asn, 88; Awded a grant for field res in Jordan by the Nat Geographic Soc, 99. **MEMBERSHIPS** Am Anthropol Asn, Middle East Studies Asn of North Am. **RESEARCH** Pastoral peoples, ritual, kinship and social organization, social construction of gender. **SELECTED PUBLICATIONS** Auth, The Rashaayda Bedouin: Arab Pastoralists of Eastern Sudan, Fort Worth, TX: Harcourt Brace Col Pubs (96); auth, "Families and the Handicapped in Northern Jordan," J of Comp Family Studies, 28, 2 (97): 151-169; auth, "From Many, One: The Social Reconstruction of the

Rashayida Tribe in Eastern Sudan," Northeast African Studies, 4, 1 (98): 71-108; auth, "Women's Performance in Ritual Context: Weddings among the Rashayda of Sudan," in S. Zuhur, ed, Images of Enchantment: Visual and Performing Arts of the Modern Middle East, Cairo: Am Univ in Cairo Press (98): 46-69; auth, "The Background to the U. S. Bombing of Khartoum: the Sudanese Civil War," Al-Jadid, 4, 25 (98); "Review of Dawn Chatty, Development Planning and Social Change in Oman," Anthropol Forum, Perth, Western Australia, Vol 8, 1-2 (98): 111-113; auth, "Anthropologists and the Problematic of Human Rights Activism in the Middle East," Human Peace and Human Rights, 12, 1 (99): 3-9; auth, "Are 'Arabs' Fighting 'Africans' in Sudan? Cultural Factors that Divide North from South, " Al-Jadid, 5, 26 (99): 6-7, 28, 30; auth, "Comments on Salzman, 'Is Inequality Universal?' " Current Anthropol, 40, 1 (99): 54-55; "Review of Brunner and Janssee, Al-Nakba: Palestinian Catastrophe of 1948," Middle East Studies Asn Bull, 32, 2 (99): 277-278. **CONTACT ADDRESS** Dept Anthropol & Sociol, Georgia So Univ, PO Box 8051, Statesboro, GA 30460-8051. **EMAIL** wcyoung@gsaix2.cc.gasou.edu

YOUNG-EISENDRATH, POLLY
PERSONAL Born 02/04/1947, Akron, OH, m, 1985, 3 children **DISCIPLINE** PSYCHOLOGY: DEVELOPMENTAL & CLINICAL **EDUCATION** Ohio Univ, AB, 65-69; Goddard College, MA, 72-74; Washington Univ, MSW, 76; diploma in Jungian Analysis, Inter-Regional Soc of Jungian Analysts, 78-86; Washington Univ, PhD, 80. **CAREER** Asst prof, 80-86, Visit lectr 86-89, Advisor for Doc dissertations 86-94, Bryn Mawr College; Adv for Doc dissertations Union Grad Inst and Fielding Inst, 94-; Jungian psychoanalyst, private practice, 94-; Clinical assoc prof Medical Coll of the Univ Vermont, 96-. **HONORS AND AWARDS** Phi Beta Kappa; Mortar Board; Phi Kappa Phi; Teaching Fel and Assistantships; Research Assistantships; Washington Univ Graduate Tuition Awds; Goddard Coll Graduate Fel; Madge Miller Awd for Faculty Research, Bryn Mawr Coll; Junior Faculty Research Awd, Bryn Mawr Coll. **MEMBERSHIPS** Intl Assn for Analytical Psychology; Amer Psychological Assn, member of Divisions 24, 29, 35 and 39; Vermont Psychological Assn; NY Assn for Analytical Psychology; Philadelphia Assc of Jungian Analysts (founding member); C.G. Jung Inst of Pittsburgh; Independent Soc for Analytical Psychology (founding member). **SELECTED PUBLICATIONS** Coauth, Jung's Self Psychology: A constructivist Perspective, 91; auth, You're Not What I Expected: Learning to Love the Opposite Sex, 93; The Cambridge Companion to Jung, 97; The Resilient Spirit: Transforming Suffering Into Insight, Compassion and Renewal, 97; Gender and Desire: Uncursing Pandora, 97; auth, Contrasexuality and the Dialect of Desire, in The Post-Jungians Today, 98; Jungian Constructivism and the Value of Uncertainty, The Journal of Analytical Psychology, 97; The Self in Analysis, Journal of Analytical Psychology, 97. **CONTACT ADDRESS** 93 A Calais Rd., Worcester, VT 05682. **EMAIL** pye@together.net

YOUNGMAN, C. VAN
PERSONAL Born 06/17/1938, PA, m, 1979, 1 child **DISCIPLINE** PSYCHOLOGY **EDUCATION** Tufts, BS, 59; Dickinson Sch Law, LLB, 62; JD, 65. **CAREER** Instr to adj prof, Community Col of Philadelphia 72-; prof, Art Inst of Philadelphia, 90-. **HONORS AND AWARDS** Teaching Excellence Awd, 98. **MEMBERSHIPS** NCTE; AAUP; APA. **RESEARCH** Consciousness. **CONTACT ADDRESS** Dept Psychology, Art Inst of Philadelphia, 2300 Market St, Philadelphia, PA 19103.

YOUNISS, JAMES
PERSONAL Born 12/20/1936, WI, m, 1959, 4 children **DISCIPLINE** PSYCHOLOGY **EDUCATION** Marquette Univ, BA, 59; Hollins Univ, MA, 60; Catholic Univ, PhD, 62. **CAREER** Asst to Prof, Catholic Univ, 88-99. **HONORS AND AWARDS** Res Awd, Alexander von Humboldt Foundation, Germany; Sen Fel, Japanese Soc for the Promotion of Sci. **MEMBERSHIPS** Soc for Res in Child Development; Soc for Res on Adolescence; Am Psychol Asn, Alexander von Humboldt Soc. **RESEARCH** Youth development; Effects of community service. **SELECTED PUBLICATIONS** Auth, "Political socialization and identity development," Journal of Social Issues, (98): 495-512; auth, "Promoting identity development: ten ideas for school-based service learning programs," in Service learning for youth empowerment and social change, new York, 99; auth, "Religion, community service, and identity, Adolescence, (99): 243-253; auth, "Catholic schools in perspective: Religious identity, achievement, and citizenship," Phi Delta Kappan, (99): 104-113; auth, "Giving the discipline new life and avoiding fruitless controversies," Human Development, (99): 145-148; auth, "Youth service and moral identity: A case for everyday morality," Educational Psychology review, (99): 363-378; co-ed, Catholic schools at the crossroads: survival and transformation, Teachers Col Press, 00; co-ed, The Catholic character of Catholic Schools, Univ of Notre Dame Press, 00; auth, "Adolescents' public discussion and collective identity," in communication: an arena of development, 00; auth, "Reflections on Piaget's 'sociological studies," New Ideas in Psychology, in press, 00. **CONTACT ADDRESS** Life Cycle Inst, Catholic Univ of America, Washington, DC 20064-0002.

YOUNT, WILLIAM R.
PERSONAL Born 07/05/1948, Clinton, IN, m, 1969, 2 children **DISCIPLINE** FOUNDATIONS OF EDUCATION **EDUCATION** Univ Md, BS, 73; Southwestern Baptist Theol Sem, MARE, 75; PhD, 78; Univ N Tex, PhD, 84. **CAREER** Adj prof, Univ N Tex; prof, Southwestern Baptist Theol Sem, 81-. **HONORS AND AWARDS** Nominated for EPCA Golden Medallion Awd for "Created to Learn," 97. **MEMBERSHIPS** N Am Prof Christian Edu. **RESEARCH** Ministry in former Soviet Union. **SELECTED PUBLICATIONS** Coauth, Teaching Ministry of the Church, Broadman Holman, 94; auth, Created to Learn, Broadman Holman, 96; auth, Christianity and Psychology: Forever Enemies?, Moscow Theol Jour, 97; auth, Called to Teach, Broadman Holman, 99. **CONTACT ADDRESS** Sch Edu Ministries, Southwestern Baptist Theol Sem, PO Box 22000, Fort Worth, TX 76122-0418. **EMAIL** yount@ swbts.edu

YOX, ANDREW
PERSONAL Born 02/22/1955, Buffalo, NY, m, 1989, 3 children **DISCIPLINE** AMERICAN CULTURAL HISTORY **EDUCATION** Valparaiso Univ, BA, 77; Univ Chicago, MA, 78; Univ Chicago, PhD, 83. **CAREER** Part-time lectr, Ball State Univ, 84-85; Vis Asst Prof, Southwest Tex State Univ, 85-89; Lectr, Univ Tex, 89-94; Assoc Prof, Northeast Tex Community Col, 94-. **HONORS AND AWARDS** Postdoctoral Fel, Ball State Univ, 85-86; Grant, Tex Commt for Humanities, 94; Who's Who Among America's Teachers, 00. **MEMBERSHIPS** Immigration and Ethnic Hist Soc. **RESEARCH** Rise and fall of the German-American community, art and the American community 1800-2000, history of popular theology. **SELECTED PUBLICATIONS** Auth, "Ethnic Loyalties of the Alsatians in Buffalo," Yearbk of German-Am Studies (85): 106-123; auth, "Bonds of Community: Buffalo's German Element 1853-1871," NY Hist (85): 141-163; auth, "When Women Dominated the Arts of Middletown U S A," in Proceedings of the 1986 Meeting of the Am Hist Asn (Ann Arbor: Univ Microfilms, 87), 1-15; auth, "Teaching the American History Survey," Perspectives: Am Hist Asn Newsletter (89): 24; auth, "An American Renaissance: Art and Community in the 1930s," Mid-Am (90): 107-118; auth, "The Parochial Context of Trusteeism: Buffalo's Saint Louis Church 1828-1855," The Cath Hist Rev (90): 712-733; auth, "The Fall of the German-American Community: Buffalo 1914-1919," in Immigration to NY (Philadelphia: Assoc UP, 91), 126-147. **CONTACT ADDRESS** Dept Soc Sci, Northeast Texas Comm Col, PO Box 1307, Mount Pleasant, TX 75456-9991. **EMAIL** ayox@ntcc. cc.tx.us

Z

ZACHARIAS, RAVI
DISCIPLINE CULTURE AND RELIGION **EDUCATION** Univ New Delhi, BA; Ontario Bible Col, BTh; Trinity Evangel Theol Sem, MDiv; Houghton Col, DD; Asbury Col, LLD; post grad stud, Ridley Hall, Cambridge Univ. **CAREER** Distinguished vis prof. **SELECTED PUBLICATIONS** Auth, Can Man Live Without God; A Shattered Visage: The Real Face of Atheism; Deliver Us From Evil; Cries of the Heart. **CONTACT ADDRESS** So Evangelical Sem, 4298 McKee Rd, Charlotte, NC 28270.

ZAKOWSKI, SANDRA
PERSONAL Born 06/04/1964, s **DISCIPLINE** PSYCHOLOGY **EDUCATION** Univ Nice, Licence, 86; Uniformed Services Univ, PhD, 93. **CAREER** Asst Prof, Chicago Med Sch, 97-. **HONORS AND AWARDS** Fetzer Young Investigator Awd, Acad of Beh Medicine Res, 95; Grant, Dept of Defense, 97. **MEMBERSHIPS** Am Psychol Asn; Soc of Beh Medicine; Soc for Personality and Social Psychol. **RESEARCH** Psychooncology; Psychoneuroimmunology; Stress and coping; Psychosocial adjustment to chronic illness. **SELECTED PUBLICATIONS** Co-auth, "Stress, stress management, and the immune system," Applied and Preventive Psychology, (92): 1-13; co-auth, "Stress, reactivity and immune function in healthy men," Health Psychology, (92): 223-232; co-auth, "Psychological stress and platelet activation: Differences in platelet reactivity in healthy men during active and passive stressors," Health Psychology, (94): 34-38; co-auth, "Differential effects of active and passive laboratory stressors on immune function," International Journal of Behavioral Medicine, (94): 163-184; auth, "The effects of stressor predictability on lymphocyte proliferation in humans," Psychology and Health, (95): 409-425; co-auth, "Stress and genetic testing for breast cancer," Health Psychology, (97): 8-19; co-auth, "Predictors of intrusive thoughts and avoidance in women with family histories of breast cancer," Annals of Behavioral Medicine, (97): 362-369; co-auth, "Emotional expressivity and intrusive cognitions in women with family histories of breast cancer: Application of a cognitive processing model," British Journal of Health Psychology, in press. **CONTACT ADDRESS** Dept Psychol, Chicago Med Sch, 3333 Green Bay Rd, Chicago, IL 60064. **EMAIL** zakowsks@mis. finchcms.edu

ZANGRANDO, JOANNA SCHNEIDER
PERSONAL Born Hastings, MN, d, 1969, 2 children **DISCIPLINE** AMERICAN SOCIAL & CULTURAL HISTORY **EDUCATION** Wayne State Univ, BA, 61, MA, 63; George Washington Univ, PhD, 74. **CAREER** Hist researcher, US Atomic Energy Comn, MD, 64-66; legis asst, US Off Educ, 66-67; lectr hist, Albertus Magnus Col, 70; instr, Univ Hartford, 70-71; lectr, Univ Akron, 71-72; NEH Mus consult, Am hist & civilization prog community mus, Nat Am Studies Fac, 72-74; vis asst prof Am studies, George Washington Univ, 74-76; asst prof, 76-80, assoc prof Am Studies, 80-88, Full Prof, 89-, Chair, Am Studies Dept, 87-99, Dir, Liberal Studies Prog, 84-87, 98-, Skidmore Col; F D Roosevelt Libr res grant, 74-75; panel mem pub progs & res, fels, and seminars, general progs, Higher Ed Curriculum Devel and Focus Grants, preservation, NEH, 76-; mem bd rev for grant proposals, Eleanor Roosevelt Inst, FDR Libr, 77-81; dir, Skidmore Col London Study Abroad Prog & vis prof, 83, 90, 95; Scholar in Residence, NYU, 98. **HONORS AND AWARDS** Endowed Chair: Douglas Professor of American Culture, History, Literary & Interdisciplinary. **MEMBERSHIPS** AHA; Orgn Am Historians; Am Studies Asn; Am Asn State & Local Hist; Conf Group Women's History. **RESEARCH** American culture, technology and aesthetics; women's studies and women labor union organizers, 1930's to 1950's; American material culture and museum studies; women reformers; civil rights. **SELECTED PUBLICATIONS** Coauth, Black protest: A rejection of the American dream, J Black Studies, 12/70; Law, the American value system, and the black community, Rutgers-Camden Law J, spring 71; Black history in the college curriculum, In: New Perspectives on Black Studies, Univ Ill Press, 71; auth, Women and archives: An historian views the liberation of Clio, Am Archivist, 4/73; coauth, The object as subject: The role of museums and material culture collections in American studies, Am Quart, 8/74; contribr, For the duration: Working women and World War II, In: FDR's America, Forum Press, 76; auth, Women's studies: closer to reality, In: American Studies, Topics and Sources, Greenwood, 76; Women's Studies in the U. S., in Sources in Am Studies, Greenwood, 83; coauth, Eleanor Roosevelt & Black Civil Rights, in Joan Hoff and Marjorie Lightman, eds, Without Precedent. The Life and Career of Eleanor Roosevelt, IN Press, 84; book rev, Planning a New Liberal Studies Curriculum, George Mason Univ Conference on Non-Traditional Interdisc Progs, Proceedings, 86; coed, Charlotte Perkins Gilman: The Mixed Legacy, U of Delaware Press, 00. **CONTACT ADDRESS** Am Studies Dept, Skidmore Col, 815 N Broadway, Saratoga Springs, NY 12866-1698. **EMAIL** jzangran@skidmore.edu

ZAPF, PATRICIA A.
PERSONAL Born 12/06/1971, Edmonton, Alta, Canada, m **DISCIPLINE** PSYCHOLOGY **EDUCATION** Univ Alta, BA, 93; Simon Fraser Univ, MA, 95; PhD, 99. **CAREER** Intern, Univ S Fla, 98-99; asst prof, Univ Ala, 99-. **HONORS AND AWARDS** Louise McKinney Scholar, 92; Nat Sci and Engineering Res Coun of Can Res Grant, 92, 93; Margaret Ruth Crawford Memorial Scholar, 93; Simon Fraser Univ Fel, 95; BC Med Serv Found Scholar, 95; SSHRC Fel, 95; Lorne M Kendall Memorial Scholar, 96; Dissertation Grant, Am Acad of Forensic Psychol, 97; Travel Awd, Am Psychol Asn Sci Directorate, 98; Lorne M Kendall Memorial Scholar, 99; Can Psychol Asn Excellence in Res Awd, 00. **MEMBERSHIPS** am Psychol Asn; Can Psychol Asn; Am Psychol - Law Soc; Intl Asn of Forensic Mental Health Serv; Intl Acad of Law and Mental Health; Mental Health, Law, and Policy Inst. **RESEARCH** Criminal and civil competencies; Risk assessment; Development and validation of forensic assessment instruments; Ethical and legal issues in psychology and law; Public policy. **SELECTED PUBLICATIONS** Co-auth, "Conceptualiziang and assessing competency to stand trial: Implications and applications of the MacArthur Treatment Competence Model," Psychol, Public Policy, and Law, (96): 96-113; co-auth, "Assessing fitness to stand trial: A comparison of institution-based evaluations and a brief screening interview," Can J of Community Mental Health, (97): 53-66; co-auth, The Fitness Interview Test rev ed, Simon Univ Press, 98; co-auth, "Fitness to stand trial: Characteristics of fitness remands since the 1992 Criminal Code amendments," Can J of Psychiat, (98): 287-293; co-auth, "Defining and assessing competency to stand trial," in Handbook of forensic psychology, (New York, 99), 327-349; co-auth, "The last competency: An examination of legal, ethical, and professional ambiguities regarding evaluations of competence for execution," J of Forensic Psychol Practice, (01): 1-25; auth, Suicide Assessment Manual for Inmates (SAMI), Simon Fraser Univ, in press; co-auth, "A comparison of the MacCAT-CA and the FIT for making determinations of competency to stand trial," Intl J of Law and Psychiat, in press; co-auth, "A comparison of American and Canadian conceptualizations of competence to stand trial," in Psychology in the courts: International advances in knowledge, (Harwood Acad, in press), 121-132; co-auth, "The utility of the fitness Interview Test rev ed," Can J of Psychiat, in press. **CONTACT ADDRESS** Dept Psychol, Univ of Alabama, Tuscaloosa, Box 870348, Tuscaloosa, AL 35487-0348. **EMAIL** pzapf@bama.ua.edu

ZASTROW, CHARLES H.
PERSONAL Born 07/30/1942, Wausau, WI, m, 2000 **DISCIPLINE** SOCIAL WORK **EDUCATION** Univ Wisc, Madison, BS, 64, MS, 66, PhD, 71. **CAREER** Asst dir and psychotherapist, Whitewater Community and Campus Coun Center, 85-86; soc Worker II, Central State Hosp, Waupun, Wisc, summer 66; proj assoc, Bureau of Res, State Dept of Health & Soc Services, Madison, Wisc, summer 67; teaching analyst, Univ Wisc, Madison, 66-69; res analyst, Madison Community Welfare Coun, 68-69; res dir, Dane County Social Planning Agency, 69-71; asst to full prof, Univ Wisc, Whitewater, 71-. **HONORS AND AWARDS** Recipient of several scholarships and nine grants; Teacher of the Year Awd, Univ Wisc, Whitewater, 87; Researcher of the Year, Univ Wisc, Whitewater, 93; member of the commission on Accreditation Coun on Social Work Ed, 97-. **MEMBERSHIPS** Nat Asn Soc Workers, Acad of Certified Soc Workers, Wisc Coun on Soc Work Ed, Coun on Soc Work Ed, NASW Register of Clinical Social Workers, Asn for the Advancement of Soc Work with Groups, Independent Clinical Soc Worker in Wisc. **RESEARCH** Social work practice, self-talk psychotherapy. **SELECTED PUBLICATIONS** Coauth with Dae Chang, et al, The Personal Problem Solver, Englewood Cliffs, NJ: Prentice-Hall (77); auth, The Outcome of Black Children-White Parents Transracial Adoption, Palo Alto, CA: R & E Res Assocs (77); auth, Talk to Yourself: the Power of Self-Talk, Englewood Cliffs, NJ: Prentice-Hall (79); auth, You Are What You Think: A Guide to Self-Realization, Chicago: Nelson-Hall (93); auth, Social Work with Groups, 4th ed, Chicago: Nelson-Hall, Inc (97); auth, The Practice of Social Work, 6th ed, Pacific Grove, CA: Brooks/Cole, Wadsworth (2000); auth, Introduction to Social Work and Social Welfare, 7th ed, Pacific Grove, CA: Brooks/Cole, Wadsworth (2000); coauth with Karen Kirst-Ashman, Understanding Human Behavior and the Social Environment, 5th ed, Pacific Grove, CA: Brooks/Cole, Wadsworth (2001); over thirty-five articles in professional journals. **CONTACT ADDRESS** Dept Soc Work, Univ of Wisconsin, Whitewater, 800 W Main, Whitewater, WI 53190.

ZAVESTOSKI, STEPHEN
DISCIPLINE SOCIOLOGY **EDUCATION** Univ Notre Dame, BA, 94; Wash State Univ, MA, 96; PhD, 98. **CAREER** Asst prof, Providence Col, 98-. **RESEARCH** Environmental sociology, sociology of consumption, social theory **CONTACT ADDRESS** Dept Sociol, Providence Col, 549 River Ave, Providence, RI 02918-0001.

ZECKER, STEVEN G.
DISCIPLINE PSYCHOLOGY **EDUCATION** Univ Mich, BA, 74; Wayne State Univ, MA, 78; PhD, 81. **CAREER** Grad Asst to Instr, Wayne State Univ, 75-80; Vis Instr to Vis Asst Prof, Hamilton Col, 80-83; Vis Asst Prof, Colgate Univ, 83-85; Asst Prof to Assoc Prof, Northwestern Univ, 85-. **HONORS AND AWARDS** High Distinction, Univ Mich, 74; Nat Inst of Mental Health Trainee, 75-78; Psi Chi Distinguished Service Awd, 83 **MEMBERSHIPS** Am Psychol Asn, Learning Disabilities Asn of Am, Soc for Applied Res in Memory and Cognition, children and Adults with Attention Deficit Disorder, Midwest Neuropsychol Group, Midwestern Psychol Asn, Eastern Psychol Asn, Professionals in Learning Disabilities **SELECTED PUBLICATIONS** Co-auth, "The time course of auditory learning: neurophysio changes during speech-sound training," Proceeding of the 16th International Congress on Acoustics, (98): 2023-2024; co-auth, "Oral sensory discrimination of fluid viscosity," Dysphasia, (97): 68-73; co-auth, "Auditory neurophysiologic responses and discrimination deficits in children with learning problems," Science, (96): 971-973; co-auth, "Dyslexic observers show a backward time shift in masking or patterns of low spatial frequency," Optical Society of America, in press; co-auth, "Visual processing and dyslexia," in Vision and visual dysfunction, Macmillan, 91 **CONTACT ADDRESS** Dept Comm Disorders, Northwestern Univ, 633 Clark St, Evanston, IL 60208-0001. **EMAIL** zecker@nwu.edu

ZEHR, HOWARD
PERSONAL Born 07/02/1944, Freeport, IL, m, 1966, 2 children **DISCIPLINE** SOCIOLOGY **EDUCATION** Morehouse Col, BA, 66; Univ Chicago, MA, 67; Rutgers Univ, PhD, 74. **CAREER** Assoc Prof, Talladega Col, 71-78; Dir, House of Simon Half-Way House, 78; Dir & Founder, Elkhart Co Center for Community Justice, , 78-82; Dir, Mennonite Central Committee, 79-98; Prof, Mennonite Univ, 96-. **RESEARCH** Criminal justice. **SELECTED PUBLICATIONS** Auth, Changing Lenses: A New Focus for Crime and Justice, Herald Pr (Scottdale, PA), 90, 95; auth, Doing Life: Reflections of Men and Women Serving Life Without Parole, Good Books (Intercourse, PA), 96; auth, "Restorative Justice: The Concept," in Corrections Today (Am Correctional Asn, 97); auth, "Restorative Justice: When Justice and Healing Go Together," in Track Two (98); auth, "Justice Alternative: A Restorative Approach," in The Corrections Psychologist, vol 30, no 1 (98); coauth, "Fundamental Concepts of Restorative Justice," in Contemp Justice Rev, vol 1, no 1 (98); auth, "Justice as Restoration, Justice as Respect," in The Justice Prof, vol 11 (98): 71-87; auth, "'Us and Them': A Photographer Looks at Police Pictures: The Photograph as Evidence," in Contemp Justice Rev, vol 1 (98): 377-385; auth, "The Meaning of Life: Working at the Healing Edge," Offender Prog Report, vol 3, no 1 (99): 3-4; coauth, "A Restorative Framework for Community Justice Practice," in Criminology and Conflict Resolution (forthcoming). **CONTACT ADDRESS** Dept Sociol & Restorative Justice, Eastern Mennonite Univ, 1200 Park Rd, Harrisonburg, VA 22802.

ZEHR, STEPHEN C.
PERSONAL Born 02/07/1959, Lowville, NY, s **DISCIPLINE** SOCIOLOGY **EDUCATION** State Univ NY, Potsdam, BA, 81; Indiana Univ, MA, 83; PhD, 90. **CAREER** Vis asst prof, Union Col, 88-90; asst prof, IL Inst of Tech, 90-94; asst prof to assoc prof, chair, Univ of S Ind, 94-. **MEMBERSHIPS** Am Sociol Assoc; Soc for Social Studies of Science; Int Visual Sociol Assoc. **RESEARCH** Sociology of Science, Sociology of the Environment. **SELECTED PUBLICATIONS** Coauth, "Professionalization of American Scientists: Public Science and the Creation/Evolution Trials", Am Sociol Rev 50 (85):392-409; auth, "Demolition Derbies and the Ritual Destruction of Technology", Science as Culture 4.4, (94):481-501; auth, "Method, Scale and Socio-Technical Networks: Problems of Standardization in Acid Rain, Ozone Depletion and Global Warming Research", Science Studies 7.1 (94):47-58; auth, "Flexible Interpretations of 'Acid Rain' and the Construction of Scientific Uncertainty in Political Settings", Politics and the Life Sciences 13.2 (94):205-216; auth, "Accounting for the Ozone Hole: Scientific Representations of an Anomaly and Prior Incorrect Claims in Public Settings", the Sociol Quarterly 35.4 (94):603-619; auth, "The Centrality of Scientists and the Translation of Interests in the U.S. Acid Rain Controversy", Can Rev of Sociol and Anthrop 31.3 (94):325-353; auth, "Scientists' Representation of Uncertainty" in Communicating Uncertainty: Media Coverage of New and Controversial Science, ed Sharon M. Friedman, Sharon Dunwoody and Carol L. Rogers, (Mahwah, NY: Erlbaum Pr), 99; ed, Syllabi and Instructional Materials for the Sociology of Science, Knowledge and Technology, 3rd Ed, ASA Teaching Res Center (wash, DC, 99); auth, "Public Representations of Scientific Uncertainty About Global Climate Change", Public Understanding of Science 9 (00):1-20. **CONTACT ADDRESS** Dept Sociol, Univ of So Indiana, 8600 Univ Blvd, Evansville, IN 47712. **EMAIL** szehr@usi.edu

ZEITLIN, MAURICE
PERSONAL Born 02/24/1935, Detroit, MI, m, 1959, 3 children **DISCIPLINE** SOCIOLOGY **EDUCATION** Wayne St Univ, BA, 57; UCLA, Berkeley, PhD, 64. **CAREER** Instr, 61-64, Princeton Univ; asst prof, assoc prof, prof, 64-76, Univ Wisc; prof, 76-, UCLA. **HONORS AND AWARDS** John Simon Guggenheim Fel, 81-82; Ford Fels, 59-60, 60-61, 65-67, 70-71; Dist Contr to Scholar Awd, polit sociol, Amer Soc Assn, 92, 96, labor sect, soc for the stud of social problems 97. **MEMBERSHIPS** Amer Sociol Assn. **RESEARCH** Political economy; socio-historical development. **SELECTED PUBLICATIONS** Coauth, Cuba: An American Tragedy, 64; auth, Revolutionary Politics and the Cuban Working Class, 67, 70; auth, The Civil Wars in Chile, 84; coauth, Landlords and Capitalists, 88; auth, The Large Corporation and Contemporary Classes, 89; coauth, Talking Union, 96. **CONTACT ADDRESS** Dept of Sociology, Univ of California, Los Angeles, Los Angeles, CA 90095-1551. **EMAIL** zeitlin@aoc.ucla.edu

ZELLER, RICHARD A.
PERSONAL Born 10/05/1944, Elgin, IL, m, 1965, 2 children **DISCIPLINE** SOCIOLOGY **EDUCATION** Univ LaVerne, BA, 66; Univ Wisc, MA, 67; PhD, 72. **CAREER** Instructor, Univ Minn, 69-71; Asst Prof, SUNY, 71-76; Asst Prof to Full Prof, Bowling Green State Univ, 76-. **HONORS AND AWARDS** Cmty Leaders of Am, 89; Intl Leaders in Achievemnet, Cambridge, 89; dictionary of Intnl biography, 90; Who's Who in am Educ, 90; who's Who in the Midwest, 91; Who's Who in Am Educ, 92; Awd, Bowling Green State Univ Stud Support Services, 97 **MEMBERSHIPS** Am Sociol Asn; Am Statistical Asn; N Cent Sociol Asn; Soc for the Sci Study of Sex; Intl Sociol Asn; Nat Asn of Scholars; OH Asn of Scholars. **RESEARCH** Statistical analysis of Social data; Measurement reliability and validity; comparison and Contrast of experimental, survey, and field research designs; Focus group research. **SELECTED PUBLICATIONS** Co-auth, "Psychometric Analysis of the Self-Coherence Survey," archives of Psychiatric Nursing, (97): 276-281; auth, "Political correctness: sociology's Achilles Heel,: Social Facts, (97): 5-7; co-auth, "Development and Testing of a Measure of Perceived Caregiver Rewards in Adults," Journal of Nursing Measurement, (97): 33-51; co-auth, "Depression and codependency in women," archives of Psychiatric Nursing, (98): 326-334; co-auth, "Development and t4esting of the codependency Assessment tool," Archives of Psychiatric Nursing, (98): 264-272; co-auth, "clinical Symptoms of Myocardial Infarction and Delayed Treatment-Seeking Behavior in blacks and Whites," Journal of Applied Biobehavioral Research, (98): 135-159; auth, Education: The complete encyclopedia on CD-ROM, Oxford, 98; co-auth, "Measuring Subgroup Variation in Social Judgment research: A Factorial Survey approach," Social Science Research, in press; co-auth, Quantitative data analysis in Criminology and Criminal Justice, Allyn and Bacon, forthcoming. **CONTACT ADDRESS** Dept Sociol, Bowling Green State Univ, 1001 E Wooster St, Bowling Green, OH 43403-0001. **EMAIL** rzeller@bgnet.bgsu.edu

ZERAI, ASSATA
PERSONAL Born 04/23/1964, Ogden, UT, m, 1996, 2 children **DISCIPLINE** SOCIOLOGY **EDUCATION** Anderson Univ, BA, 86; Univ Chicago, MA, 88; PhD, 93. **CAREER** Visiting Scholar and Lecturer, Obafemi Awolowo Univ, 93-94; Post-doct Trainee, Univ NCar, 93-94; Sen Res Assoc to Asst Prof, Syracuse Univ, 94-. **HONORS AND AWARDS** Trustees Fel, Univ Chicago, 86-88; Harris Fel, Univ Chicago, 88-90; Dorothy Danforth-Compton Dissertation Fel, 90-91; Fel, Nat Inst of Child Health and Human Dev, 91-92; Mellon Fel, 91-92, 93-94. **MEMBERSHIPS** Am Sociol Asn; Asn of Black Sociol; E Sociol Soc; Population Asn of Am. **RESEARCH** Multilevel analyses of maternal and child health; Cross cultural health and mortality issues; race, class and gender analyses; anti-drug policy laws. **SELECTED PUBLICATIONS** Co-auth, "Understanding the Proximate Determinants of Fertility of a Nigerian Ethnic Group," Genus, (96): 67-87; auth, "Preventive Health Strategies and child Survival in Zimbabwe,' African Population studies, (96): 29-62; co-auth, "Maternal Drug Abuse and Infant Health: A Proposal for a Multilevel Model," in African Americans and the Public Agenda: The Paradoxes of Public policy, (Sage, 97), 53-67; co-auth, "Maternal cocaine Use and Barriers to Prenatal Care: How the Intersection of Race, Class and Gender Creates Hostile Environments for African American Women," Race, Gender and Class: An Interdisciplinary and Multicultural Journal, 99; auth, "Agents of Knowledge and Action: Selected Africana Scholars and their Contributions to the Understanding of Race, class and Gender Intersectionality," Cultural Dynamics, forthcoming; auth, "Making a Way Outta No Way: Grandparenting Cocaine Exposed Grandchildren," in Care Work: Gender, Labor and the Welfare State, Routledge, forthcoming; co-auth, American Public Discourse, Social Policy and anti-Drug Law: A Crack Mother's Nightmare, Ashgate Pub, forthcoming. **CONTACT ADDRESS** Dept Sociol, Syracuse Univ, 426 Eggers Hall, Syracuse, NY 13244-1090. **EMAIL** azerai@mailbox.syr.edu

ZHOU, XUEGUANG
PERSONAL Born 02/15/1959, China, m, 1987, 1 child **DISCIPLINE** SOCIOLOGY **EDUCATION** Fudan Univ China, BA 81; Stanford Univ, MA, 85; PhD, 91. **CAREER** Instr, Fudan Univ China, 82-83; Asst Prof, Cornell Univ, 91-94; from Asst Prof to Assoc Prof, Duke Univ, 94-. **HONORS AND AWARDS** Spencer Fel, Nat Acad of Educ, 93-94; NSF Grant, 94-97; Citicorp Behav Sci Res Coun grant, 98-00. **MEMBERSHIPS** Am Sociol Asn, Asn for Asian Studies, Am Polit Asn. **RESEARCH** Sociology of organizations, comparative sociology, social stratification. **SELECTED PUBLICATIONS** Ed, State and Society in Contemporary China, Gui Guan Press (Taipei), 92; auth, "Organizational Decision Making as Rule Following," in Organizational Decision Making, ed. Zur Shapira (Cambridge Univ Press, 96), 257-281; coauth, "Institutional Change and Patters of Job Shifts in Urban China, 1949-1994," Am Sociol Rev 62 (97): 339-365; coauth, "Review Essay: Chinese Sociology in a Transitional Society," Contemp Sociol 26 (97): 569-572; coauth, "Educational Stratification in Urban China: 1949-1994," Sociol of Educ 71 (98): 199-222; coauth, "Children of the Cultural Revolution: the State and the Life Course in the People's Republic of China," Am Sociol Rev 64 (99): 12-36; auth, "Studies of Chinese Organizations and Institutional Changes in the English Literature: A Survey," in Social Change in China's Reform Era, ed. Edward Tu and Yi-min Lin (HK: Oxford Univ Press, 99), 139-169; auth, "Economic Transformation and Income Inequality in Urban China: Evidence from a Panel Data," Am J of Sociol 105 (00): 1135-1174; coauth, The Dynamics of Rules: Quantitative Studies of Change in Written Organizational Codes, Stanford Univ Press (Stanford), 00; coauth, "Redistribution under State Socialism: A USSR and PRC Comparison," Res in Soc Stratification and Mobility (forthcoming). **CONTACT ADDRESS** Dept Sociol, Duke Univ, PO Box 90088, Durham, NC 27708. **EMAIL** xzhou@soc.duke.edu

ZIGLER, EDWARD
PERSONAL Born 03/01/1930, Kansas City, MO, m, 1 child **DISCIPLINE** PSYCHOLOGY **EDUCATION** Univ Mo, BA, 54; Univ Tex, PhD, 58. **CAREER** Psychol intern, Worcester, Mass State Hospital, 57-59; asst prof, Univ Mo, 58-59; fac member, Yale Univ, 59-; prof, Psychol & Child Study Ctr, 67-; head, Psychol Section, Yale Child Study Ctr, 67-; Sterling Prof, Yale Univ, 76-; dir, Child Development Prog at Yale Univ, 61-76; chair of Dept of Psychol, Yale Univ, 73-74; dir, Bush Ctr in Child Development and Soc Policy, 77-. **HONORS AND AWARDS** Founders Awd, 95; Kurt Lewin Memorial Awd, Soc Psychol Study Soc Issues, 95; Dolly Madison Awd, Zero to Three, 95; Outstanding Leadership Awd, Puerto Rican Head Start Asn, 95; True Father of Head Start Recognition Awd, 96; Distinguished Fel Awd, S Conn State Univ Chapter Phi Delta Kappa, 97; Gold Medal for Lifetime Contribution, Am Psychol Found, 97; Lifetime Achievement Awd, Am Asn Applied and Preventive Psychol, 98; Bronfenbrenner Lifetime Contribution Awd Division 7, Am Psychol Asn, 98; PARENTS Child Care Awd for Advocacy, 98; Awd of Recognition, Coun for Early Childhood Professionals, 99. **MEMBERSHIPS** Joint Appointee of Yale Univ Sch of Medicine, Parents as Teachers, Nat Head Start Asn, Head Start Res & Evaluation for Admin for Children and Families. **RESEARCH** Motivational determinants of children's performance and the influence of life circumstances on children's behavior and development. **CONTACT ADDRESS** Dept Psychol, Yale Univ, PO Box 208205, New Haven, CT 06520-8205. **EMAIL** edward.zigler@yale.edu

ZIGLER, RONALD L.
PERSONAL Born 12/14/1948, Cincinnati, OH, m, 1990, 1 child **DISCIPLINE** EDUCATION **EDUCATION** Univ Cincinnati, BA, 71; Univ Cincinnati, Med, 74; Univ Cincinnati, EdD, 77. **CAREER** Asst Prof, Maharishi Int Univ, 79-83; Teacher, Prince George's Co Public Schs, 86-92; Asst Prof, Grandview Col, 92-96; Asst Prof, Pa State Univ, 96-. **HONORS AND AWARDS** Kappa Delta Pi; Five Year Serv Awd, Prince George's Co Public Schs. **MEMBERSHIPS** Philos of Educ Soc, Assoc of Moral Educ. **RESEARCH** Philosophy of moral education, John Dewey. **SELECTED PUBLICATIONS** Auth, "Reason and Emotions Revisited: Achilles, Arjuna and Moral Conduct," Educ Theory, vol 44, no 1 (94): 63-79; auth, "Moral Character and Moral Conduct: Dewey's Neglected Legacy," Proceedings of the Midwest Philos of Educ Soc 1993," Midwest Philos of Educ Soc Pr (95): 156-167; auth, "The Four Domains of Moral Education: The Contributions of Dewey, Alexander and Goleman to a Comprehensive Taxonomy," J of Moral Educ, vol 27, no 1 (98): 19-33; auth, "The Stress of Adversity, Samadhi and Spiritual Development," J of Beliefs and Values, vol 19, no 2 (98): 201-210; auth, "Spiritual Values and Public Education: A Case for Reductionism," Philos of Educ 1998, Philos of Educ Soc Pr (98): 170-178; auth, "From the Critical Post-Modern to the Post-Critical Pre-Modern: Philip Wexler, Religion and the Transformation of Social-Educational Theory," Educ Theory, vol 49, no 3 (99): 401-414; auth, "Tacit Knowledge and Spiritual Pedagogy," J of Beliefs and Values, vol 20, no 2 (99): 162-172; auth, "The Formation and Transformation of Moral Impulse," J of Moral Educ, vol 28, no 4 (99): 445-457. **CONTACT ADDRESS** Dept Educ, Pennsylvania State Univ, Abington-Ogontz, 1600 Woodland Rd, Abington, PA 19001. **EMAIL** rlz2@psu.edu

ZILFI, MADELINE CAROL
PERSONAL Born Norwood, MA, m, 1979, 1 child **DISCIPLINE** MIDDLE EAST, OTTOMAN EMPIRE, ISLAM, GENDER ISSUES **EDUCATION** Mt Holyoke Col, AB, 64; Univ Chicago, MA, 71, PhD(hist), 76. **CAREER** Asst prof Hist, Univ MD, Col Park, 76- **HONORS AND AWARDS** Recipent of grants and awards from Fulbright, the Social Sci Res Coun, and the Am Res Institute in Turkey as well as the University's Graduate Res Bd. **MEMBERSHIPS** AHA; Mid East Studies Asn; Turkish Studies Asn; Mid East Inst. **RESEARCH** Ottoman institutional history; Islamic law; Islamic fundamentalism. **SELECTED PUBLICATIONS** Auth, "The Kadizadelis: Discordant Revivalism in Seventh-Century Istanbul," Journal of Near Eastern Studies 45, 86; auth, The Politics of Piety: The Ottoman Ulema in the Post-Classical Age; ed, Women in the Ottaman Empire: Middle Eastern Women in the Early Modern Era, 97; auth, "We Don't Get Along: Women and Hul Divorce in the Eighteenth Century," 97. **CONTACT ADDRESS** Dept of Hist, Univ of Maryland, Col Park, College Park, MD 20742-0001. **EMAIL** mz11@umail.umd.edu

ZIMMER, JOSEPH E.
PERSONAL Born 05/22/1963, Buffalo, NY, m, 1991, 1 child **DISCIPLINE** EDUCATION **EDUCATION** SUNY, PhD, 96. **CAREER** Asst Prof, St Bonaventure Univ, 92-. **HONORS AND AWARDS** Finalist, Intl Reading Asn Dissertation of the Year, 96. **MEMBERSHIPS** NCTE; IRA; PDK. **RESEARCH** History of Reading. **CONTACT ADDRESS** Sch of Educ, St. Bonaventure Univ, 0 St Bonaventure Univ, Saint Bonaventure, NY 14778. **EMAIL** jezimmer@sbu.edu

ZIMMERMAN, ZORA DEVRNJA
PERSONAL Born 05/12/1945, Marienbad, Czechoslovakia, m, 1976, 2 children **DISCIPLINE** COMPARATIVE LITERATURE, FOLKLORE **EDUCATION** State Univ of NY (Buffalo), BA, 67, PhD, 74. **CAREER** Asst prof, 74-79, assoc prof, 80-84, Prof English, Iowa State Univ, 85-90; assoc dean, Col of Liberal Arts and Sci, IA State Univ, 90-. **HONORS AND AWARDS** NEH summer fel. **MEMBERSHIPS** AAASS; Am Folklore Soc; CCAS; Nat Asn Ethnic Studies; NAASS. **RESEARCH** Serbian traditional narrative and lyric, dynamics of change and persistence in folklore, English and European Romanticism, Orality theory, folk belief, contemporary literature in Eastern Europe. **SELECTED PUBLICATIONS** Co-ed, The Arc from Now (poems), Iowa State Univ, 78; auth, Moral vision in the Serbian folk epic: The foundation sacrifice of Skadar, Slavic & East Europ J, Vol 23, 79; The changing roles of the Vila in Serbian traditional literature, J of Folklore Inst, Vol 26, 79; Metrics of passion: The poetry of Carl Dennis, Poet & Critic, Vol 12, 80; Teaching folklore in Iowa, in Teaching Folklore, Am Folklore Soc Inc, 84, rev ed, 89; Tradition and change in a ritual feast: The Serbian Krsna Slava in America, Great Lakes Rev, fall 85; auth & trans & ed, Serbian Folk Poetry: Ancient Legends, Romantic Songs, Kosovo Publ Co, 86; On the hermeneutics of oral poetry: The Kosovo Mythos, Serbian Studies, fall 90; The building of Skadar, in The Walled-Up Wife Casebook, Univ Wisc Press, 96; auth Revisiting the Muse: Oral Tradition and the Legacy of Vuk Stefanovic Karadzic in a Foreign Harbor: Essays in hone of Vasa D Mihailovich, Slavica, 00. **CONTACT ADDRESS** Col of Lib Arts & Sci, Iowa State Univ of Science and Tech, Ames, IA 50011-0002. **EMAIL** zdzimme@iastate.edu

ZIOLKOWSKI, MARGARET C.
PERSONAL Born 09/14/1952, Birmingham, AL, m, 1979, 2 children **DISCIPLINE** RUSSIAN LANGUAGE, LITERATURE, & FOLKLORE **EDUCATION** Princeton Univ, AB, 73; Yale Univ, PhD, 78. **CAREER** Lectr, Univ Tex at El Paso, 84-87; from asst prof to prof, Miami Univ, 87-. **HONORS AND AWARDS** Postdoctoral Fel, Int Res & Exchanges Board, 78-79; Mellon Postdoctoral Fel, Emory Univ, 79-80; NEH Summer Stipend, 90. **MEMBERSHIPS** Am Asn for the Advancement of Slavic Studies, Am Asn of Teachers of Slavic and E European Lang. **RESEARCH** Russian Literature. **SELECTED PUBLICATIONS** Auth, Hagiography and Modern Russian Literature, Princeton Univ Pr (Princeton, NJ), 88; auth, Literary Exorcisms of Stalinism: Russian Writers and the Soviet Past, Camden House (Columbia, SC), 98; auth, The Tale of Boiarynia Morozova: A Seventeeth-Century Religious Life, Lexington Books (Lanham, Md), forthcoming. **CONTACT ADDRESS** Dept For Lang, Miami Univ, 211 North Ridge Dr, Oxford, OH 45056. **EMAIL** ziolkom@muohio.edu

ZOLBERG, VERA L.
PERSONAL Born 09/22/1932, Vienna, Austria, m, 1953, 2 children **DISCIPLINE** SOCIOLOGY **EDUCATION** Hunter Col, AB, 53; Boston Univ, AM, 56; Univ Chicago, PhD, 74. **CAREER** Asst to assoc prof, Purdue Univ, 74-83; lectr, New School for Soc Res, 83-. **HONORS AND AWARDS** Phi Beta Kappa; Pi Delta Phi; Grant, ACLS; Grant, 94; Rockefeller Found, 98-01; Grant, Lilly Found; Grant, New School Univ. **MEMBERSHIPS** ASA; ESS; ISA; AISLF; STPA. **RESEARCH** Culture, The Arts, cultural Policy, Inequality, Race, Gender, Colonial and Postcolonialism. **SELECTED PUBLICATIONS** Auth, Constructing a Sociology of the Arts, Cambridge Univ, Pr, 90; auth, "All things to All People: Success at What Price?", Museum Int 186. (95); auth, "Museum Culture and the Threat to National Identity in the Age of the GATT", J of Arts Management, Law and Society 25.1 (95): 5-16; auth, "Cultura de Nova York: Ascendente ou Descendente", Cultura Vozes 91.3 (Brazil, 97): 172-194; coed, Outsider Art: Contested Boundaries in Contemporary Culture, Cambridge Univ Pr, 97; coed, Theory and Society 27.4 (August 98); auth, "The Sociology of Art", Encyclopedia of Aesthetics, ed Michael Kelly, Oxford Univ Pr, (98); auth, "The Happy Few - en Masse: Franco-American Comparisons in Cultural Democratization", The Arts of Democracy: Culture, Civil Society, and the State, ed Casey N. Blake, Woodrow Wilson Center Pr, (forthcoming); auth, "Privatization: Threat or Promise for the Arts and Humanities?", Int J of Cultural Policy (forthcoming); auth, "Artistic Change in the Twentieth Century", Enciclopedia Italiana, (Rome), (forthcoming). **CONTACT ADDRESS** Dept Sociol, New Sch for Social Research, 65 Fifth Ave, New York, NY 10003. **EMAIL** zolbergv@newschool.edu

ZOLLWEG, WILLIAM
PERSONAL Born 10/02/1952, Detroit, MI, m, 1990, 2 children **DISCIPLINE** SOCIOLOGY, ANTHROPOLOGY **EDUCATION** Univ Northern Colo, BA, 78; MA, 79; Western Mich Univ, PhD, 84. **CAREER** Prof, Univ of Wis La Crosse, 83-. **HONORS AND AWARDS** Who's Who in Am's Teachers, 95-00; Teaching Excellence Awd, 99. **RESEARCH** Autism, Sexual Assault and Evaluation Research. **SELECTED PUBLICATIONS** Auth, Sexual Assault and Harassment Report, The Univ of Wis La Crosse, 87; auth, Evaluation: The Coulee Council on Alcohol and Chemical Abuse; High Risk Youth Project, Office of Alcohol and Drug Abuse State of Wis, 90; auth, The La Crosse River Marsh Study, The La Crosse River Marsh Coalition, 90; auth, "Mineral Wars," Humanity and Society Issue 15-1 (91); auth, The Sexual Awareness of La Crosse Teenagers, Lutheran Hosp - Teen Health La Crosse, 92; coauth, Wisconsin's Repeat Intoxicated Driving Problem: A Study of the Offender, Hwy Safety Contract, Wis Dept of Transp, 92; coauth, "The Efficacy of Auditory Integration Training: A Double Blind Study, " AM J of Audiol 6-3 (97); auth, "The Efficacy of Phytonutritional Dietary Supplements for the Treatment of Autism," Proceedings 1-3 The Fischer Inst of Med res (99). **CONTACT ADDRESS** Dept Sociol and Anthrop, Univ of Wisconsin, La Crosse, 1725 State St, La Crosse, WI 546001. **EMAIL** zollweg.will@uwlax.edu

ZONGO, OPPORTUNE MARIE
PERSONAL Born 04/21/1961, Burkina Faso, Africa, m, 1975, 2 children **DISCIPLINE** WOMEN'S STUDIES, LITERATURE **EDUCATION** Univ de Ouagadougou, Lic, 86; Univ Calif Santa Cruz, MA, 88; PhD, 92. **CAREER** Asst prof to assoc prof to dir to int dir, Bowling Green State Univ, 92-. **HONORS AND AWARDS** NEH; James B. Grubb Fel; ISCS Fel. **MEMBERSHIPS** ALA; AAWS; ASA; CIEF; MLA; ATWS; CAAS, Women in Fr. **RESEARCH** Feminist theories; literary and cultural theories; non-western women's and cultural studies; postcolonial theory. **SELECTED PUBLICATIONS** Auth, "Rethinking African Literature: Obioma Nnaemeka," Res Afro Lit 27 (96): 176-184; auth, Cartographies of Power in Colonial African Literature: Ferdinand Oyono's The Old Man and the Medal," in Col Lang Asn J 61 (97): 24-43. **CONTACT ADDRESS** Romance Lang Dept, Bowling Green State Univ, Bowling Green, OH 43403-0001. **EMAIL** ozongo@bgnet.bgsu.edu

ZOOK, DONNA M.
PERSONAL Born 05/08/1949, Chicago, IL, m, 1972 DISCI-PLINE PSYCHOLOGY EDUCATION Univ Calif Riverside, PhD, 84; US Intl Univ, PhD, 94. CAREER Asst Prof, Univ Great Falls, 96-. HONORS AND AWARDS Fac Merit Grant, 98; Sister Mary Wilson Grant, 99; Rhodes Scholar, 98-. MEMBERSHIPS Am Psychol Asn; MT Psychol Asn; Am Col of Forensic Examiners; Am Brd of Psychol Specialties; Sigma Xi. RESEARCH Mental Disorders vs. Psychopathy and malingering. CONTACT ADDRESS Dept Grad Studies, Univ of Great Falls, 1301 20th St, Great Falls, MT 59405. EMAIL dzook@ugf.edu

ZUCKER, ARNOLD H.
PERSONAL Born 07/29/1930, Brooklyn, NY, m, 1962, 4 children DISCIPLINE PSYCHOLOGY, PSYCHIATRY EDUCATION Brooklyn Col, BA, 50; State Univ NY, Col Med, MA, 54. CAREER Asso prof, Iona Col, Dept Pastoral and Family Coun, 68-. HONORS AND AWARDS Phi Beta Kappa; Who's Who in Am; Who's Who in Med and Healthcare; Who's Who in Am Jewry; Life Fel Am Psychiat Asn. MEMBERSHIPS Am Psychiat Asn, Am Psychoanalytic Asn, Am Acad of Psychoanalysis. RESEARCH Psychiatry and Religion, Pastoral Counseling. SELECTED PUBLICATIONS Auth, "Treatment of a Corrupted Family by Rabbi and Psychiatrist," J of Relig and Health (70); auth, "Conflict, Crisis, and Resolution in Life of Maimonines," J of Am Acad Psychoanalysis (72); auth, "Parents, Progeny and power in corpus psychoanalytican," Psychiatric Opinion (72). CONTACT ADDRESS Dept Pastoral and Family Coun, Iona Col, 715 N Ave, New Rochelle, NY 10801.

ZUCKERMAN, MARVIN
PERSONAL Born 03/21/1928, Chicago, IL, d, 2 children DISCIPLINE PSYCHOLOGY EDUCATION NY Univ, BA, 49; PhD, 54. CAREER Res Assoc, Asst Prof, Inst of Psychiat Res, Ind Univ Med Center, 56-60; Asst Prof, Brooklyn Col, 60-62; Assoc Prof, Adelphi Univ, 62-63; Res Labs, A. Einstein Med Center, Philadelphia, 63-69; Prof, Univ of Del, 71- HONORS AND AWARDS Res Fel, Netherlands Inst for Advanced Studies; Distinguished Lect, Univ of Del, 93. MEMBERSHIPS Am Psychol Asn, Am Psychol Soc, Int Soc for the Study of Individual Differences. RESEARCH Personality, Psychopathology, and their biosocial bases. SELECTED PUBLICATIONS Coauth, Test Manual for the Multiple Affect Adjective Check List (MAACL), Educ and Indust Testing Serv (San Diego, CA), 65; coauth, Emotions and Anxiety: New Concepts, Methods and Applications, Lawrence Erlbaum Assocs (Hillsdale, NJ), 76; auth, Sensation Seeking: Beyond the Optimal Level of Arousal, Lawrence Erlbaum Assocs (Hillsdale, NJ), 79; auth, Biological Bases of Sensation Seeking, Impulsivity, and Anxiety, Lawrence Erlbaum Assocs (Hillsdale, NJ), 83; coauth, "Manual for MAACL-R: The Multiple Affect Adjective Check List-Revised, Educ and Indust Testing Serv (San Diego, CA), 85, 99; auth, Psychobiology of Personality, Cambridge Univ Press (Cambridge), 91; auth, Behavioral Expressions and Biosocial Bases of Sensation Seeking, Cambridge Univ Press (NY), 94; auth, "An alternative five-facts model for personality," in The developing structure of personality and temperament from infancy to adulthood, ed. C.S. Halverson, G.A. Kohnstamm, and R.P. Martin (Hillsdale, NJ: Erlbaum), 53-58; auth, "The psychobiological model for impulsive, unsocialized sensation seeking," Neuropsychobiology 34 (96): 125-129; auth, Vulnerability to psychopathology: A biosocial model, Am Psychol Asn (Wash, DC), 99; CONTACT ADDRESS Dept Psychology, Univ of Delaware, Newark, DE 19716.

ZULFACAR, MALIHA
PERSONAL Born Kabul, Afghanistan, 2 children DISCIPLINE SOCIOLOGY EDUCATION Western Col for Women, Oxford, Ohio, BA, 70; Univ Cincinnati, MA, 72, MS, 72; Univ Paderborn, Germany, PhD, 72. CAREER Full-time lect, Calif State Univ, San Luis Obispo, 80-95, 98-; Adminr of state funded prog for srs, County of Santa Barbara, 87-90; adminr of state funded prog for srs, SCAN, 85-87. HONORS AND AWARDS Assoc prof, Kabul Univ; consult to ministry for education, establishment of new classes in girls schs; Outstanding Recognition, based on peer and student evaluation at Cal-Poly, Allan Hancock Community Col; Outstanding Recognition by SCAN and Sr Scis Dept. MEMBERSHIPS Am Sociol Asn, Amnesty Int, Am Aging Soc, Int Progs on Campus. RESEARCH Racial ethnicity- immigration and labor transformation; ethnic stratification. SELECTED PUBLICATIONS Auth, publication on gender issues in recherche magazine, Germany (93-97); auth, Comparative Analysis of Afghan Refugees in Germany and USA. CONTACT ADDRESS Dept Soc Sci, California Polytech State Univ, San Luis Obispo, 1 Grand Ave, San Luis Obispo, CA 93407. EMAIL mzulfaca@calpoly.edu

ZURAVIN, SUSAN
PERSONAL Born 02/11/1944, Frederick, MD, m, 1969 DISCIPLINE SOCIAL WORK EDUCATION Hood Col, BS, 67; Univ Md, MSW, 76; PhD, 80. CAREER Prof, Univ of Md, 85-. HONORS AND AWARDS Young Scholar of the Year, Univ of Md, 90; Res Career Achievement Awd, Am Prof Soc on Child Abuse, 98. RESEARCH Child abuse and neglect. SELECTED PUBLICATIONS Coauth, "The adult functioning of former foster children: A comparative study, Kinship Care, eds R. Hegar and M. Scannapieco, Oxford Univ Pr, (Cambridge, MA), 98; coauth, "Rates, patterns and frequency of child maltreatment recurrences among families known to CPS", Child Maltreatment 3.1, (98): 129-138; coauth, "Bias in child maltreatment reporting: Revisiting the myth of classlessness", Am J of Orthopsychiatry 68.2 (98): 295-304; coauth, "Social support, therapy, and changes in attributions for child sexual abuse", J of Child Sexual Abuse 7.2 (98): 1-15; coauth, "the epidemiology of child maltreatment recurrences", Soc Serv Rev 73.2 (99): 218-239; coauth, "The relationship between child sexual abuse and major depression among low-income women: A function of growing up experiences?", Child Maltreatment 4.1 (99): 3-12; coauth, "Parenting Behaviors and Perceived Parenting Competence of Child Sexual Abuse Survivors: Relationships Mediated by Maternal Depression?", Child Abuse and Neglect 23.7, (99): 623-632; coauth, "Predicting child maltreatment recurrences during treatment", Child Abuse and neglect 23.8, (99): 729-743; auth, "Child neglect: A review of definitions and measurement research", Neglect, ed H. Dubowitz, Sage Pr, (Sherman Oaks, CA), 99; coauth, "Decisionmaking by child protective service caseworkers", Foster Care Crisis: Translating Research into Practice and Policy, eds, G. Dale and P. Curtis, Univ of Nebr Pr, (Omaha), 00. CONTACT ADDRESS Sch of Soc Work, Univ of Maryland, Baltimore, 525 W Redwood St, Baltimore, MD 21201. EMAIL czuravin@aol.com

ZUSS, MARK
PERSONAL Born 11/24/1948, New York, NY, m DISCIPLINE EDUCATION EDUCATION CUNY, PhD, 93. CAREER Assoc Prof, CUNY, 93-. HONORS AND AWARDS Professional Staff Congress grant. MEMBERSHIPS Am Educ Res Asn. RESEARCH History of reading; Politics of education; Critical pragmatism; Life-writing genre. SELECTED PUBLICATIONS Auth, Subject present: Life-writings and Strategies of Representation, Peter Lang Pub, 99; auth, "Desire and Diaspora," Review of Education Pedagogy Cultural Studies, 98; auth, "Strategies of Representation: Autobiographical Metissage and Critical Pragmatism," Educational Theory, 97; auth, "Literacy as Cognitive Practice: an Interfunctional Approach," in Trends and Issues in Theoretical Psychology, Springer Pub, 95; auth, "The Politics of Autobiographical Metissage: A Critical Encounter," Education and Culture, the Journal of the John Dewey Society, 95; auth, "Reconfiguring Knowledge Relations," in Theories of Learning: Teaching for Understanding and Creativity, 95. CONTACT ADDRESS Dept Educ, Lehman Col, CUNY, 250 Bedford Park W, Bronx, NY 10468. EMAIL zuss@earthlink.net

Geographic Index

ALABAMA

Auburn
Burson, Herbert I.
Cameron, Mary M.
Cashwell, Susan T.
Katz, Jeffrey S.
O'Leary, Virginia
Starr, Paul D.
Vazsonyi, Alexander T.
Vuchinich, Rudolph E.
Wilson, David

Birmingham
Brown, John Andrew
Fitzptrick, Kevin Michael
Johnson, Leroy
Long, Ada
Lueschen, Guenther
Taub, Edward
Taylor, Christopher C.
Valentine, P. V.

Decatur
Blalock, Carmen Fountain

Florence
Wakefield, John F.

Huntsville
Reaves, Benjamin Franklin

Livingston
Smith, Louis R.

Marion
Comer, John

Montgomery
Bell, Katie Roberson
Brackett, Kimberly P.
Harris, Sandra M.
Harris, Willa Bing
Thurber, Karl T.

Muscle Shoals
Stone, Ruth J.

Normal
Fennessee, W. T.
Wilson, Patricia I.

Selma
Garcia, William Burres

Tuscaloosa
Bindon, James R.
Boles, David B.
Johnson, Rhoda E.
Oths, Kathryn S.
Pierman, Carol J.
Zapf, Patricia A.

Tuskegee
Lewis, Meharry Hubbard

ALASKA

Anchorage
Andes, Nancy
Mtika, Mike M.

Fairbanks
Geist, Charles R.

ARIZONA

Chandler
Sullivan, Deborah A.

Flagstaff
Cox, Joseph W.
Cunningham, Keith K.
Enders, Victoria L.
Mahmoudi, Kooros M.
Sexton, James D.
Willeto, Agela A.

Glendale
Brandt-Williams, Ann
Christie, Alice
Diaz-Lefebvre, Rene
Jenkins, Carol A.
Levy, Emanuel
Stage, Sarah J.
Wosinska, Wilhelmina

Hope
Ramsay, Carol

Phoenix
Doyel, D.

Scottsdale
Bruhn, John Glyndon

Sierra Vista
Madril, Jim

Tempe
Conrad, Cheryl D.
Eachron, Ann Mac
Foster, David W.
Harris, Walter, Jr.
Hegmon, Michelle
Hudak, Thomas John
Johanson, Donald C.
Kintigh, Keith W.
Kronenfeld, Jennie Jacobs
Laner, Mary Riege
Luecken, Linda
McBeath, Michael K.
Nilsen, Alleen Pace
Russo, Nancy Felipe
Steadman, Lyle B.
Warren, Morrison Fulbright
Winkelman, Michael

Tucson
Alonso, Ana Maria
Bechtel, Robert
Bollong, Charles A.
Coan, Richard W.
Croissant, Jennifer L.
Dinnerstein, Myra
Glisky, Elizabeth Louise
Gonzales, Gail
Gonzalez, Norma E.
Hilpert, Bruce
Kolodny, Annette
Longacre, William A., II
Lord-Maes, Janiece
McPherson, Miller
Parezo, Nancy Jean
Rowe, David C.
Sanchez, Mary Ann M.
Schiffer, Michael B.
Schulz, Renate A.
Wildner-Bassett, Mary E.

ARKANSAS

Arkadelphia
Steinmiller, Georgine

Batesville
Lankford, George E.

Conway
Atkins, Kathleen
Spatz, K. Christopher
Wilson, Janet

Fayetteville
Bolsterli, Margaret Jones
Cochran, Robert
Farley, Roy C.
Goforth, Carol R.
Kahf, Mohja
Morgan, Gordon D.
Wavering, Michael J.
Williams, Nudie Eugene

Forrest City
Souheaver, Harold G.

Little Rock
Benda, Brent B.
Briscoe, David L.
Rittenhouse, Robert K.
Strickland, Johnye
Wang, Guang-zhen

Nature View
Mcneil, William Kinneth

Pine Bluff
Littlejohn, Walter L.

Siloam Springs
Habermas, Ronald T.

State University
Lord, George F.

CALIFORNIA

Alameda
Quivik, Fredric L.

Alhambra
Banerjee, Leena
Lindsay, Cindy

Alta Loma
Rodriguez, Juan A.

Aptos
Wood, Corrine Shear

Arcata
Bartlett, Maria
Figone, Albert J.
Johnson, Ronald William
Oliner, Samuel P.
Taylor, Jennifer F.

Azusa
Battle-Walters, Kimberly

Bakersfield
Wildman, Louis Robert

Belmont
Gavin, Rosemarie Julie
Joseph, Cheryl
McCracken, Blair

Berkeley
Banks, William Maron, III
Clark, VeVe A.
Clifford, Geraldine Joncich
Coleman, John Aloysius
Dundes, Alan
Edwards, Harry
Eyal, Gil
Gifford, Bernard R.
Gumperz, John J.
Hartsough, Carolyn
Heinze, Ruth-Inge
Irschick, Eugene Frederick
Joyce, Rosemary A.
Kim, Elaine
Kirch, Patrick V.
Kupers, Terry
Laguerre, Michel S.
Liu, Xin
Messinger, Sheldon L.
Munoz, Carlos, Jr
Newton, Peter M.
Peng, Kaiping
Potts, D. Malcolm
Scheiffele, Eberhard
Segal, Steve P.
Shackley, M. Steven
Slobin, Dan Isaac

Carmel
Sarbin, Theodore R.

Carpenteria
Paris, Ginette

Carson
Orellana, Sandra

Chico
Burr, Carol E.
Caldwell, Sarah
Farrer, Claire Rafferty
Kimball, Gayle H.
Maneker, Jerry S.
Quaytman, Joyce A.
Singelis, Theodore M.
Willey, Patrick S.

Claremont
Csikszentmihalyi, Mihaly
Granrose, Cherlyn Skromme
Jackson, Agnes Moreland
Kopp, Claire
Levin, Shana
Seizer, Susan
Werner, Cynthia

Culver City
Gelhart, Robert

Cypress
Kaplan, Francene E.

Davis
Aldwin, Carolyn M.
Arnett, Carlee
Bettinger, Robert L.
Gilbert, Sandra Mortola
Hall, John R.
Lacy, William B.
McCarthy, William
McHenry, Henry M.
Montejo, Victor
Sandoval, Jonathan H.
Shaver, Phillip R.
Simonton, Dean K.

Encinitas
Beyer, David W.

Escondido
Neihoff, Arthur H.

Fillmore
Whitley, David S.

Fresno
Basden, B. H.
Freeman, Yvonne
Huff, Delores J.
Sharps, Matthew J.
Templer, Donald I.

Fullerton
De Rios, Marlene Dobkin
Kanel, Kristi L.
Parman, Susan
Runco, Mark
Segal, N. L.

Glendale
Kabateck, Gladys

275

Glendora
Tolen, W. Christopher

Hayward
Bowser, Benjamin Paul
Leavitt, Fred I.
Pitts, Vera L.
Rasmusson, D. X.

Irvine
Beevi, Mariam
Burton, Michael L.
Gold-Neil, Valerie L.
Grofman, Bernard N.
Leonard, Karen Isaksen
Mauss, Armand
Mazumdar, Sanjoy
Ogunseitan, Oladele
Romney, A. Kimball
Rubel, Arthur J.
Stepan-Norris, Judith
Walsh, Roger
White, Douglas R.

La Jolla
Bailey, Frederick George
Briggs, Charles L.
Johns, Adrian
Kirkpatrick, Susan
Klatch, Rebecca
Konecni, Vladimir J.
Schudson, Michael

La Mirada
Alexander, George P.
Grace, Christopher R.
Hayward, Douglas
Menjares, Pete

La Miranda
Steffen, Tom

La Verne
Burris-Kitchen, Deborah J.

LaJolla
Deak, Gedeon O.

LaVerne
Ayala-Alcantar, Christina

Long Beach
Cash, Robert W.
Fiebert, Martin S.
Griffin, Wendy
Guthrie, Sharon R.
Kennett, Douglas
Marshall, Suzanne G.
Person, Dawn Renee
Tharp, Louis
Wiley, Juniper

Los Angeles
Alexander, Theodore Thomas, Jr.
Beniger, James R.
Berk, Bernard B.
Binder, Amy J.
Borer, Hagit
Bruno, James Edward
Coombs, Robert H.
Cutter, William
Dresser, N.
Emigh, Rebecca Jean
Freeman, Stephanny Fumi
Georges, Robert A.
Glasco, Anita L.
Glaser, Daniel
Goldberg, Herbert
Jones, Michael Owen
Liebig, Phoebe
Light, Ivan
Lu, Zhong-Lin
MacDonald, Maryellen
Miller, Donald
Miller, Laura L.
Nunis, Doyce Blackman, Jr.
Orenstein, Gloria Feman
Oring, Elliott
Patti, Rino J.
Perrott, David R.
Phinney, Jean S.
Roy, William G.
Sears, David O.
Seidenberg, Mark
Singer, Laurienne
Snodgrass, Jon
Stacey, Judith
Torrecilla, Jesus

Trevizo, Dolores
Ward, Thomas W.
Wehrli, Mary Brent
Wilcox, Rand R.
Wittrock, Merlin Carl
Zeitlin, Maurice

Malibu
Martinez, Thomas
Miller-Perrin, Cindy

Mission Viejo
Quickel, Kim
Wilson, Dick

Monterey
Nitsche, Richard

Moraga
Boyd, Candy Dawson

Newhall
Johnson, Robert C.

Northridge
Bartle, Elizabeth E.
Krissman, Fred
Magliocco, Sabina
Shaw, Victor
Tarver-Behring, Shari
Tohidi, Nayereh E.

Oakland
Anderson, Robert T.
Goring, William S.
Micco, Melinda
Potter, Elizabeth
Russell, Diana Elizabeth H.
Santana, Deborah Berman
Stuckey, Priscilla F.
Williams, Bruce

Orange
Larsen, Nick
Mc Grane, Bernard

Palo Alto
Braud, William
Frager, Robert
Wade, Jenny

Pasadena
Brennan, Linda
Gorsuch, Richard L.
King, Roberta R.
Reid, Joel Otto
Shaw, R. Daniel
Vande Kemp, Hendrika

Placerville
Klimes, Rudolf

Pleasant Hill
Daley, James

Pomona
Sturges, James W.

Poway
von Borstel, Federico

Redding
Rocca, Al M.

Richmond
McSpadden, Lucia

Riverside
Arrizon, Alicia
Baker, David V.
Chang, Edward T.
Hendrick, Irving Guilford
Kposowa, Augustine
Kronenfeld, David B.
Ness, Sally A.
Robertson, Patricia
Stokes, H. Bruce
Turk, Austin T.
Turner, Jonathan H.

Rohnert Park
Castillo, Ed
Hillier, Susan
Martinez, Elizabeth Coonrod
Parker, Sue T.
Phillips, Peter
Praetzellis, Adrian

Wautischer, Helmut

Sacramento
Burger, Mary Williams
Hampton, Grace
Kando, Thomas M.
Moftakhar, Hossein
Scott, Otis L.
Stolba, Soheir
Tumminia, Diana

San Bernardino
Barkan, Elliott Robert
Downs, Louis
Everson, George D.
Freischlag, Jerry A.
Henry, Mildred M. Dalton

San Clemente
Goodman-Delahunty, Jane

San Diego
Berger, Bennet Maurice
Borstel, Frederico Von
Chang, Mei-I
Donadey, Anne
Gevirtz, Richard N.
Hinkes, Madeline J.
Hutchinson, George
Kantor, John
Lauzen, Martha M.
Lustig, Myron W.
Meadows, Eddie
Mohamed, A. Rafil
Reilly, Michael S.
Shapiro, Lewis P.
Storer, Norman William

San Francisco
Boucher, Jerry
Chope, Robert C.
Ciena, Mel
Cuellar, Jose
De Vries, Brian
Hanson, Marci J.
Jaimes-Guerrero, Mariana
Johnson, Don Hanlon
Leroux, Jeffrey
MacKinnon, Patricia L.
Murray, Stephen O.
Seely, Gordon M.
Soh, C. Sarah
Staples, Robert Eugene
Wong, Bernard P.

San Gabriel
Chen, John C.

San Jose
Callaghan, Glenn McKee
Easter, Marilyn
Murray, S. B.
Reckmeyer, William J.

San Luis Obispo
Frantz, Barbara
Jones, Terry L.
Mori, Barbara L.
Zulfacar, Maliha

San Mateo
Witt, Irving M.

Santa Barbara
Carlisle, Harry J.
Cooley, Timothy
Flacks, Richard
Jorden, Crystal W.
Lundell, Torborg Lovisa
Roof, Wade Clark
Scheff, Thomas

Santa Clara
Gelber, Steven Michael
Sullivan, Kieran
Urdan, Timothy C.

Santa Cruz
Aronson, Elliot
Crow, Ben
Fukurai, Hiroshi
Linger, Daniel T.
Pettigrew, Thomas Fraser
Roby, Pamela A.
Wilson, Carter

Santa Monica
Lundgren, Amy
Yablonsky, Lewis

Saratoga
Cubie, Michael

Seal Beach
LeMoncheck, Linda

Seaside
Mendoza, Ruben

Stanford
Bell, Susan Groag
Bower, Gordon
Carlsmith, Lyn
Delaney, Carol L.
Olzak, Susan
Scott, William Richard
Steele, Claude Mason

Stockton
Lewis, George H.

Turlock
Chu, Mayling M.

Ukiah
Hock, Roger R.

Venice
Becker-Slaton, Nellie Frances
Rosenberg, Jack L.

Watsonville
Omosupe, Ekua Rashida

Woodland Hills
Follick, Edwin D.
Rowe, Bruce M.

COLORADO

Boulder
Banich, Marie T.
Belknap, Joanne
Bourne, Lyle E.
Harvey, Lewis O., Jr.
Johnson, Thomas E.
Kintsch, Walter
McGilvray, Dennis B.
Miklowitz, David J.
Nathan, Mitchell J.
O'Reilly, Randall C.
Regoli, Robert M.
Taylor, Lucien
Walker, Deward E.

Colorado Springs
Dukes, Richard L.
Ferber, Abby L.
Fink, Virginia
Levine, Victoria Lindsay
Roeder, Bea
Watts, Linda K.

Denver
Adler, Peter
Cohen, Jonathan Allan
Curet, Luis Antonio
Furman, David M.
Gardner, Rick M.
Glenn, Cecil E.
Hayes, Edward L.
Jones, John F.
Jordan, Karin B.
King, Edith
Miller, Robert D.
Monnett, John
Robyn, Elisa
Smith, Glenn R.
Watson, Mary Ann
Watt, Norman F.

Durango
Hossain, Ziarat

Fort Collins
Galvin, Kathleen
Johnson, Marion L.
Suinn, Richard Michael
Swanson, Louis E.
Theodoratus, Robert James
Unnithan, N. Prabha

Grand Junction
Bailey, Velda

Greeley
Baldo, Tracy D. Bostwick
Hardgrave, Billy D.
Keaten, James A.
Moore, Melanie
Schlewitt-Haynes, Lora D.
Stukas, Arthur A.

Gunnison
Drake, Roger A.

Littleton
Walker, T. B.
Williams, James Hiawatha

Pueblo
Forsyth, Dan W.
Keller, Robert L.
Kulkosky, Paul
Mo, Suchoon S.
Taylor, Cindy

Steamboat Springs
Bagwell, George

United States Air Force Academy
Porter, David B.

CONNECTICUT

Bridgeport
Soares, Anthony T.

Danbury
Kuther, Tara
Manes, Averell

Fairfield
Cross, Dolores E.
Manning, Christel
Rosner, Stanley

Gales Ferry
Waterman, Thelma M.

Hartford
Desmangles, Leslie Gerald

Manchester
Wynn, Jean M.

Middletown
Johnston, William
Pomper, Philip
Walker, Willard

Miles City
Engel, Scott

New Britain
Feder, Kenneth L.
Shmurak, Carole B.

New Haven
Blatt, Sidney Jules
Dillon, Michele
Dittes, James Edward
Forte, Allen
French, Richard Frederic
Joy, Stephen
McGuire, William J.
Wallerstein, Immanuel
Wheeler, Stanton
Zigler, Edward

New Heaven
Sternberg, Robert

New London
Chrisler, Joan C.
Murstein, Bernard I.
Winter, Jerry Alan

Niantic
Jackson, Joseph Hollister

Norwalk
Bontatibus, Donna
Goodman, William

Southbury
Wescott, Roger Williams

Stamford
Tec, Nechama

Storrs
Allen, Irving L.
Berleant, Riva
Dashefsky, Arnold
Gugler, Josef
Hagan, Willie James
Meyers, Diana Tietjens
Shivers, Jay Sanford

Waterbury
O'Donnell, Kim

West Hartford
Johnson, Harriette C.
Keteku, Oheneba E.
Simmons, Louise

West Simsbury
Stevenson, Catherine Barnes

Willimantic
Carter, David G., Sr.
McGowan, Marcia Phillips
Tapia, Elena

DELAWARE

Dover
Austin, John
Caldwell, M. Milford
Hobler, Bruce
Suri, Kul Bhushan

Newark
Bergstrom, Anna
DiRenzo, Gordon James
Gates, Barbara Timm
Schwartz, Norman B.
Scott, Bonnie Kime
Sharf, Richard S.
Smith, G.
Zuckerman, Marvin

DISTRICT OF COLUMBIA

Washington
Barlow, William B.
Beck, Sylven S.
Bell, Diane
Bellamy, Everett
Birnbaum, Norman
Cahn, Edgar S.
Calhoun, Lee A.
Chambliss, William J.
Comor, Edward
D'Antonio, William
Deutscher, Irwin
Dillon, Wilton Sterling
Engel, Martin
Fisher, Leona W.
Gary, Lawrence E.
Goodman, Louis
Grimsted, David Allen
Hanson, Sandra L.
Harre, H. Romano
Hoge, Dean R.
Johnson, Ronald Maberry
Karp, Stephen A.
Kim-Renaud, Young-Key
Leigh, Irene W.
Loewen, James W.
Macharia, Kinuthia
Marthaler, Berard Lawrence
McNamara, Dennis
McNicol, Sharon-Ann
Morris, Bonnie J.
Myers, Ernest R.
Norris, Deborah Olin
Pruitt, Anne Smith
Rathnam, Mahadev
Sabat, Steven
Samarasinghe, Vidyamali
Shanks, Hershel
Silber, David E.
Spencer, Patricia
Stephens, William Richard

Studzinski, Raymond James
Sullins, Donald Paul
Trapp-Dail, Rosa Lee
Van Dam, Deedee
Weitzer, Ronald
Wickham-Crowley, Timothy P.
Yamauchi, Joanne
Youniss, James

FLORIDA

Boca Raton
Caputi, Jane

Coral Gables
Mundy, Peter

Daytona Beach
Mootry, Russell

Deland
Blum, Toni L.
Long, Lynn Landis

Fort Lauderdale
Segal, Marilyn

Fort Myers
Mayers, Marvin K.
Sawyer, William Gregory

Fort Pierce
Lett, James W.

Ft Lauderdale
Doan, James E.

Gainesville
Allington, Richard Lloyd
Ardelt, Monika
Berardo, Felix Mario
Borg, Marian J.
Dewsbury, Donald A.
Du Toit, Brian M.
Feagin, Joe R.
Hackett, David H.
Hausenblas, Heather Ann
Janelle, Christopher M.
Margolis, Maxine Luanna
McKeen, William
Schlenker, Barry R.
Shepperd, James A.
Smith, Walter L.
Stansbury, James P.
Sussman, Stephan
Thompson, Roger Mark

Jacksonville
Adams, Afesa M.
Beaman, Marian L.
Borsky, Susan
Greek, Morgan S. J.
Parker, Sidney Baynes
Urbina, Susana P.

Key West
Chandler, Theodore Alan

Lakeland
Mc Leod, Ann M.

Miami
Antoni, Michael H.
Demko, David
Dunham, Roger
Johnson, Sheri L.
Judd, Catherine
Page, John Bryan
Taylor, Linda L.
Verschoor, Charles V.
Waugh, Butler Huggins

Miami Shores
Lenaghan, Donna D.

Naples
Sutter, Leslie E.

North Miami
Salekin, Randall T.

Orlando
Baird-Olson, Karren P.
Congdon, Kristin G.
Dziegielewski, Sophia

Lehmann, Timothy J.

Oviedo
Rupp, Gary

Pensacola
Biasco, Frank
McLeod, Stephen G.
Sansone, Frank A.
Stanny, Claudia J.

Pompano Beach
Nash, Peggy

Port Orange
Riegner, Elizabeth Jane

Saint Augustine
Gamache, Gerald L.

Saint Leo
Cronin, Christopher

Saint Petersburg
Carter, Nancy Corson
Goss, Theresa Carter
Whitney, Ruth

Sarasota
Andrews, Anthony P.
Deitrick, Lynn

Tallahassee
Bower, Beverly Lynne
Darling, Carol
Ericsson, K. Anders
Gayles-Felton, Anne Richardson
Hazelrigg, Lawrence E.
Isaac, Larry
Pichugin, Valentina
Pullen, Daniel J.

Tampa
Dembo, Richard
Ellis, Carolyn Sue
Follman, John C.
Himmelgreen, David
Johanningmeier, Erwin
Mariotti, Arleen
Mauser, August J.
Poythress, N. G.
Purcell, Trevor W.
Turner, Stephen
Tykot, Robert

Wellington
Terrero, Irene

GEORGIA

Albany
Reed, William

Athens
Amir, Nader
Castenell, Louis Anthony, Jr.
Cooney, Mark
Doyle, Charles Clay
Frasier, Mary Mack
Heslep, Robert Durham
Huberty, Carl J.
Hudson, Charles M.
Ingersoll, Richard
Morris, Kenneth Earl
Pollack, Robert
Rice, Berry
Roberts, Bryndis Wynette

Atlanta
Bakeman, Roger
Bell, Linda A.
Bradley, Josephine
Brownley, Martine Watson
Burrison, John A.
Carter, Barbara Lillian
Clayton, Obie
Colatrella, Carol
Crim, Alonzo A.
Davis, Edward L.
DeFilipis, Nick A.
Ethridge, Robert Wylie
Gouinlock, James
Guy-Sheftall, Beverly
Hajjar, Lisa
Harpold, Terry

Haskell, Guy H.
L'Abate, Luciano
Lilenfeld, Lisa
Marsh, Clifton
McWilliams, Alfred E., Jr.
Nersessian, Nancy
Neu, Joyce
Rauch, Alan
Riso, Lawrence P.
Ross, Peter A.
Valiante, Giovanni
Watts, Anne Wimbush
Werum, Regina

Augusta
Carter, Judy L.
Davies, Kimberly A.
Gemmill, Robert H.
Jackson, Charles C.

Carrollton
Aanstoos, Christopher
Helminiak, Daniel A.
Morgan, Harry
Snipes, Marjorie M.

Clarkston
Sims, Toni Y.

Dalton
Elnajjar, Hassan

Decatur
Nunnally, David H., Sr.

Demorest
Andrews, Donna G.
Uhde, Anna P.
Vance, Cynthia Lynn

La Grange
Freeman, Bernice

Milledgeville
Barron, Sheree S.

Mount Vernon
Rhoades, Vance

Savannah
Jordan, Abbie H.
Scott, Vann

Stateboro
Kinsella, Susan

Statesboro
Burke, Kevin
Nielsen, Michael
Smith, William L.
Wilson, Janie Hamn
Young, William C.

Toccoa
Atkinson, Harley

Toccoa Falls
Ratcliff, Donald

Valdosta
Brown, Ola M.
Whatley, Mark A.

GUAM

Mangilao
Klitzkie, Lourdes Palomo

HAWAII

Hilo
Brown, Susan G.
Doudna, Martin Kirk

Honolulu
Bilmes, Jack
Finney, Ben Rudolph
Forman, Michael Lawrence
Graves, Michael W.
Hatfield, Elaine
Hefner, Carl
Sheridan, Mary

Yen, D. E.

Kailua
Johnson, Ronald C.

Laie
Winstead, Roy

Pearl City
Falgout, Suzanne

IDAHO

Boise
Hourcade, Jack
Petlichkoff, Linda M.

Caldwell
Attebery, Louie Wayne

Lewiston
Jolley, Jerry

Moscow
Fischer, Jerome M.
Putsche, Laura
Stoll, Sharon

Pocatello
Cowles, Lois Anne Fort
Ellis, Susan

ILLINOIS

Alsip
Altalib, Omar

Aurora
Garth, Phyllis Ham
Strassberg, Barbara

Bloomington
Rundblad, Georganne

Carbondale
Corruccini, Robert
Falvo, Donna R.
Hill, Jonathan D.
Jurkowski, Elaine
Kawewe, Saliew
Kilpatrick, Thomas L.
Schneider, Mark A.
Williams, Rhys H.

Champaign
Dulany, Don E.
Espelage, Dorothy
Olney, Marjorie F.

Charleston
Kashefi, Mahmoud
Weasmer, Jerie
Yen, Shu-Chen

Chicago
Albrecht, Gary Louis
Bidwell, Charles E.
Bottoms, Bette L.
Broudy, Harry S.
Burton, J. D.
Clark, Terry Nichols
Cohn, Bernard Samuel
Comaroff, Jean
Cooper, Chris
Craig, John Eldon
Danzer, Gerald
DePillars, Murry Norman
Dietler, Michael
Dominowski, Roger L.
Dunn, Ivy D.
Dust, Margaret C.
Elsbernd, Mary
Floyd, Samuel A., Jr.
Friedrich, Paul
Fry, Christine L.
Garner, Roberta
Gittins, Anthony
Gordon, Milton A.
Graff, Gerald E.
Greeley, Andrew M.
Green, Jesse Dawes
Gutek, Gerald Lee
Heinz, John P.

Henly, Julia
Hockings, Paul E.
Jordan, J. Scott
Keys, Christopher
Kipper, David A.
Knight, Eileen Q.
Laubscher, Leswin
Laumann, Edward O.
Lee, Johng O.
Lee, Shoou-Yih D.
Leroy Conrad, Robert
Lopata, Helena Z.
Marriott, Mc Kim
McCloskey, Michael
Mcneill, David
Miller, Bernice Johnson
Moseley, Michael Edward
Nelson, Judith C.
O'Connell, Daniel C.
Overbeck, T. Jerome
Patton, Gerald Wilson
Primous, Dianella
Reitz, Miriam
Roosevelt, Anna C.
Rychlak, Joseph F.
Saari, Carolyn
Sassen, Saskia
Schwartz, Mildred A.
Sizemore, Barbara A.
Smith, Raymond T.
Taub, Richard P.
Terrell, Melvin C.
Tuttle, Russell H.
Usiskin, Zalman
Waite, Linda J.
Walsh, Joseph A.
Warner, R. Stephen
Weinstein, Deena A.
Wolach, Allen H.
Worrill, Conrad W.
Wyrick, Floyd I.
Zakowski, Sandra

Chicago Heights
Calgaro, W.

Danville
Rediehs, Robert E.

De Kalb
Johannesen, Richard Lee
Thurman, Alfonzo
Williams, Eddie R., Jr.

Decatur
Mittal, Sushil

Deerfield
Benson, Warren S.

Dekalb
Anderson, Kevin
Kourvetaris, George A.
Sheehan-Holt, Jan

Edwardsville
Blain, Robert R.
Browne, Dallas L.
Lox, Curt L.
Pogatshnik, Lee Wolfram
Wilson, Rudolph George

Elgin
Broad, David B.

Elmhurst
Noice, Helga

Evanston
Brown, John A.
Eagly, Alice H.
Lassner, Phyllis
Launay, Robert G.
Leonard, William R.
Lewis, Dan A.
Moskos, Charles C.
Seymour, Jack L.
Waxman, Sandra R.
Wilkins, Leona B.
Zecker, Steven G.

Glen Ellyn
Bollendorf, Robert F.
Pierson, Steven J.
Slocum, Patricia

Kankakee
Walker, Connie

Lake Forest
Sadri, Ahmad

Lincoln
Gaddy, Stephanie

Macomb
Hurh, Won Moo
Majeres, Raymond L.
Mathes, Eugene W.
McClure, Kimberley A.
Na'allah, Abdul-Rasheed
Radosh, Mary F.
Tang, Shengming

Monmouth
Grahe, Jon E.

Naperville
Gems, Gerald R.
Kelley, Karl Neal

Normal
Beneson, Wayne A.
Brosnahan, Leger
Davis, Gloria-Jeanne
Giles, Linda
Moghadam, Valentine M.
Reeder, Glenn D.
Snyder, David W.
Unrau, Yvonne A.
Wortham, Anne

Oak Park
Kim, Kwang Chung

Orland Park
Antia, Kersey H.

Palos Hills
Silk, William

Park Forest
Blevins, Gregory A.
Mc Master, Michele

Peoria
Mather, Patricia L.

Rock Island
Hauck, Paul A.
Kivisto, Peter J.

Springfield
Molfese, Dennis L.
Shaidian, Hammed
Van Der Slik, Jack Ronald
Van Dyke, Annette

Techny
Luzbetak, Louis Joseph

University Park
Kennedy, Joyce S.

Urbana
Ackerson, Barry J.
Berube, Michael
Bruner, Edward M.
Carringer, Robert L.
Copeland, Robert M.
Lie, John J.
Nikelly, Arthur G.
Pauketat, Timothy
Salamon, Sonya
Toby, Ronald P.
Violas, Paul Constantine

Wheaton
Allen, Henry L.
Arnold, Dean E.

Wilmette
Ornstein, Allan

INDIANA

Anderson
Chiang, Linda H.

Bloomington
Adams, William
Brown, Mary Ellen
Bull, Barry L.

Clark, Gracia
Davies, Ivor Kevin
Graham, Cynthia A.
Gronbjerg, Kirsten Anderson
Hansen, William F.
Janelli, Roger L.
Pietsch, Paul Andrew
Sailes, Gary
Weinberg, Martin
Yan, Margaret M.

Evansville
Blake, Michelle
Zehr, Stephen C.

Fort Wayne
Bickel, Julia M.
Crismore, Avan G.
Fox, Linda Chodosh

Gary
Boland, James M.
O'Dell, Cynthia D.

Goshen
Meyers, Thomas J.

Greencastle
Warren, Stanley

Hanover
Roberts, Keith A.

Indianapolis
Colburn, Kenneth
Harris, Edward E.
Iwamasa, Gayle
Kapoor, Jitendra M.
Miller, James Blair
Plascak-Craig, Faye D.
Whitchurch, Gail

Kokomo
Shively, Marsha L.
Wysong, Earl

Marion
Boivin, Michael

Muncie
De Ollos, Ione Y.
Dolan, Ronald
Dolon, Ronald
Greenwood, Theresa M. Winfrey
Hicks, Ronald E.
Keith, Rebecca M.
Lassiter, Eric
Lassiter, Luke E.
McCord, Beth K.
Mertens, Thomas R.
Stevenson, Michael R.
Swartz, Benjamin K., Jr

New Albany
French, Sandra

Notre Dame
Aldous, Joan
Chang, Patricia
Dasilva, Fabio B.
Gaffney, Patrick D.
Spillman, Lynette P.
Weigert, Andrew

Richmond
Osborne, Randall E.
Wilde, Jerry

South Bend
Bender, Eileen Teper
Block, Joyce
Keen, Mike F.

Terre Haute
Baker, Ronald Lee
DeMarr, Mary Jean
Robinson, Ruth
Steiger, Thomas L.

West Lafayette
Babrow, Austin S.
Deflem, Mathieu
Ferraro, Kenneth K.
Garfinkel, Alan
Harper, William
Hislope, Kristi A.
Lemelle, Anthony J.

Martinez, Jacqueline M.
May, Jill P.
McGee, Reece Jerome
Ogles, Robert M.
Seigfried, Charlene
Swensen, Clifford Henrik

Westville
Sheehy, John

IOWA

Ames
Avalos, Hector
Dow, James Raymond
Epperson, Douglas
Fink, Deborah R.
Schwieder, Dorothy Ann
Zimmerman, Zora Devrnja

Cedar Falls
Crew, B. Keith
Dilly, Barbara J.
Gilgen, Albert R.
Hobson, Matthew L.
Kopper, Beverly A.

Cedar Rapids
Allen, Linda
Hensley, Robert B.
Mettlin, Connie
Snell, Joel C.

Council Bluffs
Hill, Michael R.

Decorah
Kunkel, Charlotte A.

Des Moines
King, C. Richard
Lu, Min-Zhan
Wirth-Cauchon, Janet

Dubuque
Jones, Carroll J.
Kearns, Emily
Mamali, Catalin
Swiderski, Suzanne M.

Fairfield
Travis, Fred

Grinnell
Whittaker, John

Iowa City
Boos, Florence Saunders
Ciochon, Russell L.
Di Pardo, Anne
Diaz-Duque, Ozzie Francis
Duck, Steve
Hunnicutt, Benjamin K.
Jones, Phillip Erskine
Levin, Irwin P.
Markovsky, Barry
Stone, Gerald L.
Stratton, John Ray
Troyer, Lisa L.
Woodard, Fredrick

Mount Vernon
Crowder, Diane Griffin

Orange City
Druliner, Marcia M.

Pella
Ybarrola, Steven J.

Waterloo
Schweer, Kathryn

KANSAS

Baldwin City
Buzzell, Timothy

Emporia
Bonner, Mary Winstead
Terrell, Nathaniel E.

Haviland
Landon, Michael Lee

Hays
Markley, Robert

Kansas City
Baeza, J.
Lucas, Wayne L.

Lawrence
Antonio, Robert
Hanson, Allan
Harrington, Robert
Katzman, David Manners
Roberts, Michael C.
Yetman, Norman Roger

Manhattan
Benton, Stephen L.
Chattopadhyay, Arpita
Neely, Margery A.
Prins, Harald E.
Schumm, Walter R.

Murray
Miller, Thomas W.

North Newton
Hart, Julie

Overland Park
Foster, Mark A.
Li, Jian

Pittsburg
Morgan, Lyle W., II

Shawnee-Mission
Gilson, Joan

Topeka
Altman, Joanne
Besthorn, Fred H.
Hoard, R. J.

Wichita
Huber, Tonya
Konek, Carol Wolfe
Lawless, Robert
Stuber-McEwen, Donna

KENTUCKY

Ashland
D'Aoust, Jean-Jacques

Bowling Green
Olmsted, Jane
Onyekwuluje, Anne B.

Campbellsville
Howell, J. Susan

Crestview Hills
Mcnutt, James Charles

Cumberland
Thomas, Katherine

Frankfort
Griffin, Betty Sue

Henderson
Hughes, Kathy L.

Highland Heights
Washington, Michael Harlan

Lexington
Alvey, Richard Gerald
Anderman, Eric M.
Clark, James J.
Freehling, William W.
Harris, Joseph John, III
Heath, Robin L.
Helweg-Larsen, Marie
Humble, Jeanne
Robinson, Andrew
Stilwell, William E., III
Wachtel, David
Wilkinson, Doris

Ann Arbor
Antonucci, Tony C.
Bryant, Bunyan I.
Burling, Robbins
Collins, Derek B.
Cotera, Maria E.
Ellsworth, Phoebe C.
Harrison, Don K., Sr.
Holter, Mark Clark
House, James S.
Jackson, James S.
Malm, William P.
McKeachie, William M.
Moody, Charles David, Sr.
Ness, Gayl DeForrest
Sameroff, Arnold
Smith-Rosenberg, Carroll
Williams, Melvin D.
Winter, David G.
Wolowitz, Howard M.

Battle Creek
Taylor, Charles Avon

Berrien Springs
Diaz, Hector L.
LaBianca, Oystein S.

Beulah
Tanner, Helen Hornbeck

Big Rapids
Ball, Richard E.
Pisacreta, Richard J.
Thorp, John P.

Dearborn
Rosenthal, Marilynn M.

Detroit
Barrett, Barnaby B.
Black, Beverly M.
Byars, Jackie L.
Crabtree, Clarie
Gordon, Aaron Z.
Hale, Janice Ellen
Hughes, Carl D.
Kiah, Ruth Josephine
Meisse, Tom
Mika, Joseph John
Sengstock, Mary C.
Simon, Georgianna
Slovenko, Ralph
Somers, Cheryl L.
Trix, Frances
Woodroffe, Annette

Douglas
Miller, Sharon L.

East Lansing
Achmitt, Neal W.
Busch, Lawrence M.
Hall, Ronald
Hawthorne, Berton J.
Imamura, Shigeo
Karon, Bertram Paul
LeBlanc, Albert
Lee, Robert E.
Manning, Peter K.
Perlstadt, Harry
Pyle, Ralph
Smitherman, Geneva
von Eye, Alexander A.
Wright, Robert L.

Farmington Hills
Ellens, Jay Harold

Flint
Blakely, Everett

Garden City
Settles, Rosetta Hayes

Grand Rapids
Becker, Gary J.
Garofalo, V. James
Romanowski, William D.
Shoemaker, Allen L.
Suggs, Robert Chinelo

Holland
Andre, Maria Claudia
Inman, M. L.
Motiff, James P.

Houghton
Erikson, Fritz John

Jackson
Scott, James J.

Kalamazoo
Dube, Thomas M. T.
Heller, Janet
Helweg, Arthur W.
Mathews, Gary
Phillips, Romeo Eldridge
Rudge, David W.
Washington, Earl Melvin

Mount Pleasant
Bechtold, Brigitte
Colarelli, Stephen Michael
Dornan, Reade W.
Malonebeach, Eileen
McLean, Athena H.
Ronan, George F.
Toms-Robinson, Dolores C.

Rochester
Atlas, John Wesley
Brown, Judith K.
Eberly, Mary B.
Harrison, Algea Othella
Stamps, Richard B.
Wiggins, Jacqueline D.

Sault Ste. Marie
Hines, Virginia E.

Spring Arbor
Dibaba, Mamo

University Center
Baskind, David

Waterford
James, David L.

Ypsilanti
Cao, Liqun
Friedman, Monroe P.
Leighton, Paul S.
Perry, Robert Lee
Westman, Alida S.

MINNESOTA

Brooklyn Park
Johnston, Barbara J.

Collegeville
Makepeace, James

Duluth
Kramer, Joyce Marie
Maypole, Donald E.
Rallis, Helen
Wilson, Janelle L.

Hopkins
Affinito, Mona Gustafson

Mankato
Jindra, Michael
Langston, Donna Hightower

Marshall
Butler, J. Corey

Minneapolis
Brustein, William
Clark, Anna
Cohen, Andrew D.
Doyle, Kenneth
Eckart, Michelle
Erickson, Martha F.
Hartmann, Douglas R.
Johnson, Willie J.
Klee, Carol A.
Knoke, David
Nagar, Richa
Nelson, Charles A.
Overmier, J. Bruce
Prell, Riv-Ellen
Sarles, Harvey Burton
Savelsberg, Joachim
Sera, Maria D.
Sroufe, L. Alan
Taborn, John Marvin

Houghton *(continued column)*
Tennyson, Robert
Uggen, Chris
Westermeyer, Joseph John

Moorhead
Benson, John S.
Schoen, Jill

Northfield
Boling, Becky
Fisher, James F.
Kutulas, Judy
Saiedi, Nader

Owatonna
Orton, Arlene

Saint Cloud
Andrzejewski, Julie
Daneshpour, Manijeh
Havir, Linda
Medhi, Abbas
Tripp, Luke S.
Tripp, Michael

Saint Paul
Berg, James J.
Boychuk, Terry
Herman, Randolph W.
Johnson, Eric L.
Nelson, Randolph A.
Reagan, Mary Jane
Schweigert, Francis J.
Watson, Dwight C.

White Bear Lake
Hinrichs, Bruce

MISSISSIPPI

Alcorn State
Idleburg, Dorothy

Cleveland
Abrahams, Caryl

Clinton
Fant, Gene C., Jr.

Columbus
Bean, Suzanne M.
Donat, Patricia

Courtland
Lindgren, C. E.

Decatur
Pouncey, Alice

Fulton
Mattison, William H.

Hamilton
Lancaster, Jane Fairchild

Hattiesburg
Eells, Gregory T.
Fortunato, Vincent J.
Goggin, William

Itta Bena
Nelson, Dorothy J. Smith

Jackson
Curry, Allen
Harris, William McKinley, Sr.
Hurley, James
Kocel, Katherine
Middleton, Richard Temple, III
Richardson, William
Sallis, Charles
Thaw, Kurt A.

Lowell
Chorajian, Levon

Meridian
Gilbert, James L.

Mississippi State
Bartkowski, John
Boyd, Robert
Obringer, Stephen
Person, William Alfred

Houghton *(continued column)*
Williams, Carolyn Chandler
Woodrow-Lafield, Kare

West Point
Codling, Jim

MISSOURI

Cape Girardeau
Keys, Paul
Lloyd, Paul J.
Parette, Howard P.
Petch-Hogan, Beverly M.
Snell, William, Jr
Stennis-Williams, Shirley

Chesterfield
Te, Jordan

Columbia
Bank, Barbara J.
Cooper, Harris M.
Geary, David
Gilbert, Bennie Ruth
Hessler, Richard M.
Lyman, R. Lee
Neff, Hector
Pigg, Kenneth E.
Prahlad, Sw. Anand
Rowlett, Ralph M.
Sheldon, Kennon

Joplin
Costley, Kevin
Murdock, Gwendolyn K.

Kansas City
Capra, Carl J.
Eubanks, Eugene E.
Garavalia, Linda
Kisthardt, Walter E.
Lubin, Bernard
Lumin, Bernard
Price, Tanya Y.
Reitz, Charles
Singelmann, Peter

Kirksville
Graber, Robert

Lees Summit
Westra, Matthew R.

Liberty
David, Keith R.
Garrison, Ronilue B.
Miller, Mara

Maryville
Edwards, Carla

Nevada
Lutke, Debi Reed

Parkville
McClelland, Patricia

Point Lookout
Clemmer, Linda
Kneeshaw, Stephen

Saint Louis
Akca, Zeynep
Barry, Bert
Beck, Lois
Berg-Weger, Marla
Browman, David L.
Brownell, Susan E.
Bush, Harry H.
Dzuback, Mary Ann
Harvey, Richard D.
Miles, Dorothy D.
Patterson, Miles L.
Resick, Patricia A.
Ritts, Vicki
Roediger, Henry L.
Rosenthal, Howard
Ross, Stephanie A.
Sherraden, Margaret
Stake, Jayne E.
Sussman, Robert W.
Thompson, Vetta L.
Thumin, Fred J.
Wernet, Stephen P.

Saint Peters
Feng-Checkett, Gayle

Springfield
Daley, James G.
Davis, James O.
DeAngelo, LeAnna M.
McClennen, Joan
Syler, Eleanor G.

Warrensburg
Fernquist, Robert M.

MONTANA

Bozeman
Stadtlander, Leann (Lee) M.
Wessel, Thomas Roger
Witkin-New Holy, Alexandra

Great Falls
Zook, Donna M.

Havre
Gilmartin, Brian G.

Missoula
Campbell, Gregory R.
Deaton, Robert L.

NEBRASKA

Boys Town
Larzelere, R. E.

Kearney
Borchard, Kurt
Briner, Wayne
Counts, M. Reid
Glazier, Stephen D.
Mosig, Yozan Dirk
Pigott, Ruth
Ramage, Jean C.

Lincoln
Andreasen, Nancy C.
Courtney, Sean
Deegan, Mary Jo
Honey, Maureen
Lehmann, Jennifer M.

Omaha
Burch, Hobart
Christensen, John E.
Dendinger, Donald
Dickel, Charles Timothy
Irvin, Deborah M.
Sharma, Manoj
Thorson, James A.

York
Wheeler, Kathleen B.

NEVADA

Las Vegas
Babbitt, Beatrice C.
Bell, Barbara Mosallai
Crank, Joe N.
Dil, Nasim
Donohue, Bradley C.
Filler, John W.
Hall, Gene E.
Hausbeck, Kate
Healey, William C.
Kyle Higgins, Amanda
Meana, Marta
Miller, Susan P.
Pierce, Thomas B.
Shuman, R. Baird
Stitt, J. Michael
Strawser, Sherri C.
Taylor, Susan L.

Reno
Elliott, Marta
Fruzzetti, Alan
Hayes, Steven C.
Piercy, Earl
Stewart, Mary W.

NEW HAMPSHIRE

Durham
Baum, William M.
Clark, Mary Morris
Cook, Anne E.
Drugan, Robert C.
Fitzpatrick, Ellen
Gullace, Nicoletta F.
Palmer, Stuart
Straus, Murray A.

Hanover
Kleck, Robert E.

Henniker
Crafts, Amy

Keene
Frink, Helen

Manchester
Piotrowski, Thaddeus M.

Plymouth
Funk, Joel D.
Sandy, Leo

Rindge
Picchi, Debra

NEW JERSEY

Blackwood
Curtis, William H.

Caldwell
Bar, Rosann
Spano, Rina Gangemi

Cherry Hill
Butler, Rebecca Batts

Edison
Nagy, Karoly

Ewing
Li, Rebecca

Garden City
Varacalli, Joseph A.

Glassboro
Wiltenburg, Joy

Hawthorne
Scott, Kieran

Hewitt
Mollenkott, Virginia Ramey

Jersey City
Daane, Mary
Marshood, Nabil
Ohiwerei, Godwin

Lakewood
Smorra, Mary A.

Madison
Calcagnetti, Daniel J.
Cowen, John Edwin
Gadsden, Gloria Y.
Weimer, Joan Myers

Mahwah
Frundt, Henry
Johnson, Roger N.
Sineshaw, T.

Montclair
Flint, Marcha
Haupt, Edward
Lang, Gerhard
Townsend, David J.

New Brunswick
Adams, Kimberly V.
Aronoff, Myron J.
Cobble, Dorothy Sue
Crystal, Stephen
Demone, Harold Wellington

Diamond, Elin
Gossy, Mary S.
Horowitz, Irving Louis
Kubey, Robert W.
Neugeboren, Bernard
Oppenheimer, Martin
Phillips, Julie
Popenoe, David
Strickland, Dorothy S.
Turnbull, Barbara
White, Helene R.

Newark
Kijne, Hugo
Liu, Zili
Rosenblatt, Jay
Schweizer, Karl W.
Stieglitz, Robert R.

Paramus
Ahn, Timothy Myunghoon
Skau, George
Woodland, Calvin Emmanuel

Piscataway
Borocz, Jozsef
Falk, John L.
Jussim, Lee
Sass, Louise A.
Waxman, Chaim I.

Pomona
Ashton, Nancy
Ince, Elizabeth
Lester, David

Princeton
Cooper, Joel
Curran, Sara R.
Garibaldi, Antoine Michael
Geertz, Clifford
Jasper, James M.
McLanahan, Sara S.
Nabokov, Isabelle
Rosen, Lawrence
Taylor, Howard F.
Wallace, Walter L.
Webb, Ruth H.
Western, Bruce
Wrong, Dennis H.

Sewell
Dumont, Lloyd F.
Lawson-Briddell, Lois Y.

Springfield
Stern, Frances Meritt

Teaneck
Schaefer, Charles

Toms River
Atanda, Alfred W.
MacDonald, Jane
Trevisan, Carey

Trenton
Collins, Elsie

Union
Kaplowitz, Henry L.

Wayne
Chao, Paul K.
Glassman, Ronald
Hayes, Leola G.
Korgen, Kathleen
Kressel, Neil
Lesikin, Joan
Makerec, Katherine
Seal, Robert

West Long Branch
Mitchell, William P.

NEW MEXICO

Albuquerque
Bock, Philip K.
Hill, Kim R.
Huaco, George
Jameson, Elizabeth
Keller, Robert J.
Lonewol, Ted
Mazumdar, Rinita

Power, Mary
Rodriguez, Sylvia
Straus, Lawrence G.
Wood, Richard L.
Woodward, Carolyn

Gallup
Glowienka, Emerine Frances

Las Cruces
Del Campo, Robert L.
Hart, Susan J.
Robinson, William I.
Sallee, Alvin L.
Vaughan, Stephanie L.
Winfree, L. Thomas, Jr

Portales
Lockman, Paul

Santa Fe
Bornet, Bruno
Dybowski, Brian
Schwartz, Douglas W.

Silver City
French, Laurence

NEW YORK

Albany
Alba, Richard
Bologna, M.
Carmack, Robert M.
Crowley-Long, Kathleen
Fetterley, Judith
Fortune, Anne E.
Frye, Cheryl A.
Leibo, Steve
Ley, Ronald
Loneck, Barry Martin
Moore, Gwen L.
Morehead, Joseph Hyde
Richter, Maurice N.
Smith, Michael E.
Tedeschi, James

Alfred
Greil, Arthur L.
Lovelace, Eugene A.
Walker, Gail

Bayside
Tricarico, Donald

Binghamton
Burright, Richard B.
Devitis, Joseph
Horowitz, Michael M.
Malin, Jo E.

Brentwood
Guthman, Christine A.

Brockport
Kramer, John E.
Lloyd, Jennifer
Turley, Alan

Bronx
Danzger, M. Herbert
Dytell, Rita
Friedenberg, Jay
Lavin, David E.
Mbabuike, Michael C.
Rogler, Lloyd H.
Strieby, H. Reid
Zuss, Mark

Bronxville
Doyle, Charlotte
Maida, Lori

Brooklyn
Allen, Rhianon
D'Angelo, Raymond
David, Gerald
Gielen, Uwe P.
Glazer, Ilsa M.
Haring, Lee
Kasper, Loretta F.
McLaughlin, Andree Nicola
Meyers, Barton
Monteiro, Thomas
Nishi, Setsuko Matsunaga

Ramirez, Paul
Russo, Donald T.
Schuman, Elliott Paul
Verbit, Mervin F.

Buffalo
Cummings, William K.
Dentan, Robert K.
Emihovich, Catherine A.
Gottdiener, Mark
Hart, Stephen
Johnstone, D. Bruce
Keil, Charles M. H.
Lewis, Lionel Stanley
Magdol, Lynn
Mathiot, Madeleine
McNutt, Paula M.
Otterbein, Keith F.
Palmer, Robert L., II
Pruitt, Dean
Thompson, Sanna J.

Centereach
Seifman, Eli

Clinton
Kanipe, Esther Sue

Cobleskill
Descartes, Rene

Cortland
Ba-Yunus, Ilyas
Lickona, Thomas E.
McDowell-Loudan, Ellis

Dobbs Ferry
D'heurle, Adma J.

Flushing
Eisenstein, Hester
Friedman, Norman
Heilman, Samuel C.
Pecorino, Philip Anthony
Roberts, Michael J.

Forest Hills
Gover, Yerah

Fredonia
Harper, Gary F.
Regelski, Thomas Adam

Garden City
Eisner, Wendy
Skidell, Myrna
Steil, Janice M.

Geneseo
Bailey, Charles Randall
Doan, Laura L.
Pacheco, Paul J.

Great Neck
Marcus, Paul

Greenvale
Araoz, Daniel L.
Hill-Miller, Katherine Cecelia
Reiter, Henry H.

Hamilton
Bolland, O. Nigel
De Boer, George E.
Harsh, Constance D.
Kerber, Jordan E.
Shiner, Rebecca

Hempstead
Atwood, Joan Delores
Bowe, Frank
Dobrin, Arthur
Satler, Gail R.
Serper, Mark R.

Huntington Station
Douglass, Melvin Isadore

Ithaca
Benson, LeGrace
Darlington, Richard B.
Evans, Gary W.
Greenwood, Davydd J.
Kennedy, Kenneth Adrian Raine
Krumhansl, Carol L.
Leeder, Elaine
Lurie, Alison

Mcbride, Paul Wilbert
Pinch, Trevor J.
Spivey, Michael
Turner, Terence S.
Williams, Robin M.

Jamaica
Baruch, Elaine Hoffman
Biafora, Frank
Ekbantani, Glayol
Rosenthal, Beth
Seitz, Jay

Jamestown
Victor, Jeffery

Long Island City
Feifer, Irwin

Loundonville
Murray, Paul

Middletown
Byrne, William

Mount Vernon
Brown, Beatrice S.

New Paltz
Knapp, Ronald G.

New Rochelle
Salamone, Frank A.
Solomon, Barbara Hochster
Zucker, Arnold H.

New York
Abramovitz, Mimi
Aiello, T.
Alexander, Aley E.
Alfonso, Vincent C.
Andreassi, John L.
Arafat, Ibtihaj
Ariker, Shirley
Aull, Felice
Bailey, Adrienne Yvonne
Barstow, Anne Llewellyn
Blount, Marcellus
Brooks-Gunn Brooks-Gunn, Jeanne
Brown, Steven M.
Cantor, Norman Frank
Cohen, Burton I.
Cohen, Myron L.
Conigliaro, Vincent
Creed, Gerald
Cullinan, Bernice Ellinger
Dane, Barbara
Daniel, E. Valentine
Dasgupta, Nilanjana
Dash, Irene Golden
Denmark, Florence L.
Diamond, Sigmund
Donohue, John Waldron
Eigen, Michael
Farganis, James
Fisherkeller, JoEllen
Fosshage, James L.
Friedlander, Judith
Gans, Herbert J.
Gerson, Kathleen
Globerman, Erma
Goldberg, Steven
Goldberger, Leo
Goldfarb, Jeffrey C.
Greenbaum, Michael B.
Halperin, D.
Hampton, Barbara L.
Handel, Gerald
Heyns, Barbara
Holloway, Ralph L.
Holtz, Barry
Hopkins, John Orville
Ivanoff, Andre
Jackson, Robert Max
Jasso, Guillermina
Kattago, Siobhan
Kostelanetz, Richard
Kurzman, Paul
Laderman, Carol
Lagemann, Ellen Condliffe
Lauer, Rachel M.
Lay, Nancy
Lazreg, Marnia
Lefkowitz, Joel M.
Liberopoulos, Maura H.
London, Clement B. G.
Lynch, Owen

Martin, Randy
McKay, Diane L.
McRae, Mary B.
Mikhail, Mona
Mueller, Claus
Murnion, Philip Joseph
Nash, June C.
Nelkin, Dorothy
Njoku, John
Nolan, Mary
Oates, John F.
Olitzky, Kerry M.
Ortner, Sherry B.
Penrod, Steven D.
Polk, Robert L.
Poll, Carol
Rajagopal, Arvind
Rettig, Salomon
Richardson, Richard C., Jr.
Rodriguez, Clara
Schlesinger, Yaffa
Schneider, Mareleyn
Stimpson, Catharine R.
Strand, Virginia
Straussner, Shulamith Lala
Takooshian, Harold
Tarr, Zoltan
Tartter, Vivien
Taylor, James Coleridge
Terry, James L.
Torosyan, Roben
Torres, Louis
Trope, Yaacov
Turkcwitz, Gerald
Ulanov, Ann Belford
Varderi, Alejandro
Velting, Drew
Yoshioka, Marianne R.
Zolberg, Vera L.

Nyack
Saxby, William R.

Oakdale
Nimbark, Ashakant

Oakland Gardens
Altman, Ira

Oswego
Stuck, Mary Frances
Thibault, Edward

Plattsburgh
Agne, Karen J.
Scanlon, Jennifer

Port Jefferson
Rosenthal, Naomi

Potsdam
Beauchamp, Heather
Emery, Kitty
Hanson, David J.
O'Bireck, Gary M.

Poughkeepsie
Staples, S. L.

Purchase
Dubin, S. C.
Foner, Nancy
Howard, John Robert
Newton, Esther

Rochester
Anderson, David Atlas
Bassett, Rodney
Carmel, Simon J.
Cartwright, Lisa
Deci, Edward
Doty, Dale V.
Gordon, Lynn Dorothy
Herzbrun, Michael B.
Kirschenbaum, Howard
Locke, Ralph Paul
Smith, Marshall L.

Saint Bonaventure
Adekson, Mary Olufunmilayo
Zimmer, Joseph E.

Sanborn
McWhorter, Kathleen T.

Saratoga Springs
Hassenger, Robert
Karp, David

Zangrando, Joanna Schneider

Scarsdale
Nag, Moni

Schenectady
Gmelch, George
Gmelch, Sharon Bohn

Selden
Huang, Zhen
Stewart, Cisley P.

Slingerlands
Fenton, William Nelson

Southampton
Ganesan, Indira

Staten Island
Chen, Sheying
Groth, Miles

Stony Brook
Cole, Stephen
McWorter, Gerald A.
Rachlin, Howard C.
Rivers, Elias Lynch

Syracuse
Chin, Jeffrey C.
Comstock, George Adolphc
Gold, Ann G.
Hovendick, Kelly B.
Kriesberg, Louis
Smith, Corrine
Timberlake, Constance Hector
Zerai, Assata

Tarrytown
Goldin, Milton
Lawry, John

Troy
Restivo, Sal

Uniondale
Naylor, Natalie A.

Utica
Coughlan, Reed

Valhalla
Courage, Richard A.

White Plains
Serels, M. Mitchell

Riverhead
Stewart, Cisley P.

NORTH CAROLINA

Asheville
Locke, Don C.

Belmont
Cote, Nathalie

Boiling Springs
Rainer, Jackson P.

Boone
Claassen, Cheryl
Dorgan, Howard
Hay, Fred J.
Keefe, Susan E.
Mulgrew, John

Buies Creek
Kledaras, Constantine G.

Chapel Hill
Blau, Judith R.
Brown, Frank
Smith, C. S.

Charlotte
Fullmer, Elise M.
Kaplan, Laura Duhan
Pollack, Bonnie N.
Rashotte, Lisa Slattery

Shenk, Dena
Terry, William S.
Williams, Nancy M.
Zacharias, Ravi

Concord
McLean, Mable Parker

Cullowhee
Kowalski, Robin Marie
Randolph, Mickey M. K.

Davidson
Sabaratnam, Lakshmanan

Durham
Baker, Lee D.
Davies, James
Malpass, Leslie Frederick
Page, Patricia
Rodkin, Philip C.
Tiryakian, Edward A.
Zhou, Xueguang

Fayetteville
Andrews-McCall, Maxine Ramseur
Mutisya, Phillip

Greenboro
Gould, Daniel

Greensboro
Baber, Ceola Ross
Dickerson, Joyce
Gill, Diane L.
Hayes, Charles Leonard
Jacks, Julia Zuwerink
Jennings, Robert Ray
Khopkar, Asha D.
Kirk, Wyatt D.
Pasley, B. Kay
Purkey, William Watson
Scott, Roxanna
Shoffner, Marie F.

Greenville
Chestnut, Dennis Earl
Chia, Rosina
Hall, Cathy W.
Holsey, Lilla G.

Henderson
Powell, Lydia C.

Hickory
Baker, Linda D.
Painter, Lorene H.

High Point
Adams, Jeffrey

Jacksonville
Barton, Beth

Jamestown
Schmid, Carol L.

Pembroke
Ho, Truc-Nhu
Marson, Stephen

Raleigh
Cofield, Elizabeth Bias
Crumbley, Deidre H.
Huber, R. John
Moxley, Robert L.
Ting, Siu-Man R.
Tomaskovic-Devey, Barbara A.
Vick, Laura G.

Research Triangle Park
Gatewood, Algie C.

Shelby
Bolich, Greg

Tarboro
Waters, Sharon

Wilmington
Kimmel, Richard H.

Winston-Salem
Cook, Sharon
Hattery, Angela J.
Milner, Joseph O'Beirne
Sadler, Wilbert L., Jr.

NORTH DAKOTA

Dickinson
McGarva, Andrew R.

Fargo
Goreham, Gary
Slobin, Kathleen

Grand Forks
Hume, Wendelin M.
Williams, John

OHIO

Akron
Erickson, Rebecca J.
Feltey, Kathryn M.
Lo, Celia C.
McClain, Andrew Bradley
Smith, Priscilla R.
Yoder, Janice

Ashtabula
Murray, Ed

Athens
Childs, Francine C.
Myers, Lena Wright
Rao, Nagesh
Safran, Joan
Safran, Stephen P.
Sarnoff, Susan
Sweeney, Thomas John

Berea
Ahmed, Ansaruddin

Bluffton
Nath, Pamela S.

Bowling Green
Adetunji, Jacob
Chen, Yiwei
Ludlow, Jeannie
Luibheid, E.
Martin, Michael T.
Rao, K. Vaninadha
Scott, John Sherman
Stockwell, Edward G.
Tweney, Ryan D.
Zeller, Richard A.
Zongo, Opportune Marie

Canton
Camp, David A.
McClain, Shirla R.

Cedarville
Henning, Nelson
Wiggins, Robert R.

Cincinnati
Alexander, Jonathan F.
Atkinson, Michael
Conyne, Robert
Hansen, Barbara L.
Hershey, Daniel
Kidwell, R. Jay
Matthews, G.
Schefft, Bruce K.
Smith, Paul M., Jr.
Stoffregen, Thomas
Tang, Mei
Wingard, Edward L.
Yager, Geoffrey

Cleveland
Bate, Brian R.
Beatie, Bruce A.
Biegel, David E.
Bonder, Bette R.
Bynum, David Eliab
Chirayath, Verghese J.
Clark, Sanza Barbara
Freedheim, Donald K.
Johnson, Alice K.
Long, Susan O.
Oster, Judith
Reminick, Ronald A.
Santilli, Nicholas R.
Swenson, Elizabeth V.
Varallo, Sharon

Columbus
Alberts, Darlene J.
Aman, Michael G.
Barnes, Daniel Ramon
Bartle-Haring, Suzanne
Bourguignon, Erika Eichhorn
Cooksey, Elizabeth C.
Evans, Donna Browder
Hamilton, Richard Frederick
Jang, Sung Joon
Jarvis, Gilbert Andrew
Julia, Maria C.
Kitch, Sally L.
Price-Spratlen, Townsand
Richards, Constance S.
Richardson, Laurel
Rojahn, Johannes
Rupp, Leila J.
Sagaria, Mary Ann D.
Slomczynski, Kazimietz M.
Stewart, Mac A.
Taylor, Verta
Tripodi, Tony

Dayton
Sudzina, Mary

Delaware
Mahdi, Akbar

East Liverpool
Miller, Eric D.

Fremont
Stallkamp, Ray H., III

Gambier
Kipp, Rita

Kent
Chandler, Theodore A.
Hobfoll, Steven E.
Meindl, Richard S.
Reinberg, Richard
Scott, Ellen

Lima
Page, Roger A.

Middletown
Lewiecki-Wilson, Cynthia B.

New Philadelphia
Andrews, Gregg L.

Newark
MacDonald, William L.

Oberlin
Gorfain, Phyllis
White, Clovis L.

Orrville
Beyeler, Julia M.
Kristofco, John P.

Oxford
Biran, Mia W.
Joseph, Alfred
Stiles, William B.
Ziolkowski, Margaret C.

Painesville
Borchert, Susan D.

Portsmouth
Pambookian, Hagop S.

Silver Lake
Poloma, Margaret Mary

Springfield
Davis, Robert Leigh
Kaminski, Patricia

Toledo
Al-Marayati, Abid Amin
Hovey, Joseph
Mc Guire, Patrick
Metress, Seamus

University Heights
Seaton, Shirley Smith

Westerville
Luckey, Evelyn F.

Wilmington
Gerritz, E. Keith

Yellow Springs
Amos, Oris Elizabeth Carter
Keen, Cheryl
Whelchel, Marianne

Youngstown
Friedman, Saul S.
Shale, Rick

OKLAHOMA

Ada
Sukholutskaya, Mara

Alva
Fear, Marcia B.

Durant
Flippen, J. Brooks
Kennedy, Elizabeth

Edmond
Green, Malinda Hendricks

Langston
Manning, Jean Bell
Sagini, Meshack

Lawton
Xie, Xiaolin

Norman
Dharwadker, Aparna
Henderson, George
Kennison, Shelia
Sturm, Circe

Oklahoma City
Hardeman, Carole Hall
Thornton, Jeri

Seminole
Ousley, Charles

Stillwater
Brown, Robert
Henry, Carolyn S.

Stilwater
Hershey, Douglas

Tulsa
Lindstrom, Lamont
Nicholson, Robert A.
Sloan, Tod Stratton
Stromberg, Peter G.

Weatherford
Nail, Paul R.

OREGON

Bend
Minor-Evans, Leslie

Corvallis
Cardinal, Bradley J.
Helle, Anita

Eugene
Connolly, Thomas J.
Dugaw, Dianne M.
Dumond, D. E.
Liberman, Kenneth B.
Porter, Samuel C.
Sherman, Sharon R.
Simonds, Paul E.
Wojcik, Daniel

Forest Grove
Hersen, Michel

Newberg
Bufford, Rodger K.
Gathercoal, Kathleen
Koch, Chris
Linzey, Sharon
Lloyd, Carl

Portland
Halverson, Susan E.
Heflin, John F.
Henry, Samuel Dudley
Hillis, Rick
Kovacs, Edna M.
Miller-Jones, Dalton
Thomas, Jay

PENNSYLVANIA

Abington
Zigler, Ronald L.

Allentown
Cameron, Catherine M.
McVeigh, Frank J.

Altoona
Balch, William

Bethlehem
Spokane, Arnold R.
Washington, Mary L.

Bloomsburg
Armstrong, Christopher
Bryan, Jesse A.
Lindenfeld, Frank

Blue Bell
Baron, Steven H.

Bryn Athyn
Werner, Sonia S.

Bryn Mawr
Lassek, Yun Ja
Lichtenberg, Phillip

California
Schweiker, William F.

Carlisle
Jacobs, Norman G.
Silva, Christopher

Chester
Edgette, J. Joseph

Cheyney
McCummings, LeVerne

Collegeville
Oboler, Regina

Dallas
La Jeunesse, Charles A.

Doylestown
Dimond, Roberta R.
Wiseman, Mary Bittner

East Stroudsburg
Mercado, Juan Carlos
Rochedecoppens, Peter

Easton
Smith, Andrea L.

Edinboro
Iutcovich, Mark

Elizabethtown
Ruscio, J.

Erie
Adovasio, J. M.
Baker, Parris

Glenside
Johnston, Norman

Grantham
Kraybill, Donald B.
Tettah, Joshua

Greensburg
Barriga, Alvaro

Grove City
Arnold, Edwin P.
Kring, Hilda Adam
Smith, Gary

Throckmorton, E. Warren

Huntingdon
Wiinamaki, Lizabeth

Indiana
Darling, Rosalyn
Ferro, Trenton R.
Jalongo, Mary
Worzbyt, John C.

Johnstown
Haslett, Tammy

Kutztown
Rains, G. Dennis

Lancaster
Hartley, Loyde Hobart
Kaye, Howard

Latrobe
Clough, Wulfstan

Lewisberg
Keen, J. Ernest

Lewisburg
Evans, David
Murray, Joseph L.

Mansfield
Sidell, Nancy

Meadville
Heuchert, J. W.
McKinley, Nita Mary
Ozorak, Elizabeth Weiss

Media
Cole, Phillis B.

Millersville
Winter, John Ellsworth

Minersville
Walters, Glenn D.

Newtown
Eyer, Diane E.

Philadelphia
Aiken, Linda H.
Azzolina, Davis S.
Barakat, Lamia
Chapman, Judith G.
Cotter, John Lambert
Crane, Diana
Dyson, Robert Harris, Jr.
Estes, Richard J.
Ferere, Gerard Alphonse
Fittipaldi, Silvio Edward
Fullard, William
Hyatt, Susan Brin
Kopytoff, Igor
Lefkovitz, Lori Hope
Metz, Brent E.
Miller, Naomi F.
Morawska, Ewa
Moss, Roger W.
Myrick, Howard A., Jr.
Rouse, Donald E.
Ruby, Jay W.
Schuyler, Robert L.
Solomon, P.
Soven, Margot
Van De Walle, Etienne
Walker, Valaida Smith
Watson, Wilbur H.
Youngman, C. Van

Pittsburgh
Abrams, Janice K.
Achenbaum, W. Andrew
Bart, Benjamin Franklin
Biggs, Shirley Ann
Blee, K. M.
Boneva, Bonka
Brooke, Roger
Burston, Daniel
Casile, William
Davis, Nathan T.
Dawes, Robyn M.
Drennan, Robert D.
Fararo, Thomas J.
Feldman, Heidi M.
Freed, Barbara

Kaufman, Terrence Scott
Klahr, David
Koda, Keiko
Kraft, William F.
Krause, Corinne Azen
Maguire, Lambert
Markoff, John
Perrucci, Alissa
Porter, Curtiss E.
Richardson, Cordell
Schofield, Janet W.
Simms, Eva-Maria
Simon, Herbert A.

Radnor
Rosnow, Ralph Leon
Sicoli, Mary L.

Reading
Gilbert, Edward R.
Ingram-Wallace, Brenda
Voigt, David Quentin

Scranton
Baker, Thomas E.
Norcross, John C.
Wolfer, Loreen T.

Shippensburg
James, Alice
Mehiel, Ronald

Slippery Rock
Bhatia, Kundan Lai

State College
Lyon, Janet W.

Swarthmore
Blake, J. Herman
Morgan, Kathryn L.

Uniontown
Hovanec, Evelyn Ann

University Park
Castonguay, Louis G.
Firebaugh, Glenn
Jacobs, Janis E.
Makward, Christiane Perrin
Show, Dean R.
Snow, D. R.
Stevens, Robert
Ulmer, Jeffery T.
Walker, Alan Cyril

Upper Black Eddy
Regney, Gabrielle

Verona
Matthews, Jack

Villanova
Durnin, John H.
Pattnayak, Satya R.

Washington
Miller, Stuart J.

West Chester
Dzamba, Anne
Gutwirth, Madelyn
McNairy, Francine G.
Siegel, Peter E.
Treadwell, Thomas
Voss, Richard W.

Wilkes-Barre
O'Brien, Jean

PUERTO RICO

Rio Piedras
Irizarry, Maria A.

San German
Hernandez, Juan E.

RHODE ISLAND

Kingston
Cunnigen, Donald
Rossi, Joseph S.
Stein, Karen F.
Turnbaugh, William A.
Velicer, Wayne F.

Lincoln
Thakur, Parsram S.

Newport
Martasian, Paula J.

Providence
Abramson, David M.
Allen, Peter S.
Davis, Robert Paul
Filinson, Rachel
Guido, Joseph
Heath, Dwight Braley
Kertzer, David Israel
Lieberman, Philip
Lopes, William H.
Rosenberg, Bruce
Zavestoski, Stephen

Wakefield
Coffin, Tristram Potter

SOUTH CAROLINA

Charleston
Kaiser, Charles F.
Marshall-Bradley, Tina
Sinisi, Christina S.

Clemson
Alley, Thomas R.
Crosby, Margaree Seawright
Hawdon, James E.

Clinton
Freymeyer, Robert H.
Presseau, Jack R.

Columbia
Appel, James B.
Ginsberg, Leon
Morris, Robin K.
Raymond, Frank B.
Rickert, Edward J.

Denmark
Wong, Eugene F.

Florence
Anastasi, Jeffrey S.
Diggs, William P.
Dorsel, Thomas N.
Hunter, Laurie Sullivan

Gaffney
Lundy, Duane

Greenville
Grisel, Judith E.
Siegel, Brian V.

Greenwood
Bethel, Elizabeth Rauh

Hartsvill
Culyer, Richard

Hartsville
Rubenstein, Joseph H.

Mount Pleasant
Hewett, Stephenie M.

Orangeburg
Grimes, Tresmaine
Heggins, Martha Jean Adams
Rogers, Oscar Allan, Jr.

Rock Hill
Fortner-Wood, Cheryl
Green, Ronald K.
Marx, Jonathan I.

Spartanburg
Mathews, Spencer R.

Sumpter
McCauley, Terita

SOUTH DAKOTA

Aberdeen
Coxwell, Margaret
Geier, Connie

Brookings
Phelps, Brady
White, Joseph

Sioux Falls
Harris, J. Gordon

Vermillion
Evans, Wayne
Nienonen, Jack E.

Yankton
Ferris, Alan

TENNESSEE

Blountville
O'Dell, Earlene R.

Chattanooga
Bodkin, Thomas E.

Collegedale
Coombs, Robert Stephen
Liu, Ruth A.
McClarty, Wilma King- Doering

Cookeville
Wheeler, John

Dyersburg
Seibert-McCauley, Mary F.

Gallatin
Sherrill, Vanita Lytle

Jackson
Davenport, Gene Looney
McClure, Wesley Cornelious

Johnson City
Sherrill, Catherine Anne

Knoxville
Burghardt, Gordon M.
Hunt, Barbara Ann
Jalata, Asafa
Leki, Ilona
Maland, Charles J.
Rocha, Cynthia
Speidell, Todd

Lebanon
Markert, John P.

Maryville
Simpson, Terry L.

McKenzie
Lollar, Laddie H.

Memphis
Melancon, Donald
Shadish, W. R.
Strauser, David
Ward, Jeannette P.

Murfreesboro
Anton, Harley F.
Bader, Carol H.

Nashville
Ascencao, Erlene M.
Barrett, Tracy
Blasi, Anthony J.
Church, Dan M.
Deal, Terrance E.
Enterline, Lynn
Fields, Milton
Goddu, Teresa

Grantham, D. Wesley
Harrod, Howard L.
Insignares, Harriette B.
Jackson, Andrew
Lubinski, David
Myers, Charles Bennett
Sherkat, Darren E.
Tichi, Cecelia
Winbush, Raymond A.

Sewanee
Coleman, Priscilla K.

TEXAS

Arlington
Bernstein, Ira H.
Callicutt, James W.
Harrold, Francis B.
Hoefer, Richard
Jordan, Catheleen

Austin
Blockley, Mary Eva
Denbow, James R.
Erdener, Yildiray
Goosman, Stuart
Hayman, Carol
Hester, Thomas R.
Holden, George W.
Lopreato, Joseph
Nelson, Wanda Lee
Padilla, Yolanda C.
Raley, R. Kelly
Springer, David W.
Sutherland, Kay
Webb-Johnson, Gwendolyn

Beaumont
Love, James

Brownsville
Green, George

Canyon
Kunz, Jennifer

Cedar Hill
Konditi, Jane

College Station
Marshall, Alicia A.
Peters, William H.
Sharf, Barbara F.
Street, Richard L., Jr.

Commerce
Grissett, Barbara
Thompson, William
Trusty, Jerry

Corpus Christi
Myers, Elwin R.

Dallas
Brettell, Caroline B.
Davis, Ronald Leroy
James, H. Rhett
Merrifield, William R.
Mount, George
Wendorf, D. Fred

Denton
Altekruse, Michael
Bean, Judith M.
Cissell, William B.
Cobb, Jeanne B.
Cogan, Karen D.
Gibbs, Tyson
Guarnaccia, Charles A.
Hildreth, Gladys Johnson
Marshall, Linda
Naylor, Larry L.
Quinn, James F.
Rubin, Linda J.
Sadri, Malmoud
Scobie, Ingrid Winther
Williams, Joyce E.

Edinburg
Jou, Jerwen
Raajpoot, Uzzer A.

El Paso
Campbell, Howard B.
Coleman, Karen J.
Johnson, Steve
Natalicio, Diana

Fort Worth
Bell, Reva Pearl
Black, Wesley O.
Edwards, Joy
Eldridge, Daryl
Newman, J. R.
Overstreet, Charles
Yount, William R.

Galveston
Hoskins, Billie

Georgetown
Neville, Gwen K.

Hawkins
Hawkins, Dorisula Wooten

Houston
Akubukwe, David
Atang, Christopher
Bell, Linda
Cunningham, James J.
Dworkin, Anthony G.
Elfimov, Alexei
Jefferson, Joseph L.
Kierstead, Fred P.
Lewis, Mary R.
Lindahl, Carl
McMullen, Mike
Osterberg, Susan
Rasmussen, S. J.
Robbins, Susan P.
Schiff, Frederick
Tyler, Stephen
Waldner-Haugrud, Lisa

Jacksonville
Johnson, Ronnie J.

Keene
England, Micheal

Kilgore
Ludewig, Larry M.

Killeen
Gladden, John W.

Kingsville
Ponder, Fred T.

Laredo
Cardenas, Maria de la Luz
Rodriguez

Livingston
O'Day, Edward Francis

Lubbock
Miner, Madonne
Young, Andy

McAllen
Evans, James L.

Mesquite
Evans, John

Midland
Goodyear, Russell

Mount Pleasant
Yox, Andrew

Nacogdoches
Scharff, Lauren F.
Watson, Jack B.
Wilson, Wayne J.

Odessa
Thompson, Spencer K.

Pasadena
Hall, Wayne W.

Richardson
Alexander, Bobby C.
Burton, Charles E.
Leaf, Murray J.

Stott, Deborah
Van Beveren, Toosje T.

San Antonio
Adams, Richard E. W.
Aspell, Patrick Joseph
Diem, Richard A.
Firestone, Juanita M.
Gelo, Daniel J.
Hernandez, Arthur E.
Jacobson, Rodolfo
Lampe, Philip
Mendoza, Louis

San Marcos
Chase Hankins, June
Fite, Kathleen E.
Frost, Christopher J.
Smith, Joanne Hamlin

Stephenville
Gibson, Jennifer

Tyler
Jedlicka, Davor
Rogers, Jack E.

Waco
Barker, Lewis M.
Hail, Jim G.

Wharton
Loessin, Jonathan K.
Soderstrom, Doug

UTAH

Logan
Fawcett, Bill
Glass-Cofin, Bonnie
Wilson, William Albert

Ogden
Sharpes, Donald Kenneth
Wei-Arthus, Huiying

Orem
Bennion, J.

Provo
Barton, Sally H.
Burlingame, Gary M.
Hawkins, John P.
Jacobson, Cardell K.
Lambert Brigham Young Univ,
Michael J.
Madsen, Carol Cornwall
Pedersen, Darhl M.
Shumway, Larry V.
Slife, Brent D.
Walton, Elaine
Worthen, Vaughn E.

Salt Lake City
Barlow, K. Renee
Barusch, Amanda S.
Brunvand, Jan Harold
Bullough, Robert V., Jr.
Derezotes, David S.
Fiema, Zbigniew
Giles, Jerry
Gringeri, Christina E.

VERMONT

Burlington
Berkowitz, Stephen David
Doyle, Mary Beth
Joffe, Justin M.
McCann, Harold G.
Sandoval, Dolores S.

Castleton
Acheson, Julianna

Middlebury
DiGiacomo, Susan
Margolis, Gary

Northfield
Shernock, Stanley K.

Tunbridge
Wolfe, David L.

Washington
George, Luvenia A.
Hamilton, Edwin
Mason, Donna S.
Saunders, Mauderie Hancock

Worcester
Young-Eisendrath, Polly

VIRGINIA

Alexandria
Bochnowski, Michael
Gearey, Amelia J.
Petraglia, Michael

Arlington
Oglesby, James Robert

Blacksburg
Assar, Nandini Narain
Barr, Marleen Sandra
Fine, Elizabeth C.

Charlottesville
Kauffman, James M.
Kett, Joseph Francis
Kubovy, Michael
Perdue, Charles L.
Turner, Edith
Wagner, Roy

Danville
Laughlin, John C. H.

Fairfax
Bateson, Mary Catherine
Colvin, Mark
Davis, Molly F.
Dennis, Rutledge M.
Dietz, Thomas
Jacobs, Mark D.
Kalof, Linda E.
Schunn, C.
Starosta, William J.
Tavani, Nicholas J.
Yocom, Margaret Rose

Farmville
Simmons, Betty Jo

Fredericksburg
Smith, Roy H.

Glen Allen
Tesmer, Floyd S.

Hampton
Benjamin, Lois
Noel, Melvina
Norwood, Margaret M.

Harrisonburg
Bland, Sidney Roderick
Couch, James
Halonen, Jane S.
Zehr, Howard

Lynchburg
Adams, Beverly C.

Manassas
Archer, Chalmers, Jr.

Norfolk
Berube, Maurice R.
Fellman, Anita C.
Gainey, Randy R.
Miller, Sheila D.
Raver-Lampman, Sharon
Tyler, Gerald DeForest

Radford
Edwards, Grace Toney
Jackson, Pamela A.
Parker, Jacqueline
Pribram, Karl H.
Servaty, Heather
Stanley, Paula H.

The Only Other
CRAZY CAR
Book

Sloan
Walker

Andrew
Vasey

WALKER AND COMPANY

New York, New York

This book is dedicated to our families.

First published in the United States of America in 1983 by the Walker Publishing Company, Inc.

Published simultaneously in Canada by John Wiley and Sons Canada, Limited, Rexdale, Ontario.

Library of Congress Catalog Card Number: 83-6546

Printed in the United States of America

10 9 8 7 6 5 4 3 2 1

Library of Congress Cataloging in Publication Data

Walker, Sloan.
     The only other crazy car book.

     Summary: Photographs and brief text introduce a variety of custom-made cars and hot-rods.
     1. Automobiles—Juvenile literature. [1. Automobiles. 2. Automobiles—Customizing] I. Vasey, Andrew. II. Title.
TL147.W35 1983   629.2'222   83-6546
ISBN 0-8027-6504-1
ISBN 0-8027-6517-3 (lib. bdg.)

Introduction

Most people think of the car as nothing more than a way to get to the grocery store. But a few think of the car as a way to be creative. They use their imaginations to create interesting cars that are fun to look at and would be fun to drive. These creations give people something new to wonder about. What would it be like to go over 630 miles per hour in the Budweiser Rocket or park a hot dog on a city street? Who would have thought two small Volkswagens could be combined to make a spacious limousine? Anything is possible when a car and a crazy idea come together.

This book further explores the world of unusual autos first seen in the One and Only Crazy Car Book. This is a world full of supercharged engines, chrome exhaust pipes, and wide racing tires. But here you will find more than just fast cars; each one of these cars proves that the automobile can be much more than something to get you to the grocery store.

Sloan Walker
Andrew Vasey

Roach Coach

This car was built for Roach Industries, the iron-on T-shirt transfer company. It took more than six years to build and cost over $100,000. The chassis and engine are just like the one used in Indy cars. This is one fast bug. It can go almost 200 miles per hour! The driver sits behind the bug-eyed windshield. The body was hand-made out of fiberglass and painted "Roach" red. The Roach Coach is loaded with shiny chrome from its grille to its exhaust pipes. The gas tank, which is made of a very light metal called titanium, was once used in an Atlas space rocket.

Volkswagen Double Bug Cabriolet

So you thought all VW Bugs were the same. Here's one Volkswagen that thinks it is a Rolls-Royce. The Double Bug was dreamed up by Carl Schneider one day as he sat at his desk toying with two model Volkswagens. Since he works for a Volkswagen dealership, it was easy for him to bring his idea to life.

Two convertible VW Bugs were cut in half. Then, the front end of one was joined to the back end of another. This may be the limousine of the future, if gas prices keep going up. Imagine a millionaire saying to his chauffeur: ''Forget the Rolls-Royce today, Jeeves. We'll be taking the Volkswagen.''

Pinball Wizard

Carl Casper's Pinball Wizard is a crazy car that would be fun in your gameroom or your garage! The power is supplied by a big Chrysler engine with a supercharger, but the real fun is in the back. This little pickup hauls a pinball machine which is gold-plated and is decorated with diamonds and rubies. It must have taken a lot of quarters to build this car!

New York Mets Pitching Buggy

This crazy car started out as an ordinary golf cart. It now carries major-league pitchers between the bullpen and the pitcher's mound at New York's Shea Stadium: A special fiberglass baseball body was added to the frame of the golf cart. Then a large Mets baseball hat was made and snapped on to the roof. The roof is held up by real baseball bats and the headlights rest in real gloves.

Although this crazy car doesn't have a big engine or go over 10 miles per hour, it is seen by over one million New York Mets fans every year!

Pool Hustler

The Pool Hustler is made out of a 70-year-old pool table, on which you can actually play. The pool cues are in racks on the side of the car. The hubcaps are in the shape of pool balls and the car is painted pooltable green.

It is powered by a 600-horsepower engine. It has four racing slicks in the back for good traction. The Pool Hustler is another crazy car that would be fun in your gameroom or your garage!

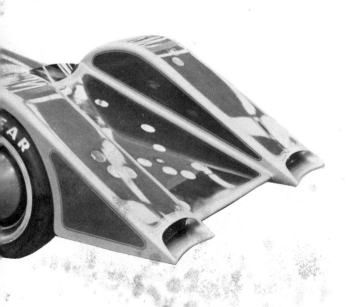

Disco "T"

The Disco "T" started out as a 1929 Model T Roadster, but Harry Willet's magic wrench turned it into a prize-winning show car. He jazzed up the old Ford by adding a chromed turbocharged engine and Firestone racing tires. The roof looks like a record-player arm. The windshield is attached to the end of the arm.

The headlights and radiator have been replaced with the front end of a racing car. And, in the back, there is a wing like the Indianapolis cars use to help press the back tires onto the track at high speeds. The Disco "T" is painted orange and is covered with black musical notes.

Geoffreymobile

The Geoffreymobile was built to carry the Toys-R-Us family of giraffes in parades. The truck runs on "potato chip power" which means that kids can put potato chips in the back and watch them fly around in a glass box over the engine in front. Actually, a Chevrolet engine powers the front-wheel-drive Geoffreymobile. The giraffes climb into the back by using a circular stairway. When the truck moves, the "eye" headlights move around. The front windshield is tinted to keep the sun off the driver during the parades.

11

Budweiser Rocket

The Budweiser Rocket holds the world's record for the highest land speed. The Rocket car was clocked at 739.666 miles per hour during tests at Edwards Air Force Base in California, which is also where the Space Shuttle lands. The Rocket car uses metal tires because rubber tires would melt at such high speed. If you put wings on the Rocket car its 48,000-horsepower engine would make it fly faster than most airplanes! On the underside of the car, the body forms a wedge to deflect air that could lift the car off the ground. This is the only car that makes driving faster than flying!

1911 Stutz-Marion

When your grandparents were young, this Stutz was the fastest car a person could buy. Its top speed was an amazing 60 miles per hour, which made it the first car to go "a mile a minute." The Budweiser Rocket, going 739.666 miles per hour, covers 12 miles in a minute. But in 1911, when most people rode in horse-and-buggies that couldn't go faster than about 20 miles per hour, the Stutz-Marion was very, very fast.

The Stutz has the steering wheel on the right hand side like English cars built today. With no top and only a small windshield on the driver's side, this early sports car certainly wouldn't be much fun in the rain!

Indy Racers

The Indianapolis 500, which has been run every year since 1911, is one of the biggest– and fastest– automobile races in America. All Indy racers are special, but here are a few that are really unusual.

Stein Twin Porsche

The Stein Twin Porsche was one of the few four-wheel-drive Indy racers. Each set of wheels is driven by a separate engine. Although it is faster than any Jeep, it would sure have trouble in the sand!

1967 STP Turbine

Driven by Parnelli Jones, the STP Turbine was the first car with a turbine engine to race in the Indianapolis 500. The turbine in this car is a lot like those in jet plane engines. Air rushes into the car through the hole in front of the driver. This air spins the turbine, which looks like a fan. The addition of the turbine makes the engine more powerful than ordinary engines. A piece of metal pops up behind the driver to slow the car down in the turns. This brake sometimes frightened the other drivers—they thought the turbine car was falling apart.

The STP Turbine is now on display at the Smithsonian Institution in Washington, D.C.

Eagle Aircraft Special

Ken Hamilton's Eagle Aircraft Special was designed to slice through the air like an airplane, but the fins around the wheels press the car down onto the track so it does not "take off" at high speeds.

Jack Adams' Aircraft Turbine Special

Jack Adams' racer combines airplane design and turbine engine power.

Hurst Sidecar

This car was built by Smokey Yunick. Instead of sitting in the center of the car in front of the engine as in most racing cars, the driver of this car sits in the sidecar beside the engine. This car can go through curves faster than many other racing cars because this design gives it better balance.

Pat Clancy Six-Wheeler

The Pat Clancy Special was built in 1948. It was the only car to have six wheels. Except for that, it looks like most of the Indy racers of those days. Notice some of the differences between this car and the Ken Hamilton Aircraft racer. The Clancy car has much narrower tires. It is higher off the track and is not designed to cut through the air as well as the Aircraft racer. The old racers were also more dangerous than the new ones because the drivers were more exposed.

Pink Panther Limo

The Pink Panther's limo is the most luxurious of all the crazy cars. The Pink Panther can enjoy the television, use the telephone or listen to the stereo in the back while his chauffeur drives in front.

The limo is based on an Oldsmobile Toronado because that car has front-wheel-drive and has a lot of room in back. The engine is right behind the driver's seat. You can see the air scoop for the engine there also.

When you see this car, you have to "think pink" since everything from the paint on the outside to the carpet on the inside is pink.

19

Cruisin' Merc

This is a 1951 Mercury that was customized for the movie The Junkman. First it was ''chopped;'' the roof was cut off and lowered to give the car a sleeker look. Then it was ''channelled;'' anything that stuck off of the body was removed to make the sides look smoother. Notice that the Cruisin' Merc has no doorhandles or side view mirrors.

After this bodywork the original two headlights were replaced with four and a custom grille was added. The finishing touches were a candy-apple red paint job and a Chevrolet 426 engine.

Munster Coach and Dragula

Here is one of America's strangest fictional families, the Munsters. The black coach is their family car. It is made from the bodies of three Model-T Fords. The interior is covered with black velvet. Herman sits in front and drives while Grandpa works behind him in his chemistry lab. Eddie can sit outside on his special bench seat in back.

Grandpa likes to drag race. He uses the sporty Dragula, which is built with a real coffin. Grandpa lifts up the lid of the coffin to get in. A Ford Cobra 289 engine provides him with plenty of power. A tombstone cutter designed the Dragula's grille.

21

1958 Corvette

The 1958 Corvette in this photograph is from the animated cartoon movie Heavy Metal. Since it was drawn by an artist, it can look very different and do very different things.

The Corvette looks like it is getting ready to land on some kind of strange planet. The parachutes in the back help it make a soft landing. Some pretty incredible things can happen in an animated movie!

Barrister

The Barrister is a car for the stars built by world-famous car designer George Barris. Only eight of these cars were built. This one was used in the movie "Smorgasbord."

To build this car, Barris started out with a Corvette chassis and engine. He then added a hand-made body and interior. The seats are filled with goose down and the instruments on the dashboard are digital. The polished chrome exhaust pipes come out of the side of the car just like they did in early sports cars. It also has wire wheels that resemble the ones on early sports cars. This car is sure to become a classic!

Star Wars' Land Speeder and Sand Crawler

What would you drive if you were on a planet with no roads? Well, if you were on the desert-like planet of Tatooine in the movie Star Wars, you could drive a landspeeder or a sandcrawler.

The landspeeder is a hover vehicle; it floats above the ground on a cushion of air. It is Tatooine's version of a convertible sports car. One advantage that the landspeeder has over a regular sports car is that it can never get a flat tire.

The sandcrawler is Tatooine's version of a family station wagon. In the movie, the evil jawas did not load the sandcrawler up with groceries; they used this huge transporter to kidnap little robots like R2-D2 and C-3PO. A vehicle as large and heavy as the sandcrawler could not hover over the ground like the landspeeder. Instead, it uses wide treads just the way tanks on our planet do.

Oscar Mayer Wienermobile

This is the world's only air-conditioned hot dog and the world's only bun with headlights. Actually, Oscar Mayer has six of these fiberglass-bodied wienermobiles that are used in promotions across the country.

The first wienermobiles were built around 1932. They have gone through some changes since then to help them last longer. For example, the old metal hot dog bodies were replaced with fiberglass ones because fiberglass doesn't rust or rot like metal does. It also is lighter, so the wienermobiles get better gas mileage. Pass the mustard!

Popcorn Wagon

The sign on the window says "Popcorn, 5 cents." Why is it so cheap? Because you first have to catch the speedy Popcorn Wagon! The Popcorn Wagon is powered by a Ford engine with two chrome superchargers.

The chrome and brass parts alone cost $4,000! The popcorn popper in the back actually works, too. Wouldn't this car be great at a drive-in movie?

27

V-8 Roadster

Most of the time, "V-8" means that a car's engine has 8 cylinders arranged in a "V" shape. This car does have a V-8 engine, but that isn't where its name comes from. The 350-horsepower engine in the V-8 Roadster is from a Ford Mustang. The outside of the car is painted to look like a can of Campbell's V-8 juice. It even has V-8 cans for hubcaps and V-8 juice in the spare tire. Wow! Now you can have a V-8!

28

President's Rod

This car is called the President's Rod in honor of former president Jimmy Carter, who owned a peanut farm in Georgia. Harry Willet, the builder, picked the 1909 Cartercar because it had the same name as the president. Unlike many other crazy cars in this book, the President's Rod doesn't have a huge engine. Instead, it has a small four-cylinder engine that gets over 50 miles to the gallon!

The interior is covered with purple velvet. The 80-year-old peanut roaster is in a hand-built oak cabinet. You can see the roasted peanuts in the trunk behind the driver's seat. This car is worth over $25,000. That's not peanuts!

Plymouth Roadrunner Superbird

Once upon a time, anyone who wanted a new car could buy one that was as fast as most racing cars. The 1970 Plymouth Roadrunner Superbird is one of the fastest American-made production cars ever built. The 425 horsepower Plymouth 426 Hemi engine in the Superbird enabled it to go faster than 120 miles per hour. The pointed nose in the front and the huge fin over the trunk help keep the tires firmly pressed on the ground at very high speeds.

The car in this photo is the standard model that anyone could buy. Plymouth only made a little more than 500 of these. Some of these cars came with horns that went "beep, beep," just like the little cartoon character they were named after. And also like that little bird, they could outrun almost anything else on the road!

With only a few small changes in the engine, and a number painted on the side, Richard Petty (43) and Pete Hamilton (40) drove Superbirds like these that won 38 out of 48 stock car races in 1970.

Dodge Super Charger

This two-seat sports car was created by the same people who built the Plymouth Roadrunner Superbird. Only one Super Charger was built. It was designed to cut through the wind. The windshield has been "chopped" and all the parts that usually stick out from a car's body, such as the door handles, have been removed. This makes the outside of the car smooth so it can go faster.

Cadillac Ranch

You probably believe that Cadillacs are built in Detroit just like all of the other American-made cars. But after seeing this you just might think that they are grown on a small farm in Texas. Actually this unusual sight is a sculpture in Amarillo, Texas, done by three men who call themselves "The Ant Farm." The artists probably had to visit many used-car lots to find these old Cadillacs. There must have been some interesting conversations between the Ant Farm sculptors and the used-car salesman:

Salesman: I can get that dent out of the front fender if you like.

Ant Farmer: Oh, don't worry about it. I don't think anyone will notice!

The Cadillacs used in this sculpture were built between 1949 and 1963. They all were in running order when they were sunk into a cement foundation. This foundation keeps the cars at the correct angles.

What do you think this sculpture says about America and its love for the automobile?

33

Anycar III

Buying a new car these days can be difficult because of all the different makes and models to choose from. But the Anycar III solves that problem: you get forty cars in one!

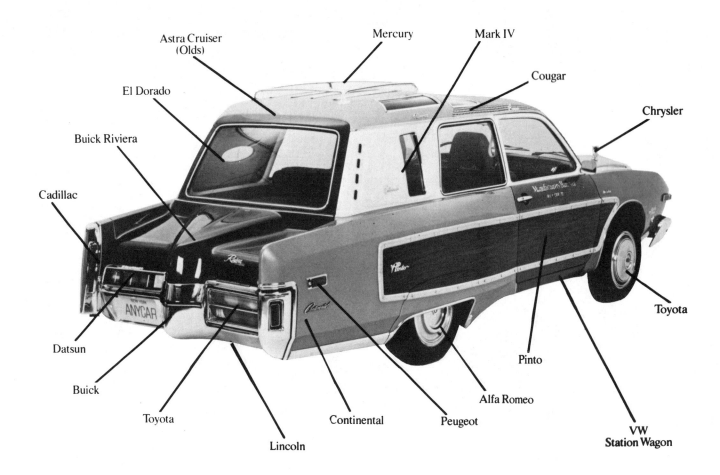

Astra Cruiser (Olds)
Mercury
Mark IV
Cougar
Chrysler
El Dorado
Buick Riviera
Cadillac
Datsun
Buick
Toyota
Lincoln
Continental
Peugeot
Alfa Romeo
Pinto
Toyota
VW Station Wagon

Created by George Barris, who designed the Anycars I and II for Manufacturers Hanover Trust, Anycar III is actually a 1974 Volkswagen station wagon with parts of forty separate cars attached to its body. It also has a mini-Anycar under its hood that comes out automatically when the driver presses a button. The interior is also made up from pieces of several different cars. The mini-Anycar can be used in heavy city traffic and it never needs a fill-up because it runs on batteries.

Texaco's Split Car

This car is a 1980 Chevrolet Citation that is used by
Texaco in television commercials. The car splits into two
pieces and each half of the car can operate by itself. Small
wheels were hidden under each half and a small engine
was added to the back half. A driver steers the back half
from the small space behind the back seat. The driver
looks through a small hole in the seat to see where the
front half is going. The two halves also can be hooked
together to make it look like a normal car again.

If your parents think that you are sometimes too noisy when you ride with them in your car, this might be the perfect car for your family. You could ride in the back half and follow your parents in the front half. Just be sure that you don't get separated in traffic!

Detroit's Experimental Cars

Most of the other cars in this book started out as normal cars and were changed into crazy ones. The crazy cars on this page and the next were built for special experiments by the major car companies.

Ford Cockpit

The Cockpit car was built by Ford in 1982 and introduced at car shows in 1983. It is a crazy car that you may be able to buy some day. It weighs only 770 pounds. Because it is so light, it can get over 75 miles per gallon. The Cockpit seats two people, one in front, one in back, like a double bicycle. Just like a fighter plane, this Ford car has a roof that pops up and lets the riders in or out.

Firebird 1

The white Firebird 1 was built by General Motors in 1954. General Motors never planned to sell cars like this. It was built to test a powerful turbine engine that they had designed.

Firebird 2

The Firebird 2 was a family car that also had a powerful turbine engine. It was designed to be used on special highways with electronic radar to control its speed. That made the Firebird 2 safer than a regular car.

Question: How do you keep some of the faster crazy cars, like the Roach Coach, the Dodge Super Charger, or the Pinball Wizard from going over the speed limit? Well, here are a few answers.

Top Kop Kar

If police cars were all built like Steve Tansy's Top Kop Kar, they would have no trouble catching up to quick little sports cars. This Plymouth Satellite police car is powered by a supercharged 350-horsepower engine. The car is painted black and white like many real police cars are. The red lights really work and the siren is under the hood.

Inside, the seats are decorated with buttons from real police uniforms. There is a chrome gun on the dashboard, and between the front and back seats there is a chrome divider to separate the good guys from the bad guys.

The Top Kop Kar has a parachute attached to the rear bumper to help it make quick stops. The sticker on the front door shows a policeman sitting on a spinning tire above the words, "What, me worry?" No way.

Kop-Ter Rod

If the Top Kop Kar can't catch the speeders, then maybe Dick Tracy's Kop-Ter Rod can. In a chase Dick Tracy climbs into the Kop-Ter Rod, which has a fiberglass body molded to look like a helicopter. He starts up the Mazda rotary engine that turns the helicopter blades and the wheels. The siren screams and the red lights flash as he drives off, steering with a helicopter stick rather than a steering wheel. They will know its Dick Tracy chasing them when they see the real detective badges on the front grille, which is from a Lincoln Continental.

Paddy Wagon

What do you do with the speeders when you catch them? Carl Casper solves that problem with the Paddy Wagon. This car started out as a 1910 Ford. Mr. Casper added a hand-built body with a cage for the criminals.

The bars on the windows are made of brass. The old-fashioned gas lights and the horn are also brass. The criminals sit in the back on hard wooden benches, while the driver sits on a comfortable "Police Blue" velvet seat. The powerful Ford engine is fully chromed and can get the Paddy Wagon to the court house in no time.

Spinner

If the Spinner is anything like the police cars of the future, then speeders will be in a lot of trouble. You might recognize the Spinner from the 1982 movie Blade Runner. The man standing in front of the car is the designer, George Barris.

What does the future hold for police cars? The Spinner might give you some ideas. The police cars of tomorrow might be guided by computers that will pick the fastest route to the scene of a crime. They may also be powered by sports car engines like the Porsche engine that is in the Spinner. the engine would serve two purposes, providing power for the wheels and power for the car to float on air when it would have to go off the road.

Hard Hat Hauler

This hot rod was built in honor of America's workers. Look at the presidents on the hubcaps; they must get very dizzy when the car moves.

The driver of this car sits on a wooden bench. From there, the driver can also control the forklift in front. There is a steel girder holding up the chrome hard hat and the trunk looks like a lunchbox.

The Hard Hat Hauler is powered by a Chevrolet 390 engine topped with three superchargers. It produces about 450 horsepower. With this car nobody has an excuse for being late to work!

Ricksha

The Ricksha is the new American version of an old Japanese vehicle. In the old days in Japan, one person would pull another along in a two-wheeled buggy called a ricksha. This American ricksha is pulled by 300 "horses" coming from the Ford engine.

The three-wheeled hot rod still looks Japanese. The header exhaust pipes look like Japanese noodles. The taillights are authentic Japanese lanterns. The dragon ornament on the top of the engine is also from Japan. The car is steered with a samurai sword.

Bed Buggy

After a hard day of work or school, there is no better way to relax than in the Bed Buggy. It combines the comforts of a real brass bed with the fun of a dune buggy. The pillows and sheets on the bed are made out of soft leopard-skin material. The Bed Buggy is even equipped with a telephone and a television! The taillights are made out of old lanterns and rest on nightstands. There are also lights near the top of the brass poles holding up the roof that look like old-fashioned candles.

The back tires have special ribs on them that dig into the sand so that the Bed Buggy can drive on the beach. The wheelie-bars at the very back of the car keep the front tires from lifting off of the ground when the car makes fast starts.

Acknowledgements

Roach Coach Roach Incorporated

Volkswagen Double Bug Cabriolet Delta Import Motors, Inc., La Crosse, Wisconsin. Conceived by Carl Schneider.

Pinball Wizard, Popcorn Wagon, Paddy Wagon Show Cars, Inc. Owned and built by Carl Casper.

New York Mets Pitching Buggy New York Mets Baseball Club. Photo by Brian Vasey.